BAKER'S
BIOGRAPHICAL DICTIONARY OF
MUSICIANS

CREDITS

Laura Kuhn
Classical Editor

Dennis McIntire
Associate Classical Editor

Lewis Porter
Jazz Editor

William Ruhlmann
Pop Editor

Key to Contributors

AB	Andrew Barlett	ETA	E. Taylor Atkins	NAL	Nancy Ann Lee
AG	Andrew Gilbert	GB	Greg Baise	NC	Norene Cashen
BH	Brock Helander	GBr	Gig Brown	NS	Nicolas Slonimsky
BJH	B. J. Huchtemann	GJ	Gregg Juke	PK	Peter Keepnews
BM	Bill Moody	GK	Gregory Kiewiet	PM	Patricia Myers
BP	Bret Primack	GM	Garaud MacTaggart	PMac	Paul MacArthur
BR	Bryan Reesman	HB	Hank Bordowitz	RB	Ralph Burnett
BW	Bill Wahl	JB	Joshua Berrett	RC	Richard Carlin
CH	Chris Hovan	JC	John Chilton,	RI	Robert Iannapolto
DB	Dan Bindert		*Who's Who of Jazz*	SC	Safford Chamberlain
DCG	David C. Gross	JC-B	John Chilton,	SH	Steve Holtje
DD	David Demsey		*Who's Who of British Jazz*	SKB	Susan K. Berlowitz
DDD	Dean D. Dauphinais	JE	James Eason	SP	Sam Prestianni
DK	Dan Keener	JM	Jeff McMillan	TP	Ted Panken
DM	Dennis McIntire	JO	Jim O'Rourke	TS	Tom Smith
DO	David Okamoto	JTB	John T. Bitter	WB	Will Bickart
DPe	Damon Percy	LK	Laura Kuhn	WF	Walter Faber
DPr	David Prince	LP	Lewis Porter	WKH	W. Kim Heron
DR	Dennis Rea	MF	Michael Fitzgerald	WR	William Ruhlmann
ED	Eric Deggans	MM	*Music Master Jazz*		
EH	Ed Hazell		*and Blues Catalogue*		
EJL	Eric J. Lawrence	MS	Matthew Snyder		

BAKER'S
BIOGRAPHICAL DICTIONARY OF
MUSICIANS

VOLUME 4
LEVY - PISA

Centennial Edition

NICOLAS SLONIMSKY
Editor Emeritus

LAURA KUHN
Baker's Series Advisory Editor

Schirmer Books
an imprint of the Gale Group
New York • Detroit • San Francisco • London • Boston • Woodbridge, CT

Schirmer Books
1633 Broadway
New York, New York 10019

Gale Group
27500 Drake Road
Farmington Hills, Michigan 48331-3535

Library of Congress Catalog Card Number: 00-046375

Printed in the United States of America

Printing number
1 2 3 4 5 6 7 8 9 10

Library of Congress Cataloging-in-Publication Data

Baker's biographical dictionary of musicians.—Centennial ed. / Nicolas Slonimsky, editor emeritus.
     p. cm.
   Includes bibliographical references and discographies.
   Enl. ed. of: Baker's biographical dictionary of musicians. 8th ed. / rev. by Nicolas Slonimsky.
   ISBN 0-02-865525-7 (set : alk. paper) — ISBN 0-02- 865526-5 (vol. 1) — ISBN 0-02-865527-3 (vol. 2) — ISBN 0-02-865528-1 (vol. 3) — ISBN 0-02-865529-X (vol. 4) — ISBN 0-02-865530-3 (vol. 5) — ISBN 0-02-865571-0 (vol. 6)
    1. Music—Bio-bibliography—Dictionaries. I. Slonimsky, Nicolas, 1894- II. Slonimsky, Nicolas, 1894- Baker's biographical dictionary of musicians.

ML105.B16 2000
780'.92'2—dc21
  [B]
                                                          00-046375

ABBREVIATIONS

A.B.	Bachelor of Arts
ABC	American Broadcasting Company
A.M.	Master of Arts
ASCAP	American Society of Composers, Authors, and Publishers
assn./Assn.	association/Association
assoc.	associate
aug.	augmented
b.	born
B.A.	Bachelor of Arts
bar.	baritone
BBC	British Broadcasting Corporation
bjo.	banjo
B.M.	Bachelor of Music
brs.	brass
bs.	bass
CBC	Canadian Broadcasting Corporation
CBS	Columbia Broadcasting System
Coll.	College
cons./Cons.	conservatory/Conservatory
d.	died
dept./Dept.	department/Department
diss.	dissertation
D.M.A.	Doctor of Musical Arts
drm.	drums
ed(s).	edit(ed), editor(s), edition(s)
enl.	enlarged
f.	formed
flt.	flute
gtr.	guitar
har.	harmonica
H.S.	High School
IRCAM	Institut de Recherche et de Coordination Acoustique/Musique
ISCM	International Society for Contemporary Music
inst./Inst.	institute/Institute

kybd.	keyboards
M.A.	Master of Arts
mdln.	mandolin
M.M.	Master of Music
MS(S)	manuscript(s)
Mus.B.	Bachelor of Music
Mus.D.	Doctor of Music
Mus.M.	Master of Music
NAACP	National Association for the Advancement of Colored People
NBC	National Broadcasting Company
n.d.	no date
NEA	National Endowment for the Arts
NHK	Japan Broadcasting Company
no(s).	number(s)
N.Y.	New York
org.	organ
op(p).	opus
orch./Orch.	orchestra/Orchestra
p(p).	page(s)
PBS	Public Broadcasting Service
perc.	percussion
perf.	performance
Ph.D.	Doctor of Philosophy
phil./Phil.	philharmonic/Philharmonic
pno.	piano
posth.	posthumously
prof.	professor
publ.	publish(ed)
RAI	Radiotelevisione Italiana
rds.	reeds
rec.	recorded
rel.	released
rev.	revised
RIAS	Radio in the American Sector
S.	San, Santo, Santa
sax.	saxophone
sop.	soprano
Ss.	Santi, Sante
St(e).	Saint(e)
sym(s).	symphony (-ies)
synth.	synthesizer
tamb.	tamborine
ten.	tenor
tr.	translate(d), translation
trmb.	trombone
trpt.	trumpet
univ./Univ.	university/University
vln.	violin
voc.	vocals
vol(s).	volume(s)
WDR	Westdeutscher Rundfunk (West German Radio)
wdwnd.	woodwinds

L

(CONTINUED)

Lévy, Alexandre, Brazilian composer of French descent; b. São Paulo, Nov. 10, 1864; d. there, Jan. 17, 1892. He studied harmony with Emile Durand at the Paris Cons. His compositions include a Sym., which received a Columbus Celebration prize in 1892, *Comala*, symphonic poem, *Suite brasileira* for Orch., chamber music, and piano works (*Schumanniana, suite, Allegro appassionato*, etc.). Although his music was steeped in the European Romantic tradition and his technique was limited, he appears an important figure in Brazilian music because of his contribution to the nationalist movement in music. He was one of the earliest Brazilian composers to use native folk material in instrumental works.

BIBL.: G. Pimenta, *A. L.* (São Paulo, 1911).—NS/LK/DM

Lévy, Ernst, distinguished Swiss pianist, pedagogue, and composer; b. Basel, Nov. 18, 1895; d. Morges, April 19, 1981. He studied in Basel with Huber and Petri, and in Paris with Pugno. He was head of the piano master class at the Basel Cons. (1917–21), then founder-conductor of the Choeur Philharmonique in Paris (1928). In 1941 he went to the U.S., where he taught at the New England Cons. of Music in Boston (1941–45), Bennington (Vt.) Coll. (1946–51), the Univ. of Chicago (1951–54), the Mass. Inst. of Technology (1954–59), and Brooklyn Coll. of the City Univ. of N.Y. (1959–66). In 1966 he returned to Switzerland. He composed 15 syms. (1920–67), many choral works, chamber music, various pieces for solo instruments, etc. Among his publications are *Tone: A Study in Musical Acoustics* (with S. Levarie; Kent, Ohio, 1968; second ed., rev., 1980), *Des rapports entre la musique et l société suivi de réflexions* (Neuchâtel, 1979), *Musical Morphology: A Discourse and a Dictionary* (with S. Levarie; Kent, Ohio, 1983), and *A Theory of Harmony* (Albany, N.Y., 1985). —NS/LK/DM

Levy (originally, Lévy), Frank, Swiss-American cellist and composer, son of **Ernst Lévy**; b. Paris,

Oct. 15, 1930. He went to America with his father, and studied at the Juilliard School of Music in N.Y. (B.S., 1951) and at the Univ. of Chicago (M.A., 1954); also studied cello with Leonard Rose and Janos Starker in N.Y. He was a cellist in various orchs.

WORKS: *Ricercar* for 4 Cellos (1958); Sonata for Unaccompanied Cello (1959); Quintet for Flute and Strings (1959); Bassoon Concerto (1961); Trio for Clarinet, Horn, and Bassoon (1961); Sonata for Bassoon and Piano (1963); *Fantasy* for Tuba, Harp, Timpani, and Strings (1965); choruses and solo songs. —NS/LK/DM

Lévy, Heniot, Polish-American pianist, teacher, and composer; b. Warsaw, July 19, 1879; d. Chicago, June 16, 1946. He was a pupil at the Hochschule für Musik in Berlin, and of Bruch (composition). He made his debut as a pianist with the Berlin Phil. (1899); in 1900 he emigrated to America, and became a piano teacher at the American Cons. in Chicago. Among his works were *24 Variations on an Original Theme* for Orch. (Chicago, April 9, 1942), Piano Concerto, String Sextet, String Quintet, 2 piano quintets, 4 string quartets, 2 piano trios, Cello Sonata, numerous piano pieces, and songs. —NS/LK/DM

Levy, Jules, Bulgarian conductor and composer; b. Salonika, June 19, 1930. He studied in Sofia with Stoyanov at the Bulgarian State Cons., graduating in 1957. He then was active as a theater conductor.

WORKS: DRAMATIC: M u s i c a l s : *The Girl I Was in Love With* (1963); *The World Is Small* (1970); *The Phone Which...* (1975). B a l l e t : *Fair in Sofia* (1968). C h o r e o g r a p h i c O r a t o r i o : *Onward to the Rising World* (1973). ORCH.: *Youth Concerto* for Violin and Orch. (1953); 3 syms.: No. 1, *Life and Death* (1958), No. 2 (1970), and No. 3 (1976); *Divertimento-Concertante No. 1* for Trumpet and Pop Orch. (1961) and *No. 2* for Flute and Orch. (1971); *Overture-Poem* (1962); *The Blacksmith*, symphonic fantasy (1964); *Pirin Mountain Rhapsody* for Jazz and

Sym. Orchs. (1972). **OTHER**: *Masks,* string quartet (1974), and other chamber pieces; choral songs; popular music. —**NS/LK/DM**

Lévy, Lazare, distinguished French pianist and pedagogue; b. Brussels (of French parents), Jan. 18, 1882; d. Paris, Sept. 20, 1964. He studied piano with Diémer at the Paris Cons. (1894–98), where he was awarded first prize for piano; also studied harmony with Lavignac and composition with Gédalge there. He gave concerts with the principal orchs. of Europe; in 1920, succeeded Cortot as a prof. at the Paris Cons. He publ. numerous piano pieces.—**NS/LK/DM**

Levy, Marvin David, American composer; b. Passaic, N.J., Aug. 2, 1932. He studied composition with Philip James at N.Y.U., and with Luening at Columbia Univ. He was awarded 2 Guggenheim fellowships (1960, 1964) and 2 American Prix de Rome fellowships (1962–63; 1965). Levy showed a particular disposition toward the musical theater. In his vocal and instrumental writing, he adopted an expressionistic mode along atonal lines, in an ambience of cautiously dissonant harmonies vivified by a nervously asymmetric rhythmic pulse.

> **WORKS: DRAMATIC: O p e r a :** *Sotoba Komachi* (N.Y., April 7, 1957); *The Tower* (Sante Fe, Aug. 2, 1957); *Escorial* (N.Y., May 4, 1958); *Mourning Becomes Electra,* after O'Neill (N.Y., March 17, 1967). **M u s i c a l :** *The Balcony* (1981–87). **ORCH.:** *Caramoor Festival Overture* (1959); Sym. (Los Angeles, Dec. 15, 1960); *Kryos,* dance poem for Chamber Orch. (1961); Piano Concerto (Chicago, Dec. 3, 1970); *Trialogues I* and *II* (1972); *In memoriam W.H. Auden* (1974); *Arrows of Time* (Orlando, Fla., Oct. 3, 1988). **CHAMBER:** String Quartet (1955); *Rhapsody* for Violin, Clarinet, and Harp (1956); *Chassidic Suite* for Horn and Piano (1956). **VOCAL:** *Echoes* for Soprano and Ensemble (1956); *For the Time Being,* Christmas oratorio (1959); *One Person,* cantata for Alto and Orch. (1962); *Sacred Service* for the Park Avenue Synagogue in N.Y. (1964); *Masada,* oratorio for Narrator, Tenor, Chorus, and Orch. (1973; rev. version, Chicago, Oct. 15, 1987); *Canto de los Marranos* for Soprano and Orch. (1977). —**NS/LK/DM**

Lévy, Michel-Maurice, French composer; b. Ville-d'Avray, June 28, 1883; d. Paris, Jan. 24, 1965. He studied at the Paris Cons. with Lavignac and Leroux. From 1920 to 1932 he was popular as a musical parodist in vaudeville under the name of **Bétove** (i.e., Beethoven), under which name he wrote operettas *Pom-Pom* (1928), *Les Exploits galants du Baron de Crac* (1932), and *D'Artagnan* (1945). Under his own name he wrote the operas *Le Cloître* (Lyons, 1932) and *Dolores* (Paris, 1952), the operettas *Lydia* (Brussels, 1936) and *La Demoiselle de Carentan* (Paris, 1951), and *Les Trois Pantins de bois,* ballet suite for Orch., *Le Chant de la terre,* symphonic poem (1945), *Moïse,* "fresque lyrique" (Mulhouse, 1955), film music, choral works, and songs. —**NS/LK/DM**

Lewandowski, Louis, eminent German Jewish scholar; b. Wreschen, near Posen, April 3, 1821; d. Berlin, Feb. 3, 1894. He studied at the Academy of Music in Berlin. He was music director of the Berlin Synagogue from 1840, and established himself as a voice teacher. His greatest accomplishment was the compilation of the Jewish service music for use by Berlin's Jewish community; in his arrangements of the traditional tunes, Lewandowski applied the technique of German Romantic music, and often reduced the exotic and asymmetrical pattern of the Jewish cantilena to simple song meters; his compositions for organ also employed ordinary 19th-century harmonies. This treatment contributed to the popularity of Lewandowski's service music, but at the same time traduced the true spirit of Jewish cantillation, so that the more nationalistic Jewish scholars refused to accept it.—**NS/LK/DM**

Lewenthal, Raymond, American pianist; b. San Antonio, Tex., Aug. 29, 1926; d. Hudson, N.Y., Nov. 21, 1988. He was taken to Los Angeles as a child and studied piano with local teachers. He then enrolled at the Juilliard School of Music in N.Y. as a student of Samaroff; continued his studies in Europe with Cortot. Returning to the U.S., he devoted himself to performing the piano music of neglected Romantic composers, among them Thalberg, Hummel, and Henselt. Particularly meritorious was his redemption from undeserved oblivion of the voluminous output of Alkan. —**NS/LK/DM**

Lewin, David (Benjamin), American music theorist, teacher, and composer; b. N.Y., July 2, 1933. He studied piano, harmony, and composition with Steuermann (1945–50), mathematics at Harvard Univ. (B.A., 1954), and theory and composition with Sessions, Babbitt, Kim, and Cone at Princeton Univ. (M.F.A., 1958); also undertook further graduate work at Yale Univ. (M.A., 1980). He taught at the Univ. of Calif. at Berkeley (1961–67), the State Univ. of N.Y. at Stony Brook (1967–80), and Yale Univ. (1979–85), and then was a prof. at Harvard Univ. (from 1985). He held a Guggenheim fellowship (1983–84). He was president of the Soc. for Music Theory (1985–88). Lewin wrote numerous articles for various learned journals.

> **WORKS:** 4 Short Pieces for String Quartet (1956; rev. 1969); Viola Sonata (1957–58); *Essay on a Subject by Webern* for Chamber Orch. (1958); *Classical Variations on a Theme by Schoenberg* for Cello and Piano (1960); 2 Studies for Computer (1961); Fantasia for Organ (1962); *5 Characteristic Pieces* for 2 Pianos (1964); *Fantasy-Adagio* for Violin and Orch. (1963–66); *Quartet Piece* for String Quartet (1969); Woodwind Trio (1969); *Computer Music* for Computer (1970–71); *Just a Minute, Roger* for Piano (1978); *Fanfare* for Bass Clarinet, Cello, and Piano (1980); *For Piano* for Piano (1982); songs.—**NS/LK/DM**

Lewis, Sir Anthony (Carey), eminent English conductor, musicologist, composer, and teacher; b. Bermuda, March 2, 1915; d. Haslemere, June 5, 1983. He became an organ scholar at Peterhouse, Cambridge (1932); continued his studies with Dent at Cambridge (B.A. and Mus.B., 1935); also took courses with Boulanger in Paris (1934). He joined the music staff of the BBC (1935); then was the creator of its Third Programme (1946). From 1947 to 1968 he was a prof. of music at the

Univ. of Birmingham; also was dean of the faculty of fine arts there (1961–64). From 1968 to 1982 he served as principal of the Royal Academy of Music in London. In 1967 he was made a Commander of the Order of the British Empire. He was knighted in 1972. His specialty was the music of the Baroque period; he ed., conducted, and recorded works by Purcell, Rameau, and Handel. He publ. *The Language of Purcell* (Hull, 1968); was a founder and ed. of the prestigious series Musica Britannica (1951). His compositions include *Choral Overture* (1938), *Elegy and Capriccio* for Trumpet and Orch. (1947), Trumpet Concerto (1950), *A Tribute of Praise* for Voices (1951), and Horn Concerto (1959).—**NS/LK/DM**

Lewis, Daniel, American conductor and pedagogue; b. Flagstaff, Ariz., May 10, 1925. He studied composition with Marcelli in San Diego (1939–41) and received violin lessons in Boston. During World War II, he saw military service in Hawaii, where he was concertmaster of the Honolulu Sym. Orch., first violinist in the U.S. Navy String Quartet, and a conductor of navy ensembles. After the War, he pursued his education at San Diego State Coll. (B.M., 1949) and at the Claremont (Calif.) Graduate School (M.A., 1950). He was asst. conductor (1954–56) and assoc. conductor and concertmaster (1956–59) of the San Diego Sym. Orch. In 1959 he held a Fulbright scholarship and studied with Eugen Jochum at the Munich Hochschule für Musik and with Karajan in Salzburg. After conducting the La Jolla (Calif.) Sym. Orch. (1961–69) and the Orange County (Calif.) Sym. Orch. (1966–70), he was music director of the Pasadena (Calif.) Sym. Orch. (1972–84). He also appeared as a guest conductor with major American orchs. He taught at Calif. State Univ. at Fullerton (1963–70) and at the Univ. of Southern Calif. in Los Angeles (from 1970).—**NS/LK/DM**

Lewis, (Big) Ed (actually, **Edward**), jazz trumpeter; b. Eagle City, Okla., Jan. 22, 1909; d. Sept. 18, 1985. His father was trumpeter Oscar Lewis. The family moved to Kansas City, Mo., before Ed started school. He began on baritone horn and marched alongside his father in Shelly Bradford's Brass Band. He ceased playing temporarily until 1924, then again took up baritone horn and joined a band led by Jerry Westbrook for a year. He switched to trumpet, spent two months in Paul Bank's Band, then worked with pianist-singer Laura Rucker before spending six years with Bennie Moten (1926–32). He left in February 1932 and joined the newly formed Thamon Hayes and his Kansas City Skyrockets, which did extensive touring and residencies in Chicago. Lewis returned to Kansas City and worked for various leaders including Pete Johnson and Jay McShann. He joined Count Basie in February 1937 and remained until September 1948. After that, he left music and worked as a cab driver in N.Y., and later became motorman on a N.Y. subway. He resumed playing again in 1954, and soon organized his own 12-piece band which gigged in and around N.Y. He continued to play gigs in N.Y. through the early 1960s.—**JC/LP**

Lewis, George (originally **Zeno, George Louis Francis**), early New Orleans clarinetist, alto saxophonist; b. New Orleans, La., July 13, 1900; d. there,

Dec. 31, 1968. The family name was originally Zenon. He bought a toy fife at the age of seven, then saved to buy his first clarinet at 16. By 1917 he was playing in the young musicians' band the Black Eagles. For the succeeding five years he worked with various leaders, including Buddie Petit, Henry "Kid" Rena, Kid Ory, Chris Kelly, Leonard Parker, among others and also played in the Pacific Brass Band. He formed his own band in 1923 and that same year began a long association with the Eureka Brass Band. In 1928 he had to stop playing temporarily because of a broken leg, but he then joined Arnold DuPas's Olympia Band and remained until 1932. He played briefly with trumpeter Evan Thomas's Band in Crowley, La. (Bunk Johnson played second trumpet), until the leader was murdered on the stand at a dance in Rayne (1932). After returning to New Orleans, he worked as a stevedore, continued to gig, and played in parades with Kid Howard and the Eureka; he subsequently played a residency at the Harmony Inn (New Orleans), mainly on alto sax. In 1942 he took part in the first Bunk Johnson recordings, which placed him at the forefront of the traditional revival. He continued to lead his own band in New Orleans, including a residency at the Gypsy Pea Room in 1943. He left New Orleans in September 1945 to work in N.Y. with Bunk Johnson's Band. They disbanded in 1946 and George returned home and continued to lead his own small groups. In the summer of 1946 Lewis (with Kid Howard's Brass Band) took part in the filming of *New Orleans*, but the sequence was not used in the film. He had a residency at Manny's Tavern (1947–48), playing clarinet and alto sax. From 1949 until 1951 he worked mainly at the El Morocco Club on Bourbon Street with the trumpeter Elmer Talbot, and at the Dream Room, which was broadcast over WDSU in 1950 and 1951. In 1952 he worked at the Hangover Club in San Francisco with Lizzie Miles, then began regular touring, leading his own band and occasionally working as a soloist. By this time he was considered by many to be the central figure in the "traditional" jazz revival. The George Lewis Ragtime Band earned regular work in New Orleans (at Preservation Hall 1961–68) as well as long residencies on the West coast, festival work, and tours to Europe and Japan several times. Though he had to contend with failing health for many of his later years, he continued to play regularly until late 1968, and last worked at the Preservation Hall (New Orleans). His style was a major influence on Sammy Rimington, Tommy Sancton, and Woody Allen, among others.

DISC.: *Echos of New Orleans, Vol. 1* (1943); *G. L.'s New Orleans Stomp* (1943); *G. L. with Kid Shots Mad* (1944); *With Kid Shots* (1944); *American Music by G. L.* (1945); *G. L. of New Orleans* (1946); *At Herbert Otto's Party* (1949); *Jazz in the Classic New Orleans* (1950); *G. L. Jam Session* (1950); *G. L. and His New Orleans* (1951); *G. L.'s Ragtime Band of New Orleans* (1952); *Beverly Caverns Sessions* (1953); *G. L. at Club Hangover* (1953); *G. L.'s Ragtime Band of New Orleans* (1953); *Hot Creole Jazz: 1953* (1953); *Sounds of New Orleans, Vol. 7* (1953); *G. L. Concert!* (1954); *G. L.'s Ragtime Band of New Orleans* (1954); *Jazz at Vespers* (1954); *Jazz at the Ohio Union* (1954); *New Orleans Music* (1954); *G. L. & His New Orleans* (1955); *G. L. with Guest Artist* (1955); *G. L.'s New Orleans Stomp* (1955); *New Orleans Stompers* (1955); *G. L. in Hi-Fi* (1956); *G. L., Vol. 1* (1956); *On Stage: G. L. Concert* (1956); *Spirituals in*

Ragtime (1956); *Doctor Jazz* (1957); *G. L./Paul Barbarin* (1957); *G. L. and Turk Murphy* (1957); *On Parade* (1958); *Perennial G. L.* (1958); *Singing Clarinet* (1958); *Oh, Didn't He Ramble!* (1959); *Blues from the Bayou* (1960); *G. L.'s Dixieland Band* (1960); *Hot Time in the Old Town Tonight* (1960); *G. L. Band* (1962); *Jazz at Preservation Hall* (1962); *At the San Jacinto Hall* (1964); *G. L. in Japan* (1964); *In Concert* (1965); *Reunion with Don Ewell* (1966).

BIBL.: Tom Bethell, *G. L.: A Jazzman from New Orleans* (Berkeley, London, 1977); Ann Fairbairn, *Call Him George* (N.Y., 1969); Eberhard Kraut, *G. L.: Streifzug durch ein Musikerleben* (Menden, Germany, 1980).—JC/MM/LP

Lewis, Henry, black American conductor; b. Los Angeles, Oct. 16, 1932; d. N.Y., Jan. 26, 1996. He learned to play piano and string instruments as a child, and at the age of 16 he was engaged as a double-bass player in the Los Angeles Phil. From 1955 to 1959 he played double bass in the 7th Army Sym. Orch. overseas, and also conducted it in Germany and the Netherlands. Returning to the U.S., he founded the Los Angeles Chamber Orch.; in 1963, traveled with it in Europe under the auspices of the State Dept. From 1968 to 1976 he was music director of the N.J. Sym. Orch. in Newark; subsequently conducted opera and orch. guest engagements. From 1989 to 1991 he was chief conductor of the Radio Sym. Orch. in Hilversum. He married **Marilyn Horne** in 1960, but they were separated in 1976. —NS/LK/DM

Lewis, Jerry Lee, one of the most outrageous figures of 1950s rock 'n' roll who later transitioned into being a country star; b. Ferriday, La., Sept. 29, 1935. Jerry Lee Lewis began playing at the age of eight, making his first public appearance at a Natchez Ford dealership in 1949 at the age of 14. Performing on weekends for four years, he built a solid regional following. In February 1956 Lewis traveled to Memphis to audition for Sun Records, recording a demonstration tape for Jack Clement in the absence of owner Sam Phillips. Returning to Memphis a month later, he discovered that Phillips liked the recordings, resulting in a recording contract. His first single, "Crazy Arms," became a moderate country hit. On Dec. 4, 1956, Elvis Presley joined Lewis and Sun stalwarts Carl Perkins and Johnny Cash in informally singing and playing a number of gospel songs. Unknown to them, the performance was recorded. Those recordings by the so-called "Million Dollar Quartet" were bootlegged for years and available in Europe for years before their eventual release in the U.S. in 1990.

In 1957, Jerry Lee Lewis's second single, "Whole Lotta Shakin' Going On," became a smash country-and-western, R&B and pop hit, bolstered by his appearance on the Steve Allen television show. Supported by backup musicians such as guitarists Hank Garland and Roland Janes and bassist Billy Lee Riley, Lewis quickly scored smash three-way crossover hits with "Great Balls of Fire" and "Breathless" (both written by Otis Blackwell), and the title song to the film *High School Confidential*. He also appeared in the 1957 film *Jamboree*.

In May 1958, Jerry Lee Lewis arrived in England for his first British tour, but it was canceled by the fifth day after the British press revealed, in rather lurid terms, that he was traveling with his 13-year-old second cousin–wife, Myra. Back home, he managed a minor pop hit with "Break-Up," but subsequent records were banned by many radio stations. Lewis was unable to score even a moderate hit until 1961 when his version of Ray Charles's "What'd I Say" made all three charts. Despite the fading fortunes of Sun Records, Lewis continued to record for the label until 1963.

Jerry Lee Lewis subsequently switched to the Smash subsidiary of Mercury Records, but commercial success eluded him as he criss-crossed the country playing county fairs, package shows, gymnasiums, and roadhouses. His dynamic stage show was captured on several live albums, including *Live at the Star Club* (recorded in 1964 with The Nashville Teens and eventually released on Rhino in 1992) and *The Greatest Live Show on Earth*. Finally, in 1968, Lewis scored the first of a series of major country-and-western hits with "Another Place Another Time," followed by the classic "What's Made Milwaukee Famous (Made a Loser Out of Me)." Subsequent top country-only hits on Smash included "She Still Comes Around (To Love What's Left of Me)," "To Make Love Sweeter for You," "One Has My Name (The Other Has My Heart)" (a top country hit for Jimmy Wakely in 1948), "She Even Woke Me Up to Say Goodbye" and "Once More with Feeling."

In 1970 Jerry Lee Lewis moved to the parent label Mercury for smash country hits such as "There Must Be More to Love Than This," "Touching Home," "Would You Take Another Chance on Me" backed with Kris Kristofferson's "Me and Bobby McGee" (a moderate pop hit), "Sometimes a Memory Ain't Enough" and "He Can't Fill My Shoes." In 1973 he recorded his best-selling album, *The Session*, in London with guitarists Peter Frampton, Rory Gallagher, Albert and Alvin Lee. Lewis's late-1970s country hits included "Let's Put It Back Together Again" and the classic "Middle Age Crazy."

In 1978 Jerry Lee Lewis switched to Elektra Records, where he scored a major country hit with the autobiographical "Rockin' My Life Away" and a smash country hit (his last) with "Thirty Nine and Holding." His three Elektra albums were later anthologized by Warner Brothers as *Rockin' My Life Away*. In the early 1980s, Lewis moved to MCA Records for two albums. Live performances with guitarist James Burton, recorded at The Palomino Club in L. A. in 1979–81 and 1985, were released on Tomato Records in the 1990s. In 1982 Lewis joined Johnny Cash and Carl Perkins to record *The Survivors* for Columbia Records, and the three later joined Roy Orbison to record *Class of '55* for Columbia in 1986.

During the 1980s Jerry Lee Lewis endured declining health, the deaths of wives numbers four and five, and protracted tax disputes with the Internal Revenue Service. He was inducted into the Rock and Roll Hall of Fame in its inaugural year, 1986. The 1989 movie *Great Balls of Fire*, starring Dennis Quaid, portrayed the early years of his career, and the soundtrack album included eight newly recorded versions of his classics. In the 1990s, Lewis opened the nightclub Jerry Lee Lewis's

Spot in Memphis, and opened his home to tourists in order to pay off his tax debt. In 1995 Sire Records released Lewis's first full studio album in more than ten years, *Young Blood*, recorded with guitarists James Burton and Al Anderson.

DISC.: *Jerry Lee Lewis* (1958); *Jerry Lee's Greatest* (1962); *Rockin' with Jerry Lee Lewis* (1963); *Golden Hits* (1964); *The Greatest Live Show on Earth* (1964); *The Return of Rock!* (1965); *The Return of Rock* (1967); *Unlimited* (1968); *The Legend of Jerry Lee Lewis* (1969); *Live at the International, Las Vegas* (1970); *Country Songs for City Folks* (1970); *In Loving Memories* (1971); *There Must Be More to Love Than This* (1971); *Touching Home* (1971); *Would You Take Another Chance of Me?* (1971); *Who's Gonna Play This Old Piano* (1972); *The "Killer" Rocks On* (1972); *The Session* (1973); *Sometimes a Memory Ain't Enough* (1973); *Southern Roots* (1974); *I-40 Country* (1974); *Boogie Woogie Country Man* (1975); *Odd Man In* (1976); *Country Class* (1976); *Country Memories* (1977); *Keeps Rockin'* (1978); *Jerry Lee Lewis* (1979); *When Two Worlds Collide* (1980); *Killer Country* (1980); *My Fingers Do the Talkin'* (1983); *I Am What I Am* (1984); *I'm on Fire* (1985); *Wild One: Rare Tracks from Jerry Lee Lewis* (rec. 1957–1963; rel. 1989); *Great Balls of Fire* (music from soundtrack, 1989); *The Complete Palomino Club Club Recordings* (rec. 1979–81, 1985; rel. 1991); *Honky Tonk Rock 'n' Roll* (1991); *Rockin' My Life Away* (rec. at the Palomino Club; 1992); *Heartbreak* (1992); *Rocket 88* (rec. at the Palomino Club; 1992); *Live at the Star Club, Hamburg, 1964* (with Nashville Teens, 1992); *Young Blood* (1995); *Solid Gold Rock 'n' Roll, Vol. 2*; *Live at the Vapors Club* (rec. in Memphis, 1994); *Piano Man* (1997); *Pretty Much Country*. **JERRY LEE LEWIS AND LINDA GAIL LEWIS:** *Together* (1969). **JERRY LEE LEWIS AND JOHNNY CASH:** *Sunday Down South* (1971); *Sing Hank Williams* (1971). **JERRY LEE LEWIS, CARL PERKINS, ELVIS PRESLEY, AND JOHNNY CASH:** *The Million Dollar Quartet* (1990). **JERRY LEE LEWIS, JOHNNY CASH, AND CARL PERKINS:** *The Survivors* (1982). **JERRY LEE LEWIS, JOHNNY CASH, ROY ORBISON, AND CARL PERKINS:** *Class of '55* (1986).

BIBL.: R. J. Cain, *Whole Lotta Shakin' Goin' On* (N.Y., 1981); R. Palmer, *Jerry Lee Lewis Rocks!* (N.Y., 1981); M. Lewis with M. Silver, *Great Balls of Fire: The Uncensored Story of J. L. L.* (N.Y., 1982); N. Tosches, *Hellfire: The J. L. L. Story* (N.Y., 1982); J. Guterman. *Rockin' My Life Away: Listening to J. L. L.* (Nashville, Tenn., 1991).—**BH**

Lewis, John (Aaron), seminal jazz pianist, composer; b. LaGrange, Ill., May 3, 1920. His family moved to Albuquerque when he was quite young. Lewis saw Lester Young there with the Young family's band in 1926. He studied anthropology and music at the Univ. of N.Mex. He moved to N.Y. by the mid-1940s. Drummer Kenny Clarke recommended that Lewis replace Thelonious Monk in Dizzy Gillespie's band in 1946; Milt Jackson was also in the band. After the band's demise, Lewis and Clarke stayed in Paris in 1947. Lewis was a steady freelance player and arranger in the late 1940s and early 1950s, working with Illinois Jacquet, Charlie Parker (1948), Miles Davis (nonet broadcasts in 1948 and recordings in 1949–51), and Lester Young. It is said that he wrote "Milestones" for Davis's first recording session as a leader in 1948. He completed his studies at the Manhattan School of Music (M.A., 1953). Jackson led sessions with Lewis and Clarke in 1947 and 1951, and in April 1952, with Percy Heath playing bass. After these

last recording sessions, Lewis accompanied Ella Fitzgerald on tour. Upon his return, Lewis, Jackson, Heath, and Clarke began recording in December of 1952 as the Modern Jazz Quartet (MJQ), a group that over the course of 22 years became one of the focal points of both "cool" and "classical" jazz, a merger known as Third Stream. To this end he composed and arranged works that, while leaving room for jazz improvisation, included such formal devices as fugal counterpoint. He also composed extended compositions, requiring the additional forces of string quartet or orch., several movie scores (*Odds Against Tomorrow, No Sun in Venice,* a.k.a. *One Never Knows,* in 1958; *A Milanese Story*), and a ballet, *Original Sin* (San Francisco Ballet, March 1961). Significantly, the MJQ abandoned the usual nightclub habitat of jazz in favor of formal, tuxedoed performances in concert halls. The personnel were stable except that in 1955 Connie Kay replaced Kenny Clarke. The MJQ disbanded in 1974, but reformed in 1981, and have had several reunion concerts. In between Lewis led a sextet. He taught at the Lenox School of Jazz in the summers of 1958–61, and He has been a professor of music at City Coll. of N.Y. since 1977. The MJQ owed much of its success to John Lewis's compositions. As a soloist he is capable of creating ecstatic intensity on the blues. His interests in classical music, though often publicized, appear to be confined to the lighter dance aspects of Baroque and Renaissance music. He was the cofounder with Gary Giddins and conductor of the American Jazz Orch. from 1986–90.

DISC.: *Modern Jazz Society* (1955); *Afternoon in Paris* (1956); *Grand Encounter* (1956); *J. L. Piano* (1956); *European Windows* (1958); *Improvised Meditations and Excursions* (1959); *Odds Against Tomorrow* (1959); *Golden Striker* (1960); *Jazz Abstractions* (1960); *Wonderful World of Jazz* (1960); *Original Sin* (1961); *Animal Dance* (1962); *Essence* (1962); *European Encounter* (1962); *Milanese Story* (1962); *P.O.V.* (1976); *Evening with Two Grand Pianos* (1979); *Kansas City Breaks* (1982); *Bridge Game* (1984); *Chess Game, Vols. 1 & 2* (1987); *Garden of Delight* (1987); *Midnight in Paris* (1988); *Private Concert* (1991).

BIBL.: Nat Hentoff, *John Lewis* (N.Y., 1960); Thierry Lalo, *John Lewis* (Donzere, France, 1992).—**NS/LP**

Lewis, Keith, New Zealand tenor; b. Methven, Oct. 6, 1950. Following training in New Zealand, he pursued studies at the London Opera Centre. In 1976 he won the Kathleen Ferrier Memorial Scholarship and in 1979 the John Christie Award. He appeared with the Chelsea Opera Group and at the English Bach Festival in 1976. In 1977 he made his debut as Don Ottavio with the Glyndebourne Touring Opera, and then sang that role for his first appearance at the Glyndebourne Festival in 1978. In the latter year he also sang Tebaldo in *I Capuleti e i Montecchi* at London's Covent Garden. After appearing as Tamino at the English National Opera in London in 1982, he made his U.S. debut as Don Ottavio in San Francisco in 1984. In 1989 he sang for the first time at the Salzburg Festival as Berlioz's Faust with the Chicago Sym. Orch. under Solti's direction. In 1993 he appeared as Oedipus Rex in N.Y. He was engaged as Alwa in *Lulu* at the Berlin State Opera in 1997. As a concert artist,

Lewis has appeared with major orchs. on both sides of the Atlantic, principally in works by Bach, Handel, Beethoven, Haydn, Mozart, Berlioz, and Mendelssohn. —NS/LK/DM

Lewis, Ramsey, pianist who charted with his own brand of pop jazz through the 1960s and 1970s (b. Chicago, May 27, 1935). Ramsey Lewis turned a couple of instrumental covers of pop tunes into a career that has spanned five decades and helped spawn the careers of artists ranging from Maurice White to Minnie Ripperton. He started playing piano at four, learning the standard classical repertoire. In his teens, he played in church and was asked by one of his fellow church musicians if he wanted to sit in with his jazz band, called the Cleffs. Lewis had previously only limited exposure to jazz, but working with the Cleffs, it became a major force in his life.

While at the Chicago Coll. of Music, Lewis formed a trio with Eldee Young and Redd Holt. The trio signed to Chess Records's Argo imprint and started recording and playing regularly enough that Lewis could leave his job as a record store manager. Their music reflected Lewis's passions for jazz, gospel, and the classical repertoire, with the emphasis on the former two. In 1965, the trio recorded an instrumental version of Dobie Gray's "The 'In' Crowd." With its gospel phrasing, jazzy chords, and breezy rhythm, it became a major hit during the summer of 1965, reaching #5 and propelling the album of the same name to #2. The song won a Grammy Award for Best Jazz Instrumental, Individual/Group. Several months later he took a cover of the McCoys' chart topper "Hang On Sloopy" to #11 (another version of the song would win a Best R&B Instrumental Grammy several years later) and the Beatles "A Hard Day's Night": to #29, with the album *Hang On Ramsey!* rising to #15. Another track on the album, "Hold It Right There," took the Grammy Award for Best R&B Group—Vocal/Instrumental. Young and Holt left to form their own trio, releasing a few funk hits as Young Holt Unlimited on Brunswick. Lewis replaced them with Cleveland Eaton on bass and drummer Maurice White. With the new rhythm section, he cut an instrumental version of the gospel standard "Wade in the Water." Taking off from the covers, he cut *Mother Nature's Son*, a collection of Beatles songs recorded with a symphony orchestra. Late in the 1960s, he became one of the first jazz musicians to include synthesizers in his music.

White left to form his own band, Earth Wind and Fire, but worked with Lewis on 1975's *Sun Goddess*, the entire EWF band joining Lewis on two of the tracks. That album hit #12 and went gold. Through the 1970s and 1980s, Lewis continued to record in a variety of formats, from records with large orchestras to trio dates. He participated in the Jazz Explosion All-Stars tour in 1986, working with a band that included Stanley Clarke, Roy Ayers, Freddie Hubbard, Noel Pointer, Tom Browne, and numerous others. In the 1990s, he signed with GRP, working extensively with his son Frayne. Another son, Bobby, has played drums for the group Immature and Tupac Shakur. In addition to an active schedule of recording and tours, Lewis has hosted the morning show on WNUA, winning a *Radio and Records* Personality of the Year award in 1999. A weekly version of the show is syndicated nationally, and he hosts a weekly jazz program for BET cable television.

Disc.: *Ramsey Lewis and His Gentlemen of Swing* (1958); *Lem Winchester and the Ramsey Lewis Trio* (1958); *Down to Earth* (1958); *An Hour with the Ramsey Lewis Trio* (1959); *Sound of Christmas* (1960); *Stretchin' Out* (1960); *Ramsey Lewis Trio in Chicago* (live; 1960); *More Music from the Soil* (1961); *Never on Sunday* (1961); *Bossa Nova* (1962); *Country Meets the Blues* (1962); *Sound of Spring* (1964); *Pot Luck* (1964); *Barefoot Sunday Blues* (1964); *The Ramsey Lewis Trio at the Bohemian Caverns* (1964); *Bach to the Blues* (1964); *You Better Believe Me* (1964); *Choice* (1965); *Hang On Ramsey* (1965); *More Sounds of Christmas* (1965); *The In Crowd* (live; 1965); *Swingin'* (1966); *Wade in the Water* (live; 1966); *Goin' Latin* (1967); *Movie Album* (1967); *Dancing in the Street* (1968); *Ramsey Lewis Trio* (1968); *Up Pops Ramsey* (1968); *Mother Nature's Son* (1968); *Maiden Voyage* (1968); *Them Changes* (1970); *Back to the Roots* (1971); *Another Voyage* (1971); *Upendo Ni Pamoja* (1972); *Piano Player* (1972); *Inside* (1972); *Tobacco Road* (1972); *Funky Serenity* (1973); *Groover* (1974); *Sun Goddess* (1974); *Don't It Feel Good* (1975); *Solid Ivory* (1975); *Live in Tokyo* (1975); *Salongo* (1976); *Love Notes* (1977); *Tequila Mockingbird* (1977); *Ramsey* (1979); *Solar Wind* (1980); *Routes* (1980); *3 Piece Suite* (1981); *Live at the Savoy* (1981); *Chance Encounter* (1982); *Les Fleurs* (1983); *The Two of Us* (1984); *Keys to the City* (1987); *We Meet Again* (1988); *A Classic Encounter* (1988); *Urban Renewal* (1989); *Fantasy* (1991); *Ivory Pyramid* (1992); *Sky Islands* (1993); *Between the Keys* (1995); *Dance of Your Soul* (1997); *Hang On Sloopy* (1998); *In Concert 1965* (live; 1998); *Appassionata* (1999).—HB

Lewis, Richard (real name, **Thomas Thomas**), noted English tenor; b. Manchester, May 10, 1914; d. Eastbourne, Nov. 13, 1990. He studied with T.W. Evans, then with Norman Allin at the Royal Manchester Coll. of Music (1939–41) and at the Royal Academy of Music in London (1945). He made his operatic debut with the Carl Rosa Opera Co. in 1939. From 1947 he sang at the Glyndebourne Festivals and at London's Covent Garden. He sang with the San Francisco Opera (1955–60), then appeared there as a guest artist (1962–68). He toured extensively as a concert and oratorio singer. In 1963 he was named a Commander of the Order of the British Empire. His repertoire was extensive, including roles in operas ranging from Monteverdi and Mozart to Schoenberg, Britten, and Tippett.

Bibl.: N. Ross-Russell, *There Will I Sing: The Making of a Tenor: A Biography of R. L. CBE* (London, 1996).—NS/LK/DM

Lewis, Robert Hall, American composer and teacher; b. Portland, Ore., April 22, 1926; d. Baltimore, March 22, 1996. He studied with Rogers and Hanson at the Eastman School of Music in Rochester, N.Y. (B.M., 1949; M.M., 1951; Ph.D., 1964), Boulanger and Bigot in Paris (1952–53), and Apostel, Krenek, and Schiske in Vienna (1955–57), and also received instruction in conducting from Monteux in Hancock, Maine (1954). He taught at Goucher Coll. and the Peabody Cons. of Music in Baltimore (from 1958); also was on the faculty of Johns Hopkins Univ. (1969–80). He held 2 Fulbright scholarships (1955–57) and 2 Guggenheim fellowships (1966, 1980).

Works: ORCH.: *Poem* for Strings (1949); *Concert Overture* (1951); *Sinfonia, Expression for Orchestra* (1955); *Prelude and*

Finale (1959); *Designs* (1963); 4 syms. (1964; 1971; 1982–85; 1990); *Music* for 12 Players (1965); *3 Pieces* (1965; rev. 1966); Concerto for Chamber Orch. (1967; rev. 1972); *Intermezzi* (1972); *Nuances II* (1975); *Osservazioni II* for Winds, Keyboard, Harpsichord, and Percussion (1978); *Moto* (1980); *Atto* for Strings (1981); Concerto for Strings, 4 Trumpets, Harps, and Piano (1984); *Destini* for Strings and Winds (1985); *Invenzione* (1988); *3 Movements on Scenes of Hieronymous Bosch* (1989); *Images and Dialogues* (1992); *Ariosi* (1995); *Scena* for Strings (1995). **CHAMBER:** 4 string quartets (1956, 1962, 1981, 1993); Trio for Clarinet, Violin, and Piano (1966); *Monophonies I-IX* for Winds (1966–77); *Tangents* for Double Brass Quartet (1968); Violin Sonata (1968); *Inflections I* for Double Bass (1969) and *II* for Piano Trio (1970); *Serenades I* for Piano (1970), *II* for Flute, Piccolo, Cello, and Piano (1976), and *III* for Brass Quintet (1982); *Fantasiemusik I* for Cello and Piano (1973), *II* for Clarinet and Piano (1978), and *III* for Saxophone, Piano, and Percussion (1984); *Combinazioni I* for Clarinet, Violin, Cello, and Piano (1974), *II* for 8 Percussion and Piano (1974), *III* for Narrator, Oboe, English Horn, and Percussion (1977), *IV* for Cello and Piano (1977), and *V* for 4 Violas (1982); *Osservazioni I* for Flutes, Piano, and Percussion (1975); *A due I* for Flute, Piccolo, Alto Flute, and Harp (1981), *II* for Oboe, English Horn, and Percussion (1981), *III* for Bassoon and Harp (1985), *IV* for Soprano and Piano (1986), and *VII* for Bassoon and Trumpet (1991); Wind Quintet (1983); Duo for Cello and Percussion (1987); *Dimensioni* for Clarinet, Violin, Viola, Cello, and Piano (1988); *9 Visions* for Piano Trio (1992); *Monologo* for Timpanist (1992); *Ottetto* (1994). **VOCAL:** *Acquainted with the Night* for Soprano and Chamber Orch. (1951); 5 Songs for Soprano, Clarinet, Horn, Cello, and Piano (1957); 2 madrigals for Chorus (1972); *3 Prayers of Jane Austen* for Small Chorus, Piano, and Percussion (1977); *Kantaten* for Chorus and Piano (1980); *Monophony X* for Soprano (1983).—**NS/LK/DM**

Lewis, Sabby (William Sebastian), jazz pianist, leader, arranger; b. Middleburg, N.C., Nov. 1, 1914; d. Boston, Mass., July 9, 1994. A legend in Boston, yet little known elsewhere, his fine band featured Big Nick Nicholas and Paul Gonsalves. Sabby was raised in Philadelphia. As a child he hated playing the piano, but his mother insisted that he learn. When, as a teenager, he discovered that the piano was a good way to attract girls, he became enthusiastic. He moved to Boston in 1932 and began gigging on piano. His first professional work came with Tasker Crosson's Ten Statesmen (1934). In 1936 he formed his own seven-piece band for a residency in Wilmington, Mass., then led a small band in Boston and N.Y., before augmenting it in the early 1940s. He led his own big band for several years, including a residency at Club Zanzibar, N.Y. (1944). He also became Boston's first black disc jockey in the late 1940s. During the 1950s he reverted to a small group. Throughout the 1960s continued to lead his own band, mainly active in Boston. He was temporarily absent from music in 1963 due to injuries sustained in a car crash. He worked primarily in New England during the 1970s. He died at Mass. General Hospital after a brief illness.—**JC/LP**

Lewis, Sam(uel) M., American lyricist; b. N.Y., Oct. 25, 1885; d. there, Nov. 22, 1959. Lewis was one of the most successful lyricists writing in Tin Pan Alley from 1910 through the 1930s. His hit songs included "Rock-a-Bye Your Baby with a Dixie Melody," "My Mammy," "Dinah," and "Five Foot Two, Eyes of Blue (Has Anybody Seen My Girl)?" (all cowritten with his longtime partner, Joe Young). He was particularly adept at catching the tone of the times, whether that meant reflecting the patriotism of World War I in "Just a Baby's Prayer at Twilight (For Her Daddy over There)," the optimism of the 1920s in "I'm Sitting on Top of the World," or the pessimism of the Depression years of the 1930s in "Gloomy Sunday."

Lewis was the son of a tailor. He had a public-school education that ended in his teens, after which he held three jobs: he worked as a runner at a Wall Street brokerage until the stock exchange closed in mid-afternoon, then at a Broadway ticket office until the theaters opened in the evening; then at night he sang at such clubs as the Brighton Café in the Bowery district.

Lewis wrote his first successful song, "Never Do Nothing for Nobody that Does Nothing for You," at 16; it was popularized by May Irwin and Sis Hopkins. By the age of 18 he was writing both songs and vaudeville skits for such entertainers as George Jessel, Lew Dockstader, and Van and Schenck. He had his first song interpolated into a Broadway musical when "Mother Pin a Rose on Me" (music by Bob Adams and Paul Schindler, lyrics also by Adams) was used in *Coming thro' the Rye* (N.Y., Jan. 9, 1906). In 1910 he opened an office in the Shubert building in the Times Square area. Around the same time, he married Ann O'Brien; she died in 1955.

Lewis wrote several lyrics to tunes by Kerry Mills for *The Fascinating Widow* (N.Y., Sept. 11, 1911). In 1914 the Haydn Quartet scored its final record hit with his "'Cross the Great Divide (I'll Wait for You)" (music by George W. Meyer). Later the same year, Henry Burr had a hit with "When You're a Long, Long Way from Home" (music by Meyer), the first successful song on which Lewis collaborated with Joe Young (1889–1939).

The year 1915 brought two more hits: "My Little Girl" (music by Albert Von Tilzer, lyrics also by Will Dillon), which had popular recordings by the duos of Burr and Albert Campbell and Ada Jones and Will Robbins, and "There's a Little Lane without a Turning on the Way to Home Sweet Home" (music by Meyer), another big seller for Burr. Burr also scored a hit with "My Mother's Rosary (or, Ten Baby Fingers and Ten Baby Toes)" (music by Meyer) in the spring of 1916. By then Lewis, working for music publishers Waterson, [Irving] Berlin, and Snyder, had formed long-standing alliances with two men who would share his enormous success, Young and Al Jolson.

Lewis and Young launched a lyric-writing team that lasted until 1930, and they contributed the comic song "Where Did Robinson Crusoe Go with Friday on Saturday Night?" (music by Meyer) to the Jolson show *Robinson Crusoe Jr.* (N.Y., Feb. 17, 1916). Jolson recorded the hit version of the song, the first of many Lewis-Young lyrics he would sing. Also in 1916, Lewis and Young wrote "If I Knock the 'L' Out of Kelly (It Would Still Be Kelly to Me)" (music by Bert Grant) for the musical *Step This Way* (N.Y., May 29, 1916). The biggest hit recording was by Marguerite Farrell, though Jones also recorded it successfully. Outside of the theater, Lewis and Young had hits during the year with "Arrah Go On (I'm Gonna Go Back to Oregon)" (music by Grant), introduced by Maggie Cline and recorded by the Peerless Quartet, and "I'm Gonna Make Hay While the Sun Shines in Virginia" (music by Archie Gottler), the first hit for Marion Harris. Van and Schenck had a best-selling record in 1917 with "Huckleberry Finn" (music and lyrics by Lewis, Young, and Cliff Hess).

Early in 1918, Irving Kaufman scored a hit with "I'm All Bound 'Round with the Mason-Dixon Line" (music by Jean Schwartz). A couple of months later Jolson had an even bigger hit with it. By then he was interpolating songs with Lewis-Young lyrics into his latest show, *Sinbad* (N.Y., Feb. 14, 1918), songs that would be identified with him for the rest of his career. Chief among these was "Rock-a-Bye Your Baby with a Dixie Melody" (music by Schwartz), which became a massive hit in the summer and was also successfully recorded by Arthur Fields. The timely World War I ditty "Hello, Central, Give Me No Man's Land" (music by Schwartz) was also a big hit for Jolson. After *Sinbad*'s 164-performance run in N.Y., Jolson took it on tour around the country, continuing to interpolate new songs into it. Meanwhile, Burr recorded the World War I–themed "Just a Baby's Prayer at Twilight (For Her Daddy Over There)" (music by M. K. Jerome) and realized the biggest hit of his career with it, earning a gold record. Prince's Orch. and Edna White's Trumpet Quartet had instrumental hits with the song, and Charles Hart also recorded it successfully; it sold a million copies of sheet music. Also in 1918, Lewis was a co-librettist and cast member in the show *Hello America*, which closed before reaching N.Y.

Shortly after the end of the war, Burr followed up the success of "Just a Baby's Prayer" with "Oh, How I Wish I Could Sleep Until My Daddy Comes Home" (music by Pete Wendling), another big hit that sold a million copies of sheet music. *Monte Cristo Jr.* (N.Y., Feb. 12, 1919) sounded like a Jolson show and opened at his Broadway home, the Winter Garden, but he wasn't in it. Nevertheless, Lewis and Young contributed several songs in the Jolson style, notably "Who Played Poker with Pocahontas When John Smith Went Away?" (music by Fred E. Ahlert). The lyricists continued to mine the subject of World War I and its aftermath with "How Ya Gonna Keep 'Em Down on the Farm (After They've Seen Paree)?" (music by Walter Donaldson), which was introduced by Nora Bayes, who had the first hit recording, and was also featured by Sophie Tucker and Eddie Cantor and successfully recorded by Fields and by Byron G. Harlan. It was then interpolated into the *Ziegfeld Follies of 1919* (N.Y., June 16, 1919), along with other Lewis-Young songs. The team also tried writing a show of their own, contributing the lyrics for *The Water's Fine* (N.Y., 1919) with lyrics by Ted Snyder, but little was heard of this effort.

"Old Pal, Why Don't You Answer Me?" (music by Jerome) was a hit for both Ernest Hare and Lewis James in the last quarter of 1920, though Burr scored the biggest hit with it in early 1921. Continuing the "mammy" theme of "Rock-a-Bye Your Baby with a Dixie Melody," Lewis and Young also had a hit with "I'd Love to Fall Asleep and Wake Up in My Mammy's Arms" (music by Ahlert), recorded by the Peerless Quartet in the fall of 1920. Jolson, on tour with *Sinbad*, interpolated another Lewis-Young mammy song, simply titled "My Mammy" (music by Donaldson), into the show at the end of January 1921. It became an enormous hit, successfully recorded in instrumental versions by Paul Whiteman and His Orch., Isham Jones and His Orch., and the Yerkes Jazarimba Orch., and in vocal versions by the Peerless Quartet and Aileen Stanley. (Curiously, Jolson did not record it at this time, though he did later.) Lewis and Young's other hits of 1921 were "Singin' the Blues (Till My Daddy Comes Home)" (music by Con Conrad and J. Russel Robinson), successfully recorded by Stanley and featured in an instrumental medley with "Margie" by the Original Dixieland Jazz Band, and "Tuck Me to Sleep in My Old 'Tucky Home" (music by Meyer), introduced by Jolson, popularized by Cantor, and successfully recorded by Hare, Billy Jones, and Vernon Dalhart.

Lewis and Young's next significant hit came in early 1925 with "Put Away a Little Ray of Golden Sunshine (for a Rainy Day)" (music by Ahlert), recorded by James. Their song "Home Pals" (music by Jerome) was used in the play *The Jazz Singer* (N.Y., Sept. 14, 1925), presaging the success they would enjoy with the film version two years later. With composer Harry Akst they wrote the songs for the Plantation Café Nightclub's *New Plantation Revue* (1925), including "Dinah," sung by Ethel Waters. In 1926, Waters became the first person to record this standard, though there were also successful early versions by the Revelers, Cliff Edwards, and Fletcher Henderson and His Orch. in an instrumental recording.

Lewis and Young also had two other major hits during 1926, songs that epitomized the Flapper era of the Roaring Twenties: "I'm Sitting on Top of the World" (music by Ray Henderson), the most popular recording of which was by Jolson, though it was also successfully recorded by Roger Wolfe Kahn and His Orch. (as an instrumental) and by Frank Crumit, and "Five Foot Two, Eyes of Blue (Has Anybody Seen My Girl?)" (music by Henderson), a best-seller for Gene Austin and also recorded by Ernie Golden and by Art Landry and His Orch.

Lewis and Young began 1927 with "In a Little Spanish Town" (music by Mabel Wayne), which was a massive hit for Whiteman, also successfully recorded by Ben Selvin's Cavaliers and by Sam Lanin and His Orch. The writing team tried another full-scale musical, writing the songs for *Lady Do* (N.Y., April 18, 1927) with composer Abel Baer, but it lasted only 56 performances. Frankie Trumbauer and His Orch. revived "Singin' the Blues (Till My Daddy Comes Home)" that spring in a hit instrumental version with a famous solo by cornetist Bix Beiderbecke, a recording later enshrined in the NARAS Hall of Fame. Later that year Trumbauer scored a hit with "There's a Cradle in Caroline" (music by Ahlert), though the most popular recording was by Austin.

The film version of *The Jazz Singer*, the first sound motion picture, opened in N.Y. on Oct. 6, 1927, and featured its star, Jolson, singing "My Mammy." Jolson finally recorded the song at the end of March 1928 and scored a hit with it in June. Also that spring, Lewis and Young had hits with "Keep Sweeping Cobwebs off the Moon" (the first published composition by Oscar Levant), recorded by Ruth Etting with Ted Lewis and His Band, and "Laugh, Clown, Laugh" (music by Ted Fiorito, based on a theme from Leoncavallo's opera I Pagliacci), recorded by Lewis, though the most popular version was by Fred Waring's Pennsylvanians. In the fall, Ted Lewis scored a hit with "King for a Day" (music by Fiorito).

Adding English words to a German song written by Ralph Erwin, Lewis and Young fashioned "I Kiss Your Hand, Madame," which was used in the show Lady Fingers (N.Y., Jan. 31, 1929) and enjoyed hit recordings by the orchestras of Smith Ballew and Leo Reisman. The arrival of sound films led the lyricists to write songs for some of the early talkies, including Looping the Loop, Wolf Song, and She Goes to War (originally titled The War Song), while "Sweeping Cobwebs off the Moon" was used in The Dance of Life and "Rock-a-Bye Your Baby with a Dixie Melody" in The Show of Shows; all five films opened in 1929.

But Lewis and Young's most substantial work for film came with the screen adaptation of Richard Rodgers and Lorenz Hart's musical Spring Is Here, released in 1930. Their contributions, with music by Harry Warren, included "Have a Little Faith in Me," which became a record hit for Guy Lombardo and His Royal Canadians; "Cryin' for the Carolines," which generated hits for Lombardo, Etting, Waring, and Ben Bernie and His Orch.; and "Absence Makes the Heart Grow Fonder (for Somebody Else)," a hit for Bernie Cummins and His Orch. Meanwhile, Ted Lewis revived "Dinah" as a hit record.

Spring Is Here marked the end of the Lewis-Young partnership. Writing lyrics by himself, Lewis immediately scored a hit with "Telling It to the Daisies" (music by Victor Young), recorded by Nick Lucas in the spring of 1930. Early in 1932, Kate Smith, backed by Lombardo, had a hit with "Too Late" (music by Victor Young). The song had been introduced on radio by Bing Crosby, who recorded another version of "Dinah" with The Mills Brothers and scored the biggest hit with it yet at the end of January. (Later in the year he sang it in his first starring film, The Big Broadcast.) "Just Friends" (music by John Klenner) was a hit for Russ Columbo and for Selvin in the spring of 1932, and in the same season Lombardo and Louis Armstrong each scored with "Lawd, You Made the Night Too Long" (music by Victor Young).

At the start of 1933, Lombardo, Selvin, and Crosby each had hit recordings of "Street of Dreams" (music by Victor Young). In September, Lombardo and Isham Jones both hit with "This Time It's Love" (music by J. Fred Coots). Morton Downey introduced "For All We Know" (music by Coots) on his radio show; the hit recordings in August 1934 were by the orchestras of Hal Kemp and Isham Jones. "I Believe in Miracles" (music by Meyer and Wendling) was a big hit for the Dorsey Brothers Orch. with Bob Crosby on vocals and for Fats Waller in February 1935. "Dinah," that perennial favor-

ite, had been used in the film The Lemon Drop Kid in the fall of 1934; The Boswell Sisters made it a hit record yet again in February 1935. Jeanette MacDonald then interpolated it into the film adaptation of Victor Herbert's Rose Marie in early 1936; it was sung in the Shirley Temple feature Poor Little Rich Girl that summer; and Waller had a hit recording in December. The next summer it was back onscreen in the Gene Autry film Round-Up Time in Texas.

Lewis's next newly written hit was "A Beautiful Lady in Blue" (music by Coots), which was in the hit parade in the winter and spring of 1936 for Jan Garber and His Orch. and was also recorded by the orchestra of Ray Noble. Also that spring, Kemp scored a hit with "Gloomy Sunday," a Hungarian song (original title "Szomoru Vasarnap") composed by Rezsó Seress with Hungarian lyrics by Laszlo Javor. Lewis's pessimistic English lyrics caused it to be dubbed a "suicide song," and it was banned from radio play by the BBC in England and by some American stations. It nevertheless went on to become a standard, recorded by Paul Robeson, Billie Holiday, and others. Lewis closed out the year with "Close to Me" (music by Peter De Rose), a hit for Tommy Dorsey and His Orch.

Lewis seems to have been less active after 1936, though his songs continued to be covered by the swing bands. Benny Goodman and His Orch. had a hit with "What's the Matter with Me?" (music by Terry Shand) in the late winter of 1940. For the most part, however, record and film producers preferred to mine Lewis's back catalog of hits for new cover versions and interpolations. "Five Foot Two, Eyes of Blue (Has Anybody Seen My Girl)?" became a minor hit for Tiny Hill and His Orch. in August 1940; "Dinah" was used in the film Hit Parade of 1941 in the fall of 1940; Dorsey, with vocals by Frank Sinatra and the Pied Pipers, had a hit with "Street of Dreams" in the summer of 1942; and "How Ya Gonna Keep 'Em Down on the Farm (After They've Seen Paree)?" was used in the film For Me and My Gal that year, while "In a Little Spanish Town" was heard in the film Ridin' Down the Canyon. The exuberant tone of many of Lewis's World War I–era songs was appropriate to the patriotic spirit of World War II, and they turned up repeatedly in Hollywood films made during the conflict.

After the war, Lewis's songs began to return to the charts as well. Sam Donohue and His Orch. had a Top Ten hit with "Dinah" in the summer of 1946. Jolson, who had sung "My Mammy" and "Rock-a-Bye Your Baby with a Dixie Melody" in the period film Rose of Washington Square in 1939, sang them again dubbing for Larry Parks in the film The Jolson Story (1946), and when he recorded "My Mammy" again, he was rewarded with a gold record in early 1947. (He sang it again in the film Jolson Sings Again [1949].) Crosby, who had recorded "I Kiss Your Hand, Madame" early in his career, sang it in the film The Emperor Waltz (1948), and it was used in the Grace Moore film biography So This Is Love (1953). Benny Strong and His Orch. had a minor hit with "Five Foot Two, Eyes of Blue (Has Anybody Seen My Girl)?" the following year, and, appropriately enough, the song was used in the film Has Anybody Seen My Gal?

in 1952. "Singin' the Blues (Till My Daddy Comes Home)" was a chart hit for Connee Boswell in 1953, the same year that Les Paul and Mary Ford enjoyed a Top Ten hit with "I'm Sitting on Top of the World," also used in the Ruth Etting film biography *Love Me or Leave Me* (1955), starring Doris Day. "In a Little Spanish Town" was revived as a chart record by David Carroll and His Orch. in 1954. In 1956 comedian Jerry Lewis scored a Top Ten gold record with "Rock-a-Bye Your Baby with a Dixie Melody," which he sang straight.

In the years after Lewis's death, his songs were used primarily to set a period mood in musical revues and films and on television, though Aretha Franklin had a Top 40 hit with "Rock-a-Bye Your Baby with a Dixie Melody" in 1961 and the Happenings took "My Mammy" into the Top 40 in 1967, testifying to the songs' enduring appeal.—**WR**

Lewis, Ted (originally, **Friedman, Theodore Leopold**), stylized bandleader, singer, and clarinetist; b. Circleville, Ohio, June 6, 1892; d. N.Y., Aug. 25, 1971. With his cane and the battered top hat that he liked to roll off his head and down his arm, his archly spoken delivery of lyrics, and his catch-phrase, "Is everybody happy?," Lewis had enough trademark gimmicks to seem mannered to many. But if entertaining consists of constructing a popular persona and sticking to it, he was unquestionably a successful entertainer in vaudeville, nightclubs, theater, and movies, and he was among the best-selling recording artists of the 1920s.

He learned to play the clarinet in public school, and he and his brother Edgar played in a local band, after which he was part of the vaudeville act Rose, Young and Friedman. While appearing in vaudeville in S.C., he adopted his stage name as part of the duo Lewis and Lewis with comedian Eddie Lewis. Arriving in N.Y. in 1915, he performed at the Coll. Arms Cabaret, then joined Earl Fuller's Band in Coney Island. That same year he married dancer Adah Becker; the marriage lasted 56 years, until his death. He formed his own five-piece group, The Ted Lewis Nut Band, in 1917, opening at Rector's Restaurant. After his first number he asked the audience, "Is everybody happy?" The reaction caused him to repeat the question in his performances from then on.

When he won a top hat from a cabbie in a crap game, it became a stage prop. In 1918 he opened his own club, Bal Tabarin (the first of several), and introduced his theme song, "When My Baby Smiles at Me," which he wrote with Bill Munro and Andrew B. Sterling; he sang it in the 1919 edition of *The Greenwich Village Follies* (N.Y., July 15, 1919) and recorded it for Columbia Records, resulting in his first best-selling disc in July 1920. He next appeared in the second 1919 edition of the *Ziegfeld Midnight Frolic* (N.Y., Oct. 2, 1919) with Fanny Brice and W. C. Fields. He and his band were then in the 1921 edition of *The Greenwich Village Follies* (N.Y., Aug. 31, 1921), and his next big record hit came with "All by Myself" in October. He also appeared in the 1922 edition of *The Greenwich Village Follies* (N.Y., Sept. 12, 1922). "O! Katharina" was his next major record hit in May 1925.

On Nov. 15, 1926, Lewis and his band backed Sophie Tucker on a new recording of her theme song, "Some of These Days"; it became a gold-selling hit in March 1927. Lewis appeared in two Broadway revues that year, *Rufus Le Maire's Affairs* (N.Y., March 28, 1927) and *Artists and Models* (N.Y., Nov. 15, 1927). Ruth Etting fronted his band for the hit recording of "Is Everybody Happy Now?" (music and lyrics by Lewis, Maurice Rubens, and Jack Osterman), which he had introduced in *Artists and Models*, in March 1928. He made his film debut in *Is Everybody Happy?* (1929), following it the same year with *The Show of Shows*.

Lewis's most successful recordings of the early 1930s were "Just a Gigolo" in February 1931, "In a Shanty in Old Shanty Town" in June 1932, and "Lazybones" in July 1933. He made film appearances in *Here Comes the Band* (1935); *Manhattan Merry-Go-Round* (1937); *Hold That Ghost* (1941; performing another of his signature songs, "Me and My Shadow"); *Is Everybody Happy* (1943; his film biography, in which he played himself); and *Follow the Boys* (1944). He continued to perform with his band into the 1960s.

Though disdained by jazz critics, Lewis employed many excellent jazz musicians in his band and on his records over the years, including Mugsy Spanier, George Brunis, Benny Goodman, Fats Waller, Frank Teschemacher, Jimmy Dorsey, and Jack Teagarden.—**WR**

Lewisohn, Adolph, German-American businessman and philanthropist; b. Hamburg, May 27, 1849; d. Saranac Lake, N.Y., Aug. 17, 1938. The principal services to music and education performed by this prominent industrialist were the erection in 1914 of the Lewisohn Stadium, which he donated to the Coll. of the City of N.Y., and the inauguration of summer concerts by the N.Y. Phil. there (1918). He also founded the Lewisohn chamber music foundation at Hunter Coll. in N.Y. (1932).—**NS/LK/DM**

Lewkowitch, Bernhard, Danish organist and composer; b. Copenhagen (of Polish parents), May 28, 1927. He studied organ, theory, and music history at the Royal Danish Cons. of Music in Copenhagen (graduated in theory, 1948; organ degree, 1949), then completed his studies of composition and orchestration there with Jersild and Schierbeck (1950). He was organist and choirmaster at Copenhagen's St. Ansgar Catholic Church (1947–63), and also founded the Schola Cantorum choral society (1953), with which he performed medieval and Renaissance music. He served as director of music at Copenhagen's Church of the Holy Sacrament (1973–85). In 1963 he was awarded the Carl Nielsen Prize; in 1966 he was given a lifetime Danish government pension. His music is primarily choral, to Latin texts, and is derived essentially from the Renaissance paradigms of modal counterpoint; it has an affinity with sacred works of Stravinsky, but is otherwise sui generis in its stylized archaisms; several of these works have become repertoire pieces in Denmark, and were also performed at various international festivals.

WORKS: *Mariavise* for Chorus (1947); *2 salmi* for Chorus (1952); *3 motets* for Chorus (1952); *Mass* for Chorus (1952); *Mass* for Chorus, Harp, and Woodwinds (1954); *Tre madrigali di Torquato Tasso* for Chorus (1954–55); *Tres orationes* for Tenor, Oboe, and Bassoon (1958); *Cantata sacra* for Tenor and Instrumental Ensemble (1959); *Improperia per voci* (1961); *Il cantico delle creature* for 8 Voices, after St. Francis of Assisi (1962–63); *Veni creator spiritus* for Chorus and 6 Trombones (1967); *Laudi a nostra Signora* for Chorus (1969); *Stabat Mater* for Chorus (1969); *Sub vesperum* for Chorus (1970); 65 organ chorales (1972); *Folk Mass* for Unison Voices and Organ (1974); 32 motets for Chorus (1975–76); *De Lamentatione Jeremiae Prophetae* for Chorus and Orch. (1977); *Memoria apostolorum* for Chorus (1978); *Mass for Chorus and 2 Horns* (1978); *Vesper in Advent* for Tenor, Chorus, and Organ (1979); 12 organ chorales (1979); *Ad nonam* for Chorus and Orch. (1980); *Requiem* for Baritone, Chorus, and Orch. (1981); *Tenebrae-Responsoria* for Chorus (1983); *Magnificat* for Chorus and Orch. (1983); *Pater noster* for Chorus and 6 Wind Instruments (1983); *Deprecations* for Tenor, Horn, and Trombone (1984); *Songs of Solomon* for Tenor, Clarinet, Horn, and Trombone (1985); *Preacher and Singer* for Tenor and Piano (1986); 6 partitas for Brass (1986–88); *Via Stenonis* for Chorus and Brass Quintet (1987); *6 Partitas* for Organ (1990).—**NS/LK/DM**

Ley, Salvador, Guatemalan pianist and composer; b. Guatemala City, Jan. 2, 1907; d. there, March 21, 1985. He studied at the Berlin Hochschule für Musik (1922–30), concurrently studying piano with Georg Bertram (1922–30) and theory and composition with Klatte (1923–25) and Leichtentritt (1928–29). He was director of the National Cons. in Guatemala City (1934–37; 1944–53), and then taught at the Westchester (N.Y.) Cons. (1963–70).

WORKS: *Lera*, opera (1959); *Danza exotica* for Piano (1959); Suite for Flute and Piano (1962); *Concertante* for Viola and String Orch. (1962); *Toccatina* for Piano (1965); *Introduction and Movement* for Cello (1965); other piano pieces; songs.—**NS/LK/DM**

Leybach, Ignace (Xavier Joseph), Alsatian pianist, organist, and composer; b. Gambsheim, July 17, 1817; d. Toulouse, May 23, 1891. He studied in Paris with Pixis, Kalkbrenner, and Chopin, and in 1844 became organist at the Toulouse Cathedral. He publ. some 225 piano pieces, in a facile and pleasing manner. His 5th Nocturne, op.52, became famous, and its popularity continued among succeeding generations of piano students; it was reprinted in countless anthologies of piano music. Other piano compositions are *Boléro brillant, Ballade, Valse poétique, Les Batelières de Naples,* etc. He also publ. an extensive organ method (3 vols.; 350 pieces). —**NS/LK/DM**

Leyden, Norman, American conductor; b. Springfield, Mass., Oct. 17, 1917. He studied at Yale Univ. (B.A., 1938; Mus.B., 1939) and at Teachers Coll. of Columbia Univ. (M.A., 1965; Ed.D., 1968). He organized the Westchester Youth Sym. Orch. in White Plains, N.Y., in 1957, which he led until 1968. In 1974 he became assoc. conductor of the Ore. Sym. Orch. in Portland. He also pursued a successful career as a guest conductor with leading U.S. orchs. in concerts of popular fare. —**NS/LK/DM**

Leygraf, Hans, Swedish pianist, teacher, and composer; b. Stockholm, Sept. 7, 1920. He appeared as a soloist with the Stockholm Orch. at the age of 10, and then studied at the Stockholm Cons., in Munich, and in Vienna. He acquired a fine reputation as a concert pianist, becoming particularly noted as a Mozart interpreter. In 1944 he married the Austrian pianist Margarete Stehle (b. Vienna, April 26, 1921). In 1956 he joined the faculty of the Salzburg Mozarteum. He wrote a Piano Concerto, chamber music, and piano pieces. —**NS/LK/DM**

Lhérie (real name, **Lévy**), **Paul,** French tenor, later baritone; b. Paris, Oct. 8, 1844; d. there, Oct. 17, 1937. He was a pupil of Obin in Paris. In 1866 he made his operatic debut in the tenor role of Reuben in *Joseph* at the Paris Opéra-Comique, where he sang until 1868 and again from 1872. On March 3, 1875, he created the role of Don José there. In 1882 he turned to baritone roles, and in 1884 he appeared as Posa in the rev. version of *Don Carlos* at Milan's La Scala. In 1887 he sang Rigoletto at London's Covent Garden, returning there as Luna and Germont. Following his retirement from the stage in 1894, he was active as a voice teacher in Paris. —**NS/LK/DM**

Lhéritier, Jean, French composer; b. c. 1480; d. after 1552. He studied with Josquin Des Prez. He was active at the Estense court in Ferrara (1506–8), and later was capellanus and maestro di cappella at Rome's St.-Louis-des-Français (1521–22). Cardinal François de Clermont, the papal legate in Avignon, was his major patron, and Lhéritier received several benefices. He was a particularly notable composer of motets. L. Perkins ed. his *Opera omnia* in Corpus Mensurabilis Musicae, XLVIII/1–2 (1969).

BIBL.: L. Perkins, *The Motets of J. L.* (diss., Yale Univ., 1965). —**NS/LK/DM**

Lhévinne, Josef, celebrated Russian pianist and pedagogue, husband of **Rosina Lhévinne** (née **Bessie**); b. Orel, Dec. 13, 1874; d. N.Y., Dec. 2, 1944. After some preliminary study in his native town, he was taken to Moscow, and entered Safonov's piano class at the Cons. (1885). At the age of 15, he played the *Emperor Concerto*, with Anton Rubinstein conducting; he graduated in 1891. Lhévinne won the Rubinstein Prize in 1895. He taught piano at the Tiflis Cons. (1900–1902), and then at the Moscow Cons. (1902–06). During this period, he also toured Europe. He made his American debut in N.Y. with the Russian Sym. Orch., conducted by Safonov (Jan. 27, 1906); afterward he made numerous concert tours in America. He lived mostly in Berlin from 1907 to 1919; was interned during World War I, but was able to continue his professional activities. In 1919 he returned to the U.S.; appeared in recitals, and with major American orchs.; also in duo recitals with his wife, whom he married in 1898. They established a music studio, where they taught numerous pupils; also taught at the Juilliard Graduate School in N.Y. (from 1922). He publ. *Basic Principles in Pianoforte Playing* (Philadelphia, 1924). Lhévinne's playing was distinguished not only by its virtuoso quality, but by an intimate understanding of the music, impeccable phrasing, and fine gradations of singing tone. He was at his best in the works of the Romantic school, his performances of the concertos of Chopin and Tchaikovsky being particularly notable.

BIBL.: R. Wallace, *A Century of Music-Making: The Lives of J. and Rosina L.* (Bloomington, Ind., 1976).—NS/LK/DM

Lhévinne, Rosina (née Bessie), distinguished Russian pianist and pedagogue; b. Kiev, March 28, 1880; d. Glendale, Calif., Nov. 9, 1976. She graduated from the Moscow Cons. in 1898, winning the gold medal, the same year she married **Josef Lhévinne.** She appeared as a soloist in Vienna (1910), St. Petersburg (1911), and Berlin (1912), then remained in Berlin with her husband through World War I. In 1919 they went to the U.S., where they opened a music studio. She also taught at the Juilliard Graduate School in N.Y. (from 1922), and later privately. Among her famous students were Van Cliburn, Mischa Dichter, John Browning, and Garrick Ohlsson.

BIBL.: R. Wallace, *A Century of Music-Making: The Lives of Josef and R. L.* (Bloomington, Ind., 1976).—NS/LK/DM

Lhotka, Fran, Croatian composer and teacher of Czech descent, father of **Ivo Lhotka-Kalinski;** b. Wožice, Dec. 25, 1883; d. Zagreb, Jan. 26, 1962. He took lessons with Dvořák, Klička, and Stecker in Prague (1899–1905). After teaching in Ekaterinoslav (1908–09), he settled in Zagreb as a member of the Opera orch. He then was conductor of the Lisinski Chorus (1912–20), and subsequently a prof. at the Academy of Music (1920–61), where he also served as rector (1923–40; 1948–52). He publ. a harmony manual (Zagreb, 1948). His music followed in the late Romantic style.

WORKS: DRAMATIC: Opera: *Minka* (Zagreb, 1918); *The Sea* (Zagreb, 1920). Ballet: *The Devil of the Village* (Zürich, Feb. 18, 1935); *Ballad of Medieval Love* (Zürich, Feb. 6, 1937); *Luk* (Munich, Nov. 13, 1939). ORCH.: Sym.; Violin Concerto (1913); Concerto for String Quartet and Orch. (1924). OTHER: Chamber music; choral works; songs.—NS/LK/DM

Lhotka-Kalinski, Ivo, Croatian composer, son of **Fran Lhotka;** b. Zagreb, July 30, 1913; d. there, Jan. 29, 1987. He studied composition with his father and also voice at the Zagreb Academy of Music. After further composition lessons with Pizzetti in Rome (1937–39), he was active as a teacher. He then was prof. of singing at the Zagreb Academy of Music (from 1951), becoming its regional director in 1967. He had a natural flair for stage composition in the folk style, and wrote several brilliant musical burlesques, among them *Analfabeta* (The Illiterate; Belgrade, Oct. 19, 1954), *Putovanje* (The Journey), the first television opera in Yugoslavia (Zagreb, June 10, 1957), *Dugme* (The Button; Zagreb, April 21, 1958), *Vlast* (Authority; Zagreb TV, Oct. 18, 1959), and *Svjetleći grad* (The Town of Light; Zagreb, Dec. 26, 1967). Other works include a children's opera, *Velika coprarija* (The Great Sorcerer; 1952), Sym. (1937), *Jutro* (Morning), symphonic poem (1941–42), *Misli* (Thoughts) for Clarinet and Strings (1965), chamber music, choral works, songs, and piano pieces.—NS/LK/DM

Liadov, Anatoli (Konstantinovich), prominent Russian conductor, teacher, and composer, son of

Konstantin (Nikolaievich) Liadov; b. St. Petersburg, May 11, 1855; d. Polynovka, Novgorod district, Aug. 28, 1914. He began his musical training with his father, then entered the St. Petersburg Cons. (1870), where he took courses in piano and violin. He then studied counterpoint and fugue with J. Johannsen and composition with Rimsky-Korsakov. However, he was expelled for failing to attend classes (1876), but after his readmission, obtained his diploma with a highly successful graduation piece, the final scene from Schiller's *Die Braut von Messina* (1878). He became an instructor of theory (1878), advanced counterpoint (1901), and composition (1906) at the Cons., and also taught theory at the Court Chapel (from 1885). He was active as a conductor. With Balakirev and Liapunov, he collected folk songs for the Imperial Geographic Soc. (publ. in 1897). He was a teacher of Prokofiev and Miaskovsky. As a composer, Liadov was fascinated by variation techniques and canonic writing; many of his works possess the imaginative quality of Russian fairy tales. Among his most popular works were the orch. pieces *Baba Yaga, The Enchanted Lake,* and *Kikimora.*

WORKS: ORCH.: *Scherzo* (1879–86); *Village Scene by the Inn,* mazurka (1887); *Polonaise* (1899); *Polonaise* in D major (1902); *Baba Yaga* (1891–1904; St. Petersburg, March 18, 1904); *8 Russian Folk Songs* (1906); *The Enchanted Lake* (St. Petersburg, March 18, 1909); *Kikimora* (St. Petersburg, Dec. 8, 1912); *Danse de l'Amazone* (1910); *From the Apocalypse* (1910–12; St. Petersburg, Dec. 8, 1912); *Nenie* (1914). OTHER: Numerous piano pieces, including études, preludes, intermezzos, mazurkas, bagatelles, etc.; choral works; songs; numerous arrangements of folk songs.

BIBL.: V. Vasina-Grossman, *A.K. L.* (Moscow and Leningrad, 1945); N. Zaporozhets, *A.K. L.: Zhizn i tvorchestvo* (Life and Works; Moscow, 1954); M. Mikhailov, *A.K. L.: Ocherk zhizni i tvorchestva* (Life and Works; Leningrad, 1961).—NS/LK/DM

Liadov, Konstantin (Nikolaievich), Russian conductor, father of **Anatoli (Konstantinovich) Liadov;** b. St. Petersburg, May 10, 1820; d. there, Dec. 19, 1868. He studied at the St. Petersburg Theatrical School, and in 1850 became conductor of the St. Petersburg Imperial Opera. He resigned shortly before his death, and was succeeded by Napravnik. Liadov was an efficient drillmaster, and did much to raise the standard of performance. He premiered several Russian operas, and was instrumental in encouraging Russian music. He was also greatly appreciated by his co-workers, and Glinka often sought his advice on details of production of his operas.—NS/LK/DM

Liapunov, Sergei (Mikhailovich), noted Russian pianist, conductor, teacher, and composer; b. Yaroslavl, Nov. 30, 1859; d. Paris, Nov. 8, 1924. He began piano studies with his mother, a talented pianist, then took courses at the Russian Musical Soc. in Nizhny-Novgorod; later studied piano with Klindworth, Pabst, and Wilborg and composition with Hubert, Tchaikovsky, and Taneyev at the Moscow Cons. (1878–83). He went in 1884 to St. Petersburg, where he entered the Balakirev circle; was asst. director of the Imperial Chapel (1894–1902), inspector of music at St. Helen's Inst. (1902–10), and director of the Free Music School

(1905–11); was prof. of piano and theory at the Cons. (1910–17) and a lecturer at the State Inst. of Art (1919). Liapunov toured widely as a pianist in Europe, and also appeared as a conductor; he spent his last years in Paris. He wrote a number of virtuoso pieces for piano, including the *12 études d'exécution transcendante* in sharp keys, written in emulation of Liszt's similarly titled works in flat keys. He also wrote some attractive character pieces for piano and songs. With Balakirev and Liadov, he was commissioned by the Imperial Geographic Soc. in 1893 to collect folk songs from the regions of Vologda, Viatka, and Kostroma; 30 of his arrangements of them for voice and piano were publ. by the society in 1897. He also utilized original folk songs in several of his works.

WORKS: ORCH.: *Ballada*, overture (1883; rev. 1894–96); 2 syms.: No. 1 (1887; St. Petersburg, April 23, 1888) and No. 2 (1910–17; Leningrad, Dec. 28, 1950); 2 piano concertos (1890, 1909); *Solemn Overture on Russian Themes* (St. Petersburg, May 6, 1896); *Polonaise* (1902); *Rhapsody on Ukrainian Themes* for Piano and Orch. (1907; Berlin, March 23, 1908); *Zelazowa Wola*, symphonic poem named after Chopin's birthplace, commemorating his centennial (1909); *Hashish*, symphonic poem (1913); Violin Concerto (1915; rev. 1921). **OTHER:** Numerous piano pieces, including *12 études d'exécution transcendante* (1900–1905) and a Sonata (1906–08); many songs.

BIBL.: M. Shifman, *S.M. L.: Zhizn i tvorchestvo* (S.M. L.: Life and Works; Moscow, 1960).—**NS/LK/DM**

Liatoshinsky, Boris (Nikolaievich), significant Ukrainian composer and pedagogue; b. Zhitomir, Jan. 3, 1895; d. Kiev, April 15, 1968. He studied jurisprudence at the Univ. of Kiev, simultaneously taking lessons in composition at the Kiev Cons. with Gliere, graduating in 1919. He was an instructor (1919–35) and then a prof. (1935–68) at the Kiev Cons.; also taught at the Moscow Cons. (1936–37; 1941–43). Liatoshinsky was awarded State Prizes in 1946 and 1952. His style of composition followed the broad outlines of national music, with numerous thematic allusions to folk songs.

WORKS: DRAMATIC: Opera: *The Golden Hoop* (1929; Odessa, March 26, 1930); *Shchors* (1937; Kiev, Sept. 1, 1938; rev. version, Kiev, Feb. 18, 1970). **ORCH.:** 5 syms.: No. 1 (1918–19), No. 2 (1935–36; rev. 1940), No. 3 (1951; rev. 1954), No. 4 (1963), and No. 5 (1965–66); *Poem of Reunification* (1949–50); *Slavonic Concerto* for Piano and Orch. (1953); *Grazina*, ballad (Kiev, Nov. 26, 1955); *On the Banks of the Vistula*, symphonic poem (1958); *Solemn Overture* (1967). **CHAMBER:** 4 string quartets (1915, 1922, 1928, 1943); 2 piano trios (1922, rev. 1925; 1942); Violin Sonata (1926); *Ukrainian Quintet* for Piano (1942; rev. 1945); *Suite on Ukrainian Folk Themes* for String Quartet (1944); other piano pieces. **VOCAL:** Choral works; songs; many folk song arrangements.

BIBL.: I. Boelza, *B.M. L.* (Kiev, 1947); V. Samokhvalov, *B. L.* (Kiev, 1970; second ed., 1974).—**NS/LK/DM**

Liberace (in full, Wladziu Valentino Liberace), popular American pianist of Italian-Polish parentage; b. West Allis, Wisc., May 16, 1919; d. Palm Springs, Calif., Feb. 4, 1987. He received musical training from his father, a horn player, then studied piano, exhibiting so natural a talent that no less a master than Paderewski encouraged him to try for a concert career. However, he was sidetracked from serious music by jobs at silent-movie houses and nightclubs, where he was billed as Walter Busterkeys. In 1940 he moved to N.Y. and soon evolved a facile repertoire of semiclassical works, such as a synthetic arrangement of the first movement of Beethoven's *Moonlight Sonata* and Rachmaninoff's Prelude in C-sharp minor, taking advantage of the fact that both works are in the same key. He prospered and made lucrative inroads into television (1951–55; 1958–59), and also made numerous recordings and toured extensively overseas. He built himself a house in Calif., complete with a piano-shaped swimming pool. Inspired by a popular movie on Chopin, he placed a candelabrum on the piano at his public appearances. This decorative object identified him as a Romantic musician, an impression enhanced by his dress suit of white silk mohair and a wardrobe of glittering cloaks, which he removed with theatrical flair before performing. In 1959 he won a lawsuit for defamation of character against the London *Daily Mirror* and its columnist "Cassandra" (William Neil Connor) for suggesting in print that he was a practitioner of the inverted mode of love. But then in 1982 his former chauffeur-bodyguard-companion sued him for $380 million for services rendered in "an exclusive non-marital relationship." In 1984 most of the suit was quashed, and in 1986 Liberace settled out of court for $95,000. When he died of AIDS in 1987, his multimillion-dollar estate containing valuable curiosa was sold at auction. A large percentage of the sale price was bequeathed to charities, for Liberace was a generous man. In spite of his critics, he once said, he cried all the way to the bank. His autobiography was publ. in 1973.

BIBL.: B. Thomas, *L.* (N.Y., 1988); S. Thorson, with A. Thorleifson, *Behind the Candelabra: My Life with L.* (N.Y., 1988).—**NS/LK/DM**

Liberati, Antimo, Italian music theorist and composer; b. Foligno, April 3, 1617; d. Rome, Feb. 24, 1692. He received training in the fine arts and law in Foligno, where he became a notary. After service with the Viennese court (1637–43), he took minor orders in Foligno (1644). About 1650 he went to Rome and studied music with Allegri and Benevoli. From 1661 to 1692 he was an alto in the papal choir, serving as its maestro di cappella in 1674–75. He also was organist and maestro di cappella at S. Maria dell'Anima, Ss. Trinità del Pellegrini, and Ss. Stimate di S. Francesco. Liberati was an influential music theorist. As a staunch defender of the Roman liturgical tradition, he opposed all liberal trends at the Sistine Chapel. He also opposed the stile nuovo and the secondo prattica. His major treatises comprise *Epitome della musica* (1666?) and *Lettera...in risposta ad huna del Signor Ovidio Persapegi, 15 Ottobre 1684* (Rome, 1685). His extant compositions consist mainly of arias found in MSS of his era.—**LK/DM**

Libert, Henri, French organist, teacher, and composer; b. Paris, Dec. 15, 1869; d. there, Jan. 14, 1937. He studied at the Paris Cons. with Marmontel and Diémer (piano), Franck and Widor (organ), and Massenet and Godard (composition), taking first organ prize (1894).

He was titular organist at the Basilica of St. Denis in Paris, and a prof. of organ at the American Cons. in Fontainebleau. He wrote many organ works, including *Variations symphoniques, Chorals, Préludes et fugues*, piano pieces, motets, and songs. He also publ. didactic works. —NS/LK/DM

Libon, Philippe, French violinist and composer; b. Cadiz (of French parents), Aug. 17, 1775; d. Paris, Feb. 5, 1838. He was a student of Viotti in London, with whom he appeared in concerts there, and then of Cimador. He subsequently served as court violinist in Lisbon (1796–98), Madrid (1798–1800), and Paris (from 1800). He publ. 6 violin concertos, 6 string trios, duets, 2 vols. of *Airs variés*, and *30 caprices* for Violin.—NS/LK/DM

Licad, Cecile, Filipino pianist; b. Manila, May 11, 1961. She studied piano with Rosario Picazo, and made her public concert debut at the age of 7. She then went to the U.S., and enrolled at the Curtis Inst. of Music in Philadelphia in the classes of Rudolf Serkin, Seymour Lipkin, and Mieczyslaw Horszowski. In 1979 she was soloist with the Boston Sym. Orch. at the Berkshire Music Center in Tanglewood, and in 1981 she won the Leventritt Gold Medal, which launched her on a fine career. She subsequently appeared with major orchs. on both sides of the Atlantic. She married **António Meneses.**

BIBL.: R. Licad, *My Daughter C.* (Manila, 1994). —NS/LK/DM

Licette, Miriam, English soprano; b. Chester, Sept. 9, 1892; d. Twyford, Aug. 11, 1969. She was trained in Milan and Paris, her principal mentors being Marchesi, Jean de Reszke, and Sabbatini. In 1911 she made her operatic debut in Rome as Cio-Cio-San. From 1916 to 1920 she sang with the Beecham Opera Co., and from 1919 to 1929 she appeared in the international seasons at London's Covent Garden. She also was a member of the British National Opera Co. from 1922 to 1928. She won particular praise as a Mozartian. Among her other roles were Eurydice, Gutrune, Eva, Desdemona, Juliette, and Louise.—NS/LK/DM

Lichnowsky, Prince Karl (actually, **Carl Alois Johann Nepomuk Vinzenz Leonhard) von,** Austrian patron of music of Polish descent; b. Vienna, June 21, 1761; d. there, April 15, 1814. He received the title of nobility from the Russian government in 1773, but spent most of his life in Vienna. He was a pupil of Mozart, who accompanied him on a visit to Prague, Dresden, Leipzig, and Berlin in 1789. Beethoven's opp. 1, 13, 26, and 36 are dedicated to Lichnowsky. In his home, Lichnowsky presented regular chamber music concerts with a quartet composed of Schuppanzigh, Sina, Weiss, and Kraft. His brother, Count Moritz (Josef Cajetan Gallus) von Lichnowsky (b. Vienna, Oct. 17, 1771; d. there, March 17, 1837), was a pianist and composer; he was also a patron and friend of Beethoven and Chopin. Beethoven dedicated his opp. 35, 51, and 90 to the Count and his wife.—NS/LK/DM

Lichtenstein, Karl August, Freiherr von, German theater manager, conductor, and composer; b. Lahm, Franconia, Sept. 8, 1767; d. Berlin, Sept. 10, 1845. He studied in Gotha and then in Göttingen with Forkel. He gained attention as composer of the opera *Glück und Zufall* (Hannover, 1793) and the Singspiel *Knall und Fall* (Bamberg, 1795), and then was made manager of the Dessau Opera, where his opera *Bathmendi* opened its new theater (Dec. 26, 1798). Then followed his popular Singspiel *Die steinerne Braut* (1799). He was made conductor and artistic director of the Vienna Court Theater (1800). After a period in the diplomatic service, he resumed his musical career as director of the Bamberg theater (1813–14). He was music director in Strasbourg (1814–17), then went to Berlin (1823), where he was music director of the Royal Opera (1825–32). He wrote 17 works for the stage.—NS/LK/DM

Lichtenthal, Peter, Austrian composer and writer on music; b. Pressburg, May 10, 1780; d. Milan, Aug. 18, 1853. He was a doctor by profession, and composed music as an avocation. He settled in Milan in 1810 as a government censor. Lichtenthal produced 3 operas and 7 ballets at La Scala. He also publ. a String Quartet, 2 piano trios, and piano pieces. His chief writings are *Cenni biografici intorno al celebre maestro Wolfgang Amadeus Mozart* (1814), *Dizionario e bibliografia della musica* (4 vols., 1826), *Estetica, ossia Dottrina del bello e delle belle arti* (1831), and *Mozart e le sue creazioni* (1842).—NS/LK/DM

Lichtenwanger, William (John), learned American librarian; b. Asheville, N.C., Feb. 28, 1915. He studied at the Univ. of Mich. at Ann Arbor (B.Mus., 1937; M.Mus., 1940), and played double bass, oboe, and other instruments in the band and orch. He wrote pieces with whimsical titles, e.g., *Phrygidair* (in Phrygian mode, naturally). He served as asst. reference librarian of the Music Division at the Library of Congress in Washington, D.C. (1940–53, except for service in the U.S. Army, 1941–45), then asst. head (1953–60) and head (1960–74) of the music reference section there. He was assoc. ed. of *Notes* of the Music Library Assn. (1946–60), then its ed. (1960–63); in 1975 he was made a member emeritus. In addition, he was music ed. of *Collier's Encyclopedia* (1947–50), consultant for the biographical dictionary *Notable American Women* (1971), and a contributor to supplements II and III of the *Dictionary of American Biography*. He was chairman and compiler of *A Survey of Musical Instrument Collections* in the U.S. and Canada (1974). A polyglot and a polymath, Lichtenwanger is fluent in German, French, and Turkish, nearly fluent in Japanese, and fairly fluent in personalized Russian. With his wife, Carolyn, he ed. an analytic index to *Modern Music* (N.Y., 1976). Among his scholarly achievements, perhaps the highest is his incandescent essay "The Music of The Star-Spangled Banner—From Ludgate Hill to Capitol Hill," in the *Quarterly Journal of the Library of Congress* (July 1977), in which he furnishes documentary proof that the tune of the American national anthem was indeed composed by John Stafford Smith, all demurrings by various estimable historians to the contrary notwithstanding. To the 6ᵗʰ ed. of *Baker's*

Biographical Dictionary of Musicians he contributed incalculably precious verifications, clarifications, rectifications, and refutations of previous inadvertent and/or ignorant fabrications and unintentional prevarications; he also ed. *Oscar Sonneck and American Music* (Urbana, Ill., 1984) and compiled *The Music of Henry Cowell: A Descriptive Catalog* (Brooklyn, 1986).—NS/LK/DM

Lichtveld, Lou (actually, **Lodewijk Alphonsus Maria**), Dutch composer; b. Paramaribo, Surinam, Nov. 7, 1903. He went to Amsterdam in 1922 and was active as an organist and music critic. In 1936 he joined the International Brigade on the Loyalist side in the Spanish Civil War. During the Nazi occupation of the Netherlands, he served in the resistance movement, and became its representative in the emergency parliament of 1945. He returned to Surinam in 1949, and served as Minister of Education and Public Health and later President of the Exchequer; organized the facilities for musical education. From 1961 to 1969 he was in the diplomatic service of the Netherlands, stationed in Washington, D.C., and at the United Nations. He wrote about 2 dozen novels and essays under the pen name of Albert Helman. His musical works include an oratorio, *Canciones* (1934; MS lost in the Spanish Civil War), Piano Concertino (1932), Flute Sonata (1930), Violin Sonata (1931), *Triptych* for Piano (1925), and Piano Sonata (1927), as well as experimental pieces employing oriental scales. He used a 24-tone scale for 2 Dutch documentary films produced by Joris Ivens: *Regen* (1929; musical score added in 1932) and *Philips-Radio* (1930; also known as *Industrial Symphony*). He also composed several choruses.—NS/LK/DM

Lickl, Johann Georg, Austrian conductor and composer; b. Korneuburg, Lower Austria, April 11, 1769; d. Fünfkirchen, May 12, 1843. He studied music with the Korneuburg church organist Witzig, then went to Vienna (1785), where he continued his studies with Albrechtsberger and Haydn. He subsequently was active as a teacher and as organist at the Carmelite Church in the Leopoldstadt. He became associated around 1789 with Schikaneder's Freihaus-Theater auf der Wieden, where he contributed numbers to popular Singspiels or wrote entire scores for them. His *Der Brigitten-Kirchtag* (July 3, 1802) was composed for the new Theater an der Wien, and his comic opera *Slawina von Pommern* (Feb. 29, 1812) for the Leopoldstadt Theater. He served as regens chori at Fünfkirchen Cathedral (from 1805), producing much sacred music. He publ. arrangements for piano and harmonium of popular classics in *Wiener Salon-Musik*. He had 2 sons: Karl Georg Lickl (b. Vienna, Oct. 28, 1801; d. there, Aug. 3, 1877), a civil servant who became well known as a physharmonica player and composer for the instrument, and Aegidius (Ferdinand) Karl Lickl (b. Vienna, Sept. 1, 1803; d. Trieste, July 22, 1864), who studied with his father, appeared as a pianist, and then settled in Trieste as a teacher, conductor, and composer; he wrote the opera *La disfida Berletta* (1848) and sacred music.

WORKS: DRAMATIC (all first perf. in Vienna): *Die verdeckten Sachen*, Singspiel (Sept. 25, 1789; in collaboration with F.

Gerl and B. Schack): *Der Zauberpfeil, oder Das kabinett der Wahrheit*, opera (June 9, 1793); *Das Zingeunermädchen*, Lustspiel mit Gesang (Nov. 10, 1793); *Die Haushaltung nach der Mode, oder der 30–jährige Bernhardl*, Singspiel (March 15, 1794); *Der Bruder von Kagran*, comic opera (June 2, 1797); *Der Kampf mit dem Fürsten der Finsternis*, comic opera (April 20, 1799); *Fausts Leben, Taten und Höllenfahrt*, romantisches Schauspiel mit Gesang (June 28, 1799); *Der vermeinte Hexenmeister*, ländliche Operette (March 29, 1800); *Der Orgelspieler, oder Die Abenteuer im Gebirge*, komisches Singspiel (Aug. 2, 1800); *Der Durchmarsch*, Singspiel (Dec. 27, 1800); *Der Brigitten-Kirchtag*, Singspiel (July 3, 1802); *Slawina von Pommern*, comic opera (Feb. 29, 1812).—NS/LK/DM

Lidarti, Christian Joseph, Austrian composer of Italian descent; b. Vienna, Feb. 23, 1730; d. probably in Pisa, after 1793. He studied at the Cistercian monastery in Klagenfurt and at the Jesuit seminary in Leoben, and then pursued training in philosophy and law at the Univ. of Vienna; he also studied harpsichord and harp but was autodidact in composition. In 1751 he settled in Italy. After completing his studies with Jommelli in Rome (1757), he played in the chapel of the Cavalieri di S. Stefano in Pisa (1757–84?). Among his well-crafted instrumental works were several sonatas and duets. —LK/DM

Lidholm, Ingvar (Natanael), prominent Swedish composer; b. Jönköping, Feb. 24, 1921. He studied violin with Hermann Gramms and orchestration with Natanael Berg in Södertälje, then received violin training from Alex Ruunqvist and conducting lessons from Tor Mann at the Stockholm Musikhögskolan (1940–45); also studied composition with Hilding Rosenberg (1943–45). He was a violinist in the orch. of the Royal Theater in Stockholm (1943–47). He received a Jenny Lind fellowship and pursued his studies in France, Switzerland, and Italy (1947), and later studied in Darmstadt (summer, 1949) and with Seiber in England (1954). He served as director of music in Örebro (1947–56) and as director of chamber music for the Swedish Radio (1956–65). After holding the position of prof. of composition at the Stockholm Musikhögskolan (1965–75), he returned to the Swedish Radio as director of planning in its music dept. (1975). In 1960 he was elected a member of the Royal Swedish Academy of Music in Stockholm. He became active in Swedish avant-garde circles, contributing greatly to the formulation of methods and aims of contemporary music. In his works, he applies constructivist methods with various serial algorithms.

WORKS: DRAMATIC: *Cyrano de Bergerac,* incidental music (1947); *Riter,* ballet (1959; Stockholm, March 26, 1960); *Holländarn,* television opera (Swedish TV, Dec. 10, 1967); *Ett drömspel,* opera (1990). **ORCH.:** *Toccata e canto* for Chamber Orch. (1944); Concerto for Strings (1945); *Music for Strings* (1952); *Ritornello* (1955; Stockholm, Feb. 17, 1956); *Mutanza* (Örebro, Nov. 15, 1959); *Motus Colores* (Cologne, June 13, 1960); *Poesis* (1963; Stockholm, Jan. 14, 1964); *Greetings (from an Old World)* (N.Y., Nov. 10, 1976); *Kontakion,* hymn (1978; Moscow, Feb. 6, 1979). **CHAMBER:** String Quartet (1945; Stockholm, March 9, 1946); Sonata for Solo Flute (1945); *Little String Trio* (1953); Concertino for Flute, Oboe, English Horn, and Cello (Stockholm, Oct. 16, 1954); *Invention* for Clarinet and Bass

Clarinet, or Viola and Cello, or Piano (1954); *4 Pieces* for Cello and Piano (Stockholm, May 16, 1955); *Fanfare* for 2 Trumpets, 2 to 4 Horns, and 2 Percussion (Stockholm, June 1956); *Fantasia sopra Laudi* for Cello (Swedish Radio, June 21, 1977); *Amicizia* for Clarinet (1980); *Tre elegier-Epilog* for String Quartet (1982–86; Stockholm, Oct. 23, 1986). KEYBOARD: Piano: *Rosettas visa* (1942); Sonata (Stockholm, Oct. 25, 1947); 2 sonatinas (1947, 1950); *10 Miniatures* (1948); *Klavierstück 1949* (1949). Organ: *Variazioni sopra Laudi* (Stockholm, Oct. 27, 1982; in collaboration with K.-E. Welin). VOCAL: *Laudi* for Chorus (1947); Cantata for Baritone and Orch. (1949–50); *Canto LXXXI* for Chorus, after Ezra Pound (1956; Stockholm, Feb. 24, 1957); *Skaldens natt* (The Night of the Poet) for Soprano, Chorus, and Orch. (1958; North German Radio, Hamburg, April 6, 1959; rev. version, Swedish Radio, Oct. 23, 1981); *Nausikaa einsam* (Nausikaa Alone) for Soprano, Chorus, and Orch., after a section of Eyvind Johnson's novel *Return to Ithaca* (Ingesund, June 2, 1963); *Stamp Music I* for Soprano and Tam-tam (1971; score printed on a Swedish postage stamp) and *II* for Chorus and Piano (1971; score printed on a Swedish postage stamp); *Och inga träd skall väcka dig* for Soprano, Chorus, String Quartet, and Electronics (1973–74; Swedish TV, March 12, 1974); *Perserna* for Tenor, Baritone, Narrator, and Men's Chorus (Uppsala, April 29, 1978); *2 Madrigals* for Chorus (1981; Minneapolis, Sept. 12, 1982); *De profundis* for Chorus (Stockholm, Oct. 23, 1983); *Inbillningens värld* for Men's Chorus (1990); other choral pieces; songs.—NS/LK/DM

Lídl, Václav, Czech composer; b. Brno, Nov. 5, 1922. He studied with Kvapil at the Brno Cons., graduating in 1948. In addition to writing numerous film scores, he also composed 4 syms. (1965, 1974, 1975, 1979), *Radostná predehra* for Orch. (1981), *Balada o červnovém ránu (Lidice 1942)* for Orch. (1982), *Serenade* for Orch. (1982), chamber music, and choral works.—NS/LK/DM

Lidón, José, Spanish organist and composer; b. Béjar, June 2, 1748; d. Madrid, Feb. 11, 1827. He studied at Madrid's Réal Colegio di Niños Cantores. After serving as organist at Orense Cathedral, he was made fourth organist (1768) and first organist (1787) of Madrid's royal chapel; was master there and rector of the Réal Colegio (1805–27). He wrote an opera, *Glauca y Coriolano* (Madrid, 1791), about 60 sacred vocal works, chamber music, and organ pieces; also wrote several theoretical works.—NS/LK/DM

Lie, Erika
 See **Lie-Nissen, Erika**

Lie, Harald, Norwegian composer; b. Christiania, Nov. 21, 1902; d. there (Oslo), May 23, 1942. He studied piano at the Christiania Cons., and later received training in composition from Valen (1930). He was stricken with tuberculosis in 1932. His works were written in a late Romantic style. He withdrew a number of his scores: among those acknowledged are 2 syms. (1934, 1937), a *Symphonic Dance*, the scherzo from his unfinished 3rd Sym. (1942), several fine songs with orch., and choral pieces.—NS/LK/DM

Lie, Sigurd, Norwegian composer; b. Drammen, May 23, 1871; d. there, Sept. 29, 1904. He began his

musical training with the Kristiansand Cathedral organist August Rojahn. After studies with Gudbrand Bøhn (violin) and Iver Holter (theory and composition) at Lindeman's Cons. in Christiania, he studied with Reinecke and Rust (theory and composition) and with Arno Hilfs (violin) at the Leipzig Cons. (1891–93) before completing his training with Urban (composition) in Berlin (1894–95). He was active in Bergen as conductor of the Musikforening, but his career was hampered by poor health. In 1902 he became conductor of the Handelsstand Sangforening in Christiania.

WORKS: ORCH.: Violin Concerto (Bergen, Feb. 13, 1896); *Oriental Suite* (Christiania, Oct. 28, 1899); Sym. (Christiania, Feb. 28, 1903). CHAMBER: String Quartet; Violin Sonata; piano pieces. VOCAL: *Erling Skjalgson* for Baritone, Men's Chorus, and Orch. (Christiania, Oct. 28, 1899); songs.—NS/LK/DM

Liebermann, Lowell, American composer, pianist, and conductor; b. N.Y., Feb. 22, 1961. He began piano lessons at the age of 8, becoming a student of Ada Sohn Segal by age 11; at 14, began piano and composition lessons with Ruth Schonthal. In 1977 he made his debut at N.Y.'s Carnegie Recital Hall. In 1978 he commenced private composition lessons with Diamond, who continued as his mentor at the Juilliard School in N.Y. from 1979; also studied there with Lateiner (piano), Halasz (conducting), and Persichetti (composition), taking a B.Mus. (1982), a M.Mus. (1984), and a D.M.A. (1987). In 1986 he won the Victor Herbert/ASCAP Award, and in 1990 the Charles Ives fellowship of the American Academy and Inst. of Arts and Letters and ASCAP's Young Composers Competition. Liebermann's output demonstrates a deft handling of both traditional and modern elements in an accessible style.

WORKS: DRAMATIC: Opera: *Dorian Gray* (1993–94; Monte Carlo, May 8, 1995). ORCH.: Concertino for Cello and Chamber Orch. (1982); Sym. (1982; N.Y., Feb. 19, 1988); 2 piano concertos: No. 1 (1983; Lake Forest, Ill., Oct. 28, 1988) and No. 2 (Washington, D.C., June 11, 1992); *The Domain of Arnheim* (1990; N.Y., Jan. 12, 1991); Flute Concerto (St. Louis, Nov. 6, 1992). CHAMBER: Cello Sonata (1978); *2 Pieces* for Violin and Viola (1978; N.Y., Oct. 25, 1986); String Quartet (1979); Viola Sonata (1984; N.Y., April 29, 1985); Flute Sonata (1987; Charleston, S.C., May 20, 1988); Contrabass Sonata (1987; Washington, D.C., March 18, 1989); Sonata for Flute and Guitar (1988; N.Y., March 15, 1989); Quintet for Piano, Clarinet, and String Trio (Washington, D.C., Nov. 13, 1988); *Fantasy on a Fugue by J.S. Bach* for Flute, Oboe, Clarinet, Horn, Bassoon, and Piano (N.Y., March 21, 1989); Concerto for Violin, Piano, and String Quartet (Charleston, S.C., May 28, 1989); *Fantasy for Bass Koto* (1989; N.Y., June 1, 1992); Trio for Piano, Violin, and Cello (Cape Cod, Mass., Aug. 8, 1990); Quintet for Piano and Strings (1990; Greenville, S.C., Feb. 2, 1991); *Soliloquy* for Flute (New Orleans, Jan. 30, 1993); Violin Sonata (N.Y., Dec. 1, 1994). KEYBOARD: Piano: 2 sonatas: No. 1 (N.Y., May 15, 1977) and No. 2, *Sonata Notturna* (Wavendon, England, July 7, 1983); *Variations on a Theme by Anton Bruckner* (1986; Charleston, S.C., June 3, 1987); 4 nocturnes: No. 1 (Washington, D.C., Nov. 21, 1986), No. 2 (N.Y., March 28, 1990), No. 3 (San Antonio, Oct. 20, 1991), and No. 4 (London, Nov. 22, 1992); *Variations on a Theme by Mozart* for 2 Pianos (1993); *Album for the Young* (1993). Organ: *De Profundis* (1985; N.Y., Jan. 16, 1986). VOCAL: *2 Choral Elegies* (Stony Brook, N.Y., April 29, 1977); *War Songs* for Bass and

Piano (1980; also for Bass and Orch., 1981); *3 Poems of Stephen Crane* for Baritone, String Orch., 2 Horns, and Harp (1983); *Sechs Gesange nach Gedichten von Nelly Sachs* for Soprano and Piano (1985; N.Y., March 19, 1986; also for Soprano and Orch., 1986; N.Y., April 7, 1987); *Missa Brevis* for Tenor, Baritone, Chorus, and Organ (1985; N.Y., March 29, 1986); *Final Songs* for Baritone and Piano (N.Y., Nov. 23, 1987); *Night Songs* for Baritone and Piano (1987); *A Poet to His Beloved* for Tenor, Flute, String Quartet, and Piano (N.Y., Feb. 13, 1993); *Out of the Cradle Endlessly Rocking* for Mezzo-soprano and String Quartet (Lawrence, Kans., April 2, 1993).—NS/LK/DM

Liebermann, Rolf, esteemed Swiss opera administrator and composer; b. Zürich, Sept. 14, 1910; d. Paris, Jan. 2, 1999. He studied law at the Univ. of Zürich and received private instruction in music from José Berr (1929–33). He took a conducting course with Scherchen in Budapest (1936), serving as his assistant in Vienna (1937–38), and also had composition studies with Vogel (1940). He was a producer at Radio Zürich (1945–50), then director of the orch. section of the Schweizerische Rundspruchgesellschaft in Zürich (1950–57). Subsequently he was director of music of the North German Radio in Hamburg (1957–59). He was Intendant of the Hamburg State Opera (1959–73), where he pursued a policy of staging numerous 20th century operas, including specially commissioned works from leading contemporary composers; then was general administrator of the Paris Opéra (1973–80), bringing enlightened leadership to bear on its artistic policies; subsequently was recalled to his former post at the Hamburg State Opera in 1985, remaining there until 1988. From 1983 to 1988 he also was director of the International Summer Academy of the Salzburg Mozarteum. He was made a Commandeur de la Légion d'honneur of France in 1975. His autobiography was publ. in English as *Opera Years* (1987). As a composer, he worked mostly in an experimental idiom, sharing the influence of hedonistic eclecticism, French neo-Classicism, and Viennese dodecaphony; he became particularly attracted to theatrical applications of modernistic procedures.

WORKS: DRAMATIC: Opera: *Leonore 40/45* (1951–52; Basel, March 25, 1952); *Penelope* (1953–54; Salzburg, Aug. 17, 1954); *The School for Wives* (1954–55; Louisville, Dec. 3, 1955; rev. as *Die Schüle der Frauen*, Salzburg, Aug. 17, 1957); *La Forêt* or *Der Wald* (1985–86; Geneva, April 11, 1987); *Non lieu pour Medea* (1992); *Freispruch für Medea* (Hamburg, Sept. 24, 1995).

BIBL.: I. Scharberth and H. Paris, eds., *R. L. zum 60. Geburtstag* (Hamburg, 1970).—NS/LK/DM

Lieberson, Goddard, English-American recording executive and composer, father of **Peter Lieberson;** b. Hanley, Staffordshire, April 5, 1911; d. N.Y., May 29, 1977. He was taken to the U.S. as a child, and studied composition with George Frederick McKay at the Univ. of Wash. in Seattle and with Bernard Rogers at the Eastman School of Music in Rochester, N.Y. In 1939 he joined the Masterworks division of Columbia Records in N.Y. He was its president (1955–66; 1973–75), during which period he recorded many contemporary works as well as those of the standard repertoire. In 1964 he was named president of the Record Industry Assn. of America; in 1978 the American Academy and Inst. of

Arts and Letters set up the Lieberson fellowships to assist young composers. He composed a Sym., a ballet, *Yellow Poodle*, chamber music, choral works, and piano pieces.—NS/LK/DM

Lieberson, Peter, American composer, son of **Goddard Lieberson;** b. N.Y., Oct. 25, 1946. He took a degree in English literature at N.Y.U. (1972). After studies with Babbitt, he trained with Wuorinen at Columbia Univ. (M.A. in composition, 1974), then studied Vajrayana Buddhism with Chögyam Trungpa of the Shambhala tradition. After completing his doctoral studies with Martino and Boykan at Brandeis Univ., he taught at Harvard Univ. (1984–88). He then settled in Halifax, Nova Scotia, as international director of Shambhala training, while continuing to pursue his career as a composer. His compositions are written in a well-crafted 12-tone system.

WORKS: DRAMATIC: Opera: *Ashoka's Dream* (Santa Fe, N.Mex., July 26, 1997). **ORCH.:** 2 piano concertos: No. 1 (1980–83; Boston, April 21, 1983) and No. 2, *Red Garuda* (1998–99; Boston, Oct. 14, 1999); *Drala* (Boston, Oct. 9, 1986); *The Gesar Legend* (Boston, June 12, 1988); *World's Turning* (1990–91; San Francisco, Feb. 6, 1991); Viola Concerto (Toronto, Feb. 18, 1993); *Fire* (1995). **CHAMBER:** *Flute Variations* for Flute (1971); Concerto for 4 Groups of Instruments (1972–73); Concerto for Cello and 4 Trios (1974); *Accordance* for 8 Instruments (1975–76); *Tashi Quartet* for Clarinet, Violin, Cello, and Piano (1978–79); *Lalita- Chamber Variations* for 10 Instrumentalists (1983–84); *Feast Day* for Flute, Oboe, Piano or Harpsichord, and Cello (Washington, D.C., Sept. 21, 1985); *Ziji* for 6 Instruments (1987; N.Y., Jan. 17, 1988); *Raising the Gaze* for 8 Instrumentalists (San Francisco, March 28, 1988); *Elegy* for Violin and Piano (1990); *Wind Messengers* for 13 Instruments (1990); *A Little Fanfare I* for Flute, Trumpet, Violin, and Harp (1991) and *II* for Clarinet, Piano, Violin, Viola, and Cello (1993); *Variations* for Violin and Piano (1993); *Rumble* for Viola, Double Bass, and Percussion (1994); String Quartet No. 1 (Halifax, June 5, 1994). **Piano:** *Piano Fantasy* (1975); (3) *Bagatelles* (1985); *Scherzo No. 1* (1989); (3) *Fantasy Pieces* (1989); *Garland* (1994). **VOCAL:** *Motetti di Eugenio Montali* for Soprano, Alto, and 4 Instruments (1971–72); *Double Entendre* for Soprano and 3 Instruments (1972); *3 Songs* for Soprano and 13 Instruments (1981); *King Gesar* for Narrator and 8 Instrumentalists (1991–92; Munich, May 20, 1992).—NS/LK/DM

Liebert, Reginaldus, Burgundian composer who flourished in the early 15th century. He most likely was master of the boy choristers at Cambrai Cathedral in 1425. He was the composer of the *Missa De Beata Virgine* for 5 Voices (see G. Reaney, ed., *Early Fifteenth Century Music*, Corpus Mensurabilis Musicae, III, 1966), historically significant as a summation of the Franco-Flemish style of the preceding 14th century in its treatment of counterpoint and cantus firmus and as a harbinger of the great cyclic masses of the 15th century in its display of a unified musical structure. His other extant works comprise a Kyrie for 4 Voices and 2 secular chansons.—LK/DM

Liebig, Karl, German conductor; b. Schwedt, July 25, 1808; d. Berlin, Oct. 6, 1872. He was oboist in the

Alexander Grenadier Regiment in Berlin. In 1843 he organized the Berlin Symphoniekapelle, which under his leadership attained a very high standard of performance. In 1867 the orch. elected another conductor, and Liebig's attempts to form a rival organization proved futile.—NS/LK/DM

Liebling, Emil, German-American pianist and composer, brother of **Georg Liebling** and uncle of **Leonard Liebling**; b. Pless, Silesia, April 12, 1851; d. Chicago, Jan. 20, 1914. He studied piano with Theodor Kullak in Berlin, Dachs in Vienna, and Liszt in Weimar, and also composition with Dorn in Berlin. In 1867 he went to America and lived in Chicago from 1872, where he was actively engaged as a concert pianist and teacher. He wrote a number of effective piano pieces in a light vein (*Florence Valse, Feu follet, Albumblatt, 2 Romances, Cradle Song, Canzonetta, Menuetto scherzoso, Mazurka de concert, Spring Song*). He ed. *The American History and Encyclopedia of Music* and co-ed. a *Dictionary of Musical Terms*.—NS/LK/DM

Liebling, Estelle, American soprano and pedagogue, sister of **Leonard Liebling**; b. N.Y., April 21, 1880; d. there, Sept. 25, 1970. She studied with Marchesi in Paris and Nicklass-Kempner in Berlin. She made her operatic debut as Lucia at the Dresden Court Opera; then appeared at the Stuttgart Opera, the Opéra-Comique in Paris, and the Metropolitan Opera in N.Y. (debut Feb. 24, 1902, as Marguerite in *Les Huguenots*); was again on the Metropolitan's roster in 1903–04. She was a soloist with leading orchs. in the U.S., France, and Germany; also with Sousa. From 1936 to 1938 she was a prof. at the Curtis Inst. of Music in Philadelphia; then settled in N.Y. as a vocal teacher. Her most famous pupil was Beverly Sills. She publ. *The Estelle Liebling Coloratura Digest* (N.Y., 1943). Her brother, Leonard Liebling (b. N.Y., Feb. 7, 1874; d. there, Oct. 28, 1945), was a pianist, music critic, and editor; her uncle, Georg Liebling (b. Berlin, Jan. 22, 1865; d. N.Y., Feb. 7, 1946), was a pianist and composer.—NS/LK/DM

Liebling, Georg, German-American pianist and composer, brother of **Emil Liebling** and uncle of **Leonard Liebling**; b. Berlin, Jan. 22, 1865; d. N.Y., Feb. 7, 1946. He studied piano with Theodor and Franz Kullak and Liszt and composition with Urban and Dorn. He toured Europe (1885–89), and then was court pianist to the Duke of Coburg (1890). From 1894 to 1897 he directed his own music school in Berlin, and from 1898 to 1908 he was a prof. at the Guildhall School of Music in London. He settled in the U.S. in 1924, making his N.Y. debut that same year. He used the pseudonym **André Myrot**.

WORKS: *Great Mass* for Soloists, Chorus, Orch., and Organ (Los Angeles, 1931); *Concerto eroico* for Piano and Orch. (1925); 2 violin concertos; 2 violin sonatas; 3 Preludes for Violin and Piano; *Aria e Tarantella* for Cello and Piano; *Légende* for Violin and Piano; etc.; piano pieces; songs.

BIBL.: G. Braun, *Hofpianist G. L.* (Berlin, 1896). —NS/LK/DM

Liebling, Leonard, American pianist, music critic, and editor, nephew of **Georg Liebling** and **Emil Lie-**

bling and brother of **Estelle Liebling**; b. N.Y., Feb. 7, 1874; d. there, Oct. 28, 1945. He studied at City Coll. in N.Y., and privately with Leopold Godowsky (piano), then in Berlin with Kullak and Barth (piano) and Urban (composition); toured Europe and America as a pianist. In 1902 he joined the staff of the *Musical Courier* in N.Y., and in 1911 became its ed.-in-chief; his weekly columns on topical subjects were both entertaining and instructive. He also served as music critic of the *N.Y. American* (1923–34; 1936–37). He wrote some chamber music, piano pieces, and songs, as well as librettos of several light operas, including Sousa's *The American Maid*. —NS/LK/DM

Liebman, Dave (actually, **David**), jazz soprano and tenor saxophonist, composer, educator, author, flutist, drummer, pianist; b. Brooklyn, N.Y., Sept. 4, 1946. He is one of the leading players and teachers of jazz. He first came to prominence during his period with Elvin Jones and Miles Davis (1971–74). Since then he has recorded in every context, from free jazz to fusion to standards, and has taught all over the world.

His parents were N.Y.C. public school teachers. He began classical piano lessons at age nine and played saxophone at 12, also studying clarinet and flute. At 13 he began performing in Catskills resorts with a band called the Impromptu Quartet and playing club dates around N.Y. He saw John Coltrane many times and was profoundly inspired by him. He made his first jazz recording in 1967, with a group of Swedish musicians, whom he had met during his first trip in Europe. Mike Garson, his first jazz friend, connected him with Lennie Tristano. Lonnie Ruthstein, the first true jazz drummer he knew, became a mentor for Liebman and others doing gigs at Catskills resorts. Liebman was also mentored through Jazz Interactions, a program run by Alan Pepper, who presented Liebman in concert at Red Garter near N.Y.U. in 1968, with a prize-winning, all-star youth quintet including Randy Brecker, Cameron Brown, and probably Garson and Ruthstein. Later in 1968 this group played opposite Roland Kirk and Elvin Jones in Town Hall, Liebman's first big concert. Besides Tristano, he studied with Joe Allard and Charles Lloyd and in 1968 graduated from N.Y.U. with a degree in American History and a teaching diploma, so he could occasionally substitute-teach. In 1969 he began freelancing with Pete LaRoca, Chick Corea, and Steve Swallow. Immersed in the N.Y. loft jazz scene with a place on 19th St., he played a key role in founding Free Life Communication, a musicians' cooperative. In 1970 he founded the Open Sky Trio with Bob Moses and began in the rock/jazz band Ten Wheel Drive. He worked with Elvin Jones from 1971–73. In 1973 he got a call from Teo Macero asking that he come immediately to a studio on 52nd St., where Miles Davis had him play without any instruction (or even headphones) for what became *On the Corner*, but when Davis asked him to leave Jones, Liebman declined. Six months later, however, Davis came to the Village Vanguard and asked Jones directly to let him go. Liebman's first gig with Davis was the following weekend, on the last night of the Fillmore East. After playing with Davis, he formed Lookout Farm with Richard Bierach and toured India, Japan,

Europe, and the U.S. The group co- authored a book in which they analyzed their own performances, a prototype for a much needed style of criticism. No one has yet followed their example. The 1976 *Down Beat* International Critics' Poll selected Lookout Farm as the "Group Most Deserving of Wider Recognition."

After this, Liebman took a totally different course, forming a commercial band with ex–James Brown saxophonist Pee Wee Ellis; they were situated on the West Coast with a big record deal, but the group was unsuccessful. In 1978, after returning from a world tour with Chick Corea which featured a string quartet and a brass section, Liebman formed a quintet, featuring at times John Scofield, Kenny Kirkland, and others. After several world tours and recordings with the group, Liebman reunited with Beirach. They began performing and recording as a duo before forming Quest with George Mraz and Al Foster in 1981. (Around this time, Liebman began playing soprano sax exclusively). In 1984 Quest took on a new form, when Ron McClure and Billy Hart joined the group. Over the course of the next seven years, the band toured extensively, and conducted many workshops around the world. In addition to playing with his bands, he has made numerous appearances in Europe, where he performs with Joachim Kuhn, Daniel Humair, Jon Christensen, Bobo Stenson, Albert Mangelsdorf, and Michel Portal. Playing with the WDR Sym. Orch. (Germany) as well as several chamber ensembles and big bands, he has recorded a number of works specially written to feature his soprano saxophone style. He has received two NEA grants, for composition (1980) and performance (1991). Since 1991, he has led the The Dave Liebman Group, with Vic Juris, Jamey Haddad, and Tony Marino on bass. The band has toured Europe, Japan, and Israel. Working prolifically, he has recorded dozens of albums under his own leadership and nearly 200 as a sideperson. A dedicated teacher, Liebman has run a master saxophone class at East Stroudsburg Univ. every summer since the late 1980s. In 1989, he founded the International Association of Schools of Jazz (IASJ). With members in 40 different countries, this organization is a jazz-school network connecting educators and students from around the globe through periodic meetings, exchange programs, and newsletters. He has written and published books on a variety of subjects, produced instructional videos, and contributed regularly to various periodicals such as the *Saxophone Journal* and the *Jazz Educators' Journal*. In recognition of his talents and accomplishments, the Sibelius Academy in Helsinki, Finland, bestowed him with an honorary doctorate in May, 1997. In 1996 he began performing on the tenor again.

Disc. *Open Sky* (1972); *Drum Ode* (1975); *Forgotten Fantasies* (1975); *Lookout Farm* (1975); *Sweet Hands* (1975); *Father Time* (1976); *First Visit* (1977); *Light'n up Please!* (1977); *Omerta* (1978); *Pendulum* (1978); *Dedications* (1979); *Doin' It Again* (1979); *In Australia* (1979); *Lieb: Close Up* (1979); *Opal Heart* (1979); *If Only They Knew* (1980); *What It Is* (1980); *One of a Kind* (1981); *Quest* (1981); *Sweet Fury* (1984); *Double Edge* (1985); *Loneliness of a Long-Distance Runner* (1985); *Quest II* (1986); *Homage to John Coltrane* (1987); *Energy of the Chance* (1988); *Plays Cole Porter* (1988); *Quest/Natural Selection* (1988); *Trio + One* (1988); *Blessing of the Old Long Sound* (1989); *Chant* (1989); *Nine Again* (1989);

Classic Ballads (1990); *Tree* (1990); *West Side Story Today* (1990); *Joy* (1992); *Setting the Standard* (1992); *Songs for My Daughter* (1995); *Meditations* (1995; new interpretation of Coltrane's suite); *Return of the Tenor* (1996); *New Vista* (1996); *The Elements: Water—Giver of Life* (1998, with Pat Metheny, Billy Hart, Cecil McBee).

Writings: *Self-Portrait of a Jazz Artist: Musical Thoughts and Realities* (Rottenberg, Germany, 1988); *A Chromatic Approach to Jazz Harmony and Melody* (Rottenberg, Germany, 1991); *The Improviser's Guide to Transcription* (Stroudsburg, Pa., 1991); *The Complete Guide to Saxophone Sound Production* (Stroudsburg, Pa., 1989).—LP

Lie-Nissen (originally, **Lie**), **Erika,** Norwegian pianist; b. Kongsvinger, Jan. 17, 1845; d. Christiania, Oct. 27, 1903. She studied with Kjerulf in Christiania, T. Kullak in Berlin, and Tellefsen in Paris, then taught at Kullak's Academy in Berlin. She toured throughout Europe, becoming noted for her performances of Chopin. She was prof. of piano at the Copenhagen Cons. (1870–74), then married Dr. Oscar Nissen and settled in Christiania.—NS/LK/DM

Lier, Bertus van
See **Van Lier, Bertus**

Lier, Jacques van
See **Van Lier, Jacques**

Lierhammer, Theodor, Austrian baritone and teacher; b. Lemberg, Nov. 18, 1866; d. Vienna, Jan. 6, 1937. He was a practicing physician when he began to study singing with Ress in Vienna, Carafa in Milan, and Stockhausen in Frankfurt am Main. He made his debut at Vienna in 1894 in a concert with Fritz Kreisler; toured Austria and Hungary (1896), Germany (1898), Russia (1899), France and England (1900), and the U.S. (1904). From 1904 to 1914 he was a prof. of singing at the Royal Academy of Music in London. He served as an army physician during World War I. From 1922 to 1924 he was in London as a singer and teacher; in 1924 he was named prof. of singing at the Academy of Music in Vienna; from 1932 to 1935, he taught at the Austro-American Summer Cons. in Mondsee (Salzburg). One of his American pupils was Roland Hayes.—NS/LK/DM

Lieurance, Thurlow (Weed), American composer; b. Oskaloosa, Iowa, March 21, 1878; d. Boulder, Colo., Oct. 9, 1963. He learned to play the cornet. After serving as a bandmaster during the Spanish-American War, he took courses in harmony and arranging at the Cincinnati Coll. of Music. His visit to the Crow Indian reservation in 1903 prompted him to develop an intense interest in American Indian music and customs. From 1911 he made field recordings of his travels. He later taught at the Municipal Univ. in Wichita, Kans., where he served as dean of its music dept. (1940–57). His collection of American Indian music is housed in the Archive of Folk Culture at the Library of Congress in Washington, D.C. In his compositions, Lieurance found inspiration in the music of the American Indian. His song *By the Waters of Minnetonka* or *Moon Deer* (1917) achieved tremendous popularity.

WORKS: DRAMATIC: *Drama of the Yellowstone.* **ORCH.:** *Minisa* (1930); *Paris, France,* symphonic sketches (1931); *Trails Southwest* (1932); *The Conquistador* (1934); *Colonial Exposition Sketches; Medicine Dance; Water Moon Maiden.* **CHAMBER:** More than 200 salon pieces for various instrumental combinations, including piano pieces (1904–55); numerous arrangements. **VOCAL: C h o r a l :** *Queen Esther,* oratorio (1897); (11) *Indian Love Songs* (1925); (10) *Indian Songs* (1934); part songs; numerous arrangements. **S o n g s F o r V o i c e a n d P i a n o :** *5 Songs* (1907); *9 Indian Songs* (1913); *By the Waters of Minnetonka* or *Moon Deer* (1917); *Songs of the North American Indian* (1920); *Songs from the Yellowstone* (1920–21); *8 Songs from Green Timber* (1921); *Forgotten Trails* (1923); *3 Songs, Each in His Own Tongue* (1925); *6 Songs from Stray Birds* (1937); *From the Land in the Sky* (1941); *Singing Children of the Sun* (1943).—NS/LK/DM

Ligabue, Ilva, Italian soprano; b. Reggio Emilia, May 23, 1932; d. Palermo, Aug. 19, 1998. She studied at the Milan Cons. and at the opera school of Milan's La Scala, where she made her operatic debut as Marina in Wolf-Ferrari's *I quattro Rusteghi* in 1953. She subsequently sang in other Italian and German music centers. From 1958 to 1961 she appeared at the Glyndebourne Festivals, where she was heard as Alice Ford, Fiordiligi, Donna Elvira, and Anna Bolena. In 1961 she made her U.S. debut as Boito's Margherita. In 1963 she sang with the American Opera Soc. in N.Y., at the Vienna State Opera, and at London's Covent Garden, returning to the latter in 1974. Her guest engagements took her to many other U.S. and European music centers.—NS/LK/DM

Ligendza, Catarina (real name, **Katarina Beyron**), Swedish soprano; b. Stockholm, Oct. 18, 1937. Her parents sang at Stockholm's Royal Theater. She studied at the Würzburg Cons., in Vienna, and with Greindl in Saarbrücken. She made her debut as Countess Almaviva in Linz (1965); then sang in Braunschweig and Saarbrücken (1966–69); subsequently became a member of the Deutsche Oper in West Berlin and of the Württemberg State Theater in Stuttgart. In 1970 she sang for the first time at Milan's La Scala and at the Salzburg Easter Festival. She made her Metropolitan Opera debut in N.Y. as Leonore in *Fidelio* on Feb. 25, 1971; that summer she appeared at the Bayreuth Festival; her Covent Garden debut in London followed as Senta in 1972. In subsequent years, she sang in principal operatic centers of Europe before retiring from the operatic stage in 1988. Her other roles included Agathe, Isolde, Brünnhilde, Desdemona, Chrysothemis, and Ariadne.—NS/LK/DM

Ligeti, György (Sándor), eminent Hungarian-born Austrian composer and pedagogue; b. Dicsöszentmárton, Transylvania, May 28, 1923. The original surname of the family was Auer; his great-uncle was **Leopold Auer.** He studied composition with Farkas at the Kolozsvar Cons. (1941–43) and privately with Kadosa in Budapest (1942–43). He then continued his training with Veress, Járdányi, Farkas, and Bárdos at the

Budapest Academy of Music (1945–49), where he subsequently was a prof. of harmony, counterpoint, and analysis (from 1950). After the Hungarian revolution was crushed by the Soviet Union in 1956, he fled his homeland for the West. In 1967 he became a naturalized Austrian citizen. He worked at the electronic music studio of the West German Radio in Cologne (1957–58); from 1959 to 1972 he lectured at the Darmstadt summer courses in new music; from 1961 to 1971 he also was a visiting prof. at the Stockholm Musikhögskolan. In 1972 he served as composer-in- residence at Stanford Univ., and in 1973 he taught at the Berkshire Music Center at Tanglewood. From 1973 to 1989 he was a prof. of composition at the Hamburg Hochschule für Musik. He has received numerous honors and awards. In 1964 he was made a member of the Royal Swedish Academy of Music in Stockholm, in 1968 a member of the Akademie der Künste in Berlin, and in 1984 an honorary member of the American Academy and Inst. of Arts and Letters; in 1986 he received the Grawemeyer Award of the Univ. of Louisville; in 1988 he was made a Commandeur in the Ordre National des Arts et Lettres in Paris; in 1990 he was awarded the Austrian State Prize; in 1991 he received the Praemium imperiale of Japan; in 1993 he won the Ernst von Siemens Music Prize of Munich; in 1996 he received the Music Prize of the Wolf Foundation in Jerusalem and the Music Prize of UNESCO. In his bold and imaginative experimentation with musical materials and parameters, Ligeti endeavors to bring together all aural and visual elements in a synthetic entity, making use of all conceivable effects and alternating tremendous sonorous upheavals with static chordal masses and shifting dynamic colors. He describes his orch. style as micropolyphony.

WORKS: DRAMATIC: *Le Grand Macabre,* opera (1974–77; Stockholm, April 12, 1978; rev. version, Salzburg, July 28, 1997); *Rondeau* for Actor and Tape (1976; Stuttgart, Feb. 26, 1977). **ORCH.:** *Romanian Concerto* for Small Orch. (1951); *Sechs Miniaturen* for Wind Ensemble (1953–75; Schwetzingen, May 16, 1976); *Apparitions* (1958–59; Cologne, June 19, 1960); *Atmosphères* (Donaueschingen, Oct. 22, 1961); *Fragment* for Chamber Orch. (1961; Munich, April 1962); Cello Concerto (1966; Berlin, April 19, 1967); *Lontano* (Donaueschingen, Oct. 22, 1967); *Ramifications* for String Orch. or 12 Solo Strings (1968–69; first version, Berlin, April 23, 1969; second version, Saarbrücken, Oct. 10, 1969); Chamber Concerto for 13 Instruments (Ottawa, April 2, 1970); *Melodien* (Nuremberg, Dec. 10, 1971); Double Concerto for Flute, Oboe, and Orch. (Berlin, Sept. 16, 1972); *San Francisco Polyphony* (1973–74; San Francisco, Jan. 8, 1975); *Mysteries of the Macabre* for Trumpet and Orch. (1974–77; 1992; Paris, Jan. 20, 1994); Piano Concerto (1985–88; movements 1–3, Graz, Oct. 23, 1986; movements 4–5, Vienna, Feb. 29, 1988); *Macabre Collage* (1991; Florence, May 16, 1992; arranged from the opera *Le Grand Macabre* by E. Howarth); Violin Concerto (first version, Cologne, Nov. 3, 1990; second version, Cologne, Oct. 8, 1992). **CHAMBER:** Cello Sonata (1948–53); *Andante und Allegretto* for String Quartet (1950; Salzburg, July 28, 1994); *Sechs Bagatellen* for Wind Quintet (1953; Södertälje, Sweden, Oct. 6, 1969); 2 string quartets: No. 1, *Métamorphoses nocturnes* (1953–54; Vienna, May 8, 1958) and No. 2 (1968; Baden-Baden, Dec. 14, 1969); 10 Pieces for Wind Quintet (1968; Malmö, Jan. 20, 1969); Trio for Violin, Horn, and Piano (Hamburg-Bergedorf, Aug. 7, 1982); Sonata for Solo Viola (1991–94; Gütersloh, April 23, 1994).

KEYBOARD: P i a n o : *Frühe Stücke* for Piano, 4-hands (1942–51); *Musica ricercata* (1951–53); *Trois bagatelles* (1961); *Monument, Selbstportrait, Bewegung* for 2 Pianos (Cologne, May 15, 1976); *13 Études* (1985–93). O r g a n : *Volumina* (1961–62); 2 studies: No. 1, *Harmonies* (1967) and No. 2, *Coulée* (1969). H a r p s i c h o r d : *Continuum* (1968); *Hungarian Rock (Chaconne)* (1978); *Passacaglia ungherese* (1978). VOCAL: *Ifúsági kantáta* (Cantata for Youth) for Soprano, Contralto, Tenor, Baritone, Chorus, and Orch. (1949); *Pápainé* for Chorus (1953); *Éjszaka* (Night) and *Reggel* (Morning) for Chorus (1955); *Aventures* for 3 Singers and 7 Instruments (1962; Hamburg, April 4, 1963); *Nouvelles aventures* for Aventures Ensemble (1962–65; Hamburg, May 26, 1966); *Aventures & Nouvelles aventures*, theater piece based on the 2 preceding works (Stuttgart, Oct. 19, 1966); *Requiem* for Soprano, Mezzo-soprano, 2 Choruses, and Orch. (1963–65; Stockholm, March 14, 1965); *Clocks and Clouds* for Women's Chorus and Orch. (1972–73; Graz, Oct. 15, 1973); *Lux aeterna* for 16 Voices (Stuttgart, Nov. 2, 1966); *Drei Phantasien* for 16 Voices (Stockholm, Sept. 26, 1983); *Magyar etüdök* (Hungarian Studies) for 16 Voices (1983); *Nonsense Madrigals* for 6 Men's Voices (1988–93). ELECTRONIC: *Glissandi* (1957); *Artikulation* (1958); *Pièce électronique* No. 3 (1957–58). OTHER: *Poème symphonique* for 100 Metronomes (1962; Hilversum, Sept. 13, 1963).

BIBL.: E. Salmenhaara, *Das musikalische Material und seine Behandlung in den Werken "Apparitions," "Atmosphères," "Aventures" und "Requiem" von G. L.* (Helsinki and Regensburg, 1969); O. Nordwall, *G. L.: Eine Monographie* (Mainz, 1971); P. Griffiths, *G. L.* (London, 1983); E. Restagno, ed., *L.* (Turin, 1985); H. Sabbe, *G. L.: Studien zur kompositorischen Phänomenologie* (Munich, 1987); R. Richart, *G. L.: A Bio-Bibliography* (N.Y., 1990); P. Peterson, ed., *Für G. L.: Die Referate des L.-Kongresses Hamburg 1988* (Laaber, 1991); W. Burde, *G. L.: Eine Monographie* (Zürich, 1993); U. Dibelius, *G. L.: Eine Monographie in Essays* (Mainz, 1994); C. Floros, *G. L.: Jenseits von Avantgarde und Postmoderne* (Vienna, 1996); F. Sallis, *An Introduction to the Early Works of G. L.* (Cologne, 1996); C. Engelbrecht, W. Marx, and B. Sweers, *Lontano-"Aus weiter Ferne:" Zur Musiksprache und Assoziationsvielfalt G. L.s* (Hamburg, 1997).—NS/LK/DM

Ligeti, Lukas, Austrian composer and percussionist; b. Vienna, June 13, 1965. He began playing percussion at the age of 18, then studied with Erich Urbanner (composition) and Fritz Ozmec (jazz drums) at the Vienna Academy of Muisc (diploma, 1993); also attended summer courses in new music at Darmstadt, taking improvisation workshops with John Zorn (1988) and David Moss (1991) and in composition with Crumb (1991). In 1994 he became a visting scholar at the Center for Computer Research in Music and Acoustics at Stanford Univ. Among his awards are composition grants from the city of Vienna (1989, 1993), a Foerderungspreis of the city of Vienna (1990), an Austrian state grant for composition (1991), and a prize of the Austrian Ministry for Science and Research (1993). Ligeti has been strongly influenced by jazz, rock, and traditional musics; he developed a new way of playing drums based on movement patterns derived from central and east African practices, as well as a new tablature. He has also devoted much time to the art of improvisation.

WORKS: *Pattern Transformation* for 4 Percussionists on 2 Marimbas (1988); *Oblique Narratives*, 3 pieces for 2 Pianos (1989–90); *Frozen State of Song* for Saxophone Quartet (1990–93); *Seeking Scapegoat* for Violin, Soprano Saxophone, 2 Electric Guitars, and Drums (1991); *The Chinese Wall* for Orch. (1992); *Groove Magic* for 11 Musicians and Computer-controlled Click Tracks (1992–93); *Tonga Tango* for Chorus (1993).—NS/LK/DM

Light, Enoch (Henry), American orchestra conductor, violinist, and record company executive; b. Canton, Ohio, Aug. 18, 1907; d. N.Y., July 31, 1978. Though his career dated back to the 1930s, when he became a bandleader and fronted a successful dance orchestra in hotels, Light gained his greatest fame for a series of albums primarily in the early 1960s that exploited the sonic possibilities of stereo sound, notably *Persuasive Percussion* and *Stereo 35/MM*.

Light was the son of Morris and Rose Feiman Light; his father was a musician. He earned a B. A. from Johns Hopkins Univ. in 1926. He attended the Dana Musical Inst., then moved to N.Y., where he studied violin with Michael Banner and Arthur Lichstein and piano and harmony with Modena Scoville in 1928–29. He married Mary Danis on Nov. 18, 1929; they had two daughters. He went to Europe in 1930 and attended the Mozarteum in Salzburg, then made his conducting debut with the Salzburg Symphony. He returned to the U.S. in 1931 and earned an M. A. from N.Y.U., then organized his own band, The Light Brigade, which performed in theaters and enjoyed residencies in several N.Y. hotels, notably the Taft.

Light was involved in a serious automobile accident while touring with his band, and during his recuperation he resolved to focus his activities on conducting and producing records. He formed his own label, Grand Award, which enjoyed its first successes with a series of albums devoted to the music of the 1920s, *The Roaring 20's*, two of which reached the charts in 1957, credited to the Charleston City All-Stars. As Enoch Light and the Light Brigade he scored a Top 40 hit with "I Want to Be Happy Cha Cha" (music by Vincent Youmans, lyrics by Irving Caesar) in the fall of 1958, and he charted with an identically titled LP in the spring of 1959.

Light sold Grand Award to ABC Records and stayed on as the label's managing director while launching the stereo sister label Command Records. The initial Command release, *Persuasive Percussion*, credited to Terry Snyder and the All-Stars, hit #1 in April 1960, remained in the charts more than two years, and went gold. Light also put five more albums into the charts in 1960, under such names as the Command All-Stars and Los Admiradores as well as Enoch Light and the Light Brigade. He returned to #1 in November 1961 with *Stereo 35/MM*, the title referring to the procedure of recording on film stock rather than audio tape for greater fidelity. The albums *Stereo 35/MM, Volume Two* (1962), and *Big Band Bossa Nova* (1962) also reached the Top Ten.

In 1965, Light left Command Records and founded a new label, Project 3, with which he continued to issue frequent instrumental albums. The last of these to reach the charts was *Big Band Hits of the '30s & '40s* in July 1971. He died at age 70 in 1978.—WR

Lightfoot, Gordon, prolific folk-style singer-songwriter; b. Orillia, Ontario, Canada, Nov. 17, 1938.

Gordon Lightfoot was first known in the United States as the composer of "For Lovin' Me" and "Early Morning Rain," recorded by Ian and Sylvia and Peter, Paul and Mary in the 1960s. Finally established in his own right in the United States with 1970's *Sit Down Young Stranger* (reissued as *If You Could Read My Mind*, after the title hit), Lightfoot enjoyed considerable success in the mid-1970s, only to fade from popularity during the 1980s. The author of some five hundred compositions, Gordon Lightfoot has seen his songs covered by a wide variety of artists, including Bob Dylan, Elvis Presley, Barbra Streisand, and Waylon Jennings.

Gordon Lightfoot started piano lessons at age eight and taught himself guitar while in high school. Writing his first song at 17, he studied composition at Westlake Coll. in Los Angeles before returning to Toronto to play bars, clubs, and coffeehouses. In 1963 he hosted a country-music television show in England, later returning to Canada to work on the CBC television series *Country Hoedown*. He recorded for Chateau and ABC-Paramount and performed with Jim Whalen as the Two Tones in the mid-1960s. Fellow Canadians Ian and Sylvia (Tyson) were the first to record any of Lightfoot's songs, but Peter, Paul and Mary were the act that first scored hits with his "For Lovin' Me" and "Early Morning Rain," in 1965.

Signed to United Artists Records, Gordon Lightfoot recorded four albums for the label before registering a chart entry with 1969's *Sunday Concert*. Quickly recognized in Canada, he remained virtually unknown in the United States through the late 1960s, despite his having recorded a number of his own excellent compositions such as "The Way I Feel," "Ribbon of Darkness," "Canadian Railroad Trilogy," "The Last Time I Saw Her," and "Did She Mention My Name?"

Switching to Warner Bros.' Reprise label at the end of 1969, Gordon Lightfoot's debut for the label yielded the smash hit "If You Could Read My Mind" while containing other outstanding songs such as "Approaching Lavender," "Saturday Clothes," and "Sit Down Young Stranger." Following several modest-selling albums, Lightfoot established himself with 1973's *Sundown*, which featured "The Watchman's Gone" and the poignant "Too Late for Praying" and produced the top title hit and near-smash "Carefree Highway." "Rainy Day People" became a major hit in 1975, followed by the dirgelike smash "The Wreck of the Edmund Fitzgerald." Lightfoot hit with "The Circle Is Small (I Can See It in Your Eyes)" in 1978 on Warner Bros., for whom he continued to record into the mid-1980s. His popularity faded during the 1980s, but he eventually reemerged in 1993 with *Waiting for You*.

DISC.: *Lightfoot* (1966); *The Way I Feel* (1967); *Did She Mention My Name?* (1968); *Back Here on Earth* (1969); *Sunday Concert* (1969); *Best* (1970); *Classic Lightfoot—Best, Vol. 2* (1971); *Very Best* (1974); *The United Artists Collection* (1993); *Sit Down Young Stranger* (1970); *Summer Side of Life* (1971); *Don Quixote* (1972); *Old Dan's Record* (1972); *Sundown* (1973); *Cold on the Shoulder* (1975); *Gord's Gold* (1975); *Summertime Dream* (1976); *Endless Wire* (1978); *Dream Street Rose* (1980); *Shadows* (1982); *Salute* (1983); *East of Midnight* (1986); *Gord's Gold, Vol. II* (1989); *Songbook* (1986); *Best* (1991); *Waiting for You* (1993).

BIBL.: Alfrieda Gabiou, *G. L.* (N.Y., 1979).—**BH**

Lightsey, Kirk, American pianist; b. Detroit, Mich., Feb. 15, 1937. He was born in one of the American hotbeds of bop pianism and it is no surprise that the style forms a substantial portion of his musical persona. It was there that he learned piano at an early age before spending some time in his high school band as a clarinet player. After a stint in the Army, he made a career of accompanying singers such as Ernestine Anderson, Damita Jo, and O.C. Smith before finally getting the chance to record with Sonny Stitt in 1965. Shortly after that, he joined Chet Baker's band, recording a series of well- received albums with the trumpeter/singer. His next marquee setting was with saxophonist Dexter Gordon, and he has also worked and recorded with a wide variety of, others players, including Don Cherry, Jimmy Raney, Clifford Jordan, and James Moody. Living in Europe since the 1980s, he is an important cog in jazz supergroups the Leaders and Roots.

DISC.: *Lightsey 1* (1983); *Everything Happens to Me* (1983); *Isotope* (1983); *Lightsey 2* (1985); *Shorter by Two* (1985); *Everything Is Changed* (1986); *Lightsey Live* (1986); *Kirk 'n Marcus* (1987); *Heaven Dance* (1988); *Temptation* (1991); *From Kirk to Nat* (1991); *First Affairs* (1993); *Saying Something* (1995).—**GM**

Lilburn, Douglas (Gordon), notable New Zealand composer and teacher; b. Wanganui, Nov. 2, 1915. He was a student of J.C. Bradshaw at Canterbury Univ. Coll., Christchurch (1934–36). As winner of the Grainger Competition with his symphonic poem *Forest* (1936), he was able to pursue his studies in London with Vaughan Williams at the Royal Coll. of Music (1937–40). He was composer-in-residence at the Cambridge Summer Music Schools (1946–49; 1951). In 1947 he began teaching at Victoria Univ. in Wellington, where he was a lecturer (1949–55), senior lecturer (1955–63), assoc. prof. (1963–70), and prof. (1970–79). In 1966 he founded New Zealand's first electronic music studio there, serving as its director until 1979. In 1967 he founded the Wai-te-ata Press Music Editions. His Lilburn Trust has done much to encourage the promotion of music in New Zealand. He publ. the lectures *A Search for Tradition* (Wellington, 1984) and *A Search for a Language* (Wellington, 1985). In 1988 Lilburn was made a member of the Order of New Zealand. In his early works, Lilburn found inspiration in traditional forms of expression. About 1953 he embraced an eclectic style, primarily influenced by Stravinsky, Bartók, the Second Viennese School, and modern American composers. By 1962 he pursued a more adventuresome path as a proponent of electronic music.

WORKS: DRAMATIC: *Landfall in Unknown Seas*, incidental music (1942). **ORCH.:** *Forest*, symphonic poem (1936); *Drysdale Overture* (1937; rev. 1940 and 1986); *Festival Overture* (1939); *Aotearoa Overture* (London, April 16, 1940); *Introduction and Allegro* for Strings (1942); *4 Canzonas* for Strings (1943–50); *A Song of Islands* or *Song of the Antipodes* (1946; Wellington, Aug. 20, 1947); *Cambridge Overture* (1946); *Diversions* for Strings (1947); 3 syms.: No. 1 (1949; Wellington, May 12, 1951), No. 2 (1951; rev. 1974), and No. 3 (1961); Suite (1955; rev. 1956); *A Birthday Offering* (1956). **CHAMBER:** *Fantasy* for String Quartet (1939); *Allegro concertante* for Violin and Piano (1944; rev.

1945); Trio for Violin, Viola, and Cello (1945); String Quartet (1946; rev. 1981); Clarinet Sonatina (1948); Violin Sonata (1950); *Duos* for 2 Violins (1954); Quartet for 2 Trumpets, Horn, and Trombone (1957); Wind Quintet (1957); *17 Pieces* for Guitar (1962–70). **KEYBOARD: P i a n o :** *3 Sea Changes* (1945–72; rev. 1981); *Chaconne* (1946); 2 sonatinas (1946, 1962); Sonata (1949); *9 Short Pieces* (1965–66; rev. 1967). **O r g a n :** *Prelude and Fugue* (1944). **VOCAL:** *Prodigal Country* for Baritone, Chorus, and Orch. (1939); *Elegy: In memoriam Noel Newson* for 2 Voices and Strings (1945); *3 Songs* for Voice and Piano (1947–54); *Elegy* for Baritone and Piano (1951); *Sings Harry* for Baritone and Piano, or Tenor and Guitar (1954); *3 Poems of the Sea* for Narrator and Strings (1958); *3 Songs* for Baritone and Viola (1958). **ELECTRONIC:** *The Return* (1965); *Poem in Time of War* (1967); *Summer Voices* (1969); *Expo '70 Dance Sequence* (1970); *3 Inscapes* (1972); *Carousel* (1976); *Winterset* (1976); *Of Time and Nostalgia* (1977); *Triptych* (1977); *Soundscape with Lake and River* (1979).

BIBL.: V. Harris and P. Norman, eds., *D. L.: A Festschrift for D. L. on His Retirement from the Victoria University of Wellington* (Wellington, 1980); P. Norman, *The Beginnings and Development of a New Zealand Music: The Life and Work of D. L., 1940–65* (diss., Univ. of Canterbury, Christchurch, 1983).—**NS/LK/DM**

Liliencron, Rochus, Freiherr von, eminent German music scholar; b. Plön, Dec. 8, 1820; d. Koblenz, March 5, 1912. He began his studies in Plön and after further training in Lübeck, he took courses in theology, law, and philology at the univs. of Kiel and Berlin (Ph.D., 1846, with the diss. *Über Neidharts höflische Dorfpoesie*; publ. in the *Zeitschrift für deutsche Altertum*, VI, 1848). He subsequently pursued Old Norse studies in Copenhagen and qualified as a Privatdozent in Bonn. In 1851 he became a teacher of Old Norse language and literature at the Univ. of Kiel. After teaching philology in Jena (from 1852), he was in the service of the court of the Duke of Saxe-Meiningen (1855–58). In 1858 the Royal Bavarian Academy of Science commissioned him to collect German folk songs, which he publ. as *Die historischen Volkslieder der Deutschen vom 13. bis 16. Jahrhundert* (4 vols. and appendix, Leipzig, 1865–69). With F. von Wegele, he then ed. the valuable *Allgemeine deutsche Biographie* (53 vols., Leipzig, 1875–1907). In 1876 he was made prelate and prior at St. John's Monastery in Schleswig. In 1909 he went to Berlin, and then settled in Koblenz in 1911. In 1894 he became head of the editorial commission of the Denkmäler deutscher Tonkunst, and was responsible for overseeing about 45 of its vols. for publication. Liliencron was one of the foremost music scholars of his day. His scholarly pursuits were complemented by his extensive knowledge of philology, literature, and theology. He publ. an autobiography, *Frohe Jugendtage, Lebenserrinnerungen, Kindern und Enkeln erzählt* (Leipzig, 1902). H. Kretzschmar ed. a Festschrift in honor of his 90th birthday (Leipzig, 1910).

WRITINGS: With W. Stade, *Lieder und Sprüche aus det letzten Zeit des Minnesangs* (Weimar, 1854); *Deutsches Leben im Volkslied um 1530* (Berlin and Stuttgart, 1885); *Die horazischen Metren in deutschen Kompositionen des XVI. Jahrhunderts* (Leipzig, 1887); *Liturgisch- musikalische Geschichte der evangelischen Gottesdienste von 1523 bis 1700* (Schleswig, 1893); *Die Aufgaben des Choregesanges im heutigen Gottesdienste* (Oppeln, 1895); *Chorodnung für die Sonn-und Festtage des evangelischen Kirchenjahres*

(Gütersloh, 1900); *Volksliederbuch für Männerchöre* (Leipzig, 1906).

BIBL.: A. Bettelheim, *Leben und Wirken des Freiherrn R. v. L.* (Berlin, 1917).—**NS/LK/DM**

Lili'uokalani (Lydia Kamaka'eha Paki), Hawaiian queen and composer; b. Honolulu, Sept. 2, 1838; d. there, Nov. 11, 1917. She entered the Chief's Children's School to study music when she was 4. She became a skillful pianist, organist, and choral director, and composed a number of attractive songs, including the popular *Aloha 'oe* (1878). She also wrote the Hawaiian national anthem, *He mele lahui Hawaii*. Her reign as queen was brief (1891–93); she was removed by American interests.—**NS/LK/DM**

Liljeblad, Ingeborg, Finnish soprano; b. Helsinki, Oct. 17, 1887; d. there, Feb. 28, 1942. She studied in Berlin with Etelka Gerster, and in Paris with Félia Litvinne. She was engaged at the Mannheim Opera (1911–13) and the Hamburg Opera (1913–14). Returning to Helsinki in 1927, she taught at the Sibelius Academy. She was married to the conductor Leo Funtek.—**NS/LK/DM**

Liljefors, Ingemar (Kristian), Swedish pianist and composer, son of **Ruben (Mattias) Liljefors**; b. Göteborg, Dec. 13, 1906; d. Stockholm, Oct. 14, 1981. He studied at the Royal Academy of Music in Stockholm (1923–27; 1929–31) and in Munich (1927–29). He taught piano (1938–43) and harmony (from 1943) at the Stockholm Musikhögskolan. From 1947 to 1963 he was chairman of the Assn. of Swedish Composers. He publ. a manual on harmony from the functional point of view (1937) and one on harmonic analysis along similar lines (1951). His compositions frequently employed elements of Swedish folk music with a later infusion of some modernistic techniques.

WORKS: DRAMATIC: O p e r a : *Hyrkusken* (The Coachman; 1951). **ORCH.:** *Rhapsody* for Piano and Orch. (1936); Piano Concerto (1940); Sym. (1943); Piano Concertino (1949); Violin Concerto (1956); *Sinfonietta* (1961); *2 Intermezzi* for Strings (1966); *Divertimento* for Strings (1968). **CHAMBER:** 2 piano trios (1940, 1961); Violin Sonatina (1954); 3 piano sonatinas (1954, 1964, 1965); Cello Sonatina (1958); String Quartet (1963); Sonatina for Solo Violin (1968). **VOCAL:** *En Tijdh-Spegel* (A Mirror of the Times) for Soloists, Chorus, and Orch. (1959; Swedish Radio, April 16, 1961).—**NS/LK/DM**

Liljefors, Ruben (Mattias), Swedish composer and conductor, father of **Ingemar (Kristian) Liljefors**; b. Uppsala, Sept. 30, 1871; d. there, March 4, 1936. He studied in Uppsala; then with Jadassohn at the Leipzig Cons.; later in Dresden with Draeseke and with Reger in Leipzig. Returning to Sweden, he was conductor of the Göteborg Phil. (1902–11) and the Gavleborg Orch. Soc. (1912–31). His works, which included a Piano Concerto (1899; rewritten 1922), Sym. (1906), *Sommer-Suite* for Orch. (1920), choral works, chamber music, piano pieces, and songs, followed in the Romantic tradition.—**NS/LK/DM**

Lill, John (Richard), English pianist; b. London, March 17, 1944. He studied at the Royal Coll. of Music in London (1955–64); also with Kempff in Positano. He made his debut at a concert in the Royal Festival Hall in London in 1963; was joint first prizewinner at the Tchaikovsky Competition in Moscow (1970), which was the beginning of his successful international career. In 1978 he received the Order of the British Empire. While Lill's repertoire ranges from the classics to the moderns, he has won particular distinction for his cycles of the music of Beethoven.—NS/LK/DM

Lillo, Giuseppe, Italian composer and teacher; b. Galatina, Lecce, Feb. 26, 1814; d. Naples, Feb. 4, 1863. He began his training with his father. After taking counterpoint lessons with Carnovale in Lecce, he settled in Naples and studied with Francesco Lanaza (piano), Furno (harmony and counterpoint), and Zingarelli (composition) at the Reale Collegio di Musica (later the Cons. di S. Pietro a Majella). In 1846 he joined its faculty as prof. of harmony, and then was prof. of counterpoint and composition from 1859 until mental illness compelled him to resign in 1861. His compositions include the operas *La moglie per 24 ore ossia L'ammalato di buona salute* (Naples, 1834) and *L'osteria i Andujar* (Naples, Sept. 1840), syms., chamber music, piano pieces, and sacred choral works.—NS/LK/DM

Lima, Jeronymo Francisco de, Portuguese organist, pedagogue, and composer; b. Lisbon, Sept. 30, 1743; d. there, Feb. 19, 1822. He received training at the Seminário Patriarcal in Lisbon (1751–61) and at the Cons. di S. Onofrio in Naples (1761–67). Returning to Lisbon, he became a member of the Brotherhood of St. Cecilia in 1767. He also taught music at the Seminário Patriarcal. In 1785 he was made mestre and in 1798 mestre de capela at the Cathedral, as well as organist of the royal chamber in 1800. Among his works were several stage pieces and numerous sacred works. His brother, Braz Francisco de Lima (b. Lison, May 3?, 1752; d. there, Sept. 15, 1813), was also a composer. He studied at the Cons. di S. Onofrio in Naples and at the Seminário Patriarcal in Lisbon. He eventually abandoned his musical career to pursue business interests. All the same, he composed many sacred works. —LK/DM

Lima, Luis, Argentine tenor; b. Córdoba, Sept. 12, 1948. He was trained in Buenos Aires and at the Madrid Cons. After taking prizes in the Toulouse (1972) and Francisco Viñas (1973) competitions, he took first prize in the Lauri-Volpe competition (1973). In 1974 he made his operatic debut as Turiddu in Lisbon, and then appeared throughout Germany. He made his U.S. debut in a concert performance of Donizetti's *Gemma di Vergy* at N.Y.'s Carnegie Hall in 1976. In 1977 he sang for the first time at Milan's La Scala as Donizetti's Edgardo. On March 16, 1978, he made his N.Y.C. Opera debut as Alfredo, which role he also chose for his Metropolitan Opera debut in N.Y. on Sept. 20, 1978. He appeared as Cavaradossi at the Teatro Colón in Buenos Aires in 1982. In 1984 he made his debut at London's Covent Garden

as Nemorino. He sang Cavaradossi at the Salzburg Easter Festival in 1988. In 1992 he appeared as Don Carlos at the San Francisco Opera. After singing Rodolfo at Covent Garden in 1996, he portrayed Don Carlos at the Metropolitan Opera in 1997. In 1999 he portrayed Pinkerton at the San Francisco Opera. Among his other roles were Berlioz's and Boito's Faust, Verdi's Riccardo, Bizet's Don José, Gounod's Faust and Roméo, and Puccini's Rodolfo.—NS/LK/DM

Limnander de Nieuwenhove, Armand Marie Ghislain, Belgian composer; b. Ghent, May 22, 1814; d. Moignanville, near Paris, Aug. 15, 1892. He studied in Freiburg with Lambillotte and in Brussels with Fétis. In 1835 he became a choral director in Mechelen. In 1845 he settled in Paris.

WORKS: DRAMATIC: Grand Opera: *Le Maître-chanteur* (Paris, 1853). Comic Opera: *Les Monténégrins* (Paris, 1849); *Le Château de la Barbe- Bleue* (1851); *Yvonne* (1859). OTHER: Sym., *La Fin des Moisson*; *Scènes druidiques* for Orch.; String Quartet; Cello Sonata; church music; songs; etc. —NS/LK/DM

Lin, Cho-Liang, outstanding Chinese-born American violinist; b. Hsin-Chu, Taiwan, Jan. 29, 1960. He began to study the violin as a child and won the Taiwan National Youth Violin Competition at age 10. When he was 12, he became a pupil of Robert Pikler at the New South Wales State Conservatorium of Music in Sydney, and when he was 15, he went to the U.S., where he enrolled at the Juilliard School in N.Y. as a scholarship student of Dorothy DeLay (graduated, 1981). He won wide notice when he was chosen to play at the inaugural concert in Washington, D.C., for President Jimmy Carter in 1977; that same year, he won first prize in the Queen Sofia International Competition in Madrid. In subsequent years, he pursued a highly rewarding career as a virtuoso, touring throughout the world; he appeared as a soloist with virtually every major orch., and also was active as a recitalist and chamber music player. In 1988 he became a naturalized U.S. citizen. His extensive repertoire ranges from the standard literature to specially commissioned works. In his performances, he combines effortless technique with a beguiling luminosity of tone.—NS/LK/DM

Lincke, (Carl Emil) Paul, German conductor and composer; b. Berlin, Nov. 7, 1866; d. Klausthal-Zellerfeld, near Göttingen, Sept. 3, 1946. After studies with Rudolf Kleinow in Wittenberge (1880–84), he was active in Berlin as a bassoonist in and later conductor of theater orchs. He also became active as a composer of small operettas and other light theater pieces, scoring his first success with *Venus auf Erden* (June 6, 1897). After a sojourn at the Folies-Bergère in Paris (1897–99), he returned to Berlin and brought out such works as *Frau Luna* (May 1, 1899), *Im Reiche des Indra* (Dec. 18, 1899), *Fräulein Loreley* (Oct. 15, 1900), *Lysistrata* (April 1, 1902; best known for its *Glühwürmchen*-[Glowworm] *Idyll*), *Nakiris Hochzeit* (Nov. 6, 1902), and *Berliner Luft* (Sept. 28, 1904). Among his later works, only *Gri-gri* (Cologne, March 25, 1911) and *Casanova* (Chemnitz, Nov. 5, 1913) attracted much attention. He subsequently devoted himself mainly to conducting and overseeing his own publishing firm, Apollo Verlag. During the Nazi era, Lincke's works were successfully revived and the composer was granted various honors. His new-won fame, however, did not survive the collapse of the Third Reich.

BIBL.: E. Nick, *P. L.* (Hamburg, 1953); O. Schneidereit, *P. L. und die Entstehung der Berliner Operette* (Berlin, 1974). —NS/LK/DM

Lincke, Joseph, Silesian cellist and composer; b. Trachenberg, June 8, 1783; d. Vienna, March 26, 1837. He studied violin with his father and cello with Oswald. He settled in Vienna, where he was cellist in Schuppanzigh's quartet (1808–16). After serving as chamber musician to Countess Erdődy in Pancovecz, near Zagreb (1816–18), he returned to Vienna as first cellist of the orch. at the Theater an der Wien. He composed concertos, variations, capriccios, etc.—NS/LK/DM

Lincoln, Abbey (Wooldridge, Anna Marie) (Aminata Moseka), talented jazz singer, composer, actress; b. Chicago, Ill., Aug. 6, 1930. Lincoln is an intuitive and often compelling singer who is able to overcome her occasional problems with intonation and range. Her delivery makes her one of the most striking singers ever, and few can match her way with lyrics and moods. Her repertory is consistently nontraditional and provocative.

The tenth child in her family, she could pick out melodies on the piano at age five and eventually learned to sing accompaniment to her piano playing. At 19 she got her first job, playing piano and singing in the basement of the A.M.E. Church in Jackson, Mich., for which she was paid five dollars per week. She began singing in dance bands in Chicago, then moved to the West Coast in 1951. In L.A. in 1954, she allowed the producers at the famous Moulin Rouge to change her name. Her first mentor, lyricist Bob Russell, named her Abbey Lincoln and produced her first recording with Benny Carter and Marty Paitch. He was also instrumental in securing Lincoln a featured performance in the Jayne Mansfield movie, *The Girl Can't Help It* (1957), where her sultry looks earned her some brief notoriety as the "Black Marilyn Monroe." After meeting Max Roach that year, Lincoln changed her image and became a serious singer and political activist. Their "Freedom Now Suite," released in 1960, was one of the harbingers of changing sentiments in the Black community. Her album *Straight Ahead* was criticized by Ira Gitler for being too overtly political, leading to a published panel discussion on jazz and race in *Down Beat* (March 1962). In her début as a lead actress in the independently produced *Nothing But a Man* (1964; dir. Michael Roehmer), her performance is sensitive and luminous. In 1968 she played the title role with Sidney Poitier in *For Love of Ivy*. She changed her name to Aminata Moseka in 1975, following a trip to Africa. She had a period of inactivity in the early 1980s, but resurfaced in the 1990s. She writes more of her own songs now, and they are poetic and haunting. In 1992 her band was Rodney

Kendrick, Michael Bowie, and Aaron Walker (a fine D.C.-based drummer); by 1996 the only change was Marc Cary replacing Kendrick on piano. She has performed on BET-TV, and is the subject of a documentary, *You Gotta Pay the Band*.

DISC.: *Affair...A Story of a Girl in Love* (1956); *That's Him* (1957); *It's Magic* (1958); *Abbey Is Blue* (1959); *Straight Ahead* (1961); *People in Me* (1973); *Golden Lady* (1981); *Talking to the Sun* (1983); *A Tribute to Billie Holiday* (1987); *Abbey Sings Billie, Vol. 1, 2* (1987); *World Is Falling Down* (1990); *You Gotta Pay the Band* (1991); *Devil's Got Your Tongue* (1992); *When There Is Love* (1992); *A Turtle's Dream* (1994); *Who Used to Dance* (1996).—LP

Lind, Eva, Austrian soprano; b. Innsbruck, June 14, 1965. She received vocal training in Vienna. In 1983 she made her debut as a Flower Maiden in *Parsifal* in Innsbruck. In 1986 she sang Lucia in Basel and at the Vienna State Opera, and also the Italian Singer in *Capriccio* at the Salzburg Festival. She appeared as the Queen of the Night in Paris in 1987. In 1988 she made her British debut as Nannetta at the Glyndebourne Festival. She was engaged as Gounod's Juliet in Zürich in 1990, and in 1993 she sang Weber's Aennechen in Bonn. She appeared as Blondchen in Catania in 1996. —NS/LK/DM

Lind, Jenny (actually, **Johanna Maria**), famous Swedish soprano, called the "Swedish Nightingale"; b. Stockholm, Oct. 6, 1820; d. Wynds Point, Herefordshire, Nov. 2, 1887. She made her first stage appearance in Stockholm at the age of 10 (Nov. 29, 1830), the same year that she entered the Royal Opera School there, where she studied with C. Craelius and I. Berg; during this period, she also sang in many comedies and melodramas. She continued her studies with A. Lindblad and J. Josephson at the school, and then made her formal operatic debut as Agathe in *Der Freischütz* at the Royal Opera in Stockholm (March 7, 1838); later that year appeared as Pamina and Euryanthe there, and then as Donna Anna (1839) and Norina (1841). In 1840 she was appointed a regular member of the Royal Swedish Academy of Music, and was also given the rank of court singer. However, she felt the necessity of improving her voice, and went to Paris to study with Manuel García (1841–42). Upon her return to Stockholm, she sang Norma (Oct. 10, 1842); later appeared there as the Countess in *Le nozze di Figaro*, Anna in *La Sonnambula*, Valentine in *Les Huguenots*, and Anna Bolena. Although Meyerbeer wrote the role of Vielka in his opera *Ein Feldlager in Schlesien* for her, the role was first sung by Tuczec in Berlin (Dec. 7, 1844); Lind first essayed it there on Jan. 4, 1845. She also sang in Hannover, Hamburg, Cologne, Koblenz, Frankfurt am Main, Darmstadt, and Copenhagen. She appeared at the Leipzig Gewandhaus (Dec. 4, 1845) and made her Vienna debut as Norma at the Theater an der Wien (April 22, 1846); subsequently sang throughout Germany, returning to Vienna as Marie in 1847 and creating a sensation. Lind made a phenomenally successful London debut as Alice in *Robert le diable* at Her Majesty's Theatre in London (May 4, 1847); her appearances in *La Sonnambula* (May 13, 1847) and *La Fille du régiment* (May

27, 1847) were acclaimed; she then created the role of Amalia in Verdi's *I Masnadieri* there (July 22, 1847).

After touring the English provinces, Lind decided to retire from the operatic stage, making her farewell appearance as Norma in Stockholm (April 12, 1848) and as Alice at London's Her Majesty's Theatre (May 10, 1849). If her success in Europe was great, her U.S. concert tour exceeded all expectations in public agitation and monetary reward. Sponsored by P.T. Barnum, she was seen as a natural phenomenon rather than an artist; nonetheless, her outstanding musicality made a deep impression upon the musical public. She made her N.Y. debut on Sept. 11, 1850, subsequently giving 93 concerts in all, her final one in Philadelphia (1851). On Feb. 5, 1852, she married her accompanist, Otto Goldschmidt, in Boston; they returned to Europe, settling permanently in England in 1858. She continued to appear in concert and oratorio performances until her retirement in 1883, when she became prof. of singing at London's Royal Coll. of Music. She also devoted much time to charitable causes. Lind possessed an extraordinary coloratura voice, with a compass reaching high G. She was, without question, one of the greatest vocal artists of her era. A letter written by her, entitled "Jenny Lind's Singing Method," was publ. in *Musical Quarterly* (July 1917).

BIBL.: J. Lyser, *G. Meyerbeer and J. L.* (Vienna, 1847); C. Rosenberg, *J. L. in America* (N.Y., 1851); H. Holland and W. Rockstro, *Memoir of Mme. J. L.-Goldschmidt* (2 vols., 1893); W. Rockstro and O. Goldschmidt, *J. L.-Goldschmidt: A Record and Analysis of the Method of the Late J. L.-Goldschmidt* (London, 1894); T. Norlind, *J. L.* (Stockholm, 1919); R. Maude, *The Life of J. L.* (London, 1926); G. Humphrey, *J. L.* (Philadelphia, 1928); E. Wagenknecht, *J. L.-Goldschmidt* (Boston, 1931); L. Benet, *Enchanting J. L.* (N.Y., 1939); H. Headland, *The Swedish Nightingale: A Biography of J. L.* (Rock Island, Ill., 1940); M. Pergament, *J. L.* (Stockholm, 1945); K. Rotzen and T. Meyer, *J. L.* (Stockholm, 1945); J. Bulman, *J. L.* (London, 1956); G. Schultz, *J. L.: The Swedish Nightingale* (Philadelphia, 1962); A. Dunlop, *The Swedish Nightingale* (N.Y., 1965); W. Ware and T. Lockard Jr., translators and eds., *The Lost Letters of J. L.* (London, 1966); E. Myers, *J. L.: Songbird from Sweden* (Champaign, Ill., 1968).—NS/LK/DM

Lindberg, Christian, extraordinary Swedish trombonist; b. Stockholm, Feb. 12, 1958. He took up the trombone at the age of 17; after playing in the Royal Opera Orch. in Stockholm (1977–78), he studied at the Stockholm Musikhögskolan, in London, and in Los Angeles (1978–82). His remarkable mastery of his instrument led to a career as a trombone virtuoso, and he subsequently appeared as a soloist with the major orchs., a recitalist, and a chamber music player in the principal music centers the worldover; also gave master classes and designed new instruments. Lindberg's repertoire is vast, embracing Baroque works on original instruments, Classical and Romantic scores, and a provocative cornucopia of contemporary pieces, including those by Berio, Cage, Dutilleux, Hindemith, Kagal, and Stockhausen. He also commissioned works, including the trombone concertos of Sandstrom, Xenakis, and Takemitsu.—NS/LK/DM

Lindberg, Magnus (Gustaf Adolf), Finnish composer; b. Helsinki, June 27, 1958. He began playing the piano at age 11, then at 15 entered the Sibelius Academy in Helsinki, where he studied composition with Rautavaara and Heininen (graduated, 1981), and also received instruction in electronic music there with Lindeman and took courses with Grisey and Globokar in Paris, Donatoni in Siena, and Ferneyhough in Darmstadt. His works are cast in a decisive contemporary idiom. He won the Prix Italia for his *Faust* in 1986 and the Nordic Council Music Prize for his *Kraft* in 1987.

WORKS: ORCH.: *Ritratto* (1979–83; Milan, Feb. 27, 1983); *Drama* (1980–81; Helsinki, Feb. 8, 1981); *Sculpture II* (1981; Helsinki, Oct. 13, 1982); *Tendenza* (1982; Paris, Jan. 27, 1983); *Kraft* (1983–85; Helsinki, Sept. 4, 1985); *Trois sculptures* (1988; Helsinki, March 13, 1989); *Marea* for Chamber Orch. (London, April 26, 1990); *Joy* for Large Chamber Ensemble (Frankfurt am Main, Dec. 9, 1990); Piano Concerto (Helsinki, Sept. 4, 1991); *Corrente I* for Chamber Orch. (1991–92; Helsinki, Feb. 5, 1992) and *II* (1991–92; London, Nov. 27, 1992); *Coyote Blues* (Stockholm, March 27, 1993); *Aura: Im Memoriam Witold Lutosławski* (1993–94; Tokyo, June 11, 1994); *Arena I* (1995) and *II* (London, June 30, 1996); *Engine* (Aldeburgh, June 21, 1996); *Feria* (London, Aug. 11, 1997); *Fresco* (1997; Los Angeles, March 12, 1998); *Campana in Aria* for Horn and Orch. (Amsterdam, June 6, 1998); *Piece* (1998–99; Cleveland, April 1, 1999); Cello Concerto (1998–99; Paris, May 6, 1999). **CHAMBER:** *Tre stycken* (3 Pieces) for Horn, Violin, Viola, and Cello (1976; Helsinki, May 25, 1977); *Arabesques* for Wind Quintet (1978; Helsinki, Oct. 5, 1980); *Espressione I* for Cello (1978) and *II* for Violin (1979); *Quintetto dell'estate* for Flute, Clarinet, Violin, Cello, and Piano (1979; Helsinki, May 24, 1980); *Sonatas* for Violin and Piano (1979; Helsinki, Jan. 27, 1981); *...de Tartuffe, je crois* for String Quartet and Piano (Kuhmo, July 27, 1981); *Linea d'ombra* for Flute, Saxophone, Guitar, and Percussion (1981; Milan, March 17, 1983); *Action-situation- signification* for Horn or Clarinets, Piano, Percussion, Cello, and Tape (Jyväskylä, July 6, 1982); *Ablauf* for Clarinet and 2 Percussion ad libitum (Helsinki, April 15, 1983; rev. 1988); *Zona* for Cello, Alto Flute, Bass Clarinet, Percussion, Harp, Piano, Violin, and Double Bass (Hilversum, Dec. 2, 1983); *Metal Work* for Accordion and Percussion (1984; Joensuu, June 18, 1985); *Stroke* for Cello (Helsinki, Dec. 30, 1984); *UR* for 5 Players and Live Electronics (Paris, Oct. 11, 1986); *Moto* for Cello and Piano (1990; Paris, April 13, 1991); *Steamboat Bill JR* for Clarinet and Cello (1990); Duo Concertante for Clarinet, Cello, and 8 Instruments (Witten, April 15, 1992); Clarinet Quintet (Kuhmo, July 16, 1992); *Decorrente* for Clarinet, Guitar, Vibraphone, Piano, and Cello (1992); *Away* for Clarinet, Percussion, Piano, and Strings (1994); *Related Rocks* for 2 Pianos, 2 Percussion, and Electronics (Paris, June 24, 1997). **Piano:** *Music* for 2 Pianos (1976); *Klavierstück* (1977); *3 pieces* (1978); *Play I* for 2 Pianos (1979); *Twine* (Bremen, May 19, 1988). **VOCAL:** *Jag vill breda vingar ut* for Mezzo-soprano and Piano (1977–78); *Untitled* for 20 Voices (1978); *Songs from North and South* for Children's Chorus (1993). **TAPE:** *Etwas zarter* (1977); *Ohne Ausdrück* (1978; Helsinki, April 15, 1983); *Faust*, radiophonic score (1985–86; Finnish Radio, Aug. 17, 1986). —NS/LK/DM

Lindberg, Oskar (Fredrik), Swedish composer and organist; b. Gagnef, Feb. 23, 1887; d. Stockholm, April 10, 1955. He studied at the Stockholm Cons. with Andreas Hallén and Ernst Ellberg. He was a church organist in Stockholm (1906–55). In 1919 he was appointed a teacher of harmony at the Stockholm Cons., becoming a prof. there in 1936.

WORKS: DRAMATIC: Opera: *Fredlös* (1936–42; Stockholm, Nov. 25, 1943). ORCH.: Sym. (1909); *Dalmålningar* (Pictures from Dalarna; 1908); 5 symphonic poems: *Florez och Blanzeflor, Från de stora skogarna, Hemifrån, Vildmark,* and *Gesunda;* overtures; orch. suites. OTHER: Piano Quartet; Piano Quintet; Requiem; choral works; piano pieces; songs. —NS/LK/DM

Lindblad, Adolf Fredrik,

important Swedish composer; b. Skännige, Feb. 1, 1801; d. Löfvingsborg, Aug. 23, 1878. He learned to play the piano and flute in his youth, and at age 15 he had a flute concerto performed in Norrköping. After receiving instruction in harmony from Haeffner in Uppsala (1823–25), he went to Berlin to study composition with Zelter. In 1827 he settled in Stockholm, where he ran his own piano school until 1861. Among his pupils were Jenny Lind, with whom he had an affair, and members of the royal family. In 1831 he beame a member of the Royal Swedish Academy of Music. Lindblad was a gifted composer who gained fame in his lifetime as the "father of Swedish song." His first collection of songs appeared in 1824, and he went on to compose some 215 songs with a third of them set to his own texts. A major edition of his songs was publ. in 9 vols. in Stockholm (1878–90). Lindblad aspired to make a name for himself as a symphonist in the Viennese Classical tradition. His First Sym. received its first complete performance in Stockholm on March 25, 1832, but was cooly received by the public and the critics. However, a subsequent performance of the work by the Leipzig Gewandhaus Orch. under Mendelssohn won the critical approbation of Schumann. His Second Sym. (Stockholm, May 6, 1855) also failed to please his auditors. However, today these finely honed scores are recognized as major additions to the Swedish orchestral repertoire. Lindblad also composed the opera *Frondörerna* (The Frondists; Stockholm, May 11, 1835), at least 7 string quartets, 2 string quintets, a Piano Trio, and piano pieces.

BIBL.: K. Linder, *Den unge A.F. L. (1801–27)* (diss., Univ. of Uppsala, 1973).—NS/LK/DM

Lindblad, Otto (Jonas),

Swedish conductor and composer; b. Karlstop, March 31, 1809; d. Norra Mellby, Jan. 24, 1864. He first studied at the Växjö Cathedral school, and later at the Univ. of Lund. He also studied music in Lund with Mathias Lundholm (1832–36). Following training in composition with K.-A. Krebs in Hamburg (1841), he completed his education at the Univ. of Lund (filosofie magister, 1844), where he conducted its men's chorus. After conducting his own men's vocal quartet, he served as a parish clerk in Norra Mellby, where he also conducted 2 parish church choirs. In 1857 he was made a member of the Swedish Royal Academy of Music in Stockholm. Lindblad wrote much vocal music, distinguishing himself particularly with his a cappella works for men's voices.

BIBL.: G. Feuk, *O. L. och hans sångare 1840–1846* (O. L. and his singers 1840–46; Lund, 1882); T. Nerman, *O. L.: Ett sångaröde* (Uppsala, 1930).—NS/LK/DM

Linde, (Anders) Bo (Leif),

Swedish composer, pianist, and music critic; b. Gävle, Jan. 1, 1933; d. there, Oct. 2, 1970. Following initial training with Bengtsson and Bökman, he studied at the Stockholm Musikhögskolan (1948–52) with Larsson (composition) and Wibergh (piano) before pursuing studies in conducting in Vienna (1953–54). He taught theory at the Stockholm Citizens' School (1957–60), and then returned to Gävle as a pianist, music critic, and composer. He composed in a well- crafted style notable for its adherence to classical forms in an accessible idiom.

WORKS: DRAMATIC: *Ballet blanc* (1953; Gävle, May 11, 1969); *Slotts-skoj* (Fun in the Castle), children's opera (1959). ORCH.: *Sinfonia fantasia* (1951); 2 piano concertos (1954, 1956); *Suite in an Old Style* (1954); *Preludium and Final* for Strings (1955); Violin Concerto (1957); Suite (1959); *Sinfonia* (1960); *Concerto for Orchestra* (1961–62); *Concert Music* for Small Orch. (1963); Cello Concerto (1964); *Suite Boulogne* (1966); *Little Concerto* for Wind Quintet and Strings (1966); *Pensieri sopra un cantico vecchio* (1967; Gävle, Jan. 1, 1968); *Pezzo concertante* for Bass Clarinet and Strings (Gävle, Sept. 9, 1970). CHAMBER: 2 piano trios (1953, 1969); String Quartet (1953); Violin Sonata (1953); *Serenata nostalgica* for 11 Strings (1965); *Quartet in Miniature* for Clarinets (1965); String Trio (1968); piano pieces. VOCAL: *Varbilder* (Spring Scenes) for Soloists, Chorus, and Orch. (1963); songs.—NS/LK/DM

Linde, Hans-Martin,

German-born Swiss flutist, recorder player, conductor, pedagogue, and composer; b. Werne, May 24, 1930. He was a student of Gustav Scheck (flute) and Konrad Lechner (composition) at the Freiburg im Breisgau Hochschule für Musik (1947–51). He played solo flute in the Cappella Coloniensis of the West German Radio in Cologne, and from 1955 he toured as a soloist throughout Europe and abroad. In later years, he appeared with his own Linde Consort. From 1957 he was active in Basel, where he served on the faculty of the Academy of Music. He served as director of its Cons. (1976–79), and then director of its choral music department at its Inst. He also was conductor of its Hochschule chorus (to 1991) and chamber chorus (to 1995). From 1980 he pursued an active career as a conductor. In 1993 he was awarded the German Handel Prize. He publ. *Kleine Anleitung zum Verzieren alter Musik* (1958) and *Handbuch des Blockflötenspiels* (1962; Eng. tr., 1967).

WORKS: Trio for Recorder, Transverse Flute, and Harpsichord (1963); *Serenata a tre* for Recorder, Guitar, and Cello (1966); *Consort Music* for 4 Instrumentalists (1972); *Fairy Tale* for Recorder (1981); *Music for 2* for Recorder and Guitar (1983); 5 *Studies* for Recorder and Piano (1985); *Browning* for Recorder Quintet (1986); *Una Follia Nuova* for Recorder (1989); Suite for Recorder Quartet (1991); *Carmina pro Lassum* for 5 Recorders and Percussion (1992); 3 *Sketches* for Recorder, Violin, and Piano (1993); Concerto for Recorder and String Orch. (1994). —NS/LK/DM

Lindegren, Johan,

Swedish organist, teacher, and composer; b. Ullared, Jan. 7, 1842; d. Stockholm, June 8, 1908. He settled in Stockholm, where he was a student at the Cons. (1860–65) of van Boom (piano), Randel (violin), and Behrens (composition). He was chorus master at the Royal Theater (from 1861), a teacher of counterpoint at the Cons. (from 1876), a music teacher at the Jacobshögskolan (from 1881), and cantor at the Storykrkan (from 1884). He ed. *Tidning för kyrkomusik* (1881–82) and publ. a *Koralbok* (1905). As a composer, he was best known for his piano music.—NS/LK/DM

Lindeman, family of Norwegian musicians:

(1) Ole Andreas Lindeman, organist, teacher, and composer; b. Surnadal, Jan. 17, 1769; d. Trondheim, Feb. 26, 1857. He was a student at the Trondheim cathedral school. After studying law in Copenhagen, he received music instruction from I. Wernicke. He then was organist of the church of Our Lady in Trondheim (1799–1857). He ed. the first book of Norwegian chorales (1835), which was given official sanction (1838). He also wrote some piano pieces and songs. He had 3 sons:

(2) Fredrik Christian Lindeman, organist; b. Trondheim, Dec. 4, 1803; d. there, July 29, 1868. He studied in Christiania and was organist of the church of Our Savior there. He then was organist of the church of Our Lady in Trondheim (1857–68).

(3) Ludvig Mathias Lindeman, organist, folk-song collector, teacher, and composer; b. Trondheim, Nov. 28, 1812; d. Christiania, May 23, 1887. He studied with his father in Trondheim, becoming his deputy organist at the church of Our Lady when he was 12. He then went to Christiania to study theology (1833), but subsequently resumed his interest in music. He was organist at the church of Our Savior in Christiania (1839–87), and also made tours as a concert artist. He taught at the Christiania theological seminary (1849–87). With his son Peter Brynie Lindeman, he founded an organ school in Christiania (1883), which became the Cons. (1894). He also spent much time collecting folk songs and editing church music. He prepared a chorale book for the Norwegian church that was officially sanctioned in 1877 and was used until being superseded in 1926. It contained his harmonizations of earlier hymn tunes and a number of his own. He also composed other sacred music, works for organ, and piano pieces.

WRITINGS: EDITIONS (all publ. in Christiania): **F o l k M u s i c :** *Norske fjeldmelodier harmonisk bearbeidede* (1841); *Norske folkeviser udsatte for fire mandstemmer* (1850); *Aeldre og nyere norske fjeldmelodier: Samlede og bearbeidede for pianoforte* (1853–67); *Halvhundrede norske fjeldmelodier harmoniserede for mandsstemmer* (1862); *30 norske kjaempevise-melodier harmoniserede for 3 lige stemmer* (1863); *Norske kjaempevise-melodier harmoniserede for blandede stemmer* (1885); O. Sandvik, ed., *Kingo-Tona: Fra Vang, Valdres* (Oslo, 1939–40). **C h u r c h M u s i c :** *Melodier til W.A. Wexels christelige psalmer* (1840); *Martin Luthers aandelige sange* (1859); *Norsk messebog* (1870; second ed., 1885); *Melodier til Landstads Salmebog* (1873); *Koralbog: Indeholdende de i Landstads salmebog forekommende melodier* (1878). **BIBL.:** O. Sandvik, *L. M. L. og folkemelodien* (Oslo, 1950).

(4) Just Riddervold Lindeman, organist and composer; b. Trondheim, Sept. 26, 1822; d. there, Jan. 21, 1894. He was organist of Trondheim Cathedral (1858–94). He wrote works for organ, piano pieces, and songs.

(5) Peter Brynie Lindeman, organist, teacher, and composer, son of (3) Ludvig Mathias Lindeman; b. Christiania, Feb. 1, 1858; d. there (Oslo), Jan. 1, 1930. He studied with his father and at the Stockholm Cons. He

was organist in Christiania (1880–1923), where, with his father, he founded an organ school (1883), which became the Cons. (1894). He was its director for many years. He ed. the periodical *Musikbladet* (1908–21). He wrote sacred music, chamber music, organ works, and piano pieces. His son, Kristian Theodor Madsen Lindeman (b. Christiania, March 8, 1870; d. Trondheim, Nov. 15, 1934), was an organist and composer. He was Trondheim Cathedral organist (1894–1934), and also wrote numerous choral works.—NS/LK/DM

Lindeman, Osmo (Uolevi), Finnish composer; b. Helsinki, May 16, 1929; d. there, Feb. 15, 1987. He studied with Linnala and Fougstedt at the Sibelius Academy in Helsinki (1956–59). In 1959 he was awarded a UNESCO grant to the Hochschule für Musik in Munich, where he studied for a year with Orff; upon returning to Finland, he taught at the Sibelius Academy (1961–84). In his works, he at first adopted a traditional Romantic manner, but after 1968 devoted himself to electronic music.

WORKS: DRAMATIC: *Huutokauppa* (Auction), ballet (1967); film scores. **ORCH.:** 2 syms. (*Sinfonia inornata*, 1959; 1964); 2 piano concertos (1963, 1965); *Music* for Chamber Orch. (1966); Concerto for Chamber Orch. (1966); *Variabile* (1967). **CHAMBER:** String Trio (1958); *Partita* for Percussion (1962); *2 Expressions* for Vibraphone and Marimba (1965); String Quartet (1966). **TAPE:** *Kinetic Forms* (1969); *Mechanical Music* (1969); *Tropicana* (1970); *Midas* (1970); *Ritual* (1972).—NS/LK/DM

Lindholm, Berit (real name, Berit Maria Jonsson), Swedish soprano; b. Stockholm, Oct. 18, 1934. She studied with Britta von Vegesack and Käthe Sundström in Stockholm. She made her debut as Mozart's Countess at the Royal Opera there in 1963. She first appeared at London's Covent Garden as Chrysothemis in *Elektra* (1966), and then sang at the Bayreuth Festivals (1967–74). She made her U.S. debut as Brünnhilde with the San Francisco Opera (1972); her Metropolitan Opera debut followed in N.Y. in the same role on Feb. 20, 1975. She became best known for her Wagnerian roles.—NS/LK/DM

Lindley, Robert, English cellist; b. Rotherham, Yorkshire, March 4, 1776; d. London, June 13, 1855. He studied cello with Cervetto. From 1794 to 1851 he was first cellist at the Royal Opera in London. In 1822 he became prof. of cello at the Royal Academy of Music there. He wrote pieces for the cello.—NS/LK/DM

Lindpaintner, Peter Joseph von, German conductor and composer; b. Koblenz, Dec. 9, 1791; d. Nonnenhorn, Lake Constance, Aug. 21, 1856. He studied violin and piano in Augsburg and theory in Munich with Winter and Joseph Gratz. In 1812 he became music director of the Isarthor Theater in Munich. From 1819 until his death he was conductor of the Court Orch. at Stuttgart, where his ability made the orch. famous.

WORKS: DRAMATIC: 28 operas, including *Der Bergkönig* (Stuttgart, Jan. 30, 1825), *Der Vampyr* (Stuttgart, Nov. 21, 1828), *Die Genueserin* (Vienna, Feb. 8, 1839), and *Lichtenstein* (Stuttgart, Aug. 26, 1846); three ballets (*Joko*, etc.); five melodramas; five oratorios. **OTHER:** Syms.; overture to *Faust*; incidental music to *Lied von der Glocke*; six masses; *Stabat Mater*; songs.

BIBL.: R. Hansler, *P. L. als Opernkomponist* (diss., Univ. of Munich, 1928).—NS/LK/DM

Lindsey, John, early jazz bassist, trombonist; b. New Orleans, La., Aug. 23, 1894 (the 1900 census says September 1891); d. Chicago, Ill., July 3, 1950. His lively, swinging bass work is prominently featured on such Jelly Roll Morton recordings as "Grandpa's Spells," basically in a two feel but with some measures of walking as well. His father was a guitarist, his brother Herb a violinist. During his early teens John began playing bass in the family band. After serving in the U.S. Army during World War I he began working in New Orleans on trombone. He played with the John Robichaux Orch. at the Lyric Theatre, then joined Armand Piron and traveled with them to N.Y. In 1924 he left Piron to tour with King Oliver. He subsequently played with Dewey Jackson (late 1925), and settled in Chicago. Throughout the 1920s Lindsay doubled on trombone and string bass with various leaders including Willie Hightower, Carroll Dickerson, Lil Hardin, and Jimmy Bell. During this period he made a series of recordings with Morton. He was on tour with Louis Armstrong from March 1931 to March 1932, including a residency in New Orleans. He returned to Chicago and worked with Jimmie Noone, Art Short, Richard M. Jones, and the Harlem Hamfats during the 1930s. During the last 10 years of his life he worked on string bass, led his own quartet at Music Bar (Chicago), and worked regularly with Darnell Howard and with guitarist Bob Tinsley's Orch., among others.—JC/LP

Ling, Jahja, Indonesian conductor and pianist of Chinese descent; b. Jakarta, Oct. 25, 1951. He received piano training at the Jakarta School of Music. After winning the Jakarta Piano Competition at 17, he was awarded a Rockefeller grant and pursued his studies at the Juilliard School in N.Y. (M.A.), where he was a pupil of Meczyslaw Munz and Beveridge Webster (piano) and of John Nelson (conducting). He also held a Leonard Bernstein Conducting Fellowship at the Berkshire Music Center at Tanglewood (summer, 1980), where he studied with Bernstein, Sir Colin Davis, Ozawa, Previn, Schuller, and Silverstein. He completed his conducting studies with Mueller at Yale Univ. (D.M.A., 1985). From 1981 to 1984 he was the Exxon/Arts Endowment Conductor of the San Francisco Sym., and also was founder-music director of its youth orch. and music director of the San Francisco Cons. of Music orch. He then was resident conductor of the Cleveland Orch. (from 1984), where he also was founder-music director of its youth orch., and later director of its Blossom Music Center (from 2000). He concurrently served as music director of the Fla. Orch. (from 1988) and artistic director of the National Sym. Orch. of Taiwan in Taipei (from 1998). In 1988 he received a Seaver-NEA Conductor's Award. A guest conductor, he appeared with many leading North American orchs. In 1988 he made his European debut with the Gewandhaus Orch. in Leipzig. At his N.Y. Phil. debut on Feb. 26, 1993, he conducted the premiere of Zwilich's 3rd Sym.—NS/LK/DM

Lingle, Paul, pop-jazz pianist; b. Denver, Colo., Dec. 3, 1902; d. Honolulu, Hawaii, Oct. 30, 1962. His father, Curt Lingle, was a professional cornet player. He began on piano at age six, and by 13 was working a variety of circuits accompanying his father. During the 1920s he settled on West Coast, working with many bands including Tom Gerun's, Jimmie Grier's, and Coffee Dan's. He accompanied singer Al Jolson in several films including *The Jazz Singer* (1927), *Mammy*, and *Sonny Boy*. During the 1930s he did studio work and resident spots on KPO radio station in San Francisco. He played occasionally with Lu Watter's Band at the Mark Twain Hotel (San Francisco) in 1940, but for the next 12 years he worked mainly as a ragtime soloist in West Coast night clubs, with long residencies at Hambone's in San Francisco and the Jug in Oakland. He moved to Honolulu in 1952, played in various clubs, organized his own band and taught piano and harmony; he died there a decade later.—JC/LP

Linike, family of German musicians:

(1) Ephraim Linike, violinist; b. 1665; d. Berlin (buried), Dec. 24, 1726. He became a violinist in the electoral chapel in Berlin in 1690, where he was a royal chamber musician (1701–04) and then in Schwedt (1704–11). Subsequently he returned to Berlin.

(2) Christian Bernhard Linike, cellist; b. June 3, 1673; d. Cöthen (buried), Jan. 3, 1751. He was a cellist and chamber musician in Berlin until the court chapel disbanded in 1713. He then became a member of the chapel of the Margrave Christian Ludwig of Cöthen where he was associated with J.S. Bach and C.F. Abel.

(3) Johann Georg Linike, violinist and composer; b. c. 1680; d. Hamburg, after 1737. He received training from Johann Theile in Berlin. By 1710 he was second violinist in the court chapel there. After it was disbanded in 1713, he went to the Weissenfels court as director of music. In 1725 he became first violinist in the orch. of the Hamburg Opera. Among his works were a Concerto for Harpsichord, Violin, and Strings, 3 concertos for Flute, Violin, Viola, and Basso Continuo, sonatas, and cantatas.—LK/DM

Linjama, Jouko (Sakari), Finnish organist and composer; b. Kirvu, Feb. 4, 1934. He studied composition with Merikanto and Kokkonen at the Sibelius Academy in Helsinki (1954–60) and musicology and literature at the Univ. of Helsinki. He continued his composition training with Zimmermann and Koenig at the Cologne Staatliche Hochschule für Musik (1962–64) and also worked with Stockhausen in the Cologne course for new music (1963). He was organist at St. Henrik's Catholic Church (1958–60) and then in the Tuusula parish (from 1964); also taught at the Sibelius Academy (1964–68). A prominent composer of sacred music, he was awarded the composition prize of the

Finnish church in 1979. In his works, he attempts to fuse Burgundian strict counterpoint with serial techniques.

WORKS: ORCH.: *La Migration d'oiseaux sauvages* (1977). CHAMBER: *5 Metamorphosen für 5 Instrumente über 5 Canons Op. 16 von Anton Webern* for Celesta, Vibraphone, Guitar, Harpsichord, and Piano (1963); *...lehtiä...* (*...leaves...*) for Cello and Piano (1974); *Hommage à Dandriaeu* for 2 Cellos or 2 Men's Voices and Organ (1977); 2 string quartets: No. 1, *Cantiones* (1978) and No. 2, *Variazioni* (1979); Concerto for Organ, Marimba, Vibraphone, and 2 Wind Quartets (1981). O r g a n : *Sonatina supra b-a-c-h* (1961); *Partita-sonata Veni Creator Spiritus* (1968); *Intrada* (1969); *Magnificat* (1970); Concerto (1971); *Triptychon* for 2 Organs (1971); *Partita* (1973); *Piae cantiones per organo piccolo* (1976); *Missa cum jubilo* (1977); *Consolation pour l'orgue* (1978); *Toccatina, danza e contradanza per organo piccolo* (1981); *Organum supra b-a-c-h* (1982); *Roccata* (1985); *Reflections* for Organ Duet (1991). VOCAL: *Millaista on* (How it is), oratorio for Baritone, 6 Men's Voices, Orch., and 3 Tape Recorders (1964–68); *Homage to Aleksis Kivi*, symphonic oratorio for Narrator, Baritone, Women's Chorus, Men's Chorus, Children's Chorus, and Orch. (1970–76); *La sapienza*, chamber oratorio for 2 Choruses (1980); cantatas; song cycles; solo songs. —NS/LK/DM

Linko, Ernst, Finnish composer and pianist; b. Helsinki, July 14, 1889; d. there, Jan. 28, 1960. He studied piano at the Helsinki School of Music (1909–11), and then in Berlin, St. Petersburg, and Paris. He was director of the Sibelius Academy in Helsinki (1939–59) and, for many years, active as a concert pianist. He wrote 4 piano concertos (1916, 1920, 1931, 1957), *Symphonie chevaleresque* (1949), *Ariette* for Wind Ensemble, *Rigaudon* for Strings, Piano Trio, String Quartet, and numerous piano pieces.—NS/LK/DM

Linley, family of English musicians:

(1) Thomas Linley Sr., English harpsichordist, concert director, singing teacher, and composer; b. Badminton, Gloucestershire, Jan. 17, 1733; d. London, Nov. 19, 1795. He began his studies with the Bath Abbey organist Thomas Chilcot; later studied with William Boyce in London. From the mid-1750s he was active as a concert director and singing teacher in Bath, and also wrote for the London stage from 1767. He was made joint director (with John Stanley) of London's Drury Lane Theatre in 1774; then continued in that capacity (with Samuel Arnold) from 1786; was also its joint manager (with his son-in-law, the dramatist Richard Brinsley Sheridan) from 1776. With his son Thomas Linley Jr., he composed the music for Sheridan's comic opera *The Duenna, or The Double Elopement* (1775). He was made a member of the Royal Soc. of Musicians in 1777. Of his 12 children, the succeeding five entries should be noted.

WORKS: DRAMATIC (all first perf. in London): *The Royal Merchant*, opera (Dec. 14, 1767); *The Duenna, or The Double Elopement*, comic opera (Nov. 21, 1775; in collaboration with his son Thomas Linley Jr.); *Selima and Azor*, comic opera (Dec. 5, 1776); *The Beggar's Opera*, ballad opera (Jan. 29, 1777); *The Camp*, musical entertainment (Oct. 15, 1778); *Zoraida*, tragedy (Dec. 13, 1779); *The Generous Imposter*, comedy (Nov. 22, 1780); *The Gentle Shepherd*, pastoral (Oct. 29, 1781); *The Carnival of Venice*, comic opera (Dec. 13, 1781); *The Spanish Rivals*, musical farce (Nov. 4, 1784); *The Strangers at Home*, comic opera (Dec. 8, 1785); *Love in*

the East, or Adventures of Twelve Hours (Feb. 25, 1788). OTHER: He also publ. *Six Elegies* (London, 1770) and *Twelve Ballads* (London, 1780); 14 pieces appeared in *The Posthumous Vocal Works of Mr. Linley and Mr. T. Linley* (London, c. 1798).

BIBL.: E. Green, *T. L., Richard Brinsley Sheridan, and Thomas Matthews: Their Connection with Bath* (Bath, 1903); C. Black, *The L.s of Bath* (London, 1911; 3rd ed., aug., 1971).

(2) Elizabeth Ann Linley, soprano; b. Bath, Sept. 5, 1754; d. Bristol, June 28, 1792. She received training from her father. After singing in concerts in Bath and Bristol, she made her debut at London's Covent Garden in Thomas Hull's masque *The Fairy Favour* in 1767. She subsequently sang in oratorios in London (1769–73) and at the Three Choirs Festival (1770–73). In 1772 she eloped with Richard Brinsley Sheridan to France, where the two were married in 1773. In subsequent years, she gave only private concerts in her home.

BIBL.: M. Bor and L. Clelland, *Still the Lark, A Biography of E. L.* (London, 1962).

(3) Thomas Linley Jr., violinist and composer; b. Bath, May 5, 1756; d. [drowned] Grimsthorpe, Aug. 5, 1778. He was a gifted child and began his music studies at an early age with his father. On July 29, 1763, he made his public debut performing a violin concerto in Bristol. Following further training from Boyce in London (1763–68), he studied violin with Nardini in Florence (1768–71), where he met Mozart in 1770 and became his close friend. From 1771 Linley performed at his father's concert presentations in Bath. From 1773 to 1778 he was concertmaster of London's Drury Lane Theatre orch. His tragic death deprived England of one of its most promising instrumentalists and composers.

WORKS: DRAMATIC (all first perf. in London): *The Duenna, or The Double Elopement*, comic opera (Nov. 21, 1775; in collaboration with his father); *The Tempest* (Jan. 4, 1777); *The Cady of Bagdad*, comic opera (Feb. 19, 1778). INSTRUMENTAL: About 20 violin concertos; violin sonatas. VOCAL: *Let God Arise*, anthem for Soloists, Chorus, and Orch. (Worcester Festival, Sept. 8, 1773); *The Song of Moses*, oratorio (London, March 12, 1777); secular choral works; songs.

BIBL.: M. Cooke, *A Short Account of the late Mr. T. L., Junior* (MS, 1812); G. Beechey, *T. L., Junior: His Life, Work and Times* (diss., Univ. of Cambridge, 1964).

(4) Mary Linley, soprano; b. Bath, Jan. 4, 1758; d. Clifton, Bristol, July 27, 1787. she was a pupil of her father. She appeared as a concert and oratorio singer, often with her sister Elizabeth. From 1771 to 1776 she sang at the Three Choirs Festival, and also in London until her marriage in 1780.

(5) Ozias Thurston Linley, organist and clergyman; b. Bath, Aug. 1765; d. London, March 6, 1831. He studied with his father and with William Herschel, graduating from Oxford in 1789. He was active as a clergyman and also was an organist fellow at Dulwich Coll. (from 1816). Among his works were anthems and chants.

(6) William Linley, composer; b. Bath, Feb. 1771; d. London, May 6, 1835. He received training from his father and from C.F. Abel. He was a civil servant in India (1790–95; 1800–07). Linley composed 2 operas, songs, and glees.—NS/LK/DM

Linn, Robert, American composer; b. San Francisco, Aug. 11, 1925; d. Los Angeles, Oct. 28, 1999. He studied with Milhaud at Mills Coll. in Oakland, Calif. (1947–49), and with Sessions, Stevens, and Dahl at the Univ. of Southern Calif. in Los Angeles (M.M., 1951); taught there (from 1958) and served as chairman of the theory and composition dept. (from 1973). In his output, Linn made effective use of traditional forms.

WORKS: ORCH.: *Overture for Symphony Orchestra* (1952); Sym. in 1 Movement (1956; rev. 1961); *Hexameron* for Piano and Orch. (1963; reconstruction of Liszt's orchestration of *Hexaméron*, variations on a theme by Bellini); Sinfonia for Strings (1967; rev. 1972); Concertino for Oboe, Horn, Percussion, and Strings (1972); *Fantasia* for Cello and Strings (1975–76); Concertino for Woodwind Quintet and Strings (1981–82). **Woodwind Orch.:** *Elevations* (1964); *Propagula* (1970); Concerto for Flute and Woodwind Orch. (1980); *Partita* (1980); Concerto for Piano and Woodwind Orch. (1984). **CHAMBER:** Clarinet Sonata (1949); String Quartet No. 1 (1951); Quartet for 4 Saxophones (1953); 2 piano sonatas (1955, 1964); Quartet for 4 Horns (1957); *Prelude and Dance* for 4 Saxophones (1960); Brass Quintet (1963); Woodwind Quintet (1963); *Dithyramb* for 8 Cellos (1965); Concertino for Violin and Wind Octet (1965); *Vino* for Violin and Piano (1975); *12* for Chamber Ensemble (1976–77); *Saxifrage Blue* for Baritone Saxophone and Piano (1977); *Trompe l'oeil* for Bass Trombone and Piano (1978); *Diversions* for 6 Bassoons (1979); *Trombosis* for 12 Trombones (1979); *Serenade* for Flute, Clarinet, Cello, and Guitar (1982). **VOCAL:** *An Anthem of Wisdom* for Chorus and Orch. (1958); *Pied Piper of Hamlin*, oratorio (1968); choruses; songs. —NS/LK/DM

Linnala, Eino (Mauno Aleksanteri), Finnish composer and teacher; b. Helsinki, Aug. 19, 1896; d. there, June 8, 1973. He studied composition with Melartin (1915–20), at the Univ. of Helsinki, in Berlin (1922), and with Willner in Vienna (1924–27). Linnala taught theory and analysis at the Univ. of Helsinki (1927–66), and was also chairman of the Finnish Composers' Copyright Bureau (1960–68). He publ. several textbooks on theory. His compositions, all composed in the Romantic tradition, included 2 syms. (1927, 1935), *Dance Suite* for Orch. (1931), *Suomalainen rapsodia* for Orch. (1932), *Overture* (1933), *Elegia* for Orch. (1945), 4 cantatas (1932–40), more than 100 choral songs, chamber music, and about 50 songs.—NS/LK/DM

Lioncourt, Guy de, French composer and teacher; b. Caen, Dec. 1, 1885; d. Paris, Dec. 24, 1961. He studied Gregorian chant with Gastoué, counterpoint with Roussel, and composition with his uncle, d'Indy, at the Paris Schola Cantorum (graduated, 1916), and in 1918 he won the Grand Prix Lasserre with his *La Belle au bois dormant* (1912–15). He became prof. of counterpoint (1914) at the Schola Cantorum; at d'Indy's death in 1931, he became subdirector and prof. of composition. He helped to found the École César Franck in Paris (1935), and then was its director. He publ. an autobiography, *Un Témoignage sur la musique et sur la vie au XXᵉ siècle* (Paris, 1956).

WORKS: DRAMATIC: Drama: *Jan de la lune* (1915–21). **Liturgical Dramas:** *Le Mystère de l'Emmanuel* (1924); *Le Mystère de l'Alléluia* (1925–26); *Le Mystère de l'Esprit* (1939–40). **CHAMBER:** Piano Quintet (1908); Piano Quartet (1925); String Quartet (1933). **KEYBOARD:** Piano pieces; organ music. **VOCAL: Soloists, Chorus, and Orch.:** *Hyalis, le petit faune aux yeux bleus* (1909–11); *La Belle au bois dormant* (1912–15); *Le Réniement de St.-Pierre* (1928); *Le Navrement de Notre Dame* (1943). **Other:** 3 masses (1914–22; 1942; 1948); *Les Dix Lépreux* for Voice, Women's Chorus, and Orch. (1918–19); *Le Dict de Mme. Saincte Barbe* for Soloists, Chorus, Harp, and Strings (1937); motets.—NS/LK/DM

Lipatti, Dinu (actually, **Constantin**), outstanding Romanian pianist and composer; b. Bucharest, April 1, 1917; d. Chêne-Bourg, near Geneva, Dec. 2, 1950. His father was a violinist who had studied with Sarasate, and his mother, a pianist; his godfather was Enesco. He received his early training from his parents; then studied with Florica Musicescu at the Bucharest Cons. (1928–32). He received a second prize at the International Competition at Vienna in 1934, a judgment that prompted Cortot to quit the jury in protest; Lipatti then studied piano with Cortot, conducting with Munch, and composition with Dukas and Boulanger in Paris (1934–39). He gave concerts in Germany and Italy, returning to Romania at the outbreak of World War II. In 1943 he settled in Geneva as a teacher of piano at the Cons. After the war, he resumed his career; played in England 4 times (1946–48). His remarkable career was tragically cut short by lymphogranulomatosis, which led to his early death. He was generally regarded as one of the most sensitive interpreters of Chopin, and was also praised for his deep understanding of the Baroque masters; was also a fine composer. Lipatti was married to the pianist and teacher Madeleine Cantacuzene.

WORKS: ORCH.: *Şătrarii*, symphonic poem (1934; Bucharest, Jan. 23, 19363); *Concertino in the Classic Style* for Piano and Chamber Orch. (1936; Bucharest, Oct. 5, 1939); *Symphonie concertante* for 2 Pianos and Strings (1938; Bucharest, May 4, 1941). **CHAMBER:** Violin Sonatina (1933); *Improvisation* for Piano, Violin and Cello (1939); Concerto for Organ and Piano (1939); *Introduction and Allegro* for Flute (1939); *Aubade* for Wind Quartet (1949). **Piano:** Sonata (1932); *3 Dances* (1937); nocturnes (1937, 1939); Sonatina for Piano, Left Hand (1941); *Romanian Dances* for 2 Pianos (1943; also for Piano and Orch., Geneva, Oct. 11, 1945). **VOCAL:** Songs.

BIBL.: M. Lipatti, ed., *Hommage à D. L.* (Geneva, 1952); A. Lipatti, *La Vie du pianiste D. L., écrite par sa mère* (Paris, 1954); T. Dragos, *L.* (Bucharest, 1965); C. Păsculescu-Florian, *Vocaţie Şi destin, D. L.* (Bucharest, 1986); D. Tanasescu and G. Bargauanu, *L.* (London, 1988); C. Păsculescu-Florian, *D. L.: Pagini din jurnalul unei regăsiri* (Bucharest, 1989); G. Bargauanu and D. Tanasescu, *D. L.* (Lausanne, 1991).—NS/LK/DM

Lipawsky or **Lipavský, Joseph,** Bohemian pianist and composer; b. Hohenmauth, Feb. 22, 1769; d. Vienna, Jan. 7, 1810. He received training in organ from Ignác Haas in Hradec Králové. After studying philosophy in Prague, he settled in Vienna and received instruction in piano and composition from G. Pasterwiz and J.B. Wanhall. Lipawsky was befriended by Mozart, who may have given him additional instruction. After serving as tutor to the daughters of Count Adam Teleky, Lipawsky was employed in the imperial Privy Chamber

Treasury. He also made appearances as a pianist. While he was best known for his piano music, he also composed Singspiels, orch. pieces, chamber music, and songs.—NS/LK/DM

Lipiński, Carl (actually, **Karol Józef**), esteemed Polish violinist, conductor, teacher, and composer; b. Radzyń, Oct. 30, 1790; d. Urłów, near Lemberg, Dec. 16, 1861. He received training in violin and music from his father. In 1809 he became concertmaster of the Lemberg Theater orch., where he conducted from 1811 to 1815. In 1817 Lipiński traveled to Italy to hear Paganini. In 1818 the two met in Padua, and Paganini was so impressed with his talent as a violinist that the two performed together in Piacenza. Between 1819 and 1828 Lipiński made tours of Poland, Germany, and Russia, and then toured throughout the whole of Europe. On April 25, 1836, he appeared as soloist in his own *Military Concerto* for Violin and Orch. in London. In 1839 he settled in Dresden as concertmaster of the Court Orch., a position he retained until his retirement in 1861. He also was active as a conductor, performed with his own string quartet, and taught. Among his most famous pupils were Joachim and Wieniawski. While Lipiński was praised as the equal in technical virtuosity to Paganini, he became best known for upholding the classical ideals of violin playing espoused by Viotti and Spohr. He composed a comic opera, *Kłótnia przez zakład* (Lemberg, May 27, 1814), and other stage works, 3 syms., 4 violin concertos, pieces for Violin and Piano, *Caprices* for Violin, and numerous technical studies for violin.

BIBL.: J. Powroźniak, *K. L.* (Kraków, 1970).—NS/LK/DM

Lipkin, Malcolm (Leyland), English composer, pianist, and teacher; b. Liverpool, May 2, 1932. He studied piano with Gordon Green in Liverpool. Following further piano training from Kendall Taylor at the Royal Coll. of Music in London (1949–53), he studied composition privately with Seiber (1954–57). He later received his doctorate from the Univ. of London (1972). In 1951 he made his debut as a pianist performing his 3rd Piano Sonata at the Gaudeamus Foundation Music Week in the Netherlands; in 1952 he made his London debut playing the same score. He served as a tutor for the external dept. of the Univ. of Oxford (1965–75) and for the School of Continuing Education at the Univ. of Kent (from 1975).

WORKS: ORCH.: 2 violin concertos: No. 1 (1952) and No. 2 (1960–62; Bournemouth, Oct. 17, 1963); *Movement* for Strings (1956–57; rev. 1960); Piano Concerto (1957; Cheltenham, July 16, 1959); 3 syms.: No. 1, *Sinfonia di Roma* (1958–65; Liverpool, Jan. 18, 1966), No. 2, *The Pursuit* (1975–79; Manchester, Feb. 9, 1983), and No. 3, *Sun* (1979–86; Manchester, Jan. 6, 1993); *Pastorale* for Horn and Strings (1963; also for Horn and String Quintet, or Horn and Piano, or Oboe and Piano); *Mosaics* for Chamber Orch. (London, Oct. 23, 1966; rev. 1969); Concerto for Flute and Strings (1974); Oboe Concerto (1988–89; London, Jan. 16, 1991); *From Across La Manche* for Strings (Canterbury, Nov. 8, 1998). **CHAMBER:** String Quartet (1951); 2 violin sonatas: No. 1 (1957) and No. 2 (1997; Tunbridge Wells, Sept. 20, 1998); Suite for Flute and Cello (1961); String Trio (1963–64); *Capriccio* for Piano and String Quartet (1966); *Interplay* for Treble Recorder,

Viola da Gamba, Harpsichord, and Percussion (London, March 5, 1976; also for Flute, Cello, and Piano); *Recollections* for Percussion (1976); *Clifford's Tower* for 8 Instruments (1977; Cheltenham, July 11, 1980); Trio for Flute, Viola, and Harp (Rye, Sept. 7, 1982); *Naboth's Vineyard* for Recorder, Cello, and Harpsichord (1982); Wind Quintet (1985; London, July 14, 1986); *Prelude and Dance* for Cello and Piano, in memory of Jacqueline DuPré (1987; London, July 5, 1988); *Idyll* for Violin (1988); Piano Trio (1988; London, March 22, 1989); *Bartók Variations* for String Quartet (1989; Newbury, May 5, 1992); *5 Bagatelles* for Oboe and Piano (1993; London, Oct. 26, 1994); Duo for Violin and Cello (1994); *Little Suite* for Flute and Piano (2000). **KEYBOARD: Piano:** 5 sonatas, including No. 3 (Bilthoven, Sept. 6, 1951; rev. 1979), No. 4 (Cheltenham, July 17, 1955; rev. 1987), and No. 5 (1986; Kent, July 21, 1989); *Nocturne No. 1* (1987; Bristol, Dec. 18, 1989), *No. 2* (1995; London, Oct. 22, 1999), and *No. 3* (1998). **Harpsichord:** *Metamorphosis* (1974). **VOCAL:** *Psalm 96* for Chorus and Orch. (London, Dec. 17, 1969); *Psalm 117* for Chorus (1969); *4 Departures* for Soprano and Violin (1972); *5 Songs* for Soprano and Piano (1978).—NS/LK/DM

Lipkin, Seymour, American pianist, conductor, and teacher; b. Detroit, May 14, 1927. He studied piano as a child and appeared as soloist in Beethoven's First Piano Concerto with the Detroit Civic Orch. (1938). He then studied formally at the Curtis Inst. of Music in Philadelphia with Saperton (1938–41) and with Serkin and Horszowski (B.Mus., 1947), and also studied conducting with Koussevitzky at the Berkshire Music Center in Tanglewood (summers, 1946; 1948–49) and was apprentice conductor to Szell and the Cleveland Orch. (1947–48). After winning first prize in the Rachmaninoff Piano Competition (1948), he played the Tchaikovsky First Piano Concerto with Koussevitzky and the Boston Sym. Orch. that same year and subsequently appeared as a soloist with major U.S. orchs. He made his formal conducting debut with the N.Y.C. Opera leading Bernstein's *Trouble in Tahiti* (1958); then was an asst. conductor of the N.Y. Phil. (1959–60) and music director of the Long Island Sym. Orch. (1963–79). He was also music director of N.Y.'s Joffrey Ballet (1966–68), then its principal guest conductor (1968–72), and once again its music director (1972–79). He taught at Marymount Coll. in Tarrytown, N.Y. (1963–72; chairman of the music dept., 1968–71), the Curtis Inst. of Music (from 1969), the Manhattan School of Music (1972–87), the New England Cons. of Music in Boston (1984–86), and the Juilliard School in N.Y. (from 1986); also served as artistic director of the Univ. of Md. International Piano Festival and William Kapell Piano Competition (1988–92). —NS/LK/DM

Lipkovska, Lydia (Yakovlevna), Russian soprano; b. Babino, Bessarabia, May 10, 1882; d. Beirut, Jan. 22, 1955. She studied with Iretzkaya in St. Petersburg and Vanzo in Milan. She made her debut as Gilda at the St. Petersburg Imperial Opera (1907), singing there until 1908 and again from 1911 to 1913. She appeared in Diaghilev's season in Paris (1909), as well as at the Opéra and the Opéra-Comique. Her American debut took place with the Boston Opera on Nov. 12, 1909, when she sang Lakmé; on Nov. 18, 1909, she made her Metropolitan Opera debut in N.Y. as Violetta, singing there until 1911 and in Chicago in 1910–11; also appeared at London's Covent Garden as Mimi (July 11, 1911). After the Russian Revolution of 1917, she was active in Paris. In 1920 she toured the U.S. and in 1921–22 appeared at the Chicago Grand Opera. She sang at the Odessa Opera (1941–44) and then returned to Paris. Her last years were spent as a teacher in Beirut.—NS/LK/DM

Lipman, Samuel, American pianist, teacher, and music critic; b. Los Gatos, Calif., June 7, 1934; d. N.Y., Dec. 17, 1994. He commenced piano studies in his youth, making his debut at age 9. He attended L'École Monteux in Hancock, Maine (summers, 1951–57), and the Aspen (Colo.) Music School (summers, 1959–61), and completed his piano training with Rosina Lhévinne at the Juilliard School of Music in N.Y. (1959–62). He also took courses in government at San Francisco State Coll. (B.A., 1956) and pursued graduate work in political science at the Univ. of Calif. at Berkeley (M.A., 1958). His tours as a pianist took him all over the U.S. and Europe; he also served as music critic of *Commentary* (from 1976) and publ. the *New Criterion* (from 1982); taught at the Aspen Music School (from 1971) and at the Waterloo Music Festival in Stanhope, N.J. (from 1976), where he was artistic director (1985–93). In 1977 he won the ASCAP-Deems Taylor Award for music criticism, and in 1980 for his vol. of essays *Music after Modernism* (1979). He also wrote *The House of Music: Art in an Era of Institutions* (1982), *Arguing for Music, Arguing for Culture: Essays* (1990), and *Music and More: Essays, 1975–1991* (1992). Lipman was a prominent figure in the American neo-conservative movement.—NS/LK/DM

Lipovšek, Marjana, distinguished Yugoslav mezzo-soprano; b. Ljubljana, Dec. 3, 1946. She received her training in Ljubljana, Graz, and Vienna. In 1979 she became a member of the Vienna State Opera, where she developed a notably successful career. In 1981 she made her first appearance at the Salzburg Festival. In 1982 she sang for the first time at the Hamburg State Opera and at Milan's La Scala. In 1983 she joined the Bavarian State Opera in Munich. She made her London debut as a soloist in *Das Lied von der Erde* with the London Sym. Orch. in 1988, returning to London in 1990 to make her Covent Garden debut as Clytemnestra. On Nov. 25, 1993, she made her North American debut as Fricka in *Die Walküre* at the Lyric Opera of Chicago. In 1995 she made her first appearance at the San Francisco Opera as Brünnhilde, and then sang Clytemnestra in Florence in 1996. She made a major recital tour of the U.S. in 1998. In 1999 she returned to the San Francisco Opera to sing both Waltraute and Fricka. In addition to her operatic career, Lipovšek has pursued an extensive following as a concert and lieder artist. She has appeared as a soloist with the leading orchs. of Europe and North America, and at many festivals. Among her many roles of note are Gluck's Orfeo, Mistress Quickly, Amneris, Azucena, Brangäne, Orlofsky, Strauss's Composer and Octavian, and Berg's Marie.—NS/LK/DM

Lipp, Wilma, esteemed Austrian soprano; b. Vienna, April 26, 1925. She was a student in Vienna of Sindel, Novikova, Bahr- Mildenburg, and Jerger, and in Milan of Dal Monte. In 1943 she made her operatic debut in Vienna as Rosina, and then was a member of the State Opera there from 1945. She also appeared at the Salzburg Festival from 1948. In 1950 she made her debut at Milan's La Scala as the Queen of the Night, a role she made her own. In 1951 she made her first appearance at London's Covent Garden singing Gilda. In 1953 she sang the Queen of the Night at her debut at the Paris Opéra. She appeared at the Glyndebourne Festival for the first time in 1957 as Constanze. Her U.S. debut followed in 1962 as Nannetta in *Falstaff* at the San Francisco Opera. In 1982 she became a prof. of voice at the Salzburg Mozarteum. She was honored as an Austrian Kammersängerin. Lipp was equally adept in coloratura and lyric roles, ranging from the operas of Mozart to Richard Strauss.—NS/LK/DM

Lipphardt, Walther, German musicologist; b. Wiescherhofen bei Hamm, Oct. 14, 1906; d. Frankfurt am Main, Jan. 17, 1981. He studied musicology with Moser at the Univ. of Heidelberg and with Gurlitt at the Univ. of Freiburg im Breisgau, then took additional courses at the Univ. of Heidelberg with Besseler, graduating with a Ph.D. in 1931 with the diss. *Über die altdeutschen Marienklagen.* He subsequently was on the faculty of the Hochschule für Musik in Frankfurt am Main (1946–70). He publ. numerous valuable papers on liturgical music and ed. works of Renaissance composers.

WRITINGS: *Die Weisen der lateinischen Osterspiele des 12. und 13. Jahrhunderts* (Kassel, 1948); *Die Geschichte des mehrstimmigen Proprium Missae* (Heidelberg, 1950); *Der karolingische Tonar von Metz* (Münster, 1965); *Gesangbuchdrucke in Frankfurt am Main vor 1569* (Frankfurt am Main, 1974).—NS/LK/DM

Lippincott, Joan, American organist and teacher; b. East Orange, N.J., Dec. 25, 1935. She studied piano and organ with William Jancovius, then organ with Alexander McCurdy at Westminster Choir Coll. in Princeton, N.J. (B.M., 1957; M.M., 1961) and at the Curtis Inst. of Music in Philadelphia (diploma, 1960), where she also received instruction in piano from Vladimir Sokoloff; subsequently she pursued graduate studies at the School of Sacred Music at the Union Theological Seminary in N.Y. She made many tours as a recitalist in the U.S. and overseas. She also taught at Westminster Choir Coll. (from 1960), where she served as head of the organ dept. (from 1967). In addition to the standard organ literature, Lippincott has played much contemporary music for her instrument.—NS/LK/DM

Lippius, Johannes, Alsatian music theorist and theologian; b. Strasbourg, June 24, 1585; d. Speyer, Sept. 24, 1612. After training in music from his father, he studied at the univs. of Jena, Leipzig, and Wittenberg; he also pursued studies in music with Calvisius in Leipzig. His most significant treatise was the *Synopsis musicae novae omino verae atque methodicae universae* (Strasbourg, 1612; Eng. tr., 1977, by B. Rivera), a departure from Renaissance theory. In his treatise, he treated the subject of 4- part writing over a bass, with the triad serving as the important symbolic representation of the Trinity.

BIBL.: B. Rivera, *German Music Theory in the Early 17th Century: The Treatises of J. L.* (Ann Arbor, 1979).—**LK/DM**

Lippman, Edward A(rthur), American musicologist; b. N.Y., May 24, 1920. He was educated at the City Coll. of N.Y. (B.S., 1942), N.Y.U. (M.A., 1945), and Columbia Univ. (Ph.D., 1952, with the diss. *Music and Space: A Study in the Philosophy of Music*). He held a Guggenheim fellowship (1958–59). Lippman taught at Columbia Univ. (from 1954), where he was a prof. (from 1969).

WRITINGS: *Musical Thought in Ancient Greece* (N.Y., 1964); *A Humanistic Philosophy of Music* (N.Y., 1977); *Musical Aesthetics: A Historical Reader* (3 vols., N.Y., 1986–90); *A History of Western Musical Aesthetics* (Lincoln, Nebr., 1992).—**NS/LK/DM**

Lipsius, Marie (pen name, **La Mara**), German writer on music; b. Leipzig, Dec. 30, 1837; d. Schmölen, near Wurzen, March 2, 1927. She received her academic training from her father, Adalbert Lipsius, rector of the Thomasschule in Leipzig, and also studied music with Richard Muller in Leipzig. Through R. Pohl, she was introduced to Liszt (1856), and in Liszt's circle at Weimar she had the happy fortune of meeting the foremost musicians of the time. Her writings on Liszt and Wagner, and on other German composers of the Romantic school, possess a stamp of authority and intimate understanding. In addition to a number of popular biographies of composers, she wrote *Musikalische Studienköpfe* (5 vols., Leipzig, 1868; second ed., aug., 1875–82), *Musikerbriefe aus fünf Jahrhunderten* (2 vols., Leipzig, 1886), *Beethovens Unsterbliche Geliebte: Das Geheimnis der Gräfin Brunsvik und ihre Memoiren* (Leipzig, 1909), *Liszt und die Frauen* (Leipzig, 1911; second ed., 1919), *An der Schwelle des Jenseits: Letzte Erinnerungen an die Fürstin Carolyne Sayn-Wittgenstein* (Leipzig, 1925), and her autobiography, *Durch Musik und Leben im Dienst des Ideals* (2 vols., Leipzig, 1917; second ed., 1925). —**NS/LK/DM**

Lipton, Martha, American mezzo-soprano and teacher; b. N.Y., April 6, 1913. She was educated at the Juilliard School of Music in N.Y. On Nov. 27, 1944, she made her debut as Siebel with the Metropolitan Opera in N.Y. and remained on its roster until 1960; also sang with the N.Y.C. Opera (1944, 1958, 1961) and at the Chicago Lyric Opera (1956). In Europe she sang in Amsterdam and The Hague, and at the Holland and Edinburgh festivals, the Vienna State Opera, and the Paris Opéra; also made appearances in South America. In 1960 she became a prof. of voice at the Ind. Univ. School of Music in Bloomington. Among her prominent roles were Cherubino, Ulrica, Orlovsky, Herodias, and Octavian. She also appeared extensively as a concert artist.—**NS/LK/DM**

Lirou, Jean François Espic, Chevalier de, French composer and music theorist; b. Paris, 1740; d. there, 1806. He was an officer in the "Mousquetaires du roi," for whom he wrote *Marche des Mousquetaires*,

which was performed until the Revolution. He publ. *Explication du système de l'harmonie* (1785), the first French theory of harmony that opposed Rameau's system and sought to establish the laws of chord progressions from the inherent affinities of tonality.—**NS/LK/DM**

Lisa Lisa and Cult Jam, chart-topping group on the cusp of new jack swing dance pop (f. 1984). **MEMBERSHIP:** Lisa Lisa (real name, Lisa Velez), voc. (b. N.Y., Jan. 15, 1967); Spanador (real name, Alex Moseley), gtr. (b. N.Y., 1962); Mike Hughes, drm. (b. N.Y., 1963).

The youngest of ten children brought up in an apartment in Hell's Kitchen, just a block off Broadway, Lisa Velez sang in the church choir, worked in community theater productions, and acted in high school musicals. After high school, she folded sweaters for Benetton by day and hung out at the Fun House by night, because she heard that Madonna had been "discovered" there. She met drummer Mike Hughes, who worked with hip-hop impresarios Full Force. He told her they were looking for a girl singer to front a new group. She auditioned and at 16 years old she got the job. The group redubbed her Lisa Lisa (after their first major hit, "Roxanne Roxanne") and within a week she was in the studio with Full Force, Hughes, and guitarist Alex "Spanador" Mosely. They cut "I Wonder If I Take You Home," which topped the dance charts, eked its way into the Top 40 at #34, and went gold. The next single, "Can You Feel the Beat" didn't fare quite as well, but the ballad "All Cried Out" broke the group pop, hitting #3 on the R&B charts, #8 on the pop charts, and going gold. The group's 1985 eponymous album, collecting all these hits, eventually went platinum.

Full Force released their next album, *Spanish Fly*, less than a year after the first single hit. The lead off single from the new album, the breezy dance tune "Head to Toe" topped the pop and R&B charts and went gold, as did the next single "Lost in Emotion."

"Somebody to Love Me for Me" went Top Ten R&B, as did "Everything Will B-Fine." *Spanish Fly* also went platinum, topping out at #7 on the album charts. This represented the peak in the band's fortunes. Their next album *Straight for the Sky*, produced just one pop single, "Little Jackie Wants to Be a Star" which went to #29 pop (#3 R&B), and a pair of minor R&B hits. For their next album, they hedged their bets, with Full Force producing half the tracks and the hot dance pop team of Cole and Clivilles producing the other. The C&C hit "Let the Beat Hit Them" topped the R&B charts, scratched into the pop Top 40 at #37, and became the group's fifth gold single. The album, however, didn't sell well.

In 1993, Lisa Lisa went solo with the album *LL77*, but the album only produced a couple of minor R&B hits. She kept busy, continuing to work with Full Force, as well as doing voice over work in both English and Spanish. "All Cried Out" resurfaced in a cover version by Allure in 1997. Lisa Lisa still lives in her mother's apartment in Hell's Kitchen.

DISC.: *Lisa Lisa & Cult Jam with Full Force* (1985); *Spanish Fly* (1987); *Straight to the Sky* (1989); *Straight Outta Hell's Kitchen* (1991); *LL 77* (1993); *Head to Toe* (1995).—**HB**

Lisinski, Vatroslav (real name, **Ignacije Fuchs**), important Croatian composer; b. Zagreb, July 8, 1819; d. there, May 31, 1854. He was a student of Sojka and Wiesner von Morgenstern in Zagreb. As late as 1847, he went to Prague to study with Pitsch and Kittl. Although he never acquired a solid technique of composition, he was notable in that he tried to establish a national style in dramatic writing. He was the composer of the first Croatian opera, *Ljubav i zloba* (Love and Malice), for which he wrote only the vocal score; it was orchestrated by Wiesner von Morgenstern, and performed in Zagreb on March 28, 1846. His second opera, *Porin* (1848–51), also in Croatian, was given many years after his death, in Zagreb, on Oct. 2, 1897. He further wrote 7 overtures, a number of choruses and songs, and piano pieces.

BIBL.: V. Novák, *V. L.* (Belgrade, 1925); L. Zupanović, *V. L. (1819–1854), život—djelo—znacenje* (V. L. [1819–1854], Life—Work—Significance; Zagreb, 1969).—NS/LK/DM

Lisitsyan, Pavel (Gerasimovich) (actually, **Pogos Karapetovich**), Armenian baritone; b. Vladikavkaz, Nov. 6, 1911. He studied in Leningrad. He sang at the Maly Theater there (1935–37); then was a member of the Armenian Opera Theater in Yerevan (1937–40); in 1940 he joined the Bolshoi Theater in Moscow, remaining on its roster until 1966, but in the interim filled engagements all over Europe, in India, and in Japan; also made his debut at the Metropolitan Opera in N.Y. as Amonasro (March 3, 1960). From 1967 to 1973 he was on the faculty of the Yerevan Cons. He was best known for his roles in Russian operas. —NS/LK/DM

Liška, Zdeněk, Czech composer; b. Smečno, March 16, 1922; d. Prague, July 13, 1983. He studied at the Prague Cons., and beginning in 1945 was active as a composer for the State Studios of Documentary Films. For the Czech spectacle *Laterna Magica*, he wrote a modernistic violin concerto in which actors and musicians alternate with their screen images without loss of continuity. This work, first performed in Leningrad on Dec. 5, 1960, was featured in the presentation of *Laterna Magica* in N.Y. in the summer of 1964.—NS/LK/DM

Lissa, Zofia, distinguished Polish musicologist; b. Lemberg, Oct. 19, 1908; d. Warsaw, March 26, 1980. She studied piano and organ at the Lemberg Cons., and then musicology with Chybiński at the Univ. of Lemberg (1925–29), where she also took courses in philosophy, psychology, and art history (Ph.D., 1930, with the diss. *O harmonice Aleksandra Skriabina*; publ. in *Kwartalnik Muzyczny*, II, 1930); subsequently completed her Habilitation at the Univ. of Poznań with her *Oistocie komizmu muzycznege* (The Essence of Musical Humor; publ. in Kraków, 1938) and later took a second Ph.D. there in 1954 with the diss. *Podstawy estetyki muzycznej* (Questions of Music Aesthetics; publ. in Warsaw, 1953). She taught at the Lwów Cons. (1931–41); later was reader (1948–51), prof. (1951–57), and director (from 1957) of the musicological inst. of the Univ. of Warsaw. She was a leading proponent of socialist realism as a critical method of musical evaluation.

WRITINGS: *Zarys nauki o muzyce* (A Short Music Textbook; Lwów, 1934; fourth ed., aug., 1966); *Muzykologia polska na przelomie* (A Turning Point in Polish Musicology; Kraków, 1952); with J. Chomiński, *Muzyka polskiego odrodzenia* (Music of the Polish Renaissance; Warsaw, 1953; 3rd ed., rev., 1958, in *Odrodzenie w Polsce*, V); *Historia muzyki rosyjskiej* (History of Russian Music; Kraków, 1955); *Estetyka muzyki filmowej* (Kraków, 1964); *Skice z estetyki muzycznej* (A Sketch of Musical Aesthetics; Kraków, 1965); *Polonica Beethovenowskie* (Kraków, 1970); *Studia nad twórczością Fryderyka Chopina* (Studies of Frédéric Chopin's Works; Kraków, 1970).

BIBL.: *Studia musicologica aesthetica, theoretica, historica: Z. L. w 70. roku urodzin* (Kraków, 1979).—NS/LK/DM

Lissenko, Nikolai (Vitalievich), notable Ukrainian composer, pianist, conductor, and folk song collector; b. Grinki, near Kremenchug, March 22, 1842; d. Kiev, Nov. 6, 1912. Following piano lessons from his mother, he was taken at age 9 to Kiev to study with Panochini (piano) and Nejnkevič (theory). He pursued training in the natural sciences at the univs. of Kharkov and Kiev (1860–64). After further music training with Wolner, Dmitriev, and Wilczyk, he was a student at the Leipzig Cons. (1867–69) of Reinecke (piano) and Richter (theory and composition). In 1869 he returned to Kiev as a piano teacher, and also became associated with its branch of the Russian Musical Soc. His ardent espousal of Ukrainian nationalism, however, led him to later break with the Soc. After studies in orchestration with Rimsky-Korsakov in St. Petersburg (1874–76), Lissenko returned once more to Kiev and established himself as its principal figure in the musical life of the city. In addition to his activities as a composer, pianist, conductor, and folk song collector, he founded a school of music and drama in 1904, which was posthumously named in his honor in 1918. His support of the 1905 revolution led to his brief imprisonment in 1907. Lissenko's life-long interest in folk songs is reflected in his works. His most significant scores comprise the operas *Taras Bulba* (1880–91; Kharkov, Oct. 4, 1924) and *Natalka Poltava* (Odessa, Nov. 24, 1889). A complete ed. of his extensive output was publ. in Kiev (20 vols., 1950–59).

WORKS: DRAMATIC: *Harkushka,* opera (1864; fragment); *Andrashiada,* opera-satire (1866; fragment); *Utoplena, abo Mayska nich* (The Drowned Maiden, or May Night), opera (1871–83; Odessa, Jan. 14, 1885); *Chernomortsy* (Black Sea Sailors), operetta (1872–73; Kharkov, June 13, 1883); *Rizdvyana nich* (Christmas Eve), comic-lyric opera (1877–82; Kharkov, Feb. 8, 1883); *Taras Bulba,* opera (1880–91; Kharkov, Oct. 4, 1924); *Koza-Dereza* (The Nanny-Goat), children's comic opera (1888; Kiev, April 21, 1901); *Natalka Poltavka,* opera (Odessa, Nov. 24, 1889); *Pan Kotskiy* (Sir Cat), children's comic opera (1891; Kharkov, May 8, 1955); *Zima i vesna, abo Snigova kralya* (Winter and Spring, or The Snow Maiden), children's opera (1892; Kiev, June 29, 1956); *Volshebniy son* (The Magic Dream), musical fairy tale (1894); *Sappho,* opera (1896–1900); *Eneida* (Aeneid), musical comedy (Kiev, Dec. 6, 1910); *Letney nochyu,* opera (1912; unfinished); *Noktyurin* (Nocturne), opera (1912; Kiev, Feb. 16, 1914); incidental music. **ORCH.:** *Moldavskaya, Russian Pizzicato* for Strings (1859–60); Sym. (1869); *Ukrainian Cossack Song* (1872–73). **CHAMBER:** String Quartet (1869); String Trio (1869); *Fantasy on Ukrainian Themes* for Violin or Flute and Piano (1872–73); *Elegiac Capriccio* for Violin and Piano (1894); *Ukrainian Rhapsody* for Violin and Piano (1897); *Elegy in Memory of Shevchenko* for

Violin and Piano (1912); many piano pieces. **VOCAL:** Cantatas; hymns; choruses; songs; over 20 vols. of folk song arrangements.

BIBL.: M. Starytsky, *K biogrfii N.V. L.: Vospominaniya* (Toward a Biography of N.V. L.: Reminiscences, Kiev, 1904); K. Kvitka, *N. L. yak zbirach narodnikh posen* (N. L. as a Folk Song Collector; Kiev, 1923); V. Chagovets, *N.V. L.* (Kiev, 1949); L. Arkimovich and N. Hordiychuk, *N.V. L.: Zhittya-tvoristvo* (N.V. L.: Life and Works; Kiev, 1952); A. Gozenpud, *N.V. L. i russkaya muzïkalnaya kultura* (N.V. L. and Russian Musical Culture; Moscow and Leningrad, 1954); Z. Vasylenko, *Folkloritichna diyalnist N.V. L.* (N.V. L.'s Work as a Folklorist; Kiev, 1972); R. Sawycky, *N. L. in Western Sources: Bibliographic Essay* (Cranford, N.J., 1992).—NS/LK/DM

List (real name, **Fleissig**), **Emanuel,** noted Austrian-born American bass; b. Vienna, March 22, 1886; d. there, June 21, 1967. He was a boy chorister at the Theater-an-der-Wien. Following voice training with Steger in Vienna, he toured Europe as a member of a comic vocal quartet. He went to the U.S. and appeared in vaudeville, burlesque, and minstrel shows. After further vocal studies with Zuro in N.Y., he returned to Vienna in 1920 and in 1922 made his operatic debut as Gounod's Méphistophélès at the Volksoper. He then sang at Berlin's Städtische Oper (1923–25) and State Opera (1925–33), London's Covent Garden (1925; 1934–36), the Salzburg Festivals (1931–35), and the Bayreuth Festival (1933). List made his Metropolitan Opera debut in N.Y. on Dec. 27, 1933, as the Landgrave. While remaining on its roster until 1948, he also appeared in San Francisco and Chicago (1935–37) and gave lieder recitals. He was again on the Metropolitan Opera's roster in 1949–50. In 1952 he returned to Vienna. List was especially admired for the rich vocal resources he brought to such roles as Osmin, the Commendatore, Sarastro, Rocco, King Marke, Hagen, Pogner, Hunding, and Baron Ochs.—NS/LK/DM

List, Eugene, American pianist; b. Philadelphia, July 6, 1918; d. N.Y., March 1, 1985. He was taken to Los Angeles when a year old; studied there at the Sutro-Seyler Studios and made his debut with the Los Angeles Phil. at the age of 12; later studied in Philadelphia with Samaroff, and at the Juilliard Graduate School in N.Y. He played the solo part in the American premiere of Shostakovich's Piano Concerto No. 1 with the Philadelphia Orch. (Dec. 12, 1934). As a sergeant in the U.S. Army, he was called upon to play the piano at the Potsdam Conference in July 1945, in the presence of Truman, Churchill, and Stalin. Subsequently he appeared as a soloist with many American orchs. and as a recitalist. In 1964 he was appointed a prof. of piano at the Eastman School of Music in Rochester, N.Y.; left there in 1975 and then joined the faculty of N.Y.U. His repertoire ranged from Mozart to contemporary composers. He championed the cause of Gottschalk, and in later years oversaw a series of "monster concerts" à la Gottschalk in which 10 or more pianos and various pianists were involved. In 1943 he married **Carroll Glenn.**—NS/LK/DM

List, Garrett, American composer; b. Phoenix, Sept. 10, 1943. He studied with Bertram McGarrity at Calif.

State Univ. in Long Beach, and in N.Y. with Hall Overton and at the Juilliard School (B.M., 1968; M.M., 1969). He became proficient as a trombonist and was active with various new-music groups, both as performer and as composer. He was music director of N.Y.'s Kitchen (1975–77) and also taught at the Liège Cons. (from 1980).

WORKS: DRAMATIC: *Time and Desire,* dance piece (1984–85). **ORCH.:** *Orchestral Études* (1972–79); *9 Sets of 7* for Chamber Orch. (1975); *Songs* for Chamber Orch. (1975); *I Am Electric* for Jazz Band (1976); *The Girls* for Narrator and Small Orch. (1977); *Escape Story* for Soloists and Orch. (1979); *Fear and Understanding* for Jazz Band (1981). **Other Instrumental:** *2 Wind Studies* for 9 to 16 Winds (1971); *Songs* for 7 to 12 Instruments (1972); *Your Own Self* for Any Instrument(s) (1972); *Elegy: To the People of Chile* for Any Instrument(s) (1973); *Requiem for Helen Lopez* for Piano and 4 to 6 Instruments (1981); *Flesh and Steel* for Piano, Guitar(s), and Instrument(s) (1982); *Baudelaire* for Instrument(s) (1983); *Hôtel des étrangers* for 5 to 21 Instruments (1983); trombone pieces. **VOCAL:** *American Images,* cantata for Voice and Instrument(s) (1972); *Standard Existence* for Voice and Instrument(s) (1977); many songs. —NS/LK/DM

Listemann, Bernhard, German-American violinist, conductor, and teacher; b. Schlotheim, Aug. 28, 1841; d. Chicago, Feb. 11, 1917. He was a student of David in Leipzig, Joachim in Hannover, and Vieutemps in Brussels. After serving as court Kammervirtuos in Rudolstadt (1859–67), he emigrated to the U.S. and made his debut at N.Y.'s Steinway Hall in Nov. 1867. In 1868 he made his first appearance in Boston as soloist in Joachim's *Hungarian Concerto* at a Harvard Musical Assn. concert, and then was active in that city's musical life until serving as concertmaster of Theodore Thomas's orch. in N.Y. (1871–74). Returning to Boston, he was active as a soloist, chamber music player, and conductor. He was founder- director of the Boston Phil. Club and Orch., and then first concertmaster of the newly organized Boston Sym. Orch. (1881–85). He was also active with his own Listemann Club and Listemann String Quartet, and later with his own Bernard Listemann Co. (1885–93). In 1893 he settled in Chicago as a teacher at the Coll. of Music. He authored a *Modern Method of Violin Playing* (1869). His brother, Fritz Listemann (b. Schlotheim, March 25, 1839; d. Boston, Dec. 28, 1909), was a violinist and composer. He also had two sons who were musicians, Paul Listemann (b. Boston, Oct. 24, 1871; d. Chicago, Sept. 20, 1950), a violinist, and Franz Listemann (b. N.Y., Dec. 17, 1873; d. Chicago, March 11, 1930).—NS/LK/DM

Listov, Konstantin, Russian composer; b. Odessa, Sept. 19, 1900; d. Moscow, Sept. 6, 1983. He learned music by ear, then studied piano in Tsaritsin and in Saratov. In 1923 he went to Moscow and began to write music for the theater. His Red Army song *Tachanka* became immensely popular. He also wrote a Sym. in commemoration of the centennial of Lenin (1970).

BIBL.: A. Tishchenko, *K. L.* (Moscow, 1962).—NS/LK/DM

Liszt, Franz (actually, **Ferenc;** baptized **Franciscus**), greatly celebrated Hungarian pianist and composer; b. Raiding, near Odenburg, Oct. 22, 1811;

d. Bayreuth, July 31, 1886. His father was an amateur musician who devoted his energies to the education of his son; at the age of 9, young Liszt was able to play a difficult piano concerto by Ries. A group of Hungarian music-lovers provided sufficient funds to finance Liszt's musical education. In 1822 the family traveled to Vienna. Beethoven was still living, and Liszt's father bent every effort to persuade Beethoven to come to young Liszt's Vienna concert on April 13, 1823. Legend has it that Beethoven did come and was so impressed that he ascended the podium and kissed the boy on the brow. There is even in existence a lithograph that portrays the scene, but it was made many years after the event by an unknown lithographer and its documentary value is dubious. Liszt himself perpetuated the legend, and often showed the spot on his forehead where Beethoven was supposed to have implanted the famous kiss. However that might be, Liszt's appearance in Vienna created a sensation; he was hailed by the press as "child Hercules." The link with Beethoven was maintained through Liszt's own teachers: Czerny, who was Beethoven's student and friend and with whom Liszt took piano lessons, and the great Salieri, who was Beethoven's early teacher and who at the end of his life became Liszt's teacher in composition.

On May 1, 1823, Liszt gave a concert in Pest. Salieri appealed to Prince Esterházy for financial help so as to enable Liszt to move to Vienna, where Salieri made his residence. Apparently Esterházy was sufficiently impressed with Salieri's plea to contribute support.

Under the guidance of his ambitious father, Liszt applied for an entrance examination at the Paris Cons., but its director, Cherubini, declined to accept him, ostensibly because he was a foreigner (Cherubini himself was a foreigner, but was naturalized). Liszt then settled for private lessons in counterpoint from Antoine Reicha, a Parisianized Czech musician who instilled in Liszt the importance of folklore. Liszt's father died in 1837; Liszt remained in Paris, where he soon joined the brilliant company of men and women of the arts. Paganini's spectacular performances of the violin in particular inspired Liszt to emulate him in creating a piano technique of transcendental difficulty and brilliance, utilizing all possible sonorities of the instrument. To emphasize the narrative Romantic quality of his musical ideas, he accepted the suggestion of his London manager, Frederick Beale, to use the word "recital" to describe his concerts, and in time the term was widely accepted by other pianists.

In his own compositions, Liszt was a convinced propagandist of program music. He liked to attach descriptive titles to his works, such as *Fantasy, Reminiscence,* and *Illustrations.* The musical form of Rhapsody was also made popular by Liszt, but he was not its originator; it was used for the first time in piano pieces by Tomaschek. A true Romantic, Liszt conceived himself as an actor playing the part of his own life, in which he was a child of the Muses. He was fascinated by a popular contemporary novel that depicted a fictional traveler named Oberman, and he wrote a suite of piano compositions under the general title *Années de pèlerinage,* in which he followed in music the imaginary progressions of Oberman.

Handsome, artistic, a brilliant conversationalist, Liszt was sought after in society. His first lasting attachment was with an aristocratic married woman, the Comtesse Marie d'Agoult; they had 3 daughters, one of whom, Cosima, married Liszt's friend Hans von Bülow before abandoning him for Richard Wagner. D'Agoult was fluent in several European languages and had considerable literary talents, which she exercised under the nom de plume of Daniel Stern. Liszt was 22 when he entered his concubinage with her; she was 28. The growing intimacy between Liszt and d'Agoult soon became the gossip of Paris. Berlioz warned Liszt not to let himself become too deeply involved with her. D'Agoult rapidly established herself as a salon hostess in Paris; she was a constant intermediary between Liszt and his close contemporary Chopin. Indeed, the book on Chopin publ. under Liszt's name after Chopin's early death was largely written by d'Agoult, whose literary French was much superior to Liszt's. His second and final attachment was with another married woman, Carolyne von Sayn-Wittgenstein, who was separated from her husband. Her devotion to Liszt exceeded all limits, even in a Romantic age.

Liszt held a clerical title of Abbé, conferred upon him by Pope Pius IX, but his religious affiliations were not limited to the Catholic church. He was also a member of the order of Freemasons and served as a tertiary of the Order of St. Francis. In 1879 he received the tonsure and 4 minor orders (ostuary, lector, exorcist, and acolyte) and an honorary canonry. But he was never ordained a priest, and thus was free to marry if he so wished.

Liszt fully intended to marry Sayn-Wittgenstein, but he encountered resistance from the Catholic church, to which they both belonged and which forbade marriage to a divorced woman. His own position as a secular cleric further militated against it. Thus, Liszt, the great lover of women, never married. (The legend of Liszt as a man of fantastic sexual powers persisted even after his death. It found its most exaggerated expression in a film directed by Ken Russell under the title *Lisztomania.* In one scene, Liszt is portrayed with a grotesquely extended male organ on which a bevy of scantily dressed maidens obscenely disported themselves.)

Liszt's romantic infatuations did not interfere with his brilliant virtuoso career. One of his greatest successes was his triumphant tour in Russia in 1842. Russian musicians and music critics exhausted their flowery vocabulary to praise Liszt as the miracle of the age. Czar Nicholas I himself attended a concert given by Liszt in St. Petersburg, and expressed his appreciation by sending him a pair of trained Russian bears. Liszt acknowledged the imperial honor, but did not venture to take the animals with him on his European tour; they remained in Russia.

Liszt was a consummate showman. In Russia, as elsewhere, he had 2 grand pianos installed on the stage at right angles, so that the keyboards were visible from the right and the left respectively and he could alternate his playing on both. He appeared on the stage wearing a long cloak and white gloves, discarding both with a spectacular gesture. Normally he needed eyeglasses, but he was too vain to wear them in public.

It is not clear why, after all his triumphs in Russia and elsewhere in Europe, Liszt decided to abandon his career as a piano virtuoso and devote his entire efforts to composition. He became associated with Wagner, his son-in-law, as a prophet of "music of the future." Indeed, Liszt anticipated Wagner's chromatic harmony in his works. A remarkable instance of such anticipation is illustrated in his song *Ich möchte hingehen*, which prefigures, note for note, Wagner's theme from the prelude to *Tristan und Isolde*. Inevitably, Liszt and Wagner became objects of derision on the part of conservative music critics. A pictorial example of such an attack was an extraordinary caricature entitled "Music of the Future," distributed by G. Schirmer in N.Y. in 1867. It represented Liszt with arms and legs flailing symmetrically over a huge orch. that comprised not only human players but also goats, donkeys, and a cat placed in a cage with an operator pulling its tail. At Liszt's feet there was placed a score marked "Wagner, not to be played much till 1995."

In 1848 Liszt accepted the position of Court Kapellmeister in Weimar. When Wagner was exiled from Saxony, Liszt arranged for the production of Wagner's opera *Lohengrin* in Weimar on Aug. 28, 1850; he was also instrumental in supervising performances in Weimar of Wagner's operas *Der fliegende Holländer* and *Tannhäuser*, as well as music by Berlioz and a number of operas by other composers.

Liszt never wrote a full-fledged opera, but he composed several sacred oratorios that were operatic in substance. In his secular works he was deeply conscious of his Hungarian heritage, but he gathered his material mainly from Gypsy dances that he heard in public places in Budapest. In a strange show of negligence, he borrowed a theme for one of the most famous of his Hungarian Rhapsodies from an unpubl. work by an obscure Austrian musician named Heinrich Ehrlich, who had sent him a MS for possible inclusion in one of Liszt's recitals. He explained this faux pas as an oversight.

As a composer, Liszt made every effort to expand the technical possibilities of piano technique; in his piano concertos, and particularly in his *Études d'exécution transcendante*, he made use of the grand piano, which expanded the keyboard in both the bass and the extreme treble. He also extended the field of piano literature with his brilliant transcriptions of operas, among them those by Mozart, Verdi, Wagner, Donizetti, Gounod, Rossini, and Beethoven. These transcriptions were particularly useful at the time when the piano was the basic musical instrument at home.

Although Liszt is universally acknowledged to be a great Hungarian composer, he was actually brought up in the atmosphere of German culture. He spoke German at home, with French as a second language. His women companions conversed with him in French, and most of Liszt's own correspondence was in that language. It was not until his middle age that he decided to take lessons in Hungarian, but he never acquired fluency. His knowledge of Hungarian folk songs came through the medium of the popular Gypsy dance bands that played in Budapest. He used to refer to himself jocularly as "half Gypsy and half Franciscan monk." This self-identification pursued him through his life, and beyond; when the question was raised after his death in Bayreuth regarding the transfer of his body to Budapest, the prime minister of Hungary voiced objection, since Liszt never regarded himself as a purely Hungarian musician.

Liszt was an eager correspondent; his letters, written in longhand, in French and in German, passed upon his death into the possession of Sayn-Wittgenstein; after her death in 1887, they were inherited by her daughter, Marie Hohenlohe- Schillingsfürst. She, in turn, left these materials to the Weimar court; eventually they became part of the Liszt Museum in Weimar.

Liszt was a great musical technician. He organized his compositions with deliberate intent to create music that is essentially new. Thus he abandons the traditional succession of two principal themes in sonata form. In his symphonic poem *Les Préludes*, the governing melody dominates the entire work. In his popular 3rd *Liebestraum* for Piano, the passionate melody modulates by thirds rather than by Classically anointed fifths and fourths. The great *Faust* sym. is more of a literary essay on Goethe's great poem than a didactic composition. His piano concertos are free from the dialectical contrasts of the established Classical school. The chromatic opening of the first Concerto led Hans von Bülow to improvise an insulting line to accompany the theme, "Sie sind alle ganz verrückt!," and the introduction of the triangle solo aroused derisive whoops from the press. Liszt was indifferent to such outbursts. He was the master of his musical fate in the ocean of sounds.

WORKS: DRAMATIC: O p e r a : *Don Sanche, ou Le Château d'amour* (1824–25; Paris, Oct. 17, 1825; in collaboration with Paër). ORCH.: 2 syms.: *Eine Faust-Symphonie in drei Charakterbildern* for Tenor, Men's Voices, and Orch. (1854–57; Weimar, Sept. 5, 1857) and *Eine Symphonie zu Dantes Divina commedia* (1855–56; Dresden, Nov. 7, 1857); 13 symphonic poems: *Ce qu'on entend sur la montagne* or *Bergsymphonie* (1848–49; orchestrated by Raff; Weimar, Feb. 1850; rev. 1850 and 1854), *Tasso: Lamento e trionfo* (1841–45; orchestrated by Conradi; Weimar, Aug. 28, 1849; rev. 1850–51 and 1854), *Les Préludes* (1848; Weimar, Feb. 23, 1854), *Orpheus* (1853–54; Weimar, Feb. 16, 1854), *Prometheus* (1850; orchestrated by Raff; Weimar, Aug. 24, 1850; rev. 1855), *Mazeppa* (1851; orchestrated by Raff; Weimar, April 16, 1854), *Festklänge* (1853; Weimar, Nov. 9, 1854), *Héroide funèbre* (1849–50; orchestrated by Raff; rev. c. 1854; Breslau, Nov. 10, 1857), *Hungaria* (1854; Budapest, Sept. 8, 1856), *Hamlet* (1858; Sondershausen, July 2, 1876), *Hunnenschlacht* (1857; Weimar, Dec. 29, 1857), *Die Ideale* (1857; Weimar, Sept. 5, 1857), and *Von der Wiege bis zum Grabe—Du berceau jusqu'à la tombe* (1881–82); 4 piano concertos: No. 1, in E- flat major (1832; rev. 1849 and 1853; Weimar, Feb. 17, 1855; rev. 1856), No. 2, in A major (1839; various revisions; Weimar, Jan. 7, 1857), E-flat major (c. 1839; Chicago, May 3, 1990), and *Piano Concerto in the Hungarian Style* (1885); *Malédiction* for Piano and Strings (1833); *Grande fantaisie symphonique* on themes from Berlioz's *Lélio* for Piano and Orch. (1834; Paris, April 1835); *Fantasie über Motive aus Beethovens Ruinen von Athen* for Piano and Orch. (c. 1837; rev. 1849; Budapest, June 1, 1853); *Totentanz* for Piano and Orch. (1849; rev. 1853 and 1859; The Hague, April 15, 1865); *Festmarsch zur Goethejubiläumsfeier* (1849; orchestrated by Conradi; Weimar, Nov. 8, 1860); *Fantasie über ungarische Volksmelodien* for Piano and Orch. (Budapest, June 1, 1853); *Künstlerfestzug zur Schiller-feier 1859* (1857; Weimar, Nov. 8, 1860); *Festmarsch nach Motiven von E.H. zu S.-C.- G.* on themes from Duke Ernst of Saxe-Coburg-Gotha's *Diana von Solange* (c. 1860); 2 episodes from Lenau's *Faust* (1860–61; No. 2, Weimar, March 8, 1861); *Salve Polonia* (1863; Weimar, 1884); *Rákóczy March* (1865; rev. 1867; Budapest, Aug. 17, 1875); *Trois odes funèbres*: No. 1 (1860–66; Weimar, May 21, 1912), No. 2 (1863–64; Weimar, Dec. 6, 1912), and No. 3 (1866; N.Y., March 1877); *Ungarischer Marsch zur Krönungsfeier in Ofen-Pest am 8. Juni 1867* (1870); *Ungarischer Sturmmarsch* (1875); *Second Mephisto Waltz* (1880–81; Budapest, March 9, 1881). **P i a n o :** *Variation über einen Walzer von Diabelli* (1822); *Huit variations* (c. 1824); *Sept variations brillantes sur un thème de Rossini* (c. 1824); *Impromptu brillant sur des thèmes de Rossini et Spontini* (1824); *Allegro di bravura* (1824); *Rondo di bravura* (1824); *Étude en douze exercices* (1826); *Scherzo* in G minor (1827); *Grandes études de Paganini* (1831); *Harmonies poétiques et religieuses* (1833; rev. 1835); *Apparitions* (1834); *Fantaisie romantique sur deux mélodies suisses* (1836); *Vingt-quatre grandes études* (1837); *Album d'un voyageur* (3 vols., 1835–38); *Études d'exécution transcendante d'après Paganini* (1838–39); *Mazeppa* (1840); *Morceau de salon, étude de perfectionnement* (1840); *Venezia e Napoli* (c. 1840; rev. 1859); *Albumblatt* in E major (c. 1841); *Feuilles d'album* in A-flat major (1841); *Albumblatt in Walzerform* in A major (1841); *Feuille d'album* in A minor (1842); *Élégie sur des motifs du Prince Louis Ferdinand de Prusse* (1842; rev. c. 1851); *Madrigal* (1844); *Tre sonetti del Petrarca* (1844–45); 19 Hungarian Rhapsodies: No. 1, in C-sharp minor (1846), No. 2, in C-sharp minor (1847), No. 3, in B-flat major (1853), No. 4, in E-flat major (1853), No. 5, in E minor (1853), No. 6, in D-flat major (1853), No. 7, in D minor (1853), No. 8, in F-sharp minor (1853), No. 9, in E-flat major (1848), No. 10, in E major (1853), No. 11, in A minor (1853), No. 12, in C-sharp minor (1853), No. 13, in A minor (1853), No. 14, in F minor (1853), No. 15, in A minor, *Rákóczy March* (1851; rev. 1871), No. 16, in A minor (1882), No. 17, in D minor (1886), No. 18, in C-sharp minor (1885), and No. 19, in D minor (1885); 6 *Consolations* (1844–48); *Ballade* No. 1, in D-flat major (1845; rev. 1848); *Hymne de la nuit; Hymne du matin* (1847); *Trois études de concert* (c. 1848); *Romance* (1848); *Années de pèlerinage: Deuxième année, Italie* (1837–49); *Grosses Konzertsolo* (c. 1849); *Études d'exécution transcendante* (1851); *Scherzo und Marsch* (1851); *Harmonies poétiques et religieuses* (1840–52); *Ab irato* (1852); *Ballade* No. 2, in B minor (1853); Sonata in B minor (1851–53); *Années de pèlerinage: Première année, Suisse* (1848–52); *Berceuse* (1854; rev. 1862); *Weinen, Klagen, Sorgen, Zagen, Präludium* (1859); *Klavierstück* in F-sharp minor (c. 1861); *Zwei Konzertetüden*: No. 1, *Waldesrauschen*, and No. 2, *Gnomenreigen* (1862–63); *Variationen über das Motiv von Bach* (1862); *Ave Maria* (1862); *Alleluja et Ave Maria* (1862); *Légendes* (1863); *Urbi et orbi, bénédiction papale* (1864); *Vexilla regis prodeunt* (1864); *Weihnachtsbaum—Arbre de Noël* (1866; rev. 1876); *La Marquise de Blocqueville, portrait en musique* (1868); *Mosonyi gyázmenete—Mosonyis Grabgeleit* (1870); *Impromptu* (1872); *Elegie* (1874); *Années de pèlerinage, troisième année* (1867–77); *Sancta Dorothea* (1877); *Resignazione* (1877); *Petofi szellemenek—Dem Andenken Petofis* (1877); *Zweite Elegie* (1877); *Fünf kleine Klavierstücke* (1865–79); *Technische Studien* (12 vols., 1868–80); *In festo transfigurationis Domini nostri Jesu Christi* (1880); *Wiegenlied—Chant du berceau* (1880); *Toccata* (1879–81); *Nuages gris* (1881); *La Lugubre gondola* (1882; rev. 1885); *R.W.—Venezia* (1883); *Am Grabe Richard Wagners* (1883); *Schlaflos, Frage und Antwort* (1883); *Historische ungarische Bildnisse—Magyar törtenelmi arcképek* (1870–85); *Trauervorspiel und Trauermarsch* (1885); *En rêve* (1885); *Ruhig* (1883–86); *Recueillement* (1887); also numerous arrange-

ments and transcriptions. **C H O R A L : S a c r e d :** *Pater noster* for Men's Voices (1846; also for 4 Equal Voices and Organ, c. 1848); *Ave Maria* for Chorus and Organ (1846; also for 4 Voices and Organ, c. 1852); *Hymne de l'enfant à son réveil* for Women's Voices, Harmonium or Piano, and Harp ad libitum (1847; rev. 1862, 1865, and 1874; Weimar, June 17, 1875); Mass for 4 Men's Voices and Organ (1848; Weimar, Aug. 15, 1852; rev. 1859; Second version, 1869; Jena, June 1872); *Pater noster* for Mixed Voices and Organ (1850); *Te Deum* for Men's Voices and Organ (c. 1853); *Domine salvum fac regem* for Tenor, Men's Voices, and Organ or Orch. (1853; orchestrated by Raff); *Missa solemnis zur Einweihung der Basilika in Gran* for Soprano, Alto, Tenor, Bass, Chorus, and Orch. (1855; Gran, Aug. 31, 1856; rev. 1857–58); *Psalm XIII* for Tenor, Chorus, and Orch. (Berlin, Dec. 6, 1855; rev. 1858 and 1862); *Festgesang zur Eröffnung der zehnten allgemeinen deutschen Lehrerversammlung* for Men's Voices and Organ (Weimar, May 27, 1858); *Die Seligkeiten* for Baritone, Mixed Voices, and Organ (1855–59; Weimar, Oct. 2, 1859); *Christus*, oratorio for Soprano, Alto, Tenor, Baritone, Bass, Chorus, Organ, and Orch. (1855; 1859; rev. 1862–66; Weimar, May 29, 1873); *Psalm XXIII* for Tenor or Soprano, Men's Voices, and Instrumental Accompaniment (1859; rev. 1862); *Psalm CXXXVII* for Soprano, Women's Voices, Violin, Harp, and Organ (1859; rev. 1862); *An den heiligen Franziskus von Paula* for Solo Men's Voices, Men's Chorus, Harmonium or Organ, 3 Trombones, and Timpani ad libitum (c. 1860; rev. c. 1874); *Pater noster* for 4 Voices and Organ (c. 1860; Dessau, May 25, 1865); *Psalm XVIII* for Men's Voices and Instrumental Accompaniment (1860; Weimar, June 25, 1861); Responses and antiphons for 4 Voices (1860); *Cantico del sol di S. Francesco d'Assisi* for Baritone, Men's Chorus, Orch., and Organ (1862; rev. 1880–81); *Die Legende von der heiligen Elisabeth*, oratorio for Soprano, Alto, 3 Baritones, Bass, Chorus, Orch., and Organ (1857–62; Budapest, Aug. 15, 1865); *Christus ist geboren* (5 versions, c. 1863); *Slavimo slavno slaveni!* for Men's Voices and Organ (Rome, July 3, 1863; rev. 1866); *Missa choralis* for Chorus and Organ (1865; Lemberg, 1869); *Crux!* for Men's Voices Unaccompanied, or Women's or Children's Voices and Piano (1865); *Ave maris stella* for Mixed Voices and Organ (1865–66; also for Men's Voices and Organ or Harmonium, 1868); *Dall'alma Roma* for 2 Voices and Organ (1866); *Hungarian Coronation Mass* for Soprano, Alto, Tenor, Bass, Chorus, and Orch. (Budapest, June 8, 1867); *Te Deum* for Mixed Voices, Organ, Brass, and Drums ad libitum (1867); *Mihi autem adhaerere* for Men's Voices and Organ (1868); *Requiem* for 2 Tenors, 2 Basses, Men's Voices, Organ, and Brass ad libitum (1867–68; Lemberg, 1869); *Psalm CXVI* for Men's Voices and Piano (1869); *Ave Maria* for Mixed Voices and Organ (1869); *Inno a Maria Vergine* for Mixed Voices, Harp, and Organ (1869); *O salutaris hostia* for Women's Voices and Organ (1869); *Pater noster* for Mixed Voices, and Organ or Piano (1869; also for Men's Voices and Organ); *Tantum ergo* for Men's Voices and Organ (1869; also for Women's Voices and Organ); *O salutaris hostia* for Mixed Voices and Organ (c. 1870); *Libera me* for Men's Voices and Organ (1870); *Ave verum corpus* for Mixed Voices and Organ ad libitum (1871); *Anima Christi sanctifica me* for Men's Voices and Organ (1874); *Die heilige Cäcilia*, legend for Mezzo-soprano, Chorus ad libitum, and Orch. or Piano (1874; Wiemar, June 17, 1875); *Die Glocken des Strassburger Münsters* for Mezzo-soprano, Baritone, Chorus, and Orch. (1874; Budapest, March 10, 1875); *Der Herr bewahret die Seelen seiner Heiligen, Festgesang zur Enthüllung des Carl-August-Denkmals in Weimar* (Weimar, Sept. 3, 1875); *O heilige Nacht*, Christmas carol for Tenor, Women's Chorus, and Organ or Harmonium (c. 1877; Rome, Dec. 25, 1881); *Septum sacramenta*, responsories for Mezzo-soprano, Baritone, Mixed Voices, and Organ (1878); *Gott sei uns gnädig und barmherzig* for Mixed Voices and Organ (1878); *O Roma nobilis* for Mixed Voices and Organ ad libitum (1879); *Ossa arida* for Unison Men's Voices and Organ, 4- hands, or Piano, 4-hands (1879); *Rosario* (1879); *Cantantibus organis*, antiphon for the feast of St. Cecilia for Solo Voices, Chorus, and Orch. (1879); *Zwölf alte deutsche geistliche Weisen* (1878–79); *Via Crucis, Les 14 Stations de la croix* for Solo Voices, Chorus, and Organ or Piano (1878–79); *Psalm CXXIX* for Baritone, Men's Voices, and Organ, or Baritone or Alto and Piano or Organ (1880–81); *Sankt Christoph*, legend for Baritone, Women's Voices, Piano, Harmonium, and Harp ad libitum (1881); *In domum Domini ibimus* for Mixed Voices, Organ, Brass, and Drums (c. 1881); *O sacrum convivium* for Alto, Women's Voices ad libitum, and Organ or Harmonium (c. 1881); *Pro Papa* (c. 1881); *Nun danket alle Gott* (1883); *Mariengarten* for Chorus and Organ (c. 1884); *Qui seminant in lacrimis* for Mixed Voices and Organ (1884); *Pax vobiscum!* for Men's Voices and Organ (1885); *Qui Mariam absolvisti* for Baritone, Unison Mixed Voices, and Organ or Harmonium (1885); *Salve regina* for Mixed Voices (1885).

S e c u l a r : *Das deutsche Vaterland* for 4 Men's Voices (1839; Leipzig, Dec. 1841); *Vierstimmige Männergesänge* (1841–42); *Das düstre Meer umrauscht mich* for Men's Voices and Piano (1842); *Über allen gipfeln ist Ruh* for Men's Voices (1842; also for Men's Voices and 2 Horns, 1849); *Titan* for Baritone, Men's Voices, and Piano (1842; rev. 1845 and 1847); *Trinkspruch* for Men's Voices and Piano (1843); *Festkantate zur Enthüllung des Beethoven-Denkmals in Bonn* for 2 Sopranos, 2 Tenors, 2 Basses, Chorus, and Orch. (Bonn, Aug. 13, 1845); *Le Forgeron* for Men's Voices, and Piano or Orch. (1845); *Les Quatre Élémens* for Men's Voices, and Piano or Orch. (1839–45); *Die lustige Legion* for Men's Voices and Piano ad libitum (1846); *A patakhoz* (To the Brook) for Men's Voices (1846); *Arbeiterchor* for Bass, 4 Men's Voices, Men's Chorus, and Piano (c. 1848); *Hungaria 1848*, cantata for Soprano, Tenor, Bass, Men's Voices, and Piano or Orch. (1848; orch. version, Weimar, May 21, 1912); *Es war einmal ein König* for Bass, Men's Voices, and Piano (1849); *Licht, mehr Licht* for Men's Voices and Brass (1849); *Chor der Engel* for Mixed Voices, and Harp or Piano (1849); *Festchor zur Enthüllungs des Herder-Denkmals in Weimar* for Men's Voices, and Piano or Orch. (orchestrated by Raff; Weimar, Aug. 25, 1850); *Chöre zu Herders Entfesseltem Prometheus* for Soprano, Alto, 2 Tenors, 2 Basses, Double Chorus, and Orch. (orchestrated by Raff; Weimar, Aug. 24, 1850; rev. 1855); *An die Künstler* for 2 Tenors, 2 Basses, Men's Chorus, and Orch. (1853; orchestrated by Raff; Karlsruhe, June 1853; rev. 1856); *Weimars Volkslied* (Weimar, Sept. 3, 1857); *Morgenlied* for Women's Voices (1859); *Mit klingendem Spiel* for Children's Voices (c. 1859); *Für Männergesang* (1842–49); *Gaudeamus igitur* for Solo Voices ad libitum, Men's or Mixed Voices, and Orch. (1869); *Zur Säkularfeier Beethovens*, cantata for Soprano, Alto, Tenor, Bass, Double Chorus, and Orch. (1869–70; Weimar, May 29, 1870); *A lelkesedés dala—Das Lied der Bergeisterung* (1871; rev. 1874); *Carl August weilt mit uns, Festgesang zur Enthüllung des Carl-August- Denkmals in Weimar* for Men's Voices, Brass, Drums, and Organ ad libitum (Weimar, Sept. 3, 1875); *Magyar király dal—Ungarisches Königslied* (1883); *Grüss* for Men's Voices (c. 1885). He also wrote numerous solo songs and some chamber music. For his works, see F. Busoni, P. Raabe et al., eds., *Franz Liszt: Musikalische Werke* (Leipzig, 1907–36), and *Franz Liszt: Neue Ausgabe sämtlicher Werke/New Edition of the Complete Works* (Kassel and Budapest, 1970 et seq.).

WRITINGS: *De la fondation Goethe à Weimar* (Leipzig, 1851); *Lohengrin et Tannhäuser de R. Wagner* (Leipzig, 1851); *F. Chopin* (Paris, 1852); *Des bohémiens et de leur musique en Hongrie* (Paris,

1859); *Über John Fields Nocturne* (Leipzig, 1859); *R. Schumanns musikalische Haus-und Lebensregeln* (Leipzig, 1860). L. Ramann edited his *Gesammelte Schriften* (Leipzig, 1880–83); a new critical ed. of his writings, under the general editorship of D. Altenburg, began to appear in 1987.

BIBL.: SOURCE MATERIAL: F. Liszt, *Thematisches Verzeichnis der Werke von F. L.* (Leipzig, 1855); idem, *Thematisches Verzeichnis der Werke, Bearbeitungen und Transkriptionen von F. L.* (Leipzig, 1877); E. Waters, *L. Holographs in the Library of Congress* (Washington, D.C., 1979); M. Saffe, *F. L.: A Guide to Research* (N.Y., 1991). **ICONOGRAPHIES:** D. Bartha, *F. L., 1811–1886: Sein Leben in Bildern* (Leipzig, 1936); R. Bory, *La vie de L. par l'image* (Paris, 1936); W. Füssmann and B. Mátéka, *F. L.: Ein Künstlerleben in Wort und Bild* (Langensalza, 1936); Z. László and B. Mátéka, *F. L.: Sein Leben in zeitgenossischen Bildern* (Budapest, 1967; Eng. tr., 1968). **CORRESPONDENCE** F. Hueffer, ed., *Briefwechsel zwischen Wagner und L.* (Leipzig, 1887; fourth ed., 1919; Eng. tr., 1888); La Mara, ed., *F. L.'s Briefe* (Leipzig, 1893–1902); C. Bache, ed., *Letters of F. L.* (London, 1894); La Mara, ed., *Briefe hervorragender Zeitgenossen an F. L.* (Leipzig, 1895–1904); idem, ed., *Briefwechsel zwischen F. L. und Hans von Bülow* (Leipzig, 1898); A. Stern, ed., *L.s Briefe an Carl Gille* (Leipzig, 1903); La Mara, ed., *Briefwechsel zwischen F. L. und Carl Alexander, Grossherzog von Sachsen* (Leipzig, 1909); V. Csapó, ed., *L. F. levelei baró Augusz A.* (F. L.'s Letters to the Baron Augusz; Budapest, 1911; Ger. tr., 1911); N. de Gutmansthal, *Souvenirs de F. L.: Lettres inédites* (Paris, 1913); La Mara, ed., *F. L.: Briefe an seine Mutter* (Leipzig, 1918); D. Ollivier, ed., *Correspondance de L. et de la comtesse d'Agoult 1833–1840* (Paris, 1933–34); idem, ed., *Correspondance de L. et de sa fille Mme. Émile Ollivier* (Paris, 1936); H. Hugo, ed., *The Letters of F. L. to Marie zu Sayn-Wittgenstein* (Cambridge, Mass., 1953); M. Prahacs, ed., *F. L.: Briefe aus ungarischen Sammlungen 1835–1886* (Kassel, 1969); W. Tyler and E. Waters, eds., *Letters of F. L. to Olga von Meyendorff* (Washington, D.C., 1979); D. Legány, *F. L.: Unbekannte Presse und Briefe aus Wien (1822–1886)* (Budapest, 1984). **BIOGRAPHICAL:** J. Christern, *F. L., nach seinem Leben und Werke, aus authentischen Berichten dargestellt* (Hamburg, 1841); L. Rellstab, *F. L.: Beurteilungen-Bericht-Lebensskizze* (Berlin, 1842; Second ed., 1861); G. Schilling, *F. L.: Sein Leben und Werken aus nächster Beschauung* (Stuttgart, 1844); R. de Beaufort, *F. L.: The Story of His Life* (Boston and London, 1866; Second ed., 1910); J. Schubert, *F. L.s Biographie* (Leipzig, 1871); L. Ramann, *F. L. als Künstler und Mensch* (3 vols., Leipzig, 1880–94; Eng. tr. of vol. I, 1882); O. Lessmann, *F. L.: Eine Charakterstudie* (Berlin, 1881); L. Nohl, *F. L.* (Leipzig, 1882–88); R. Pohl, *F. L.* (Leipzig, 1883); B. Vogel, *F. L.: Abriss seines Lebens und Würdigung seiner Werke* (Leipzig, 1898); O. Lüning, *F. L.: Ein Apostel der Ideale* (Zürich, 1896); E. Reuss, *F. L.* (Dresden, 1898); R. Louis, *F. L.* (Berlin, 1900); A. von Pozsony, *L. und Hans von Bülow* (Munich, 1900); M.-D. Calvocoressi, *F. L.* (Paris, 1905; Eng. tr. in the *Musical Observer*, N.Y., 1910–11); A. Göllerich, *F. L.* (Berlin, 1908); J. Kapp, *F. L.* (Berlin, 1909; 20th ed., 1924); idem, *L.- Brevier* (Leipzig, 1910); idem, *R. Wagner und F. L.: Eine Freundschaft F. L.* (Berlin, 1910); J. Chantavoine, *L.* (Paris, 1911; 6th ed., 1950); A. Hervey, *F. L. and His Music* (London, 1911); J. Huneker, *F. L.* (N.Y. and London, 1911); J. Kapp, *F. L. und die Frauen* (Leipzig, 1911); La Mara, *L. und die Frauen* (Leipzig, 1911; Second ed., 1919); H. Thode, *F. L.* (Heidelberg, 1911); P. Bekker, *F. L.* (Bielefeld, 1912); B. Schrade, *F. L.* (Berlin, 1914); P. Raabe, *Grossherzog Karl Alexander und L.* (Leipzig, 1918); R. Bory, *Une Retraite romantique en Suisse: L. et la Comtesse d'Agoult* (Geneva, 1923; Second ed., 1930); K. Grunsky, *F. L.* (Leipzig, 1924); F. Corder, *L.* (London, 1925; Second ed., 1933); R. Wetz, *F. L.*

(Leipzig, 1925); G. de Pourtalès, *La Vie de F. L.* (Paris, 1926; Second ed., 1950; Eng. tr., 1926); W. Wallace, *L., Wagner and the Princess* (London, 1927); C. van Wessem, *F. L.* (The Hague, 1927); M. d'Agoult, *Erinnerungen an F. L.* (ed. by S. Wagner; 1928); G. de Pourtalès, *L. et Chopin* (Paris, 1929); M. Herwegh, *Au banquet des dieux: F. L., Richard Wagner et leurs amis* (Paris, 1931); R. Raabe, *F. L.* (Stuttgart, 1931; Second ed., rev., 1968); E. Newman, *The Man L.* (London, 1934; Second ed., 1970); S. Sitwell, *L.* (London, 1934; 3rd ed., rev., 1966); R. Bory, *L. et ses enfants: Blandine, Cosima et Daniel* (Paris, 1936); H. Engel, *F. L.* (Potsdam, 1936); Z. Harsányi, *Magyar Rapszódia: F. L.* (Budapest, 1936; Eng. tr., London, 1936, as *Hungarian Melody*, and N.Y., 1937, as *Immortal Franz*); A. Hevesy, *L., ou Le Roi Lear de la musique* (Paris, 1936); R. Hill, *L.* (London, 1936; Second ed., 1949); L. Nowak, *F. L.* (Innsbruck, 1936); B. Ollivier, *L., le musicien passionné* (Paris, 1936); E. von Liszt, *F. L.* (Vienna, 1937); M. Tibaldi Chiesa, *Vita romantica di L.* (Milan, 1937; Second ed., 1941); P. Raabe, *Wege zu L.* (Regensburg, 1944); A. Pols, *F. L.* (Bloemendaal, 1951); J. Vier, *La Comtesse d'Agoult et son temps* (Paris, 1955–63); B. Voelcker, *F. L., der grosse Mensch* (Weimar, 1955); W. Beckett, *L.* (London, 1956; Second ed., 1963); Y. Milstein, *F. L.* (Moscow, 1956; Second ed., rev., 1971); B. Szabolcsi, *L. F. estéje* (The Twilight of F. L.; Budapest, 1956; Eng. tr., 1959); C. Rostand, *L.* (Paris, 1960; Eng. tr., 1972); J. Rousselot, *F. L.* (London, 1960); W. Armando, *F. L.: Eine Biographie* (Hamburg, 1961); M. Bagby, *L.'s Weimar* (N.Y., 1961); J. Hankiss, *Wenn L. ein Tagebuch geführt hätte* (Budapest, 1961); P. Rehberg and G. Nestler, *F. L.* (Zürich, 1961); K. Hamburger, *L. F.* (Budapest, 1966); E. Haraszti, *F. L.* (Paris, 1967); A. Leroy, *F. L.* (Lausanne, 1967); A. Walker, ed., *F. L.: The Man and His Music* (London, 1970; Second ed., 1976); idem, *L.* (London, 1971); E. Perényi, *L.: The Artist as Romantic Hero* (Boston, 1974); F. Légany, *L. F. Magyaronszagon 1869–1873* (F. L. and His Country 1869–1873; Budapest, 1976; Eng. tr., 1983); idem, *L. F. Magyaronszagon 1874–1886* (F. L. and His Country 1874–1886; Budapest, 1986; Eng. tr., 1992); K. Hamburger, ed., *F. L.: Beiträge von ungarischen Autoren* (Leipzig, 1978); E. Horvath, *F. L.:* vol. I, *Kindheit, 1811–27* (Eisenstadt, 1978), and vol. II, *Jugend* (Eisenstadt, 1982); R. Rehberg, *L.: Die Geschichte seines Lebens, Schaffens und Wirkens* (Munich, 1978); B. Gavoty, *L.: Le Virtuose, 1811–1848* (Paris, 1980); A. Walker, *F. L.: Vol. I, The Virtuoso Years, 1811–1847* (London, 1983; rev. ed., 1987); idem, *F. L.: Vol. II, The Weimar Years, 1848–1861* (London, 1989); W. Dömling, *F. L. und seine Zeit* (Laaber, 1986); E. Burger, *F. L.: Eine Lebenschronik in Bildern und Dokumenten* (Munich, 1986; Eng. tr., 1989); R. Taylor, *F. L.: The Man and the Musician* (London, 1986); K. Hamburger, *L.* (Budapest, 1987); L. Chiappari, *L. a Firenze, Pisa e Lucca* (Pisa, 1989); S. Gut, *F. L.* (1989); D. Watson, *L.* (London, 1989); A. Williams, *Portrait of L.: By Himself and His Contemporaries* (Oxford, 1990); G. Erasmi and A. Walker, *L., Carolyne, and the Vatican: The Story of a Thwarted Marriage* (Stuyvesant, N.Y., 1991); M. Saffle, *L. in Germany, 1840–1845: A Study in Sources, Documents, and the History of Reception* (Stuyvesant, N.Y., 1994); M. Haine, *Franz Servais et F. L.: Une amitié filiale* (Liège, 1996); P. Autexier, *La lyre maçonne: Haydn, Mozart, Spohr, L.* (Paris, 1997); F. Bastet, *Helse liefde: Biografisch essay over Marie d'Agoult, Frédéric Chopin, F. L., George Sand* (Amsterdam, 1997); C. Rueger, *F. L.: Des Lebens Widerspruch: Die Biographie* (Munich, 1997); M. Saffle and J. Deaville, eds., *New Light on L. and His Music: Essays in Honor of Alan Walker's 65th Birthday* (Stuyvesant, N.Y., 1997); I. and P. Załuski, *Young L.* (Chester Springs, Pa., 1997); R. de Candé, *La vie selon F. L.: Biographie* (Paris, 1998). CRITICAL, ANALYTICAL: R. Wagner, *Ein Brief über L.s symphonische Dichtungen* (Leipzig, 1857); E. Segnitz, *F. L.s Kirchenmusik* (Langensalza, 1911); P. Roberts, *Études sur Boieldieu, Chopin et L.* (Rouen, 1913); P. Raabe, *Die Entstehungsgeschichte der ersten Orchesterwerke F. L.s* (diss., Univ. of Jena, 1916); J. Wenz, *F. L. als Liederkomponist* (diss., Univ. of Frankfurt am Main, 1921); G. Galston, *Studienbuch: F. L.* (Munich, 1926); J. Weber, *Die symphonischen Dichtungen F. L.s* (diss., Univ. of Vienna, 1928); H. Arminski, *Die ungarischen Phantasien von F. L.s* (diss., Univ. of Vienna, 1929); J. Heinrichs, *Über den Sinn der L.schen Programmusik* (diss., Univ. of Bonn, 1929); J. Bergfeld, *Die formale Struktur der "Symphonischen Dichtungen" F. L.s* (diss., Univ. of Berlin, 1931); Z. Gárdonyi, *Die ungarischen Stileigentümlichkeiten in den musikalischen Werken F. L.s* (diss., Univ. of Berlin, 1931); H. Dobiey, *Die Klaviertechnik des jungen F. L.s* (diss., Univ. of Berlin, 1932); I. Philipp, *La Technique de L.* (Paris, 1932); B. Bartók, *L. problémák* (Budapest, 1936); Z. Gárdonyi, *L. F. magyar stilusa/Le Style hongrois de F. L.* (Budapest, 1936); D. Presser, *Studien zu den Opern-und Liedbearbeitungen F. L.s* (diss., Univ. of Cologne, 1953); H. Searle, *The Music of L.* (London, 1954; Second ed., rev., 1966); B. Hansen, *Variationen und Varianten in den musikalischen Werken F. L.s* (diss., Univ. of Hamburg, 1959); L. Bárdos, *L. F. a jövö zenésze* (F. L. the Innovator; Budapest, 1976); E. Heinemann, *F. L.s Auseinandersetzung mit der geistlichen Musik* (Munich, 1978); B. Ott, *L. et la pédagogie du piano* (Issy-les-Moulineaux, 1978; Eng. tr., 1993); D. Torkewitz, *Harmonisches Denken im Frühwerk F. L.s* (Munich, 1978); S. Winklhofer, *L.'s Sonata in B Minor: A Study of Autograph Sources and Documents* (diss., Univ. of Mich., 1980); P. Merrick, *Revolution and Religion in the Music of L.* (Cambridge and N.Y., 1987); A. Hartmann, *Kunst und Kirche: Studien zum Messenschaffen von F. L.* (Regensburg, 1991); K. Johns, *The Symphonic Poems of F. L.* (Stuyvesant, N.Y., 1995); K. Hamilton, *L.: Sonata in B minor* (Cambridge, 1996); D. Altenburg, *L. und die Weimarer Klassik* (Laaber, 1997); M. Saffle, ed., *International L. Conference (1993: Va. Polytechnic Inst. and State Univ.)* (Stuyvesant, N.Y., 1998).—NS/LK/DM

Litaize, Gaston, blind French organist, pedagogue, and composer; b. Ménil-sur-Belvitte, Vosges, Aug. 11, 1909; d. Says, Vosges, Aug. 5, 1991. Following initial training at the Institut National des Jeunes Aveugles in Paris (1926–31), he pursued his studies at the Paris Cons. with Dupré (organ), Caussade (fugue), Büsser (composition), and Emmanuel (music history), taking premiers prix for organ and improvisation (1931), fugue (1933), and composition (1937). In 1938 he won the Second Prix de Rome and the Prix Rossini with his musical legende *Fra Diavolo*. From 1946 he served as organist at St.-François-Xavier in Paris, and he also made tours as a recitalist in Europe and abroad. He was a prof. at the Institut National des Jeunes Aveugles. Among his works were various organ pieces and a number of vocal works, including a *Missa solemnior* (1954), a *Missa Virgo gloriosa* (1959), and a *Messe solennelle en français* (1966).

BIBL.: S. Duran, *G. L.: 1909–1991: Un vosgien aux doigts de lumière* (Metz, 1996).—NS/LK/DM

Literes Carrión, Antonio, Spanish composer; b. Arta, Majorca, June 18, 1673?; d. Madrid, Jan. 18, 1747. He was a composer and bass-viol player at the Royal Choir School in Madrid under Charles II, Philip V, and Ferdinand VI. In 1693 he was appointed to the royal chapel as bassist. After the fire at the old Alcazar in Madrid on Christmas Eve of 1734, Literes and Nebra were charged with the reconstruction of musical MSS that were damaged or completely burned. They also wrote new music for church services to replace the material destroyed. He wrote an opera, *Los elementos*, and several zarzuelas, including *Accis y Galatea* (Madrid, Dec. 19, 1708), as well as various sacred works. His son, Antonio Literes Montalbo (d. Madrid, Dec. 2, 1768), was a composer and organist under Ferdinand VI.—NS/LK/DM

Litinsky, Genrik, distinguished Russian composer; b. Lipovetz, March 17, 1901; d. Moscow, July 26, 1985. He studied composition with Glière at the Moscow Cons., graduating in 1928. He subsequently taught there (1928–43), numbering among his students Khrennikov, Zhiganov, Arutiunian, and other Soviet composers. In 1945 he went to Yakutsk as an ethnomusicologist. In collaboration with native Siberian composers, he produced the first national Yakut operas, based on authentic folk melorhythms and arranged in contemporary harmonies according to the precepts of socialist realism: *Nurgun Botur* (Yakutsk, June 29, 1947), *Sygy Kyrynastyr* (Yakutsk, July 4, 1947), and *Red Shaman* (Yakutsk, Dec. 9, 1967). He wrote 3 Yakut ballets: *Altan's Joy* (Yakutsk, June 19, 1963), *Field Flower* (Yakutsk, July 2, 1947), and *Crimson Kerchief* (Yakutsk, Jan. 9, 1968). Other works include: Sym. (1928), *Dagestan Suite* for Orch. (1931), Trumpet Concerto (1934), *Festive Rhapsody* for Orch. (1966), 12 string quartets (1923–61), String Octet (1944), 12 concert studies for Cello (1967), 12 concert studies for Trumpet and Piano (1968), and 15 concert studies for Oboe and Piano (1969). He publ. the valuable manuals *Problems of Polyphony* (3 vols., 1965, 1966, 1967), ranging from pentatonic to dodecaphonic patterns and from elementary harmonization to polytonality; also *Formation of Imitation in the Strict Style* (1970). He also collected, transcribed, and organized the basic materials of several Soviet Republics; altogether he compiled musical samples from as many as 23 distinct ethnic divisions of folkloric elements. He was in time duly praised by the Soviet authorities on aesthetics, but not until the policy of the Soviet Union itself had changed. In the meantime, Litinsky became the target of unconscionable attacks by reactionary groups within Soviet musical organizations who denounced him as a formalist contaminated by Western bourgeois culture. In one instance, his personal library was ransacked in search of alleged propaganda. In 1964 he was named a People's Artist of the Yakut S.S.R. and of the Tatar Autonomous S.S.R.—NS/LK/DM

Litolff, Henry (Charles), prominent French pianist, conductor, music publisher, and composer; b. London, Feb. 6, 1818; d. Bois-Colombes, near Paris, Aug. 5, 1891. He was a precocious child and received training in piano from his father until he was 12, at which time he continued his studies with Moscheles (1830–35). On July 24, 1832, he made his professional debut as a pianist in London. His early marriage at the age of 17 compelled him to seek his fortunes in Paris, where he first attracted attention as a pianist. Following a sojourn in Brussels (1839–41), he went to Warsaw and conducted the National Theater orch. He toured as a pianist in Germany

and Holland (1844–45), and then throughout Europe. While in Vienna in 1848, he participated in the revolutionary uprising. When it failed, he made his way to Braunschweig in 1849. Following a divorce from his first wife, he married Julie Meyer in 1851, the widow of the music publisher Meyer, and acquired the firm. His Collections Litolff was one of the pioneering publications of inexpensive eds. of classical music. In 1855 Litolff was named conductor at the court of Saxe-Coburg-Gotha. After divorcing his second wife in 1858, he went to Paris to pursue his conducting career. In 1860 was married for a third time to Comtese de Larochefoucauld, and turned his publishing business over to his adopted son, Theodor Litolff. Following the Comtesse's death in 1870, Litolff took as his fourth wife a 15-year-old girl. Litolff's most significant works are his four extant concertos symphoniques (1844, 1846, 1852, 1867), which are actually syms. with piano obbligato. They made a deep impression on Liszt.

WORKS: DRAMATIC: O p e r a : *Catherine Howard* (Brussels, April 1847); *Die Braut von Kynast* (Braunschweig, Oct. 3, 1847); *Rodrigo von Toledo* (c. 1848); *Le chevalier, Nahal, ou La gageure du diable,* opéra-comique (Baden-Baden, Aug. 10, 1866); *La boîte de Pandore* (Paris, Oct. 1871); *Héloïse et Abélard* (Paris, Oct. 17, 1872); *La belle au bois dormant* (Paris, April 4, 1874); *La fiancée du roi de Garbe* (Paris, Oct. 19, 1874); *La mandragore,* opéra-comique (Brussels, Jan. 29, 1876); *Les templiers* (Brussels, Jan. 25, 1886); *L'escadron volant de la reine* (Paris, Dec. 14, 1888); *Le roi Lear* (n.d.). **ORCH.:** 4 extant concertos symphoniques (1844, 1846, 1852, 1867); 4 overtures: *Maximilian Robespierre* (1856; Paris, Feb. 2, 1870), *Das Welflied von Gustav von Meyern* (1856), *Chant des Belges* (1858?), and *Die Girdondisten* (1870?). **OTHER:** Chamber music; numerous piano pieces; *Ruth et Boaz,* oratorio (1869); *Szenen aus Goethes Faust* for Soloists, Chorus, and Orch. (1875?); songs.

BIBL.: T. Blair, *H.C. L. (1818–1891): His Life and Piano Music* (diss., Univ. of Iowa, 1968); R. Hagemann, *H. L.* (Herne, 1977). —NS/LK/DM

Litta, Giulio, Italian composer; b. Milan, 1822; d. Vedano, near Monza, May 29, 1891. A composer of precocious talent and excellent training, he produced an opera at 20, *Bianca di Santafiora* (Milan, Jan. 2, 1843), followed by 6 more: *Sardanapalo* (Milan, Sept. 2, 1844), *Maria Giovanna* (Turin, Oct. 28, 1851), *Edita di Lorno* (Genoa, June 1, 1853), *Il Viandante* (Milan, April 17, 1873), *Raggio d'amore* (Milan, April 6, 1879), and *Il violino di Cremona* (Milan, April 18, 1882). He also wrote an oratorio, *La Passione,* church music, and songs. —NS/LK/DM

Little Anthony and The Imperials, one of the few 1950s black vocal groups to survive and prosper in the 1960s. **MEMBERSHIP:** "Little" Anthony Gourdine, lead voc. (b. Brooklyn, N.Y., Jan. 8, 1940); Tracy Lord, 1st ten.; Ernest Wright, 2nd ten.; Clarence Collins, bar.; and Gloucester "Nate" Rogers, bs. voc. Sammy Strain (b. Dec. 9, 1940) joined in 1964.

In 1954 "Little" Anthony Gourdine formed a vocal quartet in Brooklyn to perform at local shows. Becoming The Duponts in 1955, the group recorded their first single, "You," for Winley Records. They later recorded for Royal Roost Records and performed at Alan Freed's Easter Show at N.Y.'s Paramount Theater in 1957.

Later in 1957 Gourdine formed The Chesters with tenor Tracy Lord, second tenor Ernest Wright, baritone Clarence Collins and bass singer Gloucester "Nate" Rogers. Initially recording for Apollo Records, The Chesters were signed by Richard Barrett to George Goldner's End label, where they scored a smash pop and R&B hit with "Tears On My Pillow" in 1958 as The Imperials. As Little Anthony and The Imperials, they managed a major R&B hit with "So Much" in 1959 and a major pop and R&B hit with "Shimmy, Shimmy, Ko-Ko-Bop" at year's end.

By late 1961 Anthony Gourdine had left The Imperials to pursue a solo career. Neither The Imperials nor Anthony Gourdine solo enjoyed much success, and Gourdine reunited with The Imperials in 1963. Brought to songwriter Teddy Randazzo, the group was signed to DCP Records. Now comprised of Gourdine, Wright, Collins, and first tenor Sammy Strain, the group recorded a series of pop and R&B hits with songs written and produced by Randazzo through 1966. These included "I'm on the Outside (Looking In)," the pop smash "Goin' Out of My Head," the pop and R&B smash "Hurt So Bad," and "Take Me Back."

During the late 1960s, Little Anthony and The Imperials recorded for Veep and United Artists Records, managing their last major R&B hit with "I'm Falling in Love with You" in 1974 on Avco Records. Sammy Strain joined The O'Jays in 1975, and Little Anthony and The Imperials subsequently disbanded. By 1980 Anthony Gourdine had begun pursuing a career as a lounge entertainer and gospel recording artist. In 1992 Little Anthony and The Imperials reunited with Anthony Gourdine, Ernest Wright, Clarence Collins and Sammy Strain.

DISC.: THE IMPERIALS: *We Are Little Anthony and The Imperials* (1959); *Shades of the 40s* (1960). **LITTLE ANTHONY AND THE IMPERIALS:** *I'm on the Outside (Looking In)* (1964); *Goin' Out of My Head* (1965); *Best* (1966); *Payin' Our Dues* (1967); *Reflections* (1967); *Movie Grabbers* (1967); *Best, Vol. 2* (1968); *Forever Yours* (1969); *Out of Sight, Out of Mind* (1969); *Little Anthony and The Imperials* (1970); *On a New Street* (1974); *Shimmy, Shimmy Ko-Ko-Bop* (1995). **LITTLE ANTHONY:** *Daylight* (1980); *Little Anthony Sings the Gospel* (1996).—BH

Little Feat, recognized by musicians and critics in the early 1970s as the best "unknown" band in America. **MEMBERSHIP:** Lowell George, gtr., voc. (b. Hollywood, Calif., April 13, 1945; d. Arlington, Va., June 29, 1979); Bill Payne, kybd., perc., voc. (b. Waco, Tex., March 12, 1949); Roy Estrada, bs. (b. Santa Ana, Calif.); Richie Hayward, drm., voc. (b. Ames, Iowa). Roy Estrada left in 1972; Paul Barrere, gtr., voc. (b. Burbank, Calif., July 3, 1948); Ken Gradney, bs. (b. New Orleans, La.); Sam Clayton perc., voc. (b. New Orleans, La.) joined.

Little Feat was led during the 1970s by Lowell George, often regarded as one of the most underrated singers, songwriters, and guitarists of the era. Considered one of rock music's finest slide-guitar players, George wrote such classics as "Willin'," "Truck Stop

Girl," and "Dixie Chicken" for Little Feat. Breaking through with 1974's *Feats Don't Fail Me Now*, Little Feat enjoyed considerable success as an album act until George's departure and death in 1979. The group reformed in 1988 for the best-selling album *Let It Roll*.

Lowell George made his show-business debut on television's *Ted Mack Amateur Hour* at age six. Taking up guitar at 11, he haunted Southern Calif. coffeehouses and clubs before forming his first rock band, the Factory, with drummer Richie Hayward around 1966. When that group broke up, George played for a time with the Standells ("Dirty Water"), the Seeds ("Pushin' Too Hard"), and the Mothers of Invention. In late 1969 he formed Little Feat with former Mothers bassist Roy Estrada, keyboardist Bill Payne, and Hayward, who in the meantime had been a member of the Fraternity of Man ("Don't Bogart That Joint").

Signed to Warner Bros. on the strength of Lowell George's songwriting, Little Feat's debut album featured an acoustic version of George's oft-covered truck-driving classic "Willin'," and "Truck Stop Girl," cowritten with Payne. Although embraced by musicians and critics alike, the album failed to sell, as did *Sailin' Shoes*, regarded by many as the group's finest album. It included an electrified version of "Willin'" and George songs such as "Trouble," "Easy to Slip," and "Teenage Nervous Breakdown." Estrada left to join Captain Beefheart, and the group added guitarist Paul Barrere, bassist Ken Gradney, and percussionist Sam Clayton. *Dixie Chicken*, produced by George, proved another commercial failure, despite the inclusion of the barroom classic title song, yet it did reveal the ascendancy of Payne and Barrere as songwriters and George as singer and musician.

Having earlier produced albums for Bonnie Raitt and others, Lowell George pursued session work as Little Feat broke up for a time. They regrouped for 1974's *Feats Don't Fail Me Now*, their commercial breakthrough. The album featured Payne's "Oh Atlanta" and George's "Rock and Roll Doctor" and the title song. Successfully touring America and Europe in support of the album, Little Feat next recorded *The Last Record Album*, which contained "Mercenary Territory" and "Long Distance Love." *Time Loves a Hero*, from 1977, featured George's "Rocket in My Pocket" and Terry Allen's "New Delhi Freight Train." The live set *Waiting for Columbus* became the group's best-selling album of the Lowell George era. George produced the Grateful Dead's *Shakedown Street*, and then left the group in April 1979.

Lowell George's debut solo album, *Thanks, I'll Eat It Here*, failed to sell significantly, and while on tour with a new band to promote the album, George died of drug-related heart failure in Arlington, Va., on June 29, 1979, at age 34. Paul Barrere and Bill Payne completed the overdubs and mixing of Little Feat's next album, *Down on the Farm*, which featured "Straight from the Heart" and "Front Page News," written by Payne and George.

During the 1980s Barrere recorded two solo albums for Mirage and played and recorded with the Bluesbusters, while Payne toured for five years with James

Taylor. Little Feat eventually regrouped in 1988 with Barrere, Payne, Richie Hayward, Ken Gradney, and Sam Clayton, plus guitarist Fred Tackett and vocalist Craig Fuller (Pure Prairie League, American Flyer). *Let It Roll* sold remarkably well, staying on the album charts nearly eight months, yet by 1991 the group was recording for the small Morgan Creek label. In 1994 Shaun Murphy replaced Craig Fuller as lead vocalist in Little Feat, who recorded 1995's *Ain't Had Enough Fun* for Zoo Records.

DISC.: **LITTLE FEAT:** *L. F.* (1971); *Sailin' Shoes* (1972); *Dixie Chicken* (1973); *Feats Don't Fail Me Now* (1974); *The Last Record Album* (1975); *Time Loves a Hero* (1977); *Waiting for Columbus* (1978); *Down on the Farm* (1979); *Hoy-Hoy!* (1981); *Let It Roll* (1988); *Representing the Mambo* (1990); *Shake Me Up* (1991); *Ain't Had Enough* (1995). **LOWELL GEORGE:** *Thanks, I'll Eat It Here* (1979). **LOWELL GEORGE AND THE FACTORY:** *Lightning-Rod Man* (1993). **PAUL BARRERE:** *On My Own Two Feet* (1983); *Real Lies* (1984); *If the Phone Don't Ring* (1995).—BH

Little Richard (originally, **Penniman, Richard**),

the self-styled "King of Rock 'n' roll," Little Richard personified the music's wildness and danger, and probably was the first to gain widespread popularity on the basis of a frantic and furious presence in recording and performance; b. Macon, Ga., Dec. 5, 1932.

Little Richard was singing on the streets of Macon by the age of seven. He became the lead singer in a local church choir at the age of 14 and later joined Dr. Hudson's Medicine Show and Sugarfoot Sam's Minstrel Show. He began performing R&B at Macon's Tick Tock Club and won an Atlanta talent contest in 1951 that led to a recording contract with RCA. His blues-based recordings (which surfaced on Camden Records in 1958 and 1970) failed to sell. He switched to the Houston-based Peacock label for recordings in 1953, again with little success, and worked with The Tempo Toppers in 1953 and 1954.

In 1955, with the encouragement of Lloyd Price, Little Richard sent a demonstration record to Art Rupe of the L. A.–based Specialty label that resulted in a new recording contract. Recording under producer Robert "Bumps" Blackwell at Cosimo Matassa's J & M Studios in New Orleans, accompanied by saxophonists Lee Allen and Alvin "Red" Tyler and drummer Earl Palmer, Little Richard's first session yielded the smash R&B and major pop hit classic "Tutti Frutti," quickly covered by Pat Boone. Following the top R&B / smash pop hit "Long Tall Sally" (also covered by Pat Boone) backed with "Slippin' and Slidin'," Little Richard achieved a major crossover hit with "Rip It Up" backed by "Ready Teddy," and an R&B near-smash with "She's Got It" (recorded in L. A.). In 1956–57 he appeared in the early rock 'n' roll films *Don't Knock the Rock*, *The Girl Can't Help It* (with its hit title song) and *Mister Rock 'n' Roll*. The hits continued into 1958 with "Lucille," backed by the unusually soulful "Send Me Some Lovin'," "Jenny, Jenny," "Keep a Knockin'" (recorded in Washington, D.C.), and "Good Golly, Miss Molly."

While touring Australia in October 1957, Little Richard announced his intention to leave rock 'n' roll in

favor of the ministry. He subsequently enrolled in Ala.'s Oakwood Coll. Seminary to study theology and was ordained a minister of the Seventh Day Adventist Church in 1961. Sessions in N.Y. in 1959 produced gospel recordings later issued on 20th Century–Fox Records, Goldisc, Crown, Custom, Spin-O-Rama, and Coral. Early 1060s sessions for Mercury yielded the gospel album *It's Real*.

Little Richard returned to rock 'n' roll in 1963, touring Europe with The Beatles and The Rolling Stones. He subsequently recorded for Specialty, where he managed a minor crossover hit with "Bama Lama Bama Loo," then VeeJay, Modern, Okeh, and Brunswick. During this period Jimi Hendrix was briefly Little Richard's guitar accompanist. Enjoying renewed popularity with the rock 'n' roll revival of the late 1960s, Little Richard signed with Reprise Records in 1970 and scored a moderate pop and R&B hit with "Freedom Blues." For *The Second Coming*, he was reunited with Bumps Blackwell, Lee Allen and Earl Palmer. In 1976 Little Richard returned to Christianity and, by 1979, he had recorded *God's Beautiful City* for World Records and become a full-time evangelist. In October 1985, he was seriously injured in an automobile accident in West Hollywood.

Little Richard was inducted into the Rock and Roll Hall of Fame in its inaugural year, 1986, the year he appeared in the hit comedy movie *Down and Out in Beverly Hills*—which included his first moderate hit in 16 years, "Great Gosh A'Mighty"—and recorded *Lifetime Friend* for Warner Bros. He dueted with Phillip Bailey on the title song to the 1988 film *Twins* and sang background vocals on the minor U2–B.B. King hit "When Love Comes to Town" in 1989. In 1993 Little Richard performed at Bill Clinton's presidential inaugural.

Little Richard was, along with Chuck Berry, one of rock 'n' roll's first composers, with his 1956 hit "Tutti Frutti" one of the first important rock 'n' roll hits (coming shortly after Chuck Berry's "Maybellene"). His boisterous stage act influenced everyone from Jerry Lee Lewis and James Brown to Mick Jagger and Jimi Hendrix. Moreover, his use of outrageous costumes and makeup, a practice later taken up by the likes of David Bowie, Boy George and Prince, made him perhaps the first androgynous rock star. Little Richard's intensely sexual persona, with its thinly veiled homosexuality, predated the open homosexuality of Bowie, Boy George and Queen by decades. One of rock 'n' roll's most erratic characters, Little Richard later denounced the music and retreated into Christian fundamentalism, only to return to secular music in the 1970s and again in the late 1980s.

DISC.: *Here's Little Richard* (1957); *Little Richard* (1958); *Little Richard, Vol. 2* (1958); *The Fabulous Little Richard* (1959); *Little Richard Is Back* (1964); *Greatest Hits/Recorded Live* (1966); *Wild and Frantic Little Richard* (1966); *Explosive* (1967); *Greatest Hits Recorded Live* (1967); *Forever Yours* (1968); *The Rill Thing* (1970); *The King of Rock and Roll* (1971); *Cast a Long Shadow* (1971); *The Second Coming* (1972); *Little Richard Live* (1976); *Lifetime Friend* (1986); *Shag on Down by the Union Hall* (rec. 1955–64; rel. 1996). **GOSPEL RECORDINGS:** *Little Richard Sings Gospel* (1960); *Pray Along with Little Richard* (1960); *Pray Along with Little Richard, Vol. 2* (1960); *Clap Your Hands* (1960);

It's Real (1961); *Coming Home* (1963); *Little Richard with Sister Tharpe* (1963); *King of the Gospel Singers* (1964); *God's Beautiful City* (1979); *Little Richard Sings the Gospel* (1995). **CHILDREN'S ALBUM:** *Shake It All About* (1992).

BIBL.: C. White, *The Life and Times of L. R.: The Quasar of Rock* (N.Y., 1984; N.Y., 1985; N.Y., 1994).—**BH**

Litton, Andrew, American conductor; b. N.Y., May 16, 1959. He studied piano with Reisenberg and conducting with Ehrling at the Juilliard School in N.Y., and also received lessons in conducting from Weller at the Salzburg Mozarteum, Järvi in Hilversum, and Edoardo Müller in Milan. In 1982 he won the BBC/Rupert Foundation International Conductors' Competition; then was the Exxon-Arts Endowment asst. conductor of the National Sym. Orch. in Washington, D.C. (1982–85), where he subsequently was assoc. conductor (1985–86); also appeared as a guest conductor in North America and Europe. On March 9, 1989, he made his Metropolitan Opera debut in N.Y. conducting *Eugene Onegin*. In 1988 he assumed the position of principal conductor and artistic adviser of the Bournemouth Sym. Orch., with which he established a fine reputation. In 1994 he took it on its first tour of the U.S. before concluding his tenure with it that year to become music director of the Dallas Sym. Orch.—**NS/LK/DM**

Litvinenko-Wohlgemut, Maria (Ivanova), Russian soprano; b. Kiev, Feb. 6, 1895; d. there, April 4, 1966. She was a student of Alexeyeva- Yunevich and Ivanitsky at the Kiev Music Inst. (graduated, 1912). In 1912 she made her operatic debut as Oxana in Gulak-Artemovsky's *The Cossack Beyond the Danube* in Kiev. She was a member of the Petrograd Music Drama Theater (1914–16), the Kharkov Opera (1923–25), and the Kiev Opera (1935–51). From 1946 she taught at the Kiev Cons. In 1936 she was honored as a People's Artist of the U.S.S.R. In addition to her portrayals of Russian roles, she was admired for her Aida and Tosca.

BIBL.: A. Polyakov, *M.I L.-W.* (Kiev, 1956).—**NS/LK/DM**

Litvinne, Félia (real name, **Françoise-Jeanne Schütz**), noted Russian soprano; b. St. Petersburg, Aug. 31, 1860?; d. Paris, Oct. 12, 1936. She studied in Paris with Barth-Banderoli, Viardot-García, and Maurel; made her debut there in 1882 at the Théâtre-Italien as Maria Boccanegra; then sang throughout Europe. In 1885 she made her first appearance in the U.S. with Mapleson's company at N.Y.'s Academy of Music; after singing at the Théâtre Royal de la Monnaie in Brussels (1886–88), at the Paris Opéra (1889), and at Milan's La Scala, in Rome, and in Venice (1890), she appeared at the imperial theaters in St. Petersburg and Moscow (from 1890). She made her Metropolitan Opera debut in N.Y. as Valentine in *Les Huguenots* on Nov. 25, 1896, but remained on the roster for only that season. In 1899 she first appeared at London's Covent Garden as Isolde, and made several further appearances there until 1910. She made her farewell to the operatic stage in Vichy in 1919, but continued to give concerts until 1924. In 1927 she became prof. of voice at the American Cons. in Fontainebleau. Her pupils included Nina Koshetz

and Germain Lubin. She publ. her memoirs as *Ma vie et mon art* (Paris, 1933). Her most outstanding roles included Gluck's Alceste, Donna Anna, Aida, Kundry, Brünnhilde, and Selika.—**NS/LK/DM**

Liuzzi, Fernando, Italian composer and pedagogue; b. Senigallia, Dec. 19, 1884; d. Florence, Oct. 6, 1940. He received training in piano and composition with Fano in Bologna, where he also attended the Univ. (fine arts degree, 1905), and then pursued his studies with Falchi at Rome's Accademia di Santa Cecilia and with Reger and Mottl in Munich. Liuzzi was prof. of theory at the Parma Cons. (1910–17), and also was a teacher of composition at the Naples Cons. (1912–14). After serving as prof. of theory at the Florence Cons. (1917–23), he was prof. of musical aesthetics at the univs. of Florence (1923–27) and Rome (1927–38). With the promulgation of the Fascist racial laws, he went to Belgium in 1939. After a sojourn in N.Y., he returned to his homeland in 1940. Among his writings were *Estetica della musica* (Florence, 1924) and *Musicista italiani in Francia* (Rome, 1946).

WORKS: *L'augellin bel verde,* puppet opera (Rome, 1917); *Le vergini savie e le vergini folli,* liturgical drama after a 12th-century French MS (Florence, 1930); *La Passione* for Soloists, Chorus, and Orch. (1930); orch. music; chamber pieces; songs.—**NS/LK/DM**

Liverati, Giovanni, Italian tenor, conductor, teacher, and composer; b. Bologna, March 27, 1772; d. Florence, Feb. 18, 1846. He studied voice with Giuseppe and Ferdinando Tibaldi in Bologna, then voice with Lorenzo Gibelli and composition with Stanislao Mattei there (1786–90). He was made first tenor of the Italian theaters in Barcelona and Madrid (1792), and then Kapellmeister of the Italian Opera in Potsdam (1796) and the Prague National Theater (1799). After teaching voice in Vienna (1805–11), he was music director and composer of the King's Theatre in London (1815–17); later taught at the Royal Academy of Music there. He returned to Italy about 1835, becoming a prof. at Florence's Accademia di Belle Arti.

WORKS: DRAMATIC: Opera: *Il divertimento in campagna* (Bologna, 1790); *Enea in Cartagine* (Potsdam?, 1796); *La prova generale al teatro* (Vienna?, 1799); *Il convito degli dei* (Vienna, c. 1800); *La presa d'Egea* (Vienna, 1809); *Il tempio d'eternità* (Vienna, 1810); *David, oder Goliaths Tod* (Vienna, 1813); *I Selvaggi* (London, 1815); *Gli amanti fanatica* (London, 1816); *Gastone e Bajardo* (London, 1820); *The Nymph of the Grotto* (London, 1829); *Amore e Psiche* (London, 1831). **OTHER:** Sacred and secular vocal music.—**NS/LK/DM**

Liviabella, Lino, Italian composer; b. Macerata, April 7, 1902; d. Bologna, Oct. 21, 1964. He studied with Respighi at the Accademia di Santa Cecilia in Rome. He was director of the Pesaro Cons. from 1953 to 1959, and then taught at Parma.

WORKS: DRAMATIC: *Conchiglia,* musical play (1955). **ORCH.:** *L'usignola e la Rosa* for Chamber Orch. (1926); *I canti dell' amore,* triptych for Strings (1929); *Suite per una fiaba* (1933); *Il Vincitore,* for the Berlin Olympiad (1936); *Il Poeta e sua moglia* (1938); *La mia terra* (1942). **CHAMBER:** 3 violin sonatas; String Quartet. **VOCAL:** 3 oratorios: *Sorella Chiara* (1947), *Caterina da Siena* (1949), and *O Crux Ave* (1953); songs. —**NS/LK/DM**

Living Colour, popular hard rock band of the 1980s who reclaimed rock as a genre for black artists (f. 1983). **MEMBERSHIP:** Vernon Reid, gtr. (b. London, England, Aug. 22, 1958); William Calhoun, drm. (b. Brooklyn, N.Y., July 22, 1964); Corey Glover, voc. (b. Brooklyn, Nov. 6, 1964); Manuel "Muzz" Skilling, bs. (b. Queens, N.Y., Jan. 6, 1960); Doug Wimbush, bs. (b. Hartford, Conn., Sept. 22, 1956).

Living Colour reclaimed rock music in the names of Chuck Berry, Johnnie Johnson, Jimi Hendrix, and all other black rockers. Guitarist Vernon Reid, together with journalists like Greg Tate and other African-American musicians, spearheaded the Black Rock Coalition, attacking the racial barriers of AOR (which they occasionally referred to as Apartheid Oriented Radio) and creating art with a socio-political as well as a musical agenda.

A versatile musician, Reid had worked with jazz funk groups Defunkt and Ronald Shannon Jackson's Decoding Society in the mid-1980s as well as writing regular music criticism for the *Village Voice*. He hooked up with Skillings, a music student from City Coll., and Calhoun, a Berklee alumnus, and they started playing as Living Colour around N.Y. Initially, they fused funk and jazz along with Reid's emerging hard-rock chops. Reid met Corey Glover, who had just finished filming a role in Oliver Stones's *Platoon* and was impressed with how he sang "Happy Birthday" to a mutual friend. He asked Glover to work with the band, and with his vocal presence, the group reshaped themselves as a power trio in the Van Halen mold. Mick Jagger saw them play a show at the legendary Bowery club CBGB's and asked them to help him with his solo album. He then helped them cut demos that landed them a contract with Epic. Their debut record, 1988's *Vivid* produced two hit singles. "Cult of Personality" with its samples of President Kennedy, hard-pop sound, and stunning video rose to #13, winning a Grammy for Best Hard Rock Performance with Vocal. The second single, "Glamour Boys," rose to #31. The band toured with the Rolling Stones on their Steel Wheels tour. With all that exposure, *Vivid* went to #6 and sold double platinum.

The release of their 1990 sophomore effort *Time's Up* didn't garner the band any additional hit singles, but did earn the band their second consecutive Best Hard Rock with Vocal Grammy. It got up to #13 and went gold. They continued to tour, and while they were on the road Epic released *Biscuits*, an album of studio outtakes and live tracks. Skillings left the band and was replaced with Doug Wimbush from the decidedly funkier Tackhead. He played on the band's final album, 1993's *Stain*. The album, while well-received critically, only got to #26. The band broke up shortly after.

Reid released an outstanding solo album in 1996, *Mistaken Identity*, that brought together De La Soul's Prince Paul with legendary jazz producer Teo Macero in the control room and rapper Chubb Rock, noted jazz player Don Byron, and actor Laurence Fishburne in the grooves. The album fused all of Reid's interests including sampling. He also wrote music for several dance companies and produced music for Malian virtuoso Salif Keita. Glover released his *Hymns* album in 1998. A stylistically diverse record, it included Living Colour style hard rock, blues, and funk.

DISC.: *Vivid* (1988); *Time's Up* (1990); *Biscuits* (1991); *Stain* (1993).—**HB**

Livingston, Fud (Joseph Anthony), pop-jazz tenor saxophonist, clarinetist, arranger, composer; b. Charleston, S.C., April 10, 1906; d. N.Y., March 25, 1957. His brother Walter (d. 1931) was also a professional saxophonist. Their parents owned a retail shoe business in Charleston. Fud played accordion and piano during childhood, then took up sax, and worked with Talmadge Henry in Greensboro during the summer of 1923. He joined the Ben Pollack band at the Venice Beach Ballroom, L.A., but left by summer 1925. He worked with the California Ramblers from October 1925, then joined Jean Goldkette (late 1925). He rejoined Ben Pollack in Chicago during summer of 1926, but left in autumn 1927 to join Nat Schilkret in N.Y. During 1928, he did prolific freelance work in N.Y. including recording sessions (usually on tenor and clarinet), with Red Nichols, Miff Mole, Joe Venuti, etc. In early 1929, he briefly returned to Ben Pollack, then went to London in March 1929 to join Fred Elizalde at the Savoy Hotel, returning to N.Y. in June. He played for the *Almanac* revue that September, and then freelanced until joining Paul Whiteman from June–September 1930. He continued to arrange for Whiteman after leaving the group. During early 1930s he was mainly active as an arranger, scoring for the Ben Pollack, Al Goodman shows, etc. From 1935–37, he returned to full-time playing with Jimmy Dorsey, and then worked as an arranger for various bands including Bob Zurke's short-lived Big Band, and staff work for Pinky Tomlin (1940). During the 1940s, he worked mainly in Hollywood. In the early 1950s, he returned to N.Y., and did occasional arranging, but excessive drinking led to a deterioration in his health. He worked occasionally as a pianist in N.Y. bars until shortly before his death.—**JC/LP**

Livingston, Jay (originally, **Levison, Jacob Harold**), and **Ray(mond Bernard) Evans,** American songwriting team. Livingston (b. McDonald, Pa., March 28, 1915) composed the music and cowrote the lyrics with Evans (b. Salamanca, N.Y., Feb. 4, 1915) for their songs, which were used in at least 90 feature films between 1944 and 1976. Their efforts brought them seven Academy Award nominations and three Oscars, for "Buttons and Bows," "Mona Lisa," and "Whatever Will Be, Will Be (Que Será, Será)." Their other hits included "G'Bye Now," "To Each His Own," and "Tammy," and they also wrote the holiday standard "Silver Bells."

Evans was the son of Philip Evans and Frances Lipsitz Evans; his father was a junk dealer. He played saxophone and clarinet in his school orchestra. In 1933, while attending the Univ. of Pa., he met Livingston, the son of Maurice Levison, a shoe store owner, and Rose Wachtel Levison. Livingston had studied harmony and piano with Harry Archer and orchestration with Harl McDonald, played in his school orchestra, and worked in a band while attending high school. In 1934, Evans recommended Livingston as pianist for a band in which he was playing that had been hired to work on a cruise ship crossing the Atlantic. The two spent their Easter and summer vacations from college traveling the world on such cruises. Evans graduated in 1936 with a B. S. in economics. Livingston graduated in 1937 with a B. A. in journalism. After a final cruise to Scandinavia in the summer of 1937, the two moved to N.Y. to become songwriters.

The team struggled for several years. Livingston worked as a pianist and arranger for radio, while Evans became an accountant. Livingston was hired as a rehearsal pianist for the musical comedy revue *Hellzapoppin* (N.Y., Sept. 22, 1938) starring the comedians Ole Olsen and Chic Johnson, and he and Evans began to write special material for them. Their first successful song, "G'Bye Now" (music and lyrics also by Olsen and Johnson), was written for, but not used in, the film version of *Hellzapoppin*; nevertheless, it became a Top Ten hit for Horace Heidt and His Musical Knights in May 1941. Livingston and Evans then contributed to the next Olsen and Johnson stage revue, *Sons o' Fun* (N.Y., Dec. 1, 1941).

Livingston and Evans's progress was interrupted by the U.S. entry into World War II; Livingston joined the service in 1942, and Evans took a job in a defense plant. Livingston was discharged in 1943 and went back to work as a pianist and arranger, while Evans began writing for radio. In February 1944 they moved to Calif. to concentrate on songwriting for the movies. There Livingston attended UCLA, studying orchestration and film scoring with Leith Stevens and Earle Hagen. The songwriters began to find work with the independent studio the Producers Releasing Corporation (PRC), starting with the 1944 film *Swing Hostess*. In April 1945, Betty Hutton peaked in the Top Ten with her recording of their song "Stuff Like That There," and it was used in the Universal film *On Stage Everybody*, released in July. The PRC August release *Why Girls Leave Home* included "The Cat and the Canary," which earned Livingston and Evans their first Academy Award nomination. That month, they were contracted to Paramount Pictures.

Livingston and Evans had songs in three Paramount features released in 1946, but their most successful song for the year was one written to promote a film. "To Each His Own" was not actually used in the movie of that name issued by Paramount in May, but in June Eddy Howard and His Orch. reached the charts with their recording of the song, hitting #1 in August and selling a million copies. Remarkably, a cover version by Freddy Martin and His Orch. also topped the charts, as did The Ink Spots' million-selling recording, while Tony Martin scored a Top Ten million-seller with the song, and there was a fifth Top Ten record by the Modernaires with Paula Kelly.

Livingston and Evans were both married in 1947, Livingston to Lynne Gordon on March 19, Evans to Wyn Ritchie on April 19. Livingston adopted his wife's daughter from a previous marriage; the Evanses remained childless. (After the death of his first wife, Livingston married actress Shirley Mitchell on May 16, 1992.) The songwriters had songs in four films released

by Paramount during the year, notably the title song for the December release *Golden Earrings*, for which they wrote the lyrics to music by Victor Young. It was recorded by Peggy Lee for a Top Ten hit. They had songs in five Paramount features in 1948, scoring a massive success with "Buttons and Bows," used in the Bob Hope comedy *The Paleface*. Prior to the release of the film in December, the song was given six chart recordings, among them Dinah Shore's #1 version, which was the biggest hit of the year and sold a million copies. The song also won the 1948 Academy Award.

Livingston and Evans had songs in six films released in 1949 and in another six in 1950. They wrote "Mona Lisa" for *Captain Carey, U.S.A.*, released in March 1950. Though the song was never sung in its entirety—or in English—in the film, it inspired seven chart records, the most successful of which was Nat "King" Cole's chart-topping, million-selling rendition. The song won the 1950 Academy Award. Dean Martin sang Livingston and Evans's "I'll Always Love You" in *My Friend Irma Goes West*, released in August, and his recording made the charts in September. That month, Bing Crosby and Carol Richards recorded the team's seasonal song "Silver Bells" from the forthcoming Bob Hope film *The Lemon Drop Kid*, which opened in March 1951. Their recording took seven years to reach the charts, but "Silver Bells" became a perennial Christmas favorite.

In addition to *The Lemon Drop Kid*, Livingston and Evans had songs in nine other films released in 1951 and in another five in 1952. Their next chart record came in October 1952 with a song later featured in their first film of 1953, *Thunder in the East*, "The Ruby and the Pearl," recorded by Nat "King" Cole. It was one of six films to feature Livingston and Evans songs during 1953. The songwriters contributed to only three films in 1954, but they also scored a television musical, *Satins and Spurs*, broadcast in September.

After 1954, with Hollywood's interest in making original movie musicals on the wane, Livingston and Evans tended to place only one or two songs in non-musical films; frequently, these were title songs. They had songs in only two features released in 1955 and in only three in 1956. In April 1956, Paramount released *The Scarlet Hour*, which featured their "Never Let Me Go," recorded for a chart entry by Nat "King" Cole. In May the studio issued the Alfred Hitchcock–directed thriller *The Man Who Knew Too Much*, in which Doris Day sang "Whatever Will Be, Will Be (Que Será, Será)." Day's recording hit the Top Ten and sold a million copies, becoming her signature song. She sang it in two subsequent films and used it as the theme for her television series, *The Doris Day Show*, from 1968 to 1973. It also won the songwriters their third Academy Award.

"Whatever Will Be, Will Be" marked a considerable comeback for Livingston and Evans; it also marked the end of their tenure at Paramount Pictures. They wrote songs for four films released by three different studios in 1957, scoring another major hit with "Tammy" from Universal's June release *Tammy and the Bachelor* starring Debbie Reynolds, who recorded it for a #1 million-seller. The song also earned an Academy Award nomination.

Livingston and Evans's recent success led to a busy 1958 in which they contributed songs to nine motion pictures and saw their first Broadway musical staged. The show, *Oh Captain!*, opened in February and ran 192 performances. From the score, Johnny Mathis recorded "All the Time" for a Top 40 hit. The songwriters' title song for the May film *Another Time, Another Place* was heard only instrumentally in the picture, but Patti Page recorded it for a Top 40 hit. Sam Cooke sang "Almost in Your Arms" in *Houseboat*, released in November, but the chart version was by Johnny Nash. The song was nominated for an Academy Award.

Livingston and Evans enjoyed two Top 40 revivals of "Mona Lisa" in 1959, by Carl Mann and Conway Twitty, and they wrote songs for three films during the year. But their chief success came on television. In February their second TV musical, *No Man Can Tame Me*, was broadcast, and they wrote the title songs for two series that debuted in the fall. The Western drama *Bonanza* ran for more than 13 years, making its theme one of Livingston and Evans's most familiar tunes. Al Caiola and His Orch. had a Top 40 hit with an instrumental version of it in 1961, and Johnny Cash took a vocal version into the charts in 1962. A *Bonanza* album featuring performances by the show's stars also reached the charts in 1962. The team contributed lyrics to Henry Mancini's music for the theme from *Mr. Lucky*, which ran for a year. Mancini's instrumental recording of the song became a Top 40 hit.

Livingston and Evans were less active in the early 1960s. The Platters scored a Top 40 hit with a revival of "To Each His Own" in October 1960. The duo wrote the theme for the 1961 television comedy series *Mr. Ed*, and it was sung on the program by Livingston; the show ran five years. *Let It Ride!*, the team's second Broadway musical, opened in October 1961 and ran 68 performances. The High Keyes had a chart revival of "Whatever Will Be, Will Be (Que Será, Será)" in July 1963, and the Tymes revived "To Each His Own" for a chart entry in March 1964.

In the mid-1960s, Livingston and Evans frequently set lyrics to movie themes written by the composers who wrote the film scores. In the fall of 1964, Andy Williams, Jack Jones, and Henry Mancini each reached the charts with competing versions of the title song for the film *Dear Heart* (music by Mancini, lyrics by Livingston and Evans) in advance of its March 1965 release; the Williams and Jones versions hit the Top 40 and the song was nominated for an Academy Award. Livingston and Evans also wrote the lyrics for "Angel" (music by Max Steiner), which reached the charts for Johnny Tillotson in February 1965, two months before the release of the film *Those Calloways*, in which it was featured. In July 1965, Bobby Vinton reached the charts with "Theme from *Harlow* (Lonely Girl)" (music by Neal Hefti, lyrics by Livingston and Evans), used in the film biography of actress Jean Harlow, released that month. *This Property Is Condemned*, released in August 1966, included the song "Wish Me a Rainbow" (music and lyrics by Livingston and Evans); the Gunter Kallmann Chorus recorded it for a chart entry. The same month saw the release of *What Did You Do in the War, Daddy?*,

which featured "In the Arms of Love" (music by Henry Mancini, lyrics by Livingston and Evans), recorded for a chart entry by Andy Williams. Mancini also reached the charts with his instrumental soundtrack album.

Frankie Laine revived "To Each His Own" for a chart entry in January 1968. Livingston and Evans wrote the title song for the TV series *To Rome with Love*, which premiered in September 1969 and ran two years. Mary Hopkin reached the charts with a revival of "Whatever Will Be, Will Be (Que Será, Será)" in July 1970. The duo wrote English lyrics for the Spanish hit "Eres Tu (Touch the Wind)" (music by Joan Calderon Lopez), which hit the Top Ten for Mocedades in March 1974. Willie Nelson revived "Mona Lisa" for a Top 40 country hit in 1981.

WORKS (only works for which Livingston and Evans were primary, credited songwriters are listed): **FILMS:** *Swing Hostess* (1944); *I Accuse My Parents* (1944); *Why Girls Leave Home* (1945); *Monsieur Beaucaire* (1946); *Double Rhythm* (1946); *My Favorite Brunette* (1947); *Golden Earrings* (1947); *Isn't It Romantic?* (1948); *The Paleface* (1948); *Bride of Vengence* (1949); *Sorrowful Jones* (1949); *My Friend Irma* (1949); *The Great Lover* (1949); *My Friend Irma Goes West* (1950); *Fancy Pants* (1950); *The Lemon Drop Kid* (1951); *Rhubarb* (1951); *Here Comes the Groom* (1951); *Anything Can Happen* (1952); *Aaron Slick from Punkin Crick* (1952); *What Price Glory?* (1952); *Somebody Loves Me* (1952); *Son of Paleface* (1952); *The Stars Are Singing* (1953); *Off Limits* (1953); *Here Come the Girls* (1953); *Red Garters* (1954); *The Man Who Knew Too Much* (1956); *Omar Khayyam* (1957); *A Private's Affair* (1959); *All Hands on Deck* (1961); *The Oscar* (1966). **TELEVISION:** *Satins and Spurs* (Sept. 12, 1954); *No Man Can Tame Me* (Feb. 1, 1959). **MUSICALS** (dates refer to N.Y. openings): *Oh Captain!* (Feb. 4, 1958); *Let It Ride!* (Oct. 12, 1961).—WR

Ljungberg, Göta (Albertina), Swedish soprano; b. Sundsval, Oct. 4, 1893; d. Lidingö, near Stockholm, June 28, 1955. She studied at the Royal Academy of Music and the Royal Opera School in Stockholm; later was a student of Mme. Cahier, of Fergusson in London, of Vanza in Milan, and of Bachner and Daniel in Berlin. In 1918 she made her operatic debut as Elsa at the Royal Stockholm Opera, remaining there until 1926. She was a member of the Berlin State Opera (1926–32), and also appeared at London's Covent Garden (1924–29), creating the title role there of Goossens's *Judith* (1929). She made her Metropolitan Opera debut in N.Y. as Sieglinde in *Die Walküre* on Jan. 20, 1932. She remained on the roster until 1935, and created the role of Lady Marigold Sandys in Hanson's *Merry Mount* in its first stage production there in 1934. She subsequently taught voice in N.Y., and later in Sweden. Among her notable roles were Isolde, Brünnhilde, Salome, and Elektra.—NS/LK/DM

Llobet, Miguel, famous Catalan guitarist; b. Barcelona, Oct. 18, 1875; d. there, Feb. 22, 1938. He began his career as a painter, then turned to music and studied with Alegre and Tarrega. He lived in Paris (1900–14), and toured in Argentina (1910), Chile (1912), the U.S. (1915–17), and throughout Europe. From 1918 he toured extensively in Latin America. He often appeared in a duo with his former pupil, Maria Luisa Anido. Falla composed his *Homenaje* (for the *Tombeau de Debussy*) for him, and Llobet himself made many outstanding transcriptions and arrangements for the guitar.—NS/LK/DM

Llongueras y Badia, Juan, Catalan composer; b. Barcelona, June 6, 1880; d. there, Oct. 13, 1953. He studied in Barcelona with Morera, Millet, and Granados, and with Jaques-Dalcroze in Dresden and Geneva. He founded the Inst. Catala de Rítmica i Plástica in Barcelona for the exposition in Spain of the Dalcroze methods, and was also a music critic, writer, and prof. of music education in Barcelona. His compositions include piano pieces (*La vida sencilla, L'estiu efímer*, etc.), a quantity of *Canciones y juegos infantiles*, and other songs; he also wrote *Les cançuons de Nadal* (Catalan Christmas songs). He publ. a book of reminiscences, *Evocaciones y recuerdos de mi primera vida musical en Barcelona* (Barcelona, 1944).—**NS/LK/DM**

Lloyd, A(lbert) L(ancaster), English ethnomusicologist; b. London, Feb. 29, 1908; d. Greenwich, Sept. 29, 1982. He became interested in folk-song research while working on an Australian sheep farm (1926–35). His interest was furthered by his commitment to Socialism. In 1937–38 he collected whaling songs while working as a whaling fisherman in the Antarctic, and then traveled in South America and the Middle East. From 1950 he concentrated his research in southeastern Europe. He gave lectures in England and the U.S., and produced radio programs and documentary films. In his research, he placed special importance upon socio-economic factors.

WRITINGS: *The Singing Englishman: An Introduction to Folk Songs* (London, 1944); *Folk Song in England* (London, 1967). EDITIONS: *Come All Ye Bold Miners: Songs and Ballads of the Coalfields* (London, 1952); with R. Vaughan Williams, *The Penguin Book of English Folk Song* (Harmondsworth, 1959). —**NS/LK/DM**

Lloyd, Charles Harford, English organist, conductor, and composer; b. Thornbury, Gloucestershire, Oct. 16, 1849; d. Slough, Oct. 16, 1919. He attended Magdalen Hall, Oxford (Mus.Bac., 1871; B.A., 1872; M.A., 1875; Mus.Doc., 1892). From 1887 to 1892 he was a teacher of organ and composition at the Royal Coll. of Music in London, and from 1892 at Eton Coll. From 1914 until his death he was organist at the Chapel Royal, St. James's.

WORKS: VOCAL: C a n t a t a s : *Hero and Leander* (Worcester, 1884); *The Song of Balder* (Hereford, 1885); *Andromeda* (Gloucester, 1886); *A Song of Judgment* (Hereford, 1891); *Sir Ogie and Lady Elsie* (Hereford, 1894). OTHER: 7 services; Organ Concerto (1895) and other organ works; piano pieces. —**NS/LK/DM**

Lloyd, David, American tenor; b. Minneapolis, Feb. 29, 1920. He was educated at the Minneapolis Coll. of Music (B.A., 1941) and studied voice with Bonelli at the Curtis Inst. of Music in Philadelphia. On Oct. 13, 1950, he made his operatic debut as David in *Die Meistersinger von Nürnberg* at the N.Y.C. Opera, where he sang regularly until 1958; he appeared there again in 1965 and 1976. His other operatic engagements took him to Boston, Washington, D.C., New Orleans, and St. Paul. In 1955 he sang at the Athens Festival and in 1957 at the Glyndebourne Festival. He also pursued an active career as a concert and oratorio singer. He taught at the Univ. of Ill. in Urbana (from 1971) and was director of the Lake George Opera Festival in N.Y. (from 1974). Lloyd was particularly admired for his roles in operas by Mozart, Rossini, and Richard Strauss.—**NS/LK/DM**

Lloyd, David (John) de, Welsh composer and teacher; b. Skewen, April 30, 1883; d. Aberystwyth, Aug. 20, 1948. He studied at the Univ. Coll. of Wales, Aberystwyth (B.A., 1903; B.Mus., 1905), the Leipzig Cons. (1906–07), and the Univ. of Dublin (Mus.D., 1915). He served as a lecturer (1919–26) and a prof. (1926–48) at the Univ. Coll. of Wales. Among his works were the operas *Gwenllian* (1924) and *Tir na n-og* (1930), *Cylch corawl o ganeuon gwerin* (Choral Folksong Cycle) for Chorus and Orch. (1938), *Requiem cymraeg* (Welsh Requiem) for Soloists and Chorus (1947), and other choral pieces and songs.—**NS/LK/DM**

Lloyd, Edward, noted English tenor; b. London, March 7, 1845; d. Worthing, March 31, 1927. He was a chorister at Westminster Abbey in London until 1860, and then sang in the chapels of Trinity and King's colleges, Cambridge (1866–67), and then in the choir of St. Andrew's, London. From 1869 to 1871 he was a Gentleman of the Chapel Royal. After scoring a fine success as soloist in Bach's *St. Matthew Passion* at the Gloucester Festival in 1871, he devoted himself to a distinguished career as a concert artist. Lloyd sang in the premieres of many works by English composers, most notably as Elar's Gerontius (Birmingham, Oct. 3, 1900). He sang throughout Europe and the U.S. in programs ranging from the great masterworks to popular songs.—**LK/DM**

Lloyd, George (Walter Selwyn), English composer and conductor; b. St. Ives, Cornwall, June 28, 1913; d. London, July 3, 1998. He began violin lessons at 5 and commenced composing at 10. He later was a student of Albert Sammons (violin), C.H. Kitson (counterpoint), and Harry Farjeon (composition). In 1933 he attracted notice as a composer with the premiere of his First Sym. in Bournemouth, and then had further success with his operas *Iernin* (1933–34) and *The Serf* (1936–38). His career was interrupted when he enlisted in the Royal Marines in 1939. He served on Arctic convoy duty until he was severely shell-shocked in the attack on the HMS Trinidad in 1942. Following a long and arduous recuperation, he resumed composition with great earnestness. He was also active as a conductor and served as principal guest conductor and music advisor of the Albany (N.Y.) Sym. Orch. (1989–91). In his compositions, which included the operas *Iernin* (1933–34; Penzance, Nov. 6, 1934), *The Serf* (1936–38; London, Oct. 20, 1938), and *John Socman* (1949–51; Bristol, May 15, 1951), Lloyd embraced an unabashedly Romantic style of pleasurable accessibility.—**NS/LK/DM**

Lloyd, John, English or Welsh composer; b. c. 1475; d. London, April 3, 1523. He became a priest in the Chapel Royal in 1505. About 1510 he was made a Gentlemen there. In 1520 he went to France, and then journeyed to the Holy Land. Lloyd was the composer of a distinguished Mass, *O quam suavis.*—**LK/DM**

Lloyd, Jonathan, English composer; b. London, Sept. 30, 1948. He took composition lessons in London with Emile Spira (1963–65), and with Edwin Roxburgh (1965–66) and John Lambert (1966–69) at the Royal Coll. of Music; also worked with Tristram Cary at the electronic music studio there and then completed his training with György Ligeti at the Berkshire Music Center in Tanglewood (summer, 1973). He was composer-in-residence at the Dartington Coll. Theatre Dept. (1978–79). He has produced a number of compositions of considerable and lasting value, distinguished by a variety of forms and styles. His music theater work *Scattered Ruins* won the Koussevitzky Composition Prize in 1973.

WORKS: DRAMATIC: *Scattered Ruins*, music theater (Tanglewood, Aug. 1973); *Musices genus*, masque (1974); *The Adjudicator*, "community opera" (1985; Blewbury, April 15, 1986); *Blackmail*, music for Hitchcock's silent film (1992–93; Paris, March 13, 1993). ORCH.: *Cantique* for Small Orch. (1968; rev. 1970); *Time Caught by the Tail* for Strings and Percussion (1969); Concerto for Viola and Small Orch. (1979–80; London, Nov. 10, 1981); *Fantasy* for Violin and Orch. (1980); *Rhapsody* for Cello and Orch. (1982); 5 syms.: No. 1 (1983; Birmingham, Jan. 19, 1989), No. 2 (1983–84; Baden-Baden, Feb. 12, 1988), No. 3 for Chamber Orch. (Wilde Festival, June 27, 1987), No. 4 (London, July 26, 1988), and No. 5 (1989; Birmingham, Jan. 14, 1990); *Wa Wa Mozart* for Piano and Chamber Orch. (London, Dec. 5, 1991); *There* for Guitar and Strings (1991; Aldeburgh, Jan. 1, 1992); *Tolerance* (1993). ENSEMBLE: *Won't It Ever Be Morning* (1980); *Waiting for Gozo* (1981; London, Jan. 15, 1982); *3 Dances* (Reykjavík, June 18, 1982); *Don't Mention the War* (1982; Montepulciano, Aug. 2, 1983); *The Shorelines of Certainty* (Aldeburgh Festival, June 17, 1984; incorporated in *Songs from the Other Shore*, 1984–86; London, May 11, 1986); *Time between Trains* (Wilde Festival, June 30, 1984); *The New Ear* (Colchester, Sept. 28, 1985); *Almeida Dances* (London, June 25, 1986); *Dancing in the Ruins* (Warwick, July 12, 1990). CHAMBER: *John's Journal* for Saxophone and Piano (1980); 2 string quintets: No. 1 for 2 Violins, 2 Violas, and Cello (1982) and No. 2 for Mandolin, Lute, Guitar, Harp, and Double Bass (1982); Brass Quintet for 2 Trumpets, 2 Trombones, and Tuba (1982); Wind Quintet for Flute, Oboe, Clarinet, Bassoon, and Horn (1982; London, Jan. 5, 1984); String Quartet No. 1, "Of Time and Motion" (1984; London, June 25, 1986); Oboe Sonata (1985); *The 5 Senses* for Flute and Guitar (1985); *True Refuge* for Clarinet and Piano (1985); *Feuding Fiddles* for 2 Violins (1986); *1 Step More* for Flute, Oboe, Cello, and Harpsichord (1986); *Airs and Graces* for Violin (1987); *He Will Make It* for Cello (1988); *Restless Night* for Wind Quintet (Bournemouth, June 29, 1991); *There and Then* for Guitar Duo (1991–92; Exeter, June 20, 1992. VOCAL: *Coming into Gone* for Chanters and Orch. (1974); *The Other Shore* for Chorus and Orch. (1975); *Everything Returns* for Wordless Soprano and Orch. (1977–78; BBC, Oct. 4, 1979); *3 Songs* for Voice, Viola, and Piano (1980); *Toward the Whitening Dawn* for Chorus and Chamber Orch. (1980; London, March 4, 1981); *If I Could Turn You On* for High Soprano and Chamber Orch. (1981); *No Man's Land* for Chorus and Orch. (1982); *Mass* for 6 Solo Voices (1983; London, April 10, 1984); *Missa Brevis* for Double Chorus (1984); *Revelation* for Chorus (London, Nov. 4, 1990); *Marching to a Different Song* for Soprano and Chamber Orch. (1990; Bracknell, April 14, 1991).—NS/LK/DM

Lloyd, Robert (Andrew), esteemed English bass-baritone; b. Southend-on-Sea, March 2, 1940. He studied history at Keble Coll., Oxford, then voice with Otakar Kraus at the London Opera Centre (1968–69), making his debut at London's Collegiate Theatre as Beethoven's Fernando (1969). He was a member of Sadler's Wells (1969–72) and the Royal Opera at Covent Garden (1972–83) in London; also made guest appearances in Berlin, Paris, Hamburg, Milan, Munich, San Francisco, Salzburg, and Vienna. On Oct. 26, 1988, he made his Metropolitan Opera debut in N.Y. as Rossini's Basilio. In 1990 he became the first English singer to appear as Boris Godunov at the Kirov Opera in Leningrad. In 1991 he was made a Commander of the Order of the British Empire. Among his best roles are Sarastro, the Commendatore, Oroveso, Banquo, Boris Godunov, King Philip, and Gurnemanz (he appeared as the latter in the Syberberg film version of *Parsifal* in 1981). —NS/LK/DM

Lloyd-Jones, David (Mathias), English conductor; b. London, Nov. 19, 1934. He studied at Magdalen Coll., Oxford. He appeared as a guest conductor with the leading British opera houses, including Covent Garden, the English National Opera, the Scottish Opera, and the Welsh National Opera. Iin 1978 he was named music director of the newly organized English National Opera North in Leeds, which was renamed Opera North in 1981, and retained this post until 1990. In 1989 he became artistic adviser of the Guildhall School of Music and Drama in London. He conducted the English premieres of works from the traditional and modern operatic repertoire. He ed. the full score of Mussorgsky's *Boris Godunov* (1975) and Borodin's *Prince Igor* (1982), and served as general ed. of the William Walton Edition (23 vols., Oxford, 1999 et seq.).—NS/LK/DM

Lloyd Webber, Sir Andrew, tremendously successful English composer, brother of **Julian Lloyd Webber**; b. London, March 22, 1948. His father, William Southcombe Lloyd Webber, was the director of the London Coll. of Music and his mother was a piano teacher. Inspired and conditioned by such an environment, Lloyd Webber learned to play piano, violin, and horn, and soon began to improvise music, mostly in the style of American musicals. He attended Westminster School in London, then went to Magdalen Coll., Oxford, the Guildhall School of Music in London, and the Royal Coll. of Music in London. In college he wrote his first musical, *The Likes of Us*, dealing with a philanthropist. In 1967, at the age of 19, he composed the theatrical show *Joseph and the Amazing Technicolor Dreamcoat*, which was performed at St. Paul's Junior School in London in 1968; it was later expanded to a full-scale production (Edinburgh, Aug. 21, 1972), and achieved considerable success for its amalgam of a biblical subject with rock music, French chansonnettes, and country-western songs. In 1970 it was produced in America and in 1972 was shown on television. He achieved his first commercial success with *Jesus Christ Superstar*, an audacious treatment of the religious theme in terms of jazz and rock. It was premiered in London on Aug. 9, 1972, and ran for 3,357 performances; it was as successful in America. Interestingly enough, the "rock opera," as it was called, was first released as a record album, which eventually sold 3 million copies. *Jesus Christ Superstar* opened on Broadway on Oct. 12, 1971, even before the London production. There were protests by religious groups against the irreverent treatment of a sacred subject; particularly offensive was the suggestion in the play of a carnal relationship between Jesus and Mary Magdalen; Jewish organizations, on the other hand, protested against the implied portrayal of the Jews as guilty of the death of Christ. The musical closed on Broadway on June 30, 1973, after 720 performances; it received 7 Tony awards. In 1981 the recording of *Jesus Christ Superstar* was given the Grammy Award for best cast show album of the year. The great hullabaloo about the musical made a certainty of his further successes. His early musical *Joseph and the Amazing Technicolor Dreamcoat* was revived at the Off-Broadway Entermedia Theatre in N.Y.'s East Village on Nov. 18, 1981, and from there moved to the Royale Theater on Broadway. In the meantime, he produced a musical with a totally different chief character, *Evita*, a semi-fictional account of the career of the first wife of Argentine dictator Juan Perón; it was first staged in London on June 21, 1978; a N.Y. performance soon followed, with splendid success. It was followed by the spectacularly successful *Cats*, inspired by T.S. Eliot's *Old Possum's Book of Practical Cats*; it was premiered in London on May 11, 1981, and was brought out in N.Y. in Oct. 1982 with fantastic success; *Evita* and *Joseph and the Amazing Technicolor Dreamcoat* were still playing on Broadway, so that Lloyd Webber had the satisfaction of having 3 of his shows running at the same time. Subsequent successful productions were his *Song and Dance* (London, March 26, 1981) and *Starlight Express* (London, March 19, 1984). His series of commercial successes reached a lucrative apex with the production of *The Phantom of the Opera* (London, Oct. 9, 1986), a gothically oriented melodramatic tale of contrived suspense. On April 17, 1989, his musical *Aspects of Love* opened in London. His musical setting of the 1950 Billy Wilder film *Sunset Boulevard* was first staged in London on July 12, 1993. Apart from popular shows, Lloyd Webber wrote a mini- opera, *Tell Me on a Sunday*, about an English girl living in N.Y., which was produced by BBC Television in 1980. Quite different in style and intent were his *Variations* for Cello and Jazz Ensemble (1978), written for his brother, and his *Requiem Mass* (N.Y., Feb. 24, 1985). He was knighted in 1992.

BIBL.: G. McKnight, *A. L.W.* (London and N.Y., 1984); J. Mantle, *Fanfare: The Unauthorized Biography of A. L.W.* (London, 1989); M. Walsh, *A. L.W.: His Life and Works* (N.Y., 1989); H. Mühe, *Die Musik von A. L. W.* (Hamburg, 1993).—**NS/LK/DM**

Lloyd Webber, Julian, talented English cellist, brother of **Andrew Lloyd Webber**; b. London, April 14, 1951. He studied with Douglas Cameron (1964–67), at the Royal Coll. of Music in London (1967–71), and with Pierre Fournier in Geneva (1973). He made his London debut as soloist in the Bliss Cello Concerto in 1972, and subsequently played many engagements as a soloist with English orchs. He made his American debut in N.Y. in 1980. In 1978 he became prof. of cello at the Guildhall School of Music in London. He publ. an account of his career, *Travels with My Cello* (1984), and also ed. *Song of*

the Birds: Sayings, Stories and Impressions of Pablo Casals (London, 1985). His exhaustive repertoire embraces both traditional and contemporary works, ranging from Haydn to Rodrigo.—**NS/LK/DM**

Lobaczewska (Gerard de Festenburg), Stefania, Polish musicologist; b. Lemberg, July 31, 1888; d. Kraków, Jan. 16, 1963. She studied piano with V. Kurc at the Lemberg Cons., then musicology with Adler at the Univ. of Vienna and with Chybiński at the Univ. of Lemberg (1914–18; Ph.D., 1929, with the diss. *O harmonice Klaudiusza Achillesa Debussy' ego w pierwszym okresie jego twórczosci* [Claude Achille Debussy's Harmony in His First Creative Period]; publ. in Kwartalnik Muzyczny, II/5, 1929–30); completed her Habilitation at the Univ. of Poznań in 1949, with his *Karol Szymanowski: Życie i twórczość (1882–1937)* (Karol Szymanowski: Life and Works [1882–1937]; publ. in Kraków, 1950). She taught at the Szymanowski School of Music in Lwów (1931–39) and at the Lwów Cons. (1940–41), then went to Kraków (1945), where she became a prof. at the State Coll. of Music; later served as its rector until 1955; was also head of the musicology dept. at the Univ. of Kraków (1952–63).

WRITINGS: *Zarys estetyki muzycznej* (Outline of Music Aesthetics; Lwów, 1937); *Tablice do historii muzyki* (Kraków, 1949); *Zarys historii form muzycznych: Próba ujecia socjologicznego* (Outline of the History of Musical Form: Attempt at a Sociological Approach; Kraków, 1950); *Ludwik van Beethoven* (Kraków, 1953; second ed., 1955); *W klad Chopina do romantyzmu europejskiego* (Chopin's Contribution to European Romanticism; Warsaw, 1955); *Style muzyczne* (Kraków, 1960–62).—**NS/LK/DM**

Lobanov, Vassily, Russian composer and pianist; b. Moscow, Jan. 2, 1947. He studied piano with Naumov and composition with Balasanyan and Schnittke at the Moscow Cons. (1963–71). After 1976 piano performing became increasingly important, and he subsequently appeared in touring recitals with such major Russian instrumentalists as Natalia Gutman, Oleg Kagan, and Ivan Monighetti. In 1985 he played a joint program of modern music with Richter in Tours, France. In 1997 he joined the piano faculty at the Hochschule für Musik in Cologne. His compositions, often dark and written mostly in traditional forms, merge the aura of Shostakovich with thoroughly contemporary harmonies and techniques.

WORKS: DRAMATIC: Opera: *Antigone*, after Sophocles (1983–85); *Father Sergius*, after Tolstoy (1990–95). **ORCH.:** Double Concerto for Cello, Piano, and Orch. (1969); *Krasnojarskie Pesni* (1976); 2 syms.: No. 1 for 4 Flutes, Trumpet, Percussion, and Strings (1977) and No. 2 (1981); Triple Concerto for Violin, Cello, Piano, and Orch. (1978); 2 piano concertos (1981, 1993); Cello Concerto (1984–85); *Aria* for Violin and String Orch. (1986); *Sinfonietta* for Chamber Orch. (1986); 2 viola concertos (1989, 1998); Double Concerto for Violin, Clarinet, and Chamber Orch. (1995); Concerto for Trumpet, Percussion, and Strings (1997). **CHAMBER:** Sonata for Solo Cello (1963); 1 unnumbered string quartet (1964); 5 numbered string quartets (1965; 1968; 1978; 1987–88; 1986–88); Piano Trio (1967); 2 cello sonatas (1971, 1989); 2 violin sonatas (1973, 1975); Sonata for Solo Flute (1974); *7 Pieces* for Cello and Piano (1978); Trio for

Flute, Clarinet, and Bassoon (1979); *Variations* for 2 Trumpets (1979); *Adagio* for Piano Trio (1980); Flute Sonata (1983); *Ode to the Wind* for Violin and Piano (1984); Clarinet Sonata (1985); *Exorcism* for Clarinet and Piano (1988); *Sonata in 6 Fragments* for Violin and Piano (1989); Viola Sonata (1990); *Fantasy* for Horn and Piano (1991); Piano Quintet (1991); Trio for Clarinet, Viola, and Piano (1992); *Offertorium* for Piano Quartet and Percussion (1995); Piano Quartet (1996); String Trio (1996); Clarinet Quintet (1999). **P i a n o :** *6 Preludes* (1964); *24 Preludes* (1964–65); Sonatina (1966); *Plato* for 2 Pianos (1972); 2 sonatas (1973, 1980); *Ode to Grass* (1982); *2 Preludes* (1986); *3 Fragments* (1989); *6 Prayers* (1994–97). **V O C A L :** *Autumn*, 3 haikus for Mezzo-soprano, Oboe, and Viola (1964); *Lieutenant Schmidt*, oratorio for Soprano, Bass, Chorus, and Orch., after Pasternak (1979); *God-Nightingale*, cantata for Baritone and Chamber Ensemble (1991).—**LK/DM**

Lobe, Johann Christian, German flutist, violist, writer on music, and composer; b. Weimar, May 30, 1797; d. Leipzig, July 27, 1881. He received training in flute and violin in Weimar, his principal mentor being A.E. Müller. In 1808 he became a flutist in the Weimar ducal orch., where he later was a violist until being pensioned in 1842. He then ran his own music school until settling in Leipzig, where he ed. the *Allgemeine musikalische Zeitung* (1846–48) and *Fliegende Blätter für Musik* (1855–57), and subsequently was music ed. of the *Illustrierte Zeitung*. During his years in Weimar, he became a friend of Goethe. He championed the cause of Weimar classicism and German romanticism.

WORKS: D R A M A T I C : O p e r a (all first perf. in Weimar): *Wittekind, Herzog von Sachsen* (1819); *Die Flibustier* (Sept. 5, 1829); *Die Fürstin von Granada, oder Der Zauberblick* (Sept. 28, 1833); *Der rote Domino* (1835; April 22, 1837); *König und Pächter* (1844). O R C H . : 2 syms.; overtures; concertos. C H A M B E R : Piano quartets; variations and solos for flute.

WRITINGS (all publ. in Leipzig unless otherwise given): *Compositionslehre oder umfassende Lehre von thematische Arbeit* (Weimar, 1844); *Lehrbuch der musikalischen Composition* (4 vols., 1850–67; rev. ed., 1884–87, by H. Kretzschmar); *Handbuch der Musik* (n.d.; ed. by R. Hofmann; 31st ed., 1926); *Katechismus der Musik* (1851; Eng. tr., 1886); *Aus dem Leben eines Musikers* (1859); *Consonanzen und Dissonanzen* (1869).

BIBL.: W. Bode, *Goethes Schauspieler und Musiker: Erinnerungen von Eberwein und L.* (Berlin, 1912).—**NS/LK/DM**

Lobkowitz, Bohemian family of the nobility and patrons of music:

(1) Philipp Hyacinth (Filipp Hyacint) Lobkowitz, lutenist and composer; b. Neustadt an der Waldnab, Feb. 25, 1680; d. Vienna, Dec. 21, 1734. In 1729 he settled in Vienna, where he sponsored private concerts at the Lobkowitz-Althan palace; Gluck commenced his career as a composer at these concerts (c. 1735–36). Lobkowitz's only extant work is a Suite in B-flat major.

(2) Ferdinand Philipp Joseph (Ferdinand Filipp Josef) Lobkowitz, composer, son of the preceding; b. Prague, April 27, 1724; d. Vienna, Jan. 11, 1784. He became the ruling prince of the family in Vienna in 1743. He was a patron of Gluck, who accompanied him to London in 1745. Lobkowitz was later made a member of the Berlin Academy of Sciences, where he studied violin with F. Benda. All of his music is lost.

(3) Joseph Franz Maximilian (Josef František Maximilian) Lobkowitz, singer, violinist, and cellist, son of the preceding; b. Roudnice nad Labem, Dec. 7, 1772; d. Trebon, Dec. 15, 1816. He was active in the administration of the Vienna court theaters (1807–14), and also founder of the Gesellschaft der Musikfreunde there. He was a patron of Haydn and Beethoven. Haydn dedicated his String Quartet, op.77, to him, and Beethoven his 3rd, 5th, and 6th syms., the Triple Concerto, the string quartets, opp. 18 and 74, and the song cycle *An die ferne Geliebte.*

(4) Ferdinand Joseph Johann (Ferdinand Josef Jan) Lobkowitz, music patron, son of the preceding; b. Oberhollabrunn, Lower Austria, April 13, 1797; d. Vienna, Dec. 18, 1868. He had a private orch. in Vienna, and also founded a private music school in Eisenberg (1831). He was the patron of Gyrowetz. Beethoven wrote the *Lobkowitz Cantata* for his birthday in 1823. —**NS/LK/DM**

Lobo, Alonso, Spanish composer; b. Osuna, c. 1555; d. Seville, April 5, 1617. He was a choirboy at Seville Cathedral, and obtained the degree of licenciado at Osuna Univ. He was canon of the collegiate church in Osuna by 1591, assistant to the maestro de capilla at Seville Cathedral (1591–93), and then maestro de capilla at Toledo Cathedral (1593–1604) and subsequently at Seville Cathedral. He publ. *Liber primus missarum* for 4 to 8 Voices (Madrid, 1602), containing 6 masses and 7 motets. Other works include *Credo romano* (his most famous piece), 3 Passions, Lamentations, Psalms, and hymns.—**NS/LK/DM**

Lobo, Duarte (Latinized as **Eduardus Lupus**), noted Portuguese composer; b. Alcáçovas, c. 1565; d. Lisbon, Sept. 24, 1646. He was a pupil of Manuel Mendes at Evora, and served as choirmaster there before moving to Lisbon where, in 1594, he became master of the chapel at the Cathedral. As a composer of church music, he enjoyed considerable renown; his mastery of polyphony inspired respect. See M. Joaquim, ed., *Duarte Lobo: Composicoes polifonicas* (Lisbon, 1945 et seq.).

WORKS: *Natalitiae noctis responsoria* for 4 to 8 Voices, *missa eiusdem noctis* for 8 Voices, *Beatae Mariae Virginis antiphonae* for 8 Voices ...*virginis Salve* for 3 Choirs and 11 Voices (Antwerp, 1602); *Cantica Beatae Mariae Virginis, vulgo Magnificat* for 4 Voices (Antwerp, 1605); 2 books of masses (Antwerp, 1621, 1639).

BIBL.: A. Borges, *D. L. (156?-1646): Studien zum Leben und Schaffen des portugesischen Komponisten* (Regensburg, 1986). —**NS/LK/DM**

Locatelli, Pietro Antonio, important Italian violinist and composer; b. Bergamo, Sept. 3, 1695; d. Amsterdam, March 30, 1764. As a youth, he played violin at S. Maria Maggiore in Bergamo. He then went to Rome, where he performed in the basilica of S. Lorenzo in Damaso (1717–23). After serving as virtuoso da camera at the Mantuan court, he traveled in Italy; then played at the Bavarian court in Munich and at the Prussian court in Berlin (1727) and in Kassel (1728). He settled in Amsterdam, where he devoted himself principally to leading an amateur ensemble and teaching; also made occasional tours abroad. As a virtuoso, he amazed his auditors with his technical feats, particularly in double stops; by changing the tuning of his violin, he produced marvelous effects; Paganini is said to have profited by his innovations. Among his works were *XII concerti grossi a 4 e a 5 con 12 fughe* for 2 Violins, 1 or 2 Violas, and Basso, op.1 (1721; corrected ed., 1729); *XII sonate* for Flute and Basso Continuo, op.2 (1732); *L'arte del violino: XII concerti...con XXIV capricci ad libitum* for Violin, 2 Violins, Viola, Cello, and Bass, op.3 (1733); *Parte I7: VI introduttioni teatrali; Parte II7: VI concerti* for 2 Violins, Viola, and Cello, and for 2 Violins, Viola, and Bass, op.4 (1735); *VI sonate a 3* for 2 Violins, or Flute and Basso Continuo, op.5 (1736); *XII sonate de camera* for Violin and Basso Continuo, op.6 (1737); *VI concerti* for 4 Violins, 2 Violas, and Bass, op.7 (1741); and *X sonate*, op.8 (1744; second ed., 1752; 6 for Violin and Basso Continuo and 4 for 2 Violins and Basso Continuo). See A. Koole, ed., *Pietro Antonio Locatelli: Gesamtausgabe*, Monumenta Musicae Neerlandicae, IV (1961).

BIBL.: A. Koole, *Leven en werken van P.A. L. da Bergamo* (Amsterdam, 1949); A. Meli, *Gli esodi in patria di P.A. L.* (Bergamo, 1971); A. Dunning, ed., *Intorno a L.: studi in occasione del tricentenario della nascita di P.A. L.: 1695–1764* (2 vols., 1995); M. Eynard, *Il musicista P.A. L.: Un itinerario artistico da Bergamo ad Amsterdam* (Bergamo, 1995).—**NS/LK/DM**

Locke, Joe, American vibraphonist; b. Palo Alto, Calif., March 18, 1959. Locke is also a fine arranger who has developed a stimulating group concept for his instrument. Having worked in a wide variety of contexts, from mainstream jazz settings to more edgy situations, he has incorporated far-flung influences in his explorations of film-related themes. Strongly influenced by saxophone lines, he often plays long, flowing, harmonically open passages, while his rich, bell-like tone is highly effective on ballads. He started playing piano and drums at age eight and vibraphone at 13. As a teenager, he participated in the Eastman School of Music's preparatory department and studied privately with bassist Steve Davis and pianists Phil Markowitz and Bill Dobbins. Right out of high school, he went on the road with Davis and Spider Martin, and was soon recording with saxophonist Pepper Adams and drummer Billy Hart and working alongside saxophonists Sal Nistico and Joe Romano. He made the move to N.Y. in 1981 and has worked and recorded with a wide variety of musicians, from Kenny Barron, Walter Davis Jr., and Eddie Henderson to Marvin "Smitty" Smith, Bob Moses, and Byard Lancaster. He has also worked with Jerry Gonzalez's Fort Apache Band and the Mingus Big Band, participating in the recording and tour of *Epitaph*. He has recorded a number of excellent albums for SteepleChase, including a brilliant duo session with Kenny Barron, *Longing*, and contributed four strong arrangements to the Milestone all-star Miles Davis tribute album *Dream Session*.

DISC.: *Moment to Moment* (1996); *Sound Tracks* (1997).—**AG**

Locke (also **Lock**), **Matthew,** noted English composer; b. Exeter, c. 1621; d. London, Aug. 1677. He was a chorister at Exeter Cathedral, where he studied with Edward Gibbons, William Wake, and John Lugge. He was in the Netherlands (c. 1646–51), and at the Restoration he was made private composer-in-ordinary to the King, composer for the wind music, and composer for the band of violins (1660). He was also made organist to the Queen (c. 1662). Locke particularly distinguished himself as a composer of dramatic works and chamber music, and was a major influence on Purcell. However talented as composer, as an individual he was vain and given to polemics. See T. Dart, ed., *Matthew Locke: Keyboard Suites* (London, 1959; second ed., rev., 1964), M. Tilmouth, ed., *Matthew Locke: Chamber Music: I, II*, Musica Britannica, XXXI-XXXII (1971–72), and P. le Huray, *Matthew Locke: Anthems and Motets*, ibid., XXXVIII (1976).

WORKS: DRAMATIC: Opera: *The Siege of Rhodes* (London, 1656; in collaboration with others; music not extant); *The Tempest*, after Shakespeare as adapted by Davenant and Dryden (London, 1674; in collaboration with others); *Psyche* (London, March 9, 1675). **Other:** Various other dramatic works, including music to Shirley's masque *Cupid and Death* (March 26, 1653; in collaboration with C. Gibbons; not extant; rev. 1659) and to Shakespeare's *Macbeth* (c. 1663–74). **INSTRUMENTAL:** Many dances and suites for strings, wind music (most notable being the music for "His Majesty's Sagbutts and Cornetts"), and keyboard pieces. **VOCAL:** Over 35 English anthems, some 15 Latin motets, several services, 6 sacred canons, 4 sacred songs, and over 25 secular songs.

WRITINGS: *Observations upon a Late Book, Entitled, An Essay to the Advancement of Musick, etc., written by Thomas Salmon, M.A. of Trinity Coll. in Oxford: by Matthew Locke* (London, 1672); *The Present Practice of Musick Vindicated against the Exceptions; and New Way of Attaining Musick lately published by Thomas Salmon M.A. etc. by Matthew Locke...to which is added Duellum Musicum by John Phillips...together with a Letter from John Playford to Mr. T. Salmon by way of Confutation of his Essay* (London, 1673); *Melothesia, or, Certain General Rules for Playing upon a Continued-Bass, with a Choice Collection of Lessons for the Harpsichord and Organ of all Sorts: Never before published* (London, 1673).

BIBL.: W. Sleeper, *The Harmonic Style of the Four-part Viol Music of Jenkins, L. and Purcell* (diss., Univ. of Rochester, N.Y., 1964); A. Kooiker, *L's "Melothesia": Its Place in the History of Keyboard Music in Restoration England* (diss., Univ. of Rochester, N.Y., 1965); R. Harding, *A Thematic Catalogue of the Works of M. L. with a Calendar of the Main Events of His Life* (Oxford, 1971). —**NS/LK/DM**

Lockhart, James (Lawrence), Scottish conductor; b. Edinburgh, Oct. 16, 1930. He studied at the Univ. of Edinburgh and at the Royal Coll. of Music in London. He served as apprentice conductor of the Yorkshire Sym. Orch. (1954–55), asst. conductor at Münster (1955–56), the Bavarian State Opera in Munich (1956–57), Glyndebourne (1957–59), and Covent Garden in London (1959–68). Intercalatorily, he was music director of the Opera Workshop of the Univ. of Tex. in Austin (1957–59), and conductor of the BBC Scottish Sym. Orch. in Glasgow (1960–61). From 1968 to 1973 he was music director of the Welsh National Opera in Cardiff; from 1972 to 1980 he served as Generalmusikdirektor of the State Theater in Kassel; from 1981 to 1991 he was Generalmusikdirektor of the Rheinische Phil. in Koblenz and at the Koblenz Opera. He was head of the opera school at the Royal Coll. of Music (1986–92) and director of opera at the London Royal Schools Vocal Faculty (1992–96).—NS/LK/DM

Lockhart, Keith, American conductor; b. Poughkeepsie, N.Y., Nov. 7, 1959. He received instruction in piano at the Juilliard School's preparatory division in N.Y., and at the Vienna Hochschule für Musik (1979). Following studies in piano (B.Mus., 1981) and German (B.A., 1981) at Furman Univ. in Greenville, S.C., he took his M.F.A. degree in conducting at Carnegie-Mellon Univ. in Pittsburgh (1983). He also studied conducting at the Aspen (Colo.) Music School (summer, 1980), the American Sym. Orch. League conductor's workshops in Morgantown, W.Va. (summers, 1982–83), and the Dutch Radio's master classes in Hilversum (1988). In 1989 he was a conducting fellow of the Los Angeles Phil. Inst. He was resident conductor (1983–86) and director of orch. activities (1986–89) at Carnegie-Mellon Univ. From 1985 to 1990 he was music director of the Pittsburgh Civic Orch. He was asst. conductor of the Akron (Ohio) Sym. Orch. (1988–90), and concurrently was music director of the Akron Youth Sym. In 1990 he joined the staff of the Cincinnati Sym. Orch. and the Cincinnati Pops Orch., where he was asst. conductor (to 1992), assoc. conductor (1992–95), and artistic director of education and outreach (1995–96). From 1992 he also was music director of the Cincinnati Chamber Orch. In 1995 he became conductor of the Boston Pops Orch. As a guest conductor, he has appeared with various North American orchs.—NS/LK/DM

Locklair, Dan (Steven), American composer, organist, and teacher; b. Charlotte, N.C., Aug. 7, 1949. He studied organ at Mars Hill (N.C.) Coll. (B.M., 1971), took courses with Joseph Goodman (composition), Robert Baker (organ), and Eugenia Earle (harpsichord) at the Union Theological Seminary School of Sacred Music (S.M.M., 1973), and completed his education with Samuel Adler and Joseph Schwantner (composition) and David Craighead (organ) at the Eastman School of Music in Rochester, N.Y. (D.M.A., 1981). From 1973 to 1982 he was a church musician in Binghamton, N.Y., and an instructor in music at Hartwick Coll. in Oneonta, N.Y. In 1982 he became an asst. prof., in 1988 an assoc. prof., in 1990 composer-in-residence, and in 1996 a prof. of music at Wake Forest Univ. in Winston-Salem, N.C. From 1981 he received annual ASCAP awards, in 1989 he won the Barlow International Competition, and in 1996 he was named Composer of the Year by the American Guild of Organists.

WORKS: DRAMATIC: *Good Tidings from the Holy Beast*, opera (Lincoln, Nebr., Dec. 21, 1978); *Instant Culture*, choral drama for 2 Choruses, Soloists, and Piano (Hartford, Conn., April 26, 1985); *Scintillations*, ballet (1986; Winston-Salem, N.C., March 13, 1987). ORCH.: *Prism of Life* (1980–81; Charlotte, N.C., May 12, 1982); *Dances* (1981; Binghamton, N.Y., May 15, 1982); *Phoenix and Again*, overture (1983; Winston-Salem, N.C., Jan. 29, 1984); *In the Autumn Days*, sym. for Chamber Orch. (1984; Omaha, April 20, 1985); *When Morning Stars Begin to Fall*, tone poem (1986; Knoxville, Tenn., April 23, 1987); *Creation's*

Seeing Order (1987; Charlotte, N.C., April 13, 1988); *Dayspring*, fanfare/concertino for Guitar and Orch. (1988; Winston-Salem, N.C., June 13, 1989); Concerto Grosso for Harpsichord, Strings, and Percussion (1990–92; Lohja, Finland, Jan. 16, 1997); *Hues* (1993; Fayetteville, N.C., Oct. 27, 1994); *Since Dawn*, tone poem for Narrator, Chorus, and Orch. (1995; Winston-Salem, N.C., Sept. 28, 1996); *"Ere long we shall see..."*, concerto brevis for Organ and Orch. (1995–96; N.Y., July 9, 1996). CHAMBER: *Constellations*, concerto for Organ and Percussionists (1980); *Music of Quince* for Flute, Clarinet, Violin, and Piano (1981; New Milford, Conn., Aug. 15, 1984); *Petrus: In Bright Array* for Brass Quintet (1988–89); *Through the Winds* for Wind Quintet and Piano (1989; Winston-Salem, N.C., April 14, 1990); *Dream Steps*, dance suite for Flute, Viola, and Harp (choreographed version, Raleigh, N.C., Oct. 16, 1993; concert version, Washington, D.C., Oct. 24, 1993); *Diminishing Returns* for 7 Percussionists and Piano (1994); *Sonata da chiesa* for Flute and Organ (1998; Knoxville, Tenn., June 29, 1999). KEYBOARD: P i a n o : *Visions in the Haze* (1982); Sonata (1987); *6 Interval Inventions* (1988). O r g a n : *Inventions* (1978); *Rubrics* (1988; Pittsburgh, April 16, 1989); *Voyage*, fantasy (1991; Atlanta, July 1, 1992); *Windows of Comfort* (2 vols., 1996; Topeka, Kans., April 6, 1997). H a r p s i c h o r d : *The Breakers Pound* (1985); *Fantasy Brings the Day* (1989). VOCAL: *Lairs of Soundings* for Soprano and Double String Orch. (Binghamton, N.Y., Nov. 13, 1982); *Tapestries* for Chorus, Handbells, and Piano (1982; N.Y., Jan. 31, 1987); *Missa Brevis*, "The Brass Mass" for Chorus and Brass Quintet (1985–87; Oneonta, N.Y., Nov. 14, 1987); *"changing perceptions" and Epitaph* for Chorus and Piano (Portland, Maine, Oct. 25, 1987); *The Columbus Madrigals* for Treble Voices (Stroudsburg, Pa., June 16, 1991); *Windswept (the trees)* for Chorus, Wind Quintet, and Piano (1992; Charlotte, N.C., Feb. 25, 1994); *For Amber Waves* for 5 Choruses (1992); *Brief Mass* for Chorus (1993; Portland, Maine, March 5, 1995); *Poems 'n Pairs* for Children's Voices and Piano (1994); *Holy Canticles* for Chorus (Winston-Salem, N.C., Oct. 18, 1996); *Gloria* for Chorus, Brass Octet, and Percussion (Portland, Maine, Dec. 4, 1999).—NS/LK/DM

Lockspeiser, Edward, English writer on music; b. London, May 21, 1905; d. Alfriston, Sussex, Feb. 3, 1973. He went to Paris in 1922, where he studied with Tansman. After studies with Boulanger (1925–26), he returned to London and completed his training at the Royal Coll. of Music (1929–30) with Kitson and Sargent. He was on the staff of the BBC (1942–51). Lockspeiser distinguished himself as a writer on French music.

WRITINGS (all publ. in London unless otherwise given): *Debussy* (1936; 5th ed., rev., 1980); *Berlioz* (1939); *Bizet* (1951); ed. *Lettres inédites de Claude Debussy à Andre Caplet (1908–1914)* (Monaco, 1957); *The Literary Clef: An Anthology of Letters and Writings by French Composers* (1958); *Debussy et Edgar Poe: Manuscrits et documents inédits* (Monaco, 1961); *Debussy: His Life and Mind* (2 vols., 1962, 1965; second ed., rev., 1978); *Music and Painting: A Study in Comparative Ideas from Turner to Schoenberg* (1973).—NS/LK/DM

Lockwood, Annea (actually, **Anna Ferguson**), New Zealand composer and instrument builder; b. Christchurch, July 29, 1939. She studied at Canterbury Univ. in New Zealand (B.Mus., 1961), and then went to London, where she took courses with Fricker (composition) and E. Kendall Taylor (piano) at the Royal Coll. of Music (diplomas in both, 1963). She also attended courses in new music in Darmstadt (1961– 62), had lessons with Koenig at the Hochschule für Musik in Cologne (1963–64), studied at the Bilthoven (Netherlands) Electronic Music Center (1963–64), worked in computer composition at the Electronic Music Studio in Putney, England (1970), and undertook research at the Univ. of Southampton's Inst. for Sound and Vibration Research (1969–72). In 1968 she gave non-lectures at the Anti-Univ. of London, and later taught at Hunter Coll. of the City Univ. of N.Y. (1973–83) and at Vassar Coll. (from 1982), where she subsequently became a prof. and head of the music dept. In 1968, with her then husband, Harvey Matusow, she undertook a series of experiments in total art, including aural, oral, visual, tactile, gustatory, and olfactory demonstrations and sporadic transcendental manifestations. Since the mid-1970s, her concerns have been with aural perception and the utilization of sounds found in nature and the environment in participatory or on-site installations and performance pieces. For a decade from the mid-1980s she concentrated on writing for acoustic instruments and voices, and then returned to electroacoustic performance and installation works with *Duende* (1998) and *floating world* (1999).

WORKS: Violin Concerto (1962); *À Abélard, Heloïse*, chamber cantata for Mezzo-soprano and 10 Instruments (1963); *Glass Concert* for 2 Performers and Amplified Glass (1966); *River Archives*, recordings of select world rivers and streams (1966–); *Tiger Balm*, tape collage of sensual and erotic sounds (1972); *Malaman*, Solo Chant (1974); *World Rhythms*, 10-channel live mix of Sounds and Biorhythm of a Gong Player (1975); *Spirit Songs Unfolding* for Tape and Slides (1977); *Delta Run*, mixed-media work for Tape, Slide Projection, and Movement (1982); *A Sound Map of the Hudson River*, installation work (1982–83); *Night and Fog* for Baritone, Baritone Saxophone, Percussion, and Tape, after Osip Mandelstam and Carolyn Forché (1987); *The Secret Life* for Amplified Double Bass (1989); *Amazonia Dreaming* for Snare Drum (1989); *Red Mesa* for Amplified Piano (1989); *Thousand Year Dreaming* for Conch Shells, 4 Didjeridus, Winds, Trombones, Frame Drums and Other Percussion, and Projections (1990); *The Angle of Repose* for Baritone, Alto Flute, and Khaen (1991); *I Give You Back* for Mezzo-soprano, after Joy Harjo (1992); *Western Spaces* for Flutes, Zoomoozophone, and Percussion (1995); *Monkey Trips* for Strings, Winds, Percussion, and Non-Western Instruments (1995; in collaboration with the California E.A.R. Unit); *Shapeshifter* for Chamber Orch. (1996); *Far- Walking Woman* for Prepared Piano (1997); *Tongues of Fire, Tongues of Silk* for Women's Chorus and Percussion (1997); *Duende* for Baritone and Tape (1998; in collaboration with Thomas Buckner); *floating world* for Tape (1999).—NS/LK/DM

Lockwood, Lewis (Henry),

distinguished American musicologist; b. N.Y., Dec. 16, 1930. He was a student of Lowinsky at Queens Coll. in N.Y. (B.A., 1952) and of Strunk and Mendel at Princeton Univ. (M.F.A., 1955; Ph.D., 1960). In 1957–58 he was a cellist in the U.S. Seventh Army Sym. Orch. In 1958 he joined the faculty of Princeton Univ., where he was an assoc. prof. (1965–68), prof. (1968–80), and chairman of the music dept. (1970–73). In 1980 he became prof. of music at Harvard Univ., where he served as the Fanny Peabody Prof. of Music from 1984. He also was chairman of the music dept. (1988–90). In 1973–74 and 1984–85 he was an NEH Senior Fellow. In 1977–78 he held a Guggen-heim fellowship. In 1984 he was elected a member of the American Academy of Arts and Sciences. He served as president of the American Musicological Soc. in 1987–88, was made an honorary member in 1993, and received the society's Einstein and Kindeley awards. In 1991 he was awarded an honorary doctorate by the Università degli Studi in Ferrara. In addition to his studies of music of the Italian Renaissance, Lockwood has devoted himself to the elucidation of Beethoven's life and works with special emphasis on his creative process as revealed in his sketches and autographs. He publ. the valuable books *Music in Renaissance Ferrara, 1400–1505: The Creation of a Musical Center in the Italian Renaissance* (1984) and *Beethoven: Studies in the Creative Process* (1992), the latter the winner of the ASCAP-Deems Taylor Award in 1993. He also served as general ed. of the series Studies in Musical Genesis and Structure (1984–98) and as co-ed. of the series Studies in Music History (from 1981), *Beethoven Essays: Studies in Honor of Elliot Forbes* (1984), *Essays in Musicology: A Tribute to Alvin Johnson* (1990), and the yearbook *Beethoven Forum* (from 1991).

BIBL.: J. Owens and A. Cummings, eds., *Music in Renaissance Cities and Courts: Studies in Honor of L. L.* (Warren, Mich., 1997).—NS/LK/DM

Lockwood, Normand,

American composer and teacher; b. N.Y., March 19, 1906. He studied at the Univ. of Mich. (1921–24), and with Respighi in Rome (1925–26) and Boulanger in Paris (1926–28); he was a Fellow at the American Academy in Rome (1929–31). Upon his return to America, he was an instructor in music at the Oberlin (Ohio) Cons. (1932–43); from 1945 to 1953, was a lecturer at Columbia Univ., then at Trinity Univ. in San Antonio (1953–55); later taught at the Univ. of Hawaii and at the Univ. of Ore. (1955–61). In 1961 he was appointed a member of the faculty of the Univ. of Denver; became prof. emeritus in 1974. Lockwood's compositions are well crafted in an accessible style.

WORKS: DRAMATIC: Opera: *The Scarecrow* (N.Y., May 19, 1945); *Early Dawn* (Denver, Aug. 7, 1961); *The Wizards of Balizar* (Denver, Aug. 1, 1962); *The Hanging Judge* (Denver, March 1964); *Requiem for a Rich Young Man* (Denver, Nov. 24, 1964). **ORCH.:** 2 syms. (1935; 1978–79); *Moby Dick* for Chamber Orch. (1946); 2 concertos for Organ and Brass (1950, 1970); Oboe Concerto (1966); *Symphonic Sequences* (1966); *From an Opening to a Close* for Wind Instruments and Percussion (1967); *Panegyric* for Horn and Strings (1978–79); Concerto for 2 Harps and Strings (1981); *Prayers and Fanfares* for Brass, Strings, and Percussion (1982). **CHAMBER:** 7 string quartets (1933–50); Piano Quintet (1940); *6 Serenades* for String Quartet (1945); Clarinet Quintet (1960); Sonata for 4 Cellos (1968); *Excursions* for 4 String Basses (1976); *Tripartito* for Flute and Guitar (1980); Piano Trio (1985). **VOCAL:** *The Closing Doxology* for Chorus, Symphonic Band, and Percussion (1952); *Prairie* for Chorus and Orch. (1952); *Magnificat* for Soprano, Chorus, and Orch. (1954); oratorios, including *Children of God* (1956; Cincinnati, Feb. 1, 1957), *Light out of Darkness* (1957), *Land of Promise* (1960), and *For the Time Being* (1971); cantatas; choruses; song cycles; solo songs.

BIBL.: K. Norton, *N. L.: His Life and Music* (Metuchen, N.J., 1993).—NS/LK/DM

Loder, Edward (James), English composer, cousin of **George Loder**; b. Bath, 1813; d. London, April 5, 1865. He was the son of the English violinist and music publisher John David Loder (b. Bath, 1788; d. London, Feb. 13, 1846). After training from his father, he went to Frankfurt am Main to study with Ries. Returning to England, he had an initial success with the opera *Nourjahad* (London, July 21, 1834). However, much hackwork followed. In 1846 he became musical director of the Princess's Theatre in London, where success returned with his opera *The Nights Dancers, or The Wilis,* which was first performed on Oct. 28 of that year. He went to Manchester in 1851 as musical director of the Theatre Royal, where his most important opera, *Raymond and Agnes,* was premiered on Aug. 14, 1855. Soon thereafter Loder was stricken with a brain malady and returned to London. In 1861 he became comatose and died four years later almost totally forgotten. Among his other works were several overtures, chamber music, sacred and secular vocal pieces, and various arrangements.—**LK/DM**

Loder, George, English double bass player, conductor, and composer, cousin of **Edward (James) Loder**; b. Bath, c. 1816; d. Adelaide, July 15, 1868. He went to the U.S. in 1836, and in 1839–40 was active as a conductor and composer in N.Y. In 1842 he helped to organize the N.Y. Phil. Sym. Soc., playing double bass with it until 1847. He conducted it in the U.S. premiere of Beethoven's 9th Sym. on May 20, 1846, and returned as an occasional conductor with it until 1853. From 1844 he also served as the principal of the N.Y. Vocal Inst. In 1856 Loder settled in Australia as an opera conductor. He composed the comic operettas *Pets of the Parterre* and *The Old House at Home.* He also publ. *The New York Glee Book* (1843; includes many of his own part songs) and *The Philadelphia and New York Glee Book* (1857).—**LK/DM**

Loeffler, Charles Martin (Tornow), outstanding Alsatian-born American composer; b. Mulhouse, Jan. 30, 1861; d. Medfield, Mass., May 19, 1935. His father was a writer who sometimes used the nom de plume Tornow, which Loeffler later added to his name. When he was a child, the family moved to Russia, where his father was engaged in government work in the Kiev district; later they lived in Debrecen, and in Switzerland. In 1875 Loeffler began taking violin lessons in Berlin with Rappoldi, who prepared him for study with Joachim; he studied theory with Kiel; also took lessons with Bargiel at the Berlin Hochschule für Musik (1874–77). He then went to Paris, where he continued his musical education with Massart (violin) and Guiraud (counterpoint and composition). He was engaged briefly as a violinist in the Pasdeloup Orch.; then was a member of the private orch. of the Russian Baron Paul von Derwies at his sumptuous residences near Lugano and in Nice (1879–81). When Derwies died in 1881, Loeffler went to the U.S., with letters of recommendation from Joachim; he became a naturalized American citizen in 1887. He played in the orch. of Leopold Damrosch in N.Y. in 1881–82. In 1882 he became second concertmaster of the newly organized Boston Sym. Orch., but was able to accept other engagements during late spring and summer months; the summers of 1883 and 1884 he spent in Paris, where he took violin lessons with Hubert Leonard. He resigned from the Boston Sym. Orch. in 1903, and devoted himself to composition and farming in Medfield. He was married to Elise Burnett Fay (1910). After his death, she donated to the Library of Congress in Washington, D.C., all of his MSS, correspondence, etc.; by his will, he left the material assets of his not inconsiderable estate to the French Academy and the Paris Cons. He was an officer of the French Academy (1906); a Chevalier in the French Legion of Honor (1919); a member of the American Academy of Arts and Letters; Mus. Doc. (*honoris causa*), Yale Univ. (1926).

Loeffler's position in American music is unique, brought up as he was under many different national influences, Alsatian, French, German, Russian, and Ukrainian. One of his most vivid scores, *Memories of My Childhood*, written as late as 1924, reflects the modal feeling of Russian and Ukrainian folk songs. But his aesthetic code was entirely French, with definite leanings toward Impressionism; the archaic constructions that he sometimes affected, and the stylized evocations of "ars antiqua," are also in keeping with the French manner. His most enduring work, *A Pagan Poem*, is cast in such a neo-archaic vein. He was a master of colorful orchestration; his harmonies are opulent without saturation; his rhapsodic forms are peculiarly suited to the evocative moods of his music. His only excursion into the American idiom was the employment of jazz rhythms in a few of his lesser pieces.

WORKS: DRAMATIC: Opera: *The Passion of Hilarion* (1912–13); *Les Amants jaloux* (1918); *The Peony Lantern* (c. 1919). **Incidental Music:** *Ouverture pour le T.C. Minstrel Entertainment* (Boston, 1906?); *The Countess Cathleen* (Concord, Mass., May 8, 1924; not extant); *The Reveller* (Boston, Dec. 22, 1925). **ORCH.:** *Les Veillées de l'Ukraine* for Violin and Orch. (1888?–91; Boston, Nov. 20, 1891; rev. version, Boston, Nov. 24, 1899); *Morceau fantastique: Fantastic Concerto* for Cello and Orch. (1893; Boston, Feb. 2, 1894); *Divertissement* for Violin and Orch. (1894; Boston, Jan. 4, 1895); *La Mort de Tintagiles* for 2 Violas d'Amore and Orch. (1897; Boston, Jan. 7, 1898; rev. for Viola d'Amore and Orch., 1900; Boston, Feb. 15, 1901); *Divertissement espagnol* for Saxophone and Orch. (1900; Boston, Jan. 29, 1901); *Poem (La Bonne Chanson; Avant que tu ne t'en ailles*; 1901; Boston, April 11, 1902; rev. 1915; Boston, Nov. 1, 1918); *La Villanelle du diable* (1901; Boston, April 11, 1902; revision of his 3rd song in the set *Rapsodies*, 1898); *A Pagan Poem* (1904–06; Boston, Oct. 29, 1907; revision of *Poème païen* for 13 Instruments, 1901–02; *Memories of My Childhood* (Life in a Russian Village) (Evanston, Ill., May 30, 1924); *Intermezzo (Clowns)* for Jazz Band (Boston, Feb. 19, 1928). **CHAMBER:** *Danse bizarre* for Violin (1881); String Sextet (c. 1885–92; Boston, Feb. 27, 1893); Violin Sonata (1886); String Quartet (1889); Quintet for 3 Violins, Viola, and Cello (1894?; Boston, Feb. 18, 1895); Octet for 2 Clarinets, 2 Violins, Viola, Cello, Double Bass, and Harp (1896?; Boston, Feb. 15, 1897); *Le passeur d'eau* for 2 Violins, 2 Violas, and 2 Cellos (1900; Boston, Dec. 10, 1909); *Deux Rapsodies* for Oboe, Viola, and Piano (Boston, Dec. 16, 1901); *Poème païen (d'après Virgil)* for 2 Flutes, Oboe, Clarinet, English Horn, 2 Horns, Viola, Double Bass, Piano, and 3 Trumpets (1901–02; also as *Poème antique d'après Virgil* for 2 Pianos and 3 Trumpets, 1902–03; Boston, April 13, 1903; rev. 1904–06 as *A Pagan Poem* for

Orch.); *Ballade carnavalesque* for Flute, Oboe, Saxophone, Bassoon, and Piano (1902; Boston, Jan. 25, 1904); *Poème (Scène dramatique)* for Cello ad Piano (1916; N.Y., Jan. 27, 1917); *Music for 4 Stringed Instruments* for String Quartet (1917; rev. 1918–19; N.Y., Feb. 15, 1919; rev. 1920); *Historiettes* for String Quartet and Harp (1922); pieces for violin and piano; various unfinished works. **VOCAL**: *L'Archet* for Soprano, Women's Chorus, Viola d'Amore, and Piano (c. 1897–99; Boston, Feb. 4, 1902); *The Sermon on the Mount* for Women's Chorus, 2 Violas d'Amore, Viola da Gamba, Harp, and Organ (1901?; unfinished); *Psalm 137 (By the Rivers of Babylon)* for Women's Chorus, Organ, Harp, 2 Flutes, and Cello Obbligato (1901?; Boston, Feb. 28, 1902); *Ave maris stella* for Boy's Voices, Soprano, Strings, Piano, and Organ (c. 1906–12); *For One Who Fell in Battle* for Chorus (Boston, Dec. 13, 1906; rev. as *Ode for One Who Fell in Battle* for Chorus, 1911; Boston, March 21, 1912); *Poème mystique* for Boy's Chorus, Chorus, 4 Horns, 2 Contrabasses, Harp, and Organ (1907; also for Baritone, Chorus, 4 Horns, and 2 Contrabasses; unfinished); *Hora mystica* for Men's Chorus and Orch. (1915; Norfolk, Conn., June 6, 1916); *Beat! Beat! Drums!* for Men's Voices and Piano (1917; also 3 other versions, including one for Men's Voices and Band, 1927–32; Cleveland, Dec. 17, 1932); *5 Irish Fantasies* for Voice and Orch. (1920; numbers 2, 3, and 5, Boston, March 10, 1922; numbers 1 and 4, Cleveland, Nov. 7, 1929); *Canticum fratris solis (Canticle of the Sun)* for Voice and Chamber Orch. (Washington, D.C., Oct. 28, 1925); *Evocation* for Women's Voices and Orch. (1930; for the opening of Severance Hall, Cleveland, Feb. 5, 1931); over 45 songs.

BIBL.: W. Damrosch, *C.M. L.* (N.Y., 1936); H. Colvin, *C.M. L.: His Life and Works* (diss., Univ. of Rochester, 1959); E. Henry, *Impressionism in the Arts and Its Influence on Selected Works of C.M. L. and Charles Tomlinson Griffes* (diss., Univ. of Cincinnati, 1976); E. Knight, *C.M. L.: A Life Apart in American Music* (Urbana, 1993).—**NS/LK/DM**

Loeillet (also spelled L'Oeillet, Luly, Lulli, Lullie, Lully), noted family of Flemish musicians:

(1) Jean Baptiste Loeillet, oboist, flutist, harpsichordist, and composer, known as **John Loeillet of London**; b. Ghent (baptized), Nov. 18, 1680; d. London, July 19, 1730. He studied in Ghent and Paris, then went about 1705 to London, where he joined the orch. at Drury Lane (1707); was principal oboe and flute in the orch. at the Queen's Theatre, Haymarket (1709). He popularized the German transverse flute in England. His compositions follow Italian models, showing thorough understanding of the virtuoso possibilities of his instruments.

WORKS: *Lessons* for Harpsichord or Spinet (London, c. 1712; ed. in Monumenta Musicae Belgicae, I, 1932); (6) *Sonatas for Variety of Instruments*, op.1 (London, 1722); *6 Suits of Lessons* for Harpsichord or Spinet (London, 1723; ed. in Monumenta Musicae Belgicae, I, 1932); *12 Sonatas in 3 Parts*, op.2 (London, c. 1725); *12 Solos*, op.3 (London, 1729).

(2) Jacques (Jacob) Loeillet, oboist and composer, brother of the preceding; b. Ghent (baptized), July 7, 1685; d. there, Nov. 28, 1748. He was an oboist in the service of the Elector of Bavaria in the Netherlands and at his court in Munich (1726) and later hautbois de la chambre du roi in Versailles. He returned to Ghent in 1726. He publ. *6 Sonates* for 2 Flutes or Violin, op.4 (Paris, 1728), and *6 Sonates* for Flute or Violin and Basso Continuo (Paris, 1728).

(3) Jean Baptiste Loeillet, composer, cousin of the two preceding, known as **Loeillet de Gant**; b. Ghent (baptized), July 6, 1688; d. Lyons, c. 1720. He was in the service of the archbishop of Lyons. He publ. 3 books of 12 sonates each for Recorder and Basso Continuo, opp. 1, 2, and 4 (Amsterdam, c. 1710, 1714, 1716); also 2 books of 6 Sonates each for Flute, Oboe or Violin, and Basso Continuo, op.5 (1717).—**NS/LK/DM**

Loeschhorn, (Carl) Albert
See **Löschhorn, (Carl) Albert**

Loesser, Arthur, esteemed American pianist, teacher, and writer on music, half-brother of **Frank (Henry) Loesser**; b. N.Y., Aug. 26, 1894; d. Cleveland, Jan. 4, 1969. He studied with Stojowski and Goetschius at the Inst. of Musical Art in N.Y. He made his debut in Berlin (1913). He first played in N.Y. in 1916, and after touring the Orient and Australia (1920–21), he appeared widely in the U.S. In 1926 he was appointed a prof. of piano at the Cleveland Inst. of Music. In 1943 he was commissioned in the U.S. Army as an officer in the Japanese intelligence dept.; mastered the language and, after the war, gave lectures in Japanese in Tokyo; was the first American musician in uniform to play for a Japanese audience (1946). He publ. *Humor in American Song* (N.Y., 1943) and an entertaining vol., *Men, Women and Pianos: A Social History* (N.Y., 1954).—**NS/LK/DM**

Loesser, Frank (Henry), American songwriter; b. N.Y., June 29, 1910; d. there, July 28, 1969. Artistic growth was the chief characteristic of the career of Frank Loesser, whose restless imagination saw him continually expanding his range and challenging himself with different kinds of projects. Enormously productive, he wrote songs used in at least 80 feature films between 1935 and 1955, at first contributing only lyrics in collaboration with such composers as Burton Lane, Hoagy Carmichael, Jimmy McHugh, Louis Alter, Jule Styne, Joseph J. Lilley, and Arthur Schwartz. These efforts included such hits as "Says My Heart," "I Don't Want to Walk without You," and "Jingle, Jangle, Jingle." By the early 1940s he began to write both music and lyrics, resulting in such hits as "Praise the Lord and Pass the Ammunition!," "I Wish I Didn't Love You So," and "On a Slow Boat to China." Later in the decade he hit the Broadway stage with the successful show *Where's Charley? Guys and Dolls*, another hit, was followed by the near-operatic *The Most Happy Fella*. His last show to reach Broadway, *How to Succeed in Business without Really Trying*, was the longest-running of his career.

Loesser's parents were Henry and Julia Erlich Loesser; his father was a piano teacher and accompanist, his older half-brother Arthur a pianist, teacher, and music critic. Loesser showed an early interest in music and composition, though he was attracted to popular music and was largely self-taught. He attended the Coll. of the City of N.Y. briefly in his mid-teens, then spent the second half of the 1920s at a variety of occupations outside music. By the start of the 1930s he was writing song lyrics and vaudeville sketches, and he worked for a music publisher. In 1931 he had his first song published, "In Love with a Memory of You" (music by William Schuman), but he did not score a hit until several artists, notably Fats Waller and Emil Coleman and His Orch., recorded popular versions of "I Wish I Were Twins" (music by Joseph Meyer, lyrics also by Edgar DeLange) in the spring of 1934.

Loesser formed a songwriting partnership with composer Irving Actman, and they began performing their songs at the Back Drop nightclub. Some of the songs were featured in the short-lived Broadway revue *The Illustrators' Show* in January 1936, which led to the team being signed to Universal Pictures; they left for Hollywood in the spring. In the fall, Loesser married singer Lynn Garland (real name Mary Alice Blankenbaker). They had two children; their daughter, Susan Loesser, later wrote her father's biography. Loesser and Actman wrote songs for only a few films during their six-month tenure at Universal, after which Loesser freelanced during most of 1937, finally landing a deal at Paramount, where he remained under contract until 1949. His first Paramount film, *Blossoms on Broadway*, was released in December 1937.

Loesser came into his own as a lyricist for the movies in 1938. He contributed to eight feature films released during the year and scored six entries on the hit parade. *College Swing*, released in April, contained two hits, "How'd Ja Like to Love Me" (music by Burton Lane) and "I Fall in Love with You Every Day" (music by Manning Sherwin and Arthur Altman); both were recorded by Jimmy Dorsey and His Orch. "Says My Heart" (music by Lane), which topped the hit parade in June for Red Norvo and His Orch. with Mildred Bailey on vocals and became one of the biggest hits of the year, came from the film *Cocoanut Grove*. In August, Bing Crosby sang "Small Fry" (music by Hoagy Carmichael) in *Sing, You Sinners*, scoring a record hit with it in a duet with Johnny Mercer in October. That same month, Loesser and Carmichael's independent song "Heart and Soul" entered the hit parade for the first of ten weeks in a recording by Larry Clinton and His Orch., and in November their "Two Sleepy People" from the film *Thanks for the Memory* began a 12– week run in the chart for Fats Waller.

In 1939, Loesser had songs in 15 motion pictures. *Some Like It Hot*, released in May, brought him a hit in "The Lady's in Love with You" (music by Burton Lane), which was recorded by Glenn Miller and His Orch. and spent nine weeks in the hit parade, while *Man about Town*, released in June, featured "Strange Enchantment" (music by Frederick Hollander), sung by Dorothy Lamour, whose recording reached the hit parade that month. Loesser wrote songs for another 15 films released in 1940, resulting in the hit "Say It" (music by Jimmy McHugh) for Glenn Miller, which was in the April release *Buck Benny Rides Again*. He had songs in 11 films released during 1941, among them the Oscar-nominated "Dolores" (music by Louis Alter) from the March release *Las Vegas Nights*, in which it was performed by Tommy Dorsey and His Orch. featuring Frank Sinatra on vocals; it was given Top Ten recordings by both

Dorsey and Bing Crosby. He also provided the title song for the August release *Kiss the Boys Goodbye* (music by Victor Schertzinger), another hit for Dorsey.

The two hit songs featured in the July 1942 release *Sweater Girl*, on which Loesser collaborated with Jule Styne, both made the charts long before the film appeared: "I Said No!" peaked in the Top Ten for Alvino Rey and His Orch. in February, and "I Don't Want to Walk without You" was a Top Ten hit for Harry James and His Orch. in March. Loesser's next hit, "Jingle Jangle Jingle" (music by Joseph J. Lilley), also scored in advance of the film in which it was featured. The song reached #1 in July for Kay Kyser and His Orch., selling a million copies, then was used in *The Forest Rangers* in October. That month, Kyser scored a million-selling Top Ten hit with the war-themed "Praise the Lord and Pass the Ammunition!," Loesser's first notable song for which he wrote both music and lyrics. Collaborating with Jimmy McHugh on the songs for the film *Seven Days' Leave*, released in December, he scored three minor hits, "Can't Get Out of This Mood," which was recorded by Kyser, and "A Touch of Texas" and "I Get the Neck of the Chicken," both recorded by Freddy Martin and His Orch.

Loesser joined the army in 1942. He spent World War II writing songs for radio broadcasts and service shows that were performed at bases in the U.S. and England. He still managed to work on the occasional movie, however, at least during the first year of his enlistment when he was stationed on the West Coast. Collaborating with Jimmy McHugh, he contributed to the March 1943 release *Happy Go Lucky*, including the Top Ten hits "'Murder,' He Says" (for Dinah Shore) and "Let's Get Lost" (for Kay Kyser) and the minor hits "The Fuddy Duddy Watchmaker" (for Kyser) and "Sing a Tropical Song" (for The Andrews Sisters). "In My Arms" (music by Ted Grouya) peaked in the Top Ten for Dick Haymes in August, then turned up in the film *See Here, Private Hargrove* in March 1944. The all-star film *Thank Your Lucky Stars*, released in the fall of 1943, found Loesser collaborating with Arthur Schwartz and scoring Top Ten hits with the Academy Award nominee "They're Either Too Young or Too Old" (for Jimmy Dorsey), and "The Dreamer" and "How Sweet You Are" (both for Kay Armen and the Balladiers).

Perry Como scored a minor hit in January 1944 with "Have I Stayed Away Too Long?," for which Loesser wrote both music and lyrics; in March, Hildegarde had a minor hit with "Leave Us Face It (We're in Love)," which Loesser and Abe Burrows wrote for the radio series *Duffy's Tavern*. "Feudin' and Fightin'," a Burton Lane song featured in the Broadway revue *Laffing Room Only* (N.Y., Dec. 23, 1944), to which Loesser contributed some lyrics, went on to become a Top Ten hit for Dorothy Shay in September 1947. But Loesser, now stationed in N.Y., spent most of 1944 and 1945 writing such service revues as *About Face!* (Camp Shanks, N.Y., May 26, 1944) and *Hi, Yank!* (Fort Dix, N.J., Aug. 7, 1944).

Back in Hollywood after his discharge in 1946, Loesser worked at MGM with Johnny Green on *The Day Before Spring*, which was not produced. In March, "Wave to Me, My Lady" (music and lyrics by Loesser and William Stein) reached the pop and country charts for Elton Britt, becoming a Top Ten country hit. Thereafter, Loesser rarely wrote with a musical collaborator. His first released film for which he wrote both music and lyrics was the box office hit *The Perils of Pauline*, which appeared in July 1947. Betty Hutton, who starred in the film, recorded one of the four Top Ten versions of "I Wish I Didn't Love You So," though the more popular records were by Vaughn Monroe and His Orch. and Dinah Shore; the song was nominated for an Academy Award. Also in July, "Bloop-Bleep," an independent song by Loesser, was a minor hit for Alvino Rey. *Variety Girl*, released in October, was the second film with an all-Loesser score; from it, "Tallahassee" became a Top Ten hit for Bing Crosby and The Andrews Sisters.

Loesser was hired to write songs for the Broadway musical *Where's Charley?*, which opened in the fall of 1948. It ran 792 performances and featured "My Darling, My Darling," which became a #1 hit for Jo Stafford and Gordon MacRae, and "Once in Love with Amy," a hit for the show's star, Ray Bolger. In November, Kay Kyser sold a million copies with the most popular of four Top Ten versions of Loesser's "On a Slow Boat to China," an independent song.

Returning to Hollywood, Loesser contributed a few songs to the box office hit *Neptune's Daughter*, released in June 1949, among them "Baby, It's Cold Outside" (a duet of seduction he'd actually written years earlier as a piece to perform with his wife at parties), which was given Top Ten treatments by the teams of Dinah Shore and Buddy Clark, Margaret Whiting and Johnny Mercer, and Ella Fitzgerald and Louis Jordan, and won the Academy Award for Best Song. He also appeared in and wrote songs for the October 1949 release *Red, Hot and Blue*, including "(Where Are You) Now That I Need You," which Doris Day and Frankie Laine each recorded for minor hits.

In 1950, Loesser wrote the lyrics for the independent song "Hoop-De-Doo" (music by Milton DeLugg), with which Perry Como topped the charts in June. He wrote a film score for the Fred Astaire–Betty Hutton vehicle *Let's Dance*, then returned to Broadway for *Guys and Dolls*. Opening in November, the show ran 1,194 performances, one of the longest runs for a musical up to that time; it also won the Tony Award for Best Musical. The original cast album, which featured such favorites as "I'll Know" and "Sit Down, You're Rockin' the Boat," hit #1 in March 1951, and the biggest hits to emerge from the score were "A Bushel and a Peck," taken into the Top Ten by the team of Perry Como and Betty Hutton, and "If I Were a Bell," with which Frankie Laine reached the charts.

A film version of *Where's Charley?*, using most of Loesser's score, was released in June 1952. In October the Four Aces had a chart revival of "Heart and Soul." The box office hit *Hans Christian Andersen*, the last original movie musical for which Loesser wrote music, appeared in November. From the score, Julius LaRosa hit the Top Ten with "Anywhere I Wander" and the duo of Doris Day and Donald O'Connor charted with "No Two People," while "Thumbelina" earned Loesser his fifth Academy Award nomination.

Loesser spent most of the period 1953–56 working on the ambitious musical *The Most Happy Fella*, for which he wrote the libretto as well as the music. But he also wrote a title song (not used in the film itself) to promote the October 1955 release *The Trouble with Harry*; it reached the charts in January 1956 for Alfi and Harry (actually comedian David Seville, whose real name was Ross Bagdasarin). And he added a few new songs to the film version of *Guys and Dolls*, a box office hit upon its release in November 1955, among them "A Woman in Love," which the Four Aces took into the Top 40, and "Pet Me, Poppa," a chart record for Rosemary Clooney. (Concurrent with the film's distribution, Sammy Davis Jr. reached the charts with a revival of "I'll Know.")

The Most Happy Fella opened in the spring of 1956 and ran 676 performances. Prior to the opening, the Four Lads had recorded "Standing on the Corner," which reached the Top Ten in May, and Peggy Lee had recorded "Joey, Joey, Joey," also a chart record. Frankie Laine's version of "Don't Cry" reached the charts in July. The original cast album, an unprecedented triple-LP box set containing the complete score, spent the month of August in the charts. The show had been coproduced by Loesser's wife, Lynn. On March 4, 1957, the couple was divorced. On April 29, 1959, Loesser married Jo Sullivan, who had been the female lead in *The Most Happy Fella*. They remained married until his death, and had two daughters; Emily, the younger, became a singer.

Loesser was next heard from in March 1960, when *Greenwillow* opened. The musical was a flop, running only 97 performances. "Heart and Soul" enjoyed two Top 40 revivals in recordings by the Cleftones and Jan and Dean in the summer of 1961. Loesser returned to Broadway in October 1961 with the satirical *How to Succeed in Business without Really Trying*, which ran 1,417 performances, winning the Tony Award for Best Musical and the Pulitzer Prize for Best Play of the Year. The cast recording spent 11 months in the charts and won the Grammy Award for Best Original Cast Show Album. Loesser wrote the instrumental score for the film adaptation, which was released in March 1967 with a soundtrack album that charted for several weeks.

Loesser's subsequent efforts did not succeed. *Pleasures and Palaces* (Detroit, March 11, 1965) closed before reaching Broadway, and he worked on but abandoned another musical later in 1960s. He died of lung cancer in 1969 at the age of 59. He has been remembered primarily for his four successful musicals. All were mounted by the N.Y.C. Light Opera during the spring and summer of 1966. *Guys and Dolls* has had two major Broadway revivals. The first (July 10, 1976) featured an all-black cast; the second (April 14, 1992) ran 1,144 performances—almost as long as the original—and generated a cast album that made the charts. *The Most Happy Fella* also has had two Broadway revivals, a full-scale version (Oct. 11, 1979) and a two-piano intimate production (Feb. 13, 1992) that ran 244 performances. The Broadway revival of *How to Succeed in Business without Really Trying* opened March. 23, 1995, and ran 548 performances. A stage version of *Hans Christian Andersen*, titled *Hans Andersen*, was mounted in London in 1974.

There have been two revues devoted to Loesser's work: *Perfectly Frank*, which ran on Broadway in 1980, and *Together Again for the First Time* (Feb. 27, 1989), featuring Jo Sullivan Loesser and Emily Loesser, which ran Off-Broadway. Barry Manilow reached the Top 40 with a revival of "I Don't Want to Walk without You" in 1980, and Don Henley's rendition of "Sit Down, You're Rockin' the Boat," featured in the film *Leap of Faith*, spent six months in the adult contemporary charts beginning in September 1993.

WORKS (only works for which Loesser was a credited, primary songwriter are listed): **FILMS:** *Poetic Gems* (1935); *Postal Inspector* (1936); *The Man I Marry* (1936); *Blossoms on Broadway* (1937); *College Swing* (1938); *Spawn of the North* (1938); *Zaza* (1939); *St. Louis Blues* (1939); *Man about Town* (1939); *Hawaiian Nights* (1939); *Destry Rides Again* (1939); *The Llano Kid* (1940); *Seventeen* (1940); *Buck Benny Rides Again* (1940); *Dancing on a Dime* (1940); *Youth Will Be Served* (1940); *Seven Sinners* (1940); *At Good Old Siwash* (1940); *A Night at Earl Carroll's* (1940); *Las Vegas Nights* (1941); *Sis Hopkins* (1941); *Manpower* (1941); *Kiss the Boys Goodbye* (1941); *Aloma of the South Seas* (1941); *Glamour Boy* (1941); *Sailors on Leave* (1941); *Mr. Bug Goes to Town*, aka *Hoppity Goes to Town* (1941); *This Gun for Hire* (1942); *True to the Army* (1942); *Beyond the Blue Horizon* (1942); *Sweater Girl* (1942); *Priorities on Parade* (1942); *Seven Days' Leave* (1942); *Happy Go Lucky* (1943); *Thank Your Lucky Stars* (1943); *The Perils of Pauline* (1947); *Variety Girl* (1947); *Neptune's Daughter* (1949); *Red, Hot and Blue* (1949); *Let's Dance* (1950); *Where's Charley?* (1952); *Hans Christian Andersen* (1952); *Guys and Dolls* (1955); *How to Succeed in Business without Really Trying* (1967). **MUSICALS/ REVUES** (all dates refer to N.Y. openings unless otherwise indicated): *The Illustrators' Show* (Jan. 22, 1936); *Where's Charley?* (Oct. 11, 1948); *Guys and Dolls* (Nov. 24, 1950); *The Most Happy Fella* (May 3, 1956); *Greenwillow* (March 8, 1960); *How to Succeed in Business without Really Trying* (Oct. 14, 1961); *Hans Andersen* (London, Dec. 17, 1974); *Perfectly Frank* (Nov. 30, 1980).

BIBL.: *F. L. Song Book* (N.Y., 1972); S. Loesser, *A Most Remarkable Fella: F. L. and the Guys and Dolls in His Life: A Portrait by His Daughter* (N.Y., 1993).—**WR**

Loevendie, Theo, Dutch composer and teacher; b. Amsterdam, Sept. 17, 1930.

He received training in composition and clarinet at the Amsterdam Cons. (1956–61). He began his career as a jazz musician and appeared with his own group at many European festivals. From 1968 he devoted increasing attention to composing serious music. He served as prof. of composition at the Rotterdam Cons. (1970–88), the Royal Cons. of Music at The Hague (1988–97), and at the Sweelinck Cons. in Amsterdam (from 1995). He also led many master classes around the world. In 1984 he was co-winner of the Koussevitzky International Record Award, in 1986 he received the Matthijs Vermuelen Prize, and in 1988 the 3M Music Award for his entire creative life's work.

WORKS: DRAMATIC: O p e r a : *Naima* (1985); *Gassier, the Hero*, chamber opera (1990; Boston, May 1991); *Esmée* (1994). **ORCH.:** *Confluxus* for Jazz and Sym. Orchs. (1966); *Scaramuccia* for Clarinet and Orch. (1969); *Incantations* for Bass Clarinet and Orch. (1975); *Orbits* for Horn and Orch. (1976); *Flexio* (1979; rev. 1981); *Bons* for Improviser on Any Instrument and Chamber Orch. (1991); Piano Concerto (1995); *Vanishing Dances*, violin concerto (1998). **CHAMBER:** *3 Pieces* for 3 Clarinets (1968); *10

Easy Sketches for Clarinet and Piano (1970); *Music for Bass Clarinet and Piano* (1971); *Aulos* for 1 or More Instruments (1972; rev. 1975); *2 Trios* for 3 Percussion (1973); *Timbo* for 6 Percussion (1974); *Prelude* for 6 Percussion (1974; rev. 1980); *Music* for Flute and Piano (1979); *Nonet* (1980); *Venus and Adonis Suite* for Clarinet, Violin, Mandolin, Guitar, and Percussion (1981); *Back Bay Bicinium* for 7 Instruments (1986); *Plus One* for Flute, Bass Clarinet, and Piano (1988); *Cycles* for Violin, Clarinet, and Piano (1992); *Que pasa en la calle?* for 4 Trumpets (1996); *The Young Violinist (Shuffle, Blues, Aksak)* for Violin and Piano (1997); *2 Mediterranean Dances* for Clarinet, Trumpet, and Bassoon (1998); *Golliwogg's Other Dances* for Clarinet, Trumpet, and Bassoon (1998); *Twins* for Marimba and Vibraphone (1999); *Brothers* for Marimba and Vibraphone (1999). **P i a n o :** *Strides* (1976); *Voor Jan, Piet en Klaas* for 2 Pianos (1979); *Walk* (1985). **VOCAL:** *6 Turkish Folk Poems* for Soprano or Mezzo-soprano and 7 Instruments (1977); *De nachtegaal* for Reciter and 7 Instruments (1979); *Oh oor o hoor: Herfst der muziek, Spreken praten..., Visser van Ma Yuan, Nocturne, Het einde* for Bass-baritone and Orch. (1987); *A Nightingale from Echternach* for Soprano or Mezzo-soprano and Piano (1989); *Sonate voor stem* for Man's or Woman's Voice (1990).—**NS/LK/DM**

Loewe, Ferdinand
See **Löwe, Ferdinand**

Loewe, Frederick, German-born American composer and pianist; b. Berlin, June 10, 1901; d. Palm Springs, Calif., Feb. 14, 1988.

Loewe's music, steeped in the tradition of Viennese operetta, proved surprisingly adaptable to the various settings of the stage and film musicals he wrote with lyricist/librettist Alan Jay Lerner, among them the enormously popular *My Fair Lady*, as well as *Gigi*, *Camelot*, and *Brigadoon*; the duo's shows featured such song hits as "Almost Like Being in Love," "On the Street Where You Live," and "I Could Have Danced All Night." Achieving success relatively late in life, Loewe also retired relatively early, but the Lerner-and-Loewe musicals ranked second only to those of Richard Rodgers and Oscar Hammerstein II as the most significant work for the musical theater in the 1940s and 1950s.

Loewe's parents were Austrian. His father, Edmund Loewe, was an opera tenor; Rosa, his mother, was an actress. He showed an early interest in music and attended Stern's Cons. in Berlin. He claimed to have studied piano with Ferruccio Busoni and Eugène d'Albert, and composition with Emil Nikolaus von Reznicek. At 13 he became the youngest piano soloist to appear with the Berlin Symphony Orch.; at 15 he wrote "Katrina," which became a song hit in Europe.

Around 1924, Loewe moved with his parents to N.Y. He spent the rest of the 1920s and early 1930s at a variety of occupations primarily outside music. In 1931 he married Ernestine Zwerleine; they separated in 1947 and later divorced.

Loewe's song "Love Tiptoed through My Heart" (lyrics by Irene Alexander) was used in the Broadway play *Petticoat Fever* in 1935. "A Waltz Was Born in Vienna" (lyrics by Earle Crooker) was in the revue *The Illustrators' Show* (N.Y., Jan. 22, 1936). Loewe and

Crooker wrote the songs for the musical *Salute to Spring* (St. Louis, July 12, 1937), which was mounted by the St. Louis Municipal Opera but did not go to N.Y. Their next effort, the operetta *Great Lady*, did reach N.Y., though for only 20 performances, in late 1938.

In 1942, Loewe enlisted Alan Jay Lerner, whom he had met at the Lambs Club, to revise some of the lyrics to the songs from *Salute to Spring* for use in the musical *Life of the Party*. The show opened in Detroit on Oct. 8 but closed after this tryout. Lerner and Loewe's first full score, *What's Up?*, made it to Broadway the following year for 63 performances, and *The Day Before Spring* (1945) lasted 165 performances. But the team's first hit came with the original romantic fantasy *Brigadoon*, which ran 581 performances, making it the biggest hit of the 1946–47 Broadway season. The original cast album, featuring "Almost Like Being in Love," "Come to Me, Bend to Me," and "The Heather on the Hill," reached the Top Ten.

Notwithstanding this success, Lerner and Loewe broke up. They reunited for *Paint Your Wagon* (1951), set during the Calif. gold rush, which missed making a profit with a 289-performance run, although its cast album, featuring "They Call the Wind Maria," was a Top Ten hit.

Lerner and Loewe were approached to create a musical version of George Bernard Shaw's play *Pygmalion* in 1952 but initially were unable to find a way to adapt it and again separated. They resumed their partnership in 1954 and returned to work on it. Meanwhile, *Brigadoon* was released as a film in September 1954, and its soundtrack album reached the charts. The Shaw adaptation, titled *My Fair Lady*, finally opened in 1956, won the Tony Award for Best Musical, and became the longest-running musical in Broadway history up to that time, with 2,717 performances. The show made Julie Andrews a Broadway star, and the cast album hit #1 and stayed in the charts more than nine years, selling six million copies worldwide and becoming the best-selling cast album in history up to that time. Five songs were covered for hits: "On the Street Where You Live" reached the Top Ten for Vic Damone; Sylvia Sims took "I Could Have Danced All Night" into the Top 40; and there were chart entries of "I've Grown Accustomed to Her Face" (as "I've Grown Accustomed to Your Face," by Rosemary Clooney), "With a Little Bit of Luck" (by Percy Faith and His Orch.), and "Get Me to the Church on Time" (by Julius LaRosa).

Lerner and Loewe next turned to writing a movie musical, adapting Colette's novel *Gigi*. The film was released in May 1958 and became one of the top box office hits of the year. It won nine Academy Awards, including Best Picture and Best Song ("Gigi"). The soundtrack LP hit #1 and remained in the charts more than three years; it won the Grammy Award for Best Soundtrack Album.

Loewe suffered a massive heart attack in February 1959 but recovered and collaborated with Lerner on the 1960 musical *Camelot*, based on T. H. White's novel about King Arthur and the Knights of the Round Table, *The Once and Future King*. With a cast including Julie Andrews and newcomer Robert Goulet, the show was the biggest hit of the 1960–61 Broadway season, running 873 performances; its million-selling cast album hit #1 and stayed in the charts more than five years.

Loewe retired from full-time composing but collaborated with Lerner occasionally thereafter. October 1964 saw the release of a lavish two-hour-and-50-minute film version of *My Fair Lady* that won eight Academy Awards, including Best Picture, and was one of the top-grossing films of the year but failed to break even because of its enormous production cost. The million-selling soundtrack album reached the Top Ten and stayed in the charts more than two years, while Andy Williams took a revival of "On the Street Where You Live" into the Top 40. Three years later, an equally sumptuous three-hour film version of *Camelot* was released, and like *My Fair Lady* it lost money despite being one of the highest grossing movie musicals of the decade. But the soundtrack album sold a million copies and stayed in the charts more than a year and a half. *Paint Your Wagon* finally came to the screen in October 1969, although it had been drastically altered from its stage version; the two-and-three-quarter-hour film had a newly written libretto by Lerner and five new songs cowritten by Lerner and André Previn while retaining seven of Loewe's compositions from the original show. It also had a reported budget of $20 million, making it the most expensive movie musical yet. The result was a commercial disaster, but the soundtrack album spent more than a year in the charts and went gold.

Lerner and Loewe reunited for two projects in the 1970s. The first was a 1973 stage version of *Gigi*, for which they wrote five new songs. The show ran only 103 performances but won the Tony Award for Best Score. The second was a 1974 musical film adaptation of Antoine de Saint-Exupery's childrens' story *The Little Prince*, which earned the songwriters Academy Award nominations for their score and the title song.

The major Lerner and Loewe musicals enjoyed frequent revivals for the rest of the century. Michael Johnson finally made "Almost Like Being in Love" a Top 40 hit in 1978. Loewe died of a heart attack in 1988 at 86.

WORKS (only works for which Loewe was a primary, credited composer are listed): **MUSICALS/REVUES/ PLAYS** (dates refer to N.Y. openings): *Petticoat Fever* (March 4, 1935); *Great Lady* (Dec. 1, 1938); *What's Up?* (Nov. 11, 1943); *The Day before Spring* (Nov. 22, 1945); *Brigadoon* (March 13, 1947); *Paint Your Wagon* (Nov. 12, 1951); *My Fair Lady* (March 15, 1956); *Camelot* (Dec. 3, 1960); *Gigi* (Nov. 13, 1973). **FILMS:** *Brigadoon* (1954); *Gigi* (1958); *My Fair Lady* (1964); *Camelot* (1967); *Paint Your Wagon* (1969); *The Little Prince* (1974).

BIBL.: A. Sirmay, ed., *The Lerner and L. Songbook* (N.Y., 1962); G. Lees, *Inventing Champagne: The Worlds of Lerner and L.* (N.Y., 1990).—**WR**

Loewe, (Johann) Carl (Gottfried),

outstanding German composer of lieder; b. Löbejün, near Halle, Nov. 30, 1796; d. Kiel, April 20, 1869. His father, a schoolmaster and cantor, taught him the rudiments of music. When he was 12 he was sent to the Francke Inst. in Halle, where his attractive manner, excellent high voice, and early ability to improvise brought him to the attention of Jérôme Bonaparte, who granted him a stipend of 300 thalers annually until 1813. His teacher was Türk, the head of the Francke Inst.; after Türk's death in 1813, Loewe joined the Singakademie founded by Naue. He also studied theology at the Univ. of Halle, but soon devoted himself entirely to music. He had begun to compose as a boy; under the influence of Zelter, he wrote German ballades, and developed an individual style of great dramatic force and lyrical inspiration; he perfected the genre, and was regarded by many musicians as the greatest song composer after Schubert and before Brahms. His setting of Goethe's *Erlkönig* (1818), which came before the publication of Schubert's great song to the same poem, is one of Loewe's finest creations; other songs that rank among his best are *Edward, Der Wirthin Töchterlein, Der Nöck, Archibald Douglas, Tom der Reimer, Heinrich der Vogler, Oluf,* and *Die verfallene Mühle.* Loewe was personally acquainted with Goethe, and also met Weber. In 1820 he became a schoolmaster at Stettin, and in 1821 music director there and organist at St. Jacobus Cathedral. He lived in Stettin, except for frequent travels, until 1866, when he settled in Kiel. He visited Vienna (1844), London (1847), Sweden and Norway (1851), and Paris (1857), among other places. Loewe was an excellent vocalist, and was able to perform his ballades in public. He publ. the pedagogic works *Gesang-Lehre, theoretisch und practisch für Gymnasien, Seminarien und Bürgerschulen* (Stettin, 1826; 5th ed., 1854), *Musikalischer Gottesdienst: Methodische Anweisung zum Kirchengesang und Orgelspiel* (Stettin, 1851, and subsequent eds.), and *Klavier-und Generalbass-Schule* (Stettin, second ed., 1851). Among his other works are 6 operas: *Die Alpenhütte* (1816), *Rudolf der deutsche Herr* (1825), *Malekadhel* (1832), *Neckereien* (1833), *Die drei Wünsche* (Berlin, Feb. 18, 1834), and *Emmy* (1842). He also composed several cantatas, 2 syms., 2 piano concertos, 4 string quartets, Piano Trio, piano sonatas, and 368 ballades for Voice and Piano. M. Runze ed. a *Gesamtausgabe der Balladen, Legenden, Lieder und Gesange* (17 vols., Leipzig, 1899–1905).

BIBL.: C. Bitter, ed., *Dr. C. L.'s Selbstbiographie* (Berlin, 1870); K. König, *K. L.: Eine aesthetische Beurteilung* (Leipzig, 1884); A. Wellmer, *K. L.: Ein deutscher Komponist* (Leipzig, 1887); M. Runze, *L. redivivus* (Berlin, 1888); A. Bach, *The Art-Ballad: L. and Schubert* (London, 1890; 3rd ed., 1891); M. Runze, *Ludwig Giesebrecht und C. L.* (Berlin, 1894); W. Wossidlo, *C. L. als Balladenkomponist* (Berlin, 1894); A. Niggli, *C. L.* (Zürich, 1897); H. Bulthaupt, *C. L., Deutschlands Balladenkomponist* (Berlin, 1898); H. Draheim, *Goethes Balladen in L.s Komposition* (Langensalza, 1905); K. Anton, *Beiträge zur Biographie C. L.s* (Halle, 1912); H. Kleemann, *Beiträge zur Ästhetik und Geschichte der L.schen Ballade* (diss., Univ. of Halle, 1913); L. Hirschberg, *C. L.s Instrumentalwerke* (Hildburghausen, 1919); O. Altenburg, *C. L.* (Stettin, 1924); H. Engel, *C. L.: Überblick und Würdigung seines Schaffens* (Greifswald, 1934); G. Dallmann, *C. L.: Ein Leben für die Musik: Lebensskizze eines romantischen Musikers* (Gützkow, 1996); H. Kühn, *J.G.C. L.: Ein Lesebuch und eine Materialsammlung zu seiner Biographie* (Halle, 1996); J. Salmon, *The Piano Sonatas of C. L.* (N.Y., 1996).—NS/LK/DM

Loewe, Sophie (Johanna), German soprano; b. Oldenburg, March 24, 1815; d. Budapest, Nov. 28, 1866.

She studied in Vienna with Ciccimarra and in Milan with Lamperti, making her debut as Elisabetta in *Otto mesi in due ore* at Vienna's Kärnthnertortheater in 1832. She sang in London in 1841, the same year she appeared at La Scala in Milan, where she created Donizetti's Maria Padilla; also created Verdi's Elvira in *Ernani* (1844) and Odabella in *Attila* (1846) at the Teatro La Fenice in Venice. She retired from the stage in 1848. —NS/LK/DM

Loewenberg, Alfred, German-born English musicologist; b. Berlin, May 14, 1902; d. London, Dec. 29, 1949. He studied at the univs. of Berlin and Jena (Ph.D., 1925), settling in London in 1934. His unique achievement is the compilation of *Annals of Opera: 1597–1940* (Cambridge, 1943; new ed., Geneva, 1955; rev. and corrected, 1978), tabulating in chronological order the exact dates of first performances and important revivals of some 4,000 operas, with illuminating comments of a bibliographical nature. He also publ. *Early Dutch Librettos and Plays with Music in the British Museum* (London, 1947) and *The Theatre of the British Isles, Excluding London: A Bibliography* (London, 1950).—NS/LK/DM

Lofton, Cripple Clarence (Albert Clemens), boogie-woogie pianist, singer; b. Kingsport, Tenn., March 28, ca. 1896; d. Chicago, Ill., Jan. 9, 1957. A consummate entertainer, he helped to spearhead the boogie-woogie movement in the Windy City, influencing everyone from Meade "Lux" Lewis to John Mayall in the bargain. He lived in Chicago from 1918 and worked professionally during the 1920s and early 1930s, usually as a solo pianist. He left full-time playing, then recommenced regular work until he was knocked down by a taxi in 1940. He occasionally made guest appearances during the last decade of his life.—JC/LP

Logar, Mihovil, Croatian composer; b. Rijieka, Oct. 6, 1902. He went to Prague to study with Jirák and then attended Suk's master classes. In 1927 he settled in Belgrade, where he was a prof. of composition at the Academy of Music (1945–72). In his works, he employed a restrained modern idiom.

WORKS: DRAMATIC: Opera: *Sablazan u dolini šentflorijansko* (Blasphemy in the Valley of St. Florian; 1937); *Pokondirena tikva* (Middle Class Noblewoman; Belgrade, Oct. 20, 1956); *Četrdesetprva* (The Year of 1941; Sarajevo, Feb. 10, 1961). **Ballet:** *Zlatna ribica* (The Golden Fish; Belgrade, Nov. 11, 1953). **ORCH.:** *Rondo rustico* (1945); Violin Concerto (1954); Clarinet Concerto (1956); *Kosmonauti* (Cosmonauts), overture (Belgrade, June 8, 1962); *Sinfonia italiana* (Belgrade, Nov. 24, 1964); *Doppio Concerto* for Clarinet, Horn, and Orch. (Belgrade, April 5, 1968). **OTHER:** Vocal music; piano pieces. —NS/LK/DM

Loggins and Messina, initially formed in 1971 as an informal arrangement of Kenny Loggins with producer Jim Messina, the duo's *Sittin' In* album proved so popular that they formed a road band to tour and record as Loggins and Messina. **MEMBERSHIP:** Kenny Loggins, gtr., voc. (b. Everett, Wash., Jan. 7, 1948); Jim Messina, gtr., bs., voc. (b. Maywood, Calif., Dec. 5, 1947).

Messina was a veteran record engineer, producer, and former member of two of America's early country-rock bands, the Buffalo Springfield and Poco, whereas Loggins was a professional songwriter. With Messina providing the harder-edged songs and Loggins gentle, melodic classics such as "Danny's Song" and "A Love Song," Loggins and Messina enjoyed considerable success as an album act until their breakup in 1976. As a solo act Loggins became one of the most popular singer-songwriters of the 1980s, establishing himself with both FM radio and easy-listening audiences.

Jim Messina formed several surf bands while still in high school and later recorded an obscure surf-and-dragster album in 1964. After high school he moved to Hollywood, where he learned the fundamentals of studio engineering at Harmony Recorders and Sunset Sound. Messina was introduced to the burgeoning local folk-rock scene when David Crosby asked him to record Joni Mitchell's first demonstration tape. Word of Messina's prowess as an engineer made its way to Neil Young, who enlisted Messina for "Hung Upside Down" and "Broken Arrow" from *Buffalo Springfield Again*. With the departure of Bruce Palmer, Messina was recruited to play bass for the Buffalo Springfield, and to engineer and produce *Last Time Around*, to which he contributed "Carefree Country Day."

The stormy career of the Buffalo Springfield ended in summer 1968, and members Messina and Richie Furay formed Poco, with Messina staying on for the group's first three albums. Leaving Poco in November 1970, Messina became a staff producer at Columbia Records. The following month he met songwriter Kenny Loggins. Loggins had grown up in the Los Angeles suburb of Alhambra and started singing as a child. He took up guitar in high school and performed in the bands Gator Creek and Second Helping, later dropping out of Pasadena City Coll. to concentrate on songwriting. Serving as a staff writer for ABC/Wingate, Loggins saw one of his compositions, "House at Pooh Corner," become a minor hit for the Nitty Gritty Dirt Band in early 1971.

Jim Messina was assigned to produce Kenny Loggins's debut solo album for Columbia, but Messina suggested that they record it together, with Messina informally *Sittin' In*. The album yielded the minor hit "Vahevala" and contained excellent songs by both artists, including Messina's "Nobody but You" and "Peace of Mind," and Loggins's "House at Pooh Corner" and the gently celebratory "Danny's Song," a near-smash hit for Anne Murray in early 1973. *Sittin' In* sold so well (staying on the album charts more than two years) that Loggins and Messina decided to join forces, officially inaugurating their duo career with *Loggins and Messina*. That album included the smash hit "Your Mama Can't Dance" (cowritten by the two), the major hit "Thinking of You" (by Messina), and the duo's "Angry Eyes."

Touring regularly, Loggins and Messina eventually played more than seven hundred engagements in five years. *Full Sail* produced their last major hit, "My Music," and contained Loggins's "Love Song" and Messina's "You Need a Man." After *Mother Lode*, which yielded minor hits with "Changes" and "Growin'," and *Native Sons*, Loggins and Messina agreed to part com-

pany, completing their farewell tour in September 1976. Columbia soon issued the anthology set *The Best of Friends*.

Jim Messina eventually recorded three solo albums. Kenny Loggins quickly recorded his solo debut album, *Celebrate Me Home*, for Columbia. The album yielded a minor hit with "I Believe in Love," and Loggins toured as opening act to Fleetwood Mac in 1977. He performed at a wide variety of venues, including auditoriums, supper clubs, and casinos, in support of 1978's *Nightwatch*, which produced a smash hit with "Whenever I Call You Friend," cowritten with Melissa Manchester and sung as a rather incongruous duet with Fleetwood Mac's Stevie Nicks. *Keep the Fire* yielded a moderate hit with the title song and a near-smash with "This Is It," with Michael McDonald on backing vocal.

During the 1980s Kenny Loggins initiated a highly successful career as a soundtrack performer with the near-smash "I'm Alright" from the movie *Caddyshack*. Following the major hits "Don't Fight It" (cowritten and sung with Journey's Steve Perry), "Heart to Heart" (with backing vocals by Michael McDonald), and "Welcome to Heartlight," Loggins scored two bits from the movie *Footloose*, the top hit title song and the major hit "I'm Free (Heaven Helps the Man)." The Tom Cruise movie *Top Gun* included the Loggins's smash "Danger Zone," whereas Sylvester Stallone's *Over the Top* produced the major hit "Meet Me Halfway," and *Caddyshack II* the near-smash "Nobody's Fool." The latter two hits were also included on *Back to Avalon*, which yielded minor hits with "I'm Gonna Miss You" and "Tell Her," a remake of the Exciters' 1963 hit "Tell Him."

Loggins's 1991 album *Leap of Faith* produced hits with "Real Thing," "If You Believe," and "Conviction of the Heart," an environmental song featured in campaigns in American public schools and used by the National Park Service. Kenny Loggins's *Outside from the Redwoods* was recorded with Michael McDonald and Shanice, and his 1994 album *Return to Pooh Corner* produced a major easy listening hit with the title song.

DISC.: **KENNY LOGGINS AND JIM MESSINA:** *Sittin' In* (1972); *L. and M.* (1972); *Full Sail* (1973); *On Stage* (1974); *Mother Lode* (1974); *So Fine* (1975); *Native Sons* (1976); *The Best of Friends* (1976); *Finale* (1977). **KENNY LOGGINS:** *Celebrate Me Home* (1977); *Nightwatch* (1978); *Keep the Fire* (1979); *Alive* (1980); *High Adventure* (1982); *Vox Humana* (1985); *Back to Avalon* (1988); *Leap of Faith* (1991); *Outside from the Redwoods* (1993); *Return to Pooh Corner* (1994). **JIM MESSINA:** *Oasis* (1979); *Messina* (1981); *One More Mile* (1983).—**BH**

Logier, Johann Bernhard, German pianist, teacher, inventor, and composer; b. Kassel, Feb. 9, 1777; d. Dublin, July 27, 1846. After studying with his father, he went to England in 1791. In 1794 he became a flutist in the Marquis of Abercorn's regimental band, and later its music director. He continued in that capacity afer it was removed to Ireland. Following his discharge in 1807, he conducted a band in Kilkenny and at the Royal Hiberian Theatre in Dublin. He ran his own music store (1810–17) and was active as a teacher. Logier invented the chiroplast or hand-director for holding the hands in the most convenient positions during piano practice. He patented his invention in 1814 and promoted it with fanatic persistence in the face of great controversy. It enjoyed great success in England and Germany. After teaching his method in Berlin (1822–26), he was active in London (1826–29) before settling in Dublin. Logier also promoted the practice of group piano teaching. In reply to numerous polemical attacks on his method, he publ. equally bitter assaults on his detractors.

WRITINGS (all publ. in London unless otherwise given): *An Explanation and Description of the Royal Patent Chiroplast, or Hand-Director for Pianoforte* (1814?; second ed., 1816); *A Companion to the Royal Patent Chiroplast* (1815?); *Sequel to the Chiroplast Companion* (1815?); *Logier's Theoretical and Practical Studies for the Pianoforte* (1816); *An Authentic Account of the Examination of Pupils Instructed on the New System of Musical Education, by J.B. Logier* (1818); *A Refutation of the Fallacies and Misrepresentations* (1818); *Logier's Thorough-bass* (1818); *System der Musik-Wissenschaft und der praktischen Komposition mit Inbegriff dessen was gewöhnlich unter dem Ausdruck General-Bass verstehen wird* (Berlin, 1827; Eng. tr., 1827); *Nachträgliche Sammlung von Aufgaben und Beispielen zu J.B. Logier's System der Musik-Wissenschaft und der praktischen Komposition* (Berlin, 1827).

BIBL.: G. Pügner, *J.B. L.: Ein Musikerzieher des 19. Jahrhunderts* (diss., Univ. of Leipzig, 1959).—NS/LK/DM

Logothetis, Anestis, Bulgarian-born Austrian composer of Greek parentage; b. Burgas, Oct. 27, 1921; d. Lainz, Jan. 6, 1994. He went to Vienna in 1942 and studied at the Technischen Hochschule until 1944, and then received training in theory and composition from Ratz and Uhl and in piano and conducting from Swarowsky at the Academy of Music, graduating in 1951. In 1952 he became a naturalized Austrian citizen. He worked with Koenig at the electronic music studio of the West German Radio in Cologne (1957). In 1960 and 1963 he was awarded the Theodor Körner Prize; in 1986 he received the honorary gold medal of the city of Vienna. He exhibited in Vienna galleries a series of polymorphic graphs capable of being performed as music by optional instrumental groups. He employed a highly personalized "integrating" musical notation, making use of symbols, signs, and suggestive images, playing on a performer's psychological associations.

WORKS: DRAMATIC: O p e r a : *Daidalia* (1976–78); *Waraus ist der Stein des Sisyphos?* (1982–84). M u s i c T h e a t e r : *Im Gespinst* (1976). M u s i c a l R a d i o P l a y s : *Anastasis* (1969); *Manratellurium* (1970); *Kybernetikon* (1971–72); *Kerbtierparty* (1972–73); *Sommervögel* or *Schmetterlinge* (1973); *Menetekel* (1974); *Vor! stell! Unk!* (1980); *Bienen' Binom* (1980). B a l l e t : *Himmelsmechanik* (1960); *5 Porträts der Liebe* (1960); *Odyssee* (1963). ORCH.: *Agglomeration* for Violin and Orch. (1960); *Koordination* for 5 Orch. Groups (1960); *Kulmination I* and *II* for 2 Orch. Groups (1961); *Mäandros* (1963); *Dynapolis* (1963); *Seismographie I* and *II* (1964); *Enoseis* (1965); *Diffusion* (1965); *Linienmodulationen* (1965); *Integration* (1966); *Enklaven* (1966); *Oasi* (1967); *Desmotropie* (1967); *Polychronon* (1967); *Styx* for Plucked Strings (1968); *Zonen* (1969); *Mensuren* for Chamber Orch. (1969); *Kollisionen 70* (1970); *Komplementäres* (1970); *Klangräume I, II,* and *III* (1972); *Wellen* (1972); *Volant* (1972); *Ghia tin ora* (1975); *Geomusik 76* for Clarinet and Orch. (1976); *Rondo* (1979); *Brunnenburg-Hochzeit- Symphionetten* (1981); *Meridiane I*

und Breitengrade (1981). O T H E R : Many works for variable instrumentation; chamber pieces; piano music; *Wellenformen 1981*, computer piece.—NS/LK/DM

Logroscino, Nicola Bonifacio, Italian composer; b. Bitonto (baptized), Oct. 22, 1698; d. Palermo, after 1765. He was a pupil of Veneziano and Perugino (1714–27) at the Cons. di S. Maria di Loreto in Naples. From 1728 to 1731 he was organist at Conza (Avellino); then was active in Naples to about 1756. He subsequently went to Palermo, where he taught at the Ospedale dei Figliuoli Dispersi (c. 1758–64). Of his many works, the comic opera *Il Governatore* (Naples, Carnival 1747) and the heroic opera *Giunio Bruto* (Rome, Jan. 1748) are the only 2 in which the music is extant in full.

BIBL.: U. Prota-Giurleo, *N. L.: "il dio dell'opera buffa'"* (Naples, 1927). M. Belluci La Salandra, *Triade musicale Bitontina, Brevi cenni biografici di N.B. L., 1698–1760* (Bitonto, 1936). —NS/LK/DM

Löhlein, Georg Simon, German music theorist and composer; b. Neustadt an der Heide, near Coburg (baptized), July 16, 1725; d. Danzig, Dec. 16, 1781. On account of his tall stature (6 feet, 2 inches), he was seized on a journey and forced into the Prussian Guard when he was 16; he was stationed at Potsdam and served at the palace of Frederick the Great. He was severely wounded at the battle of Collin (1757) during the Seven Years' War, but recovered. He then studied at the Univ. of Jena (1760), where he was made director of its Academy Concerts and principal of the Collegium Musicum (1761); subsequently studied philosophy, ethics, and poetry at the Univ. of Leipzig (1763), and also received instruction in music from J.A. Hiller. He served as music director of the Grosses Konzert there. He became Kapellmeister at Danzig's Marienkirche (1781), but suffered from the rigors of the climate, and died a few months after his arrival. Löhlein wrote a Singspiel, *Zemire und Azor* (Leipzig, 1775), several instrumental concertos, chamber music, etc., but he became known mainly through his pedagogical work, *Clavier-Schule* (2 vols., Leipzig and Züllichau, 1765 and 1781; many subsequent eds.). He also publ. *Anweisung zum Violinspielen...mit 24 kleinen Duetten erläutert* (Leipzig and Züllichau, 1774; 3rd ed., aug., 1797 by J. Reichardt).

BIBL.: F. von Glasenapp, *G.S. L.* (Halle, 1937). —NS/LK/DM

Löhner, Johann, German organist, tenor, and composer; b. Nuremberg (baptized), Nov. 21, 1645; d. there, April 2, 1705. After the death of his parents, he was adopted by his brother-in-law, G.C. Wecker, who made it possible for him to study music. He was active in Nuremberg as an organist and tenor in various churches, where he was made organist of the Spitalkirche in 1682 and then of St. Lorenz in 1694. He composed over 300 songs for devotional use in the home, the most important of which are found in his collection *Auserlesene Kirch-und Tafel-Musik* for Voice, 2 Violins, and Basso Continuo (Nuremberg, 1682). Löhner also composed 3 operas, but only 2 collections of arias are extant.—LK/DM

Löhse, Otto, German conductor and composer; b. Dresden, Sept. 21, 1858; d. Baden-Baden, May 5, 1925. He was a pupil at the Dresden Cons. of Richter (piano), Grützmacher (cello), Draeseke, Kretschmer, and Rischbieter (theory), and Wüllner (conducting). He began his conducting career in Riga (1882); was first conductor there (1889–93). In 1893 he was in Hamburg, where he married Katharina Klafsky. In 1895–96 both artists were members of the Damrosch Opera Co. in N.Y., with Lohse as conductor. From 1897 to 1904, Löhse conducted opera in Strasbourg; from 1904 to 1911, in Cologne; from 1911 to 1912, at the Théâtre Royal de la Monnaie in Brussels; from 1912 to 1923, at the Leipzig Stadttheater; from 1923 to 1925, in Baden-Baden. He composed an opera, *Der Prinz wider Willen* (Riga, 1890), and songs.

BIBL.: E. Lert, *O. L.* (Leipzig, 1918).—NS/LK/DM

Lokshin, Alexander, Russian composer; b. Biisk, Altai Region, Sept. 19, 1920; d. Moscow, June 11, 1987. He studied with Miaskovsky at the Moscow Cons. (graduated, 1941). The major portion of his output is devoted to his 11 syms., 10 of them vocal, which promote their often poetic and profound expressions through a unique blend of lyricism and contemporary compositional techniques.

WORKS: ORCH.: *Wait for Me*, symphonic poem for Voice and Orch. (1943); *Hungarian Fantasia* for Violin and Orch. (1952); 11 syms.: No. 1, *Requiem*, for Chorus and Orch. (1958), No. 2, *Greek Epigrams*, for Voices and Orch., after ancient Greek poets (1963), No. 3 for Baritone, Men's Chorus, and Orch., after Kipling (1966), No. 4, *Sinfonia stretta* (1967), No. 5, *Sonnets for Shakespeare*, for Baritone, Harp, and Strings (1969), No. 6 for Baritone, Chorus, and Orch., after Alexander Blok (1971), No. 7 for Contralto and Chamber Orch., after Japanese poets of the 7th to the 13th century (1972), No. 8 for Tenor and Orch., after Pushkin (1973), No. 9 for Baritone and Strings, after Martynow (1975), No. 10 for Contralto, Organ, and Orch., after Zabolotsky (1976), and No. 11 for Soprano and Chamber Orch., after Camoëns (1977); *Speaking Out Loud*, symphonic poem for Bass, Organ, and Orch., after Mayakovsky (1968). CHAMBER: *Variations* for Piano (1953); Clarinet Quintet (1955); String Quintet (1978). VOCAL: *The Giant Cockroach*, comic oratorio (1962); *Songs of Margaret* for Soprano and Chamber Orch., after Goethe's *Faust* (1973); *Mater dolorosa*, cantata (1977).—NS/LK/DM

Lolli, Antonio, notable Italian violinist and composer; b. Bergamo, c. 1725; d. Palermo, Aug. 10, 1802. He was named solo violinist to the court of the Duke of Württemberg in Stuttgart in 1758. He also commenced touring as a virtuoso, appearing with great success in Vienna (c. 1760) and at the Concert Spirituel in Paris (1764, 1766). As a result of incurring debts, the Stuttgart court allowed him to tour extensively in order to recoup his losses. His tours took him to Frankfurt am Main and Utrecht (1769), Italy (1771), and northern Germany (1773). Lolli's Stuttgart contract was abrogated due to his debts in 1774. He then went to St. Petersburg, where he was a favorite of Catherine II in the capacity of chamber virtuoso (1774–83). He also found favor with Potemkin. Lolli continued to tour, and absented himself from the court between 1777 and 1780. Having dissi-

pated 10,000 florins he had accumulated from gambling, he returned to St. Petersburg in 1780 and succeeded in regaining his social and artistic position. He appeared in concerts at Potemkin's palace there, and also in Moscow. Despite his frequent derelictions of duty, he was retained at the court until his contract was terminated in 1783. In 1784 he gave his last public concerts in Russia. He then appeared in Stockholm, Hamburg, and Copenhagen (1784), London (1785), and Italy. After visits to Copenhagen, Hamburg, and Stettin (1791), Palermo (1793), and Vienna (1794), he settled in Palermo, where he spent his last years in poverty. Lolli was greatly admired for his commanding technique as a virtuoso, and his violin concertos and sonatas were widely admired in his day.

WORKS: ORCH: Violin Concertos (all publ. in Paris): *Deux concerto*, op.2 (1764); (2) Concerto, op.4 (1766); (2) Concerto, op.5 (1768); *Septième concerto* (1775); *Huitième concerto* (1776); etc. CHAMBER: *Sei sonate* for Violin and Bass, op.1 (Amsterdam, 1760?); *Sei sonate* for Violin and Bass, op.2 (Amsterdam, 1769); *Sei sonate* for Violin and Bass, op.3 (Paris, c. 1767); *Cinq sonates & un divertissement* for Violin and Bass, op.3 (Berlin, 1776); 6 sonates for 2 Violins, op.9 (Paris, c. 1785).

BIBL.: N. Nunamaker, *The Virtuoso Violin Concerto Before Paganini: The Concertos of L., Giornovicchi and Waldemar* (diss., Ind. Univ., 1968).—NS/LK/DM

Lomakin, Gavriil Yakimovich, Russian singer, choral conductor, teacher, and composer; b. Boriskovka, April 6, 1812; d. Gatchina, May 21, 1885. At 10, he entered the choir of Count Sheremetev in St. Petersburg, where he received training in theory from Sapienza. In 1830 he became a singing teacher with the choir, and later was its director (1850–72). He also served as conductor of the court chapel (1848–59). With Balakirev, he established the Free Music School in 1862 and was head of the singing classes until 1870. He publ. a singing tutor (St. Petersburg, 1858; 3rd ed., 1882), and composed sacred songs and made choral arrangements of early Russian hymns.—NS/LK/DM

Lomax, Alan, American ethnomusicologist, son of **John Avery Lomax**; b. Austin, Tex., Jan. 31, 1915. He acquired his métier from his father, then studied at Harvard Univ. (1932–33), the Univ. of Tex. in Austin (B.A., 1936), and at Columbia Univ. (graduate work in anthropology, 1939). He joined his father as a researcher in 1933, and they collected folk songs in the Southwestern and Midwestern regions of the U.S. They also supervised field recordings of rural and prison songs, discovering Leadbelly; they also "discovered" Jelly Roll Morton and recorded interviews with him at the Library of Congress in Washington, D.C. (1938). He also collected folk songs in Europe. In 1963 he was made director of the Bureau of Applied Social Research; also of the cantometrics project at Columbia Univ. (1963). Among his eds., compiled with his father, are *American Ballads and Folksongs* (N.Y., 1934); *Negro Folk Songs as Sung by Leadbelly* (N.Y., 1936); *Our Singing Country* (N.Y., 1941); *Folk Song: U.S.A.* (N.Y., 1947; fourth ed., 1954); *Leadbelly: A Collection of World Famous Songs* (N.Y., 1959; second ed., aug., 1965 as *The Leadbelly Legend*); he also prepared *The Folk Songs of North America in the English Language* (N.Y., 1960); *The Penguin Book of American Folk Songs* (Harmondsworth, 1966); *Hard-Hitting Songs for Hard-Hit People* (N.Y., 1967); *Folk Song Style and Culture* (Washington, D.C., 1968).

WRITINGS: With S. Cowell, *American Folk Song and Folk Lore: A Regional Bibliography* (N.Y., 1942); *Mr. Jelly Roll* (N.Y., 1950; second ed., 1973); *Harriett and Her Harmonium* (London, 1955); *The Rainbow Sign* (N.Y., 1959); *Cantometrics: A Handbook and Training Method* (Berkeley, 1976); *Index of World Song* (N.Y., 1977); *The Land Where the Blues Began* (N.Y., 1993).—**NS/LK/DM**

Lomax, John Avery, American ethnomusicologist, father of **Alan Lomax**; b. Goodman, Miss., Sept. 23, 1867; d. Greenville, Miss., Jan. 26, 1948. He began collecting and notating American folk songs in his early youth. He studied music at the Univ. of Tex. in Austin, and founded the Tex. Folklore Soc. In 1933 his son joined him in his research; for the eds. they publ., see the entry on his son. He publ. an autobiography, *Adventures of a Ballad Hunter* (N.Y., 1947).

BIBL.: N. Porterfield, *Last Cavalier: The Life and Times of J.A. L., 1867–1948* (Urbana, Ill., 1996).—**NS/LK/DM**

Lombard, Alain, French conductor; b. Paris, Oct. 4, 1940. He was only 9 when he entered Poulet's conducting class at the Paris Cons., making his debut with the Pasdeloup Orch. when he was 11; later studied with Fricsay. He conducted at the Lyons Opera (1960–64), and won the gold medal at the Mitropoulos Competition in N.Y. (1966). He then was music director of the Miami Phil. (1966–74). He made his Metropolitan Opera debut in N.Y. conducting *Faust* on Dec. 24, 1966, and continued to appear there until 1973. He was chief conductor of the Strasbourg Phil. (1972–83), artistic director of the Opera du Rhin (1974–80), and music director of the Paris Opéra (1981–83). From 1988 to 1995 he was artistic director of the Orchestre National Bordeaux Aquitaine.—**NS/LK/DM**

Lombardi, Luca, Italian composer and teacher; b. Rome, Dec. 24, 1945. He was educated at the Univ. of Vienna and the Univ. of Rome (graduated with a thesis on Eisler; publ. in Milan, 1978). He also studied composition with Renzi, Lupi, and Porena at the Pesaro Cons. (graduated, 1970). He also was in Cologne to take courses with Zimmermann and Globokar (1968–72) and to attend the courses in new music with Stockhausen, Pousseur, Kagel, Schnebel, and Rzewski (1968–70). After training in electronic music from Eimert in Cologne and Koenig in Utrecht, he studied with Dessau in Berlin (1973). He taught composition at the Pesaro Cons. (1973–78) and the Milan Cons. (1978–93). From 1983 to 1986 he was one of the artistic directors of the Cantiere Internazionale d'Arte in Montepulciano. With W. Gieseler and R. Weyer, he publ. the orchestration treatise *Instrumentation in der Musik des 20. Jahrhunderts* (Celle, 1985). In his compositions, he pursues an advanced course notable for its eclectic stylistic manifestations.

WORKS: DRAMATIC: O p e r a : *Faust, un travestimento* (1986–90; Basel, Dec. 21, 1991). **ORCH.:** 3 syms.: No. 1 (1974–75), No. 2 (1981), and No. 3 for Soprano, Baritone, Chorus, and Orch. (1992–93); *Variazioni* (1977); *Tre pezzi* for 2 Pianos and Chamber Orch. (1978–87; Cologne, Oct. 25, 1987); *Framework* for 2 Pianos and Orch. (1983); *Due Ritratti* (1987–88; Lugano, June 13, 1989); *Con Faust* (1990); *La Notte di Valpurga* for Orch. and Chorus ad libitum (1990); *Atropos* (Milan, April 20, 1991); Viola Concerto (1995). **CHAMBER:** *Elegia* for Violin and Piano (1965); *Proporzioni* for 4 Trombones (1968–69); *Non Requiescat* for 13 Instruments (1973); *Canzone* for 13 Instruments (1974–75); *Essay I* for Double Bass (1975) and *II* for Bass Clarinet (1979); *Gespräch über Bäume* for 9 Instrumentalists (1976); *Einklang* for Oboe and 7 Instruments (1980); *Winterblumen* for Flute and Harp (1982); *Sie bagatelle di fine estate* for 1 to 11 Instrumentalists (1983); *Schattenspiel* for Bass Flute (1983); *Sisyphos I* for 8 Instruments (1983) and *II* for 14 Instruments (1984); *Thamar y Amnòn* for Guitar (1983); *Schegge* for Flute, Clarinet, and Horn (1984); *Mirium* for 4 Trombones (1984); *Sisifo felice* for 8 Instruments (1985); *Ai piedo del faro* for Double Bass and 8 Instruments (1986); *Für Flori* for Violin and Piano (1990); *Psalmus VI di Josquin Desprez* for 9 Instruments (1991); String Quartet (1991–92); *Jahreswechsel* for 16 Instruments (1994); *Gruss* for Cello (1994); piano pieces. **VOCAL:** *Hasta que caigan las puertas del odio* for 16 Voices (1976–77); *Alle fronde dei salici* for 12 Voices (1977); *Mayakowski*, cantata for Bass, Chorus, and 7 Instruments (1979–80); *Mythenasche* for Soprano, Baritone, Chorus, and Orch. (1980–81); *Ophelia-Fragmente* for Soprano and Piano (1982; Berlin, Feb. 21, 1983); *Nel tuo porto quiete*, requiem for Soprano, Bass, Chorus, and Orch. (1984); *Canto di Eros* for 5 Voices (Cologne, April 29, 1986); *La canzone di Greta* for Soprano and String Quartet (RAI, Rome, May 11, 1987); *Ein Lied* for Soprano and 3 Instruments (1988; Berlin, Feb. 26, 1989); *Sisyphos III* for Reciter and Ensemble (1988–89; Frankfurt am Main, March 3, 1989); *Tum Balalaike* for Soprano and 3 Instruments (1988–89; Witten, April 21, 1989); *Giocate al giuoco mio, grassi giganti* for Chorus (1992); *A chi fa notte il giorno* for Reciter and Double Bass (1993); *Yedid Nefesh* for Mezzo-soprano and Guitar (1994). —**NS/LK/DM**

Lombardo, Guy (actually, **Gaetano Alberto**), Canadian-born American bandleader; b. London, Ontario, June 19, 1902; d. Houston, Nov. 5, 1977. Lombardo's Royal Canadians were the most popular big band on records in the 1930s, and, with sales of upwards of 100 million records, among the most successful recording artists of the first half of the 20th century. Anchored by the Lombardo brothers—Guy, Carmen, Lebert, and Victor—the Royal Canadians were a remarkably stable unit, many of the members staying for most or all of the group's 50 continuous years of prominence. Their music was just as stable, the epitome of the "sweet" band sound of the 1920s and 1930s, with melody preeminent and carried largely by vibrato-laden saxophones, and tempos that were danceable without being frantic. This identifiable sound brought them 26 years' worth of hits, the biggest of which were "Charmaine!" (1927), "September in the Rain" (1937), and "The Third Man Theme" (1950). The group's annual New Year's Eve performances on radio and television, culminating in midnight performances of their theme song, "Auld Lang Syne," defined the holiday.

Lombardo's parents were Gaetano Lombardo, an Italian-born tailor, and Angelina Paladino Lombardo. Encouraged by his parents, Lombardo began to study violin as a child; he attended St. Peter's Catholic School in London, Ontario, from 1909 to 1920. At the age of 12 he formed a band with his brothers Carmen on flute and Lebert on drums, and with Fred Kreitzer on piano. By the time he was 21 the band had nine members and was called The Lombardo Brothers Orch. Carmen had switched to saxophone and become musical director, Lebert was playing trumpet, and the band also included drummer George Gowans, trombonist Jim Dillon, and guitarist Muff Henry, all of whom would stay with it for decades. Long-time members Fred Higman (sax), Bernard Davies (tuba), and Larry Owen (sax, clarinet, arrangements) joined later.

The group came to the U.S. in 1924, settling in Cleveland, and broadcast over local radio station WTAM, then appeared at the Claremont Café where they were billed as Guy Lombardo and His Royal Canadians; later, they had a residency at the Music Box restaurant. Lombardo married Lilliebell Glenn on Sept. 9, 1926.

The Lombardo orchestra had made its first recordings for tiny Gennett Records in 1924. By 1927 the group had achieved enough prominence to earn a contract with Columbia Records, a major label, and "Charmaine!" (music by Erno Rapee, lyrics by Lew Pollack) became their first best-seller in October. Meanwhile, Carmen Lombardo had become the band's vocalist. He also wrote many of the songs the orchestra played.

Guy Lombardo and His Royal Canadians moved to Chicago, opening at the Granada Café in October 1927. On Nov. 16 they began to broadcast from the club on WBBW, and other stations soon signed on, forming a network and vastly increasing the band's renown. They had a second top-selling record with "Sweethearts on Parade" (music by Carmen Lombardo, lyrics by Charles Newman) in January 1929.

On Oct. 3, 1929, the Royal Canadians moved to the Roosevelt Hotel Grill in N.Y., which would be their headquarters for much of the next 33 years. Since their radio show was sponsored by Robert Burns Panatella Cigars, they adopted as their theme song "Auld Lang Syne," an 18th-century Scottish tune with words by poet Robert Burns; when they played it on New Year's Eve, 1929, they began a tradition. (The youngest Lombardo brother, Victor, joined the band on saxophone in 1930.)

The Royal Canadians became the best-selling band of the early 1930s, their major hits including "You're Driving Me Crazy! (What Did I Do?)" (music and lyrics by Walter Donaldson; December 1930), "By the River Sainte Marie" (music by Harry Warren, lyrics by Edgar Leslie; March 1931), "(There Ought to Be a) Moonlight Saving Time" (music and lyrics by Irving Kahal and Harry Richman; June 1931), "Good Night, Sweetheart" (music and lyrics by Ray Noble, James Campbell, Reg Connelly, and Rudy Vallée; December 1931), "River, Stay 'Way from My Door" (vocals by Kate Smith; music by Harry Woods, lyrics by Mort Dixon; January 1932), "Too Many Tears" (music by Warren, lyrics by Al Dubin; March 1932), "Paradise" (music by Nacio Herb Brown, lyrics by Brown and Gordon Clifford; May 1932), "We Just Couldn't Say Goodbye" (music and lyrics by Woods; August 1932), "You're Getting to Be a Habit with Me" (vocals by Bing Crosby; music by Warren,

lyrics by Dubin; March 1933), and "The Last Round-Up" (music and lyrics by Billy Hill; November 1933).

For three years starting in 1933, Lombardo and The Royal Canadians moved to the West Coast, appearing at the Cocoanut Grove in L. A. While there, they made their first film appearance in *Many Happy Returns* (though the music was dubbed by Duke Ellington and His Orch.!), released in June 1934. Their biggest hit of the year came in November with "Stars Fell on Alabama" (music by Frank Perkins, lyrics by Mitchell Parish).

Lombardo's first entry on the newly created hit parade in April 1935 was "What's the Reason?" (music and lyrics by Coy Poe, Jimmie Grier, Truman "Pinky" Tomlin, and Earl Hatch); it went to the top in May. Lombardo returned to the #1 spot with "Red Sails in the Sunset" (music by Will Grosz, lyrics by Jimmy Kennedy) in November. In 1936 he topped the hit parade with "Lost" (music by Phil Ohman, lyrics by Johnny Mercer and Macy O. Teetor) in April and with "When Did You Leave Heaven?" (music by Richard A. Whiting, lyrics by Walter Bullock) in October.

In 1937, the year he became an American citizen, Lombardo had an amazing six #1 records on the hit parade, four of which were among the ten biggest hits of the year, including the two most popular songs. "When My Dreamboat Comes Home" (music and lyrics by Cliff Friend and Dave Franklin) had a week at the top in March; "Boo Hoo" (music by John Jacob Loeb and Carmen Lombardo, lyrics by Edward Heyman), the fifth biggest hit of the year, was #1 for six weeks in April and May; "September in the Rain" (music by Warren, lyrics by Dubin), the biggest hit of the year, took over the top spot for five weeks in May and June; "It Looks Like Rain in Cherry Blossom Time" (music by Joe Burke, lyrics by Edgar Leslie), the second biggest hit of the year, spent six weeks at #1 in July and August; "Sailboat in the Moonlight" (music and lyrics by John Jacob Loeb and Carmen Lombardo), the sixth biggest hit of the year, had three weeks on top of the hit parade in August; and "So Rare" (music by Jerry Herst, lyrics by Jack Sharpe) was #1 for a week in September.

In the wave of sweet swing bands influenced by the Royal Canadians, Lombardo was unable to maintain his dominance of the record charts in the late 1930s; he returned to #1 in April 1944 with "It's Love-Love-Love" (music and lyrics by Alex Kramer, Joan Whitney, and Mack David) and in March 1947 with "Managua—Nicaragua" (music by Irving Fields, lyrics by Albert Gamse), and his recordings of "Humoresque" (music by Anton Dvorák; 1944), "Christmas Island" (music and lyrics by Lyle Moraine; vocals by The Andrews Sisters; 1946), and "Easter Parade" (music and lyrics by Irving Berlin; 1947) were reported to be million-sellers. He also had three Top Ten albums in the late 1940s, *Lombardoland* (1946), *Guy Lombardo Featuring the Twin Pianos* (1947), and *Lombardo—Waltzes* (1947).

Lombardo enjoyed his last #1 hit, and the biggest hit of his long career, with the million-seller "The Third Man Theme" (music by Anton Karas) in May 1950. Two of his albums, *Guy Lombardo Featuring the Twin*

Pianos—Vol. 2 and *Guy Lombardo and His Royal Canadians Silver Jubilee, 1925–50,* were Top Ten hits during the year.

Lombardo branched out into television in 1953, hosting the music show *Guy Lombardo & His Royal Canadians* on a local station in N.Y., and he took his New Year's Eve broadcast to TV for the first time in 1954. That year he also began producing musical shows at an outdoor theater at Jones Beach on Long Island, continuing for 24 summers. His nationally broadcast TV series *Guy Lombardo's Diamond Jubilee* ran during the spring of 1956. He returned to the album charts with *Your Guy Lombardo Medley* in 1957 and *Berlin by Lombardo* in 1958.

Lombardo moved his New Year's Eve appearance from the Roosevelt Hotel to the Waldorf-Astoria in 1962 (and ushered in 1964 from Grand Central Station), but otherwise his activities remained unchanged through the 1960s. The band suffered a major loss when Carmen Lombardo died in 1971, but Guy Lombardo continued to lead it until his own death from a heart attack at the age of 75, after which it continued for a time under the leadership of Lebert Lombardo, and then Lebert's son Bill.

WRITINGS: With J. Altshul, *Auld Acquaintance: An Autobiography* (Garden City, N.Y., 1975).

BIBL.: B. Herndon, *The Sweetest Music This Side of Heaven: The Story of G. L.* (N.Y., 1964); B. Cline, *The L. Story* (Don Mills, Ontario, 1979); S. Richman, *G.: The Life and Times of G. L.* (N.Y., 1980).—**WR**

Lomon, Ruth, Canadian-born American composer, pianist, and teacher; b. Montreal, Nov. 8, 1930. She studied at McGill Univ. in Montreal. In 1960 she went to the U.S. and continued her training with Frances Judd Cooke and Miklos Schwalb at the New England Cons. of Music in Boston. In 1964 she took a course with Lutoslawski at the Dartington Summer School of Music in England, and she also attended the Darmstadt summer courses in new music. In 1965 she became a naturalized American citizen. From 1971 to 1983 she was half of the duo-piano team of Lomon and Wenglin, specializing in the performance of works by women composers. Several of her most important works have been inspired by Native American ceremonials.

WORKS: DRAMATIC: Chamber Opera: *The Fisherman and His Soul* (1963). **ORCH.:** Bassoon Concerto (1979; rev. 1993); *Terra Incognita* (1993). **CHAMBER:** Trio for Horn, Cello, and Piano (1961); *Dialogue* for Vibraphone and Harpsichord (1964); *Shapes* for Violin, Cello, Guitar, and Piano (1964); *Phase I* for Cello and Piano (1969); *The Furies: Erinnyes* for Oboe, Oboe d'Amore, and English Horn (1977); *Equinox* for Brass (1978); *Solstice* for Brass Quartet (1978); *Celebrations* for 2 Harps (1978); *Vitruvian Scroll* for String Quartet (1981); *Diptych* for Woodwind Quintet (1983); *Iatiku:"bringing to life..."* for Bass Clarinet, Marimba, Vibes, Harp, Harpsichord, and Piano (1983); *Janus* for String Quartet (1984); *Desiderata* for Oboe, Marimba, and Optional Bow Chime (1984); *Spells* for Piano, Woodwind Quintet, String Quartet, Trumpet, and Percussion (1985); *Imprints,* concerto for Piano and 4 Percussion (1987; Columbus, Ohio, May 15, 1989); *The Talisman* for B-flat and Bass Clarinets, Violin, Viola, Cello, and Synthesizer (1988; Boston, Feb. 12, 1989); *The Butterfly Effect* for String Quartet (1989); *Shadowing* for Piano Quartet (1993). **KEYBOARD: Piano:** *Soundings* for Piano, 4-hands (1975); *Triptych* for 2 Pianos (1978); *5 Ceremonial*

Masks (1980); *Esquisses* (1986); *Dreams and Drama* (1994). **Organ:** *7 Portals of Vision* (1982); *Commentaries* (1988). **VOCAL:** *5 Songs After Poems by William Blake* for Contralto and Viola (1962); *Dartington Quintet* for Soprano, Flute, Clarinet, Violin, and Piano (1964); *Phase II* for Soprano, Cello, and Piano (1974); *Requiem* for Soprano, Chorus, and Instruments (1977); *Songs from a Requiem* for Soprano and Piano (1982); *Winnowing Song* for Chorus, Cello, and Piano (1982); *Symbiosis* for Mezzo-soprano, Percussion, and Piano (1983); *A Fantasy Journey into the Mind of a Machine* for Soprano and Saxophone (1985). **MIXED MEDIA:** *Many Moons* for Chamber Orch., Narrator, Mimes, and Dancers (Lexington, Mass., Oct. 14, 1990).—**NS/LK/DM**

Lonati, Carlo Ambrogio (real name, **Giovanni Ambrogio Leinati**), famous Italian violinist and composer, known as "Il Gobbo della Regina" ("the Queen's hunchback"); b. probably in Milan, c. 1645; d. probably there, c.1710. He was a violinist in the Naples royal chapel (1665–67). He went in 1668 to Rome, where he entered the service of Queen Christina of Sweden. Although a hunchback, he was greatly admired as a violinist, hence his sobriquet. He also appeared as a singer; likewise was principal violinist at S. Luigi dei Francesi (1673–74), and concertino violinist at the Oratorio della Stimmate at S. Francesco and the Oratorio del Crocifisso at S. Marcello (1674–75), and at the Oratorio della Pietà at S. Giovanni dei Fiorentini (1675). Having become a close friend of Stradella, he was compelled to leave Rome in 1677 after his friend's notorious conduct became general knowledge. They went to Genoa, but Lonati left the city after Stradella's murder in 1682. He then was in the service of the Mantuan court. He spent his last years in Milan. He was a distinguished composer of operas, cantatas, and instrumental music.

WORKS: DRAMATIC: Opera: *Amor per destino* (Genoa, 1678); *Ariberto e Flavio, regi di Longobardi* (Venice, 1684?); *Enea in Italia* (Milan, 1686; in collaboration with others); *I due germani (fratelli) rivali* (Modena, 1686); *Antico, principe della Siria* (Genoa, 1690); *Scipione africano* (Milan, 1692); *L'Aiace* (Milan, 1694; in collaboration with Magni and Ballarotti); *Aetna festivo* (Milan, 1696; in collaboration with others). **OTHER:** Cantatas; 12 sonates for Violin and Basso Continuo (1701).—**NS/LK/DM**

London, Edwin, American conductor, teacher, and composer; b. Philadelphia, March 16, 1929. After training in horn at the Oberlin (Ohio) Coll. Cons. of Music (B.A., 1952), he studied conducting (M.F.A., 1954) and composition (Ph.D., 1961) at the Univ. of Iowa. He also received private instruction in composition from Dallapiccola, Schuller, Bezanson, Milhaud, and Clapp, and in conducting from Perlea and Solomon. From 1960 to 1969 he taught at Smith Coll. He was a prof. at the Univ. of Ill. School of Music from 1968 to 1978, where he also was active as a conductor. In 1972–73 he was a visiting prof. of composition at the Univ. of Calif. at San Diego. He was a prof. (from 1978) and chairman of the music dept. (1978–86) at Cleveland State Univ. He was also founder-music director of the Cleveland Chamber Sym. (from 1980). In 1965, 1966, 1970, and 1974 he held MacDowell Colony fellowships. In 1969 he was awarded a Guggenheim fellowship. In 1973, 1974, and 1979 he received NEA grants. His stylistically diverse output includes theater scores, orch. music, chamber pieces, and vocal works.—NS/LK/DM

London (real name, **Burnstein**), **George,** esteemed Canadian-born American bass-baritone; b. Montreal, May 5, 1919; d. Armonk, N.Y., March 23, 1985. The family moved to Los Angeles in 1935; there he took lessons in operatic interpretation with Richard Lert; also studied voice with Hugo Strelitzer and Nathan Stewart. He made his public debut in the opera *Gainsborough's Duchess* by Albert Coates in a concert performance in Los Angeles on April 20, 1941. He appeared as Dr. Grenvil in *La Traviata* on Aug. 5, 1941, at the Hollywood Bowl, and then sang with the San Francisco Opera on Oct. 24, 1943, in the role of Monterone in *Rigoletto*. He took further vocal lessons with Enrico Rosati and Paola Novikova in N.Y.; then, anticipating a serious professional career, he changed his name from the supposedly plebeian and ethnically confining Burnstein to a resounding and patrician London. In 1947 he toured the U.S. and Europe as a member of the Bel Canto Trio with Frances Yeend, soprano, and Mario Lanza, tenor. His European operatic debut took place as Amonasro at the Vienna State Opera on Sept. 3, 1949. He made his Metropolitan Opera debut in N.Y. in the same role on Nov. 13, 1951; this was also the role he sang at his last Metropolitan appearance on March 10, 1966. From 1951 to 1964 he also sang at the Bayreuth Festivals. On Sept. 16, 1960, he became the first American to sing Boris Godunov (in Russian) at the Bolshoi Theater in Moscow. In 1967 he was stricken with a partial paralysis of the larynx, but recovered sufficiently to be able to perform administrative duties. From 1968 to 1971 he was artistic administrator of the John F. Kennedy Center for the Performing Arts in Washington, D.C.; was also executive director of the National Opera Inst. from 1971 to 1977. He was general director of the Opera Soc. of Washington, D.C., from 1975 to 1977, when he suffered a cardiac arrest that precluded any further public activities. For several years before his death, he suffered from a grave neurological disease. Among his best roles were Wotan, Don Giovanni, Scarpia, Escamillo, and Boris Godunov.

BIBL.: N. London, *Aria for G.* (N.Y., 1987).—NS/LK/DM

Long, Kathleen, English pianist and teacher; b. Brentford, July 7, 1896; d. Cambridge, March 20, 1968. She was a pupil of Herbert Sharpe at the Royal Coll. of Music in London (1910–16). Following her debut in 1915, she pursued a fine career as a soloist with orchs., as a recitalist, and as a chamber music artist. Her tours took her throughout Europe and North America. She also taught at the Royal Coll. of Music (1920–64). In 1950 she was awarded the palmes academiques of France and in 1957 was made a Commander of the Order of the British Empire. Long was an admirable interpreter of Bach, Scarlatti, Mozart, Schumann, and the French school, especially of Fauré. She also championed the cause of British music.—NS/LK/DM

Long, Marguerite (Marie-Charlotte), eminent French pianist and pedagogue; b. Nîmes, Nov. 13, 1874; d. Paris, Feb. 13, 1966. She began piano studies as a child with her sister, Claire Long. In 1883 she became a student of her sister at the Nîmes Cons., where she received a Prix d'Honneur in 1886. That same year she made her debut in Nîmes as a soloist in Mozart's D minor Concerto, K.466. In 1889 she entered the Paris Cons. in the class of Mme. Chêné, and then was Henri Fissot's student there (1890–91). After graduating in 1891 with a premier prix, she pursued private studies with Antonin Marmontel. In 1893 she made her formal Paris recital debut, and subsequently acquired a notable reputation as a recitalist and chamber music artist. On Nov. 22, 1903, she made her Paris debut as a soloist when she played Franck's *Variations Symphoniques* with Chevillard and the Orchestre Lamoureux. Her reputation was assured when she appeared for the first time as soloist with the orch. of the Société des Concerts du Conservatoire in Paris performing Fauré's *Ballade* on Jan. 19, 1908. Thereafter she appeared as a soloist with the principal French orchs. until her farewell appearance in the same work with Inghelbrecht and the Orchestre National de la Radiodiffusion Télévision Française in Paris on Feb. 3, 1959. In 1906 Long became a teacher of piano at the Paris Cons. In 1920 she was made a prof. of piano of a Classe Supérieure there, the first woman to hold that position. From 1906 she also was active with her own music school. After retiring from the Cons. in 1940, she joined Jacques Thibaud in founding the École Marguerite Long-Jacques Thibaud in 1941. They also organized the Concours Marguerite Long-Jacques Thibaud, which was first held in 1943. After World War II, it blossomed into one of the principal international competitions. Among Long's many notable students were Samson François, Nicole Henriot, Aldo Ciccolini, Philippe Entremont, and Peter Frankl. Her writings, all publ. in Paris, included *Le piano* (1959), *Au piano avec Claude Debussy* (1960; Eng. tr., 1972), *Au piano avec Gabriel Fauré* (1963; Eng. tr., 1981), and *Au piano avec Maurice Ravel* (1971; Eng. tr., 1973). She was made a Chevalier (1921), an Officier (1930), and a Commandeur (1938) of the Légion d'Honneur. She was the first woman to be accorded the latter honor. In 1965 she was the first woman to be awarded the Grand Croix de l'Ordre du Mérite. In 1906 she married **Joseph de Marliave**. As a pianist, Long won great renown for her interpretations of French music. Her performances of Fauré, Debussy, and Ravel, all of whom she came to know well, were outstanding. She gave the first performance of Ravel's *Le Tombeau de Couperin* (Paris, April 11, 1919). She also was the soloist in the premiere of his Piano Concerto in G major under the composer's direction (Paris, Jan. 14, 1932).

BIBL.: J. Weill, *M. L.: Une vie fascinante* (Paris, 1969); C. Dunoyer, *M. L., 1874–1966: Un siècle de vie musicale française* (Paris, 1993; Eng. tr., 1993, as *M. L.: A Life in Music, 1874–1966*). —NS/LK/DM

Longas, Federico, Spanish pianist and composer; b. Barcelona, July 18, 1893; d. Santiago, Chile, June 17, 1968. He was a pupil of Granados and Malats; toured widely in the U.S., South America, and Europe as accompanist to Tito Schipa and as a soloist. He founded a piano school, the Longas Academy, in Barcelona. He later went to Paris, then to the U.S., settling in N.Y. His works include effective piano pieces (*Jota, Aragon,* etc.) and over 100 songs (*Castilian Moonlight, La guinda, Muñequita,* etc.).—**NS/LK/DM**

Longo, Achille, Italian composer and teacher, son of **Alessandro Longo**; b. Naples, March 28, 1900; d. there, May 28, 1954. He studied with his father and with A. Savasta, then at the Naples Cons. (diplomas in piano, 1918, and composition, 1920), where he taught harmony (1926–30). He then taught at the Parma Cons. (1930–34), and subsequently taught composition at the Naples Cons. (1934–54).

WORKS: ORCH.: *Scenetta pastorale* (1924); Piano Concerto (Venice, 1932); *La burla del Pievano Arlotto* (1933); Violin Concerto (1937); *Notturno and Corte* (1942); *Serenata in do* (1950). **CHAMBER:** Suite for Flute, Oboe, Clarinet, Bassoon, and Piano (1926; won the Bellini Prize); Piano Quintet (1934). **VOCAL:** *Missa di requiem* (1934).—**NS/LK/DM**

Longo, Alessandro, Italian pianist, teacher, editor, and composer, father of **Achille Longo**; b. Amantea, Dec. 30, 1864; d. Naples, Nov. 3, 1945. He began his studies with his father, Achille Longo (b. Melicuccà, Feb. 27, 1832; d. Naples, May 11, 1919), a pianist and composer, and then entered the Naples Cons. (1878), where he studied piano with Cesi, composition with Serrao, and organ (diplomas in all 3, 1885). He was appointed prof. of piano there in 1897, retiring in 1934; later returned as its interim director (1944). Longo also was active as a piano soloist and, from 1909, served as pianist of the Società del Quartetto. In 1892 he founded the Circolo Scarlatti to promote the works of Domenico Scarlatti; ed. the *Opere complete per clavicembalo di Domenico Scarlatti* (11 vols., Milan, 1906–08); also became ed. of the periodical *L'Arte Pianistica* (1914), which became the *Vita Musicale Italiana*; it discontinued publication in 1926. He publ. the study *Domenico Scarlatti e la sua figura nella storia della musica* (Naples, 1913). He also was the composer of over 300 works, including numerous pieces for piano solo and piano, 4-hands, chamber music, and songs.

BIBL.: M. Limoncelli, *A. L.* (Naples, 1956).—**NS/LK/DM**

Longy, (Gustave-) Georges (-Léopold), French oboist, conductor, music educator, and composer; b. Abbeville, Aug. 28, 1868; d. Moreuil, March 29, 1930. He studied oboe with Georges Gillet at the Paris Cons. (premier prix, 1886). He was a member of the Lamoureux Orch. (1886–88) and of the Colonne Orch. (1888–98) in Paris. In 1898 he was engaged as first oboe player of the Boston Sym. Orch., and remained there until 1925. From 1899 to 1913 he conducted the Boston Orchestral Club. In 1916 he established his own music school in Boston (later the Longy School of Music in Cambridge, Mass.). In 1925 he returned to France.—**NS/LK/DM**

Lonque, Georges, Belgian composer and teacher; b. Ghent, Nov. 8, 1900; d. Brussels, March 3, 1967. He studied with Moeremans, Mathieu, and Lunssens at the Ghent Cons., and was awarded the Second Prix de

Rome for his cantatas *Le Rossignol* (1927) and *Antigone* (1929). He joined the faculty of his alma mater (1926), where he was a lecturer in harmony (1932–65). He was also director of the Renaix music academy (1938–64). His music was influenced mainly by Franck, Debussy, Fauré, and Ravel.

WORKS: ORCH.: *Impressions d'Hemelrijk* (1925); *Vieux quai* for Violin or Cello and Orch. (1928); *Aura,* symphonic poem and ballet (1930); *Wiener Walzer* for Small Orch. (1933); *Poème de la mer* for Cello and Orch. (1935); *Images d'Orient* for Saxophone or Viola and Orch. (1935); *Porcelaines de Saxe* for Small Orch. (1939); *Prélude et Aria* for Cello and Orch. (1943); *Estrelle* for Violin and Orch. (1944); Violin Concerto (1948); *Afgoden (Idoles)* for Clarinet and Orch. (1950). **CHAMBER:** Violin Sonata (1925); *Caprice* for Violin and Piano (1930); String Quartet (1937); piano pieces, including *Nuit d'automne* (1929), 2 sonatinas (1939, 1944), *Voilier* (1952), *Tableaux d'une chambre bleue* (1952), and *Nocturne* (1955). **VOCAL:** 2 cantatas: *Le Rossignol* (1927) and *Antigone* (1929); *Missa pro pace* for Men's Chorus and Organ (1941); songs.—**NS/LK/DM**

Loomis, Clarence, American pianist, teacher, and composer; b. Sioux Falls, S.Dak., Dec. 13, 1889; d. Aptos, Calif., July 3, 1965. He studied at the American Cons. of Chicago with Heniot Lévy (piano) and Adolph Weidig (composition), and subsequently took lessons with Godowsky in Vienna. Returning to the U.S., he held various positions as a music teacher. As a composer, he was mainly successful in writing light operas in a Romantic vein. Among them are *Yolanda of Cyprus* (London, Ontario, Sept. 25, 1929), *A Night in Avignon* (Indianapolis, July 1932), *The White Cloud* (1935), *The Fall of the House of Usher* (Indianapolis, Jan. 11, 1941), *Revival* (1943), and *The Captive Woman* (1953). He further wrote a comic ballet, *The Flapper and the Quarterback,* which was first performed in Kyoto, Japan, at the coronation of Emperor Hirohito, Nov. 10, 1928. Among his orch. works were *Gargoyles,* symphonic prelude (1936), *Gaelic Suite* for Strings (1953), *Fantasy* for Piano and Orch. (1954), and *Macbeth* (1954), as well as *The Passion Play* for Chorus and Orch. Other works include 2 string quartets (1953, 1963), a cantata, *Song of the White Earth* (1956), numerous sacred choruses, *Susanna Don't You Cry,* stage extravaganza (1939), piano suites, songs, and organ pieces.—**NS/LK/DM**

Loomis, Harvey Worthington, American composer; b. Brooklyn, Feb. 5, 1865; d. Boston, Dec. 25, 1930. He was a student at the National Cons. in N.Y. (1891–93) of Dvořák. In some of his works, he utilized American Indian melodies.

WORKS: *Sandalphon,* melodrama (1896); *The Traitor Mandolin,* opera (1898); 2 burlesque operas: *The Maid of Athens* and *The Burglar's Bride; The Song of the Pear Tree,* dramatic recitation (1913); Violin Sonata; much piano music; children's pieces. —**NS/LK/DM**

Loos, Armin, German-born American composer; b. Darmstadt, Feb. 20, 1904; d. New Britain, Conn., March 23, 1971. He studied law at the Univ. of Dresden, then attended the univs. of Berlin and Geneva and the École Supérieur de Commerce in Neuchâtel, Switzerland; he also had lessons in composition with Paul Buettner. In 1928 he emigrated to the U.S. After living in N.Y., he settled in New Britain, becoming a naturalized American citizen in 1940.

WORKS: ORCH.: 3 syms.: No. 1, "in memoriam Ferruccio Busoni" (1940), No. 2 for Strings (1940), and No. 3, "in canon form" (1941); *Pastoral and Perpetuum mobile* (1941); *Precepts* for Chamber Orch. (1968); *Aquarius 70* for Strings (1970); *Lento: Prelude to Easter* (1970). **CHAMBER:** 4 string quartets (1933–63); Woodwind Quintet (1964); 2 violin sonatas (1968; 1970–71); piano pieces. **VOCAL:** *Te Deum* for Chorus (1934); *Missa spiritorum* for Chorus and Orch. (1948); *Psalm CXX* for Chorus and Orch. (1963); songs.—**NS/LK/DM**

Loose, Emmy, Austrian soprano; b. Karbitz, Bohemia, Jan. 22, 1914; d. Vienna, Oct. 14, 1987. She was educated at the Prague Cons., then made her debut as Blondchen in *Die Entführung aus dem Serail* in Hannover (1939). From 1941 she sang with the Vienna State Opera; also appeared at the festivals in Salzburg, Glyndebourne, and Aix-en-Provence, at Milan's La Scala, London's Covent Garden, and in South America. From 1970 she taught at the Vienna Academy of Music. She was admired for her fine soubrette roles in the operas of Mozart and Richard Strauss.—**NS/LK/DM**

Loosemore, Henry, English organist and composer; b. probably in Devon, date unknown; d. 1670. He was organist at King's Coll., Cambridge (1627–70), where he took his Mus.B. in 1640. He also was active in the private music gatherings at the North family home in Kirtling. Among his works were service music and anthems. His brother, George Loosemore (b. Devon, date unknown; d. Cambridge, 1682), was also an organist and composer. He was organist at Jesus Coll., Cambridge (1635) and at Trinity Coll., Cambridge (1660–82), and took the Cambridge Mus.D. in 1665. He composed sacred music.—**LK/DM**

Looser, Rolf, Swiss cellist, teacher, and composer; b. Niederscherli, near Bern, May 3, 1920. He studied at the Cons. and at the Univ. of Bern, his principal teachers being Sturzenegger (cello) and Moeschinger, Zulauf, and Kurth (theory). After taking teaching (1942) and concert (1944) diplomas, he pursued his training with Frank Martin (composition) and Franz Walter (cello) in Geneva, Burkhard (counterpoint) in Zürich, and Fournier (cello) in Paris. He was a cellist in the radio orch. of Studio Monte Ceneri and first cellist in the Utrecht Sym. Orch. (1946–49), and then taught at the Bern and Biel Conservatories. He subsequently taught at the Zürich Cons. and Academy of Music (from 1975).

WORKS: ORCH.: Suite (1944–49); *Introduction et Dialogues* for Cello and Chamber Orch. (1950); *Konzertante Musik* (1951); *Musik* for Strings and Organ (1953); *Fantasie* for Violin and Orch. (1958); *Rhapsodia* for Cello and Chamber Orch. (1961); *Pezzo* (1964); *Alyssos*, 5 pieces for Strings and Percussion (1967); *Ponti* (1971); *Arche*, symphonic essay (1986–87); *Es Bilderbuech für d'Ohre* for Small Orch. (1988–89). **CHAMBER:** 6 *Stücke* for Flute and Clarinet (1958); *Variationenphantasie über ein eigenes Choralthema* for Trumpet and Piano (1958); *Rezitativ und Hymnus* for Violin (1960); 4 *Stücke* for Oboe and Harpsichord (1962);

Fantasia a quattro for String Quartet (1965); *Dialog* for Violin and Organ (1968); *Monologue, Gestes et Danse* for Cello (1976); *Partita à tre* for 2 Trumpets, Organ, and Percussion (1979–80); *Danza* for Dancer and Cello (1982); 5 *kurze Szenen* for Violin and Oboe (1984); *Fantasia à tre* for 3 Flutes (1985); 3 *Stücke* for Clarinet and Cello (1987); *Stück* for Flute, Basset Horn, and Organ (1989); *Monochromie* for 5 Clarinets (1991–92); organ music. **VOCAL:** Choral pieces; songs.—**NS/LK/DM**

Lopardo, Frank, American tenor; b. N.Y., Dec. 23, 1957. He studied at Queens Coll. and the Juilliard School in N.Y. In 1984 he made his formal operatic debut in St. Louis as Tamino. In 1988 he was engaged as Belfore in *Il viaggio a Reims* at the Vienna State Opera, Ernesto in *Don Pasquale* in Geneva, Elvino in *La sonnambula* at the Lyric Opera in Chicago, and Tamino in Dallas. After singing Don Ottavio in San Francisco in 1991, he returned there as Lindoro in 1992 and as Tonio in 1993. In the latter year he portrayed Rossini's Count Almaviva at the Metropolitan Opera in N.Y. He sang Alfredo at London's Covent Garden in 1994, and in 1996 he appeared as Lensky in Paris. In 1997 he returned to Chicago as Tamino. In 1999 he returned to the Metropolitan Opera to sing Rodolfo. In addition to his operatic engagements, Lopardo has also sung with many of the leading orchs.—**NS/LK/DM**

Lopatnikoff, Nicolai (actually, **Nikolai Lvovich**), outstanding Russian-born American composer; b. Tallinn, Estonia, March 16, 1903; d. Pittsburgh, Oct. 7, 1976. He studied at the St. Petersburg Cons. (1914–17). After the Revolution, he continued his musical training at the Helsinki Cons. with Furuhjelm (1918–20), and then studied with Grabner in Heidelberg (1920) and Toch and Rehberg in Mannheim (1921); concurrently took civil engineering at the Technological Coll. in Karlsruhe (1921–27). He lived in Berlin (1929–33) and London (1933–39) before settling in the U.S., becoming a naturalized American citizen in 1944. He was head of theory and composition at the Hartt Coll. of Music in Hartford, Conn., and of the Westchester Cons. in White Plains, N.Y. (1939–45); then was a prof. of composition at the Carnegie Inst. of Technology (later Carnegie-Mellon Univ.) in Pittsburgh (1945–69). In 1951 he married the poet Sara Henderson Hay. He was elected to the National Inst. of Arts and Letters in 1963. His music is cast in a neo-Classical manner, distinguished by a vigorous rhythmic pulse, a clear melodic line, and a wholesome harmonic investment. A prolific composer, he wrote music in all genres; being a professional pianist, he often performed his own piano concertos with orchs.

WORKS: DRAMATIC: Opera: *Danton* (1930–32; *Danton Suite* for Orch., Pittsburgh, March 25, 1967). **Ballet:** *Melting Pot* (1975; Indianapolis, March 26, 1976). **ORCH.:** *Prelude to a Drama* (1920; lost); 2 piano concertos: No. 1 (1921; Cologne, Nov. 3, 1925) and No. 2 (Düsseldorf, Oct. 16, 1930); *Introduction and Scherzo* (1927–29; first complete perf., N.Y., Oct. 23, 1930); 4 syms.: No. 1 (1928; Karlsruhe, Jan. 9, 1929), No. 2 (1938–39; 4-movement version, Boston, Dec. 22, 1939; withdrawn and rev. in 3 movements), No. 3 (1953–54; Pittsburgh, Dec. 10, 1954), and No. 4 (1970–71; Pittsburgh, Jan. 21, 1972);

Short Overture (1932; lost); *Opus Sinfonicum* (1933; rev. 1942; Cleveland, Dec. 9, 1943); *2 Russian Nocturnes* (1939; orig. the 2 middle movements of the Second Sym.); Violin Concerto (1941; Boston, April 17, 1942); Sinfonietta (Berkeley, Calif., Aug. 2, 1942); Concertino (1944; Boston, March 2, 1945); Concerto for 2 Pianos and Orch. (Pittsburgh, Dec. 7, 1951); Divertimento (La Jolla, Calif., Aug. 19, 1951); *Variazioni concertanti* (Pittsburgh, Nov. 7, 1958); *Music for Orchestra* (1958; Louisville, Jan. 14, 1959); *Festival Overture* (Detroit, Oct. 12, 1960); *Concerto for Orchestra* (Pittsburgh, April 3, 1964; orch. version of Concerto for Wind Orch.); *Partita concertante* for Chamber Orch. (1966); *Variations and Epilogue* for Cello and Orch. (Pittsburgh, Dec. 14, 1973; orchestration of 1946 chamber piece). **W i n d O r c h .:** Concerto for Wind Orch. (Pittsburgh, June 23, 1963); *Music for Band* (1963; transcribed by William Schaefer from *Music for Orchestra*). **CHAMBER:** 2 piano trios (1918, lost; 1935); 3 string quartets (1920; 1924, rev. 1928; 1955); Sonata for Violin, Piano, and Snare Drum (1927; rev. in 1967 as Sonata for Violin, Piano, and Percussion); Cello Sonata (1929); *Arabesque* for Cello or Bassoon and Piano (1931); *Variations and Epilogue* for Cello and Piano (1946; orchestration, 1973); Violin Sonata No. 2 (1948); *Fantasia concertante* for Violin and Piano (1962); *Divertimento da camera* for 10 Instruments (1965). **P i a n o :** 4 *Small Piano Pieces* (1920); *Prelude and Fugue* (1920); Sonatina (1926; rev. 1967); *2 Pieces* for Mechanical Piano (1927; lost); *2 danses ironiques* (1928; rev. 1967); *5 Contrasts* (1930); *Dialogues* (1932); *Variations* (1933); Sonata (1943); *Intervals*, 7 studies (1957). **V O C A L :** Songs.

BIBL.: W. Critser, compiler, *The Compositions of N. L.: A Catalogue* (Pittsburgh, 1979).—NS/LK/DM

Lopes-Graça, Fernando, eminent Portuguese composer, musicologist, pianist, and pedagogue; b. Tomar, Dec. 17, 1906; d. Lisbon, Nov. 28, 1994. He took piano lessons at home, then studied with Merea and da Motta (piano), Borba (composition), and de Freitas Branco (theory and musicology) at the Lisbon Cons. (1923–31); also studied at the Univ. of Lisbon. He taught at the Coimbra music inst. (1932–36). In 1937 he left his homeland for political reasons; went to Paris, where he studied composition and orchestration with Koechlin, and musicology with Masson at the Sorbonne. After the outbreak of World War II (1939), he returned to Lisbon, where he served as a prof. at the Academia de Amadores de Música (1941–54); from 1950 was director of its chorus, a position he held for 40 years; also made appearances as a pianist. In his music, he pursued an independent path in which he moved from Portuguese folk traditions to atonality in 1962. With M. Giacometti, he publ. the first vol. of the *Antologia da Música Regional Portuguesa*, the first attempt to collect, in a systematic way, the regional songs of Portugal.

WORKS: DRAMATIC: *La Fièvre du temps*, revue-ballet (1938); *D. Duardos e Flérida*, cantata-melodrama (1964–69; Lisbon, Nov. 28, 1970); *Dançares*, choreographic suite (1984). **ORCH.:** *Poemeto* for Strings (1928); *Prelúdio, Pastoral e Dança* (1929); 2 piano concertos (1940, 1942); 3 Portuguese Dances (1941); Sinfonia (1944); *5 estelas funerárias* (1948); *Scherzo heróico* (1949); *Suite rústica No. 1* (1950–51); *Marcha festiva* (1954); Concertino for Piano, Strings, Brass, and Percussion (1954); *5 Old Portuguese Romances* (1951–55); *Divertimento* for Winds, Kettledrums, Percussion, Cellos, and Double Basses (1957); *Poema de Dezembro* (1961); Viola Concertino (1962); *4 bosquejos* (4 Sketches) for Strings (1965); *Concerto da camera* for Cello and

Orch. (Moscow, Oct. 6, 1967, Rostropovich soloist); *Viagens na minha terra* (1969–70); *Fantasia* for Piano and Orch., on a religious song from Beira-Baixa (1974); *Homenagem a Haydn*, sinfonietta (1980); *Em louvor da paz* (1986). **C H A M B E R : ** *Estudo-Humoresca* for Flute, Oboe, Clarinet, 2 Violins, Viola, and Cello (1930); Piano Quartet (1939; rev. 1963); *Prelúdio, Capricho e Galope* for Violin and Piano (1941; rev. 1951); *Página esquecida* for Cello and Piano (1955); *Canto de Amor e de Morte* for Piano Quintet (1961); String Quartet (1964); *14 anotaçoes* for String Quartet (1966); *7 souvenirs for Vieira da Silva* for Wind Quintet (1966); *The Tomb of Villa-Lobos* for Wind Quintet (1970); *3 capriccetti* for Flute and Guitar (1975); *Quatro peças em suite* for Viola and Piano (1978); *Sete Apotegmas* for Oboe, Viola, Double Bass, and Piano (1981); *Homenagem a Beethoven—Três Equali* for Double-bass Quartet (1986); *Geórgicas* for Oboe, Viola, Double Bass, and Piano (1989). **P i a n o :** 6 sonatas (1934; 1939, rev. 1956; 1952; 1961; 1977; 1981); 8 *Bagatelles* (1939–48; No. 4, 1950); *Glosas* (Glosses; 1950); *24 Preludes* (1950–55); *Album do jovem pianista* (1953–63); *In Memoriam Béla Bartók*, 8 progressive suites (1960–75); 4 *Impromptus* (1961); *Piano Music for Children* (1968–76); *Melodias rústicas portuguesas No. 3* for Piano, 4-hands (1979); *Deploração na morte trágica de Samora Machel* (1986); *Pranto à memória de Francisco Miguel, uma vida heróica* (1988). **G u i t a r :** *Prelúdio e Baileto* (1968); *Partita* (1970–71); Sonatina (1974); *Quatro peças* (1979). **VOCAL:** *Pequeno cancioneiro do Menino Jesus* for Women's Chorus, 2 Flutes, String Quartet, Celesta, and Harp (1936–59); *História trágico-marítima* for Baritone, Contralto, Chorus, and Orch. (1942–59); *9 Portuguese Folk Songs* for Voice and Orch. (1948–49); *4 Songs of Federico García Lorca* for Baritone, 2 Clarinets, Violin, Viola, Cello, Harp, and Percussion (1953–54); *Cantos do Natal* for Women's Voices and Instrumental Ensemble (1958); *9 cantigas de amigo* for Voice and Chamber Ensemble (1964); *6 cantos sefardins* for Voice and Orch. (1971); *Requiem pelas vítimas do fascismo em Portugal* for Soloists, Chorus, and Orch. (1979); *Sete Predicações de "Os Lusíadas"* for Tenor, Baritone, Men's Chorus, and 12 Instruments (1980); *...meu país de marinheiros...* for Narrator, 4 Women's Voices, 4 Men's Voices, Flute, and Guitars (1981); many choruses; songs.

WRITINGS: *Sobre a evolução das formas musicais* (Lisbon, 1940; second ed., rev., 1959, as *Breve ensaio sobre a evolução das formas musicais*); *Reflexões sobre a música* (Lisbon, 1941); *Introdução à música moderna* (Lisbon, 1941; 3rd ed., 1984); *Música e músicos modernos (Aspectos, obras, personalidades)* (Oporto, 1943; second ed., 1985); *A música portuguesa e os seus problemas* (3 vols., 1944, 1959, 1973); *Bases teóricas da músicas* (Lisbon, 1944; second ed., 1984); *Talia, Euterpe e Terpsicore* (Coimbra, 1945); *Pequena história da música de piano* (Lisbon, 1945; second ed., 1984); *Cartas do Abade António da Costa (Introdução e notas)* (Lisbon, 1946; second ed., 1973, as *O Abade António da Costa, músico e epistólografo setecentista*); *Visita aos músicos franceses* (Lisbon, 1948); *Vianna da Motta (Subsídios para uma biografia, incluindo 22 cartas ao autor)* (Lisbon, 1949; second ed., 1984); *Béla Bartók (Três apontamentos sobre a sua personalidade e a sua obra)* (Lisbon, 1953); *A Canção popular portuguesa* (Lisbon, 1953; 3rd ed., 1981); *Em louvor de Mozart* (Lisbon, 1956; second ed., 1984); with T. Borba, *Dicionário de música* (Lisbon, 1956–58); *Musicália* (Baia, 1960; corrected and aug. ed., 1967); *Lieder der Welt, Portugal (Ausgewält und erlautert von...)* (Hamburg, 1961); *Nossa companheira música* (Lisbon, 1964); *Páginas escolhidas de crítica e estética musicale* (Lisbon, 1966); *Disto e daquilo* (Lisbon, 1973); *Um artista intervém/Cartas com alguma moral* (Lisbon, 1974); *A caça aos coelhos e outros escritos polémicos* (Lisbon, 1976); *Escritos musicológicos* (Lisbon, 1977); *A música portuguesa e os seus problemas* (Lisbon, 1989).

BIBL.: M. Henriques, *F. L.G. na música portuguesa contemporanea* (Sacavém, 1956); M. Vieria de Carvalo, *O essencial sobre F. L.-G.* (Lisbon, 1989).—**NS/LK/DM**

Lopez, Francis(co), French composer; b. Montbéliard, June 15, 1916; d. Paris, Jan. 5, 1995. He studied to be a dentist but after finding success writing songs, he opted for a career as a composer of light works for the French musical theater in Paris. He found an adept librettist and lyricist in Raymond Vincy; they scored an enormous success with their first outing, the operetta *Le Belle de Cadix* (Dec. 24, 1945). They subsequently collaborated on a long series of highly successful works, among them *Andlousie* (Oct. 25, 1947), *Quatre Jours à Paris* (Feb. 28, 1948), *Pour Don Carlos* (Dec. 17, 1950), *Le Chanteur de Mexico* (Dec. 15, 1951), *La Route fleurie* (Dec. 19, 1952), *À la Jamüque* (Jan. 24, 1954), *La Toison d'or* (Dec. 18, 1954), and *Méditerranée* (Dec. 17, 1956). Several of these works became classics and were made into films. Lopez and Vincy continued their collaboration until the latter's death in 1968. Among their later scores were *Maria-Flora* (Dec. 18, 1957), *La Secret de Marco Polo* (Dec. 12, 1959), *Visa pour l'amour* (Dec. 1961), *Cristobal le Magnifique* (Dec. 1963), and *Le Prince de Madrid* (March 4, 1967). In subsequent years, Lopez continued to compose prolifically but only infrequently found the inspiration of his earlier years. His autobiography was publ. as *Flamenco: La gloire et les larmes* (Paris, 1987).—**NS/LK/DM**

Lopez, Vincent (Joseph), American pianist, bandleader, and composer; b. Brooklyn, Dec. 30, 1894; d. North Miami Beach, Fla., Sept. 20, 1975. His father, of Portuguese ancestry, a bandmaster in the U.S. Navy, taught Lopez the rudiments of music. However, he sent him to St. Mary's Passionist Monastery in the hope that he would become a Roman Catholic priest. But Lopez turned to music, and as a teenager played in the beer halls of Brooklyn. Later he led restaurant orchs. in N.Y. In 1927 he inaugurated a regular broadcasting hour of dance band music over radio station WJX in Newark, on which he popularized the song *Nola*, using it as a signature, opening with a greeting, "Hello, everybody... Lopez speaking." He had the first sustaining television show, "Dinner Date with Lopez," which featured show-business personalities. Among his song hits were *Rockin' Chair Swing; Knock, Knock, Who's There?*; and *The World Stands Still*. He also gave lectures on numerology and related pseudo-sciences.—**NS/LK/DM**

López-Buchardo, Carlos, Argentine composer; b. Buenos Aires, Oct. 12, 1881; d. there, April 21, 1948. He studied piano, violin, and harmony in Buenos Aires and composition with Albert Roussel in Paris. He was founder-director of the National Cons. in Buenos Aires (1924–48); also founded the school of fine arts at the Univ. of La Plata, where he was a prof. of harmony. His music is set in a vivid style, rooted in national folk song; particularly successful in this respect is his symphonic suite *Escenas argentinas* (Buenos Aires, Aug. 12, 1922). His other works are the opera *El sueño de alma* (Buenos Aires, Aug. 4, 1914; won the Municipal Prize); 3 lyric comedies: *Madama Lynch* (1932), *La perichona* (1933), and *Amalia* (1935); several piano pieces in an Argentine folk manner; songs.—**NS/LK/DM**

López-Calo, José, learned Spanish Jesuit priest and music scholar; b. Nebra, La Coruna, Feb. 4, 1922. After graduating with degrees in philosophy and theology from the univs. of Comillas and Granada, he studied church music at the Madrid H.S. of Sacred Music and took his doctorate in musicology under Anglés at the Rome Pontifical Inst. for Sacred Music (1962, with the diss. *La música en la catedral de Granada*; publ. in Granada, 1963). He served as asst. to Anglés (1964–65), then was prof. of musicology at the Pontifical Inst. for Sacred Music (1965–70). He also was musical adviser for the Vatican Radio (1962–70) and general secretary of the International Soc. for Church Music (1964–70). In 1970 he returned to Spain to pursue research in Spanish cathedral archives. In 1973 he became prof. of music history at the Univ. of Santiago de Compostela, and was made prof. emeritus upon his retirement in 1988. His valuable research is reflected in his cataloging of musical archives and in the gathering of an immense collection of firsthand documentation on music history. His personal library of over 15,000 vols. includes many manuscripts of Spanish musical interest, incunabula, and rare old editions from the 16th to the 19th centuries, many of his are *unica*.

WRITINGS: *Canti sacri per la Santa Messa* (Rome, 1965; second ed., 1967); *Presente y futuro de la música sagrada* (Madrid, 1967; Italian tr., Rome, 1968); *Catálogo musical del archivo de la santa iglesia catedral de Santiago* (Cuenca, 1972; second ed., rev., 1992–93); *Hygini Anglès Scripta musicologica* (3 vols., Rome, 1976); *Catálogo del archivo de música de la catedral de Ávila* (Santiago de Compostela, 1978); *Francisco Valls: Missa Scala Aretina* (London, 1978); *Esencia de la música sagrada* (La Coruña, 1980); *La música en la catedral de Palencia* (2 vols., Palencia, 1981); *La música medieval en Galicia* (La Coruña, 1982); *Indices de la revista Tesoro Sacro Musical* (Madrid, 1983); *Historia de la música española en el siglo XVII* (Madrid, 1983); *The Symphony in Spain: 3 Symphonies by José Pons* (N.Y., 1983); *La música en la catedral de Zamora* (Zamora, 1985); *Las sonatas de Beethoven para piano* (Santiago de Compostela, 1985); *Melchor López: Misa de Requiem* (Santiago de Compostela, 1987); *La música en la catedral de Segovia* (2 vols., Segovia, 1988); *Catálogo del archivo de música de la catedral de Santo Domingo de La Calzada* (Logroño, 1988); *Documentario musical de la catedral de Segovia* (Santiago de Compostela, 1990); *Catálogo del archivo de música de la catedral de Granada* (3 vols., Granada, 1991); *La música en la catedral de Calahorra* (Logroño, 1991); *Obras musicales de Juan Montes* (8 vols., Santiago de Compostela, 1991); *La música en la catedral de Santiago* (12 vols., La Coruña, 1992 et seq.); *Catálogo del archivo de música de la capilla réal de Granada* (Granada, 1993); *La música en la catedral de Burgos* (12 vols., Burgos, 1995).

BIBL.: E. Casares and C. Villanueva, *De música hispana et aliis: Miscelánea en honor al Prof. Dr. J. L.-C., S.J., en su 65ª cumpleaños* (2 vols., Santiago de Compostela, 1990).—**NS /LK/DM**

López Capillas, Francesco, distinguished Mexican composer and organist, most likely of Spanish birth; b. probably in Andalusia, c. 1615; d. Mexico City, between Jan. 18 and Feb. 7, 1673. Following ordination into the priesthood, he was made organist and bassoonist at Puebla Cathedral in 1641, where he subsequently served as principal organist in 1647–48. From 1654 to 1668 he was organist and maestro de capilla at the cathedral in Mexico City. After giving up his position as organist, he continued in his capacity as maestro de capilla until his death. Among his notable works were masses, Magnificats, motets, hymns, and a *Passio Domini sec Matthauem.*—**LK/DM**

López-Chavarri y Marco, Eduardo, Spanish musicologist, music critic, and composer; b. Valencia, Jan. 29, 1871; d. there, Oct. 28, 1970. He received a law degree from the Univ. of Valencia (1900) and studied composition with Pedrell. In 1897 he became music critic of *Las provincias* in Valencia, a position he retained until shortly before his death. He also was prof. of aesthetics and music history at the Valencia Cons. (1910–21), where he conducted its orch. and chamber orch. His most important writings were *Historia de la música* (Barcelona, 1914; 3rd ed., 1929) and *Música popular española* (Barcelona, 1927; 3rd ed., 1958). He composed orch. works, choral pieces, chamber music, piano pieces, and songs.—**NS/LK/DM**

López-Cobos, Jesús, distinguished Spanish conductor; b. Toro, Feb. 25, 1940. He took a doctorate in philosophy at the Univ. of Madrid (1964), and studied composition at the Madrid Cons. (diploma, 1966) and conducting with Ferrara in Venice, Swarowsky at the Vienna Academy of Music (diploma, 1969), Maag at the Accademia Musicale Chigiana in Siena, and Morel at the Juilliard School of Music in N.Y. In 1969 he won first prize at the Besançon Competition. That same year, he conducted at the Prague Spring Festival and at the Teatro La Fenice in Venice. He subsequently was a regular conductor at the Deutsche Oper in West Berlin (1970–75). In 1972 he made his U.S. debut with the San Francisco Opera conducting *Lucia di Lammermoor,* and thereafter appeared as a guest conductor throughout the U.S. In 1975 he made his first appearance at London's Covent Garden conducting *Adriana Lecouvreur.* On Feb. 4, 1978, he made his Metropolitan Opera debut in N.Y. conducting the same score. He was Generalmusikdirektor of the Deutsche Oper in West Berlin (1980–90), principal guest conductor of the London Phil. (1982–86), chief conductor of the Orquesta Nacional de España in Madrid (1984–89), and music director of the Cincinnati Sym. Orch. (1986–2001) and of the Lausanne Chamber Orch. (1990–2000). To mark the 100th anniversary of the Cincinnati Sym. Orch. in 1995, he conducted it on a tour to Europe. In 1998 he became conductor of the Orchestre Français des Jeunes in Paris.—**NS/LK/DM**

Lo Presti, Ronald, American composer; b. Williamstown, Mass., Oct. 28, 1933; d. Tempe, Ariz., Oct. 25, 1985. He studied composition with Mennini and Rogers at the Eastman School of Music in Rochester, N.Y. (M.M., 1956), and subsequently was engaged as a clarinet teacher in public schools; in 1964 he was appointed an instructor in theory at Ariz. State Univ. in Tempe. He obtained popular success with his score *The Masks* (1955), which was commissioned for the space exhibit at the aerospace building at the Smithsonian Inst. in Washington, D.C.

WORKS: DRAMATIC: *The Birthday,* opera (1962; Winfield, May 1962); *Playback,* children's opera (Tucson, Ariz., Dec.

18, 1970). **ORCH.:** *The Masks* (Rochester, N.Y., May 8, 1955); *Nocturne* for Small Orch. (1955–56); *Nocturne* for Viola and String Orch. (1959); *Kansas Overture* (1960); *Kanza Suite* (1961); *Llano estacado* (The Staked Plain; 1961); *Port Triumphant* (1962); 2 syms. (1966, 1968); *From the Southwest* (1967); *Rhapsody* for Marimba, Vibraphone, and Orch. (1975). **Symphonic Band:** *Pageant* (1956); *Prelude* (1959); *Introduction, Chorale and Jubilee* (1961); *Tundra* (1967); *A Festive Music* (1968). **CHAMBER:** *Suite* for 8 Horns (1952); *Sketch* for Percussion (1956); *Suite* for 4 Horns (1958); *5 Pieces* for Violin and Piano (1960); *Scherzo* for Violin Quartet (1960); *Chorale* for 3 Tubas (1960); *Fanfare* for 38 Brasses (1960); *Requiescat* for Brass Ensemble (1961); *Suite* for 5 Trumpets (1961); *Miniature* for Brass Quartet (1962); *Rondo* for Timpani and Piano (1969); *Trio* for 3 Percussionists (1971); String Quartet (1970); *Suite* for 6 Bassoons (1971); *Fantasy* for 5 Horns (1972); *Cantalena* for Cello Orch. (1972); Wind Quintet (1975). **VOCAL:** *Alleluia* for Chorus, Brass, and Timpani (1960); *Kanza* for 4 Narrators, Chorus, and Orch. (1961); *Tribute* for Chorus and Orch. and/or Band (1962); *Scarecrow* for Children's Ballet Co., Mixed Voices, and Cello Orch. (1973); *Ode to Independence* for Baritone, Chorus, and Band (1974); *Requiem* for Chorus and Orch. (1975); *Memorials* for Chorus and Orch. (1975); choruses; songs.—**NS/LK/DM**

Loqueville, Richard, French composer; b. place and date unknown; d. Cambrai, 1418. He became the harp tutor to the son of the Duke of Bar in 1410, and also taught plainchant to the duke's choirboys. In 1413 he became a music teacher at Cambrai Cathedral. His extant works comprise mass movements, 2 motets, 4 rondeaux, and a ballade.—**LK/DM**

Lorber, Jeff, American keyboardist and record producer; b. Philadelphia, Pa., Nov. 4, 1952. From the late '70s his danceable blend of funk, Latin, and jazz has helped forge the popularity of modern fusion. A studio maven since the late '80s, his credits read like a Who's Who of Grammy contenders. His producing credits include Kenny G, Dave Koz, Herb Alpert, Michael Franks, Tower of Power, Sheena Easton, Karyn White, Jody Watley, Jon Lucien, Eric Marienthal, Art Porter, and the soundtrack to the movie *Another 48 Hours.* He has added his keyboard mastery to albums by such luminaries as Paula Abdul, the Pointer Sisters, Johnny Mathis, Gladys Knight, Manhattan Transfer, the Isley Brothers, Joe Cocker, and Paul Jackson Jr. He has also remixed tracks for U2, Chaka Khan, Bruce Hornsby, Luther Vandross, and Duran Duran. On his own releases, however, his abilities as a technician and a soloist leave the critics cold, and it has been suggested that his primary inspiration is drawn from machines, resulting in pre-packaged tracks that lack any emotionally convincing performances. His more recent work, on the other hand, displays a newly realized freedom and marked maturity as a jazz player.

He is a classically trained pianist who also studied bass, violin, and guitar. He played in R&B and blues bands when he was in high school and later attended Berklee Coll. of Music in Boston. After relocating to Ore., he began his recording career in 1977 with his group the Jeff Lorber Fusion, which featured a young Kenny G. His two Inner City releases, *Jeff Lorber Fusion* and *Soft Space*, became blueprints for the radio formats known today as NAC and Contemporary Jazz.

Between 1980 and 1985 he released seven albums on Arista and garnered a Best R&B Instrumental Grammy nomination for the smooth-jazz staple, "Pacific Coast Highway." Never manufactured on CD, these titles have become a rare find. Although the demand is great, it is still unclear whether his Arista catalog will be reissued on CD. His greatest commercial success came in 1986 when the vocal single "Facts of Love" introduced then-unknown singer Karyn White. The Top-10 pop hit brought him huge crossover success as a vocally oriented singles artist—a blessing and a curse to his established instrumental fusion fan base. In 1991 and 1992 he was voted Best Session Player in *Keyboard* magazine's Annual Reader's Poll, and Best Dance Keyboard Player in 1993.

DISC.: *Jeff Lorber Fusion* (1977); *Soft Space* (1978); *Water Sign* (1979); *Galaxian* (1980); *Wizard Island* (1980); *It's a Fact* (1981); *In the Heat of the Night* (1983); *Lift Off* (1984); *Step by Step* (1984); *Private Passion* (1990); *Worth Waiting For* (1993); *West Side Stories* (1994); *State of Grace* (1996).—**RB**

Lorengar, Pilar (real name, **Pilar Lorenza García**), prominent Spanish soprano; b. Saragossa, Jan. 16, 1928; d. Berlin, June 2, 1996. She studied with Angeles Ottein in Madrid, where she made her debut as a mezzo-soprano in zarzuela (1949); after becoming a soprano in 1951, she made her operatic debut as Cherubino at the Aix-en-Provence Festival in 1955. Her first appearance in the U.S. took place that same year as Rosario in a concert perf. of *Goyescas* in N.Y. She made her debut at London's Covent Garden as Violetta in 1955, making frequent appearances there from 1964; also sang at the Glyndebourne Festivals (1956–60) and the Berlin Deutsche Oper (from 1958). On Feb. 11, 1966, she made her Metropolitan Opera debut in N.Y. as Donna Elvira. She was named a Kammersängerin of the Berlin Deutsche Oper in 1963, and in 1984 lifetime member of the company on the occasion of her 25th anniversary with it. Her final appearance there was as Tosca on June 9, 1990. She received the Medallo d'Oro de Zaragoza of Saragossa and the Order of Isabella de Catolica (1965), as well as the San Francisco Opera Medal (1989). Among her finest roles were Donna Anna, Fiordiligi, Countess Almaviva, Alice Ford, Eva, and Mélisande.

BIBL.: W. Elsner and M. Busch, *P. L.: Ein Porträt* (Berlin, 1985).—**NS/LK/DM**

Lorentzen, Bent, Danish composer; b. Stenvad, Feb. 11, 1935. He studied with Knud Jeppesen at the Univ. of Århus and with Holmboe, Jersild, and Høffding at the Royal Danish Cons. of Music in Copenhagen (graduated, 1960), and worked at the Stockholm electronic music studio (1967–68). After teaching at the Århus Cons. (1962–71), he settled in Copenhagen and devoted himself to composition; in 1982 he was awarded a State Grant for Life. Among his honors are the Prix Italia (1970) and first prizes in the "Homage to Kazimierz Serocki" International Competition (1984) and the Spittal International Composition Competition

(1987). In his music, he employs a variety of quaquaversal techniques, often utilizing highly sonorous effects.

WORKS: DRAMATIC: O p e r a : *Stalten Mette* (Århus, Nov. 17, 1963; rev. 1980); *Die Schlange* (1964; rev. 1974); *Eurydike* (1965; Danish Radio, Dec. 16, 1969); *Die Musik kommt mir äusserst bekannt vor* (Kiel, May 3, 1974); *Eine wundersame Liebesgeschichte* (Munich, Dec. 2, 1979); *Klovnen Toto* (1982); *Fackeltanz* (1986). **I n s t r u m e n t a l T h e a t e r :** *Studies for 2* for Cello or Guitar and Percussion (1967); *Studies for 3* for Soprano Cello or Guitar, and Percussion (1968); *The End* for Cello (1969); *Friisholm*, film (1971); *3 Mobiles* for 3 Different Instruments (1979; rev. 1988). **ORCH.:** *Deep* (1967; rev. 1981); *Tide* (Copenhagen, March 31, 1971); *Partita popolare* for Strings (1976); Oboe Concerto (1980; Danish Radio, Feb. 18, 1982); Cello Concerto (Danish Radio, May 11, 1984); Piano Concerto (1984; Odense, Jan. 11, 1985); *Latin Suite I* (1984; also for Symphonic Band) and *II* for Symphonic or Brass Band (1987); Saxophone Concerto (1986; Danish Radio, March 6, 1987); *Regenbogen* for Trumpet and Orch. (1991). **CHAMBER:** *Quadrata* for String Quartet (1963); *Cyclus I* for Viola, Cello, and Double Bass (1966; rev. 1986), *II* for 2 Percussion and Harp (1966; rev. 1987), and *III* for Cello and Tape (1966; rev. 1981); *Syncretism* for Clarinet, Trombone, Cello, and Piano (1970); *Quartetto rustico* for String Quartet (1972); *Contorni* for Violin, Cello, and Piano (1978); *Samba* for Clarinet, Trombone, Cello, and Piano (1980); *Wunderblumen* for 12 Musicians (1982); *Mambo* for Clarinet, Cello, and Piano (1982); *Paesaggio* for Flute, Oboe, Clarinet, Bassoon, Horn, Violin, and Viola (1983); *Paradiesvogel* for Flute, Clarinet, Violin, Cello, Guitar, Percussion, and Piano (1983; Warsaw, July 7, 1984); *Dunkelblau* for Flute, Viola, and Harp (1985); *Quartetto Barbaro* for String Quartet (1990); *Farbentiegel* for Alto Saxophone and Piano (1990); *Cries* for Electric Guitar (1991); *Tears* for Accordion (1992); *Tiefe* for Double Bass (1993); piano pieces; organ music. **VOCAL:** *Genesis V* for Chorus and Orch. (1984; Århus, May 19, 1985); *Comics* for Entertainer, Amateur Tenor Saxophone, Electric Bass, Percussion Group, Children's Chorus, and Chorus (1987; Århus, Aug. 27, 1988); choruses; songs. **TAPE:** *The Bottomless Pit* (1972); *Cloud Drift* (1973); *Visions* (1978).—**NS/LK/DM**

Lorenz, Alfred (Ottokar), Austrian musicologist, composer, and conductor; b. Vienna, July 11, 1868; d. Munich, Nov. 20, 1939. He studied with Radecke (conducting) and Spitta (musicology) in Berlin. He was a conductor in Königsberg, Elberfeld, and Munich (1894–97), then became a conductor (1898) and later chief conductor (1904) in Coburg; was made director of its Opera (1917); was also director of the Musikverein in Gotha (1901–18) and Coburg (1907–20). He then gave up his conducting career and studied musicology with Moritz Bauer at the Univ. of Frankfurt am Main (graduated, 1922); lectured at the Univ. of Munich from 1923. He made a specialty of Wagnerian research; publ. the comprehensive work *Das Geheimnis der Form bei Richard Wagner* (4 vols., Berlin, 1924–33; second ed., 1966); also publ. *Alessandro Scarlattis Jugendoper* (Augsburg, 1927) and *Abendländische Musikgeschichte im Rhythmus der Generationen* (Berlin, 1928). He composed an opera, *Helges Erwachen* (Schwerin, 1896), incidental music to various plays, the symphonic poems *Bergfahrt* and *Columbus*, chamber music, and songs.—**NS/LK/DM**

Lorenz, Max, greatly admired German tenor; b. Düsseldorf, May 17, 1901; d. Salzburg, Jan. 11, 1975. He studied with Grenzebach in Berlin. He made his debut as Walther von der Vogelweide in *Tannhäuser* at the Dresden State Opera (1927), then sang at the Berlin State Opera (1929–44) and the Vienna State Opera (1929–33; 1936–44; 1954). He made his Metropolitan Opera debut in N.Y. as Walther von Stolzing in *Die Meistersinger von Nürnberg* on Nov. 12, 1931; was again on its roster in 1933–34 and from 1947 to 1950. Lorenz also sang at the Bayreuth Festivals (1933–39; 1952), London's Covent Garden (1934; 1937), the Chicago Opera (1939–40), and the Salzburg Festivals (1953–55; 1961). He was particularly esteemed as a Wagnerian, but was also a noted Florestan, Othello, and Bacchus.
BIBL.: W. Herrmann, *M. L.* (Vienna, 1976).—NS/LK/DM

Lorenzani, Paolo, Italian composer; b. Rome, 1640; d. there, Oct. 28, 1713. He was a pupil of Orazio Benevoli at the Vatican. Having failed to obtain Benevoli's position after the latter's death in 1672, he was given the post of maestro di cappella at the Jesuit church, the Gesù, and at the Seminario Romano in Rome in 1675; from 1675 to 1678, held a similar position at the Messina Cathedral. When Sicily was captured by the French, the Duc de Vivonne, who was the French viceroy, induced Lorenzani to go to Paris (1678); he found favor with Louis XIV, with whose financial support he purchased the post of Surintendant de la musique de la Reyne (1679); held that post until the Queen's death (1683), then was maître de chapelle to the Italian Théatine religious order (1685–87). He produced the Italian pastoral *Nicandro e Fileno* (Fontainebleau, Sept. 1681); having won the support of the Paris faction opposed to Lully, he produced an opera with a French libretto, *Orontée* (Paris, Aug. 23, 1687). This having failed, Lorenzani turned to the composition of motets, which proved his best works; the famous Paris publisher Ballard brought them out in an impressively printed ed. Ballard also publ. a book of Italian airs by Lorenzani. In 1694 Lorenzani returned to Italy, and was appointed maestro di cappella of the Cappella Giulia at the Vatican.
WORKS: VOCAL: Sacred: Motet for 2 Voices and Basso Continuo (1675); Motet for 3 Voices and Bsso Continuo (1675); (25) *Motets à I, II, III, IV, et V parties* (Paris, 1693); Mass for 2 Choirs and Basso Continuo; Magnificat for 2 Choirs and Basso Continuo. **Secular:** 4 airs and cantatas for Voice and Basso Continuo (publ. in the *Mercure Galant*, May 1680); (6) *Airs italiens de M. Lorenzani* (Paris, 1695); other airs, arias, and cantatas.
BIBL.: W. Gürtelschmied, *P. L. (1640–1713): Leben, Werk, thematischer Katalog* (diss., Univ. of Vienna, 1975).—NS/LK/DM

Lorenzo da Firenze, Italian composer who was also known as **Magister Laurentius de Florentia, Ser Lorenço de Firence,** and **Sir Laurentius Masii** or **Masini**; b. place and date unknown; d. Florence, Dec. 1372 or Jan. 1373. He may have been a student of Landini in Florence, where he most likely served as canonicus at S. Lorenzo from 1348 until his death.

Among his notable extant works are 5 ballate, 10 madrigals, 1 caccia, and a Sanctus. He composed in a bold, experimental style that often reveals the influence of French masters.—LK/DM

Lorenzo Fernândez, Oscar, Brazilian composer and teacher; b. Rio de Janeiro, Nov. 4, 1897; d. there, Aug. 26, 1948. He was a student of João Otaviano (piano and theory) before pursuing his training at the Instituto Nacionale de Música in Rio de Janeiro with Oswald (piano), Nascimento (harmony), and Braga (counterpoint and fugue). In 1924 he joined its faculty as prof. of harmony; later was founder-director of the Brazilian Cons. (1936–48). His works, derived from Brazilian folk songs, followed along national lines.
WORKS: DRAMATIC: Opera: *Malazarte* (1931–33; Rio de Janeiro, Sept. 30, 1941; orch. suite, 1941). **ORCH.:** Piano Concerto (1924); *Suite sinfônica sôbre 3 temas populares brasileiros* (1925); *Imbapará, poema amerindio* (1928; Rio de Janeiro, Sept. 2, 1929); *Amayo, bailado incaico* (1930; Rio de Janeiro, July 9, 1939); *Reisado do pastoreio* (Rio de Janeiro, Aug. 22, 1930); Violin Concerto (1941); 2 syms. (1945, 1947); *Variações sinfônicas* for Piano and Orch. (1948). **CHAMBER:** Piano Trio (1921); *Trio brasileiro* for Piano Trio (1924); Suite for Wind Quintet (1926); 2 string quartets; piano pieces. **VOCAL:** Songs.—NS/LK/DM

Loriod, Yvonne, distinguished French pianist and teacher; b. Houilles, Seine-et-Oise, Jan. 20, 1924. She studied at the Paris Cons., winning no less than 7 premiers prix; among her mentors were Eminger-Sivade, Lévy, Philipp, and Ciampi for piano, Estyle for piano accompaniment, Calvet for chamber music, Plé-Caussade for fugue, and Messiaen and Milhaud for composition. After World War II, she toured extensively, then made her U.S. debut in the premiere of Messiaen's *Turangalîla-Symphonie* with the Boston Sym. Orch. (Dec. 2, 1949). She taught at the Paris Cons. from 1967 to 1989. A foremost champion of the music of Messiaen, she married him in 1961. She also excelled in performances of the music of Bartók, Schoenberg, and Boulez.
—NS/LK/DM

Lortie, Louis, Canadian pianist; b. Montreal, April 27, 1959. He began piano lessons at age 7 in Montreal at the École de musique Wilfred-Pelletier, and later studied at the École normal de musique. In 1975 he won the CBC Talent Festival and International Stepping Stones of the Canadian Music Competition, and subsequently appeared as a recitalist and performed on the CBC. He also completed his training with Deiter Weber in Vienna (1975–76), Menahem Pressler at the Ind. Univ. School of Music in Bloomington, and Marc Durand. In 1978 he won distinction as one of the soloists to accompany Andrew Davis and the Toronto Sym. on their tour of Japan and China. After taking first prize in the Busoni Competition in Bolzano and fourth prize in the Leeds Competition in 1984, he made regular tours of Europe and North America. His commanding repertoire ranges from Mozart to the contemporary era.—NS/LK/DM

Lortzing, (Gustav) Albert, celebrated German composer; b. Berlin, Oct. 23, 1801; d. there, Jan. 21, 1851.

His parents were actors, and the wandering life led by the family did not allow him to pursue a methodical course of study. He learned acting from his father, and music from his mother at an early age. After some lessons in piano with Griebel and in theory with Rungenhagen in Berlin, he continued his own studies, and soon began to compose. On Jan. 30, 1823, he married the actress Rosina Regina Ahles in Cologne; they had 11 children. In 1824 he wrote his stage work, the Singspiel *Ali Pascha von Janina, oder Die Franzosen in Albanien*, which was not premiered until 4 years later (Münster, Feb. 1, 1828). He then brought out the Liederspiel *Der Pole und sein Kind, oder Der Feldwebel vom IV. Regiment* (1832) and the Singspiel *Szenen aus Mozarts Leben* (Osnabrück, Oct. 11, 1832), which were well received on several German stages. From 1833 to 1844 he was engaged at the Municipal Theater of Leipzig as a tenor. His light opera *Die beiden Schützen* was first performed there on Feb. 20, 1837, with much success. It was followed there by the work that is now considered his masterpiece, *Zar und Zimmermann, oder Die zwei Peter* (Dec. 22, 1837). It was performed with enormous success in Berlin (1839), and then in other European music centers. His next opera, *Caramo, oder Das Fischerstechen* (Leipzig, Sept. 20, 1839), was a failure; there followed *Hans Sachs* (Leipzig, June 23, 1840) and *Casanova* (Leipzig, Dec. 31, 1841), which passed without much notice; subsequent comparisons showed some similarities between *Hans Sachs* and *Die Meistersinger von Nürnberg*, not only in subject matter, which was derived from the same source, but also in some melodic patterns; however, no one seriously suggested that Wagner was influenced by Lortzing's inferior work. There followed a comic opera, *Der Wildschütz, oder Die Stimme der Natur* (Leipzig, Dec. 31, 1842), which was in many respects one of the best that Lortzing wrote, but its success, although impressive, never equaled that of *Zar und Zimmermann*. At about the same time, Lortzing attempted still another career, that of opera impresario, but it was short-lived; his brief conductorship at the Leipzig Opera (1844–45) was similarly ephemeral. Composing remained his chief occupation, and he wrote *Undine in Magdeburg* (April 21, 1845) and *Der Waffenschmied* in Vienna (May 30, 1846). He then went to Vienna as conductor at the Theater an der Wien, but soon returned to Leipzig, where his light opera *Zum Grossadmiral* was first performed (Dec. 13, 1847). The revolutionary events of 1848 seriously affected his position in both Leipzig and Vienna; after the political situation became settled, he wrote the opera *Rolands Knappen, oder Das ersehnte Gluck* (Leipzig, May 25, 1849). Although at least 4 of his operas were played at various German theaters, Lortzing received no honorarium, owing to a flaw in the regulations protecting the rights of composers. He was compelled to travel again as an actor, but could not earn enough money to support his large family, left behind in Vienna. In the spring of 1850 he obtained the post of conductor at Berlin's nondescript Friedrich-Wilhelmstadt Theater. His last score, the comic opera *Die Opernprobe, oder Die vornehmen Dilettanten*, was premiered in Frankfurt am Main on Jan. 20, 1851, while he was on his deathbed in Berlin; he died the next day. His opera *Regina*, written in 1848, was ed.

by Richard Kleinmichel, with the composer's libretto revised by Adolf L'Arronge, and performed in Berlin as *Regina, oder Die Marodeure* on March 21, 1899; the first perf. of the original version in the new critical ed. was given in Gelsenkirchen on March 22, 1998. His Singspiel *Der Weihnachtsabend* was first performed in Münster on Dec. 21, 1832. Lortzing also wrote an oratorio, *Die Himmelfahrt Jesu Christi* (Munster, Nov. 15, 1828), and some incidental music to various plays, but it is as a composer of characteristically German Romantic operas that he holds a distinguished, if minor, place in the history of dramatic music. He was a follower of Weber, without Weber's imaginative projection; in his lighter works, he approached the type of French operetta; in his best creations he exhibited a fine sense of facile melody, and infectious rhythm; his harmonies, though unassuming, were always proper and pleasing; his orchestration, competent and effective.

BIBL.: P. Düringer, *A. L.: Sein Leben und Wirken* (Leipzig, 1851); H. Wittmann, *L.* (Leipzig, 1890; second ed., 1902); G. Kruse, *A. L.* (Berlin, 1899); idem, *A. L.: Leben und Werk* (Leipzig, 1914; second ed., 1947); H. Laue, *Die Operndichtung L.s* (Würzburg, 1932); H. Killer, *A. L.* (Potsdam, 1938); G. Dippel, *A. L.: Ein Leben für das deutsche Musiktheater* (Berlin, 1951); H. Burgmüller, *Die Musen darben: Ein Lebensbild A. L.s* (Berlin, 1955); M. Hoffmann, *G.A. L.: Der Meister der deutschen Volksoper* (Leipzig, 1956); E. Lortzing, *A. L.: Zur Familienchronik L.-L.* (Starnberg, 1963); H. Schirmag, *A. L.: Ein Lebens-und Zeitbild* (Berlin, 1982); I. Capelle, *Chronologisch-thematisches Verzeichnis der Werke von G.A. L.: (LoWV)* (Cologne, 1994); idem, ed., *A. L.: Sämtliche Briefe* (Kassel, 1995); H. Schirmag, *A. L.: Glanz und Elend eines Künstlerlebens* (Berlin, 1995); P. Fischer, *Vormärz und Zeitbürgertum: G. L.s Operntexte* (Stuttgart, 1997).—NS/LK/DM

Los Angeles (real name, **Gómez Cima**), **Victoria de,** famous Spanish soprano; b. Barcelona, Nov. 1, 1923. She studied at the Barcelona Cons. with Dolores Frau. In 1941 she made her operatic debut as Mimi in Barcelona, but then resumed her training. In 1945 she made her formal operatic debut as Mozart's Countess in Barcelona. After winning first prize in the Geneva International Competition in 1947, she sang Salud in *La vida breve* with the BBC in London in 1948. In 1949 she made her first appearance at the Paris Opéra as Marguerite. In 1950 she sang at the Salzburg Festival for the first time. She made her debut at London's Covent Garden as Mimi in 1950, and continued to appear there regularly with notable success until 1961. She also sang at Milan's La Scala from 1950 to 1956. On Oct. 24, 1950, she made her first appearance in the U.S. in a Carnegie Hall recital in N.Y. She made her Metropolitan Opera debut in N.Y. as Marguerite on March 17, 1951, and remained on its roster until 1956. In 1957 she sang at the Vienna State Opera, and was again on the roster of the Metropolitan Opera from 1957 to 1961. After making her debut at the Bayreuth Festival as Elisabeth in 1961, she devoted herself principally to a concert career. However, she continued to make occasional appearances in one of her favorite operatic roles, Carmen, during the next 2 decades. Her concert career continued as she entered her 7th decade, highlighted by a well-received recital appearance at N.Y.'s Alice Tully Hall on March 7, 1994. Among her other acclaimed operatic roles were Donna Anna, Rosina, Manon, Nedda, Desdemona, Cio-Cio-San, Violetta, and Mélisande. As a concert artist, she excelled particularly in Spanish and French songs.—NS/LK/DM

Löschhorn, (Carl) Albert, German pianist, composer, and pedagogue; b. Berlin, June 27, 1819; d. there, June 4, 1905. He studied at the Royal Inst. for Church Music with L. Berger, Killitschgy, Grell, and A.W. Bach, and became a piano teacher there in 1851. He publ. a series of excellent piano studies, including *Melodious Studies, La Velocité, Universal Studies, Le Trille,* and *School of Octaves,* which became standard pedagogical works. He also wrote attractive piano solos: *La Belle Amazone, 4 pièces élégantes, Tarentelle; 2 valses,* the barcarolle *A Venise,* and 3 mazurkas; suites, sonatas, sonatinas, etc. With J. Weiss he publ. a *Wegweiser in die Pianoforte-Literatur* (1862; second ed., 1885, as *Führer durch die Klavierliteratur*).—NS/LK/DM

Los Lobos, one of the few contemporary Hispanic acts to be recognized by the English-speaking pop audience. **MEMBERSHIP:** David Hidalgo, lead voc., gtr. (b. Los Angeles, Oct. 6, 1954); Cesar Rosas, lead voc., gtr. (b. Los Angeles, Sept. 26, 1954); Conrad Lozano, bs., voc. (b. Los Angeles, March 21, 1951); Luis "Louie" Perez, drm., gtr., voc.(b. Los Angeles, Jan. 29, 1953). Steve Berlin, sax, kybd. (b. Philadelphia, Pa., Sept. 14, 1955) joined in 1983.

Along with X, one of the most challenging rock bands to emerge from the early-1980s punk scene in Los Angeles, the Mexican-American group Los Lobos has recorded several intriguing, eclectic albums that ranged from R&B to country, from rock and roll to blues, from *norteña* ("Tex- Mex") to *corridas* (ballads) and traditional Mexican folk music, using both rock and traditional instruments. Achieving a musical mélange comparable to only the Meters and the Grateful Dead, Los Lobos broke through commercially with 1987's cover of Ritchie Valens's "La Bamba," the first Spanish-sung song to top the pop charts. Yet interestingly, their brilliant and engaging 1992 *Kiko* album remained a decidedly underground hit, despite widespread critical acclaim.

Formed in East Los Angeles in November 1973 by Mexican-American graduates of Garfield High, Los Lobos performed traditional Mexican folk music on acoustic instruments for nearly eight years before taking up electric instruments in 1981. Then they started writing songs (principally by Hidalgo and Perez) and playing local colleges, community events, and clubs. Having recorded two albums of Mexican folk music on their own New Vista Productions label, Los Lobos sent a demonstration tape to Phil Alvin of the Blasters. They received their first break by opening for the Blasters at the Whisky a Go-Go, and Alvin later convinced the punk-rock label Slash to sign the group. Their first recording, a seven-song EP entitled *And a Time to Dance* was coproduced by the Blasters' Steve Berlin and T-Bone Burnett and released in 1983, the year saxophonist Berlin joined the group. The EP included the traditional folk song "Anselma," which won a Grammy Award.

Opening for acts such as The Clash and Public Image Ltd., Los Lobos garnered excellent reviews for their exciting, wide-ranging performances.

Los Lobos's first full-length album, *How Will the Wolf Survive?,* won outstanding critical reviews—called one of the best albums of the year—and featured the minor hit title song (covered by Waylon Jennings in 1986) and "A Matter of Time" (both written by Hidalgo and Perez), and a cover of the 1951 Peppermint Harris R&B hit "I Got Loaded." Los Lobos performed at a wide variety of venues in support of the album, and various members recorded with Ry Cooder, Paul Simon, Elvis Costello, and the Fabulous Thunderbirds in 1986. Their 1987 album *By the Light of the Moon* included the socially conscious "One Time One Night" (a minor country hit) and "Is That All There Is?" by Hidalgo and Perez and Rosas's "Set Me Free (Rosa Lee)."

During 1987, at the behest of the family of Ritchie Valens, Los Lobos recorded eight songs for the film biography of Valens, *La Bamba.* The best-selling soundtrack album yielded two hits for Los Lobos, with cover versions of Valens's "La Bamba" and "Come On, Let's Go." Typecast by some as an oldies band, Los Lobos sought to dispel the notion by recording *La Pistola y el Corazon* (The Pistol and the Heart), an entire album of traditional Mexican and South American folk songs sung in Spanish and performed on acoustic instruments. The album won the group another Grammy award.

Los Lobos began recording their next album, *The Neighborhood,* in 1989. Released in 1990, the album included "Take My Hand," Hidalgo's "Emily," and Rosas's "I Walk Alone." Their next, *Kiko,* was hailed as a masterpiece, yet it failed to sell in large quantities. The rich, haunting, mature album featured the ominous title song as well as "Dream in Blue," "Saint Behind the Glass," "That Train Don't Stop Here," and Rojas's "Wake Up Dolores." Performing and recording with the side group the Latin Playboys, Hidalgo and Perez contributed six original songs to the La Jolla Playhouse production of Bertolt Brecht's *Good Woman of Szechuan* in 1994. In 1995 Music for Little People Records, distributed by Warner Bros., issued Los Lobos's children's album, *Papa's Dream.*

DISC.: LOS LOBOS: *And a Time to Dance (mini)* (1983); *How Will the Wolf Survive?* (1984); *By the Light of the Moon* (1987); *La Bamba* (soundtrack; 1987); *La Pistola y el Corazon* (1988); *The Neighborhood* (1990); *Kiko* (1992); *Just Another Band from East L.A.: A Collection* (1993); *Colossal Head* (1996). **CHILDREN'S ALBUM:** *Papa's Dream* (1995). **THE LATIN PLAYBOYS:** *The Latin Playboys* (1994).—**BH**

Lothar, Mark, German composer; b. Berlin, May 23, 1902; d. Munich, April 6, 1985. He studied with Schreker (composition), Juon (harmony), and Krasselt (conducting) at the Berlin Hochschule für Musik (1919–20), and later with Meiszner (piano) and Wolf-Ferrari (composition). He was active as piano accompanist to the Dutch singer Cora Nerry, whom he married in 1934. Lothar served as director of music at Berlin's Deutsche Theater (1933–34) and Prussian State Theater (1934–44), and at the Bavarian State Theater in Munich

(1945–55). In addition to his various dramatic scores, he wrote a number of lieder.

WORKS: D R A M A T I C : O p e r a : *Tyll* (Weimar, Oct. 14, 1928); *Lord Spleen* (Dresden, Nov. 11, 1930); *Münchhausen* (Dresden, June 6, 1933); *Das kalte Herz*, radio opera (Berlin Radio, March 24, 1935); *Schneider Wibbel* (Berlin, May 12, 1938); *Rappelkopf* (Munich, Aug. 20, 1958); *Der Glücksfischer* (Nuremberg, March 16, 1962); *Liebe im Eckhaus*, Singspiel (n.d.); *Der widerspenstige Heilige* (Munich, Feb. 8, 1968); *Momo und die Zeitdiebe* (Coburg, Nov. 19, 1978); *La bocca della verità: Hommage à Baldassare Galuppi* (1982). **O t h e r :** Incidental music to many plays and radio dramas; film scores. **ORCH.:** *Verwandlung eines Barockthemas* (1958); Concertino for 4 Clarinets, Strings, Harp, and Percussion (1962); Concertino for 2 Pianos, Strings, and Percussion (1972). **OTHER:** Chamber music; piano pieces; choral works; numerous songs.

BIBL.: A. Ott, ed., *M. L.: Ein Musikerporträt* (Munich, 1968); F. Messmer et al., *M. L.* (Tutzing, 1986).—**NS/LK/DM**

Lott, Dame Felicity (Ann),

distinguished English soprano; b. Cheltenham, May 8, 1947. She studied in London at Royal Holloway Coll., Univ. of London, and at the Royal Academy of Music. In 1976 she sang at London's Covent Garden in the premiere of Henze's *We Come to the River*; she also appeared there as Anne Trulove in Stravinsky's *The Rake's Progress*, as Octavian in *Der Rosenkavalier*, and in various other roles. She appeared in Paris for the first time in 1976; made her Vienna debut in 1982 singing the *4 Letze Lieder* of Strauss; in 1984 she was engaged as soloist with the Chicago Sym. Orch. In 1986 she sang at the wedding of the Duke and the Duchess of York at Westminster Abbey. In 1990 she was made a Commander of the Order of the British Empire. On Sept. 4, 1990, she made her Metropolitan Opera debut in N.Y. as the Marschallin. She chose that same role for her San Francisco Opera debut in 1993. In 1994 she portrayed Strauss's Countess at the Lyric Opera in Chicago, and in 1998 at the Glyndebourne Festival. In 1999 she made her first appearance with the N.Y. Phil. under Previn's direction in excerpts from *Arabella* and *Capriccio*. She was made a Dame Commander of the Order of the British Empire in 1996. Among her finest roles are Pamina, Countess Almaviva, Donna Elvira, Octavian, Arabella, and Anne Trulove.—**NS/LK/DM**

Lotti, Antonio,

eminent Italian organist, pedagogue, and composer; b. probably in Venice, c. 1667; d. there, Jan. 5, 1740. He was a student of Legrenzi in Venice by 1683, then became an extra (1687) and regular (1689) singer at S. Marco; was made assistant to the second organist (1690), second organist (1692), first organist (1704), and primo maestro di cappella (1736). He visited Novara (1711) and later was in Dresden at the Crown Prince's invitation (1717–19). Lotti was one of the most important composers of the late Baroque and early Classical eras in Italy; his sacred music and madrigals are particularly notable. He was held in great esteem as a pedagogue, numbering among his students Domenico Alberti, Baldassari Galuppi, Michelangelo Gasparini, and Benedetto Marcello. His *Duetti, terzetti e madrigali a più voci*, op.1 (Venice, 1705), dedicated to Emperor Joseph I, includes the madrigal *In una siepe ombrosa*; it was arranged by Bononcini and presented as his own work in London in 1731, but Lotti successfully defended his authorship in 1732. Much of his music is not extant.

WORKS: D R A M A T I C : O p e r a (all first perf. in Venice unless otherwise given): *Il trionfo dell'innocenza* (1692); *Tirsi*, dramma pastorale (1696; Act 1 by Lotti); *Sidonio* (1706); *Achille placato*, tragedia per musica (1707); *Le rovine de Troja*, intermezzo (1707); *Dragontana e Policrone*, intermezzo (1707); *Teuzzone* (1707; rev. by G. Vignola as *L'inganno vinto dalla ragione*, Naples, Nov. 19, 1708); *Cortulla e Lardone*, intermezzo (1707); *Il Vincitor generoso* (Jan. 10, 1708); *Il comando non inteso et ubbidito* (Feb. 6, 1709); *La Ninfa Apollo*, scherzo comico pastorale (Feb. 12, 1709; in collaboration with F. Gasparini); *Ama più chi men si crede*, melodramma pastorale (Nov. 20, 1709); *Isacio tiranno* (1710); *Il tradimento traditor di se stesso* (Jan. 17, 1711; rev. by F. Mancini as *Artaserse, re di Persia*, Naples, Oct. 1, 1713); *La forza del sangue* (Nov. 14, 1711); *Porsenna* (1712; rev. by A. Scarlatti, Naples, Nov. 19, 1713); *L'infedeltà punita* (Nov. 12, 1712; in collaboration with C. Pollarolo); *Irene augusta* (1713); *Polidoro*, tragedia per musica (1714); *Ciro in Babilonia* (Reggio Emilia, April 1716); *Costantino* (Vienna, Nov. 19, 1716; in collaboration with others); *Foca superbo* (Dec. 1716); *Alessandro Severo* (Dec. 26, 1716); *Giove in Argo*, melodramma pastorale (Dresden, Oct. 25, 1717); *Ascanio, ovvero Gli odi delusi dal sangue* (Dresden, Feb. 1718); *Teofane* (Dresden, Sept. 13, 1719); *Li quattro elementi*, carosello teatrale (Dresden, Sept. 15, 1719); *Griletta e Serpillo*, intermezzo (n.d.). **O r a t o r i o s :** *La Giuditta* (1701); *Il voto crudele* (Vienna, 1712); *Triumphus fidei* (Venice, 1712); *L'umiltà coronata in Esther* (Vienna, c. 1714); *Il ritorno di Tobia* (Bologna, 1723); *Gioas, re di Giuda* (Venice, n.d.); *Judith* (Venice, n.d.). **O t h e r :** Other sacred music including masses and choral works. **INSTRUMENTAL:** Concerto for Oboe d'Amore and Strings; 6 sinfonie; 6 trios for Various Instruments; 6 sonatas for Violin and Basso Continuo; also numerous secular cantatas, [12] *Duetti*, [4] *terzetti e* [2] *madrigali à più voce* for Voices and Basso Continuo, op.1 (Venice, 1705), and *Spirito di Dio ch'essendo il mondo* for 4 Voices and Basso Continuo (Ascension Day, 1736).

BIBL.: H. Bishop, ed., *Lettres from the Academy of Ancient Music of London to Signor A. L. of Venice with his Answers and Testimonies* (London, 1732); O. Chilesotti, *Sulla lettera-critica di B. Marcello contro A. L.* (Bassano, 1885); C. Spitz, *A. L. in seiner Bedeutung als Opernkomponist* (diss., Univ. of Munich, 1918); R. Holden, *6 Extant Operas of A. L. (1667–1740)* (diss., Univ. of Conn., 1967); K. O'Donnell, *The Secular Solo Cantatas of A. L.* (diss., Iowa State Univ., 1975).—**NS/LK/DM**

Loucheur, Raymond,

French composer and pedagogue; b. Tourcoing, Jan. 1, 1899; d. Nogent-sur-Marne, Sept. 14, 1979. He was a student of Woollett in Le Havre (1915–18) and of Boulanger, Gédalge, d'Indy, Fauchet, and Vidal at the Paris Cons. (1920–23). In 1928 he won the Premier Grand Prix de Rome with his cantata *Héracles à Delphe*. He was active in Paris, where he taught (1925–40); after serving as inspector of musical education in the city schools (from 1941), he was director of the Cons. (1956–62). His music was chromatically lyrical and displayed rhythmic spontaneity.

WORKS: DRAMATIC: B a l l e t : *Hof-Frog* (1935–48; Paris, June 17, 1953). **ORCH.:** 3 syms.: No. 1 (1929–33; Paris, Dec. 15, 1936; rev. 1969), No. 2 (1944; Paris, Feb. 15, 1945), and No. 3 (1971; Paris, Oct. 17, 1972); *Défilé* (1936); *Pastorale* (1939); *Rapsodie malgache* (Paris, Oct. 10, 1945); *Divertissement* (1951); Violin Concerto (1960–63; Paris, Feb. 28, 1965); Percussion

Concertino (1963; Paris, Jan. 9, 1966); *Cortège, Interlude, et Danse* for Winds, Harp, and Percussion (1964–66); Cello Concerto (1967–68; Radio Luxembourg, July 11, 1968); *Thrène* for Flute and Strings (1971); *Hommage à Raoul Dufy* (1973; Paris, Oct. 27, 1974); *Évocations* for Wind Orch. (1974; Paris, March 7, 1976). **CHAMBER:** String Quartet (1930); *En famille* for Clarinet Sextet (1932; also for Chamber Orch., 1940); *Portraits* for Clarinet, Oboe, and Bassoon (1947); *4 pièces en quintette* for Harp, Flute, Violin, Viola, and Cello (1953); Concertino for Trumpet and Clarinet Sextet (1954; also for Trumpet and Orch., 1956); Sonata for Solo Violin (1959); *Recontres* for Oboe and Cello (1972); *Reflets* for Brass Quintet (1976). **VOCAL:** *Héracles à Delphe*, cantata (1928; Le Havre, June 12, 1929); *3 Duos* for Soprano, Chorus, and Orch. (1934); *La Ballade des petites filles qui n'ont pas de poupée* for 4 Soloists, Chorus, and Piano (1936); *L'Apothéose de la Seine* for Narrator, Mezzo-soprano, Chorus, Ondes Martenot, and Orch. (Paris, July 7, 1937); *5 poèmes de R.-M. Rilke* for Mezzo-soprano and String Quartet (1952–57); songs.—**NS/LK/DM**

Loudová, Ivana, Czech composer; b. Chlumec nad Cidlinou, March 8, 1941. After training with Kabeláč at the Prague Cons. (1958–61), she was a student of Hlobil at the Prague Academy of Arts (1961–66). She then attended the summer courses in new music in Darmstadt (1967–69), pursued postgraduate studies with Kabeláč at the Prague Academy of Arts (1968–72), and had lessons with Messiaen and Jolivet in Paris (1971). In 1980 she served as composer-in-residence of the American Wind Sym. Orch. in Pittsburgh. From 1992 she taught composition at the Prague Academy of Music. In her works, she makes use of both traditional and modern compositional procedures.

WORKS: DRAMATIC: Ballet: *Rhapsody in Black* (1966). **ORCH.:** *Fantasy* (1961); Concerto for Chamber Orch. (1962); 2 syms.: No. 1 (1964) and No. 2 for Contralto, Chorus, and Orch. (1965); *Spleen (Hommage à Charles Baudelaire)* (1971); *Hymnos* (1972); *Chorale* (1974); Concerto for 6 Percussion, Organ, and Wind Orch. (1974); *Cadenza* for Violin, Flute, and Strings (1975); *Nocturno* for Viola and Strings (1975); *Partita* for Flute, Harpsichord, and Strings (1975); *Magic Concerto* for Xylophone, Marimba, Vibraphone, and Wind Orch. (1976); *Concerto breve* for Flute or Violin and Orch. (1979); *Olympic Overture* for Wind Orch. (1979); *Dramatic Concerto* for Percussion and Wind Orch. (1979); *Luminous Voice* for English Horn and Wind Orch. (1985); Double Concerto for Violin, Percussion, and Strings (1989). **CHAMBER:** Suite for Flute (1959); Violin Sonata (1961); Clarinet Sonata (1964); two string quartets (1964, 1978); *Ballata Antica* for Trombone and Piano (1966); *Solo for King David* for Harp (1972); *Air a due boemi* for Bass Clarinet and Piano (1972); *Ritornello* for two Trumpets, Horn, Tuba, and Percussion (1973); *Agamemnon* for Solo Percussion (1973); *Romeo and Juliet*, suite for Flute, Violin, Viola, Cello, and Harp or Lute (1974); *Soli e tutti* for Flute, Oboe, Violin, Viola, Cello, and Harps (1976); *Ballata eroica* for Violin and Piano (1976); *Meditations* for Flute, Bass Clarinet, Piano, and Percussion (1977); *Mattinata* for Clarinet, Trombone, and Cello (1978); *Quintetto giubiloso* for two Trumpets, Horn, Trombone, and Tuba (1979); *Musica festiva* for three Trumpets and three Trombones (1981); *Flower for Emmanuel* (in memory of C.P.E. Bach) for Jazz Quintet (1981); *Duo concertante* for Bass Clarinet and Marimba (1982); *2 Eclogues* (in memory of Vergil) for Flute and Harp (1982); *Hukvaldy Suite* (in memory of Janáček) for String Quartet (1984); Trio for Violin, Cello, and Piano (1987); *Trio Italiano* for Clarinet, Bassoon, and

Piano (1987); *Don Giovanni's Dream* for Wind Octet (1989); *Variations on a Stamic Theme* for String Quartet (1989); *Veni etiam* for Wind Instruments (1996); *Canto amoroso* for Flute (1996); *Echoes* for Horn and Percussion (1997); *Ad caelestem harmoniam* for 8 Cellos and Voice (1998). **ELECTROACOUSTIC:** *Planeta ptáků* (Planet of the Birds; 1998). **OTHER:** Piano pieces and much choral music.—**NS/LK/DM**

Louël, Jean (Hippolyte Oscar), Belgian composer and conductor; b. Ostend, Jan. 3, 1914. He studied at the Ghent Cons. with Joseph Ryelandt (composition), and at the Brussels Cons. with Joseph Jongen (theory) and Defauw (conducting). He then studied conducting with Bigot and Paray at the Paris Cons. (diploma, 1943), winning the Belgian Prix de Rome in 1943 for his cantata *La Navigation* d'Ulysse. He became a teacher at the Brussels Cons. (1943), and was director of music academies in Alost (1945–49) and Anderlecht (1949–56). He was founder-conductor of the chamber orch. of the Concerts di Midi in Brussels (1949–70). In 1956 he became inspector of music schools in Flemish Belgium. In 1959 he became a teacher of composition at the Chapelle Musicale Reine Elisabeth, retiring in 1984.

WORKS: ORCH.: *Fantaisie sur 2 chansons de trouvères* (1942); *Suite* for Chamber Orch. or Piano (1942); *Burlesque* for Bassoon and Orch. (1943); *March funèbre* and *Triomfmarch* (1945); 2 piano concertos (1945, 1949); *Concerto da camera* for Flute and Orch. (1946–47); 2 violin concertos (1950, 1971); 3 syms.: No. 1 (withdrawn), No. 2 for Strings (1968), and No. 3 (1984–85); *Toccata and Fugue* for Winds (1974); *Rhapsody* (1975); Horn Concerto (1981); *Funeral Music* (1984); Cello Concerto (1986). **CHAMBER:** Clarinet Sonata (1935); Brass Trio (1951); Wind Quintet (1958); Violin Sonata (1960); *Suite* for Flute, Cello, Vibraphone, and Harp (1967); *L'Art d'être Grand'père*, 10 pieces for Piano (1978); Saxophone Quartet (1983); Sonata for Solo Violin (1985); Clarinet Quartet (1986).—**NS/LK/DM**

Loughran, James, Scottish conductor; b. Glasgow, June 30, 1931. He studied with Peter Maag in Bonn, where he was a répétiteur at the City Theater; also studied in Amsterdam and Milan. In 1961 he won first prize in a conducting competition sponsored by the Philharmonia Orch. in London. From 1962 to 1965 he was assoc. conductor of the Bournemouth Sym. Orch., and then was principal conductor of the BBC Scottish Sym. Orch in Glasgow (1965–71). He served as principal conductor of the Hallé Orch. in Manchester (1971–83), and chief conductor of the Bamberg Sym. Orch. (1979–83). He was chief guest conductor of the BBC Welsh Sym. Orch. in Cardiff (1987–90) and permanent guest conductor of the Japan Phil. in Tokyo (from 1993). In 1996 he became chief conductor of the Århus Sym. Orch.—**NS/LK/DM**

Louis, Rudolf, German writer on music and composer; b. Schwetzingen, Jan. 30, 1870; d. Munich, Nov. 15, 1914. He studied philosophy at the Univs. of Geneva and Vienna (Ph.D., 1893), then had instruction from Klose (composition) and Mottl (conducting) in Karlsruhe. He was conductor at the theaters in Landshut (1895–96) and in Lübeck (1896–97), and in 1897 settled in Munich, where he became critic for the influential periodical *Neueste Nachrichten* (from 1900). He wrote a symphonic fantasy, *Proteus* (1903), as well as pieces for piano, 4-hands, and songs.

WRITINGS: *Die Weltanschauung Richard Wagners* (Leipzig, 1898); *Franz Liszt* (Berlin, 1900); *Hector Berlioz* (Leipzig, 1904); *Anton Bruckner* (Munich and Leipzig, 1904); with L. Thuille, *Harmonielehre* (1907; 10th ed., 1933; abr. as *Grundriss der Harmonielehre*, 1908); *Die deutsche Musik der Gegenwart* (Munich, 1909; 3rd ed., 1912); *Aufgaben für den Unterricht in der Harmonielehre* (Stuttgart, 1911); *Schlüssel für Harmonielehre* (Stuttgart, 1912). —NS/LK/DM

Louis Ferdinand (actually, **Friedrich Christian Ludwig**), Prince of Prussia, German pianist and composer, nephew of **Frederick II (Frederick the Great)**; b. Friedrichsfelde, near Berlin, Nov. 18, 1772; d. in battle in Saalfeld, Oct. 10, 1806. He showed remarkable talent as a pianist in childhood. He was educated for a military career, entering the army in 1789; however, he continued his interest in music and later studied composition with Dussek in Hamburg, who subsequently entered his entourage (1804). That same year he met Beethoven, expressing great admiration for his music; in return, Beethoven dedicated his 3rd Piano Concerto to him. H. Kretzschmar ed. his collected works (Leipzig, 1915–17).

WORKS (all publ. in Leipzig unless otherwise given): 2 piano quintets (Paris, 1803, 1806); 2 piano quartets (1806); 3 piano trios (Berlin, 1806); *Andante with Variations* for Violin, Viola, Cello, and Piano (1806); *Larghetto with Variations* for Violin, Viola, Cello, Double Bass, and Piano (Berlin, 1806); Fugue for Piano (1807); 2 Rondos for Piano and Orch. (1808, 1823); Octet (1808); Nocturne for Flute, Violin, Cello, and Piano (1808).

BIBL.: E. Wintzer, *Prinz L. F. von Preussen als Mensch und Musiker* (Leipzig, 1915); R. Hahn, *L. F. von Preussen als Musiker* (diss., Univ. of Breslau, 1935); B. McMurty, *The Music of Prince L. F.* (diss., Univ. of Ill., 1972).—NS/LK/DM

Louis XIII, King of France from 1610 to 1643; b. Paris, Sept. 27, 1601; d. there, May 14, 1643. He was an amateur musician. Among his works are a couple of airs de cour and some motets; he also wrote the words and music for *Le Ballet de la Merlaison* (Chantilly, March 15, 1635). The well-known *Amaryllis*, arranged by Henri Ghis and widely publ. as *Air of Louis XIII*, is a misattribution; the melody first appears in print as *La Clochette* in the *Ballet-Comique de la Reine* by Balthazar de Beaujoyeux, produced in 1582. A gavotte, also entitled *Amaryllis*, with a elody totally different from the apocryphal *Air of Louis XIII* and dated 1620, may be an authentic composition of Louis XIII.—NS/LK/DM

Loulié, Etienne, French writer on music and inventor; b. probably in Paris, c. 1655; d. there, c. 1707. He was a chorister at the Sainte-Chapelle in Paris (c. 1663–73). Thanks to the patronage of Mlle. de Guise, he was able to study with Gehenault and Ouvrard. He invented the chronomètre, the precursor of the metronome, and the sonomètre, a monochord to aid in tuning.

WRITINGS: *Eléments ou principes de musique dans un nouvel ordre...avec l'estampe et l'usage du chronomètre* (Paris, 1696; second ed., 1698; Eng. tr., 1965); *Abrégé des principes de musique* (Paris, 1696); *Nouveau système de musique ou nouvelle division du monocorde...avec la description et l'usage du Sonomètre* (Paris, 1698). —NS/LK/DM

Lourié, Arthur Vincent (real name, **Artur Sergeievich Lure**), Russian-born American composer; b. St. Petersburg, May 14, 1892; d. Princeton, N.J., Oct. 13, 1966. He studied at the St. Petersburg Cons. but gave up formal training after becoming active in various modernistic groups, including the futurists. With the coming of the Bolshevik Revolution in 1917, he was made chief of the music dept. of the Commisarit for Public Instruction in 1918. In 1921 he went to Berlin, where he met Busoni. In 1924 he proceeded to Paris, where he was befriended by Stravinsky. In 1941 he emigrated to the U.S. and in 1947 became a naturalized American citizen. He was the author of the vol. *Profanation et sanctification du temps* (Paris, 1966). As early as 1915, Lourié experimented with 12-tone techniques in his piano music. He later pursued the practice of stylizing early forms à la Stravinsky.

WORKS: DRAMATIC: *The Feast During the Plague*, opera-ballet (1935; arranged for Soprano, Chorus, and Orch., Boston, Jan. 5, 1945); *The Blackamoor of Peter the Great*, opera (1961). **ORCH.:** *Sonata liturgica* for Piano, Chorus, and Orch. (1928); *Concerto spirituale* for Piano, Chorus, and Double Basses (N.Y., March 26, 1930); 2 syms.: No. 1, *Sinfonia dialectica* (1930; Philadelphia, April 17, 1931) and No. 2, *Kormtschaya* (1939; Boston, Nov. 7, 1941); *Concerto da camera* for Violin and Strings (1957). **CHAMBER:** *Dithyrambes* for Flute (1923); *The Mime* for Clarinet (1956); piano pieces. **VOCAL:** Sacred and secular choral pieces; songs.

BIBL.: D. Gojowy, *A. L. und der Russische Futurismus* (Laaber, 1993).—NS/LK/DM

Lovano, Joe, jazz tenor saxophonist; b. Cleveland, Ohio, Dec. 29, 1952. His father, Tony "Big T" Lovano (b. Sept. 21, 1925), was a barber by day and an accomplished tenor saxophonist by night; Big T played in the "Hot Sauce" Williams Blues Band (including the night Coltrane sat in on alto, in either 1949 or 1952); he mentored young Joe, taking him to see Sonny Stitt, James Moody, Lou Donaldson, and Gene Ammons. Joe got his first tenor, a King Super 20, when he was 11 years old. He played in Motown-style bands growing up, graduated H.S. in 1971, and then went to Berklee, where his classmates included John Scofield, Bill Frisell, George Garzone, Billy Pierce, Billy Drewes, and Jamey Haddad. After leaving Berklee in 1972, he began freelancing and worked with Lonnie Smith's quartet based in Detroit between 1974 and 1976. In 1975 he performed on baritone with Jack McDuff at the Club Baron in Harlem, alongside tenorists David Young and Bill Cody, altoist Willie Smith (not the famous one but a close friend of Joe's father, also from Cleveland), and Joe Dukes. He toured with Woody Herman in 1976–79. By 1978 he was living on 23rd St. in N.Y. and from 1980 played Mondays with the Mel Lewis big band, where his infrequent, but outstanding solos gained recognition; he stayed with Lewis through 1991, including some touring. Joe was a busy sideman, most notably with Paul Motian's trio, which included Bill Frissell. He played with Marc Johnson, John Scofield, the Carla Bley Band, the Charlie Haden Liberation Music Orch., and others. He played in Italy in 1995 with Steve Coleman, Bunky Green, and Craig Handy. His quintet, Symbiosis, formed in 1995, features his wife, vocalist Lisa Silvano, and Eric Friedlander on cello. In 1995 he recorded *Quartets* (released January 1996), from two distinctive sessions at the Village Vanguard; the album received a Grammy nomination. In 1996 *Down Beat*'s Annual Readers Poll awarded him "Jazz Musician of the Year" and "Jazz Album of the Year." He and Gunther Schuller collaborated on a film score for *Face Down*, a Showtime production, starring Joe Mantegna, which aired in 1997.

DISC.: *Tones, Shapes and Colors* (1985); *One Time Out* (1987); *Village Rhythm* (1988); *Landmarks* (1990); *From the Soul* (1991); *Sounds of Joy* (1991); *Universal Language* (1992); *Tenor Legacy* (1993); *Rush Hour* (1994); *Quartets* (1995); *Celebrating Sinatra* (1997).—**LP**

Love, underground L.A.–based band led by vocalist Arthur Lee who inspired a devoted following. **MEMBERSHIP:** Arthur Lee, gtr., voc. (b. Memphis, Tenn. March 7, 1945); Bryan Maclean, gtr., voc. (b. Los Angeles, 1947); John Echols, gtr. (b. Memphis, Tenn., 1945); Ken Forssi, bs. (b. Cleveland, Ohio, 1943); Alban "Snoopy" Pfisterer, drm. (b. Switzerland, 1947). Lee restructured Love with totally new members in August 1968 and disbanded the group in 1971.

Moving to L. A. as a child, Arthur Lee played with The L. A. G.s before forming Love with Bryan Maclean, John Echols, and two others in April 1965. Debuting live at the club Brave New World, the group replaced the two with Ken Forssi and Alban Pfisterer and built up an impressive local reputation through engagements in Sunset Strip clubs. The first rock group signed to Elektra Records, Love's hard-edged debut album included Lee's "Signed D. C." and an early version of "Hey Joe," yielding a minor hit with a pounding version of Burt Bacharach and Hal David's "Little Red Book." With Pfisterer switching to keyboards, Love recorded *Da Capo* with Tjay Cantrelli (flt., sax.) and Michael Stuart (drm.). The album contained the frantic hit single "Seven and Seven Is," excellent Lee songs such as "Stephanie Who Knows" and "She Comes in Colors," and the side-long "Revelation," a cunning parody of Mick Jagger's "Goin' Home."

With the departures of Cantrelli and Pfisterer, Love was reduced to Lee, Maclean, Echols, Forssi, and Stuart for their acknowledged classic, *Forever Changes*. Pervaded by brilliant existential songs such as MacLean's "Alone Again or" and Lee's "Andmoreagain," "The Daily Planet," "Bummer in the Summer," and "You Set the Scene," the album was largely acoustic rather than electric and featured the outstanding orchestral arrangements and production of Lee. However, the album sold less well than either previous release and, by August 1968, Lee had reconstitued Love with guitarist Jay Donnellan, bassist Frank Fayad, and drummer George Suranovich. *Four Sail*, the group's final album for Elektra, included Lee's "August," "Good Times," and "Always See Your Face." Switching to Blue Thumb Records, Love recorded two albums for the label, including *False*

Start, which featured a cameo appearance by Jimi Hendrix on "The Everlasting First."

Love disbanded in 1971, and Lee later recorded solo albums for A&M and RSO Records. However, Lee's songwriting had devolved into cloying self- parody. Lee reunited with Maclean in the late 1970s and recorded a solo album for Rhino Records in 1981. By the early 1990s, Lee was again performing in the L. A. region, even conducting an East and West Coast club tour in 1994. Bryan Maclean's half-sister Maria McKee (b. Los Angeles, Aug. 17, 1964) formed the country-rock band Lone Justice with guitarist Ryan Hedgecock in 1982 and initiated her solo career in 1986.

DISC.: **LOVE:** *Love* (1966); *Da Capo* (1966); *Forever Changes* (1967); *Four Sail* (1969); *Out Here* (1969); *Revisited* (1970); *False Start* (1970); *Studio/Live* (1982). **ARTHUR LEE:** *Vindicator* (1972); *Reel-to-Real* (1974); *Arthur Lee* (1981).—**BH**

Love, Shirley, American mezzo-soprano; b. Detroit, Jan. 6, 1940. She studied voice in Detroit with Avery Crew and in N.Y. with Marinka Gurewich and Margaret Harshaw, then sang with the Baltimore Opera (1962). She first appeared in a minor role at the Metropolitan Opera in N.Y. on Nov. 30, 1963; subsequently gained experience as a singer with other American opera companies; returned to the Metropolitan in 1970, remaining on its roster until 1984. She also appeared in opera in Europe, sang in concerts with major American orchs., gave recitals, and appeared in musical comedies. Her operatic repertoire included more than 100 roles. —**NS/LK/DM**

Löveberg, Aase (née **Nordmo**), Norwegian soprano; b. Målselv, June 10, 1923. She was born into a peasant family; spent her childhood on a farm near the Arctic Circle. When she was 19 she went to Oslo, where she studied voice with Haldis Ingebjart. She made her operatic debut in Oslo on Dec. 3, 1948; then sang in Stockholm, Vienna, Paris, and London. She made her first American appearance as a soloist with the Philadelphia Orch. (Dec. 6, 1957); then pursued her career mainly in Norway, later serving as manager of the Oslo Opera (1978–81).—**NS/LK/DM**

Løvenskjold, Herman Severin, Norwegian organist and composer; b. Holdensjärnbruk, July 30, 1815; d. Copenhagen, Dec. 5, 1870. At the age of 13 his parents took him to Copenhagen, where he studied music and, in 1836, brought out his ballet *Sylphiden* with much success. After the premiere of his second ballet, *Sara*, in 1839, he went to Vienna, where he took some lessons with Seyfried. Returning to Denmark in 1851, he was appointed organist at the Slottskyrka in Christiansborg. He wrote an opera, *Turandot* (Copenhagen, Dec. 3, 1854), *Fesoutvertüre* (for the coronation of Christian VIII), *Ouverture de concert idyllique*, the overture *Fra Skoven ved Furesø*, Piano Trio, Piano Quartet, and piano pieces for 2- and 4-hands.—**NS/LK/DM**

Lover, Samuel, Irish novelist, poet, painter, and composer, grandfather of **Victor (August) Herbert**; b.

Dublin, Feb. 24, 1797; d. St. Helier, Jersey, July 6, 1868. He wrote music to several Irish plays, and to many songs; publ. *Songs and Ballads* (London, 1859). Among his most popular songs (some of which are set to old Irish tunes) are *The Angel's Whisper, Molly Bawn,* and *The Low-Backed Car.* He also wrote an opera, *Grana Uile, or The Island Queen* (Dublin, Feb. 9, 1832), and devised a very successful musical entertainment, *Irish Evenings* (1844), with which he toured the British Isles and the U.S. (1846).

BIBL.: B. Bernard, *Life of S. L., R.H.A., Artistic, Literary, and Musical* (London, 1874); A. Symington, *S. L.: A Biographical Sketch* (London, 1880).—NS/LK/DM

Lovin' Spoonful, The

one of the prime movers in the N.Y. folk-rock movement of the mid-1960s. **MEMBERSHIP:** John Sebastian, gtr., autoharp, pno., har., voc. (b. Greenwich Village, N.Y., March 17, 1944); Zalman Yanovsky, lead gtr., voc. (b. Toronto, Dec. 19, 1944); Steve Boone, bs., pno., voc. (b. Camp Lejeune, N.C., Sept. 23, 1943); Joe Butler, drm., voc. (b. Glen Cove, Long Island, N.Y., Jan. 19, 1943).

John Sebastian was born the son of a renowned classical harmonica player. Taking up harmonica himself as a child and guitar at the age of 12, he later added piano and autoharp to his instrumental repertoire. Playing early recording sessions for Tom Rush, Tim Hardin, and Jesse Colin Young, Sebastian joined The Even Dozen Jug band in 1963. That band included Maria Muldaur (1974's "Midnight at the Oasis"), Stefan Grossman, and Steve Katz, who later formed The Blues Project and Blood, Sweat and Tears.

In 1964, Canadian-born Zalman Yanovsky was a member of the short-lived N.Y.–based Mugwumps with singer-songwriter Jim Hendricks, and Denny Doherty and Cass Elliot, who later became half of The Mamas and The Papas. Yanovsky and Sebastian met during recording sessions for The Mugwumps. Sebastian, with the encouragment of producer Erik Jacobsen, formed The Lovin' Spoonful at the beginning of 1965 with Yanovsky, Steve Boone, and Joe Butler.

Playing regular engagements at the Night Owl in Greenwich Village, The Lovin' Spoonful signed with Kama Sutra Records in June 1965. *Do You Believe in Magic* sported a fresh, clean, friendly sound on traditional folk and blues songs and Sebastian originals such as "Younger Girl," and the near-smash hits "Do You Believe in Magic" and "Did You Ever Have to Make up Your Mind." *Daydream* yielded a smash hit with the title song and contained a number of fine songs such as "Didn't Want to Have to Do It" and "You Didn't Have to Be So Nice." Between soundtrack albums for Woody Allen's *What's Up, Tiger Lily?* and Francis Ford Coppola's *You're a Big Boy Now,* The Lovin' Spoonful issued *Hums,* generally regarded as their most fully realized album. Producing a top hit with the summertime classic "Summer in the City," the album also contained the near-smashes "Rain on the Roof" and "Nashville Cats." Subsequent hits included "Darling, Be Home Soon," one of Sebastian's strongest and most endearing songs, "Six O'Clock" and "She's Still a Mystery."

However, in 1966, two members of The Lovin' Spoonful were arrested on drug charges in San Fran-

cisco, and Yanovsky, threatened with deportation, apparently incriminated at least one area resident. He left the group in ignominy in June 1967, and The Lovin' Spoonful's image was permanently tarnished. Jerry Yester was recruited for *Everything Is Playing,* which contained "Six O'Clock," "She Is Still a Mystery," and "Younger Generation," but John Sebastian departed the group in October 1968. Steve Boone also left, and Joe Butler reconstituted the group for one final album before dissolving the group in the summer of 1969.

In August 1969, John Sebastian reestablished himself with members of the counterculture with his renowned, stoned-out appearance at the Woodstock Festival, performing two songs. However, he had become embroiled in legal disputes among his former manager, MGM Records (the distributor of Kama Sutra), and his new label, Reprise. The release of his debut solo album was delayed for a time and, in fact, both MGM and Reprise issued *John B. Sebastian* in early 1970. The best-selling album of Sebastian's solo career, it was recorded with the assistance of Crosby, Stills and Nash, and contained several good-time uptempo songs, two gentle love songs, "She's a Lady" and "Magical Connection," and two songs of communal good will, "How Have You Been" and "I Had a Dream." He subsequently recorded *The Four of Us* and *Tarzana Kid* for Reprise. The latter album included Jimmy Cliff's "Sitting in Limbo," Lowell George's "Dixie Chicken," Sebastian and George's "Face of Appalachia," and Sebastian's own "Stories We Could Tell," recorded by The Everly Brothers in 1972. In 1976, Sebastian scored a top pop and easy-listening hit with "Welcome Back" from the ABC-TV situation comedy *Welcome Back Kotter.*

For the next decade, John Sebastian toured the concert and festival circuit, playing around 100 engagements a year. He worked on the animated movies *Charlotte's Web* and *The Care Bears Movie,* and briefly reunited The Lovin' Spoonful for Paul Simon's *One-Trick Pony* movie in 1980. Since 1991, Steve Boone, Joe Butler, and Jerry Yester have toured as The Lovin' Spoonful. In the early 1990s, Sebastian hosted *The Golden Age of Rock 'n' Roll* series on cable television's Arts and Entertainment network and recorded instructional harmonica and autoharp tapes for Happy Traum's Homespun Tapes. In 1993, he joined Shanachie Records with the help of labelmate Stefan Grossman, recording *Tar Beach,* his first album in 17 years. Sebastian later recorded *I Want My Roots* for MusicMasters with a jug band dubbed The J-Band.

DISC.: THE EVEN DOZEN JUG BAND: *The Even Dozen Jug Band* (1963). THE MUGWUMPS: *The Mugwumps* (1967). THE LOVIN' SPOONFUL: *Do You Believe in Magic* (1965); *Daydream* (1966); *What's Up, Tiger Lily* (soundtrack; 1966); *Hums of The Lovin' Spoonful* (1966); *You're a Big Boy Now* (soundtrack; 1967); *Everything Is Playing* (1967); *Revelation: Revolution '69* (1968). ZALMAN YANOVSKY: *Alive and Well in Argentina* (1969). JOHN SEBASTIAN: *John B. Sebastian* (1970); *Live* (1970); *Real Live John Sebastian* (1971); *The Four of Us* (1971); *Tarzana Kid* (1974); *Welcome Back* (1976); *Tar Beach* (1993); *John Sebastian* (rec. 1979; 1996). JOHN SEBASTIAN AND THE J-BAND: *I Want My Roots* (1996).—BH

Lowe, Edward, English organist, composer, and music copyist; b. Salisbury, c. 1610; d. Oxford, July 11, 1682. He was a chorister at Salisbury Cathedral and a pupil of John Holmes. In 1631 he became organist at Christ Church Cathedral, Oxford, which post he held until the establishment of the Commonwealth. He then devoted himself to teaching until the Restoration, when he resumed his Oxford post. He also served as co-organist of the Chapel Royal with W. Child and C. Gibbons. Lowe pub. *A Short Direction for the Performance of Cathedrall Service* (Oxford, 1661; second ed., aug., 1664 as *A Review of a Short Direction*). He prepared 2 valuable collections of vocal music by leading composers of his time. Among his own works were 10 anthems, 4 part songs, and harpsichord lessons.—**LK/DM**

Löwe, Ferdinand, noted Austrian conductor; b. Vienna, Feb. 19, 1865; d. there, Jan. 6, 1925. He studied with Dachs, Krenn, and Bruckner at the Vienna Cons., then taught piano and choral singing there (1883–96) and was conductor of the Vienna Singakademie (1896–98). In 1897 he became conductor of the Kaim Orch. in Munich; then of the Court Opera in Vienna (1898–1900) and of the Vienna Gesellschaftskonzerte (1900–1904). In 1904 he became conductor of the newly organized Vienna Konzertverein Orch., which he made one of the finest instrumental bodies in Europe. He returned to Munich as conductor of the Konzertverein Orch. (1908–14), which comprised members of the former Kaim Orch. From 1918 to 1922 he was head of the Vienna Academy of Music. He was a friend and trusted disciple of Bruckner; ed. (somewhat liberally) several of Bruckner's works, including his Fourth Sym., preparing a new Finale (1887–88); he also made a recomposed version of his unfinished 9th Sym., which he conducted in Vienna with Bruckner's *Te Deum* in lieu of the unfinished Finale (Feb. 11, 1903).

BIBL.: R. Rauner, *F. L.: Leben und Wirken: Eine Wiener Musiker zwischen Anton Bruckner und Gustav Mahler* (Frankfurt am Main, 1995).—**NS/LK/DM**

Löwe, (Johann) Carl Gottfried
See **Loewe, (Johann) Carl Gottfried**

Lowens, Irving, eminent American musicologist, music critic, and librarian; b. N.Y., Aug. 19, 1916; d. Baltimore, Nov. 14, 1983. He studied at Teachers Coll., Columbia Univ. (B.S. in music, 1939). During World War II, he served as an air-traffic controller for the Civil Aeronautics Administration. He continued in this capacity at the National Airport in Washington, D.C., and then took special courses in American civilization at the Univ. of Md. (M.A., 1957; Ph.D., 1965). In 1953 he began to write music criticism for the *Washington Star*; from 1960 to 1978 he was its chief music critic; received the ASCAP-Deems Taylor Award for the best articles on music in 1972 and 1977. From 1960 to 1966 he was a librarian in the Music Division of the Library of Congress in Washington, D.C. From 1978 to 1981 he was dean of the Peabody Inst. of the Johns Hopkins Univ. in Baltimore; also wrote music criticism for the *Baltimore News American*. A linguist, he traveled widely on nu-merous research grants in Europe. He was a founding member of the Music Critics' Assn., and from 1971 to 1975 served as its president.

WRITINGS: *The Hartford Harmony: A Selection of American Hymns from the Late 18th and Early 19th Centuries* (Hartford, 1953); *Music and Musicians of Early America* (N.Y., 1964); *Source Readings in American Music History* (N.Y., 1966); *Lectures on the History and Art of Music at the Library of Congress, 1946–63* (N.Y., 1968); *A Bibliography of American Songsters Published before 1821* (Worcester, Mass., 1976); *Haydn in America* (Washington, D.C., 1977); with A. Britton and R. Crawford, *American Sacred Music Imprints, 1698–1810: A Bibliography* (Worcester, Mass., 1990). —**NS/LK/DM**

Lowenthal, Jerome (Nathaniel), American pianist; b. Philadelphia, Feb. 11, 1932. He studied piano at an early age; made his debut with the Philadelphia Orch. at the age of 13, then took lessons with Samaroff at the Philadelphia Cons. (1947–50). While taking courses at the Univ. of Pa. (B.A., 1953), he received private piano instruction from Kapell; continued his studies with Steuermann at the Juilliard School of Music in N.Y. (M.S., 1956) and with Cortot at the École Normale de Musique (licence de concert, 1958). In 1957 he took first prize in the Darmstadt competition. He traveled to Israel, where he gave concerts and taught at the Jerusalem Academy of Music; returned to the U.S. in 1961. He made his professional debut as soloist with the N.Y. Phil. in 1963, and subsequently toured throughout North and South America, the Middle East, and the Far East. His repertoire embraces the standard piano litera-ture as well as contemporary works; among composers who wrote special works for him were George Rochberg and Ned Rorem.—**NS/LK/DM**

Löwe von Eisenach, Johann Jakob, German organist and composer; b. Vienna (baptized), July 31, 1629; d. Lüneburg, Sept. 1703. After training in Vienna and Italy, he studied with Schütz in Dresden in 1652. That same year, he was named director of music at the Altenburg court. He was Kapellmeister at the courts of Wolfenbüttel (1655) and Zeitz (1663–65). In 1683 he settled in Lüneburg as organist of the church of St. Nicolai and St. Marien, eventually dying in poverty. He publ. 2 vols. of instrumental pieces (Bremen, 1658; Jena, 1664), a vol. of sacred vocal concertos (Wolfenbüttel, 1660), and 3 vols. of secular songs (Bremen, 1657; Jena, 1665; Nuremberg, 1682).

BIBL.: R. Keuschnig, *J.J. L.v.E. als Instrumentalkomponist* (diss., Univ. of Vienna, 1971).—**LK/DM**

Lowinsky, Edward E(lias), eminent German-born American musicologist; b. Stuttgart, Jan. 12, 1908; d. Chicago, Oct. 11, 1985. He studied at the Hochschule für Musik in Stuttgart (1923–28); took his Ph.D. at the Univ. of Heidelberg in 1933 with the diss. *Das Antwerpener Motettenbuch Orlando di Lassos und seine Beziehungen zum Motettenschaffen der niederländischen Zeitgenössen* (publ. in The Hague, 1937). When the Nazis came to power in Germany in 1933, he fled to the Netherlands; when the dark cloud of anti-Semitism reached the Netherlands, he emigrated to the U.S. (1940), becoming a naturalized American citizen in 1947. He was asst. prof. of music at Black Mountain Coll. (1942–47); assoc. prof. of music at Queens Coll., N.Y. (1948–56); prof. of music at the Univ. of Calif., Berkeley (1956–61); and prof. of music at the Univ. of Chicago (1961–76), where he also held a post-retirement professorship until 1978. He held Guggenheim fellowships in 1947–48 and 1976–77; was a Fellow at the Inst. for Advanced Study at Princeton Univ. from 1952 to 1954; was made a Fellow of the American Academy of Arts and Sciences in 1973; was named Albert A. Bauman Distinguished Research Fellow of the Newberry Library in Chicago in 1982. He was general ed. of the Monuments of Renaissance Music series; publ. the valuable studies *Secret Chromatic Art in the Netherlands Motet* (N.Y., 1946) and *Tonality and Atonality in Sixteenth-Century Music* (Berkeley and Los Angeles, 1961; rev. printing, 1962; new ed. by B. Blackburn, 1990). He also prepared the vol. *Josquin des Prez. Proceedings of the International Josquin Festival-Conference* (London, 1976) and wrote the study *Cipriano de Rore's Venus Motet: Its Poetic and Pictorial Sources* (Provo, 1986). He was married to **Bonnie Blackburn**. She ed. *Music in the Culture of the Renaissance and Other Essays by Edward E. Lowinsky* (Chicago, 1989). With Lowinsky and C. Miller, she ed. and tr. *A Correspondence of Renaissance Musicians* (Oxford, 1991).—**NS/LK/DM**

Lowry, Robert, American hymn writer; b. Philadelphia, March 12, 1826; d. Plainfield, N.J., Nov. 25, 1899. He was a Baptist preacher and studied music in his middle age. He wrote the tunes for such popular hymns as *I Need Thee Every Hour* (1872) and *All the Way My Savior Leads Me* (1875), and both texts and tunes for the successful hymns *Shall We Gather at the River?* (1865), *Low in the Grave He Lay* (1875), and *Where Is My Wandering Boy Tonight?* (1877).—**NS/LK/DM**

Lualdi, Adriano, Italian composer; b. Larino, March 22, 1885; d. Milan, Jan. 8, 1971. He was a student in Rome of Falchi and in Venice of Wolf-Ferrari. In 1918 he settled in Milan and was active as a music critic and administrator. As a loyal Fascist, he served as director of the Cons. of San Pietro a Majella in Naples (1936–44). After the fall of the Fascist regime, he was forced to withdraw from public life but later resumed his career and was director of the Florence Cons. (1947–56). Lualdi was best known for his dramatic works.

WORKS: DRAMATIC: *Le nozze di Haura,* opera (1908; rev. 1913; Italian Radio, Oct. 19, 1939; stage premiere, Rome, April 18, 1943; *La figlia del re,* opera (1914–17; Turin, March 18, 1922; *Le furie di Arlecchino,* opera (Milan, May 17, 1915; rev. 1925; *Il diavolo nel campanile,* opera (1919–23; Milan, April 21, 1925; rev. 1952; Florence, May 21, 1954); *La grançeola,* opera (Venice, Sept. 10, 1932); *Lumawig e la saetta,* mimodrama (1936; Rome, Jan. 23, 1937; rev. 1956); *Eurydikes diatheke* or *Il testamento di Euridice,* opera (c. 1940–62; RAI, Nov. 22, 1962); *La luna dei Caraibi,* opera (1944; Rome, Jan. 29, 1953); *Tre alla radarstratotropojonosferaphonotheca del Luna Park,* satiric radio comedy (c. 1953–62). **ORCH.:** 2 symphonic poems: *La leggenda del vecchio marinaio* (1910) and *L'interludio del sogno* (1917); *Suite adriatica* (1932); *Africa,* rhapsody (1936); *Divertimento* (1941). **VOCAL:** *La rosa di Saron* or *Il cantico,* cantata (Milan, May 10, 1915); many choruses.

WRITINGS (all publ. in Milan): *Viaggio musicale in Italia* (1927); *Serate musicali* (1928); *Viaggio musicale in Europa* (1928); *Arte e regime* (1929); *Il rinnovamento musicale italiano* (1931); *Viaggio musicale nel Sud-America* (1934); *L'arte di dirigere l'orchestra* (1940; 3rd ed., 1958); *Viaggio musicale nell'URSS* (1941); *Tutti vivi* (1955); *La bilancia di Euripide: 10 libretti d'opera* (1969).

BIBL.: G. Confalonieri, *L'opera di A. L.* (Milan, 1932). —**NS/LK/DM**

Lubbock, John, English conductor; b. Much Hadham, Hertfordshire, March 18, 1945. He was a chorister at St. George's Chapel, Windsor (1952–59). Following studies at the Royal Academy of Music in London, he received training in conducting from Celibidache. While still a student, he founded the Camden Chamber Orch. in 1967. In 1972 it became the Orch. of St. John's, Smith Square, taking up residence at St. John's Church in Westminster with Lubbock as artistic director. In subsequent years, he conducted it on many tours of England, and also conducted it in Europe, the U.S., and Canada. As a guest conductor, he appeared with various orchs. and choral groups in England, and also appeared abroad as a guest conductor. In addition to works from the standard repertoire, Lubbock has been active in commissioning, performing, and recording contemporary scores. He also has been engaged in various educational ventures.—**LK/DM**

Lübeck, Ernst, Dutch pianist and composer, son of **Johann Heinrich Lübeck** and brother of **Louis Lübeck**; b. The Hague, Aug. 24, 1829; d. Paris, Sept. 17, 1876. He was trained as a pianist by his father, and as a youth made a voyage to America, playing concerts in the U.S., Mexico, and Peru (1849–54). He then settled in Paris, where he acquired the reputation of a virtuoso; Berlioz wrote enthusiastically about his playing. He became mentally unbalanced following the events of the Paris Commune of 1871. He wrote some pleasing salon pieces for Piano, among them *Berceuse, Tarentelle, Polonaise, Trilby the Sprite,* and *Rêverie caractéristique.*—**NS/LK/DM**

Lübeck, Johann Heinrich, Dutch violinist, conductor, and composer, father of **Ernst Lübeck** and **Louis Lübeck**; b. Alphen, Feb. 11, 1799; d. The Hague, Feb. 7, 1865. He was a Prussian regimental musician (1813–15). He studied music in Potsdam, then a player in theater orchs. in Riga and Stettin. In 1823 he settled in the Netherlands, giving violin concerts. From 1827 until his death he was director of The Hague Cons. He was also conductor of the "Diligentia" concerts there, and in 1829, became court conductor.—**NS/LK/DM**

Lübeck, Louis, Dutch cellist and composer, son of **Johann Heinrich Lübeck** and brother of **Ernst Lübeck**; b. The Hague, Feb. 14, 1838; d. Berlin, March 8, 1904. He studied with Jacquard in Paris. From 1863 to 1868, he taught cello at the Leipzig Cons. He toured Germany, the Netherlands, England, and the U.S. (1875–81), and in 1881 he settled in Berlin as a cellist in the Court Orch. He wrote 2 cello concertos, and solo pieces.—**NS/LK/DM**

Lubeck, Vincent, eminent German organist, pedagogue, and composer; b. Padingbuttel, Sept. (?) 1654; d.

Hamburg, Feb. 9, 1740. He was trained by his father in Flensburg. After serving as organist at Sts. Cosmas and Damian in Stade, near Hamburg (1675–1702), he was organist at the St. Nicolaikirche in Hamburg from 1702 until his death. Lubeck won great renown as a master organist and as a distinguished teacher. His 9 extant organ pieces, consisting mainly of preludes and fugues, reveal him as an outstanding composer of north German music. They have been ed. by K. Beckmann (Wiesbaden, 1973). Among his other works were 3 sacred cantatas and a keyboard suite (1728). See the ed. by G. Harms (Klecken, 1921).

BIBL.: P. Rubardt, *V. L.: Sein Leben und seine Werke, nebst Nachrichten über seine Familie und Beiträge zur Geschichte der Kirchenmusik in Stade und Hamburg im 17. und 18. Jahrhundert* (diss., Univ. of Leipzig, 1920).—**NS/LK/DM**

Lubimov, Alexei, esteemed Russian pianist and fortepianist; b. Moscow, Sept. 16, 1944. Following initial instruction at the Moscow Central Music School, he entered the Moscow Cons. in 1963 and studied with Neuhaus. He first attracted notice with his compelling performances of modern scores. In 1968 he gave the Moscow premieres of works by John Cage and Terry Riley, and subsequently championed the works of such masters as Schoenberg, Ives, Webern, Stockhausen, Boulez, and Ligeti, as well as many contemporary Russian composers. His interests were extensive, leading him to explore not only contemporary works but those from the standard repertoire as well as the early music repertoire for fortepiano. He made regular tours of Europe before making his North American debut as soloist with Andrew Parrott and the Classical Band in N.Y. in 1991.—**NS/LK/DM**

Lubin, Germaine (Léontine Angélique), noted French soprano; b. Paris, Feb. 1, 1890; d. there, Oct. 27, 1979. She studied at the Paris Cons. (1909–12) and with F. Litvinne and Lilli Lehmann. She made her debut at the Paris Opéra-Comique in 1912 as Antonio in *Les Contes d'Hoffmann*. In 1914 she joined the Paris Opéra, remaining on its roster until 1944; also appeared at London's Covent Garden (1937, 1939); in 1938 she became the first French singer to appear at Bayreuth, gaining considerable acclaim for her Wagnerian roles. She continued her career in Paris during the German occupation and was briefly under arrest after the liberation of Paris in 1944, charged with collaboration with the enemy; she was imprisoned for 3 years. After her release, she taught voice. Her most distinguished roles included Alceste, Ariane, Isolde, Kundry, Donna Anna, Leonore, Brünnhilde, Sieglinde, and the Marschallin.

BIBL.: N. Casanov, *Isolde 39—G. L.* (Paris, 1974).
—**NS/LK/DM**

Lubin, Steven, esteemed American pianist and fortepianist; b. N.Y., Feb. 22, 1942. After initial piano training, he studied philosophy at Harvard Univ. (B.A., 1963). He then continued his piano studies at the Juilliard School of Music in N.Y. (M.A., 1965), where his mentors included Rosina Lhévinne and Beveridge Webster, and studied musicology at N.Y.U. (Ph.D., 1974). He

made his N.Y. debut in 1977. In 1978 he organized the Mozartean Players, a chamber ensemble devoted to presenting period instrument performances; subsequently he toured with them throughout the U.S. He was equally adept in projecting discriminating interpretations of the Classical and Romantic keyboard repertoire, using the keyboard of the fortepiano modeled after the 1800 type of instrument.—**NS/LK/DM**

Luboff, Norman, American conductor, composer, and arranger; b. Chicago, May 14, 1917; d. Bynum, N.C., Sept. 22, 1987. He received his training in Chicago, where he attended the Univ., Central Coll., and American Cons. of Music, in the class of Leo Sowerby. After graduation, he was active as a singer and arranger for radio; then went to Hollywood as an arranger for films and television. He founded the Norman Luboff Choir in 1963, and subsequently conducted it on numerous tours, maintaining a vast repertoire of works ranging from classical to popular genres. As a composer, he devoted himself mainly to choral music.—**NS/LK/DM**

Luboshutz (real name, Luboshitz), Pierre, Russian-American pianist, brother of **Léa Luboshutz;** b. Odessa, June 17, 1891; d. Rockport, Maine, April 17, 1971. He studied violin with his father, then turned to the piano, and entered the Moscow Cons. as a pupil of Igumnov, graduating in 1912; also studied in Paris with Edouard Risler. Returning to Russia, he played in a trio with his 2 sisters, Léa (violin) and Anna (cello); in 1926, went to America as accompanist to Zimbalist, Piatigorsky, and others. In 1931 he married Genia Nemenoff (b. Paris, Oct. 23, 1905; d. N.Y., Sept. 19, 1989), with whom he formed a piano duo (N.Y. debut, Jan. 18, 1937). As Luboshutz-Nemenoff, they gave annual concerts with considerable success. From 1962 to 1968 they headed the piano dept. at Mich. State Univ.; then returned to N.Y. —**NS/LK/DM**

Lubotsky, Mark (Davidovich), Russian violinist and teacher; b. Leningrad, May 18, 1931. He was a pupil of Yampolsky and Oistrakh at the Moscow Cons., where he made his debut as soloist in the Tchaikovsky Violin Concerto (1950). He then performed throughout the Soviet Union and Eastern Europe. After making his British debut as soloist in Britten's Violin Concerto at the London Promenade Concerts (1970), he toured internationally. From 1967 to 1976 he taught at the Gnessin Inst. in Moscow. He became a prof. at the Sweelinck Cons. in Amsterdam in 1976. In 1986 he was made a prof. at the Hamburg Hochschule für Musik. His repertoire encompasses a vast range of works, from the Baroque to the most modern scores.—**NS/LK/DM**

Luca, Giuseppe de
   See **De Luca, Giuseppe**

Luca, Sergiu, noted Romanian-born American violinist and teacher; b. Bucharest, April 4, 1943. He began to study violin as a child, and in 1950 his parents took him to Israel, where he made his debut as a soloist with the Haifa Sym. Orch. (1952). He later continued his studies with Rostal in London, at the Bern Cons. (1958–61), and with Galamian at the Curtis Inst. of Music in Philadelphia (1961–65). He made his U.S. debut as soloist with the Philadelphia Orch. in 1965; subsequently appeared with many American and European orchs. with considerable success. In 1966 he became a naturalized American citizen. He was founder-director of the Chamber Music Northwest Festival in Portland, Ore. (1971–80); then was prof. of violin at the Univ. of Ill. (1980–83); subsequently was prof. of violin and violinist-in-residence at the Shepherd School of Music at Rice Univ. in Houston (from 1983) and also served as music director of the Tex. Chamber Orch. (1983–88). In 1988 he became founder-general director of the Houston-based arts organization Da Camera. He distinguished himself in a broad repertoire, ranging from the Baroque to the contemporary eras. His performances of early music are notable for their stylistic propriety.—NS/LK/DM

Lucas, Clarence (Reynolds), Canadian conductor, writer on music, and composer, father of **Leighton Lucas**; b. Smithville, Ontario, Oct. 19, 1866; d. Sèvres, near Paris, July 1, 1947. He received training in piano, organ, and violin in Montreal, and completed his studies in Paris with Marty and at the Cons. with Dubois. In 1888–89 he taught at the Toronto Coll. of Music, and in 1889–90 he was conductor of the Hamilton Phil. Soc. After teaching in Utica, N.Y. (1890–92), he was active in London mainly as a theater conductor. In 1903 he became the London correspondent of the *Musical Courier* of N.Y., and from 1907 to 1919 served on its editorial staff. He also conducted musicals for George M. Cohan. After another London sojourn (1919–23), he sent to Sèvres and was the Paris correspondent of the *Musical Courier* until 1933. He publ. *The Story of Musical Form* (London, 1908).

WORKS: DRAMATIC: *The Money Spider,* opera (c. 1897); *Anne Hathaway,* opera (c. 1897); *Peggy Machree,* musical play (1904); *Peer Gynt,* incidental music to Ibsen's play (1906). **ORCH.:** Sym.; 2 symphonic poems; overtures, including *As You Like It* (1899) and *Macbeth* (1900). **CHAMBER:** *Élégie* for Violin and Piano (1895); 2 ballades for Violin and Piano (1901, 1939); *Légende* for Violin and Piano (1903); *5 Lyrical Pieces* for Violin and Piano (1908); *3 Impromptus* for Violin (1938); many piano pieces; organ works. **VOCAL:** *The Birth of Christ,* cantata (1901); choral works; songs.—LK/DM

Lucas, Leighton, English conductor and composer; b. London, Jan. 5, 1903; d. there, Nov. 1, 1982. He was trained to be a dancer, and was a member of Diaghilev's Ballets Russes in Paris and in London (1918–21). Then he learned conducting and traveled with various ballet companies. From 1946 he conducted his own orch. He made arrangements of classical pieces for ballet and composed his own ballets, *The Wolf's Ride* (1935), *Death in Adagio,* after Scarlatti (1936), *The Horses* (1945–46), and *Tam O'Shanter* (1972–73). He also wrote *Missa pro defunctis* for Soloists, Voices, and Orch. (1934); *Sinfonia brevis* for Horn and 11 Instruments (1935); *Suite française* for Orch. (1940); *Divertissement* for Harp and 8

Instruments (1955); Cello Concerto (1956); Clarinet Concerto (1957); *Concert champêtre* for Violin and Orch. (1959); *Disquisition* for 2 Cellos and Piano, 4-hands (1967); String Trio (1969); etc.—NS/LK/DM

Lucas, Mary Anderson, English composer; b. London, May 24, 1882; d. there, Jan. 14, 1952. She studied piano at the Dresden Cons. and at the Royal Academy of Music in London, then had composition lessons from R.O. Morris, H. Howells, and M. Jacobson. She adopted an advanced harmonic style of composition. Her works include a ballet, *Sawdust* (1941), which had considerable success, as well as 6 string quartets, Trio for Clarinet, Viola, and Piano, Rhapsody for Flute, Cello, and Piano, and many songs.—NS/LK/DM

Lucca, Pauline, famous Austrian soprano of Italian-German parentage; b. Vienna, April 25, 1841; d. there, Feb. 28, 1908. She studied singing in Vienna and sang in the chorus of the Vienna Court Opera. Her professional debut took place in Olmütz as Elvira in *Ernani* on Sept. 4, 1859. Her appearances in Prague as Valentine and Norma (1860) attracted the attention of Meyerbeer, who arranged for her to become a member of Berlin's Royal Opera (1861–72). She made her first appearance at London's Covent Garden as Valentine (July 18, 1863), and sang there until 1867, returning from 1870 to 1872 and in 1882. After singing in the U.S. (1872–74), she was a leading member of the Vienna Court Opera until retiring from the stage in 1889. In her prime she was regarded as "prima donna assoluta," and her private life and recurring marriages and divorces were favorite subjects of sensational press stories; a curious promotional pamphlet, *Bellicose Adventures of a Peaceable Prima Donna,* was publ. in N.Y. in 1872, presumably to whip up interest in her public appearances, but it concerned itself mainly with a melodramatic account of her supposed experiences during the Franco-Prussian War. Among her finest roles were Cherubino, Selika, Carmen, and Marguerite.

BIBL.: A. Jansen-Mara and D. Weisse-Zehrer, *Die Wiener Nachtigall: Der Lebensweg der P. L.* (Berlin, 1935).—NS/LK/DM

Lucchesi, Andrea, Italian composer; b. Motta di Livenza, near Treviso, May 23, 1741; d. Bonn, March 21, 1801. He studied in Venice, then settled in Bonn as director of a traveling opera troupe (1771). He was made court Kapellmeister and Kurfürstlicher Rat (1774), and then Titularrat (1787). However, after the court left Bonn and the French occupied the city (1794), he was deprived of his positions.

WORKS: DRAMATIC: O p e r a : *L'isola della fortuna* (Venice, 1765); *Le Donne sempre donne* (Venice, Feb. 27, 1767); *Il Giocatore amoroso,* intermezzo (private perf., Venice, Feb. 13, 1769); *L'inganno scoperto, overo Il conte Caramella* (Bonn, May 13, 1773); *Il matrimonio per astuzia* (Venice, Oct. 1771); *L'improvisota, ossia La galanteria disturbata* (Bonn, 1773–74); *Die Liebe für das Vaterland* (Frankfurt am Main, April 22, 1784); *Ademira* (Venice, May 2, 1784); *L'amore e la misericordia guadagnano il giuoco* (Passua, 1794). **OTHER:** Ballet; syms.; chamber music; many sacred works.—NS/LK/DM

Lucchesini, Andrea, Italian pianist; b. Montecatini, July 8, 1965. He began studies at the age of 7 with

Maria Tipo, continuing his training at the Istituto Musicale Giuseppe Verdi. After winning the Dino Ciani Competition in Milan in 1983, he embarked upon a tour of Italy, giving a particularly noteworthy recital at Milan's La Scala; also toured in Germany, France, and Switzerland. He made his U.S. debut at the Newport (R.I.) Music Festival in 1984; also appeared elsewhere in the U.S. and throughout Europe.—NS/LK/DM

Luchetti, Veriano, Italian tenor; b. Viterbo, March 12, 1939. He studied in Milan and Rome. In 1965 he made his debut as Alfredo at the Wexford Festival, and in 1967 he appeared in Spoleto. In 1971 he sang in *L'Africaine* at the Maggio Musicale Fiorentino, where he returned in 1974 in Spontini's *Agnes von Hohenstaufen*. In 1973 he made his debut at London's Covent Garden as Pinkerton, and made appearances there until 1976. His first appearance at Milan's La Scala took place in 1975 as Foresto in Verdi's *Attila*, and in 1976 he sang Cherubini's Jason in Aix-en-Provence. He was engaged for *I Lombardi* in Verona in 1984. In 1985 he sang Macduff at the Salzburg Festival. After appearing as Foresto at the Vienna State Opera in 1988, he sang Radames in Turin in 1990. He also made many appearances as a soloist with various European orchs., especially in Verdi's *Requiem*. —NS/LK/DM

Lucia, Fernando de
See **De Lucia, Fernando**

Lucie, Lawrence (Larry), guitarist, singer; b. Emporia, Va., Dec. 18, 1907. His father played violin; his brother played saxophone. His wife, guitarist and singer Susan King, recorded under the name of Nora Lee King. Lawrence worked regularly in a family hillbilly band. He began specializing on guitar in 1931, and played guitar and banjo while working with June Clark's Band in 1931 and then with Benny Carter (1932–33). During 1934 he subbed for a week with Duke Ellington, then worked in pianist Dave Martin's Band, before joining the Mills Blue Rhythm Band. He played with Fletcher Henderson from summer 1934 until late 1934, then worked again with the Mills Blue Rhythm Band (then led by Lucky Millinder). He returned to Henderson's band (late 1936) and remained until 1938, when he rejoined Millinder. He joined Coleman Hawkins's Big Band in January 1940, then worked with Louis Armstrong's Big Band from May 1940 until 1944. He began leading his own small group at the 51 Club, N.Y., in 1944 and subsequently toured with his own band. He continued leading, then toured with a band led by drummer Louis Bellson in 1959. From late 1950 until January 1961 he worked in Cozy Cole's Band, then left to concentrate on freelance work. He regularly led his own quartet during the 1960s, and gigged with various leaders. In the 1970s he did extensive studio work and teaching. In 1998 he was living in retirement in N.Y. —JC/LP

Lucier, Alvin (Augustus Jr.), American composer; b. Nashua, N.H., May 14, 1931. He studied with Boatwright, Donovan, Kraehenbuhl, and Porter at Yale Univ. (1950–54); continued his training with Berger, Fine, and Shapero at Brandeis Univ. (1958–60); also studied with Foss (composition) and Copland (orchestration) at the Berkshire Music Center in Tanglewood (1958, 1959); then went to Rome on a Fulbright scholarship (1960–62). He was on the faculty of Brandeis Univ. (1962–70), where he served as choral director. With Robert Ashley, David Behrman, and Gordon Mumma, he founded the Sonic Arts Union (1966), an electronic music performing group with which he toured the U.S. and Europe. He joined the faculty of Wesleyan Univ. (1970); was music director of the Viola Farber Dance Co. (1972–77). He contributed many articles to music journals and other publications; with D. Simon, he publ. *Chambers* (Middletown, Conn., 1980). In 1990 he was in Berlin on a Deutscher Akademischer Austauschdienst fellowship. His works exploit virtually all known musical and non-musical resources available to the creative artist.

WORKS: *Action Music* for Piano (1962); *Music for Solo Performer* for Amplified Brain Waves and Percussion (1965); *North American Time Capsule* for Voices and Vocoder (1967); *Chambers*, realized by moving large and small resonant environments (1968); *Vespers*, acoustic orientation by means of echolocation (1969); *"I am sitting in a room"* for Voice and Electromagnetic Tape (1970); *The Queen of the South* for Players, Responsive Surfaces, Strewn Material, and Closed-circuit Television System (1972); *Still and Moving Lines of Silence in Families of Hyperbolas* for Singers, Players, Dancers, and Unattended Percussion (1973–74; Paris, Oct. 18, 1974); *Outlines of persons and things* for Microphones, Loudspeakers, and Electronic Sounds (1975); *Bird and Person Dyning* for Performer with Microphones, Amplifiers, Loudspeakers, and Sound-producing Object (1975); *Music on a Long Thin Wire* for Audio Oscillators and Electronic Monochord (1977); *Directions of Sounds from the Bridge* for Stringed Instrument, Audio Oscillator, and Sound-sensitive Lights (N.Y., Feb. 11, 1978); *Clocker* for Amplified Clock, Galvanic Skin Response Sensor, and Digital Delay System (1978–88); *Solar Sounder I*, electronic music system powered and controlled by sunlight (1979; in collaboration with John Fullemann); *Shapes of the Sounds from the Board* for Piano (1979); *Lullaby* for Unamplified or Amplified Voice (1979); *Music for Pure Waves, Bass Drums, and Acoustic Pendulums* (1980); *Reflections of Sounds from the Wall* (1981); *Crossings* for Small Orch. with Pure Wave Oscillator (Chicago, July 6, 1982); *Seesaw*, sound installation (1983); *Still and Moving Lines of Silence in Families of Hyperbolas, Part II, Nos. 1–12* (Oakland, Calif., Feb. 16, 1984); *Spinner*, sound installation (1984); *In Memoriam Jon Higgins* for Clarinet and Slow-sweep, Pure Wave Oscillator (Hartford, Conn., Dec. 8, 1984); *Serenade* for 13 Winds and Pure Wave Oscillator (Aspen, Colo., Aug. 8, 1985); *Sound on Paper*, sound installation (1985); *Septet* for 3 Strings, 4 Winds, and Pure Wave Oscillator (Middletown, Conn., Sept. 20, 1985); *Music for Men, Women, and Reflecting Walls* for Pure Wave Oscillators (N.Y., June 11, 1986); *Salmon River Valley Songs* for Soprano, English Horn, Xylophone, and Pure Wave Oscillators (Hartford, Conn., Sept. 27, 1986); *Kettles* for 5 Timpani and 2 Pure Wave Oscillators (1987); *Fideliotrio* for Viola, Cello, and Piano (1988); *Silver Streetcar for the Orchestra* for Triangle (1988); *Carbon Copies* for Piano, Saxophone, and Percussion (1988); *Amplifier and Reflector I* for Open Umbrella, Ticking Clock, and Glass Oven Dish (1991); *Navigations* for String Quartet (Frankfurt am Main, Oct. 11, 1991).—NS/LK/DM

Łuciuk, Juliusz (Mieczyslaw), Polish composer; b. Brzeźnica, Jan. 1, 1927. He studied in Kraków at the Jagiellonian Univ. (graduated in musicology, 1952) and at the State Higher School of Music (diplomas in theory, 1955, and composition, 1956). After further training in composition with Boulanger and Deutsch in Paris (1958–59), he returned to Poland and devoted himself to composition. In 1974 he won first prize in the Monaco competition. He received the Golden Cross of Merit of Poland in 1975. In 1983 he was awarded the prize of the City of Kraków. He received the Minister of Culture and Arts Award in 1995. In 1998 he was honored with the Polish Composers' Union Award. In his extensive output, Luciuk followed a sui generis compositional path.

WORKS: DRAMATIC: *Niobe,* ballet (1962; Gdańsk, May 20, 1967); *The Frock,* mimodrama (Wrocław, Oct. 25, 1965); *Brand-Peer Gynt,* mimodrama (Oslo, Sept. 28, 1967); *The Death of Euridice,* ballet (1972; Polish TV, Warsaw, Dec. 27, 1974); *When 5 Years Will Go By: The Legend of Time,* choreodrama (Amsterdam, Oct. 9, 1972); *L'Amour d'Orphée,* opera (1973; Wroclaw, Feb. 22, 1980); *Medea,* ballet (Poznań, Oct. 26, 1975); *Demiurgos,* opera (1976; Kraków, April 26, 1990). ORCH.: *4 Symphonic Sketches* (1957); *Symphonic Allegro* (1958; Katowice, June 9, 1959); *Composition* for 4 Orchs. (1960; Wrocław, Nov. 14, 1965); *Speranza Sinfonica* (1969; Częstochowa, June 17, 1972); *Lamentazioni in memoriam Grażyna Bacewicz* (1970; Częstochowa, March 4, 1971); *Warsaw Legend: Quasi Cradle-Song* (1974; Warsaw, Jan. 10, 1976); Double Bass Concerto (Kraków, June 10, 1986); *Hommage a quelque'un* for Guitar and Strings (Hannover, Aug. 28, 1993). CHAMBER: *Capriccio* for Violin and Piano (Warsaw, June 27, 1956); Clarinet Sonata (1956); Bassoon Sonata (1956; Kraków, Nov. 17, 1958); *Variations* for Cello and Piano (1980; Kraków, April 5, 1982); *3 Miniatures* for Violin and Piano (Kraków, May 25, 1984); *Ballata* for Guitar (1990; Kraków, April 30, 1991). KEYBOARD: P i a n o : *4 Miniatures* (1957; Kraków, March 19, 1962); *Arabesque No. 2* for 2 Pianos (1987; Kraków, Feb. 12, 1989). P r e p a r e d   P i a n o : *Marathon* (1963; Warsaw, Sept. 21, 1964); *Lirica di Timbri* (1963; Kraków, Dec. 16, 1964); *Pacem in terris* for 2 Players and Soprano (Poznań, May 29, 1964); *Passacaglia* (Kolonia Radio, April 3, 1968). O r g a n : *Image* (1977; Poznań, April 17, 1978); *Marienpräludiem* (1982; Kraków, June 6, 1983); *Tripticum Paschale* (1993; Kraków, May 22, 1994). VOCAL: *The Latin Mass* for Men's Chorus and Organ (1958); *Floral Dream* for Voice and Orch. (1960; Wenecja, April 25, 1961); *Pour un Ensemble* for Speaking Voice and 24 Strings (1961; Utrecht, Sept. 13, 1962); *Tool of the Light* for Baritone and Orch. (1966; Wroclaw, Jan. 21, 1968); *Poeme de Loire* for Soprano and Orch. (1968; Wrocław, Feb. 21, 1970); *Le Souffle du Vent* for Baritone and Orch. (Polish TV, Warsaw, Aug. 21, 1971); *Wings and Hands* for Baritone and Orch. (1972; Poznań, April 3, 1975); *Missa Gratiarum Actione* for Women's Chorus (Warsaw, Sept. 22, 1974); *Portraits lyriques* for Soprano and Orch. (1974; Posnań, April 5, 1976); *St. Francis of Assisi,* oratorio for Soprano, Tenor, Baritone, Chorus, and Orch. (Kraków, Oct. 3, 1976); *Hymnus de Caritate* for Chorus (1976; Poznań, April 7, 1981); *4 Antiphonae* for Men's Chorus (1980–84; Aachen, Dec. 16, 1984); *Manen Suita* for Chorus (1983; Warsaw, Nov. 21, 1984); *Polish Litany,* oratorio for Soloists, Chorus, and String Orch. (1984; Częstochowa, Jan. 27, 1985); *Apocalypsis* for Chorus (1985; Poznań, April 28, 1987); *Partes Variables* for Women's Chorus (1985; Kraków, May 13, 1986); *Assumpta est Maria* for Women's Chorus (1987; Częstochowa, Nov. 17, 1989); *Vesperae in Assumptione Beatae Mariae Virginis* for Women's Chorus (1987–89;

Aachen, June 9, 1989); *Magnificat* for Chorus (Częstochowa, May 4, 1991); *Antiphone ex Secundis Vesperis in Assumptione Beatae Mariae Virginis* for Chorus (1992); *The Polish Mass* for Mezzo-soprano, Chorus, and Orch. (Częstochowa, May 1, 1993); *Gesang am Brunnen,* oratorio for Soprano, Tenor, Baritone, Chorus, and Chamber Orch. (Hannover, Aug. 17, 1996); *Sanctus Adalbertus Flos Purpureus* for Mezzo-soprano, Tenor, Baritone, Chorus, and Orch. (Częstochowa, May 1, 1997); *Jubilee Cantata* for Soprano, Tenor, and Wind Orch. (Warsaw, Nov. 11, 1998); *Litany to the Virgin Mary of Supraśl* for Alto, Chorus, and Chamber Orch. (Kraków, May 30, 1999). OTHER: Children's pieces.—NS/LK/DM

Lucký, Štěpán, Czech composer; b. Žilina, Jan. 20, 1919. He was a student at the Prague Cons. (1936–39). During the Nazi occupation, he became active in the resistance and was imprisoned in Budapest before being sent to the concentration camps in Auschwitz and Buchenwald. Following the liberation in 1945, he resumed his training at the master school of the Prague Cons. (graduated, 1947). He also studied musicology and aesthetics at the Charles Univ. in Prague (graduated, 1948; Ph.D., 1990). From 1954 to 1959 he served as artistic director of music broadcasting of Czech-TV. He taught television opera directing at the Prague Academy of Music from 1964 to 1969. In 1972 he was made a Merited Artist by the Czech government. A progressive eye disease hampered his activities from about 1985. His music is couched in a pragmatic contemporary style without circumscription by any particular doctrine or technique.

WORKS (all first perf. in Prague unless otherwise given): DRAMATIC: *Půlnoční překvapení* (Midnight's Surprise), opera (1958–59; May 15, 1959); 40 feature film scores and over 100 short film scores; incidental music for plays, radio, and television. ORCH.: Cello Concerto (1946; Dec. 11, 1947); Piano Concerto (Dec. 16, 1947); Violin Concerto (1965; Mariánské Lázně, Feb. 17, 1967); *Ottetto* for Strings (1970; March 6, 1972); Double Concerto for Violin, Piano, and Orch. (1971; Jan. 24, 1974); *Nenia* for Violin, Cello, and Orch. (1974–75; May 21, 1976); *Concerto for Orchestra* (Suhl, Germany, May 4, 1976); *Fantasia concertante* for Bass Clarinet, Piano, and Orch. (1979–84; March 23, 1984). CHAMBER: 2 wind quintets: No. 1 (1946; April 10, 1947) and No. 2, *Deliciae Suhlenses* (1982; Suhl, June 5, 1983); *Sonata brevis* for Violin and Piano (Nov. 3, 1947); *Elegia* for Horn and Piano (1965; Nov. 30, 1966); Sonata for Solo Violin (1967–69; March 3, 1970); *Tre pezzi di Due Doemi* for Bass Clarinet and Piano (1969–70; Biberach, Germany, June 26, 1970); Double Sonata for 2 Violins (1971; March 29, 1974; Duo concertante for Violin and Guitar (1972; March 12, 1973); Flute Sonata (1973; March 9, 1975); *Divertimento* for Wind Quintet (1974; April 1, 1977); *Pastorale* for Oboe and Piano (1975; March 1, 1976); *Preludio e scherzino* for Clarinet (1975; N.Y., Nov. 29, 1976); *Balada* for Cello (1976; Brno, April 21, 1977); *Invence pro Sonatori* for Flute, Bass Clarinet, Piano, and Percussion (May 25, 1977); *Arietta* for Alto Flute or Bass Clarinet and Piano (1977; Stade an der Elbe, Germany, March 6, 1979); *Introduzione e capriccio* for Bassoon and Piano (1977; March 9, 1978); Concertino for Bass Clarinet, Piano, and Strings (1979; April 15, 1980); *Musica collegialis* for 10 Instruments (1980; March 10, 1982); String Quartet (1984; March 13, 1986); Wind Quartet (1985; Suhl, Sept. 23, 1986); Sonatina for 2 Guitars (1986; Jan. 18, 1988). KEYBOARD: P i a n o : Sonatina (1945; May 7, 1947). H a r p s i c h o r d : Toccata (Biberach, April 11, 1973). O r g a n :

Rapsodia (1981; Feb. 24, 1986). **VOCAL:** *Stesk* (Nostalgia), song cycle for Soprano and Piano (1940; Feb. 1, 1946); *Nedopěné písně* (Unsong Songs), song cycle for Soprano and Piano (1944; Jan. 14, 1947); *Jak se hladí kočička* (How to stroke a cat) for Children's Chorus (1983–84; Nov. 23, 1986).—**NS/LK/DM**

Ludecus, Matthäus, German composer, public official, and churchman; b. Wilsnach, Prignitz, Sept. 21, 1527; d. Havelberg, Prignitz, Nov. 12, 1606. He was educated in Perleberg, Pritzwalk, and Frankfurt an der Oder. He was a clerk in Prignitz (1550–54), and then town clerk in Lüneberg, and subsequently in Prenzlau, Uckermark (1556). From 1560 to 1597 he served as collector of land taxes for Prignitz. In 1562 he was made canon of Havelberg Cathedral, where he was its dean from 1573 until his death. He publ. 4 significant collections of Lutheran liturgical works (1589), which include unharmonized Latin Passions and various Latin hymns. —**LK/DM**

Luders, Gustav (Carl), German-American composer; b. Bremen, Dec. 13, 1865; d. N.Y., Jan. 24, 1913. After studies in Germany, he went to Milwaukee in 1888 and became active as a conductor of popular orchs. and a light opera company, as well as an arranger for the Witmark music publishing firm. In 1889 he went to Chicago as a theater conductor but soon began to compose light stage works. Following successful stagings of *The Burgomaster* (June 17, 1900) and *King Dodo* (1901), Luders attained his most popular success with the Boston staging of *The Prince of Pilsen* (May 1902). Among subsequent works, he had the most success with *The Sho-Gun* (Chicago, April 4, 1904) and *Woodland* (Boston, April 25, 1904).

WORKS: DRAMATIC: Music Theater: *Little Robinson Crusoe* (Chicago, June 21, 1895); *The Burgomaster* (Chicago, June 17, 1900); *King Dodo* (Chicago, 1901); *The Prince of Pilsen* (Boston, May 1902); *Mam'selle Napoleon* (N.Y., Dec. 8, 1903); *The Sho-Gun* (Chicago, April 4, 1904); *Woodland* (Boston, April 25, 1904); *A Society Circus* (N.Y., Dec. 13, 1905); *The Grand Mogul* (Chicago, Dec. 7, 1906); *Marcelle* (N.Y., Oct. 1, 1908); *The Fair Co-Ed* (Boston, 1908); *The Old Town* (N.Y., Jan. 10, 1910); *Ladies' Day* (London, Oct. 4, 1911); *The Gypsy* (N.Y., Nov. 14, 1912); *Somewhere Else* (N.Y., Jan. 20, 1913).—**LK/DM**

Ludford, Nicholas, English composer; b. c. 1485; d. c. 1557. He was one of the musicians at the Royal Free Chapel of St. Stephen's, Westminster, until it was dissolved in 1547, and in 1521 he was admitted to the Fraternity of St. Nicholas, a guild of musicians. His surviving works (all in MS) include masses, motets, and a Magnificat. His *Collected Works*, ed. by J. Bergsagel, were issued in Corpus Mensurabilis Musicae, XXVI (1965).—**NS/LK/DM**

Ludgin, Chester (Hall), American baritone; b. N.Y., May 20, 1925. After service in the U.S. Army (1943–46), he was a student of the American Theatre Wing Professional Training Program (1948–50); studied voice with Armen Boyajian. He began his career by singing in nightclubs; made his operatic debut in 1956 as Scarpia with the New Orleans Experimental Opera

Theatre of America. In 1957 he became a member of the N.Y.C. Opera; sang leading roles with the San Francisco Opera from 1964; made his European debut with the Netherlands Opera in 1977. He created major roles in Ward's *The Crucible* (N.Y., 1961), Imbrie's *Angle of Repose* (San Francisco, 1967), and Bernstein's *A Quiet Place* (Houston, 1983); also made successful appearances in productions of Broadway musicals.—**NS/LK/DM**

Ludikar (real name, **Vyskočil**), **Pavel,** Czech bass-baritone; b. Prague, March 3, 1882; d. Vienna, Feb. 19, 1970. He studied law in Prague, and then took piano lessons, acquiring sufficient proficiency to accompany singers. He then finally devoted himself to his real profession, that of opera singing, and studied with Lassalle in Paris. He made his operatic debut as Sarastro at the Prague National Theater (1904), then appeared in Vienna, Dresden, and Milan; was a member of the Boston Civic Opera (1913–14). He made his Metropolitan Opera debut in N.Y. as Timur in *Turandot* on Nov. 16, 1926; remained on its roster until 1932; also sang with Hinshaw's touring opera company. He essayed the role of Figaro in *Il Barbiere di Siviglia* more than 100 times in the U.S. He created the title role in Krenek's opera *Karl V* (Prague, June 22, 1938).—**NS/LK/DM**

Ludkewycz, Stanislaus, significant Polish composer and pedagogue; b. Jaroslav, Galicia, Jan. 24, 1879; d. Lwów, Sept. 10, 1979. He studied philosophy at the Univ. of Lemberg, graduating in 1901, then went to Vienna, where he studied composition with Gradener and Zemlinsky at the Cons. (Ph.D., 1908). He then settled in Lemberg. From 1910 to 1914 he served as director of the Inst. of Music there; then was recruited in the Austrian army, and was taken prisoner by the Russians (1915). After the Russian Revolution, he was evacuated to Tashkent; liberated in 1918, he returned to Lemberg; from 1939 to 1972 he was a prof. of composition at the Cons. there. When the city was incorporated in the Ukrainian Soviet Republic after World War II, Ludkewycz was awarded the Order of the Red Banner by the Soviet government (1949). On the occasion of his 100th birthday in 1979, he received the Order of Hero of Socialist Labor. His music followed the precepts of European Romanticism, with the representational, geographic, and folkloric aspects in evidence. Stylistically, the influence of Tchaikovsky was paramount in his vocal and instrumental compositions.

WORKS: DRAMATIC: Opera: *Dovbush* (1955). **ORCH.:** 2 piano concertos (1920, 1957); 4 symphonic poems: *Valse mélancolique* (1920), *Stone Carvers* (1926), *Dnieper* (1947), and *Moses* (1956); Violin Concerto (1945); *Carpathian Symphony* (1952). **CHAMBER:** Piano Trio (1919); *Variations on a Ukrainian Theme* for Violin and Piano (1949); piano pieces. **VOCAL:** *Eternal Revolutionary* for Chorus and Orch. (1898); *Caucasus*, ode for Chorus and Orch. (1905–13); *The Testament*, cantata (1934; rev. 1955); *Conquistadores* for Chorus and Orch. (1941); *A Testament for the Pioneers* for Chorus and Orch. (1967); songs.

BIBL.: M. Zagaikevycz, *S. L.* (Kiev, 1957); S. Pavlishin, *S. L.* (Kiev, 1974).—**NS/LK/DM**

Ludwig, Christa, celebrated German mezzo-soprano; b. Berlin, March 16, 1924. She was reared in a musical family. Her father, Anton Ludwig, was a tenor and an operatic administrator, and her mother, Eugenie Besalla, was a mezzo-soprano. She studied with her mother and in Frankfurt am Main with Hüni-Mihacsek. In 1946 she made her debut as Orlovsky there, and continued to sing there until 1952. After appearances in Darmstadt (1952–54), she made her debut at the Salzburg Festival as Cherubino in 1954. In 1954–55 she sang in Hannover. In 1955 she joined the Vienna State Opera, where she became one of its principal artists and was made a Kammersängerin in 1962. In 1959 she made her U.S. debut as Dorabella in Chicago. On Dec. 10, 1959, she made her first appearance at the Metropolitan Opera in N.Y. as Cherubino, and subsequently returned there regularly. Among the many outstanding roles she sang in Vienna and N.Y. were Octavian, the Dyer's Wife, Ortrud, Fricka in *Die Walküre*, the Marschallin, Kundry, Charlotte in *Werther*, Lady Macbeth, Didon in *Les Troyens*, and Strauss's Clytemnestra. In 1966 she sang Brangäne at the Bayreuth Festival and in 1969 made her first appearance at London's Covent Garden as Amneris. In addition to her appearances in other leading operatic centers, she pursued a remarkable career as a soloist with orchs. and as a lieder artist. Her performances of Schubert, Schumann, Brahms, Wolf, Mahler, and Strauss were noteworthy. In 1957 she married **Walter Berry,** but they were divorced in 1970. During their marriage and even afterward, they appeared together in operatic and concert settings. On March 20, 1993, Ludwig gave her last N.Y. recital at Carnegie Hall, and on April 3, 1993, made her farewell appearance at the Metropolitan Opera singing Fricka in *Die Walküre*. Her career closed with concert and operatic farewells in Vienna in 1994. In 1980 she received the Golden Ring of the Vienna State Opera, and in 1981 was made its honorary member. She also was awarded the Silver Rose of the Vienna Phil. in 1980. In 1989 she was honored by the French government as a Chevalier of the Légion d'honneur and as a Commandeur de l'Ordre des Arts et des Lettres. Her autobiography was publ. as "*...und ich wäre so gern Primadonna geworden*" (Berlin, 1994). Ludwig's fine vocal gifts and compelling musical integrity gained her a distinguished reputation as one of the outstanding operatic and concert artists of her day.

BIBL.: P. Lorenz, *C. L.—Walter Berry: Eine Künstler Biographie* (Vienna, 1968).—**NS/LK/DM**

Ludwig, Friedrich, eminent German musicologist; b. Potsdam, May 8, 1872; d. Gottingen, Oct. 3, 1930. He studied history at the Univs. of Marburg and Strasbourg (Ph.D., 1896), then musicology with G. Jacobsthal. He was a reader (1905–10) and a prof. (1910–20) at the Univ. of Göttingen. He was an authority on medieval music. His most valuable work was *Repertorium organorum recentioris et motetorum vetustissimi stili*, I: *Catalogue raisonné der Quellen*, part 1: *Handschriften in Quadrat-Notation* (Halle, 1910); part 2: *Handschriften in Mensural-Notation* (ed. by F. Gennrich in Summa Musicae Medii Aevi, VII, 1961); II: *Musikalisches Anfangs Verzeichnis des nach Tenores geordneten Repertorium* (ed. by Gennrich in ibid., VIII, 1962). He also ed. an incomplete collection of the works of Guillaume de Machaut (1926–34).

BIBL.: J. Müller-Blattau, *Dem Andenken F. L.s* (Kassel, 1931). —**NS/LK/DM**

Ludwig, Leopold, Austrian conductor; b. Witkowitz, Jan. 12, 1908; d. Lüneburg, April 25, 1979. He studied piano at the Vienna Cons., then conducted in provincial opera houses. He was made Generalmusikdirektor of the Oldenburg State Theater (1936), and then was a conductor at the Vienna State Opera (1939–43), the Berlin Städtische Oper (1943–51), and the Berlin State Opera (1945–51). From 1951 to 1970 he was Generalmusikdirektor of the Hamburg State Opera; also conducted at the Edinburgh Festivals (1952, 1956), the San Francisco Opera (1958–68), and the Glyndebourne Festival (1959). On Nov. 14, 1970, he made his Metropolitan Opera debut in N.Y. conducting *Parsifal*, and remained on its roster until 1972. He was known as an unostentatious but thoroughly competent interpreter of the Austro-German operatic and symphonic repertoire.

BIBL.: B. Wessling, *L. L.* (Bremen, 1968).—**NS/LK/DM**

Ludwig, Walther, German tenor; b. Bad Oeynhausen, March 17, 1902; d. Lahr, May 15, 1981. He studied jurisprudence and medicine before deciding on a singing career. He studied voice in Königsberg, where he made his debut in 1928. After singing in Schwerin (1929–32), he was a member of the Berlin Städtische Oper (1932–45). He also made appearances at the Glyndebourne Festival, Milan's La Scala, London's Covent Garden, the Salzburg Festival, and the Vienna State Opera; likewise toured as a concert artist. From 1952 to 1969 he was a prof. at the (West) Berlin Hochschule für Musik. He also completed his medical studies in Berlin (M.D., 1971). He was best known for his Mozart roles. —**NS/LK/DM**

Ludwig II, King of Bavaria and patron of Wagner; b. Munich, Aug. 25, 1845; d. (suicide) in the Starnberg Lake, June 13, 1886. As crown prince, he conceived an extreme adulation for Wagner, and when he became King, at 19, he declared his intention to sponsor all of Wagner's productions, an event that came at the most difficult time of Wagner's life, beset as he was by personal and financial problems. In sincere gratitude, Wagner spoke of his future plans of composition as "a program for the King." In his total devotion to Wagner, Ludwig converted his castle Neuschwanstein into a "worthy temple for my divine friend," installing in it architectural representations of scenes from Wagner's operas. His bizarre behavior caused the government of Bavaria to order a psychiatric examination, and he was eventually committed to an asylum near the Starnberg Lake. During a walk, he overpowered the psychiatrist escorting him, and apparently dragged him to his death in the lake, and drowned himself, too. Much material on Ludwig II is found in Wagner's bibliography; see also W. Blunt, *The Dream King, Ludwig II of Bavaria* (London, 1970), and C. McIntosh, *The Swan King: Ludwig II of Bavaria* (London, 1982).—**NS/LK/DM**

Luening, Otto (Clarence), noted American composer, music educator, flutist, and conductor; b. Milwaukee, June 15, 1900. His father, Eugene Luening, was a pianist, conductor, and teacher. After the family moved to Munich in 1912, he studied flute, piano, and theory (with Beer-Walbrunn) at the Akademie der Tonkunst. In 1916 he made his debut as a flutist in Munich. In 1917 he went to Zürich and studied with Jarnach and Andreae at the Cons. (until 1920). He also attended the Univ. there (1919–20) and profited from his association with Busoni. His Sextet (1918) and First String Quartet (1919–20) won him recognition as a composer in Europe and the U.S. After playing flute in the Tonhalle Orch. and the Opera orch. in Zürich, he went to Chicago in 1920. With Gilbert Wilson, he founded the American Grand Opera Co. in 1922. From 1925 to 1928 he was a faculty member at the Eastman School of Music in Rochester, N.Y. In 1929 he went to N.Y. and conducted on WOR Radio and in the theater. In 1932 he was awarded the David Bispham medal for his opera *Evangeline*. After serving as an asst. prof. at the Univ. of Ariz. in Tucson (1932–34), he was head of the music dept. at Bennington (Vt.) Coll. (1934–44). From 1935 to 1937 he was assoc. conductor of the N.Y. Phil. Chamber Orch. He was assoc. prof. and chairman of the music dept. at Barnard Coll. from 1944 to 1948, and then a prof. there from 1948 to 1964. In 1944 he became music director of the Brander Matthews Theater at Columbia Univ., where he conducted the premieres of Menotti's *The Medium* (May 8, 1946), Thomson's *The Mother of Us All* (May 7, 1947), and his own *Evangeline* (May 4, 1948). From 1949 to 1968 he was a prof. of music at Columbia Univ., where he also was a co-director of the Columbia-Princeton Electronic Music Center (1959–80) and music chairman of the School of the Arts (1968–70). From 1971 to 1973 he taught at the Juilliard School in N.Y. He helped to found the American Composers Alliance in 1937 and was its president from 1945 to 1951. In 1940 he co-founded the American Music Center and was it chairman until 1960. In 1954 he was a founder of Composers Recordings, Inc. Luening received various commissions, grants, awards, and honorary doctorates. He held 3 Guggenheim fellowships (1930–31; 1931–32; 1974–75). In 1952 he was elected to membership in the National Inst. of Arts and Letters. He was composer-in-residence at the American Academy in Rome in 1958, 1961, and 1965. His long and distinguished career in American music is recounted in his autobiography, *The Odyssey of an American Composer* (N.Y., 1980). Although a prolific composer in various genres and styles, Luening's most significant contribution to music rests upon his pioneering work as a composer of electronic music. His flute on tape pieces *Fantasy in Space, Invention in 12 Notes,* and *Low Speed,* all premiered at N.Y.'s Museum of Modern Art on Oct. 28, 1952, were the earliest such works ever written. In collaboration with Vladimir Ussachevsky, he also wrote the first work for tape and orch., the *Rhapsodic Variations* (Louisville, March 20, 1954). An Otto Luening Centennial Concert was given in N.Y. on May 24, 2000.

WORKS: DRAMATIC: *Sister Beatrice,* incidental music to Maeterlinck's play (Rochester, N.Y., Jan. 15, 1926); *Evangeline,* opera (1930–32; rev. 1947; N.Y., May 5, 1948, composer conducting); *Blood Wedding,* incidental music to García Lorca's play (Bennington, Vt., Dec. 1, 1940); *Of Identity,* ballet for Organ on

Tape (1954; N.Y., Feb. 9, 1955; in collaboration with V. Ussachevsky); *Carlsbad Caverns,* electronic television theme for *Wide, Wide World* (1955; in collaboration with Ussachevsky); *King Lear,* incidental music on tape for Shakespeare's play (1955; in collaboration with Ussachevsky); *Theatre Piece No. 2,* ballet for Narrator, Recorded Soprano, and Instrumental Ensemble (N.Y., April 20, 1956, composer conducting); *Back to Methuselah,* electronic incidental music to Shaw's play (1958; in collaboration with Ussachevsky); *Incredible Voyage,* electronic television score for the series *Twenty-First Century* (1968; in collaboration with Ussachevsky). **ORCH.:** Concertino for Flute and Chamber Orch. (1923; Philadelphia, Jan. 30, 1935, composer conducting); *Music* (1923; N.Y., May 26, 1978); *Symphonic Fantasia No. 1* (1924; Rochester, N.Y., Nov. 25, 1925), *No. 2* (1939–49; N.Y., Oct. 13, 1957), *No. 3* (1969–81; N.Y., Jan. 26, 1982), *No. 4* (1969–81; N.Y., May 14, 1984), *No. 5* (1978–85), *No. 6* (1985), *No. 7* (1986), *No. 8* (1986), *No. 9* (1989), *No. 10* (1990), *No. 11* (1991), and *No. 12* (1994); *Serenade* for 3 Horns and Strings (1927; Rochester, N.Y., Jan. 12, 1928); *Short Symphony* (1929–80); *Symphonic Interludes Nos. 1* and *2* (1935; N.Y., April 11, 1936), *3* (1975; Tanglewood, Aug. 13, 1980), *4* (1985), and *5* (1986); *Prelude to a Hymn Tune by William Billings* (N.Y., Feb. 1, 1937, composer conducting); Suite for Strings (Saratoga Springs, N.Y., Sept. 12, 1937); *Serenade* for Flute and Strings (1940; N.Y., Oct. 19, 1956); *Pilgrim's Hymn* (Saratoga Springs, N.Y., Sept. 14, 1946, composer conducting); *Prelude: World Without People* for Chamber Orch. (Saratoga Springs, N.Y., Sept. 14, 1946, composer conducting); *Legend* for Oboe and Strings (WNYC Radio, N.Y., July 1, 1951); *Louisville Concerto,* later renamed *Kentucky Concerto* (Louisville, March 5, 1951, composer conducting); *Wisconsin Suite "Of Childhood Tunes Remembered"* (N.Y., March 28, 1954); *Lyric Scene* for Flute and Strings (1958; Arlington, Va., Oct. 25, 1964); *Fantasia* for String Quartet and Orch. (N.Y., April 18, 1959); *Fantasia* for Strings (1966); *Sonority Forms No. 1* (North Bennington, Vt., Oct. 14, 1973, composer conducting) and *No. 2* (Bennington, Vt., June 4, 1983, composer conducting); *Wisconsin Symphony* (1975; Milwaukee, Jan. 3, 1976); *Potawatomi Legends* for Chamber Orch. (Parkside, Wisc., April 13, 1980, composer conducting); *Fanfare for Those We Have Lost* for Wind Orch. (1993). **CHAMBER:** *Minuet und Pollutionen Gavotte* for Cello and Piano (1917); 3 violin sonatas (1917; 1922; 1943–51); Sextet for Flute, Clarinet, Horn, Violin, Viola, and Cello (1918); *Variations on Christus der ist mein Leben* for Horn Quartet (1918); Flute Sonatina (1919); Fugue for String Quartet (1919); 3 string quartets (1919–20; 1924; 1928); Piano Trio (1921); *Variations on the National Air Yankee Doodle* for Piccolo and Piano (c. 1922); *Legend* for Violin and Piano (1924); 2 sonatas for Solo Cello (1924, 1992); *Fantasia brevis* for Flute and Piano (1929); *Short Fantasy* for Violin and Horn (1930); *Mañana* for Violin and Piano (1933); *Fantasia brevis* for Clarinet and Piano (1936); *Fantasia brevis* for Violin, Viola, and Cello (1936); *Short Ballad* for 2 Clarinets and Strings (1937); *Short Sonata No. 1* for Flute and Harpsichord or Piano (1937), *No. 2* for Flute and Piano (1971), and *No. 3* for Flute and Piano (1966); *Fuguing Tune* for Woodwind Quintet (1938–39); *Short Fantasy* for Violin and Piano (1938); *The Bass with the Delicate Air* for Flute, Oboe, Clarinet, and Bassoon (1940); *Variations on Bach's Chorale Prelude Liebster Jesu wir sind hier* for Cello and Piano (1942); *Aria* for Cello and Piano (1943); Suite for Violin, Viola, and Cello (1944–66); Suite for Cello or Viola and Piano (1946); 5 suites for Flute (1947, c. 1959, 1961, 1963, 1969); *Easy March* for Recorder, Flute, Oboe, and Piano (1950); 3 Nocturnes for Oboe and Piano (1951); Sonata for Bassoon or Cello and Piano (1952); Trio for Flute, Violin, and Piano (1952); Trombone Sonata (1953); Suite for Double Bass and Piano (1953); *Sonata*

Composed in 2 Dayturns for Cello (1958); Sonata for Solo Double Bass (1958); Sonata for Solo Viola (1958); 3 sonatas for Solo Violin (1958, 1968, 1971); *Song, Poem, and Dance* for Flute and String Quartet (1958); *3 Fantasias* for Guitar (1960–81); *Sonority Canon* for 2 to 37 Flutes (1962); *3 Duets* for 2 Flutes (1962); Trio for Flute, Cello, and Piano (1962); Duo for Violin and Viola (1963); *Elegy* for Violin (1963); *March for Diverse High and Low Instruments* (1963); *Suite for Diverse High and Low Instruments* (1963); *Entrance and Exit Music* for 3 Trumpets, 3 Trombones, and Cymbals (1964); *Fanfare for a Festive Occasion* for 3 Trumpets, 3 Horns, 3 Trombones, Timpani, Bells, and Cymbal (1965); *Fantasia* for Cello (1966); *Trio for 3 Flutists* (1966); *14 Easy Duets* for 2 Recorders (1967); *Meditation* for Violin (1968); Trio for Trumpet, Horn, and Trombone (1969); *Introduction and Allegro* for Trumpet and Piano (1971); *Easy Suite* for Strings (1971); *8 Tone Poems* for 2 Violas (1971); *Elegy for the Lonesome Ones* for 2 Clarinets and Strings (1974); *Mexican Serenades* for 11 Instruments (1974); *Prelude and Fugue* for Flute, Clarinet, and Bassoon (1974); *4 Cartoons: Short Suite* for Flute, Clarinet, and Bassoon (1974; also for String Trio); Suite for 2 Flutes, Piano, and Cello ad libitum (1976); *Triadic Canon with Variations* for Flute and 2 Violins (1976); *Potawatomi Legends No. 2: Fantasias on Indian Motives* for Flute (1978); *10 Canons* for 2 Flutes (1980); *2 Fantasias* for Violin, Cello, and Piano (1981, 1993); *Fantasia* for Clarinet (1982); *Fantasia* for Violin (1982); *Serenade* for Violin, Cello, and Piano (1983); *Fantasia and Dance in Memoriam Max Pollikoff* for Violin (1984); *Opera Fantasia* for Violin and Piano (1985); *Serenade and Dialogue* for Flute and Piano (1985); *3 Canons* for 2 Flutes (1985); Duo for Flute and Viola (1985); *3 Fantasias* for Baroque Flute (1986); Suite for Horn (1987); *3 Études* for Cello (1987); *Lament* for Cello(s) (1987); *Divertimento* for Oboe, Violin, Viola, and Cello (1988); *Divertimento* for 2 Trumpets, Horn, Trombone, and Tuba (1988); *Green Mountain Evening, July 25, 1988* for Flute, Oboe, Clarinet, 2 Cellos, and Piano (1988); *Canon with Variations* for Double Bass (1989); Flute Quartet (1989); *Dealer's Choice: Divertimento* for Oboe or Flute, Clarinet, and Bassoon (1990; also for String Trio); Cello Sonata (1992); Sonata for Solo Cello (1992); *Canonical Studies* for 2 Flutes (1993); *Canonical Variations* for String Quartet (1994); *Divertimento* for Clarinet, Violin, and Piano (1994); *Suite* for Flute (2000). K E Y - B O A R D : P i a n o : *Fuga a tre voce* (1918); *Music for Piano: A Contrapuntal Study* (1921); *Coal-Scuttle Blues* (1922–23; in collaboration with E. Bacon); *2 Bagatelles* (1924); *Hymn to Bacchus* (1926); *Dance Sonata* (1928); *8 Pieces* (1928); *Intermezzo III* (1928); *5 Intermezzi* (1932–36); *Phantasy* (1935); *Andante* (1936); *8 Preludes* (1936); *2 Inventions* (1938); *6 Inventions* (1938–39); *6 Short Sonatas* (1940, 1958, 1958, 1967, 1979, 1979, 1979); *Canonical Study* (1941); *Easy Canons* (1941); *Canon in the Octave* (1945); *10 Pieces for 5 Fingers* (1946); *In Memoriam Ferruccio Busoni*, sonata (1955–66); *Gay Picture* (1957); *The Bells of Bellagio* for Piano, 4-or 6-hands (1967); *Sonority Forms I* (1983), *II: The Right-hand Path* for Piano, Right Hand (1984), and *III* (1989); *Tango* (1985); *Song Without Words* (1987); *Chords at Night* (1988); *Image* (1989); *2 Études* (1994); *Fantasia Etudes* (1994). O T H E R : Organ music; harpsichord pieces. V O C A L : Trio for Soprano, Flute, and Violin (1923–24); *The Soundless Song* for Soprano, Flute, Clarinet, String Quartet, Piano, and Optional Movement and Light (1924); *When in the Langour of Evening* for Soprano, Chorus, String or Woodwind Quartet, and Piano (1932); Suite for Soprano and Flute (1936–37); *No Jerusalem But This*, cantata for Soloists, Chorus, and Chamber Ensemble (1982); *Lines from the First Book of Urizen and Vala, or a Dream of 9 Nights* for Soloists and Chorus (1983); many choral pieces; numerous songs for

voice and piano. E L E C T R O N I C : *Fantasy in Space* for Flute on Tape (N.Y., Oct. 28, 1952); *Invention in 12 Notes* for Flute on Tape (N.Y., Oct. 28, 1952); *Low Speed* for Flute on Tape (N.Y., Oct. 28, 1952); *Gargoyles* for Violin and Synthesized Sound (1961); *A Day in the Country* for Violin and Synthesized Sound (1961); *A Study in Synthesized Sounds* (1961); *Synthesis* for Orch. and Electronic Sound (1962; Erie, Pa., Oct. 22, 1963); *Moonflight* for Flute on Tape (1967); *Variations on Fugue and Chorale Fantasy* for Organ and Electronic Doubles (1973); in collaboration with Ussachevsky: *Incantation* (1953); *Rhapsodic Variations* for Tape and Orch. (1953–54; Louisville, March 20, 1954); *A Poem in Cycles and Bells* for Tape and Orch. (Los Angeles, Nov. 18, 1954); *Concerted Piece* for Tape and Orch. (N.Y., March 31, 1960); in collaboration with H. El-Dabh: *Diffusion of Bells* (1962–65); *Electronic Fanfare* for Recorder, Sound Synthesizer, and Percussion on Tape (1962–65).

BIBL.: R. Hartsock, *O. L.: A Bio-Bibliography* (Westport, Conn., 1991).—NS/LK/DM

Lugge, John, English organist and composer; b. Exeter, c. 1587; d. there, after 1647. He served as organist (1603–47) and lay vicar- choral (1605–47) at Exeter Cathedral. Among his works were several fine organ works as well as services and anthems.—LK/DM

Luigini, Alexandre (-Clément-Léon-Joseph), French violinist, conductor, and composer of Italian descent; b. Lyons, March 9, 1850; d. Paris, July 29, 1906. He was the son of Giuseppe Luigini (1820–98), who conducted at the Théâtre-Italien in Paris. Alexandre studied at the Paris Cons. with Massart (violin) and Massenet (composition), then became concertmaster at the Grand Théâtre in Lyons (1869), and began his very successful career as a ballet composer with the production of his first stage work, *Le Rêve de Nicette* (Lyons, 1870). In 1877 he became conductor at the Grand Théâtre at Lyons and a prof. of harmony at the Lyons Cons. After 20 years there, he went to Paris as conductor at the Opéra-Comique, where he remained until his death, except during 1903, when he conducted the orch. at the Théâtre- Lyrique. His greatest success as a composer came with the production of the *Ballet egyptien* (Lyons, Jan. 13, 1875), which was inserted, with Verdi's permission, in the second act of *Aida* at its performance in Lyons in 1886. In addition to a number of other ballets, he composed the comic operas *Les Caprices de Margot* (Lyons, April 13, 1877) and *Faublas* (Paris, Oct. 25, 1881), *Romance symphonique* for Orch., marches for Orch., 3 string quartets, and many piano pieces. —NS/LK/DM

Luisi, Fabio, Italian conductor; b. Genoa, Jan. 17, 1959. He was a student and an assistant of Milan Horvat. After serving on the staff of the Graz Opera (1984–87), he was active as a guest conductor with major opera houses in Austria, Germany, and other European countries. From 1995 to 2000 he was music director of the Niederösterreichisches Tonkünstlerorchester in Vienna. From 1997 he also was artistic director of l'Orchestre de la Suisse Romande in Geneva, and from 1999 chief conductor of the MDR (Mitteldeutscher Rundfunk) Sym. Orch. in Leipzig. In 2000 he made his U.S. debut as a guest conductor of the N.Y. Phil.—NS/LK/DM

Lukačić, (Marko) Ivan, Croatian organist and composer; b. Sibenik (baptized), April 17, 1587; d. Split, Sept. 20, 1648. He studied music in Italy, and in 1597 entered the Franciscan order. In 1620 he became prior of the Franciscan monastery and music master at the Split Cathedral. His book of *Sacrae cantiones* (Venice, 1620; destroyed in World War II) includes 27 motets that reflect the influence of the early Baroque style and employ instrumental accompaniment. Modern eds. of his works appear in D. Plamenac, ed., *Odabarani moteti* (Zagreb, 1935) and J. Andreis, ed., *Šesnaesi moteta* (Zagreb, 1970).—NS/LK/DM

Lukács, Miklós, Hungarian conductor; b. Gyula, Feb. 4, 1905; d. Budapest, Nov. 1, 1986. He took courses with A. Schnabel and Hindemith at the Berlin Hochschule für Musik. He conducted in various German theaters (1930–43), then at the Hungarian State Opera in Budapest (1943–78), where he also served as its director (1944; 1966–78).—NS/LK/DM

Lukáš, Zdeněk, Czech composer; b. Prague, Aug, 21, 1928. He studied at the Prague teachers' inst., and also had lessons with Řídký (composition) and Modr (theory). He was active with the Czech Radio in Plzeń (1953–64) and received instruction from Kabeláč in Prague (1961–70).

WORKS: DRAMATIC: O p e r a : *At žije mrtvý* (Long Live the Deceased; Prague, Dec. 11, 1968); *Domácí karneval* (Domestic Carnival; Prague, March 29, 1969); *Planeta a tiše fialovou září* (Planet with Soft Violet Glow; 1978); *Falkenštejn* (1985); *Veta za vetu* (Measure for Measure; 1986). ORCH.: Piano Concerto (1955); Violin Concerto (1956); Cello Concerto (1957); 5 syms. (1960, 1961, 1965, 1965, 1972); Concerto for Soprano Saxophone and Orch. (1964); 3 concerti grossi: No. 1 for String Quartet and String Orch. (1964), No. 2 for Flute, Violin, Orch., and Tape (1972), and No. 3 for Chamber Orch. (1977); *Symphonietta solemnis* (1965); *Sonata concertata* for Piano, Winds, and Percussion (1966); *Musica ritmica* for Percussion and Winds (1966); Concerto for Violin, Viola, and Orch. (1968); *Partita* for Chamber Orch. (1969); *Musica da concerto* for 12 Strings and Harpsichord (1974); *Variations* for Piano and Orch. (1970); *Postludium* (1971); Bassoon Concerto (1976); Clarinet Concerto (1976); *Transformations* for Piano and Orch. (1978); *Musica Boema,* 2 symphonic movements for Winds, Percussion, and Harp (1978); Flute Concerto (1981); Viola Concerto (1983); Cello Concerto (1986); Concertino for Violin, Marimba, and Strings (1991). CHAMBER: 4 string quartets (1960, 1965, 1973, 1987); Trio for Violin, Piano, and Side Drum (1962); *Partita semplice* for 4 Violins and Piano (1964); Wind Quintet (1968); *Duetti* for Chamber Ensemble (1969); *Music for a Private View* for Viola and Piano (1970); *Amoroso* for Clarinet, Bagpipes, and Double Bass (1970); *Divertimento* for Violin and Viola (1973); Trio for Violin, Cello, and Piano (1974); *Meditations* for Viola and Harpsichord (1976); *Cathedrals* for Brass Instruments and Organ (1976); *Intarsia* for Violin, Viola, and Cello (1977); *Sonata di danza* for Violin, Cello, and Piano (1980); *Canzoni da sonar* for Flute, Oboe, Violin, Viola, and Cello (1983); *Duo di basso* for Cello and Double Bass (1987); *Canto* for 4 Flutes and Harpsichord (1996). VOCAL: *Adam a Eva,* oratorio (1969); *Nezabiješ* (Thou Shalt Not Kill), oratorio (1971); 2 cantatas (1977; *To Prague,* 1982); *Vánoční mše* (Christmas Mass) for Chorus, Organ, and Orch. (1998); many choral works; songs.—NS/LK/DM

Luke, Ray, American composer, conductor, and teacher; b. Forth Worth, Tex., May 30, 1928. He received training in theory at Tex. Christian Univ. in Fort Worth (B.M., 1949; M.M., 1950), and in theory and composition at the Eastman School of Music in Rochester, N.Y. (Ph.D., 1960). In 1962 he joined the faculty of Oklahoma City Univ., where he taught for more than 35 years. He also conducted its orch. and opera productions until 1987. From 1963 to 1967 he was music director of the Lyric Theater of Okla. in Oklahoma City. He was assoc. conductor of the Oklahoma City Sym. Orch. from 1968 to 1973, and then was its music director and resident conductor in 1973–74. Thereafter he was a frequent guest conductor with it until 1979. Every year from 1962 he received ASCAP awards. His Piano Concerto won first prize in the Queen Elisabeth of Belgium International Composition Competition in 1969. In 1978 he won first prize in the Rockefeller Foundation/New England Cons. of Music Competition with his opera *Medea.* In 1997 he was awarded an honorary doctorate in music from Oklahoma City Univ. As a composer, Luke has utilized various contemporary techniques in his works.

WORKS: DRAMATIC: O p e r a : *Medea* (1978; Boston, May 3, 1979); *Drowne's Wooden Image* (1994); *Mrs. Bullfrog* (1994). B a l l e t : *Tapestry* (Oklahoma City, May 8, 1975). ORCH.: *2 Miniatures* (1957); 3 suites (1958, 1967, 1990); *Epilogue* (1958); 4 syms. (1959, 1961, 1963, 1970); Suite for 12 Orch. Woodwinds (1962); *Symphonic Dialogues I* for Violin, Oboe, and Orch. (1965) and *II* for Soprano, Violin, Oboe, Harpsichord, and Strings (1988); Bassoon Concerto (1965); *Fanfare* for Symphonic Winds and Percussion (1967); Piano Concerto (1968); *Incantation* for Cello, Harp, and Strings (1968); *Summer Music,* concert overture (1970); *Compressions I* (1972) and *II* (1973); *Celebration for the Oklahoma Diamond Jubilee* (1982); Sinfonia Concertante for Double Orch. (1989); *Fanfare* for Brass Quintet and Orch. (1990); Trumpet Concerto (2000). C o n c e r t B a n d : *Prelude and March* (1959); *Antiphonale and Toccata* (1960); *Introduction and Badinage* (1968); *New England Miniatures* (1968); *Intrada and Rondo* (1972); *Sonics and Metrics* (1973); *Design* (1976). CHAMBER: *Lament* for Horn and String Quartet (1957); Woodwind Quintet (1958); String Quartet (1966); *4 Dialogues* for Organ and Percussion (1970); Trio for Flute, Clarinet, and Piano (1974); Septet for Winds and Strings (1979); Suite for Trumpet (1986); Suite for Oboe, Bassoon, and Piano (1988); *Compressions III* for Brass Quintet (1988); *4 Scenes* for 8 Flutes (1993); *Contrasts* for Bassoon and Piano (1993); *Splinters From Old Wood* for 2 Trumpets (1994); *Wood From Old Splinters* for 2 Vibraphones (1994); Flute Sonata (1999). VOCAL: *Psalm 51* for Chorus and Concert Band (1960); *2 Odes* for Mezzo-soprano, Flute, and Piano (1965); *Symphonic Songs* for Mezzo-soprano and Orch. (1968); *Epitaphs* for 12 Voices (1979); *4 Foibles* for Voices (1980); *Plaintes and Dirges* for Chorus and Orch. (1982); *Quartz Mountain* for Voices and Orch. (1988); *Cantata Concertante* for Choruses, Instrumental Ensembles, and Orch. (1991); *Celebration* for Chorus, Brass Sextet, and Organ (1999).—NS/LK/DM

Lukomska, Halina, Polish soprano; b. Suchedniów, May 29, 1929. She studied at the Warsaw Academy of Music (graduated, 1954), with Giorgio Favaretto at the Accademia Musicale Chigiana in Siena, and with Toti dal Monte in Venice. In 1956 she captured first prize in the 's-Hertogenbosch competition. From 1960 she pursued a concert career that took her all over the world. In 1973 she toured North America as a soloist with the Cleveland Orch. She became especially noted for her performances of contemporary music, including the most daunting of avant-garde scores.—NS/LK/DM

Lulier, Giovanni Lorenzo, Italian cellist and composer; b. c. 1650; d. Rome, c. 1700. He was a pupil of Pietro Simone Agostini in Rome, where he pursued his career. He was in the service of Cardinal Pietro Ottoboni, and then director of the private orch. of Cardinal Benedetto Pamphili. Lulier was particularly esteemed as a cellist. Among his works were the operas *Il Clearco in Negroponte* (Rome, 1695; in collaboration with B. Gaffi and Cesarini) and *Fausta restituita all'impero* (Rome, Jan. 19, 1697), oratorios, cantatas, and other vocal works. —LK/DM

Lully, Jean-Baptiste (originally, **Giovanni Battista Lulli**), celebrated Italian-born French composer; b. Florence, Nov. 28, 1632; d. Paris, March 22, 1687. The son of a poor Florentine miller, he learned to play the guitar at an early age. His talent for singing brought him to the attention of Roger de Lorraine, Chevalier de Guise, and he was taken to Paris in 1646 as a page to Mlle. d'Orléans, a young cousin of Louis XIV. He quickly adapted to the manner of the French court; although he mastered the language, he never lost his Italian accent. There is no truth in the report that he worked in the kitchens, but he did keep company with the domestic servants, and it was while he was serving in Mlle. d'Orléans's court in the Tuileries that he perfected his violin technique. He also had the opportunity to hear the grande bande (the 24 Violons du Roi) and was present at performances of Luigi Rossi's *Orfeo* at the Louvre in 1647. When Mlle. d'Orléans suffered political disgrace in 1652 and was forced to leave Paris, Lully was released from her service, and early in 1653 he danced with the young Louis XIV in the ballet *La Nuit.* Shortly thereafter, he was made Compositeur de la musique instrumentale du Roi, with joint responsibility for the instrumental music in court ballets. At some time before 1656 he became conductor of Les Petits Violons du Roi, a smaller offshoot of the grand bande. This ensemble was heard for the first time in 1656 in La Galanterie du temps. Thanks to Lully's strict discipline with regard to organization and interpretation, Les Petits Violons soon came to rival the parent ensemble. The 2 groups were combined in 1664. Lully became a naturalized French citizen in 1661, the same year in which he was appointed surintendant de la musique et compositeur de la musique de la chambre; he also became maître de la musique de la famille royale in 1662. His association with Molière commenced in 1664; he provided Molière with the music for a series of comédies-ballets, culminating with *Le Bourgeois Gentilhomme* in 1670. Lully acquired the sole right to form an Académie Royale de Musique in 1672, and thus gained the power to forbid performances of stage works by any other composer. From then until his death he produced a series of tragédies lyriques, most of which were composed to texts by the librettist Philippe Quinault. The subject matter for several of these works was suggested by the King, who was extravagantly praised and idealized in their prologues. Lully took great pains in perfecting these texts, but was often content to leave the writing of the inner voices of the music to his pupils. His monopoly of French musical life created much enmity. In 1674 Henri Guichard attempted to establish an Académie Royale des Spectacles, and their ensuing rivalry resulted in Lully accusing Guichard of trying to murder him by mixing arsenic with his snuff. Lully won the court case that followed, but the decision was reversed on appeal. A further setback occurred when Quinault was thought to have slandered the King's mistress in his text of *Isis* (1677) and was compelled to end his partnership with Lully in disgrace for some time. The King continued to support Lully, however, in spite of the fact that the composer's homosexuality had become a public scandal (homosexuality at the time was a capital offense). Lully's acquisition of titles culminated in 1681, when noble rank was conferred upon him with the title Secrétaire du Roi. In his last years, he turned increasingly to sacred music. It was while he was conducting his *Te Deum* on Jan. 8, 1687, that he suffered a symbolic accident, striking his foot with a pointed cane used to pound out the beat. Gangrene set in, and he died of blood poisoning 2 months later.

Lully's historical importance rests primarily upon his music for the theater. He developed what became known as the French overture, with its 3 contrasting slow-fast-slow movements. He further replaced the Italian recitativo secco style with accompanied French recitative. Thus, through the Italian-born Lully, French opera came of age. A complete catalog of his works was ed. by H. Schneider (Tutzing, 1981). B. Gustafson and M. Leschinskie publ. a thematic catalog for Lully's works (N.Y., 1989).

WORKS: **DRAMATIC: O p e r a** (all are tragédies lyriques unless otherwise given): *Les Fêtes de l'Amour et de Bacchus,* pastorale-pastiche (Opéra, Paris, Nov. 15, 1672); *Cadmus et Hermione* (Opéra, Paris, April 27, 1673); *Alceste, ou Le Triomphe d'Alcide* (Opéra, Paris, Jan. 19, 1674); *Thésée* (Saint-Germain, Jan. 12, 1675); *Atys* (Saint-Germain, Jan. 10, 1676); *Isis* (Saint-Germain, Jan. 5, 1677); *Psyché* (Opéra, Paris, April 19, 1678); *Bellérophon* (Opéra, Paris, Jan. 31, 1679); *Proserpine* (Saint-Germain, Feb. 3, 1680); *Persée* (Opéra, Paris, April 18, 1682); *Phaëton* (Versailles, Jan. 9, 1683); *Amadis* (Opéra, Paris, Jan. 18, 1684); *Roland* (Versailles, Jan. 8, 1685); *Armide* (Opéra, Paris, Feb. 15, 1686); *Acis et Galatée,* pastorale héroïque (Anet, Sept. 6, 1686); *Achille et Polyxène* (Opéra, Paris, Nov. 7, 1687; Overture and Act 1 by Lully; Prologue and Acts 2 to 5 by Collasse). **B a l l e t** (all or most music by Lully): *Alcidiane* (Feb. 14, 1658); *La Raillerie* (Louvre, Paris, Feb. 19, 1659); *Xerxes* (Louvre, Paris, Nov. 22, 1660); *Ballet de Toulouze "au mariage du Roy"* (1660); *L'Impatience* (Tuileries, Paris, Feb. 14, 1661); *Les Saisons* (Fontainebleau, July 23, 1661); *Hercule amoureux* (Tuileries, Paris, Feb. 7, 1662); *Les Arts* (Palais Royal, Paris, Jan. 8, 1663); *Les Noces de village* (Vincennes, Oct. 3, 1663); *Les Amours déguisés* (Palais Royal, Paris, Feb. 13, 1664); 5 entrées for *Œdipe* (Fontainebleau, July 21, 1664); *La Naissance de Vénus* (Palais Royal, Paris, Jan. 26, 1665); *Les Gardes* (June 1665); *Ballet de Créquy ou Le Triomphe de Bacchus dans les Indes* (Hôtel de Créqui, Paris, Jan. 9, 1666); *Les Muses* (Saint-Germain, Dec. 2, 1666); *Le Carnaval ou Mascarade de Versailles* (Tuileries, Paris, Jan. 18, 1668); *Flore* (Tuileries, Paris, Feb. 13, 1669); *La Jeunesse* (1669); *Les Jeux pythiens* (Saint-

Germain, Feb. 7, 1670); *Ballet des ballets* (Saint-Germain, Dec. 2, 1671); *Le Carnaval* (Opéra, Paris, Oct. 17, 1675); *Le Triomphe de l'amour* (Saint-Germain, Jan. 21, 1681); *Le Temple de la paix* (Fontainebleau, Oct. 20, 1685). **B a l l e t** (music by Lully and others): *La Nuit* (Petit Bourbon, Paris, Feb. 23, 1653); *Les Proverbes* (Louvre, Paris, Feb. 17, 1654; music not extant); *Les Noces de Pelée et de Thétis* (Petit Bourbon, Paris, April 14, 1654); *Le Temps* (Louvre, Paris, Dec. 3, 1654); *Les Plaisirs* (Louvre, Paris, Feb. 4, 1655); *Les Bienvenus* (Compiègne, May 30, 1655; music not extant); *La Révente des habits de ballet* (1655?); *Psyché et la puissance de l'amour* (Louvre, Paris, Jan. 16, 1656; music not extant); *La Galanterie du temps* (Paris, Feb. 19, 1656); *L'Amour malade* (Louvre, Paris, Jan. 17, 1657); *Les Plaisirs troublés* (Louvre, Paris, Feb. 11 or 12, 1657; music not extant); *Mascarade du capitaine* (Palais Royal, Paris, 1664; music not extant). **O T H E R :** *L'Impromptu de Versailles*, comedy (Versailles, Oct. 14, 1663); *Le Mariage forcé*, comedy (Louvre, Paris, Jan. 29, 1664); *Les Plaisirs de l'île enchantée*, comédie-ballet (Versailles, May 7, 1664); *La Princesse d'Élide*, comédie-ballet (Versailles, May 8, 1664); *L'Amour médecin*, comedy (Versailles, Sept. 16, 1665); *La Pastorale comique*, pastorale (Saint- Germain, Jan. 5, 1667); *Le Sicilien, ou L'Amour peintre,* comedy (Saint-Germain, Feb. 10, 1667); *Intermèdes* for Georges Dandin's Grande divertissement royal de Versailles, comedy (Versailles, July 18, 1668); *La Grotte de Versailles*, divertissement (Versailles, Aug. 1668); *Monsieur de Pourceaugnac*, comedy (Chambord, Oct. 6, 1669); *Les Amants magnifiques*, comédie-ballet (Saint-Germain, Feb. 7, 1670); *Le Bourgeois Gentilhomme*, comédie-ballet (Chambord, Oct. 14, 1670); *Psyché*, tragédie-ballet (Tuileries, Paris, Jan. 17, 1671); *Idylle sur la paix*, divertissement (Sceaux, July 16, 1685). **I N- S T R U M E N T A L :** Overtures; suites; dances; organ pieces; etc. **C H O R A L :** *Te Deum* (1677); *De profundis* (1683); *Motets à deux pour la chapelle du Roi* (Paris, 1684); 6 grands motets for 2 Choirs and Orch. (1685); 14 petits motets.

BIBL.: H. Guichard, *Requête servant de factums contre B. L.* (Paris, 1673); T. Lajarte, *L.* (Paris, 1878); E. Radet, *L.: Homme d'affaires, propriétaire et musicien* (Paris, 1891); J. Écorcheville, *De L. à Rameau, 1690–1730* (Paris, 1906); H. Prunières, *L.* (Paris, 1909; second ed., 1927); L. de La Laurencie, *L.* (Paris, 1911; second ed., 1919); H. Prunières, *La Vie illustre et libertine de J.-B. L.* (Paris, 1929); E. Borrel, *J.-B. L.* (Paris, 1949); T. Valensi, *Louis XIV et L.* (Nice, 1952); J. Eppelsheim, *Das Orchester in den Werken J.-B. L.s* (Tutzing, 1961); M.-F. Christout, *Le Ballet de cour de Louis XIV, 1643–1672* (Paris, 1967); W. Cole, *The Motets of J.B. L.* (diss., Univ. of Mich., 1967); H. Ellis, *The Dances of J.B. L. (1632–1687)* (diss., Stanford Univ., 1967); L. Auld, *The Unity of Molière's Comedy-ballets* (diss., Bryn Mawr Coll., 1968); M. Benoit, *Musiques de cour: Chapelle, chambre, écurie, 1661–1733* (Paris, 1971); idem, *Verailles et les musiciens du Roi, 1661–1733* (Paris, 1971); P. Howard, *The Operas of L.* (diss., Univ. of Surrey, 1974); H. Schneider, *Der Rezeption der L.-Oper im 17. und 18. Jahrhundert in Frankreich* (diss., Univ. of Mainz, 1976); J. Newman, *J.-B. de L. and His Tragédies lyriques* (Ann Arbor, 1979); C. Wood, *J.-B. L. and His Successors: Music and Drama in the "Tragédie en musique," 1673–1715* (diss., Univ. of Hull, 1981); H. Schneider, *Die Rezeption der Opern L.s im Frankreich des Ancien Regime* (Tutzing, 1982); J. Heyer, ed., *J.-B. L. and the Music of the French Baroque: Essays in Honour of James R. Anthony* (Cambridge, 1988); J. de La Gorce and H. Schneider, eds., *J.-B. L.: Actes du colloque Saint-Germain-en-Laye, Heidelberg 1987* (Laaber, 1990); E. Haymann, *L.* (Paris, 1991); P. Beaussant, *L., ou, Le* *musicien du soleil* (Paris, 1992); M. Couvreur, *J.-B. L.: Musique et dramaturgie au service du Prince* (Brussels, 1992); C. Schmidt, *The livrets of J.-B. L.'s tragédies lyriques: A catalogue raisonné* (N.Y., 1995).—NS/LK/DM

Lumbye, Hans Christian, famous Danish conductor and composer; b. Copenhagen, May 2, 1810; d. there, March 20, 1874. He studied in Randers and Odense. At age 14, he became a military trumpeter. At 19, he entered the Horse Guards in Copenhagen, and in 1839 he founded his own orch. in Copenhagen. In 1843 he became music director of the Tivoli Gardens there, where he gained renown as the "Johann Strauss of the North." He retired in 1872. Lumbye composed about 400 scores, among them many waltzes, galops, polkas, and marches. He had two sons: Carl (Christian) Lymbye (b. Copenhagen, July 9, 1841; d. there, Aug. 10, 1911) was a violinist, conductor, and composer. He was a student of Stockman (violin) and Helsted (theory). He played in his father's orch and conducted orchs. Among his works were dances, marches, and songs. Georg (August) Lumbye (b. Copenhagen, Aug. 26, 1843; d. there, Oct. 29, 1922), was a conductor and composer. After training at the Paris Cons., he pursued his career in Copenhagen. He composed operettas, incidental music, and songs.

BIBL.: G. Skjerne, *H.C. L. og hans Samtid* (Copenhagen, 1912; second ed., 1946); D. Fog, *L.-katalog: Fortegnelse over H.C. L.s trykte kompositioner: Verzeichnis der gedruckten Kompositionen von H.C. L. (1820–1874)* (Copenhagen, 1995).—NS/LK/DM

Lummis, Charles F(letcher), American ethnomusicologist; b. Lynn, Mass., March 1, 1859; d. Los Angeles, Nov. 25, 1928. He received instruction in Hebrew, Greek, and Latin from his father, and later took courses at Harvard Univ. (1877–80). During a cross-country hike from Ohio to Calif., he became interested in the cultures of the American Indians and of Mexican-Americans and made pioneering recordings of American Indian music and folk songs. He was city ed. of the *Los Angeles Times* (1885–87) and also ed. of *Land of Sunshine* (1894–1901) and *Out West* (1902–9); he also wrote novels and poetry. He founded the Landmarks Club (1895) and the Sequoia Club (1902), which espoused Indian causes. In 1907 he founded the Southwest Museum in Los Angeles, which serves as the depository of his valuable collection. With A. Farwell, he publ. *Spanish Songs of Old California* (1923).

BIBL.: E. Bingham, *C.F. L.: Editor of the Southwest* (San Marino, Calif., 1955); M. Simmons, *Two Southwesterners: C. L. and Amando Chaves* (Cerillos, N.Mex., 1968); D. Gordon, *C.F. L.: Crusador in Corduroy* (Los Angeles, 1972); T. Fiske and K. Lummis, *C.F. L.: The Man and His West* (Norman, Okla., 1975); R. Fleming, *C.F. L.* (Boise, Idaho, 1981).—NS/LK/DM

Lumsdaine, David (Newton), Australian composer and teacher; b. Sydney, Oct. 31, 1931. He studied in Sydney at the New South Wales State Conservatorium of Music (piano, viola, and theory) and at the Univ. (composition with Raymond Hanson; B.A., 1953) before pursuing his studies in London with Seiber (1954–56) and at the Royal Academy of Music with Berkeley (1956–57). He was a lecturer at the Univ. of Durham (1970–81), where he was founder of an electronic music studio; he was awarded a Mus.Doc. there in 1981. In 1976 he served as a visiting prof. at the Univ. of Adelaide and in 1979 was composer-in-residence at the New South Wales State Conservatorium of Music, sharing the latter position with his wife, **Nicola LeFanu**, whom he married that year. He was a senior lecturer at King's Coll., Univ. of London, from 1981. In his music, Lumsdaine has pursued a highly complex but thoroughly individual mode of expression that ranges from the use of traditional instruments to the application of electronics.

WORKS: ORCH.: *Variations* (1960); *Short Symphony* (1961); *Bach Music* (1965); *Episodes* (1968–69); *Salvation Creek with Eagle* for Chamber Orch. (1974); *Sunflower: To the Memory of Luigi Dallapiccola* (1975); *Evensong* for Brass Band (1975); *Hagoromo* (1977); *Shoalhaven* for Small Orch. (1982); *Mandala V* (1988); *The Arc of Stars* for Strings (1990–91); *Garden of Earthly Delights*, fantasia for Cello and Orch. (1992). **CHAMBER:** *Mandala I* for Wind Quartet (1967), *II* for Flute, Clarinet, Viola, Cello, and Percussion (1969); *III* for Piano, Flute, Clarinet, Viola, Cello, and Chinese Bell (1978), and *IV* for String Quartet (1983); *Looking Glass Music* for Brass Quintet and Tape (1970); *Kangaroo Hunt* for Piano and Percussion (1971); *Caliban Trio* for Piano Trio, Tape, and Live Electronics (1972); *Bagatelles* for Flute, Clarinet, Piano, Violin, Viola, and Cello (1985); *Empty Sky, Mootwingee* for Flute, Trombone or Horn, Cello, Pitched Percussion, and 2 Pianos (1986); *A Dance and a Hymn for Alexander Maconochie* for Flute, Clarinet, Percussion, Mandolin, Guitar, Violin, and Double Bass (1988); *Round Dance* for Sitar, Tabla, Flute, Cello, and Keyboard (1989); *Sine nome* for Alto Saxophone or Clarinet and Pitched Percussion (1990); *Blue Upon Blue* for Cello (1991). **PIANO:** *Ruhe Sanfte, Sanfte Ruh'* (1964); *Kelly Ground* (1966); *Flights* for 2 Pianos (1967); *Cambewarra* (1980). **VOCAL:** *The Ballad of Perse O'Reilly* for Tenor, Men's Chorus, and 2 Pianos (1953–81); *Missa brevis* for Chorus and Organ (1964); *Annotations of Auschwitz* for Soprano, Flute or Trumpet, Horn, Violin, Cello, and Piano (1964); *Dum medium silentium* for Chorus (1964–75); *Easter Fresco* for Soprano, Flute, Horn, Harp, and Piano (1966); *Aria for Edward John Eyre* for Soprano, Narrators, Chamber Ensemble, Tape, and Live Electronics (1972); *My Sister's Song* for Soprano (1975); *Tides* for Narrator, 12 Voices, and Percussion (1979); *What Shall I Sing?* for Soprano and 2 Clarinets (1982); *Where the Lilies Grow* for Chamber Chorus (1985); *Just So Stories* for Narrator, Dancers, and Computer-generated Tape (1990); *A Tree Telling of Orpheus* for Soprano, Flute, Clarinet, Violin, Viola, and Cello (1990). **OTHER:** *Big Meeting* for Tape (1978); *Wild Ride to Heaven*, radiophonic piece (1980; in collaboration with N. LeFanu); *4 Soundscapes*, field recordings (1990); *Soundscape 5: Cambewarra* (1991).—**NS/LK/DM**

Lumsden, Sir David (James), noted English organist, harpsichordist, choirmaster, and music editor; b. Newcastle upon Tyne, March 19, 1928. He studied with Ord and Dart at the Univ. of Cambridge (Mus.B., 1951; Ph.D., 1955) and at the Univ. of Oxford (Ph.D., 1959). He was organist of the Univ. of Nottingham (1954–56); also founder-conductor of the Nottingham Bach Soc. He served as rector chori at Southwell Minster and director of music at the Univ. Coll. of North Staffordshire, Keele (1956–59). He then was organist at New Coll., Oxford (1959–78); also taught at the Royal Academy of Music in London (1960–62). He was principal of the Royal Scottish Academy of Music in Glasgow (1978–82) and of the Royal Academy of Music in London (1982–92). He was knighted in 1985. —**NS/LK/DM**

Lunceford, Jimmie (actually, **James Melvin**), highly influential jazz bandleader, composer, multi-instrumentalist; b. Fulton, Mo., June 6, 1902; d. Seaside, Ore., July 12, 1947. His father was a choirmaster in Warren, Ohio. Jimmie went to high school in Denver, Colo., where he studied music with Paul Whiteman's father (Wilberforce J. Whiteman). He learned saxophone, guitar, trombone, and flute. He played alto sax with George Morrison's Orch. at the Empress Theatre (1922). He left Denver, to gain a B.M. at Fisk Univ. (1926). During his college vacations, he played dates in N.Y. with John C. Smith, Wilbur Sweatman, Elmer Snowden, and Deacon Johnson; in the mid-1920s he also studied in N.Y. From 1926 he taught music at Manassa H.S. in Memphis; while there he formed the Lunceford Orch., a band that featured his students. The band began to do regular summer seasons, then from 1929 (with three former Fisk alums— Edwin Wilcox, Willie Smith, and Henry Wells—joining the band) became fully professional, playing residencies and broadcasts on WREC in Memphis. After touring and playing residencies in Cleveland and Buffalo, the band moved to N.Y.C. in September 1933 for dates at the Lafayette Theatre. After touring New England, in January 1934 they returned to N.Y. to take up residency at the Cotton Club, and then from the mid-1930s did widespread touring. The band gradually built up a national reputation, and after a short tour of Scandinavia in February 1937, consolidated its previous successes and became one of the most sought-after big bands in the U.S. The Lunceford Orch. was credited with 22 hits between 1934 and 1946, placing them behind only Duke Ellington and Cab Calloway among black swing bands. "Rhythm Is Our Business" and "I'm Gonna Move to the Outskirts of Town" were their signature songs.

The Lunceford Orch. was legendary for its precision that was achieved through careful sectional rehearsals (one of the first to do so); for its cheery, entertaining tone, created through writing that was full of unexpected instrumental combinations and at times surprising dissonance; and also for its showmanship that involved choreographed movements with the band members tossing their instruments around.

Lunceford rarely played with the band, instead conducting. He did, however, play trombone on the band's 1929 ("Chickasaw Syncopators") recordings, and occasionally played alto in the early 1930s. He played flute on the 1939 version of "Liza," and in 1943, during World War II when many of his bandsmen were drafted into the service, alto in the sax section. A primary arranger for the band was Sy Oliver, but some of the most interesting charts were contributed by Willie Smith, Eddie Wilcox, and, though rarely, Lunceford himself. From 1942, Gerald Wilson was also an arranger.

The band never regained its prewar popularity, but continued to work regularly. In 1947, Lunceford collapsed signing autographs during a personal appearance at a music store and died shortly afterwards. The band was soon reorganized under the joint leadership of Eddie Wilcox and tenorist Joe Thomas, and in 1948 Wilcox became the sole leader. The band continued for a short time afterward, and did a reunion album for Capitol in the mid-1950s. The Lunceford Band appeared in several short films and was also featured in *Blues in the Night*.

DISC.: *Rhythm Is Our Business* (1934); *Stomp It Off* (1934); *Harlem Shout* (1935); *For Dancers Only* (1936); *Blues in the Night* (1938); *Jubilee* (1940); *Uncollected Jimmie Lunceford* (1944). —JC/LP

Lund, Signe, Norwegian composer; b. Christiania, April 15, 1868; d. there (Oslo), April 6, 1950. She studied in Berlin, Copenhagen, and Paris, and spent several years in America. As a composer, she was completely under the lyrical domination of Grieg's music, and her works are eminently perishable. She wrote a ceremonial overture, *The Road to France*, on the occasion of America's entry into World War I in 1917; also various instrumental pieces and songs. She publ. an autobiography, *Sol gjennem skyer* (Oslo, 1944).—NS/LK/DM

Lundquist, Torbjörn (Iwan), Swedish composer and conductor; b. Stockholm, Sept. 30, 1920; d. Grillby, July 1, 2000. He received training in musicology at the Univ. of Uppsala, in composition from Wirén, and in conducting from Suitner in Salzburg and Vienna. He then was active as a conductor in Stockholm, and also appeared as a guest conductor throughout Europe. In 1978 he was awarded a government income to pursue composition. In his works, Lundquist utilized various styles and techniques, ranging from the traditional to the avant-garde, from jazz to Eastern music.

WORKS: DRAMATIC: Opera: *Sekund av evighet* (Moment of Eternity; 1971–74; Stockholm, May 27, 1974); *Jason and Medea* (1985–89). **ORCH.:** *Divertimento* for Chamber Orch. (1951); 9 syms.: No. 1 (1952–56; rev. 1971), No. 2 (1956–70), No. 3, *Sinfonia dolorosa* (1971–75; Swedish Radio, Malmö, Sept. 14, 1976), No. 4 (1974–85; Göteborg, Nov. 7, 1985), No. 5 (Halmstad, Feb. 13, 1980), No. 6 (1985–86), No. 7 for Soprano, Baritone, Chorus, and Orch. (1986–88; Stockholm, March 22, 1991), No. 8, *Kroumata* (1989–92), and No. 9, *Survival* (1996); *Concerto da camera* for Accordion and Orch. (1965); *Férvor* for Violino Grande and Orch. (1967); *Hangarmusik*, concerto sinfonico for Piano and Orch. (1967); *Intarzia* for Accordion and Strings (1967–68); *Confrontation* (Stockholm, Oct. 5, 1968); *Evoluzione* for Strings (1968); *Sogno* for Oboe and Strings (1968); *Galax* (1971); Marimba Concerto (1971–74); Concerto grosso for Violin, Cello, and Strings (1974); *Schatten* (Salzburg, Aug. 25, 1977); Violin Concerto (1978; Örebro, Feb. 11, 1979); *Landscape* for Tuba, Strings, and Piano (1978); *Poetry* for Flute, Strings, and Piano (1978); *Wind Power* for Wind. Orch. (1978); *Serenade* for Strings (1979); *Arktis* for Symphonic Band (1984). **CHAMBER:** *Movements* for Accordion and String Quartet (1966); *Duell* for Accordion and Percussion (1966); *Combinazione* for Violin and Percussion (1966); 2 string quartets (1966, 1969); *Teamwork* for Wind Quintet (1967); *Stereogram III* for Xylorimba, Electric Guitar, and Accordion (1969); *4 rondeaux* for Wind Quartet and Piano

(1969); *Tempera* for 6 Brass Instruments (1969); *Trio fiorente* for Piano, Violin, and Cello (1975); Suite for 6 Percussionists (1976); *Integration* for 5 Percussionists (1980–82); *Alla prima* for Saxophone Quartet (1989). **Piano:** *Metamorfoser* (1997). **VOCAL:** *Elegies from Bergen* for Tenor, Men's Chorus, and Orch. (1958); *Via the Emptiness* for Soloists, Chorus, and Chamber Orch. (1959); *Call* for Soprano and Orch. (1963–64); many songs. —NS/LK/DM

Lundsten, Ralph, Swedish composer, film creator, and artist; b. Ersnäs, Oct. 6, 1936. He was basically autodidact; settled in the wooden fairy-tale mansion of Castle Frankenburg (built 1878) in Saltsjö-Boo, where he founded Andromeda (1959), Sweden's best-known private electronic music studio and film center. A pioneer in electronic music in Sweden, he has gone on to secure an international following via the popularity of the "New Age" movement. In 1982 the Andromeda Fan Soc. was organized to promote his activities as a composer, artist, and "New Age" visionary. In 1984 Radio Sweden International adopted "Out in the Wide World" from his *Nordic Nature Symphony No. 4, A Summer Saga* as its theme signature for its international broadcasts. Much of his output has been recorded and performed throughout the world. In 1991–92 his work as a portrait artist was the subject of a special exhibition at Stockholm's Music Museum.

WORKS: *Aloha Arita* (1966); *Kaleidoscope* (1966); *Mums: EMS No. 1* (1967); *3 Electronic "Pop" Pieces* (1967); *Visions of Flying Saucers* (1967); *Happy Music* (1968); *Winter Music* (1968); *Mizar* (1968); *Tellus* (1969); *Blue Bird* (1969); *Suite for Electronic Accordion* (1969); *Energy for Biological Computer* (1969); *Erik XIV* (1969); *Carvings* (1969); *Ölskog: Through a Landscape of Mirrors* (1970); *Cosmic Love—Trial and Discussion* (1970); *Gustav III* (1971); *Nightmare* (1971); *Ourfather* (1972); *Nordic Nature Symphony No. 1, The Water Sprite* (1972–73); *The Midnight Hour* (1973); *Ode to a Lost Soul* (1973); *On Tottering Toes* (1973); *Feel It* (1973); *Gunnar of Lidärände* (1973); *Shangri-la* (1975); *Winter Music* (1975); *Heaven by Night* (1975); *Raped Planet* (1975); *Icelandic Dancing Pictures* (1975); *Nordic Symphony No. 2, Johannes and the Lady of the Woods* (1975); *Universe* (1977); *Discophrenia* (1978); *Alpha Ralpha Boulevard* (1979); *Paradise Symphony* (1980); *Nordic Nature Symphony No. 3, A Midwinter Saga* (1981); *The New Age* (1982); *Aspects of Nature* (1982); *Nordic Nature Symphony No. 4, A Summer Saga* (1983); *Strangers in Paradise* (1984); *Nordic Nature Symphony No. 5, Bewitched* (1984); *Dreamscape* (1984); *Welcome* (1985); *Fantasia by Starlight* (1986); *The Dream Master* (1986); *Suite amoroso* (1986); *The Gate of Time* (1988); *Nordic Nature Symphony No. 6, Landscape of Dreams* (1990); *The Symphony of Joy* (1994). —NS/LK/DM

Lundy, Carmen, American singer; b. Miami, Fla., Nov. 1, 1954. She is a gifted jazz singer who writes much of her own material. Though she draws widely from outside the jazz tradition influences as diverse as country, folk, pop, and soul, her approach is rooted in jazz rhythms and improvisation. Her wide range, including deep resonant chest tones, makes her a highly expressive singer. She is also an accomplished actor and painter. Sister of bassist Curtis Lundy, she began performing professionally while still a teenager. She enrolled at the Univ. of Miami as an opera major, but soon her gospel and blues background drew her toward jazz and she began performing around Miami, and with the school's big band. She moved to N.Y. in the late 1970s, sitting in with the Thad Jones/Mel Lewis Orch. She developed a successful stage career, playing the lead in the Duke Ellington review *Sophisticated Ladies* and the role of Billie Holiday in the Off-Broadway production *They Were All Gardenias*. Since relocating to Los Angeles in 1991, she has firmly established herself as one of jazz's most promising singers. She has recorded for Blackhawk, Arabesque, Sony/CBS, and JVC, her current label.

DISC.: *Just Be Yourself* (1985); *Good Morning Kiss* (1986); *Moment to Moment* (1992); *Self Portrait* (1995); *Old Devil Moon* (1997).—**AG**

Lunelli, Renato, Italian musicologist, organist, and composer; b. Trent, May 14, 1895; d. there, Jan. 14, 1967. He studied at the Händelhochschule in Munich (1913–14) and with Bormioli (organ) and Gianferri (harmony and counterpoint) at the Liceo Musicale in Trent. He then was organist at S. Maria Maggiore in Trent. Lunelli was an authority on the organ. With Tagliavini, he founded the journal *L'organa: Rivista di cultura organaria e organistica* in 1960. Among his compositions were sacred works and vocal pieces.

WRITINGS: *Un ventennio di attività organaria nel Trentino* (Trent, 1931); *Mistica ed estetica delle sonorità organistiche al servizio della liturgia* (Trent, 1950); *Der Oregelbau in Italien in seinen Meisterwerken vom 14. Jahrhundert bis zur Gegenwart* (Mainz, 1956); *L'arte organaria del Rinascimento in Rome e gli organi di S. Pietro in Vaticano, dalle origini a tutto il periodo frescobaldiano* (Florence, 1958); R. Maroni, ed., *Organi trentini: Notizie storiche, iconografia* (Trent, 1964); ed. with R. Maroni, *La musica nel Trentino dal XV al XVIII secolo* (Trent, 1967); ed. with R. Maroni, *Strumenti musicali nel Trentino* (Trent, 1968). —**NS/LK/DM**

Lunn, Louise Kirkby
See **Kirkby-Lunn, Louise**

Lunssens, Martin, Belgian conductor and composer; b. Molenbeek-Saint-Jean, April 16, 1871; d. Etterbeek, Feb. 1, 1944. He studied with Gevaert, Jehin, and Kufferath at the Brussels Cons., gaining the First Belgian Prix de Rome in 1895 with the cantata *Callirhoé*; then became a prof. there. He subsequently was director of the Music Academy at Courtrai (1905–16); at Charleroi (1916–21), at the Louvain Cons. (1921–24), and finally at the Ghent Cons. (from 1924). He was also known as an excellent conductor; was in charge of the Flemish Opera in Antwerp, where he conducted many Wagner operas.

WORKS: 4 syms., the first 3 with the programmatic titles *Symphonie romaine, Symphonie florentine,* and *Symphonie française*; symphonic poems (*Roméo et Juliette; Phèdre; Le Cid; Timon d'Athènes*); 3 violin concertos; Viola Concerto; Cello Concerto; much chamber music; songs.—**NS/LK/DM**

Lupi, Johannes, distinguished Franco-Flemish composer; b. c. 1506; d. Cambrai, Dec. 20, 1539. He was a choirboy at Notre Dame Cathedral in Cambrai (1514–21), then studied philosophy at the Univ. of Louvain (1522). After returning to Cambrai Cathedral as a parvus vicarius (1526), he was made master of the choristers (1527). He then was magnus vicarius and subdeacon (from 1530, except for a period of ill health [1535–37]). He excelled as a composer of motets; also wrote many chansons. Attaingnant and Jullet publ. a book of his motets in 1542, which helped to spread his fame. B. Blackburn ed. his complete works (3 vols., Stuttgart, 1980–89).

BIBL.: B. Blackburn, *The Lupus Problem* (diss., Univ. of Chicago, 1970).—**NS/LK/DM**

Lupi Second, Didier, French composer who flourished in the mid-16th century. He is believed to have resided in Lyons for the greater portion of his life. His vol. of chansons spirituelles was the first major collection of such works by a French Protestant composer.

WORKS: *Premier livre de chansons spirituelles nouvellement composées par Guillaume Guéroult* for 4 Voices (Lyons, 1548); *Tiers livre contenant trente et cinq chansons* for 4 Voices (Lyons, 1548); *Psaumes trente du royal prophète David, traduictz en vers françois par Giles Daurigny, dict le Pamphile* for 4 Voices (Lyons, 1549); many other works in contemporary collections.

BIBL.: M. Honegger, *Les chansons spirituelles de D. L. S. et les débuts de la musique protestante en France* (Lille, 1971).—**LK/DM**

Lupu, Radu, outstanding Romanian pianist; b. Galai, Nov. 30, 1945. He began his piano studies at the age of 6, making his recital debut when he was 12; then studied with Florica Muzicescu and on scholarship at the Moscow Cons. (1963), where he studied with Heinrich and Stanislau Neuhaus until 1969. In quick succession he won first prize in the Van Cliburn (1966), Enesco (1967), and Leeds (1969) competitions. In 1972 he made his American debut as soloist with the Cleveland Orch., and subsequently played with the Chicago, Los Angeles, N.Y., and Boston orchs. In Europe he made successful appearances in Berlin, Paris, Amsterdam, London, Vienna, and other cities in varied programs ranging from Classical to modern works.—**NS/LK/DM**

Lupus, Eduardus
See **Lobo, Duarte**

Lurano, Filippo de, Italian composer; b. probably in Cremona, c. 1475; d. after 1520. He served as maestro di cappella at Cividale Cathedral (1512–15) and at Aguileia Cathedral (1519–20). His 35 frottolas (34 publ. by Petrucci, 1505–09) are particularly notable. Among his other works were 2 motets and a lauda.—**LK/DM**

Luria, Juan (real name, **Johannes Lorie**), Polish baritone; b. Warsaw, Dec. 20, 1862; d. in the concentration camp in Auschwitz, 1942. He was a student of Gänsbacher in Vienna. In 1885 he made his operatic debut in Stuttgart. On Dec. 3, 1890, he made his Metropolitan Opera debut in N.Y. as Nevers in *Les Huguenots*, singing there for a season. He subsequently pursued his career in Berlin, Milan, Vienna, Munich, Paris, and other European music centers. In 1893 he sang the role of Wotan at its first performance at Milan's La Scala. From 1914 he taught voice in Berlin. As a Jew, Luria left Germany under the Hitler regime in 1937 and made his way to Holland, where he taught at the conservatories in Amsterdam and The Hague. After the Nazis occupied Holland in 1939, he was unable to flee, and in 1942 was arrested and sent to the Auschwitz concentration camp. Luria was best known as a Wagnerian. He also sang in the premiere of Pfitzner's *Die Rose vom Liebesgarten* (1901).—NS/LK/DM

Lussan, Zélie de, American soprano; b. Brooklyn, Dec. 21, 1862; d. London, Dec. 18, 1949. She was trained in singing by her mother, and made her first public appearance at Chickering Hall in N.Y. (April 2, 1878). In 1885 she joined the Boston Ideal Opera Co., and then went to London, where she made her debut as Carmen with A. Harris's Italian Opera Co. at Covent Garden (July 7, 1888); subsequently sang with the Carl Rosa Opera Co. and Mapleson's company. She sang Carmen again for her Metropolitan Opera debut in N.Y. on Nov. 26, 1894; after that season, was on its roster again from 1898 to 1900. She was particularly successful at Covent Garden (1890–93; 1895–1900; 1902–03; 1910). She was called upon to sing Carmen more than 1,000 times during her career; she was also a noted Cherubino, Zerlina, Mignon, and Nedda. Lussan was married to the pianist Angelo Fronani.—NS/LK/DM

Luther, Martin, great German religious reformer; b. Eisleben, Nov. 10, 1483; d. there, Feb. 18, 1546. His reform of the church extended to the musical services, in which he took the deepest interest. After leaving the Wartburg, near Eisenach (March 22, 1522), he gave his ideas practical shape; his *Formula missae* (1523) and *Deutsche Messe* (1526; facsimile ed. by J. Wolf, Kassel, 1934) established the new service. He changed the order of the Mass, with a German Psalm taking the place of the introit, and the German Creed substituting for the Latin Credo. The German Mass was sung for the first time in the Parish Church at Wittenberg on Christmas Day, 1524. Kapellmeister Conrad Rupsch and cantor Johann Walter aided Luther in organizing the musical part of the Mass. Walter states that Luther invented chorale melodies on the flute (he was an excellent flutist), and that these were noted down by Walter and Rupsch. It is impossible to establish with certainty which hymn tunes ascribed to Luther are really his; *Jesaia dem Propheten das geschah* is definitely Luther's; the celebrated hymn tune *Ein' feste Burg ist unser Gott* is most probably authentic. Most important, the words of many chorales were written, arranged, or tr. from Latin by Luther.

BIBL.: A. Rambach, *Über L.s Verdienst um den Kirchengesang* (Hamburg, 1813); K. von Winterfeld, *L.s deutsche geistliche Lieder* (Leipzig, 1840); K. Loewe, *L.studien* (1846; publ. in Wittenberg, 1918); M. Rade, *M. L.s Leben, Taten und Meinungen* (3 vols., Tubingen, 1883; second ed., 1901); H. von Stephen, *L. als Musiker* (Bielefeld, 1899); J. Lyra, *L.s Deutsche Messe* (1904); idem, *Die Lieder L.s in ihrer Bedeutung fur das evangelische Kirchenlied* (Gottingen, 1905); idem, *Studien zu L.s Liedern* (Gottingen, 1907); H. Lehmann, *L. im deutschen Lied* (Halle, 1910); K. Anton, *Luther und die Musik* (1918); H. Preuss, *L. der Kunstler* (1931); H. Moser, *Die Melodien der L.lieder* (Leipzig, 1935); G. Wolfram, *"Ein' feste Burg ist unser Gott"* (Berlin, 1936); C. Mahrenholz, *L. und die Kirchenmusik* (Kassel, 1937); C. Schneider, *L. poete et musicien et les Enchiridiens de 1524* (Geneva, 1942); F. Smend, *L. und Bach* (Berlin, 1947); P. Nettl, *L. and Music* (Philadelphia, 1948); W. Stapel, *L.s Lieder und Gedichte* (Stuttgart, 1950); C. Schalk, *L. on Music: Paradigms of Praise* (St. Louis, 1987).—NS/LK/DM

Lutosławski, Witold, eminent Polish composer and conductor; b. Warsaw, Jan. 25, 1913; d. there, Feb. 7, 1994. He began to play the piano when he was 6, and studied that instrument with Helena Hoffman, Józef Śmidowicz, and A. Taube. He received training in violin from Lidia Kmitowa (1926–32) and in theory and composition from Witold Maliszewski (1928–31). From 1931 to 1933 he studied mathematics at the Univ. of Warsaw. In 1932 he entered the Warsaw Cons. to continue his studies in composition with Maliszewski, and also studied piano with Jerzy Lefeld. In 1936 he graduated as a pianist and in 1937 he received his degree in composition with his *Requiem* for Soprano, Chorus, and Orch. He then served in the Polish Army, and, at the outbreak of World War II in 1939, he was taken prisoner-of-war by the invading Nazi Army but managed to escape shortly thereafter. During the Nazi occupation of his homeland, he earned his living playing piano in various venues. After the liberation in 1945, he made Warsaw the center of his activities. He helped to found the Polish Composers' Union, with which he remained active for the rest of his life. For the most part, however, he devoted himself mainly to composing. He also taught numerous master classes at home and abroad. From 1963 he made appearances as a conductor, becoming especially known as the authoritative interpreter of his own works. Lutosławski was accorded numerous honors, including the Polish State Award, first class, in 1955, 1964, and 1978, the Polish Composers' Union Award in 1959 and 1973, the Minister of Culture and Arts Award, first class, in 1962, the Gottfried von Herder Prize and the Léonie Sonning Music Prize in 1967, the Maurice Ravel Prize of Paris in 1971, the Sibelius Prize in 1973, the Ernst von Siemens Prize in 1983, the first Grawemeyer Award of the Univ. of Louisville in 1985, the Gold Medal of the Royal Phil. Soc. of London in 1985, the Polar Music Prize and the Kyoto Prize in 1993, and Poland's highest honor, the Order of the White Eagle in 1994. He also was made an honorary member of Hamburg's Freie Akademie der Künste in 1966, an extraordinary member of West Berlin's Akademie der Künste in 1968, a corresponding member of the American Academy of Arts and Letters in 1975, and an honorary member of London's Royal Academy of Music in 1976, among many other memberships. In 1990 the International Witold Lutosławski Competition for Composers was organized in his honor by the National Phil. in Warsaw. From the beginning of his career as a mature composer, Lutosławski's output demonstrated a consummate craftsmanship. After composing in a folk-inspired style, he developed his own individual 12-tone method. His growing mastery led him to employ aleatoric procedures with traditional techniques to create works of remarkable creativity and lasting significance in the orchestral, chamber, and vocal genres.

WORKS: ORCH.: Symphonic Variations (1936–38; Kraków, June 17, 1939); 4 syms.: No. 1 (1941–47; Katowice, April 6, 1948), No. 2 (1966–67; Katowice, June 9, 1967), No. 3 (1981–83; Chicago, Sept. 29, 1983), and No. 4 (1988–92; Los Angeles, Feb. 5, 1993); Overture for Strings (Prague, Nov. 9, 1949); *Little Suite* for Chamber Orch. (1950; also for Orch., Warsaw, April 20, 1951); *Concerto for Orchestra* (1950–54; Warsaw, Nov. 26, 1954); *Muzyka żałobna* (Musique fenèbre) for Strings (1954–58; Katowice, March 26, 1958); *Preludia tanceczne* (Dance Preludes) for Clarinet and Chamber Orch. (1955; Aldeburgh, June 1963; also for Clarinet and Piano, 1954; Warsaw, Feb. 15, 1955, and for 9 Instruments, Louny, Nov. 10, 1959); *Trzy postludia* (Three Postludes; 1958–60; rev. 1963; Kraków, Oct. 8, 1965); *Gry weneckie* (Venetian Games) for Chamber Orch. (Warsaw, Sept. 16, 1961); *Livre pour orchestre* (Hagen, Nov. 18, 1968); Cello Concerto (1969–70; London, Oct. 14, 1970); *Preludia i fuga* for 13 Solo Strings (1970–72; Graz, Oct. 12, 1972); *Mi-parti* (Amsterdam, Oct. 22, 1976); *Wariacje na temata Paganiniego* (Variations on a Theme of Paganini) for Piano and Orch. (1977–78; Miami, Nov. 18, 1979; also for 2 Pianos, 1941); *Novellette* (1978–79; Washington, D.C., Jan. 29, 1980); Double Concerto for Oboe, Harp, and Chamber Orch. (1979–80; Lucerne, Aug. 24, 1980); *Grave* for Cello and Strings (1981–82; Paris, Aug. 26, 1982; also for Cello and Piano, Warsaw, April 22, 1981); *Łańcuch* (Chain) 1 for 14 Players (London, Oct. 4, 1983), 2 for Violin and Orch. (1983–85; Zürich, Jan. 31, 1986), and 3 (1985–86; San Francisco, Dec. 10, 1986); *Fanfare for* (the Univ. of) *Louisville* for Winds and Percussion (Louisville, Sept. 19, 1986); Piano Concerto (1987–88; Salzburg, Aug. 19, 1988); *Partita* for Violin and Orch. (1988; Munich, Jan. 10, 1990; also for Violin and Piano, 1984; St. Paul, Minn., Jan. 18, 1985); *Prelude for the G.S.M.D.* (Guildhall School of Music and Drama) (London, May 11, 1989); *Fanfare for* (the Univ. of) *Lancaster* for Brass Ensemble and Side Drum (Lancaster, Oct. 11, 1989); *Interludium* (1989–90; Munich, Jan. 10, 1990); *Fanfare for the Los Angeles Philharmonic* for Brass and Percussion (Los Angeles, Nov. 4, 1993). **CHAMBER:** Trio for Oboe, Clarinet, and Bassoon (1944–45; Kraków, Sept. 1945); *Recitativo e arioso* for Violin and Piano (1951); *Preludia tanceczne* (Dance Preludes) for Clarinet and Piano (1954; Warsaw, Feb. 15, 1955; also for Clarinet and Chamber Orch., Aldeburgh, June 1963, and for 9 Instruments, Louny, Nov. 10, 1959); *Bukoliki* (Bucolics) for Viola and Cello (1962; also for Piano, 1952); String Quartet (1964; Stockholm, March 12, 1965); *Sacher Variation* for Cello (1975; Zürich, May 2, 1976); *Epitaphium* for Oboe and Piano (1979; London, Jan. 3, 1980); *Grave* for Cello and Piano (Warsaw, April 22, 1981; also for Cello and String Orch., 1981–82; Paris, Aug. 26, 1982); *Mini-uwertura* (Mini-overture) for Brass Quintet (Lucerne, March 11, 1982); *Partita* for Violin and Piano (1984; St. Paul, Minn., Jan. 18, 1985; also for Violin and Orch., 1988; Munich, Jan. 10, 1990); *Fanfare for CUBE* (Cambridge Univ. Brass Ensemble) for Brass Quintet (Cambridge, June 11, 1987); *Slides* for 11 Players (N.Y., Dec. 1, 1988); *Subito* for Violin and Piano (1992; WFYI-FM, Indianapolis, Sept. 16, 1994). **Piano:** Sonata (1934; Warsaw, Feb. 1935); 2 Studies (1940–41; Kraków, Jan. 26, 1948); *Wariacje na temat Paganiniego* (Variations on a Theme of Paganini) for 2 Pianos (1941; also for Piano and Orch., 1977–78; Miami, Nov. 18, 1979); *Melodie ludowe* (Folk Melodies; 1945; Kraków, July 22, 1946); *Bukoliki* (Bucolics; 1952; Warsaw, Dec. 1953; also for Viola and Cello, 1962); *Inwencja* (Invention; 1968). **VOCAL:** *Lacrimosa* for Soprano, Chorus ad libitum, and Orch. (1937; Warsaw, Nov. 1938); *Pieśni walki podziemnej* (Songs of the Underground Struggle) for Voice and Piano (1942–44); *Dwadzieścia kołęd* (Twenty Polish Christmas Carols) for Voice and Piano (1946; Kraków, Jan. 29, 1947; also for Soprano, Women's Chorus, and Chamber Orch., 1984; in Polish, London, Dec. 15, 1985; in Eng., Aberdeen, Dec. 14, 1990); *O Panu Tralalińskim* (About Mr. Tralalinski) for Chorus and Piano (1947; also for Voice and Piano, 1947–48; Kraków, Jan. 26, 1948); *Dwa słowiki* (Two Nightingales) for Chorus and Piano (1947); *Spóźniony słowik* (The Belated Nightingale) for Voice and Piano (1947–48; Kraków, Jan. 26, 1948; also for Voice and Chamber Orch., 1952); *Sześć piosenek dziecinnych* (Six Children's Songs) for Voice and Piano (1947; Kraków, Jan. 26, 1948; also for Mezzo-soprano and Chamber Orch., 1952–53, and for Children's Chorus and Orch., Warsaw, April 29, 1954); *Słomkowy łańcuszek i inne utwory* (Strawchain and Other Songs) for Soprano, Mezzo-soprano, Flute, Oboe, 2 Clarinets, and Bassoon (1950–51); *Wiosna* (Spring) for Mezzo-soprano and Chamber Orch. (1951); *Tryptyk śląski* (Silesian Triptych) for Soprano and Orch. (Warsaw, Dec. 2, 1951); *Pióreczko* (Little Feather) for Voice and Piano or Chamber Orch. (1953); 5 Songs for Woman's Voice and Piano, after Kazimiera Iłłakowiczówna (1956–57; Katowice, Nov. 25, 1569; also for Mezzo-soprano and Chamber Orch., 1958; Katowice, Feb. 12, 1960); *Bajka iskierki i inne piosenki dla dzieci* (The Tale of the Little Spark and Other Songs for Children) for Voice and Piano (1958); *Trzy poematy Henri Michaux* (Three Poems of Henri Michaux) for Chorus and Orch. (1961–63; Zagreb, May 9, 1963); *Paroles tissées* (Woven Words) for Tenor and Chamber Orch. (Aldeburgh, June 20, 1965); *Les espaces du sommeil* for Baritone and Orch. (1975; Berlin, April 12, 1978); *Chantefleurs et Chantefables* for Soprano and Orch. (1989–90; London, Aug. 8, 1991); *Tarantelle* for Baritone and Piano (London, May 20, 1990).

BIBL.: B. Varga, *L. Profile: W. L. in Conversation with Bálint András Varga* (London, 1976); S. Stucky, *L. and His Music* (Cambridge, 1981); T. Kaczyński, *Rozmowy z W. L.* (Conversations with W. L.; Wrocław, 1993); idem, *L.:Żzycie i muzyka* (L.: Life and Music; Warsaw, 1994); K. Meyer, *W. L.* (Poznań, 1994); I. Nikolska, *Conversations with W. L. (1987–92)* (Stockholm, 1994); C. Rae, *The Music of L.* (London, 1994); M. Homma, *W. L.: Zwölfton-Harmonik, Formbilding "aleatorischer Kontrapunkt": Studien zum Gesamtwerk unter Einbeziehung der Skizzen* (Cologne, 1996); J. Paja-Stach, *W. L.* (Kraków, 1996); idem, *L. i jego styl muzyczny* (L. and His Musical Style; Kraków, 1997). —NS/LK/DM

Lutyens, (Agnes) Elisabeth, important English composer; b. London, July 9, 1906; d. there, April 14, 1983. She was a daughter of the noted architect Sir Edwin Lutyens, and was brought up in an atmosphere of cultural enlightenment. She studied at the École Normale de Musique in Paris (1922–23) and with H. Darke at the Royal Coll. of Music in London (1926–30). In her vivid autobiography, *A Goldfish Bowl* (London, 1972), she recounted her search for a congenial idiom of musical expression, beginning with the erstwhile fashionable Romantic manner and progressing toward a more individual, psychologically tense writing in an atonal technique using a sui generis dodecaphonic method of composition. In 1969 she was made a Commander of the Order of the British Empire. She was married to Edward Clark.

WORKS: DRAMATIC: *the Birthday of the Infanta*, ballet (1932); *The Pit*, dramatic scene for Tenor, Bass, Women's Chorus, and Orch. (Palermo, April 24, 1949); *Penelope*, radio opera (1950); *Infidelio*, chamber opera (1956; London, April 17, 1973); *The Numbered*, opera (1965–67); *Time Off? Not a Ghost of a Chance*, charade (1967–68; London, March 1, 1972); *Isis and Osiris*, lyric drama for 8 Voices and Chamber Orch. (1969); *The Linnet from the Leaf*, musical theater for 5 Singers and 2 Instrumental Groups (1972); *The Waiting Game*, 5 scenes for Mezzo-soprano, Baritone, and Chamber Orch. (1973); *One and the Same*, scena for Soprano, Speaker, and Mimes (1973); *The Goldfish Bowl*, ballad opera (1975); *Like a Window*, extracts from letters of van Gogh (1976). **ORCH.:** *3 Pieces* (1939); 6 chamber concertos, some with Solo Instruments (1939–48); *3 Symphonic Preludes* (1942); *Viola Concerto* (1947); *Music I* (1954), *II* (1962), *III* (1964), and *IV* (1981); *Quincunx* (1960); *En voyage*, symphonic suite (London, July 2, 1960); *Symphonies* for Piano, Wind Instruments, Harps, and Percussion (London, July 28, 1961); *Music* for Piano and Orch. (1964); *Novenaria* (1967); *Plenum II* for Oboe and Chamber Orch. (1973; London, June 14, 1974); *The Winter of the World* for Cello and Chamber Ensemble (London, May 5, 1974); *Eos* for Chamber Orch. (1975); *Rondel* (1976); *6 Bagatelles* for Chamber Orch. (1976); *Nox* for Piano and 2 Chamber Orchs. (1977); *Wild Decembers* (1980). **CHAMBER:** Sonata for Solo Viola (1938); 13 string quartets (1938–82); String Trio (1939); *9 Bagatelles* for Cello and Piano (1942); *Aptote* for Violin (1948); *Valediction* for Clarinet and Piano (1954); *Nocturnes* for Violin, Cello, and Guitar (1956); *Capricci* for 2 Harps and Percussion (1956); *6 Tempi* for 10 Instruments (1957); Wind Quintet (1960); String Quintet (1963); Trio for Flute, Clarinet, and Bassoon (1963); *Scena* for Violin, Cello, and Percussion (1964); *Music for Wind* for Double Wind Quintet (1964); *Music for 3* for Flute, Oboe, and Piano (1964); *The Fall of the Leafe* for Oboe and String Quartet (1967); *Horai* for Violin, Horn, and Piano (1968); *The Tides of Time* for Double Bass and Piano (1969); *Driving Out the Death* for Oboe and String Trio (1971); *Rape of the Moone* for Wind Octet (1973); *Plenum III* for String Quartet (1974); *Kareniana* for Viola and Instrumental Group (1974); *Go, Said the Bird* for Electric Guitar and String Quartet (1975); *Mare et Minutiae* for String Quartet (1976); *Fantasia* for Alto Saxophone and 3 Instrumental Groups (1977); *O Absalom* for Oboe and String Trio (1977); *Constants* for Cello and Piano (1977); *Doubles* for String Quartet (1978); *Footfalls* for Flute and Piano (1978); *Prelude* for Violin (1979); Trio for Clarinet, Cello, and Piano (1979); *Morning Sea* for Oboe and Piano (1979); *Rapprochement* for Horn, Harp, Wind Quartet, String Quartet, Piano, and Percussion (1980); *6* for an ensemble of 6 Instruments and Percussion (1980); *Solo* for Clarinet, interchangeable with Bass Clarinet, and Double Bass (1980); *Branches of the Night and of the Day* for Horn and String Quartet (1981); *The Living Night* for Percussion (1981); *Echo of the Wind* for Viola (1981); *Triolet I* for Clarinet, Mandolin, and Cello (1982) and *II* for Cello, Marimba, and Harp (1982). **KEYBOARD: Piano:** *5 Intermezzi* (1942); *Piano e Forte* (1958); *Plenum I* (1973); *The Ring of Bone* (1975); *5 impromptus* (1977); *3 Books of Bagatelles* (1979); *La natura dell'acqua* (1981). **Organ:** *Sinfonia* (1956); *Plenum IV* (1975). **VOCAL:** *O Saisons, O Chateaux*, cantata for Soprano, Mandolin, Guitar, Harp, and Strings (1946); *Requiem for the Living* for Soloists, Chorus, and Orch. (1948); *Bienfaits de la lune* for Soprano, Tenor, Chorus, Strings, and Percussion (1952); *De Amore*, cantata (1957; London, Sept. 7, 1973); *Catena* for Soprano, Tenor, and 21 Instruments (1961–62); *Encomion* for Chorus, Brass, and Percussion (1963); *The Valley of Haisu-Se* for Soprano and Instrumental Ensemble (1965); *Akapotik Rose* for Soprano and Instrumental Ensemble (1966); *And Suddenly It's Evening* for Tenor and 11 Instruments (1967); *Essence of Our Happiness*, cantata (1968; London, Sept. 8, 1970); *Phoenix* for Soprano, Violin, Clarinet, and Piano (1968); *Anerca* for Women's Speaking Chorus, 10 Guitars, and Percussion (1970); *Vision of Youth* for Soprano, 3 Clarinets, Piano, and

Percussion (1970); *Islands* for Soprano, Tenor, Narrator, and Instrumental Ensemble (London, June 7, 1971); *The Tears of Night* for Countertenor, 6 Sopranos, and 3 Instrumental Ensembles (1971); *Requiescat*, in memoriam Igor Stravinsky, for Soprano and String Trio (1971); *Dirge* for the Proud World for Soprano, Countertenor, Harpsichord, and Cello (1971); *Counting Your Steps* for Chorus, 4 Flutes, and 4 Percussion Players (1972); *Chimes and Cantos* for Baritone and Instrumental Ensemble (1972); *Voice of Quiet Waters* for Chorus and Orch. (1972; Huddersfield, April 14, 1973); *Laudi* for Soprano, 3 Clarinets, Piano, and Percussion (1973); *Chorale Prelude and Paraphrase* for Tenor, String Quintet, and Percussion, after a letter of Keats (1977); *Cascando* for Contralto, Violin, and Strings (1977); *Elegy of the Flowers* for Tenor and 3 Instrumental Groups (1978); *Echoi* for Mezzo-soprano and Orch. (1979); *Cantata* for Soprano and Instruments (1979); *Cantata* for 3 Soloists and Instrumental Ensemble, after Baudelaire (1979); *The Roots of the World* for Chorus and Cello obbligato, after Yeats (1979); *Echoes* for Contralto, Alto Flute, English Horn, and String Quartet (1979); *Mine Eyes, My Bread, My Spade* for Baritone and String Quartet (1980); *Fleur du silence* for Tenor, Flute, Oboe, Horn, Harp, Violin, Viola, and Percussion, after Rémi de Gourmont (1980); *The Singing Birds* for Actress and Viola (1980).

BIBL.: M. and S. Harries, *A Pilgrim Soul: The Life and Work of E. L.* (London, 1989).—NS/LK/DM

Lutz, (Wilhelm) Meyer, German-born English organist, conductor, and composer; b. Männerstadt, near Kissingen, 1822?; d. London, Jan. 31, 1903. He studied with his father and later attended the Univ. of Würzburg, where his mentors in music were Eisenhöfer and Keller. In 1848 he settled in England and was an organist in churches in Birmingham, Leeds, and London. After conducting at the Surrey Theatre in London (1850–55), he was active as a conductor of touring theater companies. In 1869 he became music director of the Gaiety Theatre in London, for which he composed much light music. His barn-dance music for the pas de quatre from his burlesque *Faust Up-to-Date* (London, Oct. 30, 1888) was popular.—NS/LK/DM

Luvisi, Lee, American pianist and teacher; b. Louisville, Dec. 12, 1937. He studied at the Curtis Inst. of Music in Philadelphia with Serkin and Horszowski, and upon his graduation in 1957 joined its faculty. In 1963 he was named artist-in-residence at the Univ. of Louisville School of Music, and later became chairman of its piano dept. He appeared as soloist with many of the major American and European orchs., and also gave numerous recitals. In 1983 he became a member of the Chamber Music. Soc. of Lincoln Center in N.Y.—NS/LK/DM

Luxon, Benjamin, esteemed English baritone; b. Redruth, March 24, 1937. He studied with Walter Grünner at the Guildhall School of Music in London, then joined the English Opera Group, with which he sang Sid in *Albert Herring* and Tarquinius in *The Rape of Lucretia* on its tour of the Soviet Union (1963). He was chosen by Britten to create the title role in the opera *Owen Wingrave* (BBC-TV, May 16, 1971); then made his debut at London's Covent Garden as Monteverdi's Ulysses (1972), and subsequently sang there regularly; also appeared at the festivals in Aldeburgh, Edinburgh, and Glynde-bourne (from 1972), and with the English National Opera in London (from 1974). On Feb. 2, 1980, he made his Metropolitan Opera debut in N.Y. as Eugene Onegin. In 1986 he made his first appearance at Milan's La Scala. In 1988 he sang Wozzeck in Los Angeles. In 1992 he appeared as Falstaff at the English National Opera. His last years as a singer were aggravated by increasing deafness. His other roles included Count Almaviva, Don Giovanni, Papageno, Wolfram, and Eisenstein. He also distinguished himself as a concert artist, his repertoire ranging from the standard literature to folk songs. In 1986 he was made a Commander of the Order of the British Empire.—NS/LK/DM

Luython, Charles, Flemish composer; b. Antwerp, c. 1556; d. Prague, Aug. 1620. After receiving elementary training as a chorister, he was sent at the age of 10 to the Imperial Chapel in Vienna, where he remained until he was 15. He composed 2 masses for Emperor Maximilian II. Following studies in Italy, he was back in Vienna by 1576 as a member of the Kammermusik of the court; was made a chamber organist in 1577 by Rudolf II, whose court was moved to Prague; he composed a book of madrigals for his patron. He was made court organist in 1582, and then assumed the duties of first organist in 1593, being officially named to that post in 1596; that same year he became court composer, succeeding Philippe de Monte. With the death of the Emperor in 1612, Luython lost his positions and attendant financial security. He died in poverty. Apart from his book of madrigals (Venice, 1582), he publ. *Popularis anni jubilus* for 6 Voices (Prague, 1587), *Selectissimarum sacrarum cantionum...* for 6 Voices (Prague, 1603), *Opus musicum in Lamentationes Hieremiae prophetae* for 6 Voices (Prague, 1604), and *Liber primus missarum* for 3 to 7 Voices (Prague, 1609). Among his extant instrumental music is a *Fuga suavissima* (publ. in Woltz's *Tabulatur-Buch*, 1617). Luython was a composer of extraordinary ingenuity; Michael Praetorius recounts in his *Syntagma musicum* that Luython owned a keyboard instrument with 3 manuals, representing the diatonic, chromatic, and enharmonic intervals (18 notes to the octave), thus securing theoretically correct modulations through sharps or flats.

BIBL.: L. de Burbure, *C. L.* (Brussels, 1880); A. Smijers, *Karl L. als Motettenkomponist* (Amsterdam, 1923); C. Saas, *C. L.: Ses madrigaux et oeuvres instrumentales* (diss., Univ. of Louvain, 1958).—NS/LK/DM

Luzzaschi, Luzzasco, eminent Italian organist, pedagogue, and composer; b. Ferrara, 1545?; d. there, Sept. 10, 1607. He began studies as a child with Cipriano de Rore, remaining under his tutelage until 1558. He became a singer at the Este court (1561), and was first organist there from 1564 until the court's demise in 1597, and also directed one of its orchs.; likewise was organist at Ferrara Cathedral and at the Accademia della Morte. He also became director of Duke Alfonso's private musica da camera about 1569. He was one of the finest madrigalists of his day. He was also highly esteemed as a teacher, and was the mentor of Fresco-

baldi. Among his secular vocal works are 7 books of madrigals for 5 Voices (1571–1604), *Madrigali...per cantare, et sonare a uno, e doi, e tre soprani* (Rome, 1601; ed. in Monumenti di Musica Italiana, II/2, 1965), and others in contemporary anthologies. He also composed the sacred *Sacrarum cantionum liber primus* for 5 Voices (Venice, 1598). Included in his instrumental works are Canzona for Organ in A. Raverii, *Canzoni per sonar* (Venice, 1608), a number of ricercari, a toccata, and a dance.

BIBL.: E. Strainchamps, *L. L. and His Five-part Madrigals* (diss., Columbia Univ., 1960); A. Spiro, *The Five-part Madrigals of L. L.* (diss., Boston Univ., 1961).—NS/LK/DM

Lvov, Alexei Feodorovich, Russian violinist and composer; b. Reval, June 5, 1798; d. Romano, near Kovno, Dec. 28, 1870. His father, Feodor Petrovich Lvov (1766–1836), was director of the Imperial Court Chapel Choir in St. Petersburg (1825–36). Alexei received his primary education at home and took up the violin in early childhood. After graduating from the Inst. of Road Engineering (1818), he entered the army. In 1826 he was made adjutant to Czar Nicholas I's security chief in St. Petersburg. At the Czar's request, Lvov composed the Russian national anthem, *Bozhe, tsarya khrani* (God Save the Czar), in 1833. It was first performed on the Czar's name day in Moscow on Dec. 18, 1833, and remained the national anthem until the Revolution of 1917. Lvov succeeded his father as director of the Imperial Court Chapel Choir in 1837, a post he held until 1861. In 1840 he traveled in Europe, eliciting great praise in Leipzig for his playing by Schumann. Back in St. Petersburg, he founded a series of orch. concerts. Growing deafness forced him to abandon his musical activities in 1867.

WORKS: DRAMATIC: Opera: *Bianca und Gualtiero* (Dresden, Oct. 13, 1844); *Undina* (St. Petersburg, Sept. 20, 1847); *Starosta Boris, ili Russkiy muzhichok i frantsuzskiye marodyori* (Boris the Headman, or the Russian Peasant and the French Marauders; St. Petersburg, May 1, 1854). **ORCH.:** Violin Concerto (1840); *Divertimento* for Violin, Cello, and Orch. (c. 1841; also for Violin, Cello, and String Quartet or Piano); Overture (c. 1850). **CHAMBER:** *Le duel* for Violin and Cello (c. 1840); *Divertimento* for Violin, Cello, and Piano or Organ (c. 1840); 24 caprices for Violin (c. 1850). **VOCAL:** *Stabat Mater* for Soloists and Orch. (1851); many sacred choral pieces.—NS/LK/DM

Lybbert, Donald, American composer and teacher; b. Cresco, Iowa, Feb. 19, 1923; d. Norwalk, Conn., July 26, 1981. He studied at the Univ. of Iowa (B.M., 1946), with Ward and Wagenaar at the Juilliard School of Music in N.Y. (1946–48), with Carter and Luening at Columbia Univ. (M.A., 1950), and with Boulanger in Fontainebleau (1961). From 1954 to 1980 he taught at Hunter Coll. of the City Univ. of N.Y. With F. Davis, he wrote *The Essentials of Counterpoint* (1969). His music was freely atonal for the most part, although he utilized serial procedures in some of his scores.

WORKS: DRAMATIC: *Monica*, operetta (Amsterdam, Nov. 2, 1952); *The Scarlet Letter*, opera (1964–67). **ORCH.:** Concert Overture (1952). **CHAMBER:** Wind Octet (1947); *Introduction and Toccata* for Brass and Piano (1955); Trio for Clarinet, Horn, and Bassoon (1956); *Chamber Sonata* for Viola, Horn, and Piano (1957); *Sonorities* for 11 Instruments (1960);

Praeludium for Brass and Percussion (1962); *Variants* for 5 Winds (1971). **P i a n o :** 3 sonatas (1947, 1954, 1962); *Movement* for Piano, 4-hands (1960); Concerto for Piano and Tape (n.d.). **VOCAL:** *Leopardi Canti*, song cycle for Soprano, Flute, Viola, and Bass Clarinet (1959); *Austro terris inflente*, 3 motets (1961); *Lines for the Fallen* for Soprano and 2 Quarter Tone Tuned Pianos (1967); *Zap* for Multiantiphonal Chorus, Instruments, and Rock Group (1970); *Octagon* for Soprano and 7 Instrumentalists (1975).—**NS/LK/DM**

Lyford, Ralph, American conductor and composer; b. Worcester, Mass., Feb. 22, 1882; d. Cincinnati, Sept. 3, 1927. He began to study piano and violin as a child, and entered the New England Cons. of Music in Boston at the age of 12, studying piano with Helen Hopekirk, organ with Goodrich, and composition with Chadwick. He then went to Leipzig to study conducting with Arthur Nikisch (1906). Returning to America, he became asst. conductor of the San Carlo Opera Co. (1907–8); then was with the Boston Opera Co. (1908–14). In 1916 he settled in Cincinnati, where he taught at the Cons., and also conducted the summer seasons of opera at the Zoological Gardens. From 1925 to 1927 he was assoc. conductor of the Cincinnati Sym. Orch. He wrote an opera, *Castle Agrazant* (Cincinnati, April 29, 1926; won the David Bispham Medal), Piano Concerto (1917), chamber music, and songs.—**NS/LK/DM**

Lympany, Dame Moura (real name, **Mary Johnstone**), esteemed English pianist; b. Saltash, Aug. 18, 1916. After studies in Liège, she was a scholarship student of Coviello at the Royal Coll. of Music in London. She then continued her training in Vienna with Paul Weingarten and in London with Mathdilde Verne and Tobias Matthay. At age 12, she made her debut as soloist in Mendelssohn's G minor Piano Concerto in Harrogate. In 1938 she took second prize in the Ysaÿe Competition in Brussels. For professional purposes, she took the name Moura Lympany, the surname being a transformation of her mother's maiden name of Limpenny. In 1940 she was soloist in the first London performance of the Khachaturian Piano Concerto, which she later played throughout Europe. After making her first appearances in the U.S. in 1948, she toured throughout the world. In 1979 she was made a Commander of the Order of the British Empire and in 1992 a Dame Commander of the Order of the British Empire. With M. Strickland, she publ. *Moura Lympany, her Autobiography* (London, 1991). Lympany displayed a remarkable capacity for Russian music, particularly of Rachmaninoff. She also championed such English composers as Delius, Ireland, Cyril Scott, and Rawsthorne. —**NS/LK/DM**

Lyne, Felice, American soprano; b. Slater, Mo., March 28, 1887; d. Allentown, Pa., Sept. 1, 1935. Her family moved to Allentown when she was a child, where she studied with F.S. Hardman. She then had training in Paris with Marchesi, J. de Reszke, and L. d'Aubigne. She made a successful debut as Gilda in *Rigoletto* at Hammerstein's London Opera (Nov. 25, 1911), and appeared there 36 times that season, creating the principal soprano parts in the English premieres of Massenet's *Don Quichotte* and *Jongleur de Notre-Dame*, and Holbrooke's *Children of Don*; toured with the Quinlan Opera Co. Returning to the U.S., she became a member of the Boston Opera Co. She also appeared in concerts.—**NS/LK/DM**

Lynn, George, American choral conductor, organist, teacher, and composer; b. Edwardsville, Pa., Oct. 5, 1915; d. Colorado Springs, Colo., March 16, 1989. He was a student of Weinrich (organ), Williamson (conducting), and Harris (composition) at Westminster Choir Coll. in Princeton, N.J. (B.Mus., 1938) and of Thompson (composition) at Princeton Univ. (M.F.A., 1947). He was active as an organist and music director in various churches in N.J., Calif., Pa., Colo., and N.C. Lynn served as prof. of choral arts at Westminster Choir Coll. (1946–50) and at the Univ. of Colo. (1950–52). From 1963 to 1969 he was music director of the Westminster Choir. In 1971 he was visiting composer-in-residence at the Univ. of N.Mex. He subsequently was prof. of choral arts at the Colo. School of Mines (1971–80), Loretto Heights Coll. (1971–86), and Rice Univ. (1986–87). Lynn composed in a tonal idiom with a strong modal character. Rhythmic variation was indicative of his style and provided a firm foundation for his long melodic lines.

WORKS: DRAMATIC: O p e r a : *The Violinden Tree* (1960); *From Time to Time* (1962). **ORCH.:** Piano Concerto (1962); 2 syms. (1964, 1966). **CHAMBER:** 5 string quartets; works for Violin and Piano, Clarinet and Piano, etc.; over 100 piano pieces. **VOCAL:** *Gettysburg Address* for Baritone, Chorus, and Orch. (1941); *Greek Folk Song Rhapsody* for Contralto, Chorus, and Orch. (1958); 3 sacred syms. for Chorus (1959, 1960, 1962); *Second Inaugural* for Chorus and Orch. (1961); *Markings* for Soprano, Men's Chorus, and Orch. (1969); settings of e.e. cummings for Chorus (1984); 2 cantatas: *Under the Shadow* for Chorus, Brass, and Organ (1985) and *The Scandal of Christ* for Soloists, Chorus, and Organ (1986); many other choral pieces; over 100 songs; arrangements.—**NS/LK/DM**

Lynn, Loretta (neé **Webb**), the "coal miner's daughter" country singer/songwriter; b. Butcher Hollow, Ky., April 14, 1935. One of country music's pioneering female performers and songwriters, Lynn has a classic country voice that is perfectly suited to her to-the-point lyrics reflecting a uniquely woman's point-of-view. Perhaps the only country singer who has taken on a wide variety of issues, from birth control to the Vietnam War to wife abuse, Lynn has made an important contribution to widening the subject matter and audience for country music.

Lynn was born in a small coal-mining community, as she emphasized in her biography, *Coal Miner's Daughter* (1976, later a feature film). When she was 13, she married Oliver "Mooney" Lynn, who later became her manager. The couple relocated to Wash. state, where Lynn raised four children while she began performing her own material. Her first single was in the classic barroom mold, "I'm a Honky Tonk Girl," released in 1960 on the tiny Zero label. This brought her to the attention of Owen Bradley, the legendary producer who had worked with Patsy Cline.

Her early 1960s recordings showed the influence of Kitty Wells in their brash lyrics of lovin' and losin'. Soon, however, her vocal style softened, while her original material turned to unusual (for the time) topics, including "Don't Come Home a-Drinkin' (With Lovin' on Your Mind)," "You Ain't Woman Enough (to Steal My Man)," and "The Pill," a song in support of birth control. All of the songs were written from a woman's point-of-view; although their sound was classic honky tonk, their message was unusually liberated for the mid-1960s and early 1970s. It is also noteworthy that Lynn wrote her songs from the point-of-view of a wife, a figure not often encountered on the honky-tonk landscape (primarily peopled by wayward husbands and "honky-tonk angels," the unattached women who lured them to their dooms). This heavy dose of reality in a medium that seemed to thrive on fantasy pointed the direction for many of the more progressive songwriters of the 1970s and 1980s. Her autobiographical song, "Coal Miner's Daughter," from 1970, perfectly expressed the pride and anguish of growing up dirt poor in the mountains.

The early 1970s also saw her teamed up with Conway Twitty on a series of successful duets, including "After the Fire Is Gone" and "Louisiana Woman, Mississippi Man." Her autobiography, published in the mid-1970s, was instrumental not only in cementing her image as a "true country woman," but in reasserting country music's roots at a time when many acts were trying to crossover onto the pop and rock charts.

Sadly, the success inspired by her autobiography and the subsequent film of her life seems to have encouraged Lynn in the 1980s and early 1990s to move in a more mainstream direction. She less frequently writes her own material, and the material selected for her is weak. Her live show leans heavily on her early hits, and her many fans seem content to hear her perform the same repertory of well-known numbers.

In 1988, Lynn was elected to the Country Music Hall of Fame. From 1990 to 1996, she more or less withdrew from performing in order to nurse her ailing husband, who finally succumbed to diabetes in August 1996. She returned to performing on a limited basis thereafter, although she has also suffered from time to time with health problems of her own.

In the mid-1990s, Loretta's twin daughters, Patsy Eileen and Peggy Jean (b. 1964), began performing as The Lynns. They released their debut album in 1998, which primarily consisted of their own material, featuring upbeat tunes graced by their perky harmonies.

WRITINGS: *Coal Miner's Daughter* (N.Y., 1976).

DISC.: *Loretta Lynn Sings* (1963); *Before I'm Over You* (1964); *Songs from My Heart* (1965); *Blue Kentucky Girl* (1965); *Hymns* (1965); *I Like 'Em Country* (1966); *You Ain't Woman Enough* (1966); *A Country Christmas* (1966); *Don't Come Home A-Drinkin'* (1967); *Singin' with Feelin'* (1967); *Who Says God Is Dead* (1968); *Fist City* (1968); *Loretta Lynn's Greatest Hits* (1968); *Here's Loretta Lynn* (1968); *Your Squaw Is on the Warpath* (1969); *A Woman of the World/To Make a Man* (1969); *Here's Loretta Singing "Wings Upon Your Horns"* (1970); *Loretta Writes 'Em and Sings 'Em* (1970); *Coal Miner's Daugher* (1971); *I Want to Be Free* (1971); *You're Lookin' at Country* (1971); *One's On the Way* (1972); *God Bless America Again* (1972); *Alone with You* (1972); *Here I Am Again* (1972); *Entertainer of the Year* (1973); *Love Is the Foundation* (1973); *They Don't Make 'Em Like My Daddy* (1974); *Greatest Hits Vol. 2* (1974); *Back to the Country* (1975); *Home* (1975); *When the Tingle Becomes a Chill* (1976); *Somebody Somewhere* (1976); *On the Road with Loretta and the Coal Miners* (1976); *I Remember Patsy* (1977); *Out of My Head and Back in My Bed* (1978); *Honky Tonk Heroes* (1978); *Greatest Hits Live* (1978); *Diamond Duet* (1979); *We've Come a Long Way Baby* (1979); *Loretta* (1980); *Lookin' Good* (1980); *Making Love from Memory* (1982); *I Lie* (1982); *Lyin', Cheatin', Woman Chasin', Honky Tonkin', Whiskey Drinkin' You* (1983); *Just a Woman* (1985); *Great Country Hits* (1985); *Golden Greats* (1986); *20 Greatest Hits* (1987); *The Very Best of Loretta Lynn* (1988); *Making Believe* (1988); *Who Was That Stranger* (1989); *The Country Music Hall of Fame: Lorette Lynn* (1991); *Coal Miner's Daughter: The Best Of...* (1993); *Honky Tonk Girl: The Loretta Lynn Collection* (1994); *The Very Best of Loretta Lynn* (1997). Ernest Tubb: *And Mrs. Used to Be* (1965); *Ernest Tubb & Loretta Lynn Singin' Again* (1967); *If We Put Our Heads Together* (1969); *The Ernest Tubb/Loretta Lynn Story* (1973). Conway Twitty: *We Only Make Believe* (1971); *Lead Me On* (1971); *Louisiana Woman, Mississippi Man* (1973); *Country Partners* (1974); *The Very Best of Conway and Loretta* (1973); *Feelins'* (1975); *United Talent* (1976); *Dynamic Duo* (1977); *Two's a Party* (1981). Tammy Wynette, Dolly Parton: *Honky Tonk Angels* (1993).—**RC**

Lynne, Gloria, jazz/R&B vocalist; b. Harlem, N.Y., Nov. 23, 1931. A singer whose style blurs the distinctions of popular singing, jazz, and blues, Lynne made both straight jazz and jazz-oriented material during the 1950s and 1960s and had some hits on the R&B scene. She has also done some acting and songwriting. With great expressiveness, she is a master at telling a story, building tension, and punctuating a point. She has done more jazz- oriented work in recent years.

DISC.: *Miss Gloria Lynne* (1958); *Lonely and Sentimental* (1959); *Day In, Day Out* (1960); *Try a Little Tenderness* (1960); *I Am Glad There's You* (1961); *This Little Boy of Mine* (1961); *After Hours* (1962); *At the Las Vegas Thunderbird* (1962); *Gloria Lynne at Basin Street East* (1962); *He Needs Me* (1962); *Gloria, Marty and Strings* (1963); *Intimate Moments* (1965); *Soul Serenade* (1965); *Love and a Woman* (1966); *I Don't Know How to Love Him* (1976); *Gloria Blue* (1989); *Glorious Gloria Lynne* (1990); *No Detour Ahead* (1992); *Serenade in Blue* (1994).—**LP**

Lynyrd Skynyrd, perhaps the most popular Southern-rock band of the 1970s. **MEMBERSHIP:** Ronnie Van Zant, lead voc. (b. Jacksonville, Fla., Jan. 15, 1949; d. near Gillsburg, Miss., Oct. 20, 1977); Gary Rossington, gtr. (b. Dec. 4, 1951); Allen Collins, gtr. (b. July 19, 1952; d. Jacksonville, Fla., Jan. 23, 1990); Ed King, gtr.; Billy Powell, kybd.; Leon Wilkeson, bs.; Bob Burns, drm. Artimus Pyle replaced Bob Burns in 1974; Ed King left in 1975. Brother-and-sister team guitarist Steve (b. Sept. 14, 1949) and vocalist Cassie Gaines (both d. near Gillsburg, Miss., Oct. 20, 1977) joined in 1976.

Superseding progenitors the Allman Brothers, Lynyrd Skynyrd helped reclaim blues-based rock from British groups like Cream and Led Zeppelin. Often propelled by a *three*-guitar front line (a format otherwise utilized by only the Peter Green–era Fleetwood Mac) and featuring the strong vocal presence and prolific songwriting of leader Ronnie Van Zant, Lynyrd Skynyrd established themselves as a dynamic touring act by opening for the Who's 1973 Quadrophenia tour. Scoring a number of aggressive hits between 1974 and 1977, Lynyrd Skynyrd may be best remembered for the jam-style FM radio classic "Free Bird." However, the group disbanded in late 1977 after Van Zant and two other band members were killed in an airplane crash on Oct. 20, 1977. During the 1980s guitarist Gary Rossington persevered with the Rossington- Collins and Rossington bands. In 1987 many band members regrouped with Rossington and Ronnie Van Zant's brother Johnny for a tribute tour that eventually led to a new version of Lynyrd Skynyrd in 1991.

Vocalist Ronnie Van Zant and guitarists Gary Rossington and Allen Collins formed My Backyard, the first of a series of rock bands, in 1965. Experiencing numerous personnel and name changes, the band toured the Southern club circuit for seven years. In 1970 the group adopted the name Lynyrd Skynyrd, and by 1972 the band's membership had stabilized with Van Zant, Rossington, Collins, guitarist Ed King, keyboardist Billy Powell, bassist Leon Wilkeson, and drummer Bob Burns. (King had cowritten the 1967 psychedelic top hit "Incense and Peppermint" for his group the Strawberry Alarm Clock.)

By 1972 Lynyrd Skynyrd were making occasional forays into Atlanta, Ga., where they were "discovered" by producer/keyboardist Al Kooper. He signed the band to MCA Records and produced their debut album, usually referred to as *Pronounced Leh-nerd Skin-nerd*. Supported by a rigorous touring schedule and major promotional campaign by MCA, the album featured "Gimme Three Steps" and the underground favorites "Simple Man" and "Free Bird," all cowritten by Van Zant. "Free Bird" became a major hit when released as a single in late 1974.

Opening for the Who's late-1973 American tour supporting their album *Quadrophenia*, Lynyrd Skynyrd were exposed to their largest audiences to date, performing creditably. The Al Kooper-produced *Second Helping* contained "Workin' for MCA" and J. J. Cale's "Call Me the Breeze," and yielded a near-smash with the Southern anthem "Sweet Home Alabama," ostensibly a reply to Neil Young's "Southern Man." Touring exhaustively, Lynyrd Skynyrd's so-called Torture Tour of 1975 resulted in the departures of Ed King and Bob Burns. Kooper's final production for the band and King's final album with the band, *Nuthin' Fancy*, introduced drummer Artimus Pyle and included "I'm a Country Boy" and "Whiskey Rock-a-Roller," producing a major hit with the gun ode "Saturday Night Special."

Lynyrd Skynyrd continued with a two-guitar front line augmented by the female backing group the Honkettes, consisting of Cassie Gaines, Leslie Hawkins, and Joe Billingsley, in early 1976. *Gimme Back My Bullets*, produced by Tom Dowd, fared less well than Kooper's productions, and Cassie Gaines's guitarist-brother joined the group in June 1976. The live set *One More for the Road* produced a moderate hit with "Free Bird." After a touring respite, Lynyrd Skynyrd were back on the road in fall 1977, but on Oct. 20, 1977, their chartered plane crashed near Gillsburg, Miss., when it ran out of fuel, killing Ronnie Van Zant and Steve and Cassie

Gaines and injuring the others. *Street Survivors*, issued only three days before the crash, featured a ghastly cover (showing band members engulfed in flames) that was quickly withdrawn by MCA as being in poor taste. The album contained "I Know a Little," "I Never Dreamed," and the ominously ironic "That Smell," as well as the major hit "What's Your Name" and the minor hit "You Got That Right." As band members recovered, convalesced, and attempted to return to a normal lifestyle, MCA issued *Skynyrd's First … and Last*, recorded in 1970 and 1971, before the band had secured a recording contract.

In fall 1979, four surviving members of Lynyrd Skynyrd—Gary Rossington, Allen Collins, Billy Powell, and Leon Wilkeson—reunited as the Rossington- Collins Band, augmented by guitarist Barry Harwood, vocalist Dale Krantz Rossington (Gary's wife), and drummer Derek Hess. Formally debuting in June 1980, the group scored a minor hit with "Don't Misunderstand Me," only to disband in 1982. Collins subsequently formed the Allen Collins Band with Powell, Wilkeson, Harwood, and Hess. Collins was paralyzed in an automobile crash in 1986 and died of pneumonia on Jan. 23, 1990, at age 37.

Gary Rossington and Ronnie Van Zant's vocalist brother Johnny reassembled members of Lynyrd Skynyrd for a tribute tour in 1987, including Ed King, new guitarist Randall Hall, Powell, Wilkeson, and Pyle, plus Honkettes Dale Krantz Rossington and Carol Bristow. In 1988 Rossington formed the Rossington Band with wife Dale for a single MCA album. In 1991 Lynyrd Skynyrd officially regrouped with Rossington, Johnny Van Zant, King, Hall, Powell, Wilkeson, and Pyle for touring, and for recording *Lynyrd Skynyrd 1991* and *The Last Rebel* for Atlantic, and the acoustic *Endangered Species* for Capricorn.

DISC.: LYNYRD SKYNYRD: *Pronounced Leh-nerd Skin-nerd* (1973); *Second Helping* (1974); *Nuthin' Fancy* (1975); *Gimme Back My Bullets* (1976); *One More for the Road* (1976); *Street Survivors* (1977); *Skynyrd's First … and Last* (1978); *Gold and Platinum* (1979); *The Best of the Rest* (1982); *Legend* (1987); *Southern by the Grace of God: The L. S. Tribute Tour, 1987* (1988); *Skynyrd's Innyrds* (1989); *L. S. Box Set* (1991); *L. S., 1991* (1991); *The Last Rebel* (1993); *Endangered Species* (1994). TRIBUTE ALBUM: *Skynyrd Frynds* (1994). THE ROSSINGTON-COLLINS BAND: *Anytime, Anyplace, Anywhere* (1980); *This Is the Way* (1981). THE ROSSINGTON BAND: *Love Your Man* (1988).—**BH**

Lyon, James, American preacher, composer, and tunebook compiler; b. Newark, N.J., July 1, 1735; d. Machias, Maine, Oct. 12, 1794. He graduated from the Coll. of N.J. in Princeton on Sept. 26, 1759, at which ceremony an ode by him was performed. In 1762 he was awarded his M.A. at Princeton and received his preaching license from the Presbyterian Synod of New Brunswick, N.J. After serving a pastorate in Nova Scotia (1764–72), he was a pastor in Machias, Maine (1772–73; 1774–83; 1785–94). He also was an ardent supporter of the cause of American independence. Lyon compiled the important tunebook *Urania, or A Choice Collection of Psalm-Tunes, Anthems, and Hymns* (Philadelphia, 1761). It was the first such tunebook in America to include English anthems and fuging tunes, the first to identify native works, and the first to print pieces by Lyon and Hopkinson.

BIBL.: O. Sonneck, *Francis Hopkinson, the First American Poet-composer (1737–1791) and J. L., Patriot, Preacher, Psalmodist (1735–1794): Two Studies in Early American Music* (Washington, D.C., 1905).—**NS/LK/DM**

Lyon & Healy, American firm of instrument manufacturers and music dealers. The firm was founded in Chicago in 1864 by **George Washburn Lyon** (b. 1820; d. place and date unknown) and **Patrick Joseph Healy** (b. March 17, 1840; d. Chicago, April 3, 1905) as an outlet for the Oliver Ditson Co. of Boston. The firm soon grew to offer retail music from all publishers and musical instruments, some of which they began to manufacture themselves. After Lyon retired in 1889, Healy took sole charge of the firm and introduced the famous Lyon & Healy harp. The firm also manufactured many fine fretted instruments. About 1928 the Tonk Bros. Co. purchased the manufacturing rights from Lyon & Healy for all of their instruments except for harps and pianos. Lyon & Healy continued in the retail music business until 1979 when it became Lyon & Healy Harps. —**NS/LK/DM**

Lyons, Jimmy (actually, **James Leroy**), free-jazz alto (and soprano) saxophonist; b. Jersey City, N.J., Dec. 1, 1933; d. N.Y., May 19, 1986. At age 15, he was given an alto sax by Buster Bailey; he was also befriended and encouraged by Elmo Hope, Bud Powell, Kenny Drew, and Thelonious Monk and studied with Rudy Rutherford. In 1960 he met Cecil Taylor on return from army service in Korea, and in 1962 began his long tenure with Taylor when they made their recording debut. He played on all of Taylor's records until he began heading his own bands, and until the late 1970s Lyons's unique alto solos were the a familiar part of Taylor's music. They recorded for many labels, and Lyons adjusted to constant personnel changes, sometimes playing with other saxophonists like Sam Rivers, at other times with violinists, multiple drummers, or trumpeters. Lyons sometimes had other jobs, and worked for a period in the early 1970s as a music teacher at a N.Y. drug treatment center. He was an artist-in-residence with Taylor and Andrew Cyrille at Antioch Coll. (1970) and served with Bill Dixon at Bennington Coll. as director of the Black Music Ensemble in 1975. His late 1970s and 1980s groups usually included his wife, Karen Borca, and Paul Murphy, with assorted guest stars. Lyons also worked in a trio with singer Jeanne Lee and Andrew Cyrille, and in duos with Cyrille and Sunny Murray. During the 1980s he often led a quintet with his wife Karen Borca on bassoon. He used to write his pieces in whole notes so the rhythms could be played freely. He lived in the Bronx until, being a heavy smoker, he died of lung cancer.

DISC.: *Jump Up / What to Do About* (1980); *Something in Return* (1981); *Burnt Offering* (1982); *Wee Sneezawee* (1983); *Give It Up* (1985).—**LP**

Lysberg, Charles-Samuel
See **Bovy-Lysberg, Charles-Samuel**

Lytell, Jimmy (originally, **Sarrapede, James**), early jazz clarinetist, b. N.Y., Dec. 1, 1904; d. Kings Point, N.Y., Nov. 28, 1972. Professionally, he used the surname of film star Bert Lytell. Went to school in Brooklyn, during vacation of summer 1916 did first band work at a summer resort. With Original Indiana Five in autumn of 1921; joined the Original Dixieland Jazz Band early in 1922, then playing at The Balconades Ballroom, N.Y.; left in March 1922 to join Original Memphis Five. Toured and recorded with that quintet until 1925, then joined Capitol Theatre Orch. in N.Y., working under Eugene Ormandy. Freelanced in late 1920s, then spent many years (from 1930) on the staff of NBC, eventually becoming a musical director in the 1940s. Took part in the re-formed Original Memphis Five during summer of 1949. Throughout 1950s combined studio work with regular club and recording work with various bands. Led own band in Long Island in 1971. Died a year later.—**JC/LP**

Lytle, Johnny, American drummer and vibraphonist; b. Springfield, Ohio, Oct. 13, 1932. Though he was a drummer for Ray Charles and Gene Ammons in the early 1950s, he switched to vibes in the mid-1950s, utilizing a more percussive approach than some of his contemporaries. He has been a leader since the early 1960s and made several recordings with usually positive results. Though his music is spiced with R&B influences, he has eschewed strictly commercial dates despite obviously having keen pop sensibilities, particularly in the area of composition. He has spent most of his career on smaller labels and is known as "Fast Hands" for his rapid solos. Though not an innovator, he has consistently been a solid performer and leader for decades.

DISC.: *Easy Easy* (1980); *Possum Grease* (1995).—**PMac**

Lyttleton, Humphrey "Humph" (Richard Adeane), jazz trumpeter, clarinetist, leader, composer, author, broadcaster; b. Eton, Buckinghamshire, England, May 23, 1921. He is one of the best-loved British jazz figures. In addition to leading bands, he has hosted TV series and authored books. He has been leading his own bands from the late 1940s, first in a traditional style, and then, amid much controversy at the time, in a more swing and mainstream style, after the Ellington small group recordings. Many prominent British musicians (including, in the mid-1970s, Kathy Stobart and Bruce Turner among others) have worked with his bands, which have toured and recorded extensively. He has also made several recordings either with or using the arrangements of Buck Clayton. For many years he presented his own weekly show on national radio.

He began playing trumpet while at Eton. In 1941 he joined the Grenadier Guards. After demobilization in 1946, he studied at Camberwell School of Art, London, and sat-in with various bands at the Nut House, the Orange Tree, and others. He played in Carlo Krahmer's band; briefly led his own pick-up band (March 1947);

later that month joined George Webb's Dixielanders. He formed his own band in January 1948, which he has continued to lead through the 1990s. He appeared with Derek Neville's Band at the Nice Festival in February 1948; briefly co-led a big band with visiting Australian pianist/leader Graeme Bell in 1951; and with Freddy Grant, co-led the Paseo Band in 1952. Lyttleton's own band accompanied Sidney Bechet in London (1949) and later accompanied many visiting musicians and singers, including Buck Clayton, Buddy Tate, Henry Allen, Jimmy Rushing, and Joe Turner. Humphrey also worked as a cartoonist for the Daily Mail from 1949 until 1953, as well as writing the script for Wally Fawkes' "Flook" strip. From 1948 onwards he did regular international touring with his own band, including the U.S., the Middle East, and throughout Europe. In 1958 he formed his own big band, which performed frequently in the 1960s. He did a British tour with his own band from February to March 1975, also appeared on TV, played at the Concert Ellington Memorial RFH in June 1975 and the Armstrong Memorial RFH in July 1975. In 1977 he toured as a soloist with the "Salute to Satchmo" show, and guested with Alex Welsh's Band in 1978, when the show toured Australia.

For over 30 years, Humph has regularly guested with various British bands, including Mike Pembroke's Hot Seven, Mart Rodger's Hot Seven, Dave Morgan's Band, the Red River Jazzmen, Zenith Hot Stompers, George Huxley's Band, the Zenith Six, and others. He also made guest appearances in Canada during the 1980s. He is a prolific composer, and a successful author and broadcaster. He began his own Calligraph record label in 1984. His own band continued through the 1990s, and he also did concert tours and recordings with singer Helen Shapiro and in a group he co-led with Acker Bilk.

DISC.: *Delving Back and Forth with Hum* (1948); *A Tribute to Humph, Vol. 1* (1949); *A Tribute to Humph, Vol. 2* (1950); *A Tribute to Humph, Vol. 3* (1951); *Jazz at the Royal Festival Hall* (1951); *A Tribute to Humph, Vol. 4* (1952); *A Tribute to Humph, Vol. 5* (1952); *A Tribute to Humph, Vol. 6* (1953); *A Tribute to Humph, Vol. 7* (1955); *A Tribute to Humph, Vol. 8* (1955); *Some Like It Hot* (1955); *Back to the Sixties* (1960); *Humphrey Lyttleton and His Band* (1960); *Duke Ellington Classics* (1969); *Doggin' Around' WAM* (1971); *In Swinger* (1974); *Take It from the Top* (1975); *It Seems Like Yesterday* (1983); *Movin' and Groovin* (1983); *Humph at the Bull's Head* (1984); *This Old Gang of Ours* (1985); *Gonna Call My Children Home* (1986); *Gigs* (1987); *Beano Boogie* (1989); *Rock Me Gently* (1991); *Rent Party* (1991); *At Sundown* (1992).

WRITINGS: *I Play As I Please: The Memoirs of an Old Etonian Trumpeter* (London, 1954); *Second Chorus* (London, 1958); Lyttleton, *Take It from the Top: An Autobiographical Scrapbook* (London, 1975); *Why No Beethoven?* (London, 1984).—JC-B/LP

Lytton, Paul, English percussionist and instrument maker; b. London, England, March 8, 1947. He has been one of the figureheads in bringing the amplified world of small sounds and homemade electronic processors to the world of improvised music. Playing in both London and Aachen, Germany, in the late 1960s and early '70s, he began an important duo with saxophonist Evan Parker, a vast influence on later improvisers. This eventually turned into the Evan Parker Trio with the addition of Barry Guy on bass. He also worked in duo with percussionist Paul Lovens, based out of Aachen, and co-founded the fantastic Po-Torch label, which releases free improvised music circling around Lytton, Lovens, and Parker. He is also trained in dentistry; the cover of Derek Bailey's *Guitar Solos 2* shows some picks made by Lytton out of dental plate materials.

DISC.: *Ode* (1972); *Collective Calls (Urban)* (1972); *Live at Unity Theatre* (1975); *Ra 1+2* (1976); *Was It Me?* (1977); *The Inclined Stick* (1979); *Hook, Drift, and Shuffle* (1983); *Tracks* (1983); *Atlanta* (1986); *Binaurality* (1992); *Breaths and Heartbeats* (1994); *50th Anniversary Concert* (1994); *Natives and Aliens* (1996); *The Balance of Trade* (1996); *Two Octobers* (1996).—JO

Ma, Yo-Yo, brilliant Chinese-American cellist; b. Paris, Oct. 7, 1955. He was born into a musical family active in Paris; his father was a violinist, his mother a mezzo-soprano. He began to study violin as a small child, then graduated to the viola and finally the cello. He was taken to N.Y. when he was 7, and enrolled at the Juilliard School of Music when he was 9; his principal teachers were Leonard Rose and János Scholz. He subsequently received additional musical training at Harvard Univ. In 1978 he was awarded the Avery Fisher Prize. He quickly established a formidable reputation as a master of the cello in his appearances with the great orchs. of the world, as a recitalist, and as a chamber music player, being deservedly acclaimed for his unostentatious musicianship, his superlative technical resources, and the remarkable tone of his melodious lyricism. In order to extend his repertoire, he made a number of effective transcriptions for his instrument. In addition to commissioning various contemporary works for his instrument, Ma has broadened his audience by recording bluegrass, tangos, and other popular music genres. In 1998 his recording of the 6 Bach unaccompanied cello suites was released in conjunction with a series of films created in collaboration with several media artists. In addition to numerous Grammy awards, he received an honorary doctorate from Harvard Univ. in 1991 and in 1999 he was awarded the Glenn Gould Prize.—**NS/LK/DM**

Maag, (Ernst) Peter (Johannes), eminent Swiss conductor; b. St. Gallen, May 10, 1919. His father, Otto Maag, was the Lutheran minister, philosopher, musicologist, and critic; his mother was a violinist and a member of the Capet Quartet. He attended the univs. of Zürich, Basel, and Geneva, where his principal mentors were Karl Barth and Emil Brunner in theology and Karl Jaspers in philosophy. He also studied piano and theory with Czeslaw Marek in Zürich, and then pursued his training in piano with Cortot in Paris. His conducting mentors were Hoesslin and Ansermet in Geneva. He later profited greatly as an assistant to Furtwängler. He began his career as répétiteur at the Biel-Solothurn theater, where he then served as music director (1943–46). From 1952 to 1955 he held the title of 1st conductor at the Düsseldorf Opera. He was Generalmusikdirektor of the Bonn City Theater from 1955 to 1959. In 1958 he made his first appearance at London's Covent Garden. In 1959 he made his U.S. debut as guest conductor of the Cincinnati Sym. Orch. He was chief conductor of the Vienna Volksoper from 1964 to 1968. On Sept. 23, 1972, he made his Metropolitan Opera debut in N.Y. conducting *Don Giovanni*. He was artistic director of the Teatro Regio in Parma from 1972 to 1974 and of the Teatro Regio in Turin from 1974 to 1976. Thereafter he continued to appear frequently in Italy while continuing to make guest appearances with orchs. and opera houses in Europe, North and South America, and Japan. From 1984 to 1991 he was music director of the Bern Sym. Orch. Maag is particularly esteemed for his remarkable interpretations of the music of Mozart, and also for his efforts to revive forgotten works of the past.—**NS/LK/DM**

Maas, Joseph, English tenor; b. Dartford, Kent, Jan. 30, 1847; d. London, Jan. 15, 1886. He was a chorister at Rochester Cathedral, where he studied with the organist J.L. Hopkin, and then completed his training with Bodda-Pyne in London and San Giovanni in Milan. In 1871 he made his debut in a concert with Henry Leslie's Choir in London. His operatic debut followed in 1872 as Babil in Dion Boucicault's *Babil and Bijou* at London's Covent Garden. After touring the U.S. with Clara Kellogg's English Opera Co., he returned to England in 1878 and became principal tenor of the Carl Rosa Opera Co. He was the first to sing the role of Rienzi in England in 1879, and in 1883 he appeared as Lohengrin at Covent Garden. Maas was also active as a concert and oratorio singer. Among his other operatic roles were Des Grieux and Radames.—**NS/LK/DM**

Maasalo, Armas (Toivo Valdemar), Finnish composer and teacher; b. Rautavaara, Aug. 28, 1885; d. Helsinki, Sept. 9, 1960. He studied at the Helsinki Music Inst. (1907–10). He taught at the Helsinki Church Music Inst. (1914–51), serving as its director (1923–51). He then was director of the church music dept. of the Sibelius Academy in Helsinki (1951–55). Maasalo wrote much sacred music.

WORKS: ORCH.: *Ricordanza* for Cello, Piano, and Orch. (1919); Piano Concerto (1919); *Karelian Scenes* (1920); *Partita seria* for Strings (1934); Suite for Organ and Orch. (1945). **VOCAL:** *The Path of Man,* cantata (1926); *2 Stars* for Alto, Chorus, and Orch. (1929); *Christmas Oratorio* (1945); religious songs for chorus and solo voice.—NS/LK/DM

Ma'ayani, Ami, Israeli composer; b. Ramat-Gan, Jan. 13, 1936. He studied at the New Jerusalem Academy of Music (1951–53), with Ben-Haim (1956–60), and with Ussachevsky at Columbia Univ. in N.Y. (1961–62; 1964–65); he also studied architecture at the Israel Inst. of Technology (B.Sc., 1960) and philosophy at the Univ. of Tel Aviv (M.A., 1973).

WORKS: DRAMATIC: *The War of the Sons of Light,* opera-oratorio (1970–72); *A Legend of 3 and 4,* ballet (1978). **ORCH.:** *Divertimento concertante* for Chamber Orch. (1957); 2 harp concertos (1960, 1966); Violin Concerto (1967); Concerto for 8 Wind Instruments and Percussion (1966); Cello Concerto (1967); Concerto for 2 Pianos and Orch. (1969); *Qumran* (1970); *Symphony Concertante* for Wind Quintet and Orch. (1972); Sym. No. 2 (1975) and No. 4, *Sinfonietta on Popular Hebraic Themes,* for Chamber Orch. (1982); Viola Concerto (1975); Guitar Concerto (1976); Concertino for Harp and Strings (1980); Sinfonietta No. 1 for Chamber Orch. (1980); *Ouverture solonelle* (1982); *Scherzo Mediterranean* (1983). **CHAMBER:** *Magamat* for Harp (1960); *Toccata* for Harp (1962); *Poème* for Flute and String Trio (1965); *Improvisation variée* for Flute, Viola or Violin, and Harp (1966); *4 Preludes* for 4 Percussionists and Piano (1968); *2 Madrigals* for Harp and Wind Quintet (1969); Sonatina for Clarinet, Cello, and Piano (1985); piano pieces. **VOCAL:** *Psalms* for Soprano, Flute, Bass Clarinet, Harp, Percussion, and Strings (1965); *Festivals* for Soprano or Tenor and Orch. (1966); Sym. No. 3, *Hebrew Requiem,* for Mezzo-soprano, Chorus, and Orch. (1977). —NS/LK/DM

Maazel, Lorin (Varencove), brilliant American conductor; b. Neuilly, France (of American parents), March 6, 1930. His parents took him to Los Angeles when he was an infant. At a very early age, he showed innate musical ability; he had perfect pitch and could assimilate music osmotically; he began to study violin at age 5 with Karl Moldrem, and then piano at age 7 with Fanchon Armitage. Fascinated by the art of conducting, he went to sym. concerts and soon began to take lessons in conducting with Vladimir Bakaleinikov, who was an assoc. conductor of the Los Angeles Phil.; on July 13, 1938, at the age of 8, he was given a chance to conduct a performance of Schubert's *Unfinished Symphony* with the visiting Univ. of Idaho orch. In 1938 Bakaleinikov was appointed asst. conductor of the Pittsburgh Sym. Orch., and the Maazel family followed him to Pittsburgh. From Bakaleinikov, Maazel quickly learned to speak Russian. On Aug. 18, 1939, he made a sensational appearance in N.Y. conducting the National Music Camp Orch. of Interlochen at the World's Fair, eliciting the inevitable jocular comments (he was compared to a trained seal). Maazel was only 11 when he conducted the NBC Sym. Orch. (1941) and 12 when he led an entire program with the N.Y. Phil. (1942). He survived these traumatic exhibitions, and took academic courses at the Univ. of Pittsburgh. In 1948 he joined the Pittsburgh Sym. Orch. as a violinist, and at the same time was appointed its apprentice conductor. In 1951 he received a Fulbright fellowship for travel in Italy, where he undertook a serious study of Baroque music; he also made his adult debut as a conductor in Catania on Dec. 23, 1953. In 1955 he conducted at the Florence May Festival, in 1957 at the Vienna Festival, and in 1958 at the Edinburgh Festival. In 1960 he became the first American to conduct at the Bayreuth Festival, where he led performances of *Lohengrin.* In 1962 he toured the U.S. with the Orchestre National de France. On Nov. 1, 1962, he made his Metropolitan Opera debut in N.Y. conducting *Don Giovanni.* From 1965 to 1971 he was artistic director of the Deutsche Oper in West Berlin; from 1965 to 1975 he also served as chief conductor of the (West) Berlin Radio Sym. Orch. He was assoc. principal conductor of the New Philharmonia Orch. of London from 1970 to 1972, and its principal guest conductor from 1976 to 1980. In 1972 he became music director of the Cleveland Orch., a position he held with great distinction until 1982; was then made conductor emeritus. He led the Cleveland Orch. on 10 major tours abroad, including Australia and New Zealand (1973), Japan (1974), twice in Latin America, and twice in Europe, and maintained its stature as one of the world's foremost orchs. He was also chief conductor of the Orchestre National de France from 1977 to 1982; then was its principal guest conductor until 1988, and then its music director until 1991. In 1980 he became conductor of the famous Vienna Phil. New Year's Day Concerts, a position he retained until 1986. In 1982 he assumed the positions of artistic director and general manager of the Vienna State Opera, the first American to be so honored; however, he resigned these positions in the middle of his 4-year contract in 1984 after a conflict over artistic policies with the Ministry of Culture. He then served as music consultant to the Pittsburgh Sym. Orch. (1984–86); was its music adviser and principal guest conductor in 1986, becoming its music director that same year. In 1993 he also assumed the post of chief conductor of the Bavarian Radio Sym. Orch. in Munich. In 1994 he again conducted the Vienna Phil. New Year's Day Concert. In 1996 he stepped down as music director of the Pittsburgh Sym. Orch. after a notably distinguished tenure.

Maazel is equally adept as an interpreter of operatic and symphonic scores; he is blessed with a phenomenal memory, and possesses an extraordinary baton technique. He also maintains an avid interest in nonmusical pursuits; a polyglot, he is fluent in French, German, Italian, Spanish, Portuguese, and Russian. Maazel was the recipient of many awards; he received an honorary doctorate from the Univ. of Pittsburgh in 1965, the Sibelius Prize in Finland, the Commander's Cross of the Order of Merit from West Germany, and, for his numerous recordings, the Grand Prix de Disque in Paris and the Edison Prize in the Netherlands.—**NS/LK/DM**

Mabellini, Teodulo, Italian conductor and composer; b. Pistoia, April 2, 1817; d. Florence, March 10, 1897. He studied with Pillotti and Gherardeschi in Pistoia, then was a student at Florence's Istituto Reale Musicale (1833–36). At the age of 19, he produced there an opera, *Matilda a Toledo* (Aug. 27, 1836), which made so favorable an impression that Grand Duke Leopold II gave him a stipend to study with Mercadante at Novara. His 2nd opera, *Rolla* (Turin, Nov. 12, 1840), was no less successful; thereupon he wrote many more operas, among them *Ginevra degli Almieri* (Turin, Nov. 13, 1841), *Il Conte di Lavagna* (Florence, June 4, 1843), *I Veneziani a Costantinopoli* (Rome, 1844), *Maria di Francia* (Florence, March 14, 1846), *Il venturiero* (Livorno, Carnival 1851; in collaboration with L. Gordigiani), *Il convito di Baldassare* (Florence, Nov. 1852), and *Fiammetta* (Florence, Feb. 12, 1857). He also wrote several effective oratorios and cantatas: *Eudossia e Paolo* (Florence, 1845), *Etruria* (Florence, Aug. 5, 1849), and *Lo spirito di Dante* (Florence, May 15, 1865). Other works include a patriotic hymn, *Italia risorta* (Florence, Sept. 12, 1847), *Grande fantasia* for Flute, Clarinet, Horn, Trumpet, and Trombone, and sacred works for chorus and orch. He lived in Florence from 1843 until his death. He conducted the concerts of the Società Filarmonica (1843–59) and taught composition at the Istituto Reale Musicale (1859–87).

BIBL.: M. Giannini, *M. e la musica* (Pistoia, 1899); A. Simonatti, *T. M.* (Pistoia, 1923).—**NS/LK/DM**

Macák, Ivan, Slovak ethnomusicologist; b. Gbelce, near Nové Zámky, Aug. 26, 1935. He studied ethnomusicology at the Univ. of Bratislava, where he received his Ph.D. (1969) with the diss. *Štúdie k typológii a histórii slovenskych l'udovych nástrojov* (Studies in the Classification and History of Slovak Folk Instruments). He was ed. of *L'udová tvorivost'* (1959–65), and research fellow in music at the Slovak National Museum in Bratislava (from 1967), where he subsequently built its collection to include over 900 folk instruments and 7,000 pictorial records. He lectured in ethnomusicology at the Bratislava Academy (1962–73) and co-ed. the *Annual Bibliography of European Ethnomusicology* (Bratislava, 1967 et seq.). His chief contribution is in the area of organology, particularly the earliest history of instruments and their methodology.—**NS/LK/DM**

Macal, Zdenek (originally **Zdeněk Mácal**), prominent Czech-born American conductor; b. Brno, Jan. 8, 1936. He studied with Bakala, Jílek, and Vesélka at the Brno Cons. (1951–56), then at Brno's Janáček Academy of Music. He was conductor of the Moravian Phil. in Olomouc (1963–67). He won the Besançon (1965) and Mitropoulos (1966) competitions. In 1966 he made his first appearance as a guest conductor with the Czech Phil. in Prague, with which he then toured Europe. In 1968 he left his homeland in the wake of the Soviet-led invasion and served as chief conductor of the Cologne Radio Sym. Orch. (1970–74) and the Hannover Radio Orch. (1980–83); also appeared as a guest conductor throughout Europe and the U.S. He was principal guest conductor (1985–86) and music director (1986–95) of the Milwaukee Sym. Orch. He also was chief conductor of the Sydney Sym. Orch. (1986), principal guest conductor (1986–88) and artistic director and principal conductor (1988–92) of the San Antonio Sym. Orch., and artistic advisor (1992–93) and artistic director (from 1993) of the N.J. Sym. Orch. On Oct. 3, 1992, he became a naturalized American citizen at a special ceremony held during a concert he conducted with the Milwaukee Sym. Orch.—**NS/LK/DM**

MacArdle, Donald Wales, American musicologist; b. Quincy, Mass., July 3, 1897; d. Littleton, Colo., Dec. 23, 1964. He studied science at the Mass. Inst. of Technology, obtaining an M.S. in chemical engineering. He also took courses at the Juilliard School of Music in N.Y., and studied musicology at N.Y.U. Although he earned his living as an engineer, he devoted much time to scholarly research, mainly to the minutiae of Beethoven's biography. He contributed a number of valuable articles on the subject to the *Musical Quarterly* and other journals. He ed., with L. Misch, *New Beethoven Letters* (Norman, Okla., 1957), ed. and tr. Schindler's *Biographie von Ludwig van Beethoven*, 3rd ed., 1860, as *Beethoven as I Knew Him* (London and Chapel Hill, 1966), and also prepared *An Index to Beethoven's Conversation Books* (Detroit, 1962) and, with S. Pogodda, *Beethoven Abstracts* (Detroit, 1973).—**NS/LK/DM**

Macbeth, Florence, American soprano; b. Mankato, Minn., Jan. 12, 1891; d. Hyattsville, Md., May 5, 1966. She studied in N.Y. and Paris. In 1913 she made her operatic debut as Rosina in *Il Barbiere di Siviglia* in Braunschweig. On Jan. 14, 1914, she made her American debut with the Chicago Opera Co. and remained on its staff as prima coloratura soprano until 1930; for a season she undertook an American tour with the Commonwealth Opera Co., singing in Gilbert and Sullivan operettas. So melodious and mellifluous were her fiorituras that she was dubbed the "Minnesota Nightingale." In 1947 she married the novelist James M. Cain and settled in Md.—**NS/LK/DM**

MacCunn, Hamish (James), Scottish composer, conductor, and teacher; b. Greenock, March 22, 1868; d. London, Aug. 2, 1916. He won a composition scholarship to the Royal Coll. of Music in London when he was 15, and studied there with Parry, Stanford, and Franklin Taylor (until 1886). He remained in London and served as prof. of hamony at the Royal Academy of Music (1888–94). He also taught composition privately and later at the Guildhall School of Music (from 1912). From 1898 he was also active as a theater conductor. After working with the Carl Rosa Opera Co. and the Moody-Manners Co., he served as principal conductor of the Savoy Theatre (1902–05). Thereafter he conducted at various theaters, and in 1910 and 1915 he was a conductor with the Beecham Opera Co. MacCunn's most important work was the opera *Jeanie Deans* (Edinburgh, Nov. 15, 1894), after Scott's *The Heart of Midlothian*, but he remains best known for the overture *The Land of the Mountain and the Flood* (London, Nov. 5, 1887).

WORKS: DRAMATIC: *Jeanie Deans*, opera, after Scott's *The Heart of Midlothian* (Edinburgh, Nov. 15, 1894); *Diarmid* (London, Oct. 23, 1897); *Breast of Light* (n.d.; unfinished); *The Masque of War and Peace*, masque (London, Feb. 13, 1900); *The Golden Girl*, light opera (Birmingham, Aug. 5, 1905); *Prue*, light opera (n.d.; unfinished); *The Pageant of Darkness and Light*, stage pageant (1908); *The Sailor and the Nursemaid*, light opera (London, June 27, 1912). B a l l a d e s : *The Ship o' the Fiend* (London, Feb. 21, 1888); *The Dowie Dens o' Yarrow* (London, Oct. 13, 1888). VOCAL: C a n t a t a s : *Lord Ullin's Daughter*, after Walter Scott (London, Feb. 18, 1888); *Bonny Kilmeny* (Edinburgh, Dec. 15, 1888); *The Lay of the Last Minstrel* (Glasgow, Dec. 18, 1888); *The Cameronian's Dream* (Edinburgh, Jan. 27, 1890); *Queen Hynde of Caledon* (Glasgow, Jan. 28, 1892); *The Wreck of the Hesperus*, after Longfellow (London, Aug. 28, 1905). ORCH.: O v e r t u r e s : *Cior Mhor* (London, Oct. 27, 1885); *The Land of the Mountain and the Flood*, after Scott (London, Nov. 5, 1887). OTHER: *Highland Memories*, suite (London, March 13, 1897); *Scotch Dances* for Piano; songs; etc.—NS/LK/DM

Macdonald, Hugh (John),
English musicologist; b. Newbury, Berkshire, Jan. 31, 1940. He was educated at the Univ. of Cambridge (B.A., 1961; M.A., 1966; Ph.D., 1969), where he also was a lecturer in music (1966–71). He also was a lecturer in music at the Univ. of Oxford (1971–80), and in 1979 was a visiting prof. at Ind. Univ. After serving as the Gardiner Prof. of Music at the Univ. of Glasgow (1980–87), he became the Avis Blewett Prof. at Washington Univ. in St. Louis in 1987. Macdonald has devoted much of his time to the elucidation of 19th century music. He is especially known for his studies in French music, and is a leading authority on the life and music of Berlioz. In 1965 he became general ed. of the *New Berlioz Edition*. In 1985 and 1996 he was awarded the Grand Prix de Littérature Musicale Charles Cros for his contributions to the study of French music. He has contributed articles to many journals, and also to *The New Grove Dictionary of Music and Musicians* (1980; 2nd ed., rev., 2000) and *The New Grove Dictionary of Opera* (1992). He was an ed. of the *Correspondance générale de Hector Berlioz* (Vols. 4, 1984, 5, 1989, and 6, 1995), and also ed. *Selected Letters of Berlioz* (1995). He authored *Berlioz Orchestral Music* (1969), *Skryabin* (1978), and *Berlioz* (1982).—NS/LK/DM

MacDonald, Jeanette (Anna),
American soprano; b. Philadelphia, June 18, 1903; d. Houston, Jan. 14, 1965. She started a career as a chorus girl and model in N.Y. (1920) and unexpectedly won encomia for her starring role in the musical *The Magic Ring* (1923). She then attained wide recognition as a singing actress via 29 films, especially those in which she paired with Nelson Eddy: *Naughty Marietta* (1935), *Rose Marie* (1936), *Maytime* (1937), *The Girl of the Golden West* (1938), *Sweethearts* (1939), *New Moon* (1940), *Bittersweet* (1940), and *I Married an Angel* (1942). She made a belated operatic debut as Juliette in Montreal (May 1944); she

also sang in Chicago, but her voice was too small to meet the demands of the large opera halls.

BIBL.: S. Rich, *J. M.: A Pictorial Biography* (Los Angeles, 1973); E. Knowles, *Films of J. M. and Nelson Eddy* (South Brunswick, N.J., 1975); J. Parish, *The J. M. Story* (N.Y., 1976); L. Stern, *J. M.* (N.Y., 1977); E. Turk, *Hollywood Diva: A Biography of J. M.* (Berkeley, 1998).—NS/LK/DM

Macdonough, Harry (John S. MacDonald),
leading tenor of the early recording era and top recording artist in the U.S. during the first decade of the 20th century; b. Ontario, March 30, 1871; d. Sept. 26, 1931. Macdonough began his career as a musical comedy performer on Broadway during the 1880s and 1890s, then began to record for the Edison and Berliner labels in the late 1890s. He was an original member of the Edison Male Quartet, which scored a hit with Stephen Foster's "My Old Kentucky Home" (1898) before the group changed its name to the Haydn Quartet. With the Haydn Quartet, Macdonough sang lead on such hits as "Bedalia" (1904), "Blue Bell" (1904), and "Sunbonnet Sue" (1908). He was also a member of the Lyric Quartet and the Orpheus Quartet (billed as Harry Macdonough and the Orpheus Quartet on its biggest hit, "Turn Back the Universe and Give Me Yester Day" in 1916).

Like most Victor artists, Macdonough sang with the Victor Light Opera Co. He was heard on the hits "In the Good Old Summer Time" (1903) by Sousa's Band, "Smiles" (1918) by John C. Smith's Orch., and "Till We Meet Again" (1919) by Nicholas Orlando's Orch. But his greatest success came as a solo performer. He made nearly a hundred hit records between 1899 and 1918; the most successful included "Tell Me, Pretty Maiden" (1901) (with Grace Spencer), "Shine On, Harvest Moon" (1909) (with "Miss Walton," probably Elise Stevenson), "Where the River Shannon Flows" (1910), "Down by the Old Mill Stream" (1911), and "They Didn't Believe Me" (1915) (with Alice Green, actually Olive Kline).

After World War I, Macdonough retired from singing and became a record company executive.—WR

MacDowell, Edward (Alexander),
greatly significant American composer; b. N.Y., Dec. 18, 1860; d. there, Jan. 23, 1908. His father was a Scotch-Irish tradesman; his mother, an artistically inclined woman who encouraged his musical studies. He took piano lessons with Juan Buitrago and Paul Desvernine; also had supplementary sessions with Teresa Carreño, who later championed his works. In 1876, after traveling in Europe with his mother, MacDowell enrolled as an auditor in Augustin Savard's elementary class at the Paris Cons.; on Feb. 8, 1877, he was admitted as a regular student; he also studied piano with Antoine-François Marmontel and solfège with Marmontel's son, Antonin. Somewhat disappointed with his progress, he withdrew from the Cons. on Sept. 30, 1878, and went to the Stuttgart Cons. for a brief period of study with Sigmund Lebert. He then proceeded to Wiesbaden to study theory and composition with Louis Ehlert; in 1879 he enrolled at the newly founded but already prestigious Hoch Cons. in Frankfurt am Main as a student of Carl

Heymann in piano, of Joachim Raff (the Cons. director) in composition, and of Franz Böhme in counterpoint and fugue. During MacDowell's stay there, Raff's class had a visit from Liszt, and MacDowell performed the piano part in Schumann's Quintet, op.44, in Liszt's presence. At another visit, MacDowell played Liszt's *Hungarian Rhapsody* No. 14 for him; 2 years later he visited Liszt in Weimar, and played his own 1st Piano Concerto for him, accompanied by Eugène d'Albert at the 2nd piano. Encouraged by Liszt's interest, MacDowell sent him the MS of his *Modern Suite*, op.10, for piano solo; Liszt recommended the piece for performance at the meeting of the Allgemeiner Deutscher Musikverein (Zürich, July 11, 1882); he also recommended MacDowell to the publishers Breitkopf & Härtel, who subsequently brought out the first works of MacDowell to appear in print, the *Modern Suites* for piano, opp.10 and 14. MacDowell left the Cons. in 1880 and began teaching piano privately. However, he pursued private piano and composition lessons with Heymann and Raff.

Despite his youth, MacDowell was given a teaching position at the Darmstadt Cons. in 1881 but he resigned in 1882; he also accepted private pupils, among them Marian Nevins of Conn.; they were secretly married on July 9, 1884, in N.Y., followed by a public ceremony in Waterford, Conn., on July 21. During the early years of their marriage, the MacDowells made their 2nd home in Wiesbaden, where MacDowell composed industriously; his works were performed in neighboring communities; Carreño put several of his piano pieces on her concert programs. There were also performances in America. However, the MacDowells were beset by financial difficulties; his mother proposed that he and his wife live on the family property, but MacDowell declined. He also declined an offer to teach at the National Cons. in N.Y. at the munificent fee of $5 an hour. Similarly, he rejected an offer to take a clerical position at the American Consulate in Krefeld, Germany. In 1888 he finally returned to the U.S., making his home in Boston, where he was welcomed in artistic circles as a famous composer and pianist; musical Boston at the time was virtually a German colony, and MacDowell's German training was a certificate of his worth. On Nov. 19, 1888, MacDowell made his American debut as a composer and pianist at a Boston concert of the Kneisel String Quartet, featuring his *Modern Suite*, op.10. On March 5, 1889, he was the soloist in the premiere performance of his 2nd Piano Concerto with the N.Y. Phil., under the direction of Theodore Thomas. Frank van der Stucken invited MacDowell to play his concerto at the spectacular Paris Exposition on July 12, 1889. MacDowell had no difficulty having his works publ., although for some reason he preferred that his early piano pieces, opp.1–7, be printed under the pseudonym Edgar Thorn.

In 1896 Columbia Univ. invited MacDowell to become its first prof. of music, "to elevate the standard of musical instruction in the U.S., and to afford the most favorable opportunity for acquiring instruction of the highest order." MacDowell interpreted this statement to its fullest; by 1899, 2 assistants had been employed, Leonard McWhood and Gustav Hinrichs, but students received no credit for his courses. At the same time, he continued to compose and to teach piano privately; he

also conducted the Mendelssohn Glee Club (1896–98) and served as president of the Soc. of American Musicians and Composers (1899–1900). In the academic year 1902–03, he took a sabbatical; played concerts throughout the U.S. and in Europe; played his 2nd Piano Concerto in London (May 14, 1903). During his sabbatical, Columbia Univ. replaced its president, Seth Low, with Nicholas Murray Butler, whose ideas about the role of music in the univ. were diametrically opposed to the ideals of MacDowell. MacDowell resigned in 1904 and subsequently became a "cause célèbre," resulting in much acrimony on both sides. It was not until some time later that the Robert Center Chair that MacDowell had held at Columbia Univ. was renamed the Edward MacDowell Chair of Music to honor its first recipient.

Through the combination of the trauma resulting from this episode, an accident with a hansom, and the development of what appears to have been tertiary syphilis, MacDowell rapidly deteriorated mentally into a vegetative state. In 1906 a public appeal was launched to raise funds for his care; among the signers were Horatio Parker, Victor Herbert, Arthur Foote, George Chadwick, Frederick Converse, Andrew Carnegie, J. Pierpont Morgan, and former President Grover Cleveland. MacDowell was only 47 years old when he died. The sum of $50,000 was raised for the organization of the MacDowell Memorial Assoc. Mrs. MacDowell, who outlived her husband by nearly half a century (she died at the age of 98, in Los Angeles, on Aug. 23, 1956), deeded to the association her husband's summer residence at Peterborough, N.H. This property became a pastoral retreat, under the name of the MacDowell Colony, for American composers and writers, who could spend summers working undisturbed in separate cottages, paying a minimum rent for lodging and food. During the summer of 1910, Mrs. MacDowell arranged an elaborate pageant with music from MacDowell's works; the success of this project led to the establishment of a series of MacDowell Festivals at Peterborough.

MacDowell received several awards during his lifetime, including 2 honorary doctorates (Princeton Univ., 1896; Univ. of Pa., 1902) and election into the American Academy of Arts and Letters (1904); in 1940 a 5-cent U.S. postage stamp with his likeness was issued; in 1960 he was the second composer elected to the Hall of Fame at N.Y.U., where, in 1964, a bust was unveiled.

Among American composers, MacDowell occupies a historically important place as the first American whose works were accepted as comparable in quality and technique with those of the average German composers of his time. His music adhered to the prevalent representative Romantic art. Virtually all of his works bear titles borrowed from mythical history, literature, or painting; even his piano sonatas, set in Classical forms, carry descriptive titles, indicative of the mood of melodic resources, or as an ethnic reference. Since he lived in Germany during his formative years, German musical culture was decisive in shaping his musical development; even the American rhythms and melodies in his music seem to be European reflections of an exotic art. A parallel with Grieg is plausible, for Grieg was also a regional composer trained in Germany. But Grieg possessed a much more vigorous personality, and he succeeded in communicating the true spirit of Norwegian song modalities in his works. Lack of musical strength and originality accounts for MacDowell's gradual decline in the estimation of succeeding generations; his romanticism was apt to lapse into salon sentimentality. The frequency of performance of his works in concert (he never wrote for the stage) declined in the decades following his death, and his influence on succeeding generations of American composers receded to a faint recognition of an evanescent artistic period. MacDowell's writings were collected by W. Baltzell and publ. as *Critical and Historical Essays* (1912; reprinted, with new introduction by I. Lowens, N.Y., 1969).

WORKS: ORCH.: *Hamlet and Ophelia,* 2 tone poems, op.22 (1885; Ophelia, N.Y., Nov. 4, 1886; Hamlet, N.Y., Nov. 15, 1887; together, Chicago, March 26, 1890); *Lancelot and Elaine,* symphonic poem, op.25 (Boston, Jan. 10, 1890); *Lamia,* symphonic poem, op.29 (1889; Boston, Oct. 23, 1908); *The Saracens* and *The Lovely Alda,* 2 fragments after the *Song of Roland,* op.30 (Boston, Nov. 5, 1891); Suite No. 1, op.42 (Worcester Festival, Sept. 24, 1891; 3rd movement, "In October," op.42a, added in 1894; complete work 1st perf., Boston, 1896); Suite No. 2, *Indian,* op.48 (N.Y., Jan. 23, 1896); Piano Concerto No. 1, in A minor, op.15 (movements 2 and 3, N.Y., March 30, 1885, Adele Margulies soloist; complete version, Chicago, July 5, 1888, Teresa Carreño soloist); Piano Concerto No. 2, in D minor, op.23 (N.Y., March 5, 1889, composer soloist); *Romance* for Cello and Orch., op.35 (1888). **Piano:** *Amourette,* op.1 (1896); *In Lilting Rhythm,* op.2 (1897); *Forgotten Fairy Tales* (*Sung outside the Prince's Door, Of a Tailor and a Bear, Beauty in the Rose Garden, From Dwarfland*), op.4 (1898); *6 Fancies* (*A Tin Soldier's Love, To a Humming Bird, Summer Song, Across Fields, Bluette, An Elfin Round*), op.7 (1898); *Waltz,* op.8 (1895); *1st Modern Suite,* op.10 (1880); *Prelude and Fugue,* op.13 (1883); *2nd Modern Suite,* op.14 (1881); *Serenata,* op.16 (1883); *2 Fantastic Pieces* (*Legend, Witches' Dance*), op.17 (1884); *2 Pieces* (*Barcarolle, Humoresque*), op.18 (1884); *Forest Idyls* (*Forest Stillness, Play of the Nymphs, Reverie, Dance of the Dryads*), op.19 (1884); *4 Pieces* (*Humoresque, March, Cradle Song, Czardas*), op.24 (1887); *6 Idyls after Goethe* (*In the Woods, Siesta, To the Moonlight, Silver Clouds, Flute Idyl, The Bluebell*), op.28 (1887); *6 Poems after Heine* (*From a Fisherman's Hut, Scotch Poem, From Long Ago, The Post Wagon, The Shepherd Boy, Monologue*), op.31 (1887); *4 Little Poems* (*The Eagle, The Brook, Moonshine, Winter*), op.32 (1888); *Étude de concert* in F-sharp, op.36 (1889); *Les Orientales,* after Victor Hugo (*Clair de lune, Danse le Hamac, Danse Andalouse*), op.37 (1889); *Marionnettes,* 8 Little Pieces (*Prologue, Soubrette, Lover, Witch, Clown, Villain, Sweetheart, Epilogue*), op.38 (1888; originally only 6 pieces; *Prologue* and *Epilogue* were added in 1901); *12 Studies,* Book I (*Hunting Song, Alla Tarantella, Romance, Arabesque, In the Forest, Dance of the Gnomes*); Book II (*Idyl, Shadow Dance, Intermezzo, Melody, Scherzino, Hungarian*), op.39 (1890); Sonata No. 1, *Tragica,* op.45 (1893); *12 Virtuoso Studies* (*Novelette, Moto perpetuo, Wild Chase, Improvisation, Elfin Dance, Valse triste, Burleske, Bluette, Traumerei, March Wind, Impromptu, Polonaise*), op.46 (1894); *Air and Rigaudon,* op.49 (1894); Sonata No. 2, *Eroica,* op.50 (1895); *Woodland Sketches,* 10 pieces (*To a Wild Rose, Will o' the Wisp, At an Old Trysting Place, In Autumn, From an Indian Lodge, To a Water Lily, From Uncle Remus, A Desert Farm, By a Meadow Brook, Told at Sunset*), op.51 (1896); *Sea Pieces* (*To the Sea, From a Wandering Iceberg, A.D. 1620, Star-light, Song, From the Depths, Nautilus, In Mid-Ocean*), op.55 (1898); Sonata No. 3,

Norse, op.57 (1900); Sonata No. 4, *Keltic,* op.59 (1901); *Fireside Tales* (*An Old Love Story, Of Br'er Rabbit, From a German Forest, Of Salamanders, A Haunted House, By Smouldering Embers*), op.61 (1902); *New England Idyls,* 10 pieces (*An Old Garden, Midsummer, Midwinter, With Sweet Lavender, In Deep Woods, Indian Idyl, To an Old White Pine, From Puritan Days, From a Log Cabin, The Joy of Autumn*), op.62 (1902); *6 Little Pieces on Sketches by J.S. Bach* (1890); Technical Exercises, 2 Books (1893, 1895). **VOCAL: Choral:** 2 choruses for Men's Voices, op.3: *Love and Time* and *The Rose and the Gardener* (1897); *The Witch* for Men's Chorus, op.5 (1898); *War Song* for Men's Chorus, op.6 (1898); 3 songs for Men's Chorus, op.27 (1887); 2 songs for Men's Chorus, op.41 (1890); 2 *Northern Songs* for Mixed Voices, op.43 (1891); 3 choruses for Men's Voices, op.52 (1897); 2 *Songs from the 13th Century* for Men's Chorus (1897); 2 choruses for Men's Voices, op.53 (1898); 2 choruses for Men's Voices, op.54 (1898); *College Songs* for Men's Voices (1901); *Summer Wind* for Women's Chorus (1902). **Voice and Piano:** 2 *Old Songs,* op.9 (1894); 3 songs, op.11 (1883); 2 songs, op.12 (1883); *From an Old Garden* (6 songs), op.26 (1887); 3 songs, op.33 (1888; rev. 1894); 2 songs, op.34 (1888); 6 *Love Songs,* op.40 (1890); 8 songs, op.47 (1893); 4 songs, op.56 (1898); 3 songs, op.58 (1899); 3 songs, op.60 (1902).

BIBL.: L. Gilman, *E. M.: A Study* (N.Y., 1908; corrected reprint, N.Y., 1969); E. Page, *E. M.: His Works and Ideals* (N.Y., 1910); J. Adams, *What the Piano Writings of M. Mean to the Piano Student* (Chicago, 1913); O. Sonneck, *Catalogue of First Editions of E. M.* (Washington, D.C., 1917; reprint, N.Y., 1973); W. Humiston, *M.* (N.Y., 1921); J. Matthews, *Commemorative Tributes to M.* (N.Y., 1922); J. Porte, *A Great American Tone Poet: E. M.* (London, 1922); A. Brown, *The Boyhood of E. M.* (N.Y., 1924); J. Cooke, *E. M., A Short Biography* (Philadelphia, 1928); A. Brown, *A Mosaic of Muses of the M. Club of New York* (N.Y., 1930); *Catalogue of an Exhibition Illustrating the Life and Work of E. M.* (N.Y., 1938); M. MacDowell, *Random Notes on E. M. and His Music* (Boston, 1950); C. Kefferstan, *The Piano Concertos of E. M.* (diss., Univ. of Cincinnati, 1984); A. Levy, *E. M., an American Master* (Lanham, Md., 1998).—NS/LK/DM

Mace, Thomas, English lutenist, singer, writer on music, and composer; b. probably in Cambridge, 1612 or 1613; d. probably there, c. 1706. He served as a singing-man at Trinity Coll., Cambridge in 1635. His *Musick's Monument; or, A Remembrancer of the Best Pratical Musick* (London, 1676; facsimile ed. with transcription and commentary by J. Jacquot and A. Souris, 1958) is a valuable source for information about the musical activities and practices of the England of his time. It includes various compositions as well, including 8 of his own lute suites. Among his other works were 15 viol pieces. He also publ. a curious vol., *Riddles, Mervels and Rarities, or A New Way of Health* (Cambridge, 1698).
—LK/DM

Maceda, José, Filipino ethnomusicologist and composer; b. Manila, Jan. 31, 1917. He studied piano with Cortot at the École Normale de Musique in Paris (1937–41) and with Schmitz in San Francisco (1946–49), and pursued academic studies at Queens Coll. in N.Y., Columbia Univ., the Univ. of Chicago, Ind. Univ., and the Univ. of Calif. at Los Angeles (Ph.D., 1963). From 1952 to 1990 he taught at the Univ. of the Philippines Coll. of Music, where he built up an archive now known

as the U.P. Ethnomusicology Center that contains about 2,500 hours of field tapes of music of 51 Philippine linguistic groups. He also pursued field research throughout Southeast Asia, Brazil, East and West Africa, and later in Vietnam and the Yunnan province of China. In addition to articles in scholarly journals, he publ. *A Manual of Field Music Research with Special Reference to Southeast Asia* (Quezon City, 1980) and *Gongs and Bamboo: A Panorama of Philippine Music Instruments* (Quezon City, 1998). Maceda's compositions bely a conscious effort to veer away from current tenets of musical organization. He uses native instruments as drones played by hundreds of participants distributed in space (*Pagsamba*, a mass, 1968; *Udlot-Udlot*, outdoor music, 1975) or together with Western instruments in levels of definite and indefinite pitches (*Siasid* for Percussion, Blown Bamboo Tubes, and 5 Violins, 1983; *Strata* for 10 Buzzers, 10 Sticks, 5 Tam-tams, 5 Flutes, 5 Cellos, and 5 Guitars, 1988). In his orchestral music (*Distemperament*, 1980), combinations of practically all intervals of mixed instruments from the lowest to the highest levels result in one consonance without distinction between consonant and dissonant intervals. *Udlot-Udlot* was reduced in 1998 to a theater music piece for 5 people with durations of performance that can be doubled—10, 20, or 40 minutes—as in Javanese and Thai ensembles. Among his other works are *Ugma-Ugma* for Native Instruments and Chorus (1963), *Agungan* for Gongs (1965), *Kubing* for Bamboo Instruments and Men's Voices (1966), *Cassettes 100* for 100 Participants and Cassette Recorders (1971), *Ugnayan* for 20 Radio Stations (1974), *Ading* for 100 Instrumentalists, 100 Voices, and the Public (1978), *Aroding* for 40 Mouth Harps, 7 Men's Voices, and 3 Tiny Whistle-Flutes (1983), *Suling-Suling* for 10 Flutes, 10 Bamboo Buzzers, and 10 Flat Gongs (1985), *Dissemination* for 28 Instruments (1990), *Music* for 5 Pianos (1993), *Two Pianos and Four Winds* (1996), *Music for a Chamber Orchestra* (1997), *Music for Gongs and Bamboo* (1997), and *Colors Without Rhythm* for Orch., 10 Percussion, and 7 Keyboards (1999).
—**NS/LK/DM**

Macfarren, Sir George (Alexander), eminent English composer and pedagogue, brother of **Walter (Cecil) Macfarren**; b. London, March 2, 1813; d. there, Oct. 31, 1887. He began his studies with his father, George Macfarren, who was a dancing-master and dramatist, and with Charles Lucas, and then studied composition with C. Potter at the Royal Academy of Music in London (1829–36). He was a tutor there (1834–37), then a prof. (1837–47; 1851–75), and subsequently its principal (1875–87). He was also a prof. of music at Cambridge Univ. (1875–87). He was knighted in 1883. He suffered from eye problems from the age of 10, becoming totally blind in 1860. However, he continued to compose by dictating to an amanuensis. He had the great satisfaction of having his early overture *Chevy Chace* performed by Mendelssohn in Leipzig (1843) and by Wagner in London (1855). Macfarren's greatest ambition was to write an opera that would reflect the spirit of England, as the operas of Weber were redolent of the mythical lyricism of German folklore, but he signally failed in this endeavor. His 9 syms. enjoyed transient

favor, but attempts at their revival foundered in time. His wife, Natalia Macfarren (née Clarina Thalia Andrae; b. Lübeck, Dec. 14, 1826; d. Bakewell, April 9, 1916), was a singer who studied with Macfarren and dutifully sang in his operas. She publ. a *Vocal Method* and an *Elementary Course of Vocalising and Pronouncing the English Language.*

WORKS: DRAMATIC: Opera: *The Prince of Modena* (1833); *El Malhechor* (1837–38); *The Devil's Opera* (London, Aug. 13, 1838); *An Adventure of Don Quixote* (London, Feb. 3, 1846); *King Charles II* (London, Oct. 27, 1849); *Allan of Aberfeldy* (c. 1850); *Robin Hood* (London, Oct. 11, 1860); *Jessy Lea*, opera di camera (London, Nov. 2, 1863); *She Stoops to Conquer* (London, Feb. 11, 1864); *The Soldier's Legacy*, opera di camera (London, July 10, 1864); *Helvellyn* (London, Nov. 3, 1864); *Kenilworth* (1880); other stage works. **ORCH.:** 9 syms. (1828; 1831; 1832; 1833; 1833; 1836; 1839–40; 1845; 1874); Overture (1832); Piano Concerto (1835); Flute Concerto (1863); Violin Concerto (1871–74). **Overtures:** *The Merchant of Venice* (1834); *Romeo and Juliet* (1836); *Chevy Chace* (1836); *Don Carlos* (1842); *Hamlet* (1856); *Festival Overture* (1874). **CHAMBER:** 5 string quartets (1834, 1842, 1846, 1849, 1878); Quintet for Violin, Viola, Cello, Double Bass, and Piano (1844); Violin Sonata (1887). **KEYBOARD:** 3 piano sonatas (1842, 1845, 1880); various piano and organ pieces. **ARRANGEMENTS:** *Popular Music of the Olden Time* (1859); *Popular Songs of Scotland* (1874). **VOCAL: Oratorios and Cantatas:** *The Sleeper Awakened* (London, Nov. 15, 1850); *Lenora* (London, April 25, 1853); *Christmas* (London, May 9, 1860); *St. John the Baptist* (Bristol, Oct. 23, 1873); *The Resurrection* (Birmingham, 1876); *Joseph* (Leeds, 1877); *King David* (Leeds, 1883). **Other:** Numerous sacred and secular vocal works; choral works; part-songs; trios; duets; some 160 solo songs.

BIBL.: H. Banister, *G.A. M.: His Life, Works and Influence* (London, 1891).—**NS/LK/DM**

Macfarren, Walter (Cecil), English pianist and composer, brother of **Sir George (Alexander) Macfarren**; b. London, Aug. 28, 1826; d. there, Sept. 2, 1905. He was a chorister at Westminster Abbey (1836–41), then studied at the Royal Academy of Music in London (1842–46), with Holmes (piano) and his brother (composition). From 1846 to 1903 he was a prof. of piano there, and he also conducted its concerts (1873–80). He composed a number of overtures on Shakespearean subjects, a Piano Concerto, and many piano pieces. He also ed. Beethoven's sonatas, and several albums of piano pieces under the title *Popular Classics*. He publ. *Memories: An Autobiography* (London, 1905).—**NS/LK/DM**

Mach, Ernst, eminent German physicist and philosopher; b. Turas, Moravia, Feb. 18, 1838; d. Vaterstetten, near Munich, Feb. 19, 1916. He was prof. of mathematics at the Univ. of Graz (1864–67), of physics at the Univ. of Prague (1867–95), and of inductive philosophy at the Univ. of Vienna (1895–1901). Besides his scientific works of far-reaching importance, he publ. studies dealing with musical acoustics: *Zwei populäre Vorträge über musikalische Akustik* (1865); *Einleitung in die Helmholtz'sche Musiktheorie* (1866); *Zur Theorie des Gehörorgans* (1872); *Beitrag zur Geschichte der Musik* (1892); *Die Analyse der Empfindungen und das Verhältnis des*

Physischen zum Psychischen (5th ed., 1906); "Zur Geschichte der Theorie der Konsonanz," in *Populärwissenschaftliche Vorträge* (3rd ed., 1903). The unit of velocity of sound ("Mach") is named after him.—**NS/LK/DM**

Mácha, Otmar, Czech composer; b. Ostrava, Oct. 2, 1922. He studied with Hradil (1941–42), and then at the Prague Cons. (1943–45), where he subsequently attended Řídký's master class (1945–48). He was active with the Czech Radio (1945–62), and then devoted himself to composing. He was awarded the State Prize in 1967 and was made a Merited Artist by the Czech government in 1982.

WORKS: DRAMATIC: *Polapená nevěra* (Entrapped Faithlessness), opera (1956–57; Prague, Nov. 21, 1958); *Jezero Ukereve* (Lake Ukereve), opera (1960–63; Prague, May 27, 1966); *Růže pro Johanku (Panichyda za statečné)* (Rose for Jeanne [Homage to the Brave]), dramatic musical fantasy (1971–74); *Svatba na oko* (Feigned Wedding), comic opera (1974–77); *Kolébka pro hříšné panny* (Cradle for Sinful Maidens), musical comedy (1975–76); *Nenávistná láska* (The Hateful Love), opera (1999); film scores. ORCH.: Sym. (1947–48); *Slovak Rhapsody* (1951); *Symphonic Intermezzo* (1958); *Noc a naděje* (Night and Hope), symphonic poem (1959); *Variace na téma a smrt Jana Rychlíka* (Variations on a Theme by Jan Rychlík; 1964; Prague, March 15, 1966); *Variants*, short studies (1968); 2 sinfoniettas (1970–71; 1978–80); Double Concerto for Violin, Piano, and Orch. (1976); *Hommage a Josef Suk* for Violin and Strings (1998). CHAMBER: 2 string quartets (1943; 1981–82); 2 violin sonatas (1948, 1987); Cello Sonata (1949); Bassoon Sonata (1963); *Saxophone Cries* for Saxophone and Piano (1963–68); *Adagio* for Bass Clarinet and Piano (1969); *Variations* for Flute and Piano (1977); *Preludium, Aria, and Toccata* for Accordion (1978); *Elegy* for Violin and Piano (1982); organ music; piano pieces. VOCAL: *Odkaz J.A. Komenského* (J.A. Comenius's Legacy), oratorio (1952–55); *4 Monologues* for Soprano, Baritone, and Orch. (1965–66); *Janinka zpívá* (Janinka Sings), suite for Soprano and Orch. (1969); *Small Triptych*, 3 songs for Soprano, Flute, and Tam-tam (1971); *Oči a ruce* (Eyes and Hands), dramatic song for Mezzo-soprano, Clarinet, Viola, and Piano (1975); Concerto grosso for Vocal Soloists and Orch. (1980); choruses; songs.—**NS/LK/DM**

Machabey, Armand, French musicologist; b. Pont-de- Roide, Doubs, May 7, 1886; d. Paris, Aug. 31, 1966. He studied with d'Indy and Pirro, receiving his doctorat ès lettres from the Univ. of Paris in 1928 with the diss. *Essai sur les formules usuelles de la musique occidentale (des origines à la fin du XVe siècle)*, which was publ. in a rev. ed., Paris, 1955, as *Genèse de la tonalité musicale classique*. He was subsequently active as a music historian and essayist, and also one of the eds. of *Larousse de la musique* (Paris, 1957).

WRITINGS (all publ. in Paris unless otherwise given): *Sommaire de la méthode en musicologie* (1930); *Le théâtre musicale en France* (1933); *Précis-manuel d'histoire de la musique* (1942; 2nd ed., 1947); *La musique des Hittites* (Liège, 1945); *La Vie et l'oeuvre d'Anton Bruckner* (1945); *Maurice Ravel* (1947); *Traité de la critique musicale* (1947); *Le "bel canto"* (1948); *Portraits de trente compositeurs français* (1950); *Gerolamo Frescobaldi Ferrarensis (1583–1643)* (1952); *La Musique et la médicine* (1952); *La Notation musicale* (1952; 3rd ed., rev., 1971 by M. Huglo); *Guillaume de Machaut: La Vie et l'oeuvre musicale* (1955); *Le cantillation manichéene: Notation hypothétique, métrique analogies* (1956); *Notations musicales non*

modales des XIIe et XIIIe siècle (1957; 3rd ed., aug., 1959); *Problèmes de notation musicale* (1958); *Mélanges musicologiques d'Aristoxène à Hucbald* (1960); *La Musicologie* (1962; 2nd ed., 1969); *Embryologie de la musique occidentale* (1963); *La Musique de danse* (1966). —**NS/LK/DM**

Machado, Augusto (de Oliveira), Portuguese composer; b. Lisbon, Dec. 27, 1845; d. there, March 26, 1924. He was a pupil of Junior, Lami, and D'Almeide in Lisbon, and of Lavignac and Danhauser in Paris. From 1892 to 1908 he was director of the San Carlos Theater in Lisbon. He also taught singing at the Cons. (from 1893), serving as its director (1901–10). Besides numerous operettas, he wrote the operas *A Cruz de oiro* (Lisbon, 1873), *A Maria da Fonte* (Lisbon, 1879), *Lauriane* (Marseilles, Jan. 9, 1883; his most successful work), *Os Dorias* (Lisbon, 1887), *Mario Wetter* (Lisbon, 1898), *Venere* (Lisbon, 1905), and *La Borghesina* (Lisbon, 1909). For the 3rd centenary of the death of Camoens he wrote the symphonic ode *Camões es os Luziadas* (1880). He also wrote organ and piano pieces.—**NS/LK/DM**

Machaut (also **Machault, Machau, Mauchault**), **Guillaume de** (**Guillelmus de Mascaudio**), important French composer and poet; b. probably in Machaut, Champagne, c. 1300; d. probably in Rheims, April 13?, 1377. He entered the service of John of Luxembourg, King of Bohemia, about 1323, and was his secretary until the King's death (1346). He was granted a canonry in Verdun (1330), a second in Arras (1332), and a third Rheims (1333), retaining the first until 1335. He settled in Rheims permanently about 1340, and from 1346 was in the service of the French nobility, including the future King Charles V. His *Messe de Nostre Dame* for 4 Voices is one of the earliest polyphonic settings of the Mass. He also wrote 42 ballades, 33 virelais, 23 motets, 22 rondeaux, 19 lais, a double hocket, a complainte, and a chanson royal. An ed. of his works was prepared by F. Ludwig for the Publikationen Älterer Musik (1926–34; continued by H. Besseler, 1954) and by L. Schrade in Polyphonic Music of the Fourteenth Century (Vols. 2 and 3, Monaco, 1956).

BIBL.: A. Douce, *G. d.M., Musicien et poète rémois* (Rheims, 1948); S. Levarie, *G. d.M.* (N.Y., 1954); A. Machabey, *G. d.M.: La Vie et l'oeuvre musicale* (2 vols., Paris, 1955); W. Dömling, *Die mehrstimmigen Balladen, Rondeaux und Virelais von G. d.M.* (Tutzing, 1970); G. Reaney, *G. d.M.* (London, 1971); B. Harden, *Sharps, Flats, and Scribes: Musica ficta in the M. Manuscripts* (diss., Cornell Univ., 1983); L. Earp, *G.d. M.: A Guide to Research* (N.Y., 1995).—**NS/LK/DM**

Machavariani, Alexei (Davidovich), Russian composer; b. Gory, Sept. 23, 1913. He studied at the Tbilisi Cons., graduating in 1936, and then served on its faculty as a teacher of theory (1940–63) and as a prof. of composition (from 1963). He was made a People's Artist of the U.S.S.R. in 1958. His music is profoundly infused with Caucasian melorhythms.

WORKS: DRAMATIC: Opera: *Deda da shvili* (Mother and Son; 1944; Tbilisi, May 1, 1945); *Hamlet* (1964). Ballet: *Otello* (1957); *Knight in a Tiger's Skin* (1965). ORCH.: 3 symphonic poems: *Mumly Muhasa* (1939), *Satchidao* (1940), and *On the Death of a Hero* (1948); Piano Concerto (1944); 2 syms.

(1947, 1973); *The People's Choice*, overture (1950); Violin Concerto (1949). **VOCAL:** *For Peace, for Fatherland*, cantata (1951); *The Day of My Fatherland*, oratorio (1954); many songs.
—NS/LK/DM

Mâche, François-Bernard, French composer, musicologist, and philologist; b. Clermont-Ferrand, April 4, 1935. Following training in piano and harmony (with Emile Passani) at the Clermont-Ferrand Cons., he went to Paris and studied at the Ecole Normale Supérieure (diploma in Greek archaeology, 1957; agrégation in classical literature, 1958) and at the Cons. (composition with Messiaen, 1958–60). He later was awarded his Docteur d'Etat ès Lettres et Sciences Humaines by the Sorbonne for his diss. *L'idée de modèle en musique aujourd'hui* (1980). In 1968 he was made prof. of classical literature at the Lycée Louis-le-Grand in Paris. He became prof. of musicology at the Univ. of Strasbourg in 1983. In addition to many articles and reviews in the periodical literature, he publ. *Musique, mythe, nature ou les dauphins d'Arion* (1983; 2nd. ed., aug., 1991). In 1977 he received the Prix Italia, in 1984 he was awarded the Prix Chartier de l'Académie des beaux-Arts, and in 1988 he won the Grand Prix National de la Musique. In 1985 he was made an Officier and in 1990 a Commandeur de l'ordre des Arts et Lettres. While Mâche has been notably influenced as a composer by his study of philology, in particular structural linguistics, he finds the basis of his sound world in nature. His imaginative manipulation of that sound world embraces such procedures as imitation and transliteration, which he utilizes with more traditional compositional modes of expression.

WORKS: ORCH.: *La Peau du silence I* (1962; Tokyo, Oct. 24, 1986), *II* (1966; Warsaw, Sept. 29, 1968), and *III* (1970; Strasbourg, Jan. 12, 1971); *Synergies* (Paris, March 18, 1963); *Le Son d'une voix* for Chamber Orch. (Warsaw, Sept. 23, 1964); *Rituel d'oubli* for Chamber Orch. and Tape (1968; Strasbourg, June 11, 1970); *Répliques* (Royan, April 3, 1969); *Rambaramb* for Orch. and Tape (1972; Radio France, Paris, May 8, 1973); *Le Jonc à 3 glumes* (Seillans, July 8, 1974); *Andromède* for Orch. and 2 Choruses (1979; Radio France, Paris, June 4, 1980); *L'estuaire du temps* (Strasbourg, Sept. 17, 1993); *Planh* for Strings (Warsaw, Sept. 21, 1994); *Braises* for Amplified Harpsichord and Orch. (1994; Radio France, Paris, Feb. 12, 1995). **CHAMBER:** Duo for Violin and Piano (1956); *Canzone I* for 5 Instruments (1957), *II* for 5 Instruments (1963); *III* for 7 Instruments (1967), and *V* for 4 Instruments and Theater Set (1969); *Sporanges* for Harpsichord and Violin (1965); *Kemit* for Darboukka or Zarb (1970); *Korwar* for Modern Harpsichord and Tape (Bourges, June 30, 1972); *Temes Nevinbür* for 2 Pianos, 2 Percussion, and Tape (Royan, April 16, 1973); *Naluan* for 8 Instruments and Tape (Sudwestfunk, Baden-Baden, Feb. 28, 1974); *Maraé* for 6 Amplified Percussion and Tape (1974; Le Roche-Courbon, March 25, 1975); *Solstice* for Modern Harpsichord and Organ or Tape (La Roche-Courbon, March 28, 1975); *Kassandra* for 14 Instruments and Tape (Paris, Oct. 16, 1977); *Octuor* for 8 Instruments (Paris, June 6, 1977); *Aera* for 6 Percussionists (1978; Paris, March 30, 1979); *Amorgos* for 12 Instruments and Tape (Metz, Nov. 16, 1979); *Sopiana* for Flute, Piano, and Tape ad libitum (Pécs, Hungary, July 12, 1980); *Anaphores* for Modern Harpsichord and Percussionist (1981; Radio France, Paris, March 1, 1982); *Phénix* for Percussionist (Beijing, Sept. 28, 1982); *Aulodie* for Oboe or Soprano Saxophone or Piccolo Clarinet and Tape

(Amsterdam, June 25, 1983); *Iter memor* for Cello and Sampler (Radio France, Paris, Nov. 12, 1985); *Heol an Ankou* for Organ and 3 Trombones (Rennes, Nov. 28, 1985); *Uncas* for 9 Instruments, Voicetracker, Sequencer, and Tape (Paris, June 9, 1986); *Éridan* for 2 Violins, Viola, and Cello (1986; Radio France, Paris, Jan. 17, 1987); *Aliunde* for Clarinet or Contrabass Clarinet, Soprano, Percussion, and Sampler (London, July 4, 1988); *Tempora* for 3 Clavier Samplers and Sequencer (1988; Paris, Feb. 27, 1989); *Figures* for Bass Clarinet and Vibraphone (1989); *Guntur Madu* for Harpsichord (1990); *Khnoum* for Sampler and 5 Percussion (Strasbourg, Sept. 28, 1990); *Athanor* for 10 Instruments (1991; Brussels, March 9, 1992); *Hiérogamie* for Piccolo Flute and Percussion (1993); *Moires* for Quartet and Tape (Radio France, Paris, Dec. 2, 1994); *Ugarit* for Guitar (1998); *Brûlis* for Clarinet, Cello, and Piano (Venice, Sept. 25, 1999). **KEYBOARD: P i a n o:** *Areg* for Piano, 4–Hands (1977); *Nocturne* for Piano and Tape (1981); *Autonomie* for Piano, 4–Hands (1981; also for other instruments); *Styx* for 2 Pianos, 8–Hands (1984); *Léthè* for 2 Pianos, 8–Hands (1985); *Mesarthim* for 2 Pianos (1987). **H a r p s i c h o r d:** *Ziggurat* (1998). **O r g a n:** *Guntur Sari* (1990). **VOCAL:** *Safous Mélè* for Alto Solo, 4 Sopranos, 4 Altos, and 9 Instruments (1959; Paris, Oct. 5, 1963); *Nuit blanche* for Reciter and Tape (Warsaw, Sept. 18, 1966); *Canzone IV* for 2 Sopranos, Alto, Tenor, and Bass (1968); *Danaé* for 3 Sopranos, 3 Altos, 3 Tenors, 3 Basses, and Percussion (Persepolis, Sept. 3, 1970); *Rituel pour les Mangeurs d'Ombre* for 3 Sopranos, 3 Altos, 3 Tenors, 3 Basses, and Percussion (Bordeaux, May 16, 1979); *Temboctou* for 2 Sopranos, 2 Mezzo-sopranos, 3 Baritones, Tenor, Bass, 8 Instruments, Tape, and Electronics (Colmar, June 16, 1982); *Trois Chants Sacrés*: No. 1, *Muwatalli* for Mezzo-soprano or Baritone and Percussion (1984), No. 2, *Rasna* for Voice (1982), and No. 3, *Maponos* for Voice and Drum (1990); *Cassiopée I* (1988; Radio France, Paris, March 20, 1989) and *II* (1998) for Chorus and Percussion; *Kengir*, 5 pieces for Mezzo-soprano and Clavier Sampler (1991); *Manuel de Résurrection* for Mezzo-soprano and 2 Samplers (Radio France, Paris, April 10, 1998). **OTHER:** *Da capo* for Organ, 2 Percussion, 3 Medieval Reed Players, 10 Comedians, Sound Environment, and Tape (Avignon, July 15, 1976); many tape pieces.

BIBL.: B. Thomas, *Nature et musique dans l'oeuvre de F.-B. M.* (diss., Univ. of Paris, 1986).—NS/LK/DM

Machl, Tadeusz, Polish composer, organist, and teacher; b. Lwów, Oct. 22, 1922. He began to play the piano at age 10. After studies with Helena Kasparek at the Lwów Music School, he was organist at St. Elisabeth Church in Lwów (1944–46) and at Corpus Christi Church in Kraków (1947–50). He also studied composition with Artur Malawski, instrumentation with Feliks Wrobel, and organ with Bronisław Rutkowski at the State Higher School of Music in Kraków (1947–51). In 1952 he joined its faculty as a lecturer in composition and instrumentation, and later served as dean of its theory, composition, and conducting faculty (1967–70) and vice-rector (1970–73) before retiring in 1998. In 1976 he received the state title of prof. From 1982 to 1986 he taught at the Jagiellonian Univ. in Kraków, and again from 1999. In 1971 and 1990 he received the Minister of Culture and Arts Award, 1st Class. He received the Cavalier's Cross (1972) and the Officer's Cross (1988) of the Polonia Restituta Order.

WORKS: ORCH.: *Trzy miniatury symfoniczne* (Three Symphonic Miniatures; 1946); 6 syms.: No. 1 for Chorus and Orch.

(1947), No. 2 (1948), No. 3, *Tatry* (1948), No. 4 (1954), No. 5, *Cztery studia wirtuozowskie* (Four Virtuosic Studies) for Soprano, Women's Chorus, and Orch. (1963), and No. 6, *Sinfonia Desiderii* (1998); 7 organ concertos: No. 1 (1950; Zabrze, Sept. 29, 1951), No. 2 (1952), No. 3, *Uwertura koncertujaca* (Overture Concertante; 1953), No. 4 for Organ and Strings (1957), No. 5 for 3 Organs and Orch. (1969), No. 6 for Organ and 2 Orchs. (1979), and No. 7 (1983); *Suita liryczna* (Lyrical Suite; 1956); Concerto for Soprano and Orch. (1958); Violin Concerto (1960); Harpsichord Concerto (1962; Bydgoszcz, Sept. 25, 1964); Piano Concerto (1964); Harp Concerto (1965; Kraków, April 26, 1968); Double Concerto for Piano, Harpsichord, and Orch. (1966); Concerto for Cello or Viola and Orch. (1967); *Uwertura jubileuszowa* (Jubilee Overture; 1969); Triple Concerto for 2 Pianos, Organ, and Orch. (1969); Horn Concerto (1971); *Poemat Jubileuszowy* (Jubilee Poem; 1979); *Scherzo symfoniczne (Kontrowersje)* (Symphonic Scherzo [Controversies]; 1986); *Moje Miasto* (My City), symphonic poem (1992); *Noc na Kazalnicy* (A Night on the Pulpit), rhapsody (1996). **CHAMBER:** 4 string quartets (1950, 1957, 1961, 1972); *Suita liryczna* (Lyric Suite) for Violin and Piano (1955); *Haerbarium*, septet for Organ, English Horn, Horn, Bassoon, Cello, Harp, and Percussion (1980). **Organ:** *Pięć etiud wirtuozowskich* (Five Virtuoso Etudes; 1950); 2 Pieces (1964); *Piéce en cinque mouvements* (1965); *Mini Suita* (1967); *Tryptyk* (1968); 10 Pieces (1970); Sonata for 3 Organs (1972); *Pejzaże* (Landscapes) *I-III* (1976, 1977, 1982); *Wielka fantazja z podwójną fugą B-A-C-H* (Grand Fantasia with B-A-C-H Fugue; 1980); *Rupicaprae* (1982); *Piętnaście poematów różańcowych* (Fifteen Rosary Poems; 1983); *Dissonatio* (1989); *Poemat* (Poem; 1992). **VOCAL:** *Stabat Mater*, oratorio for 4 Soloists, Chorus, and Orch. (1945); *Requiem* for Soloists, Chorus, and Orch. (1946; unfinished); *Dzień pracy* (Work Day), cantata for 4 Soloists and Small Orch. (1948); 3 Songs for Soprano and Piano (1950–55); *Kantata młodzieżowa* (Cantata for Youth) for Soprano, Baritone, Chorus, and Orch. (1954); *Lot Ikara* (Icarus's Flight), cantata for Soprano, Reciter, Organ, and Orch. (1968); *Błękitny krzyż* (Blue Cross), cantata for Soprano, 2 Reciters, 2 Tapes, and Orch. (1974); *Requiem dla Zaginionych w Tatrach* (Requiem for Those Lost in the Tatra) for Soprano, Baritone, Reciter, Chorus, Organ, and Orch. (1980); *Krajobrazy Serdeczne* (Heartfelt Landscapes) for 4 Reciters, Quartet, and Chamber Orch. (1993). **—NS/LK/DM**

Machlis, Joseph, Latvian-born American writer on music and pedagogue; b. Riga, Aug. 11, 1906; d. N.Y., Oct. 17, 1998. He was taken to the U.S. as an infant. He studied at the Coll. of the City Univ. of N.Y. (B.A., 1927), and at the Inst. of Musical Art (teacher's diploma, 1927). He later took an M.A. in English literature from Columbia Univ. (1938). He was on the music faculty of Queens Coll. of N.Y. (1938–74), and then on the graduate faculty at the Juilliard School (from 1976). He made English trs. of a number of opera librettos, and publ. several well-written texts: the immensely popular *The Enjoyment of Music* (N.Y., 1955; 8th ed., 1999), *Introduction to Contemporary Music* (N.Y., 1961; 2nd ed., 1979), *American Composers of Our Time* (N.Y., 1963), and *Getting to Know Music* (N.Y., 1966). He also publ. 5 novels.**—NS/LK/DM**

Machover, Tod, American cellist, conductor, and composer; b. N.Y., Nov. 24, 1953. He studied composition at the Univ. of Calif. at Santa Cruz (1971–73), Columbia Univ. (1973–74), and the Juilliard School in N.Y. (B.M., 1975; M.M., 1977), numbering among his

mentors Dallapiccola (1973), Sessions (1973–75), and Carter (1975–78). He also studied computer music at the Mass. Inst. of Technology and at Stanford Univ. He was 1st cellist in the orch. of the National Opera of Canada in Toronto (1975–76), guest composer (1978–79) and director of musical research (1980–85) at IRCAM in Paris, and a teacher at the Mass. Inst. of Technology (from 1985), where he also was director of its Experimental Media Facility (from 1986). In 1986 he engaged in a project to design expanded musical instruments ("hyperinstruments") using technology to give extra power to virtuosic performance. From 1992 this project expanded into the development of interactive instruments for amateur musicians. He ed. the books *Le Compositeur et l'Ordinateur* (Paris, 1981) and *Musical Thought at IRCAM* (London, 1984), and was the author of *Quoi, Quand, Comment? La Recherche Musical* (Paris, 1985; Eng. tr., 1988, as *The Concept of Musical Research*) and *Microcomputers and Music* (N.Y., 1988). Among his honors were the Koussevitzky Prize (1984) and the Friedheim Award (1987).

WORKS: DRAMATIC: Opera: *Valis* (Paris, Dec. 2, 1987); *Brain Opera* (N.Y., July 23, 1996); *Resurrection* (1999). **ORCH.:** Concerto for Amplified Guitar and Orch. (1978); *Nature's Breath* for Chamber Orch. (1984–85); *Desires* (1985–89); *Hyperstring Trilogy* for Hypercello, Hyperviola, Hyperviolin, and Chamber Orch. (1991–93; rev. 1996–97; N.Y., July 25, 1996); *Forever and Ever*, concerto for Hyperviolin and Chamber Orch. (St. Paul, Minn., Sept. 24, 1993). **CHAMBER:** *Fresh Spring* for Baritone and 10 Instruments (1977); *Ye Gentle Birds* for Soprano, Mezzo-soprano, and 6 Instruments (1977); *Yoku Mireba* for Flute, Cello, and Piano (1977); *With Dadaji in Paradise* for Cello (1978; rev. 1983); *Light* for 15 Instruments (1979); *Winter Variations* for 9 Instruments (1981); String Quartet No. 1 (1981); *Hidden Sparks* for Violin (1984); *Song of Penance* for Hyperviola, Computer Voice, and Large Chamber Ensemble (Los Angeles, Feb. 3, 1992); *Bounce* for Hyperkeyboards (Chicago, Sept. 20, 1992). **ELECTRONIC:** *Déplacements* for Guitar and Computer Electronics (1979); *Soft Morning, City!* for Soprano, Double Bass, and Tape (1980); *Fusione Fugace* for Live Computer Electronics (1981); *Electric Études* for Cello and Computer Electronics (1983); *Spectres parisiens* for Flute, Horn, Cello, Synthesizer, 18 Instruments, and Computer (1984); *Flora* for Computer Tape (1989); *Bug-Mudra* for 2 Guitars, Percussion, Conductor with Gesture-tracking "Dataglove," and Live Computer (1989–90); *Epithalamion* for Vocal Soloists, 25 Players, and Live and Recorded Computer Electronics (1990); *He's Our Dad* for Soprano, Keyboard, and Computer-generated Sound (Boston, April 6, 1997); *Meteor Music*, electronic and computer interactive music (1998).**—NS/LK/DM**

Maciejewski, Roman, Polish-American pianist, organist, choral conductor, and composer; b. Berlin (of Polish parents), Feb. 28, 1910; d. Göteborg, April 30, 1998. His mother taught him to play piano at an early age. He then took lessons with Goldenweiser at the Berlin Cons. (1916–19) and with Zeleski at the Poznań Cons. (diploma, 1922), and also studied composition with Wiechowicz in Poznań and with Sikorski at the Warsaw Cons. He went to Paris in 1934, and studied with Boulanger; then lived in Sweden (1939–51). In 1952 he emigrated to the U.S., settling in Redondo Beach, Calif., as a church organist and director of the Roman Choir. In 1977 he returned to Sweden. Maciejewski excelled in writing lush, resonant, protracted choruses in self-confident tonal harmonies.

WORKS: ORCH.: *Allegro concertante* for Piano and Orch. (1944; Göteborg, Jan. 11, 1945); *Lullaby* for Piano and Orch. (1944); *Scenes from the Seaside* for Small Orch. (1972). **CHAMBER:** Brass Quartet (1937); String Quartet (1938); Violin Sonata (1940); String Trio (1948); *Nocturne* for Flute, Celesta, and Guitar (1951); *Variations* for Wind Quintet (1971). **Piano:** 2 sonatas (1926, 1932); *Mazurkas* (1928–90); *Bajka* (Fairy Tale), children's ballet for 2 Pianos (1931); Concerto for 2 Solo Pianos (1935). **VOCAL:** *Song of Bilitis* for Soprano and Orch. (1932); *Requiem* for Soloists, Chorus, and Orch. (1944–60; Warsaw, Sept. 1960); *Resurrection Mass* for Chorus and Organ (1966); masses; songs. —NS/LK/DM

Macintyre, Margaret, English soprano; b. in India, c. 1865; d. London, April 1943. She was a pupil of García in London. In 1885 she made her operatic debut as Mozart's Countess at St. George's Hall in London, and then sang there at Covent Garden (1888–97). She also made appearances in Milan, St. Petersburg, and Moscow. Among her other roles were Donna Elvira, Elisabeth, Senta, and Sieglinde. She also created the role of Rebecca in Sullivan's *Ivanhoe* (1891).—NS/LK/DM

Mackenzie, Sir Alexander (Campbell), distinguished Scottish conductor, educator, and composer; b. Edinburgh, Aug. 22, 1847; d. London, April 28, 1935. A scion of a musical family (there were 4 generations of musicians in his paternal line), he showed musical aptitude as a child, and was sent to Germany, where he studied violin with K.W. Ulrich and theory with Eduard Stein at the Schwarzburg-Sondershausen Realschule (1857–62). Returning to England, he studied violin with Sainton, piano with Jewson, and music theory with Charles Lucas at the Royal Academy of Music in London. He subsequently was active in Edinburgh as a violinist and teacher (1865–79). Between 1879 and 1885 he lived in Florence. In 1888 he was elected principal of the Royal Academy of Music in London, holding this post until 1924. From 1892 to 1899 he conducted the concerts of the Phil. Soc. of London. His reputation as an educator and composer was very high among musicians. He was knighted in 1895. As a composer, he was a believer in programmatic music, and introduced national Scottish elements in many of his works. His *Pibroch Suite* for Violin and Orch., first performed by Sarasate at the Leeds Festival (1889), acquired considerable popularity. Paderewski gave the first performance of his *Scottish Concerto* with the Phil. Soc. of London (1897). In 1922 Mackenzie was made a Knight Commander of the Royal Victorian Order.

WORKS (all 1st perf. in London unless otherwise given): **DRAMATIC:** *Colomba*, opera (April 9, 1883; rev. version, Dec. 3, 1912); *The Troubadour*, opera (June 8, 1886); *Phoebe*, comic opera (n.d.; not perf.); *His Majesty, or The Court of Vingolia*, comic opera (Feb. 20, 1897); *The Cricket on the Hearth*, opera (1900; June 6, 1914); *The Knights of the Road*, operetta (Feb. 27, 1905); incidental music to plays. **ORCH.:** *Larghetto and Allegretto* for Cello and Orch. (1875); *Overture to a Comedy* (Düsseldorf, 1876); *Cervantes*, overture (Sondershausen, 1877); *Scherzo* (Glasgow, 1878); *Rhapsodie ecossaise: Scottish Rhapsody No. 1* (1880); *Tempo di ballo*, overture (c. 1880); *Burns: Scottish Rhapsody No. 2* (1880); *La*

Belle Dame sans merci, ballad (1883); Violin Concerto (Birmingham Festival, Aug. 26, 1885); *12th Night*, overture (1888); *Pibroch*, suite for Violin and Orch. (Leeds Festival, Oct. 10, 1889; also for Violin and Piano); *Highland Ballad* for Violin and Orch. (1893); *Britannia*, overture (1894); *Scottish Concerto* for Piano and Orch. (March 24, 1897); *Processional March* (1899); *Coronation March* (1902); *London Day by Day*, suite (Norwich Festival, 1902); *Canadian Rhapsody* (1905); *Tam o' Shanter: Scottish Rhapsody No. 3* (1911); *Youth, Sport and Loyalty*, overture (1922). **CHAMBER:** Piano Trio (1874); String Quartet (1875); Piano Quartet (1875); *From the North*, 9 pieces for Violin and Piano (1895); *4 Dance Measures* for Violin and Piano (1915); *Distant Chimes* for Violin and Piano (1921); *2 Pieces* for Cello and Piano (1928); several piano works, including *Rustic Suite* (1876?), *In the Scottish Highlands*, 3 scenes (1880), *Odds and Ends, par ci, par là* (1916), (6) *Jottings* (1916), and *In Varying Moods* (1921). **VOCAL: Cantatas:** *The Bride* (Worcester Festival, 1881); *Jason* (Bristol Festival, 1882); *The Story of Sayid* (Leeds Festival, 1886); *The Dream of Jubal* (Liverpool, 1889); *The Witches' Daughter* (Leeds Festival, 1904); *The Sun-God's Return* (Cardiff Festival, 1910). **Oratorios:** *The Rose of Sharon* (Norwich Festival, Oct. 16, 1884; rev. 1910); *Bethlehem* (1894; also known as *The Holy Babe*); *The Temptation* (1914). **Other:** Many songs; arrangements of Scottish melodies and airs.—NS/LK/DM

Mackerras, Sir (Alan) Charles (MacLaurin), eminent American-born Australian conductor; b. Schenectady, N.Y. (of Australian parents), Nov. 17, 1925. He studied oboe, piano, and composition at the New South Wales State Conservatorium of Music in Sydney. From 1943 to 1946 he was principal oboist in the Sydney Sym. Orch. He then went to London, where he joined the orch. at Sadler's Wells and studied conducting with Michael Mudie. In 1947 he won a British Council Scholarship and pursued conducting studies with Václav Talich at the Prague Academy of Music. He was a staff conductor at Sadler's Wells from 1948 to 1954. From 1954 to 1956 he was principal conductor of the BBC Concert Orch. In 1963 he made his debut at London's Covent Garden conducting Shostakovich's *Katerina Izmailova*. From 1966 to 1969 he held the position of 1st conductor at the Hamburg State Opera. In 1970 he became music director of the Sadler's Wells Opera (renamed the English National Opera in 1974), a position he held until 1977. On Oct. 31, 1972, he made his Metropolitan Opera debut in N.Y. conducting Gluck's *Orfeo ed Euridice*. He was chief guest conductor of the BBC Sym. Orch. in London from 1976 to 1979, and from 1982 to 1985 chief conductor of the Sydney Sym. Orch. He was principal guest conductor of the Royal Liverpool Phil. from 1986 to 1988. From 1987 to 1992 he was music director of the Welsh National Opera in Cardiff, and then served as its conductor emeritus. In 1990 he made his debut at the Glyndebourne Festival conducting Verdi's *Falstaff*. From 1992 to 1995 he was principal guest conductor of the Scottish Chamber Orch. in Glasgow, and then its conductor laureate. He also was principal guest conductor of the Royal Phil. in London (1993–96) and of the San Francisco Opera (1993–96). In 1997 he became music director of the Orch. of St. Luke's in N.Y. As a guest conductor, Mackerras has appeared with many of the world's leading orchs. and opera houses, as well as at many of the leading festivals. In

1974 he was made a Commander of the Order of the British Empire, and in 1979 he was knighted. His recordings have won numerous awards, including *Gramophone* Awards (1977, 1980, 1983, 1984, 1986, 1994, 1999), a Grammy Award (1981), and the Edison, Deutscher Schallplattenpreis, and the Prix Caecilia (1999). In 1978 he was awarded the Janáček Medal. He has received honorary doctorates from the univs. of Hull (1990), Nottingham (1991), York, Brno, and Brisbane (1994), and Oxford (1997), and from the Prague Academy of Music (1999). In 1996 the Czech Republic honored him with the Medal of Merit. Mackerras has won great distinction for his performances of works from both the orch. and operatic repertoires. While he is highly regarded for his interpretations of the standard classics, he has also won renown for his authoritative performances of works by Janáček.

BIBL.: N. Phelan, *C. M.: A Musicians' Musician* (London, 1987).—NS/LK/DM

Maclean, Quentin (Stuart Morvaren),

English-Canadian organist, composer, and teacher; b. London, May 14, 1896; d. Toronto, July 9, 1962. He began his studies with Harold Osmund, F.G. Shuttleworth, and R.R. Terry (1904–07). After receiving training from H. Grädener in Vienna (1907–09), he completed his studies with Straube (organ) and Reger (composition) in Leipzig (1912–14). At the outbreak of World War I in 1914, he was interned as an enemy alien in the Ruhleben camp near Berlin until 1918. In 1919 he became asst. organist under Terry at Westminster Cathedral in London. He played in various British film theaters (from 1921) and on the BBC (from 1925). In 1939 he emigrated to Canada and played in Toronto film theaters until 1949. He also was organist-choirmaster at Holy Rosary Church in Toronto (1940–62), and was a teacher at the Toronto Cons. of Music and at St. Michael's Coll., Univ. of Toronto. He frequently appeared on the CBC. As a composer, he followed traditional paths.

WORKS: ORCH.: *Concert Piece* for Organ and Orch. (1932); *Rhapsody on 2 English Folk Tunes* for Harp and Small Orch. (1938); *Algonquin Legend* (1942); *Concerto Grosso in Popular Style* for Solovox, Electric Organ, Electric Guitar, Theremin, and Small Orch. (1942); Concerto for Electric Organ and Dance Orch. (1945); *The Well-tempered Orchestra* (1950); *Concerto Romantico* for Piano and Orch. (1953); *Rustic Rhapsody* (1954); *Theme and Variations* for Harpsichord and Orch. (1954); *Concerto Rococo* for Violin and Orch. (1957). **CHAMBER:** String Quartet (1937); Piano Trio (1937); Trio for Flute, Viola, and Guitar (1937); piano pieces; organ music. **VOCAL:** *Stabat Mater* for Tenor, Chorus, Organ, and Strings (1941); 10 masses; cantata; many choruses; songs.—NS/LK/DM

Maclennan, Francis, American tenor; b. Bay City, Mich., Jan. 7, 1879; d. Port Westminster, N.Y., July 17, 1935. He studied voice in N.Y., and later with Henschel in London and Franz Emerich in Berlin. He made his debut as Faust at London's Covent Garden (1902), and in 1904 he sang Parsifal in Savage's Opera Co. on a tour of the U.S. From 1907 to 1913 he was a member of the Berlin Royal Opera, where he had the distinction of being the first foreigner to sing Tristan in Germany. He

also performed Wagnerian roles in England, was a member of the Hamburg Opera (1913–16), and sang with the Chicago Opera (1915–17). He then taught voice. Maclennan was best known as a Wagnerian. He was married for several years to **Florence Easton**, with whom he appeared in duo recitals.—NS/LK/DM

Mac Low, Jackson, American poet, composer, painter, and multimedia performance artist; b. Chicago, Sept. 12, 1922. He studied piano, violin, and harmony at Chicago Musical Coll. (1927–32) and Northwestern Univ. School of Music (1932–36), then took courses in philosophy, poetics, and English at the Univ. of Chicago (A.A., 1941) and in classical languages at Brooklyn Coll. of the City Univ. of N.Y. (B.A., 1958). He also studied piano with Shirley Rhodes Perle (1943–44), Grete Sultan (1953–55), and Franz Kamin (1976–79), composition with Erich Katz (1948–49), recorder with Tui St. George Tucker (1948–53), experimental music with John Cage at the New School for Social Research in N.Y. (1957–60), Moog synthesizer with Rhys Chatham (1973), and voice with Pandit Pran Nath (1975–76). He taught at N.Y.U. (1966–73), the Mannes Coll. of Music in N.Y. (1966), the State Univ. of N.Y. at Albany (1984), Binghamton (1989), and Buffalo (1990), and Temple Univ. (1989); also held guest lectureships at various institutions and in 1990 was Regents Lecturer at the Univ. of Calif. at San Diego. Among his 26 books, many—e.g., *Stanzas for Iris Lezak* (1972), *21 Matched Asymmetries* (1978), *Asymmetries 1–260* (1980), *"Is That Wool Hat My Hat?"* (1982), *Bloomsday* (1984), *Representative Works: 1938–1985* (1986), *Words nd Ends from Ez* (1989), *Twenties: 100 Poems* (1991), *Pieces o' Six: Thirty-three Poems in Prose* (1992), *42 Merzgedichte in Memoriam Kurt Schwitters* (1994), and *Barnesbook* (1995)—comprise or include works realizable as musical-verbal performances. He wrote several quasi-musical plays, some with chance operations, including *The Marrying Maiden* (1958; unpubl.), *Verdurous Sanguinaria* (1961; publ. in anthologies, 1980, 1995), and *The Twin Plays: Port-au-Prince and Adams County Illinois* (1963, 1966). *The Pronouns* (1964, 1971, 1979) comprises works composed by a nonintentional method that are both poems and dance instructions, realized in the U.S., England, and Australia; he also wrote, directed, and performed in several verbal-musical Hörspiele for radio, 5 of which produced and broadcast by the Westdeutscher Rundfunk in Cologne. As both composer and writer, Mac Low adopted nonintentional procedures, including chance operations, indeterminacy, and related methods in 1954; but he has also written and composed extensively by intentional and quasi-intentional means. His many "simultaneities" include musical, verbal, and visual elements; these and other compositions are for live voices, instruments (usually variable), and/or tape multitracking; many are realized by instruction-guided performers' choices. He has performed extensively throughout North America, Europe, and New Zealand, often with his wife, the painter, composer, poet, and performance artist Anne Tardos. Others have performed his work in the U.S., England, Australia, Japan, and South America. A joint concert of his and James Tenney's works and a machine recording sounds as visual traces by Max Neuhaus was presented at N.Y.'s Town

Hall in 1966. An 8-hour retrospective concert on the occasion of his 60th birthday was given at Washington Square Church in N.Y. (1982). His awards include fellowships from N.Y. State's Creative Artists Public Service Program (1973–74; 1976–77), the NEA (1979), the Guggenheim Memorial Foundation (1985), and the N.Y. Foundation for the Arts (1988); he also received a Fulbright grant for travel in New Zealand and a composer's grant from New Zealand's Queen Elizabeth II Art Council (both 1986).

Works: Overture to Paul Goodman's *Faustina* (1949); Overture, Songs, and Incidental Music for Paul Goodman's *Jonah* (1950); *Hear, O Israel!*, choral canon (1950); *5 biblical poems* (1954–55); Songs and Incidental Music for W.H. Auden's *The Age of Anxiety* (1955); *Rush Hour* (1955); *4 Pianissimo Pieces* (1955); *Peaks & Lamas* (1958–59); *Sade Suit* (1959); *Headline Glass Material Buildings* (1959); *Stanzas for Iris Lezak* (1960); *A Piece for Sari Dienes* (1960); *Asymmetries 1–501* (1960–61); *Thanks, a simultaneity for people* (1960–61); *Nembutsu Gathas* (1961); *1ˢᵗ Aum Gatha* (1961); *Aum Field* (1961); *1ˢᵗ Mani Gatha* (1961); *An Asymmetry for La Monte Young* (1961); *A Piece for Recorder, Right Hand Moving* (1961); *F# for Simone Forti* (1961); *Pitches* (1961); *A Word Event for George Brecht* (1961); *"The text on the opposite page..."* (1961; various realizations, 1965–70); *Gate Gate Gathas* (1961–66); *Jesus Gathas* (1961–66); *Chamber Music for Barney Childs* (1963); *Jail Break* (1963–66); *Hare Krsna Gathas* (1967); *The 10 Bluebird Asymmetries* (1967); *The 6 Asymmetries for Dr. Howard Levy* (1967); *The 5 Young Turtle Asymmetries* (1967); *A Vocabulary for Carl Fernbach-Flarsheim* (1968); *LETT* (1969; quarter tone guitar realization, 1976); *Word Event(s) for Bici Forbes* (1971–72); *A Word Event for Bici Forbes on the Book Title "Lucy Church Amiably"* (1971); *A Word Event for Bici Forbes on the Word "Environmentally"* (1971); *The Black Tarantula Crossword Gathas* (1973; 8-voice multitrack tape realization, 1973); *Guru- Guru Gathas* (1973); *A Vocabulary for Michael Wiater* (1973); *A Vocabulary for Sharon Belle Mattlin* (1973); *The Tennyson Asymmetries* (1973); *Phoneme Dance for/from John Cage* (1974); *Govinda Gathas* (1974); *A Vocabulary for Vera Regina Lachmann* (1974); *A Vocabulary for Charlotte Moorman* (1974); *Counterpoint for Candy Cohen* (multitrack tapes, 1974, 1978); *A Vocabulary for Peter Innisfree Moore* (1974–75); *Heavens* (1974–75); *Mani-Mani Gatha* (1975); *Guru-Guru Gatha* (1975); *Tara Gathas* (1975); *Kaddish Gatha* (1975); *1ˢᵗ Sharon Belle Mattlin Vocabulary Crossword Gatha* (1976); *1ˢᵗ Milarepa Gatha* (1976, 1979); *A Word Event for Bici Forbes on the Word "Bicentennial"* (1976); *Homage to Leona Bleiweiss* (1976); *Stephanie Vevers Vocabulary Gatha* (1977); *Albuquerque Antiphonies* (1977); *Musicwords (for Phill Niblock)* (1977–78); *Free Gatha 1* (1978); *A Notated Vocabulary for Eve Rosenthal* (1978); *A Vocabulary Gatha for Pete Rose* (1978); *A Vocabulary for Custer LaRue* (1978–79); *A Vocabulary for Annie Brigitte Gilles Tardos* (1979; rev. 1980–82); *A Vocabulary Gatha for Anne Tardos* (1980); *"Is That Wool Hat My Hat?"* (1980); *Winds/Instruments* (1980–84); *Dream Meditation* (1980–82); *Words and Ends from Ez* (text, 1981–83; used in radio work, 1981; arranged as multitrack tape, 1985; music, "Ezra Pound" and Anagrams for Instrument[s], 1989–90); *Dialog unter Dichten/Dialog Among Poets*, radio work (1981); *Canon for the Summer Solstice* (1981); *Free Gatha 2* (1981); *Transverse Flute Mime Piece* (1981); *2ⁿᵈ Aum Gatha* (1982); *Milarepa Quartet for 4 Like Instruments* (1982); *Thanks/Danke*, radio work (1983); *Heterophonies from "Hereford Bosons 1 and 2"* (1984); *Phonemicon from "Hereford Bosons 1"* (1984); *A Bean Phonemicon for Alison Knowles* (1984); *Reisen*, radio work (1984); *Locks*, radio work (1984); *Für Stimmen, etc.*, radio work (1985); *Definitive Revised Instructions for Performing Gathas* (1985); *Wörter nd Enden aus Goethe/Words and Ends from Goethe* (arranged as radio work, 1986); *Phoneme Dance for John Cage/Phonemtanz für John Cage*, radio work (1986; in collaboration with A. Tardos); *The Birds of New Zealand* for Multitrack Tape (1986); *Iran-Contra Hearings* (1987–90); *Westron Winde 2* (1987–88); *22ⁿᵈ Merzgedicht in Memoriam Kurt Schwitters* (1988); *Westron Winde 4* (1988–89); *36ᵗʰ-42ⁿᵈ Merzgedichte in Memoriam Kurt Schwitters* (1989; arranged as voice duos, 1989–93); *Definitive Revised Performance Instructions for each of the Vocabularies* (1989–90); *Low Order Travesties*, computer-mediated poems arranged as voice duos (1989–90); *Lucas 1–29* (1990–92); *Motet on a Saying of A.J. Muste* for Chorus (1991); *S.E.M.* for Instrumentalists (1992); *1ˢᵗ, 2ⁿᵈ, and 3ʳᵈ Four-language Word Events in Memoriam John Cage*, collaborative paintings/scores for Voices (1992–93; in collaboration with A. Tardos); *Phoneme Dance in Memoriam John Cage* for Speaker-Vocalists (1993; in collaboration with A. Tardos); *Trope Market Phonemicons* for Voice and/or Instruments with Optional Tape (1993); *Phoneme Dance in Memoriam John Cage, Bob Watts, and George Maciunas* for Speaker-Vocalists (1994; in collaboration with A. Tardos); *A Forties Opera* for Speaker and Improvising Instrumentalist (1995; in collaboration with P. Oliveros).—NS/LK/DM

MacMillan, James, Scottish composer, conductor, and teacher; b. Kilwinning, July 16, 1959. He was a student of Rita McAllister at the Univ. of Edinburgh (1977–81) and then pursued postgraduate studies in composition with Casken at the Univ. of Durham (Ph.D., 1987). He was a lecturer in music at the Univ. of Manchester (1986–88). In 1989 he served as composer-in-residence of the St. Magnus Festival in Orkney. In 1990 he became affiliate composer of the Scottish Chamber Orch. in Glasgow and a teacher at the Royal Scottish Academy of Music and Drama there. In 1991 he was a visiting composer of the Philharmonia Orch. in London. In 2000 he became composer/conductor with the BBC Phil. in Manchester. He developed an accessible style of composition that found inspiration in his Roman Catholic faith and Scottish nationalism.

Works: DRAMATIC: *Búsqueda*, music theater (Edinburgh, Dec. 6, 1988); *Tourist Variations*, chamber opera (1991); *Inés de Castro*, opera (1991–95; Edinburgh, Aug. 23, 1996); *Visitatio Sepulchri*, music theater (1992–93; Glasgow, May 20, 1993). **ORCH.:** *The Keening* (1986); *Festival Fanfares* for Brass Band (Ayr, May 1986); *Into the Ferment* (Irvine, Dec. 19, 1988); *Tryst* (Kirkwall, Orkney, June 17, 1989); *The Exorcism of Rio Sumpúl* for Chamber Orch. (1989; Glasgow, Jan. 28, 1990); *The Berserking*, piano concerto (Glasgow, Sept. 22, 1990); *The Confession of Isobel Gowdie* (London, Aug. 22, 1990); *Sowetan Spring* for Wind Band (Glasgow, Sept. 23, 1990); *Sinfonietta* (1991; London, May 14, 1992); *Veni, Veni, Emmanuel*, percussion concerto (London, Aug. 10, 1992); *Epiclesis*, trumpet concerto (Edinburgh, Aug. 28, 1993); *They saw the stone had been rolled away*, fanfare for Brass and Percussion (Edinburgh, Aug. 27, 1993); *Mémoire impériale* (1993; Edinburgh, Feb. 13, 1994); *Britannia* (London, Sept. 21, 1994); *Triduum*, triptych comprising *The World's Ransoming* for Orch. and English Horn Obbligato (1995–96; London, July 11, 1996), Cello Concerto (London, Oct. 3, 1996), and Sym., *Vigil* (London, Sept. 28, 1997); *í (A Meditation on Iona)* for Strings and Percussion (1996; Glasgow, Feb. 21, 1997); *Ninian*, clarinet concerto (1996; Edinburgh, April 4, 1997). **CHAMBER:** *Study on 2 Planes* for Cello and Piano (1981; Edinburgh, March 4, 1984); *The Road to Ardtalla* for Sextet (1983; Manchester, Nov. 6, 1987); *3 Dawn Rituals* for Chamber Ensemble (1983;

London, Nov. 2, 1985); *2 Visions of Hoy* for Oboe and Chamber Ensemble (Manchester, June 16, 1986); *Litanies of Iron and Stone* for Clarinet, Soprano Saxophone, Trombone, and Tape (Glasgow, Sept. 14, 1987); *Untold* for Wind Quintet (1987; Ayr, Sept. 13, 1988; rev. 1991); *After the Tryst* for Violin and Piano (1988; Glasgow, Sept. 19, 1990); *Visions of a November Spring* for String Quartet (1988; Glasgow, May 3, 1989; rev. 1991); *The Cumnock Orcadian* for Chamber Ensemble (Kirkwall, Orkney, June 16, 1989); *...as others see us...* for Chamber Ensemble (London, April 5, 1990); *Tuireadh* for Clarinet and String Quartet (Kirkwall, Orkney, June 25, 1991); *Intercession* for 3 Oboes (Huddersfield, Nov. 26, 1991); *Kiss on Wood* for Violin and Piano (1993; Harrogate, Aug. 6, 1994); *Memento* for String Quartet (N.Y., Oct. 13, 1994); *Adam's Rib* for Brass Quintet (1994–95; Edinburgh, March 28, 1995); *A Different World* for Violin and Piano (London, July 22, 1995); *14 Little Pictures* for Piano Trio (London, May 21, 1997); *Why is this night different?* for String Quartet (1997; London, April 23, 1998). **KEYBOARD: P i a n o :** Sonata (1985; Radio Scotland, Sept. 1987); *A Cecilian Variation for J.F.K.* (Washington, D.C., Nov. 22, 1991; 2nd movement of *Kennedy Variations*, in collaboration with G. Victory, W. Mathias, and M. Berkeley); *Barncleupédie* (1992; Edinburgh, Feb. 28, 1993); *Angel* (Edinburgh, Oct. 31, 1993); *Lumen Christi* (Milan, April 11, 1997). **O r g a n :** *Wedding Introit* (1983); *White Note Paraphrase* (1994). **VOCAL:** *Beatus Vir* for Chorus and Organ (Norwich, July 2, 1983); *St. Anne's Mass* for Congregation and Organ or Piano (1985); *Variation on Johnny Faa'* for Soprano, Flute, Cello, and Harp (Edinburgh, Aug. 1988); *Cantos Sagrados* for Chorus and Organ (1989; Edinburgh, Feb. 10, 1990); *Catherine's Lullabies* for Chorus, Brass, and Percussion (1990; Glasgow, Feb. 10, 1991); *Scots Song* for Soprano and Chamber Quintet (Brighton, May 10, 1991); *Divo Aloysio Sacrum* for Chorus and Optional Organ (1991); *So Deep* for Chorus and Optional Viola and Oboe (1992); *...here in hiding...* for 4 Men's Voices (Glasgow, Aug. 10, 1993; also for Chorus); *7 Last Words from the Cross*, cantata for Chorus and Strings (1993; Glasgow, March 30, 1994); *Ballad* for Voice and Piano (Glasgow, May 15, 1994); *Christus Vincit* for Chorus (London, Nov. 23, 1994); *Màiri* for Chorus (London, May 19, 1995); *The Children* for Mezzo-soprano or Baritone and Piano (BBC Radio 3, London, July 23, 1995); *Seinte Mari moder milde* for Chorus and Organ (Cambridge, Dec. 24, 1995); *A Child's Prayer* for 2 Treble Soloists and Chorus (London, July 4, 1996); *The Galloway Mass* for Unison Voices, Chorus or Cantor, and Organ (1996; Ayr, March 25, 1997); *The Halie Speerit's Dancers* for Children's Chorus and Piano (1996; Glasgow, April 28, 1997); *On the Annunciation of the Blessed Virgin* for Chorus and Organ (1996; Cambridge, April 27, 1997); *The Gallant Weaver* for Chorus (Paisley, April 14, 1997); *The Prophecy* for Children's Chorus and Instruments (London, Oct. 11, 1997); *Raising Sparks* for Mezzo- soprano and Ensemble (London, Oct. 5, 1997). —NS/LK/DM

MacMillan, Sir Ernest (Alexander Campbell), eminent Canadian conductor and composer; b. Mimico, Aug. 18, 1893; d. Toronto, May 6, 1973. He began organ studies with Arthur Blakeley in Toronto at age 8, making his public debut at 10. He continued organ studies with A. Hollins in Edinburgh (1905–8), where he was also admitted to the classes of F. Niecks and W.B. Ross at the Univ. He was made an assoc. (1907) and a fellow (1911) of London's Royal Coll. of Organists, and received the extramural B.Mus. degree from the Univ. of Oxford (1911). He studied modern history at the Univ. of Toronto (1911–14) before receiving piano instruction from Therese Chaigneau in Paris (1914). In 1914 he attended the Bayreuth Festival, only to be interned as an enemy alien at the outbreak of World War I; while being held at the Ruhleben camp near Berlin, he gained experience as a conductor; was awarded the B.A. degree in absentia by the Univ. of Toronto (1915); his ode, *England*, submitted through the Prisoners of War Education Committee to the Univ. of Oxford, won him his D.Mus. degree (1918). After his release, he returned to Toronto as organist and choirmaster of Timothy Eaton Memorial Church (1919–25). He joined the staff of the Canadian Academy of Music (1920) and remained with it when it became the Toronto Cons. of Music, serving as its principal (1926–42); was also dean of the music faculty at the Univ. of Toronto (1927–52). He was conductor of the Toronto Sym. Orch. (1931–56) and of the Mendelssohn Choir there (1942–57); also appeared as guest conductor in North and South America, Europe, and Australia. He served as president of the Canadian Music Council (1947–66) and of the Canadian Music Centre (1959–70). In 1935 he was the first Canadian musician to be knighted, an honor conferred upon him by King George V; also received honorary doctorates from Canadian and U.S. institutions. He conducted many works new to his homeland, both traditional and contemporary. C. Morey ed. *MacMillan on Music: Essays on Music* (Toronto, 1997).

WORKS: DRAMATIC: *Snow White*, opera (1907); *Prince Charming*, ballad opera (1931). **ORCH.:** 4 overtures (*Cinderella*, 1915; *Don't Laugh*, 1915; 1924; *Scotch Broth*, 1933); *2 Sketches* for Strings (1927; also for String Quartet); *Fantasy on Scottish Melodies* (1946); *Fanfare for a Festival* for Brass and Percussion (1959); *Fanfare for a Centennial* for Brass and Percussion (1967). **CHAMBER:** String Quartet (1914; rev. 1921); *4 Fugues* for String Quartet (1917); piano pieces; organ music. **VOCAL:** *England*, ode for Soprano, Baritone, Chorus, and Orch., after Swinburne (1917–18; Sheffield, England, March 17, 1921); *2 Carols* for Soprano and String Trio (1927); *Te Deum laudamus* for Chorus and Orch. (1936); many choruses and songs; arrangements.

BIBL.: E. Schabas, *Sir E. M.: The Importance of Being Canadian* (Toronto, 1994).—NS/LK/DM

MacNeil, Cornell, noted American baritone; b. Minneapolis, Sept. 24, 1922. While working as a machinist, he appeared on the radio as an actor and sang minor parts on Broadway. He then was a scholarship student of Friedrich Schorr at the Hartt Coll. of Music in Hartford, Conn., and also studied with Virgilio Lazzari and Dick Marzollo in N.Y. and with Luigi Ricci in Rome. On March 1, 1950, he made his professional operatic debut as Sorel in the premiere of Menotti's *The Consul* in Philadelphia. On April 4, 1953, he made his N.Y.C. Opera debut as Tonio, and subsequently appeared there regularly. He first sang opera in San Francisco as Escamillo in 1955 and in Chicago as Puccini's Lescaut in 1957. On March 5, 1959, he made his debut at Milan's La Scala as Don Carlo in *Ernani*. On March 21, 1959, he made his Metropolitan Opera debut in N.Y. as Rigoletto, and remained on its roster until 1987. He became particularly successful there in Verdi roles, excelling as Amonasro, Germont, Luna, Iago, and Nabucco. In 1964 he made his debut at London's Covent Garden as

Macbeth. His other guest engagements took him to Vienna, Rome, Paris, Geneva, Florence, and other European operatic centers. In addition to his Verdi portrayals, he also had success as Barnaba in *La Gioconda*, the Dutchman in Wagner's opera, and as Scarpia. In the later years of his career, he became well known for his verismo roles.—**NS/LK/DM**

Macon, "Uncle" Dave (actually, David Harrison),

one of the most colorful and often-recorded of all the stars of Nashville's Grand Ole Opry; b. Smart Station, Tenn., Oct. 7, 1870; d. Nashville, Tenn., March 22, 1952. Uncle Dave Macon appeared on the Grand Ole Opry's stage from its opening days into the early 1950s, when he was in his early 80s, performing a combination of traditional banjo songs, sentimental songs, and his own compositions, often commenting on contemporary trends.

Macon was born outside of Nashville, but the family soon relocated to the big city, where his father operated a hotel located on downtown Nashville's main street. The rooming house was popular with vaudeville performers, and the young Macon was particularly impressed by the stunt banjo playing of one traveling star, Joel Davidson. He began to learn the instrument, and to play locally, mostly in informal settings. When Macon was a teenager, his father was stabbed in a brawl outside of the hotel, and the family moved once again. Macon's mother opened a rest stop for stage coaches in rural Readyville, and he took on the task of providing water for the horses.

As a young man, Macon established his own freight-carting business, powered by teams of mule-drawn wagons. He was an established businessman working mostly between Murfreesboro in the Northeast of the state and Woodbury. However, the coming of engine-driven trucks began to threaten Macon's business. In his 50s, he decided he could not adapt to new times, and let his business go.

Throughout this period, Macon had continued to play the banjo, mostly to amuse his customers and family. In the early 1920s, while visiting a Nashville barbershop, Macon was playing for customers when he was heard by a scout for Loew's vaudeville houses. Macon was soon performing on stage, and in early 1924 made his first recordings. A year later, he was invited to be the second member of WSM's "Barn Dance" program in Nashville, which would soon be renamed the "Grand Ole Opry."

Macon played both clawhammer and two-finger banjo styles. He was an exceptionally talented musician, but it was his ability to perform stunts like playing the banjo while swinging the instrument between his legs and other tricks that really won over his audiences. Macon's hearty vocals, good humor, and energetic banjo playing influenced an entire generation of musicians, including Stringbean and Grandpa Jones. He recorded hundreds of 78s, often accompanied by the talented McGee brothers and fiddler Sid Harkreader, going under the name The Fruit Jar Drinkers (illegal moonshine liquor was often dispensed in used fruit jars, hence the name). In the 1940s and early 1950s, he was often accompanied by his son, Dorris, in Opry appearances.

Macon's repertoire, like other early country performers, was made up of a mix of traditional songs and dance tunes, sentimental and popular songs of the late 19th and early 20th centuries, and his own off-beat adaptations of these songs along with original compositions. Macon's presentation of his material showed the influence of years of performing on the tent show circuit; his recordings often began and ended with a lusty shout of "Hot dog!" Macon's biting social commentary is illustrated in songs like "In and Around Nashville," in which he criticizes, among other things, women who chew gum and wear "knee-high" skirts. One of his popular songs, "The Cumberland Mountain Deer Chase," describes a deer hunt in the mountains; it was transformed in the 1950s by Pete Seeger into a long story-song for children that he called "The Cumberland Mountain Bear Hunt."

DISC.: *Go Along Mule* and *Country* (reissues of 1920s and 1930s recordings).—**RC**

Maconchy, Dame Elizabeth,

significant English composer of Irish descent, mother of **Nicola LeFanu;** b. Broxbourne, Hertfordshire, March 19, 1907; d. Norwich, Nov. 11, 1994. She studied composition with Charles Wood and Vaughan Williams, and counterpoint with C.H. Kitson at the Royal Coll. of Music in London (from 1923); she then pursued further training with Jirák in Prague (1929–30). Returning to England, she devoted herself to composition. She also served as chairman of the Composers Guild of Great Britain (1959–60) and as president of the Soc. for Promotion of New Music (from 1977). In 1977 she was made a Commander and in 1987 a Dame Commander of the Order of the British Empire. Maconchy developed a style peculiarly her own: tonally tense, contrapuntally dissonant, and coloristically sharp in instrumentation.

WORKS: DRAMATIC: *Great Agrippa*, ballet (1933); *The Little Red Shoes*, ballet (1935); *Puck Fair*, ballet (1940); *The Sofa*, opera (1956–57; London, Dec. 13, 1959); *The 3 Strangers*, opera (1958–67; Bishop's Stortford Coll., June 5, 1968); *The Departure*, opera (1960–61; London, Dec. 16, 1962); *Witnesses*, incidental music (1966); *The Birds*, opera (1967–68; Stortford Coll., June 5, 1968); *Johnny and the Mohawks*, children's opera (1969; London, March 1970); *The Jesse Tree*, church opera (1969–70; Dorchester Abbey, Oct. 7, 1970); *The King of the Golden River*, opera (Oxford, Oct. 29, 1975). **ORCH.:** Concerto for Piano and Chamber Orch. (1928); Concertino for Piano and Strings (1928); *The Land*, suite (1929); Suite for Chamber Orch. (1930); Viola Concerto (1937); *Dialogue* for Piano and Orch. (1940); *Theme and Variations* for Strings (1942); *Variations on a Well-Known Theme* (1942); Concertino for Clarinet and Strings (1945; Copenhagen, June 2, 1947); Sym. (1945–48); Double Concerto for Oboe, Bassoon, and Strings (1950); Concerto for Bassoon and Strings (1950); *Nocturne* (1951); Sym. for Double String Orch. (1952–53); *Proud Thames*, overture (1953); *Serenata concertante* for Violin and Orch. (1962); *Variazioni concertante* for Oboe, Clarinet, Bassoon, Horn, and Strings (1964–65); *An Essex Overture* (1966); *Music* for Winds and Brass (1966); *3 Cloudscapes* (1968); *Epyllion* for Cello and 14 Strings (1975); Sinfonietta (1975–76); *Romanza* for Viola and Chamber Orch. (1978; London, March 12, 1979); *Little Symphony* (1980; Norwich, July 28, 1981); *Music for Strings*

(London, July 26, 1983). **CHAMBER:** Quintet for Oboe and String Quartet (1932); 14 string quartets (1933; 1936; 1938; 1943; 1948; 1950; 1955–56; 1966; 1968–69; 1971–72; 1976; 1979; 1983; 1984); Duo for 2 Violins (1934); *Prelude, Interlude, and Fugue* for 2 Violins (Prague, Sept. 4, 1935); 2 violin sonatas (1938, 1944); Sonata for Solo Viola (1938); *Serenade* for Cello and Piano (1944); *Divertimento* for Piano and Cello (1944); *Duo, Theme, and Variations* for Violin and Cello (1951); *3 Pieces* for 2 Clarinets (1956); *Trios* for Strings (1957); *Variations on a Theme from Vaughan Williams's Job* for Cello (1957); *Reflections* for Oboe, Clarinet, Viola, and Harp (1960); Quintet for Clarinet and Strings (1963); Sonatina for String Quartet (1963); *6 Pieces* for Violin (1966); *Conversations* for Clarinet and Viola (1967–68); *Music for Double Bass and Piano* (1970); *3 Bagatelles* for Oboe and Harpsichord or Piano (1972); Oboe Quartet (1972); *3 Preludes* for Violin and Piano (1972); *5 Sketches* for Viola (1972–73); *Morning, Noon, and Night* for Harp (1976); *Contemplation* for Cello and Piano (1978); *Colloquy* for Flute and Piano (1978–79); *Fantasia* for Clarinet and Piano (1979); Trio for Violin, Viola, and Cello (1980); *Trittico* for 2 Oboes, Bassoon, and Harpsichord (1981); *Piccola musica* for String Trio (Cheltenham, July 13, 1981); *Tribute* for Violin and 8 Winds (1983); *Narration* for Cello (1985); *Excursion* for Bassoon (1985). **KEYBOARD: P i a n o :** *A Country Town* (1939); *Contrapuntal Pieces* (1941); *The Yaffle* (1962); *Mill Race* (1962); Sonatina (1965); *Preludio, Fugue, and Finale* for Piano, 4–Hands (1967). **H a r p s i c h o r d :** Sonatina (1965–66); *Notebook* (1965–66); *3 Pieces* (1977); Sonatina (1977). **VOCAL:** *The Voice of the City* for Women's Voices (1943); *Stalingrad* for Women's Chorus (1946); *Sonnet Sequence* for Soprano and String Orch. (1946); *A Winter's Tale* for Soprano and String Quartet (1949); *6 Yeats Settings* for Soprano, Women's Chorus, Clarinet, 2 Horns, and Harp (1951); *Christmas Morning* for Women's Voices and Piano or Small Ensemble (1962); *The Armado* for Chorus and Piano (1962); *Samson and the Gates of Gaza* for Chorus and Orch. (1963–64); *The Starlight Night* for High Voice and Orch. (1964); *Nocturnal* for Chorus (1965); *Propheta Mendax* for Boy's or Women's Chorus (1965); *I Sing of a Maiden* for Chorus (1966); *Peace* for High Voice and Orch. (1966); *And Death Shall Have No Dominion* for Chorus, 2 Horns, 3 Trumpets, and 3 Trombones (1968–69); *May Magnificat* for High Voice and Orch. (1970); *Ariadne* for Soprano and Orch. (1970); *Fly-by-Nights* for Treble Voices and Harp (1973); *Pied Beauty* for Chorus and Brass (1975); *Heavenhaven* for Chorus and Brass (1975); *The Leaden Echo and the Golden Echo* for Chorus, Alto Flute, Viola, and Harp (1978); *Heloise et Abelard*, cantata for Soprano, Tenor, Bass, Chorus, and Orch. (1978; Croydon, March 1979); *My Dark Heart* for Soprano and Instrumental Ensemble (1982); *L'Horloge* for Soprano, Clarinet, and Piano (1983); *Still Falls the Rain* for Double Chorus (1984); *Butterflies* for Voice and Harp (1986); other choral pieces, song cycles, and solo songs.—**NS/LK/DM**

Maconie, Robin (John), New Zealand composer and writer on music; b. Auckland, Oct. 22, 1942. He studied at Victoria Univ., Wellington (B.A., 1962; M.A., 1963), and later with Messiaen at the Paris Cons. (1963–64) and with Zimmermann and Eimert at the Cologne Hochschule für Musik (1964–65); also attended Stockhausen's lectures at the Darmstadt summer courses. He returned to New Zealand as a composer for film and theater, and also lectured at the Univ. of Auckland (1967–68). In 1969 he settled in England, where he engaged in music criticism and research in musical phenomenology. He publ. *The Works of Karlheinz*

Stockhausen (London, 1975; 2nd ed., 1991) and ed. *Stockhausen on Music: Lectures and Interviews* (London, 1989).

WORKS: Clarinet Sonata (1961); *Music for a Masque* for String Orch. (1962); *Basia Memoranda*, song cycle for Low Voice and String Quartet (1962); *Canzona* for Chamber Orch. (1962); *A:B:A:* for Harp (1964); *Ex evangelio Sancti Marci* for Chorus (1964); *A:D:C:* for Piano (1965); Sonata for String Quartet (1964); *Māui*, television ballet for Speaker, Dancers, and Orch. (1967–72); String Quartet (1970); *Limina*, modified sound track (1975).—**NS/LK/DM**

Macque, Giovanni (Jean) de, eminent Flemish organist, teacher, and composer; b. Valenciennes, c. 1548; d. Naples, Sept. 1614. He was a boy chorister at Vienna's imperial chapel, then studied at a Jesuit college before receiving instruction from Philippe de Monte. He was in Rome by 1574, where he was organist at S. Luigi dei Francesi (1580–81) as well as a member of the Compagnia dei Musici di Roma when it was sanctioned by the Pope (1584). He went to Naples about 1585 and became active in the affairs of the academy of Don Fabrizio Gesualdo da Venosa, father of the composer Carlo Gesualdo. He became second organist at the Santa Casa dell'Annunziata (1590), and was made organist (1594), and then maestro di cappella (1595) of the Spanish viceregal chapel. He was a distinguished composer of both vocal and instrumental music. He was also highly esteemed as a teacher, his pupils including Mayone, Trabaci, Luigi Rossi, Falconieri, Francesco Lambardi, G.D. Montella, and Spano.

WORKS: VOCAL: *Primo libro de madrigali* for 6 Voices (Venice, 1576); *Madrigali* for 4 to 6 Voices (Venice, 1579); *Madrigaletti e napolitane* for 6 Voices (Venice, 1581); *Secondo libro de madrigaletti e napolitane* for 6 Voices (Venice, 1582); *Madrigali* for 5 Voices (Venice, 1583; not extant); *Primo libro de madrigali* for 4 Voices (Venice, 1587); *Secondo libro de madrigali* for 5 Voices (Venice, 1587); *Secondo libro de madrigali* for 6 Voices (Venice, 1589); *Motectorum* for 5 to 6 and 8 Voices, *liber primus* (Rome, 1596); *Terzo libro de madrigali* for 5 Voices (Ferrara, 1597); *Quarto libro de madrigali* for 5 Voices (Naples, 1599); *Terzo libro de madrigali* for 4 Voices (Naples, 1610); *Sesto libro de madrigali* for 5 Voices (Venice, 1613); various other pieces in contemporary collections. **INSTRUMENTAL:** *Ricercate e canzone francesi, a 4* (Rome, 1586); *Secondo libro de ricercari, a 4* (not extant); other pieces in MS collections.

BIBL.: L. Anderson, *G. d.M. of Valenciennes and the Evolution of Polyphonic Music in Naples at the End of the Sixteenth Century* (diss., Univ. of Liege, 1970); W. Shindle, *The Madrigals of G. d.M.* (diss., Ind. Univ., 1970).—**NS/LK/DM**

Macurdy, John, American bass; b. Detroit, March 18, 1929. He studied engineering at Wayne State Univ. in Detroit, and then voice with Avery Crew and Boris Goldovsky. In 1952 he made his operatic debut in New Orleans in *Samson et Dalila*. After singing in Santa Fe, Houston, and Baltimore, he became a member of the N.Y.C. Opera in 1959. On Dec. 8, 1962, he made his Metropolitan Opera debut in N.Y. as Tom in *Un ballo in maschera*, and subsequently appeared there regularly. He also sang with other U.S. opera companies, including those of San Francisco and Chicago. In 1973 he appeared as Debussy's Arkel at the Paris Opéra, in 1974 as Beethoven's Pizzaro at Milan's La Scala, and in 1977 as Mozart's Commendatore at the Salzburg Festival. As a concert artist, he was engaged by many orchs. Among his other roles were Sarastro, Hagen, King Marke, Rocco, Pogner, Sparafucile, and Gounod's Méphistophélès.—NS/LK/DM

Maddy, Joe (actually, **Joseph Edgar**), American music educator and conductor; b. Wellington, Kans., Oct. 14, 1891; d. Traverse City, Mich., April 18, 1966. He received training in violin and clarinet in his youth, and then studied at Bethany Coll., Wichita Coll., and the Columbia School of Music in Chicago. He was a member of the Minneapolis Sym. Orch. (1909–14) and St. Paul Sym. Orch. (1914–18). Maddy was supervisor of instrumental music in the public schools of Rochester, N.Y. (1918–20), and Richmond, Ind. (1920–24), and instructor of public school methods at Earlham Coll. (1922–24). In 1924 he was appointed to the faculty of the Univ. of Mich. as a prof. of music education; in 1926 he founded and conducted the National H.S. Orch., for which he established, with T.P. Giddings, the National Music Camp at Interlochen, Mich., in 1928. In 1962 it became a private high school as the Interlochen Arts Academy.

BIBL.: N. Browning, *J. M. of Interlochen* (Chicago, 1963). —NS/LK/DM

Madeira, Francis, American conductor, pianist, and composer; b. Jenkintown, Pa., Feb. 21, 1917. He received training in piano and conducting at the Juilliard School of Music in N.Y. (1937–43). He was founder-conductor of the R.I. Phil. in Providence, R.I. (1945–80), and also appeared as a pianist in the U.S. and Europe. He composed several symphonic works. In 1957 he married **Jean Madeira** (née **Browning**). —NS/LK/DM

Madeira, Jean (née **Browning**), American mezzo-soprano; b. Centralia, Ill., Nov. 14, 1918; d. Providence, R.I., July 10, 1972. She studied piano with her mother; at the age of 12, she was piano soloist with the St. Louis Sym. Orch. She took vocal lessons in St. Louis, then studied both piano and voice at the Juilliard School of Music in N.Y. In 1943 she made her operatic debut as Nancy in *Martha* in Chautauqua, N.Y. In 1948 she joined the Metropolitan Opera in N.Y., where she sang minor roles. She went to Europe, where she first gained notice as Carmen in Vienna, Aix-en-Provence, and Munich in 1955; also sang Erda at her Covent Garden debut in London that same year. She then returned to the Metropolitan, where she appeared as Carmen on March 17, 1956; she remained on the Metropolitan's roster until 1971. Her European tours included appearances at the Vienna State Opera, the Bavarian State Opera in Munich, Milan's La Scala, the Paris Opéra, and Bayreuth. She married the conductor, pianist, and composer **Francis Madeira** in 1957. —NS/LK/DM

Maderna, Bruno, outstanding Italian-born German conductor, composer, and teacher; b. Venice, April 21, 1920; d. Darmstadt, Nov. 13, 1973. He commenced musical studies at 4, and soon took violin lessons; began touring as a violinist and conductor when he was only 7, appearing under the name Brunetto in Italy and abroad. He studied at the Verdi Cons. in Milan, with Bustini at the Rome Cons. (diploma in composition, 1940), and with Malipiero at the Venice Cons.; also took a conducting course with Guarnieri at the Accademia Musicale Chigiana in Siena (1941). He then served in the Italian army during World War II, eventually joining the partisan forces against the Fascists. After the war, he studied conducting with Scherchen in Darmstadt. He taught composition at the Venice Cons. (1947–50); then made his formal conducting debut in Munich (1950). He subsequently became a great champion of the avant-garde; with Berio, he helped to form the Studio di Fonologia in Milan (1954); also with Berio, he was conductor of the RAI's Incontri Musicali (1956–60). He taught conducting and composition in various venues, including Darmstadt (from 1954), the Salzburg Mozarteum (1967–70), the Rotterdam Cons. (from 1967), and the Berkshire Music Center in Tanglewood (1971–72). He was chief conductor of the RAI in Milan from 1971. In 1963 he became a naturalized German citizen. Stricken with cancer, he continued to conduct concerts as long as it was physically possible. He was held in great esteem by composers of the international avant-garde, several of whom wrote special works for him.

WORKS: DRAMATIC: *Don Perlimplin*, radio opera, after García Lorca (1961; RAI, Aug. 12, 1962); *Hyperion*, "lirica in forma di spettacolo" (Venice, Sept. 6, 1964; a composite of *Dimensioni III, Aria de Hyperion,* and tape); *Von A bis Z*, opera (1969; Darmstadt, Feb. 22, 1970); *Oedipe-Roi*, electronic ballet (Monte Carlo, Dec. 31, 1970); *Satyrikon*, opera after Petronius (1972; Scheveningen, the Netherlands, March 16, 1973). **ORCH.:** *Introduzione e Passacaglia* (1947); Concerto for 2 Pianos, Percussion, and 2 Harps (Venice, Sept. 17, 1948); *Composizioni No. 1* (1949) and *No. 2* for Chamber Orch. (1950); *Improvvisazione I* and *II* (1951, 1952); *Composizioni in 3 tempi* (North German Radio, Hamburg, Dec. 8, 1954); Flute Concerto (1954); *Dark Rapture Crawl* (1957); Piano Concerto (Darmstadt, Sept. 2, 1959); 3 oboe concertos: No. 1 (1962; rev. 1965), No. 2 (West German Radio, Cologne, Nov. 10, 1967), and No. 3 (Amsterdam, July 6, 1973); *Dimensioni III* for Flute and Orch. (Paris Radio, Dec. 12, 1963); *Stele per Diotima* for Orch. (1965; West German Radio, Cologne, Jan. 19, 1966); *Dimensioni IV* (combination of *Dimensioni III* and *Stele per Diotima*); *Amanda* for Chamber Orch. (Naples, Nov. 22, 1966); *Quadrivium* for 4 Percussionists and 4 Orch. Groups (1969); Violin Concerto (Venice, Sept. 12, 1969); *Grande aulodia* for Flute, Oboe, and Orch. (1969; Rome, Feb. 7, 1970); *Juilliard Serenade (Free Time I)* for Chamber Orch. and Tape Sounds (1970; N.Y., Jan. 31, 1971); *Music of Gaiety* for Solo Violin, Oboe, and Chamber Orch., based on pieces in the "Fitzwilliam Virginal Book" (1970); *Aura* (1971; Chicago, March 23, 1972); *Biogramma* (1972); *Giardino religioso* for Chamber Ensemble (Tanglewood, Aug. 8, 1972). **CHAMBER:** *Serenata* for 11 Instruments (1946; rev. 1954); *Musica su 2 dimensioni* for Flute and Tape (1952; rev. 1958); String Quartet (1955); *Serenata No. 2* for 11 Instruments (1957) and *No. 4* for 20 Instruments and Tape (1961); *Honey reves* for Flute and Piano (1961); *Aulodia per Lothar* for Oboe d'Amore and Guitar ad libitum (1965); *Widmung* for Violin (1967); *Serenata per un* *satellite* for 7 Instruments (1969). **P i a n o** : *B- A-C-H Variations* for 2 Pianos (1949). **VOCAL:** *3 Greek Lyrics* for Soprano, Chorus, and Instruments (1948); *Studi per "Il Processo" di Kafka* for Narrator, Soprano, and Small Orch. (1949); *4 Briefe* for Soprano, Bass, and Chamber Orch. (1953); *Aria da "Hyperion"* for Soprano, Flute, and Orch. (1964); *Hyperion II* (combination of *Dimensioni III, Cadenza* for Flute, and *Aria da "Hyperion"*); *Hyperion III* (combination of *Hyperion* and *Stele per Diotima*); *Ausstrahlung* for Soprano, Chorus, and Orch. (1971); *Boswell's Journal* for Tenor and Chamber Orch. (N.Y., March 12, 1972). **ELECTRONIC:** *Notturno* (1955); *Syntaxis* for 4 different but unspecified timbres produced electronically (1956); *Continuo* (1958); *Dimensioni II*, "invenzioni sue una voce" (1960); *Serenata No. 3* (1962); *Le Rire* (1964); *Ages* (1972; in collaboration with G. Pressburger).

BIBL.: M. Baroni and R. Dalmonte, eds., *B. M.: Documenti* (Milan, 1985); R. Fearn, *B. M.* (Chur and N.Y., 1990). **—NS/LK/DM**

Madetoja, Leevi (Antti), outstanding Finnish composer; b. Oulu, Feb. 17, 1887; d. Helsinki, Oct. 6, 1947. He was educated at the Univ. of Helsinki (M.A., 1910) and studied composition with Sibelius at the Helsinki Music Inst. (diploma, 1910). He then took courses with d'Indy in Paris (1910–11) and R. Fuchs in Vienna (1911–12) and in Berlin. After serving as deputy conductor of the Helsinki Phil. (1912–14) and as conductor of the Vyborg Music Soc. Orch. (1914–16), he taught at the Helsinki Music Inst. (1916–38). He was also music critic of the *Helsingen Sanomat* (1916–32), and in 1928 became a lecturer in music at the Univ. of Helsinki. In 1917 he founded the Finnish Musicians' Assn., with which he remained involved until his death. He was awarded a state composer's pension in 1919. He was one of Finland's leading composers; his music for the stage and his symphonic works are particularly notable.

WORKS (all 1ˢᵗ perf in Helsinki): **DRAMATIC: O p - e r a :** *Pohjalaisia* (The Bothnians; 1923; Oct. 25, 1924); *Juha* (1934; Feb. 17, 1935). **B a l l e t - p a n t o m i m e :** *Okon-Fuoko* (Feb. 12, 1930). **ORCH.:** *Symphonic Suite* (Sept. 26, 1910); *Concert Overture* (1911); *Tanssinaky* (Dance Vision; 1911–19); *Kullervo*, symphonic poem (Oct. 14, 1913); 3 syms.: No. 1 (Feb. 10, 1916), No. 2 (Dec. 17, 1918), and No. 3 (April 8, 1926); *Huvinäytelmäalkusoitto* (Comedy Overture; April 12, 1923). **CHAMBER:** Trio for Violin, Cello, and Piano (1910); Violin Sonatina (1913); *Lyric Suite* for Cello and Piano (1922); piano pieces, including the suite *Kuoleman puutarha* (Garden of Death; 1919). **VOCAL:** Much choral music; many songs.

BIBL.: K. Tuukkanen, *L. M.* (Helsinki, 1947); *L. M.: Teokset—Works* (1982); K. Karjalainen, *L. M. oopperat Pohjalaisia ja Juha: Teokset, tekstit ja kontekstit* (Helsinki, 1993).**—NS/LK/DM**

Madey, Bogusław, Polish conductor and composer; b. Sosnowiec, May 31, 1932. He received diplomas in composition, piano, and conducting from the Academy of Music in Poznan, then went to England, where he took a course in conducting with Norman del Mar at the Guildhall School of Music in London (1959–60). Returning to Poland, he was a conductor at the Warsaw Opera (1960–72) and later music director at the Grand Theater of Opera and Ballet in Łódz (1972–77). In 1982 he became artistic director of the

Baltic Phil. in Gdańsk. He composed a Piano Concerto (1957), Flute Concerto (1960), a concerto for Voice and Instruments entitled *Transfiguration* (1965), and some short piano pieces.**—NS/LK/DM**

Madge, Geoffrey Douglas, extraordinary Australian pianist; b. Adelaide, Oct. 3, 1941. He studied with Clemens Leski at the Elder Cons. of the Univ. of Adelaide (graduated, 1959), with Géza Anda in Switzerland (1964), and with Peter Solymos in Hungary (1967). He taught at the Royal Cons. of Music in The Hague from 1971. Madge's outstanding technical resources make him an ideal interpreter of the most formidable avant-garde scores. His repertoire ranges from Barraqué to Wyschnegradsky among the moderns; he performs standard works as well.**—NS/LK/DM**

Madonna (Louise Ciccone), personified the 1980s emphasis on artifice and attitude over content and commitment, and was the first music act to achieve mainstream popularity thanks to regular and frequent exposure of her music videos on cable television's MTV network; b. Bay City, Mich., Aug. 16, 1958. Her lavish videos, usually produced by movie directors, and her carefree party sound, clearly derived from disco music, reinforced the rise of a fashionable club scene based on dancing and dress, and opened the door for the success of video-dance artists such as Paula Abdul. Although exhibiting only a modicum of talent for singing, songwriting, and dancing, Madonna became the most conspicuous and commercially successful recording act of the 1980s and 1990s.

Madonna initially appealed largely to an impressionable adolescent female audience. Inspiring a fashion trend based on lace, bare midriffs, and undergarments worn as outerwear, Madonna titillated, intrigued, and outraged adults and critics unused to a strong, if superficial, female personality. Her regular changes in physical appearance invited comparisons to the periodic image shifts of David Bowie, and her puerile, voyeuristic sense of sexuality was compared with that of Prince. Additionally, Madonna projected a set of seemingly contradictory images (slut/goddess, boy-toy/dominatrix, narcissist/romantic) that confounded the media and enticed fans outside of music to follow her exploits. Madonna repeatedly fostered public controversy, whether calculated or incidental, while transcending the confines of pop music and transforming herself into an international celebrity.

Madonna dropped out of the Univ. of Mich.'s dance department to move to N.Y. in 1978, where she briefly worked with the Alvin Ailey Dance Company. She later met Dan Gilroy in France, forming the club band the Breakfast Club with him on their return to N.Y. She subsequently formed Emmy with drummer Steve Bray, and was "discovered" by nightclub disc jockey Mark Kamins, who produced her club hit "Everybody" in 1982. Signed to Sire Records, Madonna scored her first major hit with "Holiday," written and produced by John "Jellybean" Benitez. Her debut album, which remained on the album charts for more than three years, also yielded a near-smash hit, "Borderline," and the smash "Lucky Star."

In late 1984 Madonna broke through with her *Like a Virgin*, which stayed on the album charts for more than two years and sold seven million copies in the United States. The title song, written by Tom Kelly and Billy Steinberg, became a top pop and near-smash R&B hit. It was promoted through the first of a series of engaging and provocative videos popularized by the cable television network MTV. The album, produced by Chic's Nile Rodgers, featured scratchy guitar, swirling keyboards, and infectious dance rhythms, yielding smash hits with "Material Girl," "Angel," and "Dress You Up." The album and videos quickly established Madonna's image as an aggressive, spoiled, and slightly decadent chanteuse. She appeared in a cameo role in the 1985 movie *Vision Quest*; the soundtrack album produced her top hit "Crazy for You." Madonna broke through as an actress later that year in the film *Desperately Seeking Susan*, portraying an amoral, unconventional, hard-living rebel opposite Rosanna Arquette.

International celebrity quickly followed, as Madonna appeared on the cover of *Time* magazine in May 1985, performed at Live Aid in July, and married actor Sean Penn in August. Her public exposure and offbeat reputation were enhanced with the publication of nude photographs in *Playboy* and *Penthouse* magazines and the rerelease of her 1980 sleaze movie *A Certain Sacrifice*. Madonna's *True Blue* album yielded a top pop and easy-listening hit with "Live to Tell"; top pop hits with "Open Your Heart" and the simplistic yet controversial "Papa Don't Preach"; and the smashes "True Blue" and "La Isla Bonita," another top easy-listening hit. However, her next two endeavors, the films *Shanghai Surprise* (with husband Sean Penn) and *Who's That Girl*, failed critically and commercially, although the *Who's That Girl* soundtrack featured four new Madonna songs, including the top hit title song and the smash hit "Causing a Commotion." In late 1987 seven extended remixes of her dance hits were released as *You Can Dance*.

Madonna's tour in support of *Who's That Girl* showcased carefully prepared staging and choreography. She remained in the public eye through cover appearances on *Life* and *Vanity Fair*, introducing her new image as a glamour queen. In January 1989 Madonna signed a $5 million deal to globally promote Pepsi Cola with an elaborate two-minute commercial, but the advertisement, based on the video for the song "Like a Prayer," was withdrawn within two months of its debut in March. Viewers had apparently confused the commercial with the top hit single and video "Like a Prayer," which portrayed Catholic beliefs in what some viewed as a sacrilegious light. The resulting publicity helped make the album of the same name, coproduced with new collaborator Patrick Leonard, an international bestseller.

Ostensibly showing a more honest and mature side of Madonna, *Like a Prayer* represented a bid for critical acceptance among young adults rather than teenagers. The album included two songs concerned with the tenets of the Catholic religion, "Like a Prayer" and "Act of Contrition," and three songs concerned with family relationships: "Till Death Do Us Part," "Promises to Try," and "Oh Father," a major hit. Featuring a sultry duet with Prince on "Love Song," the album yielded smash hits with "Express Yourself" and "Cherish" (a top easy-listening hit), and a major hit with "Keep It Together." Madonna's performances in David Mamet's Broadway play *Speed the Plow* had drawn favorable reviews in May, but the movie *Bloodhounds of Broadway*, based on characters created by Damon Runyon, quickly failed at the box office upon release at year's end.

The year 1990 proved to be the most successful year of Madonna's career. Her "Vogue" dance video/single capitalized on the Manhattan posing-style dance trend and became a top hit. From April through August she conducted her worldwide Blond Ambition tour, which featured extravagant costuming, spectacular staging, and tight choreography. Madonna costarred with Warren Beatty in the popular movie *Dick Tracy* and released the album *I'm Breathless: Music from and Inspired by the Film Dick Tracy*, which contained "Vogue" and "Hanky Panky," a near-smash hit, as well as three songs written by Broadway master Stephen Sondheim: "Move," "Sooner or Later," and, in duet with Mandy Patinkin, "What You Can Lose." Near year's end the rap-style song "Justify My Love," cowritten with Lenny Kravitz, became a top hit, but the attendant video became the first by a major artist to be banned from airplay by MTV. Produced by Madonna and Shep Pettibone, "Justify My Love" and the near-smash "Rescue Me" were included on the anthology *The Immaculate Collection*; the album remained on the album charts for more than two years.

However, several Italian Catholic organizations subsequently sought to ban Madonna's performances as vulgar and blasphemous. The banishment of her "Justify My Love" video became international news when ABC-TV interviewed her and played the video on *Nightline*. Additionally, one of her remixes of "Justify My Love," "The Beast Within," was attacked as anti-Semitic by the Simon Wiesenthal Center in Los Angeles.

Appearing on the covers of *Glamour*, *Entertainment Weekly*, and, later, *Vanity Fair*, Madonna granted the gay-oriented magazine *Advocate* a lengthy candid interview in May 1991. That same month the tour documentary *Truth or Dare*, taken from her Blond Ambition tour, opened to brisk business in limited release, despite attacks that the film was unabashedly narcissistic, flagrantly exhibitionist, and artificially spontaneous.

In April 1992 Madonna signed a seven-year agreement with Time-Warner, the parent company of Sire Records. Worth a reported $60 million, the deal enabled her to establish her own multimedia entertainment company, named Maverick. One of the most lucrative contracts offered to a pop star, the deal was unprecedented in its value and magnitude for a female performer. In September she appeared topless at a Paris fashion show, and the following month she appeared nude in *Vanity Fair* as part of a massive campaign to promote her *Erotica* album and *Sex* picture book, her first efforts for Maverick. Returning to her disco sound and embracing the style of rap music, the album was comprised largely of songs written by Madonna and producer Pettibone. It included her celebration of oral sex, "Where Life Begins," and yielded the smash hit "Erotica," the near-smash "Deeper and Deeper," the major hit "Rain," and the moderate hit "Bad Girl." The tawdry, amateurish book *Sex* featured Madonna posing with a variety of sex partners in an apparent explication of her sexual fantasies.

Both *Erotica* and *Sex* were greeted by a harsh critical backlash, a situation exacerbated by the early 1993 release of the grim movie *Body of Evidence*, which was regarded by at least one critic as one of the worst movies ever made; in less than six months the film was available on videocassette. Madonna subsequently toured internationally with her Girlie Show tour in the fall. Performances featured scantily clad and topless dancers, sometimes simulating sexual acts, and provoked controversy in Puerto Rico and Germany. In March 1994 Madonna appeared on the *David Letterman* late-night television show, shocking viewers and her host with her frequent use of four-letter words. She later appeared in the equivocal film *Dangerous*, with Harvey Keitel.

Madonna deemphasized the feigned eroticism of her music with 1994's R&B–styled *Bedtime Stories*, cut with coproducer Shep Pettibone. The album yielded a smash hit with "Secret" and a top hit with "Take a Bow." In November the Fox cable network broadcast a biographical movie based on her early career. In 1995 Madonna canceled her tour in support of *Bedtime Stories* to work on the film musical *Evita*, based on the life of Eva Perón, the wife of Argentine dictator Juan Perón.

DISC.: *The Early Years* (1995); *M.* (1983); *Like a Virgin* (1984); *True Blue* (1986); *Who's That Girl* (soundtrack; 1987); *You Can Dance* (1987); *Like a Prayer* (1989); *I'm Breathless* (1990); *The Immaculate Collection* (1990); *The Royal Box* (1991); *Erotica* (1992); *Bedtime Stories* (1994); *Something to Remember* (1995); *Evita* (soundtrack; 1996); *Ray of Light* (1998); *Music* (2000).

BIBL.: Debbvi Voller, *M.: The New Illustrated Biography* (London, 1990); Marie Cahill, *M.* (London, 1991); Christopher Anderson, *M. Unauthorized* (N.Y., 1991); Douglas Thompson, *Like a Virgin: M. Revealed* (London, 1992).—**BH**

Maegaard, Jan (Carl Christian), Danish musicologist and composer; b. Copenhagen, April 14, 1926. He studied at the Royal Danish Cons. of Music in Copenhagen (teacher's diploma in theory and music history, 1953), at the Univ. of Copenhagen (M.A., 1957; Ph.D., 1972, with the diss. *Studien zur Entwicklung des dodekaphonen Satzes bei Arnold Schönberg*; publ. in Copenhagen, 1972), and at the Univ. of Calif. at Los Angeles (1958–59). After teaching at the Royal Danish Cons. of Music (1953–58), he joined the faculty of the Univ. of Copenhagen in 1959, where he was an assoc. prof. (1961–71) and prof. (1971–96). He also was a visiting prof. at the State Univ. of N.Y. at Stony Brook (1974) and prof. of music at the Univ. of Calif. at Los Angeles (1978–81). In 1986 he was made a member of the Royal Danish Academy of Sciences and Letters, and in 1988 a member of the Norwegian Academy of Science and Letters. As a composer, Maegaard has explored a wide range of styles, from tonal to serial.

WRITINGS (all publ. in Copenhagen): *Musikalsk Modernisme* (1964; 2nd. ed., 1971); *Praeludier til Musik af Schönberg* (1976);

Indføring i Romantisk Harmonik (2 vols., 1980, 1986; vol. I with T. Larsen); ed. *Musikalsk analyse efter Forte-metoden* (1988); with G. Busk, *Kuhlau: Kanons* (1996).

WORKS: DRAMATIC: *Don Quixote*, incidental music (1949); *Den hvide souper*, music for a radio play (1954); *Antigone*, incidental music (1966). **ORCH.:** 2 chamber concertos (1949; 1961–62); March for Strings (1956); *Due tempi* (1961); *Marineforeningens jubilaeumsmarch* for Military Orch. (1963); *Danmark trofast* (1971; also for Tenor and Piano); *De profundis* (1976; also for Men's Chorus and Piano); March for Military Orch. (1980); *Triptykon* for Violin and Strings (1984); *Sinfonietta* for Strings (1986); Cello Concerto (1994); *Jeu mosaïque* for Harp and Orch. (1995). **CHAMBER:** Suite for Violin and Piano (1949); Trio for Flute, Clarinet, and Bassoon (1950); Wind Quintet (1951); Suite for 2 Violins (1951); *Quasi una sonata* for Viola and Piano (1952); Bassoon Sonata (1952); *Variations impromptus* for Violin, Viola, Cello, and Piano (1953); *Fem praeludier* for Violin (1956); *O alter Duft aus Märchenzeit*, trio-serenade for Violin, Cello, and Piano (1960); *Octomeri* for Violin and Piano (1962); *ISCM Fanfare* for 4 Trombones (1964); *Movimento* for Clarinet, Horn, String Quartet, Percussion, and Hammond Organ (1967); *Musica riservata No. 1* for String Quartet (1970), *No. 2* for Oboe, Clarinet, Bassoon, and Saxophone (1976), and *No. 3* for Flute, Oboe, Cello, and Harpsichord (1982); *Pastorale* for 2 Clarinets (1976); Canon for 3 Flutes (1980); *Labirinto I* for Viola (1986) and *II* for Guitar (1987); Duo Phantasy for 2 Guitars (1988); *Double* for Cello (1988); *Pierrot in the Ball Room* for 2 Guitars (1988); *Kinderblicke* for Guitar (1989); *Preludio notturno d'estate e contrappunto fugato* for 2 Flutes, String Quartet, and Piano, 4–Hands (1991); *Progressive variationer* for Violin and Cello (1993). **KEYBOARD: Piano:** *Koncertetude/Passacaglia* (1949); Sonata (1955); *5 pezzi* (1959); *Danse til Marina* (1975). **Organ:** *Tre orgelkoraler* (1954); *Aus tiefer Not* (1956); *Tre orgelkoraler* (1969); *Passacaglia-fantasia-choral* (1981); *Fantasia: Indsigter—udsigter* (1983). **VOCAL:** *Pigens møde med Pan* for Soprano, Flute, Clarinet, and Piano (1947); *Legend* for Soprano, Violin, and Piano (1949); *Den gyldne harpe* for Mezzo-soprano, Oboe, Cello, and Piano (1952); *G'a udenom sletterne* for Chorus and String Orch. (1953); *Jaevndøgnselegi* (Elegy of Equinox) for Soprano, Cello, and Organ (1955); *Sic enim amavit*, motet for Chorus or Soprano, Trumpet, and Organ (1969); *Liebeslied* for Alto and 2 Guitars (1990); *Te Deum* for 2 Choruses, Children's Chorus, and Organ (1992); many other choral pieces and songs. **OTHER:** Cadenzas; orchestrations; arrangements.—**NS/LK/DM**

Maelzel, Johannes Nepomuk, German inventor; b. Regensburg, Aug. 15, 1772; d. on board the brig Otis in the harbor of La Guiara, Venezuela, en route to Philadelphia, July 21, 1838. He studied music with his father, an organ manufacturer. In 1792 he went to Vienna, where he began constructing mechanical instruments, which attracted great attention there and subsequently in other European cities; of these, the Panharmonicon, exhibited in Vienna in 1804, was particularly effective. He then purchased the "automatic chess player," which he claimed was his invention; in fact it was designed and built by Wolfgang von Kempelen. He was able to impress the public by his "scientific" miracle, but it was soon exposed by skeptical observers, among them Edgar Allan Poe, as an ingenious mechanical contrivance concealing a diminutive chess master behind its gears. He subsequently invented the automatic trumpeter, displaying it and a new version of the Panharmonicon in his Kunstabinet in 1812. In 1816 he constructed the metronome, the idea for which he obtained from Winkel of Amsterdam, who had exhibited similar instruments, but without the scale divisions indicating the number of beats per minute. Maelzel put the metronome on the market, despite a lawsuit brought by Winkel, and the initial of his last name was thenceforth added to the indication of tempo in musical compositions (M.M., Maelzel's metronome). Beethoven wrote a piece for the Panharmonicon, which he subsequently orchestrated and publ. as *Wellington's Victory*. After Maelzel declared that the composition was his property, Beethoven sued him in the Viennese courts, but nothing ever came from his legal action.

BIBL.: C. Carroll, *The Great Chess Automaton* (N.Y., 1975).
—NS/LK/DM

Maes, Jef, Belgian composer; b. Antwerp, April 5, 1905. He studied with N. Distelmans (viola), L. Mortelmans (chamber music), and Karl Candael (harmony, counterpoint, and fugue) at Antwerp's Royal Flemish Cons. of Music. He was a violist in several orchs. in Antwerp, and became a teacher of viola (1932) and director (1952) of the Boom Academy of Music. From 1942 to 1970 he was on the faculty of the Royal Flemish Cons. In his compositions, Maes continues the traditions of the Belgian national school.

WORKS: DRAMATIC: *Marise*, opera bugga (1946); *De antikwaar* (The Antique Dealer), television opera (1959; Antwerp TV, March 1963); *Tu auras nom...Tristan*, ballet (1960; Geneva, June 1963; orch. suite, 1963–64). **ORCH.:** *3 rythmen in dansvorm* (1931); *Légende* for Violin and Orch. (1933); Viola Concerto (1937); *Concertstück* (1938); *Ouvertura buffa* (1939); *Concertstück* for Trombone and Orch. (1944); Piano Concerto (1948); Violin Concerto (1951); 3 syms. (1953, 1965, 1975); Concerto for Harpsichord and Strings (1955); *Burlesque* for Bassoon and Orch. (1957); *Kempische Suite* for Orch. or Wind Orch. (1960); *Concertante ouverture* (1961); *Arabesque en scherzo* for Flute and Orch. (1963); *Praeludium, Pantomime, Scherzo*, suite (1966); *Partita* for Strings (1966); *Ouverture op een Belcanto Thema van Verdi* for Orch. or Wind Orch. (1967); *De verloofden* (1969); *Music pour le podium* for Wind Orch. (1971); *Dialogue* for Violin and Orch. (1972); *Intrada* (1980). **CHAMBER:** Sonatina for Flute and Viola (1934); Violin Sonata (1934); *Concertstück* for Trumpet and Piano (1957); *Prelude and Allegro* for 2 Trumpets, Horn, Trombone, and Tuba (1959); *Fantasia* for 2 Pianos (1960); Duo for Violin and Piano (1962); Trio for Violin, Viola, and Percussion (1964); *4 contrastes* for 4 Clarinets (1965); Suite for Percussion and Piano (1968); Piano Quartet (1970); *Studie* for Violin (1978); *Saxo-scope* for Saxophone Quartet (1979); *Adagio en allegretto* for Violin and Piano (1985). **VOCAL:** *Rosa mystica* for Soprano and Orch. or Piano (1959); *Mei 1871* for Narrator and Orch. (1971); choruses; songs.—NS/LK/DM

Maessens, Pieter, Flemish composer; b. Ghent, c. 1505; d. Vienna, Oct. 1563. He was a choirboy in the chapel of the Archduchess Margaret of Austria. Following univ. studies, he was active as a soldier of fortune with the armies of Charles V and the King of Spain. In 1529 he took part in the relief of Vienna, and in 1535 he was rewarded for bravery by the Emperor. In 1538 he served with the Spanish Army in Flanders. In 1539 he received minor orders in the priesthood in Tournai, and in 1540 he was made Kapellmeister of the chapter of Notre Dame in Courtrai. In 1543 he became 2nd Kapellmeister at the court chapel in Vienna, serving as its Kapellmeister from 1546. He was ennobled by Emperor Ferdinand I and took the name von Massenberg. Maessens composed much sacred and secular vocal music.
—LK/DM

Magalhâes, Filipe, important Portuguese composer; b. Azeitao, near Evora, c. 1571; d. Lisbon, Dec. 17, 1652. He studied with Manuel Mendes at the Evora Cathedral cloister school, where he became a singer; then joined Lisbon's royal chapel choir (1602), serving as its master from 1623 until 1641. He was one of the foremost masters of Portuguese music of his era.

WORKS: *Cantus ecclesiasticus commendandi animas corporaque* for 3 to 5 Voices (Lisbon, 1614; 3rd ed., 1691, as *Cantum ecclesiasticum*); *Missarum liber cum antiphonis domincalibus in principio, et motetto pro defunctis* for 4 to 6 Voices (Lisbon, 1636); *Cantica beatissimae virginis* (Lisbon, 1636); *Domine, probasti me* for Voices (n.d.).—NS/LK/DM

Magaloff, Nikita, distinguished Russian-born Swiss pianist and teacher; b. St. Petersburg, Feb. 21, 1912; d. Vevey, Dec. 26, 1992. His family left Russia after the Revolution. He enrolled in the Paris Cons. as a student of Isidor Philipp, graduating with a premier prix at the age of 17. He also studied composition with Prokofiev in Paris. In 1939 he settled in Switzerland, and in 1947 made his first American tour; also toured Europe, South America, South Africa, etc. From 1949 to 1960 he taught piano at the Geneva Cons., then gave summer courses at Taormina, Sicily, and at the Accademia Musicale Chigiana in Siena. In 1956 he became a naturalized Swiss citizen. He was renowned for his lyrico-dramatic interpretations of Chopin, with lapidary attention to detail. He was also a composer, numbering among his works a Piano Toccata, Violin Sonatina, songs, and cadenzas for Mozart's piano concertos. He was the son-in-law of **Joseph Szigeti.**—NS/LK/DM

Maganini, Quinto, American flutist, conductor, arranger, and composer; b. Fairfield, Calif., Nov. 30, 1897; d. Greenwich, Conn., March 10, 1974. He played flute in the San Francisco Sym. (1917–19) and in the N.Y. Sym. (1919–28). He studied flute with Barrère in N.Y. and composition with Boulanger at the American Cons. in Fontainebleau. In 1928–29 he held a Guggenheim fellowship. In 1930 he became conductor of the N.Y. Sinfonietta. In 1932 he organized his own orch., the Maganini Chamber Sym., with which he toured widely. From 1939 to 1970 he was conductor of the Norwalk (Conn.) Sym. Orch.

WORKS: *Toulumne*, "a Californian Rhapsody," for Orch., with Trumpet obbligato (N.Y., Aug. 9, 1924); *South Wind*, orch. fantasy (N.Y., April 7, 1931); *Sylvan Symphony* (N.Y., Nov. 30, 1932); *Napoleon*, orch. portrait (N.Y., Nov. 10, 1935); *The Royal Ladies*, orch. suite on airs ascribed to Marie Antoinette (Greenwich, Conn., Feb. 3, 1940); *Tennessee's Partner*, opera (WOR Radio, N.Y., May 28, 1942); numerous arrangements for small orch. of classical and modern works.—NS/LK/DM

Mager, Jörg, German music theorist and pioneer in electronic music; b. Eichstätt, Nov. 6, 1880; d. Aschaffenburg, April 5, 1939. After completing his univ. studies, he became interested in electronic reproduction of sounds; constructed several instruments capable of producing microtonal intervals by electronic means, which he named Sphärophon, Elektrophon, and Partiturophon; he was also active in visual music for film. He publ. *Vierteltonmusik* (Aschaffenburg, 1916) and *Eine neue Epoche der Musik durch Radio* (Berlin, 1924). —NS/LK/DM

Maggini, Gio(vanni) Paolo, important Italian instrument maker; b. Brescia (baptized), Nov. 29, 1579; d. there, c. 1630. He worked in the shop of Gasparo da Salo. After his marriage in 1615, he set up his own workshop and became prosperous, thanks to the excellence of his manufacture. His instruments are highly prized; among his extant instruments are violins, violas, cellos, basses, various examples of the viol family, and citterns. His label reads: Gio. Paolo Maggini, Brescia.

BIBL.: M. Huggins, *Gio P. M., His Life and Work* (London, 1892); A. Berenzi, *Di Gio P. M.* (Cremona, 1907).—NS/LK/DM

Magini-Coletti, Antonio, Italian baritone; b. Iesi, near Ancona, 1855; d. Rome, July 7, 1912. He launched his career in 1880, and subsequently appeared in various Italian operatic centers, including Milan and Rome. On Dec. 14, 1891, he made his Metropolitan Opera debut in N.Y. as Capulet in *Roméo et Juliette,* singing there until 1892. In subsequent years, he pursued his career in Europe. Among his other roles were Nevers and Amonasro.—NS/LK/DM

Magnard, (Lucien-Denis-Gabriel), Albéric, distinguished French composer; b. Paris, June 9, 1865; d. (killed by German soldiers at his home) Baron, Oise, Sept. 3, 1914. He was born into an intellectual family of means, his father being the publishing director of *Le Figaro.* He pursued training in law (graduated, 1887) and was a student at the Paris Cons., where he studied counterpoint with Dubois and attended the classes of Massenet (premier prix in harmony, 1888). He completed his training with d'Indy (1888–92), mastering fugue and orchestration. In 1896 he became a tutor in counterpoint at the Schola Cantorum in Paris. Magnard was an early victim of World War I. When a German cavalry detachment entered his estate, he opened fire upon it and killed at least one soldier. The detachment returned his fire and then torched his home. Magnard, as well as a number of his MSS, perished in the conflagration. He was a composer of discernment and a master of orchestration. His 3rd and 4th syms. are remarkable for their dramatic power and rhapsodic sweep.

WORKS: O p e r a : *Yolande* (1888–91; Brussels, Dec. 27, 1892); *Guercoeur* (1897–1900; orch. partially reconstructed by G. Ropartz; Paris, April 24, 1931); *Bérénice* (1905–09; Paris, Dec. 15, 1911). **ORCH.:** *Suite d'orchestre dans le style ancien* (1888; rev. 1889); 4 syms.: No. 1 (1889–90; Paris, April 18, 1891), No. 2 (1892–93; rev. version, Nancy, Feb. 9, 1896), No. 3 (1895–96; Paris, May 18, 1899), and No. 4 (1911–13; Paris, May 16, 1914); *Ouverture* (1894–95); *Chant funèbre* (1895); *Hymne à la justice* (1902); *Hymne à Vénus* (1903–04). **CHAMBER:** Piano Quintet (1894); Violin Sonata (1901); String Quartet (1902–03); Piano

Trio (1904–05); Cello Sonata (1909–10). **P i a n o :** *3 Pièces* (1887–88); *Promenades* (1893); *Pièces, En Dieu mon espérance et mon espée pour ma défense* (1889). **VOCAL:** *6 Poèmes* (1887–90); *A Henriette* (1890 or 1891); *4 Poèmes en musique* (1902); *12 Poèmes* (1913–14).

BIBL.: R. Barres, *Une défense heroïque: La mort d'A. M.* (Paris, 1915); M. Boucher, *A. M.* (Lyons, 1919); C. Carraud, *La Vie, l'oeuvre et la mort d'A. M.* (Paris, 1921); B. Bardet, *A. M., 1865–1914* (Paris, 1966).—NS/LK/DM

Magne, Michel, French composer; b. Lisieux, March 20, 1930; d. (suicide) Cergy-Pontase, Val d'Oise, Dec. 19, 1984. He was mainly self-taught, beginning to compose as a very young man in an ultramodern style; later took lessons with Plé-Caussade. His film score *Le Pain vivant* (1955) received critical acclaim, and he also experimented with electronic music. On May 26, 1955, he conducted in Paris his *Symphonie humaine* for 150 Performers, making use of inaudible "infrasounds" to produce a physiological reaction by powerful low frequencies. He wrote the musical score for Françoise Sagan's ballet *Le Rendez-vous manqué* (1957) and many film scores.—NS/LK/DM

Magomayev, (Abdul) Muslim, Azerbaijani conductor and composer; b. Shusha, Sept. 18, 1885; d. Baku, July 28, 1937. He studied at the Gori teachers' seminary (1899–1904), and learned to play violin and clarinet. He taught at Lenkoran Coll. (1905–11), then settled in Baku as an orch. player, conductor, and teacher at the Azerbaijani Theater. Later he was associated with the National Commissariat of Enlightenment, becoming artistic director and conductor of the musical theater (1924); was music director of the Azerbaijani Radio (from 1929). The first version of his opera *Shah Ismail* (1916; Baku, 1919) was mainly made up of improvised songs and dialogue; he later revised it with notated improvisatory sections and added recitatives (1920–23; 1930–32). His second opera, *Nergiz* (1934; Baku, Jan. 1, 1936), was fully notated. He also wrote orch. pieces, incidental music, film scores, and numerous arrangements of folk songs and dances.

BIBL.: G. Ismailova, *M. M.* (Baku, 1975).—NS/LK/DM

Mahaut, Antoine, Netherlands flutist and composer; b. c. 1720; d. c. 1785. He was active in Amsterdam from about 1737, and also made visits to Paris and Dresden. About 1760 he fled his creditors in Amsterdam, and settled in a French monastery. Mahaut excelled as a composer of symphonies and works for the flute, and also publ. a valuable flute method, *Nieuwe manier om binnen korten tijd de dwarsfluit te leeren speelen- ...nieuwe druk* (Amsterdam, 1759; Fr. tr., 1759).—LK/DM

Mahillon, Charles (-Borromée), Belgian manufacturer of wind instruments; b. Brussels, Nov. 4, 1814; d. Molenbeek-St.-Jean, Sept. 4, 1887. He received his training as an instrument maker in England, then organized his own firm in Brussels (1836), where he became esteemed as a manufacturer of clarinets. His son Victor-Charles Mahillon (b. Brussels, March 10, 1841; d.

St. Jean, Cap Ferrat, June 17, 1924) worked in his father's shop as a youth; pursued a diligent study of acoustics and publ. the periodical *L'Echo Musical* (1869–87). Upon his father's death, he took charge of the firm. He also served as curator of the Brussels Cons. Instrument Museum (from 1876), enlarging its collection from his own holdings. He publ. *Les Éléments d'acoustique musicale et instrumentale* (Brussels, 1874), *Catalogue descriptif et analytique du Musée instrumental du Conservatoire royal de musique de Bruxelles* (Ghent, 1880–1922), *Le Matériel sonore des orchestres de symphonie, d'harmonie et de fanfares, ou Vade mecum du compositeur* (Brussels, 1897; 5th ed., 1920), *Instruments à vent* (Brussels, 1906–07), *Notes théoriques et pratiques sur la résonance des colonnes d'air dans les tuyaux de la facture instrumentale* (St. Jean, Cap Ferrat, 1921), etc. His brother, Fernand Mahillon (b. Brussels, March 3, 1866; d. there, March 6, 1948), ran the London branch of the firm for some 30 years, and upon Victor-Charles's death took control of the firm, turning it over to J.A. Smits in 1936. It ceased making wind instruments in 1935.—NS/LK/DM

Mahler, Gustav, great Austrian composer and conductor; b. Kalischt, Bohemia, July 7, 1860; d. Vienna, May 18, 1911. He attended school in Iglau. In 1875 he entered the Vienna Cons., where he studied piano with Julius Epstein, harmony with Robert Fuchs, and composition with Franz Krenn. He also took academic courses in history and philosophy at the Univ. of Vienna (1877–80). In the summer of 1880 he received his first engagement as a conductor, at the operetta theater in the town of Hall in Upper Austria. He subsequently he held posts as theater conductor at Ljubljana (1881), Olmütz (1882), Vienna (1883), and Kassel (1883–85). In 1885 he served as 2nd Kapellmeister to Anton Seidl at the Prague Opera, where he gave several performances of Wagner's operas. From 1886 to 1888 he was assistant to Arthur Nikisch in Leipzig. In 1888 he received the important appointment of music director of the Royal Opera in Budapest. In 1891 he was engaged as conductor at the Hamburg Opera; during his tenure there, he developed a consummate technique for conducting. In 1897 he received a tentative offer as music director of the Vienna Court Opera, but there was an obstacle to overcome. Mahler was Jewish, and although there was no overt anti-Semitism in the Austrian government, an imperial appointment could not be given to a Jew. Mahler was never orthodox in his religion, and had no difficulty in converting to Catholicism, which was the prevailing faith in Austria. He held this position at the Vienna Court Opera for 10 years; under his guidance, it reached the highest standards of artistic excellence. In 1898 Mahler was engaged to succeed Hans Richter as conductor of the Vienna Phil. Here, as in his direction of opera, he proved a great interpreter, but he also allowed himself considerable freedom in rearranging the orchestration of classical scores when he felt it would redound to greater effect. He also aroused antagonism among the players by his autocratic behavior toward them. He resigned from the Vienna Phil. in 1901; in 1907 he also resigned from the Vienna Court Opera. It was in the latter year that he was diagnosed as suffering from a lesion of the heart. In the meantime, he became im-

mersed in strenuous work as a composer; he confined himself exclusively to composition of symphonic music, sometimes with vocal parts; because of his busy schedule as conductor, he could compose only in the summer months, in a villa on the Worthersee in Carinthia. In 1902 he married Alma Schindler; they had 2 daughters. The younger daughter, Anna Mahler, was briefly married to Ernst Krenek; the elder daughter died at the age of 5. Alma Mahler studied music with Zemlinsky, who was the brother-in-law of Arnold Schoenberg.

Having exhausted his opportunities in Vienna, Mahler accepted the post of principal conductor of the Metropolitan Opera in N.Y. in 1907. He made his U.S. debut there on Jan. 1, 1908, conducting *Tristan und Isolde*. In 1909 he was appointed conductor of the N.Y. Phil. His initial appearances at the Metropolitan Opera and with the N.Y. Phil. were generally well received by both audiences and critics, but inevitably he had conflicts with the board of trustees in both organizations, which were mostly commanded by rich women. He resigned from the Metropolitan Opera in 1910. On Feb. 21, 1911, he conducted his last concert with the N.Y. Phil. and then returned to Vienna. The N.Y. newspapers publ. lurid accounts of his struggle for artistic command with the regimen of the women of the governing committee. Alma Mahler was quoted as saying that although in Vienna even the Emperor did not dare to order Mahler about, in N.Y. he had to submit to the whims of 10 ignorant women. The newspaper editorials mourned Mahler's death, but sadly noted that his N.Y. tenure was a failure. As to Mahler's own compositions, the *N.Y. Tribune* said bluntly, "We cannot see how any of his music can long survive him." His syms. were sharply condemned in the press as being too long, too loud, and too discordant. It was not until the second half of the 20th century that Mahler became fully recognized as a composer, the last great Romantic symphonist. Mahler's syms. were drawn on the grandest scale, and the technical means employed for the realization of his ideas were correspondingly elaborate. The sources of his inspiration were twofold: the lofty concepts of universal art, akin to those of Bruckner, and ultimately stemming from Wagner; and the simple folk melos of the Austrian countryside, in pastoral moods recalling the intimate episodes in Beethoven's syms. True to his Romantic nature, Mahler attached descriptive titles to his syms.; the 1st was named the *Titan*; the 2nd, *Resurrection*; the 3rd, *Ein Sommermorgentraum*; and the 5th, *The Giant*. The great 8th became known as "sym. of a thousand" because it required about 1,000 instrumentalists, vocalists, and soloists for performance; however, this sobriquet was the inspiration of Mahler's agent, not of Mahler himself. Later in life, Mahler tried to disassociate his works from their programmatic titles; he even claimed that he never used them in the first place, contradicting the evidence of the MSS, in which the titles appear in Mahler's own handwriting. Mahler was not an innovator in his harmonic writing; rather, he brought the Romantic era to a culmination by virtue of the expansiveness of his emotional expression and the grandiose design of his musical structures. Morbid by nature, he brooded upon the inevitability of death; one of his most poignant compositions was the cycle for voice and orch. *Kindertotenlieder*; he wrote it shortly before the death of his little daughter, and somehow he blamed himself for this seeming anticipation of his personal tragedy. In 1910 he consulted Sigmund Freud in Leiden, Holland, but the treatment was brief and apparently did not help Mahler to resolve his psychological problems. Unquestionably, he suffered from an irrational feeling of guilt. In the 3rd movement of his unfinished 10th Sym., significantly titled *Purgatorio*, he wrote on the margin, "Madness seizes me, annihilates me," and appealed to the Devil to take possession of his soul. But he never was clinically insane. His already weakened heart could not withstand the onslaught of a severe bacterial infection of the blood, and he died at the lamentable age of 50.

Mahler's importance to the evolution of modern music is very great; the early works of Schoenberg and Berg show the influence of Mahler's concepts. An International Gustav Mahler Soc. was formed in Vienna in 1955, with Bruno Walter as honorary president.

WORKS: SYMS.: No. 1, in D, *Titan* (1883–88; Budapest, Nov. 20, 1889, composer conducting; a rejected movement, entitled *Blumine*, was reincorporated and perf. at the Aldeburgh Festival, June 18, 1967), No. 2, in C minor, *Resurrection*, for Soprano, Contralto, Chorus, and Orch. (1887–94; Berlin, Dec. 13, 1895, composer conducting), No. 3, in D minor, *Ein Sommermorgentraum* (1893–96; Krefeld, June 9, 1902, composer conducting), No. 4, in G (1899–1901; Munich, Nov. 25, 1901, composer conducting), No. 5, in C-sharp minor, *The Giant* (1901–02; Cologne, Oct. 18, 1904, composer conducting), No. 6, in A minor (1903–05; Essen, May 27, 1906, composer conducting), No. 7, in E minor (1904–06; Prague, Sept. 19, 1908, composer conducting), No. 8, in E-flat, "Symphony of a Thousand," for 8 Solo Voices, Adult and Children's Choruses, and Orch. (1906–07; Munich, Sept. 12, 1910, composer conducting), No. 9, in D (1909–10; Vienna, June 26, 1912, Bruno Walter conducting), and No. 10, in F-sharp minor (sketched 1909–10, unfinished; 2 movements, *Adagio* and *Purgatorio*, perf. in Vienna, Oct. 12, 1924, Franz Schalk conducting; publ. in facsimile, 1924, by Alma Mahler; a performing version, using the sketches then available and leaving the 2 scherzo movements in fragmentary form, was made by D. Cooke; it was broadcast by the BBC, London, Dec. 19, 1960; further sketches were made available, and a full performing version was premiered in London, Aug. 13, 1964; a final revision of the score was made in 1972; there are also other performing versions as well). **VOCAL:** *Das klagende Lied* for Soprano, Contralto, Tenor, Chorus, and Orch. (1878–80; ed. by R. Kubik and 1st perf. in Manchester, Oct. 12, 1997; rev. version 1896–98; Vienna, Feb. 17, 1901, composer conducting); *Lieder und Gesänge aus der Jugendzeit*, 14 songs for Voice and Piano (1880–91); *Lieder eines fahrenden Gesellen*, 4 songs with Orch. (1883–85; Berlin, March 16, 1896, composer conducting); 14 Lieder from *Das Knaben Wunderhorn* for Voice and Orch. (1892–1901); 5 songs, to poems by Rückert (1901–03); *Kindertotenlieder*, 5 songs, with Piano or Orch., to poems by Rückert (1901–04; Vienna, Jan. 29, 1905, composer conducting); *Das Lied von der Erde*, sym. for Contralto or Baritone, Tenor, and Orch. (1907–09; Munich, Nov. 20, 1911, Bruno Walter conducting). Mahler destroyed the MSS of several of his early works, among them a piano quintet (perf. in Vienna, July 11, 1878, with the composer at the piano) and 3 unfinished operas: *Herzog Ernst von Schwaben*, to a drama by Uhland; *Die Argonauten*, from a trilogy by Grillparzer; and *Rübezahl*, after Grimm's fairy tales. He also made an arrangement of Weber's *Die drei Pintos* (Leipzig, Jan. 20, 1888, composer conducting) and *Oberon* (c. 1907); also arranged Bruckner's 3rd Sym. for 2 Pianos (1878). Mahler made controversial reorchestrations of syms. by Beethoven, Schumann, and Bruckner, and a version for String Orch. of Beethoven's String Quartet in C-sharp minor, op.131.

BIBL.: L. Schiedermair, *G. M.* (Leipzig, 1901); P. Stefan, *G. M.: Eine Studie über Persönlichkeit und Werk* (Munich, 1910; 4th ed., 1921; Eng. tr., N.Y., 1913); R. Specht, *G. M.* (Berlin, 1913); G. Adler, *G. M.* (Vienna, 1916); H. Redlich, *G. M.: Eine Erkenntnis* (Nuremberg, 1919); P. Bekker, *M.s Sinfonien* (Berlin, 1921); A. Roller, *Die Bildnisse G. M.s* (Leipzig, 1922); N. Bauer-Lechner, *Erinnerungen an G. M.* (Vienna, 1923); A. Mahler, *Briefe G. M.s* (Berlin, 1924); W. Hutschenruyter, *G. M.* (The Hague, 1927); G. Engel, *G. M.* (Vienna, 1936; Eng. tr., N.Y., 1957); A. Mahler, *G. M.: Erinnerungen und Briefe* (Amsterdam, 1940; Eng. tr., London, 1946); B. Walter (with E. Krenek), *G. M.* (N.Y., 1941); D. Newlin, *Bruckner-M.-Schoenberg* (N.Y., 1947; 2nd ed., rev., 1978); N. Loeser, *G. M.* (Haarlem, 1950); H. Redlich, *Bruckner and M.* (London, 1955; 2nd ed., rev., 1963); D. Mitchell, *G. M.: I: The Early Years* (London, 1958; rev. 1980), *G. M.: II: The Wunderhorn Years* (Boulder, Colo., 1976), and *G. M.: III: Songs and Symphonies of Life and Death* (London, 1985); W. Reich, ed., *G. M.: Im eigenen Wort, im Wort der Freunde* (Zürich, 1958); T. Adorno, *M.: Eine musikalische Physiognomik* (Frankfurt am Main, 1960); S. Vestdijk, *G. M.* (The Hague, 1960); N. Cardus, *G. M.: His Mind and His Music* (London, 1965); H. Kralik, *G. M.* (Vienna, 1968); K. Blaukopf, *G. M., oder Zeitgenosse der Zukunft* (Vienna, 1969; Eng. tr., 1973); H.-L. de La Grange, *G. M.: Chronique d'une vie* (3 vols., Paris, 1973–84; also in Eng.); M. Kennedy, *M.* (London, 1974; rev. 1990); D. Holbrook, *G. M. and the Courage to Be* (N.Y., 1975); K. Blaukopf, ed., *G. M.: Sein Leben, sein Werk und seine Welt in zeitgenossischen Bildern und Texten* (Vienna, 1976; 2nd ed., 1994; Eng. tr., 1976, as *G. M.: A Documentary Study*; rev. and enl., 1991, as *M.: His Life, Work and World*); A. Shelley, ed., *G. M. in Vienna* (N.Y., 1976); C. Floros, *G. M.* (3 vols., Wiesbaden, 1977–85); P. Ruzicka, *M.: Eine Herausforderung* (Wiesbaden, 1977); E. Gartenberg, *M.: The Man and His Music* (N.Y., 1978); E. Reilly, *G. M. und Guido Adler: Zur Geschichte einer Freundschaft* (Vienna, 1978; Eng. tr., Cambridge, 1982); B. and E. Vondenhoff, *G. M. Dokumentation* (Tutzing, 1978); D. Cooke, *G. M.: An Introduction to His Music* (London, 1980); N. Del Mar, *M.'s Sixth Symphony* (London, 1980); H. Eggebrecht, *Die Musik G. M.s* (Munich, 1982); E. Seckerson, *M.: His Life and Times* (N.Y., 1982); H. Blaukopf, ed., and E. Jephcott, tr., *G. M.—Richard Strauss: Correspondence 1888–1911* (London, 1984); D. Greene, *M.: Consciousness and Temporality* (N.Y., 1984); C. Lewis, *Tonal Coherence in M.'s Ninth Symphony* (Ann Arbor, 1984); H. Lea, *G. M.: Man on the Margin* (Bonn, 1985); H. Danuser, *G. M.: Das Lied von der Erde* (Munich, 1986); H.-P. Jülg, *G. M.s Sechste Symphonie* (Munich, 1986); H. Blaukopf, ed., *M.'s Unknown Letters* (Boston, 1987); S. Namenwirth, *G. M.: A Critical Bibliography* (3 vols., Wiesbaden, 1987); K.-J. Müller, *M.: Leben, Werke, Dokumente* (Mainz, 1988); M. Oltmanns, *Strophische Strukturen im Werk G. M.s: Untersuchungen zum Liedwerk und zur Symphonik* (Pfaffenweiler, 1988); S. Filler, *G. and Alma M.: A Guide to Research* (N.Y., 1989); E. Nikkels, *"O Mensch! Gib Acht!": Friedrich Nietzsches Bedeutung für G. M.* (Amsterdam and Atlanta, 1989); Z. Roman, *G. M.'s American Years 1907–1911: A Documentary History* (Stuyvesant, N.Y., 1989); R. Hopkins, *Closure and M.'s Music: The Role of Secondary Parameters* (Philadelphia, 1990); H. Danuser, *G. M. und seine Zeit* (Laaber, 1991); P. Franklin, *M.: Symphony No. 3* (Cambridge, 1991); F. Krummacher, *G. M.s III. Symphonie: Welt im Widerbild* (Kassel, 1991); A. Neumayr, *Musik und Medizin:*

Chopin, Smetana, Tschaikowsky, M. (Vienna, 1991); P. Russell, *Light in Battle with Darkness: M.'s "Kindertotenlieder"* (Bern, 1991); E. Schmierer, *Die Orchesterlieder G. M.s* (Kassel, 1991); H. Danuser, ed., *G. M.* (Darmstadt, 1992); B. Meier, *Geschichtliche Signaturen der musik bei M., Strauss und Schöberg* (Hamburg, 1992); A. Unger, *Welt, Leben und Kunst als Themen der "Zarathustra-Kompositionen" von Richard Strauss und G. M.* (Frankfurt am Main, 1992); F. Berger, *G. M.: Vision und Mythos: Versuch einer geistigen Biographie* (Stuttgart, 1993); F. Willnauer, *G. M. und die Wiener Oper* (Vienna, 1993); H.-L. de La Grange and G. Weiss, eds., *G. M.: Ein Glück ohne Ruh': Die Briefe G. M.s und Alma: Erste Gesamtausgabe* (Berlin, 1995); P. Reed, ed., *On M. and Britten: Essays in Honour of Donald Mitchell on his Seventieth Birthday* (Woodbridge, Suffolk, 1995); R. Samuels, *M.'s Sixth Symphony: A Study in Musical Semiotics* (Cambridge, 1995); M. Schadendorf, *Humor als Formkonzept in der Musik G. M.s* (Stuttgart, 1995); A. Stenger, *Die Symphonien G. M.s: Eine musikalische Ambivalenz* (Wilhelmshaven, 1995); G. Borchardt et al., eds., *G. M., "Meine Zeit wird dommen": Aspekte der M. Rezeption* (Hamburg, 1996); M. Hansen, *G. M.* (Stuttgart, 1996); V. Karbusický, *M. in Hamburg: Chronik einer Freundschaft* (Hamburg, 1996); P. Franklin, *The Life of M.* (Cambridge, 1997); S. Hefling, ed., *M. Studies* (Cambridge, 1997); D. Krebs, *G. M.s Erste Symphonie: Form und Gehalt* (Munich, 1997); M. Flesch, *Hypothesen zur musikalischen Kreativität unter Berücksichtigung psychodynamischer Aspekte der Pathographie bei G. M. (1860–1911)* (Frankfurt am Main, 1998); A. Nicastro *Le sinfonie di G. M.* (Milan, 1998); P. Petazzi, *Le sinfonie di M.* (Venice, 1998).—**NS/LK/DM**

Mahrenholz, Christhard (actually, Christian Reinhard),

prominent German musicologist; b. Adelebsen, near Göttingen, Aug. 11, 1900; d. Hannover, March 15, 1980. He studied piano, organ, and cello, and took courses in theology. He also studied musicology with Schering at the Leipzig Cons., Abert at the Univ. of Leipzig, and Ludwig and Spitta at the Univ. of Göttingen (Ph.D., 1923, with the diss. *Samuel Scheidt: Sein Leben und sein Werk*; publ. in Leipzig, 1924). He served as a pastor in Göttingen; then taught at the Univ. there, being made honorary prof. of church music (1946). He was a member of the Hannover Landes Kirchenant (1930–65), president of the Assn. of Protestant Church Choirs in Germany (1934–73), and chairman of the Neue Bach-Gesellschaft (1949–74). Mahrenholz was co-ed. of *Musik und Kirche* (from 1929), the *Handbuch der deutschen evangelischen Kirchenmusik* (from 1935), the *Jahrbuch für Liturgik und Hymnologie* (from 1955), and the *Handbuch zum Evangelischen Kirchengesangbuch* (from 1956); was the general ed. of the complete works of Samuel Scheidt (from 1932). He was made abbot of the Amelungsborn Cloister in 1960. Mahrenholz retired from active work in 1967. His books include *Die Orgelregister: Ihre Geschichte und ihr Bau* (Kassel, 1930; 2nd ed., 1944); *Luther und die Kirchenmusik* (Kassel, 1937); *Die Berechnung der Orgelpfeifen-Mensuren vom Mittelalter bis zur Mitte des 19. Jahrhunderts* (Kassel, 1938); *Glockenkunde* (Kassel, 1949); with R. Untermöhlen, *Choralbuch zum evangelischen Kirchengesangbuch* (Kassel, 1950); *Das evangelische Kirchengesangbuch: Vorgeschichte, Werden und Grundsätze seiner Gestaltung* (Kassel, 1950); *Das Schicksal der deutschen Kirchenglocken* (Hamburg, 1952); *Kompendium der Liturgik des Hauptgottesdienstes* (Kassel, 1963). K. Müller ed. a collection of his articles as *Musicologica et liturgica: Aufsätze von Christhard Mahrenholz* (Kassel, 1960). His 70th birthday was honored by the Festschrift *Kerygma und Melos* (Kassel and Berlin, 1970).—**NS/LK/DM**

Maiboroda, Georgi,

Ukrainian composer and teacher; b. Pelekhovshchina, near Poltava, Dec. 1, 1913; d. Kiev, Dec. 6, 1992. He was a student of Revutsky at the Kiev Cons. (graduated, 1941). In 1952 he joined its faculty.

WORKS: DRAMATIC: Opera: *Milana* (1957); *The Arsenal* (1960); *Taras Shevchenko* (1964); *Yaroslav the Wise* (1975). **ORCH.:** 4 syms. (1940; 1952; 1976; *Autumn*, 1988); Concerto for Voice and Orch. (1969); Violin Concerto (1977); Cello Concerto (1984); *Joyful Overture* (1985). **OTHER:** Numerous vocal pieces, including *Friendship of Peoples*, cantata (1948).

BIBL.: O. Zinkevich, *G. M.* (Kiev, 1973).—**NS/LK/DM**

Maier, Guy,

American pianist and teacher; b. Buffalo, Aug. 15, 1891; d. Santa Monica, Calif., Sept. 24, 1956. He studied at the New England Cons. of Music in Boston (graduated, 1913) and with Schnabel in Berlin (1913–14). He made his U.S. debut in Boston (1914); in addition to solo appearances, he also toured as a duo-pianist with Lee Pattison (1916–31). He taught at the Univ. of Mich. (1924–31), the Juilliard School of Music in N.Y. (1935–42), and the Univ. of Calif. at Los Angeles (1946–56).—**NS/LK/DM**

Maikl, Georg,

Austrian tenor; b. Zell, April 4, 1872; d. Vienna, Aug. 22, 1951. After vocal training in Vienna, he made his operatic debut as Tamino at the Mannheim National Theater in 1899, singing there until 1904. From 1904 to 1944 he was a principal member of the Vienna Court (later State) Opera, where he was particularly noted for his roles in operas by Mozart and Wagner. He also sang in the premiere there of the rev. version of Strauss's *Ariadne auf Naxos* (1916). As a guest artist, he appeared in Salzburg (1906, 1910, 1937). Maikl gave his farewell performance in Pfitzner's *Palestrina* in 1950. —**NS/LK/DM**

Maillart, Pierre,

Franco-Flemish music theorist; b. Valenciennes, 1551; d. Tournai, July 16, 1622. He was a chorister at the Flemish chapel in Madrid (1563–70), where he studied with its director, Jean Bonmarché. He then entered the Univ. of Louvain (1572), and was later in Antwerp (1574) and Tournai (1581), where he became phonascus (singing master) in 1581, and later canon (1589) and chantre (1606) at the Cathedral. He publ. *Les tons, ou discours, sur les modes de musique, et les tons de l'église, et la distinction entre iceux* (Tournai, 1610; reprint, 1972).—**NS/LK/DM**

Mailman, Martin,

American composer, conductor, and teacher; b. N.Y., June 30, 1932; d. Denton, Tex., April 18, 2000. He studied composition with Mennini, Barlow, Rogers, and Hanson at the Eastman School of Music in Rochester, N.Y. (B.M., 1954; M.M., 1955; Ph.D., 1960). He taught at the U.S. Naval School of Music during his naval service (1955–57). After teaching at the

Eastman School of Music (1958–59), he was composer-in-residence of Jacksonville, Fla., under a Ford Foundation grant (1959–61). During the summers of 1960–61 and 1983, he taught at the Brevard Music Center. From 1961 to 1966 he was composer-in-residence and prof. of music at East Carolina Coll. He also taught at W.Va. Univ. (summer, 1963). In 1966 he joined the faculty of North Tex. State Univ. (later the Univ. of North Tex.) in Denton, where he served as Regents Prof. of Music (from 1987) and as composer-in-residence (from 1990). He was active as a guest conductor, composer, and lecturer at more than 80 colleges and univs. In 1982 he won the Queen Marie-Jose Prize for Composition for his Violin Concerto and an NEA grant, in 1983 he received the American Bandmasters Assn./NABIM Award for his *Exaltations*, and in 1989 he won the National Band Assn./Band Mans Award and the American Bandmasters Assn./Ostwald Award for his *For Precious Friends Hid in Death's Dateless Night*.

WORKS: DRAMATIC: *The Hunted*, opera (Rochester, N.Y., April 27, 1959); *Mirrors*, multimedia theater piece (1986). ORCH.: *Dance in 2 Moods* (1952); *Autumn Landscape* (1954); *Jubilate* (1955); *Elegy* (1955); *Cantiones* (1957); *Prelude and Fugue No. 1* (1959) and *No. 2* (1963); *Partita for Strings* (1960); *Gateway City Overture* (1960); *Suite in 3 Movements* (1961); Sinfonietta (1964); 3 syms. (1969; 1979; *Fantasies*, 1983); *Generations 2* for 3 String Orchs. and Percussion (1969); *Violin Concerto* (1982); *Elegy* for Strings (1985); *Mirror Music* (1987); *Dance Imageries* (1998). B a n d : *Partita* (1958); *Commencement March* (1960); *4 Miniatures* (1960); *Geometrics No. 1* (1961), *No. 2* (1962), *No. 3* (1965), *No. 4* (1968), and *No. 5* (1976); *Alarums* (1962); *Concertino for Trumpet and Band* (1963); *Liturgical Music* (1964); *Associations No. 1* (1968–69); *In Memoriam Frankie Newton* (1970); *Shouts, Hymns and Praises* (1972); *Night Vigil* (1980); *Exaltations* (1981); *For Precious Friends Hid in Death's Dateless Night* (1988); *Toward the 2nd Century* (1989); *Clarinet Concertino* (1990); *Bouquets* (1991); *Secular Litanies* (1993); *Concerto* (1993); *Pledges* (1998). CHAMBER: *Promenade* for Brass and Percussion (1953); *Brevard Fanfare* for Brass (1961); 2 string quartets (1962, 1995); *4 Divisions* for Percussion Ensemble (1966); *Partita No. 4* for 9 Players (1967); *2 Fanfares* for Brass (1970); *Clastics: Formations* for Cello (1977); *Clastics 2* for Euphonium and Percussion (1979); *Nocturne* for Trumpet Choir (1985); Trio for Violin, Cello, and Piano (1985); *For Precious Friends Hid in Death's Dateless Night* for Wind Ensemble (1988); *Surfaces* for Wind Quintet (1991); *Fanfare Folio* (1997). P i a n o : *Petite Partita* (1961); *Variations on a Short Theme* (1966); *Martha's Vineyard* (1969); *In Memoriam Silvio Scionti* (1974); *Clastics 3* for 2 Pianos (1980); *6 Brief Obituaries* (1988). VOCAL: *Alleluia* for Chorus and Band (1960); *Genesis Resurrected* for Narrator, Chorus, and Orch. (1961); *Leaves of Grass* for Narrator, Chorus, and Band (1963); *Shakespearean Serenade* for Chorus and 4 Instruments (1968); *Requiem, Requiem* for Chorus, Soloists, and Orch. (1970); *Let Us Now Praise Famous Men* for Voice, Narrators, and Band (1975); *Wind Across the Nations* for Voice, Piano, Percussion, Flute, and Guitar (1975); *Generations 3: Messengers* for Children's Choruses, Voice, and Stage Band (1977); *Soft Sounds for a Wordless Night* for Chorus (1979); *Secular Hours* for Chorus (1982); Cantata for Soloists, Jazz Chorus, and Large Jazz Ensemble (1984); *Love Letters from Margaret* for Soprano and Orch. (1991); *Agnus Dei* for Chorus (1994); *Colleagues Remembered* (1995); *Choral Greetings* (1998); *Vocalise* (1999).—NS/LK/DM

Mainardi, Enrico, Italian cellist, teacher, and composer; b. Milan, May 19, 1897; d. Munich, April 10, 1976. He studied cello and composition at the Milan Cons. (graduated, 1920), cello with H. Becker in Berlin, and composition with Malipiero in Venice. He made tours of Europe, both as a soloist and a chamber music player.

WORKS: ORCH.: 3 cello concertos: No. 1 (1943; Rome, May 13, 1947; composer soloist), No. 2 (1960), and No. 3, with String Orch. (1966); *Musica per archi*; *Elegie* for Cello and String Orch. (1957); Concerto for 2 Cellos and Orch. (1969; Freiburg im Breisgau, Oct. 12, 1970); *Divertimento* for Cello and String Orch. (1972). CHAMBER: 2 unnumbered string trios (1939, 1954); *Suite* for Cello and Piano (1940); Cello Sonatina (1943); *Notturno* for Piano Trio (1947); String Quartet (1951); Cello Sonata (1955); *Sonata* and *Sonata breve* for Solo Cello; *7 studi brevi* for Cello (1961); *Sonata quasi fantasia* for Cello and Piano (1962); Violin Sonata; Piano Quartet (1968); Viola Sonata (1968); *Burattini*, suite of 12 pieces for Cello and Piano (1968); Trio for Clarinet, Cello, and Piano (1969); String Quintet (1970); Piano Sonatina (1941); other piano pieces.

BIBL.: E. M.: *Bekenntnisse eines Künstlers* (Wiesbaden, 1977).—NS/LK/DM

Mainwaring, John, English churchman and writer on music; b. Drayton Manor, Staffordshire, c. 1724; d. Church Stretton, April 15, 1807. He was educated at St. John's Coll., Cambridge. After being ordained in 1748, in 1749 he became rector of Church Stretton, Shropshire and was a Fellow of St. John's Coll. from 1748 to 1788. He then became Lady Margaret Prof. of Divinity at Cambridge Univ. His biography of Handel, which utilized material provided by John Christopher Smith, appeared under the title *Memoirs of the Life of the Late George Frederic Handel* (London, 1760); a portion of the biography was written by Robert Price; it was tr. into German by J. Mattheson (Hamburg, 1761).—NS/LK/DM

Mainzer, Joseph, German singing teacher and musical journalist; b. Trier, Oct. 21, 1801; d. Salford, Lancashire, Nov. 10, 1851. He was a chorister at the Trier Cathedral, and then studied music in Darmstadt, Munich, and Vienna. Returning to Trier, he was ordained a priest in 1826 and was made singing master at the seminary in 1828. His outspoken political views compelled him to flee to Brussels in 1833. In 1834 he went to Paris and gave free singing classes from 1835 until being banned in 1839. He also ed. short- lived *Chronique Musicale de Paris* (1838). In 1841 he went to London. In 1844 he began publication of the monthly *Mainzer's Musical Times and Singing Circular*, which in 1846 became the *Musical Times* (publ. without interruption through nearly 1 1/2 centuries). In 1847 he settled in Manchester as a singing teacher. He mastered the English language to such an extent that he was able to engage in aggressive musical journalism. His methods of self-advertising were quite uninhibited; he arranged singing courses in open- air gatherings, and had pamphlets printed with flamboyant accounts of receptions tendered him.

WRITINGS: *Singschule* (Trier, 1831); *Méthode de chant pour les enfants* (Paris, 1835); *Méthode de chant pour voix d'hommes*

(Paris, 1836); *Bibliothèque élémentaire de chant* (Paris, 1836); *Méthode pratique de piano pour enfants* (Paris, 1837); *Abecedaire de chant* (Paris, 1837); *École chorale* (Paris, 1838); *Esquisses musicales, ou Souvenirs de voyage* (Paris, 1838–39); *Cent mélodies enfantines* (Paris, 1840); *Singing for the Million* (London, 1841); *The Musical Athenaeum* (London, 1841); *Music and Education* (London and Edinburgh, 1848).

BIBL.: A. Guilbert, *A Sketch of the Life and Labours of J. M.* (Glasgow, 1844).—NS/LK/DM

Maisenberg, Oleg, Ukrainian pianist; b. Odessa, April 29, 1945. He began piano studies in his youth, and later was a pupil of Alexander Joscheles at the Gnessin Inst. in Moscow (1966–71). From 1971 he was a soloist with the Moscow Phil. After making his Vienna debut in 1981, he performed throughout Europe. In 1983 he made his first appearance in the U.S. In subsequent years, he toured globally. He also made frequent appearances in duo concerts with Gidon Kremer. —NS/LK/DM

Maisky, Mischa, Russian-born Israeli cellist; b. Riga, Jan. 10, 1948. He was a pupil of Rostropovich at the Moscow Cons. In 1965 he won 1st prize in the All Russian Competition and made his formal debut as a soloist with the Leningrad Phil.; in 1966 he was a laureate at the Tchaikovsky Competition in Moscow. Despite his successful career, he got into trouble with the Soviet authorities when he bought a tape recorder without proper permission. In 1969 he was duly arrested and spent a few months in jail. Determined to leave Russia, he approached a liberal-minded psychiatrist, who, like Maisky, was of the Jewish faith, and was committed to an asylum. He was finally permitted to emigrate to Israel in 1971, where he settled and became a naturalized Israeli citizen. In 1973 he captured 1st prize at the Gaspar Cassado Competition in Florence. He also pursued further studies with Piatigorsky in the U.S. From 1975 he toured throughout the world, appearing as a soloist with orchs., as a recitalist, and as a chamber music artist.—NS/LK/DM

Maison, René, Belgian tenor; b. Frameries, Nov. 24, 1895; d. Mont-Dore, France, July 15, 1962. He was trained at the Brussels Cons. and the Paris Cons. After making his operatic debut as Rodolfo in *La Bohème* in 1920, he sang in Nice and Monte Carlo. From 1925 he sang in Paris at the Opéra and the Opéra-Comique, establishing a reputation as a Wagnerian. He also appeared at the Chicago Opera (1927–32) and the Teatro Colón in Buenos Aires (1934–37). On Feb. 3, 1936, he made his Metropolitan Opera debut in N.Y. as Walther von Stolzing, and remained on its roster until 1943. He later taught voice in N.Y. and Boston. Among his prominent roles were Lohengrin, Loge, Florestan, Samson, Herodes, and Don José.—NS/LK/DM

Maistre, Jhan, French composer; b. c. 1485; d. c. 1545. He was in the service of the Ferrara court from about 1512 until 1543, serving as maestro di cappella for several years before his departure. Maistre was one of the earliest composers of madrigals. His motets reflect

the influence of Josquin. Many of his works appeared in contemporary sources. For modern editions, see *Treize livres de motets parus chez Pierre Attaingnant* (Vol. III ed. by A. Smijers, Paris, 1936; Vol. VIII ed. by A. Merritt, Monaco, 1962), H. Zenck and W. Gerstenberg, eds., *Adriani Willaert opera omnia*, Corpus Mensurabilis Musicae, III/4, 8 (1952, 1972), and W. Kirsche, ed., *Drei Te Deum-Kompositionen des 16. Jahrhunderts*, Das Chorwerk, CII (1967).—LK/DM

Maitland, J(ohn) A(lexander) Fuller
See **Fuller Maitland, J(ohn) A(lexander)**

Maizel, Boris, significant Russian composer; b. St. Petersburg, July 17, 1907; d. Moscow, July 9, 1986. He graduated from the Leningrad Cons. in 1936 in the composition class of Riazanov. During the siege of Leningrad by the Germans in 1942, he was evacuated to Sverdlovsk. In 1944 he settled in Moscow.

WORKS: DRAMATIC: *Snow Queen*, ballet (1940; orch. suite, 1944); *Sombrero*, children's ballet (1959); *The Shadow of the Past*, opera (1964); film music. **ORCH.:** 9 syms.: No. 1 (1940), No. 2, *Ural Symphony* (1944), No. 3, *Victoriously Triumphant*, written in celebration of the victory over Germany (1945), No. 4 (1947), No. 5 (1962), No. 6 (1967), No. 7 (1970), No. 8 (1973), and No. 9 (1976); Double Concerto for Violin, Piano, and Orch. (1949); 3 symphonic poems: *Distant Planet* (1961; also as a ballet, 1962), *Leningrad Novella* (1969), and *Along Old Russian Towns* (1975); Double Concerto for Flute, Horn, Strings, and Percussion (1971); Concerto for 10 Instruments (1977); Concerto for 2 Pianos and Strings (1978). **CHAMBER:** Cello Sonata (1936); 2 string quartets (1937, 1974); Piano Trio (1951); piano pieces. **VOCAL:** Song cycles.—NS/LK/DM

Majo, Gian Francesco (de), Italian organist and composer, son of **Giuseppe de Majo,** known as **Ciccio di Majo;** b. Naples, March 24, 1732; d. there, Nov. 17, 1770. He received his primary training from his father, and also studied with his uncle Gennaro Manno and his great-uncle Francesco Feo. He was his father's assistant as organista soprannumerario at the royal chapel, being made its 2nd organist by 1758. His first opera, *Ricimero re dei Goti* (Parma, Feb. 7, 1759), scored a great success in Rome in 1759, and his next opera, *Astrea placata* (Naples, June 29, 1760), established his reputation as a composer for the theater. After further studies with Padre Martini (1761–63), he went to Vienna to produce his opera *Alcide negli orti Esperidi* (June 7, 1764) for the coronation of the emperor of the Holy Roman Empire, Joseph II. He then toured widely, returning to his birthplace the year of his death.

WORKS: DRAMATIC: Opera: *Ricimero re dei Goti* (Parma, Feb. 7, 1759); *Astrea placata* (Naples, June 29, 1760); *Cajo Fabricio* (Naples, Nov. 29, 1760); *L'Almeria* (Livorno, 1761); *Artaserse* (Venice, Jan. 30, 1762); *Catone in Utica* (Turin, Dec. 26, 1762); *Demofoonte* (Rome, Feb. 1763); *Alcide negli orti Esperidi* (Vienna, June 7, 1764); *Ifigenia in Tauride* (Mannheim, Nov. 4, 1764); *Montezuma* (Turin, Carnival 1765); *La constancia dichosa* (Madrid, 1765); *Alessandro nell'Indie* (Mannheim, Nov. 5, 1766); *Antigono* (Venice, Dec. 26, 1767); *Antigona* (Rome, Carnival 1768); *Ipermestra* (Naples, Aug. 13, 1768); *Adriano in Siria* (Rome,

Carnival 1769); *Didone abbandonata* (Venice, Dec. 26, 1769); *Eumene* (Naples, Jan. 21, 1771; finished by Insanguine and Errichelli); also arias for 3 London pasticcios: *Ezio* (1764); *Solimano* (1765); *The Golden Pippin* (Feb. 6, 1773). **OTHER:** Many oratorios, cantatas, and other sacred works.

BIBL.: D. DiChiera, *The Life and Operas of G.F. d.M.* (diss., Univ. of Calif., Los Angeles, 1962).—NS/LK/DM

Majo, Giuseppe de, Italian organist and composer, father of **Gian Francesco (de) Majo**; b. Naples, Dec. 5, 1697; d. there, Nov. 18, 1771. He studied with Nicola Fago and Andrea Basso at the Cons. della Pieta dei Turchini in Naples (1706–18), then was organista soprannumerario (1736–37), provicemaestro (1737–44), vicemaestro (1744–45), and maestro (1745–71) at the royal chapel. His most successful stage work was the serenata *Il sogno d'Olimpia* (Naples, Nov. 6, 1747), written to celebrate the birth of the heir apparent.

WORKS: DRAMATIC: *Lo vecchio avaro*, opera buffa (Naples, Carnival 1727); *La Milorda*, opera buffa (Naples, 1728); *La Baronessa, overo Gli equivoci*, opera buffa (Naples, 1729); *Arianna e Teseo*, opera seria (Naples, Jan. 20, 1747); *Il sogno d'Olimpia*, serenata (Naples, Nov. 6, 1747); *Semiramide ricono- sciuta*, opera seria (Naples, Jan. 20, 1751); *Il Napolitano nelli fiorentini*, farsa (n.d.). **OTHER:** Concerto for 2 Violins and Orch. (1726); cantatas; various sacred works.—NS/LK/DM

Majone or Mayone, Ascanio, Italian organist and composer; b. Naples, c. 1565; d. there, March 9, 1627. He was a pupil of Giovanni de Macque in Naples. He was organist (from 1593) and maestro di cappella (from 1621) at the Santa Casa dell'Annunziata there. Existing musical publications by Majone are *Primo libro di diversi capricci per sonare* (Naples, 1603), *Il primo libro di madrigali a 5 voci* (Naples, 1604), and *Secondo libro di diversi capricci per sonare* (Naples, 1609; reprinted in Orgue et Liturgie, 63 and 65; Paris, 1964). Two of his madrigals are included in the collection *Teatro di madri- gali a 5 v. de div. excell. musici Napolitani, posti in luce da Scipione Ricci, Libraro* (Naples, 1609). Majone is men- tioned in Scipione Cerreto's *Della prattica musica vocale e strumentale* (Naples, 1601) as an outstanding performer on the organ and harp. Majone's keyboard toccatas are among the earliest examples of the affective Baroque style found later in Frescobaldi.—LK/DM

Major (real name, Mayer), (Jakab) Gyula, Hungarian pianist, choral conductor, pedagogue, and composer, father of **Ervin Major**; b. Kassa, Dec. 13, 1858; d. Budapest, Jan. 30, 1925. After training at the Cons. in Buda, he was a pupil of Erkel and Liszt (piano) and Volkmann (composition) at the Academy of Music there (1877–81). He was active as a teacher in various music schools and teacher-training colleges. With Gyula Káldy and Sándor Nikolits, he founded the Hungarian Music School in Budapest in 1889. He was founder-conductor of the Hungarian Women's Choral Soc. (1894–1904). He made some tours or Europe as a pianist. His music follows in the German Romantic tradition with some infusion of original Hungarian folk melos.

WORKS: DRAMATIC: O p e r a : *Dalam* (n.d.); *Erzsike* (Budapest, Sept. 24, 1901); *Széchy Mária* (Koloszvár, 1906); *Mila*

(Pressburg, 1913). **ORCH.:** Overture (1881); 2 piano concertos (1882, n.d.); 6 syms.: No. 1 (1883–84), No. 2, *Hungarian* (n.d.), No. 3 (c. 1904), No. 4 (c. 1904), No. 5 for Soprano, Baritone, and Orch. (1910–12), and No. 6 (c. 1918; unfinished); *Concert sym- phonique* for 2 Pianos and Orch. (c. 1888); Violin Concerto (n.d.); Cello Concerto (n.d.); *Drei Konzert fantasien* for Piano and Orch. (n.d.); *Suite Balaton* (1906). **CHAMBER:** 3 piano trios (1881–1907); 4 string quartets (1882–1905); 2 violin sonatas (1907, 1907).—NS/LK/DM

Major, Ervin, Hungarian musicologist and com- poser, son of **Gyula (Jakab) Major** (real name, **Mayer**); b. Budapest, Jan. 26, 1901; d. there, Oct. 10, 1967. After initial training with his father, he studied with Kodály (composition) at the Budapest Academy of Music (1917–21), philosophy at the Budapest Scientific Univ. (1920–24), and musicology at the Univ. of Szeged (Ph.D., 1930, with the diss. *A népies magyar m"uzene és a népzene kapcsolatai* [The Relation of Hungarian Popular Music to Folk Music]; publ. in Budapest, 1930). He was ed. of the journal *Zenei szemle* (1926–28), and then taught composition, theory, and music history and was librarian at the Budapest Cons. (later known as the Béla Bartók Music School; 1928–44; 1945–63). He also taught Hungarian music history at the Budapest Academy of Music (1935–41; 1945–66). Among his compositions were chamber music, piano pieces, organ music, choral works, and arrangements of Hungarian melodies.

WRITINGS (all publ. in Budapest): *Bihari János* (1928); *Brahms és magyar zene* (Brahms and Hungarian Music; 1933); *Fáy András és a magyar zenetörténet* (András Fáy and the History of Hungarian Music; 1934); *A Rakoczi-indulo koruli kutatasok ujabb eredmenyei* (New Results of Research into the Rakoczi March; 1937); *Lizst Ferenc és a magyar zenetörtenet* (Ferenc Lizst and the History of Hungarian Music; 1940); *Bach és Magyarország* (Bach and Hungary; 1953); *Mozart és Magyarország* (Mozart and Hungary; 1956); *Fejezetek a magyar zene történetéből* (Chapters from the History of Hungarian Music; 1967).—NS/LK/DM

Makarova, Nina, Russian composer; b. Yurino, Aug. 12, 1908; d. Moscow, Jan. 15, 1976. She studied with Miaskovsky at the Moscow Cons., graduating in 1936. Her early works show a Romantic flair, not without some coloristic touches of French Impression- ism. She wrote an opera, *Zoya* (1955), a Sym. (1938), which she conducted in Moscow on June 12, 1947, a number of violin pieces, a Sonatina and 6 etudes for piano, several song cycles, and *The Saga of Lenin*, cantata (1970). She was married to **Aram Khachaturian**.

BIBL.: I. Martinov, *N. M.* (Moscow, 1973).—NS/LK/DM

Makedonski, Kiril, Macedonian composer; b. Bi- tol, Jan. 19, 1925; d. Skopje, June 2, 1984. After complet- ing his academic schooling in Skopje, he studied with Krso Odak at the Zagreb Academy of Music; later continued his composition studies with Brkanović in Sarajevo, and in Ljubljana with Škerjanc. He was the composer of the first national Macedonian opera, *Goce* (Skopje, May 24, 1954). His second opera was *Tsar Samuil* (Skopje, Nov. 5, 1968). He also wrote 4 syms., chamber music, and a number of choruses. His idiom follows the fundamental vocal and harmonic usages of the Russian national school.—NS/LK/DM

Maklakiewicz, Jan Adam, Polish composer and teacher; b. Chojnata, Mazuria, Nov. 24, 1899; d. Warsaw, Feb. 7, 1954. He was a student of Biernacki (harmony) and Szopski (counterpoint) at the Chopin Music School in Warsaw. After studies in composition with Statkowski at the Warsaw Cons. (1922–25), he completed his training in composition with Dukas at the École Normale de Musique in Paris. He served as a prof. at the Łódź Cons. (1927–29), and then at the Warsaw Cons. (from 1929). He was director of the Kraków Phil. (1945–47), the Warsaw Phil. (1947–48), and the Kraków Cons. (from 1947). Maklakiewicz composed in an advanced style before developing a highly simplified idiom.

WORKS: DRAMATIC: *Cagliostro w Warszawie* (Cagliostro in Warsaw), ballet (1938; Poznań, Oct. 1, 1946); *Złota kaczka*, ballet (1950); incidental music; film scores. **ORCH.:** 2 syms.: No. 1, *Wariacje symfoniczne* (1922) and No. 2, *Święty Boże* (O Holy Lord), for Baritone, Chorus, and Orch. (1928); Cello Concerto (1932); Violin Concerto (1933); *Grundwald*, symphonic poem (1939–44; Kraków, Sept. 1, 1945); *Uwertura praska* (Prague Overture; Prague, May 8, 1947). **OTHER:** Chamber music; *Pieśni japońskie* (Japanese Songs) for Soprano and Orch. (1930; Oxford, July 23, 1931); much sacred music; many arrangements of Polish folk songs.—NS/LK/DM

Maksimović, Rajko, Serbian composer and teacher; b. Belgrade, July 27, 1935. He studied with Predrag Miloševic at the Belgrade Academy of Music (graduated, 1961; M.A., 1965); continued his training at Princeton Univ. (1965–66), devoting himself mainly to electronic music. He taught at the Belgrade Academy of Music (from 1963). In 1998 he publ. an autobiographical book. In his works, he utilizes resources ranging from the Ars Nova to the contemporary period.

WORKS: ORCH.: Piano Concerto (1961; Belgrade, Jan. 28, 1964); *Musique de devenir* (1965; Belgrade, Dec. 15, 1967); *Partita concertante* for Violin and Strings (1965); *Not to Be or to Be?* and *Eppur si muove*, diptych (1969–70); *Concerto non grosso* for Student String Orch. (1970); *Nežno* (Tenderly) for Chamber Ensemble (1979); *Prelude a "l'avant midi" d'un faune* for Flute and Strings (Belgrade, May 17, 1994). **CHAMBER:** *Trialogue* for Clarinet, String Trio, and Piano (1968). **Piano:** Suite (1957); *Ab aqua terraque* (1966); *Jeu à quatre* for 2 Pianos, 8–Hands (1977); *Gambit* (1993). **VOCAL:** *Kad su živi zavideli mrtvima* (When the Living Envied the Dead), epic partita for Chorus and Orch. (1963; Belgrade, Feb. 2, 1967); *2 Basho's Haiku* for Voice, Ensemble, and Tape (1966); *3 Haiku* for Women's Chorus and 24 Instruments (Zagreb, May 16, 1967); *Iz tmine pojanje* (Chants out of Darkness), madrigals for Chorus (1975); *Buna protiv dahija* (Uprising against Dakhias), dramatic oratorio for 4 Actors, Choruses, Orch., and Tape (1978; Belgrade, March 20, 1979); *Palabras en piedra* for Chorus and Optional Percussion (1980); *After the Scent of the Blossomed Cherry*, 5 haiku for Voice and Ensemble (1981); *Veče na školju* (An Evening on the Reef) for Chorus (1982); *Les Proverbes de Fenis* for Chorus (1983; also for 4 Voices and Ancient Instruments, 1984, and for Women's Chorus and Orch., 1986); *Prometheus* for Chorus (1985); *Testament of the Bishop of Montenegro Peter Petrovich Nyegosh* for Chorus (1984; also for Bass, Chorus, Orch., and Tape, 1986); *The St. Prince Lazarus Passion* for Narrator, 4 Soloists, 2 Choruses, and Orch. (Belgrade, June 26, 1989); *She Sleeps Perhaps* for Mezzo-soprano and Chamber Orch. (Novi Sad, May 15, 1993; also for Mezzo-soprano and Piano); *Fate* for Chorus (1993); *This and That* for Chorus (1994); *Temptation, Feat, and Death of St. Peter of Korisha* for Narrator, 3 Soloists, Chorus, Chamber Orch., and Tape (Belgrade, Oct. 19, 1994); *Chase* for Women's Chorus, Percussion, and Piano (1996); *M* for Chorus (1999); *How Long, O Lord?* for Chorus (1999).—NS/LK/DM

Maksymiuk, Jerzy, Polish conductor and composer; b. Grodno, April 9, 1936. He studied piano with Kirjacka and Lefeld, composition with Perkowski, and conducting with Madey at the Warsaw Cons., winning several composition prizes. He conducted at Warsaw's Wielki Theater (1970–72), then in 1972 founded the Polish Chamber Orch. in Warsaw, which he led as music director. He was also conductor of the Polish Radio National Sym. Orch. in Katowice (1976–77) and principal conductor of the BBC Scottish Sym. Orch. in Glasgow (1983–93). From 1993 he was principal conductor of the Kraków Phil. He appeared as a guest conductor in North and South America. He wrote several ballets, orch. music, and choral pieces.—NS/LK/DM

Malanotte (-Montresor), Adelaide, Italian contralto; b. Verona, 1785; d. Salo, Dec. 31, 1832. She made her debut in 1806 in Verona. She created the title role in Rossini's *Tancredi* in Venice at the Teatro La Fenice in 1813. She retired from the stage in 1821.—NS/LK/DM

Malas, Spiro, American bass-baritone; b. Baltimore, Jan. 28, 1933. He studied voice with Nagy at the Peabody Cons. of Music in Baltimore and with Elsa Baklor and Daniel Ferro in N.Y.; was also coached by Ivor Chichagov. In 1959 he made his operatic debut as Marco in *Gianni Schicchi* in Baltimore, and in 1961 won the Metropolitan Opera Auditions. On Oct. 5, 1961, he made his first appearance at the N.Y.C. Opera as Spinellocchio in *Gianni Schicchi*, and continued to sing there regularly. In 1965 he toured Australia with the Sutherland-Williamson International Grand Opera Co. In 1966 he made his debut at London's Covent Garden as Sulpice in *La Fille du régiment*. He sang Assur in *Semiramide* for his first appearance at the Chicago Lyric Opera in 1971. On Oct. 8, 1983, he made his Metropolitan Opera debut in N.Y. as Sulpice, and later appeared as Zuniga in *Carmen*, as Mozart's Bartolo, as Frank in *Die Fledermaus*, and as the sacristan in *Tosca*. He also toured widely as a concert artist. In 1992 he scored a fine success on Broadway in the revival of *The Most Happy Fella.*—NS/LK/DM

Malawski, Artur, Polish violinist, conductor, teacher, and composer; b. Przemyśl, July 4, 1904; d. Kraków, Dec. 26, 1957. He was a student of Chmielewski (violin) at the Kraków Cons. (graduated, 1928), where he then taught violin and theory (1928–36). After further training with Sikorski (composition) and Bierdiajew (conducting) at the Warsaw Cons. (1936–39), he taught conducting and composition at the Kraków Cons. (1945–57) and conducting at the Katowice Cons. (1950–54). He pursued a progressive path as a composer from 1945, but in his last years he adopted a more Romantic style.

WORKS: DRAMATIC: *Wierchy* (The Peaks), ballet-pantomime (c. 1942; rev. 1950–52; concert perf., Kraków, Jan. 10,

1952); incidental music. **ORCH.**: *Allegro capriccioso* for Small Orch. (1929); *Sinfonietta* (1935); *Fuga w starym stylu* (Fugue in the Old Style; 1936); *Variations* (1937); 2 syms.: No. 1 (1938–43) and No. 2, *Dramatyczna* (1953–56); *Fantazja ukraińska* (1941); (6) *Etiudy symfoniczne* for Piano and Orch. (1947; Sopot, April 30, 1948); Toccata for Small Orch. (1947); Overture (1948–49); *Toccata and Fugue in Variation Form* for Piano and Orch. (1949); *Tryptyk góralski* (Mountaineer Triptych) for Small Orch. (1950; also for Piano); *Suite popularna* (1952); *Hungaria 1956* (1957; Warsaw, Feb. 14, 1958). **CHAMBER**: 2 string quartets (1926, destroyed; 1941–43); Sextet for 2 Violins, 2 Violas, and 2 Cellos (1932; destroyed); *Żywioly Tatr* (Elements of the Tatra) for Wind Quintet (1934; partly destroyed); *Burleska* for Violin and Piano (1940); *Sonata na tematy F. Janiewicza* for Violin and Piano (1951); Piano Trio (1951–53); *Siciliana i rondo na tematy F. Janiewicza* for Violin and Piano (1952); piano pieces. **VOCAL**: *Wyspa gorgon* (Gorgon's Island), cantata for Soprano, Baritone, Chorus, and Orch. (1939); *Stara baśń* (Old Tale), cantata (n.d.); songs.

BIBL.: B. Schaffer, ed., *A. M.: Zycie i twórczość* (Kraków, 1969).—**NS/LK/DM**

Malbecque, Guillaume, Netherlands composer; b. c. 1400; d. Soignies, Aug. 29, 1465. He was a member of the chapel of Pope Eugene IV (1431–38), and then canon of the collegiate church of St. Vincent in Soignies (1440–65). He was an inventive composer of chansons. His 4 rondeaux and a ballade are included in G. Reaney, ed., *Early Fifteenth-century Music*, Corpus Mensurabilis Musicae, XI/2 (1959).—**LK/DM**

Malcolm, George (John), esteemed English harpsichordist, pianist, conductor, and teacher; b. London, Feb. 28, 1917. He enrolled at the Royal Coll. of Music in London at the age of 7 and studied with G. Fryer; after attending Balliol Coll., Oxford (1934–37), he completed his training at the Royal Coll. of Music in London. Following military service in the Royal Air Force during World War II, he took up a distinguished career as a harpsichord virtuoso, chamber music pianist, and conductor; was also active as a teacher. He was Master of Music at Westminster Cathedral (1947–59), artistic director of the Philomusica of London (1962–66), and assoc. conductor of the BBC Scottish Sym. Orch. in Glasgow (1965–67). He was particularly associated with the Baroque revival. In 1965 he was made a Commander of the Order of the British Empire.—**NS/LK/DM**

Malcużyński, Witold, outstanding Polish-born Argentine pianist; b. Koziczyn, Aug. 10, 1914; d. Palma, Majorca, July 17, 1977. He was a student of Turczyński at the Warsaw Cons. (graduated, 1936) and took courses in law and philosophy at the Univ. of Warsaw before completing his training with Paderewski in Switzerland (1936). In 1937 he took 3rd prize in the Chopin Competition in Warsaw. In 1938 he married the French pianist Colette Gaveau and went to Paris. With the coming of World War II, he went to South America in 1940 and became a naturalized Argentine citizen. In 1942 he made his U.S. debut at N.Y.'s Carnegie Hall, and in subsequent years made regular tours of the U.S. and South America. After World War II, he toured in Europe and various other regions of the world. He became well known for his performances of the Romantic repertoire, especially of the music of Chopin.

BIBL.: B. Gavoty, *W. M.* (London, 1957).—**NS/LK/DM**

Maldeghem, Robert Julien van, Belgian organist, music editor, and composer; b. Denterghem, Oct. 9, 1806; d. Ixelles, near Brussels, Nov. 13, 1893. He studied with Fétis at the Brussels Cons., winning the Belgian Prix de Rome;. He obtained a post as church organist. He undertook a thorough research of early Flemish music, and publ. an anthology of choral works, *Tresor musical...* (29 vols., Brussels, 1865–93; reprint, 1965), an ed. of great documentary and historical importance, despite many errors of transcription; comments and rectifications were made by G. Reese, "Maldeghem and His Buried Treasure: A Bibliographical Study," in *Notes* (Dec. 1948).—**NS/LK/DM**

Maldere, Pierre van, noted South Netherlands violinist, conductor, and composer; b. Brussels, Oct. 16, 1729; d. there, Nov. 1, 1768. He became a violinist in 1746 and 1st violinist in 1749 at the Royal Chapel of Brussels; was also in the service of Prince Charles of Lorraine, the governor-general of the Netherlands. From 1751 to 1753 he was in Dublin, where he conducted its "Philharmonick Concerts." In 1754 he appeared in Paris as a violinist at the Concert Spirituel. Returning to Brussels, he became director of concerts to Prince Charles (1754); then was made his valet de chambre (1758); also conducted at the Brussels Opera, and later was director of the Grand Théâtre there (1762–67). He excelled as a composer of syms., in which he anticipated the masterpieces of Haydn and Mozart.

WORKS: DRAMATIC: Opera: *Le Déguisement pastoral* (Vienna, July 12, 1756); *Les Amours champêtres* (Vienna, Nov. 5, 1758; not extant); *Les Précautions inutiles* (1760); *Les Soeurs rivals* (1762); *La Bagarre* (Paris, Feb. 10, 1763; not extant); *Le Médecin de l'amour* (Brussels, 1766; not extant); *Le Soldat par amour* (Brussels, Nov. 4, 1766; not extant). **OTHER:** Numerous syms., many of which were publ.; overtures; chamber music.

BIBL.: S. Clercx, *P. v.M.: Virtuose et maitre des concerts de Charles de Lorraine (1729–1768)* (Brussels, 1948); W. Rompaey, *P. v.M. (1729–1768): Thematische catalogus van de instrumentale werken met voorbeelden in partituurvorm* (Aartselaar, 1990). —**NS/LK/DM**

Malec, Ivo, Croatian-born French composer, conductor, and teacher; b. Zagreb, March 30, 1925. He studied at the Univ. and at the Academy of Music in Zagreb (1945–51). He was director of the Rijeka (Fiume) Opera (1952–53). In 1955 he traveled to Paris, where he met Pierre Schaeffer (1957) and participated in his Groupe de Musique Concrète. In 1959 he settled in Paris and joined the Service de la Recherche de l'ORTF in 1960. He also worked with the Groupe de Recherche Musicale and taught at the Paris Cons. (1972–90). In 1992 he won the Grand Prix national de la musique. He has been honored by the French government as a Commandeur des Arts et Lettres. From 1956 his music has explored the extremes of timbre and complexity.

WORKS: DRAMATIC: *Operabus,* 2 scenes from the collective opera, after Schaeffer (Zagreb, May 15, 1965); *Le Roi Lear,* theater piece (Paris, May 6, 1967); *Victor Hugo—Un contre tous,* musical poster for 2 Actors, Chorus, Orch., and Tape, after Hugo (Avignon, Aug. 1, 1971); incidental music. **ORCH.:** Sym. (1951); *Maquettes* for 17 Instruments (1957); *Mouvements en couleur* (1959; Paris, March 19, 1960); *Séquences* for Vibraphone and Strings (1960; Strasbourg, Jan. 28, 1963); *Tutti* for Orch. and Tape (1962; Paris, March 18, 1963); *Sigma* (Zagreb, May 16, 1963); *Oral* for Actor and Orch. (Zagreb, May 19, 1967); *Vocatif* (Paris, Nov. 9, 1968); *Gam(m)es* (Strasbourg, June 10, 1971); *Tehrana* (Tehran, Oct. 8, 1975); *Arco- 22* for 22 Strings (Shiraz, Aug. 21, 1976); *Ottava bassa* for Double Bass and Orch. (1983; Paris, April 10, 1984); *Exempla* (1994; Geneva, May 12, 1995); *Ottava alta,* violin concerto (Luxembourg, Dec. 14, 1995); *Sonoris causa* (1997; Paris, Feb. 8, 1998); *Arc-en-cello,* cello concerto (1999–2000). **CHAMBER:** Piano Trio (Zagreb, May 1950); *Sonata brevis* for Cello and Piano (1956); *Exercice de style (baroque)* for Strings (1958; Zagreb, Feb. 22, 1960); *Trois stèles* for Instruments (1963); *Miniatures pour Lewis Carroll* for Violin, Flute, Harp, and Percussion (Opatija, Nov. 20, 1964); *Échos* for 10 Musicians (1965); *Planètes* for Instruments (1966); *Lumina* for 12 Strings and Tape (Lucerne, Sept. 7, 1968); *Kitica* for Violin, Flute, Clarinet, and Trombone (Paris, June 27, 1972); *Actuor* for 6 Percussionists (Strasbourg, April 1, 1973); *Arco- 11* for 11 Strings (Paris, June 12, 1975); *Pieris* for 2 Harps (Paris, Aug. 18, 1985); *Attacca,* concerto for Solo Percussion and Tape (1985–86; Metz, Nov. 20, 1986); *Arco-1* for Cello (Paris, June 18, 1987); *Saturnalia* for Double Bass (1996; Zagreb, April 22, 1999). **KEYBOARD: P i a n o :** Sonata (1949); *Dialogues* (1961; Zagreb, May 12, 1963; also for Harpsichord, Frankfurt am Main, Dec. 5, 1966). **O r g a n :** *Doppio coro* (Paris, June 14, 1993). **VOCAL:** *Poèmes de Radovan* for Soprano or Tenor and Piano (1952; Zagreb, Dec. 1954); *Cantate pour elle* for Soprano, Harp, and Tape (Paris, May 25, 1966); *Lied* for 18 Voices and 39 Strings (Dubrovnik, July 30, 1969); *Dodecameron* for 12 Solo Voices (1970; Bologna, Feb. 22, 1971); *Vox, vocis, f.* for 3 Women's Voices and 9 or 15 Instruments (Metz, Nov. 16, 1979). **TAPE:** *Mavena* (1956); *Reflets* (1960); *Dahovi* (1961); *Luminetudes* (1968; Bordeaux, Nov. 19, 1970); *Bizarra* (Paris, May 17, 1972); *Triola ou Symphonie pour moi-même* (Metz, Nov. 18, 1978); *Recitativo* (Paris, June 21, 1980); *Carillon Choral* (1981; Paris, March 22, 1982); *Week-end* for 3 Synthesizers and Tape (Paris, May 3, 1982; 2nd version utilizing movements 3 and 4 for Tape, 1982); *Artemisia* (Paris, May 24, 1991).—**NS/LK/DM**

Malfitano, Catherine, admired American soprano; b. N.Y., April 18, 1948. She received early training at home from her father, a violinist in the Metropolitan Opera orch., and then continued her studies at the Manhattan School of Music (B.A., 1971). In 1972 she made her professional operatic debut as Verdi's Nannetta with the Denver Central City Opera, and then appeared with the Minnesota Opera (1972–73). She made her European debut as Mozart's Susanna at the Holland Festival in 1974. On Sept. 7, 1974, she made her debut at the N.Y.C. Opera as Mimi, and remained on its roster until 1979. After making her debut at the Lyric Opera in Chicago as Mozart's Susanna in 1975, she sang that role at her Covent Garden debut in London and his Servilia at her Salzburg Festival debut in 1976. She made her first appearance at the Metropolitan Opera in N.Y. as Gretel on Dec. 24, 1979, returning there in subsequent years in such roles as Violetta, Juliette, Micaëla, and Massenet's Manon. She made her debut at the Vienna State Opera as Violetta in 1982. Following appearances

as Berg's Lulu in Munich in 1985 and as Cio- Cio-San at the Berlin Deutsche Oper in 1987, she made her debut at Milan's La Scala as Daphne in 1988. In 1993 she won acclaim as Salome in Salzburg. In 1995 she made her first appearance at the San Francisco Opera as Cio-Cio-San and won accolades as Janáček's Emilia Marty at the Lyric Opera in Chicago. Her outstanding portrayal of Salome at the Metropolitan Opera in 1996 was one of the highlights of the season. In 1998 she was engaged to sing Weill's Jenny in Salzburg and Tosca at the Netherlands Opera in Amsterdam. She sang Kát'a Kabanová at the Metropolitan Opera in 1999.—**NS/LK/DM**

Malgoire, Jean-Claude, French oboist, conductor, and musicologist; b. Avignon, Nov. 25, 1940. He studied from 1957 to 1960 at the Paris Cons., where he won 1st prizes in the categories of oboe and chamber music; in 1968 he won the International Prize of Geneva for his performances as an oboist. In 1974 he founded La Grande Écurie et La Chambre du Roy, with the avowed purpose of presenting early French music in historically authentic instrumentation; he toured with this ensemble in Europe, South America, Australia, and the U.S. From 1981 he was general director of the Atelier Lyrique in Tourcoing. He also appeared as a guest conductor, leading performances of rarely heard operas in various European music centers.—**NS/LK/DM**

Malherbe, Charles (-Théodore), French writer on music and composer; b. Paris, April 21, 1853; d. Cormeilles, Eure, Oct. 5, 1911. First he studied law, and was admitted to the bar, but he then took up music under A. Danhauser, A. Wormser, and J. Massenet. After a tour as Danhauser's secretary through Belgium, the Netherlands, and Switzerland in 1880–81 to inspect the music in the public schools, he settled in Paris. In 1896 he was appointed asst. archivist to the Grand Opéra, succeeding Nuitter as archivist in 1899. He ed. *Le Menestrel* and contributed to many leading reviews and musical journals. His collection of musical autographs, which he left to the Paris Cons., was one of the finest private collections in the world. With Saint-Saëns, he ed. an edition of the works of Rameau; also was ed., with Weingartner, of a complete edition of Berlioz's works. His own works include 4 opéras-comiques and a ballet-pantomime, *Cendrillon.*

WRITINGS (all publ. in Paris): With A. Soubies, *L'[f:]uvre dramatique de Richard Wagner* (1886); with A. Soubies, *Précis d'histoire de l'Opéra-Comique* (1887); with A. Soubis, *Mélanges sur Richard Wagner* (1891); with A. Soubies, *Histoire de l'Opéra-Comique: La seconde Salle Favart* (2 vols., 1892–93); *Centenaire de Gaetano Donizetti: Catalogue bibliographique de la section française à l'exposition de Bergame* (1897); *Programmes et concerts* (1898); *La caricature de 1830* (1898); *Auber* (1911).—**NS/LK/DM**

Malherbe, Edmond Paul Henri, French composer; b. Paris, Aug. 21, 1870; d. Corbeil-Essonnes, Seine-et-Oise, March 7, 1963. He studied at the Paris Cons. with Massenet and Fauré; in 1898, won the Premier Second Prix de Rome, and in 1899, the Deuxième Premier Grand Prix; won the Prix Trémont of the Académie des Beaux-Arts (1907, 1913, 1921); in 1950 he received the Grand Prix Musical of the City of Paris. He publ. *L'Harmonie du système musical actuel à demi-tons* (1920) and *Le Tiers-de-ton: Deux Systèmes: Tempéré et non-tempéré* (1900, 1950).

WORKS: DRAMATIC: O p e r a : *Madame Pierre* (1903; Paris, 1912); *L'Avare* (1907); *L'Emeute* (1911; Paris, 1912); *Cléanthis* (1912); *Anna Karénine* (1914); *Le Mariage forcé* (1924); *Néron* (1945). **O t h e r :** *L'Amour et Psyché*, lyric tragedy with ballet (1948); *Monsieur de Pourceaugnac*, pantomime with Chorus (1930). **OTHER:** A series of "tableaux symphoniques" after great paintings; 3 syms. (1948, 1956, 1957); Violin Concerto; Nonet; Sextet; many choruses, songs, and piano pieces. **—NS/LK/DM**

Malibran, María (Felicità née García), famous Spanish mezzo-soprano, daughter of **Manuel (del Popolo Vicente Rodriguez) García**; b. Paris, March 24, 1808; d. Manchester, Sept. 23, 1836. She was taken to Naples, where she sang a child's part in Paër's *Agnese* (1814). She studied voice with her father from the age of 15, and also studied solfeggio with Panseron. She made her debut as Rosina in *Il Barbiere di Siviglia* at the King's Theatre in London (June 7, 1825); then went to N.Y., where she sang in the same opera in her family's season at the Park Theatre, which commenced on Nov. 29, 1825. She became a popular favorite, singing in *Otello, Tancredi, La Cenerentola, Don Giovanni*, and the 2 operas written for her by her father, *L'Amante astuto* and *La Figlia dell'aria*. She married the French merchant François Eugène Malibran, but he soon became bankrupt, and she returned to Europe without him in 1827. Malibran made her Paris debut as Semiramide at the Théâtre-Italien (April 8, 1828), then alternated her appearances in Paris and London during the 1829–32 seasons. She subsequently went to Italy, singing in Bologna (1832) and Naples (1833); made her debut at Milan's La Scala as Norma (March 29, 1836). She met the violinist Charles de Bériot in 1829; they lived together until her marriage to Malibran was annulled in 1836, and then were married that same year. Malibran suffered serious injuries when thrown from her horse in 1836; since she was pregnant, complications developed and she lost her life. Her voice was of extraordinary compass, but the medium register had several "dead" tones. She was also a good pianist, and composed numerous nocturnes, romances, and chansonnettes, publ. in album form as *Dernieres pensées*.

BIBL.: I. Nathan, *The Life of Mme. M. M. de Beriot* (London, 1836); A. Pougin, *M. M.: Histoire d'une cantatrice* (Paris, 1911; Eng. tr., London, 1911); A. Flament, *Une Etoile en 1830: La M.* (Paris, 1928); P. Crump, *Musset and M.* (Cambridge, 1932); P. Larionoff, *M. M. e i suoi tempi* (Florence, 1935); A. Flament, *L'Enchanteresse errante, La M.* (Paris, 1937); S. Desternes and H. Chandet, *La M. et Pauline Viardot* (Paris, 1969); C. de Reparaz, *M. M.* (Madrid, 1976); H. Bushnell, *M. M.: A Biography of the Singer* (University Park, 1979); R. Giazotto, *M. M. (1808–1836): Una vita nei nomi di Rossini e Bellini* (Turin, 1986); A. Fitzlyon, *M. M.: Diva of the Romantic Age* (London, 1987); O. Aceves, *La pasión de M. M.: Biografía* (Madrid, 1995).—**NS/LK/DM**

Malipiero, Francesco, Italian composer, grandfather of **Gian Francesco Malipiero**; b. Rovigio, Jan. 9, 1824; d. Venice, May 12, 1887. He studied with Mel-

chiore Balbi at the Liceo Musicale in Venice. At the age of 18 he wrote an opera, *Giovanna di Napoli*, which was produced with signal success; Rossini praised it. Other operas were *Attila* (Venice, Nov. 15, 1845; renamed *Ildegonda di Borgogna*), *Alberigo da Romano* (Venice, Dec. 26, 1846; his best), and *Fernando Cortez* (Venice, Feb. 18, 1851).—**NS/LK/DM**

Malipiero, Gian Francesco, eminent Italian composer and teacher, uncle of **Riccardo Malipiero**; b. Venice, March 18, 1882; d. Treviso, near Venice, Aug. 1, 1973. His grandfather, Francesco Malipiero, was a composer, and his father, Luigi Malipiero, was a pianist and conductor. In 1898 Malipiero enrolled at the Vienna Cons. as a violin student; in 1899 he returned to Venice, where he studied at the Liceo Musicale Benedetto Marcello with Marco Bossi, whom he followed to Bologna in 1904, and took a diploma in composition at the Liceo Musicale G.B. Martini that same year; subsequently worked as amanuensis to Smareglia, gaining valuable experience in orchestration. He studied briefly with Bruch in Berlin (1908); later went to Paris (1913), where he absorbed the techniques of musical Impressionism, cultivating parallel chord formations and amplified tonal harmonies with characteristic added sixths, ninths, and elevenths. However, his own style of composition was determined by the polyphonic practices of the Italian Baroque. Malipiero was prof. of composition at the Parma Cons. (1921–23); afterwards lived mostly in Asolo, near Venice. He was made prof. of composition at the Liceo Musicale Benedetto Marcello in Venice (1932), continuing there when it became the Cons. (1940); was its director (1939–52). He ed. a complete edition of the works of Monteverdi (16 vols., Bologna and Vienna, 1926–42) and many works by Vivaldi, as well as works by other Italian composers. He was made a member of the National Inst. of Arts and Letters in N.Y. in 1949, the Royal Flemish Academy in Brussels in 1952, the Institut de France in 1954, and the Akademie der Künste in West Berlin in 1967.

WORKS: DRAMATIC: O p e r a : *Canossa* (1911–12; Rome, Jan. 24, 1914); *Sogno d'un tramonto d'autunno* (1913–14; concert perf., RAI, Milan, Oct. 4, 1963); *L'Orfeide*, in 3 parts: *La morte della maschere, 7 canzoni*, and *Orfeo* (1918–22; 1st complete perf., Düsseldorf, Nov. 5, 1925; *7 canzoni* [Paris, July 10, 1920] is often perf. separately); *3 commedie goldoniane: La bottega da caffè, Sior Todaro Brontolon*, and *Le baruffe chiozzotte* (1920–22; 1st complete perf., Darmstadt, March 24, 1926); *Filomela e l'Infatuato* (1924–25; Prague, March 31, 1928); *Il mistero di Venezia*, in 3 parts: *Le aquile di aquileia, Il finto Arlecchino*, and *I corvi di San Marco* (1925–28; 1st complete perf., Coburg, Dec. 15, 1932); *Merlino, Maestro d'organi* (1926–27; Rome Radio, Aug. 1, 1934); *Torneo notturno* (1929; Munich, May 15, 1931); *Il festino* (1930; Turin Radio, Nov. 6, 1937); *La favola del figlio cambiato* (1932–33; in German, Braunschweig, Jan. 13, 1934); *Giulio Cesare* (1934–35; Genoa, Feb. 8, 1936); *Antonio e Cleopatra* (1936–37; Florence, May 4, 1938); *Ecuba* (1938; Rome, Jan. 11, 1941); *La vita è sogno* (1940–41; Breslau, June 30, 1943); *I capricci di Callot* (1941–42; Rome, Oct. 24, 1942); *L'allegra brigata* (1943; Milan, May 4, 1950); *Mondi celesti e infernali* (1948–49; RAI, Turin, Jan. 12, 1950; 1st stage perf., Venice, Feb. 2, 1961); *Il Figliuol prodigo* (1952; RAI, Jan. 25, 1953; 1st stage perf., Florence May Festival, May 14, 1957); *Donna Urraca* (1953–54; Bergamo, Oct. 2, 1954); *Il capitan*

Spavento (1954–55; Naples, March 16, 1963); *Venere prigioniera* (1955; Florence May Festival, May 14, 1957); *Il marescalco* (1960–68; Treviso, Oct. 22, 1969); *Rappresentazione e festa del Carnasciale e della Quaresima* (1961; concert perf., Venice, April 20, 1962; 1st stage perf., Venice, Jan. 20, 1970); *Don Giovanni* (1962; Naples, Oct. 22, 1963); *Le metamorfosi di Bonaventura* (1963–65; Venice, Sept. 4, 1966); *Don Tartufo bacchettone* (1966; Venice, Jan. 20, 1970); *Gli Eroi di Bonaventura* (1968; Milan, Feb. 7, 1969); *L'Iscariota* (1970; Siena, Aug. 28, 1971); *Uno dei dieci* (1970; Siena, Aug. 28, 1971). **B a l l e t :** *Pantea* (1917–19; Venice, Sept. 6, 1932); *La mascherata delle principesse prigioniere* (1919; Brussels, Oct. 19, 1924); *Stradivario* (1947–48; Florence, June 20, 1949); *Il mondo novo* (1950–51; Rome, Dec. 16, 1951; rev. as *La lanterna magica*, 1955). **ORCH.: D i a l o g h i :** No. 1, *con M. de Falla*, for Orch., No. 2 for 2 Pianos, No. 3, *con Jacopone da Todi*, for Voice and 2 Pianos, No. 4 for Wind Quintet, No. 5 for Viola and Orch., No. 6 for Harpsichord and Orch., No. 7 for 2 Pianos and Orch., and No. 8, *La morte di Socrate*, for Baritone and Small Orch. (all 1956–57). **O t h e r :** *Sinfonia degli eroi* (1905); *Sinfonia del mare* (1906); *Sinfonie del silenzio e della morte* (1909–11); *Impressioni dal vero* in 3 parts (1910–11; 1st part, Milan, May 15, 1913; 2nd part, Rome, March 11, 1917; 3rd part, Amsterdam, Oct. 25, 1923); *Armenia*, on Armenian folk songs (1917); *Ditirambo tragico* (1917; London, Oct. 11, 1919); *Pause del silenzio* in 2 parts (1st part, 1917; Rome, Jan. 27, 1918; 2nd part, 1925–26; Philadelphia, April 1, 1927); *Per una favola cavalleresca* (1920; Rome, Feb. 13, 1921); *Oriente immaginario* for Chamber Orch. (Paris, Dec. 23, 1920); *Variazioni senza tema* for Piano and Orch. (1923; Prague, May 19, 1925); *L'esilio dell'eroe*, symphonic suite (1930); *Concerti per orchestra* (1931; Philadelphia, Jan. 29, 1932); *Inni* (1932; Rome, April 6, 1933; rev. 1934); 2 violin concertos: No. 1 (1932; Amsterdam, March 5, 1933) and No. 2 (1963; Venice, Sept. 14, 1965); *7 invenzioni* (1932; Rome, Dec. 24, 1933); *4 invenzioni* (1932; Dresden, Nov. 11, 1936); 11 numbered syms.: No. 1 (1933–34; Florence, April 2, 1934), No. 2, *Elegiaca* (1936; Seattle, Jan. 25, 1937), No. 3, *Delle campane* (1944–45; Florence, Nov. 4, 1945), No. 4, *In Memoriam* (1946; Boston, Feb. 27, 1948; in memory of Natalie Koussevitzky), No. 5, *Concertante, in eco*, for 2 Pianos and Orch. (London, Nov. 3, 1947), No. 6, *Degli archi*, for Strings (1947; Basel, Feb. 11, 1949), No. 7, *Delle canzoni* (1948; Milan, Nov. 3, 1949), No. 8, *Symphonia brevis* (1964), No. 9, *Dell'ahimè* (Warsaw, Sept. 21, 1966), No. 10, *Atropo* (1967), and No. 11, *Delle cornamuse* (1969); 6 piano concertos: No. 1 (1934; Rome, April 3, 1935), No. 2 (1937; Duisburg, March 6, 1939), No. 3 (1948; Louisville, March 8, 1949), No. 4 (1950; RAI, Turin, Jan. 28, 1951), No. 5 (1957–58), and No. 6, *Delle macchine* (1964; Rome, Feb. 5, 1966); Cello Concerto (1937; Belgrade, Jan. 31, 1939); *Concerto a 3* for Violin, Cello, Piano, and Orch. (1938; Florence, April 9, 1939); *Sinfonia in un tempo* (1950; Rome, March 21, 1951); *Sinfonia dello zodiaco* (1951; Lausanne, Jan. 23, 1952); *Passacaglie* (1952); *Fantasie di ogni giorni* (1953; Louisville, Nov. 17, 1954); *Elegy-Capriccio* (1953); *4 Fantasie concertanti* (all 1954): No. 1 for Strings, No. 2 for Violin and Orch., No. 3 for Cello and Orch., and No. 4 for Piano and Orch.; *Notturno di canti e balli* (1956–57); Concerto for 2 Pianos and Orch. (Besançon, Sept. 11, 1957); *Serenissima* for Saxophone and Orch. (1961); *Sinfonia per Antigenida* (1962); Flute Concerto (1967–68); *San Zanipolo* (1969); *Undicesima Sinfonia, delle cornamuse* (1969); *Omaggio a Belmonte* (1971). **CHAMBER:** 8 string quartets: No. 1, *Rispetti e Strombotti* (1920), No. 2, *Stornelli e Ballate* (1923), No. 3, *Cantari alla madrigalesca* (1930; also for String Orch.), No. 4 (1934), No. 5, *Dei capricci* (1940), No. 6, *L'arca di Noè* (1947), No. 7 (1949–50), and No. 8, *Per Elisabetta* (1964); *Ricercari* for 11 Instruments (Washington, D.C., Oct. 7, 1926); *Ritrovari* for 11 Instruments (1926;

Gardone, Oct. 26, 1929); *Sonata a 3* for Piano Trio (1926–27); *Epodi e giambi* for Violin, Viola, Oboe, and Bassoon (1932); *Sonata a 5* for Flute, Violin, Viola, Cello, and Harp (1934); Cello Sonatina (1942); *Sonata a 4* for 4 Winds (1954); *Serenata mattutini* for 10 Instruments (1959); *Serenata* for Bassoon and 10 Instruments (1961); *Macchine* for 14 Instruments (1963); *Endecatode*, chamber sym. for 14 Instruments and Percussion (1966; Hanover, N.H., July 2, 1967). **P i a n o :** *6 morceaux* (1905); *Bizzarrie luminose dell' alba, del meriggio e della notte* (1908); *Poemetti lunari* (1909–10); *Preludi autunnali* (1914); *Poemi asolani* (1916); *Barlumi* (1917); *Risonanze* (1918); *Maschere che passano* (1918); *3 omaggi* (1920); *Omaggio a Claude Debussy* (1920); *Cavalcate* (1921); *La siesta* (1921); *Il tarlo* (1921–22); *Pasqua di Resurrezione* (1924); *Preludi a una fuga* (1926); *Epitaffio* (1931); *Omaggio a Bach* (1932); *Preludi, ritmi e canti gregoriani* (1937); *Preludio e fuga* (1940); *Hortus conclusus* (1946); *5 studi per domani* (1959); *Variazione sulla "Pantomima" dell'Amor brujo di Manuel de Falla* (1960); *Bianchi e neri* (1964). **VOCAL:** *San Francesco d'Assisi*, mystery for Soloists, Chorus, and Orch. (1920–21; N.Y., March 29, 1922); *La Principessa Ulalia*, cantata (1924; N.Y., Feb. 19, 1927); *La cena* for Soloists, Chorus, and Orch. (1927; Rochester, N.Y., April 25, 1929); *Il commiato* for Baritone and Orch. (1934); *La Passione* for Soloists, Chorus, and Orch. (Rome, Dec. 15, 1935); *De Profundis* for Voice, Viola, Bass Drum, and Piano (1937); *Missa pro mortuis* for Baritone, Chorus, and Orch. (Rome, Dec. 18, 1938); *4 vecchie canzoni* for Voice and 7 Instruments (1940; Washington, D.C., April 12, 1941); *Santa Eufrosina*, mystery for Soloists, Chorus, and Orch. (Rome, Dec. 6, 1942); *Universa Universis* for Men's Chorus and Chamber Orch. (1942; Liviano, April 11, 1943); *Vergilii Aeneis*, heroic sym. for 7 Soloists, Chorus, and Orch. (1943–44; Turin, June 21, 1946; scenic version, Venice, Jan. 6, 1958); *Le 7 allegrezze d'amore* for Voice and 14 Instruments (1944–45; Milan, Dec. 4, 1945); *La Terra* for Chorus and Orch. (1946; Cambridge, Mass., May 2, 1947, with Organ); *I 7 peccati mortali* for Chorus and Orch. (1946; Monteceneri, Nov. 20, 1949); *Mondi celesti* for Voice and 10 Instruments (1948; Capri, Feb. 3, 1949); *La festa de la Sensa* for Baritone, Chorus, and Orch. (1949–50; Brussels Radio, July 2, 1954); *5 favole* for Voice and Small Orch. (Washington, D.C., Oct. 30, 1950); *Passer mortuus est* for Chorus (Pittsburgh, Nov. 24, 1952); *Magister Josephus* for 4 Voices and Small Orch. (1957); *Preludio e Morte di Macbeth* for Baritone and Orch. (1958); *L'asino d'oro* for Baritone and Orch., after Apuleius (1959); *Concerto di concerti ovvero Dell'uom malcontento* for Baritone, Concertante Violin, and Orch. (1960); *Abracadabra* for Baritone and Orch. (1962); *Ave Phoebe, dum queror* for Chorus and 20 Instruments (1964); *L'Aredodese* for Reciter, Chorus, and Orch. (1967).

WRITINGS: *L'orchestra* (Bologna, 1920; Eng. tr., 1920); *Teatro* (Bologna, 1920; 2nd ed., 1927); *Oreste e Pilade, ovvero "Le sorprese dell'amicizia"* (Parma, 1922); *I profeti di Babilonia* (Milan, 1924); *Claudio Monteverdi* (Milan, 1929); *Strawinsky* (Venice, 1945; new ed., 1982); *La pietra del bando* (Venice, 1945; new ed., 1990); *Anton Francesco Doni, musico* (Venice, 1946); *Cossí va lo mondo* (Milan, 1946); *L'armonioso labirinto (da Zarlino a Padre Martini, 1558–1774)* (Milan, 1946); *Antonio Vivaldi, il prete rosso* (Milan, 1958); *Il filo d'Arianna (saggi e fantasie)* (Turin, 1966); *Ti co mi e mi co ti (soliloqui di un veneziano)* (Milan, 1966); *Così parlò Claudio Monteverdi* (Milan, 1967); *Di palo in frasca* (Milan, 1967); *Da Venezia lontan* (Milan, 1968); *Maschere della commedia dell'arte* (Bologna, 1969).

BIBL.: F. Alfano, A. Casella, M. Castelnuovo-Tedesco et al., *M. e le sue "Sette canzoni"* (Rome, 1929); F. Ballo, *"I 'Capricci' di Callot" di G.F. M.* (Milan, 1942); M. Bontempelli and R. Cumar, *G.F. M.* (Milan, 1942); G. Scarpa, ed., *L'opera di G.F. M.* (Treviso,

1952); M. Labroca, *M., musicista veneziano* (Venice, 1957; 2nd ed., 1967); A. Gianuario, *G.F. M. e l'arte monteverdiana* (Florence, 1973); M. Messinis, ed., *Omaggio a M.* (Florence, 1977); J. Waterhouse, *La musica G.F. M.* (Turin, 1990); C. Palandri, ed., *G.F. M., il carteggio con Guido M. Gatti, 1914–1972* (Florence, 1997).—NS/LK/DM

Malipiero, Riccardo, prominent Italian composer, pedagogue, administrator, and writer on music, nephew of **Gian Francesco Malipiero;** b. Milan, July 24, 1914. He received training in piano at the Milan Cons. (diploma, 1932) and in composition at the Turin Cons. (diploma, 1937) before completing his studies in composition in his uncle's master classes in Venice (1937–39). Between 1945 and 1976 he was active as a music critic for various newspapers and magazines. In 1949 he organized the first congress on dodecaphonic music in Milan. From 1969 to 1984 he served as director of the Civico Liceo Musicale in Varese. He also lectured and gave master classes abroad. He was awarded the gold medals of Milan (1977) and Varese (1984) for his services to Italian music. As a composer, Malipiero adopted 12-tone procedures in 1945 but without doctrinaire proclivities. Among his books were *G.S. Bach* (Brescia, 1948), *C. Debussy* (Brescia, 1948; 2nd ed., 1958), *Guida alla dodecafonia* (Milan, 1961), and, with G. Severi, *Musica ieri oggi* (6 vols., Rome, 1970).

WORKS: DRAMATIC: *Minnie la Candida*, opera (Parma, Nov. 19, 1942); *La Donna è mobile*, opera buffa (1954; Milan, Feb. 22, 1957); *Battono alla Porta*, television opera (Italian TV, Feb. 12, 1962; 1st stage perf., Genoa, May 24, 1963); *L'ultima Eva*, opera (1992–95). **ORCH.:** 2 piano concertos: No. 1 (1937) and No. 2 for Piano and Chamber Orch. (Fulda, Oct. 11, 1955); *3 Dances* (1937); 2 cello concertos: No. 1 (1938) and No. 2 (1957; Milan, Oct. 30, 1958); *Balleto* (1939); *Piccolo concerto* for Piano and Orch. (1945); 3 syms.: No. 1 (1949), No. 2, *Sinfonia cantata*, for Baritone and Orch. (1956; N.Y., Feb. 19, 1957), and No. 3 (1959; Miami, April 10, 1960); Violin Concerto (1952; Milan, Jan. 31, 1953); *Studi* (Venice, Sept. 11, 1953); *Ouverture-Divertimento "del Ritorno"* (Milan, Oct. 30, 1953); *Concerto breve* for Ballerina and Chamber Orch. (Venice, Sept. 11, 1956); Sonata for Oboe and Strings (1961; Naples, Jan. 4, 1962; also for Oboe and Piano, 1960); *Concerto per Dimitri* for Piano and Orch. (Venice, April 27, 1961); *Nykteghersia* (Besançon, Sept. 8, 1962); *Cadencias* (1964; Geneva Radio, Jan. 13, 1965); *Muttermusik* (1965–66; Milan, Feb. 28, 1966); *Mirages* (1966; RAI, Milan, Feb. 6, 1970); *Carnet de notes* for Chamber Orch. (1967; Milan, Feb. 4, 1968); *Cassazione II* for Strings (London, Nov. 10, 1967; also for String Sextet); *Rapsodia* for Violin and Orch. (1967; Indianapolis, Nov. 16, 1972); *Serenata per Alice Tully* for Chamber Orch. (1969; N.Y., March 10, 1970); Concerto for Violin, Cello, Piano, and Orch. (1971; RAI, Milan, Jan. 16, 1976); *Capriccio* for Chamber Orch. (1972; Milan, Feb. 12, 1975); Concerto for 2 Pianos and Orch. (1974); *Requiem 1975* (1975; Florence, Nov. 6, 1976); *Due pezzi sacri* (1976–77); *Canti* for Viola and Orch. (1978; Milan, May 17, 1982); *Divertimento* for Oboe, Bassoon, and Strings (1978; Milan, Jan. 14, 1979); *Preludio e rondo* (1979); *Composizione concertata* for English Horn, Oboe, Oboe d'Amore, and Strings (Turin, Oct. 9, 1982); *Notturno* for Cello and Chamber Orch. (1983; Milan, Jan. 29, 1984); *Racconto* (1985); *Ombre* for Chamber Orch. (1986; Milan, May 14, 1988). **CHAMBER:** *Musik I* for Cello and 9 Instruments (1938); 3 string quartets: No. 1 (1941), No. 2 (Milan, Jan. 27, 1954), and No. 3 (Florence, May 14, 1960); Violin Sonata (1956; London, May 21, 1957); Piano Quintet (1957; London,

March 1, 1960); *Musica da camera* for Wind Quintet (1959; N.Y., Feb. 18, 1960); Oboe Sonata (1960; Milan, May 4, 1961; also for Oboe and String Orch., 1961); *Mosaico* for Wind and String Quintets (1961; Munich, April 21, 1964); *Nuclei* for 2 Pianos and Percussion (Venice, Sept. 7, 1966); *Cassazione* for String Sextet (1967; Siena, Sept. 2, 1968; also as *Cassazione II* for Strings); Trio for Piano, Violin, and Cello (1968; Rome, Jan. 13, 1970); *Ciaccona di Davide* for Viola and Piano (Washington, D.C., Nov. 20, 1970); *Fantasia* for Cello (1970–71); *Giber Folia* for Clarinet and Piano (1973; Milan, April 30, 1974); *Memoria* for Flute and Harpsichord (1974); *Winter Quintet* for Clarinet and String Quartet (Venice, Oct. 17, 1976); *Musica* for 4 Cellos (1979; Turin, March 24, 1980); *Diario* for Oboe and String Trio (1981); *Aprèsmirò* for 11 Instruments (1981–82; Venice, May 5, 1984); *Liebesspiel* for Flute and Guitar (1982; Milan, Feb. 16, 1983); *Diario d'Agosto* for Piano, Clarinet, and Cello (1985; Venice, March 26, 1986); *Rinelcàrlido* for Oboe and Piano (1986); *Mosaico secondo* for Violin (1987). **P i a n o :** *14 Invenzioni* (1938); *Musik* for 2 Pianos (1939); *Piccola musica* (1941); *Invenzioni* (1949); *Costellazioni* (1965); *Le Rondini de Alessandro* (1971); *Diario secondo* (1985). **VOCAL:** *Antico sole* for Soprano and Orch. (1947); *Cantata sacra* for Soprano, Chorus, and Orch. (1947); *Sette variazione su "Les Roses"* for Soprano and Piano (1951); *Cantata de natale* for Soprano, Chorus, and Orch. (Milan, Dec. 21, 1959); *6 poesie di Dylan Thomas* for Soprano and 10 Instruments (Rome, June 13, 1959); *Motivi* for Voice and Piano (1959); *Preludio, Adagio e Finale* for Voice and Percussion (Buenos Aires, Aug. 1, 1963); *In Time of Daffodils* for Soprano, Baritone, and 7 Instrumentalists (Washington, D.C., Oct. 30, 1964); *Due ballate* for Voice and Guitar (1965; Milan, June 20, 1966); *Monologo* for Voice and Strings (1969; Milan, April 22, 1971); *Go Placidly...*, cantata for Baritone and Chamber Orch. (1974–75; N.Y., Nov. 10, 1976); *Tre frammenti* for Voice and Piano (1979; Turin, Feb. 11, 1980); *Loneliness* for Voice and Orch. (1986–87; Rome, April 8, 1989); Vocal Quintet for Soprano and String Quartet (1988; Milan, Feb. 22, 1994); *Tre sonetti* for Soprano and 10 Instruments (1989); *Meridiana* for Soprano and Chamber Orch. (1989–90; N.Y., Oct. 24, 1990); *Lieder etudes* for Soprano and Piano (1989–90; Mendrisio, Jan. 31, 1991; also for Soprano and Instrumental Ensemble, 1992); *Dalla prigione un suono* for Soprano, Baritone, Violin, Piano, Chorus, and Orch. (1992).

BIBL.: C. Sartori, *R. M.* (Milan, 1957); P. Franci et al., *Piccolo omaggio a R. M.* (Milan, 1964); C. Sartori and P. Santi, *Due tempi di R. M.* (Milan, 1964); *Omaggio a R. M.* (It. and Eng., Milan, 1996).—NS/LK/DM

Maliponte (real name, Macciaïoli), Adriana, Italian soprano; b. Brescia, Dec. 26, 1938. She was a student of Suzanne Steppen at the Mulhouse Cons. and of Carmen Melis in Como. In 1958 she made her operatic debut as Mimi at Milan's Teatro Nuovo. In 1960 she won the Geneva Competition. After singing Micaëla at the Paris Opéra in 1962, she was chosen to create the role of Sardulla in Menotti's *Le dernier sauvage* at the Paris Opéra-Comique in 1963. In 1963 she made her U.S. debut as Leila in *Les Pêcheurs de perles* with the Philadelphia Lyric Opera, and thereafter sang with various U.S. opera companies. In 1970 she made her first appearance at Milan's La Scala as Massenet's Manon. On March 19, 1971, she made her Metropolitan Opera debut in N.Y. as Mimi, and continued to sing there regularly in subsequent years. In 1976 she made her debut at London's Covent Garden as Nedda. She sang at the Vienna State Opera in 1977. In 1986 she appeared as Maria Stuarda in Zürich. In 1990 she portrayed Luisa Miller in Trieste. She appeared in recital at the Salle Gaveau in Paris in 1994. Among her other roles were Gluck's Eurydice, Pamina, Luisa Miller, and Gounod's Juliet.—**NS/LK/DM**

Maliszewski, Witold, Polish composer and teacher; b. Mohylev-Podolsk, July 20, 1873; d. Zalesie, July 18, 1939. He studied piano in Warsaw and violin in Tiflis, then enrolled in the St. Petersburg Cons. in the class of Rimsky-Korsakov. He became director of the Odessa Cons. in 1908. He then went to Warsaw in 1921, where he later was director of the Chopin Music School (1925–27), head of the music dept. of the Ministry of Culture (1927–34), and prof. at the Cons. (1931–39); was also a founder of Warsaw's Chopin Inst. (1933). His most distinguished student was W. Lutosławski. After following the Russian Romantic tradition in his works, he made use of Polish folk music in his compositions from 1921. He wrote 5 syms., ballets, sacred works, chamber music, piano pieces, and songs.—**NS/LK/DM**

Malkin, Jacques, Russian-American violinist and teacher, brother of **Joseph Malkin** and **Manfred Malkin**; b. Slobodka, near Odessa, Dec. 16, 1875; d. N.Y., Dec. 8, 1964. He studied in Odessa, and later enrolled at the Paris Cons. From 1893 he played the viola d'amore in the Société des Instruments Anciens in Paris. In 1918 he settled in N.Y. as a violin teacher. He also played in a trio with his brothers.—**NS/LK/DM**

Malkin, Joseph, Russian-American cellist and pedagogue, brother of **Jacques Malkin** and **Manfred Malkin**; b. Propoisk, near Odessa, Sept. 24, 1879; d. N.Y., Sept. 1, 1969. He was trained in Odessa and at the Paris Cons. (premier prix, 1898). After touring France and Germany, he was 1st cellist in the Berlin Phil. (1902–08). On Nov. 28, 1909, he made his U.S. debut in N.Y., and then toured the country as a member of the Brussels Quartet. After playing 1st cello in the Boston Sym. Orch. (1914–19) and the Chicago Sym. Orch. (1919–22), he played with his brothers in the Malkin Trio. He was founder-director of the Malkin Cons. of Music in Boston (1933–43). From 1944 to 1949 he was a cellist in the N.Y. Phil. He publ. studies and arrangements for cello.—**NS/LK/DM**

Malkin, Manfred, Russian-American pianist and teacher, brother of **Jacques Malkin** and **Joseph Malkin**; b. Odessa, Aug. 11, 1884; d. N.Y., Jan. 8, 1966. He studied at the Paris Cons. In 1905 he went to the U.S. and established his own music school in N.Y. (1914–31). He also played in a trio with his brothers.—**NS/LK/DM**

Malko, Nicolai (actually, **Nikolai Andreievich**), eminent Russian-born American conductor and teacher; b. Brailov, May 4, 1883; d. Sydney, Australia, June 23, 1961. He went to St. Petersburg to study philology at the Univ. (graduated, 1906), composition and orchestration with Rimsky-Korsakov, Liadov, and Glazunov, and conducting with N. Tcherepnin at

the Cons. After completing his training in conducting with Mottl in Munich, he returned to St. Petersburg in 1908 to commence his conducting career. He subsequently appeared as a conductor in the major Russian music centers, and also was a prof. at the Moscow Cons. (1918–25) and the Leningrad Cons. (1925–28). From 1926 to 1928 he was chief conductor of the Leningrad Phil., with which he programmed many new works by Soviet composers. He then left Russia and was active as a guest conductor in Vienna, Prague, Buenos Aires, and Copenhagen. From 1928 to 1932 he was permanent guest conductor of the Danish State Radio Sym. Orch. in Copenhagen. He also was active as a teacher there, the King of Denmark being one of his students. In 1933 he made his London debut conducting the orch. of the Royal Phil. Soc. From 1938 he appeared as a guest conductor in the U.S. In 1946 he became a naturalized American citizen. In 1954–55 he was conductor of the Yorkshire Sym. Orch. In 1956 he became conductor of the Sydney Sym. Orch. He publ. the manual *The Conductor and His Baton* (1950; new ed., 1975, by E. Green as *The Conductor and His Score*; 2nd ed., 1985, as *The Conductor's Score*), and the memoir *A Certain Art* (1966). The Danish Radio sponsors a triennial international conducting competition in his memory. While Malko was particularly admired for his idiomatic readings of the Russian repertoire, he also acquitted himself well in the Viennese classics.—**NS/LK/DM**

Malling, Jørgen (Henrik), Danish organist, teacher, and composer; b. Copenhagen, Oct. 31, 1836; d. there, July 12, 1905. He studied with Gade, and was 1st winner of the Ancher stipend in 1861. He went to Paris and became enthusiastic over Cheve's system of vocal notation, which he tried (unsuccessfully) to introduce in various cities in Scandinavia and Russia. He was an organist in Svendborg (1869–72), then lived in Vienna (1879–82) and Munich (1882–95) before returning to Copenhagen in 1901, where he was active as a teacher and composer. He wrote the operas *Lisenka* and *Frithjof*, a cantata, *Küvala*, String Quartet, Piano Trio, numerous piano pieces, and songs.—**NS/LK/DM**

Malling, Otto (Valdemar), Danish organist, conductor, and composer; b. Copenhagen, June 1, 1848; d. there, Oct. 5, 1915. He studied with Gade, J.P.E. Hartmann, and Matthison-Hansen at the Copenhagen Cons. (1869–71). He conducted the Student's Choral Soc. (1875–84), and was an organist at various churches in Copenhagen (1878–1901), where he also was conductor of the Concert Soc. (1874–93). In 1885 he was appointed instructor of music theory at the Copenhagen Cons. and in 1899 became its director. He wrote a treatise on instrumentation (1894).

WORKS: Sym. (1884); Piano Concerto (1890); *Askepot*, ballet (Cinderella; 1908; Copenhagen, Sept. 25, 1910); Piano Trio (1889); Piano Quintet (1889); String Octet (1893); Violin Sonata (1894); Piano Quartet (1903); choral works; pieces for organ and for piano; songs.—**NS/LK/DM**

Mallinger, Mathilde (née **Lichtenegger**), noted Croatian soprano and teacher; b. Agram, Feb. 17, 1847; d. Berlin, April 19, 1920. She was a student in

Prague of Gordigiani and Vogl, and in Vienna of Loewy. On Oct. 6, 1866, she made her operatic debut as Norma in Munich, where she was chosen to create the role of Eva in *Die Meistersinger von Nürnberg* (June 21, 1868). On April 6, 1869, she made her first appearance at the Berlin Royal Opera as Elsa, where she continued as one of its principal artists until her retirement in 1882. In 1873 she sang in the U.S. She taught voice in Prague (1890–95) and thereafter in Berlin. Among her other distinguished roles were Mozart's Countess, Donna Anna, and Pamina, Beethoven's Leonore, Weber's Agathe, and Wagner's Sieglinde.—NS/LK/DM

Malm, William P(aul), American ethnomusicologist; b. La Grange, Ill., March 6, 1928. He studied composition at Northwestern Univ. (B.M., 1949; M.M., 1950) and ethnomusicology at the Univ. of Calif. at Los Angeles (Ph.D., 1959, with the diss. *Japanese Nagauta Music*). He taught at the Univ. of Ill. (1950), the U.S. Naval School of Music in Washington, D.C. (1951–53), and the Univ. of Calif. at Los Angeles (1958–60). Malm was an asst. prof. (1960–63), assoc. prof. (1963–66), and prof. (1966–95) of musicology, as well as director of the Stearns Collection of Musical Instruments (1980–95), at the Univ. of Mich. He also was a Distinguished Visiting Prof. at Baylor Univ. (1977) and the Univ. of Iowa (1982), the Ernest Bloch Prof. of Music at the Univ. of Calif. at Berkeley (1981), a research fellow at the National Univ. of Australia (1987), and the recipient of the Koizumi Fumio Prize in Ethnomusicology of Tokyo (1993). From 1978 to 1980 he served as president of the Soc. for Ethnomusicology. He has contributed many articles to reference books and learned journals.

WRITINGS: *Japanese Music and Musical Instruments* (1959); *Nagauta: The Heart of Kabuki Music* (1963); *Music Cultures of the Pacific, the Near East and Asia* (1967; 3rd ed., 1997); ed. with J. Crump, *Chinese and Japanese Music Drama* (1975); with J. Brandon and D. Shively, *Studies in Kabuki* (1977); *Six Hidden Views of Japanese Music* (1985); *Theater as Music* (1991); *Traditional Japanese Music and its Instruments* (2000).—NS/LK/DM

Malovec, Jozef, Slovak composer; b. Hurbanovo, March 24, 1933; d. Bratislava, Oct. 7, 1998. He received private instruction in harmony, counterpoint, and musical form from Zimmer before pursuing training with A. Moyzes at the Bratislava Academy of Music and Drama (1952–54) and with Řídký and Sommer at the Prague Academy of Music (1954–57). In 1965 he attended the summer course in new music in Darmstadt. From 1957 to 1981 he was program advisor and ed. of the Czechoslovak Radio in Bratislava, where he also was program advisor of its Electroacoustic Studio (1977–81). In 1980 he won the Union of Slovak Composers Award, in 1989 he was named an Artist of Merit, and in 1998 he was awarded an honorary prize from the Ministry of Culture. While dodecaphonic and electroacoustic explorations permeate his output, he infused a number of his works with Slovakian folkloristic elements.

WORKS: DRAMATIC: Incidental music; film scores; music for radio plays. **ORCH.:** *Scherzo* (1956); Overture (1957); *Bagatelles* (1961); *2 Movements* for Chamber Orch. (1963); Con-certante Music (1967); *Preludio alla valse* (1975); *Ode* for Piano and Orch. (1979); Chamber Symphony (1980); *Divertimento per archi* (1980); 2 syms. (1988, 1989). **CHAMBER:** Cassation for Wind Quartet (1953); *3 Bagatelles* for String Quartet (1962); *Little Chamber Music,* octet (1964; rev. 1970); *Cryptogram 1* for Bass Clarinet, Piano, and Percussion (1965); 4 suites for Harpsichord and Strings (1975–80); Divertimento for Wind Quintet (1976); Canzona for Flute and Guitar (1976); 7 string quartets (*Meditazioni notturne e coda,* 1976; 1979–80; 1985; 1986; *Symetric Music,* 1987; *3 Meditations on the Grave of Matúš Černák,* 1996; 1997); *Poem* for Violin, in memory of Dmitri Shostakovich (1977); *Avvenimento ricercato* for Chamber Ensemble (1978); *Melancholic Romance* for Violin and Piano (1979); *Canto di speranza* for Violin and Piano (1979); *Amoroso* for Violin and Piano (1981); *3 Inventions* for Wind Quintet (1983); *Pastorale* for Wind Trio (1984); *Epigrams* for Violin and Guitar (1984); *Little Poetical Suite* for 3 Clarinets (1985); *Balladic Impression* for Viola and Piano (1987); *Capriccio* for Violin and Viola (1987); *Yeoman Dances* for String and Other Instruments (1987–90); *Lyrical Suite* for Wind Quintet (1988); *Epitaph* for Viola and Piano (1988); *Folk Dances* for 2 Cimbaloms and Strings (1989). **KEYBOARD: P i a n o :** 3 sonatinas (1954, 1956, 1977); *5 Quiet Pieces* (1980); *Poetical Meditations* (1981); *2 Lyrical Compositions,* in memory of Casella (1983); *Partita* (1986); *4 Preludes* (1987–88). **O r g a n :** *Postludio serale* (1980); *Quasi una sonata* (1983); Prelude and Enigmatic Fantasia (1985); *Concerto da chiesa* (1988); Prelude and Toccata (1988); *Introduzione e corrente* (1988); *Summer Preludes* (1990). **VOCAL:** *Songs from Kysuce* for Chorus (1977); *Prasnica,* madrigal for Women's Chorus, Percussion, and Tape (1979); *A Year with a Song,* cycle for Children's Chorus and Percussion (1982); *In These Places* for Reciter and String Quartet (1990). **TAPE, ETC.:** *Orthogenesis* (1966); *Punctum alfa* (1967); *Putty* (1968); *Taboo* (1969); *Theorema* (1970); *B-A-C-H* (1975); *The Garden of Joy* (1981); *Elegiac Concerto* for Clarinet, Tape, and Digital Sound Processor (1988); *Ave maris stella* for Voice, Electroacoustic Sounds, and Dance (1991); *Intrada for Devín* for Trumpet, Horn, Trombone, and Electroacoustic Sounds (1996).—NS/LK/DM

Maltby, Richard Jr., and David Shire, writers of five decades of theatrical songs (f. 1958). Richard Maltby Jr., lyr. (b. Ripon, Wisc., Oct. 6, 1937); David Lee Shire, comp. (b. Buffalo, N.Y., July 3, 1937).

It seemed almost inevitable that Richard Maltby and David Shire would work together. Both were sons of bandleaders; both attended Yale, where they first collaborated in 1958 on an undergraduate musical version of *Cyrano de Bergerac.* After graduation, they staged their first professional production, *The Sap of Life,* produced Off-Broadway. When the show flopped, Shire went to L.A., where he started scoring for television and movies.

In 1977, Shire reteamed with Maltby for the Off-Broadway revue *Starting Here, Starting Now.* The show, consisting largely of songs from shows by the duo that didn't make it originally, had a successful run. In 1978, Maltby had a solo success writing the book and some lyrics for the Broadway musical *Ain't Misbehaving.* That same year, Shire's adapted score to *Saturday Night Fever* won him a Grammy Award (which he shared with a cast of dozens) for Best Album. A year later, Shire competed against himself for the best song at the Oscars, winning for "It Goes Like It Goes" from *Norma Rae.* In 1983, the duo landed their first Broadway collaboration, *Baby,* which had a modestly profitable run of over half a year, and has since been produced over 250 times around the world. Maltby also directed and wrote lyrics for the Broadway production of Andrew Lloyd Webber's *Song and Dance* and adapted the libretto and lyrics for *Miss Saigon* into English.

In 1989, Maltby and Shire collaborated on yet another Off-Broadway revue, *Closer Than Ever*. Two years later, Maltby was back on Broadway again as the lyricist for the musical *Nick and Nora*. In 1996, he and Shire were tapped to write a musical version of the film *Big*, for which they were nominated for a best score Tony Award. In 1998, Shire was nominated for an Emmy for his score to the made-for-TV remake of *Rear Window*.
—HB

Malten (real name, **Müller**), **Therese,** esteemed German soprano; b. Insterburg, June 21, 1855; d. Neuzschieren, near Dresden, Jan. 2, 1930. She was a student of Engel and Kale in Berlin. In 1873 she made her operatic debut as Pamina at the Dresden Court Opera, where she sang for some 30 years. She also made appearances in Berlin and Vienna. In 1881 Wagner heard her in Dresden and engaged her for the role of Kundry in the premiere of his *Parsifal* at Bayreuth (July 26, 1882). She continued to sing at Bayreuth until 1894. On May 24, 1882, she made her London debut as Beethoven's Leonore at Drury Lane, and in 1889 she appeared in Neumann's *Ring* cycles in St. Petersburg and Moscow. Malten's most celebrated Wagnerian roles included Elsa, Elisabeth, Eva, Kundry, and Isolde.
—NS/LK/DM

Malvezzi, Cristofano, Italian organist and composer; b. Lucca (baptized), June 28, 1547; d. Florence, Jan. 22, 1599. He most likely received musical training from his father, the organist at Lucca Cathedral and later at S. Lorenzo in Florence. It was in Florence that he pursued his career. He found a patron in Isabella de' Medici, who secured for him the position of canonico supernumerario at S. Lorenzo in 1562. After serving as organist at S. Trinità (1565–70), he was maestro di cappella at the Cathedral and at S. Giovanni Battista (from 1573). In 1574 he also succeeded his father as organist at S. Lorenzo. Malvezzi prepared some music for the intermedi of Giovanni Fedini's *Le due Persilie* (1583). He also collaborated with Alessandro Striggio and Giovanni de' Bardi in musical intermedia for Bardi's drama *L'amico fido* (1586), and contributed music for the grand intermedi for the marriage celebrations of Grand Duke Ferdinando I and Christine of Lorraine in 1589. Malvezzi compiled an ed. version of his intermedi in 1591. He also publ. *Il primo libro de recercari* for 4 Voices (Perugia, 1577; ed. in Recent Researches in the Music of the Renaissance, XXVI, 1977) and 3 vols. of madrigals (Venice, 1583, 1584, 1590). His brother, Alberigo Malvezzi (b. probably in Lucca, c. 1550; d. Florence, Dec. 29, 1615), was also an organist and composer. He was organist at S. Lorenzo (c. 1570–1615) and the Florence Cathedral (1590–1615). He publ. a vol. of madrigals (Venice, 1591).

BIBL.: F. Borromeo, *Notizie istoriche sulla vita e l'opera di C. M.* (diss., Univ. of Florence, 1966).—NS/LK/DM

Mamangakis, Nikos, Greek composer; b. Rethymnon, Crete, March 3, 1929. He studied at the Hellikon Cons. in Athens (1947–53); then composition with Orff and Genzmer at the Hochschule für Musik in Munich (1957–61) and electronic music at the Siemens Studio in Munich (1961–64). His works reflect modern quasi-mathematical procedures, with numerical transformations determining pitch, rhythm, and form.

WORKS: *Music for 4 Protagonists* for 4 Voices and 10 Instrumentalists, after Kazantzakis (1959–60); *Constructions* for Flute and Percussion (1959–60); *Combinations* for Solo Percussionist and Orch. (1961); *Speech Symbols* for Soprano, Bass, and Orch. (1961–62); "Cycle of Numbers": No. 1, *Monologue*, for Cello (1962), No. 2, *Antagonisms*, for Cello and 1 Percussionist moving in an arc along the stage (1963), No. 3, *Trittys* (Triad), for Guitar, 2 Double Basses, Santouri, and Percussion (1966), and No. 4, *Tetraktys*, for String Quartet (1963–66); *Kassandra* for Soprano and 6 Performers (1963); *Erotokritos*, ballad for 3 Voices and 5 Instruments (1964); *Ploutos*, popular opera after Aristophanes (1966); *Theama-Akroama*, visual-auditive event (happening) for Actor, Dancer, Painter, Singer, and 8 Instruments (Athens, April 3, 1967); *Scenario* for 2 Improvised Art Critics for Voice, Instruments, and Tape (1968); *Antinomies* for Voice, Flute, Electric Double Bass, 2 Harps, 4 Cellos, 2 Percussionists, Hammond Organ, 4 Basses, and 4 Sopranos (Athens, Dec. 18, 1968); *Bolivar*, folk cantata in pop-art style (1968); *The Bacchants*, electronic ballet (1969); *Parastasis* for various Flutes, Voice, and Tape (1969); *Askesis* for Cello (1969–70); *Perilepsis* for Flute (1970); *Erophili*, popular opera (1970); *Anarchia* for Solo Percussion and Orch. (Donaueschingen, Oct. 16, 1971); *Penthima*, in memory of Jani Christou, for Guitar (1970–71); *Monologue II* for Violin and Tape (1971); *Kykeon* for several Solo Instruments (1972); *Olophyrmos* for Tape (1973); *Folk Liturgy* for Women's Voices and Chamber Ensemble (1976).—NS/LK/DM

Mamas and the Papas, The, folk-rock harmonizing hit makers of the 1960s. **MEMBERSHIP:** John Phillips, gtr., bar. voc. (b. Parris Island, S.C., Aug. 30, 1935); Denny Doherty, ten. voc. (b. Halifax, Nova Scotia, Canada, Nov. 29, 1941); Cass Elliot (real name, Ellen Cohen), contralto voc. (b. Baltimore, Md., Sept. 19, 1941; d. July 29, 1974, London, England); Michelle Phillips (real name, Gilliam), sop. voc.(b. Long Beach, Calif., June 4, 1944).

John Phillips began performing in Greenwich Village folk clubs during the late 1950s with groups such as the Smoothies, which included Scott McKenzie. In 1961, Phillips, McKenzie, and Dick Weissman formed the folk trio the Journeymen, debuting at Gerde's Folk City that spring and ultimately recording three albums for Capitol Records. In 1962 Phillips met aspiring teenage model Michelle Gilliam in San Francisco, and the couple soon married.

Canadian Denny Doherty was a member of the folk group the Halifax Three and recorded two albums for Epic. Cass Elliot, her first husband James Hendricks, and Tim Rose formed the Big Three in N.Y. around 1963, recording two albums for FM Records. By the summer of 1964, the Mugwumps had assembled, with Elliot, Hendricks, Doherty, and future Lovin' Spoonful member Zalman Yanovsky. The Mugwumps recorded a single album that was eventually released in 1967.

With the dissolution of the Mugwumps, Denny Doherty joined John and Michelle Phillips as the New Journeymen in the Virgin Islands. Subsequently joined by Cass Elliot, the four worked on perfecting their vocal harmonies (Michelle had been singing only briefly) for five months during 1965 before moving to Los Angeles. There, Barry McGuire put them in touch with producer Lou Adler, who signed the group as The Mamas and the Papas to his newly formed Dunhill label.

The Mamas and the Papas recorded their debut album with studio musicians Larry Knechtel (keyboards), Joe Osborn (bass), and Hal Blaine (drums), with Adler providing slick pop-style production. The album *If You Can Believe Your Eyes and Ears* quickly yielded smash hits with John and Michelle's "California Dreamin'" and John's "Monday, Monday," and Lennon and McCartney's "I Call Your Name." *The Mamas and The Papas* produced smash hits with John and Denny's "I Saw Her Again" John's "Words of Love," and John and Michelle's "Trip Stumble and Fall." *Deliver* provided the hits "Dedicated to the One I Love" (a 1961 smash for the Shirelles) and John and Michelle's group autobiography "Creeque Alley," and the major hit "Look Through My Window."

In 1967, John Phillips and Lou Adler organized the Monterey International Pop Festival. Coinciding with the smash success of Phillips' insipid "San Francisco (Be Sure to Wear Some Flowers in Your Hair)," as recorded by former associate Scott McKenzie, the festival launched the careers of Jimi Hendrix, The Who, and Janis Joplin. The original quartet performed live for the last time to close the festival on June 18, 1967. *The Papas and the Mamas* produced a major hit with "Twelve Thirty" and the minor hit "Safe in My Garden." "Glad to Be Unhappy" became the group's last major hit, and by mid-1968, The Mamas and the Papas had broken up. The Mamas and the Papas were inducted into the Rock and Roll Hall of Fame in 1998.

Cass Elliot's debut solo album for Dunhill yielded the major hit "Dream a Little Dream of Me" and she later scored moderate hits with "It's Getting Better" and "Make Your Own Kind of Music" in 1969. Pursuing a career as a nightclub and television entertainer, she later recorded an ill-received but underrated album with Dave Mason, who was coming off the huge success of his debut solo album, *Alone Together*. John Phillips managed a moderate hit with "Mississippi" in the summer of 1970 (the year he and Michelle divorced). The Mamas and the Papas reunited briefly in 1971 for a single album on Dunhill. After successfully completing a two-week engagement at the Palladium Theater in London, Cass Elliot died of a heart attack on July 29, 1974, at age 32.

In the meantime, John Phillips composed the music for the flop Broadway musical *Man on the Moon*, produced by Andy Warhol. Michelle Phillips launched a career as an actress with 1973's *Dillinger* and later recorded a solo album for A&M Records. Years later, she was a featured player in CBS-TV's nighttime soap opera *Knots Landing*. John Phillips, mired in drug addiction during the latter part of the 1970s, was arrested on serious drug charges in N.Y. in July 1980; he was fined and sentenced to 30 days in jail in April 1981. In March 1982, he re-formed The Mamas and the Papas as a lounge act with Denny Doherty, daughter Mackenzie Phillips (b. Nov. 10, 1959), and Elaine "Spanky" McFarlane. Mackenzie was best known for her role in the CBS-TV situation comedy *One Day at a Time* (1975–1983), while McFarlane was the former lead vocalist for Spanky and Our Gang, who had major hits with "Sunday Will Never Be the Same," "Lazy Day," and "Like to Get to Know You" in 1967 and 1968. Scott McKenzie replaced Denny Doherty in 1987 and Mackenzie Phillips continued to tour with the group until 1992.

WRITINGS: J. Phillips, with J. Jerome, *Papa John: An Autobiography* (N.Y., 1986); M. Phillips, *California Dreamin': The True Story of The M. and the P.* (N.Y., 1986).

DISC.: THE MAMAS AND THE PAPAS: *If You Can Believe Your Eyes and Ears* (1966); *The Mamas and the Papas* (1966); *Monterey International Pop Festival* (1971); *The Papas and the Mamas* (1968); *People Like Us* (1971). **THE JOURNEYMEN:** *The Journeymen* (1961); *Coming Attractions—Live!* (1962); *New Directions in Folk Music* (1963). **THE HALIFAX THREE:** *The Halifax Three:* (1963); *San Francisco Bay Blues* (1963). **THE BIG THREE:** *The Big Three* (1963); *Live at the Recording Studio* (1964). **THE MUGWUMPS:** *The Mugwumps* (1967). **CASS ELLIOT:** *Dream a Little Dream* (1968); *Bubblegum, Lemonade, and Something for Mama* (1969); *Make Your Own Kind of Music* (1969); *Cass Elliot* (1972); *The Road Is No Place for a Lady* (1972); *Don't Call Me Mama Anymore* (1973). **CASS ELLIOT AND DAVE MASON:** *Dave Mason and Cass Elliot* (1971). **JOHN PHILLIPS:** *John Phillips* (1970). **DENNY DOHERTY:** *Watcha Gonna Do* (1971); *Waiting for a Sign* (1974). **MICHELLE PHILLIPS:** *Victim of Romance* (1977).—**BH**

Mamiya, Michio, Japanese composer; b. Asahikawa, Hokkaido, June 29, 1929. He was a student of Ikenouchi at the Tokyo National Univ. of Fine Arts and Music. In his works, Mamiya cultivates national Japanese music in modern forms, with inventive uses of dissonant counterpoint and coloristic instrumentation.

WORKS: DRAMATIC: *Mukashi banashi hitokai Tarobê* (A Fable from Olden Times about Tarobê, the Slave Dealer), opera (1959); *Elmer's Adventure*, musical (Tokyo Radio, Aug. 28, 1967); *Narukami*, opera (1974); *Yonagahime and Mimio*, chamber opera (1990). **ORCH.:** 4 piano concertos: No. 1 (1954), No. 2 (1970), No. 3 (1989–90; Savonlinna, July 22, 1990), and No. 4, *Scenes for an Unborn Opera* (1997); Sym. (1955); 2 violin concertos: No. 1 (Tokyo, June 24, 1959) and No. 2 (1975); *2 Tableau* (1965); *Serenade* (1974); Cello Concerto (1975); *Tableau '85* for Orch. and 8 Tenors (1985); *Antler* (1989); *Singing Birds in the Mountains* for Strings (1991). **CHAMBER:** Cello Sonata (1950); Violin Sonata (1953); Sonata for 2 Violins (1958); *Uta* for Cello and Piano (1960); *3 Movements* for Wind Quintet (1962); Quartet for Japanese Instruments (1962); 2 string quartets (1963, 1980); Sonata for Violin, Piano, Percussion, and Double Bass (1966); Sonata for Solo Cello (1966; rev. 1969); Sonata for Solo Violin (1971); Concerto for 9 Strings (1972); *4 Visions: Tomb of the Fireflies* for Chamber Ensemble (1987); *Trobriand* for Clarinet, Marimba, Percussion, and Double Bass (1997); Cello Sonata (1998). **P i a n o :** *3 Inventions* (1955); 3 sonatas (1955; 1973; *Spring*, 1987); *Diferencias* (1983); *3 Préludes* (1983); *Friends of the Earth* for Piano, 4–Hands (1985); *Piano Trail* (1986). **VOCAL:** *Composition for Chorus* Nos. 1–13 (1958–93; many with varying instrumental accompaniment); *King of Crow*, oratorio (1959); *June 15, 1960*, oratorio (1961); *Serenade I* for Soprano, String Quartet, and Piano (1971) and *II* for Soprano, Viola, and Piano (1986); *Brahma-nada* for Narrator, Soloists, 2 Pianos, Synthesizer, and Percussion (1987); *Nilch'i Ligai* for 5 Singers and 3 Percussionists (1992); *Wild Pear* for Narrator, Flute, String Quartet, and Piano (1996); *Kadha* for Singer and Cello (1998); cantatas; choruses; songs.—NS/LK/DM

Mamlok, Ursula, German-born American composer and teacher; b. Berlin, Feb. 1, 1928. She studied piano and composition in childhood in Berlin. After her family went to Ecuador, she continued her training there and then emigrated to the U.S., settling in N.Y. in 1941. In 1945 she became a naturalized American citizen. She studied with Szell at the Mannes Coll. of Music (1942–46) and with Giannini at the Manhattan School of Music (M.M., 1958); also took instruction from Wolpe, Sessions, Steuermann, and Shapey. She taught at N.Y.U. (1967–76), the Manhattan School of Music (from 1968), and Kingsborough Community Coll. (1972–75). She received grants from the NEA in 1974, the American Academy and Inst. of Arts and Letters in 1981 and 1989, and the Martha Baird Rockefeller Foundation in 1982. In 1988 she received a Koussevitzky Foundation commission. In 1989 she received the Walter Hinrichsen Award of the American Academy and Inst. of Arts and Letters. In 1995 she held a Guggenheim fellowship. Her works reveal a fine craftsmanship, lyricism, and wit; in a number of her works she utilizes serial techniques.

WORKS: ORCH.: Concerto for Strings (1950); *Grasshoppers: 6 Humoresques* (1957); Oboe Concerto (1974; also for Oboe, 2 Pianos, and Percussion); Concertino for Wind Quintet, 2 Percussion, and Strings (1987); *Constellations* (1993; San Francisco, Feb. 9, 1994). CHAMBER: Wind Quintet (1956); Sonatina for 2 Clarinets (1957); *Variations* for Flute (1961); *Designs* for Violin and Piano (1962); 2 string quartets (1962; 1996–97); *Composition* for Cello or Viola (1962); *Concert Piece for 4* for Flute, Oboe, Percussion, and Viola (1964); *Music* for Viola and Harp (1965); *Capriccios* for Oboe and Piano (1968); *Polyphony* for Clarinet (1968); *Variations and Interludes* for Percussion Quartet (1971); Sextet for Flute, Violin, Clarinet, Bass Clarinet, Double Bass, and Piano (1978); *Festive Sounds* for Wind Quintet (1978); *When Summer Sang* for Flute, Clarinet, Piano, Violin, and Cello (1980); *Panta Rhei* for Piano, Violin, and Cello (1981); *From My Garden* for Violin or Viola (1983); *Fantasie Variations* for Cello (1983); *Alariana* for Recorder or Flute, Clarinet, Bassoon, Violin, and Cello (1985); *3 Bagatelles* for Harpsichord (1987); *Bagatelles* for Clarinet, Violin, and Cello (1988); *Rhapsody*, trio for Clarinet, Viola, and Piano (1989); Violin Sonata (1989); *Girasol*, sextet for Flute, Clarinet, Violin, Viola, Cello, and Piano (1990); *Music for Stony Brook* for Flute, Violin, and Cello (1990); *5 Intermezzi* for Guitar (1991); *Polarities* for Flute, Violin, Cello, and Piano (1995). PIANO: Various didactic pieces, including *6 Recital Pieces for Children* (1983) and *4 Recital Pieces for Young Pianists* (1983). VOCAL: *Daybreak* for Soprano or Mezzo-soprano and Piano (1948); *4 German Songs* for Soprano or Mezzo-soprano and Piano (1957); *Stray Birds* for Soprano, Flute, and Cello (1963); *Haiku Settings* for Soprano and Flute (1967); *Der Andreas Garten* for Mezzo-soprano, Flute, Alto Flute, and Harp (1987). TAPE: *Sonar Trajectory* (1966). —NS/LK/DM

Mamoulian, Rouben, Russian-born director of operas, musicals, and films; b. Tiflis, Oct. 8, 1897; d. Los Angeles, Dec. 4, 1987. He showed an early interest in theater, founding a drama studio in his native city in 1918. In 1920 he toured England with the Russian Repertory Theater. Later he directed several hit plays in London during a 3-year span. In 1923 he emigrated to the U.S. to become director of operas and operettas at the George Eastman Theater in Rochester, N.Y. He was an innovator of both stage and screen, using an imaginative and bold blend of all the components of film with the new dimension of sound. He directed the noted early "talkie" *Applause* in 1929, as well as the film version of Gershwin's *Porgy and Bess* in 1935. He was the first director to use a mobile camera in a sound movie, and among the first to use a multiple-channel sound track. He directed the film of the Rodgers and Hammerstein musical *Oklahoma!* (1955), which was the first musical to utilize songs and dance as an integral part of the dramatic flow of the plot.—NS/LK/DM

Mana-Zucca (real name, **Gizella Augusta Zuckermann**), American composer, pianist, and singer; b. N.Y., Dec. 25, 1887; d. Miami Beach, March 8, 1981. She began playing piano as a child and took the name Mana-Zucca as a teenager. In 1902 she played in one of Frank Damrosch's young people's concerts at N.Y.'s Carnegie Hall. After training from Alexander Lambert, she toured as a pianist in Europe from about 1907. She also made some appearances as a singer, attracting notice in Lehár's *Der Graf von Luxemburg* in London in 1919. From 1921 she was active mainly in Fla., where she devoted herself fully to composition. She became best known as a composer of lyrically soaring songs, the most famous being *I Love Life* (1923).

WORKS: *Hypatia*, opera (c. 1920); *The Queue of Ki- Lu*, opera (c. 1920); *The Wedding of the Butterflies*, ballet; Piano Concerto (N.Y., Aug. 20, 1919); Violin Concerto (N.Y., Dec. 9, 1955); chamber music; choral pieces; over 170 songs; didactic pieces. —NS/LK/DM

Manchicourt, Pierre de, Franco-Flemish composer; b. Bethune, c. 1510; d. Madrid, Oct. 5, 1564. He was a choirboy at Arras Cathedral (1525); after serving as director of the choir at Tours Cathedral (1539) and as master of the choirboys and maitre de chapelle at Tournai Cathedral (1545), he was made a canon of Arras Cathedral in 1556; from 1559 he was master of Philip II's Flemish chapel in Madrid. He composed many fine masses, motets, and Parisian chansons.—NS/LK/DM

Mancinelli, Luigi, distinguished Italian conductor and composer; b. Orvieto, Feb. 5, 1848; d. Rome, Feb. 2, 1921. He studied organ and cello with his brother, Marino, then was a cellist in the Orvieto cappella and the orch. of the Teatro della Pergola in Florence; also studied cello with Sbola and composition with Mabellini in Florence. He then was 1st cellist and maestro concertatore at the Teatro Morlacchi in Perugia. In 1874 he made his conducting debut there in *Aida* after the regular conductor was unable to lead the performance owing to a temporarily inebriated condition. He then was called to Rome, where he was conductor of the Teatro Apollo from 1874 to 1881; subsequently he served as director of the Bologna Cons. On June 18, 1886, he made his London debut conducting a concert performance; in 1887 he conducted at Drury Lane; from 1888 to 1905 he was chief conductor at Covent Garden, and from 1887 to 1893 he conducted opera in Madrid. He joined the roster of the Metropolitan Opera in N.Y. in 1893, and continued to conduct there until 1903. On May 25, 1908, he led the first performance at the newly opened Teatro Colón in Buenos Aires, returning there in 1909, 1910, and 1913. He enjoyed a fine reputation as a competent, dependable, and resourceful opera conductor; naturally, he excelled in the Italian repertoire, but he also conducted Wagner's operas, albeit in dubious Italian translation. From his experience as an opera conductor, he learned the art of composing for the theater; his operas are indeed most effective; of these, *Ero e Leandro* became a favorite.

WORKS: DRAMATIC: O p e r a : *Isora de Provenza* (Bologna, Oct. 2, 1884); *Tizianello* (Rome, June 20, 1895); *Ero e Leandro* (Norwich Festival, Oct. 8, 1896); *Paolo e Francesca* (Bologna, Nov. 11, 1907); *Sogno di una notte d'estate*, after Shakespeare's Midsummer Night's Dream (not produced). **O r a t o r i o s :** *Isaia* (Norwich, Oct. 13, 1887); *Santa Agnese* (Norwich, Oct. 27, 1905). **OTHER:** Cinematic cantata, *Giuliano l'Apostata* (Rome, 1920); *Intermezzi sinfonici* for *Cleopatra* by Cossa, a symphonic suite.

BIBL.: L. Arnedo, *L. M. y su opera Hero y Leandro* (Madrid, 1898); G. Orefice, *L. M.* (Rome, 1921); L. Silvestri, *L. M.: Direttore e compositore* (Milan, 1966); A. Mariani, *L. M.: La vita* (Lucca, 1998).—NS/LK/DM

Mancini, Francesco, Italian composer and teacher; b. Naples, Jan. 16, 1672; d. there, Sept. 22, 1737. He became an organ student at the Cons. della Pietà dei Turchini in Naples (1688), where he later was organist (c. 1694–1702). He held the post of 1st organist at the royal chapel in Naples (1704–07), and subsequently was its director (1707–08), asst. director (1708–25), and again director (1725–37). He was also director of the Cons. di S. Maria di Loreto in Naples from 1720 until he suffered a stroke in 1735. He was held in high regard as a composer of operas and cantatas, and as a teacher.

WORKS: DRAMATIC: O p e r a (all 1st perf. in Naples unless otherwise given): *Ariovisto* (Nov. 15, 1702); (*Lucia*) *Silla* (Jan. 27?, 1703); *La costanza nell'honore* (June 1704); *Gl'amanti generosi* (Carnival? 1705; rev. as *Hydaspes* or *L'Idaspe fedele*, London, March 23, 1710); *La serva favorita* (1705); *Alessandro il Grande in Sidone* (1706); *Turno Aricino* (Feb. 4, 1708); *Engelberta, ossia La forza dell'innocenza* (Nov. 4, 1709; Act 1 and part of Act 2 by A. Orefici); *Mario fuggitivo* (Dec. 27, 1710); *Selim re d'Ormuz* (Jan. 23, 1712); *Artaserse re di Persia* (Oct. 8, 1713); *Il gran Mogol* (Dec. 26, 1713); *Il Vincislao* (Dec. 26, 1714); *Alessandro Severo* (Rome, Carnival 1718); *La fortezza* [*forza*] *al cimento* (Feb. 16, 1721); *Trajano* (Jan. 17, 1723); *L'Oront[e]a* (Carnival 1729); *Alessandro nelle' Indie* (Carnival 1732); *Don Aspremo* (1733); *Demofoonte* (Jan. 20, 1735; Act 2 in collaboration with Sarro, Leo, and Sellitto); also several intermezzos, serenatas, and over 200 secular cantatas. His sacred music includes oratorios, masses, motets, cantatas, a Magnificat, and Psalms for Vespers. He also publ. *XII Solos* for Violin or Flute and Basso Continuo, *which*

Solos are Proper Lessons for the Harpsichord (London, 1724; 2nd ed., rev., 1727, by F. Geminiani).

BIBL.: J. Wright, *The Secular Cantatas of F. M. (1672–1737)* (diss., N.Y.U., 1975); A. Romagnoli, *F. M.: I melodrammi* (diss., Univ. of Pavia, 1987).—NS/LK/DM

Mancini, Henry (Enrico Nicola), prolific American composer, conductor, and arranger; b. Cleveland, Ohio, April 16, 1924; d. Los Angeles, June 14, 1994. Mancini revolutionized film and television scoring by introducing elements of jazz and rock 'n' roll into a series of movie and TV productions during the late 1950s and 1960s, notably the *Peter Gunn* program, *Breakfast at Tiffany's*, and *The Pink Panther*. These efforts brought him Academy Award and Emmy nominations resulting in four Oscars, two of them for his songs "Moon River" and "Days of Wine and Roses." Simultaneously, he launched a recording career that found him reaching the charts with 39 albums between 1959 and 1977 and topping the singles charts with his recording of "Love Theme from *Romeo & Juliet*." His records won him 20 Grammys.

Mancini's parents, Quinto and Anna Pece Mancini, were Italian immigrants. His father worked in the steel industry in West Aliquippa, Pa., and played piccolo and flute, which he taught to his son; they played together in the local Sons of Italy band, and Mancini joined the Pa. All-State Band in 1937. Already intent upon a career as a film composer, he began taking piano lessons. When he was 14 or 15 he was sent to Pittsburgh to study piano with Homer Ochsenhardt, then began studying arranging with Max Adkins. Adkins introduced him to Benny Goodman, who accepted one of his arrangements. At the same time, having graduated from high school, he was accepted at the Juilliard School of Music, where he began attending in 1942. He majored in piano, studied with Gordon Stanley. Having turned 18 not long after the U.S. entry into World War II, he was quickly drafted into the Air Force. Glenn Miller arranged to have him assigned to a service band with which he played until 1944, when he was reassigned to the infantry and sent to Europe.

Mancini was discharged from the service on March 30, 1946, and shortly after, joined the Glenn Miller Orch. under the direction of Tex Beneke (Miller died in the war). Mancini played piano and wrote arrangements for the band. He became romantically involved with Ginny (Virginia) O'Connor, a member of the Mello-Larks, who sang with the orchestra. When she left to become a session singer in Los Angeles, he followed, marrying her on Sept. 13, 1947; they had three children, Christopher, Monica, and Felice, each of whom worked in the music industry.

Mancini spent the years 1947 to 1952 writing music and arrangements for radio shows, bands, and nightclub performers while studying at the Westlake School of Music. Also at this time, Mancini studied with Ernst Krenek, Dr. Alfred Sendry, and Mario Castelnuovo-Tedesco in preparation to become a film composer. When the Mello-Larks were hired to sing in a short film featuring Jimmy Dorsey at Universal-International Pictures, Mancini was brought in as their arranger, which led to a two-week assignment to write music for the Abbott and Costello comedy *Lost in Alaska*. He was then hired as a member of the music department, and over the next six years he composed, arranged, and adapted music for 100 films, most of them low-budget B-pictures. His experience with swing music gave him a natural affinity for the studio's film biography *The Glenn Miller Story*, one of the biggest box office hits of 1954, which earned him his first Academy Award nomination for Best Score. His score for the 1956 film *Rock, Pretty Baby* was released on a soundtrack LP by Decca Records that made the charts in 1957.

With the decline of the studio system, Mancini was laid off by Universal in 1958; but producer, director, and screenwriter Blake Edwards, with whom he worked previously, immediately hired him to write music for the television detective show, *Peter Gunn*. Mancini's theme for the show employed elements of rock 'n' roll, and his music for the individual episodes was jazz-styled. The series was successful upon its debut in September, and Ray Anthony, who had scored a hit five years earlier with the theme from the TV series *Dragnet*, recorded Mancini's "Peter Gunn" as a single that reached the Top Ten in February 1959. RCA Victor Records signed Mancini to a recording contract and had him record an album's worth of the music he had written for the series. His debut album, *The Music from Peter Gunn*, topped the charts in February 1959 and went gold. The series music earned him an Emmy nomination for Best Musical Contribution to a Television Program, and he was nominated for four of the newly instituted Grammy Awards for the album, winning for Album of the Year and Best Arrangement. He quickly followed up with a second LP, *More Music from Peter Gunn*, which reached the Top Ten in June 1959 and earned him an additional six Grammy nominations: Album of the Year; Best Jazz Performance, Group; Best Performance by an Orch.; Best Musical Composition, More Than 5 Minutes; Best Sound Track Album of Background Score for a Motion Picture or TV; and Best Arrangement.

Mancini and Edwards teamed for a second television series for the 1959–60 season, *Mr. Lucky*, about a gambler. The inevitable *Music from Mr. Lucky* album hit the Top Ten in April 1960, the same month that Mancini's instrumental recording of his theme "Mr. Lucky" (lyrics by Jay Livingston and Ray Evans) reached the Top 40. The LP was nominated for three Grammys, winning for Best Performance by an Orch. and Best Arrangement but losing out for Best Soundtrack Album or Recording of Music Score from a Motion Picture or TV. A follow-up album, *Mr. Lucky Goes Latin*, spent six months in the charts and earned a Grammy nomination for Best Performance by an Orch. for Dancing. *Mr. Lucky* spent only one season on TV, but Mancini and Edwards returned to filmmaking, launching a director-composer partnership that would result in 26 movies released between 1960 and 1993. The first was a Bing Crosby vehicle, *High Time*, which opened in September 1960. Marking *Peter Gunn*'s third and final season, Duane Eddy revived "Peter Gunn" for a Top 40 hit in October. Mancini's RCA contract called for three albums per year, and in addition to his versions of music he had

written for television or film, he also began to record LPs containing his arrangements of music written by others. *The Blues and the Beat*, an album of jazz and blues standards, reached the charts in November 1960 and earned two Grammy nominations: Best Performance by a Band for Dancing and Best Jazz Performance, Large Group, winning in the latter category.

Mancini scored three films released in 1961. *The Great Impostor* appeared in March, accompanied by his recording of the instrumental theme, which reached the singles charts. *Bachelor in Paradise* opened in November, and its title song, with lyrics by Mack David, was nominated for an Academy Award. But Mancini's major effort of the year was his score for the Blake Edwards-directed *Breakfast at Tiffany's*, released in October. The film was a box office hit, and Mancini's *Breakfast at Tiffany's* LP topped the charts and went gold. "Moon River" (lyrics by Johnny Mercer) was sung under the film's credits by Andy Williams and in the film itself by Audrey Hepburn. Both Mancini's instrumental recording of the song and a vocal version by Jerry Butler hit the Top Ten in November. At the Academy Awards ceremony, Mancini won best score (*Breakfast at Tiffany's*) and best song ("Moon River") Oscars. At the Grammys his *Breakfast at Tiffany's* LP was nominated for Album of the Year and won for Best Performance by an Orch. (for Other than Dancing) and Best Soundtrack Album or Recording of Score from a Motion Picture or TV; his recording of "Moon River" won for Record of the Year and Best Arrangement; "Moon River" was named Song of the Year. Andy Williams, who had not recorded "Moon River" initially, released it on an album, *Moon River & Other Great Movie Themes*, that reached the Top Ten and went gold. It became his signature song, and he used it as the theme of his television series, *The Andy Williams Show*.

Also during 1961, Mancini began to make personal appearances, eventually giving up to 50 concerts a year. He scored four films released in 1962, notably *Hatari!*, a box office hit released in July, and *Days of Wine and Roses*, released in December. Lawrence Welk scored a chart entry with "Baby Elephant Walk" from *Hatari!*, and Mancini charted with "Theme from *Hatari!*," while the *Hatari!* LP reached the Top Ten, earning four Grammy nominations: "Sounds of *Hatari!*" for Best Original Jazz Composition; "Baby Elephant Walk" for Best Instrumental Theme and Best Instrumental Arrangement; and the album as a whole for Best Performance by an Orch. or Instrumentalist with Orch. (Not Jazz or Dancing). The Blake Edwards-directed *Days of Wine and Roses* drew its greatest attention for the title song (lyrics by Johnny Mercer), which won the Academy Award for Best Song and the Song of the Year Grammy, while Mancini and Andy Williams, who sang it in the film, each scored Top 40 hits. Mancini's instrumental version won two Grammys: Record of the Year and Best Background Arrangement. In the absence of a Mancini LP of the score, Williams's *Days of Wine and Roses* album topped the charts and went gold.

Mancini had only two film scores released in 1963, which may have afforded him more time for his recordings. *Our Man in Hollywood*, which hit the Top Ten in

March, contained his versions of some of his own and others' film music; it earned a Grammy nomination for Best Performance by an Orch. or Instrumentalist with Orch. (Not Jazz or Dancing). *Uniquely Mancini*, a collection of jazz and R&B standards, was in the Top Ten in June. Mancini had a surprise Top 40 hit in July, as his instrumental "Tinpanola" from *Mr. Lucky Goes Latin* was given a lyric by Al Stillman and recorded by Perry Como as "(I Love You) Don't You Forget It." Mancini's most notable film work of the year came with the December release *Charade*, one of the year's biggest box office hits. The title song, with lyrics by Johnny Mercer, was an Academy Award nominee, and there were two instrumental versions of it in the Top 40, one by Mancini and the other by Sammy Kaye. Mancini's *Charade* LP made the Top Ten and earned a Grammy nomination for Best Performance by a Chorus.

Of Mancini's five film scores in 1964, the most memorable was Blake Edwards's *The Pink Panther*, which earned him an Academy Award nomination. His single of *"The Pink Panther* Theme" reached the Top 40 and won three Grammys, for Best Instrumental Composition (Other Than Jazz), Best Instrumental Performance (Other Than Jazz), and Best Instrumental Arrangement. His album *The Pink Panther* hit the Top Ten, went gold, and earned two Grammy nominations, for Album of the Year and Best Original Score Written for a Motion Picture or TV Show. Blake Edwards quickly followed up the film with a sequel, *A Shot in the Dark*, released in June, and Mancini's score included the title tune (lyrics by Robert Wells), which he took into the singles charts.

In July RCA released the hits collection *The Best of Mancini*, which went gold. Mancini's next notable film score came with the release of *Dear Heart* in December. The title song (lyrics by Jay Livingston and Ray Evans) earned an Academy Award nomination for Best Song, Grammy nomination for Song of the Year, and was recorded by Andy Williams and Jack Jones for Top 40 hits. Mancini's chart single of the song was nominated for a 1964 Grammy for Best Performance by a Chorus and his Top Ten LP *Dear Heart and Other Songs About Love*, released later, was nominated for the same award in 1965.

Mancini's only film score of 1965 was for Blake Edwards's box office hit *The Great Race*. From it came the song "The Sweetheart Tree" (lyrics by Johnny Mercer); it was nominated for an Academy Award. Johnny Mathis and Mancini had chart singles with the song, and Mancini earned a Grammy nomination for Best Instrumental Performance (Non-Jazz). In February 1966, Mancini released the double-album *The Academy Award Songs*, containing his renditions of Oscar-winning songs dating back to 1934; it reached the charts and earned a Grammy nomination for Best Performance by a Chorus. May brought the release of *Arabesque*, the second of three films with Mancini scores released in 1966. His *Arabesque* album charted and earned three Grammy nominations: Best Instrumental Theme and Best Instrumental Arrangement for the title tune, and Best Original Score Written for a Motion Picture or TV Show for the album itself. In August, Blake Edwards's film *What Did You Do in the War, Daddy?* was released with a Mancini score that included "In the Arms of Love" (lyrics by Jay Livingston and Ray Evans), which Andy Williams recorded for a chart entry. In September, RCA released *A Merry Mancini Christmas*, a perennial seller that eventually went gold.

Mancini's record sales declined starting in 1966, but he continued to place albums in the lower reaches of the charts and to write an average of three film scores a year. In June 1969 he scored a surprise #1, million-selling hit with his recording of "Love Theme from *Romeo & Juliet*" (music by Nino Rota) from his album *A Warm Shade of Ivory*, which went gold and hit the Top Ten. The single was nominated for Grammys for Record of the Year and Best Contemporary Instrumental Performance, and won for Best Instrumental Arrangement. By 1969 his film scores were being released as soundtrack albums by various labels rather than as Henry Mancini albums by RCA, and the film *Me, Natalie*, which opened in July 1969 with a soundtrack on Columbia Records, earned him a Grammy nomination for Best Original Score Written for a Motion Picture or TV Special.

Since his RCA contract still called for three albums a year, Mancini's work turned up with even greater frequency in record stores. In 1970, for example, eight albums containing his music were released: RCA's newly recorded *Theme from "Z" and Other Film Music*, *Mancini Country*, and *Mancini Plays the Theme from "Love Story,"* plus the compilation LP *This Is Henry Mancini* (all of which reached the charts) and soundtracks from four films that opened during the year with his scores—*The Molly Maguires* (Paramount), *The Hawaiians* (United Artists), *Darling Lili* (RCA), and *Sunflower* (Avco Embassy). During that year's Grammy competition, he won his 19th award for Best Contemporary Instrumental Performance for the *Theme from "Z" and Other Film Music* LP, his 20th for Best Instrumental Arrangement for the track "Theme from *Z*" (music by Mikis Theodorakis), and earned nominations for Best Instrumental Composition for the track "Theme from *Sunflower*" and Best Original Score Written for a Motion Picture or TV Special for the *Darling Lili* LP. (The track "Theme from *Love Story*" [music by Francis Lai], released too late to qualify for the 1970 Grammys, was nominated for a 1971 Grammy for Best Pop Instrumental Performance.) At the Oscars, he was nominated for Best Song for "Whistling Away the Dark" (lyrics by Johnny Mercer) from *Darling Lili*, Best Original Score for *Sunflower*, and Best Original Song Score for *Darling Lili*.

After doing little work on television for the previous decade, Mancini began to accepting assignments writing TV themes, such as those for the network adventure series *Cade's County*, the children's show *Curiosity Shop*, and the syndicated series *Circus!*, all in 1971. He did his next film work on *Sometimes a Great Notion*, released in November 1971, a country-styled score featuring the song "All His Children" (lyrics by Alan and Marilyn Bergman), sung on the soundtrack by Charley Pride and nominated for an Academy Award. Pride's recording hit the country Top Ten in March 1972. That year Mancini expanded his television activities, hosting and writing music for his own syndicated show, *The Mancini Generation*, for which 28 episodes were taped. His "Theme from *The Mancini Generation*" earned a Grammy nomination for Best Instrumental Arrangement, and he also got two nominations in connection with the album *Brass on Ivory*, which he did with trumpeter Doc Severinsen, Best Pop Instrumental Performance with Vocal Coloring for the LP as a whole, and Best Instrumental Composition for the title tune.

Mancini returned to film-scoring in 1973 with three movies, the most notable of which was *Oklahoma Crude*, including the song "Send a Little Love My Way" (lyrics by Hal David), sung on the soundtrack by Anne Murray, whose recording made the pop and country charts. He scored another four films released in 1974, including the MGM compilation *That's Entertainment!*, a major box office hit. Among the three films featuring his scores that were released in 1975, the box office hit *Return of the Pink Panther* marked a reunion with Blake Edwards, and the his RCA album of the film's music earned him a Grammy nomination for Best Album of Original Score Written for a Motion Picture or TV Special. He also wrote music for the TV movie *The Blue Knight* in 1975, one of several television films he would score in subsequent years. He had another four film scores in 1976, among them *The Pink Panther Strikes Again*, featuring the song "Come to Me" (lyrics by Don Black), which was nominated for an Academy Award. He also released two new albums on RCA, and two tracks from the first—*Henry Mancini Conducts the London Symphony Orch. in a Concert of Film Music*—earned Grammy nominations, for Best Instrumental Arrangement for "The Disaster Movie Suite" and Best Instrumental Composition for "The White Dawn."

Mancini's most notable work of 1977 was the score for the television miniseries *The Money Changers*. Among the three feature films and two TV movies he scored in 1978, the most successful was *Revenge of the Pink Panther*, which earned him an Academy Award nomination for the song "Move 'Em Out" (lyrics by Leslie Bricusse) and two Grammy nominations, Best Pop Instrumental Performance for "*The Pink Panther* Theme ('78)" and Best Album of Original Score Written for a Motion Picture or TV for the soundtrack LP. He left RCA after 20 years with the November release of the album *The Theme Scene*. He scored three films in 1979, notably *10*, which earned him Academy Award nominations for Best Song for "It's Easy to Say" (lyrics by Robert Wells) and Best Original Score and a Grammy nomination for Best Pop Instrumental Performance for "Ravel's *Bolero*." There were two features and a TV movie in 1980 and four features in 1981. In 1982 he won his fourth Academy Award for Best Original Song Score for *Victor/Victoria*, a film musical starring Julie Andrews and directed by Blake Edwards; the soundtrack album earned him a Grammy nomination for Best Album of Original Score Written for a Motion Picture or a TV Special. He was also up for a 1982 Grammy for Best Instrumental Composition for "*The Thorn Birds* Theme" from his score from the popular TV miniseries *The Thorn Birds*, broadcast during the 1982–83 season.

Mancini scored three films in 1983 and two in 1984. Also in 1984, he teamed with flutist James Galway for the album *In the Pink*, which earned him a Grammy nomination for Best Arrangement on an Instrumental for the track "Cameo for Flute...For James." There were three film scores in 1985 and another three in 1986, among them *That's Life!*, from which the song "Life in a Looking Glass" (lyrics by Leslie Bricusse) was nominated for an Academy Award. Also in 1986, he accompanied Johnny Mathis on the chart album *The Hollywood Musicals*, from the which the track "It Might as Well Be Spring" earned him a Grammy nomination for Best Instrumental Arrangement Accompanying Vocal(s). Among his two feature and two TV film scores of 1987, the one for the theatrical release *The Glass Menagerie* resulted in a soundtrack album that earned him two Grammy nominations, for Best Album of Original Instrumental Background Score Written for a Motion Picture or TV and for Best Instrumental Composition for the track "The Blues in Three."

Mancini scored two feature films and a TV movie in 1988. His album *Premier Pops*, recorded with the Royal Philharmonic Orch., earned him a Grammy nomination for Best Arrangement on an Instrumental for "Suite from *The Thorn Birds*"; he also was nominated for Best Instrumental Arrangement Accompanying Vocal(s) for the title track from *Volare*, an album he recorded with Luciano Pavarotti. In 1990, Mancini re-signed to RCA and recorded *Mancini in Surround: Mostly Monsters, Murders and Mysteries*, which earned a Grammy nomination for Best Arrangement on an Instrumental for the track "Monster Movie Music Suite." His next RCA album, *Cinema Italiano: Music of Ennio Morricone and Nino Rota*, released in April 1991, brought him a Grammy nomination for Best Arrangement on an Instrumental for the track "The Untouchables" (music by Ennio Morricone).

Mancini cut back somewhat on his scoring activities in the early 1990s to work on a stage musical version of *Victor/Victoria*. He died of pancreatic cancer in 1994 at age 70. *Victor/Victoria*, starring Julie Andrews and directed by Blake Edwards, opened on Broadway in 1995 and ran 738 performances. The cast album earned Mancini his 73rd Grammy nomination for Best Musical Show Album.

WRITINGS: *Sounds and Scores: A Practical Guide to Professional Orchestration* (Los Angeles, 1961); with G. Lees, *Did They Mention the Music?* (Chicago, 1989).

WORKS (only works for which Mancini was a primary, credited composer are listed): **FILM SCORES:** *Lost in Alaska* (1952); *Back at the Front* (1952); *Walking My Baby Back Home* (1953); *The Glenn Miller Story* (1954); *So This Is Paris* (1954); *Abbott and Costello Meet the Mummy* (1955); *This Island Earth* (1955); *Ain't Misbehavin'* (1955); *Foxfire* (1955); *The Second Greatest Sex* (1955); *The Benny Goodman Story* (1956); *Rock, Pretty Baby* (1956); *The Great Man* (1956); *Man Afraid* (1957); *The Kettles on Old MacDonald's Farm* (1957); *Joe Dakota* (1957); *Damn Citizen!* (1958); *Flood Tide* (1958); *Touch of Evil* (1958); *Summer Love* (1958); *Voice in the Mirror* (1958); *Never Steal Anything Small* (1959); *High Time* (1960); *The Great Impostor* (1961); *Breakfast at Tiffany's* (1961); *Bachelor in Paradise* (1961); *Experiment in Terror* (1962); *Mr. Hobbs Takes a Vacation* (1962); *Hatari!* (1962); *Days of Wine and Roses* (1962); *Soldier in the Rain* (1963); *Charade* (1963); *Man's*

Favorite Sport? (1964); *The Pink Panther* (1964); *A Shot in the Dark* (1964); *The Killers* (1964); *Dear Heart* (1964); *The Great Race* (1965); *Moment to Moment* (1966); *Arabesque* (1966); *What Did You Do in the War, Daddy?* (1966); *Two for the Road* (1967); *Gunn* (1967); *Wait Until Dark* (1967); *The Party* (1968); *Me, Natalie* (1969); *Gaily, Gaily* (1969); *The Molly Maguires* (1970); *Sunflower,* aka *I Girasoli* (1970); *The Hawaiians* (1970); *Darling Lili* (1970); *The Night Visitor* (1970); *Sometimes a Great Notion* (1971); *The Thief Who Came to Dinner* (1973); *Visions of Eight* (1973); *Oklahoma Crude* (1973); *That's Entertainment!* (1974); *99 and 44/100% Dead* (1974); *The White Dawn* (1974); *The Girl from Petrovka* (1974); *The Great Waldo Pepper* (1975); *The Return of the Pink Panther* (1975); *Once Is Not Enough* (1975); *W. C. Fields and Me* (1976); *Alex and the Gypsy* (1976); *Silver Streak* (1976); *The Pink Panther Strikes Again* (1976); *House Calls* (1978); *Revenge of the Pink Panther* (1978); *Who Is Killing the Great Chefs of Europe?* (1978); *The Prisoner of Zenda* (1979); *Nightwing* (1979); *10* (1979); *Little Miss Marker* (1980); *A Change of Seasons* (1980); *S.O.B.* (1981); *Mommie Dearest* (1981); *Condorman* (1981); *Back Roads* (1981); *Victor/Victoria* (1982); *Trail of the Pink Panther* (1982); *Better Late Than Never* (1982); *Second Thoughts* (1983); *The Man Who Loved Women* (1983); *Curse of the Pink Panther* (1983); *Angela* (1984); *Harry and Son* (1984); *That's Dancing!* (1985); *Santa Claus: The Movie* (1985); *Lifeforce* (1985); *The Great Mouse Detective* (1986); *A Fine Mess* (1986); *That's Life!* (1986); *Blind Date* (1987); *The Glass Menagerie* (1987); *Sunset* (1988); *Without a Clue* (1988); *Physical Evidence* (1989); *Welcome Home* (1989); *Ghost Dad* (1990); *Switch* (1991); *Tom and Jerry: The Movie* (1992); *Married to It* (1993); *Son of the Pink Panther* (1993). **TELEVISION SERIES:** *Peter Gunn* (1958); *Mr. Lucky* (1959); *The Richard Boone Show* (1963); *The Pink Panther* (1969); *Circus!* (1971); *Cade's County* (1971); *Curiosity Shop* (1971); *The Mancini Generation* (1972); *Columbo* (1973); *The Invisible Man* (1975); *Charlie's Angels* (1976); *What's Happening!!* (1976); *Sanford Arms* (1977); *Kingston: Confidential* (1977); *Co-Ed Fever* (1979); *Ripley's Believe It or Not* (1982); *Remington Steele* (1982); *Newhart* (1982). **TELEVISION FILM SCORES:** *Carol for Another Christmas* (1964); *The Blue Knight* (1975); *The Money Changers* (1977); *Funny Business* (1978); *A Family Upside Down* (1978); *The Best Place to Be* (1979); *The Shadow Box* (1980); *The Thorn Birds* (1983); *Hotel* (1983); *Murder by the Book* (1987); *If It's Tuesday, It Still Must Be Belgium* (1987); *Justin Case* (1988); *Peter Gunn* (1989); *Fear* (1990); *Never Forget* (1991); *Julie* (1992). **ORCH.:** *Beaver Valley '37*, symphonic suite (June 7, 1969, Philadelphia Orch., conducted by Henry Mancini). **MUSICALS/REVUES:** *Victor/Victoria* (N.Y., Oct. 25, 1995). **BIBL.:** M. Okun, ed., *The H. M. Songbook* (1981).—**WR**

Mancinus (real name, Mencken), Thomas,

German composer; b. Schwerin, 1550; d. there, 1611 or 1612. He was educated at the Univ. of Rostock. In 1572 he became Kantor in Schwerin. After serving as Kapellmeister in Güstrow in 1576, he resumed his post in Schwerin. From 1579 to 1581 he was a tenor at the Berlin court. About 1583 he entered the service of the Bishop of Halberstadt in Gröningen, becoming Kapellmeister in 1584. In 1587 he founded the Hofkantorei in Wolfenbüttel, directing it until 1604. In addition to his well known Passions according to St. Matthew and St. John (publ. in Wolfenbüttel, 1620), he publ. secular songs (1588), bicinia (1597), madrigals (1605), and motets (1608).
—**LK/DM**

Mandac, Evelyn (Lorenzana), Filipino soprano; b. Malaybalay, Mindanao, Aug. 16, 1945. After training at the Univ. of the Philippines (B.A., 1963), she pursued her studies at the Oberlin (Ohio) Coll.- Cons. of Music and then at the Juilliard School of Music in N.Y. (M.A., 1967). In 1968 she made her formal debut in Orff's *Carmina burana* in Mobile, Ala. Her operatic debut followed as Mimi in Washington, D.C., in 1969. On Dec. 19, 1975, she made her Metropolitan Opera debut in N.Y. as Lauretta in *Gianni Schicchi*, and remained with the company until 1978. She also sang opera in San Francisco, Glyndebourne, Rome, Houston, Geneva, and other cities, and she also toured as a concert artist. Among her roles were Despina, Zerlina, Susanna, Pamina, Juliet, and Mélisande. She also created roles in Pasatieri's *Black Widow* (1972) and *Inez de Castro* (1976).
—**NS/LK/DM**

Mandel, Alan (Roger), gifted American pianist and teacher; b. N.Y., July 17, 1935. He began taking piano lessons with Hedy Spielter at the incredible underage of 3–1/2, and continued under her pianistic care until he was 17. In 1953 he entered the class of Rosina Lhévinne at the Juilliard School of Music in N.Y. (B.S., 1956; M.S., 1957); later took private lessons with Leonard Shure (1957–60). In 1961 he obtained a Fulbright fellowship; went to Salzburg, where he studied advanced composition with Henze (diplomas in composition and piano, 1962); completed his training at the Accademia Monteverdi in Bolzano (diploma, 1963). He made his debut at N.Y.'s Town Hall in 1948. In later years, he acquired distinction as a pianist willing to explore the lesser-known areas of the repertoire, from early American music to contemporary scores. He taught piano at Pa. State Univ. (1963–66), was head of the piano dept. at the American Univ. in Washington, D.C. (from 1966), and founded the Washington (D.C.) Music Ensemble (1980) with the aim of presenting modern music of different nations. As a pianist, he made numerous tours all over the globe. One of Mandel's chief accomplishments was the recording of the complete piano works of Charles Ives. He composed a Piano Concerto (1950), Sym. (1961), piano pieces, and songs.
—**NS/LK/DM**

Mandelbaum, (Mayer) Joel, American composer; b. N.Y., Oct. 12, 1932. He studied with Piston at Harvard Univ. (B.A., 1953), with Fine and Shapero at Brandeis Univ. (M.F.A., 1955), and at Ind. Univ. (Ph.D., 1961, with the diss. *Multiple Division of the Octave and the Tonal Resources of 19- tone Temperament*); also studied with Dallapiccola at the Berkshire Music Center at Tanglewood and with Blacher at the Berlin Hochschule für Musik. He held a Fulbright fellowship (1957) and was a fellow at the MacDowell Colony (1968). He taught at Queens Coll. of the City Univ. of N.Y. (from 1961), where he served as director of its Aaron Copland School of Music. Many of his compositions reflect his study of microtonal music and the utilization of the Scalatron, an instrument with a color-coordinated keyboard that can be rearranged into divisions of the octave up to and including 31 tones.

WORKS: DRAMATIC: O p e r a : *The Man in the Man-made Moon* (1955); *The 4 Chaplains* (1956); *The Dybbuk* (1971; rev. 1978). **OTHER:** Light operas; musicals; incidental music; film scores. **ORCH.:** *Convocation Overture* (1951); Piano Concerto (1953); *Sursum corda* (1960); *Sinfonia Concertante* for Oboe, Horn, Violin, Cello, and Small Orch. (1962); *Memorial* for Strings (1965); Trumpet Concerto (1970). **CHAMBER:** *Moderato* for Cello and Piano (1949); Flute Sonata (1950); Wind Quintet (1957); 2 string quartets (1959, 1979); *Xenophony No. 1* for 3 Horns and Trombone (1966) and *No. 2* for Violin, Cello, Double Bass, Wind Quintet, and Organ (1979); *Romance* for String Trio (1973); *Fanfare* for Brass (1974); 3 Tonal Studies for Large Chamber Ensemble (1979); Oboe Sonata (1981); Clarinet Sonata (1983). **KEYBOARD:** Piano Sonata (1958); 9 Preludes in 19-tone temperament for 2 Specially Tuned Pianos (1961); 10 Studies for Fokker Organ based on the Conora Suler (1964); *Moderato* for 2 Pianos (1965); *Allegro agitato* for 2 Pianos (1979); 4 Miniatures in 31-tone temperament for Architone or Scalatron (1979). **VOCAL:** Mass for Men's Voices and Organ (1954); choruses; songs.—**NS/LK/DM**

Mandić, Josip, Croatian composer; b. Trieste, April 4, 1883; d. Prague, Oct. 5, 1959. He received training in Trieste, Zagreb, and Vienna. Among his works were the operas *Mirjana* (Olomouc, Feb. 20, 1937) and *Kapetan Niko* (1944), 4 syms. (1929, 1930, 1953, 1954), a Nonet, a String Quartet, *Croatian Mass*, and cantatas.—**NS/LK/DM**

Mandini, Stefano, notable Italian baritone; b. 1750; d. c. 1810. He sang in Venice (1775–76) and Parma (1776). With his wife, the soprano Maria Mandini, he made his Vienna debut with the Italian Opera in Cimarosa's *L'italiana in Londra* (May 5, 1783), where they soon established themselves as prominent figures on the operatic stage. Mandini scored a major success as Almaviva in Paisiello's *Il Barbiere di Siviglia* during the 1783–84 season. He sang the role of the Poet in Salieri's *Prima la musica e poi le parole* on Feb. 7, 1786. On May 1, 1786, he created the role of Count Almaviva in Mozart's *Le nozze di Figaro*, his wife taking the role of Marcellina. Mandini remained in Vienna until 1788, and then sang in Paris and Venice (1794–95). In 1795 he once more sang in Vienna. His brother, Paolo Mandini (b. Arezzo, 1757; d. Bologna, Jan. 25, 1842), was a tenor. He studied with Saverio Valente. After making his debut in Brescia (1777), he appeared at Milan's La Scala (1781), and in Turin, Parma, Bologna, and Rome. In 1783–84 he sang under Haydn at Esterháza. On May 6, 1785, he made his Vienna debut in Anfossi's *I viaggiatori felici*. After a sojourn in Venice (1787), he returned to Vienna in 1789. —**NS/LK/DM**

Mandrell, Barbara (Ann), multitalented country queen of the mid-1970s and early 1980s; b. Houston, Tex., Dec. 25, 1948. Born in Tex. but raised in southern Calif., Mandrell began playing with the family band at a young age, and was adept at a number of instruments, particularly the pedal steel guitar. When Mandrell was 11, she was already playing the instrument in Las Vegas shows, and two years later she toured with Johnny Cash performing for military shows in Vietnam and Korea.

After a minor hit as a vocalist on "Queen for a Day" released by the small Mosrite label, Mandrell and family moved to Nashville, where she was signed by Columbia in 1969. Her first success was covering R&B standards, beginning with "I've Been Loving You Too Long" originally recorded by Otis Redding, followed with such chestnuts as "Do Right Woman—Do Right Man" through 1973's "Midnight Oil." In mid-decade, she signed with ABC/Dot, and her first period of major success occurred, including 1977's "Married (But Not to Each Other)" and the 1978 #1 cleverly titled country hit, "Sleeping Single in a Double Bed."

Mandrell continued to be a major star in the early 1980s, thanks to increased exposure hosting a network variety program with her sisters, Irlene and Louise. A combination of *Hee Haw* and the *Bell Telephone Hour*, the show offered the girl's sweet harmonies and musical talents, as well as decidedly low-tech comedy routines. Mandrell continued to churn out solo hits, including 1981's "I Was Country When Country Wasn't Cool," 1983's "One of a Kind Pair of Fools," and 1984's duet with Lee Greenwood, "To Me."

Barbara's life and career were dealt a severe blow in 1984 when she was involved in a head-on collision, leading to a long period of hospitalization and some doubts about her ability to recover. She came back a year later with the hit "Angels in Your Arms," although her popularity on the country charts was already eroding due to the influx of new-country stars.

Through the mid-1990s, Mandrell continued to draw in big audiences at Vegas (or Branson, Mo.) like few other stars, but her chart-topping days were over, perhaps because her older style of country-meets-pop crooning seems somewhat outdated in today's return-to-roots renascence. In 1997, she gave a well-publicized farewell show, saying she wished to focus on her acting career.

DISC.: *Treat Him Right* (1971); David Houston: *A Perfect Match* (1972). *The Midnight Oil* (1973); *The Best of Barbara Mandrell and David Houston* (1974); *This Time I Almost Made It* (1974); *The Best of Barbara Mandrell* (1977); *This Is Barbara Mandrell* (1976); *Midnight Angel* (1976); *Lovers, Friends & Strangers* (1977); *Love's Ups and Downs* (1978); *Moods* (1978); *The Best of Barbara Mandrell* (1979); *Just for the Record* (1979); *Love Is Fair* (1980); *Looking Back* (1981); *Barbara Mandrell Live* (1981); *In Black and White* (1982); *He Set My Life to Music* (1982); *Spun Gold* (1983); *Clean Cut* (1984); Lee Greenwood: *Meant for Each Other* (1984). *Christmas at Our House* (1984); *Barbara Mandrell's Greatest Hits* (1985); *Get to the Heart* (1985); *Moments* (1986); *Sure Feels Good* (1987); *I'll Be Your Jukebox Tonight* (1988); *Precious Memories* (1989); *Morning Sun* (1990); *No Nonsense* (1990); *The Key's in the Mailbox* (1991); *The Best of Barbara Mandrell* (1992); *The Barbara Mandrell Collection* (1995); *Acoustic Attitude* (1995); *It Works for Me* (1995).—**HB**

Mandyczewski, Eusebius, eminent Rumanian musicologist; b. Czernowitz, Aug. 17, 1857; d. Vienna, July 13, 1929. He entered the Univ. of Vienna (1875), where his teachers included Hanslick (music history) and Nottebohm (music theory); he also studied harmony with R. Fuchs at the Vienna Cons. In 1880 he became conductor of the Vienna Singakademie and archivist of the Gesellschaft der Musikfreunde; was made a prof. of music history and composition at the

Cons. (1892). He oversaw the first complete critical ed. of Schubert's works (40 vols. in 21 series, Leipzig, 1884–97), for which he received an honorary Ph.D. from the Univ. of Leipzig (1897). In 1879 he met Brahms, and they subsequently became good friends. With H. Gal, he ed. selected works by other composers. He composed some songs and piano pieces.—NS/LK/DM

Manelli, Francesco, Italian composer and bass; b. Tivoli, Sept. 1594; d. Parma, July 1667. He became a chorister at Tivoli Cathedral about 1605, where he later was cantore ordinario (1609–24) and maestro di cappella (1627–29). During a sojourn in Rome, he married the singer Madalena in 1625. By 1637 he was in Venice, where he wrote and sang in the opera *L'Andromeda* for the opening of the Teatro S. Cassiano, the first public opera house. In 1638 he became a member of the choir at San Marco. In 1639 his opera *La Delia* inaugurated the new Teatro SS. Giovanni e Paolo. He later went to Parma as a member of the choir of S. Maria della Steccato, while his wife was in the service of the court. He also was in the service of the Duke of Parma from 1645. Although the music to his operas is lost, some librettos are extant. His vocal collection *Ciaccone et arie, libro terzo,* op.3 (Rome, 1629) survives.—NS/LK/DM

Manén, Juan, Catalan violinist and composer; b. Barcelona, March 14, 1883; d. there, June 26, 1971. He received training in solfège and piano at a very early age from his father. At 5, he began to study violin and, at 7, made his public debut as a violinist. At 9, he made his first appearances in America. Following studies with Ibarguren, he made tours of Europe from 1898. He spent some years in Germany, where his orch. compositions were influenced by Wagner and Strauss. After returning to his homeland, he devoted himself principally to composition. Much of his music was redolent of Catalan melorhythms. His writings, all publ. in Barcelona, included *Mis experiencias* (1944), *Variaciones sin tema* (1955), *El violin* (1958), *El jóven artista* (1964), and *Diccionario de celebridades musicales* (1974).

WORKS: DRAMATIC: *Juana de Nápoles,* opera (Barcelona, Jan. 1903); *Acté,* opera (Barcelona, Dec. 3, 1903; rewritten as *Neró i Akté,* Karlsruhe, Jan. 28, 1928); *Der Fackeltanz,* opera (Frankfurt am Main, 1909); *Heros,* opera (n.d.); *Camino del sol,* theater sym. (Leipzig, 1913); *Don Juan,* tragic comedy (n.d.); *Soledad,* opera (n.d.); *Triana,* ballet (1952). OTHER: Many orch. works, including pieces for violin and strings; chamber music; violin pieces; guitar music.—NS/LK/DM

Manfred Mann, British R&B-flavored rock band of the 1960s. MEMBERSHIP: Manfred Mann (real name, Michael Lubowitz), kybd. (b. Johannesburg, South Africa, Oct. 21, 1940); Paul Jones (real name, Paul Pond), voc. (b. Portsmouth, Hampshire, England, Feb. 24, 1942); Michael Vickers, gtr. (b. Southampton, Hampshire, England, April 18, 1941); Tom McGuinness, bs. (b. London, England, Dec. 2, 1941); Mike Hugg, drm. (b. Andover, Hampshire, England, Aug. 11, 1942). Later members included Jack Bruce, bs. (b. Glasgow, Scotland, May 14, 1943); Klaus Voorman, bs. (b. Berlin, Germany,

April 29, 1942); Mike D'Abo, voc. (b. Betchworth, Surrey, England, March 1, 1944).

Mike Lubowitz started studying piano at age six and moved to England from South Africa in 1961. In London, as Manfred Mann, he formed the Mann-Hugg Blues Brothers with drummer Mike Hugg in late 1962. Following the addition of vocalist Paul Jones, the group became Manfred Mann. Debuting at London's Marquee club in March 1963, the group quickly established themselves on the rhythm-and-blues club circuit, replacing their original bassist with Tom McGuinness at the beginning of 1964.

Signed to HMV Records (Ascot in the U.S.), Manfred Mann scored their first British hit with "5-4-3-2-1" in early 1964, followed by "Hubble Bubble Toil and Trouble" and Jeff Barry and Ellie Greenwich's "Do Wah Diddy Diddy," a top British and American hit. After the major hit "Sha La La," the group had a major British and minor American hit with "Come Tomorrow" and British-only hits with Carole King and Gerry Goffin's "Oh No Not My Baby" and Bob Dylan's "If You Gotta Go, Go Now."

In late 1965, Mike Vickers left Manfred Mann, as Tom McGuinness switched to guitar and Jack Bruce was recruited to play bass. Following the top British and major American hit "Pretty Flamingo," the group switched to Fontana Records (Mercury in the U.S.). By the end of July 1966, Paul Jones had left Manfred Mann for a solo career and Jack Bruce had departed to form Cream. They were replaced by singer Mike D'Abo and German bassist Klaus Voorman. Jones starred in the 1967 movie *Privilege* and managed two smash British-only hits from the film, "High Time" and "I've Been a Bad Boy." Manfred Mann continued to achieve British-only hits through 1969, including "Semi-Detached Suburban Mr. Jones," "Ha! Ha! Said the Clown," and "Fox on the Run," but only Bob Dylan's previously unrecorded "The Mighty Quinn" proved a top British and major American hit.

Manfred Mann disbanded in the middle of 1969, and Mann and Mike Hugg soon regrouped as the jazz-styled Chapter Three for one album. Mike D'Abo co- authored "Build Me Up Buttercup" (a smash British and American hit for the Foundations in 1968 and 1969) and authored "Handbags and Gladrags" (a moderate hit for Rod Stewart in 1972) and recorded two solo albums for A&M Records in the early 1970s. In 1971, Mann formed Manfred Mann's Earth Band, scoring a British-only hit with "Joybringer" in 1973 and a top American hit with Bruce Springsteen's "Blinded by the Light" from *The Roaring Silence,* their best-selling album, in 1976. Realigned in 1979, The Earth Band endured until 1986.

DISC.: MANFRED MANN: *The Manfred Mann Album* (1964); *The Five Faces of Manfred Mann* (1965); *My Little Red Book of Winners* (1965); *Mann Made* (1966); *Pretty Flamingo* (1966); *Up the Junction* (soundtrack) (1968); *The Mighty Quinn* (1968). CHAPTER THREE: *Manfred Mann's Chapter Three* (1970). EARTH BAND: *Manfred Mann's Earth Band* (1972); *Glorified, Magnified* (1972); *Get Your Rocks Off* (1973); *Solar Fire* (1974); *The Good Earth* (1974); *Nightingales and Bombers* (1975); *The Roaring Silence* (1976); *Watch* (1978); *Angel Station* (1979); *Chance* (1981); *Somewhere in Afrika* (1983).—BH

Manfredini, Francesco Onofrio, Italian violinist and composer, father of **Vincenzo Manfredini**; b. Pistoia (baptized), June 22, 1684; d. there, Oct. 6, 1762. He studied violin with Torelli and counterpoint with Perti in Bologna, then went to Ferrara (c. 1699), where he was made 1st violinist at the Church of the Holy Spirit. He then entered the orch. of S. Petronio in Bologna (1704), and also became a member of the Accademia Filarmonica in that city. He subsequently was maestro di cappella at St. Philip's Cathedral in Pistoia (1727–62).

WORKS: (12) *Concertini per camera* for Violin, and Cello or Theorbo, op.1 (Bologna, 1704); (12) *Sinfonie da chiesa* for 2 Violins, Basso Continuo (Organ), and Viola ad libitum, op.2 (Bologna, 1709); (12) *Concerti* for 2 Violins and Basso Continuo obbligato and 2 Violins, Viola, and Bass, op.3 (Bologna, 1718); 6 Sonatas for 2 Violins, Cello, and Basso Continuo (Harpsichord) (London, c. 1764); 6 oratorios.—**NS/LK/DM**

Manfredini, Vincenzo, Italian composer and writer on music, son of **Francesco Onofrio Manfredini**; b. Pistoia, Oct. 22, 1737; d. St. Petersburg, Aug. 16, 1799. After initial training from his father, he studied in Bologna with Perti and in Milan with Fioroni. In 1758 he accompanied his brother to Moscow. Moving on to St. Petersburg, he became maestro di cappella to Peter Fedorovich. When the latter became Czar, Manfredini was made maestro of the court's Italian opera company in 1762. With the arrival of Galuppi in 1765, however, Manfredini's influence waned and he was relegated to composing ballets. In 1769 he was granted a pension and settled in Bologna. For the most part, he devoted himself to writing on music. In 1798 his former pupil, now Czar Paul I, recalled him to Russia but Manfredini died before taking up any position for his patron. He publ. *Regole armoniche, o sieno Precetti ragionati* (Venice, 1775; 2nd ed., rev. and aug., 1797) and *Difesa della musica moderna* (Bologna, 1788).

WORKS: DRAMATIC: Opera: *Semiramide riconosciuta* (Oranienbaum, 1760); *Olimpiade* (Moscow, Nov. 24, 1762); *Carlo Magno* (St. Petersburg, 1763; rev. 1764); *La finta ammalata* (St. Petersburg, 1763); *La pupilla* (St. Petersburg, 1763); *Armida* (Bologna, May 1770); *Artaserse* (Venice, Jan. 1772). **Ballet:** *Amour et Psyché* (Moscow, Oct. 20, 1762); *Pygmalion* (St. Petersburg, Sept. 26, 1763); *Les Amants réchappées du naufrage* (St. Petersburg, 1766); *Le Sculpteur de Carthage* (St. Petersburg, 1766); *La Constance récompensée* (Moscow, 1767). **ORCH.:** Harpsichord Concerto (The Hague and Amsterdam, 1769?); 6 syms. (Venice, 1776). **CHAMBER:** 6 harpsichord sonatas (St. Petersburg, 1765); 6 string quartets (Florence, 1781?). **VOCAL:** Cantatas; sacred music.—**NS/LK/DM**

Mangold, Carl (Ludwig Amand), German conductor and composer, brother of **(Johann) Wilhelm Mangold**; b. Darmstadt, Oct. 8, 1813; d. Oberstdorf im Allgau, Aug. 5, 1889. He studied at the Paris Cons. with Berton and Bordogni. Returning to Darmstadt, he became a violinist in the Court Orch. and, from 1848 to 1869, was court music director and also conducted various choral societies there. He wrote an opera, *Tannhäuser*, which was produced in Darmstadt on May 17, 1846, only a few months after the premiere of Wagner's great work. In order to escape disastrous comparisons,

the title was changed to *Der getreue Eckart*, the libretto revised, and the new version was produced posthumously in Darmstadt on Jan. 17, 1892. Mangold also wrote 4 more operas, *Das Köhlermädchen, oder Das Tournier zu Linz* (1843), *Die Fischerin* (1845), *Dornröschen* (1848), and *Gudrun* (1851). Other works include 8 syms., concertos, several oratorios, masses, cantatas, various choral works, many of which were popular in his day, particularly the "concert drama" Die Hermannsschlacht (Mainz, 1845), chamber music, some 375 songs, and piano pieces.—**NS/LK/DM**

Mangold, (Johann) Wilhelm, German violinist, conductor, and composer, brother of **Carl (Ludwig Amand) Mangold**; b. Darmstadt, Nov. 19, 1796; d. there, May 23, 1875. He studied with Rinck and Abbé Vogler, then went to Paris for lessons with Cherubini, Méhul, and Kreutzer at the Cons. (1815–18). In 1825 he became a court conductor at Darmstadt. He was pensioned in 1857. Mangold wrote 3 operas, chamber music, and melodies for clarinet with piano, which were popular for a time.—**NS/LK/DM**

Mangon, Johannes, South Netherlands composer; b. c. 1525; d. Aachen, 1578. He was a duodenus in the collegiate choir school of St. Martin-en-Mont in Liège (1535–42), where he was made officiatus in 1544 and 2nd succentor in 1562; he also served as rector of the altar of St. Jean-le-Baptiste. About 1567 he became active at Aachen Cathedral, where he was succentor by 1572. Mangon composed many fine masses and motets.

BIBL.: R. Pohl, *Die Messen des J. M.* (Aachen, 1960).
—**LK/DM**

Manhattan Transfer, The, tight harmony and vocalese group gone pop. **MEMBERSHIP:** Tim Hauser (b. Troy, N.Y., Dec. 12, 1941); Alan Paul (b. Newark, N.Mex., Nov. 1949); Janis Siegel (b. Brooklyn, N.Y., Jul. 23, 1952); Laurel Massé (b. Holland, Mich., Dec. 29, 1951); Cheryl Bentyne (b. Mount Vernon, Wash., Jan. 17, 1954).

Tim Hauser had sang in doo-wop groups during his youth. He then formed a jug band under the name of Manhattan Transfer, which released the album *Jukin'*, a commercial nonstarter. Following his initial brush with failure, Hauser was driving a cab in N.Y. Coincidentally, he picked up Laurel Massé, a session singer, in his cab. She recognized his name from *Jukin'*, and he got her phone number. Not long afterward, he met Janis Siegel. She had recorded for Lieber and Stoller's Red Bird records in her teens as part of the Young Generation, and was also doing session work. He convinced them both to become part of a new Manhattan Transfer. He recruited Alan Paul from the original cast of the Broadway show *Grease*, and in 1972, the four vocalists were under way.

Through the mid-1970s they built up an audience, first playing N.Y.C.'s gay bathhouses. They started getting cabaret bookings at clubs like Trudy Heller's and even rock venues like Max's Kansas City. Atlantic records signed them in 1974, and they released their eponymous debut album in the summer of 1975. It reached #33 and eventually went platinum, helped by a summer replacement show that the band hosted on CBS-TV. The single, "Operator," hit #22.

They went into the studio with pop producer Richard Perry and released *Coming Out*. While it only hit #48 in the U.S., their French cover of "Chanson D'Amour" became a huge hit in Europe. Their next album, *Pastiche* (1978) only reached #66 in the states, but did far better in Europe. They toured Europe that spring, and an album recorded on that tour hit #4 in the U.K.

Before they went into the studio to record their next album, Masse left the band; Cheryl Bentyne replaced her. With producer Jay Graydon, they made the album *Extensions*. While it didn't chart, one of the album's standout tracks is a vocalese version of Weather Report's "Birdland," with lyrics by master jazz vocalist/songwriter John Hendricks. It won a 1980 Grammy Award for Best Vocal or Instrumental Jazz Fusion Performance. The single "Twilight Zone/Twilight Tone" reached #30; the album hit #55.

1981's *Mecca for Moderns* continued in the vein of sophisticated swing, with a jazzy update of the Ad Libs' 1965 hit "The Boy from New York City." The Manhattan Transfer version reached #7, the group's only Top Ten single in the U.S. At the 1981 Grammys, the tune won for Best Pop Performance by a Duo or Group with Vocal. Additionally, the track "Until I Met You (Corner Pocket)" won for Best Duo or Group Jazz Vocal Performance. The album topped out at #22.

The early 1980s saw a series of albums that featured further pop-jazz vocal outings. They attracted only middling sales for the group, despite numerous awards and accolades from the press. In 1985, the group hooked up again with John Hendricks. He wrote all of the lyrics for the band's next effort, *Vocalese*. The album earned 12 Grammy nominations, second only to Michael Jackson's *Thriller* in total number of nominations. They took home two awards: one for Best Duo or Group Jazz Vocal Performance, and one for Bentyne (who joined in 1979) and Bobby McFerrin's vocal arrangements. Two years later, taking a somewhat different tack, they recorded English versions of popular Brazilian songs for the album *Brasil*. It became the first entire album to earn a Grammy for Best Pop Performance by a Duo or Group with Vocal, and peaked at #96.

The 1990s again saw the group moving between experimentation and more mainstream efforts. 1991's *Offbeat of Avenues*, was an eclectic affair. With contributions from members of Steely Dan and Take 6, along with jazz greats Mark Isham and Jeff Lorber, among others, the album entered the top 200 at 179 in its first week, then disappeared. Still, they took home a Best Contemporary Jazz Performance Grammy for the tune "Sassy." They then recorded a Christmas album that featured Tony Bennett, and also did a children's record, reprising the 1945 Paul Tripp classic *Tubby the Tuba*.

The group returned to the pop arena with 1995's *Tonin'*, consisting of mostly covers of songs they sang in their teens. The album had an impressive guest list: Bette Midler, Phil Collins, Ben E King, Ruth Brown, James Taylor, B. B. King, Smoky Robinson, Laura Nyro, among others. Nonetheless, it topped off at a torpid #123. In 1998, they released *Swing*, another eclectic, star-studded affair, featuring such diverse artists as jazz violinist Stephane Grappelli, country star Ricky Skaggs, and Tex. swing band Asleep at the Wheel. Despite this talented group, the album made the jazz charts but not the pop.

Disc.: *Jukin'* (1969); *The Manhattan Transfer* (1975); *Coming Out* (1976); *Pastiche* (1976); *Extensions* (1979); *Mecca for Moderns* (1981); *Bodies and Souls* (1983); *Bop Doo-Wop* (1983); *Mantra: Live in Tokyo* (1983); *Vocalese* (1985); *Brasil* (1987); *The Offbeat of Avenues* (1991); *The Christmas Album* (1992); *The Manhattan Transfer Meets Tubby the Tuba* (1994); *Tonin'* (1995); *Swing* (1998). —HB

Mankell, (Ivar) Henning, Swedish composer, teacher, and music critic; b. Härnösand, June 3, 1868; d. Stockholm, May 8, 1930. He received piano lessons from Hilda Thegerström and Lennart Lundberg, and also studied at the Stockholm Cons. (from 1887), where he took diplomas in organ (1889) and music education (1891). As a composer, he was autodidact. After teaching in Härnösand, he settled in Stockholm in 1899 as a teacher of piano and harmony. He also wrote music criticism for the *Svenska Margonbladet* and *Stockholms-Tidningen* (1899–1907), and was active as a short-story writer. In 1917 he was elected a member of the Royal Academy of Music. Mankell's compositions, most especially his works for piano, are the work of a gifted individualist writing in a basically Romantic vein. His vast output of piano music included a Piano Concerto (1917), sonatas, ballads, nocturnes, impromptus, préludes, intermezzi, legends, miniatures, etc. He also wrote 3 string quartets, a Piano Quintet, a Piano Trio, violin sonatas, and songs.—NS/LK/DM

Mann, Alfred, German-born American musicologist and choral conductor; b. Hamburg, April 28, 1917. He was a student of Kurt Thomas, Hans Mahlke, and Max Seiffert at the Berlin Hochschule für Musik (certificate, 1937). After teaching at the Berlin Hochschule für Kirchen- und Schulmusik (1937–38), he studied at the Milan Cons. (1938). In 1938–39 he taught at the Suola Musicale di Milano. In 1939 he emigrated to the U.S. and in 1943 he became a naturalized American citizen. He studied at the Curtis Inst. of Music in Philadelphia (diploma, 1942), where he also taught (1939–42) before completing his education with Paul Henry Lang, William J. Mitchell, and Erich Hertzmann at Columbia Univ. (M.A., 1950; Ph.D., 1955, with the diss. *The Theory of Fugue*). From 1947 to 1980 he taught at Rutgers Univ. He was conductor of the Cantata Singers in N.Y. from 1952 to 1959, and of the Bach Choir in Bethlehem, Pa., from 1970 to 1980. In 1978 he was a visiting prof. at Columbia Univ. He was a prof. at the Eastman School of Music in Rochester, N.Y., from 1980 to 1987, and continued to teach there as a prof. emeritus from 1987. He served as ed. of the Rutgers Documents of Music series (1951–88) and the *American Choral Review* (1962–98), and also edited works for the critical editions of Handel, Fux, Mozart, and Schubert. His articles have appeared in many scholarly journals.

WRITINGS: Ed. J. Fux's *Gradus ad Parnassum (Die Lehre vom Kontrapunkt)* (Celle, 1938; 2nd ed., 1951; partial Eng. tr., N.Y., 1943, as *Steps to Parnassus*; 2nd ed., N.Y. and Toronto, 1965, as *The Study of Counterpoint*); *The Study of Fugue* (New Brunswick, N.J., 1958; 3rd reprint, N.Y., 1987); *Bethlehem Bach Studies* (N.Y., 1985); *Theory and Practice: The Great Composer as Student and Teacher* (N.Y. and London, 1987); ed. *Modern Music Librarianship* (Stuyvesant, N.Y., and Kassel, 1988); *Handel: The Orchestral Music* (N.Y.,1995); ed. with G. Buelow, Paul Henry Lang's *Musicology and Performance* (New Haven, N.Y., and London, 1997).

BIBL.: M. Parker, ed., *Eighteenth-Century Music in Theory and Practice: Essays in Honor of A. M.* (Stuyvesant, N.Y., 1993). —NS/LK/DM

Mann, Barry, and Cynthia Weil,

brilliant professional songwriting team of the 1960s from N.Y.'s Brill Building; Barry Mann (real name, Barry Iberman), b. Brooklyn, N.Y., Feb. 9, 1939; Cynthia Weil, b. N.Y., Oct. 18, 1937.

Barry Mann abandoned his architecture studies to become a songwriter in 1958. Achieving his first hit in collaboration with Mike Anthony in early 1959 with "She Say (Oom Dooby Doom)" as performed by The Diamonds, he was hired as a staff songwriter to Al Nevins and Don Kirshner's Aldon Music, housed at N.Y.'s famed Brill Building. Teaming with several other writers on 1960s hits, Mann co-wrote "Footsteps" for Steve Lawrence, "I Love How You Love Me" for the Paris Sisters, and the maudlin "Patches" for Dickey Lee. Encouraged by Don Kirshner, Mann recorded an album of his own for ABC Records in 1961 that yielded a near-smash hit with the novelty song "Who Put the Bomp (In the Bomp, Bomp, Bomp)," co-written with Gerry Goffin.

Barry Mann's greatest success came in collaboration with Cynthia Weil, whom he married in 1961. Their early hit compositions included "Uptown" and "He's Sure the Boy I Love" for the Crystals, both from 1962. The couple's hit songs from 1963 included "My Dad" for Paul Petersen, "Blame It on the Bossa Nova" for Eydie Gorme, "Only in America" for Jay and the Americans, and the classic "On Broadway" for the Drifters. Subsequent hit compositions were "I'm Gonna Be Strong" for Gene Pitney, "Saturday Night at the Movies" for the Drifters, and "We Gotta Get Out of This Place" for the Animals. In late 1964, the duo worked with songwriter-producer Phil Spector on "Walking in the Rain" for the Ronettes and the classic "You've Lost That Lovin' Feelin'" for the Righteous Brothers. During 1966, they provided the Righteous Brothers with "(You're My) Soul and Inspiration" and Paul Revere and the Raiders with "Kicks" and "Hungry." Other hit compositions with which they were associated through 1970 included Max Frost and The Troopers' "Shapes of Things to Come," Cass Elliot's "It's Getting Better" and "Make Your Own Kind of Music," and B. J. Thomas's "I Just Can't Help Believing."

By the late 1960s, Barry Mann and Cynthia Weil had left Aldon Music and moved to the West Coast, where Mann unsuccessfully attempted to launch a solo recording career. Another attempt in 1975 yielded the minor hit "The Princess and the Punk." Later hits with which Barry Mann was associated included "Here You Come Again" by Dolly Parton and "Sometimes When We Touch" with Dan Hill, both from 1977. Barry Mann and James Homer composed the music for the 1986 animated film *An American Tail.*

DISC.: BARRY MANN: *Who Put the Bomp* (1961); *Lay It All Out* (1972); *Survivor* (1975); *Barry Mann* (1980). **BARRY MANN AND JAMES HOMER (COMPOSERS):** *An American Tail* (soundtrack) (1987).—BH

Mann, Herbie (originally, Solomon, Herbert Jay),

flutist, bass clarinetist, tenor saxophonist; b. N.Y., April 16, 1930. Mann may have been the first jazz musician to succeed by playing the flute exclusively. He studied at the Manhattan School of Music. His flute playing is much more diatonic than typical modern jazz, perhaps to fit in with the Latin and modal world music contexts he so often uses. He has also pioneered the use of jazz with such unusual world musics as gagaku from Japan.

Mann began to specialize in flute and Latin music around 1959. With Doc Cheatham, he toured Africa, returning to N.Y. in April 1960. His touring band at the time included noted Latin musicians such as Patato Valdes. He began to investigate and record bossa-nova music in 1961 and had his first hit single and album in 1962.

Do the Bossa Nova, despite its title, was perhaps the first LP to feature an American jazz musician recorded in Brazil with Brazilian groups, including the Sergio Mendes band before they came to the U.S. His "Comin' Home Baby," a simple riffing blues written by his bassist Ben Tucker, was his biggest hit of that era. He played in Brazil and Japan and regularly topped many listener/reader polls throughout the 1960s. His album *Memphis Underground* was a monster smash and an early jazz/rock/fusion document.

During the 1970s, Mann moved into reggae and disco, had his own label, and produced sessions by Ron Carter, Miroslav Vitous, and Attila Zoller, among others. Mann's popularity waned in the 1980s, and he has never been a critical favorite. He has been living in N.Mex. since—and discovered in 1997 that he has inoperable prostate cancer.

DISC.: *Herbie Mann Plays* (1954); *Herbie Mann, Vol. 2* (1955); *Herbie Mann in Sweden* (1956); *Et Tu Flute* (1957); *Flute Flight* (1957); *Flute Souffle* (1957); *Great Ideas of Western Mann* (1957); *Mann Alone* (1957); *Sultry Serenade* (1957); *Yardbird Suite* (1957); *Just Wailin'* (1958); *African Suite* (1959); *Flautista* (1959); *Californians* (1960); *Common Ground* (1960); *Evolution of Mann* (1960); *Flute, Brass, Vibes and Percussion* (1960); *At the Village Gate* (1961); *Epitome of Jazz* (1961); *Family of Mann* (1961); *Monday Night at the Village Gate* (1961); *Nirvana* (1961); *Return to the Village Gate* (1961); *Brasil, Bossa Nova and Blue* (1962); *Do the Bossa Nova with Herbie Mann* (1962); *Latin Fever* (1962); *St. Thomas* (1962); *Herbie Mann Live at Newport* (1963); *My Kinda Groove* (1964); *Our Mann Flute* (1964); *Herbie Mann Today* (1965); *Latin Mann* (1965); *Standing Ovation at Newport* (1965); *& Tamiko Jones* (1966); *Big Band Mann* (1966); *Bongos, Conga and Flute* (1966); *Herbie Mann's Big Band* (1966); *Impressions of the Middle East* (1966); *New Mann at Newport* (1966); *Afro Jazziac* (1967); *Wailing Dervishes* (1967);

Live at the Whisky (1968); *Memphis Underground* (1968); *Windows Opened* (1968); *Concerto Grosso in D Blues* (1970); *Memphis Two Step* (1970); *Muscle Shoals Nitty Gritty* (1970); *Stone Flute* (1970); *Push Push* (1971); *At Newport* (1972); *Brazil Blues* (1972); *Hold on I'm Coming* (1972); *London Underground* (1973); *Reggae* (1974); *First Light: The Family of Mann* (1975); *Mann in Sweden* (1975); *Bird in a Silver Cage* (1976); *Gagaku and Beyond* (1976); *Surprises* (1976); *Herbie Mann and Fire Island* (1977); *Herbie Mann with Joao Gilberto* (1977); *When Lights Are Low* (1977); *Brasil* (1978); *Herbie Mann and Jasil Brazz* (1988); *Caminho De Casa* (1990); *Peace Pieces* (1995).—**LP**

Mann, Leslie (Douglas), Canadian composer and clarinetist; b. Edmonton, Alberta, Aug. 13, 1923; d. Balmoral, Manitoba, Dec. 7, 1977. He began to study clarinet at 13 and composition at 15. He was first clarinetist of the CBC Winnipeg Orch. (1958) and of the Winnipeg Sym. Orch. (1960–71). His music followed along traditional lines in an accessible manner.

WORKS: CHAMBER Opera: *The Donkey's Tale* (1971). ORCH.: *Concertino in the Old Style* for Strings (1955); Flute Concerto (1964); Clarinet Concerto (1970); *Sinfonia concertante* for Bassoon and Chamber Orch. (1971); *Concerto grosso No. 1* for Chamber Orch. (1972); *Meditations on a Chorale* for Strings (1972); 3 syms. (1973; 1974; *Typhoon*, 1976). CHAMBER: *5 Bagatelles* for Clarinet or Viola and Piano (1951); Trio for Flute, Clarinet, and Cello (1952); Cello Sonata (1953); *5 Improvisations* for Flute and Piano (1954); *Toccata alla Barocco* for Flute, Clarinet, and Cello (1956); Wind Quintet (1961); Clarinet Sonata (1962); Suite for Clarinet (1963); *Suite* for Flute (1963); Trio for Clarinet, Cello, and Piano (1967); *4 Studies in the Blues Idiom* for Wind Quintet (1969); *Music* for Clarinet, Viola, and Piano (1971); *Partita* for Violin and Bassoon (1972); Sonata for Solo Violin (1974); *Vocalise* for Oboe or Clarinet and Piano (1974); String Quartet (1975); Suite for Saxophone (1976); Flute Sonata (1977). VOCAL: *My Master Have a Garden*, cantata for Soprano and Orch. (1963); *Weep You No More Sad Fountains* for Voice and Chamber Orch., after Elizabethan poems (1974).—**NS/LK/DM**

Mann, Robert (Nathaniel), American violinist, conductor, teacher, and composer; b. Portland, Ore., July 19, 1920. He studied violin with Déthier at the Juilliard Graduate School in N.Y., and had instruction in chamber music with Betti, Salmond, and Letz. He also took courses with Schenkman in conducting, and with Wagenaar and Wolpe in composition. In 1941 he won the Naumburg Competition, and made his N.Y. debut as a violinist. From 1943 to 1946 he was in the U.S. Army; then joined the faculty of the Juilliard School and in 1948 founded the Juilliard String Quartet, in which he played 1st violin, and which was to become one of the most highly regarded chamber music groups; in 1962 it was established as the quartet-in-residence under the Whittall Foundation at the Library of Congress in Washington, D.C., without suspending its concert tours in America and abroad. As a conductor, Mann specialized in contemporary music; was associated as a performer and lecturer with the Music Festival and Inst. at Aspen, Colo., and also served with the NEA; in 1971 he was appointed president of the Walter W. Naumburg Foundation. He has composed a String Quartet (1952), Suite for String Orch. (1965), and several "lyric trios" for Violin, Piano, and Narrator.—**NS/LK/DM**

Mann, William (Somervell), English music critic, writer on music, and translator; b. Madras, Feb. 14, 1924; d. Bath, Sept. 5, 1989. He studied piano with Kabos and composition with Seiber; also studied at Magdalene Coll., Cambridge (1946–48), with Patrick Hadley, Hubert Middleton, and Robin Orr. He was on the music staff of the *Times* of London (1948–60); was its chief music critic (1960–82). He made many serviceable Eng. trs. of opera librettos and lieder texts. He publ. *Introduction to the Music of Johann Sebastian Bach* (London, 1950), *Richard Strauss: A Critical Study of the Operas* (London, 1964), and *The Operas of Mozart* (London, 1977).—**NS/LK/DM**

Manna, Gennaro, Italian composer; b. Naples, Dec. 12, 1715; d. there, Dec. 28, 1779. He was a pupil at the Cons. de S. Onofrio a Capuana in Naples, where his uncle, Francesco Feo, was primo maestro. In 1744 he was made maestro di cappella at the Naples Cathedral. He concurrently pursued a successful career as a theater composer. In 1755 he became an interim teacher at S. Maria di Loreto, where he then served on the faculty (1756–61). While continuing in his post at the Naples Cathedral, he also was maestro di cappella at the Ss. Annunziata from 1761. In later years, he devoted himself to composing sacred music. In addition to 13 stage works, he also composed 8 oratorios and more than 150 other sacred scores. His brother, Giacinto Manna (b. Naples, Sept. 13, 1706; d. there, March 11, 1768), was a harpsichordist. His son, Gaetano Manna (b. Naples, May 12, 1751; d. there, 1804), was a composer. His uncle Gennaro helped launch his career as a theater composer following his studies with Gallo and Fenaroli at S. Maria di Loreto. Upon his uncle's retirement at Ss. Annunziata, he became maestro di cappella. He also was secondo maestro at the Naples Cathedral and maestro di cappella at other churches. Among his works were an oratorio and masses.—**LK/DM**

Manneke, Daan, Dutch composer, organist, conductor, and teacher; b. Kruiningen, Nov. 7, 1939. He received training in organ from H. Houët and Louis Toebosch, and in composition from Jan van Dijk at the Brabant Cons. in Tilburg (1963–67). He completed his training in organ with Kamiel d'Hooghe in Brussels and in composition with Ton de Leeuw in Amsterdam. In 1972 he became a teacher at the Sweelinck Cons. in Amsterdam. He also was founder-conductor of the Cappella Breda chamber choir. In 1977 he was awarded the Fonteyn Tuynhout Prize and in 1999 the Culture Prize of the province of Noord Brabant.

WORKS: DRAMATIC: Opera: *De passie van Johannes Mattheus Lanckohr* (1977); *Jules*, chamber opera (1988). ORCH.: *4 Sonatas* (1972); *Sine nome* for 3 Instrumental Groups (1972); *Motet* for Orch. of Renaissance Instruments (1975); 2 sinfonias (1975, 1982); *En passant* for Small Orch. (1977); *Ruimten* for Strings (1978); *Babel* for 6 Orchs. (1985); *Organum II* (1986; also for Organ as *Organum*); *Archipel V: Les ponts* for Wind Orch. and Men's Chorus ad libitum (1992); Symphonies of Wind Instruments (1997; also for Organ, 1996). CHAMBER: *Chiasma* for Piano Quartet (1970); *Walking in Fog Patches* for Wind Quintet (1971); *Jeux* for Flute (1971); *Plein jeu* for Brass Quintet (1972); *Stages III* for Variable Ensemble (1972); *Diaphony for Geoffrey* for

Horn, Trumpet, Trombone, and Piano (1973); *Ordre* for 4 Recorders (1976); *Clair obscur* for Recorder and Organ (1978; also for Piano and Harpsichord); *Vice versa* for 5 Instruments (1979); *Ramificazioni* for Piano Trio (1979); *Wie ein Hauch...(eine kleine Nachtmusik)* for Flute (1979); *Gesti* for Clarinet (1979; also for Bass Tuba or Bass Trombone); *Rondeau* for Percussion (1979); *Gestures* for Bass Clarinet and Marimba (1981); *Archipel II* for Viola, Cello, and Double Bass (1985) and *III* for Guitar (1987); *Arc* for String Quartet (1994); *Van tijd tot tijd* for 5 Recorders (1998). O r g a n : *Diaspora* (1969); *Pneoo* (1979); *Organum* (1986; also for Orch. as *Organum II*); *Offertoire sue les grands jeux* (1996); *Symphonies of Winds* (1996; also for Wind Instruments, 1997). V O C A L : *Qui iustus est, iustificetur adhuc*, cantata for Chorus, Clarinet, Trombone, Electric Guitar, and Percussion (1970); *3 Times* for Chorus and Orch. (1975); *Job* for Baritone/Reciter, Men's Chorus, 4 Brasses, and 3 Percussionists (1976); *Chants and Madrigals* for Chorus (1980); *Trans* for Chorus and 8 Instruments (1982); *Messe de Notre Dame* for Chorus (1986); *Plenum* for Chorus and Orch. (1989); *Messa di voce* for Soprano and Organ (1990; also for Chorus and Organ, 1992, and for Women's Chorus and Organ, 1992); *Topos* for Vocal Ensemble (1995); *Vonjmem* for Soprano and Ensemble (1997); *Leçons de ténèbres* for Men's Chorus (1998); songs.—**NS/LK/DM**

Mannelli, Carlo, Italian castrato soprano, violinist, and composer; b. Rome, Nov. 4, 1640; d. there, Jan. 6, 1697. He entered the service of Prince Camillo Pamphili as a child, receiving training in voice and violin. He sang in patronal festivities at S. Luigi dei Francesi (1650, 1651), and appeared as Lerino in P. Ziani's opera *Le fortune di Rodope e Damira* (Venice, 1657). In 1660 he became a singer at S. Luigi dei Francesi, where he also was a violinist from 1665. He was its first violinist (1676–82), and then resumed his position as a singer there. From 1659 to 1664 he was also a singer at the Arciconfraternità del Ss. Crocifisso at S. Marcello, where he likewise was a violinist, later serving as its first violin (1668–90). From 1663 he also was a violinist of the Congregazione di S. Cecilia. He was much esteemed as a violinist and composer. His trio sonatas are particularly noteworthy (Rome, 1682, 1692).—**NS/LK/DM**

Manners, Charles (real name, **Southcote Mansergh**), Irish bass and opera impresario; b. London, Dec. 27, 1857; d. Dundrum, County Dublin, May 3, 1935. He studied in Dublin, then at the Royal Academy of Music in London and in Florence. In 1882 he made his stage debut with the D'Oyly Carte company in London, creating the role of Private Willis in Gilbert and Sullivan's *Iolanthe*. In 1890 he married **Fanny Moody**, with whom he organized the Moody-Manners Opera Co. (1898); it toured widely until its demise in 1916. He retired from active management of its affairs in 1913. —**NS/LK/DM**

Mannes, Clara (née **Damrosch**), German-born American pianist and teacher, daughter of **Leopold Damrosch** and mother of **Leopold Damrosch Mannes**; b. Breslau, Dec. 12, 1869; d. N.Y., March 16, 1948. She was a pupil of her father, of Scholtz in Dresden, and of Busoni in Berlin (1897). In 1898 she married **David Mannes**, with whom she toured in duo concerts throughout the U.S. In 1916 they founded the David Mannes Music School in N.Y., where she taught for many years.

BIBL.: M. Mannes, *Out of My Time* (Garden City, N.Y., 1971).—**NS/LK/DM**

Mannes, David, American pedagogue, violinist, and conductor, father of **Leopold Damrosch Mannes**; b. N.Y., Feb. 16, 1866; d. there, April 25, 1959. He was a student in violin of August Zeiss and C.R. Nicolai in N.Y., of Heinrich de Ahna and Carl Halíř in Berlin, and of Ysaÿe in Brussels. Returning to N.Y., he played in various theater orchs. In 1894 he organized the Music School Settlement. In 1895 he became a violinist in the N.Y. Sym. Soc., which he served as concertmaster from 1903 to 1912. In 1898 he married **Clara Mannes** (née **Damrosch**), with whom he subsequently made duo concert tours of the U.S. In 1912 he founded the Music School Settlement for Colored Children in Harlem. With his wife, he organized the David Mannes Music School in 1916, where he remained active for many years. In 1953 it became the Mannes Coll. of Music. He also was founder-conductor of a series of free sym. concerts at the Metropolitan Museum of Art (1918–47). His career is the subject of his memoir, publ. as *Music Is My Faith* (N.Y., 1938).

BIBL.: M. Mannes, *Out of My Time* (Garden City, N.Y., 1971).—**NS/LK/DM**

Mannes, Leopold (Damrosch), American pianist, teacher, composer, and inventor, son of **David Damrosch** and **Clara Mannes** (née **Damrosch**); b. N.Y., Dec. 26, 1899; d. Martha's Vineyard, Mass., Aug. 11, 1964. He studied at Harvard Univ. (B.A., 1920) and took courses at the Mannes School of Music and the Inst. of Musical Arts in N.Y., numbering among his teachers were Quaile, Maier, Berthe Bert, and Cortot in piano, and Johannes Schreyer, Goetschius, and Scalero in composition. He won a Pulitzer scholarship (1925) and a Guggenheim fellowship (1927). In 1922 he made his debut in N.Y. as a pianist; taught theory and composition at the Mannes School (1927–31), then worked for the Eastman Kodak Co. in Rochester, N.Y., where he invented the Kodachrome process of color photography with Loepold Godowsky, son of the pianist, in 1935. He subsequently was director (1940–48) and a teacher of theory and composition (1946–48) at the Mannes School; was its co-director (1948–52) and president (1950–64). He was also active with his own Mannes Trio (1948–55). He wrote *3 Short Pieces* for Orch. (1926), incidental music to Shakespeare's *Tempest* (1930), String Quartet (1928), Suite for 2 Pianos (1924), and songs. —**NS/LK/DM**

Manning, Jane (Marian), English soprano; b. Norwich, Sept. 20, 1938. She was a student of Greene at the Royal Academy of Music in London (1956–60), of Husler at the Scuola di Canto in Cureglia, Switzerland, and of Frederick Jackson and Yvonne Rodd-Marling in London. In 1964 she made her debut in London singing songs of Webern, Messiaen, and Dallapiccola, and subsequently established herself as a leading proponent of modern music. From 1965 she sang regularly on the

BBC, and also toured extensively around the globe. In all, she sang in more than 300 premieres of contemporary scores. In 1988 she founded her own Jane's Minstrels in London, an ensemble devoted to the furtherance of contemporary music. She was active as a lecturer, serving as a visiting prof. at Mills Coll. in Oakland, Calif. (1982–86), as a lecturer at the Univ. of York (1987), as a visiting prof. at the Royal Academy of Music (from 1995), and as an honorary prof. at the Univ. of Keele (1996–99). She publ. the book *New Vocal Repertory: An Introduction* (2 vols., Oxford, 1994, 1997). In 1990 she was made a member of the Order of the British Empire. In 1966 she married **Anthony Payne.** —NS/LK/DM

Manning, Kathleen Lockhart, American composer and singer; b. Hollywood, Oct. 24, 1890; d. Los Angeles, March 20, 1951. She was a student of Moszkowski in Paris (1908). She sang in France and England, including an engagement with the Hammerstein Opera Co. in London (1911–12), and later in the U.S. (1926), but she devoted herself principally to composition. Her output reflected her interest in oriental subjects à la the French impressionists.

WORKS: DRAMATIC: *Operetta in Mozartian Style* (n.d.); *Mr. Wu,* opera (1925–26); *For the Soul of Rafael,* opera (n.d.). ORCH.: 4 symphonic poems; Piano Concerto. CHAMBER: String Quartet; many piano pieces. SONGS: *Water Lily* (1923); *Japanese Ghost Songs* (1924); *Sketches of Paris* (1925); *Sketches of London* (1929); *Chinese Impressions* (1931); *5 Fragments* (1931); *Vignettes* (1933); *Sketches of N.Y.* (1936).—NS/LK/DM

Mannino, Franco, Italian conductor, pianist, composer, novelist, and playwright; b. Palermo, April 25, 1924. He was a student of Silvestri (piano) and Mortari (composition) at the Accademia di Santa Cecilia in Rome. At 16, he made his debut as a pianist. After the end of World War II, he toured as a pianist in Europe and the U.S. He also took up conducting and appeared as a guest conductor throughout Europe, North and South America, and the Far East. In 1968 he founded the Incontri Musicale Romani. From 1969 to 1971 he served as artistic director of the Teatro San Carlo in Naples, where he subsequently was its artistic advisor. He was principal conductor and artistic advisor of the National Arts Centre Orch. in Ottawa from 1982 to 1986, and then was its principal guest conductor from 1986 to 1989. In 1990–91 he was president of the Accademia Filarmonica of Bologna. The Italian Republic gave him its gold medal in 1968 and honored him as Commendatore ordine al merito in 1993. In his compositions, Mannino has generally followed traditional modes of expression with occasional excursions into modernistic practices. In addition to his prolific compositions, he has also written novels, plays, essays, and articles.

WORKS: DRAMATIC: *Mario e il Mago,* azione coreografia (1952; Milan, Feb. 25, 1956); *Vivì,* lyric drama (1955; Naples, March 28, 1957); *La speranza,* melodrama (1956; Trieste, Feb. 14, 1970); *La stirpe di Davide,* tragedy (1958; Rome, April 19, 1962); *La notti della paura,* melodrama (1960; RAI, Rome, May 24, 1963); *Il diavolo in giardino,* comedy (1962; Palermo, Feb. 28, 1963); *Luisella,* drama (1963; Palermo, Feb. 28, 1969); *Il quadro delle*

meraviglie, intermezzo- ballet (Rome, April 24, 1963); *Il ritratto di Dorian Gray,* drama (1973; Catania, Jan. 12, 1982); *Roma Pagana,* ballet (1978); *Il Principe Felice,* theater piece (1981; Milan, July 7, 1987); *Soltanto il rogo,* drama (1986; Agrigento, Oct. 21, 1987); *Le notte Bianche,* Liederopera (1987; Rome, April 14, 1989); *Le teste Scambiate,* legend (1988); *Anno domini 3000,* opera buffa (1993); film scores. ORCH.: *Concertino lirico* for Cello, Strings, and Piano (1938); *Tre tempi* (1951); 2 piano concertos (1954, 1974); 12 syms.: No. 1, *Sinfonia Americana* (1954; Florence, Nov. 11, 1956), No. 2 (1972), No. 3 (1978), No. 4, *Leningrad* (1981), No. 5, *Rideau Lake* (1984; Ottawa, Feb. 12, 1986), No. 6 (1986), No. 7 (1989), No. 8, *Degli Oceani* (1990), No. 9 (Rome, June 27, 1991), No. 10, *Da Colomba a Broadway,* for Baritone, Trombone, Chorus, and Orch. (1991), No. 11 for Baritone and Orch. (1993; Sanremo, Oct. 1994), and No. 12, *Panormus* (1994); *Demoniaca Ouverture* (1963); *Mottetti strumentali* (1964; Rome, June 1, 1965); *Music for Angels* for Piano and Strings (1964; RAI, Naples, Feb. 14, 1966); Concerto for 3 Violins and Orch. (1965); *Suite galante* for Flute, Trombone Obbligato, and Small Orch. (1966); *Otto commenti* (1966); *Laocoonte* (1966; RAI, Turin, April 4, 1969); *Capriccio di capricci* (1967); Concerto for Piano, 3 Violins, and Orch. (1969); *Notturno Napoletano* (1969); Concerto grosso (1970); 2 violin concertos (1970, 1993); 4 cello concertos (1974–90); *Enigma* for Strings (1975; Ottawa, April 1993); *Cinque romanze* for Viola and Orch. (1975); *Sons enchantes* for Flute, Alpine Horn, and Strings (1976); *Molto vibrato* for Violin and Orch. (1978); *Settecento* (1979); *Olympic Concert* for 6 Violins, 2 Pianos, and Orch. (1979); *Nirvana* (1980); Concerto for 6 Violins, 2 Pianos, and Orch. (1980); *Tropical Dances* for Cello Ensemble (1984; RAI, Rome, Nov. 3, 1986; also for Orch., Rome, April 10, 1987); *Piccolo concerto grosso* for Flute, Oboe, and Strings (Rome, Nov. 6, 1985); *Introduzione e aba* for Organ and Orch. (1987); *Atmosfere delle notti Bianche di Pietroburgo* for Trombone and Orch. (1987); *Inquietudini* for Clarinet and Orch. (1987); *6 Romanze senza parole* for Piano, Violin, Viola, Cello, and Orch. (1988); Concerto for Horn and Strings (1990); Concerto for Trombone and Strings (1990); *Suite Italiana* for Clarinet and Strings (1991); *Evanescenze* for Harp and Orch. (1992; Palermo, Dec. 1994; also for Harp and Piano); *La grotta della maga Circe,* overture (1995). CHAMBER: *Melodica e contrappunti* for Flute and Bamboo Pipes (1959); *Variazione capricciose* for 3 Violins (1966); *Piccolo sonata* for Viola and Piano (1966); *Melange capriccioso* for 3 Violins (1966); *Sonata breve* for Guitar (1967); *Cinque duetti* for 2 Violins (1967); *Improvvisazione* for Violin, Horn, and Piano (1969); 3 cello sonatas (1970, 1971, 1986); Sonata for Solo Viola (1970); *Ballata dramatica* for Violin, Viola, Cello, and Piano (1970); String Trio (1974); *Quattro cantabili, un intermezzo e un rondo* for Violin and Piano (1976); 3 Pieces for Viola (1983); *Suoni astrali* for 8 Violas (1985); 7 Pieces for Violin (1985); Suite for Wind Quintet (1986); 2 string quartets (1989, 1994); *Love* for Clarinet and Piano (1990); *Quindici pezzi per l'Adelchi* for Cello (1992); Trio for Violin, Cello, and Piano (1992); Violin Sonata (1994); Quintet for Clarinet and Strings (1995). Piano: 5 sonatas (1950, 1971, 1975, 1979, 1980); many other pieces. OTHER: Choral works; song cycles; solo songs; transcriptions; cadenzas for concertos by Haydn and Mozart.—NS/LK/DM

Manns, Sir August (Friedrich), prominent German-born English conductor; b. Stolzenberg, near Stetting, March 12, 1825; d. London, March 1, 1907. He learned to play the violin, clarinet, and flute in his youth. After playing in Danzig's regimental band and theater orch. (1845–48), he was 1st violinist in Gungl's orch. in Berlin (1848–49). He conducted at Kroll's Garden (1849–51) before serving as a regimental bandmaster in Königsberg and Cologne (1851–54). In 1854 he went to London as asst. conductor of the Crystal Palace band, and in 1855 he became its conductor and proceeded to enlarge it to symphonic proportions. In 1856 he founded the Saturday Concerts at the Crystal Palace, which became famous. He remained their conductor until 1901, and during his long tenure conducted the first British performances of many works. He also conducted the orch. concerts of the Glasgow Choral Union (1879–87) and 6 Triennial Handel Festivals (1883–1900). In 1894 he became a naturalized British subject and in 1903 he was knighted.

BIBL.: H. Wyndham, *A. M. and the Saturday Concerts* (London, 1909).—**NS/LK/DM**

Manojlović, Kosta, Serbian composer; b. Krnjevo, Dec. 3, 1890; d. Belgrade, Oct. 2, 1949. He studied in Munich and at the Univ. of Oxford (B.A., 1919). He wrote a Serbian liturgy, and a cantata, *By the Waters of Babylon,* as well as characteristic piano pieces and songs. He publ. several studies on Serbian folk music. His collection of 337 songs of east Serbia was publ. posthumously (Belgrade, 1953).—**NS/LK/DM**

Manoury, Philippe, French composer; b. Tulle, June 19, 1952. He studied composition with Gérard Condé and Max Deutsch and at the Paris Cons. with Ivo Malec, Claude Ballif, and Michel Philipott (premieres prix in analysis, 1977, and composition, 1978). From 1983 to 1991 he was active with IRCAM in Paris. From 1987 he was also a prof. of composition at the Lyons Cons. He publ. the vol. *La note et le son:Écrits et entretiens (1981–1998)* (Paris, 1998). He composed the opera *60e Parallèle* (Paris, March 10, 1997). Among his other works were *Puzzle* for 31 Players (1975), String Quartet (1978), *Numéro huit* for 103 Players (1980), *Zeitlauf* for 12 Voices, 13 Players, Electronics, and Tape (1983), *Instantanés III* for 5 Groups of Players (Baden-Baden, May 31, 1985), *Aleph* for 4 Speakers and Orch. (Strasbourg, Sept. 26, 1985; rev. 1987), *Les Livre des claviers* for 6 Percussionists (Strasbourg, Sept. 27, 1988), *La Partition du ciel et de l'enfer* for Orch. (1989), *Prélude* for Orch. (1992), and *Pentaphone* for Orch. (1992).—**NS/LK/DM**

Manowarda, Josef von, esteemed Austrian bass; b. Kraków, July 3, 1890; d. Berlin, Dec. 24, 1942. He studied in Graz, making his debut there (1911), then sang at the Vienna Volksoper (1915–18) and in Wiesbaden (1918–19). He then was a principal member of the Vienna State Opera (1919–42), and also appeared at the Salzburg Festivals (from 1922), the Bayreuth Festivals (1931, 1934, 1939, 1942), and the Berlin State Opera (1934–42). In addition, he taught at the Vienna Academy of Music (1932–35). Among his notable roles were Osmin, King Marke, Gurnemanz, and King Philip. He created the role of the Messenger in Strauss's *Die Frau ohne Schatten* (1919). He also pursued a fine concert career.—**NS/LK/DM**

Manrique de Lara (y Berry), Manuel, Spanish composer, folklorist, and music critic; b. Cartagena,

Oct. 24, 1863; d. St. Blasien, Germany, Feb. 27, 1929. After training with a military bandsman, he pursued music studies with Chapi in Madrid (1886). He joined the Spanish Army, attaining the rank of brigadier general. He also was active as a music critic in Madrid (1910–20) and as a folklorist, collecting Spanish ballads of the Sephardic communities in the Near East (1910–11) and in Spanish Morocco (1915–16). He composed *El ciudadano Simon,* zarzuela (1900), *Rodrigo de Vivar (El Cid),* opera (1906), Sym. (1890), *La Orestiada,* symphonic trilogy, and chamber works.—**NS/LK/DM**

Manski, Dorothée, German-American soprano and teacher; b. Berlin, March 11, 1891; d. Atlanta, Feb. 24, 1967. She studied in Berlin, where she made her debut at the Komische Oper (1911); then sang in Mannheim (1914–20) and Stuttgart (1920–24). She was a member of the Berlin State Opera (1924–27); also sang in Max Reinhardt's productions; then appeared as Isolde at the Salzburg Festival (1933) and the Vienna State Opera (1934). She made her Metropolitan Opera debut in N.Y. as the Witch in *Hänsel und Gretel* on Nov. 5, 1927, and remained on the company's roster until 1941; also sang opera in Philadelphia, Chicago, and San Francisco, and appeared as a concert singer with leading European and U.S. orchs. She was prof. of voice at the Ind. Univ. School of Music in Bloomington (1941–65). Among her other roles were Sieglinde, Venus, Gutrune, Brünnhilde, Freia, and Elsa.—**NS/LK/DM**

Manson, Marilyn (originally, **Warner, Brian**), one of the great (and most controversial) rock showmen of the 1990s; b. Canton, Ohio, Jan. 5, 1969. The son of a nurse and a Vietnam-veteran-turned-furniture-salesman, ex-Catholic schoolboy Brian Warner moved to Fla. in his late teens and started working as a music critic. In 1989, he formed a band with his friend Scott Putesky. Warner called himself "Marilyn Manson," Putesky became "Daisy Berkowitz," their stage names blending the mystique of Hollywood stardom with a fascination with serial killers (Marilyn [Monroe]/ [Charles] Manson). Adding bassist Gidget Gein, keyboard player Madonna Wayne Gacy, and drummer Sara Lee Lucas, they started playing around Fla. and selling self-produced tapes. Their show featured elaborate but homemade special effects and Gothic overtones, heavily emphasizing a nihilistic message. Their theatrics and heavy rock earned them a huge following in Fla.

In 1993, Nine Inch Nails' frontman Trent Reznor offered the group a recording deal with his newly formed Nothing Records and an invitation to open for his band. The group replaced Gein with Twiggy Ramirez, and released its first album in 1994, *Portrait of an American Family.* As with Nine Inch Nails' projects, the record was produced by Reznor and mixed in the house formerly owned by film director Roman Polansky and his late wife, actress Sharon Tate. The band hit the road with Nine Inch Nails. Antics like Manson's highly publicized ordination as a minister in the Church of Satan and his ripping up a copy of the Book of Mormon on stage in Salt Lake City earned the band notoriety for its image along with its music, a pummeling blend of industrial and goth. This mixture, along with Manson's high-visibility iconoclasm, earned him a devoted following among disaffected suburban youth.

The mainstream became more aware of Manson and his band with the release of the *Smells Like Children* EP a year later. Their send-up cover of The Eurythmics' "Sweet Dreams (Are Made of This)" became a fixture on MTV, and the EP eventually went platinum. Berkowitz left the band shortly after this, eventually suing the group for being excluded from the record (he settled out of court). Zim Zum replaced him. The band's next release, 1996's *Antichrist Superstar*, debuted on the charts at #3, shipping platinum. The more popular Manson became, the more controversial he was; his concerts often drew picket lines of concerned Christians. He wrote an autobiography, *The Long Hard Road Out of Hell*, with *New York Times* critic Neil Strauss, and appeared on the cover of *Time* magazine as a symbol of his generation's lack of a "moral center."

Severing creative ties with Reznor, the band's next album, 1998's *Mechanical Animals*, eschewed the pounding industrial sound and emphasized more glam-oriented music. It featured a photograph of Manson on the cover with artificial breasts, six fingers, and air-brushed genitalia. The song "The Dope Show" became an alternative hit. Again, the album shipped platinum. The band went on tour with Courtney Love's band, Hole, only to have an onstage war of words break out between the two bands; Hole dropped out of the bill. While they were on the road, two Columbine, Colo. teens shot up their high school, killing several teachers and students, then themselves; the boys citied Manson's website as an inspiration for their act. This put a further damper on the tour, but the group did capture several shows for a live album, *The Last Tour on Earth*.

WRITINGS: With N. Strauss, *The Long Hard Road Out of Hell* (N.Y., 1997).

DISC.: *Portrait of an American Family* (1994); *Smells Like Children* (1995); *Antichrist Superstar* (1996); *Mechanical Animals* (1998); *The Last Tour on Earth* (live; 1999).—**HB**

Mansouri, Lotfi (actually, **Lotfollah**), Iranian-born American opera director and administrator; b. Tehran, June 15, 1929. He studied psychology at the Univ. of Calif., Los Angeles (A.B., 1953). After serving as an asst. prof. on its faculty (1957–60), he was resident stage director of the Zürich Opera (1960–65) and director of dramatics at the Zürich International Opera Studio (1961–65). From 1965 to 1975 he was chief stage director of the Geneva Opera, and from 1967 to 1972 was director of dramatics at the Centre Lyrique in Geneva. In 1976 he became general director of the Canadian Opera Co. in Toronto, remaining there until 1988 when he assumed that position with the San Francisco Opera. His tenure in San Francisco was marked with the major renovation of the opera house in 1996–97, and its gala reopening concert on Sept. 5, 1997. He retired in 2001. In 1992 he was made a Chevalier of l'Ordre des Arts et Lettres de France. Mansouri's opera

productions have been staged at many of the leading opera houses of the world, and generally reflect his traditional approach to the art of stage direction. —**NS/LK/DM**

Mansurian, Tigran, prominent Armenian composer and teacher; b. Beirut, Lebanon, Jan. 27, 1939. His family moved to Soviet Armenia in 1947, where he studied with Baghdasaryan at the Yerevan Music School (1956–60) and with Sarian at the Yerevan Cons. (1960–65). After completing his postgraduate studies at the Cons. (1965–67), he taught modern theory there until being made a teacher of composition in 1986. Mansurian's music owes much to his Armenian heritage. While his early works reflect the influence of the serialists, he pursued an independent road in which Armenian and contemporary elements were effectively synthesized. In his later works, Armenian elements flourished as he infused his creative efforts with modal harmonies and folk-like melodies.

WORKS: DRAMATIC: *The Ice Queen*, ballet (1988); incidental music; film scores. **ORCH.:** Concerto for Organ and Chamber Orch. (1964); *Partita* (1965); *Preludes* (1975); 3 cello concertos: No. 1 (1976), No. 2 (1978), and No. 3 for Cello and 13 Winds (1983); *Canonical Ode* for 2 String Orchs., 4 Harps, and Organ (1977); Double Concerto for Violin, Cello, and Strings (1977); *Nachtmusik* (1980); Concerto for Violin and Strings (1981); *Postludio*, concerto for Clarinet, Cello, and Strings (1993). **CHAMBER:** 2 unnumbered string quartets (1960, 1964); 3 numbered string quartets (1983–84; 1984; 1992); Viola Sonata (1962); Flute Sonata (1963); 2 violin sonatas (1964, 1965); *Allegro barbaro* for Cello (1964); Piano Trio (1965); *Psalm* for 2 Flutes and Violin (1966); *Music* for 12 Strings (1966); *Arabesques I* for 6 Winds and Harp (1969) and *II* for 10 Instruments (1970); *Elegy* for Cello and Piano (1971); *Interior* for String Quartet (1972); *Bird's Silhouette*, suite for Harpsichord and Percussion (1973); 2 cello sonatas (1973, 1974); Quintet for Flute, Oboe, Clarinet, Bassoon, and Horn (1974); *The Rhetorician* for Harpsichord, Flute, Violin, and Double Bass (1978); *Tovem* for 15 Instrumentalists (1979); *Commemorating Stravinsky* for 15 Instruments (1981); 4 *Duets* for Violin Ensemble (1983); *Capriccio* for Cello (1984); 5 *Bagatelles* for Violin, Cello, and Piano (1985); *Le Tombeau* for Cello and Percussion (1989); *Postlude* for Clarinet and Cello (1991–92). **Piano:** Sonatina (1963); Sonata (1967); 3 *Pieces* (1971); *Nostalgia* (1976). **VOCAL:** 3 *Nairain Songs* for Baritone and Orch. (1975); 3 *Madrigals* for Voice, Flute, Cello, and Piano (1981); *Miserere* for Voice and String Orch. (1989); choruses; other songs.—**NS/LK/DM**

Mantelli, Eugenia, Italian mezzo-soprano; b. c. 1860; d. Lisbon, March 3, 1926. Following her operatic debut as Kalad in *Le Roi de Lahore* in Treviso in 1883, she appeared in Europe and South America. On Nov. 23, 1894, she made her Metropolitan Opera debut in N.Y. as Amneris, remaining on the roster until 1897. She was again on its roster from 1898 to 1900 and in 1902–03. In 1896 she sang Brünnhilde in the French-language production of *Die Walküre* at London's Covent Garden. In 1910 she made her farewell appearance in Lisbon, where she settled. Among her other roles were Urbain, Dalila, Siebel, Ortrud, and Azucena.—**NS/LK/DM**

Mantovani, (Annunzio Paolo), Italian-born British conductor and bandleader; b. Venice, Nov. 15,

1905; d. Tunbridge Wells, Kent, March 29, 1980. The most successful bandleader of the 1950s and one of the few British musicians of his time to achieve fame in America. Mantovani led a large, string- filled orchestra playing soothing instrumental music. This formula allowed him to place more than four dozen albums that reached the U.S. charts between 1952 and 1972, seven of which went gold. He also scored gold singles with his recordings of "Charmaine" and "Cara Mia."

Mantovani's father was a classical violinist at La Scala who later led the Covent Garden Orch. His family moved to England in 1912; he became a British subject in 1933. He studied at Trinity Coll. of Music and made his professional debut as a violinist at age 16. By 18 he was leading a band, and within a few years he appeared at major hotels and broadcast on the radio. His first success on records came with "Serenade in the Night" (music and lyrics by C. A. Bixio and B. Cherubini), which made the U.S. hit parade in March 1937.

In the 1940s and early 1950s, Mantovani conducted musicals in the West End, notably Noël Coward's *Pacific 1860* (London, Dec. 19, 1946) and *And So to Bed* (London, Oct. 17, 1951). At the same time, following the introduction of the LP he began to make albums of his lushly orchestrated mood music, well-suited to background listening. His initial success came with a single, "Charmaine" (music and lyrics by Erno Rapee and Lew Pollack), which had been used as the theme song for the 1926 silent film *What Price Glory?* and been a hit for Guy Lombardo and His Royal Canadians. The Mantovani revival peaked in the American Top Ten in December 1951 and sold a million copies.

Mantovani's first chart album, *Selection of Favorite Waltzes*, was in the American Top Ten in September 1952; his first U.K. Top Ten hit came with a revival of "White Christmas" in December. His next U.S. album, *Strauss Waltzes*, released as a 10-inch LP in January 1953, did not chart until 1958 when it was reissued as a 12-inch LP, and later certified gold. In May 1953, his next U.S. album, *Music of Victor Herbert*, went to #1. The same month, his single of the theme from the motion picture *Moulin Rouge* (music by Georges Auric, lyrics by William Engvick) and entered the U.S. and U.K. charts, reaching #1 in Britain and the Top Ten in America. "Swedish Rhapsody" (music by Hugo Alfven) was a U.K. Top Ten hit in the fall. In November came the U.S. album *Christmas Carols*, which did not reach the charts until its reissue as a 12-inch LP in 1957, and eventually went gold.

"Cara Mia" (music and lyrics by Tulio Trapani and Lee Lange) was an unusual Mantovani release in the summer of 1954 in that it featured a vocal, sung by David Whitfield, and was an original composition: "Tulio Trapani" was a pseudonym for Mantovani. The song reached the Top Ten in the U.S. and sold a million copies. (It was revived for a Top Ten hit by Jay and the Americans in 1965.)

Mantovani's next Top Ten album in the U.S. came with the June 1955 release *Song Hits from Theatreland*, which went gold. The gold-selling May 1957 release *Film Encores* was his biggest selling album; it remained the U.S. charts almost four and a half years, finally

going to #1 in July 1959. In the summer of 1957, Mantovani returned to the Top Ten of the U.S. singles charts with "Around the World" (music by Victor Young, lyrics by Harold Adamson). *Gems Forever...*, a follow-up to his recently successful albums of theater and film music, was released in April 1958; it went into the U.S. Top Ten, stayed in the charts two years, and was certified gold.

Mantovani made annual tours of the U.S. and other countries, and during the 1958–59 season he had a syndicated television series, *Mantovani*. But he was primarily known for his recordings, which continued to be successful as the 1950s came to a close. *Continental Encores* became his first U.K. Top Ten LP in early 1959, and the U.S. compilation *Mantovani Stereo Showcase* reached the American Top Ten later that year. Another compilation, *All- American Showcase*, reached the U.S. Top Ten in early 1960. But the conductor's major success of the year was his recording of the theme from the movie *Exodus* (music by Ernest Gold, lyrics by Pat Boone), which became a Top Ten U.S. single in December, with a companion album, *Mantovani Plays Music from Exodus and Other Great Themes* reaching the Top Ten and going gold.

While continuing to sell consistently, Mantovani's frequently released albums rarely reached such sales peaks thereafter. *Italia Mia* was a U.S. Top Ten hit in 1961, as was *American Waltzes* in 1962 and *Latin Rendezvous* in 1963. *Mantovani Magic* reached the U.K. Top Ten in 1966, as did *Mantovani's Greatest Hits* in 1967; the latter went gold in the U.S. by 1970. Two U.K. compilations, *The World of Mantovani* and *The World of Mantovani, Vol. 2*, made the U.K. Top Ten in 1969. Mantovani's last album to chart in the U.S. was his 25th anniversary album (presumably the 25th anniversary of his first 12-inch LP), *Annunzio Paolo Mantovani*, in 1972. In the U.K., the compilation *20 Golden Greats* reached the Top Ten in 1979. Mantovani died at age 74 in 1980, after which Roland Shaw led a ghost orchestra under his name that continued to perform and record.

DISC.: *Selection of Famous Waltzes* (1952); *Strauss Waltzes* (1953); *Music of Victor Herbert* (1953); *Christmas Carols* (1953); *Song Hits from Theatreland* (1955); *Film Encores* (1957); *Gems Forever* (1958); *Continental Encores* (1959); *Mantovani Stereo Showcase* (1959); *All-American Showcase* (1960); *Mantovani Plays Music from "Exodus" and Other Great Themes* (1960); *Italia Mia* (1961); *American Waltzes* (1962); *Latin Rendezvous* (1963); *Mantovani's Magic* (1966); *Mantovani's Greatest Hits* (1967); *The World of Mantovani* (1969); *The World of Mantovani, Vol. 2* (1969); *Annunzio Paolo Mantovani* (1972); *20 Golden Greats* (1979).—**WR**

Mantzaros, Nicolaos, Greek composer and pedagogue; b. Corfu, Oct. 26, 1795; d. there, March 30, 1872. He was born into a wealthy family. Following initial training with Barbatti in Corfu, he studied with Zingarelli at the Cons. di S. Sebastiano (1825–26), and its success, the Cons. di S. Pietro a Majella (1826–27), in Naples. After additional private instruction from Zingarelli (until 1832), he devoted himself to composing and teaching in Corfu. As a teacher, Mantzaros did not accept payment from his students and assisted the poorer ones financially. His most notable pupil was Spyridon Xyndas. Mantzaros was the founder-president of the Socièta Filarmonica di Corfu. As the most important Greek composer of his day, he greatly influenced his successors. His works reveal his Italian training, with some infusions of Greek folk songs and Byzantine music. Among his works are orch. pieces, choral music, part songs, and arrangements; 24 bars from his first setting of the *Hymnos is tin eleftherian* (Hymn to Liberty) for 4 Voices and Piano became the Greek national anthem.—LK/DM

Manuel, Roland
See **Roland-Manuel**

Manziarly, Marcelle de, Russian-born French conductor, pianist, and composer; b. Kharkov, Sept. 13, 1899; d. Ojai, Calif., May 12, 1989. She studied in Paris with Boulanger, in Basel with Weingartner (1930–31), and in N.Y. with Vengerova (1943). She appeared as a pianist and conductor in the U.S. and taught privately in Paris and N.Y. Her works extend the boundaries of tonality through such resources and procedures as polytonality, serialism, and atonality.

WORKS: DRAMATIC: O p e r a : *La Femme en flèche* (1954). **ORCH.:** Piano Concerto (1932); *Sonate pour Notre-Dame de Paris* (1944–45); *Musique pour orchestre* for Small Orch. (1950); *Incidences* for Piano and Orch. (1964). **CHAMBER:** String Quartet (1943); Trio for Flute, Cello, and Piano (1952); *Trilogue* for Flute, Viola da Gamba, and Harpsichord (1957); *Dialogue* for Cello and Piano (1970); *Périple* for Oboe and Piano (1972). **P i a n o :** *Mouvement* (1935); *Arabesque* (1937); *Toccata* (1939); *Bagatelle* (1940); Sonata for 2 Pianos (1946); *6 études* (1949); *Stances* (1967). **VOCAL:** *3 fables de La Fontaine* (1935); *Choeurs pour enfants* (1938); *Poèmes en trio* for 3 Women's Voices and Piano (1940); Duos for 2 Sopranos or 2 Tenors and Piano (1952); Duos for Soprano and Clarinet (1953); 3 chants for Soprano and Piano (1954); *2 odes de Grégoire de Marek* for Alto and Piano (1955); *3 sonnets de Petrarque* for Baritone and Piano (1958); *Le Cygne et le cuisinier* for 4 Solo Voices and Piano (1959). —NS/LK/DM

Manzoni, Giacomo, Italian composer, teacher, and writer on music; b. Milan, Sept. 26, 1932. He studied composition with Contilli at the Messina Liceo Musicale (1948–50); then pursued training at the Milan Cons., where he received diplomas in piano (1954) and composition (1956); also obtained a degree in foreign languages and literature at the Bocconi Univ. in Milan (1955). He was ed. of *Il Diapason* (1956), music critic of the newspaper *L'Unità* (1958–66), and music ed. of the review *Prisma* (1968); later was on the editorial staff of the review *Musica/Realtà*. He taught harmony and counterpoint at the Milan Cons. (1962–64; 1968–69; 1974–91) and composition at the Bologna Cons. (1965–68; 1969–74); also taught at the Scuola di musica in Fiesole (from 1988). In 1982 he was a guest of the Deutscher Akademischer Austauschdienst in Berlin. He contributed articles to Italian and other journals and publications; tr. works of Schoenberg and Adorno into Italian; publ. the books *Guida all'ascolto della musica sinfonica* (Milan, 1967) and *Arnold Schonberg: L'uomo, l'opera, i testi musicati* (Milan, 1975; rev. ed., 1997). Collections of his writings were ed. by C. Tempo (Florence, 1991) and A.

De Lisa (Milan, 1994). As a composer, Manzoni has embraced advanced forms of expression. While pursuing a highly individual serial path, he has explored microstructures, macrostructures, and multiphonics with interesting results.

WORKS: DRAMATIC: O p e r a : *La sentenza* (1959–60; Bergamo, Oct. 13, 1960); *Atomtod* (1963–64; Milan, March 27, 1965); *Per Massimiliano Robespierre* (1974; Bologna, April 17, 1975); *Doktor Faustus*, after Thomas Mann (1985–88; Milan, May 16, 1989). **ORCH.:** *Fantasia-Recitativo-Finale* for Chamber Orch. (1956; Milan, Jan. 21, 1957); *Studio per 24* for Chamber Orch. (Venice, April 13, 1962); *Studio No. 2* for Chamber Orch. (1962–63; Milan, April 20, 1963); *Insiemi* (1966–67; Milan, Sept. 30, 1969); *Multipli* for Chamber Orch. (1972; Washington, D.C., Feb. 23, 1973); *Variabili* for Chamber Orch. (1972–73; Bolzano, March 8, 1973); *Masse: Omaggio a Edgar Varèse* for Piano and Orch. (1976–77; Berlin, Oct. 6, 1977); *Lessico* for Strings (Piacenza, March 23, 1978); *Modulor* (1978–79; Venice, Oct. 7, 1979); *Ode* (1982; Milan, March 11, 1983); *Nuovo incontro* for Violin and Strings (Florence, June 5, 1984); *Adagio e solenne* (1990; San Marino, May 12, 1991); *Malinamusik* (1990; Rome, Sept. 14, 1991). **CHAMBER:** *2 Piccola suites* for Violin and Piano (1952–55; 1956); *Improvvisazione* for Viola and Piano (1958); *Musica notturna* for 7 Instrumentalists (1966; Venice, Sept. 12, 1967); *Quadruplum* for 2 Trumpets and 2 Trombones (1968); *Spiel* for 11 Strings (1968–69; London, April 26, 1969); *Parafrasi con finale* for 10 Instrumentalists (Bavarian Radio, Munich, June 6, 1969); Quartet for Violin, Viola, and Cello (1971); 6 pieces utilizing the title *Percorso: C* for Bassoon and Tape (1974), *a otto* for Double Wind Quartet (1975), *C2* for Bassoon and 11 Strings (1976; Graz, Oct. 15, 1977), *F* for Double Bass (1976), *GG* for Clarinet and Tape (1979), and *H* for Flute (1987); *Epodo* for Flute, Oboe, Clarinet, Horn, and Bassoon (1976); *Sigla* for 2 Trumpets and 2 Trombones (1976); *Echi* for Guitar (1977–81); *Hölderlin: Epilogo* for 10 Instrumentalists (1980); *D'improvviso* for Percussionists (1981); *Incontro* for Violin and String Quartet (Naples, Nov. 22, 1983); *Opus 50 (Daunium)* for 11 Instrumentalists (Foggia, Nov. 14, 1984); *Die Strahlen der Sonne...* for 9 Instrumentalists (Milan, April 21, 1985); *Frase* for Clarinet and Piano (1988); *To Planets and to Flowers* for Saxophone Quartet (1989); *Essai* for Flute, Bass Clarinet, and Piano (1991); *Frase 2B* for 3 Violins and Percussion (1993). **VOCAL:** *Preludio: Grave: di Waring Cuney—Finale* for Woman's Voice, Clarinet, Violin, Viola, and Cello (1956; Rome, June 30, 1958); *Cinque Vicariote* for Chorus and Orch. (1958; Turin, Nov. 29, 1968); *Tre liriche di Paul Éluard* for Woman's Voice, Flute, Clarinet, Trumpet, Violin, and Cello (Rome, May 14, 1958); *Don Chisciotte* for Soprano, Small Chorus, and Chamber Orch. (1961; Venice, Sept. 14, 1964); *Due sonetti italiani* for Chorus (1961; Siena, Aug. 5, 1987); *Quattro poesie spagnole* for Baritone, Clarinet, Viola, and Guitar (Florence, March 21, 1962); *Ombre (alla memoria di Che Guevara)* for Chorus and Orch. (1967–68; Bologna, May 10, 1968); *Parole da Beckett* for 2 Choruses, 3 Instrumental Groups, and Tape (1970–71; Rome, May 21, 1971); *Hölderlin (frammento)* for Chorus and Orch. (Venice, Sept. 17, 1972); *Omaggio a Josquin* for Soprano, Chorus, 2 Violas, and Cello (1985; Rome, Feb. 24, 1987); *Uei prea al biele stele* for Men's Chorus and Timpani (Udine, Nov. 25, 1987); *Dedica* for Bass, Flute, and Orch. (1985; Parma, May 9, 1986); *Dieci versi di Emily Dickinson* for Soprano, String Quartet, 10 Strings, and 2 Harps (1988); *Poesie dell'assenza* for Narrator and Orch. (1990; Parma, Sept. 1992); *Finale e aria* for Soprano, String Quartet, and Orch. (1991; RAI, Milan, April 23, 1992); *Il deserto cresce* for Chorus and Orch. (1992; Ravenna, July 4, 1993).

Bibl.: M. Romito, *Le composizioni sinfonico-corali di G. M.* (Bologna, 1982); J. Noller, *Engagement und Form: G. M.s Werk in kulturtheoretischen und musikhistorischen Zusammenhangen* (Frankfurt am Main, 1987); F. Dorsi, *G. M.* (Milan, 1989); *Omaggio a G. M.: 1992 sesant'annil il 26 settembre* (Milan, 1992). —NS/LK/DM

Manzuoli, Giovanni, famous Italian castrato soprano; b. Florence, c. 1720; d. there, 1782. He began his operatic career in Florence in 1731. After appearing in Verona (1735), he sang in Naples (until 1748). He appeared in Madrid (1749–52), Parma (1754), Lisbon (1755), and once again in Madrid (1755). He subsequently was active in Italy until 1764. In 1760 he made a visit to Vienna, where he scored a major success. In 1764–65 he appeared to great acclaim at the King's Theatre in London. During his London sojourn, he became friends of the Mozart family. Following further appearances in Verona, Turin, Venice, and Milan, he was made chamber singer to the Grand Duke of Tuscany in 1768. In 1771 he made his farewell public appearance in Milan.—NS/LK/DM

Mapleson, James Henry, colorful English opera impresario who dubbed himself **Colonel Mapleson**; b. London, May 4, 1830; d. there, Nov. 14, 1901. He was a student at the Royal Academy of Music in London. After playing violin in the orch. of the Royal Italian Opera at Her Majesty's Theatre there (1848–49), he pursued vocal training in Milan with Mazzucato. He sang in Lodi and Verona using the name Enrico Mariani. Returning to London, he sang under his own name in *Masaniello* at Drury Lane in a performance which proved disastrous. He subsequently abandoned his singing aspirations and opened his own musical agency in 1856. In 1858 he served as manager of E.T. Smith's Drury Lane season. He was manager of the Italian Opera at the Lyceum Theatre (1861–62), Her Majesty's Theatre (1862–67), and Drury Lane (1868). In 1869–70 he was co-manager with Gye at Covent Garden. He was manager at Drury Lane (1871–76), Her Majesty's Theatre (1877–81; 1887; 1889), and Covent Garden (1885, 1887). Between 1878 and 1897 he also presented operas at N.Y.'s Academy of Music and in other U.S. cities, his ventures fluctuating between success and disaster.

Mapleson was often the subject of news reports on both sides of the Atlantic as a result of his recurrent professional troubles and his conflicts with, and attachments to, various prima donnas. However, he succeeded in producing many operas new to British audiences and also introduced Nilsson, Nordica, and Jean de Reszke to London. He publ. a lively account of his career in *The Mapleson Memoirs* (2 vols., London, 1888; 2nd ed., rev., 1966 by H. Rosenthal). His nephew, Lionel Mapleson (b. London, Oct. 23, 1865; d. N.Y., Dec. 21, 1937), became a violinist in the orch. of the Metropolitan Opera in N.Y. in 1889. Soon thereafter he became its librarian, a position he held for 50 years. He amassed an invaluable collection of operatic memorabilia, including turn-of- the-century cylinder recordings of actual Metropolitan Opera performances. In 1985 these recordings were issued by the N.Y. Public Library.—NS/LK/DM

Mara, Gertrud (Elisabeth née **Schmeling),** famous German soprano; b. Kassel, Feb. 23, 1749; d. Reval, Russia, Jan. 20, 1833. A neglected child, she suffered from disfiguring rickets; her father exhibited her as a violin prodigy in Vienna (1755), and she later played before the Queen (1759); then studied voice with Paradisi. In 1765 she returned to Germany and became a principal singer at Hiller's concerts in Leipzig (1766); then made her operatic debut in Dresden (1767), but soon returned to Leipzig. She subsequently entered the service of Frederick the Great (1771), singing at the Berlin Royal Opera. Her marriage to the cellist Johann Baptist Mara (1746–1808) brought her grief, for Frederick opposed their union; when the couple tried to leave Leipzig, Frederick had them arrested. However, he eventually consented to their marriage after Gertrud agreed to remain at the Berlin Royal Opera; during this period, she also received instruction in harmony from Kirnberger. In 1779 she finally escaped Berlin, and subsequently sang in other German cities, in the Low Countries, and in Vienna (1780–81); appeared at the Concert Spirituel in Paris (1782), and again as a rival to Todi (1783). In 1784 she went to London, where she gained renown as a result of her participation in the Handel Commemoration performances; subsequently appeared at the King's Theatre there (1786–91) and also in Turin (1788) and Venice (1789–90; 1792); thereafter mainly in concerts and oratorios in London until 1802, when she and her lover, the flutist and composer Charles Florio, left to tour France, Germany, and Austria; they finally landed in Moscow, but soon separated. Stricken with poverty, she was forced to eke out a meager existence as a teacher. After losing everything in the French destruction of Moscow (1812), she went to Reval as a teacher. In 1819 she made a brief and unsuccessful return to London's King's Theatre, then returned to Reval. During the glory days of her career, her voice ranged from g' to e''.

Bibl.: G. Grosheim, *Das Leben der Künstlerin M.* (Kassel, 1823; reprint, 1972); G. Burkli, *G.E. M.* (Zürich, 1835); R. Kaulitz-Niedeck, *Die M.: Das Leben einer berühmten Sängerin* (Heilbronn, 1929).—NS/LK/DM

Maragno, Virtú, Argentine composer; b. Santa Fe, March 18, 1928. He studied in Buenos Aires and later in Rome with Goffredo Petrassi. Returning to Argentina, he became active as a choral conductor and teacher. He writes in a distinctly modernistic vein, leaning toward serial techniques.

Works: *Triste y Danza* for Small Orch. (1947); Divertimento for Wind Quintet (1952); *Scherzo sinfonico* (Buenos Aires, June 16, 1953); Concertino for Piano and 14 Instruments (1954); 2 string quartets (1958, 1961); *Expresion* for Double Orch. and Percussion (Rome, June 23, 1961); *Intensidad y Espacio* for Orch. (1962); *Composicion I* for Voices, Instruments, and Tape (Buenos Aires, Oct. 5, 1962); music for the theater; film scores; choruses; songs.—NS/LK/DM

Marais, Marin, great French viola da gambist and composer; b. Paris, May 31, 1656; d. there, Aug. 15, 1728. He studied bass viol with Sainte-Colombe and composition with Lully. He became a member of the royal orch. (1676); was made Ordinaire de la chambre du Roi (1679), a position he retained until his retirement (1725). Marais possessed matchless skill as a virtuoso on the viola da gamba, and set a new standard of excellence by enhancing the sonority of the instrument. He also established a new method of fingering, which had a decisive influence on the technique of performance. As a composer, he was an outstanding master of bass viol music, producing 5 extensive collections between 1686 and 1725, numbering some 550 works in all. In his dramatic music, he followed Lully's French manner; his recitatives comport with the rhythm of French verse and the inflection of the rhyme. The purely instrumental parts in his operas were quite extensive; in *Alcione* (Paris, Feb. 18, 1706) he introduced a "tempeste," which is one of the earliest attempts at stage realism in operatic music. His other operas are *Alcide* (Paris, 1693), *Ariane et Bacchus* (Paris, 1696), and *Sémélé* (Paris, 1709). He also publ. trios for violin, flute, and viola da gamba (1692) and a book of trios for violin, viol, and harpsichord under the title *La gamme et autres morceaux de simphonie* (1723). An edition of his instrumental works was ed. by J. Hsu (2 vols., N.Y., 1980, 1987). He was married in 1676 and had 19 children; his son Roland Marais was also a talented viola da gambist who publ. 2 books of pieces for his instrument with basso continuo (Paris, 1735, 1738) and a *Nouvelle méthode de musique pour servir d'introduction aux acteurs modernes* (Paris, 1711; not extant). His son-in-law was **Nicolas Bernier.**

BIBL.: C. Thompson, *M. M., 1656–1728* (diss., Univ. of Mich., 1956); M. Urquhart, *Style and Technique in the "Pieces de violes" of M. M.* (diss., Univ. of Edinburgh, 1970); B. McDowell, *M. and Forqueray: A Historical and Analytical Study of Their Music for Solo Basse de Viole* (diss., Columbia Univ., 1974); D. Teplow, *Performance Practice and Technique in M. M.'s "Pieces de viole"* (Ann Arbor, 1986)—NS/LK/DM

Mařák, Otakar, Czech tenor; b. Esztergom, Hungary, Jan. 5, 1872; d. Prague, July 2, 1939. He was a student at the Prague Cons. of Paršova-Zikeˇová. After making his operatic debut as Faust in Brünn in 1899, he sang in Prague at the Deutsches Theater (1900–01) and the National Theater (1901–07). Following guest engagements in Vienna (1903), Berlin (1906), London (Covent Garden, 1908), and Chicago (1914), he was a principal member of the National Theater in Prague (1914–34). He lost his financial security in a business venture, and went to the U.S. to seek his fortune. However, he ended up selling newspapers on Chicago streets. After funds were raised for his assistance, he was able to return to Prague to eke out his last days in straitened circumstances. At the zenith of his career, he was dubbed the Czech Caruso. Among his best roles were Turiddu, Canio, and Don José.—NS/LK/DM

Marazzoli, Marco, significant Italian composer; b. Parma, between 1602 and 1608; d. Rome, Jan. 26, 1662. In 1631 he gained the patronage of Cardinal Antonio Barberini in Rome. In 1637 he settled in Rome in the cardinal's service and became a tenor in the Papal Chapel, a position he held until his death. He also was engaged by Cardinal Mazarin in Paris in 1643; returned to Rome in 1645. In 1656 he became virtuoso di camera to Queen Christina of Sweden, who held her court in Rome at the time. Marazzoli was a prolific composer of choral music; about 375 of his cantatas and oratorios are extant. His name is also associated with that of Virgilio Mazzocchi; they collaborated on the first comic opera, *Chi soffre, speri* (Rome, Feb. 27, 1639), which was a revision of *Il facone* (Rome, Feb. 12, 1637). His other operas include *L'amore trionfante dello sdegno* (also known as *L'Armida*; Ferrara, Feb. 1641), *Gli amori di Giasone e d' Issifile* (Venice, Feb. 22, 1642; not extant), *Le pretensioni del Tebro e del Po* (Ferrara, March 4, 1642), *Il capriccio* or *Il giudizio della ragione fra la Belta e l'Affetto* (Rome, 1643), *Dal male il bene* (Rome, Feb. 12, 1653; in collaboration with A. Abbatini), *Le armi e gli amori* (Rome, Feb. 20, 1656), and *La vita humana, ovvero Il trionfo della pietà* (Rome, Jan. 31, 1656).

BIBL.: M. Grace, *M. M. and the Development of the Latin Oratorio* (diss., Yale Univ., 1974).—NS/LK/DM

Marbe, Myriam (Lucia), Romanian composer and teacher; b. Bucharest, April 9, 1931; d. there, Dec. 25, 1997. After initial studies with her mother, the piano pedagogue Angela Marbe, she pursued her training at the Bucharest Cons. (1944–54), where her mentors included Florica Musicescu and Silvia Căpăţînă (piano), Ioan Chirescu (theory), Marţian Negrea and Ion Dumitrescu (harmony), Mihail Jora and Leon Klepper (counterpoint and composition), and Theodor Rogalski (orchestration). Later she attended the summer courses in new music in Darmstadt (1968–69; 1972). From 1954 to 1988 she taught at the Bucharest Cons. She received prizes from the Romanian Composers Union (1970–71; 1973–74; 1980; 1982). In 1972 she was awarded the Bernier Prize of the Académie des Beaux-Arts in Paris. She was honored with the prize of the Romanian Academy in 1977. In her music, she pursued an advanced path in which she experimented with serialism, sonorism, and spatial music.

WORKS: ORCH.: *In memoriam* (1959); *Musica festiva* (1961); *Le temps inévitable* for Piano and Orch. (1971); *Serenata-Eine kleine Sonnenmusik* for Chamber Orch. (Braşov, June 29, 1974); *Evocări* for Strings and Percussion (Tîrgu Mureş, June 22, 1976); Viola Concerto (Braşov, Feb. 1977); *La parabole du grenier II* for Harpsichord and Chamber Orch. (Zagreb, May 13, 1977); *Trium* (1978); Concerto for Viola da Gamba or Cello and Orch. (1982; Ploieşti, May 31, 1983); Sonata for Strings (1986; also as String Quartet No. 2, 1985); Saxophone(s) Concerto (1986); Sym. No. 1, *Ur-Ariadne,* for Mezzo-soprano and Orch. (1988). **CHAMBER:** Viola Sonata (1955); Clarinet Sonata (1961); *Incantatio,* sonata for Solo Clarinet (1964); Sonata for 2 Violas (1965); *Cyclus* for Flute, Guitar, and Percussion (1974); *Vocabulaire II-Rythme* for 3 Percussion (1975); *La parabole du grenier I* for Piano, Harpsichord, and Celesta, with Glockenspiel and Bells ad libitum (1975–76); Concerto for Harpsichord and 8 Instruments (1978); *Narratio* for Flute, Violin, Viola, and Percussion (1979); 4 string quartets: No. 1, *Les musiques compatibles* (1981), No. 2 (1985; also as the Sonata for Strings, 1986), No. 3, *Lui Nau* (1988), and No. 4 (1990; also as *Preţuitorul* for String Quartet, Trombone, Percussion, Speaker, and Tenor); *Sonate per due* for Flute and Viola (1985); *Trommelbass* for String Trio and Drum Bass (1985); *Des- Cântec* for Wind Quintet (1985); *After Nau,* sonata for Cello and Organ (1987); *The World is a stage...* for

Violin, Double Bass, Clarinet, Trombone, and Percussion (1987); *Diapente* for 5 Cellos (1990); *E-Y- Thé* for Clarinet and 4 Cellos (1990); *Et in Arcadia...* for Flute, Bass Clarinet, Percussion, and Piano (1993); *Yorick* for Clarinet or Recorder, Violin, Piano, and Percussion (1993); *Haikus* for Flute and Piano (1993–94); *Le temps inévitable '94* for Chamber Ensemble (1994); *Le jardin enchanté* for Flute, Percussion, and Tape (1994); *Prophet und Vogel* for Cello and Piano (1994); *Paos* for Clarinet and Viola (1995); Suite for 4 Trumpets (1996); *The Song of Ruth* for 5 Cellos (1997); *Ariel*, sonata for Solo Cello (1997); *Renaissance* for 3 Recorders (1997). **P i a n o :** Sonata (1956); *Le temps inévitable I* and *II* (1968); *Clusterstudie I* and *II* (1970); *Accents* (1971). **V O C A L :** *Noapte ţărănească*, cantata for Chorus and Orch. (1958); *Madrigals After Japanese Haikus* for Women's Chorus (1964); *Clime* for Mezzo-soprano, Women's Chorus, Children's Chorus, and Chamber Orch. (1966); *...de aducere aminte* for Chorus and Small Orch. (1967); *Ritual pentru setea pământului* for 7 Voices and Instruments (1968); *Jocus secundus* for Small Vocal Group, Instruments, and Tape ad libitum (1969); *Vocabulaire I-Chanson* for Soprano, Clarinet, Piano, and Bells (1974); *Chiuituri* for Children's Chorus and Small Orch. (1978); *Les oiseaux artificiels* for Narrator and 6 Instruments (1979); *Timpul regăsit* for Soprano or Tenor and 7 Instruments (1982); *An die Musik* for Alto, Flute, and Organ (1983); *An die Sonne* for Mezzo-soprano and Wind Quintet (1986); *Fra Angelico-Marc Chagall-Vorone-Requiem* for Mezzo-soprano, Chorus, and Instrumental Ensemble (1990); *Stabat Mater* for 12 Voices and Instrumental Ensemble (1991); *Na Castelloza* for Mezzo-soprano, Oboe, Viola, and Percussion (1993); *Mirail-Jeu sur des fragments de poemes de femmes troubadours* for Soprano, 2 Mezzo-sopranos, Flute, Oboe, Violin, and Viola (1993); *Überzeitliches Gold* for Soprano, Percussion, and Saxophone(s) (1994); *Passages in the wind* for Tenor, Recorder, Cello, and Harpsichord (1994); *d' a Cantare-Cantarellare* for Soprano, Violin, and Percussion (1995); *Symphonia* for Mezzo-soprano and Chamber Ensemble (1996).

BIBL.: G. Gronemeyer, ed., *Klangportrait: M. L. M.* (Berlin, 1991); T. Beimel, *Vom Ritual zur Abstraktion:Über die rumänische Komponistin M. M.* (Wuppertal, 1994).—**NS/LK/DM**

Marbeck or **Marbecke, John,** English organist, composer, and writer on theology; b. probably in Windsor, c. 1505; d. 1585. He became a clerk and organist at St. George's Chapel, Windsor (1531). His interest in religion prompted him to prepare a concordance of the English Bible, as well as various theological tracts. However, he was arrested for heresy in 1543 and sentenced to die at the stake. After being saved by the intercession of Henry VIII, he resumed his duties at St. George's Chapel and returned to his theological pursuits. He brought out the first publ. concordance of the English Bible (1550). When the Act of Uniformity (1549) made the use of English services in the 1st Book of Common Prayer mandatory throughout the realm, he was commissioned to prepare a musical setting for liturgical use, which was publ. as *The Booke of Common Praier Noted* (London, 1550; facsimile ed., 1939).

BIBL.: R. Leaver, *The Work of J. Marbeck* (Oxford, 1978). —**NS/LK/DM**

Marc, Alessandra, accomplished American soprano; b. Berlin, July 29, 1957. She received her training at the Univ. of Md. In 1987 she made her operatic debut in Giordano's *La Cene delle Beffe* at the Wexford Festival in England. In 1988 she sang Maria in Strauss's *Friedenstag* at the Santa Fe Opera. During the 1988–89 season, she appeared as Leonora in *La Forza del Destino* at the Greater Miami Opera, as Madame Lidoine in *Les Dialogues des Carmélites* at the Houston Grand Opera, as Strauss's Ariadne at the Washington (D.C.) Concert Opera, and as Aida at the Lyric Opera in Chicago. On Oct. 14, 1989, she made her Metropolitan Opera debut in N.Y. as Aida. In 1992 she sang for the first time at the Philadelphia Opera as Turandot, a role she reprised at the Macerata Festival in 1996. During the 1992–93 season, she made her debut at the Berlin State Opera as Strauss's Ariadne. In 1993 she made her Italian operatic debut at the Rome Opera as Aida. During the 1994–95 season, she appeared for the first time at London's Covent Garden as Turandot. Her other opera engagements included the Vienna State Opera, the San Francisco Opera, the Cologne Opera, the Bavarian State Opera in Munich, and the Hamburg State Opera. Among her other prominent roles are Norma, Sieglinde in *Die Walküre*, and Chrysothemis in *Elektra*. As a concert artist, she has appeared with many of the finest orchs. and festivals in a repertoire ranging from classical standards to Samuel Barber.—**NS/LK/DM**

Marcel (real name, **Wasself**), **Lucille,** American soprano; b. N.Y., 1885; d. Vienna, June 22, 1921. She studied in N.Y., Berlin, and with J. de Reszke in Paris, where she made her debut as Mallika in *Lakmé* at the Opéra-Comique (1903). After marrying **Felix Weingartner** in 1907, she sang the title role in Elektra at its first Viennese staging under his direction (March 24, 1908); continued to sing at the Court Opera until 1911, then was a member of the Hamburg Opera (1912–14). She made her U.S. debut as Tosca with the Boston Opera Co. (Feb. 14, 1912), and remained on its roster until 1914. After a period in Darmstadt, she settled in Vienna. Her other roles included Eva, Marguerite, Desdemona, and Aida.—**NS/LK/DM**

Marcello, Alessandro, Italian violinist, composer, poet, and painter, brother of **Benedetto Marcello**; b. Venice, Aug. 24, 1669; d. Padua, June 19, 1747. He studied violin with his father. He publ. his compositions under the name of Eterio Stinfalico. He was the composer of the Oboe Concerto in D minor transcribed by Bach (BWV 974), formerly attributed to Vivaldi and later to Benedetto Marcello. Other extant works are (12) *Cantate di Eterio Stinfalico* for Voice and Basso Continuo (Venice, 1708), (12) *Suonate a vioolino solo di Eterio Stinfalico* (Augsburg, c. 1740), *La cetra*, [6] *concerti di Eterio Stinfalico* for 2 Flutes or Oboes, Bassoon, Strings, and Basso Continuo (Augsburg, c. 1740), Concerto No. 2 in *Concerti a cinque* for Oboe, Strings, and Basso Continuo (Amsterdam, c. 1717), other concertos, solo cantatas, arias, and canzonets.

BIBL.: E. Selfridge-Field, *The Music of Benedetto and A. M.: A Thematic Catalogue with Commentary on the Composers, Repertory, and Sources* (Oxford, 1990).—**NS/LK/DM**

Marcello, Benedetto, famous Italian composer and teacher, brother of **Alessandro Marcello**; b. Venice,

July 24 or Aug. 1, 1686; d. Brescia, July 24 or 25, 1739. He studied violin with his father; later took courses in singing and counterpoint with F. Gasparini. Having prepared for a legal career, he accepted a number of distinguished positions in public life: was made a member of the Grand Council of the Republic (1707); served on the Council of Forty for 14 years; was governor of Pola (1730–37); subsequently camarlingo (chamberlain) of Brescia (1738–39); was also active as an advocate and magistrate. Adopting the pseudonym Driante Sacreo, he became a member of Rome's Arcadian Academy; was also elected a member of Bologna's Accademia Filarmonica (1712). His distinguished students included the singer Faustina Bordoni and the composer Baldassare Galuppi. He most likely was the author of *Lettera famigliare d'un accademico filarmonico ed arcade discorsiva sopra un libro di duetti, terzetti e madrigali a più voci* (Venice, 1705), an anonymous and rather captious critique of Lotti. He publ. a famous satire on Vivaldi and his contemporaries as *Il teatro alla moda, o sia Metodo sicuro e facile per il ben comporre ed eseguire l'opere italiane in musica all'usu moderno* (Venice, c. 1720; Eng. tr. by R. Paul, *Musical Quarterly*, July 1948 and Jan. 1949). Marcello was one of the most gifted Italian composers of his time, his mastery ranging from sacred and secular vocal works to instrumental works.

WORKS: DRAMATIC: O r a t o r i o s : *Il sepolcro* (Venice?, 1705); *Giuditta* (Rome, 1709); *Gioaz* (Vienna, 1726); *Il pianto e il riso delle quattro stagioni* (Venice?, 1731); *Il trionfo della poesia e della musica* (Venice?, 1733); other sacred vocal works include *Estro poetico-armonico, parafrasi sopra li primi [secondi] 25 salmi* (Venice, 1724–26; reprint, 1967); 10 masses; 15 motets; etc. **O t h e r :** 2 serenatas: *Serenata da cantarsi ad uso di scena* (Vienna, 1725) and *La morte di Adone* (Rome, 1729); the intreccio scenico musicale *Arianna* (Florence, 1727); a cantata; etc. **SECULAR VOCAL:** (12) *Canzoni madrigalesche e [6] arie per camera* for 2 to 4 Voices, op.4 (Bologna, 1717); over 500 cantatas; about 85 duets; etc. **INSTRUMENTAL:** (12) *Concerti a cinque*, with Violin and Cello obbligato, op.1 (Venice, 1708); (12) *Suonate* for Recorder and Basso Continuo, op.2 (Amsterdam, before 1717; as op.1 for Flute or Violin and Basso Continuo, London, 1732); 6 sonatas for Cello and Basso Continuo, op.1 (Amsterdam, c. 1732; as op.2, London, 1732; as op.1, Paris, c. 1735); 6 sonatas for 2 Cellos or 2 Bass Viols and Basso Continuo or Cello, as op.2 (Amsterdam, c. 1734); Concerto for Violin and Strings; Concerto for 2 Violins and Strings; 7 sinfonias for Strings; various harpsichord sonatas (12 ed. in Le Pupitre, XXVIII, Paris, 1971); etc.

BIBL.: F. Fontana, *Vita di B. M., patrizio Veneto* (Venice, 1788); F. Caffi, *Della vita e del comporre di B. M.* (Venice, 1830); L. Busi, *B. M.* (Bologna, 1884); O. Chilesotti, *Sulla lettera critica di B. M. contro A. Lotti* (Bassano, 1885); E. Fondi, *La vita e l'opera letteraria del musicista B. M.* (Rome, 1909); A. d'Angeli, *B. M.: Vita e opere* (Milan, 1940); G. Tinctori, *L'Arianna di B. M.* (Milan, 1951); C. Sites, *B. M.'s Chamber Cantatas* (diss., Univ. of N.C., 1959); E. Selfridge-Field, *The Works of B. and Alessandro M.: A Thematic Catalogue* (Oxford, 1990); *The Music of B. and Alessandro M.: A Thematic Catalogue with Commentary on the Composers, Repertory, and Sources* (Oxford, 1990).—NS/LK/DM

Marchal, André (-Louis), distinguished blind French organist and pedagogue; b. Paris, Feb. 6, 1894; d. St. Jean-de-Luz, Aug. 27, 1980. He was blind from birth; studied at the Institution Nationale des Jeunes Aveugles; later entered the Paris Cons. in the class of Gigout. In 1915 he became organist at St. Germain-des-Près in Paris. He then served at St. Eustache from 1945 to 1963. He began a concert career in 1923, becoming greatly admired for his exhaustive repertoire and brilliance as an improviser. He was also esteemed as a teacher.—NS/LK/DM

Marchand, Louis, French organist, harpsichordist, and composer; b. Lyons, Feb. 2, 1669; d. Paris, Feb. 17, 1732. At the age of 14, he was made organist at Nevers Cathedral. He went to Paris in 1689, and in 1691 he received the post of organist of the Jesuit church in the rue St. Jacques; he was also organist at other Parisian churches. In 1708 he was named an organiste du roi, in which capacity he earned a considerable reputation, and in 1713 he made a major tour of Germany. Marchand's name is historically connected with that of Bach because both were scheduled to meet in open competition in Dresden in 1717; however, Marchand failed to appear and Bach was deemed the superior virtuoso by default. He subsequently was organist at the Cordeliers in Paris. See T. Dart, ed., *Louis Marchand: Pièces de clavecin* (Paris, 1960) and J. Bonfils, ed., *Louis Marchand: L'OEuvre d'orgue édition intégrale* (Paris 1970 et seq.).

WORKS: *Pièces de clavecin, livres 1–2* (Paris, 1702); (12) *Pièces choisies pour l'orgue* (Paris, after 1732); also 42 organ pieces in 4 books in MS and vocal works, including various airs in anthologies (1706–43).—NS/LK/DM

Marchand, (Simon-) Luc, French lutenist, violinist, organist, and composer; b. May 31, 1709; d. April 27, 1799. His father, Jean- Baptiste Marchand (b. Paris, 1670; d. there, Jan. 8, 1751), was a violinist in the royal service from 1691, and also a lutenist in the royal chamber from 1710. The younger Marchand received the reversion of his father's title of as a lutenist in 1727. However, he appears to have devoted himself to playing the violin and organ in the royal service until losing his position in 1761. He was one of the earliest composers to publ. accompanied keyboard music in France with his *Pièces de clavecin avec accompagnement de violon, hautbois, violoncelle ou viole* (Paris, 1748).—LK/DM

Marchesi, Luigi (Lodovico), celebrated Italian castrato soprano, known as "Marchesini"; b. Milan, Aug. 8, 1754; d. Inzago, Dec. 14, 1829. He studied horn with his father. After having himself castrated, he pursued vocal training with Alluzzi and Caironi. At age 11, he joined the choir at the Milan Cathedral, where he studied composition with its director Fioroni. He made his debut as Giannetta in Anfossi's *L'Incognita perseguitata* in Rome (1773); also sang in Treviso (1775), and then was a member of the Munich court (1776–78). He subsequently gained renown as a member of the Teatro San Carlo in Naples (1778–79); appeared in Florence (1780) and then again in Naples (1780–81). He sang in Milan and also in Turin, where he held the title of musico di corte (1782–98). In 1785 he was engaged by the court of Catherine the Great; on his way to St. Petersburg, he appeared in Sarti's *Giulio Sabino* in Vienna before Emperor Joseph II (Aug. 4, 1785), who ordered a medal be struck in his honor. He made his Russian debut as Rinaldo in Sarti's *Armida e Rinaldo* at the inaugural performance of the Hermitage Theater in St. Petersburg (Jan. 15, 1786). The soprano Luiza-Rosa Todi intrigued against him, however, and despite his successes, he left Russia before the expiration of his contract. He then appeared in Berlin on March 9, 1787, and subsequently scored a London triumph in *Giulio Sabino* on April 5, 1788. He made his last appearance in London on July 17, 1790, and then pursued his career mainly in Italy; also sang in Vienna again (1798, 1801). He sang in the premiere of Mayr's *Ginevra di Scozia* at the dedicatory performance of the Teatro Nuovo in Trieste on April 21, 1801. He made his farewell stage appearance in Mayr's *Lodoiska* in Milan in May 1805, but sang in public as late as 1820 in Naples. Blessed with a range of 2 1/2 octaves, Marchesi was unsurpassed in the opera seria genre of his era.—**NS/LK/DM**

Marchesi (de Castrone), Blanche, French soprano and teacher of Italian-German descent, daughter of **Salvatore Marchesi de Castrone** and **Mathilde Marchesi de Castrone** (née **Graumann**); b. Paris, April 4, 1863; d. London, Dec. 15, 1940. After studying violin, she turned to vocal training with her mother. She began her career singing in private and charity concerts in Paris, and then appeared in Berlin and Brussels in 1895. On June 19, 1896, she made her London debut in a concert and made England her home. In 1900 she made her operatic debut as Brünnhilde in *Die Walküre* in Prague, and then returned to England to sing with the Moody-Manners Co. In 1902 she appeared at London's Covent Garden as Elisabeth, Elsa, and Isolde. For the most part, however, she pursued a career on the concert stage. Later she was also active as a teacher. She made her farewell concert appearance in 1938. She publ. the memoir *A Singer's Pilgrimage* (London, 1923), and the didactic vol. *The Singer's Catechism* (London, 1932). —**NS/LK/DM**

Marchesi de Castrone, Mathilde (née **Graumann**), famous German mezzo-soprano and pedagogue, mother of **Blanche Marchesi (de Castrone)**; b. Frankfurt am Main, March 24, 1821; d. London, Nov. 17, 1913. She was a student of Ronconi in Frankfurt am Main and of Nicolai in Vienna. After making her debut in a concert in Frankfurt am Main (Aug. 31, 1844), she continued her studies with García in Paris (1844–46; 1848) and in London (1849). She subsequently appeared in concerts in London, Germany, and Holland. Her only operatic appearance was as Rossini's Rosina in Bremen in 1853. In 1852 she married **Salvatore Marchesi de Castrone**. After serving as prof. of voice at the Vienna Cons. (1854–61), she went to Paris as a private teacher and as a concert singer. She subsequently was prof. of voice at the Cologne Cons. (1865–68) and again at the Vienna Cons. (1868–78). Thereafter she taught privately in Vienna until 1881, when she returned to Paris. Following her husband's death, she settled in London. She had many celebrated students, among them Calvé, Eames, Garden, Gerster, Klafsky, Melba, Murska, Ne-

vada, and Sanderson. She publ. the autobiography *Erinnerungen aus meinem Leben* (Vienna, 1877; 4th ed., rev. and aug., 1889 as *Aus meinem Leben*; Eng. tr., 1897, as *Marchesi and Music: Passages from the Life of a Famous Singing Teacher*). She also publ. the manual *10 Singing Lessons* (N.Y., 1910; new ed., 1970, by P. Miller as *Theoretical and Practical Vocal Method*). Her niece was **Dorothea von Ertmann.**—**NS/LK/DM**

Marchesi de Castrone, Salvatore (full name and title, **Salvatore Marchesi, Cavaliere de Castrone, Marchese della Rajata**), distinguished Italian baritone and teacher, father of **Blanche Marchesi (de Castrone)**; b. Palermo, Jan. 15, 1822; d. Paris, Feb. 20, 1908. Of a noble family, he was destined for a government career and studied law in Palermo; however, he turned to music, and took lessons in singing and theory with Raimondi in Palermo, and with Lamperti in Milan. He was involved in the revolutionary events of 1848, and was compelled to leave Italy; went to N.Y., where he made his operatic debut as Carlos in *Ernani*. He then studied with Garcia in London, where he made his first British appearance in 1850. In 1852 he married **Mathilde Marchesi de Castrone** (née **Graumann**). After singing at the Berlin Royal Opera (1852–53) and in Ferrara (1853), he taught at the Vienna Cons. (1854–61). In 1863–64 he returned to London to sing at Her Majesty's Theatre. After teaching at the Cologne Cons. (1865–68) and again at the Vienna Cons. (1868–78), he settled in Paris in 1881. He wrote a book on singing as well as a number of songs. —**NS/LK/DM**

Marchetti, Filippo, Italian composer; b. Bolognola, near Camerino, Feb. 26, 1831; d. Rome, Jan. 18, 1902. After initial training with Bindi in Bolognola (1843–50), he was a student of Lillo (figured bass and harmony) and Conti (counterpoint and composition) at the Naples Cons. (1850–54). His first opera, *Gentile de Varano* (Turin, Feb. 1856), proved a fine success. However, his next opera, *La Demente* (Turin, Nov. 27, 1856), failed to please the public, and his third opera, *Il Paria*, failed even to reach the stage. Discouraged, he became active as a teacher in Rome. His next opera, *Romeo e Giulietta* (Trieste, Oct. 25, 1865), failed at its premiere but struck a responsive chord with the public at its staging at Milan's Teatro Carcano in 1867. The first performance of his opera *Ruy Blas* at Milan's La Scala (April 3, 1869) also was initially unsuccessful, but it soon was staged in Florence with notable success and then was heard throughout Europe and North and South America. A duet from the opera, "O dolce voluttà," was long popular with the public. His last operas, *Gustavo Wasa* (Milan, Feb. 7, 1875) and *Don Giovanni d'Austria* (Turin, March 11, 1880), were failures. Marchetti served as president of the Accademia di Santa Cecilia (1881–86) and as director of the Liceo Musicale (1886–1901) in Rome. Among his other works were orch. pieces, choral works, and sacred music.—**NS/LK/DM**

Marchetto da Padova, Italian music theorist and composer; b. Padua, c. 1274; d. after 1326. He was maestro di canto at Padua Cathedral (1305–07). He is known for the treatises *Lucidarium in arte musicae planae* (on plainsong, early 14th century) and *Pomerium artis musicae mensurabilis* (on mensural music, 1318); the latter is included (in part) in O. Strunk's *Source Readings in Music History* (N.Y., 1950; 2nd ed., 1998, by L. Treitler); a modern ed. is found in Corpus Scriptorum de Musica, VI (1961). He also wrote *Brevis compilatio in arte musicae mensuratae*, which was ed. by G. Vecchi, "Su la composizione del Pomerium di Marchetto de Padova e la Brevis compilatio," in *Quadrivium*, I (1956). Three motets have been ascribed to him.

BIBL.: K. Berger, *Musica Ficta: Theories of Accidental Inflections in Vocal Polyphony from M. da Padova to Gioseffo Zarlino* (Cambridge, 1987).—**NS/LK/DM**

Marchisio, Barbara, Italian contralto and teacher; b. Turin, Dec. 6, 1833; d. Mira, April 19, 1919. She studied with her brother, the composer Antonino Marchisio (1817–1875), and with L. Fabbrica in Turin, making her debut as Adalgisa in *Norma* in Vicenza (1856); she sang Rosina in Madrid that same year. Her sister, Carlotta Marchisio (b. Turin, Dec. 8, 1835; d. there, June 28, 1872), also studied with her brother and with Fabbrica in Turin; made her debut as Norma in Madrid (1856). The 2 sisters first appeared together in Turin in 1858. After singing in Trieste, they made their joint debut at Milan's La Scala in *Semiramide* (Dec. 29, 1858); this opera continued as their vehicle for their joint debut at the Paris Opéra (in French, July 9, 1860) and at Her Majesty's Theatre in London (May 1, 1862). They last appeared together in Rome in 1871. After Carlotta died in childbirth, Barbara continued her career for several more years, appearing in Milan (1872) and Venice (1876). She then devoted herself to teaching, numbering Raisa and dal Monte among her students. Rossini held the Marchisio sisters in the highest esteem.—**NS/LK/DM**

Marco, Tomás, Spanish composer; b. Madrid, Sept. 12, 1942. He studied violin and composition at the Univ. of Madrid (1959–64), and also attended the Darmstadt summer course in new music (1967). An ardent modernist, he founded in 1967 the magazine *Sonda*, dedicated to new music. His compositions are of an experimental, almost exhibitionistic, theatrical nature.

WORKS: DRAMATIC: Ballet: *Llanto por Ignacio Sanchez Mejias* (1984–85). **ORCH.:** *Los caprichos* (1959–67); *Glasperlenspiel* for Chamber Orch. (1963–64); *Vitral (Música celestial No. 1)* for Organ and Strings (1968); *Anábasis* (1968–70); *Mysteria* for Chamber Orch. (1970–71); *Angelus novus (Hommage à Mahler)* (1971); Violin Concerto, *Les Mécanismes de la mémoire* (1971–72; Royan Festival, April 19, 1973); Cello Concerto (1974–75); 5 syms.: No. 1, *Sinfonía Aralar* (1976), No. 2, *Espacio cerrado* (1985), No. 3 (1985), No. 4, *Espacio guebrado* (1987), and No. 5, *Modelos de Universo* (1988–89); *Concierto del Alma* for Violin and String Orch. (1982); *Concerto austral* for Oboe and Orch. (1982); *Pulsar* (1986); Triple Concerto for Violin, Cello, Piano, and Orch. (1987); *Settecento* for Piano and Chamber Orch. (1988); *Campo de Estrellas* (1989); *Espejo de viento* for 12 Saxophones (1989). **CHAMBER:** *Roulis-Tangage* for Trumpet, Cello, Guitar, Piano, Vibraphone, and 2 Percussionists (1962–63); *Trivium* for Piano, Tuba, and Percussion (1963); *Car en effet* for 3 Clarinets and 3 Saxophones (1965); *Schwan* for Trumpet, Trombone, Viola, Cello, and 2 Percussionists (1966); *Maya* for Cello and Piano (1968–69); *Rosa-Rosae*, quartet for Flute, Clarinet, Violin, and Cello (1969); *Floreal* for a Percussionist (1969); *Kukulcan* for Wind Quintet (1969–72); *Albor* for Flute, Clarinet, Violin, Cello, and Piano (1970); *Necronomicon*, choreography for 6 Percussionists (1971); *Jetztzeit* for Clarinet and Piano (1971); *Nuba* for Flute, Oboe, Clarinet, Violin, Cello, and Percussion (1973). **P i a n o :** *Piraña* (1965); *Evos* (1970); *Espejo Desierto* for String Quartet (1987). **VOCAL:** *Jabberwocky* for Actors, Tenor, Saxophone, Piano, 4 Percussionists, Tape, 6 Radios, Lights, and Slides (1966); *Cantos del pozo artesiano* for Actress, 3 Chamber Ensembles, and Lights (1967); *Tea Party* for 4 Vocal Soloists, Clarinet, Trombone, Cello, and Vibraphone (1969); *L'Invitation au voyage* for Soprano, optional Narrator, 3 Clarinets, Piano, and Percussion (1971); *Ultramarina* for Soprano, Clarinet, Piano, and Percussion (1975); *Concierto Coral 1* for Violin and 2 Choral Groups (1980) and *2: Espacio Sagrado* for Piano, Chorus, and Orch. (1983).—**NS/LK/DM**

Marcolini, Marietta, Italian mezzo-soprano; b. Florence, c. 1780; place and date of death unknown. By 1800 she was singing in Venice. After appearing in Naples (1803–04), Rome (1807–08), and Milan (La Scala, 1809), she won the esteem of Rossini and created his Ernestina in *Lequivoco stravagante* (1811), Ciro (1812), Clarice in *La pietra del paragone* (1812), Isabella (1813), and the title role in *Sigismondo*. She retired from the operatic stage in 1820.—**NS/LK/DM**

Marcoux, Vanni (actually, **Jean Émile Diogène**), remarkable French bass-baritone who was also known as **Vanni-Marcoux**; b. Turin (of French parents), June 12, 1877; d. Paris, Oct. 22, 1962. He received training in law at the Univ. of Turin, and in voice from Taverna and Collino in Turin and from Boyer in Paris. He was only 17 when he made his operatic debut in Turin as Sparafucile. His formal operatic debut followed in 1899 when he sang Frère Laurent in *Roméo et Juliette* in Bayonne. After singing in Nice, Brussels, and The Hague, he distinguished himself at London's Covent Garden (1905–12). In 1908 he made his debut at the Paris Opéra as Méphistophélès. On Jan. 13, 1909, he created the role of Guido Colonna in Février's *Monna Vanna* there. Massenet composed the title role of his opera *Don Quichotte* for Marcoux, who sang in its first Paris staging on Dec. 29, 1910. He appeared as a guest artist at Milan's La Scala (1910), the Boston Opera Co. (1911–12), and the Chicago Grand Opera Co. (1913–14). From 1918 to 1936 he was a principal member of the Paris Opéra-Comique. He also sang again in Chicago (1926–32) and at Covent Garden (1937). From 1938 to 1943 he taught at the Paris Cons. In 1940 he retired from the operatic stage, although he made a final appearance as Don Quichotte at the Opéra-Comique in 1947. From 1948 to 1951 he served as director of the Grand Théâtre in Bordeaux. Marcoux's outstanding repertoire consisted of over 240 roles, of which the most famous were Don Giovanni, Rossini's Don Basilio, Iago, Boris Godunov, Baron Ochs, Golaud, Scarpia, and Don Quichotte.—**NS/LK/DM**

Marcovici, Silvia, Romanian violinist; b. Bacau, Jan. 30, 1952. She studied in Bacau and at the Bucharest

Cons., her principal teacher being S. Gheorghiu. She made her professional debut in The Hague in 1967. In 1969 she won the Long-Thibaud Competition in Paris and in 1970 the Enesco Competition in Bucharest. She appeared for the first time in London in 1970, in 1977 she performed in N.Y., and she subsequently appeared with many of the world's major orchs.—NS/LK/DM

Marcuse, Sibyl, German-born American musicologist; b. Frankfurt am Main (of Swiss-English parents), Feb. 13, 1911. After studies in Europe, she lived in China (1932–35); emigrated to the U.S. with the coming of World War II, becoming a naturalized citizen in 1945; studied at a N.Y. school for piano technicians and then worked as a keyboard technician. She was curator of the Yale Univ. Collection of Musical Instruments (1953–60). She publ. *Musical Instruments, A Comprehensive Dictionary* (1964; 2nd ed., rev., 1975) and *A Survey of Musical Instruments* (1975).—NS/LK/DM

Maréchal, (Charles-) Henri, French composer; b. Paris, Jan. 22, 1842; d. there, May 12, 1924. He began his studies with Chevé (solfège) before pursuing training with Batiste (solfège), Laurent (harmony), Massé (composition), and Chollet (piano); subsequently he was a student at the Paris Cons. (1866–67) of Massé, as well as of Chauvet (counterpoint and fugue) and Benoist (organ). In 1870 he won the Grand Prix de Rome with his cantata *Le Judgement de Dieu*. In 1896 he was named inspector of music education. He publ. 2 vols. of reminiscences: *Rome: Souvenirs d'un musicien* (Paris, 1904; 2nd ed., 1913) and *Paris: Souvenirs d'un musicien* (Paris, 1907). He also publ. *Monographie universelle de l'Orphéon* (Paris, 1910) and *Lettres et Souvenirs, 1871–1874* (Paris, 1920).

WORKS: DRAMATIC: O p e r a (all 1st perf. in Paris unless otherwise given): *Les Amoureux de Catherine* (May 8, 1876); *L'étoile* (March 12, 1881); *La Taverne des Trabans* (Dec. 31, 1881); *Déidame* (Sept. 15, 1893); *Calendal* (Rouen, Dec. 12, 1894); *Ping-Sin* (1895; Jan. 25, 1918). **OTHER:** Orch. works; chamber music; piano pieces; organ music; vocal pieces, including *La Judgement de Dieu*, cantata (1870), choral works, and songs. —NS/LK/DM

Maréchal, Adolphe, Belgian tenor; b. Liège, Sept. 26, 1867; d. Brussels, Feb. 1, 1935. He studied at the Liège Cons. He made his operatic debut in Tournai in 1891, then sang in Rheims, Bordeaux, and Nice. In 1895 he became a member of the Opéra-Comique in Paris, where he remained until 1907. During that time, he created the roles of Julien in *Louise* (1901), Alain in *Grisélidis* (1901), and Danielo in *La Reine fiammette* (1903). He also created Jean in *Le Jongleur de Notre-Dame* at Monte Carlo (1902). In 1902 he appeared at London's Covent Garden as Don José, Des Grieux, and Faust. He retired in 1907 after the loss of his singing voice. —NS/LK/DM

Marek, Czeslaw (Josef), Polish-born Swiss pianist, teacher, and composer; b. Przemysl, Sept. 16, 1891; d. Zürich, July 17, 1985. He studied with Loewenhoff (piano) and Niewiadomski (harmony) at the Lemberg

Music Inst., Leschetizky (piano) and Weigl (composition) in Vienna, and Pfitzner (composition) in Strasbourg. He made his debut in Lemberg (1909), where he taught at the Music Inst. until 1915; then settled in Zürich as a pianist, teacher, and composer, becoming a naturalized Swiss citizen (1932); was also prof. of composition at the Poznań Cons. (1929–30). He publ. the manual *Lehre des Klavierspiels* (Zürich, 1972).

WORKS: ORCH.: *Méditations* (1911–13); *Scherzo symfoniczne* (1914); *Sinfonietta* (1914–16); *Serenade* for Violin and Orch. (1916–18); *Suite* (1925); *Sinfonia* (1927). **OTHER:** Violin Sonata (1914); piano pieces; songs.—NS/LK/DM

Marenzio, Luca, important Italian composer; b. Coccaglio, near Brescia, 1553 or 1554; d. Rome, Aug. 22, 1599. Little is known of his early life. He may have studied with Giovanni Contino in Brescia. About 1574 he entered the service of Cardinal Cristoforo Madruzzo in Rome. Following Madruzzo's death in 1578, he entered the service of Cardinal Luigi d'Este; he made an extended visit with the cardinal to the court of Duke Alfonso II d'Este in Ferrara, where he spent the months of Nov. 1580 to May 1581; he dedicated 2 vols. of madrigals to the duke and his sister Lucrezia. After the death of the cardinal in 1586, he entered the service of Ferdinando de' Medici, the grand duke of Florence (1588). In 1589 he returned to Rome, where he apparently received the patronage of several cardinals. About 1593 he entered the service of Cardinal Cinzio Aldobrandini, and then subsequently served at the court of Sigismund III of Poland (1596–98). He then returned to Rome, where he died the following year. Marenzio was one of the foremost madrigalists of his time; his later works in the genre are historically significant for their advanced harmonic procedures. He also composed about 75 motets. He was called by his contemporaries "il piu dolce cigno d'Italia" and "divino compositore." B. Meier and R. Jackson ed. the *Opera omnia* in Corpus Mensurabilis Musicae (1976), and S. Ledbetter and P. Myers ed. his secular works (1977 et seq.).

WORKS: VOCAL: S e c u l a r : *Il primo libro de madrigali* for 5 Voices (Venice, 1580); *Il primo libro de madrigali* for 6 Voices (Venice, 1581); *Il secondo libro de madrigali* for 5 Voices (Venice, 1581); *Il terzo libro de madrigali* for 5 Voices (Venice, 1582); *Il secondo libro de madrigali* for 6 Voices (Venice, 1584); *Madrigali spirituali* for 5 Voices (Rome, 1584; enl. ed., 1610); *Il quarto libro de madrigali* for 5 Voices (Venice, 1584); *Il primo libro delle villanelle* for 3 Voices (Venice, 1584); *Il quinto libro de madrigali* for 5 Voices (Venice, 1585); *Il terzo libro de madrigali* for 6 Voices (Venice, 1585); *Il secondo libro delle canzonette alla napolitana* for 3 Voices (Venice, 1585); *Madrigali...libro primo* for 4 Voices (Rome, 1585); *Il terzo libro delle villanelle* for 3 Voices (Venice, 1585; 4th ed., enl., 1600); *Il quarto libro de madrigali* for 6 Voices (Venice, 1587; 3rd ed., rev., 1593); *Il quarto libro delle villanelle* for 3 Voices (Venice, 1587; 4th ed., rev., 1600); *Il quinto libro delle villanelle* for 3 Voices (Venice, 1587); *Madrigali...libro primo* for 4, 5, and 6 Voices (Venice, 1588); *Il quinto libro de madrigali* for 6 Voices (Venice, 1591); *Il sesto libro de madrigali* for 5 Voices (Venice, 1594); *Il sesto libro de madrigali* for 6 Voices (Venice, 1595); *Il settimo libro de madrigali* for 5 Voices (Venice, 1595); *L'ottavo libro de madrigali* for 5 Voices (Venice, 1598); *Il nono libro de madrigali* for 5 Voices (Venice, 1599); also *Il secondo libro de madrigali* for 4 Voices, which is not extant. **S a c r e d :**

Motectorum pro festis totius anni cum Communi Sanctorum for 4 Voices (Venice, 1585); *Completorium et antiphonae* for 6 Voices (Venice, 1595; not extant); *Motetti* for 12 Voices (Venice, 1614); *Sacrae cantiones* for 5, 6, and 7 Voices (Venice, 1616).

BIBL.: P. Guerrini, *L. M., il piu dolce cigno d'Italia nel centenario della nascita* (Brescia, 1953); H. Engel, *L. M.* (Florence, 1956); D. Arnold, *M.* (London, 1965); S. Ledbetter, *L. M.: New Biographical Findings* (diss., N.Y.U., 1971); J. Chater, *L. M. and the Italian Madrigal 1577–1593* (2 vols., Ann Arbor, 1981); B. Janz, *Die Petrarca-Vertonungen von L. M.: Dichtung und Musik in späten Cinquecento- Madrigal* (Tutzing, 1992).—**NS/LK/DM**

Maresch, Johann Anton (real name, **Jan Antonín Mareš**), Bohemian horn player, cellist, and composer; b. Chotěboř, 1719; d. St. Petersburg, June 10, 1794. Following training in Chotěboř and Prague, he studied in Dresden with Hampel (horn) and Zyka (cello). In 1748 he settled in St. Petersburg as horn player in the private orch. of the Russian Grand Chancellor A.P. Bestuzhev-Ryumin. In 1752 he became horn player in the imperial court orch., where he subsequently was second cellist from 1774 to 1792. In 1752 he founded his own hunting-horn ensemble. In 1757 he was made director of the imperial hunting band, which he reorganized. He composed 3- and 4-part works for his groups, but they are not extant.—**NS/LK/DM**

Mareschall, Samuel, Swiss organist, pedagogue, and composer of South Netherlands descent; b. Tournai, May 22?, 1554; d. Basel, Dec. 1640?. He settled in Basel in the winter of 1576–77 and matriculated at the Univ. In 1577 he became organist of the Cathedral and Prof. musices at the Univ., positions he held for his entire life. He also taught music at the Gymnasium and Collegium Alumnorum. Mareschall's Psalm settings were greatly esteemed in Lutheran liturgical circles. He publ. a double vol. of vocal works as *Der gant Psalter von Herrn Ambrosio Lobwasser D. hiebevor auss der Frantzösischen Composition, mit gleicher Melodey und zahl der Syllaben in teutsche Reymen zierlich und lieblich gebract* for 4 Voices (Basel, 1606) and *Psalmen Davids, Kirchen Gesänge und geistliche Lieder von D. Martin Luther und andern gottsgelehrten Männer gestellet* for 4 Voices (Basel, 1606). His other publ. works included (12) *Melodiae suaves et concinnae psalmorum* for 4 Voices *...adjectae sunt in calce hujus libelli brevissima Musices rudimenta* (Basel, 1622) and numerous organ variations. He was the author of the teaching manual *Porta musices, das ist Eynfühung zu der edlen Kunst Musica, mit einem kurtzen Bericht und Anleitung zu den Violen, auch wie ein jeder Gesang leichtlich anzurstimmen seye* (Basel, 1589).—**NS/LK/DM**

Marescotti, André-François, Swiss composer, organist, choirmaster, and teacher; b. Geneva, April 30, 1902. Following training at the Geneva Technicum, he studied at the Geneva Cons. with Mottu (piano), Montillet (organ), Chaix (harmony, counterpoint, and composition), and Lauber (instrumentation), and in Paris with Roger-Ducasse (composition). In 1921 he became organist in Compesières. In 1924 he became choirmaster at the Sacré-Coeur, and in 1940 at the St.-Joseph Church in Geneva. He also was on the faculty of the Geneva Cons. (1931–73). He publ. the valuable folio vol. *Les Instruments d'orchestre, Leurs caractères, leurs possibilités et leur utilisation dans l'orchestre moderne* (with 900 musical examples; Paris, 1950). Marescotti's early works followed along French Impressionist lines, but he later embraced serialism.

WORKS: DRAMATIC: Ballet: *Les Anges du Grèco* (Zürich, June 1, 1947). **ORCH.:** *Ouverture pour celui qui épousa une femme muette* (1930); *Prélude au Grand Meaulnes* (1934); *Aubade* (1936); *Concert Carougeois I* (1942), *II* (1959), *III* (1964–65), and *IV* (1985); *Giboulées* for Bassoon and Orch. (1949; also for Solo Bassoon); Piano Concerto (1954–57); *Festa* (1961); *Hymnes* (1961–64); *Rondeau capriccioso* (1972); *Ballade* for Violin and Orch. (1975; also for Solo Violin); Cello Concerto (1977); *Nuage sur la vigne,* suite (1984). **CHAMBER:** *Mouvement* for Harp (1941); *Giboulées* for Bassoon (1949; also for Bassoon and Orch.); *Ballade* for Violin (1975; also for Violin and Orch.); *Méditation alternée* for Winds, Timpani, and Percussion (1979). **Piano:** *Esquisses et Croquis* (3 series, 1923–40); 3 suites (1928–44); *Fantasque* (1939); *Variations sur un thème de J.-J. Rousseau* (1978); *Ittocséram* (1980–82). **VOCAL:** *Messe St.-André* for Chorus and Organ (1925); *Réveillez-vous Pastoureaux,* 10 carols for Voices and Piano or Orch. (1944); *Vergers* for Medium Voice and Piano (1945–46); *La Lampe d'argile* for Soloists and Chorus (1947); *Insomnies* for Voice and Orch. (1950–64); *Trois Incantations* for Chorus and 4 Percussionists (1969); *Salve Regina, Regina Coeli,* 2 motets for Women's Chorus and Organ (1990).

BIBL.: A. Golea, *A.-F. M., Biographie. Études analytiques. Liste des Oeuvres. Discographie* (Paris, 1963); C. Tappolet, *A.-F. M.* (Geneva, 1986).—**NS/LK/DM**

Maretzek, Max, Czech-born American conductor, operatic impresario, and composer; b. Brünn, June 28, 1821; d. Staten Island, N.Y., May 14, 1897. He received training in medicine and law at the Univ. of Vienna and pursued musical studies with Seyfried. In 1840 he commenced his career as a conductor and composer. In 1844 he became chorus master at London's Covent Garden. He went to N.Y. in 1848 to conduct Italian opera at the Astor Place Opera House. In 1849 he launched out on his own as an operatic impresario, conducting enterprises in N.Y. and on tour throughout the U.S., Cuba, and Mexico. In addition to engaging many famous singers for the first time in the U.S., he also conducted first performances in N.Y. of many operas, most notably *Il Trovatore* (May 2, 1855), *La Traviata* (Dec. 3, 1856), and *Don Carlos* (April 12, 1877). Although he retired as an operatic impresario in 1878, he continued to be active as a conductor. Among his own works were several operas, including *Sleepy Hollow: or, The Headless Horseman* (N.Y., Sept. 25, 1879), and a number of ballets. His colorful career is related in his two books, *Crotchets and Quavers* (N.Y., 1855) and *Sharps and Flats* (N.Y., 1890).—**NS/LK/DM**

Marez Oyens, Tera de, Dutch composer, pianist, conductor, and teacher; b. Velzen, Aug. 5, 1932. She was a piano student of Jan Ode at the Amsterdam Cons., graduating when she was 20. She also took courses there in harpsichord, violin, and conducting. After further training with Henkemens (composition and orchestration), she studied electronic music with Koenig at the Inst. of Sonology at the Univ. of Utrecht. She was active as a pianist and conductor. She also was a prof. at the Zwolle Cons. (until 1988). In her music, Marez Oyens has utilized both traditional and contemporary modes of expression.

WORKS: ORCH.: *Introduzione* (1969); *Transformation* (1972); *Human* for Orch. and Tape (1975); *Shoshadre* for Strings (1976); *Episodes* for Orch. and Adaptable Ensemble (1976); *In Exile*, concertino for Piano and Strings (1977); *Litany of the Victims of War* (1985); *Structures and Dance*, violin concerto (1986; Hilversum, Jan. 22, 1987); 3 syms.: No. 1, *Sinfonia Testimonial*, for Chorus, Orch., and Tape (The Hague, Nov. 1987), No. 2, *Squaw Sachem* (1993), and No. 3, *Ceremonies* (1993); *Symmetrical Memories*, cello concerto (1988; Scheveningen, March 19, 1989); *Confrontations*, piano concerto (1990; Utrecht, Dec. 1991); *Interface* for Strings (1991); *Linzer Concert*, accordion concerto (Linz, Nov. 1991); Alto Saxophone Concerto (1992). CHAMBER: *Deducties* for Oboe and Harpsichord (1964); Wind Octet (1972); *Mahpoochah* for 7 or More Instruments (1978); *Mosaic* for Oboe, Clarinet, Horn, Bassoon, and Piano (1979); Concerto for Horn and Tape (1980); *Polskie Miasta* for Flute, Oboe, Violin, Viola, Cello, and Piano (1981); 3 string quartets, including *Contrafactus* (1981) and No. 3 (1988); *Lenaia* for Flute (1982; also as *Lenaia Quintet* for Flute, 2 Violins, Viola, and Cello); *Octopus* for Bass Clarinet and Percussion (1982); *Möbius by Ear* for Viola and Piano (1983); *Ambiversion* for Bass Clarinet and Tape (1983); *Trajectory* for Saxophone Quartet (1985); *Powerset* for Saxophone Quartet and Percussion (1986); *Free for All* for 5 Instruments (1986); *Gilgamesh Quartet* for 4 Trombones (1988); *Dublin Quartet* for Violin, Viola, Cello, and Piano (1989); *NamSan* for Marimba (1993); *A Wrinkle in Time* for Flute, Violin, Viola, and Piano (1994). KEYBOARD: Piano: Sonatine (1961); Sonatine for 2 Pianos (1963); *Ballerina on a Cliff* (1980); *Charon's Gift* for Piano and Tape (1982); *Sentenced to Dream* (1990); *The Uncarved Block* for Piano and Tape (1994). Organ: Partita (1958). VOCAL: *Zuid Afrikaanse Liederen* for Soprano or Tenor and Piano (1951); *Tragödie* for Men's Chorus (1957); *Der Chinesische Spiegel* for Tenor and Orch. (1962); *Deposuit Potentos de Sede* for Chorus (1970); *Pente Sjawoe Kost* for 7 Narrators and Chorus (1970); *Canto di Parole* for Chorus (1971); *Bist du Bist II* for Chorus (1973); *From Death to Birth* for Chorus (1974); *Ode to Kelesh* for Chorus and Instruments (1975); *The Lover* for Chorus (1975); *The Odyssey of Mr. Goodevil*, oratorio for 4 Soloists, 2 Narrators, 2 Choruses, and Orch. (1976–81); *The Fire and the Mountains*, cantata for Chorus and Orch. (1978; rev. 1984); *Takadon* for Voices and Chamber Ensemble (1978); *And Blind She Remained* for Voice, Keyboard, and Percussion (1978); 3 *Hymns* for Mezzo-soprano and Piano (1979); *Black* for Chorus (1981); *Het Lied van de Duizend Angsten* for 2 Soloists, 2 Choruses, and Orch. (1984); *Vignettes* for Soprano, Flute, Percussion, and Piano (1986); *Music for a Small Planet* for Voice, 8 Melody Instruments, and Percussion (1988); *Shadow of a Prayer* for Soprano, Flute, and Piano (1989); *From a Distant Planet* for Baritone or Alto or Mezzo-soprano and Piano (1990); *Recurrent Thoughts of a Haunted Traveller* for Soprano and Saxophone Quartet (1991); *If Only* for Soprano, Flute, Percussion, and Piano (1991); *Carichi pendenti* for Soprano, Accordion, and Cello (1993); *Strange Logic* for Contralto and Orch. (1994). ELECTRONIC: *Etude II* (1964); *Safed* (1968); *Photophonie* for 4 Tracks and 8 Light Sources (1971); *Mixed Feelings* for 4 Tracks and Percussion (1973); *Dances of Illusion*, verbosonic-electronic ballet (1985); *Lier* for Voices and Electronics (1991). OTHER: Pieces for school orch. and amateur groups.—NS/LK/DM

Margison, Richard (Charles), Canadian tenor; b. Victoria, British Columbia, July 15, 1953. He studied at the Victoria Cons. of Music, graduating in 1980. In 1976 he won the regional Metropolitan Opera auditions, and pursued further studies with Léopold Simoneau. In 1980 he made his first appearance with Pacific Opera Victoria as Count Almaviva, where he continued on its roster until 1983. He made his debut with the Vancouver Opera in 1985 as Lensky, and in 1988 he sang Don Ottavio at the Glimmerglass Opera in Cooperstown, N.Y. In 1989 he made his debut with the Canadian Opera Co. in Toronto as Vitek in the first Canadian production of Janáček's *The Makropulos Affair*. His European operatic debut followed in 1990 when he sang Verdi's Gustavus with the English National Opera in London. That same year he also appeared as Gounod's Faust at the Houston Grand Opera. In 1994 he sang Don Carlos at the San Francisco Opera, returning there in 1997 as Cavaradossi. Among his other fine roles are Alfredo, Edgardo, Rodolfo, Don José, Fenton, and Nemorino. He also sang in oratorio and concert performances throughout Canada.—NS/LK/DM

Margola, Franco, Italian composer and teacher; b. Orzinuovi, near Brescia, Oct. 30, 1908; d. Brescia, March 10, 1992. He studied violin with Romanini and composition with Guerrini, Jachino, Longo, and Casella at the Parma Cons. (diplomas in piano, 1926, and in composition, 1934), then took a course in advanced theory with Casella at the Accademia di Santa Cecilia in Rome. After serving as director of the Messina Cons. (1938–40), he taught at the conservatories in Cagliari, Bologna, Milan, Rome, and Parma. He publ. a manual, *Guida pratica per lo studio della composizione* (Milan, 1954).

WORKS: DRAMATIC: Opera: *Il mito di Caino* (Bergamo, 1940). ORCH.: Piano Concerto (1943; Florence, Feb. 12, 1944); Cello Concerto (1949); 2 syms. (1950, 1961); Children's Concerto for Piano and Small Orch. (1954); Children's Concerto for Violin and Small Orch. (1955); Concerto for Strings (1958); Concerto for Violin, Piano, and Strings (1960); Horn Concerto (1960); Double Concerto for Violin, Piano, and Strings (1960); Concerto for Oboe and Strings (1962); Passacaglia for Strings, Piano, and Percussion (1970). CHAMBER: 3 cello sonatas (1931–45); 4 violin sonatas (1932–44); 2 piano quintets (1933, 1946); 8 string quartets (1936–50); 4 *Episodi* for Flute and Guitar (1970); piano pieces.

BIBL.: R. Cresti, *Linguaggio musicale di F. M.* (Milan, 1994); idem, ed., *F. M. nella critica italiana* (Milan, 1996).—NS/LK/DM

Margulies, Adele, Austrian-born American pianist and teacher; b. Vienna, March 7, 1863; d. N.Y., June 6, 1949. She was a student of Door and Grädner at the Vienna Cons., where she took 1st prize for 3 consecutive years. On Nov. 3, 1881, she made her N.Y. recital debut. On March 30, 1885, she played the premiere of the last 2 movements of MacDowell's 2nd Piano Concerto there. In 1887 she became the first prof. of piano at the National Cons. of Music of America in N.Y., continuing in that capacity until 1936. She also was active with the Margulies Trio (1890–92; 1904–25).—NS/LK/DM

Marguste, Anti, Estonian composer and teacher; b. Are, Aug. 5, 1931. He studied with M. Saar and A.

Garshnek at the Tallinn Cons. (graduated, 1960), then taught at the Tallinn Music School from 1962. His output is marked by the use of folk elements.

WORKS: ORCH.: 6 syms. (1960, 1963, 1966, 1967, 1970, 1981); *Pieces* for Reed-pipe, Flutes, and Strings (1967); *Symphonic Runes* (1974); *Organ Tunes* for Organ and Orch. (1974). **CHAMBER:** *Concertino piccolo* No. 1 for Woodwind Quintet (1967) and No. 2 for 12 Flutes and Percussion (1979); piano pieces. **VOCAL:** *Old Proverb—Old Silver*, cycle for Children's Chorus, Women's Chorus, and Mixed Chorus (1974); *Red Data Book* for Soprano, Mezzo-soprano, Tenor, Bass, Chorus, Trumpet, Trombone, Horn, Tuba, and Piano (1980); songs.
—NS/LK/DM

Maria Antonia Walpurgis, electress of Saxony, daughter of the elector of Bavaria, later Holy Roman Emperor Charles VII; b. Munich, July 18, 1724; d. Dresden, April 23, 1780. She was not only a generous patroness of the fine arts, but a trained musician, pupil of Hasse and Porpora (1747–52). Under the pseudonym E.T.P.A. (Ermelinda Talea Pastorella Arcada, her name as member of the Academy of Arcadians) she produced and publ. 2 Italian operas to her own librettos, and sang in their premieres: *Il trionfo della Fedeltà* (Dresden, 1754) and *Talestri, regina delle Amazoni* (Nymphenburg, near Munich, Feb. 6, 1760). She also wrote texts of oratorios and cantatas for Hasse and Ristori.

BIBL.: C. von Weber, *M.A. W., Churfürstin zu Sachsen* (2 vols., Dresden, 1857); H. Drewes, *M.A. W. als Komponistin* (Leipzig, 1934).—NS/LK/DM

Mariani, Angelo (Maurizio Gaspare), eminent Italian conductor; b. Ravenna, Oct. 11, 1821; d. Genoa, June 13, 1873. He studied violin with P. Casalini and counterpoint with G. Roberti at the Ravenna Phil. Academy's music school, and also learned to play other instruments. He began his career as bandmaster of the city of Sant' Agata Feltria (1842); became a violinist and violist in the orch. in Rimini (1843). That same year he brought out a concerto and 2 overtures in Macerata, gaining the admiration and friendship of Rossini. He was 1st violinist and maestro concertatore in Messina (1844–45), then made his first appearance in Milan at the Teatro Re conducting Verdi's *I due Foscari* (July 1, 1846), winning the praise of the composer; subsequently conducted at the Teatro Carcano there, and then conducted at the Copenhagen Court Theater (1847–48). After taking part in the Italian war of independence in 1848, he was compelled to leave his homeland and went to Constantinople. He was conductor at the Pera theater there until 1850. He returned to Italy in 1851, conducting in Messina, then was appointed director and conductor of the Teatro Carlo Felice in Genoa, making his debut conducting *Robert le diable* on May 15, 1852. He led many fine performances there of operas by Rossini, Bellini, Donizetti, Meyerbeer, and Verdi, becoming a close friend of the latter; also assumed the directorship of the Teatro Comunale in Bologna, making his debut leading *Un ballo in maschera* on Oct. 4, 1860. He conducted the first Italian performances of *Lohengrin* (Nov. 1, 1871) and *Tannhäuser* (Nov. 11, 1872) in Bologna. Stricken with intestinal cancer, he was unable to accede to Verdi's request that he conduct the premiere of *Aida*

in Cairo. In spite of his grave illness, he carried out his duties in both Genoa and Bologna until his death. Mariani was one of the foremost Italian operatic conductors of his era, especially esteemed for his authoritative performances of the great masterpieces of the Italian stage. He himself wrote several cantatas, chamber music, songs, and piano pieces.

BIBL.: S. Busmanti, *Cenni su A. M.* (Ravenna, 1887); T. Mantovani, *A. M.* (Rome, 1921); U. Zoppi, *A. M., Giuseppe Verdi e Teresa Stolz in un carteggio inedito* (Milan, 1947).—NS/LK/DM

Mariani, Luciano, Italian bass; b. Cremona, 1801; d. Piacenza, June 10, 1859. He created the role of Oroe in *Semiramide* (1823), Rodolfo in *La sonnambula* (1831), and Alfonso in *Lucrezia Borgia* (1833). His sister, Rosa (b. Cremona, 1799; place and date of death unknown), was also a singer. In 1818 she made her operatic debut in Cremona. In 1823 she created the role of Arsace in *Semiramide*. She appeared at the King's Theatre in London in 1832.—NS/LK/DM

Marić, Ljubica, remarkable Serbian composer; b. Kragujevac, March 18, 1909. She studied with Josip Slavenski in Belgrade, then went to Prague, where she took composition courses with Suk and Alois Hába at the Cons. She also studied conducting with Malko in Prague (1929–32) and with Scherchen in Strasbourg (1933), and then returned to Prague for more study with Hába in his special quarter tone classes (1936–37). She subsequently taught at the Stanković School of Music in Belgrade. During the period of Nazi occupation of Serbia, she was an active participant in the resistance. After the liberation, she was a member of the teaching staff of the Belgrade Academy of Music (1945–67). In her music, she adopted a global type of modern technique, utilizing variable tonal configurations, atonal melodic progressions, and microtonal structures while adhering to traditional forms of composition.

WORKS: ORCH.: *Passacaglia* (Belgrade, April 21, 1958). **CHAMBER:** String Quartet (1931); Wind Quintet (1932); Trio for Clarinet, Trombone, and Double Bass (1937); Violin Sonata (1948); numerous piano pieces. **VOCAL:** 2 cantatas: *Pesme prostora* (Songs of Space), based on inscriptions on the graves of Bogomils, a heretical religious sect of the Middle Ages (Belgrade, Dec. 8, 1956) and *Prag sna* (Threshold of Dream), chamber cantata for Narrator, Soprano, Alto, and Instrumental Ensemble (1961; Opatija, Oct. 30, 1965); *Slovo svetlosti* (Sound of Light), oratorio, after medieval Serbian poetry (1966); songs. **OTHER:** 4 modern realizations of the Serbian Octoichos: *Muzika oktoiha No. 1* for Orch. (Belgrade, Feb. 28, 1959), *Vizantijski koncert* (Byzantine Concerto) for Piano and Orch. (Belgrade, June 4, 1963), *Ostinato super thema octoicha* for String Quintet, Harp, and Piano (Warsaw, Sept. 27, 1963), and *Simfonija oktoiha* (1964).—NS/LK/DM

Marie, Gabriel, French conductor and composer; b. Paris, Jan. 8, 1852; d. Puigcerda, Catalonia, Aug. 29, 1928. He studied at the Paris Cons. He was chorus master of the Lamoureux Concerts (1881–87), and then conductor of the orch. concerts of the Société Nationale de Musique (1887–94), of Ste.-Cécile in Bordeaux, at Marseilles, and (during the summer months) at the

Casino in Vichy. He wrote a number of melodious pieces for orch., of which *La Cinquantaine* (in arrangements for violin or cello, with piano) became immensely popular. He also wrote music criticism, collected in *Pour la musique* (Paris, 1930).—NS/LK/DM

Marie, Teena (originally, Brockert, Mary Christine),

one of the few white artists to cross over from R&B to pop; b. Santa Monica, Calif., March 5, 1956. At two years old, Mary Christine Brockert embarrassed her mother by standing up in church and belting out "The Banana Boat Song." Soon, however, her mother was encouraging her child's gift, teaching her songs and how to sing them. By the time Mary was nine, she knew over 200 tunes; she made her first public performance around that time, fronting a 36-piece orchestra at a Hollywood restaurant. She started to appear in commercials and even acted in an episode of *The Beverly Hillbillies*. By the age of 13, she fronted her own band. She continued singing and acting through high school.

While enrolled in Santa Monica City Coll., Brockert tried out for a television show called *Orphanage Children*. The show was never produced, but she impressed its producers, Motown Productions, who signed her to their record label. Unfortunately, they couldn't find a producer willing or able to handle a white woman singing heavy urban music. She languished on the Motown roster for three years before Rick James overheard her working out her voice in Stevie Wonder's office. In James's words, she was singing "her ass off. I walked in and here's this short munchkin white girl [singing soul music]." James signed on to produce her album that no one else wanted or could handle.

While working on her debut, James taught her the basics of the studio, as well as guitar and bass. He helped her explore her range. For a short time, they were romantically involved. The cover to her 1979 debut, *Wild and Peaceful*, didn't have a picture of the newly named Teena Marie, and consequently the first people to respond to this new woman singer were R&B stations. Her first single, "I'm a Sucker for Your Love," climbed to #8 on the R&B charts. Most of her listeners were unaware that she was white. Marie's next album, *Lady T*, was produced by Richard Rudolph. Rudolph had previously worked solely with his wife, Minnie Riperton; Marie was the first artist he produced after Riperton's death. This time, Marie's picture appeared on the cover, but she still primarily appealed to a black audience. The bass-and-horn workout "Behind the Groove" from the album topped out at #21 on the R&B charts.

Taking everything she had learned on her previous two projects, Marie produced her third album, 1980's *Irons in the Fire*. A commercial breakthrough, it yielded her first pop hit, the funky "I Need Your Lovin'," which peaked pop at #38, #9 on the R&B charts. The album rose to #38 on the pop charts. Similarly her next album, *It Must Be Magic*, sported the massive #3 R&B hit "Square Biz." The tune featured one of the first raps by a female artist. The album went to #23 and sold gold. Later in 1981, Rick James pulled her from a hospital bed to cut the track "Fire and Desire" for James's *Street*

Songs, another major hit. On that high note, she left the Motown fold amid acrimony and lawsuits. The label refused to issue Marie's recordings but also refused to release her from her contract; she sued, saying that Motown couldn't keep her from signing with another label if the company wouldn't issue her records. Marie won the case, resulting in the so-called "Teena Marie Law," which stated that a label can not keep an artist under contract unless it is willing to release that artist's recordings.

Marie signed with Epic records in 1983. However, her first effort for the company, *Robbery*, met with a lukewarm response. She bounced back a year later with *Starchild*. The album, infused with touches of Prince-like rock and funk, produced her biggest pop hit, "Lovergirl," her first record to go further on the pop charts (reaching #4) than it did on the R&B charts (where it stalled at #9). *Emerald City* (1986) explored more of that funk-and-roll sound, and featured guitarist Stevie Ray Vaughan on one track. Her next effort, *Naked to the World*, produced her only #1 R&B hit, the quasi-ballad "Ooo La La La." Additionally, it featured the #10 "Work It," a tune that mixed programmed drums with some amazing solo trombone. *Ivory* (1990), with tracks produced by Soul II Soul's Jazzie B., featured the soaring vocal workout "If I Were a Bell" (not the Frank Loesser standard), another R&B Top Ten tune.

However, Marie's sales never again approached the heights of *Starchild*. By 1994, Marie lacked a major label deal, and had to release her *Passion Play* album on her own. It saw little action, and she has not recorded since. As a true sign of her fading star, she was featured on VH-1's *Where Are They Now?* series in 1999.

DISC.: *Wild & Peaceful* (1979); *Lady T* (1980); *Irons in the Fire* (1980); *It Must Be Magic* (1981); *Robbery* (1983); *Starchild* (1984); *Emerald City* (1986); *Naked to the World* (1987); *Ivory* (1990); *Passion Play* (1994).—BH

Marin, Ion,

Romanian conductor; b. Bucharest, July 8, 1960. He studied at the George Enescu Music School, the Salzburg Mozarteum, the Accademia Musicale Chigiana in Siena, and the International Academy in Nice. In 1981 he became music director of the Transylvania Phil. in Cluj-Napoca. From 1987 to 1991 he served as resident conductor at the Vienna State Opera. He made his first appearance in the British capital as a guest conductor with the London Sym. Orch. in 1991, the same year he made his U.S. debut at the Dallas Opera conducting *L'Elisir d'amore*. In 1992 he conducted *Il Barbiere di Siviglia* at the San Francisco Opera and *Semiramide* at the Metropolitan Opera in N.Y. As a guest conductor, Marin appeared with many opera companies and orchs. throughout Europe, North America, Australia, and the Far East.—NS/LK/DM

Marini, Biagio,

distinguished Italian violinist and composer; b. Brescia, c. 1587; d. Venice, March 20, 1665. He was a violinist under Monteverdi at San Marco in Venice (1615–18), and then music director of the Accademia degli Erranti in Brescia (1620–21). He subsequently was a violinist in the Farnese court in Parma (1621–23), and then served at the court in Neuberg an die Donau (1623–49), where he occasionally acted as Kapellmeister; he also traveled to other cities. In 1649 he was appointed maestro di cappella at S. Maria della Scala in Milan, and in 1652–53 he was director of the Accademia della Morte in Ferrara. He was an accomplished composer of both instrumental and vocal music. His op.1, *Affetti musicali* (Venice, 1617), contains the earliest example of the Italian solo sonata with basso continuo. Among his other important collections were a vol. of sonatas and sinfonias, op.8 (Venice, 1629) and a vol. of ensemble sonatas in da camera and da chiesa forms, op.22 (Venice, 1655).—NS/LK/DM

Marini, Ignazio, outstanding Italian bass; b. Tagliuno (Bergamo), Nov. 28, 1811; d. Milan, April 29, 1873. He made his operatic debut most likely in Brescia about 1832. From 1833 to 1847 he was a leading member of Milan's La Scala, where he created the role of Guido in Donizetti's *Gemma di Vergy* (Dec. 26, 1834) and the title role in Verdi's *Oberto, Conte di San Bonifacio* (Nov. 17, 1839). He befriended the youthful Verdi, who added the Cabaletta to *Infelice* in *Ernani* for him (1844). He later created the title role in Verdi's *Attila* (Venice, March 17, 1846). From 1847 to 1849 he sang at London's Covent Garden, and then in N.Y. from 1850 to 1852. From 1856 to 1863 he appeared in St. Petersburg. Marini was greatly admired for his true basso cantante. Among his other famous roles were Rossini's Mosè and Mustafà, and Bellini's Oroveso. His wife, Antonietta Rainer-Marini, was a noted mezzo-soprano. She created the role of Leonora in Verdi's *Oberto*, as well as the Marchesa in his *Un giorno di regno* (Milan, Sept. 5, 1840). —NS/LK/DM

Marinkoví, Josef, Serbian choral conductor, teacher, and composer; b. Vranjevo, Sept. 15, 1851; d. Belgrade, May 13, 1931. He studied composition with F. Skuherský at the Prague Organ School, then was active as a choral conductor in Belgrade (1881–1924). He was the father of the Serbian lied, and the last champion of the Serbian national Romantic movement. In addition to his songs, he wrote incidental music, choral works, sacred music, and piano pieces.

BIBL.: V. Pericic, *J. M.: Zivot i dela* (J. M.: Life and Works; Belgrade, 1967).—NS/LK/DM

Marinov, Ivan, Bulgarian composer and conductor; b. Sofia, Oct. 17, 1928. He studied conducting with Goleminov and composition with V. Stoyanov and P. Khadziev at the Sofia State Cons., graduating in 1955.

WORKS: ORCH.: *Suite on 4 Folk Songs* (1955); *Ilinden*, symphonic poem (1956); *Paraphrases* (1957); *Fantastic Scenes* (1959); *Divertimento* (1961); *Festive Suite* (1968); *Ode on Liberty* (1969). VOCAL: *Dvuboj* (Duel), poem for Tenor and Orch. (1953); *Pentagram* for Bass, String Orch., Piano, and Timpani (1965–66); Sym. No. 1 for Bass and Orch. (1967); songs. OTHER: Chamber music.—NS/LK/DM

Marinuzzi, Gino, (I) noted Italian conductor and composer, father of **Gino Marinuzzi (II)**; b. Palermo, March 24, 1882; d. Milan, Aug. 17, 1945. He was a student of Zuelli at the Palermo Cons. He commenced his career conducting at the Teatro Massimo in Palermo, where he conducted the first local performance of *Tristan und Isolde* in 1909. After conducting in various Italian operatic centers, he toured in South America. In 1913 he conducted the first local performance of *Parsifal* at the Teatro Colón in Buenos Aires. From 1915 to 1918 he was director of the Bologna Liceo Musicale. On March 27, 1917, he conducted the premiere of Puccini's *La Rondine* in Monte Carlo. He was artistic director of the Chicago Grand Opera Co. from 1919 to 1921. From 1928 to 1934 he was chief conductor of the Teatro Reale dell'Opera in Rome. In 1934 he conducted at London's Covent Garden. From 1934 to 1944 he conducted at Milan's La Scala, where he served as its superintendent in 1944. Marinuzzi was especially admired as a conductor of the Italian operatic repertoire, but he also won distinction for his performances of Wagner and Strauss. Among his compositions were the operas *Barberina* (Palermo, 1903), *Jacquerie* (Buenos Aires, Aug. 11, 1918), and *Palla de' Mozzi* (Milan, April 5, 1932), a sym. (1943), and chamber music.

BIBL.: A. Garbelotto, *G. M.* (Ancona, 1965).—NS/LK/DM

Marinuzzi, Gino, (II) Italian conductor and composer, son of **Gino Marinuzzi (I)**; b. N.Y., April 7, 1920. He studied at the Milan Cons. with Calace (piano) and Paribeni and Bossi (composition), graduating in 1941. From 1946 to 1951 he was asst. conductor at the Teatro dell'Opera in Rome, and then conducted in other Italian opera houses. He was one of the first Italian composers to explore the potentialities of electronic music; in collaboration with Ketoff, he developed an electronic synthesizer, the "Fonosynth," and was a founder of an electronic studio in Rome. His compositions include a radio opera, *La Signora Paulatim* (Naples, 1966); Violin Concerto; Piano Concerto; chamber music; piano pieces; film scores; pieces for electronic tape.—NS/LK/DM

Mario (real name, **Tillotson**), **Queena,** American soprano and teacher; b. Akron, Ohio, Aug. 21, 1896; d. N.Y., May 28, 1951. She went to N.Y. to work as a journalist in order to raise funds to pursue her vocal training with Saenger and Sembrich. On Sept. 4, 1918, she made her operatic debut as Olympia in *Les Contes d'Hoffmann* with the San Carlo Opera Co. in N.Y. She remained with the company until 1920, and then was a member of the Scotti Grand Opera Co. (1920–22). On Nov. 30, 1922, she made her Metropolitan Opera debut in N.Y. as Micaëla. She remained on its roster until 1938, winning favor for her portrayals of Gilda, Juliette, Marguerite, Nedda, Sophie, and Antonia. She was particularly associated with the role of Gretel, which she sang in the first complete opera to be broadcast on radio by the Metropolitan (Dec. 25, 1931), and also at her farewell appearance with the company (Dec. 26, 1938). Mario also sang with the San Francisco Opera (1923–24; 1929–30; 1932). In 1931 she became a teacher at the Curtis Inst. of Music in Philadelphia. In 1934 she opened her own vocal studio in N.Y., and in 1942 became a teacher at the Juilliard School of Music there. She wrote 3 mystery novels, including *Murder in the Opera House*. In 1925 she married **Wilfred Pelletier**, but they divorced in 1936.—NS/LK/DM

Mario, Giovanni Matteo, Cavaliere de Candia, celebrated Italian tenor, known professionally as **Mario**; b. Cagliari, Sardinia, Oct. 17, 1810; d. Rome, Dec. 11, 1883. Born into a noble family, he studied at the Turin military academy and then joined the regiment of which his father was colonel. He eloped with a ballerina to Paris (1836), where he studied voice with Bordogni and Poncharde at the Cons. He made his debut as *Robert le diable* at the Paris Opéra (Dec. 5, 1838). He made his first London appearance as Gennaro in *Lucrezia Borgia* opposite Giulia Grisi's Lucrezia at Her Majesty's Theatre (June 6, 1839); the 2 singers remained intimate, without benefit of marriage, for 22 years. He made his debut at the Théâtre-Italien in Paris as Nemorino (Oct. 17, 1839), and soon became one of its principal members; created the role of Ernesto in *Don Pasquale* there (Jan. 3, 1843). He continued to sing in London at Her Majesty's Theatre until 1846, and then was a leading artist at the Royal Italian Opera at Covent Garden until 1871; also sang in St. Petersburg (1849–53; 1868–70), N.Y. (1854), and Madrid (1859, 1864). He retired from the stage in 1871, giving farewell appearances in Paris, London, and the U.S. Mario's beautiful voice, matched by an exquisite vocal style, handsome figure, and effective acting gifts, made him one of the most renowned operatic singers of his day; he also was greatly esteemed as a concert singer. Among his other roles were the Duke of Mantua, Faust, John of Leyden, Almaviva, Raoul, and Roméo.

BIBL.: L. Engel, *From Mozart to M.* (London, 1886); Mrs. Godfrey Pearce (M.'s daughter) and F. Hird, *The Romance of a Great Singer* (London, 1910); E. Forbes, *M. and Grisi* (London, 1985).—NS/LK/DM

Mariotte, Antoine, French composer; b. Avignon, Dec. 22, 1875; d. Izieux, Loire, Nov. 30, 1944. He was trained at the Naval Academy. In 1897 he became a pupil of d'Indy at the Schola Cantorum in Paris. In 1899 he was appointed conductor of the sym. concerts at St.-Etienne, Loire. From 1902 to 1919 he taught at the Orléans Cons., and in 1920 he was appointed its director. From 1936 to 1938 he was director of the Paris Opéra-Comique.

WORKS: DRAMATIC: O p e r a : *Salomé* (Lyons, Oct. 30, 1908); *Le Vieux Roi* (Lyons, 1911); *Léontine Soeurs* (Paris, May 21, 1924); *Esther, Princesse d'Israël* (Paris, May 5, 1925); *Gargantua* (1924; Paris, Feb. 13, 1935); *Nele Dooryn* (1940). **OTHER:** *Impressions urbaines*, symphonic suite (1921); songs; numerous teaching pieces for piano.—NS/LK/DM

Mariz, Vasco, Brazilian musicologist and diplomat; b. Rio de Janeiro, Jan. 22, 1921. He was a student of Lorenzo Fernández, Vera Janacópulos, Francisco Mignone, and Ernest Tempele at the Conservatório Brasileiro de Música in Rio de Janeiro. He also studied law at the Univ. of Rio de Janeiro (D.J., 1943). In 1945 he sang bass roles in Mozart's operas in Porto Alegre, and in 1947 made his recital debut in Rio de Janeiro. However, after entering the Brazilian diplomatic service in 1945, he devoted himself mainly to a dual career as a diplomat and musicologist. Following diplomatic posts in Oporto, Portugal (1948–49) and Belgrade (1950–51), he was consul in Rosario, Argentina (1951–54) and Naples (1956–58). From 1959 to 1962 he was cultural affairs officer at the Brazilian Embassy in Washington, D.C. In 1969–70 he was the Brazilian asst. secretary of state for cultural affairs. He subsequently served as Brazil's ambassador to Israel (1977–82), Peru (1983–84), and Germany (1985–87).

WRITINGS: *A Canção da câmara no Brasil* (Oporto, 1948; rev. and enl. ed., 1959, as *A canção brasileira: Eruita folclórica e popular*; 5th ed., 1985); *Figuras da música brasileira contemporânea* (Oporto, 1948; 2nd ed., 1970); *Dicionário bio-bibliográfico musical (brasileiro e internacional)* (Rio de Janeiro, 1948; new ed., 1985, as *Dicionário bio-bibliográfico musical: Compositores intérpretes e musicólogos*; 3rd ed., 1991); *Heitor Villa-Lobos* (Rio de Janeiro, 1949; 11th ed., 1990); *Vida musical I* (Oporto, 1950); *Alberto Ginastera, en adhesión a la fecha nacional argentina* (Rosario, 1954); *Vida musical II* (Rio de Janeiro, 1970); *História de musica no Brasil* (Rio de Janeiro, 1981; 4th ed., 1994); *Tres musicólogos brasileiros: Mário de Andrade, Renato Almeida, Luiz Heitor Correa de Azevedo* (Rio de Janeiro, 1983); *Cláudio Santoro* (Rio de Janeiro, 1994).—NS/LK/DM

Mark, Peter, American conductor; b. N.Y., Oct. 31, 1940. He studied at Columbia Univ. (B.A. in musicology, 1961) and with Jean Morel, Joseph Fuchs, and Walter Trampler at the Juilliard School of Music in N.Y. (M.S., 1963). After serving as principal violist of the Juilliard Orch. (1960–63) and the orch. of the Lyric Opera in Chicago (1964–66), he was asst. principal violist of the Los Angeles Phil. (1968–69). In 1975 he became general director of the Va. Opera. As a guest conductor, he appeared at the N.Y.C. Opera (1981), in Los Angeles (1981), at London's Covent Garden (1982), in Tulsa (1988), Mexico City (1989), Buenos Aires (1989), Orlando (1993), and other opera centers. He also was a guest conductor with various orchs. in the U.S. and abroad. In 1971 he married **Thea Musgrave**. He was awarded the Rosa Ponselle Gold Medal in 1997.—NS/LK/DM

Markevitch, Igor, greatly talented Russian-born Italian, later French composer and conductor; b. Kiev, July 27, 1912; d. Antibes, France, March 7, 1983. He was taken to Paris in his infancy; in 1916 the family settled in Vevey, Switzerland, which remained Markevitch's home for the next decade. He began to study piano with his father, and subsequently took piano lessons with Paul Loyonnet; he also took academic courses at the Collège de Vevey. In 1925 he joined the piano class of Cortot in Paris at the École Normale de Musique, and studied harmony, counterpoint, and composition with Boulanger and orchestration with Rieti. He attracted the attention of Diaghilev, who commissioned him to write a piano concerto and also to collaborate with Boris Kochno on a ballet. Markevitch was soloist in his Piano Concerto at Covent Garden in London on July 15, 1929. Diaghilev died on Aug. 19, 1929, and Markevitch interrupted his work on the ballet for him; he used the musical materials from it in his *Cantate*, which achieved an extraordinary success at its Paris premiere on June 4,

1930. On Dec. 8, 1930, his Concerto Grosso was performed for the first time in Paris with even greater acclaim. Finally, his ballet *Rébus* was produced in Paris on Dec. 15, 1931, to enthusiastic press reviews. Markevitch was hailed, only half- facetiously, as "Igor II" (the first Igor being, of course, Stravinsky). His ballet *L'Envol d'Icare* was premiered in Paris on June 26, 1933, prompting Milhaud to opine that the occasion would probably "mark a date in the evolution of music." But swift as was Markevitch's Icarus-like ascent as a composer, even more precipitous was his decline. He began to be sharply criticized for his penchant toward unrelieved dissonance. When he conducted the premiere of his oratorio *Le Paradis perdu* (London, Dec. 20, 1935), it was roundly condemned for sins of dissonance. Although he continued to compose, Markevitch turned his attention more and more to conducting. He made his professional conducting debut with the Concertgebouw Orch. of Amsterdam in 1930. In 1934–35 he took conducting lessons in Switzerland with Scherchen. During World War II, he was in Italy; after the war, he devoted himself to conducting. He conducted in Stockholm (1952–55). He made his U.S. debut as a guest conductor with the Boston Sym. Orch. (1955). Markevitch was then conductor of the Montreal Sym. Orch. (1957–61), the Havana Phil. (1957–58), and the Lamoureux Orch. in Paris (1957–62). He was founder-conductor of the Spanish Radio and Television Sym. Orch. (1965); then conducted the U.S.S.R. State Sym. Orch. in Moscow (1965), the Monte Carlo Orch. (1967–72), and the orch. of the Accademia di Santa Cecilia in Rome (1973–75). He also gave master classes in conducting in various European music centers. In 1947 he became a naturalized Italian citizen. He became a naturalized French citizen in 1982. Markevitch wrote *Introduction à la musique* (Paris, 1940), *Made in Italy* (London, 1949), and *Point d'orgue* (Paris, 1959). In addition to the Russian repertoire, he exhibited special affinity for the works of Stravinsky, Bartók, and other 20th-century composers.

WORKS: DRAMATIC: Ballet: *Rébus* (Paris, Dec. 15, 1931); *L'Envol d'Icare* (Paris, June 16, 1933; also for Piano as *La Mort d'Icare*). **ORCH.:** Sinfonietta (Brussels, Nov. 30, 1929); Piano Concerto (London, July 15, 1929, composer soloist); Concerto Grosso (Paris, Dec. 8, 1930); *Ouverture symphonique* (1931); *Hymnes* (Paris, June 26, 1933, composer conducting); *Petite suite d'après Schumann* (1933); *Hymne à la mort* for Chamber Orch. (1936); *Cantique d'amour* for Chamber Orch. (Rome, May 14, 1937); *Le Nouvel Age*, sinfonia concertante (1937; Warsaw, Jan. 21, 1938, composer conducting); *Le Bleu Danube* for Chamber Orch. (Florence, May 24, 1946, composer conducting). **CHAMBER:** Serenade for Violin, Clarinet, and Bassoon (Wiesbaden, Aug. 5, 1931); Partita (Paris, May 13, 1932); Galop for 8 Players (1932); Duo for Flute and Bassoon (1939). **Piano:** *Noces*, suite (1925); *La Mort d'Icare* (1933; also as the ballet *L'Envol d'Icare*); *Stefan le poète* (1939–40); *Variations, Fugue and Envoi on a Theme of Handel* (Rome, Dec. 14, 1941). **VOCAL:** Cantate, after Jean Cocteau (Paris, June 4, 1930); Psaume for Soprano and Chamber Orch. (Amsterdam, Dec. 3, 1933, composer conducting); *Le Paradis perdu*, oratorio, after Milton (London, Dec. 20, 1935, composer conducting); *3 poèmes* for Voice and Piano (1935); *La Taille de l'homme* for Soprano and 12 Instruments (1939; unfinished; 1st perf. as *Oraison musicale*, Maastricht, Feb. 7, 1982); *Lorenzo il magnifico*, sinfonia concer-

tante for Soprano and Orch. (1940; Florence, Jan. 12, 1941); *Inno della liberazione nazionale*, songs for the Italian underground resistance (1943–44).

BIBL.: B. Gavoty, *I. M.* (Geneva, 1954); J. Heinzelmann, *I. M.* (Bonn, 1982).—NS/LK/DM

Märkl, Jun, German conductor; b. Munich, Feb. 11, 1959. He received diplomas in violin and conducting from the Hannover Hochschule für Musik, and then had further studies in conducting with Bakels, Celibidache, Gustav Meier, Bernstein, and Ozawa. In 1989 he was named to the position of first conductor of the Darmstadt State Theater, and of the Mannheim National Theater in 1990. He became Generalmusikdirektor of the Saarland State Theater in Saarbrücken in 1992. From 1994 he served as Generalmusikdirektor of the Mannheim National Theater. As a guest conductor, he appeared with the Berlin State Opera, the Hamburg State Opera, the Bavarian State Opera in Munich, the Royal Opera, Covent Garden, London, and at the Metropolitan Opera in N.Y.—NS/LK/DM

Markova, Juliana, gifted Bulgarian pianist; b. Sofia, July 8, 1945. She studied at the Bulgarian State Cons. in Sofia (1963–65) and then with Ilonka Deckers at the Milan Cons., graduating with the highest honors in 1969. She won prizes in the Enesco Competition in Bucharest (1964) and the Long-Thibaud Competition in Paris (1965). In 1973 she made her recital debut at the Berlin Festival, and that same year her U.S. recital debut in Chicago. After appearing as soloist in the Tchaikovsky 1st Piano Concerto with the Los Angeles Phil. in 1974, she appeared as soloist with the leading orchs. of Europe and the U.S., including the London Sym., Philharmonia Orch., Royal Phil., Chicago Sym., Cleveland Orch., and Philadelphia Orch.; also toured in solo recitals. During the 1991–92 season, she toured Japan as soloist with the San Francisco Sym. She settled in London and married **Michael Roll**. A technically brilliant pianist, she excels in the Romantic and the early modern repertoire.—NS/LK/DM

Markowski, Andrzej, Polish conductor and composer; b. Lublin, Aug. 22, 1924; d. Warsaw, Oct. 30, 1986. He studied theory and composition with Malawski in Lublin (1939–41); after studies in composition with Rowley at Trinity Coll. of Music in London (1946–47), he completed his training as a composer with Rytel and Szeligowski and studied conducting with Rowicki at the Warsaw State H.S. of Music (1947–55). He conducted the Szczecin Theater (1949–50), the Poznań Phil. (1954–55), the Silesian Phil. in Katowice (1955–59), and the Kraków Phil. (1959–64), with which he toured the U.S. (1961). After conducting the Wroclaw Phil. (1965–69), he was one of the conductors of the National Phil. in Warsaw (1971–78); toured with it in Europe and Japan; then was conductor of the Artur Rubinstein Phil. in ód (1982–86), touring Italy with this orch. in 1984. He was best known as an interpreter of contemporary music. He wrote instrumental works, chamber music, film and theater scores, and electronic pieces.—NS/LK/DM

Marks, Alan, talented American pianist; b. Chicago, May 14, 1949; d. Berlin, July 12, 1995. His family moved to St. Louis when he was a child; he studied piano with Shirley Parnas Adams. In 1965 he won a prize in Interlochen, and gave his first piano recital in St. Louis in 1966. In 1967 he went to N.Y., where he studied at the Juilliard School of Music with Irwin Freundlich (B.M., 1971); then with Leon Fleisher at the Peabody Cons. of Music in Baltimore (1971–72). He took 2nd prize in the Univ. of Md. (1973) and Geza Anda (1979) competitions. In 1981 he settled in Berlin. He gave successful recitals in Boston, Washington, Philadelphia, Los Angeles, San Francisco, and other cities. In 1976 he played the first performance of *Caprichos* for Piano by Carlos Chávez; also participated in numerous concerts of chamber music. He possessed an innate virtuoso technique, and was able to interpret with perfect stylistic fidelity piano works by classical as well as modern composers.—NS/LK/DM

Marks, Edward B(ennett), American music publisher; b. Troy, N.Y., Nov. 28, 1865; d. Mineola, N.Y., Dec. 17, 1945. With Joseph Stern, he organized the music publishing concern of Joseph Stern and Co. (1894). They composed the popular song "The Little Lost Child," which became their first great publishing success. Marks bought out Stern in 1920, and the company became the Edward B. Marks Music Co. It became the Edward B. Marks Music Corp. in 1932 and subsequently brought out a considerable body of serious music by contemporary composers; it took over the catalog of the George M. Cohan Music Publishing Co. in 1967. Belwin-Mills became its distributor in 1973.—NS/LK/DM

Markull, Friedrich Wilhelm, German organist, pianist, and composer; b. Reichenbach, near Elbing, Prussia, Feb. 17, 1816; d. Danzig, April 30, 1887. He studied organ and composition with F. Schneider in Dessau. He became a church organist in Danzig (1836), and also conductor of the Gesangverein there; likewise appeared as a pianist. He wrote 3 operas for Danzig: *Maja und Alpino, oder Die bezauberte Rose* (Dec. 23, 1843), *Der König von Zion* (March 22, 1850), and *Das Walpurgisfest* (Jan. 14, 1855). Other works include syms., 2 oratorios (1845, 1856), organ pieces, piano music, and many songs.

Bibl.: W. Neumann, *F.W. M.* (Kassel, 1857).—NS/LK/DM

Markwort, Johann Christian, German tenor and voice teacher; b. Reisling, near Braunschweig, Dec. 13, 1778; d. Bessungen, near Darmstadt, Jan. 13, 1866. He took courses in theology in Leipzig, then went to Vienna to study voice. He sang opera in Munich and in Liechtenstein, and in 1810 was engaged as choirmaster in Darmstadt. In 1830 he dedicated himself entirely to teaching. He publ. pedagogical books: *Umriss einer Gesammt-Tonwissenschaft überhaupt wie auch einer Sprach- und Tonsatzlehre* (Darmstadt, 1826), *Gesang-, Ton- und Rede-Vortraglehre* (Mainz, 1827), and *Über Klangveredelung der Stimme* (Mainz, 1847); also a piano method. —NS/LK/DM

Marley, Bob (actually, **Robert Nesta**), purveyor of authentic reggae music; b. Rhoden Hall, Jamaica, April 6, 1945; d. Miami, Fla., May 11, 1981. **The Wailers: Membership:** Bob Marley, voc., gtr.; Peter Tosh (Winston Hubert Macintosh), voc., gtr. (b. Westmoreland, Jamaica, Oct. 9, 1944; d. Kingston, Jamaica, Sept. 11, 1987); Neville O'Reilly "Bunny" Livingstone, voc., perc. (b. Kingston, Jamaica, April 10, 1947); Junior (Franklin Delano Alexander) Braithwaite, voc. (b. Kingston, Jamaica, April 4, 1949; d. there, June 2, 1999); Beverly Kelso, voc.; Aston "Family Man" Barrett, bs. (b. Kingston, Jamaica, Nov. 22, 1946); Carlton Lloyd "Carly" Barrett, drm. (b. Kingston, Jamaica, Dec. 17, 1950; d. there, April 17, 1987); Al Anderson, gtr. (b. Montclair N.J.); Alvin Patterson, perc. **The I-Threes: Membership:** Rita Marley, Judy Mowatt, and Marcia Griffiths. Ziggy (David) Marley (b. Kingston, Jamaica, Oct. 17, 1968.)

Bob Marley and The Wailers were popular recording artists in Jamaica for years before securing a contract with the internationally distributed Island label in 1972. Established with the landmark *Burnin'* and *Catch a Fire* albums, The Wailers became the first reggae band to gain worldwide recognition and Bob Marley, as chief songwriter and lead vocalist, emerged as the first (and possibly only) artist from the Third World to achieve international stardom. Although their albums contained some highly personal songs, they were largely preoccupied with political repression, social injustice, and the tenets of the Rastafarian religion (which included the sacramental use of marijuana). Original members Peter Tosh and "Bunny" Livingstone left The Wailers in 1974 for their own careers, as the female vocal trio the I-Threes augmented Bob Marley and The Wailers beginning in 1975. The group achieved its biggest success with 1976's *Rastaman Vibration*. However, Marley's death in 1981 effectively coincided with the end of the first wave of reggae's popularity.

Bob Marley began recording in his native land in 1961. By 1964 he had joined fellow Jamaicans Peter Tosh and "Bunny" Livingstone in the formation of the Wailing Rudeboys. The group became the Wailin' Wailers (with Junior Braithwaite and Beverly Kelso) and later simply The Wailers for a series of recordings for small Jamaican labels, scoring their first big island hit in 1965 with "Simmer Down." Extensive local success continued into the early 1970s as the group recorded for producers such as Leslie Kong and Lee Perry. They added drummer Carlton Barrett and his bass-playing brother Aston "Family Man" Barrett around 1970, issuing four Jamaican albums by 1972. Johnny Nash used The Wailers to back his top pop hit "I Can See Clearly Now" in 1972, and Marley provided Nash with the 1972 British and 1973 American hit "Stir It Up."

Signed to Chris Blackwell's Island label in 1972, The Wailers recorded their critically acclaimed debut, *Catch a Fire*, but the album failed to sell in the United States, despite the inclusion of "Stir It Up," "No More Trouble," and Tosh's militant "400 Years." Following quiet tours of Great Britain and the United States, The Wailers recorded *Burnin'*, which was similarly overlooked, despite containing Tosh's "Get Up, Stand Up" and "One Foundation" and Marley's "I Shot the Sheriff." Eric Clapton scored a top hit with a tame version of "I Shot the Sheriff" in the summer of 1974, but by then both Tosh and Livingstone had left The Wailers.

Bob Marley and The Wailers, as they became known, finally broke through with 1975's *Natty Dread*, recorded with lead guitarist Al Anderson and the Barrett brothers. In addition to the title song the album included "Rebel Music," "Them Belly Full (But We Hungry)," "Lively Up Yourself," and the touching "No Woman, No Cry," regarded as one of Marley's finest personal songs. Successful tours of America and Britain in 1975 raised Marley to the status of cult figure as the rock press declared reggae the up-and-coming music of the 1970s.

In 1975 Bob Marley and The Wailers were augmented by the female vocal trio the I-Threes, which consisted of Marley's wife Rita, Judy Mowatt, and Marcia Griffiths. Griffiths started her career in the early 1960s, scoring her first top Jamaican hit with "Feel Like Jumping" in 1968. Judy Mowatt had her own career as early as 1970. In 1976 the group's *Rastaman Vibration* became a best-seller. Yielding their only (minor) hit with "Roots, Rock, Reggae," the album also contained "Positive Vibration," "Rat Race," and "War."

Following an assassination attempt on Dec. 3, 1976, Bob Marley went into self-imposed exile. His *Exodus* album included favorites such as "Jamming," "Exodus," and "Waiting in Vain," and the inspirational medley "One Love/People Get Ready," and sold quite well. However, *Kaya*, comprised entirely of love songs, sold only modestly. Bob Marley returned to the concert stage on April 22, 1978, for the One Love Peace Concert in Kingston, Jamaica. He induced political rivals Michael Manley and Edward Seaga to publicly shake hands during a time dominated by political turmoil and ghetto gang riots. In 1980 Marley performed at the independence ceremony in Zimbabwe and won a United Nations Peace Medal. Following *Survival* and *Uprising*, Bob Marley took ill with brain cancer. He died in Miami, Fla., on May 11, 1981, at age 36. He was inducted into the Rock and Roll Hall of Fame in 1994.

In the meantime, Peter Tosh launched a solo career on Columbia with *Legalize It* and *Equal Rights*. The debut album contained "Whatcha Gonna Do" and the classic title song, which advocated the legalization of marijuana. In 1978 Tosh became the first non–Rolling Stones act to record for Rolling Stones Records, and that summer he toured as the band's opening act. His debut album for the label included the minor hit "(You Got to Walk and) Don't Look Back," recorded in duet with Mick Jagger and originally written for the Temptations by Smokey Robinson. By 1981 Tosh had switched to EMI for *Wanted Dread and Alive* and *Mama Africa*, which contained the antiapartheid title song as well as "Where You Gonna Run" and a minor hit version of Chuck Berry's "Johnny B. Goode." He continued to record through 1987, but on Sept. 11, 1987, he was fatally shot in his Kingston home during a robbery.

"Bunny" Livingstone, born Neville O'Reilly Livingstone, took the name "Bunny Wailer" for recordings on Mango and later Shanachie. His debut, *Blackheart Man*, was considered a reggae classic yet failed to make the American charts. His popularity may have suffered due to his refusal to make public appearances until the 1980s.

Marcia Griffiths was recording on her own by 1978. She recorded extensively in the 1980s and scored a minor hit with "Electric Boogie" in late 1989. Judy Mowatt, who's 1979 *Black Woman* came to be regarded as a reggae classic, also recorded solo in the 1980s. Rita Marley, Bob's wife, recorded on her own, beginning in 1982.

Bob Marley's son David, born in 1968, began his musical career as Ziggy Marley in 1979 when his father brought him into the studio to record "Children Playing in the Streets," backed by Marley children Sharon (Rita's oldest daughter), Cedella, and Stephen. As a family group the four performed on special occasions. Ziggy began writing songs and, as The Melody Makers, the quartet recorded several albums for EMI. Switching to Virgin Records, the group recorded 1988's best-selling *Conscious Party*, which included the moderate hit "Tomorrow People," "Dreams of Home," and "Have You Ever Been to Hell." Their follow-up, *One Bright Day*, sold quite well, and with *Jahmekya*, Ziggy unveiled his modern hybrid of dance music and reggae. Despite his youth, some critics began to hail Ziggy Marley as the rightful heir to his father's legacy.

DISC.: THE WAILERS: *Catch a Fire* (1973); *Burnin'* (1973); *Talkin' Blues* (rec. 1973; rel. 1991); *One Love* (1992). **BOB MARLEY AND THE WAILERS:** *Birth of a Legend* (1976); *Birth of a Legend* (1977); *Roots of Music* (1977); *Natty Dread* (1975); *Rastaman Vibration* (1976); *Live!* (1976); *Exodus* (1977); *Kaya* (1978); *Babylon by Bus* (1978); *Survival* (1979); *Uprising* (1980); *Confrontation* (1983); *Legend (The Best of B. M. and The Wailers)* (1984); *Rebel Music* (1986); *Natural Mystic: The Legend Lives On* (1995). **ANTHOLOGIES:** *Jamaican Storm* (1982); *More of the Mighty B. M* (1990); *Birth of a Legend* (1990); *B. M.* (1990); *Saga, Vol. 2* (1991); *Reaction* (1993). **BOB MARLEY:** *Chances Are* (rec. 1968;–1972; rel. 1981); *Songs of Freedom* (1992). **TRIBUTE ALBUM:** *A Tribute to B. M.: The Riddim of a Legend* (1995). **PETER TOSH:** *Legalize It* (1976); *Equal Rights* (1977); *Bush Doctor* (1978); *Mystic Man* (1979); *Wanted Dread and Alive* (1981); *Mama Africa* (1983); *Captured Live* (1984); *No Nuclear War* (1987); *The Toughest* (1988). **BUNNY WAILER:** *Blackheart Man* (1976); *Protest* (1977); *Sings The Wailers* (1981); *Roots, Radics, Rockers, Reggae* (1983); *Peace Talks/Rockers* (1984); *Marketplace* (1985); *Rule Dance Hall* (1986); *Liberation* (1989); *Time Will Tell: A Tribute to B. M.* (1990); *Gumption* (1990); *Bunny Wailer in Concert* (1993); *Crucial!* (1994); *Retrospective* (rec. 1977–1993; rel. 1995); *Live* (1984); *Just Be Nice* (1993); *Hall of Fame: Bunny Wailer's Tribute to B. M.'s 50th Anniversary* (1995). **THE WAILERS BAND:** *I.D.* (1989). **MARCIA GRIFFITHS:** *Sweet Bitter Love* (1974); *Naturally* (1978); *Rock My Soul* (1984); *I Love Music* (1986); *Marcia* (1988); *Carousel* (1990); *Steppin'* (1991); *Indomitable* (1993). **JUDY MOWATT:** *Black Woman* (1979); *Only a Woman* (1982); *Working Wonders* (1986); *Look at Love* (1991). **RITA MARLEY:** *Who Feels It Knows It* (1982); *We Must Carry On* (1991). **ZIGGY MARLEY AND THE MELODY MAKERS:** *Play the Game Right* (1985); *Hey World* (1986); *The Time Has Come (Best)* (1988); *Conscious Party* (1988); *One Bright Day* (1989); *Jahmekya* (1991); *Joy and Blues* (1993); *Free Like We Want 2 B* (1995).

BIBL.: Adrian Boot and Vivien Goldman, *B. M.: Soul Rebel—Natural Mystic* (N.Y., 1982); Timothy White, *Catch a Fire: The Life of B. M.* (N.Y., 1983); Stephen Davis, *B. M.* (Garden City, N.Y., 1985).—**BH**

Marliani, Count Marco Aurelio, Italian composer; b. Milan, Aug. 1805; d. Bologna, May 8, 1849. He studied philosophy, and took some lessons with Rossini in Paris, where he went in 1830. Under Rossini's influence, he wrote several operas, which reached the stage in Paris: *Il Bravo* (Feb. 1, 1834), *Ildegonda* (March 7, 1837), and *La Xacarilla* (Oct. 28, 1839); also a ballet, *La Gypsy* (with A. Thomas; Jan. 28, 1839). He returned to Italy in 1847, producing another opera in Bologna, *Gusmano il Buono* (Nov. 7, 1847). He was involved in the revolutionary struggle of 1848. Wounded in a skirmish near Bologna, he died as a result of his injuries.—**NS/LK/DM**

Marliave, Joseph de, French writer on music; b. Toulouse, Nov. 16, 1873; d. (killed in battle) Verdun, Aug. 24, 1914. He wrote a valuable monograph, *Les Quatuors de Beethoven* (Paris, 1917; reprint, 1925; Eng. tr., London, 1928). He was the husband of **Marguerite Long.**—**NS/LK/DM**

Marlow, Richard (Kenneth), English conductor, organist, music scholar, and composer; b. Banstead, Surrey, July 26, 1939. He was awarded his diploma as a Fellow of the Royal Coll. of Organists in 1958, and then pursued his education at Selwyn Coll., Cambridge (B.A., 1961; Mus.B., 1962; M.A., 1965; Ph.D., 1965, with the diss. *The Life and Music of Giles Farnaby*). After serving as a Research Fellow at Selwyn Coll. (1962–65), he was a lecturer at the univs. of Southampton (1965–68) and Cambridge (1968–96). In 1968 he became a Fellow, organist, and director of music at Trinity Coll., Cambridge. In 1969 he organized the Cambridge Univ. Chamber Choir, which he conducted until 1989. In 1982 he founded the outstanding Choir of Trinity Coll., Cambridge, which he conducted in numerous concerts at home and overseas, in various radio and television broadcasts, and in many recordings. He was a visiting prof. at Dartmouth (N.H.) Coll. in 1975 and at Middlebury (Vt.) Coll. in 1990, and also was a Senior Exchange Fellow at Rice Univ. in Houston in 1988. From 1979 to 1982 he was artistic advisor of I Virtuosi di Roma. Marlow has contributed articles to various scholarly publications. While his interests range widely, he is particularly known for his work as a musican and scholar in the music of the Renaissance and Baroque eras. Among his compositions are several sacred and secular vocal works.—**LK/DM**

Marlowe (real name, **Sapira**), **Sylvia,** American harpsichordist and teacher; b. N.Y., Sept. 26, 1908; d. there, Dec. 11, 1981. She studied piano, then went to Paris to take courses with Boulanger at the École Normale de Musique. She later became a student of Landowska in harpsichord. In 1953 she joined the faculty of the Mannes School of Music in N.Y. In 1957 she founded the Harpsichord Music Soc., which commissioned works by Elliott Carter, Ned Rorem, Vittorio

Rieti, Henri Sauguet, and others. Although her primary devotion was to the Baroque style of composition, she adventurously espoused the cause of popular American music. She was a member of the pop group called Chamber Music Soc. of Lower Basin Street and even performed in nightclubs, ostentatiously proclaiming her belief in music as an art in flux.—**NS/LK/DM**

Marmontel, Antoine-François, celebrated French pedagogue and pianist, father of **Antonin Émile Louis Corbaz Marmontel**; b. Clermont-Ferrand, July 16, 1816; d. Paris, Jan. 17, 1898. He studied at the Paris Cons. with Zimmerman (piano), Dourlen (harmony), Halévy (fugue), and Le Sueur (composition), winning the premier prix for piano in 1832. In 1837 he became instructor in solfeggio at the Cons. In 1848 he succeeded Zimmerman as head of its piano class, and won enduring fame as an imaginative and efficient teacher, numbering among his pupils Albéniz, Bizet, Debussy, Diemer, d'Indy, Dubois, Pierne, and Plante. He continued to teach until 1887. He wrote numerous didactic works for piano, as well as sonatas, serenades, characteristic pieces, salon music, dances, etc.

WRITINGS (all publ. in Paris): *L'art classique et moderne du piano* (1876); *Les Pianistes célèbres* (1878); *Symphonistes et virtuoses* (1880); *Virtuoses contemporains* (1882); *Elements d'esthetique musicale, et considérations sur le beau dans les arts* (1884); *Histoire du piano et de ses origines* (1885).—**NS/LK/DM**

Marmontel, Antonin Émile Louis Corbaz, French piano teacher, son of **Antoine-François Marmontel**; b. Paris, Nov. 22, 1850; d. there, July 23, 1907. He studied at the Paris Cons. (premier prix, 1867). He was 2nd chorus master at the Paris Opéra (1878–89), and later taught at the Paris Cons. (1901–07).—**NS/LK/DM**

Maros, Miklós, Hungarian-born Swedish composer and teacher, son of **Rudolf Maros**; b. Pécs, Nov. 14, 1943. He studied composition in Budapest with Sugár at the Béla Bartók Cons. (1958–63) and with Szabó at the Franz Liszt Academy of Music (1963–67). He settled in Stockholm, where he continued his training with Lidholm and Ligeti at the Musikhögskolan (1968–72). In 1975 he became a naturalized Swedish citizen. He taught electronic music at the Stockholm Electronic Music Studio (1971–78) and at the Musikhögskolan (1976–80); also taught privately. In 1972, with his wife, the singer Ilona Maros, he founded the Maros Ensemble, which championed contemporary music. In 1980–81 he held a Deutscher Akademischer Austauschdienst fellowship in West Berlin. In 1982–83 he was composer-in-residence of the Swedish Inst. for National Concerts. In his music, Maros utilizes both traditional and experimental techniques, including electronics.

WORKS: DRAMATIC: *Jag önkar jag vore* (I Wish I Could Be), opera (1971); *Stora grusharpan* (The Huge Gravel-sifter), radio opera (1982); *Att i denna natt...* (In This Night...), church opera (1986). **ORCH.:** *Pezzo* for Chamber Orch. (1967); *Mutazioni* for Wind Orch. (1971); Concertino for Double Bass or Tuba, and 6 to 24 Instruments (1971); *Confluentia* for Strings (1972); *Proportio* for Wind Orch. (1973); 4 syms.: No. 1 (1974; Stockholm, Feb. 14, 1976), No. 2 for Wind and Percussion

(Stockholm, Sept. 22, 1979), No. 3, *Sinfonia Concertante*, for Strings (1986), and No. 4 (1998); Concerto for Harpsichord and Chamber Orch. (1978; Reykjavík, Jan. 20, 1980); *Circulation* for Strings (1980); Concerto for Wind Quintet and Orch. (1980); *Coalottino II* for Bass Clarinet and Strings (1981); *Konzertsatz* for Accordion and Strings (1982); *Fantasi* (1983); Trombone Concerto (1983; Gävle, Oct. 6, 1984); *Sinfonietta* for Chamber Orch. (1985); *Introduzione e Marcia* for Wind Orch. (1986); *Concerto grosso* for Saxophone Quartet and Orch. (1988; Wuppertal, March 2, 1990); Clarinet Concerto (1989; Stockholm, March 6, 1991); Alto Saxophone Concerto (1990; Stockholm, Jan. 19, 1991); *Vice- Concertino* for Harpsichord, Violin, and Strings (1993); *Saxazione* for 18 Saxophones (1994); *Aurora* for Double Wind Quintet and Wind Band (1995); *Lineamenti* for Strings (1999). **CHAMBER:** 2 wind quintets (1962, 1980); *Spel* (Game) for Clarinet, Trombone, Cello, and Percussion (1969); *Festeggiamento* No. 1 for Recorder, Violin, and Harp (1971) and No. 2 for Saxophones (1996); *Oolit* for 10 Instruments (1974); *Divertimento* for Wind Quintet, Violin, and Piano (1976); String Quartet No. 1 (1977); *Åtbörder* (Gestures) for Flute, Clarinet, Violin, Viola, Cello, Piano, and Percussion (1979); *Speglingar* (Reflections) for Winds, Guitars, Pianos, and Strings (1983); Saxophone Quartet (1984); *Marimbacapriccio* for Marimba or Vibraphone (1985–96); *Picchiettato* for 5 Percussionists (1986); *Aulos*, trio for Oboe, Cello, and Harpsichord (1987); *Goboj* for Oboe and Guitar (1987); *Res mobilis* for Brass Quintet (1990); *Partita* for Viola and Piano (1991); *Burattinata* for Alto Saxophone and Piano (1992); *Konzertmusik* for Chamber Ensemble (1992); *Feinschnitten* for Flute and Percussion (1993); *Lyria* for Trumpet and Harp (1993); *Ricamo* for Flute and Organ (1996); *Links* for Alto Saxophone, Cello, and Piano (1996); *Confabulation* for Flute, Viola, and Guitar (1997); *Musica da caccia* for 4 Saxophones (1997). **VOCAL:** *Prelude* for Mezzo-soprano and Orch. (1967); *Inversioni* for Soprano and Chamber Ensemble (1968); *Erotikon* for Mezzo-soprano and Orch. (1968); *Anenaika* for Soprano, Chamber Ensemble, and Tape (1970); *Denique* for Soprano and Orch. (1970); *Diversion* for Soprano, Contralto, Alto Flute, Viola, Guitar, and 3 Percussionists (1971); *Laus Pannoniae* for Soprano, Chorus, and Chamber Ensemble (1972); *Xylographia* for Soprano, Violin, Bassoon, Harp, Harpsichord, and Vibraphone (1972); *Lunovis* for Soprano, Violin, Bassoon, Harp, and Celesta (1973); *Fabula* for Alto, Cello, 2 Pianos, and Percussion (1974); *Elementen* for Soprano, Reciter, Women's Trio, and Youth Orch. (1975); *Psalm 98* for Soprano, Flute, Clarinet, Bassoon, Violin, Viola, Cello, and Percussion (1978); *4 sanger ur Gitanjali* (4 Songs from Gitanjali) for Soprano, Flute, Clarinet, and 2 Percussionists (1979); *Clusters for Clusters* for Flute, Soprano Saxophone, Guitar, and Percussion (1981); *Drehlieder* for Tenor, Hurdy-gurdy, Cello, and Harpsichord (1984); choruses; songs. **OTHER:** Live electronic pieces; electroacoustic works. —NS/LK/DM

Maros, Rudolf, Hungarian composer, father of **Miklós Maros**; b. Stachy, Jan. 19, 1917; d. Budapest, Aug. 3, 1982. He studied at the Györ teachers' training college (graduated, 1937), and then took courses in composition with Kodály and Siklós and viola with Temesváry at the Budapest Academy of Music (1938–42); later attended A. Hába's master class there (1949). He played viola in the Budapest Concert Orch. (1942–49); from 1949 to 1978 he was on the faculty of the Budapest Academy of Music. In 1971–72 he held a Deutscher Akademischer Austauschdienst scholarship in West Berlin. In 1954, 1955, and 1957 he received Erkel

prizes. In 1973 he was made a Merited Artist and in 1980 an Outstanding Artist by the Hungarian government. The early period of his music is marked by nationalistic tendencies; later he adopted serial techniques and began to explore the field of "sonorism," or sound for sound's sake, making use of all available sonorous resources, such as tone clusters and microtones.

WORKS: DRAMATIC: B a l l e t : *The Wedding at Ecser* (1950); *Bányászballada* (Miner's Ballad; 1961); *Cinque studi* (1967; after the orch. set of the same title); *Quadros soltos* (*Musica da ballo*) (1968); *Reflexionen* (1970); *Dance Pictures* (1971); *Metropolis* (1972); *The Poltroon* (1972). **ORCH.:** *Puppet Show Overture* (1944); 2 sinfoniettas (1944, 1948); Bassoon Concertino (1954); *Symphony for Strings* (1956); *Ricercare* (1959); *Musica da ballo*, suite (1962; based on the ballet *Bányászballada*); *Cinque studi* (1960; as a ballet, 1967); *3 Eufonias: I* for Strings, 2 Harps, and Percussion (1963), *II* for 24 Winds, 2 Harps, and Percussion (1964), and *III* for Orch. (1965); *Gemma* (*In Memoriam Kodály*) (1968); *Monumentum* (1969); *Notices* for Strings (1972); *Landscapes* for Strings (1974); *Fragment* (1977). **CHAMBER:** String Quartet (1948); *Serenade* for Oboe, Clarinet, and Bassoon (1952); *Musica leggiera* for Wind Quintet (1956); String Trio (1957); *Musica da camera per 11* (1966; Hanover, N.H., July 12, 1967); Trio for Violin, Viola, and Harp (1967); *Consort* for Wind Quintet (1970); *Albumblätter* for Double Bass (1973); *Kaleidoscope* for 15 Instruments (1976); *4 Studies* for 4 Percussionists (1977); *Contrasts* for Chamber Ensemble (1979). **VOCAL:** *2 Laments* for Soprano, Alto Flute, Harp, Piano, and Percussion (1962); *Lament* for Soprano and Chamber Ensemble (1967); *Messzéségek* (Remoteness) for Chorus (1975); *Strophen* for Soprano, Harp, and Percussion (1975); *Nyúlfarkkantáta* (Tiny Cantata) for Voices, Strings, and Piano (1976); *Cheremiss Folksongs* for Chorus (1977). **BIBL.:** P. Várnai, *M. R.* (Budapest, 1967).—**NS/LK/DM**

Marpurg, Friedrich, German conductor and composer, great-grandson of **Friedrich Wilhelm Marpurg**; b. Paderborn, April 4, 1825; d. Wiesbaden, Dec. 2, 1884. He played the violin and piano as a child, and studied composition later with Mendelssohn and Hauptmann at Leipzig. He became conductor at the Königsberg Theater, then at Sondershausen (1864). He succeeded Mangold as court music director at Darmstadt (1868), then was at Freiburg (1873), Laibach (1875), and Wiesbaden, where he became conductor of the Cäcilienverein. He composed the operas *Musa, der letzte Maurenkönig* (Königsberg, 1855), *Agnes von Hohenstaufen* (Freiburg, 1874), and *Die Lichtensteiner* (not perf.). —**NS/LK/DM**

Marpurg, Friedrich Wilhelm, German music theorist and composer, great-grandfather of **Friedrich Marpurg**; b. Seehof bei Seehausen, Brandenburg, Nov. 21, 1718; d. Berlin, May 22, 1795. While secretary to Generallieutenant Friedrich Rudolph Graf von Rothenburg in Paris (1746–49), he became acquainted with Rameau and his theories. After a short stay in Berlin and a prolonged sojourn in Hamburg, he joined the Prussian lottery at Berlin (1763), and was its director from 1766 until his death. In addition to editing collections of songs and keyboard works, he also composed sonatas, other pieces for keyboard, and songs.

WRITINGS: *Der critische Musicus an der Spree* (periodical; Berlin, 1749–50; publ. collectively as *Des critischen Musicus an* *der Spree erster Band*, Berlin, 1750); *Die Kunst das Clavier zu spielen, durch den Verfasser des critischen Musicus an der Spree* (Berlin, 1750; 4th ed., rev. and aug., 1762); *Abhandlung von der Fuge nach dem Grundsätzen der besten deutschen und ausländischen Meister* (2 vols., Berlin, 1753–54; 2nd ed., 1858); *Historisch-kritische Beyträge zur Aufnahme der Musik* (5 vols., Berlin, 1754–78); *Anleitung zum Clavierspielen der schönen Ausübung der heutigen Zeit gemass* (Berlin, 1755; 2nd ed., 1765); *Principes de clavecin* (Berlin, 1756); *Anfangsgründe der theoretischen Musik* (Leipzig, 1757); *An Leitung zur Singcomposition* (Berlin, 1758); *Handbuch bey dem Generalbasse und der Composition mit zwey - drey - vier - fünf - sechs - sieben - acht und mehreren Stimmen* (3 vols., Berlin, 1755–58; 2nd ed., 1762); *Kritische Einleitung in die Geschichte und Lehrsätze der alten und neuen Musik* (Berlin, 1759); *Herrn Georg Andreas Sorgens Anleitung zur Generalbass und zur Composition, mit Anmerkungen* (Berlin, 1760); *Kritische Briefe über die Tonkunst, mit kleinen Clavierstücken und Singoden begleitet, von einer musikalischen Gesellschaft in Berlin* (weekly publication; Berlin, 1760–64); *Anleitung zur Musik überhaupt und zur Singkunst besonders mit Uebungsexampeln erläutert* (Berlin, 1763); *Versuch über die musikalische Temperatur, nebst einem Anhang über den Rameau- und Kirnbergerschen Grundbass* (Breslau, 1776); *Legende einiger Musikheiligen: Ein nachtrag zur den musikalischen Almanachen und Taschenbüchern jetziger Zeit, von Simeon Metaphrastes, dem Jüngern* (Cologne [recte Breslau], 1786); *Neue Methode allerley Arten von Temperaturen dem Claviere aufs Bequemste mitzutheilen* (Berlin, 1790). **BIBL.:** E. Bieder, *Ueber F.W. M.s System der Harmonie, des Kontrapunkts und der Temperatur* (diss., Univ. of Berlin, 1923); H. Serwer, *F.W. M. (1718–1795): Music Critic in a Galant Age* (diss., Yale Univ., 1969).—**NS/LK/DM**

Marqués y García, Pedro Miguel, Spanish composer; b. Palma de Mallorca, May 20, 1843; d. there, Feb. 25, 1918. He studied in Paris with Alard and Armingaud, then at the Paris Cons. with Massart (violin) and Bazin (composition). He also studied privately with Berlioz, and in 1867 in Madrid with Monasterio. From 1870 to 1896 he was one of the most successful of the zarzuela composers, his most popular works being *El anillo de hierro* (1878) and *El monaguillo* (1891). He also wrote 4 syms., orch. variations, etc.—**NS/LK/DM**

Marriner, Sir Neville, outstanding English conductor; b. Lincoln, April 15, 1924. He studied violin with his father, and then with Frederick Mountney. He subsequently entered the Royal Coll. of Music in London when he was 13, but his studies were interrupted by military service during World War II. After resuming his training at the Royal Coll. of Music, he completed his violin studies in Paris with René Benedetti and took courses at the Cons. He was active as a violinist in chamber music ensembles, and was a prof. of violin at the Royal Coll. of Music (1949–59). He joined the Philharmonia Orch. of London as a violinist (1952), and then was principal 2nd violinist of the London Sym. Orch. (1956–58). His interest in conducting was encouraged by Pierre Monteux, who gave him lessons at his summer school in Hancock, Maine (1959). In 1958 he founded the Academy of St.-Martin-in-the-Fields; served as its director until 1978, establishing an international reputation through recordings and tours. From 1968 to 1978 he also served as music director of the Los Angeles Chamber Orch.; then was music director of the Minnesota Orch. in Minneapolis (1978–86). In 1981 he became principal guest conductor of the Stuttgart Radio Sym. Orch.; was its chief conductor from 1983 to 1989. He appeared as a guest conductor with many of the world's leading orchs. On Sept. 29, 1994, he opened the 1994–95 season of N.Y.'s Carnegie Hall conducting the Academy of St. Martin-in-the-Fields in a program featuring Cecilia Bartoli as the soloist of the evening. The concert was subsequently telecast throughout the U.S. by PBS. In 1979 he was made a Commander of the Order of the British Empire. He was knighted in 1985. Marriner has proved himself one of the most remarkable conductors of his day. His extensive activities as a chamber music player, orch. musician, and chamber orch. violinist-conductor served as an invaluable foundation for his career as a sym. conductor of the first rank. His enormous repertoire encompasses works from the Baroque era to the great masterworks of the 20th century. In all of his performances, he demonstrates authority, mastery of detail, and impeccable taste. —**NS/LK/DM**

Marrocco, W(illiam) Thomas, American violinist and musicologist; b. West New York, N.J., Dec. 5, 1909; d. Eugene, Ore., Jan. 1, 1999. After initial music studies in the U.S., he went to Italy and entered the Cons. di Musica S. Pietro a Majella in Naples, receiving his diploma di Magistero in 1930. He then studied violin and musicology at the Eastman School of Music in Rochester, N.Y. (B.M., 1934; M.A., 1940), and earned his Ph.D. at the Univ. of Calif. at Los Angeles with the diss. *Jacopo da Bologna and His Works* (1952; publ. as *The Music of Jacopo da Bologna*, Berkeley, 1954). After teaching at Elmira (N.Y.) Coll. (1936–39) and serving as a visiting lecturer at the Univ. of Iowa (1945–46), he was on the music faculty of the Univ. of Kans. in Lawrence (1946–49). He was prof. of music at the Univ. of Calif. at Los Angeles (1950–77), and also played in the Roth String Quartet. He publ. numerous informative essays dealing with early Italian and American music, and ed. Vols. VI-IX of *Polyphonic Music of the Fourteenth Century: Italian Secular Music* (Monaco, 1967–78). He also publ. *Fourteenth Century Italian Cacce* (Cambridge, Mass., 1942; 2nd ed., rev. and aug., 1961), *Music in America: An Anthology* (with H. Gleason; N.Y., 1964), *Medieval Music* (with N. Sandon; London, 1977), *Inventory of Fifteenth Century Bassedanze, Balli and Balletti in Italian Dance Manuals* (N.Y., 1981), and *Memoirs of a Stradivarius* (N.Y., 1988).—**NS/LK/DM**

Marsalis, Branford, tenor, alto, and soprano saxophonist; b. Breaux Bridge, La., Aug. 26, 1960. The oldest child of **Ellis Marsalis,** he attended Berklee. Branford and his brother, **Wynton Marsalis,** and Danny House played in Europe with Clark Terry's youth band in 1980. Branford replaced Bobby Watson on alto in Blakey's Jazz Messengers in 1981. He switched to tenor and soprano, then joined his brother's band in 1982, staying until 1985. The group toured extensively nationally and internationally and won critical applause, while selling vast numbers of records for jazz releases. But an alleged dispute over stylistic direction and

Branford's decision to join rocker Sting's tour purportedly led to the brothers' split in 1985–86. He toured and recorded with Sting and is seen in the Sting documentary *Bring on the Night*. Since then he has led his own bands, both in jazz and as Buckshot LeFonque, a fusion of hip hop and hard funk. He was the leader of the new "Tonight Show" band, but quit (at first announced as a leave) when the job turned out to be uncomfortable for him. He accidentally dedicated a number to the "late" Buddy Tate, leading him to perform and record with Tate as an apology. Marsalis is the host of the NPR series *Jazzset*. He has an endearing modesty and humor in interviews and host roles.

DISC.: *Scenes in the City* (1983); *Renaissance* (1986); *Romances for Saxophone* (1986); *Royal Garden Blues* (1986); *Random Abstract* (1987); *Steep* (1988); *Trio Jeepy* (1988); *Crazy People Music* (1990); *Beautiful Ones Are Not Yet Born* (1991); *Bloomington* (1991); *I Heard You Twice the First Time* (1992). A. Kidjo: *Oremi* (1998).—**LP**

Marsalis, Ellis,

pianist, educator; b. New Orleans, Nov. 14, 1934. He is a modern jazz artist who was well established in New Orleans before his sons Wynton, Branford, Delfeayo, and Jason became known. He also has a daughter and another son. His early experiences include playing in a Marine Corps band and working with Al Hirt. In the early 1960s, Ellis, James Black, and others played in a club called Lu and Charlie's located on Ramparts Street in New Orleans. In 1974 Ellis founded the jazz program for the New Orleans Center for the Creative Arts, which nurtured important new talent. In his classroom, there was a small group including Wynton, Branford, Donald Harrison, and Terence Blanchard. Other students included Harry Connick Jr. and Kent Jordan. Ellis and his sons have alerted the world to the existence of a modern jazz scene (not only traditional) in New Orleans (since the 1950s). He has taught at the Univ. of New Orleans since (1990). He was given the Three Key Award from International Jazz Festival of Bern, Switzerland, in 1997.

DISC.: *Classic Ellis Marsalis* (1963); *Father and Sons* (1982); *Syndrome* (1985); *Piano in E-Solo Piano* (1986); *Ellis Marsalis Trio* (1990); *Heart of Gold* (1991); *Jazzy Wonderland* (1991); *Whistle Stop* (1993); *Night in Snug Harbor, New Orleans* (1995). Nat Adderley: *In the Bag* (1962).—**LP**

Marsalis, Wynton,

trumpeter, leader, composer; b. New Orleans, Oct. 18, 1961. The most honored musician in jazz of the 1990s, Wynton (the Irish name was given in tribute to Wynton Kelly) has become a leader in the jazz field, and he wears this hat comfortably, proudly, boldly. His work is always technically astounding. He is also known for peerless performances of classical music. But his jazz trumpet style has changed dramatically over the years, as he has molded it, rather self-consciously, to reflect his changing philosophy. When he first recorded with Art Blakey in 1980 and then with Herbie Hancock, he was flashy and modern, darting in unexpected directions. Today, he pays tribute to such past masters as Louis Armstrong and Ellington's mute specialist Cootie Williams in solos that sometimes sound like patchworks rather than

coherent personal statements. Similarly his composing has gone from flexible modern jazz works such as *The Bell Ringer* (1982) to heavily scored Ellingtonian works with "old-time" church-oriented vocalizing, as on his Pulitzer prize–winning *Blood on the Fields* and his 1998 *Big Train* albums.

He has become increasingly rigid in his definition of jazz, which he and his mentor, the critic Stanley Crouch, recite often: To be considered jazz, music must have the blues, improvisation, swing feeling, and the Latin tinge. This would be his private business, but he has grown to have more and more influence in the jazz community. He is artistic director of jazz at Lincoln Center and sets the programming and hiring policies there, has hosted a radio and television series designed to introduce audiences to various aspects of jazz as he sees it. He is a regular guest on television shows, and he is routinely asked to put his imprimatur on a variety of jazz projects around the country. As a result, his rather old-fashioned and close-minded views on jazz have been attacked by a number of musicians and critics. On the other hand, a great number of young musicians say that it was Marsalis who inspired them to play.

Wynton's father, **Ellis Marsalis**, insisted that his children receive professional training. Wynton got his first trumpet at the age of six from Al Hirt. He played trumpet in Danny Barker's Fairview Baptist Church band when he was eight, playing parades, and songs such as "Over in the Glory Land," "The Second Line," "Little Liza Jane," and "Didn't He Ramble." But he didn't practice seriously until age 12. His first teacher was John Longo, a New Orleans native at Southern Univ. Longo had studied with George Janson, a transplanted New Yorker, who was his next teacher, during high school, and stressed the book *Characteristic Studies*. George Marks was his band director at Benjamin Franklin H.S. and also in the New Orleans Community Band. The late John Fernandez at Xavier Univ. was also an inspiration. William Fielder, who taught at Miss. Valley State, was good friends with Fernandez and helped Marsalis with breathing and showed him how to play piccolo trumpet. Norman Smith, who was playing in the New Orleans Philharmonic at that time, taught him about attack and orchestral style. He appeared as soloist in the Haydn Trumpet Concerto with the New Orleans Phil. when he was 14, and also performed with local groups in classical, jazz, and rock settings.

In 1974, the elder Marsalis founded the jazz program for the New Orleans Center for the Creative Arts, which nurtured important new talent. In his father's classroom, there was a small group including Wynton, Branford, Donald Harrison, and Terence Blanchard. Bert Braud was Wynton's theory teacher at the Center. He also met with Alvin Batiste and Kidd Jordan and would go over to Southern Univ. in New Orleans to play avant-garde music. He sat in with Sonny Stitt once when he was 15. He won the Harvey Shapiro Award as the most gifted brass player at the Berkshire Music Center at Tanglewood at age 17. He attended Juilliard in N.Y. for one year; there he studied with William Vaggiano, who had taught Janson. At Mikell's around this time he met Stanley Crouch, who encouraged him to study Ellington recordings. He also picked up informal tips from Sweets Edison and Clark Terry. Roy Eldridge taught him how to growl on the trumpet, and Joe Wilder gave him lessons on how to play with the hat. Dave Berger helped with composition and the study of Ellington scores.

Wynton and Branford and Danny House played in Europe with Clark Terry's youth band in 1980. He joined Art Blakey's Jazz Messengers (1980–81), playing with them at the jazz festival at Montreux, Switzerland (1980); then recorded with Herbie Hancock (1981) and toured with him in a quartet with Ron Carter and Tony Williams (1982). Hancock introduced him to Columbia, which began a major marketing campaign for the young star.

He toured internationally with his own quintet, which included Branford, from 1982–85. In 1984 and 1985 he achieved unprecedented success when he won Grammy awards in both the jazz and classical categories. He is credited with leading a jazz revival which has brought forward many talented young musicians. On Oct. 30, 1990, Marsalis hosted a benefit concert for Graham-Windham (a private child-care agency), the Autism Soc. of America, and the Immunohematology Research Foundation at Alice Tully Hall in N.Y.; featured were Ellis, Jason (making his debut on drums), Branford, and Wynton; absent was Delfeayo. They were joined by the members of Wynton's septet. Since 1987 he has been advisor to the summer concert series Classical Jazz at Lincoln Center. This expanded into a year long Jazz at Lincoln Center program, with Marsalis as artistic director. In 1996 the program became a full-fledged "consitutent" of Lincoln Center and in 1998 work began on constructing a new home for the jazz program in nearby Columbus Circle.

He was host and coauthor of the 26-part National Public Radio series *Making the Music*, and of the four-part PBS series *Marsalis on Music* (with accompanying book). He lectures at countless schools and educational conferences, tending to stress that jazz is "hard and serious," and therefore of value, and of greater value than hip hop and other pop musics—a highly specious argument which nevertheless has been effective in raising support for his program and for jazz generally. In March 1995 at the People's Music School in Chicago, he kicked off a partnership with Harman International (manufacturers of audio equipment), which sponsors his visits to inner-city schools. He coordinates the "Essentially Ellington" H.S. Jazz Band Competition through Lincoln Center, which expanded competition from three states in 1996 to 13 (and the District of Columbia) in 1997, and to all states in 1999. They also sent out clinicians to the schools to help the bands learn the music: Joe Temperley, Jon Faddis, Marcus Printup, Eric Reed, Michael Weiss, Bill Easley, Ronald Westray, Justin DiCioccio, and others. He was spokesperson for the 1997–98 NBA season, has written music for the Olympic Games, and has received several honorary degrees, including Rutgers Univ. at Newark in 1997. Starting in 1992 with *In This House, On This Morning*, he has written longer pieces, including "Jazz: Six Syncopated Movements" for the N.Y.C. Ballet (1993); the

string quartet "At the Octoroon Balls" (1995); and "Sweet Release," a jazz ballet for the Alvin Ailey American Dance Theater (1996). His evening- length composition, "Blood in the Fields," became the first jazz work to win a Pulitzer Prize in 1997 (though premiered at Lincoln Center in 1994 and recorded in 1995). He performed the work in 15 U.S. cities in 1997 before embarking on a two-week European tour in March. He now performs almost exclusively with the Lincoln Center Jazz Orch., his sextet having disbanded. Previous members included Marcus Roberts (who left to pursue a solo career), Todd Williams, Reginald Veal, Herlin Riley, Wes Anderson, Wycliffe Gordon, and pianists Farid Barron, Eric Reed, and Eric Lewis. On April 28, 1997, his quartet performed for Presidents Clinton, Bush, Carter, and Ford when they visited Independence Hall Plaza during the Presidents' Summit for America's Future. His videos inlcude the four-video set *Marsalis on Music* (1995), *Blues and Swing* (1988), and *Trumpet Kings*, which includes historical clips of various artists, hosted by Marsalis.

DISC.: *Wynton Marsalis* (1981); *Fathers and Sons* (1982); *Think of One* (1983); *Hot House Flowers* (1984); *Black Codes* (1985); *J Mood* (1985); *Standard Time, Vol. 1* (1986); *Live at Blues Alley* (1986); *Standard Time, Vol. 2: Intimacy* (1987); *Uptown Ruler: Soul Gestures in Southern Blue/Vol. III* (1988); *Levee Low Moan* (1988); *Thick in the South: Soul Gestures in Southern Blue* (1988); *Majesty of the Blues* (1988); *Blues & Swing* (1988); *Original Soundtrack from "Tune in Tomorrow"* (1989); *Crescent City Christmas Card* (1989); *Standard Time, Vol. 3* (1990); *Blue Interlude* (1991); *Citi Movement* (1992); *In This House, On This Morning* (1993); *Joe Cool's Blues* (1994); *Blood on the Fields* (1995); *Blakey's Messengers, Vol. 1, 2* (1995); *Blakey's Theme* (1995); *Live at Bubba's* (1996); *In Gabriel's Garden* (1996); *Jump Start and Jazz* (1996); *Standard Time, Vol. 5: The Midnight Blues* (1998); *One by One* (1998); *Lincoln Center Jazz Orchestra: Live in Swing City* (1998); *Standard Time, Vol. 4: Marsalis Plays Monk* (1999); *Fiddler's Tale* (1999); *At the Octoroon Balls: String Quartet No. 1* (1999); *Big Train* (1999); *Sweet Release and Ghost Story* (1999); *Standard Time, Vol. 6: Mr. Jelly Lord* (1999); *Reeltime* (1999).

WRITINGS: *Sweet Swing Blues on the Road* (1994); *Marsalis on Music* (1995).—**LP/NS**

Marschner, Heinrich (August), important German composer; b. Zittau, Saxony, Aug. 16, 1795; d. Hannover, Dec. 14, 1861. He sang in the school choir at the Zittau Gymnasium, and also studied music with Karl Hering. In 1813 he went to Leipzig, where he studied jurisprudence at the Univ. Encouraged by the cantor of the Thomasschule, J.C. Schicht, he turned to music as his main vocation. In 1816 he became a music tutor in Count Zichy's household in Pressburg, and also served as Kapellmeister to Prince Krasatkowitz. In his leisure hours he began to compose light operas; his first opera, *Titus* (1816), did not achieve a performance, but soon he had 2 more operas and a Singspiel produced in Dresden. His first signal success was the historical opera *Heinrich IV und d'Aubigné*, which was accepted by Weber, who was then music director at the Dresden Court Opera, and was produced there on July 19, 1820. In 1817 he was in Vienna, where he was fortunate enough to meet Beethoven. In 1821 Marschner moved to Dresden where his Singspiel *Der Holzdieb* was staged at the Court Opera (Feb. 22, 1825). He expected to succeed Weber as music director at the Court Opera after Weber died in London, but failed to obtain the post. He went to Leipzig, where he became Kapellmeister of the Stadttheater, and wrote for it 2 Romantic operas, in the manner of Weber: *Der Vampyr* (March 29, 1828) and *Der Templer und die Jüdin*, after the famous novel Ivanhoe by Sir Walter Scott (Dec. 22, 1829). In 1830 he received the position of Kapellmeister of the Hannover Hoftheater. His most successful opera, *Hans Heiling* (Berlin, May 24, 1833), exhibited the most attractive Romantic traits of his music: a flowing melody, sonorous harmony, and nervous rhythmic pulse; the opera formed a natural transition to the exotic melodrama of Meyerbeer's great stage epics and to Wagner's early lyrical music dramas. Historically important was his bold projection of a continuous dramatic development, without the conventional type of distinct arias separated by recitative. In this respect he was the heir of Weber and a precursor of Wagner.

WORKS: DRAMATIC: O p e r a : *Titus*, opera (1816; not perf.); *Der Kyffhäuserberg*, Singspiel (1816; Zittau, Jan. 2, 1822); *Heinrich IV und d'Aubigné*, opera (1817–18; Dresden, July 19, 1820); *Saidar und Zulima*, romantic opera (Pressburg, Nov. 26, 1818); *Der Holzdieb*, Singspiel (1823; Dresden, Feb. 22, 1825; rev. 1853 as *Geborgt*); *Lukretia*, opera (1820–26; Danzig, Jan 17, 1827); *Der Vampyr*, romantic opera (1827; Leipzig, March 29, 1828); *Der Templer und die Jüdin*, romantic opera (Leipzig, Dec. 22, 1829); *Des Falkners Braut*, comic opera (1830; Leipzig, March 10, 1832); *Hans Heiling*, romantic opera (1831–32; Berlin, May 24, 1833); *Das Schloss am Ätna*, romantic opera (1830–35; Leipzig, Jan. 29, 1836); *Der Bäbu*, comic opera (1836–37; Hannover, Feb. 19, 1838); *Kaiser Adolf von Nassau*, romantic opera (Dresden, Jan 5, 1845); *Austin*, romantic opera (1850–51; Hannover, Jan. 25, 1852); *Sangeskönig Hiarne, oder Das Tyringsschwert*, romantic opera (1857–58; Frankfurt am Main, Sept. 13, 1863). **B a l l e t :** *Die stolze Bäuerin* (Zittau, 1810). **O t h e r :** Incidental music. **OTHER:** 2 unfinished syms.; choral works.

BIBL.: W. Neumann, *H. M.* (Kassel, 1854); E. Danzig, *H. M. in seinen minderbekannten Opern und Liedern* (Leipzig, 1890); M. Wittmann, *H. M.* (Leipzig, 1897); G. Münzer, *H. M.* (Berlin, 1901); C. Preiss, *Templer und Jüdin* (Graz, 1911); H. Gaartz, *Die Opern H. M.s* (Leipzig, 1912); G. Fischer, *M. Erinnerungen* (Hannover, 1918); A. Bickel, *H. M. in seinen Opern* (diss., Univ. of Erlangen, 1929); A. Gnirs, *Hans Heiling* (Karlsbad, 1931); G. Hausswald, *H. M.* (Dresden, 1938); V. Köhler, *H. M.s Bühnenwerke* (diss., Univ. of Göttingen, 1956); A. Dean Palmer, *H.A. M., 1795–1861: His Life and Stage Works* (1980); B. Weber, *H. M.: Königlicher Hoftapellmeisters in Hannover* (Hannover, 1995); A. Behrendt and M. Vogt, eds., *H.A. M.: Bericht über das Zittauer M.-Symposium* (Leipzig, 1998).—**NS/LK/DM**

Marsh, John, English composer; b. Dorking, 1752; d. Chichester, 1828. He studied violin with Wafer in Gosport (1766–68) and then was articled to a solicitor in Ramsey. In 1774 he went to Salisbury, where he played in an amateur orch. and learned to play the organ. In 1781 he abandoned his law practice and devoted himself to music, settling in 1787 in Chichester, where he was concertmaster of several amateur groups and active as an organist. His works, which include a number of syms., overtures, concerti grossi, chamber pieces, organ voluntaries, anthems, and Psalm tunes, reflect late Ba-

roque and Classical models. Among his writings were his memoirs (MS) and *A Comparison between the Ancient and Modern Styles of Music* (1796).

BIBL.: B. Robins, ed., *The J. M. Journals: The Life and Times of a Gentleman Composer (1752–1828)* (Stuyvesant, N.Y., 1998). —**LK/DM**

Marsh, Robert C(harles), American music critic; b. Columbus, Ohio, Aug. 5, 1924. He took courses in journalism (B.S., 1945) and philosophy (A.M., 1946) at Northwestern Univ. In 1946–47 he was a Sage fellow at Cornell Univ., where he received training in theory from Robert Palmer. He pursued postgraduate studies at the Univ. of Chicago (1948), and then studied at Harvard Univ. (Ed.D., 1951), where he also attended Hindemith's lectures (1949–50). After attending the Univ. of Oxford (1952–53), he studied musicology with Thurston Dart and theory of criticism with H.S. Middleton at the Univ. of Cambridge (1953–56). He taught social sciences at the Univ. of Ill. (1947–49), was a lecturer in the humanities at Chicago City Junior Coll. (1950–51), and asst. prof. of education at the Univ. of Kans. (1951–52). After serving as visiting prof. of education at the State Univ. of N.Y. (1953–54), he taught the humanities at the Univ. of Chicago (1956–58). He was contributing ed. of *High Fidelity* magazine (1955–66; 1971–77). He served as music critic of the *Chicago Sun-Times* from 1956 to 1991. In addition to his music reviews and books, he contributed articles on music to various literary and philosophical publications. His books on music comprise *Toscanini and the Art of Orchestral Performance* (1956; 2nd ed., rev., 1962 as *Toscanini and the Art of Conducting*), *The Cleveland Orchestra* (1967), *Ravinia* (1987), *James Levine at Ravinia* (1993), and *Dialogues and Discoveries: James Levine, His Life and His Music* (1998).—**NS/LK/DM**

Marsh, Roger (Michael), English composer, conductor, writer on music, and teacher; b. Bournemouth, Dec. 10, 1949. He studied with Ian Kellam at the London Coll. of Music and privately (1966–68), and then continued his training at the Univ. of York (B.A., 1971), where he became a composition student of Bernard Rands (Ph.D., 1975). He received a Harkness fellowship to study at the Univ. of Calif. at San Diego (1976–78). Returning to England, he was a lecturer at the Univ. of Keele (1978–88), where he was founder-director of the Keele New Music Ensemble (1979–88) and head of the music dept. (1985–88). In 1988 he became a lecturer at the Univ. of York, where he now holds the personal chair in the dept. of music. He also is director of the new music ensemble Black Hair. In addition to his writings on music, he has abridged and produced the novels of James Joyce for Naxos Audiobooks.

WORKS: DRAMATIC: M u s i c T h e a t e r : *Cass* (1970); *PS* (1971); *Calypso* (1973); *Scènes de ballet* (London, Feb. 17, 1974); *Dum* (1973; rev. version, San Diego, April 29, 1977; also for Orch. as *Dum's Dream*, 1973); *Time Before* (1977; London, Jan. 19, 1979); *Bits and Scraps* (London, May 6, 1979); *Spit and Blow* (1981; Birmingham, Feb. 27, 1983); *Samson* (1983; London, Oct. 20, 1984); *Love on the Rocks* (1989); *The Big Bang* (part 1, 1989). **ORCH.:** *Dum's Dream* (1973; also a music theater version as *Dum*); *Still* (1980; Birmingham, Nov. 13, 1981; rev.

version, Liverpool, May 12, 1987); *Stepping Out* (1990); *Espace* (Huddersfield, Nov. 26, 1994); *Heathcote's Inferno* for Symphonic Wind Ensemble (Manchester, Oct. 25, 1996). **CHAMBER:** *Jesters (for sicks)* for 2 Oboes, 2 Clarinets, and 2 Bassoons (1972); *Serenade* for Amplified Double Bass and 15 Strings (London, July 16, 1974); *Sweet and Short* for Clarinet, Piano, and Double Bass (1974); *Variations* for [4] Trombones (1977; Los Angeles, Feb. 5, 1979); *Point to Point* for 2 Oboes, 2 Clarinets, 2 Horns, and 2 Bassoons (1979); *2 Movements* for 2 Flutes, 2 Clarinets, Harp, and String Quartet (London, Oct. 9, 1979); *Heaven Haven* for Harp (1982); *Music* for Piano and Wind Instruments (York, March 17, 1986); *Dying for it* for 9 Instruments (1988); *Ferry Music* for Piano, Clarinet, and Cello (1988); *Waiting for Charlie* for 15 Players (Apeldoorn, April 5, 1996); *Spin* for Piano and 9 Players (Marseilles, Nov. 21, 1997); *Slow Right Arm* for Double Bass and Baroque Violin (Huddersfield, Nov. 28, 1997); *Canto I* for String Ensemble (Huddersfield, Nov. 24, 1999). **P i a n o :** *Easy Steps* (1987). **VOCAL:** *Streim* for Soprano, Flute, Clarinet, Trumpet, and Double Bass (1972); *The Lover's Ghost,* folk song for Soprano, 2 Flutes, 2 Clarinets, and Cello (1972; also for High Voice and Harp, 1976); *On and On,* folk song for Soprano, 2 Clarinets, and Bass Clarinet (1975); *3 Hale Mairies* for 3 Sopranos, Flute, Clarinet, Trumpet, Harp, Piano, 2 Percussion, Viola, and Cello (1976; San Diego, March 17, 1977); *Another Silly Love Song* for Soprano, Clarinet, and Piano (1976); *Not a Soul but Ourselves...* for 2 Women's and 2 Men's Voices with independent amplification (San Diego, Nov. 29, 1977); *A Psalm and a Silly Love Song* for Soprano, Mezzo-soprano, Flute, Clarinet, Trumpet, Harp, Viola, and Cello (London, April 25, 1979); *The Wormwood and the Gall* for Mezzo-soprano, Flute, Clarinet, Percussion, Harp, Viola, and Cello (London, July 6, 1981); *Words of Love* for Baritone, 2 Oboes, Bassoon, and Harpsichord (1982); *Songs of Devotion* for Soprano, Clarinet, and Guitar (1983; York, March 10, 1984); *3 Biblical Songs* for Soprano, Baritone, Small Women's Chorus, and Orch. (1985); *The Song of Abigail* for Soprano and Orch. (London, March 7, 1986); *The Bodhi Tree* for Voice and Trombone (1992); *A Little Snow* for Voice (London, June 10, 1994); *Black Hair* for Voice and Piano or Ensemble (1994); *Sozu Baba* for Voice (1996; Utrecht, March 31, 1997). —NS/LK/DM

Marsh, Warne (Marion), tenor saxophonist; b. Los Angeles, Oct. 26, 1927; d. Burbank, Calif., Dec. 18, 1987. He was perhaps Lennie Tristano's most loyal long-term protege. In live performance he had an electric intensity that rarely if ever came across on records, though it is reflected in the amazingly concentrated quality of his melodic lines.

His father, Oliver T. Marsh, was a leading cinematographer, and his mother Elizabeth was a violinist who used to play music for the actors during the filming of silent movies. He studied alto saxophone in junior high school but soon switched to tenor, and played bass clarinet in the Los Angeles All-City H.S. Orch. He studied classical saxophone with Mickey Gillette and took a few lessons with Corky Corcoran. In the fall of 1942, he began performing with a youth swing band that became known as the Hollywood Canteen Kids. From 1944–46 they appeared in radio broadcasts, the short films of Junior Jive Bombers and Double Rhythm, and in the feature film *Song of the Open Road.* As part of the Teen-Agers, which included Andre Previn, he was on the *Hoagy Carmichael Show* for most of 1945. He also began sitting in at black clubs on Central Avenue and

elsewhere. In fall 1945 he enrolled as a music major at the Univ. of Southern Calif. in Los Angeles and on April 1946 he was inducted into the army and played in the band at Camp Lee, Va. There he met Don Ferrara and Ted Brown and first learned of Tristano. When he was relocated to Fort Monmouth, N.J., in Jan. 1947, he began studying with Tristano and studied clarinet with Joe Allard of Julliard. On his discharge in 1947 he returned to Los Angeles and freelanced, including an April 1948 engagement with the Tom Talbert orch. at the Trianon Ballroom. In July 1948 he joined Buddy Rich and toured the country. Marsh left the band around December 1948 in N.Y. and resumed studies with Tristano as well as performing and recording with him through August 1955. His career was hampered by recurrent drug problems. He returned to the West Coast around the beginning of 1961, and for the next nine years performed sporadically in public, working occasional jobs in electronics. In 1962 he joined the Les Elgart band briefly and moved to Las Vegas. He returned to N.Y. at the end of 1963, married Geraldyne Elmore there in 1964 (they had a son in 1968), and performed regularly with Tristano, including the TV show *Live from the Half Note* in August 1964. In the spring of 1966 he played a one-week engagement at the Cellar Club in Toronto with Tristano. He worked with Clare Fischer's big band in Los Angeles from 1968–70 and taught privately. He he emerged as a lead member of Supersax (1972–77) and recorded frequently. He became a cocaine addict during the 1980s. He died shortly after suffering a heart attack while onstage at Donte's.

DISC.: *Live in Hollywood* (1952); *Lee Konitz with Warne Marsh* (1955); *Jazz of Two Cities* (1956); *Winds of Marsh* (1956); *Music for Prancing* (1957); *Warne Marsh* (1957); *The Art of Improvising* (1959); *Jazz from the East Village* (1960); *Ne Plus Ultra* (1969); *Warne Marsh & Lee Konitz Live* (1975); *Warne Marsh Quintet* (1975); *Warne Marsh and Lee Konitz* (1975); *All Music* (1976); *Tenor Gladness* (1976); *How Deep, How High* (1977); *Warne Out* (1977); *Star Highs* (1982); *Warne Marsh Meets Gary Foster* (1982); *Ballad Album* (1983); *Newly Warne* (1985); *Posthumous* (1985); *Back Home* (1986); *Red Mitchell / Warne Marsh Big* (1987); *Two Days in the Life Of...* (1987); *Warne Marsh and Susan Chen* (1987). B. Rich: *The Legendary '47–'48 Orchestra.* Tristano: *Wow* (1949); *Crosscurrents* (1949).—SC

Marshall, Ingram D(ouglass), American composer; b. Mount Vernon, N.Y., May 10, 1942. He studied at Lake Forest (Ill.) Coll. (B.A., 1964). After studies in musicology with Lang and in electronic music with Ussachevsky at Columbia Univ. (1964–66), he pursued training with Subotnick at N.Y.'s School of the Arts (1969–70). He then continued his studies with Subotnick and with K.R.T. Wasitodipura (traditional Indonesian music) at the Calif. Inst. of the Arts in Valencia (M.F.A., 1971), where he subsequently taught (until 1974). He was active as both a composer and a music critic, receiving various grants and commissions, including 2 NEA grants (1979, 1981) and a Rockefeller Foundation grant (1982). In 1990–91 he was a visiting prof. and senior fellow at Brooklyn Coll.'s Inst. for Studies in American Music. Marshall's compositions reflect his extensive travels, as well as an artful incorporation of non-traditional instruments, live electronics, and improvisation. His highly successful *Fog Tropes* (1982) makes use of electronically manipulated taped sounds gathered around the San Francisco Bay that include not only foghorns but the falsetto keenings of seagulls and the lowing of a gambuh (a Balinese flute). His lavish *Kingdom Come* (1997) utilizes recordings made in Yugoslavia including a Croatian hymn, a liturgy from a Serbian church in Dubrovnik, and a song fragment sung by a Bosnian Muslim. It was written in memory of Marshall's brother-in-law, Francis Tomasic, a journalist who was killed in Bosnia.

WORKS: *Transmogrification* for Tape (1966); *3 Buchla Studies* for Synthesizer (1968–69); *The East is Red*, variations for Tape (1971–72); *Cortez*, text-sound piece (1973); *Ricebowlthundersock* for Prepared Piano, Percussion, and Electronics (1973); Augmented Triad Ascending for Piano, 2 Marimbas, Vibraphone, and Glockenspiel (1974); *The Emperor's Birthday*, text-sound piece (1974); *Weather Report* for Tape (1974); *Tourist Songs I-II* for Tape (1975); *Vibrosuperball* for 4 Amplified Percussion (1975); *Ikon: Ayiasma*, text-sound piece for Tape, Reciter, and Live Electronics (1976); *The Fragility Cycles* for Voice, Gambuh, Live Electronics, and Tape (1976); *Non confundar* for String Sextet, Alto Flute, Clarinet, and Electronics (1977); *Landscape Parts* for Voice, Gambuhs, Tape, and Live Electronics (1978) and II for Viola, Flute, Clarinet, Percussion, Piano, Voice, and Live Electronics (1979); *Fillmore* for Gambuh, Tape, Slides, and Live Electronics (1978); *Adendum: In aeternum* for Clarinet, Flute, and String Sextet (1979); *Gradual Requiem* for Synthesizer, Mandolin, Piano, Voice, Gambuh, Tape, and Live Electronics (1980); *Magnificat Strophes* for Synclavier (1981); *Spiritus* for 6 Strings, 4 Flutes, Harpsichord, and Vibraphone (1981; rev. for String Orch., 1983); *Fog Tropes* for Brass Sextet, Tape, and Live Electronics (1982); *Woodstone* for Gamelan (1982); *Alcatraz* for Keyboards, Tapes, Slides, and Electronics (1983–84; in collab. with J. Bengston); *Entrada (As the River)* for String Quartet with Electronic Delays (1984); *Voces resonae*, string quartet, with live electronics (1984); Piano Quartet (*In My Beginning is My End*) for String Trio (1986–87; rev. 1995 for String Quartet); *Hidden Voices* for Digitally Sampled Voices, Soprano, and Orch. (1989); *A Peaceable Kingdom* for Chamber Orch. and Tape (1990); *Kingdom Come* for Orch. and Tape (1997).—**NS/LK/DM**

Marshall, Lois (Catherine), prominent Canadian soprano, later mezzo-soprano; b. Toronto, Jan. 29, 1924; d. there, Feb. 19, 1997. She began her vocal training at age 12 with Weldon Kilburn, whom she married in 1968; also studied lieder interpretation with Emmy Heim (1947–50). She first gained notice as a soloist in Bach's *St. Matthew Passion* with Sir Ernest MacMillan and the Toronto Sym. Orch. (1947). In 1952 she made her operatic stage debut as the Queen of the Night in Toronto, won the Naumburg Award, and made her N.Y. recital debut. She appeared as a soloist in Beethoven's *Missa solemnis* with Toscanini and the NBC Sym. Orch. in 1953, and subsequently sang with many other important American orchs. She made her London debut in 1956 with Beecham and the Royal Phil., and began a series of world concert tours in 1960; began singing as a mezzo-soprano in the mid-1970s. Although she gave her official farewell performance at a Toronto concert on Dec. 10, 1982, she made occasional appearances in subsequent years. She was made a Companion of the Order of Canada (1968).—**NS/LK/DM**

Marshall, Margaret (Anne), Scottish soprano; b. Stirling, Jan. 4, 1949. She studied at the Royal Scottish Academy of Music in Glasgow, and also took voice lessons with Edna Mitchell and Peter Pears in England and with Hans Hotter in Munich. In 1974 she won 1st prize at the International Competition in Munich. She made her London concert debut in 1975, and in 1978 her operatic debut in Florence as Euridice in *Orfeo*. She then sang the role of the Countess in the 1979 Florence production of *Le nozze di Figaro*, and made her Covent Garden debut in London in the same role in 1980. In 1982 she appeared as Fiordiligi at La Scala in Milan and at the Salzburg Festival. She made her first appearances in the U.S. in 1980 as a soloist with the Boston Sym. Orch. and N.Y. Phil.; subsequently made several American tours as a concert artist. In 1988 she made her first appearance at the Vienna State Opera as Mozart's Countess. During the 1991–92 season, she appeared at the Mozart Bicentenary Gala at Covent Garden and also sang Fiordiligi in Salzburg. In 1999 she was made an Officer of the Order of the British Empire.—**NS/LK/DM**

Marshall, Mike, American mandolinist and guitarist; b. Newcastle, Pa., July 17, 1957. He studied with James Hilligoos in Lakeland, Fla. He performed in various ensembles, including the Sunshine Bluegrass Boys (1972–76), the David Grisman Quintet (1979–84), and Montreux (1984–89). In 1986 he formed, with mandolinist Dana (William) Rath (b. West Bend, Wisc., May 21, 1956), The Modern Mandolin Quartet, the first mandolin quartet, comprising mandolins, mandola, and mando-cello, corresponding to the string quartet; other members are Paul Binkley (b. Minneapolis, May 9, 1954) and John Eric Imholz (b. San Francisco, June 9, 1953). Marshall helped to spearhead the New Acoustic movement with the David Grisman Quintet and New Age music as a recording artist for Windham Hill. An accomplished international performer, he performs in bluegrass, jazz, classical, and New Acoustic Music styles. His goal as a composer and performer is to "fuse musical styles such as jazz, bluegrass, world music, and classical to form new styles reflective of a less- structured, freer world." Among his compositions are *Gator Strut, Dolphins,* and *Free D,* as well as songs.—**NS/LK/DM**

Marshall, Robert L(ewis), distinguished American musicologist; b. N.Y., Oct. 12, 1939. After training at Columbia Univ. (A.B., 1960), he studied at Princeton Univ. with Babbitt, Lockwood, Mendel, and Strunk (M.F.A., 1962; Ph.D., 1968, with the diss. *The Compositional Process of J.S. Bach: A Study of the Autograph Scores of the Vocal Works;* publ. in Princeton, 1972). In 1966 he joined the faculty of the Univ. of Chicago, where he served as chairman of the music dept. (1972–77) and then as a prof. (1977–83). He was a prof. at Brandeis Univ. from 1983 to 2000. From 1977 to 1987 he was general ed. of the series Recent Researches in the music of the Baroque Era. Marshall has particularly distinguished himself in Bach and Mozart studies, and has contributed scholarly articles to various journals. His book *The Music of Johann Sebastian Bach: The Sources, the Style, the Significance* (N.Y., 1989) won the ASCAP-Deems Taylor Award in 1990. His other books include

Mozart Speaks: Views on Music, Musicians, and the World (N.Y., 1991), *Eighteenth-Century Keyboard Music* (N.Y., 1994), and *Dennis Brain on Record* (Newton, Mass., 1996).—NS/LK/DM

Marshall-Hall, George W(illiam) L(ouis),

English-born Australian conductor, music educator, and composer; b. London, March 26, 1862; d. Melbourne, July 18, 1915. He studied in Berlin (1880) and with Grove and Parry at the Royal Coll. of Music in London (1883). After settling in Australia, he became the first Ormond Prof. at the Univ. of Melbourne in 1890 and founder of its Conservatorium in 1895. In 1900 he founded his own cons. and served as its director until his death. Between 1892 and 1913 he also conducted his own concert series. Among his works were 5 operas, 2 syms., chamber music, and songs.—LK/DM

Marshall Tucker Band, The, southern rock

band of the 1970s. **MEMBERSHIP:** Doug Gray, lead voc. (b. Spartanburg, S.C., May 2, 1948); Toy Caldwell, lead gtr., steel gtr., voc. (b. Spartanburg, S.C., 1948; d. Moore, S.C., Feb. 25, 1993); Tommy Caldwell, bs., voc. (b. Spartanburg, S.C., 1950; d. Spartanburg, S.C., April 28, 1980); George McCorkle, rhythm gtr.; Jerry Eubanks, sax., flt. (b. Spartanburg, S.C., March 9, 1950); Paul Riddle, drm. Tommy Caldwell was replaced by Franklin Wilkie; the band reformed in 1983 with Doug Gray and Jerry Eubanks enlisting new members Rusty Milner, gtr. (b. Spartanburg, S.C., June 2, 1958); Tim Lawter, bs., gtr. (b. Spartanburg, S.C., Dec. 10, 1958), along with various supporting musicians.

The Marshall Tucker Band helped bridge the gap between rock and country music with a mellow sound that featured the flute and saxophone playing of Jerry Eubanks. Established as a live band through years of touring, the Marshall Tucker Band was a popular album band, recording excellent songs such as "Can't You See" "Searchin' for a Rainbow," "Fire on the Mountain," and "Last of the Singing Cowboys," while scoring only one major pop hit, "Heard It in a Love Song."

The band centered around the musical Caldwell brothers and their Spartanburg, S.C., friends. Teenager Toy Caldwell formed a band with friend George McCorkle called the Rants; his brother Tommy played with Doug Gray in the New Generation. Both local bands were active through the mid-1960s, when various members were drafted into the Army. Toy returned to Spartanburg in 1969 and formed the Toy Factory; by 1971 brother Tommy, old buddy McCorkle, and Paul Riddle were on board and the band had a new name, the Marshall Tucker Band (Marshall Tucker owned the hall where the guys rehearsed).

The band's first album was released in 1973, and a year later they were touring as opening act for the Allman Brothers (both groups recorded for Capricorn). Although several songs received wide airplay on FM and alternative radio, the band didn't score a major hit until 1977 with "Heard It in a Love Song." That same year they played Jimmy Carter's inauguration. In 1979 the group left Capricorn for Warner Bros.

Bassist Tommy Caldwell died on April 28, 1980, from injuries sustained in an auto accident in Spartanburg six days earlier. He was replaced by former Rants and Toy Factory bassist Franklin Wilkie. The band released *Dedicated* in 1981 in memory of Tommy. Lead guitarist Toy Caldwell left the group in 1983, as did McCorkle and Riddle; Toy eventually launched a solo career in 1992, only to die on Feb. 25, 1993. Enduring many personnel changes, the Marshall Tucker Band was subsequently fronted by originals Jerry Eubanks and lead vocalist Doug Gray. By the early 1990s the band was focusing on country material.

DISC.: THE MARSHALL TUCKER BAND: *The M. T. Band* (1973); *A New Life* (1974); *Where We All Belong* (1974); *Searchin' for a Rainbow* (1975); *Long Hard Ride* (1976); *Carolina Dreams* (1977); *Together Forever* (1978); *Greatest Hits* (1978); *Running Like the Wind* (1979); *Tenth* (1980); *Dedicated* (1981) *Tuckerized* (1982); *Just Us* (1983); *Greetings from South Carolina* (1984); *Still Holdin' On* (1988); *Back to Back* (1992); *Best* (1994). **TOY CALDWELL:** *Toy Caldwell* (1992).—BH

Marsick, Armand (Louis Joseph), Belgian

conductor, teacher, and composer, nephew of Martin (-Pierre-Joseph) Marsick; b. Liège, Sept. 20, 1877; d. Haine-St.-Paul, April 30, 1959. He studied with his father, Louis Marsick, then took a course in composition with Dupuis at the Liège Cons., with Ropartz at the Nancy Cons., and d'Indy in Paris. After playing 1st violin in the Municipal Théâtre in Nancy, he became concertmaster at the Concerts Colonne in Paris (1898). In 1908 he obtained the position of instructor at the Athens Cons., where he remained until 1921. He was appointed director at the Bilbao Cons. in 1922. He was a prof. at the Liège Cons. (1927–42) and conductor of the Société des Concerts Symphoniques (1927–39).

WORKS: DRAMATIC: O p e r a : *La Jane* (1903; 1st perf. as *Vendetta corsa*, Rome, 1913; Liège, March 29, 1921); *Lara* (1913; Antwerp, Dec. 3, 1929); *L'Anneau nuptial* (1920; Brussels, March 3, 1928). **R a d i o P l a y :** *Le Visage de la Wallonie* (1937). **ORCH.:** 2 symphonic poems: *Stèle funéraire* (1902) and *La Source* (1908); *Improvisation et Final* for Cello and Orch. (1904); 2 suites: *Scènes de montagnes* (1910) and *Tableaux grecs* (1912); *Tableaux de voyage* for Small Orch. (1939); *Loustics en fête* for Small Orch. (1939); *3 morceaux symphoniques* (1950). **CHAMBER:** Violin Sonata (1900); Quartet for 4 Horns (1950); *4 pièces* for Piano (1912). **VOCAL:** Choruses; songs.—NS/LK/DM

Marsick, Martin (-Pierre-Joseph), distin-

guished Belgian violinist, pedagogue, and composer, uncle of **Armand (Louis Joseph) Marsick**; b. Jupille-sur-Neuse, near Liège, March 9, 1848; d. Paris, Oct. 21, 1924. He received training in theory at the Liège Cons. (1856–58), and then was a violin student of Désiré Hynberg, taking a medal in 1864. After further studies with Léonard at the Brussels Cons. (1865–67), he went to Paris and studied with Massart at the Cons. (1868–69; premier prix, 1869) and played in the Opéra orch. In 1870 he completed his training in Berlin with Joachim. In 1873 he made a brilliant Paris debut at the Concerts Populaires. From 1877 he toured Europe with notable success, and in 1895–96 he made a tour of the U.S. He served as a prof. of violin at the Paris Cons. from 1892 to 1900, numbering among his outstanding pupils Flesch and Thibaud. Marsick was a champion of the virtuoso violin literature, particularly of works by Vieutemps and Wieniawski. Among his own works were 3 violin concertos, chamber music, numerous solo violin pieces, and songs.—NS/LK/DM

Marteau, Henri, greatly esteemed French-born Swedish violinist and pedagogue; b. Rheims, March 31, 1874; d. Lichtenberg, Bavaria, Oct. 3, 1934. He studied violin with Léonard and Garcin at the Paris Cons. (premier prix, 1892) and began his concert career as a youth; played in Vienna when he was 10 and in London when he was 14. In 1892, 1893, 1894, 1898, and 1906 he also toured the U.S., and also gave concerts in Scandinavia, Russia, France, and Germany. In 1900 he was appointed prof. of violin at the Geneva Cons., and in 1908 succeeded Joachim as violin teacher at the Hochschule für Musik in Berlin. He conducted the Göteborg orch. (1915–20) and became a naturalized Swedish citizen (1920); then taught at the German Academy of Music in Prague (1921–24), the Leipzig Cons. (1926–27), and the Dresden Cons. (from 1928). He was greatly appreciated by musicians of Europe; Reger, who was a personal friend, wrote a violin concerto for him, as did Massenet; his teacher Léonard bequeathed to him his magnificent Maggini violin, once owned by the Empress Maria Theresa. He championed the music of Bach and Mozart. Marteau was also a competent composer, numbering among his works an opera, *Meister Schwable* (Plauen, 1921), *Sinfonia gloria naturae* for Orch. (Stockholm, 1918), 2 violin concertos, Cello Concerto, much chamber music, many choral works, numerous violin pieces, and arrangements of classical works.

BIBL.: B. Marteau, *H. M., Siegeszug einer Geige* (Tutzing, 1971); G. Weiss, ed., *Der Lehrer und Wegbereiter von H. M., Hubert Léonard* (Tutzing, 1987); K. Bangerter, *H. M. als Komponist im Spiegel der Kritik: Eine Studie zum Begriff der "Einheit" in der Musikkritik um 1900* (Tutzing, 1991).—NS/LK/DM

Martelli, Henri, French composer; b. Santa Fe, Argentina, Feb. 25, 1895; d. Paris, July 15, 1980. He studied law at the Univ. of Paris; simultaneously took courses in fugue and composition with Widor at the Paris Cons. (1912–24). From 1940 to 1944 he was head of orch. and chamber music programs of the French Radio; he was secretary of the Société Nationale de Musique (1945–67) and director of programs there from 1968; from 1953 to 1973, he also was president of the French section of the ISCM. In his compositions, he attempted to re-create the spirit of early French music using modern techniques.

WORKS: DRAMATIC: Opera: *La Chanson de Roland* (1921–23; rev. 1962–64; Paris, April 13, 1967); *Le Major Cravachon* (1958; French Radio, June 14, 1959). **Ballet:** *La Bouteille de Panurge* (1930; Paris, Feb. 24, 1937); *Les Hommes de sable* (1951). **ORCH.:** *Rondo* (1921); *Sarabande, Scherzo et Final* (1922); *Divertissement sarrasin* (1922); *Sur la vie de Jeanne d'Arc* (1923); *Scherzo* for Violin and Orch. (1925); *Mors et Juventas* (1927); *Bas-reliefs assyriens* (1928; Boston, March 14, 1930); *Passacaille sur un thème russe* (1928); *Concerto for orchestra* (1931; Boston, April 22, 1932); 3 suites: No. 1, *Suite sur un thème corse* (1936), No. 2 (1950), and No. 3 (1971); 2 concertos for Violin and Chamber Orch. (1938, 1954); *Ouverture pour un conte de Boccace* (1942); *Suite concertante*

for Wind Quintet and Orch. (1943); *Divertimento* for Wind Orch. (1945); *Fantaisie* for Piano and Orch. (1945); *Sinfonietta* (1948); 3 syms.: No. 1 for Strings (1953; French Radio, March 13, 1955), No. 2 for Strings (1956; Paris, July 17, 1958), and No. 3 (1957; Paris, March 8, 1960); Concertino for Oboe, Clarinet, Horn, Bassoon, and Strings (1955); Double Concerto for Clarinet, Bassoon, and Orch. (1956); *Le Radeau de la Meduse*, symphonic poem (1957); *Variations* for Strings (1959); *Scènes a danser* (1963); *Rapsodie* for Cello and Orch. (1966); Oboe Concerto (1971). **CHAMBER:** *Invention* for Cello and Piano (1925); Duo for Oboe and English Horn (1925); 2 string quartets (1932–33; 1944); Piano Trio (1935); Violin Sonata (1936); *Suite* for 4 Clarinets (1936); *Introduction et Final* for Violin and Piano (1937); Wind Octet (1941); *Scherzetto, Berceuse et Final* for Cello and Piano (1941); Bassoon Sonata (1941); Cello Sonatina (1941); Flute Sonata (1942); *3 esquisses* for Saxophone and Piano (1943); *Preambule et Scherzo* for Clarinet and Piano (1944); 7 Duos for Violin and Harp (1946); *Fantaisiestück* for Flute and Piano (1947); Wind Quintet (1947); Cornet Sonatina (1948); *Adagio, Cadence et Final* for Oboe and Piano (1949); 2 quintets for Flute, Harp, and String Trio (1950, 1952); Trio for Flute, Cello, and Piano (1951); *Cadence, Interlude et Rondo* for Saxophone and Piano (1952); *15 études* for Bassoon (1953); Bass Trombone Sonata (1956); Viola Sonata (1959); Suite for Guitar (1960); *Concertstück* for Viola and Piano (1962); Concertino for Cornet and Piano (1964); *Dialogue* for Trombone, Tuba or Bass Saxophone, and Piano (1966); Oboe Sonata (1972); String Trio (1973–74); Trio for Flute, Cello, and Harp (1976). **Piano:** *Suite galante* (1924); *Guitare* (1931); *3 Petites suites* (1935, 1943, 1950); Suite (1939); Sonata for 2 Pianos (1946); *Sonorités* for Piano, left-hand (1974). **VOCAL:** *Le Temps*, cantata for Voice and 8 Instruments (1945); *Chrestomathie* for Chorus (1949); songs. **OTHER:** 17 radiophonic works (1940–62).—NS/LK/DM

Martenot, Maurice (Louis Eugene), French inventor of the electronic instrument "Ondes musicales," a.k.a. "Ondes Martenot"; b. Paris, Oct. 14, 1898; d. there, Oct. 10, 1980. He studied composition at the Paris Cons. with Gédalge. He constructed an electronic musical instrument with a keyboard, which he called Ondes musicales. He gave its first demonstration in Paris on April 20, 1928, and, on Dec. 23, 1928, the first musical work for the instrument, *Poème symphonique pour solo d'Ondes musicales et orchestre*, by Dimitri Levidis, was presented in Paris. Martenot publ. *Méthode pour l'enseignement des Ondes musicales* (Paris, 1931). The instrument became popular, especially among French composers: it is included in the score of Honegger's *Jeanne d'Arc au bûcher* (1935); Koechlin's *Le Buisson ardent*, part 1 (1938); Martinon's 2nd Sym., *Hymne à la vie* (1944); and Messiaen's *Turangalila-Symphonie* (1946–48). It was used as a solo instrument in Koechlin's *Hymne* (1929), Jolivet's *Concerto* (1947), Landowski's *Concerto* (1954), Bondon's *Kaleidoscope* (1957), and Charpentier's *Concertino "alla francese"* (1961). Many other composers were attracted to it as well. Of all the early electronic instruments—Ondes Martenot, Trautonium, and Theremin—only Martenot's has proved a viable musical instrument. When Varèse's *Ecuatorial*, written in 1934 for a brass ensemble and including a Theremin, was publ. in 1961, the score substituted an Ondes Martenot for the obsolescent Theremin. Martenot's sister, Ginette Martenot (b. Paris, Jan. 27, 1902), became the chief exponent of the Ondes Martenot in concert performances in Europe and the U.S.—NS/LK/DM

Martha and the Vandellas, one of Motown Records' earliest and most exciting female vocal groups.

MEMBERSHIP: Martha Reeves (b. Eufaula, Ala., July 18, 1941); Rosalind Ashford (b. Detroit, Sept. 2, 1943); Annette Beard. Beard was replaced in late 1963 by Betty Kelly (b. Detroit, Sept. 16, 1944).

Martha Reeves moved to Detroit as a teenager and helped form the Del-Phis in 1960, recording for Checkmate Records in 1961. Spotted performing solo by Motown executive Mickey Stevenson, Reeves became secretary in the company's A&R department. Recording the occasional demonstration tape as part of her job, she first came to the attention of Berry Gordy Jr., as a substitute for an absent artist at a recording session. With high school friends Rosalind Ashford and Annette Beard, she backed Marvin Gaye's recording of "Stubborn Kind of Fellow," his first hit from 1962.

Signed to the newly formed Gordy label in September 1962 as Martha and the Vandellas, the group scored their first major pop and R&B hit in the spring of 1963 with the rather tame "Come and Get These Memories." Subsequently utilizing a harder-edged, brassy style propelled by Martha's dynamic lead vocals, Martha and the Vandellas achieved a smash pop and top R&B hit with Holland-Dozier-Holland's classic "Heat Wave" that summer. By year's end, Annette Beard had left the group, to be replaced by Betty Kelly, formerly with the Velvelettes. Martha and the Vandellas continued having smash crossover hits through early 1965 with Holland-Dozier-Holland's "Quicksand" and "Nowhere to Run," and Mickey Stevenson and Marvin Gaye's "Dancing in the Streets." Although Gordy was concentrating on the career development of the Supremes, Martha and the Vandellas achieved major pop and smash R&B hits with the less raunchy "My Baby Loves Me," "I'm Ready for Love," "Jimmy Mack" (a top R&B hit), and "Honey Chile" through 1967.

However, Martha Reeves and the Vandellas, as they were billed beginning in late 1967, never had another major hit. The group disbanded for two years, reforming in 1971 with Martha Reeves as the only original member to record *Black Magic*, which produced three moderate R&B hits. In late 1972, Martha Reeves launched a solo career, but her recordings for MCA, Arista, and Fantasy through 1980 failed to sell. The original trio reunited in 1989 for American engagements into the 1990s. Martha and the Vandellas were inducted into the Rock and Roll Hall of Fame in 1995.

WRITINGS: M. Reeves and M. Bego, *Dancing in the Streets: Confessions of a Motown Diva* (N.Y., 1994).

DISC.: MARTHA AND THE VANDELLAS: *Come and Get These Memories* (1963); *Heat Wave* (1963); *Dance Party* (1965); *Watch Out* (1966); *Live!* (1967). **MARTHA REEVES AND THE VANDELLAS:** *Ridin' High* (1968); *Sugar and Spice* (1970); *Natural Resources* (1970); *Black Magic* (1972). **MARTHA REEVES:** *Martha Reeves* (1974); *The Rest of My Life* (1976); *We Meet Again* (1978); *Gotta Keep Moving* (1980).—**BH**

Martienssen, Carl Adolf, German musicologist; b. Güstrow, Dec. 6, 1881; d. Berlin, March 1, 1955. He received training in piano from Klindworth and Berger in Berlin, and from Reisenauer in Leipzig. After teaching at the Bromber Cons., he studied with Kretzschmar, Stumpf, Wolf, and Wundt at the Univ. of Berlin. In 1914 he became a piano teacher at the Leipzig Cons. He also served as director of the piano classes at the Leipzig Inst. of Church Music, where he was made a prof. in 1932. From 1932 he was a prof. at the Berlin Musical Inst. for Foreigners. He taught at the Hochschules für Musik in Berlin (1934–45), Rostock (1945–50), and East Berlin (1950–52). Martienssen prepared Urtexts of the Haydn, Mozart, and Beethoven piano sonatas.

WRITINGS (all publ. in Leipzig): *Die individuelle Klaviertechnik auf der Grundlage des schöpferischen Klangwillens* (1930); *Die Methodik des individuellen Klavierunterrichts* (1934); *Grundlage einer deutschen Klavierlehre* (1942); *Das Klavierkunstwerk* (1950). —NS/LK/DM

Martin, Dean (originally, **Crocetti, Dino Paul**), American singer, comedian, and actor; b. Steubenville, Ohio, June 7, 1917; d. Los Angeles, Dec. 25, 1995. A relaxed, easygoing singer, Martin followed in the footsteps of his fellow Italian-American and friend, Frank Sinatra, forging a career made up of personal appearances, recordings, and radio, television, and film work. He got his start in a music-and-comedy act with Jerry Lewis that lasted 10 years, then went out on his own, finding additional success in dramatic film roles and as host of a television variety series. His extensive recordings resulted in 46 singles and numerous albums that reached the pop charts between 1948 and 1972; 12 of his albums went gold, as did the singles "That's Amore," "Memories Are Made of This," and "Everybody Loves Somebody." Of the 55 feature films in which he appeared between 1949 and 1984, 16 were musical comedies in which he co-starred with Lewis.

Martin was the child of Italian immigrant Gaetano Crocetti, a barber, and Angela Barra Crocetti. After dropping out of high school he worked a variety of jobs before he turned to singing. By 1940 he was working with Sammy Watkins's band in Cleveland. There he married Elizabeth Ann MacDonald on Oct. 2, 1941. They had four children and divorced on Aug. 24, 1949. Martin stayed with Watkins until September 1943, when he went out as a single with an extended engagement at the Riobamba nightclub in N.Y. Over the next three years he continued to perform without scoring a major success.

Martin made his first recordings for Diamond Records in July 1946. On July 25, at the 500 Club in Atlantic City, he teamed with Jerry Lewis for a zany act in which he both sang and served as straight man to Lewis's comic antics. The act grew in popularity until Martin and Lewis were among the most successful nightclub performers in the country. In April 1948 they opened at the prestigious Copacabana in N.Y., where they played for 18 weeks. During this run, on June 20, 1948, they made their television debut on the premiere broadcast of *Talk of the Town*, the variety series later called *The Ed Sullivan Show*. In August they signed contracts with Capitol Records and Paramount Pictures.

At their first Capitol recording session on Sept. 13, 1948, Martin and Lewis revived the novelty song "That Certain Party" (music by Walter Donaldson, lyrics by Gus Kahn); it became their first chart entry in December. That month Martin alone recorded "Powder Your Face with Sunshine (Smile! Smile! Smile!)" (music and lyrics by Carmen Lombardo and Stanley Rochinski); in March 1949 it became his first Top Ten hit. *The Martin and Lewis Show* premiered on network radio on April 3. It ran for the rest of the season and from November to January 1950, then returned in the fall of 1951 and ran during 1951–53.

On Sept. 1, 1949, Martin married model Jeanne Beiggers; they had three children. Martin married a third time; the couple divorced on March 29, 1973. Martin and Lewis made their first film appearance in *My Friend Irma* in September 1949 and followed it with *My Friend Irma Goes West* in August 1950. September marked the premiere of the television variety series *The Colgate Comedy Hour*, for which they served as hosts on a rotating basis with other performers, appearing about once a month. The program ran until December 1955.

Martin and Lewis's film career brought them their greatest success. Their third feature, *At War with the Army*, released in December 1950, and their fourth, *That's My Boy*, released in August 1951, were both among the ten highest grossing films of 1951; *Sailor Beware*, released in December 1951, and *Jumping Jacks*, released in July 1952, were both among the ten highest grossing films of 1952. Among their four pictures released in 1953 was *The Caddy*, in which Martin sang "That's Amore" (music by Harry Warren, lyrics by Jack Brooks). His Capitol recording of the song hit the Top Ten in December and sold a million copies. Though all of Martin and Lewis's films were comedies in which Martin got to sing at least a couple of songs, *Living It Up*, released in July 1954, was a full-fledged movie musical based on the Broadway show *Hazel Flagg*, with songs by Jule Styne (music) and Bob Hilliard (lyrics).

In January 1956, Martin hit #1 with the million-seller "Memories Are Made of This" (music and lyrics by Terry Gilkyson, Rick Dehr, and Frank Miller), a success not directly related to his partnership with Lewis and one that encouraged him to strike out on his own. Martin and Lewis gave their final performance together at the Copacabana on July 25, 1956, ten years after their first; their last film, *Hollywood or Bust*, was released in December

Martin's solo career got off to a slow start. His first film as a single, the musical comedy *Ten Thousand Bedrooms*, released in April 1957, was unsuccessful, and none of his recordings during the year reached the charts. But on Sept. 5, 1957, he starred in his first television special, followed by a second on Feb. 1, 1958, when one of his guests was Frank Sinatra. Then his third-billed, non-singing role in the epic war film *The Young Lions*, released in April, established him as a dramatic actor, and within weeks he reached the Top Ten with "Return to Me" (music and lyrics by Carmen Lombardo and Danny Di Minno). These successes set a pattern in which he effectively mixed recordings, personal appearances, and film and television work for the next quarter-century.

His film career revitalized, Martin appeared in an average of three films a year from 1959 to 1964, including his dramatic co-starring performance with John Wayne in the box office hit Western *Rio Bravo* (March 1959), and the musicals *Bells Are Ringing* (June 1960), *What a Way to Go!* (May 1964), and *Kiss Me, Stupid* (December 1964). He also appeared in a series of films with Frank Sinatra and in some cases other members of the "Rat Pack," of which they were the two most prominent members: *Some Came Running* (January 1959); *Ocean's Eleven* (August 1960); *Sergeants 3* (February 1962); *Come Blow Your Horn* (June 1963); *Four for Texas* (December 1963); and *Robin and the 7 Hoods* (August 1964).

Martin left Capitol Records at the end of 1961 and joined the Sinatra-owned Reprise Records. In May 1964, Reprise released Martin's revival of the 1948 song "Everybody Loves Somebody" (music by Ken Lane, lyrics by Irving Taylor) in a rhythmic Ernie Freeman arrangement produced by Jimmy Bowen. It hit #1 in August, selling a million copies and earning Martin his only Grammy nomination, for Best Vocal Performance, Male. It also revitalized his recording career. The album *Everybody Loves Somebody*, released in August, hit #1 in September and went gold. Also released in August was the gold album *Dream with Dean*. His next single was a revival of the 1955 R&B hit "The Door Is Still Open to My Heart" (music and lyrics by Chuck Willis); it reached the pop Top Ten and topped the easy-listening charts.

An LP titled *The Door Is Still Open to My Heart* was released in October; it reached the Top Ten in November and went gold. Martin's follow-up single, a revival of the 1944 song "You're Nobody Till Somebody Loves You" (music and lyrics by Russ Morgan, Larry Stock, and James Cavanaugh), reached the pop Top 40 and hit #1 on the easy-listening charts in January 1965.

Martin released three more gold-selling albums in 1965—*Dean Martin Hits Again* (January), *(Remember Me) I'm the One Who Loves You* (August), and *Houston* (October)—as well as four chart singles, including "I Will" (music and lyrics by Dick Glasser), which hit the Top Ten in December. He also appeared in two films, again costarring with John Wayne in the Western *The Sons of Katie Elder*, released in August, and with Frank Sinatra in the comedy *Marriage on the Rocks*, released in September. On Sept. 16 he launched *The Dean Martin Show*, a comedy-variety television series. It became a substantial success, ranking among the highest rated shows each year between 1966 and 1971 and remaining on the air until 1974.

In addition to his TV work, Martin continued to record and make films. In February 1966 he released the gold-selling album *Somewhere There's a Someone*. In March, Columbia Pictures released *The Silencers*, the first of four films in which he portrayed secret agent Matt Helm, spoofing the James Bond movies; it was one of the highest grossing films of the year. Martin released the gold-selling seasonal LP *The Dean Martin Christmas Album* in October. He also enjoyed gold albums with *Welcome to My World* (August 1967), *Dean Martin's Greatest Hits! Vol. 1* (May 1968), *Dean Martin's Greatest*

Hits! Vol. 2 (July 1968), and *Gentle on My Mind* (December 1968).

Martin's singles regularly hit the lower reaches of the pop charts and the upper reaches of the easy-listening charts: a revival of the 1936 song "In the Chapel in the Moonlight" (music and lyrics by Billy Hill) was an easy-listening #1 in August 1967, and "In the Misty Moonlight" (music and lyrics by Cindy Walker) topped the easy-listening charts in January 1968.

Martin's recording and film work had diminished by the end of the 1960s, though he was one of the featured performers in the movie *Airport* (February 1970), the highest grossing film of 1970. That year he was reported to have signed the most lucrative contract in television history to renew his series. On April 24, 1973, he married beautician Catherine Mae Hawn. He adopted her daughter from a previous marriage. They divorced on Feb. 24, 1977. For its final season, 1973–74, Martin's TV show was renamed *The Dean Martin Comedy Hour* and sometimes featured humorous "roasts" of well-known personalities. After the series went off the air, Martin continued to appear on similar programs, billed *The Dean Martin Celebrity Roasts*, as well as hosting annual Christmas specials.

Martin was gradually less active in the second half of the 1970s and 1980s. He appeared in the comedy film *The Cannonball Run* (June 1981) one of the highest grossing films of 1981, and made his final film appearance in its sequel, *Cannonball Run II* (June 1984). In 1983 he returned to record- making for the first time in five years with his final album, the country-styled *The Nashville Sessions*; it featured "My First Country Song" (music and lyrics by Conway Twitty), which became his only country singles chart entry. In the spring of 1985 he was a regular on the TV crime series *Half- Nelson*. He continued to perform live, especially in Las Vegas. In the fall of 1987 he was part of a tour with Frank Sinatra and Sammy Davis Jr., but he dropped out due to ill-health. He was inactive in his later years. He died of acute respiratory failure at age 78 in 1995.

DISC.: *Swingin' Down Yonder* (1955); *Dean Martin Sings* (1956); *Pretty Baby* (1957); *This is Dean Martin* (1958); *Sleep Warm* (1959); *A Winter Romance* (1959); *Bells Are Ringing* (soundtrack) (1960); *Cha-Cha de Amor* (1961); *Dean Martin* (1961); *This Time I'm Swingin'!* (1961); *French Style* (1962); *Country Style* (1963); *Dino Latino* (1963); *Dean 'Tex' Martin Rides Again* (1963); *The Door Is Still Open to My Heart* (1964); *Everybody Loves Somebody* (1964); *Hey Brother, Pour the Wine* (1964); *Dream with Dean* (1964); *Dean Martin Sings, Sinatra Conducts* (1965); *Holiday Cheer* (1965); *Houston* (1965); *Southern Style* (1965); *The Dean Martin TV Show* (1966); *Happy in Love* (1966); *The Hit Sound of Dean Martin* (1966); *Somewhere There's a Someone* (1966); *Christmas Album* (1966); *Relaxin'* (1966); *Songs from The Silencers* (1966); *Happiness is Dean Martin* (1967); *Welcome to My World* (1967); *Gentle on My Mind* (1968); *Favorites* (1968); *I Take a Lot of Pride in What I Am* (1969); *My Woman, My Woman, My Wife* (1970); *For the Good Times* (1971); *Dino* (1972); *Sittin' on Top of the World* (1973); *You're the Best Thing That Ever Happened to Me* (1973); *Once in a While* (1978); *The Nashville Sessions* (1983).

BIBL.: A. Marx, *Everybody Loves Somebody Sometime (Especially Himself): The Story of D. M. and Jerry Lewis* (N.Y., 1974); N. Tosches, *Dino: Living High in the Dirty Business of Dreams* (N.Y., 1992); S. Levy, *Rat Pack Confidential: Frank, D., Sammy, Peter, Joey and the Last Great Showbiz Party* (N.Y., 1998).—**WR**

Martín, Edgardo, Cuban composer and music educator; b. Cienfuegos, Oct. 6, 1915. He began his initial musical training with his maternal grandmother, the pianist Aurea Suárez, in Cienfuegos (1925–35). Settling in Havana, he studied piano with Jascha Fischermann (1936–37), attended the Univ. (1937–41), and received training in composition from José Ardévol at the Cons. (1939–46). From 1943 to 1967 he was active as a music critic. He also taught music history and aesthetics at the Cons. (1945–68) and music analysis at the Escuela nacional de Arte (1969–73). From 1962 to 1971 he was executive secretary of the National Committee of Music for UNESCO. As a Castro partisan, he was a principal figure in the reform of music teaching under the Communist regime. He composed in an accessible style.

WORKS: DRAMATIC: B a l l e t : *El Caballo de coral* (1960). **ORCH.:** 2 syms. (1947, 1948). **CHAMBER:** Concerto for 9 Winds (1944); Trio for Oboe, Clarinet, and Bassoon (1963); 2 string quartets (1967, 1968); *Recitativo y aria* for Viola and Piano (1979); guitar pieces. **P i a n o :** Sonata (1943); 2 preludes (1950); 3 *Soneras* (1950, 1971, 1975). **VOCAL:** *Los 2 abuelos* for Chorus and Instruments (1949); *Canto de héroes* for Voices and Orch. (1967); *La carta del soldado* for Narrator, Tenor, Chorus, Speaking Chorus, and Orch. (1970); *Granma* for Chorus and Instruments (1976); cantatas; songs.—**NS/LK/DM**

Martin, François, significant French cellist and composer; b. 1727; d. Paris, 1757. He became well known as a cellist and composer in Paris, and appeared at the Concert Spirituel (1747). He was an ordinaire de l'Académie Royale de Musique (1746–48), and also taught. He was granted several royal privileges to publ. his music. His place in French music rests primarily upon his syms. and overtures, which were some of the finest works of their kind written in the pre-Classical period. They were featured at the Concert Spirituel (1751–55). His motets were also performed there, including his notable *Cantate Domino*. His early death was greatly lamented.

WORKS: INSTRUMENTAL (all publ. in Paris): *6 sonates* for Cello, with duo for Violin and Cello, op.2 (1746); *6 trios ou Conversations à 3* for 2 Violins, or Flute and Cello, op.3 (1746); *Sonate da camera* for Cello and Basso Continuo, op.1 (1748); *(6) Symphonies et ouvertures* for 2 Violins, Viola, and Bass, op.4 (1751); *Symphonie à cors de chasse* (Concert Spirituel, June 10, 1751); various other works, including a Cello Concerto (Concert Spirituel, April 1747). **VOCAL: S e c u l a r :** *Le Bouquet de Thémire,* cantatille (La Planchette, July 28, 1745); *Le Soupçon amoureux,* cantatille (1747); *Le Suisse amoureux,* cantatille (1747); several other works. **S a c r e d :** *Grand Motets For Chorus and Instruments* (all perf. at the Concert Spirituel): *Laetatus sum* (April 3, 1747); *In exitu* (April 19, 1748); *Cantate Domino* (May 7, 1750); *Jubilate Deo* (April 24, 1753). **P e t i t s M o t e t s** (all 1st perf. at the Concert Spirituel): *Laetentur coeli* (Feb. 2, 1751); *Inclina Domine* (Nov. 1, 1751). **M o t e t s :** *Notum fecit dominus* (1752); *Super flumina Babilonis* (n.d.).—**NS/LK/DM**

Martin, Frank (Théodore), greatly renowned Swiss composer and pedagogue; b. Geneva, Sept. 15, 1890; d. Naarden, the Netherlands, Nov. 21, 1974. He studied privately with Joseph Lauber in Geneva (1906–14), who instructed him in the basics of the conservative idiom of Swiss music of the fin de siècle, and then had lessons with Hans Huber and Frederic Klose, who continued to emphasize the conservative foundations of the religious and cultural traditions of the Swiss establishment. However, Martin soon removed himself from the strict confines of Swiss scholasticism, encouraged in this development by Ernest Ansermet. In 1918 Martin went to Zürich, in 1921 to Rome, and in 1923 to Paris. He returned to Geneva in 1926 as a pianist and harpsichordist. Martin taught at the Inst. Jaques-Dalcroze (1927–38), was founder and director of the Technicum Moderne de Musique (1933–39), and served as president of the Assn. of Swiss Musicians (1942–46). He moved to the Netherlands in 1946, but also taught composition at the Cologne Hochschule für Musik (1950–57). His early music showed the influence of Franck and French impressionists, but soon he succeeded in creating a distinctive style supported by a consummate mastery of contrapuntal and harmonic writing, and a profound feeling for emotional consistency and continuity. Still later he became fascinated by the logic and self-consistency of Schoenberg's method of composition with 12 tones, and adopted it in a modified form in several of his works. He also demonstrated an ability to stylize folk-song materials in modern techniques. In his music, Martin followed the religious and moral precepts of his faith in selecting several subjects of his compositions. In 1944 the director of Radio Geneva asked him to compose an oratorio to be broadcast immediately upon the conclusion of World War II. He responded with *In terra pax* for 5 Soloists, Double Chorus, and Orch., which was given its broadcast premiere from Geneva at the end of the war in Europe, May 7, 1945; a public performance followed in Geneva 24 days later. He publ. *Responsabilité du compositeur* (Geneva, 1966); M. Martin ed. his *Un compositeur médite sur son art* (Neuchâtel, 1977).

WORKS: DRAMATIC: *Oedipe-Roi*, incidental music (Geneva, Nov. 21, 1922); *Oedipe à Colone*, incidental music (1923); *Le Divorce*, incidental music (Geneva, April 1928); *Roméo et Juliette*, incidental music (Mézières, June 1, 1929); *Die blaue Blume*, ballet music (1935); *Das Märchen vom Aschenbrodel*, ballet, after *Cinderella* (1941; Basel, March 12, 1942); *La Voix des siècles*, incidental music (Geneva, July 4, 1942); *Ein Totentanz zu Basel im Jahre 1943*, outdoor dance spectacle (Basel, May 27, 1943); *Athalie*, incidental music (1946; Geneva, May 7, 1947); *Der Sturm*, opera, after Shakespeare (1952–55; Vienna, June 17, 1956); *Monsieur de Pourceaugnac*, opera, after Molière (1960; Geneva, April 23, 1963). **ORCH.:** Suite (St. Gallen, June 14, 1913); *Symphonie pour orchestre burlesque* (1915; Geneva, Feb. 1916); *Esquisse* (Geneva, Oct. 30, 1920); *Entr'acte pour grand orchestre* (1924; also as a Concerto for Winds and Piano, and as the *Chamber Fox Trot*, Boston, Dec. 20, 1927; all based on the *Ouverture et foxtrot* for 2 Pianos); *Rhythmes*, 3 symphonic movements (1926; Geneva, March 12, 1927); 2 piano concertos: No. 1 (1933–34; Geneva, Jan. 22, 1936) and No. 2 (1968; ORTF, Paris, June 24, 1970); *Quatre pièces brèves* (Geneva, Nov. 21, 1934;

also for Guitar or for Piano, 1933); *Danse de la peur* for 2 Pianos and Chamber Orch. (1935; Geneva, June 28, 1944; based on the ballet music *Die blaue Blume*); Sym. (1936–37; Lausanne, March 7, 1938); *Ballade* for Alto Saxophone and Strings (1936–37); *Du Rhône au Rhin*, march for Band (Zürich, May 6, 1939); *Ballade* for Flute and Orch. (orchestrated by E. Ansermet; Lausanne, Nov. 27, 1939; based on the *Ballade* for Flute and Piano; also for Flute, Strings, and Piano, Basel, Nov. 28, 1941); *Ballade* for Piano and Orch. (1939; Zürich, Feb. 1, 1944); *Ballade* for Trombone and Chamber Orch. (1941; Geneva, Jan. 26, 1942; based on the *Ballade* for Trombone and Piano, 1940); *Petite symphonie concertante* for Harp, Harpsichord, Piano, and Double String Orch. (1944–45; Zürich, May 17, 1946; also for Full Orch. as *Symphonie concertante*, 1946; Lucerne, Aug. 16, 1947); *Ballade* for Cello and Chamber Orch. (1949; Zürich, Nov. 17, 1950; based on the *Ballade* for Cello and Piano); Concerto for 7 Winds, Percussion, and Strings (Bern, Oct. 25, 1949); Violin Concerto (1950–51; Basel, Jan. 24, 1952); Concerto for Harpsichord and Small Orch. (1951–52; Venice, Sept. 14, 1952); *Sonata da chiesa* for Viola d'Amore and Strings (1952; Turin, April 29, 1953; based on the *Sonata da chiesa* for Viola d'Amore and Organ, 1938; also for Flute and Strings, 1958; Lausanne, Oct. 15, 1959); *Passacaille* for Strings (1952; Frankfurt am Main, Oct. 16, 1953; based on the *Passacaille* for Organ, 1944; also for Full Orch., 1963; Berlin, May 30, 1963); *Pavane couleur du temps* for Chamber Orch. (1954; based on the piece for String Quintet, 1920; also for Piano, 4–Hands); *Études* for Strings (1955–56; Basel, Nov. 23, 1956; also for 2 Pianos, 1957); *Ouverture en hommage à Mozart* (Geneva, Dec. 10, 1956); *Ouverture en rondeau* (Lucerne, Aug. 13, 1958); *Inter arma caritas* (Geneva, Sept. 1, 1963); *Les Quatre éléments*, symphonic études (1963–64; Lausanne, Oct. 5, 1964); Cello Concerto (1965–66; Basel, Jan. 26, 1967); *Erasmi monumentum* for Organ and Orch. (Rotterdam, Oct. 27, 1969); *Trois danses* for Oboe, Harp, String Quintet, and String Orch. (Zürich, Oct. 9, 1970); *Ballade* for Viola and Wind Orch. (1972; Salzburg, Jan. 20, 1973); *Polyptyque: Six images de la passion du Christ* for Violin and Double String Orch. (Lausanne, Sept. 9, 1973). **CHAMBER:** 2 violin sonatas: No. 1 (1913; Thoune, July 10, 1915) and No. 2 (1931–32; Geneva, Oct. 7, 1932); Piano Quintet (1919); *Pavane couleur de temps* for String Quintet (1920; also for Piano, or for Chamber Orch., 1954); *Trio sur des mélodies populaires irlandais* for Violin, Cello, and Piano (1925; Paris, April 1926); *Quatre pièces brèves* for Guitar (1933; also for Piano, and for Orch., 1934); *Rhapsodie*, quintet for 2 Violins, 2 Violas, and Double Bass (1935; Geneva, March 10, 1936); String Trio (Brusses, May 2, 1936); *Sonata da chiesa* for Viola d'Amore and Organ (1938; Basel, Dec. 8, 1939; also for Flute and Organ, 1941, Lausanne, June 11, 1942, for Viola d'Amore and String Orch., 1952, and for Flute and String Orch., 1958); *Ballade* for Flute and Piano (1939; also for Flute and Orch., 1939, and for Flute, String Orch., and Piano, 1941); *Ballade* for Trombone and Piano (Geneva, Sept. 1940; also for Trombone and Chamber Orch., 1941); *Petite fanfare* for 2 Trumpets, 2 Horns, and 2 Trombones (1945); *Ballade* for Cello and Piano (1949; also for Cello and Chamber Orch.); String Quartet (1966–67; Zürich, June 20, 1968). **KEYBOARD: Piano:** *Overture et foxtrot* for 2 Pianos (1924; also as *Entr'acte pour grand orchestre*, as a Concerto for Winds and Piano, and as the *Chamber Fox Trot*); *Quatre pièces brèves* (1933; also for Guitar or for Orch.); *Petite marche blanche et trio noir les grenouilles, le rossignol* for 2 Pianos (1937); *Huit préludes* (1947–48; Lausanne, March 22, 1950); *Clair de lune* (1952); *Au clair de lune* for Piano, 4–Hands (1955); *Études* for 2 Pianos (Cologne, Oct. 28, 1957;

based on the *Études* for String Orch., 1955–56); *Étude rythmique* (Geneva, Feb. 22, 1965); *Esquisse* (Munich, Sept. 1965); *Fantaisie sur des rhythmes flamenco* for Piano and Dancer ad libitum (1973; Lucerne, Aug. 18, 1974). **O r g a n :** *Passacaille* (Bern, Sept. 26, 1944; also for String Orch., 1952, and for Full Orch., 1962). **VOCAL:** *Trois poèmes païens* for Baritone and Orch. (1910; Vevey, May 20, 1911); *Ode et sonnet* for 3 Treble Voices and Cello ad libitum (1912); *Les Dithyrambes* for 4 Soloists, Chorus, Children's Chorus, and Orch. (1915–18; Lausanne, June 16, 1918); *Le Roy a fait battre tambour* for Alto and Chamber Orch. (1916); *Chantons, je vous en prie* for Chorus (1920); *Quatre sonnets à Cassandre* for Mezzo-soprano, Flute, Viola, and Cello (1921; Geneva, April 7, 1923); Mass for Double Chorus (1922, 1926; Hamburg, Nov. 2, 1963); *Chanson du Mezzetin* for Soprano and Mandolin or Oboe, Violin, and Cello (1923); *La Nique à Satan* for Soprano, Baritone, Choruses, Winds, Percussion, and Piano (1928–31; Geneva, Feb. 25, 1933); *Cantate pour le temps de Noël* for Soloists, Mixed Chorus, Women's Chorus, Boy's Chorus, Strings, Harpsichord, and Organ (1929; unfinished; completed by the composer's widow, Maria Martin, and the conductor Alois Koch; Lucerne, Dec. 4, 1994); *Le Vin herbé*, secular oratorio in 3 parts (part 1, 1938; Zürich, April 16, 1940; parts 2 and 3, 1940–41; 1st complete perf., Zürich, March 28, 1942); *Cantata pour le 1er août*, secular cantata for Chorus and Piano or Organ (Geneva, Aug. 1, 1941); *Der Cornet*, song cycle for Alto and Chamber Orch., after Rilke (1942–43; Basel, Feb. 9, 1954); *Sechs Monologe aus "Jedermann,"* song cycle for Baritone and Piano, after Hofmannsthal (1943–44; Gastaad, Aug. 6, 1944; also for Baritone or Alto and Orch., 1949); *In terra pax*, oratorio brève for 5 Soloists, 2 Mixed Choruses, and Orch. (1944; radio broadcast, Geneva, May 7, 1945; 1st public perf., Geneva, May 31, 1945); *Dédicace* for Tenor and Piano (Geneva, July 6, 1945); *Golgotha*, passion oratorio for 5 Soloists, Chorus, Organ, and Orch. (1945–48; Geneva, April 29, 1949); *Quant n'ont assez fait, do-do*, song for Tenor, Guitar, and Piano, 4–Hands (Lauren, Oct. 9, 1947); *Trois Chants de Noël* for Soprano, Flute and Piano (private family perf., Amsterdam, Dec. 25, 1947); *5 Ariel Songs* for Chorus (1950; Amsterdam, March 7, 1953); *Le Mystère de la Nativité*, Christmas oratorio for 9 Soloists, Mixed Chamber Chorus, Men's Chorus, Mixed Chorus, and Orch. (1957, 1959; Geneva, Dec. 23, 1959); *Pseaumes de Genève*, cantata for Chorus, Boy's Chorus, Organ, and Orch. (1958; Geneva, May 1959); *Drey Minnelieder*, song cycle for Soprano and Piano (1960); *Ode à la musique* for Chorus, Brass, Double Bass, and Piano (1961; Bienne, June 23, 1962); *Verse à boire* for Chorus (1961; Amsterdam, June 26, 1963); *Pilate*, oratorio breve for Baritone, Mezzo-soprano, Tenor, Bass, Chorus, and Orch. (RAI, Rome, Nov. 14, 1964); *Magnificat* for Soprano, Violin, and Orch. (1967; Lucerne, Aug. 14, 1968; incorporated into the *Maria-Triptychon*); *Maria-Triptychon* for Soprano, Violin, and Orch. (1968; Rotterdam, Nov. 13, 1969); *Ballade des pendus* for 3 Men's Voices and 3 Electric Guitars (1969; incorporated into the *Poèmes de la mort*); *Poèmes de la mort* for 3 Men's Voices and 3 Electric Guitars (1969, 1971; N.Y., Dec. 12, 1971); *Requiem* for 4 Soloists, Chorus, Organ, and Orch. (1971–72; Lausanne, May 4, 1973); *Et la vie l'emporta*, chamber cantata for Alto, Baritone, Small Chorus, and Instrumental Ensemble (1974; completed by B. Reichel; private premiere, Montreux, June 12, 1975; public premiere, Lucerne, Aug. 24, 1975); a few other short choruses and songs, as well as arrangements and harmonizations.

BIBL.: R. Klein, *F. M.: Sein Leben und Werk* (Vienna, 1960); A. Koelliker, *F. M.: Biographie, les oeuvres* (Lausanne, 1963); B. Billeter, *F. M.: Ein Aussenseiter der neuen Musik* (Frauenfeld, 1970); B. Martin, *F. M. ou la réalité du rêve* (Neuchâtel, 1973); special issue of *Schweizerische Musikzeitung*, CXVI (1976); W. Misteli, ed., *F. M.: Né le 15 septembre 1890, décédé le 21 novembre 1974: Liste des oeuvres: Werkverzeichnis* (Zürich, 1981); M. Martin, ed., *Apropos de...commentaires de F. M. sur ses oeuvres* (Neuchâtel, 1984); C. King, *F. M.: A Bio-Bibliography* (Westport, Conn., 1990); D. Kämper, ed., *F. M.: Das kompositorische Werk: 13 Studien* (Mainz, 1993); K. Schüssler, *F. M.s Musiktheater: Ein beitrag zur Geschichte der Oper im 20. Jahrhundert* (Kassel, 1996).—NS/LK/DM

Martin, Freddy, American bandleader and saxophonist; b. Cleveland, Ohio, Dec. 9, 1906; d. Newport Beach, Calif., Oct. 1, 1983. Among the most popular swing bandleaders of the 1940s, Freddy Martin specialized in adapting themes from the classics into popular tunes. His biggest hits were "Piano Concerto in B-Flat," "Symphony," "To Each His Own," and "Managua, Nicaragua."

Orphaned at age four, Martin was raised in an orphanage in Springfield, Ohio, until he was 16; there he learned to play the drums and the saxophone. He got a job demonstrating saxophones in a music store in Cleveland and played in a student group at Ohio State Univ. Turning professional, he played in several groups, including Eddy Hodges and His Band of Pirates, Jack Albin's band, the Mason-Dixon Orch., and the band of Arnold Johnson. When Johnson retired, Martin took over his band and opened at the Hotel Bossert in Brooklyn on Oct. 1, 1931. He signed to Columbia Records in 1932 and held his first recording session on Aug. 24. His first successful record, "In the Park in Paree" (music by Ralph Rainger, lyrics by Leo Robin), in May 1933, was credited to the Hotel Bossert Orch. Switching to Brunswick Records, he had his first hit under his own name, "Bless Your Heart" (music and lyrics by Duke Enston, Harry Stride, and Milton Drake), in September. His first big hit was "I Saw Stars" (music and lyrics by Maurice Sigler, Al Goodheart, and Al Hoffman), which became a best-seller in September 1934.

Martin moved from the Hotel Bossert to the Roosevelt Hotel in Manhattan and subsequently to other hotels in N.Y., Chicago, and San Francisco before establishing a long-term residency at the Cocoanut Grove in the Ambassador Hotel in Los Angeles in 1938. Meanwhile, he scored a series of modest hits through the late 1930s. But he didn't top the charts until he recorded a version of Tchaikovsky's "Piano Concerto [No. 1] in B-Flat" that he had arranged with Ray Austin. The instrumental recording went to #1 in October 1941 and sold a million copies, setting off a trend of adapting the classics. Martin also recorded a vocal version of the tune with lyrics by Bobby Worth, titled "Tonight We Love," and it peaked in the Top Ten in January 1942.

Martin made a series of successful recordings during the rest of the 1940s. His 1942 version of "White Christmas" (music and lyrics by Irving Berlin) was a million-seller; the album *Tchaikowsky Nutcracker Suite* was a Top Ten hit during the holiday season of 1945; "Symphony" (music by Alex Alstone, English lyrics by Jack Lawrence) reached #1 at the start of 1946; "To Each His Own" (music and lyrics by Jay Livingston and Ray

Evans) topped the charts in August 1946; "Managua, Nicaragua" (music by Irving Fields, lyrics by Albert Gamse) was #1 in February 1947; and the album *Concerto* hit the charts in March 1947 and reached the Top Ten. Meanwhile, Martin and his band made special appearances in several films: *Mayor of 44th Street* (June 1942); *Seven Days' Leave* (December 1942); *Hit Parade of 1943* (April 1943); *Stage Door Canteen* (June 1943); and *What's Buzzin' Cousin?* (July 1943).

Merv Griffin, later a successful talk show host and casino owner, was Martin's vocalist from 1948 to 1952. In May 1948, Martin's voice was used in the Disney animated film *Melody Time*. *The Freddy Martin Show*, a musical variety series, premiered on NBC-TV on July 12, 1951, and ran weekly through Nov. 28. Martin scored his last chart record with "April in Portugal (The Whisp'ring Serenade)" (music by Raul Ferrao, English lyrics by Jimmy Kennedy) in May 1953. But unlike other bandleaders, he was able to maintain his organization long after the decline of the Swing era. He backed Elvis Presley at an engagement in Las Vegas in 1956 and appeared beside early rock 'n' roll figures in the films *The Big Beat* (June 1958) and *Senior Prom* (January 1959). Though he cut back on touring by the 1970s, he continued to work until shortly before his death at age 76 after a series of strokes.—WR

Martin, Hugh, and Ralph Blane (Uriah Hunsecker),
American songwriting team. Martin (b. Birmingham, Ala., Aug. 11, 1914) and Blane (b. Broken Arrow, Okla., July 26, 1914; d. there, Nov. 13, 1995), who both wrote music and lyrics, worked together on stage and movie musicals for 48 years, beginning with the Broadway hit *Best Foot Forward* in 1941 and ending with the Broadway adaptation of their best-known film, the 1944 hit *Meet Me in St. Louis*, in 1989, a score that contained the standard "Have Yourself a Merry Little Christmas" and the Academy Award nominee "The Trolley Song."

Martin began studying piano with Edna Gussen at the Birmingham Cons. at age 5; later he studied with Dorsey Whittington. After attending Birmingham Southern Coll., he went to N.Y. to pursue a career as a musician. Blane attended Northwestern Univ., then went to N.Y. to become a singer, studying with Estelle Liebling. He made his Broadway debut in the revue *New Faces of 1936* (N.Y., May 19, 1936).

Martin and Blane first worked together in the cast of the Broadway musical *Hooray for What!* (N.Y., Dec. 1, 1937) as part of vocal arranger Kay Thompson's singing group the Rhythm Boys. When Thompson left the show, they stepped in to finish the vocal arrangements and soon were doing the same work on other shows, together and separately. Martin was the vocal arranger for *The Boys from Syracuse* (N.Y., Nov. 23, 1938); Martin and Blane were the vocal arrangers for *Stars in Your Eyes* (N.Y., Feb. 9, 1939); and Martin was the vocal arranger for *The Streets of Paris* (N.Y., June 19, 1939) and appeared in the revue, along with comedians Bud Abbott and Lou Costello.

Martin organized a group, the Martins, with Blane as one of the singers. They performed on a bill with Judy Garland and Mickey Rooney at the Capitol Theatre in N.Y. on Aug. 17, 1939, in connection with the opening of the Garland film *The Wizard of Oz*. But their main activity continued to be vocal arranging for musicals: Martin worked on *Too Many Girls* (N.Y., Oct. 18, 1939), and Martin and Blane did *Very Warm for May* (N.Y., Nov. 17, 1939), *DuBarry Was a Lady* (N.Y., Dec. 6, 1939), and *Louisiana Purchase* (N.Y., May 28, 1940). They also appeared in *Louisiana Purchase* as part of the Martins, by now a vocal quartet completed by the sisters Jo Jean and Phyllis Rogers. Over the next two years the Martins also performed on network radio and recorded for Columbia Records.

Martin was the vocal arranger for *Walk with Music* (N.Y., June 4, 1940), and Martin and Blane were the musical arrangers for *Cabin in the Sky* (N.Y., Oct. 25, 1940). In the fall of 1941 producer/director George Abbott, who had worked on several musicals with them, gave them the chance to write the songs for the musical *Best Foot Forward*, a romantic comedy set at a boys' prep school. The songwriters took an unusual approach to their collaboration: they wrote songs separately, then polished them together. The show ran 326 performances; when MGM bought it to make a film adaptation, Martin and Blane were signed to the studio, and they moved to Calif. They wrote three new songs used in the movie version of *Best Foot Forward*, which was released in June 1943, then collaborated with Roger Edens on "The Joint Is Really Jumpin'," sung by Judy Garland in *Thousands Cheer*, released in September.

Martin and Blane next worked on MGM's adaptation of *Very Warm for May*, which was released in April 1944 under the title *Broadway Rhythm* with their newly written "Brazilian Boogie" and "What Do You Think I Am?" from *Best Foot Forward*. They then wrote three songs, along with their arrangement of the traditional "Skip to My Lou," for the Judy Garland film *Meet Me in St. Louis*, released in November. Among their contributions, "The Trolley Song" was recorded by many artists, becoming a Top Ten hit for the Pied Pipers, for Garland, and for Vaughn Monroe, it earned an Academy Award nomination for Best Song, while "Have Yourself a Merry Little Christmas" became a seasonal standard. The film ranked second only to *Going My Way* as the biggest box office hit of the year.

Martin and Blane wrote songs in 1945 for a movie version of *Huckleberry Finn* that was never produced, and for *Abbott and Costello in Hollywood*, released in November. They also worked on *Ziegfeld Follies*, not released until March 1946. But their partnership was interrupted when Martin entered the service and was sent to Europe. Blane remained at MGM, where he did vocal arrangements and wrote songs with various collaborators for such films as the box office hit *Thrill of a Romance* (May 1945), *The Harvey Girls* (January 1946), the box office hit *Easy to Wed* (July 1946), *No Leave, No Love* (October 1946), and *Two Smart People* (December 1946).

When Martin returned from Europe, he did not go to Calif. to work with Blane. Instead he went to N.Y. to work in the musical theater. He was the vocal arranger for the Broadway musicals *Barefoot Boy with Cheek* (N.Y., April 3, 1947) and *High Button Shoes* (N.Y., Oct. 9, 1947).

Blane, meanwhile, wrote lyrics to Harry Warren's melodies for an unproduced version of the film *Take Me Out to the Ball Game*. The most successful song of 1947 for either Martin or Blane was the product of their partnership on "Pass That Peace Pipe," which they wrote with Roger Edens for *Huckleberry Finn* and which had been considered for *Ziegfeld Follies*; it was finally used in the film *Good News*, released in December. Margaret Whiting recorded it for a Top Ten hit, and the song earned an Academy Award nomination.

Martin wrote the songs and did the vocal arrangements for the Broadway musical *Look Ma, I'm Dancin'* (N.Y., Jan. 29, 1948), which ran 188 performances. He was also the vocal arranger for the musicals *Heaven on Earth* (N.Y., Sept. 16, 1948) and *As the Girls Go* (N.Y., Nov. 13, 1948). Blane, meanwhile, wrote lyrics to Harry Warren's music for the film *Summer Holiday* (June 1948), including "The Stanley Steamer," which Jo Stafford recorded for a chart entry; he also wrote both music and lyrics for the songs in *One Sunday Afternoon* (December 1948), which marked his move from MGM to Warner Bros. In 1949, Blane wrote songs for the Warner Bros. films *South of St. Louis*, released in March, and *My Dream Is Yours*, released in April. Martin was the vocal arranger for the musical *Gentlmemen Prefer Blondes* (N.Y., Dec. 8, 1949).

In 1950, Blane collaborated with Harold Arlen on the lyrics for Arlen's melodies to the songs for 20th Century–Fox's *My Blue Heaven*, released in September, while Martin returned to movie work, writing *Grandma Moses Suite (New England Suite)* for the film *Grandma Moses*, released in October, and doing the vocal arrangements for *The West Point Story*, released in December. In 1951, Martin wrote the songs and did the vocal arrangements for the Broadway musical *Make a Wish!* (N.Y., April 18, 1951), which ran 102 performances, and was the vocal arranger for the musical *Top Banana* (N.Y., Nov. 1, 1951). Blane wrote the lyrics to "My Castle in the Sand" (music by Alfred Newman) for the 20th Century–Fox film *Half Angel*, released in June 1951. He then wrote the songs for the Broadway musical *Three Wishes for Jamie* (N.Y., March 21, 1952), which ran 91 performances, and set lyrics to Harry Warren's music for the film *Skirts Ahoy!*, released by MGM in May 1952.

Martin wrote the music and collaborated with Timothy Gray on the lyrics for the musical *Love from Judy* (London, Sept. 25, 1952), which ran 594 performances. Martin was the vocal arranger in 1953 for the Broadway musical *Hazel Flagg* (N.Y., Feb. 11, 1953), while Blane again collaborated on lyrics with Harold Arlen to Arlen's tunes for the 20th Century–Fox film *Down Among the Sheltering Palms*, released in June. He and Robert Wells then cowrote the lyrics to Josef Myrow's music for RKO's *The French Line*, released in May 1954.

After nearly a decade apart, Martin and Blane reunited at MGM to write the songs for *Athena*, released in December 1954, followed by *The Girl Rush*, which Paramount issued in August 1955 and which featured "An Occasional Man," recorded for a chart entry by Jeri Southern. The duo returned to performing, recording the album *Martin & Blane Sing Martin & Blane*, released by Harlequin Records in 1956. Their final cinematic collaboration came with RKO's *The Girl Most Likely*, released in December 1957. Turning to television, Martin wrote "Breezy and Easy," the theme for *The Patrice Munsel Show*, which ran during the 1957–58 season, and the songs for the TV musical *Hans Brinker or the Silver Skates*, broadcast on NBC Feb. 9, 1958.

Martin and Blane mounted a stage version of *Meet Me in St. Louis* at the Municipal Opera in St. Louis, opening June 9, 1960. Their score featured nine new songs in addition to those they had contributed to the film. In 1961, Blane collaborated with Wade Barnes on the music, lyrics, and libretto for a television musical, *Quillow and the Giant*, produced for the BBC. He and Martin teamed up again to revise *Best Foot Forward* for an Off-Broadway revival in 1963. The show, which marked the theatrical debut of Judy Garland's daughter, Liza Minnelli, opened April 2 and ran 224 performances. Martin again collaborated with Timothy Gray on the songs, book, and vocal arrangements for *High Spirits* (N.Y., April 7, 1964), a musical version of Noël Coward's play *Blithe Spirit*. It ran 375 performances and the cast album spent more than four months in the charts.

Martin and Blane worked on a new musical, *Tattered Tom*, in 1968, but it was never produced. Timothy Gray mounted *They Don't Make 'Em Like That Anymore* (N.Y., June 6, 1972), an Off-Broadway revue of his work with Martin featuring new and old songs; it ran 24 performances. In their 70s, Martin and Blane came out of retirement to write new songs for a Broadway production of *Meet Me in St. Louis* that opened in 1989 and ran 253 performances. Martin accompanied Michael Feinstein on the album *Michael Feinstein Sings the Hugh Martin Songbook*, released in September 1995. Blane died of Parkinson's Disease at age 81 in November 1995.

WORKS (only works for which Martin and Blane are credited together as primary songwriters are listed): **MUSICALS/REVUES** (dates refer to N.Y. openings): *Best Foot Forward* (Oct. 1, 1941); *Meet Me in St. Louis* (Nov. 2, 1989). **FILMS:** *Best Foot Forward* (1943); *Meet Me in St. Louis* (1944); *Abbott and Costello in Hollywood* (1945); *Athena* (1954); *The Girl Rush* (1955); *The Girl Most Likely* (1957).—**WR**

Martin, Janis, American mezzo-soprano, later soprano; b. Sacramento, Aug. 16, 1939. She studied in San Francisco and N.Y., making her operatic debut as Teresa in *La Sonnambula* at the San Francisco Opera in 1960; subsequently sang Marina, Venus, and Meg Page there. On March 25, 1962, she made her first appearance at the N.Y.C. Opera as Mrs. Grose in Britten's *The Turn of the Screw*. She won the Metropolitan Opera Auditions, making her debut as Flora in *La Traviata* on Dec. 19, 1962, in N.Y. After singing for 3 seasons as a mezzo-soprano, she returned to the Metropolitan Opera in 1973 as a soprano and sang such roles as Kundry, Sieglinde, and Berg's Marie in *Wozzeck*. In 1968 she appeared as Magdalene and as Fricka at the Bayreuth Festival. She sang Tosca at the Chicago Lyric Opera in 1971. From 1971 to 1988 she appeared at the Berlin Deutsche Oper. She made her Covent Garden debut in London as Marie in *Wozzeck* in 1973. In 1980 she sang the Woman in *Erwartung* at Milan's La Scala. She appeared as Isolde at the Geneva Opera in 1985. In 1990 she sang Beethoven's Leonore at the Deutsche Opera am Rhein in Düsseldorf. She portrayed Brünnhilde in *Götterdammerung* in Brussels in 1992. In 1996 she was engaged as Orfeo in Rome. Among her other roles are Ortrud, Brangäne, Senta, Elisabeth in *Tännhauser*, Ariadne, and Judith in *Duke Bluebeard's Castle*.—NS/LK/DM

Martin, Mary (Virginia), endearing American singer, actress, and dancer; b. Weatherford, Tex., Dec. 1, 1913; d. Rancho Mirage, Calif., Nov. 4, 1990. Martin ranked with Ethel Merman as one of the most successful musical comedy performers of the 1940s and 1950s. She starred in two long-running musicals with songs by Richard Rodgers and Oscar Hammerstein II, *South Pacific* and *The Sound of Music*, and appeared in a series of other theatrical works on Broadway, in the West End, and on tour from 1938 to 1987. She sang in a warm soprano and acted in an engaging manner that lent her characters a friendly wholesomeness, whether she was portraying the mischievous postulant in *The Sound of Music* or the kept woman who sang "My Heart Belongs to Daddy" in her first show, *Leave It to Me!* She also performed successfully in films, on radio, records, and television.

Martin's father, Preston Martin, was a lawyer. Her mother, Juanita Presley Martin, was a violin teacher, and Mary took violin lessons from age five. At age 12 she began studying voice with Helen Fouts Cahoon in Fort Worth. (She resumed studying with Cahoon in N.Y. in the late 1930s and studied with William Herman in the 1950s.) On Nov. 3, 1930, she married Benjamin Jackson Hagman, an accountant who later became a lawyer. Their son, Larry Hagman, became a successful actor on television. The couple divorced in 1937.

Martin opened a dancing school in Weatherford and began studying dance locally, then at the Fanchon and Marco School of Theatre in Hollywood. Determining to pursue a career as an entertainer, she moved to Hollywood, where she struggled for several years while studying voice with Dr. Stetson Humphrey. She sang on local radio and found minor film work, but her break did not come until she participated in a talent contest at the Trocadero nightclub where she was seen by theatrical producer Lawrence Schwab, who signed her to a contract and moved her to N.Y.

Martin was cast in the Cole Porter musical *Leave It to Me!* (N.Y., Nov. 9, 1938) and created a sensation singing the risqué song "My Heart Belongs to Daddy." She recorded the song for Brunswick Records but soon after signed to Decca. On Jan. 11, 1939, she began an eight-week engagement at the Rainbow Room nightclub while continuing to perform on Broadway.

Martin signed a contract with Paramount Pictures and returned to Hollywood, where she made three films, *The Great Victor Herbert* (released December 1939), *Rhythm on the River* (August 1940), and *Love Thy Neighbor* (December 1940). She appeared on the radio variety series *The Tuesday Night Party* from September to December 1939. Unhappy with making movies, she accepted a part in a stage musical, *Nice Goin'*, which opened a tryout in New Haven, Conn., Oct. 21, 1939, but

closed Nov. 4 in Boston without reaching Broadway. She returned to Hollywood and acted in the films *Kiss the Boys Goodbye* (August 1941), *New York Town* (November 1941), *Birth of the Blues* (December 1941), *Star Spangled Rhythm* (December 1942), *Happy Go Lucky* (March 1943), and *True to Life* (October 1943). She recorded her first album, *Mary Martin in an Album of Cole Porter Songs*, released by Decca in 1940.

On May 5, 1940, Martin married Paramount's West Coast story editor, Richard Halliday (real name, John Hope Hammond), who became her manager and co-produced some of the musicals in which she later appeared. They had a daughter, Mary Heller Halliday, who sometimes performed with her mother. Martin was a regular on the radio series *Good News of 1940* and on the *Kraft Music Hall*, starring Bing Crosby, during 1942.

Martin again left Hollywood to appear in the Broadway-bound musical *Dancing in the Streets*, which opened a tryout in Boston on March 23, 1943, and closed on April 10 without getting to N.Y. She finally achieved a starring role in a successful Broadway musical by playing the title character in Kurt Weill and Ogden Nash's *One Touch of Venus* (N.Y., Oct. 7, 1943). Martin stayed with the show for more than a year, then appeared in the national tour from February to June 1945. Meanwhile, she recorded "I'll Walk Alone" (music by Jule Styne, lyrics by Sammy Cahn), which peaked in the Top Ten in October 1944.

Martin returned to Hollywood briefly to make a featured appearance as herself in the Cole Porter film biography *Night and Day* (released July 1946), then took up her second starring role on Broadway in *Lute Song* (N.Y., Feb. 6, 1946). It ran 142 performances, after which Martin went to England to costar with Noël Coward in his show *Pacific 1860* (London, Dec. 19, 1946); it ran 129 performances. Returning to the U.S., Martin took the title role in the national tour of *Annie Get Your Gun*, which opened March 10, 1947, in Dallas and ran 11 months. She received her first Tony Award in 1948 for the performance.

Martin's third starring role on Broadway, in *South Pacific* (N.Y., April 7, 1949) brought her greatest triumph. She won the Tony Award for Outstanding Musical Actress and performed in the show for more than two years in N.Y., then, starting Nov. 1, 1951, in London. The original Broadway cast album, released by Columbia Records in May 1949, had the longest #1 run of any album in history and remained in the charts more than seven years, selling several million copies. Martin switched to Columbia as a recording artist and peaked in the Top Ten in April 1950 in a duet with Arthur Godfrey of the novelty song "Go to Sleep, Go to Sleep, Go to Sleep" (music by Fred Spielman, lyrics by Sammy Cahn). She also made a series of studio cast recreations of vintage Broadway musicals for the label, *The Band Wagon* (1951), *Anything Goes* (1951), *Girl Crazy* (1952), and *Babes in Arms* (1952).

Martin turned to television in 1951, appearing March 4 on the special *Richard Rodgers' Jubilee Show*, a tribute to the composer. On June 15, 1953, her joint appearance with Ethel Merman on *The Ford 50th Anniversary Show*, broadcast simultaneously on NBC and CBS, drew 60 million viewers, the largest television audience in history up to that time. In October 1953 she made her final film appearance, again as herself, in *Main Street to Broadway*. She returned to the N.Y. stage in a non-singing role in the comedy *Kind Sir* (N.Y., Nov. 4, 1953), which ran 166 performances, through March 27, 1954. On March 28, 1954, she emceed the TV special *The Rodgers and Hammerstein Cavalcade*, broadcast on all four networks to an audience of 70 million.

During the summer of 1954, Martin starred in the Los Angeles Civic Light Opera Company's production of a musical version of *Peter Pan*, containing songs with music by Mark "Moose" Charlap and lyrics by Carolyn Leigh. The show was revised, adding songs with music by Jule Styne and lyrics by Betty Comden and Adolph Green, for its Broadway opening on Oct. 24. On March 7, 1955, Martin and the cast performed the show live on television, again setting a record for the most-watched TV program. The broadcast curtailed ticket sales, and the show closed after 152 performances. But Martin won her third Tony Award as well as an Emmy Award for Best Actress—Single Performance. The original cast album, released by RCA Victor in March 1955, was a Top Ten hit.

Martin again took on a non-singing stage role when she appeared in a production of *The Skin of Our Teeth* in 1955. The play ran in Paris, Washington, D.C., and N.Y. before a live broadcast on television on Sept. 11. On Oct. 22, Martin was back on television, doing a special with Noël Coward, *Together with Music*. She moved to a ranch in Anápolis, Brazil, in 1955 and did not take on another long-term commitment to a stage musical for several years. On Jan. 9, 1956, she repeated her performance in *Peter Pan* live on television. She was back on television Oct. 28 starring in the straight play *Born Yesterday*. Signing to RCA Victor, she recorded the album *Mary Martin Sings, Richard Rodgers Plays* in April 1957. After appearing in *Annie Get Your Gun* and *South Pacific* in repertory in San Francisco and Los Angeles for 10 weeks starting in August, she did *Annie Get Your Gun* as a television special on Nov. 27, and the TV soundtrack album, released in December, spent several weeks in the charts.

Martin embarked on a three-month national concert tour during the winter of 1958–59. In each of the 87 cities in which she played, she performed a children's matinee, called *Magic with Mary Martin*, that featured songs with music by Linda Melnick Rogers and lyrics by Mary Rodgers, and an evening show, *Music with Mary Martin*, devoted to familiar songs from her musicals. On Easter Sunday, March 29, 1959, she performed both concerts live on television. She recorded the songs from the children's show, along with songs from the Rodgers and Hammerstein television musical *Cinderella*, for an RCA album, *Three to Make Music/Cinderella*, which was nominated for a Grammy Award for Best Recording for Children.

Martin returned to Broadway for the first time in more than four years in *The Sound of Music* (N.Y., Nov. 16, 1959), second only to *South Pacific* as her most successful venture. She was the major investor in the show, and she appeared in it for more than two years,

winning her fourth Tony Award for her performance. The original Broadway cast album became the most successful LP of 1960, topping the charts, selling more than two million copies, and winning the Grammy Award for Best Cast Album. On Dec. 8, 1960, Martin made her third live television appearance as *Peter Pan*, a performance that was taped and rebroadcast frequently thereafter.

Martin appeared in her sixth starring role in a Broadway musical with *Jennie* (N.Y., Oct. 17, 1963), containing songs with music by Arthur Schwartz and lyrics by Howard Dietz. Her least successful effort, the show ran only 82 performances, though the cast album charted for several weeks. She was nominated for a 1964 Grammy Award for Best Recording for Children for the album *A Spoonful of Sugar*. In April 1965 she embarked on a tour with *Hello, Dolly!*, performing in North America and the Far East and entertaining American troops in Vietnam before opening in London on Dec. 2. On April 3, 1966, she starred in the television special *Mary Martin at Eastertime with the Radio City Music Hall*.

Martin's final starring role in a Broadway musical came with the two- character show *I Do! I Do!* (N.Y., Dec. 5, 1966), featuring songs with music by Harvey Schmidt and lyrics by Tom Jones. The cast album spent four months in the charts. Martin toured with the show in 1968–69, then retired to Brazil. Her husband died on March 3, 1973, and she moved back to the U.S. in 1974. In 1977–78 she toured and briefly played on Broadway in the straight play *Do You Turn Somersaults?* She appeared in a television movie, *Valentine*, on Dec. 7, 1979. In 1981 she became the co-host of a daily public affairs program for senior citizens, *Over Easy*, on public television. She was injured in an automobile accident on Sept. 5, 1982, but returned to the show and acted as a guest star in television series in the mid- 1980s. In 1986–87 she toured the U.S. in the play *Legends*. In April 1989 it was announced that she would appear in a tour of *Grover's Corners*, a musical adaptation of *Our Town*, but she was diagnosed with cancer the following month. She died of the disease at age 76 in November 1990.

WRITINGS: *My Heart Belongs* (N.Y., 1976).

BIBL.: S. Newman, *M. M. on Stage* (Philadelphia, 1969); J. Kirkwood, *Diary of a Mad Playwright: How I Toured with M. M. and Carol Channing and Lived to Tell About It* (1989); B. Rivadue, *M. M.: A Bio- Bibliography* (Westport, Conn., 1991).—**WR**

Martin, (Nicolas-) Jean-Blaise, famous French baritone; b. Paris, Feb. 24, 1768; d. Ronzières, Rhone, Oct. 28, 1837. He made his debut at Paris's Théâtre de Monsieur in 1789 in *Le Marquis de Tulipano*. He sang at the Théâtre Feydeau and the Théâtre Favart from 1794 until they were united as the Opéra-Comique in 1801, remaining there until 1823; sang there again in 1826 and 1833. He was also a member of the Imperial (later Royal) Chapel from its founding until 1830. He was a prof. at the Paris Cons. (1816–18; 1832–37). He wrote an opéra-comique, *Les Oiseaux de mer* (Paris, 1796). His voice, while essentially baritone in quality, had the extraordinary range of 2 1/2 octaves, E flat to *a'*.—**NS/LK/DM**

Martin, Philip, Irish composer, pianist, and teacher; b. Dublin, Oct. 27, 1947. He went to London and studied composition (with Gardner and Reizenstein) and piano at the Royal Academy of Music, and then completed his training in composition with Berkeley, Maconchy, and Richard Rodney Bennett. He has appeared as a pianist primarily in England, but he has also appeared in the U.S., mostly notably in Pittsburgh and at Tanglewood, where he has given both recitals and master classes. He teaches composition and piano at the Birmingham Cons. in England. Martin is a member of Aosdána, the Irish state-sponsored academy of creative artists. His works favor classical formats, colorful harmonies, and concise rhythms.

WORKS: DRAMATIC: *Avebury,* sequence for radio for 2 Speakers, Children's Chorus, Orch., and Wind Effects (1991); *Thalassa,* children's/community workshop piece for Baritone, Mixed Chorus, Children's Chorus, and Instrumental Ensemble (1991–92). ORCH.: *Through Streets Broad and Narrow* for Trumpet, Piano, and Strings (1980); 2 piano concertos: No. 1 (1986) and No. 2, *A Day in the City* (Dublin, June 21, 1991); *Elegies and Dances 2* for Violin and Strings (1989); *Beato Angelico* (1990); Harp Concerto (1993; Dublin, Feb. 25, 1994). CHAMBER: Violin Sonata (1988); *Anna Livia Plurabelle: A River's Journey* for Oboe, Violin, Viola, and Cello (1990); 2 piano trios (*Serendipity,* 1993; *The Maids of Mitchelstown Fancy,* 1997); Suite for Cello (1996; rev. 1997); Sonata for 2 Violins (1997; rev. 1998); *Silver Strand* for Viola (1999). P i a n o : *Soundings* (1995); *Dialogue* for 2 Pianos (1997); *Marden Moods* (1998). VOCAL: 4 Poems for Tenor, Clarinet, Bassoon, Horn, Cello, Piano, and Percussion, after E.A. Robinson (1981); *In Dublin's Fair City* for Soloists, Chorus, and Orch. (1999–2000).—LK/DM

Martin, Riccardo (actually, **Hugh Whitfield**), American tenor, teacher, and composer; b. Hopkinsville, Ky., Nov. 18, 1874; d. N.Y., Aug. 11, 1952. He received training in composition from MacDowell at Columbia Univ. and in voice from Sbriglia in Paris (1901), Franklin Cannone in Milan, and Vincenzo Lombardi in Florence (1908). In Oct. 1904 he made his operatic debut as Gounod's Faust in Nantes under the name Richard Martin. In 1905 he appeared as Andrea Chénier in Verona under the name Riccardo Martin. After making his U.S. debut as Canio in New Orleans in 1906, he toured with the San Carlo Opera Co. (1906–07). On Nov. 20, 1907, he made his Metropolitan Opera debut in N.Y. as Boito's Faust, remaining on its roster until 1915. During his years with the Metropolitan Opera, he appeared in such roles as Pinkerton, Cavaradossi, Canio, Manrico, Rodolfo, and Turiddu; he also created the roles of Quintus in Horatio Parker's *Mona* (March 14, 1912) and Christian in Walter Damrosch's *Cyrano de Bergerac* (Feb. 27, 1913) while there. In 1910 he appeared as Pinkerton at London's Covent Garden. In 1910–11 and 1912–13 he made appearances with the Boston Grand Opera Co. In 1917–18 he was again on the roster of the Metropolitan Opera, and then sang with the Chicago Grand Opera Co. (1920–22). He also made appearances as a concert artist before settling in N.Y. as a voice teacher. Among his compositions were a ballet, orch. music, and songs. Martin possessed a beautiful spinto voice and dramatic stage gifts, but his career was overshadowed by his celebrated colleague Enrico Caruso.—NS/LK/DM

Martin, Sallie, black American gospel singer; b. Pittfield, Ga., Nov. 20, 1896; d. Chicago, June 18, 1988. She became a member of Thomas A. Dorsey's Ebenezer Baptist Church gospel choir in Chicago (1932), then helped him to found the National Convention of Gospel Choirs and Choruses that same year, remaining active with it until 1940. She subsequently toured extensively in the U.S. and Europe with her own Sallie Martin Singers. With Kenneth Morris, she also was co-founder and co-director of the Martin and Morris Music Co. in Chicago (1940–75).—NS/LK/DM

Martinelli, Caterina, Italian singer; b. Rome, 1589 or 1590; d. Mantua (buried), March 7, 1608. She entered the service of the Gonzaga family in Mantua in 1603, where her talent was appreciated by Monteverdi. After appearing as a singer there in 1608, Monteverdi was prompted to compose the title role of his opera *L'Arianna* for Martinelli. However, she was stricken with smallpox and died before the work could be mounted. Monteverdi was then moved to write his madrigal cycle *Lagrime d'amante al sepolcro dell'amata* in her memory (publ. in his 6th book of madrigals, 1614). —NS/LK/DM

Martinelli, Giovanni, famous Italian tenor; b. Montagnana, Oct. 22, 1885; d. N.Y., Feb. 2, 1969. He sang and played the clarinet in his youth. His potential as a singer was discovered by a bandmaster during Martinelli's military service. In 1908 he first appeared on the operatic stage in Montagnana as the Messenger in *Aida*. He then studied voice with Mandolini in Milan, where he made his concert debut as a soloist in Rossini's *Stabat Mater* on Dec. 3, 1910. His formal operatic debut followed there at the Teatro del Varme as Ernani on Dec. 29, 1910. Puccini was impressed with his vocal gifts and invited Martinelli to sing Dick Johnson in the European premiere of the composer's *La Fanciulla del West* in Rome on June 12, 1911. He subsequently sang that role in various Italian music centers, including Milan's La Scala in 1912. On April 22, 1912, he made his first appearance at London's Covent Garden as Cavaradossi, and sang there again in 1913–14, 1919, and 1937. Martinelli made his first appearance with the Metropolitan Opera in that same role during the company's visit to Albany, N.Y., on Nov. 18, 1913. His formal debut at the Metropolitan Opera in N.Y. followed as Rodolfo on Nov. 20, 1913, with remarkable success. He rapidly acquired distinction there and, after Caruso's death in 1921, became one of the principal tenors on the Metropolitan Opera roster. He sang there every season until 1943, winning acclaim for his portrayals of such roles as Otello, Radames, Manrico, Eléazar in *La Juive,* Don José, Canio, Faust, Samson, and Andrea Chénier. He also appeared in Boston (1914), San Francisco (1923–39), Chicago (1924–31; 1933–44), St. Louis (1934–41), and Cincinnati (1940–45). In 1944 he returned to the Metropolitan

Opera, where he made his farewell appearance as Pollione on March 8, 1945. During the 1945–46 season, he returned to the Metropolitan Opera as a concert artist. After singing in Philadelphia (1945–50), he taught voice in N.Y. while making occasional appearances as a singer. The Metropolitan Opera honored him on the 50th anniversary of his debut with the company with a gala on Nov. 20, 1963. He made his last public appearance as a singer in his 82nd year when he sang the Emperor in *Turandot* in Seattle. Martinelli's brilliant vocal and dramatic gifts made him one of the foremost singers of heroic roles of his era.—**NS/LK/DM**

Martinet, Jean-Louis, French composer; b. Ste.-Bazeille, Nov. 8, 1912. He first studied piano and harmony at the Bordeaux Cons., and then pursued training at the Paris Cons., where his mentors included Plé-Caussade (fugue), Roger-Ducasse and Messiaen (composition), and Munch, Desormière, and Fourestier (conducting), and where he took the premier prix in composition (1943). In 1952 his *Variations* for String Quartet received the Grand Prix Musical de la Ville de Paris. From 1970 to 1976 he taught at the Montreal Cons., and then returned to France.

WORKS: DRAMATIC: *La Trilogie des Prométhées*, mimodrama (1947). ORCH.: *Orphée*, symphonic poem (1944–45); *Prométhée*, symphonic fragments (1947); *Deux Images* (1953–54); *Divertissement Pastoral* for Piano and Orch. (1955); 3 symphonic movements: No. 1 for Strings (1957), No. 2, *Luttes* (1958–59), and No. 3, *Patrie* (1976–77); Sym., *In Memoriam* (1962–63); *Le Triomphe de la Mort*, dramatic sym. (1967–73); *Tristesse, Ôma Patrie* for Viola or Cello and Orch. (1976). CHAMBER: *Variations* for String Quartet (1946); Piece for Clarinet and Piano (1954); *Étude de Concert* for Harp (1984). KEYBOARD: P i -a n o : *Prélude et Fugue* for 2 Pianos (1942; rev. 1965). O r g a n : *Passacaille* (1984). VOCAL: 6 Songs for Chorus and Orch., after René Char (1948; rev. 1967); *Episodes*, cantata for Bass, Chorus, and Orch. (1949–50); *Sept poèmes de René Char* for Vocal Quartet and Orch. (1951–52); *3 Chants de France* for Chorus (1955, 1956, 1979); *Elsa*, cantata for Chorus, after Louis Aragon (1959); *Les Amours*, cantata for Chorus, after Ronsard (1959–60); *Les Douze* for Reciter, Chorus, and Orch. (1961); *Sur le Fleuve Tchou*, cantata for Soprano, Baritone, and Chamber Ensemble (1981–82).—**NS/LK/DM**

Martinez, José Daniel, Puerto Rican composer and pianist; b. San Juan, Sept. 8, 1956. He studied with Luis Antonio Ramírez and Luz N. Hutchinson at the Cons. of Music in Puerto Rico (certificate of diploma, 1975) and at the Eastman School of Music in Rochester, N.Y. (B.A. in composition, 1977; M.A. in piano, 1980). He taught piano and theory at the Hochstein School of Music in Rochester (1977–80) and at the Cons. of Music in Puerto Rico (1981–82); in 1982–83 he worked as an accompanist in N.Y. In 1985 he made a recording of Puerto Rican "Danzas" for the Círculo de Recreo de San Germán, where he subsequently taught at the Interamerican Univ. of Puerto Rico.

WORKS: *Dos preludios* for Piano (1971); *Fantasía* for Violin and Piano (1973); *Tema y variaciones* for Piano (1974); *Tiempo sinfónico* for Chamber Orch. (1976); *Impromptu* for Chamber

Ensemble (1983); *Música para la Interamericana* for Organ and Baroque Orch. (1984); *Concierto para aulos...Reflexiones sobre el retorno de un cometa* for Flute, Piccolo, Oboe, Horn, and Piano (1986); Cello Sonata (1987).—**NS/LK/DM**

Martínez, Marianne (actually, **Anna Katharina**) **von,** Austrian singer, pianist, and composer; b. Vienna, May 4, 1744; d. there, Dec. 13, 1812. She was the daughter of Nicoló Martínez, who went to Vienna as "gentiluomo" to the papal nuncio. Thanks to his privileged social position in the diplomatic circles in Vienna, her father was able to engage the best instructors for her; Metastasio was put in charge of her education, and he saw that she received lessons in singing, piano, and composition from Porpora and Haydn; she also studied counterpoint with G. Bonno. She appeared as a singer and pianist at the court while still a child, and later performed in aristocratic salons. She composed several oratorios and cantatas, a Sym., 2 piano concertos, and a group of minor instrumental pieces. None of these was in any way remarkable, but her works are of historical interest as examples of musical composition by a woman of high society who contributed to the artistic life of the Austrian capital during its greatest ascendance on the international scene. Manuscripts of some of her works are preserved in the archives of the Gesellschaft der Musikfreunde in Vienna.—**NS/LK/DM**

Martínez, Miguel Angel Gomez
See **Gomez Martínez, Miguel Angel**

Martinez, Odaline de la, Cuban-born American conductor, pianist, and composer; b. Matanzas, Oct. 31, 1949. She emigrated to the U.S. in 1961 and in 1971 became a naturalized American citizen. Following training at Tulane Univ. (B.F.A., 1972), she settled in London and studied composition with Paul Patterson at the Royal Academy of Music (1972–76) and with Reginald Smith Brindle at the Univ. of Surrey (M.M., 1977); subsequently she pursued postgraduate studies in computer music (1977–80). In 1976 she helped organize and was conductor of the chamber ensemble Lontano, with which she toured extensively. In 1981 she also organized the Contemporary Chamber Orch., for which she served as principal conductor. Among her various awards were a Guggenheim followship (1980–81) and the Villa-Lobos Medal (1987). Martinez has embraced an inclusive course as a composer in which she utilizes various styles and techniques.

WORKS: DRAMATIC: O p e r a : *Sister Aimee*, on the life of the American evangelist Aimee Semple McPherson (1978–83). ORCH.: *Phasing* for Chamber Orch. (1975). CHAMBER: *Little Piece* for Flute (1975); *A Moment's Madness* for Flute and Piano (1977); *Improvisations* for Violin (1977); *Litanies* for Flutes, Harp, and String Trio (1981); *Asonancias* for Violin (1982); Suite for English Horn and Cello (1982); String Quartet (1984–85). KEYBOARD: P i a n o : *Colour Studies* (1978). O r g a n : *Eos* (1976). VOCAL: *5 Imagist Songs* for Soprano, Clarinet, and Piano (1974); *After Sylvia* for Soprano and Piano (1976); *Absalom* for Countertenor, 2 Tenors, Baritone, and Bass (1977); *Psalmos* for Chorus, Brass Quintet, Timpani, and Organ (1977); *2 American Madrigals* for Chorus (1979); *Canciones* for Soprano, Percussion, and Piano (1983); *Cantos de amor* for Soprano, Piano, and String Trio (1985). **OTHER:** *Hallucination* for Tape (1975); *Visions and Dreams* for Tape (1977–78); *Lamento* for Amplified Soprano, Alto, Tenor, Bass, and Tape (1978); *3 Studies* for Percussion and Electronics (1980). **—NS/LK/DM**

Martini, Giovanni Battista, famous Italian pedagogue, writer on music, and composer, known as **Padre Martini;** b. Bologna, April 24, 1706; d. there, Aug. 3, 1784. He received the rudiments of musical knowledge from his father, a violinist, then took courses with Angelo Predieri, Giovanni Antonio Ricieri, and Francesco Antonio Pistocchi. A man of unquenchable intellectual curiosity, he studied mathematics with Zanotti, and took a seminar in ecclesiastical music with Giacomo Perti. In 1721 he entered the Franciscan conventual monastery in Lugo di Romagna, but abandoned monastic aspirations and returned to Bologna in 1722, where he became organist, and later maestro di cappella, at S. Francesco in 1725, and was ordained a priest in 1729. He was a prolific composer and a learned scholar; his *Storia della musica* (3 vols., Bologna, 1757, 1770, and 1781; reprinted 1967) gives an extensive survey of music in ancient Greece. But it is as a pedagogue that Padre Martini achieved lasting fame. His magnum opus in music theory was *Esemplare ossia Saggio fondamentale practico di contrappunto* (2 vols., Bologna, 1774 and 1775). J.C. Bach, Jommelli, Gretry, and Mozart were his students. A by-product of his various activities was the accumulation of a magnificent library, which Burney estimated at nearly 17,000 vols. After Martini's death, it became the foundation of the collection in the library of the Liceo Musicale (later the Civico Museo Bibliografico Musicale). He received many honors during his long life; in 1758 he became a member of the Accademia dell' Istituto delle Scienze di Bologna and of the Accademia dei Filarmonici di Bologna. In 1776 he was elected to membership in the Arcadi di Roma, where his Arcadian title was "Aristosseno Anfioneo" ("Aristoxenos Amphion"). He conducted a voluminous correspondence of about 6,000 letters, which are extant. It included communications with scholars, kings, and popes.

WORKS: *L'assunzione di Salomone al tronto d'Israello,* oratorio (1734); masses, introits, graduals, offertories, vespers, hymns; *Litaniae atque antiphonae finales B. Virginis Mariae* for 4 Voices, Organ, and Instruments, publ. in Bologna in 1734; secular vocal works, including 24 sinfonias, numerous concertos for various instruments, and about 100 keyboard sonatas.

WRITINGS: *Regola agli organisti per accompagnare il canto fermo* (Bologna, 1756); *Compendio della teoria de' numeri per uso del musico* (Bologna, 1769). **CORRESPONDENCE:** A selection of his letters was ed. by F. Parisini as *Carteggio inedito del G. Martini, coi piu celebri musicisti del suo tempo* (Bologna, 1888). A. Schnoebelen ed. *Padre Martini's Collection of Letters in the Civico Museo Bibliografico Musicale in Bologna: An Annotated Index* (N.Y., 1979).

BIBL.: A. Eximeno, *Dubbio sopra il saggio fondamentale pratico di contrappunto del P. G.B. M.* (Rome, 1775); G. Della Valle, *Memorie storiche del p. m. Giambattista M.* (Naples, 1785); G. Gandolfi, *Elogio di G.B. M.* (Bologna, 1813); F. Parisini, *Della vita*

e delle opere del P. G.B. M. (Bologna, 1887); L. Busi, *Il P. G.B. M.* (Bologna, 1891); W. Reich, *P. M. als Theoretiker und Lehrer* (diss., Univ. of Vienna, 1934); P. Pauchard, *Ein italienischer Musiktheoretiker: Pater Giambattista M.* (Lugano, 1941); P. Zaccaria, *P. M. compositore* (diss., Pontificio Istituto di Musica Sacra, Rome, 1959); H. Brofsky, *The Instrumental Music of P. M.* (diss., N.Y.U., 1963); P. Wiechens, *Die Kompositionstheorie und das kirchenmusikalische Schaffen P. M.s* (Regensburg, 1968); P. Zaccaria, *P. Giambattista M.: Compositore musicologo e maestro* (Padua, 1969). **—NS/LK/DM**

Martini, Jean Paul Egide (real name, **Johann Paul Agid Schwarzendorf**), German organist, teacher, and composer; b. Freystadt, Upper Palatinate (baptized), Aug. 31, 1741; d. Paris, Feb. 10, 1816. At the age of 10 he enrolled in the Jesuit Seminary in Neuburg an der Donau, becoming organist there. He began to tour as an organist in 1758. He went to Nancy in 1760, and was known as Martini il Tedesco. He was in the service of the former king of Poland, Prince Stanislaus Leszcynski, duke of Lorraine, in Luneville (1761–64), then went to Paris, where he won a prize for a military march for the Swiss Guard. This introduced him into army circles in France. He enlisted as an officer of a Hussar regiment, and wrote more band music. He also composed an opera, *L'Amoureux de quinze ans, ou Le Double Fête,* which was produced with extraordinary success at the Italian Opera in Paris (April 18, 1771). Leaving the army, he became music director to the Prince of Conde, and later to the Comte d'Artois. He purchased the reversion of the office of 1st Intendant of the King's Music, a speculation brought to naught by the Revolution, which caused him to resign in haste his position as conductor at the Théâtre Feydeau, and flee to Lyons in 1792. He then returned to Paris, winning acclaim with the production of his opera *Sappho* (1794). He became Inspector at the Paris Cons. in 1798, and also taught composition there (1800–02). In appreciation of his royalist record, he was given the post of Royal Intendant at the Restoration in 1814, serving as chief director of the Royal Court Orch. until his death. He wrote 13 operas, a Requiem for Louis XVI, Psalms, and other church music, but he is chiefly remembered as the composer of the popular air *Plaisir d'amour,* which was arranged by Berlioz for Voice and Orch.**—NS/LK/DM**

Martini, Johannes, Flemish composer; b. Brabant, c. 1440; d. Ferrara, 1497 or 1498. He entered the service of the Ferrara ducal chapel in 1473. After singing in the Milan ducal chapel (1474), he resumed his association with the Ferrara ducal chapel, where he was held in great esteem. He was an accomplished composer of both sacred and secular works, which included some 10 masses, about 65 Psalms, 8 hymns, and a number of chansons. See B. Disertori, ed., *J. M.: Magnificat e messe,* Archivium musices metro-palitanum mediolanense, XII (1964) and E. Evans, ed., *J. M.: The Secular Works* (Madison, Wisc., 1975 et seq.).

BIBL.: J. Brawley, *The Magnificats, Hymns, Motets, and Secular Compositions of J. M.* (diss., Yale Univ., 1968).**—LK/DM**

Martino, Al(fred Cini), American singer; b. Philadelphia, Pa., Oct. 7, 1927. A ballad singer whose style revealed his second-generation Italian roots, Martino had a brief period of success in the early 1950s with "Here in My Heart," then came back in the early 1960s for a lengthier stay in the charts that included a series of hit singles and albums including "I Love You Because," "I Love You More and More Every Day," and "Spanish Eyes."

Martino worked as a bricklayer in a construction company run by his Italian immigrant father before heeding the advice of his friend Mario Lanza to take up singing. He performed in local nightclubs and won on the amateur-contest TV show *Arthur Godfrey's Talent Scouts* in 1952, then cut "Here in My Heart" (music and lyrics by Pat Genaro, Lou Levinson, and Bill Borrelli) for the small BBS label. It hit #1 in June 1952 and he was signed to Capitol Records, for whom he recorded the chart entry "Take My Heart." Further U.S. releases were unsuccessful, but in the U.K., where "Here in My Heart" had also topped the charts and "Take My Heart" had reached the Top Ten, he had Top Ten hits with "Now" (1953), "Rachel" (1953), and "Wanted" (music and lyrics by Jack Fulton and Lois Steele; 1954).

Martino persevered, and he returned to the U.S. charts in 1959 with "I Can't Get You Out of My Heart" (music and lyrics by Danny Di Minno and Jimmy Grane) on 20th Century–Fox Records. Capitol re-signed him, and he first reached the LP charts in 1962 with *The Exciting Voice of Al Martino*. His revival of the 1950 song "I Love You Because" (music and lyrics by Leon Payne) hit the Top Ten and topped the easy-listening charts in May 1963, and an *I Love You Because* album made the Top Ten of the LP charts. This launched a successful series of recordings that lasted well into the 1970s. Notably, "I Love You More and More Every Day" (music and lyrics by Don Robertson) peaked in the Top Ten in March 1964; "Spanish Eyes" (music by Bert Kaempfert, lyrics by Charles Singleton and Eddie Snyder) peaked in the Top 40 and topped the easy-listening charts in January 1966, followed by a gold-selling, Top Ten *Spanish Eyes* LP; "Mary in the Morning" (music and lyrics by Johnny Cymbal and Mike Lendell) peaked in the Top 40 and was a #1 easy-listening hit in July 1967; and "More Than the Eye Can See" (music and lyrics by Bob Crewe and Larry Weiss) reached the pop charts and topped the easy-listening charts in the fall of 1967.

Martino played the pivotal role of singer Johnny Fontane in the 1972 film *The Godfather*. He continued to perform into the 1990s.

DISC.: *Sing Along with Al Martino* (1959); *The Exciting Voice of Al Martino* (1962); *I Love You Because* (1963); *Love Notes* (1963); *Painted, Tainted Rose* (1963); *Merry Christmas* (1964); *I Love You More and More Every Day* (1964); *Living a Lie* (1964); *My Cherie* (1965); *Somebody Else Is Taking My Place* (1965); *We Could* (1965); *Spanish Eyes* (1966); *This Is Love* (1966); *Daddy's Little Girl* (1967); *Mary in the Morning* (1967); *This Love for You* (1967); *Love Is Blue* (1968); *This Is Al Martino* (1968); *Sausalito* (1969); *Jean* (1969); *Can't Help Falling in Love* (1970); *My Heart Sings* (1970); *Love Theme from The Godfather* (1972); *To the Door of the Sun* (1975); *Al Martino Sings* (1975).—**WR**

Martino, Donald (James), American composer, clarinetist, and teacher; b. Plainfield, N.J., May 16, 1931.

He learned to play the clarinet, oboe, and saxophone in his youth, and then studied composition with Bacon at Syracuse Univ. (B.M., 1952), Babbitt and Sessions at Princeton Univ. (M.F.A., 1954), and Dallapiccola in Florence on a Fulbright scholarship (1954–56). In 1958–59 he was an instructor at Princeton Univ., and from 1959 to 1969 he taught theory and composition at Yale Univ. He then was a prof. of composition at the New England Cons. of Music in Boston (1970–80), where he served as chairman of the composition dept. He was Irving Fine Prof. of Music at Brandeis Univ. (1980–83). In 1983 he became a prof. of music at Harvard Univ., serving as Walter Bigelow Rosen Prof. of Music from 1989 until his retirement in 1993. He held 3 Guggenheim fellowships (1967, 1973, 1982). Martino was awarded the Pulitzer Prize in Music in 1974 for his chamber piece *Notturno*. In 1983 his 4th string quartet won 1st prize in the Kennedy Center Friedheim awards and in 1986 he received the Boston Sym. Orch.'s Mark M. Horblit Award. In 1981 he was made a member of the American Academy and Inst. of Arts and Letters, and in 1987 a fellow of the American Academy of Arts and Sciences.

WORKS: ORCH.: *Contemplations* (1956; Lenox, Mass., Aug. 13, 1964; originally entitled *Composition*); Piano Concerto (1965; New Haven, March 1, 1966); *Mosaic for Grand Orchestra* (Chicago, May 26, 1967); Cello Concerto (1972; Cincinnati, Oct. 16, 1973); *Ritorno* (1975; Plainfield, N.J., Dec. 12, 1976); Triple Concerto for Clarinet, Bass Clarinet, Contrabass Clarinet, and Chamber Orch. (1977; N.Y., Dec. 18, 1978); *Divertissements* for Youth Orch. (1981); Concerto for Alto Saxophone and Chamber Orch. (1987); Violin Concerto (1995). **CHAMBER:** 4 string quartets (n.d., withdrawn; 1952; 1954; 1983); Clarinet Sonata (1950–51); *A Suite of Variations on Medieval Melodies* for Cello (1952; rev. 1954); *A Set* for Clarinet (1954; rev. 1974); *Quodlibets* for Flute (1954); *Sette canoni enigmatici*, puzzle canons with various solutions for 2 Violas and 2 Cellos or 2 Bassoons, or for String Quartet, or for 4 Clarinets (1955–56); Quartet for Clarinet and String Trio (1957); 6 contrapuntal jazz pieces for Diverse Ensembles (all 1957); Trio for Clarinet, Violin, and Piano (1959); *Cinque frammenti* for Oboe and Double Bass (1961); *Fantasy-Variations* for Violin (1962); Concerto for Wind Quintet (1964); *Parisonatina al'dodecafonia* for Cello (1964); *B,A,B,B,IT,T* for Clarinet with Extensions (1966); *Strata* for Bass Clarinet (1966); *Notturno* for 6 Players (1973); *Quodlibets II* for Flute (1980); *Canzone e Tarantella sul nome Petrassi* for Clarinet and Cello (1984); *From the Other Side*, divertimento for Flute, Cello, Percussion, and Piano (1988); *15, 5, 92, A. B.: A Musical Birthday Card for Arthur Berger* for Clarinet (1992); *3 Sad Songs* for Viola and Piano (1993); *Serenata Concertante*, octet (1999); *Piccolo Studies* for Alto Saxophone (1999). **Piano:** *With Little Children in Mind* (1951); *Fantasy* (1958); *Pianississimo*, sonata (1970); *Impromptu for Roger* [Sessions] (1977); *Fantasies and Impromptus* (1978); *Suite in Old Form: Parody Suite* (1982); *12 Préludes* (1991). **VOCAL:** *Portraits: A Secular Cantata* for Mezzo-soprano, Bass, Chorus, and Orch., after Walt Whitman, Edna St. Vincent Millay, and e.e. cummings (1954); *7 Pious Pieces* for Chorus and Optional Piano or Organ, after Robert Herrick (1972); *Augenmusik: A Mixed Mediacritique* for "actress, danseuse or uninhibited female percussionist and electronic tape" (1972); *Paradiso Choruses*, oratorio for 12 Soloists, Chorus, Children's Chorus ad libitum, Tape, and Orch., after Dante's *Divine Comedy* (1974; Boston, May 7, 1975); *The White Island* for Chorus and Chamber Orch., after Robert Herrick (1985; Boston, April 8, 1987); songs. —NS/LK/DM

Martinon, Jean, significant French conductor and composer; b. Lyons, Jan. 10, 1910; d. Paris, March 1, 1976. He studied violin at the Lyons Cons. (1924–25) and at the Paris Cons. (1926–29), winning the premier prix; then took lessons in composition with Roussel and d'Indy and in conducting with Munch and Desormière; obtained his M.A. degree in arts from the Sorbonne (1932). He was in the French army during World War II; was taken prisoner in 1940 and spent 2 years in a German prison camp (Stalag IX); during imprisonment, he wrote several works of a religious nature, among them *Psalm 136, Musique d'exil ou Stalag IX,* and *Absolve Domine,* in memory of French musicians killed in the war. After his release, he appeared as a conductor with the Pasdeloup Orch. in Paris (1943); then was conductor of the Bordeaux Sym. Orch. (1943–45), asst. conductor of the Paris Cons. Orch. (1944–46), and assoc. conductor of the London Phil. (1947–49). After conducting the Radio Eireann Orch. in Dublin (1948–50), he was artistic director of the Lamoureux Orch. in Paris (1950–57). He made his American debut with the Boston Sym. Orch. on March 29, 1957, conducting the U.S. premiere of his 2nd Sym. Martinon was artistic director of the Israel Phil. (1958–60) and Generalmusikdirektor of the Düsseldorf Sym. Orch. (1960–66). In 1963 he was appointed music director of the Chicago Sym. Orch.; during the 5 years of his tenure, he conducted about 60 works by American and European composers of the modern school; this progressive policy met opposition from some influential people in Chicago society and in the press, and he resigned in 1968. He subsequently was chief conductor of the Orchestre National de la Radio Television Française in Paris (from 1968) and the Residente Orch. in The Hague (from 1974). As a conductor, he became best known for his idiomatic performances of the French repertoire. His own compositions follow the spirit of French neo-Classicism, euphonious in their modernity and expansive in their Romantic élan.

WORKS: DRAMATIC: O p e r a : *Hécube,* after Euripides (1949–54; 1st scenic perf., Strasbourg, Nov. 10, 1956). B a l l e t : *Ambohimanga ou La Cité bleue* (1946; Paris, 1947). ORCH.: 4 syms.: No. 1 (1934–36; Paris, March 1940), No. 2, *Hymne à la vie* (1942–44; Paris, Feb. 13, 1944), No. 3, *Irlandaise* (Radio Eirean, Dublin, 1949), and No. 4, *Altitudes* (Chicago, Dec. 30, 1965); *Symphoniette* for Strings, Piano, Harp, and Percussion (1935; Paris, May 30, 1938); 2 violin concertos: No. 1, *Concerto giocoso* (1937–42) and No. 2 (1958; Selle, Bavaria, May 28, 1961); *Musique d'exil ou Stalag IX,* musical reminiscence of imprisonment (1941; Paris, Jan. 11, 1942); *Divertissement* (1941); *Obsession* for Chamber Orch. (1942); *Romance bleue,* rhapsody for Violin and Orch. (1942); *Concerto lyrique* for String Quartet and Chamber Orch. (1944; transcribed as Concerto for 4 Saxophones and Chamber Orch. in 1974); *Overture for a Greek Tragedy* (1949; prelude to the 2nd act of *Hécube*); *Symphonies de voyages* (1957); *Introduction and Toccata* (1959; orchestration of the piano piece *Prelude and Toccata*); Cello Concerto (1963; Hamburg, Jan. 25, 1965); *Le Cène* (1962–63); *Hymne, Variations et Rondo* (1967; Paris, Feb. 15, 1969); Flute Concerto (1970–71); *Sonata movimento*

perpetuo (1973). C H A M B E R : 7 sonatinas: No. 1 for Violin and Piano (1935), No. 2 for Violin and Piano (1936), No. 3 for Piano (1940), No. 4 for Wind Trio (1940), No. 5 for Solo Violin (1942), No. 6 for Solo Violin (1958), and No. 7 for Flute and Piano (1958); *Domenon* for Wind Quintet (1939); String Trio (1943) *Suite nocturne* for Violin and Piano (1944); Piano Trio (1945); *Scherzo* for Violin and Piano (1945); 2 string quartets (1946; 1963–66); *Prelude and Toccata* for Piano (1947); *Duo* for Violin and Piano (1953); *Introduzione, Adagio et Passacaille* for 13 Instruments (1967); *Vigentuor* for 20 Instruments (1969); Octet (1969). V O C A L : *Absolve Domine* for Men's Chorus and Orch. (1940; perf. at Stalag IX prison camp, Nov. 2, 1940); *Appel de parfums* for Narrator, Men's or Mixed Chorus, and Orch. (1940); *Psalm 136 (Chant de captifs)* for Narrator, Soloists, Chorus, and Orch. (1942); *Ode au Soleil ne de la Mort* for Narrator, Chorus, and Orch. (1945); *Le Lis de Sharon,* oratorio (1951; Tel Aviv, 1952); songs.—NS/LK/DM

Martinpelto, Hillevi, Swedish soprano; b. Alvaden, Jan. 9, 1958. She studied at the Royal Opera School in Stockholm. After making her debut as Pamina at the Folksopera in Stockholm, she sang for the first time at the Royal Opera in Stockholm in 1987 as Cio-Cio-San. In 1989–90 she appeared as both Gluck Iphigenias at the Drottningholm Festival. She sang Fiordiligi in Brussels in 1990, and in 1991 reprised that role at the Hamburg State Opera. In 1993 she appeared as Freia in *Das Rheingold* at the Lyric Opera in Chicago, and in 1994 as Donna Anna at the Glyndebourne Festival. In 1997 she sang Agathe at the Royal Opera in Copenhagen. She also appeared as a soloist with many European orchs.—NS/LK/DM

Martins, João Carlos, Brazilian pianist; b. São Paulo, June 25, 1940. He studied piano with José Kliass. He made his professional debut at Teresopolis in 1954, after which other concerts followed in Brazilian cities. In 1960 he made his American debut at Carnegie Hall in N.Y., evoking superlatives for his "passionate subjectivity" from the critics; later he made a specialty of performing all of Bach's 48 preludes and fugues in 2 consecutive concerts. He also appeared as a soloist with orchs. in N.Y., Philadelphia, and Boston. But at the height of his successes, in 1969, he was knocked down during a soccer match, and hurt his arm to the point of a painful neuralgia, so that he had to stop playing piano. But in a surprising change of direction, he went into banking, managed a champion prizefighter, started a construction company, and became a multimillionaire in devalued Brazilian currency. An even more surprising development followed when, in 1981, he was appointed to the post of the Brazilian state secretary of culture; in this capacity, he exhibited an extraordinary knack for urban recovery in the direction of futuristic Americanization. In the meantime, his neurological ailment subsided, and he returned to his career as a virtuoso pianist.—NS/LK/DM

Martinů, Bohuslav (Jan), remarkable Czech-born American composer; b. Polička, Dec. 8, 1890; d. Liestal, near Basel, Aug. 28, 1959. He was born in the bell tower of a church in the village where his father was a watchman. He studied violin with the local tailor when he was 7; from 1906 to 1909 he was enrolled at the Prague Cons.; then entered the Prague Organ School (1909), where he studied organ and theory, but was expelled in 1910 for lack of application. He played in the 2nd violin section in the Czech Phil. in Prague (1913–14), returning to Polička (1914–18) to avoid service in the Austrian army; after World War I, he reentered the Prague Cons. as a pupil of Suk, but again failed to graduate; also played again in the Czech Phil. (1918–23). In 1923 he went to Paris and participated in progressive musical circles; took private lessons with Roussel. In a relatively short time his name became known in Europe through increasingly frequent performances of his chamber works, ballets, and symphonic pieces; several of his works were performed at the festivals of the ISCM In 1932 his String Sextet won the Elizabeth Sprague Coolidge Award. He remained in Paris until June 1940, when he fled the German invasion and went to Portugal; finally reached the U.S. in 1941 and settled in N.Y.; personal difficulties prevented him from accepting an offer to teach at the Prague Cons. after the liberation of Czechoslovakia in 1945; later was a visiting prof. of music at Princeton Univ. (1948–51). In 1952 he became a naturalized American citizen. Although Martinů spent most of his life away from his homeland, he remained spiritually and musically faithful to his native country. He composed a poignant tribute to the martyred village of Lidice when, in 1943, the Nazi authorities ordered the execution of all men and boys over the age of 16 to avenge the assassination of the local Gauleiter. Martinů immortalized the victims in a heartfelt lyric work entitled *Memorial to Lidice*. In 1953 he returned to Europe, spending the last 2 years of his life in Switzerland. On Aug. 27, 1979, his remains were taken from Schonenberg, Switzerland, to Polička, Czechoslovakia, where they were placed in the family mausoleum. Martinů's centennial was celebrated in 1990 all over Czechoslovakia. As a musician and stylist, he belonged to the European tradition of musical nationalism. He avoided literal exploitation of Czech or Slovak musical materials, but his music is nonetheless characterized by a strong feeling for Bohemian melorhythms; his stylizations of Czech dances are set in a modern idiom without losing their authenticity or simplicity. In his large works, he followed the neo-Classical trend, with some impressionistic undertones; his mastery of modern counterpoint was extraordinary. In his music for the stage, his predilections were for chamber forms; his sense of operatic comedy was very strong, but he was also capable of sensitive lyricism.

WORKS: DRAMATIC: O p e r a : *Voják a tanečnice* (The Soldier and the Dancer; 1926–27; Brno, May 5, 1928); *Les Larmes du couteau* (The Knife's Tears; 1928); *Trois souhaits, ou Les Vicissitudes de la vie*, "opera-film in 3 acts" (1929; Brno, June 16, 1971); *La Semaine de bonté* (1929; unfinished); *Hry o Marii* (The Miracle of Our Lady; 1933–34; Brno, Feb. 23, 1935); *Hlas lesa* (The Voice of the Forest), radio opera (Czech Radio, Oct. 6, 1935); *Divadlo za bránou* (The Suburban Theater), opera buffa (1935–36; Brno, Sept. 20, 1936); *Veselohra na mostě* (Comedy on a Bridge), radio opera (1935; Czech Radio, March 18, 1937; rev. 1950); *Julietta, or The Key to Dreams*, lyric opera (1936–37; Prague, March 16, 1938); *Alexandre bis*, opera buffa (1937;

Mannheim, Feb. 18, 1964); *What Men Live By* (Čím člověk žije), pastoral opera after Tolstoy (1951–52; N.Y., May 20, 1955); *The Marriage* (Ženitba), television opera after Gogol (1952; NBC- TV, N.Y., Feb. 7, 1953); *La Plainte contre inconnu* (1953; unfinished); *Mirandolina*, comic opera (1954; Prague, May 17, 1959); *Ariadne*, lyric opera (1958; Gelsenkirchen, March 2, 1961); *Řecké pašije* (Greek Passion), musical drama after Kazantzakis (1955–59; Zürich, June 9, 1961; original version reconstructed by Ales Brezina and 1st perf. in Bregenz, July 20, 1999). **B a l l e t :** *Noc* (Night), "meloplastic scene" (1913–14); *Stín* (The Shadow; 1916); *Istar* (1918–22; Prague, Sept. 11, 1924); *Who Is the Most Powerful in the World?* (Kdo je na světě nejmocnější), ballet comedy, after an English fairy tale (1922; Brno, Jan. 31, 1925); *The Revolt* (Vzpoura), ballet sketch (1922–23; Brno, Feb. 11, 1928); *The Butterfly That Stamped* (Motýl, ktery dupal), after Kipling (1926); *La Revue de cuisine* (Prague, 1927); *On tourne* (Natáčí se), for a cartoon and puppet film (1927); *Le Raid merveilleux* (Báječný let), "ballet mécanique" for 2 Clarinets, Trumpet, and Strings (1927); *Echec au roi*, jazz ballet (1930); *Špalíček* (The Chapbook), with Vocal Soloists and Chorus (1931; Prague, Sept. 19, 1933; rev. 1940; Prague, April 2, 1949); *Le Jugement de Paris* (1935); *The Strangler* (Uškreovač), for 3 Dancers (New London, Conn., Aug. 15, 1948). **ORCH.:** *Anděl smrti* (Angel of Death), symphonic poem (1910; also for Piano); *Komposition* (1913–14); *Nocturno No. 1* for Viola and Orch. (1914); *Ballada* (1915); *Míjející půlnoc* (Vanishing Midnight; 1921–22); *Half Time*, rondo (Prague, Dec. 7, 1924); Concertino for Cello, Winds, Piano, and Percussion (1924; Prague, March 24, 1949); 5 piano concertos: No. 1 (1925; Prague, Nov. 21, 1926), No. 2 (1934; Prague, 1935; rescored 1944), No. 3 (1947–48; Dallas, Nov. 20, 1949), No. 4, *Incantation* (N.Y., Oct. 4, 1956), and No. 5, *Fantasia concertante* (1957; Berlin, Jan. 31, 1959); *La Bagarre*, rondo (1926; Boston, Nov. 18, 1927); *Divertimento* for Piano, Left-Hand, and Orch. (1926; Prague, Feb. 26, 1947; rev. 1928 as the Concertino for Piano, Left-Hand, and Orch.); *Jazz Suite* for Chamber Orch. (Baden-Baden, June 7, 1928); *Allegro symphonique*, rhapsody (Boston, Dec. 14, 1928); *Praeludium* (1930); *Serenade* for Chamber Orch. (1930); 2 cello concertos: No. 1 for Cello and Chamber Orch. (1930; rev. for Full Orch., 1939; rescored 1955) and No. 2 (1944–45); Concerto for String Quartet and Orch. (1931); 2 violin concertos: No. 1 for Cello and Chamber Orch. (1931–32; Chicago, Oct. 25, 1973) and No. 2 (Boston, Dec. 31, 1943); *Sinfonia concertante* for 2 Orchs. (1932); *Partita*: Suite No. 1 (1932); *Divertimento: Serenade No. 4* for Violin, Viola, Oboe, Piano, and Strings (1932); Concertino for Piano Trio and Strings (1933; Basel, Oct. 16, 1936); *Invence* (Inventions; Venice, Sept. 1934); Concerto for Harpsichord and Chamber Orch. (1935); Concerto for Flute, Violin, and Orch. (Paris, Dec. 27, 1936); *Duo concertante* for 2 Violins and Orch. (1937); *Suite concertante* for Violin and Orch. (1937; rev. 1945); Piano Concertino (1938; London, Aug. 5, 1948); Concerto Grosso for Small Orch. (1938; Boston, Nov. 14, 1941); *3 ricercari* for Chamber Orch. (1938); Double Concerto for 2 String Orchs., Piano, and Timpani (1938; Basel, Feb. 9, 1940); *Sonata da camera* for Cello and Chamber Orch. (1940; Geneva, Nov. 25, 1943); *Sinfonietta giocosa* for Piano and Chamber Orch. (1940; rev. 1941; N.Y., March 16, 1942); *Concerto da camera* for Violin, String Orch., Piano, and Timpani (1941; Basel, Jan. 23, 1942); 6 syms.: No. 1 (Boston, Nov. 13, 1942), No. 2 (Cleveland, Oct. 28, 1943), No. 3 (1944; Boston, Oct. 12, 1945), No. 4 (Philadelphia, Nov. 30, 1945), No. 5 (1946; Prague, May 27, 1947), and No. 6, *Fantaisies symphoniques* (1951–53; Boston, Jan. 7, 1955); *Memorial to Lidice* (N.Y., Oct. 28, 1943); Concerto for 2 Pianos and Orch. (Philadelphia, Nov. 5, 1943); *Thunderbolt P-47*, scherzo (Washington,

D.C., Dec. 19, 1945); *Toccata e due canzone* for Small Orch. (1946; Basel, Jan. 21, 1947); *Sinfonia concertante* for Oboe, Bassoon, Violin, Cello, and Small Orch. (1949; Basel, Dec. 8, 1950); Concerto for 2 Violins and Orch. (1950; Dallas, Jan. 8, 1951); *Sinfonietta La Jolla* for Piano and Chamber Orch. (1950); *Intermezzo* (N.Y., Dec. 29, 1950); *Rhapsody-Concerto* for Viola and Orch. (1952; Cleveland, Feb. 19, 1953); Concerto for Violin, Piano, and Orch. (1955); *Les Fresques de Piero della Francesca* (1955; Salzburg Festival, Aug. 28, 1956); boe Concerto (1955); *The Rock*, symphonic prelude (1957; Cleveland, April 17, 1958); *The Parables* (1957–58; Boston, Feb. 13, 1959); *Estampes*, symphonic suite (1958; Louisville, Feb. 4, 1959). **CHAMBER:** 1 unnumbered string quartet (1917; Zürich, May 7, 1994); 7 numbered string quartets: No. 1 (1918; reconstructed, with the addition of a newly discovered 4th movement, by Jan Hanuš, 1972), No. 2 (1925), No. 3 (1929), No. 4 (1937; Donaueschingen, Oct. 15, 1960), No. 5 (1938; Prague, May 25, 1958), No. 6 (1946; Cambridge, Mass., May 1, 1947), and No. 7, *Concerto da camera* (1947); 2 unnumbered violin sonatas (1919; 1926, Prague, March 30, 1963); 3 numbered violin sonatas (1929, 1931, 1944); 2 string trios (1923, 1934); Quartet for Clarinet, Horn, Cello, and Drum (1924); 2 unnumbered nonets: for Violin, Viola, Cello, Flute, Clarinet, Oboe, Horn, Bassoon, and Piano (1924–25), and for Violin, Viola, Cello, Double Bass, Flute, Clarinet, Oboe, Horn, and Bassoon (1959); 2 duos for Violin and Cello (1927, 1957); *Impromptu* for Violin and Piano (1927); String Quintet (1927); Sextet for Winds and Piano (1929); *5 Short Pieces* for Violin and Piano (1929); Wind Quintet (1930); *Les Rondes*, 6 pieces for 7 Instruments (1930; Paris, March 18, 1932); 3 piano trios (*5 Brief Pieces*, 1930; 1950; 1951); Sonatina for 2 Violins and Piano (1930); *Études rythmiques* for Violin and Piano (1931); *Pastorales and Nocturnes* for Cello and Piano (both 1931); *Arabesques* for Violin or Cello and Piano (1931); String Sextet (1932); Sonata for 2 Violins and Piano (London, Feb. 1932); *Serenade* No. 1 for 6 Instruments, No. 2 for 2 Violins and Viola, and No. 3 for 7 Instruments (all 1932 and 1st perf. in Prague, Oct. 16, 1947; No. 4 is the *Divertimento* for Violin, Viola, Oboe, Piano, and String Orch.); 2 piano quintets (1933, 1944); Sonata for Flute, Violin, and Piano (1936; Paris, July 1, 1937); *4 Madrigals* for Oboe, Clarinet, and Bassoon (1937); Violin Sonatina (1937); *Intermezzo*, 4 pieces for Violin and Piano (1937); Trio for Flute, Violin, and Bassoon (1937); 3 cello sonatas (1939, 1944, 1952); *Bergerettes* for Piano Trio (1940); *Promenades* for Flute, Violin, and Harpsichord (1940); Piano Quartet (1942); *Madrigal Sonata* for Flute, Violin, and Piano (1942); *Variations on a Theme of Rossini* for Cello and Piano (1942); *Madrigal Stanzas*, 5 pieces for Violin and Piano (1943); Trio for Flute, Cello, and Piano (1944); Flute Sonata (1945); *Czech Rhapsody* for Violin and Piano (1945); *Fantasia* for Theremin, Oboe, String Quartet, and Piano (1945); 2 duos for Violin and Viola (3 Madrigals, 1947; 1950); Quartet for Oboe, Violin, Cello, and Piano (1947); *Mazurka-Nocturne* for Oboe, 2 Violins, and Cello (1949); *Serenade* for Violin, Viola, Cello, and 2 Clarinets (1951); Viola Sonata (1955); Clarinet Sonatina (1956); Trumpet Sonatina (1956); *Divertimento* for 2 Flutes-à-bec (1957); *Les Fêtes nocturnes* for Violin, Viola, Cello, Clarinet, Harp, and Piano (1959); *Variations on a Slovak Theme* for Cello and Piano (Prague, Oct. 17, 1959). **KEYBOARD: P i a n o :** *Puppets*, small pieces for children (3 sets, 1914–24); *Scherzo* (1924); *Fables* (1924); *Film en miniature* (1925); *3 Czech Dances* (1926); *Le Noël* (1927); *4 Movements* (1928); *Borová*, 7 Czech dances (1929; also for Orch.); *Préludes (en forme de...)* (1929); *Fantaisie* for 2 Pianos (1929); *Á trois mains* (1930); *Esquisses de danse*, 5 pieces (1932); *Les Ritournelles* (1932); *Dumka* (1936); *Fenêtre sur le jardin*, 4 pieces (1938); *Fantasia and Toccata* (1940); *Mazurka* (1941); *Études and*

Polkas (3 books, 1945); *The 5th Day of the 5th Moon* (1948); *3 Czech Dances* for 2 Pianos (1949); Sonata (1954); *Reminiscences* (1957). **H a r p s i c h o r d :** *2 Pieces* (1935); Sonata (1958); *Impromptus* (1959). **O r g a n :** *Vigilie* (1959). **VOCAL:** *Nipponari*, 7 songs for Woman's Voice and Chamber Ensemble (1912); *Česka rapsódie*, cantata (1918; Prague, Jan. 12, 1919); *Kouzelné noci* (Magic Nights), 3 songs for Soprano and Orch. (1918); *Le Jazz* for Voice and Orch. (1928); *Kytice* (Bouquet of Flowers), cantata on Czech folk poetry (1937; Czech Radio, May 1938); *Polní mše* (Field Mass) for Men's Chorus, Baritone, and Orch. (1939; Prague, Feb. 28, 1946); *Hora tři světel* (The Hill of 3 Lights), small oratorio for Soloists, Chorus, and Organ (1954; Bern, Oct. 3, 1955); *Hymnus k sv. Jakubu* (Hymn to St. James) for Narrator, Soloists, Chorus, Organ, and Orch. (1954; Polička, July 31, 1955); *Gilgameš* (The Epic of Gilgamesh) for Narrator, Soloists, Chorus, and Orch. (1954–55; Basel, Jan. 24, 1958); *Otvírání studánek* (The Opening of the Wells) for Narrator, Soloists, Women's Chorus, 2 Violins, Viola, and Piano (1955); *Legend from the Smoke of Potato Fires* for Soloists, Chorus, and Chamber Ensemble (1957); *Mikeš z hor* (Mikesh from the Mountains) for Soloists, Chorus, 2 Violins, Viola, and Piano (1959); *The Prophecy of Isaiah* (Proroctví Izaiášovo) for Men's Chorus, Soloists, Viola, Trumpet, Piano, and Timpani (1959; Jerusalem, April 2, 1963); numerous part-songs and choruses.

BIBL.: M. Šafránek, *B. M.: The Man and His Music* (N.Y., 1944); J. Löwenbach, *M. pozdravuje domov* (Prague, 1947); M. Šafránek, *B. M.: His Life and Works* (London, 1962); H. Halbreich, *B. M.* (Zürich, 1968); C. Martinů, *Můj život s B. M.* (My Life with B. M.; Prague, 1971); B. Large, *M.* (N.Y., 1975); J. Brabcová, ed., *B. M. anno 1981: Papers From an International Musicological Conference, 26–28 May, 1981* (Prague, 1990); G. Erismann, *M., un musicien à l'éveil des sources* (Arles, 1990).—**NS/LK/DM**

Martín y Soler, (Atanasio Martín Ignacio) Vicente (Tadeo Francisco Pellegrin),

distinguished Spanish composer; b. Valencia, May 2, 1754; d. St. Petersburg, Jan. 30, 1806. He was a choirboy in Valencia and a church organist in Alicante before going to Madrid, where he brought out his first work for the stage, the zarzuela *La Madrileña, o Tutor burlado*, most likely in 1776. He then went to Italy, where he became known as Martini lo Spagnuolo. He wrote operas for several theaters there, entering the service of the Infante, the future King Charles IV of Spain, about 1780. With Da Ponte as his librettist, he wrote the opera buffa *Il Burbero di buon cuore*, which was premiered in Vienna to much acclaim on Jan. 4, 1786. It was revived there on Nov. 9, 1789, and included 2 additional arias written expressly for the occasion by Mozart. Martín y Soler and Da Ponte then collaborated on the opera buffa *Una cosa rara, o sia Bellezza ed onestà*, a masterful stage work first given in Vienna on Nov. 17, 1786, and subsequently performed throughout Europe. Mozart used a theme from this popular work in the supper scene of his *Don Giovanni*. Martín y Soler and Da Ponte subsequently collaborated on the successful opera buffa *L'arbore di Diana* (Vienna, Oct. 1, 1787). The composer was then called to St. Petersburg to serve as court composer to Catherine II the Great, who wrote the libretto for his comic opera *Gore bogatyr Kosometovich* (St. Petersburg, Feb. 9, 1789). He then went to London, collaborating again with Da Ponte on the highly successful *La scuola dei maritati* (Jan. 27, 1795) and *L'isola del piacere* (May 26,

1795), both engaging opere buffe. He returned to St. Petersburg in 1796 and was made Imperial Russian Privy Councillor by Paul I in 1798. He was inspector of the Italian Court Theater there (1800–1804).

WORKS: DRAMATIC: O p e r a : *La Madrileña, o Tutor burlado*, zarzuela (Madrid, 1776?); *Ifigenia in Aulide*, opera seria (Naples, Jan. 12, 1779); *Ipermestra*, opera seria (Naples, Jan. 12, 1780); *Andromaca*, opera seria (Turin, Dec. 26, 1780); *Astartea*, opera seria (Lucca, Carnival 1781); *Partenope*, componimento drammatico (Naples, 1782); *L'amor geloso*, azione teatrale comica (Naples, Carnival 1782); *In amor ci vuol destrezza*, opera buffa (Venice, 1782); *Vologeso*, opera seria (Turin, Carnival 1783); *Le burle per amore*, opera buffa (Venice, Carnival 1784); *La Vedova spiritosa*, opera buffa (Parma, Carnival 1785); *Il Burbero di buon cuore*, opera buffa (Vienna, Jan. 4, 1786); *Una cosa rara, o sia Bellezza ed onestà*, opera buffa (Vienna, Nov. 17, 1786); *L'arbore di Diana*, opera buffa (Vienna, Oct. 1, 1787); *Gore bogatyr Kosometovich* (The Unfortunate Hero Kosometovich), comic opera (St. Petersburg, Feb. 9, 1789); *Pesnolyubie* (Beloved Songs), comic opera (St. Petersburg, Jan. 18, 1790); *Il castello d'Atlante*, opera buffa (Desenzano, Carnival 1791); *La scuola dei maritati*, opera buffa (London, Jan. 27, 1795); *L'isola del piacere*, opera buffa (London, May 26, 1795); *Le nozze de' contadini spagnuoli*, intermezzo (London, May 28, 1795); *La festa del villagio*, opera buffa (St. Petersburg, Jan. 26 or 30, 1798). **B a l l e t :** *La bella Arsene* (Naples, 1779 or 1780); *I Ratti Sabini* (Naples, 1779 or 1780); *La Regina di Golconda* (Lucca, 1781); *Cristiano II, rè di Danimarca* (Venice, 1782); *Aci e Galatea* (Parma, 1784); *Didon abandonée* (St. Petersburg, 1792); *L'Oracle* (St. Petersburg, 1793); *Amour et Psyché* (St. Petersburg, 1793); *Tancrède* (St. Petersburg, 1799); *Le Retour de Poliorcete* (St. Petersburg, 1799 or 1800). **OTHER:** Salve Regina; cantatas; many canzoets; ariettas; duets; canons. **—NS/LK/DM**

Martirano, Salvatore, American composer and teacher; b. Yonkers, N.Y., Jan. 12, 1927; d. Urbana, Ill., Nov. 17, 1995. He studied piano and composition at the Oberlin (Ohio) Cons. of Music (B.M., 1951), then composition at the Eastman School of Music in Rochester, N.Y., with Rogers (M.M., 1952); later took courses with Dallapiccola at the Cherubini Cons. in Florence (1952–54). He served in the U.S. Marine Corps; played clarinet and cornet with the Parris Island Marine Band. From 1956 to 1959 he held a fellowship to the American Academy in Rome, and in 1960 received a Guggenheim fellowship and the American Academy of Arts and Letters Award. In 1963 he joined the faculty of the Univ. of Ill. at Urbana. Martirano wrote in a progressive avant-garde idiom, applying the quaquaversal techniques of unmitigated radical modernism, free from any inhibitions.

WORKS: Sextet for Wind Instruments (1949); Prelude for Orch. (1950); Variations for Flute and Piano (1950); String Quartet No. 1 (1951); *The Magic Stones*, chamber opera after the *Decameron* (Oberlin Cons., April 24, 1952); *Piece for Orchestra* (1952); Violin Sonata (1952); *Contrasto* for Orch. (1954); *Chansons innocentes* for Soprano and Piano (1957); *O, O, O, O, That Shakespeherian Rag* for Chorus and Instrumental Ensemble (1958); *Cocktail Music* for Piano (1962); Octet (1963); *Underworld* for 4 Actors, 4 Percussion Instruments, 2 Double Basses, Tenor Saxophone, and Tape (1965; video version, 1982); *Ballad* for Amplified Nightclub Singer and Instrumental Ensemble (1966); *L's.G.A.* for a gas-masked Politico, Helium Bomb, 3 16mm Movie Projectors, and Tape (1968); *The Proposal* for Tapes and

Slides (1968); *Action Analysis* for 12 People, Bunny, and Controller (1968); *Selections* for Alto Flute, Bass Clarinet, Viola, and Cello (1970); *Sal-Mar Construction I-VII* for Tape (1971–75); *Fast Forward* for Tape (1977); *Fifty One* for Tape (1978); *In Memoriam Luigi Dallapiccola* for Tape (1978); *Omaggio a Sally Rand*, video piece (1982); *Thrown*, sextet for Wind and Percussion (1984); *Look at the Back of My Head for Awhile*, video piece (1984); *Sampler: Everything Goes When the Whistle Blows* for Violin and Synthetic Orch. (1985; rev. 1988); *Dance/Players I* and *II*, video pieces (1986); *3 not 2*, variable-forms piece (1987); *Phleu* for Amplified Flute and Synthetic Orch. (1988); *LON/dons* for Chamber Orch. (1989).—**NS/LK/DM**

Martland, Steve, English composer; b. Liverpool, Oct. 10, 1958. After graduating from the Univ. of Liverpool (1981), he studied composition with Louis Andriessen at the Royal Cons. of Music at The Hague (1982–85) and with Schuller at the Berkshire Music Center at Tanglewood (summer, 1984). He was active with his own Steve Martland Band, finding inspiration in the world of pop and rock music in pursuit of his own fiercely independent course as a serious composer.

WORKS: DRAMATIC: *Ghost Story*, incidental music to a television play (1989); *The Task*, incidental music (1989); *Home, Away from Home*, incidental music to a television play (1989); *Cult*, soundtrack to a dance-theater piece for television (1990). **ORCH.:** *Lotta continua* for Jazz Band and Orch. (1981; rev. 1984); *Babi Yar* (1983; Liverpool, Nov. 22, 1985); *Orc* for Horn and Small Orch. (1984; Amsterdam, Jan. 14, 1985); *Dividing the Lines* for Brass Band (1986); *Crossing the Broder* for Strings (1990–91; also for String Quartet and Tape). **CHAMBER:** *Remembering Lennon* for 7 Players (1981; rev. 1985); Duo for Trumpet and Piano (1982); *American Invention* for 13 Players (Aldeburgh, June 10, 1985); *Shoulder to Shoulder* for 13 Players (Amsterdam, Dec. 9, 1986); *Remix* for Jazz Ensemble (Amsterdam, Nov. 6, 1986); *Big Mac I* for 4 Players (The Hague, May 27, 1987) and *II* for 8 Players (1987); *Principia* for Jazz Ensemble (1989; Leeds, March 7, 1990); *Wolf-gang*, arrangements of 6 Mozart arias for Wind Octet (1991); *Crossing the Border* for String Quartet and Tape (1991; also for String Orch.); *Patrol* for String Quartet (1992); *Bach Toccata and Fugue BWV565*, arrangement for String Quartet (1992). **P i a n o :** *Kgakala* (1982); *Drill* for 2 Pianos (1987; Rotterdam, Jan. 14, 1988); *Birthday Hocket* for 2 Pianos (Amsterdam, June 6, 1989). **VOCAL:** *Canto a la Esperanza* for Soprano, Electric Guitar, and Chamber Orch. (1982); *El Pueblo unido James Sera Vencido* for Voices and 13 Players (1987); *Glad Day* for Voices and 12 Players (1988); *Skywalk* for 5 Voices or Chorus (1989); *Terra Firma* for 5 Voices, Amplification, and Video (1989); *The Perfect Act* for Voice and Amplified Ensemble (1991). **OTHER:** *Divisions* for Tape (1986–87); *Albion*, audiovisual piece (BBC-TV, Dec. 18, 1988).—**NS/LK/DM**

Marton, Eva, outstanding Hungarian soprano; b. Budapest, June 18, 1943. She studied with Endre Rösler and Jenő Sipos at the Franz Liszt Academy of Music in Budapest. She made her formal operatic debut as the Queen of Shemakha in *Le Coq d'or* at the Hungarian State Opera there in 1968, remaining on its roster until joining the Frankfurt am Main Opera in 1971. She then became a member of the Hamburg State Opera in 1977. On Feb. 23, 1975, she made her U.S. debut in N.Y. as a soloist in the world premiere of Hovhaness's folk oratorio *The Way of Jesus*, and then made her first appearance at the Metropolitan Opera there as Eva in *Die Meistersinger von Nürnberg* on Nov. 3, 1976. After singing at the Bayreuth Festivals (1977–78) and at Milan's La Scala (1978), she scored a notable success as the Empress in *Die Frau ohne Schatten* at the Metropolitan Opera in 1981; thereafter she was one of its most important artists, appearing as Elisabeth in *Tännhauser* (1982), Leonore in *Fidelio* (1983), Ortrud in *Lohengrin* (1984), Tosca (1986), and Lady Macbeth (1988). She first sang Turandot at the Vienna State Opera in 1983, and appeared as Elektra there in 1989. In 1987 she made her debut at London's Covent Garden as Turandot, and in 1990 she returned there as Elektra. In 1992 she appeared as Turandot in Chicago and as the Dyer's Wife at the Salzburg Festival. She was engaged as Turandot at the San Francisco Opera in 1993. In 1997 she sang Elektra at the Washington (D.C.) Opera. She sang the Kostelnička in *Jenůfa* at the Hamburg State Opera in 1998. On Oct. 7, 1999, she portrayed Turandot at the reopening of the restored Gran Teatre del Liceu in Barcelona. Her appearances as an oratorio and lieder artist were also well received.

BIBL.: C. Wilkens, *E. M.* (Hamburg, 1982).—NS/LK/DM

Martopangrawit, R.L., significant Indonesian composer, teacher, performer, and music theorist; b. Surakarta, Central Java, April 4, 1914; d. there, April 17, 1986. He was a descendant of many generations of royal musicians and became a member of the royal gamelan at the Kraton (palace) Surakarta at 13. In 1948 he joined the offices of the Central Javanese Ministry of Education and Culture; also taught in Surakarta at the Konservatori Karawitan (K.O.K.A.R., 1951–64) and Akademi Seni Karawiten Indonesia (A.S.K.I., from 1964; later Sekolah Tinggi Seni Indonesia [S.T.S.I.]). Considered among the finest of traditional musicians, Martopangrawit garnered fame for his inventive and stylistically diverse compositions, which numbered over 100; his earliest dated work was *Ladrang Biwadhapraja* (1939), and his last was *Ra Ngandel* (1986); others included *Ladrang Cikar Bobrok* (1943), *Ketawang ASKI, Ladrang Asri* (1946), *Ladrang Gandasuli* (1946), *Ladrang Lo Kowe Nang* (1954), *Lancaran Kebat* (1961), *Lancaran Uyal-uyel* (1962), *Ketawang Pamegatsih* (1966), *Nglara Ati* (1970), *Mijil Anglir Medung* (1981), and *Gending Parisuka* (1982). He was also active in the preservation and development of many classical music and dance forms, particularly those associated with the Kraton Surakarta, where he was promoted to "Bupati Anon-anon" and given the honorary title Raden Tumenggung Martodipura (1984). He also publ. many books on the Central Javanese gamelan; some of these comprise collections of music notation, including those of his own pieces: *Gending-gending Martopangrawit* (1968) and *Lagu Dolanan Anggitan Martopangrawit* (children's songs). Among his theoretical works is his landmark treatise *Pengetahuan Karawitan* (The Theory of Classical Javanese Music; Surakarta, 1972; Eng. tr. by M. Hatch, in J. Becker and A. Feinstein, eds., *Karawitan: Source Readings in Javanese Gamelan and Vocal Music*, vol. I, Ann Arbor, 1984). Other publications include a book of drumming notation, *Titilaras Kendangan*; a compendium of melodic patterns used by the

gender (an important instrument in the Javanese gamelan), *Titilaras Cengkok-cengkok Genderan Dengan Wiledannya* (2 vols.); and a collection of children's songs, *Lagu Dolanan Lare-lare.*—NS/LK/DM

Marttinen, Tauno (Olavi), Finnish composer, pedagogue, and conductor; b. Helsinki, Sept. 27, 1912. He received training in conducting and composition at the Viipuri Inst. of Music (1920–35), and then was a student of Peter Akimov, Ilmari Hannikainen, and Selim Palmgren at the Sibelius Academy in Helsinki (1935–37); later he studied with Vogel in Switzerland (1958). From 1949 to 1958 he was conductor of the Hämeenlinna City Orch. In 1950 he founded the Hämeenlinna Inst. of Music, serving as its director until 1975. In 1982 he was awarded an honorary prize by the Soc. of Finnish Composers and the Kalevala Soc. He received the 1st Sibelius Award in 1990. After composing in a late Romantic style, Marttinen developed a free serial mode of expression. Later he embraced free tonality before finding renewed creative resources in neo-Baroque and neo-Classical styles.

WORKS: DRAMATIC: O p e r a : *Neiti Gamardin talo* (The House of Lady Gamard; 1960–71); *Päällysviitta* (The Cloak; 1962–63); *Kihlaus* (The Engagement; 1964; Helsinki, June 12, 1966); *Apotti ja ikäneito* (The Abbot and the Old Maid; 1965); *Tulitikkuja lainaamassa* (Borrowing Matches; Helsinki, Aug. 20, 1966); *Lea* (1967; Turku, Sept. 19, 1968); *Poltettu oranssi* (Burnt Orange), television opera (1968; Finnish TV, Oct. 6, 1971; 1st stage perf., Helsinki, Nov. 3, 1975); *Mestari Patelin* (Master Patelin; 1969–72; Hämeenlinna, July 31, 1983); *Noitarumpu* (Shaman's Drum; 1974–76); *Psykiatri* (The Psychiatrist; 1974); *Laestadiuksen saarna* (Laestadius's Sermon; 1974–76; Oulu, April 29, 1976); *Meedio* (The Medium), chamber opera (1975–76); *Jaarlin sisar* (The Jarl's Sister; 1977; Hämeenlinna, April 3, 1979); *Faaraon kirje* (Pharaoh's Letter; 1978–80; Tampere, Oct. 18, 1982); *Suuren joen laulu eli Najaadi* (The Song of a Great River; 1980; Kemi, May 2, 1982); *Häät* (The Wedding), chamber opera (1984–85; Helsinki, Jan. 31, 1986); *Noidan kirous* (1987); *Seitsemän veljestä* (7 Brothers; 1989); *Mooses* (1990); *Minna Graucher* (1992). M u s i c a l : *Kullanmuru* (The Golden Treasure; 1980). B a l - l e t : *Tikkaat* (The Ladder; 1955); *Dorian Grayn muotokuva* (The Picture of Dorian Gray; 1969); *Lumikuningatar* (The Snow Queen; 1970); *Beatrice* (1970); *Päivänpäästö* (The Sun Out of the Moon; 1975–77); *Ruma ankanpoikanen* (The Ugly Duckling; 1976, 1982–83). ORCH.: 9 syms. (1958; 1959; 1960–62; 1964; *The Shaman*, 1967–72; 1974–75; 1977; 1983; 1986); *The Milky Way* (1960–61); *Rembrandt* for Cello and Orch. (1962); Violin Concerto (1962); 4 piano concertos (1964, 1972, 1981, 1984); *Birds of the Underworld* (1964); *Fauni* (1965); *Panu, God of Fire* (1966); *Dalai Lama*, cello concerto (1966; rev. 1979); *Creation of the Earth* (1966); *Mont Saint Michel* (1968); *Pentalia* (1969); *The North* for Wind Orch. (1970–71); Bassoon Concerto (1971; rev. 1983–84); Flute Concerto (1972); *On the Tracks of the Winter Moose*, clarinet concerto (1974); *Concerto espagnole* for Flute and Orch. (1978); *Night on the Fortress* for Wind Orch. (1978); *Elegia* for Harp and Strings (1979); *Voces polaris* (1979); *Sirius* for Wind Orch. (1980); Concerto for 2 Pianos and Orch. (1981); *Väinämöisen's Birth* (1981); *Adagio* (1982); *Väinämöisen's Departure for Pohjola* (1982); *The Maid of Pohjola* (1982); Concerto grosso for Violin, Viola, Cello, and Orch. (1983); *Profeetta* (1984); *A Trip to the Land of Dawn*, homage to Hermann Hesse, for Strings (1984); *Tiibetilainen fantasia* (1985); *Faustus*, violin concerto (1987); Zither Concerto (1988); *Uuden aamun soitto* for Violin and Orch. (1990);

Andante religioso for Strings (1990). **CHAMBER:** *Delta* for Clarinet and Piano (1962); *Silhouettes* for Piano and Percussion (1962); *The Conjuration* for 3 Percussionists (1963); *Alfa* for Flute and 7 Cymbals (1963); 4 nonets for Flute, Oboe, Clarinet, Bassoon, Horn, Violin, Viola, Cello, and Double Bass (1963, 1968, 1973, 1985); *Visit to the Giant Sage Vipunen* for 7 Double Basses (1969); 3 string quartets (1969, 1971, 1983); Duo for Clarinet and Percussion (1971); *Ilman, Virgin of the Air* for Piccolo (1974); *Septemalia* for 7 Double Basses (1975); *3 Preludes* for Guitar (1975); *Homage to Johann Sebastian Bach* for Guitar (1977); *Divertimento* for Oboe or English Horn and Percussion (1977); *Intermezzo* for Flute and Guitar (1977–78); *Impression* for Cello (1978); Trio for Piano, Violin, and Cello (1978); *The Old Mill Tells Its Tale* for Clarinet (1978); *Le Commencement* for Flute, Oboe, and Piano (1978); *Quo vadis* for Flute, Oboe, Bassoon, and Harpsichord (1979); *The Gnome* for Bass Clarinet (1981); Duo for Viola and Piano (1981); *Illusio* for Clarinet (1982); Trio for Violin, Viola, and Cello (1982); *Idyll* for Oboe or Clarinet (1984); Suite for Wind Quintet (1984); *Elegy* for Violin and Cello (1985); *Isis* for Violin and Guitar (1986); *Fantasia concertante* for Flute and Piano (1986); *Vedenhaltija*, trio for Violin, Cello, and Piano (1990); *Lasi* for 5 Instruments (1991). **KEYBOARD: P i a n o :** 4 Preludes (1965); *Titisee* (1965); *Taara* (1967); Sonatina (1970); *Easter* (1971); Sonata (1975); *Giant Stride* for 2 Pianos (1973); *Water Drops* (1976); *Vibrations* (1976); *Glittering* (1977); *Japanese Garden* (1983); *Faustus* (1987). **O r g a n :** *Intrada* (1967); *Adagio* (1967); *Notre Dame* (1970); *The Cupola* (1971); *Larghetto* (1972); *Orgelstück* (1972); *In the Beginning Was the Word...* (1975); *Prelude* (1978); *Largo religioso* (1980); *Fantasia on the Theme B-A-C-H* (1982); *Prophet* (1984). **VOCAL:** *Eagle, Bird of the Air* for Mezzo- soprano and Orch. (1965); *The Bow of Fire* for Bass and Piano Trio (1969); *Jesus and Peter* for Baritone and Organ (1969–70); *Sounds from Noah's Ark* for Men's Chorus (1971); *Love Songs from Ancient Times* for Voice and Orch. (1972); *Thus Was the Beginning* for Soloists, Children's Chorus, and Instruments (1977–80); *The Bosom Friend* for Bass and Wind Quintet (1977); *Cantate Jehovae canticum novum* for Mixed or Boy's Chorus, Organ, and String Orch. (1978); *Canticum canticorum* for Mezzo- soprano and Piano or Harp (1978); *Rohkea ratsastaja* for Reciter and Men's Chorus (1980); *Kaupunkini* for Voice and Orch. (1980); *The Kiss of Judas* for Bass, 2 Baritones, Tenor, Mixed Chorus, Men's Chorus, and Organ (1981); *Offenbarung Johannes* for Bass, Men's Chorus, and Organ (1981); *The Maid of Pohjola* for Reciter and Orch. (1982); *Faunit* for Voice and Orch. (1985); *Seunalan Anna* for Soprano, Speaker, Chorus, and Orch. (1989); *Lemminkäinen's Departure to the North* for Chorus and Orch. (1990–91).—**NS/LK/DM**

Martucci, Giuseppe, esteemed Italian pianist, conductor, teacher, and composer; b. Capua, Jan. 6, 1856; d. Naples, June 1, 1909. He began music training with his father, a trumpeter, and took up the piano at an early age. At 11, he entered the Naples Cons. and studied piano with Cesi and composition with Serrao. After successful engagements as a pianist in London and Dublin in 1885, he toured Europe. He also appeared in duo concerts with Alfredo Piatti. On Jan. 23, 1881, he made his conducting debut in Naples, and subsequently became well known for his championship of an expansive repertoire ranging from Lully to Richard Strauss. On June 2, 1888, he conducted the Italian premiere of *Tritan und Isolde* in Bolgona. After teaching at the Naples Cons. (1880–86), he served as director of the Bologna Liceo Musicale (1886–1902). In 1902 he became director

of the Naples Cons. Toscanini greatly admired Martucci and conducted his memorial concert in Naples on July 2, 1909. In subsequent years, he programmed Martucci's works but they failed to gain a place in the repertoire. As a composer, Martucci eschewed the traditional Italian path to success via opera, opting to concentrate on instrumental music. His works follow in the German Romantic tradition of Schumann and Brahms. His son, Paolo Martucci (b. Naples, Oct. 8, 1881; d. N.Y., Oct. 18, 1980), was a pianist and teacher.

WORKS: O R C H . : 2 piano concertos: No. 1 (1878) and No. 2 (1884–85; Naples, Jan. 31, 1886, composer pianist); 2 syms.: No. 1 (1888–95; Milan, Nov. 28, 1895, composer conducting) and No. 2 (Milan, Dec. 11, 1904, composer conducting). **CHAMBER:** Violin Sonata (1874); Piano Quintet (1878); 2 piano trios (1882, 1883); *Andante* for Cello and Piano (1888; also for Orch., 1907). **P i a n o :** Many pieces, all of them later orchestrated: *Colore Orientale-Tempo di marcia* (1875); *Danza (Tarantella)* (1875); *Minuetto* (1880); *Gigue* (1882); *Canzonetta* (1883); *Momento musicale* (1883); *Serenata* (1886); *Gavotta* (c. 1888); *Notturno* (c. 1888); *Novelletta* (1905). **VOCAL:** *Messa di Gloria* for Voices and Orch. (1871); *Samuel*, oratorio for Soloists, Chorus, and Orch. (1881; rev. 1905); *La canzone dei ricordi* for Voice and Piano (1886–87; also for Voice and Orch.); many other songs.

BIBL.: R. Prati, *G. M.* (Turin, 1914); G. Tebaldini, ed., *Capua a G. M.* (Capua, 1915); M. Limoncelli, *G. M.* (Naples, 1939); F. Fano, *G. M.* (Milan, 1950); *Comitato nazionale per la celebrazione del centenario della nascita di G. M.: Nostra di autografi, cimeli e documenti* (Naples, 1956).—**NS/LK/DM**

Martzy, Johanna, Hungarian violinist; b. Timişoara, Oct. 26, 1924; d. Glarus, Switzerland, Aug. 13, 1979. She received instruction from Hubay before entering the Budapest Academy of Music at age 10. She made her debut in Budapest when she was 13, and graduated from the Academy (1942). After winning 1st prize in the Geneva Competition (1947), she toured widely; first played in England in 1953 and in the U.S. in 1957. She acquired a fine reputation as a soloist and chamber music artist.—**NS/LK/DM**

Maruzin, Yuri, Russian tenor; b. Perm, Dec. 8, 1947. He received training in Leningrad, where he made his debut in 1972 at the Maly Theater. In 1978 he became a member of the Kirov Opera in Leningrad, with which he toured throughout Europe and North America. In 1987 he sang with the company as Lensky at London's Covent Garden. After appearing as the Czarevich in Rimsky-Korsakov's *The Tale of Czar Sultan* at Milan's La Scala in 1988, he sang Galitsin in *Khovanshchina* at the Vienna State Opera in 1989. He sang Anatol Kuragin in *War and Peace* at the San Francisco Opera and Andrei Khovansky in *Khovanshchina* at the Edinburgh Festival in 1991. In 1992 he appeared as Hermann in *The Queen of Spades* at the Glyndebourne Festival. He sang in *Lady Macbeth of the District of Mtsenek* at the New Israeli Opera in Tel Aviv in 1997. Among his other roles are Don Alvaro, the Duke of Mantua, Don Carlos, Alfredo, Faust, and Pinkerton.—**NS/LK/DM**

Marvelettes, The, vocal group that recorded Motown's first #1 single. **MEMBERSHIP:** Gladys Horton, voc. (b.1944); Georgeanna Marie Tilman, voc. (b.1944; d.

2317

Jan. 6, 1980), Wanda Young, voc. (b. 1944); Katherine Anderson, voc. (b.1944); and Juanita Cowart, voc. (b.1944).

Formed as a vocal group at Inkster High in the Detroit suburb of Inkster, the Marvelettes started life as the Casinyets (or Can't Sing Yets). They took fourth place in a school talent show that promised the top three placers an audition with the fledgling Motown label (the label had just started scoring hits with the Miracles and Barrett Strong). Their music teacher was so impressed with their Crystals-like sound that she brought them along as well. The people at Motown were impressed with their covers of current hits, as well, and asked them to come back with some original material.

The Marvelettes got the title "Please Mr. Postman" from a friend of the band. As her last act as a member, Gloria Dobbins rewrote the song and gave it to the band before dropping out of the group to take care of family matters. They performed the tune for Motown producers Brian Holland and Robert Bateman, who refined, rehearsed, and recorded it. Fifteen weeks after its release in fall 1961, it reached to top of the pop and R&B charts, going gold in the process. Trying to capitalize on the "Twist" phenomenon, the group recorded "Twistin' Postman," early in 1962, but that only managed to make it to #34. They fared better that spring with "Playboy," bringing that up to #7, and finished off the year with the #17 "Beachwood 4-5789."

The group's personnel began to change with every recording as members got married, had children, or just dropped out of show business. They went hitless in 1963. By 1964, the quintet had slimmed down to a trio and was put into the hands of songwriter/producer Smokey Robinson. Toward the end of the year, the Marvelettes were back on the charts with the #25 "Too Many Fish in the Sea." During the summer of 1965, they scraped into the Top 40 with "I'll Keep Holding On." Early in 1966, however, Robinson and the group put out "Don't Mess with Bill," which rose to #7. About a year later, they hit again with one of Robinson's most sophisticated compositions, the #13 "The Hunter Gets Captured by the Game." That spring they had another hit with the #23 "When You're Young and in Love." They took one more Robinson tune, "My Baby Must Be a Magician," to #17 in 1968.

By then, the only original member of the group left was Wanda Young. They continued playing and recording for several more years, eventually breaking up in 1971. Late in the 1980s, Young (who had married Miracle Bobby Rogers) led another session with Horton and some others for the Motor City label, producing a couple of minor disco records.

DISC.: *Please Mr. Postman* (1961); *Playboy* (1962); *The Marvelettes Sing* (1962); *The Marvelous Marvelettes* (1963); *On Stage* (1963); *Live on Stage* (1963); *The Marvelettes* (1967); *Sophisticated Soul* (1968); *In Full Bloom* (1969); *Return of the Marvelettes* (1970); *Marvelettes/Sophisticated Soul* (1977); *Compact Command Performances* (1982); *Now!* (1990); *Beechwood 4-5789* (1995).—**HB**

Marvin, Frederick, American pianist and musicologist; b. Los Angeles, June 11, 1923. He studied with

Maurice Zam (1935–39) and Milan Blanchet (1940–41; 1945–48) in Los Angeles, with Serkin at the Curtis Inst. of Music in Philadelphia (1939–40), and with Arrau (1950–54). He made his professional debut when he was 15, then made his N.Y. debut in 1948. He subsequently toured widely in North America, Europe, and India, and was a prof. and artist-in-residence at Syracuse Univ. (1968–90). As a pianist, he made it a practice to include rarely heard works on his programs; he particularly championed the music of Antonio Soler; ed. a number of Soler's works, and developed a numbering system (Marvin Verzeichnis) that was widely adopted. —**NS/LK/DM**

Marx, Adolf Bernhard, eminent German music theorist and writer on music; b. Halle, May 15, 1795; d. Berlin, May 17, 1866. Intended for the law, he matriculated at the Univ. of Halle, but also studied music with Turk, and gave up a subsequent legal appointment at Naumburg to gratify his love for art. He continued the study of composition in Berlin with Zelter. In 1824 he founded the *Berliner Allgemeine Musikalische Zeitung* (with the publisher Schlesinger), which he edited with ability, proving himself a conspicuous advocate of German music; however, the publication ceased in 1830. After taking the degree of Ph.D. at the Univ. of Marburg (1827), Marx lectured on music at the Univ. of Berlin; was appointed a prof. in 1830; became music director of the scholastic choir there in 1832. He was co-founder (with Kullak and Stern) of the Berliner Musikschule (1850), retiring in 1856 to devote himself to literary and univ. work. He was a close friend of the Mendelssohn family, and advised young Mendelssohn in musical matters. While Marx was greatly esteemed as a music theorist, his own compositions were unsuccessful. He wrote a Singspiel, *Jery und Bately*, after Goethe (1824), an oratorio, *Mose* (1841), instrumental works, songs, choral works, etc.

WRITINGS: *Die Kunste des Gesangs, theoretische-praktisch* (Berlin, 1826); *Über die Geltung Händelscher Sologesänge für unsere Zeit: Ein Nachtrag* (Berlin, 1828); *Über Malerei in der Tonkunst: Ein Maigruss an die Kunstphilosophen* (Berlin, 1828); *Die Lehre von der musikalischen Komposition, praktisch-theoretisch* (Leipzig: Vol. I, 1837; 9th ed., rev., 1887; 10th ed., 1903; Eng. tr., 1852; Vol. II, 1837; 7th ed. rev., 1890; Vol. III, 1845; 5th ed., 1879; Vol. IV, 1847; 5th ed., rev., 1888; Eng. tr., 1910); *Allgemeine Musiklehre* (Leipzig, 1839; 10th ed., 1884); *Die alte Musiklehre im Streit mit unserer Zeit* (Leipzig, 1841); *Die Musik des neunzehnten Jahrhunderts und ihre Pflege: Methode der Musik* (Leipzig, 1855; 2nd ed., 1873; Eng. tr., 1855); *Ludwig van Beethoven: Leben und Schaffen* (Berlin, 1859; 7th ed., 1907–10); *Vollständige Chorschule* (Leipzig, 1860); *Gluck und die Oper* (Berlin, 1863; 2nd ed., 1866, as *Gluck's Leben und Schaffen*); *Anleitung zum Vortrag Beethovenscher Klavierwerke* (Berlin, 1863; 5th ed., 1912; Eng. tr., 1895); *Erinnerungen: Aus meinem Leben* (Berlin, 1865); *Das Ideal und die Gegenwart* (Jena, 1867); L. Hirschberg, ed., *Musikalische Schriften uber Tondichter und Tonkunst* (Hildburghausen, 1912–22; a collection of most of his major articles from the *Berliner Allgemeine Musikalische Zeitung*); S. Burnham, ed. and tr., *Musical Form in the Age of Beethoven: Selected Writings on Theory and Method* (Cambridge, 1997).

BIBL.: G. Selle, *Aus A.B. M.'s literarischen Nachlass* (Berlin, 1898); B. Moyer, *Concepts of Musical Form in the Nineteenth Century with Special Reference to A.B. M. and Sonata Form* (diss., Stanford Univ., 1969); M. Zywietz, *A.B. M. und das Oratorium in Berlin* (Eisenach, 1996).—**NS/LK/DM**

Marx, Josef, German-American oboist, English horn player, musicologist, and music publisher; b. Berlin, Sept. 9, 1913; d. N.Y., Dec. 21, 1978. He emigrated to America in his early youth, and studied oboe with Dandois at the Cincinnati Cons. and with Goossens in London. He then took lessons in theory with Wolpe. He was an oboist in the Palestine Orch. (1936–37) and the Pittsburgh Sym. Orch. (1942–43), and then played English horn in the orch. of the Metropolitan Opera in N.Y. (1943–51). In addition, he appeared as an oboe soloist; several contemporary composers wrote special works for him. In 1945 he founded the McGinnis-Marx Edition in N.Y., which publ. works by Wolpe, Wuorinen, Sydeman, Schuller, and other contemporary composers. From 1956 to 1960 he taught oboe at the Hartt Coll. of Music in Hartford.—**NS/LK/DM**

Marx, Joseph (Rupert Rudolf), Austrian composer, pedagogue, and music critic; b. Graz, May 11, 1882; d. there, Sept. 3, 1964. He was a student of Degner and took courses in musicology at the Univ. of Graz (Ph.D., 1909, with the diss. *Über die Funktion von Intervallen, Harmonie und Melodie beim Erfassen von Tonkomplexen*). In 1914 he became a prof. of theory and composition at the Vienna Academy of Music, where he was made director in 1922. After it was made the Hochschule für Musik in 1924, he served as its first director until 1927. He continued to teach there until 1952. From 1931 to 1938 he was music critic of the *Neues Wiener Journal*. Following World War II, he was music critic of the *Wiener Zeitung*. From 1947 to 1957 he was an honorary prof. at the Univ. of Graz. Marx established his reputation as a composer early in his career with his songs, of which he wrote about 120. They are in a late Romantic vein à la Hugo Wolf.

WRITINGS (all publ. in Vienna): *Harmonielehre* (1934; 3rd ed., 1948); *Kontrapunkt-Lehre* (1935); *Betrachtungen eines romantischen Realisten* (1947); *Weltsprache Musik* (1964).

WORKS: ORCH.: *Romantische Klavierkonzert* (1919–20); *Eine Herbstsymphonie* (1920–21; Vienna, Feb. 5, 1922); *Naturtrilogie: Eine symphonische Nachtmusik, Idylle,* and *Eine Frühlingsmusik* (1922–25); *Nordlands-Rhapsodie* (1928–29); *Castelli Romani* for Piano and Orch. (1930); *Alt-Wiener Serenaden* (1941–42; Vienna, April 14, 1942); *Sinfonietta in modo classico* for Strings (1944; also as the 3rd string quartet); *Feste im Herbst* (1945); *Sinfonia in modo antico* for Strings (1947; also as the 2nd string quartet). **CHAMBER:** *Ballade* for Piano Quartet (1911); *Scherzo* for Piano Quartet (1911); *Quartett in Form einer Rhapsodie* for Piano Quartet (1911); *Frühlingssonate* for Violin and Piano (1913); *Trio Phantasie* for Piano Trio (1913); 3 string quartets: No. 1, *Quartetto in modo chromatico* (1937), No. 2, *in modo antico* (1938; also as the *Sinfonia in modo antico* for Strings), and No. 3, *in modo classico* (1941; also as the *Sinfonietta in modo classico* for Strings). **VOCAL:** *Morgengesang* for Men's Chorus, Winds, and Organ (1910; also for Men's Chorus and Orch., 1934); *Lieder und Gesänge* (3 vols., 1910–17); *Herbstchor an Pan* for Chorus, Children's Chorus, Orch., and Organ (1911); *Italienisches Liederbuch* (3 vols., 1912); *5 Lieder* for Voice and Orch. (1921); *Verklärtes Jahr,* 5 Songs for Medium Voice and Orch. (1930–32).

BIBL.: J. Bistron, *J. M.* (Vienna, 1923); A. Liess, *J. M.: Leben und Werk* (Graz, 1943); E. Werba, *J. M.* (Vienna, 1964); J. Meyers, *The Songs of J. M.* (diss., Univ. of Mo., 1972); T. Leibnitz, *Österreichische Spätromantiker: Studien zu Emil Nikolaus von Reznicek, J. M., Franz Schmidt und Egon Kornauth* (Tutzing, 1986). —**NS/LK/DM**

Marx, Karl, German composer and pedagogue; b. Munich, Nov. 12, 1897; d. Stuttgart, May 8, 1985. He served in the German army during World War I and was a prisoner of war in England; after the Armistice, he returned to Munich to study with Orff; then took courses with Beer-Walbrunn, Hausegger, and Schwickerath at the Akademie der Tonkunst (1920–24). In 1924 he joined its faculty and in 1928 he became the conductor of the Bach Soc. Chorus in Munich; from 1939 to 1946 he was instructor at the Hochschule für Musikerziehung in Graz; subsequently taught at the Hochschule für Musik in Stuttgart (1946–66). A master of German polyphony, Marx distinguished himself as a composer of both sacred and secular choral music.

WORKS: ORCH.: Concerto for 2 Violins and Orch. (1926); Piano Concerto (1929; rev. 1959); Viola Concerto (1929); *Passacaglia* (1932); Violin Concerto (1935); Concerto for Flute and Strings (1937); *15 Variations on a German Folk Song* (1938); *Musik nach alpenländischen Volksliedern* for Strings (1940); *Festival Prelude* (1956); Concerto for Strings (1964; a reworking of his 1932 *Passacaglia*); *Fantasia sinfonica* (1967; rev. 1969); *Fantasia concertante* for Violin, Cello, and Orch. (1972). **CHAMBER:** *Fantasy and Fugue* for String Quartet (1927); *Variations* for Organ (1933); *Divertimento* for 16 Winds (1934); *Turmmusik* for 3 Trumpets and 3 Trombones (1938); *Divertimento* for Flute, Violin, Viola, Cello, and Piano (1942); 6 sonatinas for various instrumental combinations (1948–51); *Kammermusik* for 7 Instruments (1955); Trio for Piano, Flute, and Cello (1962); Cello Sonata (1964); *Fantasy* for Violin (1966); *Partita über "Ein' feste Burg"* for String Quartet or String Orch. (1967); Wind Quintet (1973). **VOCAL:** Several large cantatas, including *Die heiligen drei Könige* (1936); *Rilke-Kantate* (1942); *Und endet doch alles mit Frieden* (1952); *Raube das Licht aus dem Rachen der Schlange* (1957); *Auftrag und Besinnung* (1961); chamber cantatas, including *Die unendliche Woge* (1930); also cantatas for special seasons, children's cantatas, and the like; a cappella pieces; songs, many with Orch., including *Rilke-Kreis* for Voice and Piano (1927; also for Mezzo-soprano and Chamber Orch., 1952) and *3 Songs,* to texts by Stefan George, for Baritone and Chamber Orch. (1934). —**NS/LK/DM**

Marx, Richard, unabashed pop craftsman who quietly accumulated 14 Top 40 hits; b. Chicago, Sept. 16, 1963. With a mother who sang jazz and a father who wrote and recorded jingles for companies like Nestle and Peter Pan, it's little wonder that Richard Marx developed a remarkable sense of pop craft. By age five, Marx was singing on his father's jingles; in his early teens, he was composing seriously. One of his tapes fell into the hands of Lionel Richie, who encouraged the 17-year-old Marx to come to Los Angeles, hiring him to sing backup on his first solo album. Marx continued to work as a backup singer for Madonna, Dolly Parton, Julio Iglesias, and Whitney Houston, to name but a few.

While working on a Kenny Rogers session, he overheard Rogers say he needed a new song, which Marx brought him several days later. The tune, "Crazy," went to the top of the country charts in 1984; another Marx song, "What About Me," featuring Rogers, James Ingram, and Kim Carnes topped the country and adult-contemporary charts, reaching #15 pop that same year.

While Marx tasted success with other performers, his own solo career was limited to the clubs. He received rejection notices from every record company in Los Angeles, until Bruce Lundvall heard him and signed him to his new EMI/Manhattan imprint. The first single from Marx's 1987 debut, "It Don't Mean Nothing," featured Joe Walsh on guitar, giving the tune a distinctive, recognizable sound. The song rose to #3, landing a phenomenal amount of airplay for a new artist. His next single, "Should've Known Better," also rose to #3. "Endless Summer Night" spent two weeks at #2 and the last single from the album, the power ballad "Hold On to the Night," topped the charts, making Marx the first artist to reach the Top 3 with the first four singles from a debut album. The album rose to #8 and went triple platinum. Marx went out on the road opening for REO Speedwagon, but quickly rose to headliner status. His boyish good looks no doubt added to his allure, and many a preteen girl pasted his picture on her wall.

In 1989, Marx kicked off his sophomore effort, *Repeat Offender*, with yet another chart-topping single, "Satisfied." He followed this with the biggest single of his career, the ballad "Right Here Waiting," which topped the pop charts for three weeks and the adult contemporary charts for six, and went platinum. The #4 follow-up single, "Angelia," made Marx the first solo performer to reach the Top 5 with his first seven singles. He broke the string with his next single, "Too Late to Say Goodbye," which stalled at #12. "Children of the Night," a song that took its name from a Los Angeles organization helping runaways, made it to #13. Beyond raising awareness of the organization, all the money from the song went to support it. The album topped the charts and went triple platinum. Marx toured the world again, both as a solo act and supporting Tina Turner.

As a means of promoting his next album, *Rush Street*, Marx staged a one-day, five-city "Rush In, Rush Out, Rush Street" tour in 1991. The album broke away from the ballads a bit, exploring some of the soul roots that he had put to work for Lionel Richie. The first single, "Keep Coming Back," featured Luther Vandross on backing vocals and rose to #12 pop, topping the adult-contemporary charts. "Hazard" had an almost contemporary-country feel; it reached #9 on the pop chart and again topped the adult-contemporary charts. The final single, "Take This Heart" only made it to #20. *Rush Street* hit #35 on the charts and went double platinum.

After moving his family (he had married Animotion lead singer and actress Cynthia Rhodes) back to Chicago, Marx went into the studio to cut *Paid Vacation*. Released in 1994, the first single, "Now and Forever," topped the adult-contemporary charts for 11 weeks, rising to #7 pop. The other single, "The Way She Loves Me," featured backing vocals by Vandross and Richie in

a style reminiscent of 1950s doo-wop. However, it only hit #20. The album went platinum, rising to #37.

Marx produced his next outing, 1997's *Flesh and Bone*, a hybrid of R&B and rock that featured Maurice White of Earth, Wind, and Fire on backing vocals. "Until I Find You" topped the adult-contemporary charts. Marx has yet to follow this with anything new save for the greatest hits package that ended his relationship with Capitol Records. In the later 1990s, he has produced records for artists as varied as opera/musical theater star Sarah Brightman and teen-pop sensations N'Sync, a duet with Barbra Streisand and country star Vince Gill, and country act SHeDAISY. In 1999, he made two successful tours of China.

Disc.: *Richard Marx* (1987); *Repeat Offender* (1989); *Rush Street* (1991); *Paid Vacation* (1994); *Flesh & Bone* (1997).—**HB**

Marx, Walter Burle, Brazilian-American conductor, teacher, and composer; b. São Paulo, July 23, 1902; d. Akron, Ohio, Dec. 29, 1990. He first studied piano with his mother, then pursued training in Rio de Janeiro with Enrique Oswald; in 1921, went to Berlin and studied piano with Kwast and composition with Rezniček. After touring as a pianist, he returned to Rio de Janeiro and was founder-conductor of its Phil. (1931–33); later appeared as a guest conductor in Europe and the U.S., conducting the N.Y. Phil. at the World's Fair in 1939; in 1947 he was conductor of the Rio de Janeiro Opera. In 1952 he settled in Philadelphia, where he taught piano and composition at the Settlement Music School until 1977. Among his works were 4 syms., concertos, chamber music, and vocal pieces.—**NS/LK/DM**

Marxsen, Eduard, German pianist, organist, teacher, and composer; b. Nienstadten, near Altona, July 23, 1806; d. Altona, Nov. 18, 1887. He studied with his father, an organist, in Altona, then with J.H. Clasing in Hamburg; went to Vienna (1830) to continue his training with Bocklet (piano) and I. Seyfried (composition). He settled as a teacher in Hamburg (1834), where Brahms later became his pupil. He wrote orch. music, piano pieces, songs, and other works.—**NS/LK/DM**

Maryon (-d'Aulby), (John) Edward, English composer; b. London, April 3, 1867; d. there, Jan. 31, 1954. He began to compose early in life. He went to Paris, where his first opera, *L'Odalisque*, won the Gold Medal at the Exposition of 1889; however, he regarded the work as immature and destroyed the score. In 1891 he studied with Max Pauer in Dresden; later took lessons with Wullner in Cologne. From 1914 to 1919 he was in Montclair, N.J., where he established a cons. with a fund for exchange of music students between England and America; in 1933 he returned to London. He wrote the operas *Paolo and Francesca; La Robe de plume; The Smelting Pot; The Prodigal Son; Werewolf; Rembrandt; Greater Love;* and *Abelard and Heloise.* In his *Werewolf* he applied a curious system of musical symbolism, in which the human part was characterized by the diatonic scale and the lupine self by the whole-tone scale; Maryon made a claim of priority in using the whole-tone scale consistently as a leading motive in an opera.

His magnum opus was a grandiose operatic heptalogy under the title *The Cycle of Life*, comprising 7 mystical dramas: *Lucifer, Cain, Krishna, Magdalen, Sangraal, Psyche*, and *Nirvana*. He also wrote a symphonic poem, *The Feather Robe*, subtitled *A Legend of Fujiyama* (1905), which he dedicated to the Emperor of Japan; and *Armageddon Requiem* (1916), dedicated to the dead of World War I. After Maryon's death, his complete MSS were donated to the Boston Public Library. Maryon developed a theory of universal art, in which colors were associated with sounds. An outline of this theory was publ. in his *Marcotone* (N.Y., 1915).—**NS/LK/DM**

Märzendorfer, Ernst, Austrian conductor; b. Oberndorf, May 26, 1921. He was a student in Graz and of Krauss at the Salzburg Mozarteum. In 1940 he began his conducting career in Salzburg. He conducted at the Graz (1945–51) and then Salzburg (from 1951) Landestheaters. From 1951 he taught conducting at the Mozarteum. In 1952–53 he conducted at the Teatro Colón in Buenos Aires. From 1953 to 1958 he was conductor of the Mozarteum Orch., which he led on a U.S. tour in 1956. He subsequently conducted throughout Europe. He also recorded all the Haydn syms. with the Vienna Chamber Orch. (1969–71) and prepared a completion of Bruckner's 9th Sym. (1969).—**NS/LK/DM**

Mascagni, Pietro, famous Italian composer; b. Livorno, Dec. 7, 1863; d. Rome, Aug. 2, 1945. His father was a baker who wished him to continue in that trade, but yielded to his son's determination to study music. Thanks to aid from an uncle, he was able to take some music lessons with Soffredini in Livorno and then to attend the Milan Cons., where he studied with Ponchielli and Saladino (1882). However, he became impatient with school discipline, and was dismissed from the Cons. in 1884. He then was active as a double bass player in the orch. of the Teatro dal Verme in Milan. After touring as a conductor with operetta troupes, he taught music in Cerignola, Puglia. He composed industriously; in 1888 he sent the MS of his 1-act opera *Cavalleria rusticana* to the music publisher Sonzogno for a competition, and won 1st prize. The opera was performed at the Teatro Costanzi in Rome on May 17, 1890, with sensational success; the dramatic story of village passion, and Mascagni's emotional score, laden with luscious music, combined to produce an extraordinary appeal to opera lovers. The short opera made the tour of the world stages with amazing rapidity, productions being staged all over Europe and America with never-failing success; the opera was usually presented in 2 parts, separated by an "intermezzo sinfonico" (which became a popular orch. number performed separately). *Cavalleria rusticana* marked the advent of the operatic style known as verismo, in which stark realism was the chief aim and the dramatic development was condensed to enhance the impressions. When, 2 years later, another "veristic" opera, Leoncavallo's *Pagliacci*, was taken by Sonzogno, the 2 operas became twin attractions on a single bill. Ironically, Mascagni could never duplicate or even remotely approach the success of his first production, although he continued to compose industriously and opera houses all over the world were only too eager to stage his successive operas. Thus, his opera *Le Maschere* was produced on Jan. 17, 1901, at 6 of the most important Italian opera houses simultaneously (Rome, Milan, Turin, Genoa, Venice, Verona); it was produced 2 days later in Naples. Mascagni himself conducted the premiere in Rome. But the opera failed to fire the imagination of the public; it was produced in a revised form in Turin 15 years later (June 7, 1916), but was not established in the repertoire even in Italy. In 1902 he made a tour of the U.S. conducting his *Cavalleria rusticana* and other operas, but, owing to mismanagement, the visit proved a fiasco; a South American tour in 1911 was more successful. He also appeared frequently as a conductor of sym. concerts. In 1890 he was made a Knight of the Crown of Italy; in 1929 he was elected a member of the Academy. At various times he also was engaged in teaching; from 1895 to 1902 he was director of the Rossini Cons. in Pesaro. His last years were darkened by the inglorious role that he had played as an ardent supporter of the Fascist regime, so that he was rejected by many of his old friends. It was only after his death that his errors of moral judgment were forgiven; his centennial was widely celebrated in Italy in 1963. D. Stivender ed. and tr. his autobiography into Eng. (N.Y., 1975).

WORKS: DRAMATIC: O p e r a : *Pinotta* (c. 1880; San Remo, March 23, 1932); *Guglielmo Ratcliff* (c. 1885; Milan, Feb. 16, 1895); *Cavalleria rusticana* (Rome, May 17, 1890); *L'Amico Fritz* (Rome, Oct. 31, 1891); *I Rantzau* (Florence, Nov. 10, 1892); *Silvano* (Milan, March 25, 1895); *Zanetto* (Pesaro, March 2, 1896); *Iris* (Rome, Nov. 22, 1898; rev. version, Milan, Jan. 19, 1899); *Le Maschere* (simultaneous premiere in Rome, Milan, Turin, Genoa, Venice, and Verona, Jan. 17, 1901); *Amica* (Monte Carlo, March 16, 1905); *Isabeau* (Buenos Aires, June 2, 1911); *Parisina* (Milan, Dec. 15, 1913); *Lodoletta* (Rome, April 30, 1917); *Scampolo* (1921); *Il piccolo Marat* (Rome, May 2, 1921); *Nerone* (Milan, Jan. 16, 1935); *I Bianchi ed i Neri* (1940). **O p e r e t t a :** *Il re a Napoli* (n.d.); *Sí* (Rome, Dec. 13, 1919). **OTHER:** 2 syms. (1879, 1881); *Poema leopardiano* (for the centenary of G. Leopardi, 1898); Hymn in honor of Admiral Dewey (July 1899); *Rapsodia satanica* for Orch. (music for a film, Rome, July 2, 1917); *Davanti Santa Teresa* (Rome, Aug. 1923); chamber music; choral works; songs; piano pieces.

BIBL.: G. Monaldi, *P. M.: L'Uomo e l'artista* (Rome, 1899); G. Bastianelli, *P. M.: Con nota delle opere* (Naples, 1910); G. Orsini, *L'arte di P. M.* (Milan, 1912); E. Pompei, *P. M.: Nella vita e nell'arte* (Rome, 1912); A. Donno, *M. nel 900 musicale* (Rome, 1935); A. Jeri, *M., 15 Opere, 1000 Episodi* (Milan, 1940); D. Cellamare, *M. e la "Cavalleria" visti da Cerignola* (Rome, 1941); *M. parla* (Rome, 1945); *Comitato nazionale delle onoranze a P. M. nel primo centenario della nascità* (Livorno, 1963); M. Morini, ed., *P. M.* (2 vols., Milan, 1964); G. Gavazzeni, *Discorso per M. nel centenario della nascità* (Rome, 1964); D. Cellamare, *P. M.* (Rome, 1965); R. Iovino, *M: L'avventuroso dell'opera* (Milan, 1987); C. and L. Pini, *M. a quattro mani* (Viareggio, 1992); C. Criscione and L. Andalò, eds., *M. ritrovato: 1863–1945: L'uomo, il musicista: Mostra itinierante per il cinquantenario della scomparsa del musicista livornese* (Milan, 1995); M. Morini, R. Iovino, and A. Paloscia, eds., *P. M.: Epistolario* (Lucca, 1996 et seq.).—**NS/LK/DM**

Maschera, Florentio or **Florenzo,** Italian organist, string player, and composer; b. probably in Brescia, c. 1540; d. there, c. 1584. He first studied with his father, and then was a pupil of Merulo. He served as organist at Santo Spirito in Venice. On Aug. 22, 1557, he succeeded Merulo as organist at the Brescia Cathedral. He publ. *Libro primo de canzoni da sonare a quattro voci* (Brescia, 1584), which was ed. by W. McKee in *The Music of Florentio Maschera (1540–1584)* (diss., North Tex. State Univ., 1958).—**NS/LK/DM**

Mascheroni, Edoardo, distinguished Italian conductor; b. Milan, Sept. 4, 1852; d. Ghirla, near Varese, March 4, 1941. As a boy, he showed special interest in mathematics and literature. He wrote literary essays for the journal *La Vita Nuova* before he decided to study music seriously, at which time he took lessons with Boucheron in Milan and composed various pieces. In 1880 he began a career in Brescia as a conductor, and it was in that capacity that he distinguished himself. He was first a theater conductor in Livorno; then went to Rome, where he established his reputation as an opera conductor at the Teatro Apollo (1884). From 1891 to 1894 he was chief conductor of Milan's La Scala, where Verdi chose him to conduct the premiere of his *Falstaff* (Feb. 9, 1893). After conducting in Germany, Spain, and South America, he continued his career in Italy until retiring about 1925. He wrote 2 operas, *Lorenza* (Rome, April 13, 1901) and *La Perugina* (Naples, April 24, 1909), 2 Requiems, and chamber music. His brother, Angelo Mascheroni (1855–95), was also a conductor. —**NS/LK/DM**

Mascitti, Michele, Italian-born French composer; b. S. Maria, near Naples, 1663 or 1664; d. Paris, April 24, 1760. He was a pupil of his uncle, a violinist in the Naples royal chapel. After travels throughout Europe, he settled in Paris in 1704 and became a naturalized French subject in 1739. He was in the service of the Duke of Orléans. He publ. about 100 violin sonatas (Paris, 1704–38) and other works.—**LK/DM**

Mašek, Vincenz, Bohemian pianist and organist; b. Zwikovecz, April 5, 1755; d. Prague, Nov. 15, 1831. He was a pupil of Seeger and F.X. Dussek, and became an accomplished player of the piano and harmonica. After long tours, he settled in Prague as an organist and music dealer. His brother Paul Mašek (1761–1826) was a pianist and a teacher in Vienna.—**NS/LK/DM**

Masini, Angelo, Italian tenor; b. Terra del Sole, near Forli, Nov. 28, 1844; d. Forli, Sept. 26, 1926. He studied with Gilda Minguzzi, making his debut as Pollione in *Norma* in Finale Emilia (1867). He then sang throughout Italy, Spain, and Russia. He was chosen by Verdi to sing in the Requiem, appearing under Verdi's direction in London, Paris, and Vienna in 1875. He gave his farewell stage performance in Paris in 1905. Among his finest roles were Count Almaviva, Don Ottavio, Faust, and Radames.

BIBL.: C. Rivalta, *Il tenore A. M. e Faenza* (Faenza, 1927). —**NS/LK/DM**

Masini, Galliano, Italian tenor; b. Livorno, 1896; d. there, Feb. 15, 1986. He received his training in Milan.

In 1923 he made his operatic debut as Cavaradossi in Livorno, and then sang in various Italian music centers. In 1930 he made his first appearance in Rome as Pinkerton, and continued to sing there until 1950. He also sang at Milan's La Scala, in Rio de Janeiro, Buenos Aires, Vienna, and Paris. In 1937–38 he appeared at the Chicago Opera. On Dec. 14, 1938, he made his Metropolitan Opera debut in N.Y. as Edgardo, where he remained on the roster for the season. In subsequent years, he pursued his career in Europe, making his farewell appearance in 1957. Among his other roles were Radames, Rodolfo, Turiddu, and Enzo. —**NS/LK/DM**

Maslanka, David, American composer; b. New Bedford, Mass., Aug. 30, 1943. He studied at the Oberlin (Ohio) Coll. Cons. of Music (1961–65), where he received training in composition from Joseph Wood, and at the Salzburg Mozarteum (1963–64). While at Mich. State Univ. to complete his doctorate (1965–70), he pursued further studies in composition with H. Owen Reed and Paul Harder. He taught at the State Univ. of N.Y. at Geneseo (1970–74), Sarah Lawrence Coll. (1974–80), N.Y.U. (1980–81), and Kingsborough Coll. of the City Univ. of N.Y. (1989–90). Since then, Maslanka has devoted himself fully to composition, accepting commissions in the genre of wind music, in which he is nearly peerless. After 1980 he began exploring the potential of wind instruments, promoting the explosive capabilities of their massed sonorities especially when bolstered by percussion. His Sym. No. 2 is almost volcanic in its visceral impact. On April 17, 1998, his *Sea Dreams* was premiered simultaneously on the Internet on 7 university campuses, from Ore. to N.Y., in a unique "netcast."

WORKS: DRAMATIC: *Death and the Maiden,* chamber opera (1974). ORCH.: Sym. No. 1 (1970); *Fragments* for Chamber Orch. (1971); *Intermezzo* for Chamber Orch. (1979); *A Child's Garden of Dreams,* Book 2 (1989); *Music for Strings* (1992). Symphonic Band or Wind Ensemble: Concerto for Piano, Winds, and Percussion (1974–75); *Prelude on a Gregorian Tune* (1981); *A Child's Garden of Dreams,* Book 1 (1981); Syms. No. 2 (1985), No. 3 (1991), No. 4 (1993), and No. 5 (2000); *In Memoriam* (1989); *Golden Light* (1990); Concerto for Marimba and Band (1990); *Montana Music: Chorale Variations* (1993); *Tears* (1994); *Laudamus Te* (1994); *A Tuning Piece: Songs of Fall and Winter* (1995); *Hell's Gate* for Saxophone Trio and Symphonic Wind Ensemble (1996); *Morning Star* (1997); *Sea Dreams,* concerto for 2 Horns and Wind Orch. (1997); *UFO Dreams,* concerto for Euphonium and Wind Ensemble (1998); Concerto for Saxophone and Wind Ensemble (1999). CHAMBER: String Quartet (1968); Trio for Violin, Clarinet, and Piano (1973); 4 Pieces for Clarinet and Piano (1975–79); *Variations on "Lost Love"* for Marimba (1977); *Orpheus* for 2 Bassoons and Marimba (1977); *Cello Songs* for Cello and Piano (1978); *Music for Dr. Who* for Bassoon and Piano (1979); 3 wind quintets (1981, 1986, 1999); *Arcadia I* for Cello Quartet (1982) and *II,* concerto for Marimba and Percussion Ensemble (1982); Saxophone Sonata (1988); *Little Concerto* for 6 Players (1990); *Crown of Thorns* for Keyboard Percussion Ensemble (1991); Oboe Sonata (1992); *Montana Music: 3 Dances* for Percussion (1992); *Montana Music: Fantasy on a Chorale Tune* for Violin and Viola (1993); Horn Sonata (1996; rev. 1999); *Mountain Roads* for Saxophone Quartet (1997); *Song Book* for Saxophone and Marimba (1998). VOCAL:

The Nameless Fear, or, the Unanswered Question Put Yet Another Way for Chorus, Speakers, Guitars, Harpsichord, Flute, Bassoon, and Percussion (1973); 5 Songs for Soprano, Baritone, and Chamber Orch. (1976); *Lincoln Speaks at Gettysburg* for Tenor, Alto Flute, and Contrabass (1984); *A Litany for Courage and the Seasons*, 6 songs for Chorus, Clarinet, and Vibraphone (1988); *Mass* for Soprano, Baritone, Chorus, Organ, and Symphonic Wind Ensemble (1992–96).—**LK/DM**

Masley, Michael, American instrumentalist, composer, and instrument maker; b. Trenton, Mich., Sept. 22, 1952. He studied creative writing at Northwestern Mich. Coll. (1970–72), and in 1973 began working with hammer dulcimer player Bob Spinner, who became a mentor. He played using traditional 2-hammer technique until 1979, and during months at a fishing lodge in northern Mich., he developed a 10-fingered "finger-hammer" technique. In 1982 he engaged the dulcimer maker William Webster of Detroit to make him a cymbalom; he added sections of violin bow to the finger hammers in 1983, creating his unique "bowhammers." In 1982 he moved to Palo Alto, Calif., where he met guitarist Barry Cleveland (1983) with whom he performed as the duo Thin Ice, releasing the recordings *Thin Ice Live* (1984) and *1ˢᵗ Frost* (1985). He also played on Cleveland's later albums, *Mythos* (1986) and *Voluntary Dreaming* (1990). In 1985 he settled in Berkeley, Calif. His own recordings include *Cymbalom Songs* (1985), *The Moment's River* (1987), *Bells & Shadows* (1989), *Mystery Loves Company* (1990), *Sky Blues* (1992), and *Life in the Vast Lane* (1993); also the compilation *Mystery Repeats Itself* (1994). His innovative cymbalom technique enables the player to strike, bow, or pluck notes with all 10 fingers in any combination. The resulting timbral distinctions are used to create unusually complex contrapuntal textures for a solo instrument, to which he often adds pitched and tunable percussion instruments. —**NS/LK/DM**

Mason, Daniel Gregory, eminent American composer and educator, grandson of **Lowell Mason** and nephew of **William Mason**; b. Brookline, Mass., Nov. 20, 1873; d. Greenwich, Conn., Dec. 4, 1953. A scion of a famous family of American musicians, his father, Henry Mason, was a co-founder of the piano manufacturing firm Mason & Hamlin. He entered Harvard Univ., where he studied with J.K. Paine (B.A., 1895); after graduation, he continued his studies with Arthur Whiting (piano), Goetschius (theory), and Chadwick (orchestration). Still feeling the necessity for improvement of his technique as a composer, he went to Paris, where he took courses with d'Indy (1913). In 1905 he became a member of the faculty of Columbia Univ. in N.Y.; in 1929, was appointed MacDowell Professor of Music; he was chairman of the music dept. until 1940, and continued to teach there until 1942, when he retired. As a teacher, Mason developed a high degree of technical ability in his students; as a composer, he represented a conservative trend in American music; while an adherent to the idea of an American national style, his conception was racially and regionally narrow, accept-

ing only the music of Anglo-Saxon New England and the "old South"; he was an outspoken opponent of the "corrupting" and "foreign" influences of 20th-century Afro-American and Jewish-American music. His ideals were the German masters of the Romantic school; but there is an admixture of impressionistic colors in his orchestration; his harmonies are full and opulent, his melodic writing expressive and songful. The lack of strong individuality, however, has resulted in the virtual disappearance of his music from the active repertoire.

WORKS: ORCH.: 3 syms.: No. 1 (1913–14; Philadelphia, Feb. 18, 1916; radically rev. version, N.Y., Dec. 1, 1922), No. 2 (Cincinnati, Nov. 23, 1928), and No. 3, *Lincoln* (1935–36; N.Y., Nov. 17, 1937); *Prelude and Fugue* for Piano and Orch. (1914; Chicago, March 4, 1921); *Scherzo-Caprice* for Chamber Orch. (N.Y., Jan. 2, 1917); *Chanticleer*, festival overture (1926; Cincinnati, Nov. 23, 1928); *Suite* (1933–34); *Prelude and Fugue* for Strings (1939). **CHAMBER:** Violin Sonata (1907–08); Quartet for Piano and Strings (1909–11); *Pastorale* for Violin, Clarinet or Viola, and Piano (1909–12); 3 pieces for Flute, Harp, and String Quartet (1911–12); Sonata for Clarinet or Violin and Piano (1912–15); *Intermezzo* for String Quartet (1916); *String Quartet on Negro Themes* (1918–19); *Variations on a Theme of John Powell* for String Quartet (1924–25); *Divertimento* for Flute, Oboe, Clarinet, Horn, and Bassoon (1926); *Fanny Blair*, folk-song fantasy for String Quartet (1929); *Serenade* for String Quartet (1931); *Sentimental Sketches*, 4 short pieces for Violin, Cello, and Piano (1935); *Variations on a Quiet Theme* (1939). **VOCAL:** *Russians* for Voice and Piano (1915–17; also for Baritone and Orch.); *Songs of the Countryside* for Chorus and Orch. (1923); *Soldiers* for Baritone and Piano (1948–49).

WRITINGS (all publ. in N.Y.): *From Grieg to Brahms* (1902; rev. 1930); *Beethoven and His Forerunners* (1904; 2ⁿᵈ ed., 1930); *The Romantic Composers* (1906); with T. Surette, *The Appreciation of Music* (1907) *The Orchestral Instruments and What They Do* (1909); *A Guide to Music* (1909); *A Neglected Sense in Piano Playing* (1912); with M. Mason, *Great Modern Composers* (1916; 2ⁿᵈ ed., 1968); *Short Studies of Great Masterpieces* (1917); *Contemporary Composers* (1918); *Music as a Humanity: And Other Essays* (1921); *From Song to Symphony* (1924); *Artistic Ideals* (1925); *The Dilemma of American Music* (1928); *Tune In, America!* (1931); *The Chamber Music of Brahms* (1933); *Music in My Time and Other Reminiscences* (1938); *The Quartets of Beethoven* (1947).

BIBL.: M. Klein, *The Contribution of D.G. M. to American Music* (diss., Catholic Univ. of America, 1957); R. Lewis, *The Life and Music of D.G. M.* (diss., Univ. of Rochester, 1959); D. Kapec, *The Three Symphonies of D.G. M.: Style-Critical and Theoretical Analyses* (diss., Univ. of Fla., 1982).—**NS/LK/DM**

Mason, Edith (Barnes), American soprano; b. St. Louis, March 22, 1893; d. San Diego, Nov. 26, 1973. She studied in Cincinnati, and then with Enrico Bertran and Edmond Clément in Paris. Following her operatic debut in Marseilles (1911), she sang in Boston (1912), Montreal (1912), Nice (1914), and N.Y. (Century Co., 1914–15). On Nov. 20, 1915, she made her Metropolitan Opera debut in N.Y. as Sophie in *Der Rosenkavalier*, remaining on its roster until 1917. After singing in Paris (1919–21), she was a principal member of the Chicago Opera (1921–29). She also sang at Milan's La Scala (1923), was again on the roster of the Metropolitan Opera (1934–36), and appeared at the Salzburg Festival (1935). In 1941 she made her farewell appearance in Chicago as Mimi. She was married twice to **Giorgio Polacco**. Among her other roles were Gilda, Gounod's Marguerite, Thaïs, Elsa, and Cio-Cio-San.—**NS/LK/DM**

Mason, Lowell, distinguished American organist, conductor, music educator, and composer, father of **William Mason** and grandfather of **Daniel Gregory Mason**; b. Medfield, Mass., Jan. 8, 1792; d. Orange, N.J., Aug. 11, 1872. As a youth he studied singing with Amos Albee and Oliver Shaw, and at 16 he directed the church choir at Medfield. In 1812 he went to Savannah, Ga., where he studied harmony and composition with Frederick Abel. He taught singing in schools (1813–24) and became principal of the singers (1815) and organist (1820) of the Independent Presbyterian Church. In 1827 he went to Boston and was president of the Handel and Haydn Soc. (until 1832). He established classes on Pestalozzi's system, teaching it privately from 1829 and in the public schools from 1837. He founded the Boston Academy of Music in 1833 with George J. Webb, and was superintendent of music in the Boston public schools (1837–45), remaining active as a teacher until 1851. He made 2 sojourns in Europe to study pedagogic methods (1837; 1851–53). In 1854 he settled in Orange, N.J. He received an honorary doctorate in music from N.Y.U. (1855), only the 2nd such conferring of that degree in the U.S. He publ. *Musical Letters from Abroad* (N.Y., 1853). M. Broyles ed. *A Yankee Musician in Europe: The 1837 Journals of Lowell Mason* (Ann Arbor, 1990). Mason became wealthy through the sale of his many collections of music: *Handel and Haydn Society's Collection of Church Music* (1822; 16 later eds.); *Juvenile Psalmist* (1829); *Juvenile Lyre* (1830); *Lyra Sacra* (1832); *Sabbath School Songs* (1836); *Boston Academy Collection of Church Music* (1836); *Boston Anthem Book* (1839); *The Psaltery* (1845); *Cantica Laudis* (1850); *New Carmina Sacra* (1852); *Normal Singer* (1856); *Song Garden* (3 parts; 1864–65); etc. Many of his own hymn tunes, including *Missionary Hymn (From Greenland's Icy Mountains)*, *Olivet*, *Boylston*, *Bethany*, *Hebron*, and *Olmutz*, are still found in hymnals. His valuable library, including 830 MSS and 700 vols. of hymnology, was given to Yale Coll. after his death.

BIBL.: T. Seward, *The Educational Work of Dr. L. M.* (Boston, 1885); H. Mason, *Hymn Tunes of L. M., A Bibliography* (Cambridge, Mass., 1944); idem, *L. M.: An Appreciation of His Life and Work* (N.Y., 1944); A. Rich, *L. M.: The Father of Singing among the Children* (Chapel Hill, N.C., 1946); C. Pemberton, *L. M.: His Life and Work* (Ann Arbor, 1985); idem, *L. M.: A Bio-Bibliography* (Westport, Conn., 1988).—**NS/LK/DM**

Mason, Luther Whiting, prominent American music educator and editor of school songbooks; b. Turner, Maine, April 3, 1828; d. Buckfield, Maine, July 4, 1896. He was a student of Lowell Mason at the Boston Academy of Music, who may have been a distant relative. After directing singing classes and church choirs, he went to Louisville in 1853 and pioneered the teaching of music in the primary grades of public schools. In 1856 he went to Cincinnati, where he did likewise. In 1864 he was invited to Boston to set up a curriculum for general classroom teachers to give pupils instruction in singing, a curriculum subsequently adopted by many other schools. In 1880 he was called to

Japan with the mission of organizing a national training program for music teachers. School music in Japan became known as "Mason song" due to the use of his songbooks. During his 2-year sojourn there, he also taught notation and harmony to the imperial court musicians, retuned their ancient instruments to the Western scale, and imported Western instruments. He also traveled widely in Europe. Mason's greatest success in the U.S. came with his National Music Course, which consisted of a series of music textbooks, charts, and guides based upon the labors of the German pedagogue Christian Heinrich Hohmann. The course was first issued as the *First, Second, and Third Music Readers* (1870; 2nd ed., rev., 1885) for students, *The National Music Teacher* (1870) for teacher guidance, and 3 sets of charts. *The Mason School Music Course* was publ. in 1898. He also ed. *Mason's Hymn and Tune Book* (1882).

BIBL.: O. McConathy, *L.W. M. and his Contribution to Music in the Schools of Three Continents* (MS, 1942); K. Hartley, *A Study of the Life and Works of L.W. M.* (diss., Fla. State Univ., 1960); B. Hall, *The L.W. M.—Osbourne McConathy Collection* (thesis, Univ. of Md., 1983); S. Howe, *L.W. M., International Music Educator* (Warren, Mich., 1997).—**NS/LK/DM**

Mason, Marilyn (May), American organist and pedagogue; b. Alva, Okla., June 29, 1925. She studied at Okla. State Univ. and the Univ. of Mich.; also took lessons with Boulanger, Duruflé, and Schoenberg, completing her studies at the Union Theological Seminary in N.Y. (D.S.M., 1954). She became a teacher at the Univ. of Mich. in Ann Arbor (1946); was made chairman of its organ dept. in 1962 and a prof. in 1965. She made many tours as a recitalist in North America, Europe, South America, and the Far East, performing commissioned works from such composers as Cowell, Finney, Kay, Krenek, and Sowerby.—**NS/LK/DM**

Mason, William, esteemed American pianist, pedagogue, and composer, son of **Lowell Mason** and uncle of **Daniel Gregory Mason**; b. Boston, Jan. 24, 1829; d. N.Y., July 14, 1908. He studied with his father and with Henry Schmidt in Boston. He made his debut at an Academy of Music concert there (March 7, 1846), and then went to Leipzig (1849), where he continued his studies with Moscheles, Hauptmann, and Richter. After further instruction from Dreyschock in Prague, he completed his training with Liszt in Weimar (1853–54). After appearances in Weimar, Prague, Frankfurt am Main, and other continental cities, as well as in London (1853), he toured in the U.S. (1854–55). He then settled in N.Y., where he founded the Mason and Thomas Soirees of Chamber Music with Theodore Thomas in 1855; after they were discontinued in 1868, he devoted himself mainly to teaching. In 1872 he was awarded an honorary doctorate in music from Yale Coll. He publ. *Memories of a Musical Life* (N.Y., 1901). Mason composed a *Serenata* for Cello and Piano and some 40 piano pieces. His pedagogical works include *A Method for the Pianoforte* (with E. Hoadley; N.Y., 1867), *A System for Beginners* (with E. Hoadley; Boston, 1871), *A System of Technical Exercises for the Piano-forte* (Boston, 1878), *Touch and Technique*, op.44 (Philadelphia, 1889), and *A Primer of Music* (with W. Mathews; N.Y., 1894).

BIBL.: K. Graber, *W. M. (1829–1908): An Annotated Bibliography and Catalog of Works* (Warren, Mich., 1987).—NS/LK/DM

Mason & Hamlin Co., celebrated firm of piano manufacturers. The firm was founded as the M. & H. Organ Co. in Boston in 1854 by Henry Mason, a son of **Lowell Mason** and the father of **Daniel Gregory Mason** and Emmons Hamlin. The latter, a brilliant mechanic, turned his attention to improving the quality of the reeds and obtaining great variety of tonal color, with the result that in 1861 the firm introduced the American Cabinet Organ. The firm became internationally famous when at the Paris Exposition of 1867 its organs were awarded 1st prize over numerous European competitors. In 1882 it began the construction of pianos, introducing a new system of stringing which found immediate favor; of several improvements patented by Mason & Hamlin, the most important was the Tension-Resonator (1900; described in *Scientific American*, Oct. 11, 1902), a device for preserving the tension of the sounding board. The firm subsequently became a subsidiary of the Aeolian American Corp. and eventually of the American Piano Corp. Henry Lowell Mason, son of the founder, was president of the firm until 1929. —NS/LK/DM

Massa, Juan Bautista, Argentine composer; b. Buenos Aires, Oct. 29, 1885; d. Rosario, March 7, 1938. He studied violin and composition, and became a choral conductor. He moved to Rosario, where he was active as a teacher.

WORKS: DRAMATIC: O p e r a : *Zoraide* (Buenos Aires, May 15, 1909); *L'Evaso* (Rosario, June 23, 1922); *La Magdalena* (Buenos Aires, Nov. 9, 1929). **O p e r e t t a :** *Esmeralda* (1903); *Triunfo del corazon* (1910); *La eterna historia* (1911). **B a l l e t :** *El cometa* (Buenos Aires, Nov. 8, 1932). **ORCH.:** *La muerte del Inca*, symphonic poem (Buenos Aires, Oct. 15, 1932); 2 Argentine suites; other pieces on native themes.—NS/LK/DM

Massaino (Massaini), Tiburtio, Italian composer; b. Cremona, c. 1549; d. Piacenza or Lodi, c. 1609. He was a member of the Augustinian order, in charge of music at the church of S. Maria de Populo, Salo, from 1571. In 1587 he became maestro di cappella at Salo Cathedral and, later, chaplain and singer at the court chapel of Archduke Ferdinand II in Innsbruck (c. 1589). He then entered the service of Archbishop Wolf Dietrich von Raitenau in Salzburg, where he remained until his arrest as a suspected homosexual (1591). Despite this lapse, he was highly esteemed as a composer, and later was active in Prague, Cremona, and Piacenza. He was maestro di cappella in Lodi (1608) and at Piacenza Cathedral (1609).

WORKS (all publ. in Venice unless otherwise given): **V O-CAL: S a c r e d :** *Concentus in universos psalmos...in vesperis omnium festorum per totum annum frequentatos, cum 3 Magnificat* for 5 and 9 Voices (1576; 2nd ed., 1588); *Motectorum liber primus* for 5 to 6 Voices (1576); *Missae, liber primus* for 5 to 6 Voices (1578); *Sacri cantus...liber secundus* for 5 Voices (1580); *Psalmi omnes ad vesperas per totum annum decantandi, una cum 4 Magnificat* for 8 Voices (1587); *Secundus liber missarum* for 5 Voices (1587); *Motectorum...liber tertius* for 5 Voices (1590); *Liber primus cantionum ecclesiasticarum* for 4 Voices (Prague, 1592; ed. in Denkmäler der Tonkunst in Österreich, CX, 1964); *Sacrae cantiones...liber primus* for 6 Voices (1592); *Sacri modulorum concentus* for 6 to 10 and 12 Voices (1592); *Primus liber missarum* for 6 Voices (1595); *Sacrae cantiones...liber secundus* for 5 Voices (1596); *Tertius liber missarum* for 5 Voices (1598); *Motectorum liber quartus* for 5 Voices (1599); *Musica super Threnos Ieremiae prophete in maiori hebdomada decantandas* for 5 Voices (1599); *Missarum liber primus* for 8 Voices (1600); *Sacrae cantiones...liber tertius* for 6 Voices (1601); *Sacri modulorum concentus* for 8 to 10 and 12, 15, and 16 Voices, op.31 (1606); *Musica per cantare con l'organo* for 1 to 3 Voices and Organ, op.32 (1607); *Sacrarum cantionum liber primus* for 7 Voices and Basso Continuo (organ), op.33 (1607); *Quaerimoniae cum responsoriis infra hebdomadam sanctam concinendae, et passiones pro Dominica Palmarum, et feria sexta* for 5 Voices, op.34 (1609); various other works in contemporary collections. **S e c u l a r :** *Il primo libro de madrigali* for 4 Voices (1569); *Il primo libro de madrigali* for 5 Voices (1571); *Il secundo libro de madrigali* for 4 Voices (1573); *Il secundo libro de madrigali* for 5 Voices (1578); *Trionfo di musica...libro primo* for 6 Voices (1579); *Il terzo libro de madrigali* for 5 Voices (1587); *Il quarto libro de madrigali* for 5 Voices (1594); *Madrigali...libro primo* for 6 Voices (1604); *Il secondo libro de madrigali* for 6 Voices (1604). —NS/LK/DM

Massarani, Renzo, Italian-born Brazilian composer; b. Mantua, March 26, 1898; d. Rio de Janeiro, March 28, 1975. He studied with Respighi at Rome's Accademia di Santa Cecilia (diploma, 1921), then was active as music director of Vittorio Podrecca's puppet theater Il Teatro dei Piccoli and as a music critic. He left Fascist Italy and settled in Rio de Janeiro in 1935, becoming a naturalized Brazilian citizen in 1945; was active as a music critic. Through the banning of his works during the Mussolini dictatorship, the havoc of World War II, and his own destruction of many scores, much of his output is not extant. His surviving music reveals a composer of considerable talent.

WORKS: DRAMATIC: O p e r a : *Noi due* (c. 1921); *La Donna nel pozzo* (1930); *Eliduc* (1938; unfinished). **O p e r i n a :** *Bianco e nero* (Rome, 1921); *Le nozze di Takiu* (Rome, 1927); *Gilbetto e Gherminella* (Rome, 1929); *I dolori della principessa Susina* (Rome, 1929). **B a l l e t :** *Guerin detto il meschino* (1928); *Boe* (Bergamo, 1937). **ORCH.:** Sinfonietta (1924); *Introduzione, tema e 7 variazioni* for Small Orch. (1934); *Il molinaro* for Violin and Orch. (1935); *Squilli e danze per il 18BL* (1937). **OTHER:** Chamber music; piano pieces; songs.—NS/LK/DM

Massart, (Joseph) Lambert, eminent Belgian violinist and pedagogue; b. Liège, July 19, 1811; d. Paris, Feb. 13, 1892. He studied music with his father and brother, then violin with Ambroise Delaveux. Following his debut at the Liège Theater (March 26, 1822), he received financial assistance from the King for further studies at the Paris Cons. When Cherubini refused him admission because he was a foreigner, he found a mentor in R. Kreutzer. In 1829 he was allowed to enter the Cons., where he studied theory with P. Zimmerman and counterpoint and fugue with F.-J. Fétis. He gave many successful concerts in Paris. He was prof. of violin at the Cons. (1843–90), and was also active as a chamber music artist of great distinction. He married the pianist and teacher Louise Anglaë Masson (b. Paris, June 10, 1827; d. there, July 26, 1887), with whom he performed regularly in chamber music settings. She succeeded Farrenc as a teacher at the Cons. in 1875. Among Massart's foremost pupils were Wieniawski, Marsick, Sarasate, and Kreisler.—NS/LK/DM

Massart, Nestor-Henri-Joseph, Belgian tenor; b. Ciney, Oct. 20, 1849; d. Ostend, Dec. 19, 1899. He was an officer in the Belgian army when his remarkable voice attracted the attention of the royal family, through whose influence he was granted a leave of absence for study. He then sang with success in Brussels, Lyons, Cairo, New Orleans, San Francisco, and Mexico. —NS/LK/DM

Massé, Victor (actually, Félix-Marie), French composer and teacher; b. Lorient, Morbihan, March 7, 1822; d. Paris, July 5, 1884. He entered the Paris Cons. at 12 and studied with Zimmerman (premier prix in piano, 1839). After taking premiers prix in harmony (1840) and fugue (1843), he studied composition with Halévy. In 1844 he was awarded the Grand Prix de Rome for his cantata *Le Renégat de Tanger*. While in Rome, he composed a Mass and an opera, *La Favorita e la schiava* (c. 1845; Venice, 1855). After returning to Paris, he gained his first success as an opera composer with *La Chanteuse voilée* (Nov. 26, 1850). Then followed the most successful of his light operas, *Les Noces de Jeannette* (Feb. 4, 1853). In 1866 he was named prof. of counterpoint at the Paris Cons. In 1872 he was elected a member of the Institut de France.

WORKS: DRAMATIC: O p e r a (all 1st perf. in Paris unless otherwise given): *La Favorita e la schiava* (c. 1845; Venice, 1855); *La Chambre gothique* (1849); *La Chanteuse voilée* (Nov. 26, 1850); *Galathée* (April 14, 1852); *Les Noces de Jeannette* (Feb. 4, 1853); *La Fiancée du Diable* (June 3, 1854); *Miss Fauvette* (Feb. 13, 1855); *Les Saisons* (Dec. 22, 1855); *La Reine Topaze* (Dec. 27, 1856); *Les Chaises à porteurs* (April 28, 1858); *La fee Caralosse* (Feb. 28, 1859); *La Mule de Pedro* (March 6, 1863); *Fio d'Aliza* (Feb. 5, 1866); *Le Fils du Brigadier* (Feb. 25, 1867); *Paul et Virginie* (Nov. 15, 1876); *Une Nuit de Cléopatre* (April 25, 1885); several operettas. **VOCAL:** 2 cantatas (*Le Renégat de Tanger*, 1844; 1852); Mass; more than 100 songs and romances.

BIBL.: L. Delibes, *Notice sur V. M.* (Paris, 1885); J. Ropartz, *V. M.* (Paris, 1887); H. Delaborde, *Notice sur la vie et les ouvrages de V. M.* (Paris, 1888).—NS/LK/DM

Masselos, William, American pianist and teacher; b. Niagara Falls, N.Y., Aug. 11, 1920; d. N.Y., Oct. 23, 1992. He studied at N.Y.'s Inst. of Musical Art and the Juilliard Graduate School, his principal mentors being Friedberg (piano), Salmond and Persinger (ensemble playing), and Wagenaar (theory); later he studied with Saperton and Dounis. In 1939 he made his debut in N.Y., and subsequently appeared as a soloist with orchs. and as a recitalist in the U.S. In later years he also toured in Europe. He taught at Ind. Univ. in Bloomington (1955–57), the Catholic Univ. of America in Washington, D.C. (1965–71; 1976–86), Ga. State Univ. in Atlanta (1972–75), and the Juilliard School (from 1976). Masselos acquired a fine reputation as an expo-

nent of modern music. He gave the belated premiere of Ives's 1st Piano Sonata (1949), as well as the premieres of Copland's *Piano Fantasy* (1957) and Ben Weber's Piano Concerto (1961).—NS/LK/DM

Massenet, Jules (-Émile-Frédéric), famous French composer and pedagogue; b. Montaud, near St.-Etienne, Loire, May 12, 1842; d. Paris, Aug. 13, 1912. He was 6 when he began to study piano with his mother. At 9, he was admitted to the Paris Cons. to study piano and theory. He had to leave the Cons. in 1854 when his father's ill health compelled the family to move to Chambéry. In 1855 he was able to resume his studies at the Cons., where he received instruction in piano from Laurent. In 1858 he made his public debut as a pianist in a Paris recital. In 1859 he won the premier prix for piano at the Cons., where he also pursued training with Reber (harmony), Benoist (organ), and Thomas (composition). In 1863 he won the Grand Prix de Rome with his cantata *David Rizzio*. His first major success as a composer came with the premiere of his oratorio *Marie-Magdeleine* (Paris, April 11, 1873). His next oratorio, *Éve* (Paris, March 18, 1875), won him the Légion d'honneur. His first operatic success came with the premiere of *Le roi de Lahore* at the Paris Opéra on April 27, 1877. The success of his opera *Hérodiade* (Brussels, Dec. 19, 1881) resulted in his being made a Knight of the Order of Leopold of Belgium. He scored a triumph with the first performance of his opera *Manon* at the Paris Opéra on Jan. 19, 1884. This score is generally acknowledged as his finest opera. *Werther*, another distinguished opera, added to his renown when it was premiered at the Vienna Court Opera on Feb. 16, 1892. Equally noteworthy was his opera *Thaïs* (Paris Opéra, March 16, 1894). Among his later operatic efforts, the most important were *Le jongleur de Notre-Dame* (Monte Carlo, Feb. 18, 1902) and *Don Quichotte* (Monto Carlo, Feb. 24, 1910). Of his incidental scores, that for Leconte de Lisle's drama *Les Érinnyes* (Paris, Jan. 6, 1873) was particularly notable. In 1878 Massenet was appointed prof. of composition at the Paris Cons., a position he held with distinction until 1896. He was a highly influential teacher, numbering among his students Bruneau, Charpentier, Pierné, Koechlin, and Schmitt. In 1878 he was elected a member of the Institut of the Académie des Beaux-Arts, ascending to the rank of Grand- Officier in 1900. Massenet wrote an autobiography, *Mes souvenirs* (completed by X. Leroux; Paris, 1912; Eng. tr., 1919, as *My Recollections*). He was one of the leading French opera composers of his era. His operas are the work of a fine craftsman, marked by a distinctive style, sensuous melodiousness, and lyricism that proved immediately appealing to audiences of his day. However, even before his death, developments in the lyric theater had passed him by. In succeeding years, his operas were heard infrequently, and almost disappeared from the active repertoire. Even the celebrated *Meditation* for Violin and Orch. from *Thaïs*, long a favorite concert piece with violinists and audiences, was seldom performed. Today, revivals of *Manon, Werther*, and *Thaïs* have won Massenet new audiences around the world.

WORKS: DRAMATIC: O p e r a : *Esmeralda* (1865; not

extant); *La coup du roi de Thulé* (1866?); *La grand'tante* (Paris, April 3, 1867); *Manfred* (1869?; unfinished); *Méduse* (1870; unfinished); *Don César de Bazan* (Paris, Nov. 30, 1872); *L'adorable bel'-boul'* (Paris, April 17, 1874; not extant); *Les templiers* (1875?; not extant); *Bérangère et Anatole* (Paris, Feb. 1876); *Le roi de Lahore* (Paris, April 27, 1877); *Robert de France* (1880?; not extant); *Les Girondins* (1881; not extant); *Hérodiade* (Brussels, Dec. 19, 1881); *Manon* (Paris, Jan. 19, 1884); *Le Cid* (Paris, Nov. 30, 1885); *Esclarmonde* (Paris, May 14, 1889); *Le mage* (Paris, March 16, 1891); *Werther* (Vienna, Feb. 16, 1892); *Thaïs* (Paris, March 16, 1894); *Le portrait de Manon* (Paris, May 8, 1894); *La navarraise* (London, June 20, 1894); *Amadis* (1895?; Monte Carlo, April 1, 1922); *Sapho* (Paris, Nov. 27, 1897; rev. 1909); *Cendrillon* (Paris, May 24, 1899); *Grisélidis* (Paris, Nov. 20, 1901); *Le jongleur de Notre-Dame* (Monte Carlo, Feb. 18, 1902); *Chérubin* (Monte Carlo, Feb. 14, 1903); *Ariane* (Paris, Oct. 31, 1906); *Thérèse* (Monte Carlo, Feb. 7, 1907); *Bacchus* (Paris, May 5, 1909); *Don Quichotte* (Monte Carlo, Feb. 24, 1910); *Roma* (Monte Carlo, Feb. 17, 1912); *Panurge* (Paris, April 25, 1913); *Cléopâtre* (Monte Carlo, Feb. 23, 1914). **Ballet:** *Le carillon* (Vienna, Feb. 21, 1892); *Cigale* (Paris, Feb. 4, 1904); *Espada* (Monte Carlo, Feb. 13, 1908). **Incidental Music** (all 1st perf. in Paris unless otherwise given): *Les Érinnyes* (Jan. 6, 1873); *Un drame sous Philippe II* (April 14, 1875); *La vie de Bohème* (1876); *L'Hetman* (Feb. 2, 1877); *Notre-Dame de Paris* (June 4, 1879); *Michel Strogoff* (Nov. 17, 1880); *Nana-Sahib* (Dec. 20, 1883); *Théodora* (Dec. 26, 1884); *Le crocodile* (Dec. 21, 1886); *Phèdre* (Dec. 8, 1900); *Le grillon du foyer* (Oct. 1, 1904); *Le manteau du roi* (Oct. 22, 1907); *Perce-Neige et les sept gnomes* (Feb. 2, 1909); *Jérusalem* (Monte Carlo, Jan. 17, 1914). **ORCH.:** *Ouverture de concert* (1863); 7 suites: No. 1, *Première suite d'orchestre* (1865), No. 2, *Scènes hongroises* (1871), No. 3, *Scènes dramatiques* (1873), No. 4, *Scènes pittoresques* (1874), No. 5, *Scènes napolitaines* (1876?), No. 6, *Scènes de féerie* (1879), and No. 7, *Scènes alsaciennes* (1881); *Ouverture de Phèdre* (1873); *Sarabande du XVIe siècle* (1875); *Marche héroïque de Szabady* (1879); *Parade militaire* (1887); *Visions, poème symphonique* (1890); *Devant la Madone* (1897); *Fantaisie* for Cello and Orch. (1897); *Marche solennelle* (1897); *Brumaire*, overture (1899); *Les grand violons du roi* (1900?); *Les Rosati* (1902); Piano Concerto (1903). **OTHER:** 4 oratorios: *Marie-Magdeleine* (Paris, April 11, 1873); *Éve* (Paris, March 18, 1875); *La Vierge* (Paris, May 22, 1880); *La terre promise* (Paris, March 15, 1900); the choral pieces *Narcisse* (1877) and *Biblis* (1886); secular cantatas, including *David Rizzio* (1863); part songs; about 200 songs; piano pieces; completion and orchestration of Delibes's opera *Kassya* (Paris, March 24, 1893).

BIBL.: E. de Solenière, *M.:Étude critique et documentaire* (Paris, 1897); C. Fournier, *Étude sur le style de M.* (Amiens, 1905); L. Schneider, *M.: L'homme, le musicien* (Paris, 1908; 2nd ed., 1926); H. Finck, *M. and His Operas* (London and N.Y., 1910); O. Séré, *M.* (Paris, 1911); special issue of *Musica* (Sept. 1912); A. Soubies, *M. historien* (Paris, 1913); A. Pougin, *M.* (Paris, 1914); C. Widor, *Notice sur la vie et les travaux de M.* (Paris, 1915); H. Twitchell, "M. as a Teacher," *Musician*, XXV (1920); J. Loisel, *Manon de M.:Étude historique et critique* (Paris, 1922); C. Bouvet, *M.* (Paris, 1929); J. d'Udine, *L'art du lied et le mélos de M.* (Paris, 1931); M. Delmas, *M., sa vie, ses oeuvres* (Paris, 1932); A. Bruneau, *M.* (Paris, 1935); A. Morin, *J. M. et ses opéras* (Montreal, 1944); N. Boyer, *Trois musiciens français: Gounod, M., Debussy* (Paris, 1946); P. Colson, *M.: Manon* (London, 1947); J. Bruyr, *M.* (Geneva, 1948); idem, *M., musicien de la belle époque* (Lyons, 1964); A. Coquis, *J. M.: L'homme et son oeuvre* (Paris, 1965); E. Bouilhol, *M.: Son rôle dans l'évolution du théâtre musicale* (St.-Etienne, 1969); L. Stocker, *The Treatment of the Romantic Literary Hero in Verdi's "Ernani" and in M.'s "Werther"* (diss., Fla. State Univ., 1969); J.

Harding, *M.* (London, 1970); O. Salzer, *The M. Compendium* (Fort Lee, N.J., 1984); G. Marschall, *M. et la fixation de la forme mélodique française* (Saarbrücken, 1988); D. Irvine, *M.: A Chronicle of His Life and Times* (Portland, Ore., 1993); B. Olivier, *J. M., itinéraires pour un théâtre musical* (Arles, 1996).—NS/LK/DM

Masséus, Jan, Dutch composer; b. Rotterdam, Jan. 28, 1913; d. Bilthoven, Feb. 15, 1999. He received training in piano from Callenbach and Aribo and in composition from Badings, the latter continuing as his mentor at the Rotterdam Cons.; later he worked in the electronic music studio of the Delft Technical H.S. He was a music critic in Rotterdam (1956–60), and then director of the Leeuwarden Music School (1961–72).

WORKS: ORCH.: *Sinfonietta* for Chamber Orch. (1952); Concerto for Violin and Chamber Orch. (1953); Concerto for 2 Flutes and Orch. (1956); *Cassazione*, 4 dances for Small Orch. (1960); 2 piano concertos (1966, 1994); *Iowa Serenade* (1981); *Skriabinade*, symphonic suite (1983); *Homo Ludens* (1986); *Nada Brahma* (1988); *Pandora* (1991; rev. 1992). **CHAMBER:** 2 violin sonatas (1946, 1950); Trio for Flute, Violin, and Piano (1948); *Quintetto* for Piano and String Quartet (1952); *Introduction and Allegro* for Oboe, Clarinet, and Piano (1952); *Partita* for Violin and Piano (1956); Flute Sonata (1957); *Serenade* for Oboe, Bassoon, Violin, and Viola (1958); *7 Minutes of Organized Sound* for 3 Winds, Guitar, and Percussion (1968); *Contemplations* for Brass Ensemble (1972); Concertino for 5 Accordions and Flute (1977); *Sept pièces breves* for Oboe, Clarinet, and Piano (1980); *Le secret de l'âme* for Oboe and Percussion (1989); *7 Miniaturen* for Violin, Cello, and Piano (1993); *De rieten wereld* for 12 Saxophones (1995). **Piano:** *Symphonic Fantasy* for 2 Pianos (1947); *Helicon Suite* for Piano, 4–Hands (1952); *Zoological Impressions* for Piano, 4–Hands (1954); *Balletto piccola* for 2 Pianos (1955); *Confetti* for Piano, 4–Hands (1969); *Pentatude*, 5 studies (1974); *Tango festivo* (1989). **VOCAL:** *Gezelle liederen* for Soprano, Alto, Piano, 4–Hands, and Percussion (1955); *Camphuysen-liederen* for Chorus, 3 Trumpets, 3 Trombones, and Tuba (1967); *4 Songs* for Chorus, 9 Brasses, Double Bass, and Percussion (1970); *The 7 Tile Tableaux* for Baritone, Brass Instruments, Double Bass, and Percussion (1973); *Schermutselingen* for Chorus and Orch. (Leeuwarden, Dec. 17, 1975); *Het meezennestje* for Chorus and Piano (1979); *Triptyque maconnique* for Bass, Flute, and Organ (1981); *Drentse metamorfosen* for Chorus and Orch. (1985); *In memoriam Lucia* for Soprano, Chorus, and Organ (1987); *De eenling* for Chorus (1992).—NS/LK/DM

Massey, Andrew (John), English conductor; b. Nottingham, May 1, 1946. He studied cello, flute, and trumpet while in high school, and also began to compose; then pursued musical training at the Univ. of Oxford (B.A., 1968; M.A., 1981) and at the Univ. of Nottingham (M.A., 1969); he also studied composition with Berio, Lutosawski, and Keller at the Dartington Summer School and conducting with Hurst at the Canford Summer School. He was principal conductor of the Derby Concert Orch. (1969–76), the Apollo Sym. Orch. (1969–78), and the Reading Sym. Orch. (1972–78). From 1972 to 1978 he also was senior lecturer in music at the Middlesex Polytechnic, where he was principal conductor of the Middlesex Phil. (1972–75). After serving as asst. conductor of the Cleveland Orch. (1978–80), he was assoc. conductor of the New Orleans Sym. Orch.

(1980–86) and the San Francisco Sym. (1986–88). From 1985 to 1991 he was music director of the R.I. Phil. in Providence. In 1986–87 he was music advisor of the Fresno (Calif.) Phil., and then was its music director from 1987 to 1993. He was music director designate (1990–91) and then music director (from 1991) of the Toledo (Ohio) Sym. Orch. In addition to his admirable interpretations of the standard repertory, Massey has displayed remarkable facility with works by contemporary composers, among them Ligeti, Boulez, Messiaen, Carter, Bolcom, Knussen, and Drew.—NS/LK/DM

Massol, Eugène Etienne Auguste, French baritone; b. Lodève, Aug. 23, 1802; d. Paris, Oct. 30, 1887. He received training at the Paris Cons. On Nov. 17, 1825, he made his operatic debut in the tenor role of Licinius in Spontini's *La vestale* at the Paris Opéra. After singing secondary tenor roles, he turned with success to baritone roles in the mid-1830s. He created the role of Severus in Donizetti's *Les martyrs* at the Opéra (April 10, 1840). In 1845 he went to Brussels, where he served as director of the Théâtre Royale de la Monnaie (1848–49). In 1846 he made his London debut at Drury Lane. From 1848 to 1850 he sang with the Royal Italian Opera at London's Covent Garden. He was principal baritone of the Paris Opéra from 1850 to 1858. Massol was particularly admired for his portrayals of Alfonso in *La favorite*, Pietro in *Masaniello*, and De Nevers in *Les Huguenots*. —NS/LK/DM

Másson, Áskell, Icelandic composer; b. Reykjavíik, Nov. 21, 1953. He began clarinet lessons at the age of 8. After training at the Reykjavík Coll. of Music, he went to London and studied with Patrick Savill (harmony and counterpoint) and James Blades (percussion). In 1972 he became a composer and instrumentalist with the ballet of the National Theater in Reykjavík. From 1978 to 1983 he worked as a producer for the Icelandic State Radio. He was secretary-general of the Iceland League of Composers (1983–85), then president of STEF, the association of composers and copyright owners (from 1989). Másson's output is generally marked by an intensity and brilliance of expression, complemented by a judicious infusion of lyricism.

WORKS: DRAMATIC: *Eldtröllid* (The Fire Troll), ballet (1974); *Höfudskepnurnar* (The Elements), ballet (1974); *Svart-Hvítt* (Black and White), ballet (1975); *Klakahöllin* (The Ice Palace), opera (1993); incidental music to players; music for radio and television. ORCH.: *Galda-Loftur* (The Wish; Icelandic State Radio, June 19, 1980); Clarinet Concerto (1980; Reykjavík, Jan. 31, 1981); *Konzertstück* for Snare Drum and Orch. (Reykjavík, Sept. 25, 1982); *Októ Nóvember* (Octo November for Strings (Reykjavík, Dec. 19, 1982); Viola Concerto (1983; Reykjavík, May 3, 1984); *Myndhvörf* (Metamorphoses) for Brass Orch. (Reykjavík, Nov. 29, 1983); Piano Concerto (1985; Reykjavík, Oct. 5, 1987); *Impromptu* (1986; Reykjavík, Jan. 1989); Marimba Concerto (1987; Göteborg, Oct. 1991); Trombone Concerto (1987); *Hvörf* for Strings (1992; Reykjavík, June 2, 1993); *Sinfonia Trilogia* (1992); Chamber Sym. (1997). CHAMBER: *Silja* for 3 Percussionists (1970–72); *Lafasafn* (Melodies) for 2 Flutes and Vibraphone (1974); *Vatnsdropinn* (The Drop of Water) for 2 Percussionists and Tape or 3 Percussionists (1977); *Bláa Ljósid* (The Blue Light) for 2 Flutes and 2 Percussionists (1978); *Helfró*

(Transcendental Visions) for 2 Percussionists and Tape or 4 Percussionists (1978); Sonata for Marimba and Tuned Percussion (1981; also as Sonata for Solo Marimba, 1985); Trio for Clarinet, Violin, and Viola (1983; also as *Triology* for Clarinet, Violin, and Viola, 1985); *Partita* for Guitar and Percussion (1984); *Divertimento* for Clarinet, Guitar, Percussion, and Hand Drums (1986); *Fantasy on a Chinese Poem* for Clarinet and Hand Drum (1987); *Sindur* (Sparks) for Percussion Quartet (1989); *Fantasia* for Oboe or Clarinet and Harpsichord (1991); Wind Quintet (1991); *Snow* for Violin, Cello, Vibraphone or Crotales, and Piano (1992); Violin Sonata (1993); Piano Trio (1995); Trio for Clarinet, Cello, and Piano (1999). Organ: *Elegie* (1981); *Brúdarmars* (Wedding March; 1984; also with optional trumpet); Sonata (1986); *Meditation* (1992). VOCAL: *Sýn* (Vision) for Women's Voices and Percussionist (1974–75); *Snjór* (Snow) for High Voice and Piano (1982; rev. 1992); *Introitus* for Chorus, 14 Brass Players, Timpani, and Organ (1985); *Fjörg* (The Gods) for Chorus and Percussionists (1989); *Baen* (Prayer) for High or Low Voice and Bells (1994).—NS/LK/DM

Masson, Diego, French conductor; b. Tossa, Spain, June 21, 1935. He studied percussion, harmony, and chamber music at the Paris Cons. (1953–59), and also received training in fugue, counterpoint, and composition from Leibowitz (1955–59), in composition from Maderna (1964), and in conducting from Boulez (1965). In 1966 he founded the Musique Vivante, with which he gave numerous performances of contemporary music. He also was music director of the Marseilles Opera until 1982, and of the Ballet- Théâtre Contemporain in Amiens (from 1968), which removed to Angers in 1972 under his direction as part of the Théâtre-Musical d'Angers.—NS/LK/DM

Masson, Gérard, French composer; b. Paris, Aug. 12, 1936. He studied with Stockhausen in Cologne (1965–66), and then devoted himself fully to composition.

WORKS: ORCH.: *Dans le deuil des vagues I* (1966) and *II* (1968); 2 piano concertos (1977, 1990); *Pas seulement des moments des moyens d'amour* (1980); *Offs* (1989); *Bud* (1991). CHAMBER: Piece for Chamber Ensemble (1965); *Quest I* for 10 Instruments (1967); *Bleu loin* for 12 Strings (1970); 2 string quartets (1973, 1991); Sextet (1975); *Alto-septuor* for 16 Instruments and Tape (1981); *Duo* for Viola and Violin (1982); *W3A6M4* for Chamber Ensemble (1983); *Gymnastique de l'éponge* for Piano and 10 Instruments (1984); *Alto-tambour* for Violin, Viola, and 12 Strings (1985); *Sonate Souvtchinsky* for Violin and Piano (1986); *Saxophones Fourcade* for Saxophone Quartet (1987); *Contreblanc basse* for 9 Instruments (1988); *Minutes de Saint-Simon* for Saxophone and Piano (1989); *Alors les tuyaux* for 15 Instruments (1989); *Mélisande 1 mètre 60 de désespoir* for Viola and Piano (1990); *La mort de Germanicus* for Piano and Cello (1991); *Intangibles pour punir* for 4 Instruments (1994); *Suite en fin* for 4 Instruments (2000). Piano: *Renseignements sur Apollon I* (1982), *II* (1988), and *III* (1994) for 2 Pianos; *Surimpression* for 2 Pianos (1991); *Hlet* (1991); *Smonk* (1992). VOCAL: *Quest II* for Mezzo-soprano and 13 Instruments (1969); *Hymnopsie* for Orch. and Chorus (1972); Quintet for Violin, Viola, Clarinet, Piano, and Mezzo-soprano (1978); *Après-midi d'Hamlet* for Piano and Chorus (1990).—NS/LK/DM

Masson, Paul-Marie, eminent French musicologist; b. Sète, Hérault, Sept. 19, 1882; d. Paris, Jan. 27,

1954. He studied at the lycée, the arts faculty, and the Lycée Henri IV in Montpellier before going to Paris, where he pursued his education at the Normale Superieure and concurrently was a student of Rolland and Lefranc at the École des Haute Études (agregation, 1907, with the diss. *La Musique mesurée à l'Antique au XVIe siècle*); after further training with d'Indy and Koechlin (fugue, counterpoint, and composition) at the Schola Cantorum, he completed his education at the Univ. of Paris (docteur ès lettres, 1930, with the diss. *L'opéra de Rameau*; publ. in Paris, 1930). In 1910 he served as chargé de conférences at the Univ. of Grenoble, and also taught the history of French literature and music at the Institut Français in Florence (1910–14). In 1918 he was again at the Institut Français, and then went to Naples, where he founded its Institut Français in 1919. He taught music history at the Sorbonne in Paris from 1931 to 1952. In 1951 he founded the Institut de Musicologie of the Univ. of Paris. In 1937 he was elected vice-president of the Société Française de Musicologie, and in 1949 was elected its president. He contributed numerous articles to journals and publ. the book *Berlioz* (Paris, 1923). He also composed the *Chant des peuples unis*, a cantata, *Suite pastorale* for Wind Quintet, piano pieces, and songs.

BIBL.: *Mélanges d'histoire et d'esthétique musicale offertes à P.-M. M.* (Paris, 1955).—NS/LK/DM

Massonneau, Louis, German violinist, conductor, and composer of French descent; b. Kassel, Jan. 10, 1766; d. Ludwigslust, Oct. 4, 1848. He studied violin with Jacques Heuzé and composition with Joseph-Karl Rodewald in Kassel. After playing violin and viola d'amore at the court chapel of Landgrave Friedrich II (1783–84), he was 1st violin in Forkel's Academic Concerts in Göttingen (1785–92). He then was conductor in Frankfurt am Main (1795–97), Altona (1797–99), and at the prince's chapel in Dessau (1799–1803). In 1803 he went to Ludwigslust as solo violinist, where he was asst. Kapellmeister (until 1812) and subsequently Kapellmeister (until 1837). Massonneau was an accomplished composer of instrumental music. He publ. 3 syms. in Paris (1 and 2, c. 1792; 3, 1794). His 3rd Sym., *La tempête et le calme*, is a programmatic score and is of historical interest for its seeming anticipation of Beethoven's *Pastoral* Sym. Among his other works were overtures, concertos, sacred music, chamber pieces, and songs.—NS/LK/DM

Masterson, Valerie, English soprano; b. Birkenhead, June 3, 1937. She studied at the Matthay School of Music in Liverpool and the Royal Coll. of Music in London; also in Milan. She made her debut as Frasquita in *Carmen* at the Salzburg Landestheater in 1963; then sang with the D'Oyly Carte Opera Co. in London (1966–70); became a member of the Sadler's Wells Opera in London in 1970; from 1974, sang at Covent Garden in London. She made her debut at the Paris Opéra as Marguerite (1978); made her U.S. debut as Violetta with the San Francisco Opera (1980). As a guest artist, she appeared in opera and concert around the world. In 1988 she was made a Commander of the Order of the British Empire.—NS/LK/DM

Mastilović, Danica, Yugoslav soprano; b. Negotin, Nov. 7, 1933. She was a pupil of Nikola Cvejić in Belgrade; while still a student, she sang with the Belgrade Operetta Theater (1955–59); in 1959 she made her formal operatic debut as Tosca at the Frankfurt am Main Opera, where she sang until 1969. Her guest appearances took her to Hamburg, Vienna, Munich, Bayreuth, Paris, and London. In 1963 she made her first U.S. appearance at the Chicago Lyric Opera as Abigaille, and on Nov. 25, 1975, her Metropolitan Opera debut in N.Y. as Elektra. In 1973 she made her first appearance at London's Covent Garden as Elektra. In 1978–79 she was again on the roster of the Metropolitan Opera. She became principally known for her roles in operas by Verdi, Wagner, and Strauss.—NS/LK/DM

Masur, Kurt, eminent German conductor; b. Brieg, Silesia, July 18, 1927. He received training in piano and cello at the Breslau Music School (1942–44). He then studied conducting with H. Bongartz and took courses in piano and composition at the Leipzig Hochschule für Musik (1946–48). In 1948 he commenced his career with appointments as répétiteur and conductor at the Halle Landestheater. He held the title of 1st conductor at the Erfurt City Theater (1951–53) and at the Leipzig City Theater (1953–55). He was conductor of the Dresden Phil. (1955–58), Generalmusikdirektor of the Mecklenburg State Theater in Schwerin (1958–60), and senior director of music at the Komische Oper in East Berlin (1960–64). In 1967 he returned to the Dresden Phil. as its music director, a position he retained until 1972. In 1970 he assumed the time-honored position of Gewandhauskapellmeister of Leipzig, where he served as music director of the Gewandhaus Orch. with notable distinction. He also made extensive tours with his orch. in Europe and abroad. In 1973 he made his British debut as a guest conductor with the New Philharmonia Orch. of London; his U.S. debut followed in 1974 as a guest conductor with the Cleveland Orch. On Oct. 9, 1981, he conducted the Beethoven 9th Sym. at the gala opening of the new Gewandhaus in Leipzig. In 1988 he was named principal guest conductor of the London Phil. In the autumn of 1989, during the period of political upheaval in East Germany, Masur played a major role as peacemaker in Leipzig. In 1990 he was appointed music director of the N.Y. Phil., which position he assumed in 1991 while retaining his title in Leipzig until 1998. On Dec. 7, 1992, he conducted the N.Y. Phil. in a performance of Dvořák's *New World Symphony* as part of the orch.'s 150th anniversary concert, which was televized live throughout the U.S. by PBS. In 1997 he was named honorary conductor of the Gewandhaus Orch. and was a Commandeur of the Légion d'honneur of France. From 2000 he was principal conductor of the London Phil., and from 2001 chief conductor of the Orchestre National de France in Paris. He retained his position with the N.Y. Phil. until 2002. While he has earned a reputation as a faithful guardian of the hallowed Austro-German repertoire, he frequently programs contemporary scores as well.

BIBL.: D. Härtwig, *K. M.* (Leipzig, 1975); A. Fritzsch and M. Simon, *Der Gewandhauskapellmeister K. M.* (Leipzig, 1987).—NS/LK/DM

Masurok, Yuri (Antonovich), Polish-born Russian baritone; b. Krasnik, July 18, 1931. He studied at the Lwów Inst. and the Moscow Cons., and won prizes in singing competitions in Prague (1960), Bucharest (1961), and Montreal (1967). In 1964 he made his debut as Eugene Onegin at the Bolshoi Theater in Moscow, where he later sang Prince Andrei in Prokofiev's *War and Peace*. He made his London debut at Covent Garden in 1975 as Anckarström, the same role he chose for his U.S. debut with the San Francisco Opera in 1977. In 1979 he sang Escamillo in Zeffirelli's production of *Carmen* at the Vienna State Opera, and also appeared there as Scarpia and Luna. In 1989 he portrayed Eugene Onegin in Barcelona, a role he reprised in Milwaukee in 1992. In 1991 he became a member of the Mannheim National Theater. In 1996 he sang Scarpia in Moscow. His other roles include Rossini's Figaro, Giorgio Germont, and Rodrigo in *Don Carlos*.—NS/LK/DM

Maszyński, Piotr, Polish conductor, pedagogue, and composer; b. Warsaw, July 3, 1855; d. there, Aug. 1, 1934. He was a student at the Warsaw Music Inst. of Michalowski (piano), Roguski (harmony and counterpoint), and Noskowski (composition). In 1886 he founded the Lutnia Music Soc. in Warsaw, and was conductor of its choir for the rest of his life. He also conducted other ensembles and taught choral singing. In 1902 he became a prof. at the Warsaw Music Inst. His vocal output was highly regarded in his homeland. Among his other works were syms., chamber music, and piano pieces.—LK/DM

Mata, Eduardo, Mexican conductor and composer; b. Mexico City, Sept. 5, 1942; d. in an airplane crash in Cuernavaca, Jan. 4, 1995. He studied composition with Halffter at the National Cons. of Mexico City (1954–60), then took lessons in composition and conducting with Chávez (1960–65) and Orbón (1960–63) there. In 1964 he went to the Berkshire Music Center at Tanglewood, where he attended conducting seminars led by Rudolf, Schuller, and Leinsdorf. He was conductor of the Mexican Ballet Co. (1963–64), the Guadalajara Sym. Orch. (1964–66), and the Phil. Orch. of the National Univ. of Mexico (1966–76). From 1970 to 1978 he was principal conductor of the Phoenix (Ariz.) Sym. Orch. Mata served as music director of the Dallas Sym. Orch. from 1977 to 1993. He also appeared as a guest conductor with leading orchs. throughout North America and Europe. In 1990 he became principal guest conductor of the Pittsburgh Sym. Orch. At the beginning of his career, he was active as a composer; however, he virtually abandoned composition after 1970. Among his works were 3 syms. (1962; 1963; 1966–67), the ballet music *Débora* (1963), and chamber music.—NS/LK/DM

Matačić, Lovro von, noted Slovenian conductor; b. Sušak, Feb. 14, 1899; d. Zagreb, Jan. 4, 1985. He studied with Herbst and Nedbal at the Vienna Cons., and later worked under Brechner at the Cologne Opera, where he made his debut in 1919. He then conducted in Ljubljana (1924–26), Belgrade (1926–32), and Zagreb (1932–38). He was chief conductor of the Belgrade Opera (1938–42), then conducted at the Vienna Volksoper (1942–45). Subsequently he was Generalmusikdirektor of the Dresden State Opera (1956–58), and he also conducted at the (East) Berlin State Opera. He was chief conductor of the Frankfurt am Main Opera (1961–65), the Zagreb Phil. (1970–80), and the Monte Carlo Opera (1974–78). His guest conducting engagements included appearances in Europe, the U.S., and South America.

BIBL.: E. Sedak, *M.* (Zagreb, 1996).—NS/LK/DM

Matěj, Josef, Czech composer; b. Brušperk, Feb. 19, 1922; d. there, March 28, 1992. He learned to play the trombone from his father. He studied composition with Hlobil at the Prague Cons. (1942–47) and Řídký and Janeček at the Prague Academy of Musical Arts (1947–51). His early works are characterized by folksong inflections of the Lachian region of his birth. After 1960 he introduced into his works some coloristic oriental elements; also made discreet use of dodecaphonic techniques.

WORKS: DRAMATIC: Opera: *Čtyřicet dní hory Musa Dagh* (40 Days of Musa Dagh Mountain; 1979–82). **ORCH.:** 2 trombone concertos (1947–51; 1952); *3 Symphonic Dances* (1952); 5 syms.: No. 1 for Soloists, Chorus, and Orch. (1953–55), No. 2 (1959–60), No. 3, *Sinfonia dramatica* (1969–70), No. 4 (1974), and No. 5 (1977); *Sonata da camera* for Oboe and Chamber Orch. (1955); Violin Concerto (1961); *Rhapsody* for Viola and Orch. (1962); Trumpet Concerto (1963; Prague, April 15, 1965); Concerto for Flute, Strings, and Harpsichord (1967); Concerto for Clarinet, Strings, and Piano (1970); Cello Concerto (1972; Prague, March 7, 1973); Triple Concerto for Trumpet, Horn, Trombone, and Chamber Orch. (1974). **CHAMBER:** 2 string quartets (1947–48; 1966); *Invocation* for 4 Trombones (1950); Wind Quintet (1955–56); Sonata for Trombone and Strings (1965); Violin Sonata (1971); Music for 5 Brass Instruments, *Omaggio à Leos Janáček* (1978); *Canzona* for Trumpet and Piano (1980); *Fantasia* for Organ (1981); *Inventions* for Flute and Piano (1982–83). **VOCAL:** Choral works; songs.—NS/LK/DM

Materna, Amalie, remarkable Austrian soprano; b. St. Georgen, Styria, July 10, 1844; d. Vienna, Jan. 18, 1918. She was first a church singer. She married the actor Karl Friedrich, with whom she appeared in light opera. She made her debut in Graz in 1865, and then appeared at Vienna's Carltheater. In 1869 she first sang at the Vienna Court Opera as Selika, where she was one of its principal artists until her farewell as Elisabeth in *Tannhäuser* on Dec. 31, 1894. Her dramatic talent, powerful voice, and beauteous features attracted the notice of Wagner, who selected her for the role of Brünnhilde in the first Bayreuth Festival of 1876; the following year she sang at the Wagner festival in London, under the composer's direction, and also sang in Wagner festivals in N.Y., Chicago, and Cincinnati. From 1882 to 1891 she sang regularly at Bayreuth. Her U.S. opera debut took place on Jan. 5, 1885, as Elisabeth in *Tannhäuser* during the first season of German opera at the Metropolitan Opera in N.Y.; however, she only sang there one season. In 1894 she became a member of Walter Damrosch's German company in N.Y. In 1902 she returned to Vienna and opened a singing studio there. In 1913 she came out of retirement to sing Kundry at a Wagner centennial concert in Vienna. In addition to her outstanding Wagnerian roles, she was also admired for her Rachel, Valentine, and Goldmark's Queen of Sheba, which she created in Vienna on March 10, 1875.—**NS/LK/DM**

Mather, (James) Bruce, Canadian composer, pianist, and teacher; b. Toronto, May 9, 1939. He studied at the Royal Cons. of Music of Toronto (1952–57) and at the Univ. of Toronto (B.Mus., 1959), his principal mentors being Alberto Guerrero, Earle Moss, and Uninsky in piano and Ridout, Morawetz, and Weinzweig in theory and composition. During the summers of 1957–58, he also attended the Aspen (Colo.) Music School. He then studied at the Paris Cons. (1959–61) with Milhaud (composition), Plé-Caussade (counterpoint and fugue), Messiaen (analysis), and Lévy (piano). Following further training in composition with Leland Smith at Stanford Univ. (M.A., 1964), he returned to the Univ. of Toronto to take his D.Mus. in 1967. In 1969 he studied conducting with Boulez in Basel. After teaching at the Brodie School of Music and Dance and at the Univ. of Toronto (1964–66), he taught at McGill Univ. in Montreal from 1966. From 1980 to 1996 he directed its Contemporary Music Ensemble. As a pianist, he won approbation as an interpreter of contemporary scores. He appeared in duo piano concerts with his wife, Pierrett LePage. In 1979 he won the Jules Léger Prize for his *Musique pour Champigny*, and again in 1993 for his *Yquem*. In 1987 he was one of the winners of the Micheline Coulombe Saint-Marcoux prize for his *Barbaresco*. In his music, Mather has utilized various contemporary modes of expression, ranging from serialism to microtonality. He has displayed a special affinity in composing chamber and vocal pieces.

WORKS: DRAMATIC: O p e r a : *La Princesse Blanche* (1993; Montreal, Feb. 2, 1994). **ORCH.:** Concerto for Piano and Chamber Orch. (Aspen, Colo., Aug. 20, 1958); *Elegy* for Saxophone and Strings (1959); *Symphonic Ode* (1964; Toronto, March 28, 1965); *Orchestra Piece 1967* (1966; Toronto, Jan. 11, 1967); *Ombres* (1967; Montreal, May 1, 1968); *Music for Vancouver* for Chamber Orch. (Vancouver, Sept. 17, 1969); *Musique pour Rouen* for Strings (1970; Rouen, June 9, 1971); *Musigny* (1980; Metz, Nov. 20, 1981); *Scherzo* (Toronto, Dec. 4, 1987; also for 18 Instruments, 1988; Montreal, March 16, 1989); *Dialogue* for Viola, Cello, Double Bass, and Orch. (Montreal, Nov. 4, 1988); *Tallbrem Variations* for 5 Percussion and Orch. (Toronto, March 29, 1996); *Advanced Harmony* for 12 Wind Instruments (Toronto, Jan. 18,1997). **CHAMBER:** *Étude* for Clarinet (1962); *Mandola* for Mandolin and Piano (1971); *Music* for Organ, Horn, and Gongs (Toronto, Oct. 20, 1973); *Eine kleine Bläsermusik* for Wind Quintet (1975; Ottawa, April 11, 1976); *Clos du Vougeot* for Percussion Quartet (1977; Toronto, April 3, 1978); *Barolo* for Cello and Tape (1978–85); *Ausone* for Flute, or for Flute and 2 Harps, or for Flute, 2 Harps, 2 Guitars, 2 Violins, 2 Violas, and 2 Cellos (1979); *Coulée de Serrant* for Harp and Piano (1980); *Sassicaia* for Clarinet and Piano (1981); *Gattinara* for Viola and Marimba (1982; Montreal, April 28, 1983); *Elegy* for Flute, Cello, Piano, and Percussion (Burnaby, Dec. 1, 1983); *Barbaresco* for Viola, Cello, and Double Bass (Metz, Oct. 7, 1984); *Clos d'Audignac* for Marimba and 3 Percussion (1984; Toronto, May 11, 1985); *Vourray* for Oboe and Harp (1986); Viola Duet (1987); *Vega Sicilia* for Guitar, Viola, Cello, Harp, and Marimba (1989); *Aux victimes de la guerre de Vendée* for Horn, 2 Pianos, and Tape (Metz, Nov. 17, 1990); *Yquem* for 4 Ondes Martenot and 4 Pianos (1991; Montreal, Jan. 15, 1993); *Romance* for Bassoon and Synthesizer (N.Y., Nov. 6, 1992); *Standing Ware* for Clarinet, Cello, Piano, and Percussion (1994; Vancouver, Feb. 10, 1995); Quintet for Clarinet and Strings (1995; Montreal, April 6, 1998); *Duo Basso* for Bass Flute and Bass Oboe (Ottawa, Feb. 5, 1997); *Doisy Daëne* for Flute and Piano (Montrejean, France, Aug. 26, 1998); *Tempranillo* for Guitar in 1/6 tones (Paris, Sept. 22, 1997); *Hoya de Cadenas* for Alto Flute and Guitar in 1/4 tones (Paris, March 13, 1998). **KEYBOARD: P i a n o :** *Smaragdin* (1960); *Like Snow* (1960); *Mystras* (1962); *Fantasy 1964* (CBC, Toronto, Nov. 22, 1964); Sonata for 2 Pianos (Manitoba, Oct. 14, 1970); *In Memoriam Alexandre Uninsky* (1974; Paris, Nov. 24, 1975); *Régime Onze, Type A* for 2 Pianos (Metz, Nov. 16, 1978); *Poème du Delire* for 3 Pianos (1982; Metz, April 21, 1983); *D'après un eri* (Ottawa, Oct. 17, 1997); *Hommage à Carrillo* for Piano in 1/16 tones (Enghien les Bains, June 21, 1997). **O r g a n :** *6 Études* (1982; Sinzig, Germany, March 7, 1983). **VOCAL:** 2 Songs for Bass-baritone and Orch. (1956; Toronto, April 20, 1958); *Venice* for Soprano, Clarinet, Cello, and Piano (Aspen, Colo., Aug. 23, 1957); *3 Poems of Robert Graves* for Soprano and String Orch. (1957–58); *Cycle Rilke* for Tenor and Guitar (1959; Paris, April 20, 1960); *Sick Love* for Soprano and Orch. (1960); *The Song of Blodeuwedd* for Baritone, Percussion, Harp, Piano, and Strings (1961); *Lament for Pasiphae* for Chorus and Chamber Orch. (1962; Stanford, Calif., April 28, 1963); *Orphée* for Soprano, Piano, and Percussion (San Francisco, Dec. 14, 1963); *La Lune Mince* for Chorus (1965; Montreal, April 2, 1970); *Madrigal I* for Soprano, Contralto, and 5 Instruments (Toronto, April 16, 1967), *II* for Soprano, Contralto, and 5 Instruments (Stratford, Ontario, July 27, 1968), *III* for Contralto and 3 Instruments (Toronto, July 21, 1971), *IV* for Soprano, Flute, Piano, and Tape (1972; Montreal, April 13, 1973), and *V* for Soprano, Contralto, and Chamber Orch. (Montreal, April 12, 1973); *Au Château de Pompairain* for Mezzo-soprano and Orch. (1975; Ottawa, May 4, 1977); *Musique pour Champigny* for Soprano, Mezzo-soprano, Contralto, and 5 Instruments (1976; Montreuil, France, March 3, 1977); *Les Grandes Fontaines* for Soprano and Piano (1981); *Un cri qui durerait la mer* for Mezzo-soprano or Contralto and Piano (1985; Montreal, April 25, 1986); *Travaux de Nuit* for Baritone and Chamber Orch. (1989; N.Y., June 24, 1990); *Des Laines de Lumière* for Baritone and 2 Pianos (Quebec, Dec. 7, 1998); *La Voix de l'Oiseau* for Soprano and Piano (Montreal, March 11, 1999).—**NS/LK/DM**

Matheus de Sancto Johanne, French composer who flourished in the 2nd half of the 14th century. He became a member of the chapel of Louis I of Anjou in 1378. From 1382 to at least 1386 he served as capellanus in the private papal chapel in Avignon. He most likely was the Mayshuet of the Old Hall MS. He was a significant figure in the development of the Ars Subtilior. His extant works comprise 3 ballades, 2 rondeaux, and a motet. See W. Apel, ed., *French Secular Compositions of the Fourteenth Century,* Corpus Mensurabilis Musicae, LIII/1–3 (1970–72).—**LK/DM**

Mathews, Max (Vernon), American computer scientist and composer; b. Columbus, Nebr., Nov. 13, 1926. He studied electrical engineering at the Calif. Inst. of Technology (B.S., 1950) and at the Mass. Inst. of Technology (M.S., 1952; D.Sc., 1954). He joined the Bell Telephone Laboratories in Murray Hill, N.J. (1955), and developed its MUSIC programs, the first computer sound-synthesis languages; with other scientists, he developed its GROOVE (Generated Real-time Operations on Voltage-controlled Equipment) system; he also developed electronic violins. He wrote the book *The Technology of Computer Music* (1969). His compositions for computer include *May Carol II* (1960), *Numerology* (1960), *The 2ⁿᵈ Law* (1961), *Masquerades* (1963), *Slider* (1965)l, *International Lullaby* (1966; in collaboration with O. Fujimura), and *Swansong* (1966).—NS/LK/DM

Mathews, W(illiam) S(mythe) B(abcock),

American organist, editor, and writer on music; b. London, N.H., May 8, 1837; d. Denver, April 1, 1912. Following music training in N.H., he studied piano with Lucien Southard in Boston; later he took lessons with William Mason in Binghamton, N.Y. (summers 1871–73). He began to teach music at the Appleton Academy in Mount Vernon, N.H., when he was only 15. After teaching in various states, he settled in Chicago in 1867 and served as organist of the Centenary Methodist Episcopal Church until 1893. He was also busily engaged as a teacher in various schools, including the Chicago Musical Coll. (1886–94) and the American Cons. (1889–97). He likewise was active as a music critic, contributor to various journals, including *Dwight's Journal of Music* (1859–80) and *The Etude* (1884–1911), and as ed. of the *Musical Independent* (1868–71), *Music* (1892–1902), and the *Journal of School Music* (1908–09).

WRITINGS: *An Outline of Musical Form* (Boston, 1868); *How to Understand Music* (Philadelphia, 1888); ed. *A Hundred Years of Music in America* (Chicago, 1889); *Studies in Phrasing* (Philadelphia, 1889–90); *Primer of Musical Forms* (Boston and N.Y., 1890); *A Popular History of the Art of Music* (Philadelphia, 1891); *Standard Graded Course of Studies for the Pianoforte* (Philadelphia, 1892–94); with W. Mason, *A Primer of Music* (Cincinnati, 1894); ed. *Mathew's Graded Materials* (Cincinnati, c. 1894); with E. Liebling, *Pronouncing and Defining Dictionary of Music* (Cincinnati, 1896); *Music, its Ideals and Methods* (Philadelphia, 1897); *The Masters and Their Music* (Philadelphia, 1898); *The Great in Music* (Chicago, 1900–02); *Teacher's Manual of Mason's Pianoforte Technics* (Chicago, 1901).

BIBL.: R. Groves, *The Life and Works of W.S.B. M.* (diss., Univ. of Iowa, 1981); J. Clarke, *Prof. W.S.B. M. (1837–1912): Self-made Musician of the Gilded Age (Ill.)* (diss., Univ. of Minnesota, 1983).—NS/LK/DM

Mathias, Franz Xaver,

Alsatian organist and composer; b. Dinsheim, July 16, 1871; d. Strasbourg, Feb. 2, 1939. He studied in Germany with Hugo Riemann. He was organist at the Strasbourg Cathedral (1898–1908), and then a prof. of sacred music at the Univ. of Strasbourg. Among his works, the best known is the oratorio *Mystère de Joseph*, containing an instrumental *Ballet egyptien*. He also wrote an oratorio of gigantic dimensions, *Urbem Virgo tuam serva* for 2 Choruses (with the assistance of a "crowd" of many voices), 28 cantatas, several masses, Psalms, motets, and many organ pieces. He also publ. a manual of accompaniment of Gregorian chant.—NS/LK/DM

Mathias, William (James),

prominent Welsh composer and teacher; b. Whitland, Nov. 1, 1934; d. Menai Bridge, July 29, 1992. He was a student of Ian Parrott at Univ. Coll. of Wales, Aberystwyth (B.Mus., 1956). In 1957 he went to London to continue his training with Lennox Berkeley (composition) and Peter Katin (piano) at the Royal Academy of Music, where he was made a Fellow in 1965. Upon returning to his homeland, he received his D.Mus. from the Univ. of Wales (1966). From 1959 to 1968 he lectured at Univ. Coll. of North Wales, Bangor. In 1968–69 he taught at the Univ. of Edinburgh. In 1969 he rejoined the faculty of Univ. Coll. of North Wales, where he then was a prof. and head of the music dept. from 1970 to 1988. From 1972 he also served as artistic director of the North Wales Music Festival in St. Asaph. In 1968 he received the Bax Soc. Prize and in 1981 the John Edwards Memorial Award. In 1985 he was made a Commander of the Order of the British Empire. In his music, Mathias followed a basically tonal path notable for its craftsmanship, adept handling of instrumental and vocal forces, and euphonious appeal.

WORKS: DRAMATIC: *Culhwch and Olwen*, entertainment (1966); *As You Like It*, incidental music to Shakespeare's play (1967); *The Servants*, opera (Cardiff, Sept. 15, 1980); *Jonah: A Musical Morality* (Guildford, July 6, 1988). **ORCH.:** 3 piano concertos: No. 1 (1955), No. 2 (1960), and No. 3 (Swansea, Oct. 15, 1968); *Berceuse* (1956); *Divertimento* for Strings (London, March 1958); *Music* for Strings (1960; London, Dec. 3, 1961); *Dance Overture* (Wales, Aug. 10, 1962); *Invocation and Dance* (Cardiff, March 1, 1962); *Serenade* for Chamber Orch. (Carmarthen, June 5, 1962); *Prelude, Aria, and Finale* for Strings (Caerphilly, May 23, 1964); *Concerto for Orchestra* (1965–66; Liverpool, March 29, 1966); 3 syms.: No. 1 (Llandaff, June 23, 1966), No. 2, *Summer Music* (Liverpool, May 14, 1983), and No. 3 (1991); *Sinfonietta* (Leicester, May 1, 1967); *Litanies: Concertante Music* (BBC, Feb. 28, 1968); *Festival Overture* (Caernarvon, June 1970); *Harp Concerto* (Bournemouth, June 1, 1970); *Intrada* for Small Orch. (1970–71; Aberystwyth, April 8, 1971); Concerto for Harpsichord, Strings, and Percussion (Fishguard, Aug. 26, 1971); *Holiday Overture* (Llandudno, Sept. 30, 1971); *Celtic Dances* (1972); *Laudi* (Llandaff, June 11, 1973); Clarinet Concerto (Bangor, Sept. 22, 1975); *Vistas* (Swansea, Oct. 25, 1975); *Dance Variations* (London, July 1, 1977); *Melos* for Flute, Harp, Percussion, and Strings (Abbotsham, April 24, 1977); *Vivat regina* for Brass Band (London, June 11, 1977); *Helios* (Llandaff, June 16, 1977); *Requiescat* (1977; Portmadoc, Feb. 9, 1978); *Reflections on a Theme of Tomkins* for Flute, Oboe, Organ, Harpsichord, and Strings (1980); Organ Concerto (London, Sept. 12, 1984); Horn Concerto (Llandaff, June 9, 1984; also for Horn and Piano); *Anniversary Dances* (1984; Bangor, Feb. 16, 1985); *Carnival of Wales* (Cardiff, July 24, 1987); Violin Concerto (1989–91); Oboe Concerto (Llantilio Crossenny, May 6, 1990). **CHAMBER:** *Divertimento* for Violin and Piano (n.d.); Clarinet Sonatina (1956; Cheltenham, July 13, 1957); Sextet for Clarinet, String Quartet, and Piano (1958); *Improvisations* for Harp (1958); 2 violin sonatas: No. 1 (1961; Cheltenham, July 12, 1962) and No. 2 (Swansea, Oct. 1984); Quintet for Flute, Oboe, Clarinet, Horn, and Bassoon (Cheltenham, July 4, 1963); *Divertimento* for Flute, Oboe, and Piano (1963); Piano Trio (Cheltenham, July 9, 1965); 3 string quartets: No. 1 (1967; Cardiff, April 25, 1968), No. 2 (1980; St. David's, March 6, 1981), and No. 3 (Harrogate, Aug. 7, 1986); Concertino for Flute or Recorder, Oboe, Bassoon, and Harpsichord or Piano (London, March 6, 1974); *Zodiac Trio* for Flute, Viola, and Harp (Glamorgan, Aug. 19, 1976); *Ceremonial*

Fanfare for 2 Trumpets (Whitland, Oct. 20, 1979); *Flute Sonatina* (Beaumaris, June 12, 1986); *Soundings* for Brass Quintet (1988); *Santa Fe Suite* for Harp (London, Sept. 1988). **KEYBOARD: P i a n o :** *Toccata alla danza* (1961); 2 sonatas: No. 1 (1963; Bangor, March 11, 1964) and No. 2 (1979). **O r g a n :** Postlude (1962); *Partita* (London, Oct. 26, 1962); *Variations on a Hymn Tune* (*Braint*) (Llandaff, Dec. 7, 1962); *Processional* (1964); *Invocations* (1966; Liverpool, April 4, 1967); *Toccata Giocosa* (1967); *Fantasy* (Manchester, Sept. 7, 1978); *Canzonetta* (1978); *Antiphonies* (Cardiff, May 13, 1982); *Berceuse* (Newbury, May 9, 1985); *Fenestra* (1989–90; Keele, Jan. 22, 1990); *Carillon* (1990–91). **VOCAL:** *7 Poems of R.S. Thomas* for Tenor, Harp, and Chamber Orch. (1957); *Festival Te Deum* for Chorus and Organ (1964); *3 Medieval Lyrics* for Chorus, 2 Trumpets, Percussion, and Organ (1966); *Psalm 150* for Mixed Voices, Orch., and/or Organ (Worcester, Aug. 24, 1969); *Ave Rex* for Mixed Voices and Organ or Orch. (Llandaff, Dec. 6, 1969); *Gloria* for Men's Voices and Organ (Swansea, Dec. 5, 1970); *Elegy for a Prince* for Baritone and Orch. (Llandaff, June 10, 1972); *A Vision of Time and Eternity* for Contralto and Piano (Bangor, Sept. 27, 1972); *Ceremony After a Fire Raid* for Chorus, Piano, and Percussion (London, Sept. 19, 1973); *This Worldes Joie* for Soprano, Tenor, Bass, Chorus, Boy's or Girl's Chorus, and Orch. (Fishguard, Aug. 17, 1974); *The Fields of Praise* for Tenor and Piano (1976; Bangor, March 3, 1977); *A Royal Garland* for Chorus (Paris, Sept. 1977); *A May Magnificat* for Double Chorus and Chime Bars (Cork, May 5, 1978); *Shakespeare Songs* for Chorus and Piano (Cardiff, Feb. 8, 1979); *Songs of William Blake* for Mezzo-soprano, Harp, Piano, Celesta, and Strings (Fishguard, July 29, 1979); *Rex Gloriae* for Mixed Voices (Stuttgart, May 1981); *Te Deum* for Soprano, Mezzo-soprano, Tenor, Chorus, and Orch. (Aberdeenshire, Oct. 10, 1981); *Let the People Praise Thee O Lord* for Chorus and Organ or Orch. (London, July 29, 1981); *Lux Aeterna* for Soprano, Mezzo-soprano, Contralto, Boy's Chorus, Chorus, Organ, and Orch. (Hereford, Aug. 26, 1982); *Salvator Mundi* for Women's Chorus, Piano Duet, Percussion, and String Orch. (Cheltenham, Dec. 10, 1982); *Let Us Now Praise Famous Men* for Chorus and Organ or Orch. (Worcester, Aug. 18, 1984); *Missa aedis Christi (in memoriam William Walton)* for Chorus and Organ (Oxford, June 10, 1984); *Veni Sancte Spiritus* for Chorus, Organ, 2 Trumpets, and Percussion (Hereford, Aug. 20, 1985); *Let All the World in Every Corner Sing* for Chorus, Organ, and Optional Brass (1985; London, June 25, 1987); *O Lord, Our Lord* for Chorus, Organ, and Optional Brass (Princeton, N.J., May 16, 1987); *Cantate Domino* for Chorus and Organ (Ludlow, June 1987); *Riddles* for 6 Soloists, Chorus, Piano, and Bells (1987; Vancouver, Feb. 6, 1988); *Learsongs* for Women's Chorus and Piano Duet or Clarinet, Trumpet, Piano Duet, Percussion, and Double Bass (1989); *World's Fire* for Soloists, Chorus, and Orch. (St. Asaph, Sept. 30, 1989); *Doctrine of Wisdom* for Chorus and Organ (London, May 17, 1990); various other sacred and secular pieces. **BIBL.:** S. Craggs, *W. M.: A Bio-Bibliography* (Westport, Conn., 1995).—NS/LK/DM

Mathieson, Muir, Scottish conductor and composer; b. Stirling, Jan. 24, 1911; d. Oxford, Aug. 2, 1975. He studied conducting at the Royal Coll. of Music in London with Sargent. While he made appearances as a conductor at the Sadler's Wells Opera in London, it was as a music director for films that he became best known. After working for the film producer Sir Alexander Korda (1931–39), he was music director of government film enterprises (1940–45) and then for J. Arthur Rank films. Through his efforts, such composers as Vaughan Williams, Bliss, Walton, and Britten were persuaded to write for films. In 1957 he was made an Officer of the Order of the British Empire.—NS/LK/DM

Mathieu, family of French musicians:

(1) Michel Mathieu, violinist, violist, and composer; b. Paris, Oct. 28, 1689; d. Versailles, April 7 or 9, 1768. He became a member of the orch. of the Paris Opéra in 1718, and from 1728 to 1761 he served as a musicien du roi. He publ. many instrumental and vocal works. His wife, Jacqueline-Françoise Barbier (b. 1708; d. 1773), was an esteemed soprano at the Versailles court. They had two sons, both of whom were musicians:

(2) Julien-Amable Mathieu, violinist and composer; b. Versailles, Jan. 31, 1734; d. Paris, Sept. 6 or 9, 1811. At the age of 14, he was granted a reversion of a place in the 24 violons du roi, remaining active with them until 1761. From 1765 to 1792 he was music master of the royal chapel. He wrote a number of fine sonatas and duets for violins (1756–64), and also many choral motets.

(3) Michel-Julien Mathieu, violinist, writer, and composer; b. Fontainebleau, Oct. 8, 1740; d. after 1777. He composed operas, incidental music, and many instrumental and vocal pieces. He also prepared trs. and wrote texts for several plays.—LK/DM

Mathieu, Émile (-Louis-Victor), Belgian composer and pedagogue; b. Lille, Oct. 18, 1844; d. Ghent, Aug. 20, 1932. He was a student at the Brussels Cons. of Dupont (piano), Bosselet (harmony), and Fétis (composition). In 1869 he won the 2nd Belgian Prix de Rome with his cantata *Torquato Tasso's dood*, winning the prize again in 1871 and 1873. He taught at the Louvain Music School (1867–73). After conducting at the Paris Théâtre de Châtelet (1873–75), he returned to the Louvain Music School as director in 1881. From 1898 to 1924 he was director of the Ghent Cons.

WORKS: DRAMATIC: O p e r a : *Richilde* (Brussels, Dec. 12, 1888); *L'Enfance de Roland* (Brussels, Jan. 16, 1895); *La reine Vasthi* (Brussels, 1905). **C o m i c O p e r a :** *L'Echange* (Liège, April 25, 1863); *Georges Dandin* (Brussels, Dec. 1877); *La Bernoise* (Brussels, April 1, 1880). **B a l l e t :** *Fumeurs de Kiff* (Ghent, 1876). **ORCH.:** 3 symphonic poems: *Noces féodales* (1873), *Le Lac* (1874), and *Sous bois* (1875); Violin Concerto (1899); Koncertstuk for Piano and Orch. (1905). **CHAMBER:** String Quartet (1873). **VOCAL:** 5 cantatas: *Torquato Tasso's dood* (1869), *La dernèire nuit de Faust* (1870), *Le songe de Colomb* (1872), *Debout, peuple!* (1876), and *Les Bois* (1894); *Te Deum* for Soloists, Chorus, and Orch. (1872).—NS/LK/DM

Mathieu, (Joseph) Rodolphe, Canadian composer, teacher, and pianist, father of **(René) André (Rodolphe) Mathieu;** b. Grondines, near Quebec City, July 10, 1890; d. Montreal, June 29, 1962. He went to Montreal and studied piano with Alphonse Martin and voice with Céline Marier (1906–08). After training in composition with Alexis Contant (c. 1910), he went to Paris in 1920 and studied composition with d'Indy and orchestration with Aubert at the Schola Cantorum, and conducting with Golschmann at the Collège de France. Settling in Montreal in 1927, he became a teacher at the Institut pédagogique of the Sisters of the Congregation of Notre Dame and at the convent of the Sisters of Ste. Anne in Lachine. He organized the Canadian Inst. of Music in 1929. He was also active as director of the International Soc. of Music, which became the Édition exclusive de musique canadienne in 1934 and which publ. various Canadian scores, including some by Mathieu. In addition to teaching privately, he was on the faculty of the Montreal Cons. (1955–59). He was the author of *Parlons...musique* (Montreal, 1932). His *Tests d'aptitudes musicales* (1930–56) remains in MS. In his early works, he was influenced by Debussy and more especially Wagner, but he later embraced post-Romantic elements in his output.

WORKS: CHAMBER: *Lied* for Violin and Piano (1915); String Quartet (1920); Trio for Piano, Violin, and Cello (1921); *12 Études modernes* or *Monologues* for Violin (1924); *22 Dialogues* for Violin and Cello (c. 1924); Violin Sonata (1928; also as a Cello Sonata); Quintet for Piano and String Quartet (1942). **KEYBOARD: P i a n o :** *Chevauchée* (1911); *3 Préludes* (1912–15; also orchestrated); Sonata (1927). **O r g a n :** Variations on *Venez, divin Messie!* (1910). **VOCAL:** *Un peu d'ombre* for Soprano and Orch. (1913); *Harmonie du soir* for Soprano or Tenor, Violin, and Orch. (1924); *Saisons canadiennes* for Bass and Piano (c. 1925); *Symphonie-ballet avec choeurs* for Chorus and Orch. (1927; unfinished); *Deux Poèmes* for Tenor or Soprano and String Quartet (1928); *Sanctus et Benedictus* for Chorus (1931); *Prière:"O Jésus vivant en Marie"* for Men's Voices and Organ (1933); *Lève-toi, Canadien* for Chorus and Orch. or Band (1934); *Symphonie pour voix humaines* for 12 Voices and Piano or Brass ad libitum (1960; unfinished).

BIBL.: J. Bourassa-Trépanier, *R. M., musicien canadien (1890–1962)* (diss., Laval Univ., 1972).—NS/LK/DM

Mathieu, (René) André (Rodolphe), remarkable Canadian pianist and composer, son of **(Joseph) Rodolphe Mathieu**; b. Montreal, Feb. 18, 1929; d. there, June 2, 1968. A child prodigy, he received lessons in piano and compositions at a very early age with his father; his *3 Études* for piano date from his 4th year. On Feb. 25, 1935, he created a stir in Montreal with his recital debut as a pianist at the Ritz-Carlton Hotel. In 1936 he received a Quebec government grant to pursue his studies in Paris, where he had lessons in piano with Yves Nat and in harmony and composition with Jacques de la Presle. While in Paris, he gave recitals with notable success. On Feb. 3, 1940, he made a highly successful Town Hall recital debut in N.Y.; then continued his studies in composition in N.Y. with Harold Morris while touring as a pianist in North America. In 1946–47 he was again in Paris to complete his studies with Arthur Honegger (composition) and Jules Gentil (piano). Returning to Canada, he devoted himself principally to teaching and composing. Among his works, all composed in a late Romantic vein, were 4 piano concertos; Piano Trio; Piano Quintet; pieces for Violin and Piano; numerous solo piano pieces; several vocal scores.

BIBL.: J. Rudel-Tessier, *A. M., un génie* (Montreal, 1976).—NS/LK/DM

Mathis, Edith, admired Swiss soprano; b. Lucerne, Feb. 11, 1938. She received her training at the Lucerne Cons. and from Elisabeth Bosshart in Zürich. In 1956 she made her operatic debut as the 2nd boy in *Die Zauberflöte* in Lucerne. From 1959 to 1962 she sang at the Cologne Opera. In 1960 she appeared at the Salzburg Festival, which led to engagements in Vienna and Munich. From 1960 to 1975 she appeared with the Hamburg State Opera, and in 1962 made her debut at Glyndebourne as Cherubino. From 1963 she also sang at the Berlin Deutsche Oper. On Jan. 19, 1970, she made her Metropolitan Opera debut in N.Y. as Pamina, remaining on its roster until 1974. She sang for the first time at London's Covent Garden in 1970 as Mozart's Susanna, returning there until 1972. Her frequent Munich engagements led to her being made a Kammersängerin in 1980. She appeared as the Marschallin in Bern in 1990. In addition to her operatic appearances, she won notable distinction as a concert and lieder artist. She married **Bernhard Klee**, with whom she often appeared. Her other memorable operatic roles were Zerlina, Zdenka, Nannetta, Mélisande, the Marschallin, Sophie, and Arabella. —NS/LK/DM

Mathis, Johnny, b. San Francisco, Sept. 30, 1935. If Frank Sinatra is the Chairman of the Board, Johnny Mathis must be the CEO. Mathis is not just one of the world's most successful male vocalists: he is a living bronze institution. His *Greatest Hits* LP spent over *nine years* on the best-selling album charts. The wiry crooner with the tremulous, distinctively clipped phrasing is also commonly believed to be one of the first African American millionaires, which is ironic because Mathis grew up around wealth—his parents worked as domestic help for the upper crust of San Francisco. Though he began taking opera lessons at the age of 13, Mathis was determined to become a physical education teacher; quite an athlete in his own right, he was invited to the 1956 Olympic track and field trials. But Mathis made it neither to the Olympics nor the gymnasium. His vocal talent simply could not be overlooked, and while singing at San Francisco's 440 Club he was discovered by a Columbia Records executive and signed to a recording contract. He went to N.Y. in 1956 and began his career doing jazz, but Columbia A&R chief Mitch Miller (yes, *that* Mitch Miller) convinced him to switch to the material that would ultimately make him famous: romantic pop ballads. That did the trick. A year later, Mathis scored three consecutive hits, including his unforgettable #1 "Chances Are." Mathis soon was considered the crown prince of pop music, right alongside King Frankie. Mathis landed the rest of his hits in the 1950s and 1960s, then stopped being a popular radio sensation and transformed into a cultural icon. He sold millions and millions of albums around the world and became the undisputed champion of bedroom balladry. He returned to the charts in 1978 with Deniece Williams in the duet "Too Much, Too Little, Too Late," a #1 R&B hit, and shortly thereafter joined Williams again to record "Without Us," which became the theme of the TV series *Family Ties*. His subsequent rock and dance adventures were dismal failures, sending him back to his familiar ballad turf. Mathis continues to ply his craft in

Atlantic City, Las Vegas, N.Y., and other large venues, to sellout crowds. He and his catalog of timeless romantic rhapsodies have fused into the American fabric like baseball, apple pies, or making out in the back seat of a convertible while the car stereo plays "The Twelfth of Never."

DISC: *Johnny Mathis* (1957); *Good Night, Dear Lord* (1958); *Heavenly* (1958); *Johnny's Greatest Hits* (1958); *More Johnny's Greatest Hits* (1959); *Open Fire, Two Guitars* (1959); *Merry Christmas* (1960); *I'll Buy You a Star* (1961); *Johnny* (1963); *Christmas with Johnny Mathis* (1972); *Killing Me Softly with Her Song* (1973); *That's What Friends Are For* (with Deniece Williams; 1978); *Best Days of My Life* (1979); *The Best of Johnny Mathis 1975–1980* (1980); *Silver Anniversary Album: The First 25 Years* (1981); *Friends in Love* (1982); *Johnny Mathis Live* (1983); *A Special Part of Me* (1984); *Hollywood Musicals* (with Henry Mancini; 1986); *Christmas Eve with Johnny Mathis* (1986); *16 Most Requested Songs* (1987); *You Light Up My Life* (1988); *Once in a While* (1988); *Love Songs* (1988); *Heavenly* (1989); *16 Most Requested Songs: Encore!* (1989); *In the Still of the Night* (1989); *In a Sentimental Mood: Mathis Sings Ellington* (1990); *Better Together: The Duet Album* (1991); *How Do You Keep the Music Playing?* (1993); *The Music of Johnny Mathis: Personal Collection* (1993); *This Heart of Mine* (1993); *The Christmas Music of Johnny Mathis: A Personal Collection* (1993); *The Essence of Johnny Mathis* (1994); *Heavenly/Greatest Hits/Live* (1995); *All About Love* (1996); *The Global Masters* (1997); *Because You Loved Me: Songs of Diane Warren* (1998); *The Ultimate Hits Collection* (1998); *Mathis on Broadway* (2000).

Matho, Jean-Baptiste, French composer; b. Brittany, c. 1660; d. Versailles, March 16, 1746. He was a choirboy at the French court. In 1684 he became chantre laïe de la chapelle, in 1688 maître de chante de la musique de la Dauphine, and in 1717 cantre ordinaire à la chapelle royale and chantre de la chambre. In 1722 he was made maître de musique du roi, and in 1723 maître de musique de l'Infante. With Royer, he assumed the post of maître de musique des Enfans in 1734. He was the foremost Breton composer of the age. In his works, he followed in the tradition of Lulli. He composed the opera *Arion* (Paris, April 10, 1714), ballets, divertissements, and motets.—**LK/DM**

Mátray (real name, **Róthkrepf**), **Gábor,** Hungarian music scholar, pedagogue, and composer; b. Nágykáta, Nov. 23, 1797; d. Budapest, July 17, 1875. After receiving piano lessons from his father, he went to Pest to study law. He also studied piano, theory, and voice. At 15, he composed the stage piece *Cserni György*, the earliest surviving work of its kind in Hungary. In 1816–17 he was a tutor in the service of Baron Simon Prónay, and then worked in that capacity in Vienna for Count Lajos Széchényi (1817–30). He subsequently returned to Pest to complete his law training. He ed. the journals *Regélő* and *Honművész* (1833–41). In 1837 he became music director of the Hungarian National Theater. In 1840 he was made director of the music school of the Pest-Buda Music Soc. and in 1846 curator of the Hungarian National Museum. Mátray publ. a general history of music (1828–32), the first such history in the Hungarian language. He also wrote treatises on folk

and Gypsy music. His compositions consist mainly of salon pieces, which retain historical interest for their use of native rhythms. He also prepared arrangements of folk songs.—**NS/LK/DM**

Matsudaira, Yoriaki, Japanese composer, son of **Yoritsune Matsudaira;** b. Tokyo, March 27, 1931. He studied biology at the Tokyo Metropolitan Univ. (1948–57); as a composer, he was autodidact. In 1958 he became a teacher of physics and biology at Rikkyo Univ. in Tokyo. He was also active with the composing collective Group 20.5, which he founded to promote contemporary music. In his output, Matsudaira has followed an avant-garde path in which he has utilized serialism, aleatory, tape, and electronics. He publ. the book *Conpyuta to ongaku* (Computers in Music; Tokyo, 1972).

WORKS: DRAMATIC: *Sara*, opera (Tokyo, Nov. 12, 1960); *Ishikawa no iratsume*, dance drama (Tokyo, July 1964). **ORCH.:** *Configuration* for Chamber Orch. (1961–63; Tokyo, March 29, 1967); *The Symphony* for Chamber Orch. (1971); *Messages* for Wind Orch. and Tape (1972); *Kurtosis I* (1982); *Revolution* for Piano and Orch. (1991); *Helices* (1995); *Remembrance* for Piano and Orch. (1996); *Micell* for Chamber Orch. (1998). **CHAMBER:** *Variations* for Piano Trio (Tokyo, Nov. 15, 1957); *Speed Co-Efficient* for Flute, Piano, and Keyboard Percussion (1958); *Orbits I-III* for Flute, Clarinet, and Piano (1960); *Variations on a Noh Theme* for Flute, Clarinet, 3 Percussion, Piano, Violin, Viola, and Cello (1960; in collaboration with others); *Co-Action I & II* for Cello and Piano (1962); *Parallax* for Flute, Oboe, Clarinet, Bassoon, and Saxophone (1963); *Rhymes for Severino Gazzelloni* for Flute (1965–66; Venice, Sept. 10, 1966); *Distributions* for String Quartet and Ring Modulator (1966–67; Tokyo, March 16, 1968); *Alternations* for Trumpet, Piano, Double Bass, Drums, and Ring Modulator (1967); *Gradations* for Violin, Viola, and Oscillator (1971); *Trichromatic Form* for Harp (1973); *Transient '74* for Guitar, Organ, Harp, and Percussion (1974); *Simulation* for Tuba (1974); *Coherency for Ark* for Flute, Clarinet, Percussion, Harp, and Keyboard (1976); *Brilliancy* for Flute and Piano (1978); *Extension* for Percussion Ensemble (1981); *Scroll* for Bass Clarinet (1984); *Reunion* for 2 Violins (1986); *Declaration* for Trumpet and Piano (1987); *Palindrome* for Violin and Piano (1987); *Requiem saecularum VI* and *VIII* for Horn, 2 Trumpets, 2 Trombones, and Percussion (1988); *Engraving I* and *II* for Flute and Piano (1989); *Metathesis* for Accordion (1990); *Domain* for String Quartet (1991); *Response* for Double Bass and Oboe (1992); *Dialogue* for Violin and Harpsichord (1993); *Co-existence* for Piano and Gamelan Instrument (1993); *Blessing* for Bassoon and Piano (1995); *Transliteration* for Viola (1996); *Sparkle* for Flute, 2 Violins, Piano, and Toy Piano (1997); *Theme and Variations* for Flute, Mandolin, Clarinet, Violin, Viola, and Cello (1997); *Grating* for Guitar (1998). **PIANO:** *Instruction* (1961); *Allotropy* (1970); *Erixatone* for Electric Piano (1979) *Kurtosis II* for 2 Pianos (1982); *Perspective* (1988); *Gala* (1990); *Recollection* (1990); *Multistrata* (1990); *Morphogenesis I-II* (1991–93); *Michelangelo's Pup* (1993); *To You from...* (1994); *List for Inoue Satako* (1997); *Memoriam for Kuniharu Akiyama* (1997). **VOCAL:** *What's Next?* for Soprano and 2 Noisemakers (1967–71; Graz, Oct. 12, 1972); *Wand Waves* for Narrator and Tape (1970); *Substitution* for Soprano and Piano (1972). **OTHER:** *Transient '64* for Tape (1964); *Assemblages* for Tape (1968); *Why Not?* for 4 to 5 Operators and Live Electronics (1970); *Where Now?* for 3 Dancers and Ensemble (1973); *Shift* for Dance and Tape (1976);

Monuments for Soprano, Flute, Trombone, Cello, and Electronics (1977); *Albedo* for Soprano, Viola, and Piano (1979–80); *Semiology for John Dowland* for Soprano and Tape (1991); *Card Game* for Soprano (1995).—NS/LK/DM

Matsudaira, Yoritsune, Japanese composer, father of **Yoriaki Matsudaira;** b. Tokyo, May 5, 1907. He took courses in French literature at Keio Univ. and pursued private instruction in composition with Komatsu, and with Tansman and Tcherepnin (1935–37). In 1937 he helped organize and was co-director of the Nihon Gendai Sakkyokuka Renmei, which later became the Japanese Soc. for Contemporary Music. He served the Soc. as its secretary (1953–55) and chairman (1956–60). He was the author of *Kindai waseigaku* (Harmony Today; Tokyo, 1955; rev. 1969–70). Among his honors were the Weingartner Prize (1937), the ISCM Prize (1952), the Zerboni Prize (1954), and the International Composition Competition Prize of Rome (1962). In his early works, he followed neo-Classical trends. His use of gagaku with modern methods became a hallmark of his style. He first utilized 12-tone procedures in his *Theme and Variations on Etenraku* for Piano and Orch. in 1951. Still later he explored the use of gagaku with various other avant-garde procedures.

WORKS: DRAMATIC: Opera: *Uji-Jujo* (1998). **ORCH.:** *Pastorale* (1935); *Theme and Variations on a Folk Song from the Nanbu District* for Piano and Orch. (Tokyo, Dec. 17, 1939); *Theme and Variations on Etenraku* for Piano and Orch. (1951); *Ancient Japanese Dance* (1952; Berlin, Oct. 9, 1953); *Negative and Positive Figures* (Tokyo, May 28, 1954); *Figures sonores* (1956; Zürich, June 1, 1957); *U-Mai* (Ancient Dance; 1957; Darmstadt, Sept. 11, 1958); *Samai* for Chamber Orch. (1958; Rome, June 15, 1959); *Danse sacre* (1959); *Danse finale* (1959); *Dance Suite* for 3 Orchs. (Donaueschingen, Oct. 18, 1959); *Bugaku* for Chamber Orch. (1961; Palermo, Oct. 6, 1962); *3 Movements* for Piano and Orch. (1962; Stockholm, March 20, 1964); *Ritual Dance and Finale* (1963); 2 piano concertos: No. 1 (1964; Madrid, March 20, 1965) and No. 2 (1980); *Music for 17 Performers* (1967); *Rotating Movements* for 2 Chamber Orchs. (1971; Graz, Oct. 10, 1972); *Prelude, Interlude, and Aprèslude* (1973); *2 Synthese* for Chamber Orch. (1983). **CHAMBER:** Flute Sonatina (1936); Sonatina for Flute and Clarinet (1940); Cello Sonata (1942; rev. 1947); Piano Trio (1948); 2 violin sonatas (1948, 1952); 2 string quartets (1949, 1951); Suite for Flute, Horn, and Piano (1950); *Somakusha* for Flute (1961; rev. 1970; also for Flute, Oboe, Harp, Percussion, Piano, and Strings); *Serenade* for Flute, Oboe, Percussion, and Strings (1962); Suite for 10 Instruments (1963); *Concerto da camera* for Harpsichord, Harp, and Instrumental Ensemble (1964); *Dialogue choréographique* for Wind Quintet, Harp, 2 Pianos, and Percussion (1966; Royan, April 3, 1967); *Portrait* for 2 Pianos and 2 Percussion (1967–68); *Rhapsody on a Theme of Gagaku* for Chamber Ensemble (1982); *Netori et Rôëi* for Cello and Ensemble (1985); Concertino for Piano and Chamber Ensemble (1988); *Petite Piece* for Clarinet, Piano, Marimba, and Percussion (1988); *Bonguen* for Shō, Flute, Clarinet, and Percussion (1992). **Piano:** *Lullaby and Music Box* (1928–31); 2 preludes (1934, 1940); *6 Pastoral Dances* (1939–40); Concertante for 2 Pianos (1946); Sonatina (1948); Sonata (1949); *Portrait* for 2 Pianos (1967); *Pieces for Children* (1968); *Lullabies* (1969); *Pieces for Children from Nursery Rhymes and Folk Songs* (1969–70); *Études on Japanese Melodies* (1970). **VOCAL:** *Folk Songs from the Nanbu District* for Voice and Piano (2 sets, 1928–36; 1938); *Kokin-shu* for Soprano and Piano (1939–45; also for Soprano and Orch., 1950); *Metamorphoses on an Old Japanese Melody* (*Saibara*) for Soprano and Chamber Orch. (1953; Haifa, June 3, 1954); *Koromogae* (Love Song) for Soprano and Chamber Orch. (1954; Venice, Dec. 11, 1968); *Katsura* for Soprano, Guitar, Harp, Harpsichord, and Percussion (1957; rev. 1967); *Jesei, a rôëi* (2 Stars in Vega) for Soprano, Flute, Oboe, Harp, Piano, Vibraphone, and Percussion (1967); *Kashin, a rôëi* for Women's Voices and Orch. (1969); *3 Airs du Genji Monogatari* for Soprano and Japanese Instruments (1990); *Requiem* for Soprano and Chamber Ensemble (1992).—NS/LK/DM

Matsumura, Teizo, Japanese composer and pedagogue; b. Kyoto, Jan. 15, 1929. He was orphaned at an early age. After lessons from Tsuneharu Takahashi (piano) and Toshio Nagahiro (harmony), he settled in Tokyo in 1949 to pursue his training with Ikenouchi (harmony, counterpoint, and composition) and Ifukube (composition). Between 1950 and 1955 his life was seriously threatened by tuberculosis. During his convalescence, he began to compose and in 1955 won 1st prize in the NHK-Mainichi Music Competition with his *Introduction and Allegro Concertante* for Orch. From 1970 to 1987 he was prof. of composition at the National Univ. of Fine Arts and Music. In 1994 he won the Mainichi Art Prize and the Grand Prize of the Kyoto Music Awards. Matsumura rebelled early on against dodecaphonism, the then-prevailing musical ideology in Japan. Instead, he pursued an independent course in which he combined the use of Western instruments and forms with the rich inheritance of Asian culture. Among his notable works were his Sym. (1965) and his *Prélude pour orchestre* (1968), the latter winning the Otaka Prize.

WORKS: DRAMATIC: *Flute of Devil's Passion*, mono-opera (1965); *Silence*, opera (1980–93; Tokyo, Nov. 3, 1993); incidental music; film scores. **ORCH.:** *Introduction and Allegro Concertante* (Tokyo, Oct. 22, 1955); *Cryptogame* for Chamber Orch. (1958); 2 syms.: No. 1 (Tokyo, June 15, 1965) and No. 2 for Piano and Orch. (1998); *Prélude pour Orchestre* (NHK Radio, Nov. 7, 1968); 2 piano concertos: No. 1 (NHK Radio, Nov. 4, 1973) and No. 2 (Tokyo, May 13, 1978); Cello Concerto (Tokyo, Feb. 27, 1984); *Pneuma* for Strings (Tokyo, Sept. 19, 1987); *Hommage à Akira Ifukube* (1988); *Offrande Orchesrale* (Tokyo, Sept. 21, 1989). **CHAMBER:** Music for String Quartet and Piano (1962); *Poem I* for Shakuhachi and 13-String Koto (1969) and *II* for Shakuhachi (1972); *Courtyard of Apsaras*, trio for Flute, Violin, and Piano (1971); *Poem* for Shinobue and Biwa (NHK Radio, Nov. 1979); *Fantasy* for 13-String Koto (1980); *Poem* for Alto Saxophone and Biwa (1980); *Air of Prayer* for 17-String Koto (1984; also for Cello, 1985); *Spelmatica* for Cello (1985); Trio for Violin, Cello, and Piano (1987; NHK Radio, April 1, 1988); *Nocturne* for Harp (1994); String Quartet (1996). **Piano:** *Deux Berceuses à la Grèce* (1969). **VOCAL:** *Achime* for Piano and Chamber Ensemble (1957); *Totem Ritual* for Soprano, Chorus, and Orch. (1969); *Apsaras* for Women's Voices and Small Orch. (1969); *2 Poems by the Prince of Karu* for Soprano and Piano (1973; NHK Radio, March 12, 1974); *Hymn to Aurora* for Chorus and Chamber Ensemble (Tokyo, Nov. 15, 1978); *The Drifting Reed* for Voice and Orch. (NHK-TV, July 1979); *The Patient Waters* for Chorus and Orch. (1985).—NS/LK/DM

Matsushita, Shinichi, Japanese composer; b. Osaka, Oct. 1, 1922; d. there, Dec. 25, 1990. He graduated in mathematics from the Kyushu Univ. in Fukuoka in 1947 and concurrently studied music. In 1958 he went to work in an electronic music studio in Osaka. He taught both mathematics and music at the Univ. of Osaka City. In his music, he followed cosmopolitan modernistic techniques, mostly of a functional, pragmatic nature.

WORKS: DRAMATIC: Radio Opera: *Comparing Notes on a Rainy Night* (1960); *Amayo* (1960). ORCH.: *Ouvrage symphonique* for Piano and Orch. (1957); *Isomorfismi* (1958); *Sinfonia "Le Dimensioni"* (1961); *Successioni* for Chamber Orch. (Radio Palermo, Oct. 1, 1962); *Serenade* for Flute and Orch. (1967); *Sinfonie Pol* for Orch., Harp, and Piano (1968); *Astrate Atem* for Orch., Harp, and Piano (1969–70); *Idylle*, violin concerto (1983); *Ein Neues Lied* (1984); *Ethno* (1984); *Nippon Capriccio* (1987); Sym. No. 7 (1988). CHAMBER: *Correlazioni per 3 gruppi* for 12 Players (1958); *Composizione da camera per 8* (1958); *5 tempi per undici* for 11 Instruments (1958–59); *Faisceaux* for Flute, Cello, and Piano (1959); *Cube for 3 Players* for Flute, Celesta, and Viola (1961); *Meta-Musique No. 1* for Piano, Horn, and Percussion (1962); *Uro* for Chamber Ensemble (1962); *Sinfonia "Vita"* (1963); *Fresque sonore* for 7 Instruments (1964); *Hexahedra A, B* and *C* for Piano and Percussion (1964–65); *Kristalle* for Piano Quartet (1966); *Alleluja in der Einsamkeit* for Guitar, Piccolo, and 2 Percussionists (1967); *Subject 17* for Piano, Percussion, Horn, Trumpet, and Trombone (San Francisco, Oct. 31, 1967); *Haleines astrales* for Chamber Ensemble (1968); *Musik von der Liebe* for Flute, Vibraphone, Harp, Piano, Electone, and Tape (1970); *Musik der Steinzeit* for Violin, Ondes Martenot, Tape, and the sound of Cracking Stone (1970); String Quartet (1988). KEYBOARD: Piano: *Spectra 1–4* (1964; 1967; for 2 Players, 1971; 1971); *Ostinato obbligato* (1972); *Spectra No. 6, 12 Bagatelles* (1984). Organ: *Mini- Max* for Organ, 4–Hands (1984); *Konzentrazion* (1988). VOCAL: *Le Croitre noir* for Chorus, Electronic and Musique Concrète Sounds, Piano, Harp, and Percussion (Osaka, Nov. 14, 1959); *Jet Pilot* for Narrator, Orch., String Quartet, and Women's Chorus (1960); *Musique* for Soprano and Chamber Ensemble (Osaka, Sept. 14, 1964); *Requiem on the Place of Execution* for 4 Soloists, Chorus, Orch., and Tape (1970).—NS/LK/DM

Mattei, Stanislao, Italian composer and pedagogue; b. Bologna, Feb. 10, 1750; d. there, May 12, 1825. He spent his entire life in Bologna. He was a pupil of Padre Martini. After becoming a member of the Franciscan order of Friars Minor Conventual, he began a close association with Martini at S. Francesco in 1770. In 1776 he was officially named Martini's substitute and successor, which he became upon his mentor's death in 1784. In 1789 he became maestro di cappella at S. Petronio. In 1799 he was made a member of the Accademia Filarmonica, serving as its principe in 1803, 1808, and 1818. In 1804 he was appointed prof. of counterpoint and composition at the founding of the Liceo Musicale, numbering Rossini and Donizetti among his students. He publ. the treatise *Practica d'accompagnamento sopra bassi numerati* (Bologna, c. 1824). Among his works were over 300 sacred pieces, as well as syms. and other orch. works, and secular vocal music.

BIBL.: F. Canuti, *Vita di S. M.* (Bologna, 1829); idem, *Osservazioni sulla bita di S. M.* (Reggio, 1830).—LK/DM

Mattei, Tito, Italian pianist, conductor, and composer; b. Campobasso, near Naples, May 24, 1841; d.

London, March 30, 1914. He studied with Parisi, Conti, and Thalberg, making such rapid progress that at the age of 11 he obtained a nominal appointment as "professore" of the Accademia di Santa Cecilia in Rome. He received a gold medal for playing before Pope Pius XI, and was appointed pianist to the King of Italy. About 1865 he settled in London, where he was active principally as an opera conductor. He composed the operas *Maria di Gand* (London, 1880), *The Grand Duke* (London, 1889), and *La Prima Donna* (London, 1889) and the ballet *The Spider and the Fly* (London, 1893). Other works include songs and piano pieces.—NS/LK/DM

Matteis, Nicola, Italian violinist and composer, who settled in London in 1672. He publ. there 4 books of violin pieces (airs, preludes, fugues, allemandes, sarabands, etc.) under varying Italian and English titles; also *The False Consonances of Musick, or, Instructions for playing a true Base upon the Guitarre, with* Choice Examples and Clear Directions to enable any man in a short time to play all Musicall Ayres, etc. In addition, he wrote *A Collection of New Songs* (2 vols., London, 1696). His son, also named Nicola (d. 1749), lived in Vienna and in Shrewsbury, England. He was Burney's teacher. —NS/LK/DM

Matteo da Perugia, outstanding Italian composer; b. Perugia, date unknown; d. before Jan. 13, 1418. A musicus, he was the 1st magister capellae and the only cantor at Milan Cathedral (1402–7; 1414–16); was also in the service of Petros Cardinal Filargo di Candia of Pavia, later the Antipope Alexander V. His extant works include 5 Glorias, a motet, 4 ballades, 7 virelais, 10 rondeaux, a canon, and 2 ballate. See F. Fano, ed., *La cappella musicale del duomo di Milano, I: Le origini e il primo maestro di cappella: Matteo da Perugia*, Istituzioni e Monumenti dell'Arte Musicale Italiana, new series, I (1956), and W. Apel, ed., *French Secular Compositions of the Fourteenth Century*, Corpus Mensurabilis Musicae, LIII/1–3 (1970–72).—NS/LK/DM

Mattfeld, Victor Henry, American organist, conductor, music editor, and teacher; b. Bunceton, Mo., Sept. 1, 1917. He studied at the Univ. of Chicago (B.A. in psychology, 1942), the American Cons. of Music, Chicago (B.Mus., 1944; M.Mus., 1946, both in organ), and Yale Univ. (Ph.D. in music history, 1960); also studied orch. conducting privately with Malko (1945–47) and choral conducting at the Berkshire Music Center at Tanglewood (summer, 1946). He was active as a church organist and music director in Chicago, N.Y., New Haven, and Boston (1938–63), and also ed. in chief of E.C. Schirmer Music Co. (1956–58) and the Ione Press (1963–68). He taught at the American Cons. of Music (1945–47), Yale Univ. (1952–55), and the Mass. Inst. of Technology (1957–66) before becoming associated with N.Y.'s Richmond Coll. (1967–76) and Coll. of Staten Island (1976–82). He publ. *Georg Rhaw's Publications for Vespers* (1966). He married the musicologist Jacquelyn Mattfeld (b. Baltimore, Oct. 5, 1925); she studied at Goucher Coll. (B.A., 1948) and Yale Univ. (Ph.D., 1959); taught at the Mass. Inst. of Technology (1963–65), Sarah Lawrence Coll. (1965–71), and Brown Univ. (from 1971). —NS/LK/DM

Matthaei, Karl, Swiss organist and musicologist; b. Olten, April 23, 1897; d. Winterthur, Feb. 8, 1960. He studied piano and organ at the Basel Cons., and also took courses in musicology there with Karl Nef. He then went to Leipzig, where he pursued his organ studies with Straube (1920–23). He subsequently was organist in Wadenswil. From 1925 he was organist and director of the Winterthur music school; from 1938 served also as organist of the city church. He ed. *J. Pachelbel: Ausgewählte Orgelwerke* (4 vols., Kassel, 1928–36), *M. Praetorius: Sämtliche Orgelwerke* (Wolfenbüttel, 1930), and *J.J. Froberger: Ausgewählte Orgelwerke* (Kassel, 1932). He also ed. a *Bach- Gedenkschrift* (Zürich, 1950). He publ. the books *Vom Orgelspiel* (Leipzig, 1936) and *Die Baugeschichte der Stadtkirchenorgel in Winterthur* (Winterthur, 1941).

BIBL.: *K. M.: Gedenkschrift* (Winterthur, 1960); V. Gäumann, *K. M., 1897–1960: Leben und Werk eines Schweizer Organisten* (Wilhelmshaven, 1997).—NS/LK/DM

Matthay, Tobias (Augustus), eminent English pianist and pedagogue; b. London, Feb. 19, 1858; d. High Marley, near Haslemere, Surrey, Dec. 14, 1945. He began to play the piano at the age of 6, and was taught by private teachers. In 1871 he entered the Royal Academy of Music in London as a pupil of Dorrell (piano). He won the Sterndale Bennett scholarship, and continued to study piano (with Macfarren). He took courses with Sterndale Bennett, and, after the latter's death (1875), completed his studies with Ebenezer Prout and Arthur Sullivan. He subsequently was on the faculty of the Royal Academy of Music as a sub-prof. (1876–80) and full prof. (1880–1925); in 1900 he established his own piano school in London. The Matthay System, as his teaching method was known, stressed mastery of both the psychological and physiological aspects of piano performance; it became famous not only in England but on the Continent and in America. Students flocked to him and carried his method abroad. Matthay also composed *In May*, an overture, Piano Quartet, numerous piano pieces, and songs.

WRITINGS (all publ. in London unless otherwise given): *The Art of Touch in All Its Diversity* (1903); *The First Principles of Pianoforte Playing* (1905; 2nd ed., rev., 1906); *Relaxation Studies...in Pianoforte Playing* (Leipzig, 1908); *Some Commentaries on the Teaching of Pianoforte Technique* (1911); *The Child's First Steps in Pianoforte Playing* (1912); *The Fore-arm Rotation Principle in Pianoforte Playing* (1912); *Musical Interpretation* (1913); *On Method in Teaching* (1921); *An Epitome of the Laws of Pianoforte Technique* (1931); *The Visible and Invisible in Pianoforte Technique* (1932; 2nd ed., rev., 1947); etc.

BIBL.: J. Henderson Matthay, *The Life and Work of T. M.* (London, 1945); A. Coviello, *What M. Meant* (London, 1948). —NS/LK/DM

Mattheson, Johann, famous German composer, music theorist, and lexicographer; b. Hamburg, Sept. 28, 1681; d. there, April 17, 1764. He received a thorough education in the liberal arts at the Johanneum, acquiring proficiency in English, Italian, and French; studied music there with the Kantor, Joachim Gerstenbuttel. He received private musical instruction studying keyboard music and composition with J.N. Hanff; also took singing lessons and learned to play the violin, gamba, oboe, flute, and lute. At a very early age he began to perform as an organist in the churches of Hamburg; also sang in the chorus at the Hamburg Opera. He graduated from the Johanneum in 1693, and concurrently took courses in jurisprudence. He then served as a page at the Hamburg court of Graf von Güldenlöw, who held the title of Vice-König of Norway. He made his debut as a singer in a female role with the Hamburg Opera during its visit to Kiel in 1696; from 1697 to 1705 he was a tenor with the Hamburg Opera, conducted rehearsals, and also composed works for it. He befriended Handel in 1703; together they journeyed to Lübeck to visit Buxtehude, who was about to retire as organist, and to apply for his post. The unwritten requirement for the job was marriage to one of Buxtehude's five daughters, whose attractions seemed dubious; both Mattheson and Handel declined the opportunity. In 1704 a violent quarrel broke out between Mattheson and Handel during a performance of Mattheson's opera *Cleopatra* at the Hamburg Opera. Mattheson sang the principal male role of Antonius while Handel acted as conductor from the keyboard in the capacity of maestro al cembalo. Upon the conclusion of his role on stage, Mattheson asked Handel to let him assume the position at the keyboard, since he was the composer. Handel refused and an altercation ensued. The dispute was finally decided by a duel, during which Mattheson broke his sword on a metal button of Handel's coat, or so at least the most credible report of the episode went. They were, however, soon reconciled and remained friends. In 1704 Mattheson became the tutor of Cyrill Wich, the son of Sir John Wich, British envoy at Hamburg. In 1706 he became secretary to Sir John; when the younger Wich became ambassador in 1715, he retained Mattheson as secretary, a position he held for most of his life. During this period Mattheson diligently studied English politics, law, and economics, thereby adding to his many other accomplishments. In 1715 he assumed the post of music director of the Hamburg Cathedral. He composed much sacred music for performance there, including many oratorios. In 1719 he also became Kapellmeister to the court of the duke of Holstein. Growing deafness compelled him to resign his post at the Cathedral in 1728. In 1741 he was given the title of legation secretary to the duke of Holstein, and was made counsel in 1744.

Mattheson's output as a composer was substantial, but little of his music has survived. Of his major compositions, only the MSS of one of his operas, *Cleopatra* (modern ed., by G. Buelow in Das Erbe deutscher Musik, LXIX, 1975), and one of his oratorios, *Das Lied des Lammes* (modern ed. by B. Cannon, Madison, Wisc., 1971), are extant. The bulk of his MSS, kept in the Hamburg Stadtbibliothek, were destroyed during the hideous "fire- storm" bombing of Hamburg during World War II. However, most of his numerous literary writings are preserved. Outstanding among his books is *Der vollkommene Capellmeister* (1739), an original theoretical treatise on the state of music in his era. Also valuable are his *Grosse General-Bass-Schule* (1731; based on his earlier work *Exemplarische Organisten-Probe*, 1719) and *Kleine General-Bass-Schule* (1735). Of great historical value is his biographical dictionary, *Grundlage einer Ehren-Pforte...* (1740), which contains 149 entries. Many of the entries on musicians of his own time were compiled from information provided by the subjects themselves, and several prepared complete autobiographical accounts for his lexicon.

WRITINGS (all publ. in Hamburg): *Das neu-eröffnete Orchestre, oder gründliche Anleitung, wie ein "galant homme" einen vollkommenen Begriff von der Hoheit und Würde der edlen Musik erlangen möge* (1713); *Das beschützte Orchestre* (1717); *Exemplarische Organisten-Probe im Artikel vom General-Bass* (1719; publ. in an enl. ed. as *Grosse-General-Bass-Schule, oder: Der exemplarischen Organisten-Probe zweite, verbesserte und vermehrte Auflage,* 1731); *Réflexions sur l'éclaircissement d'un problème de musique pratique* (1720); *Das forschende Orchester* (1721); *Melotheta, das ist der grundrichtige, nach jetziger neuesten Manier angeführte Componiste* (1721–22); *Critica musica* (1722–25); *Der neue gottingische, aber viel schlechter, als die alten lacedämonischen urtheilende Ephorus* (1727); *De eruditione musica, ad virum plurimum reverendum, amplissimum atque doctissimum, Joannes Christophorum Krüsike* (1732); *Kleine General-Bass-Schule* (1735); *Kern melodischer Wissenschaft* (1737); *Gültige Zeugnisse über die jüngste Matthesonisch- Musicalische Kern-Schrift* (1738); *Der vollkommene Capellmeister, das ist gründliche Anzeige aller derjenigen Sachen, die einer wissen, können und vollkommen inne haben muss, der eine Capelle mit Ehren und Nützen verstehen will* (1739; facsimile reprint, Kassel, 1954; rev. Eng. tr. by E. Harriss, 1980); *Grundlage einer Ehren-Pforte, woran die tüchtigsten Capellmeister, Componisten, Musikgelehrten, Tonkünstler, etc. Leben, Werke, Verdienste, etc., erscheinen sollen* (1740; new ed., with addenda, by M. Schneider, Berlin, 1910); *Die neuste Untersuchung der Singspiele, nebst beygefügter musicalischen Geschmacksprobe* (1744); *Das erläuterte Selah, nebst einigen andern nützlichen Anmerkungen und erbaulichen Gedanken über Lob und Liebe* (1745); *Behauptung der himmlischen Musik aus den Gründen der Vernunft, Kirchen-Lehre und heiligen Schrift* (1747); *Matthesons Mithridat wider den Gift einer welschen Satyre, genannt: La Musica* (by S. Rosa; 1749); *Matthesons bewährte Panacea, als eine Zugabe zu seinem musicalischen Mithridat, erste Dosis* (1750); *Wahrer Begriff der harmonischen Lebens. Der Panacea zwote Dosis* (1750); *Sieben Gespräche der Weisheit und Musik samt zwo Beylagen: Als die dritte Dosis der Panacea* (1751); *Philologisches Tresespiel, als ein kleiner Beytrag zur kritischen Geschichte der deutschen Sprache* (1752); *Plus ultra, ein Stüchwerk von neuer und mancherley Art* (4 vols., 1754, 1755, 1755, 1756); *Georg Friederich Händels Lebensbeschreibung* (German tr. of J. Mainwaring's biography; 1761); etc.

WORKS (all 1st perf. in Hamburg unless otherwise given): **D R A M A T I C : O p e r a :** *Die Plejades oder Das Sieben- Gestirne* (1699); *Der edelmüthige Porsenna* (1702); *Victor, Hertzog der Normannen* (pasticcio; Act 1 by Schiefferdecker; Act 2 by Matteson; Act 3 by Bronner; 1702); *Die unglückselige Cleopatra* (1704); *Le Retour du siècle d'or* (Holstein, 1705); *Boris Goudenow* (1710); *Die geheimen Begebenheiten Henrico IV* (1711); he also prepared a German version of Orlandini's *Nero* (1723), with additions. **O r a t o r i o s :** *Die heylsame Geburth und Menschwerdung unsers Herrn und Heylandes Jesu Christi* (1715); *Die gnädige Sendung Gottes des Heiligen Geistes* (1716); *Chera, oder Die Leidtragende und getröstete Wittwe zu Nain* (1716); *Der verlangte und erlangte Heiland* (1716); *Der Altonaische Hirten-Segen, nebst einer Passions-Andacht über den verlassenen Jesum* (1717); *Der reformirende Johannes* (1717); *Der für die Sünde der Welt gemartete und sterbende Jesus* (1718); *Der aller-erfreulichste Triumph oder Der überwindende Immanuel* (1718); *Die glücklich-streitende Kirche* (1718); *Die göttliche Vorsorge über alle Creaturen* (1718); *Die Frucht des Geistes*

(1719); *Christi Wunder-Wercke bey den Schwachgläubigen* (1719); *Die durch Christi Auferstehung bestägte Auferstehung aller Todten* (1720); *Das gröste Kind* (1720); *Der Blut-rünstige Kelter-Treter und von der Erden erhöhete Menschen-Sohn* (1721); *Das irrende und wieder zu recht gebrachte Sünde-Schaaf* (1721); *Die Freudenreiche Geburt und Menschwerdung unsers Herrn und Heilandes Jesu Christi* (1721); *Der unter den Todten gesuchte, und unter den lebendigen gefundene Sieges-Fürst* (1722); *Das Grosse in dem Kleinen, oder Gott in den Herzen eines gläubigen Christen* (1722); *Das Lied des Lammes* (1723); *Der liebreiche und gedultige David* (1723); *Der aus dem Löwen-Graben befreyte, himmlische Daniel* (1725); *Das gottseelige Geheimnis* (1725); *Der undanckbare Jerobeam* (1726); *Der gegen seine Brüder barmherzige Joseph* (1727); *Das durch die Fleischwerdung des ewigen Wortes erfüllte Wort der Verheissung* (1727). He also composed his own funeral oratorio, *Das fröhliche Sterbelied.* **I N S T R U M E N T A L :** *Sonate à due cembali per il Signore Cyrillo Wich gran virtuoso* (1705; ed. by B. Cannon, London, 1960); *Suite für 2 Cembali* (1705; ed. by B. Cannon, London, 1960); *XII sonates à deux et trois flûtes sans basse* (publ. in Amsterdam, 1708); *Sonate for Harpsichord* (1713); *Pièces de clavecin en deux volumes* (publ. in London, 1714; Ger. ed. as *Matthesons Harmonisches Denkmahl, aus zwölff-erwählten Clavier-Suiten* (publ. in London, 1714; reprint, 1965); *Der brauchbare Virtuoso, welcher sich...mit zwölf neuen Kammer-Sonaten* for Flute, Violin, and Harpsichord (1720); *Die wol-klingende Finger-Sprache, in zwölff Fugen, mit zwey bis drey Subjecten* (1st part, 1735; 2nd part, 1737; ed. by L. Hoffmann-Erbrecht, Leipzig, 1954).

BIBL.: L. Meinardus, *M. und seine Verdienste um die deutsche Tonkunst,* in Waldersee's *Sammlung musikalischer Vorträge* (Leipzig, 1879); H. Schmidt, *J. M.: Ein Förderer der deutschen Tonkunst, im Lichte seiner Werke* (diss., Univ. of Munich, 1897); B. Cannon, *J. M.: Spectator in Music* (New Haven, 1947); W. Braun, *J. M. und die Aufklärung* (diss., Univ. of Halle, 1952); H. Reddick, *J. M.'s Forty-eight Thorough-bass Test-Pieces: Translation and Commentary* (diss., Univ. of Mich., 1956); H. Marx, *J. M.* (Hamburg, 1982); G. Buelow and H. Marx, eds., *New M. Studies* (Cambridge, 1984).—NS/LK/DM

Matthews, Artie, black American ragtime composer; b. Braidwood, Ill., Nov. 15, 1888; d. Cincinnati, Oct. 25, 1958. He spent his formative years in Springfield, Ill., and learned ragtime from the pianists Banty Morgan and Art Dillingham. After working in the tenderloin district of St. Louis (c. 1908), he took lessons in piano, organ, and theory. He was active as a composer and arranger for local theaters. In 1915 he went to Chicago as a church organist, and after World War I settled in Cincinnati, where he obtained a degree from the Metropolitan Coll. of Music and Dramatic Arts (1918). Together with his wife, Anna Matthews, he founded the Cosmopolitan School of Music for classical training of black musicians in 1921. He was an outstanding composer of piano rags, producing 5 *Pastime* rags (1913, 1913, 1916, 1918, 1920). He also wrote a jazz classic for piano, *Weary Blues* (1915), and several songs.
—NS/LK/DM

Matthews, Colin, English composer, writer on music, record producer, and broadcaster, brother of **David (John) Matthews;** b. London, Feb. 13, 1946. He studied classics (B.A., 1967) and received instruction in composition from Arnold Whittal (M.Phil., 1969) at the Univ. of Nottingham. He also studied composition with

Nicholas Maw before completing his education at the Univ. of Sussex (Ph.D., 1977, with the diss. *Mahler at Work: A Study of the Creative Process*). With his brother, he collaborated with Deryck Cooke on a performing ed. of Mahler's 10th Sym. (1964–74). From 1971 to 1976 he was associated with Benjamin Britten, and later edited many of his early and unpubl. scores. He also worked with Imogen Holst on eds. of her father's scores (1972–84). He contributed articles to various journals and was active as a broadcaster and record producer. In 1989 he founded NMC Recordings. From 1992 to 1999 he served as assoc. composer with the London Sym. Orch.

WORKS: ORCH.: 6 sonatas, including No. 4 (1974–75) and No. 5, *Landscape* (1977–81); *Night Music* for Small Orch. (1977); *Toccata Meccanica* (1984); 2 cello concertos (1984, 1996); *Monody* (1987); *Cortège* (1988); *Quatrain* (1989); *Chiaroscuro* (1990); *Machines and Dreams: Toy Symphony* (1991); *Broken Symmetry* (1991–92); *Hidden Variables* (1992; also for 15 Players, 1988–89); *Memorial* (1993); *Unfolded Order* (1999). **CHAMBER:** *Ceres* for 3 Flutes, Guitar, Percussion, 2 Cellos, and Double Bass (1972); *Specula* for Flute, Keyed Percussion, Harp, and Viola (1976–77); *Rainbow Studies* for Flute, Oboe, Clarinet, Bassoon, and Piano (1977–78); 3 string quartets (1979; 1985; 1993–94); 2 oboe quartets (1981; 1988–89); *Divertimento* for Double String Quartet (1982); *Triptych* for Piano Quintet (1984); *Sun's Dance* for Piccolo, Oboe, Bass Clarinet, Double Bass, Horn, and String Quintet (1984–85); *3 Enigmas* for Cello and Piano (1985); *5 Duos* for Cello and Piano (1987); *2–Part Invention* for 19 Players (1987–88); *Hidden Variables* for 15 Players (1988–89; also for Orch., 1992); *3–Part Chaconne* for String Trio and Piano, Left-hand (1989); *Duologue* for Oboe and Piano (1991); *To Compose without the least Knowledge of Music...*, wind sextet (1991); *Contraflow* for 14 Players (1992); *...through the glass* for 16 Players (1994); *2 Tributes* for 15 Players (1998–99). **Piano:** *5 Studies* (1974–76); *Suite* (1977–79); *11 Studies in Velocity* (1987). **VOCAL:** *The Great Journey* for Baritone and 8 Players (1981–88); *Night's Mask* for Voice and 7 Players (1984); *Cantata on the Death of Antony* for Soprano and Chamber Ensemble (1988–89); *Strugnells Haiku* for Voice and Piano or Chamber Ensemble (1989); *Renewal* for Chorus and Orch. (1995–96); *Aftertones* for Chorus and Orch. (1998–99); choruses; solo songs.—NS/LK/DM

Matthews, David (John), English composer and writer on music, brother of **Colin Matthews;** b. London, March 9, 1943. He studied classics at the Univ. of Nottingham (1962–65) and composition with Anthony Milner. He was associated with Benjamin Britten and the Aldeburgh Festival (1966–69). With his brother, he collaborated with Deryck Cooke on a performing ed. of Mahler's 10th Sym. He wrote articles on music and publ. *Michael Tippett: An Introductory Study* (1980) and *Landscape into Sound* (1992).

WORKS: ORCH.: 5 syms.: No. 1 (Stroud Festival, Oct. 8, 1975; rev. 1978), No. 2 (1976–79; London, May 13, 1982), No. 3 (1983–85; Sheffield, Sept. 27, 1985), No. 4 for Chamber Orch. (1989–90; London, May 28, 1991), and No. 5 (1998–99; London, Aug. 21, 1999); *September Music* (1979; BBC, Glasgow, April 28, 1980; rev. 1982); *White Nights* for Violin and Small Orch. (1980; rev. 1988); *Introit* for 2 Trumpets and Strings (Windsor, Nov. 13, 1981); 2 violin concertos: No. 1 (1980–82; BBC, Manchester, Nov. 2, 1983) and No. 2 (1997–98; St.-Nazaire Festival, Sept. 23, 1998); *In the Dark Time* (1984–85; London, Dec. 11, 1985); *Variations* for Strings (1986; Uppingham, March 23, 1987); *Chaconne* (1986–87;

Manchester, Oct. 7, 1988); *The Music of Dawn* (1989–90; London, Nov. 28, 1990); *Romanza* for Cello and Chamber Orch. (1990); *Scherzo capriccioso* (1990); *Capriccio* for 2 Horns and Strings (1991); Oboe Concerto (1991–92; London, Sept. 18, 1992); *From Sea to Sky*, overture (1992); *A Vision and a Journey* (1992–93; Manchester, Oct. 21, 1993; rev. 1996); *2 Pieces* for Strings (1996–2000); *Burnham Wick* (1997; Birmingham, March 10, 1998). **CHAMBER:** 8 string quartets (1970, rev. 1980; 1976, rev. 1979; 1978, rev. 1981; 1981; 1984, rev. 1985; 1991; 1994–95; 1999); *Toccatas and Pastorals* for Oboe d'Amore, English Horn, Bassoon, and Harpsichord (1976; rev. 1979); *Duet Variations* for Flute and Piano (1982); Clarinet Quintet (1984); *Aria* for Violin and Piano (1986); *The Flaying of Marsyas* for Oboe and String Quartet (1986–87); String Trio (1989); *3 to Tango*, piano trio (1991); *A Song and Dance Sketchbook* for Piano Quartet (1994–95); piano pieces, including a sonata (1989) and variations (1997). **VOCAL:** *3 Songs* for Soprano and Orch. (1968–71); *Stars* for Chorus and Orch. (1970); *Eclogue* for Soprano and 7 Instrumentalists (1975–79); *The Golden Kingdom* for High Voice and Piano (1979–83); *Cantiga* for Soprano and Chamber Orch. (1987–88; London, July 27, 1988); *Marina* for Baritone, Basset Horn, Cello, and Piano (1988); *The Ship of Death* for Chorus (1988–89); *The Sleeping Lord* for Soprano, Flute, Clarinet, Harp, and String Quartet (1992); *Spell of Sleep* for Soprano, 2 Clarinets, Viola, Cello, and Double Bass (1992); *Vespers* for Mezzo-soprano, Tenor, Chorus, and Orch. (1993–94; Huddersfield, March 24, 1995); *Hunting in Harvest* for 6 Solo Voices (1996–97); *Winter Passions* for Baritone, Clarinet, String Trio, and Piano (1999); other songs.—NS/LK/DM

Matthews, Denis (James), English pianist, teacher, and writer on music; b. Coventry, Feb. 27, 1919; d. (suicide) Birmingham, Dec. 24, 1988. He studied with Harold Craxton (piano) and Alwyn (composition) at the Royal Academy of Music in London (1935–40). He made his London debut in 1939. During World War II, he served in the Royal Air Force while continuing to make appearances as a pianist; after the war, he toured throughout the world. Matthews was the first prof. of music at the Univ. of Newcastle upon Tyne (1971–84). In 1975 he was made a Commander of the Order of the British Empire.

WRITINGS: *In Pursuit of Music* (autobiography; London, 1966); *Beethoven's Piano Sonatas* (London, 1967); *Arturo Toscanini* (Tunbridge Wells and N.Y., 1982); *Beethoven* (London, 1985). —NS/LK/DM

Matthews, Michael (Bass), accomplished Canadian composer; b. Gander, Newfoundland, August 28, 1950. He studied composition with Aurelio de la Vega (composition) and Lawrence Christianson (conducting) at Calif. State Univ. at Northridge (B.Mus., 1975), with Ben Glovinsky (composition) at Calif. State Univ. at Sacramento (M.A. in composition, 1979), and with Larry Austin (composition) and Anshel Brusilow (conducting) at North Tex. State Univ. (Ph.D., 1982). He also attended the summer course in computer music at the Center for Computer Research in Music and Acoustics (CCRMA) at Stanford Univ. (1988). From 1979 he received numerous awards, grants, and honors, including a 1992 Media Arts Residency for the recording of *The First Sea* (1989) for its CDCM compact disc release from the Banff Centre, the 1993 International Computer Music Assn. Commission Award for one of two commissions awarded worldwide for a piece to be premiered at the International Computer Music Conference in Århus, Denmark (*In Emptiness, Over Emptiness*, 1994), a 1997 Composer Development Grant from the Manitoba Arts Council (*Toller*, 1999), and a 2000 residency at the Rockefeller Foundation Bellagio Study and Conference Center (*Cello Concerto*, 2000). He joined the music faculty of the Univ. of Manitoba, successively serving as lecturer (1982–83; 1985–87), asst. prof. (1987–90), assoc. prof. (1990–94), and prof. (from 1994); he concurrently was director of its Computer Music Studio from 1986. In 1991 he founded Goundwell, a new music series in Winnipeg. Matthews's substantial catalog includes works in virtually every genre.

WORKS: DRAMATIC: *Time Frames* for Dancers, Lights, Tape, and 2 Chamber Orchs. (Sacramento, Nov. 5, 1978); *Songs of the Masked Dancers* for Soprano, Actor, Flute, Bass Clarinet, Cello, Piano, and Tape (Winnipeg, April 25, 1990); *Madrugada* for Soprano, Actors, and Musicians (1992–95; Winnipeg, April 26, 1995); *The Raft* for Voices, Dancers, and String Quartet (Winnipeg, Dec. 11, 1997); *Ernst Toller: Requiem for an Idea* for Actor and Cello (Winnipeg, May 1, 1999). ORCH.: *Equinox* for Chamber Orch. (Northridge, Calif., Nov. 14, 1974); *Stones of the Sky* for Symphonic Wind Ensemble (1975; Sacramento, Nov. 8, 1978); *Prelude* for Symphonic Wind Ensemble (1984; Taejon, Korea, April 6, 1985); *Stone and Silence* (Taejon, Korean, Nov. 12, 1984); *The Far Field* (1987; Winnipeg, Feb. 12, 1988); *Landscape* for Piano and Strings (1990); *Three Echoes* for Strings (1990); *Between the Wings of the Earth* for Chamber Orch. (Winnipeg, March 24, 1993); *Matrix* for Concert Band (1994; Winnipeg, Feb. 23, 1995); *Two Interludes* (1996); *Velocity* for Bass Clarinet and String Orch. (1996); Sym. No. 1 (1997); *Concerto Grosso* for String Quartet, 3 Percussionists, and String Orch. (Winnipeg, May 19, 1998); Piano Concerto (1998); *Into the Page of Night* (1998; Winnipeg, Feb. 6, 1999); *Lorca Sketches* for Strings (Winnipeg, Feb. 11, 1998); Cello Concerto (2000). CHAMBER: *Games* for Chamber Ensemble (Los Angeles, April 7, 1973); *Ogdoas* for Percussion Ensemble (Northridge, Calif., Nov. 16, 1974); *Lost, Among Bright Stars* for Chamber Ensemble (1979; rev. version, Sacramento, Oct. 11, 1980); 2 string quartets: No. 1 (1979, Denton, Tex., Dec. 1, 1981; rev. 1983) and No. 2 [titled String Quartet No. 1] (Winnipeg, Oct. 24, 1999); *Sinfonia Concertante* for Wind Ensemble (1980; Banff, Alberta, July 26, 1983); *Suite* for Guitar (Denton, Tex., Dec. 1, 1981); *Mosaic* for Chamber Ensemble (1982; Winnipeg, April 21, 1983); *Four Studies* for Clarinet, Percussion, and Piano (Taejon, Korea, Dec. 6, 1984); *Fantasy* for Violin (1985; Winnipeg, March 24, 1986); *Into a Long Moment* for Flute, Clarinet, Violin, Cello, and Piano (1985; Winnipeg, Jan. 28, 1986); Piano Trio (Winnipeg, Nov. 27, 1986); *Wind Sketches* for Wind Octet (1988); *Love in a Dry Country* for Ensemble, Tape, Interactive Computer System, and Visuals (1992); *Layerings* for Vibraphone and Tape (1993; Toronto, March 11, 1994); Concerto for Percussion and Wind Ensemble (1998; Winnipeg, April 4, 2000); *Partita—Images/Fragments* for Violin and Piano (Winnipeg, Sept. 19, 1999); *...of the rolling worlds* for Bass Clarinet and Tape (Alicante, Spain, Sept. 23, 1999); *Images* for Clarinet and String Trio (Szombothely, Hungary, July 22, 1999); *Ernst Toller: Requiem for an Idea*, suite for Cello (Lviv, Ukraine, Oct. 13, 1999). PIANO: *Elegy* (1983; Taejon, Korea, June 8, 1984); *Of Time and Sky* (1990); *Scattered Mirrors* (Pinewa, Manitoba, Oct. 29, 1993); *Two Studies* (1994–95); *Bagatelle* (1997); *Postlude* (1997); *Fantasy/Nocturne* (1999). VOCAL: *The Hollow Men* for Tenor and Chamber Ensemble (Northridge, Calif., April 23, 1974);

Three Songs for Mezzo-soprano and Chamber Ensemble (1975); *if there are any heavens* for Soprano and Chamber Ensemble (Sacramento, Dec. 6, 1979); *The Wind Was There* for Soprano and Orch. (1980–82); *Rest, Heart of the Tired World* for Voice and Piano (Denton, Tex., Dec. 1, 1981; rev. 1983); *Quis Est Deus?* for Voice, Flute, and Clarinet (1983); *Folk Songs* for Soprano, Violin, Cello, and Piano (Taejon, Korea, Nov. 28, 1984); *Five Poems of Walt Whitman* for Soprano and String Quartet (Seoul, Oct. 5, 1984); *Sijo* for Soprano and Percussion (1985; Winnipeg, March 28, 1988); *Dream Songs* for Soprano, Tenor, Chorus, Piano, and Percussion (Winnipeg, Oct. 28, 1986); *Castilla* for Soprano, Recorder, Harpsichord, and Cello (Winnipeg, March 31, 1987); *Songs of Travel* for Soprano and Cello (Winnipeg, March 9, 1988); *The First Sea* for Bass, Clarinet, and Tape (Toronto, Feb. 25, 1989); *Four Songs of Japan* for Soprano, Viola, and Fortepiano (1991); *Rooms of Light* for Chorus (1992; Winnipeg, March 1, 1998); *Birds* for Soprano, Keyboard, Interactive Computer System, and Visuals (1992); *Out of the Earth* for Soprano and Ensemble (Vancouver, March 21, 1993); *In Emptiness, Over Emptiness* for Soprano and Tape (Århus, Sept. 14, 1994); *Two Night Pieces* for 4 Men's Voices (1994); *Song of the Sky Loom* for Soloists and Chorus (1995); *Deux chansons d'amour* for Voice and Piano (1996); *Two Poems* for Chorus (1999–2000). TAPE: *Study*, musique concrète (1972); *Beginnings* (1973; Santiago, Chile, June 6, 1974); *Abintra* (Hovikodden, Denmark, June 30, 1974); *Antipodes* (Glendale, Calif., Jan. 19, 1975); *Woman*, film score (1981); *The Raft*, incidental music (1991); *The North Revisited*, radio piece (1992); *Music for Ancient Spaces* (1992); *Dog and Crow*, incidental music (1992).—LK/DM

Matthews, Michael Gough, English pianist and music educator; b. Wanstead, Essex, July 12, 1931. He studied at the Royal Coll. of Music in London, where he received the Hopkinson Gold Medal (1953), and then took a course at the Accademia di Santa Cecilia in Rome. He subsequently toured as pianist in Europe and the Far East. From 1964 to 1971 he was on the staff of the Royal Scottish Academy of Music and Drama in Glasgow; then was prof. of piano at the Royal Coll. of Music (1972–75), where he was vice-director (1978–84) and director (1985–93).—NS/LK/DM

Matthison-Hansen (originally, **Matthias Hansen**), **Hans,** esteemed Danish organist and composer, father of **(Johan) Gottfred Matthison-Hansen**; b. Adelby, near Flensburg, Feb. 6, 1807; d. Roskilde, Jan. 7, 1890. He learned to play the violin, viola, and cello at the Copenhagen Academy of Art, then took general music courses with C.E.F. Weyse. In 1832 he was appointed organist of Roskilde Cathedral, a position he retained until his death. He gave solo recitals in Denmark, Norway, Sweden, and Germany (1861–62); visited London in 1864. He wrote a Sym. (1848), 2 oratorios, 2 Easter cantatas, and numerous organ works. His surname was legally changed in 1859.—NS/LK/DM

Matthison-Hansen, (Johan) Gottfred, Danish organist and composer, son of **Hans Matthison-Hansen**; b. Roskilde, Nov. 1, 1832; d. Copenhagen, Oct. 14, 1909. He studied piano with his father, and later took lessons in piano and theory with W.H. Barth; then enrolled at the Univ. of Copenhagen as a law student.

Although mainly self-taught, he trained himself so as to hold church positions as an organist at the Fredericks Church (1859), St. John's (1871), and the Trinity Church (1881) in Copenhagen; also made tours in organ recitals in Denmark and Germany. In 1867 he began teaching organ at the Copenhagen Cons., and in 1884 he also assumed the position of piano teacher there. He composed a number of works for organ which he included in his recitals. In addition to the Classical repertoire, he championed the Romantic works of the time.

—NS/LK/DM

Matthus, Siegfried,

esteemed German composer; b. Mallenuppen, April 13, 1934. He was a composition student of Wagner- Régeny at the Deutsche Hochschule für Musik (1952–58) before attending the master class of Eisler at the Akademie der Künste (1958–60) in East Berlin. From 1964 he was active as a composer and dramaturgical advisor for contemporary music at the Komische Oper in East Berlin. In 1985 he was honored with the title of Prof. In 1991 he became artistic director of the Rheinsberg Chamber Opera. Matthus was made a member of the Akademie der Künste in East Berlin in 1969, of the Akademie der Künste in West Berlin in 1976, and of the Bayerische Akademie der Schönen Künste in Munich in 1978. In 1996 he was awarded the prize of the Berlin Internationale Theaterinstitut. First and foremost, Matthus is a man of the theater. His fascination for opera has set his course as a composer, while also influencing his non-dramatic scores as well. He has effectively absorbed various avant-garde techniques and styles to create works of pronounced individuality and distinction.

WORKS: DRAMATIC: *Lazarillo vom Tormes*, opera (1960–63; Karl-Marx-Stadt, May 26, 1964); *Der letzte Schuss*, opera (1966–67; Berlin, Nov. 5, 1967); *Match*, ballet (1969; Berlin, May 1971); *Noch ein Löffel Gift, Liebling?*, comic "criminal opera" (1971; Berlin, April 16, 1972); *Omphale*, opera (1972–74; Weimar, Sept. 7, 1976); *Alptraum einer Ballerina*, ballet (1973); *Mario und der Zauberer*, ballet (1974); *Judith*, opera (1982–84; Berlin, Sept. 28, 1985); *Die Weise von Liebe und Tod des Cornets Christoph Rilke*, operatic vision (1983–84; Dresden, Feb. 16, 1985); *Graf Mirabeau*, opera (1987–88; Berlin, Karlsruhe, and Essen, July 14–15, 1989); *Farinelli oder Die Macht des Gesanges*, opera (1996–97; Karlsruhe, Feb. 28, 1998); *Crown Prince Friedrich*, opera (Rheinsberg, Dec. 30, 1999). ORCH.: *Kleines Orchesterkonzert* (1963; Dresden, Feb. 26, 1964); *Inventionen* (1964; Erfurt, Feb. 2, 1967); *Tua res agitur* (Berlin, Dec. 1965); Violin Concerto (1968; Dresden, Feb. 24, 1969); 2 syms.: No. 1, *Dresdner Sinfonie* (Dresden, Oct. 10, 1969) and No. 2 (1975–76; Berlin, Oct. 7, 1976); Piano Concerto (1970; Berlin, Feb. 18, 1971); *Orchesterserenade* (Leipzig, Nov. 26, 1974); *Werther* (1975; Potsdam, Sept. 1977); Cello Concerto (1975; Dresden, Sept. 9, 1976); *Drei Sommerbilder* (1975); *Responso*, concerto for Orch. (Dresden, Oct. 27, 1977); *Visionen* for Strings (Dresden, June 1978); Flute Concerto (1978; Leipzig, Jan. 11, 1979); Chamber Concerto for Flute, Harpsichord, and Strings (1980; Berlin, Sept. 12, 1981; based on the Flute Concerto); Concerto for Trumpet, Timpani, and Orch. (1982; Berlin, Jan. 18, 1983); *Der Wald*, timpani concerto (1984; Dresden, June 6, 1985); *Divertimento* (Salzburg, Aug. 14, 1985); Oboe Concerto (Swansea, Nov. 22, 1985); *Die Windsbraut*, concerto for Orch. (1985; Munich, June 6, 1986); *Nächtliche Szene im Park* (1987; Krefeld, April 21, 1988); *Der See*, harp concerto (Dresden, Nov. 1, 1989); Concerto for 3 Trumpets and Strings, *O namenlose*

Freude (1989–90; Kiel, July 7, 1990); Piano Concerto, after Brahms's Piano Quartet, op.25 (1992; Berlin, June 1, 1994); *Manhattan Concerto* (1993–94; N.Y., May 16, 1994); Horn Concerto (1994; Dresden, June 9, 1995); *Blow Out* for Organ and Orch. (1995; Dresden, May 4, 1996); *Das Land Phantásien* (1995–96; Frankfurt an der Oder, Sept. 6, 1996); *Ariadne* (1997–98; Berlin, Oct. 1998); Double Concerto for Flute, Harp, and Orch. (Dresden, Dec. 18, 1998); *Capriccio "Kraft Variationen"* for Violin and Orch., after Paganini (1999); *Furien-Furioso* (1999). CHAMBER: Sonata for Horn, Trumpet, Trombone, Tuba, Piano, and Timpani (1968); *Musik* for Oboes and Piano (1968); Octet for Clarinet, Bassoon, Horn, 2 Violins, Viola, Cello, and Double Bass (1970; Berlin, Oct. 28, 1971); String Quartet (1971; Berlin, Oct. 14, 1973); Trio for Flute, Viola, and Harp (1972); Octet for Flute, Oboe, Percussion, Piano, and String Quartet (1976); *Nocturno* for Flute (1977); *Adagio und Passacaglia* for Cello and Double Bass (1982; Berlin, April 18, 1984); *Impromptu* for Flute (1984); Andante for Oboe and Harp (1986); *"Ich komm einem Weg"*, octet for Clarinet, Bassoon, Horn, and String Quartet (Berlin, Oct. 19, 1989); *Unruhige Zeit*, trio for Baryton, Viola, and Cello (1990; Berlin, Feb. 24, 1991); *Die Sonne sinkt* for Speaking Voice and String Quartet, after Nietzsche (Cologne, Dec. 30, 1994); *Windspiele* for Violin, Viola, and Cello (Berlin, Oct. 15, 1995); *Lichte Spiele* for Violin, Viola, Cello, and Piano (Berlin, Oct. 26, 1996); *Das Mädchen und der Tod* for 2 Violins, Viola, and Cello (1996; Berlin, Feb. 18, 1997). P i a n o : *Variationen* (1957). VOCAL: *Liebeslieder fünfundvierzig* for Soprano, Alto, and Chorus (1960); *Die Zeit hält den Atem an* for Alto and Chorus (1964); *Kammermusik 65* for Alto, Women's Voices, and Instrumental Ensemble (1965); *Lieder* for High Voice and Piano (1965–69); *Galilei* for Voice, 5 Instruments, and Tape (1966); *Höflichkeit* for Voice and Piano (1967); *Kantate von den Beiden* for Soprano, Baritone, Speaker, and Orch. (1969); *Musica et vinum* for Chorus (1969); *Wir zwei* for Chorus (1970); *Wie die Saiten der Gitarre* for Children's or Women's Chorus (1970); *Das Jahr Zweitausend naht* for Chorus (1970); *Dorf* for High Voice and Piano (1971); *Vokalsinfonie* for Soprano, Baritone, 2 Choruses, and Orch., after the opera *Der letzte Schuss* (1972); *Fünf Liebeslieder des Catull* for Chorus (1972; Berlin, Sept. 22, 1973); *Laudate pacem*, oratorio for Soloists, 2 Mixed Choruses, Children's Chorus, Organ, and Orch. (1973–74; Berlin, April 19, 1976); *Unter dem Holunderstrauch* for Soprano, Tenor, and Orch. (Berlin, Oct. 7, 1976); *Hyperion-Fragmente* for Bass and Orch. (1979; Berlin, Feb. 23, 1980); *Holofernes* for Baritone and Orch. (Leipzig, Nov. 25, 1981); *Die Liebesqualen des Catull* for Soprano, Bass, Chorus, and Instrumental Ensemble (1985–86; Bratislava, Sept. 30, 1986); *"Der über uns"* for Voice and Piano (1986; also for Tenor and 4 Bassoons, 1986–93; Berlin, May 26, 1993); *Nachtlieder* for Baritone, String Quartet, and Harp (1987; Berlin, Sept. 12, 1988); *Wem ich zu gefallen suche* for Soprano or Tenor and Orch. (1990; also as *Feuer und Schnee* for Voice and Piano, 1990); Sym. for Soprano, Children's Chorus, Organ, and Orch., *Gewandhaus-Sinfonie* (1992–93; Leipzig, March 11, 1993); *Weisen von Liebe, Leben und Tod* for Middle Voice and Orch. (Berlin, April 6, 1995; also for Middle Voice and Piano, 1995–97); *Sappho- Fragmente* for Chorus and Harp (Netzeband, July 12, 1997; also for 4 Women's Voices and Guitar). OTHER: *Leise zieht durch mein Gemüt*, orchestration of 12 songs by Mendelssohn for High Voice and Orch. (1987–93; Berlin, April 15, 1994); String orch. version of Schubert's String Quartet No. 14, D.810, *Der Tod und das Mädchen* (1995; Berlin, Jan. 20, 1996).

BIBL.: H. Döhnert, *S. M.-für Sie porträtiert* (Leipzig, 1979).

—NS/LK/DM

Mattila, Karita (Marjatta), Finnish soprano; b. Somero, Sept. 5, 1960. She was a pupil of Liisa Linko-Malmio and Kim Borg at the Sibelius Academy in Helsinki and of Vera Rozsa in London. In 1982 she made her operatic debut as Mozart's Countess at the Finnish National Opera in Helsinki. After winning the Singer of the World Competition in Cardiff in 1983, she appeared as a soloist with many of the world's major orchs. In 1983 she sang Fiordiligi at the Munich Festival and also made her U.S. debut as Donna Elvira in Washington, D.C.; in 1986 she made her first appearance at London's Covent Garden as Fiordiligi. In 1989 she appeared as Ilia in *Idomeneo* at the San Francisco Opera. On Oct. 24, 1990, she made her Metropolitan Opera debut in N.Y. as Donna Elvira, and returned there in 1993 as Eva. She also sang at the Salzburg Festival in the latter year. In 1995 she sang Lisa in *The Queen of Spades* at the Metropolitan Opera, and in 1996 returned to San Francisco as Elsa. After singing that role and Chrysothemis at Covent Garden in 1997, she was engaged as Jenůfa in Hamburg in 1998. In 1999 she returned to the Metropolitan Opera as Emilia Grimaldi. In addition to her Mozart roles, she also became well known as a Wagnerian.—NS/LK/DM

Matton, Roger, Canadian composer and ethnomusicologist; b. Granby, Quebec, May 18, 1929. He studied with Sister Yvette Dufault (piano and theory) before pursuing his training at the Conservatoire de musique du Québec à Montréal with Champagne (composition), Delorme (solfege and harmony), and Letondal (piano). He went to Paris to study with Messiaen (analysis) at the Cons. (1950; 1953–54), and also was a student of Vaurabourg-Honegger (piano privately, 1950, and at the École Normale de Musique, 1952–53). He also studied with Boulanger (analysis, counterpoint, and composition privately, 1952–55). From 1956 to 1976 he was a researcher and ethnomusicologist at the Archives de folklore at Laval Univ. in Quebec City. He also taught there, later serving as a teacher of composition and then of the history of contemporary music at its school of music (1960–63) and finally of ethnomusicology at its Dept. of Canadian Studies and Dept. of History (1963–89). While his compositions partake of various contemporary trends, his works remain generally tonally anchored. In a number of his works, folk melos may be discerned.

WORKS: ORCH.: *Danse lente (Gymnopédie)* for Chamber Orch. (1947); Concerto for Saxophone and Strings (1948); *Pax* (1950); *L'Horoscope*, suite choregraphique (1957; CBC Radio, Oct. 12, 1958; as a ballet, CBC-TV, Nov. 6, 1958); *Mouvment symphonique I* (Quebec City, Nov. 14, 1960), *II: Musique pour un drame* (Montreal, April 17, 1962), *III* (Quebec City, May 7, 1974), and *IV* (1978); Concerto for 2 Pianos and Orch. (Quebec City, Nov. 30, 1964). CHAMBER: *Étude* for Clarinet and Piano (1946); *Esquisse* for String Quartet (1949); Concerto for 2 Pianos and Percussion (1955). KEYBOARD: P i a n o : *Berceuse* (1945); *Danse brésilienne* (1946; orchestrated 1971); *Trois Préludes* (1949). O r g a n : *Suite de Paques* (1952); *Tu es Petrus* (1984). VOCAL: *L'Escaouette* for Soprano, Mezzo-soprano, Tenor, Baritone, Chorus, and Orch. (1957); *Te Deum* for Baritone, Chorus, Orch., and Tape (1967).—NS/LK/DM

Mattox, Janis, American composer; b. St. Paul, Minn., March 18, 1949. She studied at the Univ. of Minnesota (B.A., 1972) and Northwestern Univ. in Evanston, Ill. (M.A., 1974). In 1978 she began composing and producing works involving computer music technologies and live performers at Stanford Univ.'s Center for Computer Research in Music and Acoustics (CCRMA); among the virtuoso performers she has collaborated with are jazz bassist Mel Graves (*Voice of the Ancestors*, 1983), actor Bob Ernst (*Spirits Rising*, 1984), flutist (Moroccan ney) Richard Horowitz (*Night Flyer*, 1985), and drummer George Marsh (*Adowa*, 1987); works for dance include *Song from the Center of the Earth* for belly dancer Rachel Dutton (1982) and *Beehive Suite* (1985) for Jim Self and Beehive. Mattox taught and gave lecture demonstrations on computer music at CCRMA; also lectured in Los Angeles and Venice. She is project consultant for Good Sound Foundation and a performing member (piano) of the Good Sound Band. Her other works include *Dragon's View* for Computer-generated Quadraphonic Tape (1980); *Shaman*, music theater piece for Percussionist, Belly Dancer, Bassist, Actor/Vocalist, Live Digital Processing, and Computer-generated Tape (1984); *Adowa* for Percussionist and Dancer (1987); *Book of Shadows, Part I*, for Film, 2 Pianos in just intonation, Soprano, Violin, Garden Hose, Ney, Didjeridu, Contrabass, Saxophone, Accordion in just intonation, and Live Digital Processing (1989); and Pulse for 2 Drummers (1990). She is married to **Loren Rush.**—NS/LK/DM

Matys, Jiří, Czech composer and teacher; b. Bakov, Oct. 27, 1927. He studied with František Michálek (organ) at the Cons. (graduated, 1947) and with Kvapil (composition) at the Janáček Academy of Music (graduated, 1951) in Brno. He taught at the latter, served as head of Brno's public art school Královo Pole, and was a prof. of composition at the Brno Cons.

WORKS: ORCH.: *Morning Music* for Strings, 2 Trumpets, and Percussion (1961–62); *Music* for String Quartet and Orch. (1971); Symphonic Overture (1973–74); *Music* for Strings (1982); *The Urgency of Time* for Viola and Orch. (1986–87). CHAMBER: Viola Sonata (1954); 5 string quartets (1957; 1961; 1963–64; 1973; 1989–90); Sonata for Solo Viola (1963); Violin Sonata (1964–65); Concert Piece for 2 Accordions (1968); *Inventions* for Flute and Cello (1969); *Music* for Winds (1970–71); *Allusions* for 4 Flutes (1971); Suite for Viola and Bass Clarinet (1972–73); *Suita Giocosa* for Flute and Bassoon (1974); Suite for Clarinet and Piano (1974–75); 4 sonatas for Solo Violin (1977, 1991, 1993, 1994); Suite for Flute and Guitar (1977); *Divertimento* for 4 Horns (1981); Suite for Wind Quintet (1984); *Music for 2*, suite for Violin and Marimba (1986); *The Soul of My District I* for Viola and Guitar or Cello (1987) and *II* for Viola (1988); *Scenes* for Clarinet and Piano (1989); *Visions* for Bass Clarinet and Guitar (1991); *Divertimento* for 5 Cellos (1996); piano pieces. VOCAL: *Lyrical Melodramas* for Reciter and Piano (1957); *Variations on Death* for Reciter, String Quartet, and Horn (1959); *The Red Toadstool* for Soloist, Children's Chorus, Piano, and Flute (1968); *Written by Grief into Silence...*, song cycle for Medium Voice and Orch. or Piano (1972); *4–Leaf Clover* for Reciter and Flute (1979–80); *To the Czech-Moravian Uplands* for Girl's or Women's Chorus (1991).—NS/LK/DM

Matzenauer, Margarete, celebrated Hungarian soprano and contralto; b. Temesvár, June 1, 1881; d. Van

Nuys, Calif., May 19, 1963. Her father was a conductor and her mother a soprano; she grew up in favorable musical surroundings, and began to study singing at an early age, first in Graz, then in Berlin, and finally in Munich. In 1901 she joined the staff of the Strasbourg Opera. She then sang contralto roles at the Munich Court Opera (1904–11), and also sang at Bayreuth in 1911. She made her American debut as Amneris in *Aida* at the Metropolitan Opera in N.Y. (Nov. 13, 1911) and remained one of its leading members until 1930; in the interim, she sang in opera in Germany and South America. She gave her farewell concert recital in Carnegie Hall, N.Y., in 1938, and settled in Calif. She had one of the most remarkable singing careers of her day; she sang both soprano and contralto roles until 1914, and thereafter concentrated on contralto roles. Among her many outstanding roles were Brünnhilde, Venus, Isolde, Fricka, Ortrud, Eboli, Azucena, Leonora, and Laura in *La Gioconda*.—NS/LK/DM

Mauceri, John (Francis), American conductor; b. N.Y., Sept. 12, 1945. He studied with Gustav Meier at Yale Univ. (B.A., 1967; M.Phil., 1972) and with Maderna, Colin Davis, Ozawa, and Bernstein at the Berkshire Music Center at Tanglewood (summer, 1971). He conducted the Yale Univ. Sym. Orch. (1968–74); subsequently appeared widely as a guest conductor of opera, musical theater, and sym. orchs. He was music director of the Washington (D.C.) Opera (1980–82), the American Sym. Orch. in N.Y. (1984–87), the Scottish Opera in Glasgow (1987–93), and the Hollywood Bowl Orch. (from 1990).—NS/LK/DM

Mauduit, Jacques, noted French composer; b. Paris, Sept. 16, 1557; d. there, Aug. 21, 1627. He studied humanities and philosophy, but was self-taught in music. He served as royal secretary and registrar in the judiciary. His gifts as a composer were recognized when he won the St. Cecilia's Day Competition in Evreux in 1581 for his motet *Afferte Domine* for 5 Voices. He became associated with Baïf's Académie de Poésie et de Musique in Paris, and made several settings of Baïf's poems. During the siege of Paris, he saved Baïf's unpubl. MSS and helped Le Jeune escape the city, saving the MS of his *Dodecacorde*. Many of his own works are lost.

WORKS: (23) *Chansonettes mesurées de Jean-Antoine de Baïf* for 4 Voices (Paris, 1586; ed. by H. Expert in Les Maîtres Musiciens de la Renaissance Française, X, 1899); *Psaumes mesurées à l'antique, 1 prière* for 4 and 5 Voices (publ. in M. Mersenne's *Quaestiones celeberrimae in Genesim*, 1623); *Requiem aeternum* for 5 Voices, for the funeral of Rosnard (1585; publ. by M. Mersenne, 1636–37).—NS/LK/DM

Mauersberger, Rudolf, German organist, choral conductor, teacher, and composer; b. Mauersberg, Erzgebirge, Jan. 29, 1889; d. Dresden, Feb. 22, 1971. He studied piano, organ, and composition at the Leipzig Cons. (1912–14; 1918–19), winning the Nikisch Prize for composition in 1914. He served as organist and choirmaster in Aachen (1919–25), then was in charge of church music in Thuringia (1925–30) and directing the

choir at Eisenach's Georgenkirche. In 1930 he became choirmaster of the Kreuzkirche in Dresden, and directed its famous boy's choir, taking it on numerous tours in Europe and abroad. He composed a number of choral works, including the *Dresdner Requiem* (1948), written in memory of those who lost their lives during the barbarous bombing of the beautiful porcelaneous city just a few weeks before the end of World War II.

BIBL.: M. Grun, *R. M.: Studien zu Leben und Werk* (Regensburg, 1986); M. Herrmann, *R. M. (1889–1971): Werkverzeichnis (RMWV)* (Dresden, 1991).—NS/LK/DM

Maupin, infamous French soprano; b. 1670; d. Provence, 1707. She was the daughter of the secretary to the Count of Armagnac. In 1690 she made her operatic debut as Pallas in Lully's *Cadmus et Hermione* at the Paris Opéra, where she continued to sing until 1705. She possessed a remarkable voice of great beauty, which was complemented by her physical attributes. Her life outside the theater was as exciting as any role she played on the stage. A penchant for donning men's clothing gave rise to situations in which she defended herself in duels. Her sexual appetite led to various bisexual encounters. For many years she was the mistress of the Elector of Bavaria. Her notorious life served as the basis of Gautier's novel *Mademoiselle Maupin, double amour* (Paris, 1835–36).

BIBL.: G. Letainturier-Fradin, *La M. (1760–1707): Sa vie, ses duels, ses aventures* (Paris, 1904).—NS/LK/DM

Maurel, Victor, famous French baritone; b. Marseilles, June 17, 1848; d. N.Y., Oct. 22, 1923. He studied singing at the Paris Cons., making his debut in *Guillaume Tell* in Marseilles (1867). He made his first appearance at the Paris Opéra as De Nevers in *Les Huguenots* in 1868, then sang in Italy, Spain, England, and Russia; in 1873 he made an American tour. Returning to Paris, he was on the staff of the Opéra (1879–94). He made his debut at the Metropolitan Opera in N.Y. on Dec. 3, 1894, as Iago in *Otello*; sang there until 1896, then returned in 1898–99. He was a member of the Opéra-Comique in Paris until 1904. In 1909 he emigrated to the U.S., where he remained until his death; in his last years he was active as a stage designer in N.Y. He created the role of Iago in Verdi's *Otello* (Milan, Feb. 5, 1887) and the title role in *Falstaff* (Milan, Feb. 9, 1893); also distinguished himself in Wagnerian roles. He publ., in Paris, several monographs on the aesthetics of singing and also autobiographical reminiscences, among them *Le Chant remové par la science* (1892), *Un Problème d'art* (1893), *L'Art du chant* (1897), and *Dix ans de carrière* (1897).—NS/LK/DM

Maurer, Ludwig (Wilhelm), German violinist and composer; b. Potsdam, Feb. 8, 1789; d. St. Petersburg, Oct. 25, 1878. He studied with K. Haack. A precocious child musician, he appeared in concerts at the age of 13. At 17 he went to Russia, remaining there for 10 years, giving concerts and serving as house musician to Russian aristocrats. From 1817 until 1832 he traveled in Europe, and was successful as a violinist in Berlin and in Paris. He was in Russia again (1832–45), then lived in Dresden, eventually returning to St. Petersburg. He produced 2 operas in Hannover, *Der neue Paris* (Jan. 27, 1826) and *Aloise* (Jan. 16, 1828); also wrote many stage pieces in Russia. With Aliabiev and Verstovsky, he contributed the music to Chmelnitsky's comedy *A Novel Prank, or Theatrical Combat* (1822). In addition, he wrote a curious quadruple concerto, *Symphonie concertante*, for 4 Violins with Orch. (1838), 10 violin concertos, 6 string quartets, and other chamber music. His 2 sons Vsevolod (1819–92), a violinist, and Alexis, a cellist, remained in Russia.—NS/LK/DM

Mauricio, Jose, Portuguese organist, music theorist, and composer; b. Coimbra, March 19, 1752; d. Figueira da Foz, Sept. 12, 1815. He studied theology at Coimbra Univ.; was mestre de capela at Guarda Cathedral from about 1784 to 1786; then served as organist at the Santa Cruz monastery in Coimbra. In 1791 he became director of the music school in the bishop's palace and mestre de capela of Coimbra Cathedral; in 1802 he was appointed prof. of music at Coimbra Univ. He wrote a great deal of church music and some instrumental works revealing the influence of Haydn. He also publ. a Metodo de musica (Coimbra, 1806). —NS/LK/DM

Mauro, Ermanno, Italian-born Canadian tenor; b. Trieste, Jan. 20, 1939. He emigrated to Canada in 1958 and became a naturalized Canadian citizen in 1963; after vocal training with Jean Létourneau in Edmonton, he entered the Royal Cons. Opera School in Toronto in 1964 and studied with George Lambert, Herman Geiger-Torel, and Ernesto Barbini. In 1962 he made his operatic debut as Manrico in Edmonton; after appearances in opera productions at the Royal Cons. in Toronto and with the Canadian Opera Co., he sang at London's Covent Garden (1967–72). On Feb. 3, 1975, Mauro made his debut at the N.Y.C. Opera, remaining with the company until 1979; on Jan. 6, 1978, he made his Metropolitan Opera debut in N.Y. as Canio, and returned there as Cavaradossi in 1986 and as Turiddu in 1989. After singing Manrico in Brussels in 1984, he appeared as Otello in Dallas in 1985 and as Calaf at the Deutsche Oper in Berlin in 1987. In 1990 he portrayed Manrico in Zürich, and in 1992 Turiddu at the Teatro Colón in Buenos Aires. He sang Loris in *Fedora* in Montreal in 1995. Among his other roles are Ernani, Des Grieux, Alfredo, Faust, Pinkerton, and Rodolfo. —NS/LK/DM

Maury, Lowndes, American composer; b. Butte, Mont., July 7, 1911; d. Encino, Calif., Dec. 11, 1975. He earned his B.A. degree in music at the Univ. of Mont. in 1931, then went to Los Angeles, where he studied composition with Wesley La Violette and Schoenberg. He became active in Hollywood as a pianist, arranger, and teacher. He publ. *Magic Lines and Spaces*, a series of piano instruction books in correlated notation, a system employing a 3-line staff (1974).

WORKS: *In Memory of the Korean War Dead* for Violin and Piano (1952); *Proud Music of the Storm*, cantata after Walt Whitman (1953); *Passacaglia* for String Orch. (1959); *Springtime*

Digressions for Piano, Flute, and String Quintet (1961); *Speculations* for Piano and 3 String Instruments (1964); *Summer of Green*, rhapsody for Alto Flute and String Orch. (1964); *Scène de ballet* for Piccolo and String Quartet (1965); 11 *Sketches* for Piano Trio (1968); *The Imprisoned Cellist*, suite for Cello (1973). —NS/LK/DM

Maw, (John) Nicholas, distinguished English composer and teacher; b. Grantham, Lincolnshire, Nov. 5, 1935. After studies with Berkeley (composition) and Steinitz (theory) at the Royal Academy of Music in London (1955–58), he held a French government scholarship for further training in Paris with Deutsch and Boulanger (1958–59). In 1959 he was awarded the Lili Boulanger Prize. He taught at the Royal Academy of Music (1964–66), and then was fellow commoner (composer-in-residence) at Trinity Coll., Cambridge (1966–70). He was a lecturer in music at the Univ. of Exeter, Devon (1972–74), and also served as composer-in-residence of the South Bank Summer Music series in London (1973). In 1984–85 and 1989 he was a visiting prof. of music at the Yale School of Music. From 1989 he was a prof. of music at the Milton Avery Graduate School of the Arts at Bard Coll. in Annandale-on-Hudson, N.Y. In his music, Maw pursued a personal compositional path that utilized neo-Classical and late Romantic elements before finding fulfillment in a style notable for its expansive lyrical qualities.

WORKS: DRAMATIC: *One-Man Show*, opera (London, Nov. 12, 1964; rev. 1966 and 1970); *The Rising of the Moon*, opera (1967–70; Glyndebourne, July 19, 1970); incidental music; film scores. **ORCH.:** *Sinfonia* for Small Orch. (Newcastle upon Tyne, May 30, 1966); *Severn Bridge Variations* (1967; in collaboration with M. Arnold, M. Tippett, A. Hoddinott, G. Williams, and D. Jones); Sonata for 2 Horn and Strings (Bath, June 7, 1967); *Concert Music* (London, Oct. 19, 1972; based on the opera *The Rising of the Moon*, 1967–70); *Odyssey* (1972–87; 1st complete perf., London, April 8, 1989); *Life Studies I-VIII* for 15 Solo Strings (Cheltenham, July 9, 1973; also nos. *II, III*, and *VI-VIII* for String Orch.); *Serenade* (Singapore, March 31, 1973; rev. 1977); *Summer Dances* for Youth Orch. (1980; Aldeburgh, July 27, 1981); *Toccata* (1982); *Morning Music* (1982); *Spring Music* (1982–83); *Sonata notturna* for Cello and Strings (1985; King's Lynn, May 30, 1986); *Little Concert* for Oboe, 2 Horns, and Strings (Wymondham, May 28, 1988); *The World in the Evening* (London, Oct. 21, 1988); *American Games* for Wind Band (1990–91; London, July 23, 1991); *Shahnama* (1992); Violin Concerto (N.Y., Sept. 29, 1993). **CHAMBER:** Flute Sonatina (1957); *Chamber Music* for Oboe, Clarinet, Horn, Bassoon, and Piano (1962); 2 string quartets: No. 1 (Harlow, July 12, 1965) and No. 2 (1982; London, Jan. 13, 1983); *Epitaph-Canon in Memory of Igor Stravinsky* for Flute, Clarinet, and Harp (1971); Flute Quartet (London, May 7, 1981); *Night Thoughts* for Flute (London, June 10, 1982); *Ghost Dances* for 5 Players (N.Y., May 16, 1988); *Music of Memory* for Guitar (1989). **P i a n o :** *Personae I* (1973) and *IV-VI* (1985–86). **VOCAL:** *Nocturne* for Mezzo-soprano and Chamber Orch. (1957–58); *5 Epigrams* for Chorus (1960); *Our Lady's Song* for Chorus (1961); *Scenes and Arias* for Soprano, Mezzo-soprano, Contralto, and Orch. (1961–62; London, Aug. 31, 1962; rev. 1966); *The Angel Gabriel* for Chorus (1963); *Round* for Children's Chorus, Mixed Chorus, and Piano (1963); *Corpus Christi Carol* for Chorus (1964); *Balulalow* for Chorus (1964); *6 Interiors* for High Voice and Guitar (1966; London, May 5, 1970); *The Voice of Love* for Mezzo-soprano and Piano (London, Oct. 6,

1966); *5 Irish Songs* for Chorus (1972; Cork, May 4, 1973); *Te Deum* for Treble or Soprano, Tenor, Chorus, Congregation, and Orch. (Bruton, May 29, 1975); *Reverdie* for Men's Chorus (Glasgow, Oct. 29, 1975); *20 Nonsense Rhymes* for Children's Voices and Piano (Darsham, Sept. 4, 1976); *La Vita Nuova* for Soprano and Chamber Ensemble (London, Sept. 2, 1979); *The Ruin* for Double Chorus and Horn Obbligato (Edinburgh, Aug. 27, 1980); *5 American Folksongs* for High Voice and Piano (1988); *3 Hymns* for Chorus and Organ (1989); *Roman Canticle* for Mezzo-soprano, Flute, Viola, and Harp (1989); *One Foot in Eden, Here I Stand* for Soprano, Alto, Tenor, Bass, and Chorus (1990); *The Head of Orpheus* for Soprano and 2 Clarinets (1992). —NS/LK/DM

Maxakova, Mariya (Petrovna), Russian mezzo-soprano; b. Astrakhan, April 8, 1902; d. Moscow, Aug. 11, 1974. She was a student of Maximilian Maxakov, whom she married. After singing in Astrakhan, she appeared at Moscow's Bolshoi Theater in 1923. From 1925 to 1927 she sang at the Leningrad Academy Opera. In 1927 she became a member of the Bolshoi Theater, where she sang until 1953. She also appeared as a concert artist. In addition to her distinguished Russian roles, she won particular notice for her Ortrud, Dalila, and Carmen.

BIBL.: M. Lvov, *M.P. M.* (Moscow and Leningrad, 1947). —NS/LK/DM

Maxfield, Richard (Vance), American composer; b. Seattle, Wash., Feb. 2, 1927; d. (suicide) Los Angeles, June 27, 1969. He studied at the Univ. of Calif., Berkeley, with Sessions, and at Princeton Univ. with Babbitt (M.F.A., 1955); also took courses with Krenek. He held a Fulbright fellowship (1955–57), which enabled him to continue his training with Dallapiccola in Florence and Maderna in Milan. He became deeply engaged in acoustical electronics. He taught experimental music at the New School for Social Research in N.Y. (1959–62) and then at San Francisco State Coll. He contributed essays to avant-garde publications; 2 of them, in free verse, were publ. in *Contemporary Composers on Contemporary Music*, ed. by E. Schwartz and B. Childs (N.Y., 1967). He acquired an excellent technique of composition in the traditional idiom before adopting an extreme avant-garde style. He took his own life by self-defenestration from a hotel room.

WORKS: *Classical Overture* (1942); Trio for Clarinet, Cello, and Piano (1943); Septet for 2 Flutes, 3 Clarinets, Horn, and Bassoon (1947); Sonata for Solo Violin (1949); Violin Sonata (1950); String Trio (1951); Sonata for Solo Flute (1951); *Structures* for 10 Wind Instruments (1951); *11 Variations* for String Quartet (1952); *5 Movements* for Orch. (1956); Chamber Concerto for 7 Instruments (1957); *Structures* for Orch. (1958); *Sine Music* (1959); *Stacked Deck*, opera for Tape, Actors, and Lighting (1959); *Perspectives* for Violin and Tape (1960); *Peripeteia* for Violin, Saxophone, Piano, and Tape (1960); *Clarinet Music* for 5 Clarinets and Tape (1961); *Cough Music*, with sonic materials obtained from coughs and other bronchial sound effects recorded during a modern dance recital and electronically arranged in a piece of tussive polyphony (N.Y., Jan. 13, 1961); *Toy Symphony* for Flute, Violin, Wooden Boxes, Ceramic Vase, and Tape (1962); *African Symphony* (1964); *Venus Impulses* for Electronic Sound (1967).—NS/LK/DM

Maxwell, Donald, Scottish baritone; b. Perth, Dec. 12, 1948. He studied at the Univ. of Edinburgh. In 1977 he made his operatic debut as Morton in Musgrave's *Mary, Queen of Scots* with the Scottish Opera in Glasgow, where he subsequently sang many roles. In 1982 he made his first appearance with the Welsh National Opera in Cardiff as Anckarström, and later toured with the company as Falstaff to Paris, Tokyo, and Milan. He made his debut at London's Covent Garden in the British premiere of Sallinen's *The King Goes Forth to France* in 1987, returning there in 1990 as Gunther. He portrayed Wozzeck at the English National Opera in London in 1990 and at Opera North in Leeds in 1993. In 1996 he appeared in *Lulu* at the Glyndebourne Festival. His other roles include Rossini's Figaro, Pizzaro, Don Carlo, Iago, Rigoletto, Golaud, and Scarpia.—NS/LK/DM

Maxwell Davies, Sir Peter
See **Davies, Sir Peter Maxwell**

May, Edward Collett, English organist and singing teacher, father of **Florence May**; b. Greenwich, Oct. 29, 1806; d. London, Jan. 2, 1887. He studied with C. Potter and Crivelli. He was organist of Greenwich Hospital (1837–69) and prof. of vocal music at Queen's Coll., London (1879–83). He did much to popularize singing among the masses. He publ. *Progressive Vocal Exercises for Daily Practice* (1853) and also composed songs.—NS/LK/DM

May, Florence, English pianist and writer on music, daughter of **Edward Collett May**; b. London, Feb. 6, 1845; d. there, June 29, 1923. She studied music with her father and with an uncle, Oliver May; began a promising career as a pianist in London. In 1871 she took lessons with Clara Schumann in Baden-Baden, where she made the acquaintance of Brahms, who gave her some lessons. She became his enthusiastic admirer, and upon her return to England started a vigorous campaign for performances of his music, giving many first performances of his works in London. The important result of her dedication to Brahms was her comprehensive work *The Life of Johannes Brahms* (2 vols., London, 1905; 2nd ed., 1948). She also publ. The Girlhood of Clara Schumann (London, 1912).—NS/LK/DM

Mayall, John, the "grandfather" of British blues; b. Macclesfield, Cheshire, England, Nov. 29, 1933. John Mayall became fascinated with the blues at the age of 13 and eventually learned to play guitar, keyboards, and harmonica. Forming his first group, the Powerhouse Four, while in college during the mid-1950s, he assembled the Blues Syndicate in March 1962. At the urging of Alexis Korner, he moved to London in 1963, turning professional that February and forming the Bluesbreakers with bassist John McVie. By the time of Mayall's first British-only album, the band comprised Mayall, McVie, guitarist Roger Dean, and drummer Hughie Flint. During the spring of 1965, former Yardbird Eric Clapton replaced Dean, and McVie and Jack Bruce shared bass chores through June 1966. This aggregation recorded the classic *Bluesbreakers* album, one of the most compelling blues albums ever made in Great Britain.

When Jack Bruce and Eric Clapton departed to form Cream and Hughie Flint left, Mayall recruited guitarist Peter Green and drummer Aynsley Dunbar for *A Hard Road*. By the spring of 1967, Peter Green had left the Bluesbreakers to form Fleetwood Mac with on-again, off-again Mayall drummer Mick Fleetwood. Mayall subsequently recorded *Crusade* with John McVie, guitarist Mick Taylor, drummer Keef Hartley, and two saxophonists. He recorded *The Blues Alone* as a solo album, accompanied by only Hartley. By September 1967, McVie had left to join Fleetwood Mac, and Mayall reconstituted the Bluebreakers with Taylor, Hartley, saxophonists Chris Mercer and Dick Heckstall-Smith, bassist Tony Reeves, and drummer Jon Hiseman for *Bare Wires*, consisting entirely of Mayall compositions. The album was the last album to be issued under the Bluesbreakers moniker for 18 years.

John Mayall next moved to Los Angeles, where he recorded *Blues from Laurel Canyon* with Mick Taylor. In 1969, Taylor dropped out to join the Rolling Stones. Mayall subsequently abandoned the loud electric format in favor of a revolutionary, acoustic, drummer-less aggregation with string bassist Steve Thompson, guitarist Jon Mark, and tenor saxophonist-flutist Johnny Almond. This grouping recorded the live *Turning Point* album, the best-selling album of Mayall's career, for his new label, Polydor. It featured the favorite "Room to Move" and the nine-minute "California." The group's sole studio album, *Empty Rooms*, yielded Mayall's only (minor) hit, "Don't Waste My Time."

In 1970, John Mayall made yet another stylistic shift, employing American musicians Don "Sugarcane" Harris (violin), Harvey Mandel (guitar), and Larry Taylor (bass) for the jazz-oriented *U.S.A. Union*. *Back to the Roots*, recorded with various alumni, including Clapton, Green, Taylor, Dunbar, Hartley, and Hiseman, was later remixed and rerecorded and released as *Archives to Eighties*. Mayall continued to record for Polydor through 1974, subsequently switching to ABC, then DJM Records. He conducted a brief Bluesbreakers reunion tour of America and Australia with John McVie and Mick Taylor in 1982. By 1985, he had revived the Bluesbreakers name for *Behind the Iron Curtain* for GNP Crescendo and subsequent recordings for Island. In the 1990s, John Mayall recorded for the Silvertone label.

DISC.: JOHN MAYALL *The Blues Alone* (1968); *Blues from Laurel Canyon* (1969); *The Turning Point* (1969); *Empty Rooms* (1970); *U.S.A. Union* (1970); *Back to the Roots* (1971); *Memories* (1971); *Jazz Blues Fusion* (1972); *Moving On* (1972); *Ten Years Are Gone* (1973); *The Latest Edition* (1974); *New Year, New Band, New Company* (1975); *Notice to Appear* (1976); *A Banquet of Blues* (1976); *Lots of People* (1977); *A Hard Core Package* (1977); *The Last of the British Blues* (1978); *Bottom Line* (1979); *No More Interviews* (1979); *Roadshow Blues Band* (1982); *John Mayall Plays John Mayall* (1988); *Room to Move* (1969–74) (1992); *Wake Up Call* (1993); *Spinning Coin* (1995); *Blues for the Lost Days* (1997). **JOHN MAYALL AND ERIC CLAPTON:** *Bluesbreakers* (1967). **JOHN MAYALL'S BLUESBREAKERS:** *A Hard Road* (1967); *Crusade* (1968); *Bare Wires* (1968); *Looking Back* (1969); *Primal Solos* (rec. 1966, 1968; rel. 1977); *London Blues* (rec. 1964–69; rel. 1992); *Diary of a Band* (1970); *Live in Europe* (1971); *Through the Years* (1971); *Behind the Iron Curtain* (1986); *Chicago Line* (1988); *A Sense of Place* (1990); *The 1982 Reunion Concert* (1994); *Cross Country Blues* (1994). **JOHN MAYALL AND OTHERS:** *Raw Blues* (1968).

Maybrick, Michael (pseudonym, **Stephen Adams**), English baritone and composer; b. Liverpool, Jan. 31, 1844; d. Buxton, Aug. 25, 1913. He studied at the Leipzig Cons. with Plaidy, Moscheles, and E. Richter (1866–68), and was a vocal pupil of Nava in Milan. He sang at the principal concerts in London and the provinces, and toured the U.S. and Canada in 1884. Many of his songs (sung by himself) had great vogue (e.g., *Nancy Lee*). His sacred solo *The Holy City* was sung in churches in England and America.—**NS/LK/DM**

Mayer, (Benjamin) Wilhelm, Austrian pianist, pedagogue, and composer who used the pseudonym W.A. Remy; b. Prague, June 10, 1831; d. Graz, Jan. 22, 1898. He studied with C. Pietsch, and also took a degree in law (1856). In 1862 he became conductor of the Graz Musical Soc. resigning in 1870 to apply himself to pedagogy. He taught both piano and composition, and achieved great renown, numbering among his pupils Busoni, Reznicek, and Weingartner. He wrote a concert opera, *Das Waldfraulein* (Graz, 1876), a number of syms. and other orch. works, and numerous songs. —**NS/LK/DM**

Mayer, Charles, German pianist, teacher, and composer; b. Königsberg, March 21, 1799; d. Dresden, July 2, 1862. He was taken to Russia as a child, and was taught by John Field in Moscow. He lived in Moscow until Napoleon's invasion in 1812, then went to St. Petersburg, and in 1814 to Paris. He returned to Russia in 1819 and formed a large class of pupils in St. Petersburg. In 1845 he made a tour of Scandinavia and Germany, settling in Dresden in 1850. He publ. an enormous number of piano pieces in salon style. One of his mazurkas was once misattributed to Chopin. —**NS/LK/DM**

Mayer, Sir Robert, industrious German-born English music patron; b. Mannheim, June 5, 1879; d. London, Jan. 9, 1985. His love for music was established early when he entered the Mannheim Cons. as a piano student; there he also met Brahms. His father sent him at age 17 to relatives in England to establish himself, since business opportunities were limited for Jews in Germany. So totally immersed did he become in English life that his family asserted he even spoke his native German with a British accent. He was an entrepreneur in the grand manner of the Victorian age. He never wrote music, but he promoted the art with youthful enthusiasm. In 1923, inspired by Walter Damrosch's concerts for children in N.Y., Mayer and his wife, the singer Dorothy Moulton-Mayer, began a series of children's concerts, whose first regular conductor was Adrian Boult. The tremendous success of making serious classical music available to young children everywhere in England, from slums to suburbs, encouraged a new enterprise in 1954, Youth and Music, which was specifically offered to adolescents, with the view to creating lifetime participants in musical culture. Mayer's business acumen launched this program successfully as well. In 1939 he was knighted, and in 1973 made a Companion of Honour. His centennial was gloriously celebrated, with himself as the center of festivities, at the Royal Festival Hall in London, and he was elevated to Knight Commander of the Royal Victorian Order. His autobiography was publ. as *My First Hundred Years* (London, 1979). He had the wit to proclaim that music exercised a curative power over the human body and mind, and he adjusted his entire life accordingly. —**NS/LK/DM**

Mayer, William (Robert), American composer; b. N.Y., Nov. 18, 1925. He was a student of Richard Donovan and Herbert Baumgartner at Yale Univ. (B.A., 1949), of Sessions at the Juilliard School of Music in N.Y. (summer, 1949), of Salzer at the Mannes Coll. of Music in N.Y. (1949–52), and of Izler Solomon (conducting) at the Aspen (Colo.) Music School (summer, 1960). In 1966 he held a Guggenheim fellowship. In 1980 he was secretary of the National Music Council. He received the National Inst. for Musical Theater Award in 1983.

WORKS: D R A M A T I C : *The Greatest Sound Around*, children's opera (1954); *Hello World!*, children's opera (N.Y., Nov. 10, 1956); *The Snow Queen*, ballet (1963); *One Christmas Long Ago*, opera (Philadelphia, Dec. 12, 1964); *Brief Candle*, "micro-opera" (1964); *A Death in the Family*, opera (Minneapolis, March 11, 1983); *A Sobbing Pillow of Man* (N.Y., Dec. 7, 1995). O R C H .: *Andante* for Strings (1955); *Hebraic Portrait* (1957); *Overture for an American* (1958); *2 Pastels* (1960); *Octago* for Piano and Orch. (N.Y., March 21, 1971); *Inner and Outer Strings* for String Quartet and Orch. (1982); *Of Rivers and Trains* (Albany, N.Y., Nov. 4, 1988). O T H E R : Chamber music; children's piano pieces; choruses; songs.—**NS/LK/DM**

Mayer-Serra, Otto, eminent Spanish musicologist; b. Barcelona (of German-Catalan parents), July 12, 1904; d. Mexico City, March 19, 1968. He studied in Germany with H. Abert, Curt Sachs, J. Wolf, and E. von Hornbostel; received his Ph.D. in 1929 with the diss. *Die romantische Klaviersonaten* from the Univ. of Greifswald. He returned to Spain in 1933, and was music critic of the Catalan weekly *Mirador*. In 1936, at the outbreak of the Spanish Civil War, he was appointed head of the music division of the propaganda ministry of the Catalan government; served in the Loyalist army in 1938–39; after its defeat, he fled to France. In 1940 he reached Mexico, where he became active as a writer, editor, lecturer, and manager.

WRITINGS (all publ. in Mexico City): *El romanticismo musical* (1940); *Panorama de la musica mexicana desde la independencia hasta la actualidad* (1941); *Música y músicios de Latino- América* (2 vols., 1947); *Breve diccionaria de la música* (1948); *La música contemporánea* (1954).—**NS/LK/DM**

Maynard, John, English lutenist, bass, and composer; b. St. Albans, Hertfordshire (baptized), Jan. 5, 1577; d. after 1614. He received lute training at St. Julians school in Hertfordshire. In 1588 he entered the service of King Christian IV of Denmark in Copenhagen as a bass singer, but in 1601 he absconded. He publ. the satirical collection *The XII Wonders of the World* (London, 1611), which includes 12 songs with Lute and Bass Viol, 6 dances for Lute and Basso Continuo, and 7 pavans for Lyra Viol and Bass Viol ad libitum.—**LK/DM**

Maynor, Dorothy (Leigh), noted black American soprano and music educator; b. Norfolk, Va., Sept. 3, 1910; d. West Chester, Pa., Feb. 19, 1996. She was educated at the Hampton Inst. (B.S., 1933). She began her career singing in various choirs, and later toured with the inst.'s famous chorus in Europe; subsequently studied at Westminster Choir Coll. and with William Kamroth and John Alan Haughton in N.Y. After a successful appearance at the Berkshire Music Festival at Tanglewood in 1939, she made her Town Hall debut in N.Y. on Nov. 19, 1939. In subsequent years, she toured widely in the U.S. and Europe as a concert singer, appearing with leading orchs. She founded the Harlem School of the Arts in 1963 to provide music education for underprivileged children, and served as its executive director until her retirement in 1979.

BIBL.: W. Rogers, *D. M. and the Harlem School of the Arts: The Diva and the Dream* (Lewiston, N.Y., 1993).—**NS/LK/DM**

Mayone, Ascanio, Italian organist, harpist, and composer; b. Naples, c. 1565; d. there, March 9, 1627. He spent his entire career in his native city. After training from Giovanni Domenico da Nola, he became organist of the church of the Ss. Annunziata in 1593, where, from 1595, he served as joint maestro di cappella. In 1602 he also became 2nd organist of the royal chapel of the Spanish viceroys, becoming 1st organist in 1614. Mayone was a significant composer of keyboard music. In his 2 vols. of *capricci per sonare* (Naples, 1603, 1609), his canzonas and toccatas point the way toward a more advanced style. He also publ. a vol. of madrigals (Naples, 1604).

BIBL.: R. Kelton, *The Instrumental Music of A. M.* (diss., North Tex. State Univ., 1961).—**NS/LK/DM**

Mayr, (Johannes) Simon (actually, **Giovanni Simone**), outstanding German composer; b. Mendorf, Bavaria (of Italian parents), June 14, 1763; d. Bergamo, Dec. 2, 1845. He first studied music with his father, a schoolteacher and organist, and he sang in a church choir and played organ. In 1774 he entered the Jesuit college in Ingolstadt, and in 1781 he began a study of theology at the Univ. of Ingolstadt. In 1787 a Swiss Freiherr, Thomas von Bassus, took him to Italy to further his musical education; in 1789 he commenced studies with Carlo Lenzi in Bergamo; he then was sent to Ferdinando Bertoni in Venice. He began his career as a composer of sacred music; his oratorios were performed in Venice. After the death of his patron, Count Presenti, in 1793, he was encouraged by Piccinni and Peter von Winter to compose operas. His first opera, *Saffo o sia I riti d'Apollo Leucadio*, was performed in Venice in 1794. He gained renown with his opera *Ginevra di Scozia* (Trieste, April 21, 1801), and it remained a favorite with audiences; also successful were his operas *La rosa bianca e la rosa rossa* (Genoa, Feb. 21, 1813) and *Medea in Corinto* (Naples, Nov. 28, 1813). In 1802 he became maestro di cappella at S. Maria Maggiore in Bergamo, and in 1805 he reorganized the choir school of the Cathedral as the Lezioni Caritatevoli di Musica and assumed its directorship; intractable cataracts, which led to total blindness in 1826, forced him to limit his activities to organ playing. In 1822 he founded the Societa Filarmonica of Bergamo. Mayr's operas, while reflecting the late Neapolitan school, are noteworthy for their harmonization and orchestration, which are derived from the German tradition. After 1815 he devoted most of his time to composing sacred music, which totals some 600 works in all. He was also an eminent pedagogue. Donizetti was his pupil.

WORKS: DRAMATIC: O p e r a : *Saffo o sia I riti d'Apollo Leucadio,* dramma per musica (Venice, Feb. 17, 1794); *La Lodoiska,* dramma per musica (Venice, Jan. 26, 1796; rev. for Milan, Dec. 26, 1799); *Un pazzo ne fa cento [I Rivali delusi; La Contessa immaginaria],* dramma giocoso (Venice, Oct. 8, 1796); *Telemaco nell'isola di Calipso,* dramma per musica (Venice, Jan. 16, 1797); *Il segreto,* farsa (Venice, Sept. 24, 1797); *L'intrigo della lettera [Il pittore astratto],* farsa (Venice, fall 1797); *Avviso ai maritati,* dramma giocoso (Venice, Jan. 15, 1798); *Lauso e Lidia,* dramma per musica (Venice, Feb. 14, 1798); *Adriano in Siria,* dramma per musica (Venice, April 23, 1798); *Che originali [Il trionfo della musica; Il fanatico per la musica: La musicomania],* farsa (Venice, Oct. 18, 1798); *Amor ingegnoso,* farsa (Venice, Dec. 27, 1798); *L'ubbidienza per astuzia,* farsa (Venice, Dec. 27, 1798); *Adelaide di Gueselino,* dramma per musica (Venice, May 1, 1799); *Labino e Carlotta,* farsa (Venice, Oct. 9, 1799); *L'Avaro,* farsa (Venice, Nov. 1799); *L'accademia di musica,* farsa (Venice, fall 1799); *Gli sciti,* dramma per musica (Venice, Feb. 1800); *La Locandiera,* farsa (Vicenza, spring 1800); *Il caretto del venditore d'aceto,* farsa (Venice, June 28, 1800); *L'Imbroglione e il castigamatti,* farsa (Venice, fall 1800); *L'equivoco, ovvero Le bizzarie dell'amore,* dramma giocoso (Milan, Nov. 5, 1800); *Ginevra di Scozia [Ariodante],* dramma serio eroico per musica (Trieste, April 21, 1801; inaugural perf. at the Teatro Nuovo there); *Le due giornate [Il Portatore d'acqua],* dramma eroicomico per musica (Milan, Aug. 18, 1801); *I Virtuosi [I Virtuosi a teatro],* farsa (Venice, Dec. 26, 1801); *Argene,* dramma eroico per musica (Venice, Dec. 28, 1801); *Elisa, ossia Il monte S. Bernardo,* dramma sentimentale per musica (Malta, 1801); *I misteri eleusini,* dramma per musica (Milan, Jan. 6, 1802); *I castelli in aria, ossia Gli Amanti per accidente,* farsa (Venice, May 1802); *Ercole in Lidia,* dramma per musica (Vienna, Jan. 29, 1803); *Gl'intrighi amorosi,* dramma giocoso (Parma, Carnival 1803); *Le finte rivali,* melodramma giocoso (Aug. 20, 1803); *Alonso e Cora,* dramma per musica (Milan, Dec. 26, 1803; rev. as *Cora* for Naples, 1815); *Amor non ha ritegno [La fedeltà delle vedove],* melodramma eroicomico (Milan, May 18, 1804); *I due viaggiatori,* dramma giocoso (Florence, summer 1804); *Zamori, ossia L'Eroe dell'Indie,* dramma per musica (Piacenza, Aug. 10, 1804; inaugural perf. at the Nuovo Teatro Communale); *Eraldo ed Emma,* dramma eroico per musica (Milan, Jan. 8, 1805); *Di locanda in locanda e sempre in sala,* farsa (June 5, 1805); *L'amor coniugale [Il custode di buon cuore],* dramma giocoso (Padua, July 26, 1805); *La rocca di Frauenstein,* melodramma eroicomico (Venice, Oct. 26, 1805); *Gli Americani [Idalide],* melodramma eroico (Venice, Carnival 1806); *Palmira, o sia Il trionfo della virtù e dell'amore,* dramma per musica (Florence, fall 1806); *Il piccolo compositore di musica,* farsa (Venice, 1806); *Nè l'un, nè l'altro,* dramma giocoso (Milan, Aug. 17, 1807); *Belle ciarle e tristi fatti [L'imbroglio contro l'imbroglio],* dramma

giocoso (Venice, Nov. 1807); *Adelasia e Aleramo,* melodramma serio (Milan, Dec. 25, 1807); *I cherusci,* dramma per musica (Rome, Carnival 1808); *Il vero originale,* burletta per musica (Rome, Carnival 1808); *La finta sposa, ossia Il Barone burlato,* dramma giocoso (Rome, spring 1808); *Il matrimonio per concorso,* dramma giocoso (Bologna, Carnival 1809); *Il ritorno di Ulisse,* azione eroica per musica (Venice, Carnival 1809); *Amor non soffre opposizione,* dramma giocoso (Venice, Carnival 1810); *Raùl di Créqui,* melodramma serio (Milan, Dec. 26, 1810); *Il sacrifizio d'Ifigenia [Ifigenia in Aulide],* azione seria drammatica per musica (Brescia, Carnival 1811); *L'amor figliale [Il Disertore],* farsa sentimentale (Venice, Carnival 1811); *La rosa bianca e la rosa rossa [Il trionfo dell'amicizia],* melodramma eroica (Genoa, Feb. 21, 1813); *Medea in Corinto,* melodramma tragico (Naples, Nov. 28, 1813); *Tamerlano,* melodramma serio (Milan, Carnival 1813); *Elena [Elena e Costantino],* dramma eroicomico per musica (Naples, Carnival 1814); *Atar, o sia Il serraglio d'Ormus,* melodramma serio (Genoa, June 1814); *Le due duchesse, ossia La caccia dei lupi [Le due amiche],* dramma semiserio per musica (Milan, Nov. 7, 1814); *La Figlia dell'aria, ossia La vendetta di Giunone,* dramma per musica (Naples, Lent 1817); *Nennone e Zemira,* dramma per musica (Naples, March 22, 1817); *Amor avvocato,* commedia per musica (Naples, spring 1817); *Lanassa,* melodramma eroico (Venice, Carnival 1818); *Alfredo il grande,* melodramma serio (Rome, Feb. 1818); *Le Danaide [Danao],* melodramma serio (Rome, Carnival 1819); *Fedra,* melodramma serio (Milan, Dec. 26, 1820); *Demetrio,* dramma per musica (Turin, Carnival 1824). **O r a t o r i o s :** *Iacob a Labano fugiens* (Venice, 1791), *Sisara* (Venice, 1793), *Tobia, o Tobiae matrimonium* (Venice, 1794), *La Passione* (Forli, 1794), *David in spelunca Engaddi* (Venice, 1795), *Il sacrifizio di Iefte* (Forlì; year unknown), *Samuele* (Bergamo, 1821), and *S. Luigi Gonzaga* (Bergamo, 1822); also the sacred dramas *Ifigenia in Tauride* (Florence, spring 1817) and *Atalia* (Naples, Lent 1822). **OTHER:** About 50 cantatas, 18 masses, over 200 Mass movements, 2 Requiems, 20 Requiem movements, 43 hymns, 14 antiphons, 13 motets, etc. Secular vocal works include over 40 canzonettas, arias, songs, lieder, etc. Instrumental works include 2 syms., 2 piano concertos, chamber music, and keyboard pieces.

WRITINGS: *Breve notizie storiche della vita e delle opere di Giuseppe Haydn* (Bergamo, 1809); *Regolamento delle Lezioni Caritatevoli di musica* (Bergamo, 1822); many other writings remain in MS.

BIBL.: G. Calvi, *Musica sacra di S. M.* (Milan, 1848); G. Finazzi, *Per la solenne inaugurazione del monumento eretto alla memoria del celebre maestro G.S. M. nella basilica di S. Maria Maggiore in Bergamo* (Bergamo, 1853); F. Alborghetti and M. Galli, *Gaetano Donizetti e G.S. M.: Notizie e documenti* (Bergamo, 1875); C. Schmidl, *Cenni biografici su G.S. M.* (Trieste, 1901); C. Scotti, *G.S. M.: Discorso* (Bergamo, 1903); L. Schiedermair, *Beiträge zur Geschichte der Oper um die Wende des 18. und 19. Jahrhunderts: S. M.* (2 vols., Leipzig, 1907, 1910); A. Gazzaniga, *Il Fondo musicale M. della biblioteca civica di Bergamo* (Bergamo, 1963); G. Salvetti, ed., *Aspetti dell'opera italiana fra Sette e Ottocento: M. e Zingarelli* (Lucca, 1993); J. Allit, *J.S. M.* (Shaftesbury, 1989; rev. Italian ed., 1995).—**NS/LK/DM**

Mayr, Richard, renowned Austrian bass-baritone; b. Henndorf, near Salzburg, Nov. 18, 1877; d. Vienna, Dec. 1, 1935. He studied medicine in Vienna before being persuaded by Mahler to take up music. After training at the Vienna Cons., he made his operatic debut as Hagen at the Bayreuth Festival (1902). He then was engaged by Mahler for the Vienna Opera, where he made his first appearance as Don Gomez in *Ernani* that same year. He remained on the company's roster until his death, and was also a principal singer at the Salzburg Festivals (1921–34). He made his first appearance at London's Covent Garden as Baron Ochs, his most celebrated role, on May 23, 1924, and continued to appear there until 1931. He made his Metropolitan Opera debut in N.Y. as Pogner on Nov. 2, 1927, remaining on the company's roster until 1930. Mayr possessed a rich and powerful voice, equally suited for serious and buffo roles. In addition to his remarkable portrayal of Baron Ochs, he also excelled as Figaro, Leporello, Sarastro, Wotan, Gurnemanz, and Rocco. He was chosen by Strauss to create the role of Barak in his *Die Frau ohne Schatten* (Vienna, Oct. 10, 1919).

BIBL.: H. Holz, *R. M.* (Vienna, 1923); O. Kunz, *R. M.* (Vienna, 1933).—**NS/LK/DM**

Mayseder, Joseph, distinguished Austrian violinist, pedagogue, and composer; b. Vienna, Oct. 26, 1789; d. there, Nov. 21, 1863. He was a pupil of Suche and Wranitzky (violin) and of E. Förster (piano and composition). He joined the famous Schuppanzigh Quartet as 2nd violin, and became concertmaster of the Court Theater orch. in 1810. He entered the Court Orch. in 1816, and became solo violinist at the Court Opera in 1820 and chamber violinist to the Emperor in 1835. He was music director of the court chapel in 1836–37. He never went on tours and rarely gave concerts, yet he was a finished virtuoso, admired even by Paganini. In Vienna he was very successful as a teacher. His works include 3 violin concertos, a Mass (1848), 5 string quintets, 8 string quartets, trios, and solo violin pieces.

BIBL.: E. Hellsberg, *J. M.* (diss., Univ. of Vienna, 1955). —**NS/LK/DM**

Mayuzumi, Toshirō, eminent Japanese composer; b. Yokohama, Feb. 20, 1929; d. Kawasaki, April 10, 1997. He was a student of Ikenouchi and Ifukube at the Tokyo National Univ. of Fine Arts and Music (1945–51) and of Aubin at the Paris Cons. (1951–52). With Akutagawa and Dan, he organized the contemporary music group Ars Nova Japnica, Sannin no Kai (Group of 3). In 1959 and 1962 he won the Otaka Prize, and in 1964 the Mainichi Music Prize. His style of composition embodied sonorous elements from Japanese and other Asian traditions, modified serial techniques, and electronic sounds, all amalgamated in a remarkably effective manner.

WORKS: DRAMATIC: *Bugaku*, ballet (1962; N.Y., March 20, 1963); *The Bible*, film score (1965); *Kinkakuji* (The Temple of the Golden Pavilion), opera (Berlin, June 23, 1976); *The Kabuki*, ballet (1985); incidental music; dance dramas. **ORCH.:** *Serenade Fantastic* (1946); *Rumba Rhapsody* (1948); *Symphonic Mood* (1950); *Bacchanale* (1953); *Ectoplasme* for Electronic Instruments, Percussion, and Strings (1954; Stockholm, June 5, 1956); *Phonologie symphonique* (Tokyo, May 28, 1957); *Nirvana Symphony* (Tokyo, April 2, 1958); *Manadala Symphony* (Tokyo, March 27, 1960); *Music with Sculpture* for Wind Orch. (Pittsburgh, June 29, 1961); *Samsara*, symphonic poem (Tokyo, June 12, 1962); *Textures* for Band (Pittsburgh, June 10, 1962); *Essay in Sonorities: Mozartiana* (1962; Osaka, Jan 21, 1963); *Essay* for Strings (1963);

Fireworks for Band (Pittsburgh, June 13, 1963); *Ritual Overture* for Band (Pittsburgh, July 2, 1964); *The Birth of Music*, symphonic poem (Tokyo, Oct. 10, 1964); Xylophone Concertino (1965); Concerto for Percussion and Winds (1966); *Incantation* (1967); *Ancient and Modern Music*, symphonic poem (1969–70; Tokyo, Oct. 31, 1970); *Tateyama*, symphonic poem (1974); *Aria in G* for Violin and Orch. (1978); *Capriccio* for Violin and Strings (1988); *Perpetuum mobile* (1989); *Rhapsody for the 21st Century* for Orch., Electric Piano, and Synthesizer (1991). **CHAMBER:** Violin Sonata (1946); *Divertimento* for 10 Instruments (1948); *Poem* for Violin and Piano (1950); String Quartet (1952); Sextet for Flute, Clarinet, Bass Clarinet, Horn, Trumpet, and Piano (1955); *Tone Pleromas 55* for 5 Saxophones, Musical Saw, and Pianos (1955); *Mikrokosmos* for Claviolin, Guitar, Vibraphone, Xylophone, Piano, Percussion, and Musical Saw (Karuizawa, Aug. 12, 1957); *Pieces* for Prepared Piano and String Quartet (1957); *A hun* for Japanese Flute, Kotsuzumi, and Otsuzumi (1958); *Bunraku* for Cello (1960); *Metamusic* for Violin, Saxophone, Piano, and Conductor (1961); *Prelude* for String Quartet (1961); *Showa Tenpyo-raku* for Gagaku Ensemble (1970). **PIANO:** *12 Preludes* (1946); *Poesie* (1946); *Hors d'oeuvre* (1947). **VOCAL:** *Elegy* for Soprano and Piano (1948); *Sphenogramme* for Voice, Flute, Saxophone, Marimba, Piano 4–Hands, Violin, and Cello (1950; Frankfurt am Main, June 25, 1951); *Wedding Song* for Chorus and Orch. (1959); *U-So-Ri*, oratorio for Soloists, Chorus, and Orch. (Tokyo, June 12, 1959); *Sange* for Men's Voices (1959); *Pratidesana*, Buddhist cantata for Voices (Kyoto, Sept. 5, 1963); *Mori*, cantata for Voices (1963); *Mandala* for Voice and Tape (1969); *Hymn to Japan* for Narrator, Chorus, and Orch. (1972); *Hymn to Buddha* for Chorus and Orch. (1983); *The World Prayers* for Chorus, Orch., and Tape (1991); *Kyoto 1200: Tradition and Creation*, oratorio (1994).—**NS/LK/DM**

Mazas, Jacques-Féréol, French violinist, teacher, and composer; b. Lavaur, Tarn, Sept. 23, 1782; d. Bordeaux, Aug. 25, 1849. He was a pupil of Baillot at the Paris Cons., winning 1st prize as violinist (1805). He then played in the orch. of the Italian Opera in Paris, and toured Europe (1811–27). He was a teacher in Orléans (from 1831), and director of a music school in Cambrai (1837–41). He spent the last years of his life in Bordeaux. He wrote a method for violin (new ed. by J. Hřimalý) and numerous valuable studies; also a method for viola, concertos, string quartets, trios, violin duets, fantasias, variations, romances, etc. He composed 3 operas, one of which, *Le Kiosque*, was performed in Paris in 1842. A set of 6 études was publ. in a new ed. by Hubay.—**NS/LK/DM**

Mazura, Franz, Austrian bass-baritone; b. Salzburg, April 21, 1924. He studied in Detmold. He made his operatic debut in Kassel (1949), and later appeared at the opera houses of Mainz, Braunschweig, and Mannheim. In 1963 he made his first appearance at the Berlin Städtische Oper and in 1967 at the Hamburg State Opera; also sang at the Bayreuth Festivals (from 1971). In 1979 he sang Dr. Schön in the premiere of the 3-act version of *Lulu* in Paris, which role he also sang at his Metropolitan Opera debut in N.Y. (Dec. 12, 1980). In addition to the Wagnerian repertoire, he sang Pizzaro in *Fidelio*, Jochanaan in *Salome*, and Moses in Schoenberg's *Moses und Aron.*—**NS/LK/DM**

Mazurek, Ronald, American composer and teacher; b. Perth Amboy, N.J., Dec. 2, 1943. He received training in clarinet and piano at Montclair (N.J.) Coll. (B.A., 1966) and N.Y.U. (M.A., 1967), then completed his studies there in composition with Ghezzo (Ph.D., 1986). He taught composition at N.Y.U. (from 1982) and electronic music at William Paterson Coll. of N.J. in Wayne (from 1990); served as vice president of the Composers Guild of N.J. (1983–91) and as founder-director of the Fairleigh Dickinson Univ. Concerts of Contemporary Music (1984–90). In his music, he frequently integrates acoustic and electronic elements.

WORKS: *Meditation* for Clarinet and Percussion (1978); *Voices* for Wind Quintet (1979); *Meditation* for Oboe and Percussion (1980); *Anima* for Flute, Clarinet, and Piano (1980); *Encounters* for Percussion Quartet (1981); *Dialogues* for Trumpets (1981); *Fusion/Defusion* for Clarinet (1982); *Focusing* for Alto Saxophone (1984); *Cantos* for Brass Quintet (1984); *The Voice Within* for Piano and Tape (1986); *The Mirror of Wisdom* for Wind Quintet (1987); *In Search of...* for Percussion and Tape (1987); *Yu-Chou* for Tape (1988); *Trigrams* for Clarinet, Piano, and Tape (1988); *3 Songs in Memoriam* for Soprano and Tape (1989); *3 Etudes* for Piano and Tape (1990); *Alleluia* for Chamber Orch. and Tape (1990); *Satori* for Clarinet and Tape (1991); *3 Preludes* for Piano and Tape (1992); *Visions* for Ensemble and Tape (1992). —NS/LK/DM

Mazzinghi, Joseph, English pianist and composer of Corsican descent; b. London, Dec. 25, 1765; d. Downside, near Bath, Jan. 15, 1844. He was the son of Thomas Mazzinghi, a wine merchant, who played violin at Marylebone Gardens and was active as a composer. He studied with J.C. Bach in London. Mazzinghi was a mere child when his father died, and succeeded him as organist of the Portuguese Chapel at 10. He subsequently took lessons with Bertoni, Sacchini, and Anfossi during their British sojourns. He was music director (1785–94) and harpsichordist (1785–98) at the King's Theatre in London, and then taught piano. He wrote prolifically, producing dramatic works, ballets, sonatas, piano pieces, songs, glees, etc., all of little merit. —NS/LK/DM

Mazzocchi, Domenico, Italian composer, brother of **Virgilio Mazzocchi**; b. Veja, near Città Castellana (baptized), Nov. 8, 1592; d. Rome, Jan. 21, 1665. A learned Roman lawyer, he studied music with Nanini and in 1621 entered the service of Cardinal Ippolito Aldobrandini. He publ. *Madrigali a 5 voci in partitura* (1638), in which appear, for the first time, the conventional symbols for *crescendo* (<) and *decrescendo* (>), *piano* (*p*), *forte* (*f*), and *trillo* (*tr*), which he explains in a preface. He also composed the operas *La catena d'Adone* (Rome, 1626) and *L'innocenza difesa*, several oratorios, and various pieces of church music.

BIBL.: A. Cardinali, *Cenni biografici su D. e Virgilio M.* (Subiaco, 1926).—NS/LK/DM

Mazzocchi, Virgilio, Italian composer, brother of **Domenico Mazzocchi**; b. Veja (baptized), July 22, 1597; d. there, Oct. 3, 1646. He studied music with his brother in Rome, and served as maestro di cappella at the

Chiesa del Gesù. He then was at St. John Lateran (1628–29). In 1629 he was engaged at the Cappella Giulia at St. Peter's, and served there until his death. He wrote the opera *Chi soffre, speri* with Marazzoli (Rome, Feb. 27, 1639), which was a revision of *Il facone* (Rome, Feb. 1637); excerpts from it were publ. by H. Goldschmidt. An *Argomento et allegoria* relating to it was publ. at the time of its first performance, a copy of which is in the Library of Congress in Washington, D.C.

BIBL.: A. Cardinali, *Cenni biografici su Domenico e V. M.* (Subiaco, 1926).—NS/LK/DM

Mazzoleni, Ester, Italian soprano; b. Sebenico, March 12, 1883; d. Palermo, May 17, 1982. After vocal studies, she made her operatic debut in Rome in 1906 as Leonora in *Il Trovatore*. From 1908 to 1917 she appeared at Milan's La Scala, where she sang such roles as Spontini's Giulia and Cherubini's Médée. She also sang Aida at Verona (1913) and appeared in many other Italian opera centers. Her guest engagements also took her to various European opera houses. Among her other roles were Norma, Elisabeth de Valois, and Lucrezia Borgia.—NS/LK/DM

Mazzoleni, Ettore, Canadian conductor, teacher, and composer of Italian-Swiss descent; b. Brusio, Switzerland, June 19, 1905; d. in an automobile accident in Oak Ridges, near Toronto, June 1, 1968. He studied mathematics and music at Oxford Univ. (B.A., 1927; B.Mus., 1927) and piano at the Royal Coll. of Music in London, where he later taught (1927–29). He then settled in Toronto, where he was music master and later an English instructor at Upper Canada Coll. (1929–45). He also taught music history at the Toronto Cons. (from 1932) and conducted its sym. orch. (from 1934), and was made its principal in 1945, continuing in that capacity when it became the Royal Cons. of Music of Toronto in 1952. He retired in 1966. He was assoc. conductor of the Toronto Sym. Orch. (1942–48), and also appeared as a conductor in other Canadian cities. In 1949 he became a naturalized Canadian citizen. He made several transcriptions of folk songs for various instrumental and vocal groups.—NS/LK/DM

McAllester, David P(ark), American ethnomusicologist; b. Everett, Mass., Aug. 6, 1916. He studied anthropology at Harvard Univ. (B.A., 1934) and Columbia Univ. (Ph.D., 1939). He taught anthropology at Wesleyan Univ. from 1947, and from 1972 until his retirement in 1986 he served as prof. of anthropology and music there. He devoted much time to the study of American Indian culture.

WRITINGS: *Peyote Music* (N.Y., 1949); *Enemy Way Music* (Cambridge, Mass., 1954); *The Myth and Prayers of the Great Star Chant* (Santa Fe, N.Mex., 1956); ed. *Readings in Ethnomusicology* (N.Y., 1971); with S. McAllester, *Hogans: Navajo Houses and House Songs* (Middletown, Conn., 1980).

BIBL.: C. Frisbie, ed., *Explorations in Ethnomusicology: Essays in Honor of D.P. M.* (Detroit, 1986).—NS/LK/DM

McArthur, Edwin, American conductor, pianist, and pedagogue; b. Denver, Sept. 24, 1907; d. N.Y., Feb.

2

24, 1987. He studied piano in Denver and with Rosina Lhévinne in N.Y. He toured widely as a piano accompanist to various celebrated artists of the day, becoming well known as accompanist to Kirsten Flagstad. In 1938 he made his debut as an opera conductor in Chicago, and then appeared with the San Francisco Opera in 1939. On April 1, 1940, he made his Metropolitan Opera debut in N.Y. conducting *Tristan und Isolde*, remaining on its roster until 1941. From 1945 to 1950 he was director of the St. Louis Municipal Opera. He was conductor of the Harrisburg (Pa.) Sym. Orch. from 1950 to 1974. He also served as director of the opera dept. at the Eastman School of Music in Rochester, N.Y. (1967–72) before devoting himself to private teaching. McArthur was the author of the book *Flagstad: A Personal Memoir* (N.Y., 1965).—NS/LK/DM

McBee, Cecil, jazz bassist, composer; b. Tulsa, Okla., May 19, 1935. His first instrument was clarinet on which he performed in marching bands and in duets with his sister. He took up the bass at 17, and later began playing in local nightclubs. McBee attended Central State Univ. (Wilberforce, Ohio) at various times during the 1950s and 1960s, eventually earning a B.S. in clarinet/music education. He worked with Dinah Washington in 1959, and spent a two-year stretch in the army from 1959 to 1961; there he played in a trio with Kirk Lightsey and Rudy Johnson and conducted the Fort Knox (Ky.) band. McBee moved to Detroit in 1962, where he played with the Paul Winter Sextet, then moved to N.Y. in 1964 where he gained attention through touring with Charles Lloyd and Pharoah Sanders. In the 1960s, he also performed or recorded with Graham Moncur III, Jackie McLean, Wayne Shorter, Charles Tolliver, Yusef Lateef, Sam Rivers, and Alice Coltrane. He went on to perform around the world with Elvin Jones, McCoy Tyner, Miles Davis, Bobby Hutcherson, Freddie Hubbard, and Joe Henderson. During the 1970s, McBee had extended stints with Abdullah Ibrahim, in combo and large band settings, and Chico Freeman that lasted into the 1980s; he also worked in the 1970s with Sanders, Coltrane, Sonny Rollins, and Art Pepper. When McBee began recording as a leader in the mid-1970s, he usually included Freeman in his band. The recipient of two NEA composition grants, his works have been recorded by Jones, Tyner, Sanders, and Tolliver.

DISC.: *Mutima* (1974); *Music from the Source* (1977); *Alternate Spaces* (1979); *Flying Out* (1982).—LP

McBride, Christian, bassist; b. Philadelphia, Pa., May 21, 1972. He was inspired to play the bass by his father, Lee Smith, who performed with some of the major acts of the 1970s, including the Delfonics, Billy Paul, Blue Magic, and Major Harris. His great uncle, Howard Cooper, also played acoustic bass and worked with Sunny Murray and Byard Lancaster. After studying classical bass at Philadelphia's H.S. for the Performing Arts, as well as with Neil Courtney of the Philadelphia Orch., he was awarded a scholarship to attend Juilliard. McBride began freelancing instead, first with Bobby Watson, then with Betty Carter, Wynton Marsa-

lis, Freddie Hubbard, Benny Green, and Joshua Redman. He appeared in 1995 with McCoy Tyner, Kathleen Battle, and David Sanborn, recorded with Dave Brubeck, and appeared on the live Grammy telecast with Brubeck in 1996. He had a featured musical role in Robert Altman's film *Kansas City*, and was part of Chick Corea's All Star Quintet (with Joshua Redman, Wallace Roney, and Roy Haynes) during the summer of 1996. In 1997, he toured in a trio with Redman and Brian Blade, and currently divides his time between working and recording with a vast array of musicians, and leading his own band which features Tim Warfield, Anthony Wonsey, and Carl Allen.

DISC.: *Gettin' to It* (1995); *Number Two Express* (1996); *A Family Affair* (1998); *Sci-Fi* (2000).—LP

McBride, Robert (Guyn), American composer; b. Tucson, Ariz., Feb. 20, 1911. He learned to play clarinet, saxophone, organ, and piano, and played in dance bands as a youth. He studied theory at the Univ. of Ariz. (1928–35) and was a member of the Tucson Sym. Orch. (1928–35). From 1935 to 1946 he taught wind instruments at Bennington (Vt.) Coll.; was then an arranger for Triumph Films, N.Y. (1946–57); from 1957 to 1978 he was on the music faculty of the Univ. of Ariz. An exceptionally prolific composer, he wrote over 1,000 pieces in various genres, many of them on American or Mexican themes with an infusion of jazz elements.

WORKS: ORCH.: *Mexican Rhapsody* (1934); *Side Show* (1944); Violin Concerto (1954); *Hill Country Symphony* (1964); *Symphonic Melody* (1968); *Folk-Song Fantasy* (1973); *Light Fantastic* (1976–77). **CHAMBER:** *Workout* for Oboe and Piano (1936); *Swing Stuff* for Clarinet and Piano (1938); *Jam Session* for Woodwind Quintet (1941); *Swing Foursome* for String Quartet (1957); *5 Winds Blowing* for Wind Quintet (1957); *Lament for the Parking Problem* for Trumpet, Horn, and Trombone (1968). —NS/LK/DM

McCabe, John, esteemed English pianist, music educator, and composer; b. Huyton, April 21, 1939. He learned to play piano, violin, and cello as a child. He studied with Proctor Gregg (composition) at the Univ. of Manchester and with Pitfield (composition) and Green (piano) at the Royal Manchester Coll. of Music. He later took courses at the Munich Academy of Music (1964–65) and also studied privately there with Genzmer. He was pianist-in-residence at Univ. Coll., Cardiff (1965–67), then settled in London as a pianist, excelling in the music of Haydn and contemporary composers. He was director of the London Coll. of Music from 1983 to 1990. In 1985 he was made a Commander of the Order of the British Empire.

WORKS: DRAMATIC: *The Lion, the Witch, and the Wardrobe*, children's opera (1968; Manchester, April 29, 1969); *This town's a corporation full of crooked streets*, entertainment (1969); *Notturni ed Alba*, ballet (1970; Münster, April 1976; also for Soprano and Orch., Hereford, Aug. 1970); *The Teachings of Don Juan*, ballet (Manchester, May 30, 1973); *The Play of Mother Courage*, chamber opera (Middlesborough, Oct. 3, 1974); *Mary Queen of Scots*, ballet (1975; Glasgow, March 3, 1976; Suite No. 1, London, March 16, 1987; Suite No. 2, Harlow, Essex, Oct. 23, 1988); *Shadow-Reach*, ballet after the Sym. No. 2 (Dublin, June

19, 1978); *Die Fenster*, ballet after *The Chagall Windows* for Orch. (Stuttgart, Feb. 16, 1980); *Edward II*, ballet (1994–95; Stuttgart, April 15, 1995); *Arthur, Part 1: Arthur Pendragon*, ballet (1999; Birmingham, Jan. 25, 2000); *Arthur, Part 2: Le Morte d'Arthur*, ballet (1999–2000). O R C H .: 2 violin concertos: No. 1, *Sinfonia concertante* (1959; Manchester, March 1963) and No. 2 (Birmingham, March 20, 1980); Concerto for Chamber Orch. (1962; rev. 1968); *Concerto Funèbre* for Viola and Chamber Orch. (1962; Glasgow, Sept. 1971); *Variations on a Theme of Hartmann* (1964; Manchester, Nov. 24, 1965); Chamber Concerto for Viola, Cello, and Orch. (1965); *Concertante* for Harpsichord and Chamber Ensemble (Liverpool, Dec. 18, 1965); 4 syms.: No. 1, *Elegy* (1965; Cheltenham, July 4, 1966), No. 2 (Birmingham, Sept. 26, 1971), No. 3, *Hommages* (London, July 11, 1978), and No. 4, *Of Time and the River* (1993–94; Melbourne, March 16, 1995); 3 piano concertos: No. 1 (1966; Southport, May 1967), No. 2, *Sinfonia Concertante* (1970; Middlesborough, Nov. 23, 1971), and No. 3, *Dialogues* (1976; rev. version, Liverpool, Aug. 5, 1977); *Concertante Music* (Bath, June 24, 1968); Concertino for Piano Duet and Orch. (1968; Farnham Festival, May 11, 1969); *Metamorphosen* for Harpsichord and Orch. (1968; Liverpool, Feb. 19, 1972); *Concertante Variations on a Theme of Nicholas Maw* for Strings (1970; Bristol, March 3, 1971; also for 11 Solo Strings, 1987; Southport, Feb. 7, 1989); Oboe d'Amore Concerto (Portsmouth, April 26, 1972); *Basse Danse* (1973; Guildford, May 5, 1975; also for 2 Pianos, 1970); *The Chagall Windows* (1974; Manchester, Jan. 9, 1975; also as the ballet *Die Fenster*, Stuttgart, Feb. 16, 1980); *Sonata on a Motet* for Strings (Manchester, March 20, 1976); *Jubilee Suite* (1977; 1st complete perf., London, June 14, 1986); Clarinet Concerto (1977; Glasgow, June 26, 1978); *The Shadow of Light* (London, Dec. 6, 1979); *Concerto for Orchestra* (1982; London, Feb. 10, 1983); *Tuning* ('s Hertogenbosch, July 27, 1985); Double Concerto (1987–88; London, June 25, 1988); *Fire at Durilgai* (1988; Manchester, Jan. 13, 1989); Flute Concerto (London, Sept. 20, 1990); *Red Leaves* (Istanbul, July 11, 1991); *Fizzgig* (Manchester, Oct. 1, 1994); Oboe Concerto (1994; Isle of Wight, May 7, 1995); *Pilgrim* for Double String Orch. or Chamber String Orch. (1996); *Symphony Edward II* (1997). W i n d   a n d   B r a s s   E n s e m b l e : Sym. for 10 Winds (London, Dec. 1964); *Canzona* for Winds and Percussion (1970; Farnham Festival, May 1971); *Images* for Brass Band (London, March 30, 1978; also for Wind Band, Redlands, Calif., May 14, 1978); *Desert II: Horizon* for 10 Brass Instruments (Ripon, Aug. 4, 1981; also for Brass Band, 1987; London, Oct. 8, 1988); *Rainforest I* for 10 Players (N.Y., Nov. 30, 1984) and *III: Dandernongs* (Norwich, Oct. 11, 1991); *Cloudcatcher Fells* for Brass Band (London, Oct. 6, 1985); *Centennial Fanfare* for Brass Ensemble (London, March 9, 1987); *Canyons* for Wind Band (London, July 9, 1991); *Northern Lights* for Brass Band (1992; Manchester, Jan. 25, 1993); *Salamander* (London, June 25, 1994). C H A M B E R : 5 string quartets: No. 1, *Partita* (1960), No. 2 (Macclesfield Festival, July 17, 1972), No. 3 (Goodwick, July 23, 1979), No. 4 (London, Oct. 20, 1982), and No. 5 (Fishguard Festival, July 23, 1989); *Musica Notturna* for Violin, Viola, and Piano (1964); *3 Pieces* for Clarinet and Piano (1964); *Movements* for Clarinet, Violin, and Cello (1964; rev. 1966); String Trio (1965); *Bagatelles* for 2 Clarinets (1965); *Fantasy* for Brass Quintet (1966); *Nocturnal* for Piano Quintet (1966); *Partita* for Cello (1966); *Dance-Movements* for Horn, Violin, and Piano (1967); *Rounds* for Brass Quintet (Salford, Feb. 28, 1968); *Canto* for Guitar (1968); Oboe Quartet (1968; Cardiff, Feb. 11, 1969); Sonata for Clarinet, Cello, and Piano (Macclesfield Festival, May 22, 1969); Concerto for Piano and Wind Quintet (1969; Birmingham, Feb. 1970); *Dance-Prelude* for Oboe d'Amore or Clarinet and Piano (1971); *Maze Dances* for

Violin (1973; London, May 15, 1974); *The Goddess Trilogy* for Horn and Piano (1973–75); *Star-Preludes* for Violin and Piano (Los Angeles, April 28, 1978); *Dances* for Trumpet and Piano (1980); *Portraits* for Flute and Piano (1980); *Desert I: Lizard* for Flute, Oboe, Clarinet, Bassoon, and Percussion (1981), *III: Landscape* for Violin, Cello, and Piano (Armidale, New South Wales, June 17, 1982), and *IV: Vista* for Recorder (Altrincham, May 6, 1983); *Rainforest* II for Trumpet and Strings (Ripon, Aug. 3, 1987); *Caravan* for String Quartet (Colchester, Feb. 23, 1988); *Sam Variations* for Violin, Viola, Cello, Double Bass, and Piano (1989); *January Sonatina* for Clarinet (1990; Redlands, Calif., Feb. 13, 1991); *February Sonatina* for Viola (1990); *Postcards* for Wind Quintet (Huddersfield, Nov. 23, 1991); *Harbour with Ships (Five Impressions)* for Brass Quintet (1991; Salford, Feb. 16, 1992); *...not quite a tAnGO...* for Treble Recorder and Piano (Huddersfield, Nov. 24, 1994); Cello Sonata (1999). K E Y B O A R D : P i a n o : *Variations* (1963); *5 Bagatelles* (1964); *Fantasy on a Theme of Liszt* (1967); *Intermezzi* (1968); *Capriccio* (Dublin, June 6, 1969); *Sostenuto* (Bath, Feb. 19, 1969); *Gaudi* (1970); *Aubade* (1970); *Basse Danse* for 2 Pianos (1970; also for Orch., 1973); *Paraphrase on "Mary, Queen of Scots"* (1979; Kelso, Jan. 11, 1980); *Mosaic* (St. Asaph's Wales, Sept. 25, 1980); *Afternoons and Afterwords* (1981); *Lamentation Rag* (1982); *Haydn Variations* (London, Oct. 25, 1983); *I Have a Bonnet Trimmed With Blue* for Piano Duet (1992); *Tenebrae* (1992–93; Harrogate, Aug. 11, 1994). H a r p s i - c h o r d : *The Greensleeves Ground* (1969). O r g a n : *Sinfonia* (1961); *Dies Resurrectionis* (Manchester, March 1, 1963); *Prelude* (1964); *Johannis-Partita* (1964); *Elegy* (1965); *Miniconcerto* (1966). V O C A L : 3 *Folk Songs* for High Voice, Optional Clarinet, and Piano (1963; expanded as 5 *Folk Songs* for High Voice, Horn, and Piano, 1976; Derby, July 7, 1979); *Canticles for Salisbury: Magnificat and Nunc Dimittis* for Chorus and Organ (1966); *Great Lord of Lords* for Chorus and Organ (1966; also for Chorus, Organ, and Instrumental Ensemble); *Rain Songs* for Soprano, Countertenor or Alto, Cello, and Harpsichord (1966); *Aspects of Whiteness* for Chorus and Piano (London, June 21, 1967; rev. 1969); *Notturni ed Alba* for Soprano and Orch. (Hereford, Aug. 1970; also as a ballet, Münster, April 1976); *Norwich Canticles: Magnificat and Nunc Dimittis* for Chorus (1970); *Requiem Sequence* for Soprano and Piano (1971; London, Feb. 7, 1979); *Voyage*, cantata for Soprano, Mezzo-soprano, Countertenor, Baritone, Bass, Chorus, and Orch. (Worcester, Aug. 30, 1972); *Der Letzte Gerichte* for Voice, Guitar, and Percussion (1973); *Time Remembered* for Soprano and 7 Players (Malvern, Oct. 4, 1973); *Stabat Mater* for Soprano, Chorus, and Orch. (Northampton, Oct. 28, 1976); *Reflections of a Summer Night* for Chorus and Orch. (1977); *Mangan Triptych (Motet; Siberia; Visions)* for Chorus (1979–83; 1st complete perf., Harrogate, Aug. 10, 1984); *Music's Empire* for Soloists, Chorus, and Orch. (1981; London, Oct. 6, 1982); *Scenes from America Deserta* for 6 Solo Voices (1986; London, Jan. 29, 1988); *Amen/Alleluia* for Chorus (1991; Chicago, March 27, 1992); *Wind, Sand, and Stars* for Soprano, Chorus, and Orch. (London, July 18, 1992); *Irish Songbook* for Mezzo- soprano and Piano (1993–94; Cambridge, May 5, 1994).

BIBL.: S. Craggs, *J. M.: A Bio-Bibliography* (N.Y., 1991). —NS/LK/DM

McCalla, James, American musicologist; b. Lawrence, Kans., Aug. 25, 1946. He received a B.Mus. in piano and a B.A. in French from the Univ. of Kans. in Lawrence (1968), and an M.M. in music literature from the New England Cons. of Music in Boston (1973). He then took a Ph.D. in musicology, specializing in 20th-century music, with Kerman at the Univ. of Calif. at

Berkeley (1976, with the diss. *"Between Its Human Accessories": The Art of Stéphane Mallarmé and Pierre Boulez*). He taught at the Univ. of Va. (1976–78), the State Univ. of N.Y. at Stony Brook (1978–85), and Bowdoin Coll. in Maine (from 1985). His textbooks include *Jazz: A Listener's Guide* (Englewood Cliffs, N.J., 1982) and *Chamber Music of Our Time* (1991). His research employs literary critique to analyze the interface between complex musical and textual works, with subjects including indeterminacy and jazz.—NS/LK/DM

McCann, Les(lie Coleman; aka Maxie),

jazz pianist, singer; b. Lexington, Ky., Sept. 23, 1935. A self-taught musician, McCann left the South in the early 1950s and joined the Navy. While stationed in Calif., he took every opportunity to visit San Francisco's jazz clubs, where he first heard Miles Davis and became influenced by Erroll Garner. After his discharge, he moved to Los Angeles and formed a trio, Les McCann Ltd., which became a favorite on the Sun Strip in the late 1950s. He was recommended by Miles Davis to play with Cannonball Adderley, but turned it down in favor of backing pop vocalist Gene McDaniels in 1959. In 1960, McCann signed to the Pacific Jazz label and became the label's top-selling artist; he also co-headed albums with legendary labelmates such as organist Richard "Groove" Holmes, saxman Ben Webster, The Jazz Crusaders, and the Gerald Wilson Orch. He was a hit at the 1962 Antibes Jazz Festival in Juan-les-Pins, France, where he shared the stage with Ray Charles and Count Basie. The year after, he toured Europe with Zoot Sims and Charlie Byrd. He co-produced and co-headlined Lou Rawls' debut album, and in 1967 he signed to Atlantic Records, his first major label deal. He is best known for his work in the late 1960s and early 1970s with Eddie Harris, whom he first encountered at the Montreux Jazz Festival. The resulting album, *Swiss Movement* (1970), was a top seller, and the single "Compared to What" sold platinum; that same year, he also had a hit with the ballad "With These Hands." On his album *Layers*, he helped pioneer the use of electric piano, clavinet, and synthesizer. In the early 1970s, McCann heard Roberta Flack at a nightclub in Washington D.C., and immediately became her champion, as he had earlier with Nancy Wilson. The early 1980s saw the creation of McCann's Magic Band, which recorded a number of independently released albums and featured Jeff Elliott, Keith Anderson, Tony St. James, and Abraham Laboriel. His latest release, *On the Soul Side*, once again reunited him with Eddie Harris and Lou Rawls. In the mid-1990s, his music has been sampled by hip hop artists, including Mobb Depp, De La Soul, Lords of the Underground, and Pete Rock and C.L. Smooth. His personal relationships with jazz legends such as Miles Davis, Art Blakey, and Duke Ellington, as well as many other great historical characters, have been documented in a collection of more than 8,000 photographs that McCann took over the years; he built a darkroom in his home, and has sold a significant number of pieces. In addition, he is an exhibited painter, primarily a watercolorist with a particular interest in flowers. He no longer plays the piano due to a 1995 stroke, but continues to paint and photograph.

DISC.: *In New York* (1960); *The Shout* (1960); *Plays the Truth* (1960); *Pretty Lady* (1961); *Les McCann Sings* (1961); *Plays the Shampoo at the Village Gate* (1961); *In San Francisco* (1961); *Groove* (1961); *Somethin' Special* (1962); *Stormy Monday* (1962); *Les McCann on Time* (1962); *Gospel Truth* (1963); *Jazz Waltz* (1963); *Spanish Onions* (1964); *McCann/Wilson* (1964); *New from the Big City* (1964); *McCanna* (1964); *But Not Really* (1964); *Poo Boo* (1965); *But Not Really* (1965); *Live at Shelly's Manne-Hole* (1965); *Bucket of Grease* (1966); *Plays the Hits* (1966); *More or Les McCann* (1967); *Les Is More* (1967); *Les McCann Live at the Bohemian* (1967); *From the Top of the Barrel* (1967); *Much Les* (1968); *Comment* (1969); *Swiss Movement* (1969); *Invitation to Openness* (1971); *Second Movement* (1971); *Live at Montreux* (1972); *Layers* (1972); *Talk to the People* (1972); *Another Beginning* (1974); *Hustle to Survive* (1975); *River High, River Low* (1976); *Change Change Change; Live at the Roxy* (1977); *The Man* (1978); *Tall, Dark & Handsome* (1979); *The Longer You Wait* (1983); *McCann's Music Box* (1984); *The Butterfly* (1988); *More of Les* (1989); *On the Soul Side* (1994); *Listen Up!* (1995); *Piano Jazz* (1996).—LP

McCartney, Paul,

often regarded as the Beatle who stabilized the group's appeal with audiences of all ages; b. Allerton, Liverpool, England, June 18, 1942. Paul McCartney was responsible for writing most of the group's original material, in conjunction with John Lennon. The primary author of Beatles hits such as "Michelle" and "Hey Jude," McCartney composed the classic "Yesterday," which has been recorded by more than 2,500 artists and played more than six million times, making it the most frequently performed pop song in history. Moreover, McCartney was the most proficient musician and technically accomplished vocalist in the Beatles.

Paul McCartney's first solo project outside of the Beatles was the soundtrack to the movie *Family Way*, released in 1967. He later met American photographer Linda Eastman and married her on March 12, 1969, by which time the Beatles were already suffering from internal tensions. The film of the Beatles' final album release, *Let It Be*, aptly revealed McCartney's attempt to dominate the group. The four were soon embroiled in personal and business disputes, as McCartney objected to the near-simultaneous release of *Let It Be* and his first solo album, *McCartney*, and the others sought to employ Allen Klein as financial advisor while McCartney sought the appointment of his father-in-law, Lee Eastman. In April 1970 the breakup of the Beatles was announced, and on Dec. 31, 1970, McCartney sued Klein and Apple Records for legal dissolution of the group's corporate empire.

McCartney, recorded with Linda providing harmonies and Paul playing all instruments, contained ditties by Paul such as "Every Night," "That Would Be Something," "Man, We Was Lonely," and, the one substantial song, "Maybe I'm Amazed." *McCartney* topped the album charts and remained there for nearly a year. Following the smash-hit single "Another Day," Paul and Linda McCartney recorded *Ram* with N.Y. session players. The album included "Heart of the Country" and yielded the top hit "UncleAlbert/Admiral Halsey.".

In August 1971 Paul McCartney formed his recording and touring band, Wings, with wife Linda, guitarist Denny Laine, and drummer Danny Seiwell. Session musician Seiwell had played on the *Ram* album, whereas Laine had been an original member of the Moody Blues and lead vocalist on the Moodys' first blues-inflected hit, "Go Now." *Wild Life* was generally considered to be McCartney's weakest effort, failing to yield even a minor hit. Joined in January 1972 by guitarist Henry McCullough, the band scored major hits with the singles-only releases "Give Ireland Back to the Irish," McCartney's feeble attempt at political consciousness; the inane "Mary Had a Little Lamb" and "Hi, Hi, Hi." *Red Rose Speedway* did little to establish his artistic credibility, although it did yield the top pop and easy-listening hit" My Love."

In 1973 Paul McCartney and Wings recorded the title song to the James Bond movie *Live and Let Die*, and the single became a top hit. It served as a prototype to the clever pop-style songs—replete with reprises, codas, changing time signatures, and multiple musical themes—that McCartney crafted so successfully on the subsequent album, *Band on the Run*. During 1973 Wings appeared in a British and American television special, successfully toured Europe, and scored a major hit with "Helen Wheels." However, by July Henry McCullough and Danny Seiwell had dropped out of the group.

The McCartneys and Denny Laine traveled to Lagos, Nigeria, to record their next album, *Band on the Run*, at Ginger Baker's new ARC Studio. Often regarded as McCartney's finest post-Beatles work and certainly his most consistent, the album brought the group their first critical praise and yielded the smash hits "Jet" and the title track; it also contains "Let Me Roll It," "Helen Wheels," and the ditty "Mamunia." Remaining on the album charts for more than two years and selling more than six million copies, the album effectively established McCartney as a pop-style songwriter-arranger.

Wings added Scottish guitarist Jimmy McCulloch, formerly with Thunderclap Newman and Stone the Crows, in May 1974 for the Nashville-recorded pop hits "Junior's Farm" (a smash) and "Sally G.," also a minor country hit. Drummer Joe English joined in February 1975 for the group's next album, *Venus and Mars Are Alright Tonight*, recorded primarily at Allen Toussaint's Sea Saint Studio in New Orleans. The album produced the top hit "Listen to What the Man Said," the moderate hit "Letting Go" and the major hit "Venus and Mars Rock Show." Between fall 1975 and summer 1976 Wings successfully completed their first worldwide tour, and *Wings at the Speed of Sound* was issued in spring. Considered the band's first team effort, the album included McCulloch's "Wino Junko," Laine's "Time to Hide," and Linda's first effort as a lead vocalist, "Cook of the House," as well as Paul's smash pop and easy-listening hits "Let 'Em In" and "Silly Love Songs," the latter a gentle swipe at critics had regularly attacked him for his inconsequential ditties.

The United States segment of the Wings tour, called Wings Over America, produced a live multirecord set that yielded the major hit "Maybe I'm Amazed." Otherwise largely inactive during 1977, Wings scored a smash British hit with the singles release "Mull Of Kintyre" (ostensibly the biggest-selling single in British history), whereas the flip side, "Girls School," became a

moderate American hit. *London Town*, Wings's final album of new material for Capitol Records, was recorded primarily on a chartered yacht in the Virgin Islands and produced during 1978 the hits "With a Little Luck," "I've Had Enough," and the title song. Following the album's completion, Jimmy McCulloch and Joe English left Wings, to be replaced by session musicians.

By early 1979 Paul McCartney had signed a long-term contract with Columbia Records rumored to be the most lucrative ever in the history of popular music. Wings scored a smash hit on Columbia with the disco-style "Goodnight Tonight" and their debut Columbia album, *Back to the Egg*, yielded major hits with "Getting Closer" and "Arrow Through Me." Scheduled to make his first appearance in Japan since playing there with the Beatles in 1966, McCartney was busted upon arrival on Jan. 16, 1980, for possession of nearly a half-pound of marijuana. Perhaps the most highly publicized drug bust in pop-music history, McCartney was deported after spending several days in jail. He subsequently wrote, engineered, produced, played, and sang all parts of his second "solo" album, *McCartney II*, with its hit, "Comin' Up." In April 1981 Wings officially disbanded.

For his next two albums McCartney utilized the services of George Martin, the Beatles' former producer. *Tug of War* included "Here Today" (a tribute to slain Beatle John Lennon) and yielded the top pop and easy-listening hit "Ebony and Ivory," sung in duet with Stevie Wonder, and the major hit "Take It Away." McCartney and Michael Jackson scored a smash pop, R&B, and easy-listening hit with "The Girl Is Mine" in late 1982, and McCartney's next album, *Pipes of Peace*, yielded another top pop hit for the duo with "Say Say Say" and a major hit for McCartney alone with "So Bad." McCartney's next project, his first solo feature film, *Give My Regards to Broad Street*, was a barely watchable flop, despite the inclusion of musicians Ringo Starr, Dave Edmunds, and John Paul Jones and actor Sir Ralph Richardson. The soundtrack album featured 13 rerecordings of Beatles and McCartney hits and included the smash hit "No More Lonely Nights."

In 1985 Paul McCartney returned to Capitol Records, quickly hitting with the title song to the Chevy Chase–Dan Aykroyd movie *Spies Like Us*. Eric Stewart, formerly with 10cc, collaborated on many of the songs from McCartney's debut Capitol album, as he had on *Tug of War*. *Press to Play*, however, produced only one hit, "Press." In September 1987 McCartney recorded his most spirited album in years for the Russian label Melodiya. Released exclusively in the Soviet Union in 1988, the album contained remade oldies and was eventually released outside that country in 1991.

In 1989 Paul McCartney and Elvis Costello collaborated on two songs for Costello's album *Spike*, the major hit "Veronica" and "Pads, Paws and Claws." McCartney's next effort, *Flowers in the Dirt*, included four songs coauthored by Costello: "Don't Be Careless Love," "That Day Is Done," "You Want Her Too," and the major hit "My Brave Face." McCartney subsequently conducted his first tour in 13 years with the recording band, comprised of the McCartneys, lead guitarist Robbie McIntosh (of the Pretenders), guitarist-bassist Hamish

Stuart (of the Average White Band), keyboardist Paul "Wix"Wickens, and drummer Chris Whitten. Mixing Beatles, Wings, and McCartney favorites with more recent songs, the tour helped reestablish McCartney as a pop artist and produced the live 1990 set *Tripping the Live Fantastic*, released in both double (30 songs) and single (17 songs) CD versions.

In early 1991, with Blair Cunningham replacing Chris Whitten, McCartney and band performed on MTV's *Unplugged* program. The album from the performance was the first album released from the popular, ongoing series. Later that year McCartney debuted his *Liverpool Oratorio* at Liverpool Cathedral, with mezzo-soprano Kiri Te Kanawa and a cast of more than three hundred. Written over a three-year period with American film and theater composer Carl Davis, it was politely received and later performed at Carnegie Hall. Paul McCartney toured with his band again in 1993 in support of *Off the Ground*. In 1995 another classical piece composed by McCartney, "A Leaf," for solo piano, was debuted in London at a benefit concert for the Royal Coll. of Music. McCartney reunited with ex-Beatles Ringo Starr and George Harrison in late 1995 for a video/TV program/record package on the group's history, recording two singles using demo tapes made by John Lennon in the late 1970s, "Free as a Bird" and "Real Love," both with new lyrics by McCartney and over-dubbed vocals and instruments by the trio. His 1997 album *Flaming Pie* was well-received and up for a Grammy in 1998, the year his wife, Linda, died of breast cancer.

Disc.: PAUL MCCARTNEY: *Family Way* (soundtrack; 1967); *McCartney* (1979); *McCartney II* (1980); *Tug of War* (1982) *Pipes of Peace* (1983); *Give My Regards to Broad Street* (1984); *Press to Play* (1986); *All the Best (1970–1986)* (1987); *Choba B CCCP(released in U.S.S.R. in 1988)* (1991); *Flowers in the Dirt* (1989); *Tripping the Live Fantastic* (1990); *Tripping the Live Fantastic—"Highlights"* (1990); *Unplugged* (1991); *Off the Ground* (1993); *Paul Is Live* (1993); *Standing Stone* (1997); *Flaming Pie* (1997); *Run Devil Run* (1999); *Working Classical* (1999). **PAUL AND LINDA MCCARTNEY:** *Ram* (1971). **PAUL MC-CARTNEY AND WINGS:** *Wild Life* (1971); *Red Rose Speedway* (1973); *Band on the Run* (1973); *Venus and Mars Are Alright Tonight!* (1975); *Wings at the Speed of Sound* (1976); *Wings Over America* (1976); *London Town* (1978); *Greatest Hits* (1978); *Back to the Egg* (1979). **PAUL MCCARTNEY AND CARL DAVIS:** *Liverpool Oratorio* (1991).

Bibl.: George Tremlett, *The P. M. Story* (N.Y., 1975); John Mendelsohn, *P. M.: A Biography in Words and Pictures* (N.Y., 1977); Chris Welch, *P. M.: The Definitive Biography* (London, 1984); Chris Salewicz, *McCartney* (London, 1987); Chet Flippo, *Yesterday: The Unauthorized Biography of P. M.* (Garden City, N.Y., 1988).—**BH**

McCauley, William (Alexander), Canadian conductor and composer; b. Tofield, Alberta, Feb. 14, 1917; d. Alliston, Ontario, May 18, 1999. He studied at the Univ. of Toronto (M.B., 1947), with Parsons (piano, 1947) and Willan (composition) at the Toronto Cons., and with Hanson and Rogers at the Eastman School of Music in Rochester, N.Y. (M.M., 1959; D.M.A., 1960). He also was a conducting pupil of Monteux in Hancock, Maine (summer, 1959). He was first trombone for the Ottawa Phil. and the National Film Board (1947–49), and then music director of Crawley Films (1949–60), where he composed and conducted music for over 100 television films and documentaries. He then was music director of York Univ. (1960–69), the O'Keefe Centre (1960–87), Christopher Chapman Films (1969–70), Seneca Coll. (1970–78), and the North York Sym. Orch. (1972–88).

Works: ORCH.: *Newfoundland Scene* (1952); *Saskatchewan Suite* (1956); *5 Miniatures* for Flute and Strings (1958); *Contrasts* (1958); Horn Concerto (1959); *5 Miniatures* for Bass Trombone, Harp, and Strings (1959); *Theme and Deviations* (1960); *Wilderness*, music from the film (1963); *Canadian Folk Song Fantasy* for Symphonic Band (1966); *Metropolis*, concert suite for Symphonic Band (1967); *2 Nocturnes* for Strings (1968); *Sunday Morning at Wahanowin* for Strings (1968); *Concerto grosso* for Brass Quintet and Orch. (1973); *Christmas Carol Fantasies* (1975). **CHAMBER:** *5 Miniatures* for 6 Percussionists (1962), for 10 Winds (1968), for 4 Saxophones (1972), and for Brass Quintet (1974); *Miniature Overture* for Brass Quintet (1973); *Kaleidoscope québécois* for Flute, Clarinet, Violin, Cello, and 2 Pianos (1974). **Piano:** *Space Trip* (1968). **VOCAL:** Choruses; songs.—**NS/LK/DM**

McClain, Ernest Glenn, American music scholar; b. Canton, Ohio, Aug. 6, 1918. He studied at Oberlin (Ohio) Coll. (B.Mus., 1940), Northwestern Univ. (M.Mus., 1946), and Columbia Univ. (Ed.D., 1959). He was band director at Denison Univ. (1946–47) and the Univ. of Hawaii (1947–50), and then taught at Brooklyn Coll., City Univ. of N.Y., from 1950 until his retirement in 1981. He developed an effective way of teaching tuning systems using the monochord. His articles and books are sophisticated explorations of the interface between acoustics, mathematics, philosophy, and religion in ancient and medieval cultures.

Writings: *The Myth of Invariance: The Origin of the Gods, Mathematics, and Music from the Rig-Veda to Plato* (Boulder, Colo., 1976); *The Pythagorean Plato: Prelude to the Song Itself* (York Beach, Maine, 1978); *Meditations through the Quran: Tonal Images in an Oral Culture* (1981).—**NS/LK/DM**

McClary, Susan, progressive American musicologist; b. St. Louis, Oct. 2, 1946. She studied piano at Southern Ill. Univ. (B.Mus., 1968) and musicology at Harvard Univ. (A.M., 1971; Ph.D., 1976, with the diss. *The Transition from Modal to Tonal Organization in the Works of Monteverdi*). She taught at Harvard Univ. (1969–73) and Trinity Coll. in Hartford, Conn. (1977). McClary joined the faculty of the Univ. of Minnesota in 1977, becoming a prof. in 1990. She was acting director of its Center for Humanistic Studies (1984–85) and director of its Collegium Musicum. Her early research disputed the view of 17th century music that treats it as primitive tonality, arguing instead for its theoretical integrity. From 1982 she publ. articles on the political, economic, and feminist critique of music, on subjects including Mozart, Madonna, Bach, and Laurie Anderson; these studies won her attention and infamy and led to her being called "the first radical feminist musicologist."Her books include *Feminine Endings: Music, Gender, and Sexuality* (Minneapolis, 1990), *Power and Desire in Seventeenth-Century Music* (Princeton, 1991), and *Con-*

ventional Wisdom: The Content of Musical Form (Berkeley and Los Angeles, 2000). She also ed., with R. Leppert, *Music and Society: The Politics of Composition, Performance and Reception* (Cambridge, 1987).—**NS/LK/DM**

McClure, Ron(ald Dix), bass player, composer; b. New Haven, Conn., Nov. 22, 1941. He has a B.A. from Hartt Coll. and did additional studies in arranging with Don Sebesky and composition with Hall Overton. He played in the Charles Lloyd Quartet and Fourth Way, and also was in groups led by Wynton Kelly, Buddy Rich, Marian McPartland, Most Allison, Jack De-Johnette, Dave Liebman, Thelonious Monk, and Tony Bennett; he recorded with Jerry Hahn, Julian Priester, Cal Tjader and the Pointer Sisters; and spent three years with Blood, Sweat and Tears. McClure taught full time in 1971–72, and has taught steadily since then at N.Y.U. School of Ed. and elsewhere. He has also recorded and performed with George Russell, Tom Harrell, John Scofield, John Abercrombie, Richie Bierach, and Vincent Herring. He has been active around N.Y. since the early 1970s.

DISC.: *Home Base* (1979); *Descendants* (1980); *Yesterday's Tomorrow* (1989); *McJolt* (1989); *Never Forget* (1990); *Tonight Only* (1991); *Inspiration* (1991); *Never Was* (1995).—**LP**

McConnell, Rob, Canadian trombonist; b. London, Ontario, Canada, Feb. 14, 1935. He is best known as the band leader and arranger of the Boss Brass, a potent part-time organization featuring many of Canada's best jazz musicians. He began studying music in his teens, learning valve trombone in high school. By the early 1960s, inspired by Bob Brookmeyer's smooth, harmonically sophisticated style, he had become one of Canada's premier valve trombonists. From 1965–69 he was featured in Phil Nimmons band, Nimmons 'n' Nine Plus Six. In 1968 he founded the Boss Brass as an all-brass orchestra (and rhythm section) with a repertoire of pop tunes. The group broke up briefly in the late 1980s when he moved to L.A. to teach, but reassembled in 1991 and has been together ever since. Over the years the group has featured such superior players as Moe Kaufman and Rick Wilkins (reeds), Ed Bickert and Lorne Lofsky (guitar), Ian McDougall (trombone), and Terry Clarke (drums). As a vehicle for his swinging and innovative charts, the Boss Brass is about as good an ensemble as a writer could want.

DISC.: *Mel Tormé/Rob McConnell and the Boss Brass* (1986); *The Rob McConnell Jive Five* (1990); *The Brass Is Back* (1991); *Brassy and Sassy* (1992); *Our 25th Year* (1993); *Trio Sketches* (1994); *Overtime* (1994); *Don't Get around Much Anymore* (1995); *Three for the Road* (1997); *Play the Jazz Classics* (1997).—**AG**

McCord, Castor, jazz tenor saxophonist, clarinetist; b. Birmingham, Ala., May 17, 1907; d. N.Y., Feb. 14, 1963. Twin brother of saxophonist Theodore Jobetus (Ted) McCord; both played in Edgar Hayes' Blue Grass Buddies (1924). While studying at Wilberforce Univ., Xenia, Ohio, he became a member of student band led by Horace Henderson. He took up professional music with that band, played residency in Atlantic City, then went to N.Y. From 1929–30, he played with Mills Blue

Rhythm Band and subsequently played dates with Louis Armstrong and Eubie Blake Band until, in 1932, joining Charlie Matson Orch. in N.Y. He returned to the Mills band later that year, remaining with them until journeying to Europe in a band accompanying the revue, Blackbirds of 1934 in August of that year. He settled in Paris, playing in a band accompanying Louis Armstrong and Coleman Hawkins, then spent a year and a half in the Leon Abbey Band including two trips to India in 1936. He led his own trio in Amsterdam in spring 1937; later that year played with Fletcher Allen's Band in Paris. After playing with Walter Rains' Band in Rotterdam (early in 1938), Castor returned to the U.S. and rejoined Leon Abbey in N.Y. Early in 1939, he joined the Benny Carter Big Band at Savoy, and played with Eddie Mallory during the following year. From 1941–42, he was a member of Claude Hopkins' Band. He left professional music in the 1940s and became a hairdresser, continuing in that employment until shortly before his death.—**JC/LP**

McCorkle, Donald M(acomber), American musicologist; b. Cleveland, Feb. 20, 1929; d. Vancouver, Feb. 6, 1978. He studied at Brown Univ., at Bradley Univ. (B.Mus., 1951), and with W. Apel and P. Nettl at Ind. Univ. (M.A., 1953; Ph.D., 1958, with the diss. *Moravian Music in Salem: A German- American Heritage*). He was asst. prof. of musicology at Salem Coll., Winston-Salem, N.C. (1954–64), and also director of the Moravian Music Foundation (1956–64). He then was prof. of musicology at the Univ. of Md. (1964–72), and subsequently a prof. and head of the music dept. at the Univ. of British Columbia (1972–75).—**NS/LK/DM**

McCorkle, Susannah, American singer; b. Berkeley, Calif., Jan. 1, 1946. She has developed into one of the most intelligent and incisive lyric interpreters in jazz. Though she isn't really an improvisor, she is strongly influenced by Billie Holiday and her small, warm voice packs an emotional wallop. A polyglot, she has worked as a translator from Italian, Spanish, French, and German into English, and was inspired to become a jazz singer when she first heard a Billie Holiday record while studying in Paris. Rather than pursue her budding career as a fiction writer, she threw herself into jazz, singing in Rome nightclubs. She moved to England in 1971 and hooked up with cornetist Dick Sudhalter and pianist Keith Ingham, who worked as her musical director for a number of years. Performing with Bobby Hacket, Ben Webster, and Dexter Gordon helped cement her jazz credentials, and her first N.Y. gig at the Riverboat room in 1975 spread her reputation. She has recorded a series of excellent thematic albums, first for Inner City and PA/USA and later for Concord.

DISC.: *The Songs of Johnny Mercer* (1977); *Over the Rainbow—The Songs of E.Y. "Yip" Harburg* (1980); *Thanks for the Memories—The Songs of Leo Robin* (1984); *How Do You Keep the Music Playing* (1985); *No More Blues* (1989); *Sabia* (1990); *I'll Take Romance* (1992); *From Bessie to Brazil* (1993); *From Broadway to Bebop* (1994); *Easy to Love—The Songs of Cole Porter* (1996); *Let's Face the Music* (1997).—**AG**

McCormack, John, famous Irish-born American tenor; b. Athlone, June 14, 1884; d. Booterstown County,

Dublin, Sept. 16, 1945. Straddling the classical and popular music fields, McCormack helped establish the recording medium. He reached his popular peak as a recording artist in the 1910s, when he was among the most successful singers in the world. He is reported to have sold 200 million records worldwide during his lifetime, and unlike many of the top recording stars who began in the acoustic era of recording, his work has maintained its popularity and is reissued continually.

McCormack's parents were both Scottish. He graduated from Sligo Coll. with academic honors at age 18 and went to Dublin to take the civil service examination. His budding career as a government official was sidetracked when Dr. Vincent O'Brien, choirmaster of the Palestrina Choir of Dublin's Cathedral, heard him sing and had him join the choir while giving him private lessons. He won a gold medal in Dublin at the National Irish Festival in 1903. Another gold medal winner at the festival was soprano Lily Foley. In 1904 both singers were part of the Dublin Catholic Choir that went to the U.S. to appear at the St. Louis Exposition. While there, they became engaged; married on July 2, 1906, and had two children, Cyril and Gwendolyn.

McCormack made his first recordings in London in 1904, then moved to Italy, where he studied with Vincenzo Sabbatini in Milan; he made his opera debut Jan. 13, 1906 in Savona, singing Fritz in *L'Amico Fritz*. He moved to London, and on Feb. 17, 1907, publisher Arthur Boosey heard him at a Sunday League concert and hired him to sing at his Boosey London Ballad Concerts. This led to McCormack's British opera debut at Covent Garden in *Cavalleria Rusticana* on Oct. 15, 1907. Brought back to America by impresario Oscar Hammerstein I, he made his U.S. opera debut at the Manhattan Opera House in *La Traviata* on Nov. 10, 1909. He was a member of the Boston Opera (1910–11) and the Chicago Opera (1912–14). Meanwhile, Victor Records had purchased his contract from the British Odeon label and set him to work recording a combination of opera arias, sacred music, sentimental ballads, and traditional Irish material.

He scored his first major U.S. hit with "I'm Falling in Love with Someone" from Victor Herbert's operetta *Naughty Marietta* in 1911. Such subsequent hits as "I Hear You Calling Me" (his signature song, thought to have sold nearly two million copies) (1911), "Mother Machree" (1911), and "It's a Long, Long Way to Tipperary" (1915) helped make him overwhelmingly popular, and he abandoned opera to become a full-time concert and recording artist. He also became an American citizen. He had hits with "Somewhere a Voice Is Calling" (1916), "The Sunshine of Your Love" (1916), "The Star-Spangled Banner" (released shortly after the U.S. entry into World War I in 1917), "Send Me Away with a Smile" (1917), and Irving Berlin's "All Alone" (1925), which he introduced on a radio tribute to Berlin in 1924.

McCormack appeared in one of the earliest talking motion pictures, *Song o' My Heart* (1930); his only other film was the British feature *Wings of the Morning* (1937). After a farewell tour in 1938, he retired to Ireland, where he performed for the Red Cross and on the BBC during World War II. He made his last recordings in 1942.

BIBL.: P. Key, *J. M.: His Own Life Story* (Boston, 1918); L. Strong, *J. M.* (London, 1941); L. McCormack (his widow), *I Hear You Calling Me* (Milwaukee, 1949); L. MacDermott Roe, *J. M.: The Complete Discography* (London, 1956; 2nd ed., 1972); R. Foxall, *J. M.* (London, 1963); G. Ledbetter, *The Great Irish Tenor* (London, 1977).—WR

McCoy, Seth, black American tenor and teacher; b. Sanford, N.C., Dec. 17, 1928; d. Rochester, N.Y., Jan. 22, 1997. He studied at the N.C. Agricultural and Technical Coll. (graduated, 1950), then pursued vocal training with Pauline Thesmacher at the Cleveland Music School Settlement and with Antonia Lavanne in N.Y. He first gained notice as a soloist with the Robert Shaw Chorale (1963–65), with which he toured throughout the U.S. and South America; later appeared with the Bach Aria Group (1973–80); also was a soloist with such leading U.S. orchs. as the N.Y. Phil., Boston Sym. Orch., Chicago Sym. Orch., and Los Angeles Phil. In 1978 he made his European debut at the Aldeburgh Festival. On Feb. 17, 1979, he made his Metropolitan Opera debut in N.Y. as Tamino. His London debut was as soloist in Bach's Christmas Oratorio in 1986. He taught at the Eastman School of Music in Rochester, N.Y. (from 1982). —NS/LK/DM

McCoy, William J., American composer; b. Crestline, Ohio, March 15, 1848; d. Oakland, Calif., Oct. 15, 1926. His family moved to Calif. when he was a child. He began to compose at the age of 12, and then was sent to N.Y. to study with William Mason; he later studied at the Leipzig Cons. with Reinecke and Hauptmann. His Sym. in F was conducted in Leipzig by Reinecke in 1872. He returned to Calif. and wrote some theater music for the Bohemian Club there (*Harmadryads, The Cave Man*, etc.). He also wrote an opera, *Egypt* (2 acts presented at the Berkeley Music Festival, Sept. 17, 1921), for which he received the Bispham Medal of the American Opera Soc. of Chicago. Other works include *Yosemite*, overture, Violin Concerto, a suite from *A Masque of Apollo* (*Prelude, Dance,* and *The Naiad's Idyl*), and numerous songs. He also wrote a textbook, *Cumulative Harmony.*—NS/LK/DM

McCracken, James (Eugene), remarkable American tenor; b. Gary, Ind., Dec. 16, 1926; d. N.Y., April 29, 1988. After working at the Roxy Theatre in N.Y., he sang at Radio City Music Hall and appeared in minor roles on Broadway; following formal vocal studies with Wellington Ezekiel, he made his operatic debut as Rodolfo with the Central City Opera in Colo. (1952). On Nov. 21, 1953, he made his first appearance at the Metropolitan Opera in N.Y. as Parpignol; continued to sing minor roles there until he decided to try his fortune in Europe in 1957. After further vocal training with Marcello Conati in Milan, he joined the Zürich Opera in 1959 and proved himself in major roles there. He soon gained wide recognition for his portrayal of Verdi's Otello, a role he sang to great acclaim at the Metropolitan Opera on March 10, 1963; remained on its roster until quitting the company in a dispute with the management in 1978. In 1983 he returned to the Metropolitan Opera as a participant in its Centennial Gala; he rejoined its roster in 1984, singing there with distinction until his death. He also appeared as a guest artist with major U.S. and European opera houses, and as a soloist with leading orchs. He often made joint appearances with his wife, **Sandra Warfield**. In addition to Otello, he won renown as Canio, Florestan, Don José, Radames, Samson in Saint-Saëns's opera, and Bacchus in Strauss's *Ariadne auf Naxos*. With his wife, he publ. the memoir *A Star in the Family* (ed. by R. Daley; N.Y., 1971). —NS/LK/DM

McCreesh, Paul, remarkable English conductor and music scholar; b. London, May 24, 1960. He received his education at the Univ. of Manchester, where he specialized in music, performance, and musicology (Mus.B., 1981). While still a student there, he formed his own chamber choir and period- instrument ensemble. In 1982 he founded the Gabrieli Consort and Players in London, which he molded into an outstanding choral and period-instrument ensemble, known for its extraordinary technical expertise and refinement. His best-selling recording of *A Venetian Coronation 1595* in 1990 established his reputation. He conducted his ensemble throughout England, on British radio and television, and on tours of Europe. In 1997 he conducted his ensemble on a highly successful debut tour of the U.S., and was engaged to tour the U.S. with it in 1999. As both an interpreter and music scholar, McCreesh has brought insight and erudition to his handling of works from the Venetian High Renaissance and Baroque eras. While he sometimes provokes controversy, he always elicits respect and often accolades for his imaginative performances. He has recently appeared as a guest conductor of modern orchs. and opera houses in Europe and the U.S., and has expanded his repertoire to include scores ranging from Mozart to Britten. His recordings have won a number of prestigious prizes, including *Gramophone* Awards (1990, 1993) and Diapason d'Or prizes (1994, 1999).—NS/LK/DM

McCurdy, Alexander, American organist, choirmaster, and pedagogue; b. Eureka, Calif., Aug. 18, 1905; d. Philadelphia, June 1, 1983. He was a student of Farnum (1924–27) and at the Curtis Inst. of Music in Philadelphia (graduated, 1934). In 1926 he made his debut at N.Y.'s Town Hall, and thereafter toured extensively as a recitalist, often appearing in duo recitals with his wife, harpist Flora Greenwood. From 1927 to 1972 he was organist and choirmaster at Philadelphia's Second Presbyterian Church. He was head of the organ dept. at the Curtis Inst. of Music (1935–72) and Westminster Choir Coll. in Princeton, N.J. (1940–65).—NS/LK/DM

McDaniel, Barry, American baritone; b. Lyndon, Kans., Oct. 18, 1930. He was a student at the Juilliard School of Music in N.Y. and of Alfred Paulus and Hermann Reutter at the Stuttgart Hochschule für Musik. In 1953 he made his recital debut in Stuttgart. After appearing in opera in Mainz (1954–55), Stuttgart (1957–59), and Karlsruhe (1960–62), he was a principal member of the Deutsche Oper in Berlin (from 1962). On Jan. 19, 1972, he made his Metropolitan Opera debut in N.Y. as Pelléas, remaining on the roster for that season. His guest engagements took him to most of the leading opera houses and festivals. He also appeared widely as a concert artist and recitalist. His expansive repertoire ranged from early music to contemporary scores.—NS/LK/DM

McDermott, Vincent, American composer and teacher; b. Atlantic City, N.J., Sept. 5, 1933. He studied with Rochberg at the Univ. of Pa. (B.F.A. in composition, 1959; Ph.D. in music history and theory, 1966) and took a course in music history at the Univ. of Calif. at Berkeley (M.A., 1961); also received instruction in composition from Milhaud and Stockhausen. He studied the tabla at the Ali Akbar Khan Coll. in Oakland, Calif. (1973), and the Javanese gamelan at the Akademi Seni Karawitan Indonesia in Surakarta (1971, 1978). He taught at the Hampton Inst. in Va. (1966–67), at the Wisc. Cons. of Music in Milwaukee (1967–77), and at Lewis and Clark Coll. in Portland, Ore. (from 1971). In 1980 he held the directorship of the Venerable Showers of Beauty gamelan. His music draws freely upon both Western and Eastern elements.

Works: DRAMATIC: *A Perpetual Dream*, chamber opera (1978); *Spirits among the Spires*, chamber opera (1987); *The King of Bali*, opera (Portland, Ore., April 20, 1990); *Mata Hari*, chamber opera (1994; Dallas, April 21, 1995). **ORCH.:** *Siftings upon Siftings* (1976); *Solonese Concerto* for Piano, Voice, and Orch. (1979); *Prelude, Waltz, and Chorale* for String Quartet and Chamber Orch. (1985); *Titus Magnificus*, fanfare (Cincinnati, Sept. 23, 1994). **CHAMBER:** *3 for 5* for Flute, Alto Saxophone, Vibraphone, Piano, Tabla or Bongos, and Cymbal (1970); *Komal Usha-Rudra Nisha* for Sitar, Flute, Guitar, and Double Bass (1972); *Time Let Me Plan and Be Golden in the Mercy of His Means* for Guitar and Harpsichord (1973); *Dreams, Listen* for Viola and Piano (1974); *Kagoklaras* for Prepared Piano and Gamelan (1981); *The Bells of Tajilor* for Gamelan (1984); String Quartet No. 1, *Fugitive Moons* (1991); *Price's Fancy and Gavotte* for Viola and Piano (1992). **VOCAL:** 4 numbered cantatas: *Mixes No. 1* for Voices, Violin, and Percussion (1971), No. 2, *Thou Restless Ungathered* for Soprano or Tenor, Clarinet, and Tape (1973), No. 3, *Swift Wind* for High Voice and Double Bass (1974), and No. 4, *Slayer of Time, Ancient of Days* for Soloists, Chorus, English Horn, Guitar, and Percussion (1977); *Laudamus* (1980); *The Book of the Lover, the Beloved, and the Alone* for Voice and Instruments (1980); *Tagore Songs* for Soprano and Guitar (1981); *Sweetbreathed Minstrel* for 2 Voices, Viola, and Gamelan (1982); *The Dark Laments of Ariadne and of Attis*, 2 songs for Soprano, Narrator, Viola, and Tape, after Catullus (1983); *Sir Christemas* for Men's Chorus and Percussion (1990). **TAPE AND MIXED MEDIA:** *He Who Ascends by Ecstasy into Contemplation of Sublime Things Sleeps and Sees a Dream* for Piano and Tape (1972); *Pictures at an Exhibition*, multimedia piece (1975); *Orpheus* for Tape and Video (1975); *Rain of Hollow Reeds* for Tape (1977); *A Perpetual Dream* for Voice, Tape, and 1 or 2 Dancers (1978); *Execution—what! what? what*, multimedia piece (1980). —NS/LK/DM

McDonald, Harl, American pianist, music administrator, and composer; b. near Boulder, Colo., July 27, 1899; d. Princeton, N.J., March 30, 1955. He studied at the Univ. of Southern Calif. in Los Angeles (Mus.B., 1921), then continued his studies in Leipzig at the Cons.

and the Univ. (diploma, 1922). He made tours of the U.S. as a pianist from 1923. He taught at the Philadelphia Musical Academy (1924–26) and the Univ. of Pa. (1926–46), where he later was a prof. and director of its music dept. He was also general manager of the Philadelphia Orch. (1939–55).

WORKS: ORCH (all 1st perf. in Philadelphia unless otherwise given): 4 syms.: No. 1, *The Santa Fe Trail* (1932; Nov. 16, 1934), No. 2, *The Rhumba* (1934; Oct. 4, 1935), No. 3, *Lamentations of Fu Hsuan*, for Soprano, Chorus, and Orch. (1935; Jan. 3, 1936), and No. 4, *Festival of the Workers* (1937; April 8, 1938); *3 Poems on Aramaic Themes* (1935; Dec. 18, 1936); Concerto for 2 Pianos and Orch. (1936; April 2, 1937); *San Juan Capristrano*, 2 nocturnes (1938; Boston, Oct. 30, 1939); *The Legend of the Arkansas Traveler* (1939; Detroit, March 3, 1940); *Chameleon Variations* (1940); *From Childhood* for Harp and Orch. (1940; Jan. 17, 1941); *Bataan* (Washington, D.C., July 3, 1942); *Saga of the Mississippi* (1943; April, 9, 1948); *My Country at War*, symphonic suite (1943); Violin Concerto (1943; March 16, 1945); *Song of the Nations* for Soprano and Orch. (1945); *Overture for Children* (1950). **CHAMBER**: 2 piano trios (1931, 1932); *Fantasy* for String Quartet (1932); *String Quartet on Negro Themes* (1933); numerous piano pieces. **VOCAL**: *The Breadth and Extent of Man's Empire* for Chorus (1938); *Songs of Conquest* for Chorus (1938); *Lament for the Stolen* for Women's Voices and Orch. (1939); *Dirge for 2 Veterans* for Women's Voices and Orch. (1940); *Wind in the Palm Trees* for Women's Voices and Strings (1940); *God Give us Men* for Voices and Orch. (1950); numerous other vocal pieces. **—NS/LK/DM**

McDonald, Michael, the voice behind The Doobie Brothers' second coming, and one of the great blue-eyed soulmen of the 1980s; b. St. Louis, Mo., Feb. 12, 1952. By the time he was 11, Michael McDonald started playing in local bands, working his way through the club circuit to a recording contract with RCA that sent him to Los Angeles when he was 20 years old. When the records stiffed, he started doing session work, landing a semi-permanent place with Steely Dan, playing keyboards and singing harmony vocals. In 1978, studio guitarist Skunk Baxter had joined the Doobie Brothers. When their leader Tom Johnson fell ill, Baxter suggested they hire McDonald. He and Baxter moved the band in a more Steely Dan-ish direction with hits like "Minute By Minute," "What a Fool Believes," and "Takin' It to the Streets." (For more see Doobie Brothers entry.)

When the Doobie Brothers broke up in 1982, McDonald released a solo album, *If That's What It Takes*, which went gold and rose to #6, largely on the strength of the #4 hit single, "I Keep Forgetting," a loose rewrite of an old 1960s hit written by Lieber and Stoller for Chuck Jackson. McDonald had a minor hit with the title track from his 1985 album *No Looking Back*. While his subsequent albums were commercial disasters (to the point that he quipped A&R people would rather see "[me] walk down the hall with explosives strapped to my body than another record in my hand"). However, he did have great success with other artists, reaching #19 in 1984 with "Yah Mo B There," a duet with James Ingram, and topping the charts and going gold with the 1986 Patti LaBelle duet "On My Own." He reached #7 on his own that year with "Sweet Freedom," the theme

from the Billy Crystal/Gregory Hines film *Running Scared*. In 1987, he joined the Doobie Brothers on a reunion tour. In 1991, he toured with Donald Fagan's N.Y. Rock and Soul Review, and was featured on the album culled from the tour. He continues to have success as a songwriter, studio musician, and producer. Early in 2000, he was honored with a tribute concert that featured the Doobie Brothers, Kenny Loggins, Ray Charles, Pattie LaBelle, James Ingram, Toto, Christopher Cross, Boz Scaggs, and other performers who had benefited from McDonald's artistry in the studio.

DISC.: *That Was Then* (1982); *If That's What It Takes* (1982); *No Lookin' Back* (1985); *Take It to Heart* (1990); *Blink of an Eye* (1993); *Blue Obsession* (2000).**—HB**

McDonald, Susann, noted American harpist and pedagogue; b. Rock Island, Ill., May 26, 1935. She began harp study when she was 6, then took lessons with Marcel Grandjany in N.Y. (1948) and Marie Ludwig in Chicago (1948–52). She continued her training in Paris at the École Normale de Musique and privately with Henriette Renie (1952; 1953–55), and was also a scholarship student of Lily Laskine at the Paris Cons. (1954–55), graduating with the premier prix in 1955, the first American to attain that distinction for harp. She subsequently pursued an outstanding concert career, playing with most of the leading orchs. of the world and appearing as a recitalist in the major music centers. She was artist-in-residence (1963–70) and assoc. prof. (1970–81) at the Univ. of Ariz.; was also a lecturer at the Univ. of Southern Calif. in Los Angeles (1966–81) and head of the harp dept. at the Juilliard School in N.Y. (1975–85); was chairman of the harp dept. at the Ind. Univ. School of Music in Bloomington (from 1981); served as artistic director of the World Harp Congress (from 1981). She ed. a number of works for her instrument. A remarkable virtuoso, she maintains an extensive repertoire, which ranges from early works to contemporary scores.**—NS/LK/DM**

McDonnell, Donald (Raymond), American composer and teacher; b. Helena, Mont., Feb. 14, 1952. He studied saxophone and gained practical experience as a jazz player and arranger. He pursued his education at the Berklee Coll. of Music (B.Mus., 1975), Boston Univ. (M.Mus., 1982), and Brandeis Univ. (Ph.D., 1987), his principal composition mentors being Imbrie, Del Tredici, Berger, and Boykan. In 1975 he joined the faculty of the Berklee Coll. of Music.

WORKS: Sonata for Alto Flute and Guitar (1982); *The Road Not Taken* for Soprano and Piano (1982); *Introduction and Fanfare* for 7 Brass and 2 Percussion Instruments (1982); Concertino for Alto Saxophone and Orch. (1982); *A Warm Tension From the Curved Line* for Piano (1983); Saxophone Quartet (1984); *Parvis Mundi* for Piano (1985); *Nexus/Dreamscape* for Flute, Clarinet, Bassoon, Violin, Viola, Cello, and Piano (1986); *Wall Music*, computer-realized music synthesis (1987); *Flow Gently Sweet Afton* for Chorus (1987); *Psalm XL* for Chorus, Brass Quintet, and Organ (1988); *Midwinter Sauna* for Soprano and Piano (1989).**—NS/LK/DM**

McDonough, Dick (actually, **Richard**), early jazz guitarist, banjo player; b. N.Y., July 30, 1904; d.

there, May 25, 1938. Throughout the late 1920s and 1930s, McDonough took part in hundreds of recordings with Red Nichols, Sam Lanin, Dorsey Brothers, and many others. He worked in duet with Carl Kress during the 1930s, and led his own radio and recording band; his single-string leads and imaginative chord work set a new standard for acoustic jazz guitar. McDonough collapsed while working at the NBC studios in N.Y., was taken to a hospital where an emergency operation failed to save his life

Disc.: *Chasing a Buck* (1934).—**JC/LP**

McDowell, John Herbert, American composer; b. Washington, D.C., Dec. 21, 1926; d. Scarsdale, N.Y., Sept. 3, 1985. He studied at Colgate Univ. (B.A., 1948) and at Columbia Univ. with Luening, Beeson, and Goeb (M.A., 1957), then held a Guggenheim fellowship in 1962. He devoted his energies chiefly to music for the theater and dance.

Works: *Good News from Heaven,* cantata (1957); *Four Sixes and a Nine* for Orch. (1959); *Accumulation* for 35 Flutes, Strings, and Percussion (1964); 100-odd pieces for dance, among them *Insects and Heroes* (1961); *From Sea to Shining Sea,* an homage to Ives (1965); *Dark Psalters* (1968).—**NS/LK/DM**

McEntire, Reba, country chanteuse turned actress; b. Chockie, Okla., March 28, 1954. This ropin'-and-ridin' sweetheart began her career very much in a new country-cowgirl mold, but has since veered increasingly—and very successfully—into being the ultimate country diva and an industry power-broker.

McEntire came from an authentic rodeo family; her grandfather was a celebrity on the national rodeo circuit, and her father a talented roper. Along with Reba, her brother, Pake, and two sisters, Alice and Susie, all performed in rodeos, and the four formed a family singing group. They scored a local hit in 1971 with a ballad memorializing their grandfather, "The Ballad of John McEntire." Country star Red Steagall heard Reba belt out the national anthem at the National Rodeo Finals in Oklahoma City in 1974, and invited her to come to Nashville to make a demo. Reba, her mother, and brother all ended up in music city, and both brother and sister made their first albums in late 1975.

Reba's first recordings were in a traditional style, and although they forecast the new country trends of the next decade, they failed to find much chart action. Meanwhile, she married Charlie Battles (a champion steer wrestler) and got her teaching certificate if her singing career failed to take off. In the late 1970s and early 1980s she finally began to see some chart action, covering Patsy Cline's "Sweet Dreams" and "A Poor Man's Roses;" her first #1 record came in 1983 with "Can't Even Get the Blues." McEntire's producer insisted she record the song, although she resisted cutting another ballad, preferring to try some more uptempo material.

She reached her greatest popularity in the mid-1980s. Her highly emotionally charged vocals were perfectly suited to the often melodramatic material she recorded. She did however maintain a country-influenced technique, using bends, twirls, trills, and even a slight yodel, all found in traditional mountain singing, to give her vocals added depth and authenticity. Meanwhile, her image was constantly being pushed upscale by her managers, who were steering her trying to make her a Vegas-style diva.

In 1987, McEntire divorced her first husband, and two years later wed her steel guitarist-road manager, Narvel Blackstock. The duo began building McEntire's empire, taking over the responsibility of managing and booking her act, working with the record company and producers to shape her image, and even becoming involved in the nuts and bolts of song publishing and transporting equipment for tours. Although McEntire took a more active hand in her career, there was not much change in the music that she produced; she continued to turn out finely crafted pop ballads, with the occasional, more spirited number thrown in for variety. She also began to pursue an acting career, landing some minor roles in TV and movies; but her best acting remained in her videos in which she continued to project a feisty, yet down-home and loveable personality.

Disc.: *Reba McEntire* (1977); *Out of a Dream* (1979); *Feel the Ire* (1980); *Heart to Heart* (1981); *Unlimited* (1982); *Behind the Scene* (1983); *Just a Little Love* (1984); *My Kind of Country* (1984); *Have I Got a Deal for You* (1985); *Whoever's in New England* (1986); *Reba Nell McEntire* (1986); *The Last One to Know* (1987); *Merry Christmas to You* (1987); *Reba* (1988); *Sweet 16* (1989); *Live* (1989); *Rumor Has It* (1990); *For My Broken Heart* (1991); *It's Your Call* (1992); *Read My Mind* (1994); *Starting Over* (1995); *What if it's You* (1996); *What If* (1997); *Moments and Memories* (1998); *If You See Him* (1998); *Secret of Giving* (1999); *So Good Together* (1999).—**RC**

McEwen, Sir John (Blackwood), Scottish composer and pedagogue; b. Hawick, April 13, 1868; d. London, June 14, 1948. He studied at Glasgow Univ. (M.A., 1888) and at the Royal Academy of Music in London with Corder, Matthay, and Prout. He taught piano in Glasgow (1895–98) and composition at the Royal Academy of Music in London (1898–1936); in 1924 he succeeded Alexander Mackenzie as principal, retiring in 1936. He was knighted in 1931.

Works: **ORCH.:** 2 syms.: No. 1 (1892–98) and No. 2, *Solway* (1911); 4 suites (1893, 1935, 1935, 1941); Viola Concerto (1901). **CHAMBER:** 17 string quartets (1893–1947); 7 violin sonatas (1913–39); 7 Bagatelles "Nugae" for Strings (1912); *Scottish Rhapsody* for Violin and Piano (1915); Viola Sonata (1930); piano pieces. **VOCAL:** Songs.—**NS/LK/DM**

McFerrin, Bobby (actually, **Robert**), gifted black American vocalist and conductor, son of **Robert McFerrin**; b. N.Y., March 11, 1950. He studied theory from the age of 6 and played piano in high school, forming a quartet that copied the styles of Henry Mancini and Sergio Mendes. In 1970 he heard Miles Davis's fusion album *Bitches Brew* and completely changed his musical direction. He studied music at Sacramento State Univ. and at Cerritos Coll.; then played piano professionally until 1977, when he began to develop his voice; toured in 1980 with jazz vocalist Jon Hendricks, and debuted a solo act in 1982. His recordings include *Bobby McFerrin* (1982), *The Voice* (1984), *Spontaneous Improvisation* (1986), *Simple Pleasures* (1988; includes the song *Don't Worry, Be Happy*, which made him a household name), and *Medicine Music* (1991); he also made several music videos and sang with Herbie Hancock, Yo-Yo Ma, Manhattan Transfer, and others. In 1989 he created the sound track for *Common Threads*, a 1989 documentary on the AIDS quilt. McFerrin began studying conducting in 1989, making his debut with a performance of Beethoven's Sym. No. 7 with the San Francisco Sym. on March 11, 1990. From 1994 to 1996 he held the Creative Chair of the St. Paul (Minn.) Chamber Orch. Technically, McFerrin is a virtuoso, using a remarkable range of voices with sophisticated control and accompanying them with body percussion, breath, and other self-generated sounds. Aesthetically, he fuses a number of musical styles, including jazz, rock, and New Age, in a brilliant palette; his solo and ensemble shows are based on various improvisatory structures through which he produces highly polished, expertly burnished works.

DISC.: *Bobby McFerrin* (1982); *The Voice* (1984); *Spontaneous Inventions* (1985); *Spontaneous* (1986); *Simple Pleasures* (1988); *Play* (1990); *Medicine Man* (1990); *Hush* (1991); *Paper Music* (1995); *Bang! Zoom* (1996); *Mozart Sessions* (1996); *Circlesongs* (1997).—NS/LK/DM

McFerrin, Robert,

black American baritone, father of **Bobby** (actually, **Robert**) McFerrin; b. Marianna, Ariz., March 19, 1921. He studied at Fisk Univ. in Nashville, Chicago Musical Coll. (B.M., 1948), and Kathryn Turney Long School in N.Y. In 1949 he appeared in Weill's *Lost in the Stars*, in Still's *Troubled Island* (with the N.Y.C. Opera), and as Amonasro in *Aida* (with Mary Cardwell Dawson's National Negro Opera Co.); joined the New England Opera Co. in 1950, creating roles in Marc Connelly's play *The Green Pastures* (N.Y., 1951; music by Hall Johnson) and *My Darlin' Aida* (1952), a version of Verdi's opera set in the time of the Confederacy. He won the Metropolitan Auditions of the Air in 1953; became the first black male to join the company, making his debut on Jan. 27, 1955, as Amonasro. After singing in Naples at the Teatro San Carlo, he sang the role of Porgy (played by Sidney Poitier) in the film version of Gershwin's *Porgy and Bess* (1959); also sang on the recording. He toured internationally, giving recitals of arias, art songs, and spirituals.—NS/LK/DM

MC5,

1960s-era politically conscious rock band who later inspired the British punk movement. **MEMBERSHIP:** Rob Tyner (real name, Robert Derminer), voc. (b. Detroit, Dec. 12, 1944; d. Royal Oak, Mich., Sept. 17, 1991); Wayne Kramer, gtr. (b. Detroit, April 30, 1948); Fred "Sonic" Smith, gtr. (b. W.Va., Aug. 14, 1949; d. Detroit, Nov. 4, 1994); Michael Davis, bs.; Dennis Thompson, drm.

In 1964, guitarists Wayne Kramer and Fred "Sonic" Smith formed the Bounty Hunters in Lincoln Park, Mich. The two recruited vocalist Rob Tyner, bassist Michael Davis, and drummer Dennis Thompson, and changed the group's name to the Motor City Five, moving to Detroit in 1966. Recording two local singles,

MC5 became Detroit's leading underground group by 1967. They came under the management of John Sinclair, founder of the revolutionary White Panther Party and leader of the Trans Love Energies commune. Becoming the "house band" for the Party, MC5 performed in Lincoln Park during the 1968 Chicago Democratic National Convention, which featured one of the most vicious police riots in the history of American politics.

Signed to Elektra Records, MC5 recorded their debut album live at the Grande Ballroom in Detroit in October. Yielding a minor hit with the title song, *Kick Out the Jams* also included "I Want You Right Now," "Come Together," and "Motor City Is Burning." However, the title song featured prominent use of the word "motherfucker," which led to difficulties with Elektra and their eventual dismissal from the label. Sinclair, arrested three times for marijuana possession, began a 10-year sentence for possession of two "joints" in 1969 (the conviction was overturned in 1972 after John Lennon took up his cause). Sinclair later became a poet and blues and jazz scholar and, since the 1980s, has performed poetry with his Blues Scholars band.

MC5 moved to Atlantic Records, where rock critic (and later Bruce Springsteen associate) Jon Landau produced their second album, a studio effort that drew praise but sold poorly. Following 1970's *High Time*, comprising entirely original compositions, Atlantic dropped the band. They moved to England for a while, but broke up in 1972.

Mike Davis resurfaced in the late 1970s with the Detroit-based band Destroy All Monsters with ex-Stooge Ron Asheton. Asheton later joined Dennis Thompson in the group New Race. Wayne Kramer, imprisoned for two years for dealing cocaine in the mid-1970s, returned to music around 1980, forming a short-term partnership with Johnny Thunders, one-time member of The New York Dolls, in Gang War. Kramer later led his own band, Air Raid, and eventually released a solo album on the independent label Epitaph in 1995, followed by 1996's *Dangerous Madness*. Fred "Sonic" Smith formed the band Sonic Rendezvous in the late 1970s and married Patti Smith in 1980. He played a major role in writing, playing, and recording her 1988 comeback album, *Dream of Life*. Rob Tyner died of a heart attack on Sept. 17, 1991, in Royal Oak, Mich., and Fred "Sonic" Smith died from heart failure in Detroit on Nov. 4, 1994.

DISC.: *Babes in Arms* (rec. 1966–70; rel. 1983); *Kick Out the Jams* (1969); *Back in the U.S.A.* (1970); *High Time* (1971); *Thunder Express: One Day Live in Studio* (rec. 1972; rel. 1994). **WAYNE KRAMER AND JOHNNY THUNDERS:** *Gang War* (1990); *Street Fighting* (1994); *Live at the Channel Club* (rec. 1980; rel. 1995). **WAYNE KRAMER:** *The Hard Stuff* (1995); *Dangerous Madness* (1996); *Citizen Wayne* (1997); *LLMF* (1998). **PATTI SMITH WITH FRED "SONIC" SMITH:** *Dream of Life* (1988). **SCOTS PIRATES (WITH FRED "SONIC" SMITH):** *Revolutionary Means* (1995).

BIBL.: J. Sinclair, *Guitar Army: Secret Writings, Prison Writings* (N.Y., 1972); J. Sinclair and R. Levin, *Music and Politics* (N.Y., 1971).

McGarity, (Robert) Lou(is),

trombonist, violinist, singer; b. Athens, Ga., July 22, 1917; d. Alexandria,

Va., Aug. 28, 1971. He began playing violin at the age of seven. Ten years later, he won the state high school contest on violin and shortly afterwards began specializing on trombone. He gigged with various bands while studying at the Univ. of Ga. (1934–36), then joined Kirk DeVore's Band in Atlanta (1936). During 1937 he worked with saxist Nye Mayhew's Band in N.Y. and Boston, and then with Ben Bernie from early 1938 until joining Benny Goodman in October 1940. He left Goodman in autumn 1942, and worked with Raymond Scott at CBS before serving in the U.S. Navy, beginning in the fall of 1945. He rejoined Benny Goodman from early 1946 until August 1946. He left Goodman on the West Coast, did regular studio work, and also worked with Red Nichols at the Morocco Club, Los Angeles. He moved back to N.Y. in June 1947, and worked regularly as a studio musician (including another spell with Raymond Scott). McGarity also frequently appeared with Eddie Condon's Band for club dates and recordings. Ill health temporarily curtailed his activities from 1957, but he returned to full schedule in the 1960s. He toured the Far East with Bob Crosby (late 1964), and continued to play with Crosby in N.Y. through 1966. He played with World's Greatest Jazz Band (1968–70), and then resumed studio work. He suffered a heart attack in summer 1971 while working at Blues Alley, Washington, D.C.

Disc.: *New Orleans Jazz* (1953); *Some Like It Hot* (1959); *Blue Lou* (1960).—**JC/LP**

McGegan, Nicholas, English keyboard player, flutist, and conductor; b. Sawbridgeworth, Hertfordshire, Jan. 14, 1950. He studied piano at London's Trinity Coll. of Music (1968) and also learned to play the flute, specializing in the Baroque flute; pursued his education at Corpus Christi Coll., Cambridge (B.A., 1972), and at Magdalen Coll., Oxford (M.A., 1976). He was active as a flutist, harpsichordist, fortepianist, and pianist in London, where he was also a prof. of Baroque flute (1973–79) and music history (1975–79) and director of early music (1976–80) at the Royal Coll. of Music. From 1979 to 1984 he was artist-in-residence at Washington Univ. in St. Louis; then became music director of the Philharmonia Baroque Orch. in San Francisco (1985), the Ojai (Calif.) Festival (1988), and the Göttingen Handel Festival (1991). From 1993 to 1995 he was principal conductor of the Drottningholm Court Theater in Stockholm. He also appeared widely in Europe and North America as a guest conductor.—**NS/LK/DM**

McGhee, Howard (B.; aka Maggie), jazz trumpeter, composer; b. Tulsa, Okla., March 6, 1918; d. N.Y., July 17, 1987. His family moved to Detroit during his infancy. He played clarinet in high school band, then switched to trumpet. Worked locally prior to joining Lionel Hampton for two months in September 1941. He joined Andy Kirk from November 1941–August 1942 (featured on "McGhee Special") and again during the summer of 1944; in between, he worked with Charlie Barnet. He had brief spells with Billy Eckstine and Count Basie, and then was with Coleman Hawkins in N.Y. and Calif. from November 1944 to March 1945. He led his own small band from 1945 to 1947, took part in freelance recordings, and worked with George Auld's Band. He did several "Jazz at the Philharmonic" tours in the late 1940s, and took his own small band with Jimmy Heath to Europe in May 1948. In November 1948 he led the Jimmy Heath Band under his name for a series of dates in Detroit and at the Apollo Theater in Harlem as part of a show. In December he reformed a small group with Heath which went first to N.Y. Beginning in November 1951, he toured the Pacific area, Japan, and Korea with a small band led by Oscar Pettiford, and remained briefly with the band after Pettiford was deposed in January 1952. He played occasional club dates during the 1950s, and some gigs with Machito's Band, but his problems kicking drugs led to long periods of inactivity. He also worked with rock oriented groups, one of which recorded. During the 1960s, he was again active, playing various jazz festivals, touring Europe in fall of 1964, and working briefly with Duke Ellington (1965). In 1966, he formed his own big band, but within a year was touring Europe again as a soloist. During the 1970s he arranged, composed, and performed with his own quintet and big band. By the early 1980s, heart troubles curtailed his performing, although he occasionally continued to appear; he died in 1987.

Disc.: *Howard McGhee Sextet* (1947); *Sextet with Milt Jackson* (1948); *Howard McGhee's All Stars* (1948); *Night Music* (1951); *Jazz Goes to the Battlefront, Vol. 1, 2* (1952); *Howard McGhee, Vol. 2* (1953); *Return of Howard McGhee* (1955); *Bop Master* (1955); *Life Is Just a Bowl of Cherries* (1956); *Music from "The Connection"* (1960); *Together Again!* (1961); *Sharp Edge* (1961); *Maggie's Back in Town* (1961); *Dusty Blue* (1961); *Nobody Knows You When You're Done* (1962); *House Warmin'!* (1962); *Cookin' Time* (1966); *Just Be There* (1976); *Here Comes Freddy* (1976); *Jazz Brothers* (1977); *Live at Emerson's* (1978); *Home Run* (1978); *Young at Heart* (1979); *Wise in Time* (1979).—**JC/LP**

McGibbon, William, Scottish violinist and composer; b. Edinburgh, c. 1690; d. there, Oct. 3, 1756. He studied violin in his youth with William Corbett in London, then became principal violinist of the Edinburgh Musical Soc. His extant works include 18 trio sonatas in 3 vols. (Edinburgh, 1729 and 1734; London, c. 1745), 6 sonatas for Violin and Basso Continuo (Edinburgh, 1740), 6 sonatas for 2 Flutes (London, 1748), and variations on popular tunes for Solo Violin.—**NS/LK/DM**

McGlaughlin, William, American conductor; b. Philadelphia, Oct. 3, 1943. He studied at Temple Univ. (B.M., 1967; M.M., 1969). He played trombone in the Pittsburgh Sym. Orch. and the Philadelphia Orch., and was founder-conductor of the Pittsburgh Sym. Players and the Pittsburgh Camerata (1973). He became asst. conductor of the Pittsburgh Chamber Orch. in 1975; was also a conductor with the St. Paul (Minn.) Chamber Orch. (1975–78). He was music director of the Eugene (Ore.) Sym. Orch. (1981–85) and the Tucson Sym. Orch. (1983–87). In 1986 he became music director of the Kansas City (Mo.) Sym. Orch. He also was the congenial host of the successful public radio program "St. Paul Sunday."—**NS/LK/DM**

McGlinn, John, American conductor; b. Philadelphia, Sept. 18, 1953. His academic and musical studies

led him to pursue an intensive investigation of the scores of the American musical theater. As a result, he dedicated himself to restoring the classic American musicals to their pristine state via original orchestrations and texts. In 1985 he won critical accolades when he conducted the Jerome Kern Centennial Festival at N.Y.'s Carnegie Hall. In subsequent years, he returned there with major success and also appeared as a guest conductor with various major North American orchs. His recordings were especially valuable in documenting America's golden era on Broadway. He occasionally appeared as an opera conductor as well. In 1988 he made his first appearance in London leading the London Sym. Orch.'s 70th birthday concert in honor of Leonard Bernstein. His championship of Jerome Kern, George Gershwin, Cole Porter, Vincent Youmans, and Richard Rodgers has been particularly notable.
—NS/LK/DM

McGranahan, James, American composer of Sunday-school and gospel hymns and hymnbook compiler; b. near Adamsville, Pa., July 4, 1840; d. Kinsman, Ohio, July 7, 1907. He studied with G.J. Webb, C. Zerrahn, F.W. Root, and G. Macfarren. After serving as a teacher and director of the National Normal Inst. (1875–77), he was music director for the evangelist Daniel Whittle, who provided the texts to many of his tunes. With Sankey and Stebbins, McGranahan ed. the standard compilation *Gospel Hymns and Sacred Songs* (Vols. 3–6, Cincinnati, 1878–91; the entire collection was publ. as *Gospel Hymns nos. 1–6 Complete*, 1894), which included many of his own hymns, among them *Hallelujah for the Cross* (1882), *Showers of Blessing* (1883), and *I Will Sing of My Redeemer* (1887).—LK/DM

McGuire Sisters, The, late-1950s close-harmony group that hit with covers of R&B records. Christine McGuire, b. Middletown, Ohio, July 30, 1929, Dorothy McGuire, b. Middletown, Ohio, Feb. 13, 1930, and Phyllis McGuire, Middletown, Ohio, b. Feb. 14, 1931.

Their mother was an ordained minister, so it's not surprising that the McGuire sisters started singing in the church choir. They moved on to amateur contests and the like. In 1949, they toured veteran hospitals and military bases, which brought them to the attention of a local bandleader, who got them jobs singing on a local radio program. Encouraged by this success, they went to N.Y. to try our for Arthur Godfrey's *Talent Scouts* program. Ignorant of the rules of the entertainment business, they arrived unannounced at the studio, winning an audition through their combination of innocence and audacity. While waiting for a slot to open with Godfrey, they had a further stroke of good luck when they were introduced to Kate Smith's manager. He booked them for eight weeks on Smith's radio and television shows. This opened doors at Coral Records, which signed them up as recording artists. Godfrey booked them on his show when their run with Smith ended. One of the most powerful forces in broadcasting during the early 1950s, the Godfrey show made them stars.

The McGuire's first two years as recording artists were less than successful, however. They cut a series of sides for Coral that sold marginally, right through their first chart record "Pine Tree, Pine Over Me," which reached #26 in the spring of 1954. They finally broke the Top Ten a few months later with a cover of The Spaniels' "Goodnight Sweetheart, Goodnight," which they took to #7. Four months later, they eked into the Top Ten again with "Muskrat Ramble," and finished out the year with two more minor releases. They kicked off 1955 with their first chart-topper, a cover of The Moonglows' "Sincerely" that also went gold. Over the course of the year they had half a dozen more hits. The #11 "It May Sound Silly" was another R&B cover, this one of Ivory Joe Hunter. Their #5 hit "Something's Gotta Give," on the other hand, came from the Fred Astaire film *Daddy Long Legs*. They finished the year with the #10 hit "He."

In 1956, faced with the growing success of rock 'n' roll, the McGuires still managed to land five Top 40 hits, albeit four of them didn't break the Top 30. By 1957, they hit a draught. Early in 1958, however, they had the second biggest hit of their career, the gold "Sugartime," which topped the charts for four weeks. However, although they managed to crack the Top 40 three more times, their days as charting artists were gone. They played the cabaret circuit until the late 1960s, at which point they retired. Phyllis began a solo career, continuing to play cabarets. During the mid-1980s, the McGuire Sisters came out of retirement to play places like Las Vegas. They continue to work that circuit when the mood takes them.

DISC.: *By Request* (1955); *Sincerely* (1956); *He* (1956); *S'Wonderful* (1956); *Do You Remember When?* (1956); *Children's Holiday* (1957); *Teenage Party* (1957); *Musical Magic* (1957); *When the Lights Are Low* (1957); *Greetings from the McGuire Sisters* (1958); *Sugartime* (1958); *In Harmony with Him* (1959); *May You Always* (1959); *His and Hers* (1960); *Subways Are for Sleeping* (1961); *Just for Old Times Sake* (1961); *Songs Everybody Knows* (1962); *Showcase* (1963); *The McGuire Sisters Today* (1966).—HB

McGurty, Mark, remarkably gifted American composer whose music possesses an aura of new classicism; b. Newark, N.J., April 28, 1955. He studied at the Juilliard School in N.Y., where his major teachers were Diamond and Carter. He also took lessons in violin with Frank Scocozza, piano with Frances Goldstein, and conducting with Abraham Kaplan. However, he did not at once pursue the occupation of a professional composer or performer, but had to earn a living elsewhere. He was manager of the Orquesta Filarmónica de Caracas in Venezuela (1979–83); concurrently was active as an instructor at the Simon Bolivar Univ. in Caracas, and occasional director for the Opera Nacional of Caracas. His next engagement was with the Opera of the Dominican Republic. In 1985 he moved to Calif., where he worked on the production of recordings for the Pacific Sym. Orch. During all these years, he was intensely working on a number of compositions for theater, orch., and chamber ensembles. In all cases, he favors complex ensembles of variegated instruments marked by a resilient rhythmic beat while the flow of governing melody is never muted.

WORKS: DRAMATIC: Ballet: *The Castle*, after Kafka (1974); *Journey to the Land of the Tarahumaras* (1975). **ORCH.:** *Symphonic Poem* (1975); *Variations on a Gregorian*

Chant (1976); Concerto for Viola and 24 Players (1982); Violin Concerto (1982); Sym. for Strings (1983); *Concerto grosso* for Piano and Strings (1983); *Dirige Domine* for Strings (1985); 2 piano concertos (1985, 1987); *Concerto for Orchestra* (1985); *Sinfonie pour un tombeau d'Anatole* (1987–88); *Oisin and the Gwragedd Annwn* (1988); *Denizens of the Realm Faerie* (1990). **CHAMBER:** Violin Sonata (N.Y., 1974); Quintet (N.Y., 1974); 2 piano sonatas (1975, 1985); *Partita for Violin Alone* (1976); 8 string quartets, including No. 1 (1976), No. 3 (1978), No. 4 (1981), No. 5 (1983), No. 7 (1987), and No. 8, *Armadillo Quartet* (1987); Flute Sonata (1977); *Concert Etudes* for Piano (1983); Chamber Sym. (1983); Woodwind Quintet (1985); Piano Sonata (1985); *Fantasies and Cadenzas* for Oboe Quartet (1987); *Clarinet Alone* (1987); *Sonata and Its Double* for 2 Pianos (1 pianist with midi equipment) (1987); *Whitening* for Soprano and Ensemble (1987); *Songs of the Gwrageth Anoon* for 21 Instruments (Los Angeles, 1987); *Sonata for Violin Alone* (1988); *Scene Concertante* for Flute, Harp, and Strings (Los Angeles, 1988).—**NS/LK/DM**

McHose, Allen Irvine, American music theorist and educator; b. Lancaster, Pa., May 14, 1902; d. Canandaigua, N.Y., Sept. 14, 1986. He studied at Franklin and Marshall Coll. (B.S., 1923; D.F.A., 1948), the Eastman School of Music in Rochester, N.Y. (B.M., 1928; M.M., 1929), and Oklahoma City Univ. (D.Mus., 1945). From 1930 to 1967 he was on the faculty at the Eastman School; from 1931 to 1962, he was chairman of the theory dept. there. He developed a theory of musical analysis based upon a statistical survey of works of J.S. Bach, and propounded it persuasively in his books *Contrapuntal Harmonic Technique of the 18th Century* (1947) and *Basic Principles of the Technique of 18th and 19th Century Composition* (1951). He also publ. *Sight Singing Manual* (1944; with R. Tibbs); *Keyboard and Dictation Manual* (1949; with D. White); *Teachers' Dictation Manual* (1948); and *Musical Style 1850–1920* (1950).—**NS/LK/DM**

McHugh, Jimmy (actually, **James Francis**), American song composer; b. Boston, Mass., July 10, 1894; d. Beverly Hills, Calif., May 23, 1969. McHugh worked mainly in the movies after beginning his career writing nightclub and Broadway revues. Although the productions are largely forgotten, the songs are not: "I Can't Give You Anything but Love," "On the Sunny Side of the Street," and "I'm in the Mood for Love" (all with lyrics by Dorothy Fields). Collaborating primarily with Fields and Harold Adamson, Johnny Mercer, and Frank Loesser, McHugh earned five Academy Award nominations.

McHugh's parents were James A. and Julia Ann Collins McHugh; his father was a plumber, his mother a pianist who gave him his earliest lessons. He also studied with Augustus Cuents, which led him to a job at the Boston Opera House during his high school years and while he was attending Holy Cross Coll. Initially hired as an office boy, he became a rehearsal pianist and was offered a scholarship to the New England Cons. of Music. Instead, he took a job as a song plugger at the Boston office of Irving Berlin's publishing company. His first published song was "Carolina, I'm Coming Back to You" (lyrics by Jack Caddigan; 1916). During World War I he served in the Mass. 101st Cavalry.

McHugh married after the war and fathered a son, James Francis McHugh Jr., who would marry one of Eddie Cantor's daughters and become a theatrical agent; McHugh's marriage ended in divorce. In 1921 he moved to N.Y. and became a partner at Mills Music, a publisher. He began composing material for the shows at the Cotton Club shortly thereafter.

McHugh had his first song in a Broadway musical with "How'd You Like to Be a Kid?" (lyrics by Bennett Sisters and Billy Colligan), which was interpolated into Al Jolson's *Bombo* (N.Y., Oct. 6, 1921). In 1922 he and lyricist Jack Frost updated the 1866 song "When You and I Were Young, Maggie" (music and lyrics by J. A. Butterfield and George Johnson) to create "When You and I Were Young, Maggie, Blues," which became a hit at the end of the year. McHugh's second hit also drew inspiration from an earlier model: "What Has Become of Hinky Dinky Parlay Voo?" (lyrics by Al Dubin and Irving Mills, music also by Irwin Dash), a comedy song popularized by Ernest Hare and Billy Jones in 1924, was a follow-up to the World War I song "Mademoiselle from Armentières."

In 1925, McHugh was involved in the writing of two early hits for Gene Austin. "When My Sugar Walks Down the Street" (music and lyrics by McHugh, Mills, and Austin) became a successful duet record for Austin with Aileen Stanley in the spring, and "Everything Is Hotsy Totsy Now" (lyrics by Mills), the flip side of Austin's first best-seller, "Yes Sir! That's My Baby," hit in September "I Can't Believe That You're in Love with Me" (lyrics by Clarence Gaskill) is included in the sheet music for the Broadway revue *Gay Paree* (N.Y., Aug. 18, 1925) and was performed by Aida Ward at the Cotton Club, but it did not become a record hit until two years later in an instrumental rendition by Roger Wolfe Kahn and His Orch.

McHugh and Mills themselves, billed as the Hotsy Totsy Boys, introduced "The Lonesomest Girl in Town" (lyrics by Dubin and Mills) on radio; Morton Downey had the hit recording the following January. McHugh's last notable song of 1925 was his first for the motion picture *The Big Parade*, "My Dream of the Big Parade" (lyrics by Dubin). The death of silent film star Rudolph Valentino on Aug. 23, 1926, gave McHugh the inspiration for "There's a New Star in Heaven Tonight—Rudolph Valentino" (lyrics by J. Keirn Brennan and Mills); Vernon Dalhart's recording was popular in November.

Around this time, McHugh met Dorothy Fields. They wrote songs for the next edition of the *Cotton Club Revue*, performed by Duke Ellington and His Orch. in December. They then wrote the score for the all-black Broadway revue *Blackbirds of 1928*, which ran for 519 performances and established the writing team as a success. Among the songs was "I Can't Give You Anything but Love," which they had written earlier. (Unsubstantiated rumor holds that "I Can't Give You Anything but Love" was actually written by Fats Waller and Andy Razaf and sold to McHugh.) The song generated a series of recordings, the most successful of which was by Cliff Edwards, a best-seller in October, and the show also produced hits in "Diga Diga Doo" and "Doin' the New Low-Down," released on either side of a Duke Ellington single in November, as well as "I Must Have That Man," recorded by Ben Selvin and His Orch.

McHugh and Fields's second show, *Hello, Daddy!*, starred Fields's father, comedian Lew Fields, and lasted 197 performances, with "In a Great Big Way" becoming a modest hit for Annette Hanshaw in May 1929. During that year McHugh and Fields wrote two editions of the *Ziegfeld Midnight Frolic* and placed their first song in a sound motion picture, "Collegiana," used in Warner Bros.' *The Time, the Place, and the Girl*.

McHugh and Fields began 1930 with *The International Revue*, which ran for only 96 performances on Broadway but produced hits with "On the Sunny Side of the Street" for Ted Lewis and "Exactly Like You" for Ruth Etting, among others. They then signed a $50,000 contract with MGM and went to Hollywood to write their first movie musical, *Love in the Rough*. Released in the fall, the film contained five new McHugh-Fields songs, among them "Go Home and Tell Your Mother," which became a hit for Gus Arnheim and His Orch. Back in N.Y., the team wrote *The Vanderbilt Revue*, which ran only 13 performances but included "Blue Again," a hit for Red Nichols and His Five Pennies in February 1931.

McHugh and Fields had two songs in the revue *Rhapsody in Black* (N.Y., May 4, 1931), one in the musical *Shoot the Works* (N.Y., July 21, 1931), and they wrote two of the three songs used in the play *Singin' the Blues*, which ran 46 performances in the fall. Returning to Hollywood, they contributed to two MGM films released before the end of the year: *The Cuban Love Song*, for which they wrote the title song (music also by Herbert Stothart), a hit for Jacques Renard and His Orch., and *Flying High*. The year 1932 was less busy, but the team did write "Goodbye, Blues" (lyrics also by Arnold Johnson), which became a hit for the Mills Brothers in April and was adopted as their theme song, as well as the stage show opening *Radio City Music Hall* in December, in which they also appeared.

The year 1933 saw an upsurge in McHugh and Fields's movie work, but they spent the early part of the year working on a revue, *Clowns in Clover*, which closed in Chicago but featured "Don't Blame Me," a hit for Ethel Waters and others during the summer. They contributed the title song, not used, to *Dinner at Eight*, which became a hit for Ben Selvin in October, plus songs used in *Meet the Baron*, *The Prize Fighter and the Lady*, and *Dancing Lady*. To start 1934, their "Full of the Devil" was included in the MGM film *Fugitive Lovers*. They wrote "Thank You for a Lovely Evening" for Phil Harris's nightclub act, though Don Bestor and His Orch. had the hit recording in July. "Lost in a Fog" was written for the Dorsey Brothers Orch., which was introduced at the Riviera Café in N.Y. with McHugh singing. Both songs were interpolated into the MGM feature *Have a Heart* in October.

Although McHugh and Fields maintained their partnership, Fields began working independently toward the end of 1934 while retaining McHugh's name as collaborator. Thus, "Serenade for a Wealthy Widow"

(music composed by bandleader Reginald Foresythe) has a lyric credit to McHugh and Fields; Foresythe's hit recording in November was instrumental. McHugh is also nominally co-credited as a lyricist on the Fields songs in the 1935 film version of *Roberta* composed by Jerome Kern, including the hits "Lovely to Look At," which topped the hit parade in April 1935 and was nominated for an Academy Award, and "I Won't Dance." (Both enjoyed their most popular recordings by Eddy Duchin and His Orch.).

McHugh and Fields's partnership ended with three films released in the summer of 1935. "Music in My Heart" was used in *The Nitwits* in June; *Hooray for Love*, released in July, included "I'm Livin' in a Great Big Way," which reached the hit parade in a recording by Louis Prima and His Orch.; and *Every Night at Eight*, released in August, included "I'm in the Mood for Love," which topped the hit parade for Little Jack Little and His Orch. in September.

McHugh signed a short-term contract with 20th Century–Fox. His first assignment was *King of Burlesque*, for which he collaborated with Ted Koehler, notably on "I'm Shootin' High," which reached the hit parade for Jan Garber and His Orch., and "Lovely Lady," in the hit parade for Tommy Dorsey and His Orch. He and Koehler also wrote four songs for the Shirley Temple vehicle *Dimples*. With Gus Kahn, he wrote two hit songs for two films: "With All My Heart," from Paramount's *Her Master's Voice* and "Let's Sing Again." McHugh's third collaborator of the period was his most long-lasting. With Harold Adamson he wrote songs for the 1936 releases *The Voice of Ann Bugle* (MGM), and back at Fox, *Banjo on My Knee*, featuring the hit "There's Something in the Air," which Shep Fields and His Orch. took to the hit parade in February 1937.

McHugh and Adamson signed to Universal in 1937 and the low-budget studio put them to work: They contributed to eight Universal releases for the year, their most notable efforts being *Top of the Town*, with "Where Are You?" on the hit parade for Mildred Bailey in the spring of 1937, and the title song "You're a Sweetheart" on the hit parade for Dollie Dawn in early 1938.

McHugh and Adamson contributed new songs to six Universal features in 1938. The highlights of the year came with two musicals starring Deanna Durbin. *Mad About Music* included "I Love to Whistle," which Fats Waller took to the hit parade in the spring, and *That Certain Age* included "My Own," a hit parade entry for Tommy Dorsey in the fall and McHugh's second song to be nominated for an Academy Award.

After McHugh's Universal contract expired in 1939, he went back to N.Y. and collaborated with Al Dubin, another exile from Hollywood, on a Broadway revue, *The Streets of Paris*. The show, which ran 274 performances, was notable for introducing Carmen Miranda, who sang "South American Way." McHugh returned to Hollywood on a freelance basis, writing four songs with Frank Loesser for Paramount's *Buck Benny Rides Again*, a spring 1940 release starring Jack Benny. The most successful of them was "Say It," which was in the hit parade for Glenn Miller and His Orch. McHugh and Dubin then mounted a second Broadway show with

Keep Off the Grass, but at 44 performances it was a flop. So, McHugh went back to Hollywood and collaborated with Johnny Mercer on RKO's *You'll Find Out*, featuring Kay Kyser and His Orch. Among the six songs were the hits "You've Got Me This Way," for Tommy Dorsey, and "The Bad Humor Man," for Jimmy Dorsey, but "I'd Know You Anywhere" brought McHugh his third Oscar nomination.

McHugh's most significant work of 1941 was a second effort with Mercer, six songs for Paramount's *You're the One*. In 1942 he wrote six songs with Loesser for RKO's *Seven Days' Leave*, among them the hits "Can't Get Out of This Mood," recorded by Kyser, and "A Touch of Texas" and "I Get the Neck of the Chicken," both recorded by Freddy Martin and His Orch.

McHugh enjoyed an unusually busy year in 1943, writing songs for three films and composing his most successful song that wasn't written for film or theater. His first film of the year was the Paramount musical *Happy Go Lucky*, for which he wrote five songs with Loesser, among them the hilarious "'Murder,' He Says," performed by Betty Hutton but recorded for a hit by Dinah Shore, and "Let's Get Lost" and "The Fuddy Duddy Watchmaker," both recorded by Kyser. All the recordings were made a cappella due to the musicians' union recording ban; after it ended, the Andrews Sisters had a fourth hit from the film, "Sing a Tropical Song," in July 1944.

Inspired by the words of pilot and former football star Sonny Bragg, who wrote to him that his injured plane returned from an air battle "on one engine and a prayer," McHugh renewed his partnership with Adamson and the two wrote "Comin' in on a Wing and a Prayer," one of the most successful war-themed songs of World War II. The Song Spinners had the most successful of several recordings, topping the charts in July 1943, and the song sold a million copies of sheet music. McHugh had another success with a similar subject in "Say a Prayer for the Boys Over There" (lyrics by Herb Magidson), which was interpolated into the Deanna Durbin film *Hers to Hold* and nominated for an Academy Award.

McHugh and Adamson wrote seven songs for the next Kay Kyser film, *Around the World*, which opened in November and produced a hit in "Don't Believe Everything You Dream," recorded by the Ink Spots. The duo had nine songs in *Higher and Higher*, Frank Sinatra's first feature film. Sinatra's recordings of "I Couldn't Sleep a Wink Last Night" and "A Lovely Way to Spend an Evening" became hits, as did a version of "The Music Stopped" by Woody Herman and His Orch. "I Couldn't Sleep a Wink Last Night" gave McHugh his fifth Academy Award nomination. The McHugh-Adamson partnership continued in 1944 with two major films for 20th Century–Fox, *Four Jills in a Jeep* and *Something for the Boys*. Dick Haymes, who appeared in *Four Jills in a Jeep*, scored hits with "How Many Times Do I Have to Tell You?" and "How Blue the Night." The duo also contributed to RKO's *Heavenly Days*, *The Princess and the Pirate*, and McHugh teamed with Ralph Freed to write songs for MGM's *Two Girls and a Sailor*.

McHugh and Adamson had another three films in release in 1945: *Bring on the Girls* featured six of their songs; *Nob Hill* had another four, among them the Harry James hit "I Don't Care Who Knows It"; and *Doll Face*'s five songs included two hits for its star, Perry Como—the gold-selling "Dig You Later (A-Hubba-Hubba-Hubba)" and "Here Comes Heaven Again."

McHugh's war-related activities hit a peak during this period. He wrote the songs for the seventh and eighth war-bond drives, "Buy, Buy, Buy a Bond" and "We've Got Another Bond to Buy" (both lyrics by Adamson), featured in the short films *All Star Bond Rally* and *Hollywood Bond Caravan*. He also held a bond rally in Beverly Hills that raised $28 million—a record. His efforts earned him a presidential citation from Harry Truman in February 1947.

McHugh and Adamson had only one new song in a film in 1946, "(I'm Sorry) I Didn't Mean a Word I Said" in 20th Century–Fox's *Do You Love Me?* But they scored three films in 1947: Universal's *Smash-Up: The Story of a Woman*, Republic's *Calendar Girl* and *Hit Parade of 1947*. That year, McHugh married for a second time, again fathering a son, James Francis McHugh III; McHugh and his second wife separated on Dec. 12, 1949.

In 1948, McHugh and Adamson contributed to RKO's Eddie Cantor film *If You Knew Susie* and to the MGM musical *A Date with Judy*. Later, they went to N.Y. and wrote the stage musical *As the Girls Go*, a fantasy set four years in the future after the election of a woman president. The show became a moderate hit, running 420 performances, but due to a second musicians strike its songs were not recorded.

McHugh was less frequently employed in Hollywood after the 1940s. In the spring of 1951, Bing and Gary Crosby had a major revival of "When You and I Were Young, Maggie, Blues," taking it into the Top Ten. McHugh and Adamson had a song, "You'll Know," in the RKO film *His Kind of Woman* that year. McHugh's next song in a motion picture came in 1954 with "Long...Long...Long" (lyrics by Jeannine Roger and Jean Pierre Mottier) in MGM's *The Last Time I Saw Paris*. McHugh and Adamson wrote a new musical, *Strip for Action*, which closed out of town in the spring of 1956, but one of its songs, "Too Young to Go Steady," was recorded by several artists, most successfully by Nat "King" Cole. *The Helen Morgan Story* (1957) was one of many films to use "On the Sunny Side of the Street" but the only one in which the composer appeared playing his own composition as accompaniment to Ann Blyth, portraying Morgan while being dubbed by Gogi Grant. McHugh wrote the title song for the 1958 film *Home Before Dark* with Sammy Cahn, but the song was used only as an instrumental. The songs in 1959's *A Private's Affair* had music and lyrics co-credited to McHugh, Jay Livingston, and Ray Evans.

McHugh engaged in several activities outside of songwriting during the 1950s and 1960s. Starting in late 1952, Jimmy McHugh's Song Stars of Tomorrow, which featured four female singers, an orchestra, and the composer as pianist and emcee, toured clubs throughout the country and made television appearances. During the period, McHugh was president of the Beverly

Hills Chamber of Commerce and vice president of ASCAP. He was also involved heavily in charity work.

McHugh's last work for motion pictures was in 1960 when he placed songs in the films *Let No Man Write My Epitaph* and *Where the Hot Wind Blows* and, with Pete Rugolo, wrote the score for *Jack the Ripper*. In the fall of 1961 the Everly Brothers had a Top 40 revival of "Don't Blame Me." Ten years after his death from a heart attack, McHugh scored his greatest Broadway triumph with *Sugar Babies*, a revue starring Mickey Rooney and Ann Miller made up largely of his songs. It ran 1,208 performances.

WORKS (only works for which McHugh was the primary, credited composer are listed): **MUSICALS/REVUES:** *Cotton Club Revue* (N.Y., Dec. 4, 1927); *Cotton Club Revue* (N.Y., 1928); *Blackbirds of 1928* (N.Y., May 9, 1928); *Hello Daddy!* (N.Y., Dec. 26, 1928); *Ziegfeld Midnight Frolic* (N.Y., Feb. 6, 1929); *Blackbirds of 1929* (N.Y., 1929); *Cotton Club Revue* (N.Y., 1929); *The International Revue* (N.Y., Feb. 25, 1930); *The Vanderbilt Revue* (N.Y., Nov. 3, 1930); *Singin' the Blues* (N.Y., Sept. 16, 1931); *Radio City Music Hall Opening* (N.Y., Dec. 27, 1932); *The Streets of Paris* (N.Y., June 19, 1939); *Keep Off the Grass* (N.Y., May 23, 1940); *As the Girls Go* (N.Y., Nov. 13, 1948); *Sugar Babies* (N.Y., Oct. 9, 1979). **FILMS:** *Love in the Rough* (1930); *Flying High* (1931); *Meet the Baron* (1933); *Hooray for Love* (1935); *Every Night at Eight* (1935); *King of Burlesque* (1935); *Dimples* (1936); *Banjo on My Knee* (1936); *Breezing Home* (1937); *Top of the Town* (1937); *When Love Is Young* (1937); *Merry-Go-Round of 1938* (1937); *Hitting a New High* (1937); *You're a Sweetheart* (1937); *Mad About Music* (1938); *Reckless Living* (1938); *That Certain Age* (1938); *The Road to Reno* (1938); *Buck Benny Rides Again* (1940); *You'll Find Out* (1940); *You're the One* (1941); *Seven Days' Leave* (1942); *Happy Go Lucky* (1943); *Around the World* (1943); *Higher and Higher* (1943); *Four Jills in a Jeep* (1944); *Two Girls and a Sailor* (1944); *Something for the Boys* (1944); *Hi, Beautiful* (1944); *Bring on the Girls* (1945); *Nob Hill* (1945); *Radio Stars on Parade* (1945); *Doll Face* (1945); *Ding Dong Williams* (1945); *Do You Love Me?* (1946); *Somewhere in the Night* (1946); *Smash-Up: The Story of a Woman* (1947); *Calendar Girl* (1947); *Hit Parade of 1947* (1947); with J. Livingston and R. Evans, *A Private's Affair* (1959); with P. Rugolo, *Jack the Ripper* (1960).—**WR**

McIntire, Dennis K(eith), diligent American music historian and lexicographer; b. Indianapolis, June 25, 1944. As a lexicographer, he was autodidact, being mainly inspired by the example of the great Samuel Johnson. His precocious self-assurance was such at the age of 12 he undertook a systematic attack on imperfections in reference books, beginning with misinformative vols. such as *The Lincoln Library of Essential Information.* After 10 years of badgering its eds., he was made an asst. and research ed. of the aforesaid encyclopedia in 1967. His fascination for reference books spurred him on to consume virtually the entire contents of several voluminous standard sources, among them *Baker's Biographical Dictionary of Musicians, Grove's Dictionary of Music and Musicians,* and even the monumental *Encyclopaedia Britannica.* Appalled by the surprising percentage of errors in such dignified reference publications, he undertook a systematic correspondence with their eds., suggesting corrections and additions. In the meantime, he undertook a thorough study of 20th century European history at Ind. Univ., but managed to depart the

halls of academe without a devastating critique of any deficiencies in instruction. He continued to fulfill editorial duties all the while. His capacity of total recall and indefatigability in corresponding with far corners of the musical world enabled him to make valuable additions to the 7th and 8th eds. of *Baker's Biographical Dictionary of Musicians* (1984, 1992), and also contributions to Slonimsky's *Supplement to Music since 1900* (1986) and the 5th ed. of *Music since 1900* (1994). He also lent assistance to *The Concise Oxford Dictionary of Opera* (1979), *The Oxford Dictionary of Music* (1985; 2nd ed., 1994), *The New Everyman Dictionary of Music* (1988), the French ed. of *Baker's Biographical Dictionary of Musicians* (1995), and *The Hutchinson Encyclopedia of Music* (1995). He also served as an adviser and contributor to *The New Grove Dictionary of American Music* (1986), was co-consultant ed. (with D. Cummings) of the 12th ed. of the *International Who's Who in Music* (1990), and subsequently was a contributing ed. to the 13th and 15th eds. (1992–96). He was a contributor to *The New Grove Dictionary of Opera* (1992), and, from 1996 to 1998, a member of the editorial advisory board of the *Encyclopaedia Britannica.* He served as assoc. ed. of *Baker's Biographical Dictionary of 20th Century Classical Musicians* (1997), and then of *Baker's Dictionary of Opera* (2000). He subsequently was Classical music area editor of the present volume. McIntire was also consultant ed. of the *International Authors and Writers Who's Who* (15th to 17th eds., 1997–2001) and the *International Who's Who in Poetry and Poets' Encyclopaedia* (8th to 10th eds., 1997–2001), and was a contributor to *The New Grove Dictionary of Music and Musicians* (rev. ed., 2000).—**NS/LK/DM**

McIntyre, Kalaparusha Maurice (Benford; aka Difda, Kalaparucha Abrah), tenor saxophonist, clarinetist; b. Clarksville, Ark., March 24, 1936. His family moved to Chicago when he was very young. He began playing drums at seven; he studied at the Chicago Music Coll., and performed and studied with J. Gilmore, Dave Young, Nicky Hill, Ken Chaney, Roscoe Mitchell, and Ollie Mabin. He joined R. Abrams's Experimental Band, BACM, worked with Anthony Braxton, percussionist Ajaramu, guitarist J. B. Hutto, and Little Milton. He was a founding participant of the AACM in 1965. He took the name Kalaparusha, moved to N.Y. and began playing with Warren Smith. He worked in both Chicago and N.Y. during the 1970s and 1980s, playing with Jerome Cooper, Warren Smith, Sonelius Smith, and Wilber Morris.

DISC.: *Humility in the Light of the Creator* (1969); *Forces and Feelings* (1970); *Peace and Blessings* (1979); *Ram's Run* (1981).—**LP**

McIntyre, Ken(neth Arthur; aka Makanda), jazz alto saxophonist, reeds player, educator, pianist; b. Boston, Mass., Sept. 7, 1931. He has combined playing and teaching for many years. He studied piano from 1940 to 1945, and bought an alto saxophone from a friend for $45 in June 1950. He studied with Andrew McGhee, Gigi Gryce, and Charlie Mariano. He was in the military from November 1952 until 1954; on his return, he studied at Boston Cons., eventually earning an M.A. in composition. McIntyre primarily played dances and such jobs, though he did open for Sarah Vaughan (with Richard Davis) at a Waltham festival produced by George Wein. He taught at Brandeis Univ. for two years. He formed a band in Boston, made his recording debut on Prestige, then moved to N.Y. where he met Eric Dolphy in 1960. Following a New Jazz release, McIntyre decided to become a full-time professor. In 1966, he recorded with Cecil Taylor, but declined a tour of Europe. He has taught since at SUNY in Old Westbury, Long Island. He occasionally leads his own groups and has recorded with Bill Dixon, Thierry Bruneau, and the Jazz Composers Guild Orch.

DISC.: *Stone Blues* (1960); *Looking Ahead* (1960); *Year of the Iron Sheep* (1962); *Way Way Out* (1963); *Hindsight* (1974); *Open Horizon* (1975); *Introducing the Vibrations* (1976); *Home* (1976); *Chasing the Sun* (1978); *Tribute* (1991).—**LP**

McIntyre, Sir Donald (Conroy),

esteemed New Zealand bass-baritone; b. Auckland, Oct. 22, 1934. He studied at the Guildhall School of Music in London. He made his operatic debut as Zaccaria in *Nabucco* with the Welsh National Opera in Cardiff (1959), and then was a member of the Sadler's Wells Opera in London (1960–67). In 1967 he made his debut as Pizzaro at Covent Garden in London; that same year he made his first appearance at the Bayreuth Festival as Telramund, returning there annually until 1981; sang Wotan there during the centenary *Ring* production in 1976. On Feb. 15, 1975, he made his Metropolitan Opera debut in N.Y. as Wotan. He made guest appearances with many of the leading opera houses of the world. He appeared as Prospero in the British premiere of Berio's *Un re in ascolto* in London and as Wotan in *Die Walküre* in Amsterdam in 1989. In 1990 he sang Hans Sachs in Wellington. He portrayed Gurnemanz in Antwerp in 1996 and King Marke at the Los Angeles Opera in 1997. In 1998 he sang Count Waldner in *Turandot* at the San Francisco Opera. In 1977 he was made an Officer of the Order of the British Empire, and in 1985 a Commander of the Order of the British Empire. In 1992 he was knighted. His other roles include Kaspar in *Der Freischütz*, Attila, Klingsor, Amfortas, the Dutchman, Golaud, and Escamillo.—**NS/LK/DM**

McKay, George Frederick,

American composer and teacher; b. Harrington, Wash., June 11, 1899; d. Stateline, Nev., Oct. 4, 1970. He was a student of Palmgren and Sinding at the Eastman School of Music in Rochester, N.Y., where he was the first student in composition to graduate there (B.M., 1923). In 1927 he joined the faculty of the Univ. of Wash. in Seattle, where he later was a prof. (1943–68). He publ. the book *Creative Orchestration* (1963). In his music, McKay often made use of folk melodies.

WORKS: ORCH.: 4 sinfoniettas (1925–42); *Fantasy on a Western Folk Song* (Rochester, N.Y., May 3, 1933); *From a Mountain Town* (1934); *Port Royal, 1861*, suite for Strings (1939); *Bravura Prelude* for Brass Ensemble (Rochester, N.Y., April 30, 1939); *To a Liberator: A Lincoln Tribute* (1939–40; Indianapolis, March 15, 1940); *Introspective Poem* for Strings (Philadelphia, April 3, 1941); *A Prairie Portrait* (San Francisco, Sept. 4, 1941); *Pioneer Epic* (Oakland, Calif., Feb. 17, 1942); Cello Concerto

(1942); *Music of the Americas*, suites (1947–50); *Evocation Symphony* (1951); *Song Over the Great Plains* (1954); *6 Pieces on Winter Moods and Patterns* (1961). **CHAMBER:** Wind Quintet (1930); Piano Trio (1931); *American Street Scenes* for Clarinet, Bassoon, Trombone, Saxophone, and Piano (1935); *Trombone Sonata* (1951); Suite for Chamber Ensemble (1958); Suite for Harp and Flute (1960); *Sonatina expressiva* for Brass Quintet (1966); *Andante mistico* for 8 Cellos and Piano (1968); 4 string quartets; piano pieces; organ music. **VOCAL:** Choral works; part songs; various other pieces, including works for students. —**NS/LK/DM**

McKee, Andy,

jazz bassist; Philadelphia, Nov. 11, 1953. He studied with Al Stauffer from 1975 to 1978; he played with Richard Davis (1976), and Homer Mensch (1988). In Philadelphia he worked with Hank Mobley, Johnny Hartman, "Cee" Sharp, Walt Dickerson, and Philly Joe Jones, who was a particular influence. After arriving in N.Y. in 1980, he performed with Jaki Byard, Clifford Jordan, Sal Nistico, Charlie Rouse, Billy Harper, Mike Richmond, and Brazilian drummer Edison Machado. While living in Paris in the mid-1980s, he played and toured with Mal Waldron, Clark Terry, Steve Lacy, Don Cherry, Horace Parlan, Steve Grossman, Barry Altschul, Daniel Humair, Marcial Solal, Franco D'Andrea, and others. He has been a longtime member of groups led by Philly Joe Jones, Chet Baker, Michel Petrucciani, and Elvin Jones, as well as the Mingus Dynasty, and since 1997, the Mingus Big Band. He leads Andy McKee & Next. He is a faculty member at The New School, teaches privately, and is a presenter of master-classes at conservatories around the world; he taught at Rutgers-Newark (1995–96).

DISC.: *Sound Roots* (1996).—**LP**

McKellar, Kenneth,

Scottish tenor; b. Paisley, June 23, 1927. He took a course in philology at the Univ. of Aberdeen and received a B.S. degree; then studied voice at the Royal Coll. of Music in London. He subsequently sang with the Carl Rosa Opera Co. in London; later toured the U.S. as a concert singer. He was also a fine interpreter of traditional Scottish ballads, which he included in his concert programs.—**NS/LK/DM**

McKendrick, "Big Mike" (actually, Reuben Michael),

jazz guitarist, banjoist, singer; brother of **Gilbert "Little Mike" McKendrick**; b. Paris, Tenn., 1901; d. Chicago, March 22, 1965. He worked on and off for several years with Oscar "Bernie" Young in the 1920s, with Edgar Hayes's Eight Black Pirates (April–May 1927), Dave Peyton (summer 1927), again with Bernie Young (1928 to spring 1930), and with Tiny Parham in 1929. He worked with Jerome Carrington's Orch. (early 1931), then from spring 1931 until March 1932 and again in 1933. He also acted as band manager for Louis Armstrong. McKendrick led his own band in the 1930s; he also worked with Erskine Tate (1934), Zutty Singleton, and Cleo Brown (1934–35). He continued to lead his own band, and also worked regularly in duo with Ikey Robinson. During the 1950s and early 1960s, he subbed in Franz Jackson's band, and worked with clarinetist Brian Shanley's Band (early 1962), then spent a long spell as house musician at Jazz Ltd., Chicago, until early 1965, when he was hospitalized, suffering from a circulatory ailment.—JC/LP

McKendrick, Little Mike (actually, Gilbert Michael),

jazz banjoist, guitarist, singer; brother of **Reuben Michael "Big Mike" McKendrick**; b. Paris, Tenn., c. 1903; d. Chicago, early 1961. Raised in Paducah. His father, **Gilbert Sr.**, was a violinist who doubled trombone. In the early 1920s "Little Mike" and his four brothers, Reuben Michael (guitar and banjo), Richard Michael (trombone), Daniel Michael (violin), and James Michael (piano), all moved to Chicago. To the utter confusion of discographers they all, at one time or another, worked as Mike McKendrick. "Little Mike" was with Hughie Swift's Orch. in the mid-1920s, then with Doc Cooke before joining Joe Jordan's Sharps and Flats. He briefly led his own band in Chicago, then went to Europe with Eddie South in 1928. "Little Mike" left South in Europe (c. 1931) and for the next eight years worked with international band, mainly in France and Spain. During the late 1920s he was temporarily absent from the music scene after being involved in a shooting incident with Sidney Bechet. He returned to the U.S. in October 1939, worked briefly in N.Y., then returned to Chicago where he formed his own international trio; he continued to lead his own band through the 1950s.—JC/LP

McKenzie, Red (William),

jazz singer, kazoo player, leader; b. St. Louis, Oct. 14, 1899; d. N.Y., Feb. 7, 1948. He was raised in Washington, D.C.; after both his parents died, he moved back to St. Louis. McKenzie worked at various jobs, including a spell as a professional jockey, then together with Jack Bland and Dick Slevin formed a novelty musical act which was subsequently named The Mound City Blue Blowers. At the instigation of bandleader Gene Rodemich they traveled to Chicago to make their recording debut in February 1924. Their initial release, "Arkansas Blues," was a huge seller and they began a long series of theater tours. Eddie Lang joined the group in Atlantic City and later worked with them during their trip to London. They returned to the U.S. in 1925 and recommenced touring. Despite personnel changes, McKenzie continued to lead the group until 1932, playing long residencies in N.Y. and Fla. His 1929 reccording, "(If I Could Be with You) One Hour," featured an early solo by Coleman Hawkins. He also recorded with Red Nichols and Adrian Rollini. During the late 1920s, he was active as a talent scout for recording companies, and helped land recording contracts for Bix Beiderbecke, The Chicago Rhythm Kings, and The Spirits of Rhythm. In 1932, he signed a three year contract to appear with Paul Whiteman's Orch. During his stint with Whiteman, he also led his own band and sang on various recording sessions with other leaders. He left Whiteman to reorganize The M.C.B.B. in the spring of 1933. In 1935, he opened his own club on 52nd Street, N.Y., and revived The M.C.B.B. name for recording sessions. He also recorded with the Bob Crosby band. After the death of his first wife, he left

N.Y. in 1937 and moved back to St. Louis; he returned briefly to N.Y. early in 1939 for a residency at Kelly's, then returned to St. Louis. He spent several years working for a St. Louis brewery and was musically inactive until he performed at an Eddie Condon Town Hall Concert in N.Y. in 1944. He suffered ill health during the last few years of his life; after spending six weeks in St. Clair's Hospital, N.Y., he succumbed to cirrhosis of the liver.

DISC.: *Blue Blues; Fox Trot, for Dancing* (1924); *Deep Second Street Blues: Fox Trot, for Dancing* (1925); *Best Black: Fox Trot* (1925); *There'll Be Some Changes Made* (1927); *Just Friends* (1929); *Hello Lola: Fox Trot* (1929); *Never Had a Reason to Believe in You: Fox Trot* (1929); *Just Friends* (1929); *Red McKenzie* (1935); *Timeless Historical Presents Red McKenzie* (1935); *Wouldn't I Be a Wonder* (1935); *Murder in the Moonlight: It's Love in the First Degree* (1935); *Every Now and Then* (1935); *Sing an Old Fashioned Song: To a Young Sophisticated Lady* (1936); *I Can't Get Started with You: From the Musical production "Ziegfield Follies of 1936"* (1936); *When Love Has Gone* (1936); *I Don't Know Your Name: But You're Beautiful* (1936); *Sweet Lorraine* (1937); *One Hour Fox-Trot* (1939); *Red McKenzie-Eddie Condon Chicagoans* (1944); *Through a Veil of Indifference; It's the Talk of the Town* (1944). **BUD FREEMAN:** *1928–1938* (1928); *Swingin' with the Eel* (1998). **BENNY GOODMAN:** *Early Years* (1992). **COLEMAN HAWKINS:** *Body and Soul* (1927); *1929–1934* (1929); *In the Groove 1926–1939* (1996).—JC/LP

McKibbon, Al(fred Benjamin),

jazz bassist; b. Chicago, Jan. 1, 1919. His father and brother were musicians. Raised in Detroit, he attended Cass Technical H.S. He did early gigs with McKinney's Cotton Pickers (1935), then worked with Kelly Martin, and altoist Ted Buckner before moving to N.Y. He worked with Lucky Millinder (1943), Tab Smith (1945–46), Coleman Hawkins (1946–47), J. C. Heard (1947), Dizzy Gillespie (1947–49), Count Basie (1950), George Shearing (1951–58), and Cal Tjader (1958–59). During the 1960s McKibbon worked in Los Angeles, mainly playing freelance club and concert dates, and recordings; he also worked regularly at NBC studios. He toured extensively with The Giants of Jazz in 1971–72, and also did widespread work with singer Sammy Davis in the 1970s. He remained active in the Los Angeles area through the 1980s, and returned to N.Y. in 1990 to work in the pitband of a Broadway show.

DISC.: *Tumbao Para los Conqueros Di* (1999). **CANNONBALL ADDERLEY:** *Sophisticated Swing* (1957). **LOREZ ALEXANDRIA:** *Alexandria the Great* (1964). **COUNT BASIE:** *1949: Shoutin' Blues* (1949); *Planet Jazz* (1998). **RUTH BROWN:** *Blues on Broadway:* (1989); *Fine and Mellow* (1991). **BENNY CARTER:** *Benny Carter and the Jazz Giants* (1998). **BUCK CLAYTON:** *Classic Swing of Buck Clayton* (1946); *1945–1947* (1998). **MILES DAVIS:** *Birth of the Cool* (1949); *Blue Note and Capitol Recordings* (1949); *Ballads and Blues* (1950). —JC/LP

McKinley, Carl,

American composer and organist; b. Yarmouth, Maine, Oct. 9, 1895; d. Boston, July 24, 1966. He studied with E.B. Hill at Harvard Univ., and in 1929 was appointed instructor of organ and composition at the New England Cons. of Music in Boston. Many of his works were inspired by American subjects.

He wrote *The Blue Flower*, symphonic poem (N.Y., Jan. 18, 1924), *Masquerade*, American rhapsody for Orch. (his most popular work; Chicago North Shore Festival, May 29, 1926), *Caribbean Holiday* (Boston, Nov. 18, 1948), String Quartet, Cello Sonata, and other pieces of chamber music, and organ pieces and songs.—NS/LK/DM

McKinley, Ray(mond Frederick),

jazz drummer, singer, leader; b. Fort Worth, Tex., June 18, 1910; d. Largo, Fla., May 7, 1995. His band at first was known (in 1938) as a popular boogie woogie outfit, but by 1946 was featuring the innovative works of Eddie Sauter. McKinley worked with Duncan Marion's Orch. and the Tracy Brown Band before joining Smith Ballew in 1932, then was with the Dorsey Brothers in 1934. After the brothers split up Ray remained with Jimmy Dorsey until June 1939. Together with Will Bradley, he organized a big band that made its debut in September 1939. He continued co-leading until February 1942, when he left to form his own big band. He joined the U.S.A.A.F. and served in Europe with Glenn Miller's Band. After Miller's death he acted as the band's unofficial leader until its return to the U.S. in July 1945, and then led the band until November 1945. He led his own big band 1946–50, then worked as a solo vocalist, but continued to lead his own band for specific engagements. In the spring of 1956, at the invitation of Glenn Miller's widow, he organized a new Glenn Miller Orch. During the following year he led the band on an extensive tour of Europe; and continued to lead the band with considerable success until early 1966. McKinley then resigned as leader, his place being taken by clarinetist Buddy De France. Following a period of semi-retirement in Conn., he re-formed his own band in the late 1960s. He continued to play during the 1970s and early 1980s. In the mid- 1980s, he was performing in Britain on a popular TV program, but by the 1990s was back in the U.S., playing mostly around Fla., where he died in 1995.

DISC.: *Dixieland Jazz Battle, Vol. 2* (1950); *Swingin' 30s* (1955); *Borderline* (1955); *Glenn Miller Time* (1965).

BIBL.: C. Popa, *Ray McKinley and His Orch.* (Zephyrhills, Fla., 1988).—JC/LP

McKinley, William Thomas,

American composer, pianist, and teacher; b. New Kensington, Pa., Dec. 9, 1938. He began piano lessons at 5, and began playing in local bands around age 10. At 13, he began piano studies with the jazz pianist Johnny Costa. He pursued his academic training with Lopatnikoff, Haieff, and Dorian at the Carnegie Inst. of Technology (B.F.A., 1960). After attending sessions given by Copland, Schuller, and Foss at the Berkshire Music Center at Tanglewood (summer, 1963), he completed his studies with Powell and Moss at Yale Univ. (M.M., 1968; M.F.A., 1969). He taught at the State Univ. of N.Y. at Albany (1968–69), Yale Univ. (1969), the Univ. of Chicago (1969–73), and the New England Cons. of Music in Boston (1973–92). Throughout the years, he was active as a pianist with frequent appearances in jazz settings. In 1991 he founded Master Musicians Collective recordings. Among his various honors were a BMI prize (1963), 8 NEA awards (1976–86), a Koussevitzky Music

Foundation commission (1983), and a Guggenheim fellowship (1985–86). As a composer, McKinley has developed a style that he describes as "neo-tonal," one made imaginative by his use of jazz improvisation.

WORKS: ORCH.: Triple Concerto for Piano, Double Bass, Drums, and Orch. (1970); 3 piano concertos (1974; *O'Leary*, 1987; 1994); *October Night* (1976); 6 syms.: No. 1 (1977; Minneapolis, Jan. 3, 1979), No. 2, *Of Time and Future Monuments* (1978), No. 3, *Romantic* (N.Y., May 18, 1984), No. 4 (1985; N.Y., March 25, 1986), No. 5, *Irish* (Pasadena, Calif., March 18, 1989), and No. 6 (St. Lucia, Australia, Sept. 8, 1990); Cello Concerto (1977); 3 clarinet concertos: No. 1 (1977), No. 2 (Norwalk, Conn., June 2, 1990), and No. 3, *The Alchemical* (1994); *The Mountain* (Pittsburgh, Oct. 17, 1982); *Boston Overture* (Boston, May 6, 1986); Concerto for Flute and Strings (1986); *Tenor Rhapsody* for Tenor Saxophone and Orch. (1988); *Huntington Horn Concerto* (1989); *N.Y. Overture* (1989; N.Y., May 12, 1990); *Jubilee Concerto* for Brass Quintet and Orch. (1990); *Concerto for the New World* for Wind Quintet, Strings, and Percussion (1991; N.Y., Jan. 9, 1992); Chamber Concerto No. 3 (Pittsburgh, April 29, 1991); *Concerto Domestica* for Trumpet, Bassoon, and Orch. (1991; Richmond, Va., March 6, 1992); Concerto No. 3 for Viola and Orch. (1992; N.Y., Feb. 22, 1993); *Silent Whispers* for Piano and Orch. (1992); *Andante and Scherzo* for Piano and Orch. (1993); *Fantasia Variazioni* for Harpsichord and Orch. (1993); *Concerto for Orchestra No. 2* (Seattle, Sept. 27, 1993); *Concert Variations* for Violin, Viola, and Orch. (1993; N.Y., Jan. 31, 1994); *Patriotic Variations: Reading Festival Overture* (1993; Reading, Pa., May 7, 1994); *Lightning*, overture (1993; N.Y., March 30, 1994). **CHAMBER:** 9 string quartets (1959–92); *Attitudes* for Flute, Clarinet, and Cello (1967); *Studies* for String Trio (1968); *Paintings I-VIII* for Various Instrumental Combinations (1972–86); *Tashi*, quartet for Piano, Clarinet, Violin, and Cello (1977); *August Symphony* for Flute, Clarinet, Violin, Cello, and Piano (1983); *Quintet Romantico* (1987); *Ancient Memories* for Viola and Chamber Ensemble (1989); *Glass Canyons* for Clarinet, Percussion, and Piano (1990); *Der Baum des Lebens* for 2 Violins, Viola, and Cello (1993); *Elegy* for Flute (1993); many pieces for solo instrument. **VOCAL:** *Deliverance, Amen*, oratorio for Chorus, Chamber Ensemble, and Organ (Boston, Dec. 12, 1983); *N.Y. Memories* for Soprano and Piano (1987); *When the Moon is Full* for Mezzo-soprano, Baritone, and 7 Instruments (1989); *Emsdettener Totentanz* for Soprano, Alto, Baritone, and Chamber Ensemble (1991); *Westfälischer Pan* for Mezzo-soprano, Clarinet, and Piano (1991; also for Mezzo-soprano and 6 Instruments, 1992); *Jenseits der Mauer* for Baritone, Trumpet, and Organ (1992); *3 Poems of Pablo Neruda* for Soprano and Orch. (1992).

BIBL.: J. Sposato, *W. T. M.: A Bio-Bibliography* (Westport, Conn., 1995).—NS/LK/DM

McKinley, Baylus Benjamin,

American composer and editor of gospel hymns; b. Heflink, La., July 22, 1886; d. Bryson City, N.C., Sept. 7, 1952. He was educated at Mt. Lebanon Academy in La., La. Coll., and the Southwestern Baptist Theological Seminary, where he subsequently taught (1919–32). He was music ed. for the Robert H. Coleman publishing firm in Dallas (1918–35) and for the Baptist Sunday School Board's widely used Broadman Hymnal (1941). He wrote both words and music to some 150 gospel hymns and set more than 100 texts to music.

BIBL.: W. Reynolds and A. Faircloth, *The Songs of B.B. M.* (Nashville, Tenn., 1974); T. Terry, *B.B. M.: A Shaping Force in Southern Protestant Music* (diss., North Tex. State Univ., 1981); R. Hastings, *Glorious Is Thy Name!: B.B. M., the Man and His Music* (Nashville, Tenn., 1986).—NS/LK/DM

McKinney, Nina Mae, jazz singer; b. Lancaster, S.C., 1912; d. N.Y., May 1967. She was raised in Philadelphia, came to N.Y. as a dancer, worked in *Blackbirds of 1928*, and was picked for a starring role in the film *Hallelujah*. During the late 1920s and 1930s she appeared in many films, including *Safe in Hell, Reckless, The Lost Lady,* and *In Old Kentucky.* She did extensive tours as a solo artist, first appearing in Europe from December 1932 (accompanied by Garland Wilson). During one of her visits to Britain she co-starred with Paul Robeson in *Sanders of the River.* During the early 1940s she specialized in theater and cabaret work, then returned to regular filming, appearing in *Without Love, Dark Waters,* and *Night Train to Memphis.*—JC/LP

McKinney, William, jazz band leader, drummer; b. Cynthiana, Ky., Sept. 17, 1895; d. there, Oct. 14, 1969. McKinney's Cotton Pickers, fronted by Bill McKinney, was the first modern big band of the swing era and was directed by Don Redman. It hit #1 with "If I Could Be with You One Hour Tonight" in 1930. McKinney served in U.S. Army during World War I, then worked as a circus drummer until settling in Springfield, Ohio. In Springfield he took over the leadership of the Synco Septet. The group later worked as The Synco Jazz Band. McKinney relinquished the drum chair to Cuba Austin in order to become the band's business manager. They played residencies in Mich., Toledo, Baltimore, and at the Arcadia Ballroom, Detroit (1926), before being signed by Jean Goldkette for residency at the Greystone Ballroom, Detroit. From then on the band was billed as McKinney's Cotton Pickers. Detroit was to be the band's home base for several years; they also did regular wide-ranging tours reaching N.Y., Philadelphia, Atlantic City, Ohio, Ill., and Minneapolis. In June 1927 Don Hedman was appointed musical director of the band. In 1930 the band ceased working under the auspices of Jean Goldkette. They left Detroit and toured down to Kansas City before taking up residency at Frank Sebastian's Cotton Club in Culver City, Calif. (May 1931). Then after a tour of the middle west the band split into two factions, several members leaving to form the nucleus of Don Redman's Band. Benny Carter became the new musical director in the summer of 1931. The band continued touring before taking up residencies in Detroit. After Benny Carter left (1932), the band recommenced a long spell of touring before breaking up in Baltimore (1934). Several bands began operating as The Cotton Pickers, but McKinney himself was inactive until he reformed a band for residency at the Recreation Ballroom in Boston, in January 1935. This band continued operating on and off for the next year in various locations. In 1937 McKinney began managing the Cosy Cafe in Detroit. Throughout the late 1930s he continued to act as manager-leader for bands working under his name, including one that was resident at Plantation Cafe in Detroit (1939). In the 1940s he severed his connections with the music business and worked in the Ford factory in Detroit. He retired in the 1950s and suffered from poor health for many years.

BIBL.: J. Chilton, *McKinney's Music: A Bio-Discography of McKinney's Cotton Pickers* (London, 1978).—JC/LP

McLachlan, Sarah, one of the most successful folk-rock artists of the 1990s, founder of the Lilith Fair festival of women musicians; b. Halifax, Nova Scotia, Canada, Jan. 28, 1968. Sarah McLachlan started singing seriously at the age of four; because her hands were so small, she learned to accompany herself on a ukulele. She studied voice, piano, and guitar during her school years, attending the Nova Scotia Royal Cons. of Music. By the time she was 17, her new-wave band October Game was offered a contract with Vancouver-based Nettwork Records. However, she had to get her parents to co-sign the contract because she was underage, and they refused. Sarah went off to the Nova Scotia Coll. of Art and Design. The record company, however, didn't give up and McLachlan signed up when she was 19.

Her first album, *Touch*, went gold in Canada based mostly on alternative and college airplay for the song "Vox." She signed with Arista for the U.S. and the record was released again to good reviews and minimal sales. It didn't go gold in the U.S. until 11 years later, however, in February 2000. Her high-tech folk style, exploring the darker edges of the human experience, began to coalesce with her second album *Solace*. "Drawn to the Rhythm" and "Into the Fire" became Canadian hits without stirring much notice south of the border. A live album for the Canadian audience followed.

McLachlan's breakthrough came with her 1994 album *Fumbling Towards Ecstasy*. With McLachlan touring incessantly, the album slowly rose to triple platinum, although it peaked at #50 on the charts. She followed it with the mostly live EP, the gold *Freedom Sessions*. In addition to a variety of live performances, the record contained a cover of Tom Waits's "Ol' 55" later used on the soundtrack for *Boys on the Side*.

In the summer of 1996, in response to what she saw as a boy's club atmosphere on big package tours like Lollapalooza and H.O.R.D.E. that summer, McLachlan put together her own package called the Lilith Fair tour. The show featured such notable female performers as Emmylou Harris, Lisa Loeb, and Paula Cole, along with booths featuring the work of female craftspeople and literature on women's issues. It became one of the summer's most successful bills. She married her drummer, and recorded her next album, *Surfacing*. The record came out just as the 1997 version of Lilith, featuring Jewel, Tracy Chapman, Sheryl Crow, and many others, hit the road. Beyond showcasing talented women, the tours raised hundreds of thousands of dollars for causes like battered women's shelters around the country. Nonetheless, some critics accused McLachlan of using the Lilith tours as vehicles for self-promotion.

Surfacing exceeded everyone's expectations, entering the charts in the U.S. at #2, with the single "Building a Mystery" leading the way. The single "Adia" hit the Top Ten and went gold. The album sold more than seven million copies in the U.S. alone. At the Grammys,

McLachlan took home two awards: Best Female Pop Vocal Performance for "Building a Mystery" and Best Pop Instrumental Performance for "Last Dance." In 1998, she took the most eclectic Lilith bill out on the road, touring with artists ranging from Luscious Jackson, Lauryn Hill, Erykah Badu, African star Angelique Kidjo, and Harris. She then decided to retire the Lilith concept. Her performances on the tour and several other dates were captured on a live album, *Mirrorball*, released late in 1999.

DISC.: *Touch* (1989); *Solace* (1991); *Fumbling towards Ecstasy* (1994); *The Freedom Sessions* (1995); *Surfacing* (1997); *Mirrorball* (1999).—**HB**

McLaughlin, John, innovative jazz-fusion guitarist, leader; b. Yorkshire, England, Jan. 4, 1942. An extraordinary musician, John McLaughlin was one of the first jazz guitarists to incorporate the advances and techniques of John Coltrane and Jimi Hendrix. His bold and unique compositions fuse those influences with Indian music. He has alternated, somewhat confusingly for his audience, between acoustic and electric bands, but his virtuosity and commitment are always evident.

McLaughlin played piano and guitar from age 11, and formed a band as a schoolboy. He left home when he was 15 or 16. He supported himself as a truck driver, and sold caviar to English hotels between R&B (and organ trio) gigs during the 1960s. In the early 1960s, he did studio work for 18 months but couldn't stand it, so to make money he sold his carved-top 1960 L-4C guitar with a Charlie Christian pickup, a sale he later regretted.

He worked with Georgie Fame, Alexis Korner, Brian Auger, and Graham Bond. His first known recording is in a club with Mike Carr in 1967. He emigrated to the U.S. in 1968; the next year, he issued his first album as a leader which displayed his virtuosity in a free-jazz context. On the advice of Dave Holland, Tony Williams recruited McLaughlin, and together with Larry Young, they recorded the immensely influential *Emergency*, a potent blend of jazz and rock. He played with Tony Williams's Lifetime at Newport 1970 and elsewhere. He played a significant role in the historic sessions led by Miles Davis for *In a Silent Way, Bitches Brew, A Tribute to Jack Johnson, Live-Evil, On the Corner,* and *Big Fun*.

In 1970, he sought spiritual expansion through an association with a Bengal mystic, Sri Chimnoy, cut his long hair and formed the Mahavishnu Orch. (1971–73). The name Mahavishnu was given to him by his guru. The band originally included Billy Cobham, Jerry Goodman, Jan Hammer, and Rick Laird but later, by 1973, they had added Jean Luc Ponty and Narada Michael Walden. The Mahavishnu Orch. mixed rock and jazz with Hindu religiosity. McLaughlin's striking compositions involved unusual meters and much written counterpoint. Their album *Birds of Fire* reached #20 on the British charts in 1973.

Also in 1970, he teamed up with fellow guru-inspired guitarist Carlos Santana for a duet LP entitled *Love, Devotion, and Surrender,* which reached #7 on the U.K. charts. He performed on a specially designed guitar with two necks so that he could essentially have two sounds without switching guitars. From 1974–76,

he recorded three albums credited to Mahavishnu, but other musicians were used. McLaughlin later renounced the Mahavishnu name, but in 1984 recorded an album that also featured Billy Cobham, again as "Mahavishnu."

In 1975, he had already organized an acoustic outfit known as Shakti, with Indian musicians, violinist L. Shankar and percussionists Zakir Hussein and Raghavan. Again he produced a technical innovation, supplementing his guitar with a set of resonant strumming strings similar to those found on a sitar. Around this time, he also invented a special metronome (now lost) that could produce several different beats at once; you could have 98 against 99 if so desired. Shakti was together for three years (through 1978), then McLaughlin and Shankar moved on to form the One Truth Band. By this time, he had settled in France.

In the early 1980s, McLaughlin hooked up with Al DiMeola and Paco DeLucia, touring together until 1985. In 1986, he appeared in Bertrand Tavernier's movie *Round Midnight,* and then formed a new trio with Trilok Gurtu that toured for four years and recorded two albums. He also worked with Wayne Shorter, and Larry Coryell. He wrote and performed a rather traditional classical guitar concerto in 1985, which he performed on TV. He continues to work in a variety of contexts, including a tribute to Bill Evans featuring the Aighetta Quartet and a trio with a Hammond organ. He currently lives in Monte Carlo. In 1999, he revived the group Shakti for recording and touring.

DISC.: *Extrapolation* (1969); *Where Fortune Smiles* (1970); *My Goal's Beyond* (1970); *Devotion* (1970); *Love, Devotion, and Surrender* (1972); *Shakti with John McLaughlin* (1976); *Handful of Beauty* (1977); *Natural Elements* (1978); *Electric Guitarist* (1978); *Electric Dreams* (1978); *Friday Night in San Francisco* (1981); *Belo Horizonte* (1981); *Passion, Grace, and Fire* (1982); *Music Spoken Here* (1983); *Mahavishnu* (1984); *Adventures in Radioland* (1987); *Live at the Royal Festival Hall* (1989); *Mediterranean Concerto* (1990); *Que Alegria* (1991); *Free Spirits: Tokyo Live* (1993); *Time Remembered: John McLaughlin Plays Bill Evans* (1993); *Shakti* (1994); *After the Rain* (1995); *Colaiuta, in from the Storm* (1995); *The Promise* (1996). **MAHAVISHNU ORCH.:** *Inner Mounting Flame* (1971); *Birds of Fire* (1972); *Between Nothingness & Eternity* (1973); *Apocalypse* (1974); *Visions of the Emerald Beyond* (1974); *Inner Worlds* (1976). *Mike Carr: Blues for Bells* (1967).—**LP/MM**

McLaughlin, Marie, Scottish soprano; b. Hamilton, Lanarkshire, Nov. 2, 1954. She studied at Notre Dame Coll. of Education and with Joan Alexander in Glasgow, and later at the London Opera Centre and the National Opera Studio. In 1978 she made her debut as Tatiana at the Aldeburgh Festival, and as Anna Gomez in *The Consul* at the English National Opera in London. Her debut at London's Covent Garden followed in 1980 as Barbarina, where she subsequently sang such roles as Susanna, Zerlina, Nannetta, and Britten's Tytania. After singing Ilia in Rome in 1982 and Marzelline in Berlin in 1984, she was engaged as Micaëla at the Glyndebourne Festival in 1985. On Dec. 10, 1986, she made her debut at the Metropolitan Opera in N.Y. as Marzelline. Her first appearance at the Salzburg Festival was as Susanna in 1987. In 1988 she sang Adina at Milan's La Scala and in 1990 Zerlina at the Vienna Festival. Following an engagement as Despina in Geneva and a tour to Japan with the Royal Opera, Covent Garden, as Susanna in 1992, she sang Weill's Jenny at the Opéra de la Bastille in Paris in 1995. In 1996 she appeared as Donna Elvira in Lausanne.—NS/LK/DM

McLean, Barton (Keith),
American composer; b. Poughkeepsie, N.Y., April 8, 1938. He studied music education at the State Univ. of N.Y. at Potsdam (B.S., 1960), with Cowell at the Eastman School of Music in Rochester, N.Y. (M.M., 1965), and composition at Ind. Univ. in Bloomington (Mus.D., 1972). He taught at the State Univ. of N.Y. at Potsdam (1960–66). He then was head of theory and composition and director of the electronic music center at Ind. Univ. in South Bend (1969–76). After teaching and serving as director of the electronic music center at the Univ. of Tex. in Austin (1976–83), he taught and was co-director at the I-Ear Studios at the Rensselaer Polytechnic Inst. (1987–89). In 1967 he married **Priscilla McLean**; together they toured in the U.S. and abroad as the McLean Mix electroacoustic music duo. McLean received NEA fellowships (1976, 1982), MacDowell Colony fellowships (1979, 1981, 1983, 1985), a N.Y. Foundation for the Arts fellowship (1986), Asian Cultural Council grants (1990, 1994), and Virgil Thomas Foundation grants (1996, 1999). Most of his compositional efforts have been devoted to electronic and computer music.

WORKS: ORCH.: *Metamorphosis* (1972); *Rainforest Reflections* for McLean Mix Duo and Orch. (Chico, Calif., March 6, 1993). **CHAMBER:** *Ritual of the Dawn* for 6 Players (1982); *Pathways* for Symphonic Winds (1983); *From the Good Earth*, "foot-stompin' homage to Bartók" for String Quartet (1985). **VOCAL:** *3 Songs on Sandburg Poems* for Voice and Piano (1970). **TAPE AND ELECTRONICS:** *The Sorcerer Revisited* for Tape (1975); *Mysteries from the Ancient Nahuatl* for Soloists, Chorus, Narrator, Instrumentalists, and Tape (1978); *Etunytude* for Computer (1982); *In Wilderness Is the Preservation of the World: Voices of the Wild, Passages of the Night*, electronic piece (1985); *Voices of the Wild: Primal Spirits* for McLean Mix Synthesizer, Soloists, and Orch. (1987; Troy, N.Y., Feb. 26, 1988); *Earth Music*, improvisation installation-performance computer piece (1988); *Visions of a Summer Night* for Computer (1988); *Rainforest*, environmental audience-interactive quasi-installation computer piece (1989); *Himalayan Fantasy* for Tape (1992); *Happy Days* for 2 Performers Using Music Boxes, Party Instruments, "Happy Apple," and Flexatones (1996); *Jambori Rimba* for Soprano, Woodwinds, Percussion, Tape, and Video (Sarawak, Malaysia, Nov. 1996; in collaboration with P. McLean). **OTHER:** *Rainforest Images*, audio piece (Cincinnati, Feb. 24, 1993; in collaboration with P. McLean); *Forgotten Shadows*, musical-historical installation (1994).—NS/LK/DM

McLean, Jackie (aka John Lenwood Jr.; Abdul Kareem; Omar Ahmed),
hard bop jazz alto saxophonist, composer, educator; b. N.Y., May 17, 1932. McLean was given early encouragement by Charlie Parker; he studied briefly with Foots Thomas and Cecil Scott before he began working with Sonny Rollins in the late 1940s. McLean made his recording debut with Miles Davis in the early 1950s, then played with Paul Bley, George Wallington, and Charles Mingus later in the decade. Next came a three-year stint with Art

Blakey's Jazz Messengers; he then began heading a quintet in 1958. Miles Davis and John Coltrane each recorded his composition "Little Melonae." "Dig," credited to Davis, is said to be McLean's composition also. McLean was steadily building his reputation when drug problems began to affect him. During the 1960s, his live work gradually diminished until, by the end of that decade, he had ceased performing live altogether. He was barred from many N.Y. clubs even after the problem eased. The 1970s saw him return to occasional performing. In July 1979, he achieved his only entry into the U.K. pop charts with his one fusion album—the cut "Dr. Jackyll and Mr. Funk" was a single featuring the assistance of a vocal back-up group which reached #53. McLean also became active in jazz education. He has taught since 1971 at the Hartt Coll. of Music of the Univ. of Hartford. Founded and was the first chairperson of the African-American Music Department there. Also very active in The Artists Collective, a group that he founded in 1972 which brings the arts to the youth of Hartford. In 1983, he was the recipient of the Conn. Arts Award from Conn.'s Commission on the Arts. Among other awards and honors, McLean was voted #1 in *Down Beat* Magazine's 1993 Critics Poll and the 1994 *Jazz Time* Magazine Readers' Poll and Japan's *Swing Journal*. His wife Dolly manages his career and his son Rene plays saxophone and flute and records with his father frequently. He has been often criticized for playing consistently sharp, but his heartfelt passion and unpretentious directness win over most listeners.

DISC.: *Tune Up* (1955); *Steeplechase* (1956); *McLean's Scene* (1956); *Lights Out* (1956); *Jackie's Pal* (1956); *4, 5 and 6* (1956); *Strange Blues* (1957); *Makin' the Changes* (1957); *Long Drink of the Blues* (1957); *Jackie McLean and Co.* (1957); *Jackie McLean Plays Fat Jazz* (1957); *Alto Madness* (1957); *Swing Swang Swingin* (1959); *New Soil* (1959); *Jackie's Bag* (1959); *Street Singer* (1960); *Capuchin Swing* (1960); *Fickle Sonance* (1961); *Bluesnik* (1961); *Tippin' the Scales* (1962); *Let Freedom Ring* (1962); *Jackie McLean Quintet* (1962); *Vertigo* (1963); *One Step Beyond* (1963); *Jackie McLean Sextet* (1963); *Destination Out* (1963); *It's Time* (1964); *Action* (1964); *Right Now* (1965); *Consequences* (1965); *Tune Up* (1966); *Jacknife* (1966); *High Frequency* (1966); *Dr. Jackle* (1966); *New and Old Gospel* (1967); *Hipnosis* (1967); *Demon's Dance* (1967); *Bout Soul* (1967); *Live at Montmartre* (1972); *Source* (1973); *Ode to Super* (1973); *Meeting* (1973); *Ghetto Lullaby* (1973); *N.Y. Calling* (1974); *Antiquity* (1974); *Altissimo 1974* (1974); *New Wine, Old Bottles* (1978); *Contour* (1978); *Monuments* (1979); *Dynasty* (1988); *Rites of Passage* (1991); *Jackie Mac Attack Live* (1991); *Rhythm of the Earth* (1992); *Hat Trick* (1996).—LP/MM

McLean, Priscilla (Anne née Taylor),
American composer; b. Fitchburg, Mass., May 27, 1942. She studied at Fitchburg State Coll. (B.E.E., 1963) and the Univ. of Lowell (B.M.E., 1965) in Mass., and with Heiden and Beversdorf at Ind. Univ. (M.M., 1969). She was an assoc. lecturer at Ind. Univ.'s Kokomo campus (1971–73) and at St. Mary's Coll. in Notre Dame, Ind. (1973–76); in 1975–76 she was composer-in-residence at the electronic music center at Ind. Univ.'s South Bend campus, and in 1985 served as visiting prof. of music at the Univ. of Hawaii in Manoa. In 1967 she married **Barton McLean**. From 1974 they toured as the McLean Mix electroacoustic music duo, performing in the U.S.

and abroad. Besides appearing as a pianist, percussionist, synthesist, and as a performer on native and invented instruments, she is also a virtuoso soprano using extended vocal techniques. She received numerous NEA grants (1979–87) and MacDowell Colony fellowships (1979, 1981, 1984, 1986). Her compositions make innovative use of man-made or animal sounds with synthesized music.

WORKS: ORCH.: *Holiday for Youth* for Concert Band (1965); *Variations and Mosaics on a Theme of Stravinsky* (Indianapolis, April 24, 1975); *A Magic Dwells* for Orch. and Tape (1984); *Voices of the Wild: 1 (Printemps) Rites* (Albany, N.Y., Feb. 26, 1988). **CHAMBER:** *Ah-Syn!* for Autoharp and Synthesizer (1976); *Fire and Ice* for Trombone and Piano (1977); *Beneath the Horizon I* for Tuba Quartet and Taped Whales (1978) and *III* for Tuba and Taped Whale Ensemble (1979); *The Inner Universe*, 8 tone poems for Piano and Tape (1981); *Elan! A Dance to All Rising Things from the Earth* for Instrumental Ensemble (1984); *Desert Voices* for Midi Violin, Digital Processors, and Stereo Tape (1998; Williamstown, Mass., July 1999). **VOCAL:** *4 Songs in Season* for Chorus (1963; rev. 1967); *Rainer Maria Poems*, 3 songs for Voice and Violin (1967; rev. 1974); *Messages* for 4 Soloists, Chorus, and Chamber Ensemble (1974); *Fantasies for Adults and Other Children*, 8 songs for Voice and Amplified Piano (1980); *In Wilderness is the Preservation of the World* for Soprano, Chorus, Percussion, Autoharp, and Stereo Tape (1985); *In Celebration* for Chorus, Percussion, and Stereo Tape (1987; Bennington, Vt., Feb. 1988); *Wilderness* for Soprano, Percussionist, and Tape (1989; Baltimore, April 8, 1990); *Everything Awakening Alert and Joyful!* for Narrator and Orch. (1991–92; Berkeley, Feb. 1, 1992); *In the Beginning* for Soprano, Digital Processors, Tape, and Video Projection (Akron, Ohio, March 1996); *Jambori Rimba* for Soprano, Woodwinds, Percussion, Tape, and Video (Sarawak, Malaysia, Nov. 1996; in collaboration with B. McLean). **OTHER:** *The Dance of Shiva* for Tape and Multiple Slide Projections (1989–90); *Rainforest Images*, audio piece (Cincinnati, Feb. 24, 1993; in collaboration with B. McLean).—**NS/LK/DM**

McLeod, Alice
See **Coltrane, Alice**

MC Lyte (originally, **Moorer, Lana**), one of the most successful female rappers; b. Queens, N.Y., Oct. 11, 1970. MC Lyte's father, First Priority Records head Nat Robinson, released her debut single in 1986. That record, "I Cram to Understand You (Sam)," graphically upbraided a boyfriend for pursuing other women. Her brothers, known as Milk and Gizmo of Audio Two, produced her 1988 debut album *Lyte as a Rock*. With an emphasis on social commentary accompanied by a heavy beat, the album established Lyte's signature sound. A year later, she broadened her message with her next album, *Eyes on This*, which featured "I'm Not Having It," an epic on the burgeoning AIDS epidemic. Used in a public service announcement about the disease, it also helped Lyte become the first rapper to play Carnegie Hall when she was invited to perform at an AIDS benefit.

Act Like You Know (1993) thickened her sound with soul samples. Her #14 R&B hit "When in Love," shared producers with new-jack swingers Bell Biv DeVoe. Fans saw this as softening her sound. Two years later, she responded by cranking out the nastier-in-every-way

Ain't No Other. It featured her biggest hit "Ruffneck," which rose to #35 pop, #10 R&B and went gold, the first single by a female rap artist to do so.

In the mid-1990s, Lyte started to appear as an actress, playing roles in the sitcoms *Moesha* and *In the House*, and the show *New York Undercover*. She also appeared in the film *Train Ride*. She contributed the song "Keep On Keeping On" to the *Sunset Park* soundtrack, produced by Jermaine Dupri, and it, too, went gold. She continued working with Dupri on her next album, 1996's *Bad As I Wanna Be*. The record received mixed reviews, but generated another gold single, "Cold Rock a Party," a collaboration with Missy Elliot. *Seven & Seven* was a more mature effort, featuring Elliot, LL Cool J, and Giovanni.

DISC.: *Lyte As a Rock* (1988); *Eyes on This* (1989); *Act Like You Know* (1991); *Ain't No Other* (1993); *Bad As I Wanna B* (1996); *Badder Than B-Fore* (1998); *Seven & Seven* (1998).—**BH**

McManus, Jill, jazz pianist, composer, author; b. Englewood, N.J., July 28, 1940. She incorporates Hopi themes into her music, as well as those of related Pueblo groups such as the Zuni nation. Her family moved to N.Y. when she was about six months old and to Westport, Conn., when she was about five years old where she studied at the Westport School of Music. She became interested in jazz while attending Wellesley Coll. She then moved to N.Y. where she studied jazz in the 1960s with John Mehegan at his studio. Around 1970, she also studied with Roland Hanna. McManus began as a reporter for *Time* in 1963, writing music stories and record reviews through 1971.

By 1974, she was leading the Jazz Sisters in concerts around the N.Y. area, including Town Hall in 1977 and a CBS-TV appearance. She began teaching privately in 1975 (through 1995), and from 1978 to 1980, she substituted for Kenny Barron when he was unavailable to teach at Rutgers Univ. In 1980, she led all-female groups at Symphony Space in N.Y. (the N.Y. salute to Woman in Jazz (also 1979, 1981, 1985)) and at the Women's Jazz Festival in Kansas City. She played with Pepper Adams from 1980 to 1981. In the summer of 1980, she traveled to N.Mex. where she had a life-changing experience attending a rain ceremony and meeting Hopi song composers. She returned every summer for over ten years, teaching in Santa Fe from 1982 to 1985. Her pieces have been recorded by Red Rodney and Rein DeGraaff, and she wrote the soundtrack to the documentary *In the Spirit of Haystack*. She taught at Mannes Coll. of Music (N.Y.) from 1981–91, while continuing to lead groups around N.Y. and England (1981, 1983, 1987, 1990, 1992, and 1997), though with less frequency in the late 1990s.

DISC.: *As One* (1977); *Symbols of Hopi* (1983); *Broadcast, Piano Jazz* (1992); *Broadcast, BBC Women's Hour* (1992).—**LP**

McNair, Sylvia, highly talented American soprano; b. Mansfield, Ohio, June 23, 1956. She studied with Margarita Evans at Wheaton (Ill.) Coll. (B.M., 1978) and with Virginia MacWatters (1978–80), John Wustman (1978–82), and Virginia Zeani (1980–82) at the Ind. Univ. School of Music in Bloomington (M.M., 1982). She made her formal concert debut as a soloist in *Messiah* with the

Indianapolis Sym. Orch. (1980). Her operatic debut followed as Sandrina in Haydn's *L'Infedeltà delusa* at N.Y.'s Mostly Mozart Festival (1982). In 1984 she created the title role in Kelterborn's opera *Ophelia* at her European debut at the Schwetzingen Festival, and immediately thereafter sang the role at Berlin's Deutsche Oper. In 1990 she was honored with the Marian Anderson Award. In 1993 she sang Poppea at the Salzburg Festival. On Nov. 27, 1994, she made her Alice Tully Hall recital debut in N.Y. In 1996 she sang Britten's Tytania at the Metropolitan Opera in N.Y. She was engaged as Pamina at the Salzburg Festival in 1997. In 1998 she created the role of Blanche Dubois in Previn's *A Streetcar Named Desire* at the San Francisco Opera. She portrayed Cleopatra in *Giulio Cesare* at the Metropolitan Opera in 1999. Her extensive repertoire ranges from Monteverdi to contemporary composers.—NS/LK/DM

McNeely, Jim (actually, James Harry),

jazz pianist, composer; b. Chicago, May 18, 1949. He earned his B.A. in Music from the Univ. of Ill. in 1975. He moved to N.Y. that same year and worked with Ted Curson (1976–78), Chet Baker (1978), the Thad Jones/Mel Lewis Jazz Orch. (1978–79), and the renamed Mel Lewis & the Jazz Orch. (1979–84), which overlapped with a stint from 1981–85 with the Stan Getz Quartet. He worked from 1990–95 with the Phil Woods Quintet. Starting in 1983, McNeely has also performed on occasion his own trio. In January of 1996, he re-joined The Vanguard Jazz Orch. as pianist and Composer-in-Residence. He has become a highly respected jazz composer, composing for the Carnegie Hall Jazz Band, the Metropole Orch. (Netherlands), the West German Radio Big Band, and the Stockholm Jazz Orch. He taught composition and other subjects from 1986 to 1992 at William Paterson Coll. in Wayne, N.J. From 1981 to 1998 he also taught at the jazz program of N.Y.U., and from 1991 to 1998 he was co-director of BMI Jazz Composers' Workshop for professionals. He has appeared at numerous college jazz festivals as a performer and clinician, and has been involved regularly with summer workshops such as the Stanford Jazz Workshop and Jamey Aebersold's Summer Jazz Clinics. He has also been a teaching resident at institutions in the U.S., Canada, Spain, Sweden, Finland, Germany, and Australia. In 1998, he was appointed "Permanent Chief Conductor" of the Danish Radio Jazz Orch.

DISC.: *Rain's Dance* (1976); *Plot Thickens* (1979); *From the Heart* (1984); *Winds of Change* (1989); *East Coast Blow Out* (1989); *Jigsaw* (1991); *Live at Maybeck Recital Hall, Vol. 20* (1992); *The Lickety Split Music of Jim McNeely* (1997); *Sound Bites* (1997). **M. LEWIS**: *Naturally* (1979); *Make Me Smile* (1982); *M. Lewis and the Jazz Orch.: Featuring the Music of Bob Brookmeyer* (1993); *Live at Montreux* (1997). **S. GETZ**: *Pure Getz* (1982); *Line for Lyons* (1983); *The Stockholm Concert* (1983); *Blue Skies* (1982).—LP

McNeil, John,

jazz trumpeter, flugelhornist, composer; b. March 23, 1948, Eureka, Calif. A fine player, he is sought after by musicians on all instruments for his innovative insights into lines and harmonies. He is the leader of his own ensemble, which has toured Europe and the U.S. and recorded seven albums. He has also performed with Horace Silver and the Thad Jones/Mel Lewis Orch. A respected clinician, he has led workshops throughout the U.S., Europe, Australia, and New Zealand. He is a member of the NEC Faculty, Improvisation and Jazz Studies. Since childhood, he has suffered from a neurological disease that forced him to relearn the trumpet with his left hand; he has done so successfully.

DISC.: *Embarkation* (1978); *Look to the Sky* (1979); *Glass Room* (1979); *Faun* (1979); *Clean Sweep* (1981); *Things We Did Last Summer* (1983); *I've Got the World on a String* (1983).—LP

McNeill, Lloyd,

black American artist, musician, painter, photographer, and poet; b. Washington, D.C., April 12, 1935. He studied art and zoology at Morehouse Coll. (B.A., 1961), painting and printmaking at Howard Univ. (M.F.A., 1963), lithography at the École des Beaux Arts in Paris (1964–65), and sound recording and animation at N.Y.U. (1974); also studied composition with Hale Smith and flute with Frank Albright, Eric Dolphy, Harold Jones, and others. A true Renaissance man, McNeill excels in a variety of art forms; his drawings were praised by Picasso, whom he befriended in the 1960s, and have been exhibited widely with his paintings; he also appears in readings of his own poetry. He appeared as a congo drummer with Nina Simone and in a variety of ensembles as a flutist; in 1968 he formed The Lloyd McNeill Band. He taught at Dartmouth Coll., Spelman Coll., and Howard Univ.; in 1969 he joined the visual arts faculty at Rutgers Univ. (Mason Gross School of the Arts); subsequently was a prof. there. His compositions include *Sketches* for Flute (1986); certain movements are often performed separately (e.g., *Tori Suite*, 3 pieces), while others have been arranged for different instrumental combinations, including *The Falling Snow* for Flute and Violin (1987) and *Calypso Facto* for Flute and Violin (1987; also arranged for Harpsichord). He's also recorded several albums and written and performed dance pieces and film scores.

DISC.: *Asha* (1969); *Tanner Suite* (1969); *Washington Suite* (1970); *Treasures* (1977); *Tori* (1978); *Elegia* (1980); *X.TEM.POR.E* (1997); *The Best of Lloyd McNeill* (1997).—NS/LK/DM

McPartland, Jimmy (actually, James Douggald/Douglas),

cornetist, trumpeter; brother of Dick McPartland; b. Chicago, March 15, 1907; d. Port Washington, N.Y., March 13, 1991. His father was a music teacher. Jimmy started on violin at five, then switched to cornet in the early 1920s. He formed a band with his brother and several of their friends (Jim Lanigan, Bud Freeman, Frank Teschemacher, Dave Tough, and pianist Dave North) that subsequently became known as The Austin High Gang, though they originally gigged as The Blue Friars. He got his first professional work with Al Maid's Band in 1923, subsequently playing with other local bands before moving to N.Y. to join The Wolverines. He played alongside Bix Beiderbecke for five nights until Bix left to join Jean Goldkette. McPartland left N.Y. with The Wolverines to play in Miami and Chicago; the band played in Chicago under Dick Voynow's leadership, and later Jimmy fronted the band when they were billed in Des Moines and Chicago as Husk O'Hare's Wolverines in May 1926. Jimmy then worked briefly in Detroit before joining drummer Bill Paley's Band at Friars' Inn, in Chicago in late 1926. Early in 1927, he joined Ben Pollack at The Blackhawk, Chicago, and subsequently went to N.Y. with Pollack, remaining with the group until autumn 1929. At the same time, he played on many freelance recording sessions including small group dates with Benny Goodman in 1928. McPartland worked in Broadway pit bands and with various local N.Y. groups through the early 1930s. He returned to to Chicago (c. 1934) to join his brother's Embassy Four. After a long spell of touring and residencies in New Orleans, Chicago, and other major cities, he left to form his own band. From 1937 until 1940 played mainly in Chicago, then came to Nick's in N.Y. (early 1941). McPartland briefly returned to Chicago, then played with Jack Teagarden in N.Y. until joining the U.S. Army in late 1942. He served in Europe, took part in the Normandy invasion, then played in the service show "Bandwagon" where he met and married pianist Marian Page in February 1945. Throughout the late 1940s and early 1950s, he led his own bands in Chicago and other major U.S. cities; he also visited Britain in 1949 and 1954. Beginning in 1953, he worked regularly in N.Y. He continued to work regularly throughout the 1960s–80s, mainly with his own groups, but also in spells with Bud Freeman, Peanuts Hucko, and Tony Pareti. He also made several international tours, including a tour of South Africa in 1971–72 and of Britain in 1985. He made his last concert appearance in 1990. Although he divorced Marian in 1970, they remained friendly and continued to perform togther occasionally; when he was suffering from lung cancer in 1991, she remarried him two weeks before his death.

DISC.: *Middle Road* (1956); *After Dark* (1956); *Jimmy McPartland's Dixieland* (1957); *Meet Me in Chicago* (1959); *Jimmy McPartland and His Dixieland* (1959); *Bossa Nova Plus Soul* (1963); *That Happy Dixieland Jazz* (1965); *Jimmy McPartland on Stage* (1966); *Ambiance* (1970); *McPartlands Live at the Montice* (1972); *At the Festival* (1979). **B. GOODMAN:** "A Jazz Holiday," "Wolverine Blues," "Jungle Blues" (2 takes), "Room 1411" (1928). —JC/LP

McPartland, Marian (originally, Turner, Margaret),

pianist, composer; b. Windsor, England, March 20, 1918. She played classical music as a child, just like her mother, who loved Chopin. She began playing violin and won a scholarship to the Guildhall School of Music in London, where she studied piano; in her late teens, against the vehement opposition of her parents, she switched to jazz and began gigging in London under the name "Marian Page," including work with a four-piano vaudeville act. She made joint appearances with novelty pianist Billy Mayerl, and toured entertaining Allied troops during World War II. In Belgium in 1945, she met and married **Jimmy McPartland,** who was entertaining troups for the USO. They played for Eisenhower in 1946, and moved to Chicago that year, staying until 1950, when they moved to N.Y. She lead her own trio at the Embers Club (1950) and at the Hickory House (1952–60). Starting in the late 1940s, she wrote occasionally for *Down Beat* and other publications. Her recordings from the early 1950s, especially

ballads, employ "impressionistic" voicings in the solos and arrangements that in some ways predate Bill Evans. She wrote a number of songs in the popular vein, including the successful "There'll Be Other Times." She studied the music of Monk with Hall Overton.

From 1955, she has spent much time introducing jazz to schoolchildren. She started her own label, Halcyon, in 1969 and made a triumphant return to active club and concert work in the 1970s. She and Jimmy divorced in 1970 but remained great friends and continued to work together occasionally; in 1978, they performed at the Newport Jazz Festival. They symbolically remarried shortly before his death in 1991. In 1979, McPartland began her Peabody-award-winning NPR program, *Piano Jazz,* in which she talks and plays with every style of jazz pianist; some of the roughly 400 shows have been issued on CD. She has also made extensive radio and TV appearances and served on jazz boards. She performs regularly with "pops" orchestras; in the early 1980s, she performed Grieg's Piano Concerto throughout the U.S. She gave a private performance for the Supreme Court on April 17, 1997; a major all-star concert was held at Town Hall for her 80th birthday, and broadcast on radio; the reception afterward was broadcast on BET-TV's Jazz Scene. She has won numerous awards, including *Down Beat's* Lifetime Achievement Award in 1997.

DISC.: *Great Britain's Marian McPartland* (1947); *Looking for a Boy* (1950); *Marian McPartland in Concert* (1951); *Jazz at Storyville* (1951); *Moods* (1952); *Lullaby of Birdland* (1952); *Jazz at the Hickory House* (1952); *Marian McPartland at the Hickory* (1954); *Marian McPartland Trio* (1956); *With You in Mind* (1957); *Marian McPartland at the London* (1958); *Marian McPartland Plays the Music* (1960); *Marian McPartland* (1963); *West Side Story* (1964); *Interplay* (1969); *Ambiance* (1970); *Delicate Balance* (1971); *Sentimental Journey* (1972); *McPartlands Live at the Montice* (1972); *Elegant Piano* (1972); *Plays the Music of Alec Wilder* (1973); *Maestro and Friend* (1973); *Solo Concert at Haverford* (1974); *Concert in Argentina* (1974); *Fine Performance* (1976); *Now's the Time* (1977); *Piano Jazz: McPartland/Evans* (1978); *Let It Happen* (1978); *From This Moment On* (1978); *Portrait of Marian McPartland* (1979); *Piano Jazz: McPartland/Blake* (1979); *At the Festival* (1979); *Live at the Carlyle* (1979); *Piano Jazz: McPartland/Wellstood* (1981); *Piano Jazz: McPartland/Stacy* (1981); *Piano Jazz: McPartland/Cowell* (1981); *Personal Choice* (1982); *Willow Creek and Other Ballads* (1985); *Marian Mc Partland's Piano Jazz* (1985); *Piano Jazz: McPartland/Short* (1986); *Music of Billy Strayhorn* (1987); *Piano Jazz: McPartland/Carter* (1989); *Piano Jazz: McPartland/Hyman* (1990); *Piano Jazz: McPartland/Carroll* (1990); *Marian McPartland Plays the Benny Carter Songbook* (1990); *Piano Jazz: McPartland/Richards* (1991); *Piano Jazz: McPartland/Terry* (1993); *McPartland/Burrell* (1993); *In My Life* (1993); *Plays the Music of Mary Lou Williams* (1994); *Piano Jazz: McPartland/Ellington* (1994); *At The Festival* (1994); *Piano Jazz: Amina Claudine Myer* (1995). **G. SHEARING:** *Alone Together* (1981).

WRITINGS: *All in Good Time* (N.Y., 1987).—LP/MM/NS

McPhatter, Clyde,

one of the most important and influential vocalists of R&B in the 1950s; b. Durham, N.C., Nov. 15, 1933; d. N.Y., June 13, 1972. **THE DRIFTERS: MEMBERSHIP:** Clyde McPhatter, lead ten.; Gerhart Thrasher, ten. (b. Wetumpka, Ala.); Andrew

Thrasher, bar. (b. Wetumpka, Ala.); Bill Pinckney, bass voc. (b. Sumter, S.C., Aug. 15, 1925). Later members included David Baughan, lead ten. (b. N.Y., June 28, 1937; d. Jan. 1970); Johnny Moore (b. Selma. Ala., 1934); Bobby Hendricks (b. Columbus, Ohio, 1937); Charlie Hughes, bar.; Tommy Evans, bs. voc.

Born to a Baptist preacher father, Clyde McPhatter began singing in his father's choir at age five. He later moved to the N.Y.-area with his family, turning professional at age 14 with the gospel group the Mount Lebanon Singers. In 1950 McPhatter met pianist-arranger Billy Ward and joined Ward's Dominoes as lead tenor. Signed to the King Records subsidiary, Federal, in late 1950, the Dominoes soon scored an R&B smash with "Do Something for Me." Their next hit, the lascivious top R&B hit "Sixty Minute Man," with lead vocals by bass singer Bill Brown, was one of the first R&B vocal group songs to become a major pop hit. Subsequent R&B hits for the Dominoes included "That's What You're Doing to Me," the top hit "Have Mercy Baby," and "I'd Be Satisfied" with lead vocals by McPhatter.

After training Jackie Wilson as his replacement, Clyde McPhatter left the Dominoes to form his own Drifters in May 1953. The lineup stabilized with McPhatter, brothers Gerhart and Andrew "Bubba" Thrasher, and Bill Pinckney. Signed to Atlantic Records by Ahmet Ertegun, The Drifters conducted their first successful recording session in August 1953, producing the top R&B hit and instant classic "Money Honey." Smash R&B hits continued with "Such a Night," "Honey Love" (another major pop hit), "Bip Bam," a stunning harmony version of "White Christmas" (with lead vocals by Pinckney and McPhatter), and "What'cha Gonna Do." However, in May 1954, McPhatter was drafted into the Air Force and replaced by David Baughan and later, Johnny Moore, who sang lead on the R&B hits "Adorable" and "Ruby Baby" from 1955–56. Frequent personnel changes ensued and the original Drifters broke up in June 1958. Manager George Treadwell, owner of the Drifters' name, drafted all new members for subsequent hit recordings such as "There Goes My Baby" and "Save the Last Dance for Me," which blended pop and gospel musical styles with sophisticated arrangements and orchestrations.

While on leave from the Air Force, Clyde McPhatter solo-recorded "Seven Days," and the single became a smash R&B and moderate pop hit in early 1956. Upon discharge in April, he pursued a solo career on the Atlantic Records label, scoring a top R&B and major pop hit with "Treasure of Love." Touring with Bill Haley in 1956 and the Fats Domino Caravan in 1957, McPhatter achieved R&B and pop hits with "Without Love (There Is Nothing)," "Just to Hold My Hand," "Long, Lonely Nights" (a top R&B hit), "Come What May" and "Since You've Been Gone." His biggest hit, a pop smash and top R&B hit, came in late 1958 with Brook Benton's "A Lover's Question."

Switching to MGM Records in 1959, Clyde McPhatter was subjected to inappropriate pop arrangements with the label and subsequently signed with Mercury Records through producer Clyde Otis in 1960. That summer he achieved a major pop and near-smash R&B hit with "Ta Ta," but his next didn't come until early 1962, when he scored a pop-only hit with Billy Swan's "Lover Please." His remake of "Little Bitty Pretty One" soon became a major pop hit, but it proved to be his last. He recorded his last Mercury album in 1968 and later recorded several unsuccessful singles for small labels. McPhatter went to England in 1968 to perform in small clubs, and upon his return two years later, Clyde Otis helped him secure a recording contract with Decca Records. However, *Welcome Home* failed to endear him to the record-buying public. Subsequently relegated to small clubs and the rock 'n' roll revival circuit, McPhatter died in N.Y. of complications arising from heart, liver and kidney ailments on June 13, 1972, at age 38. Clyde McPhatter was inducted into the Rock and Roll Fall of Fame in 1987.

DISC.: *Love Ballads* (1958); *Clyde* (1959); *Let's Start Over Again* (1959); *Greatest Hits* (1960); *Ta Ta* (1960); *Golden Blues Hits* (1961); *Lover Please* (1962); *Rhythm and Soul* (1963); *Greatest Hits* (1963); *Songs of the the Big City* (1964); *Live at the Apollo* (1964); *May I Sing for You* (1956); *Welcome Home* (1970). **BILLY WARD AND THE DOMINOES:** *Billy Ward with Clyde McPhatter* (1958); *Clyde McPhatter with Billy Ward and His Dominoes* (1958); *Billy Ward and the Dominoes Featuring Clyde McPhatter and Jackie Wilson* (1961). **CLYDE MCPHATTER AND THE DRIFTERS:** *Clyde McPhatter and the Drifters* (1957); *Rockin' and Driftin'* (1958).—**BH**

McPhee, Colin (Carhart), outstanding American composer and ethnomusicologist; b. Montreal, Canada, March 15, 1900; d. Los Angeles, Jan. 7, 1964. He studied piano and composition with Harold Randolph and Gustav Strube at the Peabody Cons. in Baltimore (graduated, 1921), then took piano lessons with Arthur Friedheim in Toronto (1921–24); continued his studies with Le Flem (composition) and Philipp (piano) in Paris (1924–26). Returning to the U.S. (1926), he joined the modern movement in N.Y. and was briefly a student of Varèse; wrote scores for the experimental films *H20* and *Mechanical Principles* in 1931. He became infatuated with the gamelan music of Java and Bali; moved to Indonesia in 1931 and, except for brief interruptions, remained there until 1939. He then returned to the U.S. and was a consultant to the Office of War Information during World War II; later was active with the Inst. of Ethnomusicology at the Univ. of Calif. at Los Angeles (1958–64). His *Tabuh-Tabuhan* for 2 Pianos, Orch., and Exotic Percussion, composed and premiered during an interlude in Mexico City (1936), is the quintessential work in his Bali-influenced style. He wrote the books *A House in Bali* (N.Y., 1946), *A Club of Small Men* (N.Y., 1948), and *Music in Bali* (New Haven, 1966).

WORKS: ORCH.: 2 piano concertos: No. 1, *La Mort d'Arthur* (Baltimore, May 26, 1920; not extant) and No. 2 (1923; Toronto, Jan. 15, 1924; not extant); *Sarabande* (1927); 3 syms.: No. 1 in 1 movement (1930; not extant), No. 2, *Pastorale* (1957; Louisville, Jan. 15, 1958), and No. 3 (1960–62; incomplete); *Tabuh-Tabuhan* for 2 Pianos, Orch., and Exotic Percussion (Mexico City, Sept. 4, 1936); *4 Iroquois Dances* (1944); *Transitions* (1954; Vancouver, March 20, 1955); *Nocturne* for Chamber Orch. (N.Y., Dec. 3, 1958); Concerto for Wind Orch. (1959; Pittsburgh, July 1960). **CHAMBER:** *Pastorale and Rondino* for 2 Flutes,

Clarinet, Trumpet, and Piano (1925; not extant); Concerto for Piano and Wind Octet (1928; Boston, March 11, 1929). **P i - a n o :** *4 Piano Sketches* (1916); *Invention* (1926); *Kinesis* (1930); *Balinese Ceremonial Music* for 2 Pianos (1934–38). **VOCAL:** *Sea Shanty Suite* for Baritone, Men's Chorus, 2 Pianos, and Timpani (N.Y., March 13, 1929); *From the Revelation of St. John the Divine* for Men's Chorus, 3 Trumpets, 2 Pianos, and Timpani (1935; N.Y., March 27, 1936; not extant).

BIBL.: R. Mueller, *Imitation and Stylization in the Balinese Music of C. M.* (diss., Univ. of Chicago, 1982); C. Oja, *C. M.: Composer in Two Worlds* (Washington, D.C., 1990).—**NS/LK/DM**

McPhee, Joe (actually, **Joseph J. Jr.**), avant-garde jazz saxophonist, trumpeter, cornetist, alto clarinetist, valve trombonist, bandleader, poet; b. Miami, Nov. 3, 1939. He grew up and still lives in Poughkeepsie, N.Y. He was born into a musical family; his great uncle, Al Cooper, was leader of the Savoy Sultans. His father, an accomplished trumpeter, started him on trumpet at eight; he continued through elementary and high school bands and into a stint in a U.S. Army band in Germany. During his army career, he studied harmony and theory, and began playing jazz. In 1968, he began teaching himself the saxophone. He made his debut recording in the late 1960s with Clifford Thornton. In 1969, he and painter Craig Johnson founded CJR Records; this led to a position at Vassar Coll. in Poughkeepsie, N.Y., lecturing in a Black Studies program series called "Revolution in Sound." In 1972, he appeared at the Newport Jazz Festival. He worked in N.Y. with Don Cherry, lived in Europe from 1975 to 1977, and starting in 1975 appeared at festivals in Switzerland, France, Germany, Portugal, and Canada. His recordings came to the attention of a Swiss entrepreneur, directly leading to the creation of Hat Hut Records. In 1981, he joined Hat Hut Records as Vice-President in charge of Promotion and Marketing, a position he held for four years. Later that year, he was invited to participate as a solo performer at the New Music America Festival, held in San Francisco. His work came to the attention of composer Pauline Oliveros, who inspired him to expand his investigations into extended instrumental and electronic techniques in a collaboration that continues to this day. Also in 1981, inspired by Dr. Edward de Bono's concept of lateral thinking, McPhee adapted the concept as a process to realize his own work. The result is what he calls "Po Music," a label he prefers to "jazz"; derived from words like possible, positive, poetry and hypothesis, the word "Po" is used to emphasize the process of moving from one fixed set of ideas in an attempt to discover new ones. In 1986, McPhee played live music to a screening of *L'Inhumaine*, a 1923 silent French film, in Paris; he repeated this in 1988 in Lisbon and in 1990 in Tokyo and Osaka. In 1994, he toured the U.S./Canada with Paul Plimley and Lisle Ellis; in 1995, he toured Europe with Evan Parker and Daunik Lazro. He won the Earshot Golden Ear Awards in Seattle in 1995 and 1997.

DISC.: *Underground Railroad* (1969); *Nation (Time)* (1970); *Black Magic Man* (1970); *Trinity* (1972); *Willisau Concert* (1975);

Variations on a Blue Line 'Round (1977); *Graphics* (1977); *Old Eyes and Mysteries* (1979); *Topology* (1981); *Visitation* (1983); *Po Music: Oleo* (1984); *Po Music: A Future Retrospective* (1987); *Linear B* (1990); *A Meeting in Chicago* (1996).—**LP**

McRae, Teddy (actually, **Theodore;** aka **Mr. Bear**), jazz tenor saxophonist, arranger, composer; b. Philadelphia, Jan. 22, 1908; d. N.Y., March 4, 1999. Brother of Bobby (guitar/trumpet) and Dave (alto/baritone saxes). He worked in a family band while studying medicine, also doubled regularly on guitar and trumpet. From 1926, he worked with June Clark, and also led his own band at the Club Ebony, N.Y., in 1927. After spells with Chick Webb, Charlie Johnson, and again with June Clark, he joined Elmer Snowden in 1932. After a brief time with Stuff Smith in 1934 he joined Lil Armstrong from 1935 to spring 1936, then he joined Chick Webb. He remained with Webb's group after the leader's death to work for Ella Fitzgerald (briefly as musical director) until late 1941. He then worked with Cab Calloway, then briefly with Jimmie Lunceford in late 1942. He worked as staff arranger for Artie Shaw, then two stints (on alto and tenor) with Lionel Hampton in 1943. He was musical director of Louis Armstrong's Big Band for a year from spring 1944, then formed his own band in 1945. During the 1950s and 1960s he arranged for many bands, and also for a time (in partnership with Eddie Wilcox) ran the record company RaeCox. He subsequently retired from music.

DISC.: *Chronological Chick Webb* (1935–38); *The Indispensable Artie Shaw Vol. 1–2* (1938–39); *Satisfy You* (1946); *Peek-a-Bob/The Bear Hug* (1955).—**JC/LP**

McShann, Jay (James Columbus; aka **Hootie**), jazz pianist, singer, bandleader; b. Muskogee, Okla., Jan. 12, 1916. Some sources give his birth year as 1909, which McShann himself disputes. His cousin, Pete McShann, played drums. He started playing piano from age of 12; he spent two months at Fisk Univ., returned home, then went to Tulsa to perform with the Al Dennis Band for four months. He briefly led own band in Ark. before studying for a year at Winfield Coll., Kans.; he left there to Ariz. and N.Mex. with Eddy Hill's Band. While on a trip to visit relatives in Iowa, he stopped off at Kansas City and began playing in local clubs. During the mid-1930s, he worked in many Kansas City night-spots, then after a residency at the Monroe Inn, he joined a group led by trumpeter Dee "Prince" Stewart. In 1938, he began leading his own band, which included Charlie Parker, at Martin's, Kansas City. In early 1936, he worked for four months in Chicago with his own trio, then returned to leading the band at Martin's. After a residency at the Century Room, Kansas City (February to June 1940), the band began regular touring, leading to their successful debut in N.Y. Among their hits were "Hootie Blues" (a title which gave him his nickname), "Confessin' the Blues," and "Swingmatism"; the band included Charlie Parker, Gene Ramey, Gus Johnson, and singer Walter Brown. McShann continued to lead his own big band until the Army call-up in late 1943. He was released a year later and reformed the band; in 1945, they were the resident band at The Downbeat Club in N.Y. In June 1946, he took the band to Los Angeles for various residencies including the Susie Q Club and Cobra Club. He returned to Kansas City in 1950 and has been based there since. He recorded for Vee Jay (1955–56) and backed Priscilla Bowman on her big hit, "Hands Off," for that label. During the 1950s and 1960s, he led his own group in Kansas City for long engagements at the Club Flamingo, Kismet Lounge, Barbary Coast Club, etc. After a long hiatus, he returned to recording in 1966 with the album *McShann's Piano* that rekindled interest in his work at home and make him a star touring attraction in Europe. He worked extensively in Europe during 1969, leading a specially formed band in France and Holland and subsequently appearing as a soloist at London's "Jazz Expo" in October. He embarked on worldwide touring during the 1970s, often with his own trio: Claude Williams (violin and guitar) and Paul Gunther (drums). In 1974, he toured Europe with the show *The Musical Life of Charlie Parker*; in 1975, he took part in the Montreux Jazz Festival; in 1979, he played at the Alexandra Palace Jazz Festival in London. He often appears in all-star groups and has displayed an engaging singing style more and more since the 1970s. He also appeared in the film *The Last of the Blue Devils*.

DISC.: *Jay McShann* (1954); *McShann's Piano* (1966); *Kansas City on My Mind* (1967); *Roll 'Em* (1969); *1208 Miles* (1969); *Confessin' the Blues* (1969); *Big Apple Bash* (1971); *Man from Muskogee* (1972); *Going to Kansas City* (1972); *Kansas City Memories* (1973); *Vine Street Boogie* (1974); *Crazy Legs and Friday Strut* (1976); *Last of the Blue Devils* (1977); *Tribute to Fats Waller* (1978); *Kansas City Hustle* (1978); *Tuxedo Junction* (1980); *Swingmatism* (1982); *Best of Friends* (1982); *At Cafe des Copains* (1983); *Airmail Special* (1985); *Paris All-Star Blues: A Tribute* (1989); *Some Blues* (1990); *Hootie & Hicks/Missouri Connection* (1992).—LP/NS

McTee, Cindy, American composer and teacher; b. Tacoma, Feb. 20, 1953. She studied composition at Pacific Lutheran Univ. in Tacoma (graduated, 1976), and also was an exchange fellow in composition at the State Higher School of Music in Kraków (1974–75), where she studied with Penderecki and Stachowski. She then pursued training in composition with Druckman at the Yale Univ. School of Music (M.A., 1978) before completing her studies at the Univ. of Iowa (doctorate, 1981). In 1984 she joined the faculty of the Univ. of North Tex. at Denton, where she became a full prof. in 1995. In 1992 she received the Goddard Lieberson Award of the American Academy of Arts and Letters. McTee's windsym. scores are especially notable for their cross-rhythms and sharply colored percussive sounds.

WORKS: ORCH.: *Music* for 48 Strings, Percussion, and Piano (1975); *Unisonance* (1978); *On Wings of Infinite Night* (1985); *Circuits* (1990; also for Winds); *The Twittering Machine* for Chamber Orch., after the Klee painting (Pittsburgh, Nov. 1, 1993; also as *California Counterpoint: The Twittering Machine* for Winds); *Elegy* for Strings (1994); *Pathfinder* (1999); *Timepiece* (1999; Dallas, Feb. 17, 2000; also for Winds). **W i n d s :** *Sonic Shades* (1977); *Circuits* (1990; also for Orch.); *California Counterpoint: The Twittering Machine* (1993; also as *The Twittering Machine* for Chamber Orch.); *Soundings* (1995). **CHAMBER:** 3 *Miniatures* for Clarinet (1973); Trio for Flute, Cello, and Harpsichord (1975); String Quartet No. 1 (1976); *Chord* for Flute

(1977); Wind Quintet No. 1 (1981); *Octonal Escalade* for 20 Trumpets (1985); *Images* for Horn and Piano (1987); *Circle Music I* for Viola and Piano (1988), *II* for Flute and Piano (1988), *III* for Bassoon and Piano (1988), *IV* for Horn and Piano (1988), and *V* for Trombone and Tape (1992); *8 Etudes* for 4 Instruments and Tape (1991); *Capriccio for Krzysztof Penderecki* for Violin (1993); *Fantasia* for Organ and Percussion (1993); *Changes* for Cello and Double Bass (1996); *Einstein's Dreams* for 6 Instruments (1996). **VOCAL:** *Dialogue* for Soprano and Male Vocalist (1976); *Gloria* for Chorus and Ensemble (1981); *Songs of Spring and the Moon* for Soprano and 8 Instruments (1983).—LK/DM

McVea, Jack, jazz tenor and alto saxophonist, clarinetist, leader; b. Los Angeles, Nov. 5, 1914. His father, **Isaac "Satchel" McVea** (d. 1960), was a banjoist who led his own band for many years. Jack began on banjo and by the age of 11 was playing regularly in his father's band; he began doubling on sax in 1927. After leaving high school in 1932 he played professionally with Walter "Dootsie" Williams's Harlem Dukes. From 1933 to 1935, he was in trumpeter Charlie Echols's band (except for a brief period in 1934 when he worked for Lorenzo Flennoy). He then worked with several other bands, before joining Eddie Barefield's Big Band in 1936. During the late 1930s, he played for many West Coast leaders and occasionally led his own band. Playing baritone sax, McVea worked with Lionel Hampton in N.Y. from 1940 until January 1943. He then returned to Calif., forming his own band in 1944. Over the next few years, he appeared on several of Norman Granz's "Jazz at the Philharmonic" concerts and broadcast with Count Basie. In 1946 his band scored with a commercial hit single "Open the Door Richard." McVea continued to lead through the 1950s, worked briefly on the MGM studio staff band, and played on many freelance recording dates. In 1955, he led a group in Las Vegas, then worked briefly with Benny Carter until reforming his own band. In 1959, he joined organist Perry Lee Blackwell's Trio. During the 1960s he has continued to lead his own small groups in Calif. and Ore., combining this with various recording commitments. From 1976–91, he led his own trio (on clarinet) at Disneyland. He subsequently retired in 1992, due to poor health.

DISC.: *Nothin' But Jazz* (1962); *Open the Door, Richard* (rec. in the 1940s; rel. 1985); *Come Blow Your Horn* (1985); *Two Timin' Baby* (1986); *New Deal* (1989). **RAY CHARLES:** *Blues+Jazz* (1950); *Going Down Slow* (1984); *Early Years [Zeta]* (1988).
—JC/LP

Meader, George, American tenor; b. Minneapolis, July 6, 1888; d. Los Angeles, Dec. 19, 1963. He studied law at the Univ. of Minnesota (graduated, 1908) and concurrently took vocal lessons with Anna Schoen-René; then studied with Pauline Viardot-García in Paris. He made his operatic debut as the Steersman in *Der fliegende Holländer* in Leipzig (1911), then was a member of the Stuttgart Opera until 1919. Returning to America in 1919, he gave recitals before making his operatic debut with the Metropolitan Opera in N.Y. as Victorin in Korngold's *Die tote Stadt* (Nov. 19, 1921). He left the Metropolitan in 1931 and sang in operetta, being particularly successful in Jerome Kern's *Cat and the Fiddle*.
—NS/LK/DM

Meador, Darmon (August), jazz vocalist, leader, and tenor and soprano saxophone player; b. Waterville, Maine, Aug. 26, 1961. He came from a musical family. After studying at the Univ. of Southern Mass. (1979–82) and Ithaca Coll. (1982–84), he moved to N.Y. in 1986. A year later, he formed the vocal group New York Voices along with several other Ithaca Coll. alumni. The group went through several personnel changes; originally working with instrumentalists and vocalists, the group is currently a vocal quartet. Meador has also worked as an instrumentalist and arranger, and taught at universities and jazz clinics.

DISC.: NEW YORK VOICES: *New York Voices* (1989); *Hearts of Fire* (1991); *What's Inside* (1993); *Sing the Songs of Paul Simon* (1997).—LP

Meale, Richard (Graham), notable Australian composer and teacher; b. Sydney, Aug. 24, 1932. He received training in piano, clarinet, harp, and theory at the New South Wales State Conservatorium of Music in Sydney (1946–55). As a composer, he was autodidact. In 1960 he received a Ford Foundation grant and studied non-Western music at the Inst. of Ethnomusicology at the Univ. of Calif. at Los Angeles. From 1961 to 1969 he was on the music staff of the Australian Broadcasting Corp. He was also active as a pianist and conductor of contemporary music. From 1969 to 1988 he taught at the Elder Conservatorium of Music at the Univ. of Adelaide. In 1974 he received a senior fellowship in composition from the state government of South Australia. He was awarded an Australian Creative Fellowship in 1989. In 1971 he was made a Member of the Order of the British Empire, and in 1985 a Member of the Order of Australia. By the 1960s, Meale was recognized as one of Australia's principal avant-garde composers. His visit to France and Spain, as well as his study of Japanese ritual and theater music, was influential in his development as a composer. By the close of the 1970s, Meale made a profound change of course and became one of Australia's leading composers of the neo-Romantic persuasion.

WORKS: DRAMATIC: *Voss*, opera (1979–86; Adelaide, March 1, 1986); *Mer de Glace*, opera (1986–91; Sydney, Oct. 3, 1991); ballets. ORCH.: Flute Concerto (1959); *Sinfonia* for Piano, 4–Hands, and Strings (1959); *Homage to García Lorca* for Double String Orch. (Sydney, Oct. 15, 1964); *Images (Nagauta)* (Adelaide, March 1966); *Nocturnes* for Vibraphone, Harp, Celesta, and Orch. (Sydney, April 1, 1967); *Very High Kings* (Sydney, Aug. 13, 1968); *Clouds Now and Then* (Perth, Feb. 1969); *Soon It Will Die* (Sydney, March 29, 1969); *Variations* (Brisbane, March 5, 1970); *Evocations* for Oboe, Chamber Orch., and Violin Obbligato (1973; Zürich, March 8, 1974); *Viridian* (Adelaide, May 18, 1979); Sym. (1994). CHAMBER: *Rhapsody* for Violin and Piano (1952); Quintet for Oboe and Strings (1952); *Rhapsody* for Cello and Piano (1953); Horn Sonata (1954), Sonata for Solo Flute (1957); *Divertimento* for Piano Trio (1959); Flute Sonata (1960); *Las Alborados* for Flute, Violin, Horn, and Piano (1963); *Intersections* for Flute, Viola, Vibraphone, and Piano (1965); *Cyphers* for Flute, Viola, Vibraphone, and Piano (1965); *Interiors/Exteriors* for 2 Pianos and 3 Percussion (Adelaide, March 11, 1970); Wind Quintet (1970); *Incredible Floridas (Homage to Arthur Rimbaud)* for Flute, Clarinet, Violin, Cello, Piano, and Percussion (London, June 5, 1971); *Plateau* for Wind Quintet (1971); 2 string quartets: No. 1 (London, Feb. 1975) and No. 2

(Adelaide, March 12, 1980). P i a n o : *Sonatina patetica* (1957); *Orenda* (1959); *Coruscations* (London, April 1971).—NS/LK/DM

Meat Loaf (originally, **Aday, Marvin Lee**), one of the biggest-selling (and *biggest*) solo artists in popular music; b. Dallas, Sept. 27, 1948.

Aday was raised in Tex.; his father, an alcoholic, often beat the child. This treatment worsened after his mother died of cancer. By his high school years, Aday had grown to an unusual heft, and gained his colorful nickname, probably thanks to his weighty appearance. After completing high school, he attended college for two years in Lubbock. He began working as an accountant, but quickly tired of his day job. In 1968, he moved to Los Angeles, where he befriended Gary Spragnola, a local musician whose brother, "Weasel," was lead guitarist in the garage-rock band, the Electric Prunes. Meat Loaf made some demo recordings with them, and then formed his first group, which played locally. Loaf then settled in Saginaw, Mich., where he formed another group, known as Popcorn Blizzard, releasing a single on its own. The group took up residence in Detroit's Hideout Club and then, with varying personnel and names (including Meat Loaf Soul), toured as a supporting act to such rock headliners as Iggy Pop, the Who, and Ted Nugent.

Loaf next settled in a commune outside of Los Angeles. There, he met an actor who encouraged him to try out for a touring company of the rock musical *Hair*. Loaf was hired to portray Ulysses S. Grant, and his acting career began. While in Detroit, Loaf and actress "Stoney," from the show, cut an album for Motown's Rare Earth rock label in 1971. The album produced a local hit version of "What You See Is What You Get." After touring as an opening act for other rock groups, the duo split up and Loaf returned to *Hair*, now playing in Cleveland.

Meat Loaf wound up in N.Y. during the early 1970s, working in the theater by evening and singing in clubs with various acts into the early morning hours. He appeared in Shakespeare in the Park productions of *Othello* and *As You Like It*. Off-Broadway he had roles in Sam Sheppard's *Billy The Kid and Jean Harlow*, the gospel musical *Rainbow in New York*, *The Vietnam Project*, and *More Than You Deserve*, written by a classically trained pianist named Jim Steinman. Steinman and Loaf recorded the play's title track for RSO Records, but neither the play nor the record made much of an impression. Next, Loaf joined the cast of the *Rocky Horror Picture Show*, playing Eddie in the cult favorite. Following this, he joined Steinman again, touring with the National Lampoon Show. During this tour, old friend Ted Nugent asked him to sing on his *Free for All* album. The project went double platinum.

Following this success, Meat Loaf signed with Cleveland International Records. He went into the studio with Steinman, members of Bruce Springsteen's E Street Band, actress Ellen Foley, future Baseball Hall of Famer (and voice of the N.Y. Yankees) Phil Rizzuto, and others, under the aegis of producer Todd Rundgren. The resulting album, *Bat Out of Hell*, was comprised largely of songs from Steinman's proposed musical *Neverland*, based on the Peter Pan myth, that had never been produced. The theatricality of the songs fit Loaf's big voice and over-the-top personality. While the record sold slowly at first, Meat Loaf and his band (including Steinman) toured incessantly behind it. More than a year after the record's release, during the spring of 1978, its first single, the ballad "Two out of Three Ain't Bad," broke. It went gold, despite topping out at #11 on the charts. This was followed by the album-rock standard "Paradise By the Dashboard Light." The song featured Foley as the object of Meat Loaf's affection with Rizzuto calling the seduction as if it were a baseball game ("it's a suicide squeeze, and he slides into home..."). While this hit only #39 pop, it is still played regularly wherever classic rock is heard, as is "You Took the Words Right Out of My Mouth" which fared the same on the pop charts early in 1979. When the dust cleared, *Bat Out of Hell* had sold 12 times platinum.

To keep his hand in acting, Meat Loaf took a couple of film roles: a smaller one in the 1979 film *Americathon* and the lead in the 1980 movie *Roadie*. He was slated to sing on a new album written by Steinman, *Bad for Good*, but vocal, emotional, legal, and chemical problems kept him away from the project, so Steinman went on to cut the album solo. The 1981 Meat Loaf/Steinman collaboration *Dead Ringer* failed to generate any excitement, despite (or perhaps because of) a duet with Cher on the title track. Steinman initiated legal actions against both Epic and Meat Loaf. The singer released his first Steinman-less project in 1983, *Midnight at the Lost and Found*, which fared far better in Europe than it did at home, where it was roundly ignored, as was *Bad Attitude*. He fell into a morass of lawsuits, drinking, and drugs that left him bankrupt by 1984. Meat Loaf went through physical and psychological therapy for more than a year before working with producer Frank Farian on *Blind Before I Stop*. Again, the album met with fan indifference in the U.S., but did okay in Europe. Meanwhile, Meat Loaf kept bread on the table by touring endlessly.

By 1989, rumors started circulating that Meat Loaf and Jim Steinman were working together again. However, during the early 1990s, Meat Loaf was more evident on celluloid than CD, appearing in the films *Wayne's World* and *Leap of Faith*. Finally, Loaf and Steinman released a sequel to *Bat Out of Hell*, *Bat Out of Hell II, Back into Hell* in 1993. The highly anticipated album picked up where they had left off 15 years previously. The first single, the histrionic ballad "I'd Do Anything for Love (But I Won't Do That)," topped the charts for five weeks, going platinum, taking the album to the top of the charts with it. The bombastic rocker "Rock and Roll Dreams Come Through" rose to #13. The somewhat melancholy "Objects in The Rear View Mirror May Appear Closer Than They Are" topped out at #38, but the album went quadruple platinum nonetheless.

Loaf's 1995 album, *Welcome to the Neighborhood*, featured a big hit "I'd Lie for You (And That's the Truth)." The song was written by pop tunesmith Diane Warren very much in the style of Jim Steinman. Although the song rose to #13 and went gold, taking the album to

platinum behind it, the record company dropped Meat Loaf. That year he also filed a suit against his old record company (now owned by Sony), claiming it had underpaid him some $15 million in royalties. Late in the 1990s, Loaf became an in-demand character actor, appearing in the films *Black Dog*, *The Mighty* (as *X-Files*'s star Gillian Anderson's husband), *Crazy in Alabama*, and *Fight Club*. His appearance on VH-1's *Storytellers* and the subsequent album and tour brought him back into the public eye, if not onto the charts.

WRITINGS: With D. Dalton, *To Hell and Back* (N.Y., 1988).

DISC.: *Bat Out of Hell* (1978); *Meatloaf (Featuring Stoney)* (1979); *Dead Ringer* (1981); *Midnight at the Lost & Found* (1983); *Bad Attitude* (1984); *Blind Before I Stop* (1986); *Live at Wembley* (1987); *Live* (1987); *Bat Out of Hell/Deadringer* (1993); *Bat Out of Hell II: Back into Hell* (1993); *Rock 'n' Roll Hero* (1995); *Welcome to the Neighborhood* (1995); *Live* (1996); *Live Around the World* (1996); *VH-1 Storytellers* (1999).—**HB**

Mechem, Kirke (Lewis), American composer, conductor, and lecturer on music; b. Wichita, Kans., Aug. 16, 1925. He was a pupil of Harold Schmidt, Leonard Ratner, and Sandor Salgo at Stanford Univ. (B.A., 1951) and of Walter Piston, Randall Thompson, and A. Tillman Merritt at Harvard Univ. (M.A., 1953). After serving as director of music at Menlo Coll. in Calif. (1953–56) and as a teacher and conductor at Stanford Univ. (1953–56), he was active in Vienna (1956–57; 1961–63). He was composer-in-residence at the Univ. of San Francisco's Lone Mountain Coll. (1964–65; 1966–72) and a teacher and conductor at San Francisco State Coll. (1965–66). As a composer, Mechem considers himself a conservationist, his aim being to find new ways to enlarge and enrich the tonal heritage. He maintains that music is a language, and thus cannot develop by revolution but only by evolution. He became well known as a composer of choral works and instrumental pieces. His opera *Tartuffe* (1977–80) proved an immediate success at its premiere and was subsequently performed more than 200 times, with translations into Chinese, Russian, German, and Czech.

WORKS: DRAMATIC: O p e r a : *Tartuffe*, after Molière (1977–80; San Francisco, May 27, 1980); *John Brown* (1988–89); *The Newport Rivals*, after Sheridan (in progress). **ORCH.:** 2 syms.: No. 1 (1958–59; San Francisco, Jan. 6, 1965) and No. 2 (1966; San Francisco, March 29, 1967; rev. 1968; San Francisco, Jan. 15, 1969); *Haydn's Return*, fugue and variations on Haydn's *Farewell Symphony* (1960; Santa Rosa, Calif., Feb. 12, 1961); *The Jayhawk*, overture to a mythical comedy (1974; Topeka, Kans., March 19, 1975). **CHAMBER:** Suite for 2 Violins (1952–53); Suite for Piano (1954); Trio for Oboe, Clarinet, and Bassoon (1955); Trio for Piano, Violin, and Cello (1956–57); Divertimento for Flute, Violin, Viola, and Cello (1958); String Quartet No. 1 (1962–63). **P i a n o :** Sonata (1964–65); *Whims*, 15 easy vignettes (1967; also as *Brass Buttons* for Brass Quintet, 1969). **VOCAL:** *Songs of Wisdom*, sacred cantata for 4 Soloists and Chorus (1958–59; San Francisco, March 10, 1960); *The King's Contest*, cantata for 4 Soloists, Chorus, and Orch. or Chamber Ensemble (1960–61; San Rafael, Calif., May 1, 1965; rev. 1972); *The Winged Joy: A Woman's Love by Women Poets* for Mezzo-soprano, Treble Chorus, and Piano (1963–64; Boston, Feb. 21, 1965); *7 Joys of Christmas*, sequence of carols for Soprano, Chorus, and Harp or Keyboard Instrument (San Francisco, Dec.

9, 1964; also for Soprano, Chorus, and Chamber Orch., 1974); *The Shepherd and His Love* for Chorus, Piano, Piccolo, and Viola (Cambridge, Mass., Aug. 17, 1967); *Singing is So Good a Thing: An Elizabethan Recreation*, cantata for Soprano or Tenor, Chorus, and Chamber Orch. or Instrumental Ensemble (1970–71; Elgin, Ill., Jan. 23, 1972); *Speech to a Crowd* for Baritone, Chorus, and Orch. or 2 Pianos (Anaheim, Calif., March 26, 1974); *American Madrigals* for Chorus and Instrumental Ensemble or Piano (1975; Palo Alto, Calif., Feb. 13, 1976); *Songs of the Slave* for Bass-baritone, Chorus, and Orch. (1993; Los Angeles, June 12, 1994); *3 Motets* for Chorus (1993–94); *Barter* for Women's Chorus, Trumpet, and Piano, 4–Hands (1994; Florence, July 1995); *Choral Variations on American Folk Songs* for Chorus and Piano (1995); *Earth My Song* for Chorus and Piano (1996); *Winging Wildly* for Chorus (1996); *To Music* for Chorus and Organ or Piano (1998).—**NS/LK/DM**

Měchura, Leopold Eugen, Bohemian composer; b. Prague, Feb. 2, 1804; d. Votín, near Klatovy, Feb. 11, 1870. He received training in law and philosophy at the Univ. of Prague, and in composition from Tomaschek and B. Weber. A concert of his works in Prague (March 22, 1868) brought him wide recognition. Měchura was one of the leading representatives of the Czech national school of his era. Among his works were the opera *Marie Potocká* (1869; Prague, Jan. 13, 1871), 6 syms., 16 string quartets, and the cantatas *Prořeb na Kaňku* (Burial on Kank Hill; 1866) and *Štědrý den* (Christmas Eve; 1867).—**LK/DM**

Meck, Joseph, German composer; b. probably in Knöringen, near Günzburg, 1690; d. Eichstätt, Dec. 2, 1758. Following training in Germany and Italy, he entered the service of the Eichstätt court as a violinist about 1711, where he later was made a chamber musician and valet (1714), Vice-Hofkapellmeister (1715), and Hofkapellmeister (1721). He was especially admired as a composer of instrumental music, producing finely honed works in the manner of Vivaldi. His opus 1 was the first publ. vol. of solo concertos by a German composer. In all, he composed 18 violin concertos and an oboe concerto.

BIBL.: K. Beckmann, *J. M. (1690–1758): Leben und Werk des Eichstätter-Hofkapellmeisters* (Bochum, 1975).—**LK/DM**

Meck, Nadezhda von, Russian patroness of music; b. Znamenskoye, near Smolensk, Feb. 10, 1831; d. Wiesbaden, Jan. 13, 1894. She became interested in Tchaikovsky's music through Nikolai Rubinstein, director of the Moscow Cons., of which she was a patroness. At first offering Tchaikovsky commissions, she later granted him a yearly allowance of 6,000 rubles in order that he might compose undisturbed by financial considerations. He lived for long periods in close proximity to her, at Brailov (near Kiev) and in Florence, Italy, but although they carried on an extensive and intimate correspondence (3 vols., Moscow, 1934–36), they never met face to face. Tchaikovsky's allowance was abruptly cut off in 1890 on the pretext of financial difficulties, leading to a complete break between him and Mme. von Meck in 1891. She employed the youthful Debussy as a pianist in her household.—**NS/LK/DM**

Medek, Ivo, Czech composer; b. Brno, July 20, 1956. He received training in computers and structural mechanics at the Technical Univ. in Brno, and in composition from Alois Piňos at the Janáček Academy of Music and Dramatic Art in Brno (M.A., 1989; Ph.D., 1997), where he was an asst. prof. from 1990. His output includes dramatic, orch., chamber, vocal, electroacoustic, and multimedia scores. With Piňos and Miloš Štědroň, he wrote the collaborative operas *Věc Cage aneb Anály avantgardy dokořán* (The Cage Affair, or the Avant-Garde Chronicles Flung Open; Brno, Oct. 6, 1995) and *Anály předchůdců avantgardy aneb Setkání slovansksých velikánů* (Annals of the Predecessors of the Avant-Garde, or the Meeting of the Slavonic Giants; Brno, Oct. 1997). Among his other works are *Pangea* for Clarinet, Violin, and Piano (1991), *Světy bez hranic I.* (Worlds Without Borders I.), audiovisual piece (1993), *Adam a Eva*, oratorio (1994), *Fests* for 3 Percussionists and Piano (1994), *Variace na štěsti* (Variations on Happiness) for Electrophonic Violin, Percussion, and Tape (1994), and *Persephonia* for Percussionist and String Orch. (1995). —**NS/LK/DM**

Medek, Tilo, German composer; b. Jena, Jan. 22, 1940. He went to Berlin and studied musicology at Humboldt Univ., attended the Deutsche Hochschule für Musik, and received training in composition from Wagner-Régeny at the Deutsche Akademie der Künste. Thereafter he devoted himself to composition.

WORKS: DRAMATIC: Opera: *Einzug* (1969); *Katharina Blum* (1984–91; Bielefeld, April 20, 1991). **Singspiels:** *Icke und die Hexe Yu* (1971); *Appetit auf Frühkirschen* (1971). **Ballet:** *David und Goliath* (1972). **ORCH.:** *Triade* (1964); *Porträt eines Tangos* (1968); *Das zögernde Lied* (1970); Flute Concerto (1973); *Grosser Marsch* (1974); 3 cello concertos (1978, 1984, 1992); 2 organ concertos (1979, 1994); *König Johann oder Der Ausstieg* (1980); Violin Concerto (1980); *Konzertstuck* for Timpani and Orch. (1982); *Eisenblätter* (1983); *Rheinische Sinfonie* (1986); Trumpet Concerto (1989); *Zur Lage der Nation* (1990); *Schattenbrenner* for Symphonic Wind Orch. (1991); Percussion Concerto (1993); *Sorbische Wehrstücke* (1994); *Air* for Vibraphone and Orch. (1994); Children's Piano Concerto (1994). **CHAMBER:** 4 wind quintets (1965; 1974–76; 1979; 1989); *Stadtpfeifer, ein Schwanengesang* for Clarinet, Trombone, Cello, and Piano (1973); *Tagtraum* for Flute, Oboe, Trumpet, Violin, Cello, Double Bass, and Piano (1976); *Giebichenstein* for Chamber Ensemble (1976); *Reliquienschrein* for Organ and Percussion (1980); *Spiegelszenen* for Oboe, Clarinet, Horn, Bassoon, and Piano (1986–89); *Bündelungen* for 3 Guitars (1990); *Biedermaier-Variationen* for Flute, Violin, and Cello (1991–92); *Dezett* for Double Wind Quintet (1993); piano pieces; organ music. **VOCAL:** *Altägyptische Liebslieder* for 2 Voices and Orch. (1963); *Johann Wallbergens natürliche Zauberkünste 1768* for Narrator, Soprano, and Salon Orch. (1965); *Todesfuge nach Paul Celan* for Soprano and 16 Voices (1966); *De mirabili effectu amoris/Von der wunderbaren Wirkung der Liebe* for 2 Choruses (1967); *Deutschland 1952* for Children's Chorus (1971); *Kindermesse* for Children's Chorus (1974); *Sinnsprüche des Angelus Silesius*, 12 pieces for 6 Solo Voices or Chamber Chorus (1978); *Gethsemane*, cantata for Soprano, Tenor, Chorus, and Orch. (1980); *Der Greis* for Voice, Violin, Guitar, and Percussion (1992).—**NS/LK/DM**

Meder, Johann Valentin, German singer, organist, and composer; b. Wasungen, near Meiningen (bap-

tized), May 3, 1649; d. Riga, July 1719. He studied theology in Leipzig and Jena. After serving as a court singer in Gotha (1671), Bremen (1672–73), Hamburg (1673), Copenhagen (1674), and Lübeck (1674), he was Kantor at the Reval Gymnasium (1674–80). From 1687 to 1698 he was Kapellmeister at St. Marien in Danzig. He then was Kantor at Königsberg Cathedral, and subsequently in Riga (from 1700). He composed the opera *Die beständige Argenia* (Reval, 1680), an oratorio *Passion* (1700), and many masses, cantatas, and motets.
—NS/LK/DM

Mederitsch (-Gallus), Johann (Georg Anton),

Austrian composer; b. Vienna (baptized), Dec. 27, 1752; d. Lemberg, Dec. 18, 1835. He received training from Wagenseil. In 1781–82 he served as Kapellmeister of the Olmütz Theater. After playing double bass in the orch. of the German Theater in Vienna (1782–92?), he was Kapellmeister in Ofen (Buda) from 1793 to about 1796, and again in 1798. In 1817 he settled in Lemberg. In spite of the success he attained as a composer of Singspiels for the Vienna stage, his last years were marked by poverty and neglect.

WORKS: DRAMATIC: Opera (all 1st perf. in Vienna unless otherwise given): *Der redliche Verwalter* (Aug. 26, 1779); *Arkatastor und Illiane* (Oct. 14, 1779); *Der Schlosser* (Olmütz, 1781); *Rose, oder Pflicht und Liebe im Streit* (Feb. 9, 1783); *Der letzte Rausch* (c. 1788); *Babylons Pyramiden* (Oct. 25, 1797; Act 1 by Mederitsch and Act 2 by Winter); *Krakus, Fürst von Krakau, oder Frauengrosse und Vaterliebe* (March 3, 1811). **Incidental Music**: *Macbeth* (Pest, 1793–94). **OTHER:** Syms.; concertos; chamber music; piano pieces; masses; motets.

BIBL.: T. Aigner, *J.G. M. (1752–1835): Leben und thematisches Verzeichnis der Werke* (diss., Univ. of Salzburg, 1973).—**LK/DM**

Mediņš,

family of prominent Latvian musicians, all brothers:

(1) Jāzeps Mediņš, conductor and composer; b. Kaunas, Feb. 13, 1877; d. Riga, June 12, 1947. He studied at the Riga Music Inst. (graduated, 1896), where he later was a teacher and director. He was a conductor at the Riga Theater (1906–11), the Baku Opera (1916–22), and the Latvian National Opera in Riga (1922–25), and later taught piano at the Riga Cons. (1945–47).

WORKS: DRAMATIC: Opera: *Vaidelote* (The Priestess; 1922–24; Riga, 1927); *Zemdegi* (The Zemdegs Family; 1947; completed by M. Zariņš). **OTHER:** Sym. No. 2, *Ziedoni* (In Springtime; 1937); Sym. No. 3 (1941); Violin Concerto (1911); String Quartet (1941); other chamber music; choral works; songs.

BIBL.: M. Zālīte, *J. M.* (Riga, 1951).

(2) Jēkabs Mediņš, conductor, teacher, and composer; b. Riga, March 22, 1885; d. there, Nov. 27, 1971. He studied at the Riga Music Inst. (graduated, 1905) and at the Berlin Hochschule für Musik (1910–14). He taught at the Jelgava Teachers' Inst. (1921–44), and was director of the People's Cons. there (1921–41). He later taught choral conducting at the Riga Cons. (1944–71), serving as its rector (1949–51). He wrote an autobiography, *Silueti* (Silhouettes; Riga, 1968).

WORKS: Clarinet Concerto (1948); 2 horn concertos (1949, 1962); Kokle Concerto (1952); Organ Concerto (1954); cantatas; chamber music; songs.

(3) Jānis Mediņš, conductor and composer; b. Riga, Oct. 9, 1890; d. Stockholm, March 4, 1966. He studied at the Riga Music Inst. (graduated, 1909). He was a violist and conductor at the Latvian Opera in Riga (1913–15), then a military bandmaster in St. Petersburg (1916–20). He conducted at the Latvian National Opera (1920–28), and subsequently was chief conductor of the Latvian Sym. Orch. (1928–44); was also a prof. at the Riga Cons. (1929–44). As the Soviet army approached his homeland (1944), he went to Germany, then settled in Stockholm (1948). He wrote an autobiography, *Toni un pustoni* (Tones and Semitones; Stockholm, 1964). He distinguished himself as a composer of both vocal and instrumental works.

WORKS: DRAMATIC: Opera: *Uguns un nakts* (Fire and Night; 1st written as 2 operas, 1913–19; Riga, May 26, 1921; rev. as a single opera, 1924); *Dievi un cilvēki* (Gods and Men; Riga, May 23, 1922); *Sprīdītis* (Tom Thumb; Riga, 1927); *Luteklite* (The Little Darling), children's opera (Riga, 1939). **Ballet:** *Mīlas uzvara* (Love's Victory; 1935; the 1st Latvian ballet). **ORCH.:** Cello Concerto (1928); Piano Concerto (1934); several suites for Orch., including No. 3, *Dzimtene* (The Fatherland; 1933); other orch. pieces and music for band. **CHAMBER:** 2 piano trios (1930, 1958); Cello Sonata (1945); String Quartet (1946); 2 sonatas for Violin and Piano (1946, 1954); various piano pieces. **VOCAL:** 8 cantatas; some 130 songs.
—**NS/LK/DM**

Medlam, Charles,

English conductor and cellist; b. Port-au-Prince, Trinidad, Sept. 10, 1949. He studied cello in London, and with Gendron at the Paris Cons. He also studied in Salzburg with Harnoncourt. After playing in the resident string quartet at the Chinese Univ. in Hong Kong, he settled in England. In 1978 he co-founded London Baroque, a chamber orch., which he conducted in many early music performances. In 1990 he conducted *Dido and Aeneas* at the Paris Opéra, and in 1991 he made his debut at the Salzburg Festival. In 1993 he conducted at the London Promenade Concerts. His large repertoire of orch. and vocal music includes scores by Monteverdi, Lully, Charpentier, Blow, Scarlatti, Handel, Bach, Purcell, and Rameau.—**NS/LK/DM**

Medtner, Nicolai (actually, Nikolai Karlovich),

notable Russian pianist and composer of German descent; b. Moscow, Jan. 5, 1880; d. London, Nov. 13, 1951. He first studied piano with his mother, and then with his uncle, Theodore Goedicke. In 1892 he entered the Moscow Cons., where he took courses with Sapelnikov and Safonov (piano) and Arensky and Taneyev (composition); graduated in 1900, winning the gold medal; that same year he won the Rubinstein prize in Vienna. For the next 2 years he appeared with much success as a pianist in the European capitals. Returning to Russia, he taught at the Moscow Cons. (1902–03; 1909–10; 1914–21). He then lived in Berlin and Paris before settling in London (1935). He made tours of the U.S. (1924–25; 1929–30) and the Soviet Union (1927). He publ. a collection of essays as *Muza i moda* (The Muse and Fashion; Paris, 1935; Eng. tr., 1951). In Russian music he was a solitary figure; he never followed the nationalist trend, but endeavored to create a new type of composition, rooted in both the Classical and the Romantic traditions; his sets of fairy tales in sonata form are unique examples of his favorite genre. He wrote his best compositions before he left Russia; although he continued to compose during his residence abroad, his late music lacks the verve and Romantic sincerity that distinguish his earlier works. He wrote almost exclusively for the piano and for the voice. A revival of his music was begun in Russia after his death, and a complete ed. of his works appeared in Moscow (12 vols., 1959–63).

WORKS: 3 piano concertos: No. 1 (1914–18; Moscow, May 12, 1918, composer soloist), No. 2 (1920–27; Moscow, March 13, 1927), and No. 3 (1940–43; London, Feb. 19, 1944, composer soloist); Piano Quintet (1904–49); 3 violin sonatas (1909–10; 1926; 1938); numerous piano pieces, including *34 Fairy Tales* (1905–29), 6 sonatas (1896–1915), *Sonaten-Triade* (1904–08), *Sonata romantica* (1931–32), *Sonata minacciosa* (1931–32), and *Sonata idillica* (1935); also sets of piano pieces, including *4 Lyric Fragments* (1910–11), 3 sets of *Forgotten Melodies* (1918–20), and 4 sets of *Romantic Sketches for the Young* (1932); also 107 songs.

BIBL.: V. Yakovlev, *N. M.* (Moscow, 1927); R. Holt, *M. and His Music* (London, 1948); idem, ed., *N. M. (1879–1951): A Tribute to His Art and Personality* (London, 1955); E. Dolinskaya, *N. M.* (Moscow, 1966); B. Martyn, *N. M.: His Life and Music* (Aldershot, 1995).—**NS/LK/DM**

Meester, Louis de, Belgian composer; b. Roeselare, Oct. 28, 1904; d. Ghent, Dec. 12, 1987. He was mainly autodidact as a composer. After serving as director of the Meknes Cons. in French Morocco (1933–37), he returned to Belgium and studied with Absil. From 1945 to 1961 he worked for the Belgian Radio. He was director of the Inst. for Psychoacoustics and Electronic Music at the Univ. of Ghent from 1961 to 1969.

WORKS: DRAMATIC: *Van een trotse vogel*, musical comedy (1948); *La Grande Tentation de Saint Antoine*, opera buffa (1957; Antwerp, Nov. 11, 1961); *2 is te weining, 3 is te veel* (2 is too little, 3 is too much), opera (1966; Palermo, June 13, 1969); *Paradijsgeuzen* (Beggars in Heaven), opera (1966; Ghent, March 26, 1967); incidental music. **ORCH.:** *Magreb* for Viola and Orch. (1946); *Capriccio* (1948); *Sprookjesmuziek* (1949); *Sinfonietta Buffa* (1950); 2 piano concertos (1952, 1956); *Musica per archi* (1955); *Amalgames* (1956); *Marine* (1957); Concertino for 2 String Orchs. (1965); *Serenade* for Flute, Oboe, and Strings (1967); *Tombeau voor P.-P. Rubens* (1977). **CHAMBER:** Cello Sonatina (1945); *Divertimento* for Wind Quintet (1946); 3 string quartets (1947, 1949, 1954); String Trio (1951); *Tafelmuziek* for Flute, Oboe, Violin, Viola, and Cello (1953); Sonata for Solo Guitar (1954); Violin Sonata (1957); *Serenade* for Harpsichord and 11 Strings (1958–59); *Postludium* for Organ and Brass (1959); *Divertimento* for Piano Quartet (1970); *3 Interludes* for Flute and Organ (1975); piano pieces. **VOCAL:** *La Voix du silence*, cantata for Baritone, Narrator, Women's Chorus, and Chamber Orch. (1951–54); *Ballade van de gebarste trommel* for Narrator and Orch. (1973); choruses. **OTHER:** Electronic pieces.—**NS/LK/DM**

Méfano, Paul, French composer; b. Basra, Iraq, March 6, 1937. He began his training with Andrée

Vaurabourg-Honegger, and then studied at the Paris Cons. with Milhaud and Dandelot. He also studied with Boulez, Stockhausen, and Pousseur before returning to the Paris Cons. to complete his training with Messiaen. After working in the U.S. on a Harkness Foundation grant (1966–68), he held a Berlin fellowship in 1968–69. In 1972 he co-founded the Ensemble 2e2m, a contemporary music ensemble in Paris. In 1980 he was named a Chevalier de l'Ordre National du Mérite, in 1982 he was awarded the Grand Prix National de la Musique, in 1985 he was named a Commandeur de l'Ordre des Arts et des Lettres, and in 1989 he won the Grand Prix of the SACEM.

WORKS: DRAMATIC: *Micromégas*, action musicale (Paris, July 3, 1979; rev. 1983–87; Karlsruhe, April 16, 1988). **ORCH.:** *Danse bulgare* for Strings (1959; rev. 1980); *Variations libre* for Strings (1959; rev. 1980); *Incidences* for Piano and Orch. (1960; Paris, May 19, 1967); *Signe-oubli* for 22 Players (Metz, Nov. 1972); *A Bruno Maderna* for Cello, Strings, and Tape (1980); *Voyager* (Metz, Nov. 17, 1989). **CHAMBER:** *Involutive* for Clarinet (1958); *Estampes japonaises* for Flute and Piano (1959; also for Voice and Instruments); *Captive* for Flute (1962); *Interférences* for Piano, Horn, and 10 Players (1966); *N* for Flute and Electronics (1972); *Ondes (espaces mouvants)* for 10 Players (Metz, Nov. 20, 1975); *Eventails* for Amplified Flute (1976); *Mouvement calme* for String Quartet for String Ensemble (1976); *Périple* for Saxophonist(s) and Electronics (1978); *Gradiva* for Flute (1978); *Traits suspendus* for Flute (1980); *Ensevelie* for Flute (1986; Berlin, March 3, 1988); *Tige* for Saxophone (1986; Champigny, Jan. 14, 1989); *Scintillante* for Bassoon and Electronics (1990; Gennevilliers, Jan. 25, 1991); *Asahi* for Oboe and Electronics (1992); *Matrice des vents* for Sho and Electronics (1992); *Mon ami Emile* for Flute, Clarinet, Piano, and String Quartet (1995–96; also for Flute, Clarinet, Piano, Harmonium, and String Quartet, 1998); *Cinq pièces* for 2 Violins (1998); *Hélios* for Alto Flute and String Trio (1998); *Alone* for Violin (1999). **Piano:** *Evocations à l'usage des jeunes filles* (1956); *Croquis pour un adolescent* (1957); *Mémoire de la porte blanche* (1991). **VOCAL:** *Trois Chants crépusculaires* for Soprano and Piano (1958); *Estampes japonaises* for Soprano and Instrumental Ensemble (1959; also for Soprano and Piano, and for Flute and Piano); *Madrigal* for 3 Women's Voices or 2 Women's Voices and Countertenor, and Small Instrumental Ensemble (1962); *Mélodies* for Soprano, Mezzo-soprano or Countertenor or Contralto, and Instrumental Ensemble (1962); *Que l'oiseau se déchire* for Voice, Clarinet, and Percussionist (1962); *Paraboles* for Soprano and Instrumental Ensemble (1965); *Lignes* for Bass and 15 Players (1965); *La Cérémonie*, oratorio for Soprano, Countertenor, Baritone, Chorus, and Orch. (1970); *Old Oedip* for Reciter, Tape, and Electronics (1970); *La Messe des voleurs* for Vocal Quartet, Chamber Ensemble, Electronics, and Tape (1972); *L'Age de la vie* for Soprano, Horn, and Harp (1972); *They* for Voice (1974); *Placebo domino in regione vivorum* for 6 Voices (1976); *Scène 3* for Soprano and Small Orch., after *Micromégas* (1983; Metz, Oct. 6, 1984); *Douce saveur* for Bass, English Horn, and Tuba (1984); *Dragonbass* for Bass, 2 Saxophones, and Synthesizer (1993); *Deux mélodies* for Soprano, Mezzo-soprano, Saxophone, Clarinet, and Viola (1995); *Trois chants 1958* for Soprano, 3 Saxophones, 3 Percussion, and 3 Cellos (1997). —**NS/LK/DM**

Mehegan, John, jazz educator, author, pianist; b. Hartford, Conn., June 6, 1920; d. New Canaan, Conn., April 3, 1984. He studied violin, but was a self-taught pianist. He moved to N.Y. in 1941, teaching privately at first. From 1947–57, he taught one of the few jazz courses at the Juilliard School, which grew into his noted four-volume piano method set. While clearly the largest method up to that time, and one of the largest since, it remained of limited appeal because of its reliance on classical terminology. The second volume included a generous selection of transcribed solos from a variety of instruments that are of more general usefulness. He worked as a performer in the late 1950s and early 1960s, and continued to teach through the 1970s. He died at 67 of a brain tumor.

Disc.: *Last Mehegan* (1954); *Johnny Mehegan Quartet* (1954); *First Mehegan* (1954); *From Barrelhouse to Bop* (1955); *Reflections* (1955); *Pair of Pianos* (1955); *John Mehegan Quartet* (1955); *How I Play Jazz Piano* (1956); *Casual Affair* (1959); *Act of Jazz* (1960).—**LP**

Mehlig, Anna, German pianist; b. Stuttgart, July 11, 1845; d. Berlin, July 26, 1928. She was a student of Lebert in Stuttgart and of Liszt in Weimar. On April 30, 1866, she made her London debut. From 1869 to 1875 she successfully presented the first American performances of many works in the U.S., and then returned to England. After a sojourn in Antwerp, she settled in Berlin in 1914.—**LK/DM**

Mehta, Bejun, remarkable American countertenor; b. Laurinburg, N.C., June 29, 1968. He was reared in a musical family. His father was a pianist and teacher, and a cousin of Zubin Mehta, and his mother was a singer and journalist. His precocious musical talent manifested itself at an early age, and he soon won notice as a boy soprano of great promise. At 15, he made his first CD, which was honored with the "Debut Recording Artist of the Year" citation from *Stereo Review*. He then studied cello with Aldo Parisot in New Haven (1984–90), where he also studied Germanic literature at Yale Univ. (B.A., 1990). During this period, he became active as a record producer, which led him to found Bejun Mehta Productions, Inc., a classical music audio production firm. In 1991 he began to make appearances as a baritone, and pursued vocal training with Phyllis Curtin in Boston (1991–94) and Edward Zambara in N.Y. (1994–97). In 1995 he portrayed Papageno in a N.Y.C. Opera Education production. He gave up singing as a baritone in 1997, and studied the countertenor voice with Joan Patenaude in N.Y. from 1998, the same year that he made his operatic debut as a countertenor with the N.Y.C. Opera as Armindo in *Partenope*. That same year, he made his debut as a countertenor soloist with the Arcadian Academy at the 92nd St. Y in N.Y. under Nicholas McGegan's direction, who also conducted his London debut that year at Wigmore Hall. In 1999 he made his recital debut as a countertenor in N.Y. under the auspices of the Marilyn Horne Foundation. That same year, he also appeared as Bertarido in *Rodelinda* at the Music Academy of the West in Santa Barbara, as Polinesso in *Ariodante* at the N.Y.C. Opera, as the Voice of Apollo in *Death in Venice* at the Teatro Carlo Felice in Genoa, and as a soloist with the Minnesota Orch. in Minneapolis. He portrayed Farnace in *Mitridate* at the

Théâtre du Chatelet and Andronico in *Tamerlano* with Les Talens Lyriques in Paris in 2000. In 2001 he was engaged to sing at the St. Denis Festival in France. —**LK/DM**

Mehta, Mehli, Indian violinist and conductor, father of **Zubin Mehta;** b. Bombay, Sept. 25, 1908. He studied at the Univ. of Bombay and at Trinity Coll. of Music in London (licentiate, 1929). He founded the Bombay Sym. Orch. in 1935, serving as its concertmaster (until 1945) and then its conductor (until 1955). He subsequently was asst. concertmaster of the Hallé Orch. in Manchester (1955–59). He then settled in the U.S., where he played in the Curtis String Quartet in Philadelphia (1959–64), then went to Los Angeles, where he founded the American Youth Sym. Orch. (1964). He also taught at the Univ. of Calif. there (1964–76), serving as conductor of its sym. and chamber orchs.—**NS/LK/DM**

Mehta, Zubin, notable Indian conductor; b. Bombay, April 29, 1936. His first mentor was his father, the Indian violinist and conductor **Mehli Mehta** (b. Bombay, Sept. 25, 1908). He received training in violin and piano in childhood, and at 16 had his first taste of conducting when he led a rehearsal of the Bombay Sym. Orch. He studied medicine in Bombay but the lure of music compelled him to abandon his medical training to pursue musical studies at the Vienna Academy of Music. While playing double bass in its orch., he found a conducting mentor in Swarowsky. During the summers of 1956 and 1957, he also studied conducting with Carlo Zecchi and Alceo Galliera at the Accademia Musicale Chigiana in Siena. In 1957 he made his professional conducting debut with the Niederösterreichisches Tonkünstlerorchester in Vienna. He won the 1st Royal Liverpool Phil. conducting competition in 1958, and then served for a season as its asst. conductor. In the summer of 1959 he attended the Berkshire Music Center in Tanglewood, where he took 2nd prize in conducting. He made his North American debut conducting the Philadelphia Orch. in 1960. Later that year his successful appearances with the Montreal Sym. Orch. led to his appointment as its music director in 1961. That same year he also became assoc. conductor of the Los Angeles Phil. His London debut came later in 1961 when he appeared as a guest conductor with the Royal Phil. In 1962 he became music director of the Los Angeles Phil. while retaining his Montreal post until 1967. He made his first appearance at the Salzburg Festival in 1962. He first conducted opera in Montreal in 1964 when he led a performance of *Tosca*. On Dec. 29, 1965, he made his Metropolitan Opera debut in N.Y. conducting *Aida*. In 1966 he conducted for the first time at Milan's La Scala. He was named music advisor of the Israel Phil. in 1968. His success with that ensemble led to his appointment as its music director in 1977 and as its music director for life in 1981. He led it on major tours of Europe, North and South America, and the Far East. In 1977 he made his debut at London's Covent Garden conducting *Otello*. During his tenure in Los Angeles, Mehta was glamorized in the colorful Hollywood manner. This glamorization process was abetted by his genuine personableness and his reputation as a bon vivant. As a conductor, he secured the international profile of the Los Angeles Phil. through recordings and major tours. He became particularly known for his effulgent and expansive readings of the Romantic repertoire, which he invariably conducted from memory. His success in Los Angeles led the management of the N.Y. Phil. to appoint him as music director in 1978 with the hope that he could transform that ensemble in the wake of the austere Boulez tenure. Although Mehta served as music director of the N.Y. Phil. until 1991, he was unable to duplicate the success he attained in Los Angeles. Critics acknowledged his abilities but found his interpretations often indulgent and wayward. On July 7, 1990, Mehta served as conductor of the 3 tenors extravaganza in Rome with Carreras, Domingo, and Pavarotti in a concert telecast live to the world. He returned to the N.Y. Phil. for its 150th anniversary concert on Dec. 7, 1992, when he conducted a performance of *Till Eulenspiegels lustige Streich*. On July 16, 1994, he was conductor of the Carreras, Domingo, and Pavarotti reunion when he led the Los Angeles Phil. in a concert again telecast live around the globe. In 1995 he was appointed Generalmusikdirektor of the Bavarian State Opera in Munich, which post he assumed in 1998. In 1997 he received the Great Silver Medal of Austria.

BIBL.: M. Bookspan and R. Yockey, *Z.: The Z. M. Story* (N.Y., 1978).—NS/LK/DM

Méhul, Etienne-Nicolas, famous French composer; b. Givet, Ardennes, June 22, 1763; d. Paris, Oct. 18, 1817. His father apprenticed him to the old blind organist of the Couvent des Récollets in Givet, after which he went to Lavaldieu, where he studied with the German organist Wilhelm Hansen, director of music at the monastery there. In 1778 he went to Paris, where he continued his musical studies with Jean- Frédéric Edelmann. His first opera to receive a performance was *Euphrosine, ou Le Tyran corrigé* (Théâtre Favart, Paris, Sept. 4, 1790); another opera, *Alonso et Cora* (later known as *Cora*), was staged at the Paris Opéra on Feb. 15, 1791. His next opera, *Adrien*, was in rehearsal by the end of 1791, but the revolutionary turmoil prevented a performance; it finally received its premiere at the Paris Opéra on June 4, 1799. His opera *Stratonice* was given at the Théâtre Favart in Paris on May 3, 1792, and was highly successful. Then followed his opera *Le Jeune Sage et le vieux fou*, which was performed at the same theater on March 28, 1793. In 1793 Méhul became a member of the Inst. National de Musique, which had been organized by the National Convention under the revolutionary regime. He composed a number of patriotic works during these turbulent years of French history, including the popular *Chant du départ* (1st perf. publicly on July 4, 1794). He also continued to compose for the theater, shrewdly selecting subjects for his operas allegorically suitable to the times. In 1794 he was awarded an annual pension of 1,000 francs by the Comédie-Italienne. In 1795 he became one of the 5 inspectors of the newly established Cons., and was also elected to the Institut. He became a member of the Légion d'honneur in 1804. Between 1795 and 1807 Méhul composed 18 operas, some of which were written in collaboration with other composers. His greatest opera from this period is the

biblical *Joseph* (Opéra-Comique, Feb. 17, 1807); its success in Paris led to performances in Germany, Austria, Hungary, Russia, the Netherlands, Belgium, Switzerland, England, Italy, and America. Also noteworthy is his *Chant national du 14 juillet 1800*, an extensive work calling for 2 choirs with an additional group of high voices and orchestral forces. Apart from operas, he composed several syms. In spite of poor health, he continued to teach classes at the Paris Cons.; among his students was Hérold. His last opera was *La Journée aux aventures*, which was given at the Opéra-Comique on Nov. 16, 1816. Although Méhul's operas practically disappeared from the active repertoire, his contribution to the operatic art remains of considerable historical importance. Beethoven, Weber, and Mendelssohn were cognizant of some of his symphonic works, which included 4 well-crafted syms.

WORKS: DRAMATIC (all 1st perf. in Paris): **Opera:** *Euphrosine, ou Le Tyran corrigé* (Sept. 4, 1790; rev. as *Euphrosine et Coradin*); *Alonso et Cora* (Feb. 15, 1791; later known as *Cora*); *Stratonice* (May 3, 1792); *Le Jeune Sage et le vieux fou* (March 28, 1793); *Horatius Coclès* (Feb. 18, 1794); *Le Congrès des rois* (Feb. 26, 1794; in collaboration with 11 other composers); *Mélidore et Phrosine* (May 6, 1794); *Doria, ou La Tyrannie détruite* (March 12, 1795); *La Caverne* (Dec. 5, 1795); *La Jeunesse d'Henri IV* (May 1, 1797; later known as *Le Jeune Henri*); *La Prise du pont de Lodi* (Dec. 15, 1797); *Adrien, empéreur de Rome* (June 4, 1799; later known as *Adrien*); *Ariodant* (Oct. 11, 1799); *Epicure* (March 14, 1800; in collaboration with Cherubini); *Bion* (Dec. 27, 1800); *L'Irato, ou L'Emporté* (Feb. 17, 1801); *Une Folie* (April 5, 1802); *Le Trésor supposé, ou Le Danger d'écouter aux portes* (July 29, 1802); *Joanna* (Nov. 23, 1802); *Héléna* (March 1, 1803); *Le Baiser et la quittance, ou Une Aventure de garnison* (June 18, 1803; in collaboration with Boieldieu, R. Kreutzer, and Nicolo); *L'Heureux malgré lui* (Dec. 29, 1803); *Les 2 Aveugles de Tolède* (Jan. 28, 1806); *Uthal* (May 17, 1806); *Gabrielle d'Estrées, ou Les Amours d'Henri IV* (June 25, 1806); *Joseph* (Feb. 17, 1807); *Amphion, ou Les Amazones* (Dec. 17, 1811; later known as *Les Amazones, ou La Fondation de Thèbes*); *Le Prince troubadour* (May 24, 1813); *L'Oriflamme* (Feb. 1, 1814; overture by Méhul; remainder in collaboration with H.-M. Berton, R. Kreutzer, and Paër); *La Journée aux aventures* (Nov. 16, 1816); *Valentine de Milan* (Nov. 28, 1822); the opera *Lausus* and the opéra-ballet *L'Amour et Psyché* are considered doubtful works in the Méhul canon. **Ballet:** *Le Jugement de Paris* (March 5, 1793; with music by Gluck, Haydn, and others); *La Dansomanie* (June 14, 1800; with music by Mozart and others); *Daphnis et Pandrose* (Jan. 14, 1803; with music by Gluck, Haydn, and others); *Persée et Andromède* (June 8, 1810; with music by Haydn, Paër, and Steibelt). **Other:** Incidental music. **ORCH.:** Several syms., including those numbered by Méhul as No. 1 in G minor (1809), No. 2 in D major (1809), No. 3 in C major (1809), and No. 4 in E major (1810). **CHAMBER:** *Ouverture burlesque* for Piano, Violin, 3 Mirlitons, Trumpet, and Percussion. **KEYBOARD:** 2 books of sonatas: *3 sonates*, book 1 (1783), and *3 sonates*, book 2 (1788).

BIBL.: A. Quatremère de Quincy, *Funérailles de M. M., Institut Royal de France* (Paris, 1817); P. Vieillard, *M.: Sa vie et ses oeuvres* (Paris, 1859); A. Pougin, *M.: Sa vie, son génie, son caractère* (Paris, 1889; 2nd ed., 1893); R. Brancour, *M.* (Paris, 1912). —NS/LK/DM

Mei, Girolamo, eminent Italian scholar and writer on music; b. Florence, May 27, 1519; d. Rome, July 1594. He studied with the scholar Piero Vettori, serving as his assistant in editing and annotating the works of the great Greek and Latin men of letters. Upon the founding of the Accademia de'Umidi (1540; later the Accademia Fiorentia), he became one of its first members. After settling in Rome (1559), he was a secretary to Cardinal Giovanni Ricci da Montepulciano (1561–74). He then lived in the palace of the nobleman Giovanni Francesco Ridolfi. He publ. *Discorso sopra la musica antica e moderna* (Venice, 1602; reprint, 1968, ed. by G. Massera), the first significant study of the tonoi in Greek music. He also left in MS *De modis musicis antiquorum libri IV, De nomi delle corde del monochordo,* and *Trattato di musica: Come potesse tanto la musica appresso gli antichi.* His letters to the members of Bardi's Camerata in Florence are of great historical significance, for they led to a call for the reform of music and the development of monody, which culminated in the rise of the first music dramas and the new recitative style. See C. Palisca, ed., *Girolamo Mei (1519–1594): Letters on Ancient and Modern Music to Vincenzo Galilei and Giovanni Bardi,* Musicological Studies and Documents, III (1960; 2nd ed., 1977).

BIBL.: B. Hanning, *The Influence of Humanistic Thought and Italian Renaissance Poetry on the Formation of Opera* (diss., Yale Univ., 1968).—**LK/DM**

Mei, Orazio, Italian organist and composer; b. Pisa, May 26, 1731; d. Livorno, March 1, 1788. He was a student of his father, Francesco Saverio Mei, a violinist at the church of the Cavalieri di S. Stefano in Pisa, and of his uncle, Nicola Meil, the organist of Pisa Cathedral. In 1748 he became organist at the church of Cavalieri di S. Stefano in Pisa. After serving as his uncle's successor as organist at Pisa Cathedral (1759–63), he was maestro di cappella at Livorno Cathedral from 1763 until his death. He composed both sacred and secular music, his *Stabat mater* being particularly noteworthy.—**NS/LK/DM**

Meibom (Meiboom, Meybom, Meibomius), Marcus, erudite Danish scholar; b. Tönning, Schleswig, 1620 or 1621; d. Utrecht, Feb. 15, 1710. He studied law at the Univ. of Königsberg (1644) and medicine at the Univ. of Leiden (1645), but subsequently devoted himself to philology and mathematics. He was asst. royal librarian in Stockholm (1652–53) before serving King Frederik III of Denmark in Copenhagen (1653–64), where he held the title of consilarus regius. After serving as director of customs in Elsinore (1664–68), he lived in England (1674–77) before settling in Holland. His major contribution to music was his *Antiquae musicae auctores septem, graece et latine, Marcus Meibomius restituit ac notis explicavit* (2 vols., Amsterdam, 1652), which includes treatises on music by Aristoxenos, Cleonides, Nicomachus, Alypius, Gaudentius Philosophos, Bacchius, Aristides Quintilianus, and Martianus Capella.—**NS/LK/DM**

Meier, Johanna, American soprano; b. Chicago, Feb. 13, 1938. She was a scholarship student at the Manhattan School of Music in N.Y. She made her debut with the N.Y.C. Opera in 1969 as the Countess in Strauss's *Capriccio,* and continued to appear there regularly until 1979. She made her Metropolitan Opera

debut in N.Y. as Strauss's Ariadne on April 9, 1976, and subsequently appeared there regularly; also sang opera in Chicago, Cincinnati, Pittsburgh, Seattle, and Baltimore. In Europe, she had guest engagements in opera in Zürich, Vienna, Hamburg, Berlin, and Bayreuth; also appeared in concerts.—**NS/LK/DM**

Meier, Jost, Swiss composer and conductor; b. Solothurn, March 15, 1939. He studied cello, conducting, and composition at the Bern Cons., and completed his training in composition with Frank Martin in the Netherlands. From 1969 to 1979 he was chief conductor of the Biel Orch. and Theater. After conducting in Basel (1980–83), he was active as a guest conductor throughout Europe. He also taught at the Basel Academy of Music and the Zürich Cons. His compositions follow the precepts of the second Viennese school. Among his works are the operas *Sennetuntschi* (Freiburg, April 23, 1983), *Der Drache* (Basel, May 24, 1985), *Der Zoobär* (Zürich, June 11, 1987), *Augustin* (Basel, April 21, 1988), and *Dreyfus—Die Affäre* (Berlin, May 8, 1994). —**NS/LK/DM**

Meier, Waltraud, outstanding German mezzo-soprano; b. Würzburg, Jan. 9, 1956. She was a student of Dietger Jacob in Cologne. In 1976 she made her operatic debut as Lola in *Cavalleria rusticana* at the Würzburg Opera, where she was engaged until 1978. In 1980 she appeared as Fricka at the Teatro Colón in Buenos Aires. From 1980 to 1983 she was a member of the Dortmund Opera, and then sang in Hannover (1983–84). In 1983 she made her debut at the Bayreuth Festival, where she won acclaim for her portrayal of Kundry. After singing Brangäne at the Paris Opéra in 1984, she made her first appearance at London's Covent Garden in 1985 as Eboli, returning there as Kundry in 1988. From 1985 to 1988 she sang in Stuttgart. On Oct. 9, 1987, she made her debut at the Metropolitan Opera in N.Y. as Fricka. From 1988 to 1992 she was engaged as Waltraute at Bayreuth. In 1990 she sang Venus at the Hamburg State Opera, Marguerite at the Théâtre du Châtelet in Paris, and Ortrud at the Teatro São Carlos in Lisbon. She appeared as Isolde at Bayreuth in 1993 and 1995. In 1994 she sang Sieglinde at the Vienna State Opera and at Milan's La Scala. After an engagement as Carmen at the Metropolitan Opera in 1996, she sang Beethoven's Leonore in Chicago, appeared in an all-Wagner concert in London at the Royal Festival Hall, and portrayed Waltraute at La Scala in 1998. In 1999 she sang Ortrud in Munich. Meier has been honored as a Kammersängerin of both the Bavarian State Opera in Munich and the Vienna State Opera.—**NS/LK/DM**

Meifred, Pierre-Joseph Emile, French horn player, instrument designer, and teacher; b. Colmar, Nov. 13, 1791; d. Paris, Aug. 28, 1867. He studied at the École des Arts et Métiers in Chalons, and then received training in horn from Dauprat at the Paris Cons. (premier prix, 1818). In 1819 he joined the orch. of the Paris Théâtre-Italien. From 1822 to 1850 he also was a member of the orch. of the Paris Opéra. In 1828 he helped to found the Société des Concerts du Conservatoire in

Paris. His interest in the German valve horn led him to work with the instrument maker Labbaye in improving its performance. From 1832 to 1864 he was prof. of valve horn at the Paris Cons. At his instigation, the Gymnase Militaire was founded in 1836 as a school for army musicians. In 1848 he was awarded the cross of the Légion d'honneur. He publ. *De l'étendue, de l'emploi et des ressources du cor* (Paris, 1829) and *Méthode de cor chromatique ou à pistons* (Paris, 1840; 2nd ed., rev., 1849).
—LK/DM

Meiland, Jakob, German composer; b. Senftenberg, Lausitz, 1542; d. Hechingen, Dec. 31, 1577. He was a choirboy in the Dresden Hofkapelle, and in 1558 he enrolled at the Univ. of Leipzig. In 1563 joined the Kantorei of the Protestant Margrave Georg Friedrich of Brandenburg-Ansbach, becoming its director in 1564. In 1565 founded its Hofkapelle and served as its first director. He moved to Frankfurt am Main in 1572 and to Celle in 1576. In 1577 he became Kapellmeister to Count Eitel Friedrich von Hohenzollern of Hechingen, but died that same year.

WORKS: *Cantiones sacrae cum harmonicis numeris, a 5, 6* (Nuremberg, 1564; 4th ed., 1573); *Selectae cantiones, a 5, 6* (1572); *Cantiones aliquot novae...quibus adiuncta sunt officia due, a 5* (Frankfurt am Main, 1575); *Sacrae aliquot cantiones latinae et germanicae...sequentes duas cantiones in honorem domini Sigismundi Feyerabend et Hieronymi eius filii, a 4, 5* (Frankfurt am Main, 1575); *Harmoniae sacrae selectae ac compositiones divinae, a 5* (Erfurt, 1588); *Cygneae cantiones latinae et germanicae, a 4, 5* (Wittenberg, 1590); 3 Passions; Mass; secular songs; etc.
BIBL.: R. Oppel, *J. M. (1542–1577)* (Pfungstadt, 1911).
—NS/LK/DM

Meili, Max, Swiss tenor; b. Winterthur, Dec. 11, 1899; d. Zürich, March 17, 1970. He was a student of P. Deutsch in Winterthur and of F. von Kraus in Munich. He pursued an active concert career in Europe, becoming known as an interpreter of early music. In 1933 he helped to found the Schola Cantorum Basiliensis. In 1955 he founded and subsequently served as director of the Collegium Cantorum Turicense.—NS/LK/DM

Meinardus, Ludwig (Siegfried), German conductor, composer, and writer on music; b. Hooksiel, Oldenburg, Sept. 17, 1827; d. Bielefeld, July 10, 1896. He was a pupil at the Leipzig Cons., and also studied in Berlin, in Weimar (with Liszt), and with Marx in Berlin. From 1853 to 1865 he was conductor of the Singakademie at Glogau, then was a teacher at the Dresden Cons.; from 1874 to 1887 he lived in Hamburg as a composer and critic, then went to Bielefeld. He wrote a kind of autobiography, *Ein Jugendleben* (2 vols., 1874); other writings include *Rückblick auf die Anfänge der deutschen Oper* (1878), *Mattheson und seine Verdienste um die deutsche Tonkunst* (1879), *Mozart: Ein Künstlerleben* (1882), *Die deutsche Tonkunst im 18.-19. Jahrhundert* (1887), *Klassizität und Romantik in der deutschen Tonkunst* (1893), and *Eigene Wege* (1895). Among his compositions were 2 operas and 6 oratorios, including *Luther in Worms* (Leipzig, 1876), his most successful score. He

also composed 2 syms. (c. 1875, 1879), many choral works, and much chamber music.
BIBL.: C. Kleinschmidt, *L. M., 1827–1896: Ein Beitrag zur Geschichte der ausgehenden musikalischen Romantik* (Wilhelmshaven, 1985).—NS/LK/DM

Meitus, Yuli (Sergeievich), Ukrainian composer; b. Elizavetgrad, Jan. 28, 1903; d. there (Korovograd), April 2, 1997. He received training in piano at the C.V. Neyghauza School in Elizavetgrad (graduated, 1919), and then studied in Kharkov at the Inst. of Music and Drama (graduated, 1931). For the most part, Meitus adhered to the tenets of Soviet realism in his extensive output. Among his dramatic works were the operas *Perekhop* (1938; Kiev, Jan. 20, 1939), *Gaydamaki* (1941; Ashkhabad, Oct. 15, 1943), *Leily and Medznun* (Ashkhabad, Nov. 2, 1946), *The Young Guard* (Kiev, Nov. 7, 1947), *The Sunrise Above the Dvina* (Kiev, July 5, 1955), *The Stolen Happiness* (1959; Lvov, Sept. 10, 1960), *Mukhturnkuly* (Ashkhabad, Dec. 29, 1962), *The Daughter of the Wind* (1964; Odessa, Oct. 24, 1965), *Ulyanov's Brothers* (1966; Ufa, Nov. 25, 1967), *Anna Korenina* (1970), *Yaroslau the Wise* (1972; Donetsk, March 3, 1973), *Rikkard Zorge* (1975), *Marianna Pindea* (1978), *Ivan Grozny* (1983), and *Antony and Cleopatra* (1997). He also wrote music for the theater and films, 5 orch. suites (1927, 1929, 1939, 1942, 1944), the symphonic poem *On the Way to Glory* (1945), the *Turkman Symphony* (1946), an overture (1954), chamber music, choral pieces, and some 400 romances and ballads. In 1973 he was named a National Artist of the Ukraine, and in 1991 he was awarded its T.G. Shevchenko state gratuity.—NS/LK/DM

Mekeel, Joyce, American harpsichordist and composer; b. New Haven, Conn., July 6, 1931. She studied at the Longy School of Music in Cambridge, Mass. (1952–55); received instruction in keyboard playing from Boulanger at the Paris Cons. (1955–57), from Leonhardt (1957), and from Kirkpatrick (1957–59); took courses in theory and composition at Yale Univ. (B.M., 1959; M.M., 1960) and studied privately with Earl Kim (1960–62). She completed her education at Boston Univ. (Ph.D., 1983, with the diss. *Social Influences on Changing Audience Behavior in the Mid-Victorian London Theatre*). She made appearances as a harpsichordist, and was a composer for several dance and theater companies (1961–75). She taught at the New England Cons. of Music in Boston (1964–70) and at Boston Univ. (1970–92).

WORKS: DRAMATIC: *Jaywalk* for Viola and Dancer (1969); *Moveable Feast* (1973–75; in collaboration with P. Earls and L. Davidson); *Kisses and Kazoos* (1977); *Alarums and Excursions* for Violin, Viola, Cello, Piano, Flute, Clarinet, Percussion, and Actress/Mezzo-soprano (1978); *Museum* (1980); *Sigil* for String Quintet, Clarinet, English Horn, 2 Horns, 2 Tubas, Harp, Actor, and Actress/Mezzo-soprano (1981); *Journeys of Remembrance* (1986). ORCH.: *String Figures Disentangled by a Flute* for Flute and Strings (Boston, April 2, 1969); *Vigil* (Boston, Oct. 19, 1978). CHAMBER: *Spindrift* for String Quartet (1970); *Hommages* for Brass Quintet (1973); *Rune* for Flute and Percussion (1976); *Tessera* for String Quintet, Saxophone, English Horn, Contrabassoon, Trumpet, Horn, and Harps (1981); *Fertile Vicissitudes* for Harp and Oboe (1981); *Voices* for Violin, Clarinet, and

Piano (1983); *An Insomnia of Owls* for Woodwind Quintet (1985); numerous solo works. **VOCAL:** *White Silence* for Chorus (1965); *Waterwalk* for Speaking Chorus (1970); *Corridors of Dream* for Mezzo-soprano, Flute, Clarinet, Harp, Viola, and Cello (1972); *Toward the Source* for Chorus and Orch. (1974); *Serena* for Mezzo-soprano, Speaker, and Prepared Piano (1975); songs. —NS/LK/DM

Mel, Rinaldo del, Flemish composer; b. Mechlin, c. 1554; d. c. 1598. He was a pupil of Séverin Cornet at the St. Rombaud Cathedral choir school (1562–72). About 1572 he became mestre de capela at the Lisbon court. By 1580 he was in Rome. After serving as maestro di cappella at Rieti Cathedral (1584–85), he traveled widely. In 1587–88 he was maestro di cappella to Duke Ernst of Bavaria in Liège, and then returned to Italy, where he was in the service of Paleotto Magliano (1591–96). He publ. 4 vols. of motets (1581–95) and at least 13 vols. of madrigals (1583–96).—LK/DM

Melani, family of Italian musicians, of whom the most important were the following 3 brothers:

(1) Jacopo Melani, organist and composer; b. Pistoia, July 6, 1623; d. there, Aug. 19, 1676. He became organist (1645) and maestro di cappella (1657) of Pistoia Cathedral. He excelled as a composer of comic operas, which included *Il potesta di Colognole* (Florence, 1657; also known as *La Tancia*), *Ercole in Tebe* (Florence, July 8, 1661), *Il Girello* (Rome, 1668), and *Enea in Italia* (Pisa, 1670).

(2) Atto Melani, alto and composer; b. Pistoia, March 31, 1626; d. Paris, 1714. He was a pupil of Luigi Rossi and Marc'Antonio Pasqualini in Rome. In 1664 he visited Paris, where he won the esteem of Queen Anne and Mazarin. While singing in opera there, he also secretly served as a diplomatic courier. After Mazarin's death, he entered the service of Cardinal Giulio Rospigliosi and became enmeshed in papal politics. In 1679 he returned to Paris, where he was active in politics. He composed various vocal pieces, including solo cantatas and duets.

(3) Alessandro Melani, composer; b. Pistoia, Feb. 4, 1639; d. Rome, Oct. 1703. He sang at Pistoia Cathedral (1650–60) and then served as maestro di cappella in Orvieto and Ferrara. In 1667 he succeeded his brother Jacopo as maestro di cappella of Pistoia Cathedral, but later that year went to Rome to take up that position at S. Maria Maggiore; in 1672 he obtained the same position at S. Luigi dei Francesi, which he held until his death. He composed the operas *L'empio punito* (Rome, 1669), *Il trionfo della continenza considerato in Scipione Africano* (Fano, 1677), *Le reciproche gelosie* (Siena, 1677), *Roberto ovvero Il Carceriere di se medesimo* (Florence, 1681), and *Ama chi t'ama* (Siena, 1682). He also collaborated with B. Pasquini and A. Scarlatti on the opera *S. Dinna* (Rome, 1687). His other works include oratorios, motets, and cantatas.—NS/LK/DM

Melartin, Erkki (Gustaf), Finnish composer; b. Kakisalmi, Feb. 7, 1875; d. Pukinmaki, Feb. 14, 1937. He was a pupil of Wegelius at the Helsinki Music Inst. and of Robert Fuchs in Vienna. He taught theory at the

Helsinki Music Inst. (1898; 1901–7), succeeding Wegelius as director in 1911, and remaining at this post until 1936. His compositions are marked by a lyrical strain, with thematic materials often drawn from Finnish folk songs.

WORKS: DRAMATIC: *Aino,* opera (1907; Helsinki, Dec. 10, 1909); *Sininen helmi,* ballet (The Blue Pearl, 1930); also incidental music. **ORCH.:** 8 syms. (1902; 1904; 1906–07; 1912; 1916, Sinfonia brevis; 1924–25; 2 unfinished); 3 symphonic poems; 3 lyric suites; Violin Concerto; *Serenade* for Strings; *Karjalaisia kuvia* (Karelian Pictures). **CHAMBER:** 4 string quartets; Quartet for 2 Trumpets, Trombone, and Horn; Quartet for 4 Horns; Trio for Flute, Clarinet, and Bassoon; 2 violin sonatas; Sonata for Flute and Harp; piano pieces; violin works. **VOCAL:** Choruses and about 300 songs.—NS/LK/DM

Melba, Dame Nellie (actually, **Helen Porter** née **Mitchell Armstrong**), famous Australian soprano; b. Burnley, near Richmond, May 19, 1861; d. Sydney, Feb. 23, 1931. Her father, who had decided objections to anything connected with the stage, was nevertheless fond of music and proud of his daughter's talent. When she was only 6 years old he allowed her to sing at a concert in the Melbourne Town Hall, but would not consent to her having singing lessons; instead, she was taught piano, violin, and harp, and even had instruction in harmony and composition. As she grew older she frequently played the organ in a local church, and was known among her friends as an excellent pianist, while all the time her chief desire was to study singing. Not until after her marriage in 1882 to Captain Charles Armstrong was she able to gratify her ambition, when she began to study with a local teacher, Cecchi; her first public appearance as a singer was on May 17, 1884, in a benefit concert in Melbourne. The next year her father received a government appointment in London, and she accompanied him, determined to begin an operatic career. She studied with Mathilde Marchesi in Paris. Melba gave her first concert in London (June 1, 1886). Her debut as Gilda at the Théâtre Royal de la Monnaie in Brussels (Oct. 13, 1887) created a veritable sensation; the famous impresario Augustus Harris immediately engaged her for the spring season at London's Covent Garden, where she appeared on May 24, 1888, as Lucia, to only a half-full house. However, she scored a major success at the Paris Opéra as Ophelia in Thomas's *Hamlet* (May 8, 1889); then sang with great success in St. Petersburg (1891), Milan (La Scala, 1893; immense triumph over a carefully planned opposition), Stockholm and Copenhagen (Oct. 1893), N.Y. (Metropolitan Opera, as Lucia, Dec. 4, 1893), and Melbourne (Sept. 27, 1902). From her first appearance at Covent Garden she sang there off and on until 1914; besides being one of the most brilliant stars of several seasons at the Metropolitan Opera in N.Y., she also sang with Damrosch's Opera Co. (1898) and at Hammerstein's Manhattan Opera (1906–07 and 1908–09), and made several transcontinental concert tours of the U.S. Bemberg wrote for her *Elaine* (1892), and Saint-Saëns, *Hélène* (1904), in both of which she created the title roles. In 1915 she began teaching at the Albert Street Conservatorium in Melbourne; returned to Covent Garden for appearances in 1919, 1923, and a farewell performance on June 8, 1926. Then she returned to Australia and retired from the stage. Melba was by nature gifted with a voice of extraordinary beauty and bell-like purity; through her art she made this fine instrument perfectly even throughout its entire extensive compass and wonderfully flexible, so that she executed the most difficult fioriture without the least effort. As an actress she did not rise above the conventional, and for this reason she was at her best in parts demanding brilliant coloratura (Gilda, Lucia, Violetta, Rosina, Lakmé et al.). On a single occasion she attempted the dramatic role of Brünnhilde in *Siegfried* (Metropolitan Opera, N.Y., Dec. 30, 1896), and met with disaster. In 1918 she was created a Dame Commander of the Order of the British Empire. She was a typical representative of the golden era of opera; a prima donna assoluta, she exercised her powers over the public with perfect self-assurance and a fine command of her singing voice. Among her other distinguished roles were Mimi, Else, Nedda, Aida, Desdemona, and Marguerita. As a measure of Melba's universal popularity, it may be mentioned that her name was attached to a delicious dessert (Peach Melba) and also to Melba toast, patented in 1929 by Bert Weil. A film based on her life was produced in 1953 with Patrice Munsel as Melba. She wrote an autobiography, *Melodies and Memories* (London, 1925).

BIBL.: A. Murphy, *M.: A Biography* (London, 1909); P. Colson, *M.: An Unconventional Biography* (London, 1931); J. Wechsberg, *Red Plush and Black Velvet: The Story of M. and Her Times* (Boston, 1961); G. Hutton, *M.* (Melbourne, 1962); J. Hetherington, *M.* (London, 1967); W. Moran, *N. M.: A Contemporary Review* (Westport, Conn., 1985); T. Radic, *M.: The Voice of Australia* (Melbourne and London, 1986); P. Vestey, *M.: A Family Memoir* (Melbourne, 1996).—**NS/LK/DM**

Melcer (-Szczawiński), Henryk,

esteemed Polish pianist, conductor, teacher, and composer; b. Kalisch, Sept. 21, 1869; d. Warsaw, April 18, 1928. He was a pupil of Noszkowski (composition) and Strobl (piano) at the Warsaw Music Inst. (graduated, 1890). After touring Russia as an accompanist, he received further piano training from Leschetizky in Vienna. After successful concert tours of Russia, Germany, and France, he taught at the Helsinki Cons. (1895–96) and was a prof. at the Lemberg Cons. (1896–99). He was director of the Łódź music society (1899–1902) and director-conductor of the Łódź Phil. (from 1902), as well as conductor of the Warsaw Phil. (1910–12) and Opera (1915–16). He subsequently taught at the Warsaw Cons. (from 1919), serving as head of piano studies (until 1928), orchestration (1925–26), and composition (1925–28). His works include the operas *Protasilas i Laodamia* (1902; Paris, 1925) and *Marja* (Warsaw, Nov. 16, 1904), 2 piano concertos (1895, 1898, both winning the Rubinstein prize), *Pani Twardowska*, ballad for Tenor, Chorus, and Orch. (1898), Piano Trio (1895), Violin Sonata (c. 1896), songs, and piano pieces.

BIBL.: J. Reiss, *H. M.* (Warsaw, 1949).—**NS/LK/DM**

Melchior, Lauritz (Lebrecht Hommel),

celebrated Danish-born American tenor; b. Copenhagen, March 20, 1890; d. Santa Monica, Calif., March 18, 1973.

He studied with Paul Bang at the Royal Opera School in Copenhagen, making his operatic debut in the baritone role of Silvio in *Pagliacci* at the Royal Theater there (April 2, 1913). He continued on its roster while studying further with Vilhelm Herold, and then made his tenor debut as Tannhäuser (Oct. 8, 1918). In 1921 he went to London to continue his training with Beigel, and then studied with Grenzebach in Berlin and Bahr-Mildenburg in Munich. On May 24, 1924, he made his Covent Garden debut in London as Siegmund, returning there regularly from 1926 to 1939. He was in Bayreuth in 1924 to study with Kittel; made his first appearance at the Festspielhaus there as Siegfried on July 23, 1924, and continued to make appearances there until 1931. On Feb. 17, 1926, he made his Metropolitan Opera debut in N.Y. as Tannhäuser, and quickly established himself as one of its principal artists; with the exception of the 1927–28 season, he sang there regularly until his farewell performance as Lohengrin on Feb. 2, 1950. In 1947 he became a naturalized American citizen. Melchior also appeared on Broadway and in films, and continued to give concerts. He was accorded a preeminent place among the Wagnerian Heldentenors of his era.

BIBL.: H. Hanse, *L. M.: A Discography* (Copenhagen, 1965; 2nd ed., 1972); S. Emmons, *Tristanissimo: The Authorized Biography of Heroic Tenor L. M.* (N.Y., 1990); A. Heckner, *L. M.: Die kommentierte Diskographie des Wagner-Heldentenors* (Bayreuth, 1995).—**NS/LK/DM**

Melichar, Alois,

Austrian music critic and composer; b. Vienna, April 18, 1896; d. Munich, April 9, 1976. He studied theory at the Vienna Academy of Music with Joseph Marx (1917–20) and at the Hochschule für Musik in Berlin with Schreker (1920–23). From 1923 to 1926 he was in the Caucasus, where he collected materials on Caucasian folk songs; then lived in Berlin and Vienna. As a composer, he followed the safe footpath of Reger, Pfitzner, and Graener; he wrote a symphonic poem, *Der Dom* (1934); *Rhapsodie über ein schwedisches Volkslied* (1939); *Lustspiel- Ouvertüre* (1942); lieder; film music. As a music critic, he acquired notoriety by his intemperate attacks on better composers than himself. His publications, written in his virulent, polemical manner, include *Die unteilbare Musik* (Vienna, 1952), *Musik in der Zwangsjacke* (Vienna, 1958), and (particularly vicious) *Schönberg und die Folgen* (Vienna, 1960). —**NS/LK/DM**

Melikov, Arif (Djangirovich),

Russian composer; b. Baku, Sept. 13, 1933. He studied the tar (an oriental lute) at the Baku Zeinalla Music Coll. (1948–53) and composition with Kara Karayev at the Gadjibekov Azerbaijan State Cons. (1953–58); in 1965 he joined its faculty. His early music hewed to the tenets of socialist realism, representational and stylistically inoffensive to untutored ears. In his later works, he made use of various modern techniques.

WORKS: DRAMATIC: B a l l e t : *The Legends of Love* (Leningrad, March 23, 1961); *The Two* (1969); *Poem of 2 Hearts* (1983). **M u s i c a l :** *Waves* (1967). **O t h e r :** Incidental music to plays; film scores. **ORCH.: S y m p h o n i c P o -**

e m s : *Fairy Tale* (1957); *In Memory of Fizuli* (1959); *Metamorphoses* (1963); *Motherland* for Voice and Orch. (1964); *The Last Mountain Gorge* (1976); *Remember* (1978). **O t h e r :** Flute Concertino (1956); 8 syms.: No. 1 (1958), No. 2 (1969–70), No. 3 for Chamber Orch. (1973–75), No. 4 for Strings (1977), No. 5 (1979), No. 6, *Contrasts* (1984), No. 7 (1995), and No. 8 (1996–97); *2 Suites* (1965); *Suite* for Folk Orch. (1967); *Pictures* for Folk Orch. (1967); *8 Pieces* (1968); *2 Suites* (1970); *12 Pieces* (1971); *Symphonic Dances* (1976). **C H A M B E R :** *Suite* for Violin and Piano (1954); *Scherzo* for Violin and Piano (1954); Sonata for Solo Violin (1980); *Scherzo* for 2 Pianos (1983). **VOCAL:** *Voices of the Earth*, cantata (1972); choruses; songs.—NS/LK/DM

Melik-Pashayev, Alexander (Shamilievich), noted Russian conductor; b. Tiflis, Oct. 23, 1905; d. Moscow, June 18, 1964. He studied with N. Tcherepnin at the Tiflis Cons. He was pianist and concertmaster of the Tiflis Opera orch. (1921–24), and then its conductor. After conducting studies with Gauk at the Leningrad Cons. (graduated, 1930), he returned to the Tiflis Opera as chief conductor (1930–31). He then conducted at Moscow's Bolshoi Theater, later serving as its chief conductor (1953–62). He was highly esteemed for his interpretations of Russian operas; was awarded 2 Stalin prizes (1942, 1943) and was made a People's Artist of the U.S.S.R. (1951).—NS/LK/DM

Melikyan, Romanos Hovakimi, Armenian composer; b. Kiziyar, northern Caucasus, Dec. 1, 1883; d. Yerevan, March 30, 1935. He studied at the Rostov Coll. of Music (graduated, 1905), then with Ippolitov-Ivanov, Taneyev, and Yavorsky in Moscow (1905–07); subsequently with Kalafati and Steinberg at the St. Petersburg Cons. (1910–14). He founded the Tiflis Music League (1908). He became director of music at the Armenian House of Culture in Moscow (1918), then founded the Yerevan Cons. (1923); was also founder-director of the Yerevan Theater of Opera and Ballet (1933). He was a major figure in Armenian music circles. As a composer, he was highly regarded for his songs and folk song arrangements.

BIBL.: G. Geodakyan, *R. M.* (Yerevan, 1960); K. Tordjyan, *R. M.* (Yerevan, 1960).—NS/LK/DM

Melis, Carmen, Italian soprano; b. Cagliari, Aug. 14, 1885; d. Longone al Segrino, Dec. 19, 1967. She was a student of Teresina Singer and Carlo Carignani in Milan, of Cotogni in Rome, and of Jean de Reszke in Paris. In 1905 she made her operatic debut in Novara, and then sang in Naples (1906) and Russia (1907). On Nov. 26, 1909, she made her U.S. debut as Tosca at the Manhattan Opera in N.Y., and then appeared in Boston, Chicago, and other U.S. cities. In 1913 she made her first appearance at London's Covent Garden. She later sang at Milan's La Scala, and sang regularly at the Rome Opera. Following her retirement in 1935, she taught voice. Among her most impressive roles were Musetta, Thaïs, Nedda, Zazà, Mistress Ford, Fedora, and the Marschallin.—NS/LK/DM

Melkus, Eduard, Austrian violinist, conductor, and teacher; b. Baden-bei-Wien, Sept. 1, 1928. He stud-

ied violin with Ernst Moravec at the Vienna Academy of Music (1943–53) and musicology with Schenk at the Univ. of Vienna (1951–53); continued his violin training with Firmin Touche in Paris (1953), Alexander Schaichet in Zürich (1956), and Peter Rybar in Winterthur (1958). After playing in several Swiss orchs., he became prof. of violin and viola at the Vienna Hochschule für Musik (1958). He also toured as a soloist in Europe and the U.S. He founded the Capella Academica of Vienna (1965), which he conducted in performances of works ranging from the Renaissance to the early Classical era, utilizing modern instruments as well as original instruments or reproductions.—NS/LK/DM

Mell, Davis, English violinist and composer; b. Wilton, Nov. 15, 1604; d. London, April 4, 1662. He was a violinist in the court band by 1625. In 1654 he became a violinist in Cromwell's private band. At the Restoration in 1660, he reentered the royal service as co-master of the King's Band. Some 54 of his dances for Violin and Basso Continuo were publ. in the form of 12 suites in Playford's *Courtly Masquing Ayres* (London, 1662). —LK/DM

Mell, Gertrud Maria, Swedish composer, organist, and sea captain; b. Ed, Aug. 15, 1947. She studied at the Lund Cons. (diploma in organ, 1967) and in Stockholm (music teacher's diploma, 1968), and later pursued training at the Univ. of Marine Officers in Göteborg (1978–81), passing examinations as a mate (1979), ship mechanic (1979), sea captain (master mariner, 1981), radio telephone operator (1982), and ship engineer (1985). She began her career as a church organist in Ed at age 17 and became adept at improvisation; was organist in Töftedal (1967–76) and also taught music in Ed (1969–71) and Bengtsfors (1972–76). After working as a seaperson on transatlantic ships (1976–78), she pursued both music and navigation. She served as organist of the Pater Noster Church in Göteborg (from 1982), appeared as a recitalist in concert, radio, and television settings, and even made an appearance as a pop singer in her recording *Mermaid* (1977).

WORKS: ORCH.: 4 syms. (1964, 1965, 1966, 1967); *Melodie aus dem Meer*, symphonic poem (1980; also for Violin and Piano, 1976); *Solvind* (1984; also for Flute and Piano, 1975); *Celeste cordialis* for Strings (1985); *Andante*, symphonic poem (1988); *Pacem* for Strings (1990). **OTHER:** String Quartet No. 1 (1969); piano pieces, including *Fantasie* (1961) and *Impromptu* (1971); organ music; improvisations for both piano and organ; choral works, including *Pater noster* for Soloists, Chorus, and Instruments (1983); songs; various pop pieces.—NS/LK/DM

Mellencamp, John, mainstream pop-rocker who was most successful for a decade from the mid-1980s through the mid-1990s; b. Seymour, Ind., Oct. 7, 1951. The second of five kids, John Mellencamp was born with a potentially crippling disease and spent much of his first year in the hospital, but recovered fully. The son of a Miss Indiana runner-up and an electric company worker who rose through the ranks to company vice president, Mellencamp was playing in bands by the time he was 10. In his early teens he started playing frat parties and the like. After graduating college, Mellencamp—already married with a daughter—took a job with the phone company. He promptly lost this job when he accidentally disconnected the service for a small Ind. town.

With his severance pay, Mellencamp went to N.Y. to shop his demos and was signed by David Bowie's manager, Tony DeFries. He got a generous contract with MCA and released an album of covers called *Chestnut Street Incident*. When the album came out, he was startled and upset to learn that DeFries had changed his name, losing his 10-letter appellation in favor of the zingier John Cougar. The album went nowhere and MCA dropped him. He recorded another album as part of his contract with DeFries, who held on to *The Kid Inside* until Mellencamp started to make hits.

He cut *A Biography*, which came out only in England. The *John Cougar* album that he released via Riva Records—a company run by Rod Stewart's manager—included several songs from the English release including a tune called "I Need a Lover." A slice of hard bluesy rock with an extended guitar introduction and Mellencamp's sandy voice, the tune attracted some attention at rock radio. It also became an album-rock hit for Pat Benatar. As he worked on his fourth album with producer Steve Cropper in Los Angeles, he learned that "I Need a Lover" had topped the charts in Australia. The song eventually crossed over into pop, hitting #28 in the U.S.

Building on that momentum, the Cropper-produced *Nothing Matters and What If It Did* spawned two album-rock-to-pop crossovers, "This Time" (#27) and "Ain't Even Done with the Night" (#17). The album reached #37 and went gold, solidifying Cougar as one of the Middle American rockers to be reckoned with. Reviews of his records and concerts were rife with comparisons to Tom Petty, Bruce Springsteen, and others.

In 1982, Cougar broke through in a big way with the album *American Fool*. His craggy, photogenic looks played well on MTV, and building on the popularity of his previous two records, the first single went gold, "Hurts So Good" spent four weeks at #2, rebuffed from the top by the McCartney/Wonder duet "Ebony and Ivory." His next single, "Jack and Diane," passed it on the way up the charts, as his album hit #1, making him the first artist since John Lennon to have two Top Ten hits and a chart-topping album simultaneously, a situation that lasted for a month. The album stayed at #1 for nine weeks and "Jack and Diane" topped the singles chart for four, going gold. The last single from the album, "Hand to Hold On To" hit #19. All in all, the album sold over 4 million copies. That year, he earned a Grammy for Best Rock Vocal Performance, Male, for "Hurts So Good."

With this success, Mellencamp was able to relegate "Cougar" to a middle name and start recording with his own last name finally. Thus, his next album *Uh-huh* was by John Cougar Mellencamp. He recorded the album in a bit over two weeks, and it was infused with the energy that some artists lose after a big pop hit. "Crumblin' Down," recalling his Rolling Stones roots stronger than anything he had previously done, topped out at #9. The

follow-up, "Pink Houses," notched to #8. While not his most successful song chartwise at #15, "Authority Song" became something of an anthem, a testament to the youth that got thrown off the football team in high school for smoking. The album hit #9 and went triple platinum.

Despite (or maybe because of) his success, Mellencamp chose to stay close to his Ind. roots, living most of the year (when he was home) in Bloomington. While his family was not involved in agriculture, many of his neighbors farmed for a living. Mellencamp became aware of the vast number of farms going under, and joined with other concerned artists like Willie Nelson and Neil Young to create Farm Aid in 1985. His next album reflected this as well. *Scarecrow* celebrated the ups and downs of the area. The title track, which hit #21 on the charts, laments the fall of the family farm. The album's first single, "Lonely Ol' Night" celebrated the simple joy of two lonely people coming together and no longer feeling lonely. That single rose to #6, as did the follow-up celebration of the area, "Small Town." The album also paid tribute to the music itself with the anthemic, #2 single "R.O.C.K. in the USA." Even the fifth single, "Rumbleseat," hit #28. The album sold quadruple platinum, spending three weeks at #2.

After *Scarecrow*, Mellencamp urged his band to pick up rootsy instruments to expand its musical horizons. His longtime friend, guitarist Larry Crane, sweated over the lap-steel guitar. Drummer Kenny Aronoff took lessons on the hammered dulcimer. Guitarist Mike Wanchic mastered the dobro. Fiddler Lisa Germano joined the band. The next album, *The Lonesome Jubilee*, used these instruments, along with banjos and accordions, to make an album that many described as having an Appalachian feel, though Mellencamp said he was shooting for a more gypsy rock sound. The hook of the initial single, "Paper in Fire," squealed with fiddle and squeezebox, a sound totally unlike anything else on pop radio, but went to #9 anyway. The somewhat more conventional "Cherry Bomb" hit #8. The almost whimsically lyrical "Check It Out" hit #14. The album sold a respectable 3 million copies.

In 1989, after 15 years of relentless recording and touring, Mellencamp realized that he had a daughter from his first marriage who was going to college that year. He had two other daughters who were virtually strangers. So, after the release of his next album, *Big Daddy*, Mellencamp took a break. He didn't tour, didn't do press. He spent time with his family and got heavily into painting. He made a film of a screenplay he had written with Larry McMurtry called *Falling from Grace*. He got active in the Special Olympics and Nordoff-Robbins music therapy, realizing that he could have been there had his early surgery not been successful. The album spawned the #15 single, "Pop Singer," and went platinum, rising to #7.

By 1992, though, he was ready for the grind again. He released his first album to eschew the "Cougar" altogether, *Whenever We Wanted*, and set out on a seven-month world tour. The album generated the #14 single "Get a Leg Up" and the #36 "Again Tonight." Despite the heavy touring, the album peaked at #17 and went platinum. The following year, his album *Human Wheels* got excellent reviews, but after debuting at #7 slipped rapidly down the chart, still managing to sell platinum without benefit of a hit single. For *Dance Naked*, Mellencamp recorded a duet with Me'Shell Ndeg'eOcello on Van Morrison's "Wild Night" that became a surprise hit, topping the adult-contemporary charts for eight weeks and rising to #3 on the pop charts. He hit the road again, but the tour was cut short when Mellencamp had a heart attack. He went home to Bloomington to recover. The album went to #13, and sold platinum.

Anxious to try something new again, he brought in dance producer Junior Vasquez to work with him on his next album. That record, *Mr. Happy Go Lucky*, featured samples and tape loops and the sort of studio wizardry Mellencamp had studiously avoided for the previous two decades. It generated a minor hit in "Key West Intermezzo (I Saw You First)," and went platinum. Mellencamp wanted out of his contract with PolyGram, and agreed to give them two records. The first was a greatest hits package, *The Best That I Could Do: 1978–1988*. The album became his 10th platinum record in a row.

He moved over to Columbia and released *John Mellencamp*. The album featured guest performances by Izzy Stadlin from Guns 'N' Roses and Stan Lynch from the Heartbreakers. The single "I'm Not Running Anymore" hit #22 on the adult-contemporary chart. The album rose to #41 but only went gold. Even if the album broke his string of platinum records, however, he still was in demand on the road. His tour was the #9 moneymaker of 1999, ahead of KISS.

The second record in the completion of his Mercury deal came out shortly after. *Rough Harvest* featured acoustic versions of Mellencamp's hits and favorite tunes, played as if the band performed them on the front porch. It barely broke the Top 100, peaking at #99. He also put out a book of his paintings in 1999.

DISC.: *Chestnut Street Incident* (1976); *The Kid Inside* (1977); *A Biography* (1978); *Johnny Cougar* (1979); *John Cougar* (1979); *Night Dancin'* (1980); *Nothin' Matters & What If It Did* (1980); *American Fool* (1982); *Uh- Huh* (1983); *Scarecrow* (1985); *The Lonesome Jubilee* (1987); *Big Daddy* (1989); *Whenever We Wanted* (1991); *Human Wheels* (1993); *Dance Naked* (1994); *Mr. Happy Go Lucky* (1996); *John Mellencamp* (1998); *Dance Naked* (Bonus CD; 1999).

BIBL.: M. Torgoff, *American Fool: The Roots and Improbable Rise of J. M.* (N.Y. 1986).—**HB**

Mellers, Wilfrid (Howard),

English musicologist and composer; b. Leamington, Warwickshire, April 26, 1914. He studied at the Univ. of Cambridge (B.A., 1936; M.A., 1939); was a pupil in composition of Wellesz and Rubbra; received his D.Mus. from the Univ. of Birmingham (1960). He was a lecturer in music at Downing Coll., Cambridge (1945–48); after serving as a staff tutor in the extramural dept. at the Univ. of Birmingham (1948–59), he served as Andrew W. Mellon Prof. of Music at the Univ. of Pittsburgh (1960–63); then was prof. of music at the Univ. of York (1964–81). In 1982 he was made an Officer of the Order of the British Empire.

WRITINGS: *Music and Society: England and the European Tradition* (London, 1946); *Studies in Contemporary Music* (London, 1947); *François Couperin and the French Classical Tradition* (London, 1950; 2nd ed., rev., 1987); *Music in the Making* (London, 1952); *Romanticism and the 20th Century* (London, 1957; 2nd ed., rev., 1988); *The Sonata Principle* (London, 1957; 2nd ed., rev., 1988); *Music in a New Found Land: Themes and Developments in the History of American Music* (London, 1964; 2nd ed., rev., 1987); *Harmonious Meeting: A Study of the Relationship between English Music, Poetry and Theatre, c. 1600–1900* (London, 1965); *Caliban Reborn: Renewal in Twentieth-Century Music* (N.Y., 1967); *Twilight of the Gods: The Music of the Beatles* (N.Y., 1973); *Bach and the Dance of God* (N.Y., 1980); *Beethoven and the Voice of God* (London, 1983); *A Darker Shade of Pale: A Backdrop to Bob Dylan* (London, 1984); *Angels of the Night: Popular Female Singers of Our Time* (London, 1986); *The Masks of Orpheus: Seven Stages in the Story of European Music* (Manchester, England, and Wolfeboro, N.H., 1987); *Le Jardin Parfume: Homage to Frederic Mompou* (1989); *Vaughan Williams and the Vision of Albion* (London, 1989); *Percy Grainger* (Oxford, 1992); *Francis Poulenc* (Oxford, 1994); J. Paynter, ed., *Between Old Worlds and New: Occasional Writings on Music* (London, 1997).

WORKS: DRAMATIC: O p e r a : *The Tragicall History of Christopher Marlowe* (1952); *The Shepherd's Daughter*, chamber opera (1953–54); *Mary Easter*, ballad opera (1957). **M o n o - d r a m a :** *The Ancient Wound* (Victoria, British Columbia, July 27, 1970). **ORCH.:** *Sinfonia ricercata* (1947); *Alba, in 9 Metamorphoses* for Flute and Orch. (1961); *Noctambule and Sun Dance* for Wind Sym. (1966); *Shaman Songs* for Jazz Paraphernalia (1980); *The Wellspring of Loves*, concerto for Violin and String Orch. (1981); *The Spring of the Year* for Double String Orch. (1985); *Hortus Rosarium* for 11 Solo Strings (1986). **CHAMBER:** String Trio (1945); Viola Sonata (1946); *Eclogue* for Treble Recorder, Violin, Cello, and Harpsichord (1961); Trio for Flute, Cello, and Piano (1963); *Ghost Dance* for Flute, Viola, and Harpsichord (1972); *Aubade for Indra* for Clarinet and String Quartet (1981); *The Happy Meadow*, eclogue for Flute and Guitar (1986); piano pieces. **VOCAL:** *Voice of the Earth*, cantata (1972); choruses; songs.—**NS/LK/DM**

Melles, Carl,

Hungarian conductor; b. Budapest, July 15, 1926. He received his musical training in Budapest. In 1951 he was appointed conductor of the Hungarian State Orch. and the Sym. Orch. of Hungarian Radio and Television. He was also a prof. at the Budapest Academy of Music (1954–56). After the abortive rebellion in 1956, he led the Radio Orch. of Luxembourg (1958–60); also conducted at Bayreuth and Salzburg. He eventually made his home in Vienna and became a regular conductor of the Vienna Sym. Orch. and on the Austrian Radio.—**NS/LK/DM**

Mellnäs, Arne,

Swedish composer and teacher; b. Stockholm, Aug. 30, 1933. He entered the Stockholm Musikhögskolan in 1953, where he studied composition with Koch, Larsson, Blomdahl, and Wallner (1958–61). He also was a student of Blacher at the Berlin Hochschule für Musik (1959) and of Deutsch in Paris (1961). After further training with Ligeti in Vienna (1962), he worked at the San Francisco Tape Music Center (1964). He made Stockholm the center of his activities, where he taught at the Citizen's School (1961–63) and at the Musikhögskolan (from 1963). From 1983 he also served as chairman of the Swedish section of the ISCM. In 1984 he was elected a member of the Royal Swedish Academy of Music. He was awarded the Atterberg Prize in 1994. Mellnäs is one of Sweden's most innovative composers, and has done much to advance the cause of contemporary music in his homeland.

WORKS: DRAMATIC: *Minibuff*, opera (1966); *Kaleidovision*, television ballet (1969); *Erik den helige*, church opera (1975; Stockholm, May 18, 1976); *Spöket p°a Canterville*, opera (Ume°a, April 25, 1981); *Dans p°a rosor*, opera buffa (1984); *Doktor Glas*, opera (1987–90). **ORCH.:** Concerto for Clarinet and Strings (1957); *Music* (1959); *Chiasmos* (1961); *Collage* (1962); *Aura* (Malmö, June 5, 1964); *Transparence* (1972); *Blow* for Wind Orch. (1974); *Moments musicaux* (1977; Lillehammer, March 12, 1978); *Besvärjelser* (1978); *Capriccio* (Stockholm, May 6, 1978); *Ikaros*, sym. (1986; Stockholm, March 18, 1987); *Passages* (1989; Sydney, April 21, 1990). **CHAMBER:** Oboe Sonata (1957); *Per caso* for Saxophone, Trombone, Violin, Double Bass, and 2 Percussionists (1963); *Tombola* for Horn, Trombone, Electric Guitar, and Piano (1963); *Sic transit* for Instruments and Tape (1964); *Siamfoni* for Trumpet, Horn, and Trombone (1964); *Quasi niente* for 1 to 4 String Trios (1968); *Capricorn Flakes* for Piano, Harpsichord, and Vibraphone (1970); *Cabrillo* for Clarinet, Trombone, Cello, and Percussion (1970); *Ceremus* for Flute, Clarinet, Trumpet, Trombone, Double Bass, and Percussion (1973); *The Mummy and the Hummingbird* for Flute and Harpsichord ad libitum (1974); *Riflessioni* for Clarinet or Bass Clarinet and Tape (1981); *31 Variations on C A G E* for 2 Pianos and Percussion (1982); *Rendez-vous* for 2 Flutes and Percussion (1983); *Stampede* for Saxophone Quartet (1985); *Gardens* for Flute, Clarinet, Percussion, Violin, Cello, and Piano (Stockholm, April 13, 1987); *No roses for Madame F* for Saxophone Quartet (1991); *Rolando furioso* for Violin and Harpsichord (1991); String Quartet No. 1, *Hommages* (1993); *Estampes* for Horn (1995); piano pieces. **OTHER:** Choral works; songs; electronic music. **—NS/LK/DM**

Melnikov, Ivan (Alexandrovich), noted Russian baritone; b. St. Petersburg, March 4, 1832; d. there, July 8, 1906. He was a choirboy in school. He was engaged in trade, and for a time served as inspector of Volga boats; he began to study seriously late in life; took lessons with Lomakin (1862); then went to Italy, where he studied with Repetto. He made his operatic debut as Riccardo in *I Puritani* in St. Petersburg (Oct. 6, 1867), where he sang regularly until his farewell performance in *Prince Igor* in 1890; then taught voice. He created the title role in Mussorgsky's *Boris Godunov* (St. Petersburg, Feb. 8, 1874). He was particularly esteemed for his portrayals of roles in operas by Glinka, Borodin, and Tchaikovsky.—**NS/LK/DM**

Melrose, Frank(lyn Taft), jazz pianist, leader; b. Sumner, Ill., Nov. 26, 1907; d. near Hammond, Ind., Sept. 1, 1941. His two brothers, Walter and Lester, were music publishers and talent scouts for recording companies. Frank began on violin, but later specialized on piano. He worked with various leaders in and around Chicago in the late 1920s. During this period, he recorded under the pseudonym "Kansas City Frank," and also did sessions with the Dodds Brothers, Jimmy Bertrand, and other Chicago-based musicians. He worked in N.Y., Kansas City, St. Louis, and Detroit;

played with Bud Jacobson at the Chicago World's Fair (1933). He left full-time music for several years, but returned to teaching and gigs in the late 1930s, then had a residency at Paddock and Derby Clubs in Calumet City until March 1940. This was followed by a brief spell with Pete Daily in Chicago. Melrose then worked as a machinist in a pressed-steel factory, continued to do club work, including a spell with Joe Sheets in the Cedar Lake district. After a Labor Day weekend visit to Chicago in 1941, his mutilated body was found near Hammond, Ind.

DISC.: *Kansas City Frank Melrose* (1956).—**JC/LP**

Melton, James, American tenor; b. Moultrie, Ga., Jan. 2, 1904; d. N.Y., April 21, 1961. He studied with Gaetano de Luca in Nashville and Enrico Rosati in N.Y. and then with Michael Raucheisen in Berlin. He began his career on the radio. He made his concert debut in N.Y. on April 22, 1932, and his operatic debut as Pinkerton in *Madama Butterfly* in Cincinnati on June 28, 1938. On Dec. 7, 1942, he appeared for the first time with the Metropolitan Opera in N.Y. as Tamino in *Die Zauberflöte*; remained on its roster until 1950. He also toured the U.S. as a concert singer and later appeared in films. **—NS/LK/DM**

Meluzzi, Salvatore, Italian composer; b. Rome, July 22, 1813; d. there, April 17, 1897. He was maestro di cappella at the basilica of St. Peter's in the Vatican, and for 45 years was director of the Cappella Giulia. Thoroughly versed in the art of the early Italian masters, he emulated them in writing masses, Requiems, antiphons, motets, hymns, and Psalms. Among his best pieces are a *Stabat Mater* and a *Miserere*.—**NS/LK/DM**

Membrée, Edmond, French composer; b. Valenciennes, Nov. 14, 1820; d. Château Damont, near Paris, Sept. 10, 1882. He studied at the Paris Cons. with Alkan and Zimmerman (piano) and Carafa (composition).

WORKS: DRAMATIC: Opera: *François Villon* (Paris, April 20, 1857); *L'Esclave* (Paris, July 17, 1874); *Les Parias* (Paris, Nov. 13, 1876); *La Courte Echelle* (Paris, 1879). **VOCAL:** *Fingal*, cantata (Paris, May 14, 1861); ballads; songs; etc.

BIBL.: L. Mention, *Un Compositeur valenciennois: E. M.* (Paris, 1908).—**NS/LK/DM**

Menasce, Jacques de, Austrian-born American pianist and composer; b. Bad Ischl (of a French-Egyptian father and a German mother), Aug. 19, 1905; d. Gstaad, Switzerland, Jan. 28, 1960. He studied in Vienna with Sauer (piano) and with J. Marx, Paul Pisk, and Berg (composition). From 1932 to 1940 he gave concerts in Europe as a pianist; in 1941 he went to America, living mostly in N.Y., but continued his concert career in Europe. He became a naturalized American citizen.

WORKS: DRAMATIC: Ballet: *The Fate of My People* (1945); *Status Quo* (1947). **ORCH.:** 2 piano concertos (1935, 1939); *Divertimento* for Piano and Strings (1940). **CHAMBER:** Violin Sonata (1940); Viola Sonata (1950); piano pieces. **VOCAL:** Choruses; songs.—**NS/LK/DM**

Mendel, Arthur, eminent American music scholar; b. Boston, June 6, 1905; d. Newark, N.J., Oct. 14, 1979. He studied at Harvard Univ. (A.B., 1925), and then took courses in theory with Boulanger in Paris (1925–27). Returning to America, he was literary ed. of G. Schirmer, Inc. (1930–38), and also wrote music criticism in the *Nation* (1930–33). From 1936 to 1953 he conducted in N.Y. a chorus, the Cantata Singers, specializing in Baroque music. He taught at the Dalcroze School of Music from 1938, and was its president (1947–50). Mendel also lectured at Columbia Univ. (1949) and the Univ. of Calif., Berkeley (1951). He was prof. of music and chairman of the music dept. at Princeton Univ. (1952–67), where he held the Henry Putnam Univ. Professorship from 1969 to 1973. He ed. (with H. David) *The Bach Reader* (N.Y., 1945; 2nd ed., rev., 1966; rev. and enl. ed., 1998, by C. Wolff as *The New Bach Reader*), and also ed. *Bach's St. John Passion* (1951), *Schütz's Christmas Story* (1949) and *Musicalische Exequien* (1957), and other works of the Baroque period. He publ. numerous important articles on the history of pitch, reprinted in *Studies in the History of Musical Pitch* (Amsterdam, 1969), and also promoted the possibility of music analysis with the aid of a computer, publ. in *Computers and the Humanities* (1969–70).

BIBL.: R. Marshall, ed., *Studies in Renaissance and Baroque Music in Honor of A. M.* (Kassel, 1974).—**NS/LK/DM**

Mendel, Hermann, German music lexicographer; b. Halle, Aug. 6, 1834; d. Berlin, Oct. 26, 1876. He was a pupil of Mendelssohn and Moscheles in Leipzig, and of Wieprecht in Berlin. In 1870 he founded and ed. the *Deutsche Musiker-Zeitung.* He also ed. *Mode's Opernbibliothek* (about 90 librettos, with commentaries and biographies of composers) and a *Volksliederbuch.* He publ. 2 small books on Meyerbeer (1868, 1869). His great work was the *Musikalisches Conversations-Lexikon,* which he began to publ. in 1870, but was able to continue only to the letter M. The rest was completed by August Reissmann, with the entire ed. running 11 vols. A supplementary vol. was publ. in 1883.—**NS/LK/DM**

Mendelsohn, Alfred, Romanian composer, conductor, and teacher; b. Bucharest, Feb. 17, 1910; d. there, May 9, 1966. He was a student of Schmidt and Marx (composition) and of Lach and Wellesz (music history) in Vienna (1927–31). Returning to Bucharest, he completed his training with Jora (composition) at the Cons. (1931–32). He taught harmony (1932–36) and was director (1936–40) at the E. Massini Cons. From 1946 to 1954 he was asst. music director of the Romanian Opera. From 1949 until his death he also was a prof. at the Cons. In 1945 he received the Enesco Prize and in 1949 was awarded the Romanian Academy Prize. While his music primarily reflects the influence of the Romantic Viennese School, he also probed the potentialities of motivic structures, suggesting the serial concepts of modern constructivists while remaining faithful to basic tonalitarianism.

WORKS: DRAMATIC: *Imnul iubirii* (The Love Hymn), dramatic sym. (1946); *Harap-Alb* (The White Moor), ballet (1948; Bucharest, March 30, 1949); *Meşterul Manole,* lyric drama (1949);

Călin, choreographic poem (1956; Bucharest, May 2, 1957); *Anton Pann,* operetta (1961); *Michelangelo,* opera (1964; Timişoara, Sept. 29, 1968); *Spinoza,* lyric scene (1966). **ORCH.:** *Suită concertantă în stil clasic* for Violin and Strings (1938; rev. 1961); *Divertisment* for Flute and Strings (1938); *Rapsodie* (1940); Suite for Chamber Orch. (1940); 9 syms.: No. 1, *Înainte* (1944), No. 2, *Veritas* (1947), No. 3, *Reconstrucţia* (1949), No. 4, *Apelul păcii* (1951), No. 5 (1953), No. 6 (1955), No. 7 (1960), No. 8 (1963; Bucharest, Feb. 11, 1965), and No. 9, concertante for Organ and Orch. (1964; Bucharest, July 1, 1965); 2 piano concertos (1945, 1949); Sinfonietă (1946); 2 cello concertos (1950, 1962); *Prăbuşirea Doftanei* (Doftana's Assault), poem (1950; Bucharest, May 7, 1955); 3 violin concertos (1950–54; 1957; 1963); *Eliberare* (Liberation), poem (1954); *Va înflori acel arminden* (The May Tree Will Blossom), festive poem (1956); Concerto grosso for String Quartet and String Orch. (1956); Concertino for Harp and Strings (1956); Concertino for Violin and Strings (1957); *Divertisment* for Horn and Strings (1957); Concerto for Organ and Strings (1958–59); Piano Concertino (1959); *Schiţe dobrogene* (Dobrudjan Sketches; 1960–61); *Concertino în stil clasic* for 2 Violins and Strings (1961); Concerto for 2 Violins and Orch. (1962); 6 *Schite* (Sketches; 1963); Tuba Concerto (1963); *Concerto for Orchestra* (1965); Viola Concerto (1965); *Epitaf* (1965). **CHAMBER:** 10 string quartets (1930; 1930; 1953; 1954; 1955; 1955; 1955–56; 1958; 1959–61; 1964); 4 Pieces for Clarinet and Piano (1952); Piano Quintet (1953); String Sextet (1956); 4 Pieces for Cello and Piano (1959); 2 piano trios (1957, 1960); 3 violin sonatas (all 1957); *Sonata brevis* for Violin and Organ (1960); 12 *Preludii în stil clasic* for Violin (1962); *Variatiumi rapsodice* for Cello and Piano (1963); Sonata for Solo Cello (1965); piano pieces, including a Sonata (1947). **VOCAL:** *Cantata Bucureştiului* for Reciter, Chorus, and Orch. (1953; Bucharest, Oct. 31, 1954); *Horia,* heroic oratorio for Soloists and Orch. (1954–56); *1907,* oratorio for Soloists, Chorus, and Orch. (1956; Bucharest, March 21, 1957); *Glasul lui Lenin,* cantata for Chorus and Orch. (Bucharest, Nov. 2, 1957); *Sub cerul de vară,* sym.-cantata for Soloists, 2 Reciters, Chorus, and Orch. (Bucharest, Oct. 8, 1959); *Pentru Marele Octombrie,* oratorio for Soloists, Chorus, and Orch. (Bucharest, Nov. 3, 1960).—**NS/LK/DM**

Mendelssohn, Arnold (Ludwig), distinguished German organist, pedagogue, and composer, son of a 2nd cousin of **(Jacob Ludwig) Felix Mendelssohn (-Bartholdy);** b. Ratibor, Dec. 26, 1855; d. Darmstadt, Feb. 19, 1933. He studied law at the Univ. of Tübingen (1877), then took courses with Löschhorn (piano), Haupt (organ), and Grell, Kiel, and Taubert (composition) at Berlin's Institut für Kirchenmusik (1877–80). He was organist and music director at the Univ. of Bonn (1880–82), then music director in Bielefeld (1882–85); taught composition at the Cologne Cons. (1885–90). He was Hessian master of church music and prof. at the Darmstadt Cons. (1891–1912), and thereafter a prof. at Frankfurt am Main's Hoch Cons., where his pupils included Hindemith. He championed the music of Schütz and Bach. In his own sacred works, he helped to revitalize Lutheran church music. He wrote a book on aesthetics, *Gott, Welt und Kunst* (ed. by W. Ewald; Wiesbaden, 1949).

WORKS: DRAMATIC: Opera: *Elsi, die seltsame Magd* (Cologne, 1896); *Der Bärenhäuter* (Berlin, Feb. 9, 1900); *Der Minneburg* (Mannheim, 1909). **Incidental Music To:** Goethe's *Paria* (1906) and *Pandora* (1908). **ORCH.:** 3 syms.; Violin Concerto (1922). **CHAMBER:** 3 string quartets;

Cello Sonata; 2 piano sonatas. VOCAL: Sacred choral works, including *Abendkantate* (1881) and 2 other cantatas (both 1912); *Deutsche Messe* (1923); *Geistliche Chormusik* (1926); songs.

BIBL.: W. Nagel, *A. M.* (Leipzig, 1906); A. Werner-Jensen, *A. M. als Liederkomponist* (Winterthur, 1976); J. Böhme, *A. M. und seine Klavier- und Kammermusik* (Frankfurt am Main, 1987). —NS/LK/DM

Mendelssohn (-Bartholdy), (Jacob Ludwig) Felix,

famous German composer, pianist; b. Hamburg, Feb. 3, 1809; d. Leipzig, Nov. 4, 1847. He was a grandson of the philosopher Moses Mendelssohn and the son of the banker Abraham Mendelssohn; his mother was Lea Salomon; the family was Jewish, but upon its settlement in Berlin the father decided to become a Protestant and added Bartholdy to his surname. Mendelssohn received his first piano lessons from his mother; subsequently studied piano with Ludwig Berger and violin with Carl Wilhelm Henning and Eduard Rietz; he also had regular lessons in foreign languages and in painting (he showed considerable talent in drawing with pastels); he also had piano lessons with Marie Bigot in Paris, where he went with his father for a brief stay in 1816. His most important teacher in his early youth was Carl Friedrich Zelter, who understood the magnitude of Mendelssohn's talent; in 1821 Zelter took him to Weimar and introduced him to Goethe, who took considerable interest in the boy after hearing him play. Zelter arranged for Mendelssohn to become a member of the Singakademie in Berlin in 1819 as an alto singer; on Sept. 18, 1819, his *19th Psalm* was performed by the Akademie. In 1825 Mendelssohn's father took him again to Paris to consult Cherubini on Mendelssohn's prospects in music; however, he returned to Berlin, where he had better opportunities for development. Mendelssohn was not only a precocious musician, both in performing and in composition; what is perhaps without a parallel in music history is the extraordinary perfection of his works written during adolescence. He played in public for the first time at the age of 9, on Oct. 28, 1818, in Berlin, performing the piano part of a trio by Wölffl. He wrote a remarkable octet at the age of 16; at 17 he composed the overture for the incidental music to Shakespeare's *A Midsummer Night's Dream*, an extraordinary manifestation of his artistic maturity, showing a mastery of form equal to that of the remaining numbers of the work, which were composed 15 years later. He proved his great musicianship when he conducted Bach's *St. Matthew Passion* in the Berlin Singakademie on March 11, 1829, an event that gave an impulse to the revival of Bach's vocal music. In the spring of 1829 Mendelssohn made his first journey to England, where he conducted his Sym. in C minor (seated, after the fashion of the time, at the keyboard); later he performed in London the solo part in Beethoven's *Emperor* Concerto; he then traveled through Scotland, where he found inspiration for the composition of his overture *Fingal's Cave (Hebrides)*, which he conducted for the first time during his second visit to London, on May 14, 1832; 10 days later he played in London the solo part of his G minor Concerto and his *Capriccio brillante*. He became a favorite of the English public; Queen Victoria was one of his most fervent admirers; altogether he made 10 trips to England as a pianist, conductor, and composer. From 1830 to 1832 he traveled in Germany, Austria, Italy, and Switzerland, and also went to Paris. In May 1833 he led the Lower-Rhine Music Festival in Düsseldorf; then conducted at Cologne in June 1835. He was still a very young man when, in 1835, he was offered the conductorship of the celebrated Gewandhaus Orch. in Leipzig; the Univ. of Leipzig bestowed upon him an honorary degree of Ph.D. Mendelssohn's leadership of the Gewandhaus Orch. was of the greatest significance for the development of German musical culture; he engaged the violin virtuoso Ferdinand David as concertmaster of the orch., which soon became the most prestigious symphonic organization in Germany. On March 28, 1837, he married Cécile Charlotte Sophie Jeanrenaud of Frankfurt am Main, the daughter of a French Protestant clergyman. Five children (Carl, Marie, Paul, Felix, and Elisabeth) were born to them, and their marriage was exceptionally happy. At the invitation of King Friedrich Wilhelm IV, Mendelssohn went in 1841 to Berlin to take charge of the music of the court and in the Cathedral; he received the title of Royal Generalmusikdirektor, but residence in Berlin was not required. Returning to Leipzig in 1842, he organized the famous "Conservatorium." Its splendid faculty comprised, besides Mendelssohn (who taught piano, ensemble playing, and later composition), Schumann, who taught classes in piano and composition; Hauptmann, in music theory; David, in violin; Becker, in organ; and Plaidy and Wenzel, in piano. The Conservatorium was officially opened on April 3, 1843. The financial nucleus of the foundation was a bequest from Blumner of 20,000 thaler, left at the disposal of the King of Saxony for the promotion of the fine arts. Mendelssohn made a special journey to Dresden to petition the King on behalf of the Leipzig Cons. During his frequent absences, the Gewandhaus Concerts were conducted by Hiller (1843–44) and Gade (1844–45). In the summer of 1844 he conducted the Phil. Concerts in London; this was his 8th visit to England; during his 9th visit he conducted the first performance of his oratorio *Elijah* in Birmingham, on Aug. 26, 1846. It was in England that the "Wedding March" from Mendelssohn's music to *A Midsummer Night's Dream* began to be used to accompany the bridal procession; the performance of the work was for the marriage of Tom Daniel and Dorothy Carew at St. Peter's Church, Tiverton, on June 2, 1847; the organist was Samuel Reay; it became particularly fashionable, however, when it was played at the wedding of the Princess Royal in 1858. He made his 10th and last visit to England in the spring of 1847; this was a sad period of his life, for his favorite sister, Fanny, died on May 14, 1847. Mendelssohn's own health began to deteriorate, and he died at the age of 38. The exact cause of his early death is not determined; he suffered from severe migraines and chills before he died, but no evidence could be produced by the resident physicians for either a stroke or heart failure. The news of his death produced a profound shock in the world of music; not only in Germany and England, where he was personally known and beloved, but in distant America and Russia as well, there was genuine sorrow among musicians. Mendelssohn societies were formed all over the world; in America the Mendelssohn Quintette Club was founded in 1849. A Mendelssohn Scholarship was established in England in 1856; its first recipient was Arthur Sullivan. In 1967 the Mendelssohn-Gesellschaft was founded.

Mendelssohn's influence on German, English, American, and Russian music was great and undiminishing through the years; his syms., concertos, chamber music, piano pieces, and songs became perennial favorites in concerts and at home, the most popular works being the overture *Hebrides*, the ubiquitously played Violin Concerto, the *Songs without Words* for Piano, and the "Wedding March" from incidental music to *A Midsummer Night's Dream*. Professional music historians are apt to place Mendelssohn below the ranks of his great contemporaries Schumann, Chopin, and Liszt; in this exalted company Mendelssohn is often regarded as a phenomenon of Biedermeier culture. A barbaric ruling was made by the Nazi regime to forbid performances of Mendelssohn's music as that of a Jew; his very name was removed from music history books and encyclopedias publ. in Germany during that time. This shameful episode was of but a transitory nature, however; if anything, it served to create a greater appreciation of Mendelssohn's genius following the collapse of the infamous 3rd Reich.

WORKS: DRAMATIC: *Ich, J. Mendelssohn...*, Lustspiel (1820); *Die Soldatenliebschaft*, comic opera (1820; Wittenberg, April 28, 1962); *Die beiden Pädagogen*, Singspiel (1821; Berlin, May 27, 1962); *Die wandernden Komödianten*, comic opera (1822; dialogue not extant); *Der Onkel aus Boston oder Die beiden Neffen*, comic opera (1823; Berlin, Feb. 3, 1824; dialogue not extant); *Die Hochzeit des Camacho*, op.10, opera (1825; Berlin, April 29, 1827; dialogue not extant); *Die Heimkehr aus der Fremde*, op.89, Liederspiel (1829, written for the silver wedding anniversary of Mendelssohn's parents, perf. at their home, Berlin, Dec. 26, 1829); *Der standhafte*, incidental music to Calderón's play (1833); *Trala. A frischer Bua bin i* (1833); *Ruy Blas*, incidental music to Hugo's play (1839); *Antigone*, op.55, incidental music to Sophocles's play (Potsdam, Oct. 28, 1841); *A Midsummer Night's Dream*, op.61, incidental music to Shakespeare's play (1842; Potsdam, Oct. 14, 1843); *Oedipus at Colonos*, op.93, incidental music to Sophocles's play (Potsdam, Nov. 1, 1845); *Athalie*, op.74, incidental music to Racine's play (Berlin-Charlottenburg, Dec. 1, 1845); *Lorelei*, op.98, opera (begun in childhood but unfinished; *Ave Maria*, a vintage chorus, and finale to Act I only; Birmingham, Sept. 8, 1852). **ORCH.:** 13 sinfonias for Strings: No. 1, in C major (1821), No. 2, in D major (1821), No. 3, in E minor (1821), No. 4, in C minor (1821), No. 5, in B-flat major (1821), No. 6, in E-flat major (1821), No. 7, in D minor (1821–22), No. 8, in D major (1822), No. 9, in C major (1823), No. 10, in B minor (1823), No. 11, in F major (1823), No. 12, in G minor (1823), and No. 13, in C minor (1823; one movement only); syms.: No. 1, in C minor, op.11 (1824), No. 2, in B-flat major, a sym.-cantata for Solo Voices, Chorus, and Orch., *Lobgesang* or *Hymn of Praise*, op.52 (Leipzig, June 25, 1840, composer conducting), No. 3, in A minor, *Scottish*, op.56 (1830–42; Leipzig, March 3, 1842, composer conducting), No. 4, in A major, *Italian*, op.90 (London, May 13, 1833, composer conducting), and No. 5, in D major, *Reformation*, op.107 (1830–32; Berlin, Nov. 15, 1832, composer conducting); Violin Concerto in D minor for Strings (1822; N.Y., Feb. 4, 1952); Piano Concerto in A minor for Strings (1822); Concerto in D minor for Violin, Piano, and Strings

(1823); Concerto in E major for 2 Pianos and Orch. (1823; Berlin, Nov. 14, 1824); Concerto in A-flat major for 2 Pianos and Orch. (1824; Stettin, Feb. 20, 1827); Overture in C major for Wind Instruments, op.24 (1824); *Capriccio brillant* in B minor for Piano and Orch., op.22 (1825–26; London, May 25, 1832); Overture (*Trumpet* Overture) in C major, op.101 (1826; rev. 1833); *Ein Sommernachtstraum*, overture for Shakespeare's *A Midsummer Night's Dream*, op.21 (1826; Stettin, April 29, 1827); *Meeresstille und glückliche Fahrt*, overture after Goethe, op.27 (Berlin, April 18, 1828); *Die Hebriden* or *Fingals Hohle*, overture, op.26 (1830; London, May 14, 1832); Piano Concerto No. 1, in G minor, op.25 (Munich, Oct. 17, 1831, composer soloist); *Die schöne Melusine*, overture after Grillparzer, op.32 (1833; London, April 7, 1834); *Rondo brillant* in E-flat major for Piano and Orch., op.29 (1834); *Trauermarsch* in A minor for Wind, op.103 (1836); Piano Concerto No. 2, in D minor, op.40 (Birmingham, Sept. 1837, composer soloist); *Serenade* and *Allegro giocoso*, in B minor, for Piano and Orch., op.43 (1838); *Ruy Blas*, overture after Hugo, op.95 (Leipzig, March 1839); March in D major, op.108 (1841); Violin Concerto in E minor, op.64 (1844; Leipzig, March 13, 1845, Ferdinand David, soloist, Niels Gade conducting); also a recently discovered Concerto in E minor for Piano and Orch. (n.d.). **CHAMBER:** Trio in C minor for Violin, Viola, and Piano (1820); Presto in F major for Violin and Piano (1820); Violin Sonata in F major (1820); 15 fugues for String Quartet (1821); Piano Quartet in D minor (1822); Piano Quartet No. 1, in C minor, op.1 (1822); String Quartet in E-flat major (1823); Piano Quartet No. 2, in F minor, op.2 (1823); Viola Sonata in C minor (1824); Sextet in D major for Violin, 2 Violas, Cello, Double Bass, and Piano, op.110 (1824); Clarinet Sonata in E-flat major (1824); Piano Quartet No. 3, in B minor, op.3 (1825); Violin Sonata in F minor, op.4 (1825); Octet in E-flat major for 4 Violins, 2 Violas, and 2 Cellos, op.20 (1825); Quintet No. 1, in A major, for 2 Violins, 2 Violas, and Cello, op.18 (1826; rev. 1832); String Quartet No. 2, in A major, op.13 (1827); Fugue in E-flat major for String Quartet (1827); Fugue in E-flat major for String Quartet, op.81/4 (1827); *Variations concertantes* for Cello and Piano, op.17 (1829); String Quartet No. 1, in E-flat major, op.12 (1829); *The Evening Bell* for Harp and Piano (1829); Concert Piece in F major for Clarinet, Basset Horn, and Piano or Orch., op.113 (1833); Concert Piece in D minor for Clarinet and Basset Horn, op.114 (1833); string quartets, Nos. 3–5, op.44 (1837–38); Violin Sonata in F major (1838); Cello Sonata No. 1, in B-flat major, op.45 (1838); Piano Trio No. 1, in D minor, op.49 (1839); *Capriccio* in E minor for String Quartet, op.81/3 (1843); Cello Sonata No. 2, in D major, op.58 (1843); Quintet No. 2, in B-flat major, op.87 (1845); Piano Trio No. 2, in C minor, op.66 (1845); *Lied ohne Worte* in D major for Cello and Piano, op.109 (1845); String Quartet No. 6, in F minor, op.80 (1847); *Andante* in E major for String Quartet, op.81/1 (1847); *Scherzo* in A minor for String Quartet, op.81/2 (1847). **KEYBOARD: Piano:** *Andante* in F major (1820); piano piece in E minor (1820); 2 little pieces (1820); 2 little pieces (1820); 5 little pieces (1820); *Largo-Allegro* in C minor (1820); *Recitativo (Largo)* in D minor (1820); Sonata in F minor (1820); Sonata in A minor (1820); *Presto* in C minor (1820); Sonata in E minor (1820); 2 studies (1820); *Allegro* in A minor (1821); Study in C major (1821); Sonata in G minor, op.105 (1821); *Largo-Allegro molto* in C minor/major (1821–22); 3 fugues: D minor, D minor, and B minor (1822); *Allegro* in D minor (1823); *Fantasia (Adagio)* in C minor (1823); *Rondo capriccioso* in E major, op.14 (1824); *Capriccio* in F-sharp minor, op.5 (1825); Fugue in C-sharp minor (1826); Sonata in E major, op.6 (1826); *7 charakteristische Stücke*, op.7 (1827); *Fantasia* in E major, on "The Last Rose of Summer," op.15 (1827); Sonata in B-flat major, op.106 (1827); Fugue in E minor (1827); *Scherzo* in B minor (1829); *3 fantaisies ou caprices*, op.16 (1829); *Andante* in A major (1830); *Lieder ohne Worte*: 8 books, opp.19 (1829–30), 30 (1833–34), 38 (1836–37), 53 (1839–41), 62 (1842–44), 67 (1843–45), 85 (1834–45), 102 (1842–45); *Fantasia (Sonate écossaise)* in F-sharp minor, op.28 (1833); *3 Caprices*, op.33 (1833–35); *Scherzo a capriccio* in F-sharp minor (1835–36); Study in F minor (1836); *Andante* in A-flat major (1836); *Lied* in F-sharp minor (1836); *Prelude* in F minor (1836); *3 Preludes*, op.104a (1836); *6 Preludes* and *Fugues*, op.35 (1832–37); *Gondellied (Barcarole)* in A major (1837); *Capriccio* in E major, op.118 (1837); *Albumblatt (Lied ohne Worte)* in E minor, op.117 (1837); *Andante cantabile* and *Presto agitato*, in B major (1838); *3 Studies*, op.104b (1834–38); *Prelude* and *Fugue* in E minor (1827–41); *Variations sérieuses* in D minor, op.54 (1841); *Variations* in E-flat major, op.82 (1841); *Variations* in B-flat major, op.83 (1841); *Kinderstücke (Christmas Pieces)*, op.72 (1842–47); *Perpetuum mobile* in C major, op.119; etc. **P i a n o D u e t s :** *Lento-Vivace* in G minor (1820); *Fantasia* in D minor (1824); *Allegro brillant* in A major, op.92 (1841); Variations in B-flat major, op.83a (1841). **T w o P i a n o s :** *Duo concertant:* Variations on the march from Weber's *Preciosa* (1833; with Moscheles). **O r g a n :** Several works, including *3 Preludes* and *Fugues*, op.37 (1837), and 6 sonatas, op.65 (1844–45). **VOCAL: O r a t o r i o s :** *St. Paul*, op.36 (1834–36; Düsseldorf, May 22, 1836, composer conducting); *Elijah*, op.70 (1846; Birmingham, Aug. 26, 1846, composer conducting); *Christus*, op.97 (unfinished; Boston, May 7, 1874). **O t h e r S a c r e d :** *Die Himmel erzählen* for 5 Voices (1820); *Gott, du bist unsre Zuversicht* for 5 Voices (1820); *Ich will den Herrn nach seiner Gerechtigkeit preisen* for 4 Voices (1820); *Tag für Tag sei Gott gepriesen* for 5 Voices (1820); *Das Gesetz des Herrn ist ohne Wandel* for 5 Voices (1821–22); *Er hat der Sonne eine Hütte gemacht* for 5 Voices (1821–22); *Jube Domine* for Solo Voices and Double Chorus (1822); *Psalm LXVI* for Double Women's Chorus and Basso Continuo (1822); *Magnificat* in D major for Chorus and Orch. (1822); *Kyrie* in C minor for Solo Voices and Chorus (1823); *Jesus, meine Zuversicht* for Solo Voices and Chorus (1824); *Salve Regina* in E-flat major for Soprano and Strings (1824); 2 sacred pieces for Chorus: *Wie gross ist des Allmächt'gen Güte* (1824) and *Allein Gott in der Höh' sey Ehr* (1824); *Te Deum* in D major for Double Chorus and Basso Continuo (1826); *Jesu, meine Freude*, chorale cantata for Double Chorus and Strings; *Tu es Petrus* for Chorus and Orch., op.111 (1827); *Ave Maria Stella* for Soprano and Orch. (1828); *Hora est* for 16 Voices and Organ (1828); 3 sacred pieces for Tenor, Chorus, and Organ, op.23: *Aus tiefer Not, Ave Maria,* and *Mitten; Psalm CXV* for Solo Voices, Chorus, and Orch., op.31 (1830); *Zum Feste der Dreieinigkeit (O beata et benedicta)* for 3 Sopranos and Organ (1830); 3 motets for Women's Chorus and Organ, op.39 (1830): *Hear my prayer, O Lord (Veni, Domine), O praise the Lord (Laudate pueri),* and *O Lord, thou hast searched me out (Surrexit Pastor); Verleih uns Frieden* for Chorus and Orch. (1831); *Te Deum* in A major for Solo Voices, Chorus, and Organ (1832); *Lord have mercy upon us* for Chorus (1833); 2 sacred choruses for Men's Chorus, op.115 (1833); *Responsorium et hymnus* for Men's Voices, Cello, and Organ, op.121 (1833); *Psalm XLII* for Solo Voices, Chorus, and Orch., op.42 (1837); *Psalm XCV* for Tenor, Chorus, and Orch., op.46 (1838); *Psalm V, Lord hear the voice* for Chorus (1839); *Psalm XXXI, Defend me, Lord* for Chorus (1839); *Hymn* in A major for Solo Voice, Chorus, and Orch., op.96 (1840); *Psalm CXIV* for Double Chorus and Orch., op.51 (1839); *Geistliches Lied* in E-flat major for Solo Voice, Chorus, and Organ (1840); *Psalm C, Jauchzet den Herrn* for Chorus (1842); *Herr Gott, dich loben wir* for Solo Voices, Chorus, Organ, and Orch. (1843); *Psalm XCVIII* for Double Chorus and Orch., op.91 (1843); *Ehre sei dem Vater* for 8 Voices (1844); *Hear my prayer*, hymn for Soprano, Chorus, and Organ (1844); *Ehre sei dem Vater* in C major for 4 Voices (1845); *Er kommt aus dem kindlichen Alter der Welt* for 6 Voices (1846); *Lauda Sion* for Chorus and Orch., op.73 (Liège, June 11, 1846); *Die deutsche Liturgie* for 8 Voices (1846); 3 *English Church Pieces* for Solo Voices and Chorus, op.69 (1847): *Nunc dimittis, Jubilate,* and *Magnificat*; 3 Psalms for Solo Voices and Double Chorus, op.78: *Psalm II* (1843), *Psalm XLIII* (1844), and *Psalm XXII* (1844); *6 Anthems* for Double Chorus, op.79: *Rejoice, O ye people; Thou, Lord, our refuge hast been* (1843); *Above all praises* (1846); *Lord, on our offences* (1844); *Let our hearts be joyful* (1846); *For our offences* (1844). Other works include: *Ach Gott vom Himmel sieh darein*, chorale cantata for Solo Voices, Chorus, and Orch.; *Cantique pour l'Eglise wallonne de Francfort (Venez chantez)* for 4 Voices; *Christe, du Lamm Gottes*, chorale cantata for Chorus and Orch.; *Gloria patri (Ehre sei dem Vater)* for 4 Voices; *Glory be to the Father* for 4 Voices; *Gloria* in E-flat major for Solo Voices, Chorus, and Orch. (unfinished); *Kyrie* for Chorus and Orch.; *Kyrie* in A major for 8 Voices; *Vom Himmel hoch*, chorale cantata for Solo Voices, Chorus, and Orch.; etc. **S e c u l a r C a n t a t a s :** *In feierlichen Tönen*, wedding cantata for Soprano, Alto, Tenor, Chorus, and Piano (1820); *Grosse Festmusik zum Dürerfest* for Solo Voices, Chorus, and Orch. (Berlin, April 18, 1828); *Begrüssung (Humboldt Cantata)*, festival music for Solo Men's Voices, Men's Chorus, and Winds (Berlin, Sept. 18, 1828); *Die erste Walpurgisnacht* for Chorus and Orch., op.60 (1832; Berlin, Jan. 1833; rev. 1843; Leipzig, Feb. 2, 1843); *Gott segne Sachsenland* for Men's Voices and Winds (Dresden, June 7, 1843); *An die Künstler*, festival song for Men's Voices and Brass, op.68 (Cologne, June 1846). **C h o r a l S o n g s :** *Einst ins Schlaraffenland zogen* for 4 Men's Voices (1820); *Lieb und Hoffnung* for Men's Voices (1820); *Jägerlied (Kein bess're Lust in dieser Zeit)* for 4 Men's Voices (1822); *Lob des Weines (Seht, Freunde, die Gläser)* for Solo Men's Voices and Men's Chorus (1822); *Lass es heut am edlen Ort* for 4 Men's Voices (1828); *Worauf kommt es überall an* for 4 Men's Voices (1837); *Im Freien zu singen* for Mixed Voices, op.41: 1, *Im Walde* (1838); 2, *Entflieh mit mir* (1838); 3, *Es fiel ein Reif* (1838); 4, *Auf ihrem Grab* (1834); 5, *Mailied* (1838); 6, *Auf dem See* (1838); *Der erste Frühlingstag* for Mixed Voices, op.48 (1839): 1, *Frühlingsahnung*; 2, *Die Primel*; 3, *Frühlingsfeier*; 4, *Lerchengesang*; 5, *Morgengebet*; 6, *Herbstlied; Ersatz für Unbestand* for 4 Men's Voices (1839); *Festgesang* for Men's Voices (Leipzig, June 25, 1840; No. 2 adapted by W.H. Cummings for *Hark! the Herald Angels Sing*); 6 men's choruses, op.50: 1, *Türkisches Schenkenlied* (1839–40); 2, *Der Jäger Abschied* (1840); 3, *Sommerlied* (1839–40); 4, *Wasserfahrt* (1839–40); 5, *Liebe und Wein* (1839); 6, *Wanderlied* (1842); *Nachtgesang* for 4 Men's Voices (1842); *Die Stiftungsfeier* for 4 Men's Voices (1842); *Im Grünen* for Mixed Voices, op.59: 1, *Im Grünen* (1837); 2, *Frühzeitiger Frühling* (1843); 3, *Abschied vom Wald* (1843); 4, *Die Nachtigall* (1843); 5, *Ruhetal* (1843); 6, *Jagdlied* (1843); *Sahst du ihn herniederschweben*, funeral song for Mixed Voices, op.116 (1845); *Der Sänger* (1845; Leipzig, Nov. 10, 1846); *Wandersmann* for Men's Voices, op.75: 1, *Der frohe Wandersmann* (1844); 2, *Abendständchen* (1839); 3, *Trinklied*; 4, *Abschiedstafel* (1844); 4 men's choruses, op.76: 1, *Das Lied vom braven Mann*; 2, *Rheinweinlied* (1844); 3, *Lied für die Deutschen in Lyon* (1846); 4, *Comitat*; 6 choruses for Mixed Voices, op.88: 1, *Neujahrslied* (1844); 2, *Der Glückliche* (1843); 3, *Hirtenlied* (1839); 4, *Die Waldvögelein* (1843); 5, *Deutschland* (1839–43); 6, *Der wandernde Musikant* (1840); 4 choruses for Mixed Voices, op.100: 1, *Andenken* (1844); 2, *Lob des Frühlings* (1843); 3, *Frühlingslied* (1843–44); 4, *Im Wald* (1839); 4 men's choruses, op.120: 1, *Jagdlied* (1837); 2, *Morgengruss des Thüringischen Sängerbundes* (1847); 3, *Im Süden*;

4, *Zigeunerlied; Lob der Trunkenheit (Trunken müssen wir alle sein)* for 4 Men's Voices; *Musikantenprugelei (Seht doch diese Fiedlerbanden)* for 2 Men's Voices. Also concert arias: *Che vuoi mio cor?* for Mezzo-soprano and Strings, and *Infelice* for Soprano and Orch., op.94 (1834; rev. 1843). **S o n g s** : *Ave Maria* (1820); *Raste Krieger, Krieg ist aus* (1820); *Die Nachtigall (Da ging ich hin)* (1821–22); *Der Verlassene (Nacht ist um mich her)* (1821–22); *Von allen deinen zarten Gaben* (1822); *Wiegenlied (Schlumme sanft)* (1822); *Sanft weh'n im Hauch der Abendluft* (1822); *Der Wasserfall (Rieselt hernieder)* (1823); 12 songs, op.8 (1828): 1, *Minnelied;* 2, *Das Heimweh* (by Fanny Mendelssohn); 3, *Italien* (by Fanny Mendelssohn); 4, *Erntelied;* 5, *Pilgerspruch;* 6, *Frühlingslied;* 7, *Maienlied;* 8, *Andres Maienlied (Hexenlied);* 9, *Abendlied;* 10, *Romanze;* 11, *Im Grünen;* 12, *Suleika und Hatem* (by Fanny Mendelssohn); *The Garland (Der Blumenkranz)* (1829); 12 songs, op.9 (1829–30): 1, *Frage;* 2, *Geständnis;* 3, *Wartend;* 4, *Im Frühling;* 5, *Im Herbst;* 6, *Scheidend;* 7, *Sehnsucht* (by Fanny Mendelssohn); 8, *Frühlingsglaube;* 9, *Ferne;* 10, *Verlust* (by Fanny Mendelssohn); 11, *Entsagung;* 12, *Die Nonne* (by Fanny Mendelssohn); 4 songs (1830): 1, *Der Tag (Sanft entschwanden mir);* 2, *Reiterlied (Immer fort);* 3, *Abschied (Leb wohl mein Lieb);* 4, *Der Bettler (Ich danke Gott dir); Seemanns Scheidelied* (1831); *Weihnachtslied (Auf schicke dich recht feierlich)* (1832); 6 songs, op.19a (1830–34): 1, *Frühlingslied;* 2, *Das erste Veilchen;* 3, *Winterlied;* 4, *Neue Liebe;* 5, *Gruss;* 6, *Reiselied; Mailied (Ich weiss mir'n Mädchen)* (1834); 2 romances: *There be none of beauty's daughters* (1833) and *Sun of the Sleepless* (1834); 2 songs: *Das Waldschloss* (1835) and *Pagenlied* (1835); 6 songs, op.34 (1834–36): 1, *Minnelied;* 2, *Auf Flügeln des Gesanges;* 3, *Frühlingslied;* 4, *Suleika;* 5, *Sonntagslied;* 6, *Reiselied; Lied einer Freundin (Zarter Blumen leicht Gewinde)* (1837); *Im Kahn* (1837); *O könnt ich zu dir fliegen* (1838); 6 songs, op.47 (1832–39): 1, *Minnelied;* 2, *Morgengruss;* 3, *Frühlingslied;* 4, *Volkslied;* 5, *Der Blumenstrauss;* 6, *Bei der Wiege;* 2 songs: *Todeslied der Bojaren* (1840) and *Ich hör ein Vöglein* (1841); 6 songs, op.57 (1839–43): 1, *Altdeutsches Lied;* 2, *Hirtenlied;* 3, *Suleika;* 4, *O Jugend;* 5, *Venetianisches Gondellied;* 6, *Wanderlied;* 6 songs, op.71 (1842–47): 1, *Tröstung;* 2, *Fruhlingslied;* 3, *An die Entfernte;* 4, *Schilflied;* 5, *Auf der Wanderschaft;* 6, *Nachtlied;* 3 songs, op.84 (1831–39): 1, *Da lieg' ich unter den Bäumen;* 2, *Herbstlied;* 3, *Jagdlied;* 6 songs, op.86 (1831–51): 1, *Es lauschte des Laub;* 2, *Morgenlied;* 3, *Die Liebende schreibt;* 4, *Allnächtlich im Traume;* 5, *Der Mond;* 6, *Altdeutsches Frühlingslied;* 6 songs, op.99: 1, *Erster Verlust;* 2, *Die Sterne schau'n;* 3, *Lieblingsplätzchen;* 4, *Das Schifflein;* 5, *Wenn sich zwei Herzen scheiden;* 6, *Es weiss und rät es doch keiner;* 2 sacred songs, op.112: *Doch der Herr, er leitet die Irrenden recht* and *Der du die Menschen lässest sterben;* also *Des Mädchens Klage; Warnung vor dem Rhein; Der Abendsegen (The Evening Service); Gretschen (Meine Ruh ist hin); Lieben und Schweigen (Ich flocht ein Kränzlein schöner Lieder); Es rauscht der Wald; Vier trübe Monden sind entfloh'n; Weinend seh' ich in die Nacht; Weiter, rastlos atemlos vorüber.* **V o c a l   D u e t s** : *Ein Tag sagt es dem andern* for Soprano and Alto (1821); 6 duets, op.63 (1836–45): 1, *Ich wollt' meine Lieb';* 2, *Abschiedslied der Zugvögel;* 3, *Gruss;* 4, *Herbstlied;* 5, *Volkslied;* 6, *Maiglöckchen und die Blümelein;* 3 duets, op.77 (1836–47): 1, *Sonntagsmorgen;* 2, *Das Aehrenfeld;* 3, *Lied aus "Ruy Blas";* 3 folk songs: 1, *Wie kann ich froh und lustig sein;* 2, *Abendlied;* 3, *Wasserfahrt;* also various canons.

BIBL.: COLLECTED EDITIONS, SOURCE MATERIAL: The 1st collected ed. of his works, *F. M.-B.: Werke: Kritisch durchgesehene Ausgabe,* was ed. by Julius Rietz and publ. by Breitkopf & Härtel (Leipzig, 1874–77); this ed. omits a number of works, however. A new ed. of the complete works, the *Leipziger Ausgabe der Werke F. M.-B.s,* began publication in Leipzig in 1960 by the Internationale Felix-Mendelssohn-Gesellschaft. Breitkopf & Härtel publ. a *Thematisches Verzeichnis im Druck erschienener Compositionen von F. M.-B.* (Leipzig, 1846; 2nd ed., 1853; 3rd ed., 1882). Other sources include the following: *M.-Festwoche aus Anlass der 150. Wiederkehr des Geburtstages am 3. Februar 1959* (Leipzig, 1959); M. Schneider, *M.-Archiv der Staatsbibliothek Stiftung Preussischer Kulturbesitz* (Berlin, 1965); R. Elvers, *F. M.-B.: Dokumente seines Lebens: Ausstellung zum 125. Todestag* (Berlin, 1972); P. Krause, *Autographen, Erstausgaben und Frühdrucke der Werke von F. M.-B. in Leipziger Bibliotheken und Archiven* (Leipzig, 1972); K. Schultz, ed., *F. M.B.:"Der schöne Zwischenfall in der deutschen Musik"* (Vienna, 1981); E. Klessmann, *Die M.s: Bilder aus einer deutschen Familie* (Zürich, 1990); R. Todd, ed., *M. Studies* (Cambridge, 1992); C. Schmidt, ed., *F.M. B.: Kongress-Bericht Berlin 1994* (Wiesbaden, 1997). BIOGRAPHICAL: W. Lampadius, *F. M.-B.: Ein Denkmal für seine Freunde* (Leipzig, 1848; Eng. tr., with additional articles by others, N.Y., 1865; 2nd greatly aug. Ger. ed., as *F. M.-B.: Ein Gesammtbild seines Lebens und Wirkens,* Leipzig, 1886); L. Stierlin, *Biographie von F. M.-B.* (Zürich, 1849); J. Benedict, *A Sketch of the Life and Works of the Late F. M.-B.* (London, 1850; 2nd ed., 1853); W. Neumann, *F. M.-B.: Eine Biographie* (Kassel, 1854); A. Reissmann, *F. M.-B.: Sein Leben und seine Werke* (Berlin, 1867; 3rd ed., rev., 1893); H. Barbedette, *F. M.-B.: Sa vie et ses oeuvres* (Paris, 1868); C. Mendelssohn-Bartholdy, *Goethe und F. M.-B.* (Leipzig, 1871; Eng. tr., London, 1872; 2nd ed., 1874); S. Hensel, *Die Familie M. 1729–1847, nach Briefen und Tagebüchern* (3 vols., Berlin, 1879; 18th ed., 1924; Eng. tr., 2 vols., London, 1881); J. Sittard, *F. M.-B.* (Leipzig, 1881); W. Rockstro, *M.* (London, 1884; rev. ed., 1911); E. David, *Les M.-B. et Robert Schumann* (Paris, 1886); J. Eckardt, *Ferdinand David und die Familie M.-B.* (Leipzig, 1888); J. Hadden, *M.* (London, 1888; 2nd ed., 1904); S. Stratton, *M.* (London, 1901; 6th ed., 1934); V. Blackburn, *M.* (London, 1904); E. Wolff, *F. M.-B.* (Berlin, 1906; 2nd ed., rev., 1909); C. Bellaigue, *M.* (Paris, 1907; 4th ed., 1920); J. Hartog, *F. M.-B. en zijne werken* (Leyden, 1908); P. de Stoecklin, *M.* (Paris, 1908; 2nd ed., 1927); M. Jacobi, *F. M.-B.* (Bielefeld, 1915); W. Dahms, *M.* (Berlin, 1919; 9th ed., 1922); J. Esser, *F. M.-B. und die Rheinlande* (diss., Univ. of Bonn, 1923); C. Winn, *M.* (London, 1927); J. Cooke, *F. M.-B.* (Philadelphia, 1929); E. Vuillermoz, *Une Heure de musique avec M.* (Paris, 1930); S. Kaufmann, *M.: A Second Elijah* (N.Y., 1934; 2nd ed., 1936); J. Petitpierre, *Le Mariage de M. 1837–1847* (Lausanne, 1937; Eng. tr. as *The Romance of the M.s,* London, 1947); B. Bartels, *M.-B.: Mensch und Werk* (Bremen, 1947); K. Wörner, *F. M.-B.: Leben und Werk* (Leipzig, 1947); M. Schneider, *M. im Bildnis* (Basel, 1953); P. Radcliffe, *M.* (London, 1954; 2nd ed., rev., 1967); H. Worbs, *F. M.- B.* (Leipzig, 1956; 2nd ed., 1957); idem, *F. M.-B.: Wesen und Wirken im Spiegel von Selbstzeugnissen und Berichten der Zeitgenossen* (Leipzig, 1958); H. Jacob, *F. M. und seine Zeit: Bildnis und Schicksal eines Meisters* (Frankfurt am Main, 1959–60; Eng. tr., 1963); E. Werner, *M.: A New Image of the Composer and His Age* (N.Y., 1963; 2nd ed., rev. and aug., Zürich, 1980); E. Rudolph, *Der junge F. M.: Ein Beitrag zur Musikgeschichte des Stadt Berlin* (diss., Humboldt Univ., Berlin, 1964); K.-H. Köhler, *F. M.-B.* (Leipzig, 1966; 2nd ed., rev., 1972); S. Grossmann-Vendrey, *F. M.-B. und die Musik der Vergangenheit* (Regensburg, 1969); M. Hurd, *M.* (London, 1970); W. Reich, *F. M. im Spiegel eigener Aussagen und zeitgenössischer Dokumente* (Zürich, 1970); H. Kupferberg, *The M.s: Three Generations of Genius* (N.Y., 1972); G. Marek, *Gentle Genius: The Story of F. M.* (N.Y., 1972); P. Ranft, *F. M.B.: Eine Lebenschronik* (Leipzig, 1972); Y. Tiénot, *M.: Musicien complet* (Paris, 1972); W. Blunt, *On Wings of Song: A Biography of F. M.* (N.Y., 1974); H. Worbs, *M.-B.* (Hamburg, 1974); D. Jenkins and M. Visocchi, *M. in Scotland* (London, 1978); M. Moshansky, *M.* (Tunbridge Wells, 1982); G. Schuhmacher, ed., *F. M.-B.* (Darmstadt, 1982); W. Konold, *F. M.B. und seine Zeit* (Laaber, 1984); R. Elvers, ed., *F. M.: A Life in Letters* (London, 1989); R. Todd, ed., *M. and His World* (Princeton, 1991); E. Donner, *F. M. B.: Aus der Partitur eines Musikerlebens* (Düsseldorf, 1992); A. Richter, *M.: Leben, Werke, Dokumente* (Mainz, 1994); B. Richter, *Frauen um F. M. B.* (Frankfurt am Main, 1997). **CRITICAL, ANALYTICAL:** F. Zander, *Über M.s Walpurgisnacht* (Königsberg, 1862); C. Seldon, *La Musique en Allemagne: M.* (Paris, 1867); F. Edwards, *The History of M.'s Oratorio "Elijah"* (London, 1896; 2nd ed., 1900); J. Hathaway, *An Analysis of M.'s Organ Works: A Study of Their Structural Features* (London, 1898); O. Mansfield, *Organ Parts of M.'s Oratorios and Other Choral Works Analytically Considered* (London, 1907); H. Waltershausen, *M.s Lieder ohne Worte* (Munich, 1920); J. Koffler, *Die orchestrale Koloristik in den symphonischen Werken von M.* (diss., Univ. of Vienna, 1923); H. Mandt, *Die Entwicklung des Romantischen in der Instrumentalmusik F. M.-B.s* (diss., Univ. of Cologne, 1927); R. Werner, *F. M.-B. als Kirchenmusiker* (Frankfurt am Main, 1930); C. Wilkinson, *How to Interpret M.'s "Songs without Words"* (London, 1930); T. Armstrong, *M.'s "Elijah"* (London, 1931); G. Wilcke, *Tonalität und Modulation im Streichquartett M.s und Schumanns* (Leipzig, 1933); L. Hochdorf, *M.s "Lieder ohne Worte" und der "Lieder ohne Worte"-Stil in seinen ubrigen Instrumentalwerken* (diss., Univ. of Vienna, 1938); J. Horton, *The Chamber Music of M.* (London, 1946); P. Young, *Introduction to the Music of M.* (London, 1949); D. Mintz, *The Sketches and Drafts of Three of M.'s Major Works* (*Elijah*, Sym. No. 4, and D-minor Trio; diss., Cornell Univ., 1960); S. Vendrey, *Die Orgelwerke von F. M.-B.* (diss., Univ. of Vienna, 1964); J. Werner, *M.'s "Elijah": A Historical and Analytical Guide to the Oratorio* (London, 1965); G. Friedrich, *Die Fugenkomposition in M.s Instrumentalwerk* (Bonn, 1969); F. Krummacher, *M. der Komponist: Studien zur Kompositionsweise am Beispiel der Kammermusik für Streicher* (Habilitationsschrift, Univ. of Erlangen, 1972); M. Thomas, *Das Instrumentalwerk F. M.-B.s: Eine systematisch-theoretische Untersuchung unter besonderer Berücksichtigung der zeitgenössischen Musiktheorie* (Kassel, 1972); C. Dahlhaus, ed., *Das Problem M.* (Regensburg, 1974); D. Seaton, *A Study of a Collection of M.'s Sketches and Other Autograph Material, Deutsche Staatsbibliothek Berlin "Mus. Ms. Autogr. M. 19"* (diss., Columbia Univ., 1977); F. Krummacher, *M.—der Komponist: Studien zur Kammermusik für Streicher* (Munich, 1978); A. Kurzhals-Reuter, *Die Oratorien F. M.B.s: Untersuchungen zur Quellenlage, Entstehung, Gestaltung und Überlieferung* (Tutzing, 1978); R. Todd, *The Instrumental Music of F.M.B.: Selected Studies Based on Primary Studies* (diss., Yale Univ., 1979); T. Ehrle, *Die Instrumentation in den Symphonien und Ouvertüren von F. M.B.* (Wiesbaden, 1983); R. Todd, *M.'s Musical Education: A Study and Edition of His Exercises in Composition* (Cambridge, 1982); J. Finson and R. Todd, eds., *M. and Schumann: Essays on Their Music and Its Context* (Durham, 1984); C. Jost, *M.s Lieder ohne Worte* (Tutzing, 1988); M. Pape, *M.s Leipziger Orgelkonzert 1840: Ein Beitrag zur Bach-Pflege im 19. Jahrhundert* (Wiesbaden, 1988); W. Konold, *Symphonien F. M. B.s* (Laaber, 1992); G. Vitercik, *The Early Works of F. M.: A Study in the Romantic Sonata Style* (Philadelphia, 1992); W. Dinglinger, *Studien zu den Psalmen mit Orchester F. M. B.* (Cologne, 1993); R. Todd, *M.: The Hebrides and Other Overtures* (Cambridge, 1993); T. Schmidt, *Die ästhetischen Grundlagen der Instrumentalmusik F. M. B.s* (Stuttgart, 1996); R. Wehner, *Studien zum geistlichen Chorschaffen des jungen F. M. B.* (Sinzig, 1996); W. Wüster, *F. M. B.s Choralkanten: Gestalt und Idee: Versuch einer historisch-kritischen Interpretation* (Frankfurt am Main, 1996); A. Eicchorn, *F. M.-B.: Die Hebriden, Ouvertüre für Orchester, op.26* (Munich, 1998). **CORRESPONDENCE:** P. Mendelssohn-Bartholdy, *Reisebriefe...aus den Jahren 1830–32*

(Leipzig, 1861; 5th ed., 1882; Eng. tr. by Lady Wallace as *Letters from Italy and Switzerland*, London, 1862); idem, *Briefe aus den Jahren 1833–47* (Leipzig, 1863; 8th ed., 1915; Eng. tr. by Lady Wallace, London, 1863); L. Nohl, *Musiker-briefe* (Leipzig, 1867); E. Polko, *Erinnerungen an F. M.-B.* (Leipzig, 1868; Eng. tr. by Lady Wallace, London, 1869); E. Devrient, *Meine Erinnerungen an F. M.- B. und seine Briefe an mich* (Leipzig, 1869; Eng. tr. by Lady Macfarren, London, 1869); *Acht Briefe und ein Faksimile* (Leipzig, 1871; Eng. tr. in *Macmillan's Magazine*, June 1871); F. Hiller, *F. M.: Briefe und Erinnerungen* (Cologne, 1874; Eng. tr. by M.E. von Glehn, London, 1874); S. Hensel, *The M. Family, 1729–1847, from Letters and Journals* (2 vols., 1882; reprint, N.Y., 1969); F. Moscheles, *Brief von F. M. an Ignaz und Charlotte Moscheles* (Leipzig, 1888; Eng. tr. as *Letters of F. M.*, London, 1888); E. Wolff, *F. M.-B.: Meisterbriefe* (Berlin, 1907; 2nd aug. ed., 1909); K. Klingemann, *F. M.-B.s Briefwechsel mit Legationsrat Karl Klingemann* (Essen, 1909); G. Selden-Goth, *M.'s Letters* (N.Y., 1945); R. Sietz, ed., *F. M.-B.: Sein Leben in Briefen* (Cologne, 1948); R. Elvers, ed., *M.B.: Briefe* (Frankfurt am Main, 1984); M. Citron, ed., *The Letters of Fanny Hensel to F. M.* (Stuyvesant, N.Y., 1987); P. Jones, ed. and tr., *The M.s on Honeymoon: The 1837 Diary of F. and Cécile M. B. Together With Letters to Their Families* (Oxford, 1997).—**NS/LK/DM**

Mendelssohn, Fanny (Cäcilie)
See **Hensel, Fanny (Cäcilie)**

Meneely-Kyder, Sarah, American composer, pianist, and sitar player; b. Albany, N.Y., Feb. 18, 1945. She studied theory and piano at Goucher Coll. (B.A., 1967); also had composition studies with Robert Hall Lewis (from 1966), Earle Brown at the Peabody Cons. of Music in Baltimore (M.M., 1969), and Robert Morris at the Yale School of Music (M.M.A., 1973); also studied the sitar and vina for 10 years. Her early works were serial or atonal in design; later she experimented with controlled improvisation, and spatial and proportional systems; still later she concentrated upon fusing disparate musical styles, making use of North Indian notational systems and instrumentations. She hails from a family of bell manufacturers who established the Meneely Foundry in Troy, N.Y.

WORKS: Piano Concerto (1967); *Homegrown* for Piano (1973); *Lament* for Sitar and Renaissance Instruments (1978); *Filarmonico* for Chorus, Piano, Vibraphone, and Gamelan Chimes (1980; rev. 1986, 1988); *Now I Sing Only 1 Song* for 2 Pianos (1980); *Weep, the Mighty Typhoons* for Mezzo-soprano and Piano (1982); *Narcissus* for Clarinet (1983); *Season Phases* for Piano (1987–88); *The 3 Gunas* for Piano, 4–Hands, Violin, Cello, Flute, Clarinet, and Bassoon (1989).—**NS/LK/DM**

Meneses, António, talented Brazilian cellist; b. Recife, Aug. 23, 1957. His father was 1st hornist in the opera orch. in Rio de Janeiro. António began his musical training when he was 8, then became a pupil of Janigro in Düsseldorf and Stuttgart at 16. He won 2nd prize in the Barcelona International Maria Casals Competition (1976) and in the Rio de Janeiro International Competition (1976); after winning 1st prize in the International ARD Competition in Munich (1977), he captured the prestigious gold medal at the Tchaikovsky Competition in Moscow (1982). He subsequently appeared as soloist with many major European orchs. He made his first tour of North America in 1985. His wife is **Cecile Licad**. —NS/LK/DM

Mengelberg, (Josef) Willem, celebrated Dutch conductor, uncle of **Karel (Willem Joseph) Mengelberg** and **Kurt Rudolf Mengelberg**; b. Utrecht, March 28, 1871; d. Chur, Switzerland, March 21, 1951. He studied at the Utrecht Cons., and later at the Cologne Cons. with Seiss, Jensen, and Wüllner. He was appointed municipal music director in Lucerne in 1891, and his work there attracted so much attention that in 1895 he was placed at the head of the Concertgebouw Orch. in Amsterdam, holding this post for 50 years (resigning in 1945); during his directorship, he elevated that orch. to a lofty position in the world of music. In 1898 he also became conductor of the Tonkoonst choral society in Amsterdam, and from 1908 to 1921 he was director of the Museumgesellschaft concerts in Frankfurt am Main. He appeared frequently as guest conductor in all the European countries; in England he was an annual visitor from 1913 until World War II. He first appeared with the N.Y. Phil. in 1905; then conducted it regularly from 1922 to 1930, with Toscanini serving as assoc. conductor in 1929–30. In 1928 he received the degree of Mus.Doc. at Columbia Univ. (honoris causa); in 1933 he was appointed prof. of music at the Univ. of Utrecht. During the occupation of the Netherlands by the Germans, Mengelberg openly expressed his sympathies with the Nazi cause, and lost the high respect and admiration that his compatriots had felt for him; after the country's liberation (1945), he was barred from professional activities there, the ban to be continued until 1951, but he died in that year in exile in Switzerland. Mengelberg was an outstanding representative of the Romantic tradition in symphonic conducting. His performances of the Beethoven syms. were notable for their dramatic sweep and power, if not for their adherence to stylistic proprieties. He was a great champion of many of the major composers of his era, including Mahler and Strauss; both men appeared as guest conductors of the Concertgebouw Orch., and became Mengelberg's friends. Mahler dedicated his 5th and 8th syms. to Mengelberg and the Concertgebouw Orch., and Strauss dedicated his *Ein Heldenleben* to the same forces. Mengelberg was the first to lead a major cycle of Mahler's works, in Amsterdam in 1920.

BIBL.: H. Nolthenius, *W. M.* (Amsterdam, 1920); A. Van den Boer, *De psychologische beteekenis van W. M. als dirigent* (Amsterdam, 1925); E. Sollitt, *M. and the Symphonic Epoch* (N.Y., 1930); idem, *M. spreckt* (speeches by M.; The Hague, 1935); W. Paap, *W. M.* (Amsterdam, 1960).—NS/LK/DM

Mengelberg, Karel (Willem Joseph), Dutch composer and conductor, father of **Misha Mengelberg** and nephew of **(Josef) Willem Mengelberg**; b. Utrecht, July 18, 1902; d. Amsterdam, July 11, 1984. He studied with Pijper and later took a course at the Hochschule für Musik in Berlin. He conducted theater orchs. in provincial German towns and was a musician with Berlin Radio (1930–33); subsequently was conductor of the municipal band in Barcelona (1933); then went to Kiev, where he was in charge of the music dept. in the

Ukrainian film studio. He returned to Amsterdam in 1938. In addition to his own compositions, in 1961 he completed the revision, with a simplified orchestration, of Willem Pijper's 2nd Sym. (Pijper's own rev. score was destroyed during a Nazi air raid on Rotterdam in May 1940).

WORKS: DRAMATIC: B a l l e t : *Bataille* (1922); *Parfait amour* (1945). **ORCH.:** *Requiem* (1946); *Divertimento* for Small Orch. (1948); Horn Concerto (1950); *Anion*, symphonic sketch (1950); *Serenade* for Strings (1952); *Suite* for Small Orch. (1954); *De bergen* (1982). **CHAMBER:** String Quartet (1938); Sonata for Solo Oboe (1939); Trio for Flute, Oboe, and Bassoon (1940); *Toccata* for Piano (1950); *Soliloquio* for Flute (1951); *Ballade* for Flute, Clarinet, Harp, and String Quartet (1952); *Soneria, Romanza e Mazurca* for Harp (1958). **VOCAL:** *3 songs from Tagore's "The Gardener"* for Soprano and Orch. (1925); *Jan Hinnerik* for Chorus (1950); *Recitatief* for Baritone, Viola da Gamba, and Harpsichord (1953); *Roland Holst*, cantata for Chorus and Small Orch. (1955).—NS/LK/DM

Mengelberg, Kurt Rudolf, German-born musicologist and composer of Dutch descent, nephew of **(Josef) Willem Mengelberg**; b. Krefeld, Feb. 1, 1892; d. Beausoleil, near Monte Carlo, Oct. 13, 1959. He studied piano with Neitzel in Cologne and musicology with Hugo Riemann at the Univ. of Leipzig, receiving his doctorate in 1915. He then went to Amsterdam, where he studied theory with his uncle; in 1917, through his uncle's intervention, he became artistic assistant of the Concertgebouw Orch. in Amsterdam; then was artistic manager there (1925–35), and finally director (1935–54). Among his publications were the valuable program book *Das Mahler-Fest, Amsterdam Mai 1920* (Vienna, 1920), a biography of Mahler (Leipzig, 1923), *Nederland, spiegeleener beschaving* (The Netherlands, Mirror of a Culture; Amsterdam, 1929), a commemorative publication on the semicentennial of the Concertgebouw (Amsterdam, 1938), *Muziek, spiegel des tijds* (Music, Mirror of Time; Amsterdam, 1948), and a biography of Willem Mengelberg. His compositions were mainly liturgical and included *Missa pro pace* (1932), *Stabat Mater* (1940), and *Victimae Paschali laudes* (1946). He also composed *Symphonic Variations* for Cello and Orch. (1927), Violin Concerto (1930), *Capriccio* for Piano and Orch. (1936), Concertino for Flute and Chamber Orch. (1943), piano pieces, and songs.—NS/LK/DM

Mengelberg, Misha, Russian pianist, composer; b. Kiev, Uraine, USSR, June 5, 1935. He moved at an early age to the Netherlands, where his father was a conductor. He studied composition at the Royal Cons. in The Hague but was immersed in jazz activity. In 1964 he, along with drummer Han Bennink and bassist Jacques Schols, backed U.S. reedman Eric Dolphy on his last studio session (*Last Date*). In the mid-1970s he formed the I.C.P. 10tet, followed by the I.C.P. Orch., a group that still performs works by Mengelberg and its members, as well as those of Duke Ellington, Thelonious Monk, and Herbie Nichols, all major influences on his piano and composition style. Since the early 1980s, he has also led small groups and maintained a parallel career as a composer for orchestras and chamber ensembles. His piano style stems from the percussive lineage of such players as Duke Ellington and Thelonious Monk: spare, dissonant, and effective. He will frequently mix his performances with absurdist touches that derive from an early association with the Fluxus movement.

DISC.: *Driekusman Total Loss* (1964–66); *Change of Season* (1984); *I.C.P. Orch.—Bospaadje Konijnenhol I & II* (1986–91); *Dutch Masters* (1987); *Impromptus* (1988); *Mix* (1994); *Who's Bridge* (1994); *Impromptus* (1995).—**RI**

Menges, Isolde (Marie), English violinist and teacher, sister of **(Siegfried Frederick) Herbert Menges**; b. Hove (of German parents), May 16, 1893; d. Richmond, Surrey, Jan. 13, 1976. Both her parents were violinists, and she studied at home. She then went to St. Petersburg for lessons with Auer. She made her London debut on Feb. 4, 1913, and her N.Y. debut on Oct. 21, 1916. In 1931 she was appointed to the faculty of the Royal Coll. of Music in London, where she also organized the Menges Quartet.—**NS/LK/DM**

Menges, (Siegfried Frederick) Herbert, English conductor, brother of **Isolde (Marie) Menges**; b. Hove (of German parents), Aug. 27, 1902; d. London, Feb. 20, 1972. He played violin as a child, then took piano lessons with Mathilda Verne and Arthur de Greef. He later attended courses in composition with Vaughan Williams and Holst at the Royal Coll. of Music in London. He began his conducting career in Brighton, and conducted the Brighton Phil. Soc. (which was founded by his mother) from 1925 until his death. He was also a music director of the Old Vic Theatre in London (1931–50) and of the Southern Phil. Orch. at Southsea (from 1945). In 1963 he was made an Officer of the Order of the British Empire.—**NS/LK/DM**

Mennin (real name, **Mennini**), **Peter,** eminent American composer and music educator, brother of **Louis (Alfred) Mennini**; b. Erie, Pa., May 17, 1923; d. N.Y., June 17, 1983. His family stemmed from Italy; his brother did not cut off the last letter of his name as Peter did. His early environment was infused with music, mostly from phonograph recordings. He studied piano with Tito Spampani. In 1940 he enrolled in the Oberlin (Ohio) Cons., where he took courses in harmony with Normand Lockwood. He quickly learned the basics of composition, and at the age of 18 wrote a sym. and a string quartet. In 1942 he enlisted in the U.S. Army Air Force; was discharged in 1943, and resumed his musical studies at the Eastman School of Music in Rochester, N.Y., where his teachers were Hanson and Rogers. He worked productively; wrote another sym. in 1944; a movement from it, *Symphonic Allegro,* was performed by the N.Y. Phil., Leonard Bernstein conducting, on March 27, 1945. His 3rd Sym. was performed by Walter Hendl with the N.Y. Phil. on Feb. 27, 1947. Mennin progressed academically as well; he obtained his Ph.D. from the Eastman School of Music in 1947. He received a Guggenheim fellowship grant in 1948; a 2nd Guggenheim grant followed in 1956. From 1947 to 1958 he taught composition at the Juilliard School of Music in N.Y.; in 1958 he assumed the post of director of the

Peabody Cons. of Music in Baltimore. In 1962 he received his most prestigious appointment, that of president of the Juilliard School of Music, serving in that capacity until his death. Despite his academic preoccupations, he never slackened the tempo of his activities as a composer; he diversified his syms. by adding descriptive titles; thus his 4th Sym. was subtitled *The Cycle* and was scored for chorus and orch.; his 7th Sym. was called *Variation Symphony;* the 4 movements of his 8th Sym. bore biblical titles. Increasingly also, he began attaching descriptive titles to his other works; his Concertato for Orch. was named *Moby Dick;* there followed a *Canto for Orchestra,* a *Cantata de Virtute, Voices,* and *Reflections of Emily,* after Emily Dickinson. Mennin's musical mind was directed toward pure structural forms; his music is characterized by an integrity of purpose and teleological development of thematic materials, all this despite the bold infusion of dissonant sonorities in contrapuntal passages.

WORKS: ORCH.: 9 syms.: No. 1 (1941; withdrawn), No. 2 (1944; Rochester, N.Y., March 27, 1945), No. 3 (1946; N.Y., Feb. 27, 1947), No. 4, *The Cycle,* for Chorus and Orch. (1948; N.Y., March 18, 1949), No. 5 (Dallas, April 2, 1950), No. 6 (Louisville, Nov. 18, 1953), No. 7, *Variation Symphony* (1963; Cleveland, Jan. 23, 1964), No. 8 (1973; N.Y., Nov. 21, 1974), and No. 9, *Sinfonia capricciosa* (Washington, D.C., March 10, 1981); Concertino for Flute, Strings, and Percussion (1944); *Folk Overture* (Washington, D.C., Dec. 19, 1945); *Sinfonia* for Chamber Orch. (1946; Rochester, N.Y., May 24, 1947); *Fantasia* for Strings (1947; N.Y., Jan. 11, 1948); *Canzona* for Band (1951); Concertato, *Moby Dick* (Erie, Pa., Oct. 20, 1952); Cello Concerto (N.Y., Feb. 19, 1956); Piano Concerto (Cleveland, Feb. 27, 1958); *Canto for Orchestra* (San Antonio, March 4, 1963); *Symphonic Movements,* renamed *Sinfonia* (1970; Minneapolis, Jan. 21, 1971; withdrawn); Flute Concerto (1983; N.Y., May 25, 1988). **CHAMBER:** Organ Sonata (1941; withdrawn); 2 string quartets (1941, withdrawn; 1951); *5 Pieces* for Piano (1949); *Sonata concertante* for Violin and Piano (Washington, D.C., Oct. 19, 1956); Piano Sonata (1963). **VOCAL:** *4 Songs* for Soprano and Piano (1941; withdrawn); *Alleluia* for Chorus (1941); *4 Chinese Poems* for Chorus (1948); 2 choruses for Women's Voices and Piano (1949); *The Christmas Story* for Soprano, Tenor, Chorus, Brass Quintet, Timpani, and Strings (1949); *Cantata de Virtute: Pied Piper of Hamelin* for Narrator, Tenor, Bass, Mixed Chorus, Children's Chorus, and Orch. (Cincinnati, May 2, 1969); *Voices* for Voice, Piano, Harp, Harpsichord, and Percussion, after Thoreau, Melville, Whitman, and Emily Dickinson (1975; N.Y., March 28, 1976); *Reflections of Emily* [Dickinson] for Boy's Chorus, Harp, Piano, and Percussion (1978; N.Y., Jan. 18, 1979).—**NS/LK/DM**

Mennini, Louis (Alfred), American composer and music educator, brother of **Peter Mennin;** b. Erie, Pa., Nov. 18, 1920. He studied at the Oberlin (Ohio) Cons. (1939–42), then served in the U.S. Army Air Force (1942–45); subsequently studied composition with Rogers and Hanson at the Eastman School of Music, Rochester, N.Y. (B.M., 1947; M.M., 1948). He was a prof. at the Univ. of Tex. (1948–49); then was a prof. of composition at the Eastman School of Music, receiving his doctorate in composition from the Univ. of Rochester in 1961. After serving as dean of the School of Music at the N.C. School of the Arts in Winston-Salem (1965–71), he became chairman of the music dept. at Mercyhurst Coll. in Erie, Pa., in 1973, where he founded the D'Angelo

School of Music and D'Angelo Young Artist Competition. In 1983 he founded the Va. School of the Arts in Lynchburg, serving as its head until his retirement in 1988. His music is pragmatic and functional, with occasional modernistic touches.

WORKS: DRAMATIC: O p e r a : *The Well* (Rochester, N.Y., May 8, 1951); *The Rape*, chamber opera, after Eugene O'Neill (Tanglewood, Aug. 8, 1955). **ORCH.:** *Overtura breve* (1949); *Cantilena* (1950); *Canzona* for Chamber Orch. (1950); 2 syms. (*Da Chiesa*, 1960; *Da Festa*, 1963); *Tenebrae* (1963); Concerto Grosso (1975). **CHAMBER:** Violin Sonata (1947); Cello Sonatina (1952); String Quartet (1961); many piano works. —NS/LK/DM

Menotti, Gian Carlo, remarkable Italian composer; b. Cadegliano, July 7, 1911. He was the 6th of 10 children. He learned the rudiments of music from his mother, and began to compose as a child, making his first attempt at an opera, entitled *The Death of Pierrot*, at the age of 10. After training at the Milan Cons. (1924–27), he studied with Scalero at the Curtis Inst. of Music in Philadelphia (1927–33). Although Menotti associated himself with the cause of American music, and spent much of his time in the U.S., he retained his Italian citizenship. As a composer, he is unique on the American scene, being the first to create American opera possessing such an appeal to audiences as to become established in the permanent repertoire. Inheriting the natural Italian gift for operatic drama and an expressive singing line, he adapted these qualities to the peculiar requirements of the American stage and to the changing fashions of the period; his serious operas have a strong dramatic content in the realistic style stemming from the Italian verismo. He wrote his own librettos, marked by an extraordinary flair for drama and for the communicative power of the English language; with this is combined a fine, though subdued, sense of musical humor. Menotti made no pretensions at extreme modernism, and did not fear to approximate the successful formulas developed by Verdi and Puccini; the influence of Mussorgsky's realistic prosody is also in evidence, particularly in recitative. When dramatic tension required a greater impact, Menotti resorted to atonal and polytonal writing, leading to climaxes accompanied by massive dissonances. His first successful stage work was *Amelia Goes to the Ball*, an opera buffa in 1 act (originally to an Italian libretto by the composer, as *Amelia al ballo*), staged at the Academy of Music, Philadelphia, on April 1, 1937. This was followed by another comic opera, *The Old Maid and the Thief*, commissioned by NBC, first performed on the radio, April 22, 1939, and on the stage, by the Philadelphia Opera Co., on Feb. 11, 1941. Menotti's next operatic work was *The Island God*, produced by the Metropolitan Opera, N.Y., on Feb. 20, 1942, with indifferent success; but with the production of *The Medium* (N.Y., May 8, 1946), Menotti established himself as one of the most successful composer-librettists of modern opera. The imaginative libretto, dealing with a fraudulent spiritualist who falls victim to her own practices when she imagines that ghostly voices are real, suited Menotti's musical talent to perfection; the opera had a long and successful run in N.Y., an unprecedented occurrence in the history of the American lyric theater. A short humorous opera, *The Telephone*, was first produced by the N.Y. Ballet Soc., Feb. 18, 1947, on the same bill with *The Medium*; these 2 contrasting works were subsequently staged all over the U.S. and in Europe, often on the same evening. Menotti then produced *The Consul* (Philadelphia, March 1, 1950), his finest tragic work, describing the plight of political fugitives vainly trying to escape from an unnamed country but failing to obtain the necessary visa from the consul of an anonymous power; very ingeniously, the author does not include the title character in the cast, since the consul never appears on the stage but remains a shadowy presence. *The Consul* exceeded Menotti's previous operas in popular success; it had a long run in N.Y., and received the Pulitzer Prize in Music. On Christmas Eve, 1951, NBC presented Menotti's television opera *Amahl and the Night Visitors*, a Christmas story of undeniable poetry and appeal; it became an annual television production every Christmas in subsequent years. His next opera was *The Saint of Bleecker Street*, set in a N.Y. locale (N.Y., Dec. 27, 1954); it won the Drama Critics' Circle Award for the best musical play of 1954, and the Pulitzer Prize in Music for 1955. A madrigal ballet, *The Unicorn, the Gorgon and the Manticore*, commissioned by the Elizabeth Sprague Coolidge Foundation, was first presented at the Library of Congress, Washington, D.C., Oct. 21, 1956. His opera *Maria Golovin*, written expressly for the International Exposition in Brussels, was staged there on Aug. 20, 1958. In 1958 he organized the Festival of 2 Worlds in Spoleto, Italy, staging old and new works; in 1977 he inaugurated an American counterpart of the festival in Charleston, S.C. In many of the festival productions Menotti acted also as stage director. In the meantime, he continued to compose; he produced in quick succession *Labyrinth*, a television opera to his own libretto (N.Y., March 3, 1963); *Death of the Bishop of Brindisi*, dramatic cantata with the text by the composer (Cincinnati, May 18, 1963); *Le Dernier Sauvage*, opera buffa, originally with an Italian libretto by Menotti, produced at the Opéra-Comique in Paris in a French tr. (Oct. 21, 1963; produced in Eng. at the Metropolitan Opera, N.Y., Jan. 23, 1964); *Martin's Lie*, chamber opera to Menotti's text (Bath, England, June 3, 1964); *Help, Help, the Globolinks!*, "an opera in 1 act for children and those who like children" to words by Menotti, with electronic effects (Hamburg, Dec. 19, 1968); *The Most Important Man*, opera to his own libretto (N.Y., March 12, 1971); *The Hero*, comic opera (Philadelphia, June 1, 1976); *The Egg*, a church opera to Menotti's own libretto (Washington Cathedral, June 17, 1976); *The Trial of the Gypsy* for Treble Voices and Piano (N.Y., May 24, 1978); *Miracles* for Boy's Chorus (Fort Worth, April 22, 1979); *La loca*, opera to Menotti's own libretto dealing with a mad daughter of Ferdinand and Isabella (San Diego, June 3, 1979); *A Bride from Pluto*, children's opera (Washington, D.C., April 14, 1982); *The Boy Who Grew Too Fast*, opera for young people (Wilmington, Del., Sept. 24, 1982); *The Wedding*, opera (Seoul, Sept. 16, 1988); *Singing Child*, children's opera (Charleston, S.C., May 31, 1993). Among Menotti's non-operatic works are the ballets *Sebastian* (1944) and *Errand into the Maze* (N.Y., Feb. 2, 1947); 2 piano concertos: No. 1 (Boston, Nov. 2, 1945) and No. 2 (Miami, June 23, 1982);

Apocalypse, symphonic poem (Pittsburgh, Oct. 19, 1951); Violin Concerto (Philadelphia, Dec. 5, 1952, Zimbalist soloist); *Triplo Concerto a Tre*, triple concerto (N.Y., Oct. 6, 1970); *Landscapes and Remembrances*, cantata to his own autobiographical words (Milwaukee, May 14, 1976); *First Symphony*, subtitled *The Halcyon* (Philadelphia, Aug. 4, 1976); *Nocturne* for Soprano, String Quartet, and Harp (N.Y., Oct. 24, 1982); Double Bass Concerto (N.Y. Phil., Oct. 20, 1983, James VanDemark, soloist, Zubin Mehta conducting); *For the Death of Orpheus* for Tenor, Chorus, and Orch. (Atlanta, Nov. 8, 1990). He also wrote a number of *pièces d'occasion* such as *Trio for a House-Warming Party* for Piano, Cello, and Flute (1936); *Variations on a Theme by Schumann*; *Pastorale* for Piano and Strings; *Poemetti per Maria Rosa* (piano pieces for children); etc. He is also the author of the librettos for Samuel Barber's operas *Vanessa* (Metropolitan Opera, N.Y., Jan. 15, 1958) and *A Hand of Bridge* (1959); also wrote a play without music, *The Leper* (Tallahassee, April 22, 1970).

Menotti's last years were plagued with disputes over his role as an artistic director. In 1991 a major dispute arose between the composer and the director of the Spoleto Festival USA in Charleston, but ultimately Menotti retained control. However, in 1993 he announced that he was taking the festival away from Charleston, but the city's mayor intervened and Menotti lost control of his festival. That same year he was named artistic director of the Rome Opera, but again conflicts over artistic policy between the composer and the superintendent led to Menotti's dismissal in 1994.

BIBL.: J. Gruen, *M.: A Biography* (N.Y., 1978); J. Ardoin, *The Stages of M.* (Garden City, N.Y., 1985).—**NS/LK/DM**

Menter, Joseph, German cellist, father of **Sophie Menter**; b. Teisbach, Bavaria, Jan. 23, 1808; d. Munich, April 18, 1856. He began his career as a violinist, then studied cello with Moralt in Munich. He became a member of the orch. of the Bavarian Royal Opera (1833).—**NS/LK/DM**

Menter, Sophie, esteemed German pianist and teacher, daughter of **Joseph Menter**; b. Munich, July 29, 1846; d. there, Feb. 23, 1918. She studied piano with Niest in Munich and with Lebert in Stuttgart, making her professional debut in 1867 at the Gewandhaus Concerts in Leipzig. She later took lessons with Tausig and Liszt. In 1872 she married **David Popper** (divorced, 1886). From 1883 to 1887 she taught piano at the St. Petersburg Cons., then lived mostly in the Tirol. She composed a number of attractive pieces. Tchaikovsky orchestrated her work *Ungarische Zigeunerweisen* for Piano and Orch., and she played it under his direction in Odessa, on Feb. 4, 1893.—**NS/LK/DM**

Mentzner, Susanne, American mezzo-soprano; b. Philadelphia, Jan. 21, 1957. She was a student of Norma Newton at the Juilliard School in N.Y. After making her operatic debut as Albina in *La donna del lago* at the Houston Grand Opera in 1981, she made appearances at the Washington (D.C.) Opera, the Lyric Opera in Chicago, the Opera Co. of Philadelphia, and the

N.Y.C. Opera. In 1983 she made her European operatic debut as Cherubino at the Cologne Opera, where she returned as Massenet's Cendrillon. She made her first appearance at London's Covent Garden as Rosina in 1985, where she later sang Giovanna Seymour in 1988 and Dorabella in 1989. In 1988 she portrayed Adalgisa in Monte Carlo. She made her Metropolitan Opera debut in N.Y. on Jan. 4, 1989, as Cherubino. That same year, she was engaged as Octavian at the Théâtre des Champs-Elysées in Paris. She appeared as Annius in *La clemenza di Tito* at Milan's La Scala in 1990. During the 1992–93 season, she sang Offenbach's Nicklausse and Strauss's Composer and Octavian at the Metropolitan Opera. Following an engagement as Geneviève in *Pelléas et Mélisande* at the Palais Garnier in Paris in 1997, she returned to the Metropolitan Opera as Cherubino in 1998.—**NS/LK/DM**

Menuhin, Hephzibah, American pianist, sister of **Yehudi Menuhin, Lord Menuhin of Stoke d'Abernon**; b. San Francisco, May 20, 1920; d. London, Jan. 1, 1981. She studied in San Francisco and pursued training in Paris with Ciampi. After making her public debut in San Francisco when she was only 8, she toured in recitals with her brother throughout the U.S. and Europe.—**NS/LK/DM**

Menuhin, Yehudi, Lord Menuhin of Stoke d'Abernon, celebrated American-born English violinist, conductor, and humanitarian, brother of **Hephzibah Menuhin**; b. N.Y., April 22, 1916; d. Berlin, March 12, 1999. He was born of Russian-Jewish parents whose original surname was Mnuhin. After being taken to San Francisco as a child, he studied violin with Sigmund Anker. In 1923 he became a student of Louis Persinger, the concertmaster of the San Francisco Sym. Orch. Menuhin was only 7 when he made his public debut in Oakland playing Bériot's *Scène de ballet* with Persinger as his accompanist. On Jan. 17, 1926, at the age of 9, he appeared in recital in N.Y. His European debut followed when he was 10 as soloist with Paul Paray and the Lamoureux Orch. in Paris on Feb. 26, 1927. It was in Paris that he began to study with Georges Enesco. On Nov. 25, 1927, Menuhin was soloist in the Beethoven Violin Concerto with Fritz Busch and the N.Y. Sym. Orch., garnering extraordinary acclaim from the public and critics alike. He then made tours throughout the U.S. and Europe. On April 12, 1929, he was soloist with Bruno Walter and the Berlin Phil. in a daunting program of concertos by Bach, Beethoven, and Brahms, which elicited much acclaim. His London debut followed on Nov. 10, 1929. During this time, Menuhin continued to study with Enesco, and he also received additional instruction from Adolf Busch. In 1935 he completed his first world tour, and then toured regularly around the globe. During World War II, he gave some 500 concerts for the Allies and the International Red Cross. With the end of the War in 1945, he resumed his international career. In 1950 he made his first tour of Israel. After touring Japan for the first time in 1951, he played in India for the first time in 1952. In 1957 he founded an annual music festival in Gstaad, Switzerland. In 1959 he also founded the Bath Festival in England, with which he remained active until 1968. He founded the Yehudi Menuhin School of Music in Stoke d'Abernon, Surrey, for musically gifted children in 1963. From 1969 to 1972 he was joint artistic director of the Windsor Festival. In 1971 he was president of London's Trinity Coll. of Music, a position he later held with the Young Musicians' Sym. Orch. (from 1989) and the Hallé Orch. in Manchester (from 1992).

As Menuhin's virtuosity began to decline, he turned increasing attention to conducting. In 1982 he became assoc. conductor and president of the Royal Phil. in London, with which he toured and made recordings. He also served as principal guest conductor of the Warsaw Sinfonia from 1982 and of the English String Orch. from 1988. Apart from his various musical activities, he also pursued humanitarian efforts on behalf of world peace. However, his uncompromising sense of justice often antagonized political factions of both the Left and the Right. Following Germany's defeat in World War II in 1945, the German conductor Wilhelm Furtwängler was compelled to stand trial as a Nazi collaborator by the Allies. Menuhin came to Furtwängler's defense and, after the conductor was exonerated, the two performed and recorded together in spite of the furor his defense had engendered. After being received enthusiastically by Israeli audiences following the creation of the new state of Israel in 1948, Menuhin aroused Israeli animosity when he gave benefit concerts for displaced Palestinian refugees. At a music congress in Moscow in 1971, he embarrassed his Russian hosts when he appealed to the Soviet government to respect human rights. In spite of these and other controversies, however, Menuhin served as a Good Will Ambassador of UNESCO in 1992.

Menuhin was the recipient of innumerable honors. After making his home in England, he received an honorary knighthood from Queen Elizabeth II in 1965. In 1985 he became an honorary British subject and thereby formally became Sir Yehudi, an honor he retained until 1993 when the Queen created him a Life Peer as Lord Menuhin of Stoke d'Abernon. Among his other honors were the Gold Medal of the Royal Phil. Soc. of London (1962), the Jawaharlal Nehru Award for International Understanding (1970), the Sonning Music Prize of Denmark (1972), Grand Officier de la Légion d'honneur of France (1986), Member of the Order of Merit of England (1987), the Brahms Medal of Hamburg (1987), and Grand Officer of the Order of Merit of the Republic of Italy (1987). He also was awarded many honorary doctorates, including ones from the univs. of Oxford (1962) and Cambridge (1970), and from the Sorbonne in Paris (1976), where he was the first musician to be so honored by that French center of learning.

Menuhin was the author of an interesting autobiography, *Unfinished Journey* (1977; 2ⁿᵈ ed., rev., 1996). Among his other books were *The Violin: Six Lessons by Yehudi Menuhin* (1971), *Theme and Variations* (1972), *Violin and Viola* (1976), *The Music of Man* (1980), and *Life Class* (1986).

BIBL.: B. Gavoty, *Y. M. et Georges Enesco* (Geneva, 1955); R. Magidoff, *Y. M.: The Story of the Man and the Musician* (Garden City, N.Y., 1955; 2ⁿᵈ ed., 1973); N. Wymer, *Y. M.* (London, 1961); E. Fenby, *M.'s House of Music* (London, 1969); R. Daniels, *Conversations with M.* (London, 1979); M. Menuhin, *The M. Saga* (London, 1984); D. Menuhin, *Fiddler's Moll* (London, 1985); K. Pohl and A. Zipf-Pohl, eds., *Hommage à Y. M.: Festschrift zum 70. Geburtstag am 22. April 1986* (Baden-Baden, 1986); T. Palmer, *M.: A Family Portrait* (London, 1991).—NS/LK/DM

Mercadante, (Giuseppe) Saverio (Raffaele), important Italian composer and teacher; b. Altamura, near Bari (baptized), Sept. 17, 1795; d. Naples, Dec. 17, 1870. He was born out of wedlock, and was taken to Naples when he was about 11. In 1808 he was enrolled in the Collegio di San Sebastiano. He had no means to pay for his tuition; besides, he was over the age limit for entrance, and was not a Neapolitan. To gain admission he had to change his first Christian name and adjust his place and date of birth. He studied solfeggio, violin, and flute; also took classes in figured bass and harmony with Furno and counterpoint with Tritto; subsequently studied composition with the Collegio's director, Zingarelli (1816–20). He began to compose while still a student. In 1818 he composed 3 ballets, and the success of the 3ʳᵈ, *Il flauto incantato*, encouraged him to try his hand at an opera. His first opera, *L'apoteosi d'Ercole*, had a successful premiere in Naples on Jan. 4, 1819. He wrote 5 more operas before *Elisa e Claudio*, produced at La Scala in Milan on Oct. 30, 1821, which established his reputation. Other important operas were *Caritea, regina di Spagna* (Venice, Feb. 21, 1826), *Gabriella di Vergy* (Lisbon, Aug. 8, 1828), *I Normanni a Parigi* (Turin, Feb. 7, 1832), *I Briganti* (Paris, March 22, 1836), *Il giuramento* (Milan, March 10, 1837; considered his masterpiece), *Le due illustri rivali* (Venice, March 10, 1838), *Elena da Feltre* (Naples, Dec. 26, 1838), *Il Bravo* (Milan, March 9, 1839), *La Vestale* (Naples, March 10, 1840; one of his finest), *Il Reggente* (Turin, Feb. 2, 1843), *Leonora* (Naples, Dec. 5, 1844), *Orazi e Curiazi* (Naples, Nov. 10, 1846; a major success in Italy), and *Virginia* (Naples, April 7, 1866; his last opera to be perf., although composed as early as 1845; its premiere was delayed for political reasons). Mercadante wrote about 60 operas in all, for different opera houses, often residing in the city where they were produced; thus he lived in Rome, Bologna, and Milan; he also spent some time in Vienna (where he composed 3 operas in 1824) and in Spain and Portugal (1826–31). From 1833 to 1840 he was maestro di cappella at the Cathedral of Novara. About that time he suffered the loss of sight in one eye, and in 1862 he became totally blind. In 1839 Rossini offered him the directorate of the Liceo Musicale in Bologna, but he served in that post only a short time; in 1840 he was named director of the Naples Cons. in succession to his teacher Zingarelli. Mercadante's operas are no longer in the active repertoire, but they are historically important, and objectively can stand comparison with those of his great compatriots Rossini, Bellini, and Donizetti.

WORKS: DRAMATIC: O p e r a : *L'apoteosi d'Ercole*, dramma per musica (Teatro San Carlo, Naples, Jan. 4, 1819); *Violenza e costanza, ossia I falsi monetari*, dramma giocoso (Teatro Nuovo, Naples, Jan. 19, 1820; also known as *Il castello dei spiriti*); *Anacreonte in Samo*, dramma per musica (Teatro San Carlo, Naples, Aug. 1, 1820); *Il geloso ravveduto*, melodramma buffo (Teatro Valle, Rome, Oct. 1820); *Scipione in Cartagine*, melodramma serio (Teatro Argentina, Rome, Dec. 26, 1820); *Maria Stuarda regina di Scozia [Maria Stuart]*, dramma serio (Teatro Comunale, Bologna, May 29, 1821); *Elisa e Claudio, ossia L'amore protetto dall'amicizia*, melodramma semiserio (Teatro alla Scala, Milan, Oct. 30, 1821); *Andronico, melodramma tragico* (Teatro La Fenice, Venice, Dec. 26, 1821); *Il posto abbandonato, ossia Adele ed Emerico*, melodramma semiserio (Teatro alla Scala, Milan, Sept. 21, 1822); *Amleto*, melodramma tragico (Teatro alla Scala, Milan, Dec. 26, 1822); Alfonso ed Elisa, melodramma serio (Teatro Nuovo, Mantua, Dec. 26, 1822); *Didone abbandonata*, dramma per musica (Teatro Regio, Turin, Jan. 18, 1823); *Gli sciti*, dramma per musica (Teatro San Carlo, Naples, March 18, 1823); *Costanzo ed Almeriska*, dramma per musica (Teatro San Carlo, Naples, Nov. 22, 1823); *Gli Amici di Siracusa*, melodramma eroico (Teatro Argentina, Rome, Feb. 7, 1824); *Doralice*, dramma semiserio (Kärnthnertortheater, Vienna, Sept. 18, 1824); *Le nozze di Telemaco ed Antiope*, azione lirica (Kärnthnertortheater, Vienna, Nov. 5, 1824; in collaboration with others); *Il Podestà di Burgos, ossia Il Signore del villaggio*, melodramma semiserio (Kärnthnertortheater, Vienna, Nov. 20, 1824; 2nd version as *Il Signore del villaggio*, in Neapolitan dialect, Teatro Fondo, Naples, May 28, 1825); *Nitocri*, melodramma serio (Teatro Regio, Turin, Dec. 26, 1824); *Ipermestra*, dramma tragico (Teatro San Carlo, Naples, c. 1824); *Erode, ossia Marianna*, dramma tragico (Teatro La Fenice, Venice, Dec. 27, 1825); *Caritea, regina di Spagna [Donna Caritea], ossia La morte di Don Alfonso re di Portogallo*, melodramma serio (Teatro La Fenice, Venice, Feb. 21, 1826); *Ezio*, dramma per musica (Teatro Regio, Turin, Feb. 2, 1827); *Il montanaro*, melodramma comico (Teatro alla Scala, Milan, April 16, 1827); *La testa di bronzo, ossia La capanna solitaria*, melodramma eroico comico (private theater of Barone di Quintella, Lisbon, Dec. 3, 1827); *Adriano in Siria*, dramma serio (Sao Carlos, Lisbon, Feb. 24, 1828); *Gabriella di Vergy*, melodramma serio (Sao Carlos, Lisbon, Aug. 8, 1828); *La rappresaglia*, opera buffa (Cadiz, Nov. 20?, 1829); *Don Chisciotte [alle nozze di Gamaccio]*, opera buffa (Cadiz, c. 1829); *Francesca da Rimini*, melodramma (Madrid, c. 1830); *Zaira*, melodramma tragico (Teatro San Carlo, Naples, Aug. 31, 1831); *I Normanni a Parigi*, tragedia lirica (Teatro Regio, Turin, Feb. 7, 1832); *Ismalia, ossia Amore e morte*, melodramma serio fantastico (Teatro alla Scala, Milan, Oct. 27, 1832); *Il Conte di Essex*, melodramma (Teatro alla Scala, Milan, March 10, 1833); *Emma d'Antiochia*, tragedia lirica (Teatro La Fenice, Venice, March 8, 1834); *Uggero il danese*, melodramma (Teatro Riccardi, Bergamo, Aug. 11, 1834); *La gioventù di Enrico V*, melodramma (Teatro alla Scala, Milan, Nov. 25, 1834); *I due Figaro*, melodramma buffo (1st confirmed perf., Madrid, Jan. 26, 1835); *Francesca Donato, ossia Corinto distrutta*, melodramma semiserio (Teatro Regio, Turin, Feb. 14, 1835); *I Briganti*, melodramma (Théâtre-Italien, Paris, March 22, 1836); *Il giuramento*, melodramma (Teatro alla Scala, Milan, March 10, 1837; also known as *Amore e dovere*); *Le due illustri rivali*, melodramma (Teatro La Fenice, Venice, March 10, 1838); *Elena da Feltre*, dramma tragico (Teatro San Carlo, Naples, Dec. 26, 1838); *Il Bravo [La Veneziana]*, melodramma (Teatro alla Scala, Milan, March 9, 1839); *La Vestale*, tragedia lirica (Teatro San Carlo, Naples, March 10, 1840); *La Solitaria delle Asturie, ossia La Spagna ricuperata*, melodramma (Teatro La Fenice, Venice, March 12, 1840); *Il proscritto*, melodramma (Teatro San Carlo, Naples, Jan. 4, 1842); *Il Reggente*, dramma lirico (Teatro Regio, Turin, Feb. 2, 1843); *Leonora*, melodramma semiserio (Teatro Nuovo, Naples, Dec. 5, 1844); *Il Vascello de Gama*, melodramma romantico (Teatro San Carlo, Naples, March 6, 1845); *Orazi e Curiazi*, tragedia lirica (Teatro San Carlo, Naples, Nov. 10, 1846); *La Schiava saracena, ovvero Il campo di Gerosolima*, melodramma tragico (Teatro alla

Scala, Milan, Dec. 26, 1848); *Medea*, tragedia lirica (Teatro San Carlo, Naples, March 1, 1851); *Statira*, tragedia (Teatro San Carlo, Naples, Jan. 8, 1853); *Violetta*, melodramma (Teatro Nuovo, Naples, Jan. 10, 1853); *Pelagio*, tragedia lirica (Teatro San Carlo, Naples, Feb. 12, 1857); *Virginia*, tragedia lirica (Teatro San Carlo, Naples, April 7, 1866). B a l l e t : *Il Servo balordo o La disperazione di Gilotto* (Teatro San Carlo, Naples, Feb. 1, 1818); *Il Califfo generoso* (Teatro Fondo, Naples, 1818); *Il flauto incantato o Le convulsioni musicali* (Teatro San Carlo, Naples, Nov. 19, 1818; rev. version for Teatro alla Scala, Milan, Jan. 12, 1828); *I Portoghesi nelle Indie o La conquista di Malacca* (Teatro San Carlo, Naples, May 30, 1819; in collaboration with Gallenberg). ORCH.: Sinfonias (actually free variations in the form of an overture), fantasias on themes by other composers, marches, etc. CHAMBER: Various pieces. VOCAL: Much sacred music, including masses, motets, 8 Magnificats, several Salve Reginas, 2 settings of the Tantum ergo, etc.; of particular interest is his *Le sette [ultime] parole di Nostro Signore* for 2 Sopranos, Tenor, Baritone, Mixed Voices, 2 Violas, Cello, and Double Bass (1838); also his *Christus e Miserere* for Alto, Tenor, Bass, Chorus a cappella, English Horn, Horn, Bassoon, and Harp (Cons., Naples, March 19, 1856); a number of cantatas and hymns with orch., including a hymn for Garibaldi (Naples, 1861) and another designed for the inauguration of a statue to Rossini (Pesaro, Aug. 21, 1864); songs.

BIBL.: W. Neumann, *S. M.* (Kassel, 1855); R. Colucci, *Biografia di S. M.* (Venice, 1867); O. Serena, *I musicisti altamurani… in occasione del centenario di S. M.* (Altamura, 1895); A. Pomè, *Saggio critico sull'opera musicale di S. M.* (Turin, 1925); G. de Napoli, *La triade melodrammatica altamarana: Giacomo Tritto, Vincenzo Lavigna, S. M.* (Milan, 1931); G. Solimene, *La patria e i genitori di M.* (Naples, 1940); B. Notarnicola, *S. M.: Biografia critica* (Rome, 1945; 3rd ed., rev., 1951, as *S. M. nella gloria e nella luce: Verdi non ha vinto M.*); F. Schlitzer, *M. e Cammarano* (Bari, 1945); A. Sardone, *M., le due patrie e "La gran madre Italia"* (Naples, 1954); S. Palermo, *S. M.: Biografia, epistolario* (Fasano, 1985); M. Summa, *Bravo M.: Le ragioni di un genio* (Fasano, 1995). —NS/LK/DM

Mercer, Johnny (actually, John Herndon),

idiomatic American songwriter, singer, and record company executive; b. Savannah, Ga., Nov. 18, 1909; d. Los Angeles, June 25, 1976. A prolific writer whose songs were characterized by an inventive use of rural slang and imagery. Mercer primarily was a lyricist for songs featured in motion pictures; he wrote songs for at least 73 films released between 1934 and 1973. These efforts brought him 19 Academy Award nominations, and four Oscars for "On the Atchison, Topeka, and the Santa Fe," "In the Cool, Cool, Cool of the Evening," "Moon River," and "Days of Wine and Roses." Though he worked less frequently in the theater, he contributed to 13 musicals and revues produced on Broadway and in the West End between 1930 and 1974. He also maintained a career as a singer, scoring a series of major hits in the 1940s, the most successful being his own "On the Atchison, Topeka, and the Santa Fe" and "Ac-Cent-Tchu-Ate the Positive."

A major figure in the entertainment industry, Mercer was a director of ASCAP (1940–41), a cofounder and the first president of Capitol Records, president of the Academy of Television Arts and Sciences (which bestows the Emmy Awards) (1956–57), and cofounder and the first president of the Songwriters Hall of Fame.

Mercer was the son of George A. and Lilian Mercer; his father was a lawyer who worked in real estate. He studied piano and trumpet as a child and wrote his first, unpublished, song, "Sister Susie, Strut Your Stuff," at 15. He joined a theater group in Savannah and traveled with them to N.Y. for a play competition in 1927, then stayed in the city seeking work as an actor and writer. He appeared in several Broadway plays and became a staff writer for a music publishing firm. In 1930 he auditioned for the revue *The Garrick Gaieties* (N.Y., June 4, 1930), and though he was not accepted as a performer, he placed "Out of Breath (And Scared to Death of You)" (music by Everett Miller) in the score; it became his first published song. He also met Elizabeth "Ginger" Meehan, a dancer in the show, whom he married in 1931; they had two children.

In 1932, Mercer first worked with two of his major collaborators, Harold Arlen and Hoagy Carmichael. With Arlen he wrote "Satan's Little Lamb" (lyrics also by E. Y. Harburg), one of three songs he placed in the revue *Americana* (N.Y., Oct. 5, 1932). His first major success with Carmichael came when he set a lyric to the composer's instrumental "Washboard Blues" and came up with "Lazybones," which enjoyed many recordings, including a best-seller by Ted Lewis and His Band in July 1933. This success allowed him to give up his job as a runner for a Wall Street firm and turn to songwriting and performing full-time. During this period he also appeared on the radio series *The Kraft Music Hall* as a singer and master of ceremonies with Paul Whiteman and His Orch., and he recorded with Whiteman.

Mercer began to enjoy widespread success as a songwriter in 1934. In February his song "You Have Taken My Heart" (music by Gordon Jenkins) was a hit for Glen Gray and the Casa Loma Orch.; in September, Irving Aaronson and His Commanders scored a hit with "Pardon My Southern Accent" (music by Matty Malneck); in October, The Boswell Sisters sang "If I Had a Million Dollars" (music by Malneck) in the film *Transatlantic Merry-Go-Round*, Mercer's first movie song, and Richard Himber and His Orch. recorded it for a hit; and in November, Rudy Vallée and His Connecticut Yankees had a hit with "P.S. I Love You" (music by Jenkins).

Mercer moved to Hollywood in 1935 under contract to RKO as both a writer and performer. He appeared in and wrote songs for two films released in the fall of the year, *Old Man Rhythm* and *To Beat the Band*; the latter featured "Eenie Meenie Miney Mo" (music and lyrics by Mercer and Malneck), which spent nine weeks in the hit parade for Benny Goodman and His Orch. starting in December. But the films were not successful, and Mercer returned to Tin Pan Alley. He collaborated with Fred Astaire on "I'm Building Up to an Awful Let-Down," and Astaire recorded it for a hit parade entry in February 1936.

Mercer penned "Goody Goody" (music by Malneck), which Benny Goodman took to the top of the hit parade in March. It was succeeded at #1 by "Lost" (music and lyrics by Phil Ohman, Mercer, and Macy O. Teetor), recorded by Guy Lombardo and His Royal Canadians. Mercer then collaborated with Rube Bloom on the score

for the revue *Blackbirds of 1936* (London, July 9, 1936), which ran 124 performances, and he had his first hit for which he alone wrote both music and lyrics with "I'm an Old Cowhand (From the Rio Grande)." Bing Crosby sang it in the July film release *Rhythm on the Range;* Crosby's recording took it into the hit parade in September.

The success of "I'm an Old Cowhand" brought Mercer back to Hollywood under contract to Warner Bros., where he was paired with composer Richard A. Whiting. Their first film together was *Ready, Willing and Able*, released in March 1937; it featured "Too Marvelous for Words," which Bing Crosby recorded for a hit in April. The second Mercer-Whiting outing was *Varsity Show*, released in September, which featured "Have You Got Any Castles, Baby?" in the hit parade for Tommy Dorsey and His Orch. Meanwhile, Mercer continued to write non-movie songs; "Bob White (Whatcha Gonna Swing Tonight?)" (music by Bernard Hanighen) was a hit parade entry for Bing Crosby and Connee Boswell in January 1938. The same month saw the release of the next Mercer–Whiting film *Hollywood Hotel* starring Benny Goodman, which contained no hits but featured "Hooray for Hollywood," a witty portrait of the movie business that became the industry's unofficial anthem.

Whiting died on Feb. 10, 1938, leaving Mercer without a writing partner; as the year went on he began to work with Harry Warren, whose partnership with Al Dubin was breaking down. Mercer subbed for Dubin on some of the material for *Gold Diggers of Paris*, released in June, notably "Day Dreaming," which became a minor hit for the film's star, Rudy Vallée. Mercer and Warren's score for *Hard to Get*, released in November, included "You Must Have Been a Beautiful Baby," which topped the hit parade for Bing Crosby by the end of the year and became a much-recorded standard. It was replaced at #1 in January 1939 by Mercer and Warren's "Jeepers Creepers" from *Going Places*, which was recorded by Al Donohue and His Orch. and became Mercer's first Academy Award nominee for Best Song. Maintaining his performing career, Mercer appeared as singer and master of ceremonies on the radio series *The Camel Caravan* with Benny Goodman in 1938, remaining on the show when Bob Crosby took it over from 1939 to 1940. He also made some duet recordings with Bing Crosby, among them "Small Fry" (music by Hoagy Carmichael, lyrics by Frank Loesser), which had a couple of weeks in the hit parade in October 1938.

Though Mercer continued to contribute to Warner Bros. films until the expiration of his contract with the June 1939 release *Naughty but Nice*, he turned his attention increasingly to writing for the swing bands. "Could Be" (music by Walter Donaldson) entered the hit parade for Johnny Messner and His Orch. in February 1939; "(Gotta Get Some) Shut-Eye" (music by Donaldson) was a hit for Kay Kyser and His Orch. in March; "And the Angels Sing" (music by Ziggy Elman, based on his instrumental "Frälich in Swing") topped the hit parade in May for Benny Goodman; and "Day In—Day Out" (music by Rube Bloom) went to #1 for Bob Crosby and His Orch. in October.

Meanwhile, Mercer was collaborating with Hoagy Carmichael on his first Broadway musical, *Walk with Music*, which had a long out-of-town gestation before it arrived in N.Y. in June 1940 and flopped, closing after only 55 performances. But by that time, Mercer was back in the hit parade with "Fools Rush In" (music by Rube Bloom), which went to #1 for Glenn Miller and His Orch. in July. Returning to Hollywood, Mercer collaborated with Jimmy McHugh on the Kay Kyser vehicle *You'll Find Out*, released in November, which featured two hits, "You've Got Me This Way" for Tommy Dorsey and "The Bad Humor Man" for Jimmy Dorsey and His Orch., as well as Mercer's second Oscar nominee, "I'd Know You Anywhere." He earned another Oscar nomination in the same year for "Love of My Life" (music by Artie Shaw) from the January 1941 release *Second Chorus*, for which he also cowrote the screenplay. His fourth Academy Award nomination was for "Blues in the Night" (music by Harold Arlen), from the December 1941 film of the same name, a #1 hit in February 1942 for Woody Herman and His Orch., one of five Top Ten recordings.

Mercer collaborated with Victor Schertzinger on the Jimmy Dorsey vehicle *The Fleet's In*, released in March 1942, producing three hits for Dorsey, the chart-topping "Tangerine," the Top Ten "I Remember You," and the comic "Arthur Murray Taught Me Dancing in a Hurry." Glenn Miller peaked in the Top Ten with the independent song "Skylark" (music by Hoagy Carmichael) in May. That spring, combining with record store owner Glenn Wallichs and songwriter/movie producer B. G. De Sylva, Mercer launched Capitol Records and became its president. He also became one of its first recording artists, releasing his own composition "Strip Polka," which hit the Top Ten for him, as it did for three other performers, most successfully Kay Kyser, who scored a million-seller with it in October.

Mercer had two films in release that December; first the Fred Astaire–Rita Hayworth picture *You Were Never Lovelier*, on which he collaborated with Jerome Kern, resulting in the Academy Award nominee "Dearly Beloved," recorded for a Top Ten hit by Glenn Miller, and second the all-star *Star Spangled Rhythm*, with music by Harold Arlen, which included "That Old Black Magic," a #1 hit for Glenn Miller.

From 1943 to 1944, Mercer hosted his own radio program, *Johnny Mercer's Music Shop*, an activity that, along with running Capitol Records, allowed him less time as a songwriter. In addition, the musicians' union recording ban limited his success as either a writer or performer on records. But his score for the Fred Astaire vehicle *The Sky's the Limit*, written with Harold Arlen and released in September 1943, yielded "My Shining Hour," an Academy Award nominee and Top Ten hit for Glen Gray after the ban ended, and "One for My Baby (And One More for the Road)," which became a favorite of many performers in later years.

In January 1944, Glenn Miller reached the Top Ten with "Blue Rain" (music by James Van Heusen), a Mercer song originally recorded and released in 1939 but reissued due to the recording ban. That same month Mercer himself entered the charts with the timely "G.I.

Jive," for which he had written both music and lyrics, but Louis Jordan's version outdistanced the songwriter's, going to #1 in August. Mercer's sole movie score for the year, written with Harold Arlen, was the Bing Crosby–Betty Hutton war-themed picture *Here Come the Waves*, released in December. It featured "Ac-Cent-Tchu-Ate the Positive," an Academy Award nominee that drew three Top Ten renditions, the most popular a #1 hit by Mercer himself, and "Let's Take the Long Way Home," a hit for Jo Stafford.

Mercer's next hit was his own recording of a duet with Stafford on "Candy" (music and lyrics by Mack David, Joan Whitney, and Alex Kramer), which topped the charts in March 1945. The closing theme for Mercer's radio show was his own composition, "Dream." It was picked up for a Top Ten hit by three performers in 1945, with the Pied Pipers hitting #1 in May. That same month Woody Herman peaked in the Top Ten and sold a million records with "Laura," the theme to the film noir classic released the previous autumn, to which Mercer had subsequently set a lyric; there were four other Top Ten versions as well. *Out of This World*, a film released in June, contained two Mercer-Arlen compositions, one of them the title song, with which Jo Stafford scored a Top Ten hit.

Mercer's next film score, for the Judy Garland vehicle *The Harvey Girls*, written with Harry Warren, was not released until January 1946, but his recording of its most popular song, "On the Atchison, Topeka, and the Santa Fe," appeared six months earlier, and it topped the charts starting in July, one of five Top Ten versions; it also became his first Academy Award winner. He returned to #1 as a recording artist in March 1946 with "Personality" (music by James Van Heusen, lyrics by Johnny Burke). The same month he teamed with Harold Arlen for the Broadway musical *St. Louis Woman*. It ran only 113 performances, but Margaret Whiting recorded "Come Rain or Come Shine" from the score for a minor hit and the song eventually became a standard.

After *St. Louis Woman*, Mercer focused on his singing career, hitting the Top Ten with a series of recordings in late 1946 and 1947: the seasonal "Winter Wonderland" (music by Felix Bernard, lyrics by Richard B. Smith) in December 1946; "A Gal in Calico" (music by Arthur Schwartz, lyrics by Leo Robin) and the novelty "Huggin' and a Chalkin'" (music and lyrics by Clancy Hayes and Kermit Goell) in January 1947; "Zip-a-Dee-Doo-Dah" (music by Allie Wrubel, lyrics by Ray Gilbert) in February; and "Sugar Blues" (music by Clarence Williams, lyrics by Lucy Fletcher) in November. During this period he also appeared on the radio program *Your Hit Parade*.

Mercer scored his final Top Ten hit as a recording artist in July 1949 with "Baby, It's Cold Outside" (music and lyrics by Frank Loesser), a duet with Margaret Whiting. *Texas, Li'l Darlin'*, his third attempt at a Broadway musical, opened in the fall and ran 293 performances, though it failed to turn a profit.

Returning to movie work in 1950, Mercer wrote songs for *The Petty Girl*, released in August 1950, and for *The Keystone Girl*, which was never produced. From the score for the latter, he placed "In the Cool, Cool, Cool of the Evening" (music by Hoagy Carmichael) in the Bing Crosby film *Here Comes the Groom*, released in September 1951. It became a chart hit in a recording by Crosby and his costar, Jane Wyman, and won Mercer his second Academy Award. For *Top Banana*, his fourth Broadway musical, Mercer wrote his own music. The show, a vehicle for Phil Silvers, who played a television comedian, opened in November and ran 350 performances but closed in the red. A film version, shot onstage at the Winter Garden Theater, was released in February 1954.

Mercer worked less frequently in film and in the theater in the early 1950s, but his songs continued to make the charts. Stan Kenton and His Orch. revived "Laura" for a hit in August 1951; Rosemary Clooney had a hit with "Blues in the Night" in October 1952; that same month Jo Stafford reached the charts with a million-selling version of "Early Autumn," Mercer's lyric to a late 1940s instrumental by Ralph Burns and Woody Herman; in December 1952, the Mills Brothers scored a chart-topping million-seller with "Glow-Worm," a 1902 melody from the operetta *Lysistrata* by Paul Lincke to which Mercer had set a new English lyric in 1949; the Hilltoppers revived "P.S. I Love You" for a million- selling Top Ten hit in August 1953; and the Four Aces had a chart revival of "Dream" in September 1954.

Meanwhile, Mercer teamed with Gene de Paul to write the songs for MGM's big budget movie musical *Seven Brides for Seven Brothers*, which became a box office hit upon release in July 1954 and generated a Top Ten soundtrack album, with the song "Lonesome Polecat" giving the McGuire Sisters a chart record in November. The McGuire Sisters also had the highest charting version of Mercer's next hit, "Something's Gotta Give," drawn from the soundtrack to the Fred Astaire film *Daddy Long Legs*, released in May 1955, for which he had written both music and lyrics. (The song brought Mercer his 11th Oscar nomination.) But Sammy Davis Jr. also reached the Top Ten with the song, and he followed it up with a revival of "That Old Black Magic," which entered the charts in July. In August, Roger Williams reached the charts with an instrumental version of "Autumn Leaves," Mercer's retitling of the French song "Les Feuilles Mortes" (music by Joseph Kosma), for which he had fashioned an English lyric. Williams's version went to #1, and there were five other chart recordings, with Mitch Miller's the most popular one to feature Mercer's lyrics.

In 1956, Mercer worked with Gene de Paul on *You Can't Run Away from It*, a movie musical based on the same source used for the popular 1934 film *It Happened One Night*. Released in October, it produced a hit in the title song, taken into the Top 40 by the Four Aces. Mercer and de Paul also teamed for the stage musical *Li'l Abner*, based on Al Capp's comic strip, which became Mercer's only successful Broadway show upon its opening in November. It ran 693 performances; the cast album reached the charts; and the songs "Love in a Home" (for Doris Day) and "Namely You" (for Don Cherry) became chart singles. The show was adapted into a successful film in 1959.

In May 1957, Tony Bennett belatedly made a chart record out of the much-covered "One for My Baby

(And One More for the Road)." Mercer wrote music and lyrics for two songs used in Pat Boone's film debut *Bernardine*, which was released in July 1957; the film was a box office success, and Boone's recording of the title song became a Top 40 hit. Frankie Lymon and the Teenagers revived "Goody Goody" for a Top 40 hit in August. Mercer next teamed with Saul Chaplin to write the six songs used in the movie musical *Merry Andrew*, starring Danny Kaye. Released in March 1958, it marked the last time Mercer was employed to write the complete score for a musical comedy on film. From this point on his movie work usually consisted of contributing title songs to nonmusical pictures. Louis Prima and Keely Smith performed "That Old Black Magic" in the film *Senior Prom*, released in December, and they revived the song for a Top 40 hit. Also in 1958, Mercer set a lyric to Duke Ellington and Billy Strayhorn's instrumental composition "Sophisticated Lady."

Mercer enjoyed a series of hits in the early 1960s through a combination of revivals and newly written movie themes. "Fools Rush In (Where Angels Fear to Tread)" was revived by Brook Benton for a Top 40 hit in November 1960, the same month that saw the release of the Bob Hope–Lucille Ball comedy *The Facts of Life*, which featured a Mercer title song that earned him his 12th Academy Award nomination. In 1961, Bobby Rydell's revival of "That Old Black Magic" hit the Top 40 in May; Andy Williams reached the Top 40 in June with Mercer's English language version of the 1929 Kurt Weill–Bertolt Brecht composition "The Bilbao Song"; Bobby Darin took a revival of "You Must Have Been a Beautiful Baby" into the Top Ten in October; and November saw the release of the film *Breakfast at Tiffany's*, featuring Mercer's collaboration with Henry Mancini, "Moon River." Both Mancini and Jerry Butler recorded Top Ten versions of the song, which went on to win the Academy Award for Best Song and the Grammy Award for Song of the Year.

In 1962, Frank Ifield revived "I Remember You" for a Top Ten hit in October, and in December Mercer and Mancini again found success with a movie theme, "Days of Wine and Roses," which generated Top 40 hits for Mancini and Andy Williams and repeated the feat of winning both the Academy Award and the Song of the Year Grammy. Tony Bennett reached the Top 40 in February 1963 with "I Wanna Be Around" (music and lyrics by Mercer and Sadie Vimmerstedt). Ricky Nelson revived "Fools Rush In (Where Angels Fear to Tread)" for a Top 40 hit in October. And in December, Mercer had two movie title songs in circulation: "Charade" (music by Mancini) was a Top 40 hit for Mancini and for Sammy Kaye and His Orch. and an Oscar nominee, while "Love with the Proper Stranger" became a chart record for Jack Jones.

Mercer continued to write movie themes for the rest of the 1960s, earning an additional Academy Award nomination for "The Sweetheart Tree" (music by Henry Mancini) from *The Great Race* in 1965. "Summer Wind," a German song with music by Henry Mayer to which Mercer wrote an English lyric, was a chart record for Wayne Newton in 1965 and a Top 40 hit for Frank Sinatra in 1966. The Dave Clark Five revived "You Must

Have Been a Beautiful Baby" for a Top 40 hit in 1967.

Mercer began the 1970s writing songs with Henry Mancini for *Darling Lili*, an old-fashioned musical comedy film starring Julie Andrews that was released in June 1970. It earned him two Academy Award nominations, for Song ("Whistling Away the Dark") and for Original Song Score, as well as a Grammy Award nomination for Best Original Score Written for a Motion Picture or TV Special, and the soundtrack album reached the charts. Mercer earned his final Oscar nomination for "Life Is What You Make It" (music by Marvin Hamlisch) from the 1971 film *Kotch*. In 1974 he and André Previn wrote the songs for *The Good Companions*, a stage musical mounted in London, where it played 252 performances. The Salsoul Orch. revived "Tangerine" as a disco instrumental for a Top 40 hit in February 1976. Mercer died in June at age 66 after undergoing surgery to remove a brain tumor.

In the years immediately following his death, Mercer's songs were best remembered onstage, turning up in such Broadway shows as *Dancin'* (N.Y., March 27, 1978), *42nd Street* (N.Y., Aug. 25, 1980), and *Sophisticated Ladies* (N.Y., March 1, 1981). A stage adaptation of *Seven Brides for Seven Brothers* was mounted in 1982, and *Dream*, a musical featuring Mercer's songs, ran on Broadway in 1997. In November 1997 the mystery film *Midnight in the Garden of Good and Evil*, set in Savannah, featured an all-Mercer score with his songs performed by pop and jazz artists including Tony Bennett, Rosemary Clooney, Joe Williams, k. d. Lang, and Paula Cole. The soundtrack album was a hit on the jazz charts.

WORKS (only works for which Mercer was a primary, credited songwriter are listed): MUSICALS/REVUES (dates refer to N.Y. openings unless otherwise indicated): *Blackbirds of 1936* (London, July 9, 1936); *Walk with Music* (June 4, 1940); *St. Louis Woman* (March 30, 1946); *Texas, Li'l Darling* (Nov. 25, 1949); *Top Banana* (Nov. 1, 1951); *Li'l Abner* (Nov. 15, 1956); *Saratoga* (Dec. 7, 1959); *Foxy* (Feb. 16, 1964); *The Good Companions* (London, July 11, 1974); *Seven Brides for Seven Brothers* (July 8, 1982); *Dream* (April 3, 1997). FILMS: *Old Man Rhythm* (1935); *To Beat the Band* (1935); *Ready, Willing and Able* (1937); *Varsity Show* (1937); *Hollywood Hotel* (1938); *Cowboy from Brooklyn* (1938); *Garden of the Moon* (1938); *Hard to Get* (1938); *Going Places* (1938); *Naughty but Nice* (1939); *You'll Find Out* (1940); *Second Chorus* (1941); *You're the One* (1941); *Navy Blues* (1941); *Blues in the Night* (1941); *All Through the Night* (1942); *The Fleet's In* (1942); *You Were Never Lovelier* (1942); *Star Spangled Rhythm* (1942); *The Sky's the Limit* (1943); *True to Life* (1943); *Here Come the Waves* (1944); *The Harvey Girls* (1946); *The Petty Girl* (1950); *The Belle of N.Y.* (1952); *Dangerous When Wet* (1953); *Top Banana* (1954); *Seven Brides for Seven Brothers* (1954); *Daddy Long Legs* (1955); *You Can't Run Away from It* (1956); *Bernadine* (1957); *Merry Andrew* (1958); *Li'l Abner* (1959); *How the West Was Won* (1962); *The Great Race* (1965); *Not with My Wife, You Don't!* (1966); *Darling Lili* (1970).

BIBL.: B. Bach and G. Mercer (his wife), eds., *Our Huckleberry Friend* (Secaucus, N.J., 1974; rev. as *J. M.: The Life, Times and Song Lyrics of Our Huckleberry Friend*, 1982).—WR

Mercure, Pierre, Canadian composer; b. Montreal, Feb. 21, 1927; d. in an ambulance between Avallon and Auxerres, France, Jan. 29, 1966, after an automobile crash while driving from Paris to Lyons. He studied harmony and counterpoint with Marvin Duchow and Claude Champagne and bassoon with Roland Gagnier and Louis Letellier at the Montreal Cons. (1944–49). He then studied composition with Boulanger and conducting with Barzin in Paris (1949–50), and later studied orchestration with Hoérée and Milhaud and conducting with Fournet there (1962). He also took courses with Dallapiccola at the Berkshire Music Center in Tanglewood (summer, 1951), and at Darmstadt and Dartington with Pousseur, Nono, and Berio (1962). He played bassoon with the Montreal Sym. Orch. (1947–52), then joined the CBC (1952), where he served as its first producer of television music programming (1954–59). In his music, he explored electronic sonorities in combinations with traditional instrumentation.

WORKS: ORCH.: *Kaléidoscope* (1947–48); *Pantomime* for Winds and Percussion (1948); *Divertissement* for Solo String Quartet and String Orch. (1957); *Triptyque* (1959); *Lignes et points* (1964; Montreal, Feb. 16, 1965). CHAMBER: *Emprise* for Clarinet, Bassoon, Cello, and Piano (1950); *Tetrachromie*, ballet for 3 Winds, 4 Percussionists, and Tape (1963); *H2O per Severino* for 4–10 Flutes and/or Clarinets (1965). VOCAL: *Cantate pour une joie* for Soprano, Chorus, and Orch. (1955); *Psaume pour abri*, radiophonic cantata for Narrator, 2 Choruses, Chamber Ensemble, and Tape (Montreal, May 15, 1963). TAPE: 6 pieces with optional choreography: *Improvisation, Incandescense, Structures métalliques I* and *II* (all 1961), *Manipulations* (1963), and *Surimpressions* (1964); *Répercussions*, for Japanese Wind Chimes on Tape (1961); *Jeu de Hockey* (1961); *Structures metalliques III* (1962). OTHER: 3 short choreographed pieces: *Dualité*, with Trumpet and Piano, *La Femme archaïque*, with Viola, Piano, and Timpani, and *Lucrèce Borgia*, with Trumpet, Piano, and Percussion (all 1949); film scores.—NS/LK/DM

Méreaux, family of French musicians:

(1) Nicolas-Jean Le Froid de Méreaux, organist and composer; b. Paris, 1745; d. there, 1797. After training in Paris, he was organist at St. Sauver, the Petits Augustins, and the royal capel.

WORKS: DRAMATIC: Opera (all 1st perf. in Paris): *La ressource comique* (Aug. 22, 1772); *Le retour de tendresse* (Oct. 1, 1774); *Laurette* (July 23, 1777); *Alexandre aux Indes* (Aug. 26, 1783); *Oedipe et Jocaste (Oedipe à Thèbes)* (Dec. 30, 1791); *Fabius* (Aug. 9, 1793). OTHER: 3 oratorios: *Samson* (1774), *Esther* (1775), and *La Résurrection* (1780); cantatas; motets.

(2) Jean-Nicolas Le Froid de Méreaux, organist, pianist, teacher, and composer, son of the preceding; b. Paris, June 22, 1767; d. there, Feb. 6, 1838. He was a pupil of his father. Although a Roman Catholic, he served as organist of the Protestant church of St. Louis-du-Louvre (1791–1811). Thereafter he was organist of the Chapelle de l'Oratoire St. Honoré. For Napoleon's coronation (1804), he composed a hymn for Soloist, Chorus, and Orch. Among his other works were flute sonatas, and sonatas and fantasias for piano.

(3) Jean-Amédée Le Froid de Méreaux, pianist, music scholar, and composer, son of the preceding; b. Paris, Sept. 17, 1802; d. Rouen, April 25, 1874. He was a pupil in piano of his father. After law studies at the Univ. of Paris, he received training in counterpoint from Reicha. He began his career as a pianist in 1830. After performing and teaching in London (1832–33), he settled in Rouen. He gave a series of historical concerts in Rouen in 1842 and in Paris in 1843. Méreaux devoted much time to the study of early keyboard music and ed. the collection *Les clavecinistes de 1637 à 1790* (1864–67). Among his own works were orch. pieces, chamber music, piano pieces, and vocal scores. His *Grandes études pour piano en 60 caprices* (1855) were adopted for use by the Paris Cons.—**LK/DM**

Merian, Wilhelm, Swiss musicologist; b. Basel, Sept. 18, 1889; d. there, Nov. 15, 1952. He studied with Nef at the Univ. of Basel (Ph.D., 1915, with the diss. *Die Tabulaturen des Organisten Hans Kotter: Ein Beitrag zur Musikgeschichte des beginnenden 16. Jahrhunderts*; publ. in Leipzig, 1916). He subsequently completed his Habilitation there in 1921 with his *Die Klaviermusik der deutschen Koloristen*, and joined its faculty that same year. From 1920 to 1951 he was music critic and music ed. of the *Basler Nachrichten*. With Paul Sacher, he helped to found the Schola Cantorum Basiliensis (1933).

WRITINGS: Ed. *Gedenkschrift zum 50 jährigen Bestehen der Allgemeinen Musikschule in Basel* (1917); *Basels Musikleben im XIX. Jahrhundert* (1920); *Der Tanz in den deutschen Tabulaturbuchern...* (1927); *Hermann Suter: Ein Lebensbild als Beitrag zur schweizerischen Musikgeschichte* (1936).—**NS/LK/DM**

Méric-Lalande, Henriette (Clémentine), French soprano; b. Dunkirk, 1798; d. Chantilly, Sept. 7, 1867. She studied with her father, who was the director of a provincial opera company, making her debut in Nantes in 1814. After vocal studies with García in Paris, she made her first appearance there on April 3, 1823, in Castil-Blaze's pasticcio *Les Folies amoureuses*, then continued her training with Bonfichi and Banderali in Milan and took part in the Venice premiere of Meyerbeer's *Il Crociatto in Egitto* (March 7, 1824). She created Bianca in Bellini's *Bianca e Gernando* (Naples, May 30, 1826), Imogene in *Il Pirata* (Milan, Oct. 27, 1827), and Alaide in *La Straniera* (Milan, Feb. 14, 1829), even though Bellini himself declared that she was "incapable of delicate sentiment." She made her London debut in *Il Pirata* at the King's Theatre (April 17, 1830) and appeared in Rossini's *Semiramis* (1831). She retired shortly after creating the title role in Donizetti's *Lucrezia Borgia* (Milan, Dec. 26, 1833).—**NS/LK/DM**

Merighi, Antonia Margherita, Italian soprano; b. c. 1680; d. before 1764. She was in the service of the Dowager Grand Duchess Violante Beatrice of Tuscany. After making appearances in Venice (1717–21; 1724–26; 1732–33), Bologna (1719, 1727), Naples (1721–24; 1728–29), Parma (1725), Florence (1725), and Turin (1726), she was engaged by Handel for London, where she created the role of Matilde in his *Lotario* at her debut on Dec. 2, 1729. She also created the roles of Rosmira in his *Partenope* (Feb. 24, 1730) and Erissena in his *Poro* (Feb. 2, 1731). After singing again in Florence (1732) and Modena (1735), she returned to London to sing with the Opera of the Nobility (1736–37). In 1737–38 she was a member of Heidegger's company. In 1740 she appeared in Munich, and then retired to Bologna.—**NS/LK/DM**

Merikanto, Aarre, Finnish composer and teacher, son of **(Frans) Oskar Merikanto**; b. Helsinki, June 29, 1893; d. there, Sept. 29, 1958. He studied composition with Melartin at the Helsinki Music Inst.; then in Leipzig with Reger (1912–14) and with Vasilenko in Moscow (1915–16). In 1936 he joined the faculty at the Sibelius Academy in Helsinki, and in 1951 succeeded Palmgren as head of the dept. of composition there; held this post until his death. Like his father, he wrote on themes of Finnish folklore, but some of his early works reveal Russian and French traits.

WORKS: DRAMATIC: O p e r a : *Juha* (1920–22; Finnish Radio, Helsinki, Dec. 3, 1958; 1st stage perf., Lahti, Oct. 28, 1963). **ORCH.:** 3 piano concertos (1913, 1937, 1955); 3 syms. (1916, 1918, 1953); 4 violin concertos (1916, 1925, 1931, 1954); *Lemminkainen*, symphonic suite (1916); 2 cello concertos (1919; 1941–44); *Pan*, symphonic poem (1924); Concerto for Violin, Clarinet, Horn, and String Sextet (1925); *Concert Piece* for Cello and Chamber Orch. (1926); *Symphonic Study* (1928; mutilated; reconstructed by P. Heininen, 1981; Helsinki, Aug. 26, 1982); *Notturno*, symphonic poem (1929); *Kyllikin ryöstö* (The Abduction of Kyllikki), symphonic poem (1935); *Scherzo* (1937); *3 Impressions* (1940); *Soitelma kesäyölle* (Music to the Summer Night; 1942). **CHAMBER:** 2 string quartets (1913, 1939); String Trio (1912); Piano Trio (1917); Nonet (1926); String Sextet (1932); *Partita* for Harp and Woodwinds (1936). **VOCAL:** *Genesis* for Soprano, Chorus, and Orch. (1956); *Tuhma* (Simpleton) for Men's Chorus and Orch. (1956); songs.—**NS/LK/DM**

Merikanto, (Frans) Oskar, Finnish composer, conductor, and organist, father of **Aarre Merikanto**; b. Helsinki, Aug. 5, 1868; d. Hausjärvi-Oiti, Feb. 17, 1924. After preliminary study in his native city, he studied at the Leipzig Cons. (1887–88) and in Berlin (1890–91). Returning to Finland, he became organist of St. John's Church, and from 1911 to 1922 was conductor of the National Opera in Helsinki. He wrote manuals for organ playing. He wrote the first opera in Finnish, *Pohjan Neiti* (The Maid of the North; 1899; Vyborg, June 18, 1908), as well as the operas *Elinan surma* (Elina's Death; Helsinki, Nov. 17, 1910) and *Regina von Emmeritz* (Helsinki, Jan. 30, 1920). Other works include various instrumental pieces, organ works, and numerous songs, many of which became popular in his homeland.

BIBL.: Y. Suomalainen, *O. M.* (Helsinki, 1950); S. Heikinheimo, *O. M. ja hanen aikansa* (Helsingissä, 1995).—**NS/LK/DM**

Meriläinen, Usko, Finnish composer and teacher; b. Tampere, Jan. 27, 1930. He studied with Aarre Merikanto and Funtek at the Sibelius Academy in Helsinki (1951–55); then took private lessons with Krenek in Darmstadt and with Vogel in Switzerland. In 1956–57 he was a conductor and teacher in Kuopio, and subsequently was theater conductor in Tampere (1957–60). He then taught at the music inst. there (1961–66) and from 1965 at the Univ. In his music, he adopted a pragmatic modern idiom, with structural foundations of tonal and/or dodecaphonic procedures, depending on the basic concept.

WORKS: DRAMATIC: B a l l e t : *Arius* (1958–60; also 2 suites, 1960, 1962); *Psyche* (1973). **D a n c e P a n t o - m i m e :** *Alasin* (The Anvil; 1975; also listed as his 4th Sym.).

ORCH.: 5 syms.: No. 1 (1953–55), No. 2 (1964), No. 3 (1971), No. 4, *Alasin* (The Anvil; 1975; also listed as the dance pantomime under the same name), and No. 5 (1976); 2 piano concertos (1955, 1969); Concerto (1956); Chamber Concerto for Violin, 2 Percussionists, and Double String Orch. (1962); *Epyllion* (1963); *Musique du printemps* (1969); Cello Concerto (1975); *Dialogues* for Piano and Orch. (1977); *Mobile—ein Spiel für Orchester* (1977); *A Kinetic Poem* for Piano and Orch. (1981); *Kivenmurskaajat* (The Stone Crushers; 1982); *Visions and Whispers* for Flute and Orch. (1985); *"...but this is a landscape, monsieur Dali!"* (1986); Flute Concerto (1986); *Aikaviia*, concerto (1989); *Timeline*, concerto No. 2 for Orch. (1989); Guitar Concerto (1991). CHAMBER: *Partita* for Brass (1954); *4 Bagatelles* for String Quartet (1962); 3 string quartets (1965–92); *Divertimento* for Wind Quintet, Harp, Viola, and Cello (1968); *Metamorfora for 7* for Clarinet, Bassoon, Trumpet, Trombone, Percussion, Violin, and Double Bass (1969); *Concerto for 13* for 7 Violins, 3 Violas, 2 Cellos, and Double Bass (1971); Concerto for Double Bass and Percussion (1973); *Aspects of the Ballet "Psyche"* for Tape and Instrumental Ensemble (1973); *Simultus for 4* for Flute, Alto Saxophone, Guitar, and Percussion (1979); *Kyma* for String Quartet (1979); *Suvisoitto: Summer Sounds for Flute and Grasshoppers* for Flute and Tape (1979); *Paripeli (For 2)* for Cello and Piano (1980); Alto Saxophone Sonata (1982); *Mouvements circulaires en douceur* for 4 Flutes (1985). PIANO: Suite (1955); Sonatina (1958); 5 sonatas (1960, 1966, 1972, 1974, 1992); *Tre Notturni* (1967); *Papillons* for 2 Pianos (1969). OTHER: *Yö, vene ja punaiset purjeet* (Night, a Boat and Red Sails) for Chorus (1987); 2 electroacoustic works: *The Concert Where I Dozed Off—Consciousness Streaming Free*, radiophonic poem (1982), and *Oratorio Picassolle* (1984).—NS/LK/DM

Merkel, Gustav Adolf, German organist, teacher, and composer; b. Oberoderwitz, near Zittau, Nov. 12, 1827; d. Dresden, Oct. 30, 1885. His father was an organist and teacher. He began his training at the Bautzen teacher's college, where he became Musikpräfekt. After teaching school in Dresden (1848–53), he received training in piano from Friedrich Wieck, in theory from Ernst Julius Otto, in organ from Johann Schneider, and in composition from Schumann and Reissiger. He settled in Dresden, where he was an organist at the orphanage church (1858–60), the Kreuzkirche (1860–64), and the Catholic court church (from 1864). From 1861 he also taught organ at the Cons., and, from 1867 to 1873, he was director of the Dreyssig Singakademie. Merkel was held in great esteem by his contemporaries. As an organist, he did much to preserve the Bach tradition handed down to him by Johann Schneider. His organ music, tutors, and studies were highly esteemed. Among his other works were instrumental pieces, motets, choral songs, and solo songs.

BIBL.: P. Janssen, *G. M.* (Leipzig, 1886); M. Saal, *G.A. M. (1827–1885): Leben und Orgelwerk* (Frankfurt am Main, 1993). —LK/DM

Merklin, Joseph, German organ builder; b. Oberhausen, Baden, Jan. 17, 1819; d. Nancy, France, June 10, 1905. He worked in his father's workshop in Freiburg, and in 1843 went to Brussels. In 1853 took his brother-in-law, F. Schütze, into partnership, changing the name of his firm to Merklin, Schütze & Cie. In 1855 he bought out the Ducroquet firm in Paris. In 1858 he reorganized

his partnership as the Société Anonyme pour la Fabrication des Orgues, Établissement Merklin-Schütze. The firm supplied organs to several cathedrals in Europe. Merklin publ. an interesting technical paper, *Notice sur l'électricité appliquée aux grandes orgues* (Paris, 1887), containing some surprising insights on the possible manufacture of electric organs. His nephew Albert Merklin (1892–1925) went to Madrid at the outbreak of World War I in 1914 and established a Spanish branch of the firm. Merklin's Paris factory was acquired by Guttschenritter in 1899, and his branch in Lyons was bought in 1906 by the Swiss organ builder Theodor Kuhn; it was incorporated in 1926 as Société Anonyme des Anciens Établissements Michel, Merklin & Kuhn. After several further changes of ownership, the firm was taken over in 1967 by Fredrich Jakob in Zürich.

BIBL.: M. Jurine, *J. M., facteur d'orgues européen: Essai sur l'orgue français au XIX siècle* (Paris, 3 vols., 1991).—NS/LK/DM

Merli, Francesco, Italian tenor; b. Milan, Jan. 27, 1887; d. there, Dec. 12, 1976. He studied with Borghi and Negrini in Milan. He made his first appearance at Milan's La Scala as Alvaro in Spontini's *Fernando Cortez* (1916), and subsequently sang there regularly until 1942; also appeared at the Teatro Colón in Buenos Aires; between 1926 and 1930 he sang at Covent Garden in London. He made his debut at the Metropolitan Opera in N.Y. as Radames in *Aida* on March 2, 1932; then returned to Italy. He retired from the stage in 1948 and was active mainly as a voice teacher. His other roles included Don José, Otello, Canio, Samson, Calaf, and Dick Johnson.—NS/LK/DM

Merlo, Alessandro, Italian tenor, bass, viol player, and composer, known as **Alessandro Romano** or **Alessandro della Viola**; b. Rome, 1530; d. probably there, after 1594. He most likely received his training under Willaert and Rore. He spent most of his career as an esteemed singer in the Sistine Chapel. Among his works, all publ. in Venice, are 2 vols. of madrigals (1565, 1577), 2 vols. of canzoni (1570, 1571), a vol. of villanelle (1579), and a vol. of Lamentationi (1582).—LK/DM

Merman, Ethel (originally, **Zimmermann, Ethel Agnes**), brassy American singer and actress; b. N.Y., Jan. 16, 1908; d. there, Feb. 15, 1984. Merman was the most successful musical comedy performer of her generation. Known for her loud, clear voice and excellent enunciation, she was a favorite of such songwriters as George and Ira Gershwin, Cole Porter, and Irving Berlin, and she introduced some of their most popular songs, including "I Got Rhythm," "You're the Top," "I Get a Kick Out of You," and "There's No Business Like Show Business." Merman reached her zenith as Rose, the overbearing mother of Gypsy Rose Lee in Jule Styne and Stephen Sondheim's *Gypsy*, singing such songs as "Everything's Coming Up Roses." She appeared in vaudeville and in nightclubs, gave concerts, made records, and performed on radio, on television, and in films. Her primary achievement was in the 13 roles she created on Broadway between 1930 and 1959.

Merman was the daughter of Edward Zimmermann, a bookkeeper and amateur keyboard player, and Agnes

Gardner Zimmermann. She began singing in public as a child. During World War I she entertained at local military camps. After graduating from high school she became a secretary but moonlighted as a nightclub singer. Shortening her name to Merman, she became successful in vaudeville, performing at the Palace Theatre in N.Y. in September 1930 before turning to the legitimate stage in the Gershwins' musical *Girl Crazy* (N.Y., Oct. 14, 1930). It played 272 performances, and during its run she also appeared at the Central Park Casino and began making films at the Paramount studio, then located in N.Y. Many of these films were shorts or cartoons; her first appearance in a feature film came with *Follow the Leader*, released in December 1930.

Merman's second Broadway show was the 11th edition of the revue *George White's Scandals* (N.Y., Sept. 14, 1931), which ran 202 performances. She had her first record hit with "How Deep Is the Ocean?" (music and lyrics by Irving Berlin) in November 1932. The same month, she opened in her third Broadway show, *Take a Chance* (N.Y., Nov. 26, 1932), with songs by composers Richard Whiting and Nacio Herb Brown and lyricist B. G. De Sylva. *Chance* ran 243 performances, and Merman scored a hit with "Eadie Was a Lady" from the score in January 1933.

Merman went to Hollywood in September 1933 and costarred with Bing Crosby in the film *We're Not Dressing*, released in April 1934, and with Eddie Cantor in *Kid Millions*, released in November 1934. (Her cameo in *Big Broadcast of 1936*, released in September 1935, was actually an outtake from *We're Not Dressing*.) She scored a hit in November 1934 with "An Earful of Music" (music by Walter Donaldson, lyrics by Gus Kahn) from *Kid Millions*. She returned to Broadway—and to her greatest success yet—in Cole Porter's *Anything Goes* (N.Y., Nov. 21, 1934), which ran 420 performances with a score that included "You're the Top" and "I Get a Kick Out of You," both of which she recorded for hits.

Merman left the show to return to Hollywood and make a second film with Eddie Cantor, *Strike Me Pink*, released in January 1936, and a movie adaptation of *Anything Goes* with Bing Crosby, released in February 1936. She returned to N.Y. for Cole Porter's next show, *Red, Hot and Blue!* (N.Y., Oct. 29, 1936), which ran only 183 performances, then signed a new movie contract with 20th Century–Fox and appeared in three films released in 1938: *Happy Landing* in January, the Irving Berlin anthology *Alexander's Ragtime Band* in August, and *Straight, Place and Show* in October. This marked the end of her full-time film career, though she continued to make movies occasionally.

Merman returned to Broadway with the Arthur Schwartz–Dorothy Fields musical *Stars in Your Eyes* (N.Y., Feb. 9, 1939), which ran only 127 performances. She moved on to Cole Porter's *DuBarry Was a Lady* (N.Y., Dec. 6, 1939), which became her biggest hit since *Anything Goes* with a run of 408 performances. Her fourth Porter show, *Panama Hattie* (N.Y., Oct. 30, 1940), did even better, running 501 performances.

On Nov. 15, 1940, Merman married William Jacob Smith, a theatrical agent, but the couple divorced the following year. She then married newspaperman Robert

Daniels Levitt, and they had two children: Ethel, b. July 20, 1942; and Robert Jr., b. Aug. 11, 1945. In between she starred in her fifth Cole Porter musical, *Something for the Boys* (N.Y., Jan. 7, 1943), which ran 422 performances, and she made a cameo appearance in the all-star film *Stage Door Canteen*, released in June 1943.

Merman enjoyed her longest-running musical with Irving Berlin's *Annie Get Your Gun* (N.Y., May 16, 1946), which played 1,147 performances; she stayed in it until it closed on Feb. 19, 1949. The cast album became a Top Ten hit. During 1949 she had her own network radio series, *The Ethel Merman Show*. She returned to Broadway in Berlin's *Call Me Madam* (N.Y., Oct. 12, 1950), which ran 644 performances; she won a Tony Award for her role. Since RCA Victor had rights to the cast album and Merman was contracted exclusively to Decca, she recorded the show's songs with Dick Haymes, and their *Call Me Madam* LP hit the Top Ten while "You're Just in Love" made the singles charts.

Merman and her second husband were divorced in June 1952. On March 9, 1953, she married Continental Airlines president Robert F. Six. That same month she starred in a film adaptation of *Call Me Madam*, her first major movie role in 15 years. From this point on she divided her time between the theater, television, and film. She appeared in a series of TV specials: *The Ford 50th Anniversary Show* (June 15, 1953), on which she duetted with Broadway's other leading female star, Mary Martin, and small-screen adaptations of *Anything Goes* (Feb. 28, 1954), with Frank Sinatra, and *Panama Hattie* (Nov. 10, 1954). In December 1954 she starred in another Irving Berlin anthology film, *There's No Business Like Show Business*; the soundtrack album made the Top Ten.

Merman returned to Broadway with *Happy Hunting* (N.Y., Dec. 6, 1956), which ran 412 performances. Her next Broadway show was *Gypsy* (N.Y., May 21, 1959), which ran 702 performances in N.Y. She also starred in a nine-month national tour, staying with the show until the end of 1961. The cast album was a Top Ten hit that stayed in the charts more than two years, and it won a Grammy Award for Best Show Album.

Merman divorced her third husband in December 1960. She married actor Ernest Borgnine on June 26, 1964, but they separated after 38 days and divorced in November 1965. During the 1960s she returned to nightclub performing (making her Las Vegas debut in October 1962), appeared on television, and had small roles in the films *It's a Mad, Mad, Mad, Mad World* (1963) and *The Art of Love* (1965). She also starred in a Broadway revival of *Annie Get Your Gun* (N.Y., May 31, 1966) that led to a chart album and a television adaptation (March 19, 1967), and she toured in *Call Me Madam* in the latter part of the decade.

On March 28, 1970, Merman became the eighth person to play the title role in the long-running musical *Hello, Dolly!* on Broadway, and she stayed with the show until it closed. During the 1970s and early 1980s she continued to appear on television and had a few minor movie roles (*Journey Back to Oz* [voice only; 1974], *Won Ton Ton, the Dog Who Saved Hollywood* [1976], *Airplane!*

[1980]). She also gave concerts, notably one at Carnegie Hall on May 10, 1982. She died of a brain tumor in 1984.

WRITINGS: As told to P. Martin, *Who Could Ask for Anything More* (U.K. title: *Don't Call Me Madam*; N.Y., 1955); with G. Eells, *M.—An Autobiography* (N.Y., 1978).

BIBL.: B. Thomas, *I Got Rhythm! The E. M. Story* (N.Y., 1985); G. Bryan, *E. M.: A Bio-Bibliography* (N.Y., 1992).—**WR**

Mermet, Auguste, French composer; b. Brussels, Jan. 5, 1810; d. Paris, July 4, 1889. He was a private pupil of Le Sueur and Halévy. His operatic spectacles à la Meyerbeer were popular in the Paris of his day but eventually were forgotten. Among his various stage works were *La Banniere du Roi* (Versailles, April 1835), *Le Roi David* (Paris, June 3, 1846), *Roland a Roncevaux* (Paris, Oct. 3, 1864), and *Jeanne d'Arc* (Paris, April 5, 1876). —**NS/LK/DM**

Merola, Gaetano, Italian-American conductor and opera manager; b. Naples, Jan. 4, 1881; d. while conducting a performance of the San Francisco Sym. Orch. at Sigmund Stern Grove in San Francisco, Aug. 30, 1953. He studied at the Naples Cons. He went to the U.S. in 1899, and was appointed asst. conductor at the Metropolitan Opera in N.Y.; also conducted the Henry Savage English Opera in N.Y. (1903) and at the Manhattan Opera. Merola subsequently became music director and manager of the San Francisco Opera in 1923, where he remained until his death. He also conducted opera in Los Angeles (1924–32).—**NS/LK/DM**

Merrem-Nikisch, Grete, German soprano; b. Düren, July 7, 1887; d. Kiel, March 12, 1970. She studied with Schulz-Dornburg in Cologne and Marie Hedmondt at the Leipzig Cons. In 1910 she made her operatic debut at the Leipzig Opera, where she sang until 1913. In 1911 she made her first appearance at the Berlin Royal Opera, where she was a member (1913–18), and then of its successor, the State Opera (1918–30). She was known for her lyric roles, and for her Eva and Sophie. She also sang in Dresden, where she appeared in the premieres of *Die toten Augen* (1916), *Intermezzo* (1924), and *Cardillac* (1926). From 1918 she likewise pursued a fine career as a lieder artist. In later years, she taught at the Univ. of Kiel. In 1914 she married the eldest son of Arthur Nikisch.—**NS/LK/DM**

Merriam, Alan P(arkhurst), American anthropologist and ethnomusicologist; b. Missoula, Mont., Nov. 1, 1923; d. in an airplane crash near Warsaw, March 14, 1980. He studied at the Univ. of Mont. (B.A., 1947) and took courses in anthropology from Melville Herskovits and Richard Waterman at Northwestern Univ. (M.M., 1948; Ph.D., 1951). He taught anthropology there (1953–54; 1956–62) and at the Univ. of Wisc. (1954–56); in 1962 he became a prof. of anthropology at Ind. Univ. in Bloomington; was chairman of the dept. there from 1966 to 1969. In 1976 he was engaged as a senior scholar in anthropology at the Univ. of Sydney. He was involved in field research among the Flathead Indians and the tribes in Zaire.

WRITINGS: *The Anthropology of Music* (Evanston, Ill., 1964); with F. Gillis, *Ethnomusicology and Folk Music: An International Bibliography of Dissertations and Theses* (Middletown, Conn., 1966); *Ethnomusicology of the Flathead Indians* (Chicago, 1967); *African Music on LP: An Annotated Discography* (Evanston, 1970); *The Arts and Humanities in African Studies* (Bloomington, Ind., 1972).—**NS/LK/DM**

Merrick, Frank, English pianist, pedagogue, and composer; b. Clifton, Bristol, April 30, 1886; d. London, Feb. 19, 1981. He studied piano and composition with his father; made his debut in 1895, then studied piano with Leschetizky in Vienna (1898–1901; 1905). Returning to England, he taught at the Royal Manchester Coll. of Music (1911–29), then became a prof. at the Royal Coll. of Music in London. In 1956 he joined the piano faculty of Trinity Coll. of Music in London. In 1928 he entered a rather ill-conceived contest launched by the Columbia Phonograph Co. to nail down the centenary of Schubert's death by finishing his "Unfinished" Sym. Merrick did finish it, and won a prize. He was married to the pianist Hope Squire and gave duo-piano concerts with her. He championed the music of British composers in his concerts. In 1978 he was made a Commander of the Order of the British Empire. Somewhat off-center in his propensities, proclivities, and predilections, he learned Esperanto and wrote songs to his own texts in that artificial language. He also composed 2 piano concertos and some instrumental pieces. He publ. a didactic vol., *Practising the Piano* (London, 1958), and ed. John Field's piano concertos.—**NS/LK/DM**

Merrill, Bob (originally, **Lavan, Henry Robert Merrill**), American songwriter; b. Atlantic City, N.J., May 17, 1921; d. Los Angeles, Feb. 17, 1998. Merrill had two distinct, and equally successful, careers as a songwriter. From the late 1940s to the late 1950s he displayed a facility for writing novelty songs that became pop hits, among them such light standards as "If I Knew You Were Comin' (I'd've Baked a Cake)," "The Doggie in the Window," and "Honeycomb." Then he turned his hand to writing for the musical theater, resulting in seven Broadway shows that opened between 1957 and 1993, among them such long-running hits as *Carnival* and *Funny Girl*, which featured his biggest latter-day hit, "People."

The son of James Arthur Lavan, a candy maker, and Sadie Abrahams Lavan, Merrill grew up in Philadelphia. During his teens he hitchhiked around the country, getting his earliest theatrical experience by working as a singer, impressionist, and master of ceremonies at clubs. He graduated from high school in 1938 and briefly attended Temple Univ. In 1939 he took a job at the Bucks County Playhouse, where he studied acting with Richard Bennett. He moved to N.Y. in 1940 to become an actor but was drafted into the army and spent time in the cavalry before transferring to the Special Services division, where he wrote and produced radio shows. Discharged from the army in 1942, he moved to Los Angeles, where got a job as a writer at NBC radio. In 1943 he was hired as a dialogue director at Columbia Pictures. He also had some minor acting roles in motion pictures, notably an appearance in the Universal film *Señorita from the West* in October 1945.

At Columbia, Merrill encountered comic singer Dorothy Shay, who encouraged him to try writing songs and then recorded his composition "I've Been to Hollywood" for her album *Dorothy Shay (The Park Avenue Hillbillie) Sings*, which topped the charts in July 1947. In 1948 he became a casting director at CBS television, leaving that job in 1949 to take a job as a production consultant for the Cunningham-Walsh Agency and the Liggett and Myers Tobacco Company. In December 1949 he enjoyed his first small hit, as Billy Eckstine reached the charts with his song "Fool's Paradise." His breakthrough, however, came with "If I Knew You Were Comin' (I'd've Baked a Cake)" (music and lyrics by Al Hoffman, Bob Merrill, and Clem Watts), which became a million-selling #1 hit for Eileen Barton in March 1950. The next month, Mindy Carson hit the Top Ten with Merrill's "Candy and Cake." In October, Ernest Tubb hit the country Top Ten with "You Don't Have to Be a Baby to Cry" (music and lyrics by Terry Shand and Bob Merrill).

The chief beneficiary of Merrill's writing talent in 1951 was Guy Mitchell, who reached the charts with five of his compositions. Mitchell charted in March with "Christopher Columbus" (music and lyrics by Bob Merrill and Terry Gilkyson); hit the Top Ten in April with "Sparrow in the Tree Top," narrowly besting another Top Ten rendition by Bing Crosby and the Andrews Sisters; returned to the Top Ten in June with "My Truly, Truly Fair," just ahead of a Top Ten version by Vic Damone; scored a third Merrill-composed Top Ten hit in September with "Belle, Belle, My Liberty Belle"; and reached the charts in November with "There's Always Room at Our House." Meanwhile, Guy Lombardo and His Royal Canadians charted in February with "The Chicken Song (I Ain't Gonna Take It Settin' Down)" (music and lyrics by Terry Shand and Bob Merrill), and the Fontaine Sisters with Texas Jim Robertson had the most successful of three chart versions of Merrill's "Let Me In" in March.

Guy Mitchell was responsible for three of the five chart songs Merrill enjoyed in 1952: "Pittsburgh, Pennsylvania," a Top Ten hit in April; "Feet Up (Pat Him on the Po-Po)" in August; and "('Cause I Love You) That's a-Why," a duet with Mindy Carson, in November. The year's other Merrill-penned hits were "Walkin' to Missouri," recorded by Sammy Kaye and His Orch., and "Funny (Not Much)" (music and lyrics by Hughie Prince, Bob Merrill, Philip Broughton, and Marcia Neil), by Nat "King" Cole, both in August. Guy Mitchell scored a final chart entry with a Merrill song in January 1953 with "She Wears Red Feathers," but Merrill's biggest hits of 1953 came with Patti Page, who, like Mitchell, recorded for Columbia Records under the aegis of Mitch Miller. Page hit #1 in March 1953 with the million-selling "The Doggie in the Window" and the Top Ten in August with "Butterflies." Merrill also wrote the parody "(How Much Is) That Hound Dog in the Window," which reached the charts for country comedy duo Homer and Jethro in June.

Merrill's songs continued to become hits during the mid-1950s. Rosemary Clooney reached the Top Ten with "Mambo Italiano" in December 1954; Sarah Vaughan had a Top Ten hit with "Make Yourself Comfortable" in January 1955; Perry Como made a Top Ten hit out of "Tina Marie" in June 1955; Doris Day reached the charts with "Ooh Bang Jiggilly Jang" in November 1955; "Miracle of Love" was a Top 40 hit for Eileen Rodgers in September 1956; and in July 1956, Teresa Brewer hit the Top Ten with "A Sweet Old Fashioned Girl" while Tennessee Ernie Ford revived "You Don't Have to Be a Baby to Cry" for a pop chart entry.

But Merrill had ambitions beyond the hit parade. In 1956 he signed a seven-year, ten-film contract with MGM as a composer, publisher, scriptwriter, and producer. His first assignment was to adapt Eugene O'Neill's 1921 drama *Anna Christie* into a musical to star Doris Day. Merrill had written a collection of songs by the time the project was dropped, and director George Abbott heard the songs and decided to turn it into a Broadway musical. The result was *New Girl in Town*, which opened in May 1957 and was a modest hit, running 431 performances and spawning a cast album that spent a couple of months in the charts. Eddie Fisher reached the charts with "Sunshine Girl" from the score. Meanwhile, pop singer Jimmie Rodgers revived "Honeycomb," a 1954 Merrill composition, and hit #1 with it in September 1957, selling a million copies. "When the Boys Talk About the Girls," a newly written Merrill song, became a Top 40 hit for Valerie Carr in June 1958.

Merrill's success adapting O'Neill to the musical theater made him the logical choice to replace songwriter John Latouche, who died while working on a musical version of O'Neill's comedy *Ah, Wilderness!*. Under the title *Take Me Along*, the show opened in October 1959 and ran 448 performances. Anita Bryant reached the charts with "Promise Me a Rose (A Slight Detail)" from the score. For his third musical, Merrill ambitiously tackled a stage adaptation of the 1953 film *Lili*, a musical itself with an Academy Award–winning score by Bronislau Kaper featuring the standard "Hi Lili, Hi Lo." Despite this apparent handicap, *Carnival*, which opened in April 1961, became a major hit, running 719 performances, with a cast album that topped the charts.

Merrill turned to writing songs for two children's projects in 1962. The first was a film musical employing George Pal's Puppetoon stop-action animation, *The Wonderful World of the Brothers Grimm*, released in August. Mr. Acker Bilk scored a chart entry with the instrumental "Above the Stars" from the score. The second project was a cartoon adaptation of Charles Dickens's *A Christmas Carol*, a television musical called *Mr. Magoo's Christmas Carol*, broadcast in December. For the latter, Merrill wrote lyrics to music by Jule Styne. In 1963 two of Merrill's pop hits were revived: Baby Jane and the Rockabyes released a version of "The Doggie in the Window" that made the charts in January, and the Caravelles hit the Top Ten in December with "You Don't Have to Be a Baby to Cry."

Merrill contributed a couple of songs to the musical *Hello, Dolly!*, which opened in January 1964, but his main project for the year was *Funny Girl*, a musical based on the life of singer/comedienne Fanny Brice, and starring Barbra Streisand. He again collaborated with Jule Styne on the songs, and the result was his greatest success. The show opened in March and ran 1,348 performances. The cast album reached the Top Ten, went gold, and earned the Grammy in its category. "People" was separately recorded by Streisand and became a Top Ten hit, and the song was nominated for a Grammy for Song of the Year. Streisand also scored a chart entry with a song called "Funny Girl" that Merrill and Styne had written for the show, although it was cut. Merrill married singer Dolores Marquez during the year; they later divorced. In 1965, Merrill and Styne wrote songs for a second seasonal television musical, this time a live-action effort called *The Dangerous Christmas of Little Red Riding Hood* and starring Liza Minnelli.

Merrill returned to writing his own music on his next two musicals. The first, an adaptation of Truman Capote's novella *Breakfast at Tiffany's*, tried out in Philadelphia and N.Y. in 1966 but closed without opening on Broadway. The second, an adaptation of Nora Johnson's novel *The World of Henry Orient* called *Henry, Sweet Henry*, opened on Broadway in October 1967; it was a failure, running only 80 performances. Merrill teamed up with Styne again to write a new title song for the film adaptation of *Funny Girl*, which was released in September 1968. That song earned Merrill his only Academy Award nomination, for Best Song. The film was the biggest box office hit of the year. The soundtrack album sold a million copies, and "People" was revived by the Tymes for a Top 40 hit.

Merrill was the lyricist and librettist and Styne the composer for the musical *Prettybelle*, which opened in Boston on Feb. 1, 1971; it closed without reaching Broadway. He then had greater success serving only as lyricist to Styne's melodies for the musical *Sugar*, based on the 1959 film *Some Like It Hot*. Opening on Broadway in April 1972, the show ran 505 performances, earning a Tony nomination for Best Musical; the cast album was nominated for a Grammy.

Starting in the mid-1970s, Merrill began writing screenplays, earning co- credit on *Mahogany*, released in October 1975, and sole credit on *W. C. Fields and Me*, released in March 1976. On Dec. 14, 1976, he married Suzanne Reynolds, a radio newscaster. He wrote the book as well as the music and lyrics for the musical *The Prince of Grand Street*, which tried out in Philadelphia starting on March 7, 1978, but closed in Boston on April 15, 1978, without reaching Broadway. Following this failure, he had difficulty mounting another show on Broadway.

Merrill taught at the U.C.L.A. and Loyola Univ., and worked on screenplays, notably writing the 1982 television movie *Portrait of a Showgirl*. A revue of his songs, *We're Home*, ran Off-Broadway in 1984. He wrote new songs for a Broadway revival of *Take Me Along* (N.Y., April 14, 1985), which closed after one performance. In 1987 he worked on the book, music, and lyrics to a musical adaptation of the 1968 film *The Graduate*, but it was never produced. He wrote book, music, and lyrics for *Hannah...1939*, a musical about the Nazi occupation

of Prague, and it ran Off-Off-Broadway for 46 performances in 1990. In 1993 he was brought in to replace librettist Marsha Norman as lyricist for a musical adaptation of the 1948 film *The Red Shoes*. Writing under the pseudonym Paul Stryker, he collaborated for the last time with Jule Styne, but the troubled production ran only five performances on Broadway.

Merrill's final work was the screenplay for the 1997 children's film *The Animated Adventures of Tom Sawyer*. In failing health, he committed suicide at age 76 in 1998.

WORKS (only works for which Merrill was a primary, credited songwriter are listed): **STAGE MUSICALS** (dates refer to N.Y. openings): *New Girl in Town* (May 14, 1957); *Take Me Along* (Oct. 22, 1959); *Carnival* (April 13, 1961); *Funny Girl* (March 26, 1964); *Henry, Sweet Henry* (Oct. 23, 1967); *Sugar* (April 9, 1972); *We're Home* (Oct. 11, 1984); *Hannah...1939* (May 31, 1990); *The Red Shoes* (Dec. 16, 1993). **FILM MUSICALS:** *The Wonderful World of the Brothers Grimm* (1962); *Funny Girl* (1968). **TELEVISION MUSICALS:** *Mr. Magoo's Christmas Carol* (Dec. 18, 1962); *The Dangerous Christmas of Red Riding Hood* (Nov. 28, 1965).—**WR**

Merrill, Robert, noted American baritone; b. N.Y., June 4, 1917. He first studied voice with his mother, Lillian Miller Merrill, a concert singer; subsequently took lessons with Samuel Margolis. He began his career as a popular singer on the radio; then made his operatic debut as Amonasro in Trenton, N.J., in 1944. After winning the Metropolitan Opera Auditions of the Air in N.Y., he made his debut there with the Metropolitan Opera on Dec. 15, 1945, as Germont. He remained on the roster of the Metropolitan Opera until 1976, and was again on its roster in 1983–84; he also gave solo recitals. In 1961 he made his European operatic debut as Germont in Venice; sang that same role at his Covent Garden debut in London in 1967. He became a highly successful artist through many radio, television, and film appearances; gave recitals and sang with the major American orchs.; also starred in *Fiddler on the Roof* and other popular musicals. Among his numerous roles were Don José, Iago, Figaro, Rigoletto, Ford, and Scarpia. He publ. 2 autobiographical books, *Once More from the Beginning* (N.Y., 1965) and *Between Acts* (N.Y., 1977). In 1993 he was awarded the National Medal of Arts. —**NS/LK/DM**

Merriman, Nan (actually, **Katherine-Ann**), American mezzo-soprano; b. Pittsburgh, April 28, 1920. She studied with Alexia Bassian in Los Angeles. She made her operatic debut as La Cieca in *La Gioconda* with the Cincinnati Summer Opera in 1942. From 1943 she sang with Toscanini and the NBC Sym. Orch. She also appeared in opera at Aix-en-Provence, Edinburgh, and Glyndebourne. She retired in 1965. Her best operatic roles were Gluck's Orfeo, Maddalena in *Rigoletto*, Dorabella in *Così fan tutte*, Emilia in *Otello*, Baba the Turk in *The Rake's Progress*, and Meg in *Falstaff*.—**NS/LK/DM**

Merritt, A(rthur) Tillman, American musicologist and pedagogue; b. Calhoun, Mo., Feb. 15, 1902. He studied at the Univ. of Mo. (B.A., 1924; B.F.A., 1926) and

Harvard Univ. (M.A., 1927), then went to Europe on a J.K. Paine traveling scholarship from Harvard, and studied in Paris with Boulanger and Dukas. Upon his return to America, he taught at Trinity Coll. in Hartford, Conn. (1930–32). In 1932 he joined the faculty of the music dept. of Harvard Univ., serving as its chairman from 1942 to 1952 and from 1968 to 1972, when he retired. He publ. the valuable treatise *Sixteenth-century Polyphony: A Basis for the Study of Counterpoint* (Cambridge, Mass., 1939), and also ed. works by Janequin. On his retirement, he was honored with a Festschrift, *Words and Music: The Scholar's View* (Cambridge, Mass., 1972).—NS/LK/DM

Merritt, Chris (Allan), American tenor; b. Oklahoma City, Sept. 27, 1952. Following studies at Oklahoma City Univ. and the Santa Fe Opera, he made his formal operatic debut in 1978 as Rossini's Lindoro at the Salzburg Landestheater. In 1981 he made his first appearance at the N.Y.C. Opera as Bellini's Arturo, and from 1981 to 1984 he sang at the Augsburg Opera. He made his debut at the Paris Opéra as Aaron in *Mosè in Egitto* in 1983. Following his debut at London's Covent Garden as James in *La donna del Lago* in 1985, he appeared as Rossini's Arnoldo at Milan's La Scala in 1988. He sang Gluck's Admète at the Lyric Opera in Chicago in 1990. In 1995 he sang the role of Aron in Schoenberg's *Moses und Aron* in Amsterdam. He sang in the premiere of Henze's *Venus und Adonis* in Munich in 1997. As a concert artist, Merritt has appeared with many major orchs. While he has been most notably successful in operas by Rossini, Bellini, and Donizetti, he has also been admired for his portrayals of Idomeneo, Aeneas, and Rodolfo.—NS/LK/DM

Mersenne, Marin, eminent French mathematician, philosopher, and music theorist; b. La Soultière, near Oizei, Sept. 8, 1588; d. Paris, Sept. 1, 1648. He studied at the college of Le Mans, then at the Jesuit School at La Flèche (from 1604) and at the Collège Royal and the Sorbonne in Paris from 1609. He began his novitiate at the Nigeon monastery, near Paris (1611), completing it at St. Pierre de Fublaines, near Meaux, where he took holy orders (1612). He then served the Minim monastery at the Paris Place Royale, becoming a deacon and a priest. He taught philosophy (1615–17) and theology (1618) at the Nevers monastery, and then was made correcter there. In 1619 he returned to Paris as conventual of the order. He made 3 trips to Italy between 1640 and 1645. He maintained a correspondence with the leading philosophers and scientists of his time. His writings provide source material of fundamental importance for the history of 17th-century music. An exhaustive edition of his complete correspondence was publ. in 17 vols. (Paris, 1932–88).

WRITINGS (all publ. in Paris): *Quaestiones celeberrimae in Genesim* (1623); *Traité de l'harmonie universelle* (1627); *Questions harmoniques* (1634); *Les préludes de l'harmonie universelle* (1634); *Harmonicorum libri, in quibus agitur de sonorum natura* (1635–36); *Harmonicorum instrumentorum libri IV* (1636; publ. with the preceding as *Harmonicorum libri XII*, 1648; 2nd ed., 1652); etc.

BIBL.: H. Ludwig, *M. M. und seine Musiklehre* (Halle and Berlin, 1935); F. Hyde, *The Position of M. M. in the History of Music* (diss., Yale Univ., 1954).—NS/LK/DM

Mersmann, Hans, distinguished German musicologist; b. Potsdam, Oct. 6, 1891; d. Cologne, June 24, 1971. He studied in Munich with Sandberger and Kroyer, in Leipzig with Riemann and Schering, and with Wolf and Kretzschmar at the Univ. of Berlin, where he received his Ph.D. in 1914 with the diss. *Christian Ludwig Boxberg und seine Oper "Sardanapalus" (Ansbach 1698), mit Beiträgen zur Ansbacher Musikgeschichte*; completed his Habilitation at the Berlin Technische Hochschule in 1921 with his *Grundlagen einer musikalischen Volksliedforschung* (publ. in Leipzig, 1930); was a reader there from 1927. He subsequently taught at the Stern Cons. in Berlin, and at the Technische Hochschule there, until 1933. He was in charge of the folk song archives of the Prussian Volksliederkommission (1917–33), and also organized numerous seminars on musicology and modern music; from 1924, ed. the periodical *Melos*; wrote music criticism. He was removed from all of his positions by the Nazi regime in 1933; then devoted himself to private musicological research. After the collapse of the 3rd Reich, he taught at the Staatliche Hochschule für Musik in Munich (1946–47); from 1947 to 1958 he was director of the Hochschule für Musik in Cologne. As a historian and analyst of modern music, Mersmann occupied an important position in 20th-century research.

WRITINGS: *Kulturgeschichte der Musik in Einzeldarstellungen* (4 vols., Berlin, 1921–25); *Angewandte Musikästhetik* (Berlin, 1926); *Das Musikseminar* (Leipzig, 1931); *Kammermusik* (vols. 2–4, Leipzig, 1930; vol. 1, Leipzig, 1933); *Eine deutsche Musikgeschichte* (Potsdam, 1934; 2nd ed., rev. and aug., 1955, as *Musikgeschichte in der abendländischen Kultur*; 3rd ed., 1973); *Volkslied und Gegenwart* (Potsdam, 1936); *Musikhören* (Berlin, 1938; aug. ed., 1952); *Neue Musik in den Strömungen unserer Zeit* (Bayreuth, 1949); *Die Kirchenmusik im XX. Jahrhundert* (Nuremberg, 1958); *Stilprobleme der Werkanalyse* (Mainz, 1963).

BIBL.: W. Wiora, ed., *Musikerkenntnis und Musikziehung. Dankesgaben für H. M. zu seinem 65. Geburtstag* (Kassel, 1957).—NS/LK/DM

Mertz, Caspar Joseph, Austrian guitarist and composer; b. Pressburg, Aug. 17, 1806; d. Vienna, Oct. 14, 1856. He moved to Vienna in 1840, giving concerts there and in Germany, using a 10-string guitar. His works for the guitar enjoyed a modicum of popularity, and his Concertino received 1st prize at the International Competition in Brussels in 1856. He was married to the pianist Josephine Plantin.

BIBL.: A. Stempnik, *C.J. M., Leben und Werk des letzten Gitarristen im össteichischen Biedermeier: Eine Studie über den Niedergang der Gitarre in wien um 1850* (Frankfurt am Main, 1990).—NS/LK/DM

Merula, Tarquinio, significant Italian organist and composer; b. Cremona, 1594 or 1595; d. there, Dec. 10, 1665. In 1616 he received an appointment as organist of S. Maria Incoronata in Lodi. In 1621 he went to Poland, where he served as court organist. Returning to Italy, he became provisional maestro di cappella for the

Laudi della Madonna at Cremona Cathedral in 1626. He then held a regular appointment from 1627, and also became organist of the collegiate church of S. Agata in 1628. He was appointed maestro di cappella of S. Maria Maggiore in Bergamo in 1631, but was dismissed in 1632 for "indecency" shown toward several of his pupils. He then returned to Cremona, where he became maestro di cappella for the Laudi della Madonna at the Cathedral in 1633; however, a dispute with his superiors over salary and other matters led to his resignation in 1635. By 1638 he had found a position as maestro di cappella and organist to the Cathedral in Bergamo next to S. Maria Maggiore. Disagreements with his former employers at S. Maria Maggiore soon developed, and he finally returned to Cremona in 1646 as Cathedral organist and as organist and maestro di cappella for the Laudi della Madonna, holding these positions until his death. He was a versatile composer and wrote both secular and sacred music; remarkably enough for a church organist, he also wrote instrumental music in a concertante style, his ensemble canzonas being especially fine. See A. Sutkowski, ed., *Tarquinio Merula: Opere complete*, I/i (Brooklyn, 1974).

WORKS: VOCAL: S a c r e d : *Il primo libro de motetti e sonate concertati*, op.6, for 2 to 5 Voices (Venice, 1624); *Libro secondo de concerti spirituali con alcune sonate*, op.8, for 2 to 5 Voices (Venice, 1628); *Pegaso...salmi, motetti, suonate...* for 2 to 5 Voices, *libro terzo*, op.11 (c. 1633–37); *Concerto...messi, salmi...concertati*, op.15, for 2 to 8 and 12 Voices, with Instruments (Venice, 1639); *Arpa Davidica...salmi, et messe*, op.16, a 4 (Venice, 1640); *Il terzo libro delle salmi et messa concertati*, op.18, a 3–4 (Venice, 1652). **S e c u l a r :** *La finta savia*, opera in collaboration with others (Venice, 1643); *Il primo libro de madrigaletti*, op.4, for 3 Voices and Basso Continuo (Venice, 1624); *Il primo libro de madrigali concertate*, op.5, for 4 to 8 Voices and Basso Continuo (Venice, 1624); *Satiro e Corisca dialogo musicale*, op.7, for 2 Voices and Basso Continuo (Venice, 1626); *Madrigali et altre musiche concertate a 1–5, libro secondo*, op.10 (Venice, 1633); *Curtio precipitato et altri capricii, libro secondo*, op.13, for 1 Voice (Venice, 1638); *Canzonetta a 3 et 4*, op.14? (date unknown; not extant). **I N S T R U M E N T A L :** *Il primo libro delle canzoni, a 4*, op.1 (Venice, 1615); *Il secondo libro delle canzoni da suonare*, op.9, for 3 Instruments and Basso Continuo (c. 1631–33); *Canzoni overo sonate concertate per chiesa e camera, a 2–3, libro terzo*, op.12 (Venice, 1637); *Il quarto libro delle canzoni da suonare, a 2–3*, op.17 (Venice, 1651).—**NS/LK/DM**

Merulo (real name, **Merlotti**), **Claudio,** important Italian composer, organist, and music publisher, called da Correggio; b. Correggio, April 8, 1533; d. Parma, May 4, 1604. He studied with Tuttovale Menon and Girolamo Donato. On Oct. 21, 1556, he became organist at the Cathedral in Brescia, succeeding Vincenzo Parabosco. On July 2, 1557, was chosen as 2nd organist at San Marco in Venice, and in 1566 he succeeded Padovano as 1st organist, a position he held until 1584. He composed a number of works for state occasions, including intermedi to Frangipane's *Tragedia* for the visit of Henry III of France in 1574. Active as a music publisher between 1566 and 1570, he brought out several first eds. of his own works, as well as of works by Primavera, Porta, and Wert. In 1586 he was appointed organist at the court of the Duke of Parma; in 1591

became organist to the company of the Steccata, a position he retained until his death. Merulo was one of the most famous organists of his time. As a composer, he was an important representative of the Venetian school. His organ music is of especial merit; he also composed church music and madrigals. An edition of his sacred music, ed. by J. Bastian in Corpus Mensurabilis Musicae, began publication in 1970. For his instrumental works, see S. Dalla Libera, *Claudio Merulo: Toccate per organo*, I-III (Milan, 1959).

WORKS: INSTRUMENTAL: *Ricercari d'intabolatura d'organo...libro primo* (Venice, 1567); *Messe d'intavolatura d'organo* (Venice, 1568); *Il primo libro de ricercari da cantare a 4* (Venice, 1574); *Canzoni d'intavolatura d'organo a 4 fatte alla francese* (Venice, 1592); *Toccate d'intavolatura d'organo, libro primo* (Rome, 1598); *Toccate d'intavolatura d'organo, libro secondo* (Rome, 1604); *Libro secondo di canzoni d'intavolatura d'organo a fatte alla francese* (Venice, 1606); *Ricercari da cantare a 4...libro secondo* (Venice, 1607); *Ricercari da cantare a 4...libro terzo* (Venice, 1608); *Terzo libro de canzoni d'intavolatura d'organo a 5 fatte alla francese* (Venice, 1611). **V O C A L : S a c r e d :** *Missarum liber primus* for 5 Voices (Venice, 1573); *Liber primus sacrarum cantionum* for 5 Voices (Venice, 1578); *Liber secundus sacrarum cantionum* for 5 Voices (Venice, 1578); *Il primo libro de motetti* for 6 Voices (Venice, 1583); *Il primo libro de motetti* for 4 Voices (Venice, 1584); *Il secondo libro de motetti* for 6 Voices (Venice, 1593); *Sacrorum concentuum* for 5, 8, 10, 12, and 16 Voices (Venice, 1594); *Il terzo libro de motetti* for 6 Voices (Venice, 1605); *Misse due* for 8 and 12 Voices, with Organ (Venice, 1609). **S e c u l a r :** *Il primo libro de madrigali* for 5 Voices (Venice, 1566); *Il primo libro de madrigali* for 4 Voices (Venice, 1579); *Il primo libro de madrigali* for 3 Voices (Venice, 1580); *Il secondo libro de madrigali* for 5 Voices (Venice, 1580). **OTHER:** Intermedi to L. Dolce's drama *Le Troiane* (1566) and Frangipane's *Tragedia* (Venice, July 21, 1574).

BIBL.: Q. Bigi, *Di C. M. da Correggio* (Parma, 1861); *C. M. da Correggio* (Parma, 1905; essays by 8 Italian scholars); L. Debes, *Die musikalischen Werke von C. M. (1533–1604)* (diss., Julius-Maximilians Univ., Würzburg, 1964); J. Bastian, *The Sacred Music of C. M.* (diss., Univ. of Mich., 1967).—**NS/LK/DM**

Mesangeau, René, notable French lutenist, teacher, and composer; b. place and date unknown; d. Paris, 1638. He was an equerry at the French court by 1619, serving as a musicien ordinaire du Roi to Louis XIII from 1621 until his death. Many of his lute pieces appeared in contemporary editions. See A. Souris and M. Rollin, eds., *Oeuvres de René Mesangeau*, Corpus des luthistes français (Paris, 1971).—**LK/DM**

Messager, André (Charles Prosper), celebrated French composer and conductor; b. Montiuçon, Allier, Dec. 30, 1853; d. Paris, Feb. 24, 1929. He studied at the École Niedermeyer in Paris with Gigout, Fauré, and Saint-Saëns (composition), A. Lassel (piano), and C. Loret (organ). In 1874 he became organist at St.-Sulpice. He was active as a conductor at the Folies-Bergère, where he produced several ballets. After conducting Brussels's Eden-Théâtre (1880), he returned to Paris as organist of St. Paul-St. Louis (1881) and as maître de chapelle at Ste. Marie-des-Baugnolles (1882–84). He subsequently was music director at the Opéra-Comique (1898–1903); also managed the Grand Opera Syndicate at London's Covent Garden (1901–07). He was conductor of the Concerts Lamoureux (1905) and music director of the Paris Opéra (1907–14); was also conductor of the Société des Concerts da Conservatoire from 1908 until 1919; under the auspices of the French government, he visited the U.S. with that orch., giving concerts in 50 American cities (1918); also toured Argentina (1916). Returning to Paris, he again conducted at the Opéra-Comique; led a season of Diaghilev's Ballets Russes in 1924. As a conductor, Messager played an important role in Paris musical life; he conducted the premiere of *Pelléas et Mélisande* (1902), the score of which Debussy dedicated to him. His initial steps as a composer were auspicious; his Sym. (1875) was awarded the gold medal of the Société des Compositeurs and performed at the Concerts Colonne (Jan. 20, 1878); his dramatic scene *Don Juan et Haydée* (1876) was awarded a gold medal by the Academy of St. Quentin. He wrote several other works for orch. (*Impressions orientals, Suite funambulesque*, etc.) and some chamber music, but he was primarily a man of the theater. His style may be described as enlightened eclecticism; his music was characteristically French, and more specifically Parisian, in its elegance and gaiety. He was honored in France; in 1926 he was elected to the Académie des Beaux Arts. He was married to Hope Temple (real name, Dotie Davis; 1858–1938), who was the author of numerous songs. His stage works (1st perf. in Paris unless otherwise given) included *François les-Bas-Bleus* (Nov. 8, 1883; score begun by F. Bernicat and completed after his death by Messager), *La Fauvette du temple* (Nov. 17, 1885), *La Béarnaise* (Dec. 12, 1885), *Le Bourgeois de Calais* (April 6, 1887), *Isoine* (Dec. 26, 1888), *La Basoche* (May 30, 1890; greatly acclaimed), *Madame Chrysanthème* (Jan. 26, 1893; to a story similar to Puccini's *Madame Butterfly*, produced 11 years later; but Puccini's dramatic treatment eclipsed Messager's lyric setting), *Le Chavalier d'Harmental* (May 5, 1896), *Véronique* (Dec. 10, 1898), *Les Dragons de l'impératrice* (Feb. 13, 1905), *Fortunio* (June 5, 1907), *Béatrice* (Monte Carlo, March 21, 1914), and *Monsieur Beaucaire* (Birmingham, April 7, 1919). Other stage works were *Le Mart de la Reine* (Dec. 18, 1889), *Mies Dollar* (Jan. 22, 1893), *La Fiancée* en loterie (Feb. 15, 1896), *Les Pittes Michu* (Nov. 18, 1897), *La Petite Fonctionnaire* (May 14, 1921), and *Passionnément* (Jan. 15, 1926). His ballets included *Fleur d'oranger* (1878), *Les Vins de France* (1879), *Mignons et villains* (1879), *Les Deux Pigeons* (1886), *Scaramouche* (1891), *Amants éternels* (1893), *Le Chevalier aux fleurs* (1897), *Le Procès des roses* (1897), and *Une Aventure de la guimard* (1900). He also wrote incidental music.

BIBL.: H. Février, *A. M.: Mon maître, mon ami* (Paris, 1948); M. Augé-Laribé, *A. M.: Musicien de théâtre* (Paris, 1951); J. Wagstaff, *A. M.: A Bio-Bibliography* (N.Y., 1991).—NS/LK/DM

Messchaert, Johannes (Martinus),

Dutch baritone; b. Hoorn, Aug. 22, 1857; d. Zürich, Sept. 9, 1922. He studied violin, then changed to singing, studying with Stockhausen in Frankfurt am Main and Wüllner in Munich. He began his career as a choral conductor in Amsterdam, then appeared as a singer of the German repertoire. He was prof. of voice at the Berlin Königliche Hochschule für Musik (1911–20) and at the Zürich Cons. (1920–22).

BIBL.: F. Martienssen, *J. M.: Ein Beitrag zum Verständnis echter Gesangskunst* (Berlin, 1914; 2nd ed., 1920).—NS/LK/DM

Messiaen, Olivier (Eugène Prosper Charles),

outstanding French composer and pedagogue; b. Avignon, Dec. 10, 1908; d. Clichy, Hauts-de-Seine, April 27, 1992. A scion of an intellectual family (his father was a translator of English literature; his mother, Cécile Sauvage, a poet), he absorbed the atmosphere of culture and art as a child. A mystical quality was imparted by his mother's book of verses *L'Âme en bourgeon*, dedicated to her as yet unborn child. He learned to play piano; at the age of 8, he composed a song, *La Dame de Shalott*, to a poem by Tennyson. At the age of 11, he entered the Paris Cons., where he attended the classes of Jean and Noël Gallon, Dupré, Emmanuel, and Dukas, specializing in organ, improvisation, and composition; he carried 1st prizes in all these depts. After graduation in 1930, he became organist at the Trinity Church in Paris. He taught at the École Normale de Musique and at the Schola Cantorum (1936–39). He also organized, with Jolivet, Baudrier, and Daniel-Lesur, the group La Jeune France, with the aim of promoting modern French music. He was in the French army at the outbreak of World War II in 1939; was taken prisoner; spent 2 years in a German prison camp in Görlitz, Silesia; he composed there his *Quatuor pour la fin du temps*; was repatriated in 1941 and resumed his post as organist at the Trinity Church in Paris. He was prof. of harmony and analysis at the Paris Cons. (from 1948). He also taught at the Berkshire Music Center in Tanglewood (summer, 1948) and in Darmstadt (1950–53). Young composers seeking instruction in new music became his eager pupils; among them were Boulez, Stockhausen, Xenakis, and others who were to become important composers in their own right. He received numerous honors; was made a Grand Officier de la Légion d'Honneur; was elected a member of the Institut de France, the Bavarian Academy of the Fine Arts, the Accademia di Santa Cecilia in Rome, the American Academy of Arts and Letters, and other organizations. He married **Yvonne Loriod** in 1961.

Messiaen was one of the most original of modern composers; in his music, he made use of a wide range of resources, from Gregorian chant to oriental rhythms. A mystic by nature and Catholic by religion, he strove to find a relationship between progressions of musical sounds and religious concepts; in his theoretical writing, he postulated an interdependence of modes, rhythms, and harmonic structures. Ever in quest of new musical resources, he employed in his scores the Ondes Martenot and exotic percussion instruments; a synthesis of these disparate tonal elements found its culmination in his grandiose orch. work *Turangalîla-Symphonie*. One of the most fascinating aspects of Messiaen's innovative musical vocabulary was the phonetic emulation of bird song in several of his works; in order to attain ornithological fidelity, he made a detailed study notating the rhythms and pitches of singing birds in many regions of several countries. The municipal council of Parowan, Utah, where Messiaen wrote his work *Des canyons aux étoiles*, glorifying the natural beauties of the state of Utah, resolved to name a local mountain Mt. Messiaen on Aug. 5, 1978. On Nov. 28, 1983, his opera, *St. François d'Assise*, was premiered, to international acclaim, at the Paris Opéra.

WORKS: DRAMATIC: Opera: *St. François d'Assise* (Paris Opéra, Nov. 28, 1983). **ORCH.:** Fugue (1928); *Le Banquet eucharistique* (1928); *Simple chant d'une âme* (1930); *Les Offrandes oubliées* (1930; Paris, Feb. 19, 1931); *Le Tombeau resplendissant* (1931; Paris, Feb. 12, 1933); *Hymne au Saint Sacrement* (1932; Paris, March 23, 1933); *L'Ascension* (1933; Paris, Feb. 1935); *3 Talas* for Piano and Orch. (Paris, Feb. 14, 1948); *Turangalîla-Symphonie* (1946–48; Boston, Dec. 2, 1949); *Réveil des oiseaux* for Piano and Orch. (Donaueschingen, Oct. 11, 1953); *Oiseaux exotiques* for Piano, 2 Wind Instruments, Xylophone, Glockenspiel, and Percussion (Paris, March 10, 1956); *Chronochromie* (Donaueschingen, Oct. 16, 1960); *7 Haï-kaï* for Piano, 13 Wind Instruments, Xylophone, Marimba, 4 Percussion Instruments, and 8 Violins (1962; Paris, Oct. 30, 1963); *Couleurs de la cité céleste* for Large Orch., with imitations of 2 New Zealand birds and 1 from Brazil (Donaueschingen, Oct. 17, 1964); *Et expecto resurrectionem mortuorum* for 18 Woodwinds, 16 Brass Instruments, and 3 Percussion Instruments (1964; Paris, May 7, 1965); *Des canyons aux étoiles* (1970–74; N.Y., Nov. 20, 1974); *Éclairs sur l'Au- Delà* (1987–91; N.Y., Nov. 5, 1992). **CHAMBER:** *Thème et variations* for Violin and Piano (1932); *Quatuor pour la fin du temps* for Violin, Clarinet, Cello, and Piano (Stalag 8A, Görlitz, Jan. 15, 1941, composer pianist); *Le Merle noir* for Flute and Piano (1951); *Le Tombeau de Jean-Pierre Guézec* for Horn (1971). **KEYBOARD: Piano:** *8 Préludes* (1929); *Pièce pour le tombeau de Paul Dukas* (1935); *Visions de l'Amen* for 2 Pianos (1942); *20 regards sur l'enfant Jésus* (1944); *Cantéyodjayâ* (1948); *4 études de rythme* (1949); *Catalogue d'oiseaux* (1956–58). **Organ:** *Variations écossaises* (1928); *Le Banquet céleste* (1928); *Diptyque* (1929); *Apparition de l'église éternelle* (1932); *L'Ascension* (1934; based on the orch. piece, 1933); *La Nativité du Seigneur* (1935); *Les Corps glorieux* (1939); *Messe de la Pentecôte* (1950); *Livre d'orgue* (1951); *Verset pour la fête de la dédicace* (1960); *Méditations sur le mystère de la Sainte Trinité* (1969). **VOCAL:** *2 ballades de Villon* (1921); *3 mélodies* (1930); *La Mort du nombre* for Soprano, Tenor, Violin, and Piano (1930; Paris, March 25, 1931); *Mass* for 8 Sopranos and 4 Violins (1933); *Poèmes pour Mi* for Soprano and Piano (1936; Paris, April 28, 1937; orch. version, 1937; Paris, 1946); *O sacrum convivium!* for Chorus and Organ (1937); *Chants de terre et de ciel*, song cycle for Soprano and Piano, after texts by the composer (1938); *Choeurs pour une Jeanne d'Arc* for Chorus (1941); *3 petites liturgies de la Présence Divine* for 18 Sopranos, Piano, Ondes Martenot, and Orch. (1944; Paris, April 21, 1945); *Harawi*, "chant d'amour et de mort," for Soprano and Piano (1945); *5 réchants* for Chamber Chorus (1949); *La Transfiguration de Notre Seigneur Jésus-Christ* for Chorus and Orch. (Lisbon, June 7, 1969).

WRITINGS: *20 leçons de solfèges modernes* (Paris, 1933); *20 leçons d'harmonie* (Paris, 1939); *Technique de mon langage musical* (2 vols., Paris, 1944; Eng. tr., 1957, as *The Technique of My Musical Language*).

BIBL.: B. Gavoty, *Musique et mystique: Le "Cas" M.* (Paris, 1945); V. Zinke-Bianchini, *O. M. Notice biographique; catalogue détaillé des oeuvres éditées* (Paris, 1946); C. Rostand, *O. M.* (Paris, 1958); A. Goléa, *Rencontres avec O. M.* (Paris, 1961); C. Samuel, *Entretiens avec O. M.* (Paris, 1967); S. Waumsley, *The Organ Music of O. M.* (Paris, 1969; rev. 1975); R. Johnson, *M.* (Berkeley, 1975); R. Nichols, *M.* (London, 1975; 2nd ed., 1985); C. Bell, *O. M.* (Boston, 1984); P. Griffiths, *O. M. and the Music of Time* (London, 1985); J. Gallatin, *An Overview of the Compositional Methods in Representative Works of O. M.* (diss., Univ. of Cincinnati, 1986); A.

Michaely, *Die Musik O. M.s: Untersuchungen zum Gesamtschaffen* (Hamburg, 1987); T. Hirsbrunner, *O. M., Leben und Werk* (Laaber, 1988); B. Carl, *O. M.s Orchesterwerk des Canyons aux Etoiles* (Kassel, 2 vols., 1994); P. Hill, ed., *The M. Companion* (London, 1994); J. Boivin, *La classe de M.* (Paris, 1995); S. Bruhn, *Images and Ideas in Modern French Piano Music: The Extra-Musical Subtext in Piano Works by Ravel, Debussy, and M.* (Stuyvesant, N.Y., 1997); idem, ed., *M.'s Language of Mystical Love* (N.Y., 1998); M. Pople, *M.: Quatuor pour la fin du temps* (Cambridge, 1998).—**NS/LK/DM**

Messner, Joseph, Austrian organist, conductor, and composer; b. Schwaz, Tirol, Feb. 27, 1893; d. St. Jakob Thurn, near Salzburg, Feb. 23, 1969. He studied at the Univ. of Innsbruck, and after his ordination (1918) he took courses in organ and composition with Friedrich Klose at the Munich Akademie der Tonkunst. In 1922 he was appointed Cathedral organist in Salzburg, and from 1926 to 1967 he led the concerts at the Salzburg Cathedral; at the same time, he gave a seminar in church music at the Mozarteum there. He wrote 4 operas: *Hadassa* (Aachen, March 27, 1925), *Das letzte Recht* (1932), *Ines* (1933), and *Agnes Bernauer* (1935), as well as 3 syms., Violin Concerto, Cello Concerto, String Quartet, and several sacred works, including 11 masses.—**NS/LK/DM**

Mester, Jorge, Hungarian-American conductor and teacher; b. Mexico City (of Hungarian parents), April 10, 1935. He settled in the U.S. and became a naturalized American citizen in 1968. He studied with Morel at the Juilliard School of Music in N.Y. (M.A., 1958), and also with Bernstein at the Berkshire Music Center in Tanglewood (summer, 1955) and with A. Wolff in the Netherlands. From 1956 to 1967 he taught conducting at the Juilliard School of Music. In 1967 he was appointed music director of the Louisville Orch., holding this post until 1979. Following the Louisville Orch.'s unique policy of commissioning new works and then giving their premieres, Mester conducted, during his tenure, something like 200 first performances, and made about 70 recordings of some of them. Concurrently, he served as musical adviser and principal conductor of the Kansas City Phil. (1971–74). In 1970 he became music director of the Aspen (Colo.) Music Festival. From 1980 he again taught at the Juilliard School, where he was chairman of the conducting dept. (1984–87). In 1984 he became music director of the Pasadena (Calif.) Sym. Orch. He also was concurrently music director of the West Australian Sym. Orch. in Perth (1990–93). From 1999 he was music director of the Filarmónica de la Ciudad de México in Mexico City. Equally at home in the classical and modern repertoires, in symphonic music and in opera, Mester knows how to impart a sense of color with a precision of technical detail. —**NS/LK/DM**

Mestres-Quadreny, Josep (Maria), Spanish composer; b. Manresa, March 4, 1929. He studied composition with Taltabull at the Univ. of Barcelona (1950–56). In 1960 he collaborated in the founding of Música Abierta, an organization of avant-garde musical activity; later he joined composers Xavier Benguerel, Joaquim Homs, and Josep Soler in founding the Conjunt Català de Música Contemporània, for the propagation of Catalan music. In his music, he consciously attempts to find a counterpart to Abstract Expressionism in art, as exemplified by the paintings of Miró; for this purpose he applies serial techniques and aleatory procedures.

WORKS: DRAMATIC: O p e r a : *El Ganxo* (1959). B a l l e t : *Roba i ossos* (1961); *Petit diumenge* (1962); *Vegetació submergida* (1962). M u s i c T h e a t e r : *Concert per a representar* for 6 Voices, 6 Instrumentalists, and Tape (1964); *Suite bufa* for Ballerina, Mezzo-soprano, Piano, and Electronic Sound (1966). ORCH.: *Triade per a Joan Miró* (1961; a superimposition of *Música da cámara I* for Flute, Piano, Percussion, Violin, and Double Bass, *Música da cámara II* for 3 Clarinets, English Horn, Trumpet, Trombone, Percussion, and String Trio, and *3 Moviments per a orquesta de cámara* for 15 Instruments); *Digodal* for Strings (1963); *Conversa* for Chamber Orch. (1965); *Quadre* for Chamber Orch. (1969); Double Concerto for Ondes Martenot, Percussion, and Orch. (1970). CHAMBER: Piano Sonata (1957); *3 invenció mòvils: I* for Flute, Clarinet, and Piano, *II* for Voice, Trumpet, and Electric Guitar, and *III* for String Quartet (all 1961); *Tramesa a Tàpies* for Violin, Viola, and Percussion (1961); *Quartet de Catroc* for String Quartet (1962); *3 cànons en homenatge a Galile*, in 3 versions: for Piano (1965), for Percussion (1968), and for Ondes Martenot (1969), each with Tape; String Trio (1968); *Ibemia* for 13 Instrumentalists (1969); *Micos i Papellones* for Guitar and Metal Percussion (1970); *Variacions essencials* for String Trio and Percussion (1970); *Homenatge a Joan Prats* for 6 Actors, Electroacoustical Installation, String Quartet, 4 Percussionists, Flute, Clarinet, Trumpet, 2 Trombones, and Tuba (1972); *Frigoli-Frigola* for Any Instruments (1969); *Aronada* for Any Instruments (1972). VOCAL: *Epitafios*, cantata for Soprano, Strings, Harp, and Celesta (1958); *Tríptic carnavalesc*, cantata for Soprano, Flute, Clarinet, Trumpet, Trombone, 2 Percussionists, and Piano (1966); *Música per a Anna* for Soprano and String Quartet (1967).—NS/LK/DM

Mestrino, Nicola, Italian violinist and composer; b. Milan, 1748; d. Paris, July 1789. He was a member of Prince Esterházy's orch. under Haydn (1780–85), and then was a chamber musician to Count Erdődy in Pressburg (1785–86). He subsequently settled in Paris, where he played at the Concert Spirituel in 1786. In 1789 he became concertmaster of the orch. at the Théâtre de Monsieur. He composed 12 violin concertos and other works for his instrument, but is best remembered for his didactic *Caprices ou études*.—LK/DM

Metallica, pioneers of the heavy-metal school of rock known variously as speed or thrash metal. MEM-BERSHIP: James (Alan) Hetfield, rhythm gtr., voc. (b. Los Angeles, Aug. 3, 1963); Kirk Hammett, lead gtr. (b. San Francisco, Nov. 18, 1962); Cliff(ord Lee) Burton, bs. (b. Castro Valley, Calif, Feb. 10, 1962; d. Sweden, Sept. 27, 1986); Lars Ulrich, drm. (b. Copenhagen, Denmark, Dec. 26, 1963). Cliff Burton was replaced by Jason Newsted (b. Battle Creek, Mich., March 4, 1963.

Distinguished by its speedy guitar playing and rapid tempos, Metallica achieved their earliest popularity through word-of-mouth communication. Revitalizing heavy-metal music without the pretense and image-pandering of glitter-rock groups while eschewing both the superficial and sexist party themes and pseudo-mythological concerns of their antecedents, Metallica won recognition for their sophisticated yet deafening arrangements and intelligent yet harrowing lyrics. Gradually expanding the band's commercial success without radio, video, or advertising support (drawing comparisons to the Grateful Dead), Metallica have consistently maintained their artistic integrity and fierce commitment to their music. Lauded for their socially conscious themes and brutal honesty, particularly on their album *Master of Puppets*, Metallica were the hit of the 1988 Monsters of Rock tour nominally headlined by Van Halen. Adopting a more thoughtful, mellower approach for their best-selling *Metallica* album, Metallica were one of the most popular American heavy-metal bands of the 1990s.

The evolution of Metallica began when Danish drummer Lars Ulrich recorded a demonstration tape with guitarist James Hetfield in Los Angeles in October 1981. Their first lead guitarist was replaced by Dave Mustaine in January 1982, and bassist Cliff Burton joined at the end of the year. Gaining their first recognition by playing small clubs in Los Angeles and later San Francisco, Metallica moved to Queens, N.Y., where Kirk Hammett replaced Mustaine, who later formed Megadeth in Southern Calif.

With Ulrich and Hetfield as principal songwriters, Metallica recorded their debut album, *Kill 'Em All*, in May 1983. Published and copyrighted by the band and released on the Megaforce label, the album featured earsplitting, rapid-tempo songs often characterized by sudden mood and tempo changes that drew the attention of youthful head-bangers. Their second album, *Ride the Lightning*, also on Megaforce, included "Fight Fire with Fire" and "Creeping Death," and remained on the album charts for nearly a year. Elektra Records soon picked up distribution of Metallica's albums and signed the band. Their debut for the label, *Master of Puppets*, drew praise for its stark social commentary and broke the band into the mass market. The album featured "Battery"; "Leper Messiah," which took to task television evangelists; and the title song, which decried drug addiction.

While touring Sweden, Cliff Burton was killed on Sept. 27, 1986, at age 24, when the group's van crashed on an icy road near Ljungby. He was quickly replaced by Jason Newsted, of the Phoenix-based band Flotsam and Jetsam. In 1987 the band assembled a collection of cover tunes that was issued as *The $5.98 EP: Garage Days Re-Revisited*. In summer 1988, Metallica toured with the Monsters of Rock tour, along with Van Halen, The Scorpions, Dokken, and Kingdom Come. By tour's end they had become the hit of the tour, eclipsing even the headliners. Their diverse album *...And Justice for All* featured "The Frayed Ends of Sanity," the socially conscious "Blackened," and "The Shortest Straw" and yielded their first moderate hit, the ghastly yet moving "One." The album became a best-seller.

Touring for much of 1989, Metallica next recorded the chart-topping album *Metallica*. It exhibited a more thoughtful, slower, almost gentle approach, producing five hits: "Enter Sandman," accompanied by their first video; "The Unforgiven"; the soothing "Nothing Else Matters"; the anthemic "Wherever I May Roam"; and "Sad but True." Metallica subsequently toured as single-act headliners between summer 1991 and summer 1993, playing more than three hundred engagements. In summer 1992 they conducted a seven-week tour with Guns N' Roses in one of the most anticipated tours of the year. Their *Live Sh*t* was drawn from a series of Mexico City concerts.

DISC.: *Kill 'Em All* (1983); *Ride the Lightning* (1984); *Master of Puppets* (1986); *...And Justice for All* (1988); *M.* (1991); *Live Sh*t: Binge and Purge* (1993).—**BH**

Metastasio, Pietro (real name, **Antonio Domenico Bonaventura Trapassi**), famous Italian poet and opera librettist; b. Rome, Jan. 3, 1698; d. Vienna, April 12, 1782. He was the son of a papal soldier named Trapassi, but in his professional career assumed the Greek tr. of the name, both Trapassi (or Trapassamento) and Metastasio meaning transition. He was a learned classicist. He began to write plays as a young boy, and also studied music with Porpora. He achieved great fame in Italy as a playwright. In 1729 he was appointed court poet in Vienna by Emperor Charles VI. He wrote 27 opera texts, which were set to music by Handel, Gluck, Mozart, Hasse, Porpora, Jommelli, and many other celebrated composers; some of them were set to music 60 or more times. His librettos were remarkable for their melodious verse, which naturally suggested musical associations; the libretto to the opera by Niccolo Conforto, *La Nitteti* (1754; Madrid, Sept. 23, 1756), was on the same subject as *Aida*, anticipating the latter by more than a century. Metastasio's complete works were publ. in Paris (12 vols., 1780–82) and Mantua (20 vols., 1816–20); they were ed. by F. Gazzani (Turin, 1968) and by M. Fubino (Milan, 1968); see also A. Wotquenne, *Alphabetisches Verzeichnis der Stücke in Versen ...von Zeno, Metastasio und Goldoni* (Leipzig, 1905).

BIBL.: S. Mattei, *Memorie per servire alla vita del M.* (Colle, 1785); C. Burney, *Memoirs of the Life and Letters of the Abate M.* (London, 1796); M. Zito, *Studio su P. M.* (Naples, 1904); E. Leonardi, *Il melodramma del M.* (Naples, 1909); L. Russo, *P. M.* (Pisa, 1915; 2nd ed., rev., 1921–45, as *M.*); A. della Corte, *L'estetica musicale di P. M.* (Turin, 1922); A. Vullo, *Confronto fra i melodrammi di Zeno e M.* (Agrigento, 1935); B. Brunelli, ed., *Tutte le opere di P. M.* (Milan, 1943–54); M. Muraro, *M. e il mondo musicale* (Florence, 1986); C. Maeder, *M., l'Olimpiade e l'opera del Settecento* (Bologna, 1993).—**NS/LK/DM**

Metcalf, Louis (Jr.), jazz trumpeter, singer; b. Webster Groves, Mo., Feb. 28, 1905; d. N.Y., Oct. 27, 1981. Metcalf played drums, then switched to cornet. He played in the local Knights of Phythias Brass Band, and then spent several years on and off with Charlie Creath. In the summer of 1923 he traveled to N.Y., playing in Jimmie Cooper's revue. During the following year spent several months with Willie "The Lion" Smith at the Rhythm Club. He worked with various N.Y.–based bands until joining Duke Ellington during late 1926–27. During 1928, he worked with Jelly Roll Morton in N.Y., and later that year joined the Luis Russell Orch. After working with other bands and in the Connie's Inn

Revue Orch., he spent three years in Canada during the early 1930s, mainly leading his own band. He returned to N.Y. and joined Fletcher Henderson in March 1935. After brief stints in St. Louis and Chicago, he was back in N.Y. From 1936 onwards, he led his own band (except for a brief spell with Noble Sissle in Cleveland). He also ran his own Heatwave Club in N.Y. during the late 1930s and early 1940s. He left N.Y. in 1947, moved to Canada, and organized and directed his own international band there until 1950. After a brief spell away from the music scene, he returned to N.Y. in 1951 and began leading his own small groups through the 1960s. He recovered from serious illness during 1969 and once again formed own small band, leading it until his death in 1981.

DISC.: *Louis Metcalf at the Ali Baba* (1966). **DUKE ELLINGTON:** *Early Ellington: The Complete Brunswick Recordings (1926–31)* (c. 1931); *Jungle Nights in Harlem* (1927); *Okeh Ellington* (1927); *Rockin' in Rhythm [Jazz Hour]* (1927); *Jubilee Stomp* (1928); *Beyond Category* (1994).—**JC/LP**

Metheny, Pat(rick Bruce), fusion-jazz guitarist, composer; b. Lee's Summit, Mo., Aug. 12, 1954. Growing up, almost everyone in his family played the trumpet and listened to marching band music. He played trumpet and French horn throughout high school and made his entrance into performing during football games as part of the marching band; however, he found brass instruments made his mouth sore. He was inspired to play jazz when his older brother Mike brought home Miles Davis's album *Four & More*. From age 13, when he took up the guitar, until 19, he practiced constantly, between six and twelve hours per day. He played in Kansas City with Gary Sivils, Paul Smith, Tommy Ruskin, Russ Long, and many others in bebop and post-bop settings, organ trios and the occasional free jazz groups. He left for the Univ. of Miami (Fla.) upon completing high school, did some teaching there, and appeared on a student jazz ensemble recording. Studies at Boston's Berklee Coll. of Music followed; he met Gary Burton there, who hired him to teach at Berklee and to play and record in his band (1974–77). By 1978, he formed the Pat Metheny Group with Lyle Mays, Mark Egan, and Dan Gottlieb. Besides touring and recording with the group, he has done film scores, garnered awards (*Down Beat, Rolling Stone,* Jazziz, International Musician, Recording World, and Grammy awards), and collaborated with a variety of artists including Dewey Redman, Paul Motian, Roy Haynes, Jack DeJohnette, Milton Nascimento, and Ornette Coleman. In 1996, he recorded an album of free improvisations with Derek Bailey, Paul Wertico, and Greg Bendian; he also did a U.S. and European tour with Kenny Garrett's Quartet exploring the music of John Coltrane. The Smithsonian invited him to perform with the Jim Hall Trio as part of a program on the history of the electric guitar. In 1997, he played with Michael Brecker in N.Y., at the Montreal Jazz Festival and in Japan. Among Metheny's scores are *The Search for Solutions by J.C. Crimmins,* (1979), *Walk Me to the Water* (c. 1981), *Little Sister* (1983), *Jerry Goldsmith: Under Fire O.S.T., The Falcon and the Snowman, Fandango* (1984), *It's for You,*

September 15th, Farmer's Trust, Twice in a Lifetime, Grandpa's Ghost (1986), *Lemon Sky* (1987), *Big Time* (1989), *The Silent Alarm* (1993), *Passagio Per Il Paradiso* (1997), and *A Map of the World* (1999). Composer Steve Reich wrote *Electric Counterpoint* for him.

Metheny is a remarkable musician, technically virtuosic, expert at modern technology, unaffected, and harmonically adept. His music ranges from a sweet and folksy kind of fusion, sometimes derided by purists, to straight ahead, to raucous free jazz inspired by a lifelong love of Ornette Coleman's music that culminated in a recording and tour with Coleman in 1985–86. He has also chosen regularly to play with Charlie Haden, Dewey Redman, and other musicians of the Coleman school. The music of Brazil is another lifelong influence.

DISC.: *Bright Size Life* (1975); *Watercolors* (1977); *Pat Metheny Group* (1978); *New Chautauqua* (1979); *Live on Tour* (1979); *Hour with Pat Metheny* (1979); *American Garage* (1980); *1980–81* (1980); *As Falls Wichita, So Falls Wichita Falls* (1981); *Live* (1982); *Offramp* (1982); *Travels* (1983); *Rejoicing* (1983); *First Circle* (1984); *Falcon and the Snowman* (1985); *Still Life (Talking)* (1987); *Question and Answer* (1989); *Letter from Home* (1989); *Zero Tolerance for Silence* (1992); *Secret Story* (1992); *Salt Lake* (bootleg; 1992); *Flower Hour* (live bootleg; 1992); *Secret Storm* (1993); *Road to You-Live in Europe* (1993); *Pat Metheny Group in Concert* (1993); *I Can See Your House from Here* (1993); *Sign of the Four* (1996); *Metheny-Haden* (1997); *Trio 99–00* (2000). **ORNETTE COLEMAN:** *Song X* (1985).—**LP**

Metianu, Lucian, Romanian composer; b. Cluj, June 3, 1937. He studied with Olah, Vancea, Constantinescu, and Chirescu at the Bucharest Cons. (1957–63).

WORKS: ORCH.: Concerto for Strings (1959); *2 Choreographic Tableaux* (1964); *Echo* (1966); *Ergodica* (1967); *Conexe* for Speaking Chorus and Orch. (1969); *Elogiu* (1969); *Evocare* (1972); *Evolutio II* (1976). **CHAMBER:** Piano Quintet (1960); 2 string quartets (1961, 1968); Piano Sonata (1962); *Pithagoreis* for Tape (1970–71); *Evolutio '73*, sonata for Solo Double Bass (1973); Duo for Double Bass and Cello (1974); *Evolutio '74* for Cello (1974). **VOCAL:** *Cantata de camera* for Chorus and Chamber Orch. (1953).—**NS/LK/DM**

Metner, Nikolai (Karlovich)
See **Medtner, Nicolai**

Métra, (Jules-Louis-) Olivier, French composer and conductor; b. Rheims, June 2, 1830; d. Paris, Oct. 22, 1889. He studied with E. Roche, and then at the Paris Cons. (1849–54) with Elwart. He conducted in various Parisian dance halls and theaters. His waltzes, mazurkas, polkas, quadrilles, and other light works were highly popular in his day. He also composed operettas and ballet scores.—**NS/LK/DM**

Mettenleiter, Dominicus, German music historian, brother of **Johann Georg Mettenleiter**; b. Tannhausen, near Ellwangen, May 20, 1822; d. Regensburg, May 2, 1868. He collaborated with his brother in the publication of his *Enchiridion chorale* and publ. on his own several valuable works dealing with music in Bavaria: *Aus der musikalischen Vergangenheit bayrischer*

Städte: Musikgeschichte der Stadt Regensburg (Regensburg, 1866), *Musikgeschichte der Oberpfalz* (Amberg, 1867), etc. He also wrote a biography of his brother (Brixen, 1866) and of Karl Proske (Regensburg, 1868; 2nd ed., 1895). His valuable music collection was incorporated with Proske's library in Regensburg. His cousin, Bernhard Mettenleiter (b. Wallerstein, April 25, 1822; d. Marktheidenfeld, Jan. 14, 1901), was an organist, choirmaster, teacher, and composer.—**NS/LK/DM**

Mettenleiter, Johann Georg, German organist, choirmaster, and composer, brother of **Dominicus Mettenleiter**; b. St. Ulrich, Lohntal, Württemberg, April 6, 1812; d. Regensburg, Oct. 6, 1858. He was a pupil of his uncle, the choirmaster in Wallerstein. After serving as choirmaster of the Oettingen parish church (1837–39), he was choirmaster and organist in Regensburg (1839–58). Mettenleiter was a distinguished composer of sacred music. He publ. *Manuale breve cantionum ac precum liturgicarum* (Regensburg, 1852) and *Enchiridion chorales, sive selectus locupletissimus cantionum liturgicarum* (Regensburg, 1853), both with added organ accompaniment. The latter vol. proved an important milestone in the liturgical music restoration movement. His cousin, Bernhard Mettenleiter (b. Wallerstein, April 25, 1822; d. Marktheidenfeld, Jan. 14, 1901), was an organist, choirmaster, teacher, and composer.

BIBL.: D. Mettenleiter, *J.G. M.: Ein Künstlerbild* (Brixen, 1866).—**LK/DM**

Metternich, Josef, German baritone; b. Hermuhlheim, near Cologne, June 2, 1915. He studied in Berlin and Cologne. After singing in the opera choruses in Bonn and Cologne, he made his operatic debut as Tonio at the Berlin Städtische Oper in 1945. In 1951 he sang the Dutchman at his first appearance at London's Covent Garden. On Nov. 21, 1953, he made his Metropolitan Opera debut in N.Y. as Carlo in *La forza del destino*, and remained on its roster until 1956. In 1954 he became a member of the Bavarian State Opera in Munich, where he created the role of Johannes Kepler in Hindemith's *Die Harmonie der Welt* in 1957. His guest engagements took him to Cologne, Hamburg, Vienna, Milan, Edinburgh, and other European music centers. In 1963 he sang Kothner in *Die Meistersinger von Nürnberg* at the reopening of the National Theater in Munich. He retired from the operatic stage in 1971. From 1965 he was a prof. at the Cologne Hochschule für Musik. Among his other roles were Kurwenal, Wolfram, Amfortas, Amonasro, Jochanaan, and Scarpia.—**NS/LK/DM**

Metzger, Heinz-Klaus, German writer on music; b. Konstanz, Feb. 6, 1932. He studied at the Staatliche Musikhochschule in Freiburg im Breisgau (1949–52), then studied composition with Deutsch in Paris and musicology in Tübingen (1952–54). He qualified in 1956 at the Akademie für Tonkunst in Darmstadt, where he later was active in the Darmstadt summer courses. His theoretical, philosophical, and cultural writings on modern and avant-garde music were influenced by Adorno, who recognized his talent. Metzger co-founded the journal *Musik-Konzepte* with Rainer

Riehn in 1977. His relationship with Sylvano Bussotti led to his remarkable studies of music considered unanalyzable by other writers, by composers including Bussotti, Cage, Schnebel, and Kagel.—**NS/LK/DM**

Metzger-Lattermann, Ottilie, German contralto; b. Frankfurt am Main, July 15, 1878; d. in the concentration camp in Auschwitz, Feb. 1943. She was a pupil of Selma Nicklass-Kempner and Emanuel Reicher in Berlin. In 1898 she made her operatic debut in Halle, and then appeared in Cologne (1900–03), at the Bayreuth Festivals (1901–12), the Hamburg Opera (1903–15), and the Dresden Court Opera (1915–18), and its successor, the State Opera (1918–21). In 1910 she was the first to sing Herodias in *Salome* in London under Beecham's direction. She made guest appearances in Berlin, Vienna, Munich, and other European cities, and in 1923 she toured the U.S. with the German Opera Co. As a Jew, she was forced to leave Germany in 1935 and went to Brussels, where she taught voice. In 1942 she was arrested by the Nazi henchmen and sent to Auschwitz.—**NS/LK/DM**

Metzmacher, Ingo, German conductor; b. Hannover, Nov. 10, 1957. He received training in piano and conducting in Hannover, Salzburg, and Cologne. After serving as pianist in the Ensemble Modern (1981–84), he concentrated his energies on a conducting career. In 1985 he made his debut as an opera conductor with *Le nozze di Figaro* at the Frankfurt am Main Opera. In subsequent seasons, he appeared as a guest conductor with major European opera houses. In 1997 he became Generalmusikdirektor of the Hamburg State Opera and chief conductor of the Hamburg State Phil. Orch. —**NS/LK/DM**

Meulemans, Arthur, eminent Belgian composer; b. Aarschot, May 19, 1884; d. Brussels, June 29, 1966. He was a student of Tinel at the Lemmens Inst. in Mechelen (1900–1906), and then was a prof. there until 1914. In 1916 he founded the Limburg School for organ and song in Hasselt, serving as its director until 1930. He subsequently settled in Brussels, where he was a conductor with the Belgian Radio (1930–42). In 1954 he became president of the Royal Flemish Academy of Fine Arts. Meulemans composed a prodigious body of music, excelling especially as a composer of orch. works.

WORKS: DRAMATIC: O p e r a : *Vikings* (1919); *Adriaen Brouwer* (1926); *Egmont* (1944). ORCH.: 2 cello concertos (1920, 1944); 15 syms.: No. 1 (1931), No. 2 (1933), No. 3, *Dennensymphonie* (1933), No. 4 for Winds and Percussion (1934), No. 5, *Danssymphonie,* for Women's Chorus and Orch. (1939), No. 6, *Zeesymphonie,* for Contralto, Chorus, and Orch. (1940), No. 7, *Zwaneven* (1942), No. 8, *Herfstsymphonie,* for Soloists, Chorus, and Orch. (1942), No. 9 (1943), No. 10, *Psalmen-Symphonie,* for 2 Narrators, Soloists, Chorus, and Orch. (1943), No. 11 (1946), No. 12 (1948), No. 13, *Rembrandt-Symphonie* (1950), No. 14 (1954), and No. 15 (1960); 2 horn concertos (1940, 1961); 3 piano concertos (1941, 1956, 1960); 3 violin concertos (1942, 1946, 1950); Viola Concerto (1942); Flute Concerto (1942); Oboe Concerto (1942); 2 organ concertos (both 1942); Trumpet Concerto (1943); 3 sinfoniettas (1952; 1959–60; 1960); 2 concer-tos for orch. (1953, 1956); Harp Concerto (1953); Timpani Concerto (1954); Harpsichord Concerto (1958); Concerto for 2 Pianos and Orch. (1959); Concerto grosso for Winds, Strings, Harp, and Percussion (1962); symphonic poems, suites, etc. CHAMBER: 5 string quartets (1915, 1932, 1933, 1944, 1952); Piano Quartet (1915); 2 violin sonatas (1915, 1953); 3 wind quintets (1931, 1932, 1958); 2 woodwind trios (1933, 1960); 2 brass trios (1933, 1960); Piano Trio (1941); String Trio (1941); Saxophone Quartet (1953); Viola Sonata (1953); Cello Sonata (1953); Trumpet Sonata (1959); Woodwind Quartet (1962). KEY-BOARD: P i a n o : 3 sonatas (1916, 1917, 1951); *Refleksen* (1923); 3 sonatinas (1927, 1928, 1941); *Préludes* (1951); *Atmosferiliën* (1962). O r g a n : Sonata (1915); 2 syms. (both 1949); 7 *Pieces* (1959); *Pièce heroïque* (1959). VOCAL: Oratorios; choral pieces; songs.

BIBL.: M. Boereboom, *A. M.* (Kortrijk, 1951); *Aan Meester A. M. bij zijn tachtigs verjaardag* (Antwerp, 1964).—**NS/LK/DM**

Mewton-Wood, Noel, remarkable Australian pianist; b. Melbourne, Nov. 20, 1922; d. (suicide) London, Dec. 5, 1953. After training with Seidel at the Melbourne Cons., he went to London and at age 14 was admitted to the Royal Academy of Music. Later he completed his studies with Schnabel. In 1940 he made an auspicious London debut as soloist in Beethoven's 1st Piano Concerto under Beecham's baton. Subsequently he was active as a soloist with orchs., as a recitalist, as a chamber music player, and as an accompanist. In 1947 he appeared at the London Promenade Concerts. His extensive repertoire ranged widely, from the Classics to contemporary scores.—**NS/LK/DM**

Meyer, Ernst Hermann, German musicologist and composer; b. Berlin, Dec. 8, 1905; d. there, Oct. 8, 1988. His father was a medical doctor of artistic interests who encouraged him to study music; he took piano lessons with Walter Hirschberg and played in chamber music groups. During the economic disarray in Germany in the 1920s, Meyer was obliged to do manual labor in order to earn a living. In 1926 he was able to enroll in the Univ. of Berlin, where he studied musicology with Wolf, Schering, Blume, Hornbostel, and Sachs; in 1928 he had additional studies with Besseler at the Univ. of Heidelberg, obtaining his Ph.D. in 1930 with the diss. *Die mehrstimmige Spielmusik des 17. Jahrhunderts in Nord- und Mitteleuropa* (publ. in Kassel, 1934). In 1929 he met Eisler, who influenced him in the political aspect of music. In 1930 he joined the German Communist party. He conducted workers' choruses in Berlin and composed music for the proletarian revue *Der rote Stern.* He also attended classes on film music given by Hindemith. In 1931 he took a course in Marxism- Leninism with Hermann Duncker at the Marxist Workers' School in Berlin. He also began a detailed study of works by modern composers; in his own works, mostly for voices, he developed a style characteristic of the proletarian music of the time, full of affirmative action in march time adorned by corrosive discords, and yet eminently singable. When the Nazis bore down on his world with a different march, he fled to London, where, with the help of Alan Bush, he conducted the Labour Choral Union. During World War II, he participated in the Chorus of the Free German Cultural Union in London and wrote propaganda songs; of these, *Radio Moskau ruft Frau Kramer* was widely broadcast to Germany. In 1948 he went to East Berlin, where he was a prof. and director of the musicological inst. of the Humboldt Univ. until 1970. He was acknowledged as one of the most persuasive theoreticians of socialist realism in music; he founded the periodical *Musik und Gesellschaft*, which pursued the orthodox Marxist line. He publ. *English Chamber Music: The History of a Great Art from the Middle Ages to Purcell* (London, 1946; in Ger. as *Die Kammermusik Alt- Englands*, East Berlin, 1958; new ed., rev., 1982, with D. Poulton as *Early English Chamber Music*), *Das Werk Beethovens und seine Bedeutung für das sozialistisch-realistische Gegenwartsschaffen* (East Berlin, 1970), and the autobiographical *Kontraste-Konflikte* (East Berlin, 1979). A Festschrift was publ. in his honor in Leipzig in 1973.

WORKS: DRAMATIC: Opera: *Reiter der Nacht* (1969–72; Berlin, Nov. 17, 1973). **OTHER:** Film music. **ORCH.:** Sym. for Strings (1946–47; rev. 1958); *Symphonischer Prolog* (1949); Sym. for Piano and Orch. (1961); *Poem* for Viola and Orch. (1962); Violin Concerto (1964); *Serenata pensierosa* (1965); Concerto Grosso (1966); Sym. (1967); Harp Concerto (1969); Toccata (1971); *Divertimento* (1973); Concerto for Orch. with Piano obbligato (1975); *Kontraste, Konflikte* (1977); Viola Concerto (1978); *Sinfonietta* (1980); *Berliner Divertimento* (1981); *Kammersinfonie* (1983; transcription of the 5th String Quartet); *Sinfonische widmung* for Orch. and Concertante Organ (1983). **CHAMBER:** Trio for Flute, Oboe, and Harp (1935); Clarinet Quintet (1944); Piano Trio, *Reflections and Resolution* (1948); 6 string quartets (1956, 1959, 1967, 1974, 1978, 1982); *Sonatina Fantasia* for Solo Violin (1966); Viola Sonata (1979); Piano Trio (1980); Violin Sonata (1984); piano pieces. **VOCAL: Choral:** *Mansfelder Oratorium* (1950); *Nun, Steuermann*, cantata, after Walt Whitman's *Now Voyager* (1946; rev. 1955); *Gesang von der Jugend* for Soloists, Chorus, Children's Chorus, and Orch. (1957); *Das Tor von Buchenwald* (1959); *Der Staat* for Chorus and Orch. (1967); *Lenin hat gesprochen* (1970). **Other:** More than 200 mass songs.

BIBL.: K. Niemann, *E.H. M.: Für Sie porträtiert* (Leipzig, 1975); M. Hansen, ed., *E.H. M.: Das kompositiorische und theoretische Werk* (Leipzig, 1976).—NS/LK/DM

Meyer, Kerstin (Margareta), Swedish mezzo-soprano; b. Stockholm, April 3, 1928. She studied at the Royal Academy of Music (1948–50) and at the Opera School (1950–52) in Stockholm; also at the Accademia Musicale Chigiana in Siena and at the Salzburg Mozarteum. In 1952 she made her operatic debut as Azucena at the Royal Theater in Stockholm, where she subsequently sang regularly; also made guest appearances in numerous European opera centers and toured widely as a concert artist. In 1960 she made her first appearance at London's Covent Garden as Dido in the English-language production of *Les Troyens*. On Oct. 29, 1960, she made her Metropolitan Opera debut in N.Y. as Carmen, remaining on its roster until 1963; also appeared at the Bayreuth Festivals (1962–65). In 1963 she was made a Royal Swedish Court Singer. Following her retirement, she served as director of the Opera School in Stockholm (1984–94). In 1985 she was made an honorary Commander of the Order of the British Empire. She excelled particularly in contemporary operas, most no-

tably in the works of Schuller, Searle, Henze, Maw, and Ligeti; among her standard portrayals were Orfeo, Dorabella, Fricka, Octavian, and Clytemnestra. —NS/LK/DM

Meyer, Krzysztof, remarkable Polish composer and teacher; b. Kraków, Aug. 11, 1943. He commenced piano lessons when he was 5. At 11, he began to take lessons in theory and composition with Wiechowicz. He pursued his training at the Kraków State Higher School of Music with Penderecki (composition diploma, 1965) and Frączkiewicz (theory diploma, 1966). He also studied in Fontainebleau and Paris with Boulanger in 1964, 1966, and 1968. From 1965 to 1968 he was a pianist with the contemporary music group MW-2. He was a prof. at the Kraków State Higher School of Music from 1966 to 1987, and also its vice rector from 1972 to 1975. From 1985 to 1989 he was president of the Union of Polish Composers. He was prof. of composition at the Cologne Hochschule für Musik from 1987. In addition to his various articles on contemporary music, he publ. the first monograph on the life and works of Shostakovich in Poland (Kraków, 1973; 2nd ed., 1986; Ger. tr., 1980; new ed., enl., Paris, 1994, and Bergish Gladbach, 1995). A second study on Shostakovich and his era followed (Warsaw, 1999). He prepared his own version of Shostakovich's unfinished opera *The Gamblers* (1980–81; Wuppertal, Sept. 9, 1984). His 3rd Sym. won 1st prize in the Young Polish Composers' Competition in 1968. In 1970 he won the Grand Prix of the Prince Pierre of Monaco composers' competition for his opera *Cyberiada*. He received awards from the Polish Ministry of Culture and Art in 1973 and 1975. In 1974 his 4th Sym. won 1st prize in the Szymanowski Competition in Warsaw. In 1984 he received the Gottfried von Herder Prize of Vienna. In 1987 he was made a member of the Freien Akademie der Künste in Mannheim. He received the annual award of the Union of Polish Composers in 1992. As a composer, he abandoned the early influence of Penderecki and Boulanger and pursued his own advanced course without ever transcending the practical limits of instrumental and vocal techniques or of aural perception. His scores are the product of a rare musical intelligence and acoustical acuity.

WORKS: DRAMATIC: *Cyberiada*, fantastic comic opera (1967–70; Act. 1, Polish-TV, May 12, 1971; 1st complete perf., Wuppertal, May 11, 1986); *Hrabina* (The Countess), ballet (1980; Poznań, Nov. 14, 1981); *Igroki* (The Gamblers), completion of Shostakovich's opera (1980–81; Wuppertal, Sept. 9, 1984); *Klonowi bracia* (The Maple Brothers), children's opera (1988–89; Poznań, March 3, 1990). **ORCH.:** *Concerto da camera* for Flute, Percussion, and Strings (1964; Kraków, June 25, 1965), for Oboe, Percussion, and Strings (1972; Zielona Góra, May 24, 1984), and for Harp, Cello, and Strings (1984; Cologne, Oct. 7, 1987); 6 numbered syms.: No. 1 (Kraków, June 12, 1964), No. 2, *Epitaphium Stanisław Wiechowicz in memoriam*, for Chorus and Orch. (1967; Wrocław, Feb. 15, 1969), No. 3, *Symphonie d'Orphée*, for Chorus and Orch. (1968; Warsaw, Sept. 16, 1972), No. 4 (1973; Zagreb, May 14, 1975), No. 5 for Chamber String Orch. (1978–79; Białystok, Sept. 17, 1979), and No. 6, *Polish* (Hamburg, Nov. 15, 1982); *Symphony in D major in Mozartean Style* (1976; Poznań, April 1, 1977); 2 violin concertos: No. 1 (1965; Poznań, March 22, 1969) and No. 2 (1996); 2 cello concertos: No. 1

(1971–72; Poznań, April 3, 1975) and No. 2 (1994–95; Düsseldorf, Oct. 25, 1996); Trumpet Concerto (1973; Poznań, April 2, 1976); *Fireballs* (1976; Warsaw, April 20, 1978); Piano Concerto (1979–89; Cologne, June 14, 1992) *Hommage à Johannes Brahms* (1982; Hamburg, May 15, 1983); Flute Concerto (1983; Berlin, Dec. 1, 1984); *Canti Amadei* for Cello and Orch. (Kraków, Dec. 19, 1984); *Concerto retro* for Flute, Violin, Harpsichord, and Strings (1986; Kraków, April 10, 1988); *Musica incrostata* (Cologne, June 6, 1988); *Caro Luigi* for 4 Cellos and Strings (Stuttgart, Sept. 29, 1989); *Carillon* (1992–93; Flensburg, Aug. 5, 1993); *Farewell Music* (1997; Warsaw, Feb. 20, 1998). **CHAMBER**: Sonata for Solo Cello (1959–61; Kamien Pomorski, Aug. 15, 1969); *Introspection* for 5 Cellos (1960; Kraków, May 28, 1961); *Music* for 3 Cellos, Kettledrums, and Piano (1962; Kraków, May 9, 1963); 10 string quartets: No. 1 (1963; Warsaw, Sept. 26, 1965), No. 2 (Warsaw, Sept. 28, 1969), No. 3 (1971; Warsaw, Sept. 29, 1973), No. 4 (1974; Curitiba, Jan. 29, 1975), No. 5 (1977; Białystok, March 10, 1978), No. 6 (1981; Plock, June 11, 1982), No. 7 (Wrocław, April 16, 1985), No. 8 (1985; Munich, March 16, 1986), No. 9 (1989–90; Cologne, Dec. 28, 1991), and No. 10 (1993–94; Poznań, Oct. 3, 1994); *Interludio statico* for Clarinet and 4 Cellos (1963–64; Poznań, April 19, 1967); *Hommage à Nadia Boulanger* for Flute, Viola, and Harp (1967–71; Zagreb, May 14, 1971); *Quattro colori* for Clarinet, Trombone, Cello, and Piano (1970); Sonata for Solo Violin (1975; Poznań, April 22, 1977); *Concerto retro* for Flute, Violin, Cello, and Harpsichord (1976; Curitiba, Feb. 4, 1977); *Moment musical* for Cello (1976); *3 Pieces* for Percussionist (Copenhagen, June 8, 1977); *Interludio drammatico* for Oboe and Chamber Ensemble (1980; Leipzig, Jan. 19, 1981); Piano Trio (1980; Wrocław, April 16, 1985); Sonata for Solo Flute (1980; Darmstadt, March 30, 1985); *Canzona* for Cello and Piano (1981; Hamburg, Nov. 1, 1982); *6 Préludes* for Violin (1981); *Pezzo capriccioso* for Oboe and Piano (1982; Princeton, N.J., April 18, 1983); Cello Sonata (1983; Klagenfurt, Nov. 22, 1984); Clarinet Quintet (Ulm, Nov. 2, 1986); *Capriccio per sei instrumenti* (1987–88; Lanaudière, Canada, July 10, 1989); *Wittener Kammermusik* for Flute, Oboe, and Clarinet (1988; Witten, Germany, April 22, 1989); *Monologue* for Cello (Hamburg, Oct. 5, 1990); Piano Quartet (1990–91; Cologne, May 25, 1992); String Trio (1993; Munich, March 6, 1994); *Misterioso* for Violin and Piano (Hannover, Nov. 2, 1994); *Au delà d'une absence* for String Quartet (1997; Hamburg, July 5, 1998); Trio for Clarinet, Cello, and Piano (1997–98; Hitzaker, July 31, 1999). **KEYBOARD**: **Piano**: *Aphorisms* (1961; Kraków, June 20, 1962); 5 sonatas: No. 1 (Katowice, April 26, 1962), No. 2 (Kraków, June 3, 1963), No. 3 (Kraków, May 18, 1966), No. 4 (1968; Kraków, June 5, 1969), and No. 5 (1975; Katowice, Jan. 19, 1977); *24 Préludes* (1978; Stalowa Wola, May 17, 1979). **Harpsichord**: Sonata (1972–73; Paris, Oct. 28, 1974). **Organ**: *Fantasia* (1990; Berlin, June 15, 1991). **VOCAL**: *Songs of Resignation and Denial* for Soprano, Violin, and Piano (1963; Prague, April 28, 1966); *Quartettino* for Soprano, Flute, and Cello (Szczecin, Sept. 11, 1966); *5 Chamber Pieces* for Soprano, Clarinet, and Viola (1967; Kraków, April 17, 1969); *Polish Chants* for Soprano and Orch. (1974; Bydgoszcz, Sept. 9, 1977); *Lyric Triptych* for Tenor and Chamber Orch. (1976; Aldeburgh, June 22, 1978); *9 Limericks of Stanisław Jerzy Lec* for Soprano and Piano (Baranow Sandomierski, Sept. 7, 1979); *Sunday Colloquy* for Baritone and Piano (1981; Kraków, March 26, 1987); *Mass* for Chorus and Organ (1987–92; Cologne, Jan. 24, 1993); *Wjelitchalnaja* for Chorus (1988; L'Hermitage, May 15, 1989); *Te Deum* for Chorus (Kiel, May 5, 1995); Mass for Chorus and Orch. (1995–96; Kraków, Dec. 13, 1996).—**NS/LK/DM**

Meyer, Leonard B(unce), eminent American musicologist; b. N.Y., Jan. 12, 1918. He was educated at Bard Coll. (1936–37), Columbia Univ. (B.A., 1940; M.A., 1948), and the Univ. of Chicago (Ph.D., 1954). In 1946 he joined the faculty of the Univ. of Chicago, where he served as head of the humanities section (1958–60), chairman of the music dept. (1961–70), prof. of music (1961–75), and the Phyllis Fay Horton Distinguished Service Prof. (1972–75). In 1971–72 he held a Guggenheim fellowship. From 1975 to 1988 he was the Benjamin Franklin prof. of music at the Univ. of Pa., and subsequently held its emeritus title. In 1971 he was the Ernest Bloch Prof. of Music at the Univ. of Calif. at Berkeley, and later was a senior fellow at the School of Criticism and Theory (1975–88). He was a resident scholar at the Bellagio Study and Conference Center in Italy in 1982. In 1984 he was the Tanner lecturer at Stanford Univ. and in 1985 the Patten lecturer at Ind. Univ. In 1987 he was made an honorary member of the American Musicological Soc. Many of his erudite books and articles have been tr. into various foreign languages, among them French, Italian, Spanish, Polish, Serbo-Croatian, Japanese, and Chinese.

WRITINGS: *Emotion and Meaning in Music* (Chicago, 1956); with G. Cooper, *The Rhythmic Structure of Music* (Chicago, 1960); *Music, the Arts, and Ideas: Patterns and Predictions in Twentieth Century Culture* (Chicago, 1967; with new postlude, 1994); *Explaining Music: Essays and Explorations* (Berkeley and Los Angeles, 1973); *Style and Music: Theory, History, and Ideology* (Philadelphia, 1989).

BIBL.: E. Narmour and R. Solie, eds., *Explorations in Music, the Arts, and Ideas: Essays in Honor of L. B. M.* (Stuyvesant, N.Y., 1989).—**NS/LK/DM**

Meyer, Leopold von (called **Leopold de Meyer**), celebrated Austrian pianist; b. Baden, near Vienna, Dec. 20, 1816; d. Dresden, March 5, 1883. He studied with Czerny and Fischhof. At the age of 19, he embarked on a series of pianistic tours in Europe; also toured in America (1845–47). At his concerts he invariably included his own compositions, written in a characteristic salon style. His agents spread sensational publicity about him in order to arouse interest. A *Biography of Leopold de Meyer* was publ. in London in 1845.

BIBL.: R. Lott, *The American Concert Tours of L. d.M., Henri Herz, and Sigismond Thalberg* (diss., City Univ. of N.Y., 1986).—**NS/LK/DM**

Meyer, Philippe-Jacques, Alsatian harpist, teacher, and composer; b. Strasbourg, 1737; d. London, 1819. He studied harp with Christian Hochbrucker in Paris, where made his first appearance as a soloist at the Concert Spirituel in 1761. He was active mainly in London, Paris, and Strasbourg before settling in London in 1784. Meyer publ. the harp method *Essai sur la vraie manière de jouer de la harpe, avec une méthode de l'accorder,* op.1 (Paris, 1763; 2ⁿᵈ ed., 1772). He also publ. *Nouvelle pour aprendre à jouer de la harpe avec la manière de l'accorder,* op.9 (Paris, 1774) and numerous works for solo harp and for harp with instruments.—**LK/DM**

Meyer, Sabine, gifted German clarinetist; b. Crailsheim, March 30, 1959. She began training with her father, the clarinetist Karl Meyer, and then was a student of Otto Hermann at the Stuttgart Hochschule für Musik and of Hans Deinzer at the Hannover Hochschule für Musk. After playing in the Bavarian Radio Sym. Orch. in Munich, she was engaged as solo clarinetist of the Berlin Phil. in 1982 by its chief conductor Herbert von Karajan. Karajan's appointment was made in spite of the protests of the musicians of the orch. whose self-governing charter, as well as its long- standing practice of excluding women from membership, was placed in jeopardy. The incident received international media coverage. Meyer was eventually allowed to enter the orch. on a probationary basis, but in 1984 left it and quickly demonstrated her virtuosity as a soloist, recitalist, and chamber music artist of the first rank. She made frequent tours of Europe, and also appeared in North America and Japan. As a soloist, she was engaged by many orchs. on both sides of the Atlantic. She also performed regularly with her own Trio di Clarone from 1983 and Bläserensemble Sabine Meyer from 1988. In 1994 she made her first appearances at the Ravinia Festival in Chicago and at N.Y.'s Mostly Mozart Festival. Meyer's repertoire ranges widely, and includes not only the classics but contemporary scores as well.—LK/DM

Meyerbeer, Giacomo (real name, Jakob Liebmann Beer),

famous German composer; b. Vogelsdorf, near Berlin, Sept. 5, 1791; d. Paris, May 2, 1864. He was a scion of a prosperous Jewish family of merchants. He added the name Meyer to his surname, and later changed his first name for professional purposes. He began piano studies with Franz Lauska, and also received some instruction from Clementi. He made his public debut in Berlin when he was 11. He then studied composition with Zelter (1805–07), and subsequently with B.A. Weber. It was as Weber's pupil that he composed his first stage work, the ballet-pantomime *Der Fischer und das Milchmädchen*, which was produced at the Berlin Royal Theater (March 26, 1810). He then went to Darmstadt to continue his studies with Abbé Vogler until late 1811; one of his fellow pupils was Carl Maria von Weber. While under Vogler's tutelage, he composed the oratorio *Gott und die Natur* (Berlin, May 8, 1811) and also the operas *Der Admiral* (1811; not perf.) and *Jephthas Gelübde* (Munich, Dec. 23, 1812). His next opera, *Wirth und Gast, oder Aus Scherz Ernst* (Stuttgart, Jan. 6, 1813), was not a success; revised as *Die beyden Kalifen* for Vienna, it likewise failed there (Oct. 20, 1814). However, he did find success in Vienna as a pianist in private musical settings. In Nov. 1814 he proceeded to Paris, and in Dec. 1815 to London. He went to Italy early in 1816, and there turned his attention fully to dramatic composition. His Italian operas—*Romilda e Costanza* (Padua, July 19, 1817), *Semiramide riconosciuta* (Turin, March 1819), *Emma di Resburgo* (Venice, June 26, 1819), *Margherita d'Angiù* (Milan, Nov. 14, 1820), *L'Esule di Granata* (Milan, March 12, 1821), and *Il Crociato in Egitto* (Venice, March 7, 1824)—brought him fame there, placing him on a par with the celebrated Rossini in public esteem. The immense success of *Il Crociato in Egitto* in particular led to a successful staging at London's King's Theatre (July 23, 1825), followed by a triumphant Paris production (Sept. 25, 1825), which made Meyerbeer famous throughout Europe. To secure his Paris position, he revamped *Margherita d'Angiù* for the French stage as *Margherita d'Anjou* (March 11, 1826). He began a long and distinguished association with the dramatist and librettist Eugène Scribe in 1827 as work commenced on the opera *Robert le diable*. It was produced at the Paris Opéra on Nov. 21, 1831, with extraordinary success.

Numerous honors were subsequently bestowed upon Meyerbeer: he was made a Chevalier of the Légion d'honneur and a Prussian Hofkapellmeister in 1832, a member of the senate of the Prussian Academy of Arts in 1833, and a member of the Institut de France in 1834. He began work on what was to become the opera *Les Huguenots* in 1832; set to a libretto mainly by Scribe, it was accorded a spectacular premiere at the Opéra on Feb. 29, 1836. Late in 1836 he and Scribe began work on a new opera, *Le Prophète*. He also commenced work on the opera *L'Africaine* in Aug. 1837, again utilizing a libretto by Scribe; it was initially written for the famous soprano Marie-Cornélie Falcon; however, after the loss of her voice, Meyerbeer set the score aside; it was destined to occupy him on and off for the rest of his life. In 1839 Wagner sought out Meyerbeer in Boulogne. Impressed with Wagner, Meyerbeer extended him financial assistance and gave him professional recommendations. However, Wagner soon became disenchanted with his prospects and berated Meyerbeer in private, so much so that Meyerbeer was compelled to disassociate himself from Wagner. The ungrateful Wagner retaliated by giving vent to his anti-Semitic rhetoric.

Meyerbeer began work on *Le Prophète* in earnest in 1838, completing it by 1840. However, its premiere was indefinitely delayed as the composer attempted to find capable singers. On May 20, 1842, *Les Huguenots* was performed in Berlin. On June 11, 1842, Meyerbeer was formally installed as Prussian Generalmusikdirektor. From the onset of his tenure, disagreement with the Intendant of the Royal Opera, Karl Theodor von Küstner, made his position difficult. Finally, on Nov. 26, 1848, Meyerbeer was dismissed from his post, although he retained his position as director of music for the royal court; in this capacity he composed a number of works for state occasions, including the opera *Ein Feldlager in Schlesien*, which reopened the opera house on Dec. 7, 1844, following its destruction by fire. The leading role was sung by Jenny Lind, one of Meyerbeer's discoveries. It had a modicum of success after its first performance in Vienna under the title *Vielka* in 1847, although it never equaled the success of his Paris operas. In 1849 he again took up the score of *Le Prophète*. As he could find no tenor to meet its demands, he completely revised the score for the celebrated soprano Pauline Viardot-García. With Viardot-García as Fidès and the tenor Gustave Roger as John of Leyden, it received a brilliant premiere at the Opéra on April 16, 1849, a success that led to Meyerbeer's being made the first German Commandeur of the Légion d'honneur. His next opera was *L'Étoile du nord*, which utilized music from *Ein Feldlager in Schlesien*; its first performance at the Opéra-Comique on Feb. 16, 1854, proved an outstanding success. Equally successful was his opera *Le Pardon de Ploërmel* (Opéra-Comique, April 4, 1859). In

1862 he composed a special work for the London World Exhibition, the *Fest-Ouverture im Marschstyl*, and made a visit to England during the festivities. In the meantime, work on *L'Africaine* had occupied him fitfully for years; given Scribe's death in 1861 and Meyerbeer's own failing health, he was compelled to finally complete it. In April 1864 he put the finishing touches on the score and rehearsals began under his supervision. However, he died on the night of May 2, 1864, before the work was premiered. His body was taken to Berlin, where it was laid to rest in official ceremonies attended by the Prussian court, prominent figures in the arts, and the public at large. Fétis was subsequently charged with making the final preparations for the premiere of *L'Africaine*, which was given at the Paris Opéra to notable acclaim on April 28, 1865.

Meyerbeer established himself as the leading composer of French grand opera in 1831 with *Robert le diable*, a position he retained with distinction throughout his career. Indeed, he became one of the most celebrated musicians of his era. Although the grandiose conceptions and stagings of his operas proved immediately appealing to audiences, his dramatic works were more than mere theatrical spectacles. His vocal writing was truly effective, for he often composed and tailored his operas with specific singers in mind. Likewise, his gift for original orchestration and his penchant for instrumental experimentation placed his works on a high level. Nevertheless, his stature as a composer was eclipsed after his death by Wagner. As a consequence, his operas disappeared from the active repertoire, although revivals and several recordings saved them from total oblivion in the modern era.

WORKS: DRAMATIC: Opera: *Jephthas Gelübde* (Munich, Dec. 23, 1812); *Wirth und Gast, oder Aus Scherz Ernst*, Lustspiel (Stuttgart, Jan. 6, 1813; rev. as *Die beyden Kalifen*, Vienna, Oct. 20, 1814; later known as *Alimelek*); *Das Brandenburger Tor*, Singspiel (1814; not perf.); *Romilda e Costanza*, melodramma semiserio (Padua, July 19, 1817); *Semiramide riconosciuta*, dramma per musica (Turin, March 1819); *Emma di Resburgo*, melodramma eroico (Venice, June 26, 1819); *Margherita d'Angiù*, melodramma semiserio (Milan, Nov. 14, 1820; rev. as *Margherita d'Anjou*, Paris, March 11, 1826); *L'Almanzore* (1821; not perf.); *L'Esule di Granata*, melodramma serio (Milan, March 12, 1821); *Il Crociato in Egitto*, melodramma eroico (Venice, March 7, 1824); *Robert le diable*, grand opéra (Paris, Nov. 21, 1831); *Les Huguenots*, grand opéra (Paris, Feb. 29, 1836); *Ein Feldlager in Schlesien*, Singspiel (Berlin, Dec. 7, 1844; later known as *Vielka*); *Le Prophète*, grand opéra (Paris, April 16, 1849); *L'Étoile du nord*, opéra-comique (Paris, Feb. 16, 1854; much of the music based on *Ein Feldlager in Schlesien*); *Le Pardon de Ploërmel*, opéra-comique (Paris, April 4, 1859; also known as *Le Chercheur du trésor* and as *Dinorah, oder Die Wallfahrt nach Ploërmel*); *L'Africaine*, grand opéra (Paris, April 28, 1865; originally known as *Vasco da Gama*). He also left a number of unfinished operas in various stages of development. **Other:** *Der Fischer und das Milchmädchen, oder Viel Lärm um einen Kuss* (*Le Passage de la rivière*, or *La Femme jalouse*; *Le Pêcheur et la laitière*), ballet-pantomime (Berlin, March 26, 1810); *Gli amori di Teolinda* (*Thecelindens Liebschaften*), monodrama (Genoa, 1816); *Das Hoffest von Ferrara*, masque (Berlin, Feb. 28, 1843); *Struensee*, incidental music for a drama by Michael Beer, Meyerbeer's brother (Berlin, Sept. 19, 1846); etc. **ORCH.:** Sym. in E-flat major (1811); Piano Concerto (1811); Concerto for Piano and Violin (1812); 4 *Fackeltänze* for Military Band or Orch. (1844, 1850, 1856, 1858); *Festmarsch* for the centenary of Schiller's birth (1859); *Krönungsmarsch* for 2 Orchs. (for the coronation of Wilhelm I, 1861); *Fest-Ouverture im Marschstyl* (for the opening of the World Exhibition in London, 1862); etc. **CHAMBER:** Piano pieces. **VOCAL: Sacred:** *Gott und die Natur*, oratorio (Berlin, May 8, 1811); *Geistliche Gesänge*, 7 odes after Klopstock, for Soprano, Alto, Tenor, and Bass (Leipzig, 1817 or 1818); *An Gott*, hymn for Soprano, Alto, Tenor, Bass, and Piano (Leipzig, 1817); *Psalm XCI* for Soprano, Alto, Tenor, Bass, and Double Mixed Chorus a cappella (Berlin, 1853); *Prière du matin* for 2 Choirs and Piano ad libitum (Paris, 1864); etc. **Occasional and Secular Choral:** *Festgesang zur Errichtung des Gutenbergischen Denkmals in Mainz* for 2 Tenors, 2 Basses, Men's Voices, and Piano ad libitum (Mainz, 1835); *Dem Vaterland* for Men's Voices (Berlin, 1842); *Le Voyageur au tombeau de Beethoven* for Bass Solo and Women's Voices a cappella (1845); *Festhymne* for Solo Voices, Chorus, and Piano ad libitum (for the silver wedding anniversary of the King and Queen of Prussia, 1848); *Ode an Rauch* for Solo Voices, Chorus, and Orch. (in honor of the sculptor Christian Rauch; Berlin, 1851); *Maria und ihr Genius*, cantata for Soprano, Tenor, Chorus, and Piano (for the silver wedding anniversary of Prince and Princess Carl, 1852); *Brautgeleite aus der Heimat*, serenade for Chorus a cappella (for the wedding of Princess Luise, 1856); *Festgesang zur Feier des 100- jährigen Geburtsfestes von Friedrich Schiller* for Soprano, Alto, Tenor, Bass, Chorus, and Orch. (1859); *Festhymnus* for Solo Voices, Chorus, and Piano ad libitum (for the coronation of Wilhelm I, 1861); etc. **OTHER:** Songs.

BIBL.: A. Morel, *Le Prophète: Analyse critique de la nouvelle partition de G. M.* (Paris, 1849); E. Lindner, *M.s "Prophet" als Kunstwerk beurtheilt* (Berlin, 1850); E. de Mirecourt, *M.* (Paris, 1854); A. de Lasalle, *M.: Sa vie et le catalogue de ses oeuvres* (Paris, 1864); A. Pougin, *M.: Notes biographiques* (Paris, 1864); H. Blaze de Bury, *M. et son temps* (Paris, 1865); H. Mendel, *G. M.* (Berlin, 1868); J. Schucht, *M.s Leben und Bildungsgang* (Leipzig, 1869); A. Body, *M. aux eaux de Spa* (Brussels, 1885); A. Kohut, *M.* (Leipzig, 1890); E. Destranges, *L'[f:]uvre théâtral de M.* (Paris, 1893); J. Weber, *M.: Notes et souvenirs d'un de ses secrétaires* (Paris, 1898); H. de Curzon, *M.: Biographie critique* (Paris, 1910); H. Eymieu, *L'[f:]uvre de M.* (Paris, 1910); L. Dauriac, *M.* (Paris, 1913; 2nd ed., 1930); J. Kapp, *G. M.* (Berlin, 1920; 8th ed., rev., 1932); H. Strelitzer, *M.s deutsche Jugendopern* (diss., Univ. of Münster, 1920); R. Haudek, *Scribes Operntexte für M.: Eine Quellenuntersuchung* (diss., Univ. of Vienna, 1928); J. Cooke, *M.* (Philadelphia, 1929); H. Becker, *Der Fall Heine-M.: Neue Dokumente revidieren ein Geschichtsurteil* (Berlin, 1958); idem, ed., *G. M.: Briefwechsel und Tagebücher* (4 vols., Berlin, 1960–85); C. Frese, *Dramaturgie der grossen Opern G. M.s* (Berlin, 1970); H. Becker, *G. M. in Selbstzeugnissen und Bilddokumenten* (Reinbek, 1980); H. and G. Becker, *G. M.: Ein Leben in Briefen* (Wilhelmshaven, 1983; Eng. tr., 1983, as *G. M.: A Life in Letters*); S. Segalini, *M.: Diable ou prophète?* (Paris, 1985); H. and G. Becker, *G. M.: Weltbürger der Musik* (Wiesbaden, 1991); R. Zimmermann, *G. M.: Eine Biographie nach Dokumenten* (Berlin, 1991); S. Döhring and J. Schläder, eds., *Heinz Becker zum 70. Geburtstag: G. M.-Musik als Welterfahrung* (Munich, 1995); S. Döhring and A. Jacobshagen, eds., *M. und das europaische Musiktheater* (Laaber, 1998); G. Oberzaucher-Schüller and H. Moeller, eds., *M. und der Tanz* (Feldkirchen, 1998).—**NS/LK/DM**

Meyerowitz, Jan (actually, **Hans-Hermann**), German-born American composer and teacher; b. Breslau, April 23, 1913. In 1927 he went to Berlin, where he studied with Gmeindl and Zemlinsky at the Hochschule für Musik. Compelled to leave Germany in 1933, he went to Rome, where he took lessons in advanced composition with Respighi and Casella, and in conducting with Molinari. In 1938 he moved to Belgium and later to southern France, where he remained until 1946; he then emigrated to the U.S., becoming a naturalized American citizen in 1951. He married the French singer Marguerite Fricker in 1946. He held a Guggenheim fellowship twice (1956, 1958). He taught at the Berkshire Music Center in Tanglewood (summers, 1948–51) and at Brooklyn (1954–61) and City (1962–80) Colls. of the City Univ. of N.Y. He publ. a monograph on Schoenberg (Berlin, 1967) and *Der echte judische Witz* (Berlin, 1971). His music is imbued with expansive emotionalism akin to that of Mahler; in his works for the theater, there is a marked influence of the tradition of 19th-century grand opera. His technical idiom is modern, enlivened by a liberal infusion of euphonious dissonance, and he often applies the rigorous and vigorous devices of linear counterpoint.

WORKS: DRAMATIC: O p e r a : *Simoon* (1948; Tanglewood, Aug. 2, 1950); *The Barrier*, after Langston Hughes (1949; N.Y., Jan. 18, 1950); *Eastward in Eden*, later renamed *Emily Dickinson* (Detroit, Nov. 16, 1951); *Bad Boys in School* (Tanglewood, Aug. 17, 1953); *Esther*, after Langston Hughes (Urbana, Ill., May 17, 1957); *Port Town*, after Langston Hughes (Tanglewood, Aug. 4, 1960); *Godfather Death* (N.Y., June 2, 1961); *Die Doppelgängerin*, after Gerhart Hauptmann, later renamed *Winterballade* (1966; Hannover, Jan. 29, 1967). **ORCH.:** *3 Comments on War* for Band (1957); 3 syms.: *Silesian Symphony* (1957), *Esther Midrash* (N.Y., Jan. 31, 1957), and *Sinfonia brevissima* (1968); *Flemish Overture* (1959); Oboe Concerto (1962); Flute Concerto (1962); *6 Pieces* (Pittsburgh, May 27, 1967); *7 Pieces* (1974); *4 Romantic Pieces* for Band (1978). **CHAMBER:** Cello Sonata (1946); Trio for Flute, Cello, and Piano (1946); Woodwind Quintet (1954); String Quartet (1955); Violin Sonata (1960); Flute Sonata (1961). **P i a n o :** *Homage to Hieronymus Bosch* for 2 Pianos (1945); Sonata (1958). **VOCAL:** *The Glory Around His Head* for Bass, Chorus, and Orch. (N.Y., April 14, 1955); *the 5 Foolish Virgins* for Chorus and Orch. (1956); *Stabat Mater* for Chorus and Orch. (1957); *Hebrew Service* for Tenor, Mezzo-soprano, Chorus, and Organ (1962); *I rabbini* for Soloists, Chorus, and Orch. (1962); *Missa Rachel plorans* for Soprano, Tenor, Chorus, and Organ ad libitum (1962); 6 Songs for Soprano and Orch., after August von Platen (1976; Cologne, Feb. 12, 1977); other choral works and songs.—NS/LK/DM

Meyers, Anne Akiko, American violinist; b. San Diego, May 15, 1970. She began her musical training at age 4, making her public debut as a soloist with orch. at age 7. Following studies with Alice Schoenfeld at the R.D. Colburn School of Performing Arts in Los Angeles, she had advanced training with Josef Gingold at the Ind. Univ. School of Music in Bloomington and with Dorothy DeLay, Masao Kawasaki, and Felix Galimir at the Juilliard School in N.Y. In 1993 she was awarded the Avery Fisher Career Grant. She has appeared as a soloist with most of the leading orchs. of North America, and has appeared with major orchs. abroad. As a recitalist, she has performed throughout North America, Europe, and the Far East.—NS/LK/DM

Meyer-Siat, Pie, French musicologist; b. Ribeauvillé, Haut-Rhin, Oct. 15, 1913; d. Strasbourg, April 4, 1989. He was educated at the Univ. of Strasbourg, receiving a degree in philosophy in 1937, taking the agrégation in German in 1948, and being awarded his Ph.D. in musicology in 1962 with the diss. *Les Callinet, facteurs d'orgues à Rouffach, et leur oeuvre en Alsace*, publ. in Strasbourg, 1965. He was an authority on organs in Alsace, and contributed important articles for *Les Cahiers de la Société d'Histoire de Saverne.*

WRITINGS: *L'Orgue Callinet de Masevaux* (Mulhouse, 1962); *L'Orgue Joseph Callinet de Mollau (Haut-Rhin)* (Strasbourg, 1963); *Les Orgues de Niedernai et d'Obernai* (Colmar, 1972); *Stiehr-Mockers, facteurs d'orgues* (Hagenau, 1972); *Historische Orgeln im Elsass, 1489–1869* (Munich, 1983).—NS/LK/DM

Meyrowitz, Selmar, German conductor; b. Bartenstein, East Prussia, April 18, 1875; d. Toulouse, March 24, 1941. He studied at the Leipzig Cons., and later with Max Bruch in Berlin. In 1897 he became asst. conductor at the Karlsruhe Opera under Mottl, with whom he went to America as conductor at the Metropolitan Opera in N.Y. (1903); subsequently conducted at the Prague National Theater (1905–06), the Berlin Komische Oper (1907–10), the Munich Opera (1912–13), and the Hamburg Opera (1913–17). After appearing as a guest conductor with the Berlin Phil., he conducted at the Berlin Radio and the State Opera (1924–33); also toured with the German Grand Opera Co. in the U.S. (1929–31). He settled in France (1933).—NS/LK/DM

Mézeray, Louis (-Charles-Lazare-Costard) de, French baritone, conductor, and composer; b. Braunschweig, Nov. 25, 1810; d. Asnières, near Paris, April 1887. As a young man, he conducted theater orchs. in Strasbourg and elsewhere. At 17 he obtained the post of conductor at the Liège Theater, and at 20 he became conductor at the Court Theater in The Hague, where he brought out his heroic opera *Guillaume de Nassau*; subsequently he studied with Reicha in Paris. He again traveled as a theater conductor in France, and also appeared as a baritone. Finally, in 1843, he became chief conductor at the Grand Théâtre in Bordeaux, and brought the standard of performance there to a very high level.—NS/LK/DM

Mezzrow, Mezz (originally, **Mesirow, Milton**), jazz clarinetist, soprano saxophonist; b. Chicago, Nov. 9, 1899; d. Paris, Aug. 5, 1972. He first played saxophone in 1917 while serving a brief jail sentence. Around 1923, he began gigging in and around Chicago, including work with the Austin High Gang. In spring 1928, he moved to N.Y., where he gigged with several bands. In March 1929, he sailed to Europe, remaining abroad a month, including a stint leading his own band at a Parisian nightclub. On his return, he toured with Red Nichols, then worked with Jack Levy's Orch. at

Minsky's in N.Y. During the 1930s he occasionally played clarinet and tenor sax, but was also a marijuana dealer. He organized his own all-star recording bands in 1933 and 1934 and took part in 1938 sessions supervised by Hugues Panassie. In late 1937, he led a racially mixed band in N.Y., a bold move for a performing group at that time. He continued to work and lead his own small groups through 1941, when he suffered a two-year absence from the music scene due to drug addiction. He was back to work in 1943, leading his own bands and working with others, including a stint with Art Hodes (1943–44). In 1946 he published his autobiography, *Really the Blues,* which included a frank account of his struggle with opium addiction. He spent most of the 1950s touring Europe with various "all-star" bands, and eventually settled in France. He revisited N.Y. shortly before his death in the early 1970s.

He was truly unique, a Jewish man who said he wished he were black because of his love for the music. He made his living more from selling marijuana than from his modest talents as a musician. His fame as a supplier of marijuana was supposedly unmatched in his day. He carried around a shoebox full at all times, and would call a particularly potent joint a "meziroll" or "mighty mezz." The 1943 hit "The Reefer Song" by Fats Waller was an ode to his capabilities.

DISC.: *Mezz Mezzrow's Swing Session* (1954); *Mezz Mezzrow in Paris, 1955* (1955); *Mezz Mezzrow* (1955); *Schola Cantorum* (1956); *Mezz Mezzrow a La Scholas Canto* (1956).

WRITINGS: With B. Wolfe, *Really the Blues* (N.Y., 1946). —JC/LP

M'Guckin, Barton, Irish tenor; b. Dublin, July 28, 1852; d. Stoke Poges, Buckinghamshire, April 17, 1913. After serving as a choirboy at Armagh Cathedral, he went to Dublin to pursue vocal training and to sing at St. Patrick's Cathedral. In 1874 he made his concert debut in Dublin, and then sang in London in 1875. Following further vocal studies in Milan, he made his operatic debut with the Carl Rosa Opera Co. in Birmingham in 1878, remaining with it until 1887. After touring the U.S. (1887–88), he returned to England and once more sang with the Carl Rosa Opera Co. (1889–96). In addition to his roles in English operas, M'Guckin was especially admired for his portrayals of Des Grieux, which he introduced to English audiences, and of Wilhelm Meister and Don José.—NS/LK/DM

Miaskovsky, Nikolai (Yakovlevich), eminent Russian composer and teacher; b. Novogeorgievsk, near Warsaw, April 20, 1881; d. Moscow, Aug. 8, 1950. His father was an officer of the dept. of military fortification; the family lived in Orenburg (1888–89) and in Kazan (1889–93). In 1893 he was sent to a military school in Nizhny-Novgorod, and in 1895 he went to a military school in St. Petersburg, graduating in 1899. At that time he developed an interest in music, and tried to compose. He took lessons with Kazanli, his first influences being Chopin and Tchaikovsky. In 1902–03 he was in Moscow, where he studied harmony with Glière. Returning to St. Petersburg in 1903, he took lessons with Kryzhanovsky, from whom he acquired a taste for

modernistic composition in the impressionist style. In 1906, at the age of 25, he entered the St. Petersburg Cons. as a pupil of Liadov and Rimsky-Korsakov, graduating in 1911. At the outbreak of World War I in 1914, Miaskovsky was called into active service in the Russian army; in 1916 he was removed to Reval to work on military fortifications; he remained in the army after the Bolshevik Revolution of 1917; in 1918 he became a functionary in the Maritime Headquarters in Moscow; was finally demobilized in 1921. In that year he became prof. of composition at the Moscow Cons., remaining at that post to the end of his life. A composer of extraordinary ability, a master of his craft, Miaskovsky wrote 27 syms., much chamber music, piano pieces, and songs; his music is marked by structural strength and emotional elan; he never embraced extreme forms of modernism, but adopted workable devices of tonal expansion short of polytonality, and freely modulating melody short of atonality. His style was cosmopolitan; only in a few works did he inject folkloric elements. His autobiographical notes were publ. in *Sovetskaya Muzyka* (June 1936); S. Shlifstein ed. a vol. of articles, letters, and reminiscences (Moscow, 1959) and a vol. of articles, notes, and reviews (Moscow, 1960). A collected edition of his works was publ. in Moscow (12 vols., 1953–56).

WORKS: ORCH (all 1st perf. in Moscow unless otherwise given): S y m s .: No. 1 in C minor, op.3 (1908; Pavlovsk, June 2, 1914), No. 2 in C-sharp minor, op.11 (1910–11; July 24, 1912), No. 3 in A minor, op.15 (1913–14; Feb. 27, 1915), No. 4 in E minor, op.17 (1917–18; Feb. 8, 1925), No. 5 in D major, op.18 (1918; July 18, 1920), No. 6 in E-flat minor, op.23 (1922–23; May 4, 1924), No. 7 in B minor, op.24 (1922; Feb. 8, 1925), No. 8 in A major, op.26 (1924–25; May 23, 1926), No. 9 in E minor, op.28 (1926–27; April 29, 1928), No. 10 in F minor, op.30 (1927; April 7, 1928), No. 11 in B-flat minor, op.34 (1931–32; Jan. 16, 1933), No. 12 in G minor, op.35 (June 1, 1932), No. 13 in B-flat minor, op.36 (1933; Winterthur, Oct. 16, 1934), No. 14 in C major, op.37 (1933; Feb. 24, 1935), No. 15 in D minor, op.38 (1933–34; Oct. 28, 1935), No. 16 in F major, op.39 (Oct. 24, 1936), No. 17 in G-sharp minor, op.41 (Dec. 17, 1937), No. 18 in C major, op.42 (Oct. 1, 1937), No. 19 in E-flat major for Band (Feb. 15, 1939), No. 20 in E major, op.50 (Nov. 28, 1940), No. 21 in F-sharp minor, op.51 (Nov. 16, 1940; perf. as a commissioned work as *Symphonie fantaisie* by the Chicago Sym. Orch., Dec. 26, 1940), No. 22 in B minor, op.54, *Symphonie ballade* (1941; Tbilisi, Jan. 12, 1942), No. 23 in A minor, op.56, *Symphony-Suite* (1941; July 20, 1942), No. 24 in F minor, op.63 (Dec. 8, 1943), No. 25 in D-flat major, op.69 (1946; March 6, 1947), No. 26 in C major, op.79 (Dec. 28, 1948), No. 27 in C minor, op.85 (Dec. 9, 1950). O t h e r : Overture in G major for Small Orch. (1909; rev. 1949); *Molchaniye* (Silence), op.9, symphonic poem after Poe (1909; June 13, 1914); Sinfonietta in A major, op.10, for Small Orch. (1910; rev. 1943); *Alastor,* op.14, symphonic poem after Shelley (1912–13; Nov. 18, 1914); Serenade in E-flat major, op.32/1, for Small Orch. (Oct. 7, 1929); Sinfonietta in C minor, op.32/2, for Strings (May 1930); *Lyric Concertino* in G major, op.32/2, for Small Orch. (Oct. 7, 1929); Violin Concerto in D minor, op.44 (Leningrad, Nov. 14, 1938); 2 Pieces, op.46/1, for Strings (1945); 2 Pieces, op.46/2, for Violin, Cello, and Strings (1947); *Privetstvennaya uvertyura* (Salutatory Overture) in D major, op.48, for Stalin's birthday (Dec. 21, 1939); *Zvenya,* op.65, suite (1908; rev. 1945); Cello Concerto in C minor, op.66 (March 17, 1945); *Slavonic Rhapsody,* op.71

(1946); *Divertissement*, op.80 (1948). **B a n d** : 2 marches (1930); 3 marches (1941); *Dramatic Overture* (1942). **C H A M B E R**: 2 cello sonatas (1911, rev. 1945; 1948–49); 13 string quartets (1929–49); Violin Sonata (1946–47). **P i a n o** : 9 sonatas (1907–49); sets of piano pieces. **VOCAL**: 2 cantatas: *Kirov s nami* (Kirov is With Us) for 2 Soloists, Chorus, and Orch. (1942) and *Kreml nochyu* (Kremlin at Night) for Voice, Chorus, and Orch. (1947); choruses; song cycles.

BIBL.: A. Ikonnikov, *M.: His Life and Work* (N.Y., 1946); T. Livanova, *N.Y. M.* (Moscow, 1953); V. Vinogradov, *Spravochnik-putevoditel* (a guide to the syms.; Moscow, 1954); S. Shlifstein, ed., *Notograficheskii spravochnik* (list of works; Moscow, 1962). —NS/LK/DM

Míča, František Adam, Moravian composer, nephew of **František Antonín (Václav) Míča**; b. Jaromrice nad Rokytnou, Jan. 11, 1746; d. Lemberg, March 19, 1811. He studied law in Vienna, where he was active in government service. As a composer, he won the esteem of Emperor Joseph II and Mozart. His works include the Singspiel *Adrast und Isidore, oder Die Nachtmusik* (Vienna, April 26, 1781), over 25 syms., 4 violin concertos, a Harpsichord Concerto, and many string quartets and other chamber music pieces.—NS/LK/DM

Míča, František Antonín (Václav), Czech tenor, conductor, and composer, uncle of **František Adam Míča**; b. Třebíč, Sept. 5, 1694; d. Jaroměřice nad Rokytnou, Feb. 15, 1744. His father, Mikuláš Ondřej Míča (1659–1729), was organist to Count Questenberg in Jaroměřice. He studied in Vienna (1711). About 1722 he became valet and Kapellmeister of Count Questenberg's orch. He also sang in and conducted many operatic productions for the Count. He composed the opera *L'origine di Jaromeriz in Moravia* (Jaroměřice, Dec. 1730) and other stage works, as well as oratorios and cantatas.—LK/DM

Michael, family of important German musicians:

(1) Rogier Michael, tenor and composer of Netherlandish birth; b. Mons or Bergen op Zoom, c. 1552; d. Dresden, after Jan. 25, 1619. As a child, he sang in the Vienna Hofkapelle. In 1564 he entered the Graz Hofkapelle, where he came under the tutelage of the Kapellmeisters Johannes de Cleve and Annibale Padovano; he then studied under Jacob de Brouck there (1567–69). After singing in the Hofkapelle of the Margrave in Ansbach (1572–74), he went to Dresden as a singer and musician at the Hofkapelle. In 1587 he became Hofkapellmeister; his later assistants there were Michael Praetorius and Heinrich Schütz. Among his pupils was Johann Hermann Schein. Michael's output, which includes sacred histories, chorale settings, and motets, represents the Netherlands school at its best. He had 3 sons, all of whom were his pupils:

(2) Tobias Michael, composer; b. Dresden, June 13, 1592; d. Leipzig, June 26, 1657. He was a treble in the Dresden Hofkapelle, where he studied with Andreas Petermann, Prazeptor to the choirboys. After studying at the Schulpforta electoral school and at the Univ. of Leipzig, he pursued training in theology and philosophy at the Univ. of Wittenberg (1613–18). In 1619 he was made Kapellmeister of the Neue Kirche in Sondershausen, Thuringia. After holding a government post, he became Kantor of the Leipzig Thomaskirche in 1631. Among his finest works are the 2 vols. of *Musicalische Seelenlust* (Leipzig, 1634–35; 1637), of which Vol. I includes 30 German motets for 5 Voices and Continuo and Vol. II contains 50 sacred concertos. He also wrote sacred songs and occasional pieces.

(3) Christian Michael, organist and composer; b. Dresden, c. 1593; d. Leipzig, Aug. 29, 1637. He studied at the Univ. of Leipzig, and in 1633 succeeded his brother Samuel as organist of the Leipzig Nicolaikirche. He prepared the vol. *Tabulatura, darinnen etzliche Praeludia, Toccaten und Couranten uff das Clavier Instrument gesetzt* (Braunschweig, 1639; 2nd ed., 1645).

(4) Samuel Michael, organist and composer; b. Dresden, c. 1597; d. Leipzig, between Aug. 14 and 17, 1632. He studied at the Univ. of Leipzig, and in 1628 became organist at the Leipzig Nicolaikirche, where he remained until he died from the plague. He composed collections of vocal and instrumental pieces.
—NS/LK/DM

Michael, David Moritz, German violinist, clarinetist, horn player, and composer; b. Keinhausen, near Erfurt, Oct. 21, 1751; d. Neuwied, Feb. 26, 1827. He spent some years as a Hessian army musician. In 1781 he joined the Moravian church, and from 1795 to 1815 he lived in the Moravian settlements at Nazareth and Bethlehem, Pa., and was the leading spirit in the musical performances in both towns. He played violin and most winds, and as a novelty, would amuse his audience by performing simultaneously on 2 horns. A list of programs of the Collegium Musicum at Nazareth, beginning with 1796, is preserved in the Moravian Historical Soc. in Nazareth. He composed 14 woodwind *Parthien*, 2 "Water-music" suites, 18 anthems for Solo Voice or Chorus and Instruments, and *Psalm CIII* for Soloists, Chorus, and Orch. The greater portion of his MSS are housed in the Moravian Church archives in Bethlehem, and others are in the Moravian Foundation in Winston-Salem, N.C. See A. Rau and H. David, *A Catalogue of Music by American Moravians, 1742–1842* (Bethlehem, Pa., 1938).

BIBL.: D. Roberts, *The Sacred Vocal Music of D.M. M.: An American Moravian Composer* (diss., Univ. of Kentucky, 1978); K. Hahn, *The Wind Ensemble Music of D.M. M.* (thesis, Univ. of Mo., 1979).—NS/LK/DM

Michael, George (originally, **Panayiotous, Georgios Kryiacos**), 1980s teen idol whose career subsequently fizzled; (b. Bushey, England, June 25, 1963). The son of a Greek restaurateur and his English wife, Georgios Panayiotous soaked up the sounds of Motown, ska, and classic British pop that he heard in his neighborhood. He met Andrew Ridgeley, who shared his musical tastes, while they were still in grade school. When both were 18, they formed a band called the Executive, which enjoyed limited success playing in a ska style. When the band broke up, Ridgeley and Michael (as he was now known) renamed themselves Wham!, combining soulful melodies with their perky arrangements. They recorded some demo tracks in Ridgeley's basement and sent them to various record companies. They were signed to Innervision Records, which released "Wham Rap (Enjoy What You Do)" to moderate acclaim. Their second single, "Young Guns (Go for It)," went into the U.K. Top Ten. When their debut album *Fantastic* came out, it topped the U.K. charts, but was only a Brit-pop curiosity in the U.S.

Wham!'s sophomore effort, 1984's *Make It Big*, became one of the biggest hits of the 1980s. The album was propelled up the charts by its infectious pop singles like the #1 platinum "Wake Me Up Before You Go Go" and "Careless Whisper." They topped the chart a third time with the gold "Everything She Wanted" and went to #3 with "Freedom." The album topped the charts for three weeks and went sextuple platinum. It didn't hurt that MTV was at its peak influence and both Ridgeley and Michael were extremely videogenic. Michael became the youngest person ever to win the Igor Norvello Songwriter of the Year award. In presenting the award, one of Michael's musical heroes, Elton John, proclaimed Michael "the greatest songwriter of his generation."

By 1985, Michael was already inching towards a solo career. He appeared without Ridgeley on the 50th Anniversary special for the Apollo Theater, performing "Careless Whisper" with Smokey Robinson. After the mania that surrounded *Make It Big*, Wham's 1986 followup, *Music from the Edge of Heaven*, proved something of a letdown. Although it had three Top Ten singles, including the #3 "I'm Your Man," the #10 title track, and the Michael solo "A Different Corner," which went to #7, the album only managed to go platinum. Michael and Ridgeley decided to split up while they were still on top, playing a final concert at London's Wembley Stadium for 80,000 people.

Ridgeley dropped out of the music scene in favor of race-car driving and acting. Michael tried to break out of the teen-pop bag he and Ridgeley had occupied as Wham! and create something that might appeal to a broader audience. His first step was becoming the first white male to record a duet with Aretha Franklin. "I Knew You Were Waiting (For Me)" topped the pop charts in 1987, helping to set the stage for Michael's solo debut.

Michael wrote and produced *Faith*, a varied, sexy record. The first single from the album originally was heard on the *Beverly Hills Cop II* soundtrack, "I Want Your Sex," a bit of Latin funk pillow talk that was too hot for many radio stations. About one-third of U.S. radio stations refused to air it, and it could only be heard on British radio after dark. The accompanying video became an MTV sensation. The limited radio play kept the song out of the #1 position on the charts, where it topped out at #2, going platinum. The album's title track, a bit of acoustic latter-day rockabilly, topped the charts for four weeks, going gold. Michael's hip-wriggling video for the song was no doubt a big boost to its success. The ballad "Father Figure" topped the charts for two weeks, and the gold "One More Try" was #1 on the pop, R&B, and adult-contemporary charts. "Monkey" topped the charts for two weeks and "Kissing a Fool" rose to #5. "Hard Day" wasn't even released

as a single, but went to the R&B Top 30 as an album track. The album spent a dozen weeks at the top of the charts, and went ten times platinum, winning the Grammy for Album of the Year. However, when he toured to support the album, Michael was upset by the teenybopper audiences who screamed so loud that he couldn't hear himself sing. He wanted to be taken more seriously as an artist.

Michael made his case for himself as a serious performer three years after *Faith* when he released *Listen without Prejudice, Vol. 1*. Proclaiming his serious intentions, he stated he would not tour or appear in any videos to support the album; instead, he would devote his time to songwriting and improving his craft. The lead-off single "Praying for Time" topped the charts anyway. For "Freedom (90)"—a different tune than the Wham! Track—Michael's record label Columbia hired models Cindy Crawford, Christy Turlington, Naomi Campbell, and Linda Evangelista to lip synch the song on video. Several R-rated frames of Crawford had to be edited before it was shown on MTV. The single went gold and rose to #8. The final single, "Waiting for the Day," hit only #27 and the album went double platinum. Michael felt that Columbia would only promote him as a teen sex symbol; his label felt that he was doing little or nothing to help them market his music. Frustrated by the poor showing of the album that he felt represented his artistic maturation, Michael sued the label to be released from his contract. This effectively put his career on hold for four years. He could afford this, however: in 1992, the *London Times* proclaimed him one of the richest men in the U.K.

Meanwhile, Michael recorded some benefit projects, like 1991's gold, chart-topping live duet with Elton John on "Don't Let the Sun Go Down on Me," 1992's gold #10 "Too Funky" from the AIDS benefit *Red Hot and Dance* and the live #30 track from 1993, "Somebody to Love" with Michael fronting Queen for another AIDS-related benefit. In 1994, he lost the case to Columbia, and rather than appealing, he bought his way out of his contract. Michael became the first artist signed to the new Steven Speilberg/David Katzenbaum/David Geffen label Dreamworks. Six years after his last release, the 1996 album, *Older*, went only platinum, though it spawned two gold singles, "Jesus to a Child" and "Fast Love."

In 1998, Michael was arrested for "engaging in a lewd act" in a men's room in a Beverly Hills public park. He pleaded no contest to the charges, paid the $810 fine, and did 80 hours of community service. Michael had effectively outed himself, a process he finished on CNN in the wake of the incident. The arresting officer then sued Michael for damages, saying the artist had defamed him in the video for "Outside," a new track recorded for his 1998 double CD greatest hits record. The officer lost.

Michael signed with Virgin Records in 1999, releasing an album of covers produced by Phil Ramone. The songs ran from the Police's "Roxanne" to the Bono/Luciano Pavarotti duet "Miss Sarajevo." His solo career has been a slippery slope after a fast start, and it will be interesting to see if he can regain his footing.

WRITINGS: With T. Parsons, *Naked* (London, 1990).

DISC.: WHAM! *Fantastic!* (1983); *Make It Big* (1984); *Music from the Edge of Heaven* (1986). **GEORGE MICHAEL:** *Faith* (1987); *Listen without Prejudice, Vol.1* (1990); *Older* (1996); *Songs from the Last Century* (1999).—HB

Michaelides, Solon, Greek conductor, musicologist, and composer; b. Nicosia, Nov. 25, 1905; d. Athens, Sept. 9, 1979. He studied at London's Trinity Coll. of Music (1927–30) before pursuing his training in Paris with Boulanger (harmony, counterpoint, and fugue) and Maize and Cortot (piano) at the École Normale de Musique (1930–34), and with Labey (conducting) and Lioncourt (composition) at the Schola Cantorum. In 1934 he founded the Limassol Cons. in Cyprus, for which he served as director until 1956. He also taught music at its Lanitis Communal H.S. (1941–56). From 1957 to 1970 he was director of the Salonica State Cons. He also was director-general and principal conductor of the Salonica State Orch. from 1959 to 1970. As a guest conductor, he appeared in Europe and the U.S.

WRITINGS: *Synchroni angliki moussiki* (Modern English Music; Nicosia, 1939); *I kypriaki laiki moussiki* (Cypriot Folk Music; Nicosia, 1944; 2nd ed., 1956); *Harmonia tis synchronis moussikis* (Harmony of Contemporary Music; Limassol, 1945); *The Neo- Hellenic Folk-Music* (Limassol, 1948); *I neo-elleniki moussiki* (Neo- Hellenic Music; Nicosia, 1952); *The Music of Ancient Greece: An Encyclopedia* (London, 1978).

WORKS: DRAMATIC: *Nausicaa*, ballet (1950); *Ulysses*, opera (1951; rev. 1972–73); incidental music for Greek tragedies. **ORCH.:** *De profundis* (1933; rev. 1949); *2 Byzantine Sketches* for Strings (1934); *Cypriot Wedding* for Flute and Strings (1935); *2 Greek Symphonic Pictures* (1936); *Byzantine Offering* for Strings (1944); *Archaic Suite* for Flute, Oboe, Harp, and Strings (1954); *Kypriaka eleftheria* (To Cypriot Freedom; 1959); Piano Concerto (1966); *In memoriam* for Strings (1974; based on the Piano Sonata, 1934). **CHAMBER:** String Quartet (1934); Piano Sonata (1934); Piano Trio (1946); many piano pieces. **VOCAL:** *O táfos* (The Tomb) for Mezzo- soprano, Baritone, Chorus, and Orch. (1936); *I eleftheroi poliorkimenoi* (The Free Besieged) for Soprano, Baritone, Chorus, and Orch. (1955); *Hymnos stin eleftheria* (Hymn to Freedom), the Cypriot national anthem; songs.—NS/LK/DM

Michaels-Moore, Anthony, English baritone; b. Essex, April 8, 1957. He studied with Denis Matthews at the Univ. of Newcastle (B.A., 1978), at the Royal Scottish Academy of Music and Drama in Glasgow, and with Eduardo Asquez and Neilson-Taylor. After winning the Pavarotti Competition in 1985, he appeared with Opera North in Leeds in 1986. In 1987 he made his debut at London's Covent Garden in *Jenůfa* and at the English National Opera in London as Zurga in *Les Pêcheurs de perles*. He made his U.S. debut with the Opera Co. of Philadelphia in 1989 as Guglielmo. In 1992 he created the role of Don Fernando in the stage premiere of Gerhard's *The Duenna* in Madrid. Following an engagement as Posa with Opera North in 1993, he sang Licinius in *La Vestale* at Milan's La Scala that year. In 1994 he was engaged as Figaro at the Vienna State Opera and as Sharpless at the Opéra de la Bastille in Paris. In 1995 he sang Simon Boccanegra at Covent Garden. He made his Metropolitan Opera debut in N.Y. as Marcello on Dec. 28, 1996. In 1997 he portrayed Macbeth at Covent Garden. In 1999 he sang Enrico in *Lucia di Lammermoor* at the Metropolitan Opera. Among his other roles are Escamillo, Hamlet, Falke, Belcore, Lescaut, Onegin, and Scarpia.—NS/LK/DM

Michalsky, Donal, American composer and teacher; b. Pasadena, Calif., July 13, 1928; d. in a fire at his home in Newport Beach, Calif., Dec. 31, 1975. After clarinet training in his youth, he studied with Stevens (theory) and Dahl (orchestration) at the Univ. of Southern Calif. at Los Angeles (Ph.D., 1965) and on a Fulbright scholarship with Fortner in Freiburg im Breisgau (1958). From 1960 until his tragic death he was a prof. of composition at Calif. State Coll. in Fullerton. His music was marked by robust dissonant counterpoint, often in dodecaphonic technique, and yet permeated with a lyric and almost Romantic sentiment.

WORKS: DRAMATIC: Opera: *Der arme Heinrich* (unfinished MS destroyed in the fire that took his life). **ORCH.:** Concertino for Trombone and Band (1953); *6 Pieces* for Chamber Orch. (1956); Little Sym. for Band (1959); 3 syms.: No. 1, *Wheel of Time*, for Chorus and Orch. (1967), No. 2, Sinfonia concertante, for Clarinet, Piano, and Orch. (1969), and No. 3 (1975). **CHAMBER:** Quintet for 2 Trumpets, 2 Clarinets, and Piano (1951); *Divertimento* for 2 Clarinets and Bass Clarinet (1952); *Partita* for Oboe d'Amore, String Trio, and Strings (1958); Cello Sonata (1958); *Morning Music* for Chamber Ensemble (1959); *Trio Concertino* for Flute, Oboe, and Horn (1961); *Variations* for Clarinet and Piano (1962); *Fantasia alla marcia* for Brass Quartet (1963); *Partita piccola* for Flute and Piano (1964); *Allegretto* for Clarinet and Strings (1964); *3 x 4* for Saxophone Quartet (1972). **Piano:** Sonata for 2 Pianos (1957); *Sonata concertante* (1961); *Song Suite* (1970). **VOCAL:** *Cantata memoriam* for High Voice and 12 Instruments (1971); songs.—NS/LK/DM

Micheau, Janine, French soprano; b. Toulouse, April 17, 1914; d. Paris, Oct. 18, 1976. She studied in Toulouse and at the Paris Cons. In 1933 she made her operatic debut in *Louise* at the Paris Opéra-Comique, where she was a distinguished member until 1956. In 1937 she made her debut at London's Covent Garden as Micaëla. She made her U.S. debut as Mélisande in San Francisco in 1938, a role she subsequently sang with remarkable success on both sides of the Atlantic. In 1939 she appeared for the first time at the Teatro Colón in Buenos Aires. From 1940 to 1956 she was a member of the Paris Opéra. Among her other esteemed roles were Pamina, Juliet, Violetta, Gilda, Zerbinetta, Sophie, and Anne Trulove.—NS/LK/DM

Michel, Paul-Baudouin, Belgian composer; b. Haine-St.-Pierre, Sept. 7, 1930. He studied humanities at the Mons Cons., then took courses in composition with Absil at the Queen Elisabeth Music Chapel in Brussels (1959–62) and in conducting at the Royal Cons. in Brussels; attended summer courses in Darmstadt with Ligeti, Boulez, Maderna, and Messiaen. He was later appointed director of the Academy of Music in Woluwe-St.-Lambert. His music adheres to the doctrine of precisely planned structural formations in a highly modern idiom.

WORKS: DRAMATIC: *Pandora*, ballet (1961); *Jeanne la Folle*, opera (1983–87). **ORCH.:** *Variations symphoniques* (1960); *5 inframorphoses* for Strings (1963); *Symphonium* (1966); *Concaténation* for Chamber Orch. (1967); *Hors-Temps* (1970); *Confluences* for 2 Chamber Groups (1974); *Lamobylrinthe ou Dovetailed Forms*, concerto for Piano and 21 Instruments (1979); *Humoresque-Nocturne-Rondo* for Chamber Orch. (1979–80); *Trois nocturnes* (1981); Piano Concerto (1986); Harpsichord Concerto (1986); Concertinetto for Piano and Orch. (1987); *Symphonium "Jeanne la Folle"* (1988). **CHAMBER:** String Trio (1956); Violin Sonata (1960); *Hommage à François Rabelais*, wind quintet (1960); Clarinet Sonatina (1960); String Quartet (1961); *Sérénade concertante* for Violin and Piano (1962); *Quadrance* for String Quartet (1965); *Conduit et Danse hiératique* for Harp (1964); *Monologue double* for Flute and Tape (1965); *Ultramorphoses* for Flute, Clarinet, Saxophone, Percussion, Piano, Violin, Viola, and Cello (1965); *Clarbassonance* for Bass Clarinet and Tape (1966); *Bassonance* for Bassoon and Tape (1966); *Oscillonance* for 2 Violins and Piano (1967); *Colloque* for Piano, Trumpet, and Percussion (1967); *Gravures* for 2 Trumpets and Horn (1972); *Intonations* for Brass (1972); *Parelléloide* for Clavichord and Tape (1974); *Trois sur quatre* for Flute, Cello, and Piano (1979); *Décentrement* for Wind Quintet (1980); *Expansion I* for String Quartet (1981); *Versets* for 2 Ondes Martenot (1982); *Ellipse* for 4 Saxophones and 2 Harps (1983); *Poème* for Cello and Piano (1985); *Hommage à Paul Delvaux* for Saxophone and Harpsichord (1986); *Polyèdre* for 2 Percussionists (1988). **KEYBOARD: Piano:** *Partita* No. 1 (1955); *Transsonance* (1965); *Libration I* (1971; rev. 1973); *Lithophanie* for Prepared Piano (1971); *Variations concentriques* (1971); *Musicoïde* for 2 Prepared Pianos (1971); *Orbe* (1972). **Organ:** *Transphonies pour plusieurs nefs* (1969); *Puzzlephonie* (1972). **VOCAL:** *Equateur*, cantata (1962); *Motet aléatoire sur le "Veni creator"* for Chorus, 19 Instruments, and Percussion (1962); *Rex pacificus*, radiophonic motet for Bass, Chorus, Orch., and Tape (1968); *Le Feu et le monde* for Narrator, Soloists, Chorus, Organ, 12 Trumpets, and Percussion (1970); *Systoles—Diastoles* for Soprano and Instruments (1973); *Le Graal gras, ode au pétrole* for Speaker, Soprano, 10 Instruments, and Tape (1980); *Ecce Homo* for Bass and Chorus (1983); *Itinerrance* for Soprano, Clarinet, and Piano (1988).—**NS/LK/DM**

Michelangeli, Arturo Benedetti,

celebrated Italian pianist and pedagogue; b. Brescia, Jan. 5, 1920; d. Lugano, June 12, 1995. He began his training with his father and studied violin with Paolo Chiuieri at the Venturi Inst. in Brescia. When he was 10, he entered the Milan Cons. to pursue piano studies with Giuseppe Anfossi. He was awarded his diploma at age 13. In 1939 he captured 1st prize in the Geneva competition and that same year was made a prof. at the Bologna Cons. From 1941 to 1943 he served in the Italian Air Force, and then joined the anti-Fascist partisan movement. Although taken prisoner by the German occupation forces, he soon managed to escape and awaited the complete liberation of Italy to resume his career. With World War II over in 1945, he played in his homeland. In 1946 he made his first tour of Europe, and played for the first time in the U.S. in 1948. In subsequent years, he appeared in selected major music centers of the world while acquiring a legendary reputation as a virtuoso. Unfortunately, he also developed a reputation for cancelling engagements at the last minute; when he did perform, however, his concerts were invariably sold out

and accorded ovations by public and critics alike. From 1964 to 1969 he was director of his own piano academy in Brescia. In his later years, he devoted most of his time to teaching. While his technical mastery made him one of the great keyboard exponents of the Romantic repertoire, his sympathies ranged widely, from early music to the 20th century.

BIBL.: A. Sabatucci, ed., *A.B. M.: Il grembo del suono* (Milan, 1996).—**NS/LK/DM**

Micheletti, Gaston,

French tenor; b. Tavaco, Corsica, Jan. 5, 1892; d. Ajaccio, May 21, 1959. He was a student at the Paris Cons. In 1922 he made his operatic debut as Gounod's Faust in Rheims. In 1925 he became a member of the Paris Opéra-Comique, where he remained a principal artist for 2 decades. He also made guest appearances in Brussels, Nice, and Monte Carlo. In later years, he was active as a voice teacher in Paris and then in Ajaccio. Among his admired roles were Don José, Des Grieux, and Werther.—**NS/LK/DM**

Micheli, Domenico,

Italian priest and composer; b. Bologna, c. 1540; d. probably there, c. 1590. He received training at S. Petronio in Bologna. He was maestro di cappella at Udine Cathedral in 1567 and was in the service of the Malvasia family in Cesena in 1577. From 1581 to 1588 he was in the service of the Innocenzo Malvasia in Ravenna. Returning to Bologna, he became singing master (1588) and maestro di cappella (1589) at S. Pietro. Micheli was an accomplished madrigalist and publ. 6 vols. of such works in Venice (1564–84).—**LK/DM**

Micheli, Romano,

Italian composer and writer on music; b. Rome, c. 1575; d. there, after 1659. He studied with Soriano and G.M. Nanino. He was in the service of the Duke of S. Giovanni in Rome (c. 1593) and of Gesualdo in Venice (c. 1596–98), then was maestro di cappella of Tivoli Cathedral (1609–10), Concordia Cathedral, near Udine (1616), the Metropolitan Church in Aquileia, near Venice (1618–21), and S. Luigi dei Francesi in Rome (1625–36). After serving as a canon in Naples, he returned to Rome about 1644. Micheli excelled as a composer of canons, and claimed to have invented the canoni sopra le vocali di più parole ("canons on the vowels of several words"). He was a highly disputatious individual and engaged in various controversies with his contemporaries via his polemical writings.—**NS/LK/DM**

Michi, Orazio,

eminent Italian harpist and composer, known as **della Arpa** because of his virtuosity; b. Alifa Caserta, c. 1595; d. Rome, Oct. 26, 1641. From 1614 to 1623 he was in Rome, and after that, with Cardinal Maurizio of Savoy. Until 1914 his works were unknown except for 5 arias publ. in Bianchi's *Raccolta d'arie* (Rome, 1640) and a 6th one publ. by Torchi in Vol. 5 of *L'arte musicale in Italia*. Then, A. Cametti publ., in the *Rivista Musicale Italiana* (April 1914), a full description and complete thematic catalog of about 60 cantatas by Michi, which he had discovered in various Italian libraries and which prove that Michi was one of the earliest and most important Roman masters of the monodic style.—**NS/LK/DM**

Michl, Joseph (Christian) Willibald, German composer; b. Neumarkt, Upper Palatinate, July 9, 1745; d. there, Aug. 1, 1816. He was the son of the composer Johann Joseph Ildefons Michl (b. Neumarkt, 1708; d. Regensburg, 1770). After training at the electoral Gymnasium and Lyceum in Munich, he studied with Placidus von Camerloher in Freising. He played double bass at the Jesuit church of St. Michael in Munich before serving as a composer to the electoral chamber (1771–78). From 1784 to 1803 he lived at the Augustinian prebendary institute. Among his output were well-crafted orch. works, chamber pieces, and sacred music.

BIBL.: A. Zehelein, *J. M.* (Munich, 1928).—**LK/DM**

Michna, Adam Václav, notable Czech composer; b. probably in Jindřichuv Hradec, c. 1600; d. there, Nov. 2, 1676. He pursued his career in his native town. After training at the Jesuit Gymnasium, he became town organist about 1633. He also was active as a wine merchant, property owner, and civic leader. Michna particularly distinguished himself as a composer of vernacular hymns and Latin concertato works.

WORKS: *Česká mariánská muzika* for 4 to 5 Voices and Basso Continuo (Prague, 1647; ed. by J. Sehnal and L. Štukavec, Prague, 1974); *Officium vespertinum* for 5 Voices and Instruments, op.5 (Prague, 1648); *Loutna česká* for Violin, Strings, and Organ (Prague, 1653; incomplete; reconstruction ed. by E. Trolda, Prague, 1943); *Sacra et litaniae* (Prague, 1654; includes 6 masses, a Requiem, a Te Deum, and 2 litany settings for 4 to 8 Voices and Instruments); *Svatoročni muzika* for 4 to 5 Voices and Basso Continuo (Prague, 1661); *Missa Sancti Wenceslai* for 6 Voices, 2 Violins, 4 Violas, 2 Trumpets, and Organ (n.d.; ed. by J. Sehnal, Musica Antiqua Bohemia, 2nd series, I, 1966). —**LK/DM**

Mico, Richard, English composer; b. Taunton, c. 1590; d. London (buried), April 10, 1661. He became a musician at Thorndon Hall, Essex, the seat of John, 1st Lord Petre, in 1608, serving the latter's son, Sir William Petre. In 1631 he settled in London. Mico was one of the principal composers of consort music. About 40 of his works, among them 30 fantasias, are extant.—**LK/DM**

Middelschulte, Wilhelm, eminent German organist and teacher; b. Werne, near Dortmund, April 3, 1863; d. there, May 4, 1943. He studied at the Inst. für Kirchenmusik in Berlin with Löschhorn (piano), Haupt (organ), and Commer and Schröder (composition). After serving as organist at the Church of St. Luke in Berlin (1888–91), he settled in Chicago. He was organist at the Cathedral of the Holy Name (1891–95); subsequently was organist at Milwaukee's St. James's Church (1899–1919) and also a prof. of organ at the Wisc. Cons. of Music there. He was greatly distinguished for his interpretations of Bach. In 1935 he became instructor of theory and organ at the Detroit Foundation Music School. In 1939 he returned to Germany.—**NS/LK/DM**

Middleton, Hubert Stanley, English organist, teacher, and composer; b. Windsor, May 11, 1890; d. London, Aug. 13, 1959. He studied at the Royal Academy of Music in London and at the Univ. of Cambridge (M.A., 1920). He was appointed organist and director of music at Trinity Coll., Cambridge, in 1931, and also taught at the Royal Academy of Music in London. His specialty was cathedral music. He composed a number of anthems and organ pieces. He was greatly esteemed as an educator, and his teaching methods exercised profound influence on his students, many of whom became educators in their own right.—**NS/LK/DM**

Middleton, Robert (Earl), American composer and teacher; b. Diamond, Ohio, Nov. 18, 1920. He was educated at Harvard Univ. (B.A., 1948; M.A., 1954), and also studied composition with Boulanger at the Longy School of Music (1941–42), piano with Beveridge Webster at the New England Cons. of Music in Boston (1941–42), and with K.U. Schnabel (1946–49). While holding the John Knowles Paine Traveling Fellowship from Harvard Univ. (1948–50), he pursued his composition studies with Boulanger in Paris. In 1965–66 he held a Guggenheim fellowship. After teaching at Harvard Univ. (1950–53), he joined the faculty of Vassar Coll. in 1953, where he was a prof. from 1966 to 1985 and chairman of the music dept. from 1973 to 1976. He publ. *Harmony in Modern Counterpoint* (Boston, 1967). He displayed a deft handling of genres and forms throughout his basically conservative course as a composer.

WORKS: DRAMATIC: *Life Goes to a Party*, opera (1947; Tanglewood, Aug. 12, 1948); *The Nightingale is Guilty*, opera (1953; Boston, March 1954); *Command Performance*, opera-concerto (1958–60; rev. 1987–88). **ORCH.:** *Andante* (1948); Violin Concerto (1949; rev. 1984); *Concerto di Quattro Duetti* for Solo Winds and String Orch. (1962; rev. 1986); *Variations* for Piano and Orch. (1965; rev. 1984–85); *Sinfonia Filofonica* (Poughkeepsie, N.Y., May 4, 1969); *Gardens 1 2 3 4 5* (1972); *Overture to The Charterhouse of Parma* (1981). **CHAMBER:** 3 violin sonatas (n.d., 1941, 1948); 3 string quartes (1950, 1989, 1990); *Ritratti della Notte* (*Portraits of the Night*) for Flute and Piano (1966); *Approximations* for Viola and Piano (1967); *Vier Trio-Sätze in romantischer Manier* for Violin, Cello, and Piano (1970); 2 Duologues for Violin and Piano (1973); 4 Nocturnes for Clarinet and Piano (1979). **KEYBOARD: Piano:** *Passacaglia and Fugue* for Piano, 4–Hands (1940); Sonata (1957); 12 Inventions (1960–61); *Notebooks of Designs* (book 1, 1968; book 2, 1968, rev. 1978); *vARIAzioni—variAZIONI* (1970). **Organ:** 4 Preludes (1956). **VOCAL:** Choral pieces; songs.—**NS/LK/DM**

Middleton, Velma, singer; b. St. Louis, Sept. 1, 1917; d. Freetown, Sierra Leone, Feb. 10, 1961. Her brother, Emmanuel, was a string bassist. She first toured as part of Connie McLean's Orch. in the "Cotton Club Show," visiting South America with this company c. 1938. She worked mainly as a solo entertainer until joining Louis Armstrong in 1942; she sang with Armstrong's Big Band and later worked regularly with Louis's All Stars. Her comic duets with Armstrong, which also featured her dancing, were audience favorites. In January 1961, while touring Africa with Armstrong, she was taken ill and died three weeks later in a Sierra Leone hospital. She recorded two albums as a leader (1947, 1951); she was joined on the first by Earl Hines and Cozy Cole.

Disc.: ARMSTRONG: *That's My Desire* (1947); *Baby, It's Cold Outside* (1951).—**JC/LP**

Midler, Bette, an artist of remarkably wide-ranging talents as song stylist, comedienne, and cabaret performer; b. Paterson, N.J., Dec. 1, 1945. Bette Midler perfected the persona of the Divine Miss M during a long-running engagement at N.Y.'s notorious club Continental Baths. Projecting the image of a streetwise, all-around entertainer through her flamboyance, uninhibited use of gutter comedy, and command of a variety of musical styles, Midler burst into prominence in the early 1970s through television appearances, live performances, and two best-selling albums. Since then she has made her mark as a film and television actress, and as a solo star on Broadway, while continuing to perform and tour.

Bette Midler was raised in Honolulu, Hawaii, where she studied drama in college for a year before securing a minor role in the 1966 movie *Hawaii*. Traveling to the mainland with earnings from the film role, Midler moved to N.Y., where she worked a variety of mundane jobs while securing roles in several Off-Broadway productions and singing in clubs and restaurants for experience. She landed a part in the chorus of *Fiddler on the Roof* and stayed with the show for three years, eventually working her way up to the central role of Tzeitel (Tevye's daughter).

In 1970 Bette Midler decided to concentrate on the singing aspect of her career by devising a cabaret-style show that proved enormously popular at N.Y.'s Continental Baths, a group-games club largely frequented by homosexuals and transvestites. Playing piano and performing widely eclectic material, she developed the persona of the Divine Miss M, a streetwise, foul-mouthed, flamboyant singer and comedienne. She was backed by the female vocal trio the Harlettes, whose original members included Melissa Manchester and Katey Sagal (later of television's *Married ...With Children*). Her Saturday night performances became *the* cult attraction of N.Y., and led to national notoriety.

Introduced to a larger audience through regular television appearances in 1972, Bette Midler signed with Atlantic Records, where her debut album, naturally titled *The Divine Miss M*, became an instant best-seller and led to successful engagements at exclusive clubs across the country. The album, considered her definitive recorded work, yielded a major hit with a remake of "Do You Want to Dance" and a near-smash with the old Andrews Sisters' song "Boogie Woogie Bugle Boy"; it also containeed her theme, the bittersweet "Friends," and John Prine's poignant "Hello in There," Leon Russell's "Superstar," and remakes of "The Chapel of Love" and "Leader of the Pack."

Headlining lavish New Year's Eve shows at Philharmonic Hall in 1972 and 1973, Midler successfully toured throughout the United States in 1973, accompanied by the Harlettes and musical director Barry Manilow, who produced Midler's first two albums. Her second, self-titled release became a best-seller despite yielding no major hit single; it contained such diverse material as "I Shall Be Released," "In the Mood," and "Uptown/Da Doo Run Run."

Bette Midler took 1974 off, as Barry Manilow left early in the year to pursue his own successful pop career. During 1975 she returned to live performance with a cross-country tour that concluded with her *Clams on the Half-Shell Revue* on Broadway, which broke box-office records. However, 1976's *Songs for the New Depression* was greeted with negative critical reviews, sold only modestly, and failed to produce even a minor hit. Midler's next album, *Live at Last*, fared even less well. In 1977 her *Broken Blossom* was issued, and she appeared in her first television special on NBC, *Ol' Red Hair Is Back*. Spending much of 1978 working on her first feature film, Midler also recorded *Thighs and Whispers*, which yielded the moderate hit "Married Men."

Bette Midler's film debut, *The Rose*, was a great success and revived her flagging career. She won excellent critical reviews and an Academy Award nomination for her intense and sensitive portrayal of a tough but vulnerable rock star seemingly unable to escape from a maelstrom of liquor, drugs, and sex that leads to her self-destruction (the story was loosely based on the life and times of blues rocker Janis Joplin). The soundtrack album, which featured "When a Man Loves a Woman," "Stay with Me," and the smash hit "The Rose," stayed on the album charts for nearly a year.

However, Midler was unable to build on this success, and the early 1980s found her career back in the doldrums. In 1980 she released a book, *A View from a Broad*, which chronicled her world tour, and the R-rated film *Divine Madness* attempted to create, with equivocal success, the humor, compassion, and manic spontaneity of her live performances. Her 1982 film *Jinxed* proved a dismal failure, and the album *No Frills* sold only modestly while producing minor hits with Marshall Crenshaw's "Favorite Waste of Time" and the Rolling Stones' "Beast of Burden." Touring for the first time in three years in 1982–1983, Midler next recorded the all-comedy album *Mud Will Be Flung Tonight!*, another less-than-successful effort.

Midler returned to form with a series of film roles in the mid-1980s that established her as a talented comedian. In 1986 she had the starring role as a spoiled Beverly Hills matron in *Down and Out in Beverly Hills*, with Nick Nolte and Richard Dreyfuss, followed by a similar role in *Ruthless People*, with Danny DeVito. However, the identical-twin comedy, 1988's *Big Business* with Lily Tomlin, was greeted by mixed reviews. She followed this with the two-hanky weeper *Beaches*, with Barbara Hershey. Its best-selling soundtrack remained on the album charts for more than three years. It yielded a top hit with the love song "Wind Beneath My Wings" and included "Under the Boardwalk," "The Glory of Love," and Randy Newman's "I Think It's Gonna Rain Today." Her follow-up studio album, *Some People's Lives*, produced the smash hit "From a Distance," a ballad similar in style to "Wind." Midler's movie career took another nosedive with the musical *For the Boys*, although the soundtrack managed to sell despite the film's poor box-office performance.

Bette Midler returned to touring in 1993 with her Experience the Divine tour that included a record-breaking run at N.Y.'s Radio City Music Hall. She also appeared on CBS-TV in her highly rated version of the musical *Gypsy*, which yielded a soundtrack album. In late 1995 she released a new studio album.

DISC.: *The Divine Miss M* (1972); *B. M.* (1973); *Songs for the New Depression* (1976); *Live at Last* (1977); *Broken Blossom* (1977); *Thighs and Whispers* (1979); *The Rose* (soundtrack; 1979); *Divine Madness* (1980); *No Frills* (1983); *Mud Will Be Flung Tonight!* (1985); *Beaches* (soundtrack; 1989); *Some People's Lives* (1990); *For the Boys* (1991); *The Divine Collection* (1993); *Gypsy* (television soundtrack) (1993); *Bette of Roses* (1995).

BIBL.: Robb Baker, *B. M.* (N.Y., 1975).—**BH**

Midori (real name, **Goto Mi Dori**), outstanding Japanese violinist; b. Osaka, Oct. 25, 1971. She studied with her mother, Setsu Goto; in 1981, went to the U.S., where she took violin lessons with Dorothy DeLay at the Aspen (Colo.) Music School and continued her training with that mentor at N.Y.'s Juilliard School. She attracted the attention of Zubin Mehta when she was 10 years old; he subsequently engaged her as a soloist with the N.Y. Phil., with which she traveled on an extensive Asian tour that included Hong Kong, Singapore, Korea, Thailand, and her native Japan. There followed concerts with the Berlin Phil., the Boston Sym. Orch., the Chicago Sym. Orch., the Cleveland and Philadelphia Orchs., the Los Angeles Phil., the London Sym. Orch., and other European and American orchs., in programs that included not only classical concertos but also modern works, under the direction of such renowned conductors, besides Mehta, as Bernstein, Previn, Maazel, Dohnányi, Leppard, and Barenboim. She also attracted the attention of popular television programs, and appeared as a guest of President and Mrs. Reagan at the White House during the NBC-TV special Christmas in Washington (1983). Most importantly, she won the admiration of orch. members for her remarkable artistic dependability. On one occasion, when a string broke on the concertmaster's violin during an orch. introduction, she demonstrated her sangfroid; since she had a few minutes to spare before her entrance as a soloist, she handed her own violin to the player and coolly changed the broken string in time to continue the performance without pause. On Oct. 21, 1990, she made her N.Y. recital debut at Carnegie Hall. In 1992 she created the Midori Foundation to promote the cause of classical music.—**NS/LK/DM**

Miedél, Rainer, German conductor; b. Regensburg, June 1, 1937; d. Seattle, March 25, 1983. He studied cello with Navarra in Paris, and conducting with Ferrara in Siena and Kertész in Salzburg. In 1965 he became a cellist in the Stockholm Phil. That same year, he won 1st prize in the Swedish Radio conducting competition. In 1967 he made his formal conducting debut with the Stockholm Phil., and then was its asst. conductor (1969–76). He also was music director of the Gävleborgs Sym. Orch. (1969–76), and asst. conductor (1969–72) and assoc. conductor (1972–73) of the Baltimore Sym. Orch. From 1976 until his death he was music director of the Seattle Sym. Orch. He also was interim music director of the Fla. Phil. (1980–82).—**NS/LK/DM**

Mieg, Peter, Swiss composer and painter; b. Lenzburg, Sept. 5, 1906; d. there, Dec. 7, 1990. He studied composition, piano, and theory with C.A. Richter in Lenzburg, and then continued his musical training with H. Münch in Basel, E. Frey in Zürich, and Landowska in Basel. He also was drawn to painting, taking his Ph.D. in 1933 at the Univ. of Zürich with a diss. on modern Swiss art. While he devoted much of his time to composition, he also was active as a painter. In 1961 he held his first major exhibition of paintings in Zürich, Paris, Vienna, and other cities. As a composer, his output took on a pronounced individual style after 1950. His autobiography was publ. as *Laterna magica* (Lenzburg, 1986).

WORKS: DRAMATIC: Ballet: *La fête de la ligne* (1935); *Daphne* (1943). **ORCH.:** Concerto for 2 Pianos and Orch. (1939–42); 2 piano concertos (1947, 1961); Violin Concerto (1948–49); *Concerto da camera* (1952); Concerto for Harpsichord and Chamber Orch. (1953); *Concerto veneziano* for Strings (1955); Oboe Concerto (1957); Sym. (1958); Concerto for Flute and Strings (1962); *Rondeau symphonique* (1964); Cello Concerto (1966–67); Concerto for Harp and Strings (1970); Concerto for 2 Flutes and Strings (1973–74); *Combray* for Strings (1977); *Triple concerto le goût italien* for Violin, Viola, Cello, and String Orch. (1978); *Schlossbildermusik* (1980); Double Concerto for Piano, Cello, and Orch. (1983–84); *Ouverture pour Monsieur Lully* for Strings (1986). **CHAMBER:** Violin Sonata (1936); 3 string quartets (1936–37; 1944–45; 1987); *Divertimento* for Oboe, Violin, Viola, and Cello (1950); *Musik* for Harpsichord, Flute, Oboe, Violin, Viola, Cello, and Double Bass (1954); Flute Sonata (1963); Quintet for Flute, 2 Violins, Cello, and Harpsichord (1969); Wind Quintet (1977); Piano Trio (1984–85); Cello Sonata (1986); keyboard pieces, including 5 piano sonatas (1944; 1944; 1959; 1975; 1987–88), harpsichord pieces, and organ music. **VOCAL:** Choral works; songs.

BIBL.: U. Däster, W. Kläy, and W. Labhart, *P. M.: Eine Monographie* (Aarau and Frankfurt am Main, 1976). —**NS/LK/DM**

Mielck, Ernst, Finnish composer; b. Vyborg, Oct. 24, 1877; d. Locarno, Italy, Oct. 22, 1899 (2 days before his 22nd birthday). He studied piano in St. Petersburg and composition with Max Bruch in Berlin. His early death deprived Finland of a major musical talent. He left several works showing considerable technical skill and inventive power, among them a String Quartet (1895), *Macbeth Overture* (1895), String Quintet (1896–97), *Finnish Symphony* (1897), *Dramatic Overture* (1898), 2 piano concertos (1895, 1898), and *Finnish Suite* for Orch. (1899). A monograph on Mielck was publ. by W. Mauke (Leipzig, 1901).—**NS/LK/DM**

Mielczewski, Marcin, significant Polish composer; b. place and date unknown; d. Warsaw, Sept. 1651. He was a member of the royal chapel in Warsaw by 1638. From 1645 he served as director of music to Karol Ferdynand Waza, Bishop of Plock, brother to the

King. Mielczewski was a worthy composer of sacred vocal music, producing concertatos, masses, and motets of worth. He also wrote some instrumental canzonas. See Z. Szweykowski, ed., *Marcin Mielczewski; Opera omni*, Monumenta Musicae in Polonia (1976 et seq.). —**LK/DM**

Mielke, Antonia, German soprano; b. Berlin, c. 1852; d. there, Nov. 15, 1907. At first she sang chiefly coloratura roles, but gradually assumed the great dramatic parts, for which she was particularly gifted. She sang the Wagner heroines at the Metropolitan Opera in N.Y. during the season of 1890–91 (succeeding Lilli Lehmann); also toured the U.S. in concert recitals. Returning to Germany, she continued her operatic career until 1902, when she settled in Berlin as a teacher. —**NS/LK/DM**

Miereanu, Costin, Romanian-born French composer and teacher; b. Bucharest, Feb. 27, 1943. He studied in Bucharest at the School of Music (B.M., 1960) and the Cons. (M.F.A., 1966), and then attended the summer courses in new music given by Stockhausen, Ligeti, and Karkoschka in Darmstadt (1967–68). In 1968 he settled in France and in 1977 became a naturalized French citizen. He pursued training in musical semiotics at the École des Hautes Études en Sciences Sociales in Paris (D.M.A., 1978) and in the liberal arts at the Univ. of Paris (Ph.D., 1979). In 1978 he joined the faculty of the Univ. of Paris. He also was associated with Editions Salabert (from 1981), and taught at the Sorbonne in Paris (from 1982) and at the summer courses in new music in Darmstadt (from 1982). His music represents a totality of the cosmopolitan avant-garde: semiotics, structuralism, serialism, electronic sound, aleatory, musical-verbal theater, etc.

WORKS: DRAMATIC: *L'Avenir est dans les oeufs*, opera (1980); *La Porte du paradis*, lyric fantasy (1989–91); film scores. **ORCH.:** *Monostructures I* (1966) and *II* (1967); *Finis coronat opus* (1966); *Couleur du temps* for Strings (1966–68); *Espace dernier* (1966–69; also for Chorus, 6 Instrumental Groups, and Tape); *Rosario* (1973–76); *Rosenzeit* (1980); *Miroirs celestes* (1981–83); *Voyage d'hiver II* (1982–85); *Doppel(kammer)konzert* for Saxophonist, Percussion, and Chamber Orch. (1985); *Un temps sans mémoire* (1991). **CHAMBER:** *Variants* for Clarinet (1966); *Sursum corda triplum* for 7 Instruments (1967–82); *Espace au delà du dernier* for Chamber Ensemble (1968); *Dans La Nuit des temps* for Variable Ensemble and Tape (1968–69); *Polymorphies 5 x 7 (A)* for Variable Ensemble and Tape (1968–69) and *(B)* for 8 Instruments (1969–70); *Altar* for 6 Players or Singers, Tape, and Visuals ad libitum (1973); *Aquarius* for 2 Pianos and 2 Percussion (1974–80); *Musique élémentaire de concert* for Chamber Ensemble (1977); *Piano-Miroir* for Piano, Polyphonic Synthesizer or Electric Organ, Tape, and Visuals ad libitum (1978); *Do-Mi-Si-La-Do-Re* for Saxophonist and Tape (1980–81); *Variants-invariants* for Alto or Soprano Saxophone or Bass Clarinet and Korg SE 500 Echo Chamber (1982); *Bucharest-Grenade* for Guitar (1983); *Aksax* for Bass Saxophone (1983); *Bolero des Balkans (C)* for Saxophone(s) and Percussion (1984); *Gyrasol I* for Recorder Quartet, Percussion, and Tape (1984); *Ombres lumineuses* for Chamber Group and Synthesizers (1986); *Miroir liquide* for 6 Players (1986); *Tension en cycle* for 6 Percussion and Tape (1987); *Limping Rock* for Amplified Harpsichord

(1988). **OTHER:** Various vocal, tape, and electronic scores. —**NS/LK/DM**

Mies, Paul, noted German musicologist and pedagogue; b. Cologne, Oct. 22, 1889; d. there, May 15, 1976. He studied musicology, mathematics, and physics at the Univ. of Bonn, receiving his Ph.D. there in 1912 with the diss. *Über die Tonmalerei*. He then was active as a teacher of mathematics in Cologne (1919–39) while continuing his musicological work; in 1946 he became director of the Institut für Schulmusik at the Cologne Staatliche Hochschule für Musik, retaining this post until 1954.

WRITINGS: *Stilmomente und Ausdrucksstilformen im Brahmsschen Lied* (Leipzig, 1923); *Die Bedeutung der Skizzen Beethovens zur Erkenntnis seines Stiles* (Leipzig, 1925; Eng. tr., London, 1929); *Musik im Unterricht der höheren Lehranstalten* (2 vols., Cologne, 1925–26); *Skizzen aus Geschichte und Ästhetik der Musik* (Cologne, 1926); *Das romantische Lied und Gesänge aus Wilhelm Meister; Musik und Musiker in Poesie und Prosa* (2 vols., Berlin, 1926); *Schubert, der Meister des Liedes: Die Entwicklung von Form und Inhalt im Schubertschen Lied* (Berlin, 1928); *Johannes Brahms: Werke, Zeit, Mensch* (Leipzig, 1930); *Der Charakter der Tonarten: Eine Untersuchung* (Cologne, 1948); *Von Sinn und Praxis der musikalischen Kritik* (Krefeld, 1950); with N. Schneider, *Musik im Umkreis der Kulturgeschichte: Ein Tabellenwerk aus der Geschichte der Musik, Literatur, bildenden Künst, Philosophie und Politik Europas* (Rodenkirchen, 1953); *Franz Schubert* (Leipzig, 1954); *Textkritische Untersuchungen bei Beethoven* (Munich and Duisburg, 1957); *Die geistlichen Kantaten Johann Sebastian Bachs und der Hörer von heute* (3 vols., Wiesbaden, 1959–60; 2nd ed., 1964); *Bilder und Buchstaben werden Musik* (Rodenkirchen, 1964); with H. Grundmann, *Studien zum Klavierspiel Beethovens und seiner Zeitgenossen* (Bonn, 1966; 2nd ed., 1970); *Die weltlichen Kantaten Johann Sebastian Bachs und der Horer von heute* (Wiesbaden, 1967); *Das instrumentale Rezitativ: Von seiner Geschichte und seinen Formen* (Bonn, 1968); *Die Krise der Konzertkadenz bei Beethoven* (Bonn, 1970); *Das Konzert im 19. Jahrhundert: Studien zu Kadenzen und Formen* (Bonn, 1972); ed. *Reihenfolge*, a collection for school orchs.—**NS/LK/DM**

Migenes-Johnson, Julia, American soprano; b. N.Y., March 13, 1945. She studied at the H.S. of Music and Art in N.Y., and while still a student sang in a televised concert performance of Copland's *The 2nd Hurricane* under Bernstein's direction; then appeared in *West Side Story* and *Fiddler on the Roof* on Broadway. On Sept. 29, 1965, she made her operatic debut at the N.Y.C. Opera as Annina in *The Saint of Bleecker Street*. She then pursued training in Vienna, where she sang at the Volksoper, and also studied with Gisela Ultmann in Cologne. In 1978 she made her first appearance at the San Francisco Opera as Musetta. Her Metropolitan Opera debut in N.Y. took place on Dec. 10, 1979, as Jenny in *The Rise and Fall of the City of Mahagonny*. In 1983 she sang with the Vienna State Opera. She gained international acclaim for her sultry portrayal of Carmen in Francesco Rosi's film version of Bizet's opera in 1984. In 1985 she returned to the Metropolitan Opera as Berg's Lulu. She won accolades for her compelling performances as Strauss's Salome.—**NS/LK/DM**

Mignan, Edouard-Charles-Octave, French organist and composer; b. Paris, March 17, 1884; d.

there, Sept. 17, 1969. He studied at the Paris Cons. with Widor (organ) and Vidal (composition). He was church organist at Orléans and later at the Madeleine in Paris. He wrote a number of melodious orch. suites, a Sym., sacred choruses, numerous motets, and organ pieces. —NS/LK/DM

Mignone, Francisco (Paulo), eminent Brazilian composer and pedagogue; b. São Paulo, Sept. 3, 1897; d. Rio de Janeiro, Feb. 20, 1986. He studied with his father, then took courses in piano, flute, and composition at the São Paulo Cons. (graduated, 1917). He then studied with Ferroni at the Milan Cons. (1920). Returning to Brazil, he taught at the São Paulo Cons. (1929–33). He was appointed to the faculty of the Escola Nacional de Música in Rio de Janeiro (1933), and taught there until 1967. His music shows the influence of the modern Italian school of composition; his piano pieces are of virtuoso character; his orchestration shows consummate skill. In many of his works he employs indigenous Brazilian motifs, investing them in sonorous modernistic harmonies not without a liberal application of euphonious dissonances.

WORKS: DRAMATIC: O p e r a : *O Contractador dos diamantes* (Rio de Janeiro, Sept. 20, 1924); *O inocente* (Rio de Janeiro, Sept. 5, 1928); *O Chalaca* (1972). O p e r e t t a : *Mizú* (1937). B a l l e t : *Maracatú de Chico-Rei* (Rio de Janeiro, Oct. 29, 1934); *Quadros amazónicos* (Rio de Janeiro, July 15, 1949); *O guarda chuva* (São Paulo, 1954). ORCH.: *Suite campestre* (Rio de Janeiro, Dec. 16, 1918); *Congada*, from the opera *O Contractador dos diamantes* (São Paulo, Sept. 10, 1922); *Scenas da Roda*, symphonic dance (São Paulo, Aug. 15, 1923); *Festa dionisiaca* (Rome, Oct. 24, 1923); *Intermezzo lirico* (São Paulo, May 13, 1925); *4 fantasias brasilieras* for Piano and Orch. (1931–37); *Momus*, symphonic poem (Rio de Janeiro, April 24, 1933); *Suite brasileira* (Rio de Janeiro, Dec. 9, 1933); *Sonho de um Menino Travesso* (São Paulo, Oct. 30, 1937); *Seresta* for Cello and Orch. (Rio de Janeiro, March 31, 1939); *Miudinho*, symphonic dance (São Paulo, June 28, 1941); *Festa das Igrejas* (N.Y., April 22, 1942); *Sinfonia tropical* (1958); Piano Concerto (1958); Violin Concerto (1961); Concerto for Violin, Piano, and Orch. (1966); Concertino for Clarinet and Small Orch. (1957); Bassoon Concertino (1957); Concerto for Violin and Chamber Orch. (1975). C H A M B E R : 2 sextets (1935, 1968); String Octet (1956); 2 string quartets (1956, 1957); 2 wind quintets (1960, 1962); 2 sonatas for 2 Bassoons (1960, 1965); *Trifonia* for Oboe, Flute, and Bassoon (1963); *Tetrafonia* for Flute, Oboe, Clarinet, and Trumpet (1963); 3 violin sonatas (1964, 1965, 1966); Sonata for 4 Bassoons (1966); Cello Sonata (1967); 2 wind trios (1967, 1968); 2 sonatas for Flute and Oboe (1969, 1970); *Sonata à tre* for Flute, Oboe, and Clarinet (1970); Sonata for Solo Trumpet (1970); Clarinet Sonata (1971). P i a n o : 4 sonatas (1941, 1962, 1964, 1967); *Samba rítmico* for 2 Pianos (1953); *Sonata humorística* for 2 Pianos (1968); *Rondo* (1969); waltzes. VOCAL: 2 oratorios: *Alegrias de Nossa Senhora* (Rio de Janeiro, July 15, 1949) and *Santa Claus* (1962); many songs.

BIBL.: B. Kiefer, *F. M.* (Porto Alegre, 1984); V. Mariz, ed., *F. M.: O homen e a obra* (Rio de Janeiro, 1997).—NS/LK/DM

Migot, Georges, significant French composer; b. Paris, Feb. 27, 1891; d. Levallois, near Paris, Jan. 5, 1976. He began taking piano lessons at the age of 6, entering the Paris Cons. in 1909. After preliminary courses in harmony, he studied composition with Widor, counterpoint with Gédalge, and music history with Emmanuel, then orchestration with d'Indy and organ with Gigout and Guilmant. Before completing his studies at the Paris Cons., he was mobilized into the French army, was wounded at Longuyon in 1914, and was released from military service. In 1917 he presented in Paris a concert of his own works; received the Lily Boulanger Prize in 1918. He competed twice for the Prix de Rome in 1919 and 1920, but failed to win and abandoned further attempts to capture it. In the meantime, he engaged in a serious study of painting; in fact, he was more successful as a painter than as a composer in the early years of his career; he exhibited his paintings in Paris art galleries in 1917, 1919, 1923, and subsequent years. He also wrote poetry; virtually all of his vocal works are written to his own words. In his musical compositions, he endeavored to recapture the spirit of early French polyphony, thus emphasizing the continuity of national art in history. His melodic writing is modal, often with archaic inflections, while his harmonic idiom is diatonically translucid; he obtains subtle coloristic effects through unusual instrumental registration. Profoundly interested in the preservation and classification of early musical instruments, he served as curator of the Instrumental Museum of the Paris Cons. (1949–61). He wrote *Essais pour une esthétique générale* (Paris, 1920; 2nd ed., 1937), *Appoggiatures résolues et non résolues* (Paris, 1922–31), *Jean-Philippe Rameau et le génie de la musique française* (Paris, 1930), *Lexique de quelques termes utilisés en musique* (Paris, 1947), 2 vols. of poems (Paris, 1950, 1951), *Matériaux et inscriptions* (Toulouse, 1970), and *Kaléidoscope et miroirs ou les images multipliées et contraires* (autobiography; Toulouse, 1970).

WORKS: DRAMATIC: *Hagoromo*, symphonie lyrique et chorégraphique (Monte Carlo, May 9, 1922); *Le Rossignol en amour*, chamber opera (1926–28; Geneva, March 2, 1937); *Cantate d'amour*, concert opera (1949–50); *La Sulamite*, concert opera (1969–70); *L'Arche*, polyphonie spatiale (1971; Marseilles, May 3, 1974). ORCH.: 13 numbered syms.: No. 1, *Les Agrestides* (1919–20; Paris, April 29, 1922), No. 2 (1927; Besançon, Sept. 7, 1961), No. 3 (1943–49), No. 4 (1946–47), No. 5, *Sinfonia da chiesa*, for Wind Orch. (Roubaix, Dec. 4, 1955), No. 6 for Strings (1944–51; Strasbourg, June 22, 1960), No. 7 for Chamber Orch. (1948–52), No. 8 for 15 Winds and 2 Double Basses (1953), No. 9 for Strings (n.d.; unfinished), No. 10 (1962), No. 11 for Wind Orch. (1963), No. 12 (1954–64; Lille, May 29, 1972), and No. 13 (1967); 1 unnumbered sym.: *Petite symphonie en trois mouvements enchaînés* for Strings (1970; Beziers, July 23, 1971); *La Paravent de laque aux cinq images* (1920; Paris, Jan. 21, 1923); *La Fête de la bergere* (1921; Paris, Nov. 21, 1925); *Trois ciné-ambiances* (1922); *Dialogue* for Piano and Orch. (1922–25; Paris, March 25, 1926); *Dialogue* for Cello and Orch. (1922–26; Paris, Feb. 7, 1927); Suite for Violin and Orch. (1924; Paris, Nov. 14, 1925); Suite for Piano and Orch. (Paris, March 12, 1927); *Suite en concert* for Harp and Orch. (Paris, Jan. 15, 1928); *La Jungle* for Organ and Orch. (1928; Paris, Jan. 9, 1932); *Prélude pour un poète* (Paris, June 7, 1929); *Le Livre des danceries*, suite (Paris, Dec. 12, 1931); *Le Zodiaque* (1931–39); Piano Concerto (1962; Paris, June 26, 1964); *Phonie sous-marine* (1962); Concerto for Harpsichord and Chamber Orch. (Paris, Dec. 12, 1967). C H A M B E R : Trio for Oboe, Violin, and Piano (1906); *Les Parques* for 2 Violins, Viola, and Piano (1909); Violin Sonata (1911); Trio for Violin, Viola, and

Piano (1918); 3 string quartets (1921, 1957, 1966); *Dialogue No. 1* (1922) and *No. 2* (1929) for Cello and Piano; *Dialogue No. 1* (1923) and *No. 2* (1925) for Violin and Piano; Quartet for 2 Clarinets, Corno di Bassetto, and Bass Clarinet (1925); Suite for Flute (1931); Piano Trio (1935); Trio for Oboe, Clarinet, and Bassoon (1944); String Trio (1944–45); Flute Sonata (1945); *Sonate luthée* for Solo Harp (1949); *Pastorale* for 2 Flutes (1950); 2 sonatas for Solo Violin (1951, 1959); Sonata for Solo Clarinet (1953); Sonata for Solo Bassoon (1953); Quintet for Flute, Oboe, Clarinet, Horn, and Bassoon (1954); Sonata for Solo Cello (1954); Quartet for 2 Violins and 2 Cellos (1955); Saxophone Quartet (1955); Cello Sonata (1958); Sonata for Solo Cello (1958); Quartet for Flute, Violin, Cello, and Piano (1960); Guitar Sonata (1960); Quartet for Violin, Viola, Cello, and Piano (1961); Suite for 2 Cellos (1962); Suite for English Horn and Piano (1963); *Introduction pour un concert de chambre* for 5 Strings and 5 Winds (1964); Trio for Flute, Cello, and Harp (1965); piano pieces; organ music. **VOCAL:** 4 oratorios: *La Passion* (1939–46; Paris, July 25, 1957), *L'Annonciation* (1943–46), *La Mise au tombeau* (1948–49), and *La Résurrection* (1953; Strasbourg, March 28, 1969); *Mystère orphique* for Voice and Orch. (1951; Strasbourg, March 18, 1964); *La Nativité de Notre Seigneur* for Soloists, Chorus, and Instruments (1954); sacred and secular choruses; trios; quartets; etc.

BIBL.: L. Vallas, *G. M.* (Paris, 1923); P. Wolff, *La Route d'un musicien: G. M.* (Paris, 1933); M. Pinchard, *Connaissance de G. M., musicien français* (Paris, 1959); M. Honegger, ed., *Catalogue des oeuvres musicales de G. M.* (Strasbourg, 1977); C. Latham, ed. and tr., *G. M.: The Man and His Work* (Strasbourg, 1982). —NS/LK/DM

Miguez, Leopoldo (Américo), Brazilian conductor and composer; b. Rio de Janeiro, Sept. 9, 1850; d. there, July 6, 1902. He studied with Nicolau Ribas in Oporto, Portugal, then was active with a publishing firm and as a conductor in Rio de Janeiro, where he championed the cause of Wagner. He was director of the Instituto Nacional de Música there (1890–1902). He pursued Wagnerian ideas in his theater works, which included the operas *Pele amor!* (Rio de Janeiro, 1897) and *Os Saldunes* (Rio de Janeiro, Sept. 20, 1901). Other works include a Sym. (1882), overtures, symphonic poems, marches, songs, and piano pieces.—NS/LK/DM

Mihalovich, Edmund von (actually, **Ödön Péter József de**), Hungarian composer; b. Fericsancze, Sept. 13, 1842; d. Budapest, April 22, 1929. He studied with Mosonyi in Pest and with Hauptmann in Leipzig, and also took lessons with Peter Cornelius in Munich. From 1887 to 1919 he taught at the Academy of Music in Budapest. Although he remained wholly committed to the German school of composition throughout his life, he did support the efforts of Bartók, Kodály, and Weiner in their search for a distinct national school.

WORKS: DRAMATIC: O p e r a : *Hagbart und Signe* (1867–74; Dresden, March 12, 1882); *Wieland der Schmied* (1876–78); *König Fjalar* (1880–84; unfinished) *Eleane* (1885–87; Budapest, Feb. 16, 1908); *Toldi szerelme* (Toldi's Love; 1880–90; Budapest, March 18, 1893; rev. 1893–94; Budapest, Feb. 28, 1895); *A tihanyi visszhang* (The Echo of Tichany; 1903; unfinished). **ORCH.:** 4 syms. (1879; 1892; 1899–1900; 1901–2); *Hero und Leander*, ballade (1875); *La Ronde du Sabbat*, symphonic poem (1879); *Faust*, fantasy (1880). **OTHER:** Choral works; Violin Sonata; piano pieces; songs.—NS/LK/DM

Mihalovici, Marcel, significant Romanian-born French composer; b. Bucharest, Oct. 22, 1898; d. Paris, Aug. 12, 1985. After studies with Bernfeld (violin), Cuclin (harmony), and Cremer (counterpoint) in Bucharest (1908–19), he settled in Paris and completed his training with d'Indy (composition), Saint Requier (harmony), Gastoué (Gregorian chant), and Lejeune (violin) at the Schola Cantorum (1919–25). With Martinů, Conrad Beck, and Harsányi, he founded the "École de Paris" of emigrants. In 1932 he helped to organize the contemporary music society Triton. He became a naturalized French citizen in 1955. In 1964 he was elected a member of the Inst. de France. His wife was **Monique Haas.** Mihalovici's music presents a felicitous synthesis of French and Eastern European elements, tinted with a roseate impressionistic patina and couched in euphoniously dissonant harmonies.

WORKS: DRAMATIC: O p e r a : *L'Intransigeant Pluton* (1928; Paris, April 3, 1939); *Phèdre* (1949; Stuttgart, June 9, 1951); *Die Heimkehr* (Frankfurt am Main, June 17, 1954); *Krapp ou La Dernière Bande*, after Samuel Beckett (1959–60; Bielefeld, Feb. 25, 1961); *Les Jumeaux*, opera buffa (1962; Braunschweig, Jan. 23, 1963). **B a l l e t :** *Une Vie de Polichinelle* (1923); *Le Postillon du Roy* (1924); *Divertimento* (1925); *Karagueuz*, marionette ballet (1926); *Thésée au labyrinthe* (1956; Braunschweig, April 4, 1957; rev. version as *Scènes de Thésée*, Cologne, Oct. 15, 1958); *Alternamenti* (1957; Braunschweig, Feb. 28, 1958); *Variations* (Bielefeld, March 28, 1960). **OTHER:** Incidental music for plays. **ORCH.:** *Notturno* (1923); *Introduction au mouvement symphonique* (1923; Bucharest, Oct. 17, 1926); *Fantaisie* (1927; Liège, Sept. 6, 1930); *Cortège des divinités infernales* (1928; Bucharest, Dec. 7, 1930); *Chindia* for 13 Wind Instruments and Piano (1929); *Concerto quasi una Fantasia* for Violin and Orch. (1930; Barcelona, April 22, 1936); *Divertissement* (1934); *Capriccio roumain* (1936); *Prélude et Invention* for Strings (1937; Warsaw, April 21, 1939); *Toccata* for Piano and Orch. (1938; rev. 1940); *Symphonies pour le temps présent* (1944); *Variations* for Brass and Strings (1946); *Séquences* (1947); *Ritournelles* (1951); 5 syms.: *Sinfonia giocosa* (Basel, Dec. 14, 1951), *Sinfonia partita* for Strings (1952), *Sinfonia cantata* for Baritone, Chorus, and Orch. (1953–63), *Sinfonia variata* (1960), and No. 5 for Soprano and Orch., in memory of Hans Rosbaud (1966–69; Paris, Dec. 14, 1971); *Étude en 2 parties* for Piano Concertante, 7 Wind Instruments, Celesta, and Percussion (Donaueschingen, Oct. 6, 1951); *Elegie* (1955); *Ouverture tragique* (1957); *Esercizio* for Strings (1959); *Musique nocturne* for Clarinet, Strings, Harpsichord, and Celesta (1963); *Aubade* for Strings (1964); *Périples* for Piano and Orch. (1967; Paris, March 22, 1970); *Prétextes* for Oboe, Bass Clarinet, and Chamber Orch. (1968); *Variantes* for Horn and Orch. or Piano (1969); *Borne* (1970); *Rondo* (1970); *Chant premier* for Saxophone and Orch. (1973–74); *Follia* (1976–77). **CHAMBER:** 2 violin sonatas (1920, 1941); Piano Quartet (1922); 3 string quartets (1923; 1931; 1943–46); Oboe Sonatina (1924); *Serenade* for String Trio (1929); Sonata for 3 Clarinets (1933); Viola Sonata (1942); Sonata for Violin and Cello (1944); *Egloge* for Flute, Oboe, Clarinet, Bassoon, and Piano (1945); Sonata for Solo Violin (1949); Sonata for Solo Cello (1949); Wind Trio (1955); *Pastorale triste* for Flute and Piano (1958); Bassoon Sonata (1958); Clarinet Sonata (1958); *Improvisation* for Percussion (1961); *Dialogues* for Clarinet and Piano (1965); *Serioso* for Bass Saxophone and Piano (1971); *Récit* for Clarinet (1973); *Melopeia* for Oboe (1973). **P i a n o :** *3 Nocturnes* (1928); *4 Caprices* (1929); *Ricercari* (1941); *3 pièces nocturnes* (1948); Sonata (1964); *Cantus Firmus* for 2

Pianos (1970); *Passacaglia* for Piano, Left-hand (1975). **VOCAL**: *La Genèse*, cantata (1935–40); *Cascando* for Voice and Instruments (1962); *Cantilène* for Mezzo-soprano and Chamber Orch. (1972); motets; songs.

BIBL.: G. Beck, *M. M.: Esquisse biographique* (Paris, 1954). —NS/LK/DM

Mihály, András, Hungarian composer, conductor, administrator, and teacher; b. Budapest, Nov. 6, 1917; d. there, Sept. 19, 1993. He was a student of Adolf Schiffer (cello) and of Leó Weiner and Imre Waldbauer (chamber music) at the Budapest Academy of Music. He also received private instruction in composition from Pál Kadosa and István Strasser. After playing 1st cello in the orch. of the Budapest Opera (1946–48), he was general secretary of the Opera (1948–50). From 1950 to 1978 he taught chamber music at the Budapest Academy of Music. He also was a music reader with the Hungarian Radio (1962–78). From 1978 to 1986 he was director of the Hungarian State Opera in Budapest, and then of the student orch. at the Budapest Academy of Music (from 1986). In 1952, 1954, and 1964 he received the Erkel Prize, and in 1955 was awarded the Kossuth Prize. He was made a Merited Artist (1969) and an Outstanding Artist (1974) by the Hungarian government.

WORKS: DRAMATIC: *Együtt és egyedül* (Together and Alone), opera (1964–65; Budapest, Nov. 5, 1966); incidental music for plays and films. **ORCH.**: 3 syms. (1946, 1950, 1962); Cello Concerto (1953); Piano Concerto (1954); *Fantasy* for Wind Quintet and Orch. (1955); Violin Concerto (1959); *Festive Overture* (1959); *Monodia* (1971). **CHAMBER**: Piano Trio (1940); 3 string quartets (1942, 1960, 1977); *Rhapsody* for Viola and Piano (1947); *Serenade* for Wind Trio (1956); Suite for Cello and Piano (1957); *Movement* for Cello and Piano (1962); *3 Movements* for Chamber Ensemble (1969); *Musica per 15* for Chamber Ensemble (1975); *Musica* for Viola and Piano (1977). **Piano**: Sonata (1958); *Rondo* (1958); *4 Little Piano Pieces* (1958); *Ciaccona* (1961). **VOCAL**: *Liberty and Peace* for Chorus and Orch. (1942; not extant; 2nd version, 1949); *Youth! Defend Peace!* for Chorus and Orch. (1950); *My Beloved Hungarian Fatherland* for Chorus and Orch. (1952); *The Red Cart* for Chorus and Orch. (1957); *1871* for Chorus and Orch. (1960); *Apocrypha* for 3 Women's Voices, Clarinet, and Percussion (1962); *Fly, Poem!* for Chorus and Orch. (1967); choruses; songs.

BIBL.: J. Kárpáti, *M. A.* (Budapest, 1965).—NS/LK/DM

Mikhailova, Maria (Alexandrovna), Russian soprano; b. Kharkov, June 3, 1866; d. Moscow, Jan. 18, 1943. She studied in St. Petersburg, and then in Paris and Milan. In 1892 she made her debut at the Imperial Opera in St. Petersburg as Marguerite de Valois in *Les Huguenots*; she remained a member there until 1912. On Oct. 29, 1895, she created the role of Electra in Taneyev's *Oresteia*. She visited Tokyo in 1907. She made over 300 recordings, achieving a considerable reputation through the gramophone alone.—NS/LK/DM

Mikhailovich, Maxim (Dormidontovich), Russian bass; b. Koltsovka, near Kazan, Aug. 25, 1893; d. Moscow, March 30, 1971. He studied in Kazan with Oshustovich and in Moscow with Osipov. After appearing as a soloist with Moscow's All-Union Radio

(1930–32), he sang with Moscow's Bolshoi Theater (from 1932). He was admired for his many portrayals in Russian operas. In 1940 he was made a People's Artist of the U.S.S.R.

BIBL.: V. Endrzheyevsky and E. Osipov, *M. M.* (Moscow, 1957).—NS/LK/DM

Mikhashoff, Yvar (real name, **Ronald Mackay**), American pianist and composer; b. Troy, N.Y., March 8, 1941; d. Buffalo, Oct. 11, 1993. He studied at the Eastman School of Music in Rochester, N.Y., then enrolled at the Juilliard School of Music in N.Y. as a piano student of Beveridge Webster and Adele Marcus. Subsequently he studied composition on a Fulbright scholarship with Boulanger in Paris (1968–69), and also at the Univ. of Houston (B.M., 1967; M.M., 1968) and the Univ. of Tex. in Austin (D.M.A. in composition, 1973). He taught at the State Univ. of N.Y. in Buffalo (from 1973), and also toured extensively in the U.S. and Europe, being particularly noted for his championship of American music of the 19th and 20th centuries. He also appeared as a multimedia performer. In 1980 he played the principal acting role in the La Scala premiere of Bussotti's opera *La Racine* in Milan. In 1982 he organized the Holland Festival's 2-week-long celebration of 200 years of Dutch-American friendship through a series of 9 thematic concerts covering 250 years of American music.

WORKS: *Dances for Davia I-II* for Flute and Piano (1958, 1979); Concerto No. 1 for Piano, Winds, and Percussion (1965); Viola Concerto (1969); *Nocturne* for Cello and Piano (1977); *Light from a Distant Garden* for String Quartet (1983); *Grand Bowery Tango* for Flute and Ensemble (1985); *Night Dances* for String Trio (1985); *Twilight Dances* for Violin, Contrabass, Piano, and Percussion (1986); *Evening Dances* for Violin and Piano (1987); piano pieces; several vocal works, including *In Memoriam Igor Stravinsky* for Voice, Flute, Clarinet, and Cello (1971) and *Improvisations on the Last Words of Chief Seattle* for Speaker, Percussion, Mime Dancer, and Syllabist (1976).—NS/LK/DM

Miki, Minoru, Japanese composer; b. Tokushima, March 16, 1930. He studied with Ifukube and Ikenouchi at the National Univ. of Fine Arts and Music in Tokyo (1951–55). He was a founder of the Nihon Ongaku Shūdan (Pro Musica Nipponia; 1964), an ensemble dedicated to performing new music for traditional Japanese instruments, and later served as its artistic director. He lectured at the Tokyo Coll. of Music. Miki was founder-director of UTAYOMI-ZA (1986), a musical-opera theater.

WORKS: DRAMATIC: Opera: *Mendori Teishu* (A Henpecked Husband), chamber opera (1963); *Shunkin-shō* (Tokyo, 1975); *An Actor's Revenge* (London, 1979); *Toge no muko ni naniga aruka*, choral opera (1983); *Utayomizaru*, musical-opera (1983); *Joruri* (St. Louis, 1985); *At the Flower Garden*, mini-opera (1985); *Wakahime* (1991); *Orochi-den* (1992); *Shizuka and Yoshitsume* (1993); *The Tale of the Genji* (St. Louis, June 15, 2000). **CHAMBER MUSICAL**: *Yomigaeru* (1992). **Ballet**: *From the Land of Light* (1987). **ORCH.**: *Trinita sinfonica* (1953); *Sinfonia Gamula* (1957); *Symphony: Joya* (1960); Marimba Concerto (1969); *Jo-no-Kyoku*, prelude for Shakuhachi, Koro, Shamisen, and Strings (1969); *Convexity*, concerto for 3 Groups of Sankyoku and a Japanese Drum (1970); *Ha-no-Kyoku,* koto concerto (1974); *Hote* for Japanese Orch. (1976); *Symphony from Life* (1980); *Concerto Requiem* for Koto and Japanese Instruments (1980); *Kyu-no-Kyoku* (Sym. for 2 Worlds; Leipzig, Nov. 12, 1981); *3 Pieces*: 1, *March 1930*; 2, *August 1945*; 3, *September 1950* (1983); *Japan,* overture (1990); *Z Concerto* for Marimba, Percussion, and Orch. (1992); *Mai* (1992). **CHAMBER:** *Osabai* for 12 Wind Instruments and Percussion (1955); Sextet for Wind Instruments and Piano (1965); *Figures for 4 Groups* for Various Instruments (1967–69); *Ballades* for Koto (3 vols., 1969, 1976, 1983); *Tennyo* for Koto (1969); *Hakuyo* for Violin and Koto (1973); *Danses concertantes No. 1, 4 Seasons,* for Ensemble of Japanese Instruments (1973–74), *No. 2, Naruto-Hicho,* for Ensemble of Japanese Instruments (1977), *No. 3, A Tale of Hachirō,* for Ensemble of Japanese Instruments (1981), and *No. 4, Kita-no-Uta* (1984); *Yui I* for Shō and Piano (1982), *II* for Cello and Koto (1980–83), and *III, Flowers and Water,* for Shakuhachi, Koto, Shamisen, Harp, and String Quartet (1985); *Marimba Spiritual* for Marimba and 3 Percussionists (1984); Trio for Violin, Cello, and Piano (1986); *Organ Nirvana* for Organ (1988–89); String Quartet (1989). **VOCAL:** *Paraphrase after Ancient Japanese Music* for Soprano and Ensemble of 10 Japanese Instruments (1966); *Matsu-no-Kyoko* for Women's Chorus and Ensemble of Japanese Instruments (1974); *Sinfonia concertante per Wasan* for Bass, Women's Chorus, Nohkan, Koto, and Orch. (1976); *Taro,* cantata for 5 Soloists, Children's Chorus, and 17 Japanese Instruments (1977); *Awa Kitobun, I, II, III* (1981); *Beijing Requiem* (1990). **—NS/LK/DM**

Miksch, Johann Aloys, esteemed Bohemian baritone and teacher; b. Georgental, July 19, 1765; d. Dresden, Sept. 24, 1845. He was a choirboy in Dresden, then a singer at the Court Church (from 1786) and a baritone in the Italian Opera of Dresden (from 1797). He was chorus master of the German Opera (from 1820), being pensioned in 1831. He was greatly renowned as a teacher, numbering among his pupils Schröder-Devrient.

BIBL.: A. Kohut, *J. M.* (Leipzig, 1890).**—NS/LK/DM**

Mikuli, Karl (Karol), Polish pianist, conductor, teacher, and composer of Moldavian descent; b. Czernowitz, Oct. 20, 1819; d. Lemberg, May 21, 1897. He first studied medicine in Vienna, but his pronounced talent for music made him decide to go to Paris for serious study. There he became a pupil of Chopin (1844), and he also studied composition with Reicha. After the outbreak of the Revolution of 1848, he left Paris and made several tours in Russia and Austria. He was appointed director of the Lemberg Cons. (1858), and 30 years later he established a music school of his own there. His ed. of Chopin's works contains numerous emendations made by Chopin himself as marginal remarks in Mikuli's student copies. He wrote choral works, chamber music, songs, and piano pieces, the latter greatly influenced by Chopin's style.**—NS/LK/DM**

Mila, Massimo, Italian writer on music; b. Turin, Aug. 14, 1910; d. there, Dec. 26, 1988. He studied literature at the Univ. of Turin, and after graduation became a regular contributor to many Italian musical publications. He was music critic of *L'Espresso* (1955–68) and of *La Stampa* (1968–74). He taught music history at the Turin Cons. (1953–73) and at the Univ. of Turin (from 1960).

WRITINGS: *Il melodramma di Verdi* (Bari, 1933); *Cent' anni di musica moderna* (Milan, 1944); *W.A. Mozart* (Turin, 1945); *Breve storia della musica* (Milan, 1946; 2nd ed., 1963); *L'esperienza musicale e l'estetica* (Turin, 1950; 3rd ed., 1965); *"La carriera d'un libertino" di Strawinsky* (Milan, 1952); *Cronache musicale, 1955–1959* (Turin, 1959); *La musica pianistica di Mozart* (Turin, 1963); *Le sinfonie di Mozart* (Turin, 1967); *"I vespri siciliani" di Verdi* (Turin, 1973); *Lettura del Don Giovanni di Mozart* (Turin, 1988); R. Garavaglia and A. Sinigaglia, eds., *Massimo Mila alla Scala: Scritti, 1955–1988* (Milan, 1989); A. Batisti, ed., *Brahms e Wagner* (Turin, 1994; collected articles and essays); S. Monga, ed., *Guillaume Dufay* (Turin, 1997).

BIBL.: G. Pestelli, ed., *Il melodramma italiano dell'ottocento: Studi e ricerche per M. M.* (Turin, 1977); T. Berio, ed., *Intorno a M. M.* (Florence, 1994).**—NS/LK/DM**

Milán, Luis de, Spanish musician, courtier, and poet; b. Valencia, c. 1500; d. after 1561. He was a favorite at the viceregal court of Valencia under Germaine de Foix and her 3rd husband, Don Fernando of Aragón. In 1536 he brought out his most important work, *Libro de música de vihuela de mano intitulado El Maestro* (Valencia), intended as an instruction book for learning to play the vihuela. This was the first book of its kind to be publ. in Spain, and is valuable for its many musical examples (tientos, fantasias, pavanes, and solo songs with guitar accompaniment: *villancicos,* romances, and *sonetos*), which reveal Milan's high qualities as a composer. He also publ. *El cortesano* (1561), giving a description of courtly life at Valencia in his day.

BIBL.: J. Trend, *L. d.M. and the Vihuelistas* (Oxford, 1925); J. Ward, *The Vihuela de Mano and Its Music (1536–1576)* (diss., N.Y.U., 1953); L. Gásser, *L. M. on Sixteenth-Century Performance Practice* (Bloomington, Ind., 1996).**—NS/LK/DM**

Milanollo, (Domenica Maria) Teresa, Italian violinist; b. Savigliano, near Turin, Aug. 28, 1827; d. Paris, Oct. 25, 1904. She studied solfège with her father and violin with Giovanni Ferrero, Mauro Caldera, and Giovanni Morra. On April 17, 1836, she made her debut at the Mondovi Theater. After playing in Marseilles, she toured the Netherlands with Lafont. In 1837 she performed with Johann Strauss Sr., in England. Following further training with Francis Mori, she toured Wales with the harpist Bochsa in 1838. She returned to France, where she began teaching her sister, Maria (b. Savigliano, July 19, 1832; d. Paris, Oct. 21, 1848). The two continued their studies with Bériot, and subsequently Teresa honed her technique under Habeneck's guidance in Paris (1840–41). From 1842 the sisters toured with notable success, Teresa as Mlle. Adagio and Maria as Mlle. Staccato. Teresa also received some composition lessons from F. Kufferath in Brussels. After Maria's untimely death from tuberculosis, Teresa devoted herself to giving benefit concerts. In 1852 she resumed her formal concert career. Upon her marriage in 1857 she withdrew from public appearances. Among her compositions were opera transcriptions for 2 Violins and Orch. and many solo violin pieces, including the *Fantaisie élégiaque,* written in memory of her sister. **—LK/DM**

Milanov, Zinka (née Kunc), famous Croatian-American soprano; b. Zagreb, May 17, 1906; d. N.Y., May 30, 1989. She studied at the Zagreb Academy of Music, then with Milka Ternina, Maria Kostrenčić, and Fernando Carpi. She made her debut as Leonora in *Il Trovatore* in Ljubljana (1927); subsequently was principal soprano of the Zagreb Opera (1928–35), where she sang in over 300 performances in Croatian. After appearing at Prague's German Theater (1936), she was invited by Toscanini to sing in his performance of the Verdi *Requiem* at the Salzburg Festival (1937). She then made her Metropolitan Opera debut in N.Y. as Verdi's Leonora on Dec. 17, 1937; was one of the outstanding members on its roster (1937–41; 1942–47; 1950–66); gave her farewell performance there as Maddalena in *Andrea Chénier* on April 13, 1966. In addition to appearing in San Francisco and Chicago, she also sang at Buenos Aires's Teatro Colón (1940–42), Milan's La Scala (1950), and London's Covent Garden (1966–67). Her brother was **Božidar Kunc**. She married Predrag Milanov in 1937, but they were divorced in 1946; she then married Ljubomir Ilic in 1947. Blessed with a voice of translucent beauty, she became celebrated for her outstanding performances of roles in operas by Verdi and Puccini.—**NS/LK/DM**

Milanuzzi, Carlo, Italian organist and composer; b. Sanatoglia, date unknown; d. c. 1647. He became an Augustinian monk, serving as organist at the order's church in Perugia in 1619. After serving as maestro di cappella at S. Eufemia in Verona (1622–23), he was organist at Venice's S. Stefano (1623–29) and at Finale di Modena (1629–34?). In 1636 he was maestro di cappella at Camerino Cathedral, and in 1643 at S. Mauro, Noventa di Piave, where he also was organist. He was also active as a poet. His 9 vols. of secular monody (Venice, 1620–43) are particularly notable. He also publ. 10 vols. of sacred vocal music (Venice, 1619–47).—**LK/DM**

Milburn, Ellsworth, American composer; b. Greensburg, Pa., Feb. 6, 1938. He studied with Scott Huston at the Univ. of Cincinnati Coll.-Cons. of Music (1956–58), and later with Roy Travis and Henri Lazarof at the Univ. of Calif. at Los Angeles (1959–62) and at Mills Coll. in Oakland, Calif., with Milhaud (1966–68). He was a teacher at the Univ. of Cincinnati Coll.-Cons. of Music (1970–75) and at Rice Univ. in Houston (from 1975).

WORKS: DRAMATIC: Opera: *Gesualdo* (1973). ORCH.: Concerto for Piano and Chamber Orch. (1967); *Voussoirs* (1970). CHAMBER: 5 Inventions for 2 Flutes (1965); String Trio (1968); *Soli* for 5 Players on 10 Instruments (1968); String Quintet (1969); *Soli II* for 2 Players on Flutes and Double Bass (1970); *Soli III* for Clarinet, Cello, and Piano (1971); *Soli IV* for Flute, Oboe, Double Bass, and Harpsichord (1972); Violin Sonata (1972); *Lament* for Harp (1972). VOCAL: *Massacre of the Innocents* for Chorus (1965).—**NS/LK/DM**

Milde, Hans Feodor von, Austrian baritone; b. Petronell, April 13, 1821; d. Weimar, Dec. 10, 1899. He studied with F. Hauser and M. García. He was a life member of the Weimar Court Opera, and created the role of Telramund in *Lohengrin* (1850). His wife, Rosa

Agthé Milde (b. Weimar, June 25, 1827; d. there, Jan. 26, 1906), also sang in Weimar (1845–67), where she created the role of Elsa in *Lohengrin*.

BIBL.: N. von Milde, *P. Cornelius. Briefe ...an F. und R. v.M.* (Weimar, 1901).—**NS/LK/DM**

Milder-Hauptmann, (Pauline) Anna, prominent German soprano; b. Constantinople, Dec. 13, 1785; d. Berlin, May 29, 1838. She was the daughter of an Austrian diplomatic official. In Vienna she attracted the notice of Schikaneder. He recommended her to Tomaselli and Salieri, who taught her opera singing. She made her debut as Juno in Süssmayr's *Der Spiegel von Arkadien* in Vienna on April 9, 1803, and soon became so well regarded as an artist and singer that Beethoven wrote the role of Fidelio for her (Vienna, Nov. 20, 1805). After a tour in 1808, she was made prima donna assoluta at the Berlin court. In 1810 she married a Vienna merchant, Hauptmann. In 1812 she went to Berlin, where she created a sensation, particularly as Gluck's heroines (in *Iphigénie en Tauride*, *Alcestis*, and *Armida*). She left Berlin in 1829, then sang in Russia, Sweden, and Austria. Mendelssohn chose her as a soloist in his revival of *Bach's St. Matthew Passion* in Berlin (1829). She made her farewell appearance in Vienna in 1836. Her voice was so powerful that Haydn reportedly said to her: "Dear child, you have a voice like a house."—**NS/LK/DM**

Mildmay, (Grace) Audrey (Louise St. John), English soprano; b. Herstmonceux, Dec. 19, 1900; d. London, May 31, 1953. She studied in London with Johnstone Douglas and in Vienna with Jani Strasser. In 1927–28 she toured North America as Polly Peachum in *The Begggar's Opera*, and then returned to England as a member of the Carlo Rosa Opera Co. (1928–31). In 1931 she married John Christie, with whom she helped to found the Glyndebourne Festival in 1934. She sang there from 1934 to 1936 and again in 1938–39. In 1939 she appeared at the Sadler's Wells Theatre in London. She retired from the operatic stage in 1943. Mildmay was co-founder of the Edinburgh Festival with Rudolf Bing in 1947. Her finest roles were Susanna, Zerlina, and Norina.—**NS/LK/DM**

Miles, Philip Napier, English composer and conductor; b. Shirehampton, Jan. 21, 1865; d. King's Weston, near Bristol, July 19, 1935. He studied in London with Parry and Dannreuther. He organized the Shirehampton Choral Soc. on his own estate and conducted festivals in various localities in England. He wrote the operas *Westward Ho!* (London, Dec. 4, 1914), *Fire Flies* (Clifton, Oct. 13, 1924; on the same program with his opera *Markheim*), *Good Friday*, *Demeter*, and *Queen Rosamond*, some chamber music, and many songs.—**NS/LK/DM**

Miley, Bubber (James Wesley), famed jazz trumpeter, composer; b. Aiken, S.C., April 3, 1903; d. Welfare Island, N.Y., May 20, 1932. Miley was crucial to the early sound of the Ellington Group and even helped write some of their first hits. His expertise with the plunger (wa-wa) mute was an essential aspect of the Ellington sound in every trumpeter afterward. His family moved to N.Y.C. in 1909. His father, Valentine Miley, was an amateur guitarist; his three sisters, Connie, Rose, and Murdis were professional singers (known as the South Carolina Trio). Miley was taught trombone while at school, then switched to cornet. He joined the U.S. Navy as a boy in 1918, served for 18 months, then worked in N.Y. with The Carolina Five before joining Willie Gant's Band at Lee's Cabaret in N.Y. He toured with Mamie Smith (autumn 1921), and later worked at various N.Y. clubs through mid-1923. He was back on tour that spring and summer, again working with Smith. In September 1923, he joined the Washingtonians (then led by Elmer Snowden), remaining with it when Duke Ellington took over as the leader in 1924. Other than brief absences, Bubber worked with Ellington until January 1929. After leaving Ellington, he gigged in N.Y., then sailed to France with Noble Sissle in May 1929 for a two-week engagement. On his return to N.Y., he worked with Zutty Singleton's Band at the Lafayette Theatre, then joined Allie Ross Band at Connie's Inn. From early 1930 he worked occasionally for white bandleader Leo Reisman; sometimes dressed as an usher he would join the band from the audience. Where racially mixed bands were not permitted to perform, Miley played with the orchestra, but was hidden from view by a screen. In January 1931, he accompanied noted writer Roger Pryor Dodge (then a professional dancer) in the "Sweet and Low" revue, where he remained for four months. In late 1931 Miley (financed by Irving Mills) formed his own band. They played in the "Harlem Scandals" show in Philadelphia, then opened in N.Y. (January 1932). Shortly afterwards Miley, ill with tuberculosis, was forced to stop playing. He entered a N.Y. hospital on April 18, 1932, and died just over a month later.

DISC.: DUKE ELLINGTON: *Choo-choo* (1924); *Animal Crackers* (1926); *East St. Louis Toodle-oo* (1926); *Immigration Blues* (1926); *Black and Tan Fantasy* (1927); *Creole Love Call* (1927); *Jubilee Stomp* (1928); *The Mooche* (1928); *Doin' the Voom-voom* (1929); *The Ellington Trumpet Tradition* (1929).—JC/LP

Milford, Robin (Humphrey), English composer and teacher; b. Oxford, Jan. 22, 1903; d. Lyme Regis, Dec. 29, 1959. He was a student of Holst, Vaughan Williams, and R.O. Morris at the Royal Coll. of Music in London. Thereafter he was active as a composer and teacher. He was best known for his chamber music, choral pieces, and songs.

WORKS: DRAMATIC: Opera: *The Scarlet Letter* (1959). **Ballet:** *The Snow Queen* (1946). **ORCH.:** Suite for Chamber Orch. (1924); *Miniature Concerto* for Harpsichord and Chamber Orch. (1927); *Miniature Concerto* for Strings (1933); Violin Concerto (1937); *Ariel* for Small Orch. (1940); *Elegiac Meditation* for Viola and Strings (1947); *A Festival* for Strings (1951); *Fishing by Moonlight* for Piano and Strings (1952). **CHAMBER:** Flute Sonata (1944); *Fantasia* for String Quartet (1945); Violin Sonata (1945); Trio for Clarinet, Cello, and Piano (1948); Trio for 2 Violins and Piano (1949); piano pieces. **VOCAL:** *The Pilgrim's Progress*, oratorio (1932); *The Forsaken Merman* for Tenor, Women's Chorus, Strings, and Piano (1938–50); *A Liturgy to the Holy Spirit* (1947); songs.

BIBL.: I. Copley, *R. M.* (London, 1985).—NS/LK/DM

Milhaud, Darius, eminent French composer and teacher; b. Marseilles, Sept. 4, 1892; d. Geneva, June 22, 1974. He was the descendant of an old Jewish family, settled in Provence for many centuries. His father was a merchant of almonds; there was a piano in the house, and Milhaud improvised melodies as a child; then began to take violin lessons. He entered the Paris Cons. in 1909, almost at the age limit for enrollment, where he studied with Berthelier (violin), Lefèvre (ensemble), Leroux (harmony), Gédalge (counterpoint), Widor (composition and fugue), and d'Indy (conducting) and played violin in the student orch. under Dukas. He received 1st "accessit" in violin and counterpoint, and 2nd in fugue; won the Prix Lepaulle for composition. While still a student, he wrote music in a bold modernistic manner; became associated with Satie, Cocteau, and Claudel. When Claudel was appointed French minister to Brazil, he engaged Milhaud as his secretary; they sailed for Rio de Janeiro early in 1917; returned to Paris (via the West Indies and N.Y.) shortly after the armistice of Nov. 1918. Milhaud's name became known to a larger public as a result of a newspaper article by Henri Collet in *Comoedia* (Jan. 16, 1920), grouping him with 5 other French composers of modern tendencies (Auric, Durey, Honegger, Poulenc, and Tailleferre) under the sobriquet Les Six, even though the association was stylistically fortuitous. In 1922 he visited the U.S.; lectured at Harvard Univ., Princeton Univ., and Columbia Univ.; appeared as pianist and composer in his own works; in 1925 he traveled in Italy, Germany, Austria, and Russia; returning to France, he devoted himself mainly to composition and teaching. At the outbreak of World War II in 1939, he was in Aix-en-Provence; in July 1940 he went to the U.S.; taught at Mills Coll. in Oakland, Calif. In 1947 he returned to France; was appointed prof. at the Paris Cons., but continued to visit the U.S. as conductor and teacher almost annually, despite arthritis, which compelled him to conduct while seated; he retained his post at Mills Coll. until 1971; then settled in Geneva. His autobiography appeared in an Eng. tr. as *My Happy Life* (London, 1995). Exceptionally prolific from his student days, he wrote a great number of works in every genre; introduced a modernistic type of music drama, "opéra à la minute," and also the "miniature symphony." He experimented with new stage techniques, incorporating cinematic interludes; also successfully revived the Greek type of tragedy with vocal accompaniment. He composed works for electronic instruments, and demonstrated his contrapuntal skill in such compositions as his 2 String Quartets (No. 14 and No. 15), which can be played together as a string octet. He was the first to exploit polytonality in a consistent and deliberate manner; applied the exotic rhythms of Latin America and the West Indies in many of his lighter works; of these, his *Saudades do Brasil* are particularly popular; Brazilian movements are also found in his *Scaramouche* and *Le Boeuf sur le toit*; in some of his works he drew upon the resources of jazz. His ballet *La Création du monde* (1923), portraying the Creation in terms of Negro cosmology, constitutes the earliest example of the use of the blues and jazz in a symphonic score, anticipating Gershwin in this respect. Despite this variety of means and versatility of forms, Milhaud succeeded in establishing a style that was distinctly and identifiably his own; his melodies are nostalgically lyrical or vivaciously rhythmical, according to mood; his instrumental writing is of great complexity and difficulty, and yet entirely within the capacities of modern virtuoso technique; he arranged many of his works in several versions.

WORKS: DRAMATIC: Opera: *La Brebis égarée*, "roman musical" (1910–15; Paris, Dec. 10, 1923); *Le Pauvre Matelot*, "complainte en trois actes" (1926; Paris, Dec. 12, 1927); *Les Malheurs d'Orphée* (Brussels, May 7, 1926); *Esther de Carpentras*, opéra-bouffe (1925; Paris, Feb. 1, 1938); 3 "minute operas": *L'Enlèvement d'Europe* (Baden-Baden, July 17, 1927), *L'Abandon d'Ariane*, and *La Délivrance de Thésée* (Wiesbaden, April 20, 1928); *Christophe Colomb* (Berlin, May 5, 1930); *Maximilien* (Paris, Jan. 4, 1932); *Médée* (Antwerp, Oct. 7, 1939); *Bolivar* (1943; Paris, May 12, 1950); *Le Jeu de Robin et Marion*, mystery play after Adam de la Halle (Wiesbaden, Oct. 28, 1951); *David* (Jerusalem, June 1, 1954); *La Mère coupable*, to a libretto by Madeleine Milhaud, after Beaumarchais (Geneva, June 13, 1966); *Saint Louis, Roi de France*, opera-oratorio (1970–71; Rio de Janeiro, April 14, 1972). **Incidental Music:** *Agamemnon* (1913; Paris, April 16, 1927); *Les Choéphores* (concert version, Paris, June 15, 1919; stage version, Brussels, March 27, 1935); *Les Euménides* (1922; Antwerp, Nov. 27, 1927); *Jeux d'enfants*, 3 children's plays: *A propos de bottes* (1932), *Un Petit Peu de musique* (1933), and *Un Petit Peu d'exercise* (1937). **Ballet:** *L'Homme et son désir* (Paris, June 6, 1921); *Le Boeuf sur le toit* (Paris, Feb. 21, 1920); *Les Mariés de la Tour Eiffel* (Paris, June 19, 1921; in collaboration with Honegger, Auric, Poulenc, and Tailleferre); *La Création du monde* (Paris, Oct. 25, 1923); *Salade*, "ballet chanté" (Paris, May 17, 1924); *Le Train bleu*, "danced operetta" (Paris, June 20, 1924); *Polka* for the ballet *L'Éventail de Jeanne*, in homage to the music patroness Jeanne Dubost (Paris, June 16, 1927; in collaboration with Ravel, Ibert, Roussel et al.); *Jeux de printemps* (Washington, D.C., Oct. 30, 1944); *The Bells*, after Poe (Chicago, April 26, 1946); *'adame Miroir* (Paris, May 31, 1948); *Vendange* (1952; Nice, April 17, 1972); *La Rose des vents* (1958); *La Branche des oiseaux* (1965). **ORCH.:** *Suite symphonique No. 1* (Paris, May 26, 1914) and *No. 2* (from incidental music to Claudel's *Protée*; Paris, Oct. 24, 1920); 5 syms. for Small Orch.: No. 1, *Le Printemps* (1917), No. 2, *Pastorale* (1918), No. 3, *Sérénade* (1921), No. 4, *Dixtuor à cordes* (1921), and No. 5, *Dixtuor d'instruments à vent* (1922); 12 syms. for Large Orch.: No. 1 (Chicago, Oct. 17, 1940, composer conducting), No. 2 (Boston, Dec. 20, 1946, composer conducting), No. 3, *Hymnus ambrosianus*, for Chorus and Orch. (Paris, Oct. 30, 1947), No. 4 (Paris, May 20, 1948, composer conducting), No. 5 (Turin, Oct. 16, 1953), No. 6 (Boston, Oct. 7, 1955, composer conducting), No. 7 (Chicago, March 3, 1956), No. 8, *Rhodanienne* (Berkeley, Calif., April 22, 1958), No. 9 (Fort Lauderdale, Fla., March 29, 1960), No. 10 (Portland, Ore., April 4, 1961), No. 11, *Romantique* (Dallas, Dec. 12, 1960), and No. 12, *Rural* (Davis, Calif., Feb. 16, 1962); *Cinéma-Fantaisie sur Le Boeuf sur le toit* for Violin and Orch. (Paris, Dec. 4, 1920); *Caramel mou, a shimmy*, for Jazz Band (1920); 5 *études* for Piano and Orch. (Paris, Jan. 20, 1921); *Saudades do Brasil*, suite of dances (1920–21; also for Piano); *Ballade* for Piano and Orch. (1921); 3 *Rag Caprices* (Paris, Nov. 23, 1923); *Le Carnaval d'Aix* for Piano and Orch. (N.Y., Dec. 9, 1926, composer soloist); 2 *hymnes* (1927); 3 violin concertos: No. 1 (1927), No. 2 (Paris, Nov. 7, 1948), and No. 3, *Concerto royal*

(1958); Viola Concerto (Amsterdam, Dec. 15, 1929); Concerto for Percussion and Small Orch. (Paris, Dec. 5, 1930); 5 piano concertos: No. 1 (Paris, Nov. 23, 1934), No. 2 (Chicago, Dec. 18, 1941, composer soloist), No. 3 (Prague, May 26, 1946), No. 4 (Boston, March 3, 1950), and No. 5 (1955; N.Y., June 25, 1956); *Concertino de printemps* for Violin and Orch. (Paris, March 21, 1935); 2 cello concertos: No. 1 (Paris, June 28, 1935) and No. 2 (N.Y., Nov. 28, 1946); *Suite provençale* (Venice, Sept. 12, 1937); *L'Oiseau* (Paris, Jan. 30, 1938); *Cortège funèbre* (N.Y., Aug. 4, 1940); Clarinet Concerto (1941; Washington, D.C., Jan. 30, 1946); *Suite* for Harmonica and Orch. (1942; Paris, May 28, 1947, Larry Adler soloist; also for Violin and Orch., Philadelphia, Nov. 16, 1945, Zino Francescatti soloist); Concerto for 2 Pianos and Orch. (Pittsburgh, Nov. 13, 1942); *Opus americanum* (San Francisco, Dec. 6, 1943); *Suite française* (for Band, N.Y., June 13, 1945; for Orch., N.Y., July 29, 1945); *Cain and Abel* for Narrator and Orch. (Los Angeles, Oct. 21, 1945); *Le Bal martiniquais* (N.Y., Dec. 6, 1945, composer conducting); 2 *Marches* (CBS, N.Y., Dec. 12, 1945); *Fête de la Victoire* (1945); *L'Apothéose de Molière* for Harpsichord and Strings (Capri, Sept. 15, 1948); *Kentuckiana* (Louisville, Jan. 4, 1949); Concerto for Marimba, Vibraphone, and Orch. (St. Louis, Feb. 12, 1949); *West Point Suite* for Band (West Point, May 30, 1952); *Concertino d'hiver* for Trombone and Strings (1953); *Ouverture méditerranéenne* (Louisville, May 22, 1954); Harp Concerto (Venice, Sept. 17, 1954); Oboe Concerto (1957); *Aubade* (Oakland, Calif., March 14, 1961); *Ouverture philharmonique* (N.Y., Nov. 30, 1962); *A Frenchman in New York* (Boston, June 25, 1963); *Odes pour les morts des guerres* (1963); *Murder of a Great Chief of State*, in memory of President John F. Kennedy (Oakland, Calif., Dec. 3, 1963); *Pacem in terris*, choral sym. (Paris, Dec. 20, 1963); *Music for Boston* for Violin and Orch. (1965); *Musique pour Prague* (Prague, May 20, 1966); *Musique pour l'Indiana* (Indianapolis, Oct. 29, 1966); *Musique pour Lisbonne* (1966); *Musique pour Nouvelle Orléans* (commissioned by the New Orleans Sym. Orch., but unaccountably canceled, and perf. for the 1st time in Aspen, Colo., Aug. 11, 1968, composer conducting); *Musique pour l'Univers Claudelien* (Aix-en-Provence, July 30, 1968); *Musique pour Graz* (Graz, Nov. 24, 1970); *Musique pour San Francisco*, "with the participation of the audience" (1971); *Suite in G* (San Rafael, Calif., Sept. 25, 1971); *Ode pour Jerusalem* (1972). **CHAMBER:** 2 violin sonatas (1911, 1917); 18 string quartets (1912–51), of which No. 14 and No. 15 are playable together, forming an octet (1st perf. in this form in Oakland, Calif., Aug. 10, 1949); Sonata for Piano and 2 Violins (1914); *Le Printemps* for Piano and Violin (1914); Sonata for Piano, Flute, Clarinet, and Oboe (1918); Flute Sonatina (1922); *Impromptu* for Violin and Piano (1926); 3 *caprices de Paganini* for Violin and Piano (1927); Clarinet Sonatina (1927); *Pastorale* for Oboe, Clarinet, and Bassoon (1935); Suite for Oboe, Clarinet, and Bassoon (1937); *La Cheminée du Roi René*, suite for Flute, Oboe, Clarinet, Horn, and Bassoon (1939); Sonatina for 2 Violins (1940); *Sonatine à trois* for Violin, Viola, and Cello (1940); Sonatina for Violin and Viola (1941); *Quatre visages* for Viola and Piano (1943); 2 viola sonatas (1944); *Elegie* for Cello and Piano (1945); *Danses de Jacarémirim* for Violin and Piano (1945); Sonata for Violin and Harpsichord (1945); Duo for 2 Violins (1945); String Trio (1947); *Aspen Serenade* for 9 Instruments (1957); String Sextet (1958); Chamber Concerto for Piano, Wind Instruments, and String Quintet (1961); String Septet (1964); Piano Quartet (1966); Piano Trio (1968); *Stanford Serenade* for Oboe and 11 Instruments (1969; Stanford, Calif., May 24, 1970); *Musique pour Ars nova* for 13 Instruments (1969); Wind Quintet (1973). **Piano:** *Le Printemps*, suite (1915–19); 2 sonatas (1916, 1949); *Saudades do Brasil*, 12 numbers in 2 books (1921); 3 *Rag Caprices*

(1922; also for Small Orch.); *L'Automne*, suite of 3 pieces (1932); *4 romances sans paroles* (1933); 2 sets of children's pieces: *Touches noires* and *Touches blanches* (1941); *La Muse ménagère*, suite of 15 pieces (1944; also for Orch.); *Une Journée*, suite of 5 pieces (1946); *L'Enfant aimé*, suite of 5 pieces (1948; also for Orch.); *Le Candélabre à sept branches*, suite (Ein Gev Festival, Israel, April 10, 1952); *Scaramouche*, version for 2 Pianos (1939); Le Bal martiniquais, version for 2 Pianos (1944); *Paris*, suite of 6 pieces for 4 Pianos (1948); *6 danses en 3 mouvements* for 2 Pianos (Paris, Dec. 17, 1970). **VOCAL:** 3 albums of songs after Francis Jammes (1910–12); *7 poèmes de la Connaissance de l'Est*, after Claudel (1913); *3 poèmes romantiques* for Voice and Piano (1914); *Le Château*, song cycle (1914); *4 poèmes* for Baritone, after Claudel (1915–17); *8 poèmes juifs* (1916); *Child poems* (1916); *3 poèmes*, after Christina Rossetti (1916); *Le Retour de l'enfant prodigue*, cantata for 5 Voices and Orch. (1917; Paris, Nov. 23, 1922, composer conducting); *Chansons bas* for Voice and Piano, after Mallarmé (1917); *2 poèmes de Rimbaud* for Voice and Piano (1917); *Psalm 136* for Baritone, Chorus, and Orch. (1918); *Psalm 129* for Baritone and Orch. (1919); *Les Soirées de Pétrograd*, in 2 albums: *L'Ancien Régime* and *La Révolution* (1919); *Machines agricoles* for Voice and 7 Instruments, to words from a commercial catalog (1919); *3 poèmes de Jean Cocteau* for Voice and Piano (1920); *Catalogue de fleurs* for Voice and Piano or 7 Instruments (1920); *Feuilles de température* for Voice and Piano (1920); *Cocktail* for Voice and 3 Clarinets (1921); *Psalm 126* for Chorus (1921); *4 poèmes de Catulle* for Voice and Violin (1923); *6 chants populaires hébraïques* for Voice and Piano (1925); *Hymne de Sion* for Voice and Piano (1925); *Pièce de circonstance* for Voice and Piano, after Cocteau (1926); *Cantate pour louer le Seigneur* for Soloists, Choruses, and Orch. (1928); *Pan et Syrinx*, cantata (1934); *Les Amours de Ronsard* for Chorus and Small Orch. (1934); *Le Cygne* for Voice and Piano, after Claudel (1935); *La Sagesse* for Voices and Small Orch., after Claudel (1935; Paris Radio, Nov. 8, 1945); *Cantate de la paix*, after Claudel (1937); *Cantate nuptiale*, after *Song of Songs* (Marseilles, Aug. 31, 1937); *Les Deux Cités*, cantata (1937); *Chanson du capitaine* for Voice and Piano (1937); *Les Quatre Éléments* for Soprano, Tenor, and Orch. (1938); *Récréation*, children's songs (1938); *3 élégies* for Soprano, Tenor, and Strings (1939); *Incantations* for Men's Chorus (1939); *Quatrains valaisans* for Chorus, after Rilke (1939); *Cantate de la guerre* for Chorus, after Claudel (1940); *Le Voyage d'été*, suite for Voice and Piano (1940); *4 chansons de Ronsard* for Voice and Orch. (1941); *Reves*, song cycle (1942); *La Libération des Antilles* for Voice and Piano (1944); *Kaddisch* for Voice, Chorus, and Organ (1945); *Sabbath Morning Service* for Baritone, Chorus, and Organ (1947); *Naissance de Vénus*, cantata for Chorus (Paris Radio, Nov. 30, 1949); *Ballade-Nocturne* for Voice and Piano (1949); *Barba Garibo*, 10 French folk songs, for Chorus and Orch. (for the celebration of the wine harvest in Menton, 1953); *Cantate de l'initiation* for Chorus and Orch. (1960); *Cantate de la croix de charité* (1960); *Invocation à l'ange Raphael* for 2 Women's Choruses and Orch. (1962); *Adam* for Vocal Quintet (1964); *Cantate de Psaumes* (Paris, May 2, 1968); *Les Momies d'Égypte*, choral comedy (1972).

WRITINGS: *Études* (essays; Paris, 1926); *Notes sans musique* (autobiography; Paris, 1949; Eng. tr., London, 1952, as *Notes without Music*); *Entretiens avec Claude Rostand* (Paris, 1952); *Ma vie heureuse* (Paris, 1973; Eng. tr., 1995, as *My Happy Life*).

BIBL.: G. Augsbourg, *La Vie de D. M. en images* (Paris, 1935); G. Beck, *D. M.: Étude suivie du catalogue chronologique complet* (Paris, 1949; suppl., 1957); J. Roy, *D. M.* (Paris, 1968); A. Braga, *D. M.* (Naples, 1969); C. Palmer, *M.* (London, 1976); P. Collaer, *D. M.* (Geneva and Paris, 1982; Eng. tr., 1988); H. Ehrler, *Untersuchungen zur Klaviermusik von Francis Poulenc, Arthur Honegger und D. M.* (Tutzing, 1990); F. Bloch, *D. M., 1892–1974* (Paris, 1992); A. Lunel, *Mon ami D. M.: Inédits* (Aix-en-Provence, 1992); H. Malcomess, *Die opéras minute von D. M.* (Bonn, 1993); M. Kelkel, ed., *Colloque international Arthur Honegger-D. M. (1992: Sorbonne)* (Paris, 1994); J. Roy, *Le groupe des six: Poulenc, M., Honegger, Auric, Tailleferre, Durey* (Paris, 1994); D. Mawer, *D. M.: Modality and Structure in Music of the 1920s* (Aldershot, 1997).—NS/LK/DM

Miller, (Alton) Glenn, disciplined American bandleader, arranger, and trombonist; b. Clarinda, Iowa, March 1, 1904; d. en route from England to France, Dec. 15, 1944. Though Miller succeeded relatively late as a swing bandleader, he succeeded spectacularly: For three years, 1939–42, his Orch. outstripped all competitors as the most popular recording and performing act in the U.S. Developing a signature sound in which the melody was carried by a high-pitched clarinet doubled by a saxophone section playing an octave lower, he scored 17 #1 hits and at least seven million-sellers, his most popular recordings being "In the Mood," "Moonlight Cocktail," "Chattanooga Choo Choo," and "Tuxedo Junction." His progress was stopped only by World War II; he disbanded to join the military, where he organized a service band. After his death, imitators and a ghost band continued to play in his style, and unlike other stars of the Swing Era, he remained consistently popular, with his recordings continuing to chart more than 50 years later.

The son of Lewis Elmer and Mattie Lou Cavender, Miller moved with his family to Tryon, Nebr., in 1909, then to Grant City, Mo., in 1915. Music was played at home, and his first instrument was a mandolin, which he traded for a horn. He joined the town band and was given a trombone by the bandleader, paying for it by shining shoes. The family moved to Fort Morgan, Colo., by 1918, and he played in the high school band there. After graduating in May 1921, he played with Boyd Senter's Orch., then entered the Univ. of Colo. in January 1923, leaving after a year to concentrate on music. He moved to Los Angeles and joined Ben Pollack's band. He left Pollack in the summer of 1928 and spent the next several years playing and arranging in N.Y. On Oct. 6, 1928, he married Helen Burger, with whom he later adopted two children.

In the spring of 1934, Miller joined The Dorsey Brothers Orch. as trombonist and arranger, staying with them nearly a year. He then organized an American band for British bandleader Ray Noble to take into the Rainbow Room atop Rockefeller Center in N.Y. in 1935. During this period he studied theory and composition with Joseph Schillinger. He recorded a session for Columbia Records under his own name on April 25, 1935, marking his debut as a leader, but he did not organize a permanent Orch. until 1937. The group played around the country during the year but was not successful, and Miller disbanded it at the start of 1938, only to re-form with mostly new players two months later. This group continued to struggle for another year until it landed a prestigious engagement at the Glen Island Casino in New Rochelle, N.Y., for the summer of 1939. Meanwhile, Miller had signed to the discount-priced Bluebird label of RCA Victor Records.

The attention paid to the Glen Island Casino residency and regular radio broadcasts led to rapid success for the band. In June, "Wishing (Will Make It So)" (music and lyrics by B. G. De Sylva) became Miller's first record to top the hit parade. It was succeeded by "Stairway to the Stars" (music by Matty Malneck and Frank Signorelli, lyrics by Mitchell Parish) in July, which gave way to "Moon Love" (music and lyrics by Mack David, Mack Davis, and André Kostalanetz) in August, and then "Over the Rainbow" (music by Harold Arlen, lyrics by E. Y. Harburg) in September—18 straight weeks at #1. "Blue Orchids" (music and lyrics by Hoagy Carmichael) became Miller's fifth chart-topper of the year in November. But his best-selling record of 1939 and first million-seller was his own composition and theme song, "Moonlight Serenade" (lyrics by Mitchell Parish), which he had written as an exercise for Joseph Schillinger.

In December 1939, Miller took over the *Chesterfield Supper Club* radio show, which broadcast three times a week. In January 1940 he opened at the Café Rouge in the Hotel Pennsylvania in N.Y., the first of several lengthy engagements there. Simultaneously, he also appeared at the Paramount Theatre, another important venue. "Careless" (music and lyrics by Lew Quadling, Eddy Howard, and Dick Jurgens) topped the hit parade in February; that same month marked the sales peak of Miller's second million-seller and one of the definitive songs of the Swing Era, "In the Mood" (music by Joe Garland, lyrics by Andy Razaf). "When You Wish Upon a Star" (music by Leigh Harline, lyrics by Ned Washington) topped the chart in March, superseded by "The Woodpecker Song" (music by Eldo di Lazzaro, English lyrics by Harold Adamson) in May, "Imagination" (music by James Van Heusen, lyrics by Johnny Burke) in June, and "Fools Rush In" (music and lyrics by Rube Bloom, lyrics by Johnny Mercer) in July.

But Miller's biggest success of the spring of 1940 was his third million-seller, "Tuxedo Junction" (music by Erskine Hawkins, William Johnson, and Julian Dash, lyrics by Buddy Feyne). His fourth million-seller, which peaked in the Top Ten in August, was "Pennsylvania 6–5000" (music by Jerry Gray, lyrics by Carl Sigman), the phone number of the Hotel Pennsylvania. Miller continued to score numerous hits through the rest of 1940, but he did not top the charts again until March 1941 with his adaptation of the Russian folk song "Song of the Volga Boatmen."

Miller contracted with 20th Century–Fox and went to Hollywood to make *Sun Valley Serenade*, his first motion picture, with songs by Harry Warren and Mack Gordon. Released in September 1941, the film contained his 12th chart-topper and fifth million-seller, "Chattanooga Choo Choo." He returned to the top of the charts in December with "Elmer's Tune" (music and lyrics by Elmer Albrecht, Sammy Gallop, and Dick Jurgens).

Miller continued to dominate popular music in 1942, going to #1 with "A String of Pearls" (music by Jerry Gray, lyrics by Eddie DeLange) and "Moonlight Cocktail" (music by C. Luckeyth Roberts, lyrics by Kim Gannon) in February and "(I've Got a Gal in) Kalamazoo" (music by Warren, lyrics by Gordon), from his second motion picture, *Orchestra Wives*, in September, while "American Patrol" and "Kalamazoo" gave him his sixth and seventh million-sellers. On Sept. 10 he received his commission, and his civilian band played its final date on Sept. 27.

Assigned to the Army Air Force, Miller organized a service band in the spring of 1943 and played for the troops and at war-bond rallies while doing a weekly radio show, *I Sustain the Wings;* he scored a final #1 hit with "That Old Black Magic" (music by Harold Arlen, lyrics by Johnny Mercer) in May. In June 1944 he went to Great Britain, where he continued to give concerts and do radio broadcasts. He was preparing to perform in newly liberated Paris when his plane was lost over the English Channel.

In the wake of Miller's death, his band played in Europe during the final months of World War II. *Glenn Miller*, an album of 78s, topped the charts in May 1945, becoming the best-selling album of the year. After the war the Miller band was fronted by saxophonist/vocalist Tex Beneke for several years, while Miller's original recordings continued to sell well. The album *Glenn Miller Masterpieces—Vol. 2* reached #1 in October 1947.

The Glenn Miller Story, a fictionalized screen biography starring Jimmy Stewart, was released in February 1954 and became one of the top-grossing films of the year. The film's soundtrack album, featuring Miller's music but not Miller himself, topped the charts in March. RCA Victor released a ten-inch album of original Miller performances of the songs heard in the film, *Selections from the Glenn Miller Story*, and it went to #1 in May. In 1956 the album was reissued as a 12-inch LP with a slightly different track selection. It was certified gold in 1961. In 1962, RCA Victor released *Glenn Miller Plays Selections from the Glenn Miller Story and Other Hits*, with a track listing identical to the 1956 LP. This album was certified gold in 1968.

In 1956 the Glenn Miller estate established an official "ghost" version of the Glenn Miller Orch. under the direction of drummer/singer Ray McKinley, who had played with Miller. This band continued to exist under different leaders and to make recordings.

The continuing sales of Miller records inspired RCA Victor to unearth previously unissued airchecks and outtakes. The 1959 triple-LP set *For the First Time...* earned a Grammy nomination for Best Performance by a Dance Band. (Though Miller never won a Grammy, "In the Mood" and "Tuxedo Junction" have been inducted into the Grammy Hall of Fame.)

The best sales, however, continued to be achieved by the original studio recordings: the double-LP *A Memorial, 1944–69*, containing 30 of Miller's hits and released in October 1969, went gold in 1986; the ten- track single-LP *Pure Gold*, released in March 1975, went gold in 1984. RCA Victor reissued all of Miller's recordings in a series of nine double-LPs released in the last half of the 1970s and subsequently reconfigured as a 13–CD boxed set. Miller's music was heard on a gold-selling single in 1989, when "In the Mood" was sampled on the hit "Swing the Mood," by Jive Bunny and the Mastermixers. As late as 1996, RCA Victor was continuing to find unreleased Miller material for such albums as *The Lost Recordings and The Secret Broadcasts*, which sold well enough to reach the jazz charts.

WRITINGS: *G. M.'s Method for Orchestral Arranging* (1943).

BIBL.: S. Bedwell, *A G. M. Discography and Biography* (London, 1955; 2nd ed., 1956); J. Flower, *Moonlight Serenade: A Bio-Discography of the G. M. Civilian Band* (New Rochelle, N.Y., 1972); G. Simon, *G. M. and His Orchestra* (N.Y., 1974); J. Green, *G. M. and the Age of Swing* (London, 1976); G. Butcher, *Next to a Letter from Home: Major G. M.'s Wartime Band* (Edinburgh, 1986); E. Polic, *The G. M. Army Air Force Band: Sustineo Alas/I Sustain the Wings* (Metuchen, N.J., 1989).—**WR**

Miller, Dayton C(larence), American physicist and flutist; b. Strongsville, Ohio, March 13, 1866; d. Cleveland, Feb. 22, 1941. After graduation from Baldwin Coll. and Princeton Univ. (D.Sc., 1890), he was prof. of physics at the Case School of Applied Science in Cleveland (from 1893). An early interest in the flute led to his experimentation with various versions of the instrument (including a double-bass flute); he accumulated an extensive collection of flutes and various materials relating to the flute, which he left to the Library of Congress in Washington, D.C. A leading authority in the field of acoustics and light, he was president of the American Physical Soc. (1925–26) and of the Acoustical Soc. of America (1931–32), and vice-president of the American Musicological Soc. (1939). He publ. *The Science of Musical Sounds* (1916; 2nd ed., rev., 1926), *Catalogue of Books and Literary Material Relating to the Flute and Other Musical Instruments* (1935), *Anecdotal History of the Science of Sound to the Beginning of the 20th Century* (1935), *Sound Waves, Their Shape and Speed* (1937), etc.

BIBL.: H. Fletcher, *Biographical Memoir of D.C. M.* (Washington, D.C., 1944); L. Gilliam and W. Lichtenwanger, *The D.C. M. Flute Collection: A Checklist of the Instruments* (Washington, D.C., 1961).—**NS/LK/DM**

Miller, Eddie (originally, **Muller, Edward Raymond**), tenor saxophonist, clarinetist, singer; b. New Orleans, June 23, 1911; d. Los Angeles, April 1, 1991. He played his first local gigs while still in his early teens. He joined the New Orleans Owls in 1928, subsequently moved to N.Y., where he worked on his alto sax with various bandleaders for eight months. He switched to tenor sax after joining Ben Pollack's band in September of 1930, remaining with the band until it broke up in 1934. Miller became the founding member of the band that eventually became Bob Crosby's Band; he remained with the group until it disbanded in late 1942. From early 1943, he led his own band on the West Coast (featuring several ex-Bob Crosby musicians). After brief service in the army during August 1944, Miller returned to Calif. to lead his own band again, before becoming a studio musician. The band was featured in the Donald O'Connor film *You Can't Ration Love* (1943), where Miller was also prominently featured as a soloist on many film soundtracks, including: *The Girls He Left Behind, Mr. Big, You Were Meant for Me, No Way Out,* and *Panic in the Streets.* Miller took part in many Bob Crosby reunions during the 1950s and 1960s. He traveled to Japan with Bob Crosby in late 1964, and also dates in

Las Vegas and N.Y. Miller occasionally worked in New Orleans during the 1960s, and was also featured at many jazz festivals, including the first New Orleans Jazz Festival in 1969. Miller was with Pete Fountain during the early 1970s, and toured Europe with World's Greatest Jazz Band (1977). He continued to play through the mid-1980s in Calif., and was less active until his death in 1991.

DISC.: *Uncollected Eddie Miller & His Band* (1943); *Eddie Miller-George Van Eps* (1946); *Tenor of Jazz* (1967); *Portrait of Eddie* (1971); *It's Miller Time* (1979).—**JC/LP**

Miller, Jonathan (Wolfe), English opera director; b. London, July 21, 1934. He studied the natural sciences at St. John's Coll., Cambridge, taking his M.D. degree in 1959. However, his abiding interest in the arts led him to pursue work in television and the theater. Turning to opera direction, he attracted notice with his staging of Alexander Goehr's *Arden Must Die* with the New Opera Co. in 1974. From 1974 to 1981 he was an opera director with the Kent Opera, where his stagings of *Così fan tutte, Orfeo, Falstaff,* and *Evgeny Onegin* were highly praised; also worked regularly with the English National Opera in London, winning special acclaim for his stagings of *Rigoletto* (1982) and *The Mikado* (1986). In 1991 he staged *Le nozze di Figaro* at the Vienna Festival and *Kát'a Kabanová* at the Metropolitan Opera in N.Y. His *Manon Lescaut* was produced at Milan's La Scala in 1992. He mounted *Così fan tutte* at London's Covent Garden in 1995. In 1997 he staged *Ariadne auf Naxos* in Florence.

BIBL.: M. Romain, *A Profile of J. M.* (Cambridge, 1992). —**NS/LK/DM**

Miller, Marcus, jazz-fusion electric bassist, multi-instrumentalist, composer; b. N.Y., June 14, 1959. Miller was self-taught on the electric bass, which he took up at age 15. He worked in the mid-1970s as a studio musician for various pop/R&B singers and groups. He burst into public view when he wrote (and produced) the 1986 album *Tutu* for Miles Davis, performing nearly all the parts himself on synthesizers and overdubbing Davis at the end. He also toured with Davis as a bassist during 1980–82. He has also worked with many other jazz and R&B acts. Since the early 1980s, he has led the group the Jamaica Boys.

DISC.: *Sun Don't Lie* (1993); *Tales* (1994).—**LP**

Miller, Mildred, American soprano and opera administrator; b. Cleveland, Dec. 16, 1924. She studied at the Cleveland Inst. of Music (B.M., 1946) and with Sundelius at the New England Cons. of Music in Boston (diploma, 1948). In 1949 she went to Germany and began her operatic career with appearances in Stuttgart and Munich. On Nov. 17, 1951, she made her Metropolitan Opera debut in N.Y. as Cherubino. Among her later roles there were Dorabella (1952), Octavian and Carmen (1953), Nicklausse (1955), and Rossini's Rosina and Strauss's Composer (1963). She remained on the roster of the Metropolitan Opera until 1975. During her years there, Miller also appeared widely as a concert singer. In 1978 she founded the Opera Theater of Pittsburgh, which she led as artistic director until her retirement in 1999.—NS/LK/DM

Miller, Mitch(ell William),

American chorus leader, conductor, and oboist; b. Rochester, N.Y., July 4, 1911. Miller's *Sing Along* albums of choral favorites made him one of the most successful recording artists of the second half of the 1950s, after he had spent the first half of the decade producing hits for Columbia Records' roster of popular singers, including Tony Bennett, Rosemary Clooney, Jo Stafford, and Doris Day.

Miller's parents were Abram Charles and Hinda Rosenblum Miller. He took up the oboe at the age of 12 and made his professional debut at 15 with the Rochester Philharmonic Orch., of which he was a member from 1930 to 1933. From 1928 to 1933 he studied with Arthur Forman. He earned a Bachelor's degree in music from the Eastman School of Music in 1932. From 1933 to 1936 he played with various orchestras. He married Frances Josephine Alexander on Sept. 10, 1935; they had three children.

Miller was a member of the Columbia Broadcasting System Symphony Orch. from 1936 to 1947, when he became musical director of the classical music division of Mercury Records, taking over the pop music division in 1948. At Mercury he handled successful recordings by such singers as Frankie Laine, Patti Page, and Vic Damone. Columbia Records hired him away in 1950, and he also began to make his mark as a recording artist. "Tzena Tzena Tzena" (music by Issachar Miron [Michrovsky] and Julius Grossman, English lyrics by Mitchell Parish), credited to Mitch Miller and His Orch. and Chorus, peaked in the Top Ten in July 1950. He topped the charts with the million-selling "The Yellow Rose of Texas" (traditional, adaptation by Don George) in September 1955 and returned to the Top Ten with the instrumental "Theme Song from *Song for a Summer Night*" (music and lyrics by Robert Allen) in September 1956 and with "The Children's Marching Song" (music and lyrics by Malcolm Arnold, adapted from the traditional song "This Old Man") in January 1959.

Miller released his first *Sing Along* LP, *Sing Along with Mitch*, credited to Mitch Miller & the Gang, in June 1958. It featured a male chorus of 28 singing such familiar songs as "By the Light of the Silvery Moon" (music by Gus Edwards, lyrics by Edward Madden), "You Are My Sunshine" (music and lyrics by Jimmie Davis and Charles Mitchell), and "Don't Fence Me In" (music and lyrics by Cole Porter), with lyrics included so that listeners could join in. The result was phenomenal success: the album topped the charts and went gold. Miller followed with a series of similar albums, each of which reached the Top Ten and/or went gold.

On May 24, 1960, Miller had tried out the *Sing Along* concept as a television special broadcast on *Ford Startime*. *Sing Along with Mitch* the TV series began on a trial basis, running once every two weeks, in January 1961, running through April, then gained a regular weekly slot on NBC in September, running for three seasons, through September 1964. By then the *Sing Along* phe-

nomenon had run its course. Miller retired from Columbia Records but occasionally worked as a guest conductor for various orchestras.

DISC.: *Christmas Sing-Along with Mitch* (1958); *More Sing Along with Mitch* (1958); *Still More! Sing Along with Mitch* (1959); *Folk Songs Sing Along with Mitch* (1959); *Party Sing Along with Mitch* (1959); *Fireside Sing Along with Mitch* (1959); *Saturday Night Sing Along with Mitch* (1960); *Sentimental Sing Along with Mitch* (1960); *Memories Sing Along with Mitch* (1960); *Happy Times! Sing Along with Mitch* (1961); *Mitch's Greatest Hits* (1961); *TV Sing Along with Mitch* (1961); *Your Request Sing Along with Mitch* (1961); *Holiday Sing Along with Mitch* (1961).—WR

Miller, Robert,

American pianist and lawyer; b. N.Y., Dec. 5, 1930; d. Bronxville, N.Y., Nov. 30, 1981. He studied piano with Mathilde McKinney and Abbey Simon, then enrolled at Princeton Univ., where he took classes in composition with Babbitt and Cone, graduating in 1952; also studied jurisprudence at Columbia Univ. Law School, graduating in 1957. He was admitted to the bar in 1958 and became a practicing Wall Street lawyer, and among his clients were several composers. As a pianist, he made his debut in Carnegie Hall in N.Y. in 1957. He had a fairly active, though unhappily brief, career as a recitalist, excelling particularly in ultramodern music. He gave the first performance in N.Y. in 1980 of a piano concerto by John Harbison, and George Crumb wrote his *Makrokosmos* (vol. II) for him. —NS/LK/DM

Miller, Steve,

b. Milwaukee, Wisc., Oct. 5, 1943. **The Steve Miller Band. MEMBERSHIP:** Steve Miller, gtr., voc.; James "Curly" Cooke, gtr.; Jim Peterman, org.; Lonnie Turner, bs. (b. Berkeley, Calif., Feb. 24, 1947); Tim Davis, drm. Boz (William Royce) Scaggs (b. Ohio, June 8, 1944) replaced Curly Cooke in 1967–1968. Various musicians have been employed by Miller since the early 1970s.

Mistakenly identified with the psychedelic movement emerging from San Francisco in the late 1960s, the Steve Miller Band signed with Capitol Records for a huge advance and recorded two albums, often regarded as classics of the era, featuring sophisticated production, elaborate sound effects, and the singing, guitar playing, and songwriting of Boz Scaggs. The Steve Miller Band retained their reputation as an album band after Scaggs's departure, despite a series of personnel changes, to emerge wildly successful with *The Joker, Fly Like an Eagle*, and *Book of Dreams*. Their popularity was largely based on Miller's ability to manufacture consummate but inconsequential recordings of his facile, uninvolving songs. Following 1982's *Abracadabra*, Miller recorded only occasionally, while his mid-1970s hits were often revived on so-called classic-rock radio.

Steve Miller moved as an infant with his family to Dallas, where he grew up. He took up guitar at age five and formed his first blues band, The Marksmen, at age 12 with friend Boz Scaggs. Enrolling at the Univ. of Wisc.–Madison in 1961, Miller assembled the white soul group the Ardells (later the Fabulous Night Trains), again with Scaggs, and played locally for more than three years. Miller left college to move to Chicago, where he played with black bluesmen such as Muddy Waters and Buddy Guy and white blues players such as Paul Butterfield, Mike Bloomfield, and Barry Goldberg; Scaggs, meanwhile, traveled to Europe and played around Scandinavia as a folk singer. The Miller-Goldberg Band was formed and signed to Epic, but Miller soon quit and returned to Dallas before moving to San Francisco in 1966. There he formed the Steve Miller Blues Band with Curly Cooke, Jim Peterman, Lonnie Turner, and Tim Davis.

The group backed Chuck Berry on his *Live at the Fillmore* album. Miller, besieged by contract offers, carefully and slowly conducted negotiations, eventually signing with Capitol Records on highly favorable terms, which included a $60,000 advance. In September 1967 Curly Cooke dropped out of the group, by then known as simply the Steve Miller Band, and Miller summoned Boz Scaggs from Europe. This grouping went to England to record their debut album, *Children of the Future*. Although it was only minimally associated with psychedelic music and progressive rock, as some reviewers claimed, it was nonetheless well received critically. Slickly produced, the album featured Miller's title song and Scaggs's "Baby's Callin' Me Home" and "Steppin' Stone." The band quickly recorded the follow-up, *Sailor*, employing carefully produced sound effects throughout. The album contained Miller's "Song for Our Ancestors," "Living in the U.S.A." (a minor hit), and "Quicksilver Girls," as well as Scaggs's "Overdrive" and one of Miller's theme songs, "Gangster of Love."

Boz Scaggs left the Steve Miller Band in August 1968, followed soon after by Jim Peterman. Subsequently featuring himself more on stage and in recordings, Miller recruited a new keyboardist for *Brave New World* (with "Space Cowboy") and *Your Saving Grace*. After one more album, only Miller was left from the original recording band.

Steve Miller's next two albums sold poorly, but 1973's *The Joker*, recorded with a returned Lonnie Turner, yielded a top hit with its trite and self-indulgent title song. Off the concert trail for more than a year, the band reconvened with Turner, drummer Gary Mallaber, and others for *Fly Like an Eagle* and *Book of Dreams*. The former yielded the near-smash hit "Take the Money and Run" and the smashes "Rock'n Me" and "Fly Like an Eagle"; the latter produced three major hits with "Jet Airliner," "Jungle Love," and "Swingtown." Relatively inactive for a time, the Steve Miller Band reemerged in 1981 with *Circle of Love*, which included the trite, side-long "Macho City" and the major hit "Heart Like a Wheel." *Abracadabra* brought him his last Number One in 1982, the title song.

Exhausted from touring, Steve Miller retreated to Seattle and later Idaho. He recorded two albums in the mid-1980s before returning to touring in 1988 in support of *Born 2 B Blue*, with a small jazz ensemble accompanying him, including Ben Sidran, famed vibraphonist Milt Jackson, and Phil Woods on sax. A major change in direction for Miller, the album featured four Jimmy Reed songs and other standards such as "God Bless the Child." Enjoying increased popularity as his mid-1970s hits became staples of the classic-rock radio format,

Steve Miller signed with Polygram Records after being courted by the label for two years. His debut for Polydor, 1993's *Wide River*, produced a minor hit with the title song.

DISC.: *Children of the Future* (1968); *Sailor* (1968); *Brave New World* (1969); *Your Saving Grace* (1969); *Number Five* (1970); *Children of the Future/Living in the U.S.A.* (1971); *Rock Love* (1971); *Recall the Beginning: A Journey from Eden* (1972); *Anthology* (1972); *The Joker* (1973); *The Best of S. M., 1968–1973* (1991); *Fly Like an Eagle* (1976); *Book of Dreams* (1977); *Greatest Hits: 1974–1978* (1978); *Circle of Love* (1981); *Abracadabra* (1982); *S. M. Band—Live!* (1983); *Italian X-Rays* (1984); *Living in the 20th Century* (1986); *Born 2 B Blue* (1988); *Wide River* (1993); *S. M. Band Box Set* (1994).—**BH**

Millet, Luis, Catalan composer and conductor; b. Masnou, near Barcelona, April 18, 1867; d. Barcelona, Dec. 7, 1941. He studied with Vidiella and Pedrell, then became a choral conductor. In 1891 he founded the famous choral society Orfeo Catala, which he continued to lead until the last years of his life; was also director of the municipal music school in Barcelona. He composed several orch. fantasies on Catalan folk songs and many choral works, and also publ. 2 books on folk music: *De la canción popular catalana* and *Pel nostre ideal* (1917).

BIBL.: B. Sampler, *L. M.* (Barcelona, 1926).—**NS/LK/DM**

Millico, (Vito) Giuseppe, Italian castrato soprano, singing teacher, and composer; b. Terlizzi, near Bari, Jan. 19, 1737; d. Naples, Oct. 2, 1802. After singing at the St. Petersburg Imperial Court (1758–65), he was active in Italy. He became a friend of Gluck and created the role of Paris in his *Paride ed Elena* (Vienna, Nov. 3, 1770). Following appearances in London (1772–73) and Paris (1774), Millico sang in Zweibrücken and Mannheim. In 1780 he returned to Italy and became virtuoso di camera of the Naples royal chapel. Among his works were several operas and cantatas, as well as many arias, canzonettas, and duets.

BIBL.: M. Belluci La Salandria, *V.G. M.* (Baris, 1951). —**NS/LK/DM**

Millinder, Lucky (actually, **Lucius Venable**), jazz/R&B bandleader; b. Anniston, Ala., Aug. 8, 1900; d. N.Y., Sept. 28, 1966. He was a big-band leader of the 1930s and 1940s, whose bands spawned Sweets Edison, Tab Smith, Bill Doggett, Wynonie Harris, and countless others. Raised in Chicago, Millinder worked as a master of ceremonies at various ballrooms and clubs in his early 20s. He fronted a band for a tour of R.K.O. circuit in 1931; the following spring, he took over the leadership of "Doc" Crawford's Big Band and led it at the Harlem Uproar House, N.Y. In June 1933 he took different personnel to Europe and played residencies in Monte Carlo and Paris before returning to N.Y. that October. During the following year he began fronting the Mills Blue Rhythm Band, which subsequently worked under his name. He continued leading the group until the spring of 1938, then toured fronting Bill Doggett's Band, taking the group to New York. However, in September 1939, the band went bankrupt. Millinder reformed a band in September 1940 and continued leading a big band on and off until the summer of 1952; he then left full-time music and worked as a salesman for a spirit distillery. Later he reorganized bands for stints at the Apollo, N.Y., and various tours, but was also active as a disc jockey on radio WNEW and as a publicist and fortuneteller. In later years he occasionally fronted bands for specific engagements. His band played the soundtracks for the films *Paradise in Harlem* (1939) and *Boarding House Blues* (1948).

DISC.: *Lucky Days* (1941); *Lucky Millinder & His Orch.* (1942); *Let It Roll* (1972).—JC/LP

Millo, Aprile (Elizabeth), talented American soprano; b. N.Y., April 14, 1958. Her father was a tenor and her mother a soprano. After living in Europe, Millo's family moved to Los Angeles when she was 11; during her high school years she studied voice with her parents and augmented her training by listening to recordings of the great divas. In 1977 she won 1st place in the San Diego Opera competition, received the Geraldine Farrar Award, and sang in the opening concert of the new opera center there. In 1978 she won 1st prize in the Concorso Internazionale di Voci Verdiane in Busseto and received the Montserrat Caballe Award at the Francisco Vinas competition in Barcelona. In 1981 she sang with the N.Y.C. Opera and also joined the Metropolitan Opera's Young Artists Development Program; later studied with Rita Patane. On Jan. 4, 1983, she made her first appearance at La Scala in Milan as Elvira in *Ernani*, a role she repeated with the Welsh National Opera in 1984. She made her Metropolitan Opera debut in N.Y. as Amelia in *Simon Boccanegra* on Dec. 3, 1984, substituting for the ailing Anna Tomowa-Sintow. In 1985 she received the Richard Tucker Award. Subsequently she appeared at the Metropolitan Opera in such roles as Elisabetta in *Don Carlos*, Liù in *Turandot*, Luisa Miller, Leonora in *Il Trovatore*, Desdemona in *Otello*, and Aida. She also sang in concert performances with the Opera Orch. of N.Y., appearing as Giselda in *I Lombardi alla prima crociata* (1986) and as Lida in *La battaglia di Legnano* (1987). In 1992 she made her San Francisco Opera debut as Maddalena, a role she later sang at the Metropolitan Opera and in Rome in 1996.—NS/LK/DM

Millöcker, Carl, Austrian conductor and composer; b. Vienna, April 29, 1842; d. Baden, near Vienna, Dec. 31, 1899. His father was a jeweler, and Millöcker was destined for that trade, but showed irrepressible musical inclinations and learned music as a child. He played the flute in a theater orch. at 16, and later took courses at the Cons. of the Gesellschaft der Musikfreunde in Vienna. Upon the recommendation of Franz von Suppé, he received a post as theater conductor in Graz (1864). In 1866 he returned to Vienna, and from 1869 to 1883 was 2nd conductor of the Theater an der Wien. He suffered a stroke in 1894, which left him partially paralyzed. As a composer, Millöcker possessed a natural gift for melodious music; although his popularity was never as great as that of Johann Strauss or Lehár, his operettas captured the spirit of Viennese life.

WORKS: DRAMATIC: Operetta (all 1st perf. in Vienna unless otherwise given): *Der tote Gast* (Graz, Dec. 21, 1865); *Die lustigen Binder* (Graz, Dec. 21, 1865); *Diana* (Jan. 2, 1867); *Die Fraueninsel* (Budapest, 1868); *Drei Paar Schuhe* (Jan. 5, 1871); *Wechselbrief und Briefwechsel, or Ein nagender Wurm* (Aug. 10, 1872); *Ein Abenteuer in Wien* (Jan. 20, 1873); *Das verwunschene Schloss* (March 30, 1878); *Gräfin Dubarry* (Oct. 31, 1879); *Apajune der Wassermann* (Dec. 18, 1880); *Die Jungfrau von Belleville* (Oct. 29, 1881); *Der Bettelstudent* (Dec. 6, 1882; his most successful work; popular also in England and America as *Student Beggar*; N.Y., Oct. 29, 1883); *Gasparone* (Jan. 26, 1884); *Der Feldprediger* (Oct. 31, 1884); *Der Vice-Admiral* (Oct. 9, 1886); *Die sieben Schwaben* (Oct. 29, 1887); *Der arme Jonathan* (Jan. 4, 1890; new version by Hentschke and Rixner, 1939); *Das Sonntagskind* (Jan. 16, 1892); *Der Probekuss* (Dec. 22, 1894); *Nordlicht, oder Der rote Graf* (Dec. 22, 1896).—NS/LK/DM

Mills, Charles (Borromeo), American composer; b. Asheville, N.C., Jan. 8, 1914; d. N.Y., March 7, 1982. In his youth, he played in dance bands. In 1933 he went to N.Y. and engaged in serious study of composition, first with Max Garfield and then with Copland (1935–37), Sessions (1937–39), and Harris (1939–41). He wrote mostly in a severe but eloquent contrapuntal style; in virtually his entire career as a composer, he pursued the ideal of formal cohesion; his style of composition may be described as Baroque a l'americaine. His quest for artistic self-discipline led him to the decision to become a Roman Catholic. He was baptized according to the Roman Catholic rite on May 14, 1944. In 1952 he was awarded a Guggenheim fellowship. In his last works, Mills gradually adopted serial methods, which seemed to respond to his need of strong discipline.

WORKS: ORCH.: 6 syms.: No. 1 (1940), No. 2 (1942), No. 3 (1946), No. 4, *Crazy Horse* (Cincinnati, Nov. 28, 1958), No. 5 for Strings (1980), and No. 6 (1981); Piano Concerto (1948); *Theme and Variations* (N.Y., Nov. 8, 1951); Concertino for Oboe and Strings (1957); *Serenade* for Winds and Strings (1960); *In a Mule-Drawn Wagon* for Strings (1968); *Symphonic Ode* for Strings (1976). **CHAMBER:** 5 string quartets (1939–58); 6 violin sonatas (1940–77); 2 cello sonatas (1940, 1942); Piano Trio (1941); Chamber Concerto for 10 Instruments (1942); 2 suites for Solo Violin (1942, 1944); English Horn Sonata (1946); *Concerto sereno* for Woodwind Octet (1948); *Prologue and Dithyramb* for String Quartet (1951); Brass Quintet (1962); Brass Sextet (1964); *Sonata da chiesa* for Recorder and Harpsichord (1972); *The 5 Moons of Uranus* for Recorder and Piano (1972); *Duo eclogue* for Recorder and Organ (1974). **PIANO:** 2 sonatas (1941–42); 11 sonatinas (1942–45); *30 Penitential Preludes* (1945). **VOCAL:** *Canticles of the Sun* for Voice and Piano (1945); *The Ascension Cantata* for Tenor and Chorus (1954); *The 1st Thanksgiving*, cantata for Chorus and Organ (1956). **JAZZ ENSEMBLE:** *The Centaur and the Phoenix* (1960); *Summer Song* (1960); *Paul Bunyan Jump* (1964).—NS/LK/DM

Mills, Erie, American soprano; b. Granite City, Ill., June 22, 1953. She attended the National Music Camp in Interlochen, Mich., then studied voice with Karl Trump at the Coll. of Wooster, Ohio, with Grace Wilson at the Univ. of Ill., and with Elena Nikolaidi. In 1979 she made her professional operatic debut as Ninette in *The Love for 3 Oranges* at the Chicago Lyric Opera; on Oct. 13, 1982, she made her first appearance with the N.Y.C. Opera as Cunegonde in *Candide*, and subsequently sang there regularly; she made her Metropolitan Opera debut in N.Y. as Blondchen in *Die Entführung aus dem Serail* on Nov. 26, 1987. She also made guest appearances with the Cincinnati Opera, Cleveland Opera, San Francisco Opera, Minnesota Opera, Opera Soc. of Washington, D.C., Santa Fe Opera, Houston Grand Opera, Hamburg State Opera, La Scala in Milan, and Vienna State Opera. On March 17, 1989, she made her N.Y. recital debut. On Oct. 5, 1992, she sang Orazio in the U.S. premiere of Handel's *Muzio* in N.Y. She portrayed Zerlina in Milwaukee in 1996. Among her other prominent roles are Rossini's Rosina, Donizetti's Lucia, Offenbach's Olympia, Johann Strauss's Adele, and Richard Strauss's Zerbinetta. —NS/LK/DM

Mills, Kerry (real name, **Frederick Allen**), American composer and music publisher; b. Philadelphia, Feb. 1, 1869; d. Hawthorne, Calif., Dec. 5, 1948. He was active as a violinist, and taught violin at a private cons. in Ann Arbor, Mich., known as the Univ. School of Music (1892–93). Adopting the name Kerry Mills, he publ. his own cakewalk march *Rufus on Parade* (1895). Encouraged by its favorable sales, he moved to N.Y., where he became one of the most important publishers of minstrel songs, cakewalks, early ragtime, and other popular music. His own compositions were particularly successful; *At a Georgia Campmeeting* (1897) became the standard against which all other cakewalks were measured; performed in Europe by John Philip Sousa, it became popular there as well; it was roundly denounced in the *Leipzig Illustrierte Zeitung* (Feb. 5, 1903), and may well have been the inspiration for Debussy's *Golliwog's Cakewalk*. Some of his other hits also reached Europe; his *Whistling Rufus* (1899) was publ. in Berlin as *Rufus das Pfeifergigerl*. He also wrote the popular song *Meet Me in St. Louis, Louis* (1904) for the Louisiana Purchase Exposition held in St. Louis that year; it was revived for the film of that title starring Judy Garland (1944). He also wrote sacred songs as Frederick Allen Mills.—NS/LK/DM

Mills, Richard (John), Australian conductor and composer; b. Toowoomba, Queensland, Nov. 14, 1949. After initial training at the Queensland Conservatorium of Music in North Quay (1964–69), he pursued his education at the Univ. of Queensland in St. Lucia (B.A., 1969) before completing his studies at the Guildhall School of Music in London (1969–71) with Rubbra (composition) and Gilbert Webster (percussion). He was principal percussionist in the Tasmanian Sym. Orch. in Hobart (1976–79) and the Queensland Sym. Orch. in Brisbane (1980–81). He lectured in composition at the Univ. of Northern Rivers in Lismore, New South Wales (1982–84), and in composition and conducting at the Queensland Conservatorium of Music (1985–86). In 1989–90 he served as artist-in-residence of the Australian Broadcasting Corp. He was artistic director of the Adelaide Chamber Orch. (1991–92) and artistic consultant of the Queensland Sym. Orch. (1991–92). His early diatonic style evolved into one in which more complex uses of harmony and counterpoint appeared.

Works: DRAMATIC: *Snugglepot and Cuddlepie*, ballet

(1988). **ORCH.:** *Toccata* (1976); *Music* for Strings (1977); *Fantasia on a Rondel* (1981); *Overture with Fanfares* (1981); Trumpet Concerto (1982); *Soundscapes* for Percussion and Orch. (1983); *Castlemaine Antiphons* for Brass Band and Orch. (1984); *Bamaga Diptych* (1986); *Sequenzas/Concertante* (1986); *Fantastic Pantomimes* for Flute, Oboe, Clarinet, Horn, Trumpet, and Orch. (1987–88); *Aeolian Caprices* (1988); *Seaside Dances* for 18 Solo Strings (1989); Flute Concerto (1990); Cello Concerto (1990); Violin Concerto (1992). **CHAMBER:** Brass Quintet (1986); Sonatina for String Quartet (1986); *Miniatures and Refrains* for String Quartet (1986); String Quartet No. 1 (1989). **VOCAL:** *Festival Folksongs* for Tenor, Mezzo-soprano, Chorus, Children's Chorus, 2 Optional Brass Choirs, and Orch. (1985); *Voyages and Visions* for 4 Soloists, Chorus, 3 Brass Bands, 4 Percussion, Orch., and Tape (1987); *Visionary Fanfare* for Chorus, 2 Brass Bands, 6 Trumpets, 6 Trombones, and Orch. (1988); *5 Meditations on the Poetry of David Campbell* for Soprano, Baritone, Chorus, and Orch. (1988).—NS/LK/DM

Mills, S(ebastian) B(ach), outstanding English pianist; b. Cirencester, March 13, 1838; d. Wiesbaden, Dec. 21, 1898. He played before Queen Victoria at the age of 7. He studied with Cipriani Potter and Sterndale Bennett, and later was a student of Moscheles, Plaidy, Hauptmann, and Rietz at the Leipzig Cons., and finally of Liszt. He played at a Leipzig Gewandhaus concert (Dec. 2, 1858), then went to N.Y., where he obtained a decisive success with the Schumann Piano Concerto, which he performed with the Phil. Soc. on March 26, 1859. He remained in N.Y. until making his last appearance on Nov. 24, 1877. He had a significant and lasting impact upon American pianism through his presentation of first American performances of works by Hiller, Liszt, Moscheles, Reinecke et al.—NS/LK/DM

Mills Brothers, The, American vocal group. **MEMBERSHIP:** The initial quartet consisted of the four sons of John Mills (b. Bellefonte, Pa., 1882; d. there, Dec. 8, 1967), a barber who sang light opera, and his wife Ethel, a pianist: John Mills Jr. (b. Piqua, Ohio, Feb. 11, 1911; d. Bellefontaine, Ohio, Jan. 24, 1936); Herbert Mills (b. Piqua, Ohio, April 2, 1912; d. Las Vegas, Nev., April 12, 1989); Harry F. Mills (b. Piqua, Ohio, Aug. 19, 1913; d. Los Angeles, Calif., June 28, 1982); Donald F. Mills (b. Piqua, Ohio, April 29, 1915; d. Los Angeles, Calif., Nov. 13, 1999). The Mills Brothers were the prototype for all the African-American male vocal groups that followed them, their close harmonies set off by the early use of imitations of musical instruments, especially horns and reeds. Their prime period of popularity was the 1940s, but they scored hits from the 1930s to the 1960s, the biggest of them being "Tiger Rag," "Dinah," "Paper Doll, "You Always Hurt the One You Love," and "The Glow-Worm." They were the first black entertainers to have a sponsored, nationally broadcast radio series; they also appeared in a series of motion pictures.

They began singing as children, eventually developing an approach in which Herbert and Donald sang first and second tenor, Harry was a baritone, and John sang bass and accompanied the group on guitar. After performing locally they were hired by a local Cincinnati radio station in the late 1920s.

In 1931 the group joined the CBS radio network and signed to Brunswick Records; they moved to N.Y. in

September. Their Oct. 9 recording session produced a single that revived "Tiger Rag" (music by Edwin B. Edwards, Nick La Rocca, Tony Spargo, and Larry Shields, lyrics by Harry De Cost) and "Nobody's Sweetheart" (music and lyrics by Elmer Schoebel, Ernie Erdman, Gus Kahn, and Billy Meyers).

The Mills Brothers' CBS radio show gained a sponsor in December 1931, and they broadcast two 15-minute programs a week for the next 16 months. Their fourth single, containing "Dinah" (music by Harry Akst, lyrics by Sam M. Lewis and Joe Young) and "Can't We Talk It Over?" (music by Victor Young, lyrics by Ned Washington), teamed them with Bing Crosby; "Dinah" became a best-seller in January, and "Can't We Talk It Over?" was also a hit.

The Mills Brothers continued to score major hits over the next three years, notably "St. Louis Blues" (music and lyrics by W. C. Handy; July 1932), "Bugle Call Rag" (music by Jack Pettis, Billy Meyers, and Elmer Schoebel; August 1932), "Swing It, Sister" (June 1934), and "Sleepy Head" (music by Walter Donaldson, lyrics by Gus Kahn; June 1934). They appeared in the films *The Big Broadcast* (October 1932), *Twenty Million Sweethearts* (April 1934), *Operator 13* (June 1934), *Strictly Dynamite* (July 1934), and *Broadway Gondolier* (July 1935). After the end of their own radio series they were regulars on *The Bing Crosby Show* from 1933 to 1934. They toured Europe in 1934 and 1935. In 1934 they switched recording affiliations to the recently formed American Decca label.

The Mills Brothers suffered a serious setback in January 1936 when John Mills Jr. died of tuberculosis. John Mills Sr. replaced his son as the group's bass singer, and Norman Brown became their non-singing guitar accompanist. They had a transcribed radio series in 1936 and appeared in the British film *The Sky's the Limit* in 1937. In December 1938 they reached the hit parade with "Sixty Seconds Get Together" (music by Jerry Livingston, lyrics by Mack David). The group mounted a major comeback starting in 1943. They had recorded "Paper Doll" (music and lyrics by Johnny S. Black [real name, John Huber]) in February 1942 and released it in May, but the record did not begin to catch on until a year later, when it reached the R&B charts. It entered the pop charts in August 1943 and hit #1 in November, eventually selling a reported six million copies, which made it second only to Bing Crosby's "White Christmas" as the best-selling record of the 1940s.

Unable to record due to the musicians' union strike in 1942 and 1943, the Mills Brothers returned to Hollywood where they appeared in five films released during 1943: *He's My Guy*, *Reveille with Beverly*, *Rhythm Parade*, *Chatterbox*, and *Cowboy Canteen*. Back in the recording studio in 1944, they produced the single "You Always Hurt the One You Love" (music by Doris Fisher, lyrics by Allan Roberts)/"Till Then" (music and lyrics by Eddie Seiler, Sol Marcus, and Guy Wood). "Till Then" topped the R&B charts in August, while the million-seller "You Always Hurt the One You Love" went to #1 in the pop charts in October.

The group also reached the Top Ten of the pop charts with "I Wish" (music by Doris Fisher, lyrics by Allan Roberts) in June 1945; "I Don't Know Enough about You" (music and lyrics by Peggy Lee and Dave Barbour) in August 1946; "Across the Alley from the Alamo" (music and lyrics by Joe Green) in June 1947; both sides of the single "I Love You So Much It Hurts" (music and lyrics by Floyd Tillman)/"I've Got My Love to Keep Me Warm" (music and lyrics by Irving Berlin) in early 1949; and "Someday (You'll Want Me to Want You)" (music and lyrics by Jimmie Hodges) in October 1949. The albums *Barber Shop Quartet* (1946) and *The Mills Brothers Souvenir Album* (1949) reached the Top Ten on the album charts.

The Mills Brothers' popularity continued into the early 1950s. *Famous Barbershop Ballads* was a Top Ten album in January 1950, and during that year they also hit the Top Ten of the pop singles chart with "Daddy's Little Girl" (music and lyrics by Bobby Burke and Horace Gerlach) in May and "Nevertheless (I'm in Love with You)" (music by Harry Ruby, lyrics by Bert Kalmar) in December; in August they appeared in the film *When You're Smiling*.

The Brothers augmented their one-guitar backup with big band arrangements, initially with encouraging commercial results. "Be My Life's Companion" (music and lyrics by Bob Hilliard and Milton DeLugg), backed by Sy Oliver and His Orch., hit the pop Top Ten in February 1952, and "The Glow-Worm" (music by Paul Lincke, new English lyrics by Johnny Mercer) featuring Hal McIntyre and His Orch. topped the charts in December, becoming their third million-seller. "The Jones Boy" (music by Vic Mizzy, lyrics by Mann Curtis) was a Top Ten pop hit in February 1954.

The Mills Brothers faded from widespread popularity in the mid-1950s. John Mills Sr. retired from the group, which continued as a trio. They reached the pop Top 40 with "Queen of the Senior Prom" (music and lyrics by Ed Penney, Jack Richards, and Stella Lee) in June 1957. Switching to Dot Records in 1958, they had a Top 40 hit with "Get a Job" (music and lyrics by Earl T. Beal, Raymond W. Edwards, William F. Horton, and Richard A. Lewis) in March and appeared in the film *The Big Beat* in June. They were off the charts for nearly a decade before "Cab Driver" (music and lyrics by C. Carson Parks) made the pop Top 40 in March 1968 along with the LP *Fortuosity*, which spent six months in the album charts.

The group last reached the charts with the LP *Dream* in May 1969. After Harry Mills died following surgery for a tumor in 1982, Herbert Mills retired and Donald Mills teamed with his son, John Mills III, to continue performing the group's music. Donald was performing with his son up to six months before his death following brain surgery in April 1999.

DISC.: *Barber Shop Ballads* (1950); *Wonderful Words* (1951); *Meet the Mills Brothers* (1954); *Louis Armstrong and the Mills Brothers* (1954); *Singin' and Swingin'* (1956); *One Dozen Roses* (1957); *The Mills Brothers in Hi-Fi* (1958); *Mmmm, The Mills Brothers* (1958); *Harmonni' with the Mills Brothers* (1959); *Barber Shop Harmony* (1959); *Yellow Bird* (1961); *The End of the World* (1963); *Hymns We Love* (1964); *That Country Feeling* (1966); *These Are the Mills Brothers* (1966); *The Board of Directors* (1967); *Annual Report* (1968); *My Shy Violet* (1968); *The Mills Brothers Live* (1968); *Glow with the Mills Brothers* (1978); *Fortuosity* (1978).—**WR**

Mills-Cockell, John, Canadian composer; b. Toronto, May 19, 1943. He studied composition and electronic music at the Univ. of Toronto and at the Royal Cons. of Music there. In 1966 he developed, in collaboration with the writer Blake Parker, artist Michael Hayden, and designer Dick Zander, a method of composition and performance called Intersystems. He joined the rock bands Kensington Market in Toronto (1969), Hydro-Electric Streetcar in Vancouver (1969–70), and Syrinx in Toronto (1970–72), which he founded, and then devoted himself to composing and recording. He wrote numerous pieces for mixed media, works utilizing tape, electronic music for films, etc.—**NS/LK/DM**

Milner, Anthony (Francis Dominic), English composer and teacher; b. Bristol, May 13, 1925. He studied composition privately with Matyas Seiber (1944–48), and also took courses with R.O. Morris (composition) and Herbert Fryer (piano) at the Royal Coll. of Music in London (1945–47). From 1948 to 1964 he taught at Morley Coll. in London. He served as director and harpsichordist of the London Cantata Ensemble (1954–65), and also was a part-time teacher (1961–80) and principal lecturer (1980–89) at the Royal Coll. of Music, a lecturer at King's Coll., London (1965–71), and senior lecturer (1971–74) and principal lecturer (1974–80) at Goldsmiths' Coll., London.

WORKS: ORCH.: *Variations* (1958; Cheltenham, July 6, 1959); *Divertimento* for Strings (London, Aug. 17, 1961); *Overture: April Prologue* (London, Dec. 5, 1961); *Sinfonia pasquale* for Strings (1963; Dorchester, May 5, 1964); Chamber Sym. (1967; London, March 31, 1968); 3 syms.: No. 1 (1972; London, Jan. 17, 1973), No. 2 for Soprano, Tenor, Boy's Chorus, Chorus, and Orch. (Liverpool, July 13, 1978), and No. 3 (1986; London, Nov. 26, 1987); Concerto for Symphonic Wind Band (Ithaca, N.Y., Oct. 10, 1979); Concerto for Strings (1982; Wells, June 19, 1984). CHAMBER: Quartet for Oboe and Strings (1953); Quintet for Wind Instruments (1964); String Quartet No. 1 (1975); piano music; organ pieces. VOCAL: Cantatas: *Salutatio Angelica* for Contralto or Mezzo-soprano, Chorus, and Chamber Orch. (1948; London, Nov. 11, 1951); *The City of Desolation: A Cantata of Hope* for Soprano, Chorus, and Orch. (Totnes, Devon, Aug. 12, 1955); *The Harrowing of Hell* for Tenor, Bass, and Chorus (BBC, Nov. 14, 1956); *Roman Spring* for Soprano, Tenor, Chorus, and Orch. (London, Oct. 13, 1969); *Midway* for Mezzo-soprano and Chamber Orch. (London, July 10, 1974); *Emmanuel*, Christmas cantata for Countertenor, Soprano, Contralto, Tenor, Bass, Chorus, Audience, and Orch. (1974; Kingston upon Thames, Dec. 13, 1975); other vocal works, including *The Gates of Spring*, ode for Soprano, Tenor, Chorus, and String Orch. (1988), many sacred works, and songs.

BIBL.: J. Siddons, *A. M.: A Bio-Bibliography* (Westport, Conn., 1989).—**NS/LK/DM**

Milnes, Sherrill (Eustace), distinguished American baritone; b. Downers Grove, Ill., Jan. 10, 1935. He studied at Drake Univ. (B.Mus.Ed., 1957; M.Mus.Ed., 1958), pursued postgraduate studies at Northwestern Univ. (1958–61), and received training from Rosa Ponselle. In 1960 he made his formal operatic debut as Masetto with the touring Boston Opera, and then sang Gérard in *Andrea Chénier* with the Baltimore Civic Opera in 1961. On Sept. 23, 1964, he made his European debut as Rossini's Figaro at the Teatro Nuovo in Milan. He made his first appearance with the N.Y.C. Opera as Valentin on Oct. 18, 1964, and continued on its roster until 1966. On Dec. 22, 1965, he made his Metropolitan Opera debut in N.Y. as Valentin, making regular appearances there during the next 25 years during which he was honored with 16 new productions, 7 opening nights, and 10 national telecasts. In 1971 he sang Posa at his debut with the Lyric Opera of Chicago, the same year that he made his debut as Renato at London's Covent Garden. His guest engagements also took him to Vienna, Paris, San Francisco, Buenos Aires, Barcelona, and Moscow. In later years, he made appearances as a conductor. He led master classes at the Yale Univ. School of Music from 1990, and also around the world. His autobiography was publ. as *American Aria: From Farm Boy to Opera Star* (N.Y., 1998). Milnes was especially admired for his Verdi roles, which formed the central core of his 70 roles. He also sang with orchs., gave lieder recitals, and appeared on Broadway.—**NS/LK/DM**

Milojević, Miloje, Serbian conductor, musicologist, and composer; b. Belgrade, Oct. 27, 1884; d. there, June 16, 1946. He was taught piano by his mother, then entered the Serbian School of Music at Novi Sad. He subsequently studied with Mayer G'schray (piano), Mottl (conducting), and Klose (composition) at the Munich Academy of Music and took courses in musicology with Sandberger and Kroyer at the Univ. of Munich; then studied musicology with Nejedlý at the Univ. of Prague (D.Mus., 1925). He was active as a choirmaster in Belgrade, and as conductor of the Collegium Musicum at the Univ. there (1925–41). He also wrote music criticism and taught composition at the Academy of Music there (1939–46). He publ. *Osnovi muzičke umetnosti* (Elements of Music; Belgrade, 1922), *Smetana* (Belgrade, 1924), *Smetanin harmonski stil* (Smetana's Harmonic Style; Belgrade, 1926), and *Muzičke studije i članci* (Music Studies and Articles; Belgrade, 1926, 1933, 1953). As a composer, he wrote mostly in small forms. He was influenced successively by Grieg, Strauss, Debussy, and Russian modernists, and his music contains an original treatment of Balkan folk songs. His piano suite, *Grimaces rythmiques* (in a modern vein), was performed at the Paris Festival on June 26, 1937. His list of works contains choral pieces, chamber music, songs, and piano pieces.

BIBL.: P. Konjović, *M. M.: Kompozitor i muzički pisac* (Belgrade, 1954).—**NS/LK/DM**

Milstein, Nathan (Mironovich), celebrated Russian-born American violinist; b. Odessa, Dec. 31, 1903; d. London, Dec. 21, 1992. His father was a well-to-do merchant in woolen goods, and his mother was an amateur violinist who gave him his first lessons. He then began to study with Stoliarsky in Odessa, remaining under his tutelage until 1914. He then went to St. Petersburg, where he entered Auer's class at the St. Petersburg Cons. (1915–17). He began his concert career in 1919, with his sister as piano accompanist. In Kiev he met Horowitz, and they began giving duo recitals in 1921; later they were joined by Piatigorsky, and organized a trio. In 1925 Milstein went to Berlin and then to Brussels, where he met Ysaÿe, who encouraged him in his career. He gave several recitals in Paris, then proceeded to South America. On Oct. 28, 1929, he made his American debut with the Philadelphia Orch. conducted by Stokowski. In 1942 he became a naturalized American citizen. After the end of World War II in 1945, Milstein appeared regularly in all of the principal music centers of the world. He performed with most of the great orchs. and gave numerous recitals. He celebrated the 50th anniversary of his American debut in 1979 by giving a number of solo recitals and appearing as soloist with American orchs. As an avocation, he began painting and drawing, arts in which he achieved a certain degree of self- satisfaction. He also engaged in teaching; held master classes at the Juilliard School of Music in N.Y., and also in Zürich. Milstein was renowned for his technical virtuosity and musical integrity. He composed a number of violin pieces, including *Paganiniana* (1954); also prepared cadenzas for the violin concertos of Beethoven and Brahms. His autobiography was publ. as *From Russia to the West* (N.Y., 1990).

BIBL.: B. Gavoty, *N. M.* (Geneva, 1956).—**NS/LK/DM**

Milstein, Yakov (Isaakovich), Russian pianist, pedagogue, and writer on music; b. Voronezh, Feb. 4, 1911; d. Moscow, Dec. 4, 1981. He studied piano with Igumnov at the Moscow Cons. (Ph.D., 1942), where he was a member of its faculty (from 1935). His main interest was an analysis of works of masters of Romantic music. Particularly important is his biography of Liszt (Moscow, 1956; Hungarian ed., Budapest, 1965; 2nd ed., rev., 1971). He contributed an essay on the piano technique of Chopin and Liszt to *The Book of the First International Musicological Congress Devoted to the Works of Chopin* (Warsaw, 1963). He also publ. a monograph on Igumnov (Moscow, 1975).—**NS/LK/DM**

Milton, John, amateur English composer; b. Stanton St. John, near Oxford, c. 1563; d. London (buried), March 15, 1647. His son was the great poet John Milton. He was a chorister at Christ Church, Oxford (1572–77), where he apparently remained for several years. In 1585 he went to London, where he was admitted to the Scriveners' Co. in 1600; in that year he married Sarah Jeffrey. He composed 8 anthems for 4 to 6 Voices, 7 Psalm settings, 2 madrigals for 5 Voices, Motet for 6 Voices, *In Nomine* a 6, and 4 fantasias a 5 and a 6 (1 ed. in Musica Britannica, IX, 1955; 2nd ed., 1962). See G. Arkwright, ed., *John Milton: Six Anthems*, Old English Edition, XXII (1900), and C. Hill, ed., *Sir William Leighton: The Teares or Lamentations of a Sorrowful Soul*, Early English Church Music, XI (1970).

BIBL.: E. Brennecke Jr., *J. M. the Elder and His Music* (N.Y., 1938).—**NS/LK/DM**

Milveden, (Jan) Ingmar (Georg), Swedish composer, organist, and musicologist; b. Göteborg, Feb. 15, 1920. He studied cello and organ, then took a course in composition with Sven Svensson and in musicology with C.A. Moberg at the Univ. of Uppsala (graduated, 1945; Fil.lic., 1951; Ph.D., 1972, with the diss. *Zu den*

liturgischen "Hystorie" in Schweden. Liturgie- und choralgeschichtliche Untersuchungen). He was organist at Uppsala's St. Per's Church (1967–78), and lectured at the Univ. of Stockholm (1970–73) and at the Univ. of Uppsala (1972–86). He distinguished himself as a composer of church music.

WORKS: DRAMATIC: C h u r c h O p e r a : *Vid en Korsväg* (1971; Lund, Nov. 30, 1974). **ORCH.:** *Serenade* for Strings (1942); *Pezzo concertante* (1969; Uppsala, Feb. 5, 1970); *Concerto al fresco* for Clarinet and Orch. (1970; Uppsala, Nov. 25, 1971). **CHAMBER:** Piano Sonatina (1943); Duo for Flute and Piano (1953; rev. 1975); Trio for Flute, Clarinet, and Viola (1955; rev. 1973); Threnodia for 3 Cellos (1970); *Toccata* for Organ (1973); *3 assaggi* for Cello (1975). **VOCAL:** *Canticula linnaeana* for Chorus (1965); *Mässa i skördetid* (Mass of the Harvest Time) for Congregation, Liturgist, 2 Choruses, 2 Organs, 2 Orch. Groups, and Tape (1969); *Nu...,* 4 Linne quotations for Solo Voices, Chorus, and Instrumental Groups (1972; Ingesund, March 17, 1974); *Magnificat* for 2 Choral Groups, Organ, Winds, and Percussion (1973); *Musica in honorem Sanctae Eugeniae* for Voices (1982); *Alleluia "Terribilis est"* for Voices (1987); choruses; songs.—**NS/LK/DM**

Mimaroglu, Ilhan Kemaleddin, Turkish composer and writer on music; b. Constantinople, March 11, 1926. He studied law at the Univ. of Ankara. In 1955 he traveled to the U.S. on a Rockefeller fellowship, and settled in N.Y., where he studied theory with Jack Beeson and Chou Wen-Chung, musicology with Lang, and electronic music with Ussachevsky at Columbia Univ. He also took lessons in modern composition with Wolpe, and received inspiring advice from Varèse. He was subsequently a recipient of a Guggenheim fellowship (1971–72). He publ. several books in Turkish. In 1963 he began his association with the Columbia-Princeton Electronic Music Center, where he composed most of his electronic works, among them *Le Tombeau d'Edgar Poe* (1964), *Anacolutha* (1965), *Preludes* for Magnetic Tape (1966–76), *Wings of the Delirious Demon* (1969), and music for Jean Dubuffet's *Coucou Bazar* (1973). He developed compositional methods viewing electronic music in a parallel to cinema, resulting in works for tape in which recorded performance dominates individual rendition. Concurrently, he displayed a growing political awareness in his choice of texts, conveying messages of New Left persuasion in such works as *Sing Me a Song of Songmy*, a protest chant against the war in Vietnam (1971), *Tract* (1972–74), *To Kill a Sunrise* (1974), and String Quartet No. 4 with Voice obbligato on poems by Nâzim Hikmet (1978). Other works include *Pieces sentimentales* for Piano (1957); *Music Plus 1* for Violin and Tape (1970); *Still Life 1980* for Cello and Tape (1983); *Immolation Scene* for Voice and Tape (1983); *Valses ignobles et sentencieuses* for Piano (1984). He destroyed all of his non-performed compositions, as well as those not recorded for posterity within a year of completion. Since the late 1980s he has been working on a documentary film in which various composers respond to his question dealing with the condition of the contemporary composer in a cultural environment dominated by commercial determinants. —**NS/LK/DM**

Minami, Satoshi, Japanese composer; b. Tokyo, July 17, 1955. He was a student of Teruyuki Noda and Toshirō Mayazumi at the Tokyo National Univ. of Fine Arts and Music (degree, 1983). He won 2nd prize in the Japan Music Competition (1983) and at the World Buddhist Music Festival (1986). His concept of "music on the pluralistic structure" is exemplified in his *UTA no KAGE yori* (1990).

WORKS: *Reliquiae* for Cello and Piano (1976–79); *Plants II* for 2 Violins and 3 Harps (1977–79); *Fresco* for Orch. (1980; rev. 1985); *Francesco Parmigiamino's Hand* for Piano, Glockenspiel, Tubular Bells, and Tape (1984); *Tatoereba...* for Viola and Piano (1986); *Coloration Project I* for Piano (1989), *II* for Electric Organ (1989), *III* for Niju-gen (1989), *IV* for Organ (1989), *V* for Orch. (1990), *VI* for Mandolin Orch. (1991), *VII* for Percussion (1992), and *VIII* for Viola, Cello, and Double Bass (1992); *The Window by the Metaphor* for Piano (1989); *UTA no KAGE yori* for Voice, Harp, Violin, Cello, and Piano (1990); *The Autobiography for Moon* for Cello and Piano (1990); *Latticed Eye* for Violin and Piano (1991); *The Garden of Joyful Intellection* for Flute, Violin, Piano, and Chamber Orch. (1991); *The Night of the Milky Way Railroad* for Narrator, Clarinet, Cello, and Piano (1991); *Window, the Coming Florescence*, Prelude I for Orch. (1992).—**NS/LK/DM**

Mince, Johnny (originally, Muenzenberger, John Henry), jazz clarinetist, saxophonist; b. Chicago Heights, Ill., July 8, 1912. He was a powerful and brilliant soloist, which unfortunately was not obvious from many of his recordings. He joined Joe Haymes at the age of 17; went to N.Y. with Haymes in the early 1930s, and remained when the band worked under the leadership of Buddy Rogers. He was with Ray Noble's original American band (spring 1935); briefly with Bob Crosby in 1936, resumed playing for Ray Noble until March 1937, then joined Tommy Dorsey until early in 1941. He spent a short spell in Bob Strong's Band, then the U.S. Army service from spring of 1941. He played in the band for the *This Is the Army* show and did overseas tours (including playing in Britain in 1944). After demobilization he went into radio studio work, and was later featured regularly in television orchestras. He continued to play regularly during the 1960s, occasionally leading his own small band, and subbed for a few days with Louis Armstrong in April 1967. He guested at Dick Gibson's Jazz Party in Colo. (1971). From the 1970s through mid-1980s, he toured Europe.

DISC.: *Summer of '79* (1979). **LOUIS ARMSTRONG:** *Highlights from His Decca Years* (1924); *Priceless Jazz Collection* (1935); *American Icon* (1947); *Portrait of Benny Berigan* (1932). **IRVING BERLIN:** *Alexander's Ragtime Band* (1990). **TERESA BREWER:** *Live at Carnegie Hall and Montreux* (1978). **TOMMY DORSEY:** *Having a Wonderful Time* (1935); *Yes, Indeed!* (1939); *Saturday Afternoon at the Meadowbrook: 1940* (1940); *Stop, Look and Listen* (1994); *Irish American Trombone* (1996).—**JC/LP**

Minchev, Georgi, Bulgarian composer; b. Sofia, Jan. 29, 1939. He studied composition with Goleminov at the Bulgarian State Cons. in Sofia, graduating in 1963, then went to Moscow and studied with Shchedrin (1968–70). In 1972 he traveled to France, Great Britain, and the U.S. on a UNESCO scholarship. Returning to Bulgaria, Minchev became chief of productions at the Committee for Television and Radio in Sofia.

WORKS: Sym. (1967); *Music* for 3 Orch. Groups (1968); *Starobulgarski hroniky* (Old Bulgarian Chronicles), oratorio for Narrator, Soloists, Mixed Chorus, Folk Music Chorus, and Orch. (Sofia, Dec. 22, 1971); *Intermezzo and Aquarelle* for Strings, 2 Flutes, and Harpsichord (1972); *3 Poems* for Mezzo-soprano and Orch. (1973); *Concert Music* for Orch. (1975); Piano Concerto (1976); *Symphonic Prologue* (1980); choruses; solo songs; folk song arrangements.—**NS/LK/DM**

Minghetti, Angelo, Italian tenor; b. Bologna, Dec. 6, 1889; d. Milan, Feb. 10, 1957. He began his career in 1911, and then sang in various Italian music centers. After appearing in Rio de Janeiro (1921), he was a member of the Chicago Opera (1922–24). In 1923 he made his debut at Milan's La Scala as Rodolfo, and sang there until 1932. He also was a guest artist at Buenos Aires's Teatro Colón (1924) and London's Covent Garden (1926; 1930; 1933–34).—**NS/LK/DM**

Mingotti, Pietro, Italian opera impresario; b. Venice, c. 1702; d. Copenhagen, April 28, 1759. His brother, Angelo Mingotti (b. c. 1700; d. after 1767), was also an opera impresario who organized his opera troupe in Prague about 1732. In the meantime, Pietro founded his own opera troupe and from 1736 to 1740 the two brothers worked together in Graz. During the next 10 years, they continued to work together occasionally but frequently also toured with their own troupes in Germany and Austria. By 1746 **Regina Mingotti** (née **Valentini**) had joined Pietro's troupe and was briefly his wife. In 1747 Gluck became his music director, appearing with the troupe in Dresden and Copenhagen, and in 1748 in Hamburg. Pietro settled with his troupe in Copenhagen in 1748 under contract to the Danish court. Sarti became his music director in 1752. The decline in his fortunes compelled Pietro to ask that his contract with the court be dissolved in 1755. He lost everything when the court seized his assets to pay off his debts, and he spent his last days in poverty.

BIBL.: E. Müller, *Die M.schen Opernunternehmungen: 1732 bis 1756* (Leipzig, 1915); idem, *Angelo und P. M.* (Dresden, 1917). —**NS/LK/DM**

Mingotti, Regina (née Valentini), Italian soprano; b. Naples, Feb. 16, 1722; d. Neuburg an der Donau, Oct. 1, 1808. She may have been the sister of the Italian composer Michelangelo Valentini. After training at a convent in Grätz in Silesia, she was a member of **Pietro Mingotti**'s opera troupe by 1746. Her first known appearance with the troupe was in *Il tempio di Melpomene* in Hamburg on Jan. 31, 1747. She married Mingotti, but they soon parted company. In 1747 she so impressed the Saxon court in Dresden that she became a member of the court musical establishment and received training from Porpora. Her rivalry with Bordoni became celebrated. After singing in Naples, Prague, and Madrid (1751–53), she appeared in Paris and London (1754–55). With Giardini, she was co-manager of the King's Theatre in London (1756–57; 1763–64). Her feuds

with Vaneschi there were also notorious. Mingotti had her greatest success in breeches roles, where her gifts as an actress were put to particularly good use.
—NS/LK/DM

Mingus, Charles (Jr.), highly influential jazz

bassist, leader, pianist, composer; b. on a military base in Nogales, Ariz., April 22, 1922; d. Cuernavaca, Mexico, Jan. 5, 1979. His small groups (he generally had assistance when writing for big bands or orchestras) played with a wild intensity and freedom of expression never reproduced. Most notably, he was the first and still one of the only jazz composers who would have tempo and even meter changes within pieces; this is most dramatically illustrated by listening to the various performances of "Fables of Faubus" from 1959 on. (To this day, most jazz pieces are counted off and then stay at that tempo until the end.)

His bass playing was powerful, accurate, and innovative in his use of various strumming techniques and pedal point. Mingus was also an expressive pianist. A very troubled man, he was known for his dangerous temper—in a famous incident, he punched Jimmy Knepper in the mouth in the early 1960s. He also had his psychiatrist write the notes to his album *Mingus, Mingus, Mingus, Mingus, Mingus.* He was terrifically witty, as illustrated in the words to "Fable" and to titles such as "The Shoes of the Fisherman's Wife Are Some Jive-Ass Slippers." When his fan club from Tokyo came to see him in N.Y. and presented him with a gold cigarette case, he thanked them and said he would now play a song for them entitled "I Remember Pearl Harbor"; they quietly rose and left the club. When Toshiko Akiyoshi played an imitation of Bud Powell rather than finding a unique sound, Mingus slammed the piano lid down on her fingers in the middle of her solo at the Newport Festival (1961). When Clarence Beasley was hired to play piano, Mingus fired him before he even got to solo, even though his whole family flew in from Detroit to see him.

The nephew of Fess Williams, Mingus was reared in the Watts area of Los Angeles. His earliest musical influences came from the church—choir and group singing—and from hearing Duke Ellington over the radio when he was eight. During his high school years, he learned several instruments, studied bass with Red Callender and for five years with Herman Rheinschagen (principal of the L.A. Philharmonic), as well as composition and classical music with Lloyd Reese. Mingus particularly liked Claude Debussy, Igor Stravinsky, and Richard Strauss. In 1939, he wrote his first concert piece, "Half-Mast Inhibition"; this and several other early works were first recorded in (1960) by a 22-piece orchestra with Gunther Schuller conducting; other compositions appeared on his album *Let My Children Hear Music.* His early playing experience came with Lee Young (1940), Barney Bigard (1942), Louis Armstrong (1943), Kid Ory (1944), and Lionel Hampton (1947–48). An uncredited arrangement of "Body and Soul," from a Hampton broadcast, featured a bowed bass that is now known to be by Mingus. He recorded in Calif. as a leader of jazz and R&B groups, often as Baron Mingus. He gained national attention with the Red

Norvo Trio (1950–51). In 1952, he settled in N.Y., where he worked with Billy Taylor, Duke Ellington, Stan Getz, and Art Tatum. He performed in Bud Powell's trio in 1953, including regular broadcasts, and in May went with Powell to accompany Parker and Gillespie at the now legendary Massey Hall concert in Toronto; he also recorded the concert and released it (overdubbing his bass which had been underrecorded) as head of his own recording company, Debut Records. He co-founded the "Jazz Workshop," a group which enabled young composers to have their new works performed in concert and on recordings. He showed an increasing interest in composing and his early works are very classical in sound and style, with a heavy influence of Ellington; he also composed "Open Letter to Duke" in 1959 and arranged several Ellington pieces in 1960. "Revelations," which combined jazz and classical idioms, premiered at the 1955 Brandeis (Univ.) Festival of the Creative Arts. But on his album *Blues and Roots,* he talked about becoming aware of the need to always stay grounded in African-American styles. By the late 1950s, he preferred to dictate parts to players for freshness of interpretation and improvisation; he achieved a style that effectively erased the lines between jazz improvisation and notated composition. He worked with various musicians in small combos, and eventually developed a close association with Eric Dolphy who toured with him in 1960 and again in 1964. He appeared onscreen in *All Night Long,* filmed in the summer of 1961 in London. He appeared on Canadian TV twice around 1960, but it is not known if these programs survive; he was televised in Canada twice during his 1964 tour of Europe with Eric Dolphy. In one famous scene, Mingus turns to Dolphy, who had just decided to leave the band, and says on camera, "I'll miss your ass over here." This was mistakenly transcribed as "I'll miss you, asshole" and used as a repeating theme in the film *Last Date* (about Dolphy). In 1964, a major big band concert at Town Hall, Manhattan, was a disaster. He persuaded his label to record an evening-length work at an open session to be held at Town Hall. They agreed, then suddenly made the date six weeks earlier, even though so much work remained to be done that it made success impossible. Moreover, the promoters advertised the event as a concert, raising expectations among ticket-buyers of a complete, finished performance rather than the start-stops to be expected at a recording session. Some musicians walked into the hall having never seen sheet music; copyists were seated on stage, hurriedly duplicating the later parts of the score, while musicians attempted to play the early parts; parts of the concert were issued on various albums. After his second recording company, the Charles Mingus label (1964–65), folded and his financial situation became desperate, he nearly retired from the public scene (1966–69). He married Susan around this time. In 1966, he was evicted from his apartment, a heartbreaking scene captured in the documentary *Mingus.* After resuming his career, in 1971 he was awarded the Slee Chair of Music and spent a semester teaching composition at the State Univ. of N.Y. at Buffalo. He received grants from the NEA, the Smithsonian Inst., and the Guggenheim Foundation (two grants, one in 1971); he also received an honorary degree from Brandeis and an award from Yale Univ. His music was performed frequently by ballet companies; Alvin Ailey choreographed an hour program called "The Mingus Dances" during a 1972 collaboration with the Robert Joffrey Ballet Company. Mingus toured extensively throughout Europe, Japan, Canada, South America, and the U.S. until the end of 1977 when he was diagnosed as having a rare nerve disease, Amyotropic Lateral Sclerosis (Lou Gehrig's disease). In 1978, he was confined to a wheelchair; that year he collaborated with singer Joni Mitchell on an album. On June 18, 1978, he was guest of honor at President Carter's all-star concert at the White House. Producer George Wein asked those present to honor him; the musicians gave him a standing ovation, and Carter walked over and embraced him. Mingus wept, overcome by emotion, and surely by the frustration he must have felt at not being capable of speech. Although he was no longer able to write music on paper or compose at the piano, his last works were sung into a tape recorder. His ashes were scattered in the Ganges River in India. Both N.Y. and Washington, D.C., honored him posthumously with a "Charles Mingus Day."

After his death, the NEA provided grants for a Mingus foundation called "Let My Children Hear Music" which catalogued all of Mingus's works; the microfilms of these works were then given to the Music Division of the N.Y. Public Library, and the originals to the Library of Congress, where they are available for study and scholarship. He recorded over 100 albums and wrote over 300 scores. The manuscript of the 1964 Town Hall concert was discovered by Andrew Homzy while cataloguing Sue Mingus's collection. This collection of his pieces, many of which had been recorded elsewhere as independent works, was planned by Mingus, and when completed and reworked by Gunther Schuller (with the help of a grant from the Ford Foundation), it was Mingus's longest work, the two-hour "Epitaph" for 30 instruments. Schuller conducted its premiere performance at Alice Tully Hall in N.Y. on June 3, 1989, followed by a recording and several tours in the U.S. and Europe. Since Mingus's death, his widow Sue has managed his legacy. From 1979, Mingus Dynasty was established as a repertory group with rotating personnel that features the compositions and music of Mingus. It included, at one time or another, Jimmy Knepper, Dannie Richmond, and Jack Walrath; at one point, two Mingus sons, Charles and Eric, were among the personnel. Eventually it was replaced by the larger Mingus Big Band which for several years played at the Time Cafe in lower Manhattan every Thursday and then began touring and recording as it became more established. Since the mid-1990s, Steve Slagle has directed the group, which has premiered a number of unheard Mingus works and new arrangements of his small group works. Sue Mingus has also campaigned for years against bootleg recordings. Initially she would simply go to stores and take the bootlegs out of the bins; during the mid-1990s, she began to issue the same material legally in an effort to outsell the bootlegs. His grandson Kevin Mingus is a bassist who plays an instrument given to him by Buddy Collette.

DISC.: *Young Rebel* (1946); "Shuffle Bass Boogie," "Weird Nightmare" (1946); "Zoo-bab-da-oo-ee" (1947); *Body and Soul* (1948); *Strings and Keys* (1952); *Moods of Mingus* (1954); *Jazzical Moods, Vol. 1* (1954); *Jazz Experiments of Charles Mingus* (1954); *Jazz Composers Workshop* (1954); *Intrusions* (1954); *Plus Max Roach* (1955); *Mingus at the Bohemia* (1955); *Jazzical Moods, Vol. 2* (1955); *Jazz Collaborations* (1955); *Chazz* (1955); *Charlie Mingus Quintet + Max Roach* (1955); *Pithecanthropus Erectus* (1956); *Tonight at Noon* (1957); *Tijuana Moods* (1957); *Scenes in the City* (1957); *N.Y. Sketch Book* (1957); *Modern Jazz Symposium of Music* (1957); *Mingus Three* (1957); *East Coasting* (1957); *Debut Rarities, Vol. 3* (1957); *Clown* (1957); *Charles Mingus Trios* (1957); *Weary Blues* (1958); *Wonderland* (1959); *Nostalgia in Times Square* (1959); *Mingus Dynasty* (1959); *Mingus Ah Um* (1959); *Jazz Portraits* (1959); *Blues and Roots* (1959); *Pre–Bird* (1960); *Mysterious Blues* (1960); *Mingus!* (1960); *Mingus at Antibes* (1960); *Mingus Revisited* (1960); *Charles Mingus Presents Charles Mingus* (1960); *Better Git It in Your Soul* (1960); *Oh Yeah* (1961); *Town Hall Concert* (1962); *Money Jungle* (trio w. Ellington and M. Roach; 1962); *Live at Birdland* (1962); *Mingus, Mingus, Mingus, Mingus, Mingus* (1963); *Mingus Plays Piano* (1963); *Black Saint and the Sinner Lady* (1963); *Right Now: Live at Jazz Workshop* (1964); *Portrait* (1964); *Paris 1964* (1964); *Mingus in Europe, Vol. 1, 2* (1964); *Mingus at Monterey* (1964); *Meditation* (1964); *Live in Stockholm* (1964); *Live in Paris 1964, Vol. 2* (1964); *Live in Oslo* (1964); *Great Concert of Charles Mingus* (1964); *Fables of Faubus* (1964); *Concertgebouw Amsterdam, Vol. 1, 2* (1964); *Astral Weeks* (1964); *My Favorite Quintet* (1965); *Music Written for Monterey* (1965); *Charles Mingus* (1965); *Statements* (1969); *Reincarnation of a Lovebird* (1970); *Charles Mingus in Paris* (1970); *With Orch.* (1971); *Shoes of the Fisherman's Wife...* (1971); *Live in Chateauvallon* (1972); *Let My Children Hear Music* (1972); *Charles Mingus and Friends in Concert* (1971); *Mingus Moves* (1973); *Mingus at Carnegie Hall* (1974); *Changes Two* (1974); *Changes One* (1974); *Cumbia and Jazz Fusion* (1976); *Three or Four Shades of Blues* (1977); *Live at Montreux* (1977); *Lionel Hampton Presents Music of* (1977); *His Final Work* (1977); *Giants of Jazz, Vol. 2* (1977); *Soul Fusion* (1978); *Something Like a Bird* (1978); *Me, Myself an Eye* (1978); *Chair in the Sky* (1979); *Mingus Dynasty: Live at Montreux* (1981); *Reincarnation* (1982); *Live at the Village Vanguard* (1984); *Mingus Sounds of Love* (1987); *Big Band Charles Mingus, Vol. 1* (1988); *Abstractions* (1989); *Epitaph* (1990); *Stations of the Elevated* (1990); *Live at the Theatre Boulogne* (1991); *Next Generation Performs Charles Mingus* (1991); *Meditations on Integration* (1992); *Mingus Big Band 93: Nostalgia I* (1993). **L. HAMPTON AND HIS ORCH.:** "Mingus Fingers" (1947). **DINAH WASHINGTON WITH L. THOMPSON AND HIS ALL STARS:** *Mellow Mama Blues* (1945); *Wise Woman Blues* (1963).

WRITINGS: Nel King, ed., *Beneath the Underdog: His World As Composed by Mingus* (N.Y., 1971); *More Than a Fake Book.* (N.Y., 1991).

BIBL.: Coss, *Charles Mingus: A List of Compositions Licensed by B.M.I.* (N.Y., 1961); R. Wilbraham, *Charles Mingus: A Discography with Brief Biography* (London, 1970); B. Priestley, *Mingus: A Critical Biography* (London, 1982); Michel Ruppli, *Charles Mingus Discography* (Frankfurt, Germany, 1982); H. Lindemaier and H. Salewski, *The Man Who Never Sleeps: The C. M. Discography 1945–78* (Freiburg, 1983); Michel Luzzi, *Charlie Mingus* (Rome, Lato, 1983); Janet Coleman and A. Young, *Mingus/Mingus: Two Memoirs* (Berkeley, 1989).—**LP/NS**

Minkowski, Marc, French conductor; b. Paris, Oct. 4, 1962. He was educated at the Royal Cons. of Music at The Hague and at the Monteux conducting school in the U.S. In 1984 he founded Les Musiciens du Louvre in Paris, with which he championed early music. In 1991 he conducted Gluck's *Iphigénie en Tauride* at London's Covent Garden. After conducting Lully's *Phaëton* at the Lyons Opera in 1993, he conducted Handel's *Ariodante* at the Welsh National Opera in Cardiff and Handel's *Agrippina* at the Semper Opera in Dresden in 1994. In 1995 he led a performance of Purcell's *Dido and Aeneas* at the Houston Grand Opera. After conducting Mozart's *Idomeneo* at the Opéra de la Bastille in Paris and Gluck's *Orfeo ed Euridice* at the Netherlands Opera in Amsterdam in 1996, he conducted Mozart's *Die Entführung aus dem Serail* at the Salzburg Festival in 1997. Minkowski served as music director of the Flanders Opera and Sym. Orch. in Belgium from 1997 to 1999.—NS/LK/DM

Minkus, Léon (actually, **Aloisius Ludwig**), Austrian violinist and composer; b. Vienna, March 23, 1826; d. there, Dec. 7, 1917. He went to Russia in his youth, and was engaged by Prince Yusupov as concert-master of his serf orch. in St. Petersburg (1853–56). From 1862 to 1872 he was concertmaster of the Bolshoi Theater in Moscow. In 1869 the Bolshoi Theater produced his ballet *Don Quixote* to the choreography of the famous Russian ballet master Petipa; its success was extraordinary, and its appeal to the Russian audiences so durable that the work retained its place in the repertoire of Russian ballet companies for more than a century, showing no signs of diminishing popularity. Equally popular was his ballet *La Bayadère*, produced by Petipa in St. Petersburg in 1877; another successful ballet was his *La Fiametta or The Triumph of Love*, originally produced in Paris in 1864. From 1872 to 1885 Minkus held the post of court composer of ballet music for the Imperial theaters in St. Petersburg. He remained in Russia until 1891; then returned to Vienna, where he lived in semi-retirement until his death at the age of 91. The ballets of Minkus never took root outside Russia, but their cursive melodies and bland rhythmic formulas suit old-fashioned Russian choreography to the airiest *entrechat*.—NS/LK/DM

Minnelli, Liza, b. Los Angeles, March 12, 1946. Without the most showstopping of pop voices, the daughter of actress-singer Judy Garland and director Vincente Minnelli compensates with adrenaline, energy, and charisma. In concert, she whirls through songs in a variety of colorfully sequined costumes, flailing her elbows and knees in every possible choreographed direction. Her most famous part remains the awed Sally Bowles, from the Bob Fosse musical *Cabaret*, the movie version of which earned Minnelli a best actress Oscar in 1972. Having grown up in a show-biz family—Ira Gershwin was her godfather—Minnelli tried her best to distance herself from her mother's image. In fact, she refused to sing any of the late Garland's trademark songs until recently, when she unveiled a 75th birthday tribute during a concert. The goal turned out to be easy: Minnelli's good looks developed much differently from her mother's all-American pinup-girl image, but she also had a more versatile face for comedy, theater, and

energetic stage shows. Early in life, she had to deal with tending to her mother's debilitating emotional problems, plus resentment from fellow actresses who assumed she was coasting on connections. She shook all that off in the early 1960s when she started landing prominent Broadway musicals and adoring audiences; her biggest break, *Cabaret*, came in the early 1970s. Despite Valium and alcohol addiction problems, a series of divorces, and a growing public lack of interest in her specialty (musical varieties), Minnelli has remained a popular television and concert draw. She overcame most of her problems after checking into the Betty Ford Center in the late 1980s, and even wound up recording with the electronic rock band Pet Shop Boys.

DISC: *Liza! Liza!* (1964); *It Amazes Me* (1965); *Live at the London Palladium* (1965); *Come Saturday Morning* (1969); *Cabaret* (soundtrack; 1972); *Liza with a "Z"* (1972); *At Carnegie Hall* (1979); *Highlights: Carnegie Hall Concerts* (1989); *Results* (1989); *Live from Radio City Music Hall* (1992); *Gently* (1996); *Maybe This Time* (1996); *Minnelli on Minnelli: Live at the Palace* (2000); *16 Biggest Hits* (2000).

Minoja, Ambrogio, Italian composer and singing teacher; b. Ospitaletto Lodigiano, near Piacenza, Oct. 22, 1752; d. Milan, Aug. 3, 1825. He studied music in Lodi and Naples, and then served as maestro al cembalo at La Scala in Milan and at the Teatro Canobbiano there from 1780 to 1802. In 1814 he became censor of the Milan Cons., holding that position until his death. As an instructor of high repute, he publ. books of solfeggi and *Lettere sopra il canto* (Milan, 1812). He composed the operas *Tito nelle Gallie* (La Scala, Milan, Dec. 26, 1786) and *Olimpiade* (Rome, Dec. 26, 1787) as well as several syms., sacred music, and chamber pieces.—NS/LK/DM

Minter, Drew, American countertenor; b. Washington, D.C., Jan. 11, 1955. He studied at Ind. Univ. and with Marcy Lindheimer, Myron McPherson, Rita Streich, and Erik Werba. After singing with many early music ensembles, he made his stage debut as Handel's Orlando at the St. Louis Baroque Festival in 1983. In subsequent years, he appeared in performances of early operas in Boston, Brussels, Los Angeles, Omaha, and Milwaukee; also sang in the U.S. premiere of Judith Weir's *A Night at the Chinese Opera* at the Santa Fe (N.Mex.) Opera in 1989. In 1992 he was engaged as Handel's Ottone at the Göttingen Festival. He sang Endymion in Cavalli's *Calisto* at the Glimmerglass Opera in N.Y. in 1996. He is best known for his roles in operas by Monteverdi, Handel, and Landi.—NS/LK/DM

Minton, Yvonne (Fay), noted Australian mezzo-soprano; b. Sydney, Dec. 4, 1938. She studied with Marjorie Walker in Sydney and with Henry Cummings and Joan Cross in London; won the Kathleen Ferrier Prize and the 's Hertogenbosch Competition (both 1961). She sang the role of Maggie Dempster in the premiere of Maw's *One Man Show* (London, 1964). She made her Covent Garden debut in London as Lola in *Cavalleria rusticana* (1965), and subsequently sang there regularly; also sang at the Cologne Opera (from 1969) and at the Bayreuth Festivals (from 1974). She made her first appearance in the U.S. in Chicago (1970), and her Metropolitan Opera debut in N.Y. as Octavian in *Der Rosenkavalier* on March 16, 1973; also appeared in concerts with the Chicago Sym. Orch. In 1983 she retired from the operatic stage, but continued her concert career. She resumed an active career in 1990 with an engagement in Florence. In 1994 she made her debut at the Glyndebourne Festival as Madame Larina in *Eugene Onegin*. In 1980 she was made a Commander of the Order of the British Empire. Among her finest roles were Gluck's Orfeo, Cherubino, Sextus in *La clemenza di Tito*, Dorabella, Waltraube, Fricka, Dido, and Brangäne; she also created the role of Thea in Tippett's *The Knot Garden* (1970) and sang the role of the Countess in the first perf. of the complete version of Berg's *Lulu* (1979).—NS/LK/DM

Mintz, Shlomo, Russian-born Israeli violinist and conductor; b. Moscow, Oct. 30, 1957. His family emigrated to Israel when he was 2, and he became a pupil of Ilona Feher there at age 6. He gave his first recital (1966) and appeared as soloist in the Mendelssohn Concerto with Mehta and the Israel Phil. (1968). He completed his training with Dorothy DeLay at N.Y.'s Juilliard School (1973), the same year in which he made his U.S. debut in the Bruch Concerto No. 1 with Steinberg and the Pittsburgh Sym. Orch. at Carnegie Hall in N.Y. After making his European debut at the Brighton Festival in England (1976), he made a major tour of Europe (1977). In subsequent years, he appeared in all the leading music centers of the world, performing as a soloist with orchs., as a recitalist, and as a chamber music artist. In 1989 he was appointed music adviser of the Israel Chamber Orch. In 1994 he became music advisor and principal guest conductor of the Limburg Sym. Orch. in Maastricht.—NS/LK/DM

Mirecki, Franz (actually, **Franciszek Wincenty**), Polish composer, pianist, and singing teacher; b. Kraków (baptized), March 31, 1791; d. there, May 29, 1862. He first studied with his father, making his debut as a pianist at the age of 9, and later was a student of Hummel in Vienna (1814) and of Cherubini in Paris (1817). He was active as a singing teacher, conductor, and composer in Milan (1822–38) and Genoa (1826–38), and also conducted an Italian opera company on a tour of Portugal, England, and France (1825–26). He returned to Kraków in 1838, running his own school until 1841; also served as director of the local Opera (1844–47). Among his works were the operas *Cyganie* (The Gypsies; Warsaw, May 23, 1822), *Evandro in Pergamo* (Genoa, Dec. 26, 1824), *I due forzati* (Lisbon, March 7, 1826), *Cornelio Bentivoglio* (Milan, March 18, 1844), and *Nocleg w Apeninach* (A Night in the Apennines; Kraków, April 11, 1845). He also composed piano pieces.—NS/LK/DM

Miricioiu, Nelly, Romanian soprano; b. Adjud, March 31, 1952. She studied in Bucharest and Milan. Following her operatic debut in Iaşi in 1974 as the Queen of the Night, she sang with the Braşov Opera (1975–78). In 1981 she made her British debut as Tosca

with the Scottish Opera in Glasgow, and then made her first appearance at London's Covent Garden in 1982 as Nedda. She subsequently was engaged to sing in San Francisco, San Diego, Rome, Hamburg, Milan, and other music centers. In 1988 she appeared as Rossini's Armida in Amsterdam. She sang Violetta in Philadelphia in 1992. In 1996 she portrayed Elisabeth in *Don Carlos* in Brussels. She was engaged for the title role in *Semiramide* at the Grand Theatre in Geneva in 1998. Among her other roles were Lucia di Lammermoor, Manon Lescaut, Marguerite, Cio-Cio-San, and Mimi.—NS/LK/DM

Miroglio, Francis, French composer, poet, and painter; b. Marseilles, Dec. 12, 1924. He received training in composition from Milhaud at the Paris Cons. For the most part, his compositions have utilized aleatory procedures complemented by an infusion of tonal color. His artistic bent led him to collaborate with such artists as Alexander Calder and Joan Miró.

WORKS: ORCH.: *Fusions* (1974); *Magnétiques* for Violin and Orch. (1979; also for Violin and 7 Players); *Deltas* (1986). **CHAMBER:** *Brisures* for Flute (1977); *Ping-squash* for 1, 2, or 3 Percussionists (1980); *Triade* for 1, 2, or 3 Violins (1980); *Trip Through Trinity* for Percussion (1981); *Chicanes* for 10 Players (1983); *Brut millésime 1.9.8.4.* for 6 Players (1984); *Moires* for Harp (1985); *Quinconce* for Flute, Clarinet, Violin, Cello, and Piano (Radio France, Paris, Aug. 24, 1988); *Pulsars* for Vibraphone and 7 Players (1990; Radio France, Paris, June 4, 1991). **KEYBOARD: Harpsichord:** *Insertions* (1969). **Organ:** *Gravités* (1970). **VOCAL:** *Habeas corpus* for 12 Solo Voices (1984).—LK/DM

Mirouze, Marcel, French composer and conductor; b. Toulouse, Sept. 24, 1906; d. in an automobile accident in Aude, Aug. 1, 1957. He studied with Büsser at the Paris Cons. He conducted the Paris Radio Orch. (1935–40) and in Monte Carlo (1940–43). He wrote an opera, *Geneviève de Paris*, for the 2,000[th] anniversary of the founding of the city of Paris; it was produced first as a radio play with music in 1952, and then on stage in Toulouse in the same year. He also composed 2 ballets, *Paul et Virginie* (1942) and *Les Bains de mer* (1946), 2 symphonic tableaux, *Afrique* (1936) and *Asie* (1938), Piano Concerto (1948), film music, piano pieces, and songs.—NS/LK/DM

Miry, Karel, Belgian composer; b. Ghent, Aug. 14, 1823; d. there, Oct. 3, 1889. He studied violin with Jean Andries and composition with Martin Joseph Mergal at the Ghent Cons., and in 1857 was engaged as a prof. of harmony and counterpoint there; in 1871 he was appointed asst. director. From 1875 he was inspector of music in the municipal schools of Ghent, and from 1881, inspector of state-supported music schools. As a composer, Miry cultivated the national Flemish style, writing several syms. and 18 operas and operettas to French and Flemish librettos. His opera *Boucherd d'Avesnes* was first staged in Ghent on Feb. 5, 1864, obtaining considerable success. But he owes his fame to the patriotic song *De Vlaamse Leeuw*, which he wrote at the age of 22, and which became the Flemish anthem of Belgium.

BIBL.: J. Maertens, *De structuurontleding van de symfonieen van K. M. (1823–1889)* (diss., Univ. of Ghent, 1968). —NS/LK/DM

Mirzoyan, Edvard (Mikaeli), Armenian composer and pedagogue; b. Gori, Ga., May 12, 1921. He studied in Yerevan at the Music School (1928–36) and with Talyan at the Cons. (1936–41) before completing his training with Litinsky and Peyko at the House of Armenian Culture in Moscow (1946–48). Returning to Yerevan, he was a teacher (1948–65) and a prof. (from 1965) at the Cons., where he served as head of the composition dept. (1972–87). In 1981 he was made a People's Artist of the U.S.S.R. His music followed in a lucid neo-Classical style, while his thematic materials were of Armenian provenance.

WORKS: DRAMATIC: Film scores. **ORCH.:** *Sako from Lhore*, symphonic poem (1941); *Symphonic Dances*, suite (1946); Overture (1947); *Introduction and Perpetuum Mobile* for Violin and Orch. (1957); Sym. for Strings (1962); *Epitaph*, symphonic poem (1988). **CHAMBER:** String Quartet (1947); Cello Sonata (1967); piano pieces. **VOCAL:** 3 cantatas (1948, 1949, 1950) and other pieces.

BIBL.: T. Arazyan, *E. M.* (Yerevan, 1963); M. Ter-Simonyan, *E. M.* (Moscow, 1969).—NS/LK/DM

Misch, Ludwig, German-American organist, conductor, music critic, and musicologist; b. Berlin, June 13, 1887; d. N.Y., April 22, 1967. He studied theory with Max Friedlaender at the Univ. of Berlin, and simultaneously took courses in law, obtaining his D.Jur. degree at the Univ. of Heidelberg in 1911. He was music critic for the *Allgemeine Musikzeitung* (1909–13), and also conducted theater orchs. in Berlin, Essen, and Bremen. From 1921 to 1933 he was music critic of the *Berliner Lokalanzeiger*. Under the Nazi regime, he conducted a Jewish madrigal choir in Berlin until he was sent to a concentration camp. In 1947 he emigrated to N.Y., where he became active as an organist and musicologist. He publ. the valuable books *Johannes Brahms* (Bielefeld, 1913; 2nd ed., Berlin, 1922), *Beethoven- Studien* (Berlin, 1950; Eng. tr., Norman, Okla., 1953), tr. and annotated (with D. MacArdle) *New Beethoven Letters* (Norman, 1957), *Die Faktoren der Einheit in der Mehrsatzigkeit der Werke Beethovens: Versuch einer Theorie der Einheit des Werkstils* (Bonn, 1958), and *Neue Beethoven-Studien und andere Themen* (Bonn, 1967).—NS/LK/DM

Mischakoff (real name, Fischberg), Mischa, Russian-born American violinist; b. Proskurov, April 3, 1895; d. Petoskey, Mich., Feb. 1, 1981. Owing to a plethora of Russian-Jewish violinists named Fischberg, he decided to change his name to Mischakoff, formed by adding the Russian ending -koff to his first name, the Russian diminutive for Michael. He studied with Korguyev at the St. Petersburg Cons., graduating in 1912; made his debut that year in Berlin and then was active as an orch. player and teacher. He emigrated to the U.S. in 1921 and became a naturalized citizen in 1927. He was concertmaster of the N.Y. Sym. Orch. (1924–27), the Philadelphia Orch. (1927–29), the Chicago Sym. Orch. (1930–36), the NBC Sym. Orch. in N.Y.

(1937–52), and the Detroit Sym. Orch. (1952–68), and then guest concertmaster of the Baltimore Sym. Orch. (1968–69). He was also concertmaster and soloist with the Chautauqua Sym. Orch. (summers, 1925–65); likewise led his own Mischakoff String Quartet. He taught at the Juilliard School of Music in N.Y. (1940–52), at Wayne State Univ. in Detroit (from 1952), and at various other schools.—NS/LK/DM

Misón, Luis, Spanish flutist, oboist, conductor, and composer; b. probably in Barcelona, date unknown; d. Madrid, Feb. 13, 1776. He was a flutist in the Royal Chapel and the Royal Opera, Madrid (from 1748), becoming conductor there in 1756. He composed stage music, and was one of the first to introduce the "tonadilla escénica," a sort of miniature comic opera that developed from the musical interludes in early Spanish plays. He also wrote "sainetes" (dramatic dialogues), zarzuelas, and 12 sonatas for Flute, Viola, and Bass. —NS/LK/DM

Mitchell, Donald (Charles Peter), eminent English writer on music and publishing executive; b. London, Feb. 6, 1925. He studied at Dulwich Coll. in London (1939–42) and with A. Hutchings and A.E.F. Dickinson at the Univ. of Durham (1949–50). After noncombatant wartime service (1942–45), he founded (1947) and then became co-ed. (with Hans Keller) of *Music Survey* (1949–52). From 1953 to 1957 he was London music critic of the *Musical Times*. In 1958 he was appointed music ed. and adviser of Faber & Faber, Ltd.; in 1965 he became managing director, and in 1976 vice chairman; became chairman in 1977 of its subsidiary, Faber Music. He also ed. *Tempo* (1958–62); was on the music staff of the *Daily Telegraph* (1959–64); in 1963–64 he served as music adviser to Boosey & Hawkes, Ltd. From 1971 to 1976 he was prof. of music, and from 1976 visiting prof. of music, at the Univ. of Sussex; in 1973 he was awarded by it an honorary M.A. degree; received his doctorate in 1977 from the Univ. of Southampton with a diss. on Mahler. He lectured widely in the United Kingdom, U.S., and Australia; contributed articles to the *Encyclopaedia Britannica* and other reference publications. As a music scholar, Mitchell made a profound study, in Vienna and elsewhere, of the life and works of Gustav Mahler; was awarded in 1961 the Mahler Medal of Honor by the Bruckner Soc. of America and in 1987 the Mahler Medal of the International Gustav Mahler Soc. His major work is a Mahler biography: vol. 1, *Gustav Mahler: The Early Years* (London, 1958; rev. ed., 1980); vol. 2, *The Wunderhorn Years* (London, 1976); vol. 3, *Songs and Symphonies of Life and Death* (London, 1985). His other publications include: ed. with H. Keller, *Benjamin Britten: A Commentary on All His Works from a Group of Specialists* (London, 1952); *W.A. Mozart: A Short Biography* (London, 1956); with H.C. Robbins Landon, *The Mozart Companion* (N.Y., 1956; 2nd ed., 1965); *The Language of Modern Music* (London, 1963; 3rd ed., 1970); ed. and annotated Alma Mahler's *Gustav Mahler: Memories and Letters* (London, 1968; 3rd ed., rev., 1973); ed. with J. Evans, *Benjamin Britten, 1913–1976: Pictures from a Life* (London, 1978); *Britten and Auden in the Thirties* (London, 1981); *Benjamin Britten: Death in Venice* (Cambridge, 1987).

BIBL.: P. Reed, ed., *On Mahler and Britten: Essays in Honour of D. M. on his Seventieth Birthday* (Woodbridge, Suffolk, 1995). —NS/LK/DM

Mitchell, George (Little Mitch),

jazz cornetist; b. Louisville, Ky., March 8, 1899; d. Chicago, Ill., May 27, 1972. He played on many of Jelly Roll Morton's most famous recordings. He started on trumpet at the age of 12. He joined the St. Augustine School Band, then became a member of the Louisville Musical Club Brass Band (led by Wilbur Winstead), touring with the band during the summers of 1916–17. He toured with several minstrel shows, and then settled in Chicago, where he worked with various bands through 1921. He spent the next two years on the road, and then returned to Chicago in 1923 where he joined Carroll Dickerson's band; in late summer of 1924, he joined Doc Cooke, remaining with him through summer of 1925. About this time, he switched from played trumpet to cornet. He joined Lil Armstrong's Band at Dreamland, remaining with her from fall 1925–spring of 1926. Mitchell made many freelance recordings during this period, including sessions with Jelly Roll Morton's Red Hot Peppers and The New Orleans Wanderers, as well as with his own bands. After gigging with various bands, he rejoined Doc Cooke's Orch. in September 1927, remaining with him about two years. He then worked with Earl Hines from summer 1929–spring 1930, and again summer 1930–spring 1931. In the early 1930s, he left full-time music to become a bank messenger although he continued to gig around town. He retired from his day job in the early 1960s.—JC/LP

Mitchell, Howard,

American cellist and conductor; b. Lyons, Nebr., March 11, 1911; d. Ormond Beach, Fla., June 22, 1988. He studied piano and trumpet in Sioux City, Iowa; after studying cello at the Peabody Cons. of Music in Baltimore, he completed his training with Felix Salmond at the Curtis Inst. of Music in Philadelphia (1930–35). He was first cellist of the National Sym. Orch. in Washington, D.C. (1933–44), then its asst. (1944–48), assoc. (1948–49), and principal (1949–69) conductor. He then became conductor of the SODRE Sym. Orch. in Montevideo.—NS/LK/DM

Mitchell, Joni (originally, Anderson, Roberta Joan),

with her distinctive dulcimer and guitar playing and expressive, clear, and full-bodied soprano voice, touched myriads of popular-music fans with her intensely personal, often confessional style of songwriting; b. Fort McLeod, Alberta, Canada, Nov. 7, 1943. Gaining her first recognition in the late 1960s as the composer of the folk-rock classics "Circle Game" and "Both Sides Now" (as recorded by Tom Rush and Judy Collins, respectively), Joni Mitchell developed a devoted following with her first two folk-style albums. In the 1970s Mitchell's career took her through a variety of styles, always pushing the envelope of the confessional singer-songwriter style. After flirting with jazz she returned to a more rock-oriented sound in the 1980s and 1990s, although with less commercial success.

Joni Mitchell grew up in Saskatoon, Saskatchewan, where she took up informal singing at age nine and developed an interest in the visual arts. Taking up baritone ukulele during her teens and later learning guitar, she performed in Calgary, Alberta's best-known coffeehouse, The Depression, while attending the Alberta Inst. of Art. She subsequently decided to pursue folk-style music professionally and moved to Toronto, where she played at clubs in the city's famed Yorktown district. There she met and eventually married folk singer Chuck Mitchell. They moved to Detroit in 1966 and later toured the East Coast club circuit. By 1967, however, the couple had divorced, and Joni moved to N.Y.C., where she played folk clubs and struck up friendships with Judy Collins and Tom Rush, among others.

Signed to Reprise Records, Joni Mitchell gained her first recognition as a songwriter by means of Tom Rush's recording of her "Circle Game" and "Urge for Going" on his 1968 *Circle Game* album, and through Judy Collins's near-smash hit recording of her "Both Sides Now" that same year. Mitchell soon moved to Calif., and her debut album, sometimes referred to as *Song to a Seagull*, was produced in a thin and understated manner by David Crosby. Although the album sold minimally, it featured her own cover art and was entirely comprised of her own compositions, including the poignant and brilliantly sung "Michael from Mountains," "I Had a King," and "Cactus Tree."

Joni Mitchell's second album, *Clouds*, sported her colorful self-portrait and effectively established her in the forefront of the 1970s female singer-songwriter movement. The album contained her celebratory "Chelsea Morning," the ominous "The Fiddle and the Drum" and her version of "Both Sides Now," as well as moving personal songs such as "I Don't Know Where I Stand" and "Songs to Aging Children Come." Often using obscure yet sophisticated tunings on her stringed instruments, Mitchell employed a sense of harmony that went beyond the limits of both pop and rock. Her songwriting—more accurately described as song-poetry—explored the themes of romantic love, the independence achieved through love's loss, and the guarded optimism of the youthful humanitarian ethic in such fiercely personal and incisively honest terms as to be embarrassing were it not for their underlying poignancy. Her next album, *Ladies of the Canyon*, again featured her art on the jacket. Bolstered commercially by the success of Crosby, Stills, Nash and Young's version of her classic "Woodstock," the album introduced her use of the piano and included her own electrifying version of "Woodstock" (far and away superior to CSNY's rock version); the oft-recorded "Circle Game"; and her first minor hit, the wry ecology song "Big Yellow Taxi." Containing wide-ranging music and varied emotional nuances, the album also included "For Free," a joyous look back at her precommercial days; the gentle autobiographical title cut; and "Willy," written about former lover Graham Nash.

Joni Mitchell's final album for Reprise, *Blue*, showed her flowering as an arranger and continued her string of best-selling, highly personal, and exquisitely performed releases. Among the songs included are "All I Want," "California," "This Flight Tonight," "A Case of You" (her second minor hit), "Carey," and the disturbing "The Last Time I Saw Richard." Switching to Asylum Records, she recorded *For the Roses*. The album revealed jazz influences and included her first major hit, "You Turn Me On, I'm a Radio," as well as "Cold Blue Steel and Sweet Fire," "See You Sometime," and "Blonde in the Bleachers." *Court and Spark*, recorded with members of Tom Scott's jazz-style group L.A. Express, became her most popular album, remaining on the album charts for well over a year. The album yielded three hits with "Raised on Robbery," "Help Me" (a near-smash), and "Free Man in Paris"; it also contained "People's Parties" as well as the romantic title song and a version of Lambert, Hendricks and Ross's "Twisted." Touring for the first time in several years during 1974 with Scott and the L.A. Express, her live *Miles of Aisles* compiled much of her finest material and produced a major hit with its version of "Big Yellow Taxi."

With 1975's *The Hissing of Summer Lawns*, Joni Mitchell began to move beyond the restrictive role of pop-style singer-songwriter. Eschewing the confessional style in favor of songs both musically and lyrically ambitious and complex, Mitchell suffered critical disparagement for the album in the rock and pop press. Maintaining an even more reduced personal profile, she recorded *Hejira* with jazz artists such as Jaco Pastorius and Larry Carlton. Regarded by some jazz critics as a masterpiece, this album encompasses a variety of musical textures and nuances, on songs such as "Coyote," "Black Crow," and "Furry Sings the Blues." With 1977's *Don Juan's Reckless Daughter*, Mitchell firmly broke with her pop-music past, recording the album with Pastorius, Latin percussionist Airto, and several members of the fusion group Weather Report. Inspiring critics to coin yet another hyphenated label, folk-jazz, the album featured the side-long "Paprika Plains," recorded with full symphony orchestra.

"Paprika Plains," heard by ailing jazz bassist and composer Charles Mingus, so fascinated him that in spring 1978 he contacted Mitchell regarding the possibility of working together. She consented and Mingus soon turned over to her six tunes to which she was to supply lyrics, plus the Mingus standard "Goodbye Pork Pie Hat." Mitchell worked on the collaboration for more than 18 months, but it was not completed until after Mingus's death on Jan. 5, 1979. Recorded with Wayne Shorter, Jaco Pastorius, and Herbie Hancock, the resulting album was greeted by equivocal reviews. The album contained "Goodbye Pork Pie Hat," three of the six specially written tunes, and Mitchell's own tribute to Mingus, "God Must Be a Boogie Man." She subsequently toured for the first time in four years with Pastorius, percussionist Don Alias, guitarist Pat Metheny, and others.

Mainntaining a low profile in the 1980s, Joni Mitchell switched to Geffen Records for 1982's *Wild Things Run Fast*, in which she returned to standard song forms. The album yielded a moderate hit with a cover version of "(You're So Square) Baby, I Don't Care," recorded by Elvis Presley for his 1957 movie *Jailhouse Rock*. In 1985

she recorded *Dog Eat Dog* with English synthesizer wizard Thomas Dolby. The album was highly topical, decrying television evangelists ("Tax Free"), capitalism (the title track), nuclear holocaust ("Fiction"), and consumerism. Her orientation toward contemporary issues continued with 1988's *Chalk Mark in a Rain Storm* with "The Beat of Black Wings" and "Snakes and Ladders." In the early 1990s she recorded *Night Ride Home*, which was also issued in a limited edition featuring four reproductions of her collages, while pursuing her interests as a painter, photographer, and poet. In 1994 Joni Mitchell returned to Reprise Records for *Turbulent Indigo*.

Disc.: *J. M.* (1968); *Clouds* (1969); *Ladies of the Canyon* (1970); *Blue* (1971); *For the Roses* (1972); *Court and Spark* (1974); *Miles of Aisles* (1974); *The Hissing of Summer Lawns* (1975); *Hejira* (1976); *Don Juan's Reckless Daughter* (1977); *Mingus* (1979); *Wild Things Run Fast* (1982); *Dog Eat Dog* (1985); *Chalk Mark in a Rain Storm* (1988); *Night Ride Home* (1991); *Turbulent Indigo* (1994); *Hits* (1996); *Misses* (1996); *Taming the Tiger* (1998); *Both Sides Now* (2000).

Bibl.: Leonore Fleischer, *J. M.* (N.Y., 1976).—BH

Mitchell, Leona, talented black American soprano; b. Enid, Okla., Oct. 13, 1948. She was one of 15 children; her father, a Pentecostal minister, played several instruments by ear; her mother was a good amateur pianist. She sang in local church choirs, then received a scholarship to Oklahoma City Univ., where she obtained her B.Mus. degree in 1971. She made her operatic debut in 1972 as Micaëla in *Carmen* with the San Francisco Spring Opera Theater. She then received the $10,000 Opera America grant (1973), which enabled her to study with Ernest St. John Metz in Los Angeles. On Dec. 15, 1975, she made her Metropolitan Opera debut in N.Y. as Micaëla; subsequently sang there as Pamina in *Die Zauberflöte* and Musetta in *La Bohème*; she won critical acclaim for her portrayal of Leonora in *La forza del destino* in 1982. In 1987 she appeared as Massenet's Salome in Nice. She sang the 3 leading soprano roles in Puccini's *Trittico* at the Paris Opéra-Comique in 1988. She sang Verdi's Elvira in Parma in 1990. In 1992 she appeared as Aida with the New Israeli Opera. She portrayed Strauss's Ariadne in Sydney in 1997. —NS/LK/DM

Mitchell, Louis (A.), pioneering early jazz drummer, leader; b. Philadelphia, Pa., Dec. 17, 1885; d. Washington, D.C., Sept. 12, 1957. Mitchell moved to N.Y. in 1912, and formed the Southern Symphonists' Quintet, credited as the first jazz band in the city. He took the group to Europe in summer of 1914, where it had a residency at London's Piccadilly Restaurant, the first African-American band to play there. He returned to N.Y. that fall, but was back in Britain in May 1915 with Don Kildare. He returned to the U.S. to tour in a variety act called "Jordan and Mitchell," and then did a solo act playing drums. In January 1917, he formed the Syncopating Septette, which made its debut in Glasgow; it subsequently played at the London Palladium that summer before appearing in France. Mitchell returned to the U.S. in 1918, to sing with James Reese Europe's

Band. However, he soon organized his own Jazz Kings and once again was working in Europe. During the 1920s, his band played long residencies in Paris, including a five-year spell at the Casino de Paris. During the 1930s Mitchell organized several business ventures in Europe. He owned and operated the famous Paris-based Grand Duc Club, which he reportedly won in a crap game. He returned to the U.S. in the late 1930s, although by then he had abandoned music making as a career.—JC/LP

Mitchell, Roscoe (Edward Jr.),

avant-garde reeds player, composer, leader; b. Chicago, Ill., Aug. 3, 1940. Mitchell has recorded with distinction on alto, soprano, and bass saxes and a wealth of percussion and miscellaneous instruments. He played clarinet, baritone saxophone in high school, and alto saxophone in Europe as part of the army band. He worked with Byron Austin, Scotty Holt, Jack DeJohnette and in a small combo with Henry Threadgill before joining Muhal Richard Abrams's experimental band in 1961; his association with Abram's ultimately led to the creation of the Association for the Advancement of Creative Musicians (AACM) in 1965. He then led his own trio. Mitchell's 1966 album, *Sound*, is said to have led to the formation of Art Ensemble of Chicago. The album was also important because it put some of principles of John Cage into practice in jazz medium. He has performed as a member of the Art Ensemble of Chicago since 1965, including a two-year stay in Europe. Mitchell appeared playing in Morocco in the video "The World According to John Coltrane." Besides his work with the AEC, Mitchell experimented with dance music in the 1980s. He formed his own Sound Ensemble in 1980 and, in 1988, was given an award by the National Assoc. of Jazz Educators for Outstanding Service to Jazz Education. Three years later, Mitchell was awarded the Jazz Masters Award from Arts Midwest.

DISC.: *Sound* (1966); *Old/Quartet* (1967); *Congliptious* (1968); *Solo Saxophone Concerts* (1973); *Quartet* (1975); *Nonaah* (1976); *Duets with Anthony Braxton* (1977); *Roscoe Mitchell* (1978); *L-R-G / The Maze / SII Examples* (1978); *Sketches from Bamboo* (1979); *3 x 4 Eye* (1981); *And the Sound and Space Ensemble* (1983); *An Interesting Breakfast Conversation* (1984); *Live at the Muhle Hunziken* (1986); *Flow of Things* (1986); *Live at the Knitting Factory* (1987); *Roscoe Mitchell Solo* (1988); *Live in Detroit* (1988); *After Fallen Leaves* (1989); *Songs in the Wind* (1990); *Duets & Solos* (1990); *This Dance Is for Steve McCall* (1992); *Four Compositions* (1992); *Pilgrimage* (1994); *Hey Donald* (1994).—LP

Mitchell, William J(ohn),

American musicologist; b. N.Y., Nov. 21, 1906; d. Binghamton, N.Y., Aug. 17, 1971. He studied at the Inst. of Musical Art in N.Y. (1925–29), then at Columbia Univ. (B.A., 1930) and in Vienna (1930–32). Upon his return to N.Y., he was on the staff at Columbia Univ., where he received his M.A. there in 1938; became a full prof. in 1952, then served as chairman of the music dept. from 1962 to 1967. He concurrently taught at the Mannes Coll. of Music in N.Y. (1957–68), and subsequently joined the faculty of the State Univ. of N.Y. in Binghamton. He was president of the American Musicological Soc. (1965–66). He publ. *Elementary Harmony* (N.Y., 1939; 3rd ed., rev., 1965) and

ed. and tr. Herriot's *La Vie de Beethoven* (1935) and *C.P.E. Bach's Versuch über die wahre Art das Clavier zu spielen* (1949). He was co-ed. of the first 3 vols. of *Music Forum* (1967–73).—NS/LK/DM

Mitchinson, John (Leslie),

English tenor and educator; b. Blackrod, Lancashire, March 31, 1932. He studied at the Royal Manchester Coll. of Music (graduated, 1955). In 1953 he became a founding member of the BBC Northern Singers. After singing in a concert performance of *Don Giovanni* with the Chelsea Opera Group in 1955, he made his stage debut as Jupiter in Handel's *Semele* with the Handel Opera Soc. He sang with the Sadler's Wells Opera (1972–74), and its successor, the English National Opera (1974–78) in London, and then with the Welsh National Opera in Cardiff (1978–82). From 1987 to 1992 he was senior lecturer at the Royal Northern Coll. of Music in Manchester, and then was head of vocal studies at the Welsh Coll. of Music and Drama in Cardiff from 1992. Among his operatic roles, he won particular success as Florestan, Tristan, and Peter Grimes. He was especially well known for his appearances as a soloist with the principal British orchs.—NS/LK/DM

Mitch Ryder and the Detroit Wheels,

high-energy 1960s rock band. **MEMBERSHIP:** Mitch Ryder (real name, William Levise Jr.), voc. (b. Hamtramck, Mich., Feb. 26, 1945); James McCarty, gtr. (b. 1947); Joseph Cubert, gtr. (b. 1947; d. 1991); Earl Elliot, bs. (b. 1947); Johnny "Bee" Badanjek, drm. (b. 1948).

Like a V8 in a small car, Mitch Ryder and the Detroit Wheels burned high-energy tire tracks across the pop music landscape during the mid-1960s. While their careers as hit makers lasted less than two years, their effect on the future of rock, particularly rock out of the Midwest, was incalculable. They've been cited as mentors for artists as diverse as Was (Not Was), the MC5, Iggy Pop, Bob Seger, and Ted Nugent.

Mitch Ryder was born William Levise. In his early teens, Detroit became the pop/soul capital of the world, thanks to the many hits produced by Motown Records. By high school, Levise began making a name for himself in the band Tempest, playing in the black clubs in Detroit. By 17, he cut an R&B tune with a local gospel label and was fronting a black vocal trio called the Peps. He ran into a band featuring guitarists James McCarty, bassist Earl Elliot, and drummer Johnny Badanjek. They started working together as Billy Lee and the Rivieras, adding rhythm guitarist Joe Cubert to the mix. Their show was so powerful that soon no one would let them open for them. They found themselves headlining over Motown groups. This attracted the attention of Four Seasons' producer Bob Crewe, who signed them and moved them to N.Y.

The band spent a few months playing in clubs and refining its show. They had to change their name (an Ind. band called the Rivieras had a #5 hit in 1964 with "California Sun"), with Levise taking the name Mitch Ryder by pulling two random names out of the phone book. The Rivieras became the more generic Detroit Wheels. Their first single, "I Need Help," tanked. For their second, they cut "Jenny Take a Ride," a medley of Little Richard's "Jenny Jenny" and Chuck Willis's "CC Rider" (which became "See Mitch Ryder" by the second verse). Powered by the band's manic soul energy, the song hit #10 early in 1966. They followed this with another piece of high-octane rocking soul, "Little Latin Lupe Lu," which hit #17. Next, they tried to expand their sound, recording a ballad, but found their audience wouldn't accept a slow number. They came back to their forte with the medley of "Devil with a Blue Dress On/Good Golly Miss Molly" toward the end of 1966. They kicked off 1967 with "Sock It to Me Baby," a high powered bit of funky rock that hit #6. At the height of this success, bands like The Who and Cream were opening for them in concert.

However, Crewe's agenda was different than that of the band's. He had scored success by promoting Frankie Valli, lead singer of the Four Seasons, as a lounge balladeer, and had similar plans for Ryder. When the group's attempts to record ballads floundered, Crewe urged Ryder to go out on his own. In mid-1967, he convinced Ryder to cut the Wheels loose and set him up in the studio with strings and songs by Rod McKuen and Jacques Brel. Ryder cut *What Now My Love*, and the title track even reached #30. Unable to look his rock 'n' roll face in the mirror, Ryder severed his ties with Crewe (eschewing all further royalties in the bargain) and went to Memphis where he cut 1969's *The Detroit Memphis Experiment*. While a musical success, it didn't find an audience. Neither did his next band, formed with Badanjek, which they called Detroit, though he so impressed Lou Reed with a version of The Velvet Underground's "Rock and Roll" that Reed hired the band's guitarist Steve Hunter.

For the next seven years, Ryder took a day job in a Denver warehouse, worked on his songwriting, playing only occasionally, and kicked a drug habit. In 1978, he self-released the autobiographical album *How I Spent My Vacation* followed by *Naked but Not Dead*. While he only reached a few diehard fans in the U.S., the records attracted a fair bit of interest in Europe, particularly in Germany. At about the same time, Badanjek and Mc-Carty formed a band with vocalist David Gilbert called Rockets. They released five records between 1977 and 1983, even managing to score a #30 hit in 1979 with a cover of Fleetwood Mac's "Oh Well."

During the 1980s, Ryder recorded mostly for his European fans. John Mellencamp put some of his new-found stardom to work for an artist he regarded as a spiritual mentor, producing Ryder's *Never Kick a Sleeping Dog* in 1983. The album won heavy critical praise and even a modicum of airplay for a reworking of Prince's "When You Were Mine," but sold poorly. That same year, Ryder recorded the song "Bow Wow Wow Wow" on Was (Not Was)'s *Born to Laugh at Tornadoes*. Looking for a hit, during the Iran/Contra hearings, Ryder reworked "Good Golly Miss Molly" into the novelty single "Good Golly, Ask Ollie."

However, through the late 1980s and 1990s, Ryder's European records kept him busy. Between the acceptance of his new music there and the demand for his old hits on the oldies circuit here, Ryder maintained a very satisfactory musical career. Early in 2000, J-Bird records made his self-released and European albums available in the U.S.

DISC.: MITCH RYDER AND THE DETROIT WHEELS: *Take a Ride* (1966); *Breakout!!!* (1966); *Sock It to Me* (1967). **MITCH RYDER:** *What Now My Love* (1967); *Mitch Ryder Sings the Hits* (1968); *The Detroit Memphis Experiment* (1969); *Detroit with Mitch Ryder* (1971); *How I Spent My Vacation* (1978); *Rock 'n' Roll Live* (1979); *Naked but Not Dead* (1979); *We're Gonna Win* (1980); *Live Talkies* (1981); *Got Change for a Million* (1981); *Smart Ass* (1982); *Never Kick a Sleeping Dog* (1983); *In the China Shop* (1986); *Red Blood, White Mink* (1988); *Beautiful Toulang Sunset* (1995); *Rite of Passage* (1995). **ROCKETS:** *Love Transfusion* (1977); *Rockets* (1979); *No Ballads* (1980); *Back Talk* (1981); *Live Rockets* (1983).—**HB**

Mitjana y Gordón, Rafael, eminent Spanish music historian; b. Malaga, Dec. 6, 1869; d. Stockholm, Aug. 15, 1921. He studied music with Eduardo Ocón in Málaga, Felipe Pedrell in Madrid, and Saint-Saëns in Paris, then was employed in the Spanish diplomatic service in Russia, Turkey, Morocco, and Sweden. His most important work was the extensive contribution on the history of Spanish music in Lavignac's *Encyclopédie de la musique* (Paris, 1920; Part I, vol. IV). He also wrote numerous valuable works of a critical or historical nature, including *L'Orientalisme musical et la musique arabe* (Uppsala, 1907), *Catalogue critique et descriptif des imprimés de musique des 16e et 17e siècles, conservés à la Bibliothèque de l'Université d'Uppsala* (Uppsala, 1911), *Don Fernando de las Infantas, teólogo y músico* (Madrid, 1911), and *Cristóbal de Morales: Estudio crítico biográfico* (Madrid, 1920).—**NS/LK/DM**

Mitrea-Celarianu, Mihai, Romanian composer; b. Bucharest, Jan. 20, 1935. He studied with Rogalski, Mendelsohn, Vancea, and Negrea at the Bucharest Cons. (1948–53), and also took private lessons with Jora (1949–51). He was a prof. of harmony and music history in Bucharest (1954–60; 1962–68), then attended summer courses in new music given by Aloys Kontarsky, Caskel, and Karkoschka in Darmstadt (1968), and further studied with the Groupe de Recherches Musicales in Paris (1968–69) and with Schaeffer and Pousseur at the Paris Cons. (1968–69). His trademarks in composition are aleatory, electronic, and variable scoring.

WORKS: ORCH.: *Variations* (1958); *Petite histoire d'avant-monde* for Small Chamber Ensemble (1967); *Trei pentru cinci* for Aleatorily Structured Orch. (1969; in collaboration with Miereanu and Bosseur); *Milchstrassenmusik* (1983); *Jokari* for String Trio and String Orch. (1990); *Plateaux* for Strings (1990). **CHAMBER:** Violin Sonata (1957); Piano Sonata (1958); Piano Sonatina (1960); *Glosa* (Comment) for Viola (1965); *Convergences II (Colinda)* for Electronic Instruments and Percussion (1967) and *IV* for 1 Performer on Optional Instrument or Variable Ensemble (1968); *Seth* for 7 Instruments (1969); *ZN*, "idéogramme photographique" for 3, 4, or 5 Performers (1971); *Signaux (Sur l'Océan U)* for 13 Players (1971); *Inaugural 71*, "action" for a Flutist, with Electroacoustical Devices and a Projector (1971); *Piano de matin (Écoute pour Anne Frank)*, "action" for 5 Instruments, 5 Persons manipulating Divergent Sound Sources, Electroacoustical Devices, and Projectors (1972); *Natalienlied* for 10 Instrumentalists (1986); *Evian, Evian* for

Instrumental Ensemble (1987). VOCAL: *Le Chant des étoiles*, cantata for Mezzo-soprano and 33 Instruments (1964); *Convergences III (Ideophonie M)*, aleatory music for Narrator, Children's Chorus, and 19 Instruments (1968) and *V (Jeux dans le blanc)* for Chorus, Percussion, and Tape (1969); *Prérêve* for Voice, Harpsichord, Flute, and Percussion (1975); *Weil Paul Celan* for Vocal Ensemble, Chorus, and Orch. (1988); *La Reine manquante* for Soprano and 14 Performers (1991); *Par ce fil d'or* for Tenor, Baritone, and 15 Performers or Orch. (1993).—**NS/LK/DM**

Mitropoulos, Dimitri, celebrated Greek-born American conductor and composer; b. Athens, March 1, 1896; d. after suffering a heart attack while rehearsing Mahler's 3rd Sym. with the orch. of the Teatro alla Scala, Milan, Nov. 2, 1960. He studied piano with Wassenhoven and harmony with A. Marsick at the Odeon Cons. in Athens. He wrote an opera after Maeterlinck, *Soeur Béatrice* (1918), which was performed at the Odeon Cons. (May 20, 1919). In 1920, after graduation from the Cons., he went to Brussels, where he studied composition with Gilson, and in 1921 he went to Berlin, where he took piano lessons with Busoni at the Hochschule für Musik (until 1924); concurrently was répétiteur at the Berlin State Opera. He became a conductor of the Odeon Cons. orch. in Athens (1924), then was its co-conductor (1927–29) and principal conductor (from 1929); was also prof. of composition there (from 1930). In 1930 he was invited to conduct a concert of the Berlin Phil. When the soloist Egon Petri became suddenly indisposed, Mitropoulos substituted for him as soloist in Prokofiev's Piano Concerto No. 3, conducting from the keyboard (Feb. 27, 1930). He played the same concerto in Paris in 1932 as a pianist-conductor, and later in the U.S. His Paris debut as a conductor (1932) obtained a spontaneous success; he conducted the most difficult works from memory, which was a novelty at the time; also led rehearsals without a score. He made his American debut with the Boston Sym. Orch. on Jan. 24, 1936, with immediate acclaim; that same year he was engaged as music director of the Minneapolis Sym. Orch.; there he frequently performed modern music, including works by Schoenberg, Berg, and other representatives of the atonal school; the opposition that naturally arose was not sufficient to offset his hold on the public as a conductor of great emotional power. He resigned from the Minneapolis Sym. Orch. in 1949 to accept the post of conductor of the N.Y. Phil.; shared the podium with Stokowski for a few weeks, and in 1950 became music director. In 1956 Leonard Bernstein was engaged as assoc. conductor with Mitropoulos, and in 1958 succeeded him as music director. With the N.Y. Phil., Mitropoulos continued his policy of bringing out important works by European and American modernists; he also programmed modern operas (*Elektra, Wozzeck*) in concert form. A musician of astounding technical ability, Mitropoulos became very successful with the general public as well as with the musical vanguard whose cause he so boldly espoused. While his time was engaged mainly in the U.S., Mitropoulos continued to appear as guest conductor in Europe; he also appeared on numerous occasions as conductor at the Metropolitan Opera in N.Y. (debut conducting *Salome*, Dec. 15, 1954) and at various European opera theaters. He became a naturalized American citizen in 1946. As a composer, Mitropoulos was one of the earliest among Greek composers to write in a distinctly modern idiom.

WORKS: DRAMATIC: *Soeur Béatrice*, opera (1918; Odeon Cons., Athens, May 20, 1919); incidental music to *Electra* (1936) and *Hippolytus* (1937). ORCH.: *Burial* (1925); Concerto Grosso (1928). CHAMBER: Concert Piece for Violin and Piano (1913); *Fauns* for String Quartet (1915); Violin Sonata, *Ostinata* (1925–26). Piano: Sonata (1915); *Piano Piece* (1925); *Passacaglia, Preludio e Fuga* (c. 1925); *4 Dances from Cythera* (1926). VOCAL: *10 Inventions* for Soprano and Piano (1926).

BIBL.: S. Arfanis, *The Complete Discography of D. M.* (Athens, 1990); W. Trotter, *Priest of Music: The Life of D. M.* (Portland, Ore., 1995).—**NS/LK/DM**

Mitsukuri, Shukichi, Japanese composer; b. Tokyo, Oct. 21, 1895; d. Chigasaki, Kanagawa Prefecture, May 10, 1971. He graduated in applied chemistry from the engineering dept. of the Imperial Univ. in Tokyo in 1921, then went to Berlin and studied composition with Georg Schumann. Returning to Japan in 1925, he became an Imperial Navy engineering officer. In 1930 he founded a contemporary Japanese composers' society, Shinko Sakkyokuka, and in 1954 he was appointed a prof. at the Music Academy in Tokyo.

WORKS: ORCH.: *Sinfonietta classica* (Paris, March 6, 1936); *10 Haikai de Basho* (Paris, Dec. 10, 1937); *Elegy* for Chorus and Orch. (1949); 2 syms.: No. 1 (Tokyo, Aug. 22, 1951) and No. 2 (1963); Piano Concertino (Tokyo, Aug. 22, 1953); Piano Concerto (Tokyo, April 23, 1955). CHAMBER: Violin Sonata (1935); Piano Quintet (1955); piano pieces, including *Night Rhapsody* (1935). VOCAL: 3 albums of Japanese folk songs (1950, 1954, 1955).—**NS/LK/DM**

Mitterwurzer, Anton, famous Austrian baritone; b. Sterzing, April 12, 1818; d. Döbling, near Vienna, April 2, 1876. He studied with his uncle, Johann Gänsbacher. After serving as chorister at St. Stephen's, Vienna, he sang in Austrian provincial theaters. In 1839 he was engaged by the Dresden Court Opera, and remained there until he was pensioned in 1870. He was particularly notable in Wagnerian roles.—**NS/LK/DM**

Miyagi (real name, **Wakabe**), **Michio,** Japanese koto player, teacher, and composer; b. Kobe, April 7, 1894; d. in a railroad accident in Kariya, near Tokyo, June 25, 1956. He was given the surname of Suga in infancy; became blind at age 7; studied the koto with Nakajima Kengyō II and made his debut when he was 9. He went to Inchon (1908) to teach the koto and shakuhachi; then taught in Seoul. After receiving his certificate as a koto player with highest honors, he was given the professional name of Nakasuga; was known as Michio Miyagi from 1913. He settled in Tokyo (1917), and with Seiju Yoshida, he founded the New Japanese Music Movement (1920). He became a lecturer (1930) and a prof. (1937) at the Tokyo Music School, and also taught at the National Univ. of Fine Arts and Music (from 1950). He wrote more than 1,000 works for koto and other Japanese instruments as well as an opera, *Kariteibo* (1924), choral works, and solo vocal music.

BIBL.: E. Kikkawa, *Miyagi Michio den* (The Life of M. M.; Tokyo, 1962).—**NS/LK/DM**

Miyoshi, Akira, Japanese composer and teacher; b. Tokyo, Jan. 10, 1933. He joined the Jiyû-Gakuen children's piano group at the age of 3, graduating at the age of 6. He studied French literature, and in 1951 began to study music with Hirai, Ikenouchi, and Gallois-Montbrun, who was in Tokyo at the time. He obtained a stipend to travel to France and took lessons in composition with Challan and again with Gallois-Montbrun (1955–57); upon his return to Japan, he resumed his studies in French literature at the Univ. of Tokyo, obtaining a degree in 1961. In 1965 he was appointed instructor at the Toho Gakuen School of Music in Tokyo.

WORKS: DRAMATIC: Poetical Dramas: *Happy Prince* (1959); *Ondine* (1959). **ORCH.:** *Symphonie concertante* for Piano and Orch. (1954); *Mutation symphonique* (1958); *3 mouvements symphoniques* (1960); Piano Concerto (1962); Concerto (Tokyo, Oct. 22, 1964); Violin Concerto (1965); *Odes métamorphosées* (1969); Concerto for Marimba and Strings (1969); *Ouverture de fête* (1973); *Leos* (1976); *Noesis* (1978); *Distant As I Am* (1982); *En Passant* for Violin and Orch. (1986); *Fuji Litany*, symphonic poem (1988); *Etoiles à cordes* for Violin and Strings (1991); *Creation Sonore* (1991). **CHAMBER:** Sonata for Clarinet, Bassoon, and Piano (1953); Violin Sonata (1954–55); Sonata for Flute, Cello, and Piano (1955); *Torse I* for Chamber Orch. (1959), *III* for Marimba (1968), *IV* for String Quartet and 4 Japanese Instruments (1972), and *V* for 3 Marimbas (1973); 2 string quartets (1962, 1967); *Conversation*, suite for Marimba (1962); *8 poèmes* for Flute Ensemble (1969); *Transit* for Electronic and Concrete Sounds, Percussion, and Keyboard Instruments (1969); *Hommage à musique de chambre, I, II, III,* and *IV* for Flute, Violin and Piano (1970, 1971, 1972, 1974); *Nocturne* for Marimba, Percussion, Flute, Clarinet, and Double Bass (1973); *Protase de loin à rien* for 2 Guitars (1974); *Concert Étude* for 2 Marimbas (1977); *Message Sonore* for Flute, Clarinet, Marimba, Percussion, and Double Bass (1985); *Constellation noir* for String Quartet (1992). **Piano:** Sonata (1958); *In Such Time*, suite (1960); *Études en forme de Sonate* (1967); *Kyōshō* for 2 Pianos (1983). **VOCAL:** *Torse II* for Chorus, Piano, Electone, and Percussion (1962); *Duel* for Soprano and Orch. (1964); 2 works of musical poesy: *The Red Mask of Death I* for Narrator, Orch., and Electronic Sound (1969) and *II* for Voice, Chorus, Orch., and Electronic Sound (1970); *Shihenshôei* for Flute, Chorus, and Orch. (1980); *Kyōmon* for Children's Chorus and Orch. (1984); choruses; songs.—NS/LK/DM

Mizelle, (Dary) John, American composer and teacher; b. Stillwater, Okla., June 14, 1940. He studied trombone at Calif. State Univ. in Sacramento (B.A., 1965) and composition at the Univ. of Calif. at Davis (M.A., 1967) and at the Univ. of Calif. at San Diego (Ph.D., 1977); also studied computer music at Columbia Univ. (1979–83). He taught at the Univ. of South Fla. in Tampa (1973–75) and at the Oberlin (Ohio) Coll. Cons. of Music (1975–79) and in 1990 he joined the faculty of the State Univ. of N.Y. at Purchase. He served as assoc. ed. of *Source* magazine (1966–69). Interest in Mizelle's music increased greatly when a 25-year retrospective concert was given in N.Y. in 1988. His compositions, which number over 200, have been lauded for their stylistic assimilation of such disparate Western composers as Bartók, Messiaen, and Xenakis, their admixtures of ancient, traditional acoustic, and electronic instruments, the mathematical exactitude of their construction, their

generous reliance upon the improvisational skills of performers, and their varied use of extended vocal techniques.

WORKS: 3 string quartets (1964, 1975, 1983); *Green and Red*, quartet for 9 Instruments (1965); *Straight Ahead* for Violin, Flute, Trumpet, Trombone, Percussion, and Tape (1965); *Radial Energy I* for Unspecified Instruments (1967) and *II* for Orch. (1968); *Mass* for Chorus and Live Electronics (1968); *Quanta I & Hymn to Matter* for 8 Multiphonic Volcalists, Chorus, and Orch. (1972–76); Contrabass Concerto (1974–85); *Parameters* for Solo Percussion and Orch. (1974–87); *Polyphonies I* for Quadraphonic Tape, Shakuhachi, and Electronics (1975), *II* for Tape and Dance (1976), and *III* for Quadraphonic Tape and Theater (1978); *Transforms I-XIII* for Piano (1975–94); *Soundscape* for Percussion Ensemble (1976); *Polytempus I* for Trumpet and Tape (1976) and *II* for Marimba and Tape (1979); *Primavera- Heterophony* for 24 Cellos (1977); *Samadhi* for Quadraphonic Tape (1978); *Quanta II & Hymn of the Word* for Wind Ensemble, Percussion, Organ, and 2 Choruses (1979); *Lake Mountain Thunder* for English Horn and Percussion Ensemble (1981); *The Thunderclap of Time I* (1981) and *II* (1982), music for a planetarium; *Requiem Mass* for Chorus and Orch. (1982); *Sonic Adventures*, 15 process pieces for Various Multiple Instrumental Ensembles (1982); Quintet for Woodwinds (1983); Contrabass Quartet (1983); *Indian Summer* for String Quartet and Oboe (1983); *Sounds* for Orch. (1984); *Genesis* for Orch. (1985); *Blue* for Orch. (1985–86); Percussion Concerto (1985–87); *Earth Mountain Fire*, 80 minutes of music for Compact Disc (1987); *Fossy: A Passion Play*, music theater (1987); *Chance Gives Me What I Want*, dance piece (1988); *I Was Standing Quite Close to Process* for Piano (1991–92); *Sun/The Gentle (The Penetrating Wind)* for Violin and Dance (1992); *SPAMDA*, "macrocomposition" of 198 pieces (1995 et seq.).—NS/LK/DM

Mizler, Lorenz Christoph, learned German music scholar; b. Heidenheim, Franconia, July 25, 1711; d. Warsaw, March 1778. He entered the Ansbach Gymnasium when he was 13, and also took music lessons from Ehrmann in Ansbach, and learned to play the violin and flute. In 1731 he enrolled as a theology student at the Univ. of Leipzig, receiving his bachelor's degree in 1733 and his master's degree in 1734 with his *Dissertatio, Quod musica ars sit pars eruditionis philosophicae* (2nd ed., 1736; 3rd ed., 1740). He was a friend of J.S. Bach. In 1735 he went to Wittenberg, where he studied law and medicine. Returning to Leipzig in 1736, he gave his disputation *De usu atque praestantia philosophiae in theologia, jurisprudentia, medicina* (Leipzig, 1736; 2nd ed., 1740). In 1737 he joined the faculty of the Univ. of Leipzig, where he lectured on Mattheson's *Neu-eröffnete Orchestre* and music history. In 1738 he also established the Korrespondierende Sozietät der Musicalischen Wissenschaften. He likewise publ. the valuable music periodical *Neu eröffnete musikalische Bibliothek* (1739–54). In 1743 he entered the service of the Polish count Malachowski of Konshie, working as a secretary, teacher, librarian, and mathematician; he learned the Polish language and devoted much time to the study of Polish culture. In 1747 he took his doctorate in medicine at the Univ. of Erfurt. That same year, he went to Warsaw, where he was made physician to the court in 1752. He was ennobled by the Polish court as Mizler von Kolof in 1768. His vast erudition in many branches of knowledge impelled him to publ. polemical works in which he, much in the prevalent manner of 18th-century philosophers, professed omniscience. Thus he publ. the pamphlet *Lusus ingenii de praesenti bello* (Wittenberg, 1735), in which he proposed, by means of a musical game, to advise the German emperor Karl VII on the proper conduct of the war waged at the time. Pugnacious by nature, he derided "the stupidities of conceited self-grown so-called composers making themselves ridiculous" in a lampoon entitled "Musical Stabber" (*Musikalischer Starstecher, in welchem rechtschaffener musikverständigen Fehler bescheiden angemerket, eingebildeter und selbst gewachsener sogenannter Componisten Thorheiten aber lächerlich gemachet werden*, Leipzig, 1739–40). His theoretical writings include *Anfangs-Gründe des General-Basses nach mathematischer Lehr-Art abgehandelt* (an attempt to instruct figured bass by mathematical rules; Leipzig, 1739). He also translated into German Fux's *Gradus ad Parnassum*, with annotations (Leipzig, 1742). He prepared an autobiography for Mattheson's basic biographical music dictionary, *Grundlage einer Ehren-Pforte* (Hamburg, 1740; new ed. by M. Schneider, Berlin, 1910; reprint, 1969).

BIBL.: F. Wohlke, *L.C. M.: Ein Beitrag zur musikalischen Gelehrtengeschichte des 18. Jahrhunderts* (Würzburg, 1940); J. Birke, *Christian Wolffs Metaphysik und die zeitgenössische Literatur- und Musiktheorie: Gottsched, Scheibe, M.* (Berlin, 1966).
—NS/LK/DM

Mlynarski, Emil (Simon),

Polish violinist, conductor, and composer; b. Kibarty, July 18, 1870; d. Warsaw, April 5, 1935. He studied at the St. Petersburg Cons. (1880–89), taking up both the violin, with Leopold Auer, and piano, with Anton Rubinstein; also took a course in composition with Liadov. He embarked on a career as a conductor. In 1897 he was appointed principal conductor of the Warsaw Opera, and concurrently conducted the concerts of the Warsaw Phil. (1901–05); from 1904 to 1907 he was director of the Warsaw Cons. He achieved considerable success as a conductor in Scotland, where he was principal conductor of the Scottish Orch. in Glasgow (1910–16). Returning to Warsaw, he was director of the Opera (1918–29) and Cons. (1919–22). After teaching conducting at the Curtis Inst. of Music in Philadelphia (1929–31), he returned to Warsaw. He composed an opera, *Noc letnia* (Summer Night; 1914; Warsaw, March 29, 1924), Sym., *Polonia* (1910), 2 violin concertos (1897, Paderewski prize; 1914–17), and violin pieces.

BIBL.: A. Wach, *Zycie i twórczość Emila M. ego* (Life and Works of E. M.; diss., Univ. of Kraków, 1953); J. Mechanisz, *E. M.: W setną rocznicę urodzin (1870–1970)* (Warsaw, 1970).
—NS/LK/DM

Moberg, Carl Allan,

eminent Swedish musicologist; b. Östersund, June 5, 1896; d. Uppsala, June 19, 1978. He studied with Norlind at the Univ. of Uppsala (1917–24), then took some lessons with Berg in Vienna, and took a course in musicology with Wagner in Fribourg (1924–27). He received his Ph.D. in 1927 from the Univ. of Uppsala, and later studied with Handschin in Basel (1934–35). He was a reader (1928–47) and a prof. (1947–61) at the Univ. of Uppsala; as well as ed. of *Svensk tidskrift för musikforskning* (1945–61) and of *Studia musicologica upsaliensia* (1952–61). Among his achievements was a journey to Lapland in the north to collect native songs. He was honored with a Festschrift on his 65th birthday in 1961. Moberg distinguished himself particularly in the study of music history and ethnomusicology.

WRITINGS: *Kyrkomusikens historia* (Stockholm, 1932); *Tonkonstens historia i Västerlandet* (2 vols., Stockholm, 1935); *Dietrich Buxtehude* (Hälsingborg, 1946); *Die liturgischen Hymnen in Schweden* (2 vols., Uppsala, 1947, and with A.-M. Nilsson, 1991); *Musikens historia i Västerlandet intill 1600* (Oslo, 1973).
—NS/LK/DM

Moby Grape,

short-lived but nonetheless legendary psychedelic-era rock band. **MEMBERSHIP:** Alexander "Skip" Spence, gtr., voc. (b. Windsor, Ontario, Canada, April 18, 1946); Jerry Miller, lead gtr., voc. (b. Tacoma, Wash., July 10, 1943); Peter Lewis, gtr., voc. (b. Los Angeles, Calif., July 15, 1945); Bob Mosley, bs., voc. (b. Paradise Valley, Calif., Dec. 4, 1942); Don Stevenson, drm. (b. Seattle, Wash., Oct. 15, 1942).

Formed by Peter Lewis and Bob Mosley in August 1966 in San Francisco, Moby Grape added Don Stevenson and guitarists Jerry Miller and Skip Spence, the original drummer for The Jefferson Airplane. Debuting in November and playing the Fillmore in December, the group signed with Columbia Records and began recording their first album in Los Angeles in March. The album's June release was accompanied by an unprecedented wave of publicity from Columbia Records, as ten of the album's 13 songs were issued as singles. The album included the haunting "Sitting by the Window" and the countrified "8:05," yet yielded only one minor hit with "Omaha."

Performing at the Monterey International Pop Festival, Moby Grape next recorded the double-record set *Wow/Grape Jam*. One record, *Wow*, was recorded in the studio and included Spence's "Motorcycle Irene," Mosley's "Murder in My Heart for the Judge," and Miller's "Can't Be So Bad." The other record, *Grape Jam*, was an improvisational recording made with the assistance of Al Kooper and Mike Bloomfield. (Columbia later issued each of the two records as single records.) Although the album sold quite well, Skip Spence soon left the group with drug problems. He later recorded *Oar* in Nashville for Columbia, playing all the instruments and handling all composing, arranging, and production chores. The group moved to Boulder Creek, near Santa Cruz, Calif., but Mosley soon departed, leaving the remaining three to record *Truly Fine Citizen*, their final album for Columbia.

By the summer of 1969, Moby Grape had broken up. Jerry Miller and Don Stevenson played for two years in The Rhythm Dukes, which included Sons of Champlin leader Bill Champlin. The five original members of Moby Grape reunited in 1971 to record *20 Granite Creek* for Reprise but never performed live. Bob Mosley recorded a solo album and Matthew Katz, owner of the Moby Grape name, assembled his own group to record *Great Grape* for Columbia.

The members of Moby Grape played in various aggregations around Santa Cruz, Calif., during the

1970s. Mosley, Miller, and Lewis were members of another edition of Moby Grape from 1973 to 1975. In 1977, Mosley played in The Ducks, augmented by Neil Young that summer, while Miller, Lewis, and Spence formed The Grape for 1978's *Live Grape*. In 1991, the original lineup of Moby Grape (minus Skip Spence) reunited for Spring Tour West U.S.A. By 1997, the group had won legal rights to the Moby Grape name.

DISC.: MOBY GRAPE: *Moby Grape* (1967); *Wow/Grape Jam* (1968); *'69* (1969); *Truly Fine Citizen* (1969); *Omaha* (1971); *20 Granite Creek* (1971); *Live Grape* (1978). **SKIP SPENCE:** *Oar* (1969). **BOB MOSLEY:** *Bob Mosley* (1972).—**BH**

Mocquereau, Dom André, distinguished French music scholar; b. La Tessoualle, near Cholet, Maine-et-Loire, June 6, 1849; d. Solesmes, Jan. 18, 1930. In 1875 he joined the Order of Benedictines at the Abbey of Solesmes and devoted himself to the study of Gregorian chant under the direction of Dom Pothier. He took his vows (1877) and was ordained a priest (1879). He was made choirmaster (1889), then its prior (1902–08), during which period the order was expelled from France and found refuge on the Isle of Wight (1903). He later returned to Solesmes. He was the founder and ed. of the first 13 vols. of Paléographie Musicale. He publ. *Paroissien romain: Liber usualis* (Tournai, 1903; 5th ed., 1905) and *Le Nombre musical grégorien* (2 vols., Tournai, 1908, 1927; Eng. tr., 1932–51).

BIBL.: J. Ward, *De greg. Zangen naar D. M.* (Doornik, 1929); J. de Donostia, *A propos du nombre musical grégorien de D. M.* (Paris, 1930).—**NS/LK/DM**

Mödl, Martha, esteemed German mezzo-soprano, later soprano; b. Nuremberg, March 22, 1912. She studied at the Nuremberg Cons. and in Milan. She made her operatic debut as Hansel in Nuremberg (1942), then sang in Düsseldorf (1945–49) and at the Hamburg State Opera (1947–55), appearing in soprano roles from 1950 with notable success. She sang at London's Covent Garden (1949–50; 1953; 1959; 1966). She appeared as Kundry at the resumption of the Bayreuth Festival productions in 1951, and continued to sing there regularly until 1967; sang Leonore in the first performance at the rebuilt Vienna State Opera in 1955. From 1965 to 1975 she was again a member of the Hamburg State Opera. On March 2, 1957, she made her Metropolitan Opera debut in N.Y. as Brünnhilde in *Götterdämmerung*, remaining on the roster there until 1960. In 1981 she sang in the premiere of Cerha's *Baal* in Salzburg. She was made both a German and an Austrian Kammersängerin. Her distinguished career is recounted in her book *So war mein Weg: Gespräche mit Thomas Voigt* (Berlin, 1998). Among her finest mezzo-soprano roles were Dorabella, Carmen, Eboli, Octavian, the Composer, and Marie in *Wozzeck*; as a soprano, she excelled as Brünnhilde, Isolde, Gutrune, Venus, and Sieglinde.

BIBL.: W. Schäfer, *M. M.* (Hannover, 1967).—**NS/LK/DM**

Moeck, Hermann, German music publisher and instrument maker; b. Elbing, July 9, 1896; d. Celle, Oct. 9, 1982. He established his publ. business in Celle in 1930, which in 1960 he handed over to his son Hermann

Moeck Jr. (b. Lüneburg, Sept. 16, 1922). The firm was influential in the revival of the manufacture of the vertical flute (recorder) and other Renaissance and early Baroque instruments. Moeck also publ. arrangements and authentic pieces for recorders and the theretofore obsolete fidels. Hermann Moeck Jr., wrote a valuable monograph, *Ursprung und Tradition der Kernspaltflöten* (2 vols., 1951; abr. ed., 1967, as *Typen europäischer Blockflöten*).—**NS/LK/DM**

Moeller, M(athias) P(eter)
See **Möller, M(athias) P(eter)**

Moeran, E(rnest) J(ohn), English composer of Anglo-Irish descent; b. Heston, Middlesex, Dec. 31, 1894; d. Kenmare, County Kerry, Ireland, Dec. 1, 1950. His father was a clergyman, and he learned music from hymnbooks. He then studied at the Royal Coll. of Music in London. He was an officer in the British army in World War I, and was wounded. Returning to London, he took lessons in composition with John Ireland (1920–23), and also became interested in folk music. He collected numerous folk songs in Norfolk, some of which were publ. by the Folksong Soc. (1922). In his early music, he was influenced by Ireland and Delius, but later found inspiration in the works of Vaughan Williams, Holst, and Warlock.

WORKS: ORCH.: *In the Mountain Country*, symphonic impression (1921); 2 rhapsodies (1922; 1924, rev. 1941); *Whythorne's Shadow* (1931); *Lonely Waters* (1932); Sym. (1934–37; London, Jan. 13, 1938); Violin Concerto (London, July 8, 1942); *Rhapsody* for Piano and Orch. (London, Aug. 19, 1943); *Overture to a Masque* (1944); Sinfonietta (1944); Cello Concerto (Dublin, Nov. 25, 1945, with Moeran's wife, Peers Coetmore, as soloist); *Serenade* (London, Sept. 2, 1948). **CHAMBER:** Piano Trio (1920); String Quartet (1921); Violin Sonata (1930); String Trio (1931); *Fantasy Quartet* for Oboe, Violin, Viola, and Cello (1946); Cello Sonata (1947); piano pieces; organ music. **VOCAL:** Choral pieces; songs.

BIBL.: H. Foss, *Compositions of E.J. M.* (London, 1948); S. Wild, *E.J. M.* (London, 1973); G. Self, *The Music of E.J. M.* (London, 1986).—**NS/LK/DM**

Moeschinger, Albert, Swiss composer; b. Basel, Jan. 10, 1897; d. Thun, Sept. 25, 1985. He received training in piano and theory in Bern, Leipzig, and Munich (1917–23). In 1927 he returned to Bern to teach piano and theory, and later was on the faculty of the Cons. there (1937–43). After experimenting with various styles, he embraced dodecaphony in 1954.

WORKS: DRAMATIC: Ballet: *Amor und Psyche* (1955). **ORCH.:** 5 syms.; 5 piano concertos; *Erratique* (1969); *Tres Caprichos* (1972); *Homo et fatum* (1975); *Blocs sonores* (1976); *Étude* (1978). **CHAMBER:** 6 string quartets; 2 piano trios; quintets; Piano Sextet; piano pieces; organ music. **VOCAL:** *Die kleine Meerjungfrau*, dramatic cantata for Soloists, Chorus, and Orch. (1947); choral pieces; songs.

BIBL.: F. Falkner, *A. M., 1897–1985: Werkverzeichnis: Liste des oeuvres* (Zürich, 1996).—**NS/LK/DM**

Moevs, Robert W(alter), American composer and teacher; b. La Crosse, Wisc., Dec. 2, 1920. He studied with Piston at Harvard Coll. (A.B., 1942), with Boulanger at the Paris Cons. (1947–51), and at Harvard Univ. (A.M., 1952). From 1952 to 1955 he was a Rome Prize Fellow in music at the American Academy in Rome; he held a Guggenheim fellowship (1963–64). He taught at Harvard Univ. (1955–63); was composer-in-residence at the American Academy in Rome (1960–61). In 1964 he joined the faculty of Rutgers Univ. in N.J., where he was a prof. (1968–91) and chairman of the music dept. at its New Brunswick campus (1974–81). In addition to his activities as a composer and teacher, he made appearances as a pianist, often in performances of his own works. In 1978 he was awarded the Stockhausen International Prize for his Concerto Grosso for Piano, Percussion, and Orch. As a composer, he developed a compositional method based on intervallic control as opposed to specific pitch sequence that he described as systematic chromaticism.

WORKS: ORCH.: *Passacaglia* (1941); *Introduction and Fugue* (1949); Overture (1950); *14 Variations* (1952); *3 Symphonic Pieces* (1954–55; Cleveland, April 10, 1958); Concerto Grosso for Piano, Percussion, and Orch. (1960; 2nd version with Amplified Instruments, 1968); *In Festivitate* for Wind Instruments and Percussion (Dartmouth, N.H., Nov. 8, 1962); *Main-Travelled Roads, Symphonic Piece No. 4* (1973); *Prometheus: Music for Small Orchestra, I* (1980); *Pandora: Music for Small Orchestra, II* (1986). **CHAMBER:** *Spring* for 4 Violins and Trumpets (1950); 3 string quartets: No. 1 (1957; Cambridge, Mass., Feb. 17, 1960), No. 2 (1989), and No. 3 (1994–95); *Variazioni sopra una Melodia* for Viola and Cello (1961); *Musica da camera I* (1965), *II* (1972), and *III* (1992) for Chamber Ensemble; *Fanfare canonica* for 6 Trumpets (1966); *Paths and Ways* for Saxophone and Dancer (1970); Trio for Violin, Cello, and Piano (1980); *Dark Litany* for Wind Ensemble (1987); Woodwind Quintet (1988); *Echo* for Guitar (1992); *Conundrum* for 5 Percussionists (1993); solo pieces; various keyboard works. **VOCAL:** *Cantata sacra* for Baritone, Men's Chorus, Flute, 4 Trombones, and Timpani (1952); *Attis* for Tenor, Chorus, Percussion, and Orch. (1958–59; 1963); *Et Nunc, reges* for Women's Chorus, Flute, Clarinet, and Bass Clarinet (1963); *Ode to an Olympic Hero* for Voice and Orch. (1963); *Et Occidentem Illustra* for Chorus and Orch. (1964); *A Brief Mass* for Chorus, Organ, Vibraphone, Guitar, and Double Bass (1968); *The Aulos Player* for Soprano, 2 Choruses, and 2 Organs (1975); choruses; songs.—NS/LK/DM

Moffett, Charles (Mack Sr.), jazz drummer; father of Charnett Moffett; b. Fort Worth, Tex., Sept. 11, 1929; d. N.Y., Feb. 14, 1997. He was best known for his work with Ornette Coleman in the mid-1960s. He played trumpet in his high school band, and did nightclub work with Coleman, Jimmy Witherspoon, and other R&B and blues bands around Fort Worth. He studied percussion in 1945. At 19, Moffet was the welterweight champion of the U.S. Navy's Pacific Fleet. After his discharge, he earned a B.A. in Music Education and taught in Tex. high schools for eight years (1953–61), finding time to play with jazz bands and with rock singer Little Richard one year. He moved to N.Y. and joined Coleman in 1961, working with him during the years Coleman shunned public performances. He also performed with Sonny Rollins in 1963, and led a group with Pharoah Sanders, Alan Shorter, and Carla Bley in 1964. Moffet toured and recorded with Coleman and Izenon, including European tours in 1965 and 1966;

he left in 1967. He worked with Archie Shepp in the late 1960s and directed music for schools and youth organizations. He moved to Oakland in 1970, where he directed a music school and led two bands; one was a family unit with his children and another comprised his students. He played with Steve Turre, Keshavan Maslak and Prince Lasha before returning to N.Y. During the 1980s and 1990s taught and also played with Frank Lowe, Maslak, and others.

DISC.: *Beauty Within* (1957); *Gift* (1969). Archie Shepp: *Four for Trane* (1964). Ornette Coleman: *At the Golden Circle Vol.1, 2* (1965). Charnett Moffett: *Net Man* (1976); *Nettwork* (1991).—**LP**

Moffo, Anna, noted American soprano; b. Wayne, Pa., June 27, 1932. She was of Italian descent. She studied voice at the Curtis Inst. of Music in Philadelphia, and later went to Italy on a Fulbright fellowship and studied at the Accademia di Santa Cecilia in Rome. She made her debut as Norina in Spoleto in 1955, and, progressing rapidly in her career, was engaged at La Scala in Milan, at the Vienna State Opera, and in Paris. She made her U.S. debut as Mimi with the Chicago Lyric Opera in 1957; on Nov. 14, 1959, she made her debut at the Metropolitan Opera in N.Y. as Violetta, obtaining a gratifying success; sang regularly at the Metropolitan and other major opera houses in the U.S. and Europe until she suffered a vocal breakdown in 1974; then resumed her career in 1976, but then abandoned it a few years later. In her prime, she became known for her fine portrayals of such roles as Pamina, the 4 heroines in *Les Contes d'Hoffmann*, Gilda, Massenet's Manon, Mélisande, Juliet, Luisa Miller, and Gounod's Marguerite.—**NS/LK/DM**

Mohaupt, Richard, German composer; b. Breslau, Sept. 14, 1904; d. Reichenau, Austria, July 3, 1957. He studied with J. Prüwer and R. Bilke. He began his musical career as an opera conductor, and he also gave concerts as a pianist. After the advent of the Nazi regime in 1933, he was compelled to leave Germany because his wife was Jewish. He settled in N.Y. in 1939, where he continued to compose and was also active as a teacher. In 1955 he returned to Europe.

WORKS: DRAMATIC: Opera: *Die Wirtin von Pinsk* (Dresden, Feb. 10, 1938); *Die Bremer Stadtmusikanten* (Bremen, June 15, 1949); *Double Trouble* (Louisville, Dec. 4, 1954); *Der grüne Kakadu* (Hamburg, Sept. 16, 1958). **Ballet:** *Die Gaunerstreiche der Courasche* (Berlin, Aug. 5, 1936); *Max und Moritz*, dance-burlesque (1945; Karlsruhe, Dec. 18, 1950); *Lysistrata* (1946; rev. for Orch. as *Der Weiberstreik von Athen*, 1955); *The Legend of the Charlatan*, mimodrama (1949). Also incidental music. **ORCH.:** *Stadtpfeifermusik* (1939; London, July 7, 1946; rev. for Winds, 1953); Sym., *Rhythmus und Variationen* (1940; N.Y., March 5, 1942); Concerto (1942); Violin Concerto (1945; N.Y., April 29, 1954); Banchetto musicale for 12 Instruments and Orch. (1955); *Offenbachiana* (1955). **CHAMBER:** Piano pieces and other works. **VOCAL:** *Trilogy* for Alto and Orch. (1951); *Bucolica* for 4 Soloists, Chorus, and Orch. (1955); lieder; children's songs.—**NS/LK/DM**

Moholo, Louis (T.), jazz/rock drummer, percussionist, singer, cellist; b. Cape Town, South Africa,

March 10, 1940. Moholo has played in a variety of styles, from mainstream to free to rock. His father played piano, and his mother and sisters sang; he was self-taught on drums. After working with Early Mabuza, he co-founded the Cordettes (1956). He played with saxophonist Ronnie Beer's Swinging City Six then joined Chris McGregor's Blue Notes, playing Antibes (1964), and eventually in London in 1965. He worked with Steve Lacy in South America, visited the U.S., then returned to London in 1967. An integral part of the Brotherhood of Breath during 1970s, he also worked with the Mike Osborne Trio, Stan Tracey's Open Circle Quartet, Elton Dean, Harry Miller's Isipingo, Dudu Pukwana's Spear, Keith Tippett, etc. From the late 1970s, he played extensively in Europe, with Misha Mengelberg, Irene Schweizer, Peter Brotzmann, Archie Shepp, John Tchicai, Roswell Rudd, etc. International touring included visits to Africa and the U.S. From the 1980s, he worked with guitarist Russell Bermin, conga player Thebe Lipere, and Keith Tippett in various line-ups and guested with Cecil Taylor in Berlin. From the 1970s through the 1990s, he has also regularly led his own line-ups: Spirits Rejoice, African Drum Ensemble, Culture Shock and Viva Le Black.

DISC.: *Spirits Rejoice* (1978); *Tern* (1982); *Vive La Black* (1988); *Exile* (1990); *Freedom Tour: Live in South Africa* (1995). —JC-B/LP

Moiseiwitsch, Benno, outstanding Russian-born English pianist; b. Odessa, Feb. 22, 1890; d. London, April 9, 1963. He studied in Odessa, and won the Anton Rubinstein prize at the age of 9; then went to Vienna at 14 and studied with Leschetizky. He made his British debut in Reading on Oct. 1, 1908, and subsequently made London his home; made his American debut in N.Y. on Nov. 29, 1919, and toured many times in Australia, India, Japan, etc. He became a naturalized British subject in 1937. He represented the traditional school of piano playing, excelling mostly in Romantic music.

BIBL.: M. Moiseiwitsch, *B. M.* (London, 1965). —NS/LK/DM

Mojsisovics (-Mojsvár), Roderich, Edler von, Austrian composer; b. Graz, May 10, 1877; d. there, March 30, 1953. He studied with Degner in Graz, with Wüllner and Klauwell at the Cologne Cons., and with Thuille in Munich. He conducted a choral group in Brünn (1903–07), then taught in various Austrian towns. He became director of the Graz Steiermarkische Musikverein (1912). It became the Graz Cons. in 1920, and he remained as director until 1931. Fom 1932 to 1935 he taught music history at the Univ. of Graz. He then lectured at the Trapp Cons. in Munich (1935–41) and at the Mannheim Hochschule für Musik (1941–44). He returned to teach at the Graz Cons. from 1945 to 1948. He publ. *Bach-Probleme* (Würzburg, 1931). As a composer, he followed Regerian precepts. Among his stage works were 5 operas, a melodrama, a musical comedy, 5 syms.; a symphonic poem, *Stella*, 2 overtures, Violin Concerto, 3 string quartets and other chamber music, choral works, songs, piano pieces, and organ works.

BIBL.: K. Haidmayer, *R. v.M.: Leben und Werk* (diss., Univ. of Graz, 1951).—NS/LK/DM

Mokranjac, Stevan (Stojanović), Serbian conductor, musicologist, teacher, and composer; b. Negotin, Jan. 9, 1856; d. Skoplje, Sept. 28, 1914. He studied in Munich with Rheinberger, and in Leipzig with Jadassohn and Reinecke. In 1887 he became director of the Serbian Choral Soc. in Belgrade, with which he also toured. In 1899 he founded the Serbian Music School in Belgrade, and remained its director until his death. He wrote 15 choral rhapsodies on Serbian and Macedonian melodies, a Liturgy of St. John Chrysostomos (publ. in Leipzig, 1901; also with an Eng. tr. as *Serbian Liturgy*, London, 1919), and a Funeral Service ("Opelo"). He compiled a large collection of church anthems according to the Serbian usage and derived from early Byzantine modes; wrote a collection of songs for Mixed Chorus, *Rukoveti* (Bouquets).

BIBL.: P. Konjović, *S.S. M.* (Belgrade, 1956).—NS/LK/DM

Mokranjac, Vasilije, Serbian composer; b. Belgrade, Sept. 11, 1923; d. there, May 27, 1984. He was brought up in a musical enviroment (his father was a cellist, a nephew of **Stevan Mokranjać**). He studied piano and composition at the Belgrade Academy of Music. His early works are Romantic in style, but he gradually began experimenting with serial techniques, while safeguarding the basic tonal connotations.

WORKS: Incidental music; *Dramatic Overture* (1950); Concertino for Piano, 2 Harps, and Strings (Belgrade, March 15, 1960); 5 syms.: No. 1 (Belgrade, Feb. 2, 1962), No. 2 (Belgrade, April 1, 1966), No. 3 (Belgrade, Oct. 25, 1968), No. 4 (1972), and No. 5 (1979); *Lyrical Poem* for Orch. (1974); chamber music; piano pieces.—NS/LK/DM

Molchanov, Kirill (Vladimirovich), Russian composer; b. Moscow, Sept. 7, 1922; d. there, March 14, 1982. He was attached to the Red Army Ensemble of Song and Dance during World War II, and after demobilization, he studied composition with Anatoly Alexandrov at the Moscow Cons., graduating in 1949. From 1973 to 1975 he served as director of the Bolshoi Theater in Moscow and accompanied it on its American tour in 1975. He was primarily an opera composer, his musical style faithfully following the precepts of socialist realism. His most successful work, the opera *The Dawns Are Quiet Here*, to his own libretto depicting the Russian struggle against the Nazis, was first performed at the Bolshoi Theater on April 11, 1975. It became the melodramatic event of the year, accompanied by an unabashed display of tearful emotion; however, its American performance during the visit of the Bolshoi Theater to N.Y. in June 1975 met with a disdainful dismissal on the part of the critics.

WORKS: DRAMATIC: Opera: *The Stone Flower* (Moscow, Dec. 2, 1950); *Dawn* (1956); *Romeo, Juliet, and Darkness* (1963); *The Unknown Soldier* (1967); *A Woman of Russia* (1969); *The Dawns Are Quiet Here* (Moscow, April 11, 1975). ORCH.: 3 piano concertos (1945, 1947, 1953). VOCAL: *Song of Friendship*, cantata (1955); *Black Box*, suite for Voice, Recitation, and Piano (1968).

BIBL.: Y. Korev, *K. M.* (Moscow, 1971).—NS/LK/DM

Moldenhauer, Hans, German-American musicologist; b. Mainz, Dec. 13, 1906; d. Spokane, Wash., Oct. 19, 1987. He studied music with Dressel, Zuckmayer, and Rosbaud in Mainz, where he was active as a pianist and choral conductor. In 1938 he went to the U.S., and settled in Spokane, Wash. As an expert alpinist, he served in the U.S. Mountain Troops during World War II. He founded the Spokane Cons. (1942), incorporating it as an educational institution in 1946; also continued his own studies at Whitworth Coll. there (B.A., 1945) and at the Chicago Musical Coll. of Roosevelt Univ. (D.F.A., 1951). With his wife, the pianist Rosaleen Moldenhauer (1926–82), he inaugurated a series of radio broadcasts of 2-piano music; the outgrowth of this was the publication of his valuable book *Duo-Pianism* (Chicago, 1950). As a music reseacher, he became profoundly interested in the life and works of Webern; he organized 6 international Webern festivals, in Seattle (1962), Salzburg (1965), Buffalo (1966), at Dartmouth Coll., Hanover, N.H. (1968), in Vienna (1972), and at La. State Univ., Baton Rouge (1976). His major achievement in research was the formation of the Moldenhauer Archives ("Music History from Primary Sources"), embodying a collection of some 10,000 musical autographs, original MSS, correspondence, etc., of unique importance to musical biography. Particularly rich is the MS collection of works of Webern, including some newly discovered works; for this accomplishment, Moldenhauer was awarded in 1970 the Austrian Cross of Honor for Science and Art. In 1988 the archives became a part of the Library of Congress in Washington, D.C. Moldenhauer's publications concerning Webern include *The Death of Anton Webern: A Drama in Documents* (N.Y., 1961), ed. with D. Irvine, *Anton von Webern: Perspectives: 1st Webern Festival, Seattle 1962* (Seattle, 1966; catalog of the Webern Archive), *Anton von Webern: Sketches 1926–1945* (N.Y., 1968), and, with R. Moldenhauer, *Anton von Webern: Chronicle of His Life and Work* (N.Y., 1978). Moldenhauer suffered from Retinitis pigmentosa, and became totally blind in 1980. He remarried in 1982, a few months after his first wife's death.—**NS/LK/DM**

Moldovan, Mihai, Romanian composer; b. Dej, Nov. 5, 1937; d. Medgidia, Sept. 11, 1981. He studied with Toduța and Comes at the Cluj Cons. (1956–59) and with Vancea, Vieru, and Jora at the Bucharest Cons. (1959–62). He was active in various branches of Romanian radio and television. In his music, Moldovan fused a Romanian ethos with modern harmonic textures.

WORKS: DRAMATIC: O p e r a : *Trepte ale istoriei* (1972); *Micul prinț* (1977–78). ORCH.: Oboe Concerto (1964); *Texturi* (1967); *Poem* for Ondes Martenot and Chamber Orch. (1967); *Vitralii* (Stained Glass Windows; 1968); *Scoarțe* (Tapestry; 1969); *Tulnice* for 4 Flutes, 8 Horns, Harp, 4 Cellos, 4 Double Basses, and Percussion (1971); *Sinfonia* for Strings (1972); Concerto for Double Bass and Orch. (1973); *Cantemirian* (1976); *Omagiu lui Anton Pann* (1976); *Rezonante* (1976); *Memoria Putnei* for Strings (1978). CHAMBER: Violin Sonatina (1967); 2 string quartets (1968, 1978); *Incantations* for Clarinet and Piano (1968); *Cadenza I* for Trombone and Percussion, *II* for Double Bass, *III* for Flute and Percussion (all 1971), and *V* for Cello and

Trumpet (1980); *Imaginati-vă un spectacol Kabuki* for Chamber Ensemble (1978). VOCAL: C a n t a t a s : *Soare al păcii* (Sun of Peace; 1962); *Prefigurarea primăverii*, chamber cantata (1962); *Bocet* (1963); *6 stări de nuanță* (1966); *Cintare omului* (1967); *Luceafăru de ziua* (1977). O t h e r : *Rituale*, suite for Soprano and Orch. (1963); *Cîntece străbune* (Ancient Songs) for Soprano, Flute, Clarinet, Horn, Trumpet, Trombone, Piano, Vibraphone, Xylophone, and String Quintet (1972).—**NS/LK/DM**

Moldoveanu, Vasile, Romanian tenor; b. Konstanza, Oct. 6, 1935. He was a student of Badescu in Bucharest, where he made his operatic debut in 1966 as Rinuccio. In 1972 he made his first appearance in Stuttgart as Edgardo, and then sang Alfredo at the Vienna State Opera and Rodolfo at the Bavarian State Opera in Munich in 1976. In 1977 he sang at the Deutsche Oper in Berlin and at the Chicago Lyric Opera, and on May 19 of that year he made his Metropolitan Opera debut in N.Y. as Rodolfo. He appeared as Don Carlos at the Hamburg State Opera in 1978, and sang that role at his debut at London's Covent Garden in 1979. His later engagements took him to Zürich (1980), Monte Carlo (1982), Nice (1988), Rome (1990), and other European music centers.—**NS/LK/DM**

Molinari, Bernardino, eminent Italian conductor; b. Rome, April 11, 1880; d. there, Dec. 25, 1952. He studied with Falchi and Renzi at Rome's Liceo di Santa Cecilia (graduated, 1902). He was artistic director of Rome's Augusteo Orch. (1912–43); also conducted throughout Europe and South America. In 1928 he made his American debut with the N.Y. Phil., which he conducted again during the 1929–30 and 1930–31 seasons; he also appeared with other American orchs. He was head of the advanced conducting class at Rome's Accademia di Santa Cecilia (from 1936), serving as a prof. there (from 1939). Molinari championed the modern Italian school, and brought out many works by Respighi, Malipiero, and other outstanding Italian composers. He publ. a new ed. of Monteverdi's *Sonata sopra Sonata Maria* (1919), concert transcriptions of Carissimi's oratorio *Giona*, Vivaldi's *Le quattro stagioni* et al., and also orchestrated Debussy's *L'Isle joyeuse*.

BIBL.: E. Mucci, *B. M.* (Lanciano, 1941).—**NS/LK/DM**

Molinari-Pradelli, Francesco, Italian conductor; b. Bologna, July 4, 1911; d. Marano di Castenaso, Aug. 7, 1996. He studied with d'Ivaldi and Nordio in Bologna, and with Molinari at the Accademia di Santa Cecilia in Rome. In 1938 he launched his career as a conductor; in 1939 he appeared for the first time as an opera conductor, leading *L'elisir d'amore* in Bologna. He conducted at Milan's La Scala from 1946; made his first appearance at London's Covent Garden in 1955, at the San Francisco Opera in 1957, and at the Vienna State Opera in 1959. On Feb. 7, 1966, he made his Metropolitan Opera debut in N.Y. conducting *Un ballo in maschera*, and remained on the company's roster until 1973. He was also active as a pianist. He was best known as an interpreter of the Italian operatic repertoire.—**NS/LK/DM**

Molinaro, Simone, Italian composer; b. c. 1565; d. Genoa, 1615. He received training from his uncle, G. de la Gostena, whom he succeeded as maestro di cappella at S. Lorenzo in Genoa about 1602. His lutebook (Venice, 1599), which includes dances, fantasias, and arrangements, reveals him to have been an adept composer for the instrument. In addition, he publ. 4 further vols. of secular vocal music (1595–1615) and 9 vols. of sacred vocal music (1597–1616; 2 not extant).—**LK/DM**

Molique, (Wilhelm) Bernhard, noted German violinist, teacher, and composer; b. Nuremburg, Oct. 7, 1802; d. Cannstadt, near Stuttgart, May 10, 1869. He first studied with his father, making his first public appearance when he was 6. After some lessons with Spohr (1815), he studied with Rovelli in Munich (1816–17). He made his formal debut in Vienna on Dec. 28, 1817, and then became a member of the orch. of the Theater an der Wien. He was made concertmaster of the Munich Court Orch. (1820) and then of the Stuttgart orch., being granted the title of Musikdirektor. He won fame abroad with extended tours in the Netherlands, Russia, England, and France. The political crisis of 1848 caused him to settle in London, where he was prof. of composition at the Royal Coll. of Music (1861–66). After giving his farewell concert at St. James's Hall (May 3, 1866), he retired to Cannstadt. His works include 6 violin concertos (1827–46), 8 string quartets (1841–53), pieces for violin and piano and for violin and flute, fantasias, rondos, and other works for solo violin, and many songs.

BIBL.: F. Schröder, *B. M. und seine Instrumentalkompositionen* (Stuttgart, 1923).—**NS/LK/DM**

Molitor, Raphael, German musicologist; b. Sigmaringen, Feb. 2, 1873; d. Beuron, Oct. 14, 1948. He was the son of Johann Baptist Molitor, a cathedral organist. He studied philosophy and theology in the Benedictine Monastery of Beuron, and was ordained a priest in 1897. He lectured there on canon law (1898–1904), and in 1904 was appointed a member of the advisory board of the Editio Vaticana. He was one of the foremost authorities on Gregorian chant.—**NS/LK/DM**

Moll, Kurt, outstanding German bass; b. Buir, near Cologne, April 11, 1938. He learned to play the guitar and cello and sang in a school choir in his youth; then studied voice at the Cologne Hochschule für Musik and with Emmy Müller. After singing minor roles at the Cologne Opera (1958–61), he sang in Aachen (1961–63), Mainz (1963–66), and Wuppertal (1966–69); subsequently pursued a career of great distinction, appearing regularly in Hamburg, Bayreuth, Salzburg, Vienna, Paris, Milan, and London. He made his U.S. debut as Gurnemanz at the San Francisco Opera in 1974; on Sept. 18, 1978, came his Metropolitan Opera debut in N.Y., in which he essayed the role of the Landgrave; he subsequently appeared there regularly. He made his first appearance at the Chicago Lyric Opera as Daland in 1983. In 1984 he toured Japan with the Hamburg State Opera. He portrayed Osmin at London's Covent Garden in 1987, and then sang Gurnemanz at the San Francisco Opera in 1988. In 1990 he was engaged as the Commendatore at the Metropolitan Opera, and returned there in 1992 as Gurnemanz. He sang Pogner at the Munich Festival in 1997. He also sang widely as a concert artist and recitalist; made his North American recital debut at N.Y.'s Carnegie Hall in 1984. Among his other notable roles are the Commendatore, Sarastro, King Marke, Pogner, Nicolai's Falstaff, and Baron Ochs. —**NS/LK/DM**

Möllendorff, Willi von, German pianist and composer; b. Berlin, Feb. 28, 1872; d. Stettin, April 27, 1934. He studied with Bargiel at the Berlin Hochschule für Musik (1891–93), and was subsequently active as a pianist and theater conductor in Giessen, Berlin, and Stettin. He was known especially for his experimentation with quarter-tones, for the exposition of which he invented a bichromatic harmonium with a new keyboard. For this instrument he composed an *Adagio religioso* (with Cello Solo) as well as *5 kleine Stücke*. In addition, he wrote operas, a ballet, 2 syms., choral works, etc.—**NS/LK/DM**

Mollenhauer, Eduard, German-American violinist and composer, uncle of **Emil Mollenhauer**; b. Erfurt, April 12, 1827; d. Owatonna, Minn., May 7, 1914. He was a violin pupil of Ernst (1841) and Spohr (1843). After a brief concert career in Germany, he went to London, where he joined Jullien's Orch., of which an older brother, Friedrich Mollenhauer (1818–85), also a violinist, was a member. After a tour with Jullien's Orch. in the U.S. (1853), the brothers settled in N.Y. as teachers, and Eduard also appeared as a soloist with the N.Y. Phil. He wrote the operas *The Corsican Bride* (N.Y., 1861) and *Manhattan Beach, or Love among the Breakers* (1878), 3 syms., a Violin Concerto, solo pieces for violin, and songs. Another brother, Henry Mollenhauer (b. Erfurt, Sept. 10, 1825; d. Brooklyn, N.Y., Dec. 28, 1889), was a cellist and teacher. He was a member of the Stockholm Royal Orch. (1853), and toured the U.S. with Thalberg, Gottschalk, and Carlotta Patti (1856–58). He then settled in Brooklyn as a teacher, and later founded his own cons.—**NS/LK/DM**

Mollenhauer, Emil, American violinist and conductor, nephew of **Eduard Mollenhauer**; b. Brooklyn, Aug. 4, 1855; d. Boston, Dec. 10, 1927. He studied violin with his father, Friedrich Mollenhauer, and in 1872 entered Theodore Thomas's orch. He also played with the N.Y. Sym. Soc. He then went to Boston, where he played in the orch. of the Bijou Theatre (1883–84) and the Boston Sym. Orch. (1884–89). He then helped to found the Boston Festival Orch., serving as its concertmaster (1889–92) and its conductor (1892–1914); also conducted the German Band (from 1889; renamed as the Boston Band, 1904), the Boston Municipal Band, and the People's Sym. Orch. He likewise was conductor of the Handel and Haydn Soc. (1899–1927).—**NS/LK/DM**

Moller, John Christopher (real name, **Johann Christoph Möller**), German-American organist, music publisher, concert manager, and composer; b. in Germany, 1755; d. N.Y., Sept. 21, 1803. He was active in London (c. 1775–85), then emigrated to the U.S. In 1790 he appeared in N.Y. as a harpsichordist, but left immediately after his concerts for Philadelphia, where he became organist and composer for the Zion German Lutheran Church. From 1790 to 1793 he took part in the City Concerts (with Reinagle, and later Henri Capron) as both manager and performer. Apparently he was also proficient as a pianist, violinist, and performer on the glass harmonica. In 1793 he was joint proprietor, with Capron, of a music store, which he also used as a music school. Because of the destruction of the Zion Church by fire on Dec. 26, 1794, Moller's income was severely reduced, and in 1795 he returned to N.Y. He was organist of the Trinity Episcopal Church, and also active as a concert manager. In 1796 he succeeded Hewitt in the management of the N.Y.C. Concerts with the Van Hagens. His attempt to continue this subscription series by himself, when Van Hagen later left for Boston, was unsuccessful.

WORKS: 6 quartettos for Strings (London, c. 1775); 6 sonatas for Fortepiano or Harpsichord, Violin, and Cello (London, c. 1775); 6 sonatas for Harpsichord or Pianoforte, Violin, and Cello ad libitum (London, c. 1782); 2 keyboard concertos; *Dank und Gebet,* cantata (1794); various didactic works; etc.

BIBL.: E. Wolf, *Lutheran Church Music in America during the Eighteenth and Early Nineteenth Centuries* (diss., Univ. of Ill., 1960; includes text and music of *Dank und Gebet*); R. Stetzel, *J.C. M. (1755–1803) and His Role in Early American Music* (diss., Univ. of Iowa, 1965; includes complete list of works).—**NS/LK/DM**

Möller, M(athias) P(eter), Danish-American organ builder; b. Bornholm, Sept. 29, 1855; d. Hagerstown, Md., April 13, 1937. He was trained as a mechanic before emigrating to the U.S. (1872). After working for the organ-building firm of Derrick & Felgemaker in Erie, Pa., he settled in Hagerstown and founded his own company (1880), which became the largest manufacturer of pipe organs in the U.S. He installed organs throughout the U.S. and made a number of improvements in their construction; later pioneered the development of small, self-contained organs. After his death, his son, M.P. Möller Jr. (1902–61), served as president of the company; after his death, it was run by other descendants of the founder. Among its notable modern organs are those in the National Shrine of the Immaculate Conception in Washington, D.C. (1965), in Heinz Chapel at the Univ. of Pittsburgh (1970), and at Orchestra Hall in Chicago (1981).—**NS/LK/DM**

Molnár, Antal, distinguished Hungarian musicologist and composer; b. Budapest, Jan. 7, 1890; d. there, Dec. 7, 1983. He was a pupil in composition of Herzfeld at the Budapest Academy of Music (1907–10). He was a violist in the Waldbauer String Quartet (1910–13) and the Dohnányi-Hubay Piano Quartet (1915–17). After teaching music history and solfège at the Budapest Music School (1912–18), he was a prof. at the Budapest Academy of Music (1919–59), where he taught courses in music history, theory, solfège, and chamber music. In 1914 he received the Franz Joseph Prize, in 1957 the Kossuth Prize, and in 1970 was made

an Eminent Artist by the Hungarian government.

WRITINGS (all publ. in Budapest): *A zenetörténet szelleme* (The Spirit of the History of Music; 1914); *Bartók Béla—táncjátéka alkalmából* (Béla Bartók—On the Occasion of His Ballet; 1917); *Az európai zene története 1750-ig* (History of European Music Until 1750; 1920); *Bach és Händel zenéjének lelki alapjai* (Spiritual Basis of Bach's and Handel's Music; 1920); *Bartók Két elégiájának elemzése* (Two Eagles: An Analysis; 1921); *A zenetörténet: Szociológiája* (The Sociology of Music History; 1923); *Az uj zene* (New Music; 1925); *Az uj magyar zene* (The New Hungarian Music; 1926); *Bevezetés a zenekulturába* (Introduction to Musical Culture; 1928); *Bevezetés a mai muzsikába* (Introduction to Contemporary Music; 1929); *Fizika és muzsika* (Physics and Music; 1930); *A gyermek és a zene* (The Child and Music; 1931); *A zenetörténet megvilágitása* (Light on Musical History; 1933); *Zeneesztétika és szellemtudomány* (Musical Aesthetics and "Geisteswissenschaft"; 1935); *A ma zenéje* (Music Today; 1936); *Az óvodáskoru gyermek zenei nevelése* (Musical Education in the Nursery School; 1936); *Kodály Zoltán* (1936); *Zeneesztétika* (Musical Aesthetics; 1938); *Népszerü zeneesztétika* (Popular Musical Aesthetics; 1940); *Az uj muzsika szelleme* (The Spirit of the New Music; 1948); *Bartók müvészete, emlékezésekkel a müvész életére* (The Art of Bartók with Reminiscences of his Life; 1948); *Repertórium a barokk zene történetéhez* (Repertory of the History of Baroque Music; 1959); *Irások a zenéről* (Writings on Music; 1961); *A Léner- vonósnégyes* (The Léner Quartet; 1968); *A zeneszerző világa* (The World of the Composer; 1969); *Gyakorlati zeneesztétika* (Practical Musical Aesthetics; 1971); *Magamról—másokról* (On Myself—On Others; autobiography; 1974).

WORKS: DRAMATIC: *Savitri* (1912). **ORCH.:** *Grotesque March* (1914); Cello Concerto (1916); *Hungarian Dances* (1917); *Operetta Music* (1920); *Budapest,* overture (1921); *Past and Present* for Violin and Orch. (1923); Suite (1925); *Variations on a Hungarian Theme* (1928); *Hungarian Comedy Overture* (1928); *Kuruc Music* for 4 Tárogatós and Chamber Orch. (1936); *Overture to a Comedy* (1948); Harp Concerto (1952). **CHAMBER:** Various works, including piano pieces and organ music. **VOCAL:** Sacred and secular pieces; folk song arrangements. —**NS/LK/DM**

Molter, Johann Melchior, German composer; b. Tiefenort, near Eisenach, Feb. 10, 1696; d. Karlsruhe, Jan. 12, 1765. As a composer, he was typical of his Saxon contemporaries; he attended the Gymnasium in Eisenach, the same institution where Bach had studied earlier. His instrument was the violin, and it was as a violinist that he found employment with a succession of margraves. Like Bach, he was fertile and fathered 8 children. He was even more prolific as a composer than the 2 other great Saxons, Bach and Handel. He wrote something like 170 chamber syms. and is credited with 66 instrumental concertos, not to mention religious works. He traveled to Italy, where he perfected his art of virtuoso instrumental writing. He lived sufficiently long to be impressed by the elegant style of French Rococo music, and some of his works may be described as Gallic.—**NS/LK/DM**

Mombelli, Domenico, Italian tenor and composer; b. Villanova, Feb. 17, 1751; d. Bologna, March 15, 1835. He made appearances throughout Italy from 1780. In 1786 he married **Luisa Laschi,** and sang with her in

Vienna until 1788. After her death, he married Vincenza Vigarnò. She wrote the libretto for Rossini's first opera, *Demetrio e Polibio*, and her husband created its role of Demetrio (Rome, May 18, 1812). In 1816 he retired from the operatic stage and then was active as a voice teacher in Florence and Bologna.—NS/LK/DM

Momigny, Jérôme-Joseph de, Belgian-French music theorist, publisher, and composer; b. Philippeville, Namur, Jan. 20, 1762; d. Charenton, near Paris, Aug. 25, 1842. He studied music early in life, and at the age of 12 was already engaged as a church organist in St. Omer; in 1785 he went to Lyons. He became involved in the political struggle against the Jacobins in 1793. After their ouster, he was appointed provisional municipal officer, and took part in the resistance against the troops of the National Convention; when that enterprise failed, he fled to Switzerland. After the fall of Robespierre, he returned to Lyons. He then went to Paris, where he remained under Napoleon and the restoration of the monarchy. He opened there a successful music publishing business that flourished 1800–28 and publ. about 750 works by 153 composers, including a number of his own compositions and treatises on music, in which he claimed to have invented a new and unfailing system of theory and harmony. The titles alone of some of his tracts, containing such immoderate asseverations as "théorie neuve et générale," "seul système musical qui soit vraiment fondé et complet," "la seule vraie théorie de la musique," etc., reveal his uncommon faith in himself. He bolstered his self-assurance by such declarations as: there can exist only one true art of music; there is one and only one code of morals; there must be a sharp distinction between good and bad combinations of sounds, as there is between right and wrong in morality. By false analogy with order in music, he extolled monarchical rule and publ. numerous pamphlets in support of his reactionary convictions. Not finding a ready response from the authorities, he gradually sank into pathetic solitude and ended his days in an asylum. His tracts, both on music and on politics, are of interest only to investigators of material on depraved mental states, and his own compositions fell into utter desuetude during his lifetime. Riemann publ. a devastating review of Momigny's theories which drove a mortuary nail into his hopes for recognition.

WRITINGS (all publ. in Paris): *Méthode de piano* (1802); *La Première Année de leçons de pianoforte* (1802–3); *Cours complet d'harmonique et de composition* (1803–6; 2nd ed., 1808); *Exposé succinct du seul système musical qui soit partout d'accord avec la nature, avec la raison et avec la pratique* (1808); *Le Nouveau Solfège* (1808); *La Seule Vraie Théorie de la musique* (1821); *À l'Académie des Beaux-Arts* (1831); *Cours général de musique* (1834).

WORKS: DRAMATIC: O p e r a : *Le Baron de Felsheim* (Lyons, before 1800); *La Nouvelle Laitière* (before 1811); *Arlequin Cedrillon* (Paris, 1800). **OTHER:** Cantatas; songs; chamber music; piano pieces; arrangements and transcriptions.

BIBL.: A. Palm, *J.-J. d.M.* (diss., Univ. of Tübingen, 1957); idem, *J.-J. d.M.: Leben und Werk: Ein Beitrag zur Geschichte der Musiktheorie im 19. Jahrhundert* (Cologne, 1969).—NS/LK/DM

Mompou (Semblança), Federico, significant Spanish composer; b. Barcelona, April 16, 1893; d. there,

June 30, 1987. After preliminary studies at the Barcelona Cons., he went to Paris, where he studied piano with Philipp and composition with Rousseau. He returned to Barcelona in 1914, then was again in Paris from 1921 to 1941, when he once more went back to Spain. His music is inspired by Spanish and Catalan melos, but its harmonic and instrumental treatment is entirely modern. He wrote mostly for piano: *6 impressions intimes* (1911–14), *Scènes d'enfants* (1915), *Suburbis* (1916–17), *3 pessebres* (1918), *Cants magics* (1919), *Festes Llunyanes* (1920), *6 charmes* (1921), *3 variations* (1921), *Dialogues* (1923), *Canción y Danza* (1918–53), *10 preludes* (1927–51), *3 paisajes* (1942, 1947, 1960), *Música callada* (4 albums, 1959–67), and *Suite compostelana* for Guitar (1963). Other works include choral works and songs.

BIBL.: S. Kastner, *F. M.* (Madrid, 1946); A. Iglesias, *F. M.* (Madrid, 1977); C. Janés, *F. M.: Vida, textos, documentos* (Madrid, 1987); W. Mellers, *Le Jardin Parfume: Homage to F. M.* (1989); R. Paine, *Hispanic Traditions in Twentieth-Century Catalan Music with Particular Reference to Gerhard, M., and Montsalvatge* (N.Y. and London, 1989); *F.M. S. (1893–1987): Palau de la Música Catalana, 13 d'abril-13 de maig de 1993* (Madrid, 1993); L. Millet, R. Barce, and N. Bonet, *F. M.* (Barcelona, 1993).—NS/LK/DM

Monaco, Giancarlo del
See **Del Monaco, Giancarlo**

Monaco, James V., Italian-born American composer and pianist; b. Formia, Italy, Jan. 13, 1885; d. Beverly Hills, Calif., Oct. 16, 1945. Monaco made his name in N.Y. writing songs for Broadway, notably "You Made Me Love You." When sound films were introduced, he became one of the first composers to head west and contribute songs to the movies, gaining his greatest prominence through the songs he and Johnny Burke wrote for Bing Crosby's films of the late 1930s and early 1940s, among them "Only Forever."

Monaco immigrated to America with his family in 1891, initially settling in Albany, N.Y. A self-taught musician, he played piano in local cabarets during his teens. After his family moved to Chicago, he became known as a nightclub entertainer called Ragtime Jimmy.

Monaco moved to N.Y. in 1910, where he played at Café Bohemia and in Coney Island. His first published song (for which he wrote both words and music) was "Oh, Mr. Dream Man (Please Let Me Dream Some More)" (1911); it was featured in vaudeville by the trio of singing baseball pitchers Jack Coombs, Chief Bender, and Cy Morgan, and became a record hit for Ada Jones in 1912. By then he had had his first song interpolated into a Broadway show: "Row, Row, Row" (lyrics by William Jerome), used in *The Whirl of Society* (N.Y., March 5, 1912), where it was sung by emerging star Al Jolson. Widely recorded, it was a hit for Jones, for the team of Arthur Collins and Byron Harlan, and for The American Quartet. Meanwhile, the musical revue *Hanky-Panky* (N.Y., Aug. 5, 1912) introduced Monaco's "Oh! You Circus Day" (lyrics by Edith Maida Lessing), which also became a record hit for Collins and Harlan.

Jolson interpolated Monaco's "You Made Me Love You (I Didn't Want to Do It)" (lyrics by Joseph McCarthy) into *The Honeymoon Express* (N.Y., Feb. 6, 1913); it became one of Jolson's signature songs and the most widely heard song Monaco ever wrote. Jolson had a hit with it in 1913, as did William J. Halley. Bing Crosby made a chart record of it in 1940, and Harry James and His Orch. had a gold record with it in 1941. It was also featured in several motion pictures over the years, most notably in *Broadway Melody of 1938* (1937), in which a young Judy Garland, making only her second screen appearance, sang it to a picture of Clark Gable.

Monaco and McCarthy were a successful songwriting team over the next few years. Manuel Romain had a record hit with their "I Miss You Most of All" in 1914; that same year both Eddie Morton and the team of Jones and Billy Murray hit with "I'm Crying Just for You"; Irving Kaufman had a hit with "If We Can't Be the Same Old Sweethearts (We'll Just Be the Same Old Friends)" in 1915; and Jones had another hit with Monaco, Mc-Carthy, and Grant Clarke's "Beatrice Fairfax, Tell Me What to Do!" in 1916.

Monaco had not abandoned Broadway for the record stores, although he contributed interpolations rather than writing full scores. His and McCarthy's "While They Were Dancing Around" was used in the Jolson musical *Robinson Crusoe Jr.* (N.Y., Feb. 17, 1916), but a more successful insertion was "What Do You Want to Make Those Eyes at Me For?" (lyrics by McCarthy and Howard Johnson), which had been popularized in vaudeville by Emma Carus and was used in the musical *Follow Me* (N.Y., Nov. 29, 1916). It became a record hit for Jones and Murray the following year and later turned up in two 1940s films, *The Merry Monahans* and *Incendiary Blonde*, the latter leading to a 1945 chart record by the film's star, Betty Hutton.

Monaco's next successful song was the comic "Ten Little Bottles" (lyrics by Ballard MacDonald), which was a hit for Bert Williams in 1920. That same year "Caresses" (for which he wrote his own lyrics) was interpolated into the musical *Afgar* (N.Y., Nov. 8, 1920); it became a hit for Paul Whiteman and His Orch. in 1921. That year, Monaco also contributed to the revues *Snapshots of 1921* (N.Y., June 2, 1921) and *Ziegfeld Follies of 1921* (June 21, 1921), and in the fall Jolson introduced "Dirty Hands, Dirty Face" (lyrics by Edgar Leslie, Grant Clarke, and, supposedly, Jolson) in *Bombo* (N.Y., Oct. 1, 1921).

There were three hit recordings in 1923, one by Marion Harris, another by Irving Kaufman with Ben Selvin's Orch., and an instrumental version by Selvin's Orch. alone. Monaco's next few hits were reserved for singers and recording stars: "You Know You Belong to Somebody Else (So Why Don't You Leave Me Alone)" (lyrics by Eugene West) was introduced by Nora Bayes but became a hit record for Henry Burr in 1923; "Me and the Boy Friend" (lyrics by Sidney Clare) was a hit for Jane Green in 1925; and "The Only, Only One for Me" (music cowritten by Harry Warren, lyrics by Bud Green) was a hit for Gene Austin, also in 1925.

The film *The Jazz Singer* opened in N.Y. on Oct. 6, 1927. In it Jolson sang "Dirty Hands, Dirty Face," the first synchronized song performance in a motion picture. Jolson recorded the song in March 1928, and it was

a hit again by June. Meanwhile, Monaco contributed several songs to *Harry Delmar's Revels* (N.Y., Nov. 28, 1927), but his future as a songwriter was in record stores and movie theaters. His next hit was "Me and the Man in the Moon" (lyrics by Leslie), which was successfully recorded by Helen Kane, Ted Weems and His Orch., and Cliff Edwards in 1929.

By 1930, sound was an established fact in the movies, and the need for composers was great. Monaco, as the first composer whose music had been used in a sound film, was sought after by the studios. "Me and the Boy Friend" had been used in the MGM picture *Our Dancing Daughters* in 1928, but Fox gave him his first steady work. In addition to the three features on which he was credited as composer, *The Golden Calf, Not Damaged*, and *The Solid Gold Article*, he contributed songs to a remarkable 12 other films released by the company in 1930, most of which had lyrics by Cliff Friend.

The Fox contract may have been a one-year agreement, since Monaco's songs stopped turning up in the company's films after that year, although they were used by others. Warner Bros.' *Road to Singapore* (1931) included Monaco, Leslie, and Ned Washington's "Hand in Hand," while The Boswell Sisters sang Monaco and Leslie's "Crazy People" in Paramount's *The Big Broadcast* (1932), the first film to star Crosby.

Monaco continued to enjoy record hits with his songs in the early 1930s. "Lonesome Lover" (lyrics by Alfred Bryan) was a hit for Isham Jones and His Orch. in 1931; "You've Got Me in the Palm of Your Hand" (lyrics by Friend and Leslie) was successfully recorded by Gus Arnheim and His Orch. in 1932; and Jan Garber and His Orch., Glen Gray and the Casa Loma Orch., and Harry Reser's Orch. each recorded a hit version of "You're Gonna Lose Your Gal" (lyrics by Joe Young) at the end of 1933.

Monaco moved to Beverly Hills in 1936 and signed a contract with Paramount that gave him a plumb assignment: writing the music to Burke's lyrics for Crosby's pictures. As Crosby was the most successful recording artist in the country and among the most successful film stars and radio personalities as well, the job practically guaranteed Monaco a string of hits, and they were forthcoming. Shortly before the May 1938 opening of *Doctor Rhythm*, Crosby's recording of "On the Sentimental Side," a song featured in the film, became a Top Ten hit. *Sing, You Sinners*, Monaco's second assignment with Crosby, was in theaters in August, and by fall Crosby's recording of "I've Got a Pocketful of Dreams" from the picture was dueling with a competing version by Russ Morgan and His Orch. for the top of the hit parade. Crosby also scored a hit with the film's "Don't Let That Moon Get Away."

Monaco was not involved in the next Crosby film, *Paris Honeymoon* (1939), perhaps because he was on his own honeymoon, having married former *Ziegfeld Follies* girl and actress Virginia Case (real name, Esther Virginia Kaiss Greene) on Nov. 15, 1938. Crosby slyly alluded to the match in his next film, *East Side of Heaven*. Playing the part of a singing telephone messenger, he called up Mr. and Mrs. James Monaco, only to find them fighting. The film, released in April 1939, had the usual compliment of Monaco-Burke hits introduced and recorded by Crosby: the title song, "Sing a Song of Sunbeams," and "That Sly Old Gentleman (from Featherbed Lane)" were all successful.

Another three hits emerged from Monaco's fourth film with Crosby, *The Star Maker*, which appeared in August 1939. "An Apple for the Teacher" (on which Crosby duetted with Connee Boswell), "Go Fly a Kite," and "A Man and His Dream" were all in the hit parade in September and October. The only similarity between the 1931 film *Road to Singapore* and the identically titled film that opened in March 1940 was that Monaco worked on both. The later film, which marked the beginning of the successful series of films Crosby made with Bob Hope, produced a major Monaco-Burke-Crosby hit in "Too Romantic" and another success in "Sweet Potato Piper."

Monaco's sixth Crosby picture, *If I Had My Way*, resulted in three more hit records in June 1940: "April Played the Fiddle," "I Haven't Time to Be a Millionaire," and "Meet the Sun Half Way." The Monaco-Burke-Crosby team hit its peak with the songs from *Rhythm on the River*, which opened in August and featured the hits "That's for Me," "Only Forever," and "When the Moon Comes Over Madison Square." "Only Forever" topped the charts for weeks and inspired cover records by Tommy Dorsey and His Orch. and by Eddy Duchin and His Orch. before earning an Academy Award nomination.

Notwithstanding this success, Monaco had left Paramount, and thus Burke and Crosby, at the conclusion of his contract in the summer of 1940. He had already scored another hit: the title song from the upcoming Universal feature *Six Lessons from Madame La Zonga* (lyrics by Charles Newman) charted for Jimmy Dorsey and His Orch. and Charlie Barnet and His Orch. Still, suggestions that he abandoned the three-picture-a-year Crosby schedule due to failing health seem justified by his relative inactivity over the next couple of years.

Monaco placed an instrumental, "Romance and Rhumba," in the Carmen Miranda vehicle *Weekend in Havana* (1941), and enjoyed a modest hit in the fall of 1942 with "Ev'ry Night about This Time," which was recorded by the Ink Spots and by the orchestras of Jimmy Dorsey and Kay Kyser. But his next major film work did not come until 1943, when United Artists released the all-star *Stage Door Canteen*. Credited as composer, he wrote ten songs with lyrics by Al Dubin, including "We Mustn't Say Goodbye," which earned him his second Academy Award nomination.

In 1943, Monaco signed a two-year contract with 20th Century–Fox. He paired with lyricist Mack Gordon to write songs for the 1944 films *Irish Eyes Are Smiling; Pin-Up Girl*, including "Once Too Often," which became a chart record for Ella Fitzgerald; and *Sweet and Low-Down*, including "I'm Making Believe," which became a #1 gold-selling hit for Fitzgerald with the Ink Spots and was nominated for an Academy Award.

Monaco died of a heart attack just as "I Can't Begin to Tell You," his final film song, was appearing in *The Dolly Sisters*. It was also his final hit, as Crosby teamed with Carmen Cavallaro's Orch. for a #1 gold record. It garnered Top Ten hits for James in a version featuring the film's star, Betty Grable, on vocals, Andy Russell, and Sammy Kaye and His Orch. It was his fourth song to be nominated for an Academy Award.—WR

Monaco, Mario del
See **Del Monaco, Mario**

Monasterio, Jesús de, famous Spanish violinist and pedagogue; b. Potes, near Santander, March 21, 1836; d. Casar del Periedo, Sept. 28, 1903. A child prodigy, he began his training with his father and then studied in Valladolid. He played for the Queen in 1843, and she became his patroness. After making his debut in 1845 in Madrid at age 9, he studied at the Brussels Cons. with Bériot (violin) and Fétis (theory), graduating with the prix extraordinaire. He subsequently toured throughout Europe. He was made honorary violinist at Madrid's royal chapel (1854), prof. of violin (from 1857) and director (1894–97) at the Madrid Cons., and he conducted the Sociedad de Conciertos (1869–76), becoming influential in forming a taste for classical music in Spain. He publ. a number of violin pieces, including the popular *Adiós a la Alhambra*.

BIBL.: J. Alonso, *J. d.M.* (Santander, 1954).—NS/LK/DM

Moncayo García, José Pablo, Mexican composer and conductor; b. Guadalajara, June 29, 1912; d. Mexico City, June 16, 1958. He studied with Chávez at the Mexico City Cons. From 1932 he was a member of the Mexico Sym. Orch.; was conductor of the National Sym. Orch. (1949–52). In company with Ayala, Contreras, and Galindo (also pupils of Chávez), he formed the so-called Grupo de Los Cuatro for the purpose of furthering the cause of Mexican music.

WORKS: DRAMATIC: O p e r a : *La mulata de Córdoba* (Mexico City, Oct. 23, 1948). **ORCH.:** *Huapango* (1941); Sym. (1944); Sinfonietta (1945); *Homenaje a Cervantes* for 2 Oboes and Strings (Mexico City, Oct. 27, 1947); *Cumbres* (Louisville, June 12, 1954). **OTHER:** Choruses; piano pieces.—NS/LK/DM

Monckton, (John) Lionel (Alexander), English composer; b. London, Dec. 18, 1861; d. there, Feb. 15, 1924. He was educated at Oriel Coll., Oxford, where he first composed for productions of the univ. dramatic society. He was active as a drama and music critic before launching his career as a composer of musical comedies in London in 1891. With John Crook, he collaborated on his first musical, *Claude Du-Val* (Sept. 25, 1894). After contributing to successful scores by Ivan Caryll and Sidney Jones, he worked with Howard Talbot on *Kitty Grey* (Sept. 7, 1901). He then won success in his own right with the musicals *A Country Girl* (Jan. 18, 1902) and *The Cingalee* (May 14, 1904). Collaborating again with Talbot, he created his most outstanding work in *The Arcadians* (April 28, 1909), which was performed throughout the world to great acclaim. Further success followed with his *The Quaker Girl* (Nov. 5, 1910). Collaborating once more with Talbot, he produced *The Mousme* (Sept. 9, 1911). His final collaboration with Talbot brought forth the enormously successful *The Boy* (Sept. 14, 1917).—NS/LK/DM

Moncur, Grachan (Jr.), jazz bassist; father of Grachan Moncur III; b. Miami, Fla., Sept. 2, 1915. Grachan is the half-brother of Savoy Sultans' leader Al Cooper, and is best known for his work in that band. He began playing string bass, tuba, and trombone during his early teens. He worked with George Kelly's Band in Miami, then moved with his family to Newark, N.J. Following instruction from Milton Bauzea, he specialized on string bass. He began his professional career at the Star Ballroom, Newark, and subsequently worked with the Matinee Idols on Newark radio station. John Hammond heard a broadcast by this band and arranged for Grachan to take part in several all-star recordings. In 1937, he was a founder member of the Savoy Sultans and remained with the group until it disbanded in 1945. From autumn 1947, he led his own small band with pianist Ace Harris, then joined a band led by tenorist Joe Thomas (1948). He moved to Miami in the 1950s. During the late 1960s he worked regularly in the Myrtle Jones Trio in Miami Beach, Fla. He is best remembered for his recorded work with Teddy Wilson, Mildred Bailey, Billie Holiday, and other jazz performers.—JC/LP

Mondonville, Jean-Joseph Cassanéa de, distinguished French violinist, conductor, and composer; b. Narbonne (baptized), Dec. 25, 1711; d. Belleville, near Paris, Oct. 8, 1772. He assumed his wife's maiden name, de Mondonville. He played in the Holy Week program at the Concert Spirituel in Paris (1734), and after appearing at the Concert de Lille, he returned to Paris, where he was made violinist at the royal chapel and chamber (1739). He wrote motets for the Concert Spirituel, and was made sous-maître of the royal chapel (1740). He became intendant of the "musique de la chapelle" in Versailles (1744), as well as music director of the Concert Spirituel (1755–62). He composed numerous stage works, oratorios, grand motets, and instrumental pieces.

BIBL.: J.-J. Galibert, *J.-J.C. d.M.* (Narbonne, 1856); F. Hellouin, *M.: Sa vie et son oeuvre* (Paris, 1903); E. Borroff, *The Instrumental Works of J.-J.C. d.M.* (diss., Univ. of Mich., 1958).—NS/LK/DM

Monferrato, Natale, Italian organist, teacher, and composer; b. Venice, c. 1603; d. there, before April 23, 1685. He spent his entire life in Venice. After entering the priesthood, he was a singer (1639–47), vice-maestro di cappella (1647–76), and maestro di cappella (from 1676) at San Marco. He also taught at the Cons. dei Mendicanti and was active in a publing venture with Giuseppe Sala. Monferrato became best known as a composer of motets and Psalms.—LK/DM

Monfred, Avenir de, Russian composer of French descent; b. St. Petersburg, Sept. 17, 1903; d. Paris, April 11, 1974. He studied piano, organ, and composition at the Petrograd Cons., graduating in 1922. In 1924 he went to Paris and studied with d'Indy at the Schola Cantorum (1925–27). He promulgated an interesting theory of composition, "diatonic polymodality," expounded in detail in his book *The New Diatonic Modal Principle of Relative Music* (N.Y., 1970).

WORKS: DRAMATIC: *Suite New-yorkaise*, ballet (Monte Carlo, Nov. 19, 1956); film scores. **ORCH.:** *Rapsodie juive* (1926); *Vienna, 1850*, symphonic poem (1941); 2 syms. (1955, 1957); *Manhattan Sketches*, symphonic suite (1958). **CHAMBER:** 3 violin sonatas (1922, 1926, 1947); Cello Sonata (1938); String Quartet (1939); piano pieces; organ works. **VOCAL:** Choruses.—NS/LK/DM

Mongini, Pietro, admired Italian tenor; b. Rome, Oct. 29, 1828; d. Milan, April 27, 1874. He commenced his career as a bass, and then appeared as a tenor in Genoa by 1853. In 1855 he made his debut in Paris at the Théâtre-Italien as Edgardo in *Lucia di Lammermoor*. On March 11, 1858, he made his first appearance at Milan's La Scala as Arnold in *Guillaume Tell*. His London debut followed on April 25, 1859, at Drury Lane as Elvino in *La Sonnambula*. He subsequently appeared at Her Majesty's Theatre in London. On Oct. 24, 1868, he made his debut at London's Covent Garden as Gennaro in *Lucrezia Borgia*. On Dec. 24, 1871, he created the role of Radamès in *Aida* in Cairo. Among his other notable roles were Alvaro, John of Leyden, and Manrico.—NS/LK/DM

Moniuszko, Stanislaw, famous Polish composer; b. Ubiel, Minsk province, Russia, May 5, 1819; d. Warsaw, June 4, 1872. In 1827 his family went to Warsaw, where he studied piano and music with August Freyer; continued his training with Dominick Stefanowica in Minsk and with Rungenhagen in Berlin (1837). He went to Vilnius in 1840, where he served as organist at St. John's. He gained attention as a composer when he publ. vol. I of his *Śpiewnik domowy* (Songbook for Home Use; 1843), garnering the support of various Polish figures in the arts, and also winning the admiration of Glinka, Dargomizhsky, and Cui in Russia. On Jan. 1, 1848, a concert performance of the 2-act version of his opera *Halka* was given for the first time in Vilnius; after he expanded it to 4 acts, it was staged in Warsaw on Jan. 1, 1858, scoring a great success. He then settled in Warsaw (1859), becoming conductor of opera at the Grand Theater. He continued to compose for the stage, and also taught at the Music Inst. (from 1864). He publ. *Pamietnik do nauki harmonii* (Textbook on Harmony; 1871). Moniuszko holds a revered place in Polish music history as the outstanding composer of opera in his era; he also excelled as a composer of songs. A complete ed. of his works commenced publication in Kraków in 1965.

WORKS: DRAMATIC: O p e r a : *Halka* (1846–47; 2-act version, concert perf., Vilnius, Jan. 1, 1848; 4-act version, 1857; Warsaw, Jan. 1, 1858; *Sielanka* (Idyll; c. 1848); *Bettly* (Vilnius, May 20, 1852); *Flis* (The Raftsman; Warsaw, Sept. 24, 1858); *Rokiczana* (1858–59); *Hrabina* (The Countess; 1859; Warsaw, Feb. 7, 1860); *Verbum nobile* (Warsaw, Jan. 1, 1860); *Straszny dwór* (The Haunted Manor; 1861–64; Warsaw, Sept. 18, 1865); *Paria* (1859–69; Warsaw, Dec. 11, 1869); *Trea* (1872; unfinished). **O p - e r e t t a :** *Nocleg w Apeninach* (A Night's Lodging in the Apennines; Vilnius, 1839); *Ideal czyli Nowa Precioza* (Ideal or The New Preciosa; Vilnius, 1840); *Karmaniol czyli Francuzi lubi zartować* (Carmagnole or The French Like Joking; 1841); *Zólta szlafmyca* (The Yellow Nightcap; 1841); *Nowy Don Quichot czyli Sto szanlestw* (The New Don Quixote or 100 Follies; 1841; Lemberg, 1849); *Loteria* (The Lottery; Minsk, Nov. 1843); *Cyganie* (The Gypsies; 1850; Vilnius, May 20, 1852; rev. as *Jawnuta*,

Warsaw, June 5, 1860); *Beata* (1871; Warsaw, Feb. 2, 1872). **OTHER:** Incidental music to 14 plays; ballets. **ORCH.:** *Bajka* (The Fairy Tale), overture (Vilnius, May 1, 1848); *Kain*, overture (St. Petersburg, March 1856); *Polonaise de concert* (1866); *Uwertura wojenna* (Military Overture; Vilnius, March 19, 1857). **OTHER:** Chamber music; vocal works.

BIBL.: A. Walicki, *S. M.* (Warsaw, 1873); A. Poliński, *M.* (Kiev, 1914); H. Opieński, *S. M.: Zycie i dziela* (S. M.: Life and Works; Lwów, 1924); S. Niewiadomski, *S. M.* (Warsaw, 1928); F. Kecki, A *Catalogue of Musical Works of M. Karlowicz and S. M.* (Warsaw, 1936); Z. Jachimecki, *Muzyka kościelna Moniuszki* (M's Church Music; Warsaw, 1947); W. Rudziński, *S. M.* (Kraków, 1954; 4th ed., 1972); J. Prosnack, *S. M.* (Kraków, 1964; 2nd ed., 1969); W. Rudziński and M. Stokowska, eds., *S. M.: Listy zebrane* (S. M.: Collected Letters; Kraków, 1969); K. Mazur, *Pierwodruki S.a M.* (The Editions of M.'s Works; Warsaw, 1970). **—NS/LK/DM**

Monk, Meredith (Jane),

American composer, singer, and filmmaker; b. N.Y., Nov. 20, 1942. She studied eurythmics from an early age. She was educated at Sarah Lawrence Coll. (B.A., 1964), then was a pupil in voice of Vicki Starr, John Devers, and Jeanette Lovetri, in composition of Ruth Lloyd, Richard Averee, and Glenn Mack, and in piano of Gershon Konikow. She pursued an active career as a singer, filmmaker, director, choreographer, recording artist, and composer. In 1968 she organized The House in N.Y., a company devoted to interdisciplinary approaches to the arts; in 1978 she founded there her own vocal chamber ensemble, with which she toured widely in the U.S. and abroad. In 1972 and 1982 she held Guggenheim fellowships; received various ASCAP awards and many commissions; in 1995 she was awarded a MacArthur fellowship. Her unique soprano vocalizations employ a wide range of ethnic and avant-garde influences. As one of the first and most natural of performance artists, she developed a flexible, imaginative theatrical style influenced by dream narrative and physical movement.

WORKS: *16 Millimeter Earrings* for Voice and Guitar (1966); *Candy Bullets and Moon* for Voice, Electric Organ, Electric Bass, and Drums (1967; in collaboration with D. Preston); *Blueprint: Overload/Blueprint 2* for Voice, Echoplex, and Tape (1967); *Juice*, theater cantata for 85 Voices, Jew's Harp, and 2 Violins (1969); *A Raw Recital* for Voice and Electric Organ (1970); *Needle-Brain Lloyd and the Systems Kid* for 150 Voices, Electric Organ, Guitar, and Flute (1970); *Key*, album of invisible theater for Voice, Electric Organ, Vocal Quartet, Percussion, and Jew's Harp (1970–71); *Plainsong for Bill's Bojo* for Electric Organ (1971); *Vessel*, opera epic for 75 Voices, Electric Organ, Dulcimer, and Accordion (1971); *Paris* for Piano and Vocal Duet (1972); *Education of the Girlchild*, opera for 6 Voices, Electric Organ, and Piano (1972–73); *Our Lady of Late* for Voice and Wine Glass (1972–73); *Chacon* for 25 Voices, Piano, and Percussion (1974); *Anthology and Small Scroll* for Voice and Piano (1975); *Quarry*, opera for 38 Voices, 2 Pump Organs, 2 Soprano Recorders, and Tape (1976); *Venice/Milan* for 15 Voices and Piano, 4–Hands (1976); *Songs from the Hill* for Voice (1976–77); *Tablet* for 4 Voices, Piano, 4–Hands, and 2 Soprano Recorders (1977); *The Plateau Series* for 5 Voices and Tape (1977); *Dolmen Music* for 6 Voices, Cello, and Percussion (1979); *Recent Ruins* for 14 Voices, Tape, and Cello (1979); *Turtle Dreams (Waltz)* for 4 Voices and 2 Electric Organs (1980–81); *Specimen Days* for 14 Voices, Piano, and 2 Electric Organs (1981); *View No. 1* for Piano, Synthesizer, and Voice (1981) and *No. 2* for Voice and Synthesizer (1982); *Ellis Island* for 2 Pianos (1982); *Tokyo Cha-Cha* for 6 Voices and 2 Electric Organs (1983); *Engine Steps* for Tape Collage (1983); *2 Men Walking* for 3 Voices and Electric Organs (1983); *The Games* for 16 Voices, Synthesizer, Keyboards, Flemish Bagpipes, Bagpipes, Chinese Horn, and Rauschpfeife (1983); *Panda Chant I* for 4 Voices and *II* for 8 Voices (both 1984); *Graduation Song* for 16 Voices (1984); *Book of Days* for 25 Voices, Synthesizer, and Piano (1985); *Scared Song* for Voice, Synthesizer, and Piano (1986); *I Don't Know* for Voice and Piano (1986); *Double Fiesta* for Voice and 2 Pianos (1986); *String* for Voice (1986); *Window in 7's (for Nurit)* for Piano (1986); *Duet Behavior* for 2 Voices (1987); *The Ringing Place* for 9 Voices (1987); *Do You Be* for 10 Voices, 2 Pianos, Synthesizer, Violin, and Bagpipes (1987); *Book of Days*, film score for 10 Voices, Cello, Shawm, Synthesizer, Hammered Dulcimer, Bagpipe, and Hurdy Gurdy (1988); *Fayum Music* for Voice, Hammered Dulcimer, and Double Ocarina (1988); *Light Songs* for Voice (1988); *Raven* for Piano (1988); *Cat Song* for Voice (1988); *Parlour Games* for 2 Pianos (1988); *Waltz* for 2 Pianos (1988); *Processional* for Piano and Voice (1988); *Phantom Waltz* for 2 Pianos (1990); *Facing North* for 2 Voices and Tape (1990; in collaboration with R. Een); *Atlas*, opera (Houston, Feb. 22, 1991); *3 Heavens and Hells* for 4 Voices (1992); *Custom Made* for Piano and 1 or 2 Voices (1993); *American Archeology No. 1: Roosevelt Island* for 9 Voices, Organ, Bass, Medieval Drum, and Shawm (1994); *Volcano Songs* for Voice, Tape, and Piano (1994); *Nightfall* for 16 Voices (1995); *Denkai Krikiki Chants* for 4 Voices (1995); *Magic Frequencies*, chamber opera (1998).**—NS/LK/DM**

Monk, Thelonious (Sphere),

brilliant jazz pianist and bold and witty composer, father of T.S. Monk; b. Rocky Mount, N.C., Oct. 10, 1917; d. Englewood, N.J., Feb. 17, 1982. His first name is often misspelled "Thelonius"; the birth certificate says "Thelious Junior Monk" but this is probably an error for "Thelonious Monk Jr." His family moved to N.Y. when he was four, living on W. 63rd St.; later he attended the selective public Stuyvesant H.S., an indication that he must have been a good student. He began playing piano at age of 11; he accompanied his mother's singing at the local Baptist church. In the late 1930s, he performed with a travelling evangelist's show and also gigged in and around N.Y., working with Keg Purnell's quartet (c. 1939) prior to becoming house pianist at Minton's Playhouse in Harlem.

He was first recorded playing at Minton's in 1941 with Charlie Christian and Kenny Clarke. Monk also played with Don Byas, Roy Eldridge, and Helen Humes at Minton's; Cootie Williams recorded his composition "Round Midnight" that same year. After working with Kenny Clarke's small band at Kelly's Stable, N.Y. (late 1942), he played briefly with Lucky Millinder and Kermit "Scotty" Scott at Minton's (early 1943) and with Cootie Williams and Coleman Hawkins (1944, including his studio recording debut). Monk played with the Gillespie big band at the Spotlite (March–April 1946) and recorded for Blue Note under his own name beginning in 1947; he also led a quartet with Idrees Sulieman of which one broadcast survives, from 1948; the group also played at Minton's. The first recordings of many of his originals were the critical documents that began to make people aware of him.

Monk also recorded with Charlie Parker (1950) and Miles Davis and Sonny Rollins (both 1954). Because of the "cabaret card" law then in force, Monk was not able to undertake club engagements in N.Y. from 1951–57, after he was busted for drug possession. However, he kept active playing at small clubs around N.Y., at the Blue Note (Phil.) in October 1952, the Bee Hive in Chicago in 1955, at the Hi-Hat in Boston on a few occasions between 1949 and 1955, and reportedly in Baltimore, and visited Paris in 1954 where he recorded a solo album. On July 1957, he began an engagement at the Five Spot that lasted, with a few breaks, until the end of the year. On July 18 or 19, he added John Coltrane to his trio and this quartet created a sensation that boosted the careers of both men. Monk toured from then on, usually with his own quartet. He used Johnny Griffin during 1958; in October 1958 at the Five Spot, he commenced a long association with Charlie Rouse. He appeared with big bands in special concerts in 1959 at Town Hall and at Randall's Island of N.Y.; in December 1963 he appeared at Philharmonic Hall and 1964 at Carnegie Hall, with arrangements from Hall Overton because Monk did not orchestrate for big band. Steve Lacy was added for gigs in 1960, including three weeks opposite Coltrane at the Jazz Gallery in Manhattan in June–July.

By this time Monk was one of the best known and best selling artists in jazz. His name was invoked on TV in *The Many Loves of Dobie Gillis* to signify hipness. He toured Europe several times and visited Japan and Mexico, with television appearances in Japan (1963), Norway (1966), and France (1969). The latter includes a short interview that illustrates why he was considered impossible in such situations—he appears distracted, perhaps passively hostile to the whole enterprise and gives the shortest of answers. Columbia recorded him beginning in 1962, and he was a *Time* magazine cover subject in 1964. He toured Europe with an octet (his quartet plus Griffin, Phil Woods, Ray Copeland, and Jimmy Cleveland) as part of a George Wein package tour in 1967. In 1971 and 1972, he toured world with The Giants of Jazz with Dizzy Gillespie, Sonny Stitt, Kai Winding, Al McKibbon, and Blakey. Around this time, he also appeared with Blakey in Brooklyn.

Monk suffered from poor health and lived in seclusion from 1972, emerging only for special events. He was receiving Lithium treatment for manic depression at Gracie Square Hospital, a condition that was likely worsened by years of drug use that included heroin, amphetamines, and alcohol. In 1974, he performed with the N.Y. Jazz Repertory Company at Carnegie Hall, substituting for Barry Harris by making a surprise appearance just before the concert started. He appeared with a quartet at Newport, N.Y. in 1975 and at Carnegie Hall in 1976, his last public appearance. His activities were restricted in the late 1970s by immobility due apparently to increasing mental illness. He died at Englewood Hospital, where he spent the last 12 days of his life after suffering a cerebral hemorrhage.

His work was recorded by others before he became accepted as a leader and pianist in his own right. Seemingly influenced by Ellington, James P. Johnson, and perhaps Earl Hines, he in turn influenced Randy Weston, Elmo Hope, Mal Waldron, Herbie Nichols,

McCoy Tyner, Chick Corea, and many others, as well as non-pianists and composers such as Rollins, Coltrane, and Steve Lacy. Thelonious Monk's compositions are among the most played in jazz and have been the subject of an ever increasing number of tribute albums and concerts; his best known piece is probably the ballad "Round Midnight." He played piano with a hard attack and penchant for short, punchy phrases, with voicings that were sometimes disarmingly basic and spare and at others incorporated jangling dissonant notes. As a pianist he is sometimes underestimated because he doesn't play quick flowing lines in the mainstream tradition.

His compositions and playing shared a concern with developing and building motive ideas while swinging irresistibly. "Well You Needn't" and "I Mean You" are even named in "vocalese" fashion after the sound of their main motives. His solos on the same tunes, live in Paris in 1961, are playful, expressive, and powerfully swinging. When he comps behind the soloist (often he chooses not to) he creates distinctive and driving riffs, something none of the tributes have picked up on. As a composer he sometimes worked with existing chord progressions ("Just You, Just Me" "Evidence," "Sweet Georgia Brown," "Bright Mississippi," many blues pieces), and his performances of standards were unforgettable, but he often came up with unique and challenging original sequences. He also created highly unusual forms in such pieces as "Boo Boo's Birthday," and explored virtuosity in such dazzling lines as "Trinkle, Tinkle," "Gallop's Gallop," and "Four in One." Some pieces are named for family and friends; "Crepuscule with Nellie" (his wife), "Jackie-ing" (for his oldest niece, the first young person in the family to hang out in the clubs), "In Walked Bud" (for Powell), "Pannonica" (for the Nica Rothschild de Koenigswarter, a steady friend and supporter since the early 1950s).

As early as 1963, Steve Lacy ran a quartet whose main mission was to perform Monk's tunes. Thelonious was a group that Buell Neidlinger ran. The group Sphere, with Rouse, played many Monk tunes as well as others, and was active from 1981 or 1982, and in 1984 an all-star lineup of jazz and rock players cut "That's The Way I Feel Now"; numerous tributes have followed. The Beethoven Society became interested in Monk and with T.S. Jr. founded the Thelonious Monk Inst. which in the early 1990s began the first international jazz competition; it has helped launch the careers of Joshua Redman, Jackie Terrason, and others. The cul-de-sac on 63rd St. has been renamed "Thelonious Sphere Monk Circle." He was the subject of the documentaries "Straight No Chaser" (with much performance footage), "It's Monk's Time" (concert tribute), and "Thelonious Monk, American Composer."

DISC.: *More Genius* (1947); *Genius of Modern Music, Vol. 1* (1947); *Complete Genius* (1947); *Complete Blue Note Recordings* (1947); *Vibes Are On* (1948); *Thelonious Monk/Milt Jackson* (1948); *Genius of Modern Music, Vol. 2* (1951); *Thelonious Monk Trio* (1952); *Monk's Moods* (1952); *High Priest* (1952); *Blue Monk, Vol. 2* (1952); *Work* (1953); *We See* (1953); *Monk* (1953); *Thelonious Monk and Sonny Rollins* (1954); *Thelonious Monk* (1954); *Blue Monk, Vol. 1* (1954); *Pure Monk* (1955); *Plays Duke Ellington* (1955); *Unique Thelonious Monk* (1956); *Brilliant Corners* (1956);

Brilliance (1956); *Thelonious with John Coltrane* (1957); *Thelonious Himself* (1957); *Round Midnight* (1957); *N.Y. with Johnny Griffin* (1957); *Mulligan Meets Monk* (1957); *Monk's Music* (1957); *Thelonious in Action: Recorded* (1958); *Blues Five Spot* (1958); *Discovery! at the Five Spot* (1958); *Thelonious Monk Orch. at Town Hall* (1959); *In Person* (1959); *Five by Monk by Five* (1959); *Evidence* (1959); *Alone in San Francisco* (1959); *Thelonious Monk Quartet Plus Two* (1960); *At the Blackhawk* (1960); *Two Hours with Thelonious Monk* (1961); *April in Paris* (1961); *Thelonious Monk in Italy* (1961); *Monk in Italy* (1961); *Monk in France* (1961); *Monk in Bern* (1961); *Live in Stockholm* (1961); *First European Concert* (1961); *Monk's Dream* (1962); *Criss-Cross* (1962); *Always Know* (1962); *Tokyo Concerts* (1963); *Thelonious Monk 1963 in Japan* (1963); *Mysterioso* (1963); *Live at the Village Gate* (1963); *Big Band and Quartet in Concert* (1963); *Solo Monk* (1964); *Live in Paris at the Alhambra* (1964); *Live at the Jazz Workshop* (1964); *Live at the It Club* (1964); *It's Monk's Time* (1964); *Olympia* (1965); *Straight, No Chaser* (1966); *Live in Switzerland* (1966); *Underground* (1967); *On Tour in Europe* (1967); *Nonet: Live!* (1967); *Monk's Blues* (1968); *Something in Blue* (1971); *Man I Love* (1971); *London Collection, Vol. 1–3* (1971).

BIBL.: N. Hentoff, *Thelonious Monk* (N.Y., 1961); S. Isacoff, *Jazz Masters: Thelonious Monk* (N.Y., 1978); L. Bijl and F. Conte, *Monk on Record: A Discography of Thelonious Monk* (Amsterdam, 1982); T. Fitterling, *Thelonious Monk: Sein Leben, seine Musik, seine Schallplatten [Thelonious Monk: His Life and Music]* (Waakirchen, Germany,1987; rev. English edition, 1996); Y. Buin, *Thelonious Monk* (Paris, 1988); L. Wilde, *Monk* (Paris, 1996); L. Gourse, *Straight, No Chaser: The Life and Genius of T. M.* (N.Y., 1997); C. Raschka, *Mysterious Thelonious* (N.Y., 1997).—**LP/PK**

Monk, William Henry, English organist, choirmaster, music editor, and composer; b. London, March 16, 1823; d. there, March 1, 1889. He was a pupil of T. Adams, J.A. Hamilton, and G.A. Griesbach, and served as organist in various London churches. He taught music at King's Coll. in London, the School for the Indigent Blind, the National Training School, etc. He ed. for the Church of Scotland *The Book of Psalms in Metre, Scottish Hymnal, The Psalter,* and *Book of Anthems.* He was the music ed. of *Hymns, Ancient and Modern* (1861), for which he composed the tune for the beloved hymn *Abide with me.* He also composed many other popular hymn tunes, as well as anthems and service music, and likewise ed. collections of hymns and Psalms. —**NS/LK/DM**

Monkees, The, the "Pre-Fab" four pop-group created to exploit the success of The Beatles on record and film. **MEMBERSHIP:** Michael Nesmith, gtr., voc. (b. Houston, Tex., Dec. 30, 1942); Davy Jones, tamb., voc. (b. Manchester, England, Dec. 30, 1945); Peter Tork (Thorkelson), bs., voc. (b. Washington, D.C., Feb. 13, 1944); Michael "Mickey" Dolenz, drm., voc. (b. Tarzana, Calif., March 8, 1945).

The Monkees were created through auditions conducted by NBC television in September 1965. The principals were chosen from more than 400 applicants that included Stephen Stills and Jerry Yester. Mickey Dolenz had been a child actor, appearing in the TV series *Circus Boy,* using the name Mickey Braddock, from 1956 to 1958, and later was lead singer of The Missing Links. Davy Jones had been a racehorse jockey and appeared in the London and N.Y. productions of

the musical *Oliver* before unsuccessfully attempting a solo singing career. Both Peter Tork and Michael Nesmith had performed music professionally. Tork had played Greenwich Village coffeehouses, whereas Nesmith had done session work in Memphis for Stax/Volt Records and played in the duo Mike and John with John London in Los Angeles.

The Monkees television series debuted in September 1966, with Don Kirshner as musical supervisor. His songwriting staff provided the group with many of their hits, starting with Tommy Boyce and Bobby Hart's top hit "Last Train to Clarksville." The series proved enormously successful as the group continued to record with sessions musicians such as James Burton, Leon Russell, Glen Campbell, and Hal Blaine, scoring smash hits with Neil Diamond's "I'm a Believer" (backed with the major hit "I'm Not Your Steppin' Stone") and "A Little Bit Me, a Little Bit You." The members, led by Nesmith, were finally allowed to play their own instruments beginning with *Headquarters.*

Touring the U.S. in 1967, briefly with Jimi Hendrix as the opening act, The Monkees' fourth album yielded a smash hit with Carole King and Gerry Goffin's wry "Pleasant Valley Sunday," backed by the major hit "Words." *The Birds, the Bees and the Monkees* produced the top hit "Daydream Believer" (written by John Stewart) and the smash "Valleri" (by Boyce and Hart). The final episode of the television show was broadcast in March 1968 and the show was cancelled in June. Following the major hit "D. W. Washburn" (by Jerry Leiber and Mike Stoller), the group achieved only minor hits through 1970. The Monkees' late 1968 comedy film *Head,* produced by their television producer Bob Rafelson and Jack Nicholson, proved a commercial failure, although the soundtrack album contained some of the members' finest offerings, including Nesmith's "Circle Sky" and Tork's "Can You Dig It." Tork quit The Monkees in early 1969 and Nesmith left following *The Monkees Present,* which included his minor hit, "Listen to the Band." Only Dolenz and Jones remained for 1970's *Changes.* Dolenz and Jones resurfaced in 1975 and 1976 with songwriters Tommy Boyce and Bobby Hart for one album and tour.

Of the four Monkees, only Michael Nesmith was able to establish himself as a solo artist. The Paul Butterfield Blues Band recorded his "Mary, Mary" on their *East-West* album; Linda Ronstadt and The Stone Poneys scored their first and only major hit with his "Different Drum" in 1967; and The Nitty Gritty Dirt Band managed a minor hit with his "Some of Shelly's Blues" in 1971. After producing and conducting an instrumental album of his own songs for Dot while still a member of The Monkees, he signed with RCA in 1970 and formed The First National Band with old associate John London and steel guitarist Orville "Red" Rhodes. Regarded as one of the finest country-rock bands to emerge from Los Angeles, the group recorded two albums and scored a major hit in 1970 with Nesmith's haunting "Joanne." They subsequently fell into disarray during the recording of their third album, which was completed with legendary guitarist James Burton and keyboardist Glen D. Hardin, who were later members of

Emmylou Harris' Hot Band. Nesmith later formed the short-lived Second National Band and recorded the solo album *And the Hits Just Keep on Coming*, often regarded as his finest work, with stalwart Red Rhodes.

During 1972, Michael Nesmith founded his own label, Countryside, under the auspices of Elektra Records, but the label was later abandoned when David Geffen succeeded to the presidency of Elektra. After recording a final album for RCA with Red Rhodes, Nesmith allowed his contract to expire, purchased his old masters, and formed Pacific Arts Records in Carmel, Calif., in 1977. He recorded several albums for the label in the late 1970s and expanded the company's operation into the production of videos. His award-winning 1981 television special, *Elephant Parts*, was one of the first to be specifically aimed at the home VCR market, and his *Pop Clips*, for cable television's Nickelodeon network, provided the prototype for MTV months before the music network was launched. Nesmith further expanded into feature-length movies with 1983's *Timerider*, scoring his biggest film success with the cult favorite *Repo Man* in 1984. Other film, television, and video projects followed, although none proved particularly successful.

In 1986, Davy Jones, Peter Tork, and Mickey Dolenz reunited as The Monkees for a surprisingly successful national tour. Spurred on by MTV's airing of the group's television show and the reissue of their first six albums (including *Head*) on Rhino Records, the group was introduced to a new generation and enjoyed renewed popularity. Dolenz and Tork even scored a major hit with "That Was Then, This Is Now." In 1987, the three toured again and recorded all new songs for Rhino on *Pool It!*, which produced a minor hit with "Heart and Soul." In the 1990s, Mickey Dolenz recorded two children's albums and Nesmith returned to recording with Rio Records. Peter Tork recorded *Stranger Things Have Happened* for the small Beachwood label in 1994. All four original members of The Monkees reunited for 1996's *Justus* on Rhino Records and 1997's ABC-TV special *Hey, Hey It's the Monkees*. In the mid-1990s, Michael Nesmith's guitarist-son Jason was a member of Nancy Boy with Donovan's son Donovan Leitch Jr.

DISC.: THE MONKEES: *The Monkees* (1966); *More of The Monkees* (1967); *Monkees' Headquarters* (1967); *Pisces, Aquarius, Capricorn and Jones, Ltd.* (1967); *The Birds, The Bees and The Monkees* (1968); *Head* (soundtrack; 1968); *Instant Replay* (1969); *The Monkees Present* (1969); *Changes* (1970); *Barrel Full* (1971); *Live 1967* (1987); *Pool It!* (1987); *Justus* (1996). **DAVY JONES:** *David Jones* (1965); *Davy Jones* (1972). **DOLENZ, JONES, BOYCE AND HART:** *Dolenz, Jones, Boyce and Hart* (1976); *Concert in Japan* (1996). **MICHAEL NESMITH:** *The Wichita Train Whistle Sings* (1968); *And the Hits Just Keep on Comin'* (1972); *Pretty Much Your Standard Ranch Trash* (1973); *The Prison* (1974); *Rio* (1994); *From a Radio Engine to a Photon Wing* (1977); *Live at the Palais* (1978); *Infinite Rider on the Big Dogma* (1979); *Tropical Campfires* (1992); *The Garden* (1994). **MIKE NESMITH AND THE FIRST NATIONAL BAND:** *Magnetic South* (1970); *Loose Salute* (1970); *Nevada Fighter* (1971); *Michael Nesmith and The First National Band* (1993). **MICHAEL NESMITH AND THE SECOND NATIONAL BAND:**

Tantamount to Treason (1972). **MICKEY DOLENZ CHILDREN'S RECORD:** *Mickey Dolenz Puts You to Sleep* (1991); *Broadway Mickey* (1994). **PETER TORK:** *Stranger Things Have Happened* (1994).

WRITINGS: D. Jones, *They Made a Monkee out of Me* (1987); M. Dolenz and M. Bego, *I'm a Believer: My Life of Monkees, Music and Madness* (N.Y., 1993).

BIBL.: E. Lefcowitz, *The Monkees' Tale* (Berkeley, Calif., 1985, 1989); E. Reilly, M. McMannus, and B. Chadwick, *The Monkees: A Manufactured Image* (Ann Arbor, Mich., 1987).—BH

Monleone, Domenico, Italian opera composer; b. Genoa, Jan. 4, 1875; d. there, Jan. 15, 1942. He studied at the Milan Cons. From 1895 to 1901 he was active as a theater conductor in Amsterdam and in Vienna. He attracted attention by producing in Amsterdam (Feb. 5, 1907) an opera, *Cavalleria rusticana*, to a libretto by his brother Giovanni, on the same subject as Mascagni's celebrated work; after its first Italian performance (Turin, July 10, 1907), Mascagni's publisher, Sonzogno, brought a lawsuit against Monleone for infringement of copyright. Monleone was forced to change the title; his brother rewrote the libretto, and the opera was produced as *La Giostra dei falchi* (Florence, Feb. 18, 1914). Other operas were *Una novella di Boccaccio* (Genoa, May 26, 1909), *Alba eroica* (Genoa, May 5, 1910), *Arabesca* (Rome, March 11, 1913; won 1st prize at the competition of the City of Rome), *Suona la ritrata* (Milan, May 23, 1916), *Il mistero* (Venice, May 7, 1921), *Fauvette* (Genoa, March 2, 1926), and *La ronda di notte* (Genoa, March 6, 1933); also an opera in Genovese dialect, *Scheuggio Campann-a* (Genoa, March 12, 1928). For some of his works he used the pseudonym W. di Stolzing. —NS/LK/DM

Monn (originally, **Mann**), **Johann Christoph,** Austrian pianist, teacher, and composer, brother of **Matthias Georg Monn**; b. 1726; d. Vienna, June 24, 1782. He served Count Kinsky as a music teacher in Prague (1750), and later settled in Vienna as a keyboard teacher. He wrote 6 syms., 3 piano concertos (also attributed to his brother), 10 divertimentos a 3 and a divertimento for Violin and Bass, and various keyboard works, including 8 sonatas, 20 minuets and trios, and a ballo.—NS/LK/DM

Monn, Matthias Georg or **Georg Matthias** (born **Johann Georg Mann**), Austrian organist and composer, brother of **Johann Christoph Monn**; b. Vienna, April 9, 1717; d. there, Oct. 3, 1750. He became organist of Vienna's Karlskirche about 1738. His instrumental music marks a transition from the Baroque to the new style perfected by the composers of the Mannheim school. See K. Horwitz and K. Riedel, eds., *Wiener Instrumentalmusik vor und um 1750*, I, Denkmäler der Tonkunst in Österreich, XXXI, Jg. XIX/2 (1908), and W. Fischer, ed., II, ibid., XXXIX, Jg. IXI/2 (1912).

WORKS: 21 syms. (several not extant; a Sym. in E-flat major, formerly attributed to him, is now known to be by F. Pokorny); 7 harpsichord concertos; Cello Concerto (also arranged for Harpsichord); *Concertino fugato* for Violin and Strings; Divertimento for Harpsichord and Strings; 6 string quartets (2 arranged from his syms.); *Divertimento* for 3 Strings; 8 partitas for 2 Violins and Bass; 2 trios; 2 sonatas and 2 allegros for Violin and Bass; much keyboard music, including 14 sonatas; 8 sets of preludes and versetti for Organ; sacred music, including several masses and a Magnificat.

BIBL.: R. Philipp, *Die Messenkomposition der Wiener Vorklassiker G.M. M. und C.Chr. Wagenseil* (diss., Univ. of Vienna, 1938).—**NS/LK/DM**

Monnikendam, Marius, Dutch music critic, teacher, and composer; b. Haarlem, May 28, 1896; d. Heerlen, May 22, 1977. He studied composition with Dresden, and organ and piano with de Pauw at the Amsterdam Cons. In 1925 he went to Paris, where he took courses with Aubert and d'Indy at the Schola Cantorum. Returning to the Netherlands, he taught composition at the Rotterdam Cons. and in Amsterdam; also served as music critic of the newspaper combine *De Tijd* and *De Maasbode*. He wrote a number of church works, in which he revived the most ancient form of plainchant, but injected asymmetric rhythms in a modern style; in his larger works, he employed the resources of advanced harmony, including polytonality. He publ. monographs on Franck (Amsterdam, 1949) and Stravinsky (Haarlem, 1951); also *50 Masterpieces of Music* (The Hague, 1953) and *Nederlandse Componisten van heden en verleden* (Amsterdam, 1968).

WORKS: ORCH.: *Arbeid* (Labor), symphonic movement (1931); *Sinfonia super "Merck toch hoe sterck"* for Chamber Orch. (1944); *Mouvement symphonique* (1950); Concerto for Trumpet, Horn, and Orch. (1952); *Variations symphoniques super "Merck toch hoe sterck"* (1954); Concerto for Organ and Strings (1958); *Ouverture* for Organ and Orch. (1960); *Vision* for Chamber Orch. (1963); Concerto for Organ, Wind Instruments, Harp, Double Bass, and Percussion (1968); Piano Concertino (1974). **CHAMBER:** Cello Sonata (1925); *2 toccatas* for Organ (1931, 1970); Concerto for Organ, 2 Trumpets, and 2 Trombones (1956); *10 Inventions* for Organ (1959); *Suite* for Flute, Oboe, Clarinet, Bassoon, and Harp (1960); Piano Sonatina (1967); *Suite biblique* for Piano, 4–Hands (1967); *The Bells*, prelude for Organ (1971); *Toccata batalla* for Organ, 2 Trumpets, and 2 Trombones (1972); numerous small organ pieces. **VOCAL:** 2 Te Deums for Chorus and Orch. (1919, 1946); *Missa Nova* for 3 Voices and Organ (1928); *7 Boetpsalmen* (7 Penitential Psalms) for Chorus and Orch. (1934); *Noah*, oratorio (1937); *Samson*, oratorio (1938); *Solomon*, oratorio (1939); *Missa antiphonale* (1939); *Sinfonia sacra I* for Men's Chorus and Orch. (1947) and *II* (*Domine salvum fac*) for Chorus and Orch. (1952); *Passion* for Speaker, Chorus, and Orch. (1948); *Van Riebeeck- Taferelen* for 2 Speakers, Chorus, and Orch. (1952); *Noe ou La Destruction du Premier Monde*, oratorio (1955); *Magnificat* for Soprano, Men's Chorus, and Orch. without Strings (1956; transcribed for Mixed Chorus and Full Orch., 1965); *Missa festiva* for Chorus and Orch. (1956); *Lamentations of Jeremiah* for Chorus and Orch. (1956); *Hymne* for Alto, Men's Chorus, and Orch. (1957); *Missa solenissima* for Chorus, Organ, and 7 Wind Instruments (1959); *Missa pro defunctis* for 3 Soloists, Organ, and Percussion (1961); *Apocalypse* for Chorus and Organ (1966); *Madrigalesca* for Chorus, 9 Winds, and Percussion (1966); *De Kinderkruistocht* (The Children's Crusade) for Mixed or Women's Chorus, 7 Woodwinds, and Percussion (1967); *Via sacra* (Way of the Cross) for Speaker, Chorus, Organ, Percussion, and Projection Slides (1969); *3 psaumes pour le temps present* for Soloists, Chorus, and Chamber Orch. (1971); *Missa concertanta* for Soloists, Chorus, and Orch. (1971); *Elckerlyc* (Everyman),

mystery play for Chorus, Organ, and Orch. (1975; The Hague, May 28, 1976); *Heart Rhythm* for Speaker, Men's Chorus, Organ, Double Bass, and Percussion (1975); *Gloria* for Chorus, Organ, and Orch. (1976).—**NS/LK/DM**

Monod, Jacques-Louis, French pianist, conductor, music editor, and composer; b. Asnières, near Paris, Feb. 25, 1927. He was admitted to the Paris Cons. before he had reached the official entrance age of 9, later studying with Messiaen (1944) and receiving instruction in theory, composition, and analysis from Leibowitz (1944–50). He subsequently studied composition with Wagenaar at N.Y.'s Juilliard School of Music and conducting with Rudolf Thomas at Columbia Univ., and then took courses with Blacher and Rufer in Berlin. As a pianist and conductor, he became a proponent of modern music. He was married for a time to **Bethany Beardslee**, with whom he gave many song recitals. He was chief music ed. of the Boelke-Bomart firm (1952–82); was also active as a teacher at various U.S. academic institutions. He wrote orch. works, chamber music, and songs.—**NS/LK/DM**

Mononen, Sakari (Tuomo), Finnish organist, teacher, and composer; b. Korpiselkä, July 27, 1928; d. Espoo, June 7, 1997. He studied composition with Fougstedt and Englund at the Sibelius Academy in Helsinki (graduated, 1962), and then was active mainly as an organist and teacher. He composed orch. works, chamber music, and vocal pieces.—**NS/LK/DM**

Monpou, (François Louis) Hyppolite, French organist and composer; b. Paris, Jan. 12, 1804; d. Orléans, Aug. 10, 1841. He became a choirboy at Paris's St.-Germain-l'Auxerrois at age 5, then went to Notre Dame when he was 9. He entered Choron's École Royale et Speciale de Chant at age 13. Choron sent him to the Tours Cathedral to study organ; he became its organist (1819). He soon returned to Paris, where he became master accompanist at the Académie Royale. He studied harmony with Fétis at Choron's Academy (1822), then became a teacher of singing and maître de chapelle at the Coll. of St. Louis (1825); subsequently was made organist at St. Thomas d'Aquin, St. Nicolas des Champs, and the Sorbonne (1827). He was notably successful as a composer of some 75 songs. His opera *Le Planteur* (Paris, March 1, 1839) also proved a popular success. Other operas (all 1st perf. in Paris) were *Les Deux Reines* (Aug. 6, 1835), *Le Luthier de Vienne* (June 30, 1836), *Le Piquillo* (Oct. 31, 1837), *Un Conte d'autrefois* (Feb. 28, 1838), *Perugina* (Dec. 20, 1838), *La Chaste Suzanne* (Dec. 27, 1839), *La Reine Jeanne* (Oct. 13, 1840), *Lambert Simnel* (Sept. 1, 1843; completed by A. Adam), and *L'Orfèvre* (unfinished).—**NS/LK/DM**

Monrad Johansen, David
See **Johansen, David Monrad**

Monroe, Bill (actually, **William Smith**), American bluegrass singer, mandolin player, and songwriter; b. near Rosine, Ky., Sept. 13, 1911; d. Springfield, Tenn., Sept. 9, 1996. Monroe developed his own musical subgenre, the bluegrass style of country music, from folk music, Appalachian music, and gospel. It was played on acoustic string instruments—guitar, mandolin, banjo, fiddle, and bass—usually at fast tempos and in high keys, and was characterized by rapid, improvised solos and keening harmony vocals, the whole achieving a "high, lonesome sound" that influenced the evolution of country music and rock 'n' roll. Monroe wrote many of the songs he performed, including such standards as "Blue Moon of Kentucky," "Uncle Pen," and "Kentucky Waltz."

Monroe's father, James Buchanan Monroe, was a farmer, logger, and coal miner; his mother, Melissa Vandiver Monroe, sang and played fiddle, accordion, and harmonica. Monroe took up the mandolin at about the age of ten, under the instruction of Hubert Stringfield. He also learned from and played with guitarist and fiddler Arnold Schultz, and with his uncle, Pendleton Vandiver, a fiddler whom he accompanied at local performances. His older brothers, Charlie, a guitarist, and Birch, a fiddler, went north looking for work; he joined them around 1929, working at an oil refinery and living near Chicago. The brothers also played music together, and they appeared in a road show sponsored by the WLS *Barn Dance* radio series as square dancers, starting in 1932. Later they performed on local radio in Ind.

In 1934, Birch Monroe dropped out of the group. Bill and Charlie, performing as the Monroe Brothers, continued to play full-time on radio and in live performances for extended periods in Iowa, Nebr., N.C., and S.C. over the next two years. In 1935, Monroe married Caroline Brown; they had two children, Melissa and James, both of whom later performed with their father; the couple divorced in 1960.

The Monroe Brothers made their recording debut for the Bluebird label of RCA Victor Records on Feb. 17, 1936. Their first single was "What Would You Give in Exchange (For Your Soul)?" (music and lyrics by F. J. Berry and J. H. Carr). They broke up in 1938, and by 1939 Monroe was leading a quartet featuring mandolin, guitar, fiddle, and bass, billed as Bill Monroe and His Blue Grass Boys. On Oct. 28, 1939, he made his first appearance on the *Grand Ole Opry*; he remained a regular performer on the popular radio series for the rest of his career.

Monroe recorded for RCA Victor in 1940 and 1941 and signed to Columbia Records in 1942, but he was unable to record again until 1945 due to the musicians' union recording ban of 1942–44. He expanded his group to include a banjo player and an accordionist and organized a tent show that toured the South during the week, returning to Nashville for the weekly *Grand Ole Opry* broadcasts. By the end of 1945 he had assembled what was considered the classic Blue Grass Boys lineup, featuring Lester Flatt on guitar and lead vocals and Earl Scruggs on banjo and vocals. He reached the Top Ten of the country charts in March 1946 with his own composition "Kentucky Waltz" and returned to the Top Ten in December with "Footprints in the Snow" (music and lyrics by Boyd Lane). Also in 1946, he first recorded his song "Blue Moon of Kentucky."

Flatt and Scruggs left the Blue Grass Boys in 1948 to form their own band; Monroe added new players and continued, moving to Decca Records in 1949. Among his many recordings for the label was his 1950 disc "Uncle Pen" (music and lyrics by Bill Monroe), which memorialized his musical mentor. Other artists scored hits with Monroe's compositions during the 1950s: Eddy Arnold topped the country charts in May 1951 with a revival of "Kentucky Waltz"; Elvis Presley released "Blue Moon of Kentucky" as the B-side of his debut single in July 1954; and Porter Wagoner reached the country charts with a revival of "Uncle Pen" in May 1956. Monroe's career was in decline, however, until the early 1960s, when he gained a new audience as part of the folk music revival, playing the Newport Folk Festival for the first time in 1963. He launched his own annual bluegrass festival at his music park in Bean Blossom, Ind., in 1967.

Monroe was still performing and recording regularly by the 1980s when the New Traditionalist movement in country music again brought him to the fore. Ricky Skaggs topped the country charts in October 1984 with a revival of "Uncle Pen." Monroe remarried in 1985, but the marriage was short-lived. He earned his first Grammy Award nomination in 1987 for Best Country Instrumental Performance for the track "The Old Brown Country Barn" (music by Bill Monroe) on the album *Bluegrass '87*, and in 1988 he won the first Grammy Award given out for Best Bluegrass Recording for the album *Southern Flavor*. He was again nominated for the Bluegrass Grammy in 1989 for *Live at the Opry—Celebrating 50 Years on the Grand Ole Opry*.

In 1988, Kentucky named "Blue Moon of Kentucky" the official state song, displacing Stephen Foster's "My Old Kentucky Home." Monroe continued to perform in the 1990s, despite declining health. He suffered a stroke in early 1996 and died shortly before his 85th birthday.

DISC.: *The Music of Bill Monroe* (rec. 1936–94); *The Essential* (rec. 1945–49); *Country Music Hall of Fame* (rec. 1950–91); *Live Recordings* (rec. 1965–69); *Beanblossom* (1973); *Bluegrass '87* (1987); *Southern Flavor* (1988); *Live at the Opry* (1989); *Cryin' Holy unto the Lord* (1991).

BIBL.: J. Rooney, *Bossmen: B. M. and Muddy Waters* (N.Y., 1971); N. Rosenberg, *B. M. and His Blue Grass Boys: An Illustrated Discography* (Nashville, Tenn., 1974).—**WR**

Monroe, Vaughn, American singer, bandleader, and trumpeter; b. Akron, Ohio, Oct. 7, 1911; d. Stuart, Fla., May 21, 1973. As both an orchestra leader and a solo singer, Monroe successfully straddled the Swing Era and the "sing era" that followed it in popular music. His sonorous baritone did well with ballads such as "There! I've Said It Again" and "I Wish I Didn't Love You So" and worked equally well on specialty material such as the seasonal "Let It Snow! Let It Snow! Let It Snow!" and the Western-themed "Riders in the Sky (A Cowboy Legend)," both of which were chart-topping hits for him. All told, Monroe had 25 Top-Ten hits between 1940 and 1954.

The son of Ira C. and Mabel Louisa Maahs Monroe, Vaughn Monroe grew up in Wisc., where he took up the trumpet at age 11 and won a statewide contest on the instrument at 15. Although he aspired to become an opera singer, he began singing and playing in dance bands around Pittsburgh to help pay for his tuition at the Carnegie Inst. of Technology, which he attended from 1929 to 1932. He dropped out of school to play with the orchestra of Austin Wylie in Cleveland, then worked with Larry Funk's Orch. from 1933 to 1936 while taking courses at the New England Cons. of Music. He joined the orchestra of bandleader and booker Jack Marshard in Boston in 1936; in 1937 he began fronting one of Marshard's bands. In 1939 he organized his own sweet society orchestra for an engagement at Seiler's Ten Acres, a roadhouse in Wayland, Mass., then dissolved it and reorganized a more swing-oriented unit that debuted in April 1940. On April 2 he married Marian Baughman; they had two daughters.

Monroe signed to RCA Victor Records and began recording for its discount-priced Bluebird subsidiary. (After two years he was promoted to the main label.) His first hit, "There I Go" (music by Irving Weiser, lyrics by Hy Zart), peaked in the Top Ten in December 1940. In the spring of 1941 he gained national attention with an appearance at Frank Dailey's Meadowbrook in Cedar Grove, N.J., one of the premier venues for swing bands, and he performed from the hall in the first remote broadcast on the national radio series *Matinee at Meadowbrook* on May 24. He had his first regular spot on radio with the quiz show *How'm I Doin'?* from January to October 1942. That October he finally scored a second Top Ten hit with "My Devotion" (music and lyrics by Roc Hillman and Johnny Napton), then returned to the Top Ten in December with the war-themed "When the Lights Go on Again (All over the World)" (music and lyrics by Eddie Seiler, Sol Marcus, and Bennie Benjamin).

Like other recording artists, Monroe was stymied by the musicians' union recording ban that prevailed during the war years, but he paired with his female vocal group, the Four Lee Sisters, for an a cappella recording of "Let's Get Lost" (music by Jimmy McHugh, lyrics by Frank Loesser) that reached the Top Ten in June 1943. He appeared with his band in the motion picture *Meet the People*, released in September 1944. With the lifting of the ban in November 1944, he quickly scored several Top Ten hits, including a duet with his female singer, Marilyn Duke, on "The Trolley Song" (music and lyrics by Hugh Martin and Ralph Blane) in January 1945; "Rum and Coca-Cola" (music and lyrics by Morey Amsterdam, Paul Baron, and Jeri Sullivan, based on a song with music and lyrics by Massie Patterson and Lionel Belasco) in March; and "There! I've Said It Again" (music and lyrics by Redd Evans and Dave Mann), which went to #1 in May and sold a million copies. In November he topped the album charts with *On the Moonbeam*.

Monroe's recording of "Let It Snow! Let It Snow! Let It Snow!" (music by Jule Styne, lyrics by Sammy Cahn) hit #1 in January 1946 and became a seasonal standard. He returned to the Top Ten in April with "Seems Like Old Times" (music and lyrics by Carmen Lombardo and John Jacob Loeb). His popularity led to his hosting the long-running radio series *The Camel Caravan* starting on

July 4, 1946. Running for nearly eight years, it was also known as *The Vaughn Monroe Show*. The series, in turn, boosted his popularity further, and he scored many hit recordings during the next three years. His album *Vaughn Monroe's Dreamland* was a Top Ten hit in November 1946. In May 1947 he appeared in the film *Carnegie Hall*, then reached the Top Ten of the singles charts with "I Wish I Didn't Love You So" (music and lyrics by Frank Loesser), "Kokomo, Indiana" (music by Josef Myrow, lyrics by Mack Gordon) in October, and "You Do" (music by Myrow, lyrics by Gordon) in November. He then topped the charts with the million-selling "Ballerina" (music and lyrics by Bob Russell and Carl Sigman) in December.

In 1948, "How Soon? (Will I Be Seeing You)" (music and lyrics by Carroll Lucas and Jack Owens) became a Top Ten single in January. The album *Down Memory Lane* hit #1 in March, and "Cool Water" (music and lyrics by Bob Nolan) reached the Top Ten in October. Due to a second recording ban, Monroe recorded the Western-styled "Cool Water" a cappella with the Sons of the Pioneers.

Monroe enjoyed his most successful year as a recording artist in 1949. In January his album *Vaughn Monroe Sings* went to #1. In April, "Red Roses for a Blue Lady" (music and lyrics by Sid Tepper and Roy Brodsky) was in the Top Ten. The biggest hit of his career was "Riders in the Sky (A Cowboy Legend)" (music and lyrics by Stan Jones), which topped the charts in May and was the most popular song of the year. The album *Silver Lining* made the Top Ten in August. "Someday" (music and lyrics by Jimmie Hodges) hit #1 in September. "That Lucky Old Sun (Just Rolls around Heaven All Day)" (music by Beasley Smith, lyrics by Haven Gillespie) was in the Top Ten in October, and his version of "Mule Train" (music and lyrics by Johnny Lange, Hy Heath, and Fred Glickman) reached the Top Ten in December.

Monroe was back in the Top Ten with "Bamboo" (music by Nat Simon, lyrics by Buddy Bernier) in February 1950, but his success on radio and records brought him other opportunities that prevented him from doing much recording during the year. He starred in the Western film *Singing Guns*, released in June, appeared with his orchestra at the Waldorf-Astoria Hotel in N.Y. in September, and launched a television version of his *Camel Caravan* radio series in October. The show ran through the 1950–51 season.

Monroe returned to the Top Ten in the spring of 1951 with a series of novelty records: "Sound Off (The Duckworth Chant)" (music and lyrics by Willie Lee Duckworth, based on an Army marching drill), "On Top of Old Smokey" (music and lyrics by Pete Seeger, based on the traditional folk song), and "Old Soldiers Never Die" (music and lyrics by Tom Glazer, inspired by General Douglas MacArthur's speech to Congress after being dismissed from duty in Korea). He appeared in a second Western film, *The Toughest Man in Arizona*, in October 1952. He disbanded his orchestra in 1953 and began to appear as a solo singer. His radio series ended in April 1954. In August, *The Vaughn Monroe Show* went back on television as a twice-a-week, 15-minute summer replacement show; it also ran during the summer of 1955. Monroe scored a final Top Ten hit with "They Were Doin' the Mambo" (music and lyrics by Don Raye and Sonny Burke) in October 1954 and continued to reach the charts occasionally through 1959. During the 1956–57 television season he hosted the musical variety series *Air Time '57*, and he also appeared on TV as a spokesman for RCA.

By the 1960s, Monroe had largely retired from music, though he made occasional appearances, especially in Las Vegas. He owned and managed the Meadows, a club and restaurant in Framingham, Mass. He died at the age of 61 in 1973 after a long illness. In the 1990s a Vaughn Monroe ghost orchestra under the direction of Bill Davies was active.—**WR**

Monsigny, Pierre-Alexandre,

noted French composer; b. Fauquembergues, near St.-Omer, Oct. 17, 1729; d. Paris, Jan. 14, 1817. He was educated at the Jesuit college in St.-Omer, where he also received instruction in violin. Upon his father's death, he abandoned his studies in order to support his family, taking a job in the Paris offices of the receiver-general of the Clergé de France (1749). Several years later he was befriended by the Duke of Orléans, who encouraged him to pursue his musical career. After studying for 5 months with the double-bass player Gianotti, he successfully brought out his first opera, *Les Aveux indiscrets* (Théâtre de la Foire St.-Germain, Feb. 7, 1759). In quick succession, and with increasing success, the same theater brought out 3 more of Monsigny's operas: *Le Maître en droit* (Feb. 23, 1760), *Le Cadi dupé* (Feb. 4, 1761), and *On ne s'avise jamais de tout* (Sept. 14, 1761). The members of the Comédie-Italienne, alarmed at the rising prestige of the rival enterprise, succeeded in closing it, by exercise of vested privilege, and took over its best actors. Thereafter Monsigny wrote most of his works for the Théâtre-Italien and the private theaters of the Duke of Orléans, having become the latter's maître d'hôtel in 1768. After scoring a triumph with his *Félix, ou L'Enfant trouvé* (Fontainebleau, Nov. 10, 1777), he abruptly abandoned his career as a composer for the theater. His patron died in 1785 and the new duke abolished Monsigny's job, but retained him as inspector of the canals of Orléans. With the coming of the Revolution, he lost his post. He obtained a pension from the Opéra-Comique (1798) and served as Inspector of Musical Education from 1800 until the post was abolished in 1802. His last years were relieved by several pensions; he was made a Chevalier of the Légion d'honneur (1804) and was elected to Grétry's chair in the Institut de France (1813). Monsigny possessed an uncommon and natural melodic invention, and sensibility in dramatic expression, but his theoretical training was deficient; still, his works attained the foremost rank among the precursors of the French comic operas.

WORKS: DRAMATIC (all 1st perf. in Paris unless otherwise given): *Les Aveux indiscrets*, opéra-comique (Feb. 7, 1759); *Le Maître en droit*, opéra-comique (Feb. 23, 1760); *Le Cadi dupé*, opéra-comique (Feb. 4, 1761); *On ne s'avise jamais de tout*, opéra-comique (Sept. 14, 1761); *Le Roy et le fermier*, comédie (Nov. 22, 1762); *Le Nouveau Monde*, divertissement (1763; not perf.); *Rose et Colas*, comédie (March 8, 1764); *Le Bouquet de Thalie*, prologue (Bagnolet, Dec. 25, 1764); *Aline, reine de Golconde*, ballet héroïque (April 15, 1766); *Philémon et Baucis*, comédie (Bagnolet, 1766); *L'Isle sonnante*, opéra-comique (Bagnolet, June 5, 1767); *Le Déserteur*, drame (March 6, 1769); *La Rosière de Salency*, comédie (Fontainebleau, Oct. 25, 1769; in collaboration with Philidor, Blaise, and Swieten); *Pagamin de Monègue*, opéra-comique (c. 1770; not perf.); *Le Faucon*, opéra-comique (Fontainebleau, Nov. 2, 1771); *La Belle Arsène*, comédie féerie (Fontainebleau, Nov. 6, 1773; rev. for Paris, Aug. 14, 1775); *Félix, ou L'Enfant trouvé*, comédie (Fontainebleau, Nov. 10, 1777); *Robin et Marion* (n.d.; not perf.).

BIBL.: A. Quatremère de Quincy, *Notice historique sur la vie et les ouvrages de M. de M.* (Paris, 1818); P. Hédouin, *Notice historique sur P.-A. de M.* (Paris, 1821); F. de Ménil, *Les Grands Musiciens du Nord: M.* (Paris, 1893); A. Pougin, *M. et son temps* (Paris, 1908); P. Druilhe, *M.: Sa vie et son oeuvre* (Paris, 1955). —**NS/LK/DM**

Montagnana, Antonio,

Italian bass who flourished from 1730 to 1750. After singing in Rome (1730) and Turin (1731), he was engaged by Handel for his London opera company at the King's Theatre, where he created the roles of Varo in *Ezio* (Jan. 15, 1732), Altomaro in *Sosarme, Rè di Media* (Feb. 15, 1732), and Zoroastro in *Orlando* (Jan. 27, 1733). He also sang in Handel's oratorios, being the first to sing Abinoam and the Chief Priest of Israel in *Deborah* (March 17, 1733) and Abner in *Athalia* (July 10, 1733). From 1733 to 1737 he was a member of the Opera of the Nobility in London. He then appeared with Heidegger's company at the King's Theatre, where he created the roles of Handel's Gustavo in *Faramondo* (Jan. 3, 1738) and Ariodante in *Serse* (April 15, 1738). From 1740 he was a member of the royal chapel in Madrid.—**NS/LK/DM**

Montague, Stephen (Rowley),

American composer and pianist; b. Syracuse, N.Y., March 10, 1943. Following studies in piano, conducting, and composition at Fla. State Univ. (B.M., 1965; M.M., 1967), he pursued his education at Ohio State Univ. (D.M.A., 1972) and worked at the Studio for Experimental Music at the Polish Radio in Warsaw on a Fulbright scholarship (1972–74). In 1974 he made London the center of his activities as a freelance composer, but also toured widely as a pianist championing contemporary music. From 1985 he also toured with the pianist Philip Mead in the duo known as Montague/Mead Piano Plus. In 1980 he helped organize the Electro-Acoustic Music Assn. of Great Britain, later known as the Sonic Arts Network. In 1992, 1995, and 2000 he was a visiting prof. at the Univ. of Tex. at Austin, and in 1997 at the Univ. of Auckland in New Zealand. From 1993 he was a visiting guest prof. at the Royal Coll. of Music in London, and chairman (1993–97) and artistic director (1998–99) of the SPNM (Soc. for the Promotion of New Music) of Great Britain. From 1995 to 1997 he also was composer-in-residence with the Orch. of St. John's Smith Square in London. Montague's extensive output includes various electroacoustic pieces and acoustic scores.

WORKS: DRAMATIC: *Largo con moto*, graphic/text piece for Dancer and Tape (London, March 15, 1975); *Criseyde*, theater piece for Soprano Playing Ocarina, Slide, and Tape (Mexico City, Oct. 19, 1976); *Into the Sun*, ballet for 4–Channel

Tape, Percussion, and Prepared Piano (Manchester, Oct. 31, 1977); *The West of the Imagination*, music for a television drama/documentary series (1986); many other pieces. **ORCH.**: *Voussoirs* for Orch. and Tapes (1970–72); *Sound Round* for Orch. and Digital Delay (1973; Manchester, July 11, 1988); *At the White Edge of Phrygia* for Chamber Orch. (London, June 20, 1983; for Full Orch. as *From the White Edge of Phrygia*, 1984; also as part of the ballet, *Median*, 1984); *Prologue* (1984; London, Jan. 3, 1985; also as part of the ballet, *Median*, 1984); *Dark Sun* for Orch. and Tapes (1995); *Snakebite* (1995); *The Creatures Indoors* (1996); Piano Concerto (1997); *A Toy Symphony* for 6 Soloists and Chamber Orch. (Bath, June 6, 1999). **Band**: *March Militaire* (1999). **CHAMBER**: *The Eyes of Ambush* for 1 to 5 Instruments or Voices and Digital Delay (1973); *Caccia* for Trombone, Piano, Tape, and Amplification (1974); *Quiet Washes* for 3 Trombones and 3 Pianos or Harps or Pre-recorded Versions (1974); *Strummin'* for Piano, Strings, Lighting, and Tape (1974–81); *Inundations I: Trio* for 3 Amplified Pianos, 12 Pianists, and Tape (1975) and *II: Willow* for Soprano, Piano, and Tape (1976); *E Pluribus Unum*, graphic/text piece for Any Chamber Group (1976); *Introduction* for Voice, Acoustic Feedback, and Tape (1976); *Paramell I* for Muted Trombone and Muted Piano (1977), *II: Entity* for 6 Percussionists (1977), *III* for Piano, Chorus of Humming Audience, and Pre-recorded Cassette (1981), *IV* for Tuba or Bass Trombone and Tape (1979), *V* for 2 Pianos (1981), and *VI* for Piano, Flute, Clarinet, and Cello or Percussion (1981); Quintet, graphic/text piece for Any Instrument and Pre-recorded 4–Channel Tape (1978); Trio, graphic/text piece for Any Instrument and Pre-recorded Stereo Tape (1978); *Gravity's Rainbow* for Flute, Live Electronics, and Tape (1980); Duo, graphic/text piece for Any Instrument and Pre-recorded Tape (1982); *Tongues of Fire* for Piano, Live Electronics, and Tape (1983–90); *Haiku* for Piano, Flanger, and Electronic Tape (1987); 2 string quartets: No. 1, *in memoriam Barry Anderson and Tomasz Sikorski*, with Live Electronics and Tape (1989–93) and No. 2, *Shaman*, with Live Electronics and Tape (1993); *Behold a Pale Horse* for Organ (1990); *After Ives...* for Piano, Tape, Live Electronics, and Optional Flute and String Quartet (1991–93); *Vlug* for Flute, Tape, and Live Electronics (1992); *Aeolian Furies* for Accordion (1993); *Phrygian Tucket* for Harpsichord and Tape (1994); *Silence: John, Yvar and Tim* for Prepared String Quartet and Prepared Piano (1994); *Chew Chow Chatterbox* for 4 Percussion (1998). **VOCAL**: *Varshavian Spring* for Chorus and Orch. (1973–80); *Sotto Voce*, graphic/text piece for Multiphonic Chorus, Tape Recorder, and Playback System (1976); *Tigida Pipa* for Amplified Voices, Woodblocks, Claves, and Electronic Tape (1983–89); *3 Temperance Songs* for Woman's Voice and 6 Instruments or Synthesizer, Piano, and Optional Tape (1988); *Boombox Virelai* for 4 Men's Voices (1992); *Wild Nights* for Soprano, Clarinet, Viola, and Piano (1993); *Varshavian Autumn* for Chorus and Orch. (1995); *The Camel and the Crane* for Soprano, Baritone, Chorus, and Orch. (1998). **ELECTROACOUSTIC**: *Synthetic Swamp* (1969–97); *A Presto Patch* (1973); *Scythia* (1981); *Quartet* (1982); *Slow Dance on a Burial Ground* (1982–84); *Bright Interiors* (1992–96).—NS/LK/DM

Montagu-Nathan, M(ontagu) (real name, **Montagu Nathan**), English writer on music; b. Banbury, Sept. 17, 1877; d. London, Nov. 15, 1958. He legally changed his name to Montagu Montagu-Nathan on March 17, 1909. He studied in Birmingham, then took violin lessons with Ysaÿe in Brussels, with Heermann in Frankfurt am Main, and with Wilhelmj in London. He appeared as a violinist in Belfast and Leeds,

but soon abandoned concerts in favor of music journalism. He learned the Russian language and wrote several books on Russian music: *A History of Russian Music* (London and N.Y., 1914; 2nd ed., 1918); *An Introduction to Russian Music* (London and Boston, 1916); *Contemporary Russian Composers* (London, 1917); *Handbook to the Piano Works of A. Scriabin* (London, 1917); also monographs on Glinka (London, 1916; 2nd ed., 1921), Mussorgsky (London, 1916), and Rimsky-Korsakov (London, 1916). —NS/LK/DM

Montand, Yves (real name, **Ivo Livi**), popular Italian-born French singer and actor; b. Monsummano Alto, Oct. 13, 1921; d. Senlis, Nov. 9, 1991. At age 2, he was taken by his family to Marseilles. He dropped out of school when he was 11 and held down a series of jobs before winning an amateur contest in 1938 proved the decisive turn toward a career on the stage. Taking the professional name of Yves Montand, he sang in music halls until meeting Edith Piaf, who secured for him a role in her film *Étoile sans lumière* (1945). He scored a major success with his performance of the song *Autumn Leaves*, which was written for the film *Les Portes de la nuit* (1946). As a cabaret artist, Montand became one of the leading exponents of the French chansonnier tradition. He also established himself as a dramatic actor of distinction with the starring role in the film *Le Salire de la peur* (1953). In 1951 he married the actress Simone Signoret, who remained his wife until her death in 1985 despite his torrid affair with the actress Marilyn Monroe, his co-star in the film *Let's Make Love* (1960). Among his later outstanding films were *La Guerre est finie* (1966), *Z* (1969), *L'Aveu* (1970), *Jean de Florette* (1986), and *Manon des sources* (1986). Montand was a lifelong supporter of the political Left, although the Soviet Union's invasion of Czechoslovakia in 1968 led him to break with Communism. Thereafter he was an ardent spokesman for the cause of universal human rights. With H. Hamon and P. Rotman, he wrote the autobiography *You See, I Haven't Forgotten* (N.Y., 1992). —LK/DM

Monte, Philippe de (Filippo di Monte or **Philippus de Monte)**, great Belgian composer; b. Mechlin, 1521; d. Prague, July 4, 1603. He went to Italy in his youth and was active there as a singer and teacher. From 1542 to 1551 he was in Naples in the service of the Pinelli family. He then went to Rome, where he publ. his first book of madrigals (1554), and from Rome to Antwerp in 1554, and then to England, where he served as chorus praefectus in the private chapel of Philip II of Spain, the husband of the Queen, Mary Tudor. In Sept. 1555 he left England and went to Italy again; in 1567 he was in Rome. On May 1, 1568, he became Imperial Court Kapellmeister to the Emperor Maximilian II in Vienna; he held this position until his death, which occurred while the court was at Prague during the summer of 1603. In 1572 he was appointed treasurer of Cambrai Cathedral, and in 1577, also a canon (residence was not required for either position there). He was greatly esteemed as a composer, numbering among his works some 1,000 madrigals, about 40 masses, and many other works of sacred music. A complete ed. of his works was edited by C. van den Borren and G. van Doorslaer as *Philippe de Monte: Opera* (31 vols., Bruges, 1927–39; reprint, 1965). R. Lenaerts and others ed. *Philippe de Monte: New Complete Edition* (Louvain, 1975–81).

WORKS: VOCAL: M a s s e s : *Missa ad modulum "Benedicta es"* for 6 Voices (Antwerp, 1579); *Liber primus* [7] *missarum* for 5, 6, and 8 Voices (Antwerp, 1587); Mass for 5 Voices (Venice, 1590); none of his other masses were publ. in his lifetime, and most of these remain in MS. M o t e t s : *Sacrarum cantionum...liber primus* for 5 Voices (Venice, 1572); *Sacrarum cantionum...liber secundus* for 5 Voices (Venice, 1573); *Sacrarum cantionum...liber tertius* for 5 Voices (Venice, 1574); *Libro quarto de motetti* for 5 Voices (Venice, 1575); *Sacrarum cantionum...liber quintus* for 5 Voices (Venice, 1579); *Sacrarum cantionum...liber sextus* for 5 Voices (Venice, 1584; not extant); *Sacrarum cantionum...liber primus* for 6 and 12 Voices (Venice, 1585); *Sacrarum cantionum...liber secundus* for 6 Voices (Venice, 1587); *Sacrarum cantionum...liber primus* for 4 Voices (Venice, 1596); *Sacrarum cantionum...liber septimus* for 5 Voices (Venice, 1600); etc. M a d r i g a l i   S p i r i t u a l i : *Il primo libro de madrigali spirituali* for 5 Voices (Venice, 1581); *Il primo libro de madrigali spirituali* for 6 Voices (Venice, 1583); *Il secondo libro de madrigali spirituali* for 6 and 7 Voices (Venice, 1589); *Il terzo libro de madrigali spirituali* for 6 Voices (Venice, 1590); *Eccellenze di Maria vergine* for 5 Voices (Venice, 1593). M a d r i g a l s : *Madrigali ...libro primo* for 5 Voices (Rome, 1554); *Il primo libro de madrigali* for 4 Voices (Venice, 1562); *Il secondo libro de madrigali* for 5 Voices (Venice, 1567); *Il primo libro de' madrigali* for 6 Voices (c. 1568; not extant; 2nd ed., Venice, 1569); *Il secondo libro delli madrigali* for 6 Voices (Venice, 1569); *Il secondo libro delli madrigali* for 4 Voices (Venice, 1569); *Il terzo libro delli madrigali* for 5 Voices (Venice, 1570); *Il quarto libro delli madrigali* for 5 Voices (Venice, 1571); *Madrigali...libro quinto* for 5 Voices (Venice, 1574); *Il sesto libro delli madrigali* for 5 Voices (Venice, 1575); *Il terzo libro de madrigali* for 6 Voices (Venice, 1576); *Il settimo libro delli madrigali* for 5 Voices (Venice, 1578); *Il quarto libro de madrigali* for 6 Voices (Venice, 1580); *L'ottavo libro delli madrigali* for 5 Voices (Venice, 1580); *Il nono libro de madrigali* for 5 Voices (Venice, 1580); *Il terzo libro de madrigali* for 4 Voices (c. 1580; not extant; 2nd ed., Venice, 1585); *Il decimo libro delli madrigali* for 5 Voices (Venice, 1581); *Il quarto libro de madrigali* for 4 Voices (Venice, 1581); *Il primo libro de madrigali* for 3 Voices (Venice, 1582); *Il quinto libro de madrigali* for 6 Voices (Venice, 1584); *L'undecimo libro delli madrigali* for 5 Voices (Venice, 1586); *Il duodecimo libro delli madrigali* for 5 Voices (Venice, 1587); *Il terzodecimo libro delli madrigali* for 5 Voices (Venice, 1588); *Il quartodecimo libro delli madrigali* for 5 Voices (Venice, 1590); *Il sesto libro de madrigali* for 6 Voices (Venice, 1591); *Il settimo libro de madrigali* for 6 Voices (Venice, 1591); *Il quintodecimo libro de madrigali* for 5 Voices (Venice, 1592); *Il sestodecimo libro de madrigali* for 5 Voices (Venice, 1593); *L'ottavo libro de madrigali* for 6 Voices (Venice, 1594); *Il decimosettimo libro delli madrigali* for 5 Voices (Venice, 1595); *Il decimottavo libro de madrigali* for 5 Voices (Venice, 1597); *Il decimonono libro delli madrigali* for 5 Voices (Venice, 1598); *La fiammetta...libro primo* for 7 Voices (Venice, 1599); *Musica sopra Il pastor fido...libro secondo* for 7 Voices (Venice, 1600); etc.

BIBL.: G. van Doorslaer, *P. d. M.* (Mechelen, 1895); V. Eberstein, *Die Messen P. d. M., mit besonderer Berücksichtigung seiner Parodietechnik* (diss., Univ. of Vienna, 1912); P. Bergmans, *Quatorze lettres inédites du compositeur P. d. M.* (Brussels, 1921); G. van Doorslaer, *La Vie et les oeuvres de P. d. M.* (Brussels, 1921); idem, *Deux lettres nouvelles de P. d. M.* (Mechelen, 1927); P. Oberg, *The Sacred Music of P. d. M.* (diss., Univ. of Rochester, 1944); P. Nuten, *De madrigali spirituali van Filip de M.* (Brussels, 1958); G. Michael, *The Parody Mass Technique of P. d. M.* (diss., N.Y.U., 1959); R. Lindell, *Die sechs- und siebenstimmige Madrigale von Filippo di M.* (diss., Univ. of Vienna, 1977); B. Mann, *The Secular Madrigals of Filippo di M., 1521–1603* (Ann Arbor, 1983).—NS/LK/DM

Monte, Toti dal
See **Dal Monte, Toti**

Montecino, Alfonso, Chilean-born American pianist, teacher, and composer; b. Osorno, Oct. 28, 1924. He received training in composition (with Santa Cruz) and in piano at the Cons. of the Univ. of Chile in Santiago, graduating in 1945. In 1947 he went to the U.S., and pursued training in composition with Thompson at Princeton Univ., Varèse at Columbia Univ., Sessions at the Juilliard School of Music, and Martinů at the Mannes Coll. of Music until 1949. He also studied piano with Arrau and Rafael de Silva. Following his debut as a soloist at N.Y.'s Carnegie Hall in 1950, he appeared widely as a soloist and recital accompanist. He frequently appeared with his wife, the mezzo-soprano Siri Garson. From 1963 to 1988 he taught piano at the Ind. Univ. School of Music in Bloomington. Thereafter he devoted himself principally to composition while also giving master classes in South America, Asia, and Europe. In 1977 he became a naturalized American citizen. Montecino's early works followed along classical lines, but from 1980 they have revealed the influence of the Second Viennese School.

WORKS: D R A M A T I C : *ANA or Madrigal of the High Towers*, chamber opera (1993–; unfinished). O R C H . : *Obertura Concertante* (1948); Concertino (1965); Piano Concerto (1994–95). C H A M B E R : 2 string quartets (1945, 1991); 2 duos for Violin and Piano (1950, 1974); *Improvisation* for Oboe (1966); Wind Quintet (1967); *Sonata Breve* for Flute, Saxophone, and Piano (1989); 3 Pieces for Cello (1989); *Music* for Clarinet, Cello, and Piano (1994); 4 Pieces for Viola and Piano (1998); Trio for Oboe, Viola, and Piano (1999). P i a n o : Suite (1948); *Composition for the Left Hand* (1951); *Sequences*, 7 improvisations (1987); *Composition* for 2 Pianos (1991); Sonata for 2 Pianos (1993); *3 Hommages* (1995). VOCAL: Cantata for Soprano and 8 Instruments, after Hildegard von Bingen (1993); *El Hombre Alegre* for Voice, Clarinet, Violin, Cello, and Piano (1997).—LK/DM

Montéclair, Michel Pignolet de (real name, **Michel Pignolet**), distinguished French composer, teacher, and music theorist; b. Andelot, Haute-Marne (baptized), Dec. 4, 1667; d. Aumont, Sept. 22, 1737. He became a pupil at the Langres Cathedral choir school (1676), where he was taught by the choirmaster, Jean-Baptiste Moreau. He was maître de la musique to the Prince of Vaudémont, whom he followed to Italy. He went to Paris (1687), and later added the name of the fortress in his birthplace, "Montéclair," to his own. With Fedeli, he introduced the double bass to the Paris Opéra orch., where he played from 1699 until 3 months before his death. He was also active as a teacher, his students including François Couperin's daughters. Among his works were *Les Festes de l'été*, opera ballet (Paris Opéra, June 12, 1716) and *Jephté*, tragédie lyrique (Paris Opéra, Feb. 28, 1732). He also composed *Messe de Requiem*, motets, and other sacred works, all of which are lost, as well as various cantatas, several of which were ed. by J. Anthony and D. Akmajian in Recent Researches in the Music of the Baroque Era, XXIX-XXX (1978). Other works include airs, *Sérénade ou concert divisez en 3 suites* for Violins, Recorders, and Oboes (Paris, 1697), (6) *Concerts* for 2 Flutes (n.d.; ed. by R. Viollier, N.Y. and Locarno, 1962–64), (6) Concerts for Flute and Basso Continuo (n.d.), *Brunètes anciènes et modernes* for Flute or Violin (n.d.), and other instrumental music (not extant).

WRITINGS (all publ. in Paris): *Nouvelle méthode pour apprendre la musique* (1709); *Leçons de musique divisées en quatre classes* (c.1709); *Méthode facile pour apprendre à jouer du violon* (1711–12); *Petite méthode pour apprendre la musique aux enfans et même aux personnes plus avencées en âge* (c. 1735); *Principes de musique* (1736).

BIBL.: E. Voillard, *Essai sur M.* (Paris, 1879).—**NS/LK/DM**

Montella, Giovanni Domenico, Italian lutenist, organist, and composer; b. Naples, c. 1570; d. there, before July 2, 1607. He studied with Giovanni de Macque, and was a lutenist in the academy of Don Fabrizio Gesualdo. In 1591 he was engaged as lutenist in the Spanish viceroy's chapel, where he also was an organist (from 1599). He wrote Psalms and other church music, and publ. 4 vols. of *villanelles*, 2 vols. of motets, and 10 vols. of madrigals. Some of his sacred music is included in *Istituzioni e monumenti dell'arte musicale italiano* (Vol. V, 1934).—**NS/LK/DM**

Montemezzi, Italo, eminent Italian opera composer; b. Vigasio, near Verona, Aug. 4, 1875; d. there, May 15, 1952. He was a pupil of Saladino and Ferroni at the Milan Cons., and graduated in 1900; his graduation piece, conducted by Toscanini, was *Cantico dei Cantici*, for Chorus and Orch. He then devoted himself almost exclusively to opera. In 1939 he went to the U.S., living mostly in Calif., and in 1949 he returned to Italy. Montemezzi's chief accomplishment was the maintenance of the best traditions of Italian dramatic music, without striving for realism or overelaboration of technical means. His masterpiece in this genre was the opera *L'amore dei tre re* (Milan, April 10, 1913), which became a standard work in the repertoire of opera houses all over the world. Other operas were *Giovanni Gallurese* (Turin, Jan. 28, 1905), *Hellera* (Turin, March 17, 1909), *La nave* (libretto by Gabriele d'Annunzio; Milan, Nov. 1, 1918), *La notte di Zoraima* (Milan, Jan. 31, 1931), and *L'incantesimo* (NBC, Oct. 9, 1943, composer conducting).

BIBL.: L. Tretti and L. Fiumi, eds., *Omaggio a I. M.* (Verona, 1952).—**NS/LK/DM**

Monteux, Pierre, celebrated French-born American conductor; b. Paris, April 4, 1875; d. Hancock, Maine, July 1, 1964. He studied at the Paris Cons. with Berthelier (violin), Lavignac (harmony), and Lenepveu (composition), receiving 1st prize for violin (1896). He began his career as a violist in the Colonne Orch. in Paris, where he later was chorus master; also was a violist in the orch. of the Opéra-Comique in Paris. He then organized his own series, the Concerts Berlioz, at the Casino de Paris (1911); that same year, he also became conductor for Diaghilev's Ballets Russes; his performances of modern ballet scores established him as one of the finest technicians of the baton. He led the premieres of Stravinsky's *Petrouchka*, *Le Sacre du printemps*, and *Le Rossignol*; Ravel's *Daphnis et Chloé*; and Debussy's *Jeux*. Monteux conducted at the Paris Opéra (1913–14); founded the Société des Concerts Populaires in Paris (1914); appeared as guest conductor in London, Berlin, Vienna, Budapest, and other music centers. In 1916–17 he toured the U.S. with the Ballets Russes; in 1917, conducted the Civic Orch. Soc., N.Y.; from 1917 to 1919, at the Metropolitan Opera there. In 1919 he was engaged as conductor of the Boston Sym. Orch., and held this post until 1924; from 1924 to 1934 he was assoc. conductor of the Concertgebouw Orch. in Amsterdam; from 1929 to 1938 he was principal conductor of the newly founded Orch. Symphonique de Paris. From 1936 until 1952 he was conductor of the reorganized San Francisco Sym. Orch. He became a naturalized U.S. citizen in 1942. He appeared as a guest conductor with the Boston Sym. Orch. from 1951, and also accompanied it on its first European tour in 1952, and then again in 1956; likewise was again on the roster of the Metropolitan Opera (1953–56). In 1961 (at the age of 86) he became principal conductor of the London Sym. Orch., retaining this post until his death. He was married in 1927 to Doris Hodgkins (b. Salisbury, Maine, 1895; d. Hancock, Maine, March 13, 1984), an American singer who co-founded in 1941 the Domaine School for Conductors and Orchestral Players in Hancock, Maine, of which Monteux was director. She publ. 2 books of memoirs, *Everyone Is Someone* and *It's All in the Music* (N.Y., 1965). After Monteux's death, she established the Pierre Monteux Memorial Foundation. As an interpreter, Monteux endeavored to bring out the inherent essence of the music, without imposing his own artistic personality; unemotional and restrained in his podium manner, he nonetheless succeeded in producing brilliant performances in an extensive repertoire ranging from the classics to the 20th century.—**NS/LK/DM**

Monteverdi, Claudio (Giovanni Antonio), great Italian composer, brother of **Giulio Cesare Monteverdi**; b. Cremona (baptized), May 15, 1567; d. Venice, Nov. 29, 1643. His surname is also rendered as Monteverde. He was the son of a chemist who practiced medicine as a barber- surgeon. He studied singing and theory with Marc' Antonio Ingegneri, maestro di cappella at the Cathedral of Cremona, and also learned to play the organ. He acquired the mastery of composition at a very early age. He was only 15 when a collection of his 3-part motets was publ. in Venice; there followed several sacred madrigals (1583) and canzonettas (1584). In 1589 he visited Milan, and made an appearance at the court of the Duke of Mantua; by 1592 he had obtained a position at the court in the service of Vincenzo I as "suonatore" on the viol (viola da gamba) and violin (viola da braccio). He came into contact with the Flemish composer Giaches de Wert, maestro di cappella at the Mantuan court, whose contrapuntal art greatly influenced Monteverdi. In 1592 Monteverdi publ. his third book of madrigals, a collection marked by a considerable extension of harmonic dissonance. In 1595 he accompanied the retinue of the Duke of Mantua on forays against the Turks in Austria and Hungary, and also went with him to Flanders in 1599. He married Claudia de Cattaneis, one of the Mantuan court singers, on May 20, 1599; they had 2 sons; a daughter died in infancy. In 1601 he was appointed maestro di cappella in Mantua following the death of Pallavicino. The publication of 2 books of madrigals in 1603 and 1605 further confirmed his mastery of the genre. Having already composed some music for the stage, he now turned to the new form of the opera. *L'Orfeo*, his first opera, was given before the Accademia degli Invaghiti in Mantua in Feb. 1607. In this pastoral, he effectively moved beyond the Florentine model of recitative-dominated drama by creating a more flexible means of expression; the score is an amalgam of monody, madrigal, and instrumental music of diverse kinds. In 1607 Monteverdi was made a member of the Accademia degli Animori of Cremona. He suffered a grievous loss in the death of his wife in Cremona on Sept. 10, 1607. Although greatly depressed, he accepted a commission to compose an opera to celebrate the marriage of the heir-apparent to the court of Mantua, Francesco Gonzaga, to Margaret of Savoy. The result was *L'Arianna*, to a text by Rinuccini, presented in Mantua on May 28, 1608. Although the complete MS has been lost, the extant versions of the *Lamento d'Arianna* from the score testify to Monteverdi's genius in expressing human emotion in moving melodies. In 1614 he prepared a 5-part arrangement of his sixth book of madrigals, also publ. separately (Venice, 1623). He further wrote 2 more works for wedding celebrations, the prologue to the pastoral play *L'Idropica* (not extant) and the French-style ballet *Il ballo delle ingrate*. His patron, Duke Vincenzo of Mantua, died in 1612, and his successor, Francesco, did not retain Monteverdi's services. However, Monteverdi had the good fortune of being called to Venice in 1613 to occupy the vacant post of maestro di cappella at San Marco, at a salary of 300 ducats, which was raised to 400 ducats in 1616. His post at San Marco proved to be the most auspicious of his career, and he retained it for the rest of his life. He composed mostly church music, but did not neglect the secular madrigal forms. He accepted important commissions from Duke Ferdinando of Mantua. His ballet *Tirsi e Clori* was given in Mantua in 1616. In 1619 he publ. his 7th book of madrigals, significant in its bold harmonic innovations. In 1624 his dramatic cantata, *Il combattimento di Tancredi e Clorinda*, after Tasso's *Gerusalemme liberata*, was performed at the home of Girolamo Mocenigo, a Venetian nobleman. The score is noteworthy for the effective role played by the string orch. Other works comprised intermedi for the Farnese court in Parma. A great inconvenience was caused to Monteverdi in 1627 when his son Massimiliano, a medical student, was arrested by the Inquisition for consulting books on the *Index Librorum Prohibitorum*; he was acquitted. In 1630 Monteverdi composed the opera *Proserpina rapita* for Venice; of it only 1 trio has survived. Following the plague of 1630–31, he wrote a mass of thanksgiving

for performance at San Marco (the *Gloria* is extant); in 1632 he took Holy Orders. His *Scherzi musicali* for 1 and 2 Voices was publ. in 1632. Then followed his *Madrigali guerrieri et amorosi*, an extensive retrospective collection covering some 30 years, which was publ. in 1638. In 1637 the first public opera houses were opened in Venice, and Monteverdi found a new outlet there for his productions. His operas *Il ritorno d'Ulisse in patria* (1640), *Le nozze d'Enea con Lavinia* (1641; not extant), and *L'incoronazione di Poppea* (1642) were all given in Venice. (Research by Alan Curtis suggests that the latter opera owes its final form to Francesco Sacrati.) The extant operas may be considered the first truly modern operas in terms of dramatic viability. Monteverdi died at the age of 76 and was accorded burial in the church of the Frari in Venice. A commemorative plaque was erected in his honor, and a copy remains in the church to this day.

Monteverdi's place in the history of music is of great magnitude. He established the foundations of modern opera conceived as a drama in music. For greater dynamic expression, he enlarged the orch., in which he selected and skillfully combined the instruments accompanying the voices. He was one of the earliest, if not the first, to employ such coloristic effects as string tremolo and pizzicato; his recitative assumes dramatic power, at times approaching the dimensions of an arioso. In harmonic usage he introduced audacious innovations, such as the use of the dominant seventh-chord and other dissonant chords without preparation. He is widely regarded as having popularized the terms "prima prattica" and "secunda prattica" to demarcate the polyphonic style of the 16th century from the largely monodic style of the 17th century, corresponding also to the distinction between "stile antico" and "stile moderno." For this he was severely criticized by the Bologna theorist Giovanni Maria Artusi, who publ. in 1600 a vitriolic pamphlet against Monteverdi, attacking the "musica moderna" which allowed chromatic usages in order to achieve a more adequate expression.

In addition to various eds. of his works in separate format, G.F. Malipiero edited a complete ed. as *Claudio Monteverdi: Tutte le opere* (16 vols., Asolo, 1926–42; 2nd ed., rev., 1954; vol. 17, suppl., 1966). All of these are now being superseded by 2 new complete eds.: one, by the Fondazione Claudio Monteverdi, began publishing in 1970; the other, ed. by B.B. de Surcy, began issuing simultaneously critical and facsimile eds. in 1972.

WORKS: DRAMATIC: *L'Orfeo*, opera, designated "favola in musica" (Mantua, Feb. 1607; publ. in Venice, 1609); *L'Arianna*, opera (Mantua, May 28, 1608; not extant except for various versions of the *Lament*); *In ballo delle ingrate*, ballet (Mantua, 1608; publ. in *Madrigali guerrieri et amorosi*, Venice, 1638); *Prologue to L'Idropica*, comedy with music (Mantua, June 2, 1608; not extant); *Tirsi e Clori*, ballet (Mantua, 1616; publ. in *Concerto: Settimo libro*, Venice, 1619); *Le nozze di Tetide*, favola marittima (begun 1616 but unfinished; not extant); *Andromeda*, opera (begun c. 1618 but unfinished; libretto extant); *Apollo*, dramatic cantata (unfinished; not extant); *Il combattimento di Tancredi e Clorinda* (Venice, 1624; publ. in *Madrigali guerrieri et amorosi*, Venice, 1638); *La finta pazza Licori* (composed for Mantua, 1627; never perf.; not extant); *Gli amori di Diana e di Endimione* (Parma, 1628; not extant); *Mercurio e Marte*, torneo (Parma, 1628; not extant); *Proserpina rapita*, opera (Venice, 1630;

only 1 trio extant); *Volgendo il ciel*, ballet (Vienna, c. 1636; publ. in *Madrigali guerrieri et amorosi*, Venice, 1638); *Il ritorno d'Ulisse in patria*, opera (Venice, 1640); *Le nozze d'Enea con Lavinia*, opera (Venice, 1641; not extant); *La vittoria d'Amore*, ballet (Piacenza, 1641; not extant); *L'incoronazione di Poppea*, opera (Venice, 1642).

VOCAL: Secular : *Canzonette* for 3 Voices (Venice, 1584); *Il primo libro de madrigali* for 5 Voices (Venice, 1587); *Il secondo libro de madrigali* for 5 Voices (Venice, 1590); *Il terzo libro de madrigali* for 5 Voices (Venice, 1592); *Il quarto libro de madrigali* for 5 Voices (Venice, 1603); *Il quinto libro de madrigali* for 5 Voices (Venice, 1605); *Musica tolta da i madrigali di Claudio Monteverde e d'altri autori, e fatta spirituale da Aquilino Coppini* for 5 and 6 Voices (Milan, 1607); *Scherzi musicali di Claudio Monteverde, raccolti da Giulio Cesare Monteverde suo fratello* for 3 Voices (Venice, 1607); *Il secondo libro della musica di Claudio Monteverde e d'altri autori, fatta spirituale da Aquilino Coppini* for 5 Voices (Milan, 1608); *Il terzo libro della musica di Claudio Monteverde e d'altri autori, fatta spirituale da Aquilino Coppini* for 5 Voices (Milan, 1609); *Il sesto libro de madrigali* for 5 Voices, "con uno dialogo," and 7 Voices, with Basso Continuo (Venice, 1614); *Concerto: Settimo libro de madrigali, con altri generi de canti* for 1 to 4 and 6 Voices, with Basso Continuo (Venice, 1619); *Scherzi musicali cioe arie, et madrigali in stil recitativo, con una ciaccona... raccolti da Bartholomeo Magni* for 1 and 2 Voices, with Basso Continuo (Venice, 1632); *Madrigali guerrieri et amorosi con alcuni opuscoli in genere rappresentativo, che saranno per brevi episodii frà i canti senza gesto: Libro ottavo* for 1 to 8 Voices and Instruments, with Basso Continuo (Venice, 1638); *Madrigali e canzonette...libro nono* for 2 and 3 Voices, with Basso Continuo (Venice, 1651). **Sacred :** *Sacrae cantiunculae...liber primus* for 3 Voices (Venice, 1582); *Madrigali spirituali* for 4 Voices (Brescia, 1583); *Musica tolta da i madrigali di Claudio Monteverde e d'altri autori, e fatta spirituale da Aquilino Coppini* for 5 and 6 Voices (Milan, 1607); *Il secondo libro della musica di Claudio Monteverde e d'altri autori, fatta spirituale da Aquilino Coppini* for 5 Voices (Milan, 1608); *Il terzo libro della musica di Claudio Monteverde e d'altri autori, fatta spirituale da Aquilino Coppini* for 5 Voices (Milan, 1609); *Sanctissimae virgini missa senis vocibus ad ecclesiarum choros ac Vespere pluribus decantandaecum nonnullis sacris concentibus ad sacella sive principum cubicula accommodata* for 1 to 3, 6 to 8, and 10 Voices and Instruments, with Basso Continuo (Venice, 1610); *Selva morale e spirituale* for 1 to 8 Voices and Instruments (Venice, 1641); *Messa* for 4 Voices, et salmi for 1 to 8 Voices, and concertati, e *parte da cappella, et con le letanie della beata vergine* for 6 Voices (Venice, 1650).

BIBL.: S. Davari, *Notizie biografiche del distinto maestro di musica C. M.* (Mantua, 1884); G. Sommi Picenardi, *C. M. a Cremona* (Milan, 1896); L. Schneider, *Un Précurseur de la musique italienne aux XVI*e *et XVII*e *siècles: C. M.: L'Homme et son temps* (Paris, 1921); H. Prunières, *La Vie et l'oeuvre de C. M.* (Paris, 1924; Eng. tr., 1926; 2nd French ed., 1931); G. Malipiero, *C. M.* (Milan, 1929); K. Müller, *Die Technik der Ausdrucksdarstellung in M.s monodischen Frühwerken* (Berlin, 1931); H. Redlich, *C. M.: Ein formgeschichtlicher Versuch* (Berlin, 1932); W. Kreidler, *Heinrich Schütz und der Stile Concitato von C. M.* (Stuttgart, 1934); O. Tiby, *C. M.* (Turin, 1944); D. de' Paoli, *C. M.* (Milan, 1945); H. Redlich, *C. M.: Leben und Werk* (Olten, 1949; Eng. tr. and rev., London, 1952); L. Schrade, *M.: Creator of Modern Music* (London, 1950); M. le Roux, *C. M.* (Paris, 1951); C. Sartori, *M.* (Brescia, 1953); A. Abert, *C. M. und das musikalische Drama* (Lippstadt, 1954); R. Roche, *M.* (Paris, 1959); W. Osthoff, *Das dramatische Spätwerk C. M.s* (Tutzing, 1960); D. Arnold, *M.* (London, 1963; rev. ed., 1990); D. Arnold, *M. Madrigals* (London, 1967); G. Barblan et al., *C. M. nel quarto centenario della nascita* (Turin, 1967); E. Santoro,

La famiglia e la formazione di C. M.: Note biografiche con documenti inediti (Cremona, 1967); D. Arnold and N. Fortune, eds., *The M. Companion* (London, 1968; 2nd ed., rev., 1985, as *The New M. Companion*); N. Anfuso and A. Gianuario, *Preparazione alla interpretazione della Poiésis M.ana* (Florence, 1971); D. Stevens, *M.: Sacred, Secular and Occasional Music* (Rutherford, N.J., 1978); D. de' Paoli, *M.* (Milan, 1979); D. Stevens, ed. and tr., *The Letters of C. M.* (London, 1980; rev. ed., 1995); S. Leopold, *C. M. und seine Zeit* (Laaber, 1982; Eng. tr., 1991, as *M.: Music in Transition*); J. Whenham, *Duet and Dialogue in the Age of M.* (Ann Arbor, 1982); P. Fabbri, *M.* (Turin, 1985; Eng. tr., 1994); G. Tomlinson, *M. and the End of the Renaissance* (Oxford, 1986); D. Kiel and K. Adams, *C. M.: A Guide to Research* (N.Y., 1989); E. Chafe, *M.'s Tonal Language* (N.Y., 1992); I. Fenlon and P. Miller, *The Song of the Soul: Understanding Poppea* (Chicago, 1992); A. Gianuario, *L'estetica di C. M. attraverso quattro sue lettere* (Sezze Romano, 1993); E. Lax, ed., *C. M.: Lettere* (Florence, 1994); R. Tellart, *C. M.* (Paris, 1997); J. Whenham, *M.: Vespers (1610)* (Cambridge, 1997); P. Besutti, T. Gialdroni, and R. Baroncini, eds., *C. M.: Studi e prospettive: Atti del convegno, Mantova, 21–24 ottobre 1993* (Florence, 1998); S. Leopold and J. Steinheuer, eds., *Internationales Symposium "C. M. und die Folgen"* (Kassel, 1998).—**NS/LK/DM**

Monteverdi, Giulio Cesare, Italian organist, composer, and writer on music, brother of **Claudio (Giovanni Antonio) Monteverdi**; b. Cremona (baptized), Jan. 31, 1573; d. Salo, Lake Garda, during the plague of 1630–31. In 1602 he entered the service of the Duke of Mantua, where his famous brother was maestro di cappella. He composed the music for the 4th intermedio in Guarini's play *L'Idropica*, which was performed for the wedding celebration of the Mantuan heir-apparent, Francesco Gonzaga, and Margaret of Savoy in 1608. His opera *Il rapimento di Proserpina* was given in Casale Monferrato in 1611. In 1620 he was named maestro di cappella of the Cathedral in Salo. He publ. a collection of 25 motets under the title *Affetti musici, ne quali si contengono motetti a 1–4 et 6 voci, per concertarli nel basso per l'organo* (Venice, 1620). A madrigal for 3 Voices and Continuo (1605) and 2 pieces in his brother's *Scherzi musicali* (Venice, 1607) are extant. He contributed to the collection *Scherzi musicali* an important *Dichiaratione*, in which he expounded at length the musical ideas of his brother and gave a vigorous reply to the attacks on Monteverdi by Artusi; an Eng. tr. is found in O. Strunk, *Source Readings in Music History* (N.Y., 1950). —**NS/LK/DM**

Montgomery, Buddy (Charles F.), jazz pianist, vibraphonist, brother of Monk and **Wes Montgomery**; b. Indianapolis, Ind., Jan. 30, 1930. His brother Wes got him interested in music, though he didn't begin playing piano until age 18. He never learned to read or write music. His influences were Garner, Tatum, Bud Powell, and Indianapolis pianist Earl Grandy. After only six months, he was hired for a tour down South with singer Joe Turner organized by saxophonist Jimmy Coe. Into the 1950s he rehearsed and gigged with Slide Hampton and his brothers Maceo and Lucky (trumpet and tenor) in the Hampton family band. He worked with his brothers in two aggregations in 1957–62, the Mastersounds and the Montgomery Brothers. He appeared in several C.A. concerts with the Miles Davis sextit in place of Coltrane in February and March 1960 and was scheduled to go with Davis to Europe but declined, citing a fear of airplanes. He later went to Las Vegas and became fairly successful playing in pit and stage bands. He had a long residence at the Bombay Bicycle Room at Milwaukee's Mark Plaza Hotel in the 1970s with bassist Jeff Chambers and Ray Appleton.

DISC.: *Two-Sided Album* (1968); *This Rather Than That* (1969); *Ties of Love* (1986); *Of Love* (1986); *So Why Not?* (1988); *Live at Maybeck Recital Hall, Vol. 15* (1991); *Here Again* (1997); *Mastersounds: Kismet* (1958); *Jazz Showcase Introducing the Mastersounds* (1958); *Flower Drum Song* (1958); *Mastersounds in Concert* (1959); *Mastersounds Play Horace Silver* (1959); *Ballads and Blues* (1959); *Happy Holidays from Many Lands* (1960); *Swing-in with the Mastersounds* (1961); *Mastersounds on Tour* (1961); *Date with the Mastersounds* (1961); *King and I* (1964).—**LP**

Montgomery, Kenneth (Mervyn),

Irish conductor; b. Belfast, Oct. 28, 1943. He received his formal musical education at the Royal Coll. of Music in London, and then studied conducting in Siena with Celibidache, and in London with Boult; also had instruction with Pritchard and Schmidt-Isserstedt. In 1964 he joined the conducting staff of the Glyndebourne Festival, and in 1966 he conducted at the Sadler's Wells Opera in London. In 1970 he became asst. conductor of the Western Orch. Soc. at Bournemouth, in 1972, its assoc. conductor, and in 1973 he was appointed music director of the Bournemouth Sinfonietta. He was music director of the Glyndebourne Touring Opera (1975–76). From 1976 to 1980 he was principal conductor of the Netherlands Radio. In 1981 he became chief conductor of its Groot Omroep Koor. He was music director of Opera Northern Ireland in Belfast from 1985. —**NS/LK/DM**

Montgomery, Wes (John Leslie),

popular jazz guitarist, brother of Monk and **Buddy Montgomery**; b. Indianapolis, Ind., March 6, 1923 (some give 1925); d. there, June 15, 1968. He was one of the most celebrated of all jazz guitarists, for the perfection of his melodies and phrasing, his lovely soft sound (achieved partly through the use of his right thumb rather than a pick when he found the latter cumbersome), and his fluency in block chord solos. His parents were singers and regular church goers. The oldest brother, Thomas Jr., was a drummer who got Wes and his brother started in music, though he never read music; Wes in turn inspired his other brother Buddy. He began his career performing in local clubs, then toured and recorded with Lionel Hampton's band (1948–50). He didn't solo on the studio recordings but is featured briefly in the Jubilee Armed Forces radio broadcast 327 recorded around February 1949 on the titles "Jay Bird" and "Oklahoma City Boogie and Bop." After Hampton, he returned to Indianapolis. He formed a group with his brothers Buddy and Monk, originally known as the Mastersounds (1957–60), then as the Montgomery Brothers (1960–62). He also formed his own trio (1959), which recorded the successful *Wes Montgomery Trio* album that same year after Cannonball Adderley alerted his producer Orrin Keepnews to the guitarist's talents. Montgomery was a favorite of Coltrane and

they performed at the Jazz Workshop in San Francisco in September 1961. Then, on Sept. 22, they drove up to Monterey to perform that night at the festival; they never did work out as a regular group—some say because of musical differences, some say because Wes, like his brother Buddy, didn't like to fly. Wes toured widely from 1963. He won a Grammy Award for his recording of "Goin' Out of My Head" (1965); his album *A Day in the Life* (1967) was the best-selling jazz LP of the year. He appeared on the cover of *Down Beat* only a week before his premature death of a heart attack at 43.

DISC.: *Fingerpickin'* (1957); *Montgomery Brothers* (1958); *Kismet* (1958); *Far Wes* (1958); *Yesterdays* (1959); *A Dynamic New Sound* (1959); *Guitar on the Go* (1959); *Pretty Blue* (1959); *The Incredible Jazz Guitar of Wes Montgomery* (1960); *Movin' Along* (1960); *The Alternative Wes Montgomery* (1960); *Encores* (1960); *So Much Guitar* (1961); *Recorded Live at Jorgie's Jazz Club* (1961); *Wes and Friends* (1961); *Full House* (1962); *Fusion! Wes Montgomery with Strings* (1963); *Boss Guitar* (1963); *Portrait of Wes* (1963); *Movin' Wes* (1964); *Live in Paris* (1965); *Impressions* (1965); *Solitude* (1965); *Bumpin'* (1965); *Smokin' at the Half Note* (1965); *Willow Weep for Me* (1965); *Goin' Out of My Head* (1965); *Tequila* (1966); *California Dreaming* (1966); *A Day in the Life* (1967); *Down Here on the Ground* (1967); *Road Song* (1968); *Eulogy* (1970).

BIBL.: L. Garson and J. Stewart, *Wes Montgomery Jazz Guitar Method* (N.Y., 1968); S. Khan, *Wes Montgomery Guitar Folio* (N.Y., 1978); A. Ingram, *Wes Montgomery* (Newcastle-upon-Tyne, 1985); F. Sokolow, *Wes Montgomery: Artist Transcriptions for Guitar* (Milwaukee, Wisc., 1988); J. Bastian, *The Boss Guitar of Wes Montgomery: A Collection of Early Period Transcriptions* (Houston, 1995); Zafar Saalik Saood, *Mel Bay Presents Wes Montgomery: Jazz Guitar Artistry* (Pacific, Mo., 1995).—**LP**

Monti,

family of Italian musicians:

(1) Anna Maria Monti, singer; b. Rome, 1704; d. probably in Naples, after 1727. She was only 13 when she made her debut in the 2nd comedienne's role in the Piscopo-De Falco dialect opera *Lo mbruoglio d'ammore* at the Teatro dei Fiorentini in Naples, where she sang until 1727.

(2) Laura Monti, singer, sister of the preceding; b. probably in Rome, afer 1704; d. Naples, 1760. After appearing in comic roles at the Teatro Nuovo in Naples, she sang at the royal theater S. Bartolomeo in that city (1733–35), where she created roles in operas by Hasse, Leo, and Pergolesi, including the latter's Serpina in *La Serva padrona* (1733). She was active at the court until her retirement around 1746.

(3) Marianna Monti, soprano, cousin of the two preceding; b. Naples, 1730; d. there, 1814. She made her debut in the Trinchera-Conforto opera *La finta vedova* at the Teatro dei Fiorentini in 1746. She sang there and at the Teatro Nuovo until 1759, and also appeared in concerts under the patronage of the Marchese di Gerace. From 1760 to 1780 Monti was the outstanding prima buffa in Naples, creating numerous roles in operas by Cimarosa, Jommelli, Logroscino, Paisiello, Piccinni, and Sacchini. Her last years were blighted by poverty until she was granted a royal pension in 1812.

(4) Gaetano Monti, organist and composer, brother of the preceding; b. Naples, c. 1750; d. probably there, c. 1816. He was organista straordinario at the Philippine

Tesoro di S. Gennaro in Naples from 1776 to about 1788. He wrote a number of operas, many with roles composed especially for his sister. His most successful stage works were *Le donne vendicate* (Naples, Oct. 17, 1781; also known as *Il gigante*) and *Lo studente* (Naples, 1783; not extant).—NS/LK/DM

Monticelli, Angelo Maria, Italian castrato soprano; b. Milan, c. 1712; d. Dresden, 1764. He made his first stage appearance in Rome about 1730. After singing in Venice, Milan, and Florence, he was a principal member of the King's Theatre in London (1741–44; 1746). In subsequent years, he was active in various European music centers until settling in Dresden about 1755.—NS/LK/DM

Montsalvatge, (Bassols) Xavier, Spanish composer, music critic, and teacher; b. Gerona, March 11, 1911. He settled in Madrid and studied at the Cons. His mentors in composition were Morera and Pahissa. He was active as a teacher and as a music critic, writing for the newspaper *La Vanguardia* (1960–72) and serving as ed. of the newspaper *Destino* (1962–70). His autobiography was publ. in Barcelona in 1987. Montsalvatge composed in a well-crafted tonal style in which he occasionally made use of bracing dissonance.

WORKS: DRAMATIC: *El gato con botas*, magic opera (1948); *Una voce in off*, opera (1961); incidental music; film scores. **ORCH.:** 2. syms. (*Sinfonia mediterranea*, 1949; *Sinfonia da requiem*, 1986); *Concierto breve* for Piano and Orch. (1952); *Partita 1958* (1958); *Desintegración morfología de la chacona de Bach* (1962); *Laberinto* (1970); *Cinco invocaciones al Crucificado* (1970); *Reflexus obertura* (1974); *Serenata a Lydia de Cadaques* for Flute and Orch. (1974; also for Flute and Piano, 1969); *Concerto capriccio* for Harp and Orch. (1975); *Concertino 1+13* for Violin and Chamber String Orch. (1975); *Concierto del Albayzin* for Harpsichord and Orch. (1977); *Metamorfosis de concierto* for Guitar and Orch. (1982); *Música per a un diumenge* for Band (1984); *Fanfarría para la Alegría de la Paz* (1985). **CHAMBER:** *Cuarteto Indiano* for String Quartet (1952); *Sef-paragrasis* for Clarinet and Piano (1968); *Serenata a Lydia de Cadaques* for Flute and Piano (1969; also for Flute and Orch., 1974); *Sonata concertante* for Cello and Piano (1972); *Parafrasis concertante* for Violin and Piano (1975); *Questions and Answers* for Brass Quintet (1979); *Cuadrivio para tres Stradivarius* for String Trio (1984); *Fantasis* for Guitar and Harp (1984); Trio for Violin, Cello, and Piano (1987); piano pieces; organ music. **VOCAL:** *Cinco canciones negras* for Soprano and Piano or Orch. (1945); *Cant espiritual* for Chorus and Orch. (1959); *Homenaje a Manolo Hugue* for Soprano and Orch. (1973); *Sum vermis* for Voice, 2 Pianos, and 2 Percussion (1974); solo songs. **BIBL.:** M. Valls, *X. M.* (Barcelona, 1969); E. Franco, *X. M.* (Madrid, 1975); R. Paine, *Hispanic Traditions in Twentieth-Century Catalan Music with Particular Reference to Gerhard, Mompou, and M.* (N.Y. and London, 1989).—NS/LK/DM

Monza, Carlo, Italian composer; b. Milan, c. 1735; d. there, Dec. 19, 1801. He studied with G.A. Fioroni and most likely received instruction from G.B. Sammartini, whom he succeeded as organist (1768) and then as maestro di cappella (1775) at Milan's ducal court. He also held the position of maestro di cappella at the

churches of S. Maria Segreta, S. Giovanni in Conca, and the Chiesa della Rosa there. He later became maestro di cappella at Milan Cathedral (1787), but retained his position at the ducal court. Illness ended his tenure at the former (1793), and the French occupation (1796) at the latter. He was a skillful composer of both operas and sacred music.

WORKS: DRAMATIC: Opera: *Olimpiade* (Milan, May 1753); *Sesostri re d'Egitto* (Milan, Dec. 26, 1759); *Achille in Sciro* (Milan, Feb. 4, 1764); *Temistocle* (Milan, Jan. 1, 1766); *Oreste* (Turin, Carnival 1766); *Demetrio* (Rome, Jan. 3, 1769); *Adriano in Siria* (Naples, Nov. 4, 1769); *Germanico in Germania* (Rome, Jan. 7, 1770); *La Lavandara astuta*, pasticcio (Milan, July 2, 1770); *Nitteti* (Milan, Jan. 22, 1771); *Aristo e Temira* (Bologna, May 1771); *Berenice* (Turin, 1771?); *Antigono* (Rome, Carnival 1772); *Il (finto) cavalier parigino* (Milan, Sept. 3, 1774); *Alessandro nelle Indie* (Bologna, Jan. 1775); *Cleopatra* (Turin, Dec. 26, 1775); *Caio Mario* (Venice, Ascension Fair 1777); *Attilio Regolo* (1777; not perf.); *Ifigenia in Tauride* (Milan, Jan. 1784); *Enea in Cartagine* (Alessandria, Oct. Fair 1784); *Erifile* (Turin, Dec. 26, 1785). **OTHER:** Secular cantatas. **OTHER:** Much sacred music, including 13 masses, 20 Glorias, 18 offertories, many motets, 11 Magnificats, and 37 hymns; also instrumental works, including several syms., overtures, chamber music, and keyboard pieces. —NS/LK/DM

Moodie, Alma, Australian violinist; b. Brisbane, Sept. 12, 1900; d. Frankfurt am Main, March 7, 1943. She studied with Thomson in Brussels (1907–10). She played at a concert as a child prodigy (with Reger). She gave concerts in Germany, where she lived most of her life, and also taught at the Frankfurt am Main Academy of Music. Her prestige as a musician was high in Germany, and she performed many new works, including Pfitzner's Violin Concerto, which was written for her.—NS/LK/DM

Moody, Fanny, English soprano; b. Redruth, Cornwall, Nov. 23, 1866; d. Dundrum, County Dublin, July 21, 1945. She studied with Charlotte Sainton-Dolby, making her debut in a memorial concert for her teacher at Prince's Hall in London (1885). She made her operatic debut as Arline in *The Bohemian Girl* with the Carl Rosa Opera Co. in Liverpool (1887), and subsequently was the company's principal soprano until 1898; she married the Irish bass and impresario Charles Manners (1890), with whom she founded the Moody-Manners Opera Co. (1898), and thereafter toured widely with it until it was disbanded (1916). Among her best roles were Gounod's Marguerite and Juliet, Verdi's Leonora, and Santuzza.—NS/LK/DM

Moody, James, jazz alto and tenor saxophonist, flutist; b. Savannah, Ga., March 26, 1925. He is best known for a long association with Gillespie, and like Gillespie he is a witty entertainer whose comedy sometimes obscures the brilliance of his playing. He incorporated the "Giant Steps" vocabulary of Coltrane, but few realize that he was an innovator himself; on his 1955 *Hi-Fi Party* his solo goes right into a different key than the rhythm section. His family were living in Reading, P.A., but his mother went to Savannah looking for his runaway father. After Moody was born, she returned to Reading. He was put in a school for retarded children because no one believed that he had hearing problems. His mother later moved to Newark so he could attend regular public school and the teacher agreed to sit him in the front of the room. He did well and even skipped "a couple of grades" but at a regular medical inspection Moody was diagnosed as being partially deaf and was sent to Booth St. School for the Deaf, where he went for two years, graduated, then went to Arts High in Newark. He was in the air force band in 1943–46 and was stationed in Greensboro, N.C. Moody then worked with Dizzy Gillespie in 1946–48, beginning at the Spotlite Club in N.Y. and even touring Europe with him. He initially went to Europe again to stay with an uncle (while he recovered from his alcohol addiction), but he liked it there and decided to stay. He lived in Paris from 1948–51 and, while there, scored a huge hit on alto with his improvisation on "I'm in the Mood for Love" (1949). Babs Gonzales convinced Moody to return to the U.S. to capitalize on his popularity and hit. The song was a hit again in 1952, when King Pleasure wrote words to fit his solo and turned it into "Moody's Mood for Love." Moody added flute to his arsenal in the 1950s, co-led a septet in 1951–62, then played in a three-tenor unit with Sonny Stitt and Gene Ammons in 1962; he rejoined Gillespie in 1963–68. He's been a leader ever since and worked in Las Vegas pit bands behind various pop stars in the late 1970s. He is also a marvelous scat singer and often does "Moody's Mood for Love." His 70th birthday was celebrated with a week at the Blue Note in Manhattan and a resulting album. He had a small acting role as William Simon Glover in *Midnight in the Garden of Good and Evil* (1997). Moody was named an NEA American Jazz Master in 1998.

Disc.: *New Sounds* (1948); *James Moody and His Modernists* (1948); *James Moody Favorites, Vol. 1–3* (1949); *James Moody: His Saxophone* (1950); *James Moody with Strings* (1951); *James Moody in France* (1951); *Moody Story* (1952); *Moodsville* (1952); *Workshop* (1954); *Moody's Workshop* (1954); *Moody's Moods* (1954); *Moody's Mood* (1954); *James Moody's Moods* (1954); *Wail, Moody, Wail* (1955); *James Moody and His Band* (1955); *Hi-Fi Party* (1955); *Moody's Mood for Love* (1956); *Flute 'n' the Blues* (1956); *Everything You've Always Wanted* (1956); *Last Train from Overbrook* (1958); *James Moody* (1959); *Hey! It's James Moody* (1959); *Moody with Strings* (1960); *Cookin' the Blues* (1961); *Another Bag* (1962); *Great Day* (1963); *Comin' on Strong* (1963); *Running the Gamut* (1964); *Moody and the Brass Figures* (1967); *Don't Look Away Now* (1969); *Blues and Other Colors* (1969); *Teachers* (1970); *Too Heavy for Words* (1971); *Never Again* (1972); *And the Hip Organ* (1972); *Feelin' It Together* (1973); *Beyond This World* (1977); *Jazz Legacy* (1980); *Something Special* (1986); *Moving Forward* (1987); *Sweet and Lovely* (1989); *Honey* (1990); *James Moody and Frank Foster in Concert* (1995).

Bibl.: F. Vernon, *James Moody's Greatest Transcribed Flute Solos* (Milwaukee, Wisc., 1995).—**LP**

Moody Blues, The,

grandiose British rock band who combined symphonic strings with overblown songs. **Membership:** Denny Laine (real name, Brian Hines), gtr., voc. (b. Birmingham, Warwickshire, England, Oct. 29, 1944); Mike Pinder, kybd., gtr. (b. Birmingham, England, Dec. 27, 1941); Clint Warwick (real name, Clinton Eccles), bs. (b. Birmingham, England, June 25, 1949); Ray Thomas, bs. (b. Stourport-on-Severn, Hertfordshire, England, Dec. 29, 1942); Graeme Edge, drm. (b. Rochester, Kent, England, March 30, 1942).

Laine and Warwick left in 1966, to be replaced by Justin Hayward, lead voc., lead gtr., kybd., sitar (b. Swindon, Wiltshire, England, Oct. 14, 1946); and John Lodge, bs., voc. (b. Birmingham, England, July 20, 1945)s. In 1978, Pinder was replaced by Patrick Moraz, kybd. (b. Morges, Switzerland, June 24, 1948).

The Moody Blues were formed in 1964 in Birmingham, England, by Denny Laine, Mike Pinder, Clint Warwick, Ray Thomas, and Graeme Edge. Thomas and Pinder had been in the Birmingham group El Riot and The Rebels, while Laine had led Denny Laine and The Diplomats between 1962 and 1964. The Moody Blues debuted in Birmingham in May 1964, later playing at London's famed Marquee club. Signed to British Decca (London/Deram in the U.S.), the group's second single, the blues-style "Go Now!," became a smash British and major American hit in early 1965. However, the initial lineup never again achieved even another moderate hit and, in 1966, both Laine and Warwick left, with Laine eventually joining Paul McCartney's Wings in 1971.

Adding Justin Hayward and John Lodge, The Moody Blues obtained a mellotron and embarked on a totally new musical direction under producer Tony Clarke. The lineup's debut album, *Days of Future Passed*, eschewed their blues backgrounds and was hailed both as a "concept" album and for its adventurous fusion of rock and classical music. Recorded with The London Festival Orch., the album yielded a major hit with "Tuesday Afternoon" and included the classic "Nights in White Satin," a smash hit upon rerelease in 1972. For their next album, *In Search of the Lost Chord*, The Moody Blues made extensive use of the mellotron and studio overdubbing, playing more than 30 different instruments to produce their characteristic lavish sound without an orchestra. The album contained the cosmic favorites "Legend of a Mind" and "Om" and produced a minor hit with the rocking "Ride My See-Saw."

On the Threshold of a Dream yielded a minor hit with "Never Comes the Day" in 1969, the year The Moody Blues formed Threshold Records. The group's first album release on the label, *To Our Children's Children's Children*, contained band favorites such as "Higher and Higher" and "I Never Thought I'd Live to Be a Hundred/Million." Abandoning multiple overdubs beginning with *A Question of Balance*, The Moody Blues scored major hits with "Question," "The Story in My Eyes," and "Isn't Life Strange," and "I'm Just a Singer (In a Rock and Roll Band)" from *Seventh Sojourn*.

After a nine-month world tour ended in the U.S. in early 1974, the members of The Moody Blues settled down to a variety of outside projects. The first and most successful of these, Justin Hayward and John Lodge's *Blue Jays*, yielded two minor hits with "I Dreamed Last Night" and "Blue Guitar." Other projects included solo albums by Thomas, Pinder, Hayward, and Lodge, and two albums by Edge with Adrian Gurvitz.

In July 1977, The Moody Blues announced their intention to reunite for yet another album. Following the release of *Octave*, which produced minor hits with "Steppin' in a Slide Zone" and "Driftwood," The Moody Blues conducted a successful worldwide tour with Patrick Moraz (formerly of Yes) substituting for Michael Pinder, who had moved to Calif. Moraz joined the band on a permanent basis in 1978. Pinder eventually reemerged in the mid-1990s, recording one music and two children's albums for his own label, One Step Records.

The Moody Blues' 1981 *Long Distance Voyager* produced two major hits, "Gemini Dream" and "The Voice," and 1986's *The Other Side of Life*, featuring guitar, synthesizers, and electronic drums, yielded their first near-smash hit in years with "Your Wildest Dreams." They conducted a world tour in 1986, switching to Polydor Records for *Sur La Mer* and its moderate hit "I Know You're Out There Somewhere." Patrick Moraz left The Moody Blues in early 1992 and, in 1994, the group toured America performing with local symphony orchestras. Polydor's 5–CD set *Time Traveler* compiled studio recordings from *Days of Future Passed* through *Keys to the Kingdom*, as well as Justin Hayward and John Lodge's *Blue Jays*.

DISC.: *Number 1* (1965); *The Magnificent Moodies* (1965); *Days of Future Passed* (1968); *In Search of the Lost Chord* (1968); *On the Threshold of a Dream* (1969); *To Our Children's Children's Children* (1970): *A Question of Balance* (1970); *Every Good Boys Deserves Favour* (1971); *In the Beginning* (1971); *Seventh Sojourn* (1972); *Caught Live Plus Five* (1977); *Octave* (1978); *Long Distance Voyager* (1981); *The Present* (1983); *Early Blues* (1985); *The Other Side of Life* (1986); *Prelude* (1987); *Sur La Mer* (1988); *Keys of the Kingdom* (1991); *A Night at Red Rock with The Colo. Symphony Orch.* (1993).—**BH**

Moog, Robert (Arthur), American designer of electronic instruments; b. Flushing, N.Y., May 23, 1934. He studied at Queens Coll. (B.S. in physics, 1957), Columbia Univ. (B.S. in electrical engineering, 1957), and Cornell Univ. (Ph.D. in engineering physics, 1965). He founded the R.A. Moog Co. in 1954 for the purpose of designing electronic musical instruments; in 1964 he introduced the first synthesizer modules; his company was incorporated in 1968, with its headquarters at Trumansburg, N.Y. In 1970 he brought out the Minimoog, a portable monophonic instrument; in 1971 the company became Moog Music and went to Buffalo, N.Y.; in 1973 it became a division of Norlin Industries, with which Moog was associated until 1977. He founded another firm, Big Briar, in Leicester, N.C., which manufactured devices for precision control of analog and digital synthesizers. He was associated with Kurzweil Music Systems of Boston (1984–89). His synthesizers and other electronic devices were used by both classical and rock musicians.—**NS/LK/DM**

Moonglows, The, one of the most innovative of the 1950s doo-wop vocal groups and pioneers of rock and roll. **MEMBERSHIP:** Harvey Fuqua, lead bar. (b. Louisville, Ky., July 27, 1929); Bobby Lester (Robert Dallas), lead ten. (b. Louisville, Ky., Jan. 13, 1930; d. there, Oct. 15, 1980); Alexander "Pete" Graves II, ten. (b. Cleveland, Ohio, April 17, 1936); Prentiss Barnes, bs.

voc. (b. Magnolia, Miss., April 12, 1925); Billy Johnson, gtr. (b. Hartford, Conn., 1924; d. 1987).

Bobby Lester and Harvey Fuqua started singing together in high school as a duet. In 1950 Fuqua moved to Cleveland, where he formed The Crazy Sounds with Prentiss Barnes. The group later added Lester and Pete Graves, coming to the attention of disc jockey Alan Freed through Al "Fats" Thomas. Freed changed the group's name to The Moonglows and recorded one single by the group for his short-lived Champagne label. In 1953 the group signed with Chicago's Chance label, recording five singles. Adding guitarist Billy Johnson, The Moonglows moved to the Chess label in the fall of 1954. Their first single, Fuqua's "Sincerely," with Lester on lead vocals, became a top R&B and major pop hit, but The McGuire Sisters soon covered the song for Coral, scoring a top pop hit. The Moonglows also recorded for the Chess subsidiary Checker as Bobby Lester and the Moonlighters, but achieved no hits. With Lester on lead vocals, The Moonglows' R&B hits continued through 1956 with Fuqua's "Most of All," "We Go Together" and the up-tempo "See Saw" (a major pop hit), followed by Percy Mayfield's "Please Send Me Someone to Love," with Fuqua on lead vocals. The group appeared in the 1956 film *Rock, Rock, Rock* and toured throughout the 1950s.

Bobby Lester dropped out of The Moonglows in 1958 and, with Fuqua on lead vocals, the group scored a hit with "Ten Commandments of Love" as Harvey and The Moonglows. Fuqua appeared in the 1958 film *Go, Johnny, Go* without The Moonglows, and the group soon broke up. In 1959 Fuqua recruited a Washington, D.C.–based group, The Marquees, for further recordings as The Moonglows. One of the group's co-lead singers was Marvin Gaye. Although none of their recordings proved hits, they did perform background vocals on Chuck Berry's 1959 hits "Almost Grown" and "Back in the U.S.A." By 1960 this edition of The Moonglows had disbanded. Fuqua brought Etta James to Chess Records, where the two recorded the smash R&B hit "If I Can't Have You" as Etta and Harvey.

Harvey Fuqua subsequently moved to Detroit, where he met and married Barry Gordy's sister, Gwen. In 1961 Fuqua discovered The Spinners and formed the Harvey and Tri-Phi labels with Gwen Gordy, who had formed her own independent label, Anna, in 1958. On Tri-Phi, The Spinners scored a smash R&B/major pop hit with "That's What Girls Are Made Of," with Fuqua on lead vocals and Marvin Gaye on drums. In 1963 Berry Gordy purchased Harvey and Tri- Phi Records, and Fuqua went to work for Motown as songwriter, producer and head of artists development. He brought with him Marvin Gaye, The Spinners, Johnny Bristol, Shorty Long and Junior Walker, and later discovered Tammi Terrell.

Harvey Fuqua produced Marvin Gaye and Tammi Terrell's hits "Ain't No Mountain High Enough" and "Your Precious Love." While at Motown, Fuqua and Johnny Bristol co-wrote Gaye and Terrell's near-smash hit "If I Could Build My World around You," David Ruffin's "My Whole World Ended (The Moment You Left Me)," Edwin Starr's "Twenty-Five Miles," and

Junior Walker and The All-Stars' "What Does It Take (To Win Your Love)." Bristol and Fuqua coproduced Stevie Wonder's "Yester-Me, Yester-You, Yesterday"; and the original Supremes' final hit, "Someday We'll Be Together," had been written by Bristol, Fuqua and Jackie Beavers—originally recorded by Bristol and Beavers.

In the meantime, Pete Graves had formed a new edition of The Moonglows in 1964, but recordings for Lana and other labels proved unsuccessful. In 1971 Bobby Lester briefly formed his own edition of The Moonglows. Harvey Fuqua left Motown in 1970, forming a new edition of The Moonglows in 1971 with Lester, Graves, Doc Williams and Chuck Lewis for one album issued on RCA. Fuqua soon formed his own production company and brought his discovery The New Birth to RCA. The New Birth achieved a hit with "I Can Understand" in 1973 and "It's Been a Long Time" in 1974 for RCA, and a top R&B hit with "Dream Merchant" for Buddah in 1975. Bobby Lester revived another edition of The Moonglows in the late 1970s, touring and recording *One More Time*, but he died of cancer on Oct. 15, 1980. By then Fuqua had formed another production company in San Francisco, producing disco hits for Sylvester on Fantasy Records, including the 1978 R&B hit "Dance (Disco Heat)." Fuqua also produced 1980s recordings for Marvin Gaye and continued to write songs and occasionally perform with The Moonglows.

DISC.: *Look, It's The Moonglows* (1959); *The Best of Bobby Lester and The Moonglows* (1962). **THE FLAMINGOS AND THE MOONGLOWS:** *The Flamingos Meet The Moonglows* (1962).—**BH**

Moor (real name, **Mohr**), **Karel,** Czech conductor, composer, and writer; b. Bělohrad, Dec. 26, 1873; d. Prague, March 30, 1945. He studied at the Prague Cons. and in Vienna. From 1900 to 1923 he was active as a theatrical director and conductor in Bohemia and Serbia, and then he lived mainly in Prague. He achieved his first success as a composer with the operetta *Pan profesor v pekle* (Mr. Professor in Hell), produced in Brünn in 1908. His other operas, *Hjördis* (1899; rev. 1901; Prague, Oct. 22, 1905) and *Viy*, after Gogol's fantastic tale (1901; Prague, July 14, 1903), were also successful. A facile writer, Moor publ. an autobiography in the form of a novel as *Karl Martens* (Prague, 1906), a vol. of reminiscences, *Vzpomínsky* (Pilsen, 1917), and a semi-fictional book, *V dlani osudu* (In the Hands of Fate; Nový Bydżov, 1947).—**NS/LK/DM**

Moór, Emanuel, Hungarian pianist, inventor, and composer; b. Kecskemét, Feb. 19, 1863; d. Mont Pélerin, near Montreux, Switzerland, Oct. 20, 1931. He studied in Budapest and Vienna. He toured the U.S. from 1885 to 1887 as director of the Concerts Artistiques, for which he engaged Lilli Lehmann, Ovide Musin, and other celebrated artists, and also acted as their accompanist. He then lived in London, Lausanne, and Munich. He invented the Moór-Duplex piano, consisting of a double keyboard with a coupler between the two manuals (an octave apart). With the introduction of this piano, a new technique was made possible, facilitating the playing of octaves, tenths, and even chromatic glissandos. Some piano manufacturers (Steinway, Bechstein, Bösendorfer) put the Moór mechanism into their instruments. His 2nd wife, Winifred Christie (b. Stirling, Feb. 26, 1882; d. London, Feb. 8, 1965), an English pianist, aided him in promoting the Moór keyboard, and gave many performances on it in Europe and the U.S. She publ. (in collaboration with her husband) a manual of technical exercises for the instrument.

WORKS: DRAMATIC: O p e r a : *La Pompadour* (Cologne, Feb. 22, 1902); *Andreas Hofer* (Cologne, Nov. 9, 1902); *Hochzeitsglocken* (Kassel, Aug. 2, 1908; in London as *Wedding Bells*, Jan. 26, 1911); *Der Goldschmied von Paris* (n.d.); *Hertha* (unfinished). **ORCH.:** 3 piano concertos (1886, 1888, 1906); 8 syms. (1893–1910); 4 violin concertos (1905–07); 2 cello concertos (1905–06); Triple Concerto for Violin, Cello, Piano, and Orch. (1907); Harp Concerto (1913). **OTHER:** *Requiem* (1916); much chamber music; numerous songs.

BIBL.: M. Pirani, *E. M.* (London, 1959).—**NS/LK/DM**

Moore, Carman (Leroy), versatile black American composer, conductor, teacher, and writer on music; b. Lorain, Ohio, Oct. 8, 1936. He studied with Martin Morris (horn), Peter Brown (cello), and Cecil Isaacs (conducting) at the Oberlin (Ohio) Coll. Cons. of Music. After further studies at Ohio State Univ. (B.M., 1958), he went to N.Y., where he studied at the Juilliard School of Music with Persichetti and Berio (B.M., 1966); completed his studies with Wolpe (1967). He helped to launch the Soc. of Black Composers in 1968. He taught at Manhattanville Coll. (1969–71), Yale Univ. (1969–71), and Queens (1970–71) and Brooklyn (1972–74) Colls. of the City Univ. of N.Y. He presented concerts with his own group, Carman Moore and Ensemble, which he transformed into the Skymusic Ensemble in 1985. In addition to writing music criticism, he publ. a biography of Bessie Smith as *Somebody's Angel Child* (1970) and a textbook on teaching popular music (1980). In his compositions, he makes imaginative use of various genres, ranging from jazz to the avant-garde.

WORKS: DRAMATIC: O p e r a : *The Masque of Saxophone's Voice* (1981). **M u s i c T h e a t e r :** *Wild Gardens of the Loup Garou* (1983); *Distraughter, or The Great Panda Scanda* (1983); *Paradise Re-Lost* (1987). **M u s i c a l :** *Franklin and Eleanor* (1989). **B a l l e t :** *A Musical Offering* (1962); *Catwalk* (1966); *Tryst* (1966); *They Tried to Touch* (1986); *La Dea delle Acque* (Milan, March 29, 1988). **D a n c e P i e c e :** *Shipwreck* (1989). **I n t e r m e d i a :** *Broken Suite* for Instrumental Ensemble (1969); *The Illuminated Workingman* for 11 Instruments and Tape (1971); *American Themes and Variations* for Narrator and Instrumental Ensemble (1980); *Sky Dance/Sky Time* for Instrumental Ensemble, Dance Ensemble, and Sculpture (1984); *The Persistence of Green* for Dance, Dance Projections, and Instrumental Ensemble (N.Y., April 16, 1988); *The Magical Turn About Town* for Instrumental Ensemble (N.Y., July 18, 1989); *Tales of Exile* for Dancers and Instrumental Ensemble (N.Y., July 15, 1989); *Magic Circle* for Dancer, Projections, and Instrumental Ensemble (N.Y., Dec. 28, 1989). **ORCH.:** *Sinfonia* (1964); *Saratoga Festival Overture* (1966); *Gospel Fuse* for 4 Women's Voices and Orch. (San Francisco, Jan. 22, 1975); *Wildfires and Field Songs* (N.Y., Jan. 23, 1975); *Hit*, percussion concerto (1978); Concerto for Blues Piano and Orch. (1982); *Concertos (The Theme Is Freedom)* (N.Y., Nov. 11, 1985); Concerto for Jazz Violin and Orch. (1987). **CHAMBER:**

Piano Sonata (1963); Mandolin Sonata (1966); Cello Sonata (1966); *Drum Major* for Chamber Ensemble and Tape (1969); Quartet for Saxophones and Echo Device (1978); *Dawn of the Solar Age* for Brass, Percussion, and Synthesizer (1978); *Music for the Flute Alone* for Flute, Piano, Double Bass, and Tape (1981); *Deep Night with Tree* for Flute and Taped Flute (1986); *Journey to: Journey through* for 9 Instruments (1987); Concerto for Tap and Chamber Ensemble (1989). **VOCAL:** *Wedding Cantata* for Voices and Instruments (1963); *Variations on a Theme of Abraham Lincoln* for Soprano and Instrumental Ensemble (1973); *The Great American Nebula*, cantata for Narrator, Chorus, Orch., and Synthesizer (1976); *Follow Light* for Chorus, Percussion, and Double Bass (1981); *Celestial Intervals or Triptych* for Soprano, Tenor, and Instrumental Ensemble (N.Y., April 14, 1989); *Mass for the 21st Century* for Soloists, Chorus, and Orch. (N.Y., Aug. 10, 1994).—NS/LK/DM

Moore, Dorothy Rudd, black American composer; b. New Castle, Del., June 4, 1940. She studied with Mark Fax at Howard Univ. (B.Mus., 1963), with Boulanger at the American Cons. at Fontainebleau (1963), and with Chou Wen-chung in N.Y. (1965). She then taught at the Harlem School of the Arts (1965–66), N.Y.U. (1969), and Bronx Community Coll. (1971), appeared as a singer in N.Y., and wrote poetry. In 1968 she helped to found the Soc. of Black Composers. She is married to the cellist Kermit Moore, who has given premiere performances of her works.

WORKS: DRAMATIC: Opera: *Frederick Douglass* (1979–85). **ORCH.:** *Reflections* for Symphonic Winds (1962); Sym. (1963). **CHAMBER:** *Baroque Suite* for Cello (1965); *Adagio* for Viola and Cello (1965); *3 Pieces* for Violin and Piano (1967); *Modes* for String Quartet (1968); *Moods* for Viola and Cello (1969); Piano Trio (1970); *Dirge and Deliverance* for Cello and Piano (1971); *Night Fantasy* for Clarinet and Piano (1978); also piano pieces, including *Dream and Variations* (1974) and *A Little Whimsy* (1982). **VOCAL:** Numerous works, including song cycles (*12 Quatrains from the Rubaiyat* for Soprano and Oboe [1962], etc.) and solo songs.—NS/LK/DM

Moore, Douglas (Stuart), distinguished American composer and pedagogue; b. Cutchogue, N.Y., Aug. 10, 1893; d. Greenport, Long Island, July 25, 1969. After initial musical training in N.Y., he studied with D.S. Smith and Horatio Parker at Yale Univ. (B.A., 1915; B.M., 1917). He composed several univ. and popular songs, including the football song *Good Night, Harvard*, which became a favorite among the Yale student body. After serving in the U.S. Navy, he studied organ with Tournemire and composition with d'Indy and Boulanger in Paris. He was organist at the Cleveland Museum of Art (1921–23) and at Adelbert Coll., Western Reserve Univ. (1923–25). During this period, he pursued training with Ernest Bloch. In 1925 he received a Pulitzer traveling scholarship, which enabled him to study in Europe. From 1926 to 1962 he taught at Barnard Coll. and at Columbia Univ., serving as chairman of the latter's music dept. from 1940 to 1962. In 1934 he held a Guggenheim fellowship. In 1951 he won the Pulitzer Prize in Music for his opera *Giants in the Earth*. His opera *The Ballad of Baby Doe* won the N.Y. Music Critics' Circle Award in 1958. In 1941 he was elected to the National Inst. of Arts and Letters, and in 1951 to the American Academy of Arts and Letters. He was the author of the books *Listening to Music* (1932; 2nd ed., aug., 1937) and *From Madrigal to Modern Music: A Guide to Musical Style* (1942). Moore was a fine musical craftsman who applied his technical mastery to American subjects in his operas and symphonic scores. He achieved popular success with his operas *The Devil and Daniel Webster* (N.Y., May 18, 1939) and *The Ballad of Baby Doe* (Central City, Colo., July 7, 1956).

WORKS: DRAMATIC: Opera: *Jesse James* (1928; unfinished); *White Wings*, chamber opera (1935; Hartford, Conn., Feb. 9, 1949); *The Headless Horseman*, high school opera (1936; Bronxville, N.Y., March 4, 1937); *The Devil and Daniel Webster*, folk opera (1938; N.Y., May 18, 1939); *The Emperor's New Clothes*, children's opera (1948; N.Y., Feb. 19, 1949; rev. 1956); *Giants in the Earth* (1949; N.Y., March 28, 1951; rev. 1963); *The Ballad of Baby Doe*, folk opera (Central City, Colo., July 7, 1956); *Gallantry*, soap opera (1957; N.Y., March 19, 1958); *The Wings of the Dove* (N.Y., Oct. 12, 1961); *The Greenfield Christmas Tree*, Christmas entertainment (Baltimore, Dec. 8, 1962); *Carrie Nation* (Lawrence, Kans., April 28, 1966). **Musical Comedy:** *Oh, Oh, Tennessee* (1925). **Children's Operetta:** *Puss in Boots* (1949; N.Y., Nov. 18, 1950). **Ballet:** *Greek Games* (1930). **Incidental Music To:** plays and for the films *Power in the Land* (1940), *Youth Gets a Break*, and *Bip Goes to Town* (1941). **ORCH.:** *4 Museum Pieces* (1923; based on the organ piece); *The Pageant of P.T. Barnum*, suite (1924; Cleveland, April 15, 1926); *Moby Dick*, symphonic poem (1927); 2 syms.: No. 1, *A Symphony of Autumn* (1930) and No. 2 (1945; Paris, May 5, 1946); *Overture on an American Tune* (N.Y., Dec. 11, 1932); *Village Music*, suite (N.Y., Dec. 18, 1941); *In Memoriam*, symphonic poem (1943; Rochester, N.Y., April 27, 1944); *Farm Journal*, suite for Chamber Orch. (1947; N.Y., Jan. 19, 1948); *Cotillion*, suite for Strings (1952). **CHAMBER:** Violin Sonata (1929); String Quartet (1933); Wind Quintet (1942; rev. 1948); *Down East Suite* for Violin and Piano (1944; also for Violin and Orch.); Clarinet Quintet (1946); Piano Trio (1953). **KEYBOARD: Piano:** *3 Contemporaries: Careful Etta, Grievin' Annie*, and *Fiddlin' Joe* (c. 1935–40); *Museum Piece* (1939); Suite (1948); *4 Pieces* (1955); *Dance for a Holiday* (1957); *Prélude* (1957); *Summer Holiday* (1961). **Organ:** *Prélude and Fugue* (1919–22); *4 Museum Pieces* (1922; also for Orch.); *March* (1922); *Scherzo* (1923); *Passacaglia* (1939; arranged by K. Wilson as *Dirge* for Band). **VOCAL:** *Perhaps to Dream* for Women's Voices (1937); *Simon Legree* for Men's Voices and Piano (1937); *Dedication* for Chorus (1938); *Prayer for England* for Men's Voices (1940); *Prayer for the United Nations* for Alto or Baritone, Chorus, and Piano or Orch. (1943); *Western Winde*, canon for Chorus (c. 1946); *Vayechulu* for Cantor, Chorus, and Organ (1947–48); *Bird's Courting Song* for Tenor, Chorus, and Piano (c. 1953); *The Mysterious Cat* for Chorus (1960); *Mary's Prayer* for Soprano and Women's Voices (1962); many songs for Voice and Piano; arrangements of hymns and carols.—NS/LK/DM

Moore, Dudley (Stuart John), pop-jazz pianist, actor, composer; b. London, England, April 19, 1935. Though far better known as a comic actor, he is also a fine classical and jazz pianist. Moore studied at Guildhall School of Music and in 1957 earned a music degree at Magdalen Coll., Oxford, where he also gigged with fellow students. He joined Vic Lewis, played in USA with him (1959); played in the John Dankworth Quintet and Big Band (1960), then led his own trio from the summer of 1960. Moore began appearing in the successful revue Beyond the Fringe, which later played in America. He enjoyed considerable success as a comedian and actor on British television, then starred in a number of Hollywood films during the 1970s through the early 1990s. Moore occasionally led his own trio (including tours of Britain) and hosted TV programs about music in the 1990s. He has composed music for films, plays, ballets, and television. In 1999, Moore announced that he was suffering from a degenerative nerve disease.

DISC.: *Theme from "Beyond the Fringe"* (1962); *"Beyond the Fringe" and All That* (1962); *30 Is a Dangerous Age, Cynthia* (1967); *Bedazzled* (original soundtrack; 1968); *Dudley Moore at the Wavedon Festival* (1976); *Derek and Clive: Live* (1981); *Songs without Words* (1991).—**JC-B/LP**

Moore, Gerald, renowned English piano accompanist; b. Watford, July 30, 1899; d. Penn, Buckinghamshire, March 13, 1987. He first studied with Wallis Bandey at the local music school. After the family went to Canada in 1913, he continued his studies with Michael Hambourg, then made appearances as a solo recitalist and accompanist. Following his return to England (1919), he completed his training with Mark Hambourg. He began recording in 1921 and first gained distinction as accompanist to John Coates in 1925; he subsequently achieved well-nigh legendary fame as the preeminent accompanist of the day, appearing with such celebrated singers as Kathleen Ferrier, Dietrich Fischer-Dieskau, Elisabeth Schwarzkopf, Janet Baker, and others. He retired from the concert platform in 1967 but continued to make recordings. He was made a Commander of the Order of the British Empire (1954); was made an honorary D.Litt. by the Univ. of Sussex (1968) and Mus.D. by the Univ. of Cambridge (1973). As a witty account of his experiences at the piano, he publ. a sort of autobiography, *The Unashamed Accompanist* (London, 1943; rev. 1957), followed by an even more unzipped opus, *Am I Too Loud? Memoirs of an Accompanist* (London, 1962), and concluding with a somewhat nostalgic vol., *Farewell Recital: Further Memoirs* (London, 1978), and a rip-roaring sequel, *Furthermoore [sic]: Interludes in an Accompanist's Life* (London, 1983). Of a purely didactic nature are his books *Singer and Accompanist: The Performance of 50 Songs* (London, 1953), *The Schubert Song Cycles* (London, 1975), and *"Poet's Lore" and Other Schumann Cycles and Songs* (London, 1984).—**NS/LK/DM**

Moore, Grace, popular American soprano; b. Nough, near Del Rio, Tenn., Dec. 5, 1898; d. in an airplane crash near Copenhagen, Jan. 26, 1947. She studied at the Wilson Greene School of Music in Chevy Chase, Md., and with Marafioti in N.Y. She first appeared in musical comedy in N.Y. (1921–26), then continued her studies in Antibes with Richard Berthelemy. Upon returning to America, she made her operatic debut as Mimi at the Metropolitan Opera in N.Y. (Feb. 7, 1928), and sang there off and on until 1946; made successful appearances also at the Paris Opéra-Comique (1928), Covent Garden, London (1935), and other European centers; also sang with the Chicago City Opera (1937) and appeared in several films, including *One Night of Love* (1934). She publ. an autobiography, *You're Only Human Once* (1944). Her finest roles were Mimi, Tosca, Louise, Fiora, and Manon.—**NS/LK/DM**

Moore, Jerrold Northrop, American editor and writer on music; b. Paterson, N.J., March 1, 1934. He studied at Swarthmore Coll. (B.A., 1955) and Yale Univ. (M.A., 1956; Ph.D., 1959). He taught English at the Univ. of Rochester (1958–61), then was curator of historical sound recordings at Yale Univ. (1961–70). He wrote the authoritative biography *Edward Elgar: A Creative Life* (1984); was also an editor of the complete critical ed. of Elgar's works (from 1981). His other publications include *Elgar: A Life in Photographs* (1972), *Elgar on Record: The Composer and the Gramophone* (1974), *A Voice in Time: The Gramophone of Fred Gaisberg* (1976; U.S. ed. as *A Matter of Records*), *Music and Friends: Letters to Adrian Boult* (1979), *Spirit of England: Edward Elgar in His World* (1984), *Elgar and His Publishers: Letters of a Creative Life* (2 vols., 1987), *Edward Elgar: Letters of a Lifetime* (1990), and *Vaughan Williams: A Life in Photographs* (1992). —**NS/LK/DM**

Moore, John W(eeks), pioneer American musicologist and lexicographer; b. Andover, N.H., April 11, 1807; d. Manchester, N.H., March 23, 1889. He learned the printer's trade and then went to Brunswick, Maine (1828), where he publ. the first weekly newspaper in that state. After living in N.H. again (1831–38), he settled in Bellows Falls, Vt., as ed. of the *Bellows Falls Gazette* (1838–55); also ed. the *World of Music* (1843–49), a music journal. His magnum opus was the *Complete Encyclopedia of Music, Elementary, Technical, Historical, Biographical, Vocal, and Instrumental* (1852; reprint, 1972), the first comprehensive work of its kind in English. He went to Manchester (1863), where he revived the *World of Music* (1867–70). He also brought out a supplement to his encyclopedia (1875; reprint, 1972) and ed. *A Dictionary of Musical Instruments* (1876), an abridged version of his encyclopedia.—**NS/LK/DM**

Moore, Mary (Louise) Carr, American composer and teacher; b. Memphis, Tenn., Aug. 6, 1873; d. Inglewood, Calif., Jan. 9, 1957. Her father was a cavalry officer in the U.S. Army who sang; her mother authored several theater dramas; her uncle, John Harraden Pratt, was an organist. After the family went to Calif. (1885), she studied composition with her uncle and singing with H.B. Pasmore in San Francisco. She began her career as a teacher, composer, and singer; sang the lead role in her first operetta, *The Oracle* (San Francisco, March 19, 1894), but soon devoted herself fully to teaching and composition. She taught in Lemoore, Calif. (1895–1901), and in Seattle (1901–15), where she founded the American Music Center (1909); after teaching in San Francisco (1915–26), she went to Los Angeles as an instructor at the Olga Steeb Piano School (1926–43) and was prof. of theory and composition at Chapman Coll. (1928–47); was a founder of the Calif. Soc. of Composers (1936–38) and the Soc. of Native Composers (1938–44). As a composer, she devoted herself mainly to writing vocal works, particularly operas on American themes. Her most important score was *Narcissa, or The Cost of Empire* (Seattle, April 22, 1912), which was awarded the David Bispham Memorial Medal.

WORKS: DRAMATIC: Opera: *The Oracle* (San Francisco, March 19, 1894); *Narcissa, or The Cost of Empire* (1909–11; Seattle, April 22, 1912); *The Leper* (1912); *Memories* (Seattle, Oct. 31, 1914); *Harmony* (San Francisco, May 25, 1917); *The Flaming Arrow, or The Shaft of Ku'pish-ta-ya* (1919–20; San Francisco, March 27, 1922); *David Rizzio* (1927–28; Los Angeles, May 26, 1932); *Los rubios* (Los Angeles, Sept. 10, 1931); *Legende provençale* (1929–35); *Flutes of Jade Happiness* (1932–33; Los Angeles, March 2, 1934). **ORCH.:** *Ka-mi-a-kin* (1930); Piano Concerto (1933–34); *Kidnap* (1937–38). **CHAMBER:** 3 piano trios (1895, 1906, 1941); Violin Sonata (1918–19); 2 string quartets (1926, 1930); String Trio (1936); *Brief Furlough* for Quintet (1942); some 20 pieces for Various Instruments and Piano; 57 piano pieces. **VOCAL:** 57 choral works; some 250 songs (1889–1952).

BIBL.: C. Smith and C. Richardson, *M.C. M., American Composer* (Ann Arbor, 1989).—**NS/LK/DM**

Moore, Ralph, English saxophonist; b. Brixton, England, Dec. 24, 1956. He is a top-notch player who constructs cogent, highly nuanced solos. His warm but forceful style has made him one of the busiest tenor players of his generation. He attended Boston's Berklee School of Music (1975–78) where he developed strong musical relationships with guitarist Kevin Eubanks and drummer Marvin "Smitty" Smith. Moore moved to N.Y. in late 1980 and put in long stints with Horace Silver (1981–85) and J. J. Johnson. He worked and recorded with veterans such as Ray Brown, Roy Haynes, Dizzy Gillespie, Freddie Hubbard, Kenny Barron, Bobby Hutcherson, Jimmy Knepper, and toured with the Mingus Dynasty band. In the late 1980s, Moore, pianist Renee Rosnes, bassist Larry Grenadier, and drummer Billy Drummond formed the quartet Native Colours. Since 1995, he has been in Los Angeles, where he plays in the *Tonight Show* band and works regularly around Southern Calif. He has recorded a number of albums for Criss Cross, Landmark, Savoy, and Reservoir.

DISC.: *623 C Street* (1988); *Round Trip* (1988); *Rejuvenate!* (1989); *Images* (1989); *Furthermore* (1990); *Who It Is You Are* (1994).—**AG**

Moore, Thomas, famous Irish poet, ballad singer, and song composer; b. Dublin, May 28, 1779; d. Sloperton Cottage, near Devizes, Wiltshire, Feb. 25, 1852. He had no regular musical training, but learned to play the piano with the aid of the organist William Warren. He was in London from 1799 to 1803, and then received a position as a government functionary in Bermuda. However, he stayed there only a few months, returning to London by way of the U.S. and Canada. In London he became extremely popular as a ballad singer in the houses of the aristocracy. Between 1808 and 1834 he publ. *A Selection of Irish Melodies,* with music by John Stevenson. In 1817 he issued his celebrated poem *Lalla Rookh.* An ardent Irish nationalist, Moore played an important role in the creation and revival of Irish poetry and music. Among his own melodies are *Love thee,*

dearest, When midst the gay, One dear smile, and *The Canadian Boat-Song.* He freely borrowed his musical materials from popular Irish tunes and in some cases modified them sufficiently to produce apparently new songs. He also composed short concerted vocal pieces, the terzetto *O lady fair* and the 3-part glee *The Watchman* winning wide popularity. In 1895 Stanford publ. *The Irish Melodies of Thomas Moore: The Original Airs Restored.*

BIBL.: S. Gwynn, *T. M.* (London, 1905); W. Trench, *T. M.* (Dublin, 1934); J. Flannery, *T. M.: Minstrel of Ireland* (Pinellas Park, Fla., 1991).—**NS/LK/DM**

Moorhead, John, Irish violinist and composer; b. in Ireland, c. 1760; d. (suicide) near Deal, March 1804. After studying music in Ireland, he became a theater musician in England. In 1798 he joined the orch. at London's Covent Garden, but became insane and had to be committed in 1802. After his release, he became a navy bandmaster. Then, following a relapse in 1804, he took his own life. He wrote 14 stage works, including the comic operas *Il Bondocani, or The Caliph Robber* (Covent Garden, Nov. 15, 1800; in collaboration with Attwood), *The Cabinet* (Covent Garden, Feb. 9, 1802; in collaboration with Braham, Corri, Davy, and Reeve), and *Family Quarrels* (Covent Garden, Dec. 18, 1802; in collaboration with Braham and Reeve).—**NS/LK/DM**

Moorman, Joyce Solomon, black American composer and teacher; b. Tuskegee, Ala., May 11, 1946. She studied at Vassar Coll. (B.A., 1968), Rutgers Univ. (M.A., 1971), Sarah Lawrence Coll. (M.F.A., 1975), Columbia Univ. (D.Ed., 1982), and Brooklyn Coll. (1998–99). From 1982 to 1993 she taught at the Brooklyn Music School. She was an adjunct asst. prof. at the Borough of Manhattan Community Coll. (1983–88), St. John's Univ. (1984–85), York Coll. (1991–92), LaGuardia Community Coll. (1992–94; 1996–99), N.Y.C. Coll. (1998–99), and Brooklyn Coll. (1999).

WORKS: DRAMATIC: Opera: *Elegies for the Fallen* (1986–96). **ORCH.:** *The Soul of Nature* (1975; rev. version, Detroit, March 15, 1990); *Ethereal* for Strings (1976; N.Y., Jan. 14, 1977); *The Flood* for Strings and Piano (1977); *A Tone Poem for Victims of Racism and Hatred* (Olomouc, June 28, 1998). **CHAMBER:** *Drei Besonderen Klangfarben* for Bassoon, Double Bass, and Marimba (New Brunswick, N.J., May 12, 1971); Clarinet Quintet (1974); *Among the Snow-Capped Peaks* for String Quartet, Percussion, and Piano (1976; N.Y., April 27, 1977); *An Era* for Woodwind Quintet (1976; N.Y., March 21, 1988); Trio for Oboe, Basson, and Piano (1978; rev. version, N.Y., Feb. 8, 1995); Brass Quintet (1979; Flushing, N.Y., Nov. 18, 1984); *Fantasy* for Violin and Piano (1979; N.Y., May 23, 1982); Trio for Tape, Percussion, and Piano (1980); *Solo for a Seated Percussionist* (1982; N.Y., May 1, 1985); *One Day In...* for Percussion and Piano (1985; N.Y., Feb. 21, 1986); Trio for Flute, Guitar, and Drumset (1991; Teaneck, N.J., April 12, 1997); *Remembrances '68* for String Quartet (1993). **Piano:** Suite (Bronxville, N.Y., May 8, 1974); *A Young Woman's Impressions of New York City* (1976; N.Y., April 27, 1977); *A Summer Afternoon in South Carolina* (1983; N.Y., March 25, 1984); Sonata (1994); *The Backyard* (1995). **VOCAL:** *Dance of the Streets* for Soprano, Clarinet, Cello, Percussion, and Piano (1978; N.Y., May 23, 1982); *Sing My People,* cantata for Soloists, Chorus, and Chamber Ensemble (1980; Hempstead, N.Y., June 19, 1981); *In Time of Silver Rain* for Chorus and Chamber Orch. (1990;

Minneapolis, Feb. 10, 1991); *Danse Africaine* for Soprano and Piano (1991; N.Y., Jan. 9, 1996). **OTHER**: *Computer Music Study 1 and 2* (1998).—**LK/DM**

Moorman, (Madeline) Charlotte, avant-garde American cellist; b. Little Rock, Ark., Nov. 18, 1933; d. N.Y., Nov. 8, 1991. She took a B.A. degree in music at Centenary Coll. in Shreveport, La., before studying cello with Horace Britt at the Univ. of Tex. in Austin (1956–57); then completed her training at N.Y.'s Juilliard School of Music. She was a cellist in the Boccherini Players (1958–63) and in the American Sym. Orch. in N.Y. A fascination with the avant-garde led her to found the N.Y. Avant-Garde Art Festival in 1963, with which she remained active until 1982. She first attracted attention in 1965 when she performed the *Cello Sonata No. 2 for Adults Only*. In 1967 she became something of a sensation when she performed Nam June Paik's *Opéra Sextronique* in accordance with the composer's instructions, i.e. nude from the waist up. Her performance was halted by her arrest; although she was tried and convicted for unseemly exposure, her sentence was eventually suspended and she resumed her championship of the avant-garde unhindered. Among her other notable performances were *TV Bra for Living Sculpture* (1969), which called for a bra made of 2 small televisions, and Paik's *The TV Cello* (1971), in which she played a cello made out of 3 television sets. Varèse was so taken with Moorman that he dubbed her the "Jeanne d'Arc of New Music."—**NS/LK/DM**

Mooser, (Jean Pierre Joseph) Aloys, noted Swiss organist and organ builder, great-grandfather of **R(obert) Aloys Mooser**; b. Niederhelfenschwyl, June 27, 1770; d. Fribourg, Dec. 19, 1839. He studied with his father, the Alsatian organ builder Joseph Anton Mooser (1731–92), who settled in Fribourg in the 1760s. Aloys built the outstanding organ at St. Nicolas's Cathedral there (1824–34).

  BIBL.: F. Seydoux, *Der Orgelbauer A. M. (1770–1839): Leben und Werk* (Fribourg, 1996).—**NS/LK/DM**

Mooser, R(obert) Aloys, Swiss writer on music, great-grandson of **(Jean Pierre Joseph) Aloys Mooser**; b. Geneva, Sept. 20, 1876; d. there, Aug. 24, 1969. His mother was a Russian, and he acquired the knowledge of the Russian language in childhood. He studied with his father and Otto Barblan in Geneva. In 1896 he went to St. Petersburg, where he served as organist at the French church, wrote music criticism for the *Journal de St. Petersbourg*, and made an extensive study of Russian music in the archives. He took courses with Balakirev and Rimsky-Korsakov. In 1909 he returned to Geneva and wrote music criticism for the periodical *La Suisse* (1909–62); was also founder, ed., and publisher of the periodical *Dissonances* (1923–46). His reviews were collected in the vols. *Regards sur la musique contemporaine: 1921–1946* (Lausanne, 1946); *Panorama de la musique contemporaine: 1947–1953* (Geneva, 1953); *Aspects de la musique contemporaine: 1953–1957* (Geneva, 1957); and *Visage de la musique contemporaine, 1957–1961* (Paris, 1962). He wrote the following books on Russian music:

Contribution à l'histoire de la musique russe: L'Opéra comique française en Russie au XVIIIe siècle (Geneva, 1932; 2nd ed., 1954); *Violonistes-compositeurs italiens en Russie au XVIIIe siècle* (Milan, 1938–50); *Opéras, intermezzos, ballets, cantates, oratorios joués en Russie durant le XVIIIe siècle* (Geneva, 1945; 3rd ed., 1964); *Annales de la musique et des musiciens en Russie au XVIIIe siècle* (of prime importance; 3 vols., Geneva, 1948–51). He also wrote *Deux violonistes genevois: Gaspard Fritz (1716–1783) and Christian Haensel (1766–1850)* (Geneva, 1968). —**NS/LK/DM**

Morales, Carlos O., Puerto Rican composer; b. San Juan, June 17, 1953. He studied at the Cons. of Music in Puerto Rico, graduating with degrees in guitar performance (1976) and music education (1977). He subsequently taught there, and also studied at the Accademia Musicale Chigiana in Siena. In 1979 he went to Calif., where he continued his composition studies. He is known primarily for his transcriptions to guitar of music originally written for the Renaissance laud. He was a prof. of music history at the Interamerican Univ. of Puerto Rico in Germán. Among his original compositions are *Thanks after Communion* for Men's Chorus (1980), *Etapas* for Flute (1981), 2 symphonic poems, *Guanina* (1981) and *La Campana del Ingenio* (1984), and numerous works for solo guitar, including *Nocturno* (1984) and *Canción de Cuna* (1985).—**NS/LK/DM**

Morales, Cristóbal de, eminent Spanish composer; b. Seville, c. 1500; d. probably in Marchéna, between Sept. 4 and Oct. 7, 1553. He was probably a pupil of Fernández de Castilleja, the maestro de capilla at the Seville Cathedral. Morales was maestro de capilla at Avila Cathedral (1526–28), serving in the same capacity in Plasencia (1528–31). In 1535 he entered the papal choir in Rome (until 1540, and again 1541–45), during which period he composed much sacred music. After a brief journey to Spain, he returned to Rome and increased his productivity as a composer; he also traveled in the retinue of the Pope to various towns in Italy. He was maestro de capilla at Toledo Cathedral (1545–47), to the Duke of Arcos in Marchena (1548–51), and at Malaga Cathedral (1551–53). Morales was one of the outstanding masters of the polyphonic style; he was greatly esteemed by contemporary musicians; Bermudo described him as "the light of Spain in music." His works include more than 25 masses, 18 Magnificats, 2 Lamentations, and numerous motets. A modern ed. is appearing in Monumentos de la Música Espanola (Madrid, 1952–64).

  BIBL.: R. Mitjana y Gordon, *C. d.M., Estudio critico-biográfico* (Madrid, 1920); S. Rubio, *C. d.M.: Estudio critico de su polifonia* (El Escorial, 1969).—**NS/LK/DM**

Morales, Melesio, Mexican composer; b. Mexico City, Dec. 4, 1838; d. San Petro de los Pinos, May 12, 1908. He began to compose salon music for piano and soon acquired sufficient technique to write for the stage. He produced 2 operas, *Romeo y Julieta* (Mexico City, Jan. 27, 1863) and *Ildegonda* (Mexico City, Dec. 27, 1865), then went to France and Italy for additional study. Returning to Mexico, he taught and composed. His orch. fantasy, *La locomotiva*, was performed at the opening of the Mexico-Puebla railway (Nov. 16, 1869), anticipating Honegger's *Pacific 231* by more than 50 years. He later produced 2 more operas: *Gino Corsini* (Mexico City, July 14, 1877) and *Cleopatra* (Mexico City, Nov. 14, 1891). Despite his passionate advocacy of national music, he followed conventional Italian models in his own works. —NS/LK/DM

Morales, Olallo (Juan Magnus), Spanish-born Swedish conductor, music critic, and composer; b. Almería (of a Spanish father and Swedish mother), Oct. 15, 1874; d. Tällberg, April 29, 1957. Taken to Sweden as a child, he received his education there, first at Göteborg, then at the Stockholm Cons., with W. Stenhammar and others (1891–99), and in Berlin with H. Urban (composition) and Carreño (piano). In 1901 he returned to Sweden, where he was conductor of the Göteborg Orch. (1905–09) and a teacher (1917–21) and a prof. (1921–39) at the Stockholm Cons.; was also secretary of the Royal Academy of Music (1918–40). With T. Norlind, he publ. *Kungliga muskaliska akademien* (Royal Academy of Music; Stockholm; vol. I, 1771–1921 [1921]; vol. II, 1921–31 [1932]; vol. III, 1931–41 [1942]). He also publ. a handbook on conducting (Stockholm, 1946). His works include a Sym. (1901), several overtures, Violin Concerto (1943), String Quartet, Piano Sonata, *Balada andaluza* for Piano (1946), *Nostalgia* (1920) and other character pieces for piano, choral works, and songs. —NS/LK/DM

Moralt, family of German musicians, all brothers and members of the famous Moralt string quartet:

(1) Joseph Moralt, violinist and conductor; b. Schwetzingen, Aug. 5, 1775; d. Munich, Nov. 13, 1855. He was made a supernumerary musician (1787) and concertmaster (1800) in the Munich Hofkapelle. He was also concertmaster in the family string quartet, and likewise conductor at the Italian and German Operas in Munich.

(2) Johann Baptist Moralt, violinist and composer; b. Mannheim, March 10, 1777; d. Munich, Oct. 7, 1825. He studied violin with Johann Baptist Geiger and C. Cannabich and composition with Joseph Grätz. He composed 2 syms., much chamber music, and sacred vocal works.

(3) Philipp Moralt, cellist; b. Munich, Dec. 29, 1780; d. there, Jan. 10, 1830. He also played in the Munich municipal band.

(4) Georg Moralt, violist; b. Munich, 1781; d. there, 1818.—NS/LK/DM

Moralt, Rudolf, esteemed German composer, nephew of **Richard (Georg) Strauss**; b. Munich, Feb. 26, 1902; d. Vienna, Dec. 16, 1958. He studied in Munich at the Univ. and the Academy of Music, his principal teachers being Courvoisier and Schmid-Lindner. After serving as répétiteur at the Bavarian State Opera in Munich (1919–23), he was conductor at the Kaiserslautern Stadtische Oper (1923–28; 1932–34) and music director of the German Theater in Brno (1932–34). He then conducted opera in Braunschweig (1934–36) and Graz (1937–40), and subsequently was a principal conductor at the Vienna State Opera (1940–58); also appeared as a guest conductor in Europe. In addition to his natural affinity for the music of his uncle, he also conducted fine performances of Mozart, Wagner, Johann Strauss, and Pfitzner.—NS/LK/DM

Moran, Robert (Leonard), American composer; b. Denver, Jan. 8, 1937. He studied piano; went to Vienna in 1957 and took lessons in 12-tone composition with Apostel. Returning to America, he enrolled at Mills Coll. in Oakland, Calif., where he attended seminars of Berio and Milhaud (M.A., 1963); completed his training with Haubenstock-Ramati in Vienna (1963); also painted in the manner of Abstract Expressionism. He was active in avant-garde music circles; with Howard Hersh, he was founder and co-director of the San Francisco Cons.'s New Music Ensemble; was composer-in-residence at Portland (Ore.) State Univ. (1972–74) and at Northwestern Univ. (1977–78), where he led its New Music Ensemble; also appeared extensively as a pianist in the U.S. and Europe in programs of contemporary music. In his compositions, he combines the "found art" style with aleatory techniques; some of his works are in graphic notation animated by a surrealistic imagination.

WORKS: DRAMATIC: O p e r a : *Let's Build a Nut House*, chamber opera in memory of Paul Hindemith (San Jose, April 19, 1969); *Divertissement No. 3: A Lunchbag Opera* for Paper Bags and Instruments (BBC-TV, 1971); *Metamenagerie*, department store window opera (1974); *Hitler: Geschichten aus der Zukunft* (1981); *Erlösung dem Erlöser*, music drama for Tape Loops and Performers (1982); *The Juniper Tree*, children's opera (1985; in collaboration with P. Glass); *Desert of Roses* (Houston, Feb. 1992). **B a l l e t :** *Spin Again* for Amplified Harpsichord(s) and Electric Keyboards (1980); *Chorale Variations: 10 Miles High over Albania* for 8 Harps (1983). **OTHER:** *Durch Wüsten und Wolken* for Shadow Puppets and Instruments (1975); *Marketmenagerie* for Children and Musique Concrète (1975); *Es war einmal*, children's show for Film, Slides, and Musique Concrete (1976); *Music for Gamelan*, incidental music (1978); *Am 29. 11. 1780* for Tape and Dancers (1979). **ORCH.:** *Interiors* for Orch., Chamber Orch., or Percussion Ensemble (1964; San Francisco, April 12, 1965); *Bombardments No. 2* for 1 to 5 Percussion (1964); *L'Après-midi du Dracoula* for Any Group of Instruments capable of producing Any Kind of Sound (1966); *Elegant Journey with Stopping Points of Interest* for Any Ensemble (1967); *Jewel-encrusted Butterfly Wing Explosions* (1968); *Silver and the Circle of Messages* for Chamber Orch. (San Francisco, April 24, 1970); *Emblems of Passage* for 2 Orchs. (1974); *Angels of Silence* for Viola and Chamber Orch. (1975); *Enantiodromia* for 8 Orchs. and Dancers (1977). **CHAMBER:** *4 Visions* for Flute, Harp, and String Quartet (1964); *Eclectic Boogies* for 13 Percussionists (N.Y., Jan. 14, 1965); *Within the Momentary Illumination* for 2 Harps, Electric Guitar, Timpani, and Brass (Tokyo, Dec. 1, 1965); *Scream Kiss No. 1* for Harpsichord and Stereophonic Tape (1968); *Evening Psalm of Dr. Dracula* for Prepared Piano and Tape (1973); *The Last Station of the Albatross* for 1 to 8 Instruments (1978); *BASHA* for 4 Amplified Clavichords (1983); *Survivor from Darmstadt* for Bass Oboes (1984). **OTHER:** *Smell Piece for Mills Coll.* for Frying Pans and Foods (Mills Coll., Nov. 20, 1967; originally intended to produce a conflagration sufficiently thermal to burn down the college); *39 Minutes for 30 Skyscrapers, 39*

Auto Horns, Moog Synthesizer, and Players, employing 100,000 Persons, directed from atop Twin Peaks in San Francisco, and making use of Autos, Airplanes, Searchlights, and local Radio and Television Stations (San Francisco, Aug. 20, 1969); *Titus* for Amplified Automobile and Players (1969); *Hallelujah*, "a joyous phenomenon with fanfares" for Marching Bands, Drum and Bugle Corps, Church Choruses, Organs, Carillons, Rock- 'n'- Roll Bands, Television Stations, Automobile Horns, and Any Other Sounding Implements, commissioned by Lehigh Univ. for the city of Bethlehem, Pa., with the participation of its entire population of 72,320 inhabitants (Bethlehem, April 23, 1971); *Pachelbel Promenade* for Guitar Ensemble, Folk Instruments, String Ensemble, and Jazz Ensemble (1975); *From the Market to Asylum* for Performers (1982); *Music for a Fair* (1984). **—NS/LK/DM**

Morand, Herb, early jazz trumpeter, singer; b. New Orleans, La., 1905; d. there, Feb. 23, 1952. His brother was Maurice (drums); their stepsister was singer Lizzie Miles. Morand began playing trumpet at the age of 13. At 18, he did first his professional work with Nat Towle's Creole Harmony Kings, and worked in O.K. with this New Orleans Band for almost a year. After a brief return to New Orleans he left to tour Mexico in a band he co-led with bassist Charlie Towles (Nat's father). Around 1924–25, he settled in N.Y., playing jobs accompanying Lizzie Miles and spent several months in Cliff Jackson's Krazy Cats. Later in the decade, he returned to New Orleans, working with Chris Kelly's band, and also leading his own small groups and playing in parade bands. He moved to Chicago in the late 1920s to join J. Frank Terry's Chicago Nightingales. From 1932–34, he was a member of W. McDonald and his Chicago Ramblers, and then began nearly a year- long job with pianist William Barbee and drummer "Little" Joe Lindsey playing at Tony's Tavern. From 1936, Morand played regularly in the Harlem Hamfats (mostly in Chicago); this group made many recordings over the next two years. During this period, he also played on the lake steamer S.S. North Shore and at Bratton's Rendezvous with Meade "Lux" Lewis. In 1941, Morand teamed up with Jimmy Bertrand for residency at The Firehouse, Chicago, then returned to New Orleans. He led his own band through the 1940s, including residencies at Mama Lou's, Lake Pontchartrain, and at the Rainbow Inn, but also gigged with George Lewis, becoming a regular member of his band in spring 1948 for job at Manny's Tavern. He continued to be active until 1950, when ill health caused his retirement. For most of his later life he was beset by weight problems—at one time he tipped the scales at over 300 pounds.

DISC.: *Herb Morand and His New Orleans Band* (1950). **—JC/LP**

Moran-Olden (real name, **Tappenhorn**), **Fanny,** German soprano; b. Oldenburg, Sept. 28, 1855; d. Berlin, Feb. 13, 1905. She studied with Haas in Hannover and Götze in Dresden, making her concert debut at the Leipzig Gewandhaus (1877). She made her operatic debut under the name Fanny Olden as Norma in Dresden (1878), then sang at the Frankfurt am Main Opera (1878–84), the Leipzig City Theater (1884–91),

and the Munich Court Opera (1891–95). She made her Metropolitan Opera debut in N.Y. on Nov. 28, 1888, as Valentine in *Les Huguenots*; was on its roster until 1889 and again in 1900–01. In 1896 she toured Europe. After retiring from the stage (1902), she taught voice at Berlin's Klindworth-Scharwenka Cons. She married the tenor Karl Moran (1879) and the baritone Theodor Bertram (1897).**—NS/LK/DM**

Moravec, Ivan, distinguished Czech pianist and pedagogue; b. Prague, Nov. 9, 1930. He studied with Grünfeld at the Prague Cons. (graduated, 1948), and after further training with Štěpánova-Kurzova in Prague (1952–53), he attended Michelangeli's master classes in Arezzo (1957, 1958). He made his debut with the Prague Radio (1946), and later toured in Europe, making his London debut in 1959. He first appeared in the U.S. as soloist with the Cleveland Orch. in N.Y. (Jan. 30, 1964). He taught at the Prague Academy of Music (from 1967), where he headed its master class in piano (from 1969). Moravec is particularly noted for his performances of the standard 19th- and 20th-century repertoires.**—NS/LK/DM**

Morawetz, Oskar, significant Czech-born Canadian composer; b. Světlá nad Sázavou, Jan. 17, 1917. He studied with Jaroslav Křička at the Univ. of Prague (1933–36); after the invasion of Czechoslovakia by the Nazis in 1938, he went to Vienna, where he studied with Julius Isserlis, and then to Paris, where he had lessons with Lévy; emigrated to Canada in 1940, becoming a naturalized citizen in 1946; completed his training at the Univ. of Toronto (B.M., 1944; D.Mus., 1953). He taught at the Royal Cons. of Music of Toronto (1946–51) and at the Univ. of Toronto (1951–82). In 1989 he received the Order of Canada. His music is Classical in format, Romantic in spirit, impressionistic in coloring, and modernistic in harmonic usage.

WORKS: ORCH.: *Carnival Overture* (1945; Montreal, July 1, 1947); *Divertimento* for Strings (1948; rev. 1954); 2 syms.: No. 1 (1950–53; 1st complete perf., Toronto, March 5, 1956; each movement is titled for separate perf.: *Fantasy, Dirge,* and *Scherzo*) and No. 2 (1959; Toronto, Feb. 2, 1960); *Overture to a Fairy Tale* (Halifax, Feb. 8, 1957); *Capriccio* (1960); Piano Concerto (1962; Montreal, April 23, 1963); *Sinfonietta* for Strings (1963; rev. 1983, 1989); *Passacaglia on a Bach Chorale* (Toronto, Nov. 24, 1964); *Sinfonietta* for Winds and Percussion (1965; Montreal, Feb. 22, 1966); Concerto for Brass Quintet and Chamber Orch. (Toronto, March 28, 1968); *Memorial to Martin Luther King,* elegy for Cello and Orch. (1968; the last movement employs the popular spiritual *Free at Last*; rev. 1973); *Reflections after a Tragedy* (1968); Harp Concerto (1976); Concerto for Clarinet and Chamber Orch. (1989). **CHAMBER:** 5 string quartets (1944; 1952–55; 1959; 1978; 1990); Duo for Violin and Piano (1947; rev. 1959); 3 violin sonatas (1956; 1965, rev. 1976; 1985); Trio for Flute, Oboe, and Harpsichord or Piano (1960); *2 Fantasies* for Cello and Piano (1962; rev. 1970); *2 Preludes* for Violin and Piano (1965); Flute Sonata (1980); Horn Sonata (1980); Oboe Sonata (1980–81); Clarinet Sonata (1981); Bassoon Sonata (1981); Sonata for Viola and Harp (1985–86); Trumpet Sonata (1986). **PIANO:** *Sonata tragica* (1945); *Ballade* (1946; rev. 1982); *Scherzo* (1947); *Fantasy in D minor* (1948); *Fantasy on a Hebrew Theme* (1951); *Scherzino* (1953); *Fantasy, Elegy and Toccata*

(1956); *10 Preludes* (1961); *Suite* (1968); *Fantasy* (1973); *4 Contrasting Moods* (1985–86). **VOCAL**: *Keep Us Free* for Chorus and Orch. (1951); *From the Diary of Anne Frank* for Soprano or Mezzo-soprano, and Orch. (CBC, May 20, 1970); *A Child's Garden of Verses* for Mezzo-soprano or Alto or Baritone and Orch., after R.L. Stevenson (Toronto, Feb. 10, 1973); *Psalm 22: God, Why Have You Forsaken Me?* for Baritone or Mezzo-soprano or Contralto, and Piano or Orch. (1980; orch. version, Toronto, Jan. 4, 1984); *5 Biblical Songs* for Chorus (1981; Vancouver, Sept. 12, 1982); solo songs.—**NS/LK/DM**

Morawski-Dbrowa, Eugeniusz, Polish composer and pedagogue; b. Warsaw, Nov. 2, 1876; d. there, Oct. 23, 1948. He was a student of Noskowski at the Warsaw Music Inst., and then of Gédalge (counterpoint) and Chevillard (orchestration) in Paris. In 1930 he became director of the Poznań Cons. From 1932 to 1939 he was director and prof. of composition at the Warsaw Cons. His music followed the precepts of late Romanticism, He wrote the operas *Aspazja, Lilla Weneda,* and *Salammbô,* as well as ballets, 6 syms., 2 piano concertos, Violin Concerto, symphonic poems, 7 string quartets, 2 violin sonatas, and 8 piano sonatas.—**NS/LK/DM**

Mordden, Ethan, American writer on music; b. Heavensville, Pa., Jan. 27, 1949. He studied piano at an early age, and was educated in Quaker schools, including Friends Academy in Locust Valley, N.Y. He then studied at the Univ. of Pa. (B.A. in history, 1969). He worked as a musical director and coach in N.Y. (1971–74), then was asst. ed. of *Opera News* (1974–76) and a visiting fellow at Yale Univ. (1980). He is a regular contributor to the *New Yorker,* winning a National Magazine Award in 1989; also wrote for the *N.Y. Times* and *Christopher Street,* among other publications. In addition to his numerous books on music, film, and theater, he publ. fiction on gay life, especially the *Buddies Trilogy* (*I've a Feeling We're Not in Kansas Anymore* [1985], *Buddies* [1986], and *Everybody Loves You* [1988]). He also composed *Reminiscences de Mahagonny* for Piano (1986).

WRITINGS: *Better Foot Forward: The Story of America's Musical Theatre* (1976); *Opera in the Twentieth Century* (1978); *That Jazz!: An Idiosyncratic Social History of the American Twenties* (1978); *A Guide to Orchestral Music* (1979); *The Splendid Art of Opera: A Concise History* (1980); *The Hollywood Musical* (1983); *Demented: The World of the Opera Diva* (1985); *Opera Anecdotes* (1986); *A Guide to Opera Recordings* (1987).—**NS/LK/DM**

Moreau, Jean-Baptiste, French composer; b. Angers, 1656; d. Paris, Aug. 24, 1733. He was a chorister at Angers Cathedral, then was maître de musique at the cathedrals of Langres (1681–82) and Dijon. By Jan. 1687 he was in Paris. He was introduced at the French court by the Dauphine, and was commissioned by Louis XIV to write several divertissements, among them *Les Bergers de Marly* (1687). He won great success with his musical interludes (recitatives and choruses) for Racine's *Esther* (1698) and *Athalie* (1691), performed at the school for young noblewomen at St.-Cyr, where he was musicien ordinaire. He also wrote music for Racine's *Cantiques spirituels,* for performance at St.-Cyr. His success at court was marred by his dissolute habits; however, he was greatly esteemed as a teacher of singing and composition, numbering among his pupils Montéclair, J.F. Dandrieu, Clérambault, and the singers Louise Couperin and his own daughter Marie-Claude Moreau. The music to *Esther* and *Athalie,* and the *Cantiques spirituels,* were publ. in the music supplement to P. Mesnard's *OEuvres de J. Racine* (Paris, 1873).—**NS/LK/DM**

Moreira, António Leal, Portuguese composer; b. Abrantes, 1758; d. Lisbon, Nov. 21, 1819. He studied with João de Sousa Carvalho at the Lisbon Seminario Patriarcal, becoming his assistant in 1775. In 1787 he was appointed mestre de capela of the royal chapel, then served as music director of the Italian Opera Theater (1790–93) and the Teatro San Carlo (1793–1800) in Lisbon. He composed numerous stage works, his opera buffa *Il disertore francese* being given at the Turin Carnival in 1800. Other works include 4 masses, 2 Magnificats, and 5 villancicos.—**NS/LK/DM**

Morel, Jean (Paul), French-American conductor and pedagogue; b. Abbeville, Jan. 10, 1903; d. N.Y., April 14, 1975. He was a student of Philipp (piano), N. Gallon (theory), Emmanuel (music history), Pierné (composition), and Hahn (lyric repertoire) in Paris. From 1921 to 1936 he taught at the American Cons. in Fontainebleau. He conducted the Orchestre National (1936–39) and the Orchestre Symphonique de Paris (1938). In 1939 he emigrated to the U.S. He taught at Brooklyn Coll. of the City Univ. of N.Y. (1940–43). From 1949 to 1971 he was a teacher and conductor at the Juilliard School of Music in N.Y., where he proved influential in producing a generation of musicians. On Nov. 12, 1944, he made his debut at the N.Y.C. Opera conducting *La Traviata.* He made his Metropolitan Opera debut in N.Y. on Dec. 21, 1956, conducting *La Périchole.* He remained on the roster there until 1962, and then returned for the 1967–68 and 1969–71 seasons.—**NS/LK/DM**

Morel, (Joseph Raoul) François (d'Assise), Canadian composer, teacher, pianist, and conductor; b. Montreal, March 14, 1926. After private instruction in piano (1935–43), he pursued his training at the Cons. de Musique de Québec à Montréal (1944–53) with Champagne (composition), Papineau-Couture (acoustics), Delorme (harmony, counterpoint, and fugue), and Letondal, Malépart, and Trudel (piano). He also received some training in conducting from Gagnier. From 1954 he was active in contemporary music circles. In 1956 he helped found the new music group Musique de notre temps. Between 1956 and 1979 he was active with the CBC Radio. After teaching at the Inst. Nazareth in Montreal (1959–61), he was director of the Académie de musique de Québec (1972–78). In 1979–80 he taught at the Univ. of Montreal. He was on the faculty of Laval Univ. in Montreal from 1979. Morel's music parallels the aesthetic fashions of modern times, from Debussyan coloristic imagism to motoric neo-Classicism to the organized sound world of Varèse with a circumspect handling of serial procedures.

WORKS: ORCH.: *Esquisse* (1946); *Antiphonie* (1953); *Boréal* (1959); *L'Étoile Noire (Tombeau de Borduas)* (1962); *Radiance*

(1970); *Mélisma* for Piano and Orch. (1980); *Die Stelle der Zwillinge (la position des jumeaux): Hommage à Paul Klee* (1992); *Et le Crépuscule...se trouva libre* (1996); *Métamorphoses* (1998). **W i n d   O r c h .** : *Dyptique* (1948–54); *Le Mythe de la Roche Percée* (1961); *Requiem* (1965–66); *Neumes d'Espace et Reliefs* (1967); *Prismes-Anamorphoses* (1967); *L'Oiseau-Demain* (1981–82); *Aux Couleurs du Ciel* (1985–87); *De Subitement lointain* (1989); *Strophes, Séquences, Mouvements* (1999). **B r a s s   E n s e m b l e** : *Symphonies* (1956); *Aera* (1986); *Les Voix de l'ombre* (1987); *Lumières sculptées* (1992). **P e r c u s s i o n   E n s e m b l e** : *Rythmologue* (1970); *Lyre de Cristal* (1985–86). **CHAMBER:** 2 string quartets (1952, 1963); Wind Quintet (1962); *Nuvattuk* for Flute (1967); *Iikkii (Froidure)* for Chamber Group (1971); *Me Duele España* for Guitar (1974–77); *Divergence* for Violin and Guitar (1983); *Taléa (couleur)* for Wind Trio (1984); *Paysage dépaysé*, string quintet (1990); *Figures, Segments, Ellipses* for Clarinet and String Quartet (1990); *Distance intime* for Flute and Piano (1991); *Stèle* for Clarinet (1991); *Ekleipsis* for Marimba (1993); *Les Ephémères* for 4 Horns and Tuba (1995); *Imaginaire* for Guitar (1996–99). **KEYBOARD: P i a n o** : *Deux études de Sonorité* (1954). **O r g a n** : *Prière* (1954); *Alleluias* (1968). —NS/LK/DM

Morell, Barry, American tenor; b. N.Y., March 30, 1927. He received his training in N.Y. On March 26, 1955, he made his first appearance at the N.Y.C. Opera as Pinkerton. He chose that same role for his Metropolitan Opera debut in N.Y. on Nov. 1, 1958, and continued to make occasional appearances there until 1979. As a guest artist, he also sang in Europe and South America. He was best known for his roles in Italian opera. —NS/LK/DM

Morelli (real name, **Zanelli**), **Carlo,** Chilean baritone; b. Valparaiso (of an Italian father and a Chilean mother), Dec. 25, 1897; d. Mexico City, May 12, 1970. He studied voice in Bologna with Angelo Queize and in Florence with Leopoldo Mugnone. He sang at La Scala, Milan (1922); toured South America (1925–31). He made his first U.S. appearence with the Chicago Opera in 1932, making his debut at the Metropolitan Opera in N.Y. on Dec. 21, 1935, as Marcello. He remained there until 1940, and then sang with the San Carlo Opera at the City Center, N.Y. (1940–49). In 1949 he settled in Mexico.—NS/LK/DM

Morena (real name, **Meyer**), **Berta,** noted German soprano; b. Mannheim, Jan. 27, 1878; d. Rottach-Egern, Oct. 7, 1952. Her buxom beauty attracted the attention of the famous painter von Lenbach, who persuaded her to study voice with Sophie Röhr-Brajnin and Aglaja von Orgeni in Munich; after additional training with Regina de Sales, she made her operatic debut as Agathe in *Der Freischütz* at the Munich Court Opera (1898); remained on its roster until 1927. She made her American debut with the Metropolitan Opera in N.Y. as Sieglinde (March 4, 1908), remaining on its roster until 1909; then returned from 1910 to 1912 and in 1924–25. She was regarded in Germany as an intelligent and musicianly singer, excelling particularly in Wagnerian roles, including Elisabeth, Elsa, Eva, Isolde, and the 3 Brünnhildes.

BIBL.: A. Vogl, *B. M. und ihre Kunst* (Munich,1919). —NS/LK/DM

Moreno (Andrade), Segundo Luis, Ecuadorian musicologist and composer; b. Cotacachi, Aug. 3, 1882; d. Quito, Nov. 18, 1972. He played the clarinet in a civil band in Quito. He studied at the Quito Cons., and then was active as a military band leader in various localities in Ecuador. In 1937 he took over the newly established Cons. Nacional de Música in Cuenca, and later was director of the Guayaquil Cons. (1940–45). He composed mostly for military band; many of his pieces celebrate various patriotic events in Ecuador, as the cantata *La emancipación* (1920), the overture *9 de Julio* (1925), and various pieces on native motifs, among them *3 suites ecuatorianas* for Orch. (1921, 1944, 1945). He publ. *Música y danzas autoctonas del Ecuador* (Quito, 1949) and *La música de los Incas* (Quito, 1957).—NS/LK/DM

Morera, Enrique (Enric), Spanish composer; b. Barcelona, May 22, 1865; d. there, March 11, 1942. As a child, he was taken to Argentina, and studied in Buenos Aires. He then took courses at the Brussels Cons. Returning to Barcelona, he studied piano with Albéniz and harmony with Felipe Pedrell. In 1895 he founded the choral society Catalunya Nova, which he conducted until 1909; then taught at the Escuela Municipal de Música in Barcelona (1910–28). He was an ardent propagandist of Catalan music, and wrote a number of songs to Catalan words; also collected 193 melodies of popular origin. His opera *Emporium*, originally to a Catalan text, was performed first in Italian (Barcelona, Jan. 20, 1906). He wrote more than 50 other stage works (lyric comedies, zarzuelas, operettas, intermezzos, etc.), as well as several symphonic poems, including *Introducció a l'Atlántida* (1893), Cello Concerto (1917), *Poema de la nit i del dia* for Orch. (1919), chamber music, much choral music, and many sardanas.

BIBL.: I. Iglesias, *Enric M.* (Barcelona, 1921); J. Pena, *Enric M.* (Barcelona, 1937).—NS/LK/DM

Morère (real name, **Couladère**), **Jean,** French tenor; b. Toulouse, Oct. 6, 1836; d. Paris, Feb. 1887. He studied with Paul Laget in Toulouse, making his debut as *Manrico* at the Paris Opéra in 1861, where he sang until 1869. He created the title role in Verdi's *Don Carlos* there in 1867, and also appeared in Brussels at the Théâtre Royal de la Monnaie (1865–66; 1869–70). He suffered a mental derangement in the wake of the Franco-Prussian War in 1871.—NS/LK/DM

Moreschi, Alessandro, Italian castrato soprano; b. Montecompatri, near Rome, Nov. 11, 1858; d. Rome, April 21, 1922. He studied with Capocci in Rome, and from 1883 to 1913 sang at the Vatican's Sistine Chapel. The last of the castrati, he had a voice of such purity and beauty that he was nicknamed "l'angelo di Roma." —NS/LK/DM

Moret, Norbert, Swiss composer and teacher; b. Ménières, Nov. 20, 1921; d. Fribourg, Nov. 17, 1998. He received training in piano and theory at the Fribourg Cons. before pursuing training with Messiaen, Honegger, and Leibowitz in Paris (1948–50) and with Furtwängler in Vienna (1950–51). From 1965 to 1982 he was a prof. of instrumental music at the Teacher's Training Coll. in Fribourg. Moret turned to full-time composition late in life, but his music gained almost immediate international attention. His Violin Concerto and Cello Concerto were commissioned and premiered by, respectively, Anne-Sophie Mutter and Mstislav Rostropovich.

WORKS: DRAMATIC: O p e r a : *Visitations* (1981–82). **ORCH.:** *Hymne de silence* for Organ, Percussion, and Orch. (1977); *Suite à l'image* for 2 String Orchs. (1978); Double Concerto for Violin, Cello, and Orch. (1981); *Tragiques* (1982–83); Triple Concerto for Flute, Oboe, Harp, and Strings (1984); Cello Concerto (1985); *Mille et un soleils de joie* for Chamber Orch. (1986); *En rêve*, concerto for Violin and Chamber Orch. (1988); *Trois pièces* for Chamber Orch. (1988); *Symphonies pour une fête académique* (1989); *Divertimento* for Oboe, Horn, Cello, Percussion, and Strings (1991–92); *Sensations*, concerto for Guitar and Chamber Orch. (1994); Horn Concerto (1995); Concerto No. 1 for Organ and Orch. (1996). **CHAMBER:** *Sacher Serenade* for Vibraphone, Clarinet, and 2 Organs (1982); *Sur le berceau d'un Chérubin* for Violin and Harp (1992); *Forêt enchantée* for Cello (1993). **VOCAL:** *Germes en éveil* for Soprano, Chorus, Flute, and Percussion (1973); *Cinq pièces* for Soprano, Piano, and Brass (1976); *Temps* for Baritone and Strings (1978); *2 Love Poems* for Soprano, Cello, and Orch., after Whitman (1978–79); *Mendiant de ciel bleu* for Baritone, Soprano, Chorus, and Orch. (1980); *Ave-Maria* for Tenor and Organ (1984); *Diotimas Liebeslieder* for Soprano and Orch. (1986–87); *Deux mélodies* for Baritone and Piano (1992–93).—**LK/DM**

Morgan, Al(bert), jazz bassist, tuba player, singer; b. New Orleans, La., Aug. 19, 1908; d. Los Angeles, Calif., April 14, 1974. Morgan came from a musical family; his older brothers, clarinetist/saxophonist Andrew (b. Pensacola, Fla., March 13, 1901; d. Sept. 19, 1972), and trumpeters Isaiah (b. Bertrandville, La., April 7, 1897; d. May 11, 1966) and Sam (b. Bertrandville, La., Dec. 18, 1887; d. Feb. 25, 1936), were all talented musicians. Al's early efforts were on the clarinet and drums; then he started playing on a three-string bass (c. 1918), and then took lessons with Simon Marrero. He had his first professional jobs working with his brother, Isaiah, and then traveled to Pensacola, Fla., in 1923 with Lee Collins. He was back in New Orleans a year later, playing with Davey Jones's Astoria Strutters on string bass then, after instruction from Jones, began doubling on double B-flat tuba. From 1925–29, he worked summer seasons with Fate Marable on the steamboat S.S. Capitol, during which time he studied under St. Louis bassist Cecil Scott. In fall 1929, he returned to New Orleans, and recorded with Jones-Collins Astoria Eight. In 1930, he journeyed to N.Y., and recorded with the Mound City Blue Blowers. He was with Otto Hardwick's Band at the Hot Feet Club, N.Y. (c. 1930), then with Vernon Andrade's Orch. until joining Cab Calloway from June 1932 until the spring of 1936 (including tour of Europe, 1934). He left Cab in Calif. and organized a band with Eddie Barefield; he later led his own band and worked with Fats Waller and with Louis Armstrong in the film *Going Places*. In the late 1930s, he

joined Les Hites's band, travelling with it back to N.Y. in 1940. He left Hite in spring 1941 to join Zutty Singleton's Trio and also did many freelance recordings in various small groups. He played two long stints with the Sabby Lewis Band in Boston (March 1942–March 1944, and then 1946–57), taking a year off in 1945 to work with Louis Jordan. He moved to Calif. in February 1957, and worked with Joe Darensbourg, Jack McVea, and Nellie Lutcher. He also appeared in the films *The Gene Krupa Story (Drum Crazy)* and *King Creole*. Throughout the 1960s, he worked with pianist Buddy Banks as the resident duo at the Tudor Inn, in Norwalk, Calif.—**JC/LP**

Morgan, (Edward) Lee, trumpeter, flugelhornist, composer; b. Philadelphia, July 10, 1938; d. N.Y., Feb. 19, 1972. Known to his intimates as "Howdy Doody" due to his oversized ears, he was the youngest of four children. He studied trumpet privately and at Mastbaum Vocational Technical H.S. Around 1954 he began by playing weekends with his own group around town. Playing in a series of jazz workshop conclaves at Music City, he met and/or sat in with many of the big names, such as Miles Davis and Clifford Brown. He was a childhood friend of McCoy Tyner; they used to have jam sessions in Morgan's neighborhood in North Philly, and in West Philly, where Tyner lived. They played Atlantic City several summers together and fraternity dances. In the summer of 1956, Morgan spent two weeks with Art Blakey's Jazz Messengers. In November of that year he made his first album for the Blue Note record label. He joined Dizzy Gillespie's big band at age 18 (October 1956) and played one of Gillespie's bent trumpets for a while. He was a key member of Art Blakey's Jazz Messengers from 1958–61. In 1962, troubled by drug-related problems, he decided to take a break, and went back home. In November of 1962, Morgan appeared in N.Y. for an engagement at Birdland (co-leading a group with Jimmy Heath). He achieved pop success with "The Sidewinder," recorded in 1963. From 1964–65, he played with Art Blakey again, then led his own groups with Billy Higgins and others. Morgan was shot and killed between sets by his ex-girlfriend after a quarrel at Slug's, on the lower east side of Manhattan. His widow, Kiko Yamamoto, from whom he had been separated, manages his legacy.

DISC: *Candy* (1958); *Expoobident* (1960); *The Sidewinder* (1963); *Cornbread* (1965); *Sonic Boom* (1967); *Caramba* (1968); *The Last Session* (1971); *The Best of Lee Morgan* (1988); *Here's Lee Morgan* (2000).—**LP/JM**

Morgan, Justin, American composer; b. West Springfield, Mass., Feb. 28, 1747; d. Randolph, Vt., March 22, 1798. He settled in Vt. in 1788, although he pursued an active life as a traveling singing master. Morgan was a composer of decided talent. His extant works comprise *Despair*, a lament on the death of his wife, *Judgment Anthem*, 5 fuguing-tunes, including the popular *Montgomery*, and 2 plain tunes. With the lament excepted, all were publ. in *Benham's Federal Harmony* (1790).

BIBL.: B. Bandel, *Sing the Lord's Song in a Strange Land: The Life of J. M.* (Rutherford, N.J., 1981).—**LK/DM**

Morgan, Russ, American bandleader, trombonist, and composer; b. Scranton, Pa., April 29, 1904; d. Las Vegas, Nev., Aug. 7, 1969. In the spring of 1949, Morgan's sweet band placed four songs in the Top Ten, culminating more than 25 years of effort for a musician who had worked in nearly every capacity in popular music, including sideman, arranger, songwriter, bandleader, singer, recording artist, radio personality, and movie performer. In the wake of his belated breakthrough, Morgan continued to score hits for a few years, and he appeared on television, in films, and in live performances increasingly concentrated in Las Vegas over the next two decades. But his greatest success derived from the 1949 hits, "Cruising Down the River" (a million-seller), "Forever and Ever," "So Tired," and "Sunflower."

As a youth, Morgan worked in a coal mine to earn money for music lessons. He initially played the piano but took up the trombone as a means of strengthening a broken arm and eventually also learned saxophone, guitar, vibes, and organ. In 1921 he joined Billy Lustig's Scranton Sirens, which featured Jimmy Dorsey on saxophone. When he left the group in 1922 to join Paul Specht's band in Detroit, Tommy Dorsey replaced him.

Specht went to N.Y., where Morgan was able to find work arranging for John Philip Sousa and Victor Herbert. After a tour of Europe with Specht, Morgan returned to Detroit, where he performed in the Detroit Symphony and joined the main orchestra of band organizer Jean Goldkette, then briefly became music director of radio station WXYZ. At the start of the 1930s he returned to N.Y. and wrote arrangements for The Boswell Sisters, Fletcher Henderson, Louis Armstrong, Chick Webb, the Dorsey Brothers Orch., and others. He also played in various bands, ultimately joining Freddy Martin's Orch. in 1934, where he developed a distinctive "wah-wah" trombone sound. He also served as recording director for the American Record Company's Brunswick label.

Morgan left Martin in 1935 and started his own band, which gained a residency at the Biltmore Hotel in N.Y. He first reached the hit parade in July with "Love Me Forever" (music by Victor Schertzinger, lyrics by Gus Kahn), followed in August by "The Rose in Her Hair" (music by Harry Warren, lyrics by Al Dubin). He returned to the hit parade in November 1936 with "Midnight Blue" (music by Joe Burke, lyrics by Edgar Leslie), then had five chart entries in 1937: "When the Poppies Bloom Again" in April; "The Merry-Go-Round Broke Down" (music and lyrics by Cliff Friend and Dave Franklin) in June; "Stop, You're Breaking My Heart" (music by Burton Lane, lyrics by Ted Koehler) in August; "So Many Memories" in October; and "Farewell, My Love" in November. "I Double Dare You" (music by Terry Shand, lyrics by Jimmy Eaton) entered the hit parade in January 1938 and became Morgan's first chart-topper in February, but he didn't return to the hit parade until October with "Lambeth Walk" (music by R. M. Armitage under the pseudonym Noel Gay, lyrics by Douglas Furber and L. Arthur Rose), his last hit for several years. Following an earlier marriage, he married his secretary, Shirley Gray, on July 21, 1939;

they had four children.

In the early 1940s, Morgan was based on the West Coast, where he played at the Claremont Hotel in Berkeley, Calif. Also a songwriter, he had cocomposed his theme song, "Does Your Heart Beat for Me?" (music also by Arnold Johnson, lyrics by Mitchell Parish), and his next Top Ten hit came with another of his tunes, "Somebody Else Is Taking My Place" (music and lyrics by Morgan, Dick Howard, and Bob Ellsworth), which had been written in 1937 but did not become successful until it was featured in the Universal film *Strictly in the Groove* early in 1942. (Morgan and his Orch. later performed the song in the 1947 film *Sarge Goes to Coll.*).

Morgan returned to the Top Ten periodically during the mid-1940s, with "Good Night, Wherever You Are" (music and lyrics by Dick Robertson, Al Hoffman, and Frank Weldon) in July 1944; "Dance with a Dolly (With a Hole in Her Stockin')" (music and lyrics by Terry Shand, Jimmy Eaton, and David Kapp, based on the public domain song "Buffalo Gals [Won't You Come Out Tonight?]) in December 1944; "There Goes That Song Again" (music by Jule Styne, lyrics by Sammy Cahn) in January 1945; "Let It Snow! Let It Snow! Let It Snow!" (music by Vaughn Monroe, lyrics by Cahn), accompanying Connee Boswell, in February 1946; and a revival of the 1927 song "I'm Looking over a Four Leaf Clover" (music by Harry Woods, lyrics by Mort Dixon), with vocals by the Ames Brothers, in March 1948. But he never placed among the top recording artists of the period until his surprising run of hits in 1949.

It began with the fall 1948 release of "So Tired" (music and lyrics by Russ Morgan and Jack Stuart), which peaked in the Top Ten in early April, by which time "Cruising down the River" (music and lyrics by Eily Beadell and Nell Tollerton) had hit #1 and "Forever and Ever" (music by Franz Winkler, English lyrics by Malia Rosa) was also in the Top Ten. Within weeks, "Sunflower" (music and lyrics by Mack David), the B-side of "Cruising down the River," reached the Top Ten, giving Morgan a remarkable set of simultaneous hits and making him one of the most successful performers of the year at a time when the big bands were in decline. A revival of the 1917 song "Johnson Rag" (music by Guy G. Hall and Henry Kleinhauf, lyrics by Jack Lawrence), released late in 1949, became another Top Ten hit for him in February 1950.

Just prior to his breakthrough, in the fall of 1948, Morgan and his Orch. had been regulars on the television series *Welcome Aboard*. With his new success, Morgan was given a second chance at TV with *In the Morgan Manner*, which debuted on March 1, 1950, and ran until July 30. Meanwhile, he scored his last Top Ten hit with "Sentimental Me" (music and lyrics by James T. Morehead and James Cassin) in June.

Morgan toured extensively during the 1950s, pausing to make the occasional film (*Disc Jockey* in 1951, *The Great Man* in 1956, *The Big Beat* in 1958) and to take another stab at TV with the summer replacement program *The Russ Morgan Show,* broadcast live from July to September 1956. In 1960 he reorganized his band, which by now featured his sons Jack and David, into a smaller unit and concentrated on playing in and around Los

Angeles. In 1965 he settled in Las Vegas, playing at the Dunes Hotel. He remained active until his death following a stroke at the age of 65 in 1969, after which his son Jack led the band.

DISC.: *Russ Morgan & His Orchestra Play 22 Original Big Band Recordings* (1937); *Music in the Morgan Manor* (1941).—**WR**

Morgan (Riggins), Helen, American torch singer and actress; b. Danville, Ill., Aug. 2, 1900; d. Chicago, Ill., Oct. 8, 1941.

Morgan was the preeminent singer of plaintive romantic ballads in the 1920s. Though she was primarily a nightclub performer, she also appeared in vaudeville, on Broadway, and in films, and she made popular recordings. She was best known for her stage and screen portrayal of the doomed mulatto Julie Dozier in Jerome Kern and Oscar Hammerstein II's *Show Boat*, in which she sang "Can't Help Lovin' Dat Man" and "Bill."

There are conflicting accounts of Morgan's early years. Most biographical sources state that she was the daughter of French-Canadian parents and that her father died when she was a child. Her mother then married Thomas Morgan, a railroad fireman, and Morgan took her stepfather's name. But Gilbert Maxwell, Morgan's biographer, writes that Morgan's parents were Americans of Irish descent from N.Y. state, that Thomas Morgan was Helen Morgan's father, and that, after he deserted his pregnant wife, she found a job as a waitress in a railroad yard in Toronto, where Helen Morgan was born in October 1900. According to Maxwell, Thomas Morgan returned when his daughter was four and the family moved to Danville, Ill., where he again abandoned them sometime during her childhood.

In 1912, Morgan was discovered singing in the railroad yard in Danville by Chicago *Daily News* writer Amy Leslie, who booked her into the French Trocadero in Montreal. There she was hoisted on top of an upright piano so that she could be seen, thus beginning a trademark of her performing career. That career was briefly curtailed by the Gerry Society, which discouraged child labor, and Morgan attended high school in Chicago in 1913, after which she worked at menial jobs for a number of years. When she was 18 she returned to performing, at the Green Mill Club in Chicago. She won beauty contests as Miss Illinois and Miss Mount Royal at the 1918 Winter Sports Festival in Montreal, the latter leading to a trip to N.Y., where she studied singing with Edward Petri.

Morgan made her legitimate theatrical debut in the chorus of the hit musical *Sally* (N.Y., Dec. 21, 1920), produced by Florenz Ziegfeld, which ran 570 performances. After *Sally* closed in February 1922, she appeared at the Café Montmartre in Chicago and then returned to N.Y., where she sang at the Backstage Club. She was in the 1925 edition of the revue *George White's Scandals* (N.Y., June 22, 1925) and had a featured part in the 1926 edition of the revue *Americana* (N.Y., July 26, 1926), in which she sang "Nobody Wants Me" It was during this performance thay she was spotted by Jerome Kern, who was looking for someone to play Julie in *Show Boat*. That musical was delayed, however, and meanwhile Morgan reached the pinnacle of vaudeville

success, playing the Palace in N.Y. in January 1927. She also signed to Brunswick Records and scored a hit in September 1927 with "A Tree in the Park" from the Richard Rodgers–Lorenz Hart musical *Peggy-Ann*. By this time Morgan was so successful that her name was used in a succession of speakeasies—Helen Morgan's 54th Street Club, Chez Morgan, and Helen Morgan's Summer House—at which she appeared.

Show Boat (N.Y., Dec. 27, 1927) marked the peak of Morgan's career. The initial production ran 572 performances on Broadway. Morgan had a double-sided record hit with her two songs from the show, "Bill" (music by Kern, lyrics by P. G. Wodehouse) and "Can't Help Lovin' Dat Man" (music by Kern, lyrics by Hammerstein). Within days of *Show Boat*'s opening, her prominence in the speakeasy business led to her arrest for violation of the Prohibition law; she was later cleared, but was arrested again in June 1928, to be acquitted at a jury trial in April 1929. She gave up nightclub performing for the remainder of the Prohibition era.

In May 1929, Morgan was seen in the first film version of *Show Boat*. She scored a hit record with "Mean to Me" (music by Fred E. Ahlert, lyrics by Roy Turk) in June. She returned to Broadway with *Sweet Adeline* (N.Y., Sept. 3, 1929), which had been written for her by Kern and Hammerstein, singing "Why Was I Born?" (which she recorded for a hit), "Don't Ever Leave Me," and "Here Am I." *Adeline* ran 234 performances. Before the end of the year, Morgan had made her dramatic-film debut, starring in *Applause*; she also appeared in the Ziegfeld-produced film *Glorifying the American Girl*. Early in 1930 she had another dramatic role, as the star of the film *Roadhouse Nights*.

Morgan returned to vaudeville after *Sweet Adeline* closed, again playing the Palace in March 1930 and February 1931. In November 1930 she scored a hit with "Body and Soul" (music by John Green, lyrics by Edward Heyman, Robert Sour, and Frank Eyton). She starred in the *Ziegfeld Follies of 1931* (N.Y., July 1, 1931), which ran 165 performances, then appeared in the first Broadway revival of *Show Boat* (N.Y., May 19, 1932), which ran 192 performances, followed by a North American tour that starred Morgan and played until February 1933; the show also produced one of the first cast albums ever made, featuring Morgan and Paul Robeson.

Morgan married attorney Maurice Mashke Jr. on May 15, 1933, but divorced him two years later. She returned to nightclub work in N.Y. in November 1933. In 1934 she appeared on the radio program *Broadway Melodies*, and in May of that year she starred in the play *Memory* in Los Angeles. She then made several films: she had a starring role in *You Belong to Me*, released in September, and featured parts in *Marie Galante* (November 1934), *Sweet Music* (February 1935), *Go into Your Dance* (May 1935), and *Frankie and Johnny* (briefly released in 1935, then given wide release in May 1936).

By the mid-1930s, Morgan's career was becoming hampered by her alcoholism. She repeated her role as Julie in the May 1936 film version of *Show Boat*, her final film appearance. She was part of a national tour of

George White's Scandals during the summer and fall of 1936. In 1937 she was a regular on the *Ken Murray Show* radio series. She toured in vaudeville in 1939 and worked in nightclubs in N.Y. and Miami in 1940 and 1941.

Morgan married car dealer Lloyd Johnson on July 25, 1941, and in September again went on tour with *George White's Scandals*. She was hospitalized after only one performance in Chicago and died of cirrhosis of the liver at the age of 41. On April 16, 1957, CBS-TV broadcast a dramatic treatment of her life on its *Playhouse 90* series, starring Polly Bergen. *The Helen Morgan Story*, a largely fictionalized feature film starring Ann Blyth, with her singing dubbed by Gogi Grant, followed in October, and a soundtrack album reached the charts in January 1958.

BIBL.: G. Maxwell, *H. M.: Her Life and Legend* (N.Y., 1974). **—WR**

Mori, Frank (Francis), English conductor and composer, son of **Nicolas Mori**; b. London, March 21, 1820; d. Chaumont, France, Aug. 2, 1873. He was educated by his father. He wrote light music, his operetta *The River-Sprite* (London, Feb. 9, 1865) being fairly successful.**—NS/LK/DM**

Mori, Nicolas, English violinist and music publisher, father of **Frank (Francis) Mori**; b. London (of Italian descent), Jan. 24, 1796; d. there, June 14, 1839. He studied with Barthelemon and appeared as a soloist in one of the latter's concertos when he was 8. He then continued his studies with Viotti (1808–14). He was a soloist at a Phil. Soc. concert in London (1814), and then became one of its concertmasters (1816); was also concertmaster at the King's Theatre until his death. He married Elizabeth Lavenu, widow of the publisher Lewis Lavenu, in 1819; the firm was known as Mori & Lavenu from about 1818 to 1839. He brought out the English eds. of works by Mendelssohn, and other music, and also wrote music for violin. An eccentric, he wrote flamboyant advertisements about his career, and shortly before his death announced his own memorial concert, punning on his name ("Memento Mori").

BIBL.: E. Duffin, *Particulars of the Illness and Death of the Late Mr. M. the Violinist* (London, 1839).**—NS/LK/DM**

Moriani, Napoleone, outstanding Italian tenor; b. Florence, March 10, 1806; d. there, March 4, 1878. He studied with C. Ruga, making his operatic debut in Pacini's *Gli Arabi nelle Gallie* in Pavia in 1833. He then sang throughout Italy, garnering great praise for his interpretations of Bellini, Donizetti, and Verdi; he created the role of Enrico in Donizetti's *Maria di Rudenz* in Venice in 1838, and that of Carlo in *Linda di Chamounix* in Vienna in 1842. He sang in Madrid (1844–46) and London (1844–45); made his Paris debut at the Théâtre-Italien (1845), where he returned in 1849–50 before appearing again in Madrid. He retired from the stage in 1851. Having sung so many death-laden tenor roles, he became known as "il tenore della bella morte." **—NS/LK/DM**

Mörike, Eduard, German conductor; b. Stuttgart, Aug. 16, 1877; d. Berlin, March 14, 1929. He was a great-nephew of the poet Eduard Friedrich Mörike. He studied at the Leipzig Cons. with Ruthard and Sitt, and received private piano instruction from Siloti. In 1899 he went to the U.S. and made appearances as a pianist. After working as a coach at the Metropolitan Opera in N.Y., he returned to Germany and conducted in various theaters. From 1906 to 1909 he was an asst. conductor at the Bayreuth Festivals. He held the post of 1st conductor at the Deutsches Opernhaus in Berlin from 1912 to 1922, and also made appearances as a guest conductor with the Berlin Phil. He subsequently was active as a conductor in Europe and the U.S. From 1924 until his death he was chief conductor of the Dresden Phil.**—NS/LK/DM**

Morillo, Roberto García, Argentine composer and music critic; b. Buenos Aires, Jan. 22, 1911. He studied composition with Aguirre and Juan José Castro; later took courses with Gaito and Ugarte. From 1926 to 1930 he was in Paris. Returning to Argentina, he taught at the National Cons. in Buenos Aires and wrote music criticism for *La Nación*. He publ. monographs on Mussorgsky (1943), Rimsky-Korsakov (1945), and Carlos Chávez (1960); also *Julian Bautista en la música española contemporánea* (1949). His music is marked by propulsive rhythms and a strong sense of dissonant counterpoint.

WORKS: ORCH.: *Berseker*, symphonic poem (Buenos Aires, Dec. 29, 1932); Piano Concerto (Buenos Aires, Nov. 7, 1940); *The Fall of the House of Usher*, after Poe (Buenos Aires, May 12, 1943); 3 syms. (1948, 1955, 1961); *Variaciones olímpicas* (1958); *3 pinturas de Piet Mondrian* (1960); *Ciclo de Dante Alighieri* for Chamber Orch. (1970); *Dionysos* (1971); *Concerto a 9* for 3 Clarinets and Strings (1943). **CHAMBER:** Quartet for Violin, Cello, Clarinet, and Piano (1937); *Las pinturas negras de Goya* for Piano, Violin, Cello, Flute, Clarinet, and Bassoon (Montevideo, May 27, 1940); String Quartet (1951). **Piano:** 5 sonatas (1935–62); *Divertimento sobre temas de Paul Klee* for Wind Quintet (1967; orchestrated 1971). **VOCAL:** *Cantata de los caballeros* for Soprano and Orch., after García Lorca (1965); *Cantata festiva* for Chorus (1971). **OTHER:** Film music.**—NS/LK/DM**

Morini (real name, Siracusano), Erica, Austrian-born American violinist; b. Vienna, Jan. 5, 1904; d. N.Y., Oct. 30, 1995. Her father was Italian and her mother Austrian. She first studied at her father's music school in Vienna. At 7, she became a student of Ševčik at the Vienna Cons. She was 12 when she made her professional debut in Vienna, and then was invited to appear as a soloist with the Leipzig Gewandhaus Orch. and the Berlin Phil. On Jan. 26, 1921, she made her U.S. debut as soloist in 3 concertos with Bodanzky and the Metropolitan Opera orch. in N.Y. She subsequently appeared as a soloist with various U.S. orchs. until returning to Europe in 1924 to pursue her career. After the Anschluss in 1938, she emigrated to the U.S. and in 1943 became a naturalized American citizen. After World War II ended in 1945, she toured extensively at home and abroad.**—NS/LK/DM**

Morison, Elsie (Jean), Australian soprano; b. Ballarat, Aug. 15, 1924. She studied with Clive Carey at the Melbourne Cons. She made her London debut at the Royal Albert Hall in London in 1948; then sang with the Sadler's Wells Opera (1948–54) and at Covent Garden (1953–62). She married **Rafael Kubelik** in 1963. Her roles included Pamina, Susanna, Marzelline, Micaëla, and Anne Trulove.—**NS/LK/DM**

Moritz, Landgrave of Hessen-Kassel, German patron of the arts and composer, called Moritz "der Gelehrte" (the learned); b. Kassel, May 25, 1572; d. Eschwege, March 15, 1632. He succeeded his father in 1592, remaining as landgrave until abdicating in favor of his son during the 30 Years' War in 1627. Having studied music with the court Kapellmeister Georg Otto, he took a deep interest in all the arts and gained a reputation as a great patron of enlightened views and noble generosity. He built the first court theater in Germany, the Ottoneum (1605), which he named for his Kapellmeister. He was the patron of Heinrich Schütz. In 1955 the musicological inst. in Kassel was named in his honor as the Landgraf-Moritz-Stiftung. He wrote much sacred music and some instrumental pieces, most of which have not survived.

BIBL.: E. Zulauf, *Beiträge zur Geschichte der landgräflichhessischen Hofkapelle zu Cassel bis auf die Zeit M. des Gelehrten* (Kassel, 1902).—**NS/LK/DM**

Morlacchi, Francesco (Giuseppe Baldassare), prominent Italian conductor and composer; b. Perugia, June 14, 1784; d. Innsbruck, Oct. 28, 1841. He studied with his uncle, the Cathedral organist L. Mazzetti, and with Luigi Caruso in Perugia, then with Zingarelli in Loreto (1803–04) and Padre Mattei at Bologna's Liceo Filarmonica (1805), where he received his diploma of "maestro compositore" for the cantata *Il tempio della gloria*, written in honor of Napoleon's coronation as King of Italy. He demonstrated his contrapuntal skill by composing a *Miserere à 16* (1807). He first gained success as a composer for the stage with his operas *La Principessa per ripiego* (Rome, autumn 1809) and *Le Danaidi* (Rome, Feb. 11, 1810). He then was called to Dresden as deputy Kapellmeister of the Italian Opera in 1810, being made Kapellmeister for life in 1811; he retained the latter title until the Italian Opera was closed in 1832. During these years, he wrote some of his most successful stage works, among them *Il nuovo barbiere di Siviglia* (Dresden, May 1816), *La simplicetta di Pirna* (Dresden, Aug. 1817), *La gioventu di Enrico* (Dresden, Oct. 4, 1823), *Il Colombo* (Genoa, June 28, 1828), and *Il Rinnegato* (Dresden, March 1832); also wrote a Requiem upon the death of King Friedrich August I of Saxony (1827). In later years he divided his time between Dresden and Italy. Stricken with tuberculosis in 1839, he died on his way to his homeland.

BIBL.: G. Ricci des Ferres-Cancani, *F. M.: Un maestro italiano alla corte di Sassonia (1785–1841)* (Florence, 1956); B. Brumana and G. Ciliberti, eds., *F. M. e la musica del suo tempo (1785–1841)* (Florence, 1986).—**NS/LK/DM**

Morley, Thomas, famous English composer; b. Norwich, 1557 or 1558; d. London, Oct. 1602. He studied with William Byrd. From 1583 to 1587 he was organist and master of the choristers at Norwich Cathedral. In 1588 he received his B.Mus. from Oxford. About this time he became organist at St. Paul's Cathedral. By 1591 he had turned spy for the government of Queen Elizabeth I. In 1592 he was sworn in as a Gentleman of the Chapel Royal and was made Epistler and then Gospeller. He was also active as a printer, holding a monopoly on all music publ. under a patent granted to him by the government in 1598. In addition to publishing his own works, he acted as ed., arranger, translator, and publisher of music by other composers. Notable among his eds. was *The Triumphes of Oriana* (1601), a collection of madrigals by 23 composers. He gained distinction as a music theorist, his *A Plaine and Easie Introduction to Practicall Musicke* (1597) becoming famous as an exposition of British musical schooling of his time.

WORKS: VOCAL: Madrigals: *Canzonets, or Little Short Songs to Three Voyces* (London, 1593; 3rd ed., enl., 1602, as *Canzonets...with Some Songs added by the Author*); *Madrigalls to Foure Voyces: The First Booke* (London, 1594; 2nd ed., enl., 1600, as *Madrigalls...with Some Songs added by the Author*); *The First Booke of Balletts to Fiue Voyces* (London, 1595; 3rd ed., 1600); *The First Booke of Canzonets to Two Voyces* (London, 1595); *Canzonets or Little Short Aires to Fiue and Sixe Voyces* (London, 1597); he ed. the last 3 in Italian editions as well; he also ed. *Madrigales: The Triumphes of Oriana, to Fiue and Six Voyces Composed by Divers Seurall Aucthors* (London, 1601). **Solo Songs:** *The First Booke of Aires or Little Short Songs to Sing and Play to the Lute with the Base-Viol* (London, 1600; it contains the song "It was a lover and his lasse" from Shakespeare's *As You Like It*). Many of the preceding works were ed. by E.H. Fellowes in *The English Madrigal School* (4 vols., 1913 et seq.: I, *Canzonets to 2 Voices* [1595] and *Canzonets to 3 Voices* [1593], rev. by T. Dart, 1956; II, *Madrigals to 4 Voices* [1594], rev. by T. Dart, 1963; III, *Canzonets to 5 and 6 Voices* [1597], rev. by T. Dart, 1966; IV, *Ballets to 5 Voices* [1600], rev. by T. Dart, 1966). *The Triumphes of Oriana* was ed. by E.H. Fellowes in *The English Madrigal School, A Guide to Its Practical Use* (London, 1926; rev. by T. Dart, 1962, in *The English Madrigalists*). *The First Booke of Aires* was ed. by E.H. Fellowes in *The English School of Lutenist Song Writers* (London, 1920–32; rev. by T. Dart, 1966, in *The English Lute- Songs*). Modern eds. of additional works by Morley include H. Andrews and T. Dart, *Collected Motets* (London, 1959), and T. Dart, ed., *Keyboard Works*, in *English Keyboard Music* (London, 1959). Morley ed. *The First Booke of Consort Lessons, made by divers exquisite Authors for six Instruments to play together, viz. the Treble Lute, the Pandora, the Citterne, the Base Violl, the Flute, and the Treble Violl* (London, 1599; 2nd ed., corrected and enl., 1611; modern ed. by S. Beck, N.Y., 1959). His treatise *A Plaine and Easie Introduction to Practicall Musicke* (London, 1597) was publ. in a facsimile ed. by E.H. Fellowes (London, 1937); a modernized ed. was publ. by R. Alec Harman (London, 1952; 2nd ed., 1963).

BIBL.: O. Bekker, *Die englischen Madrigalisten William Byrd, T. M. und John Dowland* (Leipzig, 1901); J. King, *An Aesthetic and Musical Analysis of the Madrigals of T. M., with Special Reference between Text and Music and Some Comparison with the Madrigals of John Wilby, John Bennet, and the "Triumphs of Oriana"* (diss., Univ. of Toronto, 1950); J. Uhler, *M.'s Canzonets for Two Voices* (diss., Univ. of La., 1954); idem, *M.'s Canzonets for Three Voices* (Baton Rouge, 1957); C. Murphy, *T. M. Editions of Italian Canzonets and Madrigals* (Tallahassee, 1964).—**NS/LK/DM**

Mornington, Garret Wesley, First Earl of,

Irish composer; b. Dublin, July 19, 1735; d. Kensington, May 22, 1781. His son was the Duke of Wellington. He studied violin, harpsichord, organ, and composition in his youth, then studied at Trinity Coll., Dublin (B.A., 1754; M.A., 1757); was made Mus.D. (1764) and served as the 1st prof. of music at the Univ. of Dublin (1764–74). He was admired as a glee composer, winning prizes awarded by the Catch Club (1776, 1777, and 1779), the last for his *Here in cool grot.* Sir Henry Bishop ed. a complete collection of his glees and madrigals (1846). —NS/LK/DM

Moroi, Makoto,

Japanese composer and teacher, son of **Saburo Moroi;** b. Tokyo, March 12, 1930. He was a student of his father and of Ikenouchi at the Tokyo National Univ. of Fine Arts and Music (1948–52), and subsequently devoted himself to composition and teaching. He has utilized ancient Japanese elements, serial procedures, and sonorism in developing his compositional style.

WORKS: ORCH.: *Composition 1* (1951–53), *2* (1958), and *5, Ode to Arnold Schoenberg,* for Chamber Orch. (1961); *Suite classique* (1953); *Suite concertante* for Violin and Orch. (1963); Piano Concerto (1966); *Vision of Cain* (1966); Sym. (Tokyo, Nov. 7, 1968); Concerto for Shakuhachi, Strings, and Percussion (1970–71); Sym. for Voice, Percussion, Japanese Instruments, and Tape (1972); Sinfonia concertante No. 3, *Demise of Mythologies,* for Marimba, Sanjū-gen, Organ, and Orch. (1992). **CHAMBER:** *Musica da camera 3* for Viola and Wind Quintet (1951) and *4* for String Quartet (1954); *Ordre* for Cello and Piano (1958); *5 epigrammes* for 7 Instruments (1964); *Toccata, Sarabande, and Tarantella* for Strings and Piano (1964); *Les Farces* for Violin (1970); piano music; pieces for Solo Japanese Instruments. **VOCAL:** *Développements rarefiants* for Soprano and Chamber Group (1957); *Composition 3* for Narrator, Men's Chorus, and Orch. (1958) and *4* for Narrator, 3 Speaking Sopranos, Chorus, and Orch. (1960); *Stars of Pythagoras* for Narrator, Chorus, Chamber Orch., and Tape (1959); *Cantata da camera 1* for Narrator, Men's Chorus, Ondes Martenot, Harpsichord, and 3 Percussionists (1959) and *2, Blue Cylinder,* for Narrator, Soprano, Chorus, and Chamber Orch. (1959); *The Red Cocoon* for Narrator, Pantomime, 2 Choruses, Orch., and Tape (1960); *Phaeton, the Coachman* for Narrator, Voice, Chorus, and Tape (1965); *Izumo, My Home!* for Baritone, Soprano, Chorus, Orch., and Tape (1970).—NS/LK/DM

Moroi, Saburo,

Japanese composer, teacher, and writer on music, father of **Makoto Moroi;** b. Tokyo, Aug. 7, 1903; d. there, March 24, 1977. He studied literature at the Univ. of Tokyo (1926–28), and later took lessons in composition with Max Trapp, orchestration with Gmeindl, and piano with Robert Schmidt at the Hochschule für Musik in Berlin (1932–34). Upon returning to Japan, he was active as a music teacher; was inspector of music and adult education for the Ministry of Culture (1946–64) and director of Tokyo's Gakuen Academy of Music (1967–77); among his students, in addition to his son, were Dan and Irino. Among his numerous publications are *Junsui tai i ho* (Strict Counterpoint; Tokyo, 1949) and *Gakushiki no kenkyū* (Historical Research on Musical Forms; 5 vols., Tokyo, 1957–67).

WORKS: ORCH.: 2 piano concertos (1933, 1977); 5 syms.: No. 1 (Berlin, Oct. 2, 1934), No. 2 (Tokyo, Oct. 12, 1938), No. 3 for Organ and Orch. (Tokyo, May 26, 1950), No. 4 (Tokyo, March 21, 1951), and No. 5 (Tokyo, 1971); Cello Concerto (1936); Bassoon Concerto (1937); Violin Concerto (1939); 2 Symphonic Movements (1942); Sinfonietta (1943); *Allegro* for Piano and Orch. (1947). **CHAMBER:** Violin Sonata (1930); String Quartet (1933); Piano Quartet (1935); Viola Sonata (1935); Flute Sonata (1937); String Sextet (1939); String Trio (1940). **Piano:** 2 sonatas (1933, 1940); *Preludio ed Allegro giocoso* (1971). **VOCAL:** *2 Songs* for Soprano and Orch. (1935); *A Visit of the Sun,* fantasy-oratorio (Tokyo, June 30, 1969).—NS/LK/DM

Moross, Jerome,

American composer; b. N.Y., Aug. 1, 1913; d. Miami, July 25, 1983. He studied at the Juilliard School of Music in N.Y. (1931–32) and at N.Y.U. (graduated, 1932). He became associated with various ballet groups and wrote a number of scores for the dance, most of them on American subjects, all of them in a vivid folklike manner. In 1940 he went to Hollywood as an arranger; collaborated with Copland on the score for *Our Town.* He held 2 Guggenheim fellowships (1947, 1948). His first film score was *Close Up* (1948); his other film scores included *The Cardinal, The Proud Rebel,* and *The Big Country.* For Broadway he wrote music for *Parade* (1935). His works for the dance included *Paul Bunyan* (1934), *American Patterns* (1937), *Frankie and Johnny* (1938), *Guns and Castanets* (1939), *The Eccentricities of Davy Crockett* (1946), and *Robin Hood* (1946). He also wrote operas: *Susanna and the Elders* (1940), *Willie the Weeper* (1945), *The Golden Apple* (1948–50), *Gentleman, Be Seated!* (1955–56; N.Y., Oct. 10, 1963), and *Sorry, Wrong Number* (1977), and a ballet suite, *The Last Judgment* (1953). Other works include several orch. pieces, including *Beguine* (N.Y., Nov. 21, 1934), *A Tall Story* (N.Y., Sept. 25, 1938), and a Sym. (1941–42; Seattle, Oct. 18, 1943), and chamber music, including Sonatina for Clarinet Choir (1966), Sonatina for Strings, Double Bass, and Piano (1967), Sonatina for Brass Quintet (1968), Sonatina for Woodwind Quintet (1970), Sonatina for Divers Instruments (1972), Sonata for Piano Duet and String Quartet (1975), and Concerto for Flute and String Quartet (1978).—NS/LK/DM

Morris, Byron,

jazz saxophonist, flutist; b. Roanoke, Va., Jan. 7, 1941. He attended Tuskegee Univ., earning his B.S. in 1964. He studied privately with Frank Foster, Jackie McLean, Jimmy Owens, Ornette Coleman, Rahsaan Roland Kirk, John Malachi, Jimmy Heath, and Webster Young. He co-founded three musical groups: Unity with Vincent McEwan and Gerald Wise in 1972; Three Saxes for Lester (Young), in 1981 with Ron Holloway and Clyde Dickerson; and Swingin' Saxes, an out-growth of Three Saxes for Lester, with in late 1983 Orrin Hall and Charlie Young, and a broadened repertory as well. All three groups have been active in the Washington, D.C., area. He worked with Joe McPhee in 1973 and that same year also hosted radio shows in Poughkeepsie/Beacon, N.Y.; from 1977–83, he hosted shows on WPFW, Washington, D.C. He received Fellowships from the NEA in 1973, 1978 and 1983, the last to conduct educational workshops on jazz history in secondary schools and colleges. He produces his own recordings.

DISC.: BYRON AND GERALD: *Unity* (1972). **UNITY:** *Blow thru Your Mind* (1974); *Vibrations in Time* (1994); *Universal Sounds of America* (1995); *Joe McPhee and Survival Unit II 1971* (1996); *Jazzier Rhythms* (1997). **BYRON MORRIS AND UNITY:** *Vibrations, Themes and Serenades* (1979); *Honey, I Love* (1982).—**LP**

Morris, Harold, American composer, teacher, and pianist; b. San Antonio, March 17, 1890; d. N.Y., May 6, 1964. He studied at the Univ. of Tex. (B.A.) and the Cincinnati Cons. (M.M., 1922). He was on the faculty of the Juilliard School of Music (1922–39) and Teachers Coll., Columbia Univ. (1935–46). He was one of the principal founders of the American Music Guild in N.Y. (1921). In his music, he revealed himself as a Romanticist; in the main direction of his creative development, he was influenced by Scriabin. Many of his works were of programmatic content, some including American thematic material.

WORKS: ORCH.: *Poem*, after Tagore's *Gitanjali* (1915; Cincinnati, Nov. 29, 1918); *Dum-A-lum*, variations on a Negro spiritual for Chamber Orch. (1925); 3 syms.: No. 1, after Browning's *Prospice* (1925), No. 2, *Victory* (1943; Chicago, Dec. 23, 1952), and No. 3, *Amaranth*, after E.A. Robinson (1946; Houston, March 13, 1948); Piano Concerto on 2 Negro Themes (1927; Boston, Oct. 23, 1931); Suite for Chamber Orch. (1927; N.Y., Nov. 1, 1941); Violin Concerto (1938; N.Y., May 25, 1939); *Passacaglia and Fugue* (1939); *American Epic* (1942); *Heroic Overture* (1943); *Passacaglia, Adagio, and Finale* (1955). **CHAMBER: 2** piano trios (1917, 1933); Violin Sonata (1919); 2 string quartets (1928, 1937); 2 piano quintets (1929, 1937); Suite for Piano and Strings (1943); also many works for solo piano, including 4 sonatas (1915, 1915, 1920, 1939) and *Ballade* (1938). —**NS/LK/DM**

Morris, James (Peppler), outstanding American bass-baritone; b. Baltimore, Jan. 10, 1947. After studies with a local teacher, he won a scholarship to the Univ. of Md.; concurrently received invaluable instruction from Rosa Ponselle; then continued his studies with Frank Valentino at the Peabody Cons. of Music in Baltimore (1966–68). He made his debut as Crespel in *Les Contes d'Hoffmann* with the Baltimore Civic Opera (1967). After further training with Nicola Moscona at the Philadelphia Academy of Vocal Arts (1968–70), he made his Metropolitan Opera debut in N.Y. as the King in *Aida* on Jan. 7, 1971. He also appeared with the Opera Orch. of N.Y. and sang widely in Europe. In 1975 he scored a notable success as Don Giovanni at the Metropolitan. Although closely associated with the Italian and French repertoires, he appeared as Wotan in *Die Walküre* at the Baltimore Civic Opera in 1984. Morris subsequently sang that role in the San Francisco Opera's *Ring* cycle in 1985, eliciting extraordinary critical acclaim. In 1986 he appeared at the Salzburg Festival as Mozart's Guglielmo and Figaro. In 1990 he sang Méphistophélès in Cincinnati and at the Metropolitan Opera, where he also appeared as Wotan, and as the Wanderer in *Siegfried* at London's Covent Garden. He portrayed Wotan at the Lyric Opera in Chicago in 1993 and 1996. In 1995 he sang that role at the San Francisco Opera, and returned there in 1997 as Scarpia. After singing Iago at the Metropolitan Opera in 1995, he returned there as Mozart's Figaro in 1997. He portrayed Wotan at the San Francisco Opera in 1999. His other esteemed roles include Count Almaviva, Philip II, the Dutchman, the 4 villains in *Les Contes d'Hoffmann*, Timur in *Le Roi de Lahore*, Scarpia, and Claggart in *Billy Budd*. In 1987 he married **Susan Quittmeyer**.—**NS/LK/DM**

Morris, Joan (Clair), American mezzo-soprano; b. Portland, Ore., Feb. 10, 1943. She studied voice with Lyle Moore at Gonzaga Univ. (1963–65), and received training in speech and voice from Clifford Jackson at the American Academy of Dramatic Art (diploma, 1968) and then privately (1968–73). She also studied with Frederica Schmitz-Svevo in N.Y. (1968–74). In 1972 she began to concertize with **William Bolcom**, whom she married in 1975. In addition to many engagements in the U.S., they have won success abroad in Florence (1989), Moscow (1991), and London's Wigmore Hall (1993). In 1997 they celebrated their 25th anniversary as duo artists. Morris has become widely known for her performances of both serious and popular works, ranging from the early American period to scores by her husband. She has recorded 20 albums and CDs, ranging from *After the Ball: A Treasury of Turn-of-the-Century Popular Songs* (1974) to collections of Irving Berlin, George Gershwin, Rodgers and Hart, and *Cabaret Songs* by Bolcom and Arnold Weinstein. In 1981 she joined the musical theater program of the Univ. of Mich. —**NS/LK/DM**

Morris, Lawrence "Butch," American singer; b. Long Beach, Calif., Feb. 10, 1947. He played with such West Coast legends as Bobby Bradford, Horace Tapscott, and Charles Moffett. Moffett led a rehearsal band at an Oakland joint called Club 7, and sometimes would put compositions aside and cue the ensemble through group improvisations in a manner Morris had never seen before, slowing them down, or speeding them up, or giving accents for the band to play. Moving to N.Y. in 1976, he joined the energy jams on the "loft scene," where the music raged for hours, sometimes leaving him concerned that there was no way to preserve, or even to repeat in that very performance, the passing moments of brilliance. Teaching in Rotterdam, he began to build on Moffett's gestural language, progressing toward his first full-blown conduction in 1985. He continues to expand his conductions (they numbered 50 as of early 1995, when he released his opus conduction collection). He also worked on the Robert Altman film, *Kansas City* and is collaborating with Murray, folk-blues singer Taj Mahal, and former Grateful Dead guitarist Bob Weir on a Broadway musical about the life of Negro baseball league star Satchel Paige.

DISC.: *Current Trends in Racism in Modern America* (1986); *Homeing* (1989); *Dust to Dust* (1991); *Burning Cloud* (1996). —**WKH**

Morris, R(eginald) O(wen), English composer and pedagogue; b. York, March 3, 1886; d. London, Dec. 14, 1948. He studied with Charles Wood at the Royal Coll. of Music in London, where he later taught (1920–26). After teaching at the Curtis Inst. of Music in Philadelphia (1926–28), he again taught at the Royal

Coll. of Music (1928–48). He became best known as a teacher, serving as a discerning mentor to many notable students. He was the brother-in-law of **Ralph Vaughan Williams**.

WORKS: ORCH.: Violin Concerto (1930); *Concerto piccolo* for 2 Violins and String Orch. (1930); Sym. (1935). **CHAMBER:** *Fantasy* for String Quartet (1922); other chamber works. **VOCAL:** Songs; folk-song arrangements.

WRITINGS (all publ. in London unless otherwise given): *Contrapuntal Technique in the 16th Century* (Oxford, 1922); *Foundations of Practical Harmony and Counterpoint* (1925); with H. Ferguson, *Preparatory Exercises in Score Reading* (1931); *Figured Harmony at the Keyboard* (1931); *The Structure of Music* (1935); *Introduction to Counterpoint* (1944); *Oxford Harmony* (1946).
—NS/LK/DM

Morris, Robert (Daniel), English-born American composer, teacher, and music theorist; b. Cheltenham, Oct. 19, 1943. He studied composition at the Eastman School of Music in Rochester, N.Y. (B.Mus., 1965), and at the Univ. of Mich. (M.Mus., 1966; D.M.A., 1969). He taught at the Univ. of Hawaii (1968–69), and then was on the faculty of Yale Univ. (1969–77), where he was director of the electronic music studio (1972–77) and chairman of the composition dept. (1973–77). From 1976 to 1980 he served on the staff of the music dept. of the Univ. of Pittsburgh. In 1980 he joined the faculty at the Eastman School of Music, where he was prof. of theory and composition from 1985 to 1998, and then was prof. of composition and chairman of the composition dept. from 1998. In 1992 he became chairman of the editorial board of *Perspectives of New Music*. He publ. *Composition with Pitch-Classes: A Theory of Compositional Design* (New Haven, 1987) and *Class-Notes for Atonal Theory* (1990), and over 20 articles on the theory and analysis of 20th century music and Indian music.

WORKS: DRAMATIC: *Hagoromo* for Soprano, Bass, Men's Chorus, 2 Flutes, 3 Violins, String Bass, and Bells (1977); also incidental music. **ORCH.:** *Syzygy* (Ann Arbor, April 13, 1966); *Continua* (New Haven, Dec. 14, 1972); *Streams and Willows*, flute concerto (Pittsburgh, Nov. 12, 1974); *In Different Voices* for Symphonic Band (New Haven, Feb. 28, 1976); *Tapestries* for Chamber Orch. (1976); *Interiors* (Pittsburgh, March 7, 1978); *Cuts* for Large Wind Ensemble (1984; Rochester, N.Y., April 4, 1986); *Just Now and Again* (1987); *Clash* (Rochester, N.Y., May 25, 1988); Concerto for Piano and Wind Ensemble (1988); *Bad Lands*, concerto for Flute and Wind Ensemble (1991); Concerto for Piano and Strings (1994); *Pilgrimage* (1997). **CHAMBER:** *Sangita 67* for Flutes, Strings, and Percussion (1967); *Varnam* for 5 Melody Instruments and Percussion (1972); *Motet on Doo-Dah* for Alto Flute, Double Bass, and Piano (1973); *Not Lilacs* for Alto Saxophone, Trumpet, Piano, and Drums (1974); *Throughout (Anyway)* for 4 Flutes (1975); *The Dreamer Once Removed* for Carillon and 4 Trumpets (1976); String Quartet (1976); *3/4/5* for 3, 4, or 5 Players (1977); *Plexus* for Woodwind Quartet (1978); *Tigers and Lilies* for 12 Saxophones (1979); *Vira* for Tuba, Flute, Crotales, and Gongs (1980); *Tournament* for 12 or 24 Trombones (1981); *2's Company* for 8 Instruments (1982); *Saraswati's Children* for Melody Instruments, Percussion, and Drone (1985); *Arci* for String Quartet (1988); *Pari Passu* for Violin and Percussion (1988); *Out and Out* for Clarinet and Piano (1989); *3 Musicians* for English Horn, Horn, and Bass (1989); *Traces* for Flute and Piano (1990); *A Fabric of Seams* for 8 Instruments (1990); *Along a*

Rocky Path for Clarinet, Violin, and Piano (1993); *Broken Consort in 3 Parts* for 6 Players (1994); *Refrains* for Cello and Piano (1995); *Cora Chorus* for 3 Harps or Any Multiple Thereof (1996); *Tete a Tete* for 2 Guitars (1999). **PIANO:** *Trip, Tusk, Night Vapors* (1967); *Cairn* (1969); *Phrases* (1970); *Bhayanaka* for Piano, 4-Hands (1977); *Either Ether* (1978); *Allies* for Piano, 4-Hands (1979); *Variations on a Theme of Steve Reich* (1980); *Diamond* (1982); *4 Voices in 3 Voices* (1983); *Alter Egos* (1985); *Twice* (1987); *Clear Sounds Above Hills and Water* (1989); *Little Harmonic Labyrinth* (1989); *Terrane* (1990); *Doing Time*, suite (1991); *Canonic Variations* for 2 Pianos (1992); *Where a Cord Ends* (1994); *Bits and Pieces* (1994); *By Far* (1995); *Odds and Ends* (1996); *Floating Points* (1996); *Wabi* (1996); *Sabi* (1998); *Something Now* for Piano, 4-Hands (1998); *9 Pieces* (1999). **VOCAL:** *Forgotten Vibrations* for Soprano and Chamber Ensemble (1967); *...Versus...* for 5 Altos, Chamber Ensemble, Jazz Ensemble, and Double Bass obbligato (1968); *Lorelei* for Soprano, Bass, Flutes, Cellos, and Piano, 4-Hands (1970–71); *Q* for Chorus and Orch. (1976); *Haiku Cycle* for Soprano and Piano (1978); *Hamiltonian Cycle: Chorus* (1979); *4-fold Heart Sutra* for Baritone, Men's Chorus, Piano, and Vibraphone (1984); *Wang River Cycle* for Mezzosoprano and 8 Instruments (1985); *A Time* for Soprano and 8 Instruments (1987–88); (19) *Cold Mountain Songs* for Soprano and Piano (1993). **ELECTRONIC:** *Entelechy* for Voice, Cello, Piano, and Electronics (1969); *Phases* for 2 Pianos and Electronics (1970); *...Delay...* for String Trio and Tape (1971; rev. 1972); *Thunders of Spring over Distant Mountains* (1973); *Bob's Plain Bobs* for 4 Percussionists and Tape (1975); *Curtains* for Pipe Organ and Tape (1976); *Entelechy '77* for Piano and Electronics (1977); *Flux Mandala* for Tape (1977–78); *Shanti* for Clarinet and Tape (1979); *Ghost Dances* for Flutes and Tape (1980); *Aubade* for Tape (1981); *Exchanges* for Piano and Tape (1982); *Night Sky Scroll* for Tape (1984–85); *Amid Flock and Flume* for Flute and Tape (1986); *To the 9* for Guitar and Tape (1991); *Ma* (1992); *Entanglement* for Viola and Electronics (1998); *About the Same* (1999); *On the Go* for Clarinet and Electronics (1999).—NS/LK/DM

Morris, Wyn, Welsh conductor; b. Trlech, Feb. 14, 1929. He studied at the Royal Academy of Music in London and the Salzburg Mozarteum. He was apprentice conductor with the Yorkshire Sym. Orch. (1950–51) and conductor of an army band (1951–53). In 1954 he founded the Welsh Sym. Orch.; in 1957 he went to the U.S., where he led the Cleveland Chamber Orch. and other groups. In 1960 he returned to Great Britain, where he served as conductor of the choir of the Royal National Eisteddfod of Wales (1960–62), of the Royal Choral Soc. of London (1968–70), and of the Huddersfield Choral Soc. (1969–74). He then organized the Symphonica of London, with which he gave regular concerts in ambitious programs, particularly of Mahler's music.—NS/LK/DM

Morrison, Van (actually, George Ivan), lead singer of the Irish R&B band Them, then as a solo artist with a long and varied career performing his own blend of rock, blues, jazz, and folk; b. Belfast, Northern Ireland, Aug. 31, 1945. **THEM: MEMBERSHIP:** Van Morrison, voc., sax., har.; Billy Harrison, gtr. (b. Belfast, Northern Ireland, Oct. 14, 1942); Jackie McAuley, org. (b. Coleraine, Northern Ireland, Dec. 14, 1946); Alan Henderson, bs. (b. Belfast, Northern Ireland, Oct. 26, 1944); Ronnie Millings, drm.

An eccentric figure on the rock scene, like Neil Young and Bob Dylan, Morrison has been able to continue to produce music—of varying quality—on his own terms, without selling out to commercial pressures.

Born into a musical family, Van Morrison picked up guitar and saxophone as a child and was singing in local bands at age 11. In 1960, at 15, he dropped out of school to pursue a career in music. He initially played and sang with Deanie Sands and the Javelins, and joined the R&B band the Monarchs in 1961 for engagements throughout Great Britain and Europe.

Around 1964 Van Morrison formed Them in Belfast, and the group soon secured a regular engagement at a local R&B club, attracting a considerable following. Signed to British Decca (Parrot in the United States), Them traveled to London to record, scoring their first major British and American hit with producer-songwriter Bert Berns's "Here Comes the Night" in spring 1965. The group's debut album also included their second hit, "Mystic Eyes," and Morrison's rock classic "Gloria," twice a minor hit, the second time backed with "Baby, Please Don't Go," which featured studio guitarist Jimmy Page playing lead. They next recorded *Them Again* and conducted their first and only tour of the United States. Upon returning to Britain in June 1966, Van Morrison quit the band. Them recruited a new lead vocalist, but then disbanded late in the year.

Invited to the United States by record producer Bert Berns, Van Morrison initially settled in Boston and began recording for Berns's Bang Records. In summer 1967 Morrison achieved his first major solo hit with his own "Brown-Eyed Girl," and by fall Bang had assembled *Blowin' Your Mind* from songs originally recorded as singles, much to Morrison's chagrin. Nonetheless, the album did contain two songs that served as precursors to his landmark album *Astral Weeks*, "T.B. Sheets" and "Who Drove the Red Sports Car." Berns died of a heart attack on Dec. 31, 1967, and Morrison played East Coast clubs as a member of a trio for six months, until his recording contract was bought out by Warner Bros. Records.

Van Morrison's debut album for Warner Bros., *Astral Weeks*, recorded in 48 hours with a veteran jazz rhythm section, was issued before the end of 1968. Greeted by critical acclaim but poor sales, the album featured an impressionistic kind of lyricism that was at once evocative, intelligent, and undeniably compelling. Propelled by Morrison's unique vocal style and distinctive stream-of-consciousness lyrics, the album showcased his stirring "Cypress Avenue" and "Madame George" and contained "Ballerina" and "Slim Slo Slider." His next effort, *Moondance*, appeared more than a year later. Produced by Morrison, the album sported a diversity of mature original material. It yielded a moderate hit with "Come Running" and included the Morrison favorites "These Dreams of You," "Stoned Me," "Crazy Love," "Caravan," "Into the Mystic" (often regarded as one of the most finely crafted songs in rock history), and the title cut.

Established as an album artist, Van Morrison moved to Woodstock, N.Y., and quickly recorded *His Band and Street Choir*. The album produced two major hits, "Domino" and "Blue Money," and contained "I've Been Working," "Gypsy Queen," and "Call Me Up in Dreamland." In spring 1971 Morrison moved to northern Calif.'s Marin County; he dismissed his band and street choir, recording the countrified *Tupelo Honey* with guitarist Ronnie Montrose. Coproduced by Morrison, the album yielded the major hit "Wild Night" and included favorites such as "Old Woodstock," "I Wanna Roo You," and "Moonshine Whiskey."

Saint Dominic's Preview, ostensibly the first album over which Morrison exercised total artistic control, continued his best-selling ways while producing only two minor hits, "Jackie Wilson Said" and "Redwood Tree"; it included the stunning "Listen to the Lion." *Hard Nose the Highway* sold quite well without producing even a minor hit. Morrison then embarked on his first full-scale tour of Europe and America with the Caledonia Soul Orch., which resulted in the live double-record set *It's Too Late to Stop Now*.

However, in 1974 Van Morrison disbanded his group and recorded *Veedon Fleece* before "retiring" for nearly three years, including more than a year's exile in England. Eventually reemerging in 1977 with the appropriately titled *A Period of Transition*, recorded with Doctor John, Morrison took on rock impresario Bill Graham as his manager in 1978. He staged a dramatic comeback with *Wavelength*, thought to be his finest album in years, and conducted his first American tour in more than four years. The album produced his final albeit moderate hit with the title song. In 1979 Morrison recorded *Into the Music* and again toured. With 1980's *Common One*, Van Morrison began exploring new dimensions in his music as his songs began to become even more personal and esoteric.

Touring infrequently during the 1980s, Van Morrison switched to Mercury Records for 1985's *A Sense of Wonder*. He returned to Ireland and later recorded the enchanting *Irish Heartbeat* album with the Chieftains, Ireland's top Celtic music group. The album featured eight traditional folk songs arranged by Morrison and Chieftains leader Paddy Moloney, plus new versions of the previously released "Irish Heartbeat" and "Celtic Ray." Moving to Polydor for 1991's *Hymns to the Silence*, one of the most engaging albums of his career, Morrison returned to his blues roots with 1993's *Too Long in Exile*. He later recorded *A Night in San Francisco* with John Lee Hooker, Junior Wells, and Georgie Fame, and *Days Like This* with his daughter Shana. Van Morrison again surprised critics and fans with his early 1996 release, a collection of jazz standards recorded at the famous London nightclub, Ronnie Scott's.

DISC.: THEM: *Them* (1965); *Them Again* (1966); *Now and Them* (1968); *Time Out! Time In! For Them* (1968); *Them in Reality* (1970); *Them Featuring V. M.* (1972); *Backtracking* (1974); *Story of Them* (1977). **VAN MORRISON:** *Blowin' Your Mind* (1967); *Best* (1970); *T.B. Sheets* (1974); *Astral Weeks* (1968); *Moondance* (1970); *His Band and Street Choir* (1970); *Tupelo Honey* (1971); *Saint Dominic's Preview* (1972); *Hard Nose the Highway* (1973); *It's Too Late to Stop Now* (1974); *Veedon Fleece* (1974); *A Period of Transition* (1977); *Wavelength* (1978); *Into the Music* (1979); *Common One* (1980); *Beautiful Vision* (1982); *Inarticulate Speech of the Heart* (1983); *A Sense of Wonder* (1985); *Live at the Grand Opera House, Belfast* (1985); *No Guru, No Method, No Teacher* (1986);

Poetic Champions Compose (1987); *Avalon Sunset* (1989); *Best* (1990); *Enlightenment* (1990); *Hymns to the Silence* (1991); *Bang Masters* (1991); *Best, Vol. 2* (1993); *Too Long in Exile* (1993); *A Night in San Francisco* (rec. live, December 1993; rel. 1994); *Days Like This* (1995). **VAN MORRISON AND GEORGIE FAME AND FRIENDS:** *How Long Has This Been Going On?* (1996). **VAN MORRISON AND THE CHIEFTAINS:** *Irish Heartbeat* (1988).

BIBL.: Ritchie Yorke, *V. M.: Into the Music* (London, 1975); Johnny Rogan, *V. M.: The Great Deception* (London, 1982); Howard A. DeWitt, *V. M.:The Mystic's Music* (Fremont, Calif. 1983).—BH

Mortari, Virgilio, Italian composer and pedagogue; b. Passirana di Lainate, near Milan, Dec. 6, 1902; d. Rome, Sept. 6, 1993. He began his training at the Milan Cons. with Bossi and Pizzetti, and then completed his studies at the Parma Cons. (composition diploma, 1928). After appearances as a pianist, he taught composition at the Venice Cons. (1933–40). From 1940 to 1973 he was a prof. of composition at the Rome Cons. He also served as superintendent of the Teatro La Fenice in Venice from 1955 to 1959. With A. Casella, he wrote the book *Le tecnica dell'orchestra contemporanea* (Milan, 1947; 2nd ed., 1950). Mortari completed Mozart's unfinished score *L'Oca del Cairo* (Salzburg, Aug. 22, 1936).

WORKS: DRAMATIC: O p e r a : *Secchi e Sberlecchi* (1927); *La scuola delle moglie* (1930; rev. 1959); *La Figlia del diavolo* (Milan, March 24, 1954); *Il contratto* (1964). **B a l l e t :** *L'allegro piazzetta* (1945); *Specchio a tre luci* (1973). **ORCH.:** *Fantasia* for Piano and Orch. (1933); Concerto for String Quartet and Orch. (1937); *Notturno incantato* (1940); 2 piano concertos (1952, 1960); Viola Concerto (1966); Double Bass Concerto (1966); Violin Concerto (1967); *Eleonora d'Arborea*, overture (1968); Double Concerto for Violin, Piano, and Orch. (1968); Cello Concerto (1969); *Tripartita* (1972); Harp Concerto (1972). **CHAMBER:** Harp Sonatina (1938); *Piccola serenata* for Cello (1946) and for Violin (1947); *Duettini concertati* for Violin and Double Bass (1966); *Capriccio* for Violin (1967); *Les Adieux* for Flute, Violin, Viola, and Cello (1978); *Offerta musicale* for Violin, Cello, and Double Bass (1980); *Divertimento* for Bassoon and Cello (1986). **VOCAL:** 2 *Funeral Psalms* in memory of A. Casella for Voice and Instruments (1947); *Stabat Mater* (1947); *Requiem* (1959); *Alfabeto a sorpresa* for 3 Voices and 2 Pianos (1959); *Gloria* for Chorus, 2 Pianos, and Orch. (1980); *Domande e risposte* for Soprano, Baritone, and String Quartet (1983); *Missa pro pace* for Chorus and Organ (1984); songs.—NS/LK/DM

Mortaro, Antonio, Italian composer who flourished from 1585 to 1610. He became a Franciscan friar in Brescia in 1595. By 1598 he was organist at Milan's Franciscan monastery, and by 1602 at Novara Cathedral. About 1607 he returned to Brescia. His large output includes 10 vols. of sacred vocal music (1595–1610) and 5 vols. of secular vocal music (1590–1600).—LK/DM

Mortelmans, Ivo (Oscar), Belgian conductor, teacher, and composer, son of **Lodewijk Mortelmans**; b. Antwerp, May 19, 1901; d. Ostend, Aug. 20, 1984. He studied at the Antwerp Cons., and upon graduation, taught academic subjects and theory in Berchem (1925–66), Deurne (1939–70), and Mortsel (1946–67). He was also active as an opera conductor. He wrote an oratorio, *Eeuwig vlecht de bruid haar kroon* (1964), and numerous other choral works, both sacred and secular. —NS/LK/DM

Mortelmans, Lodewijk, Belgian conductor, teacher, and composer, father of **Ivo (Oscar) Mortelmans**; b. Antwerp, Feb. 5, 1868; d. there, June 24, 1952. He was a chorister in the Dominican Church, then studied with Benoit in Antwerp. In 1889 he won the 2nd Belgian Prix de Rome, gaining 1st prize with his cantata *Lady Macbeth* in 1893; then taught at the Antwerp Cons. from 1902. In 1921 he made a tour in the U.S. He was director of the Antwerp Cons. from 1924 to 1933. His finest creations were his songs to Flemish texts, which prompted Gilson to call him the "Prince of the Flemish song."

WORKS: DRAMATIC: O p e r a : *De kinderen der Zee* (Antwerp, 1920). **ORCH.:** 5 symphonic poems: *Helios* (1894), *Mythe du printemps* (1895), *Avonlied* (1928), *Weemoedig aandenken* (1942), and *Eenvoud* (1950); *Symphonie homérique* (1898); 4 elegies: *In memoriam* (1917), *Elevation du coeur* (1917), *Solitude* (1919), and *Treurdicht* (1925). **P i a n o :** 3 sets of *Miniatures*; 27 *Old Flemish Folksongs*. **VOCAL:** *Jong Vlaanderen*, church cantata (1907); songs.

BIBL.: J. Broeckx, *L. M.* (Antwerp, 1945).—NS/LK/DM

Mortensen, Finn (Einar), Norwegian teacher and composer; b. Christiania, Jan. 6, 1922; d. there (Oslo), May 21, 1983. He studied harmony with Thorlief Eken (1942) and counterpoint with Klaus Egge (1943) in Oslo, and received instruction in composition with Bentzon in Copenhagen (1956). He taught theory at the Norwegian Correspondence School (1948–66), then composition at the Oslo Cons. (1970–73). Subsequently he was prof. of composition at the Oslo Musikkhgskolan (from 1973), and he also served as chairman of the Norwegian Soc. of Composers (1972–74). In some of his compositions, he adopted a modified 12-tone idiom, supplemented by the devices of permutation and thematic rotation.

WORKS: ORCH.: Sym. (1953; Bergen, Jan. 21, 1963); *Pezzo orchestrale* (1957); *Evolution* (1961); *Tone Colors* (1961); Piano Concerto (Oslo, Sept. 11, 1963); *Fantasia* for Piano and Orch. (Oslo, May 6, 1966); *Per orchestra* (Oslo, Nov. 27, 1967); *Hedda* (1974–75); *Fantasia* for Violin and Orch. (1977). **CHAMBER:** String Trio (1950); Wind Quintet (1951); Sonata for Solo Flute (1953); Duo for Soprano and Violin (1956); Sonatina for Solo Clarinet (1957); Balalaika Sonatina (1957); 5 *Studies* for Flute (1957); Sonatina for Solo Viola (1959); Oboe Sonatina (1959); *Fantasia* for Bassoon (1959); Violin Sonata (1959); Viola Sonatina (1959); Piano Quartet (1960); 3 *Pieces* for Violin and Piano (1961–63); *Constellations* for Accordion, Guitar, and Percussion (1971); *Neoserialism I* for Flute and Clarinet (1971), *II* for Flute, Clarinet, and Bassoon (1972), and *III* for Violin, Viola, and Cello (1973); Suite for Wind Quintet (1972); *Serenade* for Cello and Piano (1972); 3 *Pieces* for Accordion (1973); *Construction* for Horn (1974–75); *Adagio and Fugue* for 16 Horns (1976); Sonata for Oboe and Harpsichord (1976); *Fantasia* for Trombone (1977); Suite for 5 Recorders and String Quintet (1978–79); String

Quartet (1981). **P i a n o :** 2 sonatinas (1943, 1949); 2 sonatas (1956, 1977); *Fantasia and Fugue* (1957–58); Sonata for 2 Pianos (1964); *Drawing* (1966); *Impressions* for 2 Pianos (1971). —NS/LK/DM

Mortensen, Otto (Jacob Hubertz), Danish pianist, teacher, and composer; b. Copenhagen, Aug. 18, 1907; d. Århus, Aug. 30, 1986. He studied with Christiansen (piano), Rung-Keller (organ), and Jeppeson (theory) at the Copenhagen Cons. (1925–29). He made his debut as a pianist in Copenhagen (1930), and continued his studies in Berlin (1930), with Milhaud and Desormière in Paris (1939), and at the Univ. of Copenhagen (M.A., 1956). He taught at the Copenhagen Cons. (1942–66) and at the Univ. of Århus (1966–74). He wrote mostly vocal music, including many songs; also a Piano Concerto (1945); Sym. (1956); 2 string quartets (1937, 1955); Quartet for Flute, Violin, Cello, and Piano (1938); Wind Quintet (1944); Oboe Sonata (1947); piano pieces. —NS/LK/DM

Morthenson, Jan W(ilhelm), Swedish composer; b. Örnsköldsvik, April 7, 1940. He studied composition with Mangs, Lidholm, and Metzger in Stockholm and aesthetics at the Univ. of Uppsala. He received instruction in electronic techniques from Koenig in Cologne and attended the new music courses in Darmstadt. He devised a "non- figurative" method in which "individual changes in sound are imperceptible," and publ. a treatise on the subject (Copenhagen, 1966).

WORKS: *Coloratura I* for Strings and Tape (1960), *II* for Orch. (1962), *III* for Chamber Orch. (1962–63), and *IV* for Orch. (1963); *3 Wechselspiel: I* for Cello (1960), *II* for Flute and 3 Loudspeakers (1961), and *III* for Piano and Percussion (1961); *Canzona* for 6 Choral Groups, Percussion, and Loudspeakers (1961); *Chains-Mirrors*, electroacoustic work for Soprano (1961); *Some of these...*, graphic music for Organ (1961); *Courante I, II, and III*, graphic music for Piano (1962); *Pour Madame Bovary* for Organ (1962); *3 Antiphonia: I* for Orch. (1963), *II* for Chamber Orch. (1963), and *III* for Chamber Orch. (1970); *Eternes* for Organ (1964); *Decadenza I* for Organ and Tape (1968) and *II* for Orch. with Tape and Film (1970; Uppsala, Jan. 18, 1972); *Colossus* for Orch. (1970; Berlin, Nov. 26, 1972); *Farewell* for Organ (1970); *Senza* for Strings (1970); *Labor* for Chamber Orch. (1971); *Life* for Tenor, Orch., and Instrumental Group (1972); *Video I* for 8 Solo Strings (1972); *Alla marcia* for Women's Chorus, Orch., Tape, and 8 Stroboscopes (1972–73; Stockholm, March 31, 1974); *5 Pieces* for Orch. (1973); *Soli* for Wind Quintet (1974); *Morendo* for Chorus, Orch., and Tape (Swedish Radio, Oct. 21, 1977); *Musica nera* for 9 Instruments, Tape, and Projection (1979); Organ Concerto (1981; Stockholm, Feb. 9, 1982); *Trauma*, radio opera (Swedish Radio, Aug. 30, 1981); *Energia I* for Symphonic Band (1984); *1984* for Orch. and Electronics (Swedish Radio, Sept. 21, 1984); *Materia* for Soprano, Chorus, Synthesizer, and Organ (1985); *Paraphonia* for Orch. (Stockholm, March 29, 1987); *Once* for Clarinet, Cello, and Piano (1988); *Silence XX* for Laser and Tape (1988); *Contra* for Chamber Orch. (1990); *Interior Drums* for 6 Percussionists (1997); *Estonia* for String Orch. (1997); *Sonora*, concerto for Guitar and String Orch. (1999); computer and electronic pieces.—NS/LK/DM

Mortier, Gérard, provocative Belgian opera administrator; b. Ghent, Nov. 25, 1943. He received training in law and journalism at the Univ. of Ghent. From 1968 to 1972 he was an administrative assistant at the Flanders Festival. After serving as artistic planner at the Deutsche Oper am Rhein in Düsseldorf (1972–73), he was asst. administrator at the Frankfurt am Main Opera (1973–77). From 1977 to 1979 he was director of artistic planning at the Hamburg State Opera, and then technical program consultant to the Paris Opéra (1979–81). In 1981 he became general director of the Théâtre Royal de la Monnaie in Brussels, where he raised standards to a new high but provoked much controversy. In 1992 he became artistic director of the Salzburg Festival and proceeded to implement a radical transformation of every facet of the festival's operations. In spite of the storm of controversy he engendered, he successfully carried out his grand plan to make the festival a viable and creative music center for the dawning of the 21st century. His tenure concluded in 2001.—NS/LK/DM

Morton, Jelly Roll (actually, **Lamothe, Ferdinand Joseph**), one of the greatest and most influential jazz composers and pianists; b. New Orleans, La., Oct. 20, 1890; d. Los Angeles, Calif., July 10, 1941. His family name Lamothe is sometimes wrongly spelled Lemott, as it was on the census of 1890. Morton's Red Hot Peppers recordings (1926–30), which comprise the bulk of his output, are universally cited as among the greatest jazz recordings for the invention of his writing, the variety of combinations he gets out of his small groups, and the effective structures with which he surrounds their improvisations. His "King Porter Stomp" was one of the most recorded pieces of the swing era, especially in Fletcher Henderson's arrangements.

Jelly Morton was a proud character, and made many enemies, but when he plays there is undeniable mastery, swing, counterpoint and sometimes amazing independence of the hands. For many years it was thought he was born in 1895; perhaps he encouraged this in order to support his claim, which even appeared on his business card, that he invented jazz in 1902—an unlikely feat for a 12- year-old. Despite this tendency to boasting, his reminiscences of specific events and persons have proven to be generally reliable. Born into a French- speaking family that proudly recalled its former days of wealth and position, Morton grew up surrounded by musical instruments and attended performances at the French Opera House. He played guitar and trombone, before specializing on piano from about age 10. He began playing in New Orleans whorehouses as early as age 12, earning the disapproval of his family but making as much as $100 a night entertaining the patrons of places such as the Hilma Burt House. He drifted to engagements in Biloxi and Meridian, Miss., then returned to New Orleans.

As a young teenager, he doubled at pool hustling and piano through La. and Miss. It has been established that Morton wrote many of his compositions in his teen years, long before they were recorded. His publication of "Original Jelly Roll Blues" (by Melrose Brothers) in 1915 was among the first jazz pieces to be published with parts. Around 1909, he joined a touring show in

Memphis. After two years' extensive touring, he quit the show in Jacksonville; some months later he began another spell of theatrical work, including a gig as comedian-pianist with McCabe's Minstrel Troubadours. He worked in St. Louis and Kansas City, then moved to Chicago for residencies at the Deluxe and Elite No. 2, where he led his own band. In 1915 Morton went to San Francisco to appear at the Exposition, returned to Chicago, and later played solo piano at the Fairfax Hotel, Detroit. He returned to Calif. (c. 1917) and played at various clubs in and around Los Angeles, including Cadillac Cafe, Baron Long's in Watts, and the U.S. Grand Hotel. He ran his own club-hotel in Los Angeles, then organized his own small band for a residency at the Regent Hotel, Vancouver. After a vacation in Ark., he worked in Caspar, Wyo., then briefly performed with George Morrison's Band in Denver.

After returning to Los Angeles, Morton organized a band that toured throughout Calif., reverting to solo piano for a brief sojourn in Tijuana; he worked in San Diego (1921), then gigged at the Jump Steady Club in Los Angeles and led a short-lived career as a boxing promoter. He moved back to Chicago in 1923, recorded with the New Orleans Rhythm Kings (July 1923) for the Gennett label, located in Richmond, Ind. At that time Ind. was the scene for a resurgence of Ku Klux Klan activity and integrated recording sessions were risky business. According to trombonist George Brunis, Jelly was passed off as a Spaniard, and apparently this was accepted without question because of the diamond inlay which the pianist flashed with his broad smile. During the next five years, Morton remained based in Chicago, regularly organizing his own recording sessions, including the first of the Red Hot Peppers, and for a time worked as staff arranger for the Melrose Publishing House. During this period he rarely played in Chicago, although he did regularly tour, usually fronting a band. He very occasionally worked as a sideman under other leaders and toured briefly as second pianist in Fate Marable's Band (c. 1924) and for one short period worked in the Midwest with W. C. Handy, who fronted Morton's Band and occasionally played cornet. Later, Morton did regular tours on the M.C.A. circuit, fronting bands led by pianist Gene Anderson, pianist Henry Crowder (summer 1927). Later that year, he fronted the Alabamians on tour.

After moving to N.Y. (c. Feb. 1928), Morton played a residency at the Rose Danceland during the summer of 1928 and recorded extensively. In late 1928 he organized his own big touring band, and toured widely during 1928–29. The band was variously billed as the Red Hot Peppers or Jelly Roll Morton and his Chicago Syncopators. Morton settled in N.Y. during the early 1930s, lost most of his money in an ill-fated cosmetics business, but continued to play regularly. He led his own orch. at the Checker Club, Harlem (April 1931), and headed his "Speeding Along" revue at the Jamaica Theatre, N.Y. (May 1931), led a band at the Lido Ballroom, N.Y. (Oct. 1932), accompanied Lillyn Brown in "Headin' for Harlem," and played briefly in Laura Prampin's Orch. at Coney Island. He performed occasionally at Pod's and Jerry's, N.Y., then became resident pianist at the Red Apple Club and while working there took part in a recording session organized by Wingy Manone (Aug. 1934). He again led his own touring band from 1935–36, before settling in Washington, D.C.

After a period of musical inactivity that included waiting tables at a shoe-box nightclub called the Band Box, he began playing at the Jungle Club in Washington from late 1936 until a brief return to N.Y. in Sept. 1938. From May until July 1938,, he took part in regular recording sessions for the Library of Congress, where he told his life story and his ideas about music, which he demonstrated brilliantly at the piano. Morton returned to N.Y. in late 1938, organized his publishing company and did several recording sessions and gigs leading own small band until health forced him to restrict his activities. He moved to Calif. in late 1940, formed a new music company and organized his own small group which led to a dispute with the local musicians union. Early in 1941, Morton's health began to fail rapidly and he entered a private sanatorium in June 1941, but soon returned home. He was subsequently admitted to the Los Angeles County General Hospital shortly before his death.

In 1991 a musical entitled *Jelly's Last Jam* opened on Broadway, starring Gregory Hines. It was a fanciful approach to Morton's life, inexplicably using none of his music and broadly changing details of his life story. Yet it was effective in its own right and helped spark interest in his music.

DISC.: *New Orleans Blues* (1902); *Jelly Roll Blues* (1905); *King Porter Stomp* (1906); *Grandpa's Spells* (1911); *The Pearls* (1919); *Big Foot Ham* (1923); *Black Bottom Stomp* (1925); *Winin' Boy Blues* (1938); *Pearls* (1938); *Kansas City Stomp: The Library of Congress Recordings* (1938); *Anamule Dance* (1938).

BIBL.: A. Lomax, *Mister Jelly Roll: The Fortunes of J. R. M., New Orleans Creole and "Inventor of Jazz"* (N.Y., 1950; 2nd ed., 1973); M. Williams, *J. R. M.* (London, 1962); J. Davis and I. Wright, *Morton's Music* (London, 1968); M. Hood and H. Flint, eds., *"J. R." M.: The Original Mr. Jazz* (N.Y., 1975); L. Wright, *Mr. Jelly Lord* (Chigwell, England, 1980); J. Dapogny, ed., *The Collected Piano Music of Ferdinand "J. R." M.* (Washington, D.C., 1982); S. Martin, *J. R. M.* (Paris, 1987).—LP

Morton, Lawrence, American music critic, impresario, and musicologist; b. Duluth, Minn., July 13, 1904; d. Santa Monica, Calif., May 8, 1987. He earned a living as a film theater organist in Chicago and N.Y. In 1937 he moved to Los Angeles, where he devoted himself mainly to music criticism. In 1954 he joined Peter Yates to organize the famous West Coast concert series Evenings on the Roof (later Monday Evening Concerts), which was devoted to the performance of modern music and lesser-known works from earlier repertoires. He championed Boulez, and, among lesser lights, Dahl, in his programs, as well as Stravinsky, Copland, Schoenberg, and other celebrated masters. The Lawrence Morton Fund was established in 1987 to facilitate the completion of his historical documentation of the above-named concert series; his rich and extensive archives were donated to the Special Collections aspect of the Research Library at the Univ. of Calif. at Los Angeles.—NS/LK/DM

Morton, Robert, English composer; b. c. 1430; d. c. 1476. He was a priest; served as clerc (1457–71 or -72) and chappellaine (1457–76) at the Burgundian court chapel choir. Only 8 of his secular works are extant; his songs *N'aray je jamais mieulx que j'ay* and *Le Souvenir de vous me tue* were widely disseminated in his day. A Atlas ed. *Robert Morton: The Collected Works* (N.Y., 1981).

BIBL.: D. Fallows, *R. M.'s Songs: A Study of Styles in the Mid-Fifteenth Century* (diss., Univ. of Calif., Berkeley, 1978). **—NS/LK/DM**

Mosca, Giuseppe, Italian composer, brother of **Luigi Mosca;** b. Naples, 1772; d. Messina, Sept. 14, 1839. He studied with Fenaroli at the Cons. of S. Maria di Loreto in Naples. He was engaged as répétiteur at the Théâtre-Italien, Paris (1803–10), then was music director at the Teatro Carolino in Palermo (1817–20). He later was director of music at a Messina theater (1827). He wrote 42 operas, ballets, and other stage pieces. **—NS/LK/DM**

Mosca, Luigi, Italian composer, brother of **Giuseppe Mosca;** b. Naples, 1775; d. there, Nov. 30, 1824. He was a pupil of Fenaroli. He served as maestro al cembalo at Naples's Teatro San Carlo and also primo maestro di canto at the Cons. (from 1813). He wrote 16 operas, of which *I Pretendenti delusi* (Milan, Sept. 7, 1811) was the most successful.**—NS/LK/DM**

Moscheles, Ignaz, eminent Czech-born pianist, conductor, pedagogue, and composer; b. Prague, May 23, 1794; d. Leipzig, March 10, 1870. Of a well-to-do family (his father was a Jewish merchant), he was trained in music as soon as his ability was discovered. His first piano teacher was Dionys Weber at the Prague Cons. (1804–08), and at the age of 14, he performed one of his own concertos at a public concert. He then went to Vienna (1808), where he continued his studies with Albrechtsberger and Salieri and earned his living by teaching; his conspicuous talents won him access to the best circles; a friend of Beethoven, he prepared the piano score of *Fidelio*. He then traveled throughout Europe as a virtuoso (from 1815), winning great applause in the leading music centers. He was a pioneer in developing various modifications of tone by touch, afterward exploited by Liszt. He made his London debut at a Phil. Soc. concert on June 11, 1821, settling in London in 1825 and becoming a teacher at the Royal Academy of Music. He was also active as a conductor, serving as co-director of the Phil. Soc. (1832–41), continued to appear as a pianist, and also founded an important series of historical concerts in which he played the works of Bach, Handel, and Scarlatti on the harpsichord. He gave Mendelssohn piano lessons in Berlin (1824); the teacher-pupil relationship between Moscheles and Mendelssohn developed into a close friendship, and the two gave the premiere of Mendelssohn's Concerto for 2 Pianos and Orch. in London (July 13, 1829). After founding the Leipzig Cons. (1842), Mendelssohn invited Moscheles to join its faculty (from 1846), where a host of pupils were trained by him with sympathetic consideration, and yet with unflinching discipline in musical matters. He was noted for his energetic, brilliant, and strongly rhythmic playing; his virtuosity equaled his emotional absorption in the music; his romantic pieces for piano expressed clearly his ideas of the extent and the limitations of the instrument. Moscheles tr. Schindler's biography of Beethoven into English (with numerous additions), publ. as *The Life of Beethoven* (2 vols., London, 1841). His wife, Charlotte (née Embden) Moscheles (b. 1805; d. Detmold, Dec. 13, 1889), wrote *Aus Moscheles' Leben* (2 vols., Leipzig, 1872; Eng. tr., London, 1873). His correspondence with Mendelssohn was publ. by his son, F. Moscheles, in 1888, who also publ. his father's memoirs as *Fragments of an Autobiography* (London, 1899). His works include a Sym. (1829), 8 piano concertos (1819–38), other works for Piano and Orch., several fine sonatas for Piano, including *Sonate melancolique* (1814), Sonata in D major (1815?), *Grosse sonate* (1816), and *2 grandes sonates* for 4–Hands (1816, 1845), many salon and didactic piano pieces, chamber music, and songs. A thematic index was publ. in 1885 (reprint, London, 1967).

BIBL.: A. Coleridge, *Recent Music and Musicians as Described in the Diaries and Correspondence of I. M.* (1873; reprint, N.Y., 1970); I. Heussner, *I. M. in seinen Klavier-Sonaten, -Kammermusikwerken, und -Konzerten* (diss., Univ. of Marburg, 1963); E. Smidak, *Isaak-Ignaz M.: The Life of the Composer and His Encounters with Beethoven, Liszt, Chopin and Mendelssohn* (Aldershot, 1989).**—NS/LK/DM**

Moscona, Nicola, Greek bass; b. Athens, Sept. 23, 1907; d. Philadelphia, Sept. 17, 1975. He studied at the Athens Cons. with Elena Teodorini. He sang opera in Greece and Eygpt, then was engaged to sing at the Metropolitan Opera in N.Y., making a successful American debut there as Ramfis in *Aida* (Dec. 13, 1937) and remaining on its roster until 1962. He then went to Philadelphia, where he taught at the Academy of Vocal Arts.**—NS/LK/DM**

Mosel, Ignaz Franz von, Austrian composer, conductor, and writer on music; b. Vienna, April 1, 1772; d. there, April 8, 1844. He was the first conductor of the musical festivals given by Vienna's Gesellschaft der Musikfreunde at the imperial riding school (1812–16); he pioneered the use of the baton in Vienna. He was vice-director of the 2 Court Theaters (1820–29), then principal custos of the Imperial Library (1829–44). He was ennobled and made a Hofrat. He composed *Die Feuerprobe*, Singspiel (April 28, 1811), *Salem*, lyric tragedy (March 5, 1813), and *Cyrus und Astyages*, heroic opera (June 13, 1818); also much incidental music. All of these works were first perf. at the Vienna Court Opera. Other works included instrumental pieces, masses, Psalms, cantatas, songs, and arrangements.

WRITINGS (all publ. in Vienna): *Versuch einer Ästhetik des musikalischen Tonsatzes* (1813); *Über das Leben und die Werke des Anton Salieri* (1827); *Geschichte der k.k. Hofbibliothek in Wien* (1835); *Über die Original-Partitur des Requiems von W.A. Mozart* (1839).**—NS/LK/DM**

Moser, Andreas, noted German violin pedagogue and music scholar, father of **Hans Joachim Moser;** b.

Semlin an der Donau, Nov. 29, 1859; d. Berlin, Oct. 7, 1925. He studied first in Zürich with Hegar, and also took courses in engineering and architecture in Stuttgart. In 1878 he became a violin pupil of Joachim in Berlin, and in 1883–84 he was concertmaster in Mannheim. He settled in Berlin in 1884, and in 1888 he was appointed a teacher at the Hochschule für Musik, a post he held until his death. He publ. valuable studies on the history of the violin.

WRITINGS: *Joseph Joachim, Ein Lebensbild* (Berlin, 1898; 5th ed., rev., 1910; Eng. tr. from 2nd Ger. ed., 1900); with Joachim, *Violinschule* (3 vols., Berlin, 1902–05; 2nd. ed., rev., 1959, by M. Jacobsen); ed. *Johannes Brahms im Briefwechsel mit Joseph Joachim* (Vols. V and VI of the complete Brahms correspondence, Berlin, 1908); ed. with Joachim, *Briefe von und an Joseph Joachim* (3 vols., Berlin, 1911–13); *Methodik des Violinspiels* (2 vols., Leipzig, 1920); *Geschichte des Violinspiels* (Berlin, 1923; 2nd ed., rev. and enl., 1966–67); *Technik des Violinspiels* (2 vols., Leipzig, 1925). —NS/LK/DM

Moser, Edda (Elisabeth), prominent German soprano, daughter of **Hans Joachim Moser**; b. Berlin, Oct. 27, 1938. She studied with Hermann Weissenborn and Gerty König at the Berlin Cons. She made her debut as Kate Pinkerton at the Berlin Städtische Oper (1962); after singing in the Würzburg Opera chorus (1962–63), she sang opera in Hagen and Bielefeld; subsequently appeared with the Frankfurt am Main Opera (1968–71) before joining the Vienna State Opera; also sang in Berlin, Salzburg, Hamburg, and other major music centers. She made her U.S. debut as Wellgunde in *Das Rheingold* at the Metropolitan Opera in N.Y. on Nov. 22, 1968, and later appeared there as Donna Anna, the Queen of the Night, and Liù. Her last appearance there was in 1984. She maintained an extensive repertoire, singing both coloratura and lyrico-dramatic roles, being equally successful in standard and contemporary works; also sang widely as a concert artist.—NS/LK/DM

Moser, Hans Joachim, eminent German musicologist, son of **Andreas Moser** and father of **Edda (Elisabeth) Moser**; b. Berlin, May 25, 1889; d. there, Aug. 14, 1967. He studied violin with his father, then took courses in musicology with Kretzschmar and Wolf at the Univ. of Berlin, with Schiedermair at the Univ. of Marburg, and with Riemann and Schering at the Univ. of Leipzig. He also studied voice with Oskar Noë and Felix Schmidt, and took courses in composition with H. van Eyken, Robert Kahn, and G. Jenner, receiving his Ph.D. from the Univ. of Rostock in 1910 with the diss. *Die Musikergenossenschaften im deutschen Mittelalter*. Returning to Berlin, he was active as a concert singer (bass-baritone), then served in the German army during World War I. He subsequently completed his Habilitation at the Univ. of Halle in 1919 with his *Das Streichinstrumentenspiel im Mittelalter* (publ. in A. Moser's *Geschichte des Violinspiels*, Berlin, 1923; 2nd ed., rev. and enl., 1966–67). In 1919 he joined the faculty of the Univ. of Halle as a Privatdozent of musicology, and then became a reader there in 1922; he then was a reader at the Univ. of Heidelberg from 1925 to 1927. He was honorary prof. at the Univ. of Berlin from 1927 to 1934, and also served as director of the State Academy for Church and School

Music in Berlin from 1927 to 1933; he received the degree of doctor of theology at Königsberg in 1931. He retired from his public positions in 1934 but continued his musicological pursuits in Berlin. He later served as head of the Reichsstelle für Musik-Bearbeitungen from 1940 to 1945. After World War II, he resumed teaching by accepting appointments as a prof. at the Univ. of Jena and the Hochschule für Musik in Weimar in 1947. He then served as director of the Berlin Cons. from 1950 until 1960. Moser was an outstanding music historian and lexicographer; his numerous writings are notable for their erudition. However, his unquestionable scholarship was marred by his ardent espousal of the Nazi racial philosophy; so ferocious was his anti-Semitism that he excluded Mendelssohn from his books publ. during the 3rd Reich. He served as ed. of a projected complete edition of Weber's works (Augsburg and Leipzig, 1926–33), but it remains unfinished. Other works he ed. include *Luthers Lieder, Werke, XXXV* (Weimar, 1923; with O. Albrecht and H. Lucke); *Minnesang und Volkslied* (Leipzig, 1925; 2nd ed., enl., 1933); *Das Liederbuch des Arnt von Aich* (Kassel, 1930; with E. Bernoulli); *Das deutsche Sololied und die Ballade, Das Musikwerk, XIV* (1957; Eng. tr., 1958); *Heinrich Schütz: Italienische Madrigale, Neue Ausgabe sämtlicher Werke, XXII* (Kassel, 1962). He also contributed countless articles to various German music journals, and likewise wrote novels, short stories, and a comedy. He also tried his hand at composing, producing the school opera *Der Reisekamerad*, choruses, and songs. He arranged operas by Handel and Weber, and also wrote an entirely new libretto for Weber's *Euryanthe* and produced it under the title *Die sieben Raben* (Berlin, March 5, 1915).

WRITINGS: *Technik der deutschen Gesangskunst* (Berlin, 1911; 3rd ed., 1955; with Oskar Noë); *Geschichte der deutschen Musik* (3 vols., Stuttgart and Berlin, 1920, 1922, and 1924; 2nd ed., enl., 1968); *Musikalisches Wörterbuch* (Leipzig and Berlin, 1923); *Paul Hofhaimer: Ein Lied- und Orgelmeister des deutschen Humanismus* (Stuttgart and Berlin, 1929; 2nd ed., enl., 1966); *Die Ballade* (Berlin, 1930); *Die Epochen der Musikgeschichte im Überblick* (Stuttgart and Berlin, 1930; 2nd ed., 1956); *Die mehrstimmige Vertonung des Evangeliums* (2 vols., Leipzig, 1931 and 1934); *Musiklexikon* (Berlin, 1932–35; 2nd ed., 1943, withdrawn; 3rd ed., 1951; 4th ed., 1955; suppl., 1963); *Corydon: das ist: Geschichte des mehrstimmigen Generalbass-Liedes und des Quodlibets im deutschen Barock* (2 vols., Braunschweig, 1933); *Die Melodien der Luther-Lieder* (Leipzig and Hamburg, 1935); *Johann Sebastian Bach* (Berlin, 1935; 2nd ed., 1943); *Tönende Volksaltertümer* (Berlin, 1935); *Heinrich Schütz: Sein Leben und Werk* (Kassel, 1936; 2nd ed., rev., 1954; Eng. tr., 1959); *Lehrbuch der Musikgeschichte* (Berlin, 1936; 13th ed., 1959); *Das deutsche Lied seit Mozart* (Berlin and Zürich, 1937; 2nd ed., rev., 1968); *Die Musikfibel* (Leipzig, 1937); *Kleine deutsche Musikgeschichte* (Stuttgart, 1938; 4th ed., 1955); *Allgemeine Musiklehr* (Berlin, 1940); *Christoph Willibald Gluck* (Stuttgart, 1940); *Kleines Heinrich-Schütz-Buch* (Kassel, 1940; Eng. tr., 1967); *Carl Maria von Weber* (Leipzig, 1941; 2nd ed., 1955); *George Friedrich Händel* (Kassel, 1941; 2nd ed., 1952); *Goethe und die Musik* (Leipzig, 1949); *Lebensvolle Musikerziehung* (Vienna, 1952); *Musikgeschichte in hundert Lebensbildern* (Stuttgart, 1952); *Die evangelische Kirchenmusik in Deutschland* (Berlin, 1953); *Musikästhetik* (Berlin, 1953); *Die Musikleistung der deutschen Stämme* (Vienna, 1954); *Die Tonsprachen des Abendlandes* (Berlin and Darmstadt, 1954); *Dietrich Buxtehude* (Berlin, 1957);

Musik in Zeit und Raum (Berlin, 1960; collected essays); *Bachs Werke: Ein Führer für Musikfreunde* (Kassel, 1964); etc.

BIBL.: *Festgabe für H.J. M.* (Kassel, 1954; with complete list of writings).—**NS/LK/DM**

Moser, Rudolf, Swiss composer; b. Niederuzwyl, Jan. 7, 1892; d. in a fall while mountain climbing in Silvaplana, Aug. 20, 1960. He studied theology at Basel Univ. and musicology with Nef there, then studied at the Leipzig Cons. (1912–14) with Reger, Sitt, and Klengel; further with Huber in Basel and Lauber in Geneva. He became conductor of the Cathedral choir in Basel, and was also active as a pedagogue.

WORKS: DRAMATIC: *Die Fischerin*, Singspiel after Goethe (1935); *Der Rattenfänger*, dance play (1950). **ORCH.:** Concerto Grosso for String Orch. (Basel, June 26, 1927); several suites; 3 violin concertos; Organ Concerto; Concerto for Violin, Viola, and Cello; Piano Concerto; Viola Concerto. **CHAMBER:** 4 string quartets; Piano Trio; String Sextet; organ pieces. **VOCAL:** *Das Lied von der Sonne* for Soloists, Chorus, Orch., and Organ; *Odes of Horace* for Baritone, Chorus, and Orch.; other works.

BIBL.: H. Buchli, *R. M.* (Zürich, 1964).—**NS/LK/DM**

Moser, Thomas, American tenor; b. Richmond, Va., May 27, 1945. After training at the Richmond (Va.) Professional Inst., he studied at the Curtis Inst. of Music in Philadelphia. He later pursued vocal training with Martial Singher, Gérard Souzay, and Lotte Lehmann. In 1974 he was a winner in the Metropolitan Opera Auditions, and in 1975 he joined the Graz Landestheater. In 1976 he appeared as Mozart's Belmonte with the Bavarian State Opera in Munich. From 1977 he sang with the Vienna State Opera, where he appeared as Mozart's Tamino, Ottavio, Titus, and Idomeneo, Strauss's Flamand and Henry, and Gluck's Achilles. He made his first appearance with the N.Y.C. Opera in 1979 as Titus. In 1983 he sang at the Salzburg Festival, returning there in 1984 to create the role of the tenor in Berio's *Un re in ascolto*. In 1985 he made his debut at Milan's La Scala as Tamino. In 1986 he sang for the first time at the Rome Opera as Achilles. In 1988 he appeared in the title role of Schubert's *Fierrabras* at the Theater an der Wien. In 1992 he sang the Emperor in *Die Frau ohne Schatten* in Geneva. He portrayed Palestrina during the visit to N.Y. of the Royal Opera of London in 1997. In 1998 he was engaged as Florestan in Chicago and as Peter Grimes in San Francisco. As a concert artist, he appeared with leading North American and European orchs. His expansive operatic and concert repertoire ranges from early music to the cosmopolitan avant-garde.
—**NS/LK/DM**

Moshinsky, Elijah, Australian opera and theater producer; b. Shanghai, Jan. 8, 1946. He was educated at the Univ. of Melbourne (B.A.) and at St. Anthony's Coll., Oxford. He began his career as a theater producer, overseeing plays of Shakespeare for BBC-TV and for plays at the National Theatre in London. In 1975 he produced his first opera at London's Covent Garden with a staging of *Peter Grimes,* and returned there with such productions as *Lohengrin* (1977), *The Rake's Progress*

(1979), *Macbeth* (1981), *Tannhäuser* (1984), *Otello* (1986), *Die Entführung aus dem Serail* (1987), *Attila* (1994), and a revival of *Lohengrin* (1997). In 1980 he worked for the first time at the Metropolitan Opera in N.Y. when he staged *Un ballo in maschera.* He oversaw the British stage premiere of Ligeti's *Le Grand Macabre* at the English National Opera in London in 1981. In 1983 he produced *Un ballo in maschera* at the Australian Opera in Sydney. His staging of *La Bohème* was seen at the Scottish Opera in Glasgow in 1988. In 1998 he produced *Lohengrin* at the Metropolitan Opera. In his productions, Moshinsky upholds the traditional approach to stage craft.
—**NS/LK/DM**

Mosko, Lucky (actually, **Stephen L.**), American composer and conductor; b. Denver, Dec. 7, 1947. He studied conducting and piano with Antonia Brico (1959–65), then entered Yale Univ. as a composition student of Donald Martino and a conducting student of Gustav Meier (B.A., 1969); also studied composition at the Calif. Inst. of the Arts with Powell, Subotnick, and Stein (M.F.A., 1972). He traveled on a Fulbright grant to Iceland to research folk and contemporary music (1974, 1978). He taught at the Calif. Inst. of the Arts (1970–90); was director of its conducting program (1976–82), conductor of its orch. (1980–82), and founder-director of its Twentieth Century Players (1974–87). He was composer-in-residence at the Aspen (Colo.) Music Festival (1986, 1987). He joined the faculty at Harvard Univ. in 1990. Mosko was principal conductor of the San Francisco Contemporary Music Players (from 1987) and the Griffen Ensemble of Boston (from 1990); also was a guest conductor with the San Francisco Sym. (from 1983) and the Los Angeles Phil. (from 1985); was director of the Ojai Music Festival in 1990. Mosko is an important conductor of new music, giving first performances of works by Cage, Scelsi, Stockhausen, Xenakis, and others. His own compositions are peculiar, somewhat abstruse, and characterized by wide-ranging fragments of sound in delicately controlled timbral contexts. He is married to the flutist Dorothy Stone, a long-time member of the Calif. E.A.R. Unit.

WORKS: *Lovely Mansions* for Chamber Ensemble (1971); *Night of the Long Knives* for Soprano and Chamber Ensemble (1974); *3 Clerks in Niches* for Chamber Ensemble (1975); *Darling* for Contrabass (1976); *Rais Murad* for Cello and Piano (1978); *Cosmology of Easy Listening* for Percussion Trio (1979); *Indigenous Music I* for Chorus (1981) and *II* for Solo Instruments and Chamber Ensemble (1984); *Superluminal Connections I* for Chamber Orch. (1985) and *II: The Atu of Tahiti* for Voices and Orch. (1986); *The Road to Tiphareth* for Chamber Ensemble (1986); *for Morton Feldman* for Flute, Cello, and Piano (1987); *Schweres Loos* for Alto, Piccolo, Bass Clarinet, and Violin (1988); *A Garden of Time* for Orch. (1989).—**NS/LK/DM**

Moskowa, Joseph Napoléon Ney, Prince de la, French statesman and composer; b. Paris, May 8, 1803; d. St.-Germain-en-Laye, July 25, 1857. He was the eldest son of Michel Ney, Duc d'Elchingen and Prince de la Moskowa, and he revealed a talent for music as child. He was made a member of the Chambre de Paris (1831), and later served as brigadier general under Napoleon III. With A. Adam, he organized the Société de Concerts de Musique Vocale, Religieuse et Classique (1843), which presented works of the Renaissance, Baroque, and Classical periods at his palace. The soc. publ. 11 vols. of these works as *Recueil des morceaux de musique ancienne.* He composed 2 comic operas, *Le Cent-Suisse* (Paris, June 7, 1840) and *Yvonne* (Paris, March 16, 1855), as well as some sacred music, including a Mass with Orch. (1831).—**NS/LK/DM**

Mosley, Snub (Lawrence Leo), jazz trombonist, slide saxophonist, singer, leader, composer; b. Little Rock, Ark., Dec. 29, 1905; d. N.Y., July 21, 1981. He studied music in Cincinnati. He first played with Eugene Crook, then joined Alphonse Trent, playing with him from 1926 until 1933. On Trent's only recording date of 1933, Mosley's playing, though poorly recorded, is astonishing for its speed and bravura. He worked with Claude Hopkins (1934–36), Fats Waller (1935), and Louis Armstrong (1937). Mosley formed his first band in 1936; from 1938, he led his own band regularly. He designed a slide saxophone, which he played to great visual effect; in 1940, he recorded a song celebrating the instrument, "The Man with the Funny Little Horn," which became his nickname. Mosley led the first all-black USO troupe in 1945, featuring blues singer Alberta Hunter. He continued to perform and record from the 1950s through the 1970s, primarily in the N.Y. area, and also made several European tours. He also co-authored the tune "Pretty Eyed Baby" with pianist Mary Lou Williams.

DISC.: *'Deed I Do* (1942); *Snub Mosley Live at the Pizza Express* (1978).—**JC/LP**

Mosolov, Alexander (Vasilievich), Russian composer; b. Kiev, Aug. 11, 1900; d. Moscow, July 12, 1973. He fought in the Civil War in Russia (1918–20), being wounded and decorated twice with the Order of the Red Banner for heroism. After the war, he studied composition with Glière in Kiev; then studied harmony and counterpoint with Glière, composition with Miaskovsky, and piano with Prokofiev and Igumnov at the Moscow Cons. (1922–25). He played his 1st Piano Concerto in Leningrad on Feb. 12, 1928. In his earliest works, he adopted modernistic devices; wrote songs to texts of newspaper advertisements. His ballet *Zavod* (Iron Foundry; Moscow, Dec. 4, 1927) attracted attention because of the attempt to imitate the sound of a factory at work by shaking a large sheet of metal. However, Mosolov's attempt to produce "proletarian" music by such means elicited a sharp rebuke from the official arbiters of Soviet music. On Feb. 4, 1936, he was expelled from the Union of Soviet Composers for staging drunken brawls and behaving rudely to waiters in restaurants. He was sent to Turkestan to collect folk songs as a move toward his rehabilitation. After settling in Moscow in 1939, he continued to make excursions to collect folk songs in various regions of Russia.

WORKS: DRAMATIC: O p e r a : *Geroy* (The Hero; 1927; Baden-Baden, July 15, 1928); *Plotina* (The Dam; 1929); *The Signal* (1941); *Maskarad* (Masquerade; 1940). **M u s i c a l C o m e d y :** *Friedrich Barbarossa.* **ORCH.:** 2 piano concertos (1927, 1932); 6 syms. (1928, 1932, 1937, 1942, 1947, 1950); 5

suites: No. 1, *Turkmenian* (1933), No. 2, *Uzbekian Dance* (1935), No. 3, *Native Lands,* with Folk Instruments (1951), No. 4 (1955), and No. 5, *Festive* (1955); Harp Concerto (Moscow, Nov. 18, 1939); *Concerto for Orchestra* (1943); Cello Concerto (1946); *Elegiac Poem* (1961). **CHAMBER:** 2 string quartets (1926, 1942); Trio for Clarinet, Cello, and Piano (1926); Piano Trio (1927); Cello Sonata (1927); Viola Sonata (1928); *Dance Suite* for Piano Trio (1928). **P i a n o :** 4 sonatas (1923, 1924, 1925, 1926). **VOCAL:** 4 oratorios, including *M.I. Kalinin* (1940) and *Moscow* (1948); cantatas, including *Minin and Pozharsky; Kirghiz Rhapsody* for Mezzo-soprano, Chorus, and Orch. (1933); *Ukraine* for Soloist, Chorus, and Orch. (1942); choruses; songs. —**NS/LK/DM**

Mosonyi, Mihály (real name, **Michael Brand**), noted Hungarian composer; b. Boldogasszonyfalva, Sept. 4, 1814; d. Pest, Oct. 31, 1870. He learned to play wind instruments and the organ in childhood, and went to Magyaróvár as a church officer when he was 15, and taught himself music by copying Hummel's piano exercises. He proceeded to Pressburg (c. 1832), where he studied piano and theory with Károly Turányi. After serving as a piano teacher in the household of Count Péter Pejachevich in Rétfalu (1835–42), during which time he honed his compositional skills through diligent study of Reicha's theoretical works, he settled in Pest as a teacher of piano and composition. He first attracted notice as a composer when his overture was premiered in April 1843. It was followed by his 1st Sym. and a Piano Concerto, the latter anticipating Liszt in the formulation of cyclic development. His first work to adopt Hungarian idioms was his 2nd Sym. (Pest, March 30, 1856). Liszt became his friend in 1856 and encouraged him in his work, proposing to produce his German Romantic opera *Kaiser Max auf der Martinswand* (1856–57); the score was never performed. Mosonyi's espousal of Hungarian nationalism led him to abandon his real name in 1859, adopting one that honored his birthplace, the county of Mosen. In his compositions, he gave increasing attention to Hungarian elements, producing his *Hódolat Kazinczy Ferenc szellemenek* (Homage to Kazinczy; 1860) for Piano (later orch.), a Hungarian rhapsody, and *Gyász hangok Széchenyi István halálára* (Funeral Music for Szechenyi; 1860) for Piano (later orch.), which employs the so-called Hungarian ostinato. His second opera, *Szép Ilonka* (Pretty Helen), was premiered at the National Theater in Pest on Dec. 19, 1861, but made little impact. His last opera, *Álmos* (1862), was not performed in his lifetime; its first performance took place at Budapest's Royal Hungarian Opera on Dec. 6, 1934.

BIBL.: K. Ábrányi, *Mosonyi Mihály élet és jellemrajza* (M. M., His Biography and Character; Pest, 1872); J. Káldor, *Michael M.* (Dresden, 1936); F. Bónis, *Mosonyi Mihály* (Budapest, 1960); idem, ed., *Magyar zenetörténeti tanulmányok Mosonyi Mihály es Bartók Béla emlékér* (Studies on the History of Hungarian Music, in Memory of M. M. and Béla Bartók; Budapest, 1973). —**NS/LK/DM**

Moss, David (Michael), avant-garde American percussionist and vocalist; b. N.Y., Jan. 21, 1949. He studied South Indian drumming with Tanjore Ranganathan (1970) and composition with Bill Dixon

(1971–73). From 1972 he toured Europe, Japan, Australia, and the U.S. as a soloist and leader of his own ensembles in more than 950 concerts; worked with David Van Tieghem, John King, John Zorn, and others. Moss has collaborated with numerous dance, visual, theater, and video artists; his recordings include *Terrain: Solo Percussion and Voice* (1980), *David Moss Dense Band 'Live' in Europe* (1988), and *The Day We Forgot* (1990); he also created and produced new music programs for radio (from 1981). Moss's solo performances combine a wide range of pitched and unpitched percussion, "found" objects, sound sculpture, and electronics with extended vocalizations.

WORKS: *Light no. 18* (1983); *Full House*, duets (1983); *King Lear*, incidental music (1983); *N.Y. Objects & Noise nos. 1 and 2* (1984); *Vox Box* (1984); *Mossmen* (1984); *Intimate Solos* (1985); *Light no. 20* (1985); *Operadio* (1986); *Slow Talking* (1987); *Slant Lines* (1987); *Operadio no. 2* (1987); *Conjuring Calvino* (1988); *Language Linkage nos. 1–3* (1988); *That Tempest* (1989); *After That Tempest* (1989); *Stolen Voice* (1990).—NS/LK/DM

Moss, Lawrence (Kenneth), American composer and teacher; b. Los Angeles, Nov. 18, 1927. He studied at the Univ. of Calif. at Los Angeles (B.A., 1949), at the Eastman School of Music in Rochester, N.Y. (M.A., 1950), and with Kirchner at the Univ. of Southern Calif. in Los Angeles (Ph.D., 1957). He held a Fulbright scholarship (1953–54), 2 Guggenheim fellowships (1959–60; 1968–69), and 3 NEA grants (1975, 1977, 1980). He taught at Mills Coll. (1956–59) and Yale Univ. (1960–68), then was a prof. and director of the composition dept. at the Univ. of Md. at Coll. Park (from 1969). In 1986 he was composer-in-residence at the Rockefeller Center in Bellagio, Italy. His style of composition tends toward polycentric tonality, with sporadic application of serial techniques and electronic sounds.

WORKS: DRAMATIC: O p e r a : *The Brute*, comic opera (1960; Norfolk, Conn., July 15, 1961); *The Queen and the Rebels* (1989). T h e a t e r : *Unseen Leaves* for Soprano, Oboe, Tapes, Slides, and Lights (Washington, D.C., Oct. 20, 1975); *Nightscape* for Soprano, Flute, Clarinet, Violin, Percussion, Dancer, Tape, and Slides (1978); *Dreamscape* for Dancer, Tape, and Lights (1980); *Images* for Clarinet, Tape, and Dancer (1981); *Rites* for Tape, Slides, Lights, and Dancers (1983); *Song to the Floor* for Dancer and Tape (1984); *That Gong-Tormented Sea* for Tape and Dance (1985); *Lesbia's Sparrow* for Singer, Tape, and Dancer (1985); *Incidental Music* for Percussion and Mime/Dancer (1986); *Blackbird* for Clarinet, Mime/Dancer, and Tape (1987); *Summer Night on the Yogahenney River* for Soprano, Dancer, and Tape (1989). ORCH.: *Suite* (1950); *Scenes* for Small Orch. (1961); *Paths* (1970); *Symphonies* for Brass Quintets and Chamber Orch. (1977); *Clouds* for Chamber Ensemble (1989); *Chinese Lullaby* for Band (1994); *Dragon and Phoenix* for Band (1997). CHAMBER: 3 string quartets (1958, 1975, 1980); Violin Sonata (1959); *Music for 5* for Brass Quintet (1963); *Patterns* for Flute, Clarinet, Viola, and Piano (1967); *Auditions* for Woodwind Quintet and Tape (1971); *B.P.: A Melodrama* for Trombone, Piano, and Tape (1976); *Chanson* for Flute Choir (1979); *Après-ludes* for Flute and Percussion (1983); *Music of Changes* for 7 Performers and Conductor (1986); *Various Birds* for Woodwind Quintet (1987); *Violaria, una dramma per musica* for Viola and Tape (1988); *Clouds* for Chamber Ensemble (1990); *Through a Window...* for Flute, Clarinet, and Contrabassoon (1991); Quartet for Flute, Cello, Percussion, and Piano (1992); *Saxpressivo* for

Alto Saxophone and Tape (1992); *6 Little Pieces* for Saxophone and Piano (1993); *Fantasy* for Harp (1996); *River Music* for Saxophone Quartet (1996); *Into the Woods* for Flute and Tape (1996); *Conversations* for Oboe, Violin, Viola, and Cello (1997); *Lifelines* for Clarinet and Tape (1998); *Dao Ditties* for Clarinet, Violin, Percussion, and Piano (1998); *Harried* for Bass Clarinet and Tape (1999); piano pieces. VOCAL: *A Song of Solomon* for Chorus and Piano (1956); *Song of Myself* for Baritone and Chamber Ensemble (1957); *Ariel* for Soprano and Orch. (1969); *Loves* for Soprano, Flute, Clarinet, Viola, Harp, and Piano (1982); *Voyages* for Tenor, Flute, Clarinet, Percussion, Violin, Viola, and Cello (1985); *Grand is the Seen* for 6 Soloists and Chorus (1989); *Love Songs* for Baritone and Harp (1990); *Songs of the Earth and Sky* for Mezzo-soprano, Clarinet, Violin, and Piano, 4–Hands (1990); *10 Miracles*, song cycle for Tenor, Oboe, and Harp (1993); *From Dawn to Dawn* for Baritone, Oboe, and Orch. (1994); *A Bird...A Sleep...A Thought...* for Chorus and Piano (1998); *3 Chinese Poems* for Soprano and Cello (1999). —NS/LK/DM

Moss, Piotr, Polish composer; b. Bydgoszcz, May 13, 1949. He studied composition with Piotr Perkowski at the State Higher School of Music in Warsaw (graduated, 1972), and with Nadia Boulanger in Paris (1976–77), where he settled in 1981. In 1978 he won 1st prize in the Weber Composers' Competition in Dresden, and in 1981 1st prize in the International Composers' Competition in Barcelona.

WORKS: DRAMATIC: O p e r a : *Karla* (1996); *Les Ailes de Jean-Pierre* (1997). ORCH.: *Charon*, sym. (1973); Cello Concerto (1975); *Music in 3 Pieces* for Harpsichord and 3 Instrumental Groups (1975); *Sinfonia* (1978); Concerto for Harpsichord and 2 String Orchs. (1980); *Incontri* (1982); *Silence* (1982); *Symphonie concertante* for Flute, Piano, and Orch. (1985); *Hymne* (1985); *Musique élégiaque* for Bassoon and Strings (1986; also for Bassoon and String Quintet); *Elegia No. 2* for Cello and Strings (1987; Warsaw, May 11, 1998); *Stylisations II* for Horn and Strings (1987); *Angst und Form*, concerto for Alto Saxophone, Orch., and Soprano Obbligato (1988); *Veillée* for Oboe and Strings (1988); *D'un silence...*, clarinet concerto (1989); *Espressioni varianti*, concerto for Harp, 2 Flutes, 2 Percussion, and 2 String Orchs. (1990; Fresnes, April 19, 1991); *Mélancolies d'automne* for Alto Saxophone and Strings (1991); *Novella* (1991); *Intrada* (1993); *Capriccio* for Piano and Strings (1994; Warsaw, May 15, 1997); *Adagio II* for Organ and Strings (1996); *Fantaisie* for Cello and Strings (1996); *Concerto-Rhapsodie* for Trombone and Orch. (1996); *Fresque* (1998). CHAMBER: *Tre istanti* for Harp (1972); Trio for Violin, Cello, and Piano (1974); *Dialogi* for Violin and Piano (1977); Quartet for 4 Cellos (1978); *Trois pensées...* for Clarinet and Chamber Ensemble (1978; Siena, Aug. 1979); Sonata for Solo Cello (1981; Paris, June 30, 1983); *Chants d'antan* for Flute and Piano (Stroud, Oct. 6, 1982); *Petites histoires* for Bassoon (1982); Sonata for String Quartet (1982; Kraków, Dec. 15, 1884); *Nostalgies I* for Clarinet and 2 String Quartets (1983); *Musique en trois mouvements* for Cello and Chamber Ensemble (Versailles, Nov. 17, 1983); *Cinque intermezzi* for 2 Violins (1983); *Musique concertante* for Piano and 4 Instruments (1983; Fresnes, April 27, 1984); Concertino for 2 Violins, 2 String Quartets, and Double Bass (1984); *Nuits...* for String Quartet (1984); *Stances*, trio for Clarinet, Cello, and Piano (1984–85); *Solo II* for Cello (1985) and *IV* for Alto Saxophone (1992); *Musique élégiaque* for Bassoon and String Quintet (1986; also for Bassoon and String Orch.); *Form III* for 2 Bass Clarinets (1986), *V* for Flute, Cello, and Piano (1987), and *XI* for 2 Alto Saxophones (1995); *Elegia*

No. 1— *Alexandre Tansman in memoriam* for 2 Cellos (1986; Paris, Feb. 5, 1987); *Maillons* for Harpsichord and String Quartet (1987); *Maximun und Reflexionen* for Piano and String Quintet (1988); *Métaphores* for Alto Saxophone and Piano (1989); Alto Saxophone Sonata (1990); *Quartettsatz* for Piano and String Trio (1990); *Récit* for Cello (1991); *Ragtime II* for 8 Cellos (1992); *Duos* for 2 Violins (1994). **VOCAL:** *Garść liści wierzbowych* (A Handful of Willow Leaves) for Baritone, 3 Cellos, and 3 Double Basses (1978); *Salve Regina* for Children's Chorus and Organ (1981; Montserrat, May 30, 1982); *Magnificat I* for Children's Chorus and Orch. (1983) and *III* for Soloists and Chorus (1985); *Der Du bist drei in Einigkeit* for Chorus and String Quintet (1984); *Défets*, oratorio (1987); *Sueños*, oratorio for Soloists, Chorus, and Orch. (1990); *Pantum* for Mezzo-soprano, Cello, and Piano (1992); *Ugui* for Reciter and Orch. (1993); *De l'amour* for Tenor and Orch. (1994); *Gédéon*, oratorio (Clermont-Ferrand, Dec. 1996).—**NS/LK/DM**

Mossman, Michael, jazz trumpeter, trombonist, composer; b. Philadelphia, Pa., Oct. 12, 1959. His father was a Theremin player; Mossman studied at Oberlin, and then privately with Vincent Cichowicz of the Chicago Symphony. He left Chicago to get his masters at Rutgers Univ. in the mid-1970s, studying arranging with Don Sebesky. His first recordings (1978–83) were with Anthony Braxton, Leo Smith, and Roscoe Mitchell. He lived in Chicago from 1982–83, working in jazz groups and with the Chicago Chamber Orch. as a classical soloist. In 1983, he settled in N.Y., and has since worked with a wide variety of groups, both jazz and classical. From 1984–90, he was a featured member of Out of the Blue, Blue Note Records' attempt at a "house" combo. He has played numerous big bands, including stints with Michael Camillo (from 1985 on), Toshiko Akiyoshi (from 1987), Horace Silver (from 1989), and Chico O'Farrill (during the 1990s). In the 1980s and 1990s, he taught part-time at Rutgers, directing the jazz ensemble there, and in fall 1997 was named head of the Jazz Dept. at Queens Coll.

DISC.: *Granulate* (1990).—**MF/LP**

Moszkowski, Moritz, famous German pianist, teacher, and composer of Polish descent; b. Breslau, Aug. 23, 1854; d. Paris, March 4, 1925. He studied at the Dresden Cons., and later at the Stern Cons. and at the Kullak Academy in Berlin; then became a teacher at the latter institution. He gave his first public concert in Berlin in 1873, then played elsewhere in Germany, and in Paris, where he established his reputation as a pianist; in 1897 he made Paris his headquarters. Among his notable pupils were Josef Hofmann, Wanda Landowska, Joaquín Nin, and Joaquín Turina. As a composer, he is most widely known by his pieces in the Spanish vein, particularly the 2 books of *Spanische Tänze* for Piano Solo or Piano Duo; also popular were his études, concert waltzes, gavottes, *Skizzen*, a tarantella, a humoresque, etc. In larger forms he essayed an opera, *Boabdil, der letze Maurenkönig* (Berlin, April 21, 1892), which contains a ballet number that became popular. He also wrote a ballet, *Laurin* (1896), a symphonic poem, *Jeanne d'Arc, Phantastischer Zug* for Orch., *Aus aller Herren Länder* for Orch., Violin Concerto, and Piano Concerto.
—**NS/LK/DM**

Moszumańska-Nazar, Krystyna, Polish composer and pedagogue; b. Lwów, Sept. 5, 1924. She was a student of Stanisław Wiechowicz (composition) and of Jan Hoffman (piano) at the State Higher School of Music in Kraków (1950–55). In 1964 she joined its faculty, where she later was a prof. (from 1981) and rector (1987–93). She received the Minister of Culture and Arts Award five times. In 1970 she received the City of Kraków Award, in 1977 the Prime Minster's Award, and in 1988 the Polish Composers' Union Award. In 1999 she was honored on her 75th birthday with the Commander's Cross of the Polonia Restituta Order. While her music is classical in formal design, she often makes use of densely dissonant harmonic writing.

WORKS: ORCH.: Piano Concertino (1954); 2 overtures (1954, 1956); *Allegro symphonique* (1957); *Cztery eseje* (Four Essays; 1958); *Hexaèdre* (1960; Kraków, June 22, 1962); *Muzyka* (Music) for Strings (1962; Warsaw, Sept. 22, 1963); *Exodus* for Orch. and Tape (1964; Wrocław, Nov. 10, 1967); *Variazioni concertanti* for Flute and Chamber Orch. (1965–66; Wrocław, Jan. 19, 1968) *Pour orchestre* (1969; Poznań, March 29, 1973); *Rhapsod* (Rhapsody) *I* (1975) and *II* (Kraków, Sept. 12, 1980); *Sinfonietta* for Chamber String Orch. (1983; Baranów, Sept. 10, 1986); *Concerto for Orchestra* (1985–86); *Fresk* (Fresco) *1* (Kraków, Nov. 25, 1988), *II* (1991), and *III* (1993; Kraków, Nov. 24, 1994); *Dwa dialogi* (Two Dialogues) for Instrumental Ensemble (Odense, Nov. 23, 1994; also for Orch., 1994; Szczecin, April 17, 1995); *Leggiero e mobile* for Wind Ensemble (1996); Percussion Concerto (Kraków, Nov. 13, 1998). **CHAMBER:** *Trzy miniatury* (Three Miniatures) for Clarinet and Piano (1957); 5 Duets for Flute and Clarinet (1959); String Trio (1960); *Interpretacje* (Interpretations) for Flute, Tape, and Percussion (1967; Kraków, Feb. 7, 1968); 3 Concert Studies for Percussion (1969); 3 string quartets: No. 1 (1973–74), No. 2 (Lusławice, Aug. 28, 1980), and No. 3 (Kraków, Dec. 6, 1995); *From End to End Percussion* (1976; Berkeley, Calif., May 24, 1978); *Warianty* (Variants) for Piano and Percussion (Stalowa Wola, May 18, 1979); *Canzona* for Violin (1985); *Fantazja* (Fantasy) for Marimbaphone (1987; Wrocław, Feb. 19, 1988); *Music for Five* for Percussion (1989; Munich, Feb. 24, 1990); *Trois moments musicaux* for Double Bass (1990; Kraków, April 30, 1991); *Quatre moments musicaux* for Cello (1990–94; Kraków, Dec. 12, 1994); *Recitativo* for Cello (1991; Kraków, Dec. 12, 1994); *Un petit cadeau*, trio for Flute, Cello, and Percussion (1993); *Kwiaty* (Flowers) for Flute, Piccolo Flute, Oboe, Clarinet, and Piano (1996–97; Kraków, May 18, 1997); *Serpentine* for Oboe (1997; Wiesbaden, April 25, 1998); *Impresja* (Impression) for String Quartet (1997–98; Rybna, Dec. 13, 1998). **KEYBOARD: Piano:** Variations (1949); *Suita tańców polskich* (Suite of Polish Dances; 1954); Sonatina (1957); Bagatelles (1971; Mannheim, Oct. 12, 1972); *Konstelacje* (Constellations; Mannheim, Oct. 12, 1972). **Organ:** *Oratio brevis* (1995; Kraków, March 10, 1996). **VOCAL:** *Intonacje* (Intonations) for 2 Choruses and Orch. (1970–71); *Bel canto* for Soprano, Celesta, and Percussion (1972; Avignon, July 1973; also for Soprano, Celesta, Cello, and Percussion); *Madonny polskie* (Polish Madonnas) for Chorus and Orch. (1974; Kraków, April 23, 1976); *Wyzwanie* (Challenge) for Baritone and Chamber Ensemble (Poznań, April 28, 1977); *Pieśń nad pieśniami* (Song of Songs) for Soprano, Reciter, Small Men's Chorus, and Chamber Instrumental Ensemble (Poznań, March 24, 1984); *Pater noster* for Men's Chorus and Organ (1997; Kraków, May 23, 1999).—**NS/LK/DM**

Motian, (Stephen) Paul, jazz drummer, composer; b. Philadelphia, Pa., March 25, 1931. He started out as a Max Roach disciple, keeping straight time on his early recordings but soon developed a way of leaving space and creating a loose, shimmering sense of time. He began recording in the mid 1950s with Lennie Tristano, Zoot Sims, Al Cohn, Stan Getz, Gil Evans, and George Russell. He worked with Bob Dorough and Miles Davis before joining Bill Evans in 1959. He and Evans worked and recorded with Don Elliott, Tony Scott and others; in late 1958, they decided to work as a trio after a stint at Basin St. East, but they didn't find steady work until late 1959, when they played at the Sutherland Lounge in Chicago and an extended engagement in Greenwich Village. They first recorded together with Tony Scott in late October 1959. Motian left the trio in 1963 to play with Paul Bley and many others before joining Keith Jarrett for two long stretches (1966–69 and 1971–75); in 1968, he appeared on the Boston TV show *Mixed Bag* with the Charles Lloyd Quartet and Jarrett. Motian was part of the Jazz Composers Orch. Association and worked in Charlie Haden's Liberation Orch. as well. During the 1970s and 1980s, he led small combos, worked in solo and trio situations, and reunited with Paul Bley on two late-1980s releases. From 1987 through the early 1990s, he led a trio with Joe Lovano and Bill Frissell.

DISC.: *Conception Vessel* (1972); *Tribute* (1974); *Dance* (1977); *Le Voyage* (1979); *Psalm* (1981); *Misterioso* (1983); *Story of Maryam* (1984); *Jack of Clubs* (1984); *It Should Have Happened Long Ago* (1984); *Circle the Line* (1986); *One Time Out* (1987); *Paul Motian on Broadway, Vol. 1* (1988); *Monk in Motion* (1988); *Paul Motian on Broadway, Vol. 2* (1989); *Bill Evans: Tribute to the Great Piano Player* (1990); *On Broadway, Vol. 3* (1991); *Paul Motian & The Electric Bebop* (1992); *Motian in Tokyo* (1992). B. Evans: *Portrait in Jazz* (1959). B. Brookmeyer: *Jazz Is a Kick* (1960); *Explorations* (1961). P. Bley: *Turning Point* (1964).—**LP**

Mötley Crüe, the band that brought decadence to heavy metal. **MEMBERSHIP:** Nikki Sixx (Frank Carlton Serafino Ferrann), bs. (b. San Jose, Calif., Dec. 11, 1958); Tommy Lee (Thomas Lee Bass), drm. (b. Athens, Greece, Oct. 3, 1962); Mick Mars (Bob Deal), gtr., voc. (b. Huntington, Ind., April 3, 1956); Vince Neil (Vince Neil Wharton), voc. (b. Hollywood, Calif., Feb. 8, 1961).

More notorious than famous, Mötley Crüe fused hard rock with glam rags and turned the rock 'n' roll lifestyle up to near-cartoon parody. Several of them have landed in jail and rehab many times, and became tabloid fodder with their marriages to starlets and mud wrestlers and *Playboy* bunnies.

The band formed in 1981 around a nucleus of Nikki Sixx and Tommy Lee as a band called Christmas. They found Mick Mars via a classified ad and enticed Vince Neil away from a tribute band. Mere months after forming, they released a do-it-yourself album that sold more than 20,000 copies, attracting the attention of Elektra records. Elektra signed them and re-released the record as *Too Fast for Love*. Sounding like the bastard child of Mott the Hoople and Black Sabbath, it sold respectably, eventually going platinum.

Shortly after the band's follow-up, *Shout at the Devil*, was released in 1983, Vince Neil was in an automobile collision while under the influence of alcohol. The crash killed the passenger in Neil's car, Hanoi Rocks' drummer Nicholas Dingley, and seriously injured the couple in the other car. Sixx was also in a car accident around the same time, injuring his shoulder. The rockers put this behind them temporarily, however. *Shout at the Devil* was about to put them on the map. Their glam image made them perfect fodder for the burgeoning MTV audience, and they became a mainstay of MTV for many years. As their audience grew, their show grew to include elaborate lights, pyrotechnics and stage sets. They became the cover boys for the slew of hard-rock magazines published at the time. The album hit #17 and eventually sold quadruple platinum. The band spent over a year on the road supporting the album. Not surprisingly, they topped most of the hard-rock magazine reader polls in 1984.

Showing a modicum of musical growth, *Theater of Pain* broke the band on Top 40 radio, with its cover of Brownsville Station's anthem to youth gone awry, "Smokin' in the Boys' Room," hitting #16. The video for "Home Sweet Home" became one of the first power ballads on MTV. The album zoomed to #6 and has sold quadruple platinum. Shortly after the record came out, Neil was convicted of vehicular manslaughter. He spent a total of 30 days in jail, did 200 hours of community service and fined nearly three million dollars. In the meantime, Lee married prime time soap opera vixen Heather Locklear, Sixx married *Playboy* playmate Brandi Brandt and Neil married mud wrestler Sharisse Rudell. Their private lives were becoming nearly as colorful (and well-covered by the media) as their music.

Crüe's next record, *Girls, Girls, Girls* came out in 1987. Rather than exploit MTV coverage, they made a video of the title track that they knew MTV would find too risqué. The song reached #12 on the charts, propelling the album to #2 and quadruple platinum sales. Sixx, however, had become addicted to heroin, and just before the band left to tour Asia, he overdosed, lying clinically dead for several minutes before being revived.

In 1988, an interim bassist hired when Sixx had hurt his shoulder sued the band for royalties on songs he claimed to have written. Unable to prove his case, however, the case was dropped. In 1989, the band released *Dr. Feelgood*. Spawning two Top Ten singles, the gold #6 title track and the #8 "Without You" and two more popular singles "Kickstart My Heart" (#27) and "Don't Go Away Mad (Just Go Away)" (#19), the album zoomed to the top of the charts, eventually selling sextuple platinum. Once again, the band took off for another extensive tour of the world. On the group's return, they went to work on a greatest hits collection. The *Decade of Decadence* album debuted on the charts at #2, eventually selling double platinum. They remixed the single "Home Sweet Home," which, though successful as a video, had stalled at #89 when first released. This time, the song rose to #37. Although disappointed by the sales of the record, Elektra signed the band to a new $25 million contract.

Shortly after the release, the band members fired Neil, claiming he no longer had the fire in his belly. They brought on a new singer, John Corabi. With him, they ushered in a new sound, incorporating industrial and modern hard rock into their sound. The new sound informed their 1994 self-titled release, which debuted at #7, went gold, but quickly fell of the music business radar. The core band and Corabi were at odds, and the next release kept getting pushed back on Elektra's release schedule. In the meantime, Locklear had left Lee, and he married another TV star (and longtime *Playboy* centerfold) Pamela Anderson. At the 1997 American Music Awards, Anderson Lee introduced her husband's band, complete with Vince Neil. The band had retained the more updated sound. It was reflected in their 1997 album *Generation Swine*. Like its predecessor, it debuted high on the charts, starting at #4, went gold and disappeared without a trace. While on the road, N.C. police accused the band of inciting a riot when Sixx encouraged the crowd to attack one of the security guards as Lee poured a drink over the guard's head.

In the meantime, a pornographic home video of Lee and Anderson, intended for their own private use, wound up on the Internet. Their relationship became more and more tumultuous, with Anderson calling the police on her husband and eventually getting him locked up for battery. However, the band continued on. They hired former Ozzy Osbourne drummer Randy Castillo to fill in for Lee, reclaimed their masters from Elektra and put out a second greatest hits project on its own label that went gold. While on the road supporting it, N.C. police arrested Sixx over the 1997 incident.

In addition to forming its own label, the group also opened a Melrose Avenue Boutique called S'Crüe. The store featured signature lines of clothing by both Sixx and Neil and a ginseng drink the band invented called Mötley Brüe. Tommy Lee introduced his new band, Methods of Mayhem, with an album just before the turn of the millennium. Combining rock and rap, the album featured such guest artists as George Clinton, Snoop Dogg, and Kid Rock.

DISC.: MÖTLEY CRUE: *Too Fast for Love* (1981); *Shout at the Devil* (1983); *Theater of Pain* (1985); *Girls, Girls, Girls* (1987); *Dr. Feelgood* (1989); *Mötley Crüe* (1994); *Generation Swine* (1997); *Greatest Hits* (1999). **METHODS OF MAYHEM:** *Methods of Mayhem* (1999).

BIBL.: D. Bonutto, *The Comedy and the Tragedy* (N.Y., 1985). —HB

Motta, José Vianna da
See **Vianna da Motta, José**

Mottl, Felix (Josef), celebrated Austrian conductor; b. Unter-Sankt Veit, near Vienna, Aug. 24, 1856; d. Munich, July 2, 1911. After preliminary studies at a seminary, he entered the Vienna Cons. and studied with Door (piano), Bruckner (theory), Dessoff (composition), and Hellmesberger (conducting), graduating with high honors. In 1876 he acted as one of the assistants at the first Wagner festival at Bayreuth. In 1881 he succeeded Dessoff as court conductor at Karlsruhe, and in 1893 he was appointed Generalmusikdirektor there. He conducted *Tristan und Isolde* at the Bayreuth Festival in 1886, led a Wagner concert in London in 1894, and conducted the premiere of part I of Berlioz's *Les Troyens à Carthage, La Prise de Troie* (in German; Karlsruhe, 6, 1890). After

conducting at London's Covent Garden (1898–1900), he made his Metropolitan Opera debut in N.Y. conducting *Die Walküre* on Nov. 25, 1903. Engaged to conduct *Parsifal* there, he withdrew after protests from the Wagner family over copyright violations. In 1903 he became Generalmusikdirektor of the Munich Court Opera; was conductor of the Vienna Phil. (1904–07). His long intimate relationship with **Zdenka Fassbender** was legalized in marriage on his deathbed. He ed. vocal scores of the works of Wagner. His own work included 4 operas, *Agnes Bernauer* (Weimar, 1880), *Graf Eberstein* (Karlsruhe, 1881), *Fürst und Sänger* (1893), and *Rama*, a String Quartet, and numerous songs. Among his arrangements, that of Chabrier's *Bourrée fantasque* enjoys continued popularity in the concert hall.—NS/LK/DM

Mott the Hoople, seminal British rock band of the early 1970s. **MEMBERSHIP:** Ian Hunter, lead voc., pno., gtr. (b. Shrewsbury, England, June 3, 1946); Mick Ralphs, gtr., voc. (b. Hereford, England, May 31, 1944); Verden Allen, org. (b. Hereford, England, May 26, 1944); Pete "Overend" Watts, bs., voc. (b. Birmingham, England, May 13, 1947); Dale "Buffin" Griffin, drm., voc. (b. Ross-on-Wye, England, Oct. 24, 1948). Verden Allen and Mick Ralphs left in 1973. Luther "James" Ariel Bender (Luther Grovesnor), gtr. (b. Evesham, England, Dec. 12, 1949) was added, but left in 1974, to be replaced by Mick Ronson (b. Hull, Yorkshire, England, May 26, 1946; d. London, England, April 30, 1993).

Mott the Hoople featured the songwriting and singing of Ian Hunter and the guitar playing of Mick Ralphs, who later formed the enormously popular Bad Company. One of the pioneering glitter-rock groups, they enjoyed their greatest success in the early 1970s before internal pressures led the group to dissolve.

In the mid-1960s Pete "Overend" Watts and Dale "Buffin" Griffin formed the group Silence in their native Herefordshire, later adding Mick Ralphs and Verden Allen. Recruiting vocalist Ian Hunter in London in 1969, the group changed their name to Mott the Hoople in June at the suggestion of manager Guy Stevens, who secured them a recording contract with Island Records (Atlantic in the United States). With Ian Hunter serving as principal songwriter as well as the visual and aural focus of the group, Mott the Hoople recorded their debut album in late 1969, but it barely made the U.S. charts upon release. *Mad Shadows* showcased Hunter's rather forceful approach on a collection of gloomy songs, whereas *Wildlife* featured Ralphs's lighter style. However, neither of these albums, nor *Brain Capers*, which included "Sweet Angeline," registered much impact.

Disbanding briefly in March 1972, Mott the Hoople re-formed later that year with the encouragement of glitter-rock star David Bowie, who produced the band's debut album for Columbia and wrote the group's only major American hit, "All the Young Dudes." With Hunter assuming leadership of the group, Verden Allen quit in January 1973, followed in July by Mick Ralphs, who subsequently joined the highly successful group Bad Company. Adding former Spooky Tooth guitarist Luther Grosvenor (using the name Ariel Bender), Mott the Hoople conducted a headlining glitter-rock tour of the United States in August 1973. Their album *Mott* was well received critically, at least in the United States, and yielded major British hits with "Honaloochie Boogie" and "All the Way from Memphis"; it also contained "Ballad of Mott the Hoople." *The Hoople* included the group's final, albeit minor, American hit, "The Golden Age of Rock'n' Roll," as well as "Roll Away the Stone."

In August 1974 Luther Grosvenor left Mott the Hoople, to be replaced by guitarist Mick Ronson. Ronson had produced and played on albums for David Bowie and had been instrumental in forming his Spiders from Mars band, providing the major musical force behind Bowie's *The Man Who Sold the World, Hunky Dory, Ziggy Stardust, Aladdin Sane*, and *Pin Ups* albums. He also had coproduced and played on Lou Reed's "Walk on the Wild Side" single. His tenure with Mott the Hoople, however, was brief. In December both Ronson and Hunter left amid unbecoming rumors and public recriminations. The group reassembled as simply Mott, with Watts, Griffin, and others for two albums before disbanding in November 1976. With vocalist John Fiddler, the remaining members reemerged as British Lions in 1977.

Ian Hunter subsequently moved to N.Y. and began working with Mick Ronson, recording *Ian Hunter* with him and touring as the Hunter-Ronson Show in 1975. The two later separated; Ronson joined Bob Dylan's late-1975 Rolling Thunder Revue, and Hunter recorded *All-American Alien Boy*. In 1976 Hunter produced Roger McGuinn's acclaimed album *Cardiff Rose*, and had his own, minor hit, "Just Another Night," in 1979. Hunter and Ronson reunited for 1989's album *YUI Orta*. Ronson also produced Morrisey's 1992 album *Your Arsenal*, but on April 30, 1993, he died in London from cancer at age 46. Released posthumously, Ronson's *Heaven 'n Hull* was recorded with Chrissie Hynde, David Bowie, John Mellencamp, and Queen.

DISC.: MOTT THE HOOPLE: *M. the H.* (1970); *Mad Shadows* (1970); *Wildlife* (1971); *Brain Capers* (1972); *All the Young Dudes* (1972); *Mott* (1973); *The Hoople* (1974); *Rock and Roll Queen* (1974); *Live* (1974); *Greatest Hits* (1976); *The Ballad of Mott: A Retrospective* (1993); *Backsliding Fearlessly: The Early Years* (1994). **MOTT:** *Drive On* (1975); *Shouting and Pointing* (1976). **MICK RONSON** *Slaughter on Tenth Avenue* (1974); *Play, Don't Worry* (1975); *Heaven 'n Hull* (1994). **IAN HUNTER:** *Ian Hunter* (1975); *All-American Alien Boy* (1976); *Overnight Angels* (1977); *Shades of Ian Hunter: The Ballad of Ian Hunter and M. the H.* (1979); *You're Never Alone with a Schizophrenic* (1979); *Live: Welcome to the Club* (1980); *Short Back 'n' Sides* (1981); *All of the Good Ones Are Taken* (1983); *Shades of Ian Hunter* (1988). **IAN HUNTER AND MICK RONSON** *YUI Orta* (1989).—**BH**

Moulaert, Pierre, Belgian composer and teacher, son of **Raymond (Auguste Marie) Moulaert**; b. Brussels, Sept. 24, 1907; d. there, Nov. 13, 1967. He studied at the Royal Cons. in Brussels with his father and Joseph Jongen, and taught there from 1937 until his death. He was not a prolific composer, and wrote mostly in small forms, but his music had a distinctive quality of fine craftsmanship.

WORKS: ORCH.: Concertino for Flute, Oboe, and Strings (1954); *Sérénade* (1956); *Petite musique concertante* (1961); *Introduction et Fugue* for Flute, Oboe, Clarinet, Bassoon, and Strings (Uccle, March 7, 1963); *Séquences* (1964). **CHAMBER:** *Passepied en Rondo* for Wind Quintet (1940); String Quartet (1956).—**NS/LK/DM**

Moulaert, Raymond (Auguste Marie), Belgian pianist, teacher, and composer, father of **Pierre Moulaert**; b. Brussels, Feb. 4, 1875; d. there, Jan. 18, 1962. He studied at the Brussels Cons. with Arthur de Greef (piano) and Edgar Tinel (theory), and then was appointed to its staff and taught composition (from 1927). He concurrently was director of his own music school in St.-Gilles (1913–38), and also lectured at the Queen Elizabeth Chapel of Music in Brussels.

WORKS: ORCH.: *Theme and Variations* for Trumpet and Orch. (1910); *Appels pour un tournoi de chevalerie* for Wind Orch. (1923); *Passacaglia* (1931); *Symphonie de valses* (1936); Trumpet Concertino (1937); Piano Concerto (1938); *Rhapsodie écossaise* for Clarinet and Orch. (1940); *Tango-caprice* for Saxophone and Orch. (1942); *Symphonie de fugues* (1942–44); *Études symphoniques* (1943); *Eroica* for Horn and Chamber Orch. (1946); *Légende* for Flute and Orch. (1951); *Variations symphoniques* (1952); Sinfonietta for Strings (1955; not extant). **CHAMBER:** *Andante* for 4 Horns (1903); *Andante, Fugue et Final* for 4 Saxophones (1907); Sextet for Wind Quintet and Piano (1925); *Passacaglia* for Double Bass (1928); *Études rythmiques* for Percussion (1929); *Divertimento* for String Trio (1936); *Choral varie* for 4 Cellos (1937); *Suite* for 3 Trombones (1939); *Sonata en forme de passacaille* for Cello and Piano (1942); Concert for Wind Quintet and Harp (1950); *Bagatelles* for 2 Violins (1960). **KEYBOARD: Piano:** Sonata (1917); *Toccata* (1938); *Ciels* (1938); *Études-paraphrases*, after Paganini (1948). **Organ:** Sonata (1907); *2 Pieces* (1910); *3 poèmes bibliques* (1916–20); *2 Fugues* (1929); *Prélude et Choral* (1948). **VOCAL:** 5 sets of *Poemes de la Vieille France* for Variable Vocal Groups (1917–43); *L'Eau passe*, song cycle for Solo Voice.—**NS/LK/DM**

Moulinié, Etienne, French composer; b. Languedoc, c. 1600; d. there, after 1669. He was a child chorister at Narbonne Cathedral. In 1624 he went to Paris, where he served as director of music to the King's younger brother, Gaston of Orléans, from 1628 to 1660. In 1661 he returned to Languedoc as director of music. Moulinié was highly regarded for his *Airs de cour à 4 et 5 parties* (5 vols., Paris, 1625–39). Among his other works were ballet music, dance pieces, and religious music.—**LK/DM**

Mount-Edgcumbe, Richard, Second Earl of, English nobleman and amateur musician; b. Plymouth, Sept. 13, 1764; d. Richmond, Surrey, Sept. 26, 1839. He was the (anonymous) author of the book *Musical Reminiscences, containing an Account of the Italian Opera in England from 1773* (1824; 4th ed., 1834). He also wrote an opera, *Zenobia* (in Italian), which was produced in London on May 22, 1800.—**NS/LK/DM**

Mouquet, Jules, French composer; b. Paris, July 10, 1867; d. there, Oct. 25, 1946. He studied at the Paris Cons. with Leroux (harmony) and Dubois (composition), winning the 1st Prix de Rome in 1896 with his cantata *Mélusine*, the Prix Trémont in 1905, and the Prix Chartier (for chamber music) in 1907. In 1913 he became prof. of harmony at the Paris Cons.

WORKS: 2 oratorios: *Le Sacrifice d'Isaac* and *Le Jugement dernier*; 2 symphonic poems: *Diane et Endymion* and *Persée et Andromède*; *Danse grecque* for Orch.; *Divertissement grec* for Flute and Harp; *Flute Sonata*; pieces for oboe and piano, bassoon and piano, saxophone and piano, etc.; *Septet for Wind Instruments*; *Études antiques* for Piano.—**NS/LK/DM**

Mouret, Jean-Joseph, noted French composer; b. Avignon, April 11, 1682; d. Charenton, Dec. 20, 1738. He is believed to have received his musical training at the Notre Dame des Doms choir school in Avignon. After settling in Paris (1707), he became maître de musique to the Marshal of Noailles; within a year or so, he was made surintendant de la musique at the Sceaux court. He was director of the Paris Opéra orch. (1714–18), and became composer-director at the New Italian Theater (1717), remaining there for 2 decades. He was also made an ordinaire du Roy as a singer in the king's chamber (1720), and served as artistic director of the Concert Spirituel (1728–34), where he brought out many of his cantatas, motets, and cantatilles. In 1718 he was granted a royal privilege to publ. his own music. Stricken with a mental disorder in 1737, he was placed in the care of the Fathers of Charity in Charenton in 1738. Among his most successful works were the opera-ballet *Les Fêtes ou Le Triomphe de Thalie* (Paris, Aug. 14, 1714), the comédie lyrique *Le Mariage de Ragonde et de Colin ou La Veillée de village* (Sceaux, Dec. 1714), various divertissements for the Italian Theater, and the *Suites de simphonies* (c. 1729; ed. by M. Sanvoisin, Paris, 1970).

BIBL.: R. Viollier, *J.-J. M., le musicien des grâces* (Paris, 1950). —**NS/LK/DM**

Moussorgsky, Modest (Petrovich)
See Mussorgsky, Modest (Petrovich)

Mouton, Jean, important French composer; b. Holluigue, near Samer, c. 1459; d. St. Quentin, Oct. 30, 1522. In 1477 he became a singer and teacher of religion (écolâtre-chantre) at the collegiate church of Notre Dame in Nesle. He became maître de chapelle in Nesle in 1483, and also entered the priesthood. In 1500 he was in charge of the choirboys at the Cathedral of Amiens. In 1501 he was director of music at the collegiate church of St. André in Grenoble, but left his position without permission in 1502. He subsequently entered the service of Queen Anne; later served Louis XII and François I. He was made canon in absentia at St. André in Grenoble, which conferred a benefice on him in 1510, and later was elected a canon at St. Quentin. Pope Leo X made him an apostolic notary. He was the teacher of Adrian Willaert. In his music he followed the precepts of Josquin Des Prez; he particularly excelled in the art of the canon. He composed more than 100 motets, some 15 masses, and over 20 chansons. About 50 of his works were publ. in his lifetime; several collections were publ. posthumously. His *Opera omnia*, ed. by A. Minor, began publication in 1967 in the Corpus Mensurabilis Musicae series of the American Inst. of Musicology.

BIBL.: A. Minor, *The Masses of J. M.* (diss., Univ. of Mich., 1951); R. Dammann, *Studien zu den Motetten von J. M.* (diss., Univ. of Freiburg, 1952); J. Shine, *The Motets of J. M.* (diss., N.Y.U., 1953); P. Kast, *Studien zu den Messen des J. M.* (diss., Univ. of Frankfurt am Main, 1955).—**NS/LK/DM**

Moyse, Louis, French-American flutist, pianist, and composer, son of **Marcel (Joseph) Moyse**; b. Scheveningen, the Netherlands, July 14, 1912. He was taken to Paris as an infant, and learned to play the piano and flute at home. He later took private piano lessons with Philipp (1925–27), and in 1930 he entered the Paris Cons., where he studied flute with Gaubert and composition with Bigot. He graduated in 1932 with the premier prix in flute, then was his father's teaching assistant at the Paris Cons., and filled in with various jobs playing at movie theaters and restaurants. He served in the French army during World War II; after the war, he organized the Moyse Trio, with his father as flutist, his wife, Blanche Honegger-Moyse, as violinist, and himself as pianist. In 1948 he went with his wife to the U.S.; became a naturalized American citizen in 1959. He was active at the Marlboro (Vt.) Music Festival (from 1950), and also prof. of flute and chamber music at the Univ. of Toronto (from 1975).

WORKS: *Suite* for 2 Flutes and Viola (1957); *4 Dances* for Flute and Violin (1958); Woodwind Quintet (1961); *Divertimento* for Double Woodwind Quintet, 2 Cellos, Double Bass, and Timpani (1961); *4 Pieces* for 3 Flutes and Piano (1965); *3 Pieces* for Flute and Guitar (1968); *Marlborian Concerto* for Flute, English Horn, and Orch. (1969); *A Ballad for Vermont* for Narrator, Soloists, Chorus, and Orch. (1971–72); Flute Sonata (1975); *Serenade* for Piccolo, 4 Flutes, Alto Flute, Bass Flute, and Piano (1977); several collections of didactic flute pieces; various arrangements for flute and instrumental groups of works by Bach, Handel, Telemann, Mozart, Beethoven, and Weber. —**NS/LK/DM**

Moyse, Marcel (Joseph), celebrated French flutist and pedagogue, father of **Louis Moyse**; b. St. Amour, Jura, May 17, 1889; d. Brattleboro, Vt., Nov. 1, 1984. He studied flute (premier prix, 1906) with Taffanel, Hennebains, and Gaubert, and chamber music with Capet at the Paris Cons. In 1908 he made his debut as soloist with the Pasdeloup Orch. in Paris. From 1913 to 1938 he played flute in the orch. of the Opéra-Comique in Paris. He also played in the Concerts Staram in Paris (1922–33). From 1932 to 1949 he was prof. of flute at the Paris Cons. In 1933 he formed the Moyse Trio with his son as pianist and his daughter-in-law Blanche Honegger Moyse as violinist. In 1949 he settled in the U.S. In 1950 he helped found the Marlboro (Vt.) Music Festival, where he was active as both a performer and teacher. He also gave master classes abroad. In 1934 Moyse was made a member of the Légion d'honneur. As a performer, he played various modern works. Ibert composed his Flute Concerto for Moyse, who gave the first performance in 1933. Moyse wrote many didactic works for the flute as well as the manual *Tone Development through Interpretation*.

BIBL.: T. Wye, *M. M.: An Extraordinary Man: A Musical Biography* (Cedar Falls, 1993); A. McCutchan, *M. M.: Voice of the Flute* (Portland, Ore., 1995).—**NS/LK/DM**

Moyzes, Alexander, Slovak composer and teacher, son of **Mikuláš Moyzes**; b. Kláštor pod Znievom, Sept. 4, 1906; d. Bratislava, Nov. 20, 1984. He studied conducting with Ostrcil, composition with Karel and Šin, and organ with Wiedermann at the Prague Cons.

(1925–28), and then studied in Novák's master class there (1929–30). He taught at the Bratislava Academy of Music and Drama (from 1929). He was chief music adviser to the Bratislava Radio and a prof. at the Bratislava Cons. (from 1941), then became a prof. of composition at the Bratislava Coll. of Musical Arts (1949), serving as its rector (1965–71). He won the State Prize (1956) and was made an Artist of Merit (1961) and a National Artist (1966). His music uses the melodic resources of Slovak folk songs; his Sym. No. 1 is the first national Slovak sym.

WORKS: DRAMATIC: Opera: *Udatný král'* (The Brave King; 1966; Bratislava, 1967). **ORCH.:** 12 syms.: No. 1 (Bratislava, Feb. 11, 1929), No. 2 (1932; rev. 1941), No. 3 (1942; orch. version of the Wind Quintet), No. 4 (1939–47), No. 5 (1948), No. 6 (1951), No. 7 (Bratislava, Oct. 23, 1955), No. 8 (1968), No. 9 (1971), No. 10 (1978), No. 11 (1978), and No. 12 (1983); *Symphonic Overture* (1929); Concertino (1933); *Jánošik's Rebels* (1933); *Nikola Šuhaj*, overture (1933); *Down the River Vah*, symphonic suite (1936; rev. 1945); *Dances from the Hron Region* (1950); *February Overture* (1952); *Dances from Gemer*, suite (1955); Violin Concerto (1958); *Sonatina giocosa* for Violin, Chamber String Orch., and Harpsichord (1962); Flute Concerto (1966); *Keeper of the House*, overture (1972); *Bonfires on the Mountains*, symphonic suite (1973); *Musica istropolitana* for Chamber String Orch. (1974); *Music to Woman*, symphonic study (1975; Bratislava, May 13, 1976); *The Tale about Jánošik*, rhapsodic suite (1976). **CHAMBER:** 4 string quartets (1928, 1969, 1981, 1983); Wind Quintet (1933); *Poetic Suite* for Violin and Piano (1948); *Duetta* for Violin and Piano (1960); *Small Suite* for Violin and Piano (1968); Sonatina for Flute and Guitar (1975). **Piano:** *Divertimento* (1929); *Jazz Sonata* for 2 Pianos (1932); Sonata (1942). **VOCAL:** 2 cantatas: *Svätopluk* (1935) and *Znejú piesne na chotari* (Songs Resound in the Meadows; 1948); 2 song cycles: *Jeseň* (In Autumn) for Mezzo-soprano and Orch. or Piano (1960) and *Morning Dew* for Mezzo-soprano and Orch. or Piano (1963).

BIBL.: L. Burlas, *A. M.* (Bratislava, 1956).—**NS/LK/DM**

Moyzes, Mikuláš,

Slovak composer and teacher, father of **Alexander Moyzes**; b. Zvolenská, Slatina, Dec. 6, 1872; d. Prešov, April 2, 1944. He was a non-resident student at the Budapest Academy of Music, then a music teacher and organist in various Slovak towns. He settled in Prešov as a teacher (1908). Moyzes was a leading figure in the development of Slovak national music.

WORKS: DRAMATIC: Melodramas: *Siroty* (Orphans; 1921); *Lesná panna* (Maid of the Woods; 1922); *Čertova rieka* (The Devil's River; 1940). **ORCH.:** 2 suites (1931, 1935); *Malá vrchovská symfónia* (Little Highland Sym.; 1937); *Naše Slovensko* (Our Slovakia), festival overture (1938). **CHAMBER:** 4 string quartets (1926, 1929, 1932, 1943); Wind Sextet (1934); organ pieces. **VOCAL:** *Missa solemnis* for Chorus (1906); *Mass* for Chorus (1929); songs; folk song arrangements.

BIBL.: Z. Bokesová, *Sedemdesiatročný M. M.* (M. M. at 70; Bratislava, 1942).—**NS/LK/DM**

Mozart, Franz Xaver Wolfgang,

Austrian pianist and composer, son of **Wolfgang Amadeus Mozart** and often called by his father's name; b. Vienna, July 26, 1791; d. Carlsbad, July 29, 1844. He studied piano with F. Niemetschek in Prague while living with the Dušek family, then continued his training with S. Neukomm, Andreas Steicher, Hummel, Salieri, G. Vogler, and Albrechtsberger in Vienna. After a period as a teacher in Lemberg and environs (1807–19), he embarked upon a major tour of Europe as a pianist (1819–21). He then returned to Lemberg as a teacher (1822), receiving additional instruction in counterpoint from Johann Mederitsch or Gallus (1826); that same year he organized the Lemberg Cäcilien-Chor. He settled in Vienna (1838) and was named honorary Kapellmeister of the Dom-Musik- Verein and the Mozarteum in Salzburg (1841); was made maestro compositore onorario of Rome's Congregazione ed Accademica Santa Cecilia (1842). As a composer, he revealed a gift for pianistic writing.

WORKS: ORCH.: 2 piano concertos: C major, op.14 (publ. in Leipzig, 1809; ed. by R. Angermüller, Salzburg, 1972), and E-flat major, op.25 (publ. in Leipzig, 1818); *Konzertvariationen* for Piano and Orch. (1820); Sinfonia in D major; 12 Minuets and Trios (1808). **CHAMBER:** Piano Quintet, op.1 (1802; ed. in *Diletto musicale*, no. 180, Vienna, 1966); *Sei piccoli pezzi* for Flute and 2 Horns, op.11 (1808); 2 violin sonatas: B-flat major, op.7 (1808), and F major, op.15 (1813); *Grande Sonate* in E major for Violin or Cello, and Piano, op.19 (1820; ed. by W. Boettcher for Cello, Mainz, 1969); *Rondo (Sonate)* for Flute and Piano (ed. by R. Ermeler, Wilhelmshaven, 1962). **Piano:** Sonata, op.10 (1808); 12 Polonaises, op.17 (c. 1815), op.22 (1820), and op.26 (c. 1821); 11 sets of variations; also 4 cantatas, including 1 for Haydn's birthday (1805; not extant); several unaccompanied choral pieces; songs.

BIBL.: J. Fischer, *W.A. M. (Sohn): Eine biographische Skizze, sowie zwei bisher unbekannte Briefe Mozart's (Vater)* (Carlsbad, c. 1888).—**NS/LK/DM**

Mozart, (Johann Georg) Leopold,

German-born Austrian composer, violinist, and music theorist, father of **Wolfgang Amadeus Mozart** and **Maria Anna Mozart**; b. Augsburg, Nov. 14, 1719; d. Salzburg, May 28, 1787. A bookbinder's son, he studied at the Augsburg Gymnasium (1727–35), then continued his studies at the Lyceum attached to the Jesuit school of St. Salvator (1735–36). In 1737 he went to Salzburg, where he studied philosophy and law at the Benedictine Univ.; he received his bachelor of philosophy degree in 1738. Subsequently he entered the service of Johann Baptist, Count of Thurn-Valsassina and Taxis, the Salzburg canon and president of the consistory, as both valet and musician. In 1743 he became fourth violinist in the Prince-Archbishop's Court Orch.; also taught violin and keyboard to the choirboys of the Cathedral oratory. In 1757 he became composer to the court and chamber, and in 1758 he was promoted to second violinist in the Court Orch.; in 1762 he was appointed Vice-Kapellmeister. He married Anna Maria Pertl of Salzburg on Nov. 21, 1747; of their 7 children, only Maria Anna and Wolfgang survived infancy. He dedicated himself to the musical education of his children, but his methods of presentation of their concerts at times approached frank exploitation, and his advertisements of their appearances were in poor taste. However, there is no denying his great role in fostering his son's career. Leopold was a thoroughly competent composer; the mutual influence between father and son was such that works long attributed to his son proved to be his. He was also important as a music theorist. He produced an influential violin method in his *Versuch einer gründlichen Violin-schule* (Augsburg, 1756; 2nd ed., rev., 1769–70; 3rd ed., enl., 1787; facsimile of 1756 ed., Vienna, 1922; also various trs., including one in Eng., London, 1939; 2nd ed., 1951). His *Nannerl-Notenbuch* is a model of a child's music album; it was publ. in 1759; ed. in part by E. Valentin (Munich, 1956; 2nd ed., 1969). M. Seiffert ed. *Leopold Mozart: Ausgewählte Werke* in Denkmäler der Tonkunst in Bayern, XVII, Jg. IX/2 (Leipzig, 1908). His vocal works include sacred cantatas, masses, litanies, school dramas, and secular lieder. He also composed syms., the famous *Kindersinfonie*, long attributed to Haydn, was in all probability a work by Leopold. On this, see E.F. Schmid, "Leopold Mozart und die Kinder-sinfonie," *Mozart Jahrbuch* 1951, and R. Münster, "Wer ist der Komponist der 'Kindersinfonie'?" *Acta Mozartiana*, XVI (1969). Other orch. works include several concertos, among them *Die musikalische Schlitten-fahrt* (1755), dances, etc. He also composed chamber music and works for the keyboard. In 1992 the Internationale Leopold Mozart Gesellschaft was founded in Augsburg.

BIBL.: CORRESPONDENCE AND NOTEBOOKS: A. Schurig, *L. M.s Reiseaufzeichnungen, 1763–1771* (facsimile ed.; Dresden, 1920); O.E. Deutsch and B. Paumgartner, *L. M.s Briefe an seine Tochter* (Salzburg and Leipzig, 1936); E. Anderson, ed. and tr., *Letters of M. and His Family* (3 vols., London and N.Y., 1938; 2nd ed., rev. by A. Hyatt King and M. Carolan, 1966; 3rd ed., rev. by S. Sadie and F. Smart, 1985); A. Kozár, *Wolfgang Amadeus M. (1756–1791) im Spiegel der Briefe seines Vaters L. M.: Ein Beitrag zur Kulturgeschichte des 18. Jahrhunderts* (diss., Univ. of Graz, 1955); W. Bauer, O.E. Deutsch, and J. Eibl, eds., *M.: Briefe und Aufzeichnungen* (contains letters, notebooks, etc., relating to Leopold; 7 vols., Kassel, 1962–75). **BIOGRAPHICAL, CRITICAL, ANALYTICAL, ETC.:** E. Theiss, *Die Instrumentalwerke L. M.s nebst einer Biographie* (diss., Univ. of Giessen, 1942); J. Kay, *Mein Sohn Wolfgang Amadeus: Glück und Tragik des Vaters L. M.* (Vienna, 1965); W. Lievense, *De familie M. in Nederland: Een reisverslag* (Hilversum, 1965); L. Staehelin, *Die Reise der Familie M. durch die Schweiz* (Bern, 1968); L. Wegele, ed., *L. M., 1719–1787: Bild einer Persönlichkeit* (Augsburg, 1969); D. Carlson, *The Sacred Vocal Works of L. M.* (diss., Univ. of Mich., 1976); A. Layer, *Eine Jugend in Augsburg—L. M. 1719–1787* (Augsburg, 1976); C. Eisen, *The Symphonies of L. M. and Their Relationship to the Early Symphonies of Wolfgang Amadeus M.: A Bibliographical and Stylistic Study* (diss., Cornell Univ., 1986); E. Schwerin, *L. M.: Profile of a Personality* (N.Y., 1987); J. Mancal and W. Plath, eds., *Beiträge des internationalen L.-M.- Kolloquiums Augsburg 1994* (Augsburg, 1997).—NS/LK/DM

Mozart, Maria Anna (Walburga Ignatia),

Austrian pianist and teacher, daughter of **(Johann Georg) Leopold Mozart** and sister of **Wolfgang Amadeus Mozart**, nicknamed "Nannerl"; b. Salzburg, July 30, 1751; d. there, Oct. 29, 1829. She was taught music by her father from her earliest childhood, and appeared in public as a pianist with her brother. After their travels together in Europe, she returned to Salzburg and eventually devoted herself mainly to teaching. In 1784 she married Baron von Berchthold zu Sonnenburg, who died in 1801. She went blind in 1825. Although nearly 5 years older than Wolfgang, she survived him by 38 years.

BIBL.: W. Hummel, ed., *Nannerl M.s Tagebuchblätter mit Eintragungen ihres Bruders Wolfgang Amadeus* (Stuttgart, 1958); E. Rieger, *Nannerl M.: Leben einer Künstlerin im 18. Jahrhundert* (Frankfurt am Main, 1991).—NS/LK/DM

Mozart, Wolfgang Amadeus (baptismal names, Johannes Chrysostomus Wolfgangus Theophilus),

great Austrian composer whose works in every genre are unsurpassed in lyric beauty, rhythmic variety, and effortless melodic invention, son of **(Johann Georg) Leopold Mozart**, brother of **Maria Anna Mozart**, and father of **Franz Xaver Wolfgang Mozart**; b. Salzburg, Jan. 27, 1756; d. Vienna, Dec. 5, 1791. He and his sister, tenderly nicknamed "Nannerl," were the only two among the seven children of Anna Maria and Leopold Mozart to survive infancy. Mozart's sister was 4–1/2 years older; she took harpsichord lessons from her father, and Mozart as a very young child eagerly absorbed the sounds of music. He soon began playing the harpsichord himself, and later studied the violin. Leopold was an excellent musician, but he also appreciated the theatrical validity of the performances that Wolfgang and Nannerl began giving in Salzburg. On Jan. 17, 1762, he took them to Munich, where they performed before the Elector of Bavaria. In Sept. 1762 they played for Emperor Francis I at his palace in Vienna. The family returned to Salzburg in Jan. 1763, and in June 1763 the children were taken to Frankfurt am Main, where Wolfgang showed his skill in improvising at the keyboard. In Nov. 1763 they arrived in Paris, where they played before Louis XV; it was in Paris that Wolfgang's first compositions were printed (4 sonatas for Harpsichord, with Violin ad libitum). In April 1764 they proceeded to London; there Wolfgang played for King George III. In London he was befriended by Bach's son Johann Christian Bach, who gave exhibitions improvising 4-hands at the piano with the child Mozart. By that time Mozart had tried his ability in composing serious works; he wrote two syms. for a London performance, and the MS of another very early sym., purportedly written by him in London, was discovered in 1980. Leopold wrote home with undisguised pride:"Our great and mighty Wolfgang seems to know everything at the age of 7 that a man acquires at the age of 40." Knowing the power of publicity, he diminished Wolfgang's age, for at the time the child was fully nine years old. In July 1765 they journeyed to the Netherlands, then set out for Salzburg, visiting Dijon, Lyons, Geneva, Bern, Zürich, Donaueschingen, and Munich on the way. Arriving in Salzburg in Nov. 1766, Wolfgang applied himself to serious study of counterpoint under the tutelage of his father. In Sept. 1767 the family proceeded to Vienna, where Wolfgang began work on an opera, *La finta semplice*; his second theater work was a Singspiel, *Bastien und Bastienne*, which was produced in Vienna at the home of Dr. Franz Mesmer, the protagonist of the famous method of therapy by "animal magnetism," which became known as Mesmerism. On Dec. 7, 1768, Mozart led a performance of his *Missa solemnis* in C minor before the royal family and court at the consecration of the Waisenhauskirche. Upon Mozart's return to Salzburg in Jan. 1769, Archbishop Sigismund von Schrattenbach named him his Konzertmeister; however, the position was without remuneration. Still determined to broaden Mozart's artistic contacts, his father took him on an Italian tour. The announcement for a concert in Mantua on Jan. 16, 1770, just a few days before Mozart's 14th birthday, was typical of the artistic mores of the time: "A Symphony of his own composition; a harpsichord concerto, which will be handed to him, and which he will immediately play prima vista; a Sonata handed him in like manner, which he will provide with variations, and afterwards repeat in another key; an Aria, the words for which will be handed to him and which he will immediately set to music and sing himself, accompanying himself on the harpsichord; a Sonata for harpsichord on a subject given him by the leader of the violins; a Strict Fugue on a theme to be selected, which he will improvise on the harpsichord; a Trio in which he will execute a violin part all' improvviso; and, finally, the latest Symphony by himself." Legends of Mozart's extraordinary musical ability grew; it was reported, for instance, that he wrote out the entire score of *Miserere* by Allegri, which he had heard in the Sistine Chapel at the Vatican only twice. Young Mozart was subjected to numerous tests by famous Italian musicians, among them Giovanni Sammartini, Piccini, and Padre Martini; he was given a diploma as an elected member of the Accademia Filarmonica in Bologna after he had passed examinations in harmony and counterpoint. On Oct. 10, 1770, the Pope made him a Knight of the Golden Spur. He was commissioned to compose an opera; the result was *Mitridate, rè di Ponto*, which was performed in Milan on Dec. 26, 1770; Mozart himself conducted three performances of this opera from the harpsichord; after a short stay in Salzburg, they returned to Milan in 1771, where he composed the serenata *Ascanio in Alba* for the wedding festivities of Archduke Ferdinand (Oct. 17, 1771). He returned to Salzburg late in 1771; his patron, Archbishop Schrattenbach, died about that time, and his successor, Archbishop Hieronymus Colloredo, seemed to be indifferent to Mozart as a musician. Once more Mozart went to Italy, where his newest opera, *Lucio Silla*, was performed in Milan on Dec. 26, 1772. He returned to Salzburg in March 1773, but in July of that year he went to Vienna, where he became acquainted with the music of Haydn, who greatly influenced his instrumental style. Returning to Salzburg once more, he supervised the production of his opera *Il Rè pastore*, which was performed on April 23, 1775.

In March 1778 Mozart visited Paris again for a performance of his "Paris" Sym. at a Concert Spirituel. His mother died in Paris on July 3, 1778. Returning to Salzburg in Jan. 1779, he resumed his duties as Konzertmeister and also obtained the position of court organist at a salary of 450 gulden. In 1780 the Elector of Bavaria commissioned from him an opera seria, *Idomeneo*, which was successfully produced in Munich on Jan. 29, 1781. In May 1781 Mozart lost his position with the Archbishop in Salzburg and decided to move to Vienna, which became his permanent home. There he produced the operatic masterpiece *Die Entführung aus dem Serail*, staged at the Burgtheater on July 16, 1782, with excellent success. On August 4, 1782, he married Constanze Weber, the sister of Aloysia Weber, with whom he had

previously been infatuated. Two of his finest syms.—No. 35 in D major, "Haffner," written for the Haffner family of Salzburg, and No. 36 in C major, the "Linz"—date from 1782 and 1783, respectively. From this point forward Mozart's productivity reached extraordinary dimensions, but despite the abundance of commissions and concert appearances, he was unable to earn enough to sustain his growing family. Still, melodramatic stories of Mozart's abject poverty are gross exaggerations. He apparently felt no scruples in asking prosperous friends for financial assistance. Periodically he wrote to Michael Puchberg, a banker and a brother Freemason (Mozart joined the Masonic Order in 1784), with requests for loans (which he never repaid); invariably Puchberg obliged, but usually granting smaller amounts than Mozart requested. In 1785 Mozart completed a set of 6 string quartets which he dedicated to Haydn; unquestionably the structure of these quartets owed much to Haydn's contrapuntal art. Haydn himself paid a tribute to Mozart's genius; Mozart's father quoted him as saying, "Before God and as an honest man I tell you that your son is the greatest composer known to me either in person or by name." On May 1, 1786, Mozart's great opera buffa, *Le nozze di Figaro*, was produced in Vienna, obtaining a triumph with the audience; it was performed in Prague early in 1787 with Mozart in attendance. It was during that visit that Mozart wrote his 38th Sym., in D major, known as the "Prague" Sym.; it was in Prague, also, that his operatic masterpiece *Don Giovanni* was produced, on Oct. 29, 1787. It is interesting to note that at its Vienna performance the opera was staged under the title *Die sprechende Statue*, unquestionably with the intention of sensationalizing the story; the dramatic appearance of the statue of the Commendatore, introduced by the ominous sound of trombones, was a shuddering climax to the work. In Nov. 1787 Mozart was appointed Kammermusicus in Vienna as a successor to Gluck, albeit at a smaller salary: he received 800 gulden per annum as against Gluck's salary of 2,000 gulden. The year 1788 was a glorious one for Mozart and for music history; it was the year when he composed his last three syms.: No. 39 in E-flat major; No. 40 in G minor; and No. 41 in C major, known under the name "Jupiter" (the Jovian designation was apparently attached to the work for the first time in British concert programs; its earliest use was in the program of the Edinburgh Festival in Oct. 1819). In the spring of 1789 Mozart went to Berlin; on the way he appeared as soloist in one of his piano concertos before the Elector of Saxony in Dresden, and also played the organ at the Thomaskirche in Leipzig. His visits in Potsdam and Berlin were marked by his private concerts at the court of Friedrich Wilhelm II; the King commissioned from him a set of 6 string quartets and a set of 6 piano sonatas, but Mozart died before completing these commissions. Returning to Vienna, he began work on his opera buffa *Così fan tutte* (an untranslatable sentence because *tutte* is the feminine plural, so that the full title would be "Thus do all women"). The opera was first performed in Vienna on Jan. 26, 1790. In Oct. 1790 Mozart went to Frankfurt am Main for the coronation of Emperor Leopold II. Returning to Vienna, he saw Haydn, who was about to depart for London. In

1791, during his last year of life, he completed the score of *Die Zauberflöte*, with a German libretto by Emanuel Schikaneder. It was performed for the first time on Sept. 30, 1791, in Vienna. There followed a mysterious episode in Mozart's life; a stranger called on him with a request to compose a Requiem; the caller was an employee of Count Franz von Walsegg, who intended to have the work performed as his own in memory of his wife. Mozart was unable to finish the score, which was completed by his pupil Sussmayr, and by Eybler.

The immediate cause of Mozart's death at the age of 35 has been the subject of much speculation. Almost immediately after the sad event, myths and fantasies appeared in the press; the most persistent of them all was that Mozart had been poisoned by Salieri out of professional jealousy; this particularly morbid piece of invention gained circulation in European journals; the story was further elaborated upon by a report that Salieri confessed his unspeakable crime on his deathbed in 1825. Pushkin used the tale in his drama *Mozart and Salieri*, which Rimsky-Korsakov set to music in his opera of the same title; a fanciful dramatization of the Mozart-Salieri rivalry was made into a successful play, *Amadeus*, by Peter Shaffer, which was produced in London in 1979 and in N.Y. in 1980; it subsequently gained wider currency through its award-winning film version of 1984. The notion of Mozart's murder also appealed to the Nazis; in the ingenious version propagated by some German writers of the Hitlerian persuasion, Mozart was a victim of a double conspiracy of Masons and Jews who were determined to suppress the flowering of racial Germanic greatness; the Masons, in this interpretation, were outraged by his revealing of their secret rites in *Die Zauberflöte*, and allied themselves with plutocratic Jews to prevent further spread of his dangerous revelations. Another myth related to Mozart's death that found its way into the majority of Mozart biographies and even into respectable reference works was that a blizzard raged during his funeral and that none of his friends could follow his body to the cemetery; this story is easily refuted by the records of the Vienna weather bureau for the day (see N. Slonimsky, "The Weather at Mozart's Funeral," *Musical Quarterly*, Jan. 1960). It is also untrue that Mozart was buried in a pauper's grave; his body was removed from its original individual location because the family neglected to pay the mandatory dues.

The universal recognition of Mozart's genius during the 2 centuries since his death has never wavered among professional musicians, amateurs, and the general public. In his music, smiling simplicity was combined with somber drama; lofty inspiration was contrasted with playful diversion; profound meditation alternated with capricious moodiness; religious concentration was permeated with human tenderness. Devoted as Mozart was to his art and respectful as he was of the rules of composition, he was also capable of mocking the professional establishment. A delightful example of this persiflage is his little piece *Ein musikalischer Spass*, subtitled "Dorf Musikanten," a "musical joke" at the expense of "village musicians," in which Mozart all but anticipated developments of modern music, two centuries in the future; he deliberately used the forbidden consecutive fifths, allowed the violin to escape upward in a whole-tone scale, and finished the entire work in a welter of polytonal triads.

The variety of technical development in Mozart's works is all the more remarkable considering the limitations of instrumental means in his time; the topmost note on his keyboard was F above the 3rd ledger line, so that in the recapitulation in the 1st movement of his famous C major Piano Sonata, the subject had to be dropped an octave lower to accommodate the modulation. The vocal technique displayed in his operas is amazing in its perfection; to be sure, the human voice has not changed since Mozart's time, but he knew how to exploit vocal resources to the utmost. This adaptability of his genius to all available means of sound production is the secret of the eternal validity of his music.

In the list of Mozart's works given below, the K. numbers represent the system of identification established by L. von Köchel in his *Chronologisch-thematisches Verzeichnis sämtlicher Tonwerke Wolfgang Amade Mozarts* (Leipzig, 1862; 6th ed., rev. by F. Giegling, A. Weinmann, and G. Sievers, Wiesbaden, 1964); the rev. K. numbers of the 6th ed. are also included.

WORKS: DRAMATIC: *Apollo et Hyacinthus*, K.38, Latin intermezzo (Salzburg Univ., May 13, 1767); *La finta semplice*, K.51; 46a, opera buffa (Archbishop's palace, Salzburg, May 1?, 1769); *Bastien und Bastienne*, K.50; 46b, Singspiel (Franz Mesmer's residence, Vienna, Sept.?-Oct.? 1768); *Mitridate, rè di Ponto*, K.87; 74a, opera seria (Regio Ducal Teatro, Milan, Dec. 26, 1770); *Ascanio in Alba*, K.111, festa teatrale (Regio Ducal Teatro, Milan, Oct. 17, 1771); *Il sogno di Scipione*, K.126, serenata (Archbishop's palace, Salzburg, May? 1772); *Lucio Silla*, K.135, opera seria (Regio Ducal Teatro, Milan, Dec. 26, 1772); *La finta giardiniera*, K.196, opera buffa (Munich, Jan. 13, 1775; also produced as a Singspiel, *Die verstellte Gartnerin*, Augsburg, May 1, 1780); *Il Rè pastore*, K.208, dramma per musica (Archbishop's palace, Salzburg, April 23, 1775); *Semiramis*, K.Anh. 11; 315e, duodrama (not extant); *Thamos, König in Ägypten*, K.345; 336a, music for Gebler's play; *Zaide*, K.344; 336b, Singspiel (unfinished; dialogue rewritten and finished by Gollmick, with overture and finale added by Anton André, Frankfurt am Main, Jan. 27, 1866); *Idomeneo, rè di Creta*, K.366, opera seria (Hoftheater, Munich, Jan. 29, 1781); *Die Entführung aus dem Serail*, K.384, Singspiel (Burgtheater, Vienna, July 16, 1782); *L'oca del Cairo*, K.422, opera buffa (unfinished); *Lo Sposo deluso*, K.430; 424a, opera buffa (unfinished); *Der Schauspieldirektor*, K.486, Singspiel (Schönbrunn Palace, Heitzing [suburb of Vienna], Feb. 7, 1786); *Le nozze di Figaro*, K.492, opera buffa (Burgtheater, Vienna, May 1, 1786); *Il dissoluto punito, ossia Il Don Giovanni*, K.527, opera buffa (National Theater, Prague, Oct. 29, 1787); *Così fan tutte, ossia La scuola degli amanti*, K.588, opera buffa (Burgtheater, Vienna, Jan. 26, 1790); *Der Stein der Weisen*, Singspiel (1790; in collaboration with Schikaneder, B. Schack, F. Gerl, and J.B. Henneberg); *Die Zauberflöte*, K.620, Singspiel (Theater auf der Wieden, Vienna, Sept. 30, 1791); *La clemenza di Tito*, K.621, opera seria (National Theater, Prague, Sept. 6, 1791). **Arias and Scenes For Voice and Orch.:** *Conservati fedele*, K.23 (1765; rev. 1766); *A Berenice...Sol nascente*, K.70; 61c (1766); *Per pièta, bell'idol mio*, K.78; 73b (1766?); *Cara se le mie pene* (1769?); *Misero tu non sei*, K.A2; 73A (1770); *Fra cento affanni*, K.88; 73c (1770); *O temerario Arbace...Per quel paterno amplesso*, K.79; 73d (1766?); *Misero me...Misero pargoletto*, K.77; 73e (1770); *Se* *ardire, e speranza,* K.82; 73o (1770); *Se tutti i mali miei,* K.83; 73p (1770); *Non curo l'affetto,* K.74b (1771); *Voi avete un cor fedele,* K.217 (1775); *Ah, lo previdi...Ah, t'invola agli'occhi miei,* K.272 (1777); *Alcandro lo confesso...Non sòo d'onde viene,* K.294 (1778); *Basta vincesti...Ah, non lasciarmi,* K.486a; 295a (1778); *Popoli di Tessaglia...Io non chiedo,* K.316; 300b (1778–79); Scena, K.A3; 315b (1778); *Warum, o Liebe...Zittre, töricht Herz,* K.A11a; 365a (1780); *Ma che vi fece...Sperai vicino,* K.368 (1779–80); *Misera! dove son...Ah! non son io,* K.369 (1781); *A questo seno...Or che il cielo,* K.374 (1781); *Der Liebe himmlisches Gefühl,* K.119; 382h (1782); *Nehmt meinen Dank,* K.383 (1782); *Mia speranza adorata...Ah, non sai qual pena,* K.416 (1783); *Ah, spiegarti, oh Dio,* K.178; 417e (1783); *Vorrei spiegarti, oh Dio,* K.418 (1783); *No, che non sei capace,* K.419 (1783); *Non più, tutti ascoltai...Non temer, amato bene,* K.490 (1786); *Ch'io mi scordi di te...Non temer, amato bene,* K.505 (1786); *Bella mia fiamma...Resta, o cara,* K.528 (1787); *Ah se in ciel, benigna stella,* K.538 (1788); *In quali eccessi...Mi tradi,* K.540c (1788); *Ohne Zwang, aus eignem Triebe,* K.569 (1789); *Al desio di chi ch'adora,* K.577 (1789); *Alma grande e nobil core,* K.578 (1789); *Un moto di gioia,* K.579 (1789); *Schon lacht der holde Frühling,* K.580 (1789); *Chi sa quai sia,* K.581 (1789); *Vado, ma dove?,* K.583 (1789). **A l t o   a n d   O r c h . :** *Ombra felice...Io ti lascio,* K.255 (1776). **T e n o r   a n d   O r c h . :** *Va dal furor portata,* K.21; 19c (1765); *Or che il dover...Tali e cotanti sono,* K.36; 33i (1766); *Ah più tremar non voglio,* K.71 (1769–70); *Si monstra la sorte,* K.209 (1775); *Con ossequio, con rispetto,* K.210 (1775); *Clarice cara,* K.256 (1776); *Se al labbro mio non credi,* K.295 (1778); *Müsst'ich auch durch tausend Drachen,* K.435; 416b (1783); *Per pietà non ricercate,* K.420 (1783); *Misero! o sogno...Aura che intorni spiri,* K.431; 425b (1783); *Dalla sua pace,* K.540a (1788). **B a s s   a n d   O r c h . :** *Così dunque tradisci...Aspri rimorsi atroci,* K.432; 421a (1783); *Alcandro, lo confesso...Non sò d'onde viene,* K.512 (1787); *Mentre ti lascio,* K.513 (1787); *Ich möchte wohl der Kaiser sein,* K.539 (1788); *Un bacio di mano,* K.541 (1788); *Rivolgete a lui lo sguardo,* K.584 (1789); *Per questa bella mano,* K.612 (1791); *Io ti lascio,* K.A245; 621a (1791). **MASSES, ORATORIOS, CANTATAS, ETC.:** Kyrie in F major, K.33 (1766); *Die Schuldigkeit des ersten Gebots,* K.35, sacred drama (1767; part 1 by Mozart, part 2 by Michael Haydn, part 3 by Adlgasser; Salzburg, March 12, 1767); *Grabmusik,* K.42; 35a, cantata (1767; Salzburg Cathedral, April 7, 1767); *Missa solemnis* in C minor, K.139; 47a, "Waisenhausmesse" (1768; Vienna, Dec. 7, 1768); *Missa brevis* in C major, K.49; 47d (1768; only fragments extant); *Missa brevis* in D minor, K.65; 61a (1769; Collegiate Church, Salzburg, Feb. 5, 1769); *Missa* in C major, K.66, "Dominicus" (1769; St. Peter, Salzburg, Oct. 15, 1769); *La Betulia liberata,* K.118; 74c, oratorio (1771); *Missa brevis* in G major, K.140; C 1.12 (1773; may not be by Mozart); *Missa* in C major, K.167, "In honorem Ssmae Trinitatis" (1773); *Missa brevis* in F major, K.192; 186f (1774); *Missa brevis* in D major, K.194; 186h (1774); *Missa brevis* in C major, K.220; 196b, "Spatzenmesse" (1775–76); *Missa* in C major, K.262; 246a (1775); *Missa* in C major, K.257, "Credo" (1776); *Missa brevis* in C major, K.258, "Spaur" (1776); *Missa brevis* in C major, K.259, "Organ Solo" (1776); *Missa brevis* in B-flat major, K.275; 272b (1777; St. Peter, Salzburg, Dec. 21, 1777); *Missa* in C major, K.317, "Coronation" (1779); *Missa solemnis* in C major, K.337 (1780); Kyrie in D minor, K.341; 368a (1780–81); *Missa* in C minor, K.427; 417a (1782–83; unfinished; Kyrie and Gloria, St. Peter, Salzburg, Oct. 25, 1783); *Dir, Seele des Weltalls,* K.429; 468a, cantata (1785; unfinished); *Davidde penitente,* K.469, oratorio (1785; music from the *Missa* in C minor, K.427; 417a, 2 arias excepted); *Die Maurerfreude,* K.471, cantata (1785; "Zur gekronten Hoffnung" Lodge, Vienna, April 24, 1785); *Die ihr des unermesslichen Weltalls Schöpfer ehrt,* K.619, cantata (1791); *Eine kleine Freimaurer-*

Kantate, K.623 (1791; "Zur neugekronten Hoffnung" Lodge, Vienna, Nov. 18, 1791); Requiem in D minor, K.626 (1791; unfinished; completed by Franz Xavier Süssmayr). Also the following: *God Is Our Refuge* in G minor, K.20, motet (1765); *Stabat Mater,* K.33c (1766; not extant); *Scande coeli limina* in C major, K.34, offertory (1767); *Veni Sancte Spiritus* in C major, K.47 (1768); *Benedictus sit Deus* in C major, K.117; 66a, offertory (1768); *Te Deum* in C major, K.141; 66b (1769); *Ergo interest* in G major, K.143; 73a, motet (1773); *Miserere* in A minor, K.85; 73s (1770); *Cibavit eos* in A minor, K.44; 73u, antiphon (1770; may not be by Mozart); *Quaerite primum* in D minor, K.86; 73v, antiphon (1770); *Regina coeli* in C major, K.108; 74d (1771); *Inter natos mulierum* in G major, K.72; 74f, offertory (1771); *Regina coeli* in B-flat major, K.127 (1772); *Exsultate, jubilate* in F major, K.165; 158a, motet (1773; Milan, Jan. 17, 1773); *Tantum ergo* in D major, K.197; C 3.05 (1774; may not be by Mozart); *Sub tuum praesidium* in F major, K.198; C 3.08, offertory (1774; may not be by Mozart); *Misericordias Domini* in D minor, K.222; 205a, offertory (1775); *Venite populi* in D major, K.260; 248a (1776); *Alma Dei creatoris* in F major, K.277; 272a, offertory (1777); *Sancta Maria, mater Dei* in F major, K.273, gradual (1777); Miserere, K.Anh. 1; 297a (1778; not extant); *Kommet her, ihr frechen Sünder* in B-flat major, K.146; 317b, aria (1779); *Regina coeli* in C major, K.276; 321b (1779?); *O Gottes Lamm; Als aus Aegypten,* K.343; 336c, 2 German sacred songs (1787?); *Ave verum corpus* in D major, K.618, motet (1791). Additional works: *Litaniae Lauretanae* in B-flat major, K.109; 74e (1771); *Litaniae de venerabili altaris sacramento* in B-flat major, K.125 (1772); *Litaniae Lauretanae* in D major, K.195; 186d (1774); *Dixit Dominus, Magnificat* in C major, K.193; 186g (1774); *Litaniae de venerabili altaris sacramento* in E-flat major, K.243 (1776); *Vesperae de Dominica* in C major, K.321 (1779); *Vesperae solennes de confessore* in C major, K.339 (1780). **ORCH.: S y m s . :** No. 1 in E-flat major, K.16 (1764–65); A minor, K.Anh. 220; 16a "Odense" (1768?; considered lost until discovered in Odense in 1982; may not be by Mozart); No. 4 in D major, K.19 (1765); F major, K.Anh. 223; 19a (1765; considered lost until discovered in 1980); C major, K.Anh. 222; 19b (1765; not extant); No. 5 in B-flat major, K.22 (1765); No. 43 in F major, K.76; 42a (1767; may not be by Mozart); No. 6 in F major, K.43 (1767); No. 7 in D major, K.45 (1767); G major, K.Anh. 221; 45a, "Old Lambach" (1768); No. 55 in B-flat major, K.Anh. 214; 45b (1768); No. 8 in D major, K.48 (1768); D major, K.Anh. 215; 66c (1769; not extant); B-flat major, K.Anh. 217; 66d (1769; not extant); B-flat major, K.Anh. 218; 66e (1769; not extant); No. 9 in C major, K.73 (1772); No. 44 in D major, K.81; 731 (1770; may be by Leopold Mozart); No. 47 in D major, K.97; 73m (1770); No. 45 in D major, K.95; 73n (1770); No. 11 in D major, K.84; 73q (1770; may not be by Mozart); No. 10 in G major, K.74 (1770); No. 42 in F major, K.75 (1771); No. 12 in G major, K.110; 75b (1771); D major, K.120; 111a (1771; finale only; perf. with the overture to *Ascanio in Alba,* K.111, forming a sym.); No. 46 in C major, K.96; 111b (1771); No. 13 in F major, K.112 (1771); No. 14 in A major, K.114 (1771); No. 15 in G major, K.124 (1772); No. 16 in C major, K.128 (1772); No. 17 in G major, K.129 (1772); No. 18 in F major, K.130 (1772); No. 19 in E-flat major, K.132 (1772; with alternative slow movements); No. 20 in D major, K.133 (1772); No. 21 in A major, K.134 (1772); No. 50 in D major, K.161, 163; 141a (1772); No. 26 in E-flat major, K.184; 161a (1773); No. 27 in G major, K.199; 161b (1773); No. 22 in C major, K.162 (1773); No. 23 in D major, K.181; 162b (1773); No. 24 in B-flat major, K.182; 173dA (1773); No. 25 in G minor, K.183; 173dB (1773); No. 29 in A major, K.201; 186a (1774); No. 30 in D major, K.202; 186b (1774); No. 28 in C major, K.200; 189k (1774); D major K.121; 207a (1774–75; finale only; perf. with the overture to *La finta giardiniera,* K.196, forming a sym.); D major (4 movements from the Serenade in D major, K.204; 213a); C major, K.102; 213c (1775; finale only; perf. with versions of the overture and 1st aria from *Il Rè pastore*, K.208); D major (4 movements from the Serenade in D major, K.250; 248b); No. 31 in D major, K.297; 300a, "Paris" (1778: with 2 slow movements); No. 32 in G major, K.318 (1779; in 1 movement); No. 33 in B-flat major, K.319 (1779); D major (3 movements from the Serenade in D major, K.320, "Posthorn"); No. 34 in C major, K.338 (1780); C major, K.409; 383f (1782; minuet only; may have been intended for the Sym. No. 34 in C major, K.338); No. 35 in D major, K.385, "Haffner" (1782); No. 36 in C major, K.425, "Linz" (1783); No. 37 in G major, K.444; 425a (1783?; only the introduction is by Mozart; remainder by Michael Haydn); No. 38 in D major, K.504, "Prague" (1786); No. 39 in E-flat major, K.543 (1788); No. 40 in G minor, K.550 (1788); No. 41 in C major, K.551, "Jupiter" (1788). A sym. listed as K.Anh. 8; 311A was never composed. **P i a n o   C o n c e r t o s :** No. 5 in D major, K.175 (1773); No. 6 in B- flat major, K.238 (1776); No. 8 in C major, K.246 (1776); No. 9 in E-flat major, K.271 (1777); No. 12 in A major, K.414; 385p (1782); No. 11 in F major, K.413; 387a (1782–83); No. 13 in C major, K.415; 387b (1782–83); No. 14 in E-flat major, K.449 (1784); No. 15 in B-flat major, K.450 (1784); No. 16 in D major, K.451 (1784); No. 17 in G major, K.453 (1784); No. 18 in B-flat major, K.456 (1784); No. 19 in F major, K.459 (1784); No. 20 in D minor, K.466 (1785); No. 21 in C major, K.467 (1785); No. 22 in E-flat major, K.482 (1785); No. 23 in A major, K.488 (1786); No. 24 in C minor, K.491 (1786); No. 25 in C major, K.503 (1786); No. 26 in D major, K.537, "Coronation" (1788); No. 27 in B- flat major, K.595 (1788?-91). Also No. 10 in E-flat major, for 2 Pianos, K.365; 316a (1779); No. 7 in F major, for 3 Pianos, K.242 (1776); Rondo in D major, K.382 (1782; new finale for No. 5 in D major, K.175); Rondo in A major, K.386 (1782). **V i o l i n   C o n c e r t o s :** No. 1 in B-flat major, K.207 (1773?); No. 2 in D major, K.211 (1775); No. 3 in G major, K.216 (1775); No. 4 in D major, K.218 (1775); No. 5 in A major, K.219 (1775). Also the following: Concertone in C major for 2 Violins, K.90; 186e (1774); Adagio in E major for Violin, K.261 (1776; for Violin Concerto No. 5); Rondo in B-flat major for Violin, K.269; 261a (1776); Sinfonia concertante in E-flat major for Violin and Viola, K.364; 320d (1779); Rondo in C major for Violin, K.373 (1781); Andante in A major for Violin, K.470 (1785; not extant). **W i n d   I n s t r u m e n t s :** Concerto for Trumpet, K.47c (1768; not extant); Concerto for Bassoon in B-flat major, K.191; 186e (1774); Concerto for Oboe, K.271k (1777; not extant; perhaps a version of K.314; 285d below); Concerto for Flute in G major, K.313; 285c (1778); Concerto for Oboe or Flute in C/D major, K.314; 285d (1778; oboe version may be for K.271k above); Andante for Flute in C major, K.315; 285e (1779–80); Sinfonia concertante for Flute, Oboe, Bassoon, and Horn, K.Anh. 9; 297B (1778?; not extant; may not have been composed); Sinfonia concertante in E-flat major for Oboe, Clarinet, Bassoon, and Horn, K.Anh. 9; C 14.01 (doubtful); Concerto for Flute and Harp in C major, K.299; 297c (1778); Sinfonia concertante in G major for 2 Flutes, 2 Oboes, and 2 Bassoons, K.320 (movements 3 and 4 of the Serenade in D major, K.320, "Posthorn"); Rondo for Horn in E-flat major, K.371 (1781; unfinished); concertos for Horn: No. 1 (old No. 2) in E-flat major, K.417 (1783); No. 2 (old No. 4) in E-flat major, K.495 (1786); No. 3 in E-flat major, K.447 (1783?); No. 4 (old No.1) in D major, K.412; 386b (1791; unfinished finale completed by Sussmayr, 1792); Concerto for Clarinet in A major, K.622 (1791). **S e r e n a d e s ,   D i v e r t i m e n t o s ,   C a s s a t i o n s ,   E t c . :** *Gallimathias musicum*, K.32 (1766); 6 divertimentos, K.41a (1767; not extant); Cassation in D major, K.100; 62a (1769); Cassation in G major, K.63 (1769); Cassation

in C major (1769; not extant); Cassation in B-flat major, K.99; 63a (1769); Divertimento in E-flat major, K.113 (1771); Divertimento in D major, K.131 (1772); Divertimento in D major, K.136; 125a (1772); Divertimento in B-flat major, K.137; 125b (1772); Divertimento in F Major, K.138; 125c (1772); Divertimento in D major, K.205; 167a (1773?); Serenade in D major, K.185; 167a (1773); Serenade in D major, K.203; 189b (1774); Serenade in D major, K.204; 213a (1775); *Serenata notturna* in D major, K.239 (1776); Divertimento in F major, K.247 (1776); Serenade in D major, K.250; 248b, "Haffner" (1776); Divertimento in D major, K.251 (1776); Notturno in D major, K.286; 269a (1776–77); Divertimento in B-flat major, K.287; 271h (1777); Serenade in D major, K.320, "Posthorn" (1779); Divertimento in D major, K.334; 320b (1779–80); Serenade in B-flat major, K.361; 370a (1781–82?); Serenade in E-flat major, K.375 (1781–82); Serenade in C minor, K.388; 384a (1782); *Maurerische Trauermusik* in C minor, K.477; 479a (1785); *Ein musikalischer Spass* in F major, K.522 (1787); *Eine kleine Nachtmusik* in G major, K.525 (1787). Also 14 divertimentos for Wind Ensemble; 15 marches (2 not extant); 56 German dances, ländler, and 58 Contredanses (10 not extant, 9 doubtful); ballet, *Les Petits Riens*, K.Anh. 10; 299b (1778; Opéra, Paris, June 11, 1778); etc. **CHAMBER: S t r i n g   Q u a r t e t s :** G major, K.80; 73f (1770); D major, K.155; 134a (1772); G major, K.156; 134b (1772); C major, K.157 (1772–73); F major, K.158 (1772–73); B-flat major, K.159 (1773); E-flat major, K.160; 159a (1773); F major, K.168 (1773); A major, K.169 (1773); C major, K.170 (1773); E- flat major, K.171 (1773); B-flat major, K.172 (1773); D minor, K.173 (1773); G major, K.387 (1782); D minor, K.421; 417b (1783); E-flat major, K.428; 421b (1783); B-flat major, K.458, "Hunt" (1784); A major, K.464 (1785); C major, K.465, "Dissonance" (1785); D major, K.499, "Hoffmeister" (1786); D major, K.575, "Prussian" (1789); B-flat major, K.589, "Prussian" (1790); F major, K.590, "Prussian"(1790); Adagio and Fugue in C minor, K.546 (1788). **S t r i n g   Q u i n t e t s** (2 Violins, 2 Violas, and Cello): B-flat major, K.174 (1773); C major, K.515 (1787); G minor, K.516 (1787); C minor, K.406; 516b (1788; an arrangement of K.388; 384a); D major, K.593 (1790); E-flat major, K.614 (1791). **S t r i n g s   a n d   W i n d   I n s t r u - m e n t s :** Duo in B-flat major for Bassoon and Cello, K.292; 196c (1775); Quartet in D major for Flute, Violin, Viola, and Cello, K.285 (1777); Quartet in G major for Flute, Violin, Viola, and Cello, K.285a (1778); Quartet in C major for Flute, Violin, Viola, and Cello, K.Anh. 171; 285b (1781–82); Quartet in A major for Flute, Violin, Viola, and Cello, K.298 (1786–87); Quartet in F major for Oboe, Violin, Viola, and Cello, K.370; 368b (1781); Quintet in E-flat major for Horn, Violin, 2 Violas, and Cello, K.407; 386c (1782); Quintet in A major for Clarinet, 2 Violins, Viola, and Cello, K.581 (1789). **S t r i n g   S o n a - t a s ,   D u o s ,   a n d   T r i o s :** Solos for Cello and Bassoon, K.33b (1766; not extant); *Nachtmusik* for 2 Violins and Bassoon, K.41g (1767; not extant); Sonata in C major for Violin and Bassoon, K.46d (1768); Sonata in F major for Violin and Bassoon, K.46e (1768); Trio in B- flat major for 2 Violins and Bassoon, K.266; 271f (1777); 4 preludes for Violin, Viola, and Cello, K.404a (1782; may not be by Mozart); Duo in G major for Violin and Viola, K.423 (1783); Duo in B-flat major for Violin and Viola, K.424 (1783); Trio in E-flat major for Violin, Viola, and Cello, K.563 (1788). **KEYBOARD AND OTHER IN- STRUMENTS:** Divertimento in B-flat major for Piano, Violin, and Cello, K.254 (1776); Trio in D minor for Piano, Violin, and Cello, K.442 (1783?-90; unfinished; completed by M. Stadler); Quintet in E-flat major for Piano, Oboe, Clarinet, Bassoon, and Horn, K.452 (1784); Quartet in G minor for Piano, Violin, Viola, and Cello, K.478 (1785); Quartet in E-flat major for Piano,

Violin, Viola, and Cello, K.493 (1786); Trio in G major for Piano, Violin, and Cello, K.496 (1786); Trio in E-flat major for Piano, Clarinet, and Viola, K.498 (1786); Trio in B-flat major for Piano, Violin, and Cello, K.502 (1786); Trio in E major for Piano, Violin, and Cello, K.542 (1788); Trio in C major for Piano, Violin, and Cello, K.548 (1788); Trio in G major for Piano, Violin, and Cello, K.564 (1788); Adagio and Rondo in C minor for Glass Harmonica, Flute, Oboe, Viola, and Cello, K.617 (1791). **K e y - b o a r d   a n d   V i o l i n   S o n a t a s :** C major, K.6 (1762–64); D major, K.7 (1762–64); B-flat major, K.8 (1763–64); G major, K.9 (1763–64); B-flat major, K.10 (1764); G major, K.11 (1764); A major, K.12 (1764); F major, K.13 (1764); C major, K.14 (1764); B-flat major, K.15 (1764); E-flat major, K.26 (1766); G major, K.27 (1766); C major, K.28 (1766); D major, K.29 (1766); F major, K.30 (1766); B-flat major, K.31 (1766); G major, K.301; 293a (1778); E-flat major, K.302; 293b (1778); C major, K.303; 293c (1778); A major, K.305; 293d (1778); C major, K.296 (1778); E minor, K.304; 300c (1778); D major, K.306; 300l (1778); B-flat major, K.378; 317d (1779?); B-flat major, K.372 (1781; unfinished; completed by M. Stadler; G major, K.379; 373a (1781); F major, K.376; 374d (1781); F major, K.377; 374e (1781); E-flat major, K.380; 374f (1781); C major, K.403; 385c (1782; unfinished; completed by M. Stadler); C major, K.404; 385d (1782?; unfinished); A major, K.402; 385e (1782; unfinished; completed by M. Stadler); C minor, K.396; 385f (1782; 1 movement only; completed by M. Stadler); B-flat major, K.454 (1784); E-flat major, K.481 (1785); A major, K.526 (1787); F major, K.547, "für Anfänger" (1788); Variations in G major, K.359; 374a (1781); Variations in G minor, K.360; 374b (1781). **S o n a t a s   F o r   K e y b o a r d   S o l o :** G major, K.Anh. 199; 33d (1766; not extant); B-flat major, K.Anh. 200; 33e (1766; not extant); C major, K.201; 33f (1766; not extant); F major, K.202; 33g (1766; not extant); C major, K.279; 189d (1775); F major, K.280; 189e (1775); B-flat major, K.281; 189f (1775); E-flat major, K.282; 189g (1775); G major, K.283; 189h (1775); D major, K.284; 205b (1775); C major, K.309; 284b (1777); D major, K.311; 284c (1777); A minor, K.310; 300d (1778); C major, K.330; 300h (1781–83); A major, K.331; 300i (1781–83); F major, K.332; 300k (1781–83); B-flat major, K.333; 315c (1783–84); C minor, K.457 (1784); F major, K.533 (1786); C major, K.545, "für Anfänger" (1788); F major, K.Anh. 135; 547a (1788; may not be by Mozart); B-flat major, K.570 (1789); D major, K.576 (1789). **V a r i a t i o n s   F o r   K e y b o a r d   S o l o :** Dutch song by C.E. Graaf, K.24 (1766); *Willem van Nassau*, Dutch national song, K.25 (1766); *Mio caro Adone* from Salieri's *La fiera di Venezia*, K.180; 173c (1773); Minuet from the finale of J.C. Fischer's Oboe Concerto No. 1, K.179; 189a (1774); *Je suis Lindor* from A.L. Baudron's *Le barbier de Séville*, K.354; 299a (1778); *Ah vous diri-je, maman*, French song, K.265; 300e (1781–82); *La belle françoise*, French song, K.353; 300f (1781–82); *Lison dormait* from N. Dezède's *Julie*, K.264; 315d (1778); *Dieu d'amour* from Grétry's *Les mariages samnites*, K.352; 374c (1781); *Salve tu, Domine* from Paisiello's *I filosofi immaginarii*, K.398; 416e (1783); *Come un agnello* from Sarti's *Fra i due litiganti*, K.460; 454a (1784); *Les hommes pieusement* from Gluck's *La rencontre imprévue*, K.455 (1784); K.500 (1786); K.54; 547b (1788); Minuet from J.P. Duport's Cello Sonata, Op.4, No.6, K.573 (1789); *Ein Weib ist das herrlichste Ding* by B. Schack or F. Gerl, K.613 (1791). **K e y b o a r d   D u o :** K.501 (1786). **K e y b o a r d   D u e t :** Sonata in C major, K.19d (1765); Sonata in D major, K.381; 123a (1772); Sonata in B-flat major, K.358; 186c (1773–74); Sonata in F major, K.497 (1786); Sonata in C major, K.521 (1787). Also: Sonata in D major for 2 Keyboards, K.448; 375a (1781); many miscellaneous pieces; 17 sonatas for Organ, most with 2 Violins and Bassoon; etc.

Since the publication of the Breitkopf & Härtel ed. of Mozart's works, the list of doubtful and spurious compositions has grown extensively. The pioneering research of Wyzewa and Saint-Foix has been followed by the important studies of Plath, Tyson, and other scholars. For detailed information, see the bibliography below. A selected compilation of doubtful and spurious works follows (those noted in the list of works above are excluded): **M a s s e s :** F major, K.116; 90a, by Leopold Mozart; E-flat major, K.Anh. 235f; C 1.02, by B. Schack; G major, K.Anh. 232; C 1.04, "12th Mass"; G major, K.deest; C 1.18, "Missa solemnis pastorita"; D minor, K.Anh. 237; C 1.90, "Requiem brevis"; Kyrie in C major, K.340; C 3.06; Kyrie in C major, K.221; A1, by Eberlin. Also: *Lacrimosa* in C minor, K.Anh. 21; A2, by Eberlin; *Justum deduxit Dominus*, hymn, K.326; A4, by Eberlin; *Adoramus te*, hymn, K.327; A10, by Q. Gasparini; *De profundis clamavi*, Psalm, K.93; A22, by Reutter; *Salve Regina*, K.92; C 3.01; *Tantum ergo* in B-flat major, K.142; C 3.04; *Offertorium sub exposito venerabili*, K.177 and 342; C 3.09, by Leopold Mozart. **S y m s .:** No. 2, in B-flat major, K.17; C 11.02; B-flat major, K.Anh. 216; C 11.03; No. 3, in E-flat major, K.18; A51, by C.F. Abel; G major, "New Lambach" (1768; by L. Mozart); F major, K.98; C 11.04; B-flat major, K.311a; C 11.05, the "2nd Paris" Sym. Also: Fugue in D major, K.291; A52, by M. Haydn, finished by S. Sechter. **P i a n o   C o n c e r t o s :** The 1st 4 piano concertos, K.37, 39, 40, and 41, are arrangements of sonata movements by Raupach, Honauer, Schobert, Eckard, and C.P.E. Bach; the Piano Concerto, K.107, consists of arrangements of 3 sonatas by Johann Christian Bach. **V i o l i n   C o n c e r - t o s :** Two violin concertos, 1 in D major, K.271a; 271i, the other in E-flat major, K.268; C 14.04, may contain some music composed by Mozart. The Violin Concerto in D major, K.Anh. 294a; C 14.05, the "Adelaide" Concerto, which was widely performed after its alleged discovery in 1931, was actually composed by the French violinist Marius Casadesus; it was supposedly dedicated to Princess Adelaide, the daughter of Louis XV, by the boy Mozart during his visit to Paris at the age of 10. Also: *Sinfonia concertante* in A major for Violin, Viola, and Cello, K.Anh. 104; 320e. **S o n a t a s   F o r   K e y b o a r d   a n d   V i o l i n :** K.55–60; C23.01–6 and K.61, by Raupach.

BIBL.: COLLECTED EDITIONS, SOURCE MATE-RIAL: The first collected edition of Mozart's works was ed. by L. von Köchel et al. as *W.A. M.s Werke*; it was publ. by Breitkopf & Härtel (74 vols. in 24 series, Leipzig, 1877–83; 11 supplementary vols., Leipzig, 1877–1910). A new critical edition, *W.A. M.: Neue Ausgabe Sämtlicher Werke*, ed. by E. Schmid et al., began publishing in Kassel in 1955; it is sponsored by the Internationale Stiftung Mozarteum Salzburg. The standard thematic catalog is L. von Köchel, ed., *Chronologisch-thematisches Verzeichnis sämtlicher Tonwerke W. Amade M.s* (Leipzig, 1862; 3rd ed., extensively rev. by A. Einstein, Leipzig, 1937; reprint, with supp., Ann Arbor, 1947; 6th ed., a major revision, by F. Giegling, A. Weinmann, and G. Sievers, Wiesbaden, 1964; the 6th ed. contains a rev. K. numbering system; further supplementary material is found in the *M.-Jahrbuch 1971–2*, as prepared by P. van Reijen). See also the following: Mozart's own *Verzeichnüss aller meiner Werke* (facsimile ed. by O. Deutsch as *W.A. M.: Verzeichnis aller meiner Werke: Faksimile der Handschrift mit dem Beiheft "M.s Werkverzeichnis 1784–1791,"* Vienna, 1938; Eng. ed., 1956; also another ed. by E. Müller von Asow as *W.A. M.: Verzeichnis aller meiner Werke und Leopold M.: Verzeichnis der Jugendwerke W.A. M.s*, Vienna, 1943; 2nd ed., 1956); A. André, *Thematischer Katalog wie M. solchen von 1784–91 eigenhändig geschrieben hat* (Offenbach, 1805; 2nd ed., aug., 1828); K. Moyses, *Systematischer Katalog der im M.eum befindlichen Autographe M.s*

(Salzburg, 1862); C. von Wurzbach, *M.-Buch* (Vienna, 1869); J. Horner, *Katalog des M.s-Museums zu Salzburg* (Salzburg, 1882; 2nd ed. by J. Engl, 1898); H. de Curzon, *Essai de bibliographie mozartienne: Revue critique des ouvrages relatifs à W.A. M. et ses oeuvres* (Paris, 1906); L. Schiedermair, *W.A. M.s Handschrift in zeitlich geordneten Nachbildungen* (Bückeburg and Leipzig, 1919); M. Blaschitz, *Die Salzburger M.-Fragmente* (diss., Univ. of Bonn, 1924); O. Keller, *W.A. M.: Bibliographie und Ikonographie* (Berlin, 1927); H. Farmer and H. Smith, *New M.iana: The M. Relics in the Zavertal Collection at the University of Glasgow* (Glasgow, 1935); A. Hyatt King, *M. in the British Museum* (London, 1956); O. Schneider and A. Algatzy, *M.-Handbuch: Chronik, Werk, Bibliographie* (Vienna, 1962); R. Angermüller and O. Schneider, *M.-Bibliographie 1971–1975 mit Nachträgen bis 1970* (Kassel, 1978); A. Hyatt King, *A M. Legacy: Aspects of the British Library Collections* (London, 1984); G. Haberkamp, *Die Erstdrucke der Werke von W.A. M.: Bibliographie* (Tutzing, 1986); R. Angermüller and O. Schneider, *M.- Bibliographie, 1981–1985: Mit Nachträgen zur M.-Bibliographie bis 1980* (Kassel and N.Y., 1987); B. Hastings, *W.A. M.: A Guide to Research* (N.Y., 1989); A. Rosenthal and A. Tyson, *M's Thematic Catalogue (British Library, Stefan Zweig MS 63: A Facsimile)* (London, 1990); F. Ziegler, *W.A. M.: Autographenverzeichnis* (Berlin, 1990); C. Eisen, ed., *M. Studies* (Oxford, 1991); idem, ed., *New M. Documents: A Supplement to O.E. Deutsch's Documentary Biography* (Stanford, 1991; rev. Ger. ed., Kassel, 1997, as *Addenda zu M.: Die Dokumente seines Lebens, Neue Folge*); W. Hildesheimer, *M.: Bibliographie* (Frankfurt am Main, 1991); R. Marshall, ed., *M. Speaks: Views on Music, Musicians, and the World: Drawn from the Letters of W.A. M. and Other Early Accounts* (N.Y., 1991); N. Zaslaw and F. Fein, eds., *The M. Repertory: A Guide for Musicians, Programmers, and Researchers* (Ithaca, N.Y., 1991); U. Konrad, *M.s Schaffensweise: Studien zu den Werkautographen, Skizzen und Entwürfen* (Göttingen, 1992); J. Morris, ed., *On M.* (Washington, D.C., 1994); C. Eisen, ed., *M. Studies 2* (Oxford, 1997); W. Pieck, *Die M.s: Porträt einer Familie* (Hamburg, 1998). **YEARBOOKS AND OTHER PUBLICATIONS:** *Jahresbericht des M.eums* (Salzburg, 1880–1917); *Mitteilungen für die M.gemeinde in Berlin* (Berlin, 1895–1925); *M.eums-Mitteilungen* (Salzburg, 1918–21); *M.-Jahrbuch* (3 vols., Munich, 1923, 1924, and 1929); *Wiener Figaro* (issued by the M.gemeinde of Vienna, 1931); *Neues M.-Jahrbuch* (3 vols., Regensburg, 1941–43); *M.-Jahrbuch* (Salzburg, 1950); *Mitteilungen der Internationalen Stiftung M.eum* (Salzburg, 1952); *Acta M.iana* (issued by the Deutschen M.-Gesellschaft of Augsburg, 1954). **CORRESPONDENCE:** L. Nohl, *M.s Briefe nach den Originalen herausgegeben* (Salzburg, 1865; Eng. tr. by Lady Wallace, London, 1866; 2nd Ger. ed., aug., Leipzig, 1877); H. de Curzon, *Nouvelles lettres des dernières années de la vie de M.* (Paris, 1898); K. Storck, *M.s Briefe in Auswahl* (Stuttgart, 1906); A. Leitzmann, *M.s Briefe ausgewählt* (Leipzig, 1910); M. Weigel, *M.s Briefe* (Berlin, 1910); H. Leichtentritt, *M.s Briefe* (Berlin, 1912); L. Schiedermair, *Die Briefe W.A. M.s und seiner Familie: Erste kritische Gesamtausgabe* (5 vols., Munich and Leipzig, 1914); E. Anderson, ed. and tr., *Letters of M. and His Family* (3 vols., London and N.Y., 1938; 2nd ed., rev. by A. Hyatt King and M. Carolan, 1966; 3rd ed., rev. by S. Sadie and F. Smart, 1985); E. Müller von Asow, ed., *Gesamtausgabe der Briefe und Aufzeichnungen der Familie M.* (5 vols., Berlin, 1942); W. Bauer, O. Deutsch, and J. Eibl, eds., *M.: Briefe und Aufzeichnungen* (7 vols., Kassel, 1962–75). **BIOGRAPHICAL:** F. Niemtschek, *Leben des k. k. Kapellmeisters W. Gottlieb M. nach Originalquellen beschrieben* (Prague, 1798; 2nd ed., aug., 1808; facsimile reprint of the latter, 1905; Eng. tr., London, 1956); I. Arnold, *M.s Geist: Seine kurze Biographie und ästhetische Darstellung* (Erfurt, 1803); idem, *Galerie*

der berühmtesten Tonkünstler des 18. und 19. Jahrhunderts...W.A. M. und Joseph Haydn: Versuch einer Parallele (Erfurt, 1810; 2nd ed., 1816); Stendhal, *Lettres...sur le célèbre compositeur Haydn: Suivies d'une vie de M. et considérations sur Métastase* (Paris, 1814; 2nd ed., rev., as *Vies de Haydn, de M. et de Métastase*; Eng. tr., 1972); P. Lichtenthal, *Cenni biografici intorno al celebre maestro W.A. M.* (Milan, 1816); G. von Nissen, *Biographie W.A. M.s nach Originalbriefen* (Leipzig, 1828); A. Oulibicheff, *Nouvelle biographie de M., suivie d'un aperçu sur l'histoire générale de la musique* (3 vols., Moscow, 1843; Ger. tr. by L. Gantter, Stuttgart, 1859; Russian tr. by M. Tchaikovsky, Moscow, 1890); E. Holmes, *The Life of M.* (London, 1845; 2nd ed., 1878); O. Jahn, *W.A. M.* (4 vols., Leipzig, 1856–59; 2nd ed., 1867; Eng. tr. by P. Townsend, London, 1882; Ger. revisions by H. Deiters, 3rd ed., 1891–93, and 4th ed., 1905–07; exhaustively rewritten and rev. by H. Abert as *W.A. M.: Neu bearbeitete und erweiterte Ausgabe von Otto Jahns "M.,"* 2 vols., Leipzig, 1919–21; further revision by A.A. Abert, 2 vols., Leipzig, 1955–56; L. Nohl, *M.* (Leipzig, 1863; 2nd ed., aug., as *M.s Leben*, 1877; Eng. tr. by Lady Wallace, London, 1877; 3rd Ger. ed., rev. by P. Sakolowski, Berlin, 1906); C. Pohl, *M. und Haydn in London* (Vienna, 1867); L. Nohl, *M. nach den Schilderungen seiner Zeitgenossen* (Leipzig, 1880); G. Nottebohm, *M.iana* (Leipzig, 1880); V. Wilder, *M., L'Homme et l'artiste* (Paris, 1880; 4th ed., 1889; Eng. tr., London, 1908); L. Meinardus, *M.: Ein Künstlerleben* (Leipzig, 1882); F. Gehring, *M.* (London, 1883; 2nd ed., 1911); L. Klasen, *W.A. M.: Sein Leben und seine Werke* (Vienna, 1897); O. Fleischer, *M.* (Berlin, 1899); R. Procházka, *M. in Prag* (Prague, 1899; rev. and aug. ed. by P. Nettl as *M. in Böhmen*, Prague, 1938); E. Breakspeare, *M.* (London, 1902); E. Prout, *M.* (London, 1903); L. Mirow, *M.s letzte Lebensjahre: Eine Künstlertragödie* (Leipzig, 1904); C. Belmonte, *Die Frauen im Leben M.s* (Augsburg, 1905); C. Bellaigue, *M.* (Paris, 1906); F. Lentner, *M.s Leben und Schaffen* (Innsbruck, 1906); H. von der Pfordten, *M.* (Leipzig, 1908); K. Storck, *M.: Sein Leben und Schaffen* (Stuttgart, 1908); W. Flower, *Stray Notes on M. and His Music* (Edinburgh, 1910); L. Schmidt, *W.A. M.* (Berlin, 1912); T. de Wyzewa and G. de Saint- Foix, *W.A. M.: Sa vie musicale et son oeuvre de l'enfance à la pleine maturité* (5 vols., Paris, 1912–46; vols. 3–5 by Saint- Foix alone); A. Schurig, *W.A. M.: Sein Leben und sein Werk* (2 vols., Leipzig, 1913; 2nd ed., 1923; Fr. tr., 1925); H. de Curzon, *M.* (Paris, 1914; 2nd ed., 1927); E. Engel, *W.A. M.* (Vienna, 1914); J. Kreitmeier, *W.A. M.: Eine Charakterzeichnung des grossen Meisters nach literarischen Quellen* (Düsseldorf, 1919); L. Schiedermair, *M.: Sein Leben und seine Werke* (Munich, 1922; 2nd ed., rev., 1948); E. Blümml, *Aus M.s Freundes und Familien Kreis* (Vienna, 1923); O. Keller, *W.A. M.* (Berlin, 1926); B. Paumgartner, *M.* (Berlin, 1927; 10th ed., 1993); D. Hussey, *W.A. M.* (London, 1928; 2nd ed., 1933); M. Morold, *M.* (Vienna, 1931); R. Tenschert, *M.* (Leipzig, 1931); M. Davenport, *M.* (N.Y., 1932); H. Ghéon, *Promenades avec M.* (Paris, 1932; 7th ed., 1948; Eng. tr., 1934, as *In Search of M.*); S. Sitwell, *M.* (N.Y., 1932); R. Haas, *W.A. M.* (Potsdam, 1933; 2nd ed., 1950); E. Schmid, *W.A. M.* (Lübeck, 1934; 3rd ed., 1955); J. Talbot, *M.* (London, 1934); E. Blom, *M.* (London, 1935; 3rd ed., rev. by J. Westrup, 1975); A. Boschot, *M.* (Paris, 1935; 2nd ed., 1949); C. Perriolat, *M.: Révélateur de la beauté artistique* (Paris, 1935); A. Kolb, *M.* (Vienna, 1937); W. Turner, *M.: The Man and His Works* (London and N.Y., 1938; 3rd ed., 1966); I. Gyomai, *Le Coeur de M.* (Paris, 1939); W. Goetz, *M.: Sein Leben in Selbstzeugnissen, Briefen und Berichten* (Berlin, 1941); E. Komorzynski, *M.* (Berlin, 1941; Vienna, 1955); G. Schaeffner, *W.A. M.* (Bern, 1941); A. Albertini, *M.: La vita, le opere* (Milan, 1942); E. Valentin, *Wege zu M.* (Regensburg, 1942); A. Einstein, *M.: His Character, His Work* (N.Y., 1945; Ger. ed., 1947; 4th ed., 1960); P. Espil, *Les Voyages de Chérubin, ou L'Enfance de M.*

(Bayonne, 1946); M. Mila, *W.A. M.* (Turin, 1946); E. Valentin, *M.* (Hameln, 1947); R. Tenschert, *W.A. M.* (Salzburg, 1951; Eng. tr., London, 1952); M. Kenyon, *M. in Salzburg* (London, 1952); K. Röttger, *W.A. M.* (Stuttgart, 1952); M. Brion, *M.* (Paris, 1955); J. Dalchow, *W.A. M.s Krankheiten, 1756–1763* (Bergisch Gladbach, 1955); N. Medici di Marignano and R. Hughes, *A M. Pilgrimage: Being the Travel Diaries of Vincent and Mary Novello in the Year 1829* (London, 1955); A. Ostoja, *M. e l'Italia* (Bologna, 1955); E. Schenk, *W.A. M.: Eine Biographie* (Vienna and Zürich, 1955; 2nd ed., rev., 1975; Eng. tr. in an abr. ed., 1959, as *M. and His Times*); G. Barblan and A. Della Corte, *M. in Italia* (Milan, 1956); C. Fusero, *M.* (Turin, 1956); F. Hadamowsky and L. Nowak, *M.: Werk und Zeit* (Vienna, 1956); J. Burk, *M. and His Music* (N.Y., 1959); J. and B. Massin, *W.A. M.: Biographie, histoire de l'oeuvre* (Paris, 1959; 2nd ed., 1970); C. Haldane, *M.* (London, 1960); O. Deutsch, *M.: Die Dokumente seines Lebens, gesammelt und erläutert* (Kassel, 1961; Eng. tr., 1965, as *M.: A Documented Biography*; 2nd ed., 1966; supp., 1978); S. Sadie, *M.* (London, 1965); C. Bär, *M.: Krankheit, Tod, Begräbnis* (Kassel, 1966; rev. ed., 1972); A. Hyatt King, *M.: A Biography with a Survey of Books, Editions and Recordings* (London, 1970); M. Levey, *The Life and Death of M.* (London, 1971); H. Schuler, *Die Vorfahren W. M.s* (Essen, 1972); A. Hutchings, *M.: The Man, the Musician* (London and N.Y., 1976); W. Hildesheimer, *M.* (Frankfurt am Main, 1977; Eng. tr., 1979); I. Keys, *M.: His Life in His Music* (St. Albans, 1980); R. Angermüller, *"Auf Ehre und Credit"L: die Finanzen des W.A. M.* (Munich, 1983); J. Féron, *M.: L'Avenir d'un enfant prodige* (Paris, 1983); K. Pahlen, *Das M.-Buch: Chronik von Leben und Werk* (Zürich, 1985); V. Braunbehrens, *M. in Vienna, 1781–1791* (Munich, 1986; Eng. tr., N.Y., 1990); P. Autexier, *M.* (Paris, 1987); J. Hocquard, *M.: L'Amour, la mort* (Paris, 1987); P. Young, *M.* (N.Y., 1987); H.C. Robbins Landon, *1791: M.'s Last Year* (London, 1988); P. Davies, *M. in Person: His Character and Health* (Westport, Conn., 1989); W. Ritter, *Wurde M. ermordet?: Ein Psychographische Studie* (Frankfurt am Main, 1989); H.C. Robbins Landon, *M.: The Golden Years* (N.Y., 1989); V. Braunbehrens and K.-H. Jürgens, *M.: Lebensbilder* (Bergisch Gladbach, 1990); G. Carli Ballola and R. Parenti, *M.* (Milan, 1990); H. Gärtner, *Folget der Heissgeliebten: Frauen um M.* (Munich, 1990); B. Hamann, *Nichts als Musik im Kopf: Das Leben von W.A. M.* (Vienna, 1990); H. Kröplin, *W.A. M., 1756–1791: Eine Chronik* (Wiesbaden, 1990); K. Küster, *M.: Eine musikalische Biographie* (Stuttgart, 1990; Eng. tr., 1996, as *M.: A Musical Biography*); R. Mann, *W.A. M.: Triumph und frühes Ende: Biographie* (Berlin, 1990); H.C. Robbins Landon, ed., *The M. Compendium* (N.Y., 1990); M. Becker, *M.: Sein Leben und seine Zeit in Texten und Bildern* (Frankfurt am Main, 1991); B. Cormican, *M.'s Death—M.'s Requiem: An Investigation* (Belfast, 1991); N. Elias, *M.: Zur Soziologie eines Genies* (Frankfurt am Main, 1991; Eng. tr., 1993, as *M.: Portrait of a Genius*); G. Knepler, *W.A. M.: Annäherungen* (Berlin, 1991; Eng. tr., 1994); D. Leonhart, *M.: Liebe und Geld: Ein Versuch zu seiner Person* (Munich, 1991); M. Publig, *M.: Ein unbeirrbares Leben: Biographie* (Munich, 1991); M. Remus, *M.* (Stuttgart, 1991); H.C. Robbins Landon, *M. and Vienna* (N.Y., 1991); W. Stafford, *The M. Myths: A Critical Reassessment* (Stanford, 1991); J. Hocquard, *M., de l'ombre à la lumière* (Paris, 1993); R. Angermüller, *Delitiae Italiae: M.s Reisen in Italien* (Bad Honnef, 1994); W. Siegmund-Schultze, *W.A. M.: Ideal-Idol-Idee* (Trier, 1994); M. Solomon, *M.: A Life* (N.Y., 1994); N. Wenborn, *M.* (N.Y., 1994); P. Buscaroli, *La morte di M.* (Milan, 1996); D. Nardo, *M.* (San Diego, 1997); A Steptoe, *M.* (N.Y., 1997); W. Weiss, *Auf den Spuren von W.A. M.: Ein biographischer Reiseführer durch Salzburg, Prag und Wien* (Vienna, 1997); R. Halliwell, *The M. Family: Four Lives in a Social Context* (Oxford, 1998); J. Rosselli, *The Life of M.* (Cambridge, 1998); R. Gutman, *M.: A Cultural Biography* (N.Y., 1999). **ICONOGRAPHY**: R. Tenschert, *W.A. M. 1756–1791: Sein Leben in Bildern* (Leipzig, 1935); R. Bory, *La Vie et l'oeuvre de W.-A. M. par l'image* (Geneva, 1948; Eng. tr, 1948, as *The Life and Works of W.A. M. in Pictures*); G. Rech, *W.A. M.: Ein Lebensweg in Bildern* (Munich and Berlin, 1955); R. Petzoldt, *W.A. M.: Sein Leben in Bildern* (Leipzig, 1956); E. Valentin, *M.: Eine Bildbiographie* (Munich, 1959; Eng. tr., 1959); O. Deutsch, *M. und seine Welt in zeitgenössischen Bildern* (Kassel, 1961; in Ger. and Eng.). **MOZART AND FREEMASONRY**: O. Deutsch, *M. und die Wiener Logen: Zur Geschichte seiner Freimaurer-Kompositionen* (Vienna, 1932); P. Nettl, *M. und die königliche Kunst: Die freimaurerische Grundlage der Zauberflöte* (Berlin, 1932; 2nd ed., 1956); P. Nettl, *M. and Masonry* (N.Y., 1957); J. Chailley, *"La Flûte enchantée," opéra maconnique: Essai d'explication du livret et de la musique* (Paris, 1968; Eng. tr., 1971, as *The Magic Flute, Masonic Opera*); K. Thomson, *The Masonic Thread in M.* (London, 1977); H.C. Robbins Landon, *M. and the Masons* (London, 1983); H. Strebel, *Der Freimaurer W.A. M.* (Stäfa, 1991); H. Schuler, *M. und die Freimaurerei: Daten, Fakten, Biographien* (Wilhelmshaven, 1992); E. Nordmann and G. Schulle, *Die freimaurersiche Idee in der Zauberflöte: Ein Spiegelbild antiker Mysterien* (Münster, 1993); H.-J. Irmen, *M.'s Masonry and The Magic Flute* (Zülpich, 1996); G. Wagner, *Bruder M.: Freimaurer im Wien des 18. Jahrhunderts* (Vienna, 1996); P. Autexier, *La lyre maçonne: Haydn, M., Spohr, Liszt* (Paris, 1997). **CRITICAL AND ANALYTICAL: General**: A. Hammerle, *M. und einige Zeitgenossen: Neue Beiträge für Salzburgische Geschichte, Literatur und Musik* (Salzburg, 1877); K. Prieger, *Urtheile bedeutender Dichter, Philosopher und Musiker über M.* (Wiesbaden, 1885–86); E. Komorzynski, *M.s Kunst der Instrumentation* (Stuttgart, 1906); A. Cametti, *M. a Roma* (Rome, 1907); G. Schünemann, ed., *M. als achtjähriger Komponist: Ein Notenbuch Wolfgangs* (Leipzig, 1909; Eng. tr., 1909); W. Nagel, *M. und die Gegenwart* (Langensalza, 1912); A. Leitzmann, *M.s Persönlichkeit* (Leipzig, 1914); R. Lach, *W.A. M. als Theoretiker* (Vienna, 1918); E. Lert, *M. auf dem Theater* (Berlin, 1918; 4th ed., 1922); H. Mersmann, *M.* (Vol. 4 of *Kulturgeschichte der Musik in Einzeldarstellungen*, Berlin, 1925); V. Heinrich, *Komik und Humor bei M.* (Vienna, 1931); W. Lüthy, *M. und die Tonartencharakteristik* (Strasbourg, 1931); C. Thieme, *Der Klangstil des M.orchesters* (Leipzig, 1936); H. Deininger, ed., *Augsburger M.buch: Zeitschrift des historischen Vereins für Schwaben*, LV-LVI (Augsburg, 1942–43); H. Socnik, *Das Pedal bei M.* (Danzig, 1943); M. Mila, *Saggi M.iani* (Milan, 1945); J. Chantavoine, *M. dans M.* (Paris, 1948); E. Schmid, *Ein schwäbisches M.buch* (Stuttgart, 1948); R. Elvers, *Untersuchungen zu den Tempi in M.s Instrumentalmusik* (diss., Univ. of Berlin, 1952); A. Hyatt King, *M. in Retrospect: Studies in Criticism and Bibliography* (London, 1955; 3rd ed., 1970); R. Giazotto, *Annali M.iani* (Milan, 1956); H.C. Robbins Landon and D. Mitchell, eds., *The M. Companion* (N.Y. and London, 1956; 2nd ed., 1965); P. Schaller and H. Kühner, eds., *M.-Aspekte* (Olten and Freiburg, 1956); H. Albrecht, ed., *Die Bedeutung der Zeichen Keil, Strich, und Punkt bei M.* (Kassel, 1957); A. Della Corte, *Tutto il teatro di M.* (Turin, 1957); W. Siegmund-Schultze, *M.s Melodik und Stil* (Leipzig, 1957); G. Massenkeil, *Untersuchungen zum Problem der Symmetrie in der Instrumentalmusik W.A. M.s* (Wiesbaden, 1962); *Neues Augsburger M.buch: Zeitschrift des historischen Vereins für Schwaben*, LXII-LXIII (Augsburg, 1962); P. Lang, ed., *The Creative World of M.* (N.Y., 1963); *M.gemeinde Wien 1913 bis 1963: Forschung und Interpretation* (Vienna, 1964); M. Flothuis, *M.s Bearbeitungen eigener und fremder Werke* (Salzburg, 1969); K. Marx, *Zur Einheit der zyklischen Form bei M.* (Stuttgart, 1971); M. Schmid, *M. und die Salzburger Tradition* (Tutzing, 1976); F. Holbock, *W.A. M.: Der*

Salzburger Domorganist und seine Beziehungen zur katholischen Kirche (Stein am Rhein, 1978); C. Floros, *M. Studien I: Zu M.s Sinfonik, Opern- und Kirchenmusik* (Wiesbaden, 1979); G. Pestelli, *The Age of M. and Beethoven* (Cambridge, 1984); G. Born, *M.s Musiksprache: Schlüssel zu Leben und Werk* (Munich, 1985); G. Gruber, *M. und die Nachwelt* (Salzburg, 1985; Eng. tr., 1994, as *M. and Posterity*); A. Tyson, *M.: Studies of the Autograph Scores* (Cambridge, Mass., 1987); J.-P. Marty, *The Tempo Indications of M.* (New Haven, 1988); J. Hocquard, *M. l'unique* (Paris, 1989); H. Gagelmann, *M. hat nie gelebt—: Eine kritische Bilanz* (Freiburg im Breisgau, 1990); G. Gruber, *M. verstehen: Ein Versuch* (Salzburg, 1990); T. Seedorf, *Studien zur kompositorischen M.-Rezeption im frühen 20. Jahrhundert* (Laaber, 1990); H. Küng, *M.: Spuren der Transzendenz* (Munich, 1991; Eng. tr., 1992, as *M.: Traces of Transcendence*); K. Küster, *Formale Aspekte des ersten Allegros in M.s Konzerten* (Kassel, 1991); C. de Nys, *La musique religieuse de M.* (Paris, 1991); E. Ruggieri, *M., l'itinéraire sentimental* (Paris, 1991); R. Larry Todd and P. Williams, ed., *Perspectives on M. Performance* (Cambridge, 1991); S. Jan, *Aspects of M.'s Music in G Minor: Toward the Identification of Common Structural and Compositional Characteristics* (N.Y., 1995); H.C. Robbins Landon, *The M. Essays* (N.Y., 1995); S. Sadie, ed., *W.A. M.: Essays on His Life and Work* (London, 1995); J. Hocquard, *M. musique de vérité* (Paris, 1996); E. Rohmer, *De M. en Beethoven: Essai sur la notion de profondeur en musique* (Arles, 1996); D. Demuth, *Des idealistische M.- Bild, 1785–1860* (Tutzing, 1997); W. Caplin, *Classical Form: A Theory of Formal Functions for the Instrumental Music of Haydn, M., and Beethoven* (N.Y., 1998); F. Ortega, *Beauté et révélation en M.* (Saint-Maur, 1998); G. Tichy, *M.s unfreiwilliges Vermächtnis: Der Genius musicae aus unbekannten Perspektiven* (Bonn, 1998); F. Degrada, *Illusione e disincanto: M. e altri percorsi settecenteschi* (Florence, 2000) **O p e r a a n d V o c a l M u s i c :** A. Oulibicheff, *M.s Opern: Kritische Erläuterungen* (Leipzig, 1848); W. Pole, *The Story of M.'s Requiem* (London, 1879); C. Gounod, *Le Don Juan de M.* (Paris, 1890; Eng. tr., 1895); A. Farinelli, *Don Giovanni: Note critiche* (Turin, 1896); A. Weltner, *M.s Werke und die Wiener Hoftheater: Statistisches und Historisches* (Vienna, 1896); K. Söhle, *M. Dramatisches Zeitbild* (Leipzig, 1907); E. Dent, *M.'s Operas: A Critical Study* (London, 1913; 2nd ed., 1947); H. Cohen, *Die dramatische Idee in M.s Operntexten* (Berlin, 1916); H. von Waltershausen, *Die Zauberflöte* (Munich, 1920); R. Dumesnil, *Le "Don Juan" de M.* (Paris, 1927; 2nd ed., 1955); O. Beer, *M. und das Wiener Singspiel* (Vienna, 1932); F. Brukner, *Die Zauberflöte: Unbekannte Handschriften und seltene Drucke aus der Frühzeit der Oper* (Vienna, 1934); P. Stefan, *Die Zauberflöte: Herkunft, Bedeutung, Geheimnis* (Vienna, 1937); P. Jouve, *Le Don Juan de M.* (Freiburg im Breisgau, 1942; 3rd ed., Paris, 1948; Eng. tr., London, 1957); L. Conrad, *M.s Dramaturgie der Oper* (Würzburg, 1943); C. Benn, *M. on the Stage* (London, 1946; 2nd ed., 1947); S. Levarie, *M.'s "Le nozze di Figaro": A Critical Analysis* (Chicago, 1952); D. Lauener, *Die Frauengestalten in M.s Opern* (Zürich, 1954); K. Fellerer, *M.s Kirchenmusik* (Salzburg, 1955); A. Greither, *Die sieben grossen Opern M.s: Versuche über das Verhältnis der Texte zur Musik* (Heidelberg, 1956; 2nd ed., enl., 1970); B. Brophy, *M. the Dramatist: A New View of M., His Operas and His Age* (London and N.Y., 1964; new ed., 1988); A. Rosenberg, *Die Zauberflöte: Geschichte und Deutung* (Munich, 1964); R. Moberly, *Three M. Operas: Figaro, Don Giovanni, The Magic Flute* (London, 1967; N.Y., 1968); E. Batley, *A Preface to The Magic Flute* (London, 1969); A. Abert, *Die Opern M.s* (Wolfenbüttel, 1970; Eng. tr. in *The New Oxford History of Music*, vol. VII, London, 1973); H. Eggebrecht, *Versuch über die Wiener Klassik: Die Tanzszene in M.s "Don Giovanni"* (Wiesbaden, 1972); S. Kunze, *Don Giovanni vor M.: Die Tradition der Don Giovanni-Opern im italienischen Buffo-*

Theater des 18. Jahrhunderts (Munich, 1972); W. Mann, *The Operas of M.* (London, 1977); F. Noske, *The Signifier and the Signified: Studies in the Operas of M. and Verdi* (The Hague, 1977); C. Osborne, *The Complete Operas of M.* (London, 1978); C. Gianturco, *M.'s Early Operas* (London, 1982); W. Allanbrook, *Rhythmic Gesture in M.: Le nozze di Figaro and Don Giovanni* (Chicago and London, 1984); S. Kunze, *M.s Opern* (Stuttgart, 1984); K. Fellerer, *Die Kirchenmusik W.A. M.s* (Laaber, 1985); S. Henze- Döhring, *Opera seria, Opera buffa und M.s Don Giovanni: Zur Gattungskonvergenz in der italienischen Oper des 18. Jahrhunderts* (Laaber, 1986); J. Hocquard, *La Clemenza di Tito K. 621* (n.p., 1986); J. Kaiser, *Who's Who in M.'s Operas: From Alfonso to Zerlina* (London, 1986); B. Blomhert, *The Harmoniemusik of "Die Entführung aus dem Serail" by W.A. M.: Study about its Authenticity and Critical Edition* (The Hague, 1987); S. Corse, *Opera and the Uses of Language: M., Verdi, and Britten* (London and Toronto, 1987); J. Kristek, ed., *M.'s Don Giovanni in Prague* (Prague, 1987); T. Bauman, *W.A. M.: Die Entführung aus dem Serail* (Cambridge, 1988); T. Carter, *W.A. M.: Le Nozze di Figaro* (Cambridge, 1988); R. Maunder, *M.'s Requiem: On Preparing a New Edition* (Oxford, 1988); A. Steptoe, *The M.-Da Ponte Operas: The Cultural and Musical Background to Le nozze di Figaro, Don Giovanni, and Così fan tutte* (Oxford, 1988); D. Heartz, *M's Operas* (Berkeley, 1990); P. Branscombe, *W.A. M.: Die Zauberflöte* (Cambridge, 1991); J. Eckelmeyer, *The Cultural Context of M.'s Magic Flute: Social, Aesthetic, Philosophical* (Lewiston, N.Y., 1991); C. Ford, *Così?: Sexual Politics in M.'s Operas* (Manchester, 1991); J. Rice, *W.A. M.: La Clemenza di Tito* (Cambridge, 1991); P. Alcalde, *Strukturierung und Sinn: Die dramatische Funktion der musikalischen Form in Da Pontes and M.s Don Giovanni* (Frankfurt am Main, 1992); N. Till, *M. and the Enlightenment: Truth, Virtue and Beauty in M.'s Operas* (London, 1992); J. Rushton, *W.A. M.: Idomeneo* (Cambridge, 1993); C. Wolff, *M.'s Requiem: Historical and Analytical Studies, Documents, Score* (Berkeley, 1993); B. Brown, *W.A. M.: Così fan tutte* (Cambridge, 1995); J. Hocquard, *Les opéras de M.* (Paris, 1995); P. Adlung, *M.s Opera seria "Mitridate, rè di Ponto"* (Eisenach, 1996); W. Osthoff and R. Wiesend, eds., *M. und die Dramatik des Veneto* (Tutzing, 1996); W. Willaschek, *M. Theater: Vom "Idomeneo" bis zur "Zauberflöte"* (Stuttgart, 1996); G. Splitt, *M.s Musiktheater als Ort der Aufklärung: die Auseinandersetzung des Komponisten mit der oper im josephinischen Wien* (Freiburg im Breisgau, 1998). **O r c h e s t r a l :** D. Schultz, *M.s Jugendsinfonien* (Leipzig, 1900); A. Dickinson, *A Study of M.'s Last Three Symphonies* (London, 1927; 2nd ed., 1940); G. de Saint-Foix, *Les Sinfonies de M.* (Paris, 1932; Eng. tr., 1947); C. Girdlestone, *W.A. M. et ses concertos pour piano* (2 vols., Paris, 1939; 3rd ed., 1978; Eng. tr., 1948); A. Hutchings, *A Companion to M.'s Piano Concertos* (London, 1948; 2nd ed., 1950); G. Hausswald, *M.s Serenaden: Ein Beitrag zur Stilkritik des 18. Jahrhunderts* (Leipzig, 1951; 2nd ed., rev., 1975); J. David, *Die Jupiter-Sinfonie: Eine Studie über die thematisch-melodischen Zusammenhänge* (Göttingen, 1953); H. Tischler, *A Structural Analysis of M.'s Piano Concertos* (N.Y., 1966); D. Forman, *M.'s Concerto Form: The First Movements of the Piano Concertos* (London, 1971); A. Hyatt King, *M. Wind and String Concertos* (London, 1978); R. Dearling, *The Music of W.A. M.: The Symphonies* (Rutherford, N.J., 1982); E. Smith, *M. Serenades, Divertimenti and Dances* (London, 1982); L. Ferguson, *"Col Basso" and "Generalbass" in M.'s Keyboard Concertos: Notation, Performance, Theory, and Practice* (diss., Princeton Univ., 1983); C. Eisen, *The Symphonies of Leopold M. and Their Relationship to the Early Symphonies of W.A. M.: A Bibliographical and Stylistic Study* (diss., Cornell Univ., 1986); S. Sadie, *M. Symphonies* (London, 1986); J. Larsen and K. Wedin, eds., *Die Sinfonie KV 16a "del Sigr. M.": Bericht über das Symposium in Odense anlässlich der Erstauf-*

führung des wiedergefundenen Werkes Dezember 1984 (Odense, 1987); R. Levin, *Who Wrote the M. Four-Wind Concertante?* (Stuyvesant, N.Y., 1989); N. Zaslaw, *M.'s Symphonies: Context, Performance Practice, Reception* (Oxford, 1990); E. Sisman, *M.: The "Jupiter" Symphony* (Cambridge, 1993); J. Brügge, *Zum Personalstil W.A. M.s: Untersuchungen zu Modell und Typus am Beispiel der "Kleinen Nachtmusik," KV 525* (Wilhelmshaven, 1996); C. Lawson, *M.: Clarinet Concerto* (Cambridge, 1996); P. Gülke, *Im Zyklus eine Welt: M.s letzte Sinfonien* (Munich, 1997). **C h a m b e r   M u s i c :** T. Dunhill, *M.'s String Quartets* (London, 1927; 2nd ed., 1948); A. Hyatt King, *M. Chamber Music* (London, 1968); W. Hummeke, *Versuch einer strukturwissenschaftlichen Darstellung der ersten und vierten Sätze der zehn letzten Streichquartette von W.A. M.* (Münster, 1970); I. Hunkemöller, *W.A. M.s frühe Sonaten für Violine und Klavier* (Bern and Munich, 1970); C. Wolff, ed., *The String Quartets of Haydn, M., and Beethoven: Studies of the Autograph Manuscripts* (Cambridge, Mass., 1980); M. Flothuis, *W.A. M.: Streichquintett G-moll, KV 516* (Munich, 1987); J. Stuber, *M.s Haydn- Quartette: Intonationsanalyse* (Bonn, 1990); W.-D. Seiffert, *M.s frühe Streichquartett* (Munich, 1992); M. Heinzel, *Die Violinsonaten W.A. M.s* (Karlsruhe, 1996); J. Irving, *M.: The "Haydn" Quartets* (Cambridge, 1998). **K e y b o a r d :** F. Lorenz, *W.A. M. als Clavier-Componist* (Breslau, 1866); F. Marks, *Questions on M.'s Pianoforte-sonatas* (London, 1929); H. Dennerlein, *Der unbekannte M.: Die Welt seiner Klavierwerke* (Leipzig, 1951); P. and E. Badura-Skoda, *M.- Interpretation, Anregungen zur Interpretation der Klavierwerke* (Vienna and Stuttgart, 1957; rev. ed. in Eng., 1962, as *Interpreting M. on the Keyboard*); R. Rosenberg, *Die Klaviersonaten M.s: Gestalt- und Stilanalyse* (Hofheim, Hesse, 1972); E. McKay, *The Impact of the New Pianofortes on Classical Keyboard Style: M., Beethoven and Schubert* (West Hagley, West Midlands, 1987); R. Forster, *Die Kopfsätze der Klavierkonzerte M.s und Beethovens: Gesamtaufbau, Solokadenz und Schlussbildung* (Munich, 1992); M. Mercado, *The Evolution of M.'s Pianistic Style* (Carbondale, Ill., 1992); M. Brück, *Die langsamen Sätze in M.s Klavierkonzerten: Untersuchungen zur Form und zum musikalischen Satz* (Munich, 1994); S. Rampe, *M.s Claviermusik: Klangwelt und Aufführungspraxis: Ein Handbuch* (Kassel, 1995); N. Zaslaw, ed., *M.'s Piano Concertos: Text, Context, Interpretation* (Ann Arbor, 1996); J. Irving, *M.'s Piano Sonatas: Contexts, Sources, Style* (Cambridge, 1997). **MISCELLA-NEOUS:** C. Roleff, ed., *M.iana* (Tutzing, 1988); G. Snell, ed., *Viva M.: An Anthology of Appreciation* (San Jose, Calif., 1989); R. Angermüller, *Das Salzburger M.-Denkmal: Eine Dokumentation (bis 1845) zur 150-Jahre-Enthüllungsfeier* (Salzburg, 1992); H. Schützeichel, ed., *M.s Kirchenmusik* (Freiburg im Breisgau, 1992); G. Sauder, ed., *M.s Ansichten* (St. Ingbert, 1995). —**NS/LK/DM**

Mraczek (actually, **Mraček**), **Joseph Gustav,** Czech composer, violinist, conductor, and teacher; b. Brünn, March 12, 1878; d. Dresden, Dec. 24, 1944. He received his first instruction from his father, the cellist Franz (František) Mraček (1842–98), then was a chorister in various churches in Brünn before going to Vienna, where he studied with Hellmesberger, Stocker, and Lowe at the Cons. From 1897 to 1902 he was concertmaster at the Stadttheater in Brünn; then taught violin at the Cons. there (1898–1919). He settled in Dresden and conducted the Phil. (1919–24) and taught composition at the Cons. (from 1919).

WORKS: DRAMATIC: O p e r a : *Der gläserne Pantoffel* (Brünn, 1902); *Der Traum* (Brünn, Feb. 26, 1909); *Aebelö* (Breslau, 1915); *Ikdar* (Dresden, 1921); *Herrn Dürers Bild oder Madonna am* *Wiesenzaun* (Hannover, Jan. 29, 1927); *Der Liebesrat* (not perf.); *Der arme Tobias* (1936). **ORCH.:** *Rustans Traum,* symphonic poem (1911); *Max und Moritz,* symphonic burlesque (1911); *Orientalische Skizzen* for Chamber Orch. (1918); *Eva,* symphonic poem (1922); *Variété,* scenes (1928). **CHAMBER:** Piano Quintet; String Quartet; piano pieces. **VOCAL:** Choral pieces; songs.

BIBL.: E. Müller, *J.G. M.* (Dresden, 1917).—**NS/LK/DM**

Mravina (original name, **Mravinskaya**), **Evgeniya (Konstantinovna),** noted Russian soprano; b. St. Petersburg, Feb. 16, 1864; d. Yalta, Oct. 25, 1914. She studied in St. Petersburg with Pryanishnikov, and later with Désirée d'Artôt in Berlin, and then sang in Italy. After returning to Russia, she joined the Maryinsky Theater in St. Petersburg in 1886, remaining on its roster until 1900. In 1891–92 she toured in England, France, Belgium, and Germany. She had the privilege of going over the part of Marguerite in *Faust* with Gounod, and the part of Mignon in the opera of that name by Thomas with the composer himself. She gave brilliant renditions of Italian soprano roles, and also was greatly praised in Russia for her performances of the Russian operatic parts. She retired from the operatic stage in 1900 but continued to appear in recital.

BIBL.: A. Grigorieva, *E.K. M.* (Moscow, 1970). —**NS/LK/DM**

Mravinsky, Evgeni (Alexandrovich), eminent Russian conductor; b. St. Petersburg, June 4, 1903; d. there (Leningrad), Jan. 19, 1988. He studied biology at the Univ. of St. Petersburg, then joined the Imperial Ballet as a pantomimist and rehearsal pianist. In 1924 he enrolled in the Leningrad Cons., where he studied conducting with Gauk and Malko, graduating in 1931; also had courses in composition with Shcherbachev. He then was conductor of the Leningrad Theater of Opera and Ballet (1932–38). In 1938 he was appointed principal conductor of the Leningrad Phil., which position he held with imperious authority for 50 years. Mravinsky represented the best of the Soviet school of conducting, in which technical precision and fidelity to the music were combined with individual and even Romantic interpretations. He was especially noted for his fine performances of Tchaikovsky's operas, ballets, and syms., and also gave first performances of several syms. of Prokofiev and Shostakovich and conducted works by Bartók and Stravinsky. In 1973 he was awarded the order of Hero of Socialist Labor.

BIBL.: V. Bogdanov-Berezovsky, *The Soviet Conductor M.* (Leningrad, 1956); V. Fomin, *M. Conducts* (Leningrad, 1976). —**NS/LK/DM**

Mraz, George (Jiri), noted jazz bassist; b. Pisek, Czechoslovakia, Sept. 9, 1944. A top-notch musician, he benefitted from the fine training in Czechoslovakia. He began his musical studies on violin at seven and started playing jazz in high school on alto saxophone, before taking up the bass. He attended the Prague Cons. in 1961 studying bass violin and graduating in 1966; during that time, he performed in jazz nightclubs. After finishing his studies, he moved to Munich and played clubs and concerts throughout Germany and Europe with Benny Bailey, Carmell Jones, Leo Wright, Mal Waldron, Hampton Hawes, Jan Hammer and others. In 1968, he went to Berklee on a scholarship and played at Lennie's on the Turnpike and the Jazz Workshop with Clark Terry, Herbie Hancock, Joe Williams and Carmen McRae. In the winter of 1969, Mraz joined Dizzy Gillespie in N.Y. for a few weeks, then toured with Oscar Peterson for about two years. He then played with the Thad Jones/Mel Lewis Orch. for the next six years. In the late 1970s, he worked with Stan Getz, New York Jazz Quartet, Zoot Sims, Bill Evans, and John Abercrombie; he played with Tommy Flanagan for 10 years starting in the 1980s. In the mid-1990s, he performed with McCoy Tyner, Hank Jones and Joe Henderson and pursued his own projects.

DISC.: *Concord Duo Series* (1994); *Bottom Lines* (1997).—**LP**

Mshvelidze, Shalva (Mikhailovich), Russian ethnomusicologist, teacher, and composer; b. Tiflis, May 28, 1904; d. there (Tbilisi), March 4, 1984. He studied with Bagrinovsky at the Tiflis Cons., graduating in 1930, and with Shcherbachev, Tyulin, Steinberg, and Ryazanov at the Leningrad Cons. He was made a teacher (1929) and a prof. (1942) at the Tbilisi Cons. He was a leading figure in Georgian music.

WORKS: DRAMATIC: O p e r a : *Legend of Tariel* (Tbilisi, Feb. 25, 1946; rev. 1966); *The Grandmaster's Right Hand* (Tbilisi, June 3, 1961); *Widow of a Soldier* (1967); *Aluda Ketelauri* (1972). **OTHER:** Incidental music; film scores. **ORCH.:** 4 symphonic poems: *Azar* (1933), *Zviadauri* (1940), *Mindia* (1949), and *Youngling and Tiger* (1962); 5 syms. (1943, 1944, 1952, 1968, 1974). **OTHER:** Chamber music; vocal works, including 2 oratorios: *Caucasiana* (1949) and *The Legacy of Posterity*, for the centennial of Lenin's birth (1970), and songs.

BIBL.: V. Donadze, *S. M.* (Tbilisi, 1946); A. Shaverzashvili, *Fugi S. M.* (Tbilisi, 1964); A. Tsulukidze, *S. M.* (Tbilisi, 1964). —**NS/LK/DM**

Muck, Karl, eminent German conductor; b. Darmstadt, Oct. 22, 1859; d. Stuttgart, March 3, 1940. He received his first musical instruction from his father, then studied piano with Kissner in Würzburg. He later pursued academic studies (classical philology) at the univs. of Heidelberg and Leipzig (Ph.D., 1880). He also attended the Leipzig Cons., and shortly before graduation made a successful debut as pianist with the Gewandhaus Orch. However, he did not choose to continue a pianistic career, but obtained a position as chorus master at the municipal opera in Zürich; his ability soon secured him the post of conductor there. In subsequent years, he was a theater conductor in Salzburg, Brünn, and Graz; there Angelo Neumann, impresario of a traveling opera company, heard him, and engaged him as conductor for the Landestheater in Prague (1886), and then as Seidl's successor for his traveling Wagner Co. It was during those years that Muck developed his extraordinary qualities as a masterful disciplinarian and faithful interpreter possessing impeccable taste. In 1889 he conducted the Wagner tetralogy in St. Petersburg, and in 1891, in Moscow. In 1892 he was engaged as first conductor at the Berlin

Royal Opera, and also frequently conducted sym. concerts of the Royal Chapel there. From 1894 to 1911 he led the Silesian Music Festivals; in 1899 he conducted the Wagner repertoire at London's Covent Garden. He also appeared, with outstanding success, in Paris, Rome, Brussels, Madrid, Copenhagen, and other European centers. In 1901 he was selected to conduct the performances of Parsifal at Bayreuth; appeared there regularly until 1930. Muck was one of the conductors of the Vienna Phil. (1904–06); then was conductor of the Boston Sym. Orch. (1906–08) before returning to Berlin as Generalmusikdirektor. He returned to America in 1912 and again assumed the post of conductor of the Boston Sym. Orch.; held that post with the greatest distinction until the U.S. entered World War I in 1917. Muck's position then became controversial; a friend of Kaiser Wilhelm II, he saw no reason to temper his ardent German nationalism, nor was he inclined to alter certain aspects of his private life. Protests were made against his retention as conductor, but despite the efforts to defend him by Major Higginson, the founder of the Boston Sym. Orch., Muck's case proved hopeless. In order to avoid prosecution under the Mann Act, he subsequently submitted to being arrested at his home on March 25, 1918, as an enemy alien and was interned until the end of the war. In 1919 he returned to Germany; conducted the Hamburg Phil. from 1922 until his retirement in 1933. Muck was one of the foremost conductors of his era. A consummate musician, endowed with a masterful technique, he was renowned for his authoritative performances of the revered Austro-German repertoire. His sympathies were wide, however, and he programmed such contemporary musicians as Mahler, Debussy, Sibelius, and even Schoenberg and Webern at his concerts. His penchant for stern disciplinarianism and biting sarcasm made him a feared podium figure for the musicians who played under him, but the results he obtained were exemplary.

BIBL.: N. Stücker, *K. M.* (Graz, 1939).—**NS/LK/DM**

Muczynski, Robert, American composer, pianist, and teacher; b. Chicago, March 19, 1929. He received training from Walter Knupfer (piano) and A. Tcherepnin (composition) at De Paul Univ. (B.M., 1950; M.M., 1952), playing his own *Divertimento* for Piano and Orch. at his graduation, and pursued further training with Tcherepnin in Nice (summer, 1961). In 1958 he made his N.Y. recital debut, and in subsequent years continued to be active as a pianist. He taught at De Paul Univ. (1955–58) and served as chairman of the piano dept. at Loras Coll. in Dubuque, Iowa (1956–59). In 1964–65 he was a visiting lecturer at Roosevelt Univ. in Chicago. He was a prof. and head of the composition dept. at the Univ. of Ariz. in Tucson from 1965 until 1988, when he became prof. emeritus. His Alto Saxophone Concerto was nominated for the Pulitzer Prize in Music in 1982. The composer's own performances of his solo piano music appeared on CD in 2000. Muczynski is a particularly fine composer of chamber music and piano pieces, whose output reflects the influence of Bartók and Barber, among others.

WORKS: ORCH.: *Divertimento* for Piano and Orch. (1951–52); Sym. No. 1 (1953); Piano Concerto (1954; Louisville,

Jan. 12, 1955); *Galena: A Town*, suite (1957–58); *Dovetail Overture* (Oakland, Calif., March 13, 1960); *Dance Movements* for Chamber Orch. (1962–63); *Symphonic Dialogues* (Washington, D.C., Oct. 31, 1965); *Charade* (1970–74); *A Serenade for Summer* for Chamber Orch. (1976; Tucson, Sept. 15, 1978); *Symphonic Memoir* (1978; Tucson, Jan. 11, 1979); Concerto for Alto Saxophone and Chamber Orch. (Kalamazoo, Mich., Oct. 31, 1981). **CHAMBER:** *Allegro deciso* for Brass Sextet and Timpani (1952); *Fragments* for Woodwind Trio (1958); Trumpet Trio (1959); *3 Designs* for 3 Timpani (1960); Flute Sonata (1960–61); *Movements* for Wind Quintet (1962); 3 piano trios (1966–67; 1975; 1986–87); *Gallery*, suite for Cello (1966); Cello Sonata (1968); *Fantasy Trio* for Clarinet, Cello, and Piano (1969); *Voyage*, 7 pieces for Trumpet, Horn, and Trombone (1969); Alto Saxophone Sonata (1970); Trio for Violin, Viola, and Cello (1971–72); *Time Pieces* for Clarinet and Piano (1983); Wind Quintet (1985); also numerous piano pieces, including 3 sonatas (1957, 1966, 1974). **VOCAL:** *Alleluia* for Chorus (1961); *I Never Saw a Moor* for Chorus (1967). —NS/LK/DM

Mudarra, Alonso de, Spanish vihuelist and composer; b. Palencia diocese, c. 1508; d. Seville, April 1, 1580. He became a canon (1546) and was elected major domo (1568) at Seville Cathedral. He publ. the important vol. *Tres libro de música en cifras para vihuela* (Seville, 1546; ed. in Monumentos de la Musica Española, VII, 1949).—NS/LK/DM

Mueller (actually, **Müller**) **von Asow, Erich H(ermann),** noted German musicologist; b. Dresden, Aug. 31, 1892; d. Berlin, June 4, 1964. He studied with Riemann and Schering at the Univ. of Leipzig (Ph.D., 1915, with the diss. *Die Mingottischen Opernunternehmungen, 1732–1756*; publ. in Dresden, 1917, as *Angelo und Pietro Mingotti: Ein Beitrag zur Geschichte der Oper im XVIII. Jahrhundert*). During World War I, he was active as a military bandmaster. After serving as asst. director of Leipzig's Neue Theater, he was artistic director of Dresden's international festival for modern music (1917–18). He was director of the Wernow Theater (1918–19) and then was active as a music critic in Berlin and Dresden; joined the staff of Dresden's Pädagogium der Tonkunst (1926), serving as its director (1927–33). He went to Austria (1936), and after being briefly under arrest by the Gestapo (1943), he returned to Germany in 1945, where he founded the Internationales Musiker-Brief-Archiv in Berlin.

WRITINGS: *Joseph Gustav Mraczek* (Dresden, 1917); *Die Musiksammlung der Bibliothek zu Kronstadt* (Kronstadt, 1930); *Dresdner Musikstätten* (Dresden, 1931); *Egon Kornauth: Ein Bild von Leben und Schaffen des mährischen Komponisten* (Vienna, 1941); *Max Reger und seine Welt* (Berlin, 1944); *Richard Strauss: Thematisches Verzeichnis* (3 vols., Vienna and Wiesbaden, 1959–74; completed by A. Ott and F. Trenner); also ed. numerous vols.—NS/LK/DM

Mueller, Otto-Werner, German-American conductor and pedagogue; b. Bensheim, June 23, 1926. He studied at the Frankfurt am Main Musisches Gymnasium. He was made music director of the Stuttgart Radio's chamber music dept. (1945), where he founded and conducted its chamber choir; then became conduc-

tor at the Heidelberg Theater (1947). After moving to Canada in 1951, he conducted with the CBC and joined the faculty of the Montreal Cons. (1958). He was founder-director of the Victoria School of Music in British Columbia (1963–65) and music director of the Victoria Sym. Orch. (1963–67). He then went to the U.S., where he was prof. of music at the Univ. of Wisc. (1967–77) and of conducting at the Yale Univ. School of Music (1977–86); then taught at N.Y.'s Juilliard School and at Philadelphia's Curtis Inst. of Music (from 1986). —NS/LK/DM

Muench, Gerhart, German-born Mexican pianist, teacher, and composer; b. Dresden, March 23, 1907; d. Tacambaro, Nov. 9, 1988. He studied piano with his father, a prof. at the Dresden Cons. He gave a public piano recital in Dresden at the age of 9. His auspicious career was halted by the Nazi takeover in Germany; Muench was drafted into the German army, but was discharged in 1944 as physically unfit. He went to the U.S. in 1947. In 1953 he settled in Mexico City and taught at the Univ. Nacional. In his piano recitals he introduced the new music of Stockhausen, Boulez, Pousseur, and others to Mexican audiences.

WORKS: CHAMBER Opera: *Tumulus Veneris* (1950). **ORCH.:** *Concerto da camera* for Piano and Chamber Orch. (1926); *Capriccio variato* for Piano and Orch. (1941); *Vocationes* for Piano and Chamber Orch. (1951); Bassoon Concerto (1956); *Muerte sin fin* (1957); Concerto for Piano and Strings (1957); Violin Concerto (1959); *Labyrinthus Orphei* (1965); *Itinera duo* for Piano and Orch. (1965); *Oxymora* (1967); *Auditur* (1968); *Epitomae tacambarensiae* (1974); *Telesma* (1974); *Vida sin Fin* for Piano and Orch. (1976); *Sortilegios* (1979); *Noctis Texturae* (1983); *Paysages de Rêve* (1984). **CHAMBER:** Cello Sonata (1938); *Tesauras Orphei* for Oboe, Clarinet, Viola, Double Bass, and Harp (1951); *Tessellata tacambarensia*, cycle of 9 chamber pieces for various instrumental groups or soloists (1964–76); *Out of Chaos* for Cello and Piano (1975); *Signa Flexanima* for Piano Trio (1975); *Tetrálogo* for String Quartet (1977); *Mini-Dialogos* for Violin and Cello (1977); *Proenza* for Piano Trio (1977); *Yuriko* for Violin and Piano (1977); *Pentalgo* for Flute, Oboe, Clarinet, Violin, and Cello (1985). **Piano:** *Evoluta* for 2 Pianos (1961); *Pièce de résistance* (1962); *Pasos Perdidos* (1971); *Fugato* (1985). **VOCAL:** *Asociaciones* for Soprano and Instruments (1969); *Exaltacion de la Luz* for Soprano, Men's Chorus, and Orch. (1981); *Se nos ha ido la Tarde* for Chorus and Orch. (1983); 5 masses; choruses; songs. —NS/LK/DM

Muffat, Georg, eminent French-born German organist and composer of Scottish descent, father of **Gottlieb (Theophil) Muffat**; b. Mégève, Savoy (baptized), June 1, 1653; d. Passua, Feb. 23, 1704. He went to Alsace in childhood, and after studies with Lully and others in Paris (1663–69), he returned to Alsace as a student at the Jesuit college in Sélestat and continued his studies in Molsheim (from 1671), where he was made organist of the exiled Strasbourg Cathedral chapter. By 1674 he was in Ingolstadt as a law student. With war imminent, he went to Vienna and found a patron in Emperor Leopold I. After a sojourn in Prague (1677–78), he became organist and chamber musician to Archbishop Max Gandolf, Count of Kuenberg, in Salzburg; during his tenure, he was allowed a leave of absence to pursue his training with Pasquini in Rome, where he was befriended by Corelli. In 1690 he was appointed Kapellmeister at the court of Johann Philipp of Lamberg, Bishop of Passau. Muffat was a significant composer who helped introduce the French and Italian styles of his era to the German-speaking lands. He wrote the valuable treatise *Regulae concentuum partiturae* (c. 1699; ed. by H. Federhofer, Musicological Studies and Documents, IV, 1961).

WORKS: *Armonico tributo*, 5 sonatas for Strings and Basso Continuo (Salzburg, 1682); *Apparatus musico-organisticus*, 12 toccatas, a ciaccona, a passacaglia, and an aria with variations for Organ (Salzburg, 1690); *Suavoris harmoniae instrumentalis hyporchematicae florilegium primum*, 7 suites for Orch., *a* 4 or 5, and Basso Continuo (Augsburg, 1695); *Florilegium secundum*, 8 suites for Orch., *a* 4, and Basso Continuo (Passau, 1698); *Ausserlesene Instrumental-Music*, 12 concerti grossi (Passau, 1701); other extant works include a Sonata for Violin and Basso Continuo (1677) and various preludes and dances for Keyboard.

BIBL.: L. von Stollbrock, *Die Komponisten G. und Gottlieb M.* (Rostock, 1888); W. Kolneder, *G. M. zur Aufführungspraxis* (Strasbourg, 1970); I. Stampfl, *G. M.: Orchesterkompositionen: Ein musikhistorischer Vergleich der Orchestermusik, 1670–1710* (Passau, 1984).—**NS/LK/DM**

Muffat, Gottlieb (Theophil), distinguished German organist and composer, son of **Georg Muffat**; b. Passau (baptized), April 25, 1690; d. Vienna, Dec. 9, 1770. He most likely received his initial training from his father. By 1711 he was in Vienna, where he continued his education as a Hofscholar under Fux; later studied abroad. He was officially named court organist in 1717, his duties including performing for the Hofkapelle and serving as continuo accompanist for the opera. Later he became a teacher to the children of the royal family, and was made 2nd organist (1729) and 1st organist (1741), retaining the latter position until he was pensioned (1763). Muffat was a notable representative of the late Baroque era, producing a large body of fine keyboard music. He publ. *72 Verseltsammt 12 Toccaten (besonders zum Kirchen-Dienst bey Choral-Aemtern und Vesperen dienlich)* (Vienna, 1726) and *Componimenti musicali per il cembalo*, 6 suites and a ciaccona (Augsburg, c. 1739). His other works include 32 ricercari, 24 toccatas with 24 capriccios, various other capriccios, 19 canzonas, preludes, fugues, partitas, 2 organ masses, etc.

BIBL.: L. von Stollbrock, *Die Komponisten Georg und G. M.* (Rostock, 1888); J. Knoll, *Die Klavier- und Orgelwerke Theophile* (diss., Univ. of Vienna, 1916); S. Morris, *G. M.'s Clavier Suites* (diss., Boston Univ., 1959).—**NS/LK/DM**

Mugnone, Leopoldo, noted Italian conductor; b. Naples, Sept. 29, 1858; d. there, Dec. 22, 1941. He studied with Cesi and Serrao at the Naples Cons., and began to compose as a young student. When he was 16, he produced a comic opera, *Don Bizarro e le sue figlie* (Naples, April 20, 1875); other operas were *Il Biricchino* (Venice, Aug. 11, 1892; fairly successful) and *Vita Brettone* (Naples, March 14, 1905). He also composed an attractive Neapolitan song, "La Rosella," and other light music. But it was as a fine opera conductor that

Mugnone achieved fame, his performances of Italian stage works possessing the highest degree of authority and an intense musicianly ardor. He also brought out Wagner's music dramas in Italy, and conducted the first performances of Mascagni's *Cavalleria rusticana* (Rome, May 17, 1890) and Puccini's *Tosca* (Rome, Jan. 14, 1900). —**NS/LK/DM**

Mühlfeld, Richard (Bernhard Herrmann), famous German clarinetist; b. Salzungen, Feb. 28, 1856; d. Meiningen, June 1, 1907. He first studied the violin and played in the Meiningen Court Orch. then practiced on the clarinet without a teacher, and in 1876 became 1st clarinetist at the Saxe-Meiningen court. From 1884 to 1896 he was first clarinetist at the Bayreuth Festivals, and he became music director of the Meiningen Court Theater (1890). Brahms wrote for him the Trio, op.114 (for Clarinet, Cello, and Piano), the Quintet, op.115 (for Clarinet, 2 Violins, Viola, and Cello), and the 2 clarinet sonatas, op.120.—**NS/LK/DM**

Mul, Jan, Dutch organist, choral conductor, and composer; b. Haarlem, Sept. 20, 1911; d. Overveen, near Haarlem, Dec. 30, 1971. He was a student of H. Andriessen and Dresden in Amsterdam, and of the Roman Catholic School of Church Music in Utrecht. From 1931 to 1960 he was an organist and choral conductor in Overveen. He also was music ed. of the Amsterdam daily *De Volkskrant*. He orchestrated Dresden's opera *François Villon* from the vocal score (Amsterdam, June 12, 1958) and Sweelinck's *Keyboard Variations on an Old Song* (Amsterdam, June 12, 1963). Mul composed some fine sacred choral music.

WORKS: DRAMATIC: O p e r a : *De Varkenshoeder* (The Swineherd; Amsterdam, June 25, 1953); *Bill Clifford* (Hengelo, Oct. 5, 1964). ORCH.: Piano Concerto (1938); *Felicitatie* (1952); *Concerto for Orchestra* (1956); Sinfonietta (1957; based on the Piano Sonata, 1940); *Mein junges Leben* (1961); Concerto for Piano, 4–Hands, and Small Orch. (1962); *Confetti musicali* (1965); *Ik, Jan Mul* (I, Jan Mul; 1965); *Divertimento* for Piano and Orch. (1967); *Balladino* for Cello and Orch. or Piano (1968); *Variazioni "I due orsini"* (1968). CHAMBER: Quintet for Clarinet, Bassoon, Violin, Viola, and Cello (1957); Trio for 2 Violins and Double Bass (1969). KEYBOARD: P i a n o : 2 sonatinas (1928, 1942); Sonata (1940; orchestrated as the Sinfonietta, 1957); *Intervallen*, 6 inventions (1942; orchestrated 1954); Sonata for 2 Pianos (1953); *Les Donemoiselles*, 6 pieces (1968). O r g a n : Sonata (1942). VOCAL: *Stabat Mater* for Chorus and Small Orch. (1934); *4 Coplas* for Voice and Orch. (1936); *Egmont onthalsd* (Egmont Beheaded) for Chorus and Orch. (1938); Sonata for Mezzo-soprano, Baritone, and Small Orch. (1940–53); *Galant Quartet* for Soprano and Small Orch. or Flute, Cello, and Piano (1952); *Te Deum laudamus* for Chorus and Orch. (1955); *Lettre de M. l'Abbé d'Olivet à M. le President Bouhier* for Baritone and Orch. (1962); *De kwink*, ballad for Men's Chorus, Bassoon, and Percussion (1965); *L'Homme désarmé*, cantata for Chorus and Orch. (1970–71; Leiden, Sept. 25, 1973); masses. —**NS/LK/DM**

Mulder, Ernest Willem, Dutch composer, conductor, and teacher; b. Amsterdam, July 21, 1898; d. there, April 12, 1959. He was a pupil of Schulz (piano)

and Zweers (composition) at the Amsterdam Toonkunst cons., where he later was a prof. of theory and composition. From 1938 to 1947 he lectured at the Univ. of Utrecht. He also was director of the Bussum Music School and conductor of the Toonkunst Musical Soc.

WORKS: DRAMATIC: Opera: *Dafne* (1932–34). ORCH.: Piano Concerto (1935); *Sinfonia sacra III: Super psalmos* (1948) and *IV: Super passionem* (1949–50). CHAMBER: 2 violin sonatas (both 1920); *Ars contrapunctica*, 7 pieces for Various Instrumental Combinations (1938–40); *Sonata (in modo classico)* for Solo Violin (1941); Trio for 3 Bassoons (1942); String Quartet (1942); Sextet for Winds and Piano (1946); Quartet for Oboe, Bassoon, Cello, and Harp (1946). VOCAL: *3 chansons* for Soprano and Orch. (1921–28); *Sinfonia sacra I* for 6 Soloists, Chorus, and Orch. (1922–32) and *II: Dialogue mystique* for Baritone, Chorus, and Orch. (1936–40); *Requiem (Missa pro defunctis)* for Soloists, Chorus, and Orch. (1927–32); *Holland* for Chorus and Orch. (1942); *Maria-motetten*, 5 pieces for Soprano and Various Instrumental Ensembles (1945); *Stabat Mater dolorosa* for Soloists, Chorus, and Orch. (1948); *Te Deum laudamus* for Chorus and Orch. (1951); *Symphonietta* for Medium Voice and Orch. (1958); songs.—NS/LK/DM

Mulder, Herman, Dutch composer; b. Amsterdam, Dec. 12, 1894; d. there, April 28, 1989. He received training in harmony and voice. After a brief career as a singer, he became a prolific composer.

WORKS: ORCH.: 14 syms. (1940; 1952; 1954; 1959–60; 1961; 1962; 1964; 1967; 1968; 1971; 1972–73; 1974–75; 1976; 1981); Suite (1941); Piano Concerto (1943); *Concerto for Orchestra* (1956); Violin Concerto (1964); *Music for Violin and Chamber Orch.* (1967); *Ouverture* (1967–70); Concerto for 2 Pianos and Orch. (1968); *Funerailles* (1971); *Introduction, Chaconne, and Finale* (1978). CHAMBER: 13 string quartets (n.d.–1970); Piano Quintet (1947); 2 string sextets (1957, 1973); 6 violin sonatas (1958–82); Viola Sonata (1960); Trio for Flute, Oboe, and Bassoon (1960); 2 wind quintets (1961, 1966); 2 piano trios (1965, 1978); Piano Quartet (1965); 2 string trios (both 1972); *2 Divertimenti* for Violin (1978); other sonatas, including 6 for piano. VOCAL: *De snaren hebben getrild*, cantata for Soprano and Orch. (1977); songs.—NS/LK/DM

Muldowney, Dominic (John), English composer; b. Southampton, July 19, 1952. He received his training from Harvey at the Univ. of Southampton, Birtwistle in London, and Rands and Blake at the Univ. of York (1971–74). In 1976 he became music director of the National Theatre in London. He composes within tonal parameters with a penchant for adventuresome harmonic explorations.

WORKS: DRAMATIC: *An Heavyweight Dirge*, music theater (1971); *Klavier-Hammer*, music theater (1973); *Da Capo al Fine*, ballet (1975); *The Earl of Essex's Galliard*, music theater (1975–76); *Macbeth*, ballet (1979); *Carmen*, ballet (1984–85); incidental music; film scores. ORCH.: *Driftwood to the Flow* for Strings (1972); *Music at Chartres* for Chamber Orch. (1974); *Perspectives* (1975); Concerto for 4 Violins and Strings (1980); Piano Concerto (1983); Saxophone Concerto (1984); *Sinfonietta* for Small Orch. (1986); Violin Concerto (1989–90); *3 Pieces* (1990–91); Percussion Concerto (1991); Oboe Concerto (1991–92); Trumpet Concerto (1992–93). CHAMBER: 2 string quartets (1973, 1980); *Love Music for Bathsheba Everdene and Gabriel Oak* for Chamber Ensemble (1974); *Solo/Ensemble* (1974);

3-part Motet for 11 Instruments (1976); *Variations after Sweelinck* for Chamber Ensemble (1977); *Double Helix* for Octet (1977); *In a Hall of Mirrors* for Alto Saxophone and Piano (1979); Piano Trio (1980); *6 Chorale Preludes* for Chamber Ensemble (1986); *Ars subtilor* for Chamber Ensemble and Tape (1987); *Un carnaval Cubiste* for 10 Brass and Metronome (1989). PIANO: *A Little Piano Book*, 24 pieces (1979); *Paraphrase on Machaut's Hoquetus David* (1987); *The Ginger Tree* (1989). VOCAL: *Cantata* for Soloists, Speakers, 2 Cellos, and Percussion (1975); *Procurans Odium* for Soprano and 8 Instruments (1977); *5 Psalms* for Soprano, Tenor, Chorus, Wind, and Tape (1979); *5 Theatre Poems* for Mezzo-soprano and Ensemble (1980–81); *In Dark Times* for Soprano, Alto, Tenor, Bass, and Ensemble (1981); *The Duration of Exile* for Mezzo-soprano and Ensemble (1983); *A Second Show* for Contralto, Harp, Violin, Alto Saxophone, and Tape (1983); *Maxims* for Baritone and Ensemble (1986); *Lonely Hearts* for Woman's Voice and Ensemble (1988); *On Suicide* for Voice and Ensemble (1989); *Out of the East* for 2 Voices and Ensemble or Piano (1990).—NS/LK/DM

Mulè, Giuseppe, Italian composer and pedagogue; b. Termini, Imerese, Sicily, June 28, 1885; d. Rome, Sept. 10, 1951. He studied at the Palermo Cons., graduating as a cellist as well as in composition. In 1922 he was engaged as director of the Palermo Cons. (until 1925), and in 1925 he succeeded Respighi as director of the Accademia di Santa Cecilia in Rome; remained there until 1943. He wrote mostly for the stage, and was particularly successful in providing suitable music for revivals of Greek plays. He composed numerous operas in the tradition of the Italian verismo: *La Baronessa di Carini* (Palermo, April 16, 1912), *La Monacella della fontana* (Trieste, Feb. 17, 1923), *Dafni* (Rome, March 14, 1928), *Liola* (Naples, Feb. 2, 1935), *Taormina* (San Remo, 1938), and *La zolfara* (Rome, 1939). Other works include the oratorio *Il Cieco di Gerico* (1910), 2 symphonic poems, *Sicilia canora* (1924) and *La Vendemmia* (1936), *3 canti siciliani* for Voice and Orch. (1930), a String Quartet and other chamber music, and songs.—NS/LK/DM

Mulet, Henri, French organist, teacher, and composer; b. Paris, Oct. 17, 1878; d. Draguignan, Sept. 20, 1967. He studied with Delsart (premier prix in cello, 1893), Leroux and Pugno (premier prix in harmony, 1896), and Guilmant and Widor (2nd prix in organ, 1897) at the Paris Cons. He taught at the École Niedermeyer (1899–1917) and the Schola Cantorum (1924–31) in Paris, and also held various positions as an organist. In 1937 he settled in Draguignan, where he played organ at the Cathedral until entering a convent in 1958. Mulet composed various orch. and organ works but destroyed most of his MSS in 1937. His best known works are the organ pieces *Esquisses byzantines* and *Carillon sortie*.—NS/LK/DM

Müller, Adolf, Jr., Austrian composer and conductor, son of **Adolf Müller** Sr.; b. Vienna, Oct. 15, 1839; d. there, Dec. 14, 1901. After completing his education in Vienna, he was engaged as a theater conductor in the provinces. He was conductor of the German Opera at Rotterdam (1875–83), then at the Theater an der Wien, where his father had directed before him. He produced a number of operas, including *Heinrich der Goldschmidt* (Magdeburg, 1867), *Waldmeisters Brautfahrt* (Hamburg, Feb. 15, 1873), and *Van Dyke* (Rotterdam, 1877), and the Viennese operettas *Der Hofnarr* (Nov. 20, 1886; his greatest success), *Der Teufels Weib* (Nov. 22, 1890), *Der Millionen-Onkel* (Nov. 5, 1892), *General Gogo* (Feb. 1, 1896), and *Der Blondin von Namur* (Oct. 15, 1898). —**NS/LK/DM**

Müller, Adolf, Sr. (real name, **Matthias Schmid**), Austrian conductor and composer, father of **Adolf Müller Jr.**; b. Tolna, Oct. 7, 1801; d. Vienna, July 29, 1886. He was orphaned at an early age and reared by an aunt. He studied with Joseph Rieger, the Brünn Cathedral organist, and with Joseph von Blumenthal in Vienna. After appearances as a singer and actor, he became a prolific composer for the Viennese theater. He was conductor of the Theater an der Wien (1828–78) and also conducted at the Leopoldstadt Theater. He wrote almost 600 scores for the stage, some sacred music, chamber pieces, and about 400 songs.

BIBL.: A. Bauer, *Die Musik Adolph M.s in den Theaterstücken Johann Nestroys* (diss., Univ. of Vienna, 1935).—**NS/LK/DM**

Müller, August Eberhard, German organist and composer; b. Nordheim, Hannover, Dec. 13, 1767; d. Weimar, Dec. 3, 1817. He studied keyboard playing with his father, Matthäus Müller, an organist. After receiving instruction in harmony and composition from J.C.F. Bach in Bückeburg, he studied law in Göttingen (1786). He was an organist at various churches at Magdeburg and Leipzig. In 1800 he became assistant to Johann Adam Hiller at the Thomasschule in Leipzig, and succeeded him as Kantor there in 1804; also was music director of the Thomaskirche and Nikolaikirche. In 1810 he became court conductor in Weimar. He wrote a Singspiel, *Der Polterabend* (Weimar, 1813 or 1814), 11 flute concertos, 2 keyboard concertos, cantatas, 17 keyboard sonatas and other works for keyboard, and chamber music. He publ. a practical piano method (1805; actually the 6th ed. of G. Löhlein's *Clavier-Schule*, rev. by Müller; Kalkbrenner's method is based on it; Czerny publ. the 8th ed. in 1825) and a method for the flute. He also publ. cadenzas for, and a guide to the interpretation of, Mozart's concertos, and arranged piano scores of Mozart's operas, which were very popular in his time.

BIBL.: G. Haupt, *A.E. M.'s Leben und Klavierwerke* (Leipzig, 1926).—**NS/LK/DM**

Müller, George Godfrey (actually, **Georg Gottfried**), German-American minister, violinist, and composer; b. Gross Hennersdorf, Saxony, May 22, 1762; d. Lititz, Pa., March 19, 1821. He went to America in 1784, and spent the major part of his life at Lititz, as a member of the culturally important group of Moravians in America. His works are listed by A.G. Rau and H.T. David in *A Catalogue of Music by American Moravians* (Bethlehem, Pa., 1938), and his music is represented in Vol. I of the series Music by the Moravians in America (1938).—**NS/LK/DM**

Müller, Iwan, German clarinetist, basset-horn player, instrument maker, and composer; b. Reval, Estonia, Dec. 14, 1786; d. Bückeburg, Feb. 4, 1854. He toured throughout Europe, and served as a chamber musician at the St. Petersburg imperial court (1800–07). He developed an 18-key basset horn (1808) and a 13-key clarinet (1809), and also claimed for himself the invention of the alto clarinet; made Paris his headquarters (1809). Although he faced the opposition of conservative instrument makers, his improved clarinet eventually won general popularity. He spent the last years of his life at Bückeburg as a court musician. He publ. a method for his new instruments, and also composed 6 clarinet concertos and 2 clarinet quartets.—**NS/LK/DM**

Müller, Maria, Austrian soprano; b. Leitmeritz, Jan. 29, 1898; d. Bayreuth, March 13, 1958. She studied with Erik Schmedes in Vienna and Max Altglass in N.Y. She made her operatic debut as Elsa in Linz in 1919; then sang at the German Theater in Prague (1921–23) and at the Bavarian State Opera in Munich (1923–24). On Jan. 21, 1925, she made her Metropolitan Opera debut in N.Y. as Sieglinde, remaining on its roster until 1935. In 1926 she joined the Berlin Städtische Oper. From 1927 to 1943 she sang at the Berlin State Opera. She also sang at the Wagner festivals in Bayreuth (1930–44) and in Salzburg.—**NS/LK/DM**

Müller, Sigfrid Walther, German composer; b. Plauen, Jan. 11, 1905; d. in a Russian prison camp in Baku, Nov. 2, 1946. He studied at the Leipzig Cons. with Karg-Elert and Martienssen, and also church music and organ with Straube. He taught at the Leipzig Cons. (1929–32) and at the Hochschule für Musik in Weimar (1940–41), and then was in the German army on the eastern front. His output comprised 62 opus numbers, mostly chamber music and organ works. He also composed an opera, *Schlaraffenhochzeit* (Leipzig, 1937), *Böhmische Musik* for Orch., *Gohliser Schlossmusik* for Small Orch., and a Concerto for Flute and Chamber Orch. (1941).—**NS/LK/DM**

Müller, Wenzel, prominent Austrian conductor and composer; b. Tyrnau, Moravia, Sept. 26, 1767; d. Baden, near Vienna, Aug. 3, 1835. He studied with the Kornitz schoolmaster, learning to play all the instruments of the orch. and beginning to compose as a child; continued his studies at the Raigern Benedictine foundation, where he received further instruction from its choirmaster, Maurus Haberbauer, and then completed his studies with Dittersdorf in Johannisberg. In 1782 he became 3rd violinist in Waizhofer's theater company in Brünn, attracting notice with his successful Singspiel *Das verfehlte Rendezvouz, oder Die weiblichen Jäger*. After a concert tour with the Willmann family (1786), he settled in Vienna as Kapellmeister at the Leopoldstädter-Theater. His first success as a composer there came with his Singspiel *Das Sonnenfest der Braminen* (Sept. 9, 1790), which was followed by such popular stage works as *(Kaspar) Der Fagottist, oder Die Zauberzither* (June 8, 1791), *Die Schwestern von Prag* (March 11, 1794), *Das lustige Beilager* (Feb. 14, 1797), *Die zwölf schlafenden*

Jungfrauen (Oct. 12, 1797), and *Die Teufelsmühle am Wienerberg* (Nov. 12, 1799). After serving as Kapellmeister at Prague's German Opera (1807–13), he returned to the Leopoldstädter-Theater as Kapellmeister in 1815; among the subsequent popular scores he wrote for it were *Tankredi* (April 25, 1817), *Der verwunschene Prinz* (March 3, 1818), *Aline, oder Wien in einem andern Weltteil* (Oct. 9, 1822), *Der Barometermacher auf der Zauberinsel* (Dec. 18, 1823), *Die gefesselte Phantasie* (Jan. 8, 1828), and *Der Alpenkönigund der Menschenfeind* (Oct. 17, 1828). His daughter was **Therese Grünbaum.** Muller was the most successful composer of light stage works for the Vienna theater of his day, and several of his works remain a part of the Austrian repertoire. A prolific composer, he produced some 250 theatrical pieces alone. He also composed syms., sacred music, chamber pieces, piano works, and several enduring songs.

BIBL.: W. Krone, *W. M.: Ein Beitrag zur Geschichte der komischen Oper* (Berlin, 1906); L. Raab, *W. M.: Ein Tonkünstler Altwiens* (Baden, 1928).—NS/LK/DM

Müller-Blattau, Joseph (Maria),

noted German musicologist; b. Colmar, Alsace, May 21, 1895; d. Saarbrücken, Oct. 21, 1976. He studied musicology with Friedrich Ludwig at the Univ. of Strasbourg, and composition and conducting with Pfitzner and organ with Ernst Münch at the Strasbourg Cons. He served in the German army during World War I; after the Armistice of 1918, he resumed his studies in musicology with Wilibald Gurlitt at the Univ. of Freiburg im Breisgau (Ph.D., 1920, with the diss. *Grundzüge einer Geschichte der Fuge*; publ. in Königsberg, 1923; 3rd ed., rev., 1963). He then completed his Habilitation at the Univ. of Königsberg in 1922 with his *Die Kompositionslehre Heinrich Schützens in der Fassung seines Schulers Christoph Bernhard* (publ. in Leipzig, 1926; 2nd ed., 1963). He taught at the Univ. of Königsberg; was promoted to reader there in 1928; then taught at the univs. of Frankfurt am Main (1935–37) and Freiburg im Breisgau (1937–39); subsequently served in military administration (1939–42); then lectured at the Univ. of Strasbourg during the last years of World War II. From 1952 to 1958 he was director of the Staatliche Hochschule für Musik in Saarbrücken; he also taught at the Univ. of Strasbourg from 1952 to 1964. He was the editor of the abortive 12th ed. of Riemann's *Musiklexikon* (1937–39), of which only a few issues appeared before the outbreak of World War II made further publication impossible.

WRITINGS: *Das Elsass, ein Grenzland deutscher Musik* (Freiburg im Breisgau, 1922); *Geschichte der Musik in Ost- und Westpreussen von der Ordenszeit bis zur Gegenwart* (Königsberg, 1931; 2nd ed., enl., 1968); *Hamann und Herder in ihren Beziehungen zur Musik* (Königsberg, 1931); *Das deutsche Volkslied* (Berlin, 1932; 2nd ed., 1958); *Einführung in die Musikgeschichte* (Berlin, 1932; 2nd ed., 1941); *Johannes Brahms* (Potsdam, 1933); *Georg Friedrich Händel* (Potsdam, 1933; 2nd ed., 1959); *Zur Erforschung des ostpreussischen Volksliedes* (Halle, 1934); *Johann Sebastian Bach* (Leipzig, 1935; 2nd ed., Stuttgart, 1950); *Geschichte der deutschen Musik* (Berlin, 1938; 3rd ed., 1942); *Hans Pfitzner* (Potsdam, 1940; 2nd ed., rev., 1969); *Gestaltung—Umgestaltung: Studien zur Geschichte der musikalischen Variation* (Stuttgart, 1950); *Das Verhältnis von Wort und Ton in der Geschichte der Musik: Grundzüge und Probleme* (Stuttgart, 1952); *Die Volksliedsammlung des jungen*

Goethe (Kassel, 1955); *Von der Vielfalt der Musik: Musikgeschichte—Musikerziehung—Musikpflege* (Freiburg im Breisgau, 1966); *Goethe und die Meister der Musik* (Stuttgart, 1969).

BIBL.: W. Salmen, ed., *Festgabe für J. M.-B. zum 65. Geburtstag* (Saarbrücken, 1960; 2nd ed., 1962); C.-H. Mahling, ed., *Zum 70. Geburtstag von J. M.-B.* (Kassel, 1966).—NS/LK/DM

Müller-Hermann, Johanna,

Austrian composer and pedagogue; b. Vienna, Jan. 15, 1878; d. there, April 19, 1941. She studied with Nawrátil, Josef Labor, Guido Adler, Zemlinsky, and J.B. Foerster. She began to compose at an early age, in a Romantic vein, influenced chiefly by Mahler and Reger; was regarded as one of the foremost European women composers of orch. and chamber music of her time. She wrote an oratorio, *In Memoriam*, to Walt Whitman's words, a Sym. for Voices with Orch., a Symphonic Fantasy on Ibsen's play *Brand*, String Quartet, String Quintet, Piano Quintet, Violin Sonata, Cello Sonata, Piano Sonata, and several song cycles.—NS/LK/DM

Müller-Kray, Hans,

German conductor and composer; b. Essen, Oct. 13, 1908; d. Stuttgart, May 30, 1969. He studied piano, cello, and theory in Essen, then was a conductor at the theater there. He conducted in Münster (1934–41), Frankfurt am Main (1942–45), and Wiesbaden (1945–48). In 1948 he became chief conductor of the Stuttgart Radio Sym. Orch., a post he held until his death. He wrote several ballet scores and other works.—NS/LK/DM

Müller Quartets.

Two famous German string quartets, the first to undertake regular concert tours, their members being:

(1) The brothers **Karl** (1797–1873), **Gustav** (1799–1855), **Theodor** (1802–75), and **Georg** (1808–55). They were all born in Braunschweig and belonged to the orch. there, Karl as concertmaster, Theodor as cellist, Gustav as violinist, and Georg as conductor. Their artistic tours included not only all the large German cities, but also Vienna and Paris (1833), Copenhagen (1838), St. Petersburg (1845), and the Netherlands (1852).

BIBL.: L. Köhler, *Die Gebrüder M. und das Streichquartett* (Leipzig, 1858).

(2) The four sons of Karl, all born in Braunschweig (this quartet was organized in 1855, after the death of 2 members of the first one); **Karl**, first violin (b. April 14, 1829; d. Stuttgart, Nov. 11, 1907); **Hugo**, second violin (b. Sept. 21, 1832; d. Braunschweig, June 26, 1886); **Bernhard**, viola (b. Feb. 24, 1825; d. Rostock, Sept. 4, 1895); and **Wilhelm**, cello (b. June 1, 1834; d. N.Y., Sept. 1897). For 10 years they constituted the court quartet at Meiningen, then, after extended and successful travels, they settled in Rostock as members of the city orch., Karl being appointed music director. The quartet was broken up by the appointment of Wilhelm (1873) to succeed Sweerts as first cello in the Royal Orch. at Berlin, and prof. in the Hochschule für Musik. Karl lived from then on in Stuttgart and Hamburg and was also a composer.—NS/LK/DM

Müller von Kulm, Walter, Swiss composer; b. Kulm, Aug. 31, 1899; d. Arlesheim, near Basel, Oct. 3, 1967. He studied in Aarau and at the conservatories and in Basel and Zürich, and took courses in musicology, philosophy, and psychology at the Univ. of Basel. He was director of the Basel Cons. (1947–64). He publ. the manual *Grundriss der Harmonielehre* (Basel, 1948). Among his works were the opera *Der Erfinder* (1944), the ballet, *Die blaue Blume* (1936), the oratorios *Vater unser* (1945) and *Petrus* (1960), a Sym. (1928), chamber music, and keyboard pieces.—NS/LK/DM

Müller-Zürich (real name, **Müller**), **Paul,** esteemed Swiss conductor and composer; b. Zürich, June 19, 1898; d. Lucerne, July 21, 1993. He studied with Andreae and Jarnach at the Zürich Cons. (1917–19) and in Paris and Berlin, then taught in Zürich at the Cons. (1927–69) and at the Univ. (1959–70). He was active as a choral and sym. conductor, serving as director of the Elisabeth Schmid Choir (1931–39), the Lucerne Chamber Orch. (1948–55), and other ensembles. His music evolved from early Romantic influences to reflect neo-Baroque practices in a contemporary, tonal style.

WORKS: ORCH.: 4 syms.: *Little Symphony* (1920), Sym. for Strings (1944), Sym. (1947), and Sym. for Flute and Strings (1952); *Little Serenade* for Chamber Orch. (1921); *Hymnus* (1927); Concerto for Viola and Small Orch. (1934); 2 violin concertos: No. 1 for Violin and Small Orch. (1935) and No. 2 (1957); Concerto for Organ and Strings (1938); Cello Concerto (1954); *Sinfonischer Prolog* (1955); *Sinfonische Suite* (1956–57); Concerto for 2 Violins, Harpsichord, and Strings (1958); Sinfonietta (1964); *Sonata* for Strings (1967–68); *Consenso*, suite (1974). CHAMBER: String Quintet (1919); 2 string quartets (1921, 1960); 3 violin sonatas (1922, 1941, 1952); *Marienleben* for 10 Instruments (1928); *Praludium, Arie und Fuge* for Oboe, Bassoon, Horn, Trumpet, and String Quintet (1933); *Petite sonate* for Clarinet and Piano (1942); *Fantasie und Fugue* for Violin and Organ (1949); String Trio (1950); *Canzone* for String Quartet (1961); Trio for Flute, Clarinet, and Piano (1965–66); Sonata for Solo Viola (1979); *Fantasie* for Oboe and Organ (1980); *Serenata turicensis* for Basset Horn, Viola, and Cello (1981); organ music. OTHER: Dramatic works; choral music; songs.

BIBL.: F. Jakob, *P. M.: Biographie und Werkverzeichnis* (Zürich, 1963).—NS/LK/DM

Mulligan, Gerry (actually, **Gerald Joseph Mulligan**), b. Queens, N.Y., April 6, 1927; d. Darien, Conn., Jan. 20, 1996. Modern jazz certainly had its share of icons in the 1950s: Miles Davis, Dave Brubeck, Thelonious Monk, Charles Mingus, Sonny Rollins, and Ella Fitzgerald were all in their prime. Duke Ellington, Count Basie, and (for close to the first half of the decade, anyway) Charlie Parker were still around. Even so, no one was more visible and popular than the lanky baritone saxophonist Gerry Mulligan, whose "piano-less" quartet with Chet Baker caused a sensation when its initial recordings were issued in 1952. Even after his death, Mulligan remains the world's most famous jazz baritone sax player.

Before learning clarinet and various saxophones, Mulligan started out on piano, and became primarily an arranger who wrote for the Johnny Warrington radio band (1944), and bands led by Tommy Tucker and George Paxton in the 1940s. Going to and through N.Y. from 1947–51 (before settling in Calif.), he worked with drummer Gene Krupa's Orch., contributing charts as staff arranger and playing alto with the band. In 1948 he did the same with the Claude Thornhill band. On Sept. 4, 1948, the Miles Davis *Birth of the Cool* group broadcast from the Royal Roost, and by January 1949, Mulligan participated in a series of recording sessions for Capitol which helped introduce the relaxed, anti-frantic, cool-jazz, "West Coast sound" to the jazz world on recordings between 1948–50. Mulligan's other associations during this period included a group of musicians that would shape jazz for the next two decades: Stan Getz, Kai Winding, and those who would become Mulligan's favorite sidemen—Lee Konitz, Jerry Lloyd, Don Ferrara, and Zoot Sims. Again, it was his arrangements for this assemblage of "Five Brothers," that would capture the ears of his fans with their vibrant small-group format.

Early in 1952 Mulligan left N.Y., spending several months hitchhiking to Calif. where he settled in Los Angeles and had a rocky period with the Kenton band. Still known mostly as an arranger, it was the Los Angeles–based quartet he formed in the early 1950s with trumpeter Chet Baker, bassist "Red" Mitchell, and drummer Chico Hamilton that really focused attention on "Jeru," as Mulligan was also known. That "piano-less" foursome and its immediate successors had a crowd-pleasing, accessible approach to standards, comprising equal parts of Dixieland counterpoint, swing-like pacing, and boppish improvisation that translated into a winning combination. Formed through a series of circumstances that led to the omission of the piano, this quartet would make recordings, under the auspices of producer Richard Bock, that would be hailed by critics as the most innovative in modern progressive jazz. The original Gerry Mulligan Quartet was at its peak of fame in 1954 when a narcotics bust, 90 days in jail, and subsequent legal problems sidelined Mulligan for six months. Over a pay dispute, he and Baker parted and Mulligan headed back to N.Y.C., picking up musicians along the way—bassist Bill Crow, drummer Dave Bailey, and valve trombonist Bob Brookmeyer—all who would remain with him as his group fluxed and changed into various configurations throughout the next decade.

In 1960 Mulligan formed his 13-piece concert band and toured Europe and, in 1964, Japan. After this band folded he freelanced as sideman, working often with pianist Dave Brubeck between 1968 and 1972, and serving as arranger for various groups. In the 1970s Mulligan led the short-lived big band the Age of Steam, headed and toured regularly overseas with a sextet that included vibist Dave Samuels, doubled on soprano for a time, and led a 14-piece band he had assembled. During the 1980s he experimented with a big band that featured electronic instruments, but returned mid-decade to a small-group format, leading a quintet with Scott Hamilton and Grady Tate. During the 1990s he led a "Rebirth of the Cool" band, toured with his quartet, and recorded final sessions for Telarc before his death in 1996.

DISC: *Mulligan Plays Mulligan* (1951); *Gerry Mulligan Quartet Featuring Chet Baker Plus Chubby Jackson Big Band* (1952); *California Concerts, Vol. 1* (1954); *California Concerts, Vol. 2* (1954); *At Storyville* (1957); *The Gerry Mulligan Songbook* (1957); *Mulligan Meets Monk* (1957); *Mulligan Meets the Saxophonists* (1957); *What Is There to Say?* (1959); *The Concert Jazz Band* (1960); *Two of a Mind* (with Paul Desmond; 1962); *Timeless* (1963); *Something Borrowed, Something Blue* (1966); *Jazz Fest Masters* (with Paul Desmond; 1969); *Carnegie Hall Concert* (with Chet Baker; 1974); *Soft Lights and Sweet Music* (with Scott Hamilton; 1986); *Re-Birth of the Cool* (1992); *Walk on the Water* (1993); *Paraiso: Jazz Brazil* (1993); *Verve Jazz Masters, Vol. 36* (1994); *Dream a Little Dream* (1994); *Dragonfly* (1995); *The Complete Pacific Jazz Recordings of the Gerry Mulligan Quartet with Chet Baker* (1995); *Legacy* (1996); *This Is Jazz Number 18* (1996).

Mulliner, Thomas, English music anthologist and composer who flourished in the mid 16th century. He was the compiler of the valuable anthology known as the Mulliner Book (ed. by D. Stevens as *The Mulliner Book*, Musica Britannica, I, London, 1951; 2nd ed., 1954), which contains both original and arranged sacred and secular works, covering the period from about 1530 to 1575.

BIBL.: D. Stevens, *The Mulliner Book: A Commentary* (London, 1952).—**LK/DM**

Mullings, Frank (Coningsby), distinguished English tenor; b. Walsall, March 10, 1881; d. Manchester, May 19, 1953. He studied voice in Birmingham. He made his operatic debut in Coventry in 1907 as Faust, then sang Tristan in London in 1913, and performed the role of Otello in Manchester in 1916. In 1919 he was the first to sing Parsifal in English, at Covent Garden in London. From 1922 to 1926 he was the principal dramatic tenor of the British National Opera Co., and appeared with it as Apollo in the first performance, in 1924, of Rutland Boughton's *Alkestis*. He taught at the Birmingham School of Music (1927–46) and at the Royal Manchester Coll. of Music (1944–49). His other roles included Siegfried, Tannhäuser, Canio, and Radames. —**NS/LK/DM**

Mullova, Viktoria, Russian violinist; b. Moscow, Nov. 27, 1959. She began violin lessons in childhood and made her public debut as soloist in Vieutemps's 5th Concerto when she was 12. She studied in Moscow with Bronin at the Central Music School (1969–78) and with Kogan at the Moscow Cons. She won 1st prize in the Sibelius Competition in Helsinki in 1981 and took the Gold Medal in the Tchaikovsky Competition in Moscow in 1982. She then left Russia to pursue an international career, touring as a concert recitalist and appearing as soloist with major orchs.—**NS/LK/DM**

Mumma, Gordon, innovative American composer, performer, electronic-music engineer, teacher, and writer on music; b. Framingham, Mass., March 30, 1935. He received private instruction in piano, horn, and composition, and attended the Univ. of Mich. in Ann Arbor (1952–53). In 1958 he became co-founder of Ann Arbor's Cooperative Studio for Electronic Music, remaining active with it until 1966; also was co-director of the ONCE Festival and ONCE Group there (1960–66). He helped to develop a revolutionary theatrical art based on projected images, resulting in an aesthetic medium called "Manifestations: Light and Sound" and, later, "Space Theatre"; in 1964 he participated in a memorable presentation of "Space Theatre" at Venice's Biennial Exhibition, a pioneering demonstration of the electronic light show. Having attended the Inst. of Science and Technology at the Univ. of Mich. (1959–62), he returned there as a research assoc. in acoustics and seismics (1962–63). From 1966 to 1974 he was active as a composer and performer with the Merce Cunningham Dance Co. in N.Y.; also was active with the Sonic Arts Union in N.Y. (from 1966). He taught at the Univ. of Ill. at Urbana (1969–70) and at the Univ. of Calif. at Santa Cruz (1973–75), where he subsequently was a prof. of music (from 1975). He also was a visiting lecturer at Brandeis Univ. (1966–67), the State Univ. of N.Y. at Buffalo (1968), and the Ferienkurse für Neue Musik in Darmstadt (1974); in 1981 he held the Darius Milhaud Professorship at Mills Coll. in Oakland, Calif.; after serving as a visiting prof. at the Univ. of Calif. at San Diego (1985, 1987), he returned to Mills Coll. as Distinguished Visiting Composer in 1989. In 1995 he was made prof. emeritus. Mumma has contributed various articles on contemporary music to journals and other publications. He pioneered the process of "cybersonic music," the control of acoustical and electronic media by means of feedback; also applied computer techniques to composition.

WORKS: *Sinfonia* for 12 Instruments and Tape (1958–60; Ann Arbor, March 4, 1961); *Mographs*, pieces for Various Combinations of Pianos and Pianists (1962–64); *Retrospect*, stereophonic electro-acoustic music (1962–82; Santa Cruz, Calif., Oct. 6, 1982); *Megaton for William Burroughs*, live electronic piece for 10 Electronic, Acoustic, and Communication Channels (1963; Ann Arbor, Feb. 28, 1964); *Music for the Venezia Space Theatre* for 4-channel Magnetic Tape with Live Electronic Music (Venice, Sept. 1, 1964); *The Dresden Interleaf 13 February 1945*, quadraphonic electronic music on magnetic tape (Ann Arbor, Feb. 13, 1965); *Horn* for Cybersonic Horn and Voices (1965); *Mesa*, live electronic music for Cybersonic Bandoneon (St. Paul de Vence, France, Aug. 6, 1966); *Hornpipe* for Cybernetic Horn and Waldhorn (1967); *Schoolwork* for Bowed Psaltery, Piano Melodica, and Bowed Crosscut Saw (1970); *Telepos* for Dancers, Telemetry Belts, and Accelerometers (1971; N.Y., Feb. 2, 1972); *Cybersonic Cantilevers*, cybersonic electronic system with public participation (Syracuse, N.Y., May 19, 1973); *Some Voltage Drop*, variable-duration theater piece with electroacoustical implementation (Paris, Oct. 13, 1974); *Earheart: Flights, Formations, and Starry Nights* for Dancers and Electronics (Portland, Ore., Sept. 9, 1977); *Echo-BCD* for Dancers and Electronics (Portland, Ore., Oct. 15, 1978); *11 Note Pieces and Decimal Passacaglia* for Harpsichord (1979); *Pontpoint* for Dancers and Electronics (1979; Portland, Ore., March 14, 1980); *Faisandage et galimafrée*, divertimento for Trios of Diverse Instruments (Santa Cruz, Calif., June 10, 1984); *Epifont (Spectral Portrait in memoriam George Cacioppo)*, stereophonic electroacoustic music on magnetic tape (1984; Ann Arbor, April 14, 1985); *Than Particle* for Percussion and Digital Computer (Los Angeles, Nov. 7, 1985); *Aleutian*

Displacement for Chamber Orch. (1987); *Orait* for Dancers and Vocal Ensemble (Santa Cruz, Calif., June 17, 1988); *Ménages à deux* for Violin, Piano, Vibraphone, and Marimba (1989; Berkeley, Calif., Feb. 10, 1990).—**NS/LK/DM**

Munch (originally, **Münch**), **Charles,** eminent Alsatian-born French conductor, son of **Ernst Münch**; b. Strasbourg, Sept. 26, 1891; d. Richmond, Va., Nov. 6, 1968. He studied violin at the Strasbourg Cons. and with Lucien Capet in Paris. At the outbreak of World War I (1914), he enlisted in the German army. He was made a sergeant of artillery, and was gassed at Peronne and wounded at Verdun. After the end of the war (1918) and his return to Alsace-Lorraine (1919), he became a naturalized French citizen. Having received further violin training from Flesch in Berlin, he pursued a career as a soloist and was also prof. of violin at the Leipzig Cons. and concertmaster of the Gewandhaus Orch. there. On Nov. 1, 1932, he made his professional conducting debut in Paris with the Straram Orch. He studied conducting with Szendrei in Paris (1933–40). He quickly rose to prominence; was conductor of Paris's Orch. de la Société Philharmonique (1935–38) and became a prof. at the École Normale de Musique (1936). In 1938 he became music director of the Société des Concerts du Conservatoire de Paris, remaining in that post during the years of the German occupation during World War II; refusing to collaborate with the Nazis, he gave his support to the Resistance, being awarded the Legion d'honneur in 1945. He made his U.S. debut as a guest conductor of the Boston Sym. Orch. on Dec. 27, 1946; a transcontinental tour of the U.S. with the French National Radio Orch. followed in 1948. In 1949 he was appointed music director of the Boston Sym. Orch., which he and Monteux took on its first European tour in 1952; they took it again to Europe in 1956, also touring in the Soviet Union, making it the first U.S. orch. to do so. After retiring from his Boston post in 1962, Munch made appearances as a guest conductor; also helped to launch the Orch. de Paris in 1967. Munch acquired an outstanding reputation as an interpreter of the French repertoire, his performances being marked by spontaneity, color, and elegance. French music of the 20th century also occupied a prominent place on his programs; he brought out new works by Roussel, Milhaud, Honegger, and others. He wrote *Je suis chef d'orchestre* (Paris, 1954; Eng. tr., N.Y., 1955).

BIBL.: P. Olivier, *C. M.: Une Biographie par le disque* (Paris, 1987); G Honegger, *C. M.* (Strasbourg, 1992).—**NS/LK/DM**

Münch, Ernst, Alsatian organist and choral conductor, father of **Charles Munch** and uncle of **Hans Münch**; b. Niederbronn, Dec. 31, 1859; d. Strasbourg, April 1, 1928. He was appointed organist at St. Wilhelm (St. Guillaume) Church in Strasbourg in 1882, where he founded a choir which attained a great renown for its performance of Bach's cantatas and passions. Albert Schweitzer served as organist at these performances.
—**NS/LK/DM**

Münch, Hans, Alsatian-born Swiss conductor and composer, nephew of **Ernst Münch**; b. Mulhouse, March 9, 1893; d. Basel, Sept. 7, 1983. His father, Eugen Münch, was a conductor. After studying with Albert Schweitzer, he settled in Basel (1912) and became a naturalized Swiss citizen where he took courses with Hans Huber (composition), Adolf Hamm (organ), and Emil Braun (cello) at the Cons. and also played cello in the city orch. (1914–16). He then taught piano at the Cons. (1918–32) and conducted the Bach Choir (1921–26). He subsequently led the Gesangverein and the Liedertafel, was conductor of the Allgemeine Musikgesellschaft (1935–66), and served as director of the Music School and Cons. (1935–47). He composed a Sym. (1951), *Symphonische Improvisationen* (1971), and several cantatas.—**NS/LK/DM**

Münchinger, Karl, German conductor; b. Stuttgart, May 29, 1915; d. there, March 13, 1990. He studied at the Hochschule für Musik in Stuttgart; then with Abendroth at the Leipzig Cons. From 1941 to 1943 he was 1st conductor of the orch. in Hannover, and in 1945 founded the Stuttgart Chamber Orch. He toured America, Japan, and Russia; made his U.S. debut in San Francisco in 1953, and during the following season made a U.S. tour with his Stuttgart Chamber Orch.; he visited the U.S. again in 1977. In 1966 he organized the "Klassische Philharmonie" in Stuttgart, with which he gave regular performances. He retired in 1988.
—**NS/LK/DM**

Munck, (Pierre Joseph) Ernest, Chevalier de, Belgian cellist, teacher, and composer; b. Brussels, Dec. 21, 1840; d. London, Jan. 19, 1915. After studying cello with his father, he was a student of Servais at the Brussels Cons. (premier prix, 1855). He was active in London, where he pursued a concert career and taught at the Guildhall School of Music and Drama. After playing in the Maurin Quartet in Paris (1868–70), he was solo cellist of the Weimar Hofkapelle. In 1871 he married Carlotta Patti, with whom he made concert tours. In 1893 he settled in London as a prof. at the Royal Academy of Music. He wrote a *Concerto dramatique* for Cello and Orch. and other pieces for his instrument.—**LK/DM**

Munclinger, Milan, Czech flutist and conductor; b. Košice, July 3, 1923; d. Prague, March 30, 1986. He began to study the flute in his youth, then enrolled at the Prague Cons.; also studied at the Prague Academy of Musical Arts and the Univ. of Prague. He gained distinction as founder-conductor of the Ars Rediviva ensemble (1951), with which he gave performances of the Baroque and Classical repertoires with much success; also toured widely with his ensemble.—**NS/LK/DM**

Mundy, John, English organist and composer, son of **William Mundy**; b. c. 1555; d. Windsor, June 29, 1630. He received the degrees of B.Mus. (1586) and D.Mus. (1624) from Oxford. For more than 40 years, he served as organist of St. George's Chapel, Windsor. He publ. (12) *Songs and* [15] *Psalmes* for 3 to 5 Voices (London, 1594; ed. in The English Madrigalists, XXXV/2, 1924; 2nd ed., rev., 1961 by T. Dart and P. Brett). Among his other works were anthems and Latin sacred pieces, as well as some keyboard music.

BIBL.: G. Blount, *The Sacred Vocal Music of J. M.* (diss., Univ. of Calif., Los Angeles, 1974).—**LK/DM**

Mundy, William, English composer, father of **John Mundy**; b. c. 1529; d. probably in London, Oct. 1591. He became head chorister at Westminster Abbey in 1543. In 1564 he was made vicar-choral at St. Paul's Cathedral and a Gentleman of the Chapel Royal. He composed services, anthems, and Latin antiphons. See F. Harrison, ed., *William Mundy: Latin Antiphons and Psalms*, Early English Church Music, II (1963).—**LK/DM**

Munn, Zae, American composer; b. Moscow, Idaho, Jan. 3, 1953. She studied cello, piano, and voice in her youth, then completed her formal education at the Chicago Musical Coll. at Roosevelt Univ. (B.M., 1978) and the Univ. of Ill. at Champaign-Urbana (M.M., 1979; D.M.A. 1985). She held teaching positions at St. Cloud State Univ. in Minnesota (1983–84), Transylvania Univ. in Lexington, Ky. (1984–86), and Bowdoin Coll. in Brunswick, Maine (1986–89), and also held adjunct faculty positions at Moravian Coll. (1989–90) and Lehigh Univ. (1989–90) in Bethlehem, Pa. From 1990 to 1994 she was an asst. prof. at Saint Mary's Coll. in Notre Dame, Ind., becoming an assoc. prof. in 1994. She also taught summer courses at the Interlochen Arts Camp (from 1997).

WORKS: ORCH.: *Modem* (1987; rev. 1992); *Quantum Stew* for Concert Band or Wind Ensemble (1992); *It's the Soup That Animates the Noodles* for Chamber Orch. (1995). **CHAMBER:** *Provenance* for String Quartet (1978; rev. 1988); *Serendipity* for Oboe, Clarinet, Timpani, Trombone, Violin, Viola, Cello, Double Bass, and Percussion (1980); *Interface* for Viola and Marimba (1983); *Projectual* for Cello (1985); *Skit No 1, in 3 versions* for Chamber Orch., String Orch., or String Quartet (1988); *With a Vengeance* for Piano Trio (1991); *Ockeghem Today* for 3 Trumpets, 4 Horns, 3 Trombones, and Tuba (1993); *They Were Mysterious Guests, Hard to Capture* for Alto Saxophone and Piano (1996); *A Fraction of Your Grace* for Clarinet and String Quartet (1997); *Nudged Along On Time's Notched Stick* for Guitar, Flute, and Viola (1997); *Play Up A Storm* for Flute, Clarinet, Bassoon, Violin, and Cello (1997); *Tangles in the Web* for Percussion Ensemble (1997); *A Fine Garment, A Gentle Weave, Woven With Whispers and Exclamation Points* for Woodwind Quintet (1998); *No Longer Suitable for Framing* for Clarinet and Trombone (1999); *Start Dancing* for Viola and 4 Roto-Toms (1999); *Libero Arbitrio* for Oboe, Bassoon, and Piano (2000). **KEYBOARD: Piano:** *Fascination at a Distance* (1987); *Viscomp 1 and Viscomp 2* (1991); *Three Piano Pieces With Important Things for the Left Hand* (1995). **Harpsichord:** *Pronto, Lamento, Casino* (1999). **Organ:** *Yelling at God* (1998). **VOCAL: Mixed Chorus:** *Care-Charmer Sleep* for Chorus and Drone (1985); *The Whole Machine of the World* (1992); *To Be Like Music* (1993); *Certainty of Stone, a young person's guide to the chorus* for Chorus and Piano (1996); *Five Animals Songs* for Chorus and Piano (1998). **Women's Chorus:** *The Muse, the Stove, and the Willow Plate* (1988); *Grandma's Alleluia* (1989); *Memorial* (1992). **Children's Chorus:** *Come With Me* for Treble Chorus and Piano (1995). **Solo Voice and Instruments:** *Lauber Lieder*, 4 songs for Soprano and Piano (1994; also for Mezzo-soprano and Piano); *Two for Three*, 2 songs for Soprano, Flute, and Viola (1994); *What's for Supper?*, 4 songs for Soprano, Viola, and Piano (1995). **Other:** *In the Scarred Distortions of the Words* for 7 to 9 Readers, Piano, 1 to 3 Percussion, and 5 to 8 Brass (1995); *The Canvas* for Treble Chorus and Orch. (1998). **TAPE:** *Faster* (1989).—**LK/DM**

Munrow, David (John), gifted English recorder player; b. Birmingham, Aug. 12, 1942; d. (suicide) Chesham Bois, Buckinghamshire, May 15, 1976. He studied English at Pembroke Coll., Cambridge; during this period (1961–64), he founded an ensemble for the furtherance of early English music and organized a recorder consort. In 1967 he formed the Early Music Consort of London, with which he gave many successful concerts of medieval and Renaissance music; also was active with his own BBC radio program. He lectured on the history of early music at the Univ. of Leicester (from 1967) and was prof. of recorder at London's Royal Academy of Music (from 1969). He publ. the vol. *Instruments of the Middle Ages and Renaissance* (London, 1976). He killed himself for obscure reasons in his early maturity.—**NS/LK/DM**

Munsel, Patrice (Beverly), American soprano; b. Spokane, Wash., May 14, 1925. She studied in N.Y. with William Herman and Renato Bellini. She won an audition at the Metropolitan Opera and made a successful debut there on Dec. 4, 1943, in the role of Philine in Thomas's *Mignon*, being the youngest singer to appear there to that time; she remained on the staff until 1958, excepting the 1945–46 season. She subsequently made several European tours. Her best roles were Gilda, Lucia, Rosina, Violetta, and Lakme. She portrayed Melba in a film of Melba's life (1953); also made successful appearances in operetta and in Broadway musicals.—**NS/LK/DM**

Munz, Mieczyslaw, esteemed Polish-American pianist and pedagogue; b. Kraków, Oct. 31, 1900; d. N.Y., Aug. 25, 1976. He studied piano and composition at the Vienna Academy of Music, and later at the Hochschule für Musik in Berlin, where his principal teacher was Busoni. He made a brilliant debut in Berlin in 1920 as soloist in 3 works on the same program: the Brahms Piano Concerto in D minor, Liszt's Piano Concerto in A, and *Variations symphoniques* by Franck. His American debut took place in a solo recital in N.Y. on Oct. 20, 1922; he subsequently was soloist with a number of orchs. in the U.S.; also toured Europe, South America, Australia, and Japan. He taught at the Cincinnati Cons. of Music (1925–30); then was on the faculty of the Curtis Inst. of Music in Philadelphia (1930–32; 1941–63); from 1946 to 1965 he taught at the Peabody Inst. in Baltimore; also was a prof. of piano at the Juilliard School of Music in N.Y. (1963–75). In 1975 he was given a tenured appointment at the Toho Gakuen School of Music in Tokyo, but he was forced to return to the U.S. due to illness. He was highly esteemed as a teacher; his students included Emanuel Ax and Ilana Vered. His piano playing was distinguished by a fine Romantic flair supported by an unobtrusive virtuoso technique.—**NS/LK/DM**

Munzinger, Karl, Swiss conductor and composer; b. Balsthal, Sept. 23, 1842; d. Bern, Aug. 16, 1911. He studied in Basel (1859–60) and was a pupil of Hauptmann, Reinecke, E.F. Richter, and Moscheles at the Leipzig Cons. (1860–63). In 1866 he became director of the Liedertafel and Cäcilienverein in Solothurn. He was named conductor of the Musikgesellschaft concerts in Bern in 1884, introducing that city to works ranging from Bach to Brahms. Among his compositions were a mass, cantatas, a Piano Quartet, organ pieces, and piano music.—LK/DM

Muradeli, Vano (Ilyich), Russian composer; b. Gori, Ga., April 6, 1908; d. Tomsk, Siberia, Aug. 14, 1970. As a child he improvised songs, accompanying himself on the mandolin. He studied with Barchudarian and Bagrinsky at the Tiflis Cons. (graduated, 1931) and with Shekhter and Miaskovsky at the Moscow Cons. (graduated, 1934). His early compositions were influenced by his native folk music; he wrote a *Georgian Suite* for Piano (1935) and incidental music to plays on Caucasian subjects. His first important work was a sym. in memory of the assassinated Soviet dignitary Kirov (Moscow, Nov. 28, 1938); his 2nd Sym. (1946) received a Stalin prize. The performance of his opera *Great Friendship* (Moscow, Nov. 7, 1947) gave rise to an official condemnation of modernistic trends in Soviet music, culminating in the resolution of the Central Committee of the Communist Party of Feb. 10, 1948, which described the opera as "chaotic, inharmonious, and alien to the normal human ear." His reputation was rehabilitated by his subsequent works, which included *The Path of Victory*, symphonic poem for Chorus and Orch. (1950), a series of choruses (*Stalin's Will Has Led Us; Song of the Fighters for Peace;* and *Hymn to Moscow*, which received a Stalin prize in 1951), and an opera, *October* (Moscow, April 22, 1964).—NS/LK/DM

Murail, Tristan, remarkable French composer; b. Le Havre, March 11, 1947. He received training in Arabic and economics (1963–70), taking courses at the École Nationale des Langues Orientales and at the Institut d'Études Politiques in Paris. He also studied composition with Messiaen at the Paris Cons. (1967–71), taking the premier prix (1971). After winning the Prix de Rome, he pursued training at the French Academy in Rome (1971–73). Upon his return to Paris, he helped to found the contemporary instrumental music ensemble L'Intinéraire. In 1982–83 he was active at IRCAM in Paris. From 1989 to 1991 he was prof. of composition at the American Cons. in Fontainebleau. He also was a consultant at IRCAM from 1990 to 1992. In 1997 he was appointed a prof. at Columbia Univ. in N.Y. Murail has explored innovative approaches to all aspects of composition, often through imaginative uses of the computer.

WORKS: ORCH.: *Couleur de mer* for Chamber Orch. (Le Havre, May 13, 1969); *Altitude 8000* (1970; Paris, Jan. 18, 1971); *Au-delà du mur du son* (Rome, June 10, 1972); *Cosmos privé* (Rome, June 3, 1973); *La Dérive des continents* for Viola and Strings (1973; Royan, March 23, 1974); *Sables* (1974–75; Royan, March 22, 1975); *Les Courants de l'espace* for Ondes Martenot and Small Orch. (1979; Paris, Dec. 20, 1980); *Gondwana* (Darmstadt, July 21, 1980); *Désintégrations* for Chamber Orch. and Tape (1982; Paris, Feb. 15, 1983); *Sillages* (Kyoto, Sept. 9, 1985; rev.

1990); *Time and again* (1985; Birmingham, Jan. 21, 1986); *Les Sept Paroles du Christ en Croix* (1986–89; London, Oct. 28, 1989); *La Dynamique des fluides* (1990–91; Parma, June 17, 1991); *Serendib* (1991–92; Paris, June 18, 1992); *Le Partage des eaux* (1995). **CHAMBER:** *Où tremblent les contours* for 2 Violas (1970); *Les Miroirs étendus* for Ondes Martenot and Piano (1971); *Ligne de non- retour* for 7 Players (1971); *Mach 2,5* for 2 Ondes Martenot (1971; Paris, Feb. 2, 1972; also for 6 Ondes Martenot); *L'attente* for 7 Players (Paris, Nov. 18, 1972; rev. 1992); *Les Nuages de Magellan* for 2 Ondes Martenot, Electric Guitar, and Percussion (Orléans, March 23, 1973); *Tigres de verre* for Ondes Martenot and Piano (1974); *Transsahara express* for Bassoon and Piano (1974); *Mémoire- Erosion* for Horn and 9 Players (1975–76; Orléans, March 5, 1976); *C'est un jardin secret, ma soeur, ma fiancée, une fontaine close, une source scellée* for Viola (1976); *Tellur* for Guitar (Paris, April 26, 1977); *Ethers* for 6 Players (Lisbon, June 6, 1978); *Treize couleurs du soleil couchant* for 5 Players (1978; Madrid, Dec. 4, 1979); *La Conquête de l'Antactique* for Ondes Martenot (1982; Paris, March 2, 1984); *Random Access Memory* for 6 Players (1984–87); *Atlantys* for 2 Synthesizers (King's Lynn, July 26, 1986); *Vision de la cité interdite* for 2 Synthesizers (King's Lynn, July 26, 1986); *Vues aériennes* for Horn, Violin, Cello, and Piano (London, Dec. 1, 1988); *Allégories* for 6 Players and Synthesizer (1989–90; Brussels, March 13, 1990); *Le Fou à pattes bleues* for Flute and Piano (1990; Paris, Dec. 7, 1991); *Attracteurs étranges* for Cello (Radio France, Paris, Dec. 8, 1992); *La Barque mystique* for Flute, Clarinet, Piano, Violin, and Cello (1993); *L'esprit des Dunes* for 11 Players and Synthesizer (1993–94; Paris, May 28, 1994); *unanswered questions* for Flute (1995); *Bois flotte* for 5 Players and Synthesizer (1996); *Feuilles a traves les cloches* for Flute, Violin, Cello, and Piano (1998). **Piano:** *Estuaire* (1971); *Territoires de l'oubil* (1977; Rome, May 22, 1978); *Cloches d'adieu, et un sourire...in memoriam Olivier Messiaen* (1992); *La Mandragore* (Tokyo, Nov. 27, 1993). **VOCAL:** *Amaris et dulcibus aquis* for Chorus and 2 Synthesizers (1995).—NS/LK/DM

Murakumo, Ayako, Japanese composer; b. Gifu Prefecture, Feb. 25, 1949. She graduated from the Graduate School of Aichi Prefecture Univ. of the Arts (degree, 1982). She received the Nagoya City Cultural Promotion Prize (1985), the Incentive Prize for Original Theatrical Art from the Agency of Cultural Affairs (1986), and an award from the Kyūshū competition (1988).

WORKS: ORCH.: *Hishō* (1980); *Chronos* (1982); *Wave* (1982). **CHAMBER:** *Reflection* for Flute, Clarinet, Cello, and Percussion (1982); *Fuha* for Flute, Cello, and Piano (1984); *Chiku-in Sō-Sho* for Shakuhachi and Koto (1985); *Interspersion* for Viola, Cello, and Contrabass (1988); *Polymorph II* for Recorder and Guitar (1989). **VOCAL:** *Projection* for Mezzo-soprano, Cello, and Piano (1984); *Ondine* for Chorus (1985).—NS/LK/DM

Muratore, Lucien, prominent French tenor and teacher; b. Marseilles, Aug. 29, 1876; d. Paris, July 16, 1954. He studied at the Marseilles Cons., graduating with honors in 1897, but began his career as an actor. Later he studied opera at the Paris Cons. He made his operatic debut at the Paris Opéra-Comique on Dec. 16, 1902, as the King in Hahn's *La Carmélite*, with extraordinary success. Muratore also sang in the premieres of several operas by Massenet: *Ariane* (1906), *Bacchus*

(1909), and *Roma* (1912); Février's *Monna Vanna* (1909), and Giordano's *Siberia* (1911) et al. In 1913 he made his American debut with the Boston Opera Co.; on Dec. 15, 1913, he sang Faust with the Chicago Opera Co. In 1914 he joined the French army; then returned to the Chicago Grand Opera (1915–19; 1920–22). In 1922 he went back to France; for 7 years he served as mayor of the town of Biot. He was married 3 times; his first 2 marriages (to Marguerite Beriza, a soprano, and to **Lina Cavalieri**) ended in divorce; his 3rd wife was Marie Louise Brivaud. Among his finest roles were Faust, Don José, and Des Grieux.—**NS/LK/DM**

Mureşianu, Iacob, Romanian conductor, teacher, editor, and composer; b. Braşov, July 11, 1857; d. Blaj, June 6, 1917. Following training with his father, a folklorist, he studied at the Vienna Polytechnic School and with Jadassohn, Reinecke, and Weidenbach at the Leipzig Cons. He settled in Blaj as a conductor and teacher, and also was founder-editor of the periodical *Musa română* (Romanian Muse; 1888–1907). Mureşianu played a significant role in the development of Romanian national music via his utilization of folk elements in his compositions. He composed the operetta *Millo director* (Director Millo; 1910; orch. by I. Mureşianu), several vaudevilles, the overture *Ştefan cel Mare* (Stefan the Great; 1882), *Mănăstirea Argeşului* (The Monastery of Arges) for 3 Soloists, Chorus, and Orch. (1884; rev. 1895), *Erculeanul* for 4 Soloists, Chorus, and Orch. (1890), songs, and many piano pieces.

BIBL.: G. Merişescu, *I. M.: Viaţa şi opera* (I. M.: Life and Works; Bucharest, 1966)—**LK/DM**

Murio-Celli, Adelina, Italian soprano, teacher, and composer; b. Breslau, 1836; d. N.Y., April 10, 1900. She studied with Louis Ponchard, G. Bordogni, and G. Roger at the Paris Cons. After appearances in major European opera houses, she married E. Ravin d'Elpeux, the French vice-consul to the U.S., in 1867 and retired from the operatic stage. Settling in N.Y., she was active as a voice teacher, numbering Eleanora de Cisneros and Emma Juch among her outstanding pupils. She composed some instrumental works and vocal pieces, the best known of which was the song *The Soldier's Bride*. —**NS/LK/DM**

Muris, Johannes de (original French rendering may have been **Jehan des Murs, de Murs, de Meurs**, etc.), important French music theorist, astronomer, and mathematician; b. in the diocese of Lisieux, Normandy, c. 1300; d. c. 1351. He was long confused with Julian des Murs, a Master of the Children of the Sainte-Chapelle of Paris (c. 1350), who later served as secretary to Charles V of France; it seems most likely, however, that the 2 were close relatives. Johannes de Muris is listed as a baccalaureate student in the Faculty of Arts in Paris in 1318. During the next few years he was active in Evreux and Paris. He was associated with the Coll. de Sorbonne in Paris, where he achieved the academic degree of Magister. In 1326–27 he was at the monastery of Fontevrault (Maine-et-Loire); it is known that Julian des Murs was his clerk at

this time. In 1332–33 he was in Evreux, then returned to Paris, where he was again associated with the Sorbonne (1336–37). From 1338 to 1342 he was in service at the court of the King of Navarra, Philippe d'Evreux. In 1342 he was one of the 6 canons of the collegiate church in Mezieres-en-Brenne (Indre). In 1344 he went, at the invitation of Pope Clement VI, to Avignon, where he participated in the conference on the reform of the calendar. There is extant a letter in verse which he wrote to Philippe de Vitry.

The writings by Muris pose problems; titles and versions of the various works attributed to him are questionable. Those that appear authentic are as follows: *Ars novae musicae* or *Notitia artis musicae* (1321; although he gave it the title *Summa musicae*, the work is always known by the 2 preceding titles in order to avoid confusion with a spurious work of the same name); *Questiones super partes musicae* or *Compendium musicae practicae* (c. 1322; apparently a condensed version of the 2nd book of the *Ars novae musicae*); *Musica speculativa secundum Boetium* (June 1323). Some scholars also attribute to him *Libellus cantus mensurabilis* (secundum *Johannes de Muris*) (c. 1340) and *Ars contrapuncti secundum Johannes de Muris* (after 1340). The *Speculum musicae* (c. 1325), long attributed to Muris, has been proved to be a work by Jacques de Liège.

BIBL.: R. Hirschfeld, *J. d.M.: Seine Werke und seine Bedeutung als Verfechter des Classischen in der Tonkunst: Eine Studie* (Leipzig, 1884); W. Grossmann, *Die einleitenden Kapitel des Speculum Musicae von J. d.M.: Ein Beitrag zu Musikanschauung des Mittelalters* (Leipzig, 1924; erroneous in ascribing the authorship of *Speculum musicae* to Muris); U. Michels, *Die Musiktraktate des J. d.M.* (Wiesbaden, 1970).—**NS/LK/DM**

Muro, Bernardo de, Italian tenor; b. Tempio Pausanio, Sardinia, Nov. 3, 1881; d. Rome, Oct. 27, 1955. He studied at the Accademia di Santa Cecilia in Rome and with Alfredo Martinio. He made his operatic debut as Turiddu at Rome's Teatro Costanzi in 1910; in 1911 he appeared at Milan's La Scala as Folco in Mascagni's *Isabeau* and returned there in the title role of *Don Carlos* in 1912. He then sang in various Italian music centers, winning admiration for his portrayal of Otello, and also appeared in Europe and South America. After marrying the American soprano Barbara Wait, he toured in the U.S. with minor opera companies; following his retirement from the stage (1943), he devoted himself to teaching. He never became a star in the operatic firmament, yet knowledgeable critics regarded him as worthy of comparison with Caruso, both in the carrying force of his natural voice and in emotional appeal. He wrote an autobiographical vol., *Quandro ero Folco* (Milan, 1956). —**NS/LK/DM**

Murphy, Mark, American singer; b. Syracuse, N.Y., March 14, 1932. He started singing as a teenager in his brother's dance band, and landed his first major gig in 1954 opening for Anita O'Day in San Francisco. He made his first recordings for Milt Gabler on Decca in the mid-1950s, His two classic albums for Riverside in the early 1960s didn't lead to more work, and he ended up spending a decade in Europe, eventually settling in

London, working as an actor in TV and stage productions. He returned to the U.S. in the mid-1970s and began recording a series of fine albums for Muse. A true student of Brazilian music, he recorded a beautiful album of Ivan Lins tunes for Milestone, *Night Mood*. He has also turned his love of Beat-generation writer Jack Kerouac's novels into highly effective jazz/literature projects, such as his Muse album *Bop for Kerouac*. He spends part of each year teaching jazz singing at the Univ. of Graz in Austria and has developed a following on the acid jazz scene in Europe. He has recorded for Audiophile, Milestone, Fontana, Saba, and Muse.

DISC.: *Rah!* (1961); *That's How I Love the Blues!* (1962); *Mark Murphy Sings* (1976); *Satisfaction Guaranteed* (1979); *Beauty and the Beast* (1986); *September Ballads* (1988); *Night Mood* (1992); *I'll Close My Eyes* (1994); *Song for the Geese* (1997).—AG

Murphy, Paul, jazz drummer; b. Worcester, Mass., Jan. 25, 1949; d. Sao Paulo, Brazil, Aug. 17, 1994. He studied music, percussion, and timpani for nine years with Joseph Leavitt, the principle percussionist with the National Symphony, at Peabody Cons. in Baltimore. He had additional drum and musical studies with Dawson Bugg, Gene Krupa, Louis Bellson, Buddy Rich, Rashied Ali, and Jimmy Lyons. He led clinics at Berklee, and taught at San Francisco Cons. of Music. In 1972, he led his own band in San Francisco with Mary Ann Driscoll and Steve D'Amico, then led another group in N.Y. that included Driscoll, Dewey Johnson, Karen Borca, and Jay Oliver (1974–79). He played with the Jimmy Lyons Quartet and ensembles (1974–86), touring throughout Europe and the U.S. Murphy led an ensemble with Glen Spearman and Kash Killion at the Concord Jazz Festival (1988) and another with India Cooke, Kash Killion, and Glenn Spearman, at Concepts, Oakland, Calif. He was also a session drummer in Las Vegas and the principle session drummer for Mapleshade Studios (1990–94), playing with Clifford Jordan, Ran Blake, and others. He performed, often with William Parker, at various festivals, primarily in the N.Y. area.

DISC.: *Suite of Winds* (1986).—LP

Murphy, Suzanne, Irish soprano; b. Limerick, Aug. 15, 1941. She received vocal training from Veronica Dunne at the Dublin Coll. of Music (1973–76). After making her operatic debut in *La Cenerentola* at the Irish National Opera in Dublin, she was engaged as Constanze at the Welsh National Opera in Cardiff in 1976. She subsequently sang such roles there as Gilda, Norma, Leonora, Elisabeth de Valois, Violetta, Amelia Boccanegra, and Musetta. In 1985 she sang Norma in Munich. In 1987 she made her first appearance at the Vienna State Opera as Elettra. She sang Alice Ford during the Welsh National Opera's tour to N.Y. and Milan in 1989. In 1991 she portrayed Elettra at the London Promenade Concerts, and in 1992 she appeared as Tosca with the English National Opera in London. She was engaged as Leonore in Belfast in 1996. —NS/LK/DM

Murphy, Turk (Melvin Edward Alton), Dixieland-jazz revivalist trombonist, leader, composer; b. Palermo, Calif., Dec. 16, 1915; d. San Francisco, Calif.,

May 30, 1987. After studying music theory, he took up the cornet and trombone. He helped Lu Watters organize the Yerba Buena Band in the late 1930s and worked regularly with Watters until 1947. He played with Marty Marsala in 1951, then worked consistently with his own band, including long residencies in C.A. during the 1950s and dates in New Orleans, N.Y., etc. From September 1960 through February 1978, he led a band at his own club in San Francisco (Earthquake McGoon's); it became a major influence on the Bay Area traditional jazz scene. During that period, his band also played at various other venues including Disneyland, touring Australia and Europe in 1974. Murphy was featured at the St. Louis, Mo., Ragtime Festival in 1977. In January 1987, a concert was staged in his honor at Carnegie Hall, at which he made one of his last performances; soon after, his health failed and he died.

DISC.: *Turk Murphy, Vol. 1* (1949); *Favorites* (1949); *Turk Murphy's Jazz Band* (1950); *San Francisco Jazz, Vol. 1, 2* (1950); *Turk Murphy with Claire Austin* (1952); *At the Italian Village* (1952); *When the Saints Go Marching In* (1953); *Music of Jelly Roll Morton* (1953); *Barrelhouse Jazz* (1953); *Natural High* (1954); *Dancing Jazz* (1954); *New Orleans Jazz Festival* (1955); *New Orleans Shuffle* (1956); *Music for Losers* (1957); *At the Newport Jazz Festival* (1957); *Turk Murphy at Easy Street* (1958); *Turk Murphy at the Round Table* (1959); *Let the Good Times Roll* (1962); *Turk Murphy and His San Francisco Band* (1972); *Turk Murphy* (1972); *In Concert, Vol. 1, 2* (1972); *Many Faces of Ragtime* (1973); *San Francisco Memories* (1985); *Concert in the Park* (1986).

BIBL.: J. Goggi,. *Turk Murphy: Just for the Record* (San Francisco, 1982).—JC/NS

Murray, Ann, Irish mezzo-soprano; b. Dublin, Aug. 27, 1949. She studied at the Royal Manchester Coll. of Music and in London. In 1974 she made her operatic debut as Alceste at Glasgow's Scottish Opera, and then appeared regularly at London's English National Opera; in 1976 she made her Covent Garden debut in London as Cherubino, and subsequently sang there frequently. On Oct. 18, 1985, she made her Metropolitan Opera debut in N.Y. as Sextus in *La clemenza di Tito*. In 1990 she scored a notable success as Berlioz's Beatrice with the English National Opera. In 1994 she appeared as Giulio Cesare in Munich. She appeared as Xerxes at the Lyric Opera in Chicago in 1995. In 1997 she sang Giulio Cesare at Covent Garden. She also sang as a guest artist with various opera houses and festivals at home and abroad, and likewise pursued a notably successful career as a concert artist. Among her finest roles are Handel's Xerxes, Mozart's Dorabella and Zerlina, and Strauss's Composer. Her husband is **Philip Langridge.**—NS/LK/DM

Murray, Anne, Canada's gift to Nashville-pop; b. Spring Hill, Nova Scotia, June 20, 1945. Murray is one of those smooth-voiced crooners who combines good-girl looks with golly-gosh material, making her a consistent country as well as pop hitmaker in the 1970s and 1980s.

Murray was raised in the coal mining/fishing village of Spring Hill, where country music was fairly typical radio fare, although her mother and father preferred the light pop of Perry Como and Rosemary Clooney, perhaps explaining her later affinity for similar music. She began singing pop and folk music in high school, although she didn't really intend to pursue a musical career; instead, she enrolled in teacher's college majoring in physical education. However, she continued to perform in local clubs, and auditioned for local TV programs, including the popular folk-pop show, *Sing Along Jubillee*. Although her initial audition in 1964 was a failure, producer and cohost William Langstroth was sufficiently impressed to invite her to audition again two years later, when she finally made the mark. She remained with the show for four years.

Another producer associated with the show, Brian Ahern (who would later produce Emmylou Harris's successful 1970s recordings) encouraged her to pursue a full-time musical career, and produced her first album for the Canadian Arc label in 1968. Canadian Capitol was impressed, and signed her to a contract in 1969; its U.S. sister label picked up her single, "Snowbird," which became a U.S. gold record in 1970.

Capitol immediately brought her to Los Angeles, and vigorously promoted and showcased her as a pop recording star. But the hits dried up for a while, and Murray felt somewhat lost in the big Calif. city. In 1973, she finally returned to the pop charts with a cover of Kenny Loggins's "Danny's Song," and a year later had her first country hit, again produced by Ahern, a cover of Dickey Lee's "He Thinks I Still Care" (originally a 1962 hit for George Jones). Murray had learned this song during her Sing Along Jubilee days, and recorded it as something of an afterthought; it established her as a country star.

In the mid-1970s, Murray tired of the endless touring and decided to wed long-time friend William Langstroth and retire for a while. Although Capitol had plenty of material in the can, Murray actually did little recording until she returned from her self-imposed exile in 1978. She made a big splash on pop and country charts with the cloyingly sentimental "You Needed Me," following it with a #1 country hit with a cover of "I Just Fall in Love Again." Now working with mainstream country producer Jim Ed Norman, Murray churned out the hits in the late 1970s and early 1980s, including 1980's "Could I Have this Dance?," featured in the film *Urban Cowboy*, that launched an early 1980s country music renaissance. Murray became one of the most popular of the early 1980s divas, even though her musical output was no more "country" than it was "easy listening." She gained further attention with her 1983 hit "A Little Good News" that pleased such political conservatives as then–vice president George Bush, who quoted from its lyrics during campaign speeches!

In 1986, Murray decided to move into a more pop-oriented direction, working with new producer David Foster (known for his middle-of-the-road production style). Despite this attempt to storm up the pop charts, Murray scored another country #1 with "Now and Forever (You and Me)" from these sessions. A follow-up album continued with this new emphasis on mainstream pop, but Murray managed to alienate her core country audience while failing to crossover into the

more lucrative mainstream market. Since the late 1980s, when the new country style swept away the popularity of performers like Murray, she has mostly worked the Vegas-show circuit. In 1999, she released a two-record set aimed at the Christian music market, *What A Wonderful World*, which included duets with her daughter, Dawn.

DISC.: *What About Me?* (1968); *This Way Is My Way* (1969); *Honey, Wheat & Laughter* (1970); *Snowbird* (1970); *Straight, Clean & Simple* (1971); *Take It Over in the Morning* (1971); *And Glen Campbell* (1971); *Danny's Song* (1971); *Annie* (1972); *Love Song* (1974); *Country* (1974); *Highly Prized Possession* (1974); *Together* (1975); *Keepin' in Touch* (1976); *There's a Hippo in My Tub* (1977); *Let's Keep It That Way* (1978); *New Kind of Feeling* (1979); *I'll Always Love You* (1979); *Somebody's Waiting* (1980); *Where Do You Go When You Dream?* (1981); *Christmas Wishes* (1981); *The Hottest Night of the Year* (1982); *A Little Good News* (1983); *Heart over Mind* (1984); *Something to Talk About* (1986); *Harmony* (1987); *Songs of the Heart* (1987); *As I Am* (1988); *Christmas* (1988); *Love Songs* (1989); *From Springhill to the World* (1990); *You Will* (1990); *Yes I Do* (1991); *Croonin'* (1993); *The Season Will Never Grow Old* (1993); *Anne Murray* (1996); *An Intimate Evening With Anne Murray...Live* (1997); *What a Wonderful World* (1999).—RC

Murray, Bain, American composer and teacher; b. Evanston, Ill., Dec. 26, 1926; d. Cleveland, Jan. 16, 1993. He was a student of Elwell at Oberlin (Ohio) Coll. (A.B., 1951), of Thompson and Piston at Harvard Univ. (A.M., 1952), and of Boulanger in Paris. He taught at Harvard Univ. (1954–55), Oberlin Coll. (1955–60), and Cleveland State Univ. (from 1960), where he was head of its theory and composition dept. (from 1966).

WORKS: *The Legend*, opera-oratorio (1986; Cleveland, May 8, 1987); *Mary Stuart: A Queen Betrayed*, opera (Cleveland, March 1, 1991); *Peter Pan*, ballet; *Epitaph* for Strings; 2 string quartets; Trio for Flute, Cello, and Piano; Woodwind Quintet; piano pieces; many choral works; song cycles.—NS/LK/DM

Murray, Billy (actually, **William Thomas**), pervasive American singer of the acoustic recording era; b. Philadelphia, Pa., May 25, 1877; d. Jones Beach, N.Y., Aug. 17, 1954. The most successful American recording artist of the first quarter of the 20th century, Murray had a penetrating tenor voice, good enunciation, comic enthusiasm, and rapid-fire patter delivery that were well suited to the low-fidelity acoustic recording medium.

Murray was the son of Irish immigrants Patrick Murray, a blacksmith, and Julia Kelleher Murray. The family moved to Denver when he was an infant. He showed an early interest in entertainment and joined his first theatrical touring act, Harry Leavitt's High Roller's Show, at 16. He made his first recordings with his partner Matt Keefe in San Francisco in 1897, but the recording industry was just beginning, and he continued his career on the stage, joining the Al G. Field Minstrels. Field dubbed him "Billy," a more appropriate name for a comedian than William.

Murray made his first solo recordings in 1903, singing for Columbia, Victor, and Edison. His first major hit came in 1904 with "Bedalia," from the Broadway musical *The Jersey Lily*, and thereafter his hits included

"Navajo" (1904), "Meet Me in St. Louis, Louis" (1904), "Alexander" (1904), "Come Take a Trip in My Air-Ship" (1905), "In My Merry Oldsmobile" (1905), "Everybody Works but Father" (1906), "Under Any Old Flag at All" (1908), "Carrie (Carrie Marry Harry)" (1910), "I Love a Piano" (1916), "Pretty Baby" (1916), and "That Old Gang of Mine" (1923) (with Ed Smalle).

With his recording of "Yankee Doodle Boy" (1905), Murray became the most noted interpreter of the songs of George M. Cohan on record. He also made hits out of "Give My Regards to Broadway" (1905), "The Grand Old Rag" ("You're a Grand Old Flag") (1906), and "Harrigan" (1907). Murray's partnership with Ada Jones resulted in such duo hits as "Let's Take an Old-Fashioned Walk" (1907), "Wouldn't You Like to Have Me for a Sweetheart?" (1908), "When We Are M-A-Double R-I-E-D" (1908), "Cuddle Up a Little Closer, Lovey Mine" (1908), "Shine On, Harvest Moon" (1909), and "Be My Little Bumble Bee" (1912). He also recorded with The Haydn Quartet, most successfully on "Take Me Out to the Ball Game" (1908) and "By the Light of the Silvery Moon" (1910).

Murray was a founding member of The American Quartet, with whom he recorded the gold-selling "Casey Jones" (1910); "Call Me Up Some Rainy Afternoon" (1910) (with Jones); "Come, Josephine, in My Flying Machine" (1911) (with Jones); "Oh, You Beautiful Doll" (1912); "Moonlight Bay" (1912); "Everybody Two-Step" (1912); "Rebecca of Sunny-brook Farm" (1914); "It's a Long, Long Way to Tipperary" (1914); "Chinatown, My Chinatown" (1915); Oh Johnny, Oh Johnny, Oh!" (1917); "Over There" (1917) (Cohan's standard of World War I); and "Good-Bye Broadway, Hello France" (1917).

With the addition of counter-tenor Will Oakland, The American Quartet became The Heidelberg Quintet for such hits as "Waiting for the Robert E. Lee" (1912) and "By the Beautiful Sea" (1914). He also recorded with the Columbia Comedy Trio, Joseph C. Smith's Orch., The Great White Way Orch., The International Novelty Orch., and the orchestras of Jack Shilkret and Jean Goldkette, among many others.

Murray's was the first recorded voice to be heard on radio, in a test broadcast in 1907. In 1920 he signed an exclusive contract with Victor, but his bravura style was not appropriate to the electrical recording technology that came into use in mid-decade. His Victor contract expired in 1928, though he continued to record regularly until 1932. He became a radio actor in the 1930s, and enjoyed a brief comeback on records with Victor's Bluebird subsidiary in 1940 before retiring due to a heart condition that eventually led to his death.—**WR**

Murray, David (Keith), jazz tenor and soprano saxophonist, flutist, bass clarinetist, leader; b. Berkeley, Calif., Feb. 19, 1955. Murray started in the church playing gospel music alongside his brother, cousin, mother and father. He admired Sly Stone, whom he met in church when he was in Vallejo. He started playing alto sax at age nine; he saw Sonny Rollins at the Berkeley Jazz Festival when he was 11 or 12, which inspired him to switch from alto to tenor. At that time, he played guitar in addition to playing R&B saxophone

with Notations of Soul and doing steps in the horn section. In high school, he played "A Taste of Honey" and other songs with an organ player and drummer at pizza parlors all over the Bay area, and eventually began doing jazz. In college he studied with Bobby Bradford, Arthur Blythe (from whom he first learned free jazz), and Stanley Crouch, who became an important mentor and played drums in Murray's trio when they first moved to N.Y. in 1975. He formed the World Saxophone Quartet with Oliver Lake, Julius Hemphill, and Hamiet Bluiett in the mid-1970s. He has led and recorded with his own big band and small groups, and played in Jack DeJohnette's Special Edition. He has worked with Cecil Taylor, Don Cherry, Anthony Braxton, Sunny Murray, James "Blood" Ulmer, Ed Blackwell, McCoy Tyner, Fred Hopkins, and Andrew Cyrille. Since the mid-1990s, he has lived in Paris.

DISC.: *Live at the Peace Church* (1976); *Flowers for Albert* (1976); *Interboogieology* (1978); *Ming* (1980); *Murray's Steps* (1982); *Morning Song* (1983); *Spirituals* (1988); *New Life* (1988); *Ming's Samba* (1988); *Lucky Four* (1988); *Deep River* (1988); *Special Quartet* (1990); *Shakill's Warrior* (1991); *David Murray Big Band, Conducted by Butch Morris* (1991); *Black on Black* (1992); *Jazzpar Prize* (1993); *Jazzosaurus Rex* (1993); *Shakill's 2* (1994); *Live '93 Acoustic Octfunk* (1994); *Blue Monke* (1995).—**LP**

Murray, Michael, American organist; b. Kokomo, Ind., March 19, 1943. He studied with Dorothy Cleveland Hopkins in Kokomo (1958–59), Mallory Bransford in Indianapolis (1959–61), Haskell Thomson at Oberlin (Ohio) Coll. (1961; 1965), and Marcel Dupré in Paris (1961–64). He served as organist (1967–80) and music director (1970–80) at Cleveland Heights Christian Church. He formally launched his career as a concert artist with a series of the complete organ works of J.S. Bach in Cleveland (1968–69). He made his European debut in Leiden, the Netherlands, in 1972. Thereafter he regularly toured the U.S. and Europe, making his N.Y. debut at St. James Episcopal Church in 1986. He was a contributor of articles to the journals *Diapason* and *American Organist*. Murray publ. *Marcel Dupré: The Work of a Master* (Boston, 1985), *Albert Schweitzer, Musician* (Aldershot, 1994), and *French Masters of the Organ: Saint-Saëns, Franck, Widor, Vierne, Dupré, Langlais, Messiaen* (New Haven, 1998).—**NS/LK/DM**

Murray, Sunny (James Marcellus Arthur), free-jazz drummer; b. Idabel, Okla., Sept. 21, 1937. Sunny Murray is considered to be one of the true originals of free drumming. He started drums at nine, and was self-taught, encouraged by his stepbrother; he played trombone and trumpet briefly. He moved to N.Y. in 1956, and worked with Henry "Red" Allen, Willie "The Lion" Smith, Jackie McLean, Rocky Boyd, Ted Curson. He met Cecil Taylor in 1959 and they began working together; they toured Europe with Jimmy Lyons in 1963. Murray met Albert Ayler and formed trio with bassist Gary Peacock, recording and touring. He also played with Ornette Coleman, Don Cherry, John Coltrane, among others, and led his own groups in N.Y. and Philadelphia, featuring many younger players who have since become prominent. In 1968, he moved to

France; he performed in the Pan-African Fest. in Algiers with Archie Shepp. He later returned to Philadelphia where started a musical relationship with Philly Joe Jones and played with his own groups, including The Untouchable Factor, recording during the 1970s and appearing at the Wildflowers Festival in 1976. During the 1980s, he led his own quintets, including one with the unusual instrument of two saxes and two violins and drums; he also composed a few film scores.

DISC.: *Sunny's Time Now* (1965); *Sunny Murray Quintet* (1966); *Sunny Murray* (1966); *Hard Cores* (1968); *Big Chief* (1968); *Sunshine* (1969); *Never Give a Sucker an Even Break* (1969); *Homage to Africa* (1969); *In Paris: Big Chief* (1970); *Charred Earth* (1978); *Applecores* (1978); *Live at the Moers Festival* (1979). Albert Ayler: *New York Eye and Ear Control* (1964); *Spiritual Unity* (1964); *Bells* (1965); *Spirits Rejoice* (1965); *Bells-Prophecy* (1999).—LP

Murray, Thomas (Mantle), American organist and choral conductor; b. Los Angeles, Oct. 6, 1943. He studied with Clarence Mader (organ) and Howard Swan (choral conducting) at Occidental Coll. (B.A., 1965), then was organist at Los Angeles's Immanuel Presbyterian Church (1965–73) and organist and choirmaster at Boston's St. Paul's Episcopal Church (1973–80). He taught at the Yale Univ. School of Music from 1981 and toured widely as a recitalist, acquiring a fine reputation as an interpreter of the Romantic organ repertoire.—NS/LK/DM

Murray, William, American baritone; b. Schenectady, N.Y., March 13, 1935. He studied at Adelphi Univ. In 1956 he received a Fulbright scholarship and continued his training in Rome. After making his operatic debut as Count Gil in *Il segreto di Susanna* in Spoleto in 1956, he sang in Detmold, Braunschweig, Munich, Frankfurt am Main, Amsterdam, and Salzburg. In 1969 he became a member of the Deutsche Oper in Berlin, where he was made a Kammersanger. In 1970 he created the title role in Dallapiccola's *Ulisse* at Milan's La Scala. In 1973 he sang in the premiere of Nabokov's *Love's Labours Lost* in Brussels. Among his other roles were Don Giovanni, Rigoletto, Don Carlo, Wolfram, Macbeth, and Scarpia.—NS/LK/DM

Murrill, Herbert (Henry John), English organist, choral conductor, broadcasting executive, and composer; b. London, May 11, 1909; d. there, July 24, 1952. He studied at the Royal Academy of Music in London with York Bowen, Stanley Marchant, and Alan Bush (1925–28), and then was an organ scholar at Worcester Coll., Oxford (1928–31), where he took courses with Ernest Walker and Sir Hugh Allen. He occupied various posts as organist and choral director. He was prof. of composition at the Royal Academy of Music (1933–52), and also joined the staff of the BBC (1936), where he was program organizer (1942). After working in the British intelligence service (1942–46), he returned to the BBC as asst. head (1948) and head (1950) of music. His relatively small output was in a modern vein, exemplified by a "jazz opera," *Man in Cage* (London, 1930). He also wrote 2 cello concertos (1935; *El cant dels ocells*, 1950), choral works, chamber music, piano pieces, and songs.—NS/LK/DM

Murschhauser, Franz Xaver Anton, German music theorist and composer; b. Zabern, near Strasbourg (baptized), July 1, 1663; d. Munich, Jan. 6, 1738. He studied with J.K. Kerll in Munich, where from 1691 he was music director of the Frauenkirche there. He wrote the theoretical treatise *Academia musico-poetica bipartita, oder Hohe Schule der musikalischen Compositions*, the first part of which appeared in 1721, provocatively described as being intended "to give a little more light to the excellent Herr Mattheson." The latter retaliated with such devastating effect in his *Die melopoetische Licht-Scheere* (Vol. I, *Critica musica*, 1722) that Murschhauser refrained from publishing the second part of his work. His compositions for organ are reprinted in Denkmäler der Tonkunst in Bayern, XXX, Jg. XVIII (1917), ed. by M. Seiffert, with a biographical sketch. —NS/LK/DM

Mursell, James L(ockhart), English-born American music educator; b. Derby, June 1, 1893; d. Jackson, N.H., Feb. 1, 1963. Following training in England and at the Univ. of Queensland in Brisbane, Australia (B.A., 1915), he studied philosophy with Josiah Royce at Harvard Univ. (Ph.D., 1918), then pursued training for the ministry at N.Y.'s Union Theological Seminary (1918–20). He taught psychology and education at Lake Erie Coll. in Painesville, Ohio (1921–23), and then philosophy, psychology, and education at Lawrence Coll. in Appleton, Wisc. (1923–25), where he also studied at the Cons. with Gladys Brainard. In 1935 he became prof. of education at Teachers Coll., Columbia Univ., where he later was chairman of the music education dept. (1939–57). Mursell was a proponent of a humanistic approach to music education.

WRITINGS (all publ. in N.Y. unless otherwise given): *Principles of Musical Education* (1927); with M. Glenn, *The Psychology of School Music Teaching* (1931; 2nd ed., 1938); *Human Values in Music Education* (1934); *The Psychology of Music* (1937); *Music in American Schools* (1943); *Education for Musical Growth* (Boston, 1948); *Music and the Classroom Teacher* (1951); *Music Education: Principles and Programs* (Morristown, N.J., 1956).

BIBL.: L. Simutis, *J.L. M. as Music Educator* (diss., Univ. of Ottawa, 1961); D. Metz, *A Critical Analysis of the Thought of J.L. M. in Music Education* (diss., Case Western Reserve Univ., 1968); V. O'Keefe, *J.L. M.: His Life and Contributions to Music Education* (diss., Teachers Coll., Columbia Univ., 1970).—NS/LK/DM

Murska, Ilma di, Croatian soprano; b. Zagreb, Jan. 4, 1836; d. Munich, Jan. 14, 1889. She studied with Mathilde Marchesi in Vienna and Paris, making made her debut in Florence (1862). After a European tour, she was engaged at the Vienna Court Opera. She made her London debut as Lucia (May 11, 1865) and was favorably received there until 1873; toured America (debut as Amina in N.Y., Oct. 7, 1873) and Australia (1873–76), and was again in London in 1879. She was greatly admired for the quality of her voice and stage presence, but her voice and health deteriorated so rapidly that reviewers were embarrassed by her pathetic vocal display at her last N.Y. appearance (Dec. 29, 1887). She taught unsuccessfully at the National Cons. there (1888) and then returned to Germany, where she died in poverty. She also composed a few works. Her life was filled with turbulence and a fabricated background: 2 marriages, an illegitimate daughter whose legitimacy was established by fabricating a third marriage, lawsuits with opera companies, and injudicious advice from friends. Learning of her death, her daughter, with whom she was living, committed suicide.—NS/LK/DM

Musard, Philippe, famous French conductor and composer; b. Tours, Nov. 8, 1792; d. Auteuil, Paris, March 30, 1859. He studied music privately with Reicha. He organized his own Concerts-Musard in Paris, at which he presented popular works and dance music. The remarkable cornetist Dufresne became an added attraction, and Musard wrote special solo pieces for him; he also conducted balls at the Paris Opéra (1835–36), at which his orch. of 70 musicians won great acclaim. He led popular concerts at London's Drury Lane and Lyceum Theatre (1840–41), and remained a successful figure in France until his retirement in 1852. His quadrilles and galops enjoyed immense popularity, and he earned the sobriquet "le roi des quadrilles." His son Alfred Musard (1828–81) was also a composer of quadrilles, and a bandleader.—NS/LK/DM

Musgrave, Thea, remarkable Scottish composer; b. Barnton, Midlothian, May 27, 1928. She was a student of Mary Grierson (musical analysis) and Hans Gál (composition and counterpoint) at the Univ. of Glasgow (B.Mus., 1950), where she won the Donald Francis Tovey Prize. A scholarship made it possible for her to go to Paris, where she studied with Nadia Boulanger and at the Cons. (1952–54), during which time she won the Lili Boulanger Memorial Prize. She completed her studies with Copland at the Berkshire Music Center in Tanglewood (summer, 1959). From 1958 to 1965 she was a lecturer at the Univ. of London. In 1970 she was a visiting prof. at the Univ. of Calif. at Santa Barbara, and in 1987 she was a Distinguished Prof. of Music at Queens Coll. of the City Univ. of N.Y. In 1974 she received the Koussevitzky Award. She held Guggenheim fellowships in 1974–75 and 1982–83. In 1971 she married **Peter Mark.** Following an initial period of composition in which she followed the precepts of strict serial techniques, Musgrave pursued an individual course in which dramatic-abstract musical forms were utilized in both her theater and concert scores.

WORKS: DRAMATIC: O p e r a : *The Abbott of Drimock,* chamber opera (1955; concert perf., Park Lane Opera Group, June 22, 1958); *The Decision* (1964–65; London, Nov. 30, 1967); *The Voice of Ariadne,* chamber opera (1972–73; Aldeburgh, June 11, 1974); *Mary, Queen of Scots* (1975–77; Edinburgh, Sept. 6, 1977); *A Christmas Carol,* after Dickens (1978–79; Norfolk, Va., Dec. 7, 1979); *An Occurrence at Owl Creek Bridge,* radio opera after Ambrose Bierce (1981; BBC, Sept. 14, 1982); *Harriet, The Woman Called Moses* (1984; Norfolk, Va., March 1, 1985); *Simón Bolívar* (1989–92; Norfolk, Va., Jan. 20, 1995); *The Story of Harriet Tubman,* music drama after the opera *Harriet, The Woman Called Moses* (1990; Mobile, Ala., Jan. 1993). B a l l e t : *A Tale for Thieves* (1953); *Beauty and the Beast* (1968–69; London, Nov. 19, 1969); *Orfeo* (1975; BBC-TV, March 17, 1977). O t h e r : *Marko the Miser,* children's theater piece (1962; Farnham, May 16, 1963). ORCH.: *Divertimento* for Strings (1957); *Obliques* (1958); *Scottish Dance Suite* (1959; Glasgow, Aug. 17, 1961; also for

Concert Band, 1974); *Perspectives* (1961); *Theme and Interludes* (1962); *Sinfonia* (1963); *Festival Overture* (1965); *Variations* for Brass Band (Fife, July 15, 1966); *Nocturnes and Arias* (1966; Zürich, Nov. 3, 1968); *Concerto for Orchestra* (1967; London, March 8, 1968); Clarinet Concerto (1968; London, Feb. 5, 1969); *Night Music* for Chamber Orch. (1968; Cardiff, Oct. 24, 1969); *Memento Vitae (Concerto in Homage to Beethoven)* (1969–70; Glasgow, March 22, 1970); Horn Concerto (Glasgow, May 1, 1971); Viola Concerto (London, Aug. 13, 1973); *Orfeo II* for Flute and Strings (1975; Los Angeles, March 28, 1976); *From One to Another* for Viola and Strings (1980; Minneapolis, March 18, 1982; also for Viola and Tape, 1970); *Peripeteia* (London, Nov. 2, 1981); *Moving Into Aquarius* (1984; London, Jan. 23, 1985; in collaboration with R.R. Bennett); *The Seasons* (London, Dec. 4, 1988); *Rainbow* (Glasgow, Oct. 8, 1990); *Song of the Enchanter (In Homage to Sibelius)* (1990; Helsinki, Feb. 14, 1991); *Autumn Sonata,* bass clarinet concerto (1993; Cheltenham, July 13, 1994); *Journey Through a Japanese Landscape,* concerto for Marimba and Wind Orch. (1993–94; Cheltenham, July 14, 1994); *Helios,* oboe concerto (1994; Orkney, June 17, 1995); *Phoenix Rising* (1997; London, Feb. 18, 1998). CHAMBER: String Quartet (1958); *Colloquy* for Violin and Piano (Cheltenham, July 12, 1960); Trio for Flute, Oboe, and Piano (1960; London, Jan. 8, 1961); *Serenade* for Flute, Clarinet, Harp, Viola, and Cello (1961; London, March 14, 1962); Chamber Concerto No. 1 (Glasgow, April 26, 1962), No. 2 (*In Homage to Charles Ives*) (Dartington, Aug. 5, 1966), and No. 3 (1966; London, Oct. 16, 1967); *Sonata for Three* for Flute, Violin, and Guitar (Winchester, May 27, 1966); *Impromptu No. 1* for Flute and Oboe (London, April 16, 1967) and *No. 2* for Flute, Oboe, and Clarinet (1970; Cardiff, Nov. 16, 1971); *Music for Horn and Piano* (Zagreb, May 1967); *Soliloquy* for Guitar and Tape (1969; London, March 15, 1972); *Elegy* for Viola and Cello (Santa Barbara, May 19, 1970); *From One to Another* for Viola and Tape (Los Angeles, Nov. 30, 1970; also for Viola and Strings, 1980); *Space Play,* concerto for 9 Instruments (London, Oct. 11, 1974); *Orfeo I* for Flute and Tape (1975; Chichester, July 4, 1976; also as *Orfeo III* for Flute and 5 Instruments, Moscow, Oct. 11, 1993); *Fanfare* for Brass Quintet (Norfolk, Va., Dec. 3, 1982); *Pierrot* for Clarinet, Violin, and Piano (1985; Istanbul, April 13, 1986); *The Golden Echo I* for Horn and Tape (1986; also as *The Golden Echo II* for Solo Horn and 16 Accompanying Horns, 1986); *Narcissus* for Flute with Digital Delay System (1987; also for Clarinet and Digital Delay System, 1988); *Niobe* for Oboe and Tape (1987; London, Jan. 1988); *Piccolo Play: In Homage to Couperin* for Piccolo and Piano (New Orleans, Aug. 18, 1989); *Fanfare for a New Hall* for 2 Trumpets (1990; N.Y., Feb. 1992); Wind Quintet (1992; Provo, Utah, March 18, 1993); *Postcards from Spain* for Guitar (1995; Norfolk, Va., May 10, 1996); *From Spring to Spring* for Marimba and Optional Windchimes (1996); *Circe* for 3 Flutes (N.Y., Aug. 17, 1996); *Threnody* for Clarinet and Piano (London, June 20, 1997); *In the Still of the Night* for Viola (1997; Odessa, April 11, 1998); *Voices from the Ancient World* for Flute Trio and Percussion (1998; Glasgow, Jan. 23, 1999). P i a n o : *Monologue* (London, Dec. 12, 1960); *Excursions* for Piano, 4-Hands (1965; London, April 19, 1967). VOCAL: 2 Songs for Baritone and Piano (Paris, May 16, 1951); 4 Madrigals for Chorus (Fife, March 20, 1953); *A Suite o' Bairnsangs* for Voice and Piano (Braemar, Aug. 21, 1953); *Cantata for a Summer's Day* for Chorus, Narrator, and Orch. (1954; Edinburgh, Sept. 4, 1955); 5 Love Songs for Soprano and Guitar (Utrecht, Oct. 4, 1955); 4 Portraits for Baritone, Clarinet, and Piano (1956; London, Dec. 10, 1962); *A Song for Christmas* for High Voice and Piano (1958); *Triptych* for Tenor and Orch. (1959; London, Sept. 14, 1960); *Sir Patrick Spens* for Tenor and Guitar (Aldeburgh, July 7, 1961);

Make Ye Merry for Him That is Come for Women's Chorus and Children's Chorus (1961; London, Dec. 8, 1962); *The Phoenix and the Turtle* for Small Chorus and Orch. (London, Aug. 20, 1962); *John Cook* for Chorus (1963); *The Five Ages of Man* for Chorus and Orch. (1963–64; Norwich, June 6, 1964); *Memento Creatoris* for Chorus and Optional Organ (Aldeburgh, June 6, 1967); *Primavera* for Soprano and Flute (Zagreb, May 19, 1971); *Rorate Coeli* for Chorus (1973; Greenwich, Sept. 26, 1976); *O Caro M'è Il Sonno* for Chorus (1978); *The Last Twilight* for Chorus and Instruments (Santa Fe, July 20, 1980); *The Lord's Prayer* for Chorus and Organ (1983; San Francisco, June 25, 1984); *Black Tambourine* for Women's Chorus (1985); *For the Time Being: Advent* for Chorus and Narrator (1986; London, April 27, 1987); *Echoes Through Time* for Women's Chorus, Speaking Chorus, 3 Optional Dancers, and Orch. (1988; Decatur, Ga., April 25, 1989); *Midnight* for Chorus (1992; San Antonio, March 4, 1993); *Wild Winter* for Voices and Viols (Lichfield, July 16, 1993); *On the Underground, Set No. 1: On gratitude, love and madness* (Cheltenham, July 16, 1994), *No. 2: The Strange and the Exotic* (Ithaca, N.Y., Oct. 29, 1994), and *No. 3: A Medieval Summer* (London, Nov. 19, 1995) for Chorus; *Songs for a Winter's Evening* for Soprano and Orch. (1995; Dumfries, June 1, 1996). **ELEC-TRONIC:** *Time Remembered* (1979).

BIBL.: D. Hixon, *T. M.: A Bio-Bibliography* (Westport, Conn., 1984).—**NS/LK/DM**

Mushel, Georgi, Russian pianist and composer; b. Tambov, July 29, 1909. He studied piano with Oborin and composition with Miaskovsky at the Moscow Cons. During World War II, he moved to Tashkent in Uzbekistan, where he composed the first opera on Uzbek themes, *Farkhad i Shirin,* as well as other works inspired by Uzbek folklore.—**NS/LK/DM**

Musicescu, Gavriil, Rumanian choral conductor, teacher, and composer; b. Ismail, March 20, 1847; d. Iasi, Dec. 21, 1903. He studied at the Iaşi Cons. and later at the St. Petersburg Cons. In 1872 he was appointed a prof. at the Iaşi Cons., becoming its director in 1901. He composed liturgical hymns and Psalms as well as secular choral works and songs for solo voice. In his secular works, he utilized folk songs. He also made arrangements of folk songs. A selected vol. of his music was ed. by G. Breazul (Bucharest, 1958).

BIBL.: G. Breazul, *G. M.* (Bucharest, 1962).—**NS/LK/DM**

Musin, Ilya (Alexandrovich), Russian conductor and pedagogue; b. Kostroma, Jan. 6, 1904; d. St. Petersburg, June 6, 1999. He received training at the Petrograd Cons. In 1926 he joined the faculty of the Leningrad (formerly Petrograd) Cons. In 1937 he became an asst. conductor of the Leningrad Phil. under Nicolai Malko. Musin's Jewish heritage and his refusal to join the Communist Party proved to be major obstacles to his advancement, and he soon was sent to the Minsk Phil. to serve as its music director. After World War II, he was allowed to rejoin the faculty of the Leningrad Cons. However, his career as a conductor was thwarted by the Soviet authorities who allowed him only to make infrequent guest appearances with Russian orchs. After the collapse of the Soviet regime, Musin was invited to make his belated debut in the

West as a guest conductor of the Royal Phil. in London in 1996 at the age of 92. In his last years, he continued to teach at the Leningrad Cons. and gave master classes abroad.—**LK/DM**

Musin, Ovide, Belgian violinist, teacher, and composer; b. Nandrin, near Liège, Sept. 22, 1854; d. N.Y., Nov. 24, 1929. He studied with Heynberg and Leonard at the Liège Cons., taking 1st violin prize at the age of 13; he won the gold medal at 15. He toured Europe from 1874 to 1882 with remarkable success. In 1883 he went to America, and between 1892 and 1897 he made 2 world tours. From 1897 to 1908 he taught at the Liège Cons., and in 1908 he established himself in N.Y., where he opened his own school of music. He publ. a number of brilliant violin pieces as well as the instructive works *System of Daily Practice* (1899) and *The Belgian School of the Violin* (4 vols.; 1916; a combination of his own methods with those of his teacher Leonard). He also publ. a book, *My Memories* (1920). His wife, Annie Louise Tanner-Musin (b. Boston, Oct. 3, 1856; d. there, Feb. 28, 1921), was a well-known coloratura soprano. —**NS/LK/DM**

Mussorgsky, Modest (Petrovich), great Russian composer; b. Karevo, Pskov district, March 21, 1839; d. St. Petersburg, March 28, 1881. He received his first instruction on the piano from his mother; at the age of 10, he was taken to St. Petersburg, where he had piano lessons with Anton Herke, remaining his pupil until 1854. In 1852 he entered the cadet school of the Imperial Guard; composed a piano piece entitled *Porte enseigne Polka,* which was publ. (1852); after graduation (1856), he joined the regiment of the Guard. In 1857, he met Dargomyzhsky, who introduced him to Cui and Balakirev; he also became friendly with the critic and chief champion of Russian national music, Vladimir Stasov. These associations prompted his decision to become a professional composer. He played and analyzed piano arrangements of works by Beethoven and Schumann; Balakirev helped him to acquire a knowledge of form; he tried to write music in classical style, but without success; his inner drive was directed toward "new shores," as Mussorgsky expressed it. The liquidation of the family estate made it imperative for him to take a paying job; he became a clerk in the Ministry of Communications (1863), being dismissed 4 years later. During this time, he continued to compose, but his lack of technique compelled him time and again to leave his various pieces unfinished. He eagerly sought professional advice from his friends Stasov (for general aesthetics) and Rimsky-Korsakov (for problems of harmony); to the very end of his life, he regarded himself as being only half-educated in music, and constantly acknowledged his inferiority as a craftsman. But he yielded to no one in his firm faith in the future of national Russian music. When a group of composers from Bohemia visited St. Petersburg in 1867, Stasov publ. an article in which he for the first time referred to the "mighty handful of Russian musicians" pursuing the ideal of national art. The expression was picked up derisively by some journalists, but it was accepted as a challenge by Mussorgsky and his comrades-in-arms,

Balakirev, Borodin, Cui, and Rimsky-Korsakov, the "mighty 5" of Russian music. In 1869 he once more entered government service, this time in the forestry dept. He became addicted to drink, and had epileptic fits; he died a week after his 42nd birthday. The significance of Mussorgsky's genius did not become apparent until some years after his death. Most of his works were prepared for publication by Rimsky-Korsakov, who corrected some of his harmonic crudities, and reorchestrated the symphonic works. Original versions of his music were preserved in MS, and eventually publ. But despite the availability of the authentic scores, his works continue to be performed in Rimsky-Korsakov's eds., made familiar to the whole musical world. In his dramatic works, and in his songs, Mussorgsky draws a boldly realistic vocal line, in which inflections of speech are translated into a natural melody. His first attempt in this genre was an unfinished opera, *The Marriage*, to Gogol's comedy; here he also demonstrated his penetrating sense of musical humor. His ability to depict tragic moods is revealed in his cycle *Songs and Dances of Death*; his understanding of intimate poetry is shown in the children's songs. His greatest work is the opera *Boris Godunov* (to Pushkin's tragedy), which has no equal in its stirring portrayal of personal destiny against a background of social upheaval. In it, Mussorgsky created a true national music drama, without a trace of the Italian conventions that had theretofore dominated the operatic works by Russian composers. He wrote no chamber music, perhaps because he lacked the requisite training in contrapuntal technique. Of his piano music, the set of pieces *Pictures at an Exhibition* (somewhat after the manner of Schumann's *Carnaval*) is remarkable for its vivid representation of varied scenes (it was written to commemorate his friend, the painter Victor Hartmann, whose pictures were the subjects of the music); the work became famous in the brilliant orchestration of Ravel. Although Mussorgsky was a Russian national composer, his music influenced many composers outside Russia, and he came to be regarded as the most potent talent of the Russian national school. The paintings of Victor Hartmann that inspired *Pictures at an Exhibition* were reproduced by Alfred Frankenstein in his article on the subject in the *Musical Quarterly* (July 1939); he also brought out an illustrated ed. of the work (1951). A collected ed. of Mussorgsky's works was compiled by P. Lamm (8 vols., Moscow, 1928–34; 1939).

WORKS: DRAMATIC: O p e r a : *Salammbô* (1863–66; unfinished); *Zhenitba* (The Marriage), comic opera (1868; only Act 1 completed; St. Petersburg, April 1, 1909; completed and orchestrated by A. Tcherepnin; Essen, Sept. 14, 1937); *Boris Godunov* (1st version, with 7 scenes, 1868–69; Leningrad, Feb. 16, 1928; 2nd version, with prologue and 4 acts, 1871–72, rev. 1873; St. Petersburg, Feb. 8, 1874; rev. and reorchestrated by Rimsky-Korsakov, 1896; St. Petersburg, Dec. 10, 1896); *Khovanshchina* (1872–80; completed and orchestrated by Rimsky-Korsakov; St. Petersburg, Feb. 21, 1886); *Sorochinskaya yarmarka* (The Fair at Sorochinsk), comic opera (1874–80; completed by Cui, Liadov, Karatigin, and others; Moscow, Oct. 21, 1913; also arranged and orchestrated by N. Tcherepnin; Monte Carlo, March 17, 1923). **O R C H .:** *Scherzo* (1858; St. Petersburg, Jan. 23, 1860; originally for Piano); *Alla marcia notturna* (1861); *Ivanova noch' na Lisoy gore* (A Night on Bald Mountain; 1860–67;

reorchestrated by Rimsky-Korsakov; St. Petersburg, Oct. 27, 1886); *Intermezzo symphonique in modo classico* (1867; originally for Piano); *Vzyatiye Karsa* (The Capture of Kars), march (1880). **P i a n o :** *Porte-enseigne polka* (1852); *Souvenir d'enfance* (1857); 2 sonatas (1858; not extant); 2 *Scherzos* (both 1858); *Impromptu passion: Jeux d'enfants—Les Quatre Coins: Ein Kinderscherz* (1859; rev. 1860); Allegro and Scherzo for a Sonata for Piano, 4–Hands (1860); *Preludio in modo classico* (1860; not extant); *Intermezzo in modo classico* (1860–61; orchestrated 1867; rearranged for Piano, 1867); *Menuet monstre* (1861; not extant); *Iz vospominaniy detstva* (From Memories of Childhood; 1865); *La Capricieuse* (1865); *Shveyg* (The Seamstress; 1871); *Kartinki s vistavki* (Pictures at an Exhibition), suite (1874; *Promenade; Gnomus; Il vecchio castello; Tuileries; Bydlo; Ballet des poussins dans leurs coques; Deux juifs, l'un riche et l'autre pauvre; Limoges—Le Marché; Catacombae; Cum mortuis in lingua mortua; La Cabane sur des pattes de poule; La Grande Porte de Kiev*; French titles by Mussorgsky; orchestrated by Ravel, 1922); *Burya no Chernom more* (Storm on the Black Sea; 1879; not extant); *Na yuzhnom bere Krima* (On the Southern Shore of the Crimea; 1880); *Meditation* (1880); *Une Larme* (1880); *Au villa* (c. 1880); transcriptions of dances from the opera *The Fair at Sorochinsk*; many fragments from youthful works, etc. **VOCAL: C h o r a l :** *Marsh Shamilya* (Shamil's March) for Tenor, Bass, Chorus, and Orch. (1859); *Porazheniye Sennakheriba* (The Destruction of Sennacherib) for Chorus and Orch. (St. Petersburg, March 18, 1867; rev. 1874); *Iisus Navin* (Jesus Navin) for Alto, Bass, Chorus, and Piano (1874–77); 3 vocalises for 3 Women's Voices (1880); 5 Russian folksongs arranged for 4 Men's Voices (1880; No. 5 unfinished). **S o n g s :** *King Saul* (1863); *Cradle Song* (1865); *Darling Savishna* (1866); *The Seminarist* (1866); *Hopak* (1866); *On the Dnieper* (1879); *The Classicist* (satirical; 1867); *The Garden by the Don* (1867); *The Nursery*, children's song cycle (1868–72); *Rayok* (The Peep Show), musical lampoon at assorted contemporaries (1870); *Sunless*, song cycle (1874); *Forgotten* (1874); *Songs and Dances of Death*, cycle of 4 songs (1875–77); *Mephistopheles' Song of the Flea* (1879); etc.

BIBL.: V. Stasov, *M.* (St. Petersburg, 1881); V. Baskin, *M.* (Moscow, 1887); P. d'Alheim, *M.* (Paris, 3rd ed., 1896); M. Olenine-d'Alheim, *Le Legs de M.* (Paris, 1908); M.D. Calvocoressi, *M.* (Paris, 1907; 2nd Fr. ed., 1911; Eng. tr., London, 1919); M. Montagu-Nathan, *M.* (London, 1916); O. von Riesemann, *M.* (Munich, 1925; Eng. tr., N.Y., 1935); R. Godet, *En marge de Boris Godunov* (Paris, 1927); K. von Wolfurt, *M.* (Stuttgart, 1927); I. Glebov, *M.* (Leningrad, 1928); H. van Dalen, *M.* (The Hague, 1930); Y. Keldish, *Lyricism in M.'s Songs* (Moscow, 1933); V. Fedorov, *M.* (Paris, 1935); M. Tibaldi Chiesa, *M.* (Milan, 1935); C. Barzel, *M.* (Paris, 1939); G. Orlov, *Chronicle of the Life and Works of M.* (Moscow, 1940); G. Gavazzeni, *M. e la musica russa dell' 800* (Florence, 1943); M.D. Calvocoressi, *M.* (completed by G. Abraham, London, 1946; 2nd ed., rev., 1974); J. Leyda and S. Bertensson, eds., *The M. Reader* (N.Y., 1947); R. Hofmann, *M.* (Paris, 1952); M.D. Calvocoressi, *M. M.: His Life and Works* (London, 1956; ed. by G. Abraham); V. Serov, *M. M.* (N.Y., 1968); L. Hubsch, *M. M.: Bilder einer Ausstellung* (Munich, 1978); R. Oldani, *New Pespectives on M.'s Boris Godunov* (diss., Univ. of Mich., 1978); M. Schandert, *Das Problem der originalen Instrumentation des Boris Godunov von M.P. M.* (Hamburg, 1979); E. Reilly, *A Guide to M.: A Scorography* (N.Y., 1980); M. Brown, ed., *M.: In Memoriam 1881–1981* (Ann Arbor, 1982); P. Weber-Bockholdt, *Die Lieder M.s: Herkunft und Erscheinungsform* (Munich, 1982); A. Orlova, *M.'s Days and Works: A Biography in Documents* (Ann Arbor, 1983); C. Emerson, *Boris Godunov: Transpositions of a Russian Theme* (Bloomington and Indianapolis, 1986); S. Neef, *Die Russischen Fünf: Balakirew, Borodin, Cui, M., Rimski-Korsakow:*

Monographien, Dokumente, Briefe, Programme, Werke (Berlin, 1992); M. Russ, *M.: Pictures at an Exhibition* (Cambridge, 1992); S. Dennerle, *"Bilder einer Ausstellung" von Viktor Hartmann und M. M. als Beispiel für eine integrative ästhetische Erziehung im Musikunterricht der Allgemeinbildenden Schule* (Frankfurt am Main, 1993); R. Taruskin, *M.: Eight Essays and an Epilogue* (Princeton, 1993); J. Batchelor and N. John, eds., *Khovanshchina* (London, 1994); C. Emerson and R. Oldani, *M. M. and Boris Godunov: Myth, Realities, Reconsiderations* (Cambridge, 1994); G. Golovinsky, *M. i fol'klor* (M. and Folklore; Moscow, 1994); W. Karatygin et al., eds., *M. M.: Zugänge zu Leben und Werk: Würdigungen, Kritiken, Selbsdarstellungen, Erinnerungen, Polemiken* (Berlin, 1995); M. Schultner-Mäder, *Die Thematik des Todes in Schaffen M.s* (Frankfurt am Main, 1997).—NS/LK/DM

Mustafà, Domenico, Italian castrato soprano and composer; b. Sterpara, near Perugia, April 14, 1829; d. Montefalco, near Perugia, March 18, 1912. He entered the Sistine Chapel Choir in Rome in 1848, being the last castrato employed there. He later served as its maestro di cappella (until 1895). Among his compositions were much sacred music and various songs.

BIBL.: A. De Angelis, *D. M. e la Cappella Sistina* (Bologna, 1926).—NS/LK/DM

Mustel, Victor, celebrated French builder of harmoniums; b. Le Havre, June 13, 1815; d. Paris, Jan. 26, 1890. He began as a carpenter, and in 1844 went to Paris, where he worked in several shops, becoming foreman in Alexandre's harmonium factory. He established himself in 1853, and the following year invented the harmonium with "double expression," which won 1st prize at the Paris Exposition of 1855. From 1866 the firm was famous as V. Mustel & ses Fils. He also constructed an instrument consisting of graduated tuning forks in a resonance box, operated by a keyboard; this was patented in 1886 by his son Auguste Mustel (1842–1919) as the "Celesta." Tchaikovsky heard it in Paris and became so enchanted with it that he used it for the first time in any score in his ballet *The Nutcracker.*—NS/LK/DM

Mustonen, Olli, Finnish pianist, conductor, and composer; b. Helsinki, June 7, 1967. He was only 5 when he began studying piano, harpsichord, and composition. After piano lessons with Ralf Gothoni, he pursued his studies with Eero Heinonen (piano) and Einojuhani Rautavaara (composition). After making his debut in 1984, he appeared with the principal Finnish orchs. and soon performed with orchs. on the Continent. In 1986 he made his U.S. debut at the Newport (R.I.) Festival. In 1987 he appeared for the first time in London. He toured the Far East with the Stockholm Phil. in 1989. In 1991 he played at the London Promenade Concerts. In addition to his engagements with the world's leading orchs., Mustonen also pursued an active recital and chamber music career. His extraordinary technique is matched by a challenging spontaneous approach to interpretation. In later years, he pursued a career as a conductor as well. Among his compositions are 2 piano concertos. —NS/LK/DM

Müthel, Johann Gottfried, German organist and composer; b. Mölln, Jan. 17, 1728; d. Bienenhof, near Riga, July 14, 1788. He studied at Lübeck and became court organist at Schwerin in 1747. In 1750 he traveled to Leipzig to see Bach, and remained with him for a few days before Bach's death. He then journeyed to Potsdam, where he met Carl Philipp Emanuel Bach. In 1753 he went to Riga, where he became an organist at the Lutheran church in 1755. Among his extant works are 10 harpsichord concertos (6 ed. in Denkmäler Norddeutscher Musik, III-IV, Munich, 1975), a Concerto for 2 Bassoons and Strings, sonatas for Harpsichord, and organ music.

BIBL.: R. Campbell, *J.G. M.* (diss., Ind. Univ., 1966). —NS/LK/DM

Muti, Riccardo, greatly talented Italian conductor; b. Naples, July 28, 1941. His father was a physician who possessed a natural Neapolitan tenor voice. After receiving instruction in violin and piano from his father, Riccardo studied composition with Napoli and Rota at the Conservatorio di Musica San Pietro a Majella in Naples, taking a diploma in piano. He then studied conducting with Votto and composition with Bettinelli at the Verdi Cons. in Milan, and also attended a seminar in conducting with Ferrara in Venice (1965). After winning the Guido Cantelli Competition in 1967, he made his formal debut with the RAI in 1968; then conducted in several of the major Italian music centers. His success led to his appointment as principal conductor of the Teatro Comunale in Florence in 1970; also conducted at the Maggio Musicale Fiorentino, becoming its artistic director in 1977. In the meantime, he began his advancement to international fame with guest conducting appearances at the Salzburg Festival in 1971 and with the Berlin Phil. in 1972. He made his U.S. debut with the Philadelphia Orch. on Oct. 27, 1972. In 1973 he conducted at the Vienna State Opera, and that same year became principal conductor of the New Philharmonia Orch. in London (it resumed its original name of Philharmonia Orch. in 1977). In 1974 he conducted the Vienna Phil. and in 1977 appeared at London's Covent Garden. His successful appearances with the Philadelphia Orch. led to his appointment as its principal guest conductor in 1977. In 1979 he was also named music director of the Philharmonia Orch. In 1980 he succeeded Eugene Ormandy as music director of the Philadelphia Orch., and subsequently relinquished his posts in London and Florence in 1982. In 1986 he became music director of Milan's La Scala, but retained his Philadelphia position. Muti announced his resignation as music director of the Philadelphia Orch. in 1990, but agreed to serve as its laureate conductor from 1992. His brilliance as a symphonic conductor enabled him to maintain, and even enhance, the illustrious reputation of the Philadelphia Orch. established by Stokowski and carried forward by Ormandy. Unlike his famous predecessors, he excels in both the concert hall and the opera pit.

BIBL.: J. Kurnick, ed., *R. M.: Twenty Years in Philadelphia* (Philadelphia, 1992).—NS/LK/DM

Mutter, Anne-Sophie, outstanding German violinist; b. Rheinfelden, June 29, 1963. She was only 5

when she began studies with Erna Honiberger. At 6, she won "1ˢᵗ Prize with Special Distinction" in the Jungend Musiziert National Competition, the youngest winner in its annals. Her appearance at the Lucerne Festival at age 13 attracted the notice of Karajan, who invited her to be his soloist in the Mozart G major Concerto, K.216, with the Berlin Phil. at his Salzburg Easter Festival in 1977. While still young, she had the rare honor of recording several of the great violin masterworks with Karajan and the Berlin Phil., including concertos by Mozart (K.216 and K.219) and the Beethoven, Mendelssohn, and Brahms concertos, which won her critical approbation. In 1977 she made her first appearance at the Salzburg Festival with Wimberger and the Salzburg Mozarteum Orch. as soloist in Mozart's D major Concerto, K.211. Her British debut came that same year when she played the Mendelssohn Concerto at the Brighton Festival with Barenboim and the English Chamber Orch. She made her U.S. debut in the same concerto with Mehta and the N.Y. Phil. on Jan. 3, 1980. In 1985 she appeared for the first time in Moscow, and also played in a string trio with Giuaranna and Rostropovich at the Aldeburgh Festival. On Jan. 31, 1986, she was soloist in the first performance of Lutosławski Chain II with Sacher and the Collegium Musicum Orch. in Zürich. That same year, she was honored as the first holder of the International Chair in Violin Studies at the Royal Academy of Music in London. On Sept. 9, 1988, she appeared as soloist in the premiere of Moret's En Rêve in Locarno under Andreae's direction. From 1988 she played in duo recitals with Lambert Orkis and, on Dec. 14ᵗʰ of that year, she made her N.Y. recital debut at Carnegie Hall. She gave the first performance of Rihm's Gesungene Zeit in Zürich on June 13, 1992, with Sacher and the Collegium Musicum Orch. On June 24, 1995, she appeared as soloist in the premiere of Penderecki's 2ⁿᵈ Violin Concerto with the MDR Sym. Orch. in Leipzig under Jansons's direction. During 1998 she and Orkis appeared in many of the world's major music centers playing complete cycles of Beethoven's violin sonatas. Their marathon tour opened in Hannover on Jan. 26ᵗʰ, then continued on to such cities as Berlin, Zürich, Madrid, Amsterdam, Rome, N.Y., Chicago, Philadelphia, Boston, Los Angeles, Dresden, Milan, Paris, London, Shanghai, Seoul, Buenos Aires, and Vienna before concluding with a benefit concert at the Beethovenhaus in Bonn on Dec. 17ᵗʰ. In 1999 she toured the U.S. and the Far East, and also appeared as soloist with the World Youth Orch. under Masur's direction and with the Curtis Inst. of Music Sym. Orch. under Previn's direction. In 2000 she gave a series of concerts devoted to the 20ᵗʰ century violin literature, including engagements at N.Y.'s Carnegie Hall, with the N.Y. Phil. and the London Sym. Orch., both under Masur's direction, and at festivals in Europe. Mutter has been honored as a member of the Order of Merit of the Federal Republic of Germany, as well as of Bavaria and of Baden-Württemberg for her contributions to music and humanitarian causes. Her virtuoso technique is always employed as the secure foundation upon which to construct her masterful interpretations, which are invariably marked by an extraordinary musicianship, matchless integrity, and noble humanistic ideals.—NS/LK/DM

Muzio, Claudia (real name, **Claudina Muzzio**), oustanding Italian soprano; b. Pavia, Feb. 7, 1889; d. Rome, May 24, 1936. She studied with Casaloni in Turin and Viviani in Milan. She made her operatic debut as Manon in Arezzo (Jan. 15, 1910); then sang in Turin (1911; 1914–15), at Milan's La Scala (1913–14), and at London's Covent Garden (1914). She made her Metropolitan Opera debut in N.Y. as Tosca (Dec. 4, 1916), remaining on its roster until 1922; created the role of Giorgetta in Puccini's *Il tabarro* there (Dec. 14, 1918). In 1922 she made her first appearance with the Chicago Opera as Aida, and continued to sing there regularly until 1932; also sang in South America and again at La Scala (1926–27); after returning to the Metropolitan (1933–34), she pursued her career mainly in Rome. She was one of the most gifted dramatic sopranos of her time, excelling in such roles as Desdemona, Mimi, Santuzza, Margherita in *Mefistofele*, Violetta, and Madeleine de Coigny.

BIBL.: H. Barnes, *C. M.: A Biographical Sketch and Discography* (Austin, Tex., 1947).—NS/LK/DM

Muzio, (Donnino) Emanuele, Italian conductor and composer; b. Zibello, Aug. 24, 1821; d. Paris, Nov. 27, 1890. He began his studies with Ferdinando Provesi, then studied piano with Margherita Barezzi (Verdi's first wife), and composition with Verdi himself; was one of the very few pupils Verdi ever had. In 1850 he was engaged as conductor of the Théâtre du Cirque in Brussels; he later traveled to England and America, then settled in Paris in 1875 as a singing teacher. Carlotta Patti and Clara Louise Kellogg were his pupils. He wrote several operas: *Giovanna la pazza* (Brussels, April 8, 1851), *Claudia* (Milan, Feb. 7, 1853), *Le due regine* (Milan, May 17, 1856), and *La Sorrentina* (Bologna, Nov. 14, 1857); also many songs and piano pieces.

BIBL.: A. Belforti, *E. M., l'unico alievo di Giuseppe Verdi* (Fabriano, 1895); L. Garibaldi, ed., *Giuseppe Verdi nelle lettere di E. M. ed Antonio Barezzi* (Milan, 1931).—NS/LK/DM

Mycielski, Zygmunt, Polish music critic and composer; b. Przeworsk, Aug. 17, 1907; d. Warsaw, Aug. 5, 1987. He studied with Rizzi in Kraków and with Dukas and Boulanger at the Paris École Normale de Musique, where he was a member of the Soc. of Young Polish Musicians (1928–36). After World War II, he became active as a journalist; ed. the principal Polish music magazine, *Ruch Muzyczny* (1945–48; 1960–68); publ. 2 collections of essays: *Uzieczki z pieciolinii* (Flight of the Staff Lines; Warsaw, 1956) and *Notatki o muzyce i muzykach* (Notes on Music and Musicians; Kraków, 1961). His music, couched in a modern idiom, contains elements of Polish folk inflections, but dodecaphonic usages are also encountered.

WORKS: DRAMATIC: Ballet: *Zabawa w Lipinach* (Merrymaking at Lipiny; 1953). **ORCH.:** *Lamento di Tristano* for Small Orch., in memory of Szymanowski (1937); *5 Symphonic Essays* (1945); 6 syms.: No. 1 (1947), *Polish Sym.* (1951), No. 2 (1960), No. 3, *Sinfonia breve* (1967; Warsaw, Sept. 23, 1972), No. 4 (1972–73; Poznań, April 2, 1976), and No. 5 (1977); *Silesian Overture* (1948); Piano Concerto (1954); *Variations* for Strings (1980). **CHAMBER:** Piano Trio (1934); *5 Preludes* for Piano

Quintet (1967). VOCAL: *Portrait of a Muse* for Narrator, Chorus, and 15 Instruments (1947); *Nowy lirnik mazowiecki* (New Mazovian Bard), 9 songs and finale for Soprano, Baritone, Chorus, and Orch. (1955); *Psalms* for Baritone, Chorus, and Orch. (1982); *Liturgia sacra* for Chorus and Orch. (1983–84); *Fragments* for Chorus and Small Orch. (1987); songs. —NS/LK/DM

Myers, Rollo (Hugh), English music critic and writer on music; b. Chislehurst, Kent, Jan. 23, 1892; d. Chichester, Jan. 1, 1985. He was educated at Balliol Coll., Oxford, and at the Royal Coll. of Music in London. From 1919 to 1934 he was the Paris music correspondent of *The Times* and the *Daily Telegraph* of London. He was on the staff of the BBC in London from 1935 to 1944. After serving as music officer of the British Council in Paris (1944–45), he returned to London as ed. of *The Chesterian* (from 1947) and of *Music Today* (from 1949).

WRITINGS (all publ. in London unless otherwise given): *Modern Music: Its Aims and Tendencies* (1923); *Music in the Modern World* (1939; 2nd ed., rev., 1948); *Debussy* (1948); *Erik Satie* (1948); *Introduction to the Music of Stravinsky* (1950); *Ravel: Life and Works* (1960); ed. *Twentieth Century Music* (1960; 2nd ed., aug., 1968); ed. and tr., *Richard Strauss and Romain Rolland: Correspondence* (1968); *Emmanuel Chabrier and his Circle* (1969); *Modern French Music* (Oxford, 1971).—NS/LK/DM

Mykietyn, Paweł, Polish composer and clarinetist; b. Oława, May 20, 1971. He studied with Włodzimierz Kotoński at the Warsaw Academy of Music, from which he graduated in 1997. He organized Nonstrom, a contemporary music ensemble, in which he performs as a clarinetist.

WORKS: ORCH.: Piano Concerto (1996; Warsaw, Sept. 26, 1997); Cello Concerto (1998; Poznań, Oct. 15, 1999); Violin Concerto (1999). CHAMBER: *...choć dolecial Dedal...* (...though Dedalus reached...), trio for Piano, Clarinet, and Cello (1990; Warsaw, May 20, 1991); *La Strada* for 3 Instruments (Gdańsk, Oct. 11, 1991); *4 Preludes* for Piano (1992; Warsaw, April 26, 1993); *"U Radka"* ("At Radka's Place") for Clarinet, Trombone, Cello, and Piano (Warsaw, Nov. 27, 1993); *3 for 13* for 13 Performers (1994; Warsaw, April 3, 1995); *Sonatina für Alina* for Alto Saxophone and Tape (Warsaw, April 24, 1994); *Eine kleine Herbstmusik* for 11 Instruments (Warsaw, Sept. 17, 1995); *Epifora* for Piano and Tape (Warsaw, Sept. 24, 1996); *...na temat wlasny/...op eigen thema* for Chamber Ensemble (1997; Wrocław, Feb. 18, 1998); *Four for four* for Clarinet, Trombone, Cello, and Piano (1997; Warsaw, Nov. 30, 1998); String Quartet (London, Oct. 27, 1998); *Commencement de siècle* for Chamber Ensemble and Live Electronics (Warsaw, Sept. 18, 1999); *Before "Four for four"* for Clarinet, Trombone, Cello, and Piano (Warsaw, Dec. 15, 1999).—LK/DM

Mylius, Wolfgang Michael, German composer; b. Mannstedt, Thuringia, 1636; d. Gotha, late 1712 or early 1713. He pursued training in theology at the Univ. of Jena. In 1661 he was made a court musician in Altenburg, and in 1661–62 he studied music with Christoph Bernhard in Dresden. After the Altenburg Kapelle was dissolved in 1669, he joined he Gotha Kapelle, where he served as its Kapellmeister from 1676 until his death. He composed Singspiels and much sacred music. His teaching manual, *Rudimenta musices, das ist: Eine kurtze ung grundrichtige Anweisung zur Singe Kunst* (Gotha, 1686), retains its historic value.

BIBL.: J. Mylius, *Geschichte der Familien M.* (Buttstadt, 1895).—LK/DM

Mysliveček (Mysliweczek; Misliveček), Josef, famous Bohemian composer, called "Il divino Boemo" and "Il Venatorini" in Italy; b. Ober-Sárka, near Prague, March 9, 1737; d. Rome, Feb. 4, 1781. His father was a miller. He was a pupil at the Normalschule of the Dominicans of St. Jilgi (1744–47) and the Jesuit Gymnasium (1748–53), where he received his first instruction in music; also sang in the choir of St. Michal under Felix Benda. He then was apprenticed as a miller, being made a master miller in 1761. He also pursued his musical studies, taking courses in counterpoint with František Habermann and organ with Josef Seger. In 1760 he publ. anonymously a set of 6 sinfonias, named after the first 6 months of the year. Determined upon a career as a composer, he went to Venice in 1763 to study the art of operatic writing with Giovanni Pescetti. His first opera, *Medea*, was produced in Parma in 1764. While in Parma, he met the singer Lucrezia Aguiari, who became his mistress in the first of his many romantic liaisons. He was commissioned to write another opera, *Il Bellerofonte*, for the Teatro San Carlo in Naples, where it was performed with considerable success on Jan. 20, 1767. This led to other commissions from Italian theaters. His opera *Ezio* (Naples, June 5, 1775) and his oratorio *Isacco figura del Redentore* (Florence, March 10, 1776) were successfully performed in Munich in 1777; his career was blunted, however, by syphilis and disfiguring facial surgery. He returned to Italy but never regained his social standing. He succumbed at the age of 43. Mysliveček was one of the most significant Bohemian composers; his operas and oratorios were frequently performed and publ. in his lifetime. Mozart expressed admiration of his talent.

WORKS: DRAMATIC: O p e r a : *Medea* (Parma, 1764); *Il Bellerofonte* (Naples, Jan. 20, 1767); *Farnace* (Naples, Nov. 4, 1767); *Il trionfo di Clelia* (Turin, Dec. 26, 1767); *Il Demofoonte* (Venice, Jan. 1769); *L'Ipermestra* (Florence, March 28, 1769); *La Nitteti* (Bologna, spring 1770); *Montezuma* (Florence, Jan. 23, 1771); *Il gran Tamerlano* (Milan, Dec. 26, 1771); *Il Demetrio* (Pavia, Jan. 25, 1773); *Erifile* (Munich, 1773); *Romolo ed Ersilia* (Naples, Aug. 13, 1773); *La clemenza di Tito* (Venice, Dec. 26, 1773); *Antigona* (Turin, Carnival 1774); *Atide* (Padua, June 1774); *Artaserse* (Naples, Aug. 13, 1774); *Il Demofoonte* (Naples, Jan. 20, 1775); *Ezio* (Naples, June 5, 1775); *Merope* (Naples, 1775); *Adriano in Siria* (Florence, fall 1776); *Las Calliroe* (Naples, May 30, 1778); *L'Olimpiade* (Naples, Nov. 4, 1778); *La Circe* (Venice, May 1779); *Il Demetrio* (Naples, Aug. 13, 1779); *Armida* (Milan, Dec. 26, 1779); *Medonte* (Rome, Jan. 1780); *Antigono* (Rome, April 1780). O r a t o r i o s : *La famiglia di Tobia* (Padua, 1769); *Adamo ed Eva* (Florence, May 24, 1771); *Giuseppe riconosciuto* (Padua, 1771); *La Passione di Gesu Cristo* (Prague, 1773); *La liberazione d'Israele* (1775); *Isacco figura del Redentore* (Florence, March 10, 1776). OTHER: Sinfonias; Overtures; keyboard concertos; sonatas for keyboard; string quartets; trios.

BIBL.: H. Wilkemann, *Joseph Mysliweczek als Opernkomponist* (diss., Univ. of Vienna, 1915); J. Čeleda, *J. M., tvůrce pražského nářeči hudebniho rokoka tereziánského* (J. M.: Creator of the Prague Dialect of Theresian Musical Rococo; Prague, 1946); R. Pečman, *J. M. und sein Opernepilog* (Brno, 1970).—**NS/LK/DM**

Mysz-Gmeiner, Lula (née **Gmeiner**), noted Hungarian contralto; b. Kronstadt, Transylvania, Aug. 16, 1876; d. Schwerin, Aug. 7, 1948. She studied violin in her native town, and singing in Berlin with Etelka Gerster and Lilli Lehmann. She made her concert debut in Berlin in 1899; then traveled in Europe as a concert singer; was greatly praised for her interpretations of German lieder. She was a prof. at the Berlin Hochschule für Musik (1920–45), numbering among her students Peter Anders and Elisabeth Schwarzkopf.—**NS/LK/DM**

N

Nabokov, Nicolas (actually, **Nikolai**), distinguished Russian-born American composer; b. near Lubcha, Novogrudok district, Minsk region, April 17, 1903; d. N.Y., April 6, 1978. He was a scion of a distinguished Russian family; his uncle was a liberal member of the short-lived Duma (Russian parliament), and the famous writer Vladimir Nabokov was his first cousin. Nabokov received his early education with Rebikov in St. Petersburg and in Yalta. After taking courses at the Stuttgart Cons. (1920–22), he continued his studies with Juon and Busoni at the Berlin Hochschule für Musik (1922–23). Finally he moved to Paris, where he was introduced to Diaghilev, who commissioned him to write his first major score, the ballet-oratorio *Ode: Méditation sur la majesté de Dieu* (1927), for the Ballets Russes. In 1933 he went to the U.S., and in 1939 became a naturalized American citizen; taught at Wells Coll. in Aurora, N.Y. (1936–41) and at St. John's Coll. in Annapolis (1941–44); after working for the U.S. government in Berlin (1944–47), he taught at the Peabody Cons. of Music in Baltimore (1947–52). From 1951 to 1963 he was secretary-general of the Congress for Cultural Freedom; then served as artistic director of the Berlin Music Festivals (1963–68); lectured on aesthetics at the State Univ. of N.Y. at Buffalo (1970–71) and at N.Y. Univ. (1972–73). He was elected to membership in the National Inst. of Arts and Letters in 1970. In addition to writing articles for various periodicals, he wrote a book of essays, *Old Friends and New Music* (Boston, 1951), and the vols. *Igor Stravinsky* (Berlin, 1964) and *Bagazh: Memoirs of a Russian Cosmopolitan* (N.Y., 1975). In his music, he adopted a cosmopolitan style, with an astute infusion of fashionable bitonality; in works of Russian inspiration, he reverted to melorhythms of Russian folk songs.

WORKS: DRAMATIC: O p e r a : *The Holy Devil* (1954–58; Louisville, April 16, 1958; rev. version as *Der Tod des Grigorij Rasputin*, Cologne, Nov. 27, 1959); *Love's Labour's Lost* (1970–73; Brussels, Feb. 7, 1973). **B a l l e t :** *Ode: Méditation sur la majesté de Dieu*, ballet-oratorio (1927; Paris, June 6, 1928); *La vie de Polichinelle* (Paris, 1934); *Union Pacific* (Philadelphia, April 6, 1934); *The Last Flower* (1941); *Don Quixote* (1966); *The Wanderer* (1966). **ORCH.:** 3 syms.: No. 1, *Symphonie lyrique* (Paris, Feb. 16, 1930), No. 2, *Sinfonia biblica* (N.Y., Jan. 2, 1941), and No. 3, *A Prayer* (N.Y., Jan. 4, 1968); Piano Concerto (1932); *Le Fiancé*, overture (1934); Flute Concerto (1948); Cello Concerto, *Les Hommages* (Philadelphia, Nov. 6, 1953); *Symphonic Variations* (1967); *Variations on a Theme by Tchaikovsky* for Cello and Orch. (1968). **CHAMBER:** *Serenata estiva* for String Quartet (1937); Bassoon Sonata (1941); *Canzone, Introduzione, e Allegro* for Violin and Piano (1950); 2 piano sonatas (1926, 1940), and other piano pieces. **VOCAL:** *Job*, oratorio for Men's Voices and Orch. (1933); *Collectionneur d'échos* for Soprano, Bass, and 9 Percussion Instruments (1933); *The Return of Pushkin*, elegy for Soprano or Tenor and Orch. (Boston, Jan. 2, 1948); *America Was Promises*, cantata for Alto, Baritone, and Men's Voices (N.Y., April 25, 1950); *Vita nuova* for Soprano, Tenor, and Orch. (Boston, March 2, 1951); *Symboli chrestiani* for Baritone and Orch. (1953); *Quatre poèmes de Boris Pasternak* for Voice and Piano (1961; arr. for Voice and Strings, 1969); *5 Poems by Anna Akhmatova* for Voice and Orch. (1964).—**NS/LK/DM**

Nachbaur, Franz (Ignaz), German tenor; b. Giessen, near Friedrichshafen, March 25, 1830; d. Munich, March 21, 1902. He studied with Pischek in Stuttgart and Lamperti in Milan, making his debut in Passau (1857). He then sang in Basel (1857), Hannover (1859–60), Prague (1860–63), and Darmstadt (1863–68). He made his first appearance at the Munich Court Opera on June 24, 1867, in Flotow's *Alessandro Stradella*; subsequently was one of its principal members, and was chosen to create the roles of Walther von Stolzing in *Die Meistersinger von Nürnberg* (June 21, 1868) and Froh in *Das Rheingold* (Sept. 22, 1869). He made his London debut in *Euryanthe* at Drury Lane (1882). He gave his farewell performance at the Munich Court Opera as Chapelou in Adam's *Le Postillon de Longjumeau* on Oct. 13, 1890, his 1,001st appearance there.—**NS/LK/DM**

Naderman, (Jean-) François-Joseph, French harpist and composer, son of **Jean-Henri Naderman;** b.

Paris, 1781; d. there, April 2, 1835. He studied harp with J.B. Krumpholtz. After touring widely as a virtuoso, he was appointed harpist of the royal chapel in 1815. In 1825 he was made the first prof. of harp at the Paris Cons. He publ. *Ecole ou Méthode raisonnée pour la harpe* (Paris, c. 1832). His compositions included many for harp, among them 2 concertos, sonatas, and solo pieces. His études are still played by students. With his brother, Henri Naderman (b. Paris, c. 1780; d. there, after 1835), he carried on his father's firm.—**LK/DM**

Naderman, Jean-Henri, French music publisher and instrument maker, father of **(Jean-) François-Joseph Naderman;** b. Fribourg, 1735; d. Paris, Feb. 4, 1799. He became maitre jure de la corporation in 1774. In 1777 he received a publishing license, and subsequently brought out numerous works for piano and harp, much chamber music, and operas. With J.B. Krumpholtz, he constructed many single-action pedal harps, including an instrument for Marie Antoinette in 1780.—**LK/DM**

Nagano, Kent (George), remarkable American conductor; b. Morro Bay, Calif. (of Japanese-American parents), Nov. 22, 1951. He studied at the Univ. of Oxford (1969), with Grosvenor Cooper at the Univ. of Calif. at Santa Cruz (B.A., 1974), at San Francisco State Univ. (M.M., 1976), and at the Univ. of Toronto, and also had instruction in conducting from Laszlo Varga in San Francisco. He was associated with Sarah Caldwell's Opera Co. of Boston (1977–79). He then was made music director of the Berkeley (Calif.) Sym. Orch. (1978) and of the Ojai (Calif.) Music Festival (1984). While working as an asst. conductor with the Boston Sym. Orch., he was called upon to substitute for Ozawa at the last moment and led a notably successful performance of Mahler's 9th Sym. without benefit of rehearsal (Nov. 30, 1984). In 1985 he was the first co-recipient (with Hugh Wolff) of the Affiliate Artist's Seaver Conducting Award. He subsequently appeared as a guest conductor with various orchs. on both sides of the Atlantic. In 1989 he became chief conductor of the Opéra de Lyon. In 1991 he also was named principal conductor designate of the Hallé Orch. in Manchester, serving as its principal conductor from 1994 to 1998. In 2000 he became chief conductor of the Deutsches Symphonie-Orchester Berlin, and that same year was named principal conductor of the Los Angeles Opera. He was made an Officier in the Order of Arts and Letters of France in 1993. Nagano is highly regarded for his diversified repertoire, and for his rare insight into contemporary scores.—**NS/LK/DM**

Nagel, Wilibald, German pianist and musicologist; b. Mulheim-an-der-Ruhr, Jan. 12, 1863; d. Stuttgart, Oct. 17, 1929. He studied in Berlin with Ehrlich, Spitta, Bellermann, and others. In 1888 he was appointed a lecturer in music history at the Univ. of Zürich. He then lived in London (1893–96), where he studied early English music. Returning to Germany, he completed his Habilitation at Darmstadt's Grossherzogliche Technische Hochschule with his *Die Entwicklung der Musik in Frankreich und England* (1898; publ. in Berlin, 1898); then served on its faculty as a prof. from 1905 to 1913. He

then settled in Stuttgart, where he ed. the *Neue Musikzeitung* (1917–21). From 1921 he was a prof. at the Hochschule für Musik; also made frequent appearances as a concert pianist. He wrote the valuable article "Annalen der englischen Hofmusik von der zeit Heinrichs VIII. bis zum Tode Karls I., 1509–1649," *Monatshefte für Musikgeschichte*, XXVI-XXVII (1894–95).

WRITINGS: *Die dramatisch-musikalischen Bearbeitungen der Genovefa-Legende. Ein Beitrag zur Geschichte der Oper* (Leipzig, 1889); *Johannes Brahms als Nachfolger Beethoven's* (Leipzig and Zürich, 1892); *Geschichte der Musik in England* (2 vols., Strasbourg, 1894, 1897); *Annalen der englischen Hofmusik, 1509–1649* (1894); *Beethoven und seine Klaviersonaten* (2 vols., Langensalza, 1903, 1905; 3rd ed., 1933); *Der Musik im täglichen Leben: Ein Beitrag zur Geschichte der musikali schen Kultur unserer Tage* (Langensalza, 1907); *Über die Stromungen im unserer Musik: Kritische Randbemerkungen zur modernen Kunst* (Langensalza, 1913); *Die Klaviersonaten von Johannes Brahms: Technisch- ästhetische Analysen* (Stuttgart, 1915); *Wilhelm Mauke* (Vienna and Leipzig, 1919); *Johannes Brahms* (Stuttgart, 1923).—**NS/LK/DM**

Nägeli, Hans Georg, Swiss music publisher, writer on music, and composer; b. Wetzikon, near Zürich, May 26, 1773; d. there, Dec. 26, 1836. He founded a music shop and lending library, and then his own publ. firm (1792). The management of the latter passed to J.C. and Kaspar Hug in 1807, and Nägeli left it to form his own firm in 1818. He founded in Zürich the Singinstitut (1805), the Sangerverein (1826), and the Musikalischer Frauenverein (1828). He taught in a primary school and championed the Pestalozzian system, and wrote a singing manual and many pamphlets, his most significant essays appearing in *Vorlesungen über Musik mit Berücksichtigung der Dilettanten* (1826). W. Reich ed. a collection of his articles as *Von Bach zu Beethoven* (Basel, 1945). In spite of disagreements, he was a close friend of Beethoven. He publ. the periodical *Répertoire des Clavecinistes* (from 1803), in which he brought out piano pieces by contemporary composers, including the first ed. of Beethoven's op.31 sonatas. As a composer, he wrote some estimable choral works and solo songs, the latter presaging Schubert.

BIBL.: Biographical sketches by Ott (1838), Bierer (1844), Keller (1848), and Schneebeli (1873); H. Kling, *Beethoven et ses relations avec N.* (1912); R. Hunziker, *H.G. N.: Gedächtnisrede* (Winterthur, 1924); idem, *H.G. N.* (Zürich, 1938); A. Cherbuliez, *Der unbekannte N.* (Chur, 1938); J. Hassan, *Die Welt- und Kunstanschauung H.G. N.s mit besonderer Berücksichtigung der Musik* (diss., Univ. of Zürich, 1947); H. Schattner, *Volksbildung durch Musikerziehung: Leben und Wirken H.G. N.s* (diss., Univ. of Saarbrücken, 1960).—**NS/LK/DM**

Naginski, Charles, American composer; b. Cairo, Egypt, May 29, 1909; d. (drowned) Lenox, Mass., Aug. 4, 1940. He was taken to America at an early age, and studied piano with his father and other teachers. From 1928 to 1933 he held a fellowship at the Juilliard Graduate School in N.Y. as a pupil in composition of Rubin Goldmark.

WORKS: DRAMATIC: B a l l e t : *The Minotaur* (1938). **ORCH.:** *Suite* (1931); 2 syms. (1935, 1937); *1936*, symphonic poem (1936); *Sinfonietta* (1937); *3 Movements* for Chamber Orch. (1937); *Nocturne and Pantomime* (1938); *5 Pieces from a Children's*

Suite (1940); *Movement for Strings.* **OTHER:** 2 string quartets (1933); songs.—**NS/LK/DM**

Naldi, Giuseppe, Italian bass; b. Bologna, Feb. 2, 1770; d. Paris, Dec. 14, 1820. After making his debut in Milan in 1789, he made appearances throughout Italy. He sang in Lisbon (1803–06) before making his London debut at the King's Theatre in Guglielmi's *Le due nozze ed un sol marito* (April 15, 1806). He continued to sing in London until 1818, where he was the first to appear as Mozart's Don Alfonso (1811), Papageno (1811), Figaro (1812), and Leporello (1817), and as Rossini's Figaro (1818). Naldi was killed in a freak accident in Manuel García's Paris apartment when a steam cooker exploded and the lid struck him in the head. His daughter, Caroline Naldi (1809–76), was a singer who appeared in operas by Rossini and Bellini in Paris (1819–24). —**NS/LK/DM**

Nancarrow, Conlon, remarkable American-born Mexican composer, innovator in the technique of recording notes on a player-piano roll; b. Texarkana, Ark., Oct. 27, 1912; d. Mexico City, Aug. 10, 1997. He played the trumpet in jazz orchs., and then took courses at the Cincinnati Cons. of Music (1929–32). Subsequently he traveled to Boston, where he became a private student of Slonimsky, Piston, and Sessions (1933–36). In 1937 he joined the Abraham Lincoln Brigade and went to Spain to fight in the ranks of the Republican Loyalists against the brutal assault of General Franco's armies. Classified as a premature anti-Fascist after the Republican defeat in Spain, he was refused a U.S. passport and moved to Mexico City, where he remained for 40 years, eventually obtaining Mexican citizenship (1956). In 1981, with political pressures defused in the U.S., Nancarrow was able to revisit his native land and to participate in the New American Music Festival in San Francisco. In 1982 he was a composer-in-residence at the Cabrillo Music Festival in Aptos, Calif. He also traveled to Europe, where he participated at festivals in Austria, Germany, and France. An extraordinary event occurred in his life in 1982, when he was awarded the "genius grant" from the MacArthur Foundation of Chicago, enabling him to continue his work. From 1948 to 1993 Nancarrow composed a truly unique set of undated 52 *Studies for Player Piano* (Nos. 1–35 were originally titled *Rhythm Studies,* but now all are known simply as *Studies*). These pieces can be notated only by perforating player-piano rolls to mark the notes and rhythms, and can be performed only by activating such piano rolls. This method of composition gives him total freedom in conjuring up the most complex contrapuntal, harmonic, and rhythmic combinations that no human pianist or number of human pianists could possibly perform. The method itself is extremely laborious; a bar containing a few dozen notes might require an hour to stamp out on the piano roll. Some of his studies were publ. in normal notation in Cowell's *New Music Quarterly.* Copland, Ligeti, and other contemporary composers expressed their appreciation of Nancarrow's originality in high terms of praise. On Jan. 30, 1984, Nancarrow gave a concert of his works in Los Angeles, in a program including his *Prelude and Blues for Acoustic Piano* and several of his studies. An audiovisual documentary on Nancarrow was presented on slides by Eva Soltes. A number of Nancarrow's *Studies for Player Piano* that could be adequately notated were publ. in *Soundings 4* (1977), accompanied with critical commentaries by Gordon Mumma, Charles Amirkhanian, John Cage, Roger Reynolds, and James Tenney. For listeners who appreciate contrapuntal intricacy, Nancarrow's output is an unrivaled thunderbolt and delight. The music, beyond human-performance agility, is an almost insanely cross-rhythmic display of acceleration of canons, tinged at times with blues and jazz riffs. Among his works for conventional instruments are *Sarabande and Scherzo* for Oboe, Bassoon, and Piano (1930), *Blues* for Piano (1935), *Toccata* for Violin and Piano (1935), Septet (1940), Piano Sonatina (1941; also as a player- piano roll), *3 Two-Part Studies* for Piano (1941), Trio No. 1 for Oboe, Bassoon, and Piano (1942), *Piece No. 1* for Small Orch. (1943; rev. as *Piece* for Large Orch., 1945) and *No. 2* for Small Orch. (1985), 3 string quartets: No. 1 (1945, No. 2 (unfinished; fragments only), and No. 3 (1987; Cologne, Oct. 15, 1988), *Tango* for Piano (1983), *Canons for Ursula* (Oppens) for Piano (1988), and Quintet (1993; arranged from a discarded player-piano study).

BIBL.: P. Carlsen, *The Player-Piano Music of C. N.: An Analysis of Selected Studies* (Brooklyn, 1988); K. Gann, *The Music of C. N.* (Cambridge, 1995).—**NS/LK/DM**

Nance, Ray (Willis), noted jazz cornetist, trumpeter, violinist, singer; b. Chicago, Dec. 10, 1913; d. N.Y., Jan. 28, 1976. He began on piano at six, began studying violin three years later and attended Chicago Music Coll. with Max Fishel for seven years. He was a drum major at Wendell Phillips H.S., and began doubling on trumpet, instructed by Major N. Clark- Smith. At Lane Coll., Jackson, Tenn., he played and broadcast with the school band, the Rhythm Rascals. He sang and played in Chicago night clubs from 1932, and did short stints in Buffalo, East St. Louis, and other cities. Nance joined Earl Hines from February 1937 until December 1938, then worked with Horace Henderson (doubling on violin and trumpet) from January 1939 until March 1940. He played at Joe Hughe's De Luxe Club before joining Duke Ellington in November 1940. He left Ellington in 1944 to lead own small group, and also worked briefly as a single in late 1945. He returned to Ellington and was a regular member of the band until September 1963, taking a temporary absence from music in late 1961. (In 1948 Ray Nance, Duke Ellington, and singer Kay Davis toured British variety theatres.) He switched to cornet in 1961. He led his own small band in 1964, also worked for Paul Lavalle at N.Y.'s World's Fair (1964 and 1965). He made solo tour of Europe in summer of 1966, worked with Henri Chaix's Band in Switzerland (1967). From late 1966–69 he worked regularly with clarinetist Sol Yaged, occasionally also with Duke Ellington (1965–71), and George Wein (1970–71). He formed his own quartet (autumn 1971). He worked with Brooks Kerr in 1973, toured England with Chris Barber in 1974, then worked N.Y. clubs. He began to suffer from a kidney ailment, which soon curtailed his performing until he passed away in early 1976.

DISC.: *Body and Soul* (1969). D. Ellington: "Moon Mist," "Come Sunday," "Take the A-Train."—**JC/LP**

Nanino (Nanini), Giovanni Bernardino, Italian composer and teacher, brother of **Giovanni Maria Nanino;** b. c. 1560; d. Rome, 1623. He was a boy soprano at Vallerano Cathedral, and studied music with his brother. From 1591 to 1608 he was maestro di cappella at S. Luigi dei Francesi in Rome. His brother lived with him in a home maintained by the church, where they boarded and taught the boy sopranos. He subsequently was maestro di cappella at S. Lorenzo in Damaso, the small church in the home of Cardinal Montalto. He was a significant composer and teacher.

WORKS: VOCAL: S a c r e d : *Motecta* for 2 to 4 Voices (Rome, 1610); *Motecta, liber secundus* for 1 to 5 Voices, with Basso Continuo (Rome, 1611); *Motecta, liber tertius* for 1 to 5 Voices, with Basso Continuo (Rome, 1612); *Motecta, liber quartus* for 1 to 5 Voices, with Basso Continuo (Rome, 1618); *Salmi vespertini* for 4 to 8 Voices (Rome, 1620; ed. by K. Proske, *Musica divina*, I/3 and II/2, Regensburg, 1860–74); *Venite exultemus* for 3 Voices, with Basso Continuo (Assisi, 1620); etc. S e c u l a r : *Il primo libro de madrigali* for 5 Voices (Venice, 1588); *Il secondo libro de madrigali* for 5 Voices (Venice, 1599); *Il terzo libro de madrigali* for 5 Voices (Rome, 1612); etc.—**NS/LK/DM**

Nanino (Nanini), Giovanni Maria, important Italian composer and teacher, brother of **Giovanni Bernardino Nanino;** b. Tivoli, 1543 or 1544; d. Rome, March 11, 1607. He was a boy soprano at Vallerano Cathedral, and was a pupil of Palestrina in Rome. Following Palestrina's resignation as maestro di cappella at S. Maria Maggiore in 1567, Nanino was named his successor. From 1575 to 1577 he was maestro di cappella at S. Luigi dei Francesi. In 1577 he became a tenor in the papal choir, remaining a member until his death; he also was elected to the position of maestro di cappella several times after 1586. He continued an association with S. Luigi dei Francesi, and after his brother was made maestro di cappella there in 1591, he lived with him in a home maintained by the church, where they boarded and taught the boy sopranos. His pupils included Paolo Agostino, Felice Anerio, Antonio Brunelli, and other outstanding musicians. Nanino was one of the most significant composers and teachers of the Roman school. His sacred and secular works are of great merit.

WORKS: VOCAL: S a c r e d : *Motecta...nova inventione elaborata* for 3 to 5 Voices (Venice, 1586; 4 are found in K. Proske, ed., *Musica divina*, I/2, 4, Regensburg, 1854–62; 14 are in R. Schuler, *The Life and Liturgical Works of Giovanni Maria Nanino*, diss., Univ. of Minnesota, 1963); 5 Lamentations in F. Haberl, "G.M. Nanino," *Kirchenmusikalisches Jahrbuch*, VI (1891); 2 canons ed. by A. Cametti in *Rivista Musicale Italiana*, XXXV (1928); 14 motets are in R. Schuler, *G.M. Nanino: Fourteen Liturgical Works* (Madison, Wis., 1969). S e c u l a r : *Il primo libro de' madrigali* for 5 Voices (Venice, c. 1571; not extant; 2nd ed., 1579); *Madrigali* for 5 Voices (Venice, 1581; with 13 pieces by A. Stabile); *Il terzo libro de madrigali* for 5 Voices (Venice, 1586; with one piece by G.B. Nanino); *Il primo libro delle canzonette* for 3 Voices (Venice, 1593); also *157 Contrappunti e canoni a 2–11 voci* (in MS).

BIBL.: G. Radiciotti, *G.M. N., musicista tiburtino...Vita ed opere* (Pesaro, 1909); R. Schuler, *The Life and Liturgical Works of G.M. N.* (diss., Univ. of Minnesota, 1963).—**NS/LK/DM**

Nantier-Didiée, Constance (Betzy Rosabella), French mezzo-soprano; b. St. Denis, Ile de Bourbon, Nov. 16, 1831; d. Madrid, Dec. 4, 1867. She was a pupil of Duprez at the Paris Cons., where she took the premier prix in opera in 1849. In 1850 she made her stage debut in Mercadante's *La Vestale* at the Teatro Carignano in Turin. After appearing at the Salle Ventadour (1851) and the Théâtre-Italien (1852) in Paris, she made her debut at Covent Garden in London as the Chevalier de Gondi in Donizetti's *Maria di Rohan* (May 3, 1853), remaining there for 3 seasons. She also toured Spain in 1854 and North America in 1855–56. From 1856 to 1858 she performed once again at the Théâtre-Italien. She then resumed her association with Covent Garden, appearing as Urbain in *Les Huguenots* in the inaugural production of its new theater on May 15, 1858. She continued to sing there until 1864. On Nov. 10, 1862, she created the role of Preziosilla in *La forza del destino* in St. Petersburg.—**NS/LK/DM**

Nanton, Tricky Sam, jazz trombonist; b. N.Y., Feb. 1, 1904; d. San Francisco, July 20, 1946. He was best known for his expressive use of the plunger mute ("wa-wa") and his solos often sound like a human voice. Both of his parents are from the West Indies. His first professional gig was with Cliff Jackson, and then he spent two years in pianist Earl Frazier's Harmony Five, before rejoining Cliff Jackson's Westerners in 1925. He then worked with Elmer Snowden before joining Duke Ellington in 1926. Otto Hardwicke gave him his nickname. Except for an absence due to pneumonia in October 1937, he remained with Duke until suffering a stroke in late 1945. He resumed working with Ellington (c. May 1946) and accompanied the band on a Calif. tour, but died on that tour at the Scragg's Hotel.—**JC/LP**

Naoumoff, Émile, Bulgarian-born French pianist, composer, and teacher; b. Sofia, Feb. 20, 1962. He was taken to France at an early age and began training in piano and composition as a child. His precocious talent prompted Nadia Boulanger to accept him as a pupil, and he studied with her at the American Cons. in Fontainebleau from 1971 until her death in 1979. He also studied at the Paris Cons. (diploma, 1978; Maitrise Cycle de Perfectionnement, 1982) and conducting with Pierre Dervaux at the École Normale de Musique in Paris (Licence de Concert, 1979). In 1973 and 1977 he was awarded the Lili Boulanger composition prize. He captured first prize in the Casadesus Piano Competition in 1974. Naoumoff scored a remarkable success as a soloist in Monte Carlo in 1984 when he replaced an ailing pianist and played the Tchaikovsky 1st Piano Concerto without benefit of rehearsal. In subsequent years, he was engaged by major orchs. on both sides of the Atlantic. He also appeared in recitals and chamber music settings. Following Boulanger's death, he taught her classes at the American Cons. from 1980 until 1987. He also taught at the Paris Cons. from 1982 to 1998. In

1998 he joined the faculty of the Indiana Univ. School of Music in Bloomington. Naoumoff was awarded the composition prize of the Institut de France in 1987 and the Silver Medal of the City of Paris in 1990. His repertoire rnages from Bach and Mozart to contemporary composers. In 1994 he was soloist with Rostropovich and the National Sym. Orch. of Washington, D.C., in his own effective version for piano and orch. of Mussorgsky's *Pictures at an Exhibition*.

WORKS: DRAMATIC: O p e r a : *Le Miracle et l'infant* (1975). ORCH.: 2 piano concertos (1972, 1982); *Symphonietta Concertante* for Piano and Orch. (1973); *Bulgaria 1300* for Piano and Orch. (1976); *Capriccio* for Piano and Orch. (1978); *Concerto Elegiaque* for Violin and Strings (1981). CHAMBER: *L'élan*, trio for Piano, Cello, and Viola (1974); Sonata for Solo Violin (1977); *Divertimento I* for Oboe and Piano (1977); *Poème (sur le nom de Maria)* for Violin and Piano (1977); *Prelude and Chaconne* for Cello and Piano (1978); *3 Pieces* for 2 Violins and Piano (1981); String Quartet (1982); Viola Sonata (1983); *3 Pictures from Childhood* for Flute and Piano (1984); *Petite Suite* for Viola and Piano (1984); *Dixtuor* for Woodwind and String Quintets (1985); *Un Oiseau Meurt* for Woodwind Quintet (1985); *3 Pieces* for Clarinet and Piano (1985); *Echo*, trio for Bassoon, English Horn, and Piano (1988); *3 Elegies* for Bassoon and Piano (1990); Trio for Clarinet, Viola, and Piano (1991); *Impressions* for Bassoon and Piano (1995); *Cantilene* for Bassoon and Piano (1997). P i a n o : *Music in a Child's World* (1979); Sonata (1981); *Sur le nom de Bach* (1985); *12 Pieces* (1987); *4 Preludes* (1990); *13 Anecdotes* (1991); *Rhapsody* (1995); *Valse pour Nadia* [Boulanger] for Piano, 4-Hands (1997); *Reflexions* (1998); *3 Gymnopedies* (1999). VOCAL: 4 Songs for Soprano and Piano (1979); Concerto Oratorio for Chorus and Piano (1983–99); *La fin de Satan* for Reciter and Instruments (1996).—NS/LK/DM

Napoleon, Phil (actually, Filippo Napoli),

early jazz trumpeter, leader; uncle of Marty Napoleon and **Teddy Napoleon**; b. Boston, Sept. 2, 1901; d. Oct. 1, 1990. He recorded prolifically as leader of the Memphis Five, also known as the Cotton Pickers, Bailey's Lucky Seven, and Ladd's Black Aces (though these were white groups!). Their recordings were dance-oriented, but Napoleon's early smaller groups featured fine work by the Dorsey brothers, Joe Venuti, and Eddie Lang. His brother, Ted, was a drummer and the family also included saxophonists George and Joe, and guitarist Matthew. He gave his first public performance at the age of five and recorded in 1916 as a cornet soloist. He became a founder/member of the Original Memphis Five, whose prolific recordings were issued under a variety of pseudonyms, and later led own band at Rosemont Ballroom (1927). After many years of studio work with Sam Lanin, Joe Rines, Leo Reisman, B.A. Rolfe, etc., he left NBC in 1936. From 1938 he led his own big band in N.Y., Chicago, etc., then resumed freelance studio activities and entered the instrument business. He played briefly with Jimmy Dorsey in 1943. In May 1949, he re-formed the Memphis Five at Nick's, N.Y. He led own band there for many years until moving to Florida in June 1956 where his business interests included owning a club. He returned briefly to N.Y. in July 1959, also appearing at the Newport Jazz Festival. He continued to lead own band at his Napoleon's Retreat in Miami Beach, Florida, and remained active into the 1980s.

DISC. *Two-Beat* (1950); *Dixieland by Phil Napoleon* (1954); *Dixieland Classics, Vol. 2* (1954); *Phil Napoleon and the Memphis Five* (1959); *Phil Napoleon and His Memphis Five* (1960).—JC/LP

Napoleon, Teddy (actually, Napoli, Edward George),

jazz pianist; nephew of **Phil Napoleon**, brother of Marty Napoleon; b. Brooklyn, N.Y., Jan. 23, 1914; d. Elmhurst, N.Y., July 5, 1964. He did his first professional work in 1933. He gigged with many bands, including working with his brother Marty, then worked for a long time with Tommy Tompkins's band in the mid-to-late 1930s. Napoleon was mainly with Gene Krupa from 1944 until 1958 (including overseas tours in the 1950s). In 1959, he moved to Fla., where he led his own trio and worked occasionally with Bill Harris and Flip Phillips.—JC/LP

Napoli, Gennaro,

Italian composer and teacher, father of **Jacopo Napoli**; b. Naples, May 19, 1881; d. there, June 28, 1943. He was a student of d'Arienzo and de Nardis at the Royal Cons. in Naples. In 1906 he won the Pensionato Nazionale per la Musica. He taught composition in Naples at the Liceo Musicale (1912–15) and at the Royal Cons. (from 1915), where he served as asst. director (from 1926). He ed. *L'Arte Pianistica* and publ. *Bassi imitati e fugati* (1915).

WORKS: *Jacopo Ortis*, opera; *Armida abbandonata*, dramatic scene (1906); Sym.; *In montagna*, symphonic suite (1906); *Il sole risorto* for Soloists, Chorus, and Orch. (1909); songs; piano pieces.—NS/LK/DM

Napoli, Jacopo,

Italian composer, son of **Gennaro Napoli**; b. Naples, Aug. 26, 1911. He studied at the Cons. San Pietro a Majella in Naples, with his father and S. Cesi; was subsequently appointed to the faculty, and eventually was its director (1954–62). Subsequently he was director of the Milan Cons. (1962–72) and then of the Rome Cons. (1972–76). He specialized in opera, often with a Neapolitan background, which gave him the opportunity to use Neapolitan songs in his scores. His operas include *Il Malato immaginario* (Naples, 1939), *Miseria e nobilità* (Naples, 1945), *Un curioso accidente* (Bergamo, 1950), *Masaniello* (1951; won a prize of La Scala, Milan), *I Peccatori* (1954), *Il tesoro* (Rome, 1958), *Il rosario* (Brescia, 1962), *Il povero diavolo* (Trieste, 1963), and *Il Barone avaro* (Naples, 1970).—NS/LK/DM

Nápravnik, Eduard (Francevič),

celebrated Czech-born Russian conductor; b. Byst, near Hradec Králové, Aug. 24, 1839; d. Petrograd, Nov. 23, 1916. He began his music training with Půhonný, the village school master, and then with his uncle, Augustin Svoboda, in Dašice. He subsequently went to Prague, where he took courses with Blažek and Pitsch at the Organ School; after further studies at the Maydl Inst. (1856–61), he joined its faculty; also received instruction in orchestration from Kittl. He then was engaged to conduct the private orch. of the Russian nobleman Yussupov in St. Petersburg (1861–63). After serving as répétiteur and organist at the Imperial Opera, he was named its second conductor in 1867; he subsequently was its chief conductor from 1869 until his death, and also the conductor of the concerts of the St. Petersburg branch of the Russian Musical Society (1869–81), the Red Cross Concerts (1869–87), and the Patriotic Concerts (1871–87). He became greatly renowned as a thorough musician, possessing a fabulous sense of pitch and rhythm and exceptional ability as a disciplinarian. His reputation and influence were very great in Russian operatic affairs; Dostoyevsky, in one of his novels, uses Nápravnik's name as a synonym for a guiding spirit. Nápravnik conducted the premieres of operas by Tchaikovsky, Mussorgsky, Dargomyzhsky, N. Rubinstein, and Rimsky-Korsakov, and also introduced many non-Russian works to his adopted homeland. His interpretations of the Russian repertoire established a standard emulated by other Russian conductors; yet he was deficient in emotional inspiration; his performances of symphonic works were regarded as competent but not profound. He was himself a composer of several operas in the Russian style, imitative of Tchaikovsky; one of them, *Dubrovsky* (St. Petersburg, Jan. 15, 1895), has become part of the active repertoire in Russia. His other operas, all premiered in St. Petersburg, were *Nizhegorotzy* (Jan. 8, 1869), *Harold* (Nov. 23, 1886), and *Francesca da Rimini* (Dec. 9, 1902). He also wrote 4 syms. (c. 1860; 1873; 1874, The Demon; 1879), overtures, Piano Concerto (1877), some chamber music, and piano pieces.

BIBL.: P. Weymarn, *E.F. N.* (St. Petersburg, 1881); N. Findeisen, *E.F. N.* (St. Petersburg, 1898); V. Walter, *E.F. N.: Ksoletiyu yevo artisticheskoy deyatelnosti 1863–1913* (St. Petersburg, 1914). —**NS/LK/DM**

Nardini, Pietro, Italian violinist and composer; b. Livorno, April 12, 1722; d. Florence, May 7, 1793. He was a pupil of Tartini at Padua. From 1762 to 1765 he was solo violinist in the Stuttgart Court Orch. He lived with Tartini until the latter's death in 1770, and then was maestro of the court music at Florence. Both Leopold Mozart and Schubart praised his playing. Among his works are 16 violin concertos, 6 sonatas for Violin and Bass, 6 violin solos, 6 viola duets, and 6 string quartets.

BIBL.: C. Pfafflin, *P. N.: Seine Werke und sein Leben* (Stuttgart, 1930; 2nd ed., 1936).—**NS/LK/DM**

Narell, Andy, American steel drummer; b. N.Y., March 18, 1954. He was introduced to the steel drums (pans) when his social-worker father started steel orchestras as a way of reducing tensions among street gangs in N.Y.C. Since then he has used his formidable technique on this unique instrument to bring it into the jazz fold without neglecting its Caribbean roots. A graduate of Univ. of Calif. at Berkeley, he formed his own label (Hip Pocket) to bring his recordings into the marketplace. He later contracted with Windham Hill, a label known more for new age music than jazz. This broadened his audience base while unfairly trivializing his abilities as an outstanding jazz player among unforgiving jazz "cognoscenti." His links with Windham Hill and Heads Up enabled him to hone his skills as a producer. On the pop side, he has produced albums for the Bobs and Jimmy Haslip. Narell is also an in-demand session musician, appearing on numerous dates, includ-ing releases from Patti LaBelle, Les McCann, and Paquito D'Rivera.

DISC.: *Stickman* (1981); *Slow Motion* (1985); *Light in Your Eyes* (1989); *Little Secrets* (1989); *Different Strokes* (1991); *Down the Road* (1992); *The Bach Variations* (1994); *The Long Time Band* (1995); *The Caribbean Jazz Project* (1995).—**GM**

Nares, James, English organist, teacher, and composer; b. Stanwell, Middlesex (baptized), April 19, 1715; d. London, Feb. 10, 1783. He was a chorister in the Chapel Royal under Gates, and also studied with Pepusch. After briefly serving as assistant to John Pigott, the organist of St. George's Chapel, Windsor Castle, he became organist of York Minster in 1735. In 1756 he succeeded Greene as one of the organists to the Chapel Royal. He received a Mus.D. from Cambridge Univ. in 1757, then was Master of the Children at the Chapel Royal (1757–80). He publ. a dramatic ode, *The Royal Pastoral* for Soloists, Chorus, and Orch. (c. 1769) and *A Collection of Catches, Canons and Glees* (c. 1775). —**NS/LK/DM**

Narmour, Eugene, influential American music theorist; b. Deming, N.Mex., Oct. 27, 1939. He studied at the Eastman School of Music in Rochester, N.Y. (B.M., 1961; M.A., 1962), and with Leonard Meyer, Grosvenor Cooper, and Howard M. Brown at the Univ. of Chicago (Ph.D., 1974, with the diss. *A Theory of Tonal Melody*). From 1963 to 1967 he was an asst. prof. at East Carolina Univ., and then was a lecturer at the Univ. of Chicago from 1968 to 1971. In 1971 he joined the faculty of the Univ. of Pennsylvania as an asst. prof., subsequently serving as an assoc. prof. (1976–87), chairman of the music dept. (1980–83; 1990–93), the Edmund J. Kahn Distinguished Prof. of Music (from 1993), and assoc. dean for the humanities and the social sciences in the School of Arts and Sciences (1995–98). He also was a visiting fellow at Wolfson Coll., Oxford (1984; 1989–90), a visiting lecturer at the Sibelius Academy in Helsinki (1990), a visiting prof. at the Beijing Cons. (1991), and a fellow at the Center for Advanced Study in the Behavioral Sciences in Stanford (1993–94). He has lectured widely in North America, Europe, and Asia, and his works have been translated into French, Spanish, and Chinese. From 1995 to 1998 he served as president of the Soc. for Music Perception and Cognition. Narmour's first book, *Beyond Schenkerism* (Chicago, 1977), was an important turning point in contemporary analysis, focusing on the interface between music theory and cognition, and addressing problems of both composition and perception. His articles on hierarchical structuring, style, form, content, rule-mapping, and particularly his later books, *The Analysis and Cognition of Basic Melodic Structures* (Chicago, 1990) and *The Analysis and Cognition of Melodic Complexity* (Chicago, 1991), present a formalized theory of implication-realization, and are much cited by empirical psychologists whose experimental data have found strong support for the model. —**NS/LK/DM**

Narváez, Luis de, Spanish vihuelist and composer who flourished from 1530 to 1550. He was a native of

Granada. He served as music teacher to the children in the chapel of Prince Philip (later Philip II), and had the opportunity to travel throughout northern Europe. He publ. *Los seys libros del Delphin de música de cifra para tañer vihuela* (Valladolid, 1538; in tablature), containing the earliest examples of variation form and the use of symbols for tempo indications in Spain; it was reprinted in modern notation by E. Pujol in Monumentos de la Música Española (Vol. 3, Barcelona, 1945) and G. Tarragó (Madrid, 1971).—NS/LK/DM

Nascimento, Milton, Brazilian songwriter, musician; b. Rio de Janeiro, Brazil, Oct. 26, 1942. He was raised in the Brazilian state of Minas Gerais by his adoptive parents. He played the accordion as a child but had switched to guitar and bass by the time he was a teenager. He also formed an important long-term musical relationship with keyboard player Wagner Tiso when they both played in the same band. He played area jazz clubs while attending college. His first big break as a songwriter came in 1966 when a tune he wrote called "Cangmo Do Sal" was performed by the popular Brazilian singer Elis Regina. In 1967 he was voted best performer at the International Song Festival and one of his songs, "Travessia" ("Bridges"), won second place in the writing competition. In addition to writing many of his own songs, he has been closely involved with a cadre of poets and musicians from Minas Gerais called "Clube da Esquina" or "the Corner Club." As a collective, the club released albums under the names of fellow singer/writer L. Borges and Nascimento that were as important and revolutionary in the early '70s as the collaboration between Antonio Carlos Jobim and João Gilberto was in the late '50s.

He has also been heavily involved with the New Song movement that swept Latin America in the '60s and '70s, working with major figures within the genre like Pablo Milanes, Silvio Rodriguez, and Mercedes Sosa. In addition, he sings of the Amazon, the environment, and Amnesty International. Jazz musicians started becoming aware of his prodigious talents in the late '60s, when he toured Mexico and the United States in the company of João Gilberto and Art Blakey. Nascimento's first appearance on a U.S. jazz album was on Wayne Shorter's 1974 *Native Dancer*. Shorter returned the favor on his 1976 release, *Milton*, which also featured appearances by Herbie Hancock and Raul DeSouza in addition to Brazilian stalwarts Airto Moreira and Toninho Horta. Pianist Barry Harris even wrote a lovely ballad called "Nascimento" that has been performed by Harris and Tommy Flanagan, among others.

DISC.: *Clube da Esquina* (1972); *Milton* (1976); *Sentinela* (1980); *Encontros e Despedidas* (1986); *Yauaret J* (1988); *Miltons* (1989); *Missa Dos Quilombos* (1992); *Minha Historia* (1994); *The Art of Milton Nascimento* (1995); *Amigo* (1996); *Nascimento* (1997).—GM

Nasco, Jan, Flemish composer; b. c. 1510; d. Treviso, 1561. He was in the service of the nobleman Paolo Naldi in Vicenza before serving as maestro di cappella of the Accademia Filarmonica in Verona (1547–51) and of Treviso Cathedral (1551–61). He was sometimes referred to as Metre Gian, which led to him being confused with Maistre Jhan of Ferrara. His works, which reveal the profound influence of Willaert, included both sacred and secular pieces. He wrote a fine *St. Matthew Passion*, which was formerly attributed to Maistre Jhan. Most of his MSS in Treviso were lost during World War II. —LK/DM

Nash, Heddle, admired English tenor; b. London, June 14, 1896; d. there, Aug. 14, 1961. He was a chorister at Westminster Abbey in London. After training in London, he studied with Borgatti in Milan, where he made his operatic debut at the Teatro Carcano as Rossini's Count Almaviva in 1924. Returning to London, he sang the Duke of Mantua at his first appearance at the Old Vic Theatre in 1925. From 1926 to 1929 he appeared with the British National Opera Co. In 1929 he made his debut at Covent Garden as Don Ottavio, singing there until 1939. During World War II, he appeared with the Carl Rosa Opera Co. In 1947–48 he again sang at Covent Garden. In 1957–58 he appeared with the New Opera Co. He was greatly esteemed for his roles in operas by Mozart and Rossini. Among his other distinguished roles were David in *Die Meistersinger von Nürnberg*, Gounod's Faust, and Rodolfo. He also was a notable concert singer, winning particular renown for his interpretation of Elgar's Gerontius. His son, John Heddle Nash (b. London, March 30, 1928; d. there, Sept. 29, 1994), was a baritone who sang at the Sadler's Wells Theatre and with the Carl Rosa Opera Co. —NS/LK/DM

Nasidze, Sulkhan, Russian composer; b. Tiflis, March 17, 1927. He studied piano and composition at the Tbilisi Cons., where in 1963 he joined its staff. In 1974 he became artistic director of the State Phil. of Georgia in Tbilisi. His music is imbued with Georgian melorhythms, and is set in a fairly advanced idiom. He wrote 2 piano concertos (1954, 1961), 5 syms. (1958, 1964, 1970, 1972, 1975), *Rhapsody on themes of old Tiflis* for Orch. (1964), Cello Concerto (1974), Piano Trio (1958), 2 string quartets (1968, 1971), *Polyphonic Sonata* for Piano, and many vocal works.—NS/LK/DM

Nasolini, Sebastiano, Italian composer; b. Piacenza, c. 1768; d. probably in Naples, c. 1816. He most likely studied at the ducal chapel in Venice. He was maestro al cembalo at the S. Pietro theater in Trieste (1787–90), and also maestro di cappella at the Cathedral of S. Giusto there (1788–90); then was mainly active in Venice as a composer for the theater. He was a highly successful composer of popular stage works; among his extant operas are *La morte di Semiramide* (Padua, Oct. 1790), *La morte di Cleopatra* (Vicenza, June 22, 1791), *Merope* (Venice, Jan. 21, 1796), *Il Medico di Lucca* (Venice, 1797), *Gli umori contrarii* (Venice, June 1798), *Il trionfo di Clelia* (Milan, Dec. 26, 1798), and *Achille* (Modena, June 23, 1806). He also composed pasticcios, oratorios, and cantatas.

BIBL.: E. de Giovanni, *Giuseppe Nicolini e S. N.* (Piacenza, 1927); C. Anguissola, *Geminiano Giacomelli e S. N.: Musicisti placentini* (Piacenza, 1935).—NS/LK/DM

Nastasijević, Svetomir, Serbian composer; b. Gornje Milanovec, April 1, 1902; d. Belgrade, Aug. 17, 1979. He studied engineering and architecture, and at the same time learned to play the violin. He wrote music criticism and publ. two manuals on theory. His works include the music drama *Medjuluško blago* (The Treasure of the Medjuluzje; Belgrade, March 4, 1937), *Durad Branković*, national opera from medieval Serbian history (Belgrade, June 12, 1940), and several symphonic poems and choruses. In his operas, he adopted the Wagnerian system of leitmotifs.—NS/LK/DM

Nat, Yves, French pianist, pedagogue, and composer; b. Béziers, Dec. 28, 1890; d. Paris, Aug. 31, 1956. A gifted child, he conducted his own orchestral *Fantaisie* when he was 10. After studying with Diémer at the Paris Cons. (premier prix in piano, 1907), he toured in Europe and the Americas (1909–34). He was also active as accompanist to Ysaÿe, Enesco, and Thibaud. From 1934 he was a prof. of piano at the Paris Cons. He was especially esteemed as an interpreter of Beethoven and Schumann. Among his compositions were *L'enfer* for Chorus and Orch. (1942), a Piano Concerto (1953), piano pieces, and songs.—NS/LK/DM

Nataletti, Giorgio, Italian ethnomusicologist; b. Rome, June 12, 1907; d. there, July 16, 1972. He studied at the Pesaro Cons., then pursued ethnomusicological research in Italy, the Maritime Alps, and Tunisia (from 1926). He was technical director of Le Arti di le Tradizioni Popolari dell'OND (ENAL) (1926–36; 1946–61) and secretary of the Comitato Nazionale delle Arti Popolari (1947–52). In 1948, with Pizzetti and others, he founded the Centro Nazionale Studi di Musica Popolare. In addition, he was active as broadcaster and music director of the RAI; also was artistic director of RCA Italiana and taught folk music (from 1940) and music history (from 1961) at the Rome Cons. With A. Lomax and D. Carpitella, he prepared the Italian section of *The Columbia World Library of Folk and Primitive Music* (vols. XV and XVI).

WRITINGS (all publ. in Rome unless otherwise given): With G. Petrassi, *Canti della campagna romana* (Milan, 1930); *Musica e canti della patria* (Tunis, 1933); *Trenta ninna nanne popolari italiene* (1934); *Catalogo del Museo strumentale di Tunisi* (1935); *I poeti a braccio della campagna romana* (1936); *La raccolta dei canti popolari della CIATP* (1936); *Verdi e le sue medaglie* (1941); *Il folklore musicale Italia* (1948); *La musica folklorica italiana nel cinema* (1959).

BIBL.: *1922–1962: Quaranti anni di attivita di G. N.* (Rome, 1962).—NS/LK/DM

Natanson, Tadeusz, Polish composer and pedagogue; b. Warsaw, Jan. 26, 1927; d. Wroclaw, Nov. 10, 1990. He studied composition with K. Wilkomirski, P. Perkowski, and S. Poradowski at the Wrocław Academy of Music (1952–56). He was on its faculty (from 1957), and also taught at the Warsaw Academy of Music (from 1977), where he received his Ph.D. (1977; with a diss. on music therapy as a function of music). He also taught at the Univ. of Silesia in Cieszyn (from 1983), where he

served as head of the Inst. for Music Therapy (from 1984).

WORKS: DRAMATIC: *Quo Vadis*, ballet-pantomime (1970); *Tamango*, opera (1972). ORCH.: *Toccata* (1956); 2 piano concertos (1956, 1980); *Polifonie* for 2 String Orchs. (1958); *Rondo concertante* for Violin and Orch. (1958); Double Concerto for 2 Saxophones and Orch. (1959); 7 syms.: No. 1, *Wroclaw*, for Piano and Orch. (1961), No. 2 (1964), No. 3, *"John Kennedy in Memoriam"* (1965), No. 4 (1969), No. 5 for Baritone, Chorus, and Orch. (1974), No. 6 (1980), and No. 7 (1982); *Concerto breve* for Trombone and Orch. (1963); Viola Concerto (1971); *Triptyque* (1976); *Symphoniette classique* (1979). CHAMBER: 2 wind quartets (1960, 1987); *Toccata* for 2 Clarinets, 2 Horns, and Piano (1964); 2 trios for Violin, Cello, and Piano (1965, 1966); Oboe Sonata (1977); *Sonata antiqua* for Wind Quintet (1978); Sextet for 3 Trumpets and 3 Trombones (1981). VOCAL: *Satires* for Chorus and Instrumental Ensemble (1960); *I Prayed to Jehovah* for Reciter and Orch. (1964); *Cain's Question* for Reciter and Orch. (1967; also for Reciter and Men's Voices); *A Salt Shaker Full of Pepper* for Men's Chorus (1968); *Familiale* for Reciter and Chamber Ensemble (1979).—NS/LK/DM

Nathan, Hans, German-born American musicologist; b. Berlin, Aug. 5, 1910; d. Boston, Aug. 4, 1989. He took courses in musicology at the Univ. of Berlin (Ph.D., 1934, with the diss. *Das Rezitativ der Frühopern Richard Wagners: Ein Beitrag zur Stilistik des Opernrezitativs in der ersten Hälfte des 19 Jahrhunderts*); studied piano with Rudolph Schmidt and Claudio Arrau, theory with Grete von Zieritz, and conducting with Michael Taube. He was active as a music critic in Berlin (1932–36). In 1936 he went to the U.S. and became a naturalized American citizen in 1944. From 1936 to 1938 he did postgraduate study at Harvard Univ. After a year of teaching at Tufts Univ., he joined the faculty of Mich. State Univ. in East Lansing in 1946; held a Guggenheim fellowship in 1957; was a visiting prof. at the Inst. for Advanced Study in Princeton, N.J., in 1957–58 and again in the summer of 1979; he retired in 1981. In the U.S. he devoted himself chiefly to subjects of American music; publ. the valuable books *Dan Emmett and the Rise of Early Negro Minstrelsy* (Norman, Okla., 1962) and *William Billings: Data and Documents* (Detroit, 1976). He was the ed. of vol. 2 (1977) of the complete, critical ed. of works by William Billings, in 4 vols.; contributed articles on folk music, history, and modern biography to various publications.—NS/LK/DM

Nathan, Isaac, English-born Australian composer of Polish-Jewish descent; b. Canterbury, 1790; d. Sydney, Jan. 15, 1864. He studied singing and composition with D. Corri in London. He collaborated with Byron on the *Hebrew Melodies* (1815–19), his most successful effort. He served as music librarian to George IV, and also maintained a music publishing business. In 1841 he moved to Australia, where he continued his enterprises. He also continued to compose, being the first to write operas in Australia. He publ. *An Essay on the History and Theory of Music, and on the Qualities, Capabilities and Management of the Human Voice* (1823; 2nd ed., 1836, as *Musurgia Vocalis*) and *Memoirs of Madame Malibran de Bériot* (1836).

WORKS: DRAMATIC: Comic Opera: *Sweethearts and Wives* (London, July 7, 1823); *The Alcaid, or The Secrets of the Office* (London, July 14, 1824). **O p e r a t i c   F a r c e :** *The Illustrious Stranger, or Married and Buried* (London, Oct. 1, 1827). **O p e r a :** *Don John of Austria* (Sydney, May 3, 1847). **O T H E R :** Songs; piano pieces.

BIBL.: C. Berti, *I. N.: Australia's First Composer* (Sydney, 1922); O. Phillips, *I. N.: Friend of Byron* (London, 1940); C. Mackerras, *The Hebrew Melodist: A Life of I. N.* (Sydney, 1963).—**NS/LK/DM**

Natra, Sergiu, Romanian-born Israeli composer and teacher; b. Bucharest, April 12, 1924. He studied composition with Leon Klepper at the Bucharest Cons. (1945–52). He emigrated to Israel in 1961, where he became active mainly as a teacher. He became a teacher at the Rubin Academy of Music in Tel Aviv (1975) and was prof. at the Univ. of Tel Aviv (from 1976).

WORKS: D R A M A T I C : B a l l e t : *Diary of a Choreographer* (1982). **O R C H .:** *Divertimento in a Classical Style* for Strings (1943); *March and Chorale* (1944); *Suite* (1948); *Sym. No. 1* (1952); *Sinfonia* for Strings (1960); *Toccata* (1963); *Music* for Oboe and Strings (1965); *Variations* for Piano and Orch. (1966); *Pages from a Composer's Diary* for Chamber Orch. (1978); *Development* for Viola and Chamber Orch. (1988); *Concerto a quattro* for Clarinet, Cello, Trombone, Organ, and Strings (1993). **CHAMBER:** 2 string quartets (1947, 1991); *Music* for Violin and Harp (1959); *Music* for Harpsichord and 6 Instruments (1964); Sonatina for Solo Harp (1965; rev. 1978); 3 solo sonatinas: for Trombone, for Trumpet, and for Oboe (all 1969); Piano Trio (1971); *Music for Nicanor* (Zabaleta) for Harp, Flute, Clarinet, and String Quartet (1988); *Ancient Walls* for Oboe and Trombone (1990); Sonata for 4 Harps (1993). **VOCAL:** *4 Poems* for Baritone and Orch. (1958); *Song of Deborah* for Mezzo-soprano and Chamber Orch. (1967); *Commentary on Nehemia* for Baritone, Chorus, and Orch. (1967); *Miracle of the Peoples*, cantata (1984). **O T H E R :** *Environment for an Exhibition*, sound collage on tape (1970).—**NS/LK/DM**

Nattiez, Jean-Jacques, learned French-born Canadian musicologist; b. Amiens, Dec. 30, 1945. He studied piano privately while pursuing musical training at the Amiens Cons. Following further studies in Aix-en-Provence (L.Litt. in modern languages, 1967; Licentiate in linguistics, 1968; M.Litt. in modern languages, 1968), he studied in Paris (Certificat d'aptitude pédagogique à l'enseignement secondaire, 1970; Ph.D., 1973, with a diss. on musical semiology). He also received instruction in conducting from Jacques Clément in Montreal, Fernand Quattrochi and Pierre Dervaux in Nice, and Charles Bruck in Hancock, Maine. He settled in Canada, becoming a naturalized Canadian citizen in 1975. In 1970 he became a prof. at the Univ. of Montreal, where he taught musicology (from 1972) and also was director of the Groupe de recherches en sémiologie musicale (1974–80). From 1980 to 1985 he was co-ed. of the *Canadian University Music Review/Revue de musique des universités canadiennes*. With Pierre Boulez, he became co-ed. of the series Musique/Passé/Présent of Paris in 1981. From 1984 to 1987 he was music director of the Joliette-Lanaudière Sym. Orch. In 1988 he was elected to membership in the Royal Soc. of Canada and was awarded the Dent Medal of the Royal Musical Assn. of England. In 1990 he was made a Member of the Order of Canada. Nattiez is a foremost authority on

musical semiotics. His study, *Fondements d'une sémiologie de la musique* (Paris, 1975; rev. and expanded, 1987, as *Musicologie générale et sémiologie*), is notable for its erudite investigation of structural linguistics as applied to musical analysis.

WRITINGS: *Fondements d'une sémiologie de la musique* (Paris, 1975; rev. and expanded, 1987, as *Musicologie générale et sémiologie*); *Tétralogies "Wagner, Boulez, Chéreau," essai sur l'infidélite* (Paris, 1983); *Proust musicien* (Paris, 1989); *Il discorso musicale, Per una semiologia della musica* (Turin, 1987); *De la sémiologie à la musique* (Montreal, 1988); ed. *Pierre Boulez, John Cage: Correspondance et documents* (vol. I, Basel, 1990); *Wagner adrogyne: Essai sur l'interprétation* (Paris, 1990); *Le combat de Chronos et d'Orphée: Essais* (Paris, 1993).—**NS/LK/DM**

Naudin, Emilio, Italian-born French tenor; b. Parma (of French parents), Oct. 23, 1823; d. Boulogne-sur-Mer, May 5, 1890. He was a pupil of Panizza in Milan, making his debut in Pacini's *Saffo in Cremona* (1843). He appeared in Vienna, St. Petersburg, London, Madrid, and Paris (from 1862, at the Théâtre Italien). He created the role of Vasco da Gama in *L'Africaine* (in accordance with a stipulation in Meyerbeer's will). He retired in 1879.—**NS/LK/DM**

Naudot, Jacques-Christophe, French flutist, teacher, and composer; b. c. 1690; d. Paris, Nov. 26, 1762. He pursued his career in Paris, where he became especially well known as an instrumentalist and teacher. He also was adept at composing for the flute in the Italian style. His set of flute concertos, publ. as *6 concerto en 7 parties* for Flute, 3 Violins, Viola, Cello or Bassoon, and Basso Continuo, op.11 (Paris, c. 1737), are particularly notable. He also publ. many flute sonatas for 1 or 2 flutes, various pieces for hurdy-gurdy or musette, other instrumental scores, and Masonic songs.—**LK/DM**

Naumann, Emil, German music scholar and composer, grandson of **Johann Gottlieb Naumann;** b. Berlin, Sept. 8, 1827; d. Dresden, June 23, 1888. He was a pupil of Schnyder von Wartensee in Frankfurt am Main, and then of Mendelssohn in Leipzig (1842); he studied at the Leipzig Cons. (1843–44), and later took courses at the Univ. of Bonn. He received his Ph.D. at the Univ. of Berlin in 1867 with the dissertation *Das Alter der Psalmengesänge.* In 1850 he became Hofkirchen-Musik-direktor in Berlin. In 1873 he was made a lecturer in music history at the Dresden Cons. In his works he faithfully followed the methods of his revered teacher Mendelssohn, without ever attaining the melodic grace and harmonic lucidity that made Mendelssohn's music a perennial art. Naturally, he opposed Wagner's innovations and wrote critically about "the music of the future."

WORKS: DRAMATIC: *Judith,* opera (Dresden, 1858); *Die Muhlenhexe,* Singspiel (Berlin, 1861); *Loreley,* grand opera (Berlin, 1889). **VOCAL:** *Christus der Friedensbote,* oratorio (Dresden, 1848); *Missa solennis* (1851); *Die Zerstörung Jerusalem's durch Titus,* cantata (1855); 12 Psalms in *Psalmen auf alle Sonn- und Fest-Tage des evangelischen Kirchenjahres* for *Musica sacra,* vols. VIII-X (Berlin and Posen, 1855); *Dank- und Jubel-Cantate zur Feier der Siege Preussens im Jahre 1866.* **O T H E R :** Piano Sonata; several overtures.

WRITINGS: *Über Einführung des Psalmengesanges in die evangelische Kirche* (Berlin, 1856); *Die Tonkunst in ihren Beziehungen zu den Formen und Entwickelungsgesetzen alles Geisteslebens* (2 vols., Berlin, 1869–70); *Ludwig van Beethoven: Zur hundertjährigen Geburtstagsfeier* (Berlin, 1871); *Deutsche Tondichter von Sebastian Bach bis auf die Gegenwart* (Berlin, 1871; 6th ed., 1895); *Nachklänge: Eine Sammlung von Vorträgen und Gedenkblättern* (Berlin, 1872); *Deutschlands musikalische Heroen in ihrer Rückwirkung auf die Nation* (Berlin, 1873); *Italienische Tondichter von Palestrina bis auf die Gegenwart* (Berlin, 1874–75; 2nd ed., 1883); *Das goldene Zeitalter der Tonkunst in Venedig* (Berlin, 1876); *Musikdrama oder Oper? Eine Beleuchtung der Bayreuther Bühnenfestspiele* (Berlin, 1876); *Zukunftsmusik und die Musik der Zukunft* (Berlin, 1877); *Darstellung eines bisher unbekannt gebliebenen Stylgesetzes im Aufbau des classischen Fugenthemas* (Berlin, 1878); *Illustrierte Musikgeschichte* (2 vols., Berlin and Stuttgart, 1880–85; Eng. tr. by F. Ouseley, 1882–86; 10th Ger. ed., 1934, by E. Schmitz); *Der moderne musikalische Zopf* (Berlin, 1880). —NS/LK/DM

Naumann, Johann Gottlieb, distinguished German composer and conductor, grandfather of **Emil Naumann** and **(Karl) Ernst Naumann**; b. Blasewitz, near Dresden, April 17, 1741; d. Dresden, Oct. 23, 1801. He received his first instruction in music at the Dresden Kreuzschule. In 1757 the Swedish violinist Anders Wesström took him to Italy, where he received valuable instruction from Tartini in Padua, Padre Martini in Bologna, and Hasse in Venice. His intermezzo *Il tesoro insidiato* was premiered in Venice on Dec. 28, 1762. In 1764 he returned to Dresden, where he was appointed second church composer to the court; in 1765 he was named chamber composer. He made return trips to Italy (1765–68; 1772–74), where he brought out several operas. In 1776 he was appointed Kapellmeister in Dresden. In 1777 he visited Stockholm at the invitation of Gustavus III, and was charged with reorganizing the Hofkapelle. His most popular opera, *Cora och Alonzo*, received its first complete performance in Stockholm during the consecration of the New Opera House on Sept. 30, 1782. Another important opera, *Gustaf Wasa*, was premiered there on Jan. 19, 1786, and was considered the Swedish national opera for many years. In 1785–86 he visited Copenhagen, where he carried out some reforms at the Hofkapelle and court opera. He composed the opera *Orpheus og Eurydike* for the Danish king's birthday, and it was premiered in Copenhagen on Jan. 31, 1786. He was named Oberkapellmeister for life in Dresden in 1786. At the request of Friedrich Wilhelm II, he made several visits to Berlin, where his operas *Medea in Colchide* (Oct. 16, 1788) and *Protesilao* (Jan. 26, 1789) were premiered at the Royal Opera. He also wrote masses, cantatas, oratorios, and lieder.

WORKS: DRAMATIC (all first perf. at the Kleines Kurfürstliches Theater in Dresden unless otherwise given): *Il tesoro insidiato*, intermezzo (Teatro San Samuele, Venice, Dec. 28, 1762); *Li creduti spiriti*, opera buffa (Teatro San Cassiano, Venice, Carnival 1764; in collaboration with 2 other composers); *L'Achille in Sciro*, opera seria (Teatro San Cecilia, Palermo, Sept. 5, 1767); *Alessandro nelle Indie*, opera seria (1768; unfinished); *La clemenza di Tito*, opera seria (Feb. 1, 1769); *Il villano geloso*, opera buffa (1770); *Solimano*, opera seria (Teatro San Benedetto, Venice, Carnival 1773); *L'isola disabitata*, azione per musica (Venice, Feb. 1773); *Armida*, opera seria (Teatro Nuovo, Padua, June 13, 1773); *Ipermestra*, opera seria (Teatro San Benedetto, Venice, Feb. 1, 1774); *La villanella incostante*, opera buffa (Teatro San Benedetto, Venice, Fall 1773); *L'Ipocondriaco*, opera buffa (March 16, 1776); *Amphion*, prologue and opera-ballet (Royal Theater, Stockholm, Jan. 1, 1778); *Elisa*, opera seria (April 21, 1781); *Cora och Alonzo*, opera seria (New Opera House, Stockholm, Sept. 30, 1782); *Osiride*, opera seria (Oct. 27, 1781); *Tutto per amore*, opera buffa (March 5, 1785); *Gustaf Wasa*, lyric tragedy (New Opera House, Stockholm, Jan. 19, 1786); *Orpheus og Eurydike*, opera seria (Royal Theater, Copenhagen, Jan. 31, 1786); *La reggia d'Imeneo*, festa teatrale (Oct. 21, 1787); *Medea in Colchide*, opera seria with ballet (Royal Opera, Berlin, Oct. 16, 1788); *Protesilao*, opera seria with ballet and choruses (Royal Opera, Berlin, Jan. 26, 1789; in collaboration with J.F. Reichardt); *La dama soldato*, opera buffa (March 30, 1791); *Amore giustificato*, festa teatrale (May 12, 1792); *Aci e Galatea ossia I ciclopi amanti*, opera buffa (April 25, 1801). **Oratorios** (all performed in Dresden unless otherwise given): *La passione di Gesù Cristo* (Padua, 1767); *Isacco, figura del Redentore* (1772); *S. Elena al calvario* (1775); *Giuseppe riconosciuto* (1777); *Il ritorno del figliolo prodigo* (1785); *La morte d'Abel* (1790); *Davide in Terebinto, figura del Salvatore* (1794); *I Pellegrini al sepolcro* (1798); *Il ritorno del figliolo prodigo* (1800); *Betulia liberata* (1805). **LIEDER:** *Freimaurerlieder...zum Besten der neuen Armenschule* (publ. in Leipzig, 1775); *40 Freymäurerlieder zum Gebrauch der teutschen auch französischen Tafellogen* (publ. in Berlin, 1782; 2nd ed., 1784); *Sammlung von Liedern* (publ. in Pforten, 1784); *Sechs neue Lieder* (publ. in Berlin, 1795); *25 neue Lieder verschieden Inhalts* (publ. in Dresden, 1799); etc. **INSTRUMENTAL:** Sinfonias; Keyboard Concerto; quartets; sonatas for Keyboard and Violin; sonatas for Glass Harmonica; etc.

BIBL.: A. Meissner, *Bruckstücke zur Biographie J.G. N.'s* (2 vols., Prague, 1803–04; 2nd ed., Vienna, 1814); F. Mannstein, *Vollständiges Verzeichnis aller Kompositionen des Kurfürstlich Sächsischen Kapellmeisters N.* (Dresden, 1841); G. Schweizer, *Biographie von J.G. N.* (3 vols., Zürich, 1843–45); M. Nestler, *Der kursächsische Kapellmeister N. aus Blasewitz* (Dresden, 1901); R. Englander, *J.G. N. als Opernkomponist (1741–1801)* (Leipzig, 1922).—NS/LK/DM

Naumann, (Karl) Ernst, German organist, conductor, and composer, grandson of **Johann Gottlieb Naumann**; b. Freiberg, Saxony, Aug. 15, 1832; d. Jena, Dec. 15, 1910. He studied in Leipzig with Hauptmann, Richter, Wenzel, and Langer, and received his Ph.D. in 1858 from the Univ. of Leipzig with the dissertation *Über die verschiedenen Bestimmungen der Tonverhältnisse und die Bedeutung des pythagoreischen oder reinen Quintensystems für unsere heutige Musik* (pub. in Leipzig, 1858); also took organ lessons in Dresden with Johann Schneider. In 1860 he was appointed music director and director of academic concerts at the Univ. of Jena. He also served as city organist. He was made a prof. in 1877, retiring in 1906. He ed. 6 vols. of Bach's cantatas and works for keyboard for the collected edition of the Bach Gesellschaft, and later ed. several organ works for the Neue Bach Gesellschaft. He also ed. a practical edition of Bach's organ music in 9 vols. (1899–1904). His own compositions include chamber music, sacred works, and lieder.—NS/LK/DM

Naumann, Siegfried, Swedish conductor, teacher, and composer; b. Malmö, Nov. 27, 1919. He received instruction in violin, theory, and composition from his father, then studied with Wolf (violin) and Myrtelius (instrumentation), and also took courses with Melchers, Mann, and Broström at the Stockholm Musikhögskolan (1942–45). After conducting the Örnsköldsvik Music Soc. (1945–49), he studied composition with Pizzetti at Rome's Accademia di Santa Cecilia (1949–53); also with Malipiero and Orff. He later received instruction in conducting at the Salzburg Mozarteum and with Furtwängler and Scherchen. He was conductor of the Gävleborgs Sym. Orch. (1954–55). In 1962 he founded the Musica Nova ensemble, which he conducted on tours of Scandinavia, Germany, and England; was its conductor until 1977. He taught conducting at the Stockholm Musikhögskolan (1963–83), becoming a prof. there in 1976. He then taught at the Malmö Musikhögskolan and Teaterhögskolan (from 1983). He wrote three syms. and some other works in a traditionally acceptable infra- modern idiom, but at the age of 40 decided to adopt an austere structural style governed by serial procedures and diversified by aleatory passages. To mark this decisive avatar, he designated his first serial work, *Ruoli* (Roles) for 4 Clarinets, as op.1 (1959). Among his subsequent works were: *7 Sonetti di Petrarca* for Tenor, Harp, Vibraphone, and 4 Cellos (1959); *Phaedri: 4 Fabulae* for Soloists, Chorus, and 8 Instruments (1961); *Improvviso sopra 28 strutture* for Keyboard and Percussion Instruments (1961); *Transformations* for Orch. (1962; Gävleborg, April 29, 1962); *Risposte I* for Flute and Percussion (1963), *II* for Piano, Hammond Organ, Electric Guitar, Trombone, and Percussion (1963), and *III* for Flute, Percussion, Harp, and Strings (1994); *Il cantico del sole* for Soloists, Chorus, 10 Solo Instruments, and Orch. (1963; Stockholm, Sept. 14, 1966); *Cadenza* for 9 Players (1964); *Missa in onore della Madonna de Loreto* for Chorus, Organ, and Percussion (1964); *Spettacolo I* for Soprano and Orch. (1967) and *II* for 3 Soloists, Chorus, and Orch. (1969); *Estate* for Chamber Orch. (1968); *Ljudposter* (Soundposts) for Wind Orch. (1970); *Due cori su testi latini* for Chorus, Double Bass, Hammond Organ, and Percussion (1970); *Teatro strumentale* for Chamber Ensemble (1971); *Il cielo del ponte a Moriano*, dialogue for Tenor, Chorus, and Chamber Orch. (1972); *Material-studier i improvisation* for Orch. (1974); *Fanfarer* for Wind Ensemble (1974–76); *Strutture per Giovanni*, Version B for Wind Orch. (1980); *Ljudspel/Giuoco di suono* for 3 Instrumental Groups (1984); *Och lärka slår och Skånes somrar ila* for Chorus and Orch. (Malmö, Sept. 8, 1985); *Strutture* for Orch. (1986); *Tripla* for Flute, Cello, and Piano (1987); *Arie di battaglia* for Soprano, Tenor, and Orch. (Stockholm, Nov. 26, 1989); *Il pianot della Madonna: Lauda drammatica* for Soprano, Tenor, Baritone, Chorus, and Orch. (1990); *Skåne* for Contralto and Orch. (1992); *Versi da Francesco d'Assisi* for Soprano, Flute, and Percussion (1992); *Cadenze* for Voices and Instruments (1993); *Spel Musica* for 9 Clarinets (1995); *Fanfara di nozze* for Trumpet (1996); *Quartetto* for Saxophones (1997); Concerto for Organ and Winds (1998).—NS/LK/DM

Naumburg, Walter W(ehle), American music patron; b. N.Y., Dec. 25, 1867; d. there, Oct. 17, 1959. He received cello lessons in his youth. After graduating from Harvard Univ. in 1889, he returned to N.Y. and entered the mercantile business of his father, Elkan Naumburg, who founded a series of free concerts in N.Y.'s Central Park in 1905. Walter and his brother George continued the series after their father's death in 1924. In 1925 Walter founded a series of auditions to find young talent for Town Hall debuts, an effort continued under the auspices of the Walter W. Naumburg Foundation (from 1926).—NS/LK/DM

Nauwach, Johann, German composer; b. Brandenburg, c. 1595; d. probably in Dresden, c. 1630. By 1607 he was a choirboy in Dresden, and in 1612 he was sent to Italy for further study by the Elector of Saxony. He studied in Turin and Florence, receiving instruction on the lute from Lorenzo Allegri, then returned to Dresden in 1618 where he later was made a chamber musician. His first collection of songs shows the major influence of Caccini and other Italian monodists, while the second is historically important as the first German vol. of continuo lieder.

WORKS: *Libro primo di arie passeggiate a una voce per cantar e sonar nel chitarrone* (Dresden, 1623); *Erster Theil teutscher Villanellen mit 1, 2 und Stimmen auf der Tiorba Laute, Clavicymbel und andere Instrumenta gerichtet* (Dresden, 1627).—NS/LK/DM

Navarra, André (-Nicolas), noted French cellist and pedagogue; b. Biarritz, Oct. 13, 1911; d. Siena, July 31, 1988. He studied at the Paris Cons. with J. Loeb (cello) and Tournemire (chamber music), winning a premier prix at 16. He was a member of the Krettly String Quartet (1929–35); made his debut as a soloist with the Paris Colonne Orch. (1931); in subsequent years, he appeared as a soloist with various European orchs. He was prof. of cello at the Paris Cons. (from 1949) and at the North West German Music Academy (from 1958), and also taught in Siena (1954–88). He gave premiere performances of cello concertos by Jolivet (1962) and Tomasi (1970).

BIBL.: S. Milliot, *Entretiens avec A. N.* (Béziers, 1991). —NS/LK/DM

Navarrini, Francesco, distinguished Italian bass; b. Citadella, 1853; d. Milan, Feb. 23, 1923. He studied with Giuseppe Felix and Carlo Boroni in Milan, making his debut as Alfonso in *Lucrezia Borgia* in Ferrara in 1876. From 1883 to 1900 he was a member of La Scala in Milan, where he created the role of Lodovico in Verdi's *Otello* (Feb. 5, 1887); then toured in England, France, and Russia. He made his first American appearance in 1902 as a member of Mascagni's traveling opera co. A giant of a man (he measured six-and-a-half feet), he imposed his presence in heroic and buffo bass roles, including roles in Wagner's operas.—NS/LK/DM

Navarro, Fats (actually, **Theodore**), jazz trumpeter; b. Key West, Fla., Sept. 24, 1923; d. N.Y., July 7, 1950. Navarro was mostly self-taught, starting piano at age six, trumpet at 13, and also playing tenor sax in Fla. He toured with J. J. Johnson in Snookum Russell's band (1942) and with Andy Kirk (1943–44). Gillespie recommended him as his replacement in Billy Eckstine's band in 1945, and he also played with Illinois Jacquet and Lionel Hampton. He recorded with Tadd Dameron and Bud Powell, among others. His career was cut short by tuberculosis, edged on by narcotics usage. Some discographers doubt the date of his last known session, live at Birdland with Parker, because he sounds so good so close to his death, yet it is certainly possible.

Like every trumpeter in the 1940s, Navarro was a disciple of Dizzy Gillespie, and occasionally used double-timing, especially on live broadcasts. More typically he played lyrical, perfectly phrased lines with a big, open tone. He had a marvelous sly way of connecting choruses that was picked up by Clifford Brown, specifically in his "Joy Spring" solo.

DISC.: *Fat Girl* (1946); *Be Bop Boys* (1946); *Nostalgia* (1947); *New Trends of Jazz* (1947); *New Sounds of Modern Music* (1947).

BIBL.: J. Jepsen, *Discography of Fats Navarro* (Denmark); D. Baker, *Jazz Style of Fats Navarro* (Hialeah, Fla.).—**LP/MM**

Navarro, Juan, Spanish-born Mexican composer; b. Cádiz, c. 1550; d. c. 1610. He served as a Franciscan priest, confessor, and choir singer in Michoacán, Mexico. Navarro publ. a collection of Passion settings and Lamentations (Mexico City, 1604), the earliest vol. of music to be composed and publ. in Mexico.—**LK/DM**

Navarro, (Luis Antonio) García, Spanish conductor; b. Chiva, April 30, 1941. He was educated at the Valencia Cons., where he studied oboe; also took courses at the Madrid Cons. He then went to Vienna to study conducting with Hans Swarowsky, Karl Oesterreicher, and Reinhold Schmid; also took composition lessons with Alfred Uhl. In 1967 he won first prize at the conducting competition in Besançon. He was music director of the Valencia Sym. Orch. (1970–74); then was assoc. conductor of the Noordhollands Phil. in Haarlem (1974–78), and music director of Lisbon's Portuguese Radio Sym. Orch. (1976–78) and National Opera at the São Carlos Theater (1980–82). In 1979 he made his debut as an opera conductor at London's Covent Garden, and then appeared for the first time in the U.S. in 1980. He was principal guest conductor of the Stuttgart Radio Sym. Orch. (1984–87), the Vienna State Opera (1987–91), and the Tokyo Phil. (from 1992). He was Generalmusikdirektor of the Württemberg State Theater in Stuttgart from 1987 to 1991. From 1991 to 1993 he was music director of the Barcelona Sym. Orch. In 1992 he became permanent guest conductor of the Deutsche Oper in Berlin. He served as music director and artistic director of the Teatro Real in Madrid from 1997.—**NS/LK/DM**

Navas, Juan (Francisco) de, Spanish harpist and composer who flourished in Madrid from 1659 to 1709. He was a musician in the royal chapel by 1659, and a subordinate maestro de capilla there by 1683. He wrote numerous secular works, including some interesting Pasacalles with guitar accompaniment. He also contributed Act 2 to the 3-act zarzuela *Apolo y Dafne*, and likewise wrote some sacred music.—**NS/LK/DM**

Naylor, Bernard (James), English-born Canadian organist, conductor, and composer, son of **Edward (Woodall) Naylor**; b. Cambridge, Nov. 22, 1907; d. Keswick, Cumbria, England, May 20, 1986. He studied composition with Vaughan Williams, Holst, and Ireland at the Royal Coll. of Music in London (1924–27), then served as conductor of the Oxford Univ. Opera Club (1927–31). In 1932 he went to Canada, where he was active in Winnipeg as conductor of its Male Voice Choir, Phil. Choir, and Sym. Orch. He returned to England in 1936 and was organist and director of music at Queen's Coll., Oxford, until 1939. Once more in Canada, he conducted the Little Sym. Orch. in Montreal (1942–47). He then returned again to England and taught at Oxford (1950–52) and at Reading Univ. (1952–59). He moved permanently to Canada in 1959. As a composer, he specialized in sacred choral music.

WORKS: *Variations* for Small Orch. (1960); String Trio (1960); *The Living Fountain*, cycle of 4 songs for Tenor and String Orch. (1947); *Missa da camera* for 4 Vocal Soloists, Chorus, and Chamber Orch. (1954–66); *The Resurrection According to Saint Matthew*, Easter cantata (1965); *The Nymph Complaining for the Death of Her Faun* for Mezzo- soprano, Flute, Oboe, Clarinet, Bassoon, and String Quartet (1965); *Festal Te Deum* for Chorus and Orch. (1968); *Scenes and Prophecies* for Soprano, Chorus, Brass, and Percussion (1968–69); several a cappella choruses, including 9 Motets (1952), *Magnificat & Nunc Dimittis* (1964), and *Missa sine Credo* (1969); songs.—**NS/LK/DM**

Naylor, Edward (Woodall), English organist and composer, son of **John Naylor** and father of **Bernard (James) Naylor**; b. Scarborough, Feb. 9, 1867; d. Cambridge, May 7, 1934. He studied with his father, then at Emmanuel Coll., Cambridge (B.A., 1887; Mus.B. and M.A., 1891; Mus.D., 1897) and at London's Royal Coll. of Music (1888–92). He was organist at St. Michael, Chester Square (1889–96) and St. Mary, Kilburn (1896–97), then asst. master at the Leys School and organist at Emmanuel Coll., Cambridge, where he also was a lecturer (from 1902). He publ. *Shakespeare and Music* (London, 1896; 2nd ed., 1931), *An Elizabethan Virginal Book* (London, 1905), *Shakespeare Music* (London, 1912; 2nd ed., 1928), and *The Poets and Music* (London, 1928). Among his works were an opera, *The Angelus* (London, Jan. 27, 1909; won the Ricordi prize), *Tokugawa*, overture (Tokyo, 1919), sacred music, men's choruses, and chamber music.—**NS/LK/DM**

Naylor, John, English organist and composer, father of **Edward (Woodall) Naylor**; b. Stanningley, near Leeds, June 8, 1838; d. at sea, May 14, 1897. He was a choirboy at Leeds Parish Church, and received a Mus.D. from Cambridge Univ. in 1872. He was organist at various churches in England, then in 1883 became organist and choirmaster of York Minster. From 1892 he was also conductor of the York Musical Society.

WORKS: 4 cantatas: *Jeremiah, The Brazen Serpent, Meribah,* and *Manna*; church services, anthems, hymns, part-songs, organ pieces, and a well-known book of chants.—**NS/LK/DM**

Naylor, Oliver, early jazz bandleader, pianist; b. Birmingham, Ala., Oct. 7, 1900; d. Birmingham, Ala., Jan. 21, 1990. Naylor made some fine records for Gennett in 1924–25. He formed his first band, Oliver Naylor's Seven Aces, in his native city when he was 20. It included several New Orleans natives such as Jules Bauduc, brother of drummer Ray. At the beginning of 1924 they played the Roseland Ballroom in N.Y., followed by gigs in Altoon, Pa., and elsewhere. In January 1925 they performed at Knickerbocker Grill in N.Y. as well as Roseland; that spring he expanded the group and they toured as Oliver Naylor's Orch. In 1926 they played Philadelphia, followed by Birmingham, and an end of the year gig at a Pittsburgh resort, where Jack Lacey joined. Bob Zurke joined Naylor in 1927. The band continued to tour, primarily in the Northeast with an occasional stay in N.C., until 1939, when Naylor returned to Birmingham. He managed a theater for seven years, then was an executive at WBRC-TV from 1948 to 1960, when he retired.

DISC. *O.N.'s Seven Aces* (1924).—**LP**

Nazareth, Daniel, Indian conductor; b. Bombay, June 8, 1948. He received training in piano and theory in Bombay and London, and then studied composition and conducting in Vienna and with Bernstein at the Berkshire Music Center in Tanglewood. He appeared as a guest conductor with various orchs. in Europe, and made his debut as an opera conductor with *Così fan tutte* in Spoleto in 1977. From 1982 to 1985 he was chief conductor of the Berlin Sym. Orch. In 1988 he became music director of the Teatro San Carlo in Naples. He was chief conductor of the sym. orch. of the Mitteldeutschen Radio in Leipzig from 1992.—**NS/LK/DM**

Nazareth (Nazaré), Ernesto (Júlio de), Brazilian pianist and composer; b. Rio de Janeiro, March 20, 1863; d. there, Feb. 4, 1934. He was a pioneer in fostering a national Brazilian type of composition, writing pieces in European forms with Brazilian melorhythmic inflections, pointedly entitled *Fado brasileiro, Tango brasileiro, Valsa brasileira, Marcha brasileira,* etc.; he also composed original dances in the rhythms of the samba and chôro. In his declining years, he became totally deaf.

BIBL.: J. Diniz, *N.: Estudos analíticos* (Reclife, 1963). —**NS/LK/DM**

Neander, Valentin, (I) German composer and writer on music, father of **Valentin Neander (II);** b. Treuenbrietzen, near Berlin, c. 1540; d. probably there, c. 1584. He studied at the Gymnasium in the Old Town in Magdeburg (1553–57), where he received instruction in music from Martin Agricola. Following further training at the Univ. of Wittenberg, he returned to Treuenbrietzen as a schoolmaster and later served as town clerk. In addition to his sacred music, he publ. the vol. *Elegia de praecipuis artigicibus et laude musices* (Wittenberg, 1583). —**LK/DM**

Neander, Valentin, (II) German composer, son of **Valentin Neander;** b. probably in Treuenbrietzen, near Berlin, c. 1577; d. c. 1619. He studied in Frankfurt an der Oder at the Univ. and with Bartholomäus Gesius. His collection of 89 sacred works for 4 voices (Frankfurt an der Oder, 1619) is of historical importance for its adoption of French style Psalm settings for the Lutheran church.—**LK/DM**

Neary, Martin (Gerard James), English organist and conductor; b. London, March 28, 1940. He was an organ scholar at Gonville and Caius Coll., Cambridge, and also held a conducting scholarship to the Berkshire Music Center in Tanglewood (summer, 1963). He was asst. organist (1963–65) and organist and master of music (1965–71) at St. Margaret's, Westminster. From 1963 to 1972 he was prof. of organ at Trinity Coll. of Music in London. He was conductor of the Twickenham Musical Soc. (1966–72) and founder-conductor of St. Margaret's Westminster Singers (1967–71). In 1972 he became founder-conductor of his own Martin Neary Singers. He also was organist and master of music at Winchester Cathedral (1972–87) and conductor of the Waynflete Singers (1972–88). In 1988 he became organist and master of the choristers at Westminster Abbey. As both an organist and conductor, Neary has made numerous appearances in England and has toured extensively abroad. As a conductor, he has led performances of a vast repertoire, conducting premieres of many scores by English composers.—**NS/LK/DM**

Neate, Charles, English pianist, cellist, and composer; b. London, March 28, 1784; d. Brighton, March 30, 1877. He studied music with James Windsor and later took piano lessons with John Field. He further studied cello with W. Sharp and composition with Wolff. He started his career as a pianist at London's Covent Garden in the Lenten Oratorio performances (1800). In 1813 he became one of the founders of the London Phil. Society, with which he appeared as performer and conductor. In 1815 he went to Vienna, where he succeeded in entering into a friendly relationship with Beethoven. He composed 2 piano sonatas, a Quintet for Piano, Woodwinds, and Double Bass, and 2 piano trios, and also publ. *An Essay on Fingering* (1855). Literature on Beethoven frequently mentions Neate's relationship with him.—**NS/LK/DM**

Neblett, Carol, American soprano; b. Modesto, Calif., Feb. 1, 1946. She studied voice privately with William Vennard, then with Lotte Lehmann and Pierre Bernac at the Univ. of Southern Calif. in Los Angeles. Quitting school before graduating (1965), she toured as a soloist with the Roger Wagner Chorale, then made her operatic debut as Musetta with the N.Y. City Opera (March 8, 1969). She garnered wide public exposure when she appeared as Thaïs with the New Orleans Opera (1973), choosing to disrobe at the close of Act 1; subsequently made debuts with the Chicago Lyric Opera (Chrysothemis in *Elektra*, 1975), the Dallas Civic Opera (Antonia in *Les Contes d'Hoffmann*, 1975), the Vienna State Opera (1976), and London's Covent Garden (1977); also sang widely as a soloist with U.S. orchs. On March 8, 1979, she made her Metropolitan Opera debut in N.Y. as Senta. She made occasional appearances there in subsequent years, and also sang with various opera houses in North America and Europe. In 1975 she married **Kenneth Schermerhorn.**—**NS/LK/DM**

Nebra (Blasco), José (Melchor de), Spanish composer; b. Catalayud, Zaragoza (baptized), Jan. 6,

1702; d. Madrid, July 11, 1768. He studied with his father, José (Antonio) Nebra (b. La Hoy [baptized], Nov. 23, 1672; d. Cuenca, Dec. 4, 1748), maestro de capilla of Cuenca Cathedral (1729–48). He became principal organist of the royal chapel and of the Descalzas Reales Convent in Madrid (1724), where he was made deputy director of the royal chapel and head of the royal choir school (1751). Together with Literes, he was engaged to reconstruct and compose new music when the archives of the Royal Chapel were destroyed in the fire of 1734. He was a prolific composer, numbering among his works about 20 operas and a great deal of sacred music. His Requiem for Queen Barbara (1758) is reproduced in Eslava's *Lira Sacro-Hispana.*—NS/LK/DM

Nedbal, Oskar, distinguished Czech violist, conductor, and composer; b. Tábor, Bohemia, March 26, 1874; d. (suicide) Zagreb, Dec. 24, 1930. He was a pupil of Bennewitz (violin), Knittl and Stecker (theory), and Dvořák (composition) at the Prague Cons., where he graduated in 1892. From 1891 to 1906 he played viola in the famous Bohemian String Quartet; from 1896 to 1906 he conducted the Czech Phil.; from 1906 to 1918 he was conductor of the Tonkünstler-Orch. in Vienna; later was director of the Slovak National Theater in Bratislava (1923–30) and a conductor with the Radio there (1926–30). He was a notable interpreter of Czech music, and also was admired for his fine performances of the standard repertory.

WORKS: DRAMATIC: O p e r a : *Sedlák Jakub* (Peasant Jacob; 1919–20; Brno, Oct. 13, 1922; rev. version, Bratislava, Dec. 15, 1928). O p e r e t t a : *Die keusche Barbora* (Vienna, Oct. 7, 1911); *Polenblut* (Vienna, Oct. 25, 1913); *Die Winzerbraut* (Vienna, Feb. 11, 1916); *Die schöne Saskia* (Vienna, Nov. 16, 1917); *Eriwan* (Vienna, Nov. 29, 1918). B a l l e t : *Pohádka o Honzovi* (Legend of Honza; Prague, Jan. 24, 1902); *Z pohádky do pohádky* (From Fairy Tale to Fairy Tale; Prague, Jan. 25, 1908); *Princezna Hyacinta* (Prague, Sept. 1, 1911); *Des Teufels Grossmutter* (Vienna, April 20, 1912); *Andersen* (Vienna, March 1, 1914). OTHER: *Scherzo Caprice* for Orch. (1892); piano pieces.

BIBL.: J. Květ, *O. N.* (Prague, 1947); M. Šulc, *O. N.* (Prague, 1959); A. Buchner, *O. N.: Život a dílo* (O N.: Life and Works; Prague, 1976).—NS/LK/DM

Neefe, Christian Gottlob, German composer and conductor; b. Chemnitz, Feb. 5, 1748; d. Dessau, Jan. 26, 1798. He studied music in Chemnitz with Wilhelmi, the city organist, and with C. G. Tag, the cantor of Hohenstein. He began to compose when he was 12, and studied the textbooks of Marpurg and C. P. E. Bach. He studied law at the Univ. of Leipzig (1769–71), and subsequently continued his studies in music with A. Hiller, then succeeding Hiller as conductor of Seyler's traveling opera troupe (1776). In 1779 he became conductor of the Grossmann-Hellmuth opera enterprise in Bonn. Neefe's name is especially honored in music history because about 1780 Beethoven was his pupil in piano, organ, figured-bass practice, and composition in Bonn; there is evidence that Neefe realized the greatness of Beethoven's gift even as a child. In 1782 he was named court organist. After the Grossmann theater closed in 1784, he devoted himself mainly to teaching as

a means of support. The theater was reopened in 1789, and Neefe served as its stage director until 1794, when the French army occupied Bonn and the theater was closed again. He then moved to Dessau, becoming music director of its theater in 1796. His autobiography, *Lebenslauf von ihm selbst geschrieben,* dated 1782, was revised by F. Rochlitz for publ. in the *Allgemeine musikalische Zeitung* (1798–99; Eng. tr. in P. Nettl, *Forgotten Musicians,* N.Y., 1951).

WORKS: DRAMATIC: *Die Apotheke,* comic opera (Berlin, Dec. 13, 1771); *Amors Guckkasten,* operetta (Leipzig, May 10, 1772); *Die Einsprüche,* operetta (Leipzig, Oct. 16, 1772); *Zemire und Azor* (Leipzig, March 5, 1776; not extant); *Heinrich und Lyda,* Singspiel (Berlin, March 26, 1776); *Die Zigeuner* (Frankfurt am Main, Nov. 1777); *Sophonisbe,* monodrama (Mannheim, Nov. 3, 1778); *Adelheit von Veltheim,* opera (Frankfurt am Main, Sept. 23, 1780). OTHER: Lieder; concertos; keyboard music.

BIBL.: M. Stöpgeschoff, *N. als Liederkomponist* (diss., Univ. of Bonn, 1924); I. Leux, *C.G. N., 1748–98: Biographie und Instrumentalkompositionen* (Leipzig, 1925); A. Becker, *C.G. N. und die Bonner Illuminaten* (Bonn, 1969).—NS/LK/DM

Neel, (Louis) Boyd, English-born Canadian conductor; b. Blackheath, Kent, July 19, 1905; d. Toronto, Sept. 30, 1981. He studied at the Royal Naval Coll. in Dartmouth, and after taking medical courses at Caius Coll., Cambridge (B.A., 1926; M.A., 1930), he studied theory and orchestration at the Guildhall School of Music in London (1931). In 1932 he organized the Boyd Neel Orch., which gave its first performance in London on June 22, 1933; it quickly gained a fine reputation, excelling in performances of contemporary British music; also played Baroque works. He commissioned Britten's *Variations on a Theme of Frank Bridge* and conducted its premiere at the Salzburg Festival in 1937. He remained active with his ensemble until 1952; also appeared as a conductor with various English orchs. and theaters. He conducted at the Sadler's Wells Theatre (1945–47) and with the D'Oyly Carte Opera (1948–49); was also conductor of the Robert Mayer Children's Concerts (1946–52). After serving as founder-conductor of the Hart House Orch. in Toronto (1954–71), with which he made many tours, he conducted the Mississauga Sym. Orch. (1971–78); was also dean of the Royal Cons. of Music of Toronto (1953–71). He became a naturalized Canadian citizen in 1961. He was made a Commander of the Order of the British Empire (1953) and an Officer of the Order of Canada (1973). His book, *The Story of an Orchestra* (London, 1950), recounted his years with the Boyd Neel Orch.—NS/LK/DM

Nees, Staf (Gustaaf Frans), Belgian carilloneur, teacher, and composer; b. Mechelen, Dec. 2, 1901; d. there, Jan. 2, 1965. He was a pupil of Van Nuffel, Mortelmans, and Depuydt at the Lemmens Inst. (1916–22) and of Denijn at the Carillonneurs's school (1922–24) in Mechelen. He taught at the Lemmens Inst. (1924–44), and then was director of the Carillonneurs's school (from 1944). From 1932 he also served as town carilloneur in Mechelen. Nees toured extensively throughout Europe and North America, and also gave master classes. In addition to music for the carillon, he composed choral works.—NS/LK/DM

Nef, Albert, Swiss conductor and composer, brother of **Karl Nef;** b. St. Gallen, Oct. 30, 1882; d. Bern, Dec. 6, 1966. He studied at the Leipzig Cons. and with Kretzschmar at the Univ. of Berlin (Ph.D., 1906). From 1907 he was an opera conductor in Lübeck, Neustrelitz, and Rostock; from 1912, was in Bern, and was conductor of the Orch. Society there from 1922; from 1920, was president of the Swiss Stage Artists' Alliance. He was the author of *Das Lied in der deutschen Schweiz Ende des 18. und am Anfang des 19. Jahrhunderts* (1909); also of *50 Jahre Berner Theater* (Bern, 1956). He composed a Singspiel, *Graf Strapinski* (Bern, 1928), *Appenzeller Tänze* for Orch. (1926), *Wanderschaft*, song cycle for Tenor, Chorus, and Orch. (Bern, 1924), choruses, piano pieces, and songs.—NS/LK/DM

Nef, Isabelle (Lander), Swiss harpsichordist, pianist, and teacher; b. Geneva, Sept. 27, 1898; d. Bossy, near Geneva, Jan. 2, 1976. She studied with Marie Panthès (piano) at the Geneva Cons., and with Philipp (piano), d'Indy (composition), and Landowska (harpsichord) in Paris. She made extensive concert tours of Europe, North and South America, South Africa, and Australia. In 1936 she was appointed the first prof. of harpsichord at the Geneva Cons.—NS/LK/DM

Nef, Karl, Swiss musicologist, brother of **Albert Nef;** b. St. Gallen, Aug. 22, 1873; d. Basel, Feb. 9, 1935. He entered the Leipzig Cons. in 1891, studying with Reckendorf (piano), Julius Klengel (cello), and Jadassohn (theory). He attended Kretzschmar's lectures on musicology at the Univ. of Leipzig, and in 1896 received a Ph.D. with his diss. *Die Collegia musica in der deutschen reformierten Schweiz* (publ. in St. Gallen, 1897); subsequently completed his Habilitation in 1900 at the Univ. of Basel. He settled in Basel in 1897, and from 1897 to 1925 he was music critic of the *Basler Nachrichten* and from 1898 to 1909 he ed. the *Schweizerische Musikzeitung.* In 1900 he became Privatdozent for musicology at the Univ., in 1909, assoc. prof., and in 1923, prof.

WRITINGS: *Schriften über Musik und Volksgesang* (Bern, 1908); *Einführung in die Musikgeschichte* (Basel, 1920; 3rd ed., 1945; Eng. tr., 1935, as *Outline of the History of Music*); *Geschichte der Sinfonie und Suite* (Leipzig, 1921); *Geschichte unserer Musikinstrumente* (Leipzig, 1926; new ed., 1949); *Die neun Sinfonien Beethovens* (Leipzig, 1928); *Aufsätze* (Basel, 1936).

BIBL.: *Festschrift K. N. zum 60. Geburtstag* (Zürich, 1933). —NS/LK/DM

Neglia, Francesco Paolo, Italian composer and teacher; b. Enna, May 22, 1874; d. Intra, July 31, 1932. He studied with G. Zuelli at the Parma Cons. In 1901 he went to Hamburg, where he was director of his own conservatory and a conductor at the City Theater. With the outbreak of World War I, he returned to Italy and later became director of his own music school in Legnano. He wrote an opera, an operetta, 2 syms. and other orch. works, sacred works, chamber pieces, and songs.

BIBL.: M. Barbieri, *F.P. N.: Vita, arte e pensieri di un musicista italiano* (Genoa, 1944).—LK/DM

Negrea, Marţian, Romanian composer and teacher; b. Vorumloc, Feb. 10, 1893; d. Bucharest, July 13,

1973. He studied with Timotei Popovici (theory and harmony) at the Andréien Seminary in Sibiu (1910–14) and with Mandyczewski (harmony, counterpoint, and music history) and Franz Schmidt (composition) at the Vienna Academy of Music (1918–21). He was a prof. of harmony at the Cluj Cons. (1921–41) and the Bucharest Cons. (1941–63). In his music, Negrea sought a balance between post-Romantic and Impressionist elements, to which he brought an infusion of folk melos.

WORKS: DRAMATIC: Opera: *Marin Pescarul* (Marin the Fisherman; 1933; Cluj, Oct. 3, 1934). **ORCH.:** *Fantezie simfonică* (1921); *Rapsodia romănă I* (1938) and *II* (1950; Bucharest, April 8, 1951); *Poveşti din Grui* (Fairytale from Grui; 1940; Bucharest, March 21, 1943); *Baia-Mare* (1949); *Divertisement* (1951); *Prin Munţii Apuseni* (Through the Western Mountains; 1952); *Recrutul* (The Recruit), symphonic poem (1953); *Simfonia primăverii* (Spring Sym.; 1956); *Sărbătoarea muncii* (Celebration of Work), symphonic poem (1958; Bucharest, May 6, 1961); *Concerto for Orchestra* (1963; Bucharest, Jan. 1965). **CHAMBER:** *Prélude and Fugue* for String Quartet (1920); *4 Pieces* for Harp (1945); String Quartet (1949); Suite for Clarinet and Piano (1960). **Piano:** Rondo (1920); Sonata (1921); *Impresii de la tară*, suite (1921); Sonatina (1922). **VOCAL:** *Povestea rozei* for Voice and Orch. (Bucharest, Dec. 12, 1943); *Requiem* for Soloists, Chorus, and Orch. (1957); songs.—NS/LK/DM

Negri, Gino, Italian composer; b. Milan, May 25, 1919; d. Cernusco Montevecchia, July 19, 1991. He studied at the Milan Cons. with Renzo Bossi and Paribeni, graduating in 1942. In 1959 he was appointed artistic director of the Teatro del Popolo in Milan. He wrote a number of light operas, all to his own librettos, among them *Vieni qui, Carla* (Milan, Feb. 28, 1956), *Massimo* (Milan, April 12, 1958), *Il tè delle tre* (Como, Sept. 12, 1958), *Il Circo Max* (Venice, Sept. 23, 1959), and *Publicità, ninfa gentile* (Milan, 1970).—NS/LK/DM

Negri, Maria Rosa, Italian mezzo-soprano; b. c. 1715; d. Dresden, Aug. 4, 1760. She became a member of the Dresden Court Opera in 1730, and subsequently sang in a number of Hasse's operas. From 1733 to 1736 she also sang in several operas by Handel in London. Her sister, Maria Caterina Negri, was a contralto. After training from Pasi, she sang in Prague, Venice, and Naples. She also sang in operas by Handel in London (1733–37) before pursuing her career mainly in Italy. —NS/LK/DM

Negri, Vittorio, Italian conductor, record producer, and musicologist; b. Milan, Oct. 16, 1923; d. Blonay, April 11, 1998. He was educated at the Milan Cons., graduating with a degree in composition and conducting in 1946. He began his professional career at the Salzburg Mozarteum, working with Bernhard Paumgartner. Negri then served as a guest conductor of the Orch. del Teatro alla Scala in Milan, the Orchestre National de France in Paris, the Dresden Staatskapelle, and the Boston Sym. Orch. He also made festival appearances in Salzburg, Montreux, Monte Carlo, and Versailles.—NS/LK/DM

Neidhardt (Neidhart, Nithart) von Reuenthal, German Minnesänger; b. c. 1180; d. c. 1240. Born into a knightly family, he was in the service of

Duke Otto II of Bavaria in Landshut, then went to Austria (1232). He was in all probability the earliest German musician whose songs are extant. These are found in MS collections of the late 14th century; a complete list of sources is in Hagen's *Minnesinger* (vol. 4; 1838). An ed. of Neidhardt's songs, with facsimile reproductions and transcriptions in modern notation, was brought out by W. Schmieder in Denkmäler der Tonkunst in Österreich, LXXI, Jg. XXXVII (1930). Another collection, *Neidhardt-Lieder*, ed. by F. Gennrich, was publ. as no. 9 in the series Summa Musica Medii Aevi (Darmstadt, 1962).

BIBL.: S. Singer, *Neidhartstudien* (Tubingen, 1920); E. Wiessner, *Kommentar zu Neidharts Liedern* (Leipzig, 1954); idem, *Vollständiges Worterbuch zu Neidharts Liedern* (Leipzig, 1954); A. Hatto and R. Taylor, *The Songs of Neidhart von Reuental* (Manchester, 1958); D. Boueke, *Materialien zur Neidhart-Überlieferung* (Munich, 1967).—**NS/LK/DM**

Neidlinger, Buell, multi-talented jazz-pop bassist; b. N.Y., March 2, 1936. He has played with distinction in free-jazz, traditional jazz, and bluegrass bands. He studied piano, trumpet, and cello, before finally deciding on bass. At Yale, Neidlinger led the univ. band and worked as a disc jockey. In 1955, he moved to N.Y. where he performed with Vic Dickenson, Zoot Sims, Tony Scott, Coleman Hawkins, Tony Bennett, Rex Stewart, and Eddie Condon. In 1957, he met Cecil Taylor, and worked with him (including appearing on stage in the Jack Gelber play *The Connection*). His album *N.Y. City R&B* was issued 11 years after it was recorded, and then under Taylor's name. In the 1950s, Neidlinger also worked with Steve Lacy, and later did session work on electric as an R&B player. In the 1960s, he played with Don Cherry, Jimmy Giuffre, and joined the Boston Sym. Orch. He spent two years playing part-time with the Houston Sym. Orch. while also doing club work playing soul-jazz with Arnett Cobb. In 1964, he received a Rockefeller grant, which he used to study new music at SUNY Buffalo. Then came rock sessions with Frank Zappa and jazz-rock/fusion with Jean-Luc Ponty in the late 1960s through the mid-1970s. In 1978, he formed his own K2B2 label and made jazz and contemporary music recordings, while doing freelance bluegrass and classical work. He led various groups, including Thelonious and Buellgrass, a combination bluegrass-jazz ensemble. He also performed and recorded in a trio with saxophonist Marty Krystall and drummer Peter Erskine as Aurora in the late 1980s.

DISC. *N.Y. City R&B* (1961); *Rear View Mirror* (1979); *Ready for the '90s* (1980); *Buellgrass (Swingrass)* (1980); *Locomotive* (1987); *Big Drum* (1990); *Blue Chopsticks* (1994).—**LP**

Neidlinger, Gustav, noted German bass-baritone; b. Mainz, March 21, 1910; d. Bad Ems, Dec. 26, 1991. He studied at the Frankfurt am Main Cons. In 1929 he made his operatic debut in Mainz, where he was a member of the Opera (1931–34). After singing with the Plauen Opera (1934–35), he was a member of the Hamburg Opera (1936–50). In 1950 he became a member of the Stuttgart Opera. In 1952 he made his first appearance at the Bayreuth Festival, where he won renown as Alber-

ich; among his other distinguished roles there were Kurwenal, Telramund, Klingsor, and Hans Sachs. He was made a German Kammersänger in 1952. In 1953 he sang at Milan's La Scala, and from 1956 he appeared with the Vienna State Opera. In 1963 he made his debut at London's Covent Garden as Telramund. On Nov. 17, 1972, he made his Metropolitan Opera debut in N.Y. as Alberich, but remained on the roster for only one season. He continued to sing in Europe until his retirement in 1977.—**NS/LK/DM**

Neighbour, O(liver) W(ray), English music bibliographer and musicologist; b. Merstham, Surrey, April 1, 1923. He pursued the study of modern languages at Birbeck Coll. (B.A., 1950). He joined the dept. of printed books at the British Museum (1946); then was on the music room staff (1951–76), subsequently serving as its superintendent (1976–85). He publ. *English Music Publishers: Plate Numbers in the First Half of the Nineteenth Century* (with A. Tyson; London, 1965) and *Consort and Keyboard Music*, vol. III of *The Music of William Byrd* (London, 1978); also ed. *Music and Bibliography: Essays in Honour of Alec Hyatt King* (London, 1980).

BIBL.: C. Banks, A. Searle, and M. Turner, eds., *Sundry Sorts of Music Books: Essays on the British Library Collections; Presented to O. W. M. on his 70th Birthday* (London, 1993). —**NS/LK/DM**

Neikrug, Marc (Edward), American pianist and composer; b. N.Y., Sept. 24, 1946. He was a student of Klebe at the Northwest Music Academy in Detmold (1964–68), of Schuller at the Berkshire Music Center in Tanglewood, and at the State Univ. of N.Y. at Stony Brook (M.M., 1971). In 1972 he was composer-in-residence at the Marlboro (Vt.) Music Festival. From 1975 he toured extensively in duo concert appearances with Pinchas Zukerman. From 1978 to 1986 he was a consultant on contemporary music to the St. Paul (Minn.) Chamber Orch. As a composer, Neikrug has produced both tonal and atonal scores.

WORKS: DRAMATIC: O p e r a : *Through Roses* (1979–80); *Los Alamos* (Berlin, Oct. 1, 1988). **ORCH.:** Piano Concerto (1966); Clarinet Concerto (1967); Viola Concerto (1974; Boston, Oct. 14, 1979); *Eternity's Sunrise* (1979–80); *Mobile* (1982); Violin Concerto (1984); Concerto for 2 Violins, Viola, Cello, and Chamber Orch. (1987); *Chetro Ketl* (1988); Flute Concerto (Pittsburgh, Sept. 8, 1989); Sym. No. 1 (1991); *Flamenco Fanfare* (1994). **CHAMBER:** 2 string quartets (1966, 1972); Suite for Cello and Piano (1974); Concertino for Flute, Oboe, Clarinet, Violin, Viola, Cello, and Piano (1978); *Rituals* for Flute and Harp (1978); *Kaleidoscope* for Clarinet and Piano (1978); *Continuum* for Cello and Piano (1978); Duo for Violin and Piano (1983); *Voci* for Piano, Clarinet, Violin, and Cello (1988); *Stars the Mirror* for String Quartet (1989); *Take Me T'Susan's Gift* for Percussion (1989); Sonata Concertante for Violin and Piano (1994); String Quintet (1995). **VOCAL:** *Nachtlieder* for Soprano and Orch. (1988).—**NS/LK/DM**

Neithardt, Heinrich August, German conductor and composer; b. Schleiz, Aug. 10, 1793; d. Berlin, April 18, 1861. After studying music, he served in the army (1813–15) and subsequently was bandmaster of the Garde- Schützen-Battaillon (1816–22) and the Kaiser Franz Grenadiers (1822–40). In 1839 he was named royal music director. He also founded the choir of the Berlin Cathedral in 1843, which he led on tours of Germany and other nations. As a composer, Neithardt is best remembered for the Prussian anthem *Ich bin ein Preusse, kennt ihr meine Farben?* (1826). He also wrote an opera, *Manfred und Julietta (Die schöne Dalmatinerin)* (Königsberg, 1834), much music and arrangements for band, choral works, chamber music, and piano pieces. —**LK/DM**

Nejedlý, Vít, Czech composer, conductor, and musicologist, son of **Zdeněk Nejedlý;** b. Prague, June 22, 1912; d. Dukla, Slovakia, Jan. 1, 1945. He was a student of Svěceny and Jeremías (composition) and Talich (conducting) at the Charles Univ. in Prague, obtaining his Ph.D. in musicology in 1936. From 1936 to 1938 he was a répétiteur and conductor at the Olomouc Theater. After the Nazi occupation of his homeland in 1939, he fled to the Soviet Union and served as an ed. of Czech programs for Radio Moscow's foreign broadcasts. In 1943 he joined the Czech contingent of the Red Army.

WORKS: DRAMATIC: *The Dying,* melodrama (1933); *Tkalci* (The Weavers), opera (1938; unfinished; completed by J. Hanuš; Plzeň, May 7, 1961). **ORCH.:** 3 syms.: No. 1 (1931), No. 2, *Bídy a smrti* (Poverty and Death, 1934), and No. 3, *Španělská* (Spanish, 1937–38); *Dawn,* overture (1932); *Commemoration* (1933); Sinfonietta (1937); *Dramatic Overture* (1940); *Popular Suite* (1940); military marches. **CHAMBER:** 2 *Compositions* for Wind Quintet (1934); 2 *Compositions* for Nonet (1934); *Small Suite* for Violin and Piano (1935); String Quartet (1937); *Fantasy* for Piano (1937); Concertino for Nonet (1940). **VOCAL:** 2 cantatas: *Den* (The Day; 1935) and *To You-the Red Army* (1943); choruses; songs.

BIBL.: J. Plavec, *Vzpominky na Víta Nejedlého* (Memories of V. N.; Prague, 1948); J. Jiránek, *V. N.* (Prague, 1959). —**NS/LK/DM**

Nejedlý, Zdeněk, Czech musicologist and politician, father of **Vít Nejedlý;** b. Litomyšl, Feb. 10, 1878; d. Prague, March 9, 1962. He studied in Prague with Fibich, and took courses with Jaroslav Goll (history) and Hostinský (aesthetics) at the Charles Univ., where he qualified in 1900. He was an archivist at the National Museum (1899–1909); joined the staff of the Charles Univ. (1905), serving as a reader (1908–19) and prof. (1919–39) in musicology. He joined the Czech Communist Party in 1929; after the Nazi occupation of his country (1939), he went to the Soviet Union and was a prof. of history at the Univ. of Moscow. After the liberation of Czechoslovakia (1945), he returned to Prague; was minister of education (1948–53) and deputy premier (1953).

WRITINGS (all publ. in Prague): *Zdenko Fibich, zakladatel scénického melodramu* (Zdenko Fibich, Founder of the Scenic Melodrama; 1901); *Katechismus estetiky* (A Manual of Aesthetics; 1902); *Dějinv české hudby* (A History of Czech Music; 1903); *Dějiny předhusitského v Čechách* (A History of Pre-Hussite Song in Bohemia; 1904; 2nd ed., 1954, as *Dějiny husitského zěpvu*); *Počátky husitského zěpvu* (The Beginnings of Hussite Song; 1907; 2nd ed., 1954–55, as *Dějiny husitského zpěvu*); *Zpěvohry Smetanovy* (Smetana's Operas; 1908; 3rd ed., 1954); *Josef Bohuslav Foerster*

(1910); *Dějiny husitského spěvu za válek husitských* (A History of Hussite Song during the Hussite Wars; 1913; 2nd ed., 1955–56, as *Dějiny husitského zpěvu*); *Gustav Mahler* (1913; 2nd ed., 1958); *Richard Wagner* (1916; 2nd ed., 1961); *Všeobecné dějiny hudby, I: O původy hudby, Antika* (A General History of Music, I: Origin and Antiquity; 1916–30); *Vitězslav Novák* (1921; articles and reviews); *Otakara Hostinského estetika* (Otakar Hostinsky's Aesthetics; 1921); *Smetaniana* (1922); *Bedřich Smetana* (4 vols., 1924–33; 2nd ed., 1950–54); *Zdeňka a Fibicha milostný denik* (Zdenk Fibich's Erotic Diary; 1925; 2nd ed., 1949); *Otakar Ostrčil, Vzrůst a uzráni* (Otakar Ostrčil: Growth and Maturity; 1935; 2nd ed., 1949); *Sovětská hudba* (Soviet Music; 1936–37); *Otakar Hostinský* (1937; 2nd ed., 1955); *Kritiky* (2 vols., 1954, 1965).

BIBL.: J. Teichmann, *Z. N.* (Prague, 1938); V. Pekárek, *Z. N.* (Prague, 1948); J. Jiránek, *Z. N.* (Prague, 1952); A. Sychra, *Estetika Z.a Nejedlého* (Z. N.'s Aesthetics; Prague, 1956); F. Cervinka, *Z. N.* (Prague, 1959); V. Pekárek and J. Kubát, eds., *Na pamět' Z.a Nejedlého* (In Memory of Z. N.; Prague, 1966); *Z. N.: Doba—život—dilo* (Z. N.: Times—Life—Work; Prague, 1975); M. Ransdorf, *Z. N.* (Prague, 1988).—**NS/LK/DM**

Nelhybel, Vaclav, Czech-born American composer and conductor; b. Polanka nad Odrou, Sept. 24, 1919; d. there, March 22, 1996. He studied composition and conducting with Ridký at the Prague Cons. (1938–42) and musicology at the Univ. of Prague (1938–42); in 1942, went to Switzerland and took courses in medieval and Renaissance music at the Univ. of Fribourg. He was affiliated with the Swiss Radio (1946–50); then was music director of Radio Free Europe in Munich (1950–57). In 1957 he settled in the U.S., becoming a naturalized American citizen in 1962; subsequently evolved energetic activities as a lecturer and guest conductor at American colleges and high schools. As a composer, he was especially notable for his fine pieces for symphonic band. His harmonic idiom was of a freely dissonant texture, with melorhythmic components gravitating toward tonal centers. Among his works are *A Legend,* opera (1953–54), *Everyman,* medieval morality play (Memphis, Oct. 30, 1974), and *The Station,* opera (1978); also the ballets *In the Shadow of a Lime Tree* (1946) and *The Cock and the Hangman* (Prague, Jan. 17, 1947).—**NS/LK/DM**

Nelson, Big Eye Louis (actually **DeLisle, Louis Nelson**), early jazz clarinetist; b. New Orleans, Jan. 28, c. 1880/85; d. New Orleans, Aug. 20, 1949. He learned several instruments, but specialized on clarinet from 1904, studying with Lorenzo Tio Sr., then worked in the Imperial Orch. (c. l905), Golden Rule Orch. (1907), Superior Orch. (c. 1912), Eagle Band, and with Papa Celestin. He left New Orleans in June 1916 to join the Original Creole Orch. until the following spring, then returned to New Orleans and worked on and off with John Robichaux from late 1918 until 1924. He worked in various nonmusical jobs for the next decade and a half, and then led his own quartet on and off from 1939–49. He recorded two sessions in 1949 under the name of "Louis DeLisle" in a New Orleans revival style. It is difficult to trace his influence on other New Orleans clarinetists because he did not record during his youth; he claimed to have taught Sidney Bechet, while others said that he influenced Jimmie Noone and Johnny

Dodds, but these claims are difficult to substantiate.

He is not to be confused with trombonist Louis Nelson (b. New Orleans, Sept. 17, 1902; d. April 5, 1990) who was a prominent musician in various New Orleans revival bands, including George Lewis's band and the Preservation Hall Jazz Band.

DISC. *Kid Rena* (1940).—JC/LP

Nelson, "Dave" Davidson C., jazz trumpeter, pianist, arranger; nephew of **Joe "King" Oliver;** b. Donaldsonville, La., c. 1905; d. N.Y., April 7, 1946. His first professional gig was with Marie Lucas Orch. at Lincoln Gardens in Chicago. He then worked with Ma Rainey, Jelly Roll Morton, and Richard M. Jones, who taught him arranging. He then toured with his own band before settling in N.Y. c. early 1929, where he worked with Luis Russell (1929), toured with King Oliver (1930), then primarily led his own bands, including one which toured with Mae West in *The Constant Sinner* (1931). During his last four years, he worked as a staff arranger for the Lewis Publishing Co. His trumpet playing was very much in the style of his more famous uncle.—JC/LP

Nelson, John (Wilton), American conductor; b. San Jose, Costa Rica (of American parents), Dec. 6, 1941. He studied at Wheaton (Ill.) Coll. and with Morel at the Juilliard School of Music in N.Y. He was music director of the Indianapolis Sym. Orch. (1976–87), the Caramoor Festival in Katonah, N.Y. (1983–90), and the Opera Theatre of St. Louis (1985–91). In 1998 he became music director of the Ensemble Orchestral de Paris. —NS/LK/DM

Nelson, Judith (Anne née **Manes),** American soprano; b. Chicago, Sept. 10, 1939. She studied at St. Olaf Coll. in Northfield, Minn. She sang with music groups of the Univ. of Chicago and the Univ. of Calif. at Berkeley, making her operatic debut as Drusilla in Monteverdi's *L'incoronazione di Poppea* in Brussels in 1979. She appeared widely as a soloist and recitalist. Although she is particularly noted for her performances of Baroque music, she also introduced compositions by American and English composers.—NS/LK/DM

Nelson, Oliver (Edward), jazz composer, arranger, alto and tenor saxophonist, flutist; b. St. Louis, June 4, 1932; d. L.A., Oct. 28, 1975. One of the most respected composers of the 1960s, his bold writing style employed distinctive patterns. Though he was featured less and less as a soloist, he had a searing tone and played carefully chosen notes with great intensity. Raised in a musical family, he began on piano and played in public as a child. He worked with Jeter Pillars as a teenager and in 1951 played second alto saxophone with Louis Jordan. After serving in the U.S. Marines and studying music formally with Robert Wykes at Washington Univ. in St. Louis (1954–1958), Nelson moved to N.Y., where he studied privately with Elliot Carter. He worked with Wild Bill Davis and with Louis Bellson in Calif., and was with Quincy Jones from 1960–61. He was

prolific as a jazz composer, writing for Jimmy Smith, Billy Taylor, Wes Montgomery, and many others, and was also highly regarded for his classical and studio work. In 1967, he settled in Los Angeles. He wanted to perform more and do less TV and film work, but died suddenly of a heart attack before he could realize his goal.

WORKS: *Saxophone Sonata* (1957); *Songs* for Contralto and Piano (1957); *Divertimento* for 10 Woodwinds and Double Bass (1957); *Afro-American Sketches* for Jazz Ensemble (1960); *Blues and the Abstract Truth* for Jazz Ensemble (1960); Woodwind Quintet (1960); *Dirge* for Chamber Orch. (1961); *Soundpiece* for Contralto, String Quartet, and Piano (1963); *Soundpiece* for Jazz Orch. (1964); *Patterns* for Jazz Ensemble (1965); *A Study in 5/4* for Wind Ensemble (1966); Concerto for Xylophone, Marimba, Vibes, and Wind Orch. (1967); *The Kennedy Dream Suite* for Jazz Ensemble (1967); *Jazzhattan Suite* for Jazz Orch. (N.Y., Oct. 7, 1967); Septet for Wind Orch. (1968); *Piece* for Orch. and Jazz Soloists (1969); *A Black Suite* for Narrator, String Quartet, and Jazz Orch. (1970); *Berlin Dialogue* for Jazz Orch. (Berlin, 1970); *Concert Piece* for Alto Saxophone and Studio Orch. (1972); *Fugue and Bossa* for Wind Orch. (1973); also a sterling jazz arrangement of Prokofiev's *Peter and the Wolf* (1966) and music for films and television.

DISC.: *Meet O.N.* (1959); *Takin' Care of Business* (1960); *Soul Battle* (1960); *Screamin' the Blues* (1960); *Nocturne* (1960); *Images* (1960); *Straight Ahead* (1961); *Main Stem* (1961); *Blues and the Abstract Truth* (1961); *Afro-American Sketches* (1961); *Impressions of Phaedra* (1962); *Full N.* (1962); *More Blues & Abstract Truth* (1964); *Fantabulous* (1964); *Sound Pieces* (1966); *Musical Tribute to JFK* (1967); *Live from L.A.* (1967); *Live in Berlin* (1970); *Black, Brown and Beautiful* (1970); *Berlin Dialogue for Orch.* (1970); *Swiss Suite* (1971); *Stolen Moments* (1975); *Dream Deferred* (1976).

WRITINGS: *Blues and the Abstract Thought* (E.B. Marks Music); *Patterns for Jazz* (Los Angeles, 1966; originally titled *Patterns for Saxophone*).—MM/LP

Nelson, Rick (Eric), teen pop star who matured into being one of the founders of country-rock; b. Teaneck, N.J., May 8, 1940; d. near De Kalb, Tex., Dec. 31, 1985. Born into a show business family, Eric "Ricky" Nelson joined the cast of his parents' *The Adventures of Ozzie and Harriet* radio show in March 1949 at the age of eight. The show moved to television in October 1952, where it ran for a remarkable 14 years. Ricky studied clarinet, took up drums, and later learned to play the guitar. Signed to Verve Records in 1956—with just several months' experience in singing—Ricky scored a smash pop and R&B hit with his first release, a version of Fats Domino's "I'm Walking" (fronted by "A Teenager's Romance") after performing the song at the end of the television show on April 10, 1957.

Soon signing a five-year contract with Imperial Records, Ricky Nelson launched his career with the label in October of 1957 with the gently rocking smash pop and R&B hit "Be Bop Baby," from his debut album, recorded with guitarist Joe Maphis. He next achieved a pop, R&B and country smash with "Stood Up," backed by Johnny and Dorsey Burnette's "Waitin' in School." By 1958 Nelson had formed his own touring and recording band with James Burton, one of the most dynamic guitar players of the time. He scored three-way crossover smash hits with the Burnette brothers' "Believe What You Say," backed by Hank Williams's "My Bucket's Got a Hole in It," and "Poor Little Fool" (written by Eddie Cochran's girlfriend Sharon Sheeley). Nelson costarred in the Howard Hawks-directed classic western movie *Rio Bravo* with John Wayne and Dean Martin, and continued to have near-smash pop hits with "Lonesome Town"/"I Got a Feeling," "Never Be Anyone Else but You" backed by Dorsey Burnette's "It's Late," and Johnny Burnette's "Just a Little Too Much" backed by "Sweeter Than You." In 1960 he appeared in the comedy film *The Wackiest Ship in the Army* with Jack Lemmon and achieved major pop hits with "I Wanna Be Loved," "Young Emotions," "I'm Not Afraid" and "You Are the Only One."

After the top hit "Travelin' Man," backed by the near-smash "Hello Mary Lou" (written by Gene Pitney), Ricky Nelson shortened his name to Rick on his 21st birthday. The hits continued into 1963 with "A Wonder Like You"/"Everlovin'," "the smash "Young World," the autobiographical "Teen Age Idol," and "It's Up to You." In 1963 he switched to Decca Records, where his hits included "String Along" and the standards "Fools Rush In," "For You" and "The Very Thought of You."

Overwhelmed by the myriad British acts that dominated rock music beginning in 1964, Rick Nelson began exploring country music with 1966's *Bright Lights and Country Music*, managing a minor country hit with "Take a City Bride" in 1967. In 1969 he formed The Stone Canyon Band with pedal steel guitarist Tom Brumley and bassist Randy Meisner (later a founding member of The Eagles and Poco). The group recorded the *In Concert* album, which included "I Shall Be Released," Bob Dylan's "If You Gotta Go, Go Now" and Eric Andersen's "Violets of Dawn," and yielded a moderate pop hit with Dylan's "She Belongs to Me." After recording an entire album of his own songs, *Rick Sings Nelson*, he composed the smash 1972 hit "Garden Party," which related his feelings after being booed for performing contemporary material at an oldies show in October 1971. Nelson and The Stone Canyon Band parted company in 1974.

Touring up to 200 days a year, Rick Nelson produced his *Intakes* album for Epic and conducted recording sessions in Memphis in 1979. He joined Capitol for 1981's *Playing to Win*. In 1984 Nelson starred as a school principal in the television movie *High School USA*, with his mother Harriet appearing as his secretary. Around that time he returned to his rockabilly style, touring with James Burton, but on Dec. 31, 1985, he was killed along with six others, including guitarist Bobby Neal, when his plane crashed near De Kalb, Tex.

Several of Rick Nelson's children pursued show business careers. His daughter, Tracy, became an actress and appeared in the television series *Father Dowling's Mysteries*. His twin sons Gunnar and Matthew (b. Sept. 20, 1967) began performing in Los Angeles clubs in the mid 1980s and recorded their debut album as Nelson for DGC Records in 1990. The best-selling album *After the Rain* yielded four hits, including the top hit "(Can't Live without Your) Love and Affection" and the smash hit title song.

DISC.: *Ricky* (1957); *Ricky Nelson* (1958); *Ricky Sings Again* (1959); *Songs by Ricky* (1959); *More Songs by Ricky* (1960); *Rick Is 21* (1961); *Album 7 by Rick* (1962); *It's Up to You* (1963); *A Long Vacation* (1963); *Rick Nelson Sings for You* (1964); *For Your Sweet Love* (1963); *The Very Thought of You* (1964); *Spotlight on Rick* (1964); *Best Always* (1965); *Love and Kisses* (1965); *Bright Lights and Country Music* (1966); *Country Fever* (1967); *Another Side of Rick* (1967); *Perspective* (1968); *In Concert* (1970); *Rick Sings Nelson* (1970); *Rudy the Fifth* (1971); *Garden Party* (1972); *Windfall* (1974); *Intakes* (1977); *Playing to Win* (1981); *Memphis Sessions* (rec. late 1970s; rel.1985); *Live, 1983–1985* (1989); *All My Best* (re-recordings of his hits; 1988).

BIBL.: J. Selvin, *R. N.: Idol for a Generation* (Chicago, Ill., 1990); P. Bashe, *Teenage Idol, Travelin' Man: The Complete Biography of R. N.* (N.Y., 1992).—**BH**

Nelson, Robert U(riel), American musicologist; b. Brush, Colo., Sept. 16, 1902; d. Los Angeles, Dec. 31, 1995. He studied at the Univ. of Calif. at Berkeley (A.B., 1923), with Déthier and Goetschius at the Inst. of Musical Art in N.Y. (diplomas in piano and organ, 1925), with Holst and Zador (composition), and with Piston and Apel at Harvard Univ. (M.A., 1937; Ph.D., 1944). From 1925 to 1937 he taught at Washington State Univ. In 1938 he became an instructor and in 1955 a prof. at the Univ. of Calif. at Los Angeles, from which he retired in 1970. In addition to articles in various journals, he publ. the valuable study *The Technique of Variation* (Berkeley and Los Angeles, 1948).—**NS/LK/DM**

Nelson, Ron(ald Jack), American composer and teacher; b. Joliet, Ill., Dec. 14, 1929. He studied composition with Hanson, Rogers, Mennini, and Barlow at the Eastman School of Music in Rochester, N.Y. (B.Mus., 1952; M.Mus., 1953; D.M.A., 1956) and with Aubin at the École Normale de Musique in Paris on a Fulbright grant (1955). In 1956 he joined the faculty of Brown Univ. in Providence, R.I., where he was chairman of the music dept. (1963–73) and a prof. (1968–93). In addition to numerous commissions, he received a Ford Foundation fellowship (1963), a Howard Foundation grant (1965–66), NEA grants, the Acuff Chair of Excellence in the Creative Arts (1991), and the John Philip Sousa Medal of Honor (1994). In 1993 his *Passacaglia: Homage on B-A-C-H* won all three of the major wind band contests: the National Band Assn. Prize, the ABA (American Band Assn.) Ostwald Contest, and the Sudler International Competition. His widely known scores are stylistically diverse and generally accessible.

WORKS: DRAMATIC: *Dance in Ruins*, ballet (1954). *The Birthday of the Infanta*, opera (1955–56); *Hamaguchi*, opera (1981); many documentary and educational film scores. **ORCH.:** *Sarabande: For Katharine in April* (1954); *Savannah River Holiday* (1955; also for Band, 1973); *This Is the Orchestra*, with narrator (1960); *Jubilee* (1960); *Overture for Latecomers* (1961); *Toccata* (1961); *Rocky Point Holiday* (1969; also for Band); *Trilogy: JFK-MLK- RFK* for Orch. and Tape (1969); *5 Pieces for Orchestra after Paintings by Andrew Wyeth* (1976); *Meditation and Dance* (1977); *Fanfare for a Celebration* (1983; also for Band, 1982); *Morning Alleluias* for Wind Orch. (1989); *Epiphanies I: Fanfares and Chorales* (1993; also for Band, 1994) and *II: Panels* (1996); *Resonances III* for Orch. and Brass (1997). **Band:** Concerto for Piano and Symphonic Band (1948); *Mayflower Overture* (1958); *Medieval Suite* (1982); *Aspen Jubilee* (1984); *Lauds: Praise High Day* (1991);

To the Airborne (1992); Passacaglia: Homage on B-A-C-H (1992); Chaconne: In Memoriam (1994); Sonoran Desert Holiday (1994); Country Airs and Dances (1995); Fanfare for the Kennedy Center (1996); Nightsong (1998); Fanfare for the New Millennium (1999). Other Instrumental: 6 Pieces for Chamber Ensemble (1977); Kristen's Song for Violin, Flute, and Organ (1982); Pebble Beach Sojourn for Organ, Brass, and Percussion (1983); Danza Capriccio for Alto Saxophone and Wind Ensemble (1988); Elegy II for Strings (1988); Fanfare for the Hour of Sunrise for Winds and Percussion (1989); Resonances I for Winds and Percussion (1990). VOCAL: The Christmas Story, cantata for Chorus, Organ, Brass, and Timpani (1958; also for Chorus and Orch.); Glory to God for Chorus, Organ, and Brass (1958); All Praise to Music for Chorus, Brass, and Timpani (1960); 3 Ancient Prayers for Chorus and Organ (1962); Triumphal Te Deum for Chorus, Brass, Organ, and Percussion (1963); What Is Man?, oratorio for Soprano, Baritone, Narrator, Chorus, and Orch. (1964); Meditation of the Syllable OM for Narrator and Men's Chorus (1970); Psalm 95 for Chorus and Ensemble (1971); Prayer of the Emperor of China on the Altar of Heaven, Dec. 21, 1539 for Chorus and Ensemble (1972); Prayer of St. Francis of Assisi for Chorus and Organ (1975); 4 Pieces After the Seasons for Chorus and Small Ensemble (1977); 3 Autumnal Sketches for Chorus and Small Ensemble (1980); For Freedom of Conscience for Chorus, Organ, and Trumpets (1980); Mass of St. LaSalle for Chorus and Ensemble (1981); 3 Nocturnal Pieces for Chorus, Viola, and Small Ensemble (1982); Make Music in the Lord's Honor for Chorus, Organ, and Brass (1982); Te Deum Laudamus for Chorus and Wind Ensemble (1985); Festive Anthem for Chorus, Brass, and Organ (1985); Prime: The Hour of Sunrise for Chorus and Band (1986); Another Spring for Chorus and String Quintet (1987); Invoking the Powers for Chorus, Piano, and Percussion (1990); And This Shall be for Music for Chorus and Brass Instruments or Band (1990); Songs of Praise and Reconciliation for Chorus, Piano, and Percussion (1991); many other vocal pieces.—NS/LK/DM

Nelson, Willie (actually, William Hugh),

red-headed outlaw singer/songwriter who revolutionized country music; b. Abbot, Tex., April 30, 1933. Willie Nelson was one of the most influential country songwriters (in the early 1960s) and performers (from the mid-1970s to the mid-1980s). A leader of the so-called "outlaw" movement, Nelson abandoned the slick Nashville sound of the 1960s to forge his own unique style, laying the groundwork for the explosion of "new" country in the 1980s. His reedy, sun-beaten voice and bluesy songs reflecting romantic love gone awry have become an integral part of American popular culture, beyond the confines of strictly "country" music.

Nelson was the son of a rural farmer, who began performing while still in high school. He served in the Air Force until 1952, and worked in Tex. and briefly in Vancouver, Wash., as both a performer and country deejay. After publishing his first song, he moved to Nashville, where he hooked up with Ray Price, working as bassist in his backup band, The Cherokee Cowboys. His first success was as a songwriter, penning such number-one country classics as "Crazy" for Patsy Cline and "Hello Walls" for Faron Young, both in 1961.

He signed to Liberty and then to RCA records in the 1960s as a solo artist, but his unique style was ill-suited to the heavy-handed strings and syrupy choruses typical of Nashville production of the day. When his house burned down in 1970, he returned to Austin, Tex., turning his back on the country music community. Influenced by younger performers who also were weary of the "Nashville sound," including Kris Kristofferson and Waylon Jennings, Nelson began to experiment with writing song cycles, or groups of related songs, that would be issued on a series of seminal LPs, including 1973's Shotgun Willie, 1974's Phases and Stages (telling the story of the breakup of a relationship from both the man's and woman's perspective), and 1975's landmark Red Headed Stranger, a romantic story set in the 19th-century West. He was given artistic control over his recordings, and paired down his sound often just to his own vocals and guitars, as on his first hit, 1975's cover of Fred Rose's "Blue Eyes Crying in the Rain" from the Stranger concept LP.

The outlaw movement was given a strong push by RCA when they released the compilation album Wanted: The Outlaws in 1976, featuring Willie, Jennings, Jessi Colter (then Jennings's wife), and Tompall Glaser. In typical contrary fashion, Willie followed this success with an album of covers of 1930s and 1940s pop standards, Stardust. He proved what country audiences long knew; that there was a strong following for these pop songs among country-music fans, as well as among the rock and "yuppie" audiences who were attracted to Willie's straight-ahead approach to music.

Through the late 1970s and early 1980s Willie performed as a soloist and in duets with Jennings, Leon Russell, Merle Haggard, and in the informal group, The Highwaymen, with Johnny Cash, Kristofferson, and Jennings. He even cut a duet with Spanish crooner Julio Iglesias on the saccharine "To All the Girls I Ever Loved." A brief movie career also developed, including a remake of the classic tear-jerker Impromptu, about a classical musician's love affair with his student improbably reset in the world of country music as Honeysuckle Rose (1980, yielding the hit, "On the Road Again," which has become a theme song for Nelson), and a TV version of Red Headed Stranger (1987).

Tax problems with the IRS led to one of the most unusual deals in music history: Willie recorded two solo LPs that featured just him and his guitar performing his "old songs" and then marketed them directly through late-night TV ads; the proceeds were used to pay off back taxes. He returned to more mainstream recording on his 60th birthday with a new album produced by mainstream pop producer Don Was and a TV special.

Nelson's success in broadening the country market in the 1970s and early 1980s opened up the field to influences such as country rock, Western swing, and honky-tonk sounds. He proved, along with Bob Dylan, that a songwriter could be the most expressive performer of his own material, even if his vocals were not as "polished" as those of more commercially oriented performers (although Nelson, unlike Dylan, is a talented guitarist). In a culture oriented towards youth, Nelson's well-lined face and laidback performances showed that artistry could overcome imagery.

DISC.: Shotgun Willie (1973); Phases and Stages (1974); Red Headed Stranger (1975); The Sound in Your Mind (1976); To Lefty from Willie (1977); Willie and Family Live (1978); Willie Sings

Kristofferson (1979); *One for the Road* (with Leon Russell; 1979); *San Antonio Rose* (with Ray Price; 1980); *Somewhere over the Rainbow* (1981); *Always on My Mind* (1982); *Tougher Than Leather* (1983); *Without a Song* (1983); *Old Friends* (with Roger Miller; 1983); *City of New Orleans* (1984); *Music from the Songwriter* (with Kris Kristofferson; 1984); *Me and Paul* (1985); *Half Nelson* (1985); *Partners* (1986); *Willie* (1986); *The Promiseland* (1986); *Take It to the Limit* (with Waylon Jennings; 1987); *Island in the Seas* (1987); *What a Wonderful World* (1988); *Horse Called Music* (1989); *Born for Trouble* (1990); *Clean Shirt* (with Waylon Jennings; 1991); *Who'll Buy My Memories?* (1991); *Moonlight Becomes You* (1993); *The Early Years: The Complete Liberty Recordings Plus More* (rec. 1960s; rel. 1994); *Healing Hands of Time* (1994); *Just One Love* (1995); *Spirit* (1996).—**RC**

Nelsova (real name, **Katznelson**), **Zara,** brilliant Canadian-born American cellist of Russian descent; b. Winnipeg, Dec. 23, 1918. Her father, a flutist, gave her music lessons; she later studied with Dezso Mahalek (1924–28). In 1929 she went to London, where she continued her studies with Herbert Walenn (until 1935). In 1931, at the age of 13, she appeared as soloist with the London Sym. Orch. With her 2 sisters, a pianist and a violinist, she organized a group billed as the Canadian Trio, and toured in England, Australia, and South Africa. Returning to Canada, she served as principal cellist of the Toronto Sym. Orch. (1940–43); she was also a member of another Canadian Trio, this time with Kathleen Parlow and Sir Ernest MacMillan (1941–44). In 1942 she made her U.S. debut at Town Hall in N.Y.; also continued her studies, receiving valuable instruction from Feuermann, Casals, and Piatigorsky. In 1962 she joined the faculty of the Juilliard School of Music in N.Y. In 1953 she became a naturalized American citizen. From 1963 to 1973 she was the wife of **Grant Johannesen.** She received rather rapturous press reviews for her lyrical interpretations of classical and modern cello music in a purportedly "Russian" (i.e., wonderful) style. —**NS/LK/DM**

Nelsson, Woldemar, Russian-born German conductor; b. Kiev, April 4, 1938. His father, a conductor, gave him violin lessons in Kiev. After conducting studies at the Novosibirsk Cons., he attended master classes at the Moscow Cons. and the Leningrad Cons. In 1971 he won first prize in the All-Union Conducting Competition in Moscow, and then was an asst. to Kondrashin and the Moscow Phil. He appeared as a guest conductor in Russia and Eastern Europe before emigrating to West Germany in 1977. From 1980 to 1987 he was Generalmusikdirektor of the Kassel State Theater. Thereafter he appeared as a guest conductor of various opera companies and orchs.—**NS/LK/DM**

Nemescu, Octavian, Romanian composer; b. Pascani, March 29, 1940. He studied with Jora, Mendelsohn, Vieru, Ciortea, Vancea, and Paul Constantinescu at the Bucharest Cons. (1956–63), and also attended the summer courses of new music held in Darmstadt (1972). He devoted himself to composing and teaching. In his output, he pursued an advanced course.

WORKS: Clarinet Sonata (1961–62); *Poliritmii* for Clarinet, Piano, and Prepared Piano (1962–63); *Triunghi* (Triangle) for

Orch. (1964; Bucharest, Dec. 3, 1967); *Patru dimensiuni în timp* (4 Dimensions in Time): *I* for Orch. (1965), *II* for Chorus and Orch. (1966), *III* for Orch. (1967), and *IV* for Orch. (1968); *Combinaţii în cercuri* (Combinations of Circles) for Cello, Tape, and Multimedia Action (1965); *Plurisens*, cycle for Variable Group and Multimedia Action (1965–68); *Concentric and Efemeride*, both for Variable Ensemble, Tape, and Multimedia Action (1968–69); *Memorial I-V* for various combinations of Instruments, Tape, and Multimedia Action (1968–70); *Ego*, multimedia spectacle (1970); *Le Roi va mourir* for an Instrumentalist, Clock, Tape, and Multimedia Action (1971–72); *Ulysse* for Variable Group, Tape, and Multimedia Action (1972–73); *Jeu des sens*, music for a pair of ears, eyes, hands, a nose, and a mouth (1973–74); *Pourras-tu seul?* and *Cromoson*, both "imaginary music" (1973–74); *Natural!*, space music (1973–74); *Kalendrier*, permanent music for the atmosphere of a room (1974); *Natural-Cultural* for Chamber Ensemble and Tape (1973–83); *Sugestii II* for Chamber Ensemble (1974), *III: "Cumpana porţii"* for Viola and Tape (1977–78), *IV* for Piano (1979), and *V* for Clarinet, Piano, and Tape (1981); *Combinaţii în cercuri* for Chamber Ensemble and Tape (1979–80); *Metabizantinirikon* for Clarinet and Tape (1983–84). —**NS/LK/DM**

Németh, Mária, Hungarian soprano; b. Körmend, March 13, 1897; d. Vienna, Dec. 28, 1967. She studied with Georg Anthes and Géza Laszló in Budapest, Giannina Russ in Milan, Fernando De Lucia in Naples, and Felicie Kaschowska in Vienna. She made her operatic debut as Sulamith in *Königin von Saba* in Budapest in 1923. In 1924 she became a member of the Vienna State Opera, where she remained until 1946; also made appearances at Covent Garden in London, La Scala in Milan, Munich, Rome, Paris, and Salzburg. She sang both lyric and coloratura roles during her career, excelling as the Queen of the Night, Aida, Donna Anna, and Tosca, among others.—**NS/LK/DM**

Némethy, Ella, Hungarian mezzo-soprano; b. Sátoraljaujhely, April 5, 1895; d. Budapest, June 14, 1961. She studied at the Budapest Academy of Music and with Panizza in Milan. In 1919 she made her operatic debut as Dalila at the Budapest Opera, where she remained as one of its principal artists until 1948. She was especially known as a Wagnerian, garnering particular success as Brünnhilde, Isolde, and Kundry. —**NS/LK/DM**

Nemiroff, Isaac, American composer and teacher; b. Cincinnati, Feb. 16, 1912; d. N.Y., March 5, 1977. He studied at the Cincinnati Cons., and with Stefan Wolpe at the N.Y. Coll. of Music, then taught at various music schools in N.Y. and Brooklyn.

WORKS: Duo for Violin and Cello (1939); Concerto for Oboe and String Orch. (1955); Concertino for Flute, Violin, and String Orch. (1958); *Lorca*, solo cantata for Voice, Flute, and Strings (1963); Woodwind Quintet (1968); Quintet for Flute, Clarinet, Cello, Voice, and Piano (1969); *Atomyriades* for Oboe (1972); Duo for Oboe and Bass Clarinet (1973); 2 string quartets; 2 violin sonatas; Saxophone Sonata.—**NS/LK/DM**

Nemtin, Alexander, Russian composer; b. Perm, July 13, 1936; d. Moscow, Feb. 3, 1999. He received training at the Moscow Cons., graduating in 1960. While he wrote music in various genres, he became best known for his reification of Scriabin's *Acte préalable*, the "preliminary act" of the planned *Mysterium*. Nemtim's creation was based upon the sketches left by Scriabin, supplemented by music from his late works. —**NS/LK/DM**

Nenna, Pomponio, Italian composer; b. Bari, near Naples, c. 1550. d. probably in Rome, before Oct. 22, 1613. He was in the service of Gesualdo in Naples (c. 1594–99), then in Rome by 1608. Held in high regard by his contemporaries, he was created a Knight of the Golden Spur in 1603. He publ. 6 books of madrigals for 5 Voices from 1582 to 1618, and a book of madrigals for 4 Voices (1613). Some of his madrigals were ed. by E. Dagnino in Pubblicazioni dell'Istituto Italiano per la Storia della Musica, *Monumenti*, II (1942).—**NS/LK/DM**

Nenov, Dimiter, Bulgarian composer, pianist, and teacher; b. Razgrad, Jan. 1, 1902; d. Sofia, Aug. 30, 1953. He went to Dresden to study architecture at the Technische Hochschule and piano with Feling and composition with Blumer and Bitner at the Cons. After working as an architect, he continued his studies with Petri in Zakopane (1931) and attended the Bologna Cons. (1932). He taught piano in Sofia (1930–33), then at the State Academy of Music there (1933–35), where he later was made a reader (1937) and a prof. (1943).

WORKS: ORCH.: 2 syms. (1922; 1923, unfinished); *Ballad* (1926); Piano Concerto (1932–36); *2 ballads* for Piano and Orch. (1942, 1943); *Rhapsodic Fantasy* (1942–52). **CHAMBER:** Violin Sonata (1921); Piano Sonata (1922).

BIBL.: L. Nikolov, ed., *D. N.: spomeni i materijali* (Sofia, 1969).—**NS/LK/DM**

Nepomuceno, Alberto, important Brazilian composer; b. Fortaleza, July 6, 1864; d. Rio de Janeiro, Oct. 16, 1920. He studied in Rome, Berlin, and Paris, returning to Brazil in 1895. In 1902 he was appointed director of the Instituto Nacional de Música in Rio de Janeiro, remaining only for a few months; he returned to this post in 1906, holding it until 1916. In 1910 he conducted Brazilian music at the International Exposition in Brussels. In some of his music he introduced thematic material from Brazilian folk music.

WORKS: DRAMATIC: Opera: *Artemis* (Rio de Janeiro, June 14, 1898); *O Garatuja* (Rio de Janeiro, Oct. 26, 1904); *Abul* (1899–1905; Buenos Aires, June 30, 1913). **OTHER:** Sym. (1894; publ. 1937); *Serie brasileira* for Orch. (1892; contains a popular batuque); chamber music; over 80 songs; piano and organ pieces.—**NS/LK/DM**

Neri, Giulio, Italian bass; b. Turilla di Siena, May 21, 1909; d. Rome, April 21, 1958. He studied with Ferraresi in Florence. He made his operatic debut at the Teatro delle Quattro Fontane in Rome in 1935, then sang at the Teatro Reale dell'Opera in Rome, where he soon established himself as a principal bass; also made guest appearances at La Scala in Milan, Florence, Venice, London, and Munich. An outstanding Verdi interpreter, he was equally distinguished as a Wagnerian. —**NS/LK/DM**

Neri, Massimiliano, Italian organist and composer; b. probably in Brescia, c. 1615; d. Bonn, 1666. He served in the position of first organist at San Marco in Venice from 1644 to 1664, where he also was organist of the church of SS. Giovanni e Paolo (1644–46; 1657–64) and maestro di musica at the orphanage of the Ospedaletto (from 1655). In 1664 he became organist and Kapellmeister to the elector of Cologne. In 1651 he was ennobled by the Holy Roman Emperor Ferdinand III. Neri was an accomplished composer of sonatas and canzonas.—**LK/DM**

Neri, Saint Donna Filippo, outstanding Roman Catholic churchman; b. Florence, July 21, 1515; d. Rome, May 26, 1595. He was educated in Florence, and by 1534 was in Rome. In 1548 he founded the Confraternità della Ss. Trinita, and in 1551 he took Holy Orders. He began giving lectures on religious subjects and holding spiritual exercises in his living quarters at S. Girolamo della Carita in 1552; by 1554 he was active in the oratory of the church there. These meetings invariably ended with the singing of hymns, or *laudi spirituali*, for which the poet Ancina wrote many of the texts, while Giovanni Animuccia, maestro di cappella at the Vatican and music director of the Oratory, set them to music. In 1575 the Congregation of the Oratory, as a seminary for secular priests, was officially recognized by Pope Gregory XIII, and in 1578 the Congregation transferred its headquarters to the church of Santa Maria in Vallicella. Neri, however, remained at S. Girolamo until 1583; Victoria lived with him there, serving as chaplain. Neri was also a friend and spiritual adviser of Palestrina. From the musical practice of the Oratory there eventually developed the form that we know as "oratorio." It was not until about 1635–40 that this form actually began to receive the title of oratorio, from the place where the performances were given. Neri was beatified on May 25, 1615, and canonized on March 12, 1622.

BIBL.: P. Bacci, *Vita di S.F. N., fiorentino* (Rome, 1622; Eng. tr., 2 vols., 1903); L. Ponnelle and L. Bourdet, *Saint Philippe Néri et la société romaine de son temps (1515–1595)* (Paris, 1918; Eng. tr., 1932); G. Incisa della Rocchetta and N. Vian, eds., *Il primo processo per S.F. N. nel codice vaticano latino 3789e in altri esemplari dell'archivo dell'Oratorio di Roma*, Studi e Testi, CXCI, CXCVI, CCV, CCXXIV (Rome, 1957–63); M. Trevor, *Apostle of Rome: A Life of Philip N., 1515–1595* (London, 1966).—**NS/LK/DM**

Neruda, family of Moravian musicians:

(1) Josef Neruda, organist and teacher; b. Mohelno, Jan. 16, 1807; d. Brünn, Feb. 18, 1875. He studied at the Benedictine monastery of Rajhrad, then taught piano in Olmütz (1825–32). He was organist of Brünn Cathedral (1832–44). He also appeared in concerts throughout Europe with his children, who were as follows:

(2) Amálie Nerudova, pianist and teacher; b. Brünn, March 31, 1834; d. there, Feb. 24, 1890. She studied with her father, and in addition to making tours of Europe with her family, she played in a trio with her brother Viktor and her sister Wilma (1848–52). She then was active mainly as a performer and teacher in Brünn.

(3) Viktor Neruda, cellist; b. Brünn, 1836?; d. St. Petersburg, 1852. He studied with his father, and then played in a trio with his sisters Amálie and Wilma (from 1848). He also toured Europe with his family, dying during a visit to Russia.

(4) **Wilma Maria Francisca (Vilemína Maria Franziška) Neruda,** esteemed violinist and teacher; b. Brünn, March 21, 1838?; d. Berlin, April 15, 1911. She studied with her father and with Leopold Jansa in Vienna, making her debut there (1846). After touring Germany with her family (1848), she gave concerts in London (1849); was soloist at a Phil. Soc. concert there (June 11, 1849). She played in a trio with her sister Amálie and her brother Viktor (1848–52), and subsequently pursued a distinguished solo career. She was made chamber virtuoso by the Swedish king in 1863. In 1864 she married **Ludvig Norman,** but the two were separated in 1869. She was prof. of violin at the Stockholm Cons. (1867–70). She gave annual concerts in London from 1869 and was greatly admired there; in 1876 the Duke of Edinburgh (later of Saxe-Coburg-Gotha) and the earls of Dudley and Hardwicke presented her with an outstanding Stradivarius dating from 1709. She continued to give concerts throughout Europe while remaining closely associated with the musical life of England; also appeared as a chamber music artist, and gave recitals with **Charles Hallé** from 1877, marrying him in 1888. The Prince of Wales (later Edward VII), with the support of the kings of Sweden and Denmark, launched a public subscription in her honor in 1896. She toured the U.S. in 1899, and in 1900 settled in Berlin, where she taught at the Stern Cons.; was made violinist to Queen Alexandra in 1901.

(5) **Marie (Arlbergová) Neruda,** violinist; b. Brünn, March 26, 1840; d. Stockholm, 1922. She studied with her father, then appeared in concerts on tours of Europe with her family; later settled in Stockholm.

(6) **Franz (František Xaver Viktor) Neruda,** cellist and composer; b. Brünn, Dec. 3, 1843; d. Copenhagen, March 20, 1915. He studied violin with his father, and then took up the cello on his own (1852); appeared on tours of Europe with his family. After further cello training with Brezina in Brünn and with Servais in Warsaw (1859), he made a successful tour of Scandinavia with his sisters Wilma and Marie (1861–64); then settled in Copenhagen as a member of the royal orch. (1864–76). He was a founder of the Soc. for Chamber Music and its string quartet (1868), and performed widely with it until pursuing his career in England (1876–79). He then founded his own string quartet in Copenhagen, with which he was active from 1879 to 1889. After serving as a prof. at the St. Petersburg Cons. (1889–91), he returned to Copenhagen as conductor of the concerts of the Music Soc. (1891–1915). Concurrently he conducted the concerts of the Stockholm Music Soc., and was also active as a piano teacher. He wrote 5 cello concertos, *Fra Bøhmerwald,* a set of orch. works, chamber music, pieces for Cello and Piano, organ works, piano pieces, and songs.—**NS/LK/DM**

Neruda, Johann Baptist Georg (actually, **Jan Křtitel Jiří**), Czech violinist and composer; b. probably in Rosice, c. 1707; d. Dresden, c. 1780. He received training in Prague, after which he played in a theater orch. there, becoming a member of the Dresden court orch. in 1750; he later was its Konzertmeister. He wrote the opera *Les troqueurs,* 18 syms., many concertos, trio sonatas, and church music.—**LK/DM**

Nessi, Giuseppe, Italian tenor; b. Bergamo, Sept. 25, 1887; d. Milan, Dec. 16, 1961. He studied at the Bergamo Cons. with Vezzani and Melli. In 1910 he made his operatic debut as Alfredo in Saluzzo. From 1921 to 1959 he was a valued member of Milan's La Scala, where he excelled in comprimario roles. He also sang in other Italian opera centers and at London's Covent Garden (1927–37). Among his most notable roles were Bardolfo, Spoletta, Missail, and Goro. He also created the roles of Gobrias in *Nerone* (1924) and Pong in *Turandot* (1926).—**NS/LK/DM**

Nessler, Victor E(rnst), Alsatian composer; b. Baldenheim, Jan. 28, 1841; d. Strasbourg, May 28, 1890. He studied in Strasbourg, where he produced his first opera, *Fleurette* (1864); then continued his studies in Leipzig with M. Hauptmann, being made chorusmaster at the Stadttheater (1870) and later at the Carola-Theater. He established his reputation as a composer for the theater with his opera *Der Rattenfänger von Hameln* (Leipzig, March 19, 1879). An even greater success was achieved by his opera *Der Trompeter von Säkkingen* (Leipzig, May 4, 1884), which entered the repertoire of many European opera houses. In both operas Nessler adroitly appealed to the Romantic tastes of the German audiences, even though from a purely musical standpoint these productions offered little originality. His other operas premiered in Leipzig were *Dornröschens Brautfahrt* (1867), *Irmingard* (1876), *Der wilde Jäger* (1881), and *Otto der Schütz* (1886); his last opera was *Die Rose von Strassburg* (Munich, 1890). He also wrote the operettas *Die Hochzeitsreise* (1867), *Nachtwächter und Student* (1868), and *Am Alexandertag* (1869).—**NS/LK/DM**

Nesterenko, Evgeni (Evgenievich), distinguished Russian bass; b. Moscow, Jan. 8, 1938. He went to Leningrad to pursue training in architectural engineering at the Structural Inst. (graduated, 1961) and in voice with Lukanin at the Cons. In 1963 he made his operatic debut as Prince Gremin at the Maly Theater in Leningrad, where he sang until 1967. From 1967 to 1971 he was a member of the Kirov Opera and Ballet Theater in Leningrad. In 1970 he captured first prize in the Tchaikovsky Competition in Moscow. In 1971 he became a member of the Bolshoi Theater in Moscow, with which he toured as Boris Godunov to Milan's La Scala (1973), the Vienna State Opera (1974), and N.Y.'s Metropolitan Opera (1975). In 1978 he made his debut at London's Covent Garden as Don Basilio. In subsequent years, he appeared as a guest artist with many European opera houses. His festival appearances took him to Verona (1978, 1985, 1989, 1991), Bregenz (1986), and Orange (1990). In 1993 he appeared as Verdi's *Attila* in Antwerp. In 1995 he portrayed King Philip in Helsinki. He also toured widely as a concert artist. Among his various honors are the People's Artist of the U.S.S.R.

(1976), the Vercelli Prize (1981), the Lenin Prize (1982), and the Verona Prize (1986). Among his other outstanding roles are Ruslan, Kutuzov, King Philip, Zaccaria, and Méphistophèlés.—NS/LK/DM

Nestyev, Izrail (Vladimirovich), Russian musicologist; b. Kerch, April 17, 1911. He received training in theory and composition at the Moscow Cons. (graduated, 1937), and then pursued postgraduate studies there with Ferman (1940; degree, 1946). From 1945 to 1948 he was ed. of music broadcasting in the U.S.S.R. He was on the staff of *Sovetskaya muzika* from 1949 to 1959. He also taught at the Moscow Cons. (from 1956) and was a senior research fellow at the Inst. of the History of the Arts in Moscow (from 1960), which awarded him his Ph.D. in 1971 for his study on Bartók (publ. in Moscow, 1969). His major work was a biography of Prokofiev (Moscow, 1946; Eng. tr., N.Y., 1946; rev. ed., Moscow, 1957; Eng. tr., Stanford, Calif., 1960, with a foreword by N. Slonimsky; new ed. rev. and aug., Moscow, 1973). —NS/LK/DM

Nešvera, Josef, Czech conductor and composer; b. Praskolesy, near Hořovice, Oct. 24, 1842; d. Olomouc, April 12, 1914. He studied with his father, a teacher and organist, and then took courses in piano, organ, and theory with J. Kresjčí, J.B. Foerster, and František Blažek in Prague. He served as music director of the Beroun church (1868–78), Hradec Králové Cathedral (1878–84), and Olomouc Cathedral (1884–1914).

WORKS: DRAMATIC: O p e r a : *Bratránek* (The Little Cousin; 1882); *Perdita* (The Winter's Tale), after Shakespeare (1892; Prague, May 21, 1897); *Lesní vzduch* (The Forest Beeze; 1896; Brünn, Jan. 23, 1897); *Cernokněžník* (The Magician; 1903–05; Brünn, Feb. 7, 1906); *Meerweib* (1908–10). ORCH.: Sym.; Violin Concerto. VOCAL: Much sacred music, including *České pašije* (Czech Passion; 1882); *De profundis*, oratorio (1890); *Job*, oratorio (1912); about 25 masses; secular choral works, including the popular *Moravě* (To Moravia) for Men's Voices; songs. OTHER: Chamber music; piano pieces; organ works.—LK/DM

Nettl, Bruno, distinguished Czech-born American ethnomusicologist, son of **Paul Nettl;** b. Prague, March 14, 1930. He was taken to the U.S. in 1939, where he studied at Indiana Univ. (A.B., 1950; M.A., 1951; Ph.D., 1953, with the diss. *American Indian Music North of Mexico: Its Styles and Areas*; publ. as *North American Indian Musical Styles*, Philadelphia, 1954). He also received an M.A. degree in library science from the Univ. of Mich. in 1960. He taught at Wayne State Univ. (1953–64). In 1964 he joined the faculty of the Univ. of Ill. at Urbana, becoming a prof. of music and anthropology in 1967, and in 1992 he was made prof. emeritus but continued to teach there part time. He ed. the periodical *Ethnomusicology* from 1961 to 1965, and again from 1998, serving as president of the Soc. for Ethnomusicology (1969–71). He was also ed. of the yearbook of the *International Folk Music Council* (1974–77), and contributed articles to scholarly journals.

WRITINGS: *Music in Primitive Culture* (Cambridge, Mass., 1956); *An Introduction to Folk Music in the United States* (Detroit,

1960; 3rd ed., rev. and aug. by H. Myers, 1976, as *Folk Music in the United States, an Introduction*); *Cheremis Musical Styles* (Bloomington, Ind., 1960); *Reference Materials in Ethnomusicology* (Detroit, 1961; 2nd ed., rev., 1968); *Theory and Method in Ethnomusicology* (N.Y., 1964); *Folk and Traditional Music of the Western Continents* (Englewood Cliffs, N.J., 1965; 3rd ed., rev. by V. Goertzen, 1990); with B. Foltin Jr., *Daramad of Chahargah: A Study in the Performance Practice of Persian Music* (Detroit, 1972); with C. Hamm and R. Byrnside, *Contemporary Music and Music Cultures* (Englewood Cliffs, N.J., 1975); ed. *Eight Urban Musical Cultures, Tradition and Change* (Urbana, Ill., 1978); *The Study of Ethnomusicology: 29 Issues and Concepts* (Urbana, Ill., 1983); *The Western Impact on World Music: Change, Adaptation, and Survival* (N.Y., 1985); *The Radif od Persian Music: Studies of Structure and Cultural Context* (Champaign, Ill., 1987; 2nd ed., rev., 1991); *Blackfoot Musical Thought: Comparative Perspectives* (Kent, Ohio, 1989); ed. with P. Bohlman, *Comparative Musicology and Anthropology in Music: Essays on the History of Ethnomusicology* (Chicago, 1991); with others, *Excursions in World Music* (Englewood Cliffs, N.J., 1992); ed. with others, *Community of Music: An Ethnographical Seminar in Champaign-Urbana* (Champaign, Ill., 1993); *Heartland Excursions: Ethnomusicological Reflections on Schools of Music* (Urbana, Ill., 1995); ed. with M. Russell, *In the Course of Performance* (Chicago, 1998).—NS/LK/DM

Nettl, Paul, eminent Czech-born American musicologist, father of **Bruno Nettl;** b. Hohenelbe, Bohemia, Jan. 10, 1889; d. Bloomington, Ind., Jan. 8, 1972. He studied jurisprudence (Jur.D., 1913) and musicology (Ph.D., 1915) at the German Univ. of Prague, where from 1920 to 1937 he was on the faculty. In 1939 he emigrated to the U.S., becoming a naturalized U.S. citizen in 1945. After teaching at Westminster Choir Coll. and in N.Y. and Philadelphia, he was a prof. of musicology at Indiana Univ. in Bloomington (1946–59); remained a part-time teacher there until 1963.

WRITINGS: *Vom Ursprung der Musik* (Prague, 1918); *Alte jüdische Spielleute und Musiker* (Prague, 1923); *Musik und Tanz bei Casanova* (Prague, 1924); *Musik-Barock in Böhmen und Mähren* (Brünn, 1927); *Der Prager Kaufruf* (Prague, 1930); *Das Wiener Lied im Zeitalter des Barock* (Vienna, 1934); *Mozart in Böhmen*, after Prochazka's *Mozart in Prag* (Prague, 1938); *The Story of Dance Music* (N.Y., 1947); *The Book of Musical Documents* (N.Y., 1948); *Luther and Music* (N.Y., 1948); *Casanova und seine Zeit* (Esslingen, 1949); *Goethe und Mozart: Eine Betrachtung* (Esslingen, 1949); *The Other Casanova* (N.Y., 1950); *Forgotten Musicians* (N.Y., 1951); *National Anthems* (N.Y., 1952; 2nd ed., enl., 1967); *Beethoven Encyclopedia* (N.Y., 1956; 2nd ed., rev., 1967, as *Beethoven Handbook*); *Mozart and Masonry* (N.Y., 1957); *Beethoven und seine Zeit* (Frankfurt am Main, 1958); *Georg Friedrich Handel* (Berlin, 1958); *Mozart und der Tanz* (1960); *The Dance in Classical Music* (N.Y., 1963); R. Daniel, ed., *P.N.: Selected Essays* (Bloomington, 1975).

BIBL.: T. Atcherson, *Ein Musikwissenschaftler in zwei Welten: Die musikwissenschaftlen und literarischen Arbeiten von P. N.* (Vienna, 1962).—NS/LK/DM

Neubauer, Franz Christoph, Czech violinist and composer; b. Melník, March 21, 1750; d. Bückeburg, Oct. 11, 1795. He was taught violin by the village schoolmaster and led a wandering life. He produced an operetta, *Ferdinand und Yariko*, in Munich (1784), and then proceeded to Vienna, where he met Mozart and Haydn. From 1790 to 1794 he served as Kapellmeister to

Prince Weilburg, and in 1795 he succeeded Johann Christoph Friedrich Bach as court Kapellmeister at Bückeburg. He was a prolific composer, numbering among his publ. works 10 syms. (1791–95), *La bataille* for Orch. (1794; contains sounds imitative of battle), Flute Concerto (1795), Piano Concerto (publ. 1798), Cello Concerto (n.d.), 25 quartets (1785–93), various chamber music pieces, choral works, songs, and piano pieces.

BIBL.: R. Sjoerdsma, *The Instrumental Works of F.C. N. (1760–95)* (diss., Ohio State Univ., 1970).—**NS/LK/DM**

Neuendorff, Adolph (Heinrich Anton Magnus), German-American conductor, impresario, and composer; b. Hamburg, June 13, 1843; d. N.Y., Dec. 4, 1897. He went to N.Y. in 1854 and studied violin with Matzka and Weinlich, and piano with Schilling. He appeared both as a concert violinist and pianist, and gave violin concerts in Brazil in 1861. In 1864 he went to Milwaukee, then a center of German music, and served as music director of the German theater; subsequently moved to N.Y., where he conducted German opera, including the first American performances of *Lohengrin* (April 3, 1871) and *Die Walküre* (April 2, 1877); in 1878–79 he conducted the N.Y. Phil. From 1884 to 1889 he was in Boston and became the first conductor of the Music Hall Promenade Concerts (later Boston Pops). He then conducted the Emma Juch Grand Opera Co. (1889–91). He then followed his wife, the singer Georgine von Januschowsky, to Vienna, where she was prima donna and he a conductor at the Hofoper (1893–95). Returning to N.Y., he served as director of music at Temple Emanu-El (1896) and as conductor at the Metropolitan Opera (1897). He wrote the comic operas *Der Rattenfänger von Hameln* (1880), *Don Quixote* (1882), *Prince Waldmeister* (1887), and *The Minstrel* (1892), 2 syms. (1878, 1880) and other orch. works, quartets for Men's Voices, and songs.—**NS/LK/DM**

Neuhaus, Heinrich (Gustavovich), eminent Russian pianist and pedagogue; b. Elizavetgrad, April 12, 1888; d. Moscow, Oct. 10, 1964. He studied piano with his father, Gustav Neuhaus (1847–1938); other musical members of his family were his uncle, Felix Blumenfeld, and his first cousin, **Karol Szymanowski**. Neuhaus began giving concerts at the age of 9; he made a concert tour in Germany in 1904, then studied composition with Paul Juon in Berlin; from 1912 to 1914 he took piano lessons with Leopold Godowsky in Vienna. Returning to Russia, he taught piano at the Kiev Cons. (1918–22); then was a prof. from 1922 to his death at the Moscow Cons. Among his outstanding students were Emil Gilels, Sviatoslav Richter, Yakov Zak, and Radu Lupu. He excelled as an interpreter of the Romantic and 20th-century Russian repertory. He publ. *Ob iskusstve fortepiannoy igrï* (The Art of Piano Playing; Moscow, 1958; 3rd ed., 1967; Eng. tr., London, 1973).

BIBL.: V. Delson, *H. N.* (Moscow, 1966).—**NS/LK/DM**

Neuhaus, Rudolf, German conductor and pedagogue; b. Cologne, Jan. 3, 1914; d. Dresden, March 7, 1990. He first studied violin, then took conducting lessons with Hermann Abendroth, and also studied theory with Philipp Jarnach at the Cologne Hochschule für Musik (1932–34). He was music director of the Landestheater in Neustrelitz (1934–44), then conductor of the Landestheater in Schwerin (1945–50), serving as its Generalmusikdirektor from 1950 to 1953. In 1953 he joined the Dresden State Opera, where he was deputy Generalmusikdirektor until 1975. From 1953 he was a member of the faculty of the Dresden Hochschule für Musik; in 1959, was named prof. there.—**NS/LK/DM**

Neuhold, Günter, Austrian conductor; b. Graz, Nov. 2, 1947. He studied at the Graz Hochschule für Musik (M.A., 1969) and pursued advanced training in conducting with Ferrara in Rome and Swarowsky in Vienna. He won several prizes in conducting competitions, among them first prizes in Florence (1976), San Remo (1976), and Salzburg (1977), second prize in Vienna (1977), and third prize in Milan (1977). From 1972 to 1980 he conducted in various German opera houses, and also led performances at the Salzburg Festival (1978, 1980, 1983, 1986). From 1981 to 1986 he was music director of the Teatro Regio in Parma, where he also served as chief conductor of the Orch. Sinfonica dell'Emilia Romagna "Arturo Toscanini." He was chief conductor of the Royal Phil. Orch. of Flanders in Antwerp from 1986 to 1990, with which he toured Europe. From 1989 to 1995 he was Generalmusikdirektor of the Badisches State Theater in Karlsruhe, where he oversaw a Richard Strauss cycle and Wagner's *Ring* cycle. In 1995 he became Generalmusikdirektor and artistic director of the Theater der Freien Hansestadt in Bremen. As a guest conductor, he appeared with the Vienna Phil., the Vienna Sym. Orch., the Dresden State Orch., the Vienna State Opera, the Deutsche Oper in Berlin, the Teatro alla Scala in Milan, the Opera Co. of Philadelphia, and many others.—**NS/LK/DM**

Neukomm, Sigismund, Ritter von, Austrian pianist, conductor, writer on music, and composer; b. Salzburg, July 10, 1778; d. Paris, April 3, 1858. He began his musical studies when he was 7, with Franz Xaver Weissauer, the Salzburg Cathedral organist, then studied theory with Michael Haydn. He also took courses in philosophy and mathematics at the Univ. there, being made honorary organist of the Univ. church (c. 1792) and chorus master of the court theater (1796). He continued his studies in Vienna with Joseph Haydn (1797–1804), after which he was active as a teacher. After serving as conductor of the German Theater in St. Petersburg (1804–08), he went to Paris, where he befriended Cherubini, Gossec, Grétry, Monsigny, and other prominent musicians. He was pianist to Prince Talleyrand, in which capacity he went to the Congress of Vienna (1814), where his Requiem in C minor in memory of Louis XVI was given (Jan. 21, 1815); that same year he was ennobled by Louis XVII and was made Chevalier of the Légion d'honneur. He was taken to Rio de Janeiro by the Duke of Luxembourg (1816), and became active at the court of John VI of Portugal; after the outbreak of the revolution (1821), he accompanied John VI to Lisbon, and then returned to Paris. After again serving Talleyrand, he traveled widely (from 1826); visited England in 1829, and thereafter made frequent trips between London and Paris. Many of his articles appeared in the *Revue et Gazette Musicale de Paris.* His autobiography was publ. as *Esquisses biographiques de Sigismond Neukomm* (Paris, 1859). Elisabeth Neukomm (1789–1816), his sister, gained fame in Vienna as a soprano. A prolific composer, he produced over 1,300 works.

WORKS: DRAMATIC: *Die Nachtwächter,* intermezzo (Vienna, 1804); *Die neue Oper oder Der Schauspieldirektor,* intermezzo (Vienna, 1804); *Alexander am Indus,* opera (St. Petersburg, Sept. 27, 1804); *Musikalische Malerei,* farce (Moscow, May 1, 1806); *Arkona,* melodrama (Würzburg, Sept. 21, 1808); *Niobé,* tragédie lyrique (Montbéliard, 1809); also incidental music to plays. VOCAL: S a c r e d : Oratorios; cantatas; 48 masses; 27 offertories; 2 Passions; 11 Te Deums; 73 motets and anthems; 236 hymns and chorales; 243 chants and songs; etc. O t h e r : 36 choruses, over 150 canons, over 160 quartets and trios, and over 275 arias, songs, romances, etc. INSTRUMENTAL: 2 syms.; 5 overtures; Piano Concerto; 6 phantasies for Orch.; various marches; chamber music; piano music; pieces for Harmonium; arrangements; etc.

BIBL.: G. Pellegrini-Brandacher, *S.R. v.N. (und seine Oratorien)* (diss., Univ. of Munich, 1936); A. Seebohm, *Das deutsche Klavierlied S. N.s: Ein Beitrag zur Musikgeschichte des frühen 19. Jahrhunderts* (diss., Univ. of Vienna, 1968); R. Angermüller, *S. N.: Werkverzeichnis, Autobiographie, Beziehung zu seinen Zeitgenossen* (Munich, 1977).—NS/LK/DM

Neumann, Angelo, Austrian tenor and opera administrator; b. Vienna, Aug. 18, 1838; d. Prague, Dec. 20, 1910. He began a mercantile career, but deserted it after taking vocal lessons from Stilke-Sessi. After making his debut in Berlin in 1859, he sang in Kraków, Oldenburg, Pressburg, Danzig, and at the Vienna Court Opera (1862–76). From 1876 to 1882 he was manager of the Leipzig Opera, then gathered together a traveling company for producing Wagner operas, journeying as far as Italy. From 1882 to 1885 he was manager of the Bremen Opera, then until his death, of the Prague Deutsches Theater. He publ. *Erinnerungen an Richard Wagner* (1907; Eng. tr. by E. Livermore, 1908).—NS/LK/DM

Neumann, Franz (František), Czech conductor and composer; b. Přerov, Moravia, June 16, 1874; d. Brno, Feb. 24, 1929. He was a pupil at the Leipzig Cons. He was répétiteur in Karlsruhe and Hamburg, then conductor in Regensburg, Linz, and Reichenberg. In 1904 he became second conductor in Frankfurt am Main, being subsequently named first conductor (1919) and director (1925) of the Brno National Opera. He composed the operas *Die Brautwerbung* (Linz, 1901), *Liebelei* (Frankfurt am Main, Sept. 18, 1910), *Herbststurm* (Berlin, April 9, 1919), *Beatrice Caracci* (Brno, April 29, 1922; in Czech), and *Leyer und Schwert* (publ. 1901; not produced), as well as 2 ballets, men's choruses, etc. —NS/LK/DM

Neumann, Frederick (actually, Fritz), distinguished Austrian-born American violinist and musicologist; b. Bielitz, Dec. 15, 1907; d. Richmond, Va., March 21, 1994. He studied violin with Ondříček, Ševčik, and Marteau in Prague, and also took courses at the Univ. of Berlin (Ph.D., 1934, in political science and economics); subsequently studied violin with H. Kaplan in Berlin and A. Busch in Basel. He emigrated to the U.S. in 1939, and served as head of the string dept. of the Cornish School of Music and Arts in Seattle (1939–42); during World War II (1942–45), he was in the intelligence service of the U.S. Army, becoming a naturalized U.S. citizen (1943). After the war, he studied at Teachers Coll., Columbia Univ. (M.A., 1947), and at Columbia Univ. (Ph.D., 1952). He was prof. of music and concertmaster of the orch. at the Univ. of Miami (1948–51) and prof. of music at the Univ. of Richmond (Va.) (1955–78); also was concertmaster of the Richmond Sym. Orch. (1957–64), and a visiting prof. at Princeton (1970–71), Yale (1975–76), and Indiana (1978–79) univs. He made valuable contributions to the field of 17th- and 18th-century performance practices. He publ. the books *Contemporary Violin Technique* (with F. Galamian; 2 vols., N.Y., 1966, 1977), *Violin Left Hand Technique: A Critical Survey of the Literature* (Urbana, Ill., 1969), *Ornamentation in Baroque and Post- Baroque Music* (Princeton, N.J., 1978), *Essays in Performance Practice* (Ann Arbor, 1982), *Ornamentation and Improvisation in Mozart* (Princeton, N.J., 1986), *New Essays on Performance Practice* (Ann Arbor, 1989), and *Performance Practices of the Seventeenth and Eighteenth Centuries* (N.Y., 1992).—NS/LK/DM

Neumann, Václav, prominent Czech conductor; b. Prague, Sept. 29, 1920; d. Vienna, Sept. 2, 1995. He studied violin with J. Micka and conducting with Pavel Dědeček and Metod Doležil at the Prague Cons. (1940–45). While still a student, he was active as a chamber- music player; became a founding member of the Smetana Quartet (1945); that same year he was made first violist of the Czech Phil., making his conducting debut in 1948. He was chief conductor of the Karlovy Vary Sym. Orch. (1951–54) and of the Brno Sym. Orch. (1954–56); then conducted at East Berlin's Komische Oper (1956–64), and concurrently was conductor of Prague's FOK Sym. Orch. From 1964 to 1968 he held the post of second conductor of the Czech Phil. in Prague; during that same period, he was the conductor of the Gewandhaus Orch. and Generalmusikdirektor of the Opera in Leipzig; then held the latter post at the Württemberg State Theater in Stuttgart (1969–72). He was chief conductor of the Czech Phil. (1968–90), touring widely with it in Europe and abroad.—NS/LK/DM

Neumann, Věroslav, Czech composer and music educator; b. Citoliby, near Louny, May 27, 1931. He studied with Řídký at the Prague Academy of Music (1950–54). Thereafter he was active as a composer and teacher, working in both professional and amateur circles, and with young people. In 1991 he was appointed director of the Prague Cons. and made it his goal to restore that once venerable institution to its pre-Communist days of educational distinction. In his works, Neumann has developed an accessible style with touches of leavening wit.

WORKS: DRAMATIC: *Opera o komínku* (Chimney Opera; 1965–66); *Glorie,* radio opera (1970); *Příběh se starou lenoskou* (Story of an Old Armchair), comic opera (1987). ORCH.: *Ode* (1965–66); *Invitation to a Cocktail Party* (1967); *Dedication for*

Chamber Orch. (1977); Concerto for Trumpet, Strings, and Tape (1980); *Symphonic Dances* (1984); *Soothing* (1989). **CHAMBER:** *Music* for Viola and Piano (1968); *5 Pieces* for 2 Violins (1968); String Quartet (1969); *5 Dramatic Sequences* for Cello and Piano (1978); *Proclamation* for Tuba and Piano (1981); *Portraits of a Man* for Violin and Piano (1987); *An Aging Elegant Gentleman's Afternoon in a Spa* for Clarinet and Piano (1987). **VOCAL:** *Panorama of Prague* for Baritone and Orch. (1962); Chamber Sym. for 16 Singers and 13 Instrumentalists (1972); *Christmas for Young Singers* for Children's Chorus and Chamber Orch. (1976); *In Bohemia*, cantata for Girl's Chorus and Orch. (1983); *Elements* for Medium Voice, Cello, and Organ (1989); various choruses; other songs. **OTHER:** Didactic pieces.—**NS/LK/DM**

Neumann, Werner, respected German musicologist; b. Königstein, Jan. 21, 1905; d. Leipzig, April 24, 1991. He studied piano and theory at the Leipzig Cons., and musicology with Kroyer and Zenck at the Univ. of Leipzig (Ph.D., 1938, with the diss. *J. S. Bachs Chorfuge: Ein Beitrag zur Kompositions-Technik Bachs*; publ. in Leipzig, 1938; 2nd ed., 1950), where he also took courses in psychology and philosophy. He taught at the Leipzig Hochschule für Musik; in 1950 he founded the Leipzig Bach Archive, and in 1953 became co-ed. of the *Bach-Jahrbuch* and the *Neue Bach- Ausgabe*, retiring in 1973. The vol. *Bach-Studien, V* (Leipzig, 1975), was publ. as a Festschrift in his honor.

WRITINGS: *Handbuch der Kantaten Johann Sebastian Bachs* (Leipzig, 1947; 4th ed., 1971); *Auf den Lebenswegen Johann Sebastian Bachs* (Berlin, 1953; 4th ed., 1962); *Johann Sebastian Bach: Sämtliche Kantatatexte* (Leipzig, 1956; 2nd ed., 1967); *Bach: Eine Bildbiographie* (Munich, 1960; 2nd ed., 1961; Eng. tr., 1961, as *Bach and His World*; 2nd ed., 1969); ed. with H.-J. Schulze, *Schriftstücke von der Hand Johann Sebastian Bachs, Bach-Dokumente, I* (Leipzig, 1963); ed. with H.-J. Schulze, *Fremdschriftliche und gedruckte Dokument zur Lebensgeschichte Johann Sebastian Bachs 1685–1750*, Bach-Dokumente, II (Leipzig, 1969); ed. *Bilddokumente zur Lebensgeschichte Johann Sebastian Bachs*, Bach- Dokumente, IV (Leipzig, 1978).—**NS/LK/DM**

Neumann, Wolfgang, Austrian tenor; b. Waiern, June 20, 1945. He received training in Essen and Duisburg. In 1973 he made his operatic debut as Weber's Max in Bielefeld, and sang there until 1978. Following appearances in Augsburg (1978–80), he sang at the Mannheim National Theater from 1980. As a guest artist, he was engaged in Hamburg, Munich, Vienna, Zürich, Bologna, Florence, and other European music centers. In 1984 he made his first appearance in the U.S. in Dallas as Tannhäuser. He made his Metropolitan Opera debut in N.Y. on Feb. 20, 1988, as Siegfried. In 1990 he sang Rienzi in a concert perf. at the Teatro Colón in Buenos Aires. His portrayal of Tannhäuser at the Bayreuth Festival in 1995 proved memorable. Among his other roles were Tristan, Lohengrin, Erik, Loge, the Emperor in *Die Frau ohne Schatten*, the Drum Major in *Wozzeck*, the Cardinal in *Mathis der Maler*, and Schoenberg's Aron.—**NS/LK/DM**

Neumark, Georg, German poet, novelist, viol player, and composer; b. Langensalza, March 3, 1621; d. Weimar, July 8, 1681. He studied in Schleusingen and

Gotha, leading a wandering life until settling at the Weimar court as a chancellor and librarian. He wrote both sacred and secular poetry, many texts being set to his own music. His most important collection was publ. as *Georg Neumarks...Poetisch- und musikalisches Lustwäldchen* (Hamburg, 1652; aug. ed., Jena, 1657, as *Fortepflanzter musikalisch poetischen Lustwald*). His hymns *Wer nur den lieben Gott lässt walten* and *Ich lass Gott in allem walten* have become standard Lutheran chorales, the former being used by Bach in his cantata BWV 197.

BIBL.: F. Knauth, *G. N., Leben und Dichten* (Langensalza, 1881).—**NS/LK/DM**

Neumeister, Ed (actually, **Edward Paul**), jazz trombonist, composer; b. Sept. 1, 1952, Topeka, Kans. His father, Herbert Paul Neumeister, was a trumpeter and conductor in a military band before Ed was born. In 1960, the family moved to Fremont, Calif., near San Francisco. He started playing music in a private band called the Weldonians in Oakland, which mainly performed at football games. At age of 15, he and several members of the Weldonians joined the musicians union and formed their own band to play dances, proms and other functions most weekends. From 1978–80, he performed in Reconstruction with Jerry Garcia, Merl Saunders, and Gaylord Birch and from 1980–81 worked with Lionel Hampton's band, alongside Curtis Fuller. He played with Buddy Rich (1981), The Duke Ellington Orch., directed by Mercer Ellington (1981–90), the Mel Lewis Jazz Orch. (1981–91), and the Gerry Mulligan Concert Jazz Band (1982–85). He has toured Europe, Japan, and the U.S., composing for and performing as guest soloist with bands and orchestras. He also performs in small group concerts and recitals, gives improvisation, musicianship, and brass clinics and leads a quintet and an octet in N.Y. His arrangement of "A Nightingale Sang in Berkeley Square" was nominated for a Grammy award in 1992. He has received three fellowship grants from the NEA.—**LP**

Neusidler, Hans, eminent German lutenist, lute maker, intabulator, and composer, father of **Melchior Neusidler**; b. Pressburg, c. 1508; d. Nuremberg, Feb. 2, 1563. He settled in Nuremberg in 1530, taking the oath of citizenship in 1531. In addition to his important vols. of lute music, he was active as a lute maker. He was twice married, and fathered 17 children. Among his intabulations for lute, all of which were publ. in Nuremberg, are *Ein newgeordent künstlich Lautenbuch in zwen Theyl gethylt: Der erst für die anfahenden Schuler* (1536; 20th ed. by H. Mönkemeyer in Die Tabulatur, I, Hofheim am Taunus, 1965), *Ein newes Lautenbüchlein mit vil schonen Liedern* (1540), *Das erst Buch: Ein newes Lautenbüchlein mit vil feiner lieblichen Liedern für die jungen Schuler* (1544), *Das erst Buch: Ein newes Lautenbüchlein mit vil feiner lieblichen Liedern, für die jungen Schuler* (1547), and *Das ander Buch: Ein new künstlich Lauten Buch erst yetzo von newem gemacht für junge und alte Schuler* (1549).—**NS/LK/DM**

Neusidler, Melchior, distinguished German lutenist, intabulator, and composer, son of **Hans Neu-**

sidler; b. Nuremberg, 1531; d. Augsburg, 1590. Around 1551 he went to Augsburg, where he became a citizen in 1552. He was leader of the "stille musica," a group of musicians who played in the residences of the major members of the city; also performed with municipal musicians at public events. He was in Italy (1565–66), and also served as lutenist to Archduke Ferdinand II in Innsbruck (1580–81). His younger brother, Conrad Neusidler (b. Nuremberg [baptized], Feb. 13, 1541; d. Augsburg, c. 1604), was also a lutenist and composer; he went to Augsburg in 1562.

WORKS: INTABULATIONS FOR LUTE: *Il primo libro intabolatura di liuto di...Neysidler...ove sono madrigali, canzon francesi, pass'emezi, saltarelli & alcuni suoi ricercari* (Venice, 1566); *Il secondo libro intabolatura di liuto di Neysidler* (Venice, 1566); *Teütsch Lautenbuch, darinnenn künstliche Muteten, liebliche italienische, frantzösische, teutsch Stuck* (Strasbourg, 1574).—NS/LK/DM

Nevada (real name, Wixom), Emma,

noted American soprano, mother of **Mignon (Mathilde Marie) Nevada**; b. Alpha, near Nevada City, Calif., Feb. 7, 1859; d. Liverpool, June 20, 1940. She studied from 1877 with Marchesi in Vienna. She made her operatic debut as Amina at London's Her Majesty's Theatre (May 17, 1880); then sang in the leading Italian music centers, including Milan's La Scala (1881). Her first appearance in Paris was at the Opéra-Comique, May 17, 1883, as Zora in F. David's *Perle du Bresil*. During the 1884–85 season, she was a member of Col. Mapleson's company at the Academy of Music in N.Y., singing on alternate nights with Patti. She sang in Chicago at the Opera Festival in 1885, and again in 1889. She then sang mostly in Europe; retired in 1910.—NS/LK/DM

Nevada, Mignon (Mathilde Marie),

American soprano, daughter of **Emma Nevada**; b. Paris (of American parents), Aug. 14, 1886; d. Long Melford, England, June 25, 1971. She studied with her mother. She made her operatic debut at Rome's Teatro Costanzi as Rosina in *Il Barbiere di Siviglia* in 1907; then sang a season at the Teatro San Carlos in Lisbon; after a season at the Pergola Theater in Florence, she made her London debut at Covent Garden as Ophelia (Oct. 3, 1910), and sang there in subsequent seasons; also appeared at the Théâtre Royal de la Monnaie in Brussels, and at La Scala in Milan (1923). During World War II, she engaged in war work at Liverpool, England. From 1954 she lived in London.—NS/LK/DM

Neveu, Ginette,

brilliant French violinist; b. Paris, Aug. 11, 1919; d. in an airplane crash in San Miguel, Azores Islands, Oct. 28, 1949. She was a grandniece of **Charles-Marie Widor**. She studied with her mother, making her debut when she was 7 as soloist with the Colonne Orch. in Paris; after further studies at the Cons. there, she won the premier prix at age 11; then completed her training with Enesco and Flesch. She won the Wieniawski Competition (1935), and then embarked on an acclaimed career as a virtuoso, touring Poland and Germany that same year, the Soviet Union (1936), and the U.S. and Canada (1937). After the close of World War II, she made her London debut (1945); then appeared in South America, Boston, and N.Y. (1947). Her tragic death occurred on a flight to the U.S. for a concert tour; her brother, Jean-Paul, a talented pianist and her accompanist, also lost his life. Her performances were notable for their controlled and yet impassioned intensity, ably supported by a phenomenal technique.

BIBL.: M.-J. Ronze-Neveu, *G. N.: La Fulgurante Carrière d'une grande artiste* (Paris, 1952; Eng. tr., London, 1957).—NS/LK/DM

Neville, Chris,

jazz pianist, keyboardist; b. Boston, Oct. 15, 1955. He grew up in Boston and in West Bath, Maine; since 1987 he has lived in Boston. He studied at New England Cons. of Music (1962–71), Berklee Coll. of Music (1974–75), and Univ. of Maine–Augusta (1975–76). He performed and recorded with singer-songwriter David Mallet (1983–92) as well as leading his own groups and accompanying Dizzy Gillespie, Al Cohn, Sonny Stitt, Jimmy Heath and Richie Cole. He has worked in numerous musicals, including a yearlong tour with Donny Osmond in Andrew Lloyd Webber's *Joseph and the Amazing Technicolor Dreamcoat* (1995–96). His presence in the house band during Benny Carter's 1988 visit to Boston led to an ongoing musical relationship. He has recorded several albums with Carter, and toured with him from 1994, including dates in Japan (1995), N.Y.'s Lincoln Center, L.A., Germany, and Thailand (1996). In 1994 Carter produced and guested on Neville's debut album. Neville has also worked with the Artie Shaw Orch. (1992–95).

DISC.: *From the Greenhouse* (1994). Benny Carter: *Songbook Vol.2* (1997); *New York Nights* (1997). B. Carter and P. Woods: *My Man Benny, My Man Phil* (1990); *Harlem Renaissance* (1992); *Legends* (1993); *Another Time, Another Place* (1996); *Songbook* (1996).—LP

Neville Brothers, The,

prime musical forces in the New Orleans community for more than 30 years. **MEMBERSHIP:** Art Neville, kybd., voc. (b. New Orleans, La., Dec. 17, 1937); Aaron Neville, voc., perc. (b. New Orleans, La., Jan. 24, 1941); Charles Neville, sax., voc. (b. New Orleans, La., Dec. 28, 1938); Cyril Neville, perc., voc. (b. New Orleans, La., Jan. 10, 1948). Aaron's son Ivan Neville joined in 1979 for two years. **The Meters: MEMBERSHIP:** Art Neville, kybd.; Leo Nocentelli, gtr., voc. (b. New Orleans, La, June 15, 1946); George Porter, bs. (b. New Orleans, La., Dec. 26, 1947); Joe "Zigaboo" Modeliste, drm. (b. Dec. 28, 1948). Cyril Neville joined in 1975.

In the 1960s and 1970s Art Neville led the Meters, an influential band who appeared on many New Orleans recordings made at Allen Toussaint's famous studios. Meanwhile, brother Aaron had a major R&B hit with "Tell It Like It Is." Art and Aaron joined with brothers Charles and Cyril to form a family band in the late 1970s. The band achieved critical acclaim, if limited commercial success. Meanwhile, Aaron Neville was befriended by pop star Linda Ronstadt, who recorded a successful duet ("Don't Know Much") with the singer in 1989 and helped launch his new solo career in the early 1990s.

In the early 1950s keyboardist Art Neville joined the New Orleans group the Hawketts. In 1955 they scored a local hit with "Mardi Gras Mambo" and the song became the theme to the city's annual celebration. By that time his saxophonist brother Charles had been touring with jazz artists Tiny Grimes and George Coleman and blues artists Bobby "Blue" Bland and B. B. King. Through arranger-producer Harold Battiste, Art was signed to Specialty Records in 1956, and he and his brother Aaron worked with Larry Williams and played on package tours with the Spaniels and Screamin' Jay Hawkins. When Art was drafted into the Army in 1958, Aaron took his place in the Hawketts. Upon Art's return, Aaron launched a solo career, soon managing an R&B hit in 1960 with "Over You." At the end of 1966 Aaron Neville scored a top R&B and smash pop hit with "Tell It Like It Is" on Parlo Records. Also in that year, Aaron joined with Art and brother Charles, along with saxophonist Gary Brown and future Meters guitarist Leo Nocentelli, bassist George Porter, and drummer Joseph "Zigaboo" Modeliste, to form the Neville Sounds.

Producer Allen Toussaint hired the entire band, minus vocalists Art and Charles and Brown, to be the house band for his studio. They backed virtually every New Orleans hit of the late 1960s, including Ernie K-Doe's "Mother-in-Law," Betty Harris's "Cry to Me," and later Lee Dorsey's "Ride Your Pony," "Get Out My Life, Woman," and "Working in a Coal Mine." The Meters signed with Josie Records and recorded a number of instrumental albums, scoring smash R&B and major-to-moderate pop hits with "Sophisticated Cissy," "Cissy Strut," and "Look-Ka Py Py" in 1969. Meanwhile, Aaron, Cyril, and Brown played around New Orleans for seven years as the Soul Machine.

By 1972, with Art Neville and Leo Nocentelli taking up vocals, the Meters had signed with Reprise Records. However, their first two albums failed to sell, and it was not until 1975 that one of their albums, *Fire on the Bayou*, even charted. In the meantime, they backed Doctor John's *In the Right Place* album (which included the crossover hit "Right Place Wrong Time") and Labelle's *Nightbird* album (which included the top pop and R&B hit "Lady Marmalade"). Cyril Neville joined the Meters in 1975, and brothers Charles and Aaron contributed to the group from 1975 to 1977. The Meters opened shows for the Rolling Stones' 1975 American tour and summer 1976 European tour.

In 1976 the Meters and all four Neville brothers recorded an entire album of Mardi Gras music, backing uncle George "Big Chief Jolly" Landry and the Wild Tchoupitoulas, one of New Orleans's black Indian "tribes." In 1977 all four siblings left the Meters to form the Neville Brothers. They debuted to great acclaim with the Wild Tchoupitoulas at the 1977 Monterey Jazz Festival. They recorded one album for Capitol before switching to A&M for the excellent *Fiyo on the Bayou* album, which featured the Meters' "Hey Pocky Way" and "Fire on the Bayou," Jimmy Cliff's "Sitting in Limbo," the New Orleans classic medley "Brother John"/"Iko Iko," and "Mona Lisa," dedicated to Bette Midler.

In 1979 Aaron's son Ivan Neville joined the Neville brothers for two years. He later replaced Chaka Khan in Rufus for one album and toured with Bonnie Raitt for more than two years. He launched his solo career in 1988 with *If My Ancestors Could See Me Now*, which yielded a major hit with "Not Just Another Girl." In 1988 and again in 1992–1993 Ivan Neville toured and recorded with Keith Richards's X-Pensive Winos.

The Neville Brothers subsequently recorded the live set *Neville- ization* for the small Black Top label (reissued on Demon). In 1986 they played on the brief Amnesty International tour and opened for Huey Lewis and the News on tour. Recording *Uptown* for EMI with guests Jerry Garcia, Keith Richards, and Carlos Santana, the Neville brothers received a modicum of recognition with the 1987 compilation set *Treacherous*, released on Rhino. In 1988 they returned to A&M, where they recorded *Yellow Moon*, the best-selling album of their career, working with producer Daniel Lanois. It included Sam Cooke's "A Change Is Gonna Come," Cyril's "Sister Rosa," and "Voodoo."

In 1989–1990 Aaron Neville broke through into mass popularity thanks to Linda Ronstadt. He recorded four duets with her on her album *Cry Like a Rainstorm—Howl Like the Wind*. "Don't Know Much" and "All My Life" became smash pop and top easy-listening hits. Ronstadt coproduced Aaron's 1991 album *Warm Your Heart*, which yielded a near- smash pop and top easy-listening hit with "Everybody Plays the Fool." Meanwhile, the brothers released two other albums, 1990's *Brother's Keeper* and 1992's *Family Groove*.

After Aaron's solo career took off, Charles returned to jazz with the Diversity, while Cyril performed with his reggae band the Uptown All-Stars. Aaron reformed the Meters, replacing original member Modeliste with Russell Batiste in 1990; Nocentelli left the band in 1995, to be replaced by Brian Stoltz, who had previously toured with the Neville Brothers. In 1993 A&M Records issued Aaron Neville's *The Grand Tour*, and the Neville Brothers conducted an international tour that produced the excellent live set *Live on Planet Earth*.

DISC.: **THE NEVILLE BROTHERS:** *The N. B.* (1978); *Fiyo on the Bayou* (1981); *Neville-ization* (1984); *Treacherous: A History of the N. B. (1955–1985)* (1987); *Uptown* (1987); *Treacherous Too: A History of the N. B. (1955–1987)* (1991); *Yellow Moon* (1989); *Brother's Keeper* (1990); *Family Groove* (1992); *Live on Planet Earth* (1994). **ART NEVILLE:** *His Specialty Recordings: 1956–1958* (1993); *Mardi Gras Rock 'n' Roll* (1987). **AARON NEVILLE:** *Like It Is* (1967); *(reissued as) Tell It Like It Is* (1991); *Greatest Hits* (1990); *Golden Classics: Tell It Like It Is* (1988); *Orchid in the Storm* (1985); *The Classic: My Greatest Gift* (1990); *Warm Your Heart* (1991); *The Grand Tour* (1993); *The Tattooed Heart* (1995). **THE METERS:** *The Meters* (1969); *Look-Ka Py Py* (1970); *Struttin'* (1970); *Good Old Funky Music* (1990); *The Meters Jam* (1992); *Cabbage Alley* (1972); *Rejuvenation* (1974); *Fire on the Bayou* (1975); *Trick Bag* (1976); *New Directions* (1977); *Uptown Rulers: The Meters Live on the Queen Mary* (1992); *Funkify Your Life: The Meters Anthology* (1995). **THE WILD TCHOUPITOULAS:** *The Wild Tchoupitoulas* (1976). **IVAN NEVILLE:** *If My Ancestors Could See Me Now* (1988). **GEORGE PORTER:** *Runnin' Partner* (1990).—BH

Nevin, Arthur (Finley), American composer and pedagogue, brother of **Etherbert (Woodbridge) Nevin;** b. Edgeworth, Pa., April 27, 1871; d. Sewickley, Pa., July 10, 1943. He received musical training at home, mainly from his father, then at the New England Cons. of Music in Boston (1889–93). In 1893 he went to Berlin, where he studied piano with Klindworth and composition with Boise and Humperdinck. Returning to the U.S., he devoted himself to teaching, research, composition, and conducting. He lived with the Blackfoot Indians in Montana (summers, 1903 and 1904), and later wrote and lectured on his experiences. He was a prof. of music at the Univ. of Kansas (1915–20) and director of the municipal music dept. of Memphis, Tenn. (1920–22). In 1926 he settled in Sewickley as a private teacher.

WORKS: DRAMATIC: *A Night in Yaddo Land*, masque (1900); *Poia*, opera (Berlin, April 23, 1910); *A Daughter of the Forest*, opera (Chicago, Jan. 5, 1918). **OTHER:** 2 cantatas: *The Djinns* (N.Y., 1913) and *Roland*; *Bakawali Dances* for Orch.; 3 orch. suites, including *Lorna Doone* and *Love Dreams*; chamber music; piano pieces; songs.—**NS/LK/DM**

Nevin, Ethelbert (Woodbridge), popular American composer, brother of **Arthur (Finley) Nevin;** b. Edgeworth, Pa., Nov. 25, 1862; d. New Haven, Conn., Feb. 17, 1901. After preliminary musical studies in America, he went to Germany, where he took lessons in singing and piano with Franz Bohme in Dresden (1877–78); returning to the U.S., he studied piano with Benjamin J. Lang and harmony with Stephen A. Emery in Boston (1881–83). In 1884 he went again to Germany to study piano with Karl Klindworth in Berlin (1884–86). He then lived in Europe before finally settling in New Haven in 1897. He had a natural talent for melodious songs and piano pieces in a semi- Classical manner. His *The Rosary* (1898) achieved tremendous popularity, selling over a million copies within a decade. Another favorite was his song *Mighty Lak' a Rose* (1901), and his "Narcissus" from the piano suite *Water Scenes* (1891) was a perennial favorite in American parlors.

WORKS: *Floriane's Dream*, pantomime (N.Y., March 24, 1898); *The Quest*, cantata (1902); choruses; *Captive Memories*, song cycle for Baritone, 4 Voices, and Piano (1899); many other songs; piano suites: *Water Scenes* (1891), *Maggio in Toscana* (1896), and *A Day in Venice* (1898); other piano pieces; etc.

BIBL.: V. Thompson, *The Life of E. N.* (Boston, 1913); J. Howard, *E. N.* (N.Y., 1935).—**NS/LK/DM**

Neway, Patricia, American soprano; b. N.Y., Sept. 30, 1919. She was educated at Notre Dame Coll. for women; received vocal instruction from Morris Gesell, who later became her husband. She made her stage debut as Fiordiligi at the Chautauqua Festival in 1946. After several appearances in minor roles, she achieved her first significant success as Magda Sorel in Menotti's opera *The Consul* (Philadelphia, March 1, 1950); created the role of the Mother in another Menotti opera, *Maria Golovin*, at the Brussels World's Fair (Aug. 20, 1958). Her repertoire also included parts in operas by Berg and Britten.—**NS/LK/DM**

Newbould, Brian (Raby), English musicologist; b. Kettering, Feb. 26, 1936. He studied at the Univ. of Bristol (B.Mus., 1958; M.A., 1961). He was a lecturer at the Royal Scottish Academy of Music in Glasgow (1960–65) and at the Univ. of Leeds (1965–79). Newbould became prof. of music and head of the music dept. at the Univ. of Hull in 1979. He prepared effective realizations of Schubert's Sym. No. 7, D.729, and Sym. No. "10," D.936a. He also completed the scherzo and trio of Schubert's Sym. No. 8, D.759, "Unfinished."

WRITINGS: *Schubert and the Symphony: A New Perspective* (Surbiton, 1992); *Schubert, the Music and the Man* (Berkeley and Los Angeles, 1997); ed. *Schubert Studies* (Aldershot, 1998).—**NS/LK/DM**

New Christy Minstrels, The, American folk group. The New Christy Minstrels were a nine- or ten-member choral and instrumental group that played folk music primarily popular in the early 1960s. Led by Randy Sparks and featuring Barry McGuire, they performed in an earnest, commercial style resulting in a series of successful recordings, including the single "Green, Green" and the albums *The Early Years: The Complete Liberty Recordings Plus More* (rec. 1960s; rel. 1994); *Ramblin'* and *Today*, as well as television appearances and live performances.

Randy Sparks (b. Leavenworth, Kans., July 29, 1933) was a folk singer-songwriter and leader of The Randy Sparks Trio, which also included his wife, Jackie Miller, and Nick Woods, when he put together The New Christy Minstrels (named after the 19th-century Christy Minstrels led by Edwin P. Christy, remembered for performing the songs of Stephen Foster) in the fall of 1961. Starting with his own group, which also included backup banjo player Billy Cudmore, Sparks added another trio, The Inn Group, consisting of Karol Dugan, John Forsha, and Jerry Yester (later of The Modern Folk Quartet and The Lovin' Spoonful), as well as blues singer Terry Wadsworth and Dolan Ellis. Art Podell joined a little later.

Sparks signed this ten-member group to Columbia Records and recorded a debut album, *Presenting the New Christy Minstrels*, in April 1962. This was a studio-only ensemble, but at the behest of Columbia, Sparks organized a permanent, performing version. Sparks, Miller, Woods, Ellis, and Podell stayed on, joined by the folk duo Barry and Barry, consisting of Barry McGuire (b. Oklahoma City, Okla., Oct. 15, 1937) and Barry Kane, Peggy Connelly, Larry Ramos, and Clarence Treat. This group debuted at the Troubadour nightclub in Hollywood in July 1962. Sparks also took on business managers George Greif and Sid Garris as partners.

The New Christy Minstrels were regulars on *The Andy Williams Show* during the 1962–63 television season, beginning in September. In October, *Presenting the New Christy Minstrels* entered the charts, remaining listed more than 21 months. Also that month Connelly left, replaced by Gayle Caldwell. The group's second album, a live release called *The New Christy Minstrels in Person*, entered the charts in February 1963; their third, *Tall Tales! Legends and Nonsense*, entered in May. That month also saw them win the 1962 Grammy for Best Performance by a Chorus for their first album, which also was nominated for Best Folk Recording., while the group got a Best New Artist nomination. Also in May, Sparks retired from performing with the group, though he continued to direct it.

Dolan Ellis left the New Christy Minstrels in June 1963 and was replaced by Gene Clark. That month their single "Green, Green" (music and lyrics by Barry McGuire and Randy Sparks), on which McGuire sang lead, entered the charts, on its way to a peak in the Top 40 in August, the month that their highest charting album, *Ramblin' Featuring Green, Green*, reached the charts for a run of almost a year and a half, during which it was certified gold. It earned Grammy nominations for Best Folk Recording and Best Performance by a Chorus. The group earned its second Top 40 hit with "Saturday Night" (music and lyrics by Randy Sparks), which peaked in the charts in November. Their *Merry Christmas!* album came out for the holiday season.

Sparks wrote the songs and score for the film *Advance to the Rear*, which opened in April 1964. That month the New Christy Minstrels's sixth album, *Today*, containing songs from the film, reached the charts on its way to the Top Ten; the LP earned a Grammy nomination for Best Folk Recording. "Today" (music and lyrics by Randy Sparks) peaked in the Top 40 in June. Meanwhile, there had been more personnel changes, as Miller, Caldwell, and Clark left (Clark to join The Byrds) in February and were replaced by Ann White, Karen Gunderson, and Paul Potash.

In July 1964, Randy Sparks sold out his interest in The New Christy Minstrels to George Greif and Sid Garris. In August and September the group appeared on its own summer TV series, *The New Christy Minstrels Show*, while their seventh album, *Land of Giants*, reached the charts. In December they recorded the more pop-oriented "Chim Chim Cheree" (music and lyrics by Richard M. Sherman and Robert B. Sherman) from the film *Mary Poppins*; it became their final chart single. They toured Europe successfully in January 1965, after which McGuire and Potash left, to be replaced by Mike Whalen and Bob Buchanan. (McGuire's solo recording, "Eve of Destruction" [music and lyrics by Steve Barri and P. F. Sloan] became a #1 hit in September.)

The New Christy Minstrels suffered a commercial disappointment with their eighth album, *Cowboys and Indians*, which reached the charts in February 1965, but their ninth, *Chim Chim Cheree*, in the charts in June, was more successful and earned them another Grammy nomination for Best Performance by a Chorus. By this point, however, personnel changes were becoming rapid, and the group's tenth album, *The Wandering Minstrels*, barely reached the charts.

The New Christy Minstrels continued to perform into the 1980s, and even got back into the charts briefly in 1970 with *You Need Someone to Love*, released on Greif and Garris's Gregar label. But they are primarily remembered after their heyday as a launching pad for talent. Notably, Larry Ramos, who left in January 1966, became a prominent member of The Association. His replacement, Mike Settle (b. Tulsa, Okla., March 20, 1941), left the group a year later with three other replacement members, Kenny (Kenneth Donald) Rogers

(b. Houston, Tex., Aug. 21, 1938), Thelma Camacho, and Terry Williams (b. Hollywood, Calif., June 6, 1947), to form the First Edition, which recorded successfully and from which Rogers later emerged as a solo star.—**WR**

New Edition, the teen vocal group that spawned some of the biggest R&B acts of the 1980s and 1990s; f. 1981, Boston, Mass. **MEMBERSHIP:** Bobby Brown (b. Feb. 5, 1969); Ralph Tresvant (b. May 16, 1968); Michael Bivins (b. Aug. 10, 1968); Ricky Bell (b. Sept. 18, 1967); and Ronnie Devoe (b. Nov. 17, 1967).

All the members of New Edition grew up together in the Roxbury section of Boston. Brown was convinced they could sing their way out of the projects "and onto *Soul Train*," and they performed in talent shows into their early teens. At one of these shows, Boston-based music entrepreneur Maurice Starr signed on to manage and produce them. The result was the 1983 R&B hit "Candy Girl," a pastiche of Jackson Five harmonies and hip-hop beats, released on independent Streetwise records, better known for rap than soul. Their follow-up album spun off another R&B Top Ten single, "Is This the End." The singles and album sold well enough to come to the attention of MCA records, who signed the group.

Their self-titled 1984 major label debut kicked off with the R&B chart topper "Cool It Now," which went gold and hit #4 on the pop charts. The album went double platinum and hit #6 on the charts, spinning off another R&B chart topper, "Mr. Telephone Man" (#12 pop), in early 1985.

The group's next album, *All for Love*, didn't fare so well, only going platinum. Neither "Lost in Love" nor "A Little Bit of Love (Is All It Takes)" broke the Top 30. Brown left the group for a solo career. As a quartet, they recorded in 1986 *Under a Blue Moon*, an album of doo-wop covers, including a version of "Earth Angel" that landed in the film *The Karate Kid II*, topping out at #21.

The group replaced Brown with Johnny Gill (b. May 22, 1966, Washington, D.C.). Gill had performed since he was five in a family gospel group, Wings of Faith. Brought to Atlantic by soul singer Stacy Lattislaw, by 1983, when New Edition was charting "Candy Girl," he had a Top 30 R&B single "Super Love." "Perfect Combination," a duet with Lattislaw, went Top Ten R&B a year later. He had a couple of R&B albums under his belt, as well.

This new New Edition recorded *Heart Break* in 1988 with producers Terry Lewis and Jimmy "Jam" Harris. The album went to #12 with the hit "If It Isn't Love" rising to #7. However Bell, Bivens and Devoe felt dissatisfied, believing the group treated them like backing vocalists. They took their trio out from behind Brown, Tresvant, and then Gill, forming the group Bell Biv Devoe. They worked with some of the best producers available, including Harris and Lewis and Hank Shocklee. Their 1990 album *Poison* spent over a year on the charts, selling three million copies, with the platinum title-track single topping the R&B chart and hitting #3 pop. The single "Do Me" also hit #3, while "BBD (I Thought It Was Me)" topped the R&B chart, but only hit #26 pop. The album spawned a gold remix album

WBBD—Bootcity! that hit #18 in 1991. They topped the R&B charts again, and hit #10 pop, with 1992's "The Best Things in Life Are Free," a tune from the film *Mo Money* that paired them with Luther Vandross, Janet Jackson, and their old bandmate Ralph Tresvant.

Tresvant became the last member of the group to record a solo record in 1990. His self-titled album went platinum, hitting #17 on the strength of the #1 R&B (#4 pop) single "Sensitivity," as well as the #34 "Stone Cold Gentlemen" (which featured Brown rapping a break). Gill also scored a solo hit in 1990 with his self-titled album for Motown. The album went double platinum and rose to #8 with R&B chart toppers like the gold "Rub You The Right Way" (#3 pop) and "My, My My" (#10 pop), as well as "Fairweather Friend" (#28 pop).

Subsequent solo recordings had far less spectacular sales. Gill's 1993 *Provacative* only went gold, topping out at #14. Similarly, BBD's 1993 *Hootie Mack* went gold and hit #19. Tresvant's 1994 *It's Goin' Down* didn't even sell that well, topping out at #131. Perhaps because of their failure to generate excitement on their own, the original quintet and Gill got back together and cut the 1996 *Home Again* album, which topped the charts. The singles "Hit Me Off" charted at #3, "I'm Still in Love with You" topped out at #7 and "One More Day," #61. All the members then returned to their solo careers, though they frequently intersected with Bell Biv Devoe, touring with Gill, and so forth.

DISC.: *Candy Girl* (1983); *New Edition* (1984); *Christmas All over the World* (1985); *All for Love* (1985); *Under the Blue Moon* (1986); *Heart Break* (1989); *Vol. 1—Greatest Hits* (1991); *Home Again* (1996); *Lost in Love—Best of Slow Jams* (1998). **BELL BIV DEVOE:** *Poison* (1990); *WBBD—Bootcity!* (remix album; 1991); *Hootie Mack* (1993); *New Edition's Solo Hits* (1996). **RALPH TRESVANT:** *Ralph Tresvant* (1990); *It's Goin' Down* (1994). **JOHNNY GILL:** *Chemistry* (1985); *Provocative* (1993); *Let's Get the Mood Right* (1996); *Johnny Gill* (1983).—HB

Newlin, Dika, American writer on music and composer; b. Portland, Ore., Nov. 22, 1923. She studied piano and theory at Mich. State Univ. (B.A., 1939) and at the Univ. of Calif. at Los Angeles (M.A., 1941), and later took courses at Columbia Univ. in N.Y. (Ph.D., 1945, with the diss. *Bruckner- Mahler-Schoenberg*; publ. in N.Y., 1947; 2nd ed., rev., 1978); concurrently received instruction in composition from Farwell, Schoenberg, and Sessions, and in piano from Serkin and A. Schnabel. She taught at Western Maryland Coll. (1945–49), Syracuse Univ. (1949–51), Drew Univ. (1952–65), North Tex. State Univ. (1965–73), and Va. Commonwealth Univ. (from 1978). She ed. and tr. several books by and about Schoenberg, and also publ. *Schoenberg Remembered: Diaries and Recollections, 1938–1976* (N.Y., 1980). Her compositions follow the Schoenbergian idiom and include 3 operas, a Sym. for Chorus and Orch., a Piano Concerto, chamber music, piano pieces, and songs.

BIBL.: T. Albrecht, ed., *D. Caecilia: Essays for D. N., November 22, 1988* (Kansas City, Mo., 1988).—NS/LK/DM

Newman, Alfred, American film composer and conductor; b. New Haven, Conn., March 17, 1900; d. Los Angeles, Feb. 17, 1970. He was the uncle of the well-known popular singer, pianist, and songwriter Randy Newman (b. Los Angeles, Nov. 28, 1943). He studied piano with Sigismund Stojowski and composition with Rubin Goldmark; also had private lessons with Schoenberg in Los Angeles. He began his career in vaudeville shows billed as "The Marvelous Boy Pianist"; later, when he led theater orchs. on Broadway, he was hailed as "The Boy Conductor" and "The Youngest Conductor in the U.S." In 1930 he went to Hollywood and devoted himself entirely to writing film music; he wrote scores for about 230 films, 45 of which were nominated for Academy Awards and 9 were winners. Among his most successful scores were *The Prisoner of Zenda* (1937), *The Hunchback of Notre Dame* (1939), *Wuthering Heights* (1939), *Captain from Castille* (1947), *The Robe* (1953), and *The Egyptian* (1954; partly written by the original assignee, Bernard Herrmann). Stylistically, Newman followed an eclectic type of theatrical Romanticism, often mimicking, almost literally, the most popular works of Tchaikovsky, Rachmaninoff, Wagner, and Liszt, and amalgamating these elements in colorful free fantasia.

BIBL.: F. Steiner, *The Making of an American Film Composer: A Study of A. N.'s Music in the First Decade of the Sound Era* (diss., Univ. of Southern Calif., 1981).—NS/LK/DM

Newman, Anthony, multifaceted American organist, harpsichordist, fortepianist, conductor, and composer; b. Los Angeles, May 12, 1941. He received keyboard training before pursuing studies in Paris with Cortot, Boulanger, and Cochereau, receiving a diplome superieur from the École Normale de Musique. Following further studies at the Mannes Coll. of Music in N.Y. (B.S., 1962) and composition with Kirchner and Berio at Harvard Univ. (M.A., 1963), he completed his education at Boston Univ. (D.M.A., 1966). In 1967 he made his professional debut in a pedal harpsichord recital at N.Y.'s Carnegie Hall, and subsequently toured extensively in the U.S. and abroad as both a keyboard player and conductor. He also was active as conductor of his own period-instrument orch., the Brandenburg Collegium. After teaching at the Juilliard School in N.Y. (1968–73), he was on the faculty of the State Univ. of N.Y. at Purchase (from 1975), where he later was head of its graduate program in music. He also taught at the Indiana Univ. School of Music in Bloomington (1978–81) and gave master classes. Newman's dedication to community outreach programs led him to organize and serve as director of Hands on Outreach, which provides food to the indigent. He publ. the books *Bach and the Baroque: A Performing Guide with Special Emphasis on the Music of J. S. Bach* (1985; 2nd ed., rev., 1994) and *How Music is Composed: Models in Composition* (1995).

WORKS: DRAMATIC: Opera: *Nicole and the Trial of the Century* (1998). **ORCH.:** Violin Concerto (Indianapolis, Oct. 26, 1979); Concerto for Viola or Clarinet, Strings, Piano, and Timpani (1985); *On Fallen Heroes,* symphonic poem (1988); Piano Concerto (1989); Organ Concerto (1994; Englewood, N.J., Feb. 23, 1995); Concerto for Harpsichord, Oboe, and Strings (reconstruction of J. S. Bach's BWV 1059; Seattle, April 15, 1998); 2 syms.: No. 1, *American Classic* (1999) and No. 2 (1999). **CHAMBER:** Cello Sonata (1978); Violin Sonata (1980); *Introduction and Toccata* for Flute and Piano (1983); Piano Quintet

(1983; rev. 1995); Suite for Flute and Guitar (1985); Sonata for Viola or Clarinet and Piano (1986); String Quartet (1994); *Variations and Toccata* for Violin (1994); Trio for Violin, Cello, and Piano (1995); Bassoon Sonata (1995); Sonata for Oboe or Clarinet and Piano (1997). **KEYBOARD: Piano:** *Variations and Fugue on "BACH"* (1992); *Sonata of the Americas* (1992); *The Equal Tempered Pianoforte*, 12 preludes and fugues (1992); *Toccata and Fugue* (1995). **Harpsichord:** *Chimaeras* (1968); Suite (1989). **Organ:** 2 syms. (1985, 1991); *Concert Etude* (1990); *Preludes and Fugues* (2 vols., 1991, 1994); *Toccata and Fugue on B-A-C-H* (1999). **Guitar:** *Prelude and Grand Contrapunctus* (1989); Suite (1990); *Ride the Wind Horse* (1992). **VOCAL:** *Grand Hymns of Awakening* for Soloists, Chorus, and Orch. (1984); *Lives and Times of Angels*, oratorio (Mt. Kisco, N.Y., April 26, 1998); choruses; songs.—NS/LK/DM

Newman, Ernest (real name, William Roberts),

renowned English music critic and writer on music; b. Everton, Lancashire, Nov. 30, 1868; d. Tadworth, Surrey, July 7, 1959. He was educated at Liverpool Coll. and the Univ. of Liverpool. While employed as a bank clerk (1889–1904), he pursued various studies on his own and began to publ. books on music; assumed his *nom de plume* to symbolize an "earnest new man." In 1904 he accepted an instructorship in Birmingham's Midland Inst., and took up music as a profession; in 1905–06 he was in Manchester as critic of the *Guardian;* from 1906 to 1918 he was in Birmingham as critic for the *Daily Post;* in 1919–20 he was in London as critic for the *Observer;* from 1920 to 1958 he was on the staff of the *London Sunday Times;* from 1923 he was also a contributor to the *Glasgow Herald;* in 1924–25, was guest critic of the *N.Y. Evening Post.* One of the best equipped and most influential of English music critics, Newman continued to write his regular column in the *Sunday Times* in his 90th year.

WRITINGS (all publ. in London unless otherwise given): *Gluck and the Opera* (1895); *A Study of Wagner* (1899); *Wagner* (1904); *Musical Studies* (1905; 3rd ed., 1914); *Elgar* (1906); *Hugo Wolf* (1907); *Richard Strauss* (1908); *Wagner as Man and Artist* (1914; 2nd ed., 1924); *A Musical Motley* (1919); *The Piano-Player and Its Music* (1920); *Confessions of a Musical Critic* (1923); *Solo Singing* (1923); *A Musical Critic's Holiday* (1925); *The Unconscious Beethoven* (1927); *What to Read on the Evolution of Music* (1928); *Stories of the Great Operas* (3 vols., 1929–31); *Fact and Fiction about Wagner* (1931); *The Man Liszt* (1934); *The Life of Richard Wagner* (4 vols., 1933, 1937, 1941, 1946); *Opera Nights* (1943; U.S. ed. as *More Stories of Famous Operas*); *Wagner Nights* (1949; U.S. ed. as *The Wagner Operas*); *More Opera Nights* (1954; U.S. ed. as *17 Famous Operas*); *From the World of Music: Essays from "The Sunday Times"* (selected by F. Aprahamian; London, 1956); *More Musical Essays* (second selection from the *Sunday Times,* London, 1958); *Testament of Music* (selected essays; 1962); *Berlioz, Romantic Classic* (ed. by P. Heyworth; 1972).

BIBL.: H. van Thal, ed., *Fanfare for E. N.* (London, 1955); V. Newman, *E. N.: A Memoir by His Wife* (London, 1963).
—NS/LK/DM

Newman, Randy,

one of the most fascinating and distinctive singer-songwriters to emerge in the late 1960s; b. New Orleans, La., Nov. 28, 1943. Randy Newman achieved his first recognition when Judy Collins recorded his "I Think It's Gonna Rain Today" on her 1966 album *In My Life.* Recording his first album in 1968, Newman attracted the attention of musicians and critics and developed a cult following with his songs: alternately cynical, ironic, whimsical, and sarcastic but which nonetheless retained a deep-seated sense of humanity. Writing and recording classics such as "Living without You," "Mama Told Me Not to Come," "Political Science," and "Sail Away," Randy Newman eventually broke through to a wider audience with 1974's *Good Old Boys,* and scored his biggest commercial success with 1977's *Little Criminals,* largely on the basis of the controversy stirred by its smash hit, "Short People." Never a prolific writer, Newman concentrated on film soundtracks through the 1980s and 1990s.

Randy Newman moved with his family to Los Angeles at age five. Highly influenced by uncles Emil, Alfred, and Lionel, who composed film scores, he began playing piano at age six and studied music theory as a child. By the age of 16, while still in high school, Newman worked as a songwriter at Metric Music, a subsidiary of Liberty Records, whose board chairman was the father of his boyhood friend Lenny Waronker (who would become president of Warner Bros. Records). In the early 1960s Newman recorded demonstration tapes with session players such as Glen Campbell and Leon Russell while attending UCLA as a music major. He wrote songs for Schroeder Music; the Fleetwoods ("Come Softly to Me") recorded his "They Tell Me It's Summer" as the flip side of their moderate 1962 hit "Lovers by Night, Strangers by Day." In 1965 he scored the music for *Peyton Place,* television's first hit nighttime soap opera, and a year later Judy Collins included his tender "I Think It's Gonna Rain Today" on her *In My Life* album.

In 1967 Randy Newman began working as a session arranger at Warner Bros., and he signed his own record contract with the label's Reprise subsidiary by 1968. Recorded with an orchestra playing his arrangements under producers Lenny Waronker and Van Dyke Parks, his eponymous debut album featured "I Think It's Gonna Rain Today" and the touching "Living without You," as well as the American profile "Beehive State" and the satirical "Davy, the Fat Boy." However, despite critical acclaim, the album sold so poorly that Reprise later gave away copies as a promotional gimmick. Newman's second album, *12 Songs,* also enjoyed critical success but commercial failure. Produced by Waronker and recorded with guitarists Ry Cooder and Clarence White, the album included the wry "Yellow Man" and "Mama Told Me Not to Come," a top hit for Three Dog Night in 1970. That year Newman began performing live occasionally, usually unaccompanied, and an engagement at N.Y.'s Bitter End resulted in 1971's *Live.* In 1970 Harry Nilsson released an entire album of Newman songs.

In 1972 Randy Newman debuted *Sail Away* with the N.Y. Philharmonic. The album, generally regarded as his definitive work, includes the melodic title song, his satirical solution to the world's problems; "Political Science"; the sexual spoof "You Can Leave Your Hat On"; and the sarcastic "God's Song (That's Why I Love Mankind)." Newman's first modest album success came with *Good Old Boys*, which was debuted with the Atlanta Symphony Orch. and supported by a 20-city tour. Concerned in a vaguely conceptual way with the American South, the album contained "Birmingham" and "Louisiana 1927" as well as his sly attack on southern lower-class morality, "Rednecks," plus "Naked Man" and "Back on My Feet Again." The song "Rednecks" sparked a minor controversy with its repeated use of the word "nigger."

Generally inactive for more than two years, Randy Newman reemerged in 1977 with *Little Criminals*. The album yielded a smash hit with "Short People," his satirical assault on prejudice that some myopic listeners misconstrued as an affront to small-statured people, resulting in the song's banishment by some radio stations. The album also featured "Rider in the Rain," a minor country hit recorded with Glenn Frey and Timothy Schmit of the Eagles. The success of *Little Criminals* was probably due more to the controversy over "Short People" than to anything else, as 1979's *Born Again* sold only modestly even though it featured more fine songs like "It's Money I Love," "The Story of a Rock and Roll Band," and "Mr. Sheep."

In 1981 Randy Newman composed and performed the score for the movie *Ragtime*, based on E. L. Doctorow's best-selling novel. He recorded his next album, *Trouble in Paradise*, with Bob Seger, Don Henley, Linda Ronstadt, and Paul Simon, and the album yielded a minor hit with the Newman-Simon duet "The Blues"; it also contained "I Love L.A." (later used as a commercial jingle by Nike shoes), "My Life Is Good," "Real Emotional Girl," and the scathing "Christmas in Capetown." Newman toured for the first time in three years in 1983 and played 40 concerts in 1984 with James Taylor. In 1985 he cowrote the script to the Steve Martin–Martin Short–Chevy Chase comedy western *Three Amigos* with Martin and Lorne Michaels (producer of *Saturday Night Live*), and he composed three songs for the movie.

His next album, 1988's *Land of Dreams*, was produced by and recorded with guitarist Mark Knopfler of Dire Straits. The album included "Follow the Flag" and "Roll with the Punches," plus, for the first time, three autobiographical songs—"New Orleans Before the War," "Dixie Flyer," and "Four Eyes"—while yielding a minor hit with "It's Money that Matters." Newman toured in support of the album and subsequently composed and performed the scores to the movies *Parenthood*, *Avalon*, *Awakenings*, *The Paper*, and *Maverick*. In 1995 Reprise Records issued Randy Newman's full-length musical version of *Faust*, featuring performances by Linda Ronstadt, James Taylor, Bonnie Raitt, and Don Henley, with Newman himself portraying the Devil. Receiving critical accolades, the album did little on the commercial charts.

DISC.: THE RANDY NEWMAN ORCHESTRA: *Original Music from "Peyton Place"* (1965). **RANDY NEWMAN:** *R. N.* (1968); *12 Songs* (1970); *Live* (1971); *Sail Away* (1972); *Good Old Boys* (1974); *Little Criminals* (1977); *Born Again* (1979); *Trouble in Paradise* (1983); *The Natural* (soundtrack; 1984);

Land of Dreams (1988); *Parenthood* (soundtrack; 1989); *Avalon* (soundtrack; 1990); *Awakenings* (soundtrack; 1991); *The Paper* (soundtrack; 1994); *Maverick* (soundtrack; 1995); *Faust* (1995).
—**BH**

Newman, William S(tein), distinguished American music scholar; b. Cleveland, April 6, 1912. He studied piano with Riemenschneider and Arthur Loesser and composition with Elwell and Shepherd in Cleveland, receiving his Ph.D. at Western Reserve Univ. in 1939 with the diss. *The Present Trend of the Sonata Idea*; then pursued postdoctoral studies with Lang and Hertzmann at Columbia Univ. in 1940. During World War II, he served in the U.S. Army Air Force Intelligence. From 1945 to 1970 he taught at the Univ. of North Carolina at Chapel Hill; became prof. emeritus in 1976. He focused most of his research on the evolution of the instrumental sonata. His chief project was *A History of the Sonata Idea* (Chapel Hill; Vol. I, *The Sonata in the Baroque Era*, 1959; 4th ed., rev., 1983; Vol. II, *The Sonata in the Classic Era*, 1963; 3rd ed., rev., 1983; Vol. III, *The Sonata since Beethoven*, 1969; 3rd ed., rev., 1983). He also publ. *The Pianist's Problems* (N.Y., 1950; 4th ed., 1984), *Understanding Music* (N.Y., 1953; 3rd ed., rev., 1967), *Performance Practices in Beethoven's Piano Sonatas* (N.Y., 1971), and *Beethoven on Beethoven: Playing His Piano Music His Way* (N.Y. and London, 1989). He contributed articles to various reference works and music journals.
—**NS/LK/DM**

Newmarch, Rosa (Harriet née **Jeaffreson),** English writer on music; b. Leamington, Dec. 18, 1857; d. Worthing, April 9, 1940. Growing up in an artistic atmosphere, she entered the Hetherley School of Art to study painting, but after a time abandoned that career for literary pursuits; settled in London in 1880 as a contributor to various journals. There she married Henry Charles Newmarch in 1883. She visited Russia in 1897 and many times afterward; established contact with the foremost musicians there; her enthusiasm for Russian music, particularly that of the Russian national school of composition, was unlimited, and she publ. several books on the subject which were of importance to the appreciation of Russian music in England, though her high-pitched literary manner was sometimes maintained to the detriment of factual material.

WRITINGS (all publ. in London unless otherwise given): *Tchaikovsky: His Life and Works* (1900; 2nd ed., 1908, ed. by E. Evans); *Henry J. Wood* (1904); *The Russian Opera* (1914); *A Quarter of a Century of Promenade Concerts at Queen's Hall* (1928); *The Concert-goer's Library of Descriptive Notes* (6 vols., 1928–48); *The Music of Czechoslovakia* (Oxford, 1942); *Jean Sibelius* (1944).
—**NS/LK/DM**

Newmark, John (real name, Hans Joseph Neumark), German-born Canadian pianist; b. Bremen, June 12, 1904; d. Montreal, Oct. 17, 1991. He studied piano with Karl Boerner in Bremen (1912–19) and Annie Eisele in Leipzig (1920–21). He began his career as an accompanist to Szymon Goldberg (1925); with August Wenzinger, he founded the Neue Kammermusik society in Bremen for the performance of modern music (1929); was director of music programs for the Bremen Radio (1930–33). After going to London (1939), he was interned as an alien (1940), and sent to Canada; after his release, he studied harmony and conducting with Mazzoleni in Toronto (1942). Following World War II, he pursued a far-flung career as an accompanist, traveling all over the world with the most celebrated artists of the day. He became a naturalized Canadian citizen in 1946, and in 1974 was made an Officer of the Order of Canada.—NS/LK/DM

Newton, Frankie (actually, **William Frank**), jazz trumpeter; b. Emory, Va., Jan. 4, 1906; d. N.Y., March 11, 1954. He moved to N.Y. after having toured the West Coast in the early and mid-1920s. From 1927–30 he worked mainly with Lloyd and then Cecil Scott in N.Y. and on tours, then worked around N.Y. with Chick Webb, Charlie Johnson, Elmer Snowden, and Sam Wooding. He recorded with Bessie Smith in 1933, and worked with Charlie Johnson from c. September 1933 until entering hospital in late 1935. After a brief return to Charlie Johnson, he played with Teddy Hill from spring 1936 until spring 1937. Complications followed a tonsillectomy sidetracked him in May 1937. He worked with John Kirby from July until September 1937, when he was sidelined by a back injury. From December 1937 until February 1938 he was with Lucky Millinder, then primarily led his own bands which he led mostly in N.Y. and Boston from the end of 1938 until about 1951. He also freelanced with James P. Johnson, Sid Catlett and Edmond Hall. In summer 1948 he suffered a serious setback when his home (and trumpet) were lost in a fire. In last years of his life did little regular playing, lived in Greenwich Village, devoting considerable time to painting and politics.

DISC.: B. Smith: "Gimme a Pigfoot." M. Mezzrow: "Mutiny in the Parlor."—JC/LP

Newton, Ivor, English pianist; b. London, Dec. 15, 1892; d. there, April 21, 1981. He studied piano with Arthur Barclay; then went to Berlin, where he studied lieder with Zur Muhlen and the art of accompaniment with Conraad van Bos. An earnest student of the history of song and the proper role of accompaniment, Newton became one of the most appreciated piano accompanists of his time, playing at recitals with celebrated singers and instrumentalists, among them Dame Nellie Melba, John McCormack, Fyodor Chaliapin, Kirsten Flagstad, Pablo Casals, Yehudi Menuhin, and Maria Callas. His career, which spanned more than 60 years, is chronicled in his interesting autobiography, *At the Piano-Ivor Newton* (London, 1966). In 1973 he was made a Commander of the Order of the British Empire.—NS/LK/DM

New York Dolls, progenitors of punk and "hair metal," the most important band that most people never heard; f. 1972. **MEMBERSHIP:** David Johansen, voc. (b. Staten Island, N.Y., Jan. 9, 1950); Sylvain Sylvain (real name, Sil Myzrahi), gtr. (b. Cairo, Egypt, 1953); Johnny Thunders (real name, John Anthony Genzale Jr.), gtr. (b., N.Y., July 15, 1952; d. New Orleans, La., April 23, 1991);

Arthur Howard Kane, bs. (b. Feb. 3, 1951); Jerry Nolan, drm. (b. N.Y., May 7, 1951; d. there, Jan. 14, 1992).

Despite two acclaimed and influential records, The New York Dolls never sold very well. It might have been their sound, which teetered dangerously on the edge of chaos, without going over (too often). It might have been their attire: They wore dresses, makeup, and platform shoes. However, many who heard and experienced the band, from Malcolm McLaren to the members of Poison, claim it changed their lives.

Sil Myzrahi came to America from Egypt after the 1956 Arab-versus-Israel war made Cairo untenable for Egyptian Jews. By the late 1960s, he was designing clothes and playing rock with his schoolmate, Billy Murcia, drm. (b. N.Y., 1951; d. London, England, Nov. 6, 1972). Their band, the Pox, recorded one never-released album. The sweaters they designed, however, were enormously popular, allowing the pair to take trips to England. There, they took in the burgeoning glam-rock scene.

After lapping up the British scene, the duo returned to N.Y. Another ex-schoolmate, Johnny Genzale, then known as Johnny Volume, joined the band. When the trio were reunited, they met under a sign for the New York Dolls Hospital (a place where they repaired valuable toys), and the three decided that the name was too cool for school. Volume became Thunders; and singer David Johansen and bassist Arthur Kane were enlisted to fill out the crew.

David Johansen's father was a light opera singer who sold insurance to pay the bills. As a teen he hooked up with The Ridiculous Theater company, introducing him to flamboyant theatrics, which would become Johansen's calling-card as a performer.

The Dolls quickly became the toast of the Mercer Arts Center and Max's Kansas City, two influential downtown N.Y. nightspots. They were beloved as much for their trashy, campy appearance as for their Rolling-Stones-run-amok music. During their first tour of England, Murcia died of asphyxiation after mixing pills and alcohol, a sign of the kind of overindulgence that would plague band members for years to come. Jerry Nolan replaced him.

Mercury signed the band. In 1973, Todd Rundgren produced their eponymous debut and, a year later, legendary Girl Group producer George "Shadow" Morton tackled their sophomore effort, *In Too Much Too Soon*. Despite great songs like "Trash" and "Personality Crisis," The Dolls were too far ahead of the curve for radio, which roundly ignored the band, as did all but a cult following of musicians and critics. Thunders and Nolan left the band to form The Heartbreakers, leaving Sylvain and Johansen to carry on as The Dolls until 1977.

Many of The Dolls had substance-abuse problems. The group would call on roadie Peter Jordan to play bass when Kane was too drunk. Thunders became such a notorious heroin addict, it became part of his act: Would he be too swacked to play on any given night?

Sylvain recorded a solo album in 1977, and when it didn't take off, his record company dropped him. Almost simultaneously, he got divorced. He drove a cab for a while, then went back to clothing design, playing only occasionally.

The Heartbreakers earned a cult following, touring as frequently as Thunder's health permitted, and recording several uneven albums. In 1991, Thunders died under mysterious circumstances in New Orleans, presumably of an overdose. Nolan died a year later of complications from pneumonia and meningitis.

The most successful of the ex-Dolls was Johansen, who went solo in 1978, although it took a fluke to launch his career. His eponymous solo debut featured such pop gems as "Funky But Chic" and "Frenchette" but again was not a mighty seller. He continued to attract crowds but, by the mid-1980s, after several more critically acclaimed albums that didn't sell, he started to get tired of the grind of the road and singing for crowds that seemed to stay 19, even as he pushed into his thirties. He once described the sight of fist-pumping, post-adolescents at a concert as reminding him of a Nazi Youth rally.

Seeking something new, Johnasen started playing one night a week at the N.Y. club Tramps, singing the old jump blues, early R&B, and Caribbean music that had captured his fancy at the time. To avoid confusion, he booked the shows as Buster Poindexter and his Banshees of Blue. He put on a tux, and put together a band that nominally played lounge music, but rocked. His martini glass and cigarettes were omnipresent. The act took off in a big way, and by 1988, Poindexter achieved the goal that had eluded Johansen for the previous decade: He scored a hit record with a cover of Arrow's soca rouser "Hot, Hot, Hot." Johnasen/Poindexter found himself on the *Tonight Show*, and in ads for Amaretto. Even Hollywood came calling, and he landed roles in the films *Scrooged* and *Tales from the Dark Side*.

Johansen continued to work as Buster Poindexter, exploring Latin music in English on *Buster's Spanish Rocketship* in 1997. In 1999, he did an acclaimed set of 1920s blues and hillbilly songs with a band called The Harry Smiths, taking its name from legendary folklorist Harry Smith's *Anthology of American Folk Music*. Meanwhile, Sylvain released his first new music in nearly two decades in 1998. The album, *(Sleep) Baby Doll*, paid tribute to both Johansen and his fallen friends in The Dolls, with covers of "Frenchette," "Trash," and one of Thunder's last songs, "Your Society Makes Me Sad."

Disc.: N.Y. D. (1973); *In Too Much Too Soon* (1974); *Rock 'n Roll* (1994); *Glam Rock Hits* (1999). **DAVID JOHANSEN:** *David Johansen* (1978); *In Style* (1979); *Here Comes the Night* (1981); *Live It Up* (1982); *Sweet Revenge* (1984). **BUSTER POINDEXTER:** *Buster Poindexter* (1987); *Buster Goes Berserk* (1989); *Buster's Happy Hour* (1994); *Buster's Spanish Rocketship* (1997). **JOHNNY THUNDERS AND THE HEART-BREAKERS:** *L.A.M.F.–Lost Mixes* (1977); *So Alone* (1978); *Live at Max's Kansas City '79* (1979); *Que Será Será* (1985); *Have Faith* (1996); *Too Much Junkie Business* (1999). **SYLVAIN SYLVAIN:** *In Teenage News* (1977); *Baby Doll* (1998).—**HB**

Ney, Elly, German pianist and pedagogue; b. Düsseldorf, Sept. 27, 1882; d. Tutzing, March 31, 1968. She was a piano student of Leschetizky and Sauer in Vienna.

She made her debut in Vienna in 1905, and gave successful recitals in Europe and America. She then devoted herself mainly to teaching, living mostly in Munich. From 1911 to 1927 she was married to **Willem van Hoogstraten;** in 1928 she married P.F. Allais of Chicago. She publ. an autobiography, *Ein Leben für die Musik* (Darmstadt, 1952; 2nd ed., 1957, as *Erinnerungen und Betrachtungen; Mein Leben aus der Musik*).

BIBL.: C. von Pidoll, *E. N.* (Leipzig, 1942); Z. Maurina, *Begegnung mit E. N.* (Memmingen, 1956); E. Valentin, *E. N., Symbol einer Generation* (Munich, 1962).—**NS/LK/DM**

Nezhdanova, Antonina (Vasilievna), distinguished Russian soprano; b. Krivaya Balka, near Odessa, June 16, 1873; d. Moscow, June 26, 1950. She studied at the Moscow Cons. (graduated, 1902). She made her operatic debut as Antonida in *A Life for the Czar* in Moscow (1902); shortly thereafter, became a principal member of the Bolshoi Theater there, remaining on its roster for almost 40 years; also appeared in other Russian music centers, as both an opera singer and a concert singer; sang Gilda in Paris (1912). She taught at the Stanislavsky Opera Studio and the Bolshoi Theater Opera Studio (from 1936); was prof. of voice at the Moscow Cons. (from 1943). Her husband was **Nikolai Golovanov.** She was made a People's Artist of the U.S.S.R. (1936). She was notably successful in lyric, coloratura, and dramatic roles, her range extending to high G; in addition to Antonida, she excelled as Tatiana, Marguerite, Marfa, Lakme, and Juliette. Her memoirs were publ. posthumously in Moscow (1967).

BIBL.: M. Lvov, *A.V. N.* (Moscow, 1952); G. Polyanovsky, *A. N.* (Moscow, 1970).—**NS/LK/DM**

Nibelle, Adolphe-André, French composer; b. Gien, Loiret, Oct. 9, 1825; d. Paris, March 11, 1895. He wrote numerous operettas for Paris, the most successful being *Le Loup-Garou* (1858), *Les Filles du lac* (1858), *L'Arche-Marion* (1868), *La Fontaine de Berny* (1869), *Le 15 août* (1869), *Les Quatre Cents Femmes d'Ali-Baba* (1872), and *L'Alibi* (1873). He also publ. *Heures musicales* (24 songs).—**NS/LK/DM**

Niblock, Phill, American composer and teacher; b. Anderson, Ind., Oct. 2, 1933. He studied economics at Indiana Univ. in Bloomington (B.A., 1956), and then settled in N.Y., where he was active as both a composer and filmmaker. From 1971 he taught at the Coll. of Staten Island of the City Univ. of N.Y. In 1978 he received a Guggenheim fellowsip; also received awards and grants from the N.Y. State Council on the Arts (1981–89), the NEA (1982–88), the City Univ. of N.Y. Research Foundation (1985–89), Meet the Composer, N.Y. (1991), and N.Y.'s Foundation for Contemporary Performance Arts (1994). Niblock's works have been heard in a variety of venues, including galleries and museums around the world, including London (1982), Holland (1989), Brussels (1989), and N.Y. (1990). He has long been associated with the important N.Y.-based organization Experimental Intermedia. In 1993 he opened an artist-in-residence house and window gallery in Gent, Belgium. In 1994 a double CD collection was released as *The Young Persons Guide to Phill Niblock*.

WORKS: *3 to 7–196* for Cello (1974); *Cello & Bassoon* (1975); *First Performance* for English Horn (1976); *261.63 + and -* for Chamber Ensemble (1976); *Tymps in E* for Percussion (1978); *Earpiece* for Bassoon (1978); *A Trombone Piece* (1978); *Twelve Tones for Bass* (1979); *Voice and Violin* (1979); *A Third Trombone* (1979); *Second 2 Octaves & a Fifth* for Oboe (1980); *Every Tune* for Clarinet (1980); *PK AND SLS* for 2 Flutes (1981); *S L S* for Flute (1981); *P K* for Flute (1981); *E for Gibson* for Cello (1982); *Held Tones* for Flute (1982); *B Poore* for Tuba (1982); *Not Untitled, Knot Untied—Old* for Chamber Ensemble (1984); *Unmentionable Piece for Trombone and Sousaphone* (1984); *New Newband Work* for (the Newband) Ensemble (1984); *Summing I, II, III, and IV* for Cello (1985); *Fall and Winterbloom* for Bass Flute (1987); *According to Guy*, versions *I, II,* and *III* (a.k.a. *Aversion I, II,* and *III*) for Accordion (1987–88); *Weld Tuned* for Computer-controlled Synthesizers (1990); *Wintergreen* for Computer-controlled Synthesizers (1990); *MTPNC* for Computer-controlled Synthesizers (1992); *Didjeridoos and Don'ts* (1992); *Early Winter* for Flute, Bass Flute (prerecorded), 38 sampled and synthesized voices (computer-controlled), and String Quartet (1991–93); *Five More String Quartets* (1991–93); *Ten Auras* and *Ten Auras Live* for Tenor Saxophone (1992).—**NS/LK/DM**

Niccolò da Perugia, Italian composer who flourished in the second half of the 14th century. He was active in Florence. His extant works comprise 24 ballate, 18 madrigals, and 4 cacce. See W. Marrocco, ed., *Italian Secular Music,* Polyphonic Music of the Fourteenth Century, VIII (1972).—**LK/DM**

Nichelmann, Christoph, German composer; b. Treuenbrietzen, Aug. 13, 1717; d. Berlin, 1761 or 1762. Following training in Treuenbrietzen, he became a student at the Leipzig Thomasschule (1730), where he found a mentor in J. S. Bach. After receiving training in keyboard playing and composition from W. F. Bach, he went to Hamburg (1733) to continue his studies with Keiser, Telemann, and Mattheson. He settled in Berlin, where he completed his training with Quantz and C. H. Graun. With C. P. E. Bach, he served as harpsichordist at the royal court from 1745 to 1756. Among his works were 3 sinfonias, Ouverture, Concerto for Violin and Strings, 16 concertos for harpsichord and strings (1740–59), various keyboard pieces, *Il sogno di Scipione,* serenata (1745), Requiem, *Zeffirretti,* cantata, and 22 Lieder.

BIBL.: H. Döllmann, *C. N.: Ein Musiker am Hofe Friedrichs des Grossen* (Löningen, 1938); D. Lee, *The Works of C. N.: A Thematic Index* (Detroit, 1971).—**LK/DM**

Nicholas, Albert (Nick), talented New Orleans-style clarinetist, saxophonist; b. New Orleans, May 27, 1900; d. Basel, Switzerland, Sept. 3, 1973. His uncle, "Wooden Joe" Nicholas (b. New Orleans, Sept. 23, 1883; d. there, Nov. 17, 1957), played cornet and clarinet, working with King Oliver in 1915, and later was active during the late 1940s–early 1950s New Orleans revival. Albert started playing clarinet at age of 10, took lessons from Lorenzo Tio Jr., and soon gigged with Buddie Petit, King Oliver (several times including 1924–26), and Manuel Perez. From August 1926 he worked with bands in Shanghai, Cairo, Alexandria, and Paris, then returned to the U.S., arriving on Nov. 9, 1928, when he joined Luis Russell until December 1933. He then worked with Chick Webb, John Kirby, Louis Armstrong (1937 until spring 1939), Zutty Singleton (December 1939 to October 1940). In late 1941, he left full-time music to work as a guard on N.Y. subway, then worked for the U.S. government in Washington, D.C. Returned to N.Y. in late 1945, and began performing with various revival bands. From 1949 until 1953, he mainly led his own groups in and around L.A. In 1953, he went to France, and spent the rest of his life touring the Continent. He returned to the U.S. for playing visits in 1959 and 1960, and visited his hometown for the last time from late 1969 to early 1970.

DISC.: "This Is Jazz" (1947); *All Star Stompers* (1959); *A.N. Quartet* (1959); *Tribute to Jelly Roll Morton* (1970).—**JC/LP**

Nicholls, Agnes, English soprano; b. Cheltenham, July 14, 1877; d. London, Sept. 21, 1959. She studied singing with Visetti at the Royal Coll. of Music in London. She made her operatic debut in Manchester on Nov. 20, 1895, as Dido in a revival of Purcell's opera. From 1901 to 1924 she sang with the Denhof, Beecham, and British National Opera companies. On July 15, 1904, she married **Sir (Herbert) Hamilton Harty.** She was quite successful in Wagnerian roles; in 1908 she sang Sieglinde in *Die Walküre* at Covent Garden in London under the direction of Hans Richter.—**NS/LK/DM**

Nichols, Herbie (actually, **Herbert Horatio**), jazz pianist, composer; b. N.Y. Jan. 3, 1919; d. N.Y., April 12, 1963. Nichols is best known for his compositions, which were respected and admired by many musicians. He began playing piano at eight, studying with Charles Beck for seven years. He performed with the Royal Baron Orch. (1937) and Floyd Williams (1938). He served in the U.S. Infantry from September 1941 until August 1943. After the war, he worked with various swing and R&B bands, including a tour with Illinois Jacquet (c. 1947) then worked on and off with John Kirby during 1948 and 1949. During the 1950s, he worked with Snub Mosley, Edgar Sampson, Milton Larkin, Arnett Cobb, Wilbur de Paris, and others. His 1955 album, *Third World,* announced a composer of distinction and talent. During the early 1960s, he played various club residencies in N.Y. In 1962, he played with Archie Shepp, and toured Scandinavia. He died of leukemia. His best-known works include "Lady Sings the Blues," written for Billie Holiday, and "Mary's Waltz," a favorite of pianist Mary Lou Williams (originally known as "The Bebop Waltz"). During the 1990s his music was championed by John Zorn, Ted Nash, and other avant-garde composer/performers; in 1994, N.Y.'s Jazz Composer's Collective staged a concert of his works.

DISC.: *M & N* (1952); *Third World* (1955); *Prophetic H.N., Vol.I* (1955); *Herbie Nichols Trio* (1955); *Art of H.N.* (1955); *Thelonious Monk and H.N.* (1956); *Love, Gloom, Cash, Love* (1957); *Bethlehem Session* (1957).—**JC/LP**

Nichols, Red (actually, **Ernest Loring**), noted early jazz cornetist, bandleader; b. Ogden, Utah, May 8, 1905; d. Las Vegas, June 28, 1965. His small group recordings between 1926 and 1929 were among the most fascinating and intelligent of their time. Recorded under a variety of names and leaders, most famously Red Nichols and his Five Pennies, they were widely admired by musicians including Lester Young. They utilized complex arrangements, whole-tone scales and, as early as December 1926, the tympani of Vic Berton. But Nichols then went into pop music and many forgot his innovative early work. He has been called a Beiderbecke clone when in fact he began recording before Bix.

His father was a college music teacher, specializing in clarinet. Red started on bugle at the age of four, cornet at five; and at 12 was featured in the family musical act and in his father's brass band. He gigged with local bandleaders, then gained scholarship to Culver Military Academy (December 1919). He played cornet, violin, and piano at the Academy until being dismissed in September 1920. Nichols returned to Utah, played in pit orchestras, then joined Ray Stilson (on cornet, doubling violin) in 1922; later that year he joined the Syncopating Five (a seven-piece group) and made his first (private) recordings. He was soon appointed leader of the band, and worked in Atlantic City (early 1923) and Lake James, Ind. In late 1924 Nichols joined Sam Lanin in N.Y., and worked for many bandleaders including Harry Reser, Benny Krueger, Ross Gorman, Vincent Lopez, Don Voorhees, and the Calif. Ramblers. From December 1926 he regularly led own recording studio groups, often with Miff Mole, Eddie Lang, Jimmy Dorsey, Artie Schutt, and Vic Berton. He also took part in countless freelance sessions. He played with Paul Whiteman during May 1927, then led his own bands and orchestras from 1928–30, also working for several Broadway shows and occasionally touring (late 1928 to early 1929). He continued to lead own studio groups until 1932: the Five Pennies, the Redheads, the Arkansas Travelers, Louisiana Rhythm Kings, Charleston Chasers, etc., now also including at times Benny Goodman, Jack Teagarden, Pee Wee Russell, Adrian Rollini, Gene Krupa, mellophone specialist Dudley Fosdick, Glenn Miller, and Joe Venuti. During the 1930s Nichols had a regular radio series and was performing fairly standard dance work by this time. Except for short breaks, he continued to lead his own band until spring of 1942, when he sold the band to Anson Weeks. Nichols then moved to Calif. and left music to do mostly defense work in the shipyards. He played with Glen Gray and the Casa Loma Band from February until June 1944, and reformed the Five Pennies as a Dixieland sextet. From September 1944 through the 1950s, the group worked mainly in L.A. and San Francisco. The movie *The Five Pennies* starring Danny Kaye was released in 1959. It was very loosely based on Nichols's career, taken from the book of the same name by Grady Johnson. Nichols was also a subject on the television show *This is Your Life* and appeared in the film *The Gene Krupa Story* In the early 1960s the group played many important residencies throughout the U.S., touring overseas in 1960 and 1964. While fulfilling a residency at the Las Vegas casino Top of the Mint, Nichols suffered a fatal heart attack at a nearby hotel.

DISC.: *Jazz Time* (1950); *Syncopated Chamber Music, Vol. 2* (1953); *R.N. and Band* (1953); *Hot Pennies* (1957); *Parade of the Pennies* (1958); *R.N. and the Five Pennies* (1959); *R.N. and His Pennies* (1960); *Blues and Old Time Rags* (1964); "Battle Hymn of the Republic" (1959).

BIBL.: R. Venables, *Complete Discography of R.N.* (Melbourne, Australia); H. Lange, *R.N.: Ein Portrat* (Wetzlar, Germany, 1960).—JC/LP

Nicholson or **Nicolson, Richard,** English composer and organist; b. place and date unknown; d. Oxford, 1639. He received his D.Mus. degree from Oxford in 1596. He served as Informator choristarum (from 1595) and as first master of the Music Praxis (from 1626) at Magdalen Coll., Oxford. His works include 2 anthems, 4 madrigals, a madrigal cycle, 5 consort songs, and 2 pavans for 5 Viols.—LK/DM

Nicholson, George (Thomas Frederick), English pianist, teacher, and composer; b. Great Lumley, Sept. 24, 1949. He was educated at the Univ. of York (B.A. in English and music, 1971; Ph.D. in composition, 1979), his mentors in music being Bernard Rands and David Blake. He then was active as a teacher and performer; from 1988 he served as lecturer in music and director of composition at the Univ. of Keele.

WORKS: ORCH.: *1132* (1976); *The Convergence of the Twain* for Chamber Orch. (1978); Chamber Concerto for 13 Instruments (1979–80); *Sea-Change* for 14 Strings (1988); Cello Concerto (1990); Flute Concerto (1993). **CHAMBER:** *Recycle* for 11 Instruments (1975–76); 2 string quartets (1976–77; 1984–85); Brass Quintet (1977); *Winter Music* for Clarinet, Harp, and Percussion (1978); *Ancient Lights* for 7 Instruments (1982); *Sound Progressions Newly Minted* for Brass Quintet (1983); *Stilleven* for 5 Instruments (1985); *Romanza* for Violin and Piano (1987); *Spring Songs* for Recorder (1991); *Muybridge Frames* for Trombone and Piano (1992). **Piano:** Sonata (1983); *Cascate* (1985); *Impromptu* (1988); *All Systems Go* (1989); *For Miles* (1991–92). **VOCAL:** *Alla Luna* for Soprano, Clarinet, and Piano (1981); *Aubade* for Soprano and 5 Instruments (1981); *The Arrival of the Poet in the City* for Narrator and 7 Instruments (1982–83); *A World of Imagination* for Chorus (1984); *Blisworth Tunnel Blues* for Soprano and Chamber Orch. (1986–87); songs.—NS/LK/DM

Nicholson, Sir Sydney (Hugo), English organist, music educator, and composer; b. London, Feb. 9, 1875; d. Ashford, Kent, May 30, 1947. He was educated at Oxford, the Royal Coll. of Music in London, and in Frankfurt am Main. He served as organist of the Lower Chapel, Eton (1900–04), acting organist of Carlisle Cathedral (1904–08), and organist of Manchester Cathedral (1908–19) and of Westminster Abbey, London (1919–28). Nicholson then founded the School of English Church Music, which became the Royal School of Church Music in 1945. In 1938 he was knighted. He composed a comic opera, *The Mermaid* (1928), an opera for boy's voices, *The Children of the Chapel* (1934), church music, and organ pieces. He publ. *Church Music: A Practical Handbook* (London, 1920), *A Manual of English Church Music* (with G. Gardner; London, 1923; 2nd ed., 1936), and *Quires and Places where they sing* (London, 1932; 2nd ed., 1942).—NS/LK/DM

Nicodé, Jean-Louis, German pianist, conductor, and composer; b. Jerczik, near Posen, Aug. 12, 1853; d. Langebruck, near Dresden, Oct. 5, 1919. He was taught by his father and by the organist Hartkas, and in 1869 he entered Kullak's Academy in Berlin, where he studied piano with Kullak, harmony with Wuerst, and counterpoint and composition with Kiel. He made a concert tour (1878) with Artot through Galicia and Rumania. From 1878 to 1885 he was a piano teacher at the Dresden Cons., and from 1885 to 1888, conductor of the Dresden Phil. He established the Nicodé Concerts in 1893, and, in order to enlarge their scope by the production of larger choral works, formed the Nicodé Chorus in 1896. In 1900 he abandoned these concerts, retired to Langebruck, and devoted himself to composition. He wrote 2 expansive symphonic works: *Das Meer* for Soloists, Men's Voices, Orch., and Organ (1889) and *Gloria! ein Sturm- und Sonnenlied* for Boy's Voices, Men's Voices, Orch., and Organ (1905), several other symphonic works, some chamber music, songs, and piano pieces.

BIBL.: T. Schäfer, *J.-L. N.: Ein Versuch kritischer Würdigung und Erläuterung seines Schaffens* (Berlin, 1907); O. Taubmann, *J.-L. N.* (Leipzig, 1909).—NS/LK/DM

Nicolai, (Carl) Otto (Ehrenfried), famous German composer and conductor; b. Königsberg, June 9, 1810; d. Berlin, May 11, 1849. He studied piano at home, and in 1827 went to Berlin, where he took lessons in theory with Zelter; also took courses with Bernhard Klein at the Royal Inst. for Church Music. On April 13, 1833, he made his concert debut in Berlin as a pianist, singer, and composer. He then was engaged as organist to the embassy chapel in Rome by the Prussian ambassador, Bunsen. While in Italy, he also studied counterpoint with Giuseppe Baini. In 1837 he proceeded to Vienna, where he became a singing teacher and Kapellmeister at the Kärnthnertortheater. In 1838 he returned to Italy; on Nov. 26, 1839, he presented in Trieste his first opera, *Rosmonda d'Inghilterra,* given under its new title as *Enrico II.* His second opera, *Il Templario,* was staged in Turin on Feb. 11, 1840. In 1841 he moved to Vienna, where he was appointed court Kapellmeister in succession to Kreutzer. Nicolai was instrumental in establishing sym. concerts utilizing the musicians of the orch. of the Imperial Court Opera Theater; on March 28, 1842, he conducted this ensemble featuring Beethoven's 7th Sym.; this became the inaugural concert of the celebrated Vienna Phil. In 1848 he was appointed Kapellmeister of the Royal Opera in Berlin. On March 9, 1849, his famous opera *Die lustigen Weiber von Windsor,* after Shakespeare, was given at the Berlin Royal Opera; it was to become his only enduring creation. Nicolai died two months after its production. In 1887 Hans Richter, then conductor of the Vienna Phil., inaugurated an annual "Nicolai-Konzert" in his memory, and it became a standard occasion.

WORKS: DRAMATIC: Opera: *Enrico II* (original title, *Rosmonda d'Inghilterra;* Trieste, Nov. 26, 1839); *Il Templario* (Turin, Feb. 11, 1840; rev. as *Der Tempelritter,* Vienna, Dec. 20, 1845); *Gildippe ed Odoardo* (Genoa, Dec. 26, 1840); *Il proscritto* (Milan, March 13, 1841; rev. as *Die Heimkehr des Verbannten,* Vienna, Feb. 3, 1846); *Die lustigen Weiber von Windsor* (Berlin, March 9, 1849). **VOCAL: Sacred:** *Pater noster* for 8 Voices,

op.33; *In assumptione Beatae Mariae Virginis, offertory* for 5 Voices, op.38; *Salve regina* for Soprano and Orch., op.39; Te Deum for Solo Voices, 4 Voices, and Orch.; Mass in D major for 4 Solo Voices, 4 Voices, and Orch.; Psalms, motets, etc. **Secular Choral:** *Preussens Stimme* for 4 Voices and Orch., op.4; 6 lieder for 4 Voices, op.6; *Verschiedene Empfindungen an einem Platz* for Soprano, 2 Tenors, Bass, and Piano, op.9; 3 *Königslieder der älteren Berliner Liedertafel* for 4 Men's Voices, op.10; *Gesänge* for 4 Men's Voices, op.17; etc. **Other:** Songs. **ORCH.:** *In morte di Vincenzo Bellini,* funeral march; syms.: No. 1, in C minor (1831), and No. 2, in D major (1835; rev. 1845); *Kirchliche Festouvertüre über...Ein feste Burg* for 4 Voices, Organ, and Orch., op.32 (1844); *Weihnachtsouvertüre über Vom Himmel hoch* for 4 Voices ad libitum and Orch. **CHAMBER:** Various works.

BIBL.: H. Mendel, *O. N.: Eine Biographie* (Berlin, 1866; 2nd ed., 1868); B. Schröder, ed., *O. N.: Tagebücher nebst biographischen Ergänzungen* (Leipzig, 1892); G. Kruse, *O. N.: Ein Künstlerleben* (Berlin, 1911); idem, *O. N.s musikalische Aufsätze* (Regensburg, 1913); W. Altmann, ed., *O. N.: Briefe an seinen Vater* (Regensburg, 1924); W. Altmann, ed., *O. N.s Tagebücher* (Regensburg, 1937); W. Jerger, ed., *O. N.: Briefe an die Wiener Philharmoniker* (Vienna, 1942); U. Konrad, *O. N., 1810–1849; Studien zu Leben und Werk* (Baden-Baden, 1986).—NS/LK/DM

Nicolai, David Traugott, German organist, organ builder, and composer; b. Görlitz, Aug. 24, 1733; d. there, Dec. 20, 1799. Following training from his father, a pupil of Bach, he took courses in law, mathematics, and physics at the Univ. of Leipzig (1753–55). In 1758 he became his father's assistant as organist at the Hauptkirche in Görlitz, succeeding him as organist in 1764. In 1775 he was made electoral court organist. Nicolai acquired a notable reputation as an organ virtuoso and as an organ builder. Among his compositions were fugues for organ, piano sonatas, and some cantatas.
—LK/DM

Nicolai, Philipp, German theologian, poet, and composer; b. Mengeringhausen, near Kassel, Aug. 10, 1556; d. Hamburg, Oct. 26, 1608. Following studies with J. à Burck and L. Helmbold in Mühlhausen and F. Beurhaus in Dortmund, he studied theology in Erfurt (1575–76), Wittenberg (1576–79), and at the Volkhardinghausen Monastery. In 1582 he was made pastor in Herdecke. He espoused the Lutheran faith and completed his training in theology with Aegidius Hunnius in Wittenberg, where he took his degree in 1594. In addition to his large output of theological works and poems, he brought out the devotional vol. *Der Freudenspiegel des ewigen Lebens* (Frankfurt am Main, 1599), which includes his celebrated songs "Wie schön leuchtet der Morgenstern" and "Wachet auf, ruft uns die Stimme."

BIBL.: L. Curtze, *D.P. N.s Leben und Lieder* (Halle, 1859); V. Schultze, *P. N.* (Mengeringhausen, 1909).—LK/DM

Nicolescu, Marianna, Romanian soprano; b. Gavjani, Nov. 28, 1948. After studies in Romania, she pursued training at the Cons. Statale di Musica di St. Cecilia in Rome and with Elizabeth Schwarzkopf and Rodolfo Celletti. She made her debut in a television concert in Milan in 1972. Following an engagement as

Beatrice di Tenda in Venice in 1975, she appeared in Florence as Violetta in 1976. On April 18, 1978, she made her Metropolitan Opera debut in N.Y. as Nedda. She made her first appearance at Milan's La Scala in the premiere of Berio's *La vera storia* in 1982, and made return visits there in 1987, 1988, and 1993. In 1984 she sang Donna Elvira at the Rome Opera. From 1986 to 1993 she made appearances at the Bavarian State Opera in Munich and at the Munich Festival. In 1990 she was engaged as Elettra at the Salzburg Festival. She sang Donizetti's Queen Elizabeth in Monte Carlo in 1992. In 1995 she returned to Munich as Anna Bolena. —NS/LK/DM

Nicolet, Aurele, prominent Swiss flutist and pedagogue; b. Neuchâtel, Jan. 22, 1926. He studied flute and theory with André Jamet and Willy Burkhard in Zürich, then pursued training with Marcel Moyse and Yvonne Drappier at the Paris Cons., where he won the premier prix for flute in 1947. In 1948 he captured first prize for flute at the Geneva Competition. After playing flute in the Zürich Tonhalle Orch. (1945–47), the Winterthur orch. (1948–50), and the Berlin Phil. (1950–59), he pursued an international career as a soloist, recitalist, and chamber music player. He also was a prof. at the Berlin Hochschule für Musik (1953–65) and later taught in Fribourg and Basel. In addition to traditional scores, he also played much modern music for his instrument, including works by Denisov, C. Halffter, Holliger, Kelterborn, Ligeti et al. He publ. a flute method (1967). —NS/LK/DM

Nicolini (real name, **Nicolo Grimaldi**), renowned Italian castrato alto; b. Naples (baptized), April 5, 1673; d. there, Jan. 1, 1732. He studied with Provenzale in Naples, making his debut there as a page in his La Stellidaura vendicata (1685); then entered the Cappella del Tesoro di S. Gennaro at Naples Cathedral (1690) and the Naples Royal Chapel (1691). He appeared in opera in Naples (1697–1724) and also in Venice (1700–1731), being made a Knight of the Order of San Marco (1705). He made his London debut at the Queen's Theatre in Haym's arrangement of A. Scarlatti's *Pirroe Demetrio* (Dec. 14, 1708), and subsequently was its leading singer until 1712; he created Handel's Rinaldo (Feb. 24, 1711). He returned to London to create Handel's Amadigi (May 25, 1715), singing there until 1717. He then pursued his career in his homeland, remaining active until his death. At the zenith of his career, he was held in the highest esteem by his contemporaries, being celebrated for his remarkable vocal gifts and dramatic abilities.—NS/LK/DM

Nicolini, Giuseppe, Italian composer; b. Piacenza, Jan. 29, 1762; d. there, Dec. 18, 1842. He studied with his father, Omobono Nicolini, organist and maestro di cappella in Piacenza. Following vocal instruction from Filippo Macedone, he studied composition at the Cons. di S. Onofrio in Naples with Insanguine. During the first two decades of the 19th century, Nicolini enjoyed great popularity as a composer for the theater, bringing out some 50 operas in all. However, with the

ascendancy of Rossini, he abandoned the theater and in 1819 was made maestro di cappella at Piacenza Cathedral. He died in poverty, long forgotten by his contemporaries. In addition to his operas, he wrote some orch. pieces, chamber music, and many sacred works. Piacenza finally honored its native son by naming the Liceo Musicale after him in 1914.

BIBL.: E. de Giovanni, *G. N. e Sebastiano Nasolini* (Piacenza, 1927).—NS/LK/DM

Niculescu, Ştefan, Romanian composer and teacher; b. Moreni, July 31, 1927. He was a student of Jora (harmony and counterpoint), Rogalski (orchestration), and Andricu (composition) at the Bucharest Cons. (1951–59), of Kagel at the Siemens Studio in Munich (1966), and of Ligeti, Stockhausen, and Karkoschka at the summer courses in new music in Darmstadt (1966–68). After serving as head of research at the Bucharest Inst. of the Arts (1960–63), he taught at the Bucharest Cons. (1963–87). He was director of the International Festival of New Music in Bucharest from 1990. In addition to his various articles on music, he publ. a vol. of reflections on music (Bucharest, 1980). He first composed in a stringent adherence to serial dictates before adopting a more freely inspired personal mode of expression in which he utilized aleatory and diatonic harmony while remaining true to nontonal precepts. He later enhanced his works with enriched melodic and harmonic elements.

WORKS: DRAMATIC: *Cartea cu "Apolodor,"* opera (Cluj-Napoca, April 13, 1975); *Le Prince né des larmes,* ballet (1982). **ORCH.:** 3 syms.: No. 1 (1955–56; Bucharest, April 12, 1960), No. 2, *Opus dacicum* (1979–80; Timişoara, Nov. 19, 1984), and No. 3, *Cantos* (Timişoara, Nov. 19, 1984); *Scenes* (1962; Cluj-Napoca, March 13, 1965); Sym. for Small Orch. (1963; Bucharest, June 16, 1964); *Hétéromorphie* (1967; Bucharest, April 12, 1968); *Formants* for Chamber Orch. (Bucharest, Aug. 15, 1968); *Unisonos I* (Mainz, Sept. 26, 1970) and *II* (1971; Ljubljana, Oct. 17, 1972); *Ison I* (1973; also for 14 Instruments) and *II*, concerto for Winds and Percussion (Romanian TV, Bucharest, Nov. 13, 1975); *Sincronie II, Omaggio a Enescu e Bartók* (Cluj-Napoca, May 22, 1981); *Undecimum* for Chamber Orch. (1997–98; also for 11 Instruments). **CHAMBER:** Clarinet Sonata (1953–55); Trio for Violin, Viola, and Cello (1957; Bucharest, Feb. 18, 1976); *Inventions* for Clarinet and Piano (1963–64; Bucharest, Jan. 29, 1965); *Invenţiuni* for Viola and Piano (1965); Sextet for Flute, 2 Clarinets, 2 Oboes, and Trumpet (1969; based on the 3rd cantata, 1960); *Triplum I* for Flute, Cello, and Piano (Royan, April 8, 1971) and *II* for Clarinet, Cello, and Piano (1972; Bucharest, April 18, 1973); *Echoes I* for Violin (1977; Bucharest, Feb. 21, 1978) and *II* for Violin and Synthesizer (1984; Turin, Oct. 1, 1985); *Sincronie I* for 2 to 12 Instruments (Bucharest, Nov. 5, 1979), *V* for Wind Quintet (1982), *III* for Flute, Oboe, and Bassoon (1985; Lugar, Spain, Feb. 22, 1986), and *IV* for Clarinet, Piano, and Percussion (1987; Bucharest, March 21, 1989); *Duplum I* for Cello and Piano or Synthesizer (Bucharest, Nov. 7, 1984) and *III* for Clarinet and Piano (1986); *Ricercare in uno* for Clarinet, Violin, and Synthesizer (Bucharest, March 27, 1984); *Sincronie per quattro* for Flute, Oboe, Violin, and Cello (1985); *Octuplum* for Chamber Ensemble (Den Bosch, the Netherlands, March 31, 1985); *Hétérofonies pour Montreux* for Flute, English Horn, Clarinet, Bassoon, and Horn (Vevey, Aug. 29, 1986); *A Due* for Clarinet and Bassoon (1986); *Monophonie* for Bassoon (1988; Bucharest, Feb. 4, 1989); *Chant-son* for Soprano or Alto

Saxophone (1989). VOCAL: *Cantata I* for Women's and/or Children's Chorus and Orch. (1959; Cluj-Napoca, June 16, 1961), *II* for Tenor, Chorus, and Orch. (1960; Warsaw, Feb. 15, 1963), and *III, Răscruce*, for Mezzo-soprano and Wind Quintet (Cluj-Napoca, Dec. 11, 1965); *Aphorismes d'Heraclite* for Chorus (Zagreb, May 1969); *Fragments I* for 12 Voices and Instruments (1977; Bucharest, March 23, 1978), *II* for Voice and Instruments (1977), and *III* for Voice and Instruments (1977); *Invocatio* for Voices (Paris, April 18, 1989).—**NS/LK/DM**

Nidecki, Tomasz Napoleon, Polish conductor and composer; b. Studzianka, Jan. 2, 1807; d. Warsaw, June 5, 1852. He studied with Alojzy Stolpe (piano), Józef Bielawski (violin), and Wilhelm Würfel (organ) before pursuing training in composition with Elsner at the Warsaw Inst. of Music and Dramatic Art and at the Higher School of Music (1824–27). After completing his studies in Vienna (1828–31), he was conductor of the Leopoldstadt Theater there from 1833 to 1838. He then returned to Warsaw as deputy conductor of the Wielki Theater, where he served as conductor and director from 1840. He wrote 9 operas, instrumental music, and sacred choral works.—**LK/DM**

Niecks, Frederick (actually, **Friedrich**), German-English writer on music; b. Düsseldorf, Feb. 3, 1845; d. Edinburgh, June 24, 1924. He studied the violin under Langhans, Grunewald, and Auer, and piano and composition with J. Tausch, making his debut (as a violinist) at Düsseldorf in 1857. He was a member of the orch. there until 1867, the last years as concertmaster. In 1868 he became organist at Dumfries, Scotland, and viola player in a quartet with A.C. Mackenzie. After teaching at the Univ. of Leipzig (1877–78) and travels in Italy, he won a position in London as critic for the Monthly Musical Record and Musical Times; in 1891, was appointed Reid Prof. of Music at Edinburgh Univ. In 1901 Niecks founded the Music Education Society. He was made a Mus.Doc. (honoris causa) by Dublin Univ. in 1898; LL.D. by Edinburgh Univ. After his retirement in 1914, he lived in Edinburgh.

WRITINGS (all publ. in London unless otherwise given): *A Concise Dictionary of Musical Terms* (2nd ed., 1884; 5th ed., rev. and enl., 1900); *Frederick Chopin as a Man and Musician* (1888; 3rd ed., 1902); *Musical Education and Culture* (Edinburgh, 1892); *Programme Music in the Last Four Centuries* (1907); *Robert Schumann* (ed. by C. Niecks; 1925).—**NS/LK/DM**

Niedermeyer, (Abraham) Louis, Swiss composer; b. Nyon, April 27, 1802; d. Paris, March 14, 1861. He was a pupil in Vienna of Moscheles (piano) and Förster (composition), in 1819 of Fioravanti in Rome, and of Zingarelli in Naples. He lived in Geneva as an admired song composer, and settled in Paris in 1823, where he brought out 4 unsuccessful operas (*La casa nel bosco*, May 28, 1828; *Stradella*, March 3, 1837; *Marie Stuart*, Dec. 6, 1844; *La Fronde*, May 2, 1853). He then bent his energies to sacred composition, and reorganized Choron's Inst. for Church Music as the École Niedermeyer, which eventually became a flourishing inst. with government subvention. He also founded (with d'Ortigue) a journal for church music, *La Maîtrise*

(1857–61); they publ. *Traité théorique et pratique de l'accompagnement du plain-chant* (Paris, 1857; 2nd ed., 1876; Eng. tr., N.Y., 1905). He wrote masses, motets, hymns, romances (*Le Lac; Le Soir; La Mer; L'Automne*; etc.), organ preludes, piano pieces, etc.

BIBL.: A. Niedermeyer, *L. N.: Son oeuvre et son école* (Paris, n.d.); *Vie d'un compositeur moderne* (by Niedermeyer's son; Fontainbleau, 1892); M. Galerne, *L'École N.* (Paris, 1928).—**NS/LK/DM**

Nielsen, Alice, American soprano; b. Nashville, Tenn., June 7, 1868?; d. N.Y., March 8, 1943. She sang in a church choir in Kansas City, then joined the Burton Stanley Opera Co., where she sang in operettas. She made her debut as a grand-opera singer in Naples as Marguerite in *Faust* (Dec. 6, 1903). She made her first American appearance in N.Y. (Nov. 10, 1905). In 1908 she toured with the San Carlo Co. in the U.S., and then achieved the status of a prima donna with the Boston Opera Co. (1909–13) and also sang concurrently with the Metropolitan Opera in N.Y. She eventually settled in N.Y. as a singing teacher.—**NS/LK/DM**

Nielsen, Carl (August), greatly significant Danish composer; b. Sortelung, near Nrre-Lyndelse, June 9, 1865; d. Copenhagen, Oct. 3, 1931. He received violin lessons in childhood from his father and the local schoolteacher, and played second violin in the village band, and later in its amateur orch. After studying cornet with his father, he played in the Odense military orch. (1879–83), serving as its signal horn and alto trombone player; also taught himself to play piano. While in Odense, he began to compose, producing several chamber pieces; then received financial assistance to continue his training at the Royal Cons. in Copenhagen, where he studied violin with Tofte, theory with J.P.E. Hartmann and Orla Rosenhoff, and music history with Gade and P. Matthison-Hansen (1884–86). He was a violinist in Copenhagen's Royal Chapel Orch. (1889–1905); in the interim, he achieved his first success as a composer with his *Little Suite* for Strings (1888); then continued private studies with Rosenhoff. In 1901 he was granted an annual pension. He was conductor of the Royal Theater (1908–14) and the Musikföreningen (1915–27) in Copenhagen; also appeared as a guest conductor in Germany, the Netherlands, Sweden, and Finland; taught theory and composition at the Royal Cons. (1916–19), being appointed its director a few months before his death. The early style of Nielsen's music, Romantic in essence, was determined by the combined influences of Gade, Grieg, Brahms, and Liszt, but later on he experienced the powerful impact of modern music, particularly in harmony, which in his works grew more and more chromatic and dissonant; yet he reserved the simple diatonic progressions, often in a folk-song manner, for his major climaxes; in his orchestration, he applied opulent sonorities and colorful instrumental counterpoint; there are instances of bold experimentation in some of his works, as, for example, the insertion of a snare-drum solo in his 5th Sym., playing independently of the rest of the orch.; he attached somewhat mysterious titles to his 3rd and 4th syms. (*Expansive* and *Inextinguishable*). Nielsen is sometimes described as the Sibelius of Denmark, despite obvious dissimilarities in idiom and sources of inspiration; while the music of Sibelius is deeply rooted in national folklore, both in subject matter and melodic derivation, Nielsen seldom drew on Danish popular modalities; Sibelius remained true to the traditional style of composition, while Nielsen sought new ways of modern expression. It was only after his death that Nielsen's major works entered the world repertoire; festivals of his music were organized on his centennial in 1965, and his syms. in particular were played and recorded in England and America, bringing him belated recognition as one of the most important composers of his time. In 1988 Queen Margrethe II dedicated the Carl Nielsen Museum in Odense. His writings include *Levende musik* (Copenhagen, 1925; Eng. tr., London, 1953, as *Living Music*) and *Min fynske barndom* (Copenhagen, 1927; Eng. tr., London, 1953, as *My Childhood*). A new ed. of his works commenced publication in Copenhagen in 1994 as *The New Carl Nielsen Edition*.

WORKS (all first perf. in Copenhagen unless otherwise given): DRAMATIC: *Saul og David*, opera (1898–1901; Nov. 28, 1902); *Maskarade*, opera (1904–06; Nov. 11, 1906); *Snefrid*, melodrama (1893; April 10, 1894; rev. 1899); incidental music to A. Munch's *En aften paa Giske* (1889; Jan. 15, 1890), G. Wied's *Atalanta* (Dec. 19, 1901), Drachmann's *Hr. Oluf han rider—* (Master Oluf Rides—; Oct. 9, 1906), L. Holstein's *Tove* (1906–08; March 20, 1908), L. Nielsen's *Willemoes* (1907–08; Feb. 7, 1908), O. Benzon's *Foraeldre* (Feb. 9, 1908), J. Aakjaer's *Ulvens sn* (Århus, Nov. 14, 1909), A. Oehlenschlaeger's *Hagbarth og Signe* (June 4, 1910) and *Sankt Hansaftenspil* (June 3, 1913), Christiansen's *Faedreland* (1915; Feb. 5, 1916), H. Rode's prologue to the Shakespeare Memorial Celebrations (Elsinore, June 24, 1916), J. Sigurjónsson's *Lgneren* (Feb. 15, 1918), Oehlenschlaeger's *Aladdin*, op.34 (1918–19; Feb. 15 and 22, 1919), Rode's *Moderen*, op.41 (1920; Jan. 30, 1921), Christiansen's *Cosmus* (1921–22; Feb. 25, 1922), H. Bergstedt's *Ebbe Skammelsen* (June 25, 1925), S. Michaelis's *Amor og Digteren*, op.54 (Odense, Aug. 12, 1930), and N. Grundtvig's *Paaske-aften* (April 4, 1931). ORCH.: *Little Suite* for Strings, op.1 (Sept. 8, 1888; rev. 1889); *Symphonic Rhapsody* (1888; Feb. 24, 1893; not extant); 6 syms.: No. 1, op.7 (1890–92; March 14, 1894), No. 2, op.16, *Die fire temperamenter* (The 4 Temperaments; Dec. 1, 1902), No. 3, op.27, *Sinfonia espansiva* (1910–11; Feb. 28, 1912), No. 4, op.29, *Det uudslukkelige* (The Inextinguishable; 1914–16; Feb. 1, 1916), No. 5, op.50 (Jan. 24, 1922), and No. 6, *Sinfonia semplice* (Dec. 11, 1925); *Helios*, overture, op.17 (Oct. 8, 1903); *Saga-drm* (Dream of Saga), op.39 (April 6, 1908); Violin Concerto, op.33 (1911; Feb. 28, 1912); paraphrase on "Naermere Gud til dig" ("Near My God to Thee") for Wind Orch. (1912; Aug. 22, 1915); *Pan og Syrinx*, op.49, pastorale (Feb. 11, 1918); Flute Concerto (Paris, Oct. 21, 1926); *En fantasirejse til Faererne* (A Fantasy-Journey to the Faroe Islands), rhapsodic overture (Nov. 27, 1927); Clarinet Concerto, op.57 (Humlebaek, Sept. 14, 1928); *Bohmisk- Dansk folketone* (Bohemian and Danish Folk Tunes), paraphrase for Strings (Nov. 1, 1928). CHAMBER: 2 numbered violin sonatas: No. 1 (1881–82) and No. 2, op.35 (1912); 1 unnumbered violin sonata, op.9 (1895); 5 string quartets: No. 1 (1882–83), No. 2, op.13 (1887–88; rev. 1897–98), No. 3, op.5 (1890), No. 4, op.14 (1897–98), and No. 5, *Piacevolezza*, op.19 (1906; rev. as the Quartet in F major, op.44, 1919); Duet for 2 Violins (1882–83); Piano Trio (1883); String Quintet for 2 Violins, 2 Violas, and Cello (1888); *Fantasistykke* for Clarinet and Piano (c. 1885); *Ved*

en ung kunstners baare (At the Bier of a Young Artist) for String Quartet and Double Bass (1910); 2 *Fantasistykker* for Oboe and Piano, op.2 (1889); *Canto serioso* for Horn and Piano (1913); *Serenata in vano* for Clarinet, Bassoon, Horn, Cello, and Double Bass (1914); Wind Quintet, op.43 (1922); *Prelude and Theme with Variations* for Violin, op.48 (1923); *Preludio e presto* for Violin, op.52 (1927–28); *Allegretto* for 2 Recorders (1931). KEYBOARD: Piano: 2 character pieces (1882–83); 5 pieces, op.3 (1890); *Symphonic Suite*, op.8 (1894); *Humoreske-bagateller*, op.11 (1894–97); *Fest-praeludium: "Ved Aarhundredskiften"* (1900); *Drmmen om "Glade Jul"* (1905); *Chaconne*, op.32 (1916); *Theme and Variations*, op.40 (1917); Suite "Den Luciferiske," op.45 (1919–20); 3 pieces, op.59 (1928); *Klaviermusik for smaa og store*, op.53 (2 vols., 1930). Organ: 29 Little Preludes, op.51 (1929); 2 Preludes (1930); *Commotio*, op.58 (1931) VOCAL: Cantatas: For the Lorens Frlich Festival (1900), the Students' Assn. (1901), the anniversary of the Univ. of Copenhagen, op.24 (1908), the commemoration of Feb. 11, 1659 (1909), the national exhibition in Århus (1909; in collaboration with E. Bangert), the commemoration of P. Kryer (1909), the centenary of the Merchants' Committee (1917), the centenary of the Polytechnic H.S. (1929), the 50th anniversary of the Danish Cremation Union (1930), the 50th anniversary of the Young Merchants' Education Assn. (1930), and *Digtning i sang og toner*, for the opening of the swimming baths (1930); also *Hymnus amoris* for Soprano, Tenor, Baritone, Chorus, and Orch., op.12 (April 27, 1897); *Svnen* (Sleep) for Chorus and Orch., op.18 (1903–4; March 21, 1905); *Fynsk foraar* (Springtime in Funen), lyrical humoresque for Soprano, Tenor, Bass, Chorus, and Orch., op.42 (1921; Odense, July 8, 1922); *Hyldest til Holberg* for Solo Voices, Chorus, and Orch. (1922); *Hymne til kunsten* for Soprano, Tenor, Chorus, and Wind Orch. (1929). Unaccompanied Choral: *Sidskensang* (1906); *Kom Guds engel* (1907); *Aftenstemning* (1908); *Paaske-liljen* (1910); *Der er et yndigt land* (1924); 2 school songs (1929); 3 Motets, op.55 (1929; April 30, 1930); *Til min fde* (1929); 6 Rounds (1930); etc. Solo Vocal: 2 melodramas: *Franz Neruda in memoriam* for Speaker and Orch. (1915) and *Island* for Speaker and Piano (1929). Songs: 5 Songs, op.4 (1891); *Viser og vers*, op.6 (1891); 6 Songs, op.10 (1894); *Du danske mand* (1906); *Strophic Songs*, op.21 (1902–07); *De unges sang* (1909); *Hymns and Sacred Songs* (1913–14); 20 Danish Songs (vol. I, 1914; in collaboration with T. Laub); 20 Danish Songs (vol. II, 1914–17; in collaboration with T. Laub); *Studie efter naturen* (1916); *Blomstervise* (1917); 20 Popular Melodies (1917–21); 4 Popular Melodies (1922); *Balladen om bjrnen*, op.47 (1923); 10 Little Danish Songs (1923–24); 4 Jutish Songs (1924–25); *Vocalise-étude* (1927); etc.

BIBL.: H. Seligmann, *C. N.* (Copenhagen, 1931); T. Meyer and F. Schandorf Petersen, *C. N.: Kunstneren og mennesket* (2 vols., Copenhagen, 1947–48); H. Riis-Vestergaard, *C. N.s symfoniske stil, dens forudsaetninger og saerpraeg* (diss., Univ. of Copenhagen, 1952); I. Mller and T. Meyer, eds., *C. N.s breve i udvalg og med kommentarer* (Copenhagen, 1954); J. Balzer, ed., *C. N. i hundredåret for hans fdsel* (Copenhagen, 1965; Eng. tr., 1965); J. Fabricius, *C. N. 1865–1931: A Pictorial Biography* (Copenhagen, 1965); D. Fog and T. Schousboe, *C. N.: kompositioner: En bibliografi* (Copenhagen, 1965); R. Simpson, *Sibelius and N.: A Centenary Essay* (London, 1965); A. Telmányi, *Mit barndomschjem* (Copenhagen, 1965); T. Schousboe, ed., *C. N.: Dagboger og brevvesling med Anna Marie Carl Nielsen* (2 vols., Copenhagen, 1983); M. Miller, *C. N.: A Guide to Research* (N.Y., 1987); J. Jensen, *C. N.: Danskeren: Musikbiografi* (Copenhagen, 1991); B. Bjrnum and K. Mllerhj, eds., *Kongelige Bibliotek (Denmark): C. N.s samling: Katalog over komponistens musikhåndskrifter i Det konge-*

lige Bibliotek: The C. N. Collection: A Catalogue of the Composer's Musical Manuscripts in the Royal Library (Copenhagen, 1992); M. Mogensen, ed., C. N.: Der dänische Tondichter: Biographischer Dokumentationsbericht (5 vols., Arbon, 1992); M. Miller, ed., The N. Companion (Portland, oreg., 1995); D. Fanning, ed., N.: Symphony No. 5 (Cambridge, 1997).—NS/LK/DM

Nielsen, (Carl Henrik) Ludolf, Danish violist, conductor, and composer; b. Nrre-Tvede, Jan. 29, 1876; d. Copenhagen, Oct. 16, 1939. He was a pupil of V. Tofte (violin), A. Orth (piano), Bondesen (harmony), and O. Malling and J.P.E. Hartmann (composition) at the Copenhagen Cons. (1896–98), and then was a violist at the Tivoli and violist and deputy conductor at the Palekoncerter. He won the Ancker stipend and traveled in Germany, Austria, and Italy (1907). He later played in the Bjrvig Quartet, and subsequently was conductor of the musical society Euphrosyne (1914–20). His music represents an expansive late Romantic style.

WORKS: DRAMATIC: Opera: Isbella (Copenhagen, Oct. 8, 1915); Uhret (The Clock; 1911–13); Lola (1917–20). Ballet: Lackschmi (1921; Copenhagen, March 4, 1922); Rejsekammeraten (1928). Also incidental music to plays; music for radio. ORCH.: 3 syms.: No. 1 (1903), No. 2 (1909; Copenhagen, April 25, 1910), and No. 3 (1913; Copenhagen, May 4, 1914); other orch. works. CHAMBER: 3 string quartets (1900, 1904, 1920); piano pieces; organ music. VOCAL: Choral works; songs.—NS/LK/DM

Nielsen, Inga, Danish soprano; b. Holbaek, June 2, 1946. She received training at the Vienna Academy of Music and at the Stuttgart Hochschule für Musik. Following her operatic debut in Gelsenkirchen in 1973, she sang in Münster (1974–75) and Bern (1975–77). From 1978 to 1983 she was a member of the Frankfurt am Main Opera. In 1980 she sang at the N.Y. City Opera. She created the role of Minette in Henze's The English Cat at the Schwetzingen Festival in 1983. After singing Donna Anna in Stuttgart in 1984, she appeared at the Wexford Festival in 1986 as Amenaide in Tancredi. Her debut at London's Covent Garden followed in 1987 as Constanze, which role she also sang at the Salzburg Festival that year. In 1990 she appeared as Christine in the Italian premiere of Strauss's Intermezzo in Bologna. In 1992 she sang Gilda in Oslo, and then returned to Covent Garden as Ursula in Hindemith's Mathis der Maler in 1995. She appeared as Chrysothemis in Amsterdam in 1996 and sang at the Vienna Festival in 1997. She married **Robert Hale.**—NS/LK/DM

Nielsen, Ludvig, Norwegian organist, conductor, and composer; b. Borge in stfold, Feb. 3, 1906. He studied with Sandvold and Lange at the Oslo Cons., then with Straube, Raphael, and Hochkofler at the Leipzig Cons. (1931–32) and with Steenberg and Walle-Hansen in Oslo. He was organist at the Hvik Church, Baerum, Akershus (1924–32), and organist and choirmaster at Trondheim Cathedral (1935–76); also taught at the Oslo Cons. (1934–35) and the Trondheim Music School (from 1942). He distinguished himself primarily as a composer of sacred music. Among his organ works are a Concerto for Organ and Strings (1965), chorales, fugues, fantasies, and other pieces; his choral works include a Te Deum (1944–45), the oratorio Draumkvedet (1962), and motets.

BIBL.: B. Moe, L. N. (diss., Univ. of Trondheim, 1974).—NS/LK/DM

Nielsen, Riccardo, Italian composer and administrator; b. Bologna, March 3, 1908; d. Ferrara, Jan. 30, 1982. He studied with Casella and Gatti. He served as director of the Teatro Comunale in Bologna (1946–50). In 1952 he became director of the Liceo Musicale (later Cons.) in Ferrara. In his early works, he was influenced by Casella. He later wrote in a 12-tone idiom, which eventually evolved into a post-Webern style.

WORKS: DRAMATIC: L'incuba, monodrama (1948); La via di Colombo, radio opera (1953). ORCH.: Sinfonia concertante for Piano and Orch. (1931); Violin Concerto (1932); 2 syms. (1933, 1935); Concerto for Orchestra (1935); Musica per archi (1946); Variations (1956); Varianti (1965); 6 + 5 fascie sonore for Strings (1968). CHAMBER: Divertimento for Clarinet, Bassoon, Trumpet, Violin, Viola, and Cello (1934); 7 aforismi for Clarinet and Piano (1958); Cello Sonata (1958); Piano Quartet (1961); Cadenza a due for Cello and Piano (1967). VOCAL: Musik für Chor und Orchester (1944); Requiem nella miniera for Soloists, Chorus, and Orch. (1957); 4 Goethelieder for Soprano and Orch. (1958); Invenzioni e sinfonie for Soprano and Orch. (1959); songs.—NS/LK/DM

Nielsen, Svend, Danish composer and teacher; b. Copenhagen, April 20, 1937. He studied theory with Holmboe at the Royal Danish Cons. of Music in Copenhagen (graduated, 1967). After advanced composition studies with Nrgård, he taught at the Jutland Cons. of Music in Århus.

WORKS: CHAMBER Opera: Bulen (1968). ORCH.: Metamorfoser for 23 Solo Strings (1968); Nuages (1972); Sym. (1978–79); Violin Concerto (1985); Concertino for Viola and Strings (1988; also for Viola and Orch., 1990); Nightfall for Chamber Orch. (1989); Aria (1991); Aubade (1994); Sinfonia concertante for Cello and Orch. (1994). CHAMBER: Rondo for Flute, Violin, Viola, Cello, and Piano (1985); String Quartet (1987); Black Velvet for Clarinet and String Quartet (1988); Variations for Chamber Ensemble (1990); Vindbilleder for 5 Instruments (1990); Akvareller for Oboe and Piano (1992); Luftkasteller for Woodwind Quintet (1992); Reflekser for Flute and Organ (1994). Piano: Fall (1987). VOCAL: Duetter for Soprano, Contralto, Flute, Cello, Vibraphone, and Percussion (1964); Prisma-suite for Contralto, Flute, Viola, and Strings (1965); Paraphrase on "Auf dem Wasser zu singen" for Soprano and Ensemble (1985); Det dybe smil I-III for Chorus (1986); Så stille for Alto and 4 Instruments (1986); Dreamsongs for Soprano, Flute, Electric Guitar, and Cello (1988); På bunden af min drom... for Mezzo-soprano, Clarinet, Piano, and Cello (1993).—NS/LK/DM

Nielsen, Tage, Danish composer, pedagogue, and administrator; b. Copenhagen, Jan. 16, 1929. He received training in music and French at the Univ. of Copenhagen (M.A., 1955). In 1951 he joined the music dept. of Radio Denmark, where he was program secretary (from 1954) and later program ed. and deputy head of the dept. (from 1957). In 1963 he became director of the Jutland Academy of Music in Århus, where he was prof. of theory and music history from 1964. From 1983 to 1989 he was director of the Accademia di Danimarca in Rome. He served as managing director of the Soc. for the Publication of Danish Music from 1989 to 1993. In 1992 he received the Schierbeck Prize. His stylistic development proceeded through neo-Classicism, expressionism, the Danish New Simplicity mode, to neo-Romanticism.

WORKS: DRAMATIC: O p e r a : *Laughter in the Dark* (1986–91). **ORCH.:** *Intermezzo gaio* (1952; rev. 1963); *Bariolage* (1965; Århus, Feb. 7, 1966); *Il giardino magico* (1967–68; Århus, Feb. 24, 1969); *Passacaglia* (1981; Copenhagen, Nov. 24, 1983). **CHAMBER:** *Variants* for Alto Flute (1963); *2 Impromptus* for Viola and Organ (1967); *Recitative and Elegy* for Guitar (1975); *Arrangement and Landscape* for Flute (1981); *Ballade* for Percussion (1984); *Salon*, trio for Flute, Viola, and Harp (1984); *3 Opera Fragments* for 13 Instruments (1986); *Tramonto* for Cello and Percussion (1989); *The Frosty Silence in the Gardens* for Guitar (1990); *Uccelli* for Clarinet (1992); *A Winter's Tale*, clarinet sonatina (1994). **KEYBOARD: P i a n o :** Sonata (1949–50); *2 Nocturnes* (1960–61); *3 Character Pieces and an Epilogue* (1972–74); *Paesaggi* for 2 Pianos (1985). **O r g a n :** Toccata (1951); *Divertimento: Fields and Meadows* (1971); *Lamento* (1993); *Chorale Fantasy* (1994–95). **VOCAL:** *5 Songs* for Mezzo-soprano and Piano (1946–70); *Attic Summer* for Soprano, Guitar, and Percussion (1974); *8 Choral Songs* (1974); *3 Shakespeare Fragments* for Soprano, Oboe, Cello, and Piano (1977–78); *3 Black Madrigals* for Chorus (1978); *5 Poems by William Blake* for Soprano and Vibraphone (1979); *3 Mexican Poems* for Soprano, Alto, Tenor, Bass, and Piano (1982); *2 Choral Songs* (1984); *In tribulatione mea*, motet for Chorus (1985); *Ritual* for Mezzo-soprano, Flute, Piano, and Percussion (1989); *3 Choral Songs* (1990); *5 Romantic Songs* for Mezzo-soprano and Guitar (1994).—**NS/LK/DM**

Niemann, Albert, greatly respected German tenor; b. Erxleben, near Magdeburg, Jan. 15, 1831; d. Berlin, Jan. 13, 1917. He began his career as an actor and dramatist. He joined the Dessau Opera (1849), where he sang in the chorus and appeared in minor roles; then had lessons with F. Schneider and Nusch. He sang in Halle from 1852 to 1854, then in Hannover; he then went to Paris, where he studied with Duprez. In 1866 he was engaged at the Berlin Royal Opera, remaining on its roster until 1888. Wagner thought highly of him, and asked him to create the role of Tannhäuser in Paris (March 13, 1861) and of Siegmund at the Bayreuth Festival (Aug. 14, 1876). From 1886 to 1888 he was a member of the Metropolitan Opera in N.Y.; his debut there was in his star role as Siegmund (Nov. 10, 1886); then he sang Tristan at the American premiere of *Tristan und Isolde* (Dec. 1, 1886) and Siegfried in *Götterdämmerung* (Jan. 25, 1888) there. He publ. *Erinnerungen an Richard Wagner* (Leipzig, 1907; Eng. tr., 1908); his correspondence with Wagner was ed. by W. Altmann (Berlin, 1924).

BIBL.: R. Sternfeld, *A. N.* (Berlin, 1904).—**NS/LK/DM**

Niemann, Walter, German writer on music and composer; b. Hamburg, Oct. 10, 1876; d. Leipzig, June 17, 1953. He was a pupil of his father, Rudolph (Friedrich) Niemann, and of Humperdinck (1897). From 1898 to 1901 he studied at the Leipzig Cons. with

Reinecke and von Bose, and at the Univ. with Riemann and Kretzschmar (musicology), receiving a Ph.D. in 1901 with the diss. *Über die abweichende Bedeutung der Ligaturen in der Mensuraltheorie der Zeit vor Johannes de Garlandia* (publ. in Leipzig, 1902; reprint, Wiesbaden, 1971). From 1904 to 1906 he was ed. of the *Neue Zeitschrift für Musik* in Leipzig, and in 1906–07 he was a teacher at the Hamburg Cons. From 1907 to 1917 he was again in Leipzig as a writer and critic of the *Neueste Nachrichten*, then gave up this position to devote himself to composition. Besides a Violin Sonata and a few works for orch. and string orch., he wrote numerous piano pieces (over 150 opus numbers).

WRITINGS (all publ. in Leipzig unless otherwise given): *Musik und Musiker des 19. Jahrhunderts* (1905); *Die Musik Skandinaviens* (1906); *Das Klavierbuch* (1907; 5th ed., 1920); with G. Schjelderup, *Edvard Grieg: Biographie und Würdigung seiner Werke* (1908); *Das Norlandbuch* (Weimar, 1909); *Die musikalische Renaissance des 19. Jahrhunderts* (1911); *Taschenlexikon für Klavierspieler* (1912; 4th ed., 1918, as *Klavierlexikon*); *Die Musik seit Richard Wagner* (1913; 5th and later eds. as *Die Musik der Gegenwart seit Wagner*); *Jean Sibelius* (1917); *Die nordische Klaviermusik* (1918); with O. Klauwell, *Die Formen der Instrumentalmusik* (2nd ed., 1918); *Die Virginalmusik* (1919); *Meister des Klaviers* (1919); *Brahms* (1920; 14th ed., 1933; Eng. tr., N.Y., 1929). —**NS/LK/DM**

Niemöller, Klaus Wolfgang, esteemed German musicologist; b. Gelsenkirchen, July 21, 1929. He was a student of Fellerer at the Univ. of Cologne (Ph.D., 1955, with the diss. *Nikolaus Wollick [1480–1541] und sein Musiktraktat*; publ. in Cologne, 1956), and continued his studies in Paris, Rome, and Freiburg im Breisgau (1955–56). In 1958 he became an asst. lecturer in the musicology dept. at the Univ. of Cologne, where he completed his Habilitation in 1964 with his *Untersuchungen zu Musikpflege und Musikunterricht an den deutschen Lateinschulen vom ausgehenden Mittelalter bis um 1600* (publ. in Regensburg, 1969). He subsequently held appointments on its faculty as a lecturer, ausserplanmässiger Professor (1969–70), and research fellow and prof. (from 1970), and, from 1983 to 1994, as director of its Musikwissenschaftlichen Inst. In 1977 he became chairman of the Joseph Haydn Inst. in Cologne. From 1989 to 1993 he was president of the Gesellschaft für Musikforschung. With A. Mayeda, he served as ed. of the new critical edition of the complete works of Robert Schumann, which began publication in 1991. In 1971 he received the Dent Medal of England, and, in 1975, was made a member of the Nordheim- westfälischen Akademie der Wissenschaften. Niemöller's learned articles have appeared in various Festschriften, series, and journals. He is an authority on sources for the study of the history of early music theory and other aspects of early music, as well as of the music of the 19th century. —**NS/LK/DM**

Niemtschek (Niemetschek, Němeček), Franz Xaver, Czech writer on music; b. Sadská, near Poděbrady, July 24, 1766; d. Vienna, March 19, 1849. He studied at the Prague Gymnasium (1776–82), then studied philosophy at the Univ. of Prague (Ph.D., 1800), where he was a prof. of philosophy (1802–20). He is known in musical annals for his biography of Mozart, whom he greatly admired and evidently knew personally: *Leben des k. k. Kapellmeisters Wolfgang Gottlieb Mozart* (Prague, 1798; 2nd ed., 1808; Eng. tr., 1956). —NS/LK/DM

Nietzsche, Friedrich (Wilhelm), celebrated German philosopher; b. Röcken, near Lützen, Oct. 15, 1844; d. Weimar, Aug. 25, 1900. He was prof. of classical philology at the Univ. of Basel (1869–79). He was at first a warm partisan of Wagner, whom he championed in *Die Geburt der Tragödie aus dem Geiste der Musik* (1872; 2nd ed., 1874) and *Richard Wagner in Bayreuth* (1876). However, in *Der Fall Wagner* and *Nietzsche contra Wagner* (both 1888) and in *Götzendämmerung* (1889), he turned against his former idol and became a partisan of Bizet. Nietzsche tried his hand at composition, producing both sacred and secular choral works, songs, and piano pieces. See C. Jang, ed., *Friedrich Nietzsche: Der musikalische Nachlass* (Kassel, 1977).

BIBL.: E. Förster-Nietzsche, *Das Leben F. N.s* (2 vols., Leipzig, 1895–1904; Eng. tr. [condensed], 1912–15); J. Zeitler, *N.s Ästhetik* (Leipzig, 1900); T. Lessing, *Schopenhauer, Wagner, N.* (Munich, 1906); H. Bélart, *F. N. und Richard Wagner* (Berlin, 1907); P. Lasserre, *Les Idées de N. sur la musique. La Période Wagnérienne (1871–76)* (Paris, 1907; new ed., 1930); H. Bélart, *F. N.s Freundschaftstragödie mit R. Wagner* (Dresden, 1912); E. Förster-Nietzsche, *Wagner und N. zur Zeit ihrer Freundschaft* (Munich, 1915); W. Dahms, *Die Offenbarung der Musik. Eine Apotheose F. N.s* (1922); L. Griesser, *N. und Wagner* (1923); K. Hildebrandt, *Wagner und N., Ihr Kampf gegen das 19. Jahrhundert* (Breslau, 1924); J. Verweyen, *Wagner und N.* (Stuttgart, 1926); E. Gürster, *N. und die Musik* (1929); J. Huneker, *Essays* (N.Y., 1929); E. Eckertz, *N. als Künstler* (Munich, 1930); G. Foster, *F. N.* (N.Y., 1931); P. Dippel, *N. und Wagner* (1934); E. Ruprecht, *Der Mythos bei Wagner und N.* (Berlin, 1938); F. Love, *Young N. and the Wagnerian Experience* (Chapel Hill, 1963); D. Fischer-Dieskau, *Wagner und N.: Der Mystagogue und sein Abtrünniger* (Stuttgart, 1974; Eng. tr. as *Wagner and N.*, N.Y., 1976 and London, 1978); B. Schmidt, *Der esthische Aspekt der Musik: N.s "Geburt der Tragödie und die Weiner klassische Musik* (Wützburg, 1991); G. Liébert, *N. et la musique* (Paris, 1995); G. Pöltner and H. Vetter, eds., *N. und die Musik* (Frankfurt am Main, 1997).—NS/LK/DM

Nigg, Serge, prominent French composer and teacher; b. Paris, June 6, 1924. He entered the Paris Cons. at age 17, where he studied harmony with Messiaen and then counterpoint and fugue with Plé-Caussade (until 1945). He subsequently studied dodecaphonic composition with Liebowitz. His *Variations* for Piano and 10 Instruments (1946) was the first strictly dodecaphonic score to be composed in France. In 1956 he was made a member of the music committee of Radiodiffusion Française. From 1967 to 1982 he was inspector of the French lyrical theaters for the Ministry of Culture. He served as prof. of composition (1978–82) and of instrumentation and orchestration (1982–89) at the Paris Cons. From 1982 to 1989 he was president of the Société National de Musique. Among his honors are 6 grands Prix du Disque (1957–89), the Italia Prize (1958), the Musical Grand Prix of the City of Paris (1974), 3 grands Prix de l'Académie des Beaux Arts (1976; Prix Florence Gould, 1983; Prix René Dumesnil, 1987), and the Grand Prix of the SACEM (1978). In 1989 he was elected a member of the Institut de France (Académie des Beaux-Arts), becoming president in 1995. After composing orthodox serial pieces, Nigg opted for a synthesis of nondoctrinal serial writing and accessible French refinement.

WORKS: DRAMATIC: Ballet: *Billard* (1950). **ORCH.:** *Timour,* symphonic poem (Paris, Feb. 1944); *Pour un poète captif,* symphonic poem (1950; Prague, May 1951); 2 piano concertos: No. 1 (1954) and No. 2 (Strasbourg, June 10, 1971); Violin Concerto (1957; Paris, May 27, 1960); *Musique funèbre* for Strings (1959); *Jérôme Bosch Symphonie* (1959; Strasbourg, June 21, 1960); Concerto for Flute and Strings (Vichy, July 26, 1961); *Visages d'Axël* (1965–67; Besançon, Sept. 4, 1967); *Fulgur* (Paris, Oct. 7, 1969); *Fantes de l'Imaginaire* (Paris, June 1974); *Scènes concertantes* for Piano and Strings (1975; French Radio, Paris, March 26, 1976); *Mirrors for William Blake,* sym. for Orch. and Piano (1978; French Radio, Paris, Oct. 25, 1979); *Millions d'oiseaux d'or* (1980–81; Boston, March 20, 1981); Viola Concerto (1988); *Poème* (1989; Quebec, Feb. 12, 1990). **CHAMBER:** *Variations* for Piano and 10 Instruments (1946; Paris, Jan. 29, 1947); Suite for Violin, Viola, Cello, and Harp (1952); Sonata for Solo Violin (N.Y., Nov. 10, 1965); *Pièce* for Trumpet and Piano (1972); *Pièce* for Flute and Piano (1976); String Quartet (1982; Radio France, Paris, April 11, 1983); *Duo élégiaque* for Cello and Piano (1985); *Arioso* for Violin and Piano (1987); Violin Sonata (1994). **Piano:** 3 sonatas (1943, 1964, 1984); *Deux pièces* (1947); *Deux images de nuit* (1997); *Tumultes* (1998). **VOCAL:** *Quatre mélodies sur des poèmes de Paul Eluard* for Soprano and Piano (1948); *Prière pour le Premier Jour de l'Eté* for Baritone, Reciter, Chorus, Children's Chorus, and Orch. (1956); *L'Etrange Aventure de Gulliver a Lilliput* for Reciter, Children's Chorus, and Instrumental Ensemble (1958); *La Croisade des Enfants* for Chorus, Children's Chorus, and Instrumental Ensemble (1959); *Histoire d'Oeuf* for 2 Reciters, 6 Percussion, Piano, and Celesta (1961; Strasbourg, Jan. 17, 1962; choreographed version, 1977); *Le Chant du dépossédé* for Baritone, Reciter, and Orch. (Strasbourg, June 25, 1964); *Du clair au sombre* for Soprano and Chamber Orch. (1986; French Radio, Paris, March 7, 1987). —NS/LK/DM

Niimi, Tokuhide, Japanese composer; b. Nagoya, Aug. 5, 1947. After graduating from the Univ. of Tokyo (1970), he studied composition with Miyoshi, Noda, Yashiro, and Mamiya at the Tokyo National Univ. of Fine Arts and Music (1971–78). He taught at the Toho Gakuen School of Music in Tokyo and served on the board of directors of the Japanese Composers Society.

WORKS: ORCH.: Percussion Concerto (1973); 2 syms. (1981; with chorus, 1986); *Waving* for Japanese Drums and Orch. (1982); 2 piano concertos (1984; *Eyes of the Creator,* 1993); *Ohju* (1986); *Heteorhythmix* (1991); *Chain of Life* for Small Orch. (1993); *Fu Sui-win* for Strings, Percussion, and Celesta (1995); *Fujin-Raijin* for Japanese Drum, Organ, and Orch. (1995–97); *The Cosmic Tree* for Japanese Instrument and Orch. (1996); *Towards the Silence* (1998). **CHAMBER:** *Enlaçage II* for 3 Percussionists (1978) and *III* for 2 Marimbas and 2 Percussionists (1980); *Fuin I* for Saxophone and Cello (1987) and *II* for 3 Shakuhachis (1988); *Ohju* for Cello (1987); *Kazane* for Clarinet, Violin, and Cello (1989); *Far Away from the Far Past,* concerto for 17-String Koto and Koto Ensemble (1987); *Planets Dance* for 6 Percussionists (1993); String Quartet (1994); *Tree in a Dream* for Marimba and String Quartet (1996); *Garden in the Light* for Piano and

String Quartet (1997); *Fairy Ring* for Clarinet and Piano (1998). **KEYBOARD: Piano**: *In the Twilight,* preludes for 2 Pianos (1983); *Various Divines* (1983); *3 Valses* for Piano Duet (1986); *Preludes of the Wind* (1992). **Organ**: *Wind Spiral* (1991). **VOCAL**: *Enlaçage I* for Chorus and Orch. (1977); *Under Blue Skies* for Children's Chorus, Mixed Chorus, and Orch. (1986); *Au-Mi* for Soprano, Violin, Cello, and Piano (1989); also choruses; songs.—**NS/LK/DM**

Nikiprowetzky, Tolia, Russian-born French composer, ethnomusicologist, and broadcasting administrator; b. Fyodosia, Crimea, Sept. 25, 1916; d. Paris, May 5, 1997. He was taken by his parents to France when he was 7, and began his training in music in Marseilles. In 1937 he settled in Paris and studied counterpoint and fugue with Simone Plé-Caussade and music history with Louis Laloy. In 1946 he pursued training in composition with René Leibowitz. In 1956 he became head of the Discothèque Centrale de la Société de Radiodiffusion de la France d'Outre-mer (SOR-AFOM), and also was active with the Office de Coopération radiophonique (OCORA). He pursued ethnomusicological missions to Mauritania in 1960, Senegal in 1962, Niger in 1963, and Cameroun in 1965. From 1969 he was active with the French Radio. He was a contributor to *La musique dans la vie* (2 vols., Paris, 1967, 1969).

WORKS: **DRAMATIC:** *Les Noces d'ombre* (concert perf., Paris, Dec. 12, 1957; stage perf., Toulouse, May 4, 1974; new version as the choregraphique divertissement *Danse des reflets minéraux,* 1974; Paris, Jan. 12, 1975); *La fête et les Masques,* opera (1970; French Radio, Paris, Dec. 19, 1973); *Le Sourire de l'Autre* (1979; suite, Bordeaux, Dec. 12, 1980); *Auto-Stop,* opera-film (1981); *La Veuve du Héros* (1983). **ORCH.:** *Sinfonietta* (1954; Algiers, Feb. 23, 1955); *Adagio* for Strings (1955; French Radio, Paris, June 2, 1957; concert perf., Paris, Nov. 25, 1962); *Diptyque* for Strings (Paris, March 17, 1963); Sym., *Logos 5* (1964; Strasbourg, April 1965); *Hommage à Antonio Gaudi* (1965; Paris, Dec. 5, 1967); *Naturae divisio* (1973; Paris, July 10, 1975); *Tetraktys* for Saxophones and Chamber Orch. (1975; London, July 30, 1976); Piano Concerto (1977; Paris, Feb. 24, 1979); *Fleuves impassibles* (1978; Paris, Feb. 24, 1979); Violin Concerto (1981; Paris, Oct. 19, 1982); Trumpet Concerto (1986; Paris, July 7, 1988). **CHAMBER:** String Quartet (1961); Sonatine for Solo Flute (1962); *Recitatif et Scène* for Cello and Piano (1985; Paris, Sept. 15, 1986); *Anaphora* for Cello and Piano (1987); *La vie fragile* for Guitar (1989). **Piano**: *Deux pièces* (1948); Sonata (1960); *Treize études* (1966); *Une Quète du Seuil* (1990–94). **VOCAL:** *Quatre mélodies* for Soprano and Piano (1949); *Les chants de la fille seule* for Mezzo-soprano and Orch. (1959; French Radio, Paris, July 9, 1962); *Trois poèmes d'Yves Bonnefoy* for Vocal Ensemble and Piano (1962); *Numinis Sacra* for Tenor, Chorus, Organ, and Percussion (1967); *Voix nocturnes* for Soprano, Flute, Horn, Cello, and Harpsichord (1978); *Ode Funèbre* for Soprano, Baritone, Chorus, and Orch. (1985; Paris, Nov. 4, 1988).—**LK/DM**

Nikisch, Arthur, famous Austrian conductor of Moravian and Hungarian descent; b. Lébényi Szent-Miklós, Oct. 12, 1855; d. Leipzig, Jan. 23, 1922. His father was head bookkeeper to Prince Lichtenstein. Nikisch attended the Vienna Cons., studying with Dessoff (composition) and Hellmesberger (violin), graduating in 1874. While still a student, he had the honor of playing among the first violins under Wagner's direction at the laying of the cornerstone of the Bayreuth Theater (1872). He was at first engaged as a violinist in the Vienna Court Orch. (1874–77), then was chorusmaster (1877–78), second conductor (1878–79), and first conductor (1879–89) of the Leipzig City Theater. In 1889 he was engaged as conductor of the Boston Sym. Orch., with excellent success, remaining at this post until 1893. Returning to Europe, he was music director of the Budapest Opera (1893–95). He also conducted the Phil. Concerts there, and from 1895 was conductor of the Gewandhaus Orch. in Leipzig, and of the Berlin Phil. From 1897 he was in constant demand as a visiting conductor, and made a number of extended tours with the Berlin Phil.; he directed many of the concerts of the London Phil. Society, and works of Wagner and Richard Strauss at Covent Garden; in 1912 he made a tour of the U.S. with the London Sym. Orch. From 1902 to 1907, he was director of studies at the Leipzig Cons., and in 1905–06 general director of the Stadttheater. As a sym. conductor, Nikisch possessed an extraordinary Romantic power of musical inspiration. He was the first of his profession to open the era of "the conductor as hero," exercising a peculiar magnetism on his audiences equal to that of virtuoso artists; his personal appearance, a poetic-looking beard and flowing hair, contributed to his success. His son Mitja Nikisch (b. Leipzig, May 21, 1899; d. Venice, Aug. 5, 1936) was an excellent pianist who toured South America in 1921. He made his U.S. debut in N.Y., Oct. 23, 1923.

BIBL.: F. Pfohl, *A. N. als Mensch und als Künstler* (Leipzig, 1900; 2nd ed., 1925); E. Segnitz, *A. N.* (Leipzig, 1920); H. Chevalley, ed., *A. N., Leben und Wirken* (Berlin, 1922; 2nd ed., 1925); A. Dette, *A. N.* (Leipzig, 1922).—**NS/LK/DM**

Nikolais, Alwin (Theodore), American choreographer, stage director, and composer; b. Southington, Conn., Nov. 25, 1912; d. N.Y., May 8, 1993. He studied piano and played in movie houses for the silent films. In 1929 he began to study dance with a pupil of Mary Wigman; became director of the Hartford (Conn.) Parks Marionette Theater and later chairman of the dance dept. of the Hartt School of Music there. From 1942 to 1946 he served in military counterintelligence in Europe; then studied with Hanya Holm in N.Y. He became director of the Henry Street Settlement Playhouse in N.Y. (1948), where he organized the Alwin Nikolais Dance Theatre. He wrote music for many of his dance productions, including works in the electronic medium. His principal choreographic innovation is the technique of body extension by tubular projections and disks attached to the head and upper and nether limbs, so that a biped dancer becomes a stereogeometrical figure; often in his productions clusters of dancers form primitivistic ziggurats.—**NS/LK/DM**

Nikolayeva, Tatiana (Petrovna), esteemed Russian pianist, pedagogue, and composer; b. Bezhitz, May 4, 1924; d. San Francisco, Nov. 22, 1993. She began her piano training with Goldenweiser at Moscow's Central Music School, continuing as his pupil at the Moscow Cons. (graduated, 1947); also studied composition there with Golubev (graduated, 1950). After a highly successful series of concerts in Russia, she won first prize at Leipzig's Bach festival for her performance of Bach's clavier works (1950); subsequently toured in Eastern Europe and later made visits to Western Europe; gave several highly acclaimed recitals in London (1986). She was a teacher (1959–65) and a prof. (from 1965) at the Moscow Cons. She was stricken with a cerebral hemorrhage while giving a recital in San Francisco on Nov. 13, 1993; she died 9 days later. Nikolayeva was a remarkably gifted virtuoso; Shostakovich wrote his 24 Preludes and Fugues expressly for her. She was made an Honored Artist of the R.S.F.S.R. in 1955. Among her works are several syms.; 2 piano concertos; Piano Quintet; Piano Sonata; many piano pieces.—NS/LK/DM

Nikolov, Lazar, Bulgarian composer; b. Burgas, Aug. 26, 1922. He studied composition with Vladigerov at the Bulgarian State Cons. in Sofia (1942–47) and in 1961 he joined its faculty. An experimenter by nature, Nikolov was one of the few composers in Bulgaria who adopted modern procedures of composition, melodically verging on atonality and harmonically on polytonality.

WORKS: DRAMATIC: O p e r a : *Prometheus Bound*, chamber opera (1963–69; Ruse, March 24, 1974); *Uncles* (1975). ORCH.: 2 piano concertos: No. 1 (1947–48; Ruse, Nov. 21, 1949) and No. 2 (1954–55; Sofia, Feb. 28, 1963); Concerto for Strings (1949; Ruse, Nov. 30, 1951); Violin Concerto (1951–52; Varna, March 25, 1955); 2 syms.: No. 1 (1953; Varna, Feb. 16, 1956) and No. 2 for 2 Pianos and Orch. (1960–61); Piano Concertino (1964); *Symphonies* for 13 Strings (1965); *Divertimento concertante* for Chamber Orch. (1968); Cello Concertino (1973). CHAMBER: Violin Sonata (1953–54); Viola Sonata (1955); Piano Quintet (1958–59); Flute Sonata (1962); Cello Sonata (1962); Clarinet Sonata (1962); 2 string quartets (1965, 1970); Sonata for 2 Harps (1971); Double Bass Sonata (1972); Bassoon Sonata (1976); Oboe Sonata (1976). P i a n o : 4 sonatas (1950, 1952, 1955, 1964); Sonata for 2 Pianos (1952). VOCAL: *Chants* for Soloists, Chorus, and Chamber Instrumental Group (1969). —NS/LK/DM

Nikolovski, Vlastimir, Macedonian composer; b. Prilep, Dec. 20, 1925. Both his parents were professional musicians from whom he received elementary musical education. In 1944 he obtained a baccalaureate in Prilep; subsequently studied theory with Evlahov at the Leningrad Cons. In 1955 he returned to Yugoslavia, where he took courses at the Belgrade Academy of Music. Upon graduation, he settled in Skopje and became active as a teacher and as director of musical programming for the state radio. In 1976 he was appointed a corresponding member of the Academy of Arts of Macedonia. In his music he makes use of a number of native instruments, particularly percussion. Among his works are 3 syms., a Piano Concerto, 2 oratorios, a Violin Sonata, a Cello Sonata, a Piano Sonata, a String Quartet, and a number of choruses on Macedonian themes.—NS/LK/DM

Niles, John Jacob, American folksinger, folk-music collector, and composer; b. Louisville, Ky., April 28, 1892; d. at his Boot Hill farm, near Lexington, Ky., March 1, 1980. He began collecting and transcribing Appalachian songs when he was 15, and subsequently traveled throughout the Southern Appalachians; studied at the Cincinnati Cons. (1919), and later took courses at the Univ. of Lyons and at the Paris Schola Cantorum. After making his operatic debut in Massenet's *Manon* with the Cincinnati Opera (1920), he devoted himself to teaching, performing folk music, collecting, and composing. His own works include such favorites as *I Wonder as I Wander, Go 'way from my Window*, and *Black Is the Color of My True Love's Hair*. With Douglas Moore, he also brought out *Songs My Mother Never Taught Me* (1929). Many of his works were included in the collection *The Songs of John Jacob Niles* (1975). The greater part of his MSS, field notebooks, instruments, etc., are housed in the John Jacob Niles Collection at the Univ. of Kentucky. Among his publications are *7 Kentucky Mountain Songs* (1929), *7 Negro Exultations* (1929), *Songs of the Hill Folk* (1934), *10 Christmas Carols* (1935), *More Songs of the Hill Folk* (1936), *Ballads and Tragic Legends* (1937), *The Anglo-American Ballad Study Book* (1945), *The Anglo-American Carol Study Book* (1948), and *The Shape-Note Study Book* (1950).—NS/LK/DM

Nilsson (family surname **Svensson**), **(Märta) Birgit,** greatly renowned Swedish soprano; b. Västra Karup, May 17, 1918. She began singing at an early age and was a member of the local church choir. At age 15, she began vocal studies with a nearby choirmaster. In 1941 she entered the Royal Academy of Music in Stockholm, her principal mentors being Hislop and Sunnegaard. Upon graduation in 1946, she made her operatic debut at the Royal Opera in Stockholm as Agathe. Following her success as Lady Macbeth there in 1947, she joined its roster and sang leading roles in Italian and German operas with increasing success. On June 20, 1951, she made her British debut as Mozart's Elettra at the Glyndebourne Festival. In 1954 she sang Elsa at the Bayreuth Festival and at the Vienna State Opera. That same year, she was accorded the title of a Swedish Court Singer and sang Brünnhilde in *Götterdämmerung* that Dec. at the Royal Opera. After singing Isolde at the Teatro Colón in Buenos Aires in 1955, she won critical acclaim for her portrayal of Brünnhilde in *Siegfried* at the Maggio Musicale Fiorentino in Florence in 1956. On Aug. 9, 1956, Nilsson made her U.S. debut singing excerpts from *Tristan und Isolde* and *Götterdämmerung* with the Los Angeles Phil. at the Hollywood Bowl. Her U.S. operatic debut followed on Oct. 5, 1956, when she appeared as Brünnhilde in *Die Walküre* at the San Francisco Opera, a role she then sang at the Chicago Lyric Opera. In 1957 she portrayed Brünnhilde in the *Ring* cycle at her first appearance at London's Covent Garden, where she won outstanding critical acclaim. Another remarkable success followed in 1958 when she sang Turandot at her debut at Milan's La Scala. On Dec. 18, 1959, Nilsson scored a triumph at her Metropolitan Opera debut in N.Y. as Isolde, and immediately established herself as one of its foremost artists. Her subsequent critically acclaimed portrayals there included Brünnhilde in *Die Walküre* in 1960, Turandot, Aida, and Brünnhilde in *Götterdämmerung* in 1961, Tosca in 1962, Salome in 1965, and Elekra in 1966. She remained on the roster there until 1975. On Oct. 9, 1976, she celebrated the 30th anniversary of her operatic debut singing Isolde at the Royal Opera in Stockholm. In 1979 she rejoined the roster of the Metropolitan Opera, where she portrayed Elektra in 1980 and the Dyer's Wife in *Die Frau ohne Schatten* in 1981 with little evidence of any serious diminution of her vocal powers. Her final appearance there came on Oct. 22, 1983, as a participant in its 100th anniversary gala. In subsequent years, Nilsson devoted herself to giving master classes in the vocal art. She publ. *Mina minnesbilder* (Stockholm, 1977; Eng. tr., 1981, as *My Memoirs in Pictures*).

Nilsson was one of the foremost vocal artists of the 20th century, universally acknowledged as one of the greatest Wagnerian sopranos of all time. In addition to Wagner, she also excelled in operas by Verdi and Strauss. Her resplendent vocal and dramatic gifts made her portrayals unforgettable. She was accorded numerous honors. In 1968 she was made an Austrian Kammersängerin, and in 1970 a Bavarian Kammersängerin. She was made a Commander of the Vasa Order, 1st Class, of Sweden in 1974, and was named a Commandeur des Arts et des Lettres of France in 1991. In 1999 she was made an honorary member of the Vienna Phil.

BIBL.: *La N.* (Stockholm, 1995).—**NS/LK/DM**

Nilsson, Bo, Swedish composer; b. Skellefteå, May 1, 1937. He attended seminars in new music in Cologne and Darmstadt but was mainly autodidact. He publ. his memoirs as *Livet i en mössa* (Life in a Cap; 1984).

WORKS: ORCH.: *Buch der Veränderungen* (1957); *Plexus* (1959); *Szene I-III* for Chamber Orch. (1961); *Versuchungen* for 3 Orch. Groups (1961); *Entrée* for Tape and Orch. (1963); *Litanei über das verlorene Schlagzeug* for Orch. without Percussion, to conform to the title (1965); *Revue* (1967); *Quartets* for 36 Winds, Percussion, and Tape (1969); *Caprice* (1970); *Exit* for Tape and Orch. (1970); *Eurythmical Voyage* for Piano, Tape, and Orch. (1970); *Kaleidoskop* for Flute, Vibraphone, and Chamber Orch. (1997). **CHAMBER:** *Frequenzen* for Piccolo, Flute, Percussion, Guitar, Xylophone, Vibraphone, and Double Bass (1955–56); *Zeiten im Umlauf* for 8 Woodwinds (1957); *Kreuzungen* for Flute, Vibraphone, Guitar, and Xylophone (1957); *20 Gruppen* for Piccolo, Oboe, and Clarinet, or any 3 Instruments (1958); *Stenogramm* for Percussion or Organ (1959); *Reaktionen* for 1 to 4 Percussionists (1960); *Szene I* for 2 Flutes, 2 Trumpets, Piano, Harp, and 2 Percussionists (1960) and *II* for 6 Trumpets, 6 Violins, 4 Percussionists, Piano, Harp, Celesta, and Vibraphone (1961); *Déjà-vu* for Wind Quartet (1967); *Attraktionen* for String Quartet (1968); *Design* for Violin, Clarinet, and Piano (1968); *Déjà-connu* for Wind Quintet (1973); *Déjà connu, déjà entendu* for Wind Quintet (1976); Piano Quintet (1979); *Wendepunkt* for Brass and Live Electronics (1981); *Carte postale a Sten Frykberg* for Brass Quintet (1985). **Piano:** *Bewegungen* (1956); *Schlagfiguren* (1956); *Quantitäten* (1958); *Rendezvous* (1968). **VOCAL:** *Ett blocks timme,* chamber cantata for Soprano and 6 Instrumentalists (1957–58); *Szene IV* for Saxophone, Orch., and Chorus (1974–75); *La Bran* for Chorus and Orch. (1961); *La Bran* for Saxophone, Chorus, and Orch. (1963–76; Stockholm, March 19, 1976); *Nazm* for Speakers, Vocal Soloists, Chorus, Orch., and Tape (1972–73). **TAPE:** *Audiogramme* (1957–58).—**NS/LK/DM**

Nilsson, Christine (real name **Kristina Törnerhjelm**), admired Swedish soprano; b. Sjoabol, near Vaxjo, Aug. 20, 1843; d. Stockholm, Nov. 22,

1921. Her teachers were Baroness Leuhausen, and F. Berwald in Stockholm; with him she continued study in Paris, and on Oct. 27, 1864, made her debut, as Violetta in *La Traviata*, at the Théâtre-Lyrique, where she was engaged for 3 years. After successful visits to London, she was engaged from 1868 to 1870 at the Paris Opéra; then made long tours with Strakosch in America (1870–72), and sang in the principal continental cities. In 1872 she married Auguste Rouzaud (d. 1882); her second husband (married 1887) was the Spanish count Angel Vallejo y Miranda. She revisited America in the winters of 1873, 1874, and 1883, making her debut on the opening night of the Metropolitan Opera House in N.Y. on Oct. 22, 1883, as Marguerite in *Faust*. Her voice was not powerful, but it was brilliant. She excelled as Marguerite and Mignon.

BIBL.: B. Carlsson, *K. N.* (Stockholm, 1922); T. Norlind, *K. N.* (Stockholm, 1923); H. Headland, *C. N.: The Songbird of the North* (Rock Island, Ill., 1943).—**NS/LK/DM**

Nilsson, Harry, perhaps best remembered for his hit recordings of Fred Neil's "Everybody's Talkin'" (from the movie *Midnight Cowboy*) and Badfinger's "Without You,"; b. Brooklyn, N.Y., June 15, 1941; d. Agoura Hills, Calif., Jan. 15, 1994. Brooklyn- born Harry Nilsson achieved success as a songwriter with Blood, Sweat and Tears' recording of his "Without Her" in 1968 and Three Dog Night's smash-hit recording of his "One" in 1969. Recording for RCA between 1967 and 1980, his output included an entire album of Randy Newman songs, the soundtrack to *The Point* (one of television's first full-length animated movies), and the best-selling album *Nilsson Schmilsson*, considered to be his finest work. Retaining the curious distinction of never having performed in public, Nilsson became known for his associations with Ringo Starr, Keith Moon, and John Lennon in the mid 1970s. He also composed and performed the soundtracks to *Son of Dracula* and *Popeye*, but withdrew from recording in the 1980s. Harry Nilsson eventually returned to the studio in 1993, but on Jan. 15, 1994, he died at his home in the Agoura Hills above Los Angeles of a heart attack at age 52.

DISC.: NILSSON: *Spotlight* (1969); *Early Tymes* (1977); *Pandemonium Shadow Show* (1967); *Aerial Ballet* (1968); *Skidoo* (soundtrack; 1968); *Harry* (1969); *Nilsson Sings Newman* (1970); *The Point* (1971); *Aerial Pandemonium Ballet* (1971); *Nilsson Schmilsson* (1971); *Son of Schmilsson* (1972); *A Little Touch of Schmilsson in the Night* (1973); *Son of Dracula* (soundtrack; 1974); *Pussycats* (1974); *Duit on Mon Dei* (1975); *Sandman* (1976); *... That's the Way It Is* (1976); *Best* (1977); *Knnillssonn* (1977); *World's Greatest Lover* (soundtrack; 1978); *Greatest Hits* (1978); *All Time Greatest Hits* (1989); *Everybody's Talkin' and Other Hits* (1990); *Songwriter* (1992); *Personal Best: The H. N. Anthology* (1995); *Popeye* (soundtrack; 1980).—**BH**

Nilsson, Leo, Swedish composer; b. Malmö, Feb. 20, 1939. He studied organ and music pedagogy at the Stockholm Musikhögskolan (1958–62). After working at the electronic-music studio of the ORTF in Paris, he returned to Sweden and was active in electronic-music circles; collaborated with Ralph Lundsten for a time, and also organized his own electronic-music studio in

Skåne; taught at the Stockholm Musikshögskolan (from 1982). He composed various experimental works utilizing electronics.

WORKS: *Vilda livet fortsätter*, electronic score (1974); *Star–75*, multimedia piece (1975); *Zoo*, intermedia piece (1975); *String Play Video*, video piece (1976); *Vad speglar ögat själens spegel*, electronic score (1976); *Identitet* for Trombone, Violin, Double Bass, Synthesizer, and Electronics (1978); *Incostante* for Instrument and Electronics (1978); *Musica mobile*, electronic score (1978); *Signs of Presence*, sonographic piece (1978); *Sonata grafica Y* for Brass Quintet and Live Electronics (1978); *Va-et-vient monsieur Satie* for Piano and Live Electronics (1979); *Lek*, electronic score (1979); *Stenens hjärta*, electronic score (1979); *Animagica* (1980); *Sonata infernale*, electronic score (1981); *Early Ear*, electronic score (1982); *An der Quelle* for Piano (1983); *Musique d'ameublement* for 16 Winds, Cello, and Tape (Stockholm, Oct. 5, 1983); *Niente subito* for Cello and Tape (1983); *Svart vår-vår tiger* for Narrator, Piano, Cello, Live Electronics, and Tape (1983); *Voice of Glass*, electroacoustic piece (1985); *Passage* for Amplified Viola and Percussion (1986).—NS/LK/DM

Nilsson, Sven, Swedish bass; b. Gävle, May 11, 1898; Stockholm, March 1, 1970. He studied with Gillis Bratt and Hjaldis Ingebjarth in Stockholm, and then with Ivar Andresen in Dresden (1928–30). From 1930 to 1944 he was a member of the Dresden State Opera, where he became well known for his Mozart and Wagner portrayals, and also sang in the premieres of Strauss's *Arabella* (1933) and *Daphne* (1938). He likewise sang Wagner in Zoppot from 1934 to 1942. In 1946 he became a member of the Royal Theater in Stockholm, where he appeared until his death. On Nov. 9, 1950, he made his Metropolitan Opera debut in N.Y. as Daland, remaining there on the roster for a season. His guest engagements also took him to London, Milan, Amsterdam, Brussels, Barcelona, and other European music centers. Among his other roles were Osmin, Sarastro, Pogner, and Baron Ochs.—NS/LK/DM

Nilsson, Torsten, Swedish organist, choirmaster, teacher, and composer; b. Höör, Jan. 21, 1920; d. Stockholm, Sept. 24, 1999. He studied church music and pedagogy at the Stockholm Musikhögskolan (1938–42) and also had instruction in organ from Alf Lindner and in organ and composition from Anton Heiller in Vienna (1961, 1965). He was organist in Köping (1943–53), Hälsingborg (1953–62), and at the Oscar Church in Stockholm (1962–79), and also was conductor of the Oscar Motet Choir. He taught theory at the Stockholm Citizen's School (1962–73) and liturgical singing at the Stockholm Theological Inst. (1964–70) and the Univ. of Uppsala (1966–70). He excelled in liturgical works, and in his organ music introduced many innovations, such as static tone-clusters and specified periods of thematic improvisation.

WORKS: DRAMATIC: Church Opera-oratorios: *Ur jordens natt* (Out of the Night of the Earth) for Improvising Soloists and Vocal Groups, with Organ (Stockholm, April 12, 1968); *Dantesvit* (Dante Suite) for Soloists, Vocal Group, Percussion, Organ, Harpsichord, and Tape (Stockholm, April 23, 1969); *Skapelse* (The Creation) for Narrator, Chorus, Organ, and Instruments (Stockholm, May 11, 1970); *Ur jordens natt. Del 2* (Out of the Night of the Earth, Part 2; Stockholm,

April 12, 1974); *Den sista natten* (The Last Night) for 2 Actors, Mixed and Children's Chorus, Flute, Harp, Organ, and Percussion (Stockholm, Nov. 25, 1973). O p e r a : *Malin: The Doors of History Open Wide* (1983–90; first complete perf., Stockholm, Aug. 30, 1991). ORCH.: 2 concertos: No. 1 for Piano and Strings (1974–77) and No. 2, *On the Threshold*, for Piano, Wind Instruments, and Percussion (1975); Concerto for Trombone and Strings (1978); *Om ett brev*, lyric suite for Strings (1983); *A Lyric Suite* for Strings (1986–87). CHAMBER: Concertino for Trombone and Organ (1978); *Verwerfungen* for Organ and Percussion (1980); *Rondo* for Trombone (1981); Concertino for Trombone and Organ (1981–85); Concertino for Horn and Brass Quartet or Organ (1983); *Signals with 7 Structures* for Organ and 5 Percussionists (1985); *Rondo Sueziae* for Trombone and Piano (1987); *Revelations*, concerto for Organ and Piano (1988); *Barrage: Marche de dressage (marche surréaliste)* for 4 Trombones (1990); *Musica* for Winds (1992); organ music; piano pieces.—NS/LK/DM

Nimsgern, Siegmund, German bass-baritone; b. Stiring-Wendel, Jan. 14, 1940. He was a student in Saarbrücken of Sibylle Fuchs, Jakob Stämpfli, and Paul Lohmann. In 1965 he made his debut as a concert artist, and his operatic debut followed in 1967 when he appeared as Lionel in Tchaikovsky's *The Maid of Orleans* in Saarbrücken, where he sang until 1971. In 1970 he made his Salzburg Festival debut. From 1971 to 1974 he was a member of the Deutsche Oper am Rhein in Düsseldorf. He made his British debut in 1972 as a soloist in *La Damnation de Faust*. In 1973 he made his first appearance at London's Covent Garden as Amfortas, and he also made debuts as Milan's La Scala and the Paris Opéra. In 1974 he made his U.S. debut as Jokanaan at the San Francisco Opera. He made his Metropolitan Opera debut in N.Y. as Pizarro on Oct. 2, 1978, and returned there as Jochanaan in 1981. From 1983 to 1985 he appeared as Wotan at the Bayreuth Festivals. Among his other roles were Telramund, Alberich, Günther, the Dutchman, Macbeth, Iago, and Luna.—NS/LK/DM

Nin-Culmell, Joaquín (María), Cuban-American composer, pianist, and teacher, son of **Joaquín Nin (y Castellanos);** b. Berlin, Sept. 5, 1908. He went to Paris and studied piano at the Schola Cantorum and composition with Dukas at the Cons. From 1930 to 1935 he pursued training in composition with Falla in Granada. He also continued piano studies with Cortot and Viñes. In 1938 he emigrated to the U.S., where he taught at Williams Coll. in Williamstown, Mass. (1940–50) and the Univ. of Calif. at Berkeley (1950–74). He ed. and annotated the Spanish Choral Tradition (1975 et seq.), a series devoted to secular music of the Renaissance. His own music exhibits Spanish influence in its basic lyricism and vital rhythmic energy, but it combines these elements with 20th century harmonies in transparent textures that are essentially homophonic and tonal.

WORKS: DRAMATIC: *Yerma*, incidental music to García Lorca's play (1956); *El burlador de Sevilla*, ballet (1957–65); *La Celestina*, opera (1965–85); *Le rêve de Cyrano*, ballet (1978); *Cymbeline*, incidental music to Shakespeare's play (1980). ORCH.: *Homenaje a Falla* (1933–90); Piano Concerto (1946); *3 Piezas antiguas españolas* (1959–61); *Diferencias* (1962); Cello

Concerto (1962; also as a Guitar Concerto, 1992). **CHAMBER:** Piano Quintet (1934–36); *Celebration for Julia* for String Quartet and Glockenspiel (1981). **Guitar:** *6 Variations and Theme by Luis de Milán* (1945); *La Matilda y El Emilio* (1990). **KEYBOARD: Piano:** *Tres impresiones* (1929); *Sonata brève* (1932); *3 Homages* (1941–90); *Tonadas* (4 vols., 1956–61); *Alejandro y Luis* (1983); *12 Danzas Cubanas* (1985). **Organ:** *Variations on a Theme by Bach* (1987); *Sinfonia de los Misterios* (1993–94). **VOCAL:** Cantata for Voice, Harpsichord, and Strings (1965–66); *Dedication Mass* for Chorus and Organ (1970); *6 Popular Sephardic Songs* for Voice and Orch. or Piano (1982); *10 de Octubre!* for Chorus and Brass (1985–90); *Ragpicker's Song* for Chorus and Piano (1995); art songs; 49 Spanish and Cuban folk songs.—NS/LK/DM

Nini, Alessandro, Italian composer; b. Fano, near Pesaro, Nov. 1, 1805; d. Bergamo, Dec. 27, 1880. He studied with Luigi Palmerini at the Liceo Musicale in Bologna. In 1830 he accepted the post of director of the singing school in St. Petersburg, returning to Italy in 1837. Eventually he moved to Bergamo, where he was maestro di cappella at S. Maria Maggiore (1847–77) and director of the Istituto Musicale. He wrote 7 operas as well as syms., some chamber music, and cantatas. He was commended as a composer by Rossini and Verdi. —NS/LK/DM

Ninot le Petit (real name, **Johannes Baltazar**), Franco-Netherlands composer who flourished in the late 15th century. He was a member of the Sistine Chapel Choir at the Vatican in Rome from 1488 until his death about 1501. He was especially admired as a composer of chansons. Among his other extant works are a mass and 4 motets.—LK/DM

Nin (y Castellanos), Joaquín, Spanish-born Cuban pianist and composer, father of **Joaquin (María) Nin-Culmell;** b. Havana, Sept. 29, 1879; d. there, Oct. 24, 1949. He studied with Carlos Vidiella (piano) in Barcelona and with Moszkowski (piano) and d'Indy (composition) at the Paris Schola Cantorum, teaching piano at the latter (1905–08). After living in Berlin, Havana, and Brussels, he settled in Paris. He was a member of the French Légion d'honneur and a corresponding member of the Spanish Academy. He was especially noted as an interpreter of early piano music. He championed the music of the Bach family and works by early Spanish composers, advocating their performance on the piano as opposed to the harpsichord. He wrote articles on aesthetics; ed. 2 valuable collections of keyboard music: *16 sonatas anciennes d'auteurs espagnols* (Paris, 1925) and *17 sonates et pièces anciennes d'auteurs espagols* (Paris, 1929); these 2 collections contained the first contemporary eds. of Padre Antonio Soler, and led to the rediscovery of Spain's outstanding 18th-century master; also ed. *Sept chants lyriques espagnols anciens* (1926) and *Sept chansons picaresques espangoles anciennes* (1926), both for Voice and Piano, 10 pieces by Herrando for Violin and Piano (1937), and *Vocalise (Chant elégiaque)* for Voice and Piano.

WORKS: *20 cantos populares españoles* for Voice and Piano (1923); *10 noëls espagnols* for Voice and Piano (1932); *Aus jardín de Lindaraja* for Violin and Piano (1927); *5 commentarios* for Violin and Piano (1929); many solo piano pieces, including *Danza ibérica* (1926), *Mensaje a Claude Debussy* (1929), *Cadena de valses* (1929), *"1830" variaciones* (1930), and *Canto de cuna para los huérfanos de España* (1939).—NS/LK/DM

Nirvana, first grunge-rock band to achieve international popularity. **MEMBERSHIP:** Kurt Cobain, gtr., voc. (b. Hoquiam, Wash., Feb. 20, 1967; d. Seattle, Wash., April 5, 1994); Krist Novoselic, bs. (b. Los Angeles, May 16, 1965); David Grohl, drm. (b. Warren, Ohio, Jan. 14, 1969). **Hole: MEMBERSHIP:** Courtney Love (Harrison), gtr., voc. (b. San Francisco, July 9, 1964); Eric Erlandson, gtr. (b. Los Angeles, Jan. 9, 1963); Melissa Auf der Maur, bs. (b. Montreal, Canada, March 17, 1972); Patty Schemel, drm. (b. Seattle, Wash., April 24, 1967). Bassist Kristen Pfaff (b. ca. 1968; d. Seattle, Wash, June 16, 1994) joined in 1993; after Pfaff's death, Auf der Maur returned to the band.

Nirvana produced a surprisingly melodic yet deafeningly loud, guitar-based sound behind stark and unsettling lyrics that reflected a deep-seated sense of anger, alienation, and hopelessness regarding contemporary life and culture. Their success, along with that of rivals Pearl Jam, brought attention to Seattle as one of the most vital musical centers in the country, opening the door for similar acts such as Soundgarden, Stone Temple Pilots, and Alice in Chains. The popularity of Nirvana inspired a fashion craze, favoring dirty, baggy jeans, flannel shirts, and combat boots.

Kurt Cobain and Krist Novoselic grew up in Aberdeen, Wash., where Cobain took up drums and fraternized with the local group the Melvins. Kicked out of his mother's house after quitting high school, Cobain experimented with guitar and formed Nirvana with Novoselic in 1987. They played club engagements in Olympia, Tacoma, and Seattle, and with Melvins' drummer Dale Crover recorded a 10-song demonstration tape that they submitted to Seattle's underground label, Sub Pop. Signed to the label, the two recorded *Bleach* with drummer Chad Channing and guitarist Jason Everman. The album featured their debut single, "Love Buzz" and "Negative Creep," and gained Nirvana their first underground following. They toured Europe as an opening act in 1989 and signed with DGC Records in 1990. With the departures of Everman and Channing, Nirvana recruited David Grohl as their drummer for *Nevermind.* An angry, raw, yet melodic work, the album yielded the band's barely intelligible theme song and first (smash) hit, the anthemic "Smells like Teen Spirit"; *Nevermind* became an instant best-seller. It also produced the moderate hit "Come as You Are" and the minor hit "Lithium."

The underground reputation won by Nirvana led to a major-label recording contract with DGC Records. The abrasive yet compelling album *In Utero* was banned by several major chain stores but nonetheless sold quite well, although not to the level of *Nevermind.* It featured the disconcerting "Rape Me," "Serve the Servants," "Dumb," and the surprisingly tender "All Apologies." In 1992 Cobain wed Courtney Love, singer-songwriter for the band Hole, and the two became tabloid darlings during their brief, stormy marriage.

During 1993 Nirvana performed a benefit in San Francisco for rape victims of the ongoing war in Bosnia and appeared on the MTV cable series *Unplugged*. By this time the band was one of rock's major attractions, an achievement that left Cobain feeling conflicted, at best. He fell into a coma in Rome after ingesting champagne and sedatives in March 1994, but he recovered. In less than a month he was found dead in his Seattle home, having shot himself in the head with a shotgun on April 5. Krist Novoselic and Dave Grohl called it quits as Nirvana and subsequently assembled Nirvana's recordings from *Unplugged* for 1995 release. Switching to lead vocals and rhythm guitar, Grohl formed Foo Fighters, recording much of the band's debut album by himself.

Courtney Love grew up in Eugene, Ore., and moved to San Francisco in 1983, where she formed Sugar Baby Doll with Kathy Bjelland (now with Babes in Toyland) and Jennifer Finch (now with L7), and briefly sang with the band Faith No More. Subsequently moving to Los Angeles, she appeared in two Alex Cox movies, *Sid and Nancy* and *Straight to Hell*, but decided to concentrate on a career in rock music. She learned guitar and moved to Minneapolis, N.Y., and Seattle before returning to Los Angeles, where she formed Hole with Eric Erlandson, Melissa Auf der Maur, and Patty Schemel in 1989. Their debut album, *Pretty on the Inside*, on Caroline Records, won Love a reputation as an adamant, outspoken, and independent young woman vocalist and songwriter, and one of the first so-called riot grrrls. She became Kurt Cobain's companion in late 1991 and married him on Feb. 24, 1992, giving birth to their child Frances Bean on Aug. 18, 1992. She put her career on hold, eventually returning to touring in late 1993. With new bassist Kristen Pfaff, Hole recorded *Live Through This*, which featured "Miss World," "Doll Parts," "Asking for It," and "I Think that I Would Die." However, on June 16, 1994, Pfaff was found dead in Seattle of an apparent drug overdose at age 26. Melissa Auf der Maur subsequently rejoined Hole. Courtney Love served as executive music coordinator of the soundtrack to the 1995 cult movie *Tank Girl*, which featured performances by Hole, L7, Veruca Salt, Ice-T, and Joan Jett with Paul Westerberg. Later that year Hole toured as part of the Lollapalooza tour with Sonic Youth and Beck.

DISC.: NIRVANA: *Bleach* (1989); *Nevermind* (1991); *Insecticide* (1993); *In Utero* (1993); *Unplugged in New York* (1994). **KURT COBAIN AND WILLIAM S. BURROUGHS:** *The "Priest" They called Him* (1995). **HOLE:** *Pretty on the Inside* (1991); *Live Through This* (1994); *Ask for It.* **FOO FIGHTERS:** *Foo Fighters* (1995).

BIBL.: Gina Arnold, *Route 666: On the Road to N.* (N.Y., 1993).—BH

Nisard, Théodore (pen name of **Abbé Théodule-Eléazar-Xavier Normand**), Belgian organist and writer on music; b. Quaregnon, near Mons, Jan. 27, 1812; d. Jacqueville, Seine- et-Marne, Feb. 29, 1888. He was a chorister at Cambrai, and also studied music at Douai. He attended the priests' seminary at Tournai and was ordained in 1835. In 1839 he was appointed director of the Enghien Gymnasium, occupying his leisure with the study of church music. In 1842 he became second chef de chant and organist at St. Germain des Prés in Paris, but he soon devoted himself wholly to literary work. Nisard publ. the first transcription of the Antiphonary of Montpellier (neumes and Latin letter notation from A to P), discovered by Danjou in 1847. Of his numerous books on plainchant the most important are a revised ed. of Jumilhac's *La Science et la pratique du plain-chant* (1847; with Le Clercq) and *Dictionnaire liturgique, historique et pratique du plain-chant et de musique d'église au moyen âge et dans les temps modernes* (1854; with d'Ortigue). He also publ. *De la notation proportionelle au moyen âge* (1847), *Etudes sur les anciennes notations musicales de l'Europe* (1847), *Etudes sur la restauration du chant grégorien au XIXe siècle* (1856), *Du rythme dans le plain chant* (1856), *Les Vrais Principes de l'accompagnement du plain-chant sur l'orgue d'après les maîtres des XVe et XVIe siècles* (1860), *Des chansons populaires chez les anciens et chez les Français* (1867), and *L'Archéologie musicale et le vrai chant grégorien* (1890; 2nd ed., 1897). All of these works were publ. in Paris. —NS/LK/DM

Nishimura, Akira, Japanese composer; b. Osaka, Sept. 8, 1953. He studied with Ikenouchi, Yashiro, and Mamiya at the Tokyo National Univ. of Fine Arts and Music (1973–80). He taught at the Tokyo Coll. of Music and served on the board of the Japanese Composers Soc. In 1993–94 he was composer-in-residence of the Kanazawa Orch. Ensemble. He won the Queen Elisabeth of Belgium International Music Competition (1977), the Dallapiccola Composition Award (1977), and the Otaka Prize (1988, 1992, 1993). His energetic and colorfully chromatic music explores the universe of sound and its transfigurations, with a special affinity for percussion.

WORKS: DRAMATIC: *Hot Rain in August*, television opera (1986). **ORCH.:** *Prelude* (1974); 2 syms. (1976, 1979); *Mutazioni* (1977); 2 piano concertos (*Guren*, 1979; 1982); *Nostalgia* (1983); *Heterophony* for 2 Pianos and Orch. (1987); *Navel of the Sun* for Hichiriki and Orch. (1989); Cello Concerto (1990); *Into the Light of the Eternal Chaos* (1990); *Tapas*, concerto for Bassoon, Percussion, and Strings (1990); *A Ring of Lights*, double concerto for Violin, Piano, and Orch. (1991); *Music of Dawn* for Japanese Instruments and Orch. (1991); *Hoshi-Mandala* (1992); *Astral Concerto: A Mirror of Lights* for Ondes Martenot and Orch. (1992); *Birds Heterophony* (1993); *Birds in Light* (1993–94); *Fugaku* (1994); *A Mirror of Mist* for Violin and String Ensemble (1995); *Melos Aura* (1995); *Vision in Twilight* (1995); *Canticle of Light* (1996); *Flame and Shadow*, viola concerto (1996); *Monody* (1996); *Padma Incarnation* (1997); *A Stream—After Dark* for Piano and Chamber Orch. (1997); *River of Karuna I* for Violin and Strings (1997) and *II* for Clarinet and Chamber Orch. (1997); *After Glow*, violin concerto (1998). **CHAMBER:** 3 string quartets (*Heterophony*, 1975, rev. 1987; *Pulse of the Lights*, 1992; *Avian*, 1997); *Kecak* for 6 Percussionists (1979); *Tāla* for 6 Percussionists (1982); *Khyāl* for Flute and Piano (1985); *Mātra* for Marimba, Timpani, and 5 Percussionists (1985); *Gaka I: Concrete of Heterophony* for Shakuhachi, Flute, Koto, and Cello (1987), *III: Generalize of Heterophony* for Violin and 2 Pianos (1987), and *IV: Heterophony* *on Drone* for Violin and Cello (1988); *Padma in Meditation* for 6 Percussionists (1988); Timpani Concerto for Timpani and 5 Percussionists (1988); *Kāla* for Marimba and 6 Percussionists (1989); *Organums* for Flute, Clarinet, Violin, Piano, and Vibraphone (1989); *Pipa* for 3 Guitars (1989); *Honey of Lights* for Nonet (1990); *Voice of the Sun* for Marimba, Oboe, Soprano Saxophone, and 2 Percussionists (1991); *Ektāl* for 3 Marimba Players and 2 Percussionists (1992); *Silver Cord* for Ondes Martenot and Cello (1993); *Mirror of the Moon* for Yokobue and 6 Percussionists (1995); *Fragment and Echo* for Piano Trio (1996); *Acquatic Aura* for Clarinet and Piano (1996); *Light of Padma* for Violin and Organ (1996); *Duologue* for Timpani and Piano (1996); Concerto for Flute, Winds, and Percussion (1997); *Lamento* for Saxophone and Piano (1997); *Halos* for Trumpet and Piano (1998). **P i a n o :** Sonata (1972); *Tritrope* (1978); *Penguin Suite* (1983; rev. 1989); *Vibrancy Mirrors* for 2 Pianos (1985); *Because* (1991); *Mirror of the Stars* (1992). **VOCAL:** *Ceremony* for 2 Sopranos and Orch. (1973); *Gaka II: Abstraction of Heterophony* for Soprano, Clarinet, Violin, and 2 Pianos (1987); *Mana II* for Mezzo-soprano and 5 Percussionists (1989); *Mantra of the Light* for Women's Chorus and Orch. (1993); *5 Lyrics from "The Blue Cat"* for Women's Chorus, Clarinet, Violin, Cello, and Piano (1996). —NS/LK/DM

Nishizaki, Takako, Japanese violinist; b. Aichi Prefecture, April 14, 1944. She was born to musical parents and received early instruction from her father. He then was the first student of Suzuki, and subsequently pursued training with Broadus Erle (violin) and Saito (cello) at the Toho Gakuen School of Music in Tokyo (1960–63). In 1962 she was accepted as a violin student of Joseph Fuchs at the Juilliard School of Music in N.Y., where she took first prize in its concerto competition in 1967. After winning second prize in the Leventritt competition in 1964, she toured extensively in the Far East, North America, and Europe. In addition to the standard repertoire, she has won particular notice for her championship of rarely performed concertos by Spohr, Bériot, Joachim, Cui, Anton Rubinstein, and Respighi. She has also acquired a notable reputation as a performer of scores by Chinese composers. —NS/LK/DM

Nissen, Georg Nikolaus, Danish statesman and music scholar; b. Haderslev, Jan. 22, 1761; d. Salzburg, March 24, 1826. He entered the diplomatic service in 1792, becoming the Danish chargé d'affaires in Vienna in 1793. He commenced a friendship with Mozart's widow, Constanze (1797), and later became her husband (1809). After a period in Copenhagen (1810–20), he settled in Salzburg. He collected materials for a biography of Mozart, which was completed and publ. by Johann Feurstein as *Biographie W.A. Mozarts: Nach Originalbriefen, Sammlungen alles über ihn Geschriebenen, mit vielen neuen Beylagen, Steindrucken, Musikblättern und einem Facsimile* (Leipzig, 1828; suppl., 1829; 2nd ed., 1849).—NS/LK/DM

Nissen, Hans Hermann, distinguished German bass-baritone; b. Zippnow, near Marienwerder, West Prussia, May 20, 1893; d. Munich, March 28, 1980. He studied with Julius von Raatz-Brickmann in Berlin, where he made his concert debut (1920); then made his operatic debut as the Caliph in *Der Barbier von Bagdad* at the Berlin Volksoper (1924); subsequently joined the Bavarian State Opera in Munich (1925). In 1930 he went to the U.S., where he was a member of the Chicago Civic Opera (until 1932); on Nov. 23, 1938, he made his debut with the Metropolitan Opera in N.Y. as Wotan and remained with it for a season. He then rejoined the Bavarian State Opera in Munich, retiring in 1967. He remained in Munich as a voice teacher.—NS/LK/DM

Nissman, Barbara, American pianist; b. Philadelphia, Dec. 31, 1944. She was educated at the Univ. of Mich. (B.M., 1966; M.M., 1966; D.M.A., 1969), her principal mentor being György Sandor. In 1971 she made her U.S. orch. debut as soloist with Ormandy and the Philadelphia Orch. She subsequently appeared as soloist with leading orchs. throughout the U.S. and Europe, and also gave concerts in Latin America and the Far East. She has become particularly known for her performances of contemporary music, most especially the works of Ginastera, who dedicated his third piano sonata to her.—NS/LK/DM

Nivers, Guillaume Gabriel, French organist, music theorist, and composer; b. probably in Paris, c. 1632; d. there, Nov. 30, 1714. He most likely received his education at the Univ. of Paris (M.A., 1661). He was organist of St. Sulpice from the early 1650s, and was also made one of the 4 organists of the royal chapel (1678), master of music to the queen (1681), and head of music at the Maison Royale de St. Louis, the convent school in St. Cyr for young women of the nobility. He was a leading figure in the development of the French organ school.

WRITINGS: *Traité de la composition de musique* (Paris, 1667; 4th ed., 1712; Eng. tr. ed. by A. Cohen in Music Theorists in Translation, III, Brooklyn, 1961); *Dissertation sur le chant grégorien* (Paris, 1683); *L'art d'accompagner sur la basse continue* (see *Motets à voix seule... below); *Méthode certaine pour apprendre le plein-chant de l'Église* (Paris, 1699). **EDITIONS:** *Graduale romanum juxta missale...in usum et gratiam monialum ordinis Augustini* (Paris, 1658); *Antiphonarium romanum juxta breviarum* (Paris, 1658); *Passiones D. N. J. C. cum benedictione cerei paschalis* (Paris, 1670); *Lamentationes Jeremiae prophetae* (Paris, 1689); *Graduale monasticum juxta missale...in usum et gratiam monialum ordinis S. Benedicti* (Paris, 1696); *Antiphonarium monasticum juxta breviarum* (Paris, 1696); *Le Processionel avec les saluts suivant l'antiphonaire des religieuses* (Paris, 1706).

WORKS: SACRED VOCAL: *Motets à voix seule...et quelques autres motets à deux voix propres pour les religieuses avec L'Art d'accompagner sur la basse continue, pour l'orgue et le clavecin* (Paris, 1689; 4th ed., 1741); with Clérambault, *Chants et motets à l'usage de l'église et communauté des Dames de la Royale Maison de St.-Louis à St.-Cyr* (Paris, 1692); etc. **ORGAN:** *Livre d'orgue contenant cent pièces de tous les tons de l'Église* (Paris, 1665); 2: *Livre d'orgue contenant la messe et les hymnes de l'Église* (Paris, 1667); 3: *Livre d'orgue des huit tons de l'Église* (Paris, 1675).

BIBL.: W. Pruitt, *The Organ Works of G.G. N.* (diss., Univ. of Pittsburgh, 1969).—NS/LK/DM

Nixon, Marni (née **Margaret Nixon Mc Eathron**), American soprano; b. Altadena, Calif., Feb. 22, 1930. She studied with Carl Ebert at the Univ. of

Southern Calif. in Los Angeles, Jan Popper at Stanford Univ., and Boris Goldovsky and Sarah Caldwell at the Berkshire Music Center at Tanglewood. She pursued a multifaceted career; sang on the soundtrack of the films *The King and I, West Side Story*, and *My Fair Lady*, and also starred in her own children's program on television; appeared in musical comedy and opera; was a soloist with major orchs. in the U.S. and abroad. She taught at the Calif. Inst. of the Arts (1969–71) and the Music Academy of the West in Santa Barbara (from 1980).—NS/LK/DM

Nixon, Roger, American composer and teacher; b. Tulare, Calif., Aug. 8, 1921. He studied clarinet with a local teacher, and in 1940 attended a seminar in composition with Bliss at the Univ. of Calif. at Berkeley, and in 1941, with Bloch. From 1942 to 1946 he was in the U.S. Army. He then returned in 1947 to Berkeley, where he studied with Sessions (M.A., 1949; Ph.D., 1952); in the summer of 1948 he took private lessons with Schoenberg. In 1960 he joined the faculty of San Francisco State Coll. (later Univ.), where he retired as prof. emeritus in 1991. A prolific composer, Nixon writes in a consistent modern idiom anchored in fluctuating tonality and diversified by atonal protuberances. His music is marked by distinctly American melorhythms; his miniature opera, *The Bride Comes to Yellow Sky*, is an exemplar of adroit modernistic Westernism fashioned in a non-ethnomusicological manner.

WORKS: DRAMATIC: O p e r a : *The Bride Comes to Yellow Sky* (Charleston, Ill., Feb. 20, 1968; rev. version, San Francisco, March 22, 1969). ORCH.: *Air* for Strings (1953); *Violin Concerto* (1956); *Elegiac Rhapsody* for Viola and Orch. (1962); *3 Dances* (1963); *Viola Concerto* (1969; San Francisco, April 29, 1970); *San Joaquin Sketches* for Orch. or Band (1982); various works for Band, including *Chamarita!* (1980), *California Jubilee* (1982), *Golden Jubilee* (1985), *Flower of Youth* (1989–90), and *A Centennial Overture* (1993). CHAMBER: String Quartet No. 1 (1949); *Conversations* for Violin and Clarinet (1981); *Music for Clarinet and Piano* (1986); *Variations* for Clarinet and Cello (1991). VOCAL: *Christmas Perspectives* for Chorus (1980); *Festival Mass* for Chorus (1980); *Chaunticleer* for Men's Voices (1984); *The Canterbury Tales* for Chorus (1986); *The Daisy* for Chorus (1987); *Wonders of Christmas* for Chorus (1988); other choral works; song cycles and songs; etc.—NS/LK/DM

Niyazi (real name, **Taghi-zade-Khadzhibekov**), Russian conductor and composer; b. Tiflis, Aug. 20, 1912; d. Baku, Aug. 2, 1984. His father was the composer Zulfugar Khadzhibekov. He studied music in Moscow, Yerevan, and Baku. From 1937 to 1965 he served, off and on, as conductor of the Azerbaijani Ballet. In 1961 he was named principal conductor of the Leningrad Theater of Opera and Ballet. He conducted a number of first performances of works by Azerbaijani composers. Among his works are *Hosrov and Shirin*, opera (1942), *Chitra*, ballet, after Rabindranath Tagore (1961), *In Combat*, symphonic poem (1944), popular concert pieces, and songs.

BIBL.: E. Abasova, *N.* (Baku, 1965).—NS/LK/DM

Nketia, J(oseph) H(ansen) Kwabena, Ghanaian ethnomusicologist; b. Mampong Ashanti, near Kumasi, June 22, 1921. He attended the Teacher Training Coll. in Akropong-Akwapim (1937–40); then taught music and languages at Presbyterian Training Coll. there (1942–44; 1949–52), where he made his first collection of Akan songs (publ. 1949), and composed original works and arrangements of Ghanaian music. He also studied at the School of Oriental and African Studies, Univ. of London (1944–46; B.A., 1949), where he developed an interdisciplinary approach to ethnomusicology. He taught at the Univ. of Ghana (1951–81) and at the Univ. of Calif. at Los Angeles (1969–83); became Andrew Mellon Prof. of Music at the Univ. of Pittsburgh in 1983; also was director of the Inst. of African Studies at the Univ. of Ghana (1965–80). His numerous publications include collections and studies of African music and performance (publ. in Ghana), as well as the important *Music of Africa* (N.Y., 1974; won the ASCAP-Deems Taylor Award).—NS/LK/DM

Nobel, Felix de, Dutch choral conductor, pianist, and teacher; b. Haarlem, May 27, 1907; d. Amsterdam, March 25, 1981. He studied with Martha Autengruber (piano) and Dresden (composition) at the Amsterdam Cons. He was a piano accompanist with the Dutch Radio and was a pianist in the Concergebouw Quintet. From 1939 to 1973 he conducted the Netherlands Chamber Choir, which he led on numerous tours abroad. He also taught at the Amsterdam Cons. and the Royal Cons. of Music at The Hague. As a choral conductor, his expansive repertoire extended from Obrecht to contemporary Dutch composers.—NS/LK/DM

Noble, Dennis (William), English baritone; b. Bristol, Sept. 25, 1899; d. Jávea, Spain, March 14, 1966. He was trained as a chorister at Bristol Cathedral. In 1924 he made his operatic debut at London's Covent Garden as Marullo in *Rigoletto*, and then sang there until 1938 and again in 1947. He also appeared with the British National Opera Co. and the Carl Rosa Opera Co. In 1931 he was soloist in the premiere of Walton's *Belshazzar's Feast* in Leeds. In 1936–37 he appeared in Cleveland. In addition to his various French and Italian roles, he also sang in many contemporary British operas.—NS/LK/DM

Noble, Ray(mond Stanley), English bandleader, songwriter, and arranger; b. Sussex, England, Dec. 17, 1903; d. London, April 3, 1978. Thirty years before The Beatles arrived in America, Ray Noble mounted his own British Invasion, becoming one of the few English musicians of his time to achieve substantial success in the U.S. In addition to scoring hits like "Isle of Capri" with his accomplished dance band, he also wrote many popular songs, notably "Goodnight, Sweetheart," "The Very Thought of You," and "Love Is the Sweetest Thing."

Noble's father was a surgeon; his uncle Thomas Noble was a composer and organist. Initially intending to follow his father into medicine, he studied at Dulwich Coll. and Cambridge Univ., later transferring to the Royal Academy of Music. His first published song was "Nobody's Fault but Your Own" (lyrics by Alan Murray) in 1928. In 1929 he won an arranging competition sponsored by *Melody Maker*, which led to a job as arranger with Jack Payne's BBC Dance Orch. In July he moved to a job as staff arranger with HMV Records, eventually replacing Carroll Gibbons as head of Light Music. In this position he directed the New Mayfair Orch., a studio-only band made up of top musicians from various English orchestras.

"Goodnight, Sweetheart" (music and lyrics by Noble, Jimmy Campbell, and Reg Connelly) was featured briefly in the 1930 edition of the Broadway revue *Earl Carroll's Vanities* (N.Y., July 1, 1930) without attracting notice. But after it was used again in the next edition of the *Vanities* (N.Y., Aug. 27, 1931) and introduced on radio by Rudy Vallée (who earned a songwriting credit for adapting it for U.S. consumption), it became a bestseller for Wayne King and His Orch. in October 1931 and again for Guy Lombardo and His Royal Canadians in December, making it the biggest hit of the year. Meanwhile, Noble's recordings, initially credited to the London Mayfair Orch., had begun to earn U.S. distribution, with his first stateside hit, "Lady of Spain," coming in September 1931.

"By the Fireside" (music and lyrics by Noble, Jimmy Campbell, and Reg Connelly) became a U.S. hit for George Olsen and His Orch. in April 1932. Also in 1932, Noble earned his first screen credit, when his music was used in the British film *Say It with Music*, notably "Love Is the Sweetest Thing" (music and lyrics by Noble), which also became his first U.S. best- seller as a recording artist in August 1933. "The Old Spinning Wheel" (music and lyrics by Billy Hill) became his next bestseller in January 1934, but the following month British bandleader (Bert) Ambrose and His Orch. had a more successful version of Noble's composition "Love Locked Out" (lyrics by Max Kester) than Noble himself.

Noble had songs in four films released in England in 1934, notably *Brewster's Millions* and *Princess Charming*, both of which earned American distribution the following year. He had another U.S. best-seller in July 1934 with "The Very Thought of You" (music and lyrics by Noble). In August he left his position with HMV, and in September he crossed the Atlantic to launch a career in America, taking with him only his vocalist, Al Bowlly, and his manager and drummer, Bill Harty. "It's All Forgotten Now," another of his compositions, became a hit for him in October. "Isle of Capri" (music by Will Grosz, lyrics by Jimmy Kennedy) was a best-seller in January 1935 and one of the biggest hits of the year.

Noble initially went to Hollywood, where he wrote songs for Paramount Pictures. All of his compositions were cut from the final print of *Love in Bloom* when it was released in April 1935, but the film is notable for introducing him to the comedy team of George Burns and Gracie Allen, with whom he would work later on the radio. All of them appeared in *The Big Broadcast of 1936*, which was released in September 1935.

Noble hired former Dorsey Brothers Orch. arranger Glenn Miller to organize a band for him, and he opened with it at the Rainbow Room in N.Y. on June 1, 1935, staying at the club through the following year. In August he reached the top of the hit parade with "Paris in the Spring" (music by Harry Revel, lyrics by Mack Gordon). In addition to his own recordings, he also got into the hit parade via Bing Crosby's recording of his song "The Touch of Your Lips" in the spring of 1936.

Noble returned to Hollywood in 1937 to work on the Fred Astaire film *A Damsel in Distress*, appearing in a comic role and backing Astaire on the George and Ira Gershwin score, both on screen and in the recording studio; the Astaire/Noble recording of "Nice Work If You Can Get It" became a hit upon the movie's release in November. Noble returned to the hit parade in the summer of 1938 with his composition "I Hadn't Anyone Till You" and again backed Astaire on studio recordings of the songs from the film *Carefree*, among them "Change Partners" (music and lyrics by Irving Berlin), which topped the hit parade in the fall. Also in 1938, Noble wrote the instrumental "Cherokee," which Charlie Barnet recorded and used as his theme song; it became a standard of the Swing Era.

Noble wrote several songs for the MGM film *Honolulu*, released in February 1939. In early 1940 he became the musical director of the *Burns and Allen* radio show, later holding the same position on *The Edgar Bergen and Charlie McCarthy Show*. His recording of the 1909 song "By the Light of the Silv'ry Moon" (music by Gus Edwards, lyrics by Edward Madden) became a hit twice, once in May 1942 and again when it was reissued during the recording ban in 1944; eventually it sold over a million copies.

Noble made a series of film appearances during the 1940s, in *Here We Go Again* (1942), *Lake Placid Serenade* (1944), and *Out of This World* (1945). In May 1947 he returned to the top of the charts with "Linda" (music and lyrics by Jack Lawrence). September saw the release of the animated Disney film *Fun and Fancy Free*, for which Noble wrote songs.

After *The Edgar Bergen and Charlie McCarthy Show* went off the air in the 1950s, Noble retired, living in Santa Barbara for a time, and also on the Isle of Jersey off the English coast. He died of cancer at the age of 74 in 1978, survived by his wife.—**WR**

Noble, (Thomas) Tertius, English organist and composer, uncle of **Ray(mond Stanley) Noble;** b. Bath, May 5, 1867; d. Rockport, Mass., May 4, 1953. He studied organ with Parratt at the Royal Coll. of Music in London, where he also took courses in music theory with Bridge and Stanford. He was subsequently employed as a church organist in Colchester and Cambridge. In 1898 he organized the York Sym. Orch., which he conducted until 1912. He then emigrated to America and served as organist at St. Thomas's Episcopal Church in N.Y. until 1947; he gave his final organ recital, playing his own works, in N.Y. on Feb. 26, 1947. He publ. *The Training of the Boy Chorister* (N.Y., 1943). —**NS/LK/DM**

Nobre, Marlos, notable Brazilian composer, pianist, and conductor; b. Recife, Feb. 18, 1939. He studied piano and theory at the Pernambuco Cons. of Music (1948–59). Following studies in composition with Koellreutter and Guarnieri (1960–62), he held a Rockefeller Foundation scholarship to pursue training with Ginastera, Messiaen, Copland, and Dallapiccola at the Latin American Center in Buenos Aires (1963–64). In 1969 he worked with Goehr and Schuller at the Berkshire Music Center in Tanglewood and studied at the Columbia-Princeton Electronic Music Center in N.Y. From 1971 to 1976 he was music director of Radio MEC and the National Sym. Orch. in Rio de Janeiro, and then was the first director of the National Inst. of Music (1976–79). In 1982–83 he was in Berlin under the sponsorship of the Deutscher Akademischer Austauschdienst. He held a Guggenheim fellowship in 1985–86. In 1986–87 he was president of the international Music Council of UNESCO. In 1992 he was a visiting prof. at Yale Univ. As a pianist and conductor, he appeared in South America and Europe. In 1988 he was made an Officer of the Order of Merit of Brasilia, in 1989 an Officer of the Rio Branco Order of Brazil, and in 1994 an Officier de l'Ordre des Arts et des Lettres of France. Nobre has developed a strong, individual style in which various contemporary techniques are effectively complemented by his inventive handling of native musical elements.

WORKS: DRAMATIC: B a l l e t : *Football* (1980); *Saga Marista* (1992; Recife, April 2, 1998). ORCH.: Concertino for Piano and Strings (Rio de Janeiro, Nov. 23, 1959); *Divertimento* for Piano and Orch. (1963; Rio de Janeiro, Nov. 10, 1965); *Convergências* (Rio de Janeiro, June 11, 1968; rev. version, Maracaibo, Nov. 20, 1977); *Desafio I* for Viola and Strings (1968; Rio de Janeiro, Oct. 30, 1974; also for Viola and Piano), *II* for Cello and Strings (1968; Porto Alegre, Nov. 17, 1978; also for Cello and Piano), *III* for Violin and Strings (1968; Recife, May 11, 1978; also for Violin and Piano), *IV* for Double Bass and Strings (1968; also for Double Bass and Piano), *VI* for Strings (1968–79), *VII* for Piano and Strings (1968–80; Fribourg, May 26, 1980), *VIII* for Alto Saxophone and Strings (1982; also for Saxophone and Piano), *IX* for Flute and Strings (1983; also for Flute and Piano), *X* for Oboe and Strings (1986; also for Oboe and Piano), *XI* for Clarinet and Strings (1985; also for Clarinet and Piano), *XII* for Bassoon and Strings (1986; also for Bassoon and Piano), *XIII* for Horn and Strings (1987; also for Horn and Piano), *XIV* for Trumpet and Strings (1988; also for Trumpet and Piano); *XV* for Trombone and Strings (1989; also for Trombone and Piano), *XVI* for Tuba and Strings (1990; also for Tuba and Piano), and *XVII* for Bass Clarinet and Strings (1992; also for Bass Clarinet and Piano); *Concerto breve* for Piano and Orch. (Rio de Janeiro, May 27, 1969); *Ludus instrumentalis* for Chamber Orch. (Tanglewood, Aug. 18, 1969); *Biosfera* for Strings (1970; Lisbon, Jan. 27, 1971); *Mosaico* (Rio de Janeiro, May 12, 1970); *In memoriam* (1973–76; Rio de Janeiro, Sept. 18, 1976); Concerto I (1976) and II (Bloomington, Ind., Aug. 6, 1981) for Strings; Guitar Concerto (1980); *Elegia* for Strings (Recife, Dec. 21, 1981); *Abertura festiva* (Rio de Janeiro, Oct. 10, 1982); Concerto for Piano and Strings (Nice, July 24, 1984); *4 Latin American Dances* for Chamber or Full Orch. (1989); Concerto for Trumpet and Strings (1989); *Concertante do imaginário* for Piano and Strings (Rio de Janeiro, Dec. 15, 1989); *Xingú* (1989); Double Concerto for 2 Guitars and Orch. (1995; São Paulo, Sept. 10, 1998); *Passacaglia* (Recife, Oct. 20, 1997); *Amazonia* for Winds, Brass, Piano, Guitar, Double Basses, and Percussion (Belém, June 6, 1998); *Chacona Amazonica* for Winds, Brass, Percussion, Double Basses, and Piano (São Paulo, July 15, 1999). CHAMBER: Trio for Violin, Cello, and Piano (Rio de Janeiro, Nov. 28, 1960); *Musicamera* for Chamber Ensemble (1962; N.Y., April 29, 1981); Sonata for Solo Viola (1963; Rio de Janeiro, Dec. 16, 1968); *Variações ritmicas* for Piano and Percussion (Buenos Aires, Nov. 25, 1963); 2 string quartets: No. 1 (Madrid, Oct. 23, 1967) and No. 2 (1985); *Canticum instrumentale* for Flute, Harp, Piano, and Timpani (1967); Wind Quintet (1968); *Tropicale* for Piccolo, Clarinet, Piano, and Percussion (Rio de Janeiro, March 15, 1968); *Sonâncias I* for Piano and Percussion (Munich, Aug. 4, 1972), *II* for Flute, Guitar, Piano, and Percussion (1980), and *III* for 2 Pianos and Percussion (Geneva, Oct. 27, 1980); *Solo I* for Flute (Rio de Janeiro, May 23, 1984), *II* for Bass Clarinet (1994), and *III* for Vibraphone (1994); *Circulos magicos* for Bass Clarinet and Percussion (1989); Duo for Guitar and Percussion (1989); *Sonante I* for Marimba (Oviedo, April 19, 1994), *II* for Mallet Percussion (1995), and *III* for Flute, Clarinet, Bass Clarinet, Violin, Cello, Piano, and Guitar (1995); also numerous guitar pieces, including *Momentos I-VII* (1974–84), *Homenagem a Villa-Lobos* (1977; N.Y., April 17, 1978), *Fandango* for Guitar Ensemble (1985), *Reminiscencias* (1990; London, Sept. 8, 1991), *Relembrando* (1990), and *Re-memórias* (1993). P i a n o : *Nazarethiana* (1960); *16 Variations on a Theme by Frutuoso Vianna* (1962; Brasilia, Aug. 7, 1970); 2 sonatas: No. 1, *Sonata breve* (1966), and No. 2 (on a theme by Bartók; 1977); *Tango* (Toronto, Sept. 25, 1984). VOCAL: *Ukrinmakrinkrin* for Soprano, Piccolo, Oboe, Horn, and Piano (Buenos Aires, Nov. 20, 1964); *O canto multiplicado* for Voice and String Orch. (Rio de Janeiro, Aug. 5, 1972; also for Voice and Piano); *Yanománi* for Tenor, Chorus, and Guitar (1980; Fribourg, Feb. 6, 1981); *Cantata do Chimborazo* for Soloists, Chorus, and Orch. (1982; Maracaibo, Oct. 24, 1983); *Columbus*, cantata for Soloists, Chorus, and Orch. (1990); *Amazonia (Desafio XVIII)* for Voice and Guitar (1993; N.Y., April 4, 1994); *Canto a García Lorca* for Voice and Cello Octet (1998; Amsterdam, Sept. 13, 1999); *Beiramar* for Voice and Cello Octet (Amsterdam, Sept. 13, 1999); *Tres Canciones Negras* for Voice and Cello Octet (Assen, Oct. 10, 1999); other choral pieces; songs.—NS/LK/DM

Noda, Ken, American pianist and composer; b. N.Y., Oct. 5, 1962. He studied piano with Adele Marcus at the Juilliard School in N.Y., and also had lessons in composition with Sylvia Rabinof and Thomas Pasatieri. In 1977 he made his professional debut as a soloist with the Minnesota Orch. in Minneapolis, followed by his London debut as soloist with the English Chamber Orch. in 1979. After further studies with Barenboim in Paris (1979–83), he made appearances on both sides of the Atlantic until 1990. In 1991 he became musical assistant to the artistic director, artistic administration, at the Metropolitan Opera in N.Y. He again appeared in public as a pianist in 1997. Among his works were several operas, song cycles, and piano pieces. —NS/LK/DM

Noda, Teruyuki, Japanese composer; b. Mie Prefecture, June 15, 1940. He was a pupil of Ikenouchi and Yashiro at the Tokyo Univ. of Fine Arts and Music.

WORKS: ORCH.: 4 syms.: *Symphony in One Movement* (1963), Choral Sym. (Tokyo, July 10, 1968), Sym. No. 2 (1983), and *Mie Ode* (1990); *A Mirror or a Journey* (1968); *Dislocation* (Tokyo, Feb. 10, 1971); *Mutation* for 4 Japanese Instruments and Orch. (1971); Piano Concerto (1977); Guitar Concerto (1984); *Fresque Symphonique* (1987); *Rapsodie Adriatique* for Guitar and Strings (1988); *Carnaval* (1989); *Liturgical Overture* for Winds (1991); *Forest Echoes* for Marimba, 2 Percussionists, and Strings

(1992). **CHAMBER:** Trio for Violin, Horn, and Piano (1963); Quartet for Horn, Cello, Timpani, and Piano (1965); *Morning Song* for Marimba, 3 Flutes, and Contrabass (1968); 2 quartets for Japanese Instruments (1969, 1973); *Poems I* and *II* for 7 Instruments (1980); *Novelette* for String Quartet (1983); String Quartet (1985); *In the Garden* for Violin and Piano (1986); *Ode Capricious* for Piano (1986); *Consonance* for Wind Quintet (1993). **VOCAL:** Choral music.—**NS/LK/DM**

Noehren, Robert, American organist, organ builder, and composer; b. Buffalo, Dec. 16, 1910. He studied at the Inst. of Musical Art in N.Y. and at the Curtis Inst. of Music in Philadelphia. He served in the U.S. Army in World War II. After demobilization, he studied at the Univ. of Mich. (B.Mus., 1948). He taught at Davidson Coll. in N.C. (1946–49) and at the Univ. of Mich. (1949–76); also toured extensively as a recitalist in North America and overseas. He built organs for churches in Milwaukee, Buffalo, San Francisco, and other cities. Among his works are a number of solo organ pieces, including 2 sonatas.—**NS/LK/DM**

Noetel, Konrad Friedrich, German composer; b. Posen, Oct. 30, 1903; d. Berlin, April 9, 1947. Following training in engineering and law, he studied music in Hannover and Königsberg. He completed his studies with Hindemith at the Berlin Hochschule für Musik, where he subsequently was on the faculty (1936–47). Noetel's works were in a late Romantic idiom. He composed a Sym., Suite for Chamber Orch. (1934), Concerto for Flute, Violin, and Strings (1942), *Konzertmusik* for Strings (1944), Concerto for Flute, Oboe, and Strings (1947), chamber music, choral pieces, and songs. —**NS/LK/DM**

Nohl, (Karl Friedrich) Ludwig, German writer on music; b. Iserlohn, Westphalia, Dec. 5, 1831; d. Heidelberg, Dec. 15, 1885. He studied jurisprudence at Bonn (1850), Heidelberg, and Berlin, and entered the legal profession against his own desire, to please his father. In music he was instructed by Dehn, and later (1857–58) by Kiel, in Berlin. Having embraced music as his profession, he took his Ph.D. at Heidelberg in 1860. He subsequently went to Munich (1861), where he was an honorary prof. at the Univ. (1865–68). After living in Badenweiler (1868–72), he settled in Heidelberg as a private lecturer, becoming a prof. at the Univ. in 1880. He publ. biographies and eds. of letters of several great composers, but these have been superseded by modern scholarship. Among his writings are *Musikalisches Skizzenbuch* (1866); *Musiker-Briefe* (1867); *Beethovens Leben* (3 vols., 1867–77); *Neues Skizzenbuch* (1869); *Gluck und Wagner* (1870); *Die Beethoven-Feier und die Kunst der Gegenwart* (1871); *Beethoven, Liszt, Wagner* (1874); *Beethoven nach den Schilderungen seiner Zeitgenossen* (1877; Eng. tr., 1880, as *Beethoven as Depicted by His Contemporaries*); *Mozart nach den Schilderungen seiner Zeitgenossen* (1880); *Richard Wagners Bedeutung für die nationale Kunst* (1883); *Das moderne Musikdrama* (1884), and *Die geschichtliche Entwickelung der Kammermusik* (1885).—**NS/LK/DM**

Nola, Giovanni Domenico del Giovane da, distinguished Italian composer; b. Nola, c. 1515; d. Naples, May 1592. He was made maestro di cappella at Naples's Ss. Annunziata (1563). He excelled as a composer of both sacred and secular vocal music.

WORKS: VOCAL: S a c r e d : *Liber primus motectorum* for 5 Voices (Venice, 1549); *Cantiones vulgo motecta appellatae-...monis generis instrumentis cantatu commodissimae...liber primus* for 5 to 6 Voices (Venice, 1575; not extant). **S e c u l a r :** *Canzoni villanesche...liber primo et secondo* for 3 Voices (Venice, 1541; not extant; 2nd ed. publ. separately as 2 books, Venice, 1545); *Madrigali* for 4 Voices (Venice, 1545); *Il secondo libro de madrigali* for 5 Voices (Rome, 1564); *Il primo libro delle villanelle alla napolitana* for 3 to 4 Voices (Venice, 1567); *Il quarto libro di madrigali* for 5 to 6 Voices (not extant).

BIBL.: L. Cammarota, *Gian Domenico del Giovane da Nola: I documenti biografici d'l'attivita presso la SS. Annunziata con l'opera completa* (Rome, 1973).—**NS/LK/DM**

Nolte, Ewald V(alentin), American organist, choirmaster, teacher, and composer; b. Utica, Nebr., Sept. 21, 1909; d. Winston-Salem, N.C., March 31, 1991. He studied at Concordia Teachers Coll. in Seward, Nebr. (certificate, 1929) and later was a student of Albert Noelte at Northwestern Univ. in Evanston, Ill. (M.Mus., 1945; Ph.D., 1954, with the diss. *The Instrumental Works of Johann Pachelbel*). He also studied with Hindemith and Schrade at Yale Univ. (1950–51). From 1929 to 1944 he was a Lutheran church organist and choirmaster in Ill. and Ohio. He was an asst. prof. of music at Northwestern Univ. from 1944 to 1964, and then was a prof. of music at Salem Coll. in Winston-Salem from 1964 to 1980. From 1964 to 1972 he also was executive director of the Moravian Music Foundation and ed. numerous works in its archive. He composed sacred choral music, supplied accompaniments to hymns, and arranged American folk songs.—**NS/LK/DM**

Noni, Alda, Italian soprano; b. Trieste, April 30, 1916. After studies in piano and voice in Trieste, she pursued vocal training in Vienna. In 1937 she made her operatic debut as Rossini's Rosina in Ljubljana, and then sang in Zagreb, Belgrade, and Trieste. She was a member of the Vienna State Opera (1942–44), where she sang the role of Zerbinetta at Strauss's 80th birthday celebration in 1944. In 1946 she appeared as Norina in London. In 1949 she sang with the Glyndebourne Opera at the Edinburgh Festival, and then appeared at Glyndebourne (1950; 1952–54). From 1949 to 1953 she also sang at Milan's La Scala. Among her notable roles were Despina, Papagena, Zerlina, Nannetta, Clorinda in *La Cenerentola*, and Oscar.—**NS/LK/DM**

Nono, Luigi, remarkable Italian composer who earned a unique place in the history of modern music through his consistent devotion to social problems; b. Venice, Jan. 29, 1924; d. there, May 8, 1990. He became a student at the Venice Cons. (1941), where he received instruction in composition with Malipiero (1943–45); also studied law at the Univ. of Padua (graduated, 1946); later had advanced harmony and counterpoint lessons with Maderna and Scherchen. A man of extraordinary courage, he joined the Italian Communist Party while the country was still under the dictatorship of Mussolini, and was an active participant in the Italian

Resistance Movement against the Nazis. In 1975 he was elected to the Central Committee of the Communist Party, and remained a member until his death. Although his works were extremely difficult to perform and practically all of them were devoted to Leftist propaganda, he found support among a number of liberal composers and performers. At the end of his life, he acquired an enormous reputation as a highly original composer in the novel technical idiom as well as a fearless political agitator. In his technique of composition, he followed the precepts of Schoenberg without adhering to the literal scheme of dodecaphonic composition. As a resolutely "engaged" artist, Nono mitigated the antinomy between the modern idiom of his music and the conservative Soviet ideology of Socialist Realism by his militant political attitude and his emphasis on revolutionary subjects in his works, so that even extreme dissonances may be dialectically justified as representing the horrors of Fascism. He made several visits to Russia, the last in 1988, but his works were rarely performed there because of the intransigence of his idiom. He made use of a variety of techniques: serialism, "sonorism" (employment of sonorities for their own sake), aleatory and concrete music, and electronics. Perhaps his most militant composition, both politically and musically, is his opera *Intolleranza 1960*, utilizing texts by Brecht, Eluard, Sartre, and Mayakovsky; the work is a powerful protest against imperialist policies and social inequities. At its premiere in Venice on April 13, 1961, a group of neo-Fascists showered the audience with leaflets denouncing Nono for his alleged contamination of Italian music by alien doctrines, and even making a facetious allusion to his name as representing a double negative. Nono was married to Schoenberg's daughter, Nuria, in 1955; they separated on friendly terms after several years; they had 2 daughters. Nuria settled in her father's last residence in Los Angeles, while Nono traveled widely in Europe. He died of a liver ailment at the age of 66.

WORKS: *Variazioni canoniche* for Orch., based on the 12-tone row of Schoenberg's *Ode to Napoleon Buonaparte* (Darmstadt, Aug. 27, 1950); *Polifonica, monodia, ritmica* for Flute, Clarinet, Bass Clarinet, Saxophone, Horn, Piano, and Percussion (Darmstadt, July 10, 1951); *España en el corazón* for Voices and Instruments, to words by García Lorca (Darmstadt, July 21, 1952); *Der rote Mantel*, ballet (Berlin, Sept. 20, 1954); *La Victoire de Guernica* for Voices and Orch. (1954); *Canti* for 13 Instruments (Paris, March 26, 1955); *Incontri* for 24 Instruments (Darmstadt, May 30, 1955); *Varianti* for Violin, Strings, and Woodwinds (Donaueschingen, Oct. 20, 1957); *La terra e la compagna* for Soloists, Chorus, and Instruments (Hamburg, Jan. 13, 1958); *Il canto sospeso* for Solo Voices, Chorus, and Orch., to texts from letters by young men and women condemned to death by the Fascists (Cologne, Oct. 24, 1956); *Intolleranza 1960*, opera (1960–61; Venice, April 13, 1961); *Sarà dolce tacere* for 8 Solo Voices, to texts from "La terra e la morte" by Cesare Pavese (Washington, D.C., Feb. 17, 1961); *La fabbrica illuminata* for Voice and Magnetic Tape (1964); music for the documentary play *Die Ermittlung* by Peter Weiss, dealing with the trial of Nazi guards (Frankfurt am Main, Oct. 19, 1965); *Sul ponte di Hiroscima* for 2 Soloists and Orch., commemorating the victims of the atomic bomb attack on Hiroshima (1962); *A Floresta é jovem e cheja de vida*, oratorio to texts from declarations by the Vietnam guerrilla

fighters (1966); *Per Bastiana* for Electronic Tape and 3 Orch. Groups (1967); *Non consumiano Marx* for Electronic Sound (1968); *Voci destroying Muros* for Women's Voices and Instruments in Mixed Media, featuring a machine gun pointed toward the audience (1970); *Y entonces comprendió* for Voices and Magnetic Tape, dedicated to Ché Guevara (1970); *Ein Gespenst geht um in der Welt* for Voice and Orch., to words from the Communist Manifesto (Cologne, Feb. 11, 1971); *Como una ola de fuerza y luz* for Singer, Piano, Magnetic Tape, and Orch. (1972); 2 piano concertos (1972, 1975); *Al gran sole carico d'amore*, opera (1974); *...sofferte onde serene...* for Piano and Tape (1976); *Con Luigi Dallapiccola* for 6 Percussionists and Live Electronics (1979); *Fragmente- Stille, an Diotima* for String Quartet (1979–80); *Das atmende Klarsein* for Bass Flute, Chorus, and Live Electronics (1980–81); *Quando stanno morendo...* for 4 Women's Voices, Bass Flute, Cello, and Live Electronics (1982); *Omaggio a György Kurtág* for Trombone and Live Electronics (1983); *A C. Scarpa architetto, ai suo infiniti possibili* for Orch. (1984); *Guai ai gelidi mostri* for 2 Altos, Flute, Clarinet, Tuba, Viola, Cello, Double Bass, and Live Electronics (1984); *Prometeo, Tragedia dell'ascolto* (1984; rev. 1985); *A Pierre: Dell'azzurro silenzio, inquietum* for Chorus, Flute, Clarinet, and Live Electronics (1985); *Risonanze erranti a M. Cacciari* for Alto, Flute, Tuba, Percussion, and Live Electronics (1986); *Découvrir la subversion: Omaggio a E. Jabés* for Mezzo-soprano, Narrator, Tuba, Horn, and Live Electronics (1987); *No hay caminos, hay que caminar...A. Tarkovsky* for Orch. (1987).

BIBL.: J. Stenzl, ed., *L. N.: Texte: Studien zu seiner Musik* (Zürich, 1975); F. Spangemacher, *L. N., die elektronische Musik* (Regensburg, 1983); C. Henius, *Schnebel, N., Schönberg, oder, Die wirkliche und die erdachte Musik: Essays und autobiographisches* (Hamburg, 1993); M. Taibon, *L. N. und sein Musiktheater* (Vienna, 1993); L. Jeschke, *Prometeo: Geschichtskonzeptionen in L. N.'s Hörtragödie* (Stuttgart, 1997); J. Stenzl, *L. N.* (Reinbek, 1998). —NS/LK/DM

Noone, Jimmie, New Orleans clarinetist, soprano and alto saxophonist, leader; b. Cut Off, La., April 23, 1895; d. L.A., April 19, 1944. Benny Goodman considered Noone to be one of the finest technicians among New Orleans stylists. He also influenced Buster Bailey, Barney Bigard, Joe Marsala, Omer Simeon, saxophonist Bud Freeman and even Eric Dolphy. Born on family farm ten miles from New Orleans, Noone started playing guitar from age of 10 and clarinet from 15. His family moved into New Orleans in late 1910, and he began taking lessons from Sidney Bechet. His first paid work was subbing for Bechet in Freddie Keppard's Band (1913), and he subsequently worked with Keppard for a year afterwards. Together with Buddie Petit, he formed the Young Olympia Band, and gigged with Kid Ory and Papa Celestin. In late 1917, he moved to Chicago to join Keppard in the Original Creole Band, and toured until the group disbanded in spring 1918. After gigging in New Orleans, he returned to Chicago in autumn 1918 (with King Oliver) and joined the band at the Royal Gardens then led by bassist Bill Johnson. From the summer of 1920 until autumn 1926, and later again in 1927, he performed with Doc Cooke's Orch., as well as leading his own small groups. He then led resident band at the Apex Club, which included Earl Hines for a while, until it closed in spring of 1928. From then through the 1930s, except for engagements in N.Y. in 1931 and 1935, he remained in Chicago leading small groups at various clubs. At some point he studied with Franz Schoepp, a classically trained clarinetist. In the early 1940s, he played in Omaha, Neb., and San Antonio, Tex. He moved to Calif., where he led a group in Hollywood from August 1943. He did radio and record dates with Kid Ory, Zutty Singleton, Jack Teagarden, and others in San Francisco and L.A. Shortly before his death, he joined an all-star revival band organized for Orson Welles's CBS variety show. He died in his home from a sudden heart attack. Noone appeared with the East Side Kids in the 1944 film *The Block Busters*.

His son, Jimmie Noone Jr. (b. James Fleming N., Chicago, April 21, 1938; d. San Diego, March 29, 1991), is also a clarinetist. After spending much of his career in obscurity in San Diego, in the 1980s he commenced an active recording and international touring schedule, which he pursued until his death in 1991.

DISC.: "I Know That You Know" (1928); *Four or Five Times* (1928); *Apex Blues* (1928); *The Blues Jumped a Rabbit* (1936); *Oh Sister, Ain't That Hot* (1928). O. Powers: *Play That Thing* (1923). K. Oliver: *Chattanooga Stomp/New Orleans Stomp* (1923); *Camp Meeting Blues* (1923). Capitol Jazzmen: *Clambake in B Flat* (1943).—**JC/LP**

Noordt, Anthoni van, Dutch organist and composer; b. place and date unknown; d. Amsterdam (buried), March 23, 1675. He was organist of Amsterdam's Nieuwe-Zijds-Kapel (1638–64) and Nieuwe Kerk (1664–73). Several of his organ works were publ. in *Tabulatuur-boeck van psalmen en fatasyen* (Amsterdam, 1659).—**LK/DM**

Nopitsch, Christoph Friedrich Wilhelm, German organist, teacher, and composer; b. Kirchensittenbach, near Nuremberg, Feb. 4, 1758; d. Nördlingen, May 22, 1824. He received training in organ, harpsichord, and composition from Johann Siebenkäs and G.W. Gruber in Nuremberg, Joseph Riepel in Regensburg, Eberhard Beck in Passau, and Georg Benda and Anton Schweitzer in Gotha. From 1781 he was organist and music director in Nördlingen, where he also was Kantor of the gymnasium from 1800. He publ. a singing method in 1784. Nopitsch was especially admired as a lieder composer. He also wrote a comic opera, 3 syms., piano concertos, chamber music, an oratorio, and a cantata.

BIBL.: J. Mlynarczyk, *C.F.W. N.: Ein Nördlinger Kantatenmeister (1758 bis 1824)* (Leipzig, 1928).—**LK/DM**

Norberg-Schulz, Elizabeth, Norwegian soprano; b. Oslo, Jan. 1959. She studied at the Accademia di Santa Cecilia in Rome, the Pears-Britten School in Snape, and with Schwarzkopf in Zürich. After singing Britten's *Les Illuminations* in Snape in 1981, she was active as a concert and lieder artist. She also appeared at Milan's La Scala, touring with the company to Japan in 1988 as Musetta. In 1989 she sang Barbarina at the Rome Opera and Ilia at the Maggio Musicale Fiorentino. After portraying Pamina in Salzburg in 1991, she returned there as Servilia in 1992, the same year she sang Norina in Naples. In 1994 she made her debut at London's Covent Garden as Liù. Her Metropolitan Opera debut

followed in N.Y. on Nov. 10, 1995, as Verdi's Oscar. She appeared as Cimarosa's Carolina in Rome in 1996. In 1998 she sang Adele at the Metropolitan Opera. —**NS/LK/DM**

Norby, Erik, Danish composer; b. Copenhagen, Jan. 9, 1936. He studied with Kayser at the Royal Danish Cons. of Music in Copenhagen (diploma in composition and theory, 1966) and with Nrgård at the Jutland Cons. He taught at the Alborg Cons. until 1975. His music reveals deft handling of styles ranging from the late Romantic to Darmstadt schools.

WORKS: ORCH.: *Folkesang-suite* (1962); *Variations* (1963); *Music for 8 Sextets* (1966); *Nocturne* (1969); *Corps celeste*, symphonic poem (1970); *Regnbueslangen* (Rainbow Snake), symphonic poem (Copenhagen, Nov. 20, 1975); *Illuminations*, capriccio for Flute and Strings (1978); *3 Dances* for Wind Orch. (1983); Concerto for 2 Sopranos and Orch. (1987); *Cortège II* (1992). **CHAMBER:** *Illustrations* for 6 Percussion (1965); *Schubert Variations* for 4 Flutes (1974); *Kuhlau Metamorphoses* for 4 Flutes (1978); *Partita* for Flute and Organ (1981); *Tivoli Collage* for 5 Percussion (1983); organ pieces. **VOCAL:** *Edvard Munch Triptych* for Chorus and Orch. (Danish Radio, Oct. 11, 1979); Cantata for the 150th anniversary of the Copenhagen Cathedral (1979); *Abendstern* for Soprano, English Horn, Harp, and Cello (1984); *Södergran-Lieder* for Alto and Orch. (1992).—**NS/LK/DM**

Nordal, Jón, Icelandic composer; b. Reykjavík, March 6, 1926. He studied with Kristjánsson and Thórarinsson at the Reykjavík Coll. of Music, then in Zürich with Burkhard (1949–51), and finally in Paris and Rome (1956–57) and in Darmstadt (1957). He taught at the Reykjavík Coll. of Music before becoming its director in 1959. In 1968 he became a member of the Royal Swedish Academy. His early works are in the neo-Classical mold, but in the course of time he adopted colorism in the French impressionist vein.

WORKS: ORCH.: *Concerto Grosso* (1950); Concerto (1954); *Sinfonietta seriosa* (1954); Piano Concerto (1957); *Brotaspil* (A Play of Fragments; 1963); *Adagio* for Flute, Harp, Piano, and Strings (1965); *Stiklur* (1969); *Canto elegiaco* for Cello and Orch. (1971); *Leidsla* (Rapture; 1973); *Epitafion* (1974); *Langnaetti* (The Winter Night; 1976); *Tvisong* (Twinsong), double concerto for Violin, Viola, and Orch. (1979); *Tileinkun* (Dedication; 1981); *Choralis* (Washington, D.C., Nov. 23, 1982); Cello Concerto (1983). **CHAMBER:** Violin Sonata (1952); *Rórill* for Flute, Oboe, Clarinet, and Bass Clarinet; Duo for Violin and Cello (1983); *Carvings* for Clarinet and Piano (1985); *Piccolo musica notturna* for Viola and Piano (1995); *Frá Draumi til Draums* for String Quartet (1996); *Andad á Sofinn Streng* for Violin, Cello, and Piano (1998); organ music. **VOCAL:** Choral pieces; songs. —**NS/LK/DM**

Nordblom, Johan Erik, Swedish organist, bass, teacher, and composer; b. Uppsala, April 12, 1788; d. there, Dec. 25, 1848. He was a student of J.C.F. Haeffner in Uppsala, whom he succeeded as director musices of the Univ. orch. and as organist of the Cathedral there (1833). He also was active as a concert singer and vocal teacher in Stockholm. Nordblom's songs for men's chorus and his solo songs were much admired in Sweden. His daughter, Johanna Maria Nordblom (1827–1909), was a singer. She married the composer P.A. Ölander in 1853.—**LK/DM**

Nordgren, Pehr Henrik, Finnish composer; b. Saltvik, Jan. 19, 1944. He studied composition with Kokkonen and musicology at the Univ. of Helsinki, and composition and traditional Japanese music at the Tokyo Univ. of Arts and Music (1970–73). In his works, he utilizes traditional and advanced harmonies and both Western and traditional Japanese instruments.

WORKS: D R A M A T I C : *Den svarte munken* (The Black Monk), chamber opera (1981; Stockholm, March 20, 1984); *Alex*, television opera (1983; Helsinki, Sept. 6, 1986). ORCH.: *Epiphrase* (1966); *Koko maailma valittanee* (The Whole World Will Lament) for Strings (1966–74); *Euphonie I* (Helsinki, Feb. 25, 1967), *II* (1967; Helsinki, Jan. 30, 1969), *III* (Lahti, April 12, 1975), and *IV* (1981); *Minore* (1968); 3 violin concertos: No. 1 (1969; Helsinki, Feb. 12, 1970), No. 2 for Violin and Strings (Helsinki, Nov. 15, 1977), and No. 3 for Violin and Strings (1981; Kaustinen, Jan. 31, 1982); 3 viola concertos: No. 1 (1970), No. 2 (Helsinki, Dec. 7, 1979), and No. 3 for Viola and Chamber Orch. (Vaasa, July 2, 1986); Concerto for Clarinet, Folk Instruments, and Small Orch. (1970; Helsinki, April 22, 1971); *The Turning Point* (1972; Helsinki, March 12, 1974); *Autumnal Concerto* for Traditional Japanese Instruments and Orch. (Helsinki, Aug. 28, 1974); 2 syms.: No. 1 (Turku, Oct. 10, 1974) and No. 2 (1990); Piano Concerto (Helsinki, April 22, 1975); *Pelimannimuotokuvia* (Portraits of Country Fiddlers) for Strings (Seinäjoki, April 5, 1976); *Summer Music* (Kaustinen, July 18, 1977); Sym. for Strings (1978; Kokkola, Jan. 14, 1979); 3 cello concertos: No. 1 for Cello and Strings (Kuhmo, July 28, 1980), No. 2 (Helsinki, March 21, 1984), and No. 3 (1992); Concerto for Strings (1982; Kokkola, Nov. 27, 1983); *Elegy to Vilho Lampi* (1984; Oulu, Feb. 21, 1985); Concerto for Kantele and Small Orch. (Joensuu, June 19, 1985); *Tanse-Choral* for 15 Strings (Kokkola, Jan. 6, 1986); *HATE-LOVE* for Cello and Strings (1987); *Cronaca* (1991). CHAMBER: 7 string quartets (1967–92); *Nachtwache*, suite from the music to the radio play by Nelly Sachs, for Chamber Ensemble (1967); *Neljä kuolemankuvaa* (4 Pictures of Death) for Chamber Ensemble (1968); *Kolme maanitusta* (3 Enticements): 2 wind quintets: No. 1 (1970) and No. 2 (1975); 2 quartets for Traditional Japanese Instruments (1974; *Seita*, 1978); Piano Quintet (1978); Piano Trio (1980); *Equivocations* for Kantele and String Trio (1981). V O C A L : *Agnus Dei* for Soprano, Baritone, Chorus, and Orch. (1970; Helsinki, May 11, 1971); *Kuninkaan kämmenella* (In the Palm of the King's Hand), cantata for Soprano, Baritone, Chorus, and Orch. (1979; Kokkola, Feb. 24, 1980); *Taivaanvalot* (The Lights of Heaven) for Soprano, Tenor, Chorus, Children's Chorus, and Orch. (Kaustinen, Feb. 3, 1985).—NS/LK/DM

Nordheim, Arne, significant Norwegian composer; b. Larvik, June 20, 1931. He studied at the Oslo Cons. (1948–52). His principal mentors in composition were Andersen, Baden, and Brustad. Following further studies with Holmboe in Copenhagen, he returned to Oslo and wrote music criticism for the *Morgenpost* (1959–63) and *Dagbladet* (1963–69). In 1960 he was awarded the Bergen Festival prize. His *Eco* for Soprano, Choruses, and Orch. took the Nordic Council Music Prize in 1972. He was made a member of the Royal Swedish Academy of Music in Stockholm in 1975 and in 1982 he was named a knight first class in the Royal Norwegian Order of St. Olav. In 1990 he received the Norwegian Cultural Council's prize. Nordheim is one of Norway's most important composers, one long in the forefront of avant-garde developments in his country. His works are marked by extraordinary craftsmanship

and imagination, and are notable for their experimental use of pointillistic tone colors and for their motivic method of seemingly spontaneous melorhythmic structures.

WORKS: D R A M A T I C : B a l l e t : *Katharsis* (1962); *Stages* (1971); *Strender* (1974); *Stoolgame* (1974); *Greening* (1975); *Ariadne* (1977); *The Tempest* (1979; also as a suite for Soprano, Baritone, and Orch.). O t h e r : Incidental music; film scores. ORCH.: *Nachruf* for Strings (1956); *Canzona* (1961); *Epitaffio* for Chamber Orch. and Tape (1964); *Floating* (Graz, Oct. 20, 1970); *Greening* (Los Angeles, April 12, 1973); *Spur* for Accordion and Orch. (1975); *Tenebrae*, cello concerto (Washington, D.C., Nov. 23, 1982); *Boomerang* for Oboe and Chamber Orch. (1985); *Rendezvous* for Strings (1986; orchestration of the String Quartet, 1956); *Tractatus* for Flute and Chamber Ensemble (1986); *Magma* (1988); *Monolith* (1990); *Acantus Firmus Olympiadis* for Hardanger Fiddle, Trumpets, Strings, and Electroacoustic Sounds (1992; Lillehammer, Jan. 1993); *Ad fontes* for Orch. and Electroacoustic Sounds (1993); *Adieu* for Strings and Bells (Warsaw, Sept. 9, 1994); *Jubel* for Winds, Percussion, and Carillon (1995). CHAMBER: String Quartet (1956; orch. as *Rendezvous* for Strings, 1986); *Response* for 2 Percussionists and Tape (1966; also for Organ, 4 Percussionists, and Tape, 1967–75, Percussionist and Tape, 1968, and 4 Percussionists and Tape, 1977); *Signals* for Accordion, Percussion, and Electric Guitar (1968); *Partita II* for Electric Guitar (1969); *Dinosauros* for Accordion and Tape (1971); *Listen* for Piano (1971); *The Hunting of the Snark* for Trombone (1976); *Clamavi* for Cello (1980); *Partita für Paul* for Violin and Electronic Delay (1985); *Flashing* for Accordion (1986); *Duplex* for Violin and Viola (1990). V O C A L : *Aftonland* (Evening Land) for Soprano and Chamber Ensemble (1959); *Eco* for Soprano, Chorus, Children's Chorus, and Orch. (1968); *Doria* for Tenor and Orch. (1975); *Tempora Noctis* for 2 Sopranos and Orch. (1979); *Aurora* for 4 Singers, Chotales, and Tape (1983; also for 4 Singers, Chorus, Percussion, and Tape); *Wirklicher Wald* for Soprano, Cello, Chorus, and Orch. (1983); *Music to 2 Fragments to Music by Shelley* for Women's Chorus (1985); *Tres Lamentationes* for Chorus (1985); *Tre Voci* for Soprano and Chamber Ensemble (1988); *Be Not Afeard* for Soprano, Baritone, and Orch. (1989); *Draumkvedet* for 9 Voices, Chorus, and Electroacoustic Sounds (Oslo, Feb. 1, 1994); *Lacrimosa*, a movement for the international *Requiem of Reconciliation*, for Soprano, Chorus, and Orch. (Stuttgart, Aug. 16, 1995). ELECTRONIC: *Evolution* (1966); *Warszawa* (1968); *Solitaire* (1968); *Pace* (1970); *Lux et tenebrae* (1971).—NS/LK/DM

Nordica (real name, Norton), Lillian, distinguished American soprano; b. Farmington, Maine, Dec. 12, 1857; d. Batavia, Java, May 10, 1914. She studied with John O'Neill at the New England Cons. of Music in Boston (graduated, 1876), then with Marie Maretzek in N.Y. (1876), where she made her formal debut as soloist with Gilmore's Grand Boston Band (Sept. 30, 1876); toured with it in the U.S. and later in Europe (1878). After coaching from Francois Delsarte and Emilio Belari in Paris, she studied with Antonio Sangiovanni at the Milan Cons., who suggested she adopt the stage name Nordica. It was under that name that she made her operatic debut as Donna Elvira at the Teatro Manzoni there (March 8, 1879). In St. Petersburg, she sang for Czar Alexander II a week before he was assassinated in March 1881. After making appearances in several German cities, she went to Paris to study with Giovanni Sbriglia (1881–82); she made her Paris debut on July 22,

1882, as Marguerite *(Faust)*, at the Opéra. On Jan. 22, 1883, she married Frederick A. Gower. With him she returned to America and made her American debut as Marguerite with Mapleson's company at N.Y.'s Academy of Music on Nov. 26, 1883. In 1884 she began proceedings for divorce from her first husband, but he mysteriously disappeared while attempting to cross the English Channel in a balloon. She made her debut at Covent Garden in London on March 12, 1887, as Violetta; sang there again in 1898, 1899, and 1902. She first sang at the Metropolitan Opera in N.Y. on Dec. 18, 1891, as Valentine in *Les Huguenots*. She was heard for the first time as Isolde at the Metropolitan on Nov. 27, 1895, scoring an overwhelming success. From then on she sang chiefly Wagnerian roles; she continued to appear off and on at the Metropolitan until 1909, when she began to make extended concert tours. Her farewell appearance was at a concert in Melbourne on Nov. 25, 1913. In 1896 she married the Hungarian tenor Zoltan Doeme, from whom she was divorced in 1904; in 1909 she married the banker George W. Young in London. She died while on a trip around the world.

BIBL.: I. Glackens, *Yankee Diva: L. N. and the Golden Days of Opera* (N.Y., 1963).—**NS/LK/DM**

Nordin, Lena, Swedish soprano; b. Visby, Feb. 18, 1956. She studied at the Malmö Musikhögskolan and the Stockholm Musikhögskolan, and in Salzburg, Florence, and Siena. In 1984 she attracted notice with her performance of Rameau's Aricie at the Swedish Baroque Festival. In 1986 she made her debut at the Royal Opera in Stockholm as Luisa Miller and in 1987 she was awarded the Birgit Nilsson Prize. In subsequent years, she appeared at the Royal Opera in such roles as Cleopatra, Donna Anna, Constanze, Maria Stuarda, Marguerite, and Sophie. Her portrayal of Norma there in 1997 was acclaimed. That same year, she was awarded the Jussi Björling Prize. As a guest artist, she sang in Copenhagen, Wexford, London, Dresden, Moscow, and other European cities. She also toured as a concert artist in Europe and the U.S.—**NS/LK/DM**

Nordine, Ken, American singer; b. Des Moines, Iowa, April 13, 1920. He grew up in Chicago during the glory days of television and radio. His rich, sonorous voice was well-suited for storytelling and poetry readings, which he would also perform in local clubs with the accompaniment of some of his musician friends during the '50s. Coming to the attention of Dot Records, he was invited to appear on a track from easy-listening bandleader Billy Vaughn titled "The Shifting, Whispering Sands," providing an epic monologue that drove the song to the top of the charts. Throughout the late '50s, he released a series of his own records that featured his surreal stories read over a musical backdrop provided by session musicians like Fred Katz, Richard Marx, Paul Horn, and others. Ad-libbing his way through tracks like "The Sound Museum" and "Faces in the Jazzamatazz," he created a unique mix of witty recitation and jazzy music that was unforgettable, making him an obvious choice to be a pitchman for products ranging from Taster's Choice coffee to Levi's Jeans. Over the next three decades, he worked consistently, doing several hundred commercials a year, and releasing the occasional record, often on his own cassette-only label. His work continues to be fresh, whimsical, and laced with the soul of bebop bass.

DISC.: *The Best of Word Jazz, Vol.1* (1990); *Colors* (1995). —**EJL**

Nordoff, Paul, American composer and music therapist; b. Philadelphia, June 4, 1909; d. Herdecke, Germany, Jan. 18, 1977. He studied piano with Olga Samaroff at the Philadelphia Cons. (B.M., 1927; M.M., 1932) and composition with Rubin Goldmark at the Juilliard School of Music in N.Y. (1928–33); later received his bachelor's degree in music therapy at Combs Coll. (1960). In 1993–94 and 1935–36 he held Guggenheim fellowships. He taught composition at the Philadelphia Cons. (1937–42), Mich. State Coll. (1945–49), and Bard Coll. (1949–59). From 1959 he devoted himself mainly to music therapy for handicapped children. With C. Robbins, he publ. *Music Therapy for Handicapped Children: Investigations and Experience* (N.Y., 1965), *Music Therapy in Special Education* (N.Y., 1971), *Therapy in Music for Handicapped Children* (N.Y., 1971), and *Creative Music Therapy: Individualized Treatment for the Handicapped Child* (N.Y., 1977).

WORKS: DRAMATIC: O p e r a : *Mr. Fortune* (1936–37; rev. 1956–57); *The Sea Change* (1951). **O p e r e t t a :** *The Masterpiece* (1940; Philadelphia, Jan. 24, 1941). **B a l l e t :** *Every Soul Is a Circus* (1937); *Salem Shore* (1943); *Tally Ho* (1943). **ORCH.:** *Prelude and 3 Fugues* for Chamber Orch. (1932–36); Piano Concerto (1935); Suite (1938); Concerto for Violin, Piano, and Orch. (1948); Violin Concerto (1949); *The Frog Prince* for Narrator and Orch. (1954); *Winter Symphony* (1954); *Spring Symphony* (1956); *Gothic Concerto* for Piano and Orch. (1959). **CHAMBER:** Piano Quintet (1936); Quintet for Winds and Piano (1948); Violin Sonata (1950); Flute Sonata (1953); piano pieces. **VOCAL:** Choral pieces; songs. **OTHER:** Many pieces for handicapped children.—**NS/LK/DM**

Nordqvist, Gustaf (Lazarus), Swedish organist, teacher, and composer; b. Stockholm, Feb. 12, 1886; d. there, Jan. 28, 1949. He studied organ (diploma, 1903), piano (with Lundberg), and composition (with Ellberg) at the Stockholm Cons. (1901–10) before completing his training with Willner in Berlin (1913–14). Returning to Stockholm, he served as organist of the Adolf Fredrik Church (1914–49), as a teacher (1925–44) and a prof. (1944–49) of harmony at the Cons., and as a teacher of organ at Wohlfart's music school (1926–49). In 1932 he was made a member of the Royal Swedish Academy of Music in Stockholm. He composed some chamber music, piano pieces, organ music, and choral works, but it was as a composer of art songs that he established his reputation in Sweden.—**NS/LK/DM**

Nordqvist, (Johan) Conrad, Swedish conductor, organist, and composer; b. Vänersborg, April 11, 1840; d. Charlottenlund, April 16, 1920. He was a pupil of the Stockholm Cons. (1856), then joined the court orch. in 1859 as a viola player. In 1864 he became regimental bandmaster, and in 1876 chorus master at the Royal Opera. He then was court conductor (1885–92; 1897–1908). From 1870 to 1872, from 1880 to 1900, and from 1910 to 1916 he taught at the Stockholm Cons. He then occupied various posts as organist and conductor. He wrote a funeral march for the obsequies of Charles XV (1872) and a festival march for the golden wedding anniversary of Oscar II (1897), besides ballets, piano pieces, and songs.—NS/LK/DM

Nordraak, Rikard, Norwegian composer; b. Christiania, June 12, 1842; d. Berlin, March 20, 1866. He was a pupil of Kiel and Kullak in Berlin, becoming a composer with a strong Norwegian nationalist tendency. He was a close friend of Grieg, upon whom he exerted a considerable influence, and who wrote a funeral march in his memory. He wrote the Norwegian national anthem, *Ja, vi elsker dette landet* (Yes, We Love This Land), which was first sung on Norway's national day (May 17, 1864). His other works include incidental music to Björnson's *Maria Stuart i Skotland* (1864–65; Christiania, 1867) and *Sigurd Slembe: Kaares sang* (Copenhagen, 1865), several unaccompanied men's choruses, songs, and piano pieces. His death at the age of 23 was a grievous loss to Norway's music.

BIBL.: L. Greni, *R. N.* (Oslo, 1941); A. van E. Sein, *R. N.* (Oslo, 1942).—NS/LK/DM

Noren, Heinrich (real name, **Heinrich Suso Johannes Gottlieb**; in 1916 he added his wife's name, **Noren**, to his own), Austrian violinist and composer; b. Graz, Jan. 5, 1861; d. Rottach, Bavaria, June 6, 1928. He studied violin with Vieuxtemps in Brussels (1878) and with Massart in Paris (1883), and composition with Gernsheim and Bussler in Berlin. In 1895 he settled in Krefeld, where he founded his own music school. He then taught at the Stern Cons. in Berlin (1901–07). In 1915 he moved to Rottach. His name attracted attention with the performance of his orch. variations, *Kaleidoskop* (Dresden, July 1, 1907), in which the last movement, dedicated to "a famous contemporary," was a variation on a theme from *Ein Heldenleben* by Richard Strauss. The publishers of Strauss instituted a lawsuit against Noren, which created a ripple of excitement in musical circles. Noren also composed an opera, *Der Schleier der Beatrice*, Sym., Violin Concerto, and some chamber music.—NS/LK/DM

Norena, Eidé (real name, **Kaja Andrea Karoline Hansen- Eidé**), Norwegian soprano; b. Horten, April 26, 1884; d. Lausanne, Nov. 19, 1968. She studied voice with Ellen Gulbranson in Christiania, and later in Weimar, London, and Paris; was a pupil of Raimund von Zur Mühlen. She began her career as a concert singer in Scandinavia. She made her operatic debut as Amor in Gluck's *Orfeo* in Christiania (1907), subsequently singing at the National Theater there (1908–18). After appearances at Stockholm's Royal Theater, she sang at La Scala in Milan (1924), Covent Garden in London (1924–25; 1930–31; 1934; 1937), and at the Paris Opéra (1925–37). She was a member of the Chicago Opera (1926–28); from 1933 to 1938, of the Metropolitan Opera in N.Y. (made her debut as Mimi,

on Feb. 9, 1933); toured the U.S. in concert. Among her finest roles were Mathilde in *Guillaume Tell*, Violetta, Marguerite in *Les Huguenots*, the 3 heroines in *Les Contes d'Hoffmann*, and Desdemona.—NS/LK/DM

Nørgård, Per, prominent Danish composer and pedagogue; b. Gentofte, near Copenhagen, July 13, 1932. He began piano lessons when he was 8. In 1949 he became a private composition pupil of Holmboe. After entering the Royal Danish Cons. of Music in Copenhagen (1952), he continued his training with Holmboe there and also took courses with Hffding (theory), Koppel (piano), and Jersild (solfège), passing his examinations in theory, composition, and pedagogy (1955). Following further studies with Boulanger in Paris (1956–57), he was awarded the Lily Boulanger Prize in 1957. He was a music critic for Copenhagen's *Politiken* (1958–62), and also taught at the Odense Cons. (1958–60). After teaching at the Royal Danish Cons. of Music in Copenhagen (1960–65), he joined the faculty of the Århus Cons. in 1965, where he was made prof. of composition in 1987. In 1988 he was awarded the Henrik-Steffens-Preis of Germany. In 1995 he was made an honorary member of the ISCM, the first Dane ever to be accorded that distinction. In 1996 he received the Léonie Sonning Music Prize of Denmark. After a period of adolescent emulation of Sibelius, Nrgård plunged into the mainstream of cosmopolitan music-making, exploring the quasi- mathematical serial techniques based on short tonal motifs, rhythmic displacement, metrical modulation, pointillism, graphic notation, and a "horizontal" invariant fixing certain notes to specific registers; then shifted to a pointillistically impressionistic colorism evolving in a tonal bradykinesis.

WORKS: DRAMATIC: O p e r a : *The Labyrinth* (1963; Copenhagen, Sept. 2, 1967); *Gilgamesh* (1971–72; Århus, May 4, 1973); *Siddharta* (1977–79; Stockholm, March 18, 1983); *The Divine Tivoli*, chamber opera (1982). **B a l l e t :** *Le Jeune Homme à marier* (1964; Danish TV, April 2, 1965; first stage perf., Copenhagen, Oct. 15, 1967); *Tango Chicane* (Copenhagen, Oct. 15, 1967); Trio for 3 Dancers and Percussion (Paris, Dec., 1972). **ORCH.:** *Metamorphose* for Strings (1952); 6 syms.: No. 1, *Sinfonia austera* (1954; Danish Radio, Aug. 19, 1958), No. 2 (Århus, April 13, 1970), No. 3 (1972–75; Copenhagen, Sept. 2, 1976), No. 4, *Indian Rose Garden and Chinese Witch Lake* (Hamburg, Oct. 30, 1981), No. 5 (1990), and No. 6 (1999; Danish Radio, Jan. 6, 2000); *Constellations*, concerto for 12 Solo Strings or 12 String Groups (Copenhagen, Nov. 3, 1958); *Lyse Danse* for Chamber Orch. (1959); *Fragment VI* for 6 Orch. Groups: Winds, Brass, Percussion, Harp, Pianos, and Timpani (1959–61; Århus, Feb. 12, 1962); *Iris* (Copenhagen, May 19, 1967); *Luna, 4 Phases* (Danish Radio, Sept. 5, 1968); *Recall* for Accordion and Orch. (1968); *Voyage into the Golden Screen* for Chamber Orch. (Copenhagen, March 24, 1969); *Mosaic* for 16 Winds (1969); *Doing* for Wind Orch. (1969); *Dream Play* for Chamber Orch. (1975); *Twilight* for Orch. and Conga Player Obbligato with Dancer ad libitum (1976–77); *For a Change*, percussion concerto (1982); *Burn* (Glasgow, Sept. 17, 1984); *Between* for Cello and Orch. (Copenhagen, Aug. 30, 1985); *Prelude to Breaking* (Göteborg, Sept. 26, 1986); *Remembering Child* for Viola and Chamber Orch. (St. Paul, Minn., Sept. 12, 1986); *Helle Nacht*, violin concerto (1987); *Pastorale* for Strings (1988); *King, Queen, and Ace* for Harp and Chamber Ensemble (1989); *Night Symphonies, Day Breaks* (1991); *Spaces of Time* (1991); Piano Concerto (1995). **CHAM-**

BER: Quintet for Flute, Violin, Viola, Cello, and Piano (1951–52); *Suite* for Flute and Piano (1952); 7 string quartets: No. 1, *Quartetto Breve* (1952), No. 2, *Quartetto Brioso* (1952–58), No. 3, *3 Miniatures* (1959), No. 4, *Dreamscape* (1969), No. 5, *Inscape* (1969), No. 6, *Tintinnabulary* (1986), and No. 7 (1993); *Solo intimo* for Cello (1953); *Diptychon* for Violin and Piano (1953); 2 trios for Clarinet, Cello, and Piano (1955, 1974); *Songs from Aftonland* for Contralto, Flute, Harp, Violin, Viola, and Cello (1956); *Waves* for Percussion (1969); *Returns* for Guitar (1976); *I Ching* for Percussion (1982); *9 Friends* for Harmonica or Piano (1985); *Lin* for Clarinet, Cello, and Piano (1986); *Hut ab* for 2 Clarinets (1988); *Syn* for Brass Quintet (1988); *Swan Descending* for Harp (1989); *Nemo Dynamo* for Percussion and Computer (1991); *Tjampuan* for Violin and Cello (1992). **KEYBOARD: Piano:** 2 sonatas (1952, 1957); *Sketches* (1959); *9 Studies* (1959); *4 Fragments* (1959–60); *Grooving* (1967–68); *Turn* (1973); *Achilles and the Tortoise* (1983). **Organ:** *Canon* (1971); *Triapartita* (1988). **VOCAL:** *Triptychon* for Mixed Voices and Wind Instruments or Organ (1957); *Nocturnes*, suite for Soprano and Piano or 19 Instruments (1961–62); *3 Love Songs* for Contralto and Orch. (1963); *Prism* for 3 Vocalists and Instrumental Ensemble (1964); *The Fourth Day* for Chorus and Orch. (1984–85; 4th movement of a collaborative work, *Hexaemeron*, depicting the 7 days of creation); *Entwicklungen* for Alto and Instrumental Ensemble (1986); *L'Enfant et l'aube* for Soprano, Tenor, and Chamber Ensemble (Radio France, Paris, June 7, 1988). —NS/LK/DM

Nørholm, Ib, Danish composer, organist, and teacher; b. Copenhagen, Jan. 24, 1931. He studied theory with Holmboe, music history with Hjelmborg, and form and analysis with Bentzon and Hffding at the Royal Danish Cons. of Music in Copenhagen (1950–54), passing his examinations in theory and music history (1954), organ and teaching (1955), and sacred music (1956). He was active as a music critic (1956–64). He was a church organist in Elsinore (1957–63) and then at Copenhagen's Bethlemskirken (from 1964). He also taught part-time at the Royal Danish Cons. of Music in Copenhagen (from 1961) and at the Odense Cons., and subsequently taught theory at the Royal Danish Cons. of Music in Copenhagen (from 1973). His musical idiom is permeated with Scandinavian lyricism, even when he introduces modernistic devices.

WORKS: DRAMATIC: *Invitation to a Beheading*, opera after Nabokov (1965, Danish TV, Oct. 10, 1967); *The Young Park*, chamber opera (Århus, Oct. 14, 1970); *The Garden Wall*, choral opera (1976); *The Revenge of the Truth*, chamber opera (1985). **ORCH.:** 9 syms.: No. 1 (Danish Radio, Aug. 13, 1959), No. 2, *Isola Bella* (Copenhagen, April 27, 1972), No. 3, *Day's Nightmare* (Copenhagen, Oct. 9, 1973), No. 4, *Modskabelse*, for Soloists, Chorus, and Orch. (1979), No. 5 (1981), No. 6 (1982), No. 7, *Ecliptical Instincts* (Copenhagen, May 20, 1983), No. 8, *Faith and Longing* (1989–90), and No. 9, *The Sun Garden in 3 Shades of Light* (1990); *Fluctuations* for 34 Solo Strings, 2 Harps, Harpsichord, Mandolin, and Guitar (1962); *Relief I* and *II* for Chamber Ensemble (both 1963) and *III* for Orch. (1964); *Serenade of Cincinnatus* for Chamber Orch. (1964); *Exile* (Copenhagen, Sept. 8, 1966); *Efter Ikaros* (After Icarus), suite (1967); *Heretic Hymn*, fresco (1974); Violin Concerto (1974); *Idylles d'Apocalypse* for Organ and 20 Instruments (1980); *Spirales* for Accordion and Orch. (1986–87); Cello Concerto (1989). **CHAMBER:** *Rhapsody* for Viola and Piano (1955); 8 string quartets: No. 1, *In Vere* (1955), No. 2, *5 Impromptus* (1965), No. 3, *From My Green*

Herbarium (1966), No. 4, *September—October—November* (1966), No. 5 (1976), No. 6, *Skygerne Frosner* (1978), No. 7, *En passant* (1985), and No. 8, *Memories* (1988); *Tombeau* for Cello and Piano (1956); Violin Sonata (1956–57); Trio for Clarinet, Cello, and Piano (1957); *Mosaic Fragments* for Flute and String Trio (1958); Piano Trio (1959); *Signature from a Province* for Piano (1970); *Dialogue in 3 Courses* for Guitar, Accordion, and Percussion (1975); Guitar Sonata (1976); *Essai prismatique* for Piano Trio (1979); *The Garden with Paths That Part* for 7 Instruments (1982); 6 Short Motets (1986); Saxophone Quartet (1992). **VOCAL:** *Jongleurs—69* for Soloists, Chorus, Ensembles, Loudspeaker Voice, and Orch. (Odense, Nov. 25, 1969); *Tys og lovsang* (Light and Hymn of Thanksgiving) for Soloists, Chorus, Organ, and Instrumental Ensemble (Copenhagen, Dec. 5, 1972); *Day's Nightmare II* for Soloists, Chorus, and Orch. (Copenhagen, Nov. 29, 1973); *Proprium Missae Dominicae Pentacostis* for 2 Choruses, Winds, and Organ (1977); *Lux Secunda* for Soprano, Baritone, Chorus, and Small Orch. (1984); songs.—NS/LK/DM

Norlind, (Johan Henrik) Tobias, distinguished Swedish musicologist; b. Vellinge, May 6, 1879; d. Stockholm, Aug. 13, 1947. He studied piano and music in Lund, then took courses in composition with Jadassohn at the Leipzig Cons. (1897–98) and with Thuille in Munich (1898–99); he also studied musicology with Sandberger at the Univ. of Munich, and subsequently with Friedlaender at the Univ. of Berlin. Returning to Sweden in 1900, he attended Univ. of Uppsala and Univ. of Lund, obtaining the degree of Ph.D. in 1909. He then held several positions as an instructor in colleges and univs., and taught music history at the Stockholm Cons. (1918–45).

WRITINGS (all publ. in Stockholm unless otherwise given): *Svensk musikhistoria* (Hälsingborg, 1901; 2nd ed., 1918; abr. Ger. tr., 1904); *Allmänt musiklexikon* (1912–16; 2nd ed., 1927–28); *Jenny Lind: en minnesbok till hundraårsdagen* (1919); *Allmän musikhistoria* (1922); *Kristina Nilsson, sångerskan och konstärinnan* (1923); *Beethoven och hans tid* (1924–25); with E. Trobäck, *Kunglia hovkapellets historia 1526–1926* (1926); *Systematik der Saiteninstrumente*: Vol. I, *Geschichte der Zither* (1936), and Vol. II, *Geschichte des Klaviers* (1939; 2nd ed., 1941); *Bilder ur svenska musikens historia från äldsta tid till medeltidens slut* (1947). —NS/LK/DM

Norman, (Fredrik Vilhelm) Ludvig, notable Swedish conductor, pianist, and composer; b. Stockholm, Aug. 28, 1831; d. there, March 28, 1885. He began piano lessons as a child with Vilhelmina Josephson. While still young, he received training in theory with Adolf Fredrik Lindblad and in piano with Theodor Stein and Jan van Boom. At 14, he made his first public appearance as a pianist. In 1848 he went to Leipzig to pursue training at the Cons. with Moscheles (piano), Hauptmann (counterpoint), and Rietz (composition). Upon his return to Stockholm in 1852, he became active as a pianist, teacher, and composer. From 1858 to 1861 he taught at the Cons. of the Swedish Academy of Music. In 1860 he helped to organize the New Harmonic Soc. and established himself as a conductor. In 1861 he became conductor of the Royal Opera, a position he held with great distinction until 1878. During his tenure there, he also conducted sym. concerts with its orch. that developed into regular sym. concerts from 1878. Norman introduced many works to the Swedish public, among them operas by Wagner, Verdi, Gounod, and Bizet. In 1880 he founded the Music Soc., which he served as conductor until his death. In 1864 he married **Wilma Neruda**, but they separated in 1870. As a composer, Norman was respected but little appreciated by his contemporaries. He is now acknowledged as one of the principal Swedish symphonists of the second half of the 20th century. He was an able craftsman who revealed secure handling of instrumentation set off by a gift of inventive melodic writing.

WORKS: ORCH.: Overture (1849); Concert Piece for Piano and Orch. (1850; rev. 1875 and 1880): Concerto Overture (1856; Stockholm, Feb. 1857); 3 syms.: No. 1 (1858–59; Stockholm, April 4, 1875), No. 2 (1870–71; Stockholm, Jan. 4, 1873), and No. 3 (1881; Stockholm, Nov. 14, 1885); *Funeral March* in memory of August Söderman (1876); Overture to Shakespeare's *Antony and Cleopatra* (1881); *Festival Overture on National Themes* (1882). **CHAMBER:** Violin Sonata (1848); 2 piano trios (1849; 1871–72); *5 Tonbilder in Zusammenhange* for Violin and Piano (1851); String Sextet (1854); Piano Quartet (1856–57); *10 karaktärsstycken* for Violin and Piano (1863–83); String Octet (1866–67); Cello Sonata (1867); Sextet for Piano, 2 Violins, Viola, Cello, and Double Bass (1868–69; rev. 1873); Viola Sonata (1869); String Quintet (1870); 5 string quartets; many piano pieces. **VOCAL:** Several cantatas; songs.

BIBL.: J. Bagge, *Förteckning öfver L. N.'s tonverk* (Stockholm, 1886).—**NS/LK/DM**

Norman, Jessye, exceptionally gifted black American soprano; b. Augusta, Ga., Sept. 15, 1945. She received a scholarship to study at Howard Univ. in Washington, D.C. (1961), where she had vocal lessons from Carolyn Grant; continued her training at the Peabody Cons. of Music in Baltimore and at the Univ. of Mich., where her principal teachers were Pierre Bernac and Elizabeth Mannion. She won the Munich Competition (1968), and then made her operatic debut as Elisabeth in *Tannhäuser* at the Berlin Deutsche Oper (1969); appeared in the title role of *L'Africaine* at Florence's Maggio Musicale (1971), and the following year sang Aida at Milan's La Scala and Cassandra in *Les Troyens* at London's Covent Garden; subsequently made major recital debuts in London and N.Y. (1973). After an extensive concert tour of North America (1976–77), she made her U.S. stage debut as Jocasta in *Oedipus rex* and as Purcell's Dido on a double bill with the Opera Co. of Philadelphia on Nov. 22, 1982. She made her Metropolitan Opera debut in N.Y. as Cassandra on Sept. 26, 1983. In 1986 she appeared as soloist in Strauss's *Vier letzte Lieder* with the Berlin Phil. during its tour of the U.S. On Sept. 20, 1989, she was the featured soloist with Zubin Mehta and the N.Y. Phil. in its opening concert of its 148th season, which was telecast live to the nation by PBS. In 1992 she sang Jocasta at the opening operatic production at the new Saito Kinen Festival in Matsumoto. On Sept. 20, 1995, Norman was again the featured soloist with the N.Y. Phil., this time under Kurt Masur's direction, in a gala concert telecast live to the nation by PBS marking the opening of the orch.'s 53rd season. In 1996 she appeared as Emilia Marty at the Metropolitan Opera.

Norman's extraordinary repertory ranges from Purcell to Richard Rodgers; she commended herself in Mussorgsky's songs, which she performed in Moscow in the original Russian; in her recitals she gave performances of the classical German repertory as well as contemporary masterpieces, such as Schoenberg's *Gürrelieder* and the French moderns, which she invariably performed in the original tongue. This combination of scholarship and artistry contributed to her consistently successful career as one of the most versatile concert and operatic singers of her time.—**NS/LK/DM**

Norrington, Sir Roger (Arthur Carver), scholarly English conductor; b. Oxford, March 16, 1934. He was educated at Clare Coll., Cambridge, and the Royal Coll. of Music in London; was active as a tenor. In 1962 he founded the Schütz Choir in London, with which he first gained notice as a conductor. From 1966 to 1984 he was principal conductor of the Kent Opera, where he produced scores by Monteverdi utilizing his own performing eds. He served as music director of the London Baroque Players (from 1975) and the London Classical Players (from 1978); also was principal conductor of the Bournemouth Sinfonietta (1985–89). On April 2, 1989, he made an auspicious N.Y. debut at Carnegie Hall conducting Beethoven's 8th and 9th syms. In 1990 he became music director of the Orch. of St. Luke's in N.Y., which post he held until 1994. In 1980 he was made an Officer of the Order of the British Empire; in 1990, a Commander of the Order of the British Empire; in 1996 he was knighted. In 1990 he conducted *Die Zauberflöte* at the Promenade Concerts in London. In 1997 he conducted Mozart's *Mitridate* in Salzburg, where he also became chief conductor of its Camerata Academica that year. In 1998 he also became chief conductor of the Stuttgart Radio Sym. Orch.

Norrington entered controversy by insisting that the classical tempo is basic for all interpretation. He also insisted that Beethoven's metronome markings, not usually accepted by performers, are in fact accurate reflections of Beethoven's inner thoughts about his own music. He obtained numerous defenders of his ideas (as one critic put it, "inspired literalism") for the interpretation of classical music, which aroused sharp interest as well as caustic rejection. However that might be, his performances, especially in the U.S., received a great deal of attention, and he was particularly praised for the accuracy and precision of his interpretations. —**NS/LK/DM**

Norris, David Owen, English pianist and teacher; b. Northampton, June 16, 1953. He studied at Keble Coll., Oxford (1972–75) and was an organ scholar at the Royal Academy of Music in London (1975–77). Following the completion of his training in Paris (1977–78), he returned to London as a prof. at the Royal Academy of Music (from 1978). In 1982 he won third prize in the Geneva competition. He secured his reputation as both a pianist and broadcaster via frequent appearances with the BBC; also made extensive tours of Europe and North America. In 1991 he was honored as the first recipient of the Gilmore Artist Award of

Kalamazoo, Mich. In 1992 he became chairman of the faculty of the Steans Inst. for Singers in Chicago and artistic director of the Cardiff Festival in Wales. In 1993 he was honored with the Gresham professorship in music in London. Norris has eschewed the usual path of the virtuoso, opting instead for a steady enhancement of his interpretive powers in a varied repertoire ranging from the classics to the contemporary era.—**NS/LK/DM**

Norris, Walter, free-jazz pianist; b. Little Rock, Ark., Dec. 27, 1931. He played on the West Coast and performed briefly with Ornette Coleman during the 1950s. He came to N.Y. in 1960, where he lead the orch. at the Playboy Club from 1963–70. In the early 1970s, he toured with The Thad Jones–Mel Lewis Orch. He went to Europe in 1976, and has been living and teaching in Berlin at the Hochschule fur Musik since 1984. He gained new attention in the 1990s thanks to a series of albums for Concord Jazz. His rhythmic creativity is deceptive; in fact his beat is quite sure.

DISC.: *Drifting* (1974); *Winter Rose* (1978); *Synchronicity* (1978); *Stepping on Cracks* (1978); *Live at Maybeck Recital Hall, IV* (1990); *Lush Life* (1990); *Sunburst* (1991); *Love Every Moment* (1992); *Hues of Blues* (1995); *From Another Star* (1998).

North, Alex, gloriously gifted American composer and conductor with a predilection for uniquely colored film music; b. Chester, Pa., Dec. 4, 1910; d. Pacific Palisades, Calif., Sept. 8, 1991. His father, a blacksmith, was an early immigrant from Russia. North studied piano and theory at the Curtis Inst. of Music in Philadelphia, and later received a scholarship to study at the Juilliard School of Music in N.Y., where he took courses in composition (1929–32). A decisive change in his life came with his decision to go to Russia as a technology specialist at a time when Russia was eager to engage American technicians. He became fascinated with new Russian music and received a scholarship to attend the Moscow Cons., where he studied composition with Anton Weprik and Victor Bielyi (1933–35). He also was music director of the propaganda group of German Socialists called "Kolonne Links" (Column to the Left!). He mastered the Russian language and acquired a fine reputation in Russia as a true friend of Soviet music. Returning to the U.S., he took additional courses in composition with Copland (1936–38) and Toch (1938–39). In 1939 he conducted 26 concerts in Mexico as music director of the Anna Sokolow Dance Troupe; during his stay in Mexico City, he had some instruction from Silvestre Revueltas. In 1942 North entered the U.S. Army; promoted to captain, he became responsible for entertainment programs in mental hospitals. He worked closely with the psychiatrist Karl Menninger in developing a theatrical genre called "psychodrama," which later became an accepted mode of psychological therapy. During his Army years, North also worked with the Office of War Information, composing scores for over 25 documentary films. During all these peregrinations he developed a distinct flair for theater music, while continuing to produce estimable works in absolute forms. His concerto, *Revue* for Clarinet and Orch., was performed by Benny Goodman in N.Y. under the baton of Leonard Bernstein on Nov. 18, 1946. He further expanded his creative talents to write a number of modern ballets. The result of these multifarious excursions into musical forms was the formation of a style peculiarly recognizable as the specific art of North. His concentrated efforts, however, became directed mainly toward the art of film music, a field in which he triumphed. John Huston stated in 1986 that "it is the genius of Alex North to convey an emotion to the audience"; other directors praised North's cinemusical abilities in similar terms. Among the writers with whom he worked were Tennessee Williams, John Steinbeck, and Arthur Miller. But no success is without disheartening frustration. North was commissioned to write the score for *2001: A Space Odyssey*, on which he worked enthusiastically. But much to his dismay, the director, Stanley Kubrick, decided to replace it by a pasticcio that included such commonplaces as Strauss's *The Blue Danube Waltz*. North refused to be downhearted by this discomfiture and used the discarded material for his 3rd Sym. He was nominated 15 times for an Academy Award for best film music, but it was not until 1986 that the Academy of Motion Picture Arts and Sciences finally awarded him an Oscar for lifetime achievement. Among his outstanding scores are *A Streetcar Named Desire* (1951), *Death of a Salesman* (1951), *Viva Zapata!* (1952), *The Rose Tattoo* (1955), *The Bad Seed* (1956), *The Rainmaker* (1956), *The Sound and the Fury* (1959), *Spartacus* (1960), *The Children's Hour* (1961), *The Misfits* (1961), *Cleopatra* (1963), *The Agony and the Ecstasy* (1965), *Who's Afraid of Virginia Woolf?* (1966), *The Shoes of the Fisherman* (1968), *Shanks* (1973), *Bite the Bullet* (1975), *Dragonslayer* (1981), *Under the Volcano* (1984), *Prizzi's Honor* (1985), *The Penitent* (1986), *The Dead* (1987), and *Good Morning, Vietnam* (1988). His song *Unchained Melody* (1955) became a popular hit in its rendition by The Righteous Brothers.

WORKS: DRAMATIC: B a l l e t : *Ballad in a Popular Style*, for Anna Sokolow (1933); *Case History* (1933); *War Is Beautiful* (1936); *Slaughter of the Innocents* (N.Y., Nov. 14, 1937); *American Lyric*, for Martha Graham (N.Y., Dec. 26, 1937); *Inquisition* (1938); *Lupe* (1940); *Design for 5* (1941); *Exile* (Mansfield, March 3, 1941); *Golden Fleece*, for Hanya Holm (Mansfield, March 17, 1941); *Clay Ritual* (Hartford, Conn., May 20, 1942); *Intersection* (1947); *A Streetcar Named Desire* (Montreal, Oct. 9, 1952); *Daddy Long Legs Dream Ballet* (1955; for Fred Astaire and Leslie Caron in the film *Daddy Long Legs*); *Mal de siècle* (Brussels, July 3, 1958). C h i l d r e n ' s O p e r a a n d T h e a t e r : *The Hither and Thither of Danny Dither* (1941); *Little Indian Drum* for Narrator and Orch. (N.Y., Oct. 19, 1947). ORCH.: *Rhapsody* for Piano and Orch. (N.Y., Nov. 11, 1941); *Revue* for Clarinet and Orch. (N.Y., Nov. 18, 1946); 3 syms.: No. 1 (1947), No. 2 (1968), and No. 3 (1971; based upon the unused original score for *2001: A Space Odyssey*); *Holiday Set* (Saratoga, N.Y., July 10, 1948). OTHER: *Morning Star Cantata* for Chorus and Orch. (N.Y., May 18, 1947); *Negro Mother Cantata* for Chorus and Orch. (N.Y., May 17, 1948); chamber music.—**NS/LK/DM**

North, Roger, English lawyer and writer on music; b. probably in Tostock, Suffolk, c. 1651; d. Rougham, March 1, 1734. He was a member of Parliament, and served as Queen's Attorney General under James II until the Revolution of 1688. His writings were not publ.

during his lifetime and have only recently been recognized as significant contributions to music. See J. Wilson, ed., *Roger North on Music: Being a Selection from His Essays Written during the Years c. 1695–1728* (London, 1959), M. Chan and J. Kassler, eds., *Roger North's Cursory Notes of Musicke (c. 1698-c. 1703): A Physical, Psychological and Critical Theory* (Kensington, N.S.W., 1986), idem and J. Hine, *Roger North's Writings on Music to c. 1703: A Set of Analytical Indexes* (Kensington, N.S.W., 1986), and idem, *Roger North's The Musical Grammarian and Theory of Sounds* (Kensington, N.S.W., 1988).—NS/LK/DM

Norup, Bent, Danish baritone; b. Hobro, Dec. 7, 1936. He received vocal training in Copenhagen from Kristan Rils, in Munich from Karl Schmitt-Walter, and in N.Y. from Herta Sperber. In 1970 he made his operatic debut in Copenhagen as Kurwenal, where he subsequently sang at the Royal Theater. He also made guest appearances in Hamburg, Berlin, Düsseldorf, Paris, Vienna, and the U.S. His concert engagements took him to leading music centers of the world. Among his roles of note were Hans Sachs, Wotan, Telramund, Klingsor, Amfortas, Jochanaan, Iago, and Scarpia.—NS/LK/DM

Norvo, Red (actually, **Norville Kenneth**), innovative jazz xylophonist, vibraphonist, marimba player, pianist, leader; b. Beardstown, Ill., March 31, 1908; d. Santa Monica, Calif., April 6, 1999. Norvo showed a consistent interest in inventive writing and innovations, working with Paul Whiteman, who emphasized writing, and later hiring Eddie Sauter to write for his band. He recorded in 1945 with Parker and Gillespie, then formed a trio with Charles Mingus in the early 1950s and recorded third stream classical works in 1956.

Norvo played piano from early childhood, then studied xylophone. Mallet instruments were widely regarded as novelties when he first encountered them in his early teens. He began playing professionally at 17 in territory bands and vaudeville acts like the Flaming Youth Revue. In 1925, he toured the Middle West with a marimba band called The Collegians but left them in Chicago to work with the established dance bands of Paul Ash (who changed Red's name to Norvo) and Ben Bernie. He played regularly in local radio stations and also had a solo vaudeville act that including tap-dancing. He then enrolled as a student and studied mine engineering at Univ. of Mo. (1926–27). Norvo returned to full- time music, led his own band on Station KSTP (c. 1929) and worked with Victor Young's Radio Orch. (NBC) in Chicago. Two solos recorded for Brunswick in 1929 were never issued. His four-mallet virtuosity on Bix Beiderbecke's "In a Mist" attracted the attention of Paul Whiteman, whose band already boasted Mildred Bailey. Norvo was regularly featured with Whiteman until mid-1932. In late 1933, he and Bailey married. Norvo attracted notice performing with Whiteman; Bernard Addison dragged Rex Stewart through a blizzard to hear him play with the band in Paterson, N.J. He made extensive freelance recordings and worked occasionally with Charlie Barnet. His unusual 1933 recording "Dance of the Octopus," with

Benny Goodman on bass clarinet, lost him further Brunswick dates, but attracted John Hammond who bought two dozen copies of the 78 and offered Norvo additional recording dates. More significantly, the records prompted Eddie Sauter to seek him out. From October 1935, he led a piano-less, drummer-less octet (recorded by Decca) at 52nd Street's Famous Door with Sauter, Dave Barbour, and Herbie Haymer. In May 1936, encouraged by the William Morris Agency, he expanded the group from six to 10 pieces for a Hotel Commodore engagement. Bailey was doing well in radio in N.Y., but, when she and Norvo's band were simultaneously booked into Chicago's Blackhawk, they realized they were an irresistible combination. "Mr. and Mrs. Swing," as George Simon dubbed them, led a subtly swinging unit that Ellington called "Superleviathanic." During 1936, Norvo made several recordings on piano under the pseudonym Ken Kenny. Recording under both Norvo's and Bailey's names, their band waxed dozens of tracks between 1936 and 1939. From 1937–44, they led bands of varying sizes including a 10-piece unit at Palisades, N.Y., in 1940. His Overseas Spotlight octet (organized to play for servicemen) featured Flip Phillips and Ralph Burns in two recording sessions for V-Disc. From about 1943 onwards, he worked mainly on vibraphone. In late 1944, he disbanded his current group, a sextet, and joined Benny Goodman. By this time he and Bailey were working separately again and in 1945 they divorced but remained close. During 1945, he led a celebrated date with Parker, Gillespie, and Teddy Wilson. Norvo left Goodman in December 1945 and worked with Woody Herman until December 1946. He moved to southern Calif. in 1947, working as a freelance and leading own group. He did studio work and continued to experiment with recording bands of all configurations for various labels, playing with guests including Benny Carter and Dexter Gordon. He recorded for Capitol in 1948 with Stan Hasselgard and then returned to N.Y. in September 1949 to lead a sextet with Tony Scott, Dick Hyman, and Mundell Lowe. In 1950, he formed a trio, first with Red Mitchell and Mundell Lowe, then with Charles Mingus and Tal Farlow. His trio later included Jimmy Raney and Red Mitchell. He first toured Europe early in 1954, then led his own small groups in U.S. and recorded for numerous labels. He reunited with his brother-in-law Shorty Rogers; remade Sauter charts with Helen Humes replacing Bailey; experimented with third stream works, notably Bill Smith's Divertimento. After touring Australia in 1956, he opened own club in Santa Monica, Calif., and worked in Las Vegas from 1957–58. After he guested with Goodman on TV in 1958, Frank Sinatra prompted him to expand his group into a sextet for a 1959 tour that traveled as far as Australia. His quintet joined Goodman and four others for a 10-piece tour in late 1959 and also worked in the Goodman Sextet in spring 1961. During the 1960s and 1970s he rarely played in N.Y., working mainly in Calif. and Nev, including a long residencies at the Sands Hotel. An ear operation left him out of action from March-July 1968, but he was able to tour Europe as a soloist in late 1968. Norvo worked with George Wein's Newport All Stars (1969), led his own group (1970–72), took a year's sabbatical, then resumed playing. His hearing continued to deteriorate and he had a stroke about 1986, and didn't play again, except once on a jazz cruise, where he performed with one hand, in late 1990.

DISC.: "Dance of the Octopus" (1933); "Just a Mood" (1937); "Smoke Dreams" (1937); *R. N. and Mildred Bailey* (1938); "Wartime Vibe-rations" (1943); *Legendary V-Disc Masters* (1943); *Fabulous Jam Session* (1945); *Town Hall Concert, Vol. 1, 2* (1944); *Improvisations on Keynote* (1944); *R. N. Trio with Tal Farlow* (1950); *Move! With Tal Farlow and Charlie Mingus* (1950); "September Song," "Move," "Budo" (1950); *With Jimmy Raney and Red Mitchell* (1954); *R. N. Trio* (1955); *R. N. Ad Lib Featuring Buddy Collette* (1956); *Music to Listen to R. N. By* (1957); *Forward Look* (1957); *Pretty Is the Only Way to Fly* (1962); *R. N. and His All Stars* (1968); *Swing That Music* (1969); *N....Naturally* (1972); *Vibes a la Red* (1974); *Second Time Around* (1975); *R. in N.Y.* (1977); *Live at Rick's Cafe Americain* (1978); *R. and Ross* (1979); *Just Friends* (1983). **FRANK SINATRA:** *Frank Sinatra with the R. N. Quintet: Live in Australia, 1959* (1997).—**JC/MM/LP**

Noske, Frits (Rudolf), Dutch musicologist; b. The Hague, Dec. 13, 1920; d. Ariolo, Switzerland, Sept. 15, 1993. He studied cello and theory at the Amsterdam Cons. and at the Royal Cons. in The Hague (1940–45), then pursued musicological training with Bernet Kempers and Smits van Waesberghe at the Univ. of Amsterdam (Ph.D., 1954, with the diss. *La Mélodie française de Berlioz à Duparc*; publ. in Amsterdam, 1954; Eng. tr., rev., 1970); also had lessons with Masson at the Sorbonne in Paris (1949–50). He taught music history at the Amsterdam Cons. and at the Bussum Toonkunst Music School; was librarian at the Amsterdam Music Library (1951–54), and subsequently was its director (1954–68); also was a reader in musicology at the Univ. of Leiden (1965–68) and prof. of musicology at the Univ. of Amsterdam (from 1968).

WRITINGS: *Forma formans: Een strutuuranalytische methode, toegepast op de instrumentale muziek van Jan Pieterszoon Sweelinck* (Amsterdam, 1969; Eng. tr., rev., 1976, in the *International Review of the Aesthetics and Sociology of Music*, VII); *The Signifier and the Signified: Studies in the Operas of Mozart and Verdi* (The Hague, 1977); *Sweelinck* (Oxford, 1988); *Saints and Sinners: The Latin Musical Dialogue in the Seventeenth Century* (Oxford, 1992).—**NS/LK/DM**

Noskowski, Zygmunt, significant Polish conductor and composer; b. Warsaw, May 2, 1846; d. there, July 23, 1909. He studied at the Warsaw Music Inst., then became an instructor in a school for the blind, and devised a music notation for the blind. He subsequently studied composition with Kiel in Berlin. After a brief period of professional activities in Western Europe, he returned to Warsaw and was director of the Music Soc. (1881–1902); in 1888 he was appointed a prof. at the Warsaw Cons., and later was director of the Warsaw Phil. (1905–08) and Opera (1907–09). He wrote the operas *Livia Quintilla* (Lemberg, Feb. 1, 1898), *Wyrok* (The Judgement; Warsaw, Nov. 15, 1906), and *Zemsta za mur graniczny* (Revenge for the Boundary Wall), after A. Fredro's *Zemsta* (Warsaw, 1909), as well as 3 syms.: No. 1 (1874–75); No. 2, *Elegiac* (1875–79); No. 3, *Od wiosny do wiosny* (From Spring to Spring; 1903), *Morskie Oko*, symphonic overture (1875), *Step* (The Steppe), sym-

phonic poem (1896–97), *Z zycia narodu* (From the Life of the Nation), symphonic variations (1901), chamber music, and songs.

BIBL.: A. Sutkowski, *Z. N.* (Kraków, 1957); W. Wrónski, *Materialy z zycia i twórczości Z. N.ego* (Kraków, 1960).—**NS/LK/DM**

Notari, Angelo, Italian composer; b. Padua, Jan. 14, 1566; d. London, Dec. 1663. After settling in England, he entered the service of Prince Henry about 1610. By 1618 he was in the service of Prince Charles, continuing in his patron's service as Charles I (1625–49). With the Restoration of 1660, he again was in the royal service until his death. He publ. *Prime musiche nuove* (London, c. 1613), which contains settings of Italian poems in various styles.—**LK/DM**

Noté, Jean, Belgian baritone; b. Tournai, May 6, 1859; d. Brussels, April 1, 1922. He studied at the Ghent Cons., making his debut in a concert in Ghent in 1883. He then sang opera in Lille, Brussels, Lyons, Marseilles, etc. He made his N.Y. Metropolitan Opera debut on Dec. 3, 1908, as Escamillo. In 1913 he joined the Paris Opéra, and remained on its roster until his death. Among his finest roles were Hamlet, Beckmesser, Rigoletto, and Wolfram.—**NS/LK/DM**

Notker "Balbulus" (the latter nickname meaning "stammerer"), music theorist and composer; b. Elgg, near Zürich (or Jonschwyl, near St. Gallen), c.840; d. April 6, 912. He was a monk at the St. Gallen monastery. He was one of the earliest and most important writers of sequences, his *Liber hymnorum* (sequence texts of the year 884) being of particular interest. Several short treatises on music ascribed to him are most likely by others, including Notker Labeo (b. c.950; d. St. Gallen, June 29, 1022), a monk at St. Gallen, known as Notker the German.

BIBL.: A. Henschel, *Zehn Sequenzen des N. B., aus den ältesten Quellen übertragen und mit der Überlieferung verglichen* (diss., Univ. of Erlangen, 1924); R. van Doren, *Etude sur l'influence musicale de l'Abbaye de St. Gall* (1925).—**NS/LK/DM**

Notorious B.I.G. (originally, **Wallace, Christopher**), successful, if shortlived, rap star of the 1990s; b. Brooklyn, N.Y., May 21, 1972; d. Los Angeles, March 9, 1997. Although his mother was a teacher, Chris Wallace grew up in awe of the street hustlers in his Brooklyn neighborhood, and started selling drugs in his teens. After serving his second term in prison, he borrowed a friend's DJ setup and started making tapes of his articulate yet streetwise raps. Ironically, the perspective he took was not that of the insider who had done time for his gangsta ways but as an observer describing the conditions from the outside. His tapes started circulating and wound up at *The Source* magazine. The editors liked one of them so much, they put it into the "Unsigned Hype" column and a compilation CD of unsigned artists. Sean "Puffy" Combs, at the time Uptown Records' director of A&R, signed B.I.G. on the basis of his performance on this CD. Before recording B.I.G. (Wallace was 6 foot, 3 inches and weighed close to 300 pounds) as a solo artist, Combs hooked him up on records with Jodeci and Mary J. Blige, earning a big hit with his rap on the remix of Blige's "What's the 411." He also was given a track on the soundtrack to *Who's the Man*.

When Combs left Uptown to start his own label, Bad Boy, Uptown cut many of the artists he had signed. Before long, Combs had signed several of them, including B.I.G. His debut album, *Ready to Die*, captured the East Coast gangsta sound perfectly, with its heavy R&B tracks and clear rhymes. The album featured guest spots by reggae star Diana Kind and Method Man from the Wu Tang Clan. The album spun off three double-sided singles: the gold "Juicy," "Unbelievable," which rose to #27 pop; the platinum "Big Poppa," with heavy samples of the Isley Brothers's "Between the Sheets"; "Warning," which hit #6 pop; the platinum "One More Chance/Stay with Me," which sampled DeBarge's "Stay with Me"; and his duet with Method Man, "The What," which topped the R&B charts for nine weeks and spent three weeks at #2 on the pop charts. Another single, "Can't You See," from the soundtrack to *New Jersey Drive*, hit #13 and went gold. Within a year, the album was double platinum and to date has passed the quadruple-platinum mark.

While the album was running its course, B.I.G. married singer Faith Evans and had several run-ins with the law, including allegedly beating a promoter who canceled a concert without paying the guarantee. He and Combs were also placed on a list of suspects when rapper Tupac Shakur was robbed and shot in N.Y. They both vehemently denied this accusation and charges were never brought. B.I.G. produced L'il Kim's *Hardcore* album, and appeared on records by R. Kelly and even Michael Jackson. He joined M.C. Lyte and several other rappers who played themselves in an episode of the TV show *New York Undercover*.

After finishing the sessions for his second album, *Life After Death*, B.I.G. went to the *Soul Train* Awards in Los Angeles. While sitting in an SUV, he was shot several times and died instantly. His funeral set off riots in the streets of Brooklyn. A week after he died, *Life After Death* was released, lodging at #1 for three weeks and shipping sextuple platinum on its way to diamond status (over 10 million sales). The album also spawned the platinum singles "Hypnotize," "No Money Mo Problems," and the gold "Sky's The Limit." B.I.G. was also the subject of Combs's hit single, "I'll Be Missing You." Another posthumous project, *Born Again*, was issued late in 1999. It also topped the charts in its first week, shipping double platinum.

DISC.: *Ready to Die* (1994); *Life After Death* (1997); *Born Again* (1999).—HB

Nottara, Constantin, Romanian violinist, conductor, teacher, and composer; b. Bucharest, Oct. 13, 1890; d. there, Jan. 19, 1951. He studied with Klenck (violin), Kiriac (theory), and Castaldi (composition) at the Bucharest Cons. (1900–07), with Enesco and Bethelier (violin) in Paris (1907–09), and with Klinger (violin) and Schatzenhalz (composition) at the Berlin Royal Academy (1909–13). His career was centered in Bucha-

rest, where he was a violinist in the Phil. (1905–07; 1918–20) and first violinist in a string quartet (1914–33). From 1916 to 1947 he taught at the Cons. He also was a conductor with the Municipal Orch. (1929–32) and the Radio Sym. Orch. (1933–38).

WORKS: DRAMATIC: *Iris*, drama (1926; Moravska Ostrava, Nov. 13, 1931); *La drumul mare* (In the Highway), opera (1931; Cluj-Napoca, Oct. 3, 1934); *Cu dragostea nu se glumeşte* (Love is Not a Joke), comic opera (1940; Bucharest, Feb. 8, 1941); *Ovidiu* (Ovid), opera (1941–43; unfinished; completed by W. Berger); *Se face ziuă* (At Dawn), opera (1943); ballets. **ORCH.:** 3 suites: No. 1 (1917; Iaşi, Feb. 28, 1918), No. 2 (1930), and No. 3 (1930; Bucharest, Dec. 9, 1932); *Poem elegiac* for Cello and Orch. (1919); *Poem* for Violin and Orch. (1920; Bucharest, April 10, 1932); *Schiţă simfonică oltenească* (1943); *Variaţiuni pe un cîntec popular bihorean* (1943); *Poemul păcii* (1947); *Poemul pentru pace* (1948); Violin Concerto (1950; Bucharest, Oct. 10, 1951). **CHAMBER:** 2 violin sonatas (1914, 1949); *Suită românească* for Viola and Piano (1945); Suite for Piano, Violin, and Cello (1949); *Suită în stil românesc* for Cello and Piano (1949); Nonet (1950); piano pieces, including *Rapsodie olteana* (1943) and a Sonata (1947). **VOCAL:** *Mircea şi Baiazil* for Baritone and Orch. (1931); many solo songs.—NS/LK/DM

Nottebohm, (Martin) Gustav, distinguished German musicologist; b. Lüdenscheid, Westphalia, Nov. 12, 1817; d. Graz, Oct. 29, 1882. He studied with Berger and Dehn in Berlin (1838–39), with Mendelssohn and Schumann in Leipzig (1840–45), and finally with Sechter in Vienna (1846), where he settled as a music teacher. He revised the Beethoven ed. publ. by Breitkopf & Härtel, prepared thematic catalogues of the works of Beethoven and Schubert, and edited some of the works of Mozart. Of particular importance are his studies of Beethoven's sketchbooks.

WRITINGS (all publ. in Leipzig unless otherwise given): *Ein Skizzenbuch von Beethoven* (1865; 2nd ed., 1924, by P. Mies, as *Zwei Skizzenbücher von Beethoven aus den Jahren 1801 bis 1803*); *Thematisches Verzeichniss der im Druck erschienenen Werke von Ludwig van Beethoven* (2nd ed., 1868, reprint, 1969); *Beethoveniana* (1872; 2nd ed., 1925); *Beethovens Studien* (1873; includes Beethoven's exercise books under Haydn, Albrechtsberger, and Salieri); *Thematisches Verzeichniss der im Druck erschienenen Werke von Franz Schubert* (Vienna, 1874); *Mozartiana* (1880); E. Mandyczewski, ed., *Zweite Beethoveniana* (1887; 2nd ed., 1925). —NS/LK/DM

Nouguès, Jean, French composer; b. Bordeaux, April 25, 1875; d. Auteuil, Aug. 28, 1932. He showed remarkable precocity as a composer, having completed an opera, *Le Roi du Papagey*, before he was 16. After regular study in Paris, he premiered his opera *Yannha* at Bordeaux in 1897. The next 2 operas, *Thamyris* (Bordeaux, 1904) and *La Mort de Tintagiles* (Paris, 1905), were brought out without much success; but after the production of his spectacular *Quo Vadis?* (libretto by H. Cain, after Sienkiewicz's famous novel; Nice, Feb. 9, 1909), he suddenly found himself famous. The work was given in Paris on Nov. 26, 1909, and in N.Y. on April 4, 1911; had numerous revivals in subsequent years. His later operas, not nearly so successful, included *L'Auberge rouge* (Nice, Feb. 21, 1910), *La Vendetta* (Marseilles, 1911), *L'Aiglon* (Rouen, Feb. 2, 1912), and *Le Scarabée bleu* (1931).—NS/LK/DM

Nourrit, Adolphe, celebrated French tenor, son of **Louis Nourrit;** b. Montpellier, March 3, 1802; d. (suicide) Naples, March 8, 1839. He studied voice with the elder Manuel García. At the age of 19, he made his debut as Pylaides in Gluck's *Iphigénie en Tauride* at the Paris Opéra (Sept. 10, 1821), with excellent success. He soon became known in Paris as one of the finest tenors of his generation, and famous opera composers entrusted him with leading roles at the premieres of their works; thus, he appeared in the title role of Meyerbeer's *Robert le diable* (Paris, Nov. 21, 1831) and as Raoul in *Les Huguenots* (Paris, Feb. 29, 1836); in the title role in Rossini's *Le Comte Ory* (Paris, Aug. 20, 1828) and as Arnold in his *Guillaume Tell* (Paris, Aug. 3, 1829); as Masaniello in Auber's *La Muette de Portici* (Paris, Feb. 29, 1828); as Eléazar in Halévy's *La Juive* (Paris, Feb. 23, 1835); and others. He then traveled in Italy in Dec. 1837, and was particularly successful in Naples. His career seemed to be assured, but despite all these successes, vocal problems and a liver ailment led to depression, and he killed himself by jumping from the roof of his lodging in Naples.

BIBL.: M. Quicherat, *A. N.: Sa vie* (3 vols., Paris, 1867); E. Boutet de Monvel, *Un Artiste d'autrefois, A. N.* (2 vols., Paris, 1903); H. Pleasants, ed. and annotator, *The Great Tenor Tragedy: The Last Days of A. N. as Told (Mostly) by Himself* (Portland, Ore., 1995).—NS/LK/DM

Nourrit, Louis, French tenor, father of **Adolphe Nourrit;** b. Montpellier, Aug. 4, 1780; d. Brunoy, Sept. 23, 1831. He was a pupil of Garat at the Paris Cons. On March 3, 1805, he made his debut at the Paris Opéra as Renaud in Gluck's *Armide.* He sang there regularly thereafter, serving later as its principal tenor from 1812 until his retirement in 1826.—NS/LK/DM

Novães, Guiomar, extraordinary Brazilian pianist; b. São João da Bôa Vista, Feb. 28, 1895; d. São Paulo, March 7, 1979. She was the 17th of 19 offspring in a highly fecund family. She studied piano with Luigi Chiafarelli, and soon began performing in public recitals. The Brazilian government sent her to France to take part in a competition for entering the Paris Cons. She won first place among 389 contestants from a jury that included Debussy and Fauré, and Debussy praised her for "the power of total inner concentration, rare among artists." She enrolled in the class of Philipp, who later described her as a true "force of nature." She graduated from the Paris Cons. in 1911, and made a successful concert tour in France, England, and Italy. She made her U.S. debut at a N.Y. recital on Nov. 11, 1915, and subsequently made numerous tours of the U.S. Reviewing one of her concerts, James Huneker described her as "the Paderewska of the Pampas." In 1922 she married **Octavio Pinto.** She made her home in São Paulo, with frequent sojourns in N.Y. In 1956 the Brazilian government awarded her the Order of Merit as a goodwill ambassador to the U.S. She made her last U.S. appearance in 1972. She was especially praised for her interpretations of the music of Chopin, Schumann, and other composers of the Romantic era; she also played pieces by South American composers, including some works

written for her by her husband. Her playing was notable for its dynamic colors; she exuded a personal charm, while often disregarding the more pedantic aspects of the music.—NS/LK/DM

Novák, Jan, Czech composer; b. Nová Říše na Morave, April 8, 1921; d. Ulm, Germany, Nov. 17, 1984. He studied composition with Petrželka at the Brno Cons. (1940–46; interrupted by the Nazi occupation) and Bořkovec at the Prague Academy of Musical Arts (1946–47), then with Copland at the Berkshire Music Center at Tanglewood (summer, 1947) and Martinů in N.Y. (1947–48). He subsequently made his home in Brno; being outside his homeland at the time of the Soviet invasion (1968), he chose not to return, and went to Denmark before settling in Rovereto, Italy (1970), where he taught piano at the municipal music school. Predictably, his works ceased to be performed in his native land until the Communist regime collapsed in 1989. His early music is influenced by Martinů; with the Concertino for Wind Quintet (1957) and the *Capriccio* for Cello and Orch. (1958), he adopted jazz elements; beginning in 1958 he applied dodecaphonic techniques, and after 1960 his interest in all things Latin and vocal almost completely dominates his output.

WORKS: DRAMATIC: *Svatební Košile* (The Specter's Bride), ballet-ballad (1954; Plzeň, 1955); *Komedie o umučenie a slavném vzkříšení Pána a spasitele našeho Ježíše Krista* (Play of the Passion and Glorious Resurrection of the Lord Our Savior Jesus Christ; Brno, 1965); *Dulcitius,* lyric drama (1977); *Aesopia,* fable-cantata with introit and exit (1981; version for 2 Pianos and Orch. as *Aesopia minora*). ORCH.: Oboe Concerto (1953); Concerto for 2 Pianos and Orch. (1954); *Capriccio* for Cello and Orch. (1958); *Variations on a Theme of Martinů* (1959; orchestration of a 1949 piece for 2 Pianos); *Musica Caesariana* for Wind Orch. (1960); *Concentus Eurydicae* for Guitar and Strings (1971); *Odarum contentus,* 5 Meditations for Strings (1973); *Concentus biiugis* for Piano, 4-Hands, and Small Orch. (1976); *Ludi symphoniaci I* (1978); *Choreae vernales* for Flute, Harp, Celesta or Piano, and Small Orch. (1980); *Ludi concentantes* for 18 Instruments (1981); *Symphonia bipartita* (1983). CHAMBER: *Ioci pastorales* for Oboe, Clarinet, Horn, and Bassoon (1974); *Rosarium,* 9 divertimenti for 2 Guitars (1975); *Quadricinium fidium I* for String Quartet (1978); *Sonata solis fidibus* for Solo Violin (1980); *Sonata da chiesa I* for Violin and Organ and *II* for Flute and Organ (both 1981); *Sonata rustica* for Accordion and Piano (1982); *Aeolia* for 2 Flutes and Piano (1983); piano pieces, including *Variations on a Theme of Martinů* for 2 Pianos (1949; orchestrated 1959); harpsichord and organ works. VOCAL: *Píseň Závišova* (Songs of Zavis) for Tenor and Orch. (1957); *Passer Catulli* for Bass and 9 Instruments (1961); *Ioci vernales* for Bass, 8 Instruments, and Bird Songs on Tape (1964); *Testamentum* for Chorus and 4 Horns (1966); *Dido,* oratorio (1967); *Ignis pro Ioanne Palach,* cantata (1968; Prague, April 15, 1969); *Planctus Troadum,* chamber cantata for Contralto, Women's Chorus, 8 Cellos, 2 Double Basses, and 2 Percussionists (1969); *Vernalis temporis symphonia* for Soloists, Chorus, and Orch. (1982); songs and choruses.—NS/LK/DM

Novák, Johann Baptist (actually, **Janez Krstnik**), Slovenian composer; b. Ljubljana, c. 1756; d. there, Jan. 29, 1833. He served as a government clerk and at the same time studied music. In 1799–1800 he was conductor, and from 1808 to 1929 music director, of the Phil. Society in Ljubljana; he gave concerts as a singer and violinist. A close contemporary of Mozart, he composed in a Mozartean manner. His historical importance lies in his incidental music to T. Linhart's play *Ta veseli dan, ali Matiček se ženi* (A Happy Day, or Maticek Is Getting Married; 1790), which is based on Beaumarchais's comedy that served for Mozart's great opera *Le nozze di Figaro*. Novak later renamed his work *Figaro*. His music forms a striking parallel to Mozart's procedures and yet contains some original traits.—**NS/LK/DM**

Novák, Milan, Slovak composer; b. Trahovice, Aug. 12, 1927. He studied piano with Kafenda, composition with Alexander Moyzes, and conducting with Talich at the Bratislava Cons. In 1955 he was appointed conductor of the Military Artistic Ensemble in Bratislava.

WORKS: DRAMATIC: B a l l e t : *Where the Play Ends* (1964); *Ballad about a Tree* (1967). OTHER: Music for theater and films. ORCH.: Concertino for Trumpet, Strings, Piano, 4-Hands, and Percussion (1964); *Reminiscences* for Cello and Orch. (1969); Concerto for Harp and Chamber Orch. (1972); 4 Preludes for Orch. (1981); *Music for Trumpet and Strings* (1984). CHAMBER: Clarinet Sonatina (1959); Cello Sonatina (1961); String Quartet (1975); *Music for Flute and String Quartet* (1975); *Divertimento* for Oboe, Clarinet, and Bassoon (1980). VOCAL: *Mountains and the Heart*, song cycle for Bass and Orch. (1973); *30 Happy Years*, cantata for Children's Chorus and Orch. (1975); *So that There Is Life on Earth*, cantata (1976).—**NS/LK/DM**

Novák, Vítězslav (actually, **Viktor Augustín Rudolf**), eminent Czech composer and pedagogue; b. Kamenitz, Dec. 5, 1870; d. Skuteč, July 18, 1949. He received lessons in violin and piano as a child in Počátky, and then was a student of Vilím Pojman in Jindřichův Hradec. In 1889 he went to Prague, where he studied law and philosophy at the Univ. but concentrated his studies on music at the Cons., where he was a student of Knittl, Stecker, and Dvořák. After graduating from the Cons. in 1892, he continued to study piano there with Jiránek until 1896. He also remained a student at the Univ. until 1895. He then taught privately and was active as a folk song collector. Through such orch. works as *V tatrách* (In the Tatras; 1902), *Slovácká svita* (Slovak Suite; 1903), and *O věcne touzé* (Eternal Longing; 1903–05), the cantata *Bouře* (The Storm; 1910), and the piano tone poem *Pan* (1910), he acquired a notable reputation as a composer. He also was actively engaged in teaching, serving as a prof. at the Prague Cons. (1909–39). His importance as a composer was enhanced in later years by such works as the *Podzimní symfonie* (Autumn Sym.; 1931–34) and *Jihočeská svita* (South Bohemian Suite) for Orch. (1936–37). He was honored with the title of National Artist of the Czech Republic in 1945. The first vol. of his unfinished autobiography, *O sobě a jiných*, was publ. in Prague in 1946. Novák's earliest works followed the general line of German Romanticism; Brahms was so impressed with them that he recommended Novák to his own publisher, Simrock. Novák's interest in folk music made a substantial impact on his music, although he rarely incorporated original folk material in his compositions. His late works espoused patriotic themes.

WORKS (all first perf. in Prague unless otherwise given): DRAMATIC: *Zvíkovský rarášek* (The Zvikov Imp), comic opera (1913–14; Oct. 10, 1915); *Karlštejn*, opera (1914–15; Nov. 18, 1916); *Lucerna* (The Lantern), musical fairy tale (1919–22; May 13, 1923); *Dědův odkaz* (Grandfather's Legacy), opera (1922–25; Brno, Jan. 16, 1926); *Signorina Gioventù*, ballet pantomime (1926–28; first concert perf., Feb. 10, 1929; first stage perf., March 8, 1930); *Nikotina*, ballet pantomime (1929; March 8, 1930; concert suite, Nov. 3, 1930); incidental music to F. Rachlík's play *Žižka* (1948; Ostrava, Oct. 28, 1949). ORCH.: *Korzár* (The Corsair), overture (1892; Nov. 20, 1927; rev. 1943); *Serenade* in F major for Small Orch. (Sept. 27, 1895); Piano Concerto (1895; Nov. 21, 1915); *Maryša*, dramatic overture (1898; Jan. 28, 1899); *V Tatrách* (In the Tatras), symphonic poem (Nov. 25, 1902); *Slovácká svita* (Slovak Suite) for Small Orch. (1903; Feb. 4, 1906); *O věcné touze* (Eternal Longing; 1903–05; Feb. 8, 1905); Serenade for Small Orch. (1905; March 6, 1906); *Toman a lesní panna* (Toman and the Wood Nymph), symphonic poem (1906–07; April 5, 1908); *Lady Godiva*, overture to J. Vrchlický's play (Nov. 24, 1907); *Podzimní symfonie* (Autumn Sym.) for Men's Chorus, Women's Chorus, and Orch. (1931–34; Dec. 18, 1934); *Jihočeská svita* (South Bohemian Suite; Dec. 22, 1937); *De profundis*, symphonic poem for Orch. and Organ (Brno, Nov. 20, 1941); *Svatováclavský triptych* (St. Wenceslas Triptych) for Orch. and Organ (1941; Oct. 8, 1942); *Májová symfonie* (May Sym.) for Solo Voices, Chorus, and Orch. (1943; Dec. 5, 1945). CHAMBER: Violin Sonata (1891; July 8, 1892); Trio in G minor for Piano, Violin, and Cello (1892; July 8, 1893); Quartet for Violin, Viola, Cello, and Piano (1894; rev. version, Brünn, Feb. 5, 1899); Quintet for Piano, 2 Violins, Viola, and Cello (1896; rev. version, April 26, 1905); 3 string quartets: No. 1 (1899; Nov. 19, 1900), No. 2 (Berlin, Nov. 1905), and No. 3 (1938; Jan. 23, 1939); Trio in D minor, *quasi una ballata* (Brünn, April 6, 1902); Cello Sonata (1941; Brno, Feb. 27, 1942). P i a n o : *Sonáta eroica* (1900; March 1, 1905); *Pan*, tone poem (1910; Nov. 14, 1911; orch. 1912; Jan. 12, 1913); *Dva valašské tance* (Two Valachian Dances; 1904; orch. 1936; Dec. 13, 1936); 6 sonatinas (1919–20; Dec. 11, 1920). VOCAL: *Údolí Nového království* (Valley of the New Kingdom), 4 songs for High Voice and Piano (1903; Chrudim, Dec. 26, 1904); *Melancholické písně o lásce* (Melancholy love songs about love), song cycle for Voice and Piano (1906); *Notturna* for Voice and Piano (1906–08; Nov. 19, 1908); *Bouře* (The Storm), sea fantasy for Soloists, Chorus, and Orch. (1908–10; Brünn, April 17, 1910); *Svatební košile* (The Spectre's Bride), ballad for Soloists, Chorus, and Orch. (1912–13; Dec. 3, 1913); *Dvě romance* (Two romances) for Voice and Orch. (1934; March 26, 1936); *In memoriam*, song cycle for Mezzo-soprano, String Orch., Harp, and Tom-tom (1936–37; March 17, 1938); *Dvě legendy na slova lidové poezie moravské* (Two legends to words of Moravian folk poetry) for Mezzo-soprano and Piano or Orch. (1944; Oct. 5, 1949).

BIBL.: Z. Nejedlý, *V. N.: Studie a kritiky* (Prague, 1921); B. Vomáčka and S. Hanuš, eds., *Sborník na počest 60 narozenin V.a N.a* (Prague, 1930); A. Srba, ed., *V. N.: Studie a vzpomínky* (Prague, 1932; supplements, 1935, 1940); A. Hába, *V. N.: K 70 narozeninám* (Prague, 1940); V. Štěpán, *N. a Suk* (Prague, 1945); K. Hoffmeister, *Tvorba V.a N.a z let 1941–1948* (Prague, 1949); V. Lébl, *V. N.: Život a dílo* (Prague, 1964; Eng. tr., 1968); K. Padría and B. Štědroň, eds., *Národní umělec V. N., Studie a vzpomínky k 100. výroči narozeni* (Studies and Reminiscences on the 100th Anniversary of V. N.'s Birth; České Budějovice, 1972).—**NS/LK/DM**

Novello, Clara (Anastasia), outstanding English soprano, daughter of **Vincent Novello** and sister of **(Joseph) Alfred Novello;** b. London, June 10, 1818; d. Rome, March 12, 1908. Having studied piano and singing in London, she entered the Paris Institution de Musique Religieuse in 1829, but returned home the following year because of the revolution. She won the approbation of Rossini, and became his friend for life. After a successful concert debut on Oct. 22, 1832, at Windsor, she was engaged for the Phil. Society, the Antient Concerts, and the principal festivals. In 1837 Mendelssohn engaged her for the Gewandhaus concerts in Leipzig. Following additional studies in Milan (1839), she made her operatic debut as Rossini's Semiramide in Bologna (1841); sang with great success in the principal Italian cities. On Nov. 22, 1843, she married Count Gigliucci, withdrawing to private life for several years; she reappeared in 1850, singing in concert and opera (chiefly in England and Italy). After her farewell appearance in London in 1860, she retired to Rome. Schumann greatly admired her, and coined the term Novelette for some of his pieces as an affectionate homage to her.

BIBL.: V. Gigliucci, *C. N.'s Reminiscences, compiled by her daughter* (London, 1910; with memoir by A. Coleridge); A. Mackenzie- Grieve, *C. N., 1818–1908* (London, 1955). —NS/LK/DM

Novello, (Joseph) Alfred, prominent English music publisher, son of **Vincent Novello** and brother of **Clara (Anastasia) Novello;** b. London, Aug. 12, 1810; d. Genoa, July 16, 1896. He joined his father's music publishing venture when he was 19 and was instrumental in making it a commercial success as Novello & Co.; the firm prospered by bringing out eds. of the classics, most notably of choral music. He was also active as a bass singer, organist, choirmaster, and composer. He retired to Genoa in 1856.—NS/LK/DM

Novello, Vincent, English organist, conductor, editor, music publisher, and composer, father of **Clara (Anastasia) Novello** and **(Joseph) Alfred Novello;** b. London, Sept. 6, 1781; d. Nice, Aug. 9, 1861. He was a chorister at the Sardinian Embassy Chapel in London, where he studied organ with Samuel Webe. He later was deputy organist to Webbe and Danby, and from 1797 to 1822, organist at the chapel of the Portuguese Embassy. He was pianist to the Italian Opera in 1812; was a founder of the Phil. Society in 1813, sometimes conducting its concerts. From 1840 to 1843 he was organist at the Roman Catholic Chapel in Moorfields. In 1811 he founded the great London music publishing firm of Novello & Co. Himself a composer of sacred music (masses, motets, anthems, Kyries, etc.), he gathered together and publ. excellent collections: *A Collection of Sacred Music* (1811; 2 vols.); *Purcell's Sacred Music* (1829; 5 vols.); *Croft's Anthems; Greene's Anthems; Boyce's Anthems;* masses by Haydn, Mozart, Beethoven; etc. He retired to Nice in 1848.

BIBL.: M. Cowden-Clarke, *Life and Labours of V. N.* (London, 1864); N. Medici and R. Hughes, *A Mozart Pilgrimage* (London, 1955; travel diaries of V. N. and his wife); M. Hurd, *V. N.—and Company* (Borough Green, 1981).—NS/LK/DM

Novello & Co., one of the world's leading music publishing firms. **Vincent Novello** began editing and publishing works at his own expense in London in 1811. His son, **(Joseph) Alfred Novello,** became active with his father at age 19, and the two developed their activities into the successful commercial enterprise known as Novello & Co. The firm prospered by publishing affordable eds. of the classics, concentrating on the choral literature. Henry Littleton (b. London, Jan. 2, 1823; d. there, May 11, 1888) joined the business in 1841. Following the retirement of the younger Novello in 1856, he became manager of the firm; subsequently was made a partner (1861) and sole proprietor (1866). He acquired the business of Ewer and Co. in 1867, creating the firm of Novello, Ewer & Co. On his retirement in 1887 he was succeeded by his sons, Alfred H. and Augustus J. Littleton, and his sons-in-law, George T.S. Gill and Henry W. Brooke. In 1898 the firm became Novello & Co., Ltd. It became a part of the Granada group of companies in 1970. In addition to bringing out works by leading English composers of the 20th century, it also publ. the highly respected music journal *Musical Times;* founded in 1844 by Joseph Mainzer, it was acquired by Novello in 1846 and remains the oldest continuously issued music periodical in the world. It was publ. by Orpheus Publications from 1988.

BIBL.: J. Bennett, *A Short History of Cheap Music as Exemplified in the Records of the House of N., Ewer & Co.* (London, 1887); M. Hurd, *V. N.—and Company* (Borough Green, 1981). —NS/LK/DM

Novello-Davies (real name, Davies), Clara, Welsh singer, choral conductor, and composer; b. Cardiff, April 7, 1861; d. London, March 1, 1943. Her father (who was also her first teacher) called her "Clara Novello" after the celebrated singer of that name, and she adopted the combined name professionally. She sang at concerts; in 1881 she turned to choral conducting; organized a Royal Welsh Ladies' Choir, with which she traveled with fine success in Great Britain, France, America, and South Africa; at the World's Fair in Chicago (1893) and at the Paris Exposition (1900) the chorus was awarded first prize. She was commended by Queen Victoria (1894) and by King George V and Queen Mary (1928). She publ. a number of successful songs (*A Voice from the Spirit Land, The Vigil,* and *Comfort*); authored *You Can Sing* and an autobiography, *The Life I Have Loved* (London, 1940). Her son, Ivor Novello (real name, David Ivor Davies) (b. Cardiff, Jan. 15, 1893; d. London, March 6, 1951), was a composer, playwright, and actor who, at his mother's request, wrote the popular World War I song *Till the Boys Come Home (Keep the Home Fires Burning;* 1914). He wrote musical comedies and revues, and was also active as an actor. After working as a playwright, he resumed composing for the stage, his most successful musical being *The Dancing Years* (London, March 23, 1939).

BIBL.: S. Wilson, *I.* (London, 1975).—NS/LK/DM

Noverre, Jean-Georges, Swiss-French choreographer; b. Paris, April 29, 1727; d. St.-Germain-en-Laye, Oct. 19, 1810. He studied in Paris. He danced in Fontainebleau (1743) and then in Berlin, and subsequently was principal dancer in Strasbourg (1750–54) and at the Paris Opéra- Comique (1754–55). He later was active in London (1755–57), Lyons (1757–60), Stuttgart (1760–67), Vienna, and Milan (1774–76), Vienna again (1776), the Paris Opéra (1776–81), and London once more (1781–82; 1787–89). He retired in 1794. He is credited with introducing dramatic action into the ballet (ballet-pantomime). He publ. *Lettres sur la danse, et sur les ballets* (Lyons and Stuttgart, 1760; 2nd ed., 1783; Eng. tr., 1782).

BIBL.: C. Noverre, *Life and Works of the Chevalier N.* (London, 1882); H. Niedecken, *J.G. N.: Sein Leben und seine Beziehungen zur Musik* (Halle, 1914); D. Lynham, *The Chevalier N.: Father of Modern Ballet* (London, 1950); P. Tugal, *J.-G. N. der grosse Reformator des Tanzes* (Berlin, 1959).—**NS/LK/DM**

Novotná, Jarmila, Czech soprano; b. Prague, Sept. 23, 1907; d. N.Y., Feb. 9, 1994. She studied with Destinn in Prague; made her operatic debut as Mařenka in *The Bartered Bride* there (1925), then continued her studies in Milan. She sang in Berlin (from 1928); was a member of the Vienna State Opera (1933–38), where she gained distinction as Octavian; also created the title role in Lehár's Giuditta (1934). She made her American debut at San Francisco as Madama Butterfly (Oct. 18, 1939); first sang at the Metropolitan Opera in N.Y. as Mimi in *La Bohème* on Jan. 5, 1940; remained on its roster until 1951; was there again from 1952 to 1956; also appeared in films and on Broadway. Her other fine roles included Pamina, Donna Elvira, Violetta, Mélisande, and various roles in Czech operas. She was the author of *Byla jsem stastná* (Prague, 1991).—**NS/LK/DM**

Novotný, Václav Juda, Czech writer on music and composer; b. Wesetz, Sept. 17,1849; d. Prague, Aug. 1, 1922. He attended Ambros's lectures in music history, studied violin with Bennewitz, singing with Pivoda and harmony with F. Blažek, and received instruction from Skuherský in Prague. After playing violin in the orch. of the Provisional Theater there, he contributed to various publications, including the journal *Dalibor*, which he edited (1875; 1979–80). Novotný prepared translations into Czech of some 100 opera libretti. Among his works were 2 operas, sacred music, choruses, vocal duets, songs, and about 300 folk song arrangements.—**LK/DM**

Nowak, Leopold, eminent Austrian musicologist; b. Vienna, Aug. 17, 1904; d. there, May 27, 1991. He studied piano and organ with Louis Dité and counterpoint with Franz Schmidt at the Vienna Academy of Music, then took courses in musicology with Guido Adler and Robert Lach at the Univ. of Vienna; received his Ph.D. there in 1927 with the diss. *Das deutsche Gesellschaftslied bei Heinrich Finck, Paul Hofhaymer und Heinrich Isaac*; publ. in an aug. version as "Das deutsche Gesellschaftslied in Österreich von 1480 bis 1550," *Studien zur Musikwissenschaft*, XVII, 1930. He completed his Habilitation in 1932 with his *Grundzüge einer Geschichte des Basso ostinato* (publ. in Vienna, 1932). He lectured at the Univ. of Vienna from 1932 until 1973; in 1945 he became ed. of the critical edition of Bruckner's works, a position he held until 1990; from 1946 to 1969 he was

director of the music division of the Nationalbibliothek in Vienna, where he compiled valuable catalogues for special exhibitions on Bruckner, Bach, Mozart, Haydn, and others. His exhaustive studies on the life and music of Bruckner are of prime value.

WRITINGS: *Franz Liszt* (Innsbruck, 1936); *Te Deum laudamus: Gedanken zur Musik Anton Bruckners* (Vienna, 1947); *Joseph Haydn* (Vienna, 1951; 3rd ed., 1965); with F. von Reznicek, the composer's daughter, *Gegen den Strom: Leben und Werk von Emil Nikolaus von Reznicek* (Vienna, 1960); *Anton Bruckner: Musik und Leben* (a brief study; Vienna, 1964); *Reden und Ansprachen* (Vienna, 1964); *Anton Bruckner: Musik und Leben* (a voluminous pictorial biography; Linz, 1973); *Das Geburtshaus Anton Bruckners [Ansfelden]: Führer* (Linz, 1975).

BIBL.: F. Grasberger, ed., *Bruckner-Studien: L. N. zum 60. Geburtstag* (Vienna, 1964).—**NS/LK/DM**

Nowak, Lionel (Henry), American pianist, teacher, and composer; b. Cleveland, Sept. 25, 1911. He studied piano with Beryl Rubinstein and Edwin Fischer, and took courses in composition with Elwell, Sessions, and Porter at the Cleveland Inst. of Music (B.Mus., 1933; M.Mus., 1936). In 1924 he made his formal debut as a soloist with the Cleveland Orch.; was director of music at Fenn Coll. in Cleveland (1932–38) and of the Doris Humphrey-Charles Weidman Modern Dance Co. (1938–42). He was prof. of music at Converse Coll. in Spartanburg, S.C. (1942–46), and also conducted the Spartanburg Sym. Orch. (1942–45). He was prof. of music at Syracuse Univ. (1946–48) and at Bennington (Vt.) Coll. (from 1948). Following a stroke in 1980, he composed works for piano, right-hand, and also commissioned such scores from other composers. He wrote some effective dance pieces.

WORKS: DRAMATIC: Dance: *Square Dances* (1938); *Danzas mexicanas* (1939); *On My Mother's Side* (1939); *The Green Land* (1941); *Flickers* (1942); *House Divided* (1944); *Story of Mankind* (1946). **ORCH.:** Piano Concerto (1944); *Concert Piece* for Timpani and Strings (1961). **CHAMBER:** Oboe Sonata (1949); *Orrea Pernel*, sonata for Violin (1950); 3 cello sonatas (1950, 1951, 1960); *Diptych* for String Quartet (1951); Quartet for Oboe and Strings (1952); Piano Trio (1954); *Soundscapes*: for Piano (1964), String Quartet (1970), Bassoon and Piano (1971), Violin, Piano, and Percussion (1971), and Woodwind Trio (1973); Suite for 2 Cellos (1981); Suite for Flute and Harpsichord (1989). **VOCAL:** Various pieces.—**NS/LK/DM**

Nowakowski, Józef, Polish pianist, teacher, and composer; b. Miniszek, Sept. 16, 1800; d. Warsaw, Aug. 27, 1865. He studied at the Cistercian school in Wachock and continued his training with Würfel (piano) and Elsner (composition) at the Warsaw Cons. (1821–26). Following a tour of Germany, Italy, and France in 1833, he settled in Warsaw and taught piano privately and at the Aleksandryjski Inst. (1840–44) and the Music Inst. (1861–64). He publ. a piano manual (Warsaw, 1850). His works included 2 syms. (1830, 1846), 4 overtures, 2 piano quintets, a String Quartet, songs, and numerous piano pieces.—**LK/DM**

Nowowiejski, Felix, Polish organist, conductor, and composer; b. Wartenburg, Feb. 7, 1877; d. Poznań,

Jan. 18, 1946. He studied in Berlin with Bussler at the Stern Cons., with Bruch at the Königliche Musikakademie, and with Friedlaender, Ballermann, and Dessoir at the Univ.; also received some instruction from Dvořák in Prague, winning the Paderewski Prize in 1903. He was director of the Kraków Music Soc. (1909–14) and a prof. at the Poznań Cons. (1920–27). A competent composer, he followed the line of German Romanticism.

WORKS: DRAMATIC: 2 operas: *Emigranci* (The Emigrants; 1917) AND *Legenda Bałtyku* (Baltic Legend; Poznań, 1924); several ballets. **ORCH.:** 5 syms. (1903–41; 1st not extant); Cello Concerto (1938); Piano Concerto (1941). **KEYBOARD:** Piano pieces; organ works. **VOCAL:** Much choral music, including oratorios, masses, cantatas, patriotic works, etc.; songs.

BIBL.: J. Boehm, *F. N.* (Olsztyn, 1968).—NS/LK/DM

Nozzari, Andrea, Italian tenor; b. Vertrova, near Bergamo, 1775; d. Naples, Dec. 12, 1832. He studied with Petrobelli in Bergamo, making his operatic debut in 1794. He made appearances in Rome, Milan, and Paris; was a principal tenor in Naples (1811–25), where he created tenor roles in several operas of Rossini. He then retired and taught singing.—NS/LK/DM

Nucci, Leo, prominent Italian baritone; b. Castiglione dei Pepuli, near Bologna, April 16, 1942. He studied with Giuseppe Marchesi and Ottaviano Bizzarri. He made his operatic debut as Rossini's Figaro in Spoleto (1967). After singing in the chorus of Milan's La Scala (1969–75), he attracted attention with his portrayal of Schaunard in *La Bohème* at Venice's Teatro La Fenice (1975); then was engaged as a member of La Scala, where he appeared as Rossini's Figaro, Rodrigo in *Don Carlos*, Miller in *Luisa Miller*, Marcello, and Sharpless. In 1978 he made his first appearance at the Vienna State Opera and at London's Covent Garden; he made his Metropolitan Opera debut in N.Y. as Renato in *Un ballo in maschera* on Feb. 22, 1980. He first sang at the Paris Opera and the Chicago Lyric Opera in 1981. In 1985 he appeared as Rigoletto in Wiesbaden. In 1991 he sang Iago in concert performances of *Otello* in Chicago and N.Y. He was engaged as Dulcamara in Turin in 1994, and in 1996 as Rossini's Figaro in Verona. He also sang in San Francisco, Berlin, Rome, Hamburg, and Geneva.—NS/LK/DM

Nucius (Nucis, Nux), Johannes, German composer and music theorist; b. Görlitz, c. 1556; d. Himmelwitz, March 25, 1620. He studied music with Johannes Winckler, the cantor of the Görlitz Gymnasium, and in c. 1586 he took Holy Orders at the monastery of Rauden. In 1591 he was made abbot of the monastery of Himmelwitz in Silesia. He publ. 50 *Modulationes sacrae modis musicis* for 5 and 6 Voices (Prague, 1591; 2nd ed., 1609, as *Cantionum sacrarum liber primus*), 52 *Cantionum sacrarum diversarum vocum, liber secundus*, some for 7, others for 8, Voices (Liegnitz, 1609), and a theoretical work, *Musices poeticae sive De compositione cantum praeceptiones ultissimae* (Neisse, 1613). A selected ed. of his motets was brought out by J. Kendermann in *Das Erbe Deutscher Musik*, 2nd series, V (1968).

BIBL.: B. Widmann, *J. N., Abt von Himmelwitz* (Bregenz, 1921); E. Kirsch, *Von der Personlichkeit und dem Stil des schlesischen Zisterzienser-Komponisten J. N.* (Breslau, 1926).
—NS/LK/DM

Nugent, Ted, touring act and album artist with bombastic, feedback-laden, high-decibel playing, blatantly sexist lyrics, and manic onstage antics; b. Detroit, Dec. 13, 1948. Scoring his first national hit with the psychedelic "Journey to the Center of the Mind" in 1968 as lead guitarist for the Amboy Dukes, Ted Nugent established the band in the American Midwest through years of heavy touring, despite numerous personnel changes. The Amboy Dukes continued to tour and record through 1974, but in 1975 Nugent went solo. Recording heavy-metal favorites such as "Stranglehold," "Dog Eat Dog," "Free-for-All," "Death By Misadventure," and "Wang Dang Sweet Poontang," Nugent managed his only major hit with a live version of "Cat Scratch Fever" in 1977.

In 1989 Nugent formed Damn Yankees with bassist-vocalist Jack Blades of Night Ranger (1984's "Sister Christian") and guitarist-vocalist Tommy Shaw of Styx. The group scored a smash hit with "High Enough" in 1990 and a major hit with "Where Are You Goin' Now" in 1992. A rabid conservative, Nugent has spoken out in favor of bow-hunting and is a champion of the National Rifle Association, adding to his neanderthal image. By 1995 Nugent had returned to Atlantic for *Spirit of the Wild*, releasing independently a single from the record, "Fred Bear, The American Hunter's Theme Song," which sold more than 100,000 copies, primarily to Nugent's fringe fans.

DISC.: THE AMBOY DUKES: *The Amboy Dukes* (1968); *Journey to the Center of the Mind* (1968); *Migration* (1969); *Best of the Original Amboy Dukes* (1971). **TED NUGENT AND THE AMBOY DUKES:** *Survival of the Fittest/Live* (1971); *Call of the Wild* (1974); *Tooth, Fang and Claw* (1974). **TED NUGENT:** *T. N.* (1975); *Free-for-All* (1976); *T. N./Free-for-All* (1986); *Cat Scratch Fever* (1977); *Double Live Gonzo* (1978); *Weekend Warriors* (1978); *State of Shock* (1979); *Scream Dream* (1980); *Intensities in Ten Cities* (1981); *Great Gonzos! The Best of T. N.* (1981); *Out of Control* (1993); *Nugent* (1982); *Penetrator* (1984); *Little Miss Dangerous* (1986); *If You Can't Lick 'Em...Lick'Em* (1988); *Spirit of the Wild* (1995). **DAMN YANKEES:** *Damn Yankees* (1990); *Don't Tread* (1992).

BIBL.: Robert Holland, *The Legendary T. N.* (London, 1982).
—BH

Nummi, Seppo (Antero Yrjönpoika), Finnish composer, music critic, and festival administrator; b. Oulu, May 30, 1932; d. Tampere, Aug. 1, 1981. He studied at the Univ. of Helsinki and at the Sibelius Academy, and his private composition teacher was Yrjö Kilpinen. He began writing music criticism for the newspaper *Uusi Suomi* in 1953. In 1967 he founded the Savonlinna Opera Festival. He then was executive director of the Helsinki Festival (1969–77). As a composer, he is best known for his many songs in a fine lyrical mode, in the tradition of Hugo Wolf and Kilpinen; he also wrote some chamber music. He publ. *Musica fennica* (with T. Makinen; Helsinki, 1965) and *Modern Musik* (Stockholm, 1966).—NS/LK/DM

Nunes, Emmanuel, Portuguese-born French composer and teacher; b. Lisbon, Aug. 31, 1941. He studied at the Lisbon Academy of Music (until 1964), at the summer courses in new music at Darmstadt (1963–65), with Pousseur and Stockhausen at the Cologne Staatliche Hochschule für Musik (1965–67), and with Marcel Beaufils at the Paris Cons. (premier prix in aesthetics, 1970). In 1978–79 he was in Berlin under the auspices of the Deutscher Akademischer Austauschdienst. He taught at the Freiburg im Breisgau Hochschule für Musik and lectured at the Paris Cons. His works are technically assured and inventive. They have become increasingly compact, tense, and extreme in character.

WORKS: ORCH.: *Seuils I* and *II* (1966–67; rev. 1977–78); *Un calendrier révolu* for Chamber Orch. (1968); *Purieu* for 21 Strings (1971); *Down Wo* for 13 Winds (1971–72); *Omens I* (1972) and *II* (1975); *Fermata* (1973); *Es webt* (1974–75; rev. 1977); *Ruf* (1975–77); *Chessed I* for 4 Orch. Groups (1979), *II* for 16 Solo Instruments (1979), and *IV* for String Quartet and Orch. (1992); *Tif ereth* for 6 Solo Instruments, 6 Orch. Groups, and 2 Conductors (1978–85); *Musik der Frühe* for 18 Instruments (1980; rev. 1984–86); *Nachtmusik II* (1981); *Stretti* for 2 Orchs. (1982–83); *Wandlungen* for 25 Instruments and Electronics (1986); *Lichtung* for Orch. and Electronics (1988–92); *Quodlibet* for 3 Instrumental Ensembles (1990–91). **CHAMBER:** *Degrés* for String Trio (1965); *Esquisses* for String Quartet (1967; rev. 1980); *Impromptu pour un voyage I* for Trombone, Flute, Viola, and Harp (1973) and *II* for Alto Flute, Viola, and Harp (1974–75; rev. 1992); *The Blending Season* for Flute, Alto, Clarinet, Electric Organ, and Amplification (1973; rev. 1976–77 and 1992); *Nachtmusik I* for Viola, Cello, English Horn, Bass Clarinet, Trombone, and Modulation (1977–78); *Einspielung I* for Violin (1979), *II* for Cello (1980), and *III* for Viola (1981); *Grund* for Flute and Tape (1982–83); *Aura* for Flute (1983–89); *Sonate a tre* for String Trio (1986); *Clivages I* (1987); and *II* (1988) for 6 Percussionists; *Chessed III* for String Quartet (1990–91). **VOCAL:** *Minnesang* for 12 Voices (1975–76); *Vislumbre* for Chorus (1981–86); *Machina Mundi* for Chorus and Orch. (1991–92).—**NS/LK/DM**

Nunez, Alcide "Yellow", pioneering jazz clarinetist; b. New Orleans, March 17, 1884; d. New Orleans, Sept. 2, 1934. Originally a guitarist, he switched to clarinet in 1902 and worked regularly with Papa Jack Laine, Tom Brown. In March 1916, he went to Chicago with drummer Johnny Stein's band. He left with three other members of that band to form the Original Dixieland Jazz Band. After a dispute with Nick LaRocca he ceased working with the O.D.J.B. on Oct. 31, 1916. He led his own band for a while, then toured in vaudeville with Bert Kelly's Band, and then joined Anton Lada's Louisiana Five, appearing on their recordings of 1919–20. During the mid-1920s, he toured with own quartet, and then returned to New Orleans in 1927, where he worked for a while with the local police band. —**JC/LP**

Nurimov, Chari, Russian composer; b. Buiramali, Turkmenia, Jan. 1, 1941. He studied with Litinsky at the Gnessin Inst. in Moscow (graduated, 1964); returning to Turkmenia, he worked for the Ashkhabad radio and taught at the music inst. He received awards as a national Turkmenian composer; his Trumpet Concerto became popular.

WORKS: DRAMATIC: Ballet: *The End of Sukhovei* (1967); *Immortality* (1972); *A Kughitang Tragedy* (1976). **Other:** Film scores. **ORCH.:** 3 overtures (1959, 1961, 1974); Sym. No. 1 (1963); Trumpet Concerto (1968); *Concerto-Poem* for Voice and Orch. (1971); Piano Concerto (1973); *Ghazels* for Oboe, Percussion, Piano, and Strings (1976); *The Flame of October*, poem (1979); *Sinfonietta* (1981); *Destan Concerto* for Flute, Oboe, Percussion, Piano, and Strings (1983). **CHAMBER:** Suite for String Quartet (1960); Violin Sonata (1961); *Partita* for String Quartet (1963); Oboe Sonatina (1964); *The Tekin Frescoes* for 11 Instruments (1969); *Concert Piece* for Trombone and Piano (1971); *Pastoral* for Flute and Piano (1973); Woodwind Quintet (1979); String Quartet (1980). **Piano:** 2 sonatinas (1960, 1965); 3 Fugues (1962); *Impromptu-Fantasia* (1964); 12 Polyphonic Pieces (1968). **VOCAL:** Over 70 songs.—**NS/LK/DM**

Nurock, Kirk, innovative American composer and originator of "natural sound"; b. Camden, N.J., Feb. 28, 1948. He held scholarships for study at the Juilliard School in N.Y. and at the Eastman School of Music in Rochester, N.Y. His teachers in composition were Persichetti, Sessions, and Berio. He was awarded the Elizabeth Sprague Coolidge Prize in chamber music in 1970. From his earliest essays in composition, he adhered to extraordinary and unusual sound production; became active as a conductor of idiosyncratic theater productions, among them the temporarily objectionable musical *Hair*, which aroused indignant protests on the part of tender-minded listeners. He further developed a natural ability to perform advanced keyboard jazz music. In 1971 he developed an experimental vocal technique which he called "natural sound," founded on the assumption that every person's vocal cords, as well as other parts of their bodies, are capable of producing variegated sound. In several works he annexed animal noises; the most challenging of them being *Sonata for Piano and Dog* (1982) and *Gorilla, Gorilla* for Piano (1988). Audience participation is welcomed as an integral part of "natural sound" productions. Several of Nurock's works are specifically scored for untrained, improvisatory participants. Interestingly enough, many newspaper reviews of his presentations seem to revive the alarmed outcries of shocked innocence that greeted first performances of the now-recognized works of Prokofiev, Stravinsky, Schoenberg, and Varèse.

WORKS: DRAMATIC: Music Theater: *Mowgli*, after Kipling, with 12 Singing Actors and 6 Musicians (1978–84). **ORCH.:** *Accumulations* (1968); *Assemblage* (1969). **CHAMBER:** Clarinet Chant for 6 Clarinets and Bass Clarinet (1970); *Creature Memory* (1979). **"NATURAL SOUND," INCLUDING ANIMALS:** *Elemental Chant* (1972); *Audience Oratorio*, with Audience Participation (1975); *Howl* for 20 Voices and 4 Canines (N.Y., Jan. 15, 1980); *Bronx Zoo Events* (Bronx Zoo, N.Y., Oct. 24, 1980); Sonata for Piano and Dog (1982; N.Y., March 16, 1983); *Expedition* for Jazz Trio and Siberian Husky (N.Y., Jan. 14, 1984); *Sendings* for 5 Winds and 4 Creatures (N.Y., March 17, 1984); *Haunted Messages* for Piano and Barking Audience (1984; N.Y., March 20, 1990); *Listening Bach* for Orch., Chorus, Narrator, and Animals (1986–88); *Gorilla, Gorilla* for Piano (N.Y., March 19, 1988). **OTHER:** *The Incurable Dorothy Parker*, song cycle for Soprano and Piano (Philadelphia, Nov. 10, 1986); *3 Screams* for 2 Amplified Pianos (N.Y., March 20, 1990); numerous ensemble numbers for plays.—**NS/LK/DM**

Nussbaum, Adam, jazz drummer; b. N.Y., Nov. 29, 1955. He was raised in Norwalk, Conn., from age four. He studied piano from ages seven to 12 with a woman who had been a student of Bartok. He was originally self-taught on drums. After attending Emerson Coll. for a year, he returned to N.Y. at age 18 to study at City Coll. while sitting in and gigging around the city. He has long been in demand around N.Y. and has recorded with John Scofield (playing with him starting in 1977), Michael Brecker, and others. He has led his own trio with John Abercrombie and Dan Wall since 1991. He teaches at N.Y.U., the New School, and Long Island Univ.—**LP**

N.W.A., controversial rap group of the late 1980s and early 1990s. **MEMBERSHIP:** Ice Cube (O'shea Jackson), (b. Los Angeles, June 15, 1969); Dr. Dre (Andre Young), (b. Los Angeles, Feb. 18, 1965); Eazy-E (Eric Wright), (b. Compton, Calif., Sept. 7, 1963; d. Los Angeles, March 26, 1995); MC Ren (Lorenzo Patterson), (b. Los Angeles, June 16); DJ Yella (Antoine Carraby), (b. Los Angeles, Dec. 11).

N.W.A. (Niggaz Wit Attitude) was led by rappers Eazy-E, Ice Cube, and Dr. Dre. Although recording together only briefly, the group helped popularize gangsta rap and aroused widespread controversy with their brutal and cynical profanity-filled raps, particularly the anthemic "Fuck tha Police." Through his Ruthless Records label, group leader Eazy-E became one of the most important producers/promoters in rap before his tragically early death from AIDS. Ice Cube and Dr. Dre have both gone on to be successful solo artists.

Eric Wright dropped out of high school in the 10th grade and started Ruthless Records in 1986 with money earned selling drugs. In 1988, as Eazy-E, he recorded the trailblazing rap album *Eazy-Duz-It*, which included "Boyz-n-the Hood," written by O'shea Jackson and Andre Young. Jackson had begun writing his own raps at 14. Eazy-E formed N.W.A. (Niggaz Wit Attitude) with Jackson ("Ice Cube"), Young ("Dr. Dre"), Lorenzo Patterson ("MC Ren"), and disc jockey Antoine Carraby ("DJ Yella") for recordings on his Ruthless label. The group recorded the landmark album *Straight Outta Compton*, which stirred controversy with the antiauthoritarian "Fuck tha Police" and included "Gangsta Gangsta" and "Dopeman." The album sold more than two million copies, but Ice Cube soon left the group amidst royalty disputes.

Ice Cube's debut album for Priority Records, *AmeriKKKa's Most Wanted*, included "Better Off Dead," "The Drive-By," and "It's a Man's World," stark portrayals of street life in South Central Los Angeles. In 1990 Ice Cube formed his own record label and production company, Street Knowledge, producing female rapper Yo Yo's *Make Way for the Motherlode*, issued on EastWest Records. Ice Cube recorded *Kill at Will*, which included "Dead Homiez" and "The Product," in 1991, and appeared in the film *Boyz n the Hood*. In the meantime, N.W.A. recorded the misogynist *Efil4zaggin* (backward: niggaz 4 life), which topped the album charts and sold more than one million copies. The album contained "Findum, Fuckum & Flee," "I'd Rather Fuck You," and "To Kill a Hooker," as well as an attack on Ice Cube, "Message to B.A." At the end of 1991 Ice Cube's album *Death Certificate* raised protests over the anti- Korean "Black Korea" and seemingly anti-Semitic "No Vaseline." *Billboard* magazine denounced the album as racist and hate-mongering, and Rabbi Abraham Cooper of the Simon Wiesenthal Center urged retailers to pull the record from their shelves.

In 1992 Ice Cube appeared with Ice-T in the film *Trespass*, participated in the Lollapalooza tour, and recorded *The Predator*, often regarded as his most powerful and cohesive album. It produced major pop hits with "It Was a Good Day" and "Check Yo Self" and included his response to the Los Angeles riots in the wake of the Rodney King verdict, "We Had to Tear This Mothafucka Up." In 1992 MC Ren recorded his solo debut album and Dr. Dre formed Death Row Records, launching his own solo career the following year with *The Chronic*. Dr. Dre scored two smash pop hits with "Nuthin' but a "G" Thang" and "Dre Day," which featured rapper Snoop Doggy Dogg. In 1994 Priority issued Ice Cube's *Bootlegs and B-Sides*, which included three new tracks, and Hitman released *Concrete Roots— Anthology*, a compilation of songs performed, produced, or written by Dr. Dre and recorded by acts such as N.W.A., Michel'le, and the World Class Wreckin' Cru. On March 26, 1995, Eazy-E died in Los Angeles at age 31 from complications brought on by AIDS. Ice Cube cowrote, coproduced, and costarred in the comedy film *Friday* and costarred in the drama *The Glass Shield*, both released in 1995.

DISC.: EAZY-E: *Eazy-Duz-It* (1988). **N.W.A.:** *Straight Outta Compton* (1989); *100 Miles and Runnin'* (1990); *Efil4zaggin* (1991). **ICE CUBE:** *AmeriKKKa's Most wanted* (1990); *Kill at Will* (1991); *Death Certificate* (1991); *The Predator* (1992); *Bootlegs and B-Sides* (1994). **DR. DRE:** *The Chronic* (1993); *Concrete Roots—Anthology* (1994). **MC REN:** *Kizz My Black Azz* (1992). **—BH**

Nygaard, Jens, American conductor; b. Longview, Tex., Oct. 26, 1931. He went to N.Y., where he studied with Katharine Bacon (1954–56) and took his B.Sc. (1957) and M.Sc. (1958) at the Juilliard School of Music. In 1966 he founded the Westchester Chamber Chorus and Orch. in White Plains, serving as conductor until 1979. In 1979 he founded and became conductor of the Jupiter Sym. in N.Y., which he led in enterprising programs embracing an extensive repertory. As a guest conductor, he appeared in the U.S. and abroad, including engagements with the Seoul Phil. (1987), the Cape Town Sym. Orch. (1988), and the Orquesta Sinfónica de Xalapa in Vera Cruz (1997).—**LK/DM**

Nyiregyházi, Erwin, remarkable and eccentric Hungarian- American pianist; b. Budapest, Jan. 19, 1903; d. Los Angeles, April 13, 1987. He absorbed music by a kind of domestic osmosis, from his father, a professional tenor, and his mother, an amateur pianist. An exceptionally gifted *Wunderkind*, he had perfect pitch and a well-nigh phonographic memory as a very small child; played a Haydn sonata and pieces by Grieg, Chopin, and himself at a concert in Fiume at the age of 6. In 1910 he entered the Budapest Academy of Music, studying theory with Siklós and Weiner, and piano with Thomán. In 1914 the family moved to Berlin, where he became a piano student of Dohnányi. He made his debut in Germany playing Beethoven's 3rd Piano Concerto with the Berlin Phil. (Oct. 14, 1915). In 1916 he began studying with Frederic Lamond, a pupil of Liszt, who was instrumental in encouraging Nyiregyházi to study Liszt's music, which was to become the most important part of his concert repertoire. In 1920 he went to the U.S.; his American debut (Carnegie Hall, N.Y., Oct. 18, 1920) was sensationally successful; the word "genius" was freely applied to him by critics usually restrained in their verbal effusions. Inexplicably, his American career suffered a series of setbacks; he became involved in a lawsuit with his manager; he married his next manager, a Mrs. Mary Kelen, in 1926, but divorced her a year later. He then went to Calif., where he became gainfully employed as a studio pianist in Hollywood; in 1930 he made a European tour; then lived in N.Y. and in Los Angeles. Beset by personal problems, he fell into a state of abject poverty, but resolutely refused to resume his concert career; he did not even own a piano. He married frequently, and as frequently divorced his successive wives. In 1972 he married his 9th wife, a lady 10 years his senior; she died shortly afterward. Attempts were made in vain by friends and admirers in Calif. to induce him to play in public; a semi-private recital was arranged for him in San Francisco in 1974; a recording of his playing of Liszt was issued in 1977; it was greeted with enthusiastic reviews, all expressing regret for his disappearance from the concert stage. Nyiregyházi composed several hundred works, mostly for piano; they remain in MS. As a child, Nyiregyházi was the object of a "scientific" study by Géza Révész, director of the Psychological Laboratory in Amsterdam, who made tests of his memory, sense of pitch, ability to transpose into different keys at sight, etc.; these findings were publ. in German as *Psychologische Analyse eines musikalisch hervorragenden Kindes* (Leipzig, 1916; Eng. tr., 1925), but the examples given and the tests detailed in the book proved to be no more unusual than the capacities of thousands of similarly gifted young musicians.—NS/LK/DM

Nyman, Michael (Laurence), notable English composer, conductor, and writer on music; b. London, March 23, 1944. He studied with Alan Bush at the Royal Academy of Music in London (1961–65) and with Thurston Dart at King's Coll., London (B.Mus., 1967). From 1964 to 1976 he wrote extensively on music for *The Listener, New Statesman,* and *The Spectator.* He also publ. the important study *Experimental Music: Cage and Beyond* (1974; 2nd ed., 1995). In 1977 he founded his own Michael Nyman Band, which served as a showcase for his music via concerts and recordings. He won his first great success as a composer with his film score to Peter Greenaway's *The Draughtsman's Contract* (1982). In subsequent years, he became widely known for his many dramatic works. In his output, Nyman attempts to bridge the chasm between art and popular music.

WORKS: DRAMATIC: The *Masterwork/Award-Winning Fishknife,* performance art/theater piece (1979); *Basic Black,* ballet (1984); *The Kiss,* opera (Channel 4 TV, London, Oct. 13, 1984); *Portraits in Reflection,* ballet (1985; N.Y., Feb. 1986); *The Man Who Mistook his Wife for a Hat,* chamber opera, after Oliver Sacks (London, Oct. 27, 1986); *And Do They Do,* ballet (London, Nov. 25, 1986); *Vital Statistics,* opera (London, June 3, 1987); *Orpheus' Daughter,* opera (Rotterdam, Dec. 13, 1988); *The Fall of Icarus,* dance piece (Brussels, Oct. 1989); *La princese de Milan,* opera (Avignon, July 24, 1991); *Letters, Riddles, and Writs,* television opera (BBC TV, Nov. 10, 1991; first stage perf., London, June 24, 1992); *Noises, Sounds, and Sweet Airs* for Soprano, Alto, Tenor, and Instrumental Ensemble (Tokyo, Dec. 7, 1994); *The Only Witness,* opera (1999–2000). **F i l m : :** *Keep It Up Downstairs* (1976); *The Draughtsman's Contract* (1982); *Brimstone and Treacle* (1982); *Nelly's Version* (1983); *The Cold Room* (1984); *A Zed and Two Noughts* (1985); *Drowning by Numbers* (1988); *The Cook, the Thief, His Wife and Her Lover* (1989); *Monsieur Hire* (1989); *Prospero's Books* (1991); *Le Mari de la Coiffeuse* (1991); *The Piano* (1992); *À La Folie* (1994); *Carrington* (1994); *The Diary of Anne Frank* (1995); *The Ogre* (1996). **ORCH.:** *A Handsom, Smooth, Sweet, Smart, Clear Stroke: or Else Play Not at All* (1983); *Taking a Line for a Second Walk* (1983; Houston, Jan. 1984); *Where the Bee Dances,* concerto for Soprano Saxophone and Chamber Orch. (Cheltenham, July 13, 1991); *MGV (Musique à Grande Vitesse)* (Lille, Sept. 26, 1993); *The Piano Concerto* (Lille, Sept. 26, 1993; also for 2 Pianos and Orch.); *Prospero's Books* (1994; Edinburgh, Jan. 19, 1995); *Carrington* (London, April 29, 1995); Concerto for Harpsichord and Strings (London, April 29, 1995); Trombone Concerto (Las Vegas, May 30, 1995); *Purcell Practices* (London, Nov. 9, 1995); Double Concerto for Saxophone, Cello, and Orch. (1996–97; London, March 8, 1997); *Strong on Oaks, Strong on the Causes of Oaks* (1997; London, April 14, 1998); *Cycle of Disquietude (Coisas, Vozes, Lettras)* (1997–98; Lisbon, May 19, 1998); *Drowning by Numbers* for Chamber Orch. (Warwick, Dec. 9, 1998). **CHAMBER:** *Bell Set No. 1* for Multiple Metal Percussion (1974); *In Re Don Giovanni* for 9 Players (1977); *Five Orchestral Pieces Opus Tree* for 9 Players (1981); *M-Work* for 9 Players (1981); *Think Slow, Act Fast* for 10 Players (1981); *Four Saxes* for Saxophone Quartet (1982); *I'll Stake My Cremona to a Jew's Crump* for Electronically Modified Violin and Viola (1983); 4 string quartets: No. 1 (London, Nov. 3, 1985), No. 2 (London, Sept. 15, 1988), No. 3 (1989; London, Feb. 16, 1990), and No. 4 (London, April 21, 1995); *Zoo Caprices* for Violin (1985; Paris, April 8, 1986); *Shaping the Curve* for Soprano Saxophone and Piano (1990); *Masque Aria* for Brass Quintet (1991); *Time will Pronounce* for Violin, Cello, and Piano (Cheltenham, July 14, 1992); *The Upside-Down Violin* for 9 Players (Seville, Sept. 21, 1992); *For John Cage* for Brass Ensemble (Ashford, Nov. 16, 1992); *The Final Score* for 14 Players (Channel 4 TV, London, Dec. 8, 1992); *Songs for Tony* for Saxophone Quartet (London, May 1, 1993); *On the Fiddle* for Violin and Piano (Vale of Glamorgan Festival, Aug. 27, 1993); *Yamamoto Perpetuo* for Violin (Tokyo, Dec.20, 1993); *Three Quartets* for Saxophone Quartet, String Quartet, and Brass Quartet (Tokyo, July 15, 1994); *H.R.T.* for Chamber Ensemble (1995); *Viola and Piano* (London, Nov. 19, 1995); *A.E.T.* for Chamber Ensemble (Salisbury Festival, June 5, 1996). **KEYBOARD: P i a n o :** *1-100* (1976). **H a r p s i c h o r d :** *The Convertibility of Lute Strings* (London, Nov. 17, 1992); *Tango for Tim* (1994); *Elisabeth Gets Her Way* (1995–96). **VOCAL:** *Bird List Song* for Soprano and 9 Players (1979); *A Neat Slice of Time* for Chorus and Amplified Piano, after Leonardo da Vinci (1980); *Bird Anthem* for Chorus and 9 Players (1981); *Love is Certainly as Least Alphabetically Speaking* for Soprano and 9 Players (1983); *The Abbess of Andouillets* for Chorus (1984); *L'Orgie Parisienne* for Soprano or Mezzo-soprano and 14 Players (1989); *Six Celan Songs* for Low Woman's Voice and 14 Players (1990; Amsterdam, Feb. 1, 1992); *Mozart on Mortality* for Soprano and 6 Instruments (London, June 7, 1992); *Self-Laudatory Hymn of Inanna and Her Omnipotence* for Countertenor and Viols (London, June 11, 1992; also for Contralto and Strings, London, April 29, 1995, and for Countertenor and Wind Ensemble, Amsterdam, Jan. 21, 1999); *Anne de Lucy Songs* for Soprano and Piano (Huddersfield, Nov. 24, 1992); *To Morrow* for Soprano and Organ (Bath, June 8, 1994); *The Waltz Song* for Unison Voices and Piano (Lincoln, Oct. 14, 1995).—**NS/LK/DM**

Nyro, Laura, singer/songwriter of the 1960s; b. Laura Nigro, Bronx, N.Y., Oct. 18, 1947; d. Danbury, Conn., April 9, 1997. Laura Nyro began playing piano at a very early age, ostensibly writing her first song at the age of eight. After attending Manhattan's H.S. of Music and Art, she signed with Verve Records in 1966 and made her first extended professional appearance at San Francisco's hungry i in early 1967. Her debut album, *More Than a New Discovery* (reissued by Columbia as *The First Songs*), contained "Wedding Bell Blues," "And When I Die," "Stoney End," "Blowin' Away," and "He's a Runner," yet was sorely overlooked by the record-buying public. At 1967's celebrated Monterey International Pop Festival, she played with a trio of black female backup singers as a soul revue, but the experiment proved less than successful and she was nearly booed off the stage.

Switching to Columbia Records, Laura Nyro's debut for the label, *Eli and the Thirteenth Confession*, was greeted by highly favorable critical reviews but barely sold despite the inclusion of "Sweet Blindness," "Eli's Coming," "Stoned Soul Picnic," and the overlooked "Woman's Blues." Although the public failed to recognize her exceptional songwriting, dynamic delivery, and fine piano accompaniment, a number of acts began recording her songs with astounding success. In 1968, The Fifth Dimension scored a smash with her "Stoned Soul Picnic," followed by "Sweet Blindness," the top hit "Wedding Bell Blues," and the major hits "Blowin' Away" and "Save the Country" through 1970. Blood, Sweat and Tears had a smash hit with "And When I Die" in 1969 and recorded "He's a Runner" on their third album. Three Dog Night hit with "Eli's Coming" and Barbra Streisand scored a smash with "Stoney End" in late 1970.

Laura Nyro's second Columbia album, *N.Y. Tendaberry*, with "You Don't Love Me When I Cry" and "Sweet Lovin' Baby," became her best-selling album, yet *Christmas and the Beads of Sweat* sold less well despite yielding her only (minor) hit with a remake of Gerry Goffin and Carole King's "Up on the Roof." In 1971, under producers Kenny Gamble and Leon Huff, Nyro recorded *It's Gonna Take a Miracle*, an album of soul/rhythm-and-blues classics, with the Labelle trio, but she soon retired from the music business. She reemerged in 1975, recording the jazz-flavored *Smile* and touring again, but again withdrew in 1979. She recorded the neglected *Mother's Spiritual* for 1984 release and later wrote "Broken Rainbow," used as the title song to an award-winning documentary about the Native Americans' loss of their land. Nyro resumed touring in 1988, recorded *Live at the Bottom Line* for Cypress Records, and returned to Co-

lumbia Records for 1993's *Walk the Dog and Light the Light*. Laura Nyro died of ovarian cancer on April 9, 1997, in Danbury, Conn., at the age of 49.

DISC.: LAURA NYRO: *More Than a New Discovery* (1967); *Eli and the Thirteenth Confession* (1968); *N.Y. Tendaberry* (1969); *Christmas and the Beads of Sweat* (1970); *It's Gonna Take a Miracle* (1971); *Smile* (1976); *Season of Lights* (1977); *Nested* (1978); *Mother's Spiritual* (1984); *Live at the Bottom Line* (1989); *Walk the Dog and Light the Light* (1993); *Stoned Soul Picnic* (1997).—**BH**

Nystedt, Knut, esteemed Norwegian choral conductor, organist, pedagogue, and composer; b. Christiania, Sept. 3, 1915. He studied organ with Sandvold, conducting with Fjeldstad, and composition with Per Steenberg and Brustad at the Oslo Cons. (1931–43), and then pursued training with Ernest White (organ) and Copland (composition) in N.Y. (1947). From 1946 to 1982 he was organist at Oslo's Torshov Church, and also a prof. of choral conducting at the Oslo Cons. (1964–85). In 1950 he founded Det Norske Solistokor (the Norwegian Soloist Choir), which he conducted for the first time in Oslo on May 23, 1951. In subsequent years, he developed it into one of the finest choral groups in the world, conducting it in a comprehensive literature with a special regard for contemporary scores. In 1960 he conducted it for the first time in the U.S.; later led it on tours of Japan, Korea, Hong Kong, and Thailand (1978), China (1982), and Israel (1984, 1988). On March 18, 1990, he conducted his farewell concert as its conductor in Oslo. In 1966 he was made a Knight of the Order of St. Olav, in 1978 he was awarded the Spellemannsprisen, and in 1980 he received the music prize of the Norwegian Council for Cultural Affairs. Nystedt is an outstanding composer of choral music; his orch. works have also won approbation both at home and abroad.

WORKS: DRAMATIC: O p e r a : *Med krone og stjerne* (With Crown and Star), Christmas opera (1971); *Salomos hoysang* (The Song of Songs), church opera (1989). **ORCH.:** *Hgfjell* (The Mountains), suite (1940–41); Concerto grosso for 3 Trumpets and Strings (1946); *Spenningens land* (Land of Suspense), symphonic fantasy (1947; Oslo, Sept. 29, 1948); *Festival Overture* (1950); Sym. for Strings (1950); Concertino for English Horn, Clarinet, and Strings (1952); *De syv segl* (The 7 Seals), visions (1958–60); *Collocations* (1963); *Mirage* (1974); *Fisken* (Fish; 1976); *Exsultate* (1980; Oslo, Sept. 5, 1985; also for Organ); *Sinfonia del mare* (1983); Horn Concerto (Helsinki, Oct. 13, 1986); *Concerto Arctandriae* for Strings (1991); *Apocalypsis Joannis*, sym. for Soloists, Chorus, and Orch. (1998); band music. **CHAMBER:** 5 string quartets (1938; 1948; 1956; 1966, Norwegian Radio, Feb. 6, 1989; 1988); *The Moment* for Soprano, Celesta, and Percussion (1962); *Pia memoria*, Requiem for 9 Brass Instruments (1971); *Rhapsody in Green* for Brass Quintet (1978); *Music for 6 Trombones* (1980); organ pieces. **VOCAL: C h o r a l :** *Ndevegen*, oratorio for Soloists, Chorus, and Orch. (1943–46); *Norge mitt land* (Norway, My County) for Baritone, Chorus, and Orch. (1944); *De profundis* (1964); *Spes Mundi* (The Hope of the World), Mass for Chorus, Drama Group, Trumpet, Organ, Percussion, Narrator, and Congregation (1970); *Dies Irae* for 4 Choruses, Wind, and Percussion (1976); *A Hymn of Human Rights* for Chorus, Organ, and Percussion (1982; Des Moines, Iowa, March 6, 1983); *For a Small Planet* for Chorus, String Quartet, Harp, and Narrator (1983; Eugene, Ore., July 13, 1984); *Missa Brevis* (1984; Bergen, June 17, 1985); *The Lamentations of Jeremiah* (1985); *Stabat*

Mater for Chorus and Cello (1986); *Salomo* (Song of Songs) for Soloists, Chorus, Dancers, Instruments, and Organ (1990); *One Mighty Flowering Tree* for Chorus and Brass Orch. (1994); *Kristnikvede* for Chorus and Orch. to celebrate the 1,000th anniverary of Christianity in Norway (1994; Moster, June 4, 1995); *Libertas Vincit* for Reciter, Chorus, and Chamber Orch. to celebrate the 50th anniversary of the liberation of Norway from Nazi occupation (1994; Oslo, May 10, 1995); *A Song as in the Night* for Soloists, Chorus, and Orch. (1996); *Salve Regina* for Chorus (1999).—**NS/LK/DM**

Nystroem, Gösta, Swedish composer; b. Silvberg, Oct. 13, 1890; d. Särö, near Göteborg, Aug. 9, 1966. He studied piano, harmony, and composition with his father, then piano and harmony with Lundberg and Bergenson in Stockholm. He took courses at the Cons. there (1913–14), and also studied composition with Hallén. After further training in Copenhagen and Germany, he went to Paris (1920) and studied composition and instrumentation with d'Indy and Sabaneyev and conducting with Chevillard. He subsequently wrote music criticism in Göteborg (1932–47). After following neo-Baroque practices, he developed an independent mode of composition.

WORKS: DRAMATIC: *De Blinda* (The Blind), radio drama (1949); *Ungersvennen och de sex prinsessorna* (The Young Lad and the 6 Princesses), ballet (1951); *Herr Arnes penningar* (Sir Arne's Hoard), opera (Swedish Radio, Nov. 26, 1959); incidental music. **ORCH.:** *Rondo capriccioso* for Violin and Orch. (1917; rev. 1920); 2 symphonic poems: *Is havet* (The Arctic Ocean; 1924) and *Babels torn* (The Tower of Babel; 1928); 2 concertos for Strings (1930, 1955); 6 syms.: No. 1, *Sinfonia breve* (1931; Göteborg, Oct. 19, 1932), No. 2, *Sinfonia espressiva* (1932–35; Göteborg, Feb. 18, 1937), No. 3, *Sinfonia del mare*, for Soprano and Orch. (1947–48; Stockholm, March 24, 1949), No. 4, *Sinfonia Shakespeareana* (Göteborg, Nov. 5, 1952), No. 5, *Sinfonia seria* (Stockholm, Oct. 9, 1963), and No. 6, *Sinfonia Tramontana* (1965; Stockholm, Oct. 30, 1966); Suite for Small Orch. (1950); *Partita* for Flute, Strings, and Harp (1953); Violin Concerto (1954); *Concerto ricercante* for Piano and Orch. (1959; Stockholm, May 15, 1960). **CHAMBER:** 2 string quartets (1956, 1961); piano pieces. **VOCAL:** *3 Havsvisioner* (Visions of the Sea) for Chorus (1956); *Summer Music* for Soprano and Orch. (1964); solo songs.

BIBL.: P. Christensen, *The Orchestral Works of G. N.: A Critical Study* (diss., Univ. of Wash., 1961; publ. in London, 1965).—**NS/LK/DM**

O

Oakeley, Sir Herbert (Stanley), English composer and teacher; b. Ealing, Middlesex, July 22, 1830; d. Eastbourne, Oct. 26, 1903. He was educated at Christ Church, Oxford (B.A., 1853; M.A., 1856), where he studied organ and harmony with S. Elvey; subsequently had lessons with Plaidy, Moscheles, and Papperitz at the Leipzig Cons., J. Schneider in Dresden, and Breidenstein in Bonn. In 1865 he was appointed a prof. of music at Edinburgh Univ., and held this post until 1891. Oakeley was influential in the musical affairs of Scotland in general. He was knighted in 1876. He wrote a cantata, *A Jubilee Lyric* (1887), *Suite in the Olden Style* for Orch. (1893), church music, choruses, piano pieces, and arrangements of Scottish melodies.

BIBL.: E. Oakeley, *The Life of Sir H.S. O.* (London, 1904). **—NS/LK/DM**

Oberlin, Russell (Keys), American countertenor; b. Akron, Ohio, Oct. 11, 1928. He studied at the Juilliard School of Music in N.Y., graduating in 1951. In 1952 he joined the N.Y. Pro Musica Antiqua, appearing as a soloist in works from the medieval and Renaissance periods; in 1960 he sang the role of Oberon in Britten's *A Midsummer Night's Dream* at Covent Garden, London. In 1966 he joined the faculty at Hunter Coll. in N.Y. **—NS/LK/DM**

Oborin, Lev (Nikolaievich), Russian pianist, pedagogue, and composer; b. Moscow, Sept. 11, 1907; d. there, Jan. 5, 1974. He studied with Elena Gnessina at the Gnessin Music School in Moscow and with Igumnov at the Moscow Cons. (graduated, 1926). He made his debut in 1924; won the Chopin Competition in Warsaw (1927), then toured widely; was also on the faculty of the Moscow Cons. (1928–74). He was made a People's Artist of the U.S.S.R. in 1964. He was known for his wide sympathies as an interpreter, ranging from the classics to the Soviet school; was soloist in the premiere of Khachaturian's Piano Concerto. He wrote piano sonatas and other works for piano, as well as several orch. pieces.

BIBL.: S. Khentova, *L. O.* (Moscow, 1964).**—NS/LK/DM**

Obouhov, Nicolas (actually, **Nikolai**), remarkable Russian composer; b. Kursk, April 22, 1892; d. Paris, June 13, 1954. He studied at the St. Petersburg Cons. with Nikolai Tcherepnin and Maximilian Steinberg. After the Revolution in 1917, he emigrated to Paris, where he received instruction from Ravel. As early as 1914 he began experimenting with harmonic combinations containing 12 different notes without duplication (he called his system "absolute harmony"). In 1915 he devised a special notation for this type of harmony, entirely enharmonic, with crosses indicating sharps or flats; several composers, among them Honegger, wrote pieces in Obouhov's notation. He gave a demonstration of his works written and notated in this system in Petrograd at a concert organized by the eds. of the review *Muzykalnyi Sovremennik* on Feb. 3, 1916. He devoted his entire life to the composition of his magnum opus, *Le Livre de vie*, for Solo Voices, Chorus, 2 Pianos, and Orch. The MS score, some 2,000 pages in length, was deposited after his death at the Bibliothèque Nationale in Paris. A mystic, Obouhov signed his name "Nicolas l'illuminé" and used his own blood to mark sections in the score; the finale represented the spiritual and religious apotheosis in which both the old and the new Russian societies and political factions become reunited. In this and some other scores, Obouhov introduced shouting, screaming, sighing, and groaning sounds for the voice parts. A section of *Le Livre de vie* was performed by Koussevitzky in Paris on June 3, 1926. In quest of new sonorities, Obouhov devised an electronic instrument, the "croix sonore," in the form of a cross, and composed works for it, which were performed by Mme. Aussenac de Broglie. He publ. *Traité d'harmonie tonale, atonale et totale* (Paris, 1946), which presents an exposition of his system.

BIBL.: C. Laronde, *Le Livre de vie de N. O.* (Paris, 1932).
—NS/LK/DM

Oboussier, Robert, Swiss composer; b. Antwerp (of Swiss parents), July 9, 1900; d. (stabbed to death by his roommate) Zürich, June 9, 1957. He studied at the Zürich Cons. with Andreae and Jarnach (composition); then with Ochs (conducting) at the Berlin Hochschule für Musik. He then lived in Florence (1922–28); was music ed. of the *Deutsche Allgemeine Zeitung*; but in 1939 political conditions in Germany impelled him to leave for Switzerland; in 1942 he became director of the Central Archive of Swiss Music, and in 1948 of Suisa (the Swiss assn. of writers, composers, and publishers). Of cosmopolitan background, Oboussier combined in his music the elements of both Germanic and Latin cultures. He publ. *Der Sänger* (with others; Berlin, 1934; 2nd ed., rev., 1959) and *Die Sinfonien Beethovens* (Berlin, 1937); also a collection of critical reviews, *Berliner Musik-Chronik 1930–38* (1969).

WORKS: DRAMATIC: Opera: *Amphitryon* (1948–50; Berlin, March 13, 1951). **ORCH.:** Piano Concerto (1932–33; rev. 1944); Sym. (1935–36); *Chant de deuil* (1942–43); *Introitus* for Strings (1946); Violin Concerto (1952–53). **CHAMBER:** Several pieces, including piano music. **VOCAL:** *Trilogia sacra* for Solo Voices, Chorus, and Orch. (1925–29); *Antigone* for Voice and Orch. (1938–39); *3 Psaumes* for Solo Voices, Chorus, and Orch. (1946–47); solo songs.—NS/LK/DM

Obradović, Aleksandar, Yugoslav composer, pedagogue, writer on music, painter, and poet; b. Bled, Aug. 22, 1927. He studied with Logar at the Belgrade Academy of Music (graduated, 1952), with Berkeley in London (1959–60), and at the Columbia-Princeton Electronic Music Center in N.Y. (1966–67). From 1955 to 1991 he was prof. of composition at the Belgrade Academy of Music. He also served as rector of the Univ. of Arts from 1977 to 1983. He was general secretary of the Union of Yugoslav Composers (1962–66). In 1959 he received the Award of the City of Belgrade for his *Symphonic Epitaph* and in 1980 the award of the Republic of Serbia for his creative oeuvre. He publ. a textbook on orchestration (Belgrade, 1978; 2nd ed., 1997). Formally, his music adheres to the architectonic Classical design with discernible tonal centers, but he also experiments with atonal thematics, polytonal harmonies, and dodecaphonic formulas, also using elements of electronic and aleatoric music.

WORKS (all first perf. in Belgrade unless otherwise given): **DRAMATIC:** *Prolećni uranak* (Spring Early Outing), ballet (1948); music for 9 radio plays; 7 film scores. **ORCH.:** 8 syms.: No. 1 (1952; March 11, 1953), No. 2 (1959–61; Jan. 22, 1965), No. 3, *Microsymphony* for Tape and Orch. (1967; Opatija, Oct. 27, 1968), No. 4 (May 24, 1972), No. 5, *Intima* (Opatija, Nov. 17, 1974), No. 6, *Explicatio duplex, expressio triplex* (1977; May 12, 1978), No. 7 (1985; Oct. 6, 1987), and No. 8, *Na davnom proplanku detinjstva* (In childhood's bygone meadow), for 2 Voices, Chorus, and Orch. (1989; Nov. 26, 1991); *Prelude and Fugue* for Strings (1954); Concertino for Piano and Strings (1956); Concerto for Clarinet and Strings (1958; March 26, 1959); *Scherzo Overture* (1959); *Kroz svemir* (Through Outer Space), suite (1961); *Epitaph H* for Orch. and Tape (Berlin, Oct. 6, 1965); *Dramatična fuga* for Wind Orch. (Nov. 17, 1972); Cello Concerto (1979; April

23, 1980); *Askeza* (Ascetism) for Strings and Celesta (1991); Concerto for Violin and Strings (1991; Sept. 28, 1992; also as a Concerto for Cello and Strings); *Music* (Concerto No. 1) for Piano and Strings (1992; Sept. 24, 1993); *Diptych* (Concerto No. 2) for Piano and Strings (1999); *Diptych* (Prelude and Fugue) for Strings (1999); *Pro libertate* (Concerto No. 3) for Piano and Orch. (2000). **CHAMBER:** Quintet for Flute, Clarinet, and String Trio (1951); *Microsonata I* for Clarinet (1969) and *II* for Bassoon (1970); *Divertimento* for Wind Quintet (1983); piano pieces. **VOCAL:** *Mala horska svita* (Little choral suite; 1947); *Plameni vjetar* (Wing of Flame), song cycle for Baritone and Orch. (1955); *Symphonic Epitaph* for Reciter, Chorus, and Orch. (May 21, 1959); *Sutjeska* for 2 Reciters, Chorus, and Orch. (1968; Dec. 19, 1971); *Dačko doba Šumarica* (School Days in Šumarice) for Reciters, Chorus, Children's Chorus, and Wind Orch. (Kragujevac, Oct. 21, 1972); *Mezomed Muzi* (Mesomedes to the Muse), song cycle for Mezzo-soprano and Chamber Trio (1972); *Zeleni vitez* (The Green Knight), song cycle for Voice and Strings (1990); *Stradun*, song cycle for Voice and Piano (1990). **ELECTRONIC:** *Electronic Toccata and Fugue* (1967).—NS/LK/DM

Obraztsova, Elena (Vasilievna), outstanding Russian mezzo-soprano; b. Leningrad, July 7, 1937. Her father was an engineer who played the violin. She studied at the Leningrad Cons., graduating in 1964. She made her operatic debut as Marina in *Boris Godunov* at Moscow's Bolshoi Theater (1963). In 1970 she won first prize at the Tchaikovsky Competition in Moscow. She made her first tour of the U.S. with the Bolshoi troupe in June-July 1975; on Oct. 12, 1976, she made her Metropolitan Opera debut in N.Y. as Amneris in Verdi's *Aida*. She appeared in recital in N.Y. in 1987, and was also invited to sing again at the Metropolitan Opera after an absence of some 10 years. In 1973 she was named a National Artist of the R.S.F.S.R. and in 1976 she was awarded the Lenin prize. She possessed a remarkably even tessitura, brilliant in all registers; her roles included virtually the entire Russian operatic repertoire, and such standard roles as Norma, Carmen, Eboli, and Dalila.—NS/LK/DM

Obrecht (Obreht, Hobrecht, Obertus, Hobertus), Jacob, famous Netherlandish composer; b. probably in Bergen-op-Zoom, Nov. 22, 1450 or 1451; d. Ferrara, 1505. He is first mentioned as zangmeester in Utrecht (c. 1476–78), then became choirmaster for the Corp. of Notre Dame at St. Gertrude in Bergen-op-Zoom (1479). He took Holy Orders, and said his first Mass as an ordained priest on April 23, 1480. He was made maître des enfants at Cambrai (July 28, 1484), but was dismissed for his neglect of the choirboys as well as financial irregularities (1485); then was made succentor at St. Donatian in Bruges (Oct. 13, 1486). At the invitation of the Duke of Ferrara, he obtained a leave of absence to travel to Italy; arrived in Ferrara in Dec. 1487, returning to Bruges Aug. 15, 1488, where he was made maitre de chapelle in 1490; obtained remission from his position on Jan. 24, 1491. By 1494 he was at Notre Dame in Antwerp, serving as Capellanie magister in 1495. He returned to St. Gertrude in Bergen-op-Zoom in 1496–97, and then received a benefice connected to the altar of St. Josse in Notre Dame at Antwerp in 1498. He was again at St. Donatian in Bruges from 1499 until his retirement in 1500. He then lived in Bergen-op-Zoom and made visits to Antwerp. In 1504 he returned to the ducal court in Ferrara, where he died of the plague. Obrecht was one of the leading composers of his era, his masses and motets being of particular importance. He also wrote chansons, many to Dutch texts. Petrucci publ. *Misse Obreht* (Venice, 1503), which contained several of his finest masses. An extensive ed. of his works was prepared by J. Wolf and publ. as *Werken van Jacob Obrecht by the Vereeniging voor Noord-Nederlands Musiekgeschiedenis* (7 vols., Amsterdam and Leipzig, 1908–21). Since its appearance, additional works by Obrecht have been discovered while others formerly attributed to him have been determined to be spurious; the *Passio Domini nostri Jesu Christi* is now considered a doubtful work, since early sources attribute it to Antoine Longueval and J. a la Venture. A. Smijers ed. *Jacob Obrecht: Opera omnia, editio altera* (9 vols., 1953–64). *The New Obrecht Edition*, under general ed. C. Maas, commenced publication in 1983.

BIBL.: O. Gombosi, *J. O.: Eine stilkritische Studie* (Leipzig, 1925); M. Kyriazis, *Die Cantus firmus-Technik in den Messen O.s* (Bern, 1952); A. Salop, *The Masses of J. O. (1450–1505), Structure and Style* (diss., Ind. Univ., 1959); L. van Hoorn, *J. O.* (The Hague, 1968); M. Picker, *Johannes Ockeghem and J. O.: A Guide to Research* (N.Y., 1988); R. Wegman, *Born for the Muses: The Life and Masses of J. O.* (Oxford, 1994).—NS/LK/DM

Obretenov, Svetoslav, Bulgarian choral conductor and composer; b. Provadia, Nov. 25, 1909; d. Sofia, May 16, 1955. He studied at the Sofia Cons., then was active as a choral conductor. He wrote mostly for chorus; his oratorio *The Partisans* was performed for the first time in Sofia on June 25, 1949.

BIBL.: V. Krstev, *S. O.* (Sofia, 1959).—NS/LK/DM

O'Brien, Eugene, American composer and teacher; b. Paterson, N.J., April 24, 1945. He studied with Robert Beadell at the Univ. of Nebr. (B.M., 1967; M.M., 1969) and on a Fulbright fellowship with Zimmermann at the Cologne Staatliche Hochschule für Musik (1969–70); after further training with Eaton and Xenakis at Ind. Univ. (1970–71), he completed his studies with Erb at the Cleveland Inst. of Music (D.M.A., 1983). In the meantime, he taught composition at the Cleveland Inst. of Music (1973–81), subsequently serving as its composer-in-residence and as chairman of its composition and theory dept. (1981–85); he was assoc. prof. of music and chairman of the composition dept. at the school of music at the Catholic Univ. of America in Washington, D.C. (1985–87); then assoc. prof. of music at the Ind. Univ. School of Music in Bloomington (from 1987), where he was chairman of the composition dept. (from 1994). He held the Rome Prize Fellowship at the American Academy in Rome (1971–73); also received NEA (1977, 1979) and Guggenheim (1984–85) fellowships.

WORKS: DRAMATIC: Ballet: *Taking Measures* (Cleveland, Oct. 10, 1984). **ORCH.:** Sym. (Lincoln, Nebr., May 16, 1969); Cello Concerto (1971; Rome, Dec. 5, 1972); *Rites of Passage* (1978); *Mysteries of the Horizon* (1987; also for Chamber Orch., 1988); Alto Saxophone Concerto (1989; Bloomington, Ind., Dec. 1, 1993); *The Clouds of Magellan* for the 175th anniversary of Ind. Univ. (1995). **CHAMBER:** *Intessitura* for Cello and Piano (1975); *Embarking for Cythera* for 8 Instruments (1978); *Tristan's Lament* for Cello (1979); *Allures* for Percussion Trio (1979); *Black Fugatos* for 5 Instruments (1983); *Psalms and Nocturnes* for Flute, Viola da Gamba, and Harpsichord (1985); *Close Harmony* for 2 Pianos (1986); *Mysteries of the Horizon* for 11 Instruments (1987); *Rhyme and Reason* for Marimba (1993); *Fancies and Goodnights* for Flute, Clarinet, and Double Bass (1994). **Piano:** *Ambages* for Piano, 4-Hands (1972). **VOCAL:** *Ceremony after a Fire Raid* for Baritone and String Quartet (1965); *Requiem Mass* for Soprano, Chorus, and Wind Ensemble (1966); Nocturne for Soprano and 10 Instruments (1968); *Elegy for Bernd Alois Zimmermann* for Soprano, Trumpet, 2 Percussion, and Cello (1970); *Lingual* for Soprano, Flute, and Cello (1972); *Dédales* for Soprano and Orch. (1973; Rome, Dec. 18, 1976); *Dreams and Secrets of Origin* for Soprano and Orch. (Cleveland, Oct. 19, 1983); *Mareas* for Soprano and Orch. (1991).—NS/LK/DM

Obukhova, Nadezhda (Andreievna), Russian mezzo-soprano; b. Moscow, March 6, 1886; d. Feodosiya, Aug. 14, 1961. She studied with Masetti at the Moscow Cons., graduating in 1912. She made her operatic debut at the Bolshoi Theater there in 1916 as Pauline in *The Queen of Spades*; remained on its roster until 1948. In addition to the Russian repertoire, she was noted for her portrayals of Carmen, Dalila, Amneris, and Fricka. She was greatly esteemed in Russia; in 1943 she was awarded the State Prize of the U.S.S.R.

BIBL.: E. Grosheva, *N. O.* (Moscow, 1953).—NS/LK/DM

Ocean, Billy (originally, Charles, Leslie Sebastian), pop-soul singer who enjoyed success in the mid-1980s; b. Trinidad, West Indies, Jan. 21, 1950. One of the vast numbers of Caribbeans who immigrated to Britain, Billy Ocean was raised in England. He subsidized a career as a session singer by working days at the Ford Motor plant. He was signed as a solo artist and scored an international hit in 1976 with "Lover Really Hurts without You," which hit #22 on the U.S. pop charts. A minor hit, "Red Light Spells Danger," followed, and then he went back to the session singer/day job routine, this time as a Saville Row tailor. He moved to the United States in the late 1970s and recorded a series of less-than-commercial albums, scoring a minor dance hit with "Night (Feel Like Getting Down)."

Finally, Ocean's manager suggested he work with producer Keith Diamond. The result was Ocean's Arista-label debut, *Suddenly*. The album generated four hit singles on the way to selling double platinum. The gold chart topper "Caribbean Queen" led the charge with its raucous rock meets techno-soul sound, with Ocean's tenor reaching for the sky. The #2 "Lover Boy" had a very similar sound. The title track, a ballad in the mold of Jeffrey Osbourne and Quincy Jones, reached #4. "Mystery Lady" climbed to #24. The album topped out at #9.

Suddenly, Ocean was a hot property. He was asked to sing the theme song for *The Jewel of the Nile*, the sequel to the very successful film *Romancing the Stone*. His song, "When the Going Gets Tough, the Tough Get Going," had an almost martial feel to it, rising to #2. It presaged Ocean's own next album, *Love Zone*. The next single, the ballad "There'll Be Sad Songs (To Make You Cry)" topped the pop, adult-contemporary, and R&B charts. The title track also topped the R&B charts, going Top Ten pop. The album rose to #6 and went double platinum.

Ocean kicked off his next album, *Tear Down These Walls*, with yet another chart-topping single, the rocking "Get outta My Dreams, Get into My Car." However, the follow-up singles were disappointing: the ballad "The Colour of Love" reached #17, and "License to Chill" stalled at #32. The album reached only #18, although it did go platinum. During the 1990s, Ocean recorded several more albums, but his career never regained its forward momentum. In 1999, the boy band N'Sync covered Ocean's "When the Going Gets Tough, the Tough Get Going."

DISC.: *Billy Ocean* (1975); *City Limit* (1980); *Nights (Feel Like Getting Down)* (1981); *Inner Feelings* (1982); *Suddenly* (1984); *Love Zone* (1986); *Tear Down These Walls* (1988); *Time to Move On* (1993); *L.I.F.E.* (1997).—**HB**

Očenáš, Andrej, Slovak composer; b. Selce, near Banská Bystrica, Jan. 8, 1911. He studied composition with Alexander Moyzes at the Bratislava Academy of Music, graduating in 1937, and then took a course with Novák at the Prague Cons., graduating in 1939. He worked at the Czech Radio in Bratislava (1939–50) and was music deputy to the regional director of broadcasting there (1956–62). He taught at the Bratislava Cons. (1943–73), serving as director from 1950 to 1954. His music is imbued with a Slovak ethos.

WORKS: DRAMATIC: *At the Brigand's Ball* (1941); *Year in a Village*, musical play (Bratislava, Dec. 11, 1948); *Highlander's Songs*, ballet (1954–56); *The Romance of the Rose*, stage sym. for Narrator, Soloists, Chorus, and Orch. (1969–71). **ORCH.:** *Tales of My Native Land* (1943); *Resurrection*, symphonic trilogy (1945–53); *To My Nation*, symphonic cycle (1947); Cello Concerto (1952); *Ruralia Slovaca* for Strings, 2 Flutes, 2 Clarinets, 2 Trumpets, Horns, and Piano (1957); Piano Concerto (1959); *Concertino rustico* for Cimbalom, Strings, and Piano (1963); Sinfonietta (1966); *The Flames of May*, prelude (1972); Violin Concerto (1974); *The Depiction of Life*, symphonic cycle (1980); *Gilding of Traditions* (1984). **CHAMBER:** 2 string quartets (*Pictures of the Soul*, 1942; *Étude*, 1970); Concertino for Flute and Piano (1961–62); Piano Trio (1967); *Frescoes* for Violin and Piano (1967); *Poem of the Heart* for Violin (1968); *Don Quixote*, duo for Violin and Cello (1969). **Piano:** *Zvony* (The Bells), sonata (1972); other piano pieces. **VOCAL:** *Prophecies*, cantata tetralogy (1949–52); *About Earth and Man*, sym. for Chorus and Small Orch. (1970); choral pieces; songs.—**NS/LK/DM**

Ochman, Wieslaw, Polish tenor; b. Warsaw, Feb. 6, 1937. He studied in Kraków, Bytom, and Warsaw. He made his operatic debut as Edgardo in *Lucia di Lammermoor* in Bytom (1959), appearing there regularly until 1963, and then sang in Kraków and Warsaw. He subsequently made debuts at Berlin's Deutsche Oper (1966), the Hamburg State Opera (1967), the Chicago Lyric Opera (1972), the San Francisco Opera (1972), the Paris

Opéra (1974), and the Vienna State Opera (1975); made his Metropolitan Opera debut in N.Y. as Arrigo in *Les Vêpres siciliennes* (March 12, 1975). In 1982 he returned to the Metropolitan Opera as Grigori in *Boris Godunov*. He sang Idomeneo in San Francisco in 1989. In 1996 he portrayed Grigori at the Berlin State Opera. Among his best known roles were those in Mozart's operas as well as Count Almaviva, Ernesto, the Duke of Mantua, and Cavaradossi.—**NS/LK/DM**

Ochs, Phil, social-protest singer of the 1960s who had a troubled life and career; b. El Paso, Tex., Dec. 19, 1940; d. Far Rockaway, Queens, N.Y., April 9, 1976. Phil Ochs studied journalism at Ohio State Univ., forming the folk duo The Sundowners with Jim Glover before dropping out to move to N.Y. in the early 1960s. Ochs became involved with the *Broadside* magazine movement and debuted at Gerde's Folk City in Greenwich Village in August 1962. Signed to Elektra Records in 1964, his debut album contained "Talking Vietnam," "Too Many Martyrs," "The Power and the Glory," and his tribute to Woody Guthrie, "Bound for Glory." His second album, *I Ain't Marching Anymore*, established him at the forefront of the protest movement with its anthemic title song, "The Men Behind the Guns," and "Here's to the State of Mississippi," and included the satirical "Draft Dodger Rag." In the fall of 1965, Joan Baez scored a minor hit with Ochs's "There but for Fortune," included on his *In Concert* album, generally regarded as his finest acoustic work. The album also featured "Love Me, I'm a Liberal," "Cops of the World," "When I'm Gone," and the love song "Changes."

By 1966, the popularity of folk music was fading in favor of folk-rock, leading to a public rift between Phil Ochs and Bob Dylan, who had taken up electric guitar in 1965. Ochs moved to Los Angeles and switched to A&M Records, adapting elaborate arrangements for his debut for the label, *Pleasures of the Harbor*, which included his telling and satirical attack on apathy, "Outside a Small Circle of Friends." *Tape from California* contained "White Boots Marching in a Yellow Land" and one of the most potent antiwar songs of the 1960s, "The War Is Over." Ochs appeared at protests during the 1968 Democratic Convention in Chicago. Following *Rehearsals for Retirement* and *Greatest Hits* (actually all new material, including "Chords of Fame" and the overlooked "Gas Station Women"), Ochs recorded *Gunfight at Carnegie Hall*, issued in Canada only.

During the early 1970s, Phil Ochs lived in London and traveled extensively. He suffered damage to his vocal chords when assaulted in Africa and fell into fits of depression and bouts with alcoholism. Returning to N.Y., he organized a benefit for victims of the Chilean junta that had overthrown Salvador Allende in 1974, convincing Bob Dylan to appear. Phil Ochs last performed publicly in October 1975 and hanged himself to death at his sister's house in Far Rockaway, Queens, N.Y., on April 9, 1976, at the age of 35.

Still a revered and lamented figure, Phil Ochs's posthumous releases included early 1960s recordings on Smithsonian/Folkways and Archives Alive, Elektra's *There but for Fortune*, A&M's *Chords of Fame* (which compiled his recordings for Elektra and A&M) and *The War Is Over*, and live sets on Rhino and Vanguard.

DISC.: *All the News That's Fit to Sing* (1964); *I Ain't Marching Anymore* (1965); *Phil Ochs Live in Concert* (1966); *Pleasures of the Harbor* (1967); *Tape from California* (1968); *Rehearsals for Retirement* (1969); *"Greatest Hits"* (1970); *Gunfight at Carnegie Hall* (1974); *Songs for Broadside (Broadside #10)* (1976); *Chords of Fame* (1977); *Broadside Tapes #1 (Broadside #14)* (1980); *A Toast to Those Who Are Gone* (rec. prior to 1964; rel. 1989); *There but for Fortune* (1989); *Live at Newport* (rec. 1963–66; rel. 1996).

BIBL.: M. Eliot, *Death of a Rebel* (Garden City, N.Y., 1979, 1989); M. Schumacher, *There but for Fortune: The Life of P. O.* (N.Y., 1996).—**BH**

Ochs, Siegfried, German choral conductor and composer; b. Frankfurt am Main, April 19, 1858; d. Berlin, Feb. 5, 1929. He entered the Berlin Hochschule für Musik (1877), where his mentors were F. Kiel (theory), Joachim (ensemble playing), and Adolf Schulze (choral singing); later continued private studies with Kiel and Barth, and also attended the Univ. In 1882 he organized in Berlin a choral union under his own name, working in close collaboration with the Berlin Phil.; was known as the Phil. Choir from the 1887–88 season until being merged with the chorus of the Berlin Hochschule für Musik (1920), where Ochs served as director of the oratorio dept. He publ. *Der deutsche Gesangverein* (4 vols., Berlin, 1923–28) and *Über die Art, Musik zu Hören* (Berlin, 1926), as well as an autobiography, *Geschehenes, Gesehenes* (Leipzig, 1922). Among his works were a comic opera, *Im Namen des Gesetzes* (Hamburg, Nov. 3, 1888), 2 operettas, song cycles, and choral arrangements of German folk songs.

BIBL.: K. Singer, *S. O.: Der Bergrunder des Philharmonischen Chors* (Berlin, 1933).—**NS/LK/DM**

Ockeghem (Okeghem, Okengheim, Ockenheim, etc.), **Johannes (Jean, Jehan de),** great Flemish composer; b. c. 1410; d. probably in Tours, Feb. 6, 1497. He may have been a pupil of Binchois. He is first listed among the vicaires-chanteurs at Notre Dame in Antwerp on June 24, 1443, and served there until 1444. By 1446 he was in the service of Charles I, Duke of Bourbon, in Moulins, remaining there until at least 1448. By 1452 he was in the service of Charles VII of France as first among the singer-chaplains who were non-priests; by 1454 he was premier chapelain. He subsequently served Louis XI and Charles VIII, and in 1459 the latter made him treasurer of the church of St. Martin-de-Tours. Under Louis XI, he also was a canon at Notre Dame in Paris from 1463 to 1470. He likewise was a chaplain at St. Benoit. In Jan. 1470 he traveled to Spain at the King's expense. In 1484 he journeyed to Bruges and Dammes. Upon his death, Guillaume Cretin wrote a poetic "Deploration," and Josquin Des Prez and Lupi composed musical epitaphs. With his contemporaries Dufay and Josquin, Ockeghem ranks among the foremost masters of the Franco-Flemish style of composition in the second half of the 15th century. Among his settings of the Mass is the earliest extant polyphonic Requiem. The inventiveness displayed in his masses is only excelled in his superb motets. His achievements in the art of imitative counterpoint unquestionably make his music a milestone on the way to the a cappella style of the coming generations. A major ed. of his works is found in D. Plamenac, editor, *J. Ockeghem: Sämtliche Werke*, in the Publikationen Alterer Musik, Jg. I/2 (Leipzig, 1927), which contains eight masses; a second ed., rev., 1959, was publ. as *Masses I-VIII* in *J. Ockeghem: Collected Works*, I (N.Y.); *Masses and Mass Sections IX-XVI* appeared in the same ed. as vol. II (N.Y., 1947; 2nd ed., 1966).

BIBL.: E. Thoinan, *Déploration de Guillaume Crétin sur le trépas de J. O., musicien, premier chaplain du roi de France et trésorier de Saint-Martin de Tours* (Paris, 1864); D. Plamenac, *J. O. als Motetten- und Chansonkomponist* (diss., Univ. of Vienna, 1925); W. Stephan, *Die burgundisch-niederländische Motette zur Zeit Ockeghems* (Kassel, 1937); E. Krenek, *J. O.* (N.Y., 1953); M. Henze, *Studien zu den Messenkompositionen J. O.* (Berlin, 1968); *J. O. en zijn tijd* (Dendermonde, 1970); E. Houghton, *Rhythmic Structure in the Masses and Motets of J. O.* (diss., Univ. of Calif., Berkeley, 1971); M. Picker, *J. O. and Jacob Obrecht: A Guide to Research* (N.Y., 1988); A. Lindmayr, *Quellenstudien zu den Motetten von J. O.* (Laaber, 1990); C. Goldberg, *Die Chansons J. O.s: Ästhetik des musikalischen Raumes* (Laaber, 1992). —**NS/LK/DM**

O'Connell, Charles, American conductor and recording executive; b. Chicopee, Mass., April 22, 1900; d. N.Y., Sept. 1, 1962. He studied at the Catholic School and Coll. of the Holy Cross (B.A., 1922), and also had instruction in organ from Widor in Paris. From 1930 to 1944 he was head of the artist and repertoire dept. of the RCA Victor Red Seal label, then music director of Columbia Masterworks (1944–47). He publ. *The Victor Book of the Symphony* (1934; new ed., 1948), *The Victor Book of the Opera* (1937), *The Other Side of the Record* (1947), and *The Victor Book of Overtures, Tone Poems and Other Orchestral Works* (1950).—**NS/LK/DM**

O'Conor, John, Irish pianist; b. Dublin, Jan. 18, 1947. He was only 3 when he began lessons with his sister; after studies with Sheila Rumbold (1953–57), he attended the Dublin Coll. of Music (1957–68); also pursued his general education at Belvedere Coll., Dublin (graduated, 1965) and studied music at Univ. Coll., Dublin (B.Mus., 1969). His postgraduate studies followed with Dieter Weber at the Vienna Hochschule für Musik (1971–75); also attended master classes given by C. Zecchi at the Salzburg Mozarteum (1967–68), Agosti at the Accademia Musicale Chigiana in Siena (1972), and Kempff in Positano, Italy (1974, 1980). He took first prize in both the Beethoven (1973) and Bösendorfer (1975) competitions in Vienna. On Nov. 12, 1968, he made his formal debut in Dublin. He first played in London at the Wigmore Hall in Feb. 1974. In May 1976 he made his Tokyo debut at the Bunka Kaikan Hall. On Jan. 10, 1983, he made his first appearance in N.Y. at Alice Tully Hall. In 1985 he was awarded an honorary D.Mus. degree from the National Univ. of Ireland and in 1994 he was made a fellow of the Royal Irish Academy of Music. O'Conor is a particularly sensitive and refined interpreter of the Austro-German masters. He has also championed the music of his neglected countryman, John Field.—**NS/LK/DM**

Odak, Krsto, Croatian composer and teacher; b. Siverić, Dalmatia, March 20, 1888; d. Zagreb, Nov. 4, 1965. He studied composition with P. Hartmann in Munich (1912–13) and with Novák in his master class at the Prague Cons. (1919–22). Upon his return to Yugoslavia, he was prof. of composition at the Zagreb Academy of Music, retiring in 1961.

WORKS: DRAMATIC: O p e r a : *Dorica pleše* (Dorica Dances; Zagreb, April 16, 1934); *Majka Margarita* (Mother Margaret), radio opera (Zagreb, March 25, 1955). OTHER: Incidental music; film scores. ORCH.: 2 passacaglias (1938, 1955); 4 syms. (1940, 1951, 1961, 1965); Concertino for Bassoon and Strings (1958). CHAMBER: 4 string quartets (1923, 1927, 1934, 1956); Violin Sonata (1922); Flute Sonata (1946). VOCAL: *Radost* (Gaiety), cantata (1959); masses; motets; songs. —NS/LK/DM

O'Day, Anita (originally, **Colton, Anita Belle**), pop-jazz vocalist; b. Chicago, Ill., Dec. 18, 1919. She was part of the Chicago dance marathons as a teenager. She worked with the Max Miller Band at the Off-Beat Club in Chicago from January 1939, then at the Three Deuces Club with the same band for a year. She joined Gene Krupa in early 1941 for two years. After a brief spell with Woody Herman, O'Day sang with Stan Kenton from 1944–45, and then rejoined Krupa, leaving his band in Hollywood in Spring 1946. She recorded with Benny Goodman, Duke Ellington, Will Bradley, Ralph Burns, Benny Carter, and many others, scoring several hits. She performed mainly as a solo act in late 1940s and 1950s with several long periods of enforced absence from music primarily due to drug addiction. She had a resurgence of activity in the late 1950s, and was featured at Newport Jazz Festival in 1958, and toured Europe with Benny Goodman (1959). During the 1960s, O'Day made many tours of Europe, twice toured Japan, and played club dates throughout the U.S., including a long residency at the Half Note Club, N.Y. in 1969. She did many overseas tours during the 1970s, formed her own label, and also continued to work clubs in the U.S. In 1985 she celebrated her 50th year as a jazz singer at Carnegie Hall. She has appeared in several films, notably *Jazz on a Summer's Day.*

DISC.: *Cool Heat* (1952); *A. O. Sings Jazz* (1952); *A. O. Collates* (1953); *Tea for Two* (1958); *A. O. at Mr. Kelly's* (1958); *Jimmy Giuffre Arrangements* (1959); *Incomparable! A. O.* (1960); *A. O. and the Three Sounds* (1962); *Recorded Live at the Berlin Jazz Festival* (1970); *In Berlin* (1970); *A. O. Live in Tokyo* (1975); *Live at Mingo's* (1976); *A. O. Live* (1976); *Mello Day* (1978); *S'Wonderful (Big Band Concert)* (1985); *At Vine St.: Live* (1991); *Live in Person* (1993).

BIBL.: *A. O.: High Times, Hard Times* (N.Y., 1981; new ed. with updated discography, 1989).—JC/NS/LP

O'Dette, Paul, distinguished American lutenist, conductor, pedagogue, and music scholar; b. Pittsburgh, Feb. 2, 1954. He studied at W.Va. Univ. (1972–73) before pursuing training in Basel at the Schola Cantorum Basiliensis (1973–76). He also took courses at the Musikwissenschaftliches Institut at the Univ. of Basel. In 1974 he launched his career as a lutenist, and his recitals in N.Y., London, Paris, Berlin, Hamburg, Vienna, Munich, Boston, Philadelphia, Los Angeles, San Francisco, Chicago, and other leading cities on both sides of the Atlantic secured his reputation as one of the foremost lute virtuosos of his era. He also made frequent ensemble appearances. In 1976 he became co-director of the Musicians of Swanne Alley, and also joined the faculty of the Eastman School of Music in Rochester, N.Y., where he became assoc. prof. of conducting and ensembles, and where he served as director of early music. From 1993 he likewise was artistic director of the Boston Early Music Festival. He served as a visiting prof. of lute at the Oberlin (Ohio) Coll. Cons. of Music (1977–78), the Akademie für alte Musik in Bremen (1989–95), and the Ind. Univ. School of Music (1995–96), and was artist- in-residence at Washington Univ. (1982) and the Univ. of Calif. at Los Angeles (1989). At the Boston Early Music Festival, he conducted performances of Purcell's *King Arthur* (1995), Rossi's *L'Orfeo* (1997), and Cavalli's *Ercole Amante* (1997). He conducted Rossi's *L'Orfeo* at the Drottningholm Court Theater (1997), Cavalli's *Ercole Amante* at the Utrecht Early Music Festival (1999), and Provenzale's *Stellidaura* at the Vadstena Academy (1999). In 1999 he was a guest conductor of the Portland (Ore.) Baroque Orch. O'Dette's scholarly interests have led him to pursue work on the performance and sources of 17th century Italian and English solo song, continuo practices, and lute technique, and he has contributed articles to books and journals. His remarkable recording of the complete lute music of John Dowland was awarded the Diapason D'or de l'année (1997).—LK/DM

Odington, Walter, English music theorist and scientist who fluorished from 1298 to 1316, known as Walter of Evesham. He was a monk at Evesham, a Benedictine abbey near Worcester; was at Oxford (c. 1316). He was one of the chief medieval writers on mensural notation. His *De speculatione musices* (MS in Corpus Christi Coll., Cambridge) was printed by Coussemaker in 1864 (*Scriptores*, I; modern ed. by F. Hammond, *Walteri Odington Summa de speculatione musicae*, in Corpus Scriptorum de Musica, XIV, 1970). This work is particularly valuable for the light it throws on musical rhythm as practiced in the late 13th century; it also discusses intervals, notation, musical instruments, and musical forms (rondellus, motet, etc.). His views on consonance and dissonance are interesting for their acceptance of thirds and sixths as legitimate consonances. He was also noted as an astronomer. —NS/LK/DM

Odnoposoff, Adolfo, Argentine cellist and teacher, brother of **Ricardo Odnoposoff;** b. Buenos Aires, Feb. 22, 1917; d. Denton, Tex., March 13, 1992. He studied with Alberto Schiuma, then went to Berlin, where he took lessons with Feuermann, and to Paris, where he became a student of Diran Alexanian. He was subsequently active as a concert cellist in Palestine (1936–38), Peru (1938–40), Chile (1940–44), Havana (1944–58), and Mexico City, where he also taught at the Cons. Nacional de Música (1958–64); then was a prof. of cello and chamber music at the Cons. of Music in San Juan, Puerto Rico. In 1975 he became a prof. of cello at

North Tex. State Univ. in Denton. Several Latin American composers (Roque Cordero, Rodolfo Halffter, Eduardo Mata, Floro Ugarte, Antonio Tauriello, and others) wrote special works for him.—**NS/LK/DM**

Odnoposoff, Ricardo, Argentine violinist and teacher, brother of **Adolfo Odnoposoff;** b. Buenos Aires, Feb. 24, 1914. He studied with Aaron Klasse in Buenos Aires (1919–26), Rudolph Deman in Berlin (1927–28), and Carl Flesch at the Berlin Hochschule für Musik (1928–32). A precocious musician, he played in public as an infant. He was a soloist with the Berlin Phil. at 17, winning first prize at the Vienna (1932) and Ysaÿe (1937) competitions. He evolved a brilliant career as a concert violinist, appearing in all parts of the world. He taught at the Vienna (1956), Stuttgart (from 1964), and Zürich (1975–84) Hochschules für Musik.—**NS/LK/DM**

Odo de Cluny, composer; b. in the Maine, 878 or 879; d. Tours, Nov. 18, 942. A pupil of Remy d'Auxerre in Paris, he took Holy Orders at 19, and in 899 was canon and choir singer at Tours. In 909 he entered the Benedictine monastery at Baume, near Besançon, and then was successively abbot at Aurillac, Fleuri, and (from 927) Cluny. The famous treatise *Dialogus de musica* (also known as *Enchiridion musices*) is attributed to him without foundation (it is printed in Gerbert's *Scriptores* and, in Eng. tr., in O. Strunk's *Source Readings in Music History*, N.Y., 1950). It is most likely of north Italian origin. In the development of pitch notation through letter-names, the treatise was the first to give a complete series (2 octaves and a fifth) of letter-names (G, A, B, C, D, E, F, G, etc.) corresponding to our modern series; but whereas we change from capital to lower-case letters at c to designate the pitches of the second octave, in its system the change was made at a. The treatise was also the first to add the sign gamma (Greek "G") to designate the note corresponding to G on the first line of our bass clef. It distinguished between b flat and b natural (b *rotundum* and b *quadratum*), but only at one point in the gamut, namely, the note lying one degree below middle C in our system. Odo's only extant compositions are three hymns and 12 antiphons.

BIBL.: T. Nisard, *St.-O. d.C.* (Paris, 1866).—**NS/LK/DM**

Oehl, Kurt (Helmut), eminent German musicologist; b. Mainz, Feb. 24, 1923. He was educated at the Mainz Cons. and at the Johannes Gutenberg Univ. in Mainz, obtaining his Ph.D. (1952) with the diss. *Beitrage zur Geschichte der deutschen Mozart-Übersetzungen.* After working as a dramaturg (1952–60), he became a member of the editorial staff of the *Riemann Musiklexikon* in 1960. In this capacity, he helped to prepare the vol. on musical terms and historical subjects (*Sachteil*) for the 12th ed. (Mainz, 1967); also served as a biographical ed. for the *Supplement* (2 vols., Mainz, 1972, 1975). He then became an ed. for the *Brockhaus-Riemann Musiklexikon* (2 vols., Mainz, 1978–79; supplements, 1989 and 1995). From 1973 to 1987 he also was on the faculty of the Johannes Gutenberg Univ. With K. Pfarr, he publ. *Musikliteratur im Überblick: Eine Anleitung zum Nachschlagen* (Mainz, 1988).—**NS/LK/DM**

Oelze, Christiane, German soprano; b. Cologne, Oct. 9, 1963. She studied in Cologne and received vocal instruction from Schwarzkopf. After winning the Hugo Wolf Competition in 1987, she appeared as a concert artist. In 1990 she made her operatic debut in Ottawa as Despina. She sang Constanze in Salzburg and Anne Trulove at the Glyndebourne Festival in 1991, and in 1993 she appeared in London. In 1994 she made her U.S. debut with the Atlanta Sym. Orch. She sang Zerlina at London's Covent Garden in 1996, and in 1997 she returned to Salzburg as Mitridate. In 1999 she appeared as Mélisande at the Glyndebourne Festival. She has pursued a highly successful career as a soloist with the world's major orchs. and as a lieder artist. Among her other operatic roles are Pamina, Marzelline, Zdenka in *Arabella,* and Regina in *Mather der Maler.*—**NS/LK/DM**

Oestvig, Karl (Aagaard), Norwegian tenor; b. Christiania, May 17, 1889; d. there (Oslo), July 21, 1968. He studied in Cologne. He made his operatic debut at the Stuttgart Opera in 1914, remaining on its roster until 1919. He was then a member of the Vienna State Opera (1919–27), where he created the role of the Emperor in Strauss's *Die Frau ohne Schatten* in 1919; also sang at the Berlin State Opera (until 1926) and the Städtische Opera (1927–30), and made concert tours of Europe and North America. He retired from the stage in 1932 and devoted himself to teaching; accepted the post of director of the Oslo Opera (1941) during the Nazi occupation of Norway, an action which brought him disgrace after the liberation. He was married to the soprano Maria Rajdl. Among his finest roles were Walther von Stolzing, Lohengrin, and Parsifal.—**NS/LK/DM**

Offenbach, Jacques (actually, **Jacob**), famous French composer of German descent; b. Cologne, June 20, 1819; d. Paris, Oct. 5, 1880. He was the son of a Jewish cantor, whose original surname was Eberst; Offenbach was the town where his father lived. He studied violin before taking up the cello when he was 9. After training with Joseph Alexander and Bernhard Breuer in Cologne, he settled in Paris (1833). Following cello studies with Vaslin at the Cons. (1833–34), he played in the orch. of the Opéra-Comique; also received further instruction from Louis Norblin and Halévy. He then pursued a career as a soloist and chamber music artist (from 1838); subsequently was a conductor at the Théâtre-Français (1850–55). His *Chanson de Fortunio* for Musset's *Chandelier* (1850) proved tremendously popular. In 1855 he ventured to open his own theater, the Bouffes-Parisiens, at the Salle Marigny; late that year it moved to the Salle Choiseul, where he scored his first great success with the operetta *Orphée aux enfers* (Oct. 21, 1858). His *La Belle Hélène* (Variétés, Dec. 17, 1864) proved to be one of his most celebrated works, soon taken up by theatrical enterprises all over the world. Having abandoned the management of the Bouffes-Parisiens in 1866, he nevertheless continued to write for the stage. His *La Vie parisienne* (Palais Royal, Oct. 31, 1866), *La Grande-Duchesse de Gérolstein* (Variétés, April 12, 1867), and *La Périchole* (Variétés, Oct. 6, 1868) were notably successful. In 1873 he took over the management of the Théâtre de la Gaîté, where he brought out his rev. version of *Orphée aux enfers* as an opéra-féerique (Feb. 7, 1874). In 1876 he undertook a tour of the U.S., describing his impressions in *Notes d'un musicien en voyage* (Paris, 1877) and *Offenbach en Amérique* (Paris, 1877; Eng. tr., 1877, as *Offenbach in America*; republ. as *Orpheus in America*, Bloomington, Ind., 1957). His only grand opera, the masterpiece *Les Contes d'Hoffmann*, remained unfinished at his death; recitatives were added by E. Guiraud with the famous barcarolle from Offenbach's *Die Rheinnixen* (1864), in which the tune was used for a ghost song; the completed score was premiered at the Opéra-Comique in Paris (Feb. 10, 1881) with instantaneous success, and subsequently was performed on both sides of the Atlantic. Offenbach was a master of the operetta; his music is characterized by an abundance of flowing, rollicking melodies, seasoned with ironic humor, suitable to the extravagant burlesque of the situations. His irreverent treatment of mythological characters gave Paris society a salutary shock; his art mirrored the atmosphere of precarious gaiety during the second Empire.

WORKS: DRAMATIC (all first perf. in Paris unless otherwise given): *L'Alcôve* (April 24, 1847); *Le Trésor à Mathurin* (May 1853; rev. as *Le Mariage aux lanternes*, Oct. 10, 1857); *Pépito* (Oct. 28, 1853); *Luc et Lucette* (May 2, 1854); *Oyayaie, ou La Reine des îles* (June 26, 1855); *Entrez, messieurs, mesdames* (July 5, 1855); *Les Deux Aveugles* (July 5, 1855); *Une Nuit blanche* (July 5, 1855); *Le Rêve d'une nuit d'été* (July 30, 1855); *Le Violoneux* (Aug. 31, 1855); *Madame Papillon* (Oct. 3, 1855); *Paimpol et Périnette* (Oct. 29, 1855); *Ba-ta-clan* (Dec. 29, 1855); *Élodie, ou Le Forfait nocturne* (Jan. 19, 1856); *Le Postillon en gage* (Feb. 9, 1856); *Trombalcazar, ou Les Criminels dramatiques* (April 3, 1856); *La Rose de Saint-Flour* (June 12, 1856); *Les Dragées du baptême* (June 18, 1856); *Le "66"* (July 31, 1856); *Le Savetier et le financier* (Sept. 23, 1856); *La Bonne d'enfants* (Oct. 14, 1856); *Les Trois Baisers du diable* (Jan. 15, 1857); *Croquefer, ou Le Dernier des paladins* (Feb. 12, 1857); *Dragonette* (April 30, 1857); *Vent du soir, ou L'Horrible Festin* (May 16, 1857); *Une Demoiselle en lôterie* (July 27, 1857); *Les Deux Pêcheurs* (Nov. 13, 1857); *Mesdames de la Halle* (March 3, 1858); *La Chatte métamorphosée en femme* (April 19, 1858); *Orphée aux enfers* (Oct. 21, 1858; rev. version, Feb. 7, 1874); *Un Mari à la porte* (June 22, 1859); *Les Vivandières de la grande armée* (July 6, 1859); *Geneviève de Brabant* (Nov. 19, 1859; rev. version, Dec. 26, 1867; 2nd rev. version, Feb. 25, 1875); *Le Carnaval des revues* (Feb. 10, 1860); *Daphnis et Chloé* (March 27, 1860); *Barkouf* (Dec. 24, 1860); *La Chanson de Fortunio* (Jan. 5, 1861); *Le Pont des soupirs* (March 23, 1861; rev. version, May 8, 1868); *M. Choufleuri restera chez lui le ...* (May 31, 1861); *Apothicaire et perruquier* (Oct. 17, 1861); *Le Roman comique* (Dec. 10, 1861); *Monsieur et Madame Denis* (Jan. 11, 1862); *Le Voyage de MM. Dunanan père et fils* (March 23, 1862); *Les Bavards or Bavard et bavarde* (Bad Ems, June 11, 1862); *Jacqueline* (Oct. 14, 1862); *Il Signor Fagotto* (Bad Ems, July 11, 1863); *Lischen et Fritzchen* (Bad Ems, July 21, 1863); *L'Amour chanteur* (Jan. 5, 1864); *Die Rheinnixen* (Vienna, Feb. 4, 1864); *Les Géorgiennes* (March 16, 1864); *Jeanne qui pleure et Jean qui rit* (Bad Ems, July 1864); *Le Fifre enchanté, ou Le Soldat magicien* (Bad Ems, July 9, 1864); *La Belle Hélène* (Dec. 17, 1864); *Coscoletto, ou Le Lazzarone* (Bad Ems, July 24, 1865); *Les Refrains des bouffes* (Sept. 21, 1865); *Les Bergers* (Dec. 11, 1865); *Barbe-bleue* (Feb. 5, 1866); *La Vie parisienne* (Oct. 31, 1866); *La Grande-Duchesse de Gérolstein* (April 12, 1867); *La Permission de dix heures* (Bad Ems, July 9, 1867); *La Leçon de chant* (Bad Ems, Aug. 1867); *Robinson Crusoé* (Nov. 23, 1867); *Le Chateau à Toto* (May 6, 1868); *L'Île de Tulipatan* (Sept. 30, 1868); *La Périchole* (Oct. 6, 1868; rev. version, April 25,

1874); *Vert-vert* (March 10, 1869); *La Diva* (March 22, 1869); *La Princesse de Trébizonde* (Baden-Baden, July 31, 1869; rev. version, Paris, Dec. 7, 1869); *Les Brigands* (Dec. 10, 1869); *La Romance de la rose* (Dec. 11, 1869); *Mam'zelle Moucheron* (c. 1870; rev. version by Delibes, May 10, 1881); *Boule de neige* (Dec. 14, 1871; rev. version of *Barkouf*); *Le Roi Carotte* (Jan. 15, 1872); *Fantasio* (Jan. 18, 1872); *Fleurette, oder Näherin und Trompeter* (Vienna, March 8, 1872); *Der schwarze Korsar* (Vienna, Sept. 21, 1872); *Les Braconniers* (Jan. 29, 1873); *Pomme d'api* (Sept. 4, 1873); *La Jolie Parfumeuse* (Nov. 29, 1873); *Bagatelle* (May 21, 1874); *Madame l'archiduc* (Oct. 31, 1874); *Whittington* (London, Dec. 26, 1874); *Les Hannetons* (April 22, 1875); *La Boulangère à des écus* (Oct. 19, 1875); *Le Créole* (Nov. 3, 1875); *Le Voyage dans la lune* (Nov. 26, 1875); *Tarte à la crème* (Dec. 14, 1875); *Pierrette et Jacquot* (Oct. 13, 1876); *La Boîte au lait* (Nov. 3, 1876); *Le Docteur Ox* (Jan. 26, 1877); *La Foire Saint-Laurent* (Feb. 10, 1877); *Maître Péronilla* (March 13, 1878); *Madame Favart* (Dec. 28, 1878); *La Marocaine* (Jan. 13, 1879); *La Fille du tambour-major* (Dec. 13, 1879); *Belle Lurette* (Oct. 30, 1880; completed by Delibes); *Les Contes d'Hoffmann* (Feb. 10, 1881; completed by Guiraud). **Vaudevilles and Incidental Music:** *Pascal et Chambord* (March 2, 1839); *Le Brésilien* (May 9, 1863); *Le Gascon* (Sept. 2, 1873); *La Haine* (Dec. 3, 1874). **Ballet:** *Arlequin barbier* (July 5, 1855); *Pierrot clown* (July 30, 1855); *Polichinelle dans le monde* (Sept. 19, 1855); *Les Bergers de Watteau* (June 24, 1856); *Le Papillon* (Nov. 26, 1860); much other dance music. **OTHER:** Various works for Cello, including *Prière et Boléro* for Cello and Orch. (1840); *Musette, Air de ballet du 17me siècle* for Cello and Orch. (1843); *Hommage à Rossini* for Cello and Orch. (1843); *Concerto militaire* (1848); *Concerto Rondo* (c. 1850; discovered by A. de Almeida in 1983); *Concertino* (1851); many pieces for Cello and Piano; several works for Solo Cello; pedagogical pieces; songs; etc.

BIBL.: E. de Mirecourt, *Les Contemporains: Auber, O.* (Paris, 1869); Argus, *Célébrités dramatiques: J. O.* (Paris, 1872); A. Martinet, *O.: Sa vie et son oeuvre* (Paris, 1887); P. Bekker, *J. O.* (Berlin, 1909); R. Northcott, *J. O.: A Sketch of His Life and a Record of His Operas* (London, 1917); E. Rieger, *O. und seine Wiener Schule* (Vienna, 1920); L. Schneider, *O.* (Paris, 1923); R. Brancour, *O.* (Paris, 1929); A. Henseler, *Jakob O.* (Berlin, 1930); H. Kristeller, *Der Aufstieg des Kölners J. O.: Ein Musikerleben in Bildern* (Berlin, 1931); S. Kracauer, *J. O. und das Paris seiner Zeit* (Amsterdam, 1937; 2nd ed., 1962; Eng. tr., 1937); S. Sitwell, *La Vie Parisienne: A Tribute to O.* (London, 1937); J. Brindejont-Offenbach, *O., mon grand-père* (Paris, 1940); A. Decaux, *O., roi du Second Empire* (Paris, 1958; 3rd ed., 1975); A. Silbermann, *Das imaginäre Tagebuch des Herrn J. O.* (Berlin, 1960); O. Schneidereit, *J. O.* (Leipzig, 1966); P. Jacob, *J. O. in selbstzeugnissen und Bilddokumenten* (Hamburg, 1969); R. Pourvoyeur, *J. O.: Essay in Toengepaste Muziek-en Toneelsociologie* (Brussels, 1977); A. Faris, *J. O.* (London, 1980); P. Gammond, *O.: His Life and Times* (Tunbridge Wells, 1980; 2nd ed., rev., 1986); J. Harding et al., *O., 1819–1880: A Tribute* (London, 1980); R. Pourvoyeur, *O.: Idillio e Parodia* (Turin, 1980); T. Groepper, *Aspekte der O.iade: Untersuchungen zu den Libretti der grossen Operetten O.s* (Frankfurt am Main and N.Y., 1990); C. Dufresne, *J. O., ou, La gaîté parisienne* (Paris, 1992); R. Pourvoyeur, *O.* (Paris, 1994); A. Jacobshagen, ed., *J. O., Les Contes d'Hoffmann: Dossier de presse parisienne (1881)* (Bietigheim, 1995); C. Dufresne, *O., our, La joie de vivre* (Paris, 1998); J. Kaufman, *Isaac Offenbach und sein Sohn J. oder "Es ist nicht alle Tage Purim"* (Tübingen, 1998); P. Hawig, *J. O.: Facetten zu Leben und Werk* (Cologne, 1999).—NS/LK/DM

Ogden, Will (actually, **Wilbur Lee**), American composer and teacher; b. Redlands, Calif., April 19,

1921. He studied at the Univ. of Wisc. in Madison (B.M., 1942) and at Hamline Univ. in St. Paul, Minn. (M.A., 1947). After graduate studies at the Univ. of Calif. at Berkeley (1949–50) and at Ind. Univ. in Bloomington (1950–52), he went to Paris on a Fulbright grant and attended the École Normale de Musique (1952–53). Returning to the U.S., he obtained his Ph.D. in 1955 from Ind. Univ. with the diss. *Series and Structure: An Investigation into the Purpose of the Twelve-Note Row in Selected Works of Schoenberg, Webern, Krenek, and Leibowitz*; his teachers in the U.S. included Krenek, Sessions, Bukofzer, Apel, and P. Nettl, and in Paris, Leibowitz. He taught at the Univ. of Tex. in Austin (1947–50), at St. Catherine Coll. in St. Paul, Minn. (1954–55), and at Ill. Wesleyan Univ. in Bloomington (1956–65). Ogden then became a prof. at the Univ. of Calif. at San Diego (1966), where he served as founder-chairman of its music dept. (1966–71). He retired in 1991. His compositions display an effective utilization of serial procedures.

WORKS: CHAMBER Opera: *The Awakening of Sappho* (1976–80). ORCH.: *Movements for Dance* for Chamber Orch. (1948); *Diversions* for Wind Band (1964); *5 Comments and Capriccio* (1979); *5 Preludes* for Violin and Chamber Orch. (1985). CHAMBER: String Quartet (1947); *3 Trifles* for Cello and Piano (1958); *Palindrome and Variations* for String Quartet (1961–62); *6 Small Trios* for Marimba with Suspended Cymbal, Trumpet, and Piano (1982); 2 serenades for Wind Quintet (1986–87; 1991–94); *7 Pieces and a Capriccio* for Violin and Piano (1988–89); *13 Expressions* for Solo Violin with Oboe, Clarinet, Viola, Cello, and Piano (1993); *15 Variants* for Clarinet and Strings (1994); *Variation Suite* for Violin and Viola (1995–96); String Quartet in 3, 4, or 5 Movements (1996–99); *5 Episodes and 9 Variants* for Flute, Clarinet, and Strings (1997–98); *3 Times 3 Small Trios* for 2 Violins and Piano (1998); Violin Suite (1998). VOCAL: *3 Statements* for Chorus (1955); *3 Sea Choruses* (1959, 1960, 1976); *Orpheus Song* for Chorus (1963); *Un Tombeau de Jean Cocteau I* for Soprano and Piano (1972), *Un Tombeau II* for Soprano and Chamber Instruments (1972), and *Un Tombeau III* for Soprano, Clarinet or Oboe, Actor, Piano, Slides, and Tape (1976–77); *By the Isar* for Soprano, Alto Flute, and Double Bass (1969); *Winter Images* (1982) and *Summer Images* for Soprano, Flute, Clarinet, Trumpet, and Piano; *2 Sea Chanteys* for Soprano, Baritone, and 2 Percussionists (1987–88); *4 Chamber Songs* for Soprano, Flute, Oboe, Clarinet, Harp, Viola, and Cello (1989); songs.—NS/LK/DM

Ogdon, John (Andrew Howard), remarkable English pianist; b. Manchester, Jan. 27, 1937; d. London, Aug. 1, 1989. He studied with Iso Elinson at the Royal Manchester Coll. of Music (1945), and then pursued training with Denis Matthews, Egon Petri, and Ilona Kabos. He began his career while still a student, premiering works by Goehr and Maxwell Davies; made his London debut as soloist in the Busoni Piano Concerto (1958). After winning joint first prize (with Ashkenazy) at the Tchaikovsky Competition in Moscow (1962), he pursued a far-flung international career. He also taught at the Ind. Univ. School of Music in Bloomington (1976–80). His extraordinary talent and success were marred by the tragedy of his life, acute schizophrenia. His father, Howard Ogdon, who also had the disease, described his misfortunes in *Kingdom of the Lost*. His wife also wrote a book, *Virtuoso: The Story of John Ogdon* (London, 1981), in which she described in detail Og-

don's suffering. Physically he presented a picture of astute well-being, being large of body, powerful of manual dexterity, and sporting a spectacular triangular beard. Despite numerous stays in sanatoriums, electric shock and drug treatment, and suicide attempts, he continued to appear as a concert artist. He maintained a vast repertory. His death at the age of 52 was mourned by a multitude of friends and admirers.—NS/LK/DM

Ogihara, Toshitsugu, Japanese composer; b. Osaka, June 6, 1910; d. Odawara, June 14, 1992. He studied composition with Matsudaira at Nihon Univ., and took private lessons with A. Tcherepnin during the latter's stay in Japan. His music follows the classical models.

WORKS: DRAMATIC: Ballet: *Springtime* (1973). ORCH.: *2 Movements* for Percussion and Orch. (1942); *Sôshun no Hiroba*, symphonic poem (1955); Sym. No. 1 (1958); *Rhapsody* (1960); 2 violin concertos (1962, 1963); Violin Concertino (1962); *Capriccio* for Strings (1964); *4 Pieces* for Horn and Strings (1972); *Fancy Parade* (1983). CHAMBER: 4 string quartets (1940, 1949, 1953, 1969); 2 string trios (1947, 1961); Violin Sonata (1959); Concerto for Clarinet and String Quartet (1955); *Capriccio* for Woodwinds and Strings (1958); Trio for Clarinet, Cello, and Piano (1962); English Horn Sonata (1962); Quartet for 4 Flutes (1963); Trio for Flute, Violin, and Piano (1965); Piano Quintet (1970); *Serenade* for Cello, Violin, and Clarinet (1972); *4 Pieces* for Tuba, 3 Tenor Trombones, and Bass Trombone (1972); *2 Suites* for Flute and Piano (1974); *Duet No. 1* for Violin and Piano (1983); *Suite* for Flute and Piano (1984); piano pieces, including a *Fantasia* (1984). VOCAL: *7 Poems* for Soprano, Violin, Cello, and Piano (1971); other songs.—NS/LK/DM

Oginski, Prince Michal Kleofas, Polish composer; b. Guzow, near Warsaw, Sept. 25, 1765; d. Florence, Oct. 15, 1833. He was a Polish nobleman of a musical family; his uncle, Michal Kazimierz Oginski (b. Warsaw, 1728; d. there, May 31, 1800), was an amateur composer of some talent. He studied violin and piano with Jozef Kozlowski in Guzow (1773–78), and later with Viotti (1798) and Baillot (1810). He was active as a diplomat; he left Poland after its partition, and agitated in Turkey and France for the Polish cause. In 1799 he wrote an opera, *Zélis et Valcour ou Bonaparte au Caire*, to ingratiate himself with Napoleon. Of historical interest are his polonaises, many of which were publ.; the one in A minor, known as *Death Polonaise*, became extremely popular. He also wrote mazurkas and waltzes for Piano, and a patriotic Polish march (1825). His son, Franciszek Krawery Oginski (1801–37), was also a composer who wrote piano pieces and songs.—NS/LK/DM

Ogura, Roh, Japanese composer and teacher; b. Kitakyūshu, Jan. 19, 1916; d. Kamakura, Aug. 26, 1990. He studied with Fukai, Sugawara, and Ikenouchi, and then engaged in teaching.

WORKS: DRAMATIC: Opera: *Neta* (1957). ORCH.: 3 syms. (1941; Tokyo, April 25, 1951; 1968); Piano Concerto (Tokyo, March 24, 1946); *5 Movements on Japanese Folk Songs* (1957); Violin Concerto (1971); Cello Concerto (1980). CHAMBER: 3 string quartets (1941, 1946, 1954); Violin Sonata (1950); Violin Sonatina (1960); *Divertimento* for 7 (1964) and

8 (1972) Winds; piano music. VOCAL: *Orly—A Bugbear at Sea* for Narrator and Orch. (1963); choruses; songs.—NS/LK/DM

Ohana, Maurice, French composer and pianist; b. Casablanca (of Spanish parents), June 12, 1914; d. Paris, Nov. 13, 1992. He studied piano with Frank Marshall in Barcelona and with Lazare Lévy at the Paris Cons., and also had lessons in counterpoint with Daniel-Lesur at the Schola Cantorum in Paris (1937–40). Following service in the British Army during World War II, he completed his training with Casella at Rome's Accademia di Santa Cecilia (1944–46), then settled in Paris. In 1981 he was made a Commandeur des Arts et Lettres. He won the Prix National de Musique (1975) and the Honegger (1982) and Ravel (1985) prizes.

WORKS: DRAMATIC: O p e r a : *Syllabaire pour Phèdre* (1967; Paris, Feb. 5, 1968); *Autodafé* (Lyons, May 23, 1972); *Trois contes de l'Honorable Fleur* (Avignon, July 16, 1978); *La Célestine* (1982–86; Paris, June 13, 1988). **R a d i o p h o n i c S c o r e s :** *Les Hommes et les autres* (1955); *Histoire véridique de Jacotin* (1961); *Hélène* (1963); *Les Héraclides* (1964); *Iphigénie en Tauride* (1965); *Hippolyte* (1965–66). **O t h e r :** Film music. **ORCH.:** *Trois graphiques,* concerto for Guitar and Orch. (1950–57; BBC, London, Feb. 1961); *Synaxis* for 2 Pianos, 4 Percussionists, and Orch. (1965–66); *Chiffres de clavecin* for Harpsichord and Chamber Orch. (1967–68); *Silenciaire* for 6 Percussion and Strings (1969); *T'harân-Ngô* (Paris, Oct. 1974); *Anneau du Tamarit* for Cello and Orch. (1976); *Livre des Prodiges* (Lyons, Oct. 4, 1979); *Crypt* for Strings (1980); Piano Concerto (1980–81); Cello Concerto No. 2 (1988–89; Tokyo, May 13, 1991). **CHAMBER:** *Tiento* for Guitar (1955); *Quatre improvisations* for Flute (1961); *Cinq séquences* for String Quartet (1963); *Signes* for Flute, 2 Guitars, Piano, and 4 Percussion (1965); *Syrtes* for Cello and Piano (1970); *Sacral d'Ilx* for Harpsichord, Oboe, and Horn (1975); *Satyre* for 2 Flutes (1976); String Quartet No. 2 (1980) and No. 3 (1990); *Kypris* for 4 Instruments (1985); piano pieces; harpsichord music. **VOCAL:** *Llanto por Ignacio Sanchez Mejias* for Baritone, Reciter, Women's Voices, and Instrumental Ensemble (Paris, May 22, 1950); *Cantigas* for Soprano, Mezzosoprano, Chorus, and Instrumental Ensemble (1953); *Récit de l'ano zéro,* scenic oratorio (1958–59); *Tombeau de Claude Debussy* for Soprano, Guitar, Piano, and Chamber Orch. (1962; Paris, Jan. 8, 1964); *Cris* for 12 Voices (1968); *Stream* for Bass and String Trio (1970); *Office des oracles* for 3 Vocal Groups and Instruments (Ste. Baume, Aug. 9, 1974); *Lys de Madrigaux* for Women's Chorus and Instrumental Ensemble (Paris, June 1, 1976); *Messe* for Soprano, Mezzo-soprano, Chorus, and Instrumental Ensemble (Avignon, July 30, 1977); *Lux Noctis—Die Solis* for 4 Choral Groups and 2 Organs (1981–88; Paris, Dec. 9, 1988); *Swan Songs* for 12 Voices (1988); *Tombeau de Louise Labbé* for 12 Voices (1988–90); *Nuit de Pouchine* for 12 Voices, Solo Man's Voice, and Viola da Gamba or Cello (Leningrad, Nov. 16, 1990); *Avoaha* for Chorus, Percussion, and 2 Pianos (1991; Aix-les-Bains, Feb. 14, 1992). **BIBL.:** N. Quist, *M. O.* (diss., Univ. of Heidelberg, 1973). —NS/LK/DM

O'Hara, Betty, multi–instrumentalist; d. April 18, 2000. She played in a Hartford, Conn., big band and for the Hartford Symphony in the 1950s. She moved to Calif. in 1960, married bass trombonist Barrett O'Hara, and during the 1980s, performed numerous studio sessions for TV and film on trumpet and euphonium. She toured Japan and Brazil, and performed in the bands of Dizzy Gillespie, Bud Freeman and Tommy Newsom. O'Hara played trombone, cornet and euphonium, arranged, and sang with the West Coast all-female big band, Maiden Voyage. She also co-led a female jazz quintet, Jazz Birds, and appeared frequently as a featured soloist at U.S. festivals.

DISC.: *Horns Aplenty* (1985).—NAL

O'Hara, Geoffrey, Canadian-born American composer; b. Chatham, Ontario, Feb. 2, 1882; d. St. Petersburg, Fla., Jan. 31, 1967. He settled in the U.S. in 1904 and became a naturalized American citizen in 1919. He studied with Homer Norris and J. Vogler; then acted in vaudeville as a pianist, singer, and composer; wrote the song *Your Eyes Have Told Me* for Caruso. In 1913 he was appointed an instructor in American Indian music as part of a program of the Dept. of the Interior; in 1917, became an army song leader; was instructor in community singing at Teachers Coll., Columbia Univ. (1936–37). He wrote the operettas *Peggy and the Pirate* (1927), *Riding Down the Sky* (1928), *The Count and the Co-ed* (1929), and *The Smiling Six-pence* (1930); also about 300 songs, of which the following were extremely popular: *K-K-K-Katy, I Love a Little Cottage, The Living God, I Walked Today Where Jesus Walked,* and *Give a Man a Horse He Can Ride.* —NS/LK/DM

Ohio Players, pioneering mid-1970s funk band. **MEMBERSHIP:** Leroy "Sugar" Bonner, gtr., voc.; James "Diamond" Williams, drm., perc. (b. Brooklyn, N.Y.); Marvin Pierce, trpt.; Billy Beck, kybd.; Clarence "Satch" Satchell, sax. (d. Dayton, Ohio, Dec. 30, 1995); Marshall "Rock" Jones, bs. (Natchitoches, La., Oct. 4, 1942; d. St. Louis, Mo., Aug. 18, 1984); Ralph "Pee Wee" Middlebrooks, trmb., trpt., Walter "Junie" Morrison, kybd.; Greg Webster, drm., Clarence "Chet" Willis, gtr., voc.; Robert "Kuumba" Jones, perc.; Darwin Dortch, bs., voc.

The group began its life in the early 1960s as the Ohio Untouchables, eventually by fusing midwestern soul, rocking southern funk, and jazzy horns, they helped pioneer the self-contained funk band. The Untouchable's biggest moment came after they were signed to Lupine Records (Ward was related to one of the company's principles). In addition to cutting their own (largely ignored) sides, they backed the Falcons (featuring a very young Wilson Pickett on lead vocals) on the 1962 Top Ten R&B hit "I Found a Love." However, in 1964, Ward went solo, and the rest of the group—bassist Marshall "Rock" Jones, Clarence Satchell on saxophone, and guitarist and trumpeter Ralph Middlebrook—returned to Dayton to regroup. They added singing guitarist Leroy "Sugarfoot" Bonner, a new drummer, and a sax player, and went through a series of lead singers, including pianist Dutch Robinson and Bobby Lee Frears. By 1967, calling themselves the Ohio Players, they became the house band for Compass Records in N.Y. They had their first minor hit that year, "Trespassin'," which reached the R&B Top 50. By 1972, however, Compass had begun to fade, Frears and Robinson left, and the group again retreated to Dayton.

At this time, Sugarfoot Bonner took over lead vocals. While not a classic soul vocalist, his eccentric sound helped give the group a distinguishing presence. With the addition of keyboardist Walter "Junie" Morrision, and a couple of more horns, the group recorded the single "Pain" for a local label. Emerging Midwest funk powerhouse Westbound records, which also released records by Funkadelic, picked the single up. The West-bound version of the single "Pain" climbed to Top 40 R&B. This set the stage for the group's first stab at the Top 40, a novelty song called "Funky Worm," from the *Pleasure* album. This single topped the R&B charts, hit #15 pop, and went gold. The Players followed this with the title track from the *Ecstacy* album, which went to #31 pop. Morrison left the band, landing with label mates Funkadelic.

Flush with this success, the Players signed with major label Mercury in 1974 to take their music to the next step commercially. Jim Williams joined the band on drums and vocals and Billy Beck replaced Morrison on keyboards and vocals. Together, they added a sweet, high counterpoint to Bonner's playfully nasal voice. With their distinctive sound and look—including Bonner's drooping moustache and giant afro and Marshall's turban—they were ripe to hit. With their Mercury debut, *Skin Tight*, they did. Led by the gold, #13 pop title track along with the #6 R&B hit "Jive Turkey," a jazzy workout for the horns, and the syrupy ballad "Heaven Must Be Like This," the album went gold and hit #11.

This set the stage for the band's 1975 epochal album, *Fire*. The title track, a throw-down piece of funk propelled by Jones and Williams's lock groove and Bonner's chopped chords, bluesy lead break, and distinctive vocals, topped the pop and R&B charts, going gold. It took the album to the top of the LP charts. The group started headlining tours and playing on various TV shows. That same year, they followed *Fire* with *Honey*. The ballad "Sweet Sticky Thing" topped the R&B charts, hitting #33 pop. The funky "Fopp" went to #30 pop. But the big hit off the album was "Love Rollercoaster." With Bonner's trebly repeating chords, distinctive voice, and a controversy about a scream toward the end of the song (rumors spread that it was the sound of a woman being murdered), the tune topped the pop and R&B charts, going gold. It helped propel *Honey* to gold and #2 on the album charts. Capitalizing on the group's newfound success, Westbound put out *Rattlesnake*, an album of outtakes from the band's early years.

The year 1975 was the apex of the Ohio Players, both commercially and creatively. Their next album, *Contra-diction*, featured the #1 R&B hit "Who'd She Coo?" (#18 pop), but lacked the immediacy and fire of the previous two albums. The album rose to #12 and went gold. They followed this just a few months later with the *Ohio Players Gold* compilation, which also went gold and hit #31. From this point forward, the quality of their work began to decline. They recorded the soundtrack for the blaxploitation film *Mr. Mean* and in 1977 released the album *Angel* with the #9 R&B hit, "O-H-I-O," an extension of the chant they used to end their live show. By 1979, they had split into two groups, one retaining the Ohio Players' name, the other going by the name Shadow. By the mid-1980s, both bands

sank without a trace. Bonner released a solo album in 1975 and also did session work, lending his distinctive vocals to projects by Herbie Hancock and fellow Ohio funkster Roger Troutman. The Players reunited for a 1988 album, *Back*, but the fire had gone. They continued recording and playing on and off into the new millennium.

DISC.: *Observations in Time* (1968); *Pain* (1972); *Pleasure* (1973); *Ecstacy* (1973); *Climax* (1974); *Pain + Pleasure = Ecstacy* (1974); *Skin Tight* (1974); *Rattlesnake* (1975); *Fire* (1975); *Honey* (1975); *Ohio Players Gold* (1976); *Contradiction* (1976); *Angel* (1977); *Mr. Mean* (1977); *Jass-Ay-La-Dee* (1978); *Everybody Up* (1979); *Tenderness* (1981); *Ouch* (1982); *Graduation Century* (1984); *O-H-I-O* (1989); *Lonely Street* (1995); *Jam* (1996).—**HB**

Ohlsson, Garrick (Olof), talented American pianist; b. Bronxville, N.Y., April 3, 1948. At the age of 8, he became a pupil of Thomas Lishman at the Westchester (N.Y.) Cons. He entered the preparatory division of the Juilliard School of Music in N.Y. in 1961 as a student of Sascha Gorodnitzki and later of Rosina Lhévinne (B.Mus., 1971); also studied privately with Olga Barabini and Irma Wolpe. He won the Busoni (1966) and Montreal (1968) competitions; then made his N.Y. recital debut on Jan. 5, 1970; later that year he gained international recognition when he became the first American pianist to win the prestigious quinquennial Chopin Competition in Warsaw. A Polish writer described Ohlsson as a "bear-butterfly" for his ability to traverse the entire spectrum of 18 dynamic degrees discernible on the modern piano, from the thundering fortississimo to the finest pianississimo, with reference also to his height (6 foot, 4 inches), weight (225 lbs.), and stretch of hands (an octave and a fifth in the left hand and an octave and a fourth in the right hand). Thereafter, Ohlsson pursued a distinguished global career. In 1994 he was awarded the Avery Fisher Prize. His interpretations are marked by a distinctive Americanism, technically flawless and free of Romantic mannerisms.—**NS/LK/DM**

Ohms, Elisabeth, Dutch soprano; b. Arnhem, May 17, 1888; d. Marquardstein, Oct. 16, 1974. She studied in Amsterdam, Frankfurt am Main, and Berlin. She made her operatic debut in Mainz in 1921, and in 1922 she joined the Bavarian State Opera in Munich, of which she was a principal member until 1936. She also sang at La Scala in Milan (1927–29), Covent Garden in London (1928–29, 1935), and the Bayreuth Festival (1931). On Jan. 17, 1930, she made her debut with the Metropolitan Opera in N.Y. as Brünnhilde, remaining on its roster until 1932. She excelled in Wagner's operas; among her finest roles were Brünnhilde, Kundry, Venus, and Isolde. —**NS/LK/DM**

Oistrakh, David (Fyodorovich), great Russian violinist, outstanding pedagogue, and esteemed conductor; b. Odessa, Sept. 30, 1908; d. Amsterdam, Oct. 24, 1974. He studied violin as a child with Stoliarsky in Odessa, making his debut there at the age of 6, and then continued his studies with Stoliarsky at the Odessa Cons. (1923–26); then appeared as soloist in Glazunov's Violin Concerto under the composer's direction in Kiev in 1927. In 1928 he went to Moscow and in 1934 he was appointed to the faculty of the Cons. His name attracted universal attention in 1937 when he won first prize at the Ysaÿe Competition in Brussels, in which 68 violinists from 21 countries took part. This launched a career of great renown as a violin virtuoso. He played in Paris and London in 1953 with extraordinary success; made his first American appearances in 1955, as soloist with major American orchs. and in recitals, winning enthusiastic acclaim; also made appearances as a conductor from 1962. He died while on a visit to Amsterdam as a guest conductor with the Concertgebouw Orch. Oistrakh's playing was marked, apart from a phenomenal technique, by stylistic fidelity to works by different composers of different historical periods. Soviet composers profited by his advice as to technical problems of violin playing; he collaborated with Prokofiev in making an arrangement for violin and piano of his Flute Sonata. A whole generation of Soviet violinists numbered among his pupils, first and foremost his son Igor (Davidovich) Oistrakh (b. Odessa, April 27, 1931), who has had a spectacular career in his own right; he won first prize at the International Festival of Democratic Youth in Budapest (1949) and the Wieniawski Competition in Poznań (1952); some critics regarded him as equal to his father in virtuosity; from 1958 he taught at the Moscow Cons.

BIBL.: V. Bronin, *D. O.* (Moscow, 1954); I. Yampolsky, *D. O.* (Moscow, 1964); D. Naberin, *D. und Igor O.* (Berlin, 1968); V. Josefowitsch, *D. O.* (Stuttgart, 1977); Y. Soroker, *D. O.* (Jerusalem, 1982).—**NS/LK/DM**

Okeghem, Johannes
See **Ockeghem, Johannes**

Oki, Masao, Japanese composer; b. Iwata, Shizuoka, Oct. 3, 1901; d. Kamakura, April 18, 1971. He studied engineering and music, then devoted himself mainly to teaching and composition. He wrote six syms., including No. 5, *Atomic Bomb* (Tokyo, Nov. 6, 1953) and No. 6, *Vietnam* (1970). His other works included a cantata, *Take Back the Human* (1961–63), String Quartet, and choral works.—**NS/LK/DM**

Okoshi, Tiger (actually, **Toru**), jazz-fusion trumpeter, synthesizer player; b. Ashita, Japan, March 21, 1950. He started to play the trumpet at age 11, working in local bands. He came to the U.S. initially in 1972. He was based in Boston since the early 1970s, where he attended Berklee School of Music, graduating in 1975, and achieved local renown for his Miles Davis-like fusion approach. He recorded in Boston with Gary Burton, as well as working with Buddy Rich, Michael Franks, and John Scofield. He recorded his first solo album in 1980, and has since led his own groups. He is Associate Professor of trumpet at Berklee.

DISC.: *T.'s Baku* (1981); *Face to Face* (1989); *That Was Then, This Is Now* (1990); *Echoes of a Note* (1993); *Two Sides to Every Story* (1994).—**LP**

Olah, Tiberiu, Romanian composer; b. Arpăşel, Jan. 2, 1928. He studied at the Cluj Cons. (1946–49) and

the Moscow Cons. (1949–54), and in each of the years from 1966 to 1971, he attended the summer courses in new music at Darmstadt. In 1954 he joined the faculty of the Bucharest Cons. In his music he adopts a strong contrapuntal style, with some excursions into the atonal domain and dodecaphonic organization.

WORKS: ORCH.: *Little Suite* (1954); 2 syms. (1952–55; 1985–87); *Coloana fără sfîşit* (Endless Column), symphonic poem inspired by the works of the Romanian sculptor Constantin Brâncuşi (1962); *Poarta sărutului* (Archway of the Kiss), symphonic poem (1966); *Masa tăcerii* (The Table of Silence), symphonic poem (1967–68); *5 Pieces* (1966); *Crescendo* (1972); *Evenimente 1907* (1972); *Harmonies: No. 1* (1975), *No. 3* (1977–78), and *No. 4*, concerto for 23 Instruments (1981). **CHAMBER:** String Quartet (1952); Trio for Violin, Clarinet, and Piano (1954); Violin Sonatina (1955); 2 sonatas for Solo Clarinet (1963, 1982); *Spaţiu şi ritm* (Space and Rhythm), étude for 3 Percussion Groups (1964); *Translations* for 16 Strings (1968); *Perspectives* for 13 Instruments (1969); Sonata for Solo Cello (1971); *Invocations* for Various Instruments (1971); *Time of Memory* for Chamber Ensemble (1973; N.Y., Dec. 6, 1974); *Harmonies: No. 2* for Winds and Percussion (1976); Sonata for Solo Flute (1978); Sonata for Violin and Percussion (1985); Sonata for Saxophone and Tape (1986). **Piano:** Sonatina (1950). **VOCAL:** 4 cantatas: *Cantata for Women's Chorus, 2 Flutes, Strings, and Percussion* (1956), *Prind visele aripi* (Dreams Become Reality, 1959), *Lumina lui Lenin* (The Light of Lenin, 1959), and *Constelaţia omului* (The Galaxy of Man, 1960); *Echinocţii* (Equinoxes) for Voice, Clarinet, and Piano (1967).—**NS/LK/DM**

Ölander, Per, Swedish violinist and composer; b. Linkoping, Jan. 8, 1824; d. Stockholm, Aug. 3, 1886. He studied with his father, an organist, and with J.E. Nordblom at the Univ. of Uppsala, whose daughter, Johanna Maria Nordblom, he married in 1853. While pursuing a civil service career, he made appearances as a violinist and wrote music criticism. He composed the opera *Blenda* (1876), the operetta *Mäster Placide* (1879), a Sym., chamber music, choral works, and songs. —**LK/DM**

Olcott, Chauncey, American tenor, lyricist, and composer; b. Buffalo, July 21, 1858; d. Monte Carlo, March 18, 1932. He began his career singing with traveling minstrel shows and opera troupes. After vocal training in London, he became principal tenor of Augustus Pitou's Irish operetta productions in the U.S. in 1893. He wrote librettos, lyrics, and songs, producing the scores of *Sweet Inniscarra* (1897), *A Romance of Athlone* (1899), *Garrett O'Magh* (1901), and *Old Limerick Town* (1902). Olcott wrote the famous song "My Wild Irish Rose" (1899) and also the lyrics for the songs "Mother Machree" (1911) and "When Irish Eyes Are Smiling" (1912) by Ernest Ball.

BIBL.: R. Olcott, *Song in his Heart* (N.Y., 1939).—**LK/DM**

Olczewska, Maria (real name, **Marie Berchtenbreitner**), prominent German mezzo-soprano; b. Ludwigsschwaige bei Donauwörth, near Augsburg, Aug. 12, 1892; d. Klagenfurt, Austria, May 17, 1969. She studied with Karl Erler in Munich. She began her career singing in operetta, making her operatic debut in Krefeld (1915). She then appeared in Leipzig (1916–20), Hamburg (1920–23), and Vienna (1921–23). She was a favorite at London's Covent Garden in Wagnerian roles (1924–32); also sang in Munich (1923–25) and again in Vienna (1925–30); likewise appeared in Chicago (1928–32). She made her Metropolitan Opera debut in N.Y. as Brängane on Jan. 16, 1933, remaining on its roster until 1935. From 1947 to 1969 she taught at the Vienna Academy of Music. She had a powerful voice, which made it possible for her to master the Wagner roles; but she was also excellent in dramatic parts, such as Carmen. Furthermore, she had a genuine talent as a stage actress. She was married for a time to **Emil Schipper.**—**NS/LK/DM**

Oldberg, Arne, American composer; b. Youngstown, Ohio, July 12, 1874; d. Evanston, Ill., Feb. 17, 1962. He studied composition with Middelschulte, then went to Vienna, where he was a piano pupil of Leschetizky (1893–95); also took courses with Rheinberger in Munich. Returning to America in 1899, he became head of the piano dept. at Northwestern Univ. He retired in 1941. Most of his orch. works were performed by the Chicago Sym. Orch., among them *Paolo and Francesca* (Jan. 17, 1908), *At Night* (April 13, 1917), Sym. No. 4 (Dec. 31, 1942), Sym. No. 5 (Jan. 19, 1950), and *St. Francis of Assisi* for Baritone and Orch. (Ravinia Festival, July 16, 1954). Other works are *Academic Overture* (1909), *The Sea*, symphonic poem (1934), two piano concertos, of which the second won the Hollywood Bowl prize and was performed there (Aug. 16, 1932), Violin Concerto (1933; Chicago, Nov. 7, 1946), two rhapsodies for Orch., chamber music, and piano pieces.—**NS/LK/DM**

Oldham, Arthur (William), English pianist, chorus master, and composer; b. London, Sept. 6, 1926. He studied at the Royal Coll. of Music in London with Howells, and privately with Britten. He was music director of the Ballet Rambert, and served as chorus master of the Edinburgh Festival Chorus (1965–94) and of the Scottish Opera in Glasgow (1966–74), and was director of the London Sym. Orch. Chorus (1969–76). In 1990 he was made an Officer of the Order of the British Empire. He wrote the ballets *Mr. Punch* (1946), *The Sailor's Return* (1947), *Circus Canteen* (1951), and *Bonne-Bouche* (1952); also *The Apotheosis of Lucius*, symphonic poem (1952), *The Land of Green Ginger*, musical for children (1964), *Hymns for the Amusement of Children* for Voices and Organ (1962), and various sacred and secular choral works.—**NS/LK/DM**

Oldman, C(ecil) B(ernard), English librarian and bibliographer; b. London, April 2, 1894; d. there, Oct. 7, 1969. He studied at Exeter Coll., Oxford. In 1920 he received an appointment in the Dept. of Printed Books in the British Museum in London; from 1948 to 1959, was Principal Keeper. In 1952 he was made a Companion of the Order of the Bath and in 1958 a Commander of the Royal Victorian Order. He was an authority on Haydn, Mozart, and Beethoven bibliographical matters; annotated the letters of Constanze Mozart to J.A. André in E. Anderson's *The Letters of Mozart and His Family* (3 vols., London, 1938; 2nd ed., rev., 1966 by A. Hyatt King and M. Carolan; 3rd ed., rev., 1985 by S. Sadie and F. Smart); his essay "Musical First Editions" in J. Carter, ed., *New Paths in Book-collecting* (London 1934) was publ. separately (1938).—**NS/LK/DM**

Oldmixon, Mrs. (Georgina née Sidus), English-American soprano; b. Oxford, c. 1767; d. Philadelphia, Feb. 3, 1835. She made her debut under the name of Miss George at London's Haymarket Theatre on June 2, 1783. Following contention with Elizabeth Billington, she settled in the U.S. and became a member of the Wignell and Reinagle enterprise in Philadelphia, where she made her first appearance on May 14, 1793. After a sojourn in N.Y., she returned to Philadelphia, where she gave her farewell performance in a benefit on Feb. 19, 1814. She subsequently ran her own Female Academy.—**NS/LK/DM**

Olenin, Alexander, Russian composer, brother of **Marie (Alexeievna) Olénine d'Alheim;** b. Istomino, Riazan district, June 13, 1865; d. Moscow, Feb. 15, 1944. He studied with P. Pabst and with Erdmannsdörfer. He lived most of his life in Moscow. He wrote an opera in a folk style, *Kudeyar* (Moscow, Nov. 26, 1915), a symphonic poem, *After the Battle, Préludes prairiales* for 2 Oboes, Violin, and Piano (1927), Piano Sonata, Violin Sonata, several song cycles (*The Street, The Peasant's Son, The Autumn, Home,* etc.), and 52 songs to texts by Heine. —**NS/LK/DM**

Olénine d'Alheim, Marie (Alexeievna), Russian soprano, sister of **Alexander Olenin;** b. Istomino, Riazan district, Oct. 2, 1869; d. Moscow, Aug. 27, 1970. She studied in Russia and later in Paris, where she made her debut in 1896. Through her brother she met Stasov, Balakirev, and Cui, and became interested in Russian vocal music. In 1893 she married the French writer Pierre d'Alheim (1862–1922), tr. of the text of *Boris Godunov;* together they organized, in Moscow and in Paris, numerous concerts and lectures on Russian music, particularly on Mussorgsky. She was an outstanding interpreter of Russian songs; publ. a book, *Le Legs de Mussorgsky* (Paris, 1908). In 1935 she settled in Paris as a voice teacher. In 1949 she joined the French Communist Party and in 1959 she returned to Russia. —**NS/LK/DM**

Olevsky, Julian, German-born American violinist; b. Berlin, May 7, 1926; d. Amherst, Mass., May 25, 1985. After studies in Germany, he went with his family to Buenos Aires (1935), where he made his debut at age 10; then settled in the U.S. (1947), becoming a naturalized American citizen (1951). He made his N.Y. debut at Town Hall (1949), and then toured as a soloist, recitalist, and chamber music player. He taught at the Univ. of Mass. in Boston (1967–74), and then in Amherst. —**NS/LK/DM**

Olitzka, Rosa, German-American contralto and teacher, aunt of **Walter Olitzki;** b. Berlin, Sept. 6, 1873; d. Chicago, Sept. 29, 1949. She studied with Julius Hey in Berlin and with Désirée Artôt in Paris. She sang at Berlin (1891), then was engaged at the Hannover Opera (1892–93), at Covent Garden in London (1894), and in N.Y. with the German Opera Co. (1895–97); was also with the Metropolitan Opera (1895–97; 1899–1901). After a season with the Chicago Grand Opera (1910–11), she made guest appearances in opera and concert in Europe and North America. She later taught voice in Chicago.—NS/LK/DM

Olitzki, Walter, German-American baritone, nephew of **Rosa Olitzka;** b. Hamburg, March 17, 1903; d. Los Angeles, Aug. 2, 1949. He received his training in Germany, where he developed his career. On Dec. 2, 1939, he appeared as Beckmesser at the Metropolitan Opera in N.Y., where he remained until 1947. He specialized in Wagnerian roles.—NS/LK/DM

Oliveira, Elmar, talented American violinist; b. Waterbury, Conn., June 28, 1950. He studied violin with Raphael Bronstein on a scholarship at the Hartt Coll. of Music in Hartford, Conn. and later at the Manhattan School of Music in N.Y. He made his formal debut as a soloist with the Hartford (Conn.) Sym. Orch. (1964); appeared with Bernstein at a N.Y. Phil. Young People's Concert (1966), which was telecast to the nation; made his N.Y. recital debut at Town Hall (1973). After winning the Naumburg Award in 1975, he became the first American violinist to capture the Gold Medal at the Tchaikovsky Competition in Moscow (1978); thereafter he pursued a rewarding international career. In 1990 he joined the faculty of the Manhattan School of Music in N.Y. His enormous repertoire ranges from the standard literature to contemporary works.—NS/LK/DM

Oliveira, Jocy de, Brazilian pianist and composer of French and Portuguese descent; b. Curitiba-Parana, April 11, 1936. She studied piano in São Paulo with J. Kliass, in Paris with Marguerite Long, and at Washington Univ. in St. Louis (M.A., 1968). She appeared as a piano soloist with major orchs. in Europe and America, specializing in the modern repertoire; in 1966 she played the piano part in Stravinsky's *Capriccio* in St. Louis, under Stravinsky's direction. As a composer, she occupies the aphelion of ultra-modernism, experimenting in electronic, environmental, theatrical, cinematic, and television media, as exemplified by her *Probabilistic Theater I, II,* and *III* for Musicians, Actors, Dancers, Television and Traffic Conductor, and other environmental manifestations. Her *Polinteracões I, II, III* present the culmination of "total music," involving the visual, aural, tactile, gustatory, and olfactory senses, with an anatomic chart serving as a score for guidance of the participants, supplemented by a phonemic table indicating the proper verbalization of vocal parts. (Complete score and illustrations were reproduced in *Source,* no. 7, Sacramento, Calif., 1970.) A performance of *Polinteracoes* was attempted on the occasion of the Catalytic Celebration of the 10th Anniversary Festival of the New Music Circle in St. Louis on April 7, 1970, but was stopped by the management as a noisy, noisome nuisance. She also composed a number of advanced sambas, precipitating the vogue of the Brazilian bossa nova. Active in belles-lettres, she penned a sociological fantasy, *O 3 Mundo* (The Third World), a controversial play, *Apague meu* (Spotlight), poetical works, etc. She married **Eleazar de Carvalho.**—NS/LK/DM

Oliver, John, American conductor and teacher; b. Teaneck, N.J., June 4, 1939. He was educated at the Univ. of Notre Dame (B.M., 1961) and the New England Cons. of Music (M.M. in choral conducting, 1967). From 1964 he was on the staff of the Mass. Inst. of Technology, where he was a technical instructor (1969–77), lecturer (1977–81), and senior lecturer (from 1981). He also was conductor of its glee club (1971–74), choral society (1972–88), schola cantorum (1973–75), and chamber chorus and concert choir (from 1988). From 1970 to 1991 he was head of vocal and choral activities at the Berkshire Music Center in Tanglewood. He also was founder-conductor of the Tanglewood Festival Chorus (from 1970) and of the John Oliver Chorale (from 1977). Oliver's repertoire ranges from the 18th century to the present era.—NS/LK/DM

Oliver, King (actually, **Joe**), seminal jazz cornetist, bandleader; b. on a plantation near Abend, La., May 11, 1885; d. Savannah, Ga., April 8, 1938. He was an uncle of Dave Nelson and of classical composer Ulysses (Simpson) Kay. There is some doubt about his birthplace, but he was certainly raised in New Orleans. Oliver began playing trombone before switching to cornet and worked at a young age in Walter Kinchin's Band and the Melrose Band. During adolescence he permanently lost the sight in one eye through an accident. From 1908–17, he did parade work, gigs, and occasional tours with various bands including the Olympia, the Onward Brass Band, the Magnolia, the Eagle, the Original Superior, and Allen's Brass Band. He was also employed as a butler. Oliver worked at the Abadie Brothers' Cabaret in Richard M. Jones's Four Hot Hounds (c. 1912), with Kid Ory at Pete Lala's, and also led his own band at the same venue and at the 101 Ranch. In 1917, he acquired the nickname "King," traditionally reserved for the leading New Orleans musician. He rejoined Kid Ory in 1917, left c. March 1919, and moved to Chicago to join clarinetist Lawrence Duhe's Band, also doubling in a band led by bassist Bill Johnson. Later, he became leader of Duhe's Band and played residencies at Deluxe Cafe, Pekin Cabaret, and Dreamland (1920 to May 1921). He took the band to San Francisco, led at the Pergola Dancing Pavilion (from June 1921), and later worked in Oakland, Leak's Lake, etc.

After returning to Chicago in April 1922, Oliver led his own Creole Jazz Band at Lincoln Gardens starting in June 1922. In 1922, Louis Armstrong, who Oliver had known in New Orleans, joined the band. They subsequently toured and made their recorded debut on March (not April 1), 1923. The group's 1923 recordings are among the most celebrated in jazz, in particular Oliver's three chorus solos on two versions of "Dippermouth Blues" (named for and written with Armstrong). In keeping with the approach of the time, his solos are quite similar, but not identical. They also recorded the first and probably best-known version of "High Society," a New Orleans standard. After a solo visit to N.Y. (September 1924), Oliver returned to Lincoln Gardens until December 1924. He guested with Dave Peyton in December 1924, led his own Dixie Syncopators at the Plantation Cafe from February 1925 until Spring 1927, then played dates in Milwaukee, Detroit, and St. Louis; worked at the Savoy Ballroom, N.Y. in May 1927 and toured before disbanding in Fall 1927. He remained in N.Y., playing on Clarence Williams's recording sessions (1928), leading his own studio bands for recordings, and occasionally forming bands for specific engagements, before reforming a regular band for touring in 1930. He left N.Y. and lived for a while in Nashville. Oliver formed yet another new band in 1931, made his last recordings that year, and recommenced touring, despite personnel changes and a series of misfortunes. King Oliver continued leading bands until 1937; he then ran a fruit stall in Savannah, Ga. before working as a pool-room attendant. He died in Savannah, but was buried in N.Y.

DISC.: *King Oliver* (1950); *King Oliver Plays the Blues* (1953); *King Oliver's Uptown Jazz* (1954); *King Oliver Featuring Louis Armstrong* (1956); *King Oliver and His Orch.* (1960); *King Oliver in New York* (1965); *Complete Vocalion/Brunswick Recordings 1926–31* (1992).

BIBL.: W. Allen and B. Rust, *King Joe Oliver* (1955; London, 1957; revised ed. Chigwell, U.K., 1987); P. Bonneau, *King Oliver* (Paris); R. Bowman, "The Question of Improvisation and Head Arrangement in King Oliver's Creole Jazz Band" (thesis, York Univ., 1982).—**JC/LP**

Oliver, Stephen (Michael Harding), English composer; b. Liverpool, March 10, 1950; d. London, April 29, 1992. He was a student at Worcester Coll., Oxford (1968–72), receiving training from Leighton (composition) and Sherlaw Johnson (electronic music). Oliver revealed a special talent for composing dramatic scores.

WORKS: DRAMATIC: *Slippery Soules*, Christmas drama (Oxford, Dec. 1969; rev. 1976; orchestrated version, London, Dec. 12, 1988); *The Duchess of Malfi* (1971; rev. version, Santa Fe, N.Mex., Aug. 5, 1978); *3 Instant Operas: Paid Off, Time Flies*, and *Old Haunts* (1973); *Sufficient Beauty* (1973); *Past Tense* (1973); *Cadenus Observ'd* (1974; London, Jan. 26, 1975); *Perseverance* (1974); *Tom Jones* (1974–75; Snape, April 6, 1976); *Bad Times* (London, June 24, 1975); *The Great McPorridge Disaster* (1976); *The Waiter's Revenge*, short opera (Nottingham, June 15, 1976); *Il Giardino*, short opera (Batignano, July 27, 1977; Eng. version as *The Garden*, London, April 17, 1980); *A Stable Home*, short opera (1977); *The Girl and the Unicorn* (London, Dec. 9, 1978); *The Dreaming of the Bones* (1979); *Jacko's Play*, short opera (1979); *A Man of Feeling*, short opera (London, Nov. 17, 1980); *Nicholas Nickelby*, incidental music (London, June 1980); *The Lord of the Rings*, incidental music (1981); *Euridice*, after Peri's score of 1600 (London, March 4, 1981); *Sasha* (1982; Banff, April 7, 1983); *Peter Pan*, incidental music (London, Dec. 16, 1982); *Blondel*, musical (Bath, Sept. 5, 1983); *Britannia Preserv'd*, masque (Hampton Court, May 30, 1984); *The Ring* (Manchester, May 31, 1984); *La Bella e la bestia* (Batignano, July 26, 1984; Eng. version as *Beauty and the Beast*, London, June 21, 1985); *Exposition of a Picture* (London, June 24, 1986); *Mario ed il mago* (Batignano, Aug. 5,

1988; Eng. version as *Mario and the Magician*); *Tables Meet* (London, May 1990); *Timon of Athens* (London, May 17, 1991); *L'Oca del Cairo* (Batignano, July 30, 1991). **ORCH.:** *The Boy and the Dolphin* (1974); *Luv* (1975); Sym. (Liverpool, May 23, 1976; rev. version, Kuopio, Oct. 13, 1983); *O No* for Brass Band (London, Oct. 10, 1976; rev. 1985); Concerto for Recorder and Strings (Aldeburgh, June 19, 1988). **CHAMBER:** *Music for the Wreck of the Deutschland* for Piano Quintet (1972); *Ricercare I* for Clarinet, Violin, Cello, and Piano (1973; London, Jan. 11, 1974), *II* for 2 Oboes, 2 Clarinets, 3 Bassoons, and 2 Horns (Canterbury, June 7, 1981), *III* for Guitar, Viola, and Cello (1983; London, Jan. 7, 1984), and *V* for 2 Trumpets, Horn, Trombone, and Tuba (Sevenoaks, June 15, 1986); Guitar Sonata (1979; Ludwigsburg, May 16, 1981); *Character Pieces* for 2 Oboes, 2 Clarinets, 2 Horns, and 2 Bassoons (Glyndebourne, July 12, 1991); piano pieces; organ music. **VOCAL:** *The Elixir* for 4 Soloists, Chorus, and Melody Instrument (1976); *Magnificat and Nunc Dimittis* for Chorus (1976); *The Dong with a Luminous Nose* for Narrator and 5 String Quartets (Woodfords, July 31, 1976; rev. version, London, Oct. 17, 1989); *A Dialogue Between Mary and Her Child* for Soprano, Baritone, and Chorus (1979); *The Child from the Sea*, cantata for Treble Voice, Chorus, and Orch. (Newcastle upon Tyne, Oct. 30, 1980); *The Key to the Zoo* for Narrator, 2 Oboes, Bassoon, and Harpsichord (Anglia TV, Feb. 5, 1980); *A String of Beads*, cantata for Chorus, 2 Oboes, Bassoon, and Strings (1980; Milton Keynes, Feb. 15, 1981); *Namings*, cantata for Chorus, Brass Quintet, and Timpani (Edinburgh, Sept. 3, 1981); *Trinity Mass* for Chorus (Norwich, July 5, 1981); *7 Words*, cantata for Chorus and String Orch. (Norwich, Oct. 15, 1985); *Forth in Thy Name* for Soprano, Bass, and Chorus (St. Albans, Oct. 5, 1985); *Festal Magnificat and Nunc Dimittis* for Chorus and Organ (Norwich, July 6, 1986); *2 Songs and a Scene from Cymbeline* for Baritone and Piano (Bromsgrove, Sept. 26, 1986); *Ricercare IV* for Countertenor, 2 Tenors, and Baritone (1986); *Prometheus*, cantata for Chorus and Orch. (Guildford, Nov. 26, 1988); *The Vessel*, cantata for Soprano, Tenor, Bass, Chorus, and Orch. (Nottingham, Oct. 19, 1990).—**NS/LK/DM**

Oliver, Sy (Melvin James), jazz arranger, trumpeter, singer; b. Battle Creek, Mich., Dec. 17, 1910; d. N.Y., May 28, 1988. He is best known for his arrangements for the Jimmie Lunceford band during the 1930s. The brother-in-law of pianist Archie "Skip" Hall, Sy Oliver was raised in Zanesville, Ohio. Both his parents were music teachers. He played trumpet from age 12, performing in the local Knights of Pythias Band as a teenager. While still in high school, he joined Clin Barnett's Club Royal Serenaders and played with them on and off for about three years. He then left Ohio at age 17 to work with Zack Whyte and his Chocolate Beau Brummels (then in Huntington, W. Va.). He then played with Alphonso Trent, left after a few months to rejoin Zack Whyte briefly (1930), then settled in Columbus, Ohio, and began teaching and arranging. After submitting arrangements to Jimmie Lunceford, he was invited to join the band, and traveled to N.Y. with them in late 1933 for their debut at the Lafayette Theatre. He was Lunceford's principal arranger for six years and played regularly in trumpet section. He began working with Tommy Dorsey in summer of 1939, mainly as staff arranger-composer, though he was occasionally featured on vocals. During his Army service from 1943 until late 1945, he served as a bandmaster. He worked again as a freelance arranger, receiving regular commissions from Tommy Dorsey. He led his own big band in 1946, which toured and had a residency at the Zanzibar Club, N.Y. He spent the next 10 years as a musical director and record supervisor at leading record companies, including Decca. During the 1950s and 1960s he did regular freelance arranging and led his own recording bands. He toured extensively during the 1960s and 1970s, directing a band in Paris during 1968 and 1969 (visiting Europe the latter year). He led his own big band in N.Y. (summer 1970 and 1978), and toured Europe with Warren Covington (1974). He resumed playing trumpet and led a nonet that played at several N.Y. clubs. Oliver worked with Money Johnson, Bobby Jones, Mousey Alexander, and Chris Woods, among others. They played Oliver's arrangements and worked into the 1980s.

DISC.: O.'s Twist & Easy Walker (1960); Take Me Back (1973); "Stomp It Off," "My Blue Heaven," "Organ Grinder's Swing," "On the Beach at Bali- Bali."—JC/LP

Olivero, Magda (actually, **Maria Maddalena**), remarkable Italian soprano; b. Saluzzo, near Turin, March 25, 1912. She studied at the Turin Cons. She made her operatic debut as Lauretta in *Gianni Schicchi* in Turin in 1933; then sang in the Italian provinces. She temporarily retired from the stage when she married in 1941, but resumed her career in 1951; made successful appearances at La Scala in Milan, and in Paris and London. On Nov. 4, 1967, she made her U.S. debut in Dallas in the title role of Cherubini's *Médée*; she was 63 years old when she made her first appearance with the Metropolitan Opera in N.Y., on April 3, 1975, as Tosca; on Dec. 5, 1977, she gave a highly successful recital in a program of Italian art songs at Carnegie Hall, N.Y. Among her other notable operatic roles were Violetta, Fedora, Liù, Suor Angelica, and Minnie; she was praised mainly for her dramatic penetration of each character and her fine command of dynamic nuances. —NS/LK/DM

Oliveros, Pauline, American composer, performer, teacher, author, and philosopher; b. Houston, May 30, 1932. She received rudimentary instruction in music from her mother and grandmother, and then had lessons with William Sydler (violin), Marjorie Harrigan (accordion), and J.M. Brandsetter (horn). Following studies in composition with Paul Koepke and in accordion with William Palmer at the Univ. of Houston (1949–52), she studied with Robert Erickson (1954–60) and at San Francisco State Coll. (B.A. in composition, 1957). In 1966–67 she was director of the Mills Coll. Tape Music Center in Oakland, Calif. From 1967 to 1981 she was a prof. of music at the Univ. of Calif. at San Diego, where she also was director of its Center for Music Experiment (1976–79). In 1985 she was a prof. at the Theater School for New Dance in Amsterdam. In 1985 she founded and became president and co-artistic director of the Pauline Oliveros Foundation, Inc. Among her writings are *Pauline's Proverbs* (1976), *Initiation Dream* (1982), and *Software for Peoples* (1984). In 1973 she held a Guggenheim fellowship. She received annual ASCAP awards from 1982 to 1994. In 1984, 1988, and 1990 she held NEA composer's fellowships. In 1994 she was awarded the Foundation for Contemporary Performance Arts grant. In her life and work, Oliveros has been absorbed by the potentialities of meditation, ritual, and myth. In her music, she has extended the boundaries of her art by an innovative approach to the sound and non-sound worlds, from the use of improvisation to electronics and beyond.

WORKS: 3 Songs for Soprano and Piano (1957); *Variations for Sextet* for Flute, Clarinet, Trumpet, Horn, Cello, and Piano (1959); *Sound Patterns* for Chorus (1961); Trio for Flute, Piano, and Page Turner (1961); *Outline* for Flute, Percussion, and String Bass (1963); Trio for Accordion, Trumpet, and String Bass (1963); *Pieces of 8*, theater piece for Flute, Oboe, Clarinet, Bass Clarinet, Trumpet, Horn, and Trombone (1965); *Aeolian Partitions*, theater piece for Flute, Clarinet, Violin, Cello, and Piano (1968); *Double Basses at 20 Paces*, theater piece for 2 Basses, Their Seconds, and a Referee with Slide and Tape (1968); *Meditation on the Points of the Compass* for Chorus (1970); *To Valerie Solanas and Marilyn Monroe in Recognition of Their Desperation* for Ensemble or Orch. (1970); *Deep Listening Pieces* for Voices and Instruments (1970–90); *Bonn Feier*, environmental theater piece with knowing and unknowing performers (1971); *Sonic Meditations* for Voices and Instruments (1971); *Rose Moon*, ritual theater piece for Chorus (1977); *Spiral Mandala* for Clarinets, Tuned Crystal Glasses, and Bass Drum with 4 Players and Chant (1978); *Music for Stacked Deck* for 4 Players (1979); *El Relicario de los Animales* for Singer and 20 Players (1979); *The Witness* for Solo or Duo or Any Ensemble (1979); *Traveling Companions* for Percussion and Dancers (1980); *Tashi Gomang* for Orch. (1981); *The Wanderer* for Accordion Ensemble and Percussion (1982); *Earth Ears* for Any Ensemble (1983); *Gathering Together* for Piano, 8–Hands (1983); *Tree/Peace* for Violin, Cello, and Piano (1983); *The Well and the Gentle* for Ensemble (1983); *The Wheel of Time* for String Quartet (1983); *Wings of Dove* for Double Wind Quintet and 2 Pianos (1984); *Lion's Eye* for Javanese Gamelan and Sampler (1985); *Portraits* for Solo or Any Ensemble (1987); *Dream Horse Spiel* for Voices and Sound Effects (1988); *Dream Gates* for Solo or Ensemble (1989); *Wind Horse* for Chorus (1989); *All Fours for the Drum Bum* for Solo Drum Set (1990); *Contenders*, dance piece (1991); *Njinga the Queen King*, theater piece (1993); *Hommage a Serafina*, dance piece (1996); *Ghost Dance*, dance piece (1996).

BIBL.: H. von Gunden, *The Music of P. O.* (Metuchen, N.J., 1983).—NS/LK/DM

d'Ollone, Max(imilien-Paul-Marie-Félix), French conductor, writer on music, and composer; b. Besançon, June 13, 1875; d. Paris, May 15, 1959. He studied with Lavignac, Massenet, and Lenepveu at the Paris Cons., receiving the Grand Prix de Rome in 1897 with his cantata *Frédégonde*. He was active as an opera conductor in Paris and the French provinces. He wrote the books *Le langage musical* (Paris and Geneva, 1952) and *Le Théâtre lyrique et le public* (Paris, 1955). He wrote 5 operas: *Le Retour* (Angers, Feb. 13, 1913), *Les Uns et les autres* (Paris, Nov. 6, 1922), *L'Arlequin* (Paris, Dec. 24, 1924), *George Dandin* (Paris, March 19, 1930), and *La Samaritaine* (Paris, June 25, 1937). Other works include *Fantaisie* for Piano and Orch. (1899), *Dans la cathédrale* for Orch. (1906), chamber music, and many songs. —NS/LK/DM

Olsen, (Carl Gustav) Sparre, Norwegian composer; b. Stavanger, April 25, 1903; d. Oslo, Nov. 8, 1984.

He studied composition with Valen and Brustad in Christiania (1925–30), Butting in Berlin, in Vienna, and with Grainger in London. He was violinist in the Christiania Phil. (1923–33); was active as a music teacher, music critic, and choral conductor in Bergen (1934–40). In 1936 he received a government life pension, and in 1968 he was awarded the Order of St. Olav. He publ. the books *Percy Grainger* (Oslo, 1963), *Tor Jonsson-Minne* (Oslo, 1968), and *Sparretonar* (Oslo, 1973). His music followed in the national tradition.

WORKS: ORCH.: *Symphonic Fantasia I* (Oslo, Sept. 21, 1939), *II* (Oslo, Oct. 6, 1957), and *III* (1973; Bergen, Nov. 28, 1974); *Serenade* for Flute and Strings (1954); *Intrada* (1956); *Canticum* (1972). **CHAMBER:** Wind Quintet (1946); String Quartet (1972); *Metamorfose* for Cello (1982). **VOCAL:** *2 Edda Songs* for Voice and Orch. or Piano (1931); *Draumkvedet* (The Dream Ballad) for Narrator, Soloists, Chorus, and Orch. (Bergen, April 19, 1937); sacred choruses; other songs.—**NS/LK/DM**

Olsen, Poul Rovsing, Danish composer and ethnomusicologist; b. Copenhagen, Nov. 4, 1922; d. there, July 2, 1982. He studied law at the Univ. of Århus (1940–42) and at the Univ. of Copenhagen (1942–48); concurrently, studied harmony and counterpoint with Jeppesen and piano with Christiansen at the Copenhagen Cons. (1943–46); later studied composition with Boulanger and analysis with Messiaen in Paris (1948–49). Between 1958 and 1963 he took part in ethnomusicological expeditions to Arabia, India, Greece, and eastern Greenland and wrote numerous valuable papers on the folklore and musical cultures of the areas he visited. He worked until 1960 for the Danish Ministry of Education as a legal expert on music copyright; served as chairman of the Danish Soc. of Composers (1962–67); taught ethnomusicology at the Univ. of Lund, Sweden (1967–69), and subsequently at the Univ. of Copenhagen. He was president of the International Council of Traditional Music (formerly the International Folk Music Council) from 1977 until his death. He was a music critic for the newspapers *Morgenbladet* (1945–46), *Information* (1949–54), and *Berlingske Tidende* (1954–74). Much of his music embodies materials of non-European cultures, reflecting the influence of his travels. His *Elegy* for Organ (1953) is the first serial work written by a Danish composer.

WRITINGS: *Musiketnologi* (Copenhagen, 1974); with J. Jenkins, *Music and Musical Instruments in the World of Islam* (London, 1976).

WORKS: DRAMATIC: Opera: *Belisa*, after García Lorca (1964; Copenhagen, Sept. 3, 1969); *Usher*, after Poe (1980). **Ballet:** *Ragnarök* (Twilight of the Gods; 1948; Copenhagen, Sept. 12, 1960); *La Création* (1952; Copenhagen, March 10, 1961); *Brylluppet* (The Wedding; 1966; Copenhagen, Sept. 15, 1969); *Den Fremmede* (The Stranger; 1969; Copenhagen, July 17, 1972). **ORCH.:** *Symphonic Variations* (1953); Piano Concerto (1953–54); *Sinfonia I* (1957–58; Copenhagen, April 13, 1959) and *II: Susudil* (Copenhagen, Oct. 31, 1966); *Capriccio* (1961–62); *Et russisk bal* (The Russian Ball), 3 dances (1965); *Au Fond de la nuit* for Chamber Orch. (1968); *Randrussermarchen* (1977); *Lux Coelestis* (1978). **CHAMBER:** *2 Pieces* for Clarinet and Piano (1943); *Romance* for Cello and Piano (1943); Violin Sonata (1946); 2 string quartets (1948, 1969); *Serenade* for Violin and Piano (1949); 2 piano trios (1950, 1976); *Prolana* for Clarinet, Violin, and Piano

(1955); Cello Sonata (1956); *The Dream of Pan* for Flute (1959); *Nouba*, 6 movements for Harp (1960); *Passacaglia* for Flute, Violin, Cello, and Piano (1960); *Patet* for 9 Musicians (1966); *How to Play in D major without Caring about It*, fantasy for 2 Accordions (1967); *Arabesk* for 7 Musicians (1968); *Shangri-La* for Flute, Viola d'Amore, and Piano (1969); *Pour une Viola d'Amour* (1969); *Rencontres* for Cello and Percussion (1970); *Poème* for Accordian, Guitar, and Percussion (1973); Concertino for Clarinet, Violin, Cello, and Piano (1973); *Partita* for Cello (1974); *Nostalgie* for Guitar (1976); *Danse élégiaque* for Flute and Guitar (1978); *A Dream of Violet* for String Trio (1982). **Piano:** 3 sonatinas (1941, 1951, 1967); *Theme with Variations* (1947); 2 sonatas for Piano, 4–Hands (1948, 1967); *12 Préludes* (1948); 2 sonatas (1950, 1952); *3 Nocturnes* (1951); *Medardus*, suite (1956); *5 Inventions* (1957); *Bagatelles* (1962); *Images* (1965); *4 Innocent Sonatas* (1969); *Many Happy Returns* (1971). **VOCAL:** *Schicksalslieder*, after 4 Hölderlin poems, for Soprano or Tenor and 7 Instruments (1953); *Evening Songs* for Mezzo-soprano and Flute (1954); *Alapa-Tarana*, vocalise for Mezzo-soprano and Percussion (1959); *A l'inconnu* for Soprano or Tenor and 13 Instruments (1962); *Kejseren* (The Emperor) for Tenor, Men's Chorus, and Orch. (1963; Copenhagen, Sept. 5, 1964); *A Song of Mira Bai* for Chorus, 3 Trumpets, and Percussion (1971); *Air* for Mezzo-soprano, Saxophone, and Piano (1976); *The Planets* for Mezzo-soprano, Flute, Viola, and Guitar (1978).—**NS/LK/DM**

Olsson, Otto (Emanuel), eminent Swedish organist, pedagogue, and composer; b. Stockholm, Dec. 19, 1879; d. there, Sept. 1, 1964. He studied with Lagergren and Dente at the Stockholm Cons. (1897–1901), where he subsequently taught (1908–45). He also was organist of the Gustav Vasa Church in Stockholm (1908–56). He became a member of the Royal Academy of Music in 1915.

WORKS: *Requiem* for Soloists, Chorus, and Orch. (1903; Stockholm, Nov. 14, 1976); 3 string quartets (1903, 1906, 1947); 2 organ syms. (1903, 1918); *Te Deum* for Chorus, Strings, Harp, and Organ (1906); 3 sets of *Preludes and Fugues* for Organ (1910–11; 1918; 1935); piano pieces; choral works; songs. —**NS/LK/DM**

O'Mara, Joseph, Irish tenor; b. Limerick, July 16, 1861; d. Dublin, Aug. 5, 1927. He studied with Moretti in Milan. On Feb. 4, 1891, he made his debut as Sullivan's Ivanhoe at the Royal English Opera House in London. After further training from Perini and Edwin Holland, he toured under the auspices of Augustus Harris. From 1902 to 1908 he was the principal tenor of the Moody-Manners Opera Co. In 1910 he became a member of Beecham's Co. at London's Covent Garden. From 1912 to 1924 he was director of his own O'Mara Grand Opera Co., with which he often appeared in leading roles. —**NS/LK/DM**

Oncina, Juan, Spanish tenor; b. Barcelona, April 15, 1925. He was a student in Oran, Algeria, and of Mercedes Caspir in Barcelona. In 1946 he made his Italian operatic debut as Count Almaviva in Bologna, and subsequently appeared with leading Italian opera houses. From 1952 to 1961 he also sang at the Glyndebourne Festivals. While he was best known for his roles in operas by Mozart, Rossini, and Donizetti, he also appeared in operas by Verdi and Puccini.—**NS/LK/DM**

Ondříček, family of Czech musicians:

(1) Ignac Ondříček, violinist and conductor; b. Krusovice, May 7, 1807; d. Prague, Feb. 8, 1871. He studied with Simon Pergler, the local schoolmaster. After playing in his teacher's band, he settled in Prague (1839), where he conducted his own band (1855–70).

(2) Jan Ondříček, violinist and conductor, son of the preceding; b. Bělěc, near Bratronice, May 6, 1832; d. Prague, March 13, 1900. He studied with his father and with Mořic Mildner (violin) and Dvorak (theory), then conducted his own band. He had 15 children, including the following:

(3) František Ondříček, eminent violinist and pedagogue; b. Prague, April 29, 1857; d. Milan, April 12, 1922. He studied with his father, and then with Bennewitz at the Prague Cons. (1873–76), where he won a first prize, and then with Massart at the Paris Cons. (1879–81), where he won a premier prix. He gave the premiere of Dvořák's Violin Concerto in Prague (1883). After extensive tours of Europe, the U.S., and the Far East, he was made Kammervirtuos in Vienna (1888). He founded his own quartet (1907), taught at the New Vienna Cons. (1909–12), and gave master classes at the Prague Cons. (1919–22). He acquired a notable reputation as a virtuoso, and also composed many violin pieces, as well as cadenzas and paraphrases, fantasias, and arrangements of themes by other composers. With S. Mittelmann, he publ. *Neue Methode zur Erlangung der Meistertechnik des Violinspiels auf anatomisch-physiologischer Grundlage* (2 vols., Vienna, 1909).

BIBL.: B. Sich, *F. O.* (Prague, 1947).

(4) Emanuel Ondříček, violinist and pedagogue; b. Pilsen, Dec. 6, 1882; d. Boston, Dec. 30, 1958. He studied with his father, then with Ševčik at the Prague Cons. (1894–99). After touring Europe, he emigrated to the U.S. (1912), and taught in Boston and N.Y. He publ. *The Mastery of Tone Production and Expression on the Violin* (1931).—**NS/LK/DM**

Onégin, (Elisabeth Elfriede Emilie) Sigrid (née Hoffmann), noted German contralto; b. Stockholm (of a German father and a French mother), June 1, 1889; d. Magliaso, Switzerland, June 16, 1943. She studied in Frankfurt am Main with Resz, in Munich with E.R. Weiss, and with di Ranieri in Milan. She made her first public appearance, under the name Lilly Hoffmann, in Wiesbaden, Sept. 16, 1911, in a recital, accompanied by the Russian pianist and composer Eugene Onégin (real name, Lvov; b. St. Petersburg, Oct. 10, 1883; d. Stuttgart, Nov. 12, 1919; he was a grandnephew of Alexis Lvov, composer of the Russian Czarist hymn). She married him on May 25, 1913; after his death, she married a German doctor, Fritz Penzoldt (Nov. 20, 1920). She made her first operatic appearance as Carmen in Stuttgart on Oct. 10, 1912; made her first appearance in London in 1913; was a member of the Bavarian State Opera in Munich (1919–22). On Nov. 22, 1922, she made her Metropolitan Opera debut in N.Y. as Amneris, continuing on its roster until 1924. She subsequently sang in Berlin (1926–31), at London's Covent Garden (1927), the Salzburg Festivals (1931–32), in Zürich (1931–35), and at the Bayreuth Festivals (1933–34). She made her last appearances in the U.S. as a recitalist in 1938. Among her most distinguished roles were Gluck's Orfeo, Eboli, Fidès, Erda, Lady Macbeth, Fricka, Waltraute, and Brangäne.

BIBL.: F. Penzoldt, *Alt-Rhapsodie: S. O., Leben und Werk* (Magdeburg, 1939; 3rd ed., 1953).—**NS/LK/DM**

O'Neill, Dennis (James), Welsh tenor; b. Pontardulais, Feb. 25, 1948. He studied at the Univ. of Sheffield and at the Royal Northern Coll. of Music in Manchester. In 1973 he made his debut in *Ivan Susanin* at the Wexford Festival, and then sang with the State Opera of South Australia (1974–76) and subsequently with the Scottish Opera in Glasgow. In 1979 he sang Alfredo with the Welsh National Opera in Cardiff and Flavio at London's Covent Garden. He appeared as the Italian Singer in *Der Rosenkavalier* at the Glyndebourne Festival in 1980. After singing at the Vienna State Opera and the Hamburg State Opera in 1981, he made his U.S. debut as Edgardo at the Dallas Opera in 1983. In 1984 he sang at the San Francisco Opera, in 1985 at the Lyric Opera in Chicago, and in 1986 at the Paris Opéra. His first appearance with the Metropolitan Opera was as Alfredo during a tour by the company in 1986. In 1987 he returned to the Metropolitan Opera to make his house debut in N.Y. In 1992 he sang at the Bavarian State Opera in Munich. He was engaged as Radamès at Covent Garden in 1994, and he returned there in 1997 as Macduff.—**NS/LK/DM**

Onishi, Junko, Japanese pianist; b. Kyoto, Japan, April 16, 1967. She grew up in Tokyo and began playing piano at age four. After graduating from high school in 1986, she moved to Boston to attend Berklee Coll., where she interacted with Delfeayo Marsalis, Roy Hargrove, and Ryan Kisor (among others) in jam sessions. Her first professional gig came in 1988 when she went on tour to France in Slide Hampton's band. The following year she graduated first in her class from Berklee and moved to N.Y., where she played in the Jesse Davis Quintet, the house band at Augie's. She returned to Japan with that group, and played with small groups led by Gary Thomas, Joe Henderson, and Kenny Garrett. She has also worked with Terence Blanchard, Greg Osby, Mingus Dynasty, and the Mingus Big Band. In 1992 she moved back to Japan and formed the trio heard on her first album, *WOW*, with classmates from her Berklee days. Blue Note began licensing her albums for U.S. release after she began using American rhythm sections, and she also made an album with Jackie McLean in 1996.

DISC.: *Cruisin'* (1993); *WOW* (1993); *Live at the Village Vanguard* (1994); *Live at the Village Vanguard II* (1994); *Piano Quintet Suite* (1995); *Hat Trick* (1996).—**SH**

Ono, Yoko, Japanese-born American vocalist, songwriter, and performance artist; b. Tokyo, Feb. 18, 1933. She was born to a wealthy banking family. In 1947 she moved to N.Y., where she entered Sarah Lawrence Coll. (1953). She became active in Manhattan conceptual-art circles, and in 1966 met John Lennon of The Beatles; they became companions and collaborators, marrying in 1969. Under her influence, Lennon became interested in avant-garde ideas that drew him away from rock, contributing to the breakup of The Beatles in 1970. After Lennon's death in 1980, Ono produced several posthumous collaborations. Her solo recordings include *Yoko Ono/Plastic Ono Band* (1970), *Fly* (1971), *Approximately Infinite Universe* (1973), *Feeling the Space* (1973), *Seasons of Glass* (1981), *It's Alright* (1982), and *Every Man Has a Woman* (1984). Her recordings with Lennon include *Unfinished Music no. 1: 2 Virgins* (1968) and *no. 2: Life with the Lions* (1969), *Wedding Album* (1969), *Live Peace in Toronto 1969* (1970), *Double Fantasy* (1980), *Milk and Honey* (1982), and *Heart Play: Unfinished Dialogue* (1983). Ono's work is often bizarre, her shrill tremolo voice moving over a fluid, arrhythmic background reflecting Asian influences; some of her recordings, notably those between 1980 and 1984, are popular in style. In 1992 she released *Onobox*, a collection of 6 compact discs featuring a wide range of music, from pop to serious scores. Her musical *N.Y. Rock* was premiered in N.Y. on March 30, 1994.

BIBL.: J. Cott and C. Doudna, eds., *The Ballad of John and Yoko* (N.Y., 1982).—NS/LK/DM

Onslow, (André) Georges (Louis), noted French composer of English descent; b. Clermont-Ferrand, July 27, 1784; d. there, Oct. 3, 1853. He was the grandson of the first Lord Onslow. He studied in London with Hüllmandel, Dussek, and Cramer (piano) and in Paris with Reicha (composition). He wrote three comic operas, produced in Paris, *L'Alcalde de la Vega* (Aug. 10, 1824), *Le colporteur, ou L'enfant du bûcheron* (Nov. 22, 1827), and *Guise, ou Les états de Blois* (Sept. 8, 1837), as well as four syms. and other orch. music. However, these works failed to maintain interest. Onslow's real achievement was the composition of a great number of chamber works, in which he demonstrated an uncommon mastery of counterpoint. He wrote 34 string quintets, 35 string quartets, six piano trios, Sextet for Flute, Clarinet, Horn, Bassoon, Double Bass, and Piano, Nonet for Violin, Viola, Cello, Double Bass, Flute, Oboe, Clarinet, Bassoon, and Horn, Septet for Flute, Oboe, Clarinet, Horn, Bassoon, Double Bass, and Piano, violin sonatas, cello sonatas, piano sonatas, four- hands, and piano pieces. He was struck by a stray bullet during a hunting expedition in 1829 and became deaf in one ear; his Quintet No. 15, subtitled *Le Quintette de la balle*, was the musical rendering of this episode.

BIBL.: L. Halévy, *Notice sur O.* (Paris, 1855); C. Vulliamy, *The O. Family, 1528–1874* (London, 1953); C. Nobach, *Untersuchungen zu G. O.s Kammermusik* (Basel, 1985).—NS/LK/DM

Opie, Alan (John), English baritone; b. Redruth, Cornwall, March 22, 1945. He received training at London's Guildhall School of Music and Drama, and at the London Opera Centre. In 1969 he made his operatic debut as Papageno at the Sadler's Wells Opera in London, where he was its principal bass in 1973–74 and its successor, the English National Opera from 1974 to 1996. He made his U.S. operatic debut as Tony in *The Globolinks* at the Santa Fe Opera in 1970. In 1971 he sang for the first time at London's Covent Garden in *Il*

Barbiere di Siviglia, where his later appearances included Hector in *King Priam* (1985), Mangus in *The Knot Garden* (1988), Falke (1989), Sharpless (1993), and Faninal (1995). He made his debut at the Glyndebourne Festival as Sid in *Albert Herring* in 1985, and returned there as Mozart's Figaro in 1991 and as Birtten's Balstrode in 1992. In 1994 he sang the latter role at the Metropolitan Opera in N.Y., and in 1997 he returned there as Sharpless. On Oct. 2, 1996, he created the title role in Berio's *Outis* at Milan's La Scala.—NS/LK/DM

Opieński, Henryk, Polish conductor, music scholar, teacher, and composer; b. Kraków, Jan. 13, 1870; d. Morges, Switzerland, Jan. 21, 1942. He studied with Zeleński in Kraków, with d'Indy in Paris, and with H. Urban in Berlin, then went to Leipzig, where he studied musicology with Riemann and conducting with Nikisch. In 1907 he was appointed an instructor at the Warsaw Musical Soc. From 1908 to 1912 he conducted the Warsaw Opera. In 1912 he went again to Germany, where he took his degree of Ph.D. (Univ. of Leipzig, 1914). He spent the years of World War I in Morges, Switzerland, and, returning to Poland, was director of the Poznań Cons. (1919–26). He then settled again in Morges. He publ. several books and essays on Chopin (Lemberg, 1910; 2nd ed., 1922) and also the collected letters of Chopin in Polish, German, French, and Eng. (1931). Other writings include a history of Polish music (Warsaw, 1912; 2nd ed., 1922), *La Musique polonaise* (Paris, 1918; 2nd ed., 1929), a monograph on Paderewski (Lemberg, 1910; 2nd ed., 1928; Fr. tr., Lausanne, 1928; 2nd ed., 1948), and a valuable monograph on Moniuszko (Warsaw, 1924).

WORKS: DRAMATIC: O p e r a : *Maria* (1904; Poznań, April 27, 1923); *Jakub lutnista* (Jacob the Lutenist; 1916–18; Poznań, Dec. 21, 1927). **ORCH.:** 2 symphonic poems: *Lilla Weneda* (1908) and *Love and Destiny* (1912). **CHAMBER:** *Scènes lyriques en forme de quatuor* for String Quartet; violin pieces. **VOCAL:** *The Prodigal Son*, oratorio (1930); many songs.

BIBL.: A. Forenerod, *H. O.* (Lausanne, 1942).—NS/LK/DM

Oppens, Ursula, talented American pianist; b. N.Y., Feb. 2, 1944. She studied economics and English literature at Radcliffe Coll. (B.A., 1965), then studied with Rosina Lhévinne and Leonard Shure at the Juilliard School of Music in N.Y. She won first prize at the Busoni Competition in Italy in 1969. Returning to the U.S., she co-founded Speculum Musicae in N.Y., a chamber music ensemble devoted to performing contemporary music; also appeared with other chamber music groups, as a recitalist, and as a soloist with major U.S. orchs. In 1976 she was awarded the Avery Fisher Prize. Her expansive repertory ranges from the classics to the cosmopolitan avant-garde.—NS/LK/DM

Oppitz, Gerhard, German pianist and teacher; b. Frauenau, Feb. 5, 1953. He began piano lessons as a child and made his first public appearance when he was 12. In 1973 he pursued further training in the master class of Wilhelm Kempff. After winning first prize in the Rubinstein Competition in Tel Aviv in 1977, he appeared as a soloist with the world's major orchs. and gave recitals in the leading music centers. From 1981 he was also a prof. at the Munich Hochschule für Musik. His catholic repertoire ranges from the standard literature to the contemporary era.—NS/LK/DM

Orbán, György, Hungarian composer; b. Tîrgu-Mureş, Romania, July 12, 1947. He was a student of Toduţa and Jagamas at the Cluj Cons. (1968–73). After serving on its faculty (1973–79), he went to Budapest and was an ed. at Editio Musica Budapest and a teacher at the Academy of Music.

WORKS: ORCH.: 2 serenades (1984, 1985); Christmas Oratorio for Organ, 2 Percussionists, and Strings (1998). **CHAMBER:** Sonata for Solo Violin (1970); Triple Sextet (1980); Wind Quintet (1985); Brass Quintet (1987); Sonata Concertante for Clarinet and Piano (1987); Bassoon Sonata (1987); 3 violin sonatas (1989, 1991, 1995); 3 string quartets (1994, 1994, 1997); Sonata for String Instrument and Piano (1997); Viola Sonata (1997). **Piano:** 4 sonatas (1985, 1987, 1988, 1988). **VOCAL:** 5 *Canons to Poems by Attila József* for Soprano and Chamber Ensemble (1977); Duo No. 1 for Soprano and Clarinet (1979), No. 2 for Soprano and Double Bass (1987), No. 3 for Soprano and Cello (1989), and No. 4 for Soprano and Violin (1992); *Stabat Mater* for Chorus (1987); 7 masses (1990–93); *Rotate Coeli*, oratorio for Chorus and Orch. (1992); *Regina Martyrum*, oratorio for Chorus and Orch. (1993); *Cantico de Frate Sole* for Soprano and String Orch. (1996); several choral cycles. —NS/LK/DM

Orbison, Roy, one of the greatest and most original voices in rock and roll; b. Vernon, Tex., April 23, 1936; d. Madison, Tenn., Dec. 6, 1988. Roy Orbison was raised in Wink, Tex., where he took up guitar at the age of six and formed his own band, The Wink Westerners, in 1952. He attended North Tex. Univ. with Pat Boone and first recorded in early 1956 as leader of The Teen Kings at Norman Petty's studio in Clovis, N.Mex. Signed to the Memphis-based Sun label, Orbison's soaring voice was hardly suited to the "rockabilly" he recorded there, yet "Ooby Dooby" became a minor hit in the summer of 1956. He toured and recorded for Sun until 1958 without achieving another hit.

Roy Orbison moved to Nashville to concentrate on songwriting for Acuff-Rose Music, placing "Claudette," written for his wife, with The Everly Brothers in 1958. Briefly recording for RCA Records, he switched to Fred Foster's newly formed Monument label in late 1959. After the minor hit "Uptown," Orbison scored a smash with the classic "Only the Lonely," cowritten with Joe Melson. The song initiated a string of powerful, nearly operatic ballad hits cowritten with Melson such as "Blue Angel," "I'm Hurtin,'" and the top hit "Running Scared" (backed by Felice and Boudleaux Bryant's "Love Hurts"), recorded with string section, male backup voices, and a driving bolero-like crescendo. The smash hit "Crying" (again with Melson) was backed by the major hit "Candyman," written by Fred Neil, and Orbison's success continued with Cindy Walker's "Dream Baby," "Leah," "In Dreams," "Falling," and "Mean Woman Blues" (a near smash rhythm-and-blues hit) backed with "Blue Bayou." He first toured Great Britain in 1962 and, in 1963, he toured that country as

headliner act to The Beatles and Gerry and The Pacemakers. The hits continued with Willie Nelson's "Pretty Paper," and two songs cowritten with Bill Dees, "It's Over" and the top hit classic "Oh, Pretty Woman."

After hits with "Goodnight" and "(Say) You're My Girl," Roy Orbison switched to MGM Records, but only "Ride Away" proved to be a major hit and, by 1968, he had dropped out of the charts. Dogged by personal problems (his wife was killed in a motorcycle accident on June 6, 1966; two of his three children died when his Nashville home burned on Sept. 14, 1968), Orbison appeared in the silly 1967 movie *The Fastest Guitar Alive* and recorded entire albums of songs by Don Gibson and Hank Williams, as well as a duet effort with Hank Williams Jr. Refusing to join rock 'n' roll "revival" shows and seldom touring the U.S. after the late 1960s (although he continued to tour Europe and Great Britain regularly), Orbison eventually recorded new albums for Mercury, Monument, and Elektra in 1975, 1977, and 1979, respectively. In 1977, he returned to American touring and saw Linda Ronstadt score a smash pop and country hit with "Blue Bayou."

In 1980, Roy Orbison achieved a minor pop and smash country hit in duet with Emmylou Harris on "That Lovin' You Feelin' Again" from the film *Roadie*. The following year, Don McLean scored a smash hit with his rendition of "Crying," and Van Halen achieved a near-smash with a remake of "Oh, Pretty Woman" in 1982. In 1986, he joined Sun Records alumni Johnny Cash, Carl Perkins, and Jerry Lee Lewis for *Class of '55*. The experience renewed his vigor for writing and recording, and he soon signed with Virgin Records and rerecorded 19 of his hits for *In Dreams* under producer T-Bone Burnett. His rerecording of "In Dreams" was featured in the 1986 movie *Blue Velvet* and, on Sept. 30, he performed at an all-star tribute with Bruce Springsteen, Elvis Costello, Tom Waits, Bonnie Raitt, and others that was aired on the Cinemax cable network in December 1988 and released as an album one year later as *A Black and White Night Live*. He also scored a moderate country hit with k.d. lang on a remake of his "Crying" and later joined George Harrison, Bob Dylan, Jeff Lynne, and Tom Petty as Lefty Wilbury for The Traveling Wilburys' *Volume One* album, singing lead vocals on "Not Alone Any More."

Roy Orbison was inducted into the Rock and Roll Hall of Fame in 1987 and recorded a new album for Virgin Records in 1988. However, on Dec. 6, 1988, he died of a heart attack in Madison, Tenn., at the age of 52. The album *Mystery Girl* was released in early 1989 and became the best-selling album of his career. It featured "Careless Heart," "She's a Mystery to Me" (written by The Edge and Bono of U2), "In the Real World," and "A Love So Beautiful," and yielded a near-smash hit with "You Got It," written by Orbison, Jeff Lynne, and Tom Petty. Virgin Records later assembled *King of Hearts* for 1992 release.

DISC.: *At the Rock House* (1961); *Lonely and Blue* (1961); *Crying* (1962); *In Dreams* (1963); *There Is Only One Roy Orbison* (1965); *The Orbison Way* (1966); *Classic Roy Orbison* (1966); *Roy Orbison Sings Don Gibson* (1966); *Fastest Guitar Alive* (soundtrack; 1967); *Cry Softly, Lonely One* (1967); *Many Moods*

(1969); *Great Songs* (1970); *Roy Orbison and Hank Williams Jr.* (1970); *Hank Williams the Orbison Way* (1972); *I'm Still in Love with You* (1975); *Regeneration* (1977); *Laminar Flow* (1979/1989); *In Dreams* (1987); *Mystery Girl* (1989); *A Black and White Night* (1989); *King of Hearts* (1992).

BIBL.: A. Clayson, *Only the Lonely: R. O.'s Life and Legacy* (N.Y., 1989); E. Amburn, Ellis. *Dark Star: The R. O. Story* (N.Y., 1990).—**BH**

Orbón (de Soto), Julián, Spanish-American composer; b. Aviles, Aug. 7, 1925; d. Miami Beach, May 20, 1991. He entered the Oviedo Cons. when he was 10. In 1938 he went with his family to Havana, where he continued his training under his father (piano) and Ardévol (composition). After completing his training in composition with Copland at the Berkshire Music Center in Tanglewood (summer, 1945), he returned to Havana and became director of his father's Orbón Cons. in 1946. In the wake of the Cuban Revolution, he went to Mexico City in 1960 and worked with Chávez at the National Cons. until 1963. In 1964 he settled in the U.S. In 1964–65 he taught at the State Univ. of N.Y at Purchase and at Washington Univ. in St. Louis. He subsequently concentrated his efforts on composition. In 1959 and 1969 he held Guggenheim fellowships. In 1967 he received an award from the American Academy of Arts and Letters. After composing works revealing Spanish and Cuban stylistic traits, he turned to a more expressive Romantic style in his later scores.

WORKS: ORCH.: Sym. (1945); *Homenaje a la tonadilla* (1947); *Tres versiones sinfónicas* (1953; Caracas, Dec. 11, 1954); *Danzas sinfónicas* (1955; Miami, Nov. 17, 1957); Concerto Grosso (1958; N.Y., Nov. 8, 1961); *Partita* No. 3 (1965) and No. 4 for Piano and Orch. (1982–85; Dallas, April 11, 1985). **CHAMBER:** *Concerto da camera* for Horn, English Horn, Trumpet, Cello, and Piano (1944); String Quartet (1951); *Preludio y danza* for Guitar (1951); *Partita* No. 1 for Harpsichord (1963) and No. 2 for Harpsichord, Vibraphone, Celesta, Harmonium, and String Quartet (1964); numerous piano pieces; organ music. **VOCAL:** *Crucifixus*, motet for Chorus (1953); *Hymnus ad galli cantum* for Soprano, Flute, Oboe, Clarinet, Harp, and String Quartet (1956); *Tres cantigas del rey* for Soprano, String Quartet, Harpsichord, and Percussion (1960); *Monte Gelboe* for Tenor and Orch. (1962); *Introito* for Chorus (1967–68); *Oficios: Liturgia de tres días* for Chorus and Orch. (1970–75); *Dos canciones folklóricas* for Chorus (1972); *Libro de cantares* for Mezzo-soprano and Piano (1987).

BIBL.: V. Yedra, *J. O.: A Biographical and Critical Essay* (Miami, 1990).—**NS/LK/DM**

Ord, Boris, English organist, harpsichordist, and conductor; b. Bristol, July 9, 1897; d. Cambridge, Dec. 30, 1961. He was educated at the Royal Coll. of Music in London and was an organ scholar at Corpus Christi Coll., Cambridge. From 1929 to 1957 he was organist and choirmaster at King's Coll., Cambridge, where he made the Christmas Eve Festival of 9 Lessons and Carols celebrated via the radio. He also was a lecturer on music at the Univ. of Cambridge (1936–58) and was conductor of its Musical Soc. (1938–54). He composed the carol *Adam lay y-bounden* (1957). In 1958 he was made a Commander of the Order of the British Empire. As both a solo artist and conductor, Ord distinguished himself in an extensive repertoire.

BIBL.: P. Radcliffe, *B. O.: A Memoir* (Cambridge, 1962).—**NS/LK/DM**

Ordonez or Ordonez, Carlos d', Austrian composer of Spanish extraction; b. Vienna, April 19, 1734; d. there, Sept. 6, 1786. He was employed as a clerk, but studied violin and performed successfully at chamber music concerts. He wrote numerous Singspiels and much instrumental music, some of which was publ. during his lifetime. His Singspiel *Diesmal hat der Mann den Willen* was performed in Vienna on April 22, 1778, and his marionette opera *Alceste* was introduced by Haydn in Esterház on Aug. 30, 1775. Ordonez developed an excellent metier, and several of his syms. possessed enough merit to be misattributed to Haydn.

BIBL.: A. Brown, *Carlo d'Ordonez (1734–1786): A Thematic Catalogue* (Detroit, 1978).—**NS/LK/DM**

Ore, Cecilie, Norwegian composer; b. Oslo, July 19, 1954. She studied piano at the Norwegian State Academy of Music in Oslo and in Paris, and then pursued training in composition at the Sweelinck Cons. in Amsterdam with Ton de Leeuw and attended the Inst. of Sonology at the Univ. of Utrecht. In 1988 her *Prophyre* for Orch. was named the Norwegian composition of the year, and she was awarded the Norwegian state guaranteed income for artists. In her output, Ore creates multi-layered constructs in which sonority and rhythm play essential roles. Her use of the computer has become highly significant in her approach to composition.

WORKS: DRAMATIC: Theater: *Prologos*, electroacoustic piece (1990). **Film:** *Kald Verden*, electroacoustic music (1986). **Television** *Im-Mobile*, electroacoustic music (1984); *Contracanthus* for Double Bass (1987). **ORCH.:** *Prophyre* (1986); *Nunc et Nunc* (1994). **CHAMBER:** *Helices* for Wind Quintet (1984); *Janus* for Cello (1985); *Praesens Subitus* for Amplified String Quartet (1989); *Erat Erit Est* for Amplified Chamber Ensemble (1991); *Futurum Exactum* for Amplified String Ensemble (1992); *Lex Temporis* for Amplified String Quartet (1992); *Ictus* for 6 Percussionists (1997); *Semper Semper* for Saxophone Quartet (1998); *Non Nunquam* for Violin, Viola, and Cello (1999). **VOCAL:** *Carnatus* for Soprano and Chorus (1982); *Calliope* for Soprano (1984); *Ex Oculus* for 2 Tenors, Baritone, and Bass (1985); *Cantus Aquatoris* for Soprano, Alto, Tenor, and Bass (1987). **TAPE:** *Vacuus* (1986); *Etapper* (1988). **OTHER:** *Im-Moible (I+II+III)*, electroacoustic sculptures (1984); *Festina Lente*, electroacoustic piece (1996).—**NS/LK/DM**

Orefice, Antonio, Italian composer who flourished in the first half of the 18th century. His comic opera in Neapolitan dialect, *Patrò Calienno de la Costa* (Naples, Teatro dei Fiorentini, Oct. 1, 1709), was the first such work given on a public stage in Naples. With Mancini and Albinoni, he composed the opera seria *Engelberta, ossia La forza dell'innocenza* (Naples, Nov. 4, 1709). His 7 arias from *Le finte zingare* (1717) are the earliest extant music from a comic opera in Neapolitan dialect.
—**NS/LK/DM**

Orefice, Giacomo, Italian pianist, music critic, teacher, and composer; b. Vicenza, Aug. 27, 1865; d. Milan, Dec. 22, 1922. He studied piano with Busi and composition with Mancinelli at the Bologna Liceo Musicale (diploma, 1885). He taught at the Milan Cons. (1909–22); was also active as a music critic. He publ. the study *Luigi Mancinelli* (Rome, 1921); ed. Monteverdi's *Orfeo* (Milan, 1909) and Rameau's *Platée*. As a composer of operas, he followed in the verismo school.

WORKS: DRAMATIC: Opera: *L'oasi* (Bologna, 1885); *Mariska* (Turin, Nov. 19, 1889); *Consuelo* (Bologna, Nov. 27, 1895); *Il Gladiatore* (Madrid, March 20, 1898); *Chopin* (Milan, Nov. 25, 1901); *Cecilia* (Vicenza, Aug. 16, 1902); *Il Mosè* (Genoa, Feb. 18, 1905); *Il pane d'altrui* (Venice, Jan. 19, 1907); *Radda* (Milan, Oct. 25, 1912); *I Castello dei sogni* (not perf.). **Ballet:** *La soubrette* (Milan, 1907). **ORCH.:** 2 syms. (1892, 1911); *Sinfonia del bosco* (1898); *Anacreontiche*, suite (1917); *Laudi francescane*, suite (1920). **OTHER:** Chamber music; piano pieces; songs.

BIBL.: A. Bassi, *G. O.: Tradizione e avanguardia nel melodramma del primo '900* (Padua, 1987).—**NS/LK/DM**

Orejón y Aparicio, José de,

Peruvian composer and organist; b. Huacho, 1706; d. Lima, between May 7 and 21, 1756. He was admitted to the choir at Lima Cathedral when he was only 9, and studied organ there with its principal organist, Juan de Peralta. After his teacher's death, Orejón y Aparicio briefly served as interim organist and was recalled in 1742 as principal organist. He also was made its maestro di capilla in 1760. His sacred music was greatly esteemed in his era. —**LK/DM**

Orel, Alfred,

distinguished Austrian musicologist; b. Vienna, July 3, 1889; d. there, April 11, 1967. He studied law at the Univ. of Vienna, graduating in 1912, then was employed in the Ministry of Finance until 1918. He subsequently studied musicology with Guido Adler at the Univ. of Vienna, where he received his Ph.D. in 1919 with the diss. *Die Hauptstimme in den "Salve regina" der Trienter Codices*. He completed his Habilitation there in 1922 with his *Über rhythmische Qualität in mehrstimmigen Tonsätzen des 15. Jahrhunderts*. He was director of the music division of the Vienna Stadtbibliothek (1918–40), librarian of the Inst. of Musicology (1918–22), and a reader in music history (1929–45) at the Univ. of Vienna. He was particularly noted for his work on the life and music of Anton Bruckner.

WRITINGS: *Unbekannte Frühwerke Anton Bruckners* (Vienna, 1921); *Ein Wiener Beethoven-Buch* (Vienna, 1921); *Anton Bruckner: Das Werk—Der Künstler—Die Zeit* (Vienna and Leipzig, 1925); *Wiener Musikerbriefe aus zwei Jahrhunderten* (Vienna, 1925); *Beethoven* (Vienna, 1927); with R. Stöhr and H. Gál, *Formenlehre der Musik* (Leipzig, 1933; 2nd ed., 1954); *Anton Bruckner, 1824–1896: Sein Leben in Bildern* (Leipzig, 1936); *Kirchenmusikalische Liturgik* (Augsburg, 1936); *Franz Schubert, 1797–1828: Sein Leben in Bildern* (Leipzig, 1939); *Aufsätze und Vorträge* (Vienna and Berlin, 1939); *Ein Harmonielehrekolleg bei Anton Bruckner* (Vienna and Berlin, 1940); *Der junge Schubert* (Vienna, 1940); *Mozarts deutscher Weg: Eine Deutung aus Briefen* (Vienna, 1940; 2nd ed., 1943); *Grillparzer und Beethoven* (Vienna, 1941); *Mozart in Wien* (Vienna, 1944); *Hugo Wolf: Ein Künstlerbildnis* (Vienna, 1947); *Johannes Brahms: Ein Meister und sein Weg* (Olten, 1948); *Goethe als Operndirektor* (Bregenz, 1949); *Bruckner-Brevier: Briefe, Dokumente, Berichte* (Vienna, 1953); *Musikstadt Wien* (Vienna, 1953); *Mozart, Gloria Mundi* (Salzburg, 1956); ed.

Johannes Brahms und Julius Allgeyer: Eine Künstlerfreundschaft in Briefen (Tutzing, 1964).

BIBL.: H. Federhofer, ed., *Festschrift A. O. zum 70. Geburtstag überreicht von Kollegen, Freunden und Schülern* (Vienna and Wiesbaden, 1960).—**NS/LK/DM**

Orel, Dobroslav,

Czech ecclesiastical music scholar and choral conductor; b. Ronov, near Prague, Dec. 15, 1870; d. Prague, Feb. 18, 1942. He studied music with Novák and Hostinský in Prague, and later musicology with Adler at the Univ. of Vienna. In 1914 he received a Ph.D. there with the diss. *Der Mensuralkodex Speciálník: Ein Beiträg zur Geschichte der Mensuralmusik und der Notenschrift in Böhmen bis 1540*. He was ordained a priest. He was a prof. at the Prague Cons. (1907–19). From 1909 to 1918 he was ed. of the Prague church music periodical *Cyrill*, and from 1921 to 1938 was a prof. of musicology at the Komensky Univ., Bratislava; was active as a conductor of various choral societies. He greatly distinguished himself as an authority on Czech liturgical music.

WRITINGS (all in Czech and publ. in Bratislava unless otherwise given): *A Theoretical and Practical Manual of Roman Plainsong* (Hradec Králové, 1899); *A Czech Hymnbook* (Prague, 1921; 5th ed., 1936); *The Franus Hymnbook* (Prague, 1922); *The Beginnings of Polyphony in Bohemia* (1925); *Ján Levoslav Bella* (1924); *František Liszt a Bratislava* (1925); *Musical Sources in the Franciscan Library in Bratislava* (1930); *St. Wenceslas Elements in Music* (Prague, 1937); J. Potúček, ed., *Contributions to the History of Slovak Music* (1968).—**NS/LK/DM**

Orff, Carl,

eminent German composer and music educator; b. Munich, July 10, 1895; d. there, March 29, 1982. He began piano lessons in his fifth year, and later studied at the Munich Academy of Music (1912–14) and with Helmut Zilcher (1914). From 1915 to 1917 he conducted at the Munich Kammerspiele. In 1917 he entered military service and was sent to the Eastern front during the final stages of World War I. After the War, he conducted at the Mannheim National Theater and at the Darmstadt Court Theater in 1918. Orff completed his studies with Heinrich Kaminski in 1920–21. His interest in education led him to found, with Dorothee Günther, the Günther School in Munich in 1924 for the training of children in gymnastics, rhythm, music, and dance. His influence as a music educator was widespread. With Gunild Keetman, he publ. the *Orff-Schulwerk Elementare Musikübung* (1931–34; rev. as *Musik für Kinder*, 1950–54). In 1932–33 Orff served as conductor of the Munich Bach Soc. On June 8, 1937, his cantiones profanae, *Carmina Burana*, was premiered in Frankfurt am Main. Scored for Soprano, Tenor, Baritone, Chorus, Children's Chorus, and Orch., and set to texts in Latin and German from 13th century Goliard poems in the Benediktbeuren monastery in Bavaria, it became Orff's most celebrated work. From 1950 to 1960 he taught at the Munich Staatliche Hochschule für Musik. In 1956 he was made a member of the order Pour le mérite. He received honorary doctorates from the Univ. of Tübingen in 1959 and the Univ. of Munich in 1972. In 1972 he was awarded the Grand Cross for Distinguished Service of the Order of

Merit of the Federal Republic of Germany. Orff spent his last years preparing *Carl Orff und sein Werk* (8 vols., Tutzing, 1975–83). In his works after 1936, he attempted to develop what he described as dramatic music along the lines of total theater. While the form was freer, dramatic action was lacking and settings were static. However, the utilization of elementary rhythms and folk melodies made his works more agreeable in constituting works of total art.

WORKS: DRAMATIC: *Gisei*, music drama (1913); *Ein Sommernachtstraum*, Schauspiel after Shakespeare (1917; 2nd version, 1928; 3rd version, Frankfurt am Main, Oct. 14, 1939; 4th version, 1943; 5th version, Darmstadt, Oct. 30, 1952; 6th version, Stuttgart, March 12, 1963); *Orpheus*, new version of Monteverdi's *L'Orfeo* (1924; Mannheim, April 17, 1925; 2nd version, Munich, Oct. 13, 1929; 3rd version, 1939; Dresden, Oct. 4, 1940); *Klage der Ariadne*, new version of Monteverdi's *Lamento d'Arianna* (1925; rev. version, Gera, Nov. 30, 1940); *Tanz der Spröden*, new version of madrigals from Monteverdi's *Ballo del e Ingrate* (Karlsruhe, Dec. 28, 1925; rev. version, Gera, Nov. 30, 1940); 3 preceding works first perf. as the trittico teatrale *Lamenti* (Schwetzingen, May 15, 1958); *Carmina Burana*, cantiones profanae for Soprano, Tenor, Baritone, Chorus, Children's Chorus, and Orch. (1936; Frankfurt am Main, June 8, 1937; with *Catulli Carmina* and *Trionfo di Afrodite* as the trittico teatrale *Trionfi*, Milan, Feb. 14, 1953); *Der Mond* (1937–38; Munich, Feb. 5, 1939; rev. 1945; Munich, Nov. 26, 1950); *Die Kluge* (1941–42; Frankfurt am Main, Feb. 20, 1943); *Catulli Carmina*, ludi scaenici (Leipzig, Nov. 6, 1943; with *Carmina Burana* and *Trionfo di Afrodite* as the trittico teatrale *Trionfi*, Milan, Feb. 14, 1953); *Die Bernauerin* (1944–45; Stuttgart, June 15, 1947); *Astutuli* (1945–46; Munich, Oct. 20, 1953); *Antigonae*, Trauerspiel after Sophocles and Hölderlin (1947–48; Salzburg, Aug. 9, 1949); *Die Weihnachtsgeschichte* (Bavarian Radio, Munich, Dec. 24, 1948); *Trionfo di Afrodite*, concerto scenico (1950–51; with *Carmina Burana* and *Catulli Carmina* as the trittico teatrale *Trionfi*, Milan, Feb. 14, 1953); *Comoedia de Christi Resurrectione*, Easter play (1955; Bavarian Radio, Munich, March 31, 1956; stage perf., Stuttgart, April 21, 1957); *Oedipus der Tyrann*, Trauerspiel after Sophocles and Hölderlin (1957–58; Stuttgart, Dec. 11, 1959); *Ludus de nato Infante mirificus*, Christmas play (Stuttgart, Dec. 11, 1960); *Prometheus* (1963–67; Stuttgart, March 24, 1968). **ORCH.:** *Tanzende Faune* (1914; Munich, Dec. 6, 1995); *Kleines Konzert* for Wind Ensemble, after 16th century lute music (1927; Munich, Dec. 11, 1928; rev. 1975; also for Orch., Munich, Dec. 15, 1937); *Entrata*, after William Byrd (1928; 2nd version, Frankfurt am Main, Aug. 24, 1940; 3rd version, Frankfurt am Main, Feb. 28, 1941). **CHAMBER:** Quartet Movement (c. 1914; Altötting, July 5, 1989); piano pieces; violin works. **VOCAL:** *Zarasthustra* for Baritone, 3 Men's Choruses, and Orch., after Nietzsche (1911–12); *Frühe Lieder* for Voice and Piano (1911; 1919–21); *Des Turmes Auferstehung* for 2 Basses and Orch., after Werfel (1921; 2nd version for 2 Men's Choruses and Orch., Munich, Dec. 6, 1995); Cantata for Chorus, Piano, and Percussion, after Werfel (1930; rev. 1968); Cantata for Chorus, Piano, and Percussion, after Brecht (1930; rev. 1973); *Concento di voci* (1, *Sirmio* for Chorus, 1930; 2, *Laudes creaturarum* for Chorus, 1954; Solingen, July 21, 1957; 3, *Sunt lacrimae rerum* for Men's Chorus, 1956; Solingen, July 21, 1957); *Dithyrambi* for Chorus and Instruments, after Schiller (1, *Die Sänger der Vorwelt*, 1955; Stuttgart, Aug. 3, 1956; 2, *Nanie und Dithyrambe*, Bremen, Dec. 4, 1956; both rev. 1981; Munich, Nov. 22, 1987); *Stücke* for Speaking Chorus and Instruments (1969); *Rota* for Chorus and Instruments, after *Sumer is icumen in* (Munich, Aug. 26, 1972);

(3) *Sprechstücke* for Speaker, Speaking Chorus, and Percussion (1976).

BIBL.: W. Trittenhoff, *O.-Schulwerk: Einführung* (Mainz, 1930); A. Liess, *C. O.: Idee und Werk* (Zürich, 1955; 2nd ed., rev., 1977; Eng. tr., 1966); K. Ruppel, G. Sellner, and W. Thomas, *C. O., ein Bericht in Wort und Bild* (Mainz, 1955; 2nd ed., rev., 1960; Eng. tr., 1960); I. Kiekert, *Die musikalische Form in den Werken C. O.s* (Regensburg, 1957); M. Devreese-Papgnies, *Sur les traces du Schulwerk de C. O.: Méthodologie pour l'usage des instruments d'orchestre scolaire* (Brussels, 1968); F. Willnauer, ed., *Prometheus: Mythos, Drama, Musik: Beiträge zu C. O.s Musikdrama nach Aischylos* (Tübingen, 1968); U. Klement, *Das Musiktheater C. O.s: Untersuchungen zu einem bürgerlichen Kunstwerk* (diss., Univ. of Leipzig, 1969); G. Keetman, *Elementaria: Erster Umgang mit dem O.Schulwerk* (Stuttgart, 1970; Eng. tr., 1974); R. Münster, ed., *C. O.: Das Bühnenwerk* (Munich, 1970); H. Wolfgart, ed., *Das O.-Schulwerk im Dienste der Erziehung und Therapie behinderter Kinder* (Berlin, 1971); W. Thomas, *C. O.: De temporum fine comoedia...eine Interpretation* (Tutzing, 1973); G. Orff, *The O. Music Therapy* (London, 1980); U. Klement, *Das Musiktheater C. O.s* (Leipzig, 1982); H. Leuchtmann, *C. O.: Ein Gedenkbuch* (Tutzing, 1985); G. Orff-Büchtemann, *Mein Vater und ich: Erinnerungen an C. O.* (Munich, 1992); A. Fassone, *C. O.* (Lucca, 1994); W. Thomas, *O.s Märchenstücke: Der Mond, Die Kluge* (Mainz, 1994); idem, *Dem unbekannten Gott: Ein nicht ausgeführtes Chorwerk von C. O.* (Mainz, 1997).—NS/LK/DM

Orgad, Ben-Zion, German-born Israeli composer; b. Gelsenkirchen, Aug. 21, 1926. He went to Palestine in 1933 and studied with Ben-Haim (1942–47), and also took courses at the Rubin Academy of Music (graduated, 1947). He later studied with Copland at the Berkshire Music Center in Tanglewood (summers, 1949, 1951, 1961) and with Fine and Shapero at Brandeis Univ. (M.F.A. in musicology, 1962). From 1950 to 1988 he worked for the Israeli Ministry of Education and Culture. In 1997 he received the Israel Prize in Music.

WORKS: ORCH.: *Building the King's Stage* (1957); *Music for Horn and Orch.* (1960; rev. 1988); *Kaleidoscope* (1961); *Movement on A* (1965); *First Watch* for Strings (1969); *Melodic Dialogues on 3 Scrolls* (1969); *Ballad* (1971); *Second Watch* for Chamber Orch. (1973; rev. for Orch., 1982); *Dialogues on the First Scroll* for Chamber Orch. (1975); *A Vigil in Jerusalem: Third Watch* (1978); *Song of Praise* (1979); *Individuations I*, concertante for Clarinet and Chamber Orch. (1981; rev. 1984) and *II*, concertante for Violin, Cello, and Chamber Orch. (1990); *She'arim* for Brass Orch. (1986); *Filigrees V*, concertante for Chamber Orch. (1993) and *VI* for Strings (1993); *Toccata in Galilean Maqam: Choregraphic Tonescapes* (Tel Aviv, Nov. 24, 1994); *Toccata in a Galilean Maqam (Choreographic Tonescape)* (1994); *Ad profundos* (1998). **CHAMBER:** *Ballad* for Violin (1947); *Monolog* for Viola (1957); *Septet* for Clarinet, Bassoon, Horn, Violin, Viola, Cello, and Double Bass (1959); Duo for Violin and Cello (1960); String Trio (1961); *Tak'sim* for Harp (1962); *Landscapes* for Wind Quintet (1969); *Songs without Words* for Flute, Piano, Clarinet, Violin, Cello, Piano, and Percussion (1970); *Filigrees I* for Clarinet and String Quartet (1989–90), *II* for Oboe or English Horn and String Quartet (1990), *III* for Bassoon and String Quartet (1992), and *IV*, septet for Clarinet, Bassoon, Horn, Violin, Viola, Cello, and Double Bass (1993); *Melosalgia* for 2 Trumpets (1993); *Siphonic Movement* for Wind Quintet, Brass Quintet, 2 String Quintets, and Percussion (1999). **Piano:** *Toccata* (1946); *2 Preludes in Impressionistic Mood* (1960); *7 Variations on C* (1961); *Reshuyoth* (1978); *Martir* (1994); *Tone Alleys* (1999). **VOCAL:** *Leave Out*

My Name, song cycle for Mezzo-soprano and Flute (1947); *The Beauty of Israel*, sym. for Baritone and Orch. (1949); *Isaiah's Vision*, biblical cantata for Chorus and Orch. (1952); *The Story of the Spies*, biblical cantata for Chorus, Narrator ad libitum, and Orch. (1952); *Out of the Desert*, quintet for Mezzo-soprano or Contralto, Flute, Bassoon, Viola, and Cello (1956); *Mizmorim*, cantata for Soloists and Chamber Orch. (1966–68); (4) *Songs of an Early Morning* for Mezzo-soprano, Baritone, and Chamber Orch. (1968); *Death Came to the Wooden Horse Michael*, ballad for 2 Mezzo- sopranos and Chamber Ensemble (1968; rev. 1977); *The Old Decrees*, Passion in 5 Testimonies for Soloists, Chorus, and Chamber Orch. (1970; rev. 1987; Cologne, Nov. 3, 1990); *Story of a Pipe* for Soloists, Chorus, and Orch. (1971); *Sufferings for Redemption*, cantata for Mezzo-soprano, Women's Chorus, and Chamber Orch. (1974); *Songs Out of Hoshen Valley* for Chorus (1981); *Sh'ar Larashut* for Chorus (1988); *And This is the Blessing*, cantata for Soloists, Chorus, Trumpet, and Piano (1993); *A Personal Place* for Alto and 12 Players (1995); *Voices* for Narrator and Clarinet or Cello (1999).—**NS/LK/DM**

Orgeni, Aglaja (real name, Anna Maria von Görger St. Jorgen)

, respected Hungarian soprano and teacher; b. Roma Szombat, Dec. 17, 1841; d. Vienna, March 15, 1926. She was a pupil of Pauline Viardot-García at Baden-Baden, making her debut on Sept. 28, 1865, as Amina, at the Berlin Royal Opera. She made her first appearance in London on April 7, 1866, as Violetta, at Covent Garden; later sang in Vienna, Dresden, Berlin, Copenhagen, etc. From 1886 she taught singing at the Dresden Cons. She was made a Royal Professor in 1908, the first case of the title being conferred on a woman. In 1914 she settled in Vienna. Among her distinguished pupils were Erika Wedekind and Edyth Walker. She was held in high esteem for such roles as Agathe in *Der Freischütz*, Marguerite in *Faust*, Leonora in *Il Trovatore*, and Valentine in *Les Huguenots*.

BIBL.: E. Brand, *A. O.* (Munich, 1931).—**NS/LK/DM**

Orgitano, family of Italian musicians:

(1) **Vincenzo Orgitano**, composer; b. c. 1735; d. Naples, c. 1807. He was made music master to Maria Teresa and Maria Louisa, the daughters of King Ferdinand of Naples, about 1779. In 1782 he was named maestro di cappella soprannumerario and in 1787 primo maestro of the royal chapel. He wrote the operas *Il finto pastorello* (Naples, 1759) and *Le pazzie per amore* (Rome, Carnival 1761), much instrumental music, including 14 sinfonias, chamber music, keyboard pieces, and various sacred vocal works.

(2) **Paolo Orgitano**, organist and composer, brother of the preceding; b. Naples, c. 1740; d. there, May 1796. He was made second substitute organist in 1776 and first organist in 1779 of the royal chapel in Naples. He also served as maestro di cappella straordinario at the Tesoro di S. Gennaro in Naples from 1777.

(3) **Raffaele Orgitano**, composer, son of (1) **Vincenzo Orgitano**; b. Naples, c. 1770; d. probably in Paris, 1812. He was a student of Sala at the Cons. della Pietà dei Turchini in Naples. In 1790 he was made maestro di cappella straordinario at the Tesoro di S. Gennaro and in 1791 organista soprannumerario of the royal chapel. In 1800 he went to Palermo, and later settled in Paris. He

wrote the operas *Non credere alle apparenze, ossia L'amore intraprendente* (Venice, Oct. 10, 1801), *Adelaide e Tebaldo* (Venice, Dec. 27, 1801), *Gli amanti al cimento* (Rome, Carnival 1802), *Amore ed interesse, ossia L'infermo ad arte* (Naples, 1802), and *Arsinoe* (n.d.), as well as some sacred pieces.—**LK/DM**

Óriada, Seán

, Irish composer; b. Cork, Aug. 1, 1931; d. London, Oct. 3, 1971. He was a pupil of Fleischmann at Univ. Coll., Cork (B.Mus., 1952). After serving as asst. music director of Radio Eireann (1954–55), he was music director of Dublin's Abbey Theatre (1955–62) and a teacher at his alma mater (from 1963). He wrote a series of works entitled Nomos, the most ambitious being No. 2 for Baritone, Chorus, and Orch. (1963). Among his other works were stage music, orch. pieces, and chamber music.—**LK/DM**

O'Riley, Christopher

, talented American pianist; b. Chicago, April 17, 1956. He began piano lessons with Lilli Simon when he was only four; later studied with Russell Sherman at the New England Cons. of Music in Boston. After winning second prize in the Montreal Competition (1980), fifth prize in both the Van Cliburn and Leeds competitions (1981), and sixth prize in the Busoni Competition (1981), he made his formal recital debut in N.Y. in 1981; that same year he made his European debut in a recital in Amsterdam. He subsequently appeared as soloist with leading orchs. of the U.S. and Europe, gave recitals, and played in chamber music concerts. His programs often include rarely heard works both in the standard and the contemporary piano literature.—**NS/LK/DM**

Orkis, Lambert (Thomas)

, distinguished American pianist, fortepianist, and teacher; b. Philadelphia, April 20, 1946. He was a student of Guglielmo Sabbatini (1951–55) and Eleanor Sokoloff (1955–60), continuing his training with the latter at the Curtis Inst. of Music in Philadelphia (diploma, 1965; B.M., 1966). He also studied with Maryan Filar at Temple Univ. (M.M., 1968). In 1957 he made his debut as a soloist with the Philadelphia Orch. under the direction of William Smith. In 1968 he joined the faculty of Temple Univ., where he taught for over 30 years. From 1976 to 1987 he was the pianist of the 20th Century Consort, and from 1986 to 1989 of the American Chamber Players. He became principal keyboard player of the National Sym. Orch. in 1982 and the pianist of the Smithsonian Chamber Players in 1983 in Washington, D.C. In 1988 he also became fortepianist in the Castle Trio. In 1993 he made his European debut as a soloist in Richard Wernick's Piano Concerto with the Residentie Orch. in The Hague under the composer's direction. In addition to his various positions, Orkis has pursued an acclaimed career as a chamber music artist of the highest distinction. He has appeared regularly with Mstislav Rostropovich (from 1981), Lucy Shelton (from 1981), and Anne-Sophie Mutter (from 1988), and also with Arleen Auger (1987–90). During 1998, Orkis and Mutter appeared in various music centers of the world in compelling performances of complete cycles of the Beethoven violin sonatas. They began their tour in Hannover on Jan. 26, and then played in such cities as Berlin, Zürich, Madrid, Amsterdam, Rome, N.Y., Chicago, Philadelphia, Boston, Los Angeles, Dresden, Milan, Paris, London, Shanghai, Seoul, Buenos Aires, and Vienna before ending it with a benefit concert at the Beethovenhaus in Bonn on Dec. 17. Orkis maintains an extensive repertoire, beginning with Bach and traversing the 19th and 20th centuries. In addition to his discerning interpretations of such masters as Mozart, Beethoven, Schubert, Mendelssohn, Schumann, Liszt, Chopin, Brahms, Debussy, and Ravel, he has played much contemporary music, including works written for him by George Crumb, James Primosch, Wernick, and Maurice Wright.—**LK/DM**

Orlandi, Ferdinando, Italian composer and singing teacher; b. Parma, Oct. 7, 1774; d. there, Jan. 5, 1848. He was a pupil of Gaspare Rugarli, the Colorno organist, of Gaspare Ghiretti and Paër in Parma, and of Sala and Tritto at the Cons. della Pietà dei Turchini in Naples (1793–99). In 1800 he became a member of the ducal chapel in Parma. He then went to Milan, where he taught at the Reale Casa dei Paggi (1806–14) and at the Cons. (1814–22). After teaching in Munich (1822–23) and Stuttgart (1823–28), he served as director of singing at the Teatro Ducale in Parma from 1834 to 1848. He was also honorary maestro di cappella at the court. Among his works were 26 operas, chamber music, and sacred pieces.—**LK/DM**

Orlandini, Giuseppe Maria, prominent Italian composer; b. Florence, March 19, 1675; d. there, Oct. 24, 1760. He most likely received his musical training in Florence. He served as maestro di cappella at the court of Tuscany during most of his career, and also held that position in Florence at the Cathedral (1732–60) and at S. Michele (1734–57). His *Serpilla e Bacocco* was one of the most celebrated stage works of the 18th century.

WORKS: DRAMATIC: O p e r a : *Artaserse* (Naples, 1708; additional music by F. Mancini; *L'amor generoso* (Pratolino, 1708; additional music by R. Cerruti); *L'odio e l'amore* (Genoa, 1709); *La fede tradita e vendicata* (Genoa, 1709); *Ataulfo re de'Goti, ovvero La forza della virtù* (Rome, Carnival 1712); *L'innocenza difesa* (Ferrara, 1712); *Teuzzone* (Ferrara, 1712); *Carlo, rè d'Alemagna* (Bologna, Oct. 28, 1713); *Nerone fatto Cesare* (Venice, Carnival 1715; in collaboration with others); *Amore e maestà* (Florence, 1715; rev. as *Arsace*, London, Jan. 1, 1721); *I veri amici* (Naples, Nov. 26, 1715); *Griselda, ovvero La virtù al cimento* (Brescia, Carnival 1716); *La Merope* (Bologna, Oct. 24, 1717); *Lucio Papirio* (Naples, Dec. 11, 1717; additional music by F. Feo); *Antigona* (Venice, Carnival 1718; rev. as *La fedeltà coronata*, Bologna, 1727); *Le amazoni vinte da Ercole* (Reggio Emilia, April 1718); *Ifigenia in Tauride* (Venice, Carnival 1719); *Il carciere di se stesso* (Turin, Dec. 26, 1719); *Paride* (Venice, Carnival 1720); *Il Farasmene* (Bologna, Nov. 1720; rev. as *L'amor tirannico*, Pesaro, Carnival 1722); *Nerone* (Hamburg, 1720); *Nino* (Rome, Jan. 7, 1722; with additional music by A. Tinazzoli, Pesaro, Carnival 1723); *Semiramide* (Turin, Carnival 1722); *Ormisda* (Bologna, 1722); *Alessandro Severo* (Milan, Jan. 1723); *L'Oronta* (Milan, Jan. 1724); *Berenice* (Venice, Carnival 1725); *Adelaide* (Genoa, Carnival 1726; with additional music by others, Mantua, Carnival 1731); *La fida ninfa* (Venice, 1730); *Massimiano* (Venice, Carnival 1731); *Ifigenia in Aulide* (Florence, Carnival 1732); *Temistocle*

(Florence, Carnival 1737); *Le nozze di Perseo e Andromeda* (Florence, 1738); *Arianna* (Florence, Jan. 1739); *Venceslao* (Florence, Dec. 26, 1741); *Vologeso re de'Parti* (Florence, Jan. 1742); *Lo scialacquatore* (Florence, 1744). I n t r e m e z z o s : *Madama Dulcinea e il cuoco del Marchese del Bosco, ovvero La preziosa ridicola* (Rome, 1712); *Lisetta e Delfo* (Rome, Carnival 1713); *Il Marito giocatore e la moglie becchatona* (Venice, Jan. 1719; best known as *Serpilla e Bacocco*); *Melinda e Tiburzio* (Venice, Carnival 1721; rev. as *La Donna nobile*, Venice, Carnival 1730); *Il bottegaro gentiluomo, ovvero Larinda e Vanesio* (Florence, Carnival 1721); *L'Ammalato immaginario* (Florence, Carnival 1725); *Un vecchio innamorato* (Florence, Carnival 1732); *Porsugnacco e Grilletta* (Milan, 1727); *Grullo e Moschetta* (Venice, Carnival 1725); *Il Marito geloso* (St. Petersburg, 1734); *Balbo e Dalisa* (Rome, Carnival 1740). O t h e r : 8 oratorios (only librettos extant). —**NS/LK/DM**

Orlov, Nikolai (Andreievich), talented Russian pianist; b. Elets, Orlov district, Feb. 26, 1892; d. Grantown-on-Spey, Scotland, May 31, 1964. He studied in Moscow at the Gnessin Music School and then with Igumnov at the Cons. (graduated, 1910); also studied privately with Taneyev. He launched his career in 1912; was also a teacher at the Phil. School (1913–15) and a prof. at the Cons. (1916–21) in Moscow; then toured extensively in Europe, the U.S., and Latin America, settling in England in 1948. He was one of the finest Russian pianists of his day.—**NS/LK/DM**

Orlowski, Antoni, Polish violinist, pianist, conductor, and composer; b. Warsaw, 1811; d. Rouen, Feb. 11, 1861. He studied with Bielawski (violin), Detroit and Ernemann (piano), Lenz (organ), and Elsner (composition) in Warsaw (1824–29) before completing his training with Le Sueur in Paris. From 1835 he was active as a conductor in Rouen. He wrote two operettas, a ballet, chamber music, and piano pieces.—**LK/DM**

Ormandy, Eugene (real name, **Jenö Blau**), outstanding Hungarian-born American conductor; b. Budapest, Nov. 18, 1899; d. Philadelphia, March 12, 1985. He first studied violin at a very early age with his father, and at age 5 he was admitted to the Royal Academy of Music in Budapest. At 9, he became a student of Hubay there, receiving his artist's diploma at 13. When he was 17 he joined its faculty. He also pursued training in philosophy at the Univ. of Budapest. In 1917 he became concertmaster of the Blüthner Orch. in Germany, and also made tours as a soloist and recitalist. In 1921 he emigrated to the U.S. and in 1927 became a naturalized American citizen. He became a violinist in the pit orch. at the Capitol Theater in N.Y. in 1921, and soon thereafter became its concertmaster. In Sept. 1924 he made his debut as a conductor with the orch., and in 1926 he was named its assoc. music director. He appeared as a guest conductor with the N.Y. Phil. at the Lewisohn Stadium in 1929 and with the Philadelphia Orch. at Robin Hood Dell in 1930. Ormandy first attracted national attention when he substituted for an indisposed Toscanini at a Philadelphia Orch. concert on Oct. 30, 1931. His unqualified success led to his appointment as conductor of the Minneapolis

Sym. Orch. in 1931. In 1936 he was invited to serve as assoc. conductor with Stokowski of the Philadelphia Orch. On Sept. 28, 1938, Ormany was formally named music director of the Philadelphia Orch., a position he retained with great distinction until his retirement in 1980. Thereafter he held its title of Conductor Laureate. Ormandy's 42–year tenure as music director of the Philadelphia Orch. was the longest of any conductor of a major American orch. Under his guidance, the Philadelphia Orch. not only retained its renown from the Stokowski era but actually enhanced its reputation through many tours in North America and abroad, innumerable recordings, and radio and television broadcasts. Between 1937 and 1977 Ormandy led it on 9 transcontinental tours of the U.S. In 1949 he took it to England, in 1955 and 1958 to the Continent. In 1973 he took it to the People's Republic of China, the first U.S. orch. to visit that nation. Ormany received numerous honors. In 1952 he was made an Officier and in 1958 a Commandeur of the French Légion d'honneur. In 1970 he was awarded the U.S. Medal of Freedom by President Richard M. Nixon. In 1976 Queen Elizabeth II made him an honorary Knight Commander of the Order of the British Empire. He also received various doctorates. Ormandy excelled as an interpreter of the Romantic repertoire, in which his mastery of orch. resources was most evident. It was his custom to conduct most of his concerts from memory.—NS/LK/DM

Ornithoparchus (Greek form of his real name, **Vogelsang**), **Andreas,** German music scholar; b. Meiningen, c. 1485; d. Münster, c. 1535. He matriculated at the Univ. of Rostock (M.A., 1512) and at the Univ. of Tübingen (M.A., 1515). He was rector of the parochial school in Münster in 1515, and also matriculated at Wittenberg (1516), Leipzig (1516), and Greifswald (1518). He publ. a valuable theoretical treatise, *Musice activae micrologus* (Leipzig, 1517; 6th ed., 1540; Eng. tr. by J. Dowland, London, 1609; reprint 1977).

BIBL.: J. Lyra, *A. O. aus Meiningen...und dessen Lehre von den Kirchenaccenten* (Gütersloh, 1877).—NS/LK/DM

Ornstein, Leo, remarkable Russian-born American pianist, teacher, and composer; b. Kremenchug, Dec. 11, 1892. The son of a synagogal cantor, he studied music at home, and then with Vladimir Puchalsky in Kiev and, at the age of 10, with Essipova at the St. Petersburg Cons. As a consequence of anti-Semitic disturbances in Russia, the family emigrated to the U.S. in 1907. Ornstein studied piano with Bertha Feiring Tapper and Goetschius at the Inst. of Musical Art in N.Y. He gave his first concert in N.Y., as a pianist, on March 5, 1911, and then played in Philadelphia and other cities. About 1910 he began to compose; he experimented with percussive sonorities, in dissonant harmonies. Ornstein made a European tour in 1913–14, and appeared in London on March 27, 1914, in a piano recital announced as "futuristic music" featuring his Sonata and other works. Returning to the U.S. early in 1915, he gave a series of recitals at the Bandbox Theater in N.Y., comprising works by Debussy, Ravel, Schoenberg, Scriabin, and other modern composers as well as his own; his *Danse sauvage* excited his audiences by its declared wildness and placed him in the center of controversy; he was hailed as the prophet of a new musical era. After several years as an active virtuoso, he turned mainly to teaching; was made head of the piano dept. of the Philadelphia Musical Academy (1920); also founded the Ornstein School of Music in Philadelphia (1940), and continued to teach until 1955. In 1975 he received the Marjorie Peabody Waite Award of the National Inst. of Arts and Letters. Ornstein's longevity is unmatched by any composer of comparable magnitude.

WORKS: ORCH.: *3 Moods: Anger, Peace, Joy* (1914); *The Fog,* symphonic poem (1915); *Evening Song of the Cossack* for Chamber Orch. (1923); Piano Concerto (1923; Philadelphia, Feb. 13, 1925); *Lysistrata Suite* (1930); *Nocturne and Dance of the Fates* (St. Louis, Feb. 12, 1937). CHAMBER: 2 violin sonatas (c. 1915, c. 1918); *3 Russian Impressions* for Violin and Piano (1916); 2 cello sonatas (c. 1918, c. 1920); Piano Quintet (1927); 3 string quartets (?, c. 1929, 1976); 6 *Préludes* for Cello and Piano (1931); *Nocturne* for Clarinet and Piano (1952); *Ballad* for Saxophone and Piano (1955); *Allegro (Intermezzo)* for Flute and Piano (1959); *Fantasy Pieces* for Viola and Piano (1972); *Hebraic Fantasy* for Violin and Piano (1975); *Poem* for Flute and Piano (1979). Piano: *At Twilight* (1911); *Wild Men's Dance (Danse Sauvage)* c. 1913; *Three Moods* (c. 1914; also for Orch.); *Cossack Impressions* (c. 1914); *Impressions of Notre Dame* (c. 1914); *Suicide in an Airplane* (c. 1915); *Dwarf Suite* (1915); *9 Miniatures* (1915); *Poems of 1917* (1917); *A la Chinoise* (c. 1917); *An Allegory* (c. 1917); 8 sonatas: No.s 1–3 (unaccounted for), No. 4 (1918), No. 5, *Biography* (1974), No. 6 (1981), No. 7 (1988), and No. 8 (1990); *Impressions of the Thames* (1920); *6 Water Colors* (1921); *9 Arabesques* (1921); *Prelude Tragique* (1924); *Bagatelle* (1952); *17 Waltzes* (1958–80?); *Tarantelle Diabolique* (1960); *4 Legends* (1960–82); *A Long Remembered Sorrow* (1964); *Some New York Scenes* (1971); *Burlesca (A Satire)* (1976); *Valse Diabolique* (1977); *The Recruit and the Bugler* (1978); *Barbaro: A Pantomime* (1978); *A Reverie* (1979); *A Chromatic Dance* (1978); *The Deserted Garden* (1982); *Journal* (1987–88). VOCAL: *4 Songs* for Voice and Orch. or Piano (1928).

BIBL.: F. Martens, *L. O.: The Man, His Ideas, His Work* (N.Y., 1918); T. Darter Jr., *The Futurist Piano Music of L. O.* (diss., Cornell Univ., 1979).—NS/LK/DM

Orologio, Alessandro, Italian compoer; b. c. 1550; d. Vienna, c. 1633. He entered the service of the Emperor Rudolf II in Prague about 1579 as a trumpeter, where he later was vice-Kapellmeister (1603–13) and traveled widely. In later years he was active in Steyr and at the Garsten monastery. He publ. three books of madrigals (1586, 1589, 1595), three books of canzonettas (1593, 1595, 1596), and a book of intradas for five to six instruments (1597).—LK/DM

Orozco, Rafael, Spanish pianist; b. Córdoba, Jan. 24, 1946; d. Rome, April 24, 1996. He studied at the Córdoba Cons., at the Madrid Cons. (1960–64), and with Alexis Weissenberg at the Accademia Musicale Chigiana in Siena. In 1966 he won first prize in the Leeds Competition, and thereafter toured extensively. Orozco was best known for his interpretations of the Romantic repertoire.—NS/LK/DM

Orr, C(harles) W(ilfred), English composer; b. Cheltenham, July 31, 1893; d. Painswick, Gloucestershire, Feb. 24, 1976. He studied at the Guildhall School of Music in London. He wrote songs in the manner of German lieder, to words by English poets; his set of seven songs to texts from Housman's *A Shropshire Lad* is notable.—NS/LK/DM

Orr, Robin (actually, Robert Kemsley),

Scottish composer, organist, and teacher; b. Brechin, June 2, 1909. He studied at the Royal Coll. of Music in London (1926–29), and then was an organ scholar at Pembroke Coll., Cambridge (Mus.B., 1932); subsequently took his Mus.B. (1938) and Mus.D. (1950) at the Univ. of Cambridge; he also studied composition with Casella at the Accademia Musicale Chigiana in Siena (1934) and with Boulanger in Paris (1938). He was director of music at Sidcot School in Somerset (1933–36), and then was an asst. lecturer at the Univ. of Leeds (1936–38). From 1938 to 1941, and again from 1945 to 1951, he was organist and director of music at St. John's Coll., Cambridge. From 1947 to 1956 he was a lecturer at the Univ. of Cambridge, and from 1950 to 1956 he was a prof. at the Royal Coll. of Music in London. After serving as the Gardiner prof. of music at the Univ. of Glasgow from 1956 to 1965, he was prof. of composition at the Univ. of Cambridge from 1965 to 1976. From 1962 to 1976 he served as the first chairman of the Scottish Opera in Glasgow. He was director of the Welsh National Opera in Cardiff from 1977 to 1983. In 1972 he was made a Commander of the Order of the British Empire. As a composer, Orr has been particularly adept at investing traditional forms with an individual voice of distinction.

WORKS: DRAMATIC: *A Winter's Tale*, incidental music to Shakepeare's play (1947); *Oedipus et Colonus*, incidental music to Sophocles's play (1950); *Deirdre of the Sorrows*, incidental music (1951); *Full Circle*, opera (Perth, April 10, 1968); *Hermiston*, opera (Edinburgh, Aug. 27, 1975); *On the Razzle*, comic opera (1986; Glasgow, June 27, 1988). **ORCH.:** *The Prospect of Whitby*, overture (1948); *Italian Overture* (1952); *Rhapsody* for Strings (1956); 3 syms.: No. 1, *Symphony in 1 Movement* (Glasgow, Dec. 12, 1963), No. 2 (1970; Glasgow, March 28, 1971), and No. 3 (Llandaff, June 14, 1978); *Sinfonietta Helvetica* (1990; Glasgow, Dec. 6, 1991). **CHAMBER:** Cello Sonatina (1938); Violin Sonatina (1941); Viola Sonata (1947); *Serenade* for String Trio (1948); *Sicilienne and Chaconne* for Viola and Piano (1949); 2 serenades for Horn and Piano (1951, 1960); Duo for Violin and Cello (1953; rev. 1965); Sonata for Violin and Harpsichord or Piano (1956); *Rondeau des Oiseaux* for Recorder or Flute (1994). **KEYBOARD: Piano:** 2 Pieces (1940); 3 *Lyric Pieces* (1994). **Organ:** Toccata alla marcia (1937); 3 *Preludes on Scottish Psalm Tunes* (1958); *Elegy* (1968). **VOCAL:** 3 *Songs of Innocence* for Voice and String Quartet (1932); 4 *Romantic Songs* for Tenor, Oboe, and String Quartet (1950); *Festival Te Deum* for Chorus and Organ or Orch. (1950–51); 3 *Pastorals* for Soprano, Flute, Viola, and Piano (1951); *Te Deum and Jubilate* for Chorus and Organ (1952); *Spring Cantata* for Mezzo-soprano, Chorus, Piano, Timpani, Percussion, and Strings (1955); *Come and Let Yourselves Be Built* for Chorus and Organ (1961); *Magnificat and Nunc Dimittis (Short Service)* for Voices (1967); *From the Book of Philip Sparrow* for Mezzo-soprano and Strings (1969); *Journeys and Places* for Mezzo-soprano and String Quintet or String Orch. (1970); *Liebeslied* for Mezzo-

soprano and Piano or Organ (1978); *Versus from Ogden Nash* for Medium Voice and Strings (1978); *O God, Ruler of the World*, anthem for Chorus and Organ (1982); *Jesu, Sweet Son Dear* for Chorus (1989); other choral pieces and songs.—NS/LK/DM

Orrego-Salas, Juan (Antonio),

distinguished Chilean composer and musicologist; b. Santiago, Jan. 18, 1919. He studied composition at the National Cons. (1936–43) and architecture at the Catholic Univ. (graduated, 1943) in Santiago. In the meantime, he became a teacher of music history at the Univ. of Chile and in 1938 founder-conductor of the Catholic Univ. Chorus. After receiving a Rockefeller Foundation grant and a Guggenheim fellowship, he studied musicology with Lang and Herzog at Columbia Univ. (1944–45), and composition with Thompson at Princeton Univ. (1945–46) and Copland at the Berkshire Music Center in Tanglewood (summer, 1946). Upon returning to Santiago in 1947, he became prof. of composition at the Univ. of Chile. He also resumed his post as conductor of the Catholic Univ. Chorus. In 1949 he became ed. of the *Revista Musical Chilena* and in 1950 music critic of the newspaper *El Mercurio*. In 1953 he was made Distinguished Prof. of composition at the Univ. of Chile. In 1954 he received a second Guggenheim fellowship and revisited the U.S. Upon returning to Santiago, he was director of the Instituto de Extension Musical until 1956. He then became the first director of the music dept. at the Catholic Univ. while continuing to teach at the Univ. of Chile. In 1961 he became a prof. at the Ind. Univ. School of Music in Bloomington, where he was founder-director of its Latin American Music Center. From 1975 to 1980 he also was chairman of its composition dept. He retired as prof. emeritus in 1987. In addition to monographs on composers, Orrego-Salas publ. numerous articles in journals in the U.S., England, and Latin America. In 1956 and 1958 he won the Olga Cohen prize for composition. He was made a corresponding member of the Chilean Academy of Fine Arts in 1971. In 1988 the OAS awarded him the Inter-American Gabriela Mistral Cultural Prize. In 1992 the Chilean government honored him with the Premio Nacional de Arte. He was honored as Distinguished Prof. of the Catholic Univ. in Valparaiso, Chile, in 1999. As a composer, Orrego-Salas has revealed himself as a refined craftsman and an assured master of neo-Classical techniques.

WORKS: DRAMATIC: *Juventud*, ballet (Santiago, Nov. 19, 1948; based on Handel's *Solomon*); *El Retablo del rey pobre*, opera-oratorio (1950–52; first stage perf., Bloomington, Ind., Nov. 10, 1990); *Umbral del sueño*, ballet (Santiago, Aug. 8, 1951); *La Veta del diablo*, film score (1953); *Caleta olvidada*, film score (1959); *The Tumbler's Prayer*, ballet (concert perf., Santiago, Nov. 1960; stage perf., Santiago, Oct. 1961); *Versos de ciego*, incidental music (Santiago, June 1961); *Widows*, opera (1987–90); *The Goat That Couldn't Sneeze*, musical comedy (Bloomington, Ind., Oct. 25, 1992). **ORCH.:** *Escenas de cortes y pastores*, 7 symphonic scenes (1946; Santiago, May 16, 1947); *Obertura festiva* (Santiago, April 1948); 6 syms.: No. 1 (1949; Santiago, July 14, 1950), No. 2, *to the memory of a wanderer* (1954; Minneapolis, Feb. 17, 1956), No. 3 (Washington, D.C., April 22, 1961), No. 4, *of the distant answer* (1966; Bloomington, Ind., April 7, 1967), No. 5 (1995), and No. 6, *semper reditus* (1996); 2 piano concertos: No. 1 (Santiago, Nov. 24, 1950) and No. 2 (1985; Bloomington, Ind.,

Oct. 28, 1988); *Concierto de cámara* (Santiago, Nov. 28, 1952); *Serenata concertante* (1954; Louisville, May 14, 1955); *Jubileaus musicus* (Valparaíso, Chile, Dec. 15, 1956); *Psalms* for Wind Orch. (Pittsburgh, July 1962); *Concerto a tre* for Violin, Cello, Piano, and Orch. (1962; Washington, D.C., May 7, 1965); Concerto for Wind Orch. (1963–64; Pittsburgh, June 1964); *Quattro liriche brevi* for Saxophone and Chamber Orch. (1967; Washington, D.C., May 1, 1974; also for Alto Saxophone and Piano); *Volte* for Chamber Orch. (Rochester, N.Y., Dec. 11, 1971); *Variaciones serenas* for Strings (Santiago, Nov. 23, 1971); Concerto for Oboe and Strings (1980; Santiago, June 16, 1981); Violin Concerto (1983; Bloomington, Ind., Oct. 3, 1984); *Riley's Merriment*, scherzo (Indianapolis, Oct. 7, 1986); *Fantasia* for Piano and Wind Orch. (1986; San Antonio, April 29, 1987); Fanfare for the tenth Pan American Games (1986–87; Indianapolis, June 27, 1987); Cello Concerto (1991–92; Bloomington, Ind., Feb. 5, 1995); *Introduction and Allegro Concertante* for Piano, 4–Hands and Chamber Orch. (1999) **CHAMBER:** Violin Sonata (N.Y., April 1945); *Sonata a duo* for Violin and Viola (1945; Santiago, Aug. 1947); Bandoneon Suite (1952; Paris, June 2, 1953); Sextet for Clarinet, String Quartet, and Piano (1953; Tanglewood, Aug. 15, 1954); *Duos concertantes "in memoriam Hans Kindler"* for Cello and Piano (1955; Washington, D.C., Jan. 9, 1956); *Pastorale y scherzo* for Violin and Piano (1956; N.Y., April 1957); 2 divertimentos for Flute, Oboe, and Bassoon (Santiago, Aug. 23, 1956); 2 string quartets: No. 1 (1957; Washington, D.C., April 19, 1958) and No. 2 (1995); Concertino for Brass Quartet (Bloomington, Ind., Nov. 19, 1963); *Sonata a quattro (Edgewood Sonata)* for Flute, Oboe, Harpsichord, and Contrabass (Washington, D.C., Oct. 31, 1964); 2 trios for Violin, Cello, and Piano: No. 1 (Caracas, May 12, 1966) and No. 2 (1977; N.Y., May 13, 1981); *Quattro liriche brevi* for Alto Saxophone and Piano (1967; London, Jan. 19, 1969; also for Saxophone and Chamber Orch.); *Mobili* for Viola and Piano (1967; Santiago, Nov. 1969); *A Greeting Cadenza* for Viola (1970; Bloomington, Ind., Nov. 1, 1971); *Esquinas* for Guitar (1971; Winona Lake, Ind., March 10, 1973); *Serenata* for Flute and Cello (Columbus, Ohio, Feb. 22, 1972); *Sonata de estío* for Flute and Piano (1972; Bloomington, Ind., Oct. 27, 1974); *Presencias* for Flute, Oboe, Clarinet, Harpsichord, Violin, Viola, and Cello (1972; Washington, D.C., May 5, 1977); *De Profundis* for Tuba and Cello Quartet (1979; N.Y., Jan. 5, 1981); *Variations for a Quiet Man* for Clarinet and Piano for Copland's 80th birthday (1980; Miami, Oct. 3, 1982); *Tangos* for 11 Players (Miami, Oct. 2, 1982); *Balada* for Cello and Piano (1982–83; Bloomington, Ind., Sept. 26, 1983); *Glosas* for Violin and Guitar (1984; Buenos Aires, April 9, 1985); *Variations on a Chant* for Harp (1984; Jerusalem, July 24, 1985); *Gyrocantus* for Flute, Clarinet, Percussion, Harpsichord or Celesta, Violin, and Cello (Santiago, Sept. 1987); *Midsummer Diversions* for Cello and Tuba (Bloomington, Ind., Sept. 27, 1987); *Partita* for Alto Saxophone and Piano Trio (1988); 3 Fanfares for Brass Quintet (Santiago, Nov. 1994); *Encuentros* for Piano and String Quartet (1997); *Espacios* for Cello and Piano (1998; Washington, D.C., Nov. 17, 1999). **Piano:** 2 suites: No. 1 (N.Y., July 31, 1946) and No. 2 (Santiago, Aug. 1951); *Variaciones y fuga sobre el tema de un pregón* (Santiago, July 15, 1946); *Diez piezas simples* (1951; Santiago, Dec. 1, 1952); *Canción y danza* (1951); *Rústica* (1952; Santiago, Jan. 15, 1954); Sonata (Minneapolis, Nov. 18, 1967); *Dialogues in Waltz* for Piano, 4–Hands (1984); *Rondo- Fantasia* (Boulder, Colo., Oct. 16, 1984); *Cantango* for 2 Pianos (Bloomington, Ind., Nov. 4, 1999). **VOCAL:** *Villancico* for Chorus (1942; Santiago, June 9, 1947); *Romance a lo divino* for Chorus (1942; Washington, D.C., April 14, 1947); *Let Down the Bars, Oh Death* for Chorus (1945); *Romances pastorales* for Chorus (1945; Santiago, Sept. 28, 1950);

Canciones en tres movimientos for Soprano and String Quartet (1945); *Cantata de Navidad* for Soprano and Orch. (Rochester, N.Y., Oct. 23, 1946); *Romance a la muerte del Señor Don Gato* for Men's Voices (1946); *Cánones y rondas* for Children's Chorus (1946); *Canciones castellanas* for Soprano and 8 Instrumentalists (Santiago, Dec. 12, 1948); *Cànticos de Navidad* for Women's or Children's Chorus (N.Y., Dec. 12, 1948); *Cantos de Advenimiento* for Woman's Voice, Cello, and Piano (Santiago, June 26, 1948); *El Alba del Alhelí*, song cycle for Soprano and Piano (1950; Santiago, July 10, 1951); *Garden Songs* for Soprano, Flute, Viola, and Harp (1959; Santiago, Nov. 28, 1960); *Alabanzas a la Virgen* for Voice and Piano (1959; Valparaíso, Chile, Feb. 1960); *Alboradas* for Women's Chorus, Harp, Piano, Timpani, and Percussion (Bloomington, Ind., March 17, 1965); *América, no en vano invocamos tu nombre*, cantata for Soprano, Baritone, Men's Chorus, and Orch. (Ithaca, N.Y., May 10, 1966); *Tres madrigales* for Chorus (Bloomington, Ind., Nov. 9, 1967); *Missa "in tempore discordiae"* for Tenor, Chorus, and Orch. (1968–69; Louisville, April 20, 1979); *Palabras de Don Quijote* for Baritone and Chamber Ensemble (Washington, D.C., Oct. 31, 1970); *The Days of God*, oratorio for Soprano, Alto, Tenor, Baritone, Chorus, and Orch. (1974–76; Washington, D.C., Nov. 2, 1976); *Psalms* for Baritone and Piano (Bloomington, Ind., Aug. 3, 1977); *Un Canto a Bolivar*, cantata for Men's Voices and Folk Instruments (1980–81; Athens, Nov. 1981); *Canciones en el estilo popular* for Voice and Guitar (1981; Bloomington, Ind., Jan. 23, 1983); *Bolívar* for Narrator, Chorus, and Orch. (1981–82); *Yo digo lo que no digo* for Voices and Popular Instruments (1983); *Biografía Mínima de Salvador Allende* for Voice, Guitar, Trumpet, and Percussion (San Diego, Aug. 16, 1983); *Cinco canciones a seis* for Mezzo-soprano, 2 Violins, Clarinet, Cello, and Piano (Bloomington, Ind., Dec. 6, 1984); *Ash Wednesday*, 3 songs for Mezzo-soprano and String Orch. (1984); *Saludo* for Unison Voices (1988); *Cancion de Cuna* for Voice and Piano (1991); *La Ciudad Celeste*, cantata for Baritone, Chorus, and Orch. (1992); *3 Sacred Songs "in memoriam Alfonso Letelier"* (1994–95); *Canto a la Cordillera* for Chorus and Orch. (1997–98).—**NS/LK/DM**

Orthel, Léon, Dutch pianist, pedagogue, and composer; b. Roosendaal, North Brabant, Oct. 4, 1905; d. The Hague, Sept. 6, 1985. He studied composition with Wagenaar at the Royal Cons. of Music in The Hague (1921–26) and with Juon at the Hochschule für Musik in Berlin (1928–29). From 1941 to 1971 he taught piano and theory at the Royal Cons. of Music in The Hague, and concurrently taught composition at the Amsterdam Cons. (1949–71). He was chairman of the Composers' Section of the Royal Dutch Society of Musicians (1947–70) while continuing to appear as a pianist.

WORKS: ORCH.: *Concertstuk* for Violin and Orch. (1924); *Scherzo* for Piano and Orch. (1927); 2 cello concertos (1929, 1984); *Concertino alla burla* for Piano and Orch. (1930); 6 syms.: No. 1 (1931–33), No. 2, *Piccola sinfonia* (1940; Rotterdam, Oct. 31, 1941), No. 3 (1943), No. 4, *Sinfonia concertante* for Piano and Orch. (1949), No. 5, *Musica iniziale* (1959–60), and No. 6 (1960–61); 2 Scherzos (1954–55; 1956–57); *3 movimenti ostinati* (1971–72; Amsterdam, Sept. 1, 1973); *Album di disegni* (1976–77); *Evocazione* (1977); Suite No. 2 (1980); *Music* for Double Bass and Orch. (1981). **CHAMBER:** 2 violin sonatas (1924, 1933); 2 cello sonatas (1925, 1958); *5 pezzettini* for Clarinet and Piano (1963); String Quartet (1964); Viola Sonata (1964–65); *Ballade* for Flute and Piano (1970); *8 abbozzi* for Flute, Cello, and Piano (1971); *5 Schizzetti* for Harp (1977). **Piano:** Sonata (1923); *4 Pieces* (1923–24); 9 sonatinas (1924; Minatuure sonatine, 1942; 1945;

1953; for the left hand, 1959; 1974; *Uit 1920 en 1922*, 1975; *Sonatina capricciosa*, 1975; 1977); pieces for children. **VOCAL**: thirteen separate song cycles to texts by Rilke (1934–72). —NS/LK/DM

d'Ortigue, Joseph (-Louis), French writer on music; b. Cavaillon, Vaucluse, May 22, 1802; d. Paris, Nov. 20, 1866. He studied music with H. Blaze and Castil-Blaze, and after training for the law in Aix-en-Provence, he settled in Paris (1829), where he wrote articles on music for various journals. In 1857 he founded *La Maîtrise* (with L. Niedermeyer) and in 1862 the *Journal des Maîtrises* (with F. Clement), both periodicals for church music. In 1863 he became ed. of *Le Ménestrel*, and in 1864 he succeeded Berlioz as critic for the *Journal des Débats*. D'Ortigue exercised considerable influence on musical life in Paris.

WRITINGS (all publ. in Paris): *Le balcon de l'Opéra* (1833); *De l'école musicale italienne et de l'administration de l'Académie royale de musique à l'occasion de l'opéra de M.H. Berlioz* (1839; 2ⁿᵈ ed., 1840, as *Du Théâtre italien et de son influence sur le goût musical français*); *Abécédaire de plain-chant* (1841); *Dictionnaire liturgique, historique et théorique de plain-chant et de musique de l'église, au Moyen-Age et dans les temps modernes* (1853); *Introduction à l'étude comparée des tonalités, et principalement du chant grégorien et de la musique moderne* (1853); with Niedermeyer, *Traité théorique et pratique de l'accompagnement du plain-chant* (1857; Eng. tr., 1905); *La Musique à l'église* (1861).

BIBL.: M. Barber, *J. d'O.* (Paris, 1919).—NS/LK/DM

Ortiz, Cristina, Brazilian-born English pianist; b. Bahia, April 17, 1950. She studied in Rio de Janeiro; after training with Magda Tagliaferro in Paris, she won first prize in the Van Cliburn Competition (1969). She made her N.Y. recital debut in 1971. Following further studies with R. Serkin at the Curtis Inst. of Music in Philadelphia, she pursued an international career (from 1973). In 1977 she became a naturalized British subject. She maintains an extensive repertoire, which includes both standard and rarely heard works.—NS/LK/DM

Ortiz, Diego, Spanish music theorist and composer; b. Toledo, c. 1510; d. probably in Naples, c. 1570. He was maestro de capilla at the viceregal court in Naples (1558–65). He was one of the earliest masters of variations (divisions). His greatest work is *Trattado de glosas sobre clausulas y otros géneros de puntos en la música de violones* (Rome, 1553; modern ed. by M. Schneider, Berlin, 1913; 3ʳᵈ ed., Kassel, 1967), containing early examples of instrumental variations and ornamental cadenzas (for Viola da Gamba alone with harpsichord). An Italian version of this work was also publ. at Rome in 1553 (*Il primo libro de Diego Ortiz Toletano*, etc.). In addition, he publ. a vol. of sacred music at Venice in 1565 (hymns, motets, Psalms, etc., for 4 to 7 Voices). Some motets by him (in lute tablature) were included in Valderrabano's *Silva de Sirenas* (1547).

BIBL.: P. Strassler, *Hymns for the Church Year, Magnificats, and other Sacred Choral Works of D. O.* (diss., Univ. of N.C., 1966). —NS/LK/DM

Orto (real name, Dujardin), Marbrianus de, Franco-Flemish singer and composer; b. probably in the Tournai diocese, c. 1460; d. Nivelles, c.Feb. 1529.

He was the illegitimate offspring of a priest. He sang in the papal choir in Rome (1483–99?), and was also dean of the collegiate church of St. Gertrude in Nivelles (1489–96). In 1505 he was in the service of Philip the Fair of Burgundy, and was legitimized; went to Spain with him in 1506, and was ennobled. After Philip's death that same year, he entered the service of his son, Archduke Charles, later Emperor Charles V, being active at his chapel until at least 1518. Petrucci publ. a book of five masses by him (Venice, 1505), as well as 11 chansons for four voices in the *Odhecaton* (1500–03) and a Lamentation in *Lamentationum Jeremias prophetae liber I* (1506). —NS/LK/DM

Ory, Kid (actually **Edward**), leading New Orleans trombonist, leader, singer, string bassist, cornetist, alto saxophonist; b. La Place, La., Dec. 25, 1890 (some authorities give 1886, U.S. Census suggests 1881); d. Honolulu, Jan. 23, 1973. He was the most famous exponent of the tailgate style, which was highly rhythmic with extensive use of slurs and glissandos, and was featured on many 1920s recordings with Armstrong, Oliver, Morton, and others. When Ory was rediscovered during the 1940s New Orleans revival, he sometimes sang in Creole dialect; his generation still held to Creole customs including the spoken patois.

Ory began playing banjo from the age of 10, led boys' bands in La Place, then began doubling on valve trombone before specializing on slide trombone. He made regular visits to New Orleans before making his home there. From c. 1912 until 1919, he led one of the most successful bands in the city. A doctor advised Ory to live in a humid climate, and he moved to Calif. in 1919. He soon sent for several New Orleans musicians and formed his own band on the West Coast in November 1919. They played residencies in San Francisco, L.A., and Oakland, and in mid-1922 became the first black jazz band to have recordings issued. In late 1925, he handed over the leadership to Mutt Carey and moved to Chicago for recording dates with Louis Armstrong, then joined King Oliver where he played alto sax for six weeks until trombonist George Filhe worked out his notice. During this time he also recorded with Morton. Ory left Chicago with Oliver, played briefly with the band in N.Y. (May 1927), then returned to Chicago to join Dave Peyton, then Clarence Black, and Boyd Atkins (1929). He returned to L.A. in 1930, played in Mutt Carey's Jeffersonians for a few months, freelanced with a touring theatre band and others, then left music to help his brother run a chicken farm (1933). He visited N.Y. in September 1939, then returned to L.A. to work in a railroad office. He resumed regular playing by joining Barney Bigard's Band at Trouville Club, L.A. (summer 1942). During 1943–44 he was mainly active on string bass and alto sax, but reverted to trombone after his success on Orson Welles's radio series (1944). From then on he led his own highly successful band, primarily for West Coast residencies, and toured the U.S. in 1948. Poor health forced him to temporarily disband in the summer of 1955, but he soon re-formed and led his band on several overseas tours including visits to Europe in 1956 and 1959. From 1954 until 1961, Ory played frequently at his own club, On the Levee, San Francisco. He performed regularly during the early 1960s, but after recurring bouts of illness moved to Hawaii in the summer of 1966. Pneumonia threatened his life early in 1969. After recovering, he lived in quiet retirement. He played at New Orleans Jazz Fest (April 1971). Kid Ory appeared in several films including: *New Orleans* (with Louis Armstrong) and with own band in *Crossfire, Mahogany Magic, Disneyland After Dawn,* and *The Benny Goodman Story.* His most famous composition, "Muskrat Ramble," became the basis for one of the most pervasive protest songs of the Vietnam era: Country Joe Mac-Donald's "Feel Like I'm Fixin' to Die Rag."

DISC.: *K. O. and His Creole Band* (1948); *At the Beverly Cavern* (1951); *This K.'s the Greatest!* (1953); *Live at Club Hangover, Vol. 1* (1953); *K. O.'s Creole Jazz Band* (1954); *K. O. Favorites!* (1956); *K. O. at the Green Room, Vol. 1* (1947); *King of the Tailgate Trombone* (1948); *Edward Plays W. C. Handy* (1959); *At the Jazz Band Ball* (1959); *Original Jazz* (1961); *K. O. Storyville Nights* (1961).

BIBL.: Giltrap and Dixon, *K. O.* (London, 1957); R. Dixon, *K. O.: A Biography, Appreciation, Record Survey and Discography* (London, 1958).—JC/LP

Osborne (real name, **Eisbein**), **Adrienne,**
American contralto; b. Buffalo, Dec. 2, 1873; d. Zell am Ziller, Austria, June 15, 1951. She studied with August Götze and Max Stagemann in Leipzig; later with **Felix von Kraus,** whom she married in 1899. She sang at the Leipzig City Theater; in 1908 she settled in Munich, where she received the rank of Royal Chamber Singer. After the death of her husband in 1937, she went to Zell am Ziller.—NS/LK/DM

Osborne, George Alexander,
Irish pianist, teacher, and composer; b. Limerick, Sept. 24, 1806; d. London, Nov. 16, 1893. After theological training, he took up the piano. He taught in Brussels before going to Paris in 1826 to study with Pixis (piano) and Fétis (harmony and counterpoint), and then completed his piano studies with Kalkbrenner. He was active in the circle of such notables as Chopin, Rossini, Berlioz, and Liszt. In 1843 he settled in London as a pianist and teacher. He became particularly well- known for his championship of the music of Chopin. Osborne publ. the book *Reminiscences of Chopin* (1880). Among his compositions were 2 operas, orch. pieces, chamber music, including duos for violin and piano in collaboration with Bériot, and songs.—LK/DM

Osborne, Nigel,
English composer and teacher; b. Manchester, June 23, 1948. He received training in composition from Leighton and in 12–tone procedures from Wellesz at the Univ. of Oxford (B.Mus., 1970), and then worked in Warsaw with Rudziński and at the Polish Radio Experimental Studio (1970–71). In 1976 he became a lecturer in music at the Univ. of Nottingham. In 1990 he became prof. of music at the Univ. of Edinburgh. His *7 Words* won the International Opera Prize of the Radio Suisse Romande in 1971, his *Heaventree* received the Gaudeamus Prize in 1973, and his *I Am Goya* was honored with the Radcliffe Award in 1977. Osborne's works are in a thoroughly contemporary style pointing the way to postmodernism.

WORKS: DRAMATIC: O p e r a : *Hell's Angels* (1985; London, Jan. 4, 1986); *The Electrification of the Soviet Union* (1986–87; Glyndebourne, Oct. 5, 1987); *Terrible Mouth* (1992); *Sarajevo* (1993–94). **ORCH.:** Cello Concerto (1977); Concerto for Flute and Chamber Orch. (1980); *Sinfonia I* (1982) and *II* (1983); *Esquisse I* (Bath, June 5, 1987) and *II* (Frankfurt am Main, April 17, 1988) for Small String Orch.; *Stone Garden* (London, Feb. 18, 1988); *Eulogy* (for Michael Vyner) for Small Orch. (London, May 6, 1990); Violin Concerto (London, Sept. 21, 1990); *The Sun of Venice* (1991); *Hommage à Panufnik* (1992). **CHAMBER:** *Kinderkreuzzug* for Chamber Ensemble and Tape (1974); *Remembering Esenin* for Cello and Piano (1974); *Musica da camera* for Violin, Tape Delay, and Audience (1975); *Prélude and Fugue* for Chamber Ensemble (1975); *After Night* for Guitar (1977); *Kerenza at the Zawn* for Oboe and Tape (1978); *Quasi una fantasia* for Cello (1979); *In Camera* for Chamber Ensemble (1979); *Mythologies* for Flute, Clarinet, Trumpet, Harp, Violin, and Cello (1980); *Fantasia* for Chamber Ensemble (1983); *Wildlife* for Chamber Ensemble and Optional Live Electronics (1984); *Zansa* for Chamber Ensemble (1985); *Mbira* for Violin and Piano (1985); *Lumière* for String Quartet and 4 Children's Groups (Devon, Sept. 24, 1986); *The Black Leg Miner* for Oboe, English Horn, Bassoon, and Harpsichord (Southfields, March 6, 1987); *Zone* for Oboe, Clarinet, and String Trio (1989); *Canzona* for 4 Trumpets, Horn, 4 Trombones, and Tuba (London, July 13, 1990); *Adagio for Vedran Smailovic* for Cello (1993). **P i a n o :** *Figure/Ground* (1978; rev. 1979); Sonata (1981). **VOCAL:** *7 Words* for 2 Tenors, Bass, Chorus, Orch., and Optional Ondes Martenot (1971); *Heaventree* for Chorus (1973); *The Sickle* for Soprano and Orch. (1975); *Chansonnier* for Soprano, Alto, Tenor, Bass, Chorus, and Chamber Ensemble (1975); *Passers By* for Bass Recorder, Cello, 3 Voices, and Slides (1976); *Vienna. Zürich. Constance.* for Soprano, Violin, Cello, 2 Clarinets, and Percussion (1977); *I Am Goya* for Bass-baritone, Flute, Oboe, Violin, and Cello (1977); *Orlando furioso* for Chorus and Chamber Ensemble (1978); *Under the Eyes* for Voice, Percussion, Piano, Oboe, and Flute (1979); *Songs from a Bare Mountain* for Women's Chorus (1979); *Poem Without a Hero* for Soprano, Mezzo-soprano, Tenor, Bass, and Live Electronics (1980); *Gnostic Passion* for Chorus (1980); *The Cage* for Tenor, Chamber Ensemble, and Optional Live Electronics (1981); *For a Moment* for Women's Chorus, Cello, and Optional Kandyan Drum (1981); *Choralis I* (1981), *II* (1981; rev. 1982), and *III* (1982) for Soprano, 2 Mezzo-sopranos, Tenor, Baritone, and Bass; *Cantata Piccola* for Soprano and String Quartet (1982); *Alba* for Mezzo-soprano, Chamber Ensemble, and Tape (1984); *The 4–Loom Weaver* for Mezzo-soprano and Tape (1985); *Pornography* for Mezzo-soprano and Chamber Ensemble (1985); *Tracks* for 2 Choruses, Orch., and Wind Band (Rochester, Kent, April 21, 1990). —NS/LK/DM

Osborn-Hannah, Jane,
American soprano; b. Wilmington, Ohio, July 8, 1873; d. N.Y., Aug. 13, 1943. After vocal instruction from her mother, she studied with Marchesi and Sbriglia in Paris and with Sucher in Berlin. In 1904 she made her operatic debut as Elisabeth in *Tannhäuser* in Leipzig, and sang there until 1907. After appearances in Dresden, Munich, and Berlin, she sang at London's Covent Garden in 1908. On Jan. 5, 1910, she made her Metropolitan Opera debut in N.Y. as Elisabeth, and continued on its roster for the 1910–11 season.

She also was a member of the Chicago Grand Opera (1910–14). While she was best known as a Wagnerian, she also sang such roles as Desdemona, Cio-Cio-San, and Nedda with conviction.—NS/LK/DM

Osbourne, Ozzy (actually, John Michael),

one of the founding fathers (and perennial performers) of heavy metal; b. Birmingham, England, Dec. 3, 1948. As the lead singer for Black Sabbath, Ozzy Osbourne helped take the band's grinding blues and turn it into something louder and more sinister. Along the way he was accused of biting the heads off of small animals and birds, driving young men to suicide, and consorting with Satan.

Born into a working class family in the British steel-and-industrial zone, Osbourne's father worked in a metal factory and his mother worked on a car-assembly line. Not an especially keen student, Ozzy (as he was known since grade school) left school for a series of jobs that included tuning car horns, and working in a slaughterhouse and a crematorium. Not happy in any of these positions, Osbourne embarked on a small-time life of breaking and entering. Unfortunately, his preferred dress included sporting gloves with the fingers cut off; tracked by his tell-tale fingerprints, Osbourne was sent off for a three- month stay in prison. However, unreformed and unrepentant, on his release he returned to small-time thievery. His second prison sentence followed a botched robbery attempt after a large television fell on his head; on his release, he was involved in a brawl with a policeman, leading to yet another jail term. While in prison, he gave himself several tattoos, the first in a large collection. His grandfather, who apparently had a snake tattoo that started at his head and wound its way down to his feet, might have inspired this.

After his third prison stretch, Osbourne decided to go straight. It was the height of Beatlemania and amateur pop groups were forming left and right. One of Osbourne's friends invited him to sing with his band, and thus began a series of gigs with various bands, usually ending with Ozzy being evicted for his less-than-reliable behavior. Working under the name Ozzy Zig, he put an ad in the local music shop and hooked up with guitarist Geezer Butler. Their band Rare Breed joined forces with another band called the Rest with guitarist Tony Iommi and drummer Bill Ward. Butler took up the bass and the band became first Polka Tulk Blues Band, then Earth, and finally Black Sabbath.

After more than 10 years with Black Sabbath (see separate entry), Osbourne was asked to leave in 1978, his personal excesses beginning to get in the band's way. He secluded himself in a hotel room frequented by delivery people from local food and liquor establishments, and his various drug connections. Finally, the daughter of Black Sabbath's manager (and owner of its record company) suggested he start a band of his own. He pulled together former Rainbow bassist Bob Daisley, former Uriah Heap drummer Lee Kerslake, and former Quiet Riot guitarist Randy Rhoads. Largely due to Rhoads's style and flash, Osbourne's 1981 solo debut *Blizzard of Ozz* offered a fresh take on the whole metal sound. Osbourne achieved immediate success, outstripping Black Sabbath as his first album went triple platinum.

The band's tour in support of the album is the stuff of rock legend. During part of the show, Osbourne began throwing raw meat into the audience. As word spread, people started throwing things back at Osbourne: dead animals of all descriptions wound up on stage. At a Des Moines, Iowa, show, someone tossed onto the stage a live bat. Thinking it was a toy, Osbourne picked it up and bit the head off, before realizing that it was a living thing. Beyond freaking himself and the audience out, Osbourne needed a series of rabies shots over the next week. The incident entered rock 'n' roll folklore. At a stop in San Antonio, Tex., Osbourne got drunk and relieved himself on the Alamo, for which he was arrested; as a member of Black Sabbath, he peed on Hitler's Shrine in Berlin.

Later in the tour, as the band traveled between dates in Tenn. and Fla,. the band took a rest stop at a northern Fla. airstrip. There the bus driver (who also happened to be a pilot) started taking band and crew members on airplane rides. During one of these rides, Rhoads, a member of the crew, and the driver were killed when the plane hit a building and exploded. Several guitarists passed through the band to fill in for Rhoads during remainder of the tour. Despite this loss, Osbourne managed to release two more albums, 1981's *Diary of a Madman* and the double live album *Speak of the Devil* a year later, both charting in the Top 20 and selling extremely well.

Still in shock from losing Rhoads, Osbourne married his manager, Sharon Arden, and retreated after the 1982 tour. To make a break with the past, he left his old label and signed with CBS. During an event to introduce him to CBS executives, Sharon suggested releasing a pair of doves to make a grand entrance. Drunk and feeling like a piece of merchandise, Osbourne released one dove and bit the head off of another; the stunt was immortalized on film. This stunt landed Osbourne in rehab at the Betty Ford Clinic. There he began work on his next album, *Bark at the Moon*. Once again he was joined by Daisley on bass, and he finally found another compatible young guitarist in Jake E. Lee. The album went double platinum in 1983 and rose to #19.

Following a relatively uneventful tour, the band set to work on the *The Ultimate Sin* album. The album hit #6 and sold double platinum after its release in 1986. During that year, Osbourne made news again when the father of a young man who committed suicide while listening to *Diary of a Madman* accused Osbourne of causing the tragedy. In his complaint, the father focussed on the song "Suicide Solution," which was actually a cautionary tale inspired by the death by alcohol and exposure of AC/DC vocalist Bon Scott. The prosecution brought in "experts" from the Inst. for Bio-Acoustic Research who claimed that lyrics recorded faster than normal, yet still audible, subliminally urged the listener to "get the gun and try it." They further asserted that the album contained "hemisync tones," a means of using sound waves to influence mental acuity. Ignoring these claims, Osbourne won the case largely on First Amendment grounds. However, defending himself kept him off the road and out of the studio.

Despite these problems, Osbourne made his acting debut in 1987, ironically playing a preacher in the horror film *Trick or Treat*. Earlier in the year, he had sent some unreleased tapes featuring Rhoads to an engineer to see if they could be brought up to releasable quality. The result was the #6 platinum *Tribute* album.

In 1988, with yet another new young guitarist, Zakk Wylde, joining Daisley and drummer Randy Castillo, Osbourne recorded *No Rest for the Wicked*. The album went platinum and hit #13. The tour took the band to the Moscow Music Peace Festival. Osbourne next recorded a duet "Close My Eyes Forever" with Lita Ford, and in 1989, it became the first Top Ten hit of his solo career, reaching #8 and going gold. Early in 1990, Daisley left the band and was replaced by Osbourne's old friend Geezer Butler. Osbourne also finally quit abusing substances, making a concerted effort to get healthy. In this frame of mind, he created *No More Tears*. The album was a departure, going beyond the heavy metal sound to include softer numbers. "Mama, I'm Coming Home" became his only solo Top 40 hit, topping out at #28. Another song on the album, "I Don't Want to Change the World" won the Grammy Award for Best Heavy Metal Performance. The album hit #7 and went triple platinum. He called the subsequent live jaunt "No More Tours," claiming that at 44 he was getting to old to spend his life on the road. As a special treat during the last two shows, Tony Iommi, Bill Ward, and Geezer Butler joined him on the encore. The tour was taped and released in 1993 as *Live and Loud*.

A few weeks into his retirement, however, Osbourne decided that the life of a country squire would bore him to death. He started working on a new project with former David Lee Roth guitarist Steve Vai. With Vai, Wylde, former Yes keyboardman Rick Wakeman, and Butler in tow, they recorded dozens and dozens of tracks, winnowing them down to the 10 that appeared on 1995's *Ozzmosis*. The most daring record Osbourne ever made, with shades of progressive rock and psychdelia, it eventually went double platinum. He called the subsequent tour "Retirement Sucks." Replacing Wylde with one of Rhoads's former students Joe Holmes, the tour began during the spring of 1996. That summer marked the height of the multi-artist Lollapalooza festival and the advent of the all-woman Lilith festival. Inspired by these, Osbourne and his wife came up with Ozzfest, a touring metal caravan featuring Danzig, Sepultura, and a half-dozen other bands that fell into the abyss of heavy metal. It proved one of the year's most successful tours, second only to Lilith. A live album from the festival came out in 1997.

Into his 50s, Osbourne continues to rule the heavy metal roost with even more authority than he did at its inception some 30 years earlier. During 1999, he toured again with Black Sabbath. An updated version of "Iron Man" from the subsequent *Reunion* album won the band Best Metal Performance Grammy.

DISC.: *Blizzard of Ozz* (1981); *Diary of a Madman* (1981); *Speak of the Devil* (1982); *Bark at the Moon* (1983); *The Ultimate Sin* (1986); *Tribute* (1987); *No Rest for the Wicked* (1989); *Ten Commandments* (1990); *Just Say Ozzy* (live; 1990); *No More Tears* (1991); *Ozzmosis* (1995); *OzzFest, Vol.1: Live* (1997).—**HB**

Osmond, Donny and Marie, wholesome teen idols who became stars of stage and television. Donny Osmond (real name, Donald Clark Osmond), b. Ogden, Utah, Dec. 9, 1957; and Marie Osmond (real name, Olive Marie Osmond), b. Ogden, Utah, Oct. 13, 1959.

George and Olive Osmond were devout Mormons who raised their nine children to be musicians. The oldest brothers were the first to begin performing, forming a barbershop/gospel quartet. They were discovered on a trip to Disneyland, which in turn led to their first TV appearance. This earned them a regular place on the Andy Williams and Jerry Lewis variety shows from 1963 through 1971. Donny started working with the group at the age of four. With the ascent of the Jackson Five, the Osmonds tried to capitalize on that success and sound, moving from barbershop harmonies to a slightly more soulful sound that set the hearts of teenage girls of the early 1970s aflutter. With 15-year-old Donny up front, their initial hit "One Bad Apple" topped the charts for five weeks during the winter of 1971, going gold, and starting a teenybopper avalanche that became the family business. A phenomenal string of hits followed both for the group and for Donny as a solo act. Their second major hit, "Yo-Yo," rose to #3 and went gold. Then Donny took the ballad "Go Away Little Girl"—a #1 for Steve Lawrence a generation earlier—back to #1 for three weeks. Jazzing up one of their barbershop tunes, the Osmonds returned with the gold #4 "Down By the Lazy River," and then had two #14 hits with "Hold Her Tight" and "Crazy Horses" before 1972 ended. Donny took Paul Anka's "Puppy Love" to #3 and gold, Nat "King" Cole's "Too Young" to #13, and Frankie Avalon's "Why" to #13. The Osmonds became a cottage industry, with an animated cartoon series (they all provided their own voices) added to the spate of gold singles and albums.

While most teen sensations petered out after a few months or a year, the Osmonds continued to go strong; their youngest brother Jimmy joined the act in 1972 and finally the only girl in the family, Marie, joined in. More interested in country than the curious hybrid of pop, rock, soul, and MOR her brothers were performing, she covered Anita Bryant's Top 5 hit from 1960, "Paper Roses," and took it to #5, gold, and a #1 country hit in 1973. While the brothers only managed two #36 hits that year ("Goin' Home" and "Let Me In"), Donny continued to go strong with four Top 40 hits, including the gold #8 cover of Johnny Mathis's "Twelfth of Never." He took "A Million to One" to #23 and the B-side, "Young Love," to #25, finishing off the year with a cover of a 1927 hit that Elvis Presley had previously popularized, "Are You Lonesome Tonight." Osmond's version reached #14.

As the chart numbers started to dwindle, a fresh line-up seemed in order, so Donny started to work with his sister Marie. The move helped recharge their careers. They rode a cover of Don and Dewey's "I'm Leaving It All Up to You" to gold and #4 in 1974, topping the adult-contemporary chart. They topped the adult chart again several months later with "Morning Side of the Mountain," which rose to #8 pop. In the meantime, the larger group was only able to land one hit in 1974, the #10 "Love Me for a Reason."

The Osmonds' teenybopper appeal started to wane around 1975. However, as their chart fortunes diminished, they started to invade another medium, where they really got started: Television. Donny and Marie were offered a variety special in 1975. It was successful enough that they were given a regular slot for the 1976 season. This time the teenyboppers had to share them with their parents (though Marie had appealed in that direction all along). Donny's purple socks became national objects of derision. She was "a little bit country," he "a little bit rock 'n' roll." And they were both as wholesome as freshly pasteurized milk. They took a pair of notable duet covers to the charts that year, Nino Tempo and April Stevens's "Deep Purple," to #14 and Marvin Gaye and Tammy Terrell's "Ain't Nothing Like the Real Thing" to #21. Donny also scored his first solo hit in two and a half years with "C'mon Marianne," albeit a minor one with a peak of #38.

In 1978, Donny and Marie tried to parlay their newfound fame into success in the only medium that had eluded them thus far: film. They made the ill-advised *Going Coconuts*, a film described (kindly) in one review as "smarmy" The film marked another ebb in their popularity. By the end of 1979, their variety show had been cancelled. Donny retreated from the business for a couple of years, coming back behind the scenes as producer of the syndicated TV show *Blue Jean Network*. Marie kept busy with a line of sewing patterns for Butterick. She also took on some more acting projects, staring in the TV movie *The Gift of Life* in 1979. During the 1981 season, she had a solo variety show. The older brothers started performing as a country band.

By 1982, both Donny and Marie's music careers had taken a back seat to acting. Donny made the "comedy western" *The Wild Women of Chastity Gulch*, and then made his Broadway debut in a remake of George M. Cohan's *Little Johnny Jones* that closed after one night. After that, he pretty much dropped off the radar for seven years. Marie did somewhat better. Returning to performing country music, she had hits with "Back to Believing" in 1981, the country chart topper "Meet Me in Montana," a 1984 duet with Dan Seals, her own chart-topper "There's No Stopping Your Heart," the Top 5 country hit "Read My Lips," and the 1990 "Like a Hurricane." In 1983, she co-founded the Children's Miracle Network. She also started acting, playing her mother in a TV biopic of the family in 1982, starring in the TV movie *I Married Wyatt Earp* in 1983, and hosting the weekly show *Ripley's Believe It or Not* during the 1985 season.

In 1992, a more mature Donny Osmond came back with a new album. With a sound reminiscent of George Michael (who had just sold 10 million records), *Donny Osmond* spawned three singles, but failed to break the album Top 40, despite one of those singles, "Soldier of Love," hitting #2 on the pop charts. "Sacred Emotion" clocked in at #13 and "My Love Is a Fire" hit #21. However, he wasn't able to sustain his new career in adult pop. His follow-up album, *Eyes Don't Lie*, stiffed. Rather than retreat, he took the stage again, and spent five years, from 1992–97 touring in Andrew Lloyd Webber and Tim Rice's *Joseph and the Amazing Techni-*

color Dreamcoat. By 1994, Marie was on the road, too, playing Maria in *The Sound of Music*. In 1998, she followed Donny's run in *Joseph* on Broadway, taking over the role of Anna in *The King and I*. Donny also provided the singing voice of Shang in the Disney movie *Mulan*.

Back in the public eye, Donny and Marie decided to join the syndicated talk show circus of the late 1990s, bringing their wholesome, good-humored point of view as an alternative to the increasingly sleazy programming in the genre. The show was a moderate success. In 1999, they co-hosted the Miss America pageant.

DISC.: DONNY AND MARIE OSMOND: *I'm Leaving It All Up to You* (1974); *Make the World Go Away* (1975); *Greatest Hits* (1993). **DONNY OSMOND:** *The Donny Osmond Album* (1971); *To You with Love, Donny* (1971); *Too Young* (1972); *Alone Together* (1973); *Donny Osmond Superstar* (1973); *A Time for Us* (1973); *Donny* (1974); *I'm Leaving It All up to You* (1974); *Make the World Go Away* (1975); *Disco Train* (1976); *Donald Clark Osmond* (1977); *Winning Combination* (1978); *Donny Osmond* (1989); *Eyes Don't Lie* (1991); *Christmas at Home* (1998). **MARIE OSMOND:** *Paper Roses* (1973); *In My Little Corner of the World* (1974); *Who's Sorry Now* (1975); *This Is the Way I Feel* (1977); *Steppin' Stone* (1985); *There's No Stopping Your Heart* (1986); *I Only Wanted You* (1987); *All in Love* (1988). **OSMONDS:** *Osmonds* (1970); *Homemade* (1971); *Phase III* (1972); *Live* (1972); *Crazy Horses* (1972); *The Plan* (1973); *Love Me for a Reason, The Proud One* (1975); *Around the World: Live in Concert* (1975); *Brainstorm* (1976); *The Osmond Christmas Album* (1976); *Osmond Family Christmas* (1991); *Second Generation* (1992).

WRITINGS: D. Osmond, *Life Is Just What You Make It: My Life So Far* (N.Y., 1999).—**HB**

Ossman, Vess L. (actually, Sylvester Louis), American ragtime banjo player; b. Hudson, N.Y., Aug. 21, 1868; d. Fairmont, Minn., Dec. 8, 1923. The leading ragtime musician on records, billed as the King of the Banjo, Ossman began his recording career with a string of major hits at the dawn of the recording era, including "Yankee Doodle" (1894), "Coconut Dance" (1895), and "A Hot Time on the Levee" (1896), the last with singer Len Spencer. His signature tune was his own "A Bunch of Rags" (1899). (It was his good fortune that the banjo recorded particularly well on the earliest recording equipment.)

Ossman's records brought him international fame: he toured England to acclaim in 1900 and 1903. He also recorded with the Dudley brothers, George (harp-guitar) and Audley (mandolin), as the Ossman-Dudley Trio. Their hits included "St. Louis Tickle" (1906) and "Panama Rag Two-Step" (1907).

Ossman continued to score hits through 1912, his final popular recordings being accompaniments of Arthur Collins on "When Uncle Joe Plays a Rag on His Old Banjo" and "In Ragtime Land." At the time of his death he was on tour with his son, also named Vess Ossman. They were billed as the Ossmans, World's Great Banjo Players. The younger Ossman went on to form the vaudeville duo Ossman and Schepp with Rex Schepp, performing into the 1930s.—**WR**

Osten, Eva von der, German soprano; b. Insel, Aug. 19, 1881; d. Dresden, May 5, 1936. She studied with

August Iffert and Marie Söhle in Dresden. She made her operatic debut as Urbain in *Les Huguenots* in Dresden in 1902, and then was a principal member of the Dresden Court (later State) Opera until 1927, where she created the role of Octavian in *Der Rosenkavalier* in 1911. She also appeared at London's Covent Garden (1912–14) and in the U.S. with the German Opera Co. (1923–24). After her retirement from the stage, she became a producer of opera in Dresden. She was married to **Friedrich Plaschke**. Among her other outstanding roles were Kundry, Isolde, Senta, Ariadne, and Tosca.—**NS/LK/DM**

Osterc, Slavko, Slovenian composer and teacher; b. Veržej, June 17, 1895; d. Ljubljana, May 23, 1941. He began his training with Beran in Maribor, then studied at the Prague Cons. (1925–27). He subsequently taught at Ljubljana's Cons. and Academy of Music. He experimented with various techniques, including quarter tone writing.

WORKS: DRAMATIC: O p e r a : *Salome* (1919–30); *Krst pri Savici* (Baptism at the Savica; 1921); *Iz komične opere* (1928); *Krog s kredo* (The Chalk Circle; 1928–29); *Medea* (1930); *Dandin v vicah* (Dandin in Purgatory; 1930). **B a l l e t :** *Iz Satanovega dnevnika* (From Satan's Diary; 1924); *Maska rdeče smrti* (The Masque of the Red Death; 1930); *Illusions* (1938–40); *Illegitimate Mother* (1940). **ORCH.:** Sym. (1922); Concerto (1932); Concerto for Piano and Winds (1933; Prague, Sept. 1, 1935); *Passacaglia and Chorale* (Warsaw, April 14, 1934); *Mouvements symphonique* (1936; London, June 24, 1938); *Nocturne* for Strings (1940). **CHAMBER:** 2 string quartets (1927, 1934); Sonata for 2 Clarinets (1929); Wind Quintet (1932); Saxophone Sonata (1935); piano pieces; organ music.—**NS/LK/DM**

Osthoff, Helmuth, distinguished German musicologist, father of **Wolfgang Osthoff;** b. Bielefeld, Aug. 13, 1896; d. Würzburg, Feb. 9, 1983. He studied music in Bielefeld and in Münster. He served in the German army during World War I. After the Armistice, he resumed his studies at the Univ. of Münster (1919), and later (1920–22) took courses with Wolf et al. at the Univ. of Berlin, where he received his Ph.D. in 1922 with the diss. *Der Lautenist Santino Garsi da Parma: Ein Beitrag zur Geschichte der oberitalienischen Lautenmusik der Spätrenaissance* (publ. in Leipzig, 1926). He subsequently studied conducting with Brecher, composition with Klatte, and piano with Kwast at Berlin's Stern Cons. (1922–23). From 1923 to 1926 he served as répétiteur at the Leipzig Opera; in 1926 he became assistant to Arnold Schering in the dept. of musicology at the Univ. of Halle; in 1928 he was appointed chief assistant to Schering in the dept. of music history at the Univ. of Berlin; completed his Habilitation there in 1932 with his treatise *Die Niederländer und das deutsche Lied 1400–1640* (publ. in Berlin, 1938). In 1938 he became a prof. and director of the inst. of musicology at the Univ. of Frankfurt am Main, positions he held until his retirement in 1964. He was especially noted for his astute studies of Renaissance music. His publications include *Adam Krieger: Neue Beiträge zur Geschichte des deutschen Liedes in 17. Jahrhundert* (Leipzig, 1929; 2nd ed., 1970); *Johannes Brahms und seine Sendung* (Bonn, 1942); *Josquin Desprez* (2 vols., Tutzing, 1962–65). A Festschrift was

publ. in Tutzing in 1961 to honor his 65th birthday, a second in 1969 for his 70th birthday (contains a bibliography of his writings), and a third in 1977 for his 80th birthday.—**NS/LK/DM**

Osthoff, Wolfgang, eminent German musicologist, son of **Helmuth Osthoff;** b. Halle, March 17, 1927. He studied piano and theory at the Frankfurt am Main Staatliche Hochschule für Musik (1939–43), and then took lessons in conducting with Kurt Thomas and in theory with Kurt Hessenberg (1946–47). He subsequently studied musicology with his father at the Univ. of Frankfurt am Main (1947–49) and with Georgiades at the Univ. of Heidelberg (1949–54), taking his Ph.D. there in 1954 with the diss. *Das dramatische Spätwerk Claudio Monteverdis* (publ. in Tutzing, 1960). He taught at the Univ. of Munich (1957–64) and completed his Habilitation there in 1965 with his *Theatergesang und darstellende Musik in der italienischen Renaissance* (publ. in Tutzing, 1969). He became a lecturer at the Univ. of Munich in 1966. In 1968 he was named a prof. of musicology at the Univ. of Würzburg. In addition to many scholarly articles dealing with music history from the 15th to the 19th centuries, he also contributed to many music reference works.

WRITINGS (all publ. in Tutzing unless otherwise given): With J. Ruile-Dronke, *Colloquium Alessandro Scarlatti* (1979); with P. Cahn and J. Vogel, *Gerhard Frommel: Der Komponist und sein Werk* (1979); *Symposium Hans Pfitzner* (1984); with R. Wiesend, *Bach und die italienische Musik (Bach e la musica italiana)* (Venice, 1987); with R. Wiesend, *Colloquium Klassizität, Klassizismus, Klassik in der Musik 1920–1950* (1988); *St. George und "Les deux Musiques"—Tönende und vertonte Dichtung im Einklang und Widerstreit* (Stuttgart, 1989); *Briefwechsel Hans Pfitzner–Gerhard Frommel 1925–1948* (1990); *Hans Pfitzner und die musikalische Lyrik seiner Zeit* (1994); with R. Wiesend, *Mozart und die Dramatik des Veneto* (1996); with P. Cahn, *Hans Pfitzner-"Das Herz" und der Übergang zum Spätwerk* (1997); with B. Guthmüller, *Carlo Gozzi: Letterature e musica* (Rome, 1997).

BIBL.: M. Just and R. Wiesend, eds., *Liedstudien: W. O. zum 60. Geburtstag* (Tutzing, 1989).—**NS/LK/DM**

Östman, Arnold, Swedish conductor; b. Malmö, Dec. 24, 1939. He received training in art history at the Univ. of Lund and in music history at the univs. of Paris and Stockholm. From 1969 to 1979 he was artistic director of the Vadstena Academy, where he attracted notice with his productions of operas of the 17th and 18th centuries. He then was artistic director of the Drottningholm Court Theater in Stockholm from 1980 to 1992, where he mounted performances of early operas utilizing period instruments, costumes, and stagings. He also appeared frequently with the Cologne Opera, taking its productions of *Il matrimonio segreto* on tour to London (1983) and Washington, D.C. (1986). In 1984 he conducted *Don Giovanni* at London's Covent Garden. In 1985 he conducted *Le Siège de Corinthe* at the Paris Opéra. He conducted *Lucio Silla* at the Vienna State Opera in 1990. Östman also appeared as a guest conductor with various European orchs. While he has become best known for his performances of early operas, he has also commissioned and conducted the premieres of many contemporary works.—**NS/LK/DM**

Ostrčil, Otakar, eminent Czech conductor and composer; b. Smichov, near Prague, Feb. 25, 1879; d. Prague, Aug. 20, 1935. He studied languages at the Univ. of Prague, and then taught at a school in Prague (until 1919). At the same time, he took courses in piano with Adolf Mikeš (1893–95) and studied composition privately with Fibich (1895–1900). From 1908 to 1922 he conducted the amateur orch. assn. in Prague; also conducted opera there (from 1909). In 1920 he succeeded Karel Kovařovic as principal conductor at the Prague National Theater; also taught conducting at the Prague Cons. (1926–29). In his compositions, Ostrčil continued the Romantic tradition of Czech music, with some modern elaborations revealing the influence of Mahler.

WORKS: DRAMATIC: O p e r a : *Vlasty skon* (The Death of Vlasta; 1900–03; Prague, Dec. 14, 1904); *Kunálovy oči* (Kunala's Eyes; Prague, Nov. 25, 1908); *Poupě* (The Bud; 1909–10; Prague, Jan. 25, 1911); *Legenda z Erinu* (The Legend of Erin; 1913–19; Brno, June 16, 1921); *Honzovo královstvi* (Honza's Kingdom; 1928–33; Brno, May 26, 1934). **ORCH.:** Sym. (1905); Sinfonietta (1921); *Léto* (Summer), symphonic poem (1925–26); *Křízová cesta* (Way of the Cross), symphonic variations (1928). **CHAMBER:** String Quartet; Trio for Violin, Viola, and Piano. **VOCAL:** Choral pieces; song cycles.

BIBL.: Z. Nejedlý, *O. O.: vzrůst a uzrání* (O. O.: Development and Maturity; Prague, 1935); J. Bartos, *O. O.* (Prague, 1936).—**NS/LK/DM**

O'Sullivan, Denis, American baritone; b. San Francisco, April 25, 1868; d. Columbus, Ohio, Feb. 1, 1908. He was a student of Ugo Talbot and Karl Formes in San Francisco, Vannuccini in Florence, Stanley and Shakespeare in London, and Sbriglia in Paris. Following an engagement at a London concert in 1895, he made his operatic debut as Ferrando in *Il trovatore* with the Carl Rosa Co. in Dublin on Aug. 25, 1895. He was notably successful as the hero in Stanford's *Shamus O'Brien* (London, March 2, 1896). From 1897 to 1899 he sang on both sides of the Atlantic.—**NS/LK/DM**

Oswald, Henrique, Brazilian pedagogue and composer of Swiss descent; b. Rio de Janeiro, April 14, 1852; d. there, June 9, 1931. He studied with Gabriel Giraudon in São Paulo, and then in Florence with Buonamici (piano) and Maglioni (composition). After serving as vice-consul for Brazil in Le Havre and Genoa, he returned to Rio de Janeiro and was director of the National Inst. of Music (1903–06). Thereafter, he taught privately until becoming prof. of piano at the National Inst. of Music in 1911.

WORKS: DRAMATIC: O p e r a : *La croce d'oro* (1872); *Il nel* (1902); *Le fate* (1902). **ORCH.:** Suite (1884–87); Piano Concerto (1888); Violin Concerto (1888); *Sinfonietta* (1890); Sym. (1910). **CHAMBER:** Piano Quintet; 4 string quartets; 3 piano trios; Violin Sonata; many piano pieces.—**LK/DM**

Oswald, James, Scottish composer and music publisher; b. Scotland, 1711; d. Knebworth, Hertfordshire, 1769. He went to Edinburgh in 1736, where he was active as a singer and concert producer. He also composed, publishing his works anonymously or as David Rizzio. In 1741 he went to London, where he founded his own publishing firm in 1747 and subsequently brought out editions of popular works. He also composed music for the stage. In 1761 King George III made him his chamber composer. Oswald was most effective as a composer of works in Classical forms infused with a Scottish melos.—**LK/DM**

Oswald, John, provocative Canadian composer and sound engineer; b. Kitchener-Waterloo, May 30, 1953. In 1989 he produced and distributed, free of charge, *Plunderphonic*, a CD anthology of original pieces made up of "plunderphones" ("electroquotes or macrosamples of familiar sound") derived from revised performances of recordings by well-known artists, including James Brown, Lorin Maazel with the Cleveland Orch., George Harrison, Dolly Parton, Glenn Gould, Bing Crosby, Michael Jackson, and Count Basie. Oswald's "plunderphones" are the substance of each of his 24 tracks, themselves sequenced into typical genre groupings, with the exception of "compilation tracks of a particular performer, juxtapositions of complimentary performances by unrelated performers, unusual rearrangements of existing compositions, and the James Brown tracks, which are vehicles for various types and sources of appropriation." Virtually no extraneous music is added, all of the sounds heard being accurate, unprocessed reproductions of the originals. The overall effect is both less and more complicated than Oswald's explanation—repelling and compelling, with referential musical modules flitting around like bytes of information in the bowels of a computer. Oswald is actively involved in the issue of copyright morality; he has lectured widely on the subject and also wrote extensively for a variety of publications (*Keyboard, The Whole Earth Review, Grammy Pulse*, etc.). *Plunderphonic* itself carries no copyright warning; in its place is a "shareright" insignia, which encourages reproduction but prohibits sale. Since 1980 Oswald has been director of Mystery Laboratory of Toronto, the "aural research, production, and dissemination facility" where Plunderphonic was produced; he is also music director of the North American Experience Dance Co. (from 1987) and co-founder of *Musicworks*, an informative Canadian journal which emphasizes the experimental and avantgarde. Oswald is currently designing the soundtrack for *Stress*, an 8–screen movie by Bruce Mau, and also composing a one-note electroacousmatic work entitled *Jues* for the Rien a Voir festival in Montreal. He himself also appeared in two feature films, John Greyson's *un©ut* and Craig Baldwin's *Sonic Outlaws*. Oswald has been critically touted as both "Canada's most important composer-musician" (*Montreal Mirror*) and "the maddest man on the planet" (*London Observer*).

WORKS: *VT*, monophonic recording (1973); *Burrows*, monostomatic recording (1974); *Go, Stop* for 2 Musicians (1975); *Mrs. Schultz Overdubbing*, stereo recording (1976); *Animal Voices Human*, monostomatic recording (1977); *Moose and Salmon*, stereo recording (1978); *Warm Wind Pressure and Aura* for Ensemble without Instruments (1979); *Alto Sax*, monostomatic recording (1980); *Beat*, recording for dance (1981); *Jazz Edit*, monophonic recording (1981); *Jazz Edit*, monophonic recording (1982); *Bell Speeds*, stereo recording (1983); *Pitch*, environment

(1976–84); *Fossils*, monostomatic recording (1985); *Para De*, stereo recording for dance (1986); *Skindling Shades*, stereo recording for dance (1987); *Wounded* for Miming Musicians with Recording (1988); *Zorro* for Soprano and Bass Vocalists for dance (19889); *Plunderphonic*, recordings (1979–89); *Spectre* for String Quartet with Stereo Recording (1990); *Acupuncture*, sextet (1991); *Fence*, recording for dance (1991); *Pitch Pivot*, dark edifice (1991); *die Offnüng*, trompe l'oreille recording for dance (1992; also an orch. arrangement as *Classic*, 1994); *Plexure*, stereo recording (1992–93); *Mach* for String Quartet with Recording (1993; rev. 1995); *(m)utterD & (m)utterK* for Mezzo-soprano and Recording (1993; rev. 1995); *Aphasia* for Silent Woodwind Quintet (1994); *Early 20th Century Woodwind Quintet* (1994); *Orchestral Tunning Arrangement* for Orch. (1994); *Exquisite Corpse*, stereo recording for dance (1994–95); *Gray Folded*, stereo recording (1994–95); *Senacade*, sonic motorcade (1994–95); *24f/s*, stereo recording for dance (1994–95); *Bildbescreibung/Surveillance*, trilingual play (1996); *Brazilianaires*, quadralingual radio play recording (1996); *Metropolis*, recording for silent play (1996); *Fore* for String Quartet (1997); *Homonymy* for Mixed Ensemble and Bilingual Cinema (1998); */(delta gradient)* for Ondes Martinot and Brass Octet (1999); *The Idea of This* for Vocal Recordings, Piano, and Orch. (1999); *Janéad O'Jakriel*, vision (Moving Stills) (2000); *Jues*, octophonal recording (2000); *Stress*, dodecaphonal recording for 8 cinemas (2000).—**NS/LK/DM**

Otaka, Hisatada, Japanese conductor and composer; b. Tokyo, Sept. 26, 1911; d. there, Feb. 16, 1951. While still a teenager, he studied in Vienna. Following composition lessons with Pringsheim in Tokyo (1932–34), he returned to Vienna and studied with J. Marx (composition) and Weingartner (conducting) at the Academy of Music (1934–38); he also studied privately with Franz Moser. In 1940 he returned to Japan. From 1942 until his death he was conductor of the Nippon Sym. Orch. in Tokyo.

WORKS: ORCH.: *Sinfonietta* for Strings (1937); *Japanese Suite* No. 1 (Budapest, Nov. 8, 1938) and No. 2 (Vienna, Nov. 3, 1939); *Midare* (Berlin, Dec. 10, 1939); Cello Concerto (Tokyo, May 23, 1943); *Rhapsody* for Piano and Orch. (Tokyo, Dec. 10, 1943); *Fatherland* (Tokyo, Oct. 22, 1945); Sym. (1948); Flute Concerto (Tokyo, March 5, 1951). **CHAMBER:** Violin Sonata (1932); 2 string quartets (1938, 1943); Piano Trio (1941); many piano pieces. **VOCAL:** Songs.—**NS/LK/DM**

Otaka, Tadaaki, Japanese conductor; b. Kamakura, Nov. 8, 1947. He received training at the Toho Gakuen School of Music in Tokyo and at the Hochschule für Musik in Vienna. In 1970 he joined the faculty of the Toho Gakuen School of Music. From 1974 to 1981 he was principal conductor of the Tokyo Phil., and then of the Sapporo Sym. Orch. from 1981 to 1986. In 1987 he became principal conductor of the BBC Welsh Sym. Orch. in Cardiff, which position he retained when it was renamed the BBC National Orch. of Wales in 1993. In 1991 he became principal conductor of the Yomiuri Nippon Sym. Orch. in Tokyo, leaving his Cardiff post in 1995. From 1998 he was principal conductor of the Sapporo Sym. Orch. and director of the Britten-Pears Orch. As a guest conductor, he appeared with various orchs. in Japan and abroad.—**NS/LK/DM**

Otescu, Ion (Nonna), Romanian conductor, teacher, and composer; b. Bucharest, Dec. 15, 1888; d.

there, March 25, 1940. He was a student of Kiriac (theory) and Castaldi (composition) at the Bucharest Cons. (1903–07), and then completed his training in composition in Paris with d'Indy at the Schola Cantorum and with Widor at the Cons. (1908–11). Returning to Budapest, he was a teacher of harmony and composition (1913–40) and director (1918–40) of the Cons. He also was a conductor of the National Theater (1921–39) and the Bucharest Phil. (from 1927). In 1920 he helped to organize the Soc. of Romanian Composers, serving as its vice-chairman until his death. In 1913 he won the Enesco Prize and in 1928 the National Prize for composition. Otescu's music followed along traditional lines with infusions of folk and French elements.

WORKS: DRAMATIC: *Buby*, musical comedy (1903); *Ileana Cosinzeana*, ballet (1918; to a libretto by Queen Marie of Romania); *Rubinul miraculos*, ballet (1919); *Iderim*, opera (1920); *De la Matei cetire*, opera buffa (1926–38; completed by A. Stroe; Cluj, Dec. 27, 1966). **ORCH.:** *Le temple de Gnid*, symphonic poem (1908; Bucharest, March 2, 1914); Overture (1908); *Narcisse*, symphonic poem (Bucharest, Dec. 9, 1912); *Cuvente din betrani*, symphonic sketch (1912; Bucharest, April 5, 1913); *Impresiuni de iarnă*, symphonic tableau (1913; Bucharest, March 2, 1914); *Vrăjile Armidei*, symphonic poem for Violin and Orch. (1915; Bucharest, Nov. 20, 1922); *Scherzo* (1923; Bucharest, Nov. 19, 1939). **OTHER:** Chamber music; songs.—**NS/LK/DM**

Othmayr, Caspar, celebrated German composer; b. Amberg, March 12, 1515; d. Nuremberg, Feb. 4, 1553. He was a choirboy at the courts in Neumarkt and Amberg, and matriculated at the Univ. of Heidelberg (1533), subsequently receiving the degrees of Bachelor, Licentiate, and Master of Arts there. He became Rektor of the Lateinschule at Heilbronn's Cistercian monastery (1545) and then provost of the St. Gumbertus monastery in Ansbach (1547). He was greatly esteemed not only for his sacred works but also for his ingenious polyphonic settings of secular songs. See H. Albrecht, ed., *Caspar Othmayr: Ausgewähtle Werke*, Das Erbe Deutscher Musik, 1st series, XVI (1941) and XXVI (1956).

WORKS (all publ. in Nuremberg): (10) *Cantilena aliquot elegantes ac piae* for 4 to 5 Voices (1546); (2) *Epitaphium D. Martini Lutheri* for 5 Voices (1546); (34) *Symbola illustrissimorum principum, nobilium, aliorumque...virorum* for 5 Voices (1547); (41) *Bicinia sacra* (1547); (30) *Tricinia* (1549); (50) *Reutterische und jegerische Liedlein* for 4 to 5 Voices (1549); other songs and motets in various contemporary collections.

BIBL.: H. Albrecht, *C. O.: Leben und Werk* (Kassel, 1950). —**NS/LK/DM**

Otis, Johnny (John Veliotes), American R&B bandleader, songwriter, and multi-instrumentalist; b. Vallejo, Calif., Dec. 8, 1921. Otis fostered the development of R&B music in crucial and varied ways. He led a band that showcased performers and as a talent scout discovered others. He wrote songs, among them his hit "Willie and the Hand Jive" and "Dance with Me Henry (Wallflower)." He also founded clubs and record companies, and hosted radio and television programs on which the music was performed.

Otis was the son of Greek immigrants Alexander and Irene Veliotes, who ran a grocery in Berkeley, Calif., where he was raised. He was fascinated by African-American culture and came to consider himself black. In 1939 he taught himself to play the drums and began performing in local and then territory bands. He married Phyllis Walker in 1941; they had five children, among them Shuggie (Johnny Otis Jr.) and Nicky, who became musicians and played with their father.

In 1945, Otis formed his own big band to play at the Club Alabam in Los Angeles. That September he made his first recordings as a leader for Excelsior Records. With the decline of swing music, he cut his group down and turned to a more blues-oriented sound, opening the Barrel House club in Los Angeles in 1948. In the fall of 1948 "That's Your Last Boogie," credited to Joe Swift with Johnny Otis and His Orch., reached the Top Ten of the R&B charts.

Otis signed to Savoy Records and scored a remarkable number of R&B hits in the early 1950s. "Double Crossing Blues" (music and lyrics by Johnny Otis) by the Johnny Otis Quintette with vocals by the Robins and Little Esther, hit #1 in March 1950, succeeded by "Mistrustin' Blues" (music and lyrics by Johnny Otis) by the Johnny Otis Orch. with vocals by Little Esther and Mel Walker. He had a third R&B chart-topper in July with "Cupid Boogie" (music and lyrics by Johnny Otis); he also had another six Top Ten R&B hits during the year, four more in 1951 and two in 1952.

Moving to the joint Duke and Peacock labels, Otis produced and, under the pseudonym Kansas City Bill, accompanied Willie Mae "Big Mama" Thornton on "Hound Dog" (music and lyrics by Jerry Leiber and Mike Stoller), which topped the R&B charts in April 1953. He also produced Johnny Ace's "Pledging My Love" (music and lyrics by Ferdinand Washington and Don D. Robey), a #1 R&B hit in February 1955. It was succeeded at #1 in April by Etta James's recording of "The Wallflower" (aka "Roll with Me Henry"; music and lyrics by Hank Ballard, Johnny Otis, and Etta James), written as an answer record to the #1 R&B hit "Work with Me Annie" (music and lyrics by Hank Ballard) recorded by Hank Ballard's group the Midnighters. Georgia Gibb covered it as "Dance with Me Henry (Wallflower)" for a #1 million-selling pop hit in May 1955.

In the mid-1950s Otis gave up touring, founded his own Dig Records label, and became a disc jockey on a Los Angeles radio station, later launching a local television program. In 1957 he signed to Capitol Records and began recording as the Johnny Otis Show. His revival of the 1921 song "Ma (He's Making Eyes at Me)" (music by Con Conrad, lyrics by Sidney Clare) with vocals by Marie Adams and the Three Tons of Joy became a Top Ten hit in Great Britain in November 1957. In the U.S. his recording of "Willie and the Hand Jive" (music and lyrics by Johnny Otis) became a Top Ten pop hit in August 1958 (he performed it in the film Juke Box Rhythm in March 1959), and he scored three more pop chart entries through 1960. Meanwhile, the Fiestas scored a Top 40 pop hit with his composition "So Fine" in April 1959, and the Pips, later known as Gladys Knight and the Pips, revived his ten-year-old song "Every Beat of My Heart" for a Top Ten pop hit in June 1961.

Otis spent much of the 1960s working as a political aide, but in 1968 he signed to Kent Records and recorded the album Cold Shot, featuring the single "Country Girl," which became an R&B chart entry in March 1969. He then signed to the Epic Records subsidiary of CBS Records and made Cuttin' Up, released in March 1970. Reforming his revue, he performed at the Monterey Jazz Festival in September 1970 and the concert was recorded for an album, The Johnny Otis Show Live at Monterey!, released in the spring of 1971; it featured Joe Turner, Little Esther, and other R&B singers. In September 1971, Otis appeared in the film Play Misty for Me.

Eric Clapton revived "Willie and the Hand Jive" for a Top 40 hit in 1974. That year Otis formed another record label, Blues Spectrum, to record veteran R&B performers such as himself and Louis Jordan. In 1975 he was ordained as a minister and in 1978 founded a nondenominational church in Los Angeles, though he continued to perform and record music occasionally. In 1981 he signed to the blues-oriented independent label Alligator Records and released The New Johnny Otis Show, which was nominated for a 1982 Grammy for Best Traditional Blues Recording. In the early 1990s he moved from Los Angeles to Sebastopol, Calif., where he opened a grocery that doubled as a nightclub, marketed his own apple juice, painted and made sculptures, hosted a radio program, and occasionally recorded. His album Spirit of the Black Territory Bands, released by Arhoolie Records in November 1992, was nominated for a Grammy for Best Big-Band Jazz Album.

WRITINGS: Listen to the Lambs (N.Y., 1968); Upside Your Head! Rhythm and Blues on Central Avenue (Middletown, Conn., 1993); Red Beans & Rice and Other Rock 'n' Roll Recipes (1997).

DISC.: The Johnny Otis Show (1958); The Original Johnny Otis Show (1945–1951) (1978); Rock and Roll Hit Parade, Vol. 1 (1957); The Johnny Otis Show (1958); Cold Shot (1968); Snatch and The Poontangs (1970); Cuttin' Up (1970); Live at Monterey (1971); Back to Jazz (1977); The New Johnny Otis Show (1982); Otisology (1986); The Capitol Years (rec. 1957–59; rel. 1989); The Spirit of the Black Territory Bands (1992).

BIBL.: L. Hildebrand and M. O'Neal, Colors and Chords: The Art of J. O. (1995).—WR

Ots, Charles, South Netherlands teacher and composer; b. Brussels, May 13, 1776; d. there, 1845. He was active as a teacher in Ghent, where he wrote 3 operas: La ruse villageoise (Jan. 2, 1796), Jean II ou Charles-Quint dans les murs de Gand (Dec. 18, 1816), and David Teniers (Oct. 28, 1818). Among his other works were instrumental pieces, the cantata La rose enlevée, and sacred music.—LK/DM

Ott, David, American composer; b. Crystal Falls, Mich., July 5, 1947. He studied at the Univ. of Wisc., Platteville (B.S. in music education, 1969). After training in piano with Alfonso Montecino at the Ind. Univ. School of Music (M.M., 1971), he took courses in theory and composition at the Univ. of Ky. (D.M.A., 1982). He taught at Houghton (N.Y.) Coll. (1972–75), the Univ. of Ky., Lexington (1976–77), Catawba Coll., Salisbury, N.C. (1977–78), Pfeiffer Coll., Misenheimer, N.C. (1978–82), and DePauw Univ., Greencastle, Ind. (from 1982). He also was active as an organist and conductor. In 1991 he became composer-in-residence of the Indianapolis Sym. Orch.

WORKS: DRAMATIC: *Lucinda Hero*, opera (1985); *Visions: The Isle of Patmos*, ballet (1988). **ORCH.:** *Genesis II* (1980); Piano Concerto (1983); 4 numbered syms.: No. 1, *Short Symphony*, for Chamber Orch. (1984), No. 2 (1990; Grand Rapids, Mich., Jan. 18, 1991), No. 3 (1991; Grand Rapids, Mich., Oct. 9, 1992), and No. 4 (Fort Wayne, Ind., Oct. 15, 1994); Percussion Concerto (1984); Cello Concerto (1985); *Water Garden* (1986); *Celebration at Vanderburgh* (1987); Saxophone Concerto (1987); Viola Concerto (1988); Concerto for 2 Cellos and Orch. (1988); *Vertical Shrines* (1989); *Music of the Canvas* (Indianapolis, Oct. 11, 1990); *String Symphony* (1990); Triple Brass Concerto for Trumpet, Trombone, Horn, and Orch. (1990); Violin Concerto (Reading, Pa., Oct. 17, 1992); Trombone Concerto (1992; San Diego, April 22, 1993); *Overture on an American Hymn* for Chamber Orch. (1992); *Indianapolis Concerto for Orchestra* (1992–93; Indianapolis, Sept. 30, 1993); *The 4 Winds* (1993); *Improvisation on "Freudvoll und Leidvoll" (Egmont)* (1993); Triple Concerto for Clarinet, Violin, Piano, and Orch. (Grand Rapids, Mich., Nov. 4, 1993); Double Concerto for Violin, Cello, and Orch. (1995; Indianapolis, Feb. 26, 1996). **CHAMBER:** Viola Sonata (1982); *Sabado* for Woodwind Quintet (1985); Trombone Sonata (1986); *DodecaCelli* for 12 Cellos (1988); String Quartet No. 1 (1989); *5 Interludes* for Cello and Piano (1990); organ pieces. **VOCAL:** Choral works; songs.—NS/LK/DM

Ottani, Bernardo, Italian composer, brother of **Gaetano Ottani;** b. Bologna, Sept. 8, 1736; d. Turin, April 26, 1827. He was a pupil of Padre Martini. In 1765 he was elected a member of the Accademia Filarmonica in Bologna. He was made maestro di cappella at the basilica of S. Giovanni in Monte in Bologna in 1769, and later held similar appointments in that city at the church of S. Luca and at the Collegio degli Ungheri. In 1779 he became maestro di cappella at Turin Cathedral. Ottani wrote 13 operas, including *L'amore senza malizia* (Venice, Carnival 1767–68), *Le virtuose ridicole* (Dresden, Carnival 1769), and *L'amore industrioso* (Dresden, Nov. 21, 1769). He also wrote much sacred music.—NS/LK/DM

Ottani, Gaetano, Italian tenor, brother of **Bernardo Ottani;** place and date of birth unknown; d. Turin, 1808. After singing in Bologna (1747) and Lucca (1748), he appeared in Turin in 1750, where he served as primo uomo at the court opera from 1754 to 1768. He also sang in Milan in 1752 and in 1770. In addition to his career as a tenor, Ottani was active as a landscape painter.—NS/LK/DM

Otte, Hans (Günther Franz), German composer and pianist; b. Plauen, Dec. 3, 1926. He was a student of Hindemith and J.N. David (composition), Pozniak and Gieseking (piano), Germani (organ), and Abendroth, conducting). In 1959 he won the Prix de Rome. From 1959 to 1984 he served as head of music for Radio Bremen, where he was a proponent of contemporary music. As a composer, he pursued an experimental course which ranged from serial and aleatoric techniques to electronic pieces and sound installations.

WORKS: DRAMATIC: *voicing*, radiophonic piece (1988); *jetzt*, theater piece (1992); *im garten den klänge*, vocal theater (1993). **ORCH.:** *realisationen* for Piano and Orch. (1956); *momente* (1958; Paris, May 1960); *ensemble* for Strings (Palermo, Sept. 1961); *passages* for Piano and Orch. (1965–66); *Buch* (1968); *zero* for Orch. and Chorus (North German Radio, Hamburg, Jan. 1971); *terrain* (Bavarian Radio, Munich, Dec. 1974). **CHAMBER:** *montaru* for 2 Pianos, Brass, and Percussion (South German Radio, Stuttgart, Dec. 1955); *folie et sens* for Piano Trio (1955–56; South German Radio, Stuttgart, May 1956); *daidalos* for Piano, Guitar, Harp, and 2 Percussionists (1960); *valeurs* for Winds (1969); *rendezvous* for Chamber Ensemble (Rome, Oct. 1969); *text* for Percussionist (Stuttgart, May 1972); *orient: occident* for 2 Winds and Tape (1978); *einklang* for Acoustic and Electronic Strings (South West Radio, Baden-Baden, April 1979; also for 2 Wind Groups and Tape, South West Radio, Baden-Baden, April 1979); *wassermann-musik* for Harp (1984); *text* for Vibraphone (1986); *eins* for Alto Flute (1987); *septuor* for Flute, Clarinet, Percussion, Piano, Violin, Cello, and Harp (1988); *phoenix-piece* for Clarinet (1989); *alltagsmusik* for Violin (1992). **KEYBOARD: Piano:** *dromenon* for 3 Pianos (1957; North German Radio, Hamburg, Jan. 1960); *tropismen* (1959; South German Radio, Stuttgart, April 1960); *interplay* for 2 Pianists (1962); *face à face* for Piano and Tape (1965); *intervall* (Buenos Aires, June 1974); *biographie* for Piano and Tape (South West Radio, Baden-Baden, Jan. 1976); *das buch der klänge* (1979–82). **Organ:** *touches* (1965); *minimum: maximum*, simultaneous piece for 2 Organists on 2 Organs (Swedish Radio, Stockholm, and Radio Bremen, Oct. 1973); *sounds* (1992). **VOCAL:** *tasso concerti* for Soprano, Flute, Piano, and Percussion (1961); *schrift* for Chorus, Lights, Loudspeaker, and Organ (1976); *siebengesang* for 3 Singers, Piano, and 3 Winds (1985); *philharmonie* for Chorus and Orch. (1986); *das lied der welt* for 10 Choruses in 10 Countries (European Broadcasting Union, Dec. 1, 1986). —NS/LK/DM

Otter, Anne Sofie von, outstanding Swedish mezzo-soprano; b. Stockholm, May 9, 1955. She began her training at the Stockholm Musikhögskolan, and then studied with Erik Werba in Vienna and Geoffrey Parsons in London, and later with Vera Rozsa. In 1982 she joined the Basel Opera; in 1984 she sang at the Aix-en-Provence Festival. She made her first appearance at London's Covent Garden in 1985 as Cherubino; that same year, she made her U.S. debut as soloist in Mozart's C-minor Mass with the Chicago Sym. Orch. In 1987 she sang at La Scala in Milan and at the Bavarian State Opera in Munich. In 1988 she appeared as Cherubino at the Metropolitan Opera in N.Y. In 1989 she made her first appearance at the Salzburg Festival as Marguerite in *La Damnation de Faust* with Solti and the Chicago Sym. Orch. In 1992 she returned to Salzburg to sing Ramiro. In 1996 she sang in the Metropolitan Opera Gala, and returned there in 1997 as Mozart's Sesto. On May 6, 1998, she made her Carnegie Hall recital debut in N.Y. She sang widely as a soloist with major orchs. and as a recitalist. Her other operatic roles include Gluck's Orfeo, Mozart's Idamantes and Dorabella, Tchaikovsky's Olga, and R. Strauss's Octavian. Otter was acclaimed for her extraordinary vocal mastery, from opera to lieder.—NS/LK/DM

Otterloo, (Jan) Willem van, prominent Dutch conductor; b. Winterswijk, Dec. 27, 1907; d. in a automobile accident in Melbourne, Australia, July 27, 1978. He studied with Orobio de Castro (cello) and Sem Dresden (composition) at the Amsterdam Cons. In 1932 he became a cellist in the Utrecht Sym. Orch.; from 1933 to 1937, served as its asst. conductor, and from 1937 to 1949, as its chief conductor. He was chief conductor of the Residente Orch. in The Hague (1949–73); took it on a tour of the U.S. in 1963. He was also chief conductor (1967–68) and principal guest conductor (1969–71) of the Melbourne Sym. Orch.; then was chief conductor of the Sydney Sym. Orch. from 1973 until his tragic death; was also Generalmusikdirektor of the Düsseldorf Sym. Orch. (1974–77). His unmannered readings of the classics were esteemed. He also composed, producing a Sym., suites for Orch., chamber music, etc.—NS/LK/DM

Ottman, Robert W(illiam), American music theorist and pedagogue; b. Fulton, N.Y., May 3, 1914. He studied theory with Rogers at the Eastman School of Music in Rochester, N.Y. (M.Mus., 1943). He served in U.S. Army infantry (1943–46), and then took lessons in composition with Alec Rowley at Trinity Coll. of Music in London. In 1946 he was engaged as a lecturer in music at North Tex. State Univ., from which he also received his Ph.D. (1956). Ottman became prof. emeritus in 1980.

WRITINGS (all publ. in Englewood Cliffs, N.J., unless otherwise given): *Music for Sight Singing* (1956; 3rd ed., 1986); with P. Kreuger, *Basic Repertoire for Singers* (San Antonio, 1959); *Elementary Harmony, Theory and Practice* (1961; 5th ed., 1998); *Advanced Harmony, Theory and Practice* (N.Y., 1961; 4th ed., 1992); with F. Mainous, *The 371 Chorales of J.S. Bach* (N.Y., 1966; with Eng. texts); with F. Mainous, *Rudiments of Music* (1970; 2nd ed., 1987); *Workbook for Elementary Harmony* (1974; 2nd ed., 1983); with F. Mainous, *Programmed Rudiments of Music* (N.Y., 1979; 2nd ed., 1994); *More Music for Sight Singing* (1981); with P. Dworak, *Basic Ear Trining Skills* (1991).—NS/LK/DM

Otto, (Ernst) Julius, German choral conductor and composer; b. Königstein, Sept. 1, 1804; d. Dresden, March 5, 1877. He studied with Weinlig in Dresden, then was a teacher there. In 1830 he was appointed cantor at the Kreuzkirche, and held this position for 45 years, his choir becoming one of the most celebrated in Germany; he also conducted several choral societies. His best works are the excellent male choruses in his collection *Ernst und Scherz*, which became extremely popular (*Burschenfahrten, Gesellenfahrten, Soldatenleben, Der Spinnabend, Der Sängersaal*, etc.). He also composed two grand operas and four comic operas for amateur performance (*Die Mordgrundbruck bei Dresden* is the best), three oratorios, many songs for Solo Voice (*In die Ferne, Des deutschen Rheines Braut*, etc.), piano sonatas, rondos, etc.

BIBL.: A. Scheumann, *J. O.* (Dresden, 1904).—NS/LK/DM

Otto, Georg, German composer; b. Torgau, 1550; d. Kassel (buried), Nov. 30, 1618. He was educated at the monastery school in Schulpforta (1564–68) and at the Univ. of Leipzig (1568–69). After serving as municipal Kantor in Langensalza (1569–86), he was Kapellmeister at the court of the Landgrave of Hessen-Kassel (from 1586). Germany's first court theater, the Ottoneum in Kassel (1605), was named in his honor. Among his students were Moritz, the Landgrave's heir, and Schütz. He publ. 3 vols. of sacred vocal music (1574, 1588, 1604). Some of his works remain in manuscript collections.

BIBL.: H. Grössel, *G.ius O.: Ein Motettenkomponist des 16. Jahrhunderts* (Kassel, 1935).—LK/DM

Otto, Lisa, German soprano; b. Dresden, Nov. 14, 1919. She was educated at the Hochschule für Musik in Dresden. She made her operatic debut as Sophie in 1941 at the Landestheater in Beuthen. In 1945–46 she sang at the Nuremberg Opera. She was a member of the Dresden State Opera (1946–51); then joined the Berlin Städtische Opera (1952); also sang in Salzburg (from 1953), and made tours of the U.S., South America, and Japan. She was made a Kammersängerin in 1963. She became best known for her roles in Mozart's operas. —NS/LK/DM

Ötvös, Gábor, Hungarian-born German conductor; b. Budapest, Sept. 21, 1935. He began his training at the Franz Liszt Academy of Music in Budapest. Following the abortive Hungarian Revolution in 1956, he pursued studies in Venice and Rome. In 1958 he became a conductor at the Teatro Verdi in Trieste, and served as its music director in 1960–61. From 1961 to 1967 he was chief conductor of the Hamburg Sym. Orch. He held the title of first conductor and deputy Generalmusikdirektor of the Frankfurt am Main Opera from 1967 to 1972. In 1969 he made his debut with the N.Y.C. Opera. On Oct. 27, 1971, he made his first appearance with the Metropolitan Opera in N.Y. conducting *Carmen*, returning there in 1973 and 1974. From 1972 to 1981 he was Generalmusikdirektor of Augsburg. In subsequent years, he appeared as a guest conductor with opera companies and orchs. In 1998 he became principal conductor of the Orquesta Filarmónica de Santiago in Chile.—NS/LK/DM

Oudin, Eugène (Espérance), American baritone of French descent; b. N.Y., Feb. 24, 1858; d. London, Nov. 4, 1894. He studied law at Yale Univ. He made his debut in N.Y., on Aug. 30, 1886, in an operetta. On Jan. 31, 1891, he created the role of Ivanhoe in London in Arthur Sullivan's opera of that name, and won immediate acclaim. He remained in England most of his life, but also made several appearances in Europe, including Russia. He scored notable successes in Wagnerian roles, especially Wolfram and Telramund.—NS/LK/DM

Oudrid (y Segura), Cristóbal, Spanish conductor and composer; b. Badajoz, Feb. 7, 1825; d. while conducting a rehearsal at the Teatro Real in Madrid, March 12, 1877. He studied music with his father, acquiring his craft by arranging works of Haydn and Mozart for wind instruments. In 1844 he went to Madrid, where he conducted Italian opera (from 1867) and was director of the Teatro Real (from 1870). He showed a decided talent for writing melodious zarzuelas, among them *Buenas noches, Señor Don Simon* (Madrid, April 16, 1852), *El postillon de la Rioja* (Madrid, June 7, 1856), and *El último mono* (Madrid, May 30, 1859).—NS/LK/DM

Oue, Eiji, Japanese conductor; b. Hiroshima, Oct. 3, 1956. He was a student of Saito at the Toho School of Music in Tokyo (B.M., 1978) and of Larry Livingston at the New England Cons. of Music in Boston (Artist Diploma, 1981), and also worked with Ozawa (1978–84), Bernstein (1980–90), and Calibidache (1982–83). In 1980 he received the Koussevitzky Prize at Tanglewood, in 1981 he took first prize at the Salzburg conducting competition, and in 1982 he was a fellow at the Los Angeles Phil. Inst. He was music director of the New Bedford (Mass.) Sym. Orch. (1982–84) and the Boston Mozarteum Orch. (1982–89). Oue was also music director of the Greater Boston Youth Sym. Orch. (1982–88), the Brown Univ. Orch. (1985–86), and the Empire State Youth Sym. Orch. (1986–88). From 1986 to 1990 he was assoc. conductor of the Buffalo Phil. In 1990 he took the London Sym. Orch. on a tour of Japan, and in 1990 and 1991 he served as resident conductor of the new Pacific Music Festival in Sapporo. From 1990 he was music director of the Erie (Pa.) Phil. In 1995 he became music director of the Minn. Orch. in Minneapolis, a position he held until 2002. He became chief conductor of the Radio-Philharmonie Hannover in 1998. As a guest conductor, he appeared with leading orchs. throughout North America, Europe, and the Far East.—NS/LK/DM

Oulibicheff, Alexander Dmitrievich, Russian government official and writer on music; b. Dresden, April 13, 1794; d. Lukino, near Nizhny-Novgorod, Feb. 5, 1858. He studied violin at home in Dresden, where his father was Russian ambassador, and then was educated in Germany. When the family returned to Russia in 1810, he was employed in the Ministry of Finance (1812), and later in the Ministry of Foreign Affairs (1816–30). He was the ed. of the periodical *Journal de St. Petersbourg* (1812–30); retired to his estate at Lukino in 1841. Oulibicheff's greatest admiration was for Mozart, which resulted in his magnum opus, *Nouvelle biographie de Mozart, suivie d'un aperçu sur l'histoire générale de la musique et de l'analyse des principales oeuvres de Mozart* (3 vols., Moscow, 1843; second Ger. tr., Stuttgart, 1859; Russian tr., Moscow, 1890). By way of praising Mozart, he inserted deprecating remarks on Beethoven's later style; when he was taken to task for this lack of appreciation (by Lenz and others), he publ. *Beethoven, ses critiques et ses glossateurs* (Leipzig and Paris, 1857), in which he emphatically reiterated his sharp criticism of Beethoven's harmonic and formal procedures.—NS/LK/DM

Oundjian, Peter, Canadian conductor; b. Toronto, Dec. 21, 1955. He received training in violin from Parikian and received the Gold Medal of the Royal Coll. of Music in London. He pursued violin studies with Galamian, Perlman, and DeLay at the Juilliard School in N.Y., and also attended master classes in conducting given by Karajan. After winning first prize in the Vina del Mar Violin Competition in Chile in 1980, he distinguished himself as first violinist in the Tokyo String Quartet (1981–95). In 1995 he made his conducting debut with the Orch. of St. Luke's at the Caramoor Festival in Katonah, N.Y. He was named artistic director of the Caramoor Festival in 1997, the same year that he

made his German debut as guest conductor with the Saarbrücken Radio Sym. Orch. and his Scottish debut as guest conductor with the Scottish Chamber Orch. at the Edinburgh Festival. In 1998 he became music director of the Niew Sinfonietta in Amsterdam. He made his British debut as guest conductor with the City of Birmingham Sym. Orch. in 2000.—LK/DM

Oury, Anna Caroline (née de Belleville), German pianist and composer; b. Landshut, June 24, 1808; d. Munich, July 22, 1880. Her father, a French nobleman, was director of the Bavarian Court Opera in Munich. She studied with Czerny in Vienna, where she made her debut. She then gave concerts in Munich and in Paris. She settled for many years in London, where she married **Antonio James Oury** in 1831; toured with him in Russia, Germany, Austria, and France. She wrote a number of piano pieces in the salon style, of which nearly 200 were publ.—NS/LK/DM

Oury, Antonio James, English violinist of Italian descent; b. London, 1800; d. Norwich, July 25, 1883. After studying violin at an early age with his father, he took lessons with Mori, Spagnoletti, and Kiesewetter; later studied violin with Baillot, Kreutzer, and Lafont and conducting with Fétis in Paris. He made his London debut at a benefit concert for Kiesewetter's widow and children (Feb. 20, 1828), and later that year played at a Phil. Soc. concert; also was active as a theater musician. After marrying **Anna Caroline Oury** (née de Belleville) (1831), he toured widely with her in Europe until 1847. He also was a prof. at London's Royal Academy of Music.—NS/LK/DM

Ouseley, Sir Frederick (Arthur) Gore, English organist, pianist, music theorist, and composer; b. London, Aug. 12, 1825; d. Hereford, April 6, 1889. He was the son of Sir Gore Ouseley, ambassador to Persia and Russia. He studied classics and theology with James Joyce, vicar of Dorking (1840–43). He inherited his father's title of baronet (1844) and his considerable wealth, then completed his education at Christ Church, Oxford (B.A., 1846; M.A., 1849; D.Mus., 1854). He was ordained a priest in 1849. Ouseley was curate at St. Barnabas, Pimlico (1849–51), and also founded the Coll. of St. Michael and All Angels, Tenbury (1854), serving as warden and vicar of the new parish. He was also made precentor of Hereford Cathedral (1855), and later canon residentiary there (1886); likewise was prof. of music at the Univ. of Oxford (1855–89). He was a fine organist, and excelled in fugal improvisation. Among his compositions are an opera, *L'isola disabitata* (1834), and other secular vocal works, three overtures, two oratorios, numerous anthems, church services, chamber music, organ works, and piano pieces. He publ. *A Treatise on Harmony* (1868), *A Treatise on Counterpoint, Canon, and Fugue, based on Cherubini* (1869), and *A Treatise on Musical Form and General Composition* (1875). He left his fine music library to St. Michael's Coll., Tenbury.

BIBL.: F. Havergal, *Memorials of F.A.G. O., Bart.* (London, 1889); F. Joyce, *Life of Rev. Sir F.A.G. O., Bart., etc.* (London, 1896); W. Shaw, ed., *Sir F. O. and St Michael's, Tenbury: A Chapter in the History of English Church Music and Ecclesiology* (Birmingham, 1988).—NS/LK/DM

Ousset, Cécile, French pianist; b. Tarbes, Jan. 23, 1936. A child prodigy, she made her public debut when she was only 5. She studied with Marcel Ciampi at the Paris Cons., where she graduated with the premier prix at age 14. In 1953 she won the Claire Pagès Prize. She subsequently won prizes in several competitions, including the Geneva (second prize co-winner, 1954), Queen Elisabeth of Belgium (fourth prize winner, 1956), Busoni (second prize co-winner, 1959), and Van Cliburn (fourth prize winner, 1962) competitions. She appeared regularly as a soloist with French orchs. and as a recitalist. In 1980 she made her British debut at the Edinburgh Festival. In 1984 she made her U.S. debut as a soloist with the Los Angeles Phil., and that same year she made her first tour of Japan. In subsequent years, she pursued an international career. In addition to her idiomatic interpretations of the French repertoire, she has also won distinction in the Austro-German repertoire.—NS/LK/DM

Ouvrard, René, French ecclesiastic, man of letters, and composer; b. Chinon, Indre-et-Loire, June 16, 1624; d. Tours, July 19, 1694. He received training in theology and music in Tours. In 1655 he went to Italy, where he met Carissimi in Rome. Upon his return to France, he was made maître de chapelle at Bordeaux Cathedral about 1657. About 1660 he became chef de la maîstrise at St. Just Cathedral in Narbonne. He went to Paris about 1663 to assume the duties of maître de musique at Saint-Chapelle. In 1679 he became canon at St. Gatien in Tours. Although Ouvrard's music is not extant, his writings have been preserved, among them *Secret pour composer en musique* (Paris, 1658, under the pseudonym Du Reneau; 2nd ed., 1660), *L'art et la science des nombres* (Paris, 1677), and *Architecture harmonique* (Paris, 1679). His important correspondence with the French ecclesiastic Claude Nicaise remains in MS.—LK/DM

Ovchinnikov, Viacheslav, Russian composer and conductor; b. Voronezh, May 29, 1936. He studied composition with Khrennikov at the Moscow Cons. (graduated, 1962), and also received training in conducting from Lev Ginzburg.

WORKS: DRAMATIC: *Sulamith*, ballet (1962); *On the Dawn of Misty Youth*, opera (1974–78); *Song of Songs*, ballet (1988); film scores, including *War and Peace* (1961–67). ORCH.: 6 symphonic suites (1955–72); 5 syms.: No. 1 (1955–57), No. 2, *Yuri Gargarin* (1956; rev. 1972–73), No. 3 (1964), No. 4 for Chorus and Orch. (1986), and No. 5 (1991); *Piece to the Memory of Ravel* (1956); Cello Concerto (1989–90). CHAMBER: *Ave Maria* for 2 Harps, Violins, and Cellos (1960); piano pieces. VOCAL: *Sergei of Radonezh*, oratorio (1958; rev. 1978 and 1985); *Elegy in Memory of Rachmaninoff* for Soprano, Chorus, and Orch. (1973); *Hymn to the Fatherland*, oratorio (1974); *The Seasons*, oratorio (1982); choruses; songs.—NS/LK/DM

Overton, Hall (actually, **Franklin**), American pianist, teacher, and composer; b. Bangor, Mich., Feb. 23, 1920; d. N.Y., Nov. 24, 1972. He studied piano at the Chicago Musical Coll. and counterpoint at the Juilliard School of Music in N.Y. (1940–42). He served in the U.S. Army overseas (1942–45). After WWII, he studied com-position with Perischetti at Juilliard, graduating in 1951; he also took private lessons with Riegger and Milhaud. At the same time, he filled professional engagements as a jazz pianist and contributed articles to the magazine *Jazz Today*. He was awarded two Guggenheim fellowships (1955, 1957). Overton taught at Juilliard (1960–71), the New School for Social Research in N.Y. (1962–66), and at the Yale Univ. School of Music.

WORKS: DRAMATIC: Opera: *The Enchanted Pear Tree*, after Boccaccio's *Decameron* (N.Y., Feb. 7, 1950); *Pietro's Petard* (N.Y., June 1963); *Huckleberry Finn*, after Mark Twain (N.Y., May 20, 1971). ORCH.: 2 syms.: No. 1 for Strings (1955) and No. 2 (1962); *Interplay* (1964); *Sonorities* (1964); *Rhythms* for Violin and Orch. (1965); *Pulsations* for Chamber Orch. (1972). CHAMBER: 3 string quartets (1950, 1954, 1967); String Trio (1957); Viola Sonata (1960); Cello Sonata (1960); various piano works, including *Polarities Nos. 1* (1959) and *2* (1971), and a Sonata (1963). VOCAL: Songs.—NS/LP

Owen, Morfydd Llywn, Welsh composer, pianist, and singer; b. Treforest, Oct. 1, 1891; d. Gowerton, near Swansea, Sept. 7, 1918. She studied with David Evans at the Univ. of South Wales in Cardiff (B.M., 1912), then with F. Corder at the Royal Academy of Music in London (1912–17), where she later taught. On Feb. 4, 1917, she married Ernest Jones, the Welsh disciple and biographer of Sigmund Freud. Her early death from complications following an operation for appendicitis was greatly lamented, for she had already established herself as a promising composer of vocal works. Her *Nocturne* for Orch. received the Lucas Prize in Composition from the Royal Academy of Music. She appeared frequently at the semi-annual Eisteddfods, both as a vocalist and as a composer. A 4–vol. ed. of her works, containing a biographical memoir by Jones, was publ. in London (1924).

WORKS: ORCH.: *Nocturne* (1913; Dallas, June 23, 1987); *Morfa Rhuddlan*, tone poem (1914); *The Passing of Branwen* (1917). CHAMBER: *Romance* for Violin and Piano (1911); Piano Trio (1912). Piano: Sonata (1910); *Étude* (1911); *Rhapsody* (1911); *Prélude after the Style of Bach* (1912); *Fantasie appassionata* (1912); *Rhapsodie* (1913); *Prélude* (1913); 3 préludes: *Waiting for Eirlys*, *Beti Bwt*, and *Nant-y-ffrith* (1914–15); *Preludio e Fuga grotesca* (1914); *Little Eric*, humoresque (1915); *Talyllyn* (1916); 3 *Welsh Impressions*: *Llanbynmair*, *Glantaf*, and *Beti Bwt* (1917). VOCAL: *Ave Maria* for Soprano, Chorus, and Orch. (1912); *Choric Songs* for Chorus and Orch. (1913); *Towards the Unknown Region*, vocal scena after Walt Whitman for Tenor and Orch. (1915); *Pro Patria*, cantata (1915); choral pieces, including *The Refugee*, after Schiller (1910), *Fierce Raged the Tempest*, after Thring (1911), *Sweet and Low*, after Tennyson (1911), *Sweet and Low* (1911), and *Jubilate* (1913); songs; hymns.

BIBL.: R. Davies, *Yr eneth ddisglair annwyl: M. O. (1891–1918), ei bywyd mewn Iluniau: Never so Pure a Sight: M. O. (1891–1918), a Life in Pictures* (Welsh and Eng., Llandysul, 1994). —NS/LK/DM

Owen, Richard, American lawyer, judge, and composer; b. N.Y., Dec. 11, 1922. He graduated from Dartmouth Coll. in 1947 and from Harvard Law School in 1950. He subsequently served as a senior trial attorney, and then was appointed to the bench by President Nixon to the U.S. District Court in N.Y. (1974). In between he attended night school at the Mannes School of Music, took courses in harmony and counterpoint with Vittorio Giannini and Robert Starer, and attended the Berkshire Music Center at Tanglewood. He wrote several operas deeply influenced by Puccini and Menotti, including *Dismissed with Prejudice* (1956), *A Moment of War* (1958), *A Fisherman Called Peter* (1965), *Mary Dyer* (dealing with a woman Quaker who was hanged in Boston on June 1, 1660; N.Y., June 12, 1976, with Owen's wife singing the title role), *The Death of the Virgin* (N.Y., March 31, 1983), *Abigail Adams* (N.Y., March 18, 1987), and the children's opera *Tom Sawyer* (N.Y., April 2, 1989).—NS/LK/DM

Oxinaga, Joaquin de, Spanish organist and composer; b. Bilbao (baptized), Oct. 26, 1719; d. Madrid, Oct. 24, 1789. He served as organist at Burgos Cathedral (1740) and in Bilbao (1742). From 1747 to 1749 he was third organist at the royal chapel in Madrid. From 1750 to 1754 he was organist at Toledo Cathedral. Oxinaga was esteemed for his organ compositions, most particularly his masterful fugal writing.—LK/DM

Oxley, Tony, English drummer; b. Sheffield, England, June 15, 1938. He initially made his impact as the house drummer at Ronnie Scott's club in London in the mid-1960s, backing many visiting U.S. musicians. His early discography finds him behind such unexpected players as pianist Bill Evans and violinist Sugarcane Harris. He was also a drummer on what is arguably guitarist John McLaughlin's best album *Extrapolation*. He was concurrently involved in the early British free jazz experiments (from 1966) and had an early trio with guitarist Derek Bailey and then-bassist (now composer) Gavin Bryars.

His first recordings were for CBS and RCA and he used these opportunities to record decidedly modern works using such musicians as Bailey, saxophonist Evan Parker, trumpeter Kenny Wheeler, and trombonist Paul Rutherford. His most high- profile collaboration has been with pianist Cecil Taylor, an association that lasted from 1988 to 1992.

DISC.: *Ichnos* (1971); *Tony Oxley* (1992); *The Enchanted Messenger* (1994).—RI

Ozawa, Seiji, eminent Japanese conductor; b. Fenytien, China (of Japanese parents), Sept. 1, 1935. His father was a Buddhist, his mother a Christian. The family returned to Japan in 1944, at the end of the Japanese occupation of Manchuria. Ozawa began to study piano; at 16, he enrolled at the Toho School of Music in Tokyo, where he studied composition and conducting; one of his teachers, Hideo Saito, profoundly influenced his development as a musician; he graduated in 1959 with first prizes in composition and conducting. By that time he had already conducted concerts with the NHK (Japan Broadcasting Corp.) Sym. Orch. and the Japan Phil.; upon Saito's advice, he went to Europe; to defray his expenses, he became a motor-scooter salesman for a Japanese firm, and promoted the product in Italy and France. In 1959 he won first prize at the international competition for conductors in Besançon,

and was befriended by Charles Munch and Eugène Bigot; he then studied conducting with Bigot in Paris. Munch arranged for Ozawa to go to the U.S. and to study conducting at the Berkshire Music Center in Tanglewood; in 1960 he won its Koussevitzky Prize, and was awarded a scholarship to work with Karajan and the Berlin Phil. Bernstein heard him in Berlin and engaged him as an asst. conductor of the N.Y. Phil. On April 14, 1961, he made his first appearance with the orch. at Carnegie Hall; later that year, he accompanied Bernstein and the orch. on its tour of Japan. In 1962 he was invited to return as a guest conductor of the NHK Sym. Orch., but difficulties arose between him and the players, who objected to being commanded in an imperious manner by one of their own countrymen; still, he succeeded in obtaining engagements with other Japanese orchs., which he conducted on his periodic visits to his homeland.

After serving as sole asst. conductor of the N.Y. Phil. (1964–65), Ozawa's career advanced significantly. From 1964 to 1968 he was music director of the Ravinia Festival, the summer home of the Chicago Sym. Orch. In 1969 he served as its principal guest conductor, and from 1965 to 1969 he also was music director of the Toronto Sym. Orch., which he took to England in 1965. From 1970 to 1976 he was music director of the San Francisco Sym. Orch., and then its music adviser (1976–77); took it on an extensive tour of Europe in 1977, garnering exceptional critical acclaim. Even before completing his tenure in San Francisco, he had begun a close association with the Boston Sym. Orch.; with Schuller, he became co-artistic director of its Berkshire Music Center in 1970; in 1972 he assumed the post of music adviser of the Boston Sym. Orch., and in 1973 he became its music director, and sole artistic director of the Berkshire Music Center, an astonishing event in American music annals, marking the first time an oriental musician was chosen solely by his merit to head the Boston Sym. Orch., which was for years since its foundation the exclusive preserve of German, and later French and Russian, conductors. In 1976 Ozawa took the Boston Sym. Orch. on a tour of Europe; in 1978 he escorted it to Japan, where those among Japanese musicians who had been skeptical about his abilities greeted his spectacular ascendance with national pride. Another unprecedented event took place in the spring of 1979, when Ozawa traveled with the Boston Sym. Orch. to the People's Republic of China on an official cultural visit; in Aug. 1979 Ozawa and the orch. went on a tour of European music festivals. The centennial of the Boston Sym. Orch. in 1981 was marked by a series of concerts, under Ozawa's direction, which included appearances in 14 American cities and a tour of Japan, France, Germany, Austria, and England. On Sept. 24, 1991, he conducted the Saito Kinen Orch. of Japan at its first appearance in the U.S. at N.Y.'s Carnegie Hall. On Sept. 5, 1992, he inaugurated the Saito Kinen Festival in Matsumoto. He made his Metropolitan Opera debut in N.Y. on Dec. 4, 1992, conducting *Eugene Onegin*. In 1994 the Boston Sym. Orch.'s new concert hall at Tanglewood was named the Seiji Ozawa Hall in his honor.

After Ozawa consolidated his music directorship of the Boston Sym. Orch., he retained that position for 29 years, the longest tenure in the orch.'s history. His last years at its helm did not equal his early success, but he contrived to demonstrate his capacity for interpretations of occasional brilliance. In 2002 he relinquished his Boston position to become chief conductor of the Vienna State Opera. He was married twice: first to the Japanese pianist Kyoko Edo, and second, to a Eurasian, Vera Ilyan. He received an honorary doctorate in music from the Univ. of San Francisco in 1971, and one from the New England Cons. of Music in 1982. His remarkable career was the subject of the documentary film *Ozawa*, which was telecast by PBS in 1987.

BIBL.: S. Tan, *S. O.* (Austin, Tex., 1997); L. Russell, *S.: An Intimate Portrait of S. O.* (Boston, 1998).—**NS/LK/DM**

Ozi, Etienne, French bassoonist, teacher, and composer; b. Nîmes, Dec. 9, 1754; d. Paris, Oct. 5, 1813. He settled in Paris about 1779, where he made many successful appearances at the Concert Spirituel. He was in the service of the Duke of Orléans (1783–86), and also played in the concert series of the Masonic Loge Olympique de la Paraite Estime (from 1783). From 1786 to 1788 he was first bassoonist in the musique du roi. With the coming of the Revolution, Ozi became a member of the National Guard Band and a teacher of its music school, the École Gratuite de Musique de la Garde Nationale Parisienne. He remained with it when it became the Institut Nationale de Musique in 1793 and then the Conservatoire National de Musique in 1795. From 1797 he also was director of its publishing activities. From 1797 to 1806 he was a member of the Opéra orch.'s virtuoses d'elite and in 1806 he was first bassoonist in Napoleon's chapelle-musique. Ozi was the author of the pedagogical works *Méthode nouvelle et raisonnée pour le basson* (1787), *Méthode de basson...avec des airs et des duos* (1788), and *Nouvelle méthode de basson adoptée par le Conservatoire* (1803). Among his compositions were 8 bassoon concertos (1785–1801), 4 syms. concertantes, many pieces for wind band, and much chamber music.—**LK/DM**

Ozim, Igor, Slovenian violinist and teacher; b. Ljubljana, May 9, 1931. He studied with Leon Pfeifer at the Ljubljana Academy of Music and with Rostal in London (1949–51), then won the Flesch (1951) and Munich (1953) competitions. He toured widely in Europe and the U.S.; also taught at the Ljubljana Academy of Music (1960–63) and then at the Cologne Hochschule für Musik. In 1990 he served on the jury of the International Violin Competition of Indianapolis. He was a notable advocate of contemporary music.—**NS/LK/DM**

P

Paap, Wouter, eminent Dutch musicologist and composer; b. Utrecht, May 7, 1908; d. Lage Vuursche (Baarn), Oct. 7, 1981. He studied piano and theory at the Utrecht School of Music (1928–32). He taught at the Netherland's Inst. for Catholic Church Music (1934–47); was founder-editor of the journal *Mens en Melodie* (1946–75).

WRITINGS: *Anton Bruckner* (Bilthoven, 1936); *Toscanini* (Amsterdam, 1938); *Mens en melodie: Inleiding tot de muziek* (Utrecht, 1940); *Ludwig van Beethoven* (Amsterdam, 1941); with E. Reeser, *Moderne kerkmuziek in Nederland* (Bilthoven, 1942); *De symfonieen van Beethoven* (Utrecht, 1946); *Die kunst van het moduleren* (Utrecht, 1948); *Eduard van Beinum* (Baarn, 1956); *De symfonie* (Bilthoven, 1957); ed. with A. Corbet, *Algemene muziekencyclopedie* (6 vols., Amsterdam, 1957–63; suppl. ed. by J. Robijns, Ghent, 1972); *Willem Mengelberg* (Amsterdam and Brussels, 1960); *Muziek, moderne en klassiek* (Utrecht, 1961); *Mozart: Portret van een muziekgenie* (Utrecht, 1962); *Honderd jaar muziekonderwijs te Utrecht* (Utrecht, 1974); *Een eeuw koninklijke Nederlandse toonkunstenaars vereniging* (Amsterdam, 1975).

WORKS: ORCH.: Sinfonietta for Chamber Orch. (1938); *Wals* for Chamber Orch. (1940); *Passacaglia* (1943); *Studentenmuziek* for Strings (1948); *Guirlanden van Muziek* for Strings (1951); *Ballet Suite* for Chamber Orch. (1953); *Overture Electora* (1956); *Trompetten en klaretten*, 3 pieces for Wind Orch. (1960). **CHAMBER:** *Luchtige suite* for Carillon (1955); Carillon Sonatina (1963); various pieces for Wind Instruments. **VOCAL:** *Sterre der zee* for Soprano, Chorus, and Orch. (1937); *Declamatorium* for Reciter and Orch. (1940); *Muziek ter Bruiloft*, cantata for Tenor and Orch. (1945); 5 Liederen for Voice and Orch. (1956).—**NS/LK/DM**

Pablo (Costales), Luís (Alfonso) de, eminent Spanish composer and teacher; b. Bilbao, Jan. 28, 1930. He commenced his musical training in Fuenterrabía when he was 8. After settling in Madrid, he pursued the study of law at the Universidad Complutense (graduated, 1952) while continuing his musical training on his own. In 1958 he joined the Nueva Música group. In 1959 he organized the Tiempo y Música group, with which he presented concerts of contemporary chamber music

until 1963. He founded the Forum Musical in 1963 for the purpose of giving concerts of contemporary music. In 1964 he served as the artistic organizer of the first gathering of the Música Contemporánea of Madrid. He founded the new music group Alea and the first electroacoustic music laboratory in Spain in 1965. In 1967 he was in Berlin as a guest of the Deutscher Akademischer Austauschdienst. In 1968 he founded Alea, Música electronica libre, a group that presented performances of live electroacoustic music. He became a prof. of contemporary music analysis at the Madrid Cons. in 1971. With José Luis Alexanco, he served as co-director of the Encuentros de Arts in Pamplona in 1972. In 1973 he was the Visiting Slee Prof. at the State Univ. of N.Y. at Buffalo, and in 1974 he was a prof. of contemporary music analysis at the univs. of Ottawa and Montreal. In subsequent years, he lectured widely on contemporary music in Spain and abroad. He became president of the Spanish section of the ISCM in 1981. In 1983 he was made director of the Centro para la Difusión de la Música Contemporánea of the Ministry of Culture. In 1994 he was composer-in-residence at the Spanish Academy in Rome, and in 1998–99 at the Strasbourg Cons. In 1973 the French government honored him with the title of Chevalier des Arts et des Lettres, and in 1986 it bestowed upon him the Médaille d'Officier de l'Ordre des Arts et des Lettres. In 1986 King Juan Carlos of Spain presented him with the Medalla de Oro al Mérito en las Bellas Artes españolas. He was made a full member of the Real Academia de Bellas Artes de San Fernando of Madrid and a corresponding member of the Academy of Granada in 1988. In 1991 he was awarded the Premio Nacional de Música by the Ministry of Culture, and in 1993 he was awarded its diploma of the Consejo Internacional de la Música. He was awarded an honorary doctorate in fine arts and music from the Univ. of Madrid in 1997. In his compositions, he has demonstrated a remarkable versatility in handling various techniques. All the while, he has remained true to himself by finding his own compositional path in which each score becomes a thoroughly new adventure in sound. This is so whether he utilizes traditional instruments or ranges into other sound worlds, such as electronic manifestations.

WORKS: DRAMATIC: *Per diversos motivos* for 2 Actors, Soprano, 12 Voices, and Piano (1969); *Berceuse* for Actor, Soprano, 3 Flutes, 2 Percussionists, and Hammond Organ (1973–74; Buffalo, Jan. 26, 1975); *Sólo un paso* for Actor and Flute (Bremen Radio, May 1974); *Very Gentle* for Soprano, Countertenor, and 2 Instrumentalists (Royan, April 3, 1974); *Kiu*, opera (1979–82; Madrid, April 16, 1983); *El viajero indiscreto*, opera (1984–88; Madrid, March 12, 1990); *La madre invita a comer*, opera (1992; Venice, June 19, 1993); *La Señorita Cristina*, opera (1997–99); incidental music; film scores. **ORCH.:** *Sinfonías* for Chamber Orch. (1954–66; Madrid, Dec. 17, 1966); *Invenciones* (1955; rev. 1959–60; Madrid, June 15, 1960); *Radial* for 24 Instruments (1960); *Tombeau* (1962–63); *Iniciativas* (1965–66); *Módolus II* for 2 Orchs. (1966; Madrid, Oct. 24, 1967); *Imaginario II* (1967); *Quasi una fantasía* for String Sextet and Orch. (1969); *Oroitaldi* (1971; Monte Carlo, Dec. 3, 1972); *Éléphants ivres I* (1972; Madrid, April 27, 1973), *III* (1973), and *IV* (1973); *Je mange, tu manges* for Chamber Orch. (1972); *Latidos* (1974–80; Radio France, Paris, Jan. 23, 1981); *Tinieblas del agua* (Metz, Nov. 18, 1978); 2 piano concertos: No. 1 (1978–79; Madrid, March 1, 1980; also as *Concierto de cámara* for Piano and Chamber Orch., 1979; Quebec, Dec. 11, 1980) and No. 2 (1979–80; Santander, Aug. 5, 1982; also as Concerto for Harpsichord, 2 Percussion, and Strings, Naples, Dec. 16, 1983); *Adagio* (1983; Hilversum, March 2, 1984); *Adagio-Cadenza-Allegro spiritoso* for Oboe and Orch. (Murcia, April 18, 1987); *Fiesta* for 6 Percussionists and Orch. (1987; Rennes, Feb. 1988; also for 6 Percussionists, 1989); *Senderos del aire* (1987; Tokyo, Nov. 4, 1988); *Une couleur* for Saxophone and Orch. (1988; Fontenai, Jan. 20, 1989); *Figura en el mar* for Flute and Orch. (1989; Metz, Nov. 17, 1990); *Cinco impromptus* (1990; San Sebastian, Jan. 28, 1991); *Las orillas* (1990; Tenerife, Jan. 7, 1991); *Sueños* for Piano and Orch. (1991; Parma, June 5, 1992); *Vendaval* (1994; Brussels, Feb. 12, 1995); *Tréboles* (1995; Valladolid, Feb. 1996); *Rostro* for Chamber Orch. (1995; Cadaqués, Aug. 1996); Violin Concerto (1997–98; Madrid, Nov. 19, 1999). **CHAMBER:** *Coral* for 7 Instruments (1954; rev. 1958); *Polar* for 11 Instruments (1961); *Prosodía* for 6 Instruments (1962); *Condicionado* for Flute (1962); *Recíproco* for Flutes, Piano, and Percussion (Venice, April 13, 1963); *Cesuras* for 6 Instruments (Madrid, Dec. 11, 1963); *Módulos I* for 11 Instruments (1964–65; Darmstadt, July 31, 1965), *IV* for String Quartet (1965–67), *III* for 17 Instruments (1967; North German Radio, Hamburg, Jan. 9, 1968), and *V* for Organ (1967); *Imaginario I* for Harpsichord and 3 Percussion (1967); *Paráfrasis* for 12 Instruments (1968); *La libertad sonríe* for 15 Instruments (Salamanca, May 7, 1971); *Promenade sur un corps* for Flute and Percussion (1971); *Éléphants ivres II* for Chamber Ensemble (1972); *Historia natural* for 2 Organs, Percussion, and Tape (1972); *Pardon* for Clarinet and Trombone (Warsaw, Sept. 1972); *Soirée* for Clarinet and Violin (1972); *Le prie-dieu sur la terrasse* for Percussionist (1973; Barcelona, Feb. 22, 1974); *Vielleicht* for 6 Percussionists (1973; Royan, March 27, 1975); *Déjame hablar* for Strings (1974; Royan, March 27, 1975); *Visto de cerca* for 3 Instrumentalists and Tape (1974); *A modo concierto* for Percussion and Instruments (1975–76); *Credo* for 2 Flutes, 2 Oboes, 2 Clarinets, 2 Bassoons, and 2 Horns (1976; Madrid, April 30, 1977); *Invitación a la memoria* for Chamber Ensemble (1976–77; Saintes, July 18, 1978); *Lerro* for Flute (1977); *Oculto* for Bass Clarinet or Saxophone (1977); Trio for Violin, Viola, and Cello (1978; Madrid, Nov. 3, 1980); *Dibujos* for Flute, Clarinet, Violin, and Cello

(1979–80; Madrid, April 29, 1980); *Tornasol* for 2 Flutes, 2 Clarinets, Violin, Viola, Cello, Double Bass, and Tape (1980–81; Marseilles, Feb. 23, 1982); *Ofrenda (Seis piezas a la memoria de Manuel Azaña)* for Cello (1980–82; N.Y., April 1983); *Saturno* for 2 Percussionists (1983); *Cinco meditaciones* for Chamber Ensemble (1983–84; San Sebastián, Aug. 26, 1984); *J. H.* for Clarinet and Cello (1983–84); *Cuatro fragmentos de Kiu* for Violin and Piano (1984–86; also for Flute and Piano, 1985–86; Madrid, June 18, 1986); *Caligrafías (Federico Mompou in memoriam)* for Piano, Violin, and Cello (1987; Santander, Aug. 9, 1988); *Notturnino* for Chamber Ensemble (1987); *Il violino spagnolo* for Violin (1988); *Compostela* for Violin and Cello (1989); *Fiesta* for 6 Percussionists (1989; also for 6 Percussionists and Orch., 1987); *Metáforas* for Piano, 2 Violins, Viola, and Cello (1989–90; Madrid, Nov. 7, 1990); *Melisma furioso* for Flute (Tokyo, Sept. 1, 1990); Sextet, *Paráfrasis e interludio*, for 2 Violins, 2 Violas, Cello, and Double Bass (1990; Reykjavík, Feb. 1991); *Monólogo* for Viola (1990–92); *Libro de imágenes* for 9 Instruments (Amsterdam, June 1992); *Fábula* for Guitar (1991–92; Madrid, March 12, 1992); *Paraíso y Tres danzas macabras* for Chamber Ensemble (1992); *Parodia* for 2 Violins, Viola, and Cello (Madrid, Dec. 6, 1992); *Ritornello* for 8 Cellos (1992–93; Santander, Aug. 22, 1993); *Segunda lectura* for 10 Instruments (1992–93); *Umori* for Flute, Oboe, Clarinet, Trumpet, and Bassoon (1992–93; Bologna, April 28, 1993); *Caligrafía serena* for 2 Violins, Viola, and Cello (1993); Trio for Violin, Cello, and Piano (1993); *Monos y liebres* for Bass Clarinet and Marimba (1995); *Flessuoso* for String Quartet (1996; Bilbao, Dec. 1997); *Soliloquio* for Flute (1997–98; Asiago Festival, Aug. 1998); *Corola* for Saxophone Quartet, Piano, and Percussion (1997–98; London, Dec. 1998); Clarinet Quintet (1998–99; Madrid, April 1999). **Piano:** *Móvil* for 2 Pianos (1957) and *II* for Piano, 4-Hands (1959–67); Sonata (1958; Madrid, March 6, 1960); *Libro para el pianista* (1961–62); *Comme d'habitude* for 1 Pianist on 2 Pianos (1970); *Affettuoso* (1973); *Cuaderno* (1982); *Retratos y transcripciones* (2 books, 1984–92, 1996); *Amable sombra* for 2 Pianos (1989). **VOCAL:** *Comentarios a dos textos de Gerardo Diego* for Soprano or Tenor, Piccolo, Vibraphone, and Double Bass (1956; Barcelona, May 11, 1960); *Escena* for Chorus, 2 Percussion, and 15 Strings (1964); *Ein Wort* for Soprano, Piano, Violin, and Clarinet (1965); *Heterogéneo* for 2 Reciters, Hammond Organ, and Orch. (1967); *Yo lo vi* for Chorus (1970); *Visto de cerca* for 3 Men's Voices and Electronics (1974); *Al son que tocan* for Soprano, 4 Basses, 8 Instruments, and Tape (1974–75; Madrid, Nov. 18, 1975); *Portrait imaginé* for Chorus, Chamber Orch., and Tape (1974–75; Ottawa, Oct. 1, 1975); *Zurezko olerkia* for Chorus, 2 Txalapartas, and 4 Percussionists (1975; Bonn, May 24, 1976); *Bajo el sol* for Chorus (1977; Cuenca, March 25, 1978); *Ederki* for Soprano, Viola, and Percussion (1977–78; Naples, June 17, 1978); *Canción* for Soprano, Oboe, Trumpet, Celesta, and Harp (1979); *Pocket zarzuela* for Mezzo-soprano, 2 Flutes, Clarinet, Violin, Cello, and Piano (Bonn, Oct. 9, 1979); *Retratos de la conquista* for Chorus (Lille, Nov. 15, 1980); *Sonido de la guerra* for Soprano, Tenor, Reciter, Small Women's Chorus, Flute, Harp, Celesta, 2 Percussionists, and Cello (1980; Madrid, Dec. 17, 1981); *Una cantata perdida* for Soprano, Double Bass, and Percussion (N.Y., Nov. 1981); *Viatges i flors* for Soprano, Reciter, Chorus, and Orch. (1981–84; Brussels, Oct. 10, 1985); *El manantial* for Soprano, Flute, Celesta, Harp, Piano, and 2 Violins (Valladolid, Nov. 12, 1982); *Malinche* for Soprano, Percussion, and Tape (1983; Naples, Sept. 1984; also for Soprano and Piano, Rome, April 25, 1985); *Serenata* for Chorus and Band (1984–85; Lille, Dec. 1990); *Zu Strassburg auf der Schanz* for Baritone and Orch. (Radio France, Paris, Feb. 28, 1985); *Tarde de poetas* for Soprano, Baritone, Chorus, and Chamber Orch. (1985–86; *Com* *um epilog* for Men's Chorus and Orch. (1988; Paris, May 1989); *Antigua fe* for Soprano, Men's Chorus, and Orch. (1990; Madrid, Jan. 28, 1992); *Ricercare recordare* for Reciter, Chorus, and Chamber Ensemble (1990); *De la América pretérita* for Soprano and Orch. (1991); *Variaciones de Léon* for 2 Sopranos, Contralto, Tenor, Baritone, and Bass (1992–93; Royaumont, Sept. 11, 1993); *Romancero* for 12 Voices (1994; Venice, Aug. 1995); *Relámpagos* for Tenor and Orch. (Madrid, Nov. 1996); *Puntos de amor* for Soprano and Clarinet (Strasbourg, Oct. 1999); *Tre frammenti sacri* for Chorus, 2 Trumpets, and Trombone (Milan, Dec. 1999). ELECTROACOUSTIC: *We* (1969–70; Paris, Oct. 1970; 2nd version, 1984; Madrid, Jan. 28, 1985); *Tamaño natural* (Paris, Oct. 1970); *Soledad interrumpida* (Buenos Aires, July 20, 1971); *Chamán* (1975–76; Ottawa, Feb. 1, 1976).

BIBL.: T. Marco, *L.d. P.* (Madrid, 1976); J. García del Busto, *L.d. P.* (Madrid, 1979); idem, *Escritos sobre L.d. P.* (Madrid, 1987); P. De Volder, *Encuentros con L.d. P.* (Madrid, 1998).—**NS/LK/DM**

Pacchiarotti, Gasparo,

famous Italian castrato soprano; b. Fabriano, near Ancona (baptized), May 21, 1740; d. Padua, Oct. 28, 1821. He studied with Bertoni at San Marco in Venice, where he was principal soloist (1765–68). He then was primo uomo in Palermo (1770–71) before singing in Naples (1771–76). After appearing throughout Italy, he was engaged for the inaugural operation productions at Milan's La Scala (Aug.-Sept. 1778). He sang at the King's Theatre in London (1778–80), returning there 1781–84; also appeared at the Tuileries before the French court (1782). Having served as primo uomo at Venice's Teatro S. Benedetto (1784–91), he once more sang in London (1791), appearing in concert as well as opera. He sang in the inaugural season at Venice's Teatro La Fenice (1792–93) before retiring to his estate in Padua. He later sang for Napoleon in Padua (1796) and at Bertoni's funeral at San Marco (June 28, 1814). Pacchiarotti was acclaimed as the greatest castrato of his day, his voice ranging from C' to B flat. A. Calegari publ. *Modi generali del canto premessi alle maniere parziali onde adornace o rifiorice le nude o semplici melodie o cantilene giusta il metodo di Gasparo Pacchiarotti* (Milan, 1836).

BIBL.: G. Pacchiarotti (his adopted son), *Cenni biografici intorno a G. P.* (Padua, 1844); R. Sassi, *Un celebre musico fabrianese, G. P. (col testamento)* (Fabriano, 1935).—**NS/LK/DM**

Pacchioni, Antonio Maria,

Italian priest and composer; b. Modena (baptized), July 5, 1654; d. there, July 15, 1738. He spent his entire life in Modena, where he studied with Marzio Erculeo (singing), Agostino Bendinelli (counterpoint), and G.M. Bononcini (violin and compostion). In 1677 he became a priest at S. Carlo, where he was admitted to its mensa comune, a congregation of musician priests in 1679. From 1694 he was maestro di cappella at the Cathedral, and also vice-maestro di cappella (1699–1722) and maestro di cappella (from 1722) at the ducal court. Among his works were 3 oratorios (1677–82), masses and other liturgical pieces, and secular music.—**LK/DM**

Pace, Pietro,

Italian organist and composer; b. Loreto, 1559; d. there, April 15, 1622. He was organist of the Santa Casa, Loreto (1591–92), and subsequently was in the service of Giuliano della Rovere in Urbino. In 1597 he was organist at Pesaro Cathedral, and then again at the Santa Casa, Loreto, from 1611. He composed music for Iganazio Bracci's *L'ilarocosmo ovvero Il mondo lieto* (Urbino, April 29, 1621), and publ. various vols. of madrigals, motets, and other vocal works (1597–1619).—**LK/DM**

Pacelli, Asprilio,

Italian composer; b. Vasciano, 1570; d. Warsaw, May 4, 1623. He went to Rome, where he was active at the churches of S. Maria de Monserrato (1589–93) and Trinità dei Pellegrini (1594). From 1595 to 1602 he was maestro di cappella at the Collegio Germanico, and in 1602 at St. Peter's. He then was called to Warsaw by King Sigismund to serve as director of his royal chapel in 1603. Among his works were Psalms, motets and other sacred vocal works, and madrigals.

BIBL.: M. Gliński, *A. P., insigne maestro di cappella della corte reale de Polonia (1570–1623)* (Vatican City, 1941).—**LK/DM**

Pachelbel, Charles Theodore (actually, Carl Theodor),

German-American organist, harpsichordist, teacher, and composer, son of **Johann Pachelbel** and brother of **Wilhelm Hieronymus Pachelbel**; b. Stuttgart (baptized), Nov. 24, 1690; d. Charleston, S.C. (buried), Sept. 15, 1750. He emigrated to Boston c. 1732; served as organist at Trinity Church in Newport, R.I. He then went to N.Y. and appeared in concerts as a harpsichordist (Jan. 21 and March 8, 1736), and then was organist at St. Philip's Church in Charleston (1737–50). He gave his first public concert in his home there (Nov. 22, 1737). In 1749 he founded his own singing school. His only extant work, a Magnificat for 8 Voices (modern ed., N.Y., 1937), was written before his emigration to the U.S.—**NS/LK/DM**

Pachelbel, Johann,

celebrated German organist, pedagogue, and composer, father of **Charles Theodore (Carl Theodor) Pachelbel** and **Wilhelm Hieronymus Pachelbel**; b. Nuremberg (baptized), Sept. 1, 1653; d. there (buried), March 9, 1706. He studied music in Nuremberg with Heinrich Schwemmer, received instruction in composition and instrumental performance from G.C. Wecker, and pursued his academic studies at the local St. Lorenz school; also attended the lectures at the Auditorium Aegidianum. He then took courses briefly at the Univ. of Altdorf (1669–70), and served as organist at the Lorenzkirche there. He subsequently was accepted as a scholarship student at the Gymnasium Poeticum in Regensburg, and took private music lessons with Kaspar Prentz. In 1673 he went to Vienna as deputy organist at St. Stephen's Cathedral. In 1677 he assumed the position of court organist in Eisenach. In 1678 he became organist at the Protestant Predigerkirche in Erfurt, where he established his reputation as a master organist, composer, and teacher. He was a friend of the Bach family, and was the teacher of Johann Christoph Bach, who in turn taught Johann Sebastian Bach. On Oct. 25, 1681, Pachelbel married Barbara Gabler; she and their infant son died during the plague of 1683. He then married Judith Drommer on Aug. 24, 1684, with whom he had 5 sons and 2 daughters. In addition to Carl and Wilhelm, their son Johann Michael became an instrument maker and their daughter Amalie became a painter. In 1690 he accepted an appointment as Wurttemberg court musician and organist in Stuttgart. However, with the French invasion in the fall of 1692, he fled to Nuremberg; in Nov. of that year he became town organist in Gotha. In 1695 he succeeded Wecker as organist at St. Sebald in Nuremberg, a position he held until his death. Pachelbel was one of the most significant predecessors of Johann Sebastian Bach. His liturgical organ music was of the highest order, particularly his splendid organ chorales. His non-liturgical keyboard music was likewise noteworthy, especially his fugues and variations (of the latter, his *Hexachordum Apollinis* of 1699 is extraordinary). He was equally gifted as a composer of vocal music. His motets, sacred concertos, and concertato settings of the Magnificat are fine examples of German church music. He was a pioneer in notational symbolism of intervals, scales, and pitch levels arranged to correspond to the meaning of the words. Thus, his setting of the motet *Durch Adams Fall* is accomplished by a falling figure in the bass; exaltation is expressed by a rising series of arpeggios in a major key; steadfast faith is conveyed by a repeated note; satanic evil is translated into an ominous figuration of a broken diminished-seventh-chord. Generally speaking, joyful moods are portrayed by major keys, mournful states of soul by minor keys, a practice which became a standard mode of expression through the centuries. In addition to various separate editions of his works, major publications include M. Seiffert and A. Sandberger, eds., *Johann Pachelbel: Klavierwerke*, in Denkmäler der Tonkunst in Bayern, II, Jg. II/1 (1901), M. Seiffert, ed., *Johann Pachelbel: Orgelkompositionen*, in Denkmäler der Tonkunst in Bayern, VI, Jg. IV/1 (1903), and K. Matthaei and W. Stockmeier, eds., *Johann Pachelbel: Ausgewählte Orgelwerke* (vols. 1–4 by Matthaei, Kassel, 1928–36; vols. 5–6 by Stockmeier, Kassel, 1972–74).

WORKS: CHORALES FOR ORGAN: *8 Choräle zum Praeambulieren* (Nuremberg, 1693). **FUGUES:** *Ach Gott, vom Himmel sieh darein; Ach Herr, mich armen Sünder; Christe, der du bist Tag und Licht; Da Jesus an dem Kreuze stund* (may not be by Pachelbel); *Der Herr ist mein getreuer Hirt* (2 versions); *Dies sind die heil'gen zehn Gebot; Es woll uns Gott genädig sein* (2 versions); *In dich hab' ich gehoffet, Herr; Wo Gott zum Haus nicht gibt sein Gunst.* **THREE-PART CANTUS FIRMUS:** *Allein Gott in der Höh sei Ehr* (may not be by Pachelbel); *Christ unser Herr zum Jordan kam; Durch Adams Fall; Erbarm dich mein, o Herre Gott; Erhalt uns Herr, bei deinem Wort* (may not be by Pachelbel); *Gelobet seist du, Jesu Christ; Gott Vater, der du deine Sonn; Herr Gott, dich loben alle wir; Ich hab' mein' Sach' Gott heimgestellt; Ich ruf zu dir; Jesus Christus, unser Heiland, der den Tod* (2 versions); *Kommt her zu mir, spricht Gottes Sohn; Lob sei Gott in des Himmels Thron; Meine Seele erhebt den Herren [tonus peregrinus]* (2 versions); *Nun freut euch, lieben Christen g'mein'; O Mensch bewein dein Sünde gross; Vom Himmel hoch da komm ich her; Warum betrübst du dich, mein Herz; Was mein Gott will, das g'scheh allzeit; Wenn wir in höchsten Nöten sein; Wie schön leuchtet der Morgenstern; Wo Got der Herr nicht bei uns halt* (2 versions); *Wo Gott zum Haus nicht gibt sein Gunst.* **FOUR-PART CANTUS FIRMUS:** *Gott hat das Evangelium; Gott Vater, der du deine Sonn'; Komm, Gott Schöpfer, heiliger Geist; Mag ich Unglück nicht widerstahn; Nun lasst uns Gott dem Herren; Vater unser im Himmelreich.*

COMBINATION-FORM: *Ach Gott, vom Himmel sieh darein; Ach Herr, mich armen Sünder; Ach wie elend ist unsre Zeit; Allein Gott in der Höh sei Ehr* (may not be by Pachelbel); *An Wasserflüssen Babylon* (2 versions); *Auf meinen lieben Gott; Christ lag in Todesbanden; Der Tag der ist so freudenreich; Durch Adams Fall; Ein feste Burg; Es spricht der Unweisen Mund wohl; Herr Christ, der einig Gott's Sohn; Herr Jesu Christ, ich weiss gar wohl; Ich ruf zu dir; Nun komm der Heiden Heiland; O Lamm Gottes unschuldig; Vater unser im Himmelreich; Vom Himmel hoch da komm ich her; Warum betrübst du dich, mein Herz; Wenn mein Stundlein vorhanden ist; Wenn wir in höchsten Nöten sein; Wo Gott der Her nicht bei uns halt.* **BICINIA:** *Durch Adams Fall; Es spricht der unweisen Mund wohl* (may not be by Pachelbel); *Jesus Christus, unser Heiland, der von uns; Was mein Gott will, das g'scheh allzeit.* **OTHER KINDS:** *Allein zu dir, Herr Jesu Christ* (2 versions); *Nun lob, mein' Seel', den Herren; Wir glauben all' an einen Gott.* **OTHER:** 95 Magnificat fugues; non-liturgical music for organ, including 26 fugues, 16 toccatas, 7 preludes, 6 fantasias, 6 ciacconas, 3 ricercari, etc.; additional keyboard music, including arias with variations known as *Hexachordum Apollinis, sex arias exhibens...quam singulis suae sunt subjectae variationes* (Nuremberg, 1699), about 17 suites, and the following chorale variations: *Ach was soll ich Sünder machen, Alle Menschen müssen sterben, Christus, der ist mein Leben, Freu dich sehr, o meine Seele [Treuer Gott, ich muss dir klagen], Herzlich tut mich verlangen, Was Gott tut, das ist wohlge-tan,* and *Werde munter, mein Gemüte.* **CHAMBER:** *Canon and Gigue* in D major for 3 Violins and Basso Continuo (the *Canon* is one of his most famous works, being extremely popular with modern audiences; it has been publ. and republ. in numerous arrangements for various instruments); *Musicalische Ergötzung bestehend in 6 verstimten Partien* for 2 Violins and Basso Continuo (Nuremberg, 1695); *Partie* in G major for 2 Violins, 2 Violas, Cello, and Basso Continuo. **VOCAL: Motets For 2 4-part Choruses:** *Der Herr ist König, darum toben die Volker; Der Herr ist König und herrlich geschmückt; Gott ist unser Zuversicht; Jauchzet dem Herrn; Jauchzet Gott, alle Lande; Nun danket alle Gott; Singet dem Herrn; Tröste uns Gott;* also the unfinished *Der Herr ist König und herrlich geschmückt* for 5 Voices and Basso Continuo. **Other:** 2 Latin motets: *Exsurgat Deus* and *Paratum cor meum.* **Sacred Concertos:** *Christ lag in Todesbanden* for 4 Voices, 2 Violins, 3 Violas, and Basso Continuo; *Der Name des Herren sei gelobet* for 3 Voices, 2 Violins, and Basso Continuo; *Gott ist unser Zuversicht* for 4 Voices, 2 Violins, 2 Violas, Bassoon, and Basso Continuo; *Gott sei uns gnädig* for 5 Voices, 5 Trumpets, Timpani, 2 Violins, 4 Violas, Bassoon, Basso Continuo, and Organ; *Jauchzet dem Herrn, alle Welt* for 5 Voices, 2 Oboes, 2 Violins, 3 Violas, Viole, and Basso Continuo; *Jauchzet dem Herrn, alle Welt* for 5 Voices, 4 Trumpets, Timpani, 2 Violins, 3 Violas, Bassoon, and Basso Continuo; *Kommt her zu mir* for 4 Voices, 2 Violins, 2 Cornets, and Basso Continuo; *Lobet den Herrn in seinem Heiligtum* for 5 Voices, 2 Flutes, Bassoon, 5 Trumpets, Trombone, Timpani, Cymbal, Harp, 2 Violins, 3 Violas, Basso Continuo, and Organ; *Meine Sünde betrüben mich* for Voice, Chorus of 4 Voices, 4 Viole da Gamba, Bassoon/Viole, and Basso Continuo (fragment only extant); etc. **Arias:** *Auf, werte Gäst* for Voice, 2 Violins, and Basso Continuo; *Augen, streuet Perlen-Tränen* for 2 Voices, 4 Violas, Viola pro Basso, and Organ; *Das angenehmste Wetter* for Voice, 2 Violins, and Basso Continuo (unfinished); *Das Gewitter* for Voice, 2 Violins, and Basso Continuo; *Das Jahr fängt an* for Voice, 2 Violins, 2 Violas, and Basso Continuo; *Der Widder Abrahams* for 2 Voices, 2 Violins, and Basso Continuo; *Die freudenfüllten Abendstunden* for Voice, 2 Violins, 2 Violas, and Basso Continuo; *Es muss die Sinne ja erfreuen* for Voice, 2 Violins, and Basso Continuo; *Geliebtes Vaterherz* for Voice, 2 Violins, 2 Violas, and Basso Continuo/Viole; *Guter Walter unsers Rats* for Voice, 2 Violins, 2 Violas, and Basso Continuo; *Hör, grosser Mäcenat* for Voice, 2 Violins, 2 Violas, and Basso Continuo; *Mäcenas lebet noch* for Voice, 2 Violins, 2 Violas, Trumpet, and Basso Continuo; *Mein Leben, dessen Kreuz* for Voice, 4 Violas, Viola pro Basso, and Organ; *O grosses Musenlicht* for Voice, 2 Violins, 2 Viole da Gamba, and Basso Continuo; *So ist denn dies der Tag* for Voice, Chorus of 4 Voices, 2 Violins, 3 Violas, 4 Trumpets, Timpani, and Basso Continuo; *So ist denn nur die Treu* for 2 Voices, Chorus of 5 Voices, 2 Flutes, 2 Violins, 3 Violas, and Basso Continuo; *Voller Wonder, voller Kunst* for 4 Voices and Basso Continuo (unfinished); *Wie nichtig, ach* for Voice, 3 Violas, and Basso Continuo; *Wohl euch, die ihr in Gott verliebt* for 4 Voices (unfinished). **M u s i c F o r V e s p e r s**: *Ingressus* in C major for 4 Voices, 2 Violins, Viola, and Basso Continuo; *Ingressus* in C major for 4 Voices, 2 Violins, 3 Violas, Bassoon, and Basso Continuo; *Ingressus* in C major for 5 Voices, 4 Trumpets, Timpani, 2 Violins, 3 Violas, Bassoon, Basso Continuo, and Organ; *Ingressus* in D major for 4 Voices, 2 Violins, Viola, and Basso Continuo; *Ingressus* in D major for 4 Voices, 2 Violins, 3 Violas, Bassoon, and Basso Continuo; *Ingressus* in D minor for 5 Voices, 2 Violins, 3 Violas, Bassoon, and Basso Continuo; *Ingressus* in F major for 5 Voices, 2 Violins, 4 Violas, Bassoon, and Basso Continuo; *Ingressus* in G major for 4 Voices, 2 Violins, 3 Violas ad libitum, Bassoon ad libitum, and Basso Continuo; *Ingressus* in G minor for 4 Voices, 2 Violins, Bassoon, and Basso Continuo; *Ingressus* in G minor for 5 Voices, 2 Violins, Viola, 2 Viole da Gamba, Bassoon, and Basso Continuo; *Ingressus* in A major for 5 Voices, 2 Violins, 3 Violas, Bassoon, and Basso Continuo; *Ingressus* in A minor for 5 Voices, 2 Violins, 3 Violas, Bassoon, and Basso Continuo; *Magnificat* in C major for 5 Voices, 2 Oboes, 2 Violins, 3 Violas, Bassoon, and Basso Continuo; *Magnificat* in C major for 5 Voices, 4 Trumpets, Timpani, 2 Violins, Viola, 2 Viole da Gamba, Bassoon, Basso Continuo, and Organ; *Magnificat* in C major for 4 Voices, 2 Trumpets, 2 Violins, 2 Violas, and Basso Continuo; *Magnificat* in C major for 5 Voices, 4 Trumpets, Timpani, 2 Violins, Viola, 2 Viole da Gamba, Bassoon, and Basso Continuo; *Magnificat* in D major for 5 Voices, 2 Violins, 2 Cornets/Oboes, 3 Violas, Bassoon, and Basso Continuo; *Magnificat* in D major for Double Chorus of 5 Voices and Double Orch., each with 2 Violins, 3 Violas, Bassoon, and Basso Continuo; *Magnificat* in D major for 4 Voices and 4 Violas ad libitum; *Magnificat* in E-flat major for 4 Voices, 2 Violins, 3 Violas, Bassoon, Basso Continuo, and Organ; *Magnificat* in F major for 4 Voices, 2 Violins, Bassoon, and Basso Continuo; *Magnificat* in F major for 5 Voices, 2 Violins, and Basso Continuo; *Magnificat* in G major for 4 Voices, 2 Violins, and Basso Continuo; *Magnificat* in G minor for 4 Voices; *Magnificat* in B-flat major for 5 Voices, 2 Oboes, 2 Violins, 3 Violas, Bassoon, Basso Continuo, and Organ. **O t h e r**: *Missa* in C major for 4 Voices, 2 Violins, Clarino, and Basso Continuo; *Missa brevis* in D major for 4 Voices.

BIBL.: E. Born, *Die Variation als Grundlage handwerklicher Gestaltung im musikalischen Schaffen J. P.s* (Berlin and Frankfurt am Main, 1941); H. Woodward, *A Study of the Tenbury Manuscripts of J. P.* (diss., Harvard Univ., 1952); E. Nolte, *The Instrumental Works of J. P.* (diss., Northwestern Univ., 1954). —NS/LK/DM

Pachelbel, Wilhelm Hieronymus, German organist, harpsichordist, and composer, son of **Johann Pachelbel** and brother of **Charles Theodore (Carl Theodor) Pachelbel;** b. Erfurt (baptized), Aug. 29, 1686; d. Nuremberg, 1764. His only known teacher was his father, who gave him instruction in both keyboard instruments and composition. He is believed to have begun his career as an organist in Furth. He then was organist of the Predigerkirche in Erfurt. In 1706 he became organist of the Jakobikirche in Nuremberg, and that same year was named organist at St. Egidien there. In 1719 he became organist at St. Sebald, a post he held until his death. Little of his music is extant, all of it being for keyboard instruments. He publ. *Musicalisches Vergnügen bestehend in einem Praeludio, Fuga und Fantasia, sowohl auf die Orgel als auch auf das Clavier...vorgestellt und componiert* in D major (Nuremberg, 1725?) and *Praeludium und Fuga* in C major (Nuremberg, 1725?). He also composed *Fantasia super "Meine Seele, lass es gehen," Fantasia* in B-flat major, *O Lamm Gottes unschuldig* for Clavier, and *Toccata* in G major. See H.J. Moser and T. Fedtke, *Wilhelm Hieronymus Pachelbel: Gesamtausgabe der erhaltenen Werke für Orgel und Clavier* (Kassel, 1957). —NS/LK/DM

Pachler-Koschak, Marie Leopoldine, Austrian pianist; b. Graz, Oct. 2, 1792; d. there, April 10, 1855. She was an enthusiastic admirer of Beethoven, who wrote to her in 1817: "I have found no one, not excepting the great pianists, who interprets my compositions as well as you." In 1816 she married Dr. Karl Pachler, a lawyer in Graz. In their house Franz Schubert spent several weeks in the summer of 1827. Schubert wrote a little 4-hand march for their son, Faust Pachler, who publ. *Beethoven und M. Pachler-Koschak* (Berlin, 1866), which contains valuable details concerning Beethoven's last days.—NS/LK/DM

Pachmann, Vladimir de, eccentric Russian-born Italian pianist; b. Odessa, July 27, 1848; d. Rome, Jan. 6, 1933. He received his primary music education at home from his father, an Austrian lawyer and amateur musician; his mother was Turkish. He then was a pupil of J. Dachs at the Vienna Cons. (1866–68), graduating with the Gold Medal. He began his concert career with a tour of Russia in 1869, but he was 40 years old before he made a decisive impact on the international scene. His first American tour, in 1891, was sensationally successful, and it was in America that he began exhibiting his curious eccentricities, some of them undoubtedly calculated to produce shock effect: he made grimaces when he did not like his own playing and shouted "Bravo!" when he played a number to his satisfaction; even more bizarre was his crawling under the grand piano after the concert, claiming that he was looking for the wrong notes he had accidentally hit; all this could be explained as idiosyncratic behavior, but he also allowed himself to mutilate the music itself, by inserting arpeggios between phrases and extra chords at the end of a piece. Most American critics were outraged by his shenanigans, but some, notably Philip Hale, found mitigation in the poetic quality of his interpretations. Pachmann was particularly emotional in playing Chopin, when his facial contortions became quite obnoxious; James Huneker dubbed him "Chopinzee." Pachmann did not lack official honors; in 1885, on his tour of Denmark, he was made a Knight of the Order of Danebrog, and in

1916 the Royal Phil. Society of London awarded him its Gold Medal. He made his last tour of the U.S. in 1925, then spent his last years in Italy, becoming a naturalized Italian citizen in 1928. His personal life was turbulent; he married frequently (the exact number of his wives is in dispute). His first wife was his pupil, the Australian Maggie Oakey (1864–1952), who toured as Marguerite de Pachmann from the time of their marriage (1884) until their divorce (1895); she later married a French lawyer, becoming known as Marguerite de Pachmann-Labori. Pachmann and his first wife had a son, Adrian de Pachmann (c. 1893–1937), who also became a pianist. **—NS/LK/DM**

Pachymeres, Georgios, Byzantine scholar, church and government official, and music theorist; b. Nicaea, 1242; d. Constantinople, c. 1310. He was an influential figure in Constantinople church and government circles, and also a teacher at the Univ. there. He wrote a valuable treatise on the Quadrivium, *Syntagma tōn tessarōn mathēmaton, artihmētikēs, mousikēs geōmetrias kai astronomias* (modern ed. by P. Tannéry, Rome, 1940).

BIBL.: F. Magos, *Etude sur le système parfait chez G. P.* (diss., Univ. of Louvain, 1961–62).**—LK/DM**

Pacini, Andrea, Italian castrato alto and composer; b. Lucca, c. 1690; d. there, March 1764. He made his debut in Albinoni's *Astarto* in Venice in 1708, and returned to sing there (1714–16; 1726). He also appeared in Naples (1713–14; 1722–23), Turin (1719), and Genoa (1720). In 1721 he was elected to membership in the Accademia Filarmonica in Bologna, in which city he sang in 1722. From 1720 to 1730 he was virtuoso to Prince Antonio of Parma. On Oct. 31, 1724, he made his London debut creating the title role in Handel's *Tamerlano*. Handel also wrote the role of Unulfo for him. Following appearances in Florence (1725–26; 1731–32) and Parma (1729), he was active as a priest.**—NS/LK/DM**

Pacini, Antonio Francesco Gaetano Saverio, Italian-born French composer and music publisher; b. Naples, July 7, 1778; d. Paris, March 10, 1866. He studied harmony and counterpoint with Fenaroli at the Cons. della Pietà de' Turchini in Naples. After directing an orch. and teaching there, he went to Nîmes. In 1804 he settled in Paris and taught singing until about 1822. With Momigny, he founded a publishing firm in 1806. In addition to music, they publ. the *Journal des troubadours* (c. 1806–14), *Le troubadour ambulant* (1817–20?), and *L'écho lyrique* (1827–30). Among his compositions were the opéras-comiques *Isabelle et Gertrude* (Nîmes?, 1801?), *Point d'adversaire* (Paris, April 8, 1805), *Le voyage impromptu* (Paris, April 5, 1806?), and *Amour et mauvaise tête* (Paris, May 17, 1808), and many songs. **—LK/DM**

Pacini, Giovanni, Italian composer; b. Catania, Feb. 17, 1796; d. Pescia, Dec. 6, 1867. He was a pupil of Marchesi and Padre Mattei at Bologna, and of Furlanetto at Venice. His first opera was *Don Pomponio* (1813; not perf.), followed by *Annetta e Lucinda* (Milan, Oct. 17, 1813); by 1835 he had produced over 40 operas on

various Italian stages, when the failure of *Carlo di Borgogna* (Feb. 21, 1835) at Venice temporarily checked the flow of dramatic composition. He went to Viareggio, near Lucca, and established a very successful school of music, for which he wrote several short treatises, *Corso teoretico-pratico di lezioni di armonia* (Milan, c. 1844), and *Cenni storici sulla musica e trattato di contrappunto* (Lucca, 1864), and built a private theater. Later he removed the school to Lucca. In 1840 Pacini, who prided himself on rapid work, wrote his dramatic masterpiece, *Saffo*, in 28 days (Naples, Nov. 29, 1840). Forty more operas followed to 1867, the best of which were *Medea* (Palermo, Nov. 28, 1843), *La Regina di Cipro* (Turin, Feb. 7, 1846), and *Niccolò de Lapi* (1857; Florence, Oct. 29, 1873). He also wrote numerous oratorios. He excelled in melodic invention, although his early style prompted Rossini to exclaim "God help us if he knew music: no one could resist him." He was also an active contributor to several musical papers. He publ. memoirs as *Le mie memorie artistiche* (Florence, 1865; enl. by Cicconetti, 1872; rev. by F. Magnani, 1875). His brother, Emilio Pacini (b. 1810; d. Neuilly, near Paris, Dec. 2, 1898), was a distinguished librettist.

BIBL.: M. Davini, *Il maestro G. P.* (Palermo, 1927).**—NS/LK/DM**

Paciorkiewicz, Tadeusz, Polish composer, teacher, and organist; b. Sierpc, Oct. 17, 1916; d. Warsaw, Nov. 21, 1998. He studied organ with Rutkowski at the Warsaw Cons. (graduated, 1942) and composition with Sikorski at the Łódź State Higher School of Music (graduated, 1951). He taught in music schools in Plock (1945–49) and Łódź (1949–59). He also taught at the Warsaw State Coll. of Music (from 1954), becoming a permanent faculty member (1959), dean of its composition, theory, and conducting dept. (1963–69), and then its rector (1969–71).

WORKS: DRAMATIC: Opera: *Ushico*, radio opera (1962); *The Maiden from the Dormer Window* (1964); *Ligea*, radio opera (1967). **Ballet:** *Warsaw Legend* (1959). **ORCH.:** 2 piano concertos (1952, 1954); 4 syms. (1953, 1957, 1989, 1992); Violin Concerto (1955); *Duet koncertujacy* for Organ and Orch. (1962); 2 organ concertos (1967, 1988); *Divertimento* for Clarinet and Strings (1968); Trombone Concerto (1971); Viola Concerto (1975–76); *Concerto alla Barocco* (1979); Concerto for Harp, Flute, and Strings (1980); Oboe Concerto (1982); Concerto for 2 Violins and Orch. (1983); Horn Concerto (1986); Concerto for Viola, Organ, and Orch. (1990); Concerto for Cello and Chamber Orch. (1991). **CHAMBER:** Wind Quintet (1951); Violin Sonata (1954); 2 string quartets (1960, 1982); 4 caprices: *Quasi una sonata* for Clarinet and Piano (1960); Trio for Flute, Viola, and Harp (1966); *6 Miniatures* for 4 Trombones (1972); Piano Quintet (1972); *Concertante Duet* for Clarinet and Piano (1973); Cello Sonata (1974–75); *3 Musical Moments* for 5 Clarinets (1985); *Duo Serenade* for Flute and Piano (1987); *Decet* for Wind Quintet and String Quintet (1988); Viola Sonata (1988); Flute Quintet (1988); *Klangdialog* for Mandolin and Guitar (1989); *Klanspiele* for 6 to 7 Percussionists; organ pieces, including a Sonata (1946–47); piano works. **VOCAL:** *De Revolutionibus*, oratorio for 4 Solo Voices, Reciter, Boy's Chorus, Chorus, Organ, and Orch. (1972); *2 Psalms* for Soprano and Organ (1985); *Psalm 150* for 5 Solo Voices and Organ (1990).**—NS/LK/DM**

Pacius, Fredrik (actually, **Friedrich**), significant German-born Finnish conductor, teacher, and composer; b. Hamburg, March 19, 1809; d. Helsinki, Jan. 8, 1891. He studied violin with Spohr and composition with Hauptmann in Kassel. After playing violin in Stockholm's Royal Chapel (1828–34), he settled in Helsinki (1835) as a lecturer at the Univ., being promoted to prof. (1860); also founded a choral society (1835) and regular sym. concerts (1845). Pacius is acknowledged as the father of Finnish music, and his works owe much to the German Romanticists, especially Spohr and Mendelssohn, and to Finnish folk music. His setting of J. Runeberg's Swedish poem *Vart land* became the Finnish national anthem in 1843; it was set to Finnish words as *Maamme* in 1848. He also wrote the first Finnish opera, *Kung Karls jakt* (to a Swedish libretto; Helsinki, March 24, 1852), as well as the opera *Loreley* (Helsinki, April 28, 1887) and incidental music to *Prinsessan af Cypern* (1860), both to Swedish texts. Other works include one movement of a sym., a Violin Concerto (1845), other orch. works, part-songs, and songs.

BIBL.: M. Colan-Beaurain, *F. P.* (Helsinki, 1921); O. Andersson, *Den unge P. och musiklivet i Helsingfors på 1830-talet* (Helsinki, 1938); J. Rosas, *F. P. som tonsättare* (Turku, 1949). —NS/LK/DM

Packe, Thomas, English composer who flourished from about 1480 to 1520. He was the composer of 2 masses, a Te Deum, a Nunc dimittis, and a motet. —LK/DM

Padbrué, Cornelis Thymanszoon, Netherlands composer and schalmei player, nephew of **David Janszoon Padbrué**; b. Haarlem, c. 1592; d. there (buried), Jan. 18, 1670. He spent his entire life in Haarlem, where he was made a city musician in 1610. In 1629 he was named to the position of 1st schalmei player, being granted the title of master. He also served as a harpsichord teacher to the blind at the Reformed church. A contentious individual by nature, Padbrué was dismissed from his municipal duties in 1635. He publ. 7 vols. of music (1631–46), the most significant being his *De tranen Petri ende Pauli* for 2 to 5 Voices and Basso Continuo (Amsterdam, 1646).—LK/DM

Padbrué, David Janszoon, Netherlands singer, lutenist, and composer, uncle of **Cornelis Thymanszoon Padbrué**; b. Haarlem, c. 1553; d. Amsterdam (buried), Feb. 19, 1635. His father, Jan Janszoon Padbrué, "Jenning de Sangher" (b. c. 1520; d. 1582), was a countertenor at St. Baaf's, and his brother, Thyman Janszoon Padbrué (b. c. 1555; d. 1627), was a town piper. He sang in the choir at St. Baaf's as a child, and from 1562 to 1570 he was a member of the Capilla Flamenca in Madrid. He held prebends in Delft, The Hague, and Haarlem. Following studies in literature at the Univ. of Leiden (1580), he settled in Amsterdam and was active as a flax merchant from 1587. Several pieces in the *Thysius Lutebook* are attributed to him.—LK/DM

Paderewski, Ignacy (Jan), celebrated Polish pianist and composer; b. Kurylowka, Podolia (Russian Poland), Nov. 18, 1860; d. N.Y., June 29, 1941. His father was an administrator of country estates; his mother died soon after his birth. From early childhood, Paderewski was attracted to piano music, and he received some musical instruction from Peter Sowinski, who taught him 4-hand arrangements of operas. His first public appearance was in a charity concert at the age of 11, when he played piano with his sister. His playing aroused interest among wealthy patrons, who took him to Kiev. He was then sent to Warsaw, where he entered the Cons., learned to play trombone, and joined the school band. He also continued serious piano study; his teachers at the Warsaw Cons. were Schlözer, Strobl, and Janotha. In 1875 and 1877 he toured in provincial Russian towns with the Polish violinist Cielewicz; in the interim periods, he took courses in composition at the Warsaw Cons., and upon graduation in 1878 was engaged as a member of the piano faculty there. In 1880 he married a young music student named Antonina Korsak, but she died 9 days after giving birth to a child, on Oct. 10, 1880. In 1882 he went to Berlin to study composition with Kiel; there he met Anton Rubinstein, who gave him encouraging advice and urged him to compose piano music. He resigned from his teaching job at the Warsaw Cons. and began to study orchestration in Berlin with Heinrich Urban. While on a vacation in the Tatra Mountains (which inspired his *Tatra Album* for piano), he met the celebrated Polish actress Modjeska, who proposed to finance his further piano studies with Leschetizky in Vienna. Paderewski followed this advice and spent several years as a Leschetizky student. He continued his career as a concert pianist. On March 3, 1888, he gave his first Paris recital, and on Nov. 10, 1888, played a concert in Vienna, both with excellent success. He also began receiving recognition as a composer. Anna Essipova (who was married to Leschetizky) played his piano concerto in Vienna under the direction of Hans Richter. Paderewski made his London debut on May 9, 1890. On Nov. 17, 1891, he played for the first time in N.Y., and was acclaimed with an adulation rare for pianists; by some counts he gave 107 concerts in 117 days in N.Y. and other American cities and attended 86 dinner parties; his wit, already fully developed, made him a social lion in wealthy American salons. At one party, it was reported, the hostess confused him with a famous polo player who was also expected to be a guest, and greeted him effusively. "No," Paderewski is supposed to have replied, "he is a rich soul who plays polo, and I am a poor Pole who plays solo." American spinsters beseeched him for a lock of his luxurious mane of hair; he invariably obliged, and when his valet observed that at this rate he would soon be bald, he said, "Not I, my dog." There is even a story related by a gullible biographer that Paderewski could charm beasts by his art and that a spider used to come down from the ceiling in Paderewski's lodgings in Vienna and sit at the piano every time Paderewski played a certain Chopin etude. Paderewski eclipsed even Caruso as an idol of the masses. In 1890 he made a concert tour in Germany; also toured South America, South Africa, and Australia. In 1898 he purchased a beautiful home, the Villa Riond-Bosson on Lake Geneva, Switzerland; in 1899 he married Helena Gorska, Baroness von Rosen. In 1900, by a deed of trust, Paderewski established a fund of $10,000 (the original trustees were William Steinway, Henry Lee Higginson, and William Mason), the interest from which was to be used for triennial prizes given "to composers of American birth without distinction as to age or religion" for works in the categories of syms., concertos, and chamber music. In 1910, on the occasion of the centennial of Chopin's birth, Paderewski donated $60,000 for the construction of the Chopin Memorial Hall in Warsaw; in the same year, he contributed $100,000 for the erection of the statue of King Jagiello in Warsaw, on the quinquecentennial of his victory over the Teutonic Knights in 1410. In 1913 he purchased a ranch in Paso Robles in Calif.

Although cosmopolitan in his culture, Paderewski remained a great Polish patriot. During the First World War he donated the entire proceeds from his concerts to a fund for the Polish people caught in the war between Russia and Germany. After the establishment of the independent Polish state, Paderewski served as its representative in Washington; in 1919 he was named prime minister of the Polish Republic, the first musician to occupy such a post in any country at any period. He took part in the Versailles Treaty conference; it was then that Prime Minister Clemenceau of France welcomed Paderewski with the famous, if possibly apocryphal, remark: "You, a famous pianist, a prime minister! What a comedown!" Paderewski resigned his post on Dec. 10, 1919. He reentered politics in 1920 in the wake of the Russian invasion of Poland that year, when he became a delegate to the League of Nations; he resigned on May 7, 1921, and resumed his musical career. On Nov. 22, 1922, he gave his first concert after a hiatus of many years at Carnegie Hall in N.Y. In 1939 he made his last American tour. Once more during his lifetime Poland was invaded, this time by both Germany and Russia. Once more Paderewski was driven to political action. He joined the Polish government-in-exile in France and was named president of its parliament on Jan. 23, 1940. He returned to the U.S. on Nov. 6, 1940, a few months before his death. At the order of President Roosevelt, his body was given state burial in Arlington National Cemetery, pending the return of his remains to Free Poland. While his body was buried at Arlington National Cemetery, his heart was buried in Brooklyn and finally entombed at the Shrine of Our Lady of Czestochowa in Doylestown, Pa., in 1986. His body was finally removed from Arlington National Cemetery and returned to Free Poland, where a Mass and state burial was accorded him at the St. John the Baptist Cathedral in Warsaw on July 5, 1992, with President Bush of the U.S. and President Walesa of Poland in attendance. Paderewski received many honors. He held the following degrees: Ph.D. from the Univ. of Lemberg (1912); D.Mus. from Yale Univ. (1917); Ph.D. from the Univ. of Kraków (1919); D.C.L. from the Univ. of Oxford (1920); LL.D. from Columbia Univ. (1922); Ph.D. from the Univ. of Southern Calif. (1923); Ph.D. from the Univ. of Poznań (1924); and Ph.D. from the Univ. of Glasgow (1925). He also held the Grand Cross of the French Legion of Honor (1922). A postage stamp with his picture was issued in Poland in 1919, and 2 postage stamps honoring him in the series "Men of Liberty" were issued in the U.S. in 1960.

As an artist, Paderewski was a faithful follower of the Romantic school, which allowed free, well-nigh improvisatory declensions from the written notes, tempi, and dynamics; judged by 20th-century standards of precise rendering of the text, Paderewski's interpretations appear surprisingly free, but this very personal freedom of performance moved contemporary audiences to ecstasies of admiration. Also, Paderewski's virtuoso technique, which astonished his listeners, has been easily matched by any number of pianists of succeeding generations. Yet his position in the world of the performing arts remains undiminished by the later achievements of younger men and women pianists. As a composer, Paderewski also belongs to the Romantic school. At least one of his piano pieces, the *Menuet in G* (a movement of his set of *6 Humoresques de concert*), achieved enormous popularity. His other compositions, however, never sustained a power of renewal and were eventually relegated to the archives of unperformed music. His opera *Manru* (1897–1900), dealing with folk life in the Tatra Mountains, was produced in Dresden on May 29, 1901, and was also performed by the Metropolitan Opera in N.Y. on Feb. 14, 1902. Another major work, a Sym. in B minor, was first performed by the Boston Sym. Orch. on Feb. 12, 1909. His other works included a Piano Concerto in A minor (1888); *Fantaisie polonaise* for Piano and Orch. (1893); Violin Sonata (1880); songs; and the following compositions for piano solo: *Prelude and Capriccio; 3 Pieces (Gavotte, Mélodie, Valse mélancholique); Krakówiak; Élégie; 3 Polish Dances; Introduction and Toccata; Chants du voyageur* (5 pieces); *6 Polish Dances; Album de mai* (5 pieces), *Variations and Fugue; Tatra Album* (also arr. for Piano, 4-Hands); *6 Humoresques de concert* (which includes the famous *Menuet in G*); *Dans le désert; Miscellanea* (7 pieces); *Légende*; Sonata in E-flat minor (1903). A complete list of Paderewski's works was publ. in the *Bolletino bibliografico musicale* (Milan, 1932).

BIBL.: F. Buffen, *I. P.* (N.Y., 1891); C. Tretbar, *P.: A Biographical Sketch* (N.Y., 1892); H. Finck, *P. and His Art* (N.Y., 1895); A. Nossig, *P.* (Leipzig, 1901); E. Baughan, *I. P.* (London, 1908); A. Chybiński, *P.* (Warsaw, 1910); S. Popielowna, *I. P.* (Tarnow, 1919); F. Martens, *P.* (N.Y., 1923); B. Sidorowicz, *I. P.* (Poznań, 1924); J. Cooke, *P.* (Philadelphia, 1928); H. Opieński, *I.J. P.* (Warsaw, 1928; 3rd ed., rev. and aug., 1960); C. Philips, *P.* (N.Y., 1933); R. Landau, *I. P.: Musician and Statesman* (N.Y., 1934); *P.'s Diamond Anniversary* (N.Y., 1936); M. Lawton, *The P. Memoirs* (to 1914 only; N.Y., 1938); E. Ligocki, *Homage to P.* (Edinburgh, 1941); A. Gronowicz, *P.: Pianist and Patriot* (Edinburgh, 1943); B. Sarrazin, *Imageries de P.* (Annonay, 1945); A. Baumgartner, *La Vérité sur le prétendu drame P.* (Geneva, 1948); S. Giron, *Le Drame P.* (Geneva, 1948); A. Strakacz, *P. as I Knew Him* (New Brunswick, N.J., 1949); C. Kellogg, *P.* (N.Y., 1956); J. Cieplinski, *I. P.* (N.Y., 1960); R. and P. Hume, *The Lion of Poland: The Story of P.* (N.Y., 1962); R. Halski, *P.* (London, 1964); W. Dulaba, *I. P.* (Kraków, 1966); A. Zamoyski, *P.* (N.Y., 1982); J. Hoskins, *I.J. P., 1860–1941: A Biographical Sketch and a Selective List of Reading Materials* (Washington, D.C., 1984); E. Lipmann, *P., l'idole des années folles* (Paris, 1984); M. Perkowska, *Diariusz koncertowy I.ego J.a. P.ego* (Kraków, 1990).—**NS/LK/DM**

Padilla, Juan Gutiérrez de, significant Spanish-born Mexican composer; b. Malaga, c. 1590; d. Puebla, Mexico, c. April 22, 1664. He received instruction from Francisco Vázquez as a member of the cathedral choir in Malaga. By 1613 he was maestro de capilla in Jérez de la Frontera. After entering the priesthood, he served as maestro di capilla at Cádiz Cathedral (1616–20?). He subsequently went to Mexico, where he was a singer and co-adjutor maestro at Pueblo Cathedral (1622–29) and later its maestro de capilla. Padilla was a master of polyphony. Among his works were about 50 sacred vocal pieces and many secular villancicos.—LK/DM

Padilla, Lola Artôt de, Spanish soprano, daughter of **Mariano Padilla y Ramos** and **Désirée Artôt;** b. Sevres, near Paris, Oct. 5, 1876; d. Berlin, April 12, 1933. After vocal training with her mother, she sang in salons and concerts and made her operatic debut at the Paris Opéra-Comique in 1903. Later she toured as a concert singer through Europe. She was engaged at the Komische Oper in Berlin from 1905 to 1908 as prima donna, and from 1909 to 1927 she was a member of the Royal (later State) Opera in Berlin.—NS/LK/DM

Padilla y Ramos, Mariano, Spanish baritone, father of **Lola Artôt de Padilla;** b. Murcia, 1842; d. Auteuil, near Paris, Nov. 23, 1906. He studied with Mabellini and Ronconi in Florence, making his debut in Messina. He sang in opera with great success in Italy, Austria, Germany, and Russia. In 1869 he married **Désirée Artôt.**—NS/LK/DM

Padlewski, Roman, Polish violinist, choral conductor, music critic, and composer; b. Moscow, Oct. 7, 1915; d. in the Warsaw uprising, Aug. 16, 1944. He went to Poznań and studied with Jahnke (violin) and Wiechowicz (composition) at the Cons. (1927–29) and with Kamienski (musicology) at the Univ. (1932–35). He was active as an orch. musician, choral conductor, and music critic until being taken prisoner by the Nazis at the outbreak of World War II in 1939. However, he managed to escape to Warsaw, where he resumed his studies in 1943 with Rutkowski (organ), Bierdiajew (conducting), and Sikorski (composition). Many of his MSS were destroyed during the Warsaw uprising, but a Suite for Violin and Orch., 2 string quartets, a Violin Sonata, and several vocal pieces are extant. These reveal Padlewski as a composer of marked talent.—NS/LK/DM

Padovano, Annibale, Italian organist and composer; b. Padua, 1527; d. Graz, March 15, 1575. He was an organist at San Marco in Venice from 1552 to 1565. In 1566 he became organist at the court of Archduke Karl II of Austria in Graz, where he was made chief musician in 1567 and director of music in 1570. He distinguished himself as a composer of organ music and publ. fine ricercares and toccatas (1556, 1604). Among his other publ. works were madrigals (1561, 1564) and sacred pieces (1567, 1573).

BIBL.: G. del Valle de Paz, *A. P. nella storia della musica* (Turin, 1933).—LK/DM

Paër, Ferdinando, significant Italian composer; b. Parma, June 1, 1771; d. Paris, May 3, 1839. He studied with Francesco Fortunati and Gaspare Ghiretti in Parma, producing his first stage work, the prose opera *Orphée et Euridice,* there in 1791. On July 14, 1792, he was appointed honorary maestro di cappella to the court of Parma, bringing out his opera *Le astuzie amorose* that same year at the Teatro Ducale there. His finest work of the period was *Griselda, ossia La virtù al cimento* (Parma, Jan. 1798). In 1797 he was appointed music director of the Kärnthnertortheater in Vienna. While there, he made the acquaintance of Beethoven, who expressed admiration for his work. It was in Vienna that he composed one of his finest operas, *Camilla, ossia Il sotteraneo* (Feb. 23, 1799). Another fine opera was his *Achille* (Vienna, June 6, 1801). After a visit to Prague in 1801, he accepted the appointment of court Kapellmeister in Dresden. Three of his most important operas were premiered there: *I Fuorusciti di Firenze* (Nov. 27, 1802), *Sargino, ossia L'Allievo dell'amore* (May 26, 1803), and *Leonora, ossia L'amore conjugale* (Oct. 3, 1804), a work identical in subject with that of Beethoven's *Fidelio* (1805). In 1806 he resigned his Dresden post and accepted an invitation to visit Napoleon in Posen and Warsaw. In 1807 Napoleon appointed him his maître de chapelle in Paris, where he also became director of the Opéra-Comique. Following the dismissal of Spontini in 1812, he was appointed director of the Théâtre-Italien. One of his most successful operas of the period, *Le Maître de chapelle* (Paris, March 29, 1821), remained in the repertoire in its Italian version until the early years of the 20th century. Paër's tenure at the Théâtre-Italien continued through the vicissitudes of Catalani's management (1814–17) and the troubled joint directorship with Rossini (1824–27). After his dismissal in 1827, he was awarded the cross of the Légion d'honneur in 1828; was elected a member of the Inst. of the Académie des Beaux Arts in 1831. He was appointed director of music of Louis Philippe's private chapel in 1832. Paer was one of the most important Italian composers of opera in his era. His vocal writing was highly effective, as was his instrumentation. Nevertheless, his operas have disappeared from the active repertoire. His *Leonora,* however, was revived and recorded in the 1970s by the Swiss conductor Peter Maag.

BIBL.: T. Masse and A. Deschamps, *De MM. P. et Rossini* (Paris, 1820); F. Paër, *M. P.: Ex-directeur du Théâtre- Italien, a MM les dilettans* (Paris, 1827); C. de Colobrano, *Funerailles de F. P.* (Paris, 1893).—NS/LK/DM

Paganelli, Giuseppe Antonio, Italian composer; b. Padua, March 6, 1710; d. probably in Madrid, c. 1762. He was employed as a harpsichordist in an Italian opera company. He was in Venice (1732), then at Bayreuth (1737–38). In 1755 he went to Madrid. His *Divertisement de le Beau Sexe* (6 sonatas) was ed. by G. Tagliapietra (Milan, 1936). In addition to 11 operas, he composed a number of instrumental works which were popular in his day.

BIBL.: E. Schenk, *G.A. P.* (Salzburg, 1928).—NS/LK/DM

Paganini, Niccolò, legendary Italian violinist; b. Genoa, Oct. 27, 1782; d. Nice, May 27, 1840. His father, a poor dockworker, gave him his first lessons on the mandolin and violin, after which he studied with Giovanni Servetto, a violinist in the theater orch. By this time the young Paganini was already composing; he also began to study harmony with Francesco Gnecco, and subsequently studied violin with Giacomo Costa, who arranged for him to play in local churches. His first documented public appearance took place at the church of S. Filippo Neri on May 26, 1794. It was about this time that he was indelibly impressed by the Franco-Polish violin virtuoso Auguste Frédéric Durand (later billed as Duranowski), who was a brilliant showman. Having made phenomenal progress in his studies, he was sent to Parma in 1795 to study with Alessandro Rolla. To defray the costs of the journey, he gave a special concert on July 31, 1795. Upon his arrival in Parma, Rolla is reported to have told him that there was nothing left to teach him and suggested that he study composition with Paër instead. Paër, in turn, sent him to his own teacher, Gasparo Ghiretti. After study with both Ghiretti and Paër, Paganini returned to Genoa (1796), appearing as a violinist in private performances. With Napoleon's invasion of Italy, the family moved to Ramairone. By 1800 he was with his father in Livorno, where he gave concerts; he also appeared in Modena. They returned to Genoa in 1801; that same year, in the company of his older brother Carlo, who was also a violinist, he went to Lucca to play at the Festival of Santa Croce. His appearance there on Sept. 14, 1801, was a brilliant success. He settled there, becoming concertmaster of the National Orch.

As a soloist, Paganini captivated his auditors by his pyrotechnics. During an engagement in Livorno he so impressed a wealthy French merchant that he was rewarded with a valuable violin. With the arrival of Princess Elisa Baciocchi, the sister of Napoleon, as ruler of Lucca (1805), musical life there was reorganized. The 2 major orchs. were dissolved and replaced by a chamber orch. Paganini was retained as 2nd violinist, and then was made solo court violinist (1807). After the chamber orch. itself was dissolved (Jan. 1, 1808), he played in the court string quartet and also served as violin teacher to Prince Felix Baciocchi. Dissastisfied with his position, he broke with the court in Dec. 1809, and pursued a career as a virtuoso. He came to national prominence in 1813 with a series of sensationally successful concerts in Milan. He subsequently toured throughout Italy, his renown growing from year to year and his vast technical resources maturing and augmenting such that he easily displaced the would-be rivals Lafont in Milan (1816) and Lipinski in Piacenza (1818). In 1824 he met the singer Antonia Bianchi, who became his mistress; she bore him a son, Achilles, in 1825, whom Paganini had legitimized in 1837. In 1827 he was made a Knight of the Golden Spur by Pope Leo XII. When he left Italy for his 1st tour abroad in 1828, he immediately gained a triumph with his opening concert in Vienna (March 29). He gave 14 concerts during his stay in Vienna, and was accorded the honorary title of chamber virtuoso by the Emperor and presented with the city's medal of St. Salvator. He made his first appearance in Berlin on March 4, 1829. He also played in Frankfurt am Main, Darmstadt, Mannheim, and Leipzig. In 1831 he

made his Paris (March 9) and London (June 3) debuts. He subsequently gave concerts throughout Great Britain (1831–33).

Paganini's artistic fortunes began to decline in 1834; his long- precarious health was ruined, but he had managed to retain his fame and considerable wealth. He continued to give sporadic concerts in subsequent years, but he spent most of his time at his villa in Parma, making occasional visits to Paris. A critical illness in Oct. 1838 led to the loss of his voice; in Nov. 1839 he went to Nice for his health, and died there the following spring.

Paganini's stupendous technique, power, and control, as well as his romantic passion and intense energy, made him the marvel of his time. He also was not above employing certain tricks of virtuosity, such as tuning up the A string of his violin by a semitone or playing the *Witches' Dance* on one string after severing the other 3 on stage, in sight of his audience, with a pair of scissors. He was also a highly effective composer for the violin, and gave regular performances of his works at his concerts with great success. Outstanding among his compositions are the 24 *Caprices* for Solo Violin, the *Moto perpetuo* for Violin and Orch., and several of the violin concertos. His collected works are being publ. in an Edizione Nazionale, ed. by L. Ronga et al. (1976–). See also M. Moretti and A. Sorento, *Catalogo tematico delle musiche di Niccolò Paganini* (1983). Paganini prepared a brief autobiography, which was publ. in the *Allgemeine musikalische Zeitung*, XXXII (1830). His letters were ed. by E. Neill (Genoa, 1982).

Works: VIOLIN CONCERTOS: E minor (1815?); No. 1, in E-flat major, op.6 (1817?); No. 2, in B minor, op.7 (1826); No. 3, in E major (1826); No. 4, in D minor (1830); No. 5, in A minor (1830); various other works for Violin and Orch. **CHAMBER:** 3 string quartets (1800–1805); 21 quartets for various combinations of instruments (1806–20); *Centone di sonate*, 18 sonatas; other sonatas; works for Solo Violin, including 24 *Caprices* (1805).

BIBL.: Valuable information may be found in *Quaderno dell'Istituto di studi P.ani* (1972–); see also K. Guhr, *Über P.s Kunst, die Violine zu spielen* (Mainz, 1830; Eng. tr. by S. Novello, 1831); G. Imbert de Laphalèque, *Notice sur le célèbre violoniste N. P.* (Paris, 1830); J. Schottky, *P.s Leben und Treiben als Künstler und als Mensch* (Prague and Hamburg, 1830; 2nd ed., 1909); F. Schütz, *Leben, Charakter und Kunst des Ritters N. P.* (Ilmenau, 1830); G. Conestabile, *Vita di N. P.* (Perugia, 1851; 2nd ed., rev., 1936, by F. Mompellio); F.-J. Fétis, *Notice biographique sur N. P.* (Paris, 1851; Eng. tr., 1852; 2nd ed., 1876); O. Bruni, *N. P., Racconto storico* (Florence, 1873; new ed., 1903); J.-G. Prod'homme, *P.* (Paris, 1907; Eng. tr., 1911; 2nd French ed., 1927); S. Stratton, *N. P.: His Life and Work* (London, 1907); A. Bonaventura, *P.* (Modena, 1911; 4th ed., 1939); J. Kapp, *N. P.* (Berlin, 1913; 15th ed., rev., 1969); E. Istel, *N. P.* (Leipzig, 1919); J. Siber, *P.* (Berlin, 1920); L. Day, *P. of Genoa* (N.Y., 1929); A. Günther, *P. in Lucca* (Munich, 1929); A. Montanelli, *P. a Forlì* (Forlì, 1930); A. Codignola, *P. intimo* (Genoa, 1935); J. Pulver, *P., the Romantic Virtuoso* (London, 1936); R. de Saussine, *P. le magicien* (Paris, 1938; Eng. tr., 1954); I. Pizzetti, *N. P.* (Turin, 1940); M. Tibaldi Chiesa, *P.: La vita e l'opera* (Milan, 1940; 2nd ed., 1944); N. Podenzani, *Il Romanzo di N. P.* (Milan, 1944); H. Spivacke, *P.ana* (Washington, D.C., 1945); T. Valensi, *P.* (Nice, 1950); G. de Courcy, *P.: The Genoese* (2 vols., Norman, Okla., 1957; 2nd ed., rev., 1977); R. de Saussine, *P.* (Milan, 1958); A. Armando, *P.: Eine Biographie* (Hamburg, 1960);

A. Codignola, *Arte e magio di N. P.* (Milan, 1960); D. Botti, *P. e Parma* (Parma, 1961); G. de Courcy, *Chronology of N. P.'s Life* (Wiesbaden, 1961); P. Berri, *P.: Documenti e testimonianze* (Genoa, 1962); A. Kendall, *P.* (London, 1982); J. Sugden, *P.* (N.Y., 1982; 2nd ed., rev., 1986); X. Rey, *N. P.: Le romtique italien* (Paris, 1999).—**NS/LK/DM**

Page, Christopher (Howard),

English choral conductor and scholar; b. London, April 8, 1952. He was educated at the Univ. of Oxford (B.A.) and the Univ. of York (Ph.D.). As an academician, he served as a lecturer in Medieval English at the Univ. of Cambridge. He became widely known, however, via his role as founder and conductor of the esteemed musical vocal ensemble Gothic Voices. In addition to many concerts, he conducted his ensemble in many broadcasts and recordings. Page's performances of music of the Middle Ages are notable for their informed and high standard of performance practice. In addition to his articles in learned journals, he publ. the tome *Music and Instruments of the Middle Ages* (London, 1997).—**LK/DM**

Page, Hot Lips (actually, Oran Thaddeus),

talented jazz trumpeter, mellophone player, singer; b. Dallas, Tex., Jan. 27, 1908; d. N.Y., Nov. 5, 1954. Page had his first music lessons from his mother, a former schoolteacher. After early efforts on clarinet and saxophone, he specialized on trumpet from the age of 12. He joined a kids' band, but then left music, attended high school in Corsicana, Tex., but left to work in Seminole oil fields in Tex. In 1923, he became a regular member of the band accompanying Ma Rainey; he made his first visit to N.Y. with Rainey, then toured with a T.O.B.A. circuit band, accompanied Bessie Smith, Ida Cox, and learned how to sing the blues. He joined the Troy Floyd Band in San Antonio, and worked in Tex. with Sugar Lou and Eddie's Hotel Tyler Band. Page was heard with this band by bassist/bandleader Walter Page (no relation) and was invited to join Page's Blue Devils early in 1928. He left the band in 1931 to join Bennie Moten's Band, and worked mainly with Moten until 1935; after Moten's death (April 1935), he led his own quintet in and around Kansas City. Page worked as a specialty act with Count Basie at the Reno Club, Kansas City (l936), was signed by manager Joe Glaser and moved to N.Y. He formed his own big band, which opened at Small's Paradise, N.Y., in August 1937, and led that group and smaller ones through late 1939. Featured on tour with Bud Freeman's Big Band and with Joe Marsala in 1940, then from November 1940 led own groups again until he joined Artie Shaw from Aug. 15, 1941 until January 1942. He primarily led big and small bands in N.Y., Boston, and Chicago, from then until early 1949. In May 1949 made his first trip to Europe for the Paris Jazz Festival, returned to U.S.A., and continued leading own small band in N.Y., Chicago, Minneapolis. He shared a highly successful recorded single with Pearl Bailey, "The Hucklebuck"/"Baby it's Cold Outside" (1949). He worked mainly as a single from then on and from July until October 1951 and the summer of 1952, he toured Europe. He suffered a heart attack on Oct. 27, 1954, and died in the Harlem Hospital nine days later.

DISC.: *After Hours in Harlem* (1941); *Dr. Jazz Series, Vol. 6* (1951); *Americans in Sweden: H.L.P.* (1951).—**JC/LP**

Page, Patti (originally, Fowler, Clara Ann),

American singer; b. Muskogee, Okla., Nov. 8, 1927. Page was the most successful recording artist of the first half of the 1950s, and the most successful female recording artist of that entire decade. Her frequently country-tinged ballads and novelty songs were notable for an early double-tracking process that allowed her to harmonize with herself. Among her 79 pop chart entries between 1948 and 1968, her biggest hits were "The Tennessee Waltz," "I Went to Your Wedding," and "The Doggie in the Window." In the 1970s and 1980s she focused on the country market and placed an additional 16 songs in the country charts.

Page grew up in Tulsa in a large family and first sang in the church choir, later in a trio with two of her sisters. As a teenager she was hired to sing with Al Klauser and His Oklahomans on a local radio station, acquiring her stage name as the singer on the *Meet Patti Page* show, sponsored by the Page Milk Company. In 1946 saxophonist Jack Rael, road manager for the Jimmy Joy band, which was playing in Tulsa, heard her on the radio and arranged for her to join the group in Chicago in December. She spent only a brief time with Joy, but Rael became her manager and arranged radio appearances and club work for her. In May and early June 1948 she sang with Benny Goodman. Signed to Mercury Records, she charted her first single, "Confess" (music and lyrics by Bennie Benjamin and George David Weiss), in late June.

Page had a series of minor chart entries from 1948 to 1950, finally reaching the Top Ten for the first time in July 1950 with "I Don't Care If the Sun Don't Shine" (music and lyrics by Mack David). Her next single, "All My Love (Bolero)" (music by Paul Durand, French lyrics by Henri Contet, English lyrics by Mitchell Parish), did even better, hitting #1 in October. But the recording that inadvertently established her was her revival of the 1948 country song "The Tennessee Waltz" (music and lyrics by Redd Stewart and Pee Wee King), an intended B-side to her 1950 Christmas single "Boogie Woogie Santa Claus" that took off and hit #1 in December, selling a million copies and becoming the biggest hit of the year.

Page had eight chart entries in 1951, five of which made the Top Ten, the most successful of them being the million-seller "Mockin' Bird Hill" (music and lyrics by Vaughn Horton). Her eight chart entries in 1952 included another five Top Tens, among them the chart-topping "I Went to Your Wedding" (music and lyrics by Jesse Mae Robinson), which was her third million-selling single. That year she broke into television, hosting the twice-a-week, 15-minute series *Music Hall* during the summer, then becoming a regular on the weekly series *Scott Music Hall* during the 1952–53 season. There were seven chart entries in 1953, three of them in the Top Ten, including her third #1 and fourth million-seller, "The Doggie in the Window" (music and lyrics by Bob Merrill), and her fifth million-seller, "Changing Partners" (music by Larry Coleman, lyrics by Joe Darion). There were another six chart entries in 1954, four in the Top Ten and one of them, "Cross Over the Bridge" (music and lyrics by Bennie Benjamin and George David Weiss), her sixth million-seller.

In June and July 1956, Page starred on television in *The Patti Page Show*, a one-hour musical variety series that served as one of the summer replacement programs for *The Perry Como Show*. She returned to television during the 1957–58 season as the hostess of the music series *The Big Record*, then during the 1958–59 season as the star of *The Patti Page Olds Show*, a series that earned her an Emmy nomination for Best Performance by an Actress (Continuing Character) in a Musical or Variety Series. With the rise of rock 'n' roll in the mid-1950s, she had fewer hits, although she continued to reach the singles charts regularly and returned to the Top Ten with the million-seller "Allegheny Moon" (music and lyrics by Al Hoffman and Dick Manning; 1956), "Old Cape Cod" (music and lyrics by Claire Rothrock, Milt Yakus, and Allan Jeffrey; 1957), and "Left Right Out of Your Heart (Hi Lee Hi Lo Hi Lup Up Up)" (music by Mort Garson, lyrics by Earl Shuman; 1958).

Page tried film acting in the early 1960s, appearing in *Elmer Gantry* (1960), *Dondi* (1961), and *Boys' Night Out* (1962), but did not continue it. She maintained her career primarily as a club performer in the 1960s. Moving to the Columbia Records label as of 1963, she scored a final Top Ten hit in 1965 with the movie theme "Hush, Hush, Sweet Charlotte" (music by Frank DeVol, lyrics by Mack David). She had stopped reaching the pop charts by the end of the 1960s, and in 1970 she returned to Mercury Records, where she began to record country music with modest success, reaching the country charts with a series of singles through the mid-1970s and again in the early 1980s on a succession of labels, Epic, Avco, and Plantation.

From the 1980s, she alternated between country music and performances of her pop hits, sometimes appearing with pops orchestras. She won the 1998 Grammy for Best Traditional Pop Vocal Performance for her album *Live at Carnegie Hall—The 50th Anniversary Concert*, issued by DRG Records.

Page was married to and divorced from Charles O'Curran, after which she married Jerry Filiciotto. She had two children.

DISC.: *Folksong Favorites* (1951); *Patti Sings for Romance* (1954); *Just Patti* (1954); *In the Land of Hi-Fi* (1956); *Christmas with Patti Page* (1959); *Golden Hits* (1960); *Go on Home* (1962); *Patti Page on Stage* (1963); *Hush, Hush, Sweet Charlotte* (1965); *Sings America's Favorite Hymns* (1966); *Gentle on My Mind* (1968); *Greatest Hits* (1987); *16 Most Requested Songs* (1989); *The Uncollected Patti Page with Lou Stein's Music '49* (1990); *The Patti Page Collection: The Mercury Years, Vol. 1* (1991); *The Patti Page Collection: The Mercury Years, Vol. 2* (1991); *Hits of—Vol. 1* (1992); *A Touch of Country* (1993); *Fallen Angels* (1993); *Just a Closer Walk with Thee* (1995); *Greatest Hits—Finest Performances* (1995); *Greatest Songs—Legendary Artist Series* (1995); *Christmas with Patti Page* (1996); *Dreaming* (1996); *Tennessee Waltz* (1996); *Golden Greats* (1996); *A Golden Celebration* (1997); *Tennessee Waltz* (1997); *Live at Carnegie Hall: The 50th Anniversary Concert* (1998); *Cocktail Hour: Patti Page* (2000).

WRITINGS: *Once Upon a Dream.*—WR

Page, Robert, esteemed American conductor and pedagogue; b. Abilene, Tex., April 27, 1927. Following studies at Abilene Christian Coll. (B.A., 1948) and Ind. Univ. (M.M., 1951), he pursued graduate training at N.Y.U. (1955–59). He was director of choral activities at Eastern N.Mex. Univ. in Portales (1951–55) and at Temple Univ. in Philadelphia (1956–75). From 1964 to 1976 he was music director of the Mendelssohn Club of Philadelphia. He served as director of choruses for the Cleveland Orch. from 1971 to 1989. He also was director of the Blossom Festival Chorus (1973–89) and asst. conductor of the Cleveland Orch. (1979–89). From 1975 to 1980 he was head of the music dept. at Carnegie-Mellon Univ. in Pittsburgh. In 1979 he became music director of the Mendelssohn Choir of Pittsburgh. He also was a conductor and chorus master of the Cleveland Opera (1980–86), founder-music director of the Robert Page Singers (1982–98), director of choral studies of Carnegie-Mellon Univ. (from 1988), and director of special projects and choral activities of the Pittsburgh Sym. Orch. (from 1989). He likewise served as president of Chorus America (1990–93). Page has won notable distinction as a choral conductor and teacher. In 1998 he was named Pa. Artist of the Year.—NS/LK/DM

Page, Walter (Sylvester), noted jazz bassist, bandleader; b. Gallatin, Mo., Feb. 9, 1900; d. N.Y., Dec. 20, 1957. He is praised, and quite rightly, for his firm, propulsive beat, but he should also be noted for his creative ways of breaking up the beat (as on "He's Funny That Way," 1938) and even for double-timing, which was unheard of in that era. He played tuba and bass drum in local brass bands and in high school, and was taught string bass by Major N. Clark Smith. While taking a teachers' course at Kans. Univ., he began playing in a band, and later worked with Bennie Moten in Kansas City. He regularly doubled on baritone sax throughout the 1920s. In January 1923 he joined Billy King's Road Show, working in a band led by trombonist Emir Coleman. During 1925 the outfit disbanded in Oklahoma City and Page took the nucleus of the band to form his Blue Devils (Emir Coleman remaining to work for a while with Page). In 1931 he turned the band over to trumpeter James Simpson and worked with small bands in and around Kansas City before rejoining Bennie Moten. The Original Blue Devils (as they were then called) continued to work under various leaders including drummer Earnest Williams, Buster Smith, and trumpeter Leroy "Snake" White. Page remained with Moten until 1934, then worked in a band led by Count Basie before joining Jeter-Pillars' Band in St. Louis (autumn 1934). Page returned to Kansas City to rejoin Count Basie (c. early 1936) and remained with him until September 1942. He toured with Nat Towle's Band (spring 1945), then worked with Jesse Price's Band in Joplin, Mo. he returned to Count Basie from summer 1946 until spring 1949, then joined Hot Lips Page, Worked with Jimmy Rushing (1951), then did extensive freelance work, mainly in N.Y. with Jimmy McPartland, at Eddie Condon's Club, and with Ruby Braff, Wild Bill Davison (touring in summer 1956), Roy Eldridge (late 1956). He continued to work regularly until shortly before his death. He contracted pneumonia, and resultant complications caused his death. He is not related to Hot Lips Page, trumpeter Dave Page, or tuba-player Vernon Page.—JC/LP

Pagliardi, Giovanni Maria, Italian composer; b. Genoa, 1637; d. Florence, Dec. 3, 1702. He entered the priesthood and served as maestro di cappella at the church of the Gesu in Genoa, to the Grand Duke of Tuscany, at S. Lorenzo in Florence, at the Tuscan court (from 1681), and at the Florence Cathedral (from 1701). He wrote several operas, the most successful being *Caligula deleriante* (Venice, Dec. 18, 1672), an oratorio, chamber cantatas, motets, arias, and spiritual madrigals.—LK/DM

Pagliughi, Lina, American-born Italian soprano; b. N.Y., May 27, 1907; d. Rubicone, Oct. 2, 1980. She was encouraged to pursue a career as a singer by Tetrazzini, and studied voice in Milan with Manlio Bavagnoli. She made her operatic debut at the Teatro Nazionale in Milan as Gilda in 1927, then made appearances throughout Italy. She sang at La Scala in Milan in 1930, and continued to make appearances there until 1947. She then sang with the RAI until her retirement in 1956. She was married to the tenor Primo Montanari. She was best known for her roles in operas by Rossini, Bellini, and Donizetti.—NS/LK/DM

Pahissa, Jaime, Catalan-born Argentine writer on music, teacher, and composer; b. Barcelona, Oct. 7, 1880; d. Buenos Aires, Oct. 27, 1969. He was a practicing architect for 4 years before turning to music as a profession; studied composition with Morera in Barcelona. He associated himself with the Catalan nationalist movement in art, obtaining his first important success in 1906 with the Romantic opera *La presó de Lledida* (The Prison of Lérida), which had 100 consecutive performances in Barcelona; it was later revised and produced in Barcelona on Feb. 8, 1928, as *La Princesa Margarita,* again obtaining a notable success. Other operas produced in Barcelona were *Gala Placidía* (Jan. 15, 1913) and *Marianela* (March 31, 1923). Among his orch. works, the most remarkable is *Monodía* (Barcelona, Oct. 12, 1925), written in unisons, octaves, double octaves, etc., without using any other intervals, and depending for its effect only on instrumental variety; in a different vein is his *Suite Intertonal* (Barcelona, Oct. 24, 1926), based on his own method of free tonal and polytonal composition. In 1935 Pahissa emigrated to Argentina, settling in Buenos Aires, where he continued to compose; he also established himself as a teacher and writer. He publ. in Buenos Aires the books: *Espíritu y cuerpo de la música* (1945), *Los grandes problemas de la música* (1945; 2nd ed., 1954), *Vida y obra de Manuel de Falla* (1947; Eng. tr., London, 1954), and *Sendas y cumbres de la música española* (1955). **BIBL.:** X. Aviñoa, *J. P.: Un estudi biogràfic i critic* (Barcelona, 1996).—NS/LK/DM

Pahud, Emmanuel, Swiss flutist; b. Geneva, Jan. 27, 1970. He began his music training when he was 6.

After winning the Belgian National Competition in 1985, he made his professional debut that Oct. in a recital at the Palais des Beaux Arts in Brussels. He pursued studies with Michel Debost, Alain Marion, and Pierre-Yves Artaud at the Paris Cons., where he was awarded the premier prix in 1990. Even before his graduation, he was appointed principal flutist of the Basel Radio Sym. Orch. at the age of 19, a position he held until 1992. He also pursued advanced studies with Aurèle Nicolet in Paris. In 1992 he captured 1st prize in the Geneva competition, and then made his U.S. debut as a soloist in the U.S. premiere of Corghi's *Suite Dodo* for Soprano, Flute, and Orch. at N.Y.'s Alice Tully Hall. In 1993 he became principal flutist of the Berlin Phil. While retaining this position, he has pursued a highly successful career as a soloist and recitalist. He made his Paris recital debut in 1994, followed by recital appearances in London and N.Y. in 1998. His engagements have taken him to major music centers on both sides of the Atlantic. Pahud's repertoire ranges from C.P.E. Bach, Haydn, Mozart, Beethoven, Schubert, and Weber to Fauré, Debussy, Ravel, Prokofiev, Berio, Ligeti, and Penderecki.—LK/DM

Paich, Marty (actually, **Martin Louis**), arranger, composer, pianist, leader; b. Oakland, Calif., Jan. 23, 1925. He is best known for tasteful jazz-oriented arrangements in the 1950s for artists such as Mel Torme and Ella Fitzgerald on the Verve label. Later, he did arrangements for Ray Charles, Sammy Davis Jr., Lena Horne, and many others. He recorded most of his LPs during the second half of the 1950s, before he turned to lucrative studio and session work, as well as television and film soundtrack work.

DISC.: *M.P. Octet* (1955); *Jazz City Workshop* (1955); *M.P. Quartet, Vol. 9* (1956); *Picasso of Big Band Jazz* (1957); *M.P. Trio* (1957); *M.P. Quartet* (1957); *M.P. Big Band* (1958); *Revel without Pause* (1959); *Moanin'* (1959); *Piano Quartet* (1960); *N.Y. Scene* (1991); *Hot Piano* (1991).—MM/LP

Paik, Byung-Dong, Korean composer and pedagogue; b. Seoul, Jan. 26, 1936. He studied at Seoul National Univ. (B.A., 1959), and later with Fritz von Block and Alfred Koerppen (theory) and Isang Yun (composition) at the Hannover Staatliche Hochschule für Musik (1969–71). In 1976 he became a prof. at the Coll. of Music at Seoul National Univ., where he also was head of its composition dept. (1981–87). Among his awards are the Annual Korean New Composer's Prize (1962, for his *Symphony in 3 Movements*), the 5th Wolgan Musicians Prize (1975), the 1st Korean National Composer's Prize (1977, for his *Zweite Streichquartett*), and the Cultural Prize of Seoul (1983). Several of his works combine Korean musical traditions and instruments with contemporary Western instruments and practices. His style of composition tends toward strict formal procedures utilizing academic musical vocabularies.

WORKS (all 1st perf. in Seoul unless otherwise given): **ORCH.:** *Symphony in 3 Movements* (1962; July 9, 1963); Cello Concerto (Oct. 30, 1969); *Stimmung* (1971; March 28, 1974); Viola Concerto (Oct. 11, 1972); Piano Concerto (March 26, 1974); *Metamorphosen für 83 Spieler* (Oct. 23, 1974); *Requiescat* for 3

Oboes and Orch. (1974; Feb. 11, 1976); *Youlmok* for Strings (June 23, 1982); *Sansudo* (Sept. 22, 1983); *Pogu* (Pusan, May 2, 1986); *In September* (1987). **CHAMBER:** *Zeite Streichquartett* (Nov. 29, 1977); *Sori* for Flute, Guitar, and Cello (Tokyo, Feb. 26, 1981); Piano Trio (June 30, 1985); *Zweite Kammerkonzert* (March 11, 1988); *Contra* for Marimbaphone and 2 Percussion (Tokyo, June 21, 1988); *5 Pieces* for Cello and Contrabass (March 9, 1989). **TRADITIONAL KOREAN INSTRUMENTS:** *Shin Byul Gock* (April 18, 1972); *Un-Rack* (April 14, 1976); *3 Essays of GAYO* (Dec. 13, 1985); *Hwan Myung* (May 17, 1988). **OTHER:** Numerous works for Solo Instruments; dance music. **VOCAL:** Numerous works, including songs.—NS/LK/DM

Paik, Kun-Woo, Korean pianist; b. Seoul, March 10, 1946. He studied music with his father, making his public debut when he was 8. He went to the U.S. in 1960 to continue his studies at the Juilliard School of Music in N.Y. with Rosina Lhévinne; won the Naumburg Award, and also studied with Ilona Kabos in London and Wilhelm Kempff in Italy. He subsequently developed a fine concert career, appearing as soloist with leading orchs. of North America as well as in Europe. —NS/LK/DM

Paik, Nam June, innovative avant-garde Korean-American composer and visual arts; b. Seoul, July 20, 1932. He studied first at the Univ. of Tokyo, and then took courses in theory with Georgiades in Munich and with Fortner in Freiburg im Breisgau. He then attended the summer courses in new music in Darmstadt (1957–61) and worked at the Cologne Electronic Music Studio (1958–60). In his showings, Paik pursues the objective of total art as the sum of integrated synesthetic experiences, involving all sorts of actions: walking, talking, dressing, undressing, drinking, smoking, moving furniture, engaging in quaquaversal commotion intended to demonstrate that any human or inhuman action becomes an artistic event through the power of volitional concentration of an ontological imperative. Paik attracted attention at his duo recitals with the topless cellist Charlotte Moorman, at which he acted as a surrogate cello, with his denuded spinal column serving as the fingerboard for Moorman's cello bow, while his bare skin provided an area for intermittent pizzicati. About 1963 Paik began experimenting with videotape as a medium for sounds and images; his initial experiment in this field was *Global Groove,* a high-velocity collage of intermingled television bits, which included instantaneous commercials, fragments from news telecasts, and subliminal extracts from regular programs, subjected to topological alterations. His list of works (some of them consisting solely of categorical imperatives) includes *Ommaggio a Cage* for piano demolition, breakage of raw eggs, spray painting of hands in jet black, etc. (Düsseldorf, Nov. 13, 1959); *Symphony for 20 Rooms* (1961); *Variations on a Theme of Saint-Saëns* for Cello and Piano, with the pianist playing *Le Cygne* while the cellist dives into an oil drum filled with water (N.Y., Aug. 25, 1965, composer at the keyboard, cellist Moorman in the oil drum); *Performable Music,* wherein the performer is ordered to make with a razor an incision of no less than 10 centimeters on his left forearm (Los Angeles, Dec. 2, 1965); *Opéra sextron-ique* (1967); *Opéra électronique* (1968); *Creep into the Vagina of a Whale* (c. 1969); and *Young Penis Symphony,* a protrusion of 10 erectile phalluses through a paper curtain (c. 1970; first perf. at "La Mamelle," San Francisco, Sept. 21, 1975, under the direction of Ken Friedman, who also acted as one of the 10 performers). Of uncertain attribution is a sym. designated as No. 3, which Paik delegated to Friedman, who worked on it in Saugus, Calif., the epicenter of the earthquake of Feb. 9, 1971, and of which the earthquake itself constituted the finale. Among his subsequent works were *Video Buddha* (1974); *VIDEA* (1980), *The More the Better* (1988), *My Faust/The Stations* (1988–91), and *Video Opera* (1993). —NS/LK/DM

Pailliard, Jean-François, noted French conductor; b. Vitry-le-François, April 12, 1928. He received his musical training at the Paris Cons., and later took courses in conducting with Markevitch at the Salzburg Mozarteum. In 1953 he founded the Jean-Marie Leclair Instrumental Ensemble, which became the Jean-François Pailliard Chamber Orch. in 1959, with which he toured widely; also appeared extensively as a guest conductor. He ed. the series Archives de la Musique Instrumentale, and publ. the study *La musique française classique* (Paris, 1960).—NS/LK/DM

Paine, John Knowles, prominent American composer and pedagogue; b. Portland, Maine, Jan. 9, 1839; d. Cambridge, Mass., April 25, 1906. His father ran a music store, and conducted the band in Portland. He studied organ, piano, harmony, and counterpoint with Hermann Krotzschmar, then took courses with K. Haupt (organ), W. Wieprecht (orchestration and composition), and others in Berlin (1858–61); concurrently appeared as an organist and pianist in Germany and England. He settled in Boston, becoming organist of the West Church (1861). He joined the faculty of Harvard Univ. (1862), where he also was organist at its Appleton Chapel; was prof. of music at Harvard (1875–1906), the first to hold such a position at a U.S. univ.; was made a member of the National Inst. of Arts and Letters (1898), and was awarded the honorary degrees of M.A. from Harvard (1869) and Mus.D. from Yale (1890). He greatly distinguished himself as a teacher, serving as mentor to J.A. Carpenter, F.S. Converse, A. Foote, E.B. Hill, D.G. Mason, W. Spalding, and many others. He publ. *The History of Music to the Death of Schubert* (Boston, 1907). His complete organ works were ed. by W. Leupold (Dayton, Ohio, 1975) and his complete piano works were ed. by J. Schmidt (N.Y., 1984).

WORKS: DRAMATIC: *Il pesceballo,* comic opera (1862; music not extant); *Azara,* grand opera (1883–98; concert perf., Boston, May 7, 1903); incidental music to Sophocles's *Oedipus tyrannus* (1880–81; Cambridge, Mass., May 17, 1881; rev. 1895) and to Aristophanes's *The Birds* (1900; Cambridge, May 10, 1901). **ORCH.:** 2 syms.: No. 1 (1875; Boston, Jan. 26, 1876) and No. 2, *In the Spring* (1879; Cambridge, March 10, 1880); *As You Like It,* overture (c. 1876); 2 symphonic poems: *The Tempest* (c. 1876) and *An Island Fantasy* (c. 1888); Duo Concertante for Violin, Cello, and Orch. (c. 1877); *Lincoln: A Tragic Tone Poem* (c. 1904–06; unfinished). **CHAMBER:** String Quartet (c. 1855); Piano Trio (c. 1874); Violin Sonata (1875; rev. c. 1905); *Romanza* *and Scherzo* for Cello and Piano (c. 1875); *Larghetto and Scherzo* for Violin, Cello, and Piano (c. 1877); piano music; organ works. **VOCAL: C h o r a l :** *Domine salvum fac* for Men's Chorus and Orch. (1863); Mass for Soloists, Chorus, Organ, and Orch. (1865; Berlin, Feb. 16, 1867); *St. Peter*, oratorio for Soloists, Chorus, Organ, and Orch. (1870–72; Portland, Maine, June 3, 1873); *Centennial Hymn* for Chorus, Organ, and Orch. (Philadelphia, 1876); *The Realm of Fancy*, cantata for Soloists, Chorus, and Orch. (1882); *Phoebus, Arise!*, cantata for Tenor, Men's Chorus, and Orch. (1882); *The Nativity*, cantata for Soloists, Chorus, and Orch. (1883; rev. 1903); *Song of Promise*, cantata for Soprano, Chorus, Organ, and Orch. (1888); *Columbus March and Hymn* for Chorus, Organ, and Orch. (1892; Chicago, 1893); *Hymn of the West* for Chorus and Orch. (1903; St. Louis, 1904). **O t h e r :** Songs.

BIBL.: J K. Roberts, *J.K. P.* (thesis, Univ. of Mich., 1962); J. Huxford, *J.K. P.: Life and Works* (diss., Fla. State Univ., 1968); J. Schmidt, *The Life and Works of J.K. P.* (Ann Arbor, Mich., 1980). —NS/LK/DM

Paisible, James, French-born English recorder player, oboist, and composer; b. place and date unknown; d. London, Aug.?, 1721. He was in England by 1674 where he became active in court circles. In 1685 he was officially named a member of the King's Musick. After serving as an instrumentalist in James II's private chapel, he was one of the musicians in the service of Prince George. He also played in the band at the Theatre Royal, Drury Lane. His works included music for the stage, sonatas, and songs.—LK/DM

Paisible, Louis Henri, French violinist and composer; b. St. Cloud, near Paris, July 21, 1748; d. (suicide) St. Petersburg, March 19, 1782. He studied with Gaviniès, played in the orch. of the Concert Spirituel in Paris, and then traveled through Europe. In 1778 he was engaged at the Russian court in St. Petersburg. Although well received at first, he was unable to make headway with a series of concerts for which he solicited subscriptions; deprived of resources, he shot himself. Twelve of his string quartets and 4 violin concertos have been publ. in Paris and London.—NS/LK/DM

Paisiello, Giovanni, famous Italian composer; b. Roccaforzata, near Taranto, May 9, 1740; d. Naples, June 5, 1816. He studied at the Jesuit school in Taranto, and then at the Cons. di S. Onofrio in Naples (1754–63). He began his career as an opera composer by writing works for the Marsigli-Rossi Theater in Bologna in 1764. He settled in Naples in 1766, and proceeded to write over 40 operas during the next decade. Outstanding works from this period include *Le finte contesse* (Rome, Feb. 1766), *L'idolo cinese* (Naples, 1767), and *La Frascatana* (Venice, 1774). In 1776 he was invited to Russia, where he was appointed maestro di cappella to the Empress Catherine II in St. Petersburg. He composed one of his most celebrated operas there, *Il Barbiere di Siviglia* (Sept. 26, 1782), which remained popular in Italy until the appearance of Rossini's masterpiece in 1816. In 1783 Ferdinand IV of Naples made him compositore della musica de' drammi. In 1784 he left Russia for Naples, making a stop in Vienna, where he brought out one of his finest scores, *Il Re Teodoro in Venezia* (Aug. 23, 1784). His success in Naples led to his additional appointment in 1787 as maestro della real camera, in which capacity he was responsible for secular music at the court. Between 1784 and 1799 he composed several noteworthy operas, including *Le gare generose* (Naples, 1786), *L'amore contrastato* (Naples, 1788), *Nina, o sia La Pazza per amore* (Caserta, June 25, 1789), and *I Zingari in fiera* (Naples, Nov. 21, 1789). After Republican troops took control of Naples in Jan. 1799, Paisiello was named maestro di cappella nazionale by the new government on May 4, 1799. However, with the return of the Royalists in June 1799, he fell into disfavor with the court; was eventually granted a pardon, and restored to his posts on July 7, 1801. Ferdinand subsequently allowed him to serve as Napoleon's maitre de chapelle in Paris from April 1802 until his return to Naples in Aug. 1804. He was made a member of the Légion d'honneur in 1806. He was further honored with membership in the Institut, taking the place of the deceased Haydn in 1809. After Joseph Bonaparte became King of Naples in 1806, Paisiello was appointed director of secular and sacred music at the court; he continued to hold these positions under Joachim Murat, Joseph's successor as King (1808–15); he also served as one of the directors of the new college of music (1807–13). In 1815 Ferdinand returned to the throne, and Paisiello lost all of his posts with the exception of that of maestro della real cappella.

Paisiello's success as a composer of comic operas equaled that of Piccini and Cimarosa. He was extraordinarily prolific; his operas alone number over 90, a few of which have been revived in the 20th century. Although he employed instrumental effects that were rare in Italy, he avoided the over-elaborate numbers in his operas which marked the works of many of his contemporaries, obtaining his results by melodic invention, and by the grace, beauty, and dramatic faithfulness of his conceptions.

BIBL.: I. Arnold, *G. P.: Seine kurze Biographie* (Erfurt, 1810); J. Le Sueur, *Notice sur P.* (Paris, 1816); Quatremère de Quincy, *Notice historique de P.* (Paris, 1817); G. de Dominicis, *Saggio su la vita del Cavalier Don G. P.* (Moscow, 1818); F. Schizzi, *Della vita e degli studi di G. P.* (Milan, 1833); C. Pupino, *P.* (Naples, 1908); S. Panareo, *P. in Russia* (Trani, 1910); U. Prota-Giurleo, *P. ed i suoi primi trionfi a Napoli* (Naples, 1925); A. Cametti, *P. e la corte di Vienna* (Rome, 1929); G. Speziale, *G. P.* (Naples, 1931); E. Faustini-Fasini, *L'ultima opera di P., I pittagorici* (Taranto, 1937); idem, *Opere teatrali, oratori e cantate di G. P.* (Bari, 1940); A. Ghislanzoni, *G. P.: Valutazioni critiche rettificate* (Rome, 1969); J. Hunt, *G. P.: His Life as an Opera Composer* (N.Y., 1975); M. Robinson and U. Hoffmann, *G. P.: A Thematic Catalogue of His Music* (2 vols., Stuyvesant, N.Y., 1991, 1994).—NS/LK/DM

Paita, Carlos, Argentine conductor; b. Buenos Aires, March 10, 1932. He studied piano with Juan Neuchoff, composition with Jacobo Fischer, and conducting with Rodzinski; greatly impressed by Fürtwangler's concerts in Argentina, he became determined to pursue a conducting career. After appearances in Buenos Aires, he conducted in Europe; made his U.S. debut as a guest conductor with the Houston Sym. Orch. (1979). He was active mainly in South America and Europe; recorded with an orch. in London created especially for him. A conductor of passionate Latin tempermant, he won both fervent admirers and intrepid detractors with his supercharged performances of the Romantic repertory.—NS/LK/DM

Paiva, Heliodoro de, Portuguese organist and composer; b. Lisbon, 1502; d. Coimbra, Dec. 21, 1552. He was the son of the king's wardrobe master and superintendent of public works. It is probable that he was educated at the court, for his interests included theology, philosophy, Hebrew, Greek, and Latin. He became well known as a scribe, keyboard artist, and singer. As a composer, he excelled in writing tientos. Paiva was so admired in his day that such composers as Palestrina and Scheidt freely borrowed from his works.—LK/DM

Paix, Jakob, German organist and composer; b. Augsburg, 1556; d. probably in Hiltpolstein, after 1623. He was the son of Peter Paix, organist at St. Anna in Augsburg, with whom he studied. He served as organist at St. Martin, Lauingen an der Donau, Swabia (1576–1609), and also was a teacher at the royal Gymnasium and at the Lateinschule. From 1609 to about 1617 he was organist at the ducal court in Neuburg an der Donau. Paix publ. *Ein schön nutz und gebreüchlich Orgel Tabulaturbuch* (Laungingen an der Donau, 1583), which includes works by other composers as well. It is a valuable source of German keyboard music of his era. Several of his sacred vocal works are also extant.—LK/DM

Pakhmutova, Alexandra (Nikolaievna), Russian composer; b. Beketovka, near Stalingrad, Nov. 9, 1929. She studied at the Moscow Cons. with Shebalin, graduating in 1953. She was particularly successful in the genre of urban ballads, close to contemporary reality. Among them, especially popular were her *Songs of Turbulent Youth* (1961), *Cuba, My Love* (1962), *Keep Your Heart Young* (1963), *Young Eagles Learn to Fly* (1965), *A Coward Will Not Play Hockey* (1968), *Let Us Embrace the Sky* (1966), *Gagarin's Constellation* (1971), *Sport Heroes* (1972), and *Hope* (1974). Her Trumpet Concerto acquired great popularity in Russia.

WORKS: DRAMATIC: Ballet: *Lucid Vision* (1973). ORCH.: *Russian Suite* (1952); Trumpet Concerto (Moscow, June 11, 1955); Concerto (1971). CHAMBER: *4 Miniatures on Russian Folk Themes* for String Quartet (1950); *Nocturne* for Horn and Piano (1956). VOCAL: *Lenin Is in Our Hearts*, suite for Narrator, Children's Chorus, and Orch. (1957); *Young Pioneer Songs*, cantata (1972); choruses; songs.

BIBL.: E. Dobrynina, *A. P.* (Moscow, 1973).—NS/LK/DM

Paladilhe, Emile, French composer; b. Montpellier, June 3, 1844; d. Paris, Jan. 6, 1926. He entered the Paris Cons. in 1853, and was a pupil of Marmontel (piano), Benoist (organ), and Halévy (counterpoint). He won 1st prize for piano and organ in 1857, and the Grand Prix de Rome in 1860 with the cantata *Le Czar Ivan IV* (Paris Opéra, 1860). He brought out the comic opera *Le Passant in Paris* (April 24, 1872), followed by *L'Amour africain* (May 8, 1875), *Suzanne* (Dec. 30, 1878), *Diana* (Feb. 23, 1885), the opera *Patrie* (Dec. 20, 1886),

and *Les Saintes Maries de la mer*, a sacred lyric drama (Montpellier, 1892). He also produced 2 masses, Sym., and numerous songs (*Mandolinata, Premières pensées, Mélodies écossaises*). In 1892 he succeeded Guiraud as member of the Institut de France.—NS/LK/DM

Palange, Louis S(alvador), American conductor, composer, and arranger; b. Oakland, Calif., Dec. 17, 1917; d. Burbank, Calif., June 8, 1979. He played the clarinet and bassoon in school bands, and also studied composition with his father and at Mills Coll. in Oakland, Calif. with Domenico Brecia before going to Los Angeles (1936), where he continued his studies with Wesley La Violette. He subsequently pursued a varied career as a conductor, composer, and arranger, working mainly in Los Angeles from 1946.

WORKS: ORCH.: 2 tone poems: *Evangeline* (1943) and *The Plagues of Egypt* (1945); 2 syms.: No. 1, *Invasion* (1946) and No. 2 (1950; Los Angeles, March 22, 1968); *Pictures* for Flute and Orch. (1948); *Poker Deck Ballet Suite* (1949; Redondo Beach, Calif., Dec. 9, 1960); *A Romantic Concerto* for Piano and Orch. (1949); 2 violin concertos (1950, n.d.). Symphonic Band: *Symphony in Steel* (1940; Los Angeles, March 8, 1941); *Hollywood Panorama*, tone poem (1950; Burbank, Sept. 21, 1952); various other pieces. CHAMBER: *Classical Trio* for Flute, Violin, and Viola (1942); *4 Generations* for String Quartet (1950). OTHER: Film scores; arrangements for Band or Orch.—NS/LK/DM

Palau Boix, Manuel, Spanish conductor, teacher, and composer; b. Alfara de Patriarca, Jan. 4, 1893; d. Valencia, Feb. 18, 1967. He studied first at the Valencia Cons., and later in Paris, where he took lessons from Koechlin and Ravel. Returning to Valencia, he established himself as a teacher, conductor, and composer. Most of his thematic material is inspired by Catalan folk songs; his instrumental music usually bears programmatic content; his technique of composition follows the French impressionist procedures.

WORKS: ORCH.: *Poemas de juventud* (1926); *Gongoriana* (1927); *Siluetas* (1928); *Homenaje a Debussy* (1929); *Valencia* for Piano and Orch. (1936); *Marcha burlesca* (1936); *Divertimento* (1938); *Poemes de Ilum* (1939); 3 syms. (1945, 1946, 1950); *Concierto dramático* for Piano and Orch. (1948); *Mascarada sarcastica* (1949). OTHER: Zarzuelas; chamber works; piano pieces; choral music; songs.

BIBL.: A. Mingote, *M. P.* (Valencia, 1946); F. León Tello, *La obra pianistica de M. P.* (Valencia, 1956).—NS/LK/DM

Palazzesi, Matilde, Italian soprano; b. Montecarotto, March 1, 1802; d. Barcelona, July 3, 1842. She studied with Giacomo Solarto in Pesaro, making her debut in the title role of Rossini's *Zelmira* in 1824 in Dresden. She sang with the Italian Opera there until 1833, then appeared at La Scala in Milan and other Italian opera houses. She went to Barcelona, where she sang at the Opera from 1841. She was a leading interpreter of Mozart, Rossini, Bellini, Donizetti, and Spontini.

BIBL.: B. Padovano, *M. P.* (1953).—NS/LK/DM

Palazzotto e Tagliavia, Giuseppe, admirable Italian compoer; b. Castelvetrano, Sicily, c. 1587; d. after

1633. He was born of a noble family. He became a cleric and, in 1606, entered the Congregazione dell'Oratorio dei Filippini in Palermo. In 1608 he was ordained a priest in Tusa. After serving as a full member of his order (1609–13), he was active in Naples, Palermo, and Messina before becoming archdeacon and synodal inquisitor at Cefalù Cathedral. He was one of the principal Sicilian composers of his era, excelling as a madrigalist. In addition to 3 vols. of madrigals (116, 1617, 1620), he also composed masses and motets.—**LK/DM**

Palella, Antonio, Italian composer; b. Naples, Oct. 8, 1692; d. there, March 7, 1761. He served as 2nd harpsichordist at the Teatro San Carlo in Naples from its opening in 1737. His operas, all written for Naples, included *L'Origelle* (Dec. 8, 1740), *L'incanti per amore* (Oct. 2, 1741), *Il trionfo del valore* (1741; in collaboration with G. Signorille, Porpora, and G. Paolo), *Il chimico* (1742), *Tigrane* (Nov. 4, 1745; a major reworking of Hasse's 1725 opera), and *Il geloso* (1751). Among his other works were a Sinfonia, a Concerto a 4 for Flute, 2 Violins, and Bass, and cantatas.—**LK/DM**

Pálenícek, Josef, Czech pianist, pedagogue, and composer; b. Travnik, July 19, 1914; d. Prague, March 7, 1991. He made his debut as a pianist at 11. After training with Hoffmeister (piano) and Šín and Novák (composition) at the Prague Cons., he studied in Paris with Alexanian and Fournier (chamber music), Roussel, and Cortot. Returning to Prague, he co-founded the Smetana Trio in 1934, which later became the Czech Trio. He toured widely from 1935. In 1963 he became a teacher at the Prague Academy of Music. In 1967 he was made an Artist of Merit and in 1977 was awarded the State Prize by the Czech government. As a solo pianist, he distinguished himself as an interpreter of Janáček.

WORKS: DRAMATIC: **B a l l e t :** *Kytice* (Bouquet; 1980–82). **O R C H .:** Concertino (1937–45); 3 piano concertos (1939, 1953, 1961); Saxophone Concerto (1944); Flute Concerto (1955); *Concertino da camera* for Clarinet and Orch. (1957); *Symphonic Variations on an Imaginary Portrait of Ilya Ehrenburg* (1971); Cello Concerto (1973); Sinfonietta for Strings (1977). **C H A M B E R :** Piano Quintet (1933); *Preludium a capriccio* for Violin and Piano (1935); Clarinet Sonatina (1936); *Choral Variations* for Cello and Piano (1942); *Little Suite* for Clarinet and Piano (1943); String Quartet (1954); *Masks* for Saxophone and Piano (1957); *Little Suite* for Violin and Piano (1958); *Variations* for Cello and Piano (1972); *Rondo concertante* for Cello and Piano (1972); *Suita in modo antico* for Cello and Piano (1973); *Concertant Etudes* for Double Bass and Piano (1975); *Pictures* for Flute, Bass, Clarinet, Piano, and Percussion (1976); *Tre concertini* for Clarinet and Piano (1977); piano pieces. **V O C A L :** *Song of Man,* oratorio (1952–58); Trio Sonata for Mezzo-soprano, Oboe, and Piano (1965).—**NS/LK/DM**

Palester, Roman, Polish composer; b. Śniatyń, Dec. 28, 1907; d. Paris, Aug. 25, 1989. After training in piano from Soltysowa at the Lwów Cons., he entered the Warsaw Cons. in 1925 and studied composition with Sikorski. He subsequently pursued the study of art history at the Univ. of Warsaw. In 1931 he obtained diplomas in composition and theory. After dividing his time between Poland and France, he taught at the Warsaw Cons. from the end of World War II until 1948, when he settled in Paris. In 1981 he was reinstated as a member of the Polish Composers Union. In his music, he was particularly influenced by French music but sought to preserve elements of Polish folk melos in the thematic structure of his scores. Harmonically he did not choose to transcend the limit of enhanced tonality.

WORKS: DRAMATIC: **O p e r a :** *Zywe kamienie* (The Living Stones; 1944; unfinished); *La Mort de Don Juan* (1959–60). **B a l l e t :** *Piesn o ziemi* (Song of the Earth; 1937). **ORCH.:** *Muzyka symfoniczna* (1930; London, July 27, 1931; not extant); Piano Concerto (1935; not extant); *Danse polonaise* (1935; Barcelona, April 22, 1936); 5 syms.: No. 1 (1935; not extant), No. 2 (1942), No. 3 for Chamber Orch. (1949), No. 4 (1940–51; rev. 1972), and No. 5 (1977–81; Warsaw, Sept. 23, 1988); Saxophone Concertino (1937); *Suita symfoniczna* (1938); Violin Concerto (1941; London, July 14, 1946); Piano Concertino (1942); *Notturno* for Strings (1947); *Serenade* for 2 Flutes and Strings (Kraków, Nov. 9, 1947); *Passacaglia* (1950); *Variations* (1955); Concertino for Harpsichord and Instrumental Ensemble (1955); *Adagio* for Strings (1956); *Music* for 2 Pianos and Orch. (1957); *Study 58* for Chamber Orch. (1958); Sonata for Strings (1959); Piccolo Concerto for Chamber Orch. (1959); *Metamorphosen* (1965–66); Viola Concerto (1977–78). **C H A M B E R :** Sonatina for Violin and Cello (1930; not extant); 3 string quartets (1932, not extant; 1935; 1943); Sonata for 2 Violins and Piano (1939); 2 string trios (1945, 1958); *Divertimento* for 9 Instruments (1949); Trio for Flute, Viola, and Harp (1969); Duo for 2 Violins (1972); *Suite à quatre* for Oboe and String Trio (1973); Trio for Flute, Viola, and Harp (1985). **P i a n o :** 2 sonatas (1970, 1980); *Passacaille et Variations* (1974). **V O C A L :** *Psalm V* for Baritone, Chorus, and Orch. (1931); *Requiem* for Soloists, Chorus, and Orch. (1945); *Wisla,* cantata for Chorus (1945–48); *Missa brevis* for Chorus (1948); *Sonnets for Orpheus* for Voice and Chamber Ensemble (1952); *Songs* for Soprano and Chamber Orch. (1976); *Te Deum* for 3 Choruses and Instruments (1978–79).—**NS/LK/DM**

Palestrina, Giovanni Pierluigi da, great Italian composer; b. probably in Palestrina, near Rome, 1525 or 1526; d. Rome, Feb. 2, 1594. In his letters he customarily signed his name as Giovanni Petraloysio. He is first listed as a choirboy at S. Maria Maggiore in 1537, and it is likely that he studied with each of the maestri of the period, Robin Mallapert, one Robert, and Firmin Lebel. In 1544 he was appointed organist of the cathedral of S. Agapit in Palestrina, where his duties also included teaching music to the canons and choirboys. On June 12, 1547, he married Lucrezia Gori, with whom he had 3 sons, Rodolfo (1549–72), Angelo (1551–75), and Iginio (1558–1610). In 1550 the bishop of Palestrina, Cardinal Giovanni Maria Ciocchi del Monte, was elected pope, taking the name of Julius III. On Sept. 1, 1551, he appointed Palestrina maestro of the Cappella Giulia in succession to Mallapert; Palestrina dedicated his first book of masses to him in 1554. On Jan. 13, 1555, the pope rewarded him by making him a member of the Cappella Sistina even though he was a married man; he was admitted without taking the entrance examination and without receiving the approval of the other singers. In Sept. 1555 Pope Paul IV dismissed Palestrina and 2 other singers after invoking the celibacy rule of the chapel, although he granted each of them a small pension. On Oct. 1, 1555, Palestrina became maestro di cappella of the great church of St. John Lateran, where his son Rodolfo joined him as a chorister. Palestrina's tenure was made difficult by inadequate funds for the musical establishment, and he resigned his post in July 1560. From 1561 to 1566 he was maestro di cappella of S. Maria Maggiore. In 1562–63 the Council of Trent took up the matter of sacred music. Out of its discussions arose a movement to advance the cause of intelligibility of sacred texts when set to music. Palestrina's role with this Council remains a matter of dispute among historians, but his *Missa Pape Marcelli* is an outstanding example of a number of its reforms. From 1564 he was also in charge of the music at the summer estate of Cardinal Ippolito II d'Este in Tivoli, near Rome. He apparently took up a full-time position in the Cardinal's service from 1567 to 1571. From 1566 to 1571 he likewise taught at the Seminario Romano, where his sons Rodolfo and Angelo were students. In 1568 the court of Emperor Maximilian II offered him the position of imperial choirmaster in Vienna, but Palestrina demanded so high a salary that the offer was tacitly withdrawn. In April 1571, upon the death of Giovanni Animuccia, he resumed his post as maestro of the Cappella Giulia. In 1575 his salary was increased to forestall his move to S. Maria Maggiore. In 1577, at the request of Pope Gregory XIII, Palestrina and Annibale Zoilo began the revision of the plainsongs of the Roman Gradual and Antiphoner. Palestrina never completed his work on this project; the revision was eventually completed by others and publ. as *Editio Medicaea* in 1614. In 1580, having lost his eldest sons and his wife to the plague, he made a decision to enter the priesthood; he soon changed his mind, however, and instead married Virginia Dormoli, the widow of a wealthy furrier, on Feb. 28, 1581. In succeeding years he devoted much time to managing her fortune while continuing his work as a musician. In 1583 he was tendered an offer to become maestro at the court of the Duke of Mantua, but again his terms were rejected as too high. In 1584 he publ. his settings of the *Song of Solomon*. In 1593 he began plans to return to Palestrina as choirmaster of the cathedral, but he was overtaken by death early the next year. He was buried in the Cappella Nuova of old St. Peter's Church.

With his great contemporaries Byrd and Lassus, Palestrina stands as one of the foremost composers of his age. He mastered the polyphonic style of the Franco-Flemish school, creating works of unsurpassing beauty and technical adroitness. His sacred music remains his most glorious achievement. Highly prolific, he composed 104 masses, over 375 motets, 68 offertories, over 65 hymns, 35 Magnificats, over 140 madrigals (both sacred and secular), Lamentations, litanies, and Psalms. The first complete edition of his works, *Giovanni Pierluigi da Palestrina: Werke*, was ed. by F.X. Haberl et al. (33 vols., Leipzig, 1862–1903). A new complete edition, *Giovanni Pierluigi da Palestrina: Le opere*, ed. by R. Casimiri and his successors, began publication in Rome in 1939.

BIBL.: G. Baini, *Memorie storico-critiche della vita e delle opere di G.P. d.P.* (Rome, 1828; reprint, 1966); C. von Winterfeld, *J.P. v.P.* (Breslau, 1832); F. Kandler, *Über das Leben und die Werke des G.P. d.P....nach den Memorie storico-critiche des Abbate G. Baini*

verfasst (Leipzig, 1834); G. Campori, *Delle relazioni di Orlando di Lasso e G.P. d.P. coi principi estensi* (Rome, 1870); P. Wagner, *P. als weltlicher Komponist* (Strasbourgh, 1890); A. Cametti, *Cenni biografici di G.P. d.P.* (Milan, 1894); G. Cascioli, *La vita e le opere di G.P. d.P.* (Rome, 1894); G. Félix, *P. et la musique sacrée (1594–1894)* (Lille, 1896); C. Respighi, *G.P. d.P. e l'emendazione del Graduale romano* (Rome, 1900); M. Brenet, *P.* (Paris, 1905; 3rd ed., 1910); J. Gloger, *Die "Missa Prima." Eine Studie über den P.stil* (Leobschutz, 1910); E. Schmitz, *G.P. P.* (Leipzig, 1914; 2nd ed., 1954); K. Weinmann, *P.s Geburtsjahr* (Regensburg, 1915); R. Casimiri, *Il Codice 59 dell' Archivio musicale lateranense, autografo di G.P. d.P.* (Rome, 1919); Z. Pyne, *P.: His Life and Times* (London, 1922); K. Jeppesen, *P.stil med saerligt henblik paa dissonansbehandlingen* (Copenhagen, 1923; Ger. tr., 1925; Eng. tr., 1927; 2nd ed., 1946, as *The Style of P. and the Dissonance*); A. Cametti, *P.* (Milan, 1925); K. Fellerer, *Der P.stil und seine Bedeutung in der vokalen Kirchenmusik des 18. Jahrhunderts* (Augsburg, 1929); idem, *P.* (Regensburg, 1930; 2nd ed., 1960); H. Coates, *P.* (London, 1938); J. Samon, *P., ou La Poésie de l'exactitude* (Geneva, 1940); E. Paccagnella, *P.: Il linguaggio melodico e armonico* (Florence, 1957); H. Andrews, *An Introduction to the Technique of P.* (London, 1958); E. Ferraci, *Il P.* (Rome, 1960); S. Klyce, *P. and His "Missa Pape Marcelli": An Analysis for Performance* (diss., Ind. Univ., 1969); T. Day, *P. in History* (diss., Columbia Univ., 1970); L. Lockwood, *Norton Critical Score ed. of the Pope Marcellus Mass* (N.Y., 1975; includes background and analysis); A. Monterosso Vacchelli, *La messa L'Homme armé di P.: Studio paleografico ed edizione critica*, Vol. VII, Istituta et Monumenta (1979); J.-F. Gautier, *P., ou, L'esthétique de l'âme du monde* (Arles, 1994); M. Heinemann, *G.P. d.P. und seine Zeit* (Laaber, 1994); R. Stewart, *An Introduction to Sixteenth-Century Counterpoint and P.'s Musical Style* (N.Y., 1994); L. Bianchi, *P. nella vita nelle opere nel suo tempo* (Rome, 1995); G. Rostirolla, ed., *Bibliografia degli scritti su G.P. d.P. (1568–1996)* (1997).—NS/LK/DM

Paliashvili, Zakhari (Petrovich), significant Georgian composer and pedagogue; b. Kutaisi, Aug. 16, 1871; d. Tiflis, Oct. 6, 1933. His father was a singer and his siblings were active in Georgian music. He studied with his older brother Ivan, and later, in 1887, he went to Tiflis, where he joined a Georgian national chorus. He also studied horn with Mosko (1891–95) and theory with Klenovsky (1895–99) at the music school there, then took a course with Taneyev at the Moscow Cons. (1900–03). Returning to Tiflis (1903), he assisted in the founding of the Georgian Phil. Soc. (1905) and directed its music school (1908–17). He publ. 2 collections of folk songs with native harmonies in 5 Georgian dialects under the pseudonym Palia (1910). Following the revolution, he became affiliated with the Tiflis Cons. (1917; prof., 1919; director, 1919; 1923; 1929–32). He was one of the founders of the nationalistic school of Georgian music, and, with Arakishvili and Balanchivadze, incorporated native elements into established musical formulas. Their operas were the first to use the Georgian language. His own opera *Abesalom and Eteri* (1919) was based upon a Georgian epic. He was awarded many honors during his life, including that of being made a National Artist of Georgia (1925). The Tbilisi opera house was named for him (1937), as was the Georgian State Prize (1971).

WORKS: DRAMATIC: O p e r a : *Abesalom and Eteri* (Tiflis, Feb. 21, 1919); *Daisi* (Twilight; Tiflis, Dec. 19, 1923); *Latavra* (Tiflis, March 16, 1928). **OTHER:** *Georgian Suite* for Orch. (1928); choruses; many songs for Voice and Piano.

BIBL.: S. Kashmadze, *Z. P.* (Tbilisi, 1948); V. Donadze, *Z. P.* (Moscow, 1958; 2nd ed., 1971); S. Aslanishvili, *The Road to "Abesalom"* (Tbilisi, 1971); A. Tsulukidze, *Z. P.* (Tbilisi, 1971); P. Khuchua, *Z. P.* (Tbilisi, 1974).—NS/LK/DM

Palisca, Claude V(ictor), esteemed American musicologist; b. Fiume, Yugoslavia, Nov. 24, 1921. He was taken to the U.S. as a child and in 1929 he became a naturalized American citizen. He was a student of Rathaus (composition) at Queens Coll. of the City Univ. of N.Y. (B.A., 1943), and of Piston and Thompson (composition) and Kinkeldey, Gombosi, and Davison (musicology) at Harvard Univ. (M.A., 1948; Ph.D., 1954, with the diss. *The Beginnings of Baroque Music: Its Roots in Sixteenth-century Theory and Polemics*). In 1949–50 he held a John Knowles Paine Traveling fellowship, and then studied in Italy on a Fulbright grant (1950–52). From 1953 to 1959 he taught at the Univ. of Ill. in Urbana. He was assoc. prof. (1959–64) and prof. (1964–80) of the history of music at Yale Univ., where he then was the Henry L. and Lucy G. Moses Prof. of Music from 1980 until being made a prof. emeritus in 1992. He also served as chairman of the music dept. (1969–75), and later as director of its graduate studies (1987–92). From 1966 he was ed. of the Yale Music Theory Translation Series. In 1971–72 he was president of the American Musicological Soc. In 1960–61 and 1981–82 he held Guggenheim fellowships. In 1972–73 he was a senior fellow of the NEH. He became a member of the American Academy of Arts and Sciences in 1986 and of the Accademia filarmonica of Bologna in 1987. In 1991 he was made an honorary member of the American Musicological Soc.

WRITINGS: *Girolamo Mei: Letters on Ancient and Modern Music to Vincenzo Galilei and Giovanni Bardi* (Rome, 1960; 2nd ed., 1977); with others, *Seventeenth Century Science and the Arts* (Princeton, N.J., 1961); with others, *Musicology* (Englewood Cliffs, N.J., 1963); *Baroque Music* (Englewood Cliffs, N.J., 1968; 3rd ed., 1991); *Music in Our Schools: A Search for Improvement* (Washington, D.C., 1964); with D. Grout, *A History of Western Music* (3rd ed., N.Y., 1980; 5th ed., 1995); ed. *Norton Anthology of Western Music* (2 vols., N.Y., 1980; 3rd ed., 1995); *Humanism in Italian Renaissance Musical Thought* (New Haven, 1985); *The Florentine Camerata: Documentary Studies and Translations* (New Haven, 1989); *Studies in the History of Italian Music and Music Theory* (Oxford, 1994).

BIBL.: N. Baker and B. Hanning, *Musical Humanism and Its Legacy: Essays in Honor of C. V. P.* (Stuyvesant, N.Y., 1992).—NS/LK/DM

Palkovský, Oldřich, Czech composer, father of **Pavel Palkovský;** b. Brušperk, Feb. 24, 1907; d. Gottwaldov, March 15, 1983. He studied with Petrželka at the Brno Cons. (1925–31) and Suk at the Prague Cons. (1931–33). He was director of the State Testing Commission for Music (1939–54), and taught at the Kromriz branch of the Brno Cons. (1950–67).

WORKS: ORCH.: 6 syms. (1933–34; 1939; 1944; 1947; 1956–57; 1962); Concerto for Cimbalom and Small Orch. (1952–53); *Scherzo capriccio* (1953); *Morvarian Dances* (1956); *Variations and Fugue* for Cimbalom, Strings, and Timpani (1959); Flute Concerto (1959); Oboe Concerto (1961); Accordion Concerto (1961); *3 Symphonic Movements* (1971); *Sinfonietta* (1978);

Small Suite (1981). **CHAMBER:** 10 string quartets (1931–81); 2 piano trios (1940, 1968); Violin Sonata (1942); 2 viola sonatas (1944, 1966); Concertino for Winds (1945); Cello Sonata (1946); Clarinet Sonata (1947); 4 wind quintets (1949–79); Quartet for Flute, Violin, Viola, and Cello (1950); Horn Sonata (1963); *Chamber Music* for 8 Instruments (1964); *Balladic Sonata* for Bassoon and Piano (1969); *Sonnets* for Flute, Bass Clarinet, and Piano (1969); Tuba Sonata (1978); Trumpet Sonata (1980); Sextet for Wind Instruments (1981); Wind Quartet (1982); piano pieces. **VOCAL:** Songs.—NS/LK/DM

Palkovský, Pavel, Czech composer, son of **Oldřich Palkovský;** b. Zlín, Dec. 18, 1939. He studied composition with Schaefer at the Brno Cons. (graduated, 1960), and with Kapr at the Janáček Academy of Music in Brno (graduated, 1964).

WORKS: ORCH.: 2 syms.: No. 1 (1964) and No. 2 for Piano and Orch. (1968–69); *Chamber Music I* for Strings, Piano, and Percussion (1964). **CHAMBER:** Cello Sonata (1963); *Chamber Music II* for Piano, Organ, Celesta, and Percussion (1968); Horn Sonata (1967); *3 Studies* for Accordion and 9 Winds (1969); Trio for 3 Accordions (1969); Suite for Tuba and Piano (1979); *Musica polyphonica* for Clarinet and Piano (1983). —NS/LK/DM

Pallandios, Menelaos, Greek composer and pedagogue; b. Piraeus, Feb. 11, 1914. He studied with Mitropoulos in Athens and with Casella in Rome. In 1936 he became an instructor at the Athens Cons., and in 1962 was appointed its director. In 1969 he was elected to the Athens Academy. He wrote music to several ancient Greek tragedies, endeavoring to re-create the classical modes in modern investiture.

WORKS: DRAMATIC: Opera: *Antigone* (1942). **Ballet:** *Pombi ston Aheronta* (Procession Towards Acheron; 1942); *Prosefhi se archaeo nao* (Prayer in the Ancient Temple; 1942); *Electra* (1944); *Penthesilea* (1944); *3 Archaic Suites* (1949); *Greek Triptych* (1960). **Other:** Incidental music to Greek dramas; film scores. **ORCH.:** *Suite in Ancient Style* for Strings (1941); *Prosefhi stin Akropoli* (Prayer on the Akropolis; 1942); *Narcissus* (1942); *Greek Classical Overture* (1944); Sym. (1948); *Divertimento* (1952); Piano Concerto (1958). **CHAMBER:** *5 Character Pieces* for Oboe, Clarinet, and Bassoon (1962); piano music.

BIBL.: M. Pallandios, ed., *M.G. P., moussourgos* (Athens, 1968).—NS/LK/DM

Pallavicino, Benedetto, Italian composer; b. Cremona, 1551; d. Mantua, Nov. 26, 1601. He was a court musician in Mantua from 1583 and maestro di cappella to the Duke from 1596. Monteverdi mentions Pallavicino's death in a letter applying for his post to the Duke of Mantua (Nov. 28, 1601). Pallavicino was a particularly distinguished composer of madrigals.

WORKS: VOCAL: Sacred: *Liber primus missarum* for 4 to 6 Voices (Venice, 1603); *Sacrae Dei laudes* for 8, 12, and 16 Voices (Venice, 1605); motet for 5 Voices, etc. **Secular:** *Il primo libro de madrigali* for 4 Voices (Venice, 1579); *Il primo libro de madrigali* for 5 Voices (Venice, 1581); *Il secondo libro de madrigali* for 5 Voices (Venice, 1584); *Il terzo libro de madrigali* for 5 Voices (Venice, 1585); *Il primo libro de madrigali* for 6 Voices (Venice, 1587); *Il quatro libro de madrigali* for 5 Voices (Venice,

1588); *Il quinto libro de madrigali* for 5 Voices (Venice, 1593); *El sesto libro de madrigali* for 5 Voices (Venice, 1600); *Il settimo libro de madrigali* for 5 Voices (Venice, 1604); *L'ottavo libro de madrigali* for 5 Voices (Venice, 1612).

BIBL.: T. Bridges, *The Madrigals of B. P.* (diss., Univ. of Calif., 1952); P. Flanders, *The Five-Part Madrigals of B. P.* (diss., N.Y.U., 1972); idem, *A Thematic Index to the Works of B. P.* (Hackensack, N.J., 1974).—**NS/LK/DM**

Pallavicino, Carlo, Italian composer; b. Salo, near Brescia, date unknown; d. Dresden, Jan. 29, 1688. He served as an organista ai concerti at S. Antonio in Padua in 1665–66, and in 1673–74 was maestro dei concerti there. He became a Vice-Kapellmeister at the Dresden court in 1667; was named Kapellmeister in 1672. In 1674 he was named maestro di coro of the Ospedale degli Incurabili in Venice. In succeeding years he became one of the leading opera composers in Venice. In 1685 he accepted an invitation from the Elector Johann Georg III of Saxony to resume his former post as Dresden Kapellmeister. On Jan. 1, 1687, he assumed his duties as director of theater and chamber music. Thirteen of his operas are extant.—**NS/LK/DM**

Pallo, Imre, Hungarian-American conductor; b. Budapest, May 15, 1941. He was a student of Kodály at the Budapest Academy of Music and of Swarowsky at the Vienna Academy of Music. After conducting in Europe, he made his U.S. debut as a guest conductor with the National Sym. Orch. in Washington, D.C., in 1973. He subsequently conducted at the N.Y.C. Opera. From 1976 to 1991 he was music director of the Hudson Valley Phil. in Poughkeepsie, N.Y. He also held the post of 1st conductor of the Frankfurt am Main Opera from 1987. In 1994 he joined the faculty of the Ind. Univ. School of Music in Bloomington.—**NS/LK/DM**

Palm, Siegfried, noted German cellist, pedagogue, and operatic administrator; b. Barmen, April 25, 1927. He studied cello with his father, a member of the City Orch. in Wuppertal. After playing in the City Orch. in Lübeck (1945–47), he joined the North German Radio Sym. Orch. in Hamburg (1947). He served as a member of the Cologne Radio Sym. Orch. (1962–67); in 1962, joined the faculty of the Cologne Hochschule für Musik; was appointed its director in 1972. From 1977 to 1981 he was Intendant of the Deutsche Oper in West Berlin, while continuing his career as a cellist. From 1981 to 1988 he was president of the ISCM. He traveled widely in Africa and Asia with the purpose of studying native music. He commissioned several modern composers, among them Blacher, Kagel, Keleman, Ligeti, Penderecki, Xenakis, and Zimmermann, to write special works which he premiered. He also contributed scholarly treatises on the new techniques of string instruments.—**NS/LK/DM**

Palma, Athos, Argentine composer and teacher; b. Buenos Aires, June 7, 1891; d. Miramar, Jan. 10, 1951. He studied with C. Troiani (piano) and other teachers in Buenos Aires; in 1904, went to Europe, returning to Buenos Aires in 1914. There he was busily engaged as a teacher. He publ. *Teoría razonada de la música* (5 vols., n.d.) and *Tratado completo de armonía* (1941). His music follows the Italian tradition, although the subject matter is derived from South American history and literature.

WORKS: DRAMATIC: Opera: *Nazdah* (Buenos Aires, June 19, 1924); *Los Hijos del Sol* (Buenos Aires, Nov. 10, 1928). **ORCH.:** *Cantares de mi tierra* for Strings (1914); 2 symphonic poems: *Jardines* (1926) and *Los Hijos del Sol* (1929). **CHAMBER:** Cello Sonata (1912); Violin Sonata (1924); Piano Sonata. **VOCAL:** Many songs.

BIBL.: N. Lamuraglia, *A. P.: Vida, arte, educación* (Buenos Aires, 1954).—**NS/LK/DM**

Palma, Silvestro, Italian composer; b. Barano d'Ischia, March 15, 1754; d. Naples, Aug. 8, 1834. He studied at the Cons. San Maria di Loreto in Naples and with Paisiello. Palma was particularly successful as a composer of comic operas.

WORKS: DRAMATIC (all are commedie per musica and were 1st perf. in Naples unless otherwise given): *La finta Matta* (1789); *Gli amanti dell dote*, dramma giocoso (Florence, 1791); *Le nozze in villa*, intermezzo (Rome, Carnival 1792); *Chi mal fa, mal aspetti, ovvero Lo scroccatore smascherato*, dramma tragicomico (Venice, 1792); *L'ingaggiatore di campagna*, intermezzo (Florence, 1792); *La pietra simpatica* (1795); *Gli amanti ridicoli* (1797); *Il pallone aerostatico* (1802); *Le sequaci di Diana* (1805); *L'erede senza eredità* (Sept. 29, 1808); *Lo scavamento* (April 29, 1810); *I furbi amanti* (1810); *Il palazzo delle fate* (1812); *I vampiri* (1812); *Le miniere di Polonia*, melodramma (1813). **OTHER:** Several sacred works.—**LK/DM**

Palmer, Felicity (Joan), admired English soprano; b. Cheltenham, April 6, 1944. She received her training at the Guildhall School of Music in London (1962–67) and from Marianne Schech at the Munich Hochschule für Musik. She first sang in the John Alldis Choir and the Purcell Consort in London. In 1970 she won the Kathleen Ferrier Memorial Scholarship and made her formal debut in Purcell's *Dioclesian* at London's Queen Elizabeth Hall. She made her operatic debut as Dido with the Kent Opera in 1971. In 1973 she made her U.S. operatic debut as Mozart's Countess with the Houston Grand Opera. In 1975 she made her first appearance with the English National Opera in London as Pamina. She continued to make regular appearances in opera in London in subsequent years. She also pursued a highly successful career as a soloist with orchs. and as a recitalist. In 1973, 1977, and 1984 she toured Europe as soloist with the BBC Sym. Orch. After singing opera in Bern (1977), Frankfurt am Main (1978), and Zürich (1980), she made her Glyndebourne debut as Florence in *Albert Herring* in 1985. In 1986 she appeared as Kabanicha in *Kát'a Kabanová* at the Chicago Lyric Opera. In 1987 she sang in the first perf. of Testi's *Riccardo III* at Milan's La Scala. She made her debut at the Salzburg Festival in 1988 as a soloist in *Messiah*. In 1992 she sang the title role in the stage premiere of Roberto Gerhard's *The Duenna* in Madrid. She portrayed Clytemnestra at Covent Garden in 1997. Palmer's operatic and concert repertoire is notable for its range, from early music to the avant-garde. In 1993 she was made a Commander of the Order of the British Empire. —**NS/LK/DM**

Palmer, Larry, American harpsichordist, organist, and teacher; b. Warren, Ohio, Nov. 13, 1938. He studied at the Oberlin (Ohio) Coll. Cons. of Music and with David Craighead (organ) at the Eastman School of Music in Rochester, N.Y. (D.M.A., 1963). He also received training in harpsichord from Ahlgrimm at the Salzburg Mozarteum and from Leonhardt in Haarlem. In 1969 he became the harpsichord ed. of *The Diapason*. From 1970 he served as prof. of harpsichord and organ at Southern Methodist Univ. in Dallas. He also toured widely as a harpsichordist and organist in the U.S. and Europe. He publ. the vols. *Hugo Distler and his Church Music* (1967) and *Harpsichord in America: A 20th Century Revival* (1989; 2nd ed., 1992). Palmer has championed the organ music of Distler and has performed an extensive repertoire of harpsichord music, ranging from the 17th century to the present era.—NS/LK/DM

Palmer, Robert (Alan), British blue-eyed soul singer and hit maker of the 1980s; b. Batley, England, Jan. 19, 1949. After spending his early years on Malta, where his father served as a naval intelligence officer, Robert Palmer first enjoyed fame as the lead singer and guitarist for Vinegar Joe, a late 1960s–early 1970s English blues–influenced band in the Allman Brothers mold. Although they were a popular live band, opening for Jimi Hendrix, The Who, and others, their fans didn't buy their records, and after three albums they went their separate ways.

In the mid-1970s, Palmer went to America, where he recorded his first solo album *Sneakin' Sally through the Alley* with The Meters's New Orleans funk rhythm section and members of Little Feat. While critically well-received, the album sold poorly, as did his next two albums *Pressure Drop* and *Some People Can Do What They Like*. In 1978 Palmer moved to the sunny climes of Nassau in the Bahamas, where he cut *Double Fun*. The album yielded his first pop hit, the Marvin Gaye–ish "Every Kinda People," which reached #16 on the pop chart. His next album, *Secrets*, found his version of the bar-band raunchy "Bad Case of Loving You (Doctor Doctor)" playing leapfrog in the charts with the Moon Martin original. Palmer's version eventually became the pop hit, rising to #14. His version of Todd Rundgren's "Can We Still Be Friends" from the same album also garnered rock airplay. The album went to #19.

Palmer followed this with an album of electro-pop featuring Gary Numan and members of Talking Heads, 1980's *Clues*. While the title track garnered some rock airplay in the U.S., the album was a much bigger hit in England, with the title track, "Johnny and Mary" and the single-only "Some Guys Have All the Luck" becoming hits. He then released a live album that also sold poorly.

Palmer had not had a U.S. hit in more than four years when John and Andy Taylor from Duran Duran asked him to join them, along with the Chic rhythm section of Bernard Edwards and Tony Thompson, in the group Power Station in 1983. Palmer had already started working on his next album, but couldn't pass up the offer. The exposure he gained was priceless. The group had two Top Ten singles, the #6 "Some Like It Hot" and

the #9 cover of T. Rex's "Get It On." This gave Palmer pop radio exposure as well as putting him all over MTV. This exposure helped launch his next and first widely successful album, 1985's *Riptide*. The first single from the album, the crunchy, high-gloss rock tune "Addicted to Love" zoomed to the top of the pop charts, going gold. This was no doubt aided by the promotional video for the song, which featured a group of instrument-wielding models in little black dresses "accompanying" Palmer. While the follow-up, "Hyperactive," didn't break the Top 30, his cover of Cherelle's modern funk tune "I Didn't Mean to Turn You On" rose to #2. The album went to #8 and sold platinum, eventually going double platinum. In the course of a year, Palmer had gone from middling success to stardom.

Palmer moved his family to Switzerland, and then recorded *Heavy Nova*, released in 1988. This album explored his interests in Brazilian pop and heavy metal, without losing his funky edge. The first single, "Simply Irresistible," covered similar ground as that of "Addicted to Love" (even the video mirrored the earlier hit, with another bevy of well-endowed babes), with similar results, rising to #2. A cover of The Gap Band's 1982 funk hit "Early in the Morning" followed, peaking at #19. The album rose to #13 and also went platinum.

Palmer followed this with *Don't Explain*, an eclectic selection featuring the soca-flavored "Housework," "People Will Say We're in Love" from *Oklahoma*, a cover of Antonio Carlos Jobim's "Aeroplane," and a reggae version of Bob Dylan's "I'll Be Your Baby Tonight" recorded with UB40. Such an eclectic mix was bound to confuse his fans. The single "You're Amazing" reached only #28, however, while his medley of Marvin Gaye's "Mercy Mercy Me/I Want You" rose to #16.

Palmer has been unable to equal his earlier chart success since then, although he continues to have a strong cult following. His 1992 release, *Ridin' High*, explored his early fondness for singers like Nat King Cole and the music of Tin Pan Alley. Two years later, *Honey* brought Palmer together with legendary jazz producer Teo Macero and hard-rocking guitarist Nuno Bettencourt (albeit on acoustic guitar). In an attempt to regain some chart steam, Palmer reunited with The Power Station, but the reunion fizzled. He returned as a solo act in 1999 with *Rhythm and Blues*, a set that reunited him with members of Little Feat.

Disc.: *Sneakin' Sally through the Alley* (1974); *Pressure Drop* (1976); *Some People Can Do What They Like* (1976); *Double Fun* (1978); *Secrets* (1979); *Clues* (1980); *Maybe It's Live* (1982); *Pride* (1983); *Riptide* (1985); *Heavy Nova* (1988); *Don't Explain* (1990); *Ridin' High* (1992); *True Romance* (1993); *Honey* (1994); *Rhythm and Blues* (1999).—HB

Palmer, Robert (Moffat), American composer and teacher; b. Syracuse, N.Y., June 2, 1915. He studied at the Eastman School of Music in Rochester, N.Y., with Hanson and Rogers (B.M., 1938; M.M., 1940), and also studied with Harris (1939), Copland (1940), and Porter. He held 2 Guggenheim fellowships (1952–53; 1960–61) and a Fulbright Senior fellowship for study in Italy (1960–61). From 1940 to 1943 he was on the faculty at the Univ. of Kans., and from 1943 to 1980 he taught at

Cornell Univ. In his music, he generally adhered to neo-Classical principles while producing works of a distinctive originality.

WORKS: ORCH.: *Poem* for Violin and Chamber Orch. (1938); Concerto for Small Orch. (1940); *K 19*, symphonic elegy for Thomas Wolfe (1945); Chamber Concerto for Violin, Oboe, and Strings (1949); *Variations, Chorale and Fugue* (1947; rev. 54); 2 syms. (1953, 1966); *Memorial Music* (1960); *Centennial Overture* (1965); *Choric Songs and Toccata* for Band (1968); Piano Concerto (1971); *Overture on a Southern Hymn* for Symphonic Band (1979); Concerto for 2 Pianos, 2 Percussion, Strings, and Brass (1984). CHAMBER: 4 string quartets (1939; 1943, rev. 1947; 1954; 1959); 2 piano quartets (1947, 1973); Piano Quintet (1950); Viola Sonata (1951); Quintet for Clarinet, Strings, and Piano (1952; rev. 1953); Violin Sonata (1956); Piano Trio (1958); *Organon I* for Flute and Clarinet (1962) and *II* for Violin and Viola (1975); Trumpet Sonata (1972); *Sinfonia Concertante* for 9 Instruments (1972); 2 cello sonatas (1978, 1983). P i a n o : 3 sonatas (1938, rev. 1946; 1942, rev. 1948; 1979); Sonata for 2 Pianos (1944); Sonata for Piano, 4-Hands (1952); *Evening Music* (1956); *7 Epigrams* (1957–59); *Morning Music* (1973). VOCAL: *Abraham Lincoln Walks at Midnight* for Chorus and Orch. (1948); *Carmina amoris* for Soprano, Clarinet, Violin, and Piano (1951; also for Soprano and Chamber Orch.); *Of Night and the Sea*, chamber cantata (1956); *Nabuchodonosor*, dramatic oratorio (1964); *Portents of Aquarius (Visions and Prophecies)* for Narrator, Chorus, and Organ (1975).—NS/LK/DM

Palmgren, Selim, eminent Finnish composer and teacher; b. Björneborg, Feb. 16, 1878; d. Helsinki, Dec. 13, 1951. He studied piano and composition at the Helsinki Cons. (1895–99), then went to Berlin, where he continued his piano studies with Ansorge, Berger, and Busoni. Returning to Finland, he became active as a choral conductor in Helsinki (1902–04), and from 1909 to 1912 he was director of the Music Soc. in Turku. In 1921 he made a tour of the U.S. as a pianist. From 1923 to 1926 he taught piano and composition at the Eastman School of Music in Rochester, N.Y. He then returned to Helsinki, becoming a prof. of harmony and composition at the Sibelius Academy in 1936, remaining there until his death. He was married to the Finnish soprano Maikki Pakarinen in 1910, after her divorce from Armas Järnefelt. He publ. *Minusta tuli muusikko* (Helsinki, 1948). He excelled in piano compositions, often tinged with authentic Finnish colors; some of his pieces are marked by effective impressionistic devices, such as whole-tone scales and consecutive mild dissonances. Among his piano miniatures, *May Night* enjoyed considerable popularity with music students and their teachers.

WORKS: DRAMATIC: O p e r a : *Daniel Hjort* (Turku, April 15, 1910; rev. version, Helsinki, 1938); *Peter Schlemihl.* ORCH.: 5 piano concertos: No. 1 (1903), No. 2, *Virta* (The Stream; 1913), No. 3, *Metamorphoses* (1915), No. 4, *Huhtikuu* (April; 1924–26), and No. 5 (1939–41); *Pastorale* (1920); *Ballet Music* (1944); *Concert Fantasy* for Violin and Orch. (1945). P i a n o : 2 sonatas; *Fantasia*; *24 Preludes*; *Ballade*; *Finnische Lyrik* (12 pieces); *Finnische Suite (The Seasons)*; *Maskenball*, suite; *24 Etudes* (1921–22); etc. VOCAL: *Turun lilja* (The Lily of Turku), cantata (1929); songs and men's choruses.—NS/LK/DM

Palombo, Paul (Martin), American composer; b. Pittsburgh, Sept. 10, 1937. He was trained in electron-

ics; studied composition at the Peabody Cons. of Music in Baltimore and at the Eastman School of Music in Rochester, N.Y. (Ph.D., 1969), with Barlow and Rogers. In 1969 he was appointed to the faculty of the Univ. of Cincinnati (Ohio) Coll.-Cons. of Music; in 1973, assumed the direction of the electronic music studio there; then was director of the music school of the Univ. of Wash. in Seattle (1978–81); in 1981 he became dean of the Coll. of Fine Arts at the Univ. of Wisc. in Stevens Point.

WORKS: DRAMATIC: B a l l e t : *Proteus* (1969). ORCH.: *Serenade* for Strings (1964); Sinfonietta for Chamber Orch. (1965); *Movement* (1967); *Variations* (1967–68). CHAMBER: Cello Sonata (1966); String Quartet No. 1 (1966–67); *Metatheses* for Flute, Oboe, Double Bass, and Harpsichord (1970); *Montage* for Violin and Piano (1971); *Ritratti anticamente* for Viola and Piano (1972; rev. 1974); *4 Sonos: I* for Harpsichord and Tape (1972), *II* for Harp and Tape (1972), *III* for Double Bass and Tape (1973), and *IV* for String Trio and Tape (1974); *Variatione da camera* for Flute, Clarinet, Viola, Cello, Piano, and 2 Percussion (1980). KEYBOARD: Piano Sonata (1965); *Variants* for Harpsichord (1975). VOCAL: *Moody Blues* for Voices and Dance Band (1981); *Morning Memories* for Voice and Piano (1981); *It's Over* for Voice and Piano (1981). ELECTRONIC: *Morphosis*, ballet (1970); *Crystals*, multimedia score (1971); *Etcetera*, ballet (1973); *Stegowagenvolkssaurus*, music for a sculpture (1973–74); *Music for Triceratops Americus* (1977). OTHER: *Laser Music* for Tape (1975); *The Dance* for Dance Band (1980). —NS/LK/DM

Palomino, José, Spanish composer; b. Madrid, 1755; d. Las Palmas, April 9, 1810. He became a violinist in the Spanish royal chapel at an early age, and received training from Rodriguez de Hita. He first gained notice as a composer of tonadillas, his *El canapé* (Madrid, 1769) being particularly well received. In 1774 he went to Lisbon and entered the S. Cecilia brotherhood. By 1785 he was a violinist in the Portuguese royal chapel. His opera *Il ritorno di Astrea in terra* (June 15, 1785), presented in honor of the double marriages of the Portuguese and Spanish infantes, was a notable success. After the royal family fled in the face of Napoleon's invasion, Palomino settled in Las Palmas as maestro de capilla in 1808.—LK/DM

Palsa, Johann, esteemed Bohemian horn player; b. Jemeritz, June 20, 1752; d. Berlin, Jan. 24, 1792. He received training in Prague, and by 1770 he was in Paris, where he performed in duos with Carl Türrschmidt. They also were members in the private orch. of the Prince of Monaco. In 1783 they joined the orch. of the Landgrave of Hessen-Kassel. After appearing in London in 1786, they joined the Berlin court musical establishment the same year.—LK/DM

Pálsson, Páll (Pampichler), Icelandic composer and conductor; b. Graz (of Icelandic parents), May 9, 1928. He studied with Michl, Mixa, and Brugger in Graz and conducting at the Hamburg Hochschule für Musik (1959–60). He was active as a conductor in Reykjavík, where he led both choral and instrumental ensembles.

WORKS: ORCH.: Bassoon Concerto (1961); *Divertimento* (1965); *Suite Arctica* (1969); *Dialoge* (1974); *Hugleiding um L*

(1977); *Faein Haustlaug* (1979); *Fléttuleikur* for Orch. and Jazz Quartet (1981); Clarinet Concerto (1982); *Tonlist á Tyllidögum* (1984); *Sinfonietta Concertante* (1988); *Concerti di Giubileo* (1989); Violin Concerto (1998). CHAMBER: *Sextet 1949* (1949); Wind Quartet (1954); *Kristallar* for Chamber Ensemble (1970); *Mixed Things* for Flute and Piano (1976); *Lantao* for Oboe, Harp, and Percussion (1979); *Music* for 6 Instruments (1982); Nonet (1984); *Capriccio* for Saxophone Quartet (1992); *Expromptu* for Violin and Piano (1997). VOCAL: *Requiem-Kyrie-Dies irae* for Chorus (1968); choruses; songs.—NS/LK/DM

Paminger, Leonhard, Austrian composer; b. Aschach an der Donau, March 25, 1495; d. Passau, May 3, 1567. His education commenced in Vienna in 1505, where he matriculated at the Univ. (1513–16) and sang in the Stadtkantorei at St. Stephen's. As a composer, he was autodidact. In 1516 he settled in Passau and soon became schoolmaster at St. Nikola's. In 1529 he became its Rektor, a position he lost when he espoused the Lutheran faith in 1557. However, he was allowed to retain the position of secretary there until his death. Paminger's music was widely known in his day, and was included in various French and Italian anthologies. Among his works were Latin antiphons, responsories, motets, Psalms, and hymns, as well as German Lutheran hymns.

BIBL.: C. Hirsch, *De vita P. orum commentarius* (Oettingen, c. 1764); I. Roth, *L. P.: Ein Beitrag zur deutschen Musikgeschichte des 16. Jahrhunderts* (Munich, 1935).—LK/DM

Pampani, Antonio Gaetano, Italian composer; b. Modena, c. 1705; d. Urbino, Dec. 1775. He was a student of Salviati in Urbino. From 1726 to 1734 he was maestro di cappella at Fano Cathedral. He served as director of the chorus and orch. at the Ospedaletto orphanage in Venice from 1749 to 1764. In 1767 he was made maestro di cappella at Urbino Cathedral. He composed some 18 stage works, mainly opere serie (1730–68). Among his other works were various oratorios, solo motets, concertos, and sonatas.—NS/LK/DM

Pampanini, Rosetta, Italian soprano; b. Milan, Sept. 2, 1896; d. Corbola, Aug. 2, 1973. She studied with Emma Molajoli in Milan. She made her operatic debut as Micaëla in Rome in 1920, and then continued her vocal studies. In 1925 she joined La Scala in Milan, remaining on its roster until 1937, with the exception of the 1931–33 seasons; also sang at Covent Garden in London (1928, 1929, 1933) and in Chicago (1931–32). After retiring in 1942, she taught voice. She was particularly admired for her Puccini roles, most notably Manon, Cio-Cio-San, and Mimi.—NS/LK/DM

Pandolfini, Angelica, Italian soprano, daughter of **Francesco Pandolfini**; b. Spoleto, Aug. 21, 1871; d. Lenno, July 15, 1959. She studied with Jules Massart in Paris. She made her debut as Marguerite in 1894 in Modena; after singing in the Italian provinces, she appeared at La Scala in Milan (1897–99; 1906). She created the title role in *Adriana Lecouvreur* at the Teatro Lirico in Milan in 1902; retired from the stage in 1908. She was best known for her convincing portrayals of verismo roles.—NS/LK/DM

Pandolfini, Francesco, Italian baritone, father of **Angelica Pandolfini**; b. Termini Imerese, Palermo, Nov. 22, 1836; d. Milan, Feb. 15, 1916. He studied with Ronconi and Vannuccini in Florence, making his debut in Gemma di Vergy in Pisa in 1859; then sang throughout Italy. In 1871 he appeared with notable success at La Scala in Milan, creating the role of Arnoldo in *I Lituani* by Ponchielli there in 1874. He also sang at Covent Garden in London (1877, 1882). He retired from the stage in 1890.—NS/LK/DM

Pane, Domenico dal
See **Dal Pane, Domenico**

Panenka, Jan, Czech pianist and teacher; b. Prague, July 8, 1922. He was a student of Maxián in Prague and of Serebryakov in Leningrad. In 1944 he made his debut in Prague. After winning the Prague Piano Competition in 1951, he toured widely as a soloist. He devoted much time to chamber music, serving as a member of the Suk Trio of Prague from 1957. He also taught at the Prague Academy of Music. In 1972 he was made an Artist of Merit by the Czech government.—NS/LK/DM

Panerai, Rolando, Italian baritone; b. Campi Bisenzio, near Florence, Oct. 17, 1924. He studied at the Florence Cons. with Frazzi and also with di Armani and Tess in Milan. After winning 1st prize in the voice competition in Spoleto, he made his debut as Faraone in *Mosè in Egitto* in Naples (1947). In 1951 he joined La Scala in Milan; also sang at Covent Garden in London, the Vienna State Opera, and the Salzburg Festivals. He specialized in the Italian repertoire.—NS/LK/DM

Panizza, Ettore, Argentine conductor and composer of Italian descent; b. Buenos Aires, Aug. 12, 1875; d. Milan, Nov. 27, 1967. He studied at the Milan Cons., graduating in 1898 with prizes for piano and composition. From 1907 to 1914 and again in 1924 he conducted at London's Covent Garden. He made his first appearance at the Teatro Colón in Buenos Aires (1908), conducting there regularly from 1921. He joined the roster of Milan's La Scala (1916), serving as assistant to Toscanini (1921–29); was a regular conductor there (1930–32; 1946–48); also conducted at the Chicago Civic Opera (1922–24) and N.Y.'s Metropolitan Opera (1934–42). He publ. an autobiography, *Medio siglo de vida musical* (Buenos Aires, 1952).

WORKS: DRAMATIC: Opera: *Il Fidanzato del mare* (Buenos Aires, Aug. 15, 1897); *Medio evo latino* (Genoa, Nov. 17, 1900); *Aurora* (Buenos Aires, Sept. 5, 1908); *Bisanzio* (Buenos Aires, July 25, 1939). OTHER: *Il Re della foresta* for Soloists, Chorus, and Orch.; *Tema con variaciones* for Orch.; Violin Sonata; Cello Sonata; String Quartet; piano pieces; songs.—NS/LK/DM

Pankiewicz, Eugeniusz, Polish pianist and composer; b. Siedlce, Dec. 15, 1857; d. Tworki, near Warsaw, Dec. 24, 1898. He studied piano in Lublin, then went to Warsaw to study with J. Wieniawski. He later took master classes with Leschetizky in St. Petersburg, and also studied composition with W. Zelenski

(1880–81) and Z. Noskowski (1881–83) in Warsaw. He subsequently taught piano at the Warsaw Music Inst. He was confined to a mental hospital (from 1895). He became best known for his attractive songs and piano miniatures, the latter revealing the influence of Chopin.

BIBL.: W. Poźniak, *E. P.* (Kraków, 1958; with thematic catalogue of works).—**NS/LK/DM**

Pannain, Guido, distinguished Italian musicologist and composer; b. Naples, Nov. 17, 1891; d. there, Sept. 6, 1977. He studied composition with C. de Nardis at the Naples Cons. (graduated, 1914). He was prof. of music history at the Naples Cons. (1915–61), and also wrote music criticism. As a musicologist, he devoted much of his time to the study of Neapolitan music.

WRITINGS: *La teoria musicale di Giovanni Tinctoris* (Naples, 1913); *Le origini della scuola musicale napoletana* (Naples, 1914); *Le origini e lo sviluppo dell'arte pianistica in Italia dal 1500 fino al 1730 circa* (Naples, 1917); *Lineamenti di storia della musica* (Naples, 1922; 9ᵗʰ ed., rev., 1970); *Musica e musicisti in Napoli nel secolo XIX* (Naples, 1922); *Musicisti dei tempi nuovi* (Milan, 1932; Eng. tr., 1932, as *Modern Composers*; 2ⁿᵈ Italian ed., 1954); with A. della Corte, *Storia della musica* (Turin, 1936; 4ᵗʰ ed., 1964); *Il Conservatorio di musica di S. Pietro in Maiella* (Florence, 1942); *La vita del linguaggio musicale* (Milan, 1947; 2ⁿᵈ ed., 1956); *Ottocento musicale italiano: Saggi e note* (Milan, 1952); *L'opera e le opere ed altri scritti di letteratura musicale* (Milan, 1958); *Giuseppe Verdi* (Turin, 1964); *Richard Wagner: Vita di un artista* (Milan, 1964).

WORKS: DRAMATIC: Opera: *L'Intrusa* (1926; Genoa, 1940); *Beatrice Cenci* (Naples, Feb. 21, 1942); *Madame Bovary* (Naples, April 16, 1955). **ORCH.:** 2 violin concertos (1930, 1960); Viola Concerto (1955); Harp Concerto (1959); Piano Concerto (1969). **VOCAL:** *Requiem* (1912); *Stabat Mater* (1969). —**NS/LK/DM**

Panseron, Auguste-Mathieu, French singing teacher and composer; b. Paris, April 26, 1795; d. there, July 29, 1859. His father, who orchestrated many operas for Grétry, taught him until he entered the Paris Cons. in 1804, where he studied under Gossec, Levasseur, and Berton, winning the Prix de Rome in 1813. After study in Bologna, Rome, Naples, Vienna (with Salieri), and Munich, he returned to Paris in 1818, taught singing, was an accompanist at the Opéra-Comique, and wrote 4 one-act operas. He became a prof. of solfeggio at the Cons. in 1826, of vocalization in 1831, and of singing in 1836. From 1825 to 1840 he brought out some 200 *romances*. He also composed church music, but attained real eminence as a vocal teacher and as a writer of instructive works on singing.—**NS/LK/DM**

Pantaleoni, Adriano, Italian baritone, brother of **Romilda Pantaleoni;** b. Udine, Oct. 7, 1837; d. there, Dec. 18, 1908. He studied in Udine and Milan. He was a principal member of La Scala in Milan (1871–77; 1896), and also sang in London and the U.S. (1879). After his retirement, he taught voice in Udine and Trieste. He was particularly noted for his roles in Verdi's operas. —**NS/LK/DM**

Pantaleoni, Romilda, Italian soprano, sister of **Adriano Pantaleoni;** b. Udine, 1847; d. Milan, May 20, 1917. She studied with Prati, Rossi, and Lamperti in Milan, making her debut at the Teatro Carcano in Milan in Foroni's *Margherita* in 1868. She then sang in Turin and at La Scala in Milan, where she created the role of Desdemona in Verdi's *Otello* in 1887 and Tigrana in Puccini's *Edgar* in 1889.—**NS/LK/DM**

Panufnik, Sir Andrzej, eminent Polish-born English conductor and composer; b. Warsaw, Sept. 24, 1914; d. London, Oct. 27, 1991. His father was a Polish manufacturer of string instruments, his mother an Englishwoman who studied violin in Warsaw. He began his musical training with his mother; after studying composition with Sikorski at the Warsaw Cons. (diploma, 1936), he took conducting lessons with Weingartner at the Vienna Academy of Music (1937–38); subsequently completed his training with Gaubert in Paris, and also studied in London (1938–39). He returned to Warsaw in 1939, remaining there during the Nazi occupation, playing piano in the underground. After the liberation, he conducted the Kraków Phil. (1945–46) and the Warsaw Phil. (1946–47); he then left his homeland in protest of the Communist regime (1954), settling in England, where he became a naturalized British subject (1961). After serving as music director of the City of Birmingham Sym. Orch. (1957–59), he devoted himself to composition. His wife, Scarlett Panufnik, publ. *Out of the City of Fear* (London, 1956), recounting his flight from Poland; his autobiography was publ. as *Composing Myself* (London, 1986). In 1988 he appeared as a guest conductor of his own works with the N.Y. Chamber Sym. and in 1990 with the Chicago Sym. Orch. In 1991 he was knighted. In his early years, he belonged to the vanguard group of Polish composers. He made use of advanced techniques, including quarter tones, and made certain innovations in notation; in several of his orch. works, he left blank spaces in the place of rests to indicate inactive instrumental parts. In his later music, he adopted a more circumspect idiom—expressive, direct, and communicative. His compositions to 1944 were destroyed during the Warsaw uprising.

WORKS: ORCH.: *Tragic Overture* (1942; Warsaw, 1943; reconstructed 1945; rev. 1955); *Nocturne* (1947; Paris, 1948; rev. 1955); *Lullaby* for 29 Strings and 2 Harps (1947; Kraków, 1948; rev. 1955); *Divertimento* for Strings, after trios by Felix Janiewicz (1947; Kraków, 1948; rev. 1955); 10 syms.: No. 1, *Sinfonica Rustica* (1948; Kraków, 1949; rev. 1955), No. 2, *Sinfonica Elegiaca* (Houston, Nov. 21, 1957; rev. 1966), No. 3, *Sinfonia Sacra* (1963; Monte Carlo, Aug. 12, 1964), No. 4, *Sinfonia Concertante*, for Flute, Harp, and Strings (1973; London, May 20, 1974), No. 5, *Sinfonia di Sfere* (1974–75; London, April 13, 1976), No. 6, *Sinfonia Mistica* (1977; Middlesborough, England, Jan. 17, 1978), No. 7, *Metasinfonia*, for Organ, Timpani, and Strings (Manchester, England, Sept. 9, 1978), No. 8, *Sinfonia Votiva* (1981; Boston, Jan. 28, 1982; rev. 1984), No. 9, *Sinfonia di Speranza* (1986; London, Feb. 25, 1987), and No. 10 (1989; Chicago, Feb. 1, 1990); *Old Polish Suite* for Strings (1950; Warsaw, 1951; rev. 1955); *Concerto in modo antico* for Trumpet and Orch. (Kraków, 1951; rev. 1955); *Heroic Overture* (Helsinki, July 27, 1952; rev. 1969); *Rhapsody* (1956; BBC, London, Jan. 11, 1957); *Polonia* (London, Aug. 21, 1959); Piano Concerto (Birmingham, England, Jan. 25, 1962; rev. 1970, 1972, and 1982); *Landscape* for Strings (1962; rev. version,

Twickenham, Nov. 13, 1965); *Autumn Music* (1962; rev. 1965; Paris, Jan. 16, 1968); *Jagiellonian Triptych* for Strings (London, Sept. 24, 1966); *Katyn Epitaph* (1967; N.Y., Nov. 17, 1968; rev. 1969); Concerto for Violin and String Orch. (1971; London, July 18, 1972); *Concerto Festivo* (London, June 17, 1979); Concertino for Timpani, Percussion, and Strings (1979–80; London, Jan. 24, 1981); *A Procession for Peace* (1982–83; London, July 16, 1983); *Arbor Cosmica*, 12 evocations for 12 Strings or String Orch. (1983; N.Y., Nov. 14, 1984); Concerto for Bassoon and Small Orch. (1985; Milwaukee, May 18, 1986); *Harmony* (N.Y., Dec. 16, 1989); Cello Concerto (1991; London, June 24, 1992). **CHAMBER:** Piano Trio (1934; Warsaw, 1935; reconstructed 1945; rev. 1977); *Quintetto Accadèmico* for Flute, Oboe, 2 Clarinets, and Bassoon (1953; rev. 1956); *Triangles* for 3 Flutes and 3 Cellos (BBC-TV, April 14, 1972); 3 string quartets: No. 1 (London, Oct. 19, 1976), No. 2, *Messages* (St. Asaph's Cathedral, North Wales, Sept. 25, 1980), and No. 3, *Wycinanki* (1990; London, April 15, 1991); String Sextet, *Trains of Thought* (1987; London, Feb. 21, 1988). **Piano:** *12 Miniature Studies* (1947; rev. 1955–64); *Reflections* (1968; London, April 21, 1972); *Pentasonata* (1984; Aldeburgh, June 23, 1989). **VOCAL:** *5 Polish Peasant Songs* for Soprano or Treble Voices, 2 Flutes, 2 Clarinets, and Bass Clarinet (1940; reconstructed 1945; Kraków, 1945; rev. 1959); *Song to the Virgin Mary* for Chorus or 6 Solo Voices (London, April 26, 1964; rev. 1969); *Universal Prayer* for Soloists, Chorus, 3 Harps, and Organ (1968–69; N.Y., May 24, 1970); *Thames Pageant*, cantata for Young Players and Singers (1969; Twickenham, Feb. 7, 1970); *Winter Solstice* for Soprano, Baritone, Chorus, 3 Trumpets, 3 Trombones, Timpani, and Glockenspiel (Kingston-upon-Thames, Dec. 16, 1972); *Invocation for Peace* for Treble Voices, 2 Trumpets, and 2 Trombones (Southampton, England, Nov. 28, 1972); *Love Song* for Mezzo-soprano and Harp or Piano (1976; also for Mezzo-soprano, Harp or Piano, and Strings, London, Nov. 28, 1991); *Dreamscape* for Mezzo- soprano and Piano (London, Dec. 12, 1977); *Prayer to the Virgin of Skempe* for Voice or Chorus, Organ, and Piano or Instruments (1990; 1st perf. at the composer's funeral, St. Mary's Church, Twickenham, Nov. 5, 1991). **BIBL.:** T. Kaczyński, *A. P. i jego muzyka* (Warsaw, 1994). —NS/LK/DM

Panula, Jorma, Finnish conductor, pedagogue, and composer; b. Kauhajoki, Aug. 10, 1930. He studied in Helsinki at the School of Church Music and with Leo Funtek at the Sibelius Academy (1948–53); then pursued conducting studies with Dean Dixon in Lund (1953), and with Albert Wolff (1957) and Franco Ferrara (1958) in Hilversum. He conducted theater orchs. in Lahti (1953–55), Tampere (1955–58), and Helsinki (1958–62); after conducting the Finnish National Opera (1962–63), he conducted the Turku Phil. (1963–65), the Helsinki Phil. (1965–72), the Århus Sym. Orch. in Denmark (1972–75), and the Espoo City Orch. (1986–88); also appeared as a guest conductor throughout Europe and in North America. He served as a prof. of conducting at the Sibelius Academy (from 1972), the Stockholm Musikhögskolan (1980–86), and the Copenhagen Royal Danish Cons. of Music (1986–91).

WORKS: DRAMATIC: 2 folk operas: *Jaakko Ilkka* (1978) and *Jokiooppera* (The River Opera; 1982); *Vallan Miehet* (Men of Power), television opera (1987); musicals; scores for films, radio, and television. **ORCH.:** Violin Concerto (1954); *Adagio and Allegro* (1957); *Orkesteriisittely* (Orchestral Introduction; 1965); *Jazz Capriccio* for Piano and Orch. (1965); Concertino

(1972). **OTHER:** Choral music; numerous arrangements of folk music.—NS/LK/DM

Panzéra, Charles (Auguste Louis), noted Swiss-born French baritone and teacher; b. Geneva, Feb. 16, 1896; d. Paris, June 6, 1976. He studied at the Paris Cons. He made his operatic debut as Albert in *Werther* at the Paris Opéra-Comique in 1919, and then gave concerts in Europe and America; also taught at the Juilliard School of Music in N.Y. In 1949 he was appointed a prof. at the Paris Cons. He excelled in the interpretation of French songs. He publ. *L'Art de chanter* (Paris, 1945), *L'Amour de chanter* (Paris, 1957), *L'Art vocal: 30 leçons de chant* (Paris, 1959), and *Votre voix: Directives générales* (Paris, 1967).—NS/LK/DM

Paoli, Antonio (real name, **Ermogene Imleghi Bascaran**), Puerto Rican tenor; b. Ponce, April 14, 1871; d. San Juan, Aug. 24, 1946. He studied in Spain and at the Milan Cons. In 1899 he made his operatic debut as Arnold in Rossini's *Guillaume Tell* at the Paris Opéra. After appearances in Caracas, Havana, and N.Y. (1901), he toured the U.S. with Mascagni's opera troupe (1902) and then pursued his career in Europe and South America. From 1928 he taught at the Univ. of Puerto Rico. Among his best roles were Verdi's Manrico and Otello, Meyerbeer's Vasco da Gama, and Saint-Saëns's Samson.—NS/LK/DM

Paolo da Firenze, Italian composer and music theorist; b. place and date unknown; d. Arezzo, September 1419. He was a member of the Camaldolese order, and died in its monastery of S. Viti. Among his extant works are 11 madrigals, 22 ballate, and 2 sacred pieces. He was the author of the treatise *Ars ad adiscendum contrapunctum.*—LK/DM

Papaioannou, Yannis (Andreou), Greek composer and teacher; b. Kavala, Jan. 6, 1911; d. Athens, May 11, 1989. He studied piano and theory at the Hellenic Cons. in Athens (1922–34), then had some composition lessons with Honegger in Paris (1949). In 1953 he was appointed to the staff of his alma mater. His music traversed from a fairly conservative neo-Classical idiom to dodecaphony and eventually integral serialism.

WORKS: DRAMATIC: Theater music, including the ballet *Winter Fantasy* (1950). **ORCH.:** *Idyll* (1938); *Choreographic Prelude* (1939); 7 symphonic poems: *The Corsair* (1940), *Poem of the Forest* (1942), *Vassilis the Albanian* (1945), *Matins of Souls* (1947), *Pygmalion* (1951), *Hellas* (1956), and *Symphonic Tableau* (1968); 5 syms. (1946, 1951, 1953, 1963, 1964); *Triptych* for Strings (1947); Piano Concerto (1950); *Concerto for Orchestra* (1954); 3 suites (Nos. 1 and 2, *Pictures from Asia*; No. 3, *Egypt*, 1961); Concertino for Piano and Strings (1962); *India*, suite (1969); Concerto for Violin and Chamber Orch. (1971); Concerto for Violin, Piano, and Orch. (1972–73). **CHAMBER:** Violin Sonata (1947); String Quartet (1959); Suite for Guitar (1960); Sonatina for Flute and Guitar (1962); Quartet for Flute, Clarinet, Guitar, and Cello (1962); Trio for Oboe, Clarinet, and Bassoon (1962); *Archaic* for 2 Guitars (1962); String Trio (1963); Trio for Flute, Viola, and Guitar (1967); Quartet for Oboe, Clarinet, Viola, and

Piano (1968); *5 Characters*, brass quintet (1970); *Aphigissis* (Narration) for Violin (1970); *The Harlequin's Prattling* for Tuba (1971); *Portrait* for Tuba (1972); *Syneirmoi* (Associations) for 9 Instruments (1973); *Echomorphes* (Sound-figures) for Violin (1975); *Rhythms and Colors* for Cello (1976); *Puck* for Cello (1976); Piano Trio (1977). **P i a n o** : Several pieces, including a sonata (1958). **VOCAL:** *Daphnis and Chloe* for Chorus and Orch. (1934); *Sarpidon's Funeral*, cantata (1965); *3 Byzantine Odes* for Soprano and Chamber Ensemble (1966); *Electra Monologues* for Soprano and Instrumental Ensemble (1968); *Footsteps* for Mezzo-soprano, Narrator, Chorus, and Instrumental Ensemble (1969); *4 Orphic Hymns* for Narrator and Instrumental Ensemble (1971); choruses; songs.—**NS/LK/DM**

Papandopulo, Boris, Croatian conductor and composer; b. Bad Honnef am Rhein, Feb. 25, 1906; d. Zagreb, Oct. 17, 1991. He studied in Zagreb and Vienna. Returning to his homeland, he was active as a conductor and composer. In 1959 he was appointed conductor of the National Theater in Zagreb, and from 1964 to 1968 he conducted in Split and Rijeka; later filled engagements as a guest conductor in Yugoslavia. His operas and most of his instrumental works were written in a national Croatian idiom; but he also experimented with the 12-tone techniques, as exemplified by his pointedly titled *Dodekafonski concert* for 2 Pianos (1961).

WORKS: **DRAMATIC: O p e r a :** *Amiftrion* (Zagreb, Feb. 17, 1940); *Sunčanica* (The Sun Girl; Zagreb, June 13, 1942); *Rona* (Rijeka, May 25, 1955); *Marulova Pisan* (Marul's Song; Split, Aug. 14, 1970); *Madame Buffault* (1972). **B a l l e t :** *Zlato* (Gold; Zagreb, May 31, 1930); *Žetva* (The Harvest; Sarajevo, March 25, 1950); *Intermezzo* (Sarajevo, May 25, 1953); *Beatrice Cenci* (Gelsenkirchen, 1959); *Gitanella* (1965); *Doktor Atom: Qu + H³ + H² = He⁴ + n + 9* (Rijeka, Oct. 29, 1966); *Ljudi u hotelu* (People in a Hotel; Vienna, May 27, 1967); *Teuta* (1973). **ORCH.:** 2 syms.: No. 1 (1930) and No. 2 (Zagreb, May 8, 1946); Sinfonietta (1938); 4 piano concertos (1938, 1942, 1947, 1958); Concerto for Harpsichord and Strings (1962); Double Bass Concerto (1968); Concerto for 4 Timpani and Orch. (1969). **CHAMBER:** 5 string quartets (1927, 1933, 1945, 1950, 1970); Piano Quartet (1938); Clarinet Quintet (1940); Viola Sonata (1956); *Mozaik* for Strings and Jazz Quartet (1963); piano pieces. **VOCAL:** Many cantatas; choruses; songs;—**NS/LK/DM**

Papavoine, French violinist and composer; b. probably in Normandy, c. 1720; d. probably in Marseilles, 1793. Little is known about him, not even his first name. He spent the greater portion of his life in Paris, where he played in the orch. of the Comédie-Italienne (1760–62). With N.-M. Audinot, he founded the Théâtre de l'Ambigue-Comique about 1767, and was active with it until at least 1789. His wife, Mlle. Pellecier, was also a musician and composer. Papavoine was one of the earliest French symphonists. His *6 simphonies*, op.1 (Paris, 1752) and the Symphonie in D major (c. 1765) are extant. He also composed 4 operas, incidental music, pantomimes, and chamber music.—**LK/DM**

Pape, René, German bass-baritone; b. Dresden, Sept. 4, 1964. After singing in the Dresden Kreuzchor (1974–81), he pursued vocal training at the Dresden Hochschule für Musik. In 1987 he made his debut as the Speaker in *Die Zauberflöte* at the Berlin State Opera, where he also sang Capellio in 1993. In 1994 he appeared as Hunding in Philadelphia and as Masetto at the Bavarian State Opera in Munich. He portrayed Rocco, Ramfis, and Fafner in Berlin in 1995, and then was engaged as Sarastro in Bonn in 1996. In 1997 he sang Pope Pius IV in *Palestrina* and King Heinrich in *Die Meistersinger von Nürnberg* at London's Covent Garden. —**NS/LK/DM**

Papi, Gennaro, Italian-American conductor; b. Naples, Dec. 21, 1886; d. N.Y., Nov. 29, 1941. He received training in piano, organ, violin, and theory at the Naples Cons. (graduated, 1904). He was a chorus master at S. Severo (1906), Warsaw (1909–10), Turin (1911), and London's Covent Garden (1911–12). After serving as Toscanini's assistant on a tour of Argentina (1912), Toscanini made him his assistant at the Metropolitan Opera in N.Y. On April 29, 1915, he made his debut there conducting *Rigoletto*. He was on the conducting roster there from 1916 to 1926, and again from 1935 until his death. He also conducted at Chicago's Ravinia Festival (1916–31) and Civic Opera (1925–32). —**NS/LK/DM**

Papier, Rosa, Austrian mezzo-soprano; b. Baden, near Vienna, Sept. 15, 1858; d. Vienna, Feb. 9, 1932. She sang at the Vienna Court Opera, and later taught at the Vienna Cons. In 1881 she married the pianist Hans Paumgartner. Their son was the conductor and musicologist **Bernhard Paumgartner.**—**NS/LK/DM**

Papineau-Couture, Jean, prominent Canadian composer, teacher, and administrator; b. Montreal, Nov. 12, 1916. He was the grandson of the Canadian musician Guillaume Couture. At 6, he commenced piano lessons with his mother. From 1926 to 1939 he was a student of Françoise D'Amour, receiving instruction in piano, harmony, sight reading, and music history. He also studied counterpoint with Gabriel Cusson (1937–40). His training continued with Léo-Pol Morin (piano; 1939–40), and then at the New England Cons. of Music in Boston (B.Mus., 1941), where he was a student of Quincy Porter (composition), Francis Findlay (conducting), and Beveridge Webster (piano). He completed his studies with Boulanger at the Longy School in Cambridge, Mass. (1941–43) and in Madison, Wisc., and Lake Arrowhead, Calif. (1944–45). He taught at the Jean-de-Brébeuf Coll. in Montreal (1943–44; 1945–46), and then was on the faculty of the Cons. de Musique de Québec à Montréal (1946–63). From 1951 to 1982 he also taught at the Univ. of Montreal, where he was dean of the music faculty from 1968 to 1973. He served as president of the Canadian League of Composers (1957–59; 1963–66), the Académie de musique de Québec (1962–63), the Sociétè de Musique Contemporaine du Québec (1966–72), the Canadian Music Council (1967–68), the Canadian Music Centre (1973–74), and the Humanities Research Council of Canada (1977–78). In 1962 he received the Prix de musique Calixa- Lavallée. He was made an Officer of the Order of Canada in 1968. In 1973 he was awarded the Canadian Music Council Medal. In 1986 the Canadian Conference of the Arts honored him with its

Diplôme d'honneur. He was made a Grand Officier of the Ordre national du Québec in 1988. After composing works in an impressionist and neo-Classical manner, he adopted a personal style in which structuralist, chromatic, and symmetrical writing predominated.

WORKS: DRAMATIC: *Papotages*, ballet (1949; Montreal, Nov. 20, 1950); puppet shows. **ORCH.:** Concerto Grosso for Chamber Orch. (1943; rev. 1955; Montreal, April 10, 1957); Sym. No. 1 (1948; Montreal, Feb. 20, 1949; rev. 1956); *Aria* (1949; Vancouver, Jan. 22, 1960; from the Suite for Piano, 1942–43); Concerto for Violin and Chamber Orch. (1951–52; Montreal, Feb. 3, 1954); *Marche de Guillaumet* (Montreal, Dec. 1952); *Ostinato* for Harp, Piano, and Strings (1952); *Poème* (1952; Montreal, Jan. 27, 1953); *Prélude* (Montreal, May 25, 1953); *Piéce concertante No. 1: Repliement* for Piano and Strings (Montreal, April 6, 1957), *No. 2: Eventails* for Cello and Chamber Orch. (1959), *No. 3: Variations* for Flute, Clarinet, Violin, Cello, Harp, and Strings (Montreal, March 24, 1959), *No. 4: Additions* for Oboe and Strings (1959), and *No. 5: Miroirs* (Montreal, Sept. 21, 1963); *Trois Piéces* (1961; Saskatoon, Nov. 25, 1962); Piano Concerto (1965; Toronto, Feb. 6, 1966); *Suite Lapitsky* (1965; Montreal, Feb. 2, 1966); *Oscillations* for Chamber Orch. (Vancouver, Sept. 27, 1969); *Obsession* for Small Orch. (Montreal, Oct. 18, 1973); *Clair-obscur* for Contrabassoon, Double Bass, and Orch. (Montreal, Dec. 10, 1986); *Célébrations* (Toronto, Feb. 24, 1991). **CHAMBER:** Violin Sonata (1944; Montreal, April 1946; rev. 1953); Suite for Flute and Piano (1944–45); *Aria* for Violin (1946); Suite for Flute, Clarinet, Bassoon, Horn, and Piano (1947; Montreal, Jan. 31, 1955); 2 string quartets: No. 1 (Forest Hill, Ontario, Dec. 8, 1953) and No. 2 (1967; Orford Arts Centre, June 24, 1970); Rondo for 4 Recorders (1953); Suite for Violin (1956); *Éclosion* for Piano, Violin, and Tape (Montreal, April 1961); *Trois Caprices* for Violin and Piano (Orford Arts Centre, July 5, 1962); *Fantaisie* for Wind Quintet (Winnipeg, June 1963); Canons for Brass Quintet (1964); *Dialogues* for Violin and Piano (Montreal, Aug. 19, 1967); Sextet for Horn, Clarinet, Bassoon, Violin, Viola, and Cello (Montreal, Aug. 15, 1967); *Nocturnes* for Flute, Clarinet, Violin, Cello, Guitar, Harpsichord, and Percussion (Montreal, Nov. 28, 1969); *Trio in 4 Movements* for Viola, Clarinet, and Piano (Montreal, March 15, 1974); *Départ* for Alto Flute (1974; Montreal, April 17, 1980); *Verségères* for Bass Flute (Vancouver, May 29, 1975); *J'aime les tierces mineures* for Flute (1975; Orford Arts Centre, July 6, 1976); *Slano* for String Trio (1975; Paris, Dec. 2, 1976); *Exploration* for Guitar (London, Sept. 1983); *Prouesse* for Viola (1985; Montreal, Nov. 21, 1986); *Arcadie* for 4 Flutes (1986); *Thrène* for Violin and Piano (1988; Montreal, Feb. 7, 1991); *Les Arabesques d'Isabelle* for Flute, English Horn, Clarinet, Bassoon, and Piano (1989; Winnipeg, Feb. 13, 1990); *Automne* for 10 Instruments (1992); *Vents capricieux ser le clavier* for Flute, Oboe, Clarinet, Bassoon, and Piano (1993; Montreal, April 11, 1994); *Chocs sonores* for Marimba (1994); *Fantasque* for Cello (1995). **KEYBOARD: Piano:** Suite (1942–43; Montreal, June 1957); *Mouvement perpétuel* (1943; WNYC Radio, N.Y., Feb. 22, 1947); *Deux valses* (1943–44; Montreal, Feb. 17, 1950); *Étude* (1944–45); Rondo for Piano, 4-Hands (1945); *Aria* (1960); *Complémentarité* (1971; Toronto, Jan. 24, 1972); *Nuit* (1978; Toronto, Jan. 20, 1981); *Idée* (1982; Ottawa, Sept. 1984). **Harpsichord:** *Dyarchie* (Boston, March 30, 1971). **Organ:** *Vers l'extinction* (1987; Montreal, Nov. 1, 1989); *Courbes* (1988; Montreal, Nov. 1, 1989); *Quasapassacaille* (1988; Paris, April 26, 1990); *Autour du Dies Irae* (1991); *C'est bref* (1991); *Tournants* (1992). **VOCAL:** *Églogues* for Alto, Flute, and Piano (1942; Cambridge, Mass., Feb. 23, 1943); *Pater noster* for Mezzo-soprano or Baritone and Organ (Montreal, June 15, 1944); *Ave Maria* for Mezzo-soprano or Baritone or Organ (Montreal, June 23, 1945); *Complainte populaire* for Soprano, Bass, and Piano (1946; Montreal, March 21, 1953); *Quatrains* for Soprano and Piano (1947; Montreal, May 14, 1948); *Offertoire "Père, daignez recevoir"* for Tenor and Organ or Harmonium (1949); *Psaume CL* for Soprano, Tenor, Chorus, Winds, and Organ (1954; Montreal, April 11, 1955); *Mort* for Alto and Piano (Montreal, Nov. 15, 1956); *Te mater* for 3 Voices (1958); *À Jésus, mon roi, mon grand ami, mon frère* for 2 Soloists and Chorus (Montreal, May 1960); *Viole d'amour* for Chorus (1966); *Paysage* for 8 Voices, 8 Speakers, and Chamber Orch. (1968; Zagreb, May 9, 1969); *Contraste* for Voice and Orch. (1970); *Chanson de Rahit* for Voice, Clarinet, and Piano (1972; Montreal, March 3, 1973); *Le Débat du coeur ed du corps de Villon* for Speaker, Cello, and Percussion (1977; Montreal, Feb. 22, 1979); *Nuit polaire* for Contralto and 10 Instruments (1986; Montreal, Jan. 29, 1987); *Glanures* for Soprano and Chamber Orch. (Ottawa, Nov. 5, 1994).

BIBL.: L. Bail-Milot, *J. P.-C.: La vie, la carrière et l'oeuvre* (Montreal, 1986).—NS/LK/DM

Pappano, Antonio, Italian-born American conductor; b. London, Dec. 30, 1959. He went to the U.S. and pursued training in piano with Norma Verrilli, in composition with Arnold Franchetti, and in conducting with Gustav Meier. After working as a répétiteur and asst. conductor in several opera houses, he conducted at the Norwegian Opera in Oslo, the English National Opera in London, the Royal Opera, Covent Garden, London, the San Francisco Opera, the Lyric Opera in Chicago, the Théâtre du Châtelet in Paris, and the Berlin State Opera. From 1992 to 2003 he served as music director of the Théâtre Royal de la Monnaie in Brussels. In 1993 he made an acclaimed debut at the Vienna State Opera when he conducted on short notice a performance of *Siegfried*. He conducted *Eugene Onegin* at his Metropolitan Opera debut in N.Y. on Jan. 13, 1997. In 1998 he was made principal guest conductor of the Israel Phil. He was engaged to conduct *Lohengrin* at the Bayreuth Festival in 1999. In 2002 he became music director of the Royal Opera House at London's Covent Garden. As a guest conductor, Pappano appeared with the Orchestre de Paris, the Chicago Sym. Orch., the Cleveland Orch., the Orch. of La Scala in Milan, the Berlin Phil., the Los Angeles Phil., the London Sym. Orch., and the Philharmonia Orch. in London.
—NS/LK/DM

Pâque, (Marie Joseph Léon) Désiré, remarkable Belgian-born French conductor, teacher, and composer; b. Liège, May 21, 1867; d. Bessancourt, Val d'Oise, Nov. 20, 1939. He began to compose as a child, writing a Mass at the age of 12. He studied at the Liège Cons., where he was a prof. of music theory until 1897. He was a conductor and prof. of composition in Athens (1900–03), then was a prof. of organ at the Lisbon Cons. (1904), and also conducted at the Portuguese court. He subsequently traveled throughout Europe (from 1909), settling in Paris in 1914. He wrote 144 opus nos., his production falling into 3 periods: cosmopolitan and formal (1886–1908), freely episodic, in an *adjonction constante* of recurrent themes (1909–18), and atonal and polytonal (1919–39). His last manner was exemplified by *10 pièces atonales pour la jeunesse* for Piano (1925). The bulk of his music remains in MS. Other works include an opera, *Vaima* (1903; Ostend, 1904), 8 syms. (1895, 1905, 1912, 1916, 1919, 1927, 1934, 1936), 2 piano concertos (1888, 1935), Cello Concerto (1893), *Ouverture sur 3 thèmes bulgares* (Ostend, Aug. 17, 1895), *Ouverture libre* (1899; Munich, Dec. 29, 1911), Requiem (1900), 10 string quartets (1892–1939), 3 piano quintets (1896, 1924, 1938), 2 sextets (1909, 1919), 5 suites for Piano, Violin, and Viola (1891–96), 3 piano trios (1903–30), 4 violin sonatas (1890–1934), 4 piano sonatas (1911), Viola Sonata (1915), 13 albums of piano pieces, and choral works. —NS/LK/DM

Parabosco, Girolamo, Italian organist and composer; b. Piacenza, c. 1524; d. Venice, April 21, 1557. His father, Vincenzo Parabosco, was an organist. He was a student of Willaert in Venice, where he later held the position of 1st organist at San Marco from 1551. Among his extant works are *21 Madrigali* for 5 Voices (Venice, 1546) and 2 instrumental pieces. See F. Bussi, ed., *Girolamo Parabosco: Composizioni* (Piacenza, 1961).

BIBL.: G. Bianchini, *G. P., scrittore e organista del secolo XVI* (Venice, 1899); F. Bussi, *Umanità e arte di G. P.* (Piacenza, 1961). —LK/DM

Paradies (originally **Paradisi**), **(Pietro) Domenico,** Italian composer and harpsichordist; b. Naples, 1707; d. Venice, Aug. 25, 1791. He was a pupil of Porpora. He brought out several operas in Italy. In 1746 he went to London, where he earned a living mainly as a teacher of harpsichord playing, but also produced several operas, including *Fetonte* (London, Jan. 17, 1747) and *La forza d'amore* (London, Jan. 19, 1751); also composed several symphonic overtures, 2 organ concertos, and cantatas. He publ. *12 sonate di gravicembalo* (London, 1754). Toward the end of his life he returned to Italy. Some of his MSS are preserved in the Fitzwilliam Museum at Cambridge. His sonatas were brought out by G. Benvenuti and D. Cipollini in Milan (1920). —NS/LK/DM

Paradis, Maria Theresia von, noted Austrian pianist, organist, singer, and composer; b. Vienna, May 15, 1759; d. there, Feb. 1, 1824. She was the daughter of Josef von Paradis, the imperial court secretary. She studied piano with L. Koželuh, singing with Richter, singing and dramatic composition with Salieri, dramatic composition with Vogler, and theory with Friberth. She appeared in concerts in Vienna (from c. 1775). She was blind from her 5th year; Mesmer became interested in her condition and attempted to cure her, without effect (1777–78). She set out on a major concert tour in 1783, visiting Salzburg, Frankfurt am Main, Mainz, and other cities. In 1784 she arrived in Paris, where she was highly praised for her appearances as both a keyboard artist and a singer at the Concert Spirituel; Mozart composed a concerto for her. She went to London in late 1784 and appeared at court and in public concerts, then returned to Vienna in 1786, where she continued to make tours until founding her own music inst. (1808). Her friend and librettist, Johann Riedinger, invented a notation system for her, and she

became a skilled composer. Much of her music is not extant.

WORKS: DRAMATIC: *Ariadne und Bacchus*, melodrama (Laxenburg, June 20, 1791); *Der Schulkanditat*, ländliches Singspiel (Vienna, Dec. 5, 1792); *Rinaldo und Alcine, Die Insel der Verführung*, comic opera (Prague, June 30, 1797). ORCH.: 2 piano concertos. CHAMBER: Piano Trio (Vienna, 1800). PIANO: 4 sonatas (Amsterdam, 1778); 12 sonatas (Paris, 1792); other pieces. VOCAL: Cantatas; songs; etc.—NS/LK/DM

Paranov, Moshe (real name, **Morris Perlmutter**), American pianist, conductor, and music educator; b. Hartford, Conn., Oct. 28, 1895; d. West Hartford, Conn., Oct. 7, 1994. He began his musical studies as a child and sang in synagogues. At 14, he commenced piano playing in theaters and hotels. He was 17 when he made his formal debut as a pianist in Hartford. He pursued training in piano with Julius Hartt and Harold Bauer, and in composition with Ernest Bloch and Rubin Goldmark. After making his N.Y. recital debut as a pianist at Aeolian Hall in 1920, he made appearances as a soloist with orchs. and as a recitalist. With Hartt and others, he founded a music school in Hartford in 1920 as Julius Hartt, Moshe Paranov, and Associated Teachers, which soon became the Hartt School of Music. In 1934 Paranov became its director and proceeded to develop it into one of the finest schools of its kind. After it became a part of the Univ. of Hartford in 1957, he continued to preside over the school until 1971. He also served as music director of WTIC Radio in Hartford (1938–49), and as conductor of the Hartt Opera Theater, the Hartford Sym. Orch. (1947–53), and the Brockton (Mass.) Sym. Orch. (1954–64). His 95th birthday was marked by a special celebration at the Univ. of Hartford on May 16, 1991, at which occasion he conducted a sprightly rendition of Offenbach's overture to *Orpheus in the Underworld*. An endowed chair was also created in his honor to further his efforts in promoting music education.—NS/LK/DM

Paratore, Anthony (b. Boston, June 17, 1944) and his brother, **Joseph Paratore** (b. Boston, March 19, 1948), outstanding American duo-pianists. They followed separate courses of study as pianists, graduating from the Boston Univ. School of Fine and Applied Arts; both entered the Juilliard School of Music in N.Y., in the class of Rosina Lhévinne, who suggested that they try a career as duo-pianists; they subsequently appeared as duo-pianists with Arthur Fiedler and the Boston Pops Orch., and then made their N.Y. recital debut in 1973. In 1974 they won 1st prize at the Munich International Competition, and thereafter scored international successes as duo-pianists. In addition to the standard repertory, they also perf. contemporary works; commissioned and gave the premiere of Michael Schelle's Concerto for 2 Pianos and Orch. (Indianapolis, Jan. 14, 1988). They also gave the premiere of William Bolcom's Sonata for 2 Pianos (Lafayette, Ind., April 6, 1994). —NS/LK/DM

Paray, Paul, distinguished French conductor and composer; b. Le Tréport, May 24, 1886; d. Monte Carlo,

Oct. 10, 1979. He began his musical education with his father, a church organist. In 1904 he entered the Paris Cons. as a composition student of Leroux, Caussade, Lenepveu, and Vidal, receiving the Premier Grand Prix de Rome with his cantata *Yanitza* (1911). He was drafted into the French army during World War I and was taken prisoner by the Germans; composed a String Quartet while interned at Darmstadt; after the Armistice (1918), he became conductor of the orch. of the Casino de Cauterets. Substituting for an ailing Caplet, Paray made his Paris debut on Feb. 20, 1920, and soon became asst. conductor of the Lamoureux Orch., succeeding Chevillard as 1st conductor in 1923; was appointed conductor of sym. concerts in Monte Carlo in 1928, and in 1932 succeeded Pierné as conductor of the Concerts Colonne, remaining until the orch. was disbanded by the Nazi occupiers of Paris in 1940. He conducted briefly in Marseilles and, following the liberation of Paris, resumed his duties with the Concerts Colonne (1944–52). Paray made his American debut in N.Y. on July 24, 1939, in a program of French music. In 1952 he became music director of the reorganized Detroit Sym. Orch., and on Oct. 18, 1956, inaugurated the new Ford Auditorium in Detroit in a program that included his own *Mass for the 500th Anniversary of the Death of Joan of Arc*, a work first heard in the Rouen Cathedral in France in 1931; he resigned in 1963 and returned to France, although he continued to guest-conduct internationally. In July 1977, at the age of 91, he conducted an orch. concert in honor of Marc Chagall's 90th birthday celebration in Nice, and, at age 92, made his last conducting appearance in the U.S., leading the orch. of the Curtis Inst. of Music in Philadelphia. As a conductor, he concentrated on the Classics and Romantics, and French music. He was the composer of several highly competent works, including, besides *Yanitza* and his *Mass*, a ballet entitled *Artémis troublée* (Paris, April 28, 1922, perf. as a symphonic poem, *Adonis troublé*); *Fantaisie* for Piano and Orch. (Paris, March 25, 1923); 2 syms. (1935, 1940); Sym. for Strings; String Quartet (1918); Violin Sonata (1908); Cello Sonata (1919); piano pieces.

BIBL.: W. Landowski, *P. P.* (Lyons, 1956); J.-P. Mousnier, *P. P.* (1998).—**NS/LK/DM**

Parelli (real name, **Paparella**), **Attilio**, Italian conductor and composer; b. Monteleone d'Orvieto, near Perugia, May 31, 1874; d. there, Dec. 26, 1944. He studied at the Accademia di Santa Cecilia in Rome, graduating in 1899. He held various posts as a conductor in Italy and France; went to the U.S. as asst. conductor to Campanini at the Manhattan Opera in N.Y. (1906); also conducted for the Chicago Grand Opera Co. In 1925 he returned to Europe. He wrote the operas *Hermes* (Genoa, Nov. 8, 1906), *I dispettosi amanti* (Philadelphia, March 6, 1912), and *Fanfulla* (Trieste, Feb. 11, 1921), as well as a Sym., *Rapsodia umbra*, orch. suite, *La Chimera*, symphonic poem, and songs.—**NS/LK/DM**

Parenti, Tony (actually, **Anthony**), jazz clarinetist, saxophonist, uncle of **August Schellang;** b. New Orleans, La., Aug. 6, 1900; d. N.Y., April 17, 1972. Both parents were from Sicily. He played in an Italian band in New Orleans, then gigged in theater orchs., and with Papa Laine, Nick LaRocca, and drummer Johnny Stein, Johnny De Droit (c. 1916), and led his own successful band (record debut: January 1925). He moved to N.Y. in the late 1920s, and worked through the mid-1930s as a CBS staff musician; during this period, he led his own saxophone quartet on radio and in short Warner Bros. film. He spent four years with Radio City Symp. Orch. (1935–39), and then left to join Ted Lewis until the summer of 1945. In the late 1940s, he worked with several Dixieland-style revivalists, including Eddie Condon (January–June 1946) and Georg Brunis (June 1946), and, in Chicago, with Muggsy Spanier (late 1947) and Miff Mole (January 1948–June 1949). During the early 1950s, he worked for four years in Fla., mainly with Preacher Rollo Laylan's Five Saints, briefly with the Dukes of Dixieland in 1952. He moved back to N.Y. in 1954, toured with his own band in N.Y. State, Boston, and Canada. He led his own group at Jimmy Ryan's from late 1963 until 1969, and appeared at the first New Orleans Jazz Fest in June 1969. Parenti remained active in N.Y. area until his death.

DISC.: *Tony Parenti and His New Orleans Band* (1949); *Jazz, That's All* (1955); *Ragtime* (1956); *Two Beat Bash* (1957); *Tony Parenti and His Downtown Band* (1961); *Night at Jimmy Ryan's* (1967).—**JC/LP**

Parepa-Rosa, Euphrosyne (née **Parepa de Boyescu**), prominent Scottish soprano; b. Edinburgh, May 7, 1836; d. London, Jan. 21, 1874. Her father was Baron Georgiades de Boyescu of Bucharest, and her mother the soprano Elizabeth Seguin. After studying with her mother, she made her debut as Amina in *La Sonnambula* in Malta (1855); then sang in Italy, Madrid, and Lisbon. She made her first London appearance as Elvira in *I Puritani* with the Royal Italian Opera at the Lyceum Theatre (May 21, 1857); appeared at Covent Garden and Her Majesty's Theatre (1859–65), becoming a great favorite of the English public; also sang in Germany. She then toured the U.S. with Theodore Thomas's orch. and with Carl Rosa (1865). She married Rosa in 1867, and together they formed an opera company in which she starred as the principal soprano. She returned to Covent Garden (1872), but illness forced her to give up her career the following year. Her husband founded the Parepa-Rosa Scholarship at the Royal Academy of Music in her memory.—**NS/LK/DM**

Pareto, Graziella (actually, **Graciela**), Spanish soprano; b. Barcelona, March 6, 1888; d. Rome, Sept. 1, 1973. She studied with Vidal in Milan. She made her operatic debut as Micaëla in Barcelona in 1906; then sang at the Teatro Colón in Buenos Aires, in Turin, and in St. Petersburg. In 1914 she appeared at La Scala in Milan; subsequently sang at Covent Garden in London (1920), in Chicago (1923–25), and in Salzburg (1931). Among her prominent roles were Rosina, Ophelia, Marguerite de Valois, Violetta, and Norina.—**NS/LK/DM**

Pari, Claudio, Italian composer of Burgundian birth who flourished in the early 17th century. He was active in Sicily, garnering a reputation as one of the finest madrigalists of his time. He publ. 5 vols. of madrigals, 3 of which are extant (1611, 1617, 1619). —LK/DM

Paribeni, Giulio Cesare, Italian music critic, teacher, and composer; b. Rome, May 27, 1881; d. Milan, June 13, 1960. He studied at the Univ. of Rome and at the Liceo di S. Cecilia of Rome. He was first a conductor, then, from 1911 to 1915, head of the publishing firm of Sonzogno; from 1914, was a teacher of composition and harmony at the Royal Cons. in Milan; from 1922, an opera critic of *L'Ambrosiano* in Milan. He was the author of *Storia e teoria della antica musica greca* (Milan, 1912) and *Muzio Clementi* (Milan, 1921). Among his compositions were orch. works, chamber pieces, and church music.—NS/LK/DM

Parík, Ivan, Slovak composer and pedagogue; b. Bratislava, Aug. 17, 1936. Following private instruction from Alexander Albrecht (1951–53), he studied with Očenáš (composition) and Schimpl (conducting) at the Bratislava Cons. (until 1958). He completed his composition studies with Moyzes at the Bratislava Academy of Music and Drama (1958–62). From 1959 to 1968 he worked as a program director for the Czechoslovak TV in Bratislava. He was a part-time teacher at the Bratislava Academy of Music and Drama from 1962 to 1968, and then taught there full time. In 1984 he became head of its theory dept. In 1990 he was made a prof. and vice-rector of the Academy. From 1993 until his retirement in 1997 he served as its rector. In his output, Parík has made use of both tonal and serial resources with excursions into the realm of electroacoustic music.

WORKS: DRAMATIC: *Fragment,* ballet (1969); film music. ORCH.: *Overture* (1962); *Tower Music* for 12 Winds and Tape (1968); *Music to Ballet* (1968); *Introduction to Haydn's Sym. No. 102 in B major* (1971); *Music for Winds, Double Basses, and Percussion* (1981); *Musica pastoralis* (1984); *Music for Flute, Viola, and Orch.* (1987). CHAMBER: *Meditation* for Viola and Piano (1956); *Music for 4 Strings* (1958); *Epitaph in the Style of Improvisations,* trio for Flute, Viola, and Cello (1961); Flute Sonata (1962); *Song About a High, Old Tree* for Cello and Piano (1962); *Microstudies* for Flute, Viola, and Harpsichord (1963); *Music for 3* for Flute, Oboe, and Clarinet (1964); Trumpet Sonata (1965); Cello Sonata (1967); Oboe Sonata (1973); Clarinet Sonata (1974); Bassoon Sonata (1975); *Epitaph II* for Flute and Guitar (1976); Violin Sonata (1976); *Nocturne* for Violin and Piano (1979); *Music for Miloš Urbásek* for String Quartet (1981); Duet for 2 Violas (1981); Viola Sonata (1983); *Quadrophony* for 4 Cellos (1987); *Chant* for Flute (1991); piano pieces. VOCAL: *Seen Closely Above the Lake* for Speaker, Wind Quintet, Piano, and String Quartet or Orch. (1979); *2 Arias* on fragments of the *Stabat mater* for High Voice and Orch. (1989; also for High Voice and Piano or Organ); *How One Drinks from a Well* for Speaker and Chamber Orch. (1990); choruses; solo songs. ELECTROACOUSTIC: *Hommage to William Croft* (1969); *Variations on Pictures by Miloš Urbásek* (1970); *Sonata-Canon* for Cello and 4 Electronic Voices (1971); *Tower Music* (1971); *In memoriam Ockeghem* (1971); *Outside the Door* (1974); *Sonata pastoralis 44* (1974); *Cantica ferialia* (1975); *Hommage to Hummel* (1980); *Concerto grosso* (1990).—NS/LK/DM

Parikian, Manoug, Turkish-born English violinist and teacher of Armenian descent; b. Mersin, Sept. 15, 1920; d. Oxford, Dec. 24, 1987. He was a student of Louis Pecsaki at London's Trinity Coll. of Music (1936–39). In 1947 he made his debut as a soloist in Liverpool, and then was concertmaster of the Liverpool Phil. (1947–48) and the Philharmonia Orch. in London (1949–57). From 1957 he made tours of Europe as a soloist. He also was active as a performer in chamber music groups and as a duo recitalist. From 1980 to 1984 he was music director of the Manchester Camerata. He taught in London at the Royal Coll. of Music (1954–56) and the Royal Academy of Music (1959–87). Parikian became well known as an advocate of contemporary British music.—NS/LK/DM

Pâris, Alain, French conductor and writer on music; b. Paris, Nov. 22, 1947. He had a conducting course with Dervaux at the École Normal de Musique in Paris (Licence de concert, 1967), where he also was a student of Dandelot (1965–68); then studied conducting with Fourestier. In 1968 he won 1st prize in the Besançon conducting competition; subsequently appeared as a guest conductor with various French orchs. In 1976–77 he was asst. conductor of the Orchestre de Capitole de Toulouse. In 1980 he organized the Ensemble à Vent in Paris, which he led in programs of rarely heard works as well as premiere performances of many contemporary scores. From 1983 to 1987 he was permanent conductor of the Opéra du Rhin in Strasbourg. From 1986 to 1989 he was a prof. of conducting at the Strasbourg Cons. As a guest conductor, he appeared throughout Europe. He publ. the *Dictionnaire des interprètes et de l'interprétation musicale au XXᵉ siècle* (Paris, 1982; 4th ed., rev., 1995) and *Les Livrets d'opéra* (Paris, 1991); also made French translations of the *New Oxford Companion to Music* (Paris, 1988) and *Baker's Biographical Dictionary of Musicians* (Paris, 1995).—NS/LK/DM

Paris, Guillaume-Alexis, South Netherlands conductor and composer; b. Liège, c. 1756; d. St. Petersburg, Jan. 30, 1840. He began his career at the Maastricht theater in 1776. From 1780 to 1782 he was conductor at the Théâtre de la Monnaie in Brussels. After conducting in Ghent (1782–83), Lyons (1784), Liège (1786), and Amsterdam (1787–88), he was again conductor at the Théâtre de la Monnaie (1790–92). When the French invaded his homeland, he fled to Hamburg in 1794. He was called to St. Petersburg to take charge of the French opera company at the imperial court (1799–1804). From 1801 to 1821 he was conductor of the St. Petersburg Phil. Soc., where he introduced a number of masterworks to Russia. He composed the opera *Le nouveau sorcier* (Liège, Jan. 9, 1786), several ballets, and other stage works.—LK/DM

Parish-Alvars, Elias, remarkable English harpist; b. Teignmouth, Feb. 28, 1808; d. Vienna, Jan. 25, 1849. He studied with F. Dizi and N. Bochsa, and after a tour of Germany when he was 15, he completed his studies with T. Labarre. He made tours of Europe from 1834, making his home in Vienna. He appeared in the Far East (1838–42), then played in Leipzig and London (1842), in

Dresden and Prague (1843), and again in London (1844, 1846); subsequently was made a chamber musician at the Viennese court (1847). He wrote an opera, a Sym., 2 piano concertos, and many works for harp, including 2 concertos, a Concertino for 2 Harps, duos for harp and piano, and some 80 virtuoso pieces for solo harp. —NS/LK/DM

Parke, family of English musicians:

(1) William Thomas Parke, oboist and composer; b. London, 1762; d. there, Aug. 26, 1847. He began flute studies at age 10 and oboe training at 11 with his brother. When he was 13 he began piano lessons with Charles Rousseau Burney, and later took composition lessons with Baumgarten. He was only 14 when he began to play the viola at Vauxhall Gardens and at Drury Lane. In 1783 he was made 1st oboist at Covent Garden. With his brother, he was among the musicians who played in Haydn's concerts at the Hanover Square Rooms in London. He publ. the valuable *Musical Memoirs* (London, 1830). Among his works were pieces for the theater, oboe concertos, and many songs.

(2) John Parke, oboist, brother of the preceding; b. London, 1745; d. there, Aug. 2, 1829. After studying with Simpson, he was active as an oboist in various theater orchs. and gave concerts in London.

(3) Maria Hester Park(e), singer, pianist, and composer, daughter of **(1) William Thomas Parke;** b. London, 1775; d. there, Aug. 15, 1822. She studied with her father and then became well known as a concert singer. Among her works were a Concerto for Piano or Harpsichord and Strings (London, c. 1792), 3 sonatas for Piano or Harpsichord (c. 1795–96), 2 sonatas for Piano and Violin Accompaniment (c. 1801), and a set of glees (c. 1790).—LK/DM

Parkening, Christopher (William), outstanding American guitarist; b. Los Angeles, Dec. 14, 1947. He began guitar lessons when he was 11 with Celedonio and Pepe Romero in Los Angeles, making his public recital debut in 1959. When he was 15, he entered Andrés Segovia's master class at the Univ. of Calif., Berkeley; also received instruction from cellist Gregor Piatigorsky and harpsichordist Malcolm Hamilton. He attended the Univ. of Calif., Los Angeles (1964–65), then entered the Univ. of Southern Calif. as a cello student of Gabor Retjo (there were no guitar teachers on its faculty). By the close of his sophomore year, he was asked by the Univ. to teach guitar, thus initiating its guitar studies; was head of its guitar dept. (1971–75). In the meantime, he launched a brilliant career as a guitar virtuoso; after his first major tour of North America (1969), he regularly performed throughout the U.S. and Canada; also made extensive tours throughout the world, garnering acclaim as one of the foremost masters of his instrument. He publ. a valuable guitar method (1973) and made effective transcriptions of works by Bach, Dowland, Debussy, Ravel, and others. —NS/LK/DM

Parker, (Charles) Stephen (Lawrence), English-born Irish composer, writer, painter, and jazz pianist; b. Melton Mowbrey, Leicestershire, March 29, 1961. He received training in music from Frederick Rogan in Kettering, Northamptonshire (1969–79), and also played with chamber groups and jazz ensembles. After private studies in composition with Oliver Knussen (1978–79), he studied with Ruth Gerald (piano) and John Lambert (composition) at the Royal Coll. of Music in London (1979–82). In 1982 he emigrated to Ireland, where he taught piano and gave numerous piano recitals, often programming contemporary works. From 1990 he devoted himself to composition, writing, painting, and making appearances as a jazz pianist. Among his works are a number of orch. scores, including a *Sinfonietta* (1996), *The Walk to Poolbeg Lighthouse* (1997), 2 violin concertos (1997–98; 1999), *First Light on Skellig Rock* (1998), *Dance the Magic Isle* (1999), a Jazz Trumpet Concerto (1999), *Amazon* (1999), and an Organ Concerto (2000). He has also written film music.—LK/DM

Parker, Charlie (actually, **Charles Jr.**; aka **Bird**; **Yardbird**; and **Charlie Chan**), brilliant alto saxophonist and the single most influential jazz musician after Louis Armstrong, stepfather of **Kim Parker**; b. Kansas City, Kans., Aug. 29, 1920; d. N.Y., March 12, 1955. He got the name "Yardbird" because of his liking for fried chicken. This was later shortened to "Bird." He did not have a middle name, though Christopher has been given. His father, Charles Parker Sr., was born in Miss. and raised in Memphis and was a pianist, dancer and singer in Kansas City; by the late 1920s he worked in railroad dining cars. His mother, Adelaide "Addie" Bailey (b. c. 1888), was part Choctaw and lived in Okla. before coming to Kans. She cleaned in private homes and for the Western Union office. She was a Baptist but sent Charlie to a Catholic school. The family moved to Kansas City, Mo. in the late 1920s, settling eventually at 1516 Olive St. (his mother later bought the house at 1535), and the parents separated around 1932. Probably also in 1932, Parker Jr.'s first musical experience was in the band at Lincoln H.S. under Leo Davis and Alonzo Lewis, first on alto horn, then baritone horn. He began teaching himself on a used alto saxophone that his mother bought later in 1932 for $45. He said that hearing Rudy Vallee got him interested in the saxophone, but he didn't become serious at the time and even loaned the instrument to a friend, he said, for two years.

By 1934, Parker was apparently playing alto with Mary Kirk's trio and with other students (some of whom were probably later in the Deans of Swing), was studying chords on a piano at home, but sometime after that he sat in with Jimmie Keith's band at the High Hat and got laughed off the stage. He said that this drove him to practice seriously, all day long, over the next three or four years. He had tried alcohol and "pills" as early as 1932, but in 1935 he became a heroin addict, which was to shape the rest of his short life and also, perversely, to help initiate a vogue for the destructive drug among his legions of disciples in the late 1940s. He had never been interested in school and finally dropped out in June 1935, after playing with the high school orch. He worked for the next year and a half with the Deans of Swing, initially a student band led by pianist Lawrence Keyes that included singer Walter Brown;

around the end of 1935, he played briefly with Oliver Todd. On July 25, 1936, he married Rebecca Ellen Ruffin (b. Feb. 23, 1920), who with her mother and six siblings had been boarders in the Parker home since April 1934, but who had moved out that spring at Addie's request when the courtship became serious. Sometime around mid-1936, in a famous incident, Parker was jamming at the Reno Club with Count Basie's group, which included his idol Lester Young, when Jo Jones "rang the gong" on him by dropping a cymbal on the floor. On Nov. 28, 1936, he was injured in a serious auto accident (one passenger died) on the way to a gig in the Ozarks. He continued to freelance; he played baritone and tenor as needed but specialized on alto saxophone. Like all self-taught musicians he was not in isolation; he picked up many pointers from colleagues such as Tommy Douglas, with whom he worked in 1936. In the summer of 1937, while working with George E. Lee at Muesser's Ozarks Tavern in Eldon, Mo., he learned some of Young's solos by heart—probably including "Oh Lady Be Good" and "Shoe Shine Boy" (1936 recordings)—and returned two months later a much improved musician. That fall he played in the band of Buster Smith, a significant mentor, which included Jay McShann, at Lucille's Paradise (making some radio broadcasts that were not preserved) and at the Antler Club. During the latter engagement, Smith moved to N.Y., leaving Parker and a tenorist to lead the band. After a while, Parker led his own quintet at Lucille's. He worked for perhaps three months at Martin's-on-the-Plaza with McShann's band; McShann later fired him for unreliability. During this gig, Parker wrote "What Price Love?," a vocal number which the group performed; it was later known as the instrumental "Yardbird Suite." Sometime in 1938, he had his first of several brushes with the law when he stabbed a taxi driver in a fight over his inability to pay the fare. Rebecca gave birth to Francis Leon (after Leon "Chu" Berry) Parker on Jan. 10, 1938, but Parker spent less and less time at home and she did not accompany him on his trips out of town. In January 1939, he worked with Harlan Leonard for perhaps two weeks, then went to Chicago where he sat in and maybe even gigged for money, then went to stay with Buster Smith in N.Y. While he looked for gigs, he supported himself by cleaning up for two weeks at a little club, and then for three months washed dishes at Jimmy's Chicken Shack, where Tatum often sat in. Though Parker was never asked about Tatum, it seems likely that he learned from the pianist's innovations in voicings and chord substitutions, and possibly from his fondness for inserting clever quotations; Parker also worked at a dance hall, the Parisien. Parker said that while sitting in with guitarist Biddy Fleet at Dan Wall's Chili House on Seventh Ave. in Harlem he experimented with new chords and different keys and one night had a breakthrough when he played on the higher intervals of "Cherokee" while Fleet tried backing him with related harmonies.

At the end of 1939, Parker and Fleet were working with Banjo Burney in Annapolis, Md., when his father was killed, stabbed by a lover in a drunken quarrel, and he returned to Kansas City for the funeral around the beginning of 1940. Sometime after, perhaps in February,

he joined McShann's touring band, with which he made his first recordings in Wichita, Kans. in November 1940 (not counting an undated solo demo disk from around this time); these private discs were not issued until 1974. While with McShann he got the nickname "Yardbird" (later "Bird"). He first recorded commercially with McShann on April 30, 1941, in Dallas. Afterward the band had a break between gigs and Parker and Walter Brown became violently ill while staying with Gene Ramey and family in Austin because they could not locate a source of heroin. They soon resumed touring with McShann; in November 1941, the band went to Chicago and they debuted at the Savoy Ballroom in Harlem on Jan. 9, 1942, followed by touring. Soon after a recording session in N.Y. on July 2, Parker chose to remain there when the band went out on another tour. He began appearing at jam sessions at Monroe's and Minton's, then rejoined McShann briefly, finally leaving to join Earl Hines on tenor in December 1942. While the Hines band was in Chicago from Feb. 14 to March 2, 1943, Parker was recorded privately in jam sessions with Gillespie and others; these were first issued in 1986. On April 10, 1943, while the band was in Washington, D.C., he married Geraldine "Gerri" Scott, whom he had apparently known back home; he never went through a legal divorce from his first wife, though. During this visit, or another one to D.C. later in the year, he left Hines to work with Charles Thompson, then returned to Kansas City without Gerri, the relationship having quickly ended, and performed at Tutty's Mayfair Club.

In early 1944 Gillespie sent Parker a telegram offering to hire him for his group, but he never received it; soon he had rejoined McShann. In the spring, he was fired for passing out on the bandstand in Detroit, rode from there with Andy Kirk's band, and joined Noble Sissle in N.Y. When Sissle arrived in St. Louis in the summer of 1944, Parker transferred to the Billy Eckstine band. On Sept. 15, 1944, he recorded in N.Y. accompanying Tiny Grimes. Later that year, he worked briefly with Andy Kirk, and then joined Cootie Williams at the end of 1944, including gigs in N.Y. at the Apollo (Jan. 12–17, 1945) and the Savoy Ballroom (mid-February 1945). In 1945 he began recording regularly with Gillespie, and performing with him at the three Deuces in N.Y. in March and in concerts at Town Hall (May 22 and June 30; one of which was recorded) and Philadelphia's Academy of Music (June 5, 1945). He and Gillespie practiced together and became leaders of the new music, bebop. At times, Parker and Gillespie would even turn practice compositions upside down and play them that way for relief. Parker became the acknowledged leader of bebop as he developed an improvising technique characterized by virtuosic speed, intense tone, complex harmonies, and florid melodies having irregular rhythmic patterns and asymmetric phrase lengths. During the 1940s and 1950s, he also wrote a number of seminal tunes, among them "Ornithology," "Scrapple from the Apple," "Parker's Mood," and "Yardbird Suite." As a composer, he usually worked with the 12-bar blues patterns (but always in an nonstereotypical manner; he made 175 blues recordings, all markedly different) or with chord progressions of well-known "standard" tunes: his "Ornithology," for instance, is based on the progression of "How High the Moon."

Around this time he studied Islam and Arabic with Argonne Thornton (later Sadik Hakim) and was sometimes known as Saluda Hakim among his Muslim friends. Late in 1945, he began living with Doris Sydnor, but she stayed behind when he went to L.A. with Gillespie's group for an engagement at Billy Berg's lasting from Dec. 10, 1945, through Feb. 3, 1946. Radio broadcasts survive, but a silent home movie clip of the band remains unconfirmed. On Feb. 5, 1946, Parker and Gillespie made the first recording session for the new Dial label; it had been hoped that Lester Young would join them but he was out on tour. The Gillespie group then returned to N.Y. but Parker remained in L.A. He was briefly in a hospital for withdrawal; in February, he was visited by a lover from N.Y., Chan Richardson (born Beverly Dolores Berg). He led a group at the Finale Club with Miles Davis (of which broadcasts survive), recorded again for Dial, was recorded live with Young and others at J.A.T.P., and led Sunday jam session at Billy Berg's; he also met his early idol Rudy Vallee. In April, the Finale closed after a raid and his drug connection, Emery "Moose the Mooche" Byrd was arrested. Parker was soon in withdrawal, drinking alcohol as a substitute, broke, and crashing in a converted garage. In May, Chan left: she was pregnant with another man's child and gave birth in N.Y. to Kim, who became known as Parker's daughter. Howard McGhee hired Parker for an engagement at the Hi-De-Ho and recorded with him on July 29, 1946. But at that infamous "Lover Man" session Parker was in poor condition (he later said it "should never have been released"); Elliott Grennard, who was present, wrote a romanticized short story based on the session, "Sparrow's Last Jump."

That night while sitting naked, Parker accidentally started a fire in his room at the Civic Hotel with a cigarette, failed to get dressed when the firefighters came, made a scene and was arrested. He was taken to a hospital, then placed in the psychiatric wing of the L.A. county jail and finally sentenced to be confined at Camarillo State Hospital, where he was broken of his addiction. In September, Doris moved to L.A. to lend support and visit him regularly. Upon his release on Jan. 31, 1947, in the custody of and partly through the efforts of Dial producer Ross Russell, he moved into a furnished room with Doris and immediately resumed his career. He was already becoming a cult figure and numerous private recordings were made of him in clubs and even jam sessions, almost all of them were eventually issued. After a stint at the Hi-De-Ho in March, he returned to N.Y. and soon returned to heroin and alcohol, often failing to pay his sidepeople, and sometimes engaging in outrageous behaviors, such as urinating in a nightclub's phone booth. Tragically, his heroin habit was copied by many younger musicians, among whom heroin use became a social norm. Still, Parker managed to lead a productive and increasingly successful career. He won first place in the alto saxophone category of the Metronome Poll from 1947 through 1952, and in the *Down Beat* Readers Poll from 1950 through 1954. From 1947 through 1950, he led a quintet, first with Miles Davis (followed by Kenny Dorham, then Red Rodney) and Max Roach (followed by Roy Haynes). In 1948, he and Doris married. In May 1949, he appeared at the jazz festival in Paris. The Manhattan club Birdland, named for him, opened Dec. 15, 1949. In early 1950, his marriage with Doris broke up and by May he moved in with Chan, who became known as Chan Parker though they never legally married. He served as a father to Kim and titled a recording for her; they had a daughter Pree and a son Baird (for whom he wrote "Laird Baird").

In 1950, Parker's quintet broke up. He performed live with strings plus oboe added to his rhythm section. He also began touring as a "single," accompanied by local musicians in each city. His playing between 1950 and at least 1952 revealed an even more developed technique—a smoothness of sound in all registers, cleanness of execution, and an increased ease at the fastest tempos. His innovative patterns, incorporating bitonality, presaged at times Dolphy and other later disciples. His style is most evident in live recordings, such as those from Sweden (1950) and from the Rockland Palace in 1952 ("Lester Leaps In," "The Rocker (2)"). His studio recordings for Norman Granz were generally highly arranged affairs featuring voices, strings, and various bands; they did however serve to bring him a wider audience, and he was especially proud of the string group because of his interests in modern classical music. He used Slonimsky's Thesaurus of Scales and Melodic Patterns and studied scores of Stravinsky. He met Stefan Wolpe and wrote to Varése and Schoenberg, with the intent of studying with them, but never followed through. In November 1950, he toured Sweden and Denmark but did not appear for a scheduled performance while in Paris. In N.Y., he was hospitalized for a stomach ulcer caused by drinking. Because of narcotics possession, he was arrested in July 1951. He was only given a three-month suspended sentence, but his cabaret card was revoked, denying him the right to work in most N.Y. nightclubs. He was not prevented from concert halls, and he did work frequently in Philadelphia and elsewhere. His card was restored in 1953 after he wrote a letter requesting clemency. In 1953, King Pleasure set lyrics to his solo on "Parker's Mood" (1948 recording); it was a hit but Parker disliked the lyrics which (presciently) told of him dying and going back to Kansas City. (Eddie Jefferson had set it to more typical "miss my baby" lyrics in 1949 as "Bless My Soul," but his recording remains little known.) On May 15, 1953 he appeared in Massey Hall, Toronto with Gillespie, Powell, Mingus and Roach. Poorly attended at the time, it resulted in a celebrated recording. From Feb. 28 through March 28, 1954, he and Gillespie were on a package tour where they were accompanied by the Stan Kenton Orch.

His health and mental condition were deteriorating. He still had ulcers, and Chan referred to a "heart attack" of some kind while in Philadelphia. He was grief-stricken when Pree died on March 6, 1954 of a congenital heart problem, while he was performing at the Tiffany Club in L.A. He was fired from the Tiffany for his erratic behavior. That summer his family vacationed in East Brewster on Cape Cod and though he was touring he probably spent some time there before they returned to N.Y. But his relationship with Chan was suffering and after a row he attempted suicide on Aug. 30, 1954 by drinking iodine, and subsequently entered Bellevue Hospital until Sept. 10. On Sept. 28, he voluntarily returned to Bellevue to get help with depression and alcoholism; he was released on Oct. 15 and continued to report there for psychotherapy. Chan separated from him and he lived in the apartment of Ahmed Basheer in Greenwich Village; his last gig was on March 4 and 5, 1955 at Birdland. The second night was disastrous, with Parker and Bud Powell arguing on stage and both Powell and Charles Mingus storming off. On March 9, before going to a gig in Boston, he stopped in the Stanhope Hotel apartment of jazz patron Pannonica de Koenigswarter. Seeing that he was vomiting blood, she had him stay for several days under a doctor's supervision. He choked and died while watching television there. It seems that alcoholism, not heroin, was the immediate cause due to the cirrhosis of his liver and stomach ulcers. Chan arranged for him to be buried near Pree at Mt. Hope Cemetery in Westchester County, N.Y., but his legal wife Doris intervened and scheduled services for March 21 at the Abyssinian Baptist Church on 138th St. before flying his body to Kansas City for burial. Soon after his death there were memorial concerts, and the graffiti "Bird Lives" began showing up around N.Y., a tribute to his powerful impact.

Parker's life with Chan was the main subject of the 1988 film, *Bird*, directed by Clint Eastwood. He is also the subject of the documentary *Celebrating Bird*, and an animated short by Peter Bodge. He appeared in a Noman Granz JATP film in 1950; the film was never edited but the two performances on which he appears (and others without him) were released in the late 1990s, without synch sound. The only footage of Parker with "live" sound is a performance of "Hot House" with Gillespie from a television variety program, Feb. 24, 1952. The films clearly illustrate that he played with perfect composure and a minimum of movement, far from the laughable wiggling of neck and fingers as portrayed in *Bird*. Only audio survives of other television appearances in N.Y. and Montreal. Doris's daughter Kim was raised by Phil Woods and is a jazz singer.

DISC.: *First Recordings* (1940); *Early Bird* (1940); *Birth of the Bebop* (1943); *Yardbird in Lotus Land* (1945); *Every Bit of It* (1945); *C.P. on Verve* (1946); *Lullaby in Rhythm* (1947); *Dial Masters, Vols. 1 & 2* (1947); *Dean Benedetti Recordings of Charlie Parker* (1947); *Complete Dial Sessions* (1946–47); *Bird on 52nd Street* (1948); *Band That Never Was* (1948); *Complete Savoy Studio Sessions* (1948); *Rara Avis* (1949); *Live at Carnegie Hall* (1949); *Charlie Parker & Stars of Modern Jazz* (1949); *Jazz at the Philharmonic* (1949); *Bird in Paris* (1949); *At the Roost, Vols. 1–4* (1949); *One Night in Chicago* (1950); *One Night at Birdland* (1950); *Bird in Sweden* (1950); *Evening at Home with the Bird* (1950); *Bird with Strings* (1950); *Bird at the Roost, Vol. 3* (1950); *Bird at St. Nick's* (1950); *Bird You Never Heard* (1950); *Apartment Sessions* (1950); *Summit Meeting at Birdland* (1951); *Happy Bird* (1951); *Bird with The Herd* (1951); *Sept. 26, 1952* (1952); *Inglewood Jam* (1952); *Live at Rockland Palace* (1952); *Yardbird: DC–53* (1953); *One Night in Washington* (1953); *Jazz at Massey Hall* (1953); *C.P. at Storyville* (1953); *C.P. Plays South of the Border* (1953); *Bird at the Hi-Hat* (1953); *Big Band* (1953).

BIBL.: M. Harrison, *C. P.* (London, 1960); R. Reisner, *Bird: The Legend of C. P.* (N.Y., 1961); J. Jepsen, *A Discography of C. P.* (Copenhagen, 1968); D. Morgenstern et al., *Bird and Diz: A Bibliography* (N.Y., 1973); R. Russell, *Bird Lives: The High Life and Hard Times of C. (Yardbird) P.* (N.Y., 1973/4); P. Koste, D. Bakker, *C. P.* (Alphen aan den Rijn, the Netherlands, 1976); C. Parker and F. Paudras, *To Bird with Love* (Poitiers, France, 1981); B. Priestley, *C. P.* (N.Y., 1984); G. Giddins, *Celebrating Bird: The Triumph of C. P.* (N.Y., 1987); L. Koch, *Yardbird Suite: A Compendium of the Music and Life of C. P.* (Bowling Green, Ohio, 1988/89); M. Miller, *Cool Blues: C.P. in Canada 1953* (London, 1989).—LP

Parker, Graham, originally accompanied by The Rumour, one of the most compelling singer-songwriters of the British New Wave scene; b. East London, England, Nov. 18, 1950. The Rumour, rock band involved in London's early 1970s pub scene. **MEMBERSHIP:** Graham Parker, voc.; Brinsley Schwarz, gtr. (b. Woodbridge, England, March 25, 1949); Martin Belmont, gtr. (b. Dec. 21, 1948); Bob Andrews, kybd. (b. June 20, 1949, June 20, 1949); Andrew Bodnar, bs.; Stephen Goulding, drm.

By writing songs with a personalized vision that dealt with anger, frustration, and defiance in a variety of styles, from rockabilly to reggae, Graham Parker and The Rumour garnered critical praise for their early albums. Although they failed to sell, their albums presaged punk's rebellion against the pomposity of progressive rock and the slick, bland, complacent commercialism of many 1970s groups. Achieving his biggest commercial and critical success with 1979's *Squeezing Out Sparks*, Parker eventually recorded for many labels with only modest success. His 1988 *The Mona Lisa's Sister* was hailed as a triumphant comeback, but he was unable to successfully follow it up.

Graham Parker grew up in Deep Cut, Surrey, a small town south of London, and formed his first band, the Deep Cut Three, at age 13. After a stint with the R&B–styled Blackrockers band, he dropped out of high school to travel around Europe by working a variety of mundane jobs and manning several bands. Years later, in 1975, Parker recorded a demonstration tape that led to a connection with The Rumour, an outstanding band comprised of veterans of England's declining pub-rock scene. Bob Andrews and Brinsley Schwarz had been members of the cult band Brinsley Schwarz, whereas Martin Belmont had been with Ducks Deluxe, and Andrew Bodnar and Stephen Goulding with Bontemps Roulez.

Signed to Mercury Records, Graham Parker and The Rumour recorded two well-received but poor-selling albums released in 1976. With Parker singing his songs in a gruff, raspy voice, *Howlin' Wind* featured such powerful and vituperative songs as "Between You and Me," "Back to School Days," and "Don't Ask Me Questions." *Heat Treatment*, which included "That's What They All Say," the excellent "Pourin' It All Out," and "Fool's Gold," became their first American album-chart entry, sparked by two American tours.

Scoring a minor hit with "Hold Back the Night" in spring 1977, Graham Parker and The Rumour recorded *Stick to Me* under producer Nick Lowe, another veteran of the band Brinsley Schwarz. However, the album was not well received, as Lowe's use of complex arrangements and a horn section was criticized, yet it contained a number of outstanding songs, including the title song as well as "Soul on Ice" and the ominous "Thunder and Rain." Their next album, the double-record set *The Parkerilla*, contained three live sides and one studio side. Switching to Arista Records, Parker and the group recorded *Squeezing Out Sparks* with veteran producer Jack Nitzche. Projecting a simpler, guitar-based sound unmuddled by horns, the album was critically lauded for containing Parker's best compositions and vocal performances to date. It included "Local Girls," "Nobody Hurts You," the passionate "You Can't Be Too Strong," and the potent "Passion Is No Ordinary Word," as well as "Mercury Poisoning" and "No Protection." Supported by a three-month American tour, the album sold far better than previous releases. In 1979 Dave Edmunds covered Parker's "Crawling from the Wreckage," while Parker recorded *The Up Escalator* with guest keyboardists Nicky Hopkins and Danny Federici. The album featured "Stupefaction," "No Holding Back," "Love without Greed," and "Endless Night," with harmony vocals by Bruce Springsteen.

Graham Parker and The Rumour split company in 1981, and Parker recorded his next three albums as a solo artist while retaining guitarist Brinsley Schwarz. Moving in a softer direction, *Another Grey Area* included "Crying for Attention," "Temporary Beauty," and "No More Excuses," whereas *The Real Macaw* contained "Just Like a Man," "You Can't Take Love for Granted," and the minor hit "Life Gets Better." Switching to Elektra Records, Parker scored a moderate hit with "Wake Up (Next to You)" from *Steady Nerves*, which included the political "Break Them Down" and "Lunatic Fringe." He next signed with Atlantic Records, but no recordings were ever released. By 1988 Parker had moved to RCA Records, where his debut for the label, *The Mona Lisa's Sister*, was hailed as a brilliant return to form. The album contained his attack on Atlantic, "Success," plus "The Girl Isn't Ready," "Start a Fire," "Don't Let It Break You Down," "Back in Time," and the soothing "Blue Highways."

In 1990 Graham Parker joined Dave Edmunds, 1960s rocker Dion, and Kim Wilson of the Fabulous Thunderbirds for a nine-week tour as Dave Edmunds's Rock and Roll Revue. Following two more modest-selling studio albums for RCA, Parker switched to Capitol for 1992's *Burning Questions*. Parker toured in support of the album, and in 1993 Rhino Records issued the stunning anthology set *Passion Is No Ordinary Word*. By 1995 Graham Parker had moved to the independent label Razor & Tie for *12 Haunted Episodes*.

DISC.: GRAHAM PARKER AND THE RUMOUR: *Howlin' Wind* (1976); *Heat Treatment* (1976); *Stick to Me* (1977); *The Parkerilla* (1978); *Pourin' It All Out: The Mercury Years* (1985); *Squeezing Out Sparks* (1979); *The Up Escalator* (1980); *Best* (1982). **THE RUMOUR:** *Max* (1977); *Frogs, Sprouts, Clogs and Krauts* (1979); *Purity of Essence* (1982). **GRAHAM PARKER:** *Another Grey Area* (1982); *The Real Macaw* (1983); *Steady Nerves* (1985); *The Mona Lisa's Sister* (1988); *Human Soul* (1990); *Struck by Lightning* (1991); *Best, 1988–1991* (1992); *Burning Questions* (1992); *Passion Is No Ordinary Word: The G. P. Anthology, 1976–1991* (1993); *12 Haunted Episodes* (1995).—BH

Parker, Henry Taylor, American critic and writer on music; b. Boston, April 29, 1867; d. there, March 30, 1934. He attended Harvard Univ., then served as N.Y. correspondent of the *Boston Evening Transcript* and later as its London correspondent. In 1905 he became the newspaper's principal drama and music critic, holding this position until his death. Although not trained as a musician (he could not read notes), Parker possessed an extraordinary sense of aesthetic values, and often gave unstinting praise to composers of the modern school who were disdained by the musical establishment; he was equally capable of appreciating fresh talents among performers. He wrote a curiously antiquated prose, employing archaic turns of phrase, but his articles, often very long, were uniquely artistic. He signed his name H.T.P., which was facetiously deciphered by some as an acronym for "Hard To Please," or "Hell To Pay." He publ. a collection of essays on music, *Eighth-Notes* (N.Y., 1922).

BIBL.: D. McCord, *H.T. P.; Portrait of a Critic* (N.Y., 1935). **—NS/LK/DM**

Parker, Horatio (William), eminent American composer and pedagogue; b. Auburndale, Mass., Sept. 15, 1863; d. Cedarhurst, N.Y., Dec. 18, 1919. He studied piano with John Orth, theory with Emery, and composition with Chadwick in Boston, and then went to Germany, where he took courses in organ and composition with Rheinberger in Munich (1882–85); under his tutelage he wrote a cantata, *King Trojan* (1885). Returning to the U.S., he settled in N.Y. and taught at the cathedral schools of St. Paul and St. Mary (1886–90), at the General Theological Seminary (1892), and at the National Cons. of Music (1892–93). He was organist and choirmaster at St. Luke's (1885–87), St. Andrew's (1887–88), and the Church of the Holy Trinity (1888–93); in 1893 he went to Boston as organist and choirmaster at Trinity Church, remaining there until 1902. He attracted attention with the first performance of his oratorio *Hora novissima* (N.Y., May 3, 1893), in which he demonstrated his mastery of choral writing, while his harmonic and contrapuntal style remained securely tied to German practices. In 1894 he was engaged as a prof. of theory at Yale Univ.; in 1904 he became dean of its School of Music, and remained there until his death. Many American composers received the benefit of his excellent instruction, among them Charles Ives, who kept his sincere appreciation of Parker's teaching long after he renounced Parker's conservative traditions. In 1895 he founded the New Haven Sym. Orch., which he conducted until 1918. Parker conducted performances of his works in England in 1900 and 1902, and received an honorary degree of Mus.Doc. at Cambridge Univ. in 1902. Returning to the U.S., he served as organist and choirmaster at the collegiate church of St. Nicholas in Boston from 1902 to 1910. He continued to compose industriously, without making any concessions to the emerging modern schools of composition; his choral works are particularly notable. In 1911 his opera *Mona* won the $10,000 prize offered by the Metropolitan Opera in N.Y., and was produced there on March 14, 1912; he also won a prize offered by the National Federation of Women's Clubs for his 2nd opera, *Fairy-*

land, which was produced in Los Angeles on July 1, 1915. Neither of the operas possessed enough power to survive in the repertoire.

WORKS: DRAMATIC: O p e r a : *Mona* (1910; N.Y., March 14, 1912); *Fairyland* (1914; Los Angeles, July 1, 1915). I n c i d e n t a l   M u s i c   T o : *The Eternal Feminine* for Chorus and Orch. (1903–04; New Haven, Nov. 7, 1904; not extant); *The Prince of India* for Voice, Chorus, and Orch. (1905; N.Y., Sept. 24, 1906). O t h e r : *Cupid and Psyche,* masque (New Haven, June 16, 1916); *The Legend of St. Christopher,* dramatic oratorio for Solo Voices, Chorus, and Orch. (1897; N.Y., April 15, 1898); *Morven and the Grail,* oratorio for Solo Voices, Chorus, and Orch. (Boston, April 13, 1915). ORCH.: Concert Overture (Munich, July 7, 1884); *Regulus,* overture héroique (1884); *Venetian Overture* (1884); Sym. in C major (Munich, May 11, 1885); *Count Robert of Paris,* overture (N.Y., Dec. 10, 1890); *A Northern Ballad,* symphonic poem (Boston, Dec. 29, 1899); Organ Concerto (Boston, Dec. 26, 1902); *Vathek,* symphonic poem (1903); *Collegiate Overture,* with Men's Chorus (Norfolk Festival, June 7, 1911). CHAMBER: String Quartet (1885; Detroit, Nov. 29, 1887); Suite for Piano, Violin, and Cello (1893); String Quintet (1894; Boston, Jan. 21, 1895); Suite for Piano and Violin (1894; Boston, Jan. 15, 1895). VOCAL: C h o r a l : *Psalm* for Soprano, Women's Chorus, Organ, and Harp (Munich, Dec. 23, 1884; publ. as *The Lord Is My Shepherd,* 1904); *Ballade* for Chorus and Orch. (Munich, July 7, 1884; publ. as *The Ballad of a Knight and His Daughter,* 1891); *König Trojan,* ballad for Tenor, Baritone, Chorus, and Orch. (Munich, July 15, 1885; publ. as *King Trojan,* 1886); *Idylle,* cantata for Tenor, Bass, Chorus, and Orch. (1886); *Normannenzug,* cantata for Men's Chorus and Orch. (1888; publ. as *The Norsemen's Raid,* 1911); *Dream-King and His Love,* cantata for Tenor, Chorus, and Orch. (1891; N.Y., March 30, 1893); *The Holy Child,* Christmas cantata for Soprano, Tenor, Bass, Chorus, and Piano or Organ (1893); *The Legend of St. Christopher,* dramatic oratorio for Solo Voices, Chorus, and Orch. (1897; N.Y., April 15, 1898); *Adstant angelorum chori,* motet for 8 Voices (N.Y., March 16, 1899); *A Wanderer's Psalm,* cantata for Solo Voices, Chorus, and Orch. (Hereford, England, Sept. 13, 1900); *Hymnos Andron* for Solo Voices, Men's Chorus, and Orch. (New Haven, Oct. 23, 1901; publ. as *Greek Festival Hymn,* 1901); *A Star Song,* lyric rhapsody for Solo Voices, Chorus, and Orch. (1901; Norwich, England, Oct. 23, 1902); *King Gorm the Grim,* ballad for Chorus and Orch. (1907; Norfolk Festival, June 4, 1908); *A Song of Times,* cantata for Soprano, Chorus, Bugle Corps, Band or Orch., and Organ (Philadelphia, Dec. 1, 1911); *Morven and the Grail,* oratorio for Solo Voices, Chorus, and Orch. (Boston, April 13, 1915); *The Dream of Mary,* morality for Solo Voices, Children's Chorus, Chorus, Congregation, Organ, and Orch. (Norfolk Festival, June 4, 1918). O t h e r : Cantatas, choruses, part-songs, anthems, and services.

BIBL.: G. Chadwick, *H. P.* (New Haven, 1921); W. Kearns, *H. P. 1863–1919: A Study of His Life and Music* (diss., Univ. of Ill., 1965).—NS/LK/DM

Parker, Jamie (real name, **James Edward Kimura**), Canadian pianist, brother of **Jon Kimura Parker**; b. Burnaby, British Columbia, May 31, 1963. He began his studies with his uncle, Edward J. Parker, and later was a pupil of Marek Jablonski at the Banff School of Fine Arts (1978–87) and of Kum-Sing Lee at the Vancouver Academy of Music (performance certificate, 1981). After obtaining his B.Mus. at the Univ. of British Columbia (1985), he completed his training with Adele Marcus at the Juilliard School in N.Y. (M.Mus., 1987). In

1981 he made his debut as a soloist in Prokofiev's 1st Piano Concerto with the Calgary Phil., and thereafter performed with principal Canadian orchs. and was active as a recitalist and chamber music artist. In addition to the standard repertoire, Parker also programs the works of contemporary Canadian composers.
—NS/LK/DM

Parker, Jon Kimura (real name, **John David Kimura**), Canadian pianist, brother of **Jamie Parker**; b. Vancouver, Dec. 25, 1959. He studied with Jessie Morrison and was only 5 when he appeared as soloist with the Vancouver Youth Orch. After further training with his uncle, Edward J. Parker, with Kum-Sing Lee at the Vancouver Academy of Music (performance certificate, 1977), and with Marek Jablonski at the Banff School of Fine Arts, he completed his studies with Adele Marcus at the Juilliard School in N.Y. (B.Mus. and M.Mus., 1981; D.M.A., 1989). In 1982 he won the Viña del Mar Competition in Chile, and in 1983 toured Europe as a soloist with the Juilliard Orch. After capturing 1st prize in the Leeds Competition in 1984, he appeared as a soloist with principal orchs. the world-dover and as a recitalist. His commanding technical resources are notably refined by a gift for poetic lyricism, which serves him well as an interpreter of the Romantic repertoire. He has also played much out-of-the-ordinary music, ranging from rags to contemporary Canadian works.—NS/LK/DM

Parker, Kim, jazz vocalist; stepdaughter of **Charlie Parker**; b. N.Y., Aug. 22, 1946. After the famous saxophonist's death, she was raised by her mother and her stepfather, Phil Woods. She performed with her stepfather's and Quincy Jones's orchs. in the late 1950s; while studying drama at Hofstra Univ. (graduating in 1964), won "best vocalist" award at Villanova's Intercollegiate Jazz Festival. She left the music scene from 1967–79; she has since recorded and toured throughout the world with various accompanists. She has also acted in a number of films, most of them in French.

DISC.: *Language of Blue* (1980); *Havin' Myself a Time* (1981); *Good Girl* (1982); *Sometimes I'm Blue* (1985).—LP

Parker, Leon (Evans Jr.), eclectic jazz drummer; b. White Plains, N.Y., Aug. 21, 1965. A tasteful, swinging performer and a purist of sorts who uses a very small drum set, he slowly developed a reputation around N.Y. in the late 1980s and 1990s. He began drumming on household objects at three, performing solo improvisations at age six. As a teenager, Parker performed with a youth jazz ensemble and then went on to work in local dance bands; for his senior high school recital he composed a concerto using orchestral percussion instruments. Inspired by native drummers of Spain, he began reducing his drum set to fewer and fewer parts; by the late 1980s, he was only using the ride cymbal; he worked with Tom Harrell and even went out with Kenny Barron and Dewey Redman with the lone cymbal. He was house drummer at N.Y.'s Augies jazz club from 1987–88, and then led groups in N.Y., mostly at the Village Gate's sidewalk level from 1989–94. During this time, he brought back the bass drum and snare and added hand drumming, including congas, bell, rattle, clave, marimba, ashiko and caxixi, gong and bowl. His second album, *Belief*, was awarded "1996 Album of the Year" by the N.Y. Jazz Critics' Circle. That same year, he worked with the performance group Urban Bush Women, with whom he toured Brazil and Australia. He has also begun teaching vocal/body movement and rhythm workshops to dance students in conservatories and universities, including at the Univ. of Mich. He sometimes solos entirely by slapping and tapping his body, and by shaking various percussion objects. He often works with his wife, Lisa, who is a flutist.

DISC.: *Above and Below* (1994); *Belief* (1996); *Awakening* (1998).—**LP**

Parker, William, American baritone; b. Butler, Pa., Aug. 5, 1943; d. N.Y., March 29, 1993. He took German language and literature courses at Princeton Univ. (B.A., 1965); after singing in the U.S. Army Chorus in Washington, D.C., he pursued serious vocal training with Bernac and Ponselle. He won 1st prize in the Toulouse Competition and the special Poulenc Prize in the Paris Competition, then gained wide recognition in 1979 when he took 1st prize in the Kennedy Center-Rockefeller Foundation International Competition for Excellence in the Performance of American Music. In subsequent years, Parker acquired a fine reputation as a concert singer; also sang with various opera companies in the U.S. and abroad. He was especially admired for his cultured approach to art song interpretation and for his advocacy of contemporary American music. After contracting AIDS, he commissioned a number of composers to contribute selections to *The AIDS Quilt Songbook*. With the baritones Kurt Ollman, William Sharp, and Sanford Sylvan, he gave the premiere of the cycle at N.Y.'s Alice Tully Hall in 1992. Parker continued to make appearances until his last public concert in Minneapolis on Jan. 1, 1993.—**NS/LK/DM**

Parker, William, jazz bassist; b. Bronx, N.Y., Jan. 10, 1952. His earnest playing and personality have made him a favorite on the new music scene in N.Y. since the early 1980s. He originally studied cello, switching to bass in the last year of high school. He played with various pop and folk bands, and also studied with Richard Davis, and J. Garrison. For more than 10 years, Parker performed and recorded with Cecil Taylor (1980–91). During this same period and through the 1990s, Parker collaborated with a wide variety of contemporary musicians, including David S. Ware, Peter Brotzmann, Matthew Shipp, Rashied Ali, Roscoe Mitchell, Clifford Jordan, Melodic Art-tet, and Muhal Richard Abrams. He has composed music for dance and dramas, and has played in big bands and small ensembles. Since the mid-1990s, he has led his own small combo, In Order to Survive, and a big band, the Little Huey Creative Music Orch.; he also tours as a soloist.

DISC.: *Through Acceptance of the Mystery* (1981); *Flowers Grow in My Room* (with the Little Huey Creative Music Orch.; 1995); *Testimony* (1995); *In Order to Survive* (1995); *Comparison Seizes Bed-Stuy* (with In Order to Survive; 1996); *Invisible Weave* (1997); *Sunrise in a Tone World* (1997).—**LP**

Parlan, Horace (Louis), jazz pianist; b. Pittsburgh, Pa., Jan. 19, 1931. A pianist discovered by Charles Mingus, Parlan has overcome disability and made it an asset. His right hand was partially crippled by polio when he was a child, yet he has made kinetic, rhythmic right-hand phrases part of his attack, contrasting them with striking left-hand chords. He filters blues and R&B influences through solos that are stark, sometimes somber, but never dull. Parlan began playing in R&B bands during the 1950s, then moved from Pittsburgh to N.Y. and joined Mingus's group, where he received considerable attention (1957–59). He worked with Booker Ervin (1960–61), then was a regular pianist with the Eddie "Lockjaw" Davis-Johnny Griffin quintet in 1962. He played with Rahsaan Roland Kirk (1963–66), and recorded with Tubby Hayes, Slide Hampton, Dexter Gordon, and others. He had a string of Blue Note releases in 1960–63, but encountered tough times near the end of the decade. He left the U.S. for Copenhagen in 1973, and during the 1970s and 1980s gained international recognition for some superb releases, including a pair of duet sessions with Archie Shepp. In 1986, he led his own trio on a tour of Japan, and in 1991 he played in Moscow with Red Mitchell.

DISC.: *Us Three* (1960); *Speakin' My Piece* (1960); *Movin' and Groovin'* (1960); *Headin' South* (1960); *Up and Down* (1961); *On the Spur of the Moment* (1961); *Happy Frame of Mind* (1963); *Back from the Gig* (1963); *Arrival* (1973); *No Blues* (1975); *Frankly Speaking* (1977); *Blue Parlan* (1978); *Pannonica* (1981); *Like Someone in Love* (1983); *Musically Yours* (1979); *Maestro* (1979); *Going Home* (1979); *Glad I Found You* (1984); *Little Esther* (1987).—**LP**

Parlow, Kathleen, Canadian violinist and teacher; b. Calgary, Alberta, Sept. 20, 1890; d. Oakville, Ontario, Aug. 19, 1963. Her family moved to San Francisco when she was a child, where she had early instruction in violin; in 1906 she was sent to St. Petersburg, where she was accepted by Leopold Auer in his violin class at the Cons. She subsequently developed an extensive concert career, playing in England, Scandinavia, the U.S., and the Orient. From 1929 to 1936 she was a violin instructor at Mills Coll. in Oakland, Calif., and in 1941 she joined the faculty of the Royal Cons. of Music of Toronto, where she organized in 1941 the Parlow String Quartet. She was head of the string dept. at the London (Ontario) Coll. of Music (from 1959). The Kathleen Parlow Scholarship was established at the Univ. of Toronto from proceeds from her estate.

BIBL.: M. French, *K. P.: A Portrait* (Toronto, 1967). —**NS/LK/DM**

Parmeggiani, Ettore, Italian tenor; b. Rimini, Aug. 15, 1895; d. Milan, Jan. 28, 1960. He was a pupil of Mandolini in Milan, making his operatic debut there in 1922 at the Teatro dal Verme as Cavaradossi. In 1927 he made his first appearance at Milan's La Scala as Max in *Der Freischütz*, and continued to sing there for a decade. In addition to his Wagnerian roles, he appeared in the premieres of Mascagni's *Nerone* (1935) and Respighi's *Lucrezia* (1937) there. In 1936 he also sang in the premiere of Malipiero's *Giulio Cesare* in Genoa. In later years, he taught voice in Milan and led the claque at La Scala.—**NS/LK/DM**

Parnas, Leslie, American cellist and teacher; b. St. Louis, Nov. 11, 1931. He studied with Piatigorsky at the Curtis Inst. of Music in Philadelphia (1948–53). He won a number of prizes, including 2nd prize in the Geneva Competition (1957), the Prix Pablo Casals in the International Cello Competition in Paris (1957), and the joint 2nd prize (no 1st prize was given) in the Tchaikovsky Competition in Moscow (1962). He was 1st cellist in the St. Louis Sym. Orch. (1954–62), and then appeared worldwide as a soloist with orchs., recitalist, and chamber music player. He taught at Boston Univ. (from 1962) and the St. Louis Cons. of Music (from 1982). —NS/LK/DM

Parratt, Sir Walter, eminent English organist, teacher, and composer; b. Huddersfield, Feb. 10, 1841; d. Windsor, March 27, 1924. He was a pupil of his father, the organist of the Huddersfield Parish Church, then became a pupil of George Cooper (1851), and also began playing the organ in various churches. He was made organist of Great Witley Church and private organist to the Earl of Dudley (1864), at the Wigan Parish Church (1868), at Magdalen Coll., Oxford (1872), and finally at St. George's Chapel, Windsor (1882); was also made private organist to the Queen (1892). He was prof. of organ at the Royal Coll. of Music in London (1883–1923), prof. of music at Oxford Univ. (1908–18), and dean of music at London Univ. (1916–24). Parratt served as Master of the Queen's (later King's) Music (1893–1924). A distinguished recitalist and teacher, he received honorary doctorates in music from the Univs. of Oxford (1894), Cambridge (1910), and Durham (1912); was knighted (1892); became a Member (1901), Commander (1917), and Knight Commander (1921) of the Royal Victorian Order. Among his compositions were the Obitt Service, 4 anthems, and other sacred works, incidental music, songs, organ pieces, and piano music.

BIBL.: D. Tovey and G. Parratt, *W. P., Master of Music* (London, 1941).—NS/LK/DM

Parris, Herman, Russian-American physician and composer; b. Ekaterinoslav, Oct. 30, 1903; d. Philadelphia, Jan. 14, 1973. He was taken to America in his infancy. He studied at the Jefferson Medical Coll. in Philadelphia, obtaining his M.D. in 1926. Concurrently he studied music at the Univ. of Pa., and graduated in 1921. He was a diligent and competent composer; wrote 4 syms. (1946, 1947, 1949, 1952), 8 piano concertos (1946–53), 4 string quartets (1946, 1948, 1960, 1964), 22 piano sonatas (1946–65), 115 piano preludes (1946–65), *Hebrew Rhapsody* for Orch. (1949), *Lament* for Strings (in memory of O. Downes; 1956), and various pieces of chamber music. He gained a flickering moment of notoriety with his orch. piece entitled *Hospital Suite*, realistically portraying bloody events in the sickroom; it was brought to light in a collegiate spirit by the Doctors' Orch. Society in N.Y. on May 13, 1948. Unfortunately, no further performances were given (all the patients in the suite died).—NS/LK/DM

Parris, Robert, American composer, pianist, and teacher; b. Philadelphia, May 21, 1924; d. Washington, D.C., Dec. 5, 1999. He studied piano in his youth and later pursued his education at the Univ. of Pa. (B.S., 1945; M.S., 1946). He then studied composition with Mennin at the Juilliard School of Music in N.Y. (B.S., 1948), Ibert and Copland at the Berkshire Music Center in Tanglewood (summers, 1950–51), and Honegger at the École Normale de Musique in Paris on a Fulbright fellowship (1951–52). After teaching at Washington State Coll. in Pullman (1948–49) and the Univ. of Md. (1961–62), he joined the faculty of George Washington Univ. in Washington, D.C., in 1963, where he was a prof. from 1976. Between 1961 and 1975 he also acted as an occasional music critic for the *Washington Post* and the *Washington Evening Star*. In his early compositions, Parris pursued a tonal path but in his later works he adopted atonal procedures.

WORKS: ORCH.: *Symphonic Movement No. 1* (N.Y., June 1948) and *No. 2* (1951); *Harlequin's Carnival* (1949; Tanglewood, Aug. 11, 1951); Sym. (1952); Piano Concerto (1954); Concerto for 5 Kettle Drums and Orch. (1955; Washington, D.C., March 25, 1958); Viola Concerto (1956; Washington, D.C., May 20, 1971); Violin Concerto (1958); *Lamentations and Praises* for Brass and Percussion (1962; Philadelphia, May 24, 1966); Sinfonia for Brass (1963); Flute Concerto (1964); Concerto for Trombone and Chamber Orch. (Washington, D.C., Sept. 19, 1964); *The Golden Net* for Chamber Orch. (1968); *The Phoenix*, timpani concerto (1969; Detroit, Jan. 2, 1970); *The Messengers*, later renamed *Angels* (1974; Albany, N.Y., March 14, 1975); *Rite of Passage* for Clarinet, Electric Guitar, and Chamber Orch. (1978); *The Unquiet Heart* for Violin and Orch. (1981); *Chamber Music for Orchestra* (1984; Glasgow, Feb. 12, 1985); *Symphonic Variations* (1987; Washington, D.C., Jan. 28, 1988). **CHAMBER:** Cello Sonata (c. 1946); 2 string trios (1947, 1951); Sonatina for Brass Quintet (1948; Pullman, Wash., May 1, 1949); 2 string quartets: No. 1 (1951; Washington, D.C., May 11, 1958) and No. 2 (1952); Sonatina for Winds (1954); *Fantasy and Fugue* for Cello (1955); Violin Sonata (1956); Viola Sonata (1957); Quintet for Violin, Cello, Flute, Oboe, and Bassoon (1957); Trio for Clarinet, Piano, and Cello (1959); *Cadenza, Caprice, and Ricercar* for Piano and Cello (1961); Sonatina for Recorder Quartet (1964); Duo for Flute and Violin (1965); Sonata for Solo Violin (1965); *4 Pieces* for Brass or Wind Trio (1965); *St. Winefred's Well* for 6 Players (1967); Concerto for Percussion, Violin, Cello, and Piano (1967); *The Book of Imaginary Beings I* for Flute, Violin, Cello, Piano, and Percussion (1972) and *II* for Clarinet, Violin, Viola, Cello, and Percussion (1983); 3 Duets for Electric Guitar and Amplified Harpsichord (1985); *Metamorphic Variations* for Flute, Clarinet, Violin, Cello, and Percussion (1986); *13 Pieces* for Trumpet, Violin, Viola, Cello, and Percussion (1989); *2 Small Duets and a Solo* for Violin and Piano (1989); *Nocturnes I* for Flute, Violin, Viola, Cello, and Percussion (Washington, D.C., Nov. 2, 1992) and *II* for Clarinet, Viola, Cello, Bass, and Percussion (1994). **Piano:** *Toccata* for 2 Pianos (1950); *Variations* (1952); *6 Little Studies* (1960). **VOCAL:** 3 Songs for Baritone, Piano, and Celesta (1947); *The Hollow Men* for Tenor, Men's Chorus, and Chamber Ensemble (1949; N.Y., Feb. 16, 1951); *Night* for Baritone, String Quartet, and Clarinet (1951; Washington, D.C., Oct. 31, 1958); *Alas, for the Day*, cantata for Chorus (1954); *3 Passacaglias* for Soprano, Violin, Harpsichord, and Cello (1957); *Mad Scene* for 2 Baritones, Soprano, and Chamber Orch. (1960); *The Raids* for Soprano, Piano, and Violin (1960); *The Leaden Echo and the Golden Echo* for Baritone and Orch. (1960; Washington, D.C., Jan. 10, 1962); *Hymn for the Nativity* for Chorus and Brass Ensemble (1962); *Reflections on Immortality* for Chorus and Brass

(1966); *Jesu duclis memoria* for Voices (1966); *Dirge for the New Sunrise* for Chorus (1970); *Walking Around* for Chorus, Clarinet, Violin, Piano, and 2 Percussionists (1973); *Dreams* for Soprano and Chamber Orch. (1976); *Cynthia's Revells* for Baritone and Guitar or Piano (1979); *3 Lyrics by Ben Jonson* for Baritone and Piano (1979).—NS/LK/DM

Parrish, Avery, jazz pianist, arranger; b. Birmingham, Ala., Jan. 24, 1917; d. N.Y. Dec. 10, 1959. He was best known for his work with the Erskine Hawkins band and will always be remembered for his creative blues solo "After Hours" (1940). His cousin was pianist-vocalist Gladys Palmer. Parrish attended Ala. State Coll. and while there began working with Erskine Hawkins. He went with the band to N.Y. in 1934, and continued to work with them until early 1941. He relocated to Calif., where he worked as a soloist until suffering severe injuries in a L.A. bar skirmish in 1942, suffered partial paralysis, and never again played professionally. He worked day jobs for the rest of his life that ended under mysterious circumstances in N.Y.—JC/LP

Parrish, Carl, American musicologist and composer; b. Plymouth, Pa., Oct. 9, 1904; d. (as a result of injuries incurred in an automobile accident) Valhalla, N.Y., Nov. 27, 1965. He studied at the American Cons. in Fontainebleau (1932), the MacPhail School of Music (B.M., 1933), Cornell Univ. (M.A., 1936), and Harvard Univ. (Ph.D, 1939, with the diss. *The Early Piano and Its Influences on Keyboard Technique and Composition in the Eighteenth Century*). He taught at Wells Coll. (1929–43), Fisk Univ. (1943–46), Westminster Choir Coll. (1946–49), and Pomona Coll. (1949–53); from 1953 to 1965 he was a prof. at Vassar Coll. He publ. *The Notation of Medieval Music* (N.Y., 1957; 2nd ed., 1959) and *A Treasury of Early Music* (N.Y., 1958). With J. Ohl, he publ. *Masterpieces of Music before 1750* (N.Y., 1951). He wrote orch. pieces, choral music, a String Quartet, a song cycle, piano pieces, and folk song arrangements for chorus. —NS/LK/DM

Parrott, Andrew (Haden), distinguished English conductor and musicologist; b. Walsall, March 10, 1947. He was educated at Merton Coll., Oxford (B.A., 1969), where he served as director of music (1969–71). In 1973 he founded the Taverner Choir, and subsequently the Taverner Consort and Players, with which he acquired a notable reputation as a conductor of works from the medieval era to the late 18th century. In 1977 he made his first appearance at London's BBC Promenade Concerts conducting Monteverdi's *Vespers*. He made his debut at Milan's La Scala in 1985, and at the Salzburg Festival in 1987. In 1993 he made his first appearance at London's Covent Garden conducting *Die Zauberflöte*. He was named Honorary Resident Fellow at Royal Holloway, Univ. of London, in 1995. In 2000 he became music director of the London Mozart Players. Parrott has appeared as a guest conductor with both period and modern instrument orchs., as well as chamber orchs. and opera companies. His repertoire embraces music from the medieval period to the present. In addition to articles in scholarly journals, he ed., with H. Keyte, *The New Oxford Book of Carols* (Oxford, 1992).—NS/LK/DM

Parrott, (Horace) Ian, English composer, teacher, and writer on music; b. London, March 5, 1916. At 12, he began lessons in harmony with Benjamin Dale. Following studies at the Royal Coll. of Music in London (1932–34), he completed his education at New Coll., Oxford (D.Mus., 1940; M.A., 1941). From 1940 to 1945 he saw service in the Royal Signals. He was a lecturer at the Univ. of Birmingham from 1947 to 1950. From 1950 to 1983 he was the Gregynog Prof. of Music at the Univ. Coll. of Wales in Aberystwyth. In his music, Parrott remained faithful to the tonal tradition. In a number of his works, he was inspired by the culture of Wales.

WRITINGS: *Pathways to Modern Music* (1947); *A Guide to Musical Thought* (1955); *Method in Orchestration* (1957); *The Music of "An Adventure"* (1966); *The Spiritual Pilgrims* (1969); *Elgar* (1971); *The Music of Rosemary Brown* (1978); *Cyril Scott and His Piano Music* (1992); *The Crying Curlew: Peter Warlock: Family & Influences: Centenary 1994* (1994).

WORKS: DRAMATIC: O p e r a : *The Sergeant- Major's Daughter*, burlesque opera (1942–43); *The Black Ram* (1951–53; Aberystwyth, March 9, 1966); *Once Upon a Time*, comic opera (1959; Christchurch, New Zealand, Dec. 3, 1960); *The Lady of Flowers*, chamber opera (1981; Colchester, Sept. 17, 1982). **ORCH.:** *Malvern Music* (1937); *Malvern March* (1938); *De l'Estuaire à la source* (1939); *Russian Dance* for Small Orch. (1941); *A Dream* for Small Orch. (1941); *Scherzo No. 2* (1941–43); 5 syms.: No. 1 (1943–46), No. 2, *Round the World* (1960–61), No. 3 (1966), No. 4, *Sinfonietta* (1978), and No. 5 (1979; Coventry, May 23, 1981); *El Alamein* (1944; Guildford, Oct. 1945); *Miniature Concerto* for Violin and Small Orch. (1945); *Luxor* (1947; London, Oct. 17, 1950); *Piano Concerto* (1948–49); *Maid in Birmingham* (1949); *Pensieri*, concerto grosso for Strings (1950); *Solemn Overture: Romeo and Juliet* (1951–53; Bournemouth, Oct. 24, 1957); *Flourish for a Royal Visit* for Small Orch. (1955); *Orchestral Variations on Dufay's Se la face ay pale* (1955); *4 Shakespeare Dances* (1956); English Horn Concerto (1956; Cheltenham, July 18, 1958); *The Three Ladies (Cwyn Mam 'n Y'nghyfraith, Hen Ferchetan,* and *Mae 'Nghariad i'n Fenws*; 1958); *Seithenin*, overture (1959); Cello Concerto (1961; Newtown, May 2, 1963); *Ian Parrott's Attempt* for Strings (1962); *Broncastell* (1964); Suite for Violin and Orch. (1965); Concerto for Trombone and Winds (1967; based on the Sonatina for Trombone and Piano, 1958); *Fantasia on Welsh Tunes* for Brass Band (1968); *Homage to 2 Masters* (1970; also for Organ); *Harrow March* for Brass (1970); *Reaching for the Light* (Attingham Park, Aug. 21, 1971); Concertino for 2 Guitars and Small Orch. (1973); *Rumbustuoso VERNONcello Am GRIFFbrett* for Strings (Christchurch, New Zealand, Feb. 1, 1974); Fanfare-Overture (Montacute, July 3, 1993). **CHAMBER:** Oboe Sonata (1935); Trio for Flute, Violin, and Piano (1937); 5 string quartets: No. 1 (1946; London, May 2, 1950), No. 2 (1954–55), No. 3 (1957; Bangor, May 1961), No. 4 (1963), and No. 5 (1994); Duet for 2 Flutes (1946); Oboe Quartet (1946; Oxford, Oct. 19, 1947); 2 wind quintets: No. 1 (1947–48; Birmingham, May 6, 1949) and No. 2 (1970; Cardiff, May 14, 1971); *Fantasy* for Cello and Piano (Birmingham, Oct. 8, 1948); *Fantasy Trio* for Violin, Cello, and Piano (1950; Birmingham, May 24, 1951); *Hobos Riding* for Oboe, Oboe d'Amore, English Horn, and Heckelphone (1951); *Dafydd y Garreg Wen* for Viola and Piano (1951); *Capriccio* for Trumpet and Piano (1956); *Ceredigion* for Harp (1957); *Rhapsody* for Violin and Piano (1957); Trombone Sonatina (1958; reworked as the Concerto for Trombone and Winds, 1967); *Fantasy for James Blades* for Percussion (1959); *Blackbird Piece* for Flute, Oboe, Clarinet, Horn, Bassoon, and Piano (Bournemouth, Feb. 22, 1960); *Septet 1962* (1961–62;

Cheltenham, July 10, 1962); *Abergenny* for Crwth and Optional Clarinet (1965); *Big Hat Guy* for Violin and Piano (1965); *Partita on 2 Welsh Tunes* for Harp (1967); *Pant Glas* for Violin, Glockenspiel, and Piano (1967); *4 Silhouettes* for Flute (1969); *2 Dances* for Flute and Harp (1969); *Arabesque and Dance* for Treble Recorder and Harpsichord or Piano (1972); *Fanfare and March* for 2 Trumpets, Trombone, and Bass Tuba (1973); *Devil's Bridge Jaunt* for Cello and Piano (1974); *Gleaming Brass* for Brass Quintet (1976); *Duo fantastico I* (1976) and *II* (1990) for Violin and Piano; *Rhapsody* for Trumpet and Organ (1977); *Arfon* for Harp (1978); *Fantasy Sonata* for Clarinet and Piano (1979; New Haven, Conn., Oct. 1986); *Reflections* for Violin and Piano (1982); *Suite for Stefan Popov* for Cello and Piano (1982; London, Feb. 5, 1985); Duo for Clarinet and Trumpet (1983; London, May 17, 1984); *Autumn Landscape* for Oboe and Piano (1983; BBC, March 6, 1986); Duo for 2 Guitars (1988); *3 North Wales Tunes* for 2 Guitars (1993); *Fantasising* (on a Welsh Tune) for Flute, Oboe, and Piano (1993); *Awel Dyfi* for Treble Recorder (1996); *The Wrexham Pipers meet the Machynlleth Marchers* for Recorder and Guitar (1996); *Rondo Giocoso* for Bassoon and Piano (1998); *Portraits* for Treble Recorder and Piano (1999). **KEYBOARD: P i a n o :** *Siberian March* (1928); *Scherzo No. 1* (1933); *Foursome* for Piano, 4-Hands (1935–39); *Caprice* (1937); *Nocturne* (1937); *Malvern Hills* (1938); *Betinka* (1939); *Westerham* (1940); *Fuga giocosa* (1942); *Impromptu* (1942); *Theme and 6 Variants* (London, Oct. 17, 1946); *Fantasy and Allegro* for 2 Pianos (1946; London, May 1, 1947); *The Birds of Glanyrafon* (1953); *By the Ystwyth* (1954); *Little Fugato* (1954); *Fantasy* (1964; Bangor, March 8, 1965); *Aspects* (1975; Copenhagen, March 12, 1976); *Humoresque* (1993). **O r g a n :** Sonata (1933); *Agincourt* (1948); *Elegy* (1957); *Toccata* (Cambridge, May 13, 1962); *Mosaics* (1968); *Fantasia* (1974); 2 suites: No. 1 (1977; London, June 1, 1978) and No. 2 (BBC, April 13, 1991); *Hands Across the Years: In Memoriam Gerald Finzi* (1980; Harrogate, Aug. 8, 1983). **VOCAL:** *2 Nature Pieces* for Chorus and Orch. (1936–37); *Jolly Good Ale & Old* for Basses (1939); *Earth Rejoices* for Chorus (1939); *Psalm 91* for Bass, Chorus, and Orch. (1946–47; Belfast, March 16, 1951); *All the Woods Answer* for Voices (1949); *Money Talks* and *Song in a Saloon Bar* from *Voices in a Giant City* for Men's Voices and Piano (1949); *3 Kings Have Come* for Women's Voices or Soprano or Baritone or Chorus, Piano, and Strings (1951; Cambridge, Nov. 22, 1952); *Magnificat and Nunc Dimittis* for Voices and Organ (1961); *Cantata jubilate Deo* for Soloists, Chorus, and Orch. (1963; London, Oct. 20, 1967); *The 3 Moorish Princesses* for Narrator and Orch. (1963–64); *The Song of the Stones of St. David's* for Chorus and Organ (1968); *Offertory Motet: Diffusa est gratia in labiis tuis* for Voices (1968; London, March 20, 1969); *Cymun bendigaid* for Voice(s) and Organ or Piano or Guitar and Percussion Band (1972; also as the *Folksong Mass*); *Song for Dyfed* for 2 Narrators, Chorus, and Piano (1973–74); *Master Hugues of Saxe-Gotha* for Men's Voices and Piano (1975); *My Cousin Alice* for Mezzo-soprano, Tenor, Chorus, Piano, and Tape of Birds (1982; Aberystwyth, May 16, 1983); *Eastern Wisdom* for Voice and Chamber Orch. (1987; Machynlleth, May 6, 1990); *Arglwydd ein Ior ni* for Voices (Lower Machen, June 30, 1991); various solo songs, including *The Christ Child* (1987), *Aphorisms and Arias* for Soprano and Baritone (1995), and *Songs of Renewal* (1995). —NS/LK/DM

Parry, John, Welsh instrumentalist, writer on music, and composer, known as "Bardd Alaw" ("master of song"); b. Denbigh, Feb. 18, 1776; d. London, April 8, 1851. He became a member (1793) and master (1795) of the Denbighshire militia band. In 1807 he settled in London, where he taught the flageolet; was made composer to Vauxhall Gardens (1809). He wrote various works for the stage (from 1814), and also appeared as a conductor of the Welsh cymrodorio and eisteddfodau in various locales for many years, being named Bardd Alaw at the Powys Eisteddfod (1820); likewise was music critic for the *Morning Post* (1834–49). His most successful stage work was the musical drama *Ivanhoe or The Knight Templar* (Covent Garden, London, March 2, 1820), which included the popular song "The Lullaby." He also wrote incidental music, harp sonatas, part-songs, glees, songs, etc. He ed. a collection of Welsh music as *The Welsh Harper* (1839–48). His writings, all publ. in London, include *Il Puntello, or The Supporter* (1832), *An Account of the Rise and Progress of the Harp* (1834), and *An Account of the Royal Musical Festival Held in Westminster Abbey in 1834* (1834). His son, John Orlando Parry (b. London, Jan. 3, 1810; d. East Molesey, Surrey, Feb. 20, 1879), was a pianist and comic singer who studied harp with Bochsa and later voice with Lablache in Naples. After a successful career as a singer, he retired from the stage (1853), and was active as organist at St. Jude's, Southsea, and as a teacher. He wrote glees and dances for piano.

BIBL.: C. Andrews and J. Orr-Ewing, *Victorian Swandsdown: Extracts from the Early Travel Diaries of J.O. P.* (London, 1935).—NS/LK/DM

Parry, Joseph, Welsh composer; b. Merthyr Tydfil, May 21, 1841; d. Penarth, near Cardiff, Feb. 17, 1903. His parents emigrated to America, but he returned to Britain. He won Eisteddfod prizes for songs, and entered the Royal Academy of Music in 1868, studying under Bennett, Garcia, and Steggall; received his Mus.Bac. degree from Cambridge in 1871. He was prof. of music at the Univ. of Wales in Aberystwyth (1873–79). After receiving his Mus.D. from Cambridge (1878), he ran his own music school in Swansea (1881–88); subsequently lectured at the Univ. Coll. of South Wales and Monmouthshire in Cardiff. In addition to his dramatic works, he wrote some 400 hymn tunes, the most celebrated being *Aberystwyth* (1877). He also ed. and harmonized *Cambrian Minstrelsie* (6 vols., Edinburgh, 1893).

WORKS: DRAMATIC: O p e r a : *Blodwen* (Aberdare, 1878); *Virginia* (Aberdare, 1883); *Arianwen* (Cardiff, 1890); *Sylvia* (Cardiff, 1895); *King Arthur* (1897); *Ceridwen* (Liverpool, 1900); *The Maid of Cefn Ydfa* (Cardiff, 1902). **O r a t o r i o s :** *The Prodigal Son* (Chester, 1866); *Emmanuel* (London, 1880); *Saul of Tarus* (Rhyl and Cardiff, 1892). **C a n t a t a s :** *The Birds* (Wrexham, 1873); *Jerusalem* (Cambridge, 1878); *Joseph* (Swansea, 1881); *Nebuchadnezzar* (London, 1884); *Cambria* (Llandudno, 1896). **OTHER:** Syms.; overtures; String Quartet; anthems; songs; piano pieces.

BIBL.: E. Evans et al., *Cofiant Dr. J. P.* (Cardiff and London, 1921).—NS/LK/DM

Parry, Sir C(harles) Hubert H(astings), eminent English composer, pedagogue, and writer on music; b. Bournemouth, Feb. 27, 1848; d. Rustington, Oct. 7, 1918. While attending a preparatory school in Twyford, near Winchester, he began piano lessons with a local organist. He then had training in piano, harmony, and counterpoint with Edward Brind, the organist at Highnam Church. In 1861 he entered Eton, where he became active in its musical society. During this time, he also had composition lessons with George Elvey, organist at St. George's Chapel, Windsor. In 1866 he took his B.Mus. exercise at New Coll., Oxford, with his cantata *O Lord, Thou hast cast us out*. In 1867 he entered Exeter Coll., Oxford, to study law and history. During the summer of that year, he pursued training in instrumentation and composition with Pierson in Stuttgart. After graduating from Exeter Coll. in 1870, he had a few lessons with Sterndale Bennett. Between 1873 and 1877 he was engaged in business in London, but he also pursued training in piano with Dannreuther (from 1873) and in composition with Macfarren (1875–77). In 1875 Grove made him sub-editor of his *Dictionary of Music and Musicians*, to which Parry contributed a number of the major articles. In 1883 he was named prof. of music history at the newly organized Royal Coll. of Music in London and was awarded an honorary Doc.Mus. from Trinity Coll., Cambridge. In 1884 he was elected Choragus at the Univ. of Oxford, where he received an honorary doctorate. In 1894 Parry was elevated to the directorship of the Royal Coll. of Music, a position he retained with distinction for the rest of his life. He also served as the Heather Prof. of Music at the Univ. of Oxford from 1900 to 1908. In 1898 he was knighted and in 1905 he was made a Commander of the Royal Victorian Order. Parry secured his reputation as a composer with his distinguished choral ode *At a Solemn Music: Blest Pair of Sirens* (1887). There followed a series of ethical choral works in which he attempted to build upon the British choral tradition. His coronation anthem *I was glad* (1902) is a masterwork in the genre. Also notable is his *Ode on the Nativity* (1910). His unison song *Jerusalem* (1916) quickly established itself as a national song. Among his other fine works are his *Songs of Farewell* and his collections of *English Lyrics*. In his orchestral music, Parry played a significant role in the fostering of the British symphonic tradition. While his orchestral works owe much to the German Romanticists, particularly Mendelssohn, Schumann, and Brahms, he nevertheless developed a personal style notable for its fine craftsmanship and mastery of diatonic writing. His 5 syms. reveal a growing assurance in handling large forms. He also wrote some effective incidental music and fine chamber pieces.

WRITINGS (all publ. in London unless otherwise given): *Studies of the Great Composers* (1887); *The Art of Music* (1893; enl. ed., 1896, as *The Evolution of the Art of Music*); *Summary of the History and Development of Medieval and Modern European Music* (1893; 2nd ed., 1904); *The Music of the Seventeenth Century*, vol. III of *The Oxford History of Music* (1902); *Johann Sebastian Bach* (1910); *Style in Musical Art* (1911); *Instinct and Character* (c. 1915–18; MS); H. Colles, ed., *College Addresses* (1920).

WORKS: DRAMATIC: Opera: *Guenever* (1886). **Ballet:** *Proserpine* (London, June 25, 1912). **Incidental Music To:** Aristophanes' *The Birds* (Cambridge, Nov. 27, 1883; rev. 1903); Aristophanes' *The Frogs* (Oxford, Feb. 24, 1892; rev. version, Oxford, Feb. 19, 1909); S. Ogilvie's *Hypatia* (London, Jan. 2, 1893; orch. suite, London, March 9, 1893); P. Craigie's *A Repentance* (London, Feb. 28, 1899); Aeschylus'

Agamemnon (London, Nov. 16, 1900); Aristophanes' *The Clouds* (Oxford, March 1, 1905); Aristophanes' *The Acharnians* (Oxford, Feb. 21, 1914). **ORCH.:** *Allegretto Scherzando* (1867); *Intermezzo Religioso* (Gloucester, Sept. 3, 1868); *Vivien*, overture (1873); Concertstück (1877); Piano Concerto (1878–80; London, April 3, 1880; rev. 1895); *Guillem de Cabestanh*, overture (London, March 15, 1879); 5 syms.: No. 1, in G major (1880–82; Birmingham, Aug. 31, 1882), No. 2, in F major, *Cambridge* (Cambridge, June 12, 1883; rev. version, London, June 6, 1887; 2nd rev. version, London, May 30, 1895), No. 3, in C major, *English* (London, May 23, 1889; rev. version, Leeds, Jan. 30, 1895; 3rd rev. version, Bournemouth, Dec. 18, 1902), No. 4, in E minor (London, July 1, 1889; rev. version, London, Feb. 10, 1910), and No. 5, *Symphonic Fantasia 1912* (London, Dec. 5, 1912); *Suite Moderne* or *Suite Symphonique* (Gloucester, Sept. 9, 1886; rev. 1892); *An English Suite* for Strings (1890–1918; London, Oct. 20, 1922); *Overture to an Unwritten Tragedy* (Worcester, Sept. 13, 1893; rev. 1897 and 1905); *Lady Radnor Suite* for Strings (London, June 29, 1894; also for Piano, 1905, and for Violin and Piano, 1915); *Elegy for Brahms* (1897; London, Nov. 9, 1918); *Symphonic Variations* (London, June 3, 1897); *From Death to Life*, symphonic poem (Brighton, Nov. 12, 1914). **Wind Band:** *Foolish Fantasia* (n.d.). **CHAMBER:** 3 movements for Violin and Piano (1863); 2 string quartets (1867, c. 1879); 2 *Duettinos* for Cello and Piano (1868); *Short Trios* for Violin, Viola, and Piano (1868); *Freundschaftslieder*, 6 pieces for Violin and Piano (1872); 3 violin sonatas (1875; *Fantasie Sonate*, 1878; 1889, rev. 1894); Nonet for Winds (1877); 3 piano trios (1878, 1884, 1890); Piano Quartet (1879); Cello Sonata (1880); String Quintet (1884; rev. 1896 and 1902); *Partita* for Violin and Piano (1886); *12 Short Pieces* for Violin and Piano (1895); Piece for Violin and Piano (1896); *Romance* for Violin and Piano (1896); 2 suites for Violin and Piano (1907, 1907). **KEYBOARD: Piano:** 4 fugues (1865); *Andante non troppo* (1865); Overture for Piano Duet (1865); Sonata for Piano Duet (1865); *Andante* (1867); *Sonnets and Songs Without Words*, 3 sets (1868; 1867–75; 1870–77); 7 *Charakterbilder* (1872); *Variations on an air by Bach* (1873–75); *Grosses Duo* for 2 Pianos (1875–77); 2 sonatas (1877; 1876–77); *Theme and 19 Variations* (1878); *Shulbrede Tunes* (1914); *Hands across the Centuries*, suite (1918). **Organ:** Fugue (1865); Fantasia and Fugue (1877; new Fantasia, 1882; new Fugue, 1912); Chorale Preludes, 2 sets (1912, 1916); Toccata and Fugue, *Wanderer* (1912–18); *Elegy* (1913); 3 Chorale Fantasias (1915). **VOCAL: Choral** (all with orch. unless otherwise given): *O Lord, Thou hast cast us out*, cantata (Eton Coll., Dec. 8, 1867); *Scenes from Shelley's "Prometheus Unbound"*, dramatic cantata (Gloucester, Sept. 7, 1880; rev. 1881 and 1885); *The Contention of Ajax and Ulysses: The Glories of Our Blood and State*, ode (Gloucester, Sept. 4, 1883; rev. 1908 and 1914); *At a Solemn Music: Blest Pair of Sirens*, ode (London, May 17, 1887); *Judith* or *The Regeneration of Manasseh*, oratorio (Birmingham, Aug. 29, 1888); *Ode on St. Cecilia's Day*, ode (Leeds, Oct. 11, 1889); *L'Allegro ed Il Penseroso*, cantata (Norwich, Oct. 15, 1890; rev. 1909); *Eton*, ode (Eton Coll., June 28, 1891); *De Profundis* (Hereford, Sept. 10, 1891); *The Lotos-Eaters*, choric song (Cambridge, June 13, 1892); *Job*, oratorio (Gloucester, Sept. 8, 1892); *Hear my words ye people*, anthem for Chorus, Organ, Brass, and Timpani (Salisbury Cathedral, May 10, 1894); *King Saul*, oratorio (Birmingham, Oct. 3, 1894); *Invocation to Music*, ode (Leeds, Oct. 2, 1895); *Magnificat* (Hereford, Sept. 15, 1897); *A Song of Darkness and Light* (Gloucester, Sept. 15, 1898); *Thanksgiving Te Deum* (Latin version, Hereford, Sept. 1900; Eng. version, rev., Gloucester, Sept. 11, 1913); *Ode to Music* (London, June 13, 1901); *I was glad*, coronation anthem (London, Aug. 9, 1902; rev. version, London, June 23, 1911); *War* *and Peace*, symphonic ode (London, April 30, 1903); *Voces Clamantium*, motet (Hereford, Sept. 10, 1903); *The love that casteth out fear*, sinfonia sacra (Gloucester, Sept. 7, 1904); *The Pied Piper of Hamelin*, cantata (Norwich, Oct. 26, 1905; rev. 1910); *The Soul's Ransom: A Psalm of the Poor*, sinfonia sacra (Hereford, Sept. 12, 1906); *The Vision of Life*, symphonic poem (Cardiff, Sept. 26, 1907; rev. 1914); *Beyond these voices there is peace*, motet (Worcester, Sept. 9, 1908); *Eton Memorial Ode* (Eton Coll., Nov. 18, 1908); *Coronation Te Deum* (London, June 23, 1911); *Ode on the Nativity* (Hereford, Sept. 12, 1912); *God is our hope* (London, April 24, 1913); *The Chivalry of the Sea*, naval ode (London, Dec. 12, 1916). **L i t u r g i c a l :** *Te Deum* (c. 1864); *Magnificat and Nunc Dimittis* (1864); *Te Deum and Benedictus* (1868); Communion, Morning, and Evening Services (1869); *Te Deum* (1873); Evening Service (1881); 10 anthems; 28 hymns, etc. **O t h e r :** Part songs; unison songs, including the famous *Jerusalem* (1916); numerous solo songs, including 12 sets of *English Lyrics* (publ. 1885–1920); *Songs of Farewell*, 6 motets (1916–17).

BIBL.: C. Graves, *H. P.: His Life and Works* (2 vols., London, 1926); J. Dibble, *C. H. H. P.: His Life and Music* (Oxford, 1992); B. Benoliel, *P. Before Jerusalem: Studies of His Life and Music With Excerpts From His Published Writings* (Aldershot, 1997). **—NS/LK/DM**

Parsch, Arnošt, Czech composer and teacher; b. Bučovice, Moravia, Feb. 12, 1936. He was a pupil of J. Podešva and M. Ištvan. He later took courses at the Janáček Academy of Music in Brno, and subsequently served on its faculty.

WORKS: ORCH.: *Suite* for Strings (1963); Concerto for Winds, Percussion, and Piano (1964); Sonata for Chamber Orch. (1967); 2 syms. (1967, 1973); *Musica concertante con ommagio* (1970); *The Flight* (1973); *The Bird Flew above the Clouds* for Oboe and Orch. (1975); Double Concerto for Flute, Trumpet, and Orch. (1977); *The Message* for 2 String Orchs. (1978); *Divisi. Non divisi!* (1979); Sym.- Concerto for Horn and Orch. (1982); *Rondo* for Orch. with Concertante Violin (1983); *2 Rondos* for Strings (1984); *Poema*, concerto for Cimbalom and Orch. (1986); Concerto for Bass Clarinet, Piano, and Orch. (1989); *Rapsodietta* for 11 Strings (1991); *Wells* for Chamber Orch. (1992); *Rose Garden*, concerto for Piano and Chamber Ensemble (1997). **CHAMBER:** *Music* for String Quartet and Percussion (1964); *Trasposizioni I* for Flute, Oboe, Clarinet, Bassoon, and Horn (1967); Organ Sonata (1968); 3 string quartets (1970, 1973, 1994); *Esercizii per uno, due, tre e quatro* for 2 Flutes, Guitar, and Cello (1971); *Quatro pezzi per quatro stromenti* for Violin, Clarinet, Double Bass, and Piano (1972); *Early Spring* for Reciter, Flute, Bass Clarinet, and Piano (1972); *Hold Fast!* for 2 Trumpets, Horn, 2 Trombones, and Tuba (1979); *Drawings* for Violin, Clarinet, and Piano (1989–94); *Distant Skylines* for Flute, Bass Clarinet, and Piano (1990); *Musica per i montanari* for 2 Horns (1991); *Meditation* for Guitar (1993); *The Voice of the River* for 9 Players (1994); *Hillside* for Violin and Percussion (1995). **VOCAL:** *Simple Truths* for Soprano, 2 Flutes, Guitar, and Cello (1973); *The Sun Rose Once*, cantata for Chorus, Clarinet, Saxophone, and Jazz Orch., after a text by Sitting Bull (1974); *Kings' Ride* for Tenor, Bass, Chorus, and Chamber Ensemble (1984); *Invocation of Love*, 5 songs for Tenor and Piano (1987); *Spring Rites* for Mezzo-soprano, Tenor, Bass-baritone, Chorus, Children's Chorus, and Orch. (1990); *Lullabies* for Woman's Voice, 2 Cymbals, Double Bass, and Chimes (1991); *Etudes Amoureuses* for Mezzo-soprano, Violin, Marimba, and Percussion (1995).

ELECTROACOUSTIC: *Poetica No. 3* (1967); *Trasposizioni II* (1969) and *III* (1970); *Rotae rotarum* (1971); *Prologos* (1971); *Labyrinthos* (1972); *In High Mountains* (1973); *Daybreak* (1983); *Metamorphoses of Time* (1989).**—NS/LK/DM**

Parsley, Osbert, English singer and composer; b. 1511; d. Norwich, 1585. He was a "singing-man" at Norwich Cathedral for some 50 years. He wrote both Latin and English sacred music, excelling in the former, and several of his instrumental pieces are also extant. See E. Fellowes, *Tudor Church Music*, X (1929). **—NS/LK/DM**

Parsons, Alan, progressive rocker famous for his many "Projects"; b. in England, Dec. 20, 1949. Alan Parsons studied piano, guitar, and flute in his youth, but found working in a recording studio more lucrative than trying to make it as a musician. He rose through the ranks at EMI's London studios. As an assistant staff engineer at Abby Road Studios, he worked on The Beatles's *Let It Be* and *Abbey Road*. When The Beatles split up, Parsons engineered projects for Wings, as well as hits for The Hollies. His main claim to fame as an engineer came with the pristine, ground- breaking recording of Pink Floyd's *Dark Side of the Moon*. Suddenly artists sought him out as an engineer and a producer.

Producing Al Stewart's conceptual *Time Passages* put him in mind of his own, earlier endeavors as a musician. Parsons consulted with one of his compatriots at Abbey Road, Eric Woolfson. While the relationship started off as a business venture, they soon started collaborating musically. Choosing Edgar Allen Poe's *Tales of Mystery and Imagination* as their first concept, they called on musician friends, like Arthur Brown, The Hollies' Allan Clarke, and former Zombie Colin Blunstone, among many others to work on the album. Parsons played guitar and keyboards and Woolfson provided keyboards and vocals. In their off-hours from the studio, they created the album. Taking much of its lead from his work with Pink Floyd, The Alan Parsons Project had a sound that fit neatly into the progressive pop-rock genre, increasingly popular in the wake of *Dark Side of the Moon*. To everyone's mild surprise, the album generated the minor hit "(The System of) Doctor Tarr and Professor Fether" which scratched into the Top 40, as did the album, in 1975.

Encouraged, Parsons and Woolfson took on Isaac Asimov's *I Robot* as their next source. The Project's music followed a similar, almost comforting formula with simple songs couched in the highest-tech sound available. The hit "I Wouldn't Want to Be Like You" became a favorite at rock radio and rose to #36 on the pop charts in 1977; the album went to #9 and platinum. Parsons followed this with more general topics for his "Projects." *Pyramid* (1978) dealt with mysticism, and without benefit of a major hit still managed to reach #26 and go gold. A year later, *Eve* dealt with the battle of the sexes. The single "Damned If I Do" rose to #26 and the album hit #13 and went gold. *Turn of a Friendly Card* dealt with luck. It generated two singles during 1980, the #16 "Games People Play" and the #15 "Time." The album went platinum, peaking at #13. The 1982 album

Eye in the Sky earned the Project its first Top Ten hit with the #3 title track. The album went to #7 and platinum. Two years later, *Ammonia Avenue* also generated two hits, the #15 "Don't Answer Me" and the #34 "Prime Time." The album rose to #15 and went gold, becoming the group's sixth album in a row to go either gold or platinum.

In the three years between *Ammonia Avenue* and the Project's next release, 1987's *Gaudi*, the pop music landscape changed. Instead of reaping the kind of pop success they had previously, Parsons and Woolfson were now releasing records for their fans. Trying a new direction, they hooked up with Brian Brolly in the late 1980s, an erstwhile partner in Andrew Lloyd Webber's Really Useful Group, and tried to create an Alan Parsons Project musical. The theme they chose was Freud, creating the musical *Freudiana*. The play ran in Vienna, but was never staged anywhere else, and became the subject of a lawsuit between the theatrical producer and his partners. A studio and a cast album of the project were released, but didn't generate much attention.

During the making of *Freudiana*, Woolfson became enamored with the theater. He split with Parsons to pursue that goal. Parsons continued as a musician, engineer, and producer, creating the soundtrack for the 1996 film *Ladyhawke*. He also made a series of audio-analyzing CDs. He also continued to make Projects for his loyal coterie of fans, although without Woolfson, they became Alan Parsons albums. He was named head of EMI Studios in 1997, but found the time to tour with Yes in 1998. He released his impressions of Jules Verne's *The Time Machine* in 1999.

DISC.: *Tales of Mystery & Imagination* (1975); *I Robot* (1977); *Pyramid* (1978); *Eve* (1979); *The Turn of a Friendly Card* (1980); *Eye in the Sky* (1982); *Ammonia Avenue* (1984); *Stereotomy* (1985); *Vulture Culture* (1985); *Gaudi* (1987); *Try Anything Once* (1993); *Ladyhawke* (1995); *On Air* (1996); *Sound Check 2 without Response Analyzer* (1999); *Sound Check 2 with Response Analyzer* (1999); *The Time Machine* (1999).—**HB**

Parsons, Geoffrey (Penwill), notable Australian piano accompanist and teacher; b. Sydney, June 15, 1929; d. London, Jan. 26, 1995. He received his training from Winifried Burston at the New South Wales State Conservatorium of Music in Sydney (1941–48) and from Wührer in Munich (1956). In 1948 he made his first tour of Australia. In 1950 he first appeared in London, where he settled. In subsequent years, he pursued an international career as a piano accompanist to many of the leading artists of the day. He toured Australia some 30 times and performed in more than 40 nations. He also gave master classes in the art of piano accompaniment. In 1977 he was made an Officer of the Order of the British Empire.—**NS/LK/DM**

Parsons, Robert, English singer and composer; b. probably in Colyton, Devon, 1596; d. Exeter, July 1676. He became a lay vicar in 1621 and priest-vicar in 1640 at Exeter Cathedral. From 1634 he also was rector of St. Martin's in Exeter. He composed anthems and services. —**LK/DM**

Parsons, William, English composer who flourished in the mid 16th century. He was active at Wells Cathedral, where he served as vicar-choral in 1555. Parsons contributed 81 of the 141 settings found in John Day's *The Whole Psalmes in Foure Parts* (1563). He also wrote anthems, services, and motets, but few have survived in full.—**LK/DM**

Pärt, Arvo, outstanding Estonian-born Austrian composer; b. Paide, Sept. 11, 1935. He was a student of Heino Eller at the Tallinn Cons., graduating in 1963. From 1958 to 1967 he worked for the Estonian Radio in Tallinn. In 1980 he emigrated to the West, becoming a naturalized Austrian citizen. In his early works, Pärt followed a modern path in which he utilized serial, aleatoric, and collage techniques. This course, along with his deeply felt spiritual convictions, caused him difficulties with Soviet officialdom. Pärt's intense interest in medieval and Renaissance music led to a remarkable change of course in the mid-1970s as he developed a tintinnabular technique that resulted in scores notable for their beauty, strong character, and spirituality. In 1978 he was awarded the Estonian Music Prize for his *Tabula rasa*, a score that established his international reputation. He was elected a member of the American Academy of Arts and Letters in 1997. In 1998 he won the Moscow Triumph Award.

WORKS: ORCH.: *Nekrolog* (1960); 3 syms. (1963, 1966, 1971); *Perpetuum mobile* (1963); *Pro et contra*, cello concerto (1966); *Wenn Bach Bienen gezüchtet hätte* for Piano, Wind Quintet, and Strings (1976–84); *Cantus in Memory of Benjamin Britten* for Strings and Bell (1977); *Tabula rasa*, double concerto for 2 Violins or Violin and Viola, Strings, and Prepared Piano (1977); *Fratres* for Strings and Percussion (1977; rev. 1991; also for Violin, String Orch., and Percussion, 1992); *Spiegel im Spiegel* for Violin, Piano, and Strings (1980; also for Violin and Piano, 1978); *Summa* for Strings (1980–91); *Dreiklang*, concerto for Violin, Cello, and Chamber Orch. (1981); *Festina lente* for Strings and Harp ad libitum (1988; rev. 1990); *Silouan's Song: My Soul Yearns After the Lord...* for Strings (1991); *The Introductory Prayers* for Strings (1992; rev. 1995). **CHAMBER:** String Quartet (1959); Wind Quintet (1964); *Musica syllabica* for 12 Instruments (1964); *Collage über B-A-C-H* for Strings, Oboe, Harpsichord, and Piano (1964); *Fratres* for Chamber Ensemble (1977; also for Violin and Piano, 1977–80, for 4, 8, or 12 Cellos, 1977–83, for String Quartet, 1977–85, etc.); *Arbos* for 7 Flutes and 3 Triangles ad libitum (1977; also for 8 Brass and Percussion, 1977–86); *Spiegel im Spiegel* for Violin and Piano (1978; also for Violin, Piano, and String Orch., 1980); *Pari intervallo* for 4 Flutes (1980; also for Organ); *Summa* for Violin, 2 Violas, and Cello (1980–90; also for String Quartet, 1980–91); *Psalom* for String Quartet (1986–91; rev. 1997); *Adagio* for Violin, Cello, and Piano (1992); *Darf ich...* for Violin, Tubular Bells ad libitum, and Strings (1995). **KEYBOARD: Piano:** 2 sonatinas (1958, 1959); *Partita* (1959); *Diagrams* (1964); *Für Alina* (1976); *Variationen zur gesundung von Arinuschka* (1977). **Organ:** *Trivium* (1976); *Pari intervallo* (1980; also for 4 Flutes); *Annum per annum* (1980); *Mein Weg hat Gipfel und Wellentäler* (1985). **VOCAL:** *Meie aed* (Our Garden) for Children's Chorus and Orch. (1958); *Maailma samm* (The World's Stride), oratorio for Chorus and Orch. (1961); *Solfeggio* for Chorus and String Quartet (1964); *Credo* for Chorus, Piano, and Orch. (1968); *Laul armastatule* (Song for the Beloved) for 2 Solo Voices, Chorus, and Orch. (1973); *Calix* for Chorus and Instruments (1976); *By the Waters of Babylon*, Psalm 137 for Voices and Instruments (1976–84; rev. 1994); *Modus* for Soprano and Instruments (1976); *In spe* for 4 Voices and

Instruments (1976); *Sarah was 90 Years Old* for 3 Voices, Percussion, and Organ (1977–90); *Cantate Domino Canticum Novum*, Psalm 95 for Voices and Instruments (1977–91); *Missa Syllabica* for Voices and Instruments (1977–96); *Summa* for Chorus or 4 Soloists (1980–90); *De profundis* for Men's Chorus, Organ, and Optional Percussion (1980); *Passio Domini nostri Jesu Christi secundum Joannem* for Tenor, Bass, Vocal Quartet, Chorus, Instrumental Quartet, and Organ (1982); *2 Slavic Psalms* (117 and 131) for Soprano, Alto, Countertenor, Tenor, and Bass (1984); *Ein Wallfahrtslied*, Psalm 121 for Tenor or Baritone and String Quartet (1984; rev. 1996); *Es sang vor Langen Jahren* for Alto or Countertenor, Violin, and Viola (1984); *Te Deum* for 3 Choruses, Piano, Strings, and Tape (1984–85; rev. 1986); *Stabat Mater* for Soprano, Alto, Tenor, Violin, Viola, and Cello (1985); *7 Magnificat-Antiphonen* for Chorus (1988; rev. 1991); *Magnificat* for Chorus (1989); *Nun eile ich zu euch* for Chorus or Soloists (1989); *Miserere* for Soloists, Chorus, Ensemble, and Organ (1989; rev. 1992); *Mother of God and Virgin* for Chorus (1990); *Beatus Petronius* for 2 Choruses and 2 Organs (1990); *Statuit ei Dominus* for 2 Choruses and 2 Organs (1990); *The Beatitudes* for Chorus or Soloists and Organ (1990; rev. 1991); *Berliner Messe* for Chorus or Soloists and Organ or String Orch. (1990; rev. 1997); *And One of the Pharisees...* for 3 Voices (1992); *Litany: Prayers of St. John Chrysostom for Each Hour of the Day and Night* for Soloists, Chorus, and Orch. (1994); *Dopo la vittoria* for Chorus (Milan, Dec. 6, 1997); *Kanon pokajanen* for Chorus (Cologne, March 17, 1998); *Triodion* for Chorus (London, April 30, 1998); *Como anhela la cierva* for Soprano and Orch. (1998; Santa Cruz, Feb. 3, 1999); *Cantiques des degrés* for Chorus and Orch. (Monte Carlo, Nov. 19, 1999).

BIBL.: P. Hillier, *A. P.: The Book* (Oxford, 1997).
—NS/LK/DM

Partch, Harry, innovative American composer, performer, and instrument maker; b. Oakland, Calif., June 24, 1901; d. San Diego, Sept. 3, 1974. Largely autodidact, he began experimenting with instruments capable of producing fractional intervals, which led him to the formulation of a 43-tone scale; he expounded his findings in his book, *Genesis of a Music* (1949; 2nd ed., rev. and aug., 1974). Among new instruments constructed by him were elongated violas, a chromelodeon, kitharas with 72 strings, harmonic canons with 44 strings, boos (made of giant Philippine bamboo reeds), cloud- chamber bowls, blow-boys (a pair of bellows with an attached automobile horn), etc. Seeking intimate contact with American life, he wandered across the country, collecting indigenous expressions of folkways, inscriptions on public walls, etc., for texts in his productions. T. McGeary ed. a vol. devoted to Partch as *Bitter Music: Collected Journals, Essays, Introductions, and Librettos* (Urbana, Ill., 1991).

WORKS: *17 Lyrics by Li Po* for Voice and Adapted Viola (1930–33; San Francisco, Feb. 9, 1932); *2 Psalms* for Voice and Adapted Viola (1931; San Francisco, Feb. 9, 1932; rev. 1941); *The Potion Scene from Romeo and Juliet* for Voice and Adapted Viola (1931; San Francisco, Feb. 9, 1932; rev. 1955); *The Wayward Barstow: 8 Hitchhiker Inscriptions from a Highway Railing at Barstow, California* for Voice and Adapted Guitar (1941; N.Y., April 22, 1944; rev. 1954); *U.S. Highball: A Musical Account of a Transcontinental Hobo Trip* for Voices, Guitar I, Kithara, and Chromelodeon (1943; N.Y., April 22, 1944; rev. 1955); *San Francisco: A Setting of the Cries of 2 Newsboys on a Foggy Night in the 20s* for 2 Baritones, Adapted Viola, Kithara, and Chromelo-deon (1943; N.Y., April 22, 1944); *The Letter: A Depression Message from a Hobo Friend* for Intoning Voices and Original Instruments (1943; N.Y., April 22, 1944); *Dark Brother* for Voice, Chromelodeon, Adapted Viola, Kithara, and Bass Marimba (1942–43); *2 Settings from Joyce's Finnegans Wake* for Soprano, Kithara, and 2 Flutes (1944); *Yankee Doodle Fantasy* for Soprano, Tin Flutes, Tin Oboes, Flex-a-tones, and Chromelodeon (N.Y., April 22, 1944); *11 Intrusions* for Large Ensemble of Original Instruments (1946–50); *Plectra and Percussion Dances* for Voices and Original Instruments (1949–52; Berkeley, Calif., Nov. 19, 1953); *Oedipus*, dance music for 10 Solo Voices and Original Instruments, after Sophocles (1951; Oakland, Calif., March 14, 1952; rev. 1952–54); *2 Settings from Lewis Carroll* for Voice and Original Instruments (Mill Valley, Calif., Feb. 13, 1954); *Ulysses at the Edge* for Alto Saxophone or Trumpet, Baritone Saxophone, and Original Instruments (1955; adapted to *The Wayward*); *The Bewitched*, dance satire for Soprano and Ensemble of Traditional and Original Instruments (1955; Urbana, Ill., March 26, 1957); *Windsong*, film score (1958; rev. as the ballet *Daphne of the Dunes*, 1967); *Revelation in the Courthouse Park* for 16 Solo Voices, 4 Speakers, Dancers, and Large Instrumental Ensemble (1960; Urbana, Ill., April 11, 1962); *Rotate the Body in All Its Planes*, film score (Urbana, Ill., April 8, 1961); *Bless This Home* for Voice, Oboe, and Original Instruments (1961); *Water! Water!*, farcical "intermission" (1961; Urbana, Ill., March 9, 1962); *And on the 7th Day Petals Fell in Petaluma* for Large Ensemble of Original Instruments (1963–66; Los Angeles, May 8, 1966); *Delusion of the Fury: A Ritual of Dream and Delusion*, dramatic piece for Large Ensemble (1965–66; Los Angeles, Jan. 9, 1969); *The Dreamer That Remains: A Study in Loving*, film score (1972).

BIBL.: G. Hackbarth, *An Analysis of H. P.'s "Daphne of the Dunes"* (Ann Arbor, 1979); T. McGeary, *The Music of H. P.: A Descriptive Catalog* (Brooklyn, 1991); B. Gilmore, *H. P.: A Biography* (New Haven, 1998).**—NS/LK/DM**

Partenio, Gian Domenico, Italian singer and composer; b. Spilimberg, Friuli, c. 1649; d. Venice, 1701. He pursued his career in Venice, where he was a tenor (1666–85), vicemaestro di cappella (1685–91), and maestro di cappella (from 1691) at San Marco. He also was a priest and served at the parish church of San Martino, where he formed the guild of St. Cecilia for performers and music teacher. His operas, first perf. in Venice, included *Genserico* (1669), *Iphide greca* (1671; Act 1 by Partenio, Act 2 by Freschi, and Act 3 by Sartorio), *La costanza trionfante* (1673), *Fionisio, overo La virtù trionfante del vitio* (Jan. 12, 1681; Act 1 by P. Franceschini), and *Flavio Cuniberto* (1682; rev. 1687). He also wrote sacred music.**—LK/DM**

Parton, Dolly (Rebecca), a larger-than-life-size figure (in more ways than one) on the American musical scene; b. Locust Ridge, Tenn., Jan. 19, 1946. Dolly Parton is hardly the "aw-shucks," country-bred, dumb blond personality that she often projects. A talented singer and songwriter, she has shown a unique ability to market herself and mold an image, while at the same time producing unique, personal music that continues the great traditions of previous generations of singer/songwriters.

The fourth of 12 children raised in poverty in rural Tenn., Dolly's first recordings were made in 1959 for Goldband; in 1964, she traveled to Nashville, signing with Monument Records, and scoring her first hit with "Dumb Blond" in 1967. The same year, she joined forces with country legend Porter Wagoner, a savvy business-man who ran a large country revue. He recorded a string of duets with the younger singer, beginning with a cover of Tom Paxton's "Last Thing on My Mind" that helped launch her career.

Dolly's solo recordings from RCA in the late 1960s and early 1970s established her as a sensitive singer/songwriter who could reflect on her own rural heritage. In songs like 1971's "Coat of Many Colors," she honored the memory of her mother who made her a patchwork coat out of fabric remnants. Many of her songs were based on childhood memories, presenting in a straightforward, unembarrassed way the often hard times that she endured as a child. In 1974, Parton permanently split from Wagoner, who was bitterly jealous of his younger rival's talent and success, and her songs began to be covered by folk-rock artists from Linda Ronstadt ("I Will Always Love You," later a 1992–93 #1 hit for pop singer Whitney Houston) and Maria Muldaur ("My Tennessee Mountain Home"). This encouraged Parton to attempt her own crossover recordings for the pop charts, beginning with the bouncy 1977 hit, "Here You Come Again."

In 1980, Parton's everywoman personality was per-fectly exploited in the working class/feminist movie 9 to 5. This depiction of a group of secretary's revenge on their domineering and sexist boss appealed to working women and helped cement Parton's image as "just another gal." Her title composition for the film was a pop and country hit. This success led to a decade of minor and major film roles, plus continued recordings in a pop-country vein. A longtime friendship with pop stars Linda Ronstadt and Emmylou Harris resulted in the 1987 LP Trio, a rather subdued folk- country outing that produced a minor hit in their cover of Phil Spector's "To Know Him Is to Love Him." In 1989, in an attempt to return to her roots, she recorded a more country-oriented LP called White Limozeen produced by new country star Ricky Skaggs, an artistic if not a great chart success.

Parton also showed savvy as a businesswoman, opening her own theme park, Dollywood, to celebrate Tenn. mountain crafts and culture. This somewhat er-satz recreation of an idealized mountain life has proved to be quite successful, helping the economic revitaliza-tion of her childhood region and, not incidentally, also making a good deal of money for the singer.

In 1999, Parton was finally recognized by the country world by being elected into the Country Music Hall of Fame. That same year, she issued an album accompa-nied by a bluegrass band, working with new bluegrass star, Alison Krauss.

Dolly's sister Stella (b. 1949) had some minor coun-try hits in the mid-1970s, including 1975's "Ode to Olivia," in which she defended Olivia Newton-John against her country music critics.

DISC.: Hello, I'm Dolly (1967); Just Because I'm a Woman (1968); In the Good Old Days (1969); My Blue Ridge Mountain Boy (1969); The Fairest of Them All (1970); As Long As I Love (1970); A Real Live Dolly (1970); Golden Streets of Glory (1971); Joshua (1971); Coat of Many Colors (1971); Touch Your Woman (1972); Just the Way I Am (1972); Dolly Parton Sings, My Favorite Songwriter, Porter Wagoner (1972); My Tennessee Mountain Home (1973); Bubbling Over (1973); Mine (1973); Jolene (1974); Love Is Like a Butterfly (1974); The Bargain Store (1975); Dolly: The Seeker We Used To (1975); All I Can Do (1976); New Harvest—First Gathering (1977); Here You Come Again (1977); Heartbreaker (1978); Great Balls of Fire (1979); Dolly, Dolly, Dolly (1980); 9 to 5 (And Odd Jobs) (1980); Heartbreak Express (1982); The Best Little Whorehouse in Texas (soundtrack; 1982); Burlap and Satin (1983); The Great Pretender (1984); Rhinestone (soundtrack; 1984); Once upon a Christmas Dolly Parton/Kenny Rogers (1984); Real Love (1985); Think about Love (1986); Rainbow (1987); White Limozeen (1989); Home for Christmas (1990); Eagle When She Flies (1991); Straight Talk (soundtrack; 1992); Slow Dancing with whe Moon (1993); Heartsongs: Live from Home (1994); Something Special (1995); Treasures (1996); Hungry Again (1998); The Grass Is Blue (1999). Porter Wagoner: Just Between You and Me (1968); Just the Two of Us (1968); Always, Always (1969); Porter Wayne and Dolly Rebecca (1970); Once More (1970); Two of a Kind (1971); Together Always (1972); We Found It (1973); Love and Music (1973); Porter 'n Dolly (1974); Say Forever You'll Be Mine (1975). Emmylou Harris and Linda Ronstandt: Trio (1987); Trio II (1999). Loretta Lynn and Tammy Wynette: Honky Tonk Angels (1994).—**RC**

Partos, Oedoen (actually, Ödön),

Hungarian-born Israeli violinist, violist, pedagogue, and composer; b. Budapest, Oct. 1, 1907; d. Tel Aviv, July 6, 1977. He was a student of Hubay (violin) and Kodály (composi-tion) at the Budapest Academy of Music (1918–24). He served as concertmaster of the Lucerne City Orch. (1924–26) and the Budapest Concert Orch. (1926–27; 1937–38), and also toured throughout Europe as a soloist. In 1938 he emigrated to Israel, where he was 1st violinist in the Palestine Orch. (later the Israel Phil.) until 1956. He also was the violist in the Israel Quartet (1939–54). In 1951 he became director of the Tel Aviv Academy of Music (later the Rubin Academy of Music of the Univ. of Tel Aviv), where he was a prof. from 1961. In 1954 he was awarded the 1st Israel State Prize for composition for his symphonic fantasy Ein Gev. In many of his works, he utilized eastern Jewish folk modalities. In 1960 he embraced 12-tone composition. Late in his life he experimented with the 31-tone scale.

WORKS: ORCH.: Rondo on a Sephardic Theme for Strings (1939); Yizkor (In memoriam) for Viola or Violin or Cello and Strings (1947; also for Viola or Violin or Cello and Piano); 2 viola concertos: No. 1, Shir Tehillah (Song of Praise; 1948; Tel Aviv, Jan. 22, 1949) and No. 2 (1957); Ein Gev, symphonic fantasy (1951–52; Ein Gev, Oct. 1, 1953); Mourning Music (Oriental Ballad) for Viola or Cello and Chamber Orch. (1956; also for Cello or Viola and Piano); Violin Concerto (1958); Iltur (Impro-visation) for 12 Harps (1960); Dmuyoth (Images; 1960); Tehilim (Psalms) for Strings (1960; also as String Quartet No. 2); Sinfonia concertante for Viola and Orch. (1962); Symphonic Movements (1966); Netivim (Paths), symphonic elegy (1969); Shiluvim (Fu-sions) for Viola and Chamber Orch. (Tel Aviv, June 21, 1970); Music for Chamber Orch. (1971); Arabesque for Oboe and Chamber Orch. (1975). **CHAMBER:** 2 string quartets: No. 1, Concertino (1932; rev. 1939; N.Y., May 24, 1941) and No. 2, Tehilim (Psalms; 1960; also for String Orch.); Rondo for Violin and Piano (1947); 4 Israeli Tunes for Violin or Viola or Cello and Piano (1948); Maqamat for Flute and String Quartet (1959); Agada (A Legend) for Viola, Piano, and Percussion (1960;

London, June 6, 1962); *Arpiliyot* (Nebulae) for Wind Quintet (1966); Concertino for Flute and Piano (1969); *3 Fantasies* for 2 Violins (1972; composed in the 31-tone system); *Elegy* for Violin and Piano (1973); *Ballad* for Piano Quartet (1977); *Fantasia* for Violin, Cello, and Piano (1977); *Invenzione a 3 (Homage a Debussy)* for Flute, Harp, and Viola (1977). **P i a n o :** *Prelude* (1960); *Metamorphoses* (1971). **VOCAL:** *4 Folk Songs* for Alto and String Quartet (1939); *Daughter of Israel*, cantata for Soprano or Tenor, Chorus, and Orch. (1961); *5 Israeli Songs* for Tenor, Oboe, Piano, and Cello (1962); choruses; other songs.

BIBL.: W. Elias, *O. P.* (Tel Aviv, 1978).—NS/LK/DM

Partridge, Ian (Harold), English tenor; b. Wimbledon, June 12, 1938. He was a chorister at New Coll., Oxford, and a music scholar at Clifton Coll. before pursuing his training in London at the Royal Coll. of Music and the Guildhall School of Music. He commenced his career as a piano accompanist while singing in the Westminster Cathedral Choir (1958–62). In 1958 he made his formal debut as a singer in Bexhill, and from 1962 he pursued a solo career. In 1969 he made his debut at London's Covent Garden as Iopas in *Les Troyens*. He appeared as a soloist with many major orchs. in England and abroad, gave many recitals, and sang on radio and television. In 1989 he made his debut at the Salzburg Festival in Bach's *St. John Passion*. In 1991 he was made a Commander of the Order of the British Empire. His sister, Jennifer Partridge (b. New Malden, June 17, 1942), is a pianist who has often served as his accompanist.—NS/LK/DM

Partridge Family, The, TV version of a family rock band. **MEMBERSHIP:** Shirley Jones, voc. (b. Smithton, Pa., March 31, 1934); David Cassidy, voc. (b. N.Y.C., April 12, 1950). Like The Monkees before it, The Partridge Family turned pop music into a TV situation comedy. Also like The Monkees, none of the people on the screen actually played an instrument—and only two of them really sang. Also like The Monkees, the Family's ersatz pop was immediately successful and reaped enormous benefit to the Screen Gems TV studio.

Loosely based on a real family band, The Cowsills, the show cast Shirley Jones as Shirley Partridge, a widowed mother of five who lets her kids convince her that the family should be a band. Jones came from a musical theater background, and acted in the filmed version of *Oklahoma!* and *The Music Man*, among others. She starred with her own stepson, David Cassidy—the only other singing Partridge—as Keith. The rest of the actors included Susan Dey, Danny Bonaduce, Suzanne Crough and Jeremy Gelbwaks, who was replaced by Brian Foster after the first season. The program debuted in the fall of 1970. Like *The Monkees*, every episode featured two full songs, written by Brill Building stalwarts like Barry Mann, Gerry Goffin, and Mike Appel (several years before he'd manage Bruce Springsteen). The material was a slight cut above the standard bubblegum issue, but definitely geared to the prepubescent girls the Keith Partridge character was created to attract. The first episode featured the group cutting a demo of "I Think I Love You." The song zoomed to the top of the charts and stayed there for three weeks, going

gold. It propelled *The Partridge Family Album* to #4 and gold.

During the show's first season, the "group" had two more hits: "Doesn't Somebody Want to Be Wanted" also went gold and rose to #6; "I'll Meet You Halfway" went to #9. The album *Up to Date* also went gold and hit #3. Even before the fall season began in 1971, the song "I Woke up in Love This Morning" started getting airplay, but it only reached #13. "It's One of Those Nights (Yes Love)" fared poorer still, reaching #20. However, the album *The Partridge Family Sound Magazine* went to #9 and gold, and the show's ratings continued to be high.

Cassidy's character, Keith, proved so popular he released a solo recording. His first single, "Cherish," topped the adult-contemporary chart, hit #9 pop, and went gold. But what really brought in the big bucks was the enormous amount of licensing and merchandising opportunities the show presented. By the second season, there were Partridge Family products of every description, generating half a billion dollars. While negotiating with Screen Gems for a piece of this action, Cassidy spent his time acting on the show by weekday and touring for his solo career weekends. Eventually, he and Screen Gems came to terms that made him one of his time's best-paid performers.

The hits kept coming through the early 1970s for both the "group" and Cassidy, though not with the strength of their early hits. Cassidy scored with "Could It Be Forever" (#37) and "How Can I Be Sure" (#25) before the end of the show's second season in the spring of 1972. At the same time, *The Partridge Family Shopping Bag* went gold and rose to #18. During the 1972–73 season, Cassidy only managed one hit, "Rock Me Baby," which stalled at #38. The Partridges scored two hits that season, "Breaking up Is Hard to Do" in the fall of 1972 and "Looking through the Eyes of Love" in the winter of 1973. Their *Greatest Hits* album went gold, topping out at #21.

After the fourth season, Cassidy—already at odds with his character—left the show. The producers decided that without him, there was no show, and pulled the plug. Cassidy tried a dramatic role, but the Keith Partridge image ran too deep. He withdrew even further after his father died in a fire in 1975. Six years later, he came out of seclusion to tour in a revival of the George M. Cohan show *Little Johnny Jones* in 1981. He followed this with a role in *Joseph and the Amazing Technicolor Dreamcoat* in 1983. In 1990, Cassidy released *Didn't You Used to Be*, a solo album of more mature material that met with lukewarm success, taking the minor hit "Lying to Myself" to #27 in the pop charts. In 1993, he returned to the stage with his half-brother (and fellow former teen idol) Shaun Cassidy and Petula Clark in the show *Blood Brothers*. He signed a long-term contract to appear in a show in Las Vegas called EFX in the late 1990s, releasing a record on his own label called *Old Trick, New Dog* in 1998.

Susan Dey fared better in drama, making several feature films and TV movies before landing a role in the series *L.A. Law* during the 1980s. Danny Bonaduce endured his own post-stardom substance-abuse problems, but came out of them with his sharp wit intact. He spent much of the 1990s as a radio personality, and even had his own syndicated TV talk show. To date, The Partridge Family has sold some 25 million records worldwide.

DISC.: *The Partridge Family Album* (1970); *The Partridge Family Sound Magazine* (1971); *Up to Date* (1971); *The Partridge Family Shopping Bag* (1972); *The Partridge Family Notebook* (1972); *Crossword Puzzle* (1973); *Bulletin Board* (1973); *The World of The Partridge Family* (1974); *The Partridge Family* (1971); *A Partridge Family Christmas Card* (1992).—**HB**

Pasatieri, Thomas, talented American composer; b. N.Y., Oct. 20, 1945. He began to play the piano by spontaneous generation, and picked up elements of composition, particularly vocal, by a similar subliminal process; between the ages of 14 and 18 he wrote some 400 songs. He persuaded Boulanger to take him as a student by correspondence between Paris and N.Y. when he was 15, and at 16 he entered the Juilliard School of Music in N.Y., where he became a student of Giannini and Persichetti. He also took a course with Milhaud in Aspen, Colo., where his first opera, *The Women*, to his own libretto, was performed when he was only 19. It became clear to him that opera was his natural medium, and that the way to achieve the best results was by following the evolutionary line of Italian operatic productions characterized by the felicity of *bel canto*, facility of harmonic writing, and euphonious fidelity to the lyric and dramatic content of the subject. In striving to attain these objectives, Pasatieri ran the tide of mandatory inharmoniousness; while his productions were applauded by hoi polloi, they shocked music critics and other composers; one of them described Pasatieri's music as "a stream of perfumed urine." This attitude is akin to that taken by some toward Giannini and Menotti (interestingly, all 3 are of Italian genetic stock). From 1967 to 1969 Pasatieri taught at the Juilliard School; then was engaged at the Manhattan School of Music (1969–71); from 1980 to 1983 he was Distinguished Visiting Prof. at the Univ. of Cincinnati (Ohio) Coll.-Cons. of Music.

WORKS: DRAMATIC: O p e r a : *The Women* (Aspen, Aug. 20, 1965); *La Divina* (N.Y., March 16, 1966); *Padrevia* (N.Y., Nov. 18, 1967); *Calvary* (Seattle, April 7, 1971); *The Trial of Mary Lincoln,* television opera (Boston, Feb. 14, 1972); *Black Widow* (Seattle, March 2, 1972); *The Seagull,* after Chekhov (Houston, March 5, 1974); *Signor Deluso,* after Molière's *Sganarelle* (Vienna, Va., July 27, 1974); *The Penitentes* (Aspen, Aug. 3, 1974); *Inez de Castro* (Baltimore, April 1, 1976); *Washington Square,* after Henry James (Detroit, Oct. 1, 1976); *Three Sisters,* after Chekov (1979; Columbus, Ohio, March 13, 1986); *Before Breakfast* (N.Y., Oct. 9, 1980); *The Goose Girl,* children's opera (Fort Worth, Tex., Feb. 15, 1981); *Maria Elena* (Tucson, April 8, 1983). **P i a n o :** 2 sonatas (1976); other works. **VOCAL:** *Heloise and Abelard* for Soprano, Baritone, and Piano (1971); *Rites de passage* for Voice and Chamber Orch. or String Quartet (1974); *3 Poems of James Agee* for Voice and Piano (1974); *Far from Love* for Soprano, Clarinet, and Piano (1976); *Permit Me Voyage,* cantata for Soprano, Chorus, and Orch. (1976); *Mass* for 4 Solo Voices, Chorus, and Orch. (1983).—**NS/LK/DM**

Pasdeloup, Jules-Étienne, famous French conductor; b. Paris, Sept. 15, 1819; d. Fontainebleau, Aug.

13, 1887. He studied piano with Laurent and Zimmerman at the Paris Cons., winning premiers prix for solfege (1832) and piano (1834), and then was on its faculty (1841–68). He organized the Société des Jeunes Artistes' sym. concerts in Paris, where he conducted for the first time on Feb. 20, 1853; these became the Société des Jeunes Artistes du Conservatoire Imperial de Musique concerts, which he conducted from 1856 to 1865. He founded the Concerts Populaires de Musique Classique, conducting its first concert on Oct. 27, 1861, and with it championed the works of the great masters as well as those by contemporary French composers. He also founded the Société des Oratorios (1868), and was a conductor at the Théâtre-Lyrique (1868–70). His Concerts Populaires gradually lost ground in competition with the concerts of Colonne and Lamoureux, and were abandoned in 1884; they were revived in 1886–87. A grand popular music festival at the Trocadero (1884), instituted for his benefit, netted him nearly 100,000 francs.

Pasero, Tancredi, noted Italian bass; b. Turin, Jan. 11, 1893; d. Milan, Feb. 17, 1983. He studied in Turin. He made his operatic debut in 1917 as Rodolfo in *La Sonnambula* in Vicenza. From 1924 to 1930 he sang at the Teatro Colón in Buenos Aires, and in 1926 he joined La Scala in Milan, remaining on its roster until 1952. He made his Metropolitan Opera debut in N.Y. on Nov. 1, 1929, as Alvise in *La Gioconda*; continued on its roster until 1933. He also had guest engagements at London's Covent Garden (1931) and the Paris Opéra (1935). His repertoire was extensive and included Italian, German, French, and Russian operas; he excelled in Verdi's operas, and made a distinctive appearance as Mussorgsky's Boris Godunov.

BIBL.: C. Clerico, *T. P.: Voce verdiana* (Scomegna, 1985). —**NS/LK/DM**

Pashchenko, Andrei (Filippovich), prolific Russian composer; b. Rostov, Aug. 15, 1883; d. Moscow, Nov. 16, 1972. He studied with Wihtol and Steinberg at the St. Petersburg Cons., graduating in 1917. He occupied various clerical positions, including librarian of the St. Petersburg Court Orch. (from 1911), remaining with it when it became the State Orch. (1917) and the Leningrad Phil. (1924). He left his post in 1931. In 1961 he went to live in Moscow. An exceptionally fertile composer, he wrote some 14 operas and 15 syms. The style of his music is a natural continuation of the traditions of the Russian national school. In his later works he allowed a certain influx of impressionistic harmonies and unresolved dissonant combinations.

WORKS: DRAMATIC: O p e r a : *Eagles in Revolt* (Leningrad, Nov. 7, 1925); *King Maximilian* (1927); *The Black Cliff* (Leningrad, June 12, 1931); *The Pompadours* (1939); *Jester Balakirev* (1949); *The Capricious Bride* (1956); *Radda and Loyko* (1957); *Nila Snishko* (1961); *The Great Seducer* (1966); *Woman, This Is the Devil* (1966); *African Love* (1966); *The Horse in the Senate* (1967); *Portrait* (1968); *Master and Margarita* (1971). **ORCH.:** 15 syms. (1915, 1929, 1933, 1938, 1952, 1954, 1956, 1957, 1958, 1963, 1964, 1966, 1969, 1969, 1970); 4 sinfoniettas (1943, 1945, 1953, 1964); *Volga Fantasy* (1961); *Ukrainiada,* symphonic poem (1963); *Icarus,* symphonic poem (1964); *Dance Triptych* (1965); *The Voice of Peace*, symphonic poem (1971); *Poem of Stars*, symphonic poem (1971); Cello Concerto (1964). **CHAMBER:** 9 string quartets. **VOCAL:** Numerous works for chorus.

BIBL.: Y. Meylikh, *A.F. P.* (Leningrad, 1960).—NS/LK/DM

Pashkevich, Vasily (Alexeievich), Russian violinist and composer; b. c. 1740; d. St. Petersburg, March 20, 1797. In 1763 he was admitted as a violinist to the 2nd court orch. in St. Petersburg. His Russian opera *A Carriage Accident* was performed in St. Petersburg on Nov. 7, 1779; in 1782 he presented 2 comic operas in Russian: *The Miser* (Moscow) and *The Pasha of Tunis* (St. Petersburg). In 1783 he became a violinist in the first court orch. In 1786 he was commissioned by Catherine the Great to write a comic Russian opera, *Fevey*, for which the Empress herself wrote the libretto. It was produced in St. Petersburg on April 19, 1786, and Pashkevich received an award of 1,000 rubles. He was then made chief of ball music at the Imperial Palace and concertmaster of the first court orch. (1786); received the honorary rank of colonel. In 1790 he collaborated with Sarti and Canobbio on another Russian opera to a text of Catherine the Great, *The Early Reign of Oleg*, which was first produced at the palace, and publicly performed in St. Petersburg on Nov. 2, 1790. In collaboration with Martin y Soler, he wrote still another comic opera to a text by the Empress, *Fedul and His Children* (perf. at the palace, Jan. 27, 1791; publicly, St. Petersburg, March 2, 1791). His Mass according to the Russian Orthodox liturgy was publ. in Moscow in 1796.—NS/LK/DM

Pasini, Laura, Italian soprano; b. Gallarate, Jan. 28, 1894; d. Rome, Sept. 30, 1942. She studied piano with Appiano at the Milan Cons., and made her debut as a pianist in Rome in 1912. After vocal training from Pietro at the Accademia di Santa Cecilia in Rome, she made her operatic debut as Zerlina in *Fra Diavolo* at Milan's Teatro Eden in 1921. She sang in Rome (1922–23), at Milan's La Scala (1923–26; 1930–31) and Buenos Aires's Teatro Colón (1925), and in Turin (1925–27), Salzburg (1931), and Florence (1933) before settling in Cagliari as a voice teacher.—NS/LK/DM

Pasini (-Vitale), Lina, Italian soprano; b. Rome, Nov. 8, 1872; d. there, Nov. 23, 1959. She studied in Rome. She made her operatic debut in 1893 as Cecilia in Cilea's *Tilda* at the Teatro dal Verme in Milan; then sang at La Scala in Milan, Turin, the Teatro Colón in Buenos Aires, Rome, and Naples; retired from the stage in 1928. She married the conductor Edoardo Vitale in 1897. At the height of her career, she was widely regarded as one of the finest Wagnerian sopranos on the Italian stage. Her sister, Camilla Pasini (b. Rome, Nov. 6, 1875; d. there, Oct. 29, 1935), was also a soprano who studied in Rome. She created the role of Musetta in *La Bohème* (Turin, Feb. 1, 1896). She retired from the stage in 1905. —NS/LK/DM

Paskalis, Kostas, Greek baritone; b. Levadia, Sept. 1, 1929. He received training in voice in Athens, where he concurrently took courses in piano and composition at the Cons. In 1951 he made his operatic debut as Rigoletto at the National Opera in Athens, where he sang until 1958. In 1958 he made his debut at the Vienna State Opera as Renato, and continued to appear there regularly until 1979. He made his British debut as Macbeth at the Glyndebourne Festival in 1964. On Feb. 17, 1965, he made his Metropolitan Opera debut in N.Y. as Carlo in *La forza del destino*. He made occasional appearances there until 1975. In 1965–66 he sang in Rome. In 1966 he appeared as Pentheus in the premiere of *The Bassarids* at the Salzburg Festival. In 1967 he made his first appearance at Milan's La Scala as Valentin. He first sang at London's Covent Garden in 1969 as Macbeth, returning there in 1971–72. From 1988 he was director of the National Opera in Athens. Among his other roles were Don Giovanni, Donizetti's Alfonso, Posa, Nabucco, Iago, and Escamillo.—NS/LK/DM

Pasquali, Francesco, Italian composer; b. Cosenza, c. 1590; d. after 1635. He studied in Rome, and remained there for most of his life. Between 1615 and 1633 he brought out 3 books of madrigals for 1 to 5 Voices, and several vols. of secular and sacred songs for 1, 2, 3, 4, and 5 voices.—NS/LK/DM

Pasquali, Niccolò, Italian violinist and composer; b. c. 1718; d. Edinburgh, Oct. 13, 1757. He went to Edinburgh (1740) and then to London (c. 1743); was in Dublin (1748–49), again in London (1750–51), again in Dublin (1751–52), and then settled in Edinburgh, where he publ. the valuable treatise *Thorough-bass made easy* (1757); also publ. *The Art of Fingering the Harpsichord* (Edinburgh, 1758). His extant works include 12 overtures (London, 1751), 6 sonatas for Violin and Basso Continuo (1744), 2 sets of 3 sonatas for 2 Violins, Viola, and Basso Continuo (1750), many minuets, and numerous songs.—NS/LK/DM

Pasquini, Bernardo, eminent Italian organist, harpsichordist, pedagogue, and composer; b. Massa di Valdinievole, near Lucca, Dec. 7, 1637; d. Rome, Nov. 21, 1710. He settled in Rome (1650), where he studied with Vittori and Cesti. He was organist at Chiesa Nuova (1661–63), S. Maria Maggiore (1663), S. Maria in Aracoeli (1664–1710), and S. Luigi dei Francesi (1673–75); was also first organist at the Oratory of SS. Crocifisso (1664–85). He served as harpsichordist and music director to Prince Giambattista Borghese, and was the teacher of Della Ciaja, Durante, and G. Muffat. In 1706 he became a member of the Arcadian Academy. Although greatly esteemed as a keyboard player, little of his music was publ. in his lifetime; many of his vocal works are lost. He excelled as a composer of keyboard suites and variations. See M. Haynes, ed., *Bernardo Pasquini: Collected Works for a Keyboard*, Corpus of Early Keyboard Music, V/1–7 (1964–68).

WORKS DRAMATIC (all 1st perf. in Rome unless otherwise given): **Opera:** *La sincerità con la sincerità, overo Il Tirinto* (Ariccia, 1672); *La forza d'amore* (Rome, 1672; rev. as *Con la forza d'amor si vince amore*, Pratolino, near Florence, 1679); *L'amor per vendetta, overo L'Alcasta* (Jan. 27, 1673); *Tespolo tutore* (1675); *La Donna ancora è fidele* (Carnival 1676); *La caduta del* *regno dell'Amazzoni* (1678); *Dov'è è pietà* (Carnival 1679); *L'Idalma, overo Chi la duca la vince* (Carnival 1680); *Il Lisimaco* (Carnival 1681); *La Tessalonica* (Jan. 31, 1683); *L'Arianna* (Carnival 1685); *Santa Dinna* (Carnival 1687; in collaboration with A. Melani and A Scarlatti); *L'Eudossia* (Feb. 6, 1692). **VOCAL: O r a t o r i o s :** *L'Agar* (March 17, 1675); *L'Assuero* (April 15, 1675); *Sant'Alessio* (1676); *Sant'Agnese* (1677); *Sant'Eufrasia* (c. 1677); *Salutazione angelica* (Messina, 1681); *Divae clarae triumphus* (March 20, 1682); *L'idolatria di Salomone* (1686); *I fatti di Mosè nel deserto* (Modena, 1687); *Il martirio dei santi* (Modena, 1687); *L'Abramo* (Palermo, 1688); *La sete di Christo* (1689); *La caduta di Salomone* (Florence, 1693); *L'Ismaele* (Florence, 1693); *David trionfante contro Goliath* (Florence, 1694). **O t h e r :** Some 60 cantatas, of which 50 are for Solo Voice, 2 canzonettas, solo motets and arias, etc. **KEYBOARD:** Sonatas, dances, toccatas, variations, etc.

BIBL.: V. Virgili, *B. P.* (Pescia, 1908); A. Bonaventura, *B. P.* (Ascoli Piceno, 1923); E. Luin, *B. P. e il suo tricentenario* (Rome, 1939); W. Heimrich, *Die Orgel- und Cembalo-Werke B. P.s* (diss., Free Univ. of Berlin, 1958); M. Haynes, *The Keyboard Works of B. P.* (diss., Ind. Univ., 1960); G. Crain, *The Operas of B. P.* (diss., Yale Univ., 1965).—**NS/LK/DM**

Pasquini, Ercole, significant Italian organist and composer; b. Ferrara, c. 1550; d. Rome, between 1608 and 1619. He studied with Alessandro Milleville. He was organist in Ferrara and then at the Cappella Giulia at St. Peter's in Rome (1597–1608), and also organist at S. Spirito in Saxia (1604). He was one of the leading masters of keyboard composition in his era. In addition to some 30 keyboard pieces, several sacred vocal works are extant. See W. Shindle, ed., *Ercole Pasquini: Collected Keyboard Works*, Corpus of Early Keyboard Music, XII (1966).

BIBL.: W. Shindle, *The Keyboard Works of E. P.* (diss., Ind. Univ., 1963).—**NS/LK/DM**

Pasquotti, Corrado, Italian composer; b. Vittorio Veneto, March 11, 1954. He studied in Padua, Venice, and Milan. In 1977 he received the diploma of merit of the Teatro Angelicum in Milan. He subsequently taught at the Rossini Cons. of Pesaro. In his works, he strives to achieve intimate synergy of visual images and auditory projections; his written scores literally follow the parameters of a given painting, with notes corresponding to the lines of the design and rests occupying the spaces of the object; depending on a chart for such correspondences, different musical versions are achieved in actual performances. A typical product of this method is *Forma Magistra Ludi* for Chamber Orch., to images by Yasmin Brandolini d'Adda (1980). He also composed a string quartet, *Quartet "i reflessi"* (1983).—**NS/LK/DM**

Pass, Joe (originally, **Passalaqua, Joseph Anthony Jacobi**), famed jazz guitarist; b. New Brunswick, N.J., Jan. 13, 1929; d. Los Angeles, Calif., May 23, 1994. He took up the guitar as a schoolboy, cutting short his education to pursue a career in music; he played guitar in Tony Pastor's band while still in his teens. Unfortunately, he succumbed to drug addiction, was caught, and sentenced to prison; after spending years in halfway houses and hospitals, he was placed at

the famous Synanon Foundation clinic in Santa Monica, Calif., where he was finally cured. As a souvenir of this confinement, he recorded a jazz album with his fellow inmates, *Sounds of Synanon* (1962). He recorded and toured in the 1960s with George Shearing, Sarah Vaughan, Carmen McRae, and others, but became better known with his first solo album, *Virtuoso* (1973). He went on to several successful collaborations with Oscar Peterson, Ella Fitzgerald, Count Basie, Duke Ellington, and Herb Ellis, and released several more solo recordings in addition to extensive live performing as a solo artist. Pass remained active on tour and record from the 1970s through the early 1990s. He worked in a duo with classical guitarist Elliot Fisk, and they were about to record when Pass died.

DISC.: *Sound of Synanon* (1962); *Complete* Catch Me! *Sessions* (1963); *Joy Spring* (1964); *For Django* (1964); *Virtuoso, Vol. 4* (1973); *Virtuoso, Vol. 1* (1973); *Two for the Road* (1974); *At Akron Univ.* (1974); *Montreux '75* (1975); *Virtuoso, Vol. 2* (1976); *Virtuoso, Vol. 3* (1977); *Montreux '77: Live!* (1977); *Chops* (1978); *Northsea Nights* (1979); *Checkmate* (1981); *We'll Be Together Again* (1984); *Live at Long Bay Beach Coll.* (1984); *Univ. of Akron Concert* (1985); *Virtuoso: Live!* (1991); *Live at Yoshi's* (1992); *My Song* (1993); *Finally: Live in Stockholm* (1993); *Roy Clark & J.P. Play* (1994). —**NS/LP**

Passereau, Pierre, French composer who flourished in the first half of the 16th century. He was chapel singer to the Duke of Angoulême, and later of later Francis I. Twenty-three of his chansons were publ. in contemporary anthologies (1533–47). G. Dottin ed. his complete works (1967).—**NS/LK/DM**

Passy, (Ludvig Anton) Edvard, Swedish pianist, organist, teacher, and composer; b. Stockholm, Sept. 3, 1789; d. Drottningholm, Aug. 16, 1870. He received his first music instruction from his brother, then studied with L. Piccinni in Stockholm, John Field in St. Petersburg, and Eggert in Stockholm. After several successful tours of Germany, he settled in his native city as a highly esteemed teacher, and pianist in the royal orch. (1818–23) and organist of the royal chapel (1833–66). He wrote 2 operas, 2 piano concertos, Fantasy for Piano and Orch., 4 string quartets, Piano Trio, choruses, songs, organ works, and many virtuoso piano pieces.—**NS/LK/DM**

Pasta, Giuditta (Maria Costanza née **Negri),** famous Italian soprano; b. Saronno, near Milan, Oct. 28, 1797; d. Blevio, Lake Como, April 1, 1865. She studied with Asioli at the Milan Cons. and with Giuseppe Scappa, making her debut in his *Le tre Eleonore* at the Teatro degli Accademici Filodrammatici in Milan (1815). She then made her Paris debut in Paër's *Il Principe di Taranto* (1816) and her London debut as Telemachus in Cimarosa's *Penelope* at the King's Theatre (Jan. 11, 1817). After further studies with Scappa, she sang in Venice, Padua, Rome, Brescia, Trieste, and Turin. She then returned to Paris and made a sensational appearance as Desdemona in Rossini's *Otello* at the Théâtre-Italien (June 5, 1821), her voice being acclaimed as a vocal phenomenon and her dramatic abilities without equal. She continued to sing there, appearing in the premiere of Rossini's *Il viaggio a Reims* (June 19, 1825); also sang in London from 1824. She created the title role in Pacini's *Niobe* at Naples's Teatro San Carlo (Nov. 19, 1826). After singing in Vienna (1829), she created the title role in Donizetti's *Anna Bolena* (Milan, Dec. 26, 1830) and Amina in Bellini's *La Sonnambula* (Milan, March 6, 1831); then created the title role in Bellini's *Norma* at Milan's La Scala (Dec. 26, 1831) and Beatrice di Tenda in Venice (March 16, 1833). Following appearances in London (1837) and St. Petersburg (1840), she virtually abandoned the stage due to the wretched condition of her voice. At the apex of her career, she astounded her auditors by the range of her voice, which encompassed A in the low register to D in the high treble; combined with her rare dramatic gifts, she had few equals on the operatic stage.

BIBL.: M. Ferranti-Giulini, *G. P. e i suoi tempi* (Milan, 1935). —NS/LK/DM

Pasterwitz, Georg (actually **Robert) von,** Austrian composer; b. Bierhutten, near Passau, June 7, 1730; d. Kremsmünster, Jan. 26, 1803. He studied music with Eberlin in Salzburg, and after touring Europe, entered the order of the Benedictines in 1755. He was choirmaster at the monastery in Kremsmünster (1767–83), then lived in Vienna (1785–94). In 1794 he became dean of his monastery's Upper School (until 1801). He publ. 24 *Fughe* for Organ or Harpsichord and 300 *Themata und Versetten* for Organ or Piano. In MS there exists about 20 masses, numerous Psalms, offertories, vespers, motets, etc., as well as several operas, intermezzi, and detached arias interpolated in various operas of other composers.

BIBL.: W. Kaas-Cornelius, *G. v.P. als Kirchenkomponist* (diss., Univ. of Vienna, 1925).—NS/LK/DM

Pastor, Tony (originally, **Pestritto, Anthony/Antonio**), pop band leader, vocalist, saxophonist; b. Middletown, Conn., Oct. 26, 1907; d. New London, Conn., Oct. 31, 1969. From about 1927, he worked with various local bands, then played with Irving Aaronson (1928–30). He led his own band in Hartford, Conn. (1931–34), and became a mainstay of Artie Shaw's bands (1936–40). He became a star with Shaw (his zany vocal on "Indian Love Call" was on the other side of Shaw's hit "Begin the Beguine" in 1938). He formed his own band in late 1940 and achieved considerable success, having had more than a dozen top 20 hits in the 1940s, and continued to lead his own band until 1959. From then onwards, he appeared with his family vocal group, which also featured his sons Tony Jr., Guy, and John. In the spring of 1968 he was forced to retire through ill health; he died a year later.

DISC.: *Tony Pastor* (1949); *Dance Date Series* (1950).—JC/LP

Pastorius, Jaco (John Francis), jazz-fusion electric bassist who helped redefine bass in modern popular music; b. Norristown, Pa., Dec. 1, 1951; d. Fort Lauderdale, Fla., Sept. 21, 1987. He began playing electric bass in local bands in Fort Lauderdale, going on to back visiting stars such as the Supremes, the Temp-

tations and Nancy Wilson. Soaking up both country and Caribbean music, he developed enormous technical skill and a distinctive gorgeous sound. He played with Blood, Sweat & Tears, Ira Sullivan, Paul Bley, Joni Mitchell and Pat Metheny, once sat in with Chick Corea's Return to Forever, and played in Herbie Hancock's Headhunters, taking Paul Jackson's place for two or three weeks. He joined Weather Report in 1976; he played with them for several years and developed an international following for his playing and for writing such pieces as "Teen Town" and "Punk Jazz." He then toured with his own group Word of Mouth from (1980–83), recording in 1984. At one point, he was interested in playing acoustic bass and asked George Mraz for lessons. Pastorius suffered from depression and endured several financial setbacks. He was assaulted by a club manager in Fort Lauderdale and hospitalized in a coma for nine days before he died.

DISC.: *J.* (1974); *J.P.* (1976); *The Birthday Concert* (1981); *Word of Mouth* (1981); *Holiday for Pans* (1982); *Twins I & II* (1982); *Invitation* (1983); *Blackbird* (1984); *Live in N.Y. City, Vols. 1–4* (1985); *PDB* (1986); *Live in Italy* (1986); *Jazz Street* (1986); *Honestly: Solo Live* (1986); *Curtain Call* (1986); *Heavy N' Jazz* (1986). **WEATHER REPORT:** *Black Market* (1976); *Italian Weather* (1976); *Heavy Weather* (1977); *Mr. Gone* (1978); *Live Weather* (1978); *8:30* (1979); *Night Passage* (1980); *Weather Report* (1982). **ESSENCE FEATURING J.P.:** *Last Flight* (1984). —LP/MM

Pastrana, Pedro de, Spanish compoer; b. c. 1480; d. after 1559. He was a chaplain and singer at the chapel of Ferdinand the Catholic in Aragon in 1500. From 1527 to 1541 he was chaplain to Charles V. He also was abbot of the Cistercian monastery of S. Bernardo near Valencia (from 1530) and maestro de capilla to the Duke and Duchess of Calabria in Valencia. In 1547 he was made maestro de capilla to Prince Philip and in 1548 royal chaplain to Charles V, making his residence in Valladolid. He composed a Mass, 3 Magnificats, motets, Psalms, and sacred and secular villancicos.—LK/DM

Pásztory, Ditta, Hungarian pianist; b. Rimaszombat, Oct. 31, 1903; d. Budapest, Nov. 21, 1982. She studied piano with Bartók at the Budapest Academy of Music (1922–23); on Aug. 28, 1923, she became his second wife. Although she subsequently abandoned her solo career, she was encouraged by her husband to appear with him in duo performances. She joined him in the premiere of his Sonata for 2 Pianos and Percussion in Basel on Jan. 16, 1938, after which they made tours of Europe and the U.S.; they settled in the U.S. in 1940. After her husband's death in 1945, Pásztory returned to Hungary (1946), where she championed a number of her husband's piano works on recordings. Her will provided for the establishment of the Bartók-Pásztory Award, the most important annual Hugarian prize for composers and performers.—NS/LK/DM

Patachich, Iván, Hungarian composer; b. Budapest, June 3, 1922; d. there, May 11, 1993. He studied with Albert Siklós, János Viski, and Ferenc Szabó at the Budapest Academy of Music. After working as a theater conductor, he became music director of the Budapest Film Studio in 1952. In 1971 he established the electronic music studio EXASTUD (Experimentum Auditorii Studii) in Budapest.

WORKS: DRAMATIC: O p e r a : *Theomachia* (1962); *Fuente ovajuna* (1969); *Brave New World* (1988–89). **B a l l e t :** *Fekete-fehér* (Black and White; 1958); *Bakaruhában* (Sunday Romance; 1963); *Mngongo and Mlaba* (1965); *Studio sintetico* (1973). **P a n t o m i m e :** *Möbius tér* (Mobius Space; 1980). **ORCH.:** 2 harp concertos (1956, 1968); *Poema sinfonico* (1958); Flute Concerto (1958); Viola Concerto (1959); Oboe Concerto (1959); *Serenata* for Strings (1960); Guitar Concerto (1961); *Concerto breve* for Cello and Orch. (1962); 2 divertimentos (1962, 1969); 2 piano concertos (1963, 1968); *Sinfonietta Savariensis* (1964); Violin Concerto (1964); 2 syms. (1965, 1966); *Quadri di Picasso* (1965); Bassoon Concerto (1965); Concerto for 3 Percussionists and Orch. (1966); Concerto for Violin, Piano, and Strings (1969); Organ Concerto (1972); *Presentazioni*, concertino for Cimbalom or Marimba, and Orch. (1975); *Coordinate* (1979); Trumpet Concerto (1985); *Naconxypan szigeten* (On the Island of Naconxypan), 5 symphonic poems (1986); *DX7 Reports No. 2* for Synthesizer and Orch. (1987); Trombone Concerto (1988). **CHAMBER:** 2 violin sonatas (1948, 1964); Sextet for Harp and Winds (1957); Quintet for Harp, Flute, and Strings (1958); Trio for Violin, Viola, and Harp (1958); Wind Quintet (1960); Quartet for 2 Harps, Viola, and Double Bass (1962); 2 piano trios (1962, 1967); Viola Sonata (1962); Cello Sonata (1963); Sonata for Harp and Horn (1964); Wind Trio (1965); String Trio (1965); *Elementi* for Percussion (1966); *Quattro studii* for 6 Percussionists (1968); *Costruzioni* for 4 Percussionists (1969); Sonata for Oboe and Harp (1971); *Bagatelli* for Organ, Flute, and Horn (1971); *Proporzioni* for 4 Percussionists (1972); *Ja amidohele*, quintet for 5 Cellos (1976); *Quintetto* for Trombone and Tuba (1981); Trio for Bassoons (1982); *Terzettino* for Saxophones (1987); *Quartettino* for Trombones (1988); *Anpro-Sifi* for Percussion Quartet (1988); *Play 88* for Saxophone Quartet (1988); also piano pieces, including a Sonata (1965) and Sonatina (1966). **VOCAL: C a n t a t a s :** *Szirtország* (Country of Cliffs) for Chorus and Orch. (1953); *Music of the Bible* for Tenor, Chorus, and Orch. (1968); *Cantus Profani Silvae* for Chorus and Tape (1978); *Canti stravaganti* for Chorus and Tape (1981); *Az éjszaka csodái* (Miracles of the Night) for Chorus, Orch., and Tape (1985); *Cantus discipulus* for Chorus and Tape (1986); *Miracle of the Hermit Thrush* for Chorus, Orch., and Tape (1987). **O t h e r V o c a l :** *Missa simplex* for Chorus and Organ (1949); *Messe di Santa Marguerita* for Chorus and Orch. (1967); *Canticum Canticorum* for Chorus and Instruments (1985). **OTHER:** Live electronic scores; tape pieces.—NS/LK/DM

Pataky, Kálmán, Hungarian tenor; b. Alsolenda, Nov. 14, 1896; d. Los Angeles, March 3, 1964. He studied in Budapest. In 1922 he made his operatic debut as the Duke of Mantua at the Budapest Opera, where he subsequently appeared regularly. From 1926 he also sang at the Vienna State Opera. He made guest appearances at the Paris Opéra (1928), the Glyndebourne Festival (1936), the Salzburg Festival (1936), and at Milan's La Scala. He also appeared frequently at the Teatro Colón in Buenos Aires. After the Anschluss in Austria in 1938, he sang mainly in Hungary. After World War II, he settled in the U.S. Pataky was admired for his Mozart roles, particularly his Belmonte, Ottavio, and Tamino. He was a fine concert artist. Strauss dedicated several of his lieder to him.

BIBL.: V. Somogyi and I Molnár, *P. K.* (Budapest, 1968).—NS/LK/DM

Patanè, Giuseppe, Italian conductor; b. Naples, Jan. 1, 1932; d. (fatally stricken while conducting *Il Barbiere di Siviglia* at the Bavarian State Opera) Munich, May 30, 1989. He was a son of Franco Patane (1908–68), a conductor. He studied at the Cons. S. Pietro a Majella in Naples and made his debut as a conductor at the age of 19, when he led a performance of *La Traviata* at the Teatro Mercadante in Naples. He was subsequently 2nd conductor at the Teatro San Carlo in Naples (1951–56); became principal conductor of the Linz Landestheater in 1961, and in 1962 to 1968 was a conductor of the Deutsche Oper in Berlin; he further filled engagements at La Scala in Milan, at the Vienna State Opera, and in Copenhagen. On Oct. 18, 1975, he made his Metropolitan Opera debut in N.Y. conducting *La Gioconda*. In 1982 he was appointed co-principal conductor of the American Sym. Orch. in N.Y., remaining at this post until 1984; then was chief conductor of the Mannheim National Theater (from 1987) and of the Munich Radio Orch. (from 1988).—NS/LK/DM

Patey, Janet (Monach née Whytock), greatly esteemed Scottish contralto; b. London, May 1, 1842; d. Sheffield, Feb. 28, 1894. She studied with Wass, making her debut under the name Ellen Andrews in Birmingham in 1860, and then continued her studies with Mrs. Sims Reeves and Ciro Pinsuti. In 1866 she married the baritone John (George) Patey (b. Stonehouse, Devon, 1835; d. Falmouth, Dec. 4, 1901; he studied in Paris and Milan, and then made his London debut (1858); appeared in light roles at Covent Garden and the Italian Opera at the Lyceum Theatre. The 2 then traveled extensively together, both at home and overseas. She became duly recognized as the leading British contralto by 1870. She made a tour of the U.S. in 1871.—NS/LK/DM

Patinkin, Mandy, American singer and actor; b. Chicago, Nov. 30, 1952. He grew up on Chicago's South Side, the son of a scrap-metal dealer, and began singing in temple when he was 8, later becoming involved in community theater. He spent 2 years at the Univ. of Kans., then went to the Juilliard School in N.Y., where he studied acting. His first important Broadway appearance was as Che Guevara in *Evita* (1978), for which he won a Tony Award. He created the title role in Sondheim's *Sunday in the Park with George* (1984), and delivered a virtuoso performance in the concert version of Sondheim's *Follies* in 1985, performing the trio *Buddy's Blues* as a solo. He has performed extensively with the N.Y. Shakespeare Festival in classical and contemporary roles, and his film appearances have included *Yentl* (1983), *The Princess Bride* (1987), and *Dick Tracy* (1990). In the 1990s he had a starring role on the popular television series, *Chicago Hope*. His solo album *Mandy Patinkin* (1989) includes American popular tunes such as "Sonny Boy" among the more expected Sondheim and contemporary songs. He is an expressive actor with an extraordinarily beautiful tenor voice, and one of the most skilled performers in musical theater.—NS/LK/DM

Patiño, Carlos, eminent Spanish composer; b. Santa Maria del Campo, date unknown; d. Madrid, Sept. 5, 1675. He settled in Madrid, where he became chaplain and maestro de capilla at the Monasterio de la Encarnacion (1628), holding the latter title at the royal chapel (from 1633); was rector of the college of choirboys (from 1648). He holds an important place in Spanish music history for supplanting the Italian madrigal style for one of Spanish provenance. He produced a large body of sacred music, numbering among his finest works 6 masses for 4 and 8 Voices and 2 masses for 12 Voices, 17 sacred Latin works, and 24 sacred Spanish compositions (tonos and villancicos). He also wrote theater pieces, most notably cuatros de empezar, which were sung as preludes to dramatic works. —NS/LK/DM

Paton, Mary Ann, distinguished Scottish soprano; b. Edinburgh, Oct. 1802; d. Bulcliffe Hall, Chapelthorpe, July 21, 1864. Of a musical family, she sang in concerts as a child, making her first operatic appearance as Susanna in *Le nozze di Figaro* (London, Aug. 3, 1822). She sang the part of Rezia in the premiere of Weber's *Oberon* in London (April 12, 1826) and was praised by Weber himself. She had a very fine voice, and could sing lyric and coloratura parts with equal brilliance. She was married to the tenor Joseph Wood.

BIBL.: J. Wood, *Memoir of Mr. and Mrs. Wood* (Philadelphia, 1840).—NS/LK/DM

Patorzhinsky, Ivan (Sergeievich), noted Ukrainian bass; b. Petrovo-Svistunovo, March 3, 1896; d. Kiev, Feb. 22, 1960. He studied at the Ekaterinoslav Cons., graduating in 1922. From 1925 to 1935 he was a member of the Kharkov Opera, and from 1935 to 1960 of the Kiev Opera. He also pursued a concert career. From 1946 he taught at the Kiev Cons. In 1944 he was made a People's Artist of the U.S.S.R. Patorzhinsky was the leading Ukrainian bass of his day, excelling particularly in roles in Ukrainian operas. He also was a fine Don Basilio, Boris Godunov, and Méphistophélès.

BIBL.: M. Stefanovich, *I.S. P.* (Moscow, 1960).—NS/LK/DM

Patterson, Paul (Leslie), English composer and teacher; b. Chesterfield, June 15, 1947. He studied with Richard Stoker at the Royal Academy of Music in London (1964–68), and also received instruction from Elizabeth Lutyens, Hans Keller, and Harrison Birtwistle. He pursued private training with Richard Rodney Bennett (1968–70). In 1971 he became the Manson Fellow at the Royal Academy of Music, where he served as head of composition and 20th-century music from 1985. From 1974 to 1980 he also was director of contemporary music at the Univ. of Warwick. In 1989 he became composer-in- residence of the Southwark Festival. In 1990–91 he was composer-in-residence of the Exeter Festival, and in 1991 its artistic director. Patterson has developed a compositional style that combines such contemporary usages as aleatory and electronics with more accessible means of expression.

WORKS: DRAMATIC: Film scores; television music. ORCH.: Trumpet Concerto (1968; Bristol, Nov. 19, 1969); *Symphonic Study II* (1968); Chamber Concerto (1969); *Partita* for

Chamber Orch. (Nottingham, March 5, 1970); *Piccola sinfonia* for Strings (1970; Oakham, March 11, 1971); Concerto for Horn and Strings (Nottingham, July 21, 1971); *Fiesta sinfonica* (1971; Nottingham, July 22, 1972); *Sonors* (1972; Southend, Jan. 10, 1973); *Fusions* for Orch. and Tape (Croydon, March 9, 1974); *Chromascope* for Brass Band (Harrogate, Aug. 9, 1974); *Count Down* for Brass Band (1974; London, Oct. 11, 1975); *Strange Meeting* for Orch. and Tape (Croydon, May 5, 1975); *Cataclysm* for Brass Band (Hull, Aug. 9, 1975); *The Circular Ruins* (Exeter, Dec. 10, 1975); *Wildfire* for Orch. and Tape (London, March 27, 1976); Concerto for Clarinet and Strings (London, May 19, 1976); *Concerto for Orchestra* (Birmingham, Nov. 13, 1981); *Sinfonia* for Strings (1982; Warsaw, Sept. 22, 1983); *Europhony* for Chamber Orch. (Cardiff, June 11, 1985); *Upside-Down-Under-Variations* (London, March 3, 1985); *Propositions* for Harmonica and Strings (London, April 25, 1987); *White Shadows on the Dark Horizon* (1988); *Fanfare for the Future* for Brass and Percussion (London, Oct. 29, 1989); Sym. (1989–90); *Little Red Riding Hood* for Narrators and Orch. (1992); Concerto for Violin and Strings (1992); *Festivo* (1993). CHAMBER: Wind Quintet (San Remo, Aug. 4, 1967); Wind Trio (London, Oct. 16, 1968); *Monologue* for Oboe (1969; London, May 5, 1970); *Fanfares for Great Occasions* for 3 Trumpets, 2 Trombones, Bass Trombone, and Tuba (1969–75; 1, *Chichester Fanfare*, Chichester, June 6, 1975; 2, *Warwick Fanfare*, Warwick, Sept. 11, 1974; 3, *St. Bartholomew's Fanfare*, London, June 21, 1973; 4, *Exeter Fanfare*, Exeter, July 19, 1969); *Comedy* for 5 Winds (Mayfield, May 15, 1972); *Intersections* for Chamber Ensemble (N.Y., July 8, 1973); *Conversations* for Clarinet and Piano (London, Nov. 18, 1974); *Floating Music* for Flute, Clarinet, Violin, Cello, Piano or Celesta, and Percussion (London, Oct. 21, 1974); *Shadows* for Clarinet and Tape (Cincinnati, April 6, 1975); *Diversions* for Saxophone Quartet (1975); *Cracowian Counterpoint* for Chamber Ensemble (London, June 3, 1977); *At the Still Point of the Turning World* for 8 Instruments (1979; Stockholm, Jan. 5, 1980); *Deception Pass* for Brass Ensemble (Cheltenham, July 5, 1980); *Spiders* for Harp (St. Asaph, Wales, Sept. 27, 1983); *Duologue* for Oboe and Piano (Christchurch, July 20, 1984); *Luslawice Variations* for Violin (Luslawice, Sept. 10, 1984); *Mean Time* for Brass Quintet (London, June 16, 1985); String Quartet (Chester, July 24, 1986); *Memories of Quiberville* for Trombone Quartet (1986; Manchester, Feb. 7, 1987); Suite for Cello (Bristol, Nov. 19, 1987); *Tides of Mananan* for Viola (1987). KEYBOARD: P i a n o : *Country Search* (1974); *3 Portraits* (1984); *A Tunnel of Time* (1988). O r - g a n : *Jubilate* (1969); *Intrada* (1969); *Visions* (1972); *Interludium* (1972); *Fluorescence* (1973); *Games* (1977). VOCAL: *Rebecca* for Speaker and Chamber Ensemble (1965; Dartington, Aug. 21, 1966); *Kyrie* for Chorus and Piano, 4-Hands (1971; N.Y., March 21, 1972); *Time Piece* for Men's Voices (1972; London, March 10, 1973); *Gloria* for Chorus and Piano, 4-Hands (1972); *The Abode of the Dead/You'll Never be Alone* for Voices and Chamber Orch. (BBC, Oct. 10, 1973); *Requiem* for Chorus, Boy's Chorus, and Orch. (1974; Coventry, June 21, 1975); *Spare Parts* for Chorus (1976; London, Jan. 18, 1978); *Brain Storm* for Soprano, Alto, Tenor, Bass, and Live Electronics (London, Feb. 9, 1978); *Voices of Sleep* for Soprano, Chorus, and Orch. (Washington, D.C., April 19, 1979); *The Canterbury Psalms* for Chorus and Orch. or Organ (Canterbury, April 15, 1981); *Vampireen* for 6 Men's Voices (St. Albans, June 5, 1983); *Mass of the Sea* for Soprano, Bass, Chorus, and Orch. (Gloucester, Aug. 22, 1983); *Christ is the King* for Chorus (Chichester, July 19, 1984); *Missa brevis* for Chorus (1985); *Stabat mater* for Mezzo-soprano, Chorus, and Orch. (1985–86; Huddersfield, March 27, 1986); *Magnificat and Nunc Dimittis* for Chorus and Organ (Norwich, July 4, 1986); *Te*

Deum for Soprano, Chorus, Boy's Chorus, and Orch. (Hereford, Aug. 25, 1988); *The End* for Chorus (1989); *O be Joyful* for Chorus and Organ (1991); *Revolting Rhymes* for Narrator and Ensemble (1992).—NS/LK/DM

Patti, family of prominent Italian singers:

(1) Salvatore Patti, tenor; b. Catania, 1800; d. Paris, Aug. 21, 1869. He was 2nd tenor at Palermo's Teatro Carolino (1825–26). After singing throughout Sicily, Italy, and Spain, he settled in N.Y. (1844), where he became active as an opera manager. His wife was the soprano Caterina Chiesa Barilli-Patti (b. Rome, date unknown; d. there, Sept. 6, 1870). She studied with her first husband, Barilli, and created the role of Eleanora in Donizetti's *L'assedio di Calais* (Naples, Nov. 19, 1836); later sang in N.Y. before retiring to Rome. She had 4 children by her first husband, all of whom became singers. She had 3 daughters by her 2nd husband:

(2) Amalia Patti, singer; b. Paris, 1831; d. there, Dec. 1915. She appeared in opera and concert in the U.S. until marrying **Maurice Strakosch.**

(3) Carlotta Patti, soprano; b. Florence, Oct. 30, 1835; d. Paris, June 27, 1889. She studied with her parents and with Henri Herz in Paris, making her concert debut in N.Y. (1861). She sang opera at the Academy of Music there (1862), but due to lameness decided to pursue a concert career, and toured in the U.S. and Europe. After marrying the cellist Ernest de Munck (1871), she settled in Paris as a voice teacher.

(4) Adelina (actually, **Adela Juana Maria) Patti,** greatly celebrated soprano; b. Madrid, Feb. 19, 1843; d. Craig-y-Nos Castle, near Brecon, Wales, Sept. 27, 1919. She was taken to N.Y. (1844), where she began study with her half-brother, Ettore Barilli, and made her first public appearance at a charity concert at Tripler's Hall when she was 7. She then toured the U.S. as a child prodigy with her brother-in-law **Maurice Strakosch,** and with Ole Bull, and later toured with Gottschalk (1857). As the "little Florinda," she made her formal debut as Lucia in N.Y. on Nov. 24, 1859; her European debut followed at London's Covent Garden as Amina in *La Sonnambula* on May 16, 1861. She was hailed as the true successor of Grisi, and subsequently returned to Covent Garden each season for the next 25 years. She sang in Berlin (1861), then in Brussels, Amsterdam, and The Hague (1862). She appeared as Amina at the Théâtre-Italien in Paris (Nov. 19, 1862), a role she sang at Vienna's Karlstheater (1863); made her first tour of Italy in 1865–66. She married the Marquis de Caux in Paris in 1868; soon after their divorce in 1885, she married the tenor **Nicolini;** after his death in 1898, she married the Swedish nobleman Baron Rolf Cederstrom in 1899. Patti made her first appearance at Milan's La Scala as Violetta on Nov. 3, 1877. She returned to the U.S. for a concert tour in 1881–82, then sang in opera there under the auspices of J.H. Mapleson during the next 3 seasons, earning as much as $5,000 per performance. In 1886–87 she again toured the U.S. under the auspices of H.E. Abbey, who presented her at the Metropolitan Opera in N.Y. in the spring of 1887, and then again in 1890 and 1892; her final tour of the U.S. followed in 1903. She made her last appearance at Covent Garden in 1895, and

her operatic farewell took place in Nice in 1897. Her official farewell concert was given at London's Albert Hall on Dec. 1, 1906. Her last public appearance was at a benefit concert for the Red Cross in that same hall on Oct. 20, 1914. Patti was one of the greatest coloraturas of the 19th century. Although her voice was not one of great power, it possessed a wide range, wonderful flexibility, and perfect evenness. In addition to Amina and Lucia, she was renowned for such roles as Zerlina, Rosina, Norina, Elvira, Martha, Adina, and Gilda; she was also esteemed as Aida and Gounod's Marguerite.

BIBL.: T. de Grave, *Le Biographie d'A. P.* (Paris, 1865); G. de Charnace, *A. P.* (Paris, 1868); G. Dalmazzo, *A. P.'s Life* (London, 1877); L. Lauw, *Fourteen Years with A. P.* (London, 1884); H. Klein, *The Reign of P.* (N.Y., 1920).—NS/LK/DM

Pattiera, Tino, Croatian tenor; b. Čavtat, near Ragusa, June 27, 1890; d. there, April 24, 1966. He studied at the Vienna Academy of Music with Ranieri. In 1915 he joined the Dresden Court (later State) Opera, where he was a principal member of the company until 1941. He also sang with the Berlin State Opera (1924–29), and was a guest artist in Chicago, Vienna, Budapest, Paris, Prague, and other music centers. He gave his farewell concert in Dresden in 1948. From 1950 he taught voice at the Vienna Academy of Music. He was most renowned for the lyric roles in Verdi's operas.—NS/LK/DM

Pattison, Lee, American pianist; b. Centralia, Wisc., July 22, 1890; d. Claremont, Calif., Dec. 22, 1966. He first studied at the New England Cons. of Music in Boston, and then later in Berlin with Schnabel. In 1916 he formed a duo-piano team with Guy Maier; they gave a number of successful concerts until 1931, when the partnership was dissolved. From 1932 to 1937 he was head of the piano dept. at Sarah Lawrence Coll.; also taught at the Juilliard Summer School; lived mostly in N.Y. His compositions include *Florentine Sketches* for Piano and a piano suite of 7 pieces, *Told in the Hills.*—NS/LK/DM

Patzak, Julius, distinguished Austrian tenor; b. Vienna, April 9, 1898; d. Rottach-Egern, Bavaria, Jan. 26, 1974. He studied musicology and conducting with Adler, Schmidt, and Mandyczewski at the Univ. of Vienna, but was autodidact as a singer. He made his operatic debut as Radamès in Reichenberg (1923). After singing in Brno (1927–28), he was a principal member of the Bavarian State Opera in Munich (1928–45) and the Vienna State Opera (1945–59); first appeared at London's Covent Garden as Tamino (1938), returning there with the visiting Vienna State Opera (1947), and then singing there regularly (1951–54). He was a teacher at the Vienna Academy of Music and the Salzburg Mozarteum, retiring from the stage in 1966. Patzak was noted for his roles in Mozart's operas, but he became best known for his compelling portrayals of Beethoven's Florestan and Pfitzner's Palestrina.—NS/LK/DM

Pauer, Ernst, Austrian pianist, teacher, editor, and composer, father of **Max von Pauer;** b. Vienna, Dec. 21,

1826; d. Jugenheim, near Darmstadt, May 9, 1905. He studied piano with Mozart's son, F.X.W. Mozart, and composition with Sechter. In 1851 he went to London, where he later taught at the Royal Academy of Music (1859–64). In 1861 he began a series of historical performances of harpsichord and piano music in chronological order, which attracted considerable attention. After a number of concerts in Germany and Austria, he was appointed pianist to the Austrian court (1866). He served as prof. of piano at London's National Training School for Music (from 1876), remaining there when it became the Royal Coll. of Music (1883); retired to Jugenheim (1896). He publ. in London a number of educational works, among them *The Art of Pianoforte Playing* (1877), *Musical Forms* (1878), and *The Elements of the Beautiful in Music* (1877), as well as *The Birthday Book of Musicians and Composers* (1881) and *A Dictionary of Pianists and Composers for the Pianoforte* (1895). He further brought out collections for piano students: *The New Gradus ad Parnassum, Classical Companion: Celebrated Concert-studies*, and *Cultures of the Left Hand*. He made excellent arrangements of syms. by Beethoven and Schumann, for piano solo, piano, 4-hands, and piano, 8-hands, and also arranged Mendelssohn's orch. works for piano, 4-hands and 8-hands; these arrangements were widely used in the 19th century and were extremely useful for young pianists until the advent of the phonograph administered a lethal blow to this type of musical activity.—NS/LK/DM

Pauer, Jíří, Czech composer and arts administrator; b. Libušín, near Kladno, Feb. 22, 1919. He studied composition with Otakar Šin, then with Alois Hába at the Prague Cons. (1943–46) and with Bořkovec at the Prague Academy of Musical Arts (1946–50). He occupied various administrative posts with the Ministry of Education and Culture and with the Czech Radio. He was artistic director of the Opera of the National Theater in Prague (1953–55; 1965–67; 1979–89), and also taught at the Prague Academy. He was director of the Czech Phil. from 1958 to 1980. His music followed the pragmatic precepts of socialist realism in its modern application, broadly lyrical and tensely dramatic by turns.

WORKS: DRAMATIC: O p e r a : *Žvanivý Slimejš* (Prattling Snail; 1949–50; Prague, April 5, 1958); *Zuzana Vojířová* (1954–57; Prague, May 11, 1958); *Červená Karkulka* (Little Red Riding Hood; 1959; Olomouc, 1960); *Manželské kontrapunkty* (Marital Counterpoints; 1961; 3 operatic satirical sketches, Ostrava, 1962; 2nd version as 5 satires, Liberec, 1967); *Zdravý nemocný* (The Imaginary Invalid), after Molière (1966–69; Prague, May 22, 1970). M o n o d r a m a : *Labutí píseň* (The Swan Song; 1973). B a l l e t : *Ferda Mravenec* (Ferdy the Ant; 1975). ORCH.: *Comedy Suite* (1949); Bassoon Concerto (1949); *Youth Suite* (1951); *Scherzo* (1951); *Children's Suite* for Chamber Orch. (1953); *Rhapsody* (1953); Oboe Concerto (1954); Horn Concerto (1958); Sym. (1963); *Commemoration*, symphonic picture (1969); *Canto festivo* (1970–71); Trumpet Concerto (1972); *Initials* (1974); *Aurora*, overture for Large Wind Orch. (1976; also for Orch., 1978); Sym. for Strings (1978); Concerto for Marimba and Strings (1984); Suite (1987). CHAMBER: *Partita* for Harp (1947); *Divertimento* for 3 Clarinets (1949); *Capriccio* for Flute or Oboe or Clarinet or Bassoon and Piano (1952); Violin Sonatina

(1953); Cello Sonata (1954); 4 string quartets (1960, 1969, 1970, 1976); *Divertimento* for Nonet (1961); Wind Quintet (1961); Piano Trio (1963); *Concertant Music* for 13 Winds (1971); *Intrada* for 3 Pianos, 3 Trumpets, and 3 Trombones (1975); *Characters* for Brass Quintet (1977–78); Episodes for String Quartet (1980); Trio for 3 Horns (1986); Violin Sonata (1987); Nonet No. 2 (1988–89); piano pieces. VOCAL: Cantatas; choruses; songs.
—NS/LK/DM

Pauer, Max von, eminent Austrian pianist and teacher, son of **Ernst Pauer**; b. London, Oct. 31, 1866; d. Jugenheim, May 12, 1945. He studied with his father and with V. Lachner, and then embarked on several successful concert tours in Germany. In 1887 he was appointed prof. of piano at the Cologne Cons., and in 1897 he became a prof. at the Stuttgart Cons.; was its director from 1908 to 1920; in 1920 it became the Hochschule für Musik, which he directed until 1924. He then he was director of the Leipzig Cons. (1924–32) and of the Mannheim Hochschule für Musik (1933–34). He made an American tour in 1913–14. Following his father's excellent example in arranging Classical syms. for piano, he made transcriptions of syms. by Mozart and Haydn for piano solo and piano, 4-hands. He publ. an ironic autobiography, *Unser seltsames Ich: Lebensschau eines Künstlers*—NS/LK/DM

Pauk, György, distinguished Hungarian-born English violinist and pedagogue; b. Budapest, Oct. 26, 1936. He began violin studies when he was 5, and at 13 he entered the Franz Liszt Academy of Music in Budapest, where he was a student of Zathureczky Weiner and Zoltán Kodály. He made his debut as a soloist with orch. when he played the Khatchaturian Violin Concerto in Budapest when he was 14, and then toured Eastern Europe. Following the suppression of the Hungarian revolution in 1956, he left his homeland and won the Paganini (Genoa, 1956), Munich (1957), and Long-Thibaud (Paris, 1959) competitions. In 1961 he settled in England and in 1967 he became a naturalized British subject. In 1962 he made his London recital debut, and also his London debut as a soloist in Mozart's A major Violin Concerto, K.219, with the London Sym. Orch. conducted by Maazel. Thereafter he was engaged by all of the principal British orchs. and festivals, and also toured abroad as a soloist with British orchs. In 1970 he made his U.S. debut as soloist in the Stravinsky Violin Concerto with Solti and the Chicago Sym. Orch., the same year that he made his first appearance as a soloist in Vienna playing the Beethoven Violin Concerto with the Vienna Sym. Orch. under Melles's direction. He made his N.Y. debut in 1972 in the Brahms Violin Concerto with Doráti and the National Sym. Orch. of Washington, D.C. With the pianist Peter Frankl and the cellist Ralph Kirshbaum, he formed a trio in 1972. It celebrated its 25th anniversary in 1997. In 1976 he made his Berlin debut as a soloist in the Dvořák Violin Concerto with the Berlin Radio Sym. Orch. conducted by Wakasugi. In 1979 he made his Japanese debut in Tokyo in Pederecki's 1st Violin Concerto with the NHK Sym. Orch. under the composer's direction. He made his debut at N.Y.'s Carnegie Hall as soloist in the Brahms Violin Concerto with the American Sym. Orch.

under Comissiona in 1981, and in 1982 he appeared with the Boston Sym. Orch. under Sir Colin Davis's direction in the Tippett Violin Concerto. He also played with many other orchs. around the world, and at many festivals. In 1991 he served as artistic director of the Mozart Bicentenary Festival at London's Wigmore Hall, where he appeared as both a violinist and a violist. Pauk taught at the Royal Manchester Coll. of Music (1964–67), and later in London at the Guildhall School of Music and Drama (1984–87) and the Royal Academy of Music (from 1987). He has also given master classes in England and abroad. In 1998 he was awarded the Order of the Hungarian Republic for his services to music. In addition to his admired performances of the standard repertoire, he has also won distinction for his interpretations of contemporary works.—NS/LK/DM

Paul, Les (originally, Polfuss, Lester William),

American guitarist and inventor; b. Waukesha, Wisc., June 9, 1915. As a guitarist, Paul performed without regard to style, gaining recognition in the genres of country, jazz, and pop music and, with Mary Ford, scoring such hits as "Mockin' Bird Hill," "How High the Moon," and "Vaya con Dios (May God Be with You)." As an inventor he pioneered the development of the electric guitar and sophisticated recording techniques that had a broad impact on the sound of popular music from the 1940s onward.

Paul was the son of George William Polfuss (real name Polsfuss), the owner of a car-repair service, and Evelyn Stutz Polfuss. He began to play the harmonica at about the age of eight, then taught himself piano, banjo, and, at 12, guitar. In his teens he began performing as Red Hot Red and soon embarked on a career as a radio musician, first at local stations, then in the major cities of the Midwest. Billed as Rhubarb Red, at first he played country music, then pop and jazz. He married Virginia Webb in 1938 and they had two children; they divorced in 1948.

By 1938, Paul had formed a jazz trio that played on the *Fred Waring Show* out of N.Y. through 1941. He then worked in radio in Chicago and moved to Calif. in 1943, where he formed another trio and performed on various radio shows as well as appearing in a cameo role in the June 1944 film *Sensations of '45*. While serving in the U.S. Army in 1944 he performed on various military radio programs. Upon his discharge he re-formed his trio and signed to Decca Records.

Paul and his trio backed Bing Crosby on his recording of "It's Been a Long, Long Time" (music by Jule Styne, lyrics by Sammy Cahn), which hit #1 in December 1945. On his own he accompanied the Andrews Sisters on "Rumors Are Flying" (music and lyrics by Bennie Benjamin and George David Weiss), which peaked in the Top Ten in December 1946. During the 1940s he developed his own amplified guitars and experimented with overdubbing in his own home-recording studio. In January 1948 he was severely injured in an automobile accident and endured a long recovery. He formed a musical partnership with singer-guitarist Mary Ford (real name Iris Colleen Summers

Watson), and they married on Dec. 29, 1949. They had two children and adopted one.

In 1950, signed to Capitol Records, Paul began to score hits with the results of his musical experiments, records on which his electric guitar was overdubbed multiple times to create unusual musical textures. His instrumental revival of the 1916 tune "Nola" (music by Felix Arndt) peaked in the Top Ten in August 1950. He also made recordings on which Mary Ford sang, and their "Tennessee Waltz" (music and lyrics by Redd Stewart and Pee Wee King) peaked in the Top Ten in January 1951, beginning a year in which they became the most successful recording artists in the U.S. Ten other recordings were in the charts during 1951 (some of them Paul instrumentals), including the #1 million-selling hits "Mockin' Bird Hill" (music and lyrics by Vaughn Horton) and "How High the Moon" (music by Morgan Lewis, lyrics by Nancy Hamilton)—the latter inducted into the Grammy Hall of Fame in 1979—and a million-selling Top Ten revival of the 1919 song "The World Is Waiting for the Sunrise" (music by Ernest Seitz, lyrics by Eugene Lockhart). They also reached the Top Ten of the LP charts with *New Sound—Vol. 1* and *New Sound—Vol. 2*.

In 1952 the Gibson guitar company introduced the Les Paul solid-body electric guitar, which went on to revolutionize popular music. During the year, Paul alone or Paul and Ford had another nine singles chart entries, among them a Top Ten revival of the 1918 song "Tiger Rag" (music by Edwin B. Edwards, Nick La Rocca, Tony Spargo, and Larry Shields, lyrics by Harry Da Costa), and another Top Ten album, *Bye Bye Blues*. Their five singles chart entries in 1953 included the biggest hit of their career, "Vaya con Dios (May God Be with You)" (music and lyrics by Larry Russell, Inez James, and Buddy Pepper), which hit #1 in August, selling a million copies and becoming the biggest hit of the year. They also reached the Top Ten of the LP charts with *Hit Makers*.

Les Paul and Mary Ford were less successful after 1953, though they hit the Top Ten three more times in 1954 and 1955. They switched to Columbia Records in 1958 and continued to reach the charts until 1961. They split up as a performing duo in 1963 and divorced in December 1964.

Paul largely gave up performing, concentrating on developing new recording techniques and improving his line of guitars, though he released the album *Les Paul Now!* in 1968. In the early 1970s he returned to performing occasionally. In 1976 he released a duo guitar album with Chet Atkins, *Chester and Lester*, which won the Grammy Award for Best Country Instrumental Performance. The two were nominated for the Best Pop Instrumental Performance Grammy for their follow-up album, *Guitar Monsters*, in 1978.

Following heart surgery, Paul retired in the early 1980s, but in March 1984 he began playing a weekly show at the jazz club Fat Tuesday's in N.Y. Later he moved to another club, Iridium, where he continued to play on Monday nights into the late 1990s.

DISC.: LES PAUL AND MARY FORD: *The New Sound* (1955); *The New Sound, Vol. 2* (1955); *Bye Bye Blues* (1955);

The Hit Makers (1955); *Les and Mary* (1955); *Time to Dream* (1957); *Lovers' Luau* (1959); *The Hits of Les Paul and Mary Ford* (1960); *Warm and Wonderful* (1961); *Bouquet of Roses* (1962); *Swingin' South* (1963); *The Fabulous Les Paul and Mary Ford* (1965); *The World Is Still Waiting for the Sunrise* (1974). **LES PAUL AND CHET ATKINS:** *Chester and Lester* (1976); *Guitar Monsters* (1978). **LES PAUL:** *Les Paul Now!* (1968; resissued as *The Genius of Les Paul-Multi-Trackin'*; 1979); *Tiger Rag* (1984); *Masters of the Guitar Together* (1989)*Les Paul and Mary Ford* (1992); *The Legend and the Legacy* (1991); *The Best of The Capitol Masters* (1992); *Greatest Hits!* (1994); *16 Most Requested Songs* (1996).

BIBL.: M. Shaughnessy, *L. P.: An American Original* (N.Y., 1993).

Paul, Oskar, German music scholar; b. Freiwaldau, April 8, 1836; d. Leipzig, April 18, 1898. He studied with Plaidy, Richter, and Hauptmann at the Univ. of Leipzig (Ph.D., 1860). He was prof. of music history, piano, and composition at the Leipzig Cons. (from 1869) and prof. extraordinarius at the Univ. of Leipzig (from 1872), and also music critic of the *Leipziger Tagblatt*. He adapted Hauptmann's *Lehre von der Harmonik* for practical usages and publ. the result under the title *Lehrbuch der Harmonik* (Leipzig, 1880; Eng. tr., N.Y., 1885). He also publ. *Geschichte des Klaviers* (Leipzig, 1869), *Handlexikon der Tonkunst* (Leipzig, 1871–73), and *Musikalische Instrumente* (Braunschweig, 1874).—NS/LK/DM

Paul, Thomas (Warburton), distinguished American bass; b. Chicago, Feb. 22, 1934. He studied viola with Robert Gross and voice with Howard Swan at Occidental Coll. in Los Angeles (B.A., 1956), and then pursued graduate studies in conducting with Jean Morel and Frederic Waldman at the Juilliard School of Music in N.Y. (1956–57). After studying voice with Themy Georgi in Washington, D.C. (1957–59), he returned to N.Y. to continue vocal training with Hans Joachim Heinz (1961–64) and Beverley Johnson (1964–69). Still later he pursued vocal studies in N.Y. with Ted Puffer (from 1999). On Oct. 4, 1962, he made his formal operatic debut as Monterone at the N.Y.C. Opera, where he continued to sing until 1971. He made his first appearance as a soloist with orch. in 1962 when he sang with the Boston Sym. Orch. under Leinsdorf's direction. In subsequent years, he appeared as a soloist with several major U.S. orchs. From 1971 to 1987 he sang at the Rochester (N.Y.) Opera Theatre, and from 1971 to 1996 at the Washington (D.C.) Opera. He also was active as a singer and teacher at the Aspen (Colo.) Music Festival from 1971 to 1990, and from 1971 to 1998 he was a prof. of voice at the Eastman School of Music in Rochester, N.Y. On April 3, 1976, he made his European debut in Zürich as a soloist in Bach's St. Matthew Passion. In Dec. 1980 he made his recital debut at N.Y.'s Alice Tully Hall. From 1981 to 1986 he was a member of the Bach Aria Group. Paul's extensive operatic and concert repertoire ranges from the Baroque era to the contemporary period. In addition to the standard works, he has sung in premieres of scores by Elliott Carter, Sir Peter Maxwell Davies, Carlisle Floyde, Bernard Rands, Robert Ward, and many others. —NS/LK/DM

Paull, Barberi, avant-garde American composer; b. N.Y., July 25, 1946. She began to play piano as an infra-adolescent, in private and in public, and with the awakening of consciousness, she opted for jazz and multimedia forms of self-expression. However, she went through the motions of academic training at the Juilliard School of Music in N.Y., where she studied composition with Overton and Druckman (1970–71); later she took courses with Wuorinen at the Manhattan School of Music (1972) and attended the Musical Theatre Workshop conducted by Lehman Engel (1973). She founded the Barberi Paull Musical Theatre, Inc., with which she presented a series of mixed-media events. In her compositions, she elevates eclecticism to an article of democratic faith, embracing jazz, pop tunes, and electronic sound in a context of ostentatious and unapologetic cosmic sentimentality.

WORKS: *Time,* electronic ballet (1971); *Earth Pulse,* choreographic cantata, making use of musique concrète (1971); *The Mass* for Tape, Percussion, and Visual Projections (1974); *A Land Called The Infinity of Love* for Multimedia (1975); *Sheer Silver Sheen Flower Sky* for Chorus (1971–74); *O Wind* for Mezzosoprano and String Quartet (1975); *Song for Orchestra* (1977); *A Christmas Carol* for Chorus and Instrumental Trio, after Dickens (1977; also in a jazz version); many unabashed pop tunes. —NS/LK/DM

Paulli, Holger Simon, Danish violinist, conductor, and composer; b. Copenhagen, Feb. 22, 1810; d. there, Dec. 23, 1891. He studied violin with Schall and Wexschall, and at the age of 12, entered the court orch. in Copenhagen, where he was later its concertmaster (1849–63) and principal conductor (1863–83). In 1866 he was appointed co-director, with Gade and Hauptmann, of the newly founded Copenhagen Cons. He was an admirer of Wagner, and conducted the first performances in Denmark of *Lohengrin* (1870) and *Die Meistersinger von Nürnberg* (1872). He composed a Singspiel, *Lodsen* (The Pilot), which was produced in Copenhagen on Sept. 25, 1851. Other works include some ballet music, violin pieces, and songs.—NS/LK/DM

Paul Revere and The Raiders, pop-rock hitmakers of the 1960s; **MEMBERSHIP:** Paul Revere, kybd. (b. Boise, Idaho, Jan. 7, 1942); Mark Lindsay, lead voc., sax. (b. Cambridge, Idaho, March 9, 1942); Drake Levin, gtr.; Mike Holiday, bs.; Mike Smith, drm. In 1964, Philip "Fang" Volk replaced Holiday. Freddie Weller (b. Atlanta, Ga., Sept. 9, 1947) was lead guitarist from 1967 to 1971.

Starting out in Idaho in 1959 as The Downbeats, with Paul Revere and Mark Lindsay, the group became Paul Revere and The Raiders in 1960. They achieved their first moderate hit with the instrumental "Like, Long Hair" on the Gardena label in 1961. Regrouping in Portland, Ore., around 1962 with Revere, Lindsay, and Mike Smith, the group enjoyed considerable regional success and recorded an early version of the raunchy Richard Berry classic "Louie, Louie." Nonetheless, another local group, The Kingsmen, scored the national hit in 1963. Realigning with Revere, Lindsay, Smith, Drake Levin, and Mike "Doc" Holiday, the group secured a

Columbia Records recording contract, replacing Holiday with Phil "Fang" Volk in 1964.

Moving to Los Angeles in 1965, Paul Revere and The Raiders' first big break came when they became the house band for Dick Clark's daily ABC-TV show *Where the Action Is* in June. That fall, they had a moderate hit with "Steppin' Out," followed by the major hit "Just Like Me," both written by Revere and Lindsay. They subsequently scored smash hits with two Barry Mann and Cynthia Weil songs, "Kicks" and "Hungry," and two songs written by Lindsay and producer Terry Melcher, "Good Thing" and "Him or Me—What's It Gonna Be?." "The Great Airplane Strike" and "Ups and Downs," cowritten by Melcher and Lindsay, became major hits. In 1967, Drake Levin, Mike Smith, and Phil Volk formed Brotherhood (later Friendsound), as Freddy Weller joined the Raiders on lead guitar. The group had their own Saturday morning ABC-TV show *Happening*, produced by Dick Clark, in 1968 and 1969 as the major hits continued with "I Had a Dream," "Talk Too Much," "Mr. Sun, Mr. Moon," and "Let Me." Lindsay's parallel solo career produced major hits with "Arizona" and "Silver Bird" around the same time.

Experiencing frequent personnel changes, the group became The Raiders in 1970 and managed a top hit with John D. Loudermilk's "Indian Reservation" and a major hit with "Birds of a Feather." Paul Revere and The Raiders subsequently remained nominally intact under the direction of Paul Revere, establishing themselves on the state fair and oldies circuit and securing a long-standing engagement at Harrah's Reno (Nev.). In 1988, Paul Revere and erstwhile Righteous Brother Bill Medley opened the oldies dance club Kicks in Reno.

DISC.: PAUL REVERE AND THE RAIDERS: *Like, Long Hair* (1961); *Paul Revere and The Raiders* (1963); *In the Beginning* (1966); *Here They Come!* (1965); *Just Like Us!* (1966); *Midnight Ride* (1966); *The Spirit of '67* (1966); *Revolution!* (1967); *Christmas Present...and Past* (1967); *Goin' to Memphis* (1968); *Something Happening* (1968); *Hard 'n' Heavy* (1969); *Alias Pink Puzz* (1969); *Special Edition* (1982). **THE RAIDERS:** *Collage* (1970); *Indian Reservation* (1971); *Country Wine* (1972). **THE BROTHERHOOD (WITH PHIL VOLK, DRAKE LEVIN AND MIKE SMITH):** *The Brotherhood* (1968); *Brotherhood, Brotherhood* (1969). **FRIENDSOUND (WITH PHIL VOLK, DRAKE LEVIN AND MIKE SMITH):** *Joyride* (1969). **MARK LINDSAY:** *Arizona* (1970); *Silverbird* (1970); *You've Got a Friend* (1971).—**BH**

Paulson, Gustaf, Swedish composer and organist; b. Hälsingborg, Jan. 22, 1898; d. there, Dec. 17, 1966. He studied composition in Copenhagen with Peder Gram. From 1929 until his death, served as church organist in Hälsingborg. He was an extraordinarily prolific composer. His music reflected the type of Scandinavian Romanticism associated with Sibelius and Nielsen, pervaded by streaks of coherent polyphony.

WORKS: ORCH.: 13 syms.: No. 1 (1928), No. 2 (1933), No. 3, *Sinfonia da chiesa* (1945), No. 4, *Uppstandelse* (The Resurrection; 1947), No. 5, *Aron Bergenson in memoriam* (1948), No. 6 (1952), No. 7 (1953), No. 8 (1954), No. 9 (1956), No. 10 (1957), No. 11, *Stabat Mater* (1959; Halsingborg, March 26, 1961), No. 12 (1963; Hälsingborg, Nov. 28, 1963), and No. 13 (1966); 2 sinfo-

nias for Strings (1953, 1954); 19 concertos: 2 for Piano (1940, 1961), 2 for Cello (1944, 1957), 2 for Oboe (1950, 1957), 2 for English Horn and Strings (1958, 1959), 2 for Clarinet (1958, 1959), and one each for Bassoon (1959), Saxophone (1959), Violin (1960), Flute and Women's Chorus, *Arets tider* (1962), Horn (1964), Trombone (1965), Trumpet (1965), Viola (1965), and Double Bass (1965–66); *Symphonic Variations* (1934); *Metamorphoses on a Theme by Clementi* (1951); *Passion* for Cello and Orch. (1961). **CHAMBER:** 5 string quartets; Violin Sonata (1958); Cello Sonata (1960); piano pieces; organ pieces. **VOCAL:** *Stabat Mater* for Soloists, Women's Chorus, Strings, and Percussion (1956; Hälsingborg, March 17, 1957); *Vid korset*, oratorio (1957); songs.—**NS/LK/DM**

Paulus, Olaf, Norwegian organist and composer; b. Christiania, Jan. 25, 1859; d. Stavanger, June 29, 1912. He was a pupil of C. Cappelen and J. Svendsen, and also studied at the Leipzig Cons. From 1889 he was organist at the Cathedral in Stavanger, making a trip to the U.S. in 1902 and directing choral concerts in Minneapolis and St. Paul. In his native country he was highly esteemed as a national composer, and his men's choruses were in the repertoire of all Norwegian societies. He also wrote songs and piano pieces, and ed. a collection of songs, *De 1,000 hjems sange* (Home Songs; 1888).—**NS/LK/DM**

Paulus, Stephen (Harrison), American composer; b. Summit, N.J., Aug. 24, 1949. He studied with Paul Fetler and Dominick Argento at the Univ. of Minn. (B.M., 1971; M.M., 1974; Ph.D., 1978). In 1973 he founded the Minn. Composers Forum in Minneapolis with Libby Larsen, and was managing composer until 1984. He served as composer-in-residence of the Minn. Orch. (1983–87), the Santa Fe Chamber Music Festival (1986), the Atlanta Sym. Orch. (1988–92), the Dale Warland Singers (1991–92), and the Aspen (Colo.) Music Festival (1992). In 1987 his Violin Concerto No. 1 won the Kennedy Center Friedheim 3rd Prize. In 1983 he held a Guggenheim fellowship. Paulus has demonstrated fine craftsmanship in both vocal and instrumental writing.

WORKS: DRAMATIC: Opera: *The Village Singer* (1977; St. Louis, June 9, 1979); *The Postman Always Rings Twice* (1981; St. Louis, June 19, 1982; also an orch. suite, Minneapolis, July 26, 1986); *The Woodlanders* (1984; St. Louis, June 13, 1985); *Harmoonia*, children's opera (1991); *Summer*, after Edith Wharton (1997–99; Pittsfield, Mass., Aug. 28, 1999). **ORCH.:** *Spectra* for Small Orch. (Houston, April 12, 1980); *Translucent Landscapes* (Peninsula Music Festival, Aug. 6, 1982); *7 Short Pieces* (1983; Minneapolis, Feb. 9, 1984); *Divertimento* for Harp and Chamber Orch. (1983); *Concerto for Orchestra* (Minneapolis, April 6, 1983); *Ordway* Overture (1984); *Reflections: 4 Movements on a Theme of Wallace Stevens* (1984; St. Paul, Minn., March 22, 1985); *Symphony in 3 Movements (Soliloquy)* (1985; Minneapolis, Jan. 15, 1986); *Ground Breaker*, overture (Minneapolis, Oct. 7, 1987); 2 violin concertos: No.1 (Atlanta, Nov. 5, 1987) and No. 2 (1992); *Night Speech* (Spokane, Wash., April 21, 1989); *Concertante* (Atlanta, April 27, 1989); *Symphony for Strings* (Ore. Bach Festival, July 5, 1989); *Street Music* (1990); *Ice Fields* for Guitar and Orch. (1990; in collaboration with L. Kottke); *Sinfonietta* (1991); Trumpet Concerto (1991); Organ Concerto (1992); *The Veil of Illusion*, concerto for Violin, Cello, and Orch. (1994); 3

Places of Enlightenment, concerto for String Quartet and Orch. (1995); *Manhattan Sinfonietta* (1995). **CHAMBER: En-semble:** *Exploration* (1974); *Village Tales: A Tree of Life* (1975); *Graphics* (1977); *Lunar Maria* (1977). **Other Chamber:** *Colors* for Brass Quintet (1974); *Wind Suite* for Woodwind Quartet (1975); 2 string quartets: No. 1, *Music for Contrasts* (1980) and No. 2 (1987); *Courtship Songs for a Summer's Eve* for Flute, Oboe, Cello, and Piano (1981); *Partita* for Violin and Piano (1986); *American Vignettes* for Cello and Piano (1988); *Fantasy in 3 Parts* for Flute and Guitar (1989); *Bagatelles* for Violin and Piano (1990); *Quartessence* for String Quartet (1990); Concerto for Brass Quintet (1991); *Air on Seurat: The Grand Canal* for Cello and Piano (1992); *Music of the Night* for Violin, Cello, and Piano (1992). **KEYBOARD: Piano:** *Translucent Landscapes* (1979); *Dance* (1986); *Preludes* (1992). **Organ:** *The Triumph of the Saint* for Organ Duet (1994); *Meditations of the Spirit* (1995). **VOCAL:** *Personals* for Chorus, Flute, and Percussion (1975); *Canticles: Songs and Rituals for Easter and the May* for Soloists, Chorus, and Orch. (1977); *North Shore* for Soloists, Chorus, and Orch. (1977); *Letters for the Times* for Chorus and Chamber Ensemble (1980); *Echoes between the Silent Peaks* for Chorus and Chamber Ensemble (1984); *Letters from Colette* for Soprano and Chamber Ensemble (1986); *Madrigali di Michelangelo* for Chorus (1987); *Voices* for Chorus and Orch. (1988); *Canticum Novum* for Chorus, Flute, Oboe, Percussion, and Harp (1990); *Sacred Songs* for Chorus, Flute, Oboe, Percussion, and Organ (1990); *Visions of Hildegard* for Chorus and Instruments (1992–95); *Whitman's Dream* for Double Chorus and Instruments (1994); *The Earth Sings* for Women's Voices, Percussion, and Piano (1995). **—NS/LK/DM**

Pauly, Rosa (actually, **Rose** née **Pollak**), noted Hungarian soprano; b. Eperjes, March 15, 1894; d. Kfar Shmaryahn, near Tel Aviv, Dec. 14, 1975. She studied voice with Rosa Papier in Vienna, and made her operatic debut at the Vienna State Opera as Desdemona in Verdi's *Otello* in 1918. She subsequently sang in Hamburg, Cologne, and Mannheim. From 1927 to 1931 she was a member of the Kroll Opera in Berlin; also of the Vienna State Opera (1929–35); in 1934 she sang the challenging role of Elektra in Strauss's opera in Salzburg, gathering encomiums; in 1935 she appeared at La Scala in Milan. She made her American debut as Elektra in a concert performance with the N.Y. Phil. on March 21, 1937, a role she reprised at her first appearance with the Metropolitan Opera in N.Y. on Jan. 7, 1938; appeared there until 1940; also sang at the Teatro Colón in Buenos Aires in 1939. In 1946 she went to Palestine, and devoted herself to teaching in Tel Aviv. She was esteemed for her roles in the operas of Mozart, Verdi, and Wagner, but most particularly for her compelling portrayals of such Strauss roles as Elektra, the Dyer's Wife, and Helena.—**NS/LK/DM**

Paumann, Conrad, significant German organist and composer; b. Nuremberg, between 1410 and 1415; d. Munich, Jan. 24, 1473. He was blind from birth. Through the patronage of Ulrich Grundherr, and later his son Paul Grundherr, he was able to obtain instruction in music. By 1446 he was appointed organist at St. Sebald in Nuremberg, and in 1447 he became town organist. In 1450 he was called to Munich to serve as court organist to Duke Albrecht III of Bavaria. He won

great renown as an organist, and traveled to Austria and Italy. He also achieved mastery as a player on the harp, the lute, and the recorder, being particularly noted for his improvisations. Some of his extant works have been publ. in *Das Erbe deutscher Musik*, 1st series (1958); see also the *Fundamentum organisandi magistri Conradi Paumanns ceci de Nurenberga anno 1452* as ed. by W. Apel in *Keyboard Music of the Fourteenth and Fifteenth Centuries*, Corpus of Early Keyboard Music, I (1963).—**NS/LK/DM**

Paumgartner, Bernhard, eminent Austrian musicologist and conductor; b. Vienna, Nov. 14, 1887; d. Salzburg, July 27, 1971. He was a son of the pianist Hans Paumgartner (1843–96) and the mezzo-soprano Rosa Papier. He learned to play the horn, violin, and piano in his youth; began to conduct while still in school. After receiving a doctorate in law from the Univ. of Vienna (1911), he studied musicology privately with Adler. He was répétiteur at the Vienna Court Opera (1911–12), and then director of the Salzburg Mozarteum (from 1917), which he headed until 1938, and again from 1945 to 1959. He was also closely associated with the Salzburg Festival from its founding (1920), serving as its president (1960–71). He also composed. Among his works were the operas *Die Hohle von Salamanca* (Dresden, 1923) and *Rossini in Neapel* (Zürich, March 27, 1936), various other stage pieces, including several ballets, orch. music, and songs.

Writings: *Mozart* (Berlin, 1927; 6th ed., Aug. 1967); *Franz Schubert: Eine Biographie* (Zürich, 1943; 3rd ed., 1960); *Johann Sebastian Bach: Leben und Werk, I: Bis zur Berufung nach Leipzig* (Zürich, 1950); *Erinnerungen* (Salzburg, 1969); G. Croll, ed., *Bernhard Paumgartner: Vorträge und Essays* (Salzburg, 1972).

Bibl.: E. Preussner, ed., *Wissenschaft und Praxis: Eine Festschrift zum 70. Geburtstag von B. P.* (Zürich, 1957); G. Croll, ed., *B. P.* (Salzburg and Munich, 1971).—**NS/LK/DM**

Paunović, Milenko, Serbian composer; b. Šajkaš, Nov. 28, 1889; d. Belgrade, Oct. 1, 1924. He studied in Leipzig with Reger and Riemann, and became a choral conductor in Novi Sad. In his music he followed Wagnerian concepts, and wrote several music dramas to his own texts; also a *Yugoslav Symphony* (Ljubljana, March 17, 1924).—**NS/LK/DM**

Paur, Emil, Austrian conductor; b. Czernowitz, Bukovina, Aug. 29, 1855; d. Mistek, Bohemia, June 7, 1932. He was trained in the rudiments of music by his father, and played the violin and piano in public at the age of 8. At 11 he entered the Vienna Cons., where he studied violin with J. Hellmesberger Sr., and composition with Dessoff, graduating in 1870. He was 1st court conductor in Mannheim (1880–91), where he also led the sym. concerts, then conductor of the Leipzig Stadttheater (1891–93). He achieved an excellent reputation as a competent drillmaster, and in 1893 was engaged as conductor of the Boston Sym. Orch. to succeed Nikisch; he held this post for 5 seasons; from 1898 to 1902 he conducted the N.Y. Phil.; during the season of 1899–1900, he led the Wagner repertoire at the Metropolitan Opera in N.Y.; from 1899 to 1902 he served as director of the National Cons. in N.Y., succeeding

Dvorak; from 1902 to 1904 he filled engagements in Europe; in 1904 he was again engaged in the U.S., as conductor of the Pittsburgh Sym. Orch. (until 1910). In 1912 he returned to Berlin, but failed to impress the fastidious concert audiences there; after a brief tenure as director of the Berlin Royal Opera (1912), he pursued a career as a guest conductor in Europe. He also composed, numbering a sym., *In der Natur*, a Violin Concerto, and chamber music among his works.
—NS/LK/DM

Pauwels, Jean-Englebert, South Netherlands violinist, conductor, and composer; b. Brussels, Nov. 24?, 1768; d. there, June 3, 1804. He was a chorister at the royal chapel, where he was a student of Van Maldere (violin) and Vitzthumb (composition). He continued his training in composition in Paris with Le Sueur. After playing in the Théâtre Feydeau orch. there, he went to Strasbourg as director of its theater in 1790. About 1791 he returned to Brussels, where he was 1st violinist in the orch. of the Théâtre de la Monnaie. In 1794 he was made director of its orch. With L. Godecharle, he founded the Société du Concert in 1799. His dramatic works, all first perf. at the Théâtre de la Monnaie, included *La maisonnette dans les bois* (Aug. 3, 1796), *L'auteur malgré lui* (Nov. 2, 1801), *L'arrivée du heros* (c. 1803), and *Léontine et Fonroe* (April 13, 1804). He also wrote much instrumental music and various sacred and secular vocal works.
—LK/DM

Pavageau, Alcide "Slow Drag," jazz bassist; b. New Orleans, La., March 7, 1888; d. there, Jan. 19, 1969. He was known in New Orleans during his early days as a guitarist and a spectacular dancer (the "slow drag" is a dance). During the late 1920s he took up string bass and worked with Buddie Petit, Herb Morand, worked regularly with George Lewis from 1943, went to N.Y. with Bunk Johnson in 1945, and worked regularly with George Lewis, with whom he made overseas tours. During the last few years of his life he regularly marched in parades as the Grand Marshal and played at Preservation Hall. His wife, Anne, recorded as a pianist and vocalist.—JC/LP

Pavarotti, Luciano, greatly renowned Italian tenor; b. Modena, Oct. 12, 1935. His father, a baker by trade, sang in the local church choir; Luciano learned to read music and began singing with the boy altos; later joined his father in the choir, and also sang in the chorus of the local Teatro Comunale and the amateur Chorale Gioacchino Rossini. To prepare himself for a career as a schoolteacher, he attended the local Scuola Magistrale; then taught in an elementary school, augmenting his income by selling insurance. In the meantime, he began vocal studies with Arrigo Polo in Modena (1955), then went to Mantua, where he continued his training with Ettore Campogalliani (1960). He made his operatic debut as Rodolfo in *La Bohème* at the Teatro Municipale in Reggio Emilia on April 29, 1961. He obtained his first major engagement when he appeared as the Duke of Mantua at the Teatro Massimo in Palermo (March 15, 1962). His first important appearance outside his home-

land was as Edgardo with the Netherlands Opera in Amsterdam (Jan. 18, 1963). On Feb. 24, 1963, he made his Vienna State Opera debut as Rodolfo, a role he also sang for his first appearance at London's Covent Garden (Sept. 21, 1963). On Feb. 15, 1965, he made his U.S. debut as Edgardo opposite Joan Sutherland's Lucia with the Greater Miami Opera. After his first appearance at Milan's La Scala as Alfredo (April 28, 1965), he made a summer tour of Australia with the Sutherland Williamson International Grand Opera Co., a venture featuring the celebrated diva. He subsequently scored his first triumph on the operatic stage when he essayed the role of Tonio in *La Fille du régiment* at Covent Garden (June 1, 1966); with insouciant aplomb, he tossed off the aria *Pour mon âme*, replete with 9 successive high C's, winning an ovation. He was dubbed the "King of the High C's," and a brilliant international career beckoned. He made his debut at the San Francisco Opera as Rodolfo (Nov. 11, 1967), a role he chose for his first appearance at the Metropolitan Opera in N.Y. (Nov. 23, 1968). In subsequent seasons, he became a mainstay at both houses, and also appeared regularly with other opera houses on both sides of the Atlantic. He also made frequent appearances in solo recitals and concerts with orchs. In 1977 he starred as Rodolfo in the first "Live from the Met" telecast by PBS. In 1978 he made an acclaimed solo recital debut at the Metropolitan Opera, which was also telecast by PBS. In 1980 he founded the Opera Co. of Philadelphia/Luciano Pavarotti International Voice Competition. On Oct. 22, 1983, he was one of the featured artists at the Metropolitan Opera Centennial Gala. In 1984 he gave a concert before 20,000 admirers at N.Y.'s Madison Square Garden, which was also seen by millions on PBS. He celebrated the 25th anniversary of his operatic debut by singing his beloved Rodolfo at the Teatro Comunale in Modena on April 29, 1986. In 1988 he sang Nemorino at the Berlin Deutsche Oper, eliciting thunderous applause and no less than 15 curtain calls. On Jan. 9, 1989, he appeared in concert with the N.Y.C. Opera orch. in a special program at Avery Fischer Hall at N.Y.'s Lincoln Center for the Performing Arts, which was televised live by PBS. In 1990 he appeared at the Bolshoi Theater in Moscow. On July 7, 1990, he made an unprecedented concert appearance with fellow tenors José Carreras and Plácido Domingo in Rome in an extravaganza telecast to the world. In subsequent years, the "three tenors" appeared in concert in various cities around the globe. Pavarotti celebrated the 30th anniversary of his career with a special concert at London's Hyde Park on July 30, 1991, which event was telecast throughout Europe and overseas. On July 26, 1993, he gave a concert before some 500,000 people in N.Y.'s Central Park, which was seen by countless others via a live telecast by PBS. He celebrated the 25th anniversary of his debut at the Metropolitan Opera on Sept. 27, 1993, singing Otello in the first act of Verdi's opera in a live radio broadcast heard around the world. On July 6, 1994, he again appeared with Carreras and Domingo in concert in Los Angeles, an event telecast live around the globe. On Nov. 22, 1998, he celebrated the 30th anniversary of his Metropolitan Opera debut in a gala performance with the company.

The most idolized tenor since Caruso, Pavarotti made such roles as Nemorino in *L'elisir d'amore*, Riccardo in *Un ballo in maschera*, Fernando in *La Favorite*, Manrico in *Il Trovatore*, Cavaradossi in *Tosca*, and Radames in *Aida*, as well as the ubiquitous Rodolfo, virtually his own. Indeed, through recordings and television appearances, he won an adoring global following, which he retained into his sixth decade in spite of health problems and the breakup of his marriage in 1995 following the revelation of his affair with a young assistant. His autobiography was publ. as *Pavarotti: My Own Story* (with W. Wright; Garden City, N.Y., 1981).

BIBL.: M. Mayer, *Grandissimo P.* (Garden City, N.Y., 1986; with career chronology and discography by G. Fitzgerald); A. Pavarotti and W. Dallas, *P.: Vivere con L.* (Trento, 1992; Eng. tr., 1992, as *P.: Life with L.*); C. Bonvicini, *The Tenor's Son: My Days with P.* (N.Y., 1993); L. Magiera, *P.: Mythos, Methode und Magie* (Zürich, 1993); E. Ruggieri, *P.* (Paris, 1993); M. Lewis, *The Private Lives of the Three Tenors: Behind the Scenes With Plácido Domingo, L. P., and José Carreras* (N.Y., 1996).—**NS/LK/DM**

Pavesi, Stefano,

Italian composer; b. Casaletto Vaprio, near Crema, Jan. 22, 1779; d. Crema, July 28, 1850. He was a pupil of Piccinni in Naples (1795–97) and of Fenaroli there at the Cons. di S. Onofrio, later S. Maria di Loreto (1797–99). After being expelled for his revolutionary sentiments, he was deported to Marseilles, joined Napoleon's Army, and fought in the Italian campaign. He then completed his vocal training with Gazzaniga, whom he succeeded as maestro di cappella at Crema Cathedral (1818–50). From 1826 to 1830 Pavesi also served as music director of the Vienna Court Opera. He composed about 70 operas, winning notable success with *La fiera* (Florence, 1804), *La festa della rosa* (Venice, May 21, 1808), *Ser Marcantonio* (Milan, Sept. 26, 1810), and *Fenella, ovvero La muta Portici* (Venice, Feb. 5, 1831). Among his other compositions were sacred pieces, songs, and 6 harpsichord sonatas.

BIBL.: F. Sanseverino, *Notizie intorno alla vita e alle opere del Maestro S. P.* (Milan, 1851).—**NS/LK/DM**

Paxton, Stephen,

English composer; b. London, 1735; d. there, Aug. 18, 1787. He was a pupil of William Savage. His 6 Solos for Cello and Bass, op.1 (London, 1772) are particularly admirable, as are many of his glees. He also composed Latin liturgical music.—**LK/DM**

Payen, Nicolas,

South Netherlands composer; b. Soignies, c. 1512; d. Madrid, after April 24, 1559. He studied at St. Vincent's in Soignies. After serving as a choirboy in Charles V's Spanish chapel, he was his clerc d'oratoire, chapelain des hautes messes (from 1540) and his maestro de capilla (from 1556). In 1558 he was awarded a canonry in the Tournai collegiate church. His extant works comprise 11 motets and 5 chansons. —**LK/DM**

Payne, Anthony (Edward),

English composer and music critic; b. London, Aug. 2, 1936. He studied at Dulwich Coll. and the Univ. of Durham (1958–61). He was a music critic for the London *Daily Telegraph* (1965–87) and the *Independent* (from 1987). In 1966 he

married **Jane Manning**. Payne made a realization of the unfinished sketches of Elgar's 3rd Sym. (1933) in 1998. His style of composition is structurally disciplined, but inwardly Romantic and inspired by northern moods and modes.

WRITINGS (all publ. in London): *Schoenberg* (1968); with L. Foreman, *Frank Bridge* (1976); *Frank Bridge: Radical and Conservative* (1984); *Elgar's Third Symphony: The Story of the Reconstruction* (1998).

WORKS: DRAMATIC: Ballet: *Fresh Dances for the Late Tchaikovsky* (London, Oct. 20, 1993). **ORCH.:** *Suite from a Forgotten Ballet* (1955; rev. 1986; BBC Radio 3, Feb. 1, 1989); *Contrapuncti* for String Quartet and String Orch. (1958; rev. 1979); *Concerto for Orchestra* (1974; London, Jan. 8, 1975); *Song of the Clouds* (1979–80; Cheltenham, June 29, 1980); *Spring's Shining Wake* (1980–81; BBC Radio 3, Dec. 21, 1983); *Songs and Seascapes* for Strings (London, June 6, 1984); *The Spirit's Harvest* (London, July 31, 1985); *Half-Heard in the Stillness* (Derby, Sept. 17, 1987); *Time's Arrow* (London, July 24, 1990); *Symphonies of the Wind and Rain* (1992; London, April 25, 1993); *A Hidden Music* (London, June 16, 1992); *The Seeds Long Hidden...*, orchestral variations (London, Nov. 22, 1994); Elgar/Payne Sym. No. 3 (realization of Elgar's unfinished sketches, 1998). **Brass:** *Fire on Whaleness* (York, June 25, 1976); *Fanfares and Processional* (London, Sept. 19, 1986); *Echoes of Courtly Love* (1987; London, May 13, 1988); *River-race* (Norwich, Oct. 9, 1990). **CHAMBER:** *Paraphrases and Cadenzas* for Clarinet, Viola, and Piano (London, Nov. 20, 1969; rev. 1979); *Sonatas and Ricercars* for Flute, Oboe, Clarinet, Bassoon, and Horn (1970; 1st complete perf., BBC Radio 3, May 28, 1974); String Quartet (London, Dec. 4, 1978); *Footfalls Echo in the Memory* for Violin and Piano (1978; Three Choirs Festival, Aug. 22, 1980); *The Stones and Lonely Places Sing* for Flute, Clarinet, Horn, Piano and String Trio (London, Sept. 2, 1979); *A Day in the Life of a Mayfly* for Flute, Clarinet, Percussion, Piano, Violin, and Cello (London, Sept. 25, 1981); *The Song Streams in the Firmament* for Clarinet, String Quartet, and Double Bass (N.Y., April 19, 1986); *A 1940's Childhood* for Flute and Guitar (London, April 10, 1987; also for Flute and Harp, London, Feb. 19, 1989); *Consort Music* for 2 Violins, 2 Violas, and Cello (Cambridge, July 27, 1987); *Sea-Change* for Flute, Clarinet, Harp, and String Quartet (Islington, June 12, 1988); *Amid the Winds of Evening* for Viola (1988; London, April 26, 1989); *The Enchantress Plays* for Bassoon and Piano (1990; London, Jan. 8, 1991); *Empty Landscape—Heart's Ease* for Oboe, Clarinet, Horn, Violin, Viola, and Cello (London, March 21, 1995); Piano Trio (1998). **KEYBOARD: Piano:** *Paean* (London, Dec. 9, 1971); *Miniature Variations on a Theme of E. L.* (1980; London, March 6, 1981). **Organ:** *Reflections in the Sea of Glass* (1983). **VOCAL:** *Phoenix Mass* for Chorus, 3 Trumpets, and 3 Trombones (1965–72; BBC Radio 3, Oct. 2, 1973); *2 Songs Without Words* for Men's Vocal Quintet (1970; London, Feb. 4, 1971); *4 Little Cantatas* for Chorus (1974–83; rev. 1984); *First Sight of Her and After* for 16 Solo Voices (London, Dec. 11, 1975; also for Chorus and Chamber Ensemble, London, April 27, 1989); *The World's Winter* for Soprano, Flute, Oboe, and Clarinet (Cheltenham, July 4, 1976); *The Sea of Glass* for Chorus and Organ (St. Albans Abbey, July 2, 1977); *Evening Land* for Soprano and Piano (Norwich, April 4, 1981); *Alleluias and Hockets* for Chorus and 10 Instruments (London, Sept. 3, 1987); *Adlestrop* for Soprano and Piano (Aldeburgh, June 10, 1989; also for Soprano and Piano Quintet, 1993); *Aspects of Love and Contentment* for Soprano and Ensemble (London, June 16, 1991); *Break, break, break* for Chorus (1996); *Scenes From the Woodlanders* for Soprano, 2 Clarinets, Violin, and Cello (1998).—**NS/LK/DM**

Payne, Bennie (actually, **Benjamin E.**), jazz pianist, vocalist; b. Philadelphia, Pa., June 18, 1907; d. Los Angeles, Calif., Sept. 2, 1986. He studied with Fats Waller, and freelanced from about 1926, including work with Wilbur Sweatman (1928) and Elizabeth Welch. He joined *Blackbirds of 1929* and came to Europe with this revue in 1929. Returning to N.Y., he played in the *Hot Chocolates* show, then joined Cab Calloway in November 1931 through 1946, including a European tour in 1934, and excepting his service in U.S. Army beginning late 1943. He was with Pearl Bailey, and from 1950 toured as accompanist and musical director for vocalist Billy Daniels, with whom he worked for over two decades. He retired in L.A.

DISC.: *Benny Payne Plays and Sings* (1955).—JC/LP

Payne, Jim, jazz drummer; b. Bridgeport, Conn., Feb. 25, 1943. After receiving his B.A. (Yale, 1965), he moved to N.Y., got an M.B.A. (Columbia, 1968) and began studying drums privately with Sonny Igoe, Henry Adler, and Philly Joe Jones. He also began teaching at Adler's studios on 46th St. along with Ed Shaunessey and Andrew Cyrille. During this time, he also played with Mike and Randy Brecker, Esther Phillips, and Esther Satterfield, and many jazz and rock groups. In 1978, he moved to the Bay Area for constant five-nights-a-week work with various R&B and funk bands including a stint as musical director for Motown star Mary Wells. He also played with a short-lived group led by David Liebman and Alfred "Pee Wee" Ellis. After moving back to N.Y. in 1981, he again taught at the Henry Adler Studios and also began teaching at the Drummers Collective. He took extension classes at the Manhattan School of Music and the Julliard School, studying music theory and songwriting. He played in Broadway shows, the Radio City Music Hall Orch., and had a five-year association with a jazz/funk band, Slickaphonics, which included many European tours and five albums. In 1989, he moved to Orlando, Fla., where he was a staff drummer and producer for King Snake Records and became a producer and songwriter with the J.B. Horns, touring Japan with them. He has done master classes at SUNY Purchase and at the Percussive Arts Convention and produced the first Medeski, Martin & Wood record, as well as several other funk and R&B-oriented records. He is on the Adjunct faculty of SUNY Purchase.—LP

Payne, Maggi (actually, **Margaret Ducé**), American composer and recording engineer and editor; b. Temple, Tex., Dec. 23, 1945. She studied at Northwestern Univ. (B.M., 1968), the Univ. of Ill. (M.M., 1970) and Mills Coll., in Oakland, Calif. (M.F.A.), numbering among her mentors Walfrid Kujala (flute) and Gordon Mumma, Robert Ashley, and David Behrman (composition); also took courses at Yale Univ. (1969). In 1972 she became a recording engineer in the multi-track facilities at the Center for Contemporary Music at Mills Coll., later being named co-director (1992); from 1983 to 1985 she was artist-in-residence at San Francisco's Exploration, and from 1983 to 1994 also a production engineer for the Northern Calif. radio station KSFO/KYA. Her works, largely electroacoustic, have been performed in various venues throughout the U.S. and Europe. Among her awards are three NEA fellowships (1979–80; 1987; 1989–90) and video grants from both the Mellon Foundation (1983) and the Western Regional Media Arts Fellowships Program (1983–84). In 1998 her *Apparent Horizon* was distinguished with an Honorary Mention from Prix Ars Electronica competition, and in 2000 her *Sweet Dreams* was accorded the same from the 27th annual Les Concours International de Musique Electroacoustique de Bourges competition.

WORKS: *Inflections* for Flute (1970); *Orion* for Film and Electronic Sound Track (1973); *HUM* for Tape and Live Flutist (or 7 Live Flutists) (1973); *VDO* for Film with Electronic Sound Track (1973); *Allusions* for Tape, Dancers, Lighting, and Film (1974); *Farewell* for Tape and Slides (1975); *Transparencies* for Tape and Slides (1976); *Spheres* for Tape and Slides (1977); *Spirals* for Tape and Slides (1977); *Lunar Earthrise* for Tape and Slides (1978); *Lunar Dusk* for Tape and Slides (1979); *Blue Metallics* for Tape and Slides or Film (1980); *Rising* for Tape and Slides and/or Dancers (1980); *Circular Motions* for Tape and Video (1981); *Ling* for Tape and Slides (1981); *Crystal* for Tape and Videomicrography (1982); *Io* for Tape and Videomicrography (1982); *Scirocco* for Live Flute with Digital Delay and Tape (1983); *Solar Wind* for Tape and Video or Slides (1983); *White Night* for Tape (1984); *Shimmer* for Tape (1985); *Subterranean Network* for Tape and Staging (1985); *Back to Forth* for Tape (1986); *Airwaves (realities)* for Tape and Video (1987); *Ahh-Ahh (ver 2.1)* for Tape (1988); *Song of Flights* for Soprano and Piano (1988); *Phase Transitions* for Tape (1989); *Desertscapes* for 2 Spatially separated Treble Choruses (1991); *Heavy Water* for Tape (1991); *Resonant Places* for Tape (1992); *Aolian Confluence* for Tape (1993); *Liquid Metal* for Tape and Video (1994); *Apparent Horizon* for Tape and Video (1996); *Minutiae 0–13* for 1–3 Pianos (1996); *Moiré* for Tape (1996); *Raw Data* for Tape (1998); *Close-ups* for Tape (1999); *Sweet Dreams* for Tape (1999); *HUM 2* for 8 Trombones or Solo Trombone and 7 Channels of Tape (2000; also for Solo Trombone and Quadraphonic or Stereo Diffusion); *White Turbulence 2000*, electroacoustic piece for quadraphonic diffusion (2000).—LK/DM

Paz, Juan Carlos, significant Argentine composer; b. Buenos Aires, Aug. 5, 1901; d. there, Aug. 25, 1972. He studied composition with Constantino Gaito in Argentina and later with d'Indy in Paris. In 1929, with several young composers of radical tendencies, he organized in Buenos Aires the "Grupo Renovacion," and in 1937 inaugurated a series of concerts of new music. He became a music critic and author of several books. His early works, after 1921, are marked by strong polyphony, in a neo-Classical style; about 1927 he adopted atonal and polytonal procedures; in 1934 he began to compose almost exclusively in the 12-tone idiom; after 1950 he modified his musical language, adopting a less rigid and more personal style of composition.

WORKS: ORCH.: *Canto de Navidad* (1927; orchestrated 1930); *Movimiento sinfonico* (1930); Suite for Ibsen's *Juliano Emperador* (1931); *3 Pieces* (1931); *Passacaglia* (1936; Paris, June 25, 1937; rev. 1952–53); *Música (Preludio y fuga)* (1940); *Passacaglia* for Strings (1944; rev. 1949); *Ritmica constante* (1952); *6 superposiciones* (1954); *Transformaciones canónicas* (1955–56); *Música* for Bassoon, Strings, and Percussion (1955–56); *Continuidad 1960* (1960–61; Caracas, May 11, 1966); *Estructuras 1962* for Chamber Orch. (1962); *Música* for Piano and Orch. (1964;

Washington, D.C., May 12, 1965). **CHAMBER:** *Tema y transformaciones* for 11 Winds (1929); Wind Octet (1930); 3 sonatinas: No. 1 for Clarinet and Piano (1930), No. 2 for Flute and Clarinet (1932), and No. 3 for Oboe and Bassoon (1933; later transcribed for Piano); *Concierto No. 1* for Flute, Oboe, Clarinet, Bassoon, Trumpet, and Piano (1932) and *No. 2* for Oboe, Trumpet, 2 Trombones, Bassoon, and Piano (1935); *4 Composiciónes dodecafónica*: No. 1 for Flute, English Horn, and Cello (1934; lost), No. 2 for Flute and Piano (1935), No. 3 for Clarinet and Piano (1937), and No. 4 for Violin (1938); Overture for 12 Instruments (1936); 4 pieces for Clarinet (1936); *3 Composiciónes en trio*: No. 1 for Flute, Clarinet, and Bassoon (1937), No. 2 for Clarinet, Trumpet, and Alto Saxophone (1938), and No. 3 for Flute, Oboe, and Bass Clarinet or Bassoon (1940; rev. 1945); 2 string quartets (1938, 1940–43); *Música* for Flute, Saxophone, and Piano (1943); *Dedalus 1950* for Flute, Clarinet, Violin, Cello, and Piano (1950–51); *Continuidad 1953* for Piano and Percussion (1953–54); *3 contrapuntos* for Clarinet, Electric Guitar, Celesta, Trumpet, Trombone, and Cello (1955); *Invención* for String Quartet (1961); *Concreción* for Flute, Clarinet, Bassoon, Horn, Trumpet, Trombone, and Tuba (1964). **KEYBOARD: P i a n o :** 3 sonatas (1923, 1925, 1935); *Tema con transformaciones* (1928); *3 movimientos de jazz* (1932); Sonatina No. 3 (1933; originally for Oboe and Bassoon); *10 piezas sobre una serie dodecafónica* (1936); *Música 1946*; *Núcleos*, 1st series (1962–64). **O r g a n :** *Galaxia 64* (1964).

BIBL.: J. Beschinsky, *J.C. P.* (Buenos Aires, 1964); J. Romano, *J.C. P.: Tribulaciones de un músico* (Buenos Aires, 1970). **—NS/LK/DM**

Pazovsky, Ariy (Moiseievich), Russian conductor; b. Perm, Feb. 2, 1887; d. Moscow, Jan. 6, 1953. He received violin training as a child, and then was a student of Krasnokutsky and Auer at the St. Petersburg Cons. (1897–1904). After conducting provincial opera companies (1905–08), he was conductor of Zimin's opera company in Moscow (1908–10), and then conducted in Kharkov, Odessa, and Kiev. He was music director of the Petrograd People's Opera (1916–18). After conducting at Moscow's Bolshoi Theater (1923–24; 1925–28), he conducted in Baku, Sverdlovsk, Kharkov, and Kiev (1926–36). He was artistic director of Leningrad's Kirov Theater (1936–43), and then of the Bolshoi Theater (1943–48). In 1940 he was made a People's Artist of the U.S.S.R. He publ. *Zapiski dirizhora* (The Writings of a Conductor; Moscow, 1966).**—NS/LK/DM**

Peabody, George, American businessman and philanthropist; b. South Danvers, Mass., Feb. 18, 1795; d. London, Nov. 4, 1869. He was the founder of George Peabody & Co., which specialized in American securities and foreign exchange. In 1837 he settled in England, where he conducted a thriving business. In 1857 he disbursed $1,500,000 for the founding of the Peabody Inst. in Baltimore, which later established the Peabody Cons. of Music.**—NS/LK/DM**

Peacock, Gary, jazz bassist; b. Burley, Idaho, May 12, 1935. He is best known for playing and touring with Bill Evans and Paul Bley, both renowned for hiring creative and interactive bassists. Peacock studied piano, then took up bass in 1956 while in the army; in Germany, he played with local musicians and visiting

Americans. In 1958, he moved to Calif. He first recorded with Clare Fischer (1962), then moved to N.Y. later in 1962, playing with Bley, Evans, Jimmy Giuffre, Albert Ayler, Roswell Rudd, Steve Lacy, Archie Shepp, Sonny Rollins, George Russell, and Don Ellis. In 1965, he toured Europe with Ayler, Don Cherry and Sonny Murray, then worked briefly with Miles Davis and Bley. He was inactive in music until the mid-1970s, playing with Bley and teaching. Since 1976, he has toured and recorded in a trio with Keith Jarrett and Jack De-Johnnette. He currently lives in upstate N.Y. In 1998, a hearing problem forced him to cut down on performing.

DISC.: *Tales of Another* (1977); *Shift in the Wind* (1980); *December Poems* (1980); *Voice from the Past: Paradigm* (1981); *Guamba* (1987); *Partners* (1989); *Tethered Moon* (1991); *Cosi Lontano–Quasi Dentro* (1991); *Oracle* (1993).**—LP**

Pearl Jam, along with Nirvana, brought attention to the music of Seattle and launched grunge rock into mainstream popularity. **MEMBERSHIP:** Eddie Vedder, lead voc. (b. Chicago, Dec. 23, 1964); Mike McCready, lead gtr. (b. Seattle, Wash., April 5, 1965); Steve "Stone" Gossard, rhythm gtr. (b. Seattle, Wash., July 20, 1966); Jeff Ament, bs. (b. Big Sandy, Mont., March 10, 1963); Dave Krusen, drm. Dave Krusen was replaced by Dave Abbruzzese in 1992; Abbruzzese was replaced by Jack Irons in 1995.

Fronted by charismatic lead vocalist-songwriter Eddie Vedder, Pearl Jam tapped the rage and frustration of youth with a sense of longing and compassion missing from the songs of Nirvana. The band debuted in 1991 with the best- selling *Ten*, and have since been one of the most popular in all of rock. They have won fans by fighting what they consider to be the monopolistic practices of ticket-seller Ticketmaster, and have been outspoken in their support of lower ticket prices.

Formed in Seattle around 1990, Pearl Jam was initially comprised of Jeff Ament and Steve "Stone" Gossard, of Green River and Mother Love Bone; Eddie Vedder and Mike McCready of the one-shot Temple of the Dog; and Dave Krusen. Temple of the Dog was convened with Ament, Gossard, Vedder, and McCready and Soundgarden's Chris Connell and Matt Cameron to record a tribute album to Mother Love Bone lead vocalist Andrew Wood, who died of a drug overdose in 1990. Signed to Epic Records, Pearl Jam broke through with their debut album, *Ten*. Ultimately selling more than five million copies in the United States, the album featured highly melodic but aggressively played songs such as "Even Flow," the energetic ballads "Jeremy" and "Alive," and the plaintive "Release." In 1992 Pearl Jam became one of the most popular attractions on the second Lollapalooza tour.

Replacing drummer Dave Krusen with Dave Abbruzzese, Pearl Jam next recorded the softer *Vs.* album. Another instant best-seller, the album included the powerful "Leash," "Rear View Mirror" and "Blood," as well as the brooding "Dissident," the acoustic guitar-based "Daughter," and the introspective "Indifference." During 1993 Vedder sang three songs with the surviving Doors at the Rock and Roll Hall of Fame induction ceremony, and Pearl Jam appeared on MTV's *Un-*

plugged. The band toured Europe with Neil Young and collaborated with him on "Rockin' in the Free World" at the MTV Video Awards show.

One of the most populist and politically committed bands in contemporary rock, Pearl Jam sought to keep ticket prices reasonable for their planned summer tour of 1994, but they were thwarted by Ticketmaster, the only nationwide ticket-service agency. In May the band filed a complaint against Ticketmaster with the U.S. Justice Department, and Jeff Ament and Stone Gossard testified at Congressional hearings investigating monopolistic business practices in the ticket-distribution industry in June. In August 1994 Dave Abbruzzese left Pearl Jam after the group had completed recording *Vitalogy,* released on vinyl two weeks prior to its release on CD and cassette. The fastest-selling album of the year, *Vitalogy* returned to the ferocity of *Ten* with songs such as "Spin the Black Circle" (their first-ever single release) and "Last Exit"; it also contained "Not for You," "Satan's Bed," and "Nothingman." In a remarkably astute move, Pearl Jam bought three hours of satellite time in January 1995 to broadcast the three-hour show *Self-Pollution* on any radio station that availed itself of the band's free offer. The group eventually toured the United States in the summer of 1995 with new drummer Jack Irons, playing venues independent of Ticketmaster. However, the tour was beset with problems, including rain in Utah and Eddie Vedder's incapacitating illness after seven songs in San Francisco's Golden Gate Park. Neil Young completed the San Francisco show, and only days later Reprise issued Young's *Mirror Ball,* on which Pearl Jam served as his backing band–it is perhaps his best effort since his early days with Crazy Horse.

Disc.: TEMPLE OF THE DOG: *Temple of the Dog* (1991). P E A R L J A M: *Ten* (1991); *Vs.* (1993); *Vitalogy* (1994); *No Code* (1996); *Yield* (1998); *Live on Two Legs* (1998); *Binaural* (2000). NEIL YOUNG AND PEARL JAM: *Mirror Ball* (1995). —BH

Pearlman, Martin, noted American conductor, harpsichordist, and composer; b. Chicago, May 21, 1945. He received training in composition, violin, piano, and theory in his youth. Following studies in composition with Husa at Cornell Univ. (B.A., 1967), he pursued training in harpsichord with Leonhardt on a Fulbright scholarship in the Netherlands (1967–68). He subsequently took his M.M. in composition under Wyner at Yale Univ. (1971), and also studied with Ralph Kirkpatrick (harpsichord) and Arel (electronic music). In 1972 he won the Erwin Bodky Award and in 1974 he was a prize winner in the Bruges Competition. In 1973 he founded and became music director of Banchetto Musicale, the first permanent Baroque orch. established in North America. In 1992 it was renamed Boston Baroque. From 1976 to 1981 he taught at the Univ. of Mass. in Boston, and also at Brandeis Univ. in 1980–81. As a harpsichordist, Pearlman has become well known for his performances of the Couperin family and of D. Scarlatti. As a conductor, he has led numerous period instrument performances and has given the American premieres of many Baroque and Classical scores, including those of Bach, Handel, Rameau, Mozart, and Beethoven. He has also appeared as a guest conductor

of modern instrument groups and sym. orchs., as well as of Baroque ensembles. In 1995 he made his Kennedy Center debut in Washington, D.C., conducting Handel's *Semele.* Pearlman has prepared performing eds. of Monteverdi's *L'incoronazione di Poppea,* Purcell's *Comical History of Don Quixote,* and Mozart's *Lo sposo deluso.* He has also prepared a complete ed. of the keyboard music of Armand-Louis Couperin.—NS/LK/DM

Pears, Sir Peter (Neville Luard), renowned English tenor; b. Farnham, June 22, 1910; d. Aldeburgh, April 3, 1986. He began his career as temporary organist at Hertford Coll., Oxford (1928–29), then was director of music at the Grange School, Crowborough (1930–34). He was a scholarship student at the Royal Coll. of Music in London (1933–34); concurrently sang in the BBC Chorus, and then was a member of the BBC Singers (1934–38) and the New English Singers (1936–38). During this period, he received vocal instruction from Elena Gerhardt and Dawson Freer. In 1936 he also met Benjamin Britten; they gave their first joint recital in 1937, and thereafter remained lifelong personal and professional companions. After singing in the Glyndebourne Chorus (1938), he accompanied Britten to the U.S. (1939); continued his vocal training with Thérèse Behr and Clytie Hine-Mundy. In 1942 he returned to England with Britten, making his stage debut that same year in the title role of *Les Contes d'Hoffmann* at London's Strand Theatre. In 1943 he joined the Sadler's Wells Opera Co., gaining fame when he created the title role in Britten's *Peter Grimes* (June 7, 1945). In 1946 he became a member of the English Opera Group, and thereafter greatly distinguished himself in operas by Britten; among the roles he created were Albert Herring, the Male Chorus in *The Rape of Lucretia,* Captain Vere in *Billy Budd,* Essex in *Gloriana,* Quint in *The Turn of the Screw,* Flute in *A Midsummer Night's Dream* (was co-librettist with the composer), the Madwoman in *Curlew River,* Sir Philip Wingrave in *Owen Wingrave,* and Aschenbach in *Death in Venice.* It was in the latter role that he made his Metropolitan Opera debut in N.Y. on Oct. 18, 1974. He was one of the founders of the Aldeburgh Festival (1948), serving as a director and as a teacher of master classes until his death. Pears also sang in several first performances of Britten's non-operatic works, including the *Serenade* for Tenor, Horn, and Strings, the *Michelangelo Sonnets,* and the *War Requiem.* He also excelled in the works of other English composers, among them Elgar, Holst, Vaughan Williams, and Walton, as well as those by Schütz, Bach, Mozart, Schubert, and Schumann. He was made a Commander of the Order of the British Empire in 1957, and was knighted in 1978. P. Reed ed. and annotated *The Travel Diaries of Peter Pears, 1936–1978* (Woodbridge, 1995).

Bibl.: M. Thorpe, ed., *P. P.: A Tribute on His 75th Birthday* (London, 1985); C. Headington, *P. P.: A Biography* (London and Boston, 1993).—NS/LK/DM

Pearsall, Robert Lucas, English antiquarian and composer; b. Clifton, March 14, 1795; d. Wartensee, Lake Constance, Aug. 5, 1856. He studied law and music, and as a boy of 13 wrote a cantata, *Saul and the Witch of*

Endor. He lived many years in Germany, where he publ. many of his compositions; was in London on several extended visits. In 1842 he purchased a castle on Lake Constance, and remained there for the rest of his life. As a composer, he was at his best in many ingenious madrigals. Particularly popular were his part-songs, *Sir Patrick Spens, The Hardy Norseman,* and *O who will o'er the downs so free.* He ed. early church music in Germany, and also publ. an *Essay on Consecutive Fifths and Octaves in Counterpoint* (London, 1876).—NS/LK/DM

Pease, James, American bass-baritone; b. Indianapolis, Jan. 9, 1916; d. N.Y., April 26, 1967. He studied at the Curtis Inst. of Music in Philadelphia. In 1941 he made his operatic debut as Gounod's Méphistophélès at the Philadelphia Opera. On May 9, 1946, he made his first appearance at the N.Y.C. Opera as Sparafucile, where he sang until 1953 and again in 1959–60 and 1967. From 1952 to 1959 he also was a member of the Hamburg State Opera. As a guest artist, Pease appeared at London's Covent Garden, the Zürich Opera, the San Francisco Opera, the Chicago Lyric Opera, and other opera centers. Among his best roles were Don Giovanni, Figaro, King Marke, Hans Sachs, and Baron Ochs. —NS/LK/DM

Pecháček, Franz Xaver, Austrian violinist and composer; b. Vienna, July 4, 1793; d. Karlsruhe, Sept. 15, 1840. He studied with his father, Franz Martin Pecháček (1763–1816), who was also a composer. After an appearance before the Viennese court when he was only 8, he received training in violin with Johann Kletzinsky and Schuppanzigh and in composition with Aloys Förster (1805–09). From 1809 to 1822 he was a member of the orch. at the Theatre an der Wien, and concurrently pursued a successful solo career. He subsequently served as concertmaster in Württemberg (1822–26) and Karlsruhe (from 1826). In addition to many virtuoso violin pieces, he also wrote 3 overtures and a quartet. —LK/DM

Pechner, Gerhard, German-American baritone; b. Berlin, April 15, 1903; d. N.Y., Oct. 21, 1969. He studied in Berlin, making his debut there in 1927. After singing at the German Theater in Prague (1933–39), he emigrated to the U.S. In 1940 he made his U.S. debut as Mozart's Bartolo at the San Francisco Opera. On Nov. 27, 1941, he made his Metropolitan Opera debut in N.Y. as the Notary in *Der Rosenkavalier,* and remained on its roster until 1965. In 1966–67 he was again on its roster. Pechner was especially admired for such roles as Alberich, Beckmesser, Melitone in *La forza del destino,* and the Sacristan in *Tosca.*—NS/LK/DM

Pedersøn, Mogens, significant Danish composer; b. c. 1583; d. probably in Copenhagen, Jan. or Feb. 1623. As a result of the patronage of King Christian IV, he was sent to Venice to study with Giovanni Gabrieli (1599–1600). Upon his return to Copenhagen, he worked under Borchgrevinck (1600–03), then became an instrumentalist in the royal chapel. After further studies in Italy (1605–9), he returned to Copenhagen to enter the

royal chapel once again; was sent by the King to England to serve his sister, Anne, queen to James I (1611). Following his return to Copenhagen (1614), he again was active in the royal chapel, becoming its asst. director (1618). Pedersøn greatly distinguished himself as a composer of both sacred and secular music.

WORKS: *Madrigali, libro primo* for 5 Voices (Venice, 1608; ed. in Dania Sonans, I, Copenhagen, 1933); *Madrigali, libro secondo* for 5 Voices (1611?; greater portion not extant except for 10 madrigals; ed. in Dania Sonans, III, Egtved, 1967); *Pratum spirituale* for 5 Voices (Copenhagen, 1620; ed. in Dania Sonans, I, Copenhagen, 1933); 2 madrigaletti for 3 Voices (1619; ed. in Dania Sonans, II, Egtved, 1966); 2 pavanes for 5 Viols (MS). —NS/LK/DM

Pederzini, Gianna, noted Italian mezzo-soprano; b. Vò di Avio, Feb. 10, 1903; d. Rome, March 12, 1988. She studied with De Lucia in Naples. She made her operatic debut as Preziosilla in 1923 in Messina; in 1930 she joined La Scala in Milan, where she sang until 1943; also appeared in Rome (1939–52), at Covent Garden, London (1931), and at the Teatro Colón in Buenos Aires (1937–39; 1946–47). She returned to La Scala in 1956–57, creating the role of the Prioress in Poulenc's *Dialogues des Carmélites.* She was an outstanding interpreter of roles in Rossini's operas; was also greatly admired for her interpretation of Carmen.—NS/LK/DM

Pederzuoli, Giovanni Battista, Italian organist and composer; b. place and date unknown; d. c. 1692. He was maestro di cappella at S. Maria Maggiore in Bergamo (1664–65). After settling in Vienna, he was organist (1677–82) and Kapellmeister (1682–86) to the Dowager Empress Eleanora. He distinguished himself as a composer of vocal music, including sepolcri and oratorios. His philosophical cantatas (1685) were the first of their kind. He also composed some sinfonias. —LK/DM

Pedrell, Carlos, Uruguayan composer, nephew of **Felipe Pedrell;** b. Minas, Oct. 16, 1878; d. Montrouge, near Paris, March 3, 1941. He studied in Madrid with his uncle, and later went to Paris, where he took lessons with d'Indy and Breville at the Schola Cantorum. Returning to South America, he was inspector of music in the Buenos Aires schools. He lectured at the Univ. of Tucumán. In 1921 he went to Paris, where he remained for the rest of his life. His works are cast in the French style, but the rhythmic elements are related to Spanish and South American sources; his songs, with richly developed accompaniments, are the best among his works.

WORKS: DRAMATIC: Opera: *Ardid de Amor* (Buenos Aires, June 7, 1917); *Cuento de Abril; La Guitare* (Madrid, 1924). **Ballet:** *La Rose et le gitan* (Antwerp, 1930); *Alleluia* (Buenos Aires, 1936). **ORCH.:** *Une Nuit de Schéhérazade* (1908); *Danza y canción de Aixa* (1910); *En el estrado de Beatriz* (1910); *Fantasia Argentina* (1910); *Ouverture catalane* (1912). **VOCAL:** *Pastorales* for Voice and Orch. (Paris, 1928); choruses; songs. —NS/LK/DM

Pedrell, Felipe, eminent Spanish musicologist and composer, uncle of **Carlos Pedrell;** b. Tortosa, Feb. 19,

1841; d. Barcelona, Aug. 19, 1922. He became a chorister at Tortosa Cathedral when he was about 7, receiving instruction from Juan Antonio Nin y Serra. In 1873 he went to Barcelona as deputy director of the Light Opera Co., where he produced his first opera, *L'ultimo Abenzeraggio* (April 14, 1874). After a visit to Italy (1876–77) and a sojourn in Paris, he settled in Barcelona (1881), where he devoted himself mainly to musicological pursuits. In 1882 he founded the journals *Salterio Sacro-Hispano* and *Notas Musicales y Literarias*, both of which ceased publication in 1883. He then was founder-ed. of the important journal *La Illustración Musical Hispano-Americana* (1888–96). During this period, he worked on his operatic masterpiece, the trilogy *Los Pirieneos/Els Pirineus* (1890–91), and also publ. the book *Por nuestra música* (1891), which served as its introduction and as a plea for the creation of a national lyric drama based on Spanish folk song. In 1894 he went to Madrid, where he was named prof. of choral singing at the Cons. and prof. of advanced studies at the Ateneo; was also elected a member of the Royal Academy of Fine Arts. Upon his return to Barcelona (1904), he devoted himself to writing, teaching, and composing. Among his outstanding pupils were Albéniz, Falla, Granados, and Gerhard. Although Pedrell was admired as a composer by his contemporaries, his music has not obtained recognition outside his homeland. His lasting achievement rests upon his distinguished as a musicologist, in which he did much to restore interest in both historical and contemporary Spanish sacred music.

WRITINGS: *Gramática musical or manual expositivo de la teoria del solfeo, en forma de diálogo* (Barcelona, 1872; 3rd ed., 1883); *Las sonatas de Beethoven* (Barcelona, 1873); *Los músicos españoles en sus libros* (Barcelona, 1888); *Por nuestra música* (Barcelona, 1891); *Diccionario técnico de la música bibliográfico de músicos y escritores de música españoles, portugueses y hispano-ameríanos antiguos y modernos* (Barcelona, 1895–97); *Emporio científico e histórico de organografía musical española antigua* (Barcelona, 1901); *Prácticas preparatorias de instrumentación* (Barcelona, 1902); *La cançó popular catalana* (Barcelona, 1906); *Documents pour servir à l'histoire de théâtre musical: La Festa d'Elche ou le drame lyrique liturgique espagnol* (Paris, 1906); *Musicalerias* (Valencia, 1906); *Catàlech de la Biblioteca musical de la Diputació de Barcelona* (Barcelona, 1909); *Músicos contemporáneos y de otros tiempos* (Paris, 1910); *Jornadas de arte* (Paris, 1911; memoirs and articles, 1841–1902); *La lírica nacionalizada* (Paris, 1913); *Tomás Luis de Victoria Abulense* (Valencia, 1918); *P. Antonio Eximeno* (Madrid, 1920); *Jornados postreras* (Valls, 1922; autobiography); *Musiquerias* (Paris, n.d.; autobiography). **EDITIONS:** *Hispaniae schola musical sacra* (Barcelona, 1894–98); *Teatro lirico español anterior al siglo XIX* (La Coruña, 1897–98); *T.L. de Victoria: Opera omnia* (Leipzig, 1902–13); *El organista litúrgico español* (Barcelona, 1905); *Antologia de organistas clásicos españoles* (Madrid, 1908); *Cancionero musical popular español* (Valls, 1918–22; 2nd ed., 1936); with H. Anglès, *Els madrigals i la missa de difunts d'en Brudieu* (Barcelona, 1921).

BIBL.: G. Tebaldini, *F. P. ed il dramma lirico spagnuolo* (Turin, 1897); R. Mitjana, *La música contemporanea en España y F. P.* (Málaga, 1901); H. de Curzon, *F. P. et "Les Pyrénées"* (Paris, 1902); L. Vilalba Muñoz, *F. P.: Semblanza y biografía* (Madrid, 1922); F. Bonastre, *F. P.: Acotaciones a una idea* (Tarragona, 1977). —**NS/LK/DM**

Pedrollo, Arrigo, Italian composer and pedagogue; b. Montebello Vicentino, Dec. 5, 1878; d. Vicenza, Dec. 23, 1964. He studied at the Milan Cons. (1891–1900); at his graduation, he wrote a Sym., which was performed by Toscanini. He was the director of the Istituto Musicale in Vicenza (1920–30), then was a prof. of composition at the Milan Cons. (1930–41); from 1942 to 1959 he was director of the Vicenza Cons. In 1914 he won the Sonzogno competition with his opera *Juana*. His other operas include *Terra promessa* (Cremona, 1908), *La Veglia* (Milan, Jan. 2, 1920), *L'Uomo che ride* (Rome, March 6, 1920), *Maria di Magdala* (Milan, 1924), *Delitto e castigo*, after Dostoyevsky (Milan, Nov. 16, 1926), *L'Amante in trappola* (Verona, Sept. 22, 1936), and *Il Giglio di Ali* (1948). He also wrote orch. pieces, chamber music, choral works, and songs.—**NS/LK/DM**

Pedrotti, Carlo, eminent Italian conductor and composer; b. Verona, Nov. 12, 1817; d. there (suicide), Oct. 16, 1893. He studied with Domenico Foroni in Verona, where he first gained success as a composer with his opera *Lina* (May 2, 1840). After serving as conductor of the Italian Opera in Amsterdam (1841–45), he returned to Verona, where he was active as a teacher, opera coach, and conductor at the Teatro Filarmonico and at the Teatro Nuovo, where he brought out his finest opera, *Tutti in maschera* (Nov. 4, 1856). In 1868 he was called to Turin as director of the Liceo Musicale and as director and conductor of the Teatro Regio, where he reorganized the musical life of the city; he also founded and conducted the weekly series of Concerti Popolari, in which he presented the Italian premieres of many historical and contemporary works. In 1882 he went to Pesaro as the first director of the newly founded Liceo Musicale, a position he held until ill health compelled him to resign in 1893; that same year he took his own life by drowning himself in the Adige River. Although Pedrotti excelled as a composer of opera buffa, his importance today rests upon his work as a conductor.

BIBL.: T. Mantovani, *C. P.* (Pesaro, 1894).—**NS/LK/DM**

Peebles, David, Scottish composer who flourished in the 16th century. He was a canon at the Augustinian Priory at St. Andrews. His extant works comprise the motet *Si quis diligit me* and 106 Protestant Psalm settings for 4 Voices.—**LK/DM**

Peellaert, Augustin-Philippe (-Marie-Ghislain), South Netherlands composer; b. Bruges, March 12, 1793; d. Brussels, April 16, 1876. He studied in Paris with Momigny. In 1832 he became a member of the executive board of the Brussels Cons. He wrote several operas, of which the following were produced in Brussels: *L'Heure du rendez-vous* (1821), *Agnes Sorel* (Aug. 30, 1823), *Le Barmècide* (1824), *Teniers ou La Noce flamande* (Feb. 21, 1825), *L'Exilé* (1827), *Faust* (1834), *Le Coup de pistolet* (1836), and *Louis de Male* (1838). His autobiography appeared as *Cinquante ans de souvenirs* (Brussels, 1867).—**NS/LK/DM**

Peerce, Jan (real name, **Jacob Pincus Perelmuth**), noted American tenor; b. N.Y., June 3, 1904; d. there, Dec. 15, 1984. He played the violin in dance bands, and sang at various entertainment places in N.Y. In 1932 he was engaged as a singer at Radio City Music Hall in N.Y. He made his operatic debut in Philadelphia as the Duke of Mantua in *Rigoletto* (May 14, 1938), and gave his first solo recital in N.Y. on Nov. 7, 1939. His lyrical voice attracted attention, and he was engaged by the Metropolitan Opera in N.Y.; made his debut there as Alfredo in *La Traviata* on Nov. 29, 1941; sang also the parts of Cavaradossi in *Tosca*, Rodolfo in *La Bohème*, and Gounod's *Faust*; remained on the staff of the Metropolitan until 1966, appearing again in 1967–68. He continued to make occasional appearances until his retirement in 1982. He was the brother-in-law of **Richard Tucker**.

BIBL.: A. Levy, *The Bluebird of Happiness: The Memoirs of J. P.* (N.Y., 1976).—**NS/LK/DM**

Peerless Quartet, The, The most successful vocal group on records in the U.S. in the first quarter of the 20th century. The Peerless Quartet was founded under the auspices of Columbia Records and initially called the Columbia Male Quartet. The original members were Henry Burr (ten.), Albert Campbell (ten.), Steve Porter (bar.), and Tom Daniels (bs.). Their first hit was "You're the Flower of My Heart, Sweet Adeline" (1904). By 1906, when Frank Stanley replaced Daniels, they had begun to record for other record labels and changed their name. Stanley became the group's lead singer and manager. Porter left in 1909 and was replaced by Arthur Collins. Stanley died in 1910 and was replaced by John Meyer, after which Burr usually sang lead as the group scored major hits with "Let Me Call You Sweetheart" (1911), "I Didn't Raise My Boy to Be a Soldier" (1915), "My Bird of Paradise" (1915), "The Lights of My Home Town" (1916), George M. Cohan's "Over There" (1917), and "I Don't Know Where I'm Going but I'm on My Way" (1918).

Collins left the group in 1918 and was replaced by Frank Croxton. This lineup continued through 1925, when it disbanded. Burr continued the group name with three new members, until the Peerless Quartet finally broke up in 1928.—**WR**

Peerson, Martin, English virginalist, organist, and composer; b. March, near Ely, c. 1572; d. (buried) London, Jan. 15, 1651. Although convicted of recusancy in 1604, he was granted his B.Mus. from Oxford in 1613. Settling in London, he was almoner and master of the choristers at St. Paul's Cathedral (1624–42), later serving in the sole capacity of almoner. He publ. *Private Musicke* (1620), which includes ayres for solo voice and 3 viols, duets, and dialogues, and *Mottects or Grave Chamber Musique* (1630), the first English music to include a figured bass part. Among his other works were 20 anthems and various keyboard pieces.—**LK/DM**

Peeters, Flor, outstanding Belgian organist, pedagogue, and composer; b. Tielen, July 4, 1903; d. Antwerp, July 4, 1986. He studied organ with Depuydt and Gregorian chant with van Nuffel at the Lemmens Inst. in Mechelen, succeeding Depuydt as prof. of organ there in 1925, and holding this position until 1952. From 1931 to 1938 he was a prof. at the Ghent Cons., and then

at the Tilbourg Cons. from 1935 to 1948. He became a prof. of organ at the Antwerp Cons. in 1948, and was its director from 1952 to 1968. He was elevated to the peerage as Baron Peeters by King Baudoin in 1971. He composed nearly 500 works for organ alone, and also wrote much sacred choral music. His works for organ include *Passacaglia and Fugue* (1938), *Sinfonia* (1940), Organ Concerto (1944), *Lied Symphony* (1948), *30 Short Chorale Preludes* (1959), *213 Hymn Preludes for the Liturgical Year* (24 installments, 1959–67), and *6 Lyrical Pieces* (1966). He also publ. several vols., including *Anthologia pro organo* (4 vols., Brussels, 1949–59), *Ars organi* (3 vols., Brussels, 1952–54), and *Little Organ Book* (Boston, 1957).

BIBL.: P. Visser, *F. P., Organist* (Turnhout, 1950); J. Hofmann, *F. P.: His Life and His Organ Works* (Fredonia, 1978). —**NS/LK/DM**

Peiko, Nikolai, Russian composer and teacher; b. Moscow, March 25, 1916; d. there, July 1, 1995. He studied with Litinsky, Rakov, and Miaskovsky at the Moscow Cons. (1933–40). From 1942 to 1959 he taught at the Moscow Cons. His music faithfully follows the precepts of socialist realism.

WORKS: DRAMATIC: O p e r a : *Aikhylu* (1943; rev. 1953). **B a l l e t :** *Spring Winds* (1950); *Jeanne d'Arc* (1957). **ORCH.:** *Suite on Yakutsk Themes* (1941); Piano Concerto (1943; rev. 1954); 7 syms.: No. 1 (1945), No. 2 (1946), No. 3 (1957), No. 4 (1965), No. 5 (1968), No. 6 (1972), and No. 7, for Russian Folk Instruments (1977); *From Russia's Remote Past*, suite (1949); *Moldavian Suite* (Moscow, Dec. 14, 1950); *Festive Overture* (1951); *2 Concert Fantasies* for Violin and Orch. (1953, 1965); *Symphonic Ballad* (1959); *Concerto-Symphony* (1974); *In the Throes of War*, 5 symphonic tableaux (1975); *Concerto-Poem* for Clarinet, Balalaika, and Orch. (1979). **CHAMBER:** Piano Quintet (1961); 3 string quartets (1964, 1965, 1966); *Decimet* for 10 Instruments (1971); Violin Sonata (1976). **P i a n o :** 2 sonatinas (1942, 1957); *Sonatina Fairy Tale* (1943); 2 sonatas (1951, 1975).

BIBL.: G. Grigorieva, *N. P.* (Moscow, 1965).—**NS/LK/DM**

Peinemann, Edith, German violinist and teacher; b. Mainz, March 3, 1937. She learned the rudiments of music from her father, concertmaster of the Mainz orch., then continued her studies with Heinz Stanske in Heidelberg (1951–53) and Max Rostal in London (1953–56), where she also took courses at the Guildhall School of Music. At the age of 19, she won the Munich International Competition, and then played with many major German orchs.; also gave duo recitals with the Austrian pianist Jorg Demus. In 1962 she made her first tour of America. She was a prof. at the Frankfurt am Main Hochschule für Musik (from 1976).—**NS/LK/DM**

Peixinho, Jorge (Manuel Rosada Marques), Portuguese composer and teacher; b. Montijo, Jan. 20, 1940. He received training in piano and composition (with Santos and Vasconcelos) at the Lisbon Cons. (1951–58). After attending the Univ. of Lisbon (1959), he studied composition with Nono in Venice (1960) and Petrassi and Porena at the Accademia di Santa Cecilia in Rome (1960–61). Between 1960 and 1970, he attended the summer courses in new music in Darmstadt, and in 1962–63 he studied at the Basel Academy of Music. In

1965–66 he taught at the Oporto Cons. In 1970 he became director of the Grupo de Música Contemporanea in Lisbon. He was prof. of composition at the National Cons. in Lisbon from 1985. In 1974 he received the Gulbenkian Prize. In 1988 he was awarded Portugal's Medal of Cultural Merit. Peixinho is one of the leading avant-garde composers of Portugal. In developing his own advanced compositional course, he has experimented with almost every resource available to the contemporary composer.

WORKS: DRAMATIC: *O gebo a sombra*, theater music (1966); *Recitativo II*, music theater (1966–70); *As quatro estações*, theater music (1968); *Shakespeare's Sonnets*, ballet (1970); *Mariana Pineda*, theater music (1975); film music. **ORCH.:** *Políptico* for Chamber Orch. (1960); *Sobreposições* (1960); Saxophone Concerto (1961); *Diafonia* for Harp, Harpsichord, Piano, Celesta, Percussion, and Strings (1962–65); *Kinetofonias* for 25 Strings and 3 Tapes (1965–69); *Nomos* (1967); *Sucessões simétricas II* (1971) and *III* for Chamber Orch. (1974); *Voix-en-jeux* (1972–76); *Retrato de Helena* (1982); *Concerto de outono* for Oboe and Orch. (1983); *Viagem da natural invenção* (1991). **CHAMBER:** *Do espressioni* for Trumpet and Harpsichord (1959); *Evocação* for Flute, Oboe, Clarinet, Harp, Vibraphone, and Xylophone (1960); *Episodios* for String Quartet (1960); *Imagens sonoras* for 2 Harps (1962); *Domino* for Flute and Percussion (1963–64); *Sequência* for Flute, Celesta, and Percussion (1963–64); *Morfocromia* for 12 Instruments (1963–68); *Situações 66* for Flute, Clarinet, Trumpet, Harp, and Viola (1966); *Recitativo III* for Flute, Harp, and Percussion (1966–69), *V* for Octet (1966–74), *I* for Harp (1971), and *IV* for 8 Instruments (1974); *As quatro estações* for Trumpet, Harp, Piano, and Cello (1968–72); *C D E* for Clarinet, Violin, Cello, and Piano (1970); *A idade do ouro* for 2 Clarinets, 2 Violins, Organ, Piano, Harp, and Harpsichord (1970–73); *Quatro pecas para setembro vermelho* for Chamber Ensemble (1972); *Ma Fin est mon commencement: Homage to Machaut* for Trombone, Viol, Viola, Harp, Recorders, Piano, and Celesta (1972); *Welkom* for Violin and Viola (1972); *Morrer em Santiago* for 6 Percussion (1973); *...e isto é só o início, hein?* for Chamber Ensemble (1975); *A aurora do socialismo: Madrigale capriccioso* for Flute, Horn, Violin, Piano, Percussion, and Short Wave Receiver (1975); *Canto da sibila* for Clarinet, Piano, Percussion, Lights, and Smells (1976); *Solo* for Double Bass (1976); *Elegia* for Trombone, Viola, Piano, and Percussion (1976); *Madrigal II* for Clarinet Quintet (1977); *Música en água e mármore* for 7 Instruments (1977); *Lov II* for Cello, Flute, Piano, and Percussion (1978); *Faites vox jeux* for Flute, Cello, Harp, and Piano (1979–81); *Mémoires...miroirs...* for Amplified Clavichord and 12 Strings (1980); *Warsaw Workshop Waltz* for Clarinet, Trombone, Cello, and Piano (1980); *Ciclo-Valsa* for Variable Instrumental Ensemble, Percussion, Velophonem, Music Boxes, and Voices ad libitum (1980–85); *Novo canto da sibila* for Clarinet, Piano, and Percussion (1981); *Sax-Blue* for Alto Saxophone or Sopranino Saxophone and Electro-acoustics (1982–85); *Serenata per A* for Flutes, Guitar, Piano, and Percussion (1983); *O jardim de Belisa* for 7 Instruments (1984); *Metaformoses* for Bass Clarinet and 7 Instruments (1984); *Remake* for Flute, Cello, Harp, and Piano (1985); *Ougam a soma dos sons que soam* for 9 Instruments (1986); *O quadrado azul* for Oboe, Viola, Double Bass, and Piano (1987); *Passage intérieur* for Saxophone and Electric Instruments (1989); *Alis* for 15 Instruments (1990); *Glosa I* for Piano, *II* for Flute, *III* for Violin, and *IV* for Cello (all 1990); *Fantasia- impromptu* for Alto Saxophone and Piano (1990); *Mediterrânea* for 7 or 8 Instruments (1991). **VOCAL:** *Fascinação* for Soprano, Flute, and Clarinet (1959); *Alba* for Soprano, Mezzo-soprano, Wom-

en's Chorus, and 11 Instruments (1959); *Triptico* for Solo Voices and Instrumental Ensemble (1959–60); *A cabeça do grifo* for Soprano, Mandolin, and Piano (1960; also for Soprano, Viola, Harp, and Piano, 1980); *Coração habitado* for Mezzo-soprano, Flute, Cello, and Piano (1965); *Euridice reamada* for Solo Voices, Chorus, and Orch. (1968); *Voix* for Mezzo-soprano and Chamber Orch. (1972); *A lira destemperada* for Soprano, Trombone, and Percussion (1973); *Madrigal* for Chorus (1975); *Leves veus celam* for Soprano, Flute, Viola, Harp, and Marimba (1980); *Canto para Anna Livia* for 3 Women's Voices and 11 Instruments (1981); *A flor das águas verdes* for 15 Voices (1982); *Ulivi aspri e forti* for Mezzo-soprano and Piano (1982; also for Mezzo- soprano, Flute, Clarinet, Trumpet, Harp, Guitar, Viola, and Cello, 1984); *Greetings* for Mezzo-soprano, Flute, Bassoon, Cello, and Percussion (1985); *Llanto por Mariana* for Soprano, Flute, Clarinet, Piano, and String Quartet (1986); *Credo* for Tenor, Alto Saxophone, Piano, Double Bass, and Percussion (1988); *A capela de Janas* for Soprano and Instrumental Ensemble (1989); *Memoria de Marília* for Soprano, Baritone, Oboe, Clarinet, 2 Guitars, Violin, and Cello (1990); *Cantos de Sophia* for Chorus (1990). **ELECTRONIC:** *Elegia a Amilcar Cabral* (1973); *Luis Vaz 73* (1973–74); *Electronicolirica* (1979); *Canto germinal* (1989).—NS/LK/DM

Pękiel, Bartłomiej, important Polish composer; b. place and date unknown; d. probably in Kraków, c. 1670. He served as organist at the Polish royal court in Warsaw, where he also was deputy director of music. In 1649 he assumed the duties of director of music, and in 1653 he was formally named to that position. In 1656 he settled in Kraków, where he was made director of music at the Wawel Cathedral Chapel in 1658. Pękiel was the principal Polish composer of his day, excelling in sacred music. He composed concertato polychoral masses, a cappella masses, motets, and organ music. His most notable work is his *Missa pulcherrima ad instar Praenestini* for 4 Voices (1669).

BIBL.: H. Feicht, *Komppzycje religijne B.a. P.a.* (The Sacred Compositions of B. P.; Lwów, 1923–24).—LK/DM

Pekinel, Güher and Süher, remarkable Turkish-Spanish duo pianist; b. identical twins, Istanbul, March 29, 1951. They were only 5 when they began piano lessons with their mother. At 6, they played for the first time in public. When they were 9 they attracted wide notice when they appeared with the Ankara Phil. in a broadcast throughout Turkey. At 12, they went to Paris to pursue training with Loriod at the Cons. They continued their studies with August Leopolder at the Frankfurt am Main Hochschule für Musik, and Güher took a degree in psychology and Süher a degree in philosophy at the Johann Wolfgang Goethe Univ. in Frankfurt am Main. Following additional studies at the Curtis Inst. of Music in Philadelphia, where they received training as soloists under Serkin and as duo artists under Horszowski, they completed their studies at the Juilliard School in N.Y. under Adele Marcus. In 1978 they captured 1st prize at the UNESCO World Music Week in Bratislava. Thereafter they pursued a highly rewarding career in appearances with major orchs. and festival throughout the world.—NS/LK/DM

Pelemans, Willem, Belgian composer; b. Antwerp, April 8, 1901; d. Brussels, Oct. 28, 1991. He studied music history at the Malines Cons. A highly prolific composer, he adopted an attractive idiom of writing music in a Romantic manner.

WORKS: DRAMATIC: *La Rose de Bakawali*, chamber opera (1938); *Het tinnen soldaatje*, musical play, after Andersen (1945); *Floris en Blancefloer*, lyric drama (1947); *Le Combat de la vierge et du diable*, chamber opera (1949); *De mannen van Smeerop* (1952); *De nozem en de nimf*, chamber opera (1960). **Ballet:** *Miles gloriosus* (1945); *Herfstgoud* (1959); *Pas de quatre* (1969). **ORCH.:** Concertos: one each for Harpsichord (1931), Violin (1954), Viola (1963), 2 Trumpets and Strings (1963), Organ (1965), 2 Pianos (1973), Saxophone (1973), and Clarinet Quartet (1983), 3 for Piano (1945, 1950, 1967), and 7 for Orch. (1948–83); 8 ballades (1933–35); 6 syms. (1936, 1937, 1937, 1938, 1938, 1939); 5 concertinos (1948–66); *Schetsen voor een buffa-opera* for Chamber Orch. (1952); *Ouvertura buffa* (1959); *Petite suite* (1962). **CHAMBER:** 3 piano trios (1932, 1942, 1972); 3 trios for Oboe, Clarinet, and Bassoon (1940, 1941, 1960); 8 string quartets (1942, 1943, 1943, 1943, 1944, 1955, 1961, 1970); 3 violin sonatas (all 1942); String Trio (1945); Viola Sonata (1945); Sonata for Cello and Bassoon (1946); Sonata for Solo Cello (1947); 2 wind quintets (1948, 1968); Quintet for Flute, Clarinet, Violin, Viola, and Cello (1950); 2 sonatas for Flute, Oboe, and Piano (1955, 1956); Sonata for Trumpet, Horn, and Trombone (1955); Sonata for Solo Violin (1955); Cello Sonata (1959); Sonata for Flute and Harpsichord or Piano (1959); 2 clarinet quartets (1961, 1976); Clarinet Sonata (1961); Quintet for Harp, Flute, Violin, Viola, and Cello (1962); Saxophone Quartet (1965); Wind Quartet (1965); Piano Quartet (1967); Sonata for Flute and Harp (1967); Sonata for 2 Guitars (1967); Brass Sextet (1968); Trio for 2 Oboes and English Horn (1971). **Piano:** 4 suites (1932–33); 19 sonatas (1935–69); *10 Banalities* (1944); 2 sonatas for 2 Pianos (1947, 1954); 3 toccatas (1948, 1951, 1951); Sonata for Piano, 4-Hands (1961). **VOCAL:** *De wandelende jood*, oratorio (1929); *Van Ostaijen*, suite for Soprano, Tenor, Women's Chorus, Men's Chorus, and Orch. (1980–81); cantatas; songs.—**NS/LK/DM**

Pélissier, Marie, French singer; b. 1707; d. Paris, March 21, 1749. She made her debut at the Paris Opéra in 1722. After marrying the theater impresario Pélissier in 1725, she appeared at his theater in Rouen until it went bankrupt. Returning to Paris, she was a principal singer at the Académie Royale (1726–34; 1735–41), where she created roles in numerous works, including Rameau's Aricia in *Hippolyte et Aricie* (1733), Emilie in *Les Indes galantes* (1735), Telaïre in *Castor et Pollux* (1737), and Iphis in both *Les fêtes d'Hébé* (1739) and *Dardanus* (1739).—**NS/LK/DM**

Pelissier, Victor, French-American horn player, arranger, and composer; b. probably in Paris, c. 1745; d. c. 1820. His name appears first in 1792 on Philadelphia concert programs as "first horn of the Theatre in Cape François." In 1793 he went to N.Y., where he lived for many years and became the principal horn player, also composer and arranger, of the Old American Co. He composed one of the earliest and most influential melodramas in the U.S., *Ariadne Abandoned by Theseus in the Isle of Naxos* (N.Y., 1797); also publ. the collection *Pelissier's Columbia Melodies* (12 vols., Philadelphia, 1811–12; ed. by K. Kroeger in Recent Researches in American Music, XIII-XIV, 1984), consisting of piano arrangements of instrumental works, dances, and

songs. His other works include the operas *Edwin and Angelina, or The Banditti* (N.Y., Dec. 19, 1796) and *Sterne's Maria, or The Vintage* (N.Y., Jan. 14, 1799), various pantomimes, most of them lost, incidental music, most notably to W. Dunlap's *The Voice of Nature* (N.Y., 1803), a number of instrumental pieces, etc.—**NS/LK/DM**

Pellegrin, Claude Mathieu, French organist and composer; b. Aix-en-Provence, Oct. 25, 1682; d. there, Oct. 10, 1763. He entered the Sauveur choir school in 1696 and studied with the maître de chapelle Poitevin, whom he succeeded as organist at Aix Cathedral in 1706. In 1717 he was ordained a priest and in 1719 he was made beneficier. After serving as chapelain ordinaire at Sainte-Chapelle in Paris (1724–31), he resumed his post at Aix Cathedral, which he retained until 1748. He composed a Te Deum (1745), 2 Magnificats, and several motets.—**LK/DM**

Pellegrini, Valeriano, Italian castrato soprano and composer; b. Verona, date unknown; d. after 1729. He was in the service of the elector palatine in Düsseldorf from about 1705 until 1716. He also was active in London, where he made his concert debut on April 9, 1712, and was principal castrato at the Queen's Theatre, where he created Handel's Mirtillo in *Il pastor fido* (Nov. 22, 1712) and Teseo (Jan. 10, 1713). From 1716 he pursued his career in Italy. He spent his last years in Rome as a priest.—**NS/LK/DM**

Pellegrini, Vincenzo, Italian composer and organist; b. Pesaro, date unknown; d. Milan, c. 1631. He became a priest, serving at Pesaro Cathedral (1594–1612), then was maestro di cappella at Milan Cathedral (1612–31). His extant works include *Canzoni de intavolatura d'organo fatte alla francese, libro primo* (Venice, 1599; ed. in Corpus of Early Keyboard Music, XXXV, 1972), Missae for 4 to 5 Voices (Venice, 1603), and sacred vocal pieces with organ accompaniment, publ. under the title *Concerti ecclesiastici da 1, 2, 3, 5 e 6 voci* (Venice, 1619). Other compositions are in the collections *Parnassus musicus Ferdinandoeus* (Venice, 1615). —**NS/LK/DM**

Pelletier, (Louis) Wilfred, noted Canadian conductor and music educator; b. Montreal, June 20, 1896; d. N.Y., April 9, 1982. His father, a baker by trade, was an amateur musician who gave Pelletier his primary instruction. At the age of 14, he played piano in the orch. of the National Theatre in Montreal, and in 1915 he won the Prix d'Europe and went to Paris, where he studied piano with Philipp, composition with Widor, and opera repertoire with Bellaigue. In 1917 he returned to America and was engaged as rehearsal pianist at the Metropolitan Opera in N.Y.; in 1921 he was appointed an asst. conductor there; from 1928 to 1950 he was a principal conductor there, specializing in the French repertoire; in 1936 he founded the popular Metropolitan Opera Auditions of the Air. He also was active as a conductor in Canada; from 1935 to 1951 he was conductor of the Société des Concerts Symphoniques de Montréal, and from 1951 to 1966, of the Orchestre Symphonique de Québec. From 1943 to 1961 he served as director of the Cons. de Musique in Montreal. In 1968 he was made a Companion of the Order of Canada. He was married consecutively to **Queena Mario** (1925–36) and **Rose Bampton** (from 1937). He publ. an autobiographical sketch, *Une Symphonie inachevée* (Quebec, 1972). —NS/LK/DM

Peñalosa, Francisco de, important Spanish composer; b. Talavera de la Reina, c. 1470; d. Seville, April 1, 1528. In 1498 he became a singer in the chapel choir of Ferdinand V. The King obtained a canonry (in absentia) for him in 1505 at the Seville Cathedral; in 1506 the Cathedral authorities revoked the appointment, but by 1510 he was able to fulfill the residence requirement. In 1511 the King made him maestro de capilla to his grandson. In 1512 he went to the royal monastery of S. Pedro de Cardena, near Burgos. In 1516 he returned to Seville, where he assumed administrative duties at the Cathedral. In 1517 he became chamberlain and singer at the papal chapel; in 1518 he resigned his canonry at Seville Cathedral to become archdeacon of Carmona. In 1521 he resumed his canonry at Seville Cathedral, where he remained until his death. Penalosa was one of the most important composers of his era, a master of polyphonic sacred and secular music. His sacred works include masses, Magnificats, motets, and hymns. Some of them are found in H. Eslava y Elizondo, ed., Lira Sacro-Hispaña (1st series, vol. I, Madrid, 1869). —NS/LK/DM

Penderecki, Krzysztof, eminent Polish composer, pedagogue, and conductor; b. Dębica, Nov. 23, 1933. He went to Kraków, where he studied composition privately with Franciszek Skołyszewski before pursuing training at the State Higher School of Music (1955–58) with Artur Malawski and Stanisław Wiechowicz. In 1958 he joined its faculty as a lecturer in composition, where he later was prof. (from 1972) and rector (1972–87). In 1959 he won the 1st, 2nd, and 3rd prizes in the Young Composers' Competition of the Polish Composers' Union. His *Tren "Ofiarom Hiroszimy"* (Threnody "to the Victims of Hiroshima") for 52 Strings (Warsaw, May 31, 1960) won the prize of the International Rostrum of Composers in Paris in 1961. From 1966 to 1968 he was an assoc. prof. at the Essen Folkwang-Hochschule. His *Passio et mors Domini Nostri Jesu Christi secundum Lucam* for Solo Voices, Speaking Voice, Boy's Chorus, Mixed Chorus, and Orch. (Münster, March 30, 1966) won the Prix Italia in 1967, and his *Dies irae Oratorium ob memoriam in perniciei castris in Oświęcim necatorum inexstinguibilem reddendam* (Dies irae Oratorio in memory of the victims of Asuchwitz) for Soloists, Chorus, and Orch. (Kraków, April 14, 1967) won another Prix Italia in 1968. In 1970 he received the award of the Polish Composers' Union. Penderecki made his conducting debut with the London Sym. Orch. in 1973, and in subsequent years appeared as a guest conductor with leading world orchs. In 1988 he became principal guest conductor of the North German Radio Sym. Orch. in Hamburg. He conducted the Sinfonia Varsovia on a tour of the U.S. in 1995. Penderecki publ. the vol. *Labirynt czasu: Pięć wykładów na koniec wieku*

(Warsaw, 1997; Eng. tr., 1998, as *Labyrinth of Time: Five Addresses for the End of the Millennium*). His honors have been numerous. In 1977 he was awarded the Gottfried von Herder Prize of the F.v.S. Foundation of Hamburg. He received the Sibelius Prize of the Wihouri Foundation in 1983. In 1985 he was honored with the Premio Lorenzo Magnifico. The Federal Republic of Germany decorated him with the Great Cross of Merit of the Order of Merit in 1990. In 1992 he received the Grawemeyer Award of the Univ. of Louisville. In 1993 he was decorated with the Commander's Cross with Star of the Polonia Restituta Order, and also received the International Music Council/UNESCO Music Prize. In addition to several honorary doctorates, he holds honorary memberships with the Royal Academy of Music in London, the Accademia Nazionale di Santa Cecilia in Rome, the Royal Academy of Music in Stockholm, and the Akademie der Künste in Berlin, among others.

Very early in his career, Penderecki assumed a leading position among the figures of the Polish avantgarde. He created a hyper-modern technique of composition in a highly individual style, in which no demarcation line was drawn between consonances and dissonances, tonal or atonal melody, traditional or innovative instrumentation; an egalitarian attitude prevailed toward all available resources of sound. While his idiom is naturally complex, he did not disdain tonality, even in its overt triadic forms. In his creative evolution, he bypassed orthodox serial procedures; his music followed an athematic course, in constantly varying metrical and rhythmic patterns. He expanded the domain of tone to unpitched elements, making use of such effects as shouting, hissing, and verbal ejaculations in vocal parts, at times reaching a climax of aleatory glossolalia; tapping, rubbing, or snapping the fingers against the body of an instrument; striking the piano strings with mallets, etc. From the 1970s he explored more conservative byways as a composer, although his works continue to challenge both performers and audiences. Indeed, his opera *Die schwarze Maske* (Salzburg, Aug. 15, 1986) demonstrates Penderecki's penchant for creating works that continue to elicit a determined response for their progressive tendencies.

WORKS: DRAMATIC: *Diabły z Loudun* (Die Teufel von Loudun; The Devils of Loudun), opera (1968–69; Hamburg, June 20, 1969); *Raj utracony* (Paradise Lost), sacra rappresentazione (1976–78; Chicago, Nov. 29, 1978); *Czarna maska* (Die schwarze Maske), opera (1984–86; Salzburg, Aug. 15, 1986); *Ubu Rex*, opera buffa (1990–91; Munich, July 6, 1991). **ORCH.:** *Epitaphium Artur Malawski in memoriam* for Strings and Timpani (1957–58; Kraków, Sept. 1958); *Emanacje* (Emanations) for 2 String Orchs. (1958–59; Darmstadt, Oct. 7, 1961); *Tren "Ofiarom Hiroszimy"* (Threnody "to the Victims of Hiroshima") for 52 Strings (1959–60; Warsaw, May 31, 1960); *Anaklasis* for Strings and Percussion (1959–60; Donaueschingen, Oct. 16, 1960); *Fonogrammi* for Flute and Chamber Orch. (Venice April 24, 1961); *Polymorphia* for 48 Strings (1961; Hamburg, April 16, 1962); *Kanon* for 52 Strings and Tape (Warsaw, Sept. 20, 1962); *Drei Stücke im alte Stil* for Strings, after the film *Die Handschrift von Saragossa* (1963; Kraków, June 11, 1988); Sonata for Cello and Orch. (Donaueschingen, Oct. 15, 1964); *Capriccio* for Oboe and 11 Strings (1964–65; Lucerne, Aug. 26, 1965); *De natura sonoris I* (Royan, April 7, 1966) and II (1970–71; N.Y., Dec. 3, 1971);

Violino Grande Concerto (1966–67; Östersund, Sweden, July 1, 1967); 2 cello concertos: No. 1 (1966–67; rev. 1971–72; Edinburgh, Sept. 2, 1972) and No. 2 (1982; Berlin, Jan. 11, 1983); *Uwertura pittsburska* (Pittsburgh Overture) for Wind Orch., Percussion, Piano, and Double Basses (Pittsburgh, June 30, 1967); *Capriccio* for Violin and Orch. (Donaueschingen, Oct. 22, 1967); *Preludium* for Winds, Percussion, and Contrabasses (Amsterdam, July 4, 1971); *Actions* for Jazz Ensemble (Donaueschingen, Oct. 17, 1971); *Partita* for Harpsichord, Electric Guitar, Bass Guitar, Harp, Double Bass, and Orch. (1971–72; Rochester, N.Y., Feb. 11, 1972; rev. 1991–92; Munich, Jan. 5, 1992); 7 syms.: No. 1 (1972–73; Peterborough, England, July 19, 1973), No. 2, *Wigilijna* (Christmas; 1979–80; N.Y., May 1, 1980), No. 3 (1988; Munich, Dec. 8, 1995), No. 4, *Adagio* (Paris, Nov. 26, 1989), No. 5, *Koreańska* (Korean; 1991–92; Seoul, Aug. 14, 1992), No. 6 (n.d.), and No. 7, *Siedem Bram Jerozolimy* (Seven Gates of Jerusalem) for Solo Voices, Chorus, and Orch. (1996; Jerusalem, Jan. 9, 1997); *Intermezzo* for 24 Strings (Zürich, Nov. 30, 1973); *Przebudzenie Jakuba* (The Awakening of Jacob; Monte Carlo, Aug. 14, 1974); 2 violin concertos: No. 1 (1976–77; Basel, April 27, 1977; rev. 1988) and No. 2, *Metamorphosen* (1992–95; Leipzig, June 24, 1995); *Adagietto z "Raju utraconego"* (Adagietto from "Paradise Lost"; Osaka, April 8, 1979); Viola Concerto (Caracas, July 21, 1983; also for Viola and Chamber Orch., 1984; Moscow, Oct. 20, 1985; as a Cello Concerto, 1984; Wuppertal, Dec. 15, 1989; as a Clarinet Concerto, 1984; Boulder, July 9, 1995); 2 sinfoniettas: No. 1 for Strings (1990–92; Warsaw, Feb. 17, 1992) and No. 2 for Clarinet and Strings (Bad Kissingen, July 13, 1994); Concerto for Flute and Chamber Orch. (1992; Lausanne, Jan. 11, 1993; as a Clarinet Concerto, 1995; Prague, March 7, 1996); *Entrata* for 4 Horns, 3 Trumpets, 3 Trombones, Tuba, and Timpani (Cincinnati, Nov. 4, 1994); *Agnus Dei z "Polskiego Requiem"* (Agnus Dei from "Polish Requiem") for Strings (Kraków, Dec. 4, 1994); Serenade for Strings (1996–97). **CHAMBER:** Violin Sonata (1953; Houston, Jan. 7, 1990); *Miniatures* for Clarinet and Piano (1954); *Miniatures* for Violin and Piano (1959; Kraków, June 1960); 2 string quartets: No. 1 (1960; Cincinnati, May 11, 1962) and No. 2 (1968; Berlin, Sept. 30, 1970); *Capriccio per Siegfried Palm* for Cello (Bremen, May 4, 1968); *Capriccio* for Tuba (1979–80; Kraków, June 20, 1980); *Cadenza* for Viola (Lusławice, Sept. 10, 1984; also for Violin, Warsaw, Oct. 28, 1986); *Per Slava* for Cello (1985–86); *Prélude* for Clarinet (1987); *Der unterbrochene Gedanke* for String Quartet (Frankfurt am Main, Feb. 4, 1988); Trio for Violin, Viola, and Cello (Kraków, Dec. 8, 1990); Quartet for Clarinet and String Trio (Lübeck, Aug. 13, 1993); *Divertimento* for Cello (Cologne, Dec. 28, 1994). **VOCAL:** *Prośba o wyspy szczęśliwe* (A Plea for the Happy Isles) for Voice and Piano (1957); *Psalmy Dawida* (Psalms of David) for Chorus, Strings, and Percussion (1958; Kraków, Sept. 1959); *Strofy* (Strophes) for Soprano, Speaking Voice, and 10 Instruments (Warsaw, Sept. 17, 1959); *Wymiary czasu i ciszy* (Dimensions of Time and Silence) for Chorus, Strings, and Percussion (1959–60; Warsaw, Sept. 18, 1960); *Stabat Mater* for 3 Choruses (Warsaw, Nov. 27, 1962); *Brygada śmierci* (The Death Brigade) for Reciter and Tape (1963); *Passio et mors Domini Nostri Jesu Christi secundum Lucam* for Soloists, Speaking Voice, Boy's Chorus, Mixed Chorus, and Orch. (1963–66; Münster, March 30, 1966); *Cantata in honorem Almae Matris Universitatis Iagellonicae sescentos abhinc annos fundatae* for Chorus and Orch. (Kraków, May 10, 1964); *Dies irae Oratorium ob memoriam in perniciei castris in Oświęcim necatorum inexstinguibilem reddendam* (Dies irae Oratorio in memory of the victims of Auschwitz) for Soloists, Chorus, and Orch. (Kraków, April 14, 1967); *Jutrznia I: Złożenie Chrystusa do grobu* (Utrenja I: The Entombment of Christ) for Soloists, 2 Choruses, and Orch. (1969–70; Altenberg, April 8, 1970) and *II: Zmartwychwstanie Pański* (The Resurrection of Christ) for Soloists, Chorus, Boy's Chorus, and Orch. (1970–71; Münster, May 28, 1971); *Kosmogonia* for Solo Voices, Chorus, and Orch. (N.Y., Oct. 24, 1970); *Canticum canticorum Salomonis quod hebraice dicitur "Sir hasirim"* for Chorus and Orch. (1970–73; Lisbon, June 5, 1973); *Ecloga VIII* for 6 Men's Voices (Edinburgh, Aug. 22, 1972); *Magnificat* for Bass, Vocal Ensemble, 2 Mixed Choruses, Boy's Chorus, and Orch. (1973–74; Salzburg, Aug. 17, 1974); *Te Deum* for Soloists, Chorus, and Orch. (1978–80; Assisi, Sept. 27, 1980); *Vorspiel, Visionen und Finale aus "Paradise Lost"* for 6 Solo Voices, Chorus, and Orch. (Salzburg, Aug. 10, 1979); *Lacrimosa z "Polskiego Requiem"* (Lacrimosa from "Polish Requiem") for Soprano, Chorus, and Orch. (Gdańsk, Dec. 16, 1980); *Polskie Requiem* (Polish Requiem) for Soloists, Chorus, and Orch. (1980–84; Stuttgart, Sept. 28, 1984; rev. version, Stockholm, Nov. 11, 1993); *Agnus Dei z "Polskiego Requiem"* (Agnus Dei from "Polish Requiem") for Chorus (Warsaw, May 31, 1981); *Pieśń Cherubinów* (Cherubim Song) for Chorus (1986; Washington, D.C., March 27, 1987); *Veni Creator* for Chorus (Madrid, April 28, 1987); *Benedicamus Domino* for Men's Chorus (1991–92; Lucerne, April 18, 1992); *Benedictus* for Chorus (1993); *Agnus Dei aus "Requiem der Versöhnung"* (Agnus Dei for the "Requiem of Reconciliation") for Soloists, Chorus, and Orch. (Stuttgart, Aug. 15, 1995); *Credo* for Soloists, Chorus, and Orch. (1996–98; Eugene, Ore., July 11, 1998); *Hymn do świętego Daniela* (Hymn to the Holy Daniel) for Chorus and Winds (Moscow, Oct. 4, 1997); *Hymn do świętego Wojciecha* (Hymn to the Holy Adalbert) for Chorus and Winds (Gdańsk, Oct. 18, 1997). **TAPE:** *Psalmus 1961* (Stockholm, April 10, 1961); *Ekecheiria* (Munich, Aug. 26, 1972).

BIBL.: K. Lisicki, *Szkice o K. P.* (Sketches on K. P.; Warsaw, 1973); L. Erhardt, *Spotkania z K. P.* (Encounter with K. P.; Kraków, 1975); R. Robinson and A. Winold, *A Study of the P. St. Luke Passion* (Celle, 1983); W. Schwinger, *K. P.: Leben und Werk* (Mainz, 1994); M. Tomaszewski, ed., *The Music of K. P.: Poetics and Reception* (Kraków, 1995); B. Malecka-Contamin, *K. P.: Style et Matériaux* (Paris, 1997); D. Mirka, *The Sonoristic Structuralism of K. P.* (Katowice, 1997); *Studies in P.* (Princeton, 1998). **—NS/LK/DM**

Penet, Hilaire, French composer; b. Poitiers diocese, c. 1501; d. place and date unknown. He was in Rome by 1514, where he was a papal choirboy. By 1516 he was a member of the papal cappella. In 1519 he entered the papal private cappella, but left Rome in 1520. His motet *Descendit angelus Domini* influenced both Porta and Palestrina. In addition to other sacred works, he also wrote several cantatas.—**LK/DM**

Penherski, Zbigniew, Polish composer; b. Warsaw, Jan. 26, 1935. He received training in composition from Stefan Poradowski at the State Higher School of Music in Poznań (1955–59) and conducting with Bohdan Wodiczko (1960–63) at the State Higher School of Music in Warsaw. In 1969 he received a Dutch government scholarship. He received the Silver Cross of Merit from the Polish government in 1975, and in 1982 the Minister of Culture and Arts Award, 1st Class.

WORKS: DRAMATIC: *Sąd nad Samsonem* (Samson Put on Trial), radio opera (1967; Warsaw, Sept. 23, 1969); *Zmierzch Peryna* (Peryn's Twilight), opera (1972; Poznań, Oct. 6, 1974); *Edgar, syn Walpora* (Edgar, Son of Walpor), opera (1982); *Wyspa* *róż* (The Island of Roses), chamber opera (1989). **ORCH.:** *Kroniki mazurski II* (Mazurian Chronicles II) for Orch. and Tape (1973; Warsaw, Sept. 27, 1985); *Anamnesis* (1975; Kraków, May 19, 1978); *Kroniki szkockie* (Scottish Chronicles; Glasgow, May 29, 1987); *Intermezzo* for Chamber Orch. (1990); *Sygnaly I* (Signals; Warsaw, Sept. 8, 1992) and *II* (Warsaw, Sept. 20, 1995); *X-Play* for 30 Flutes (1999). **CHAMBER:** Suite for Oboe and Piano (1963); *Muzyka uliczna* (Street Music) for Chamber Ensemble (1966); Quartet for Piano or Other Keyboard Instrument and 3 Optional Instruments (1970); *Incantationi I* for 6 Percussionists (1972; Berlin, Feb. 18, 1973); *Symfonia radiowa* (Radio Symphony) for 2 Players (1974); *String Play* for Strings and 3 Metronomes (Ludźmierz, March 2, 1980); *Jeux parties* for Saxophone and Percussion (Warsaw, Sept. 24, 1984); *Scherzino* for 4 Violins (1985); *Introjukcja* (Introduction) for Clarinet, Trombone, and Cello (Warsaw, Sept. 17, 1994); *Toccata* for Clarinet, Trombone, Cello, and Piano (1998); *Scherzino* for Street Bells, Flute, Clarinet, 3 Trumpets, and 2 Percussion (1988); *Liryczny walc* (Lyric Waltz) for Street Bells, Flute, 3 Trumpets, and 2 Percussion (1998); *Muzycka na koniec wieku* (Little Music for the End of the Century) for Recorder, 2 Percussion, Organ, and Tape (Warsaw, Sept. 24, 1999). **P i a n o :** 4 Preludes (1956); *Kolorowe etiudy* (Studies in Color; 1961); *Trzy łatwe utwory* (Three Easy Pieces; 1997). **VOCAL:** 2 Lullabies for Mezzo-soprano and Piano (1955); 3 Songs for Soprano and Piano (1955); *Obrazki chóralne* (Choral Pictures) for Chorus (1960); *Ostinata* for Chorus and Orch. (1960); *Trzy pieśni cygański* (Three Gypsy Songs) for Women's Chorus (1961); *Trzy pieśni do tekstów staropolskich* (Three Songs to Old Polish Texts) for Chorus (1961); *Pieśni dziecięce* (Children's Songs) for Soprano, Reciter, and Instrumental Ensemble (1962); *Kontrasty* (Contrasts) for Vocal Ensemble, Instruments, and String Orch. (1962; Lublin, March 5, 1965); *Musica humana* for Baritone, Chorus, and Orch. (1963; Warsaw, Jan. 20, 1967); *Missa abstracta* for Tenor, Reciter, Chorus, and Orch. (Kragujevac, Oct. 21, 1966); *Trzy recytatywy* (Three Recitatives) for Soprano, Piano, and Percussion (1968); *Cantatina* for Chorus and Orch. (1969); *Hymnus laudans* for Chorus and Chamber Orch. (1970; Wrocław, Feb. 24, 1972); *Trzy impresje* (Three Impressions) for Soprano, Piano, and 4 Percussionists (1985); *Cantus* for Chorus (1992). **TAPE:** *3M- HI* (1969; Warsaw, Sept. 21, 1970).—**NS/LK/DM**

Penna, Lorenzo, Italian composer; b. Bologna, 1613; d. there, Oct. 31, 1693. He studied at the Univ. of Ferrara. In 1630 he entered the Carmelite monastery of S. Martino in Bologna, becoming maestro di cappella at S. Illario in Casale Monferrato (1656). In 1665 he received his doctorate in theology from the Univ. of Ferrara. He was then maestro di cappella at S. Cassiano in Imola (1667–69), and in 1669 entered the Carmelite Order in Mantua, remaining until 1672. Subsequently he was maestro di cappella at the church of the Carmine in Parma (1672–73). In 1676 he became a member of the Accademia dei Filarmonici in Bologna, where he remained until his death.

WORKS: *Messe e salmi concertati* for 5 Voices, 2 Violins ad libitum, and Basso Continuo (1656); *Psalmorum totius anni modulatio...* for 4 to 5 Voices (1669); *Correnti francesi a quattro,* with String Instruments (1673; designated as "Sonate" in the dedication); *Il sacro Parnaso delli salmi festivi* for 4 to 8 Voices (1677); *Reggia del sacro Parnaso...* for 4 to 8 Voices (1677); *Galeria del sacro Parnaso...* for 4 to 8 Voices, with Instrumental Accompaniment ad libitum (1678).

WRITINGS: *Li primi albori musicali per li principianti della*

musica figurata (Bologna, 1672; 5th ed., 1696); *Direttorio del canto fermo* (1689).

BIBL.: J.-H. Lederer, *L. P. und seine Kontrapunkttheorie* (diss., Univ. of Graz, 1970).—**NS/LK/DM**

Pennario, Leonard, brilliant American pianist; b. Buffalo, July 9, 1924. He received instruction from Guy Maier, Isabelle Vengerova, and Olga Steeb (piano) and Ernst Toch (composition). He played in public at 7, and made his formal debut as soloist in the Grieg Concerto with the Dallas Sym. Orch. when he was 12. He made his Carnegie Hall debut as soloist in Liszt's 1st Concerto with the N.Y. Phil (Nov. 17, 1943), toured Europe for the first time (1952), and subsequently appeared throughout the world. He played chamber music with Heifetz and Piatigorsky; was active as a teacher.—**NS/LK/DM**

Pentland, Barbara (Lally), Canadian composer and teacher; b. Winnipeg, Jan. 2, 1912; d. Vancouver, Feb. 6, 2000. After taking piano lessons at a Montreal boarding school, she went to N.Y. and studied with Jacobi and Wagenaar at the Juilliard School of Music (1936–39). She also took summer courses with Copland at the Berkshire Music Center in Tanglewood (summers, 1941–42). She was an instructor at the Toronto Cons. (1943–49) and the Univ. of British Columbia in Vancouver (1949–63). In her compositions, Pentland adopted a pragmatic method of cosmopolitan modernism, employing dissonant linear counterpoint and dodecaphonic melodic structures within the framework of Classical forms.

WORKS: DRAMATIC: *Beauty and the Beast,* ballet-pantomine (1940); *The Lake,* chamber opera (1952; Vancouver, March 3, 1954). **ORCH.:** *Concert Overture* (1935); *2 Pieces* for Strings (1938); *Lament* (1939); *Holiday Suite* for Chamber Orch. (1941); *Arioso and Rondo* (1941); Concerto for Violin and Small Orch. (1942); 4 syms.: No. 1 (1945–48), No. 2 (1950; Toronto, Feb. 9, 1953), No. 3, *Symphony in 10 Parts* for Chamber Ensemble (1957; Vancouver, Sept. 18, 1959), and No. 4 (1959); *Colony Music* for Piano and Strings (1947); *Variations on a Boccherini Theme* (1948); Concerto for Organ and Strings (1949); *Ave atque vale* (1951); *Ricercar* for Strings (1955); Concerto for Piano and Strings (1956); *Strata* for Strings (1964); *Cine scene* for Chamber Orch. (1968); *Variations concertante* for Piano and Small Orch. (1970); *Res musica* for Strings (1975). **CHAMBER:** Piano Quartet (1939); Cello Sonata (1943); 5 string quartets (1945, 1953, 1969, 1980, 1985); *Vista* for Violin and Piano (1945); Violin Sonata (1946); Wind Octet (1948); *Weekend Overture* for Resort Combo of Clarinet, Trumpet, Piano, and Percussion (1949); Sonata for Solo Violin (1950); Sonatina for Solo Flute (1954); Piano Trio (1963); *Variations* for Viola (1965); *Trio con Alea* for String Trio (1966); Septet for Horn, Trumpet, Trombone, Violin, Viola, Cello, and Organ (1967); *Reflections* for Free Bass Accordion (1971); *Interplay* for Accordion and String Quartet (1972); *Occasions* for Brass Quintet (1974); *Trance* for Flute, Piano, and Harp (1978); *Eventa* for Flute, Clarinet, Trombone, 2 Percussion, Harp, Violin, and Cello (1978); *Elegy* for Horn and Piano (1980); *Tellus* for Flute, Cello, Piano, Percussion, and Celesta (1982); Piano Quintet (1983); *Tides* for Violin, Marimba, and Harp (1984); *Elegy* for Cello and Piano (1985). **P i a n o :** *Studies in Line* (1941); *Variations* (1942); Sonata (1945); *Sonata Fantasy* (1947); 2 sonatinas (1951); *Mirror Study* (1952); Sonata for 2 Pianos (1953); *Toccata* (1958); *3 Duets after Pictures by Paul Klee*

(1959); *Fantasy* (1962); *Puppet Show* (1964); *Shadows* (1964); *Signs* (1964); *Suite borealis* (1966); *Space Studies* (1967); *Arctica* for Young Pianists (1971–73); *Vita brevis* (1973); *Ephemera* (1974–78); *Tenebrae* (1976); *Vincula* (1983); *Horizons* (1985). **VOCAL:** *News* for Virtuoso Voice and Orch., after texts from the news media (1970); *Disasters of the Sun* for Mezzo-soprano, 9 Instruments, and Tape (1976); choruses; other songs.

BIBL.: S. Eastman and T. McGee, *B. P.* (Toronto, 1983). **—NS/LK/DM**

Pépin, (Jean-Josephat) Clermont,

Canadian composer; b. St.-Georges-de-Beauce, May 15, 1926. He studied piano and harmony as a child with Georgette Dionne, then piano with Arthur Letondal and harmony and counterpoint with Claude Champagne in Montreal (1937–41). He was a scholarship student of Jeanne Behrend (piano) and Rosario Scalero (composition) at the Curtis Inst. of Music in Philadelphia (diploma, 1945). After further training from Lubka Kolessa (piano) and Arnold Walter (composition) at the Toronto Cons., he won the Prix d'Europe (1949) and went to Paris to complete his composition studies with Jolivet, Honegger, and Messiaen. He taught composition at the Montreal Cons. from 1955 to 1964, and later was its director from 1967 to 1973. He taught there again from 1978 to 1987. In 1981 he was made an Officer of the Order of Canada and in 1990 an Officier of the Ordre national du Quebec. In his music, he has explored various aspects of serialism while adhering to classical forms.

WORKS: DRAMATIC: Ballet: *Les Portes de l'enfer* (1953); *L'Oiseaux-Phénix* (1956); *Le Porte-rêve* (1957–58). **ORCH.:** 2 piano concertos (1946, 1949); *Variations symphoniques* (1947); 5 syms.: No. 1 (1948), No. 2 (Montreal, Dec. 22, 1957), No. 3, *Quasars* (Montreal, Feb. 7, 1967), No. 4, *La Messe sur le monde*, for Narrator, Chorus, and Orch. (1975), and No. 5, *Implosion* (Montreal, Sept. 13, 1983); *Guernica*, symphonic poem after Picasso's painting (Quebec, Dec. 8, 1952); *Le Rite de soleil noir*, symphonic poem (Luxembourg, Sept. 1955); *Monologue* for Chamber Orch. (1961); *Nombres* for 2 Pianos and Orch. (Montreal, Feb. 6, 1963); *Monade* for Strings (1964); *Prismes et cristaux* for Strings (Montreal, April 9, 1974); *Monade* for Violin and Orch. (1972); *Chroma* (Guelph, Ontario, May 5, 1973); Marimba Concerto (1988). **CHAMBER:** Piano Sonata (1947); 5 string quartets (1948, 1955, 1956, 1960, 1976); *Musique pour Athalie* for Woodwinds and Brass (1956); Suite for Piano Trio (1958); *Sequences* for Flute, English Horn, Violin, Viola, and Cello (1972); *Monade IV-Réseaux* for Violin and Piano (1974); *Monade VI-Réseaux* for Violin (1974–76); *Interactions* for 7 Groups of Percussion and 2 Pianos (1977); Trio No. 2 for Violin, Cello, and Piano (1982); *Monade VII* for Violin and Piano (1986). **VOCAL:** *Cycle-Eluard* for Soprano and Piano (1948–49); *Hymne au vent du nord*, cantata (1960); *Paysage* for Soprano, Clarinet, Cello, and Piano (1987); *Trois incantations* for Voice and Piano (1987). **—NS/LK/DM**

Pepöck, August,

Austrian composer; b. Gmunden, May 10, 1887; d. there, Sept. 5, 1967. He studied in Vienna with Heuberger and R. Fuchs. He was active as a conductor of theater music in various provincial towns in Germany; subsequently lived mostly in Vienna. He scored great success with his operettas *Mädel ade!* (Vienna, Oct. 5, 1930) and *Der Reiter de Kaiserin* (Vienna, April 30, 1941). He also wrote some chamber music and songs.**—NS/LK/DM**

Pepper, Art(hur Edward Jr.),

famed and troubled jazz alto and tenor saxophonist, clarinetist; b. Gardena, Calif., Sept. 1, 1925; d. Panorama City, Calif., June 1, 1982. His father was of German origin; his mother was Italian. He played jazz clarinet and alto saxophone in school bands; he got married at 17 and was drafted into the U.S. Army. He played with Gus Arnheim's band as a teenager, but also frequently worked with black musicians on Central Avenue in Los Angeles. He joined Stan Kenton's band (1946–52), where he made his first recordings. He made more records, sometimes under the punning pseudonym Art Salt, with Chet Baker and others, but his highly promising career was ruined by his demonic addiction to heroin and other narcotic drugs. He squandered his earnings and, in desperate need of expensive drugs, descended into thievery and brawls. He was busted in 1952 on narcotics charges, and served time in the Los Angeles County jail; he was paroled to the U.S. Public Health Service Hospital at Fort Worth (1953–54), but got in trouble again, and was sentenced to jail in Los Angeles from 1954 to 1956. After his release, he made numerous recordings with Warne Marsh, Red Garland, and others. Unable to control his habits, Pepper was arrested as a recidivist and sent to San Quentin, where he served from 1961–64 and, after another transgression, in 1965–66. Finally freed, he played with Buddy Rich's Big Band (1968–69). From 1970–73, he was receiving treatment at the Synanon rehabilitation center, trying to kick his drug habit. In 1975, he returned to playing, working with Don Ellis. In 1977 and 1978, he completed two highly successful tours of Japan. His wife Laurie helped him to write *Straight Life* (1979), a brutally honest book, disturbing because at its end he had still not sworn off of drugs. He continued to record and tour until his death in 1982.

On such recordings as "What Is This Thing Called Love?" with Bill Perkins (1956), Pepper's bright fresh sound and improvisational clarity were truly uplifting. His later style incorporated influences from Coltrane that sat uneasily with his "cool" sound. He was the subject of the 1981 film, *Notes from a Jazz Survivor*. A film documentary on Pepper's life was presented at the Berlin Film Festival in 1982.

DISC.: *Surf Ride* (1952); *Rediscoveries* (1952); *Late Show: A Night at the Surf* (1952); *Early Show: A Night at the Surf* (1952); *Discoveries* (1952); *With Sonny Clark Trio, Vol. 1* (1953); *Return of Art Pepper: Complete* (1956); *Complete Pacific Jazz Small Group Sessions* (1956); *Meets the Rhythm Section* (1957); *Plus Eleven* (1959); *Modern Jazz Classics* (1959); *Art Pepper + Eleven: Modern Jazz Classics* (1959); *Smack Up* (1960); *Intensity* (1960); *Gettin' Together* (1960); *Art Pepper Quartet in San Francisco* (1964); *Living Legend* (1975); *I'll Remember April: Live* (1975); *Trip* (1976); *Complete Village Vanguard Sessions* (1977); *Live in Japan, Vol. 1, 2* (1978); *Complete Galaxy Recordings* (1978); *Art Pepper Today* (1978); *Among Friends* (1978); *Straight Life* (1979); *So in Love* (1979); *N.Y. Album* (1979); *Landscape* (1979); *Artworks* (1979); *One September Afternoon* (1980); *Winter Storm* (1981); *Roadgame* (1981); *Maiden Voyage Sessions* (1981); *Arthur's Blues* (1981); *Art and Zoot* (1981); *Goin' Home* (1982).

WRITINGS: *Straight Life: The Story of Art Pepper* (1979). **—NS/MM/LP**

Pepper, Jim, jazz flutist, saxophonist; b. Portland, Ore., June 17, 1941; d. there, Feb. 10, 1992. Pepper began tap dancing as a youth in Portland. His father played saxophone and he took up clarinet then saxophone. He played and recorded in Free Spirits with Larry Coryell and Bob Moses (1967) then joined Everything is Everything (1970). Through the 1980s, he worked with various leaders, including Charlie Haden's Liberation Music Orch. (1982) and Paul Motion, as well as leading his own groups. Amina Myers played with him in Austria 1991. He had Kaw Indian blood; his best-known composition, "Witchi Tai Toe," was based on an Indian chant.

DISC.: *Pepper's Pow Wow* (1971); *Comin' and Goin'* (1984); *Dakota Sound* (1987); *Path* (1988); *West End Avenue* (1989); *Camargue* (1989).—**LP**

Pepping, Ernst, distinguished German composer and pedagogue; b. Duisburg, Sept. 12, 1901; d. Berlin, Feb. 1, 1981. He studied with Gmeindl at the Berlin Hochschule für Musik. He taught at the Berlin-Spandau Church Music School (from 1934); was also a prof. at the Berlin Hochschule für Musik (1953–68). He publ. *Stilwende der Musik* (Mainz, 1934) and *Der polyphone Satz*: vol. I, *Der cantus-firmus-Satz* (Berlin, 1943; 2nd ed., 1950), and vol. II, *Übungen im doppelten Kontrapunkt und im Kanon* (Berlin, 1957). In 1989 the Ernst-Pepping- Gesellschaft was organized. By virtue of his lifelong association with Lutheran Church culture, Pepping acquired a profound understanding of German polyphonic music, both sacred and secular. He was a significant composer of German chorales; also produced 3 notable syms. A neo-Baroque penchant is discernible in all of his works.

WORKS: ORCH.: *Prelude* (1929); *Invention* (1930); *Partita* (1934); *Lust hab ich g'habt zur Musika: Variationen zu einem Liedsatz von Senfl* (1937); 3 syms.: No. 1 (1939), No. 2 (1942), and No. 3, *Die Tageszeiten* (1944); *Serenade* (1944–45); *Variations* (1949); *Piano Concerto* (1950); *2 Orchesterstücke über eine Chanson des Binchois* (1958). **CHAMBER:** String Quartet (1943); Flute Sonata (1958). **KEYBOARD: Piano:** Various pieces, including 4 sonatas (1937–45). **Organ:** *Grosses Orgelbuch* (3 vols., 1939); 2 concertos (both 1941); 3 Fugues on BACH (1943); 3 partitas: No. 1, *Ach wie flüchtig* (1953), No. 2, *Wer weiss, wie nahe mir mein Ende* (1953), and No. 3, *Mit Fried und Freud* (1953); *12 Chorale Preludes* (1958); Sonata (1958). **VOCAL** (all for a cappella chorus unless otherwise given): **Sacred:** *Deutsche Choralmesse* (1928); *Choralbuch* (30 works; 1931); *Spandauer Chorbuch* (20 vols., 1935–38; rev. by G. Grote, 4 vols., 1962); *Missa "Dona nobis pacem"* (1948); *Te Deum* for Solo Voices, Chorus, and Orch. (1956); *Die Weihnachtsgeschichte des Lukas* (1959); *Aus hartem Weh die Menschheit klagt* (1964); *Psalm CXXXIX* for Alto, Chorus, and Orch. (1964); *Deines Lichtes Glanz* (1967). **Secular:** *Sprüche und Lieder* (1930); *Lob der Träne* (1940); *33 Volkslieder* for Women's or Children's Chorus (1943); *Die wandelnde Glocke* (1952); also song cycles.

BIBL.: H. Poos, ed., *Festschrift E. P.* (Berlin, 1972); K. Hüschen, *Studien zum Motettenschaffen E. P.s* (Regensburg, 1987); M. Heinemann and H. Poos, eds., *Analysen zum Schaffen der Jahre 1926–1949: Im Auftrag der E.-P.-Gesellschaft* (Kassel, 1996).
—**NS/LK/DM**

Pepusch, John Christopher (actually, **Johann Christoph**), German-born English composer; b. Berlin, 1667; d. London, July 20, 1752. He was taught by Klingenberg (theory) and Grosse (organ). He had a position at the Prussian court in 1681–97, and then went to Holland. He was in London by 1704, where he was active as a violist and harpsichordist at Drury Lane Theatre; later as a composer, adapting Italian airs to English operas and adding recitatives and songs. In 1710 he founded (with Needler, Gates, Galliard, and others) the Academy of Ancient Music, famous for the revival of 16th-century compositions. Having received the D.Mus. degree from Oxford in 1713, he served as music director to James Brydges (later the Duke of Chandos) at Cannons. He wrote the masques *Venus and Adonis* (1715), *Apollo and Daphne* (1716), and *The Death of Dido* (1716), the ode *The Union of the Three Sister-Arts* (for St. Cecilia's Day; 1723), and arranged music to the ballad-operas *The Beggar's Opera, Polly,* and *The Wedding*. In 1730 a fortune brought him by marriage with **Marguerite de l'Epine** rendered him independent. From 1737 until his death he was organist of the Charterhouse. Pepusch was a learned, though conservative, musician who enjoyed high renown in England. His various odes and cantatas and his instrumental concertos and sonatas are of slight importance, and his name is preserved in music history mainly for his original music and some arranged numbers in *The Beggar's Opera*. He publ. a *Treatise on Harmony* (London, 1730; 2nd ed., rev., 1731).

BIBL.: H. Fred, *The Instrumental Music of J.C. P.* (diss., Univ. of N.C., 1961); J. Williams, *The Life, Work and Influence of J.C. P.* (diss., Univ. of York, 1976).—**NS/LK/DM**

Peragallo, Mario, Italian composer; b. Rome, March 25, 1910; d. there, Nov. 23, 1996. He was a student of Casella. In his early works, he followed the line of Italian traditionalism, characterized by modern but euphonious polyphony; later he adopted a radical quasi-dodecaphonic idiom, with frequent reversions to diatonic structures.

WORKS: DRAMATIC: Opera: *Ginevra degli Almieri* (Rome, Feb. 13, 1937); *Lo stendardo di S. Giorgio* (Genoa, 1941); *La collina* (Venice, 1947); *La Gita in campagna* (Milan, March 24, 1954); *La parrucca dell'imperatore* (Spoleto, 1959). **ORCH.:** Concerto for Orchestra (1939); 2 piano concertos (1949, 1951); *Fantasia* (1950); Violin Concerto (1954); *Forme sovrapposte* (1959); *Emircal* for Orch. and Tape (1980). **CHAMBER:** 3 string quartets (1933, 1934, 1937); *Vibrazioni* for Flute, "Tiptofono," and Piano (1960); *Perclopus*, chamber concerto for Clarinet, Wind Quintet, String Quintet, and Tape (1982); piano pieces; organ works. **VOCAL:** Choral pieces; songs.—**NS/LK/DM**

Perahia, Murray, outstanding American pianist of Spanish-Jewish descent; b. N.Y., April 19, 1947. He studied piano with J. Haien (1953–64), and then entered the Mannes Coll. of Music, where he studied conducting and composition (B.S., 1969); he also continued his piano studies with Balsam and Horszowski. In 1968 he made his Carnegie Hall debut in N.Y., and in 1972 he became the first American to win (by unanimous vote of the jury) the Leeds International Pianoforte Competition. In 1975 he was awarded the 1st Avery Fisher Prize, sharing it with the cellist Lynn Harrell. He appeared as soloist with the leading orchs. of the U.S. and Europe, and also gave many recitals in the U.S. and abroad. In

1982 he was appointed co-artistic director of the Aldeburgh Festival, which post he retained until 1989. In 1992 he sustained a crippling hand injury that compelled him to withdraw from public performances. In 1994 he returned to the concert stage as soloist in Beethoven's 4th Piano Concerto in London. He excels in Classical music; mastered all of Mozart's concertos, often conducting from the keyboard; he is praised also for his congenial interpretation of the standard concert repertoire.—NS/LK/DM

Peralta, Angela, Mexican soprano, known as "the Mexican Nightingale"; b. Puebla, July 6, 1845; d. Matzatlán, Aug. 30, 1883. She made her debut in *Il Trovatore* in Mexico City at the age of 15. In 1862, at age 17, she made her Italian debut as Lucia; she sang in Havana, N.Y., and Madrid. She then barnstormed throughout Mexico as the organizer of her own opera company, presenting operas by Donizetti, Bellini, and Verdi. She also appeared in the premieres of several Mexican operas, including Melesio Morales's *Ildegonda* (Jan. 27, 1866) and *Gino Corsini* (July 14, 1877) and Aniceto Ortega's *Guatimotzin* (Sept. 13, 1871). She made her last appearance in *Il Trovatore* (May 23, 1883), succumbing on tour to yellow fever, but not before marrying, on her deathbed, one of her many devotees.—NS/LK/DM

Peranda, Marco Gioseppe, important Italian composer; b. Rome or Macerata, c. 1625; d. Dresden, Jan. 12, 1675. He was taken by Christoph Bernhard to Dresden, where he was an alto in the chapel of the heir to the electorate. He sang with the chapel after it was incorporated into the court (1656), then was made vice-Kapellmeister (1661), Kapellmeister (1663), and 1st Hofkapellmeister (1672). Although a Roman Catholic at a Lutheran court, he earned the greatest esteem. He was a distinguished composer of sacred concertos and motets, and influenced many of his German contemporaries.

WORKS: DRAMATIC: O p e r a : *Dafne* (Dresden, Sept. 3, 1671; in collaboration with G.A. Bontempi); *Jupiter und Io* (Dresden, Jan. 16, 1673; in collaboration with Bontempi; only libretto extant). O r a t o r i o s : *Historia von der Geburt des Herrn Jesu Christi* (Dresden, Dec. 25, 1668; not extant); *Historia des Leidens und Sterbens unsers Hernn … Jesu Christi nach dem Evangelisten St. Marcum* (Dresden, March 20, 1668); *Il sacrificio de Jefte* (Bologna, 1675; only text extant). OTHER: 4 masses; sacred concertos; motets.—NS/LK/DM

Perera, Ronald (Christopher), American composer and teacher; b. Boston, Dec. 25, 1941. He studied with Leon Kirchner (composition) at Harvard Univ. (B.A., 1963; M.A., 1967), and while on a John Knowles Paine Traveling Fellowship, with Gottfried Koenig (electronic music and computer composition) at the Univ. of Utrecht (1967–68). He also studied privately with Randall Thompson (choral music) and Mario Davidovsky (electronic music). After teaching at Syracuse Univ. (1968–70), he was acting director of the Dartmouth Coll. Electronic Music Studio (1970–71). In 1971 he became a teacher of theory, composition, and electronic music at Smith Coll. in Northampton, Mass.,

where he was the Elsie Irwin Sweeney Prof. of Music from 1983. In 1975–76 he also was a visiting scholar at the Columbia-Princeton Electronic Music Center. With J. Appleton, he ed. *The Development and Practice of Electronic Music* (1975). He received annual ASCAP awards from 1972, and NEA grants in 1978 and 1988. In 1997 he became a permanent fellow of the Bogliasco Foundation for the Arts and Letters.

WORKS (all 1st perf. in Northampton, Mass., unless otherwise given): DRAMATIC: O p e r a : *The Yellow Wallpaper*, chamber opera (May 17, 1989); S. (Sept. 21, 1995). ORCH.: *Chanteys* (1976; Concord, Mass., Feb. 4, 1977; rev. 1979); *Chamber Concerto* for Brass Quintet, 9 Winds, Piano, and Percussion (1983; Cambridge, Mass., April 19, 1984); *The Saints* (N.Y., Dec. 4, 1990); *Music for Flute and Orchestra* (1990; Cleveland, April 14, 1997). CHAMBER: *Reverberations* for Organ and Tape (Troy, N.Y., April 12, 1970); *Reflex* for Viola and Tape (N.Y., Oct. 13, 1973); *Fantasy Variations* for Piano and Live Electronics (1975; March 30, 1976); *Bright Angels* for Organ, Percussion, and Tape (Hartford, Conn., June 6, 1977); Sonatina for Viola and Piano (1986; N.Y., April 17, 1994); Fanfare for Viola and Piano (1987; Durham, N.C., Sept. 8, 1990). KEYBOARD: P i a n o : Suite (1966; South Hadley, Mass., April 23, 1967); *Tolling* for 2 Pianos and Tape (1979; Feb. 3, 1980); *Augmented Forces* for Piano and Synthesizer (1987; May 19, 1988); *Out of Shadow* (1987; Upper Montclair, N.J., March 11, 1988). O r g a n : *5 Meditations on "Wondrous Love"* (Oct. 26, 1986); *Sun's Rising* (1986; N.Y., Feb. 9, 1987); *Triptych* (Pittsfield, Mass., June 23, 1997). VOCAL: *Mass* for Soloists, Chorus, and Orch. (1967; Washington, D.C., May 9, 1973); *Did You Hear the Angels Sing?* for Soprano, Chorus, and Organ (Cambridge, Mass., Dec. 16, 1968); *Dove Sta Amore* for Soprano and Tape (Syracuse, N.Y., April 17, 1969); *5 Summer Songs* for Medium Voice and Piano (1969–72; May 3, 1974; also for Mezzo-soprano and Chamber Orch., 1991; Cleveland, May 4, 1992); *Apollo Circling* for High Voice and Piano (Oct. 22, 1972); *3 Night Pieces* for Soprano, Alto, Women's Chorus, Cello, Piano, and Percussion (April 7, 1974); *3 Poems of Günter Grass* for Mezzo-soprano, Flute, Clarinet, Violin, Viola, Cello, Piano, and Tape (Cambridge, Mass., Nov. 19, 1974); *Children of the Sun* for Soprano, Horn, and Piano (Feb. 19, 1978); *The White Whale* for Baritone and Orch. (1981; Feb. 14, 1982); *Crossing the Meridian* for Tenor, Flute, Clarinet, Violin, Viola, Cello, Piano, and Percussion (Cambridge, Mass., Dec. 8, 1982); *Earthsongs* for Women's Chorus and Orch. (1983; May 19, 1984); *As Freedom is a Breakfastfood* for Women's Chorus and Piano (Rye, N.Y., May 10, 1984); *The Canticle of the Sun* for Narrator, Chorus, and Digitally synthesized Instruments (1984; Groton, Mass., April 21, 1985); *Sleep Now* for High Voice and Piano (1985; Oct. 19, 1986); *Shakespeare Songs* for High Voice and Piano (1985; March 1, 1987); *The Light Here Kindled* for Baritone, Chorus, Brass Quintet, Timpani, and Organ (Cambridge, Mass., Sept. 7, 1986); *The Outermost House* for Soprano, Narrator, Chorus, and Chamber Orch. (West Yarmouth, Mass., Nov. 16, 1991); *Psalm 126* for Chorus, Brass Quintet, Timpani, and Organ (May 30, 1992); *A Fondness for Music* for Women's Chorus and Piano (1993; April 17, 1994); *Visions* for 2 Sopranos and Chamber Ensemble (1993; Cambridge, Mass., Oct. 3, 1997); *The Golden Door* for Chorus and Chamber Ensemble (N.Y., June 8, 1999). ELECTRONIC: *Improvisation* for Loudspeakers (1969); *Time Machine* (1970); *Alternate Routes* (1971).—NS/LK/DM

Peress, Maurice, American conductor; b. N.Y., March 18, 1930. He studied at N.Y.U. (B.A., 1951) and with H. Freistadt and J. Cnudde (trumpet) and P. James and C. Bamberger (conducting) at N.Y.'s Mannes Coll. of Music (1955–57). After serving as asst. conductor of the N.Y. Phil. (1961–62), he was music director of the Corpus Christi (Tex.) Sym. Orch. (1962–75), the Austin (Tex.) Sym. Orch. (1970–73), and the Kans. City Phil. (1974–80).—NS/LK/DM

Pérez, David or **Davide,** significant Italian composer; b. Naples (of Spanish descent), 1711; d. Lisbon, Oct. 30, 1778. He studied counterpoint and composition with Mancini, Veneziano, and Galli at the Cons. di S. Maria di Loreto in Naples (1722–33). Between 1735 and 1752 he produced some 19 operas, establishing himself as a leading opera composer in his day. He served as vice-maestro di cappella of the Royal Chapel Palatine in Palermo (1738–39) and as maestro di cappella in Palermo (1741–48); then was called to Lisbon (1752) as maestro di cappella and music master to the royal princesses, duties he retained for the rest of his life. He continued to compose until his last days, even though he was stricken with blindness. He was a master of the opera seria, being acclaimed as a worthy rival of Hasse and Jommelli.

WORKS: DRAMATIC: Opera: *La nemica amante* (Naples, Nov. 4, 1735); *Li travestimenti amorosi,* opera buffa (Naples, July 10, 1740); *Il Siroe* (Naples, Nov. 4, 1740); *L'eroismo di Scipione* (Palermo, 1741); *Demetrio* (Palermo, June 13, 1741; 2nd version, Lisbon, 1766); *Astartea* (Palermo, 1743); *Medea* (Palermo, 1744); *Alessandro nell'Indie* (Genoa, Carnival 1744; 2nd version, Lisbon, March 31, 1755); *Merope* (Genoa, Carnival 1744); *L'isola incantata* (Palermo, 1746); *Artaserse* (Florence, 1748); *La clemenza di Tito* (Naples, 1749); *Vologeso* (Vienna, 1750); *Il Farnace* (Rome, 1750); *Andromaca* (Vienna, 1750); *Semiramide* (Rome, 1750); *Ezio* (Milan, Carnival 1751); *La Didone* (Genoa, 1751); *La Zenobia* (Milan, 1751); *Demofoonte* (Lisbon, 1752); *Adriano in Siria* (Lisbon, 1752); *L'Eroe cinese* (Lisbon, June 6, 1753); *Olimpiade* (Lisbon, 1753); *L'Impermestra* (Lisbon, 1754); *Lucio Vero* (Verona, 1754); *Solimano* (Lisbon, Carnival 1757); *Enea in Italia* (Lisbon, 1759); *La Berenice* (Verona, Carnival 1762); *Giulio Cesare* (Lisbon, 1762); *L'isola disabitata* (Lisbon, 1767); *Il Cinese* (Lisbon, 1769); *Creusa in Delfo* (Lisbon, Carnival 1774); *Il ritorno di Ulisse in Itaca* (Lisbon, 1774); *L'Eroe coronato* (Lisbon, 1775); *La pace fra la Virtù e la Bellezza* (Lisbon, Dec. 17, 1777). VOCAL: Secular: *Il trionfo di Venere,* serenata (Palermo, 1738); *L'Atlanta,* serenata (Palermo, 1739); *L'amor pittore,* componimento drammatico civile (Naples, July 24, 1740); *La vera felicità* (Lisbon, 1761). Sacred: *Mattutino de' morti* for 5 Voices and Orch. (London, 1774); *Il martirio di S. Bartolomeo,* oratorio; 8 masses for Chorus and Orch.; Mass sections; Magnificat; antiphones; motets; etc.

BIBL.: E. Soares, *D. P.: Subsidios para a biografia' do célébre mestre de musica da camera de D. José* (Lisbon, 1935); P. Jackson, *The Operas of D. P.* (diss., Stanford Univ., 1967).—NS/LK/DM

Pérez Martínez, Vicente, Spanish singer and music editor; b. Cifuentes, near Madrid, date unknown; d. Madrid, Jan. 2, 1800. He was a tenor in the Madrid royal chapel from 1770. He publ. a valuable anthology of plainsong, *Prontuario del cantollano gregoriano...segun practica de la muy santa primade iglesia de Toledo* (3 vols., 1799–1800; 2nd ed. by A. Hernandéz, 1828–29).—LK/DM

Perfall, Karl, Freiherr von, German composer and conductor; b. Munich, Jan. 29, 1824; d. there, Jan. 14,

1907. He took music lessons with Hauptmann in Leipzig (1848–49). He became conductor of the Munich Liedertafel (1850), and founded the Oratorio Society (1854). In 1864 he was appointed Intendant of the court music and abandoned his activities as a conductor. From 1867 to 1893 he was Intendant of the National Theater in Munich. Of his operas (all produced in Munich), *Raimondin* (March 27, 1881; rev. as *Melusine,* 1885) and *Junker Heinz* (April 9, 1886; rev. as *Jung Heinrich,* 1901) were successful. He publ. *25 Jahre Münchener Hoftheater-Geschichte* (1892; covering the period from 1867), *Ein Beitrag zur Geschichte des königlichen Theaters in München 25 November 1867–25 November 1892* (1894), and *Die Entwickelung des modernen Theaters* (1899).—NS/LK/DM

Pergament, Moses, Finnish-born Swedish music critic and composer; b. Helsinki, Sept. 21, 1893; d. Gustavsberg, near Stockholm, March 5, 1977. He studied violin at the St. Petersburg Cons. and conducting at Berlin's Stern Cons. In 1915 he settled in Sweden and became a naturalized Swedish citizen (1918); from 1923 to 1966 he was active as a music critic in Swedish newspapers; he publ. 4 books on music. His musical style was initially circumscribed by Russian paradigms; later he was influenced by Sibelius; still later he adopted some modernistic procedures. Several of his compositions reflect an ancestral strain of Jewish melos.

WORKS: DRAMATIC: Opera: *Himlens hemlighet* (The Secret of Heaven), chamber opera (1952); *Eli,* radio opera (1958; Swedish Radio, March 19, 1959); *Abrams Erwachen,* opera-oratorio (1970–73). Ballet: *Krelantems and Eldeling* (1920–28); *Vision* (1923). Also incidental music and film scores. ORCH.: *Romance* for Violin and Orch. (1914); *Adagio* for Clarinet and Strings (1915); *Rapsodia ebraica* (1935); *Concerto romantico* for Strings (1935); *Dibbuk,* fantasy for Violin and Orch. (1935); *Almquistiana,* 2 suites (1936, 1938); *Swedish Rhapsody* (1941); Violin Concerto (1948); *Kol Nidre* for Cello and Orch. (1949); Piano Concerto (1951); Concerto for 2 Violins and Orch. (1954); Cello Concerto (1955); *Canto lirico* for Violin and Orch. (1956); *Pezzo intimo* for 16 Solo Cellos (1957); Viola Concerto (1964–65); *Fantasia differente* for Cello and Strings (1970); *Sonatina* for Flute and Strings (1973). CHAMBER: Piano Trio (1912–13; rev. 1940); Violin Sonata (1918–20); 3 string quartets (1922, 1952, 1956); Sonata for Solo Violin (1961); Flute Sonata (1968); *Little Suite* for Woodwinds (1970). VOCAL: *Nedanförmänskliga visor* (Subhuman Songs) for Narrator, Soloists, Chorus, and Orch. (1936); *Den judiska sången* (The Jewish Song), choral sym. (1944); *De sju dödssynderna* (The 7 Deadly Sins), oratorio (1963); *4 Poems by Edith Södergran* for Soprano and Orch. (1965–66); *Årstider,* 4 songs for Baritone and Orch. (1968); *Drömmen om mullen och vindarna* (The Dream of the Earth and the Winds) for Baritone and Orch. (1969); *Biblical Cantata* for Chorus and Orch. (1974); over 100 solo songs.—NS/LK/DM

Perger, Richard von, Austrian composer and conductor; b. Vienna, Jan. 10, 1854; d. there, Jan. 11, 1911. He studied cello and theory. After serving in the Austrian army during the campaign in Bosnia (1878), he received a stipend and took lessons with Brahms (1880–82). He was director of the Rotterdam Cons. (1890–95). Returning to Vienna, he conducted the Gesellschaftskonzerte, and from 1899 to 1907 he was director of the Vienna Cons. His music bears unmistakable evidence of the profound influence of Brahms. Among his works are the text and music of a comic opera, *Der Richter von Granada* (Cologne, 1889), a Singspiel, *Die 14 Nothhelfer* (Vienna, 1891), a musical fairy tale, *Das stählerne Schloss* (Vienna, 1904). a Violin Concerto, some chamber music, and songs. He also publ. a biography of Brahms (1908; new ed. by Hernried, 1934). His *Geschichte der K. K. Gesellschaft der Musikfreunde in Wien* was publ. posthumously (1912).—NS/LK/DM

Pergolesi, Giovanni Battista,

remarkable Italian composer; b. Jesi, near Ancona, Jan. 4, 1710; d. Pozzuoli, near Naples, March 16, 1736. The original family name was Draghi; the name Pergolesi was derived from the town of Pergola, where Pergolesi's ancestors lived. He was the only surviving child of his parents, 3 others having died in infancy. His childhood seems to have been plagued by ill health; a later caricature depicts him as having a deformed leg. He first studied music with Francesco Santi, the maestro di cappella of the Jesi Cathedral. He also studied violin with Francesco Mondini. He then was given a stipend by the Marchese Cardolo Maria Pianetti, which enabled him to enter the Cons. dei Poveri di Gesù Cristo in Naples, where he studied violin with Domenico de Matteis, and composition with Gaetano Greco, its maestro di cappella, Leonardo Vinci, and Francesco Durante. Pergolesi became highly proficient as a violinist, playing at the Conservatorio and throughout Naples. His first work to be performed was the dramma sacro *Li prodigi della divina grazia nella conversione di S. Guglielmo Duca d'Aquitania*, which was given by the Cons. at the monastery of S. Agnello Maggiore in 1731. He graduated shortly thereafter, and received a commission for his first opera, *La Salustia* (Naples, Jan. 1732). He then became maestro di cappella to Prince Ferdinando Colonna Stigliano, equerry to the Viceroy of Naples, in 1732. His *Lo Frate 'nnamorato* (Naples, Sept. 27, 1732) proved highly successful. In Dec. 1732 he composed several sacred works for performance at the church of S. Maria della Stella as a votive offering following a series of severe earthquakes in Naples. He was next commissioned to write an opera seria to celebrate the birthday of the empress on Aug. 28, 1733; however, the premiere of the resulting *Il Prigionier superbo* was delayed until Sept. 5, 1733; it contained the 2-act intermezzo *La Serva padrona*, which became his most celebrated stage work. He was named deputy to the maestro di cappella of Naples in 1734. During a brief sojourn in Rome, his Mass in F major was performed at the church of S. Lorenzo in Lucina (May 16, 1734).

After returning to Naples, Pergolesi became maestro di cappella to Marzio Domenico IV Carafa, the Duke of Maddaloni. For the birthday of the king's mother, he was commissioned to write the opera *Adriano in Siria*; it was premiered, without success, in Naples on Oct. 25, 1734, with the intermezzo *La Contadina astuta* (subsequently staged under various titles). He then was commissioned to write an opera for Rome's Teatro Tordinona, resulting in his unsuccessful opera seria *L'Olimpiade* (Jan. 8 or 9, 1735). His last popular success for the stage was the commedia musicale *Il Flaminio*

(Naples, 1735). By 1735 his health had seriously declined, most likely from tuberculosis. Early in 1736 he went to the Franciscan monastery in Pozzuoli, where he soon died at the age of 26. He was buried in the common grave adjacent to the Cathedral. Following his death, his fame spread rapidly through performances of *La Serva padrona* and several other stage works. The Paris revival of the work in 1752 precipitated the so-called *querelle des bouffons* between the partisans of the Italian and French factions. His fame was further increased by performances of the *Salve regina* in C minor and the *Stabat Mater* in F minor.

The chaotic entanglement of spurious, doubtful, and authentic works attributed to Pergolesi was unraveled in M. Paymer's *G.B. P.: A Thematic Catalogue of the Opera Omnia with an Appendix Listing Omitted Compositions* (N.Y., 1976). The *Opera Omnia*, ed. by F. Caffarelli (5 vols., Rome, 1939–42), is most unreliable; it is being replaced by a critical ed., the first vol. of which appeared in 1985.

BIBL.: C. de Rosa, Marchese di Villarosa, *Lettera biografica intorno alla patria ed all vita di G.B. P. celebre compositore di musica* (Naples, 1831; 2nd ed., 1843); F. Villars, *La Serva padrona, Son apparition à Paris en 1752, son influence, son analyse* (Paris, 1863); G. Annibaldi, *Alcune delle notizie più importanti intorno al P. recentemente scoperte: Il P. in Pozzuoli: Vita intima* (Jesi, 1890); E. Faustini-Fasini, *G.B. P. attraverso i suoi biografi e le sue opere* (Milan, 1900); G. Radiciotti, *G.B. P.: Vita, opere ed influenza su l'arte* (Rome, 1910; 2nd ed., rev., 1935; Ger. tr., 1954); A. Della Corte, *G.B. P.* (Turin, 1936); R. Giraldi, *G.B. P.* (Rome, 1936); F. Schlitzer, *G.B. P.* (Turin, 1940); S. Luciani, ed., *G.B. P. (1710–1736): Note e documenti* (Siena, 1942); E. Luin, *Fortuna e influenza della musica di P. in Europa* (Siena, 1943); M. Paymer, *The Instrumental Music Attributed to G.B. P.: A Study in Authenticity* (diss., City Univ. of N.Y., 1977); A. Dunning, *Count Unico Wilhelm van Wassenaer (1692–1766); A Master Unmasked; or, The P.-Ricciotti Puzzle Solved* (Buren, 1980); H. Beckwith, *G.B. P. and the Chamber Cantata* (diss., Univ. of Md., 1983); F. Degrada, ed., *Studi P.ani/P. Studies* (4 vols., N.Y., 1986, 1988, 1999, 2000); M. Paymer and H. Williams, *G.B. P.: A Guide to Research* (N.Y., 1989).—NS/LK/DM

Peri, Achille,

Italian composer; b. Reggio Emilia, Dec. 20, 1812; d. there, March 28, 1880. He studied piano and composition with Gregori and Rabitti in Reggio Emilia, and then completed his training with Carafa in Paris. He wrote operas for several Italian theaters and also served as maestro di cappella at Reggio Emilia Cathedral. His finest opera was the biblical drama *Giuditta* (La Scala, Milan, March 26, 1860). Although a failure at its premiere, it was revived there two years later to much acclaim. His other works included chamber music, piano pieces, choral works, and songs. —LK/DM

Peri, Jacopo,

significant Italian composer, called "Il Zazzerino" for his abundant head of hair; b. Rome, Aug. 20, 1561; d. Florence, Aug. 12, 1633. He was descended from a noble Florentine family. At an early age he went to Florence, where he entered the convent of Ss. Annunziata in 1573 and became a singer; also studied music with Cristofano Malvezzi. He was organist at the Badia (1579–1605) and a singer at S. Giovanni Battista (by

1586). He entered the service of the Medici court of Grand Duke Ferdinando I (1588), and was also in the service of the Mantuan court (from the early 1600s). The Florentine Camerata met at the home of Count Giovanni de' Bardi in the 1580s, and it is likely that Peri participated in its activities. As early as 1583 he collaborated with other composers in writing music for the intermedi to Giovanni Fedini's dramatic comedy *Le due Persilie*. In the 1590s the home of Jacopo Corsi became the meeting place for many Florentine musicians, poets, and philosophers, and Peri undoubtedly attended, for Corsi collaborated with him in setting Ottavio Rinuccini's pastoral *Dafne* to music. The first known performance of this work was a private one in Florence in 1598. Later versions were given in 1599, 1600, and 1605. *Dafne* is generally recognized as the first opera in monodic style (i.e., vocal Soloists supported by instruments), which was termed *stile rappresentativo*. Peri's next opera was *Euridice*, again to a text by Rinuccini; some of the music was rewritten by Caccini for the first performance, which was given for the wedding of Maria de' Medici and Henri IV of France at the Palazzo Pitti in Florence (Oct. 6, 1600). He composed the opera *Tetide* (libretto by Cini) for Mantua in 1608, but it was not performed. His next opera, *Adone* (libretto by Cicognini), was finished by 1611; a performance scheduled for Mantua in 1620 never took place. Another work of the period, *La liberazione di Tirreno e d'Arnea* (Florence, Feb. 6, 1617), may be by Peri; it is also possible that he collaborated with M. da Gagliano on the score, or it may be totally the work of Gagliano. Peri collaborated with Marco da Gagliano on the opera *Lo sposalizio di Medoro e Angelica*. It was given in honor of the election of Emperor Ferdinand III at the Palazzo Pitti on Sept. 25, 1619. He also composed the role of Clori for the opera *La Flora*, the remainder of the music being by Gagliano. It was first performed in honor of the wedding of Margherita de' Medici and Duke Odoardo Farnese of Parma at the Palazzo Pitti on Oct. 14, 1628. Peri also collaborated with Gagliano on 3 oratorios, *La benedittione di Jacob* (Florence, Sept. 23, 1622), *Il gran natale di Christo salvator nostro* (Florence, Dec. 27, 1622), and *La celeste guida, o vero L'Arcangelo Raffaello* (Florence, Jan. 5, 1624), but these works are not extant. In addition to individual songs publ. in various collections of the time, he also brought out *La varie musiche ... for 1 to 3 Voices, con alcune spirituali in ultimo, per cantare, harpsichord, chitarrone, ancora la maggior parte di esse per sonare semplicemente, organ* (Florence, 1609; 2nd ed., 1619).

BIBL.: G. Corazzini, *J. P. e la sua famiglia* (Florence, 1895); F. Ghisi, *Alle fonti della monodia: Due nuove brani della 'Dafne'* (Milan, 1940); T. Carter, *J. P. (1561–1633): His Life and Works* (diss., Univ. of Birmingham, 1980).—**NS/LK/DM**

Pericič, Vlastimir, Serbian composer and musicologist; b. Vršac, Dec. 7, 1927. He studied in Vienna with Uhl. He became active as a pedagogue in Belgrade, and publ. manuals on harmony and form; also compiled a valuable reference work on Serbian composers, *Muzički Stvaraoci u Srbiji* (Belgrade, 1969). Among his compositions were String Quartet (1950), *Symphonic Movement* (Belgrade, Oct. 14, 1952), *Fantasia quasi una sonata* for Violin and Piano (1954), *Sinfonietta* for Strings (Zagreb, Nov. 13, 1957), and piano pieces.—**NS/LK/DM**

Perick (real name, Prick), Christof, German conductor; b. Hamburg, Oct. 23, 1946. He was a student in Hamburg of Brückner-Rüggeberg. After serving as an asst. conductor at the Hamburg State Opera, he conducted at the operas in Trier (1970–72) and Darmstadt (1972–74). He was Generalmusikdirektor in Saarbrücken (1974–77) and Karlsruhe (1977–84), and also held the title of 1st conductor at the Deutsche Oper in Berlin (1977–84). He was music director (1991–94) and music advisor (from 1994) of the Los Angeles Chamber Orch. In 1993 he became Generalmusikdirektor of the Niedersächsische State Theater and Orch. in Hannover. Perick appeared as a guest conductor of opera and sym. throughout Europe and North America.—**NS/LK/DM**

Périer, Jean (Alexis), French baritone; b. Paris, Feb. 2, 1869; d. there, Nov. 3, 1954. He studied at the Paris Cons., obtaining the premier prix for singing (1892). He made his debut at the Paris Opéra-Comique as Monostatos in *Die Zauberflöte* on Dec. 16, 1892; was engaged there until 1894, and again from 1900 to 1920. He created the role of Pélleas at the premiere of Debussy's opera (1902), and sang the leading tenor parts in several other premieres of French operas; sang at N.Y.'s Manhattan Opera House (1908). A talented comedian, Périer also appeared in variety shows in Paris. He publ. an instructive album, *Mes exercises, tirés des chansons populaires de France* (Paris, 1917).—**NS/LK/DM**

Perini, Annibale, Italian organist and compoer; b. c. 1560; d. Graz, 1596. He was active in Venice before settling in Graz about 1575. In 1579 he was made organist at the court chapel of Archduke Karl II, who made it possible for him to complete his musical training. After serving as organist at the Graz evangelical collegiate church (1590–94), he resumed his post as Graz court chapel organist. Perini composed the *Missa super Benedicite omnia opera Domini* for 8 Voices and various motets.—**LK/DM**

Perino, Fiorentino, Italian lutenist and composer; b. probably in Florence, 1523; d. 1552. He was a student of Francesco da Milano. A number of his lute pieces are extant.—**LK/DM**

Perissone, Cambio, Italian singer and composer of French or Flemish descent who flourished in the 1st half of the 16th century. He was active in Venice. Among his works are 4 vols. of secular music (Venice, 1545–49), including madrigals and villanellas. A motet is also extant.—**LK/DM**

Perkins, Carl, legendary rockabilly pioneer and composer of the rock classic "Blue Suede Shoes"; b. near Tiptonville, Tenn., April 9, 1932; d. Nashville, Tenn., Jan. 19, 1998. Carl Perkins grew up in Lake County, Tenn., and obtained his first guitar at the age of six. In 1950 he formed a family band with his older brothers Jay (rhythm gtr.) and Clayton (stand-up bs.) to play local dances and honky-tonks. Adding drummer W.S. Holland in 1953 and turning professional in 1954, the band signed with Sam Phillips's Memphis- based Flip Records for one single, before switching to Phillips's Sun Records label in 1955. Their second Sun single, "Blue Suede Shoes," became a smash hit in the country, then pop, then R&B fields in early 1956 and eventually sold two million copies. Booked to appear on the *Ed Sullivan* and *Perry Como Shows*, the band was involved in a serious auto accident near Dover, Del., enroute to N.Y. on March 22, 1956. Carl was hospitalized for a month (Jay never fully recovered and died in 1958), as Elvis Presley became the first rockabilly artist to appear on network television. Presley's follow-up to his break-through hit "Heartbreak Hotel" was a cover version of Perkins's "Blue Suede Shoes," which became a major pop-only hit in April. Carl Perkins managed near-smash country hits later in 1956 with "Boppin' The Blues" and "Dixie Fried," but he did not tour again until 1957 and was unable to reestablish his career's momentum.

On Dec. 4, 1956, a Carl Perkins recording date attended by Sun labelmates Johnny Cash and Jerry Lee Lewis turned into an informal session when Elvis Presley dropped in. Unknown to the four, the session was recorded, and bootleg copies of "The Million Dollar Quartet" circulated for years until RCA finally issued the recordings in 1990.

In 1957 Carl Perkins appeared in the film *Jamboree* and had a major country hit with "Your True Love," yet, in early 1958, he switched to Columbia Records, where he scored a major country hit with "Pink Pedal Pushers." His career subsequently languished, but, in 1964, while on his first British tour with Chuck Berry, he met The Beatles, who soon recorded his songs "Slow Down," "Matchbox" and "Everybody's Trying to Be My Baby." His career was revived, particularly in Europe, and, in 1966, he switched to the country label Dollie Records, where he achieved a major country hit with "Country Boy's Dream." He joined Johnny Cash's road show and toured with him from 1965 to 1975. In 1969 he provided Cash with the top country hit "Daddy Sang Bass" and scored a major country hit on his own with "Restless," back on Columbia. Perkins also appeared as a regular on ABC television's *The Johnny Cash Show* from 1969 to 1971.

In 1970 Carl Perkins recorded the sorely overlooked *Boppin' the Blues* with NRBQ. He later recorded an album for Mercury and left Johnny Cash to form a performing band with sons Greg (bs.) and Stan (drm.). In 1976 Perkins conducted recording sessions with his sons in Muscle Shoals, Ala., which eventually surfaced on Accord Records in 1982 and were repackaged by RCA Nashville in 1993. He recorded *Ol' Blue Suede's Back* in 1978 and joined Johnny Cash and Jerry Lee Lewis for the live set *The Survivors*, recorded in West Germany in 1981. Perkins wrote and sang on "Get It" from Paul McCartney's *Tug of War* album and later performed an HBO cable television special that featured Eric Clapton, George Harrison, Dave Edmunds and

Ringo Starr. In 1986 he recorded *The Class of '55* with Johnny Cash, Jerry Lee Lewis and Roy Orbison, contributing the autobiographical "Birth of Rock and Roll" which became a moderate country hit. Inducted into the Rock and Roll Hall of Fame in 1987, Perkins suffered from cancer and heart disease in the last years of his life. He died in 1998.

WRITINGS: With R. Rendleman, *Disciple in Blue Suede Shoes* (Grand Rapids, Mich., 1978); with D. McGee, *Go, Cat, Go!: The Life and Times of C. P., the King of Rockabilly* (N.Y., 1996).

DISC.: *Dance Album* (1957); *Whole Lotta Shakin'* (1958); *Country Boy's Dream* (1966); *On Top* (1969); *My Kind of Country* (1973); *The Carl Perkins Show* (1976); *Ol' Blue Suede's Back* (1978); *Live at Austin City Limits* (1981); *Presenting Carl Perkins* (1982); *Boppin' the Blues* (1982); *Carl Perkins* (1985); *Original Sun Greatest Hits (1955–1957)* (1986); *Honky Tonk Gal: Rare and Unissued Sun Masters* (1989); *Born to Rock* (1989); *Friends, Family and Legends* (1992); *Restless: The Columbia Years* (1992); *Carl Perkins and Sons* (1993); *Disciple in Blue Suede Shoes* (1993); *The Man and the Legend* (rec. 1985; rel. 1996). **CARL PERKINS AND NRBQ:** *Boppin' the Blues* (1970/1990). **CARL PERKINS, JOHNNY CASH, AND JERRY LEE LEWIS:** *The Survivors* (1982). **CARL PERKINS, JERRY LEE LEWIS, ROY ORBISON, AND JOHNNY CASH:** *Class of '55* (1986).

Perkins, John MacIvor, American composer and teacher; b. St. Louis, Aug. 2, 1935. He studied at Harvard Univ. (B.A., 1958), at the New England Cons. of Music in Boston (B.Mus., 1958), with Boulanger in Paris and Gerhard and Rubbra in London (1958–59), and at Brandeis Univ. (M.F.A., 1962). After teaching at the Univ. of Chicago (1962–65) and at Harvard Univ. (1965–70), he was assoc. prof. of music (from 1970) and chairman of the music dept. (1970–75) at Washington Univ. in St. Louis. In 1966 he received an American Academy and National Inst. of Arts and Letters award.

WORKS: DRAMATIC: *Divertimento*, chamber opera (1958); *Andrea del Sarto*, operatic monologue (1981). **ORCH.:** *Fantasy and Variations* (1961; orchestration of the piano pieces *Fantasy*, 1959, and *Variations*, 1960); *Music* (1965). **CHAMBER:** *Canons* for 9 Instruments (1957); *Variations* for Flute, Clarinet, Trumpet, Piano, and Percussion (1962); *Music for Carillon* (1963); *Music for 13 Players* (1964); *Music for Brass* for 3 Trumpets and 3 Trombones (1965); *After a Silence-Alpha* for 12 Instruments (1976); *Canzona* for Harpsichord and Piano (1982); *Divisions* for Bass Gamba and Harpsichord (1982); *Quartet for Strings and Tape* (1984); *Sequence* for 5 Brass Instruments (1986); *Lyric Variations* for Violin and Piano (1989); *Reflections on a Bach Fugue* for Flute and Piano (1995). **KEYBOARD: Piano:** *Fantasy* (1959), *Intermezzo* (1962), and *Variations* (1960); *Caprice* (1963); *Cadenza* (1978). **Organ:** *Fugue in C, The Relief* (1977). **VOCAL:** *7 Songs* for Voice and Piano (1955–62); *3 Studies* for Chamber Chorus (1958); *Alleluia* for Chorus (1966; also for Chorus and Percussionist, 1971); *4 Songs on Transience* for Voice and Piano (1988).—NS/LK/DM

Perkowski, Piotr, Polish composer and pedagogue; b. Oweczacze, Ukraine, March 17, 1901; d. Otwock, near Warsaw, Aug. 12, 1990. He studied composition with Statkowski at the Warsaw Cons. (1923–25), then took private lessons with Szymanowski in Warsaw and with Roussel in Paris. He was director of the Toruń Cons. (1936–39), and taught composition at the Warsaw Cons. (1946–51; 1954–73). He was artistic director of the Kraków Phil. (1949–51) and dean of the Music Academy in Wrocław (1951–55); served as councilor for cultural development for the city of Warsaw (1965–74). In his earlier years, he followed the fashionable cosmopolitan trend of absolute music without reference to national or general programmatic subjects, but under the influence of social changes he began introducing concrete, historic, and pictorial representations.

WORKS: DRAMATIC: Opera: *Garlands* (Warsaw, 1962). **Ballet:** *Swantewit* (1930; rev. 1945–47; Poznań, June 19, 1948); *Rhapsody* (1949); *Fantasia* (1950); *Clementine* (1960–63); *Balladyna* (1960–64; Warsaw, 1965). **ORCH.:** 2 syms.: No. 1 for Chorus and Orch. (1925; lost; reconstructed 1955) and No. 2 (1949); *Geometric Suite* (1930); 2 violin concertos (1933, 1960); *Warsaw Overture* (1954); *Sinfonia drammatica* (1963); *Scottish Impressions* (1968); *Amphiction* (1970); Cello Concerto (1973). **CHAMBER:** 2 string quartets (1930, 1977); *Elegia* for Cello and Organ (1945); Trumpet Sonatina (1954); Flute Sonata (1954); piano pieces. **VOCAL:** 5 cantatas: *Wisla* (1951), *Epitaphe pour Nicos Belojannis* (1952), *Suita weselna* (Merry Suite) for Soprano, Tenor, Chorus, and Orch. (1952), *Suita epicka* (1953), and *Alexiares*, with Narrator and Tape (1966–69); *Niebo w plomieniach* (The Sky in Flames), song cycle, for Voice and Orch. (1969). —NS/LK/DM

Perle, George, eminent American composer, music theorist, and pedagogue; b. Bayonne, N.J., May 6, 1915. Following training in composition and theory with La Violette at DePaul Univ. in Chicago (graduated, 1938), he pursued private lessons in composition with Krenek (1939–41) and obtained his M.M. degree at the American Cons. of Music in Chicago (1942). Later he studied musicology with Sachs, Reese, and Bernstein at N.Y.U. (Ph.D., 1956). In 1941 Perle founded the New Music Group of Chicago with Robert Erickson and Ben Weber. After teaching music history and composition at the Univ. of Louisville (1949–57), he was prof. of theory and composition at the Univ. of Calif. at Davis (1957–61) and at Queens Coll. of the City Univ. of N.Y. (1961–85). With Hans Redlich and Igor Stravinsky, he organized the International Alban Berg Soc. in 1968. He was composer-in-residence at the Berkshire Music Center in Tanglewood (summers, 1967, 1980, and 1987), of the San Francisco Sym. (1989–91), and at the Marlboro (Vt.) Music Festival (summer, 1993). Among his positions as a visiting prof. were the Birge-Cary Prof. of Music at the State Univ. of N.Y. at Buffalo (1971–72), the Visiting Ernest Bloch Prof. of Music at the Univ. of Calif. at Berkeley (1989), and the Visiting Distinguished Prof. of Music at N.Y.U. (1994). In 1966–67 and 1974–75 he held Guggenheim fellowships. In 1977 he received an award from the American Academy and Inst. of Arts and Letters, and was elected to its membership in 1978. The first vol. of his study *The Operas of Alban Berg* (Berkeley, 1980) was honored with the ASCAP-Deems Taylor Award and the Kinkeldey Award of the American Musicological Soc. in 1981. He was elected a member of the National Academy of Arts and Sciences in 1985. His 4th wind quintet was awarded the Pulitzer Prize in Music in 1986, the same year he was named a MacArthur fellow. Perle was one of the earliest American serialists, and one of the most innovative. He developed a highly personal and distinctive "12-tone tonality," one made notable by expert craftsmanship.

WRITINGS: *Serial Composition and Atonality: An Introduction to the Music of Schoenberg and Webern* (Berkeley, 1962; 6th ed., 1991); *Twelve-Tone Tonality* (Berkeley, 1977; 2nd ed., 1995); *The Operas of Alban Berg* (2 vols., Berkeley, 1980, 1985); *The Listening Composer* (Berkeley, 1990); *The Right Notes: 23 Selected Essays on 20th-Century Music* (Hillsdale, N.Y., 1994); *Style and Idea in the Lyric Suite of Alban Berg* (Hillsdale, N.Y., 1995).

WORKS: DRAMATIC: *The Birds*, incidental music to Aristophanes' play (Berkeley, Sept. 28, 1961). **ORCH.:** *3 Movements* (1960; Amsterdam, June 14, 1963); *Serenade No. 1* for Viola and Chamber Orch. (N.Y., May 10, 1962), *No. 2* for 11 Players (1968; Washington, D.C., Feb. 28, 1969), and *No. 3* for Piano and Chamber Ensemble (N.Y., Dec. 14, 1983); *6 Bagatelles* (1965; Riverhead, N.Y., Nov. 18, 1977); Cello Concerto (1966; N.Y., Nov. 14, 1987); Concertino for Piano, Winds, and Timpani (Chicago, April 20, 1979); *A Short Symphony* (Tanglewood, Aug. 16, 1980); *Dance Overture*, renamed *Dance Fantasy* (1986; Houston, May 16, 1987); *New Fanfares* for Brass Ensemble (Tanglewood, Aug. 1, 1987); *Lyric Intermezzo* for 15 Players (Seattle, Nov. 8, 1987); *Sinfonietta I* (1987; St. Paul, Minn., Jan. 29, 1988) and *II* (San Francisco, Feb. 19, 1990); 2 piano concertos: No. 1 (1990; San Francisco, Jan. 24, 1991) and No. 2 (1991; Columbus, Ohio, Jan. 28, 1992); *Adagio* (1992; N.Y., April 13, 1993); *Transcendental Modulations* (1993; N.Y., Nov. 21, 1996). **Concert Band:** *Solemn Procession* (1947). **CHAMBER:** Sonata for Solo Viola (1942); *3 Sonatas* for Solo Clarinet (1943; Chicago, Aug. 7, 1955); *Hebrew Melodies* for Cello (1945; N.Y., Jan. 24, 1947); *Lyric Piece* for Cello and Piano (1946); Sonata for Solo Cello (1947; N.Y., Feb. 22, 1949); String Quintet (1958; San Francisco, Feb. 19, 1960); 4 wind quintets: No. 1 (Berkeley, April 8, 1959), No. 2 (1960; N.Y., May 6, 1962), No. 3 (1967; Chicago, April 5, 1968), and No. 4 (1984; N.Y., Oct. 2, 1985); 2 sonatas for Solo Violin: No. 1 (1959; Davis, Calif., March 13, 1960) and No. 2 (1963; Boston, Feb. 20, 1966); String Quartet No. 5 (1960; rev. version, Tanglewood, Aug. 13, 1967), No. 7 (1973; Buffalo, March 19, 1974), and No. 8, *Windows of Order* (1988; Washington, D.C., April 6, 1989); *Monody I* for Flute (1960; N.Y., May 10, 1962) and *II* for Bass (N.Y., Nov. 2, 1962); *3 Inventions* for Bassoon (1962; N.Y., March 26, 1963); *Solo Partita* for Violin and Viola (Chicago, April 23, 1965); *Sonata quasi una fantasia* for Clarinet and Piano (Buffalo, March 19, 1972); *Sonata a quattro* for Flute, Clarinet, Violin, and Cello (N.Y., May 17, 1982); Cello Sonata (N.Y., April 13, 1985); *Sonata a cinque* for Bass Trombone, Clarinet, Violin, Cello, and Piano (1986; N.Y., Feb. 28, 1987); *For Piano and Winds* (1988; N.Y., March 19, 1989); *Nightsong* for Flute, Clarinet, Violin, Cello, and Piano (1988; N.Y., March 7, 1991); Duos for Horn and String Quartet (1995; Kalamazoo, Mich., July 10, 1996); *Critical Moments* for Flute, Clarinet, Violin, Cello, Piano, and Percussion (1996; N.Y., April 14, 1997). **Piano:** *Pantomime, Interlude, and Fugue* (1937; N.Y., Feb. 27, 1982); *Little Suite* (Chicago, Oct. 23, 1939); *6 Préludes* (1946); Sonata (1950; N.Y., Feb. 11, 1951); *Short Sonata* (1964; N.Y., May 5, 1965); *Toccata* (1969; N.Y., Nov. 20, 1972); Suite in C (1970; Washington, D.C., April 29, 1987); *Fantasy-Variations* (1971; Sacramento, Calif., Nov. 6, 1986); *6 Études* (Boston, Oct. 29, 1976); *Ballade* (1981; N.Y., Feb. 17, 1982); *6 New Études* (1984; Beijing, May 7, 1985); Sonatina (Sacramento, Calif., Nov. 6, 1986); *Lyric Intermezzo* (Seattle, Nov. 7, 1987); *Phantasieplay* (1994; N.Y., April 2, 1997); *6 Celebratory Inventions* (1995; Boston, Jan. 17, 1997); *Chansons cachées* (Boston, Dec. 8, 1997); *Musical Offerings* for Piano,

Left-Hand (1998; N.Y., Dec. 6, 1999); *9 Bagatelles* (1999). **VOCAL:** *2 Rilke Songs* for Voice and Piano (1941; N.Y., May 6, 1949); *Sonnets to Orpheus* for Chorus (1974; N.Y., Feb. 18, 1975); *Songs of Praise and Lamentation* for Soloists, Chorus, and Orch. (1974; N.Y., Feb. 18, 1975); *13 Dickinson Songs* for Voice and Piano (Princeton, N.J., June 19, 1978).—NS/LK/DM

Perlea, Jonel, Romanian-born American conductor, teacher, and composer; b. Ograda, Dec. 13, 1900; d. N.Y., July 29, 1970. He studied piano and composition in Munich (1918–20) and conducting in Leipzig (1920–23). He made his conducting debut in Bucharest in 1919, then held posts as a conductor in Leipzig (1922–23) and Rostock (1923–25). He then conducted the Bucharest Opera (1929–32; 1934–36) and the Bucharest Radio Orch. (1936–44), of which he was a founder. He led conducting classes at the Bucharest Cons. (1941–44); during the last year of World War II, he was interned in a German concentration camp. After the war, he conducted opera in Rome (1945–47); in 1950, conducted at La Scala in Milan. He made his American debut at the Metropolitan Opera in N.Y. on Dec. 1, 1949, conducting *Tristan und Isolde*; appeared at the San Francisco Opera and the Lyric Opera of Chicago; from 1955 to 1970, was conductor of the Conn. Sym. Orch. He taught conducting at the Manhattan School of Music from 1952 until shortly before his death. Perlea became a naturalized American citizen in 1960. He suffered a heart attack in 1957 and a stroke in 1958, as a result of which he lost the use of his right arm, but he continued to conduct with his left hand.

WORKS: ORCH.: *2 Sketches* (1919); *Variations on an Original Theme* (Bucharest, Dec. 5, 1935); *Don Quichotte*, symphonic scherzo (1946); Sym. (1951); *Adagio* (1952); Sinfonia Concertante for Violin and Orch. (1968); *3 Studies* (1969). **CHAMBER:** Violin Sonata (1921); Cello Sonata (1921); String Quartet (1922); piano pieces, including a Sonata (1930). **VOCAL:** Songs. —NS/LK/DM

Perlemuter, Vlado, esteemed French pianist and pedagogue of Polish descent; b. Kaunas, Lithuania, May 26, 1904. He was taken to Paris at age 3, and entered the Cons. when he was 13, taking the premier prix at 15; his principal mentors were Moszkowski and Cortot. He devoted much time to teaching while making occasional appearances principally as a recitalist. He was a prof. at the Paris Cons. (1950–77), and also gave master classes. He acquired a remarkable reputation for his insightful interpretations of Chopin and Ravel. In 1993 he gave his farewell performance. In 1968 he was made a member of the Légion d'honneur. With H. Jourdan-Morhange, he publ. *Ravel d'aprés Ravel* (Lausanne, 1953; Eng. tr., 1988, as *Ravel According to Ravel*).—NS/LK/DM

Perlis, Vivian, American musicologist and harpist; b. N.Y., April 26, 1928. She was educated at the Univ. of Mich. (B.Mus., 1949; M.Mus., 1952), and then pursued postgraduate studies in harp at the Philadelphia Academy of Music (1953–54) and in musicology at Columbia Univ. (1962–64). She taught at Berkshire Coll. (1954–56), the Westport School of Music (1957–66), and Norwalk Community Coll. (1964–66). From 1966 she was active

as a freelance harpist. In 1967 she joined the staff of Yale Univ., where she was a reference librarian in its music library until 1972, and where she served as director of the Ives oral history project from 1968 to 1971. In 1972 she became a senior research associate at its school of music, where she founded and subsequently served as director of its valuable Oral History, American Music project. From 1972 to 1974 and again from 1991 she was a lecturer in the school of music and American studies. She also was a lecturer at the Univ. of Southern Calif. in Los Angeles (1974–75), a visiting senior research fellow at Brooklyn Coll. (1976–77), and a visiting lecturer at Wesleyan Univ. (1992–93). In 1971 she received the Charles Ives Award from the National Inst. of Arts and Letters, in 1975 the Otto Kinkeledy Award from the American Musicological Soc., in 1985 the ASCAP-Deems Taylor Award, in 1987 a Guggenheim fellowship, and in 1991 the Irving Lowens Award from the Sonneck Soc. In 1993 she was made a member of the Conn. Academy of Arts and Sciences. In addition to her contributions to various publications, Perlis was co-producer and writer of the television documentaries "Memories of Eubie" (on Eubie Blake; 1980), "Aaron Copland, A Self Portrait" (1985), and "John Cage: I Have Nothing to Say and I am Saying It" (1990).

WRITINGS: *Charles Ives Remembered: An Oral History* (1974); with H. Wiley Hitchcock, *An Ives Celebration: Papers and Panels of the Charles Ives Centennial Festival-Conference* (1977); *Two Men for Modern Music* (1978); *The Charles Ives Papers* (1983); with A. Copland, *Copland: 1900 through 1942* (1984) and *Copland: Since 1943* (1989).—LK/DM

Perlman, Itzhak, eminent Israeli-born American violinist, teacher, and conductor; b. Tel Aviv, Aug. 31, 1945. He contracted polio when he was 4 but persevered in his determination to study music. After studying at the Tel Aviv Cons., he pursued training at the Juilliard School of Music in N.Y. with Galamian and DeLay. On March 5, 1963, he made his formal U.S. debut as soloist with the National Orch. Assn. in N.Y. In 1964 he won 1st prize in the Leventritt Competition in N.Y., and quickly established himself as one of the principal violin virtuosos of the day. He appeared as a soloist with all of the major U.S. orchs., and also toured widely as a recitalist and chamber music artist. In 1968 he made his London debut as soloist with the London Sym. Orch., and thereafter was engaged by all of the leading British orchs. He made his Salzburg Festival debut as soloist with the Vienna Phil. in 1972, and in succeeding years made regular tours of Europe. In 1975 he joined the faculty of Brooklyn Coll. of the City Univ. of N.Y. while continuing his international career. In 1999 he became a teacher at the Juilliard School. Perlman also became active as a conductor, and in 2001 assumed the position of principal guest conductor of the Detroit Sym. Orch. He was honored with the U.S. Medal of Freedom by President Reagan in 1986. As a violinist, Perlman has performed and recorded all of the standard concertos. He has also sought out and performed works from the non-standard repertoire, including excursions into rags and jazz.

BIBL.: C. Behrman, *Fiddler to the World: The Inspiring Life of I. P.* (White Hall, Va., 1992).—NS/LK/DM

Perlongo, Daniel, American composer and teacher; b. Gaastra, Mich., Sept. 23, 1942. He was a student of Bassett, Wilson, and Finney at the Univ. of Mich. (M.M., 1966), and of Petrassi at the Accademia di Santa Cecilia in Rome (1966–68). He won the American Prix de Rome and was in residence at the American Academy in Rome (1970–72). Upon returning to the U.S., he became an assoc. prof. of composition and theory at Ind. Univ. of Pa. In 1980 and 1995 he held NEA fellowships, and in 1982 a Guggenheim fellowship.

WORKS: ORCH.: *7 Pieces* (1965); *Myriad* (1968); *Changes* for Wind Ensemble (1970); *Ephemeron* (1972); *Variations* for Chamber Orch. (1973); *Voyage* for Chamber Orch. (1975); Concertino for Chamber Orch. (1980); *Montalvo Overture* for Wind Ensemble (1984); *Lake Breezes* for Chamber Orch. (1990); *Preludes and Variations* for Wind Ensemble (1991); Piano Concerto (1992); *Shortcut from Bratislava* (1994); *2 Movements* (1995); *Sunburst* for Clarinet and Orch. (1995); *Millennium Overture* (1999). CHAMBER: *Episodes* for Double Bass (1966); *Movement* for 8 Players (1967); *Intervals* for String Trio (1967); *For Bichi* for Percussion Quartet (1968); *Movement in Brass* for 12 Brass Instruments (1969); *Process 7, 5, 3 for 6 in 12* for Flute, Oboe, Clarinet, and 3 Percussion (1969); 2 string quartets (*Semblance*, 1973; 1983); *Tre Tempi* for Flute, Clarinet, Horn, Violin, and Cello (1971); *Solo* for Violin (1971); *Fragments* for Flute and Cello (1972); *Ricercar* for Oboe, Clarinet, and Bassoon (1976); *Summer Music* for Brass Quintet (1978); *Aureole* for Saxophone Quartet (1979); *Soliloquy* for Bass Clarinet (1980); *A Day at Xochimilco* for Wind Quintet and Piano (1987); *Novella* for Trombone and Organ (1988); *Arcadian Suite* for Horn and Harp (1993); *2 Movements* for Clarinet and String Quartet (1995); *Poppies With Butterflies* for Cello and Piano (1996); *Groznjan Souvenir* for Wind Quintet (1998); *Breezes at Yellow Creek* for Violin, Cello, and Piano (2000). KEYBOARD: Piano: Sonata (1965); *Serenade* (1977); Suite (1988); *First Set* (1990). Organ: *Tapestry* (1981). VOCAL: *Missa Brevis* for Chorus (1967); *6 Songs* for Soprano and Piano (1980); *By Verse Distills* for Mezzo-sopranc, Clarinet, Violin, and Piano (1989); *3 Songs* for Chorus (1994).—**NS/LK/DM**

Perne, François Louis, French singer, double-bass player, music historian, and composer; b. Paris, Oct. 4, 1772; d. Laon, Aisne, May 26, 1832. He studied with Abbé d'Haudimont at the maîtrise of St.-Jacques-de-la-Boucherie. He was a chorus singer at the Paris Opéra from 1792, and double-bass player in the orch. there (1799–1816). His profound skill in composition was illustrated by his writing a triple fugue, to be sung backward on reversing the page; his knowledge of early music was extraordinary. In 1813 he became a prof. of harmony at the Paris Cons., as successor to Catel; he became inspector-general of the Cons. in 1816, and librarian in 1819. In 1822 he went into retirement, at an estate near Laon, returning to Paris shortly before his death. He publ. *Exposition de la séméiographie, ou Notation musicale des Grecs* (1815), *Cours d'harmonie et d'accompagnement* (1822), *Chansons du Châtelain de Coucy* (1830), and a great number of articles on Greek and medieval music publ. in vols. I-IX of the *Revue Musicale*, ed. by Fétis. He also wrote several pieces of sacred music.—**NS/LK/DM**

Pernerstorfer, Alois, Austrian bass-baritone; b. Vienna, June 3, 1912; d. there, May 12, 1978. He took courses with Lierhammer and Josef Krips at the Vienna Academy of Music. In 1936 he made his operatic debut as Biterolf in Graz, where he sang until 1939. He was a member of the Volksoper (1939–45) and State Opera (from 1945) in Vienna. He also sang in Zürich (1947–51), and at the Salzburg Festivals (from 1948), the Glyndebourne Festival (1951), and the Metropolitan Opera in N.Y. (debut as Sparafucile, Nov. 15, 1951). He was known for such roles as Figaro, Leporello, King Marke, Alberich, Pogner, and Baron Ochs.—**NS/LK/DM**

Pernet, André, French bass; b. Rambervillers, Jan. 6, 1894; d. Paris, June 23, 1966. He studied at the Paris Cons. with Gresse. He made his operatic debut in 1921 in Nice, and was a principal member of the Paris Opéra (1928–45); appeared there again in 1948, and also sang at the Paris Opéra-Comique (1931–48). His most notable roles included Don Giovanni, Boris Godunov, and Méphistophélès, but he also sang in many contemporary operas.—**NS/LK/DM**

Perosi, Don Lorenzo, distinguished Italian composer of church music; b. Tortona, Dec. 21, 1872; d. Rome, Oct. 12, 1956. He studied at the Milan Cons. (1892–93); also took courses at Haberl's School for Church Music at Regensburg (1893). He became maestro di cappella at Imola, and then at San Marco in Venice (1894–98). He was ordained a priest in 1895; in 1898 he became music director of the Sistine Chapel and leader of the papal choir; he resigned this post in 1915 owing to a severe mental disturbance; spent some time in a sanatorium (1922–23), after which he nominally held these duties again until his death, although with many relapses. Shortly after his 80th birthday, he led a performance of his oratorio *Il natale del Redentore* at the Vatican before Pope Pius XII (Dec. 28, 1952). He was a self-denying and scholarly worker for the cause of the cultivation of a pure church style, both in composition and in performance, and was esteemed above all others as a church musician at the Vatican.

WORKS: DRAMATIC: Oratorios: *La passione di Cristo secondo San Marco* (I, *La cena del Signore*; II, *L'orazione al monte*; III, *La morte del Redentore*; Milan, Dec. 2, 1897); *La trasfigurazione del nostro Signore Gesù Cristo* (Venice, March 20, 1898); *La risurrezione di Lazaro* (Venice, July 27, 1898); *La risurrezione di Cristo* (Rome, Dec. 13, 1898); *Il natale del Redentore* (Como, Sept. 12, 1899); *L'entrata di Cristo in Gerusalemme* (Milan, April 25, 1900); *La strage degli innocenti* (Milan, May 18, 1900); *Mosè* (Milan, Nov. 16, 1901); *Dies iste* (Rome, Dec. 9, 1904); *Transitus animae* (Rome, Dec. 18, 1907); *In patris memoriam* (1909; Naples, May 15, 1919); *Giorni di tribulazione* (Milan, Oct. 1916). OTHER: Some 40 masses, with Organ; *Requiem*, with Instrumental Accompaniment; *Stabat Mater* for Solo Voices, Chorus, and Orch.; *Vespertina oratio* for Solo Voices, Chorus, and Orch.; about 150 motets, *Psalms*, etc.; 2 symphonic poems: *Dovrei non piangere* and *La festa del villaggio*; a series of 8 orch. pieces, each named after an Italian city: *Roma, Firenze, Milano, Venezia, Messina, Tortona, Genoa,* and *Torina*; Piano Concerto; 2 violin concertos; chamber music; many organ works.

BIBL.: L. Seytre, *L'Abbé P.: Sa biographie, son oeuvre* (Nice, 1901); A. Damerini, *L. P.* (Rome, 1924); A. Della Corte, *L. P.*

(Turin, 1936); A. Paglialunga, *L. P.* (Rome, 1952); M. Glinsky, *L. P.* (Milan, 1953); M. Rinaldi, *L. P.* (Rome, 1967); M. Bruni, *L. P., el cantore evangelico* (Turin, 1972); A. Bassi, *D. L. P.: L'uomo, il compositore e il religioso* (Fasano, 1994).—**NS/LK/DM**

Perotin (called **Perotinus Magnus** and **Magister Perotinus**), celebrated composer who flourished in the 12th century. His very identity, as well as a general outline of his life, remains open to speculation. Research by H. Tischler indicates that he was born between 1155 and 1160, may have studied with Leonin, carried out his major work on the revision of the *Magnus liber* between 1180 and 1190, was involved in the early development of the motet between 1190 and 1200, wrote his works for 4 voices at the close of the century, and died between 1200 and 1205. Another chronology has been propounded by Reckow, Rokseth, and Sanders, who maintain that he wrote the works for 4 voices in the 1190s, which were the early years of his career, worked on the *Magnus liber* during the first years of the new century, wrote elaborate clausulas about 1210, was instrumental in creating Latin motets between 1210 and 1220, and died about 1225. See H. Husmann, ed., *Die drei- und vierstimmigen Notre-Dame-Organa*, Publikationen Älterer Musik, XI (Leipzig, 1940), and E. Thurston, ed., *The Works of Perotin* (N.Y., 1970).

WORKS: Compositions attributed to Perotin are as follows: **4-VOICE ORGAN:** *Viderunt omnes V. Notum fecit* (gradual for Christmas and Circumcision); *Sederunt principes V. Adiuva* (gradual for St. Stephen). **3-VOICE ORGAN:** *Sancte Germane V. O. sancte Germane* (responsory for St. Germanus); *Terribilis V. Cumque* (responsory for consecration of church); *Virgo V. Sponsus* (responsory for St. Catherine); *Exiit sermo V. Sed sic* (gradual for St. John the Evangelist); *Alleluia, Pascha nostrum* (Easter); *Alleluia, Nativitas* (Nativity of the Blessed Virgin Mary); *Alleluia, Dilexit Andream* (St. Andrew); *Alleluia, Posui adiutorium* (Confessor-Bishop); *Benedicamus Domino* (1, 2, and 3). **CLAUSULAS:** *Mors* for 4 Voices; *In odorem* for 3 Voices; *Et illuminare* for 3 Voices; *Et gaudebit* for 3 Voices; *Et exaltavi* for 3 Voices; 156 clausulas for *Magnus liber* for 2 Voices. **CONDUCTUS:** *Salvatoris hodie* for 3 Voices; *Dum sigillum summi Patris* for 2 Voices; *Beata viscera* for 1 Voice.

BIBL.: R. von Ficker, ed., *Perotinus: Organum quadruplum Sederunt principes* (Vienna and Leipzig, 1930); F. Gennrich, *Perotinus Magnus: Das Organum Alleluja Nativitas gloriose virgins Marie und seine Sippe*, Musikwissenschaftliche Studien-Bibliothek, XII (Darmstadt, 1955); F. Reckow, ed., *Der Musiktraktat des Anonymus 4* (Wiesbaden, 1967).—**NS/LK/DM**

Perotti, Giovanni Agostino, Italian composer and writer on music, brother of **Giovanni Domenico Perotti**; b. Vercelli, April 12, 1769; d. Venice, June 28, 1855. He studied with his brother and then with Mattei in Bologna. In 1795 he appeared as a keyboard player at the Viennese court and was active in London (1798–1802) before returning to his homeland. In 1811 he was made maestro primo at San Marco in Venice, and subsequently its maestro di cappella in 1817. He wrote the comic opera *La contadina nobile* (Pisa, 1795), many instrumental pieces, and music sacred music. He publ. *Dissertazione...determinare in tutta la sua estensione e con*

gli opportuni confronti il gusto, e lo stato attuale della musica in Italia (Venice, 1811), *Sugli studii e sulle opere di Benedetto Marcello* (Milan, 1843), and *Guida per lo studio del canto figurato* (Milan, 1846).—**LK/DM**

Perotti, Giovanni Domenico, Italian composer, brother of **Giovanni Agostino Perotti;** b. Vercelli, Jan. 20, 1761; d. there, March 24, 825. He was a student of Fioroni in Milan and Martini and Mettei in Bologna. From 1781 he served as maestro di cappella at Vercelli Cathedral. Among his output were the operas *Zemira e Gandarte* (Alessandria, 1787), *Agesilao re di Sparta* (Rome, 1789), and *La vittima della propria vendetta* (Venice, 1808), a Sym., 2 quartets, and several sacred works.—**LK/DM**

Perrachio, Luigi, Italian pianist, teacher, writer on music, and composer; b. Turin, May 28, 1883; d. there, Sept. 6, 1966. He studied piano in Turin, and also law at the Univ. there. After piano training in Vienna, he received instruction in piano and composition (diploma, 1913) at the Bologna Liceo Musicale. He taught piano (1925–40) and composition (1940–55) at the Turin Liceo Musicale. His writings included *L'opera pianistica di Claude Debussy* (Milan, 1924), *Il "clavicembalo ben temperato" di J. S. Bach* (Milan, 1926), and treatises on harmony and composition.

WORKS: DRAMATIC: *Mirtilla*, opera (1937–40); *La calunnia*, ballet (1952). **ORCH.:** *3 notturni a Giuseppe Verdi* (1929); *Piccola*, suite (1930); *Taccuino* (1930); Piano Concerto (1931–32); Violin Concerto (1932). **CHAMBER:** 2 string quartets (1910, 1930); Piano Quintet (1919); piano pieces. **VOCAL:** Choral pieces.—**LK/DM**

Perrault, Michel (Brunet), Canadian composer, percussionist, and conductor; b. Montreal, July 20, 1925. He studied theory and timpani with Louis Decair at the McGill Cons. in Montreal (1941–43), oboe with Réal Gagnier at the Montreal Cons. (1943–44), and harmony with Gabriel Cusson (1943–46). After further training with Boulanger, Honegger, and Dandelot at the École Normale de Musique in Paris (1946–47), he returned to Montreal and completed his studies with Conrad Letendre. He was a timpanist in the Montreal Sym. Orch. (1944–46) and the Little Sym. of Montreal (1945–46). He was a percussionist with the Montreal Sym. Orch. (1949–65), and also served as its asst. conductor (1957–60). From 1949 to 1968 he was active as a composer and conductor with the CBC. He also was music director of Les Grands Ballets Canadiens (1958–62). In his music, Perrault is a convinced traditionalist who finds inspiration in Quebec folk music.

WORKS: DRAMATIC: Ballet: *Commedia del arte* (1958); *Sea Gallows* (1958); *Suite canadienne* (1965). **ORCH.:** *Les Trois Cones* for Cello and Orch. (1949); *La Belle Rose* for Cello and Orch. (1952); *Fête et parade* for Trumpet and Orch. (1952); *Monologues* for Strings (1954); *Margoton* for Harp and Orch. (1954); *Le Saucisson canadien* for 4 Saxophones and Strings (1955); *Pastiche espagnol* for Trumpet and Orch. (1956); *Pastiche tzigane* for 2 Trumpets and Orch. (1957); *Berubée* for Piano and Orch. (1959); *Jeux de quartes* for Harp and Orch. (1961); *Serenata per tre fratelli* for 3 Horns and Orch. (1962); Double Bass Concerto (1962); *Homage*, overture (1966); Horn Concerto

(1967). **CHAMBER:** Violin Sonata (1946); Saxophone Quartet (1953); Piano Trio (1954); Sextet for Clarinet, Harp, and String Quartet (1955); *Georgian Rhapsody* for Alto Saxophone and Piano (1987). **VOCAL:** *Esquisses en plein air* for Soprano and String Orch. (1954); songs. **OTHER:** Pieces for jazz ensemble.—NS/LK/DM

Perrichon, Julien, French lutenist and composer; b. Paris, Nov. 6, 1566; d. probably there, c. 1600. He received musical training at the court, and by 1595 he was valet de chambre and lutenist to King Henri I. Many of his fine lute pieces were included in contemporary collections.—LK/DM

Perrin, Pierre, French poet; b. Lyons, c. 1620; d. Paris, April 25, 1675. He took the title of Abbé, and served as introducteur des ambassadeurs for Gaston d'Orléans (1648–60). Having written the texts to 2 of Cambert's pastorals—*Pastorale d'Issy* and *Ariane, ou Le mariage de Bacchus*—he obtained the privilege to organize académies d'opéra in 1669. The Paris academy was inaugurated with the Perrin-Cambert collaboration *Pomone* (March 3, 1671), which ran for 146 performances. However, his unscrupulous business managers took flight with the proceeds, leaving Perrin to spend time in a debtors' prison (1671); later that year he sold part of his privilege to the composer Sablières and his librettist Henri Guichard, and then turned over the full privilege to Lully in 1672 in return for a pension.

BIBL.: A. Pougin, *Les Vrais Créateurs de l'opéra français, P. et Cambert* (Paris, 1881); L. Auld, *The Lyric Art of P. P., Founder of French Opera* (3 vols., Henryville, Pa., 1986).—NS/LK/DM

Perron (real name, **Pergamenter**), **Karl,** noted German bass-baritone; b. Frankenthal, June 3, 1858; d. Dresden, July 15, 1928. He studied with Hey in Berlin, Hasselbasch in Munich, and Stockhausen in Frankfurt am Main, making his debut as Wolfram in 1884 in Leipzig, where he sang until 1891. He then joined the Dresden Court (later State) Opera, remaining on its roster until 1924; during his tenure there, he created the roles of Jochanaan in *Salome*, Orest in *Elektra*, and Baron Ochs in *Der Rosenkavalier*; also appeared at the Bayreuth Festivals (1889–1904), where he was acclaimed for his fine performances of Wotan and King Marke.—NS/LK/DM

Perry, Janet, American soprano; b. Minneapolis, Dec. 27, 1944. She received piano and violin lessons at home, and appeared in local young people's theater productions; then studied voice with Eufemia Giannini Gregory at the Curtis Inst. of Music in Philadelphia (B.M., 1967). In 1969 she made her operatic debut as Zerlina at the Linz Landestheater, remaining on its roster until 1971; following guest appearances at the Gärtnerplatztheater in Munich and at the Cologne Opera, she became a member of the Bavarian State Opera in Munich. She further made guest appearances in opera and concert in Hamburg, Düsseldorf, Paris, Zürich, Vienna, Berlin, Glyndebourne, and Salzburg. In 1983 she made her formal U.S. debut as Despina in Washington, D.C. Among her most successful roles were Susanna, Pamina, Constanze, Gilda, and Sophie.—NS/LK/DM

Perry, Julia (Amanda), black American composer; b. Lexington, Ky., March 25, 1924; d. Akron, Ohio, April 29, 1979. After studying at the Westminster Choir Coll. in Princeton, N.J. (M.Mus., 1948), she took a course in composition with Dallapiccola at the Berkshire Music Center in Tanglewood (summer, 1951). She then took composition lessons, intermittently, with Boulanger in Paris and again with Dallapiccola in Italy (1952–56), and also attended classes in conducting in Siena (1956–58). She received 2 Guggenheim fellowships and an award from the National Inst. of Arts and Letters.

WORKS: DRAMATIC: Opera: *The Bottle* (n.d.); *The Cask of Amontillado* (N.Y., Nov. 20, 1954); *The Selfish Giant,* opera-ballet (1964); *3 Warnings* (n.d.). **ORCH.:** *Short Piece* (1952); 12 syms. (1959–72), including No. 11, *Soul Symphony* (1972); *Pastoral* for Flute and Strings (1959); 2 piano concertos (1964); Violin Concerto (1964); *Module* (1975). **CHAMBER:** *Homunculus C.F.* for Harp and 10 Percussion (1960); Woodwind Trio; String Quartet; etc. **VOCAL:** *Chicago,* cantata for Baritone, Narrator, Chorus, and Orch. (1948); *Ruth,* cantata for Chorus and Organ (1950); *Stabat Mater* for Alto and Strings (1951); numerous songs.—NS/LK/DM

Persen, John, Norwegian composer; b. Porsanger, Norwegian Lapland, Nov. 9, 1941. He studied composition with Finn Mortensen at the Oslo Cons. (1968–73). From 1974 to 1976 he was president of Ny Musikk, the Norwegian section of the ISCM. His music follows the lines of the cosmopolitan avant-garde, with a mixture of jazz, rock, sonorism, and special effects (*ČSV* requires 2 pistol shots to be heard at the end of the work).

WORKS: DRAMATIC: Opera: *Under Kors og Krone* (Under Cross and Crown; 1978–85). **ORCH.:** *re-Verk* (1972); *Orkesterwerk II* (Oslo, May 4, 1974); *ČSV* (1976; Oslo, March 22, 1977); *Stykket har ingen tittel* (This Piece Has No Name; 1976; Trondheim, Jan. 20, 1977); *The John Persen's Guide to the Orchestra* (1990); *Over kros og krone* (1999). **Brass Band:** *Music for Resting Marching Band* (1977). **CHAMBER:** *Loops* for Chamber Ensemble (1995); *Recycled Encores* for 2 Violins, Viola, and Cello (1996). **VOCAL:** *Sámesiidat—ČSV* for Chorus (1976); *Enn!* for Chorus, 2 Narrators, and Tape (1986); *til a'Lisa* for Mezzo-soprano, Piano, and Percussion (1995). **ELECTRONIC:** *TTT-Things Take Time* (1985); *NotaBene* (1988); *Fuglan Veit* (1988–89).—NS/LK/DM

Persiani, Fanny (née **Tacchinardi**), renowned Italian soprano and singing teacher and daughter of **Nicola (Niccolò) Tacchinardi,** known as "La Persiani"; b. Rome, Oct. 4, 1812; d. Neuilly-sur-Seine, May 3, 1867. She studied with her father, and performed at an early age in his small training theater in Florence. After marrying the composer Giuseppe Persiani in 1830, she made her professional debut as Fournier-Gorre's *Francesca da Rimini* in Livorno in 1832. Following successful appearances in Venice and Milan, she gained distinction as a leading performer of roles in operas by Bellini and Donizetti, creating the title role in Donizetti's *Lucia di Lammermoor* in Naples in 1835; she also sang in her husband's operas, including *Ines de Castro*. She made her first appearance in Paris at the Théâtre-Italien in 1837, and continued to sing there with brilliant success until 1850. She made her London debut at the King's Theatre in *La Sonnambula* in 1838, remaining a favorite there, and later at Covent Garden, until 1849; also sang in Vienna (1837, 1844). After singing at the Italian Opera in St. Petersburg (1850–52), she settled in Paris as a voice teacher. Blessed with a small but beautiful coloratura voice, she had few equals in her day.

BIBL.: Chaudesaigues, *Madame P.* (Paris, 1839); P. Ciarlantini, *Giuseppe Persiani e F. Tacchinardi: Due Protagonisti del Melodramma Romantico* (Ancona and Bologna, 1988).
—NS/LK/DM

Persiani, Giuseppe, Italian composer; b. Recanati, Sept. 11, 1799; d. Paris, Aug. 13, 1869. As a youth he played violin in theater orchs. in Rome and Naples, where he studied with Zingarelli and Tritto. In 1830 he married **Fanny Persiana** (née **Tacchinardi**), who became famous as "La Persiani"; her illustrious name completely eclipsed his, yet he was a notable composer whose dramatic opera *Ines de Castro*, produced in Naples on Jan. 27, 1835, scored great success and was performed all over Europe. The celebrated soprano Malibran sang the title role, and Czerny wrote a piano paraphrase on themes of the opera. Persiani's other operas were *Attila* (Parma, Jan. 31, 1827), *Il Solitario* (Milan, April 26, 1829), *Il Fantasma* (Paris, Dec. 14, 1843), and *Eufemio di Messina* (Lucca, Sept. 20, 1829; perf. also under the alternative titles *La distruzione di Catania* and *I Saraceni a Catania*).

BIBL.: P. Ciarlantini, *G. P. e Fanny Tacchinardi: Due Protagonisti del Melodramma Romantico* (Ancona and Bologna, 1988).
—NS/LK/DM

Persichetti, Vincent (Ludwig), remarkable American composer and pedagogue whose finely amalgamated instrumental and symphonic music created an image of classical modernity; b. Philadelphia, June 6, 1915; d. there, Aug. 13, 1987. His father was a native of Abruzzi, Italy, who emigrated to the U.S. in 1894. His mother was of German descent, hailing from Bonn. Persichetti's middle name was given to him not to honor Beethoven but to commemorate his maternal grandfather who owned a saloon in Camden, N.J. He studied piano, organ, double bass, tuba, theory, and composition as a youth; began his career as a professional musician when he was only 11 years old; became a church organist at 15. He took courses in composition with Russell King Miller at the Combs Cons. (Mus.B., 1936); then served as head of the theory and composition dept. there; concurrently studied conducting with Reiner at the Curtis Inst. of Music (diploma, 1938) and piano with Samaroff and composition with Nordoff at the Philadelphia Cons. (M.Mus., 1941; D.Mus., 1945); also studied composition with Harris at Colo. Coll. From 1941 to 1947 he was head of the theory and composition dept. of the Philadelphia Cons.; in 1947, joined the faculty of the Juilliard School of Music in N.Y.; in 1963, was named chairman of the composition dept. there. In 1952 he became director of music publishing of Elkan-Vogel, Inc. With F. Schreiber, he wrote a biography of William Schuman (N.Y., 1954). He publ. a valuable manual, *Twentieth Century Harmony: Creative Aspects and Practice* (N.Y., 1961). His music is remarkable

for its polyphonic skill in fusing the ostensibly incompatible idioms of Classicism, Romanticism, and stark modernism, while the melodic lines maintain an almost Italianate diatonicism in a lyrical manner. The skillful concatenation of ostensibly mutually exclusive elements created a style that was characteristically Persichetti's. He was not interested in program music or in any kind of descriptive tonal works (exceptionally, he wrote a piece of background music for the Radio City Music Hall organs which was performed in 1969). His significance for American music, therefore, is comprised in his 9 syms., and, most particularly, in his 12 piano sonatas and 6 piano sonatinas. Although he stood far from the turmoil of musical politics, he unexpectedly found himself in the center of a controversy when he was commissioned by the 1973 Presidential Inauguration Committee to write a work for narrator and orch. for a perf. at President Richard Nixon's 2nd inauguration. Persichetti selected the text of a speech by President Abraham Lincoln, his 2nd inaugural address, but, surprisingly, objections were raised by certain groups to the passionate denunciation of war in the narrative, at a time when the Vietnam War was very much in the news. The scheduled performance by the Philadelphia Orch. was hurriedly canceled, and the work's premiere was deferred to a performance by the St. Louis Sym. Orch. on Jan. 25, 1973. In 1987 Persichetti contracted a cancer of the lungs, but even when racked by disease he continued to work on his last opus, *Hymns and Responses for the Church Year, Vol. II.* He requested that his body be donated to medical science. His devoted wife suffered a stroke and died on Thanksgiving Day in the same year. Her monograph on her husband (1960) remains unpublished.

WORKS: DRAMATIC: O p e r a : *Parable XX: The Sibyl* (1976; Philadelphia, April 13, 1985). **ORCH.:** Piano Concertino (1941; Rochester, N.Y., Oct. 23, 1945); 9 syms.: No. 1 (1942; Rochester, N.Y., Oct. 21, 1947), No. 2 (1942), No. 3 (1946; Philadelphia, Nov. 21, 1947), No. 4 (1951; Philadelphia, Dec. 17, 1954), No. 5, for Strings (1953; Louisville, Aug. 28, 1954), No. 6, for Band (St. Louis, April 16, 1956), No. 7, *Liturgical* (1958; St. Louis, Oct. 24, 1959), No. 8 (Berea, Ohio, Oct. 29, 1967), and No. 9, *Sinfonia Janiculum* (1970; Philadelphia, March 5, 1971); *Dance Overture* (1942; Tokyo, Feb. 7, 1948); *Fables* for Narrator and Orch. (1943; Philadelphia, April 20, 1945); *The Hollow Men* for Trumpet and Strings (1944; Germantown, Pa., Dec. 12, 1946); *Serenade No. 5* (Louisville, Nov. 15, 1950); *Divertimento* for Band (N.Y., June 16, 1950); *Fairy Tale* (1950; Philadelphia, March 31, 1951); *Psalm* for Band (Louisville, May 2, 1952); *Pageant* for Band (Miami, May 7, 1953); *Serenade No. 11* for Band (1960; Ithaca, N.Y., April 19, 1961); *Bagatelles* for Band (Hanover, N.H., May 21, 1961); Piano Concerto (1962; Hanover, N.H., Aug. 2, 1964); *So Pure the Star*, chorale prelude for Band (Durham, N.C., Dec. 11, 1962); *Introit* for Strings (1964; Kansas City, Mo., May 1, 1965); *Masquerade* for Band (1965; Berea, Ohio, Jan. 23, 1966); *Turn Not Thy Face*, chorale prelude for Band (1966; Ithaca, N.Y., May 17, 1967); *Night Dances* (Kiamesha Lake, N.Y., Dec. 9, 1970); *O Cool is the Valley*, poem for Band (1971; Columbus, Ohio, Feb. 5, 1972); *Parable IX* for Band (1972; Des Moines, April 6, 1973); *A Lincoln Address* for Narrator and Orch. (1972; St. Louis, Jan. 25, 1973; also for Narrator and Band, Russelville, Arks., Feb. 1, 1974); Concerto for English Horn and Strings (N.Y., Nov. 17, 1977); *O God Unseen*, chorale prelude for Band (Winston-Salem,

N.C., Nov. 4, 1984). **CHAMBER:** *Serenade No. 1* for 10 Winds (1929), *No. 3* for Violin, Cello, and Piano (1941), *No. 4* for Violin and Piano (1945), *No. 6* for Trombone, Viola, and Cello (1950), *No. 9* for 2 Recorders (1956), *No. 10* for Flute and Harp (1957), *No. 12* for Tuba (1961), *No. 13* for 2 Clarinets (1963), and *No. 14* for Oboe (1984); 4 string quartets (1939; 1944; 1959; *Parable X*, 1972); Suite for Violin and Cello (1940); Violin Sonata (1940); *Concertato* for Piano Quintet (1940); *Fantasy* for Violin and Piano (1941); *Pastoral* for Woodwind Quintet (1943; Philadelphia, April 20, 1945); *Vocalise* for Cello and Piano (1945); *King Lear* for Woodwind Quintet, Timpani, and Piano (1948; 1st perf. as *The Eye of Anguish*, Martha Graham Dance Co., Montclair, N.J., Jan. 31, 1949); Sonata for Solo Cello (1952); Piano Quintet (1954; Washington, D.C., Feb. 4, 1955); *Little Recorder Book* (1956); *Infanta Marina* for Viola and Piano (1960); *Masques* for Violin and Piano (1965); *Parable I* for Flute (1965), *II* for Brass Quintet (1968), *III* for Oboe (1968), *IV* for Bassoon (1969), *VII* for Harp (1971), *VIII* for Horn (1972), *XI* for Alto Saxophone (1972), *XII* for Piccolo (1973), *XIII* for Clarinet (1973), *XIV* for Trumpet (1973), *XV* for English Horn (1973), *XVI* for Viola (1974), *XVII* for Double Bass (1974), *XVIII* for Trombone (1975), *XXI* for Guitar (1978), *XXII* for Tuba (1981), and *XXIII* for Violin, Cello, and Piano (1981). **KEYBOARD: Piano:** *Serenade No. 2* (1929), *No. 7* (1952), and *No. 8* for Piano, 4-Hands (1954); 12 sonatas (1939, 1939, 1943, 1949, 1949, 1950, 1950, 1950, 1952, 1955, 1965, 1980); *Poems* (3 vols., 1939, 1939, 1941); Sonata for 2 Pianos (1940); *Variations for an Album* (1947); 6 sonatinas (1950, 1950, 1950, 1954, 1954, 1954); Concerto for Piano, 4-Hands (1952); *Parades* (1952); *Little Piano Book* (1953); *Parables XIX* (1975); *Reflective Studies* (1978); *Little Mirror Book* (1978); *4 Arabesques* (1978); *3 Toccatinas* (1979); *Mirror Etudes* (1979). **Organ:** Sonatine (1940); Sonata (1960); *Shimah b'koli* (1962); *Drop, Drop Slow Tears*, chorale prelude (1966); *Parable VI* (1971); *Do Not Go Gentle* (1974); *Auden Variations* (1977); *Dryden Liturgical Suite* (1980); *Song of David* (1981). **Harpsichord:** 8 sonatas (1951, 1981, 1981, 1982, 1982, 1982, 1983, 1984); *Parable XXIV* (1982); *Little Harpsichord Book* (1983); *Serenade No. 15* (1984). **VOCAL:** *Magnificat and Nunc dimittis* for Chorus and Piano (1940); *Canons* for Chorus (1947); *2 Cummings Choruses* for 2 Voices and Piano (1948); *Proverb* for Chorus (1948); *2 Cummings Choruses* for Women's Chorus (1950); *Hymns and Responses for the Church Year* for Chorus (1955; Philadelphia, Oct. 7, 1956); *Seek the Highest* for Voices and Piano (1957); *Song of Peace* for Men's Chorus and Piano (1959); Mass for Chorus (1960; N.Y., April 20, 1961); *Stabat Mater* for Chorus and Orch. (1963; N.Y., May 1, 1964); *Te Deum* for Chorus and Orch. (1963; Philadelphia, March 15, 1964); *Spring Cantata* for Women's Chorus and Piano (1963; Boston, April 1, 1964); *Winter Cantata* for Women's Chorus, Flute, and Marimba (1964; Troy, N.Y., April 9, 1965); *4 Cummings Choruses* for 2 Voices and Piano (1964); *Celebrations* for Chorus and Wind Ensemble (River Falls, Wisc., Nov. 18, 1966); *The Pleiades* for Chorus, Trumpet, and Strings (1967; Potsdam, N.Y., May 10, 1968); *The Creation* for Soprano, Alto, Tenor, Baritone, Chorus, and Orch. (1969; N.Y., April 17, 1970); *Love* for Women's Chorus (1971); *Glad and Very* for 2 Voices (1974); *Flower Songs* (Cantata No. 6) for Chorus and Strings (1983; Philadelphia, April 20, 1984); several songs, including the major cycle *Harmonium* for Soprano and Piano, after poems of Wallace Stevens (1951; N.Y., Jan. 20, 1952). **BIBL.:** D. and J. Patterson, *V. P.: A Bio-Bibliography* (Westport, Conn., 1988).**—NS/LK/DM**

Persinger, Louis, eminent American violinist and teacher; b. Rochester, Ill., Feb. 11, 1887; d. N.Y., Dec. 31, 1966. He began his violin studies at an early age in Colo., making his public debut when he was 12; then studied with Hans Becker at the Leipzig Cons. (1900–04), with Ysaÿe in Brussels, and with Thibaud in Paris. He toured Belgium and Germany; served as concertmaster of the Berlin Phil. (1914–15) and the San Francisco Sym. Orch. (1915–16). He then led his own string quartet and served as director of San Francisco's Chamber Music Society (1916–28); subsequently devoted himself mainly to teaching; in 1930 he joined the staff of the Juilliard School of Music in N.Y. He achieved a great reputation as a teacher who subordinated technical demands to the paramount considerations of formal balance and expressiveness of the melodic line. Among his pupils were Yehudi Menuhin, Ruggiero Ricci, and Isaac Stern.

BIBL.: Y. Menuhin, "L. P.," *Juilliard Review Annual* (N.Y., 1966–67).**—NS/LK/DM**

Person, Eric, jazz alto saxophonist; b. St. Louis, Mo., May 2, 1963. His father, Thomas Person, is a saxophonist. Eric went through the Normandy H.S. music program in St. Louis, then attended the St. Louis Conservatory of Music. Since his arrival in N.Y. in the early 1980s, he has worked with the John Hicks Big Band, Ronald Shannon Jackson's Decoding Society, Chico Hamilton, McCoy Tyner Big Band, Woody Shaw, Kelvyn Bell, Jackie McLean, World Saxophone Quartet, and the rock band Living Colour; he also toured and recorded for three years with The Dave Holland Quartet. Since the formation of his current working ensemble, Meta-Four, he has performed all over the U.S. and Canada. In fall 1997, he toured Europe with Michiel Borstlap; he also appeared on singer/guitarist Ben Harper's popular album, *The Will to Live*, touring with Harper in France and performing on Quincy Jones's *Vibe* TV show. He has played on film scores with Chico Hamilton, including *A Practical Man*.

DISC.: *Prophecy* (1992); *Arrival* (1992); *More Tales to Tell* (1997). B. Harper: *The Will to Live* (1997). D. Holland: *Dream of the Elders* (1996). World Saxophone Quartet: *Moving Right Along* (1994). C. Hamilton: *Euphoria* (1988); *Arroyo* (1990); *My Panamanian Friend* (1994); *Trio!* (1993). R. S. Jackson: *When Colors Play* (1986); *Texas* (1987); *Taboo* (1990).**—LP**

Person, Houston, one of the more prolific saxophonists on the jazz scene with a style that has served him well both commercially and artistically for over three decades; b. Florence, S.C., Nov. 10, 1934. Along with Grant Green, Stanley Turrentine, Charles Earland, and Richard "Groove" Holmes, tenor saxophonist Houston Person was at the forefront of the "groove jazz" movement in the late 1960s/early 1970s. A pianist as a child, he took up tenor sax at age 17. His first major break came when he played with organist Johnny "Hammond" Smith. After he left Smith's group, he began a fruitful solo career, but continued to do extensive work as a sideman, including a long relationship with singer Etta Jones. Since the late 1970s, he has been the house producer and saxophonist for HighNote (formerly Muse) Records. As HighNote's session saxophonist of choice, he can always be counted on to deliver tasteful solos with his unique tone. His recordings are fun, and though sometimes predictable, generally filled with good playing. While he has strong R&B and blues influences, he is an excellent and underrated straight-ahead player whose funkier jazz dates feature more sophisticated playing than usually heard in such settings.

DISC.: *Goodness!* (1969); *Legends of Acid Jazz* (1970–71); *Lost & Found* (1978); *Wildflower* (1978); *Sweet Slumber* (1978); *The Complete Muse Sessions* (1989); *Person- ified* (1997); *The Opening Round* (1997); *Christmas with Houston Person & Etta Jones* (1997).—**PMac**

Persuis, Louis-Luc Loiseau de, French violinist and composer; b. Metz, July 4, 1769; d. Paris, Dec. 20, 1819. He received training in violin. After playing in the Metz theater orch., he settled in Paris in 1787. He played in the orch. of the Théâtre Montansier (1790–93) and the Opéra (from 1793). In 1820 he was made director, in 1814 inspector-general of music, and in 1817 director of the Opéra. In 1811 he also was made chef d'orchestre of Napoleon's Paris chapel. Perrichon composed a number of theater works, the most significant being his opera *Godefroy de Bouillon, ou La Jérusalem délivérée* (Paris, Sept. 15, 1812). Among his other scores were pieces for state occasions, sacred music, romances, and songs.—**LK/DM**

Perti, Giacomo or **Jacopo Antonio,** greatly significant Italian composer; b. Crevalcore, near Bologna, June 6, 1661; d. Bologna, April 10, 1756. He began to study music with his uncle, Lorenzo Perti, and with Rocco Laurenti, and later took lessons in counterpoint with Petronio Franceschini. As early as 1678 he had a Mass performed at the church of S. Tomaso al Mercato. In 1679 he collaborated on the opera *Atide*, to which he contributed the score for the 3rd act. In 1681 he was elected a member of the Accademia Filarmonica, of which he was 5 times the principe (in 1719 was named censor). He then went to Parma, where he continued his studies with Giuseppe Corso. In 1689 he had his opera *Dionisio Siracusano* performed in Parma, and another opera, *La Rosaura*, in Venice. In 1690 he succeeded his uncle as maestro di cappella at the Cathedral of S. Pietro in Bologna. In 1696 he became maestro di cappella of S. Petronio, a position he held until his death. He also held similar positions at S. Domenico (1704–55; deputized for Alberti from 1734) and at S. Maria in Galliera (1706–50). Emperor Charles VI made him a royal councillor in 1740. His students included G.B. Martini and Giuseppe Torelli.

WORKS: DRAMATIC: O p e r a : *Atide* (Bologna, June 23, 1679; incomplete; in collaboration with others); *Marzio Coriolano* (Venice, Jan. 20, 1683); *Oreste in Argo* (Modena, Carnival 1685); *L'incoronazione di Dario* (Bologna, Jan. 13, 1686); *La Flavia* (Bologna, Feb. 16, 1686); *Dionisio Siracusano* (Parma, Carnival 1689); *La Rosaura* (Venice, 1689); *Brenno in Efeso* (Venice, 1690); *L'inganno scoperto per vendetta* (Venice, Carnival 1690 or 1691); *Il Pompeo* (Genoa, Carnival 1691); *Furio Camillo* (Venice, Carnival 1692); *Nerone fatto Cesare* (Venice, 1693); *La forza della virtù* (Bologna, May 25, 1694); *Laodicea e Berenice* (Venice, 1695); *Penelope la casta* (Rome, Jan. 25, 1696); *Fausta restituita all'impero* (Rome, Jan. 19, 1697); *Apollo geloso* (Bologna, Aug. 16, 1698); *Ariovisto* (Milan, Sept. 1699; in collaboration with others);

La prosperità di Elio Sejano (Milan, Carnival 1699; in collaboration with others); *Dionisio rè di Portogallo* (Pratolino, Sept. 1707); *Il fratricida innocente* (Bologna, May 19, 1708); *Ginevra principessa di Scozia* (Pratolino, Fall 1708); *Berenice regina d'Egitto* (Pratolino, Sept. 1709); *Rodelinda regina de' Longobardi* (Pratolino, Fall 1710); *Lucio vero* (Bologna, Spring 1717); *Rosinde ed Emireno* (undated). **O r a t o r i o s :** *S. Serafina [I due gigli porporati nel martirio de S. Serafina e S. Sabina]* (Bologna, 1679); *Abramo vincitore* (Venice, 1683); *Mosè* (Modena, 1685); *Oratorio della passione di Cristo* (Bologna, 1685); *La beata Imelde Lambertini* (Bologna, 1686); *Agar* (Bologna, 1689); *La passione del Redentore* (Bologna, 1694); *S. Galgano* (Bologna, 1694); *Cristo al limbo* (Bologna, 1698); *La sepoltura di Cristo* (Bologna, 1704); *S. Giovanni* (Bologna, 1704); *Gesù al sepolcro* (Bologna, 1707); *S. Petronio* (Bologna, 1720); *L'amor divino [I conforti di Maria vergine addolorata]* (Bologna, 1723); also several undated oratorios. **OTHER SACRED:** *Messa e salmi concertati* for 4 Voices, Instruments, and Chorus (Bologna, 1735); *7 canzonette in aria marmoresca sopra le 7 principali feste di Nostra Signora* (Bologna, 1780); 120 Psalms, 54 motets, 28 masses; about 150 secular cantatas; *Cantate morali e spirituali* for 1 and 2 Voices, with Violin (Bologna, 1688).

BIBL.: L. Mancini, *J.A. P.* (Bologna, 1813); G. Vecchi, ed., *La musica barocca a Bologna ... G.A. P.* (Bologna, 1961).—**NS/LK/DM**

Pertile, Aureliano, noted Italian tenor; b. Montagnana, Nov. 9, 1885; d. Milan, Jan. 11, 1952. He studied with Orefice and Fugazzola. He made his operatic debut in *Martha* in Vicenza in 1911; then sang in Naples (1914), at Milan's La Scala (1916), and the Teatro Colón in Buenos Aires (1918); made his Metropolitan Opera debut in N.Y. as Cavaradossi in *Tosca* (Dec. 1, 1921). He then returned to La Scala, where he gained renown for his portrayal of Faust in *Mefistofele* (1922); was a leading tenor there until 1937; also appeared at London's Covent Garden (1927–31); retired from the stage (1946); taught at the Milan Cons. (from 1945). He was esteemed for such roles as Andrea Chénier, Manrico, Radames, Canio, and Don Alvaro; he created Boito's Nerone and Mascagni's Nerone.—**NS/LK/DM**

Pescetti, Giovanni Battista, Italian composer; b. Venice, c. 1704; d. there, March 20, 1766. He was the grandson of C.F. Pollarolo. Following his training with Lotti, he became active as an opera composer, frequently collaborating with Galuppi. In 1736 he went to London as director of the Opera of the Nobility, where he commenced a rivalry with Handel. Pescetti's opera *Demetrio*, first performed in Venice in 1732, was given in London in a revised version on Feb. 12, 1737. His success was short- lived, and from 1738 he prepared various pasticcios. He returned to Venice about 1745, where he wrote a number of works for the stage. In 1762 he became 2nd organist at San Marco. He wrote about 25 operas in all, as well as sacred music and instrumental pieces.—**NS/LK/DM**

Pešek, Libor, admirable Czech conductor; b. Prague, June 22, 1933. He received his training at the Prague Academy of Music, graduating in 1956. He was founder-conductor of the Prague Chamber Harmony (1959) and the Prague Sebastian Orch. (1965). From 1969 to 1975 he was music director of the Frysk Orch. in the

Netherlands, and also of the Czech State Chamber Orch. in Prague from 1969 to 1977. He was music director of the Overijssels Phil. in the Netherlands as well from 1975 to 1979. In 1981–82 he was conductor of the Slovak Phil. in Bratislava. In 1982 he was made conductor-in-residence of the Czech. Phil. in Prague. He also was principal conductor and artistic adviser of the Royal Liverpool Phil. from 1987 to 1995, which he led on its first tour of the U.S. in 1992. As a guest conductor, he appeared with many of the leading European and North American orchs. He is an especially distinguished interpreter of the 19th- and 20th-century Czech repertoire. —NS/LK/DM

Pesenti, Martino, blind Italian harpsichordist and composer; b. Venice, c. 1600; d. there, c. 1648. He was a pupil of Giovanni Battista Grillo in Venice, where he later was in the service of various families of the nobility. He publ. in Venice 7 vols. of madrigals and canzonettas (c. 1619–48), 4 vols. of dances (c. 1619–46), 3 vols. of arias (1633–39), and a vol. of sacred music (1643).—LK/DM

Pesenti, Michele, Italian singer, lutenist, and composer; b. probably in Verona, c. 1470; d. after 1524. He was in the service of the d'Este family in Ferrara. Pesenti was a notable composer of frottolas, of which 36 were publ. (1505–21). Two of his motets are also extant. —NS/LK/DM

Peskanov, Mark, Russian-born American violinist; b. Odessa, Aug. 30, 1956. He entered the Stoliarsky School of Music in Odessa at age 7, where he was a pupil of Boris Brant. In 1973 he emigrated to the U.S., where he pursued studies with Dorothy DeLay at the Juilliard School in N.Y. (B.A., 1979). On Nov. 1, 1977, he made his debut as soloist in Wieniawski's 1st Violin Concerto with Rostropovich and the National Sym. Orch. in Washington, D.C. During the 1978–79 season, he made his London debut with Rostropovich and the London Phil. In 1985 he won the Avery Fisher Career Grant and the 1st Isaac Stern Award of N.Y.'s Carnegie Hall. After appearing as soloist with the Philadelphia Orch. at the Mann Music Center in 1987, he received the 1st Frederick R. Mann Young Artist Award. Subsequently, he was engaged as soloist by many principal American orchs.; he also appeared as a chamber music artist in the U.S. and abroad. He made frequent appearances with the Chamber Music Soc. of Lincoln Center in N.Y.—NS/LK/DM

Peskó, Zoltán, Hungarian-born Italian conductor and composer; b. Budapest, Feb. 15, 1937. He studied at the Budapest Academy of Music (graduated, 1962); also took courses in composition with Petrassi and in conducting with Ferrara in Italy, and in conducting with Boulez in Switzerland (1963–66). He was asst. conductor to Maazel and the Deutsche Oper and Berlin Radio Sym. Orch. in the Western sector (1966–69); then conducted at the Berlin State Opera in East Berlin (1969–73); also served on the faculty at the Berlin Hochschule für Musik (1969–72). From 1974 to 1976 he was chief conductor of the Teatro Comunale in Bologna; subsequently was chief conductor of Venice's Teatro La Fenice (1976–77) and Milan's Orchestra Sinfonica della RAI (1978–82). From 1996 to 1999 he was chief conductor of the Deutsche Oper am Rhein in Düsseldorf. He wrote some orch. music, chamber works, and keyboard pieces. —NS/LK/DM

Pesonen, Olavi, Finnish composer and teacher; b. Helsinki, April 8, 1909; d. there, Nov. 11, 1993. He studied with Ilmari Krohn and Leevi Madetoja at the Univ. of Helsinki (M.A., 1932), and also took courses with Arthur Willner in Vienna and Seiber in London, and studied organ with Ramin in Leipzig. He then devoted himself to teaching and composing in Helsinki. His works follow along traditional lines.

WORKS: DRAMATIC: *Havahtuminen* (Awakening), melodrama for Narrator and Orch. (1936); *Huutokauppa* (Auction), music to A. Leinonen's play (1949). ORCH.: *Pieni sarja* (Little Suite; 1936); *Juhla-alkusoitto* (Festive Overture; 1938; rev. 1946); *Fuga fantastica* (1948; based on the organ piece, 1939); *Tanhusoitto* (Folk Dances; 1949); 2 syms. (1949, 1953); *Suite ancienne* (1978); *Pieces* for Strings, after Finnish folk songs (1980); *In dulci jubilo* for Strings (1981). OTHER: Various works for Chorus and Orch., including the cantatas *Ah autuus suuri* (O Great Bliss; 1939; rev. 1978), *Koulukantaatti* (School Cantata; 1941), and *Silenivät pitkospuut* (The Causeway Became Smoother; 1966); a cappella choruses; songs; organ music, including *Fuga fantastica* (1939; also for Orch., 1948) and *Jesu dulcis memoria* (1981).—NS/LK/DM

Pessard, Émile (-Louis-Fortuné), French composer; b. Paris, May 29, 1843; d. there, Feb. 10, 1917. He studied at the Paris Cons. with Bazin (harmony), Laurent (piano), Benoist (organ), and Carafa (composition), winning the 1st harmony prize in 1862, and the Grand Prix de Rome in 1866 with the cantata *Dalila* (1866). In 1881 he was appointed prof. of harmony at the Paris Cons. He enjoyed considerable regard as a composer of fine songs. As a student, Debussy copied Pessard's song *Chanson d'un fou*, and the MS in Debussy's handwriting was publ. erroneously as Debussy's own.

WORKS: DRAMATIC: O p e r a (all 1st perf. in Paris): *La Cruche cassée* (Feb. 1870); *Don Quichotte* (Feb. 13, 1874); *Le Char* (Jan. 18, 1878); *Le Capitaine Fracasse* (July 2, 1878); *Tabarin* (Jan. 12, 1885); *Tartarin sur les Alpes* (Nov. 17, 1888); *Les Folies amoureuses* (April 15, 1891); *Une Nuit de Noël* (1893); *Mam'zelle Carabin* (Nov. 3, 1893); *La Dame de trèfle* (May 13, 1898); *L'Armée des vierges* (Oct. 15, 1902); *L'Epave* (Feb. 17, 1903). OTHER: Orch. pieces; choral works; chamber music; songs; piano pieces.—NS/LK/DM

Pestalozzi, Heinrich, Swiss composer; b. Wadenswil, near Zürich, Aug. 26, 1878; d. Zürich, Aug. 9, 1940. He studied theology and music in Berlin, where he was a singing teacher (1902–12). He then was a pastor in Arosa, Switzerland, and then in 1917 became a voice teacher at the Zürich Cons. His choral works and songs acquired great popularity in his homeland. He also publ. several manuals on singing.—NS/LK/DM

Peter, John Frederick (actually, **Johann Friedrich**), significant American Moravian violinist, organist, and composer, brother of **Simon Peter;** b.

Heerendijk, the Netherlands (of German parents), May 19, 1746; d. Bethlehem, Pa., July 13, 1813. He was educated in the Netherlands and Germany, then went to the U.S. in 1770. He served the Moravian Church in various capacities in the Pa. communities of Nazareth, Bethlehem, and Lititz (until 1780), then in Salem, N.C., until 1790. He spent the rest of his life mostly in Bethlehem as organist of the church. He is widely considered the greatest of the American Moravian composers. His collection of copies of instrumental works by Stamitz, J.C.F. Bach, J.C. Bach, Abel, Boccherini, and Haydn (preserved in the Archives of the Moravian Church) proves his knowledge of contemporary music. Among his compositions are 105 concerted anthems (he excelled in the genre) and solo songs. While in Salem, he completed (1789) a set of 6 quintets for 2 Violins, 2 Violas, and Cello (his only secular works), which are the oldest preserved examples of chamber music composed in America. His MSS are preserved in the Archives of the Moravian Church in Bethlehem and the Moravian Foundation in Winston-Salem, N.C.

BIBL.: W. Schnell, *The Choral Music of Johann Friedrich P.* (diss., Univ. of Ill., 1973); C. Crews, *J.F. P. and His Times* (Winston-Salem, N.C., 1990).—NS/LK/DM

Peter, Simon, American Moravian composer, brother of **John Frederick (Johann Friedrich) Peter;** b. Heerendijk, the Netherlands (of German parents), April 2, 1743; d. Salem, N.C., May 29, 1819. With his brother, he was educated at the Moravian Brethren's schools in the Netherlands and Germany. He went to the U.S. in 1770. His ministry was spent in both the Northern and Southern Provinces of the Moravian Church (i.e., both Pa. and N.C.). From 1784 to 1819 he lived in N.C. as pastor of several congregations, and was a member of the governing board of the Church. He composed only a few sacred anthems, but one, *O Amblick, der mirs Herze bricht,* is one of the most expressive Lenten songs written in America.—NS/LK/DM

Peter, Paul and Mary, influential folk-singing trio who scored many 1960s-era hits. **MEMBERSHIP:** Peter Yarrow, gtr., ten. voc. (b. N.Y., May 31, 1938); (Noel) Paul Stookey, gtr., bar. voc. (b. Baltimore, Md., Nov. 30, 1937); Mary Travers, sop. voc. (b. Louisville, Ky., Nov. 7, 1937).

Peter, Paul and Mary were brought together by manager Albert Grossman in N.Y.'s Greenwich Village during 1961. Peter Yarrow was a Cornell Univ. graduate in psychology who had worked for a time as a solo artist and appeared at the 1960 Newport Folk Festival. Noel Paul Stookey had led a high school rock band before pursuing a career around Greenwich Village as a standup comic. He encouraged former folk group member Mary Travers to return to singing after her appearance in the flop Broadway show, *The Next President.* Conducting intensive rehearsals for seven months, Peter, Paul and Mary debuted at The Bitter End in Greenwich Village and signed with Warner Bros. Records.

Peter, Paul and Mary's debut album became a top album hit, staying on the charts for well over three years. It included standard folk material such as Reverend Gary Davis's "If I Had My Way," Hedy West's "500 Miles," and Pete Seeger's "Where Have All the Flowers Gone," and original compositions by Yarrow and Stookey. It yielded a moderate hit with "Lemon Tree" and a near-smash hit with "If I Had a Hammer," coauthored by Seeger. Quickly thrust into the forefront of the folk movement, Peter, Paul and Mary became favorites on the college circuit and frequently performed at political rallies and protest marches. Their second album, *(Moving),* also became a best-seller, remaining on the album charts for nearly two years. It produced a smash hit with "Puff, the Magic Dragon," written by Yarrow and Leonard Lipton, moderate hits with "Stewball" and "Tell It on the Mountain," and contained Woody Guthrie's "This Land Is Your Land."

With *In the Wind,* Peter, Paul and Mary began featuring songs by then-unknown contemporary songwriters. The smash successes of "Blowin' in the Wind" and "Don't Think Twice, It's All Right" introduced Bob Dylan to a wider audience and bolstered the burgeoning "folk-protest" movement. Following the live double-record set *In Concert,* the trio recorded *A Song Will Rise,* which contained the first hit version of Gordon Lightfoot's "For Lovin' Me," and *See What Tomorrow Brings,* which included Lightfoot's "Early Morning Rain" and Tom Paxton's "Last Thing on My Mind."

The *Peter, Paul and Mary Album* featured Laura Nyro's "And When I Die" and Richard Farina's "Pack Up Your Sorrows" and was followed by perhaps their finest albums, *Album 1700* and *Late Again. Album 1700* produced a near-smash hit with Stookey's collaborative tongue-in-cheek "I Dig Rock and Roll Music" while containing John Denver's "Leaving on a Jet Plane" (a top pop and easy-listening hit when released as a single two years later) and some of the group's most memorable compositions, including the touching "House Song," Yarrow's antiwar "The Great Mandella (The Wheel of Life)," and the classic "The Song Is Love." *Late Again* included "Hymn" and "Rich Man, Poor Man," coauthored by Stookey and Yarrow, respectively, and Tim Hardin's "Reason to Believe," and yielded a moderate hit with Bob Dylan's "Too Much of Nothing."

Following *Peter, Paul and Mommy* and the major hit "Day Is Done," Peter Yarrow, Paul Stookey and Mary Travers went their separate ways in 1970. Stookey fared the best of the three as a solo artist, scoring a major hit with "Wedding Song (There Is Love)" from the excellent *Paul And* album in 1971. By the mid-1970s, Paul Stookey had retreated to Maine and Peter Yarrow had become involved in television and record production work, leaving Mary Travers as the only former member to perform extensively. In 1976, Yarrow produced Mary MacGregor's best-selling *Torn Between Two Lovers* album, coauthoring the top hit title song. He also coproduced the 1978 CBS animated television special, "Puff, the Magic Dragon," based on the song. He later supervised the soundtracks to two more animated television specials based on the song.

In 1978, Peter, Paul and Mary reunited at the Survival Sunday benefit show in Calif., subsequently recording *Reunion* for Warner Bros. They performed 30 to 50 concerts a year until 1983, when they began playing around 100 engagements a year. Without a major label deal during most of the 1980s, Peter, Paul and Mary eventually recorded *No Easy Walk to Freedom* for the small Gold Castle label, followed by the Christmas album *A Holiday Celebration* Two Peter, Paul and Mary PBS television specials fared well in the late 1980s and their Gold Castle recordings were reissued by Warner Bros. in 1992. By 1995, Peter, Paul and Mary had returned to their original label, Warner Bros., for *Lifelines*, recorded with Pete Seeger, Ramblin' Jack Elliott, Holly Near, Judy Collins, and Emmylou Harris. *Lifelines Live*, from 1996, featured Odetta, Tom Paxton, and John Sebastian.

DISC.: PETER, PAUL AND MARY: *Peter, Paul and Mary (Moving)* (1962); *In the Wind* (1963); *In Concert* (1964); *A Song Will Rise* (1965); *See What Tomorrow Brings* (1965); *Album 1700* (1967); *Late Again* (1968); *Peter, Paul and Mommy* (1969); *Best (Ten Years Together)* (1970); *Reunion* (1978); *No Easy Walk to Freedom* (1987/1989); *A Holiday Celebration* (1988/1989); *Flowers and Stones* (1990); *Peter, Paul and Mommy, Too* (1993); *Lifelines* (1995); *Lifelines Live* (1996). **MARY TRAVERS:** *Mary* (1971); *Morning Glory* (1972); *All My Choices* (1973); *Circles* (1974); *It's in Every One of Us* (1978). **PAUL STOOKEY:** *Paul And* (1971); *Noel—One Night Stand* (1973); *Bodyworks* (1990). **PETER YARROW:** *Peter* (1972); *That's Enough for Me* (1973); *Hard Times* (1975); *Love Songs* (1975).—**BH**

Peters (real name, Petermann), Roberta,

outstanding American soprano; b. N.Y., May 4, 1930. She studied voice with William Pierce Hermann. At the age of 20, she made her operatic debut with the Metropolitan Opera in N.Y. as Zerlina in *Don Giovanni* on Nov. 17, 1950, as a substitute on short notice; she subsequently remained on its roster for more than 40 years. She also sang with the opera companies of San Francisco and Chicago, at Covent Garden in London, at the Salzburg Festivals, and at the Vienna State Opera. In 1998 she was awarded the National Medal of Arts. She was one of the leading coloratura sopranos of her generation; also appeared with success on television, films, and in musical comedies. She was briefly married to **Robert Merrill**. With Louis Biancolli, she wrote *A Debut at the Met* (1967).—**NS/LK/DM**

Peters, Carl Friedrich,

German music publisher; b. Leipzig, March 30, 1779; d. Sonnenstein, Bavaria, Nov. 20, 1827. In 1814 he purchased Kühnel & Hoffmeister's Bureau de Musique (founded, 1800; Hoffmeister left the firm in 1805, and Kühnel led it from 1805 until his death in 1813). It became known as Bureau de Musique C.F. Peters, but encountered difficulties as a result of the Battle of Leipzig and Peters's committal to an asylum; nevertheless, it acquired a notable reputation through its publication of the first collected ed. of the works of J.S. Bach and of a number of works by Beethoven. In 1828 the manufacturer Carl Gotthelf Siegmund Bohme (1785–1855) took charge of the firm; after his death, the town council took it over as a charity foundation. In 1860 it was purchased by the Berlin book and music seller Julius Friedländer, who took the lawyer Max Abraham (1831–1900) into partnership in 1863; Abraham became sole owner in 1880 and proceeded to build

an international reputation for the firm. In addition to publishing works by the foremost composers of the day, the firm launched the inexpensive and reliable Edition Peters in 1867, opened its large and valuable Musikbibliothek Peters to the public in 1893, and publ. the scholarly *Jahrbuch der Musikbibliothek Peters* from 1895 (it was the *Deutsches Jahrbuch der Musikwissenschaft* from 1956 to 1977; then the *Jahrbuch Peters*). Abraham's nephew, Heinrich Hinrichsen (b. Hamburg, Feb. 5, 1868; d. in the Auschwitz concentration camp, Sept. 30, 1942), became a partner in 1894 and sole owner in 1900; his son Max Hinrichsen (b. Leipzig, July 6, 1901; d. London, Dec. 17, 1965) joined the firm in 1927 and became a full partner in 1931; another son, Walter Hinrichsen (b. Leipzig, Sept. 23, 1907; d. N.Y., July 21, 1969), joined the firm in 1931, and a third son, Hans-Joachim Hinrichsen (b. Leipzig, Aug. 22, 1909; d. in the Perpignan concentration camp, Sept. 18, 1940), joined it in 1933. Walter left the firm in 1936 and founded the C.F. Peters Corp. in N.Y. in 1948; Max left the firm in 1936, and in 1938 founded the Hinrichsen Edition in London, which became the Peters Edition in 1975; Heinrich and Hans-Joachim were deprived of their ownership by the Nazis in 1939, and Johannes Petschull took control of the firm. During and after World War II, the original Leipzig firm encountered great difficulties; the German Democratic Republic took it over in 1949–50. With the Hinrichsen heirs as partners, Petschull founded a new company in Frankfurt am Main in 1950. The Leipzig firm publishes much contemporary music while issuing rev. and updated eds. of earlier scores. The London firm has brought out much English music, while the N.Y. firm has a deep commitment to modern music.—**NS/LK/DM**

Petersen, Wilhelm,

German composer and teacher; b. Athens, March 15, 1890; d. Darmstadt, Dec. 18, 1957. He studied in Germany and worked as a theater conductor, then served in the German army during World War I. In 1922 he settled in Darmstadt as a teacher. He wrote the opera *Der goldne Topf* (Darmstadt, March 29, 1941), 5 syms. (1921, 1923, 1934, 1941, 1957), 3 violin sonatas, 3 string quartets, and several sacred choruses and songs. He was highly regarded in Darmstadt as a musician and pedagogue. In 1972 a Wilhelm Petersen Society was founded to memorialize his work.

BIBL.: A. Petersen, *W. P., Skizze seines Wesens und Lebens* (Darmstadt, 1962); W. Mechsner, *W. P.: Leben und Werk: Biographie mit thematischem Werkverzeichnis* (Frankfurt am Main, 1996). —**NS/LK/DM**

Peters (Lazzara), Bernadette,

star of stage, screen, and even one hit record; b. Queens, N.Y., Feb. 28, 1948. By the time Bernadette Lazzara was five years old, she was on TV, appearing on the *Horn and Hardart Children's Hour*, imitating Sophie Tucker. By nine, she was a member of Actors Equity, performing in *The Most Happy Fella*. She toured in *Gypsy* as a teenager, and appeared Off-Broadway regularly from the age of 17 on. In 1967, she made her Broadway debut in *The Girl in the Freudian Slip*, then played Josie Cohan in the musical *George M*, starring Joel Grey. In 1968, she was proclaimed a star by reviewers of the Off-Broadway production of *Dames at Sea*. Despite this success, her next two leading roles on Broadway in 1969 and 1970 closed on their first night. She earned a Tony nomination for her work in the 1971 revival of *On the Town* and another one for her performance in *Mack and Mabel* in 1974. Leaving Broadway for a while in the mid-1970s, she moved to Hollywood and started making films, including *The Jerk* and *Pennies from Heaven*, with Steve Martin, and Mel Brooks's *Silent Movie*.

Peters also explored a mainstream singing career. In 1980, she cut *Bernadette Peters*, going to #31 with her version of Carla Thomas's "Gee Whiz," her only pop hit. By 1984, she was back on Broadway in Stephen Sondheim's *Sunday in the Park with George*. She won a Tony Award for her demanding role in Andrew Lloyd Webber's 1985 play *Song and Dance*, which featured Peters alone onstage for the entire first act. She was given star billing in a supporting role in Sondheim's 1987 musical *Into the Woods*. Back in Hollywood for the early part of the 1990s, she took on mostly dramatic roles, though she also provided the voice for Rita the Cat in the cartoon series *Animaniacs*. She returned to Broadway for the ill-fated musical version of Neil Simon's *The Goodbye Girl* in 1993, and started making concert appearances. In 1997, she gave voice to Sophie in the animated feature *Anastasia*. From 1999 through 2000, she appeared as Annie Oakley in the successful Broadway revival of *Annie Get Your Gun*. The performance won her another Tony Award.

DISC.: *Dames at Sea: Original Cast Recording* (1969); *Bernadette Peters* (1980); *Now Playing* (1981); *Bernadette* (1992); *Andrew Lloyd Webber's Song and Dance* (1995); *I'll Be Your Baby Tonight* (1996); *Sondheim, Etc.* (1997).—**HB**

Peterson, Oscar (Emmanuel),

pianist, singer, one of the most popular of all jazz musicians; b. Montreal, Quebec, Canada, Sept. 15, 1925. He was part of a very musical black community. His older sister Daisy was a legendary piano teacher. His father started him on classical piano at age six, culminating with studies with Hungarian classical pianist Paul deMarky. He quit school at 16 to pursue his career; by his teens, he was playing on a weekly radio show. In 1944–47, he was playing with the Johnny Holmes Orch. in a style reminiscent of Teddy Wilson, Erroll Garner, and Art Tatum. He had trouble reading music but overcame this by having members of his group immediately memorize the arrangements for the trios. From 1945, he recorded in Canada for RCA, and in 1949 he came to Carnegie Hall with Norman Granz's Jazz at the Philharmonic. He has been associated with Granz on the Verve and Pablo labels ever since, except for a period on European MPS in the mid-1970s when Granz was "retired." In 1950, *Down Beat* named him pianist of the year, an award he won 12 times. On at least one occasion in Cleveland, he got to jam with Tatum after hours. He led a Nat Cole–styled trio with Ray Brown on bass and Irving Ashby, succeeded by Barney Kessel, then Herb Ellis (from 1953), on guitar. In 1958, the guitar was replaced by drummer Ed Thigpen, in turn replaced in by Louis Hayes in 1965; Sam Jones took over from Brown on bass. Peterson occasionally sang, notably on *With Respect To Nat* (1965), very much in Cole's style. After 1970, he concentrated on solo piano performances and has worked with symphony orchestras since the mid 1970s. He was made an Officer of the Order of Canada (1973). In 1991, he was named chancellor of York Univ. in Toronto, where he continues to do some teaching. He toured 40 weeks a year, but always maintained a home in the Toronto area. The pace of his schedule took its toll on his personal life: his first three marriages, which produced six children, ended in divorce. He also has 11 grandchildren and one great-grandchild. In 1993, he suffered a stroke while playing at a club in N.Y. He required three months of intensive therapy at home to recover from the stroke's physical effects. Peterson says that he also needed a push from his physiotherapist to recover emotionally. It took him 14 months, until July 1994, before he felt comfortable playing publicly and touring again. The stroke partially paralyzed the left side of his body, limiting his use of the left hand, but fortunately not enough to prevent him from playing well. His playing has often been criticized for a glib excess of notes (there was a famous mutual antagonism between Peterson and Monk related to this), specifically that it lacks drama, but his music has undeniably powerful drive and swing and the light emotional tone of his work is in keeping with much of his generation. He is one of the great accompanists, and in that role he has provided a cushion of support on hundreds of recordings with great warmth and modesty. In 1997, he was living in Mississauga, a suburb of Toronto. In summer of 1997, he appeared at several jazz festivals in Europe. Since the stroke, he spends no more than eight weeks a year on the road, and the balance of his time at home with current wife Kelly, an American. When not touring, he is composing and playing in his basement, which is equipped with a grand piano, high-tech keyboards, his musical library and a recording studio. Peterson is one of the most recorded musicians, probably the most recorded pianist, with over 250 albums as a leader or sideperson. He doesn't believe in perfect pitch but says "I come as close as someone who claims to have it." He is the subject of a South Bank documentary and of *Life in the Key of Oscar*.

DISC.: *I Got Rhythm* (1945); *Complete Young Oscar Peterson* (1945); *Rockin' in Rhythm* (1947); *Oscar Peterson at Carnegie Hall* (1950); *Piano Solos* (1950); *Keyboard Music by Oscar Peterson* (1950); *Romance* (1952); *At the Stratford Shakespearean Festival* (1956); *Louis Armstrong Meets Oscar Peterson* (1957); *At the Concertgebouw* (1957); *Jazz Soul of Oscar Peterson* (1959); *Jazz Portrait of Frank Sinatra* (1959); *Harold Arlen Songbook* (1959); *George Gershwin Songbook* (1959); *Very Tall* (1961); *Trio: Live from Chicago* (1961); *Sound of the Trio* (1961); *Night Train, Vol. 1* (1962); *Live at the London House* (1962); *Affinity* (1962); *We Get Requests* (1964); *Plus One* (1964); *Oscar Peterson Trio Plus One* (1964); *Canadian Suite* (1964); *With Respect to Nat* (1965); *Eloquence* (1965); *Canadian Concert of Oscar Peterson* (1965); *Blues Etude* (1965); *Great Oscar Peterson on Prestige* (1968); *Motions and Emotions* (1969); *Tristeza on Piano* (1970); *History of an Artist, Vol. 1, 2* (1972); *Satch and Josh* (1974); *Oscar Peterson in Russia* (1974); *In Russia* (1974); *Oscar Peterson and Roy Eldridge* (1974); *Oscar Peterson and Harry Edison* (1974); *Oscar Peterson and Dizzy Gillespie* (1974); *Oscar Peterson and Clark Terry* (1975); *Oscar Peterson and Joe Pass* (1975); *Big Six* (1975); *Satch and Josh Again*

(1977); *Royal Wedding Suite* (1981); *Nigerian Marketplace* (1981); *Freedom Song* (1982); *Saturday Night at the Blue Note* (1990).

BIBL.: R. Palmer, *Oscar Peterson* (Tunbridge Wells, 1984); G. Lees, *Oscar Peterson: The Will to Swing* (Toronto, rev. ed., 1999). **—LP/NS/MM**

Peterson, Wayne, American composer and teacher; b. Albert Lea, Minn., Sept. 3, 1927. He studied with Early Rymer (piano) and with Paul Fetler, Earl George, and James Aliferis (composition) at the Univ. of Minn. (B.A., 1951; M.A., 1953; Ph.D., 1960); also with Lennox Berkeley and Howard Ferguson at the Royal Academy of Music in London. He served on the music faculty of the Univ. of Minn. (1953–54), Chico (Calif.) State Coll. (1959–60), and San Francisco State Coll. (later Univ.; from 1960). He held numerous NEA awards. In 1989–90 he held a Guggenheim fellowship (1989–90). In 1992 he won the Pulitzer Prize in Music for his orch. works *The Face of the Night, the Heart of the Dark.*

WORKS: ORCH.: *Introduction and Allegro* (1953); *Free Variations* (1954–58); *Exaltation, Dithyramb and Caprice* (1959–60); *Cataclysms* (1968); *Clusters and Fragments* for Strings (1969); *Transformations II* for Chamber Orch. (1985; San Francisco, April 11, 1986); *Trilogy* (1987; Saratoga, Calif., June 18, 1988); *The Widening Gyre* (1990; N.Y., Feb. 10, 1991); *The Face of the Night, the Heart of the Dark* (1990–91). **CHAMBER:** *Metamorphosis* for Wind Quintet (1967); *Phantasmagoria* for Flute, Clarinet, and Double Bass (1968); *Capriccio* for Flute and Piano (1973); *Transformations* for String Quartet (1974); *Encounters* for 9 Players (1976); *An Interrupted Serenade* for Flute, Harp, and Cello (1978); Sextet (1982); String Quartet (1983–84); *Ariadne's Thread* for Harp, Flute, Clarinet, Horn, Percussion, and Violin (1985); *Duodecaphony* for Viola and Cello (1986–87). **—NS/LK/DM**

Peterson-Berger, (Olof) Wilhelm, esteemed Swedish music critic, teacher, and composer; b. Ullånger, Feb. 27, 1867; d. Ostersund, Dec. 3, 1942. He studied with J. Dente and O. Bolander at the Stockholm Cons. (1886–89); then in Dresden with Scholtz (piano) and Kretzschmar (composition). He eventually settled in Stockholm, where he became active as a pedagogue and music critic of *Dagens Nyheter* (1896–1908; 1910–20; 1921–30). His opera *Arnljot* was one of the finest Swedish operas in the national tradition; his other notable works included his 3rd Sym., Violin Concerto, songs, and piano pieces.

WORKS: DRAMATIC: *Sveagaldrar,* festival play for the silver jubilee of the accession of Oscar II (1897); 4 music dramas (all 1st perf. in Stockholm): *Ran* (1899–1900; May 20, 1903), *Arnljot* (1907–09; April 13, 1910), *Domedagsprofeterna* (The Prophets of Doom; 1912–17; Feb. 21, 1919), and *Adils och Elisiv* (1921–24; Feb. 27, 1927); *Lyckan* (Luck), fairy opera (Stockholm, March 27, 1903). **ORCH.:** 5 syms.: No. 1, *Baneret* (The Banner; 1889–90; 1903; Stockholm, Feb. 23, 1904; rev. 1932–33), No. 2, *Sunnanfärd* (The Journey to the South; 1910; Göteborg, March 22, 1911), No. 3, *Same Ätnam* (Lappland; 1913–15; Stockholm, Dec. 11, 1917), No. 4, *Holmia* (1929; Stockholm, April 9, 1930), and No. 5, *Solitudo* (1932–33; Stockholm, April 11, 1934); 3 orch. suites: *I somras* (Last Summer; 1903), *Earina* (Spring; 1917), and *Italiana* (1922); *Romans* for Violin and Orch. (1915); Violin Concerto (1928; Stockholm, Feb. 6, 1929). **CHAMBER:** 2 violin sonatas (1887, 1910); Suite for Violin and Piano (1896); over 100 piano pieces. **VOCAL: Cantatas:** *Norrbotten* (1921);

Operakantaten (1922; rev. 1935–36); *Soluppgång* (1929). **Other:** 40 songs for choruses; nearly 100 solo songs.

WRITINGS: *Svensk Musikkultur* (1911); *Richard Wagner som kulturföreteelse* (Richard Wagner as a Phenomenon of Civilization; 1913; Ger. tr., 1917, as *Richard Wagner als Kulturerscheinung*). A selection of his essays was publ. in Stockholm in 2 vols. (1923); another, in one vol., in Östersund (1951). His reminiscences were publ. posthumously (Uppsala, 1943).

BIBL.: B. Carlberg, *W. P.-B.* (Stockholm, 1950); S. Beite, *W. P.-B.: En känd och okänd tondiktare* (Östersund, 1965); G. Norell, *W. P.-B. och dikten* (vol. 1, Arboga, 1991).—**NS/LK/DM**

Petit (first name unknown), French violinist and composer; b. c. 1700; d. probably in Paris, after 1753. He was a student of Tartini. On Dec. 25, 1738, he made his first appearance at the Concert Spirituel in Paris playing one of his own concertos, and performed there again in 1741–42. His contemporaries held him in the highest esteem.—**LK/DM**

Petit Jehan, Claude, French composer; b. place and date unknown; d. Metz, 1589. He became choirmaster at Metz Cathedral in 1571, and served as a canon there until his death. By 1575 he was choirmaster at Verdun Cathedral. In 1576 he won a prize at the Evreux music competition for his *Ce riz plus doux* for 4 Voices. He was long confused with Petit Jehan de Lattre. **—LK/DM**

Petkov, Dimiter, Bulgarian composer and conductor; b. Smolyan, May 4, 1919. He studied composition with Veselin Stoyanov at the State Academy of Music in Sofia, graduating in 1950; then went to Moscow for postgraduate studies in theory at the Cons. (1952–54). He taught theory at the State Academy of Music in Sofia (1949–52; 1954–58) and was director of the National Opera Theater; later served as president of the Union of Bulgarian Composers (1972–80).

WORKS: DRAMATIC: *The Winding Path,* children's operetta (1956; Michailovgrad, Oct. 29, 1975); *Restless Hearts,* musical comedy (1960). **CHAMBER:** *3 Polyphonic Pieces* for Flute, Clarinet, and Bassoon (1953). **VOCAL:** *The Sparks of October* for Soloists, Children's Chorus, and Orch. (1967); *Rozhan Comes Down from Rhodopa,* oratorio (1965); 5 cantatas: *September Legend* (1953), *Communists* (1956), *Requiem for a Sailor* (1967), *Cantata about Paissy* (1973), and *Festive Cantata* (1974); choruses; folk song arrangements.

BIBL.: E. Pavlov, *D. P.* (Sofia, 1987).—**NS/LK/DM**

Petra-Basacopol, Carmen, Romanian composer and teacher; b. Sibiu, Sept. 5, 1926. She studied philosophy at the Univ. of Bucharest (1945–49); then took courses with Jora (composition and counterpoint), Rogalski (orchestration), and Constantinescu (harmony) at the Bucharest Cons. (1949–56); attended courses in new music in Darmstadt (1968); later completed her training at the Sorbonne in Paris (Ph.D., 1976, with the diss. *L'Originalité de la musique roumaine à travers les oeuvres d'Enesco, Jora et Constantinesco;* publ. in Bucharest, 1979). She taught at the Bucharest Cons. (from 1962). She received the Order of Cultural Merit (1969) and the

Georges Enesco composition prize of the Romanian Academy (1980). Her music is lyrical, with colorful and effective instrumentation.

WORKS: DRAMATIC: B a l l e t : *Fata şi masca* (The Girl and the Mask; 1970); *Ciuleandra* (1985–86). **ORCH.:** Sym. No. 1 (1956); *Tara de piatra* (Stone Country; 1959); Piano Concerto (1961); *Symphonic Triptych* (1962); 2 violin concertos (1963, 1965); Concertino for Harp, Kettledrums, and Strings (1975); Concerto for Strings (1981); Cello Concerto (1982). **CHAMBER:** Suite for Flute and Piano (1950); Cello Sonata (1952); Trio for Violin, Cello, and Piano (1959); Sonata for Flute and Harp (1961); *Divertissement* for Harp, Wind Quintet, Double Bass, and Xylophone (1969); Trio for Flute, Clarinet, and Bassoon (1974); Quartet for Flute, Violin, Cello, and Piano (1978); Suite for Cello (1981); Trio for Flute, Clarinet, and Harp (1987); piano pieces. **VOCAL:** Choral music; songs.—NS/LK/DM

Petrassi, Goffredo, outstanding Italian composer and teacher; b. Zagarolo, near Rome, July 16, 1904. He went to Rome and had private piano lessons with Bastini, and then commenced the study of harmony with Donato (1925). He subsequently entered the Cons. di Santa Cecilia (1928), where he studied composition with Bustini (diploma, 1932) and organ with Germani (diploma, 1933). He taught at the Accademia di Santa Cecilia (1934–36), where he also received instruction from Molinari. He was general director of Venice's Teatro La Fenice (1937–40). After teaching composition at the Cons. di Santa Cecilia (1939–59), he taught again at the Accademia di Santa Cecilia (1959–74), and also taught at Siena's Accademia Musicale Chigiana (1966–67). He publ. the vol. *Autoritratto* (Rome, 1991). Despite the late beginning, Petrassi acquired a solid technique of composition; the chief influence in his music was that of Casella; later he became interested in 12-tone procedures.

WORKS: DRAMATIC: O p e r a : *Il Cordovano* (1944–48; Milan, May 12, 1949; rev. 1958; Milan, Feb. 18, 1959); *La morte dell'aria* (1949–50; Rome, Oct. 24, 1950). **B a l l e t :** *La follia di Orlando* (1942–43; Milan, April 12, 1947); *Il ritratto di Don Chisciotte* (1945; Paris, Nov. 21, 1947). **ORCH.:** *Divertimento* (1930); *Ouverture da concerto* (1931); *Passacaglia* (1931); *Partita* (1932; Rome, April 2, 1933); 8 concertos: No. 1 (1933–34; Rome, March 31, 1935), No. 2 (1951; Basel, Jan. 24, 1952), No. 3, *Récréation concertante* (1952–53; Aix-en-Provence Festival, July 23, 1953), No. 4 for Strings (1954; Rome, April 28, 1956), No. 5 (Boston, Dec. 2, 1955), No. 6, *Invenzione concertata*, for Brass, Strings, and Percussion (1956–57; London, Sept. 9, 1957), No. 7 (1961–64; Bologna, March 18, 1965), and No. 8 (1970–72; Chicago, Sept. 28, 1972); Piano Concerto (1936–39; Rome, Dec. 10, 1939); Flute Concerto (1960; Hamburg, March 7, 1961); *Estri*, chamber sym. for 15 Performers (Hanover, N.H., Aug. 2, 1967; as a ballet, Spoleto, July 11, 1968); *Frammento* (1983). **CHAMBER:** *Sinfonia, Siciliana e Fuga* for String Quartet (1929); *Introduzione e allegro* for Violin and Piano (1933; also with 11 Instruments); *Preludio, Aria e Finale* for Cello and Piano (1933); *Sonata da camera* for Harpsichord and 10 Instruments (1948); *Dialogo angelico* for 2 Flutes (1948); *Musica a 2* for 2 Cellos (1952); String Quartet (1958); *Serenata* for Flute, Viola, Double Bass, Harpsichord, and Percussion (1958); String Trio (1959); *Serenata II*, trio for Harp, Guitar, and Mandolin (1962); *Musica di Ottoni* for Brass and Timpani (1963); *3 per 7* for 3 Performers on 7 Wind Instruments (1966); *Ottetto di Ottoni* for 4 Trumpets and 4 Trombones (1968); *Souffle* for 1 Performer on 3 Flutes (1969);

Elogio per un'Ombra for Violin (1971); *Nunc* for Guitar (1971); *Ala* for Flute and Harpsichord (1972); *4 odi* for String Quartet (1973–75); *Fanfare* for 3 Trumpets (1974–76); *Alias* for Guitar and Harpsichord (1977); *Sestina d'autunno* for 6 Instruments (1981–82); *Inno* for 4 Trumpets, 4 Cornets, and Trombone (1984); *Duetto* for Violin and Viola (1985). **P i a n o :** *Siciliana e marcetta* for 2 Pianos (1930); *Toccata* (1933); *Invenzioni* for 2 Pianos (1944); *Oh les beaux jours!* (1976); *Petite pièce* (1976). **VOCAL:** *3 Choruses* for Chorus and Small Orch. (1932); *Psalm IX* for Chorus, Strings, Brass, 2 Pianos, and Percussion (1934–36); *Magnificat* for Soprano, Chorus, and Orch. (1939–40); *Coro di morti*, dramatic madrigal for Men's Chorus, Brass, Double Basses, 3 Pianos, and Percussion (Venice, Sept. 28, 1941); *2 liriche di Saffo* for Voice, and Piano or 11 Instruments (1941); *Quattro inni sacri* for Tenor, Baritone, and Organ (1942; also for Tenor, Baritone, and Orch., Rome, Feb. 22, 1950); *Noche oscura*, cantata (Strasbourg, June 17, 1951); *Nonsense* for Chorus, after Edward Lear (1952); *Propos d'Alain* for Baritone and 12 Performers (1960); *Sesto non-senso* for Chorus, after Edward Lear (1964); *Mottetti per la Passione* for Chorus (1966); *Beatitudines*, chamber oratorio for Baritone and 5 Instruments, in memory of Martin Luther King Jr. (Fiuggi, July 17, 1969); *Orationes Christi* for Chorus, Brass, 8 Violins, and 8 Cellos (1974–75; Rome, Dec. 6, 1975); *Laudes creaturarum* for Reciter and 6 Instruments (1982); *Tre cori sacri* for Chorus (1980–83); *Kyrie* for Chorus and Strings (1986; Rome, March 10, 1991).

BIBL.: J. Weissmann, *G. P.* (Milan, 1957; 2nd ed., 1980); C. Annibaldi, *G. P.: Catalogo delle opere e bibliografia* (Milan, 1971); G. Zosi, *Ricerca e sintesi nell'opera di G. P.* (Rome, 1978); E. Restagno, ed., *P.* (Turin, 1986); S. Sablich et al., *A G. P., per i suoi 90 anni* (It. and Eng.; Milan, 1994).—NS/LK/DM

Petrauskas, Kipras, Lithuanian tenor, brother of **Mikas Petrauskas;** b. Vilnius, Nov. 23, 1885; d. there, Jan. 17, 1968. He studied with his brother. He appeared in his brother's opera *Birute* (Vilnius, Nov. 6, 1906), then was a singer at the Imperial Opera in St. Petersburg (1911–20); also appeared in Berlin, Paris, and Milan, and made a tour of the U.S. He returned to Lithuania before World War II. In 1950 he received the Stalin Prize. —NS/LK/DM

Petrauskas, Mikas, Lithuanian composer, brother of **Kipras Petrauskas;** b. Kaunas, Oct. 19, 1873; d. there, March 23, 1937. He studied organ with his father and was a student at the St. Petersburg Cons. of Rimsky-Korsakov. During the abortive revolution in 1905, he was implicated in political activities and imprisoned. After his release, he brought out the opera *Birute* (Vilnius, Nov. 6, 1906). In 1907 he went to the U.S. He settled in Boston in 1914, where he founded the Lithuanian Cons. and brought out the operas *The Devil Inventor* (May 20, 1923) and *Egle, Queen of the Snakes* (May 30, 1924; he sang the role of the King of the Snakes). In 1930 he returned to Lithuania.—NS/LK/DM

Petrella, Clara, Italian soprano; b. Greco Milanese, March 28, 1918; d. Milan, Nov. 19, 1987. She studied with her sister, Micaela Oliva, and with Giannina Russ in Milan. She made her operatic debut in 1939 as Liù at the Teatro Puccini in Milan, and then sang in several provincial Italian theaters. She made her first appearance at La Scala in Milan in 1941, becoming a principal member of the company in 1947; also sang in Rome and Naples; in addition, she appeared in concerts. She was particularly noted for her performances of contemporary operas by Italian composers.—NS/LK/DM

Petrella, Errico, noted Italian composer; b. Palermo, Dec. 10, 1813; d. Genoa, April 7, 1877. He studied at the age of 8 with the violinist Del Giudice in Naples and then at the Cons. there, becoming a free boarder when he was 11; his teachers included Bellini, Furno, Ruggi, and Zingarelli. While still a student, he received a commission to write his first opera, *Il Diavolo color di rosa* (July 1829), for Naples's Teatro della Fenice; it proved a success, but led him to be expelled from the Cons. for showing such daring at his age; nevertheless, he continued to receive private instruction from Ruggi. After producing 5 more operas during the next decade, he devoted himself mainly to teaching singing. In 1851 he was named music director of Naples's Teatro Nuovo, where he successfully produced his opera *Le precauzioni* (May 20, 1851); his next opera, *Elena di Tolosa* (Teatro del Fondo, Naples, Aug. 12, 1852), proved even more successful, prompting him to compose his first serious opera, *Marco Visconti* (Teatro San Carlo, Naples, Feb. 9, 1854), which scored a brilliant success and spread his name throughout Italy; it also led to the production of his best-known serious opera, *Jone* (La Scala, Milan, Jan. 26, 1858). His greatest notoriety came with his opera *I promessi sposi* (Lecco, Oct. 2, 1869). Petrella was the last representative of the old Neapolitan school. He was at his best in buffo works, for his serious operas could not compete with the dramatic masterpieces of Verdi.

BIBL.: G. Carotti, *Cenni biografici e ritratto di E. P.* (Turin, 1877); F. Guardione, *Di E. P. e della traslazion e della salma da Genova a Palermo* (Palermo, 1908); G. Cosenza, *Vita e opere di E. P.* (Rome, 1909); G. Siciliano, *Di E. P.: Musicista palermitano* (Palermo, 1913).—NS/LK/DM

Petrelli, Eleanora (née Wigstrom), Swedish soprano; b. Simtuna, April 9, 1835; d. Chicago, Feb. 21, 1904. While touring Finland as a member of a small theatrical company, she married a wealthy Russian named Petrov, and Italianized her married name to Petrelli. She studied in Milan with Lamperti, and in Paris with Viardot-García. After her husband died in 1869, she virtually abandoned the stage, but continued to give concerts in Russia, Germany, and Scandinavian countries. In 1886 she settled in Stockholm, but soon went to Chicago, where she established a school for vocal culture. She publ. a number of songs.—NS/LK/DM

Petri, Egon, eminent German pianist and pedagogue of Dutch descent; b. Hannover, March 23, 1881; d. Berkeley, Calif., May 27, 1962. His father, Henri Wilhelm Petri (1856–1914), was a Dutch violinist who served as concertmaster in Hannover and of the Leipzig Gewandhaus Orch.; his mother was a singer. He studied violin and organ as well as piano from an early age; began piano lessons with Carreño, later studying with Buchmayer, Draeseke, and Busoni; also received composition lessons from Kretzchmar. Having pursued a career as an orch. violinist and as a member of his

father's string quartet, he launched his career as a piano virtuoso in 1902; subsequently toured extensively in Europe; was also active as a teacher, serving on the faculties of the Royal Manchester Coll. of Music (1905–11) and the Berlin Hochschule für Musik (1921–26); then taught in Zakopane. On Jan. 11, 1932, he made his U.S. debut in N.Y., then performed on both sides of the Atlantic until the outbreak of World War II; also taught at Boston's Malkin Cons. (1934–35). After World War II, he resumed his extensive tours. Having taught at Cornell Univ. (1940–46), he then settled in Calif. to teach at Mills Coll. in Oakland (1947–57) and at the San Francisco Cons. of Music (1952–62). He made his farewell concert appearance in a recital in 1960. As Busoni's foremost student, he followed in his mentor's grand manner of piano virtuosity. His performances of Bach and Liszt were formidable; he also championed the works of Alkan and Medtner as well as Busoni. —NS/LK/DM

Petri, Georg Gottfried, German composer, uncle of **Johann Samuel Petri;** b. Sorau, Dec. 9, 1715; d. Görlitz, July 6, 1795. He studied law in Halle. After teaching law there, he was active as a private tutor. He served as music director (1748–64) and asst. headmaster (1763–64) in Guben. From 1764 he was Kantor in Görlitz, where he also served as music director of the church of SS. Peter and Paul. He was a prolific composer, mainly of church music. Among his other works were keyboard pieces and songs.—LK/DM

Petri, Johann Samuel, German composer and writer on music, nephew of **Georg Gottfried Petri;** b. Sorau, Nov. 1, 1738; d. Bautzen, April 12, 1808. He taught himself to play several instruments. After teaching music at the Pädagogium in Halle (1762–63), he was Kantor and schoolteacher in Lauben (1763–70) and Bautzen (from 1770). He composed several passion cantatas and many works for chorus and orch., and publ. the treatise *Anleitung zur practischen Musik, vor neuangehende Sänger und Instrumentspieler* (Lauban, 1767; 2nd ed., Aug. 1782).—LK/DM

Petri, Michala, gifted Danish recorder player; b. Copenhagen, July 7, 1958. She began to play at the incredible age of 3 and appeared on Danish radio when she was 5. She made her concert debut as a soloist in Copenhagen in 1969. Petri formed a trio with her mother, a harpsichordist, and her cellist brother, and toured widely with it. She studied with Ferdinand Conrad at the Hannover Staatliche Hochschule für Musik (1970–76). In addition to chamber music performances, she toured extensively as a soloist. She made her U.S. debut with N.Y.'s 92nd Street Y Chamber Orch. in 1982, and first played in Japan in 1984. In 2000 she was awarded the Léonie Sonning Music Prize of Denmark. Her repertoire ranges from the early Baroque era to contemporary music; she has commissioned a number of composers to write works for her.—NS/LK/DM

Petrić, Ivo, Slovenian composer; b. Ljubljana, June 16, 1931. He received training in composition and conducting at the Ljubljana Academy of Music (1950–58). In 1962 he founded the chamber music group Ensemble Slavko Osterc for the promotion of new music. In 1970 he became ed.-in-chief of the publ. division of the Union of Slovenian Composers. He also was artistic director of the Slovenian Phil. from 1975 to 1995. In 1975 he won 1st prize in the Wieniawski Competition in Poznań for his Sonata for Solo Violin and in 1984 1st prize in the Oscar Espla Competition in Alicante, Spain, for his symphonic poem *The Picture of Dorian Gray*. His compositions are Romantic in their inspiration, and agreeably modernistic in technical presentation.

WORKS: ORCH.: 4 syms. (1954, 1957, 1960, 1996); *Concerto Grosso* for Strings (1955); Concerto for Flute and Chamber Orch. (1955–57); *Divertimento* (1956); Concerto for Clarinet and Chamber Orch. (1958); *Concertante Suite* for Bassoon and Strings (1959); *Concertante Overture* (1960); *Concertante Music* for Wind Quintet, Timpani, and Strings (1962); *Croquis sonores* for Harp and Chamber Ensemble (1963); *Mosaics* for Clarinet and Chamber Ensemble (1964); *Symphonic Mutations* (1964); *Epitaph* for Harp, Clarinet, Violin, Cello, Strings, and Percussion (1965); *Integrali v barvah* (Integrals in Colors; 1968); *Burlesque pour les temps passés* for Trombone and Orch. (1969); *Music Concertante* for Piano and Orch. (1970); *Dialogues concertants* for Cello and Orch. (1972); *3 Images* for Violin and Orch. (1973); *Nocturnes and Games* (1973); *Fresque symphonique* (1973); *Episodes lyriques* for Oboe and Chamber Orch. (1974); *Gemini Concerto* for Violin, Cello, and Orch. (1975); *Thus Played Kurent*, symphonic poem for Viola and Orch. (1976); *Jeux concertants* for Flute and Orch. (1978); *Hommage à Johannes* (1978); *Toccata concertante* for 4 Percussionists and Orch. (1979); *Concerto for Orchestra* (1982); *The Picture of Dorian Gray* (1984); Trumpet Concerto (1986); *Dresden Concerto* for 15 Strings (1987); *Moods and Temperaments* (1987); *After So Many Years*, symphonic reminiscences (1989); *Toccata* (1989); *Gallus Metamorphoses* (1992); *Spring Concertino* for Percussionist and Orch. (1993); *Jubilee Concerto for Celea* for Strings (1994); *Scottish Impressions* (1995); *Four Seasons* (1996); Saxophone Concerto (1997); Horn Concerto (1997). CHAMBER: 4 wind quintets (1953, 1959, 1974, 1999); Bassoon Sonata (1954); Oboe Sonata (1955); Flute Sonata (1955); Clarinet Sonata (1956–57); *7 Movements* for 7 Instruments (1963); *Jeux à 3* for Cello, Percussion, and Harp (1965); *Jeux à 4* for Flute, Piano, Harp, and Cello (1966); *Little Chamber Concerto* for Oboe, English Horn, Bass Clarinet, Horn, Harp, Piano, and String Quartet (1966); *5 Movements* for Oboe, and Harp or String Quartet (1967); *Intarzije* (Inlaid Work) for Wind Trio, Horn, Trumpet, Trombone, Percussion, and String Quintet (1968); *Quatuor 69* for String Quartet (1969); *Capriccio* for Cello and 8 Instruments (1974); Violin Sonata (1976); Concerto for 5 Percussionists (1978); *Episodes poetiques* for Oboe and 9 Instruments (1979); *Leipzig Chamber Music* for 5 Players (1983); *Quatuor 1985* for String Quartet (1985); *Fantasies and Nocturnes* for Violin, Clarinet, and Piano (1986); *Rondeau* for Piano Quartet (1987); Chamber Sonata No. 1, ...*meditations and nocturnos*..., for Oboe, Viola, Bass Clarinet, and Harp (1991) and No. 2, ...*capriccio*..., for Flute, English Horn, Violin, Cello, and Harpsichord (1991); *Portrait d'automne* for String Quartet (1992); *Quatres pièces d'été* for Violin and Harp (1992); Alto Saxophone Sonata (1992); *Deux portraits* for 2 Violins and Piano (1993); Trio Sonata for Flute, Viola, and Double Bass (1993); *Burlesque* for 4 Saxophones (1994); *Elegie* for English Horn and String Quartet (1994); *Hommage à Serge Prokofiev*, variations for Oboe, Clarinet, Violin,

Viola, and Double Bass (1994); *Quatuor 1996* for String Quartet (1996); *Diptykhos* for 12 Saxophones (1996); Concerto for 4 Clarinets (1999); *Autumn Encounters* for Clarinet and Piano (1999). PIANO: 2 sonatas (1993–94); *MacPhadraig's Scottish Diary* (1996); *Pagine d'album for Tatjana* (1999). VOCAL: *Pierre de la mort*, cantata (1962); *The Song of Life* for Mezzo-soprano and Orch. (1981).—NS/LK/DM

Petridis, Petros (John), eminent Turkish-born Greek composer; b. Nigdé, July 23, 1892; d. Athens, Aug. 17, 1977. He studied in Constantinople at the American Robert Coll. and received instruction in piano from Hegey and in harmony from Selvelli. He then went to Paris and read law at the Sorbonne and political science at the École Libre des Sciences Politiques (1911–14), and later studied with Wolff (1914) and Roussel (1919). He became a naturalized Greek citizen (1913). He subsequently was a music critic for English, American, and Greek publications, dividing his time between Paris and Athens. His use of Byzantine modalities, adorned with contemporary harmonies, reveals the influence of Greek culture.

WORKS: DRAMATIC: *Zefyra*, opera (1923–25; rev. 1958–64); *Iphigenia in Tauris*, incidental music to Euripides' play (Athens, Oct. 15, 1941); *O pramateftis* (The Pedlar), ballet (1941–43; Athens, May 6, 1944). ORCH.: *Kleftikoi horoi* (Cleftic Dances; 1922); 5 syms.: No. 1, *Greek* (1928–29; Athens, Jan. 16, 1933), No. 2, *Lyric* (1941; Athens, Dec. 11, 1949), No. 3, *Parisian* (1944–46; Geneva, 1949), No. 4, *Doric* (1941–43; Athens, May 20, 1945), and No. 5, *Pastoral* (1949–51; rev. 1972–73); *Concerto Grosso* for Winds and Timpani (c. 1929); *Greek Suite* (1929–30; Athens, Nov. 27, 1932); *Dighenis Akritas* (1933–39; Athens, May 17, 1940); *Studies* for Small Orch. (Athens, Jan. 29, 1934); 2 piano concertos (1934, rev. c. 1948; 1937); *Vyzantini thyssia* (Byzantine Offering; 1934–35); *Ionian Suite* (c. 1935); Cello Concerto (1936); *Chorale and Variations on Kyrie ton dynameon* for Strings (1940; Athens, June 28, 1941); *Chorale and Variations on Christos anesti* for Strings (1941–43; Athens, May 20, 1945); *Largo* for Strings (Athens, Feb. 6, 1944); *Issagoghi pentihimi ke heroiki* (Funeral and Heroic Overture; 1944; Athens, May 20, 1945); Violin Concerto (1972); Concerto for 2 Pianos (1972). CHAMBER: Piano Trio (c. 1933); String Quartet (1951; unfinished); piano pieces. VOCAL: *Hayos Pavlos*, oratorio for Narrator, Soloists, Chorus, and Orch. (1950; Athens, June 29, 1951); *Requiem ya ton aftorkratora* (Requiem for the Emperor) for Soloists, Chorus, and Orch. (1952–64); songs.—NS/LK/DM

Petrini, family of German musicians, most likely of Italian descent:

(1) Petrini (first name unknown); b. place and date unknown; d. Berlin, 1750. He served at the court of Crown Prince Friedrich (later Friedrich II the Great), where he was active as a harpist and chamber musician. He also was active at the Berlin Opera. C.P.E. Bach held him in high esteem and wrote a harp sonata for him (1740). Petrini had 2 children who became musicians:

(2) (Marie) Therese Petrini, singer and harpist; b. Berlin, 1736; d. there, after 1800. She studied voice and harp with her father. After his death, she became a harpist at the court, where she also received vocal instruction from J.F. Agricola. In 1754 she became a singer and harpist at the chapel of Margrave Karl

Albrecht of Brandenburg-Schwedt in Berlin, and also gave public concerts as a singer.

(3) Francesco Petrini, harpist, teacher, and composer; b. Berlin, 1744; d. Paris, 1819. He received instruction in harp from his father. In 1765 he became harpist and chamber musician at the Mecklenburg-Schwerin court, where he studied composition. In 1769 he settled in Paris and made his first appearance at the Concert Spirituel in 1770. He composed 4 syms., 5 harp concertos, harp sonatas, and various other harp pieces. He also publ. *Méthode de harpe* (Paris, n.d.; rev., 1796, as *Abrégé de la méthode de harpe avec la manière de l'accorder*), *Nouveau système de l'harmonie en 60 accords* (Paris, 1793), *Règles de l'harmonie, rendues plus faciles par une suite le leçons en forme de préludes,* op.51 (Paris, n.d.), and *Étude préliminaire de la composition, selon le nouveau système de l'harmonie en 60 accords* (Paris, 1810).—**LK/DM**

Petrobelli, Pierluigi, distinguished Italian musicologist; b. Padua, Oct. 18, 1932. He studied at the Univ. of Rome (Laurea in Lettere, 1957), with Strunk, Mendel, Lockwood, and Babbitt at Princeton Univ. (1959–61; M.F.A. in music, 1961), with W.G. Waite (musicology) at the Harvard Summer School (1960), and at the Univ. of Calif. at Berkeley (1962–63). From 1968 to 1971 he was ed. of the *Rivista Italiana di Musicologia*. In 1968 he became a teaching asst. at the Univ. of Padua, where he was assoc. prof. of music history from 1970 to 1972. He was librarian and teacher of music history at the Rossini Cons. in Pesaro from 1970 to 1973. After serving as a lecturer in music at King's Coll., Univ. of London from 1973 to 1977, he was a reader in musicology at the Univ. of London from 1978 to 1980. In 1980 he became director of the Istituto di Studi Verdiani in Parma, which became the Istituto Nazionale di Studi Verdiani in 1989. He became ed. of *Studi verdiani* in 1981. From 1981 to 1983 he was prof. of music history at the Univ. of Perugia, and then at the Univ. of Rome "La Sapienza" from 1983. In 1989 he was made a corresponding member of the American Musicological Soc. He became a member of the Academia Europaea in 1992, and in 1996 he served as the Lauro De Bosis Lecturer in the History of Italian Civilization at Harvard Univ. He was made a foreign honorary member of the Royal Musical Assn. of England in 1997. Petrobelli's articles, ranging in subject matter from Gregorian chant to Dallapiccola, have appeared in various learned books and journals.

WRITINGS: With V. Duckles and M. Elmer, *Thematic Catalog of an 18th-Century Collection of Italian Instrumental Music in the Music Library, University of Calif. at Berkeley* (Berkeley and Los Angeles, 1963); *Giuseppe Tartini-Le fonti biografiche* (Vienna, London, and Milan, 1967); *Tartini, le sue idee e il suo tempo* (Lucca, 1992); *Music in the Theater: Essays on Verdi and Other Composers* (Princeton, 1994; It. tr., 1998, as *La musica nel teatro: Saggi su Verdi e altri compositori*).—**NS/LK/DM**

Petrov, Andrei (Pavlovich), Russian composer; b. Leningrad, Sept. 2, 1930. He studied composition at the Leningrad Cons. with Evlakhov, graduating in 1954. In 1957 he joined the Communist party. In his music he follows the general precepts of socialist realism, ethnic in thematic material, euphonious in harmony, energetic

in rhythm, stimulating in modalities, optimistic in contemporary philosophy, and realistic in treatment.

WORKS: DRAMATIC: O p e r a : *Peter the First* (Leningrad, 1975). **B a l l e t :** *The Magic Apple Tree* (Leningrad, Nov. 8, 1953); *The Station Master,* after Pushkin (Leningrad, May 9, 1955); *The Shore of Hope* (1959); *The Creation of the World* (1971); *Pushkin* (1979). **M u s i c a l :** *We Want to Dance* (1967). **ORCH.:** *Pioneer Suite* (1951); *Sport Suite* (1953); *Radda and Lioko,* symphonic poem (1954); *Festive Overture* (1955); *Songs of Today,* symphonic cycle (1965); *Poem,* in memory of those fallen in the siege of Leningrad, for Strings, Organ, 4 Trumpets, 2 Pianos, and Percussion (1965). **VOCAL:** *The Poem of a Young Pioneer* for Soprano, Mezzo- soprano, and Orch. (1959); *Poème pathétique* for Baritone, 2 Pianos, and Percussion, commemorating the centennial of Lenin's birth, after Soviet poets (1970); *Pushkin,* vocal-poetic sym. for Narrator, Mezzo-soprano, Chorus, 2 Harps, and Orch. (1978).

BIBL.: A. Kenigsberg, *A. P.* (Moscow, 1959); L. Markhasev, *A. P., Familiar and Unfamiliar* (Leningrad, 1974).—**NS/LK/DM**

Petrov, Ivan (Ivanovich), prominent Russian bass; b. Irkutsk, Feb. 29, 1920. He studied with A. Mineyev at the Glazunov Music Coll. in Moscow (1938–39). He then joined the Kozlovsky opera group; became a soloist with the Moscow Phil. in 1941. In 1943 he joined the staff of the Bolshoi Theater in Moscow; his most celebrated interpretation was in the title role of *Boris Godunov,* inviting comparisons with Chaliapin. He made several tours as a member of the Opera of the Bolshoi Theater in Europe, Japan, and the U.S.

BIBL.: I. Nazarenko, *I. P.* (Moscow, 1957).—**NS/LK/DM**

Petrov, Nikolai (Arnoldovich), outstanding Russian pianist; b. Moscow, April 14, 1943. He studied with Tatiana Kestner at the Moscow Central Music School (1951–61), then continued his training with Yakov Zak at the Moscow Cons. (graduated, 1967). He won 2nd prize in both the Van Cliburn (1962) and Queen Elisabeth of Belgium (1964) competitions; then pursued a remarkable career as a virtuoso, touring widely in the Soviet Union and Eastern Europe; also performed in Western Europe and North America. As a result of the renewed U.S.-Soviet cultural exchange program, he appeared as soloist with Yuri Termirkanov and the N.Y. Phil. at N.Y.'s Avery Fisher Hall in 1986. His repertoire ranges from Classical to contemporary Soviet music; he has given first performances of works by Khachaturian, Khrennikov, Shchedrin, and other Soviet composers, and also tackled the original version of the Liszt transcriptions of the Paganini études.—**NS/LK/DM**

Petrov, Osip (Afanasievich), celebrated Russian bass; b. Elizavetgrad, Nov. 15, 1807; d. St. Petersburg, March 11, 1878. He joined the Zhurakhovsky opera troupe and made his debut in Cavos's *The Cossack Poet* in Elizavetgrad (1826); received instruction from Cavos. In 1830, Lebedev, the director of the St. Petersburg Imperial Opera, heard him sing with an inferior company at a fair in Kursk, and immediately engaged him. Petrov made his debut in St. Petersburg as Sarastro that same year. The enormous compass of his voice, its extraordinary power and beautiful quality, combined with consummate histrionic skill, secured for him recognition as one of the greatest of Russian bassos. He appeared on the stage for the last time on March 10, 1878, on the eve of his death. He created the roles of Susanin in Glinka's *Life for the Czar* (1836), Ruslan in *Ruslan and Ludmila* (1842), the Miller in Dargomyzhsky's *Rusalka* (1856), and Varlaam in Mussorgsky's *Boris Godunov* (1874).

BIBL.: E. Lastotchkina, *O. P.* (Moscow, 1950).—**NS/LK/DM**

Petrova-Vorobieva, Anna,

Russian contralto; b. St. Petersburg, Feb. 14, 1817; d. there, April 26, 1901. She was a student of Antonio Sapienza and Cavos in St. Petersburg, and also received some training from Glinka. Following her operatic debut as Pippo in *La gazza ladra*, she sang with the St. Petersburg Opera (1835–50), where she created the roles of Vanya in *A Life for the Czar* (1836) and Ratmir in *Ruslan and Ludmila* (1842). Glinka subsequently added the aria *In the Monastery* to his latter opera to showcase her vocal talent. Her husband was **Osip Petrov.**—**NS/LK/DM**

Petrovics, Emil,

Hungarian composer; b. Zrenjanin, Yugoslavia, Feb. 9, 1930. He went to Budapest (1941) and studied at the Academy of Music with Sugár (1949–51), Viski (1951–52), and Farkas (1952–57). He was director of the Petőfi Theater (1960–64). He taught at the Academy of Music (from 1969), and served as director of the Hungarian State Opera (1986–90). His opera *C'est la guerre* (1961) was awarded the Kossuth Prize in 1966.

WORKS: DRAMATIC: O p e r a : *C'est la guerre* (Budapest Radio, Aug. 17, 1961; 1st stage perf., Budapest, March 11, 1962); *Lysistrate*, after Aristophanes (1962; rev. 1971); *Bűn es bűnhődés* (Crime and Punishment), after Dostoyevsky (Budapest, Oct. 26, 1969). **B a l l e t :** *Salome* (1978). **ORCH.:** Flute Concerto (1957); Sym. for Strings (1962); Piano Concerto (1998–99). **CHAMBER:** *Cassazione* for Brass (1953); 2 string quartets (1958, 1991); *4 Self-Portraits in Masks* for Harpsichord (1958); Wind Quintet (1964); *Passacaglia in Blues* for Bassoon and Piano (1964; as a ballet, Budapest, 1965); *Deux mouvements* for 1 or 2 Cimbaloms (1977); *Rhapsody No. 1* for Violin (1982) and *No. 2* for Viola (1983). **VOCAL:** 9 cantatas: No. 1, *Alone in the Forest*, for Soprano and Chamber Ensemble (1956), No. 2, *Let Me Die There*, for Men's Chorus and Orch. (1972–73), No. 3, *Fanny's Legacy*, for Soprano and Chamber Ensemble (1978), No. 4, *We All Depart*, for Women's Chorus and Chamber Orch. (1980), No. 6, *"We Shall Rest!"*, for Soprano, Chorus, and Orch. (1986), No. 7, *Pygmalion* (1992), No. 8 for Voice and Piano (1995), and No. 9, *By the Danube* (1998); 2 oratorios: *Jónás könyve* (The Book of Jonah; 1966) and *Ott essem el én* (Let Me Die There) for Men's Chorus and Orch. (1972); choruses.—**NS/LK/DM**

Petrucci, Brizio,

Italian composer; b. Massalombarda, near Ferrara, Jan. 12, 1737; d. Ferrara, June 15, 1838. He studied at the Imola seminary, took courses in law at the Univ. of Ferrara (doctorate, 1758), and received training in music from Pietro Berretta, maestro di cappella at Ferrara Cathedral. After serving as coadjutor to Pietro Marzola, maestro di cappella at Ferrara Cathedral, he succeeded him in that position in 1784. He also was maestro al cembalo at the Bonacossi and Scroffa theaters in Ferrara. Among his works were the operas *Ciro riconosciuto* (Ferrara, Carnival 1765), *Demofoonte*

(Ferrara, Dec. 26, 1765), *I pazzi improvvisati* (Ferrara, Carnival 1770), and *Teseo in Creta* (Cesena, 1771), an oratorio, *La madre de' Maccabei* (Ferrara, 1763), a cantata, *La pace italica* (Ferrara, 1815), a Requiem (1822), and numerous other sacred pieces.—**LK/DM**

Petrucci, Ottaviano dei,

Italian music publisher; b. Fossombrone, June 18, 1466; d. Venice, May 7, 1539. He was the descendant of an impoverished family of the nobility. He went to Venice about 1490. He petitioned in 1498 for the exclusive privilege of printing "canto figurato" and "intabolature d'organo e de liuto" in the Venetian dominions for a period of 20 years; the privilege was granted on May 25, 1498. His first vol., *Harmonice musices odhecaton A*, was issued on May 15, 1501; it contained 96 works, mostly French chansons for 3 and 4 Voices. It was followed by *Canti B* (1501) and *Canti C* (1503), which contained 49 and 137 works, respectively. In 1507 he became the first printer to publ. lute tablature. When the war of the League of Cambrai against the Venetian Republic made further work impossible, he returned to Fossombrone (1511), leaving his associates Amedeo Scotto and Nicolò da Rafael to oversee his affairs in Venice. He was active as a publisher in Fossombrone until about 1521, bringing out eds. of both musical and non-musical works. He received a 15-year privilege from Pope Leo X in 1513 for printing mensural music and organ tablature (the privilege to publ. keyboard music was revoked in 1516); also received a 5-year extension of his Venetian privilege in 1514; ceased publishing from 1516 to 1519, again most likely due to the unsettled times. In 1520 he built a paper mill in Acqua Santa, near Fossombrone; was recalled to Venice by the senate in 1536 to supervise the publication of Latin and Italian classical texts. His eds., printed with great neatness, are rare and highly prized specimens of early presswork. In Venice he brought out eds. of works by leading composers of the Netherlands school, as well as by Italian composers. His publications in Fossombrone continued to highlight Italian music, with the French school displacing the Netherlands masters. Modern eds. of his publications include the following: K. Jeppesen, ed., *Die mehrstimmige italienische Laude um 1500: Das 2. Laudenbuch des O. d.P. (1507)* (Leipzig and Copenhagen, 1935), R. Schwartz, ed., *O. P.: Frottole, Buch I und IV*, Publikationen Älterer Musik, VIII (Leipzig, 1935), H. Hewitt, ed., *Harmonice Musices Odhecaton A* (Cambridge, Mass., 1942; 2nd ed., rev., 1946), G. Cesari, R. Monterosso, and B. Disertori, eds., *Le frottole nell' edizione principe di O. P., I: Libri, I, II, e III*, Istituta et Monumenta, i/1 (1954), B. Disertori, ed., *Le frottole per canto e liuto intabulate da Franciscus Bossinensis*, Istituzioni e Monumenti dell'arte Musicale Italiana, new series, iii (1964), and H. Hewitt, ed., *O. P.: Canti B numero cinquante (Venice, 1502)*, Monuments of Renaissance Music, II (1967).

BIBL.: D. Vernarecci, *O. d.P. da Fossombrone* (Fossombrone, 1881; 2nd ed., 1882); C. Boer, *Chansonvormen op het einde van de XVde eeuw: Een studie naar aanleiding van P.'s "Harmonice musices odhecaton"* (Amsterdam, 1938); C. Sartori, *Bibliografia delle opere musicali stampate da O. P.* (Florence, 1948).—**NS/LK/DM**

Petrucciani, Michel, jazz pianist; b. Orange, France, Dec. 28, 1962; d. N.Y., Jan. 6, 1999. He suffered from calcium deficiency osteogenesis imperfecta ("glass bones") and was about three feet tall and had to be carried to the piano. His father was a jazz guitarist. Michel played with his two older brothers, Philippe (guitarist) and Louis (bassist), in a family band. At age four, he was playing drums, but saw Duke Ellington on TV and decided to switch to piano. He was influenced by Bill Evans and Lennie Tristano. By age 15, he was playing with Kenny Clarke and accompanied touring artists such as Clark Terry. He toured France in the early 1980s; following a visit to N.Y., he moved full-time to the U.S. in 1982. His first U.S. appearance was as a guest of Lee Konitz's nonet at SUNY in Purchase, N.Y. When Konitz announced that a friend from France was coming out, the audience was pleasantly surprised to see a young woman, more surprised when she seemed to be carrying a baby, and astounded when the "baby," seated at the piano, played a terrific solo on "Cherokee"! (The woman was his wife of the time; he was married and divorced several times.) He played in Charles Lloyd's comeback band in 1982, recording and touring Europe with him, then made an infamous Blue Note appearance in 1983 and a heralded appearance at the Kool Jazz Festival in 1984. Petrucciani subsequently recorded with Wayne Shorter, Jim Hall, and cut many albums as a leader. He did a two-year solo tour all over Europe and Latin America (1995–96). He played with Lloyd again in 1996 at the Iridium in N.Y. and was in N.Y. to play at Birdland (1997) with Steve Gadd and Anthony Jackson. In July 1997, he appeared in Paris, Wiesbaden, Germany, and the Juan les Pins festival.

DISC.: *Michel Petrucciani Trio* (1981); *Date with Time* (1981); *Toot Suite* (1982); *Oracle's Destiny* (1982); *100 Hearts* (1983); *Note 'n Notes* (1984); *Live at the Village Vanguard* (1984); *Pianism* (1985); *Cold Blues* (1985); *Power of Three* (1986); *Michel Plays Petrucciani* (1987); *Music* (1989); *Playground* (1991); *Live* (1991); *Promenade with Duke* (1993); *Marvellous* (1994).—**LP/MM**

Petrus de Cruce, writer on music and composer who flourished in the late 13th century. He was the author of a *Tractatus de tonis* (ed. in Corpus scriptorum de musica, XXX, 1976). Petrus made a significant contribution to the development of mensural music by proposing a new subdivision of Franco's breve, contending that up to 7 semibreves could equal the value of a breve, and that any 2 successive groups of semibreves (equivalent to 2 breves) must be separated from one another by a puntus. Among his compositions were a number of motets.—**LK/DM**

Petrushka, Shabtai (Arieh), German-born Israeli composer; b. Leipzig, March 15, 1903; d. Jerusalem, 1997. He studied at the Inst. of Technology in Berlin-Charlottenburg, and received an engineering diploma; studied music at the Leipzig Cons. He was a violinist in various Berlin theater orchs. (1928–33). After the advent of the Nazis in 1933, he was a member of the orch. of the Jewish Kulturbund, for which he wrote incidental music. He emigrated to Palestine in 1938, where he served as an arranger and conductor of the Palestine Broadcasting Service (1938–48). He then was asst. director of music of the Israel Broadcasting Service (1948–58) and head of the music division of the Israel Broadcasting Authority (1958–68). From 1969 to 1981 he taught at the Rubin Academy of Music in Jerusalem.

WORKS: String Trio (1939); *4 Movements* for Symphonic Band (1953); *5 Oriental Dances* for Orch. (1954); *The Broken Blackboard*, children's musical (1969); *Piccolo Divertimento* for Symphonic Band (1970); *3 Jewish Melodies* for 2 Flutes and 3 Clarinets (1972); *Hebrew Melodies* for Wind Quintet (1974); Wind Quartet (1975); *Jewish Melodies* for Brass Quintet (1974); *3 Sephardic Songs* for Women's Chorus (1976); Sonatina for Horn and String Quartet (1982); *Little Suite* for Band (1986). —**NS/LK/DM**

Petrželka, Vilém, noted Czech composer and pedagogue; b. Královo Pole, near Brünn, Sept. 10, 1889; d. Brno, Jan. 10, 1967. He studied with Janáček at the Brno Organ School (1905–08) and in 1910 became his assistant at the school; subsequently took private lessons in Prague with Vítězslav Novák. He taught at the Phil. Society School in Brno (1914–19), and in 1919 became a prof. at the newly formed Brno Cons. In his compositions, he continued the national tradition of modern Moravian music; he was mainly influenced by Janáček, but expanded his resources and on occasion made use of jazz rhythms, quarter-tones, and other modernistic procedures.

WORKS: DRAMATIC: *Námořník Mikuláš* (Mariner Nicholas), symphonic drama for Narrator, Soloists, Chorus, Organ, Jazz Band, and Orch. (1928; Brno, Dec. 9, 1930); *Horník Pavel* (The Miner Paul), opera (1935–38). **ORCH.:** *Věčný návrat* (Eternal Return), symphonic poem (1922–23; Brno, Feb. 10, 1924); *Suite* for Strings (1924–25); *Dramatic Overture* (1932; Brno, March 26, 1933); *Partita* for Strings (1934); Sinfonietta (1941; Brno, Jan. 22, 1942); Violin Concerto (1943–44; rev. 1946); *Pastoral Sinfonietta* (1951–52); Sym. (1956). **CHAMBER:** 5 string quartets (1909; 1914–15; Fantasy, 1927; Suite, 1932; 1947); *Z intimních chvil* (From Intimate Moments) for Violin and Piano (1918); Sonata for Solo Cello (1930); Violin Sonata (1932); Piano Trio (1936–37); *4 Impromptus* for Violin and Piano (1939–40); *Divertimento* for Wind Quintet (1941); *Serenade* for Nonet or Chamber Orch. (1945); *2 Pieces* for Cello and Piano (1947); Violin Sonatina (1953); *Miniatures* for Wind Quintet (1953); *2 Pieces* for Viola and Piano (1959); *Fantasy* for String Quartet (1959); *Suite* for String Trio (1961). **P i a n o :** Sonata (1908); *Songs of Poetry and Prose* (1917); *Suite* (1930); *5 nálad* (5 Moods; 1954). **VOCAL:** *Modlitba k slunci* (A Prayer to the Sun), cantata (1921; Brno, Feb. 13, 1922); *Štafeta* (The Courier), 4 songs for Voice and String Quartet (1926–27); choruses, including the popular patriotic part song for Men's Chorus *To je má zem* (This Is My Land; 1940); song cycles; folk song arrangements.

BIBL.: L. Firkušný, *V. P.* (Prague, 1946).—**NS/LK/DM**

Pet Shop Boys, snide dance-pop hit makers of the late 1980s. **MEMBERSHIP:** Neil Tennant, voc. (b. North Shields, Northumberland, England, July 10, 1954); Chris Lowe, kybd. (b. Blackpool, Lancashire, England, Oct. 4, 1959).

In their teens, both Neil Tennant and Chris Lowe played in bands, Tennant working with a group called Dust, Lowe playing trombone in a dance band. Both put these pursuits behind them during college, Tennant studying history, Lowe architecture. After finishing school, Tennant took an editorial position at Marvel Comics, preparing U.S. comics for distribution in England. He took several other publishing jobs before moving to the English rock magazine *Smash Hits*. He met Lowe at an electronics shop and they discovered many common interests, especially dance music. They started to write together, initially calling themselves the West End Boys, but changing that to the Pet Shop Boys after some friends who actually worked in a pet shop. They thought the name made them sound like an English rap group.

The Boys mostly worked on tape, making demos of their clever dance tunes. Lowe discovered a talent for creating remarkable textures with synthesizers and samplers that only became keener as the group developed. Tennant brought along a demo tape on an assignment in N.Y. and gave one to producer Bobby Orlando. Orlando pioneered High NRG dance music, a genre for which Tennant and Lowe had a fondness. Orlando liked what he heard and offered to produce a record of their song "West End Girls." It became a minor club hit (in that version). The record attracted the attention of Parlophone records, and after negotiating a deal with Orlando, the duo signed to Parlophone. Tennant left his job at *Smash Hits* and they went into the studio with producer Stephan Hague, recutting "West End Girls." The single came out in the fall of 1985, reaching #1 on the English charts shortly after the first of the year. By the end of 1986, it had topped the charts in the U.S., Canada, Hong Kong, and several other countries. They released their debut album, *Please*, in the spring of 1986. With a boost from the #10 follow-up single "Opportunity (Let's Make Lots of Money)," the album rose to #7 and went platinum. Capitalizing on this success, a record of remixes was released before the year was over.

In the summer of 1987, the duo released "It's a Sin." They filmed a video with Derek Jarman, highlighting the seven deadly sins. It began a long relationship with the director. The song topped the English charts, rising to #9 in the U.S. That fall, it was on their sophomore album, *Actually*. Another track on the album featured Dusty Springfield dueting with Tennant on the track "What Have I Done to Deserve This?"— it hit #2 in the U.S. The album, however, only rose to #25, selling gold.

In August of 1987, The Pet Shop Boys performed on a British TV special commemorating the tenth anniversary of Elvis Presley's death. They performed "Always on My Mind," without plans to release it. However, the performance proved so popular that they issued it during the holiday season in England, where it reached #1 during Christmas. The single came out in the U.S. the following spring, rising to #4. It also appeared on their next album, released later that year, *Introspective*. With the help of a single that coincided with the album's release, "Domino Dancing," which hit #18, the album went gold, topping out at #34.

Over the next two years, the duo toured, produced part of an album for Dusty Springfield, and an entire album for Liza Minnelli. Tennant and Lowe both worked with the New Order/Smiths offshoot Electronic, but finally found time to put together their own

project, 1990's *Behaviour*. Original disco kingpin Harold Faltemeyer produced, with Johnny Marr from The Smiths and Electronic playing guitar. A less lyrically scabrous album than their previous releases, it didn't fare as well. However, they remained popular enough, especially in England, to be given their own custom label, Spaghetti Records. The label released several records by young dance artists through the early 1990s. In 1992, the Pet Shop Boys contributed to the soundtrack to the Neil Jordan film *The Crying Game*. At Jordan's suggestion, they produced an updated version of the 1964 Dave Berry title song, using former Culture Club frontman Boy George as the vocalist. The record and film became enormous hits around the world.

In 1993, the Boys got back together with producer Stephan Hague and recorded *Very*. While there were no pop hits from the record, it went gold and rose to #20. A companion piece of less pop-oriented dance material, *Relentless*, was released at the same time. As popular as they were performing, they were earning fame as producers as well. They worked with David Bowie on the song "Hallo Spaceboy." Tina Turner also invited them into the studio to produce the song "Confidential" for her.

During the second half of the 1990s, the Boys continued to be active both as a group and producers, although they failed to produce any major hits. Toward the end of 1996, they released their first new record in three years, *Bilingual*. With a heavy dose of various Latin American music, it was a reaction against Britpop. In 1998, Tennant produced the compilation *20th Century Blues: The Songs of Noel Coward*. A charity project for the Red Hot AIDS Trust, he spent close to a year and a half putting it together. In 1999, the duo released *Nightlife*, one of their best, if thorniest, efforts. On the tune "In Denial," Tennant duets with Kylie Minogue, singing about his being gay, at which point Minogue asks, "Can you love me anyway?" And thus the walls of pop music stretch just a little bit more.

DISC.: *Please* (1986); *Actually* (1987); *Introspective* (1988); *Behavior* (1990); *Relentless* (1993); *Very* (1993); *Bilingual* (1996); *Nightlife* (1999).—**HB**

Pettersson, Gustaf Allan, remarkable sui generis Swedish composer; b. Västra Ryd, Sept. 19, 1911; d. Stockholm, June 20, 1980. His father was a blacksmith, and his mother was a devout woman who also sang; the family moved to Stockholm, and lived in dire poverty. Pettersson sold Christmas cards and bought a violin from his meager returns. He also practiced keyboard playing on a church organ. In 1930 he entered the Stockholm Cons., studying violin and viola with J. Ruthström and theory with H.M. Melchers. From 1940 to 1951 he played viola in the Stockholm Concert Society Orch., and also studied composition with Otto Olsson, Tor Mann, and Blomdahl. In his leisure hours he wrote poetry; he set 24 of his poems to music. In 1951 he went to Paris to study with Honegger and Leibowitz. Returning to Sweden, he devoted himself to composition in large forms. His music is permeated with dark moods, and he supplied deeply pessimistic annotations to his syms. and other works. In 1963 he began suffering from painful rheumatoid arthritis; he stubbornly continued to compose while compulsively proclaiming his misfortunes in private and in public print. He described himself as "a voice crying out, drowned in the noise of the times." The Stockholm Phil. played several of his syms., but when his 7th Sym., originally scheduled for its American tour in 1968, was taken off the program, Pettersson, wrathful at this callous defection, forbade performance of any of his music in Sweden. Stylistically, Pettersson's music is related to Mahler's symphonic manner, in the grandiosity of design and in the passionate, exclamatory dynamism of utterance. Most of his syms. are cast in single movements, with diversity achieved by frequent changes of mood, tempo, meter, and rhythm. Characteristically, all, except No. 10, are set in minor keys.

WORKS (all 1st perf. in Stockholm unless otherwise given): **ORCH.**: 2 violin concertos: No. 1 for Violin, String Quartet, and Orch. (1949; March 10, 1951) and No. 2 (1977–78; Jan. 25, 1980); 3 concertos for Strings: No. 1 (1949–50; April 6, 1952), No. 2 (1956; Dec. 1, 1968), and No. 3 (1956–57; March 14, 1958); 16 syms.: No. 1 (1950–51; withdrawn with instructions to perform it only posthumously), No. 2 (1952–53; Swedish Radio, May 9, 1954), No. 3 (1954–55; Goteborg, Nov. 21, 1956), No. 4 (1958–59; Jan. 27, 1961), No. 5 (1960–62; Nov. 8, 1963), No. 6 (1963–66; Jan. 21, 1968), No. 7 (1966–67; Oct. 13, 1968), No. 8 (1968–69; Feb. 23, 1972), No. 9 (1970; Göteborg, Feb. 18, 1971), No. 10 (1971–72; Swedish TV, filmed Dec. 16, 1973, for delayed broadcast of Jan. 14, 1974), No. 11 (1971–73; Bergen, Oct. 24, 1974), No. 12, *De döda på torget* (The Dead on the Square) for Chorus and Orch., after Pablo Neruda (1973–74; Sept. 29, 1977), No. 13 (1976; Bergen, June 7, 1978), No. 14 (1978; Nov. 26, 1981), No. 15 (1978; Nov. 19, 1982), and No. 16, originally Concerto for Alto Saxophone and Orch. (Feb. 24, 1983); *Symphonic Movement* (1st perf. as *Poem*, Swedish TV, Dec. 24, 1976). **CHAMBER**: *2 Elegies* for Violin and Piano (1934); *Fantasy Piece* for Viola (1936); *4 Improvisations* for Violin, Viola, and Cello (1936); *Andante espressivo* for Violin and Piano (1938); *Romanza* for Violin and Piano (1942); *Fugue in E* for Oboe, Clarinet, and Bassoon (1948); 7 sonatas for 2 Violins (1951–52). **VOCAL**: *6 songs* for Voice and Piano (1935); *24 Barfotasånger* (24 Barefoot Songs) for Voice and Piano (1943–45); *Vox humana*, 18 songs for Soprano, Alto, Tenor, Baritone, Chorus, and String Orch., after American Indians (1974; March 19, 1976).

BIBL.: L. Aare, *A. P.* (Stockholm, 1978); P. Rapoport, *Opus Est: 6 Composers from Northern Europe* (London, 1978); idem, *A. P.* (Stockholm, 1981); M. Kube, ed., *A. P. (1911–1980): Texte-Materialien-Analysen* (Hamburg, 1994).—**NS/LK/DM**

Pettiford, Oscar, noted jazz bassist, cellist; b. on an Indian reservation, Okmulgee, Okla., Sept. 30, 1922; d. Copenhagen, Denmark, Sept. 8, 1960. He was a mixture of black and native American and grew up in Minn. At 11, he took up the piano, then turned to the bass at 14; his 10 brothers and sisters were all musicians and they all played together in the family band. He left Minn. with the Charlie Barnet Band in 1942, then went to N.Y. and joined Roy Eldridge in 1943. He did several sessions with Coleman Hawkins, Earl Hines, and Ben Webster. Pettiford co-led a group with Dizzy Gillespie in 1944, then led his own combos and big band in 1945. He relocated on the West Coast to work with Hawkins in 1945, then spent three years with Duke Ellington

(1945–48), followed by Woody Herman (1949), and Charlie Shavers and Louie Bellson's band in 1950. After that, he usually led his own bands; he also composed "Bohemia After Dark" and "Laverne Walk." He settled in Copenhagen in 1958. He had been out playing and, afterwards, didn't feel well; taken to the hospital, Pettiford died there the next day from a viral infection. He was the most influential bassist between Jimmy Blanton and Charles Mingus and the first to take up the cello as a second instrument. He tuned his cello like a bass.

DISC.: *Oscar Pettiford Memorial Album* (1949); *Discoveries* (1952); *Sextet* (1953); *New Oscar Pettiford Trio* (1953); *Oscar Pettiford Modern Quintet* (1954); *Bass by Oscar Pettiford* (1954); *Basically Duke* (1954); *Jazz Mainstream* (1955); *Another One* (1955); *Oscar Pettiford Orchestra* (1956); *Orchestra in Hi Fi* (1956); *Deep Passion* (1956); *Oscar Pettiford and His Birdland Orch.* (1957); *O.P.'s Jazz Men* (1957); *Jazz Legacy: Baden Baden* (1958); *Montmartre Blues* (1959); *Vienna Blues: The Complete Sessions* (1959); *Essen Jazz Festival* (1959); *Last Recordings by the Late, Great O.P.* (1960).

BIBL.: C. Gazdar, *First Bass: The Oscar Pettiford Discography* (Bangladore, India, 1991).—**NS/LP/MM**

Petyrek, Felix, Czech composer and teacher; b. Brünn, May 14, 1892; d. Vienna, Dec. 1, 1951. After training with Godowsky and Sauer (piano), he studied with Schrecker (composition) and Adler (musicology) at the Univ. of Vienna (graduated, 1919). He taught at the Salzburg Mozarteum (1919–21), the Berlin Hochschule für Musik (1921–23), the Athens Odeon Athenon (1926–30), the Stuttgart Cons. (1930–39), the Cons. and Univ. in Leipzig (1939–49), and the Vienna Academy of Music (1949–51). In his melodic writing, he adopted the scale of alternating whole tones and semitones as a compromise between tonality and atonality.

WORKS: DRAMATIC: *Die arme Mutter und der Tod*, musical fairy play (1923); *Der Garden des Paradieses*, opera (1923–41; Leipzig, Nov. 1, 1942); pantomimes. **ORCH.:** Sym. (1919); *Sinfonietta* (1921); 2 concertos for 2 Pianos and Orch. (1931, 1949). **CHAMBER:** String Quartet (1913); Violin Sonata (1913); String Quartet (1914); Piano Trio (1921); *Divertimento* for 8 Winds (1923); Sextet for Clarinet, String Quartet, and Piano (Donaueschingen, July 30, 1922); piano pieces. **VOCAL:** Choral music; songs.

BIBL.: L. Mahn, *F. P.: Lebensbild eines "vergessenen" Komponisten* (Tutzing, 1998).—**NS/LK/DM**

Petzold, Rudolf, German composer and teacher; b. Liverpool (of a German father and English mother), July 17, 1908; d. Michaelshoven, Nov. 17, 1991. He was a pupil of Jarnach at the Cologne Hochschule für Musik (1930–33), where he taught (1937–38). After teaching at the Frankfurt am Main Hochschule für Musik (1941–42), he again taught at the Cologne Hochschule für Musik (1946–70), where he also was its deputy director (1960–69).

WORKS: ORCH.: 3 syms.: (1942, 1953, 1956); Concerto for Violin and Strings (1960). **CHAMBER:** 4 string quartets (1932, 1948, 1955, 1972); Piano Trio (1961); Cello Sonata (1964); Sonata for Solo Violin (1965); Piano Sonata (1967); Violin Sonata (1969). **VOCAL:** Sacred cantatas; choruses.—**NS/LK/DM**

Petzoldt, Richard (Johannes), German musicologist; b. Plauen, Nov. 12, 1907; d. Leipzig, Jan. 14,

1974. He studied at the Univ. of Berlin, where his teachers were Abert, Schering, Moser, Sachs, Hornbostel, Schünemann, and Blume. He received his Ph.D. in 1933 with the diss. *Die Kirchenkompositionen und weltlichen Kantaten Reinhard Keisers* (publ. in Düsseldorf, 1935). He ed. the *Allgemeine Musikalische Zeitung* (1935–39) and the periodical *Musik in der Schule* (1949–59). He was a prof. of music history at the Univ. of Leipzig (1952–67). His publs. include *Beethoven* (Leipzig, 1938; 2nd ed., 1947); *Schubert* (Leipzig, 1940; 2nd ed., 1947); *Schumann* (Leipzig, 1941; 2nd ed., 1947); *Mozart* (Wiesbaden, 1948; 2nd ed., 1965); *Johann Sebastian Bach und Leipzig* (Leipzig, 1950); *Die Oper in ihrer Zeit* (Leipzig, 1956); iconographies of Bach (Leipzig, 1950; 2nd ed., 1970), Verdi (Leipzig, 1951), Beethoven (Leipzig, 1952; 7th ed., rev., 1968), Schubert (Leipzig, 1953), Tchaikovsky (Leipzig, 1953), Handel (Leipzig, 1954; 2nd ed., 1960), Glinka (Leipzig, 1955), Schumann (Leipzig, 1956), Mozart (Leipzig, 1956; 3rd ed., 1961), *Beethoven* (Leipzig, 1970; 2nd ed., 1973), and Schütz (Kassel, 1972). —NS/LK/DM

Peuerl (Peurl, Bäwerl, Bäurl, Beurlin), Paul, German organist, organ builder, and composer; b. probably in Stuttgart (baptized), June 13, 1570; d. after 1625. He was an organist at Horn, Lower Austria (from 1602), and of the Protestant church school in Steyer (1609–25). He is generally acknowledged to be the originator of the German variation-suite. Following the example of the lutenists, he expanded the earlier combination of pavane and galliard into a new 4-movement suite form for strings. He was also an organ builder. He ed. the following (all publ. in Nuremberg): *Newe Padouan, Intrada, Däntz und Galliarda* (1611), *Weltspiegel, das ist: Neue teutsche Gesänger* (1613), *Ettliche lustige Padovanen, Intraden, Galliarden, Couranten und Däntz sampt zweyen Canzon zu 4 Stimmen* (1620), and *Gantz neue Padouanen, Auffzüg, Balletten, Couranten, Intraden und Däntz* (1625). Selections from his works, ed. by K. Geiringer, appear in Denkmäler der Tonkunst in Österreich, LXX, Jg. XXXVI/2 (1929).

BIBL.: P. Frankl, *P. P., ein osterreichischer Vokal- und Instrumentalkomponist um 1600* (diss., Univ. of Vienna, 1915). —NS/LK/DM

Peverara, Laura, Italian singer; b. Mantua, c. 1545; d. Ferrara, Jan. 4, 1601. She was born into a wealthy merchant's family. She gained distinction as a member of the prominent group of singing ladies in Ferrara (1580–98). Tasso dedicated numerous poems to her and 3 major musical anthologies were dedicated to her, *Il Lauro secco* (Ferrara, 1582), *Il Lauro verde* (Ferrara, 1583), and a MS collection.—**LK/DM**

Pevernage, Andries, Flemish composer; b. Harelbeke, near Courtrai, 1543; d. Antwerp, July 30, 1591. He was a boy chorister in Courtrai. On Feb. 11, 1563, he became choirmaster at St. Salvator in Bruges, and on Oct. 17, 1563, he was appointed choirmaster of Notre Dame in Courtrai; due to religious upheavals, however, he fled to Antwerp in 1578, returning to Courtrai to resume his post in 1584. On Oct. 29, 1585, he took the oath as choirmaster of Notre Dame in Antwerp. Pevernage was greatly honored there, and was buried in the Cathedral. His complete chansons were ed. by G. Hoekstra in Recent Researches in the Music of the Renaissance, LX–LXIV (1983).

WORKS: [6] *Missae* for 5 to 7 Voices (Antwerp, 1602); [39] *Cantiones aliquot sacrae* for 6 to 8 Voices, *quibus addita sunt* [29] *alogia monnulla* (Douai, 1578); 14 motets, *Laudes vespertinae B. Mariae Virginis* (Antwerp, 1604); etc. *Chansons...livre premier, contenant chansons spirituelles* for 5 Voices (Antwerp, 1589); *Chansons...livre second* for 5 Voices (Antwerp, 1590); *Chansons...livre troisième* for 5 Voices (Antwerp, 1590); *Chansons...livre quatrième* for 6 to 8 Voices (Antwerp, 1591); *Chansons...tant spirituelles que prophanes* for 5 Voices (Antwerp, 1606–07); etc.

BIBL.: J. Stellfeld, *A. P.: Zijne leven, zijne werken* (Louvain, 1943).—NS/LK/DM

Peyser, Joan (née **Gilbert**), American musicologist, editor, author, and journalist; b. N.Y., June 12, 1931. She majored in music at Barnard Coll. (B.A., 1951) and studied musicology with Lang at Columbia Univ. (M.A., 1956). She then devoted herself mainly to musical journalism. Peyser publ. the popular book *The New Music: The Sense Behind the Sound* (N.Y., 1971; 2nd ed., rev., 1981 as *Twentieth Century Music: The Sense Behind the Sound*), and created considerable excitement in the music world with her biography *Boulez: Composer, Conductor, Enigma* (N.Y., 1976). From 1977 to 1984 she was ed. of the *Musical Quarterly*, the first woman to occupy this position; during her tenure, she attempted to veer away from the prevalent musicological sesquipedalianism toward plain diction. Among her other publs. are *The Orchestra: Origins and Transformations* (N.Y., 1986), *Leonard Bernstein: A Biography* (N.Y., 1987; rev. ed., 1998), and *The Memory of All That: The Life of George Gershwin* (N.Y., 1993).—NS/LK/DM

Pez or **Petz, Johann Christoph,** German singer, instrumentalist, and composer; b. Munich, Sept. 9, 1664; d. Stuttgart, Sept. 25, 1716. He first studied at the choir school of St. Peter in Munich, and then pursued studies at that city's Jesuit school, where he sang in its choir and played in its orch. After singing tenor at St. Peter, he served as its choirmaster (1687–88). He then was made a chamber musician at the court of the Elector Max Emanuel, who provided for the completion of his studies in Rome (1689–92). Following a brief return to the Munich court, he was called to Bonn by Joseph Clemens, Archbishop-Elector of Cologne and Bishop of Liège, to reorganize its music establishment in 1694. In 1696 he became Kapellmeister there. With the outbreak of the War of the Spanish Succession, he returned to the almost moribund Munich court in 1701, where he led its church music. From 1706 he served as Kapellmeister at the Wüttemberg court in Stuttgart, where he remained until his death. While his music ws greatly influenced by his Italian sojourn, his output also owes much to Kerll. He composed various dramatic scores, school operas, instrumental music, and sacred vocal pieces. He publ. a set of 12 sonatas (Augsburg, 1696) under the title *Duplex Genius sive Gallo-italus Instrumentorum Concentus*; also a Psalm. Two of his operas were produced in Bonn. —**LK/DM**

Pezel (Petzold, Petzel, Pezelius, etc.**), Johann Christoph,** German bandsman and composer; b. Glatz, Dec. 5, 1639; d. Bautzen, Oct. 13, 1694. He was made 4th Kunstgeiger in the Leipzig town band in 1664, and in 1670 was promoted to Stadtpfeifer. Because of the plague, he left Leipzig in 1681 for Bautzen, where he remained until his death. He publ. several collections: *Musica vespertina Lipsicaca* (1669), *Hora decima musicorum Lipsiensium, oder Musicalische Arbeit zum Ab-blasen* (1670), *Intraden* (1676), *Delitiae musicales, oder Lust-Music* (1678), etc. His most interesting work is *Fünffstimmigte blasende Musik* (1685).

BIBL.: E. Wienandt, *J. P.: Thematic Catalogue* (N.Y., 1983). —NS/LK/DM

Pezold or **Petzold, Christian,** German organist, teacher, and composer; b. Königstein, 1677; d. Dresden, by June 1733. He settled in Dresden, where he was organist at the court by 1697. In 1703 he became organist at the Sophienkirche, and in 1709 he was made court chamber organist and composer. He also traveled as an organ virtuoso, and made notable appearances in Paris (1714) and Venice (1716). He was the teacher of C.H. Graun. Among his works were several virtuoso keyboard pieces, chamber music, and the cantata *Meine Seufzer, meine Klagen.*—**LK/DM**

Pfeiffer, Johann, German violinist and composer; b. Nuremberg, Jan. 1, 1697; d. probably in Bayreuth, 1761. He studied at the univs. of Halle and Leipzig. He was a violinist (1720–25) and Konzertmeister (1726–33) of the Weimar court orch. From 1734 he served as Kapellmeister in Bayreuth, and also was music teacher to Margravine Wilhelmine, sister of Friedrich II the Great. In 1753 he was granted the honorary title of Hofrat. He composed 3 syms., 18 concertos for Violin and Strings, 9 concertos for Violino Picolo and Orch., 2 concertos for Lute and Strings, a Flute Concerto, chamber music, and vocal pieces.—**LK/DM**

Pfeiffer, (Johann) Michael Traugott, German-Swiss pedagogue; b. Wilfershausen, Bavaria, Nov. 5, 1771; d. Wettingen, Switzerland, May 20, 1849. He settled in Switzerland in 1792. After training in languages and philosophy in Solothurn, he served in the Aargau cantonal government. He then became the first to apply Pestalozzian methods to the teaching of music in a school setting, opening his own private school in Solothurn in 1804 and in Lenzburg in 1805. He publ. *Die Pestalozzische Gesangbildungslehre nach Pfeiffers Erdindung* (1809), *Gesangbildungslehre nach Pestalozzischen Grundsatzen paedgogisch begrundet, von Michael Traugott Pfeiffer, methodisch bearbeitet von Hans Georg Nägeli* (1810), and *Auszug der Gesangbildungslehre...* (1812). With Nägeli, he publ. *Gesangbildungslehr für den Mannerchor* (1817) and *Chorgesangschule* (1821).

BIBL.: J. Keller, *M.T. P.* (Frauenfeld, 1894).—**LK/DM**

Pfendner, Heinrich, German organist and composer; b. Hollfeld, Upper Franconia, c. 1590; d. Würzburg, c. 1631. He was a pupil of Aichinger and Erbach in Augsburg and of Cifra in Italy. After serving as organist to the Bishop of Gurk in Austria, he was court organist in Graz (1615–18). From 1618 he was organist and Kapellmeister to the Bishop of Würzburg. His admired Latin church music included 4 vols. of motets (1614, 1623, 1625, 1630).

BIBL.: M. Sack, *Leben und Werk H. P.s* (diss., Univ. of Berlin, 1954).—**LK/DM**

Pfister, Hugo, Swiss composer; b. Zürich, Sept. 7, 1914; d. Küsnacht, near Zürich, Oct. 31, 1969. After training as a schoolteacher, he taught music at the Küsnacht Teachers's Seminary. In 1956–57 he studied with Boulanger in Paris. He wrote much incidental music for the stage and radio, orch. works, chamber music, and piano pieces.

BIBL.: R. Tschupp, *H. P.* (Zürich, 1973).—**LK/DM**

Pfitzner, Hans (Erich), eminent German composer, conductor, pedagogue, and writer on music; b. Moscow (of German parents), May 5, 1869; d. Salzburg, May 22, 1949. He was a student of Kwast (piano) and Knorr (composition) at the Hoch Cons. in Frankfurt am Main (1886–90). In 1892–93 he taught at the Koblenz Cons. From 1894 to 1896 he conducted at the Mainz City Theater, where his first opera, *Der arme Heinrich*, scored a remarkable success at its premiere on April 2, 1895. He went to Berlin, where he taught at the Stern Cons. (1897–1907) and held the position of 1st conductor at the Theater des Westens (1903–06). His opera *Die Rose vom Liebesgarten* brought him further success at its first performance in Elberfeld on Nov. 9, 1901. In 1907–08 he conducted the Kaim Orch. in Munich. He then went to Strasbourg, where he served as music director of the city, and as director of the Cons. (1908–18) and of the Opera (1910–16). The premiere of his greatest work, the opera *Palestrina* (Munich, June 12, 1917), brought Pfitzner his widest recognition as a composer. In 1919–20 he was music director of the Munich Konzertverein. From 1920 to 1929 he taught a master class in composition at the Berlin Academy of Arts, and then at the Munich Akademie der Tonkunst from 1929 to 1934. In 1925 he received the order Pour le mérite for his services to German music.

Pfitzner's genuine talent as a composer in the late Romantic tradition has been overshadowed by his overwhelming sense of self worth as a creative artist, by his polemical writings, such as *Futuristengefahr* (1917) and *Die neue Ästhetik der musikalischen Impotenz* (1920), and by his craving for public recognition and honors. In 1936 he accepted an appointment by the Nazi government as a Cultural Senator of the Reich. He degraded himself by sending a devotional public address to the notorious Nazi field marshal Hermann Göring and by dedicating his *Krakauer Begrüssung*, to Hans Frank, the murderous Nazi governor general of occupied Poland. With the collapse of the Nazi regime in 1945, Pfitzner was required to explain his conduct during the Third Reich to the Denazification Court in Munich. The aging composer was exonerated in 1948, and spent his last days in Salzburg. Apart from his *Palestrina*, Pfitzner's most important works include the *Kleine Symphonie*, the Sym. in C major, the Violin Concerto, particularly remarkable for its craftsmanship and melodic invention, the cello concertos, and several fine lieder.

WORKS: DRAMATIC: Opera: *Der arme Heinrich* (1891–93; Mainz, April 2, 1895); *Die Rose vom Liebesgarten* (1897–1900; Elberfeld, Nov. 9, 1901); *Das Christ- Elflein* (Munich, Dec. 11, 1906; rev. version, Dresden, Dec. 11, 1917); *Palestrina* (1911–15; Munich, June 12, 1917); *Das Herz* (Berlin and Munich, Nov. 12, 1931). **Incidental Music:** *Das Fest auf Solhaug,* to Ibsen's play (1889–90; Mainz, Nov. 28, 1890); *Das Käthchen von Heilbronn,* to Kleist's play (Berlin, Oct. 19, 1905); *Gesang der Barden* for Kleist's play *Die Hermannsschlacht* (1906). **ORCH.:** *Scherzo* (1887; Frankfurt am Main, Nov. 8, 1888); 3 cello concertos: op. post. (1888; Würzburg, Feb. 18, 1977), G major (Hamburg, Sept. 27, 1935), and A minor (Solingen, April 23, 1944); *3 Preludes* from the opera *Palestrina* (1917); Piano Concerto (Dresden, March 16, 1921); Violin Concerto (1923; Nuremberg, June 4, 1924); 3 syms.: C- sharp minor (1932; Munich, March 23, 1933; arr. from the String Quartet No. 2, 1903), *Kleine Symphonie* (Hamburg, Nov. 17, 1939), and C major (Frankfurt am Main, Oct. 11, 1940); Duo for Violin, Cello, and Chamber Orch. (Frankfurt am Main, Dec. 3, 1937); *Elegie und Reigen* (1939; Salzburg, April 4, 1941); *Krakauer Begrüssung* (1944); *Fantasie* (1947). **CHAMBER:** 4 string quartets (1886, 1903, 1925, 1942); Cello Sonata (1890); Piano Trio (1896); Piano Quintet (1908); Violin Sonata (1918); Sextet for Clarinet, Violin, Viola, Cello, Double Bass, and Piano (1945). **Piano:** 5 Pieces (1941); *6 Studien* (1943). **VOCAL:** Over 100 lieder for Voice and Piano (1884–1931); *Der Blumen Rache* for Alto, Women's Voices, and Orch. (1888); *Herr Oluf* for Baritone and Orch. (1891); *Rudgesang zum Neuhjarsfest 1901* for Bass, Chorus, and Piano (1900); *Die Heinzelmannchen* for Bass and Orch. (1902–03); *Columbus* for Chorus (1905); *2 deutsche Gesänge* for Baritone and Men's Voices ad libitum (1915–16); *Von deutscher Seele,* cantata for 4 Soloists, Chorus, Orch., and Organ (1921); *Lethe* for Baritone and Orch. (1926); *Das dunkle Reich* for Soloists, Orch., and Organ (1929); *Fons salutifer* for Chorus, Orch., and Organ (1941); 2 men's choruses (1941); 3 songs for Men's Chorus and Small Orch. (1944); *Kantate* for 4 Soloists, Chorus, Orch., and Organ (1948–49; completed by R. Rehan).

WRITINGS: *Gesammelte Schriften* (2 vols., Augsburg, 1926, 1929); *Über musikalische Inspiration* (Berlin, 1940); *Eindrücke und Bilder meines Lebens* (Hamburg, 1947); W. Osthoff, ed., *Briefwechsel H. P.—Gerhard Frommel 1925–1948* (Tutzing, 1990); B. Adamy, ed., *H. P. Briefe* (2 vols., Tutzing, 1991).

BIBL.: P. Cossmann, *H. P.* (Munich, 1904); R. Louis, *H. P.s "Rose vom Liebesgarten"* (Munich, 1904); C. Wandrey, *H. P.* (Leipzig, 1922); E. Kroll, *H. P.* (Munich, 1924); W. Lütge, *H. P.* (Leipzig, 1924); E. Valentin, *H. P.: Werk und Gestalt eines Deutschen* (Regensburg, 1939); H. Lindlar, *H. P.s Klavier-Lied* (Würzburg, 1940); J. Müller-Blattau, *H. P.: Ein Bild in Widmungen anlässlich seines 75. Geburtstages* (Leipzig, 1944); H. Rutz, *H. P.: Musik zwischen den Zeiten* (Vienna, 1949); K. Müller, *In memoriam H. P.* (Vienna, 1950); D. Henderson, *H. P.: The Composer and His Instrumental Music* (diss., Univ. of Mich., 1963); H. Rectanus, *Leitmotivik und Form in den musikdramatischen Werken H. P.s* (Würzburg, 1967); W. Dietz, *H. P.s Lieder: Versuch einer Stilbetrachtung* (Regensburg, 1968); W. Abendroth and K.-R. Danler, eds., *Festschrift aus Anlass des 100. Geburtstags und des 20. Todestags H. P.s* (Munich, 1969); B. Cherney, *The Bekker-P. Controversy: Its Significance for German Music Criticism During the Weimar Republic* (diss., Univ. of Toronto, 1974); E. Busse, *Die Eichendorff- Rezeption im Kunstlied: Versuch einer Typologie anhand von Kompositionen Schumanns, Wolfs, und P.s* (Würzburg, 1975); W. Osthoff, ed., *Symposium H. P.* (1981: Berlin, Germany) (Tutz-

ing, 1984); R. Ermen, *Musik als Einfall: H. P.s Position im ästhetischen Diskurs nach Wagner* (Aachen, 1986); E. Wamlek-Junk, *H. P. und Wien: Sein Briefwechsel mit Victor Junk und andere Dokumente* (Tutzing, 1986); J. Vogel, *H. P.: Mit Zelbstzeugnissen und Bilddokumenten* (Reinbek bei Hamburg, 1989); G. Busch-Salmen and G. Weiss, *H. P.: Münchner Dokumente, Bilder und Bildnesse* (Regensburg, 1990); J. Williamson, *The Music of H. P.* (Oxford, 1992); W. Osthoff, *H. P. und die musikalische Lyrik seiner Zeit* (Tutzing, 1994); P. Cahn and W. Osthoff, *H. P.—"Das Herz" und der Übergang zum Spätwerk* (Tutzing, 1997); R. Mercier, *The Songs of H. P.: A Guide and Study* (Westport, Conn., 1998). —NS/LK/DM

Pfleger, Augustin, German composer; b. Schlackenwerth, near Carlsbad, c. 1635; d. probably there, after July 13, 1686. He was a pupil of Kindermann. After serving as Kapellmeister to Duke Julius Heinrich of Saxe-Lauenber in Schlackenwerth, he was vice-Kapellmeister to Duke Gustav Adolph of Mecklenburg in Güstrow (1662–65) and Kapellmeister to the Schleswig-Holstein court in Gottorf (1665–73). In 1686 he returned to Schlackenwerth to resume his former position. His output includes more than 200 compositions, both German and Latin. In the former, he anticipated the development of the German sacred cantata. He also wrote various secular odes.—LK/DM

Pflughaupt, Robert, brilliant German pianist; b. Berlin, Aug. 4, 1833; d. Aachen, June 12, 1871. He studied with Dehn in Berlin, Henselt in St. Petersburg, and Liszt in Weimar, then pursued a career as a virtuoso. He wrote a number of agreeable piano pieces. His wife, Sophie (née Shtchepin) Pflughaupt (b. Dvinsk, Russia, March 15, 1837; d. Aachen, Nov. 10, 1867), was also a pupil of Henselt and Liszt and won praise as a pianist.—NS/LK/DM

Pfundt, Ernst (Gotthold Benjamin), celebrated German timpanist and inventor; b. Dommitzsch, near Torgau, June 17, 1806; d. Leipzig, Dec. 7, 1871. He studied theology, and at the same time developed extraordinary expertise as a drummer. He was invited by Mendelssohn in 1835 to join the Gewandhaus Orch. in Leipzig, where he achieved legendary fame for his rhythmic skill. He was the inventor of the pedal kettledrums. He publ. a method for drums (1849; 3rd ed., enl. by H. Schmidt, 1894).—NS/LK/DM

Phalèse, Pierre, Flemish music publisher; b. Louvain, c. 1510; d. there, c. 1575. He established a music publishing business in 1545. The printing was done elsewhere, and it was not until 1553 that Phalèse began to print on the premises in Louvain. From 1570 he worked in association with Jean Bellère of Antwerp;. He was also assisted by his sons, Corneille and Pierre Phalèse the Younger (b. Louvain, c. 1550; d. Antwerp, March 13, 1629). Corneille left the business before his father's death and settled in Antwerp as a schoolmaster; Pierre the Younger took over the enterprise, with Bellère continuing his association until his death in 1595.

BIBL.: A. Goovaerts, *Notice biographique sur P.* (1869); idem, *De muziekdrukkers P. en Bellerus te Leuven* (Antwerp, 1882); H. Vanhulst, *Catalogue des éditions de musique publiées à Louvain par P. P. et ses fils 1545–1578* (Brussels, 1990).—NS/LK/DM

Phile (Fyles, Pfeil, Phyla, etc.), **Philip,** German-American violinist and composer; b. in Germany, c. 1734; d. Philadelphia, between Aug. 1 and Nov. 9, 1793. He served in the Pa. German Regiment during the Revolutionary War, being transferred in July 1778 to the Invalid Regiment, and discharged on Jan. 4, 1783; a pension was granted to him on July 11, 1785. He was active in Philadelphia and N.Y. He gave concerts, played in theater orchs., and conducted the orch. of the Old American Co. of Comedians. His only extant work is *The President's March,* which appears to have been written for George Washington's first inauguration (1789). Joseph Hopkinson's (son of Francis Hopkinson) text "Hail Columbia" was added to it, and it was subsequently performed for the first time on April 25, 1798.—NS/LK/DM

Philidor (real name, **Danican),** family of famous French musicians:

(1) Michel Danican; b. Dauphine, c. 1600; d. Paris, Aug. 1659. He is the earliest known member of the family, although he never used the name Philidor. He went to Paris about 1620. By 1651 he was in the service of King Louis XIII as a member of the grande ecurie (military band), in which he played the oboe, cromorne, and trompette marine.

(2) Jean Danican; b. probably in Dauphine, c. 1620; d. Versailles, Sept. 8, 1679. He most likely was a younger brother or son of **(1) Michel Danican.** He adopted the name Philidor about 1659, and by 1657 he was in the royal service. In 1659 he became a phiphre marine. He was also a composer.

(3) André Danican Philidor (l'aîné), son of **(2) Jean Danican**; b. Versailles, c. 1647; d. Dreux, Aug. 11, 1730. In 1659 he entered the grande écurie, succeeding **(1) Michel Danican,** in which he played the cromorne, trompette marine, and drums. He subsequently played the oboe, bassoon, and bass cromorne in the royal chapel and chambre du roi. In 1684 King Louis XIV appointed him royal music librarian, a position he held until his death. During his long tenure, he acquired operas, ballets, sacred music, partbooks, etc. from various periods of French history for the collection. A large portion of this collection eventually passed to St. Michael's Coll., Tenbury. It was sold at auction in London in 1978, and passed to the Bibliothèque Nationale in Paris and the Bibliothèque Municipale in Versailles. The latter library already housed 35 vols. of the royal collection. The Paris Cons. library once housed 59 vols., but through various misfortunes its collection was reduced to 34 vols. Additional vols. are housed in other library collections. Philidor continued to serve as a musician in the royal chapel until 1722, and in the royal service until 1729. By his first wife he had 16 children, and by his second, 5. His most famous son was **(7) François-André Danican Philidor.**

WORKS: DRAMATIC: O p é r a - b a l l e t : *Le Canal de Versailles* (Versailles, July 16, 1687); *Le Mariage de la couture avec la grosse Cathos* (Versailles, 1687?); *La Princesse de Crète* (Marly, 1700?); *La Mascarade du roi de la Chine* (Marly, 1700); *La Mascarade du vaisseau marchand* (Marly, Feb. 18, 1700); *La Mascarade de la noce village* (Marly, 1700). INSTRUMENTAL: Various works, including dances, marches, etc.

(4) Jacques Danican Philidor (le cadet), son of **(2) Jean Danican** and younger brother of **(3) André Danican Philidor (l'aîné);** b. Paris, May 6, 1657; d. Versailles, May 27, 1708. In 1668 he became a phiphre in the grande ecurie, and subsequently played the cromorne and trompette marine. In 1683 he became a musicien ordinaire de la chapelle, and played the oboe and bassoon. In 1690 he became a member of the chambre du roi. He composed airs, dance music, and marches (only the last are extant). Of his 12 children, 4 became musicians.

(5) Anne Danican Philidor, son of **(3) André Danican Philidor (l'aîné);** b. Paris, April 11, 1681; d. there, Oct. 8, 1728. In 1698 he became an oboist in the grande écurie. In 1704 he became a member of the royal chapel, and in 1712 of the chambre du roi. He founded the famous Paris concert series known as the Concert Spirituel, which was launched on March 18, 1725; it was disbanded in 1790. He also founded the short-lived Concerts Français (1727–33).

WORKS: DRAMATIC: *L'Amour vainqueur,* pastoral (Marly, Aug. 9, 1697); *Diane et Endymion,* pastoral (Marly, 1698); *Danae,* opera (Marly, 1701). OTHER: Mass, Te Deum, motets, and instrumental pieces.

(6) Pierre Danican Philidor, son of **(4) Jacques Danican Philidor (le cadet);** b. Paris, Aug. 22, 1681; d. there, Sept. 1, 1731. In 1697 he became a member of the grande écurie, in 1704 an oboist in the royal chapel, and in 1712 a flutist in the chambre du roi. A pastoral he composed in 1697 was given in Marly and Versailles. He also wrote 6 suites for Transverse Flutes (publ. in Paris, 1717–18), 6 suites for 3 Flutes, and Oboes or Violins (1718), and marches.

(7) François-André Danican Philidor, the greatest in the line of musicians in the family, the youngest son of **(3) André Danican Philidor (l'aîné);** b. Dreux, Sept. 7, 1726; d. London, Aug. 31, 1795. He was a page boy in the royal chapel in Versailles, where he studied music with the maître de chapelle, André Campra. It was also at that time that he learned to play chess. A motet by him was performed in the royal chapel when he was 12. In 1740 he went to Paris, where he supported himself by copying and teaching. His interest in chess continued, and he gained distinction as an outstanding player by defeating a number of celebrated chess masters of the day. He publ. a fundamental treatise on chess, *L'Analyze des échecs* (London, 1749; rev. ed., 1777, as *Analyse du jeu des échecs),* which appeared in more than 100 eds. and several translations. As a member of the St. James Chess Club in London, he gave lectures and demonstrations as a master; a famous chess opening was named after him. In the meantime, he began a successful career as a composer for the theater. His first success was *Le Maréchal ferrant* (Paris, Aug. 22, 1761), which was accorded numerous performances. His *Le Sorcier* (Paris, Jan. 2, 1764) was also a triumph. Although *Tom Jones* (Paris, Feb. 27, 1765) was an initial failure, it enjoyed great popularity after its libretto was revised by Sedaine and performed on Jan. 30, 1766. The same fate attended his *Ernelinde, princesse de Vorvège* when it was first given at the Paris Opéra on Nov. 24, 1767. It was subsequently revised by Sedaine and performed most successfully as *Ernelinde* in Versailles on Dec. 11, 1773. Philidor continued to compose for the stage until his death, but he allowed his love for chess to take more and more of his time. He made frequent trips to London after 1775 to play at the St. James Chess Club. Philidor was one of the finest early composers of opéra-comique. Although his scores are often hampered by poor librettos, his orch. writing is effective. He was an inventive composer, and introduced the novelty of a vocal quartet a cappella (in *Tom Jones*). He wrote sacred music as well. His choral work, the *Carmen saeculare*, after Horace, proved most successful at its premiere in London on Feb. 26, 1779. Other vocal works include 12 ariettes périodiques.

BIBL.: G. Baretti, *The Introduction to the Carmen Seculare* (London, 1779); G. Allen, *The Life of P., Musician and Chess Player* (Philadelphia, 1858; 2nd ed., 1863; reprint, 1971; 3rd ed., 1865); G.-E. Bonnet, *P. et l'évolution de la musique française au XVIIIe siècle* (Paris, 1921); C. Carroll, *F.-A. D.-P.: His Life and Dramatic Art* (diss., Fla. State Univ., 1960); C. Rollin, *[F.-A. D.] P.: Il musicista che giocava a sacchi* (Brescia, 1994).—NS/LK/DM

Philip de Bourbon, Duke of Chartres and Orléans, French regent (1715–23) and composer; b. St. Cloud, Aug. 2, 1674; d. Versailles, Dec. 2, 1723. He was a nephew of Louis XIV. He studied music with Charpentier, who became his intendant of music. With Charpentier, he wrote the opera *Philomèle* (1694; not extant), with his later intendant, Charles-Hubert Gervais, he wrote *Renaud et Armide* (1705), and with his captain of the guard, the Marquis de la Fare, he wrote *Penthée* (Palais Royal, July 16, 1705; rev. 1709).—LK/DM

Philipp, Franz, German organist, music educator, and composer; b. Freiburg im Breisgau, Aug. 24, 1890; d. there, June 2, 1972. He studied organ with Hamm in Basel and received training in literature and philosophy at the Univ. of Freiburg im Breisgau. He served as organist and choirmaster at St. Martin in Freiburg im Breisgau. In 1924 he became director of the Karlsruhe Cons. (later the Hochschule für Musik), a position he held until 1942. In addition to a vast number of sacred works, he also wrote a Sym., chamber music, and songs.

BIBL.: H. Baum, ed., *F. P. 70 Jahre* (Freiburg im Breisgau, 1960).—LK/DM

Philipp, Isidor, eminent French pianist and pedagogue of Hungarian descent; b. Pest, Sept. 2, 1863; d. Paris, Feb. 20, 1958. He was taken to Paris as an infant. He studied piano with Georges Mathias at the Paris Cons., winning 1st prize in 1883, then took lessons with Saint-Saëns, Stephen Heller, and Ritter. His concert career was brief, but he found his true vocation in teaching. He was a prof. at the Paris Cons. (1893–1934), where he was mentor to many notable pupils, including Albert Schweitzer. In Paris he continued to perform, mostly in chamber music groups. He formed a concert trio with Loeb and Berthelier, with which he gave a number of successful concerts. After the outbreak of World War II, he went to the U.S., arriving in N.Y. in 1941; despite his advanced age he accepted private students, not only in N.Y., but also in Montreal. At the age of 91, he played the piano part in Franck's Violin Sonata (N.Y., March 20, 1955); then returned to France.

He publ. some technical studies for piano, among them *Exercices journaliers, École d'octaves, Problèmes techniques, Études techniques basées sur une nouvelle manière de travailler*, and *La Gamme chromatique*. He made arrangements for 2 pianos of works by Bach, Mendelssohn, Saint-Saëns, and others, and also brought out *La Technique de Liszt* (2 vols., Paris, 1932).—NS/LK/DM

Philippe de Vitry
See **Vitry, Philippe de**

Philippot, Michel, French composer and teacher; b. Verzy, Marne, Feb. 2, 1925. He was a student at the Paris Cons. (1945–47) and of Leibowitz (1945–49). After working with the Radiodiffusion française (1949–59), he was associated with Schaeffer's Groupe de recherches musicales de la RTF (1959–61). From 1963 to 1975 he was active with the ORTF. He taught at the Univ. of Paris (1969–76) and was a prof. of composition at the Paris Cons. (1970–90). He also was active in Brazil, where he founded and directed the music dept. at the Univ. of São Paulo (1976–79) and was a prof. at the Univ. of Rio de Janeiro (1979–81). In 1987 he was awarded France's Grand Prix national for music. He publ. the vols. *Électronique et techniques compositionnelles* (Paris, 1956), *Pierre Boulez aujourd'hui, entre hier et demain* (Paris, 1964), *Stravinski* (Paris, 1965), *Diabolus in musica: Analyse des variations "Diabelli" de Beethoven* (São Paulo, 1978), and *Traité de l'écriture musicale* (São Paulo, 1984).

WORKS: ORCH.: *Ouverture* for Chamber Orch. (1949); *Composition No. 1* for Strings (1959) and *No. 2* for Strings, Piano, and Harp (1974), and *No. 4* (1980); *Composition* for Double Orch. (1960); *Carres mágiques* (1983); Concerto for Violin, Viola, and Orch. (1984). **CHAMBER:** Piano Trio (1953); *Variations* for 10 Instruments (1957); *Pièces* for 10 Instruments (1961); *Transformations triangulaires* for 12 Instruments (1963); *Composition No. 1* (1965) and *No. 3* (1976) for Violin; *Scherzo* for Accordion (1972); *Passacaille* for 12 Instruments (1973); Octet for Clarinet, Bassoon, Horn, String Quartet, and Double Bass (1975); 4 string quartets (1976, 1982, 1985, 1988); Septet (1977); Piano Quintet (1986); *Concerto de chambre* for Piano and 6 Instruments (1986); Wind Quintet (1988); *Composition* for Violin and Piano (1990). **KEYBOARD: Piano:** 2 sonatas (1947, 1973); *3 Compositions* (1958); *Composition No. 4* (1975), *No. 5* (1976), and *No. 6* (1977). **Organ:** Sonata (1971). **OTHER:** *Contrapunctus X* (1994).—NS/LK/DM

Philippus de Caserta, French composer and music theorist; b. c. 1360; d. c. 1435. His extant works include a Credo and 16 ballades. See W. Apel, ed., *French Secular Works of the Fourteenth Century*, Corpus Mensurabilis Musicae, LIII/I (1970). The treatises *Tractatus de diversis figuris* and *Regule Contrapuncti* have been attributed to him, but their authorship remains in dispute.—LK/DM

Philips, Peter, important English composer; b. 1560 or 1561; d. Brussels, 1628. His surname was also rendered as **Phillips** or **Phillipps**; after leaving England, he was known as **Petrus Philippus, Pietro Philippi,** and **Pierre Philippe.** He was born into a Roman Catholic family, and his name appears in the list of choirboys at

St. Paul's Cathedral in London in 1574. He was befriended by a Roman Catholic almoner of St. Paul's, Sebastian Westcote, who was in charge of the music and choirboys there. Upon Westcote's death in 1582, Philips received a bequest of "five poundes thirteen shillings fower pence." He left England in 1582, and arrived at the English Coll. at Douai on Aug. 18. He then proceeded to Rome, arriving at the English Coll. there on Oct. 20. He was its organist until 1585, and also was in the service of Cardinal Alessandro Farnese. In Feb. 1585 Lord Thomas Paget, a Roman Catholic refugee from England, arrived at the English Coll. Philips entered his service, and on March 19, 1585, they set out for Italy and Spain; they went to France in Sept. 1586, spending most of their time in Paris from early 1587 to June 1588. They subsequently went to Antwerp, remaining there until Feb. 1589; they then proceeded to Brussels. After Paget's death in early 1590, Philips went to Antwerp and maintained himself by teaching keyboard playing. In 1593 he went to Amsterdam, where he heard and met Sweelinck. On his return to Antwerp, he stopped in Middelburg due to illness. During his stay, he was accused by a fellow Englishman of complicity in a plan to assassinate Queen Elizabeth. He was arrested by the Dutch authorities and taken to The Hague for questioning. After inquiries were made in England, he was exonerated and released. He returned to Antwerp in late 1593; publ. his 1st book of 6-part madrigals in 1596. He entered the service of the Archduke Albert in Brussels in 1597, being employed as one of the 3 organists of the vice-regal chapel until his death. His collection of 8-part madrigals was publ. in 1598, and it proved highly popular. In later years he held a number of appointments as canon and chaplain, but he was never ordained. On March 9, 1610, he was appointed to a canonry at the collegiate church of St. Vincent, Soignies, but continued to reside in Brussels. On Jan. 25, 1621, he exchanged his prebend at Soignies for a chaplainship at St. Germain Tirlemont. In 1623 he is also described as canon of Bethune in the title page of his *Litaniae Beatae Mariae Virginis*. His first extensive collection of sacred works, the *Cantiones sacrae* for 5 Voices, was publ. in 1612. Other collections followed in 1613 and 1616. His last publication was a major collection of motets, *Paradisus sacris cantionibus* (Antwerp, 1628). Philips was highly esteemed as both composer and organist, his keyboard music reflecting the English style at its finest. His outstanding madrigals and motets reflect his adoption of the Roman school as a model for his vocal music.

BIBL.: P. Bergmans, *L'Organiste des archiducs Albert et Isabelle: P. P.* (Ghent, 1903); P. Lyder, *The Latin Sacred Music of P. P.* (diss., N.Y.U., 1955); F. Pearson, *The Madrigals of P. P.* (diss., Univ. of Mich., 1961); L. Pike, *The Vocal Music of P. P., Its Technique and Transcription of Selected Items* (diss., Oxford Univ., 1969–70).—NS/LK/DM

Phillipps, Adelaide, English contralto; b. Stratford-on-Avon, Oct. 26, 1833; d. Karlsbad, Oct. 3, 1882. Her family took her to America as a child. She was trained as a dancer, and made her first appearance at the Tremont Theater in Boston on Jan. 12, 1842, in a variety show. She also displayed an early gift as a vocalist, and

was introduced to Jenny Lind, who encouraged her to study singing. Accordingly she was sent to London, where she took lessons with Manuel García, making her operatic debut in Brescia (1853). She continued to sing in Italy under the name Signorina Filippi until 1855, when she returned to Boston to appear in light opera in English. Her first major appearance on the grand opera stage in America was as Azucena in Verdi's *Il Trovatore* (N.Y., March 17, 1856). After a long and successful tour in Europe (1861–62), she sang with the Boston Ideal Opera Co. from 1879 to 1881. She was advised to go to Karlsbad for her health in 1882, but died shortly after her arrival there.

BIBL.: A. Waterston, *A. P.: A Record* (Boston, 1883). —NS/LK/DM

Phillips, Barre, free-jazz bassist; b. San Francisco, Calif., Oct. 27, 1934. He began playing in 1948, studying at Berkeley, then in N.Y. with Fred Zimmerman. He worked with Don Heckman, Archie Shepp, Jimmy Giuffre, and George Russell, touring Europe with Russell (1964) and Giuffre (1965). He also performed with the N.Y. Philharmonic, Marion Brown and others. Beginning around 1967, he divided his time between Europe (primarily London and Paris) and the U.S. In 1969, he started working with British saxophonist John Surman. He has recorded on his own and with Shepp, Surman, Attila Zoller, Bob James, Brown, Siegfried Kessler, Michel Portal, and Dave Holland. He spent most of the 1980s in Montreal.

DISC.: *For All It Is* (1971); *Mountainscapes* (1976); *Journal Violone II* (1979); *Die Jungen: Random Generators* (1979); *Camouflage* (1989); *Aquarian Rain* (1991).—LP

Phillips, Burrill, American composer and teacher; b. Omaha, Nov. 9, 1907; d. Berkeley, Calif., June 22, 1988. He studied music with Edwin Stringham in Denver; then with Hanson and Rogers at the Eastman School of Music in Rochester, N.Y. (B.M., 1932; M.M., 1933). He taught at the Eastman School of Music (1933–49; 1965–66), the Univ. of Ill. in Urbana (1949–64), the Juilliard School in N.Y. (1968–69), and Cornell Univ. (1972–73). His early music was cast in a neo-Classical style; later he incorporated free serial techniques.

WORKS: DRAMATIC: Opera: *Don't We All* (1947; Rochester, N.Y., May 9, 1949); *The Unforgiven* (1981). **Ballet:** *Katmanusha* (1932–33); *Play Ball* (Rochester, N.Y., April 29, 1938); *Step into My Parlor* (1942); *La piñata* (1969). **Other:** Incidental music. **ORCH.:** *Selections from McGuffey's Reader* (1933; Rochester, N.Y., May 3, 1934); *Sinfonia concertante* (Rochester, N.Y., April 3, 1935); *American Dance* for Bassoon and Strings (Rochester, N.Y., April 25, 1940); *3 Satiric Fragments* (Rochester, N.Y., May 2, 1941); Piano Concerto (1942); *Scherzo* (1944); *Tom Paine Overture* (1946; N.Y., May 15, 1947); Concerto grosso for String Quartet and Chamber Orch (1949); Triple Concerto for Clarinet, Viola, Piano, and Orch. (1952); *Perspectives in a Labyrinth* for 3 String Orchs. (1962); *Soleriana concertante* (1965); *Yellowstone, Yates, and Yosemite* for Tenor Saxophone and Symphonic Band (1972). **CHAMBER:** Trio for 3 Trumpets (1937); 2 string quartets (1939–40; 1958); Violin Sonata (1941); *Partita* for Piano Quartet (1947); Cello Sonata (1948); *4 Figures in Time* for Flute and Piano (1952); Oboe Quintet (1967); *Intrada* for Wind Ensemble, Percussion, Piano, Violin, and Cello (1975); *Scena da camera* for Violin and Cello (1978); *Canzona VI* for Wind Quintet (1985). **P i a n o :** 4 sonatas (1942–60); *9 by 9*, a set of 9 variations, each in a meter of 9 beats (1942); *Toccata* (1944); *Commentaries* (1983). **VOCAL:** *Declaratives* for Women's Chorus and Chamber Orch. (1943); *The Return of Odysseus* for Baritone, Narrator, Chorus, and Orch. (1956); *Letters from Italy Hill* for Soprano, Flute, Clarinet, String Quartet, and Piano (1984).—**NS/LK/DM**

Phillips, Harvey (Gene), outstanding American tuba player and teacher; b. Aurora, Mo., Dec. 2, 1929. He played the sousaphone in high school. After attending the Univ. of Mo. (1947–48), he joined the Ringling Brothers and Barnum & Bailey Circus Band. He then took general music courses at the Juilliard School of Music (1950–54) and at the Manhattan School of Music (1956–58) in N.Y. He played in various ensembles there, including the N.Y.C. Ballet Orch., the N.Y.C. Opera Orch., the Goldman Band, and the Sym. of the Air. He also was a founding member of the N.Y. Brass Quintet. From 1967 to 1971 he held an administrative position at the New England Cons. of Music in Boston. In 1971 he became a prof. of music at the Ind. Univ. School of Music, being named a distinguished prof. of music there in 1979. He retired in 1994. Phillips commissioned works for tuba from Gunther Schuller, Robert Russell Bennett, Alec Wilder, and Morton Gould. With W. Winkle, he publ. *The Art of Tuba and Euphonium* (Secaucus, N.J., 1992).—**NS/LK/DM**

Phillips, Henry, English bass; b. Bristol, Aug. 13, 1801; d. London, Nov. 8, 1876. He sang as a boy soprano at the Harrowgate theater about 1807, and then proceeded to London and sang in the chorus at Drury Lane. After studying as a baritone with Broadhurst, he sang in the chorus of the English Opera House before completing his training with Smart. In 1824 he sang Artabanes in Arne's *Artaxerxes* at Covent Garden, and then garnered notable success as Caspar in *Der Freischütz* at the English Opera House that same year. In 1825 he became principal bass of the Concert of Ancient Music. He also toured as an opera and concert singer, making a visit to the U.S. in 1844–45. On Feb. 25, 1863, he gave his farewell concert in London, and then was active as a teacher in Birmingham and later in Dalston. He publ. *The True Enjoyment of Angling, with Music to the Songs* (1843), *Hints on Declamation* (1848), and *Musical and Personal Recollections during Half a Century* (1864). —**NS/LK/DM**

Phillips, Peter (Sayer), outstanding English choral conductor, music scholar, and music critic; b. Southampton, Oct. 15, 1953. He was educated at Winchester Coll. (1967–71) and was an organ scholar at St. John's Coll., Oxford (B.A., 1975). In 1973 he founded the Tallis Scholars, which he developed under his discerning conductorship into one of the world's foremost choral ensembles. After serving as editor of the *Early Music Gazette* (1980–82), he became music critic of *The Spectator* in 1983. In 1981 he co-founded and became director of Gimell Records, with which he made many

remarkable recordings with the Tallis Scholars. In 1987 they won the *Gramophone* Record of the Year Award. In 1988 Phillips conducted the Tallis Scholars for the first time on tour in the U.S., and also at the London Promenade Concerts. In 1989 he conducted them in Tokyo. In 1994 he conducted them in the Palestrina anniversary concert in Rome, returning that year to Italy to conduct them at the Sistine Chapel at the Vatican. As a guest conductor, Phillips led choral groups far and wide, including ensembles in Florence (1996), Washington, D.C., and Tokyo (1998), and Barcelona and Novosibirsk (1999). He taught at the Univ. of Oxford (1976–81), and in London at Trinity Coll. of Music (1980–84) and the Royal Coll. of Music (1981–88). In 1995 he became proprietor and advisory editor of *The Musical Times*. In addition to his vol. *English Sacred Music, 1549–1649* (1991), he has contributed articles to various journals and periodicals. He has won universal acclaim for his interpretations of the masters of Renaissance polyphony.—**NS/LK/DM**

Phillips, Philip, American singer, hymn-tune composer, and editor; b. Chautauqua County, N.Y., Aug. 13, 1834; d. Delaware, Ohio, June 25, 1895. He sang in a choir as a child, but was mainly self-taught in music. He taught in singing-schools from age 19, and in c. 1863 founded Philip Phillips & Co. in Cincinnati, which sold pianos and melodeons and publ. Sunday-school songbooks. He later was music ed. of the Methodist Books Concern in N.Y. He toured widely in the U.S. as a singing evangelist, being dubbed the "Singing Pilgrim," making an extensive tour of Europe, the Holy Land, and the Far East (1875), which he related in his book *Song Pilgrimage Around and Throughout the World* (N.Y., 1882). He also publ. gospel songs and wrote the hymn-tunes *Home of the Soul* and One Sweetly Solemn Thought.

BIBL.: A. Clark, *P. P.: His Songs and Tours* (N.Y., c. 1887). —**NS/LK/DM**

Phinot, Dominique, significant Franco-Flemish composer; b. c. 1510; d. c. 1555. He was mainly active in Italy, being in the service of the Urbino court, and also working in Pesaro. He was particularly important for his contribution to the development of the 8-voice double-choir technique. Among his works are 2 masses, 2 Magnificat settings, numerous motets, and many Psalms. He also publ. 2 books of chansons (Lyons, 1548). A complete ed. of his works was prepared by J. Hofler in Corpus Mensurabilis Musicae, LIX (1972–82).

BIBL.: P. Hansen, *The Life and Works of D. P.* (diss., Univ. of N.C., 1939).—**NS/LK/DM**

Piaf, Edith (originally, **Gassion, Edith Giovanna**), French singer, actress, and songwriter; b. Paris, Dec. 19, 1915; d. Plascassier, France, Oct. 11, 1963. An impassioned singer, Piaf was among the most popular performers in France from the 1930s to the 1960s and one of the few French musical artists to gain a significant following internationally. Famous for a troubled life, she sang dramatic songs of unhappy love, many of which contained her lyrics or were written especially for her. These included her best-known songs, "La Vie en

Rose" and "Non, Je Ne Regrette Rien." Although she sang in French for the most part (with occasional forays into English), her highly personal approach to material influenced English-speaking singers such as Judy Garland as well as a generation of French cabaret performers.

Piaf's parents were Louis-Alphonse Gassion, an acrobat, and Anetta Giovanna Maillard Gassion, who became a singer under the name Line Marsa. Her father was serving in the army when she was born, and her mother abandoned her to his care after he returned. When she was seven, he took her to live with her grandmother, a cook in a brothel in Normandy. After a year he reclaimed her, and she accompanied him in his travels around the country, singing as part of his act. When she was about 15, her father acquired a common-law wife and the family settled in Paris, where Piaf worked in a factory and began to sing in the streets. She entered into a relationship with Louis Dupont, an errand-boy, and gave birth to a daughter in February 1933, but she left him soon after to return to singing, and the child died of meningitis.

Piaf began to find work singing in cafés and nightclubs but was still singing in the street in October 1935 when she was heard by Louis Leplée, owner of Gerny's Club. He named her Piaf (Parisian slang for *sparrow*), picked songs for her, had her dress in black, and put her on at his cabaret. She rapidly became a success, earning a recording contract with Polydor before the end of the year. Leplée was robbed and murdered in the spring of 1936, which negatively affected her career. But she soon became the protégé of songwriter Raymond Asso. She made her film debut in *La Garçonne* and began making radio broadcasts in the fall. Asso wrote hit songs for her, including "Mon Légionnaire" (music by Marguerite Monnot, lyrics by Asso), and in March 1937 she debuted at the prestigious A.B.C. cabaret in Paris.

With the start of World War II in September 1939, Asso went into the army, and Piaf began living with singer Paul Meurisse. In May 1940 the two appeared in the one-act play *Le Bel Indifférent*, written for her by Jean Cocteau. She continued to perform and record after the Germans entered Paris on June 14, 1940. She had begun to write song lyrics, and she contributed four songs her next film appearance, in 1941's *Montmartre-Sur-Seine*, her first onscreen acting part. She sang for French prisoners-of-war in Germany and helped them to escape. With the end of the war in 1945 she made another film, *Etoile sans Lumière*, and switched record companies to Pathé-Marconi (EMI in the U.K.), recording for that label for the rest of her life. She toured with nine-member male vocal group Les Compagnons de la Chanson, made a film with them, *Neuf Garçons, un Coeur* (1947), and took them with her for her U.S. debut in N.Y. in October 1947. She returned to the U.S. frequently thereafter.

Piaf began a relationship with middleweight boxer Marcel Cerdan in 1947, but he was killed in a plane crash in October 1949. In June 1950 the orchestras of Victor Young and Paul Weston reached the U.S. charts with instrumental treatments of Piaf's 1946 French hit and signature song "La Vie en Rose" (music credited to R. S. Louiguy [real name Luis Guglielmi] though apparently composed by Piaf, lyrics by Piaf). Mack David wrote an English lyric, and Tony Martin scored a Top Ten hit with the song in August. Four other chart versions followed, including one by Piaf herself singing in English. In the wake of this success, other American performers recorded anglicized versions of her hits. Kay Starr peaked in the Top Ten in June 1954 with "If You Love Me (Really Love Me)" (music by Marguerite Monnot, English lyrics by Geoffrey Parsons), which Piaf had introduced in France in 1949 with her original lyrics as "Hymne à L'Amour." Patti Page reached the Top 40 with "I'll Remember Today" (music by Piaf, lyrics by William Engvick) in December 1957. And "C'Est l'Amour" (music by Marguerite Monnot, lyrics by Piaf) became "Just Come Home," a Top 40 hit for Hugo and Luigi in January 1960.

Piaf had begun living with American actor Eddie Constantine in 1950, and she appeared with him in the musical comedy *La P'tite Lili* (Paris, March 3, 1951), but the show closed after she was involved in an automobile accident in which she was severely injured, leading to an addiction to pain-killing drugs she never overcame. In June 1952 she married singer-songwriter Jacques Pills (real name Ducos); they divorced in 1957. She toured extensively during the 1950s, both in Europe and the U.S. After several minor appearances in films—*Paris Chante Toujours* (1951), *Boum sur Paris* (1952), *Si Versailles M'Était Conté* (1953), *French Cancan* (1954)—she had a larger role in her final film, *Les Amants de Demain* (1959).

In January 1959, Piaf collapsed onstage in N.Y. and underwent a four-hour operation for stomach ulcers and internal hemorrhaging. Her health steadily deteriorated during the last several years of her life. Still, she scored an international hit in the early 1960s with "Milord" (music by Marguerite Monnot, lyrics by Georges Moustaki), which reached the British charts in May 1960 and the American charts in March 1961. She mounted a major performing comeback with a four-month stand at the Olympia Music-Hall in Paris starting on Dec. 26, 1960, performing songs by composer Charles Dumont, among them a new signature song, "Non, Je Ne Regrette Rien" (No, I Regret Nothing; lyrics by Michel Vaucaire). The resulting album, *Live at the Olympia*, reportedly sold a million copies in France.

Piaf married hairdresser-turned-singer Théo Sarapo (real name Theophanis Lamboukas) on Oct. 9, 1962, and made her final public appearance with him at the Bobino Music-Hall in Paris on Feb. 21, 1963. She died at 47 of an internal hemorrhage. After her death her recordings continued to sell consistently. A sensationalized biography by Simone Berteaut—who falsely claimed to be her half-sister—was a best-seller at the end of the 1960s and served as the basis for the 1974 film *Piaf—The Early Years*. Pam Gems's biographical play *Piaf!* (London, Jan. 15, 1980) was a more reasonable account; it was revived successfully in the West End in 1993, starring Elaine Paige. The Piaf-Cerdan relationship exerted a particular fascination, and Claude Lelouch focused on it in his 1983 film *Edith et Marcel*, with Marcel Cerdan Jr. playing his father.

WRITINGS: *Au Bal de la Chance* (Geneva, 1958; Eng. tr. as *The Wheel of Fortune*, London, 1965); *Ma Vie: Texte Recueilli par Jean Nol* (Paris, 1964; 2nd ed., 1978).

BIBL.: M. Blistène, *Au Revoir, E.* (Paris, 1963); S. Berteaut, *P.* (Paris, 1969; Eng. tr., N.Y., 1972); E. Bertin, *E. P., Le Chant d'Amour* (Paris, 1973); J. Noli, *E. P.: Trois Ans pour Mourir* (1973); G. Costaz, *E. P.* (1974); D. Gassion (her half-sister), *P. Ma Soeur* (1977); M. Lange, *Histoire de P.* (1979; Eng. tr. as *P.*, N.Y., 1981); A. Le Breton, *La Môme P.* (1980); A. Fildier, ed., *E. P., 1915–1963* (1981); C. Dureau, *E. P. 20 Ans Après* (1982); E. Boissonnade, *P. et Cerdan, l'Amour Foudroyé* (1983); D. Grimault and P. Mahé, *P.-Cerdan, Un Hymne à l'Amour, 1946–1949* (1983); A. Larue, *E. P.: L'Amour Toujours* (1983); W. Laurent, *E. P.* (1983); J. Monserrat, *E. P. et la Chanson* (1983); P. Ribert, ed., *Témoignages sur E. et Chansons de P.* (1984); M. Crosland, *P.* (N.Y., 1985); D. Bret, *The P. Legend* (London, 1988).—**WR**

Piani, Giovanni Antonio,
Italian violinist and composer; b. Naples, 1678; d. probably in Vienna, after 1757. He was a student of Vinciprova and Cailò at the Cons. della Pietà dei Turchini in Naples. In 1704 he went to Paris, and by 1712 was principal violinist to Louis Alexandre de Bourbon, Count of Toulouse and admiral of the French fleet. From 1721 he was a musician at the imperial court in Vienna. He publ. a vol. of 12 sonatas, 6 for Violin and Continuo and 6 for Flute or Violin and Continuo (1712).—**LK/DM**

Piantanida, Giovanni,
Italian violinist and composer; b. Florence, 1705; d. Bologna, 1782. He went to Russia, where he entered the service of the Czarina Anna Ivanova in St. Petersburg. His wife, Costanza, known as La Pasterla, was active as a singer. After sojourns in Hamburg (1737–38) and Holland, he went to London in 1739 and appeared in many concerts, including some with Handel. In 1743 he appeared at the Concert Spirituel in Paris. He later settled in Bologna, where he was made a member of the Accademia Filarmonico in 1758. In 1770 he served as one of the judges at Mozart's examination for membership. He composed violin concertos and publ. 6 violin sonatas (London, 1742). His son, Gaetano Piantanida (b. Bologna, 1768; d. Milan, Nov. 1835), was a pianist and composer. After studying with his father and with Mattei at the Liceo Musicale in Bologna, he toured in Germany and Denmark. In 1810 he settled in Milan and taught at the Istituto Musicale. He publ. a number of piano pieces. —**LK/DM**

Piatigorsky, Gregor,
great Russian-born American cellist and pedagogue, brother of **Alexander Stogorsky;** b. Ekaterinoslav, April 17, 1903; d. Los Angeles, Aug. 6, 1976. He received his first music lessons from his father, a violinist, then took cello lessons with Alfred von Glehn at the Moscow Cons. He played in various orchs. in Moscow. In 1921 he left Russia and took cello lessons with Julius Klengel in Leipzig. After serving as 1st cellist of the Berlin Phil. (1924–28), he devoted himself to a solo career. He played the solo part in Richard Strauss's *Don Quixote* under the composer's direction many times in Europe, and was probably unexcelled in this part; Strauss himself called him "mein Don Quixote." He went to America in 1929, and made his American debut in Oberlin, Ohio, on Nov. 5, 1929; played the Dvořák Concerto with the N.Y. Phil., eliciting great praise (Dec. 29, 1929). He was regarded as the world's finest cellist after Casals; continued giving solo recitals and appearing with major European and American orchs. for many years; gave first performances of several cello works commissioned by him from Hindemith, Dukelsky, Castelnuovo-Tedesco, and others. He became a naturalized American citizen in 1942. He taught at the Curtis Inst. of Music in Philadelphia (1942–51) and at the Berkshire Music Center in Tanglewood; was a prof. at the Univ. of Southern Calif. in Los Angeles (1962–76); presented a series of trio concerts with Heifetz and Pennario. He was the recipient of honorary D.Mus. degrees from Temple Univ., Columbia Univ., the Univ. of Calif., Los Angeles, etc. He publ. an autobiographical vol., *Cellist* (N.Y., 1965).—**NS/LK/DM**

Piatti, Alfredo (Carlo),
renowned Italian cellist and teacher; b. Borgo Canale, near Bergamo, Jan. 8, 1822; d. Crocetto di Mozzo, July 18, 1901. He received his primary musical education from his father, the violinist Antonio Piatti, and his great uncle, the cellist Gaetano Zenetti, whom he succeeded as cellist in the local theater orch. when he was only 8; continued his studies with Merighi at the Milan Cons. (1832–37), playing his own concerto at a public Cons. concert (Sept. 21, 1837). He made his first tour of Europe in 1838; perf. with Liszt in Munich in 1843, making his Paris debut in 1844. On May 31 of that year he appeared in London for the first time, and soon established a remarkable reputation as a master of his instrument; also taught privately and at the Royal Academy of Music. He owned an outstanding Stradivari cello of 1720, which is now known as "The Piatti." He publ. a cello method (London, 1878), and also composed 2 cello concertos (1874, 1877), a Concertino for Cello and Orch. (1863), 6 sonatas for Cello and Piano, 12 caprices for Cello, and various arrangements of 18th-century music.

BIBL.: M. Latham, *A. P.* (London, 1901); A. Lodetti Barzanò, *Il musicista C.A. P.: Un violoncellista nell'Europa dell'800* (Bergamo, 1996).—**NS/LK/DM**

Piazzolla, Astor,
fiery Argentine bandoneón player, bandleader, composer, and arranger; b. Mar del Plata, March 11, 1921; d. Buenos Aires, July 5, 1992. He was taken to N.Y. in 1924, where he took up the bandoneón when he was 12. Upon settling in Buenos Aires in 1937, he began a career as a bandoneón player and arranger; also pursued training with Ginastera, and later was a scholarship student in Paris of Boulanger (1954–55). Upon his return to Buenos Aires, he organized his own band, and in 1960 founded the innovative Quinteto Nuevo Tango. From 1974 to 1985 he made his home in Paris; then returned to his homeland. Piazzolla was a master of the modern tango, embracing an avant-garde style incorporating classical and jazz elements with a piquant touch of modern dissonances. His other works included operas, theater music, film scores, concertos (including one for Bandoneón [1979]), and chamber music.

BIBL.: C. Kuri, *P., la música límite* (Buenos Aires, 1992; 2nd ed., 1997); O. Lopéz Ruiz, *P. loco loco loco: 25 años de labura y jodas conviviendo con un genio* (Buenos Aires, 1994).—**NS/LK/DM**

Piccaver (real name, **Peckover**), **Alfred,** English tenor; b. Long Sutton, Lincolnshire, Feb. 15, 1884; d. Vienna, Sept. 23, 1958. He studied at the Metropolitan School in N.Y. He made his operatic debut as Roméo in Prague in 1907, then continued his studies there and in Milan. In 1910 he deputized at the Vienna Court (later State) Opera in the Italian season; remained in Vienna as a leading lyric tenor until 1937. His repertoire included Don José, Florestan, Walther von Stolzing, Lensky, and Andrea Chénier; he also took part in the first Austrian performance of *La Fanciulla del West* in 1913. He appeared in Chicago (1923–25); in 1924 he sang Cavaradossi and the Duke of Mantua at Covent Garden in London. From 1937 to 1955 he taught voice in London; then returned to Vienna to attend the opening of the new building of the Staatsoper; he remained in Vienna as a voice teacher until his death.—**NS/LK/DM**

Picchi, Giovanni, Italian organist, lutenist, harpsichordist, and composer; b. Venice, 1572; d. there, May 19, 1643. He pursued his career in Venice, where he was first active as a performer and composer of dance music. About 1606 he became organist at the church of Santa Maria de' Frari, a position he retained for the rest of his life. He also served as organist of the confraternity of the Scuola Grande di San Rocco from 1623. He pub. the vols. *Intavolatura di balli d'arpicordo...novamente corrette, & ristampate* (Venice, 1st ed. not extant; 2nd ed., 1621) and *Canzoni da sonar con ogni sorte d'istromenti a due, tre, quattro, sei et otto voci, con il suo basso continuo* (Venice, 1625), both of which contain attractive scores. His fine *Toccata* for harpsichord was included in the *Fitzwilliam Virginal Book.*—**LK/DM**

Picchi, Mirto, Italian tenor; b. Florence, March 15, 1915; d. there, Sept. 25, 1980. He was a pupil of Florence of Giuseppe Armani and Giulia Tess. After making his operatic debut as Radamès in Milan in 1946, he sang in various Italian music centers. In 1947–48 he sang at London's Cambridge Theatre, appearing as Rodolfo, Cavaradossi, and the Duke of Mantua. In 1949 he appeared with the Glyndebourne company as Verdi's Riccardo during its visit to Edinburgh. In 1952 he sang at London's Covent Garden. In 1957 he appeared at Milan's La Scala, where he gave his farewell appearance as Don Basilio in 1974. Picchi was especially known for his roles in contemporary operas.—**NS/LK/DM**

Picchi, Silvano, Argentine composer; b. Pisa, Italy, Jan. 15, 1922. His family emigrated to Argentina while he was a child. He studied composition with Constantino Gaito, Alberto Ginastera, Arturo Luzzatti, Gilardo Gilardi, and Floro Ugarte in Buenos Aires. He was the music critic of *La Prensa* in Buenos Aires.

WORKS: ORCH.: *Suite irreverente* (1949); *Música para caballos* (1952); Piano Concerto (Buenos Aires, July 23, 1967); Violin Concerto (Buenos Aires, Aug. 12, 1968); *Euè,* funeral chant for Strings, on an African theme (Buenos Aires, March 18, 1969); *Sinfonia breve* (1970); *Mozartiana* for Strings (1971). CHAMBER: *Discantus* for Guitar and Bassoon (1968); 2 trios for Oboe, Violin, and Piano; guitar pieces. VOCAL: Songs.—**NS/LK/DM**

Piccinini, Alessandro, Italian lutenist, writer on music, and composer; b. Bologna, Dec. 30, 1566; d. probably there, c. 1638. He was born into a musical family. In 1582 he was called to the ducal court in Mantua, but soon thereafter he joined the rest of his family at the Este court in Ferrara. From 1597 to 1621 he was in the service of Cardinal Pietro Aldobrandini. He publ. 2 vols. of dances and toccatas for lute and chitarrone (Bologna, 1623, 1639).—**LK/DM**

Piccinni, (Vito) Niccolò (Marcello Antonio Giacomo), significant Italian composer; b. Bari, Jan. 16, 1728; d. Passy, near Paris, May 7, 1800. His father was a violinist at Bari's Basilica di San Nicola, and his maternal uncle was **Gaetano Latilla.** His precocity manifested itself at an early age; thanks to Muzio Gaeta, archbishop of Bari, he was able at 14 to enter Naples's Cons. di S. Onofrio, where he studied with Leo and Durante. Upon graduation (1754), he commenced his career as a composer for the stage with his comic opera *Le Donne dispettose* (Naples, 1754). His theatrical instinct led him to select librettos rich in dramatic content; his melodic invention was fresh, and his arias were written in a pleasing style eminently suited to the voice; he elaborated the conventional climactic scenes so that dramatic interest was sustained to the end; he varied the tempos and the harmonies in the ensembles, which further contributed to the general effect. His *Zenobia* (Naples, Dec. 18, 1756) was his first attempt at a serious opera. After several other operas for Naples, he received a commission to write an opera for Rome, *Alessandro nelle Indie* (Jan. 21, 1758); it was followed by his comic opera *La Cecchina, ossia La buona figliuola* (Rome, Feb. 6, 1760), which proved a great success at home and abroad. In subsequent years he wrote prolifically for the stage, producing well over 100 operas for the major Italian theaters. Making his home in Naples, he served as 2nd maestro di cappella at the Cathedral, was active as an organist in convents, and taught singing. Piccinni's fortunes in Rome declined with the rise of Anfossi, his former pupil and protégé, in 1773. However, he still found success in Naples with a 2nd *Alessandro nelle Indie* (Jan. 12, 1774) and *I Viaggiatori* (1775). In 1776 he was called to Paris by the French court, where his presence precipitated the "querelle célèbre" between the "Gluckists" and "Piccinnists." Piccinni's first French opera, *Roland* (Jan. 27, 1778), won considerable success. He then served as director of an Italian troupe in Paris (1778–79). Although he was promised by the Paris Opéra that his *Iphigénie en Tauride* would be produced before Gluck's masterpiece on the same subject, it was not given until Jan. 23, 1781, some 2 years after the Gluck premiere. While it was fairly successful, he gained his only major success with the opera *Didon* (Fontainebleau, Oct. 16, 1783), the same year in which he finally was granted a pension by the French court. In 1784 he was appointed maître de chant at the École

Royale de Chant et de Déclamation Lyrique in Paris. In spite of their rivalry, Piccinni held the highest regard for Gluck; indeed, he suggested that an annual memorial concert be given in Gluck's memory, but financial support was not forthcoming. Upon the death of another rival, Sacchini, Piccinni spoke in homage at his funeral. With the coming of the French Revolution, Piccinni lost his post as maître de chant and his pension. In 1791 he returned to Naples; upon his daughter's marriage to a French Jacobite, he was placed under house arrest in 1794; he finally gained freedom in 1798 and returned to Paris, where he obtained a partial restoration of his pension; his appointment as 6th inspector at the Cons. came when he was too ill to pursue an active life. Piccinni demonstrated a remarkable facility in writing both comic and serious operas. His historical importance rests upon his establishment of the Italian operatic style as the model for his French and German successors. His son Luigi (Lodovico) Piccinni (b. 1764; d. Passy, July 31, 1827) was also a composer; studied with his father and then wrote operas for Paris and several Italian cities; was Kapellmeister to the Swedish court in Stockholm (1796–1801); then taught singing. Piccinni had another son, who in turn sired an illegitimate son, Louis Alexandre (actually, Luigi Alessandro) Piccinni (b. Paris, Sept. 10, 1779; d. there, April 24, 1850), who also became a composer; studied piano with Haussmann and composition with Le Sueur; also received some instruction from his grandfather; was active as an accompanist and rehearsal pianist in several Parisian theaters, and was also active as a conductor; taught in various French cities, serving as director of the Toulouse music school (1840–44); wrote numerous works for the theater.

BIBL.: P. Ginguene, *Notice sur la vie et les ouvrages de Nicolas P.* (Paris, 1801); G. le Brisoys Desnoiresterres, *La Musique française au XVIIIe siècle: Gluck et P. 1774–1800* (Paris, 1872); E. Thoinan, *Notes bibliographiques sur la guerre musicale des Gluckistes et P.stes* (Paris, 1878); H. de Curzon, *Les Dernières Années de P. a Paris* (Paris, 1890); J. Popovici, *La buona figliuola von Nicola P.* (Vienna, 1920); A. della Corte, *P.: Settecento italiano* (Bari, 1928); P. La Rotella, *N. P.: Commemorato nel II centenario della nascità* (Bari, 1928); N. Pascazio, *L'Uomo P. e la "Querelle célèbre"* (Bari, 1951); W. Ensslin, *N.P.: Catone in Utica: Quellenüberlieferung, Aufführungsgeschichte und Analyse* (Frankfurt am Main, 1996). —NS/LK/DM

Piccioni, Giovanni, Italian organist and composer; b. Rimini, c. 1550; d. Orvieto, after June 17, 1619. He went to Conegliano, Veneto, in 1577 as maestro di musica to the "Magnifici Signori Desiosi." From 1590 he served as organist at Orvieto Cathedral, and from 1616 he was also organist and maestro di cappella in Monte Fiascone. He publ. 9 vols. of polyphonic madrigals (Venice, 1577-after 1602) and 5 vols. of sacred works (Venice, 1589–1619). —LK/DM

Pichl, Wenzel (actually **Václav**), Bohemian violinist and composer; b. Bechin, Sept. 23, 1741; d. Vienna, Jan. 23, 1805. He studied violin with the local Kantor, Jan Pokorný, and composition with Seger in Prague. He was made 1st violinist of the Vienna court theater (c. 1770), and served as music director and

Kammerdiener (valet) to Archduke Ferdinando d'Este, the Austrian governor of Lombardy, in Milan (1777–96), and then in Vienna. He wrote some 900 works, including 13 operas, over 30 masses, more than 90 syms. or symphonie concertantes, over 30 concertos or concertinos, about 20 serenatas, minuets, dances, and a vast amount of chamber music.

BIBL.: R. Kolisko, *W. P.s Kammermusik* (diss., Univ. of Vienna, 1918). —NS/LK/DM

Picka, František, Czech organist, conductor, and composer; b. Strašice, near Hořovice, May 12, 1873; d. Prague, Oct. 18, 1918. Of a musical family, he received a solid education in Prague and held several posts as a chorus master and opera conductor. His opera, *Malíř Reiner* (The Painter Reiner), was produced in Prague (April 28, 1911). The bulk of his works consists of church music, including 9 masses and many other works in an effective contrapuntal style. —NS/LK/DM

Picken, Laurence (Ernest Rowland), English zoologist, biologist, musicologist, and ethnomusicologist; b. Nottingham, July 16, 1909. He studied the natural sciences at Trinity Coll., Cambridge (B.A., 1931; M.A., 1935; Ph.D., 1935; D.Sc., 1952). In 1944 he became a Fellow at Jesus Coll., Cambridge. From 1946 to 1966 he was asst. director of research in zoology at Univ. of Cambridge, and from 1966 to 1976 he was engaged at the Faculty of Oriental Studies there. In 1944 he went to China as a member of the British Council Scientific Mission; studied the *ch'in* there with Hsu Yuan- Pai and Cha Fu-Hsi. In 1951 he took lessons in Turkish music from Nejdet Senvarol in Istanbul. In 1962 he became ed. of the *Journal of the International Folk Music* Council. He was ed. of *Musica Asiatica* (1977–84). He also ed. the series Music from the Tang Court (from 1981), and contributed articles to many learned journals. He publ. the comprehensive study *Folk Musical Instruments of Turkey* (London, 1975); also ed., with E. Dal, E. Stockmann, and K. Vetterl, *A Select Bibliography of European Folk Music* (Prague, 1966), and, with K. Pont, *Ancient Chinese Tunes* (London, 1973). —NS/LK/DM

Picker, Tobias, American composer; b. N.Y., July 18, 1954. He was a student of Wuorinen at the Manhattan School of Music (B.M., 1976) and of Carter at the Juilliard School (M.M., 1978) in N.Y. From 1985 to 1987 he served as composer-in-residence of the Houston Sym. Orch. In addition to various awards and commissions, he held a Guggenheim fellowship in 1981. In his music, Picker has generally used serial techniques without abandoning tonality.

WORKS: ORCH.: 3 piano concertos: No. 1 (1980; Manchester, N.H., Jan. 16, 1981), No. 2, *Keys to the City*, for the 100th anniversary of the Brooklyn Bridge (1982–83; Fulton Ferry Landing, Brooklyn, N.Y., May 24, 1983), and No. 3 (1986; Honolulu, Jan. 10, 1988); Violin Concerto (1981; N.Y., Feb. 1, 1982); 3 syms.: No. 1 (1982; San Francisco, April 23, 1983), No. 2, *Aussöhnung*, for Soprano and Orch. (Houston, Oct. 25, 1986), and No. 3 for Strings (1989); *Encantadas* for Narrator and Orch. (1983); *Dedication Anthem* for Band (1984); *Old and Lost Rivers* (1986; also for Piano); *Romances and Interludes*, after Schumann, for Oboe and Orch. (1990); *2 Fantasies* (1991); *Séance* (1991); *Bang!* for Piano and Orch. for the opening of the 150th anniversary season of the N.Y. Phil. (N.Y., Sept. 24, 1992); Viola Concerto (1992–94). **CHAMBER:** 4 sextets for Various Instruments (1973; 1973; 1977; *The Blue Hula*, 1981); *Rhapsody* for Violin and Piano (1979); *Nova* for Piano, Violin, Viola, Cello, and Double Bass (1979); *Serenade* for Piano and Wind Quintet (1983); String Quartet No. 1, *New Memories* (1986–87); Piano Quintet (N.Y., May 6, 1988); Violin Sonata, *Invisible Lilacs* (1992; N.Y., Jan. 8, 1993). **Piano:** *Piano-o-rama* for 2 Pianos (1984); *Old and Lost Rivers* (1986; also for Orch.).—**NS/LK/DM**

Pickett, Philip, esteemed English recorder player, conductor, and teacher; b. London, Nov. 17, 1950. He was initiated into the world of early wind instruments by Anthony Baines and David Munrow, and subsequently made that field his specialty. He mastered the recorder and learned to play other early instruments, including the shawm, crumbhorn, and rackett. He appeared as recorder soloist with the leading British ensembles. He also founded and directed the New London Consort, which he conducted throughout Europe. From 1972 he served as prof. of recorder at the Guildhall School of Music and Drama in London. In 1995 he became conductor of the Musicians of the Globe, which became well known via performances at the New Globe Theatre in London. He conducted the New London Consort in its U.S. debut at the Mostly Mozart Festival in N.Y. in 1999. As both performer and conductor, Pickett brings erudition and mastery to his vast early music repertoire.—**NS/LK/DM**

Pickett, Wilson, popular R&B songster of the 1960s; b. Prattville, Ala., March 18, 1941. Raised in rural Prattville, Ala., Wilson Pickett moved to Detroit at the age of 16 and made his professional debut as lead singer of the gospel quartet The Violinaires in the late 1950s. From 1961 to 1963, he manned the Detroit vocal group The Falcons, authoring and singing lead on their smash 1962 rhythm-and-blues hit "I Found a Love." Pickett subsequently went solo, joining Lloyd Price's Double L label, where he wrote and recorded "If You Need Me" (a smash R&B hit for Solomon Burke in 1963) and scored a near-smash R&B hit with "It's Too Late."

Signing with Atlantic Records in 1964, Wilson Pickett completed his early recordings in Memphis with Booker T. Jones and Steve Cropper of The MGs. Cropper coauthored three of his early hits, the classic "In the Midnight Hour" (a major pop and top rhythm-and-blues hit), and "Don't Fight It" (a smash R&B hit) from his debut Atlantic album, and "634–5789" (another major pop and top R&B hit) from *The Exciting Wilson Pickett*, the album that established him as a major soul star. That album also included the major R&B hit "Ninety-Nine and a Half (Won't Do)," Bobby Womack's "She's So Good to Me," and the top R&B and smash pop hit "Land of 1,000 Dances" (originally a minor hit for its author Chris Kenner in 1963), all recorded at the Fame Studios in Muscle Shoals, Ala.

Wilson Pickett subsequently scored smash R&B and major pop hits with "Mustang Sally," a remake of "I Found a Love," and Dyke and The Blazers' "Funky

Broadway," all recorded in Muscle Shoals. After the R&B smashes "I'm in Love" and "She's Lookin' Good," Pickett teamed with songwriter-producer Bobby Womack in 1968 for *Midnight Mover*, which yielded a smash R&B and major pop hit with Womack's title song. In 1969, Pickett achieved a major pop hit with The Beatles' "Hey Jude" (recorded with guitarist Duane Allman), followed in 1970 by the novelty crossover hit "Sugar Sugar." Later, in 1970, Pickett worked with producers Kenny Gamble and Leon Huff at Sigma Sound Studios in Philadelphia, and the resulting album, *In Philadelphia*, yielded two major crossover hits with "Engine Number Nine" and "Don't Let the Green Grass Fool You."

After the crossover hits "Don't Knock My Love—Part 1" and "Fire and Water," recorded in Muscle Shoals, Wilson Pickett left Atlantic Records for RCA, with minimal success. He later recorded for several different record companies, including his own Wicked label, but failed to achieve another major pop or rhythm-and-blues hit. Pickett joined Motown Records in 1987 and was inducted into the Rock and Roll Hall of Fame in 1991.

DISC.: *It's Too Late* (1964); *In the Midnight Hour* (1965); *The Exciting Wilson Pickett* (1966); *Wicked Pickett* (1967); *The Sound of Wilson Pickett* (1967); *I'm in Love* (1968); *Midnight Mover* (1968); *Hey, Jude* (1969); *Right On* (1970); *In Philadelphia* (1970); *Don't Knock My Love* (1971); *Wickedness* (1971); *Mr. Magic Man* (1973); *Miz Lena's Boy* (1973); *Pickett in the Pocket* (1974); *Join Me and Let's Be Free* (1975); *Chocolate Mountain* (1976); *A Funky Situation* (1978); *I Want You* (1979); *Right Track* (1981); *American Soul Man* (1987).—**BH**

Pick-Mangiagalli, Riccardo, Italian pianist and composer; b. Strakonice, Bohemia, July 10, 1882; d. Milan, July 8, 1949. He was of mixed Italian and Bohemian parentage; studied at the Cons. Giuseppe Verdi in Milan with Appiani (piano) and Ferroni (composition). He began his career as a successful concert pianist, but later turned exclusively to composition. In 1936 he succeeded Pizzetti as director of the Cons. Giuseppe Verdi, and held this post until his death.

WORKS: DRAMATIC: Opera: *Basi e Bote* (1919–20; Rome, March 3, 1927); *Casanova a Venezia* (Milan, Jan. 19, 1929; orch. suite as *Scene carnevalesche*, Milan, Feb. 6, 1931); *L'Ospite inatteso* (Milan-Turin-Genoa Radio, Oct. 25, 1931); *Il notturno romantico* (Rome, April 25, 1936). **Dance:** *Il salice d'oro*, ballet (1911–12; Milan, 1914); *Sumitra* (1917; Frankfurt am Main, 1922); *Mahit*, ballet-fable (Milan, March 20, 1923); *La Berceuse* (San Remo, Feb. 21, 1933); *Variazioni coreografiche* (San Remo, April 13, 1935). **ORCH.:** *Sortilegi*, symphonic poem for Piano and Orch. (Milan, Dec. 13, 1917); *Notturno e rondo fantastico* (1914; Milan, May 6, 1919); *Humoresque* for Piano and Orch. (1916); *2 preludi* (Rome, March 1, 1921); *4 poemi* (Milan, April 24, 1925); *Piccola suite* (Milan, June 12, 1927); *Preludio e fuga* (Rome, March 11, 1928); *Preludio e scherzo sinfonico* (Milan, Oct. 22, 1938); Piano Concerto (1944). **CHAMBER:** Violin Sonata; String Quartet (1909); piano pieces. **VOCAL:** Songs.—**NS/LK/DM**

Picou, Alphonse (Floristan), seminal early jazz clarinetist, composer; b. New Orleans, La., Oct. 19, 1878; d. there, Feb. 4, 1961. He was gigging from about the age of 16, during the late 1890s played in the Lyre Club

Symphony Orch., and with Oscar DuConge, Bunk Johnson, Dave Peyton, Wooden Joe Nicholas, and Manuel Perez. Between 1900 and 1915, he worked with the Excelsior Brass Band and Freddie Keppard's Olympia Band; he played briefly in Chicago with Manuel Perez at the Arsonia Cafe (c. 1917), returned to New Orleans, worked for John Robichaux, the Golden Leaf Orch., and Tuxedo Brass Band. Composed tunes for King Oliver's Creole Jazz Band. Played regularly until 1932, then returned to his original trade as a tin-smith. More active from the early 1940s, and in the late 1940s worked with Papa Celestin. Made records with Kid Rena and Papa Celestin featuring the famous clarinet solo from the march, High Society, which he had originally adapted from the piccolo part that was published in 1902. He led a small group in the 1950s and made special appearances with the Eureka Band in the late 1950s, but was mainly active in helping his daughter manage the various properties that he owned in New Orleans. He died at his daughter's home above Picou's Bar; his funeral was one of the most elaborate ever seen in the city.—JC/LP

Pieltain, Dieudonné-Pascal, South Netherlands violinist and composer; b. Liège (baptized), March 4, 1754; d. there, Dec. 10, 1833. He received his musical training in Liège. By 1773 he was in Paris as a member of the orch. at the Concert Spirituel, where he later appeared as a soloist (1776–80), sometimes in his own concertos. From 1782 until about 1792 he played in orchs. in London. By 1801 he settled in Liège. His large output included 30 violin concertos, 167 string quartets, and 6 violin sonatas.—LK/DM

Pierce, Webb, American country singer, songwriter, and guitarist; b. near West Monroe, La., Aug. 8, 1921; d. Nashville, Tenn., Feb. 24, 1991. Pierce was the most successful recording artist in country music during the 1950s. He employed a hard-edged honky-tonk style in his music, pioneering the use of the electric pedal steel guitar, and the subject matter of his songs frequently dwelled on such honky-tonk themes as drinking and infidelity, notably in the hits "There Stands the Glass" and "Back Street Affair." He scored 96 country chart entries between 1952 and 1982, including 53 that hit the Top Ten and 13 that hit #1. His biggest hits were "Slowly," "In the Jailhouse Now," and "Love, Love, Love."

Pierce was the son of Webb Mite and Florine Pierce. His father died when he was an infant. He was raised on a farm by his mother and stepfather and began playing guitar before his teens. Local performances led to his own weekly radio show, *Songs by Webb Pierce* on KMLB in Monroe, La., when he was a teenager. With the U.S. entry into World War II, his budding career was interrupted by army service. He married singer Betty Jane Lewis in June 1942. Upon his discharge in 1945, he and his wife settled in Shreveport, La., where he got a job at a department store while attempting to further his career as a singer. By 1947 he and his wife were appearing together on local radio. In 1949 he signed to the independent 4-Star Records label and secured a

berth on the KWKH radio show *Louisiana Hayride*. He and KWKH program director Horace Logan founded Pacemaker Records and a publishing company. In 1950 he and his wife divorced.

In 1951, Pierce signed to Decca Records. His first success with the major label came with a revival of the 1937 song "Wondering" (music and lyrics by Jack Werner), which entered the country charts in January 1952 and hit #1 in March. His follow-up single, the self-written "That Heart Belongs to Me," hit #1 in the country charts in July. In September he was invited to join the radio show the *Grand Ole Opry* and moved to Nashville to do so. In November he married Audrey Greisham, with whom he had two children, one of whom, Debbie Pierce, became a country singer. He scored his third straight country #1 in December with "Back Street Affair" (music and lyrics by Billy Wallace).

Pierce had seven Top Ten hits on the country charts in 1953, including the chart-toppers "It's Been So Long" (music and lyrics by Autry Inman) and "There Stands the Glass" (music and lyrics by Mary Jean Schurz, Russ Hill, and Audrey Greisham). Among his six country Top Ten hits in 1954 were the #1 songs "Slowly" (music and lyrics by Webb Pierce and Tommy Hill), "Even Tho" (music and lyrics by Webb Pierce, Willie Jones, and Curt Peeples), and "More and More" (music and lyrics by Webb Pierce and Merle Kilgore), which was enough chart success to make him the top country recording artist of the year. He repeated that ranking in 1955 with five Top Ten country hits, including the top three songs of the year: "In the Jailhouse Now" (music and lyrics by Jimmie Rodgers), "Love, Love, Love" (music and lyrics by Ted Jarrett), and "I Don't Care" (music and lyrics by Webb Pierce and Cindy Walker).

Due to the touring demands created by his enormous record success, Pierce ended his regular appearances on the *Grand Ole Opry*, though he returned to the program occasionally. In 1955 and 1956 he was one of the hosts of the weekly network television series *Ozark Jubilee*, and in 1955 he had his own syndicated TV program, *The Webb Pierce Show*. He scored six country Top Ten hits in 1956, including the #1 record "Why Baby Why" (music and lyrics by George Jones and Darrell Edwards), a duet with Red Sovine. There were another six country Top Ten hits in 1957, among them the chart-topping "Honky Tonk Song" (music and lyrics by Mel Tillis and A. R. Peddy). Four of his recordings made the country Top Ten in 1958, the most successful of which was "Cryin' Over You." Among his three country Top Ten hits in 1959, the most popular was "I Ain't Never" (music and lyrics by Mel Tillis and Webb Pierce), which also was his only pop Top 40 hit.

Pierce's record sales diminished after the end of the 1950s, although he scored 13 country Top Ten hits between 1960 and 1964, the most successful of which was "Memory #1" (music and lyrics by Wayne P. Walker and Max Powell). An album with the same title reached the country Top ten in 1965. During this period he toured and made occasional film appearances as himself, notably in *Buffalo Gun* (1961) and *Second Fiddle to a Steel Guitar* (1965). His records continued to reach the country charts regularly through 1972, when he left

Decca. He signed to the independent Plantation Records label and made some recordings in the mid-1970s, but by this time he was semiretired from performing, concentrating instead on his business interests in country radio and music publishing. He died of cancer at 69 in 1991.

DISC.: *The Wondering Boy* (rec. 1951–58; rel. 1990); *King of the Hokny-Tonk* (rec. 1952–59; rel. 1994).—**WR**

Pierné, (Henri-Constant-) Gabriel, noted French composer, conductor, and organist, cousin of **Paul Pierné;** b. Metz, Aug. 16, 1863; d. Ploujean, near Morlaix, July 17, 1937. He studied at the Paris Cons. (1871–82), where his teachers were Marmontel (piano), Franck (organ), and Massenet (composition). He won 1st prizes for piano (1879), counterpoint and fugue (1881), and organ (1882), and was awarded the Grand Prix de Rome (1882) with the cantata *Edith.* He succeeded Franck as organist at Ste.-Clotilde (1890), where he remained until 1898. He was asst. conductor (1903–10) and conductor (1910–34) of the Concerts Colonne. Pierné was elected a member of the Académie des Beaux-Arts in 1925. His music reveals the hand of an expert craftsman.

WORKS: DRAMATIC: O p e r a : *La Coupe enchantée* (Royan, Aug. 24, 1895; rev. version, Paris, Dec. 26, 1905); *Vendée* (Lyons, March 11, 1897); *La Fille de Tabarin* (Paris, Feb. 20, 1901); *On ne badine pas avec l'amour* (Paris, May 30, 1910); *Sophie Arnould,* lyric comedy, based on episodes from the life of the famous singer (Paris, Feb. 21, 1927). **B a l l e t a n d P a n - t o m i m e s :** *Le Collier de saphirs* (1891); *Les Joyeuses Commères de Paris* (1892); *Bouton d'or* (1893); *Le Docteur Blanc* (1893); *Salomé* (1895); *Cydalise et le chèvre-pied* (1919; Paris, Jan. 15, 1923; as an orch. suite, 1926); *Impressions de Music-Hall,* "ballet à l'Améri-caine" (Paris, April 6, 1927); *Giration* (1934); *Fragonard* (1934); *Images,* "divertissement sur un thème pastoral" (Paris, June 19, 1935). **O R C H.:** *Suite de concert* (1883); *Première suite d'orchestre* (1883); *Ouverture symphonique* (1885); Piano Concerto (1887); *Marche solonnelle* (1889); *Pantomime* (1889); *Scherzo-Caprice* for Piano and Orch. (1890); *Poème symphonique* for Piano and Orch. (1901); *Ballet de cour* (1901); *Paysages franciscains* (1920); *Gulliver au pays de Lilliput* (Paris, June 23, 1937). **C H A M B E R :** *Pastorale variée dans le style ancien* for Wind Instruments (also for Piano); *Berceuse* for Violin and Piano; *Caprice* for Cello and Piano; *Canzonetta* for Clarinet and Piano; *Solo de concert* for Bassoon and Piano; *Variations libres et Finale* for Flute, Violin, Viola, Cello, and Harp. **P i a n o :** *15 pièces* (1883); *Étude de concert; Album pour mes petits amis* (containing the famous *Marche des petits soldats de plomb*); *Humoresque; Rêverie; Ariette dans le style ancien; Pastorale variée; Sérénade à Colombine; Sérénade vénitienne; Barcarolle* for 2 Pianos; folk song arrangements. **V O C A L : O r a t o r i o s :** *La Croisade des enfants* for Chorus of Children and Adults (Paris, Jan. 18, 1905); *Les Enfants à Bethléem* for Soloists, Children's Chorus, and Orch. (Amsterdam, April 13, 1907); *Les Fioretti de St. François d'Assise* (1912). **S o n g C y c l e s :** *Contes* (1897); *3 Adaptations musicales* (1902); *3 mélodies* (1904); 38 other songs; folk song arrangements.

BIBL.: G. Masson, *G. P., musicien lorrain* (Nancy and Metz, 1987).—**NS/LK/DM**

Pierné, Paul, French composer, cousin of **(Henri-Constant-) Gabriel Pierné;** b. Metz, June 30, 1874; d. Paris, March 24, 1952. He studied at the Paris Cons. with

Lenepveu and Caussade. He wrote a number of works, which were occasionally performed in Paris. They included the operas *Le Diable galant* (1913), *Emilde,* and *Mademoiselle Don Quichotte,* a ballet, *Le Figurinai,* 2 syms., several symphonic poems (*Jeanne d'Arc, Cléopâtre, De l'ombre à la lumière, Nuit évocatrice, Rapsodie Lorraine,* etc.), choral works, organ pieces, a song cycle, *Schéhérazade,* and piano pieces.—**NS/LK/DM**

Piero, Italian composer; b. place and date unknown; d. c. 1350. He was active at the courts of the Visconti family in Milan and the Scala family in Verona. His canonic madrigals and cacce are the earliest such works extant. See N. Pirrotta, ed., *The Music of Fourteenth-century Italy,* Corpus Mensurabilis Musicae, VIII/2 (1960) and W. Marrocco, *Italian Secular Music,* Polyphonic Music of the Fourteenth Century, VI (1967) and VIII (1972).—**LK/DM**

Pierpont, James, American composer; b. Boston, 1822; d. Winter Haven, Fla., 1893. In 1857 he publ. a ballad entitled *One Horse Open Sleigh* (composed in 1850), which, in 1859, was publ. under the title *Jingle Bells, or The One Horse Open Sleigh* (the original music is reprinted in facsimile in R. Jackson's *Popular Songs of 19th- Century America,* N.Y., 1976); however, while the original words and the music to the verse are the same as those known today, the original music to the chorus is different. This song did not acquire its wide popular-ity as a Christmas song until the 20th century; during the 19th century, Pierpont's most popular works were *The Little White Cottage, or Gentle Nettie Moore* (1857), *We Conquer or Die* (1861), and *Strike for the South* (1863). The last two of these were rallying songs for the Confed-eracy during the Civil War (his father, in contrast, was a fiery abolitionist minister). He was the uncle of the millionaire financier John Pierpont Morgan. —**NS/LK/DM**

Pierson (real name, **Pearson**), **Henry Hugo (Hugh),** English composer; b. Oxford, April 12, 1815; d. Leipzig, Jan. 28, 1873. He was educated at Trinity Coll., Cambridge; in 1839, went to Germany, where he took courses in music with Rinck and Reissiger; also with Tomaschek in Prague. He entered the circle of Mendelssohn in Leipzig. After a brief term as Reid Prof. of music at the Univ. of Edinburgh (1844–45), he re-turned to Germany, where he remained for the rest of his life. He married Caroline Leonhardt, who wrote the German librettos for his operas. He changed his name from the original form Pearson to Pierson in order to secure proper pronunciation by Germans; used the pen name Edgar Mansfeldt for his publ. music. His music reflects the profound influence of Schumann. He won wide acceptance in Germany with his incidental music to part 2 of Goethe's *Faust,* the symphonic poem *Mac-beth,* works for men's choruses, and lieder.

WORKS: DRAMATIC: O p e r a : *Der Elfensieg* (Brünn, 1845); *Leila* (Hamburg, Feb. 22, 1848); *Contarini oder Die Ver-schwörung zu Padua* (1853; Hamburg, April 16, 1872; as *Fenice,* Dessau, April 24, 1883); also incidental music to part 2 of

Goethe's *Faust* (Hamburg, March 25, 1854) and to Shakespeare's *As You Like It* (Leipzig, Jan. 17, 1874) and *Romeo and Juliet* (1874). Oratorios: *Jerusalem* (Norwich Festival, Sept. 23, 1852); *Hezekiah* (Norwich Festival, 1869; unfinished). VOCAL: Men's choruses; lieder.—NS/LK/DM

Pietkin, Lambert, Walloon organist and composer; b. Liège (baptized), June 22, 1613; d. there, Sept. 16, 1696. He spent his entire career in Liège. He most likely received his training at St. Lambert Cathedral. After taking holy orders, he was made its second organist in 1630 and its first organist in 1632. Having served as its temporary maître de chapelle in 1633, he formally held that title from 1644 to 1674. He publ. a vol. of 32 motets as *Sacri concentus* for Voices, Instruments, and Basso Continuo (Liège, 1668). Among his other extant works are 11 further motets in *Grande livre de choeur de Saint Lambert* (1645) and 2 sonatas for 4 Instruments and Basso Continuo.

BIBL.: J. Anthony, *The Vocal Music of L. P. for the Cathedral of Liège* (diss., Univ. of Mich., 1977).—LK/DM

Piéton, Loyset, composer who flourished in the mid-16th century. His works, which reveal the influence of the Flemish masters, included a Mass, a Magnificat, and various motets.—LK/DM

Pietrobono de Burzellis, Italian lutenist and singer; b. probably in Ferrara, c. 1417; d. there, Sept. 20, 1497. He was active mainly at the Estense court in Ferrara, where he won notable distinction as a lutenist. —LK/DM

Pigott, Francis, English organist and composer; b. c. 1665; d. London, May 15, 1704. He was a chorister at the Chapel Royal. By 1685 he was organist at St. John's Coll., Oxford. After serving as organist at Magdalen Coll., Oxford (1686–88), he was made first organist at the Temple Church in London. He also was named organist-extraordinary (1695) and organist (1697) at the Chapel Royal. In 1698 he was awarded his Mus.B. from Cambridge. With Blow, Clarke, and Croft, he publ. *A Choice Collection of Ayres for the Harpsichord* (1700). —LK/DM

Pijper, Willem, renowned Dutch composer and pedagogue; b. Zeist, Sept. 8, 1894; d. Leidschendam, March 18, 1947. He received a rudimentary education from his father, an amateur violinist, then went to the Toonkunst School of Music in Utrecht, where he studied composition with Johan Wagenaar and piano with Mme. H.J. van Lunteren-Hansen (1911–16). From 1918 to 1923 he was music critic of *Utrecht Dagblad*, and from 1926 to 1929, co- ed. of the monthly *De Muziek*. He taught theory at the Amsterdam Cons. (from 1918), and was a prof. of composition there from 1925 to 1930; served as director of the Rotterdam Cons. from 1930 until his death. In his music, Pijper continued the Romantic tradition of Mahler, and also adopted the harmonic procedures of the modern French School. He postulated a "germ-cell theory," in which an opening chord or motif is the source of all succeeding harmonic and melodic development; he also cultivated the scale of alternating whole tones and semitones, regarding it as his own, not realizing that it was used abundantly by Rimsky-Korsakov (in Russian reference works it is termed the Rimsky-Korsakov scale); the "Pijper scale," as it became known in the Netherlands, was also used by Anton von der Horst and others. During the German bombardment of Rotterdam in May 1940, nearly all of Pijper's MSS were destroyed by fire, including the unpubl. reduced scoring of his large 2nd Sym. (restored in 1961 by Pijper's student Karel Mengelberg); also destroyed was the unpubl. *Divertimento* for Piano and Strings.

WORKS: DRAMATIC: Opera: *Halewijn* (1932–33; Amsterdam, June 13, 1933; rev. 1934); *Merlijn* (1939–45; incomplete; Rotterdam, June 7, 1952). Incidental Music To: Sophocles' *Antigone* (1920; rev. 1922 and 1926); Euripides' *Bacchantes* (1924) and *The Cyclops* (1925); Shakespeare's *The Tempest* (1930); Vondel's *Phaëton* (1937). ORCH.: *Orchestral Piece* for Piano and Orch. (Utrecht, Dec. 11, 1915; originally titled "Piano Concerto No. 1," causing confusion with his later and only Piano Concerto [Amsterdam, Dec. 22, 1927], in turn sometimes incorrectly referred to as "Piano Concerto No. 2"); 3 syms.: No. 1, *Pan* (1917; Amsterdam, April 23, 1918), No. 2 for Large Orch. (1921; Amsterdam, Nov. 2, 1922; reduced scoring by K. Mengelberg, 1961), and No. 3 (Amsterdam, Oct. 28, 1926); *6 Symphonic Epigrams* (Amsterdam, April 12, 1928); Cello Concerto (Amsterdam, Nov. 22, 1936; rev. 1947); Violin Concerto (1938–39; Amsterdam, Jan. 7, 1940); *6 Adagios* (1940; Utrecht, Nov. 14, 1951). CHAMBER: 2 piano trios (1913–14, 1921); 5 string quartets (1914; 1920; 1923; 1928; 1946, unfinished); *Passepied* for Carillon (1916); 2 violin sonatas (1919, 1922); 2 cello sonatas (1919, 1924); Septet for Wind Quintet, Double Bass, and Piano (1920); Sextet for Wind Quintet and Piano (1922–23); Flute Sonata (1925); Trio for Flute, Clarinet, and Bassoon (1926–27); Wind Quintet (1928–29); Sonata for Solo Violin (1931). Piano: *Theme with 5 Variations* (1913); *3 Aphorisms* (1915); 3 sonatinas (1917, 1925, 1925); *3 Old Dutch Dances* (1926); Sonata (1930); Sonata for 2 Pianos (1935). VOCAL: *Fêtes galantes* for Mezzo-soprano and Orch., after Verlaine (1916; Schweningen, Aug. 2, 1917); *8 vieilles chansons de France* for Voice and Piano (1918); *8 Noëls de France* for Voice and Piano (1919); *Romance sans paroles* for Mezzo- soprano and Orch., after Verlaine (1919; Amsterdam, April 15, 1920); *8 Old Dutch Love Songs* for Voice and Piano (1920; rev. 1943); *Heer Halewijn* for Chorus (1920); *8 Old Dutch Songs* for Voice and Piano (2 sets: 1924, 1935); *Heer Danielken* for Chorus (1925); *Hymne* for Bass-baritone and Orch., after Boutens (1941–43; Amsterdam, Nov. 1945).

BIBL.: W. Kloppenburg, *Thematisch-bibliografische Catalogus van de Werken van W. P.* (Assen, 1960); H. Ryker, *The Symphonic Music of W. P.* (diss., Univ. of Wash., 1971).—NS/LK/DM

Piket, Roberta, jazz pianist, composer; b. Flushing, Queens, N.Y., Aug. 9, 1965. Her father Frederick wrote liturgical music for Jewish services at the Free Synagogue of Flushing, where he was musical director; he died when she was eight. She began playing piano at age 11, began composing at age 15, and studied jazz at the New England Conservatory and computer science at the affiliated Tufts Univ. Piket received a lesson in voicings from Gillespie, who was a guest artist at Tufts in February 1985. She graduated with degrees in both fields in 1988, worked as a computer engineer for a year before deciding to return to Brooklyn and devote herself full time to music. She studied with Richie Beirach. She placed second out of 260 entries in the 1993 International Thelonious Monk–BMI Composers' Competition. Her band has performed as opening act for Diane Schuur at the Celebrate Brooklyn Performing Arts Festival (1994), a 1998 concert at Flushing Town Hall, and at Smalls, Metronome and the Knitting Factory, N.Y. She held the piano chair with the all-female big band, Diva, for two years (1995–97), including two weeks at Tavern on the Green, N.Y. (1995) and appearances at the Hollywood Bowl. She also performed with Winard Harper, Sam Newsome, Benny Golson, and Joe Williams. She teaches at Long Island Univ. in Brooklyn; she curated and performed in the first month-long Women Leaders in Jazz Series at Fifth House Performance Space in Brooklyn, 1997. She is a recipient of a grant from the NEA. In 1998, her trio played at the Museum of Modern Art, Cleopatra's Needle, and the Blue Note. She has written more than 40 originals and recompositions of standards, often with carefully worked out bass lines and counterpoints.

DISC.: *Unbroken Line* (1997); *Live at the Blue Note* (1999).—LP

Pilarczyk, Helga (Käthe), German soprano; b. Schöningen, March 12, 1925. She studied piano and aspired to a concert career, then took voice lessons and sang in operetta. She found her true vocation in opera, and made her debut at Braunschweig in 1951; was a member of the Hamburg State Opera from 1953 until 1968. She made a specialty of modern music, and sang Schoenberg's dramatic monologue *Erwartung*, and the leading parts in Berg's *Wozzeck* and Lulu as well as in works by Stravinsky, Prokofiev, Dallapiccola, Honegger, Krenek, and others. She appeared as a guest artist at the Bavarian State Opera in Munich, the Vienna State Opera, La Scala in Milan, the Paris Opéra, Covent Garden in London, and the Metropolitan Opera in N.Y. (debut, Feb. 19, 1965, as Marie in *Wozzeck*). She publ. an interesting essay, *Kann man die moderne Oper singen?* (Hamburg, 1964).—NS/LK/DM

Pilinski, Stanislaw, French pianist, organist, conductor, and composer of Polish descent; b. Paris, April 5, 1839; d. there, Jan. 20, 1905. After training at Nidermeyer's École de Musique Religeuse in Paris, he served as organist at Ste. Marguerite and later conducted the Polish Phil. Soc. He composed an opera, *Zmija* (The Viper, 1881), a Sym. (1896) and other orch. works, choral pieces, chamber music, and innumerable keyboard pieces.—LK/DM

Pilkington, Francis, English composer; b. c. 1570; d. Chester, 1638. He received a B.Mus. degree at Lincoln Coll., Oxford, in 1595. He became a lay clerk (or conduct) at Chester Cathedral in 1602, and then a minor canon in 1612. After taking Holy Orders, he was made a "full minister" on Dec. 18, 1614. He was active in the Cathedral choir, and was precentor there from 1623 until his death. He also held other curacies in Chester,

including his principal charge at St. Bridget's from 1616. See B. Jeffery, ed., *Francis Pilkington: Complete Works for Solo Lute* (London, 1970). In addition to the works below, he also contributed 2 songs to Sir William Leighton's collection *The Teares or Lamentacions of a Sorrowful Soule* (1614).

WORKS: *The First Booke of Songs or Ayres of 4. Parts: with tableture for the lute or orpherian, with the violl de gamba* (London, 1605; the versions for 4 voices with lute were publ. in *The Old English Edition*, XVIII-XX, London, 1897–98; the versions for voice and lute were publ. in E.H. Fellowes, ed., *The English School of Lutenist Song Writers*, London, 1920–32; rev. by T. Dart, 1971, in *The English Lute-Songs*); *The First Set of Madrigals and Pastorals of 3. 4. and 5. parts* (London, 1613–14; ed. by E.H. Fellowes in *The English Madrigal School, A Guide to Its Practical Use*, London, 1926; rev. by T. Dart, 1959, in *The English Madrigalists*); *The Second Set of Madrigals, and Pastorals, of 3. 4. 5. and 6. Parts: apt for violls and voyces* (London, 1624; ed. by E.H. Fellowes in *The English Madrigal School...*, London, 1926; rev. by T. Dart, 1958, in *The English Madrigalists*).—NS/LK/DM

Pilotti-Schiavonetti, Elisabetta, Italian soprano; b. place and date of birth unknown; d. Hannover, May 5, 1742. She married the oboist Giovanni Schiavonetti and entered the service of the Dowager Electress Sophia of Hannover, whom she also served in England. On Nov. 22, 1710, she made her first London appearance with the Queen's Theatre company in Mancini's *Idaspe fedele*. She then created the roles of Armida in *Rinaldo* (Feb. 24, 1711), Amarilli in *Il pastor fido* (Nov. 12, 1712), Medea in *Teseo* (Jan. 21, 1713), and Melissa in *Amadigi di Gaula* (May 25, 1715), all by Handel. By 1715 she was in the service of the Princess of Wales. In 1726 she sang in Stuttgart. She settled in Hannover in 1728.—NS/LK/DM

Pimsleur, Solomon, Austrian-American pianist and composer; b. Paris (of Austrian-Jewish parents), Sept. 19, 1900; d. N.Y., April 22, 1962. He was taken to the U.S. in 1903. He studied piano privately and majored in Eng. literature at Columbia Univ. in N.Y. (M.A., 1923), where he also received instruction in composition from Daniel Gregory Mason. He was a fellowship student of Rubin Goldmark at the Juilliard School of Music in N.Y. (1926), and then studied at the Salzburg Mozarteum. Returning to the U.S., he was active as a pianist and lecturer. He also ran his own artists agency and production company. His compositions followed along Romantic lines, and included an unfinished opera *The Diary of Anne Frank; Ode to Intensity*, symphonic ballad (N.Y., Aug. 14, 1933), *Shakespearean Sonnet Symphony* for Chorus and Orch., chamber music, and many piano pieces.—NS/LK/DM

Pincherle, Marc, noted French musicologist; b. Constantine, Algeria, June 13, 1888; d. Paris, June 20, 1974. He studied musicology in Paris with Pirro, Laloy, and Rolland. He served in both world wars; was taken prisoner of war in June 1940 and was interned in Germany until March 1941. He taught at the Paris École Normale de Musique; was artistic director of the Société Pleyel (1927–55) and president of the Société Française de Musicologie (1948–56). As a musicologist, he devoted himself mainly to the study of 17th- and 18th-century French and Italian music.

WRITINGS (all publ. in Paris unless otherwise given): *Les Violonistes compositeurs et virtuoses* (1922); *Feuillets d'histoire du violon* (1927; 2nd ed., 1935); *Corelli* (1933); *Les Musiciens peints par eux-mêmes* (160 letters of famous composers from his own autograph collection; 1939); *Antonio Vivaldi et la musique instrumentale* (2 vols., 1948); *Les Instruments du quatuor* (1948; 3rd ed., 1970); *L'Orchestre de chambre* (1948); *Jean- Marie Leclair l'âiné* (1952); *Petit lexique des termes musicaux d'usage courant* (1953; 2nd ed., 1973); *Corelli et son temps* (1954; Eng. tr., 1956, as *Corelli, His Life, His Work*); *Vivaldi* (1955; Eng. tr., 1957, as *Vivaldi: Genius of the Baroque*); *Fritz Kreisler* (Geneva, 1956); *Albert Roussel* (Geneva, 1957); *Histoire illustrée de la musique* (1959; 2nd ed., 1962; Eng. tr., 1959); *Le Monde des virtuoses* (1961; Eng. tr., 1963); *Musical Creation* (Washington, D.C., 1961); *L'orchestra da camera* (Milan, 1963); *Le Violon* (1966; 2nd ed., 1974).—NS/LK/DM

Pine, Courtney, jazz tenor and soprano saxophonist, bass clarinetist; b. Paddington, London, England, March 18, 1964. His parents are from Jamaica. He began on clarinet, then specialized on tenor and soprano saxes. He worked with reggae bands and dance groups such as Hi Tension, then formed his own group, Dwarf Steps (a pun on the famous John Coltrane composition, "Giant Steps"; Pine was greatly influenced by Coltrane in his early playing). He joined John Stevens's Freebop (1984–85), playing alongside Evan Parker, Harry Beckett, and Paul Rogers. From 1985–86, he played with Charlie Watts's Big Band, then joined Gail Thompson's 21-piece Jazz Warriors for its January 1986 debut. That same year, he toured with George Russell's Orch., sat in with Art Blakey and worked briefly with Elvin Jones, then guested with Art Blakey at the Apollo, N.Y. He toured the U.S. and Japan with own group in the late 1980s. In 1991, he made a concert tour with Ellis Marsalis, and worked with Marvin "Smitty" Smith. In the early 1990s, he toured Britain leading his own American band and also was featured with Gary Crosby's Jazz Jamaica. He continues to lead his own line-ups through the 1990s, featuring blends of reggae, hip-hop and jazz, as well as being featured as a soloist at international festivals.

DISC.: *Journey to the Urge Within* (1986); *Destiny's Song and the Image* (1987); *Vision's Tale* (1989); *Within the Realms of Our Dreams* (1990); *To the Eyes of Creation* (1992); *Closer to Home* (1992); *Modern Day Jazz Stories* (1996); *Underground* (1997). —JC-B/LP

Pinelli, Ettore, Italian violinist, conductor, teacher, and composer; b. Rome, Oct. 18, 1843; d. there, Sept. 17, 1915. He studied violin with his uncle, Tullio Ramacciotti. He was only 13 when he launched a promising concert career. After further training with Joachim in Hannover, he joined his uncle's Quartetto Romano. When his uncle left it in 1866, the pianist Sgambati joined its ranks and it became a quintet. Pinelli and Sgambati founded a school to teach violin and piano to poor children without tuition in 1869. Their venture proved so successful that it developed into the Liceo Musicale of the Accademia di Santa Cecilia in Rome in 1876, where Pinelli remained on the faculty for the rest of his life. Throughout the years, he continued to appear as both a soloist and chamber music player. In 1874 he founded the Orchestral Soc. in Rome, which he conducted until 1899. Among his works were a Sym., a String Quartet, and songs.—LK/DM

Pinello di Ghirardi, Giovanni Battista, Italian composer; b. Genoa, c. 1544; d. Prague, June 15, 1587. He was a tenor in the Landshut Hofkantorei in 1569–70. In 1571 he served as maestro di cappella at Vincenza Cathedral, and then was a tenor at the Innsbruck court chapel from 1576. In 1580 he was made Kapellmeister at the court of the Elector August of Saxony in Dresden, but in 1584 he was dismissed after the non-Italian musicians at the court succeeded in undermining his position. His 4 vols. of secular vocal music (1571–84) played a significant role in introducing the Italian vocal style to Germany. Among his other works were 3 vols. of sacred vocal music (1583–88). —LK/DM

Pingoud, Ernest, Russian-born Finnish composer; b. St. Petersburg, Oct. 14, 1888; d. Helsinki, June 1, 1942. He studied piano in St. Petersburg with Siloti, then went to Leipzig, where he took courses in music history with Riemann and in composition with Reger. In 1918 he settled in Finland, where he served as managing director of the Helsinki Phil. (1924–42). In his music, he was influenced by the Russian modern school, particularly by Scriabin, from whom he acquired his predilection for mystical titles, often in French.

WORKS: DRAMATIC: Ballet: *Suurkaupungin kasvot* (The Face of the Big City; 1936); *Epajumala* (The Idol; n.d.). **ORCH.:** *Prologue* (1916); *Confessions* (1916); *La Derniere Aventure de Pierrot* (1916); *Diableries galantes "Le fetiche"* (1917); 3 piano concertos (1917, 1921, 1922); *Hymneja yolle* (Hymns to the Night; 1917); *5 Sonnets* for Chamber Orch. (1918); *Ritari peloton ja moitteeton* (The Knight without Fear or Reproach), an "adventure" (1918); *Mysterium* (1919); *Flambeaux eleints* (1919); *Chantecler* (1919); *Le Sacrifice* (1919); 3 syms. (1920; 1920; 1923–27); *Profeetta* (The Prophet; 1921); *Cor ardens* (1927); *Narcissos* (1930); *Le Chant d'espace* (1931; rev. 1938); *La Flamme eternelle* (1938–39). **OTHER:** Chamber music; piano works; *Kuolemantanssi* (Danse macabre) for Chorus and Orch. (1918); songs.—NS/LK/DM

Pini-Corsi, Antonio, noted Italian baritone; b. Zara, Dalmatia, June 1858; d. Milan, April 22, 1918. He made his debut as Dandini in *La Cenerentola* in Cremona (1878), then sang throughout Italy. Verdi chose him to create the role of Ford in *Falstaff* at La Scala in Milan in 1893. He also sang at Covent Garden in London (1894–96, 1902–03). On Dec. 27, 1899, he made his Metropolitan Opera debut in N.Y. as Masetto, remaining on its roster until 1901 and returning for the 1909–14 seasons. He was one of the great buffo singers of his day, being famous for his portrayals of Dr. Bartolo, Leporello, Don Pasquale, and others.—NS/LK/DM

Pinkett, (William) Ward, early jazz trumpeter; b. Newport News, Va., April 29, 1906; d. N.Y., March 15, 1937. He is best known for his recordings with Jelly Roll Morton. He attended Hampton Inst., Va., and played in the school band; he then went to New Haven Conservatory of Music in Meridian, Miss., for further studies. He arrived in N.Y. with a travelling show and worked there with Charlie Johnson, Willie Gant (summer 1926). From 1928–30, he worked with Jelly Roll Morton, appearing on several seminal recordings; he also freelanced on record with various other leaders, including King Oliver, Bubber Miley, Clarence Williams, and James P. Johnson in this period. Around 1930, he became resident musician at James Hogan's Joyland, working with Joe Steele, Morton, Chick Webb, Bingie Madison (1931), Rex Stewart (1933), and Teddy Hill (1934). During 1935, he worked with Albert Nicholas and Bernard Addison, and also played briefly with Louis Metcalf. He died in N.Y. of pneumonia and was buried in his home town.—JC/LP

Pink Floyd, long-lived psychedelic band that has gone through many changes in leadership and direction. **MEMBERSHIP:** Roger "Syd" Barrett, lead gtr., voc. (b. Cambridge, England, Jan. 6, 1946); Rick Wright, kybd., voc. (b. London, England, July 28, 1945); Roger Waters, bs., pno., voc. (b. Great Bookham, Surrey, England, Sept. 6, 1944); Nick Mason, drm. (b. Birmingham, England, Jan. 27, 1945). Barrett was replaced in 1968 by David Gilmour (b. Cambridge, England, March 6, 1944).

Roger "Syd" Barrett attended school with Roger Waters and David Gilmour in the early 1960s in Cambridge. Barrett moved to London after school, where he took up guitar and played in several groups, including a folk duo with Gilmour. Waters moved to London to study architecture and met Rick Wright and Nick Mason in an architecture class. In 1964, Waters, Mason, and Wright formed Sigma 6, which later became The T-Set and The Abdabs. The Abdabs broke up in late 1965 and Mason, Wright, and Waters recruited guitarist Syd Barrett for a new group, dubbed Pink Floyd by Barrett. By March 1966, Pink Floyd had obtained their first regular engagement at London's Marquee club, where they experimented with feedback and lighting effects. In October, they moved to London's Sound/Light Workshop, where they were accompanied by a light show, the first of its kind in Great Britain. Becoming the house band at the UFO Club by year's end, Pink Floyd signed with EMI Records (the small, experimental Tower label in the U.S.) in March 1967.

Pink Floyd's first single, Barrett's "Arnold Layne," concerned a perverted transvestite and proved so controversial that even "underground" Radio London banned the song, yet it became a major British hit. Barrett's "See Emily Play" became a smash British hit in the spring and Pink Floyd's debut album was released in the U.S. near the end of 1967. Critically acclaimed as one of the most original albums of the 1960s, *The Piper at the Gates of Dawn* was dominated by Barrett's surreal, mystical songwriting. However, the group's next three British singles fared poorly as Pink Floyd toured America for the first time in October 1967.

Barrett's behavior, already erratic, began to deteriorate and Dave Gilmour joined the group as second guitarist in early 1968. By April, Barrett had left amid rumors of drug abuse and bizarre stories of his unpre-

dictable behavior. Between 1968 and 1970, Barrett recorded on several occasions, often with Gilmour and Wright. Two albums of his recordings were released in 1970 and eventually repackaged as a double-record set for U.S. release in 1974. Each album was issued in CD form in 1990 and 1989's *Opel* comprised alternate takes and unreleased material from the sessions. All three albums were included on 1994's *Crazy Diamond*. Inspiring a devoted cult following that persists to this day, Barrett's influence can be seen in the work of many 1980s acts, most notably Robyn Hitchcock. Syd Barrett remains a mysterious and enigmatic figure, despite seldom appearing in public.

With Barrett's departure, Pink Floyd reverted to a quartet and Roger Waters began assuming the role of chief songwriter. *A Saucerful of Secrets* contained his "Let There Be More Light" and "Set Controls for the Heart of the Sun." In the summer of 1969, they first toured with a custom-built quadraphonic sound system as their soundtrack to the film *More* was released. At the beginning of 1970, Pink Floyd's double-record set *Ummagumma* was issued on EMI's new "underground" label Harvest (and later reissued on Capitol). Their first moderately successful album in the U.S., *Ummagumma*, comprised one live album and one studio album.

In 1970, Waters recorded a soundtrack album, *Music from "The Body,"* with electronics wizard Ron Geesin. Pink Floyd's *Atom Heart Mother* was debuted at the Bath Festival in England during June and the album featured choir, orchestra, and remarkably diverse sounds under the influence of Geesin. Pink Floyd's stage shows became more elaborate and, in the summer of 1971, an outdoor concert in London utilized a 60-foot inflatable octopus. The group-produced *Meddle* included the instrumental "One of These Days" and the 23-minute-plus "Echoes," one of their most popular songs.

Following the soundtrack to the film *Le Vallee* entitled *Obscured by Clouds*, Pink Floyd spent nine months recording their next album. Premiered live in London in 1972 using more than nine tons of equipment, *The Dark Side of the Moon* comprised entirely songs written by Roger Waters and became an instant best-seller, establishing Gilmour as a guitar hero and the group as "superstars." Dealing with alienation and madness as caused by the pressures of contemporary society, the album yielded Pink Floyd's first major American hit, "Money," and included group favorites such as "Brain Damage" and "Time." The album sold millions of copies worldwide and remained on the American album charts for *more than 14 years.* The group spent much of 1973 performing the album in its entirety in an elaborately staged production.

Pink Floyd's *Wish You Were Here*, recorded for their new label Columbia, became a best-seller and featured Gilmour's title song, the classic "Welcome to the Machine," and Waters's tribute to Syd Barrett, "Shine on You Crazy Diamond." Continuing to explore the themes of repression, alienation, and loneliness, Pink Floyd's *Animals* depicted society as divided into three castes, dogs, pigs, and sheep, and the album included songs for each. Their massive tour in support of the album utilized tons of musical and lighting equipment and, in performance, featured a huge flying pig. Rick Wright and David Gilmour each recorded solo albums released in 1978 and Pink Floyd reconvened for new recordings in April 1979.

In late 1979, Pink Floyd issued their next album, *The Wall*, almost entirely composed by Roger Waters. Another bleak and gloomy view of modern society, the album was considered their most ambitious and personal work in years and stayed on the album charts for more than two years, selling more than ten million copies in the U.S. The album contained group favorites such as "Is There Anybody Out There?" "Nobody Home," and "Comfortably Numb," and produced a minor hit with "Run Like Hell" and a top hit with the controversial "Another Brick in the Wall (Part II)." The 1980 tour in support of *The Wall* was so massive that it was performed in only three cities, London, N.Y., and Los Angeles. It was one of the most elaborate rock productions ever mounted, utilizing a 30-foot-high, stage-wide wall of cardboard blocks that were toppled before the end of the shows. The production featured films, sophisticated lighting, and gigantic plastic inflatables in one of the most awesome and spectacular performances in rock history. The album later served as the basis for the grim, violent 1982 movie *The Wall*, starring Bob Geldof of The Boomtown Rats and directed by Alan Parker.

Rick Wright left Pink Floyd after the tour and Nick Mason recorded the solo album *Fictitious Sports* in 1981. Following 1983's desultory *The Final Cut*, essentially a Roger Waters solo album, Pink Floyd dissolved. Dave Gilmour and Roger Waters each recorded solo albums for Columbia Records in 1984. In 1986, Waters sued for formal dissolution of Pink Floyd, but, in 1987, Gilmour, Rick Wright, and Nick Mason reconstituted the group for *A Momentary Lapse of Reason*, entirely written by Gilmour. The album yielded a minor hit with "Learning to Fly" and remained on the album charts for more than a year. With eight-piece accompaniment, the three toured arenas in 1987 and stadiums in 1988. Waters countered with the concept album *Radio K.A.O.S.* and his own tour in 1987.

Pink Floyd toured internationally in 1989 and, in July 1990, *The Wall* was performed as a benefit for the Memorial Fund for Disaster Relief at the Berlin Wall by Roger Waters and a host of others, including Paul Carrack, Van Morrison, Sinead O'Connor, Joni Mitchell, and Levon Helm and Rick Danko of The Band. In 1991, David Palmer and The Royal Philharmonic Orch. recorded *The Music of Pink Floyd: Orchestral Maneuvers*, and, in 1992, Waters recorded *Amused to Death* with guitarist Jeff Beck. In 1994, Pink Floyd issued *The Division Bell* on Sony and toured once again. The tour produced the 1995 live set *Pulse*. Pink Floyd was inducted into the Rock and Roll Hall of Fame in 1996.

DISC.: *The Piper at the Gates of Dawn* (1967); *A Saucerful of Secrets* (1968); *More* (soundtrack; 1969); *Ummagumma* (1969); *Atom Heart Mother* (1970); *Relics* (rec. 1967–69; rel. 1971); *Meddle* (1971); *Obscured by Clouds* (1972); *The Dark Side of the Moon* (1973); *Wish You Were Here* (1975); *Animals* (1977); *The Wall* (1979); *A Collection of Great Dance Songs* (1975–1981) (1981); *Works* (rec. 1968–73; rel. 1983); *The Final Cut* (1983); *A Momentary*

Lapse of Reason (1987); *Delicate Sound of Thunder* (1988); *The Division Bell* (1994); *Pulse* (1995).

BIBL.: Miles, *P. F.: Another Brick* (London, 1980); M. Watkinson and P. Anderson, *Crazy Diamond: Syd Barrett and the Dawn of P. F.* (London, 1990); N. Schaffner, *Saucerful of Secrets: The P. F. Odyssey* (N.Y., 1991); B. McDonald, ed., *P. F.: Through the Eyes of...the Band, Its Fans, Friends, and Foes* (N.Y., 1997).—**BH**

Pinkham, Daniel (Rogers, Jr.), esteemed American composer, organist, choral conductor, and teacher; b. Lynn, Mass., June 5, 1923. He received training in organ and harmony from Carl Pfatteicher at the Phillips Academy in Andover, Mass., before pursuing his studies with Merritt, Piston, Davison, and Copland at Harvard Univ. (A.B., 1943; M.A., 1944). He also received instruction in harpsichord from Aldrich and Landowska, and in organ from Biggs. He likewise attended the composition courses given by Honegger and Barber at the Berkshire Music Center in Tanglewood, and then studied with Boulanger. Pinkham taught at Simmons Coll. in Boston, Boston Univ., and Dartington Hall in Devon, England. In 1957–58 he was a visiting lecturer at Harvard Univ. In 1958 he became music director of the King's Chapel in Boston. He also taught at the New England Cons. of Music in Boston from 1959. In 1950 he held a Fulbright fellowship and in 1962 received a Ford Foundation fellowship. He was awarded an honorary Litt.D. degree from Nebr. Wesleyan Univ. (1976) and honorary Mus.D. degrees from Adrian Coll. (1977), Westminster Choir Coll. (1979), the New England Cons. of Music (1993), Ithaca Coll. (1994), and the Boston Cons. of Music (1998). In 1990 he was named composer of the year by the American Guild of Organists. He received the Alfred Nash Patterson Foundation Lifetime Achievement Award for contributions to the choral arts in 1996. In his prolific output as a composer, Pinkham has demonstrated a fine capacity for producing versatile scores. The formal design of his music is compact and contrapuntally cohesive. The rhythmic element is often propulsive while he occasionally introduces modernistic devices without disrupting the tonal fabric of his scores.

WORKS: DRAMATIC: Theater works; chamber operas; some 20 documentary film scores. **ORCH.:** 3 sonatas for Organ and Strings (1943, 1954, 1986; also for Organ and Chamber Ensemble); 2 violin concertos: No. 1 (Falmouth, Mass., Sept. 8, 1956) and No. 2 (1968); 4 syms.: No. 1 (Washington, D.C., April 29, 1961), No. 2 (1962; Lansing, Mich., Nov. 23, 1963), No. 3 (1985), and No. 4 (Washington, D.C., Nov. 4, 1990); *Catacoustical Measures* (N.Y., May 28, 1962); *Signs of the Zodiac* for Orch. and Optional Narrator (Portland, Maine, Nov. 10, 1964); 3 organ concertos: No. 1 (1970), No. 2 (Rheinland-Pfalz, Sept. 1, 1995), and No. 3 (1997); *Serenades* for Trumpet and Wind Orch. (1979; Cambridge, Mass., March 7, 1980); *Concerto piccolo* for Piccolo, String Orch. or Quintet, and Percussion (New Orleans, Aug. 20, 1989); *Overture Concertante* (Boston, Oct. 29, 1992); *Music for an Indian Summer* for Harp and Wind Ensemble (1997); *Evening Music* for Brass Ensemble and Glockenspiel (1998). **CHAMBER:** Piano Concertino (Cambridge, Mass., May 3, 1950); Concerto for Celesta and Harpsichord (1954; N.Y., Nov. 19, 1955); Concertante for Organ, Celesta, and Percussion (1963); *Toccatas for the Vault of Heaven* for Organ and Tape (1972); *Masks* for Harpsichord and Chamber Ensemble

(1978); *Diversions* for Organ and Harp (1980); Brass Quintet (1983); *Sonata da chiesa* for Viola and Organ (1988); String Quartet (Boston, April 8, 1990); Reed Trio (Boston, Sept. 29, 1994); *Morning Music* for Organ and Brass Quintet (1994); *Sagas* for Guitar and Cello (1997); *Divertimento* for Trumpet and Harp (1997); String Trio (1998); *Odes* for English Horn and Organ (1998); *Quarries* for Piano, 4-Hands (Rocca di Cambio, Aug. 11, 1999); numerous organ pieces. **VOCAL:** *Wedding Cantata* for Optional Soprano and Tenor, Chorus, and Orch. (Cambridge, Mass., Sept. 22, 1956); *Christmas Cantata* for Chorus and Orch. (1957); *Easter Cantata* for Chorus and Orch. (1961); *Requiem* for Alto, Tenor, Chorus, and Orch. (1962; N.Y., Jan. 24, 1963); *Stabat Mater* for Soprano, Chorus, and Orch. (Lenox, Mass., Aug. 10, 1964); *St. Mark Passion* for Chorus and Orch. (Southboro, Mass., May 22, 1965); *Magnificat* for Soprano, Women's Chorus, and Orch. (1968); *Ascension Cantata* for Chorus and Orch. (Columbus, Ohio, March 20, 1970); *Daniel in the Lion's Den* for Narrator, Tenor, Baritone, Bass, Chorus, 5 Instrumentalists, and Tape (1972); *The Passion of Judas* for Soloists, Chorus, and 5 Instrumentalists (1975; Washington, D.C., June 6, 1976); *The Descent into Hell* for Soprano, Tenor, Bass, Chorus, Orch., and Tape (1979; Buckhannon, W.Va., Oct. 17, 1980); *Hezekiah* for Chorus and Orch. (1979; Shaker Heights, Ohio, April 8, 1981; rev. 1987); *When God Arose* for Chorus and Orch. (1979; Norman, Okla., Feb. 15, 1980); *Before the Dust Returns* for Chorus and Orch. (Lewisburg, Pa., Nov. 21, 1981); *In Heaven Soaring Up* for Alto, Tenor, Chorus, Oboe, and Harp (1985); *Getting to Heaven* for Soprano, Chorus, Brass Quintet, and Harp (1987); *Stabat Mater* (1990); *Advent Cantata* (Albany, N.Y., Dec. 4, 1991); *The Creation of the World* for Narrator, Chorus, Organ, and Brass Quintet (1994); *The Guiding Star* for Tenor, Chorus, Organ, and Brass Quartet (1994); *The White Raven* for Soprano, Chorus, and Orch. (1995); *Jubilee and Psalm* (1999; Boston, Jan. 1, 2000); numerous other vocal works, both sacred and secular.

BIBL.: M. Johnson, *The Choral Works of D. P.* (diss., Univ. of Iowa, 1966); M. Corzine, *The Organ Works of D. P.* (diss., Eastman School of Music, 1979); M. Stallings, *Representative Works for Mixed Chorus by D. P.: 1968–1983* (diss., Univ. of Miami, 1984); K. Deboer and J. Ahouse, *D. P.: A Bio-Bibliography* (Westport, Conn., 1988).—NS/LK/DM

Pinnock, Trevor (David), outstanding English harpsichordist and conductor; b. Canterbury, Dec. 16, 1946. He became a chorister at Canterbury Cathedral when he was 7, and after receiving instruction in piano and organ, he served as a church organist. At 19, he entered the Royal Coll. of Music in London, where he took courses in organ and later harpsichord. While still a student, he organized the Gailliard Harpsichord Trio (1966); also toured Europe with the Academy of St. Martin-in-the-Fields. In 1973 he founded the English Concert, an ensemble devoted to the performance of early music on original instruments; through numerous tours and recordings, his ensemble acquired an international reputation; toured North America with it for the first time in 1983. He also pursued a distinguished career as a harpsichord virtuoso. On Sept. 27, 1988, he made his Metropolitan Opera debut in N.Y. conducting *Giulio Cesare*. In 1989 he founded the Classical Band of N.Y., which he led in performances of the Classical repertoire from Haydn to Mendelssohn on period instruments until resigning unexpectedly in 1990. In 1991 he was named artistic director and principal conductor of the National Arts Centre Orch. in Ottawa. In 1995 he

conducted it on a critically acclaimed tour of Europe. In 1996 he stepped down from his post but served as its artistic advisor during the 1996–97 season. In 1992 he was made a Commander of the Order of the British Empire.—NS/LK/DM

Piňos, Alois Simandl, Czech composer and teacher; b. Vyškov, Oct. 2, 1925. He studied forestry at the Univ. of Brno (graduating in 1953), music with Petrželka at the Brno Cons. (1948–49) and at the Janáček Academy of Music in Brno with Kvapil and Schaeffer (1949–53); attended the summer courses of new music at Darmstadt (1965) and an electronic music seminar in Munich (1966). In 1953 he joined the faculty of the Janáček Academy of Music in Brno. In 1967 he founded in Brno a modern music group, with which he produced a number of works by the local avant-garde, some composed collectively.

WORKS: DRAMATIC: Chamber Opera: *The Criers* (1970). **Audiovisual:** *The Lattice* for Piano and Film (1970); *The Genesis* for Chamber Orch. and Film (1970); *Static Music* for Tape and Slides (1970). **ORCH.:** *Czech Dances* (1951); *Wedding Suite* (1952); Horn Concerto (1953); *Concertino* (1963); *Abbreviations* (1963); Concerto for Orch. and Tape (1964); Double Concerto for Cello, Piano, Winds, and Percussion (1965–66; Prague, March 7, 1967); Chamber Concerto for Strings (1967); *Concerto on the Name B-A-C-H* for Bass Clarinet, Cello, Piano, Strings, and Percussion (1968); *Apollo XI*, sym. (1970); *Symphonic Diptych* (1973–74); Concerto for Harp and Strings (1978); *Ballad* for Chamber Orch. and Synthesizer (1981); Organ Concerto (1985). **CHAMBER:** Cello Sonata (1950); 2 wind quintets (1951, 1959); Sonata for Viola and Cello (1960); Piano Trio (1960); Suite for String Trio (1961); *Monologues* for Bass Clarinet (1962); *Caricatures* for Flute, Bass Clarinet, and Piano (1962); 3 string quartets (1962–93); *Conflicts* for Violin, Bass Clarinet, Piano, and Percussion (1964); *3 Pieces* for Bass Clarinet and Piano (1965); *Pulsus intermissi* for Percussionist (1965); *Hyperboles*, 7 pieces for Harp (1966); *16 January 1969* for Piano Quintet and Kettledrums (1969); *Dialogues* for Bass Clarinet (1969); *2 campanari* for Bass Clarinet, Piano, and Ringing Instruments (1971); *Be Beaten* for Percussionist (1972); *Sonata Concertante* for Cello and Piano (1974); *Composition for 3* for Flute, Clarinet, and Marimbaphone (1975); Nonet (1982–83). **Piano:** *Paradoxes* (1965); *2–3–1*, 3 pieces (1969); *Esca* for Prepared Piano (1971). **VOCAL:** *Hunting Music* for Baritone and 4 Horns (1963); *2 Lyrical Sketches* for Narrator, Flute, and Violin (1964); *4 Lyrical Sketches* for Narrator, Flute, Bass Clarinet, and Piano (1965); *Ludus floralis*, 5 songs for Baritone, Women's Chorus, Percussion, and Tape (1966); *Gesta Machabaeorum* for Chorus, Flute, Trumpet, Harp, and Percussion (1967–68); *Power of Love* for Baritone and String Quartet (1974); *Acquaintance* for Soprano, Bass-baritone, and Guitar or Harpsichord, to texts from advertisements (1975); choruses; other songs. **TAPE:** *Home* (1972–73); *Speleophony* (1976).—NS/LK/DM

Pinsuti, Ciro, Italian singing teacher and composer; b. Sinalunga, near Florence, May 9, 1829; d. Florence, March 10, 1888. His talent developed so rapidly that at 11 he was elected an honorary member of the Accademia Filarmonica of Rome. Taken to England soon after by Henry Drummond, he studied piano under C. Potter and violin under Blagrove; returned to Bologna in 1845, and studied at the Liceo, also privately with

Rossini, soon becoming asst. teacher of a piano class. In 1848 he returned to England, where he was appointed a prof. of singing at London's Royal Academy of Music in 1856. He divided his time between London and Italy. He brought out an opera, *Il Mercante di Venezia*, at Bologna (Nov. 9, 1873), another, *Mattia Corvino*, at Milan (1877), and a thrid, *Margherita*, at Venice (1882). In 1871 he represented Italy at the opening of the London Exhibition, for which he composed the hymn *O people of this favoured land*. As a recipient of the order of the Italian Crown, he was styled "Cavaliere" Pinsuti. Besides his operas, he wrote some 250 songs to Eng. and Italian texts.—NS/LK/DM

Pinto, Alfredo, Italian-Argentine pianist, conductor, and composer; b. Mantua, Oct. 22, 1891; d. Buenos Aires, May 26, 1968. He studied piano with Longo and composition with De Nardis in Naples. He then went to Buenos Aires, where he became active as a pianist and conductor. He wrote the operas *La última esposa, o Sheherazade* and *Gualicho* (Buenos Aires, 1940), 3 symphonic poems: *Nostalgias* (1929), *Eros* (1930), and *Rebelión* (1939), numerous piano pieces, choruses, and songs. —NS/LK/DM

Pinto, Francisco António Norberto dos Santos, Portuguese composer; b. Lisbon, June 6, 1815; d. there, Jan. 30, 1860. He studied solfège at the royal chapel of Bemposta and horn with Justino José Garcia, the royal cavalry bandmaster. At 15, he became a player in the royal cavalry band, at 17 a cornetist in the royal police guard band, and at 18 first horn in the orch. of the Teatro Sãn Carlos in Lisbon. He received instruction in composition and orchestration from Manuel Joaquim Botelho (1833–38). In 1854 he was made prof. of brass instruments at the National Cons. and in 1857 director of the orch. at the Teatro Sãn Carlos. He composed 19 ballets, incidental music to 33 plays, a Symphonia, overtures, and many sacred pieces.—LK/DM

Pinto, George Frederick, English violinist, pianist, and composer; b. Lambeth, Sept. 25, 1785; d. Chelsea, March 23, 1806. His father's name was Saunders or Sanders, but he adopted his mother's surname as his own. He began violin lessons in early childhood, and became a student of Salomon at the age of 8, making his debut as a violinist at a benefit concert for Salvini (May 4, 1796); also became active as a pianist. His early death, at the age of 20, was regretted by his older contemporaries, who ascribed it, pietistically, to sexual indulgence and general dissipation, without offering facts. He wrote works for piano, including several sonatas, violin duets, and songs, a number of which reveal great promise.

BIBL.: M. Gordon, *Authentic Memoirs of the late celebrated G.F. P. collected by a Friend to Genius and Merit* (Edinburgh, 1807). —NS/LK/DM

Pinto, Octavio, Brazilian composer; b. São Paulo, Nov. 3, 1890; d. there, Oct. 31, 1950. He was trained as an architect and built apartment houses in Brazil. He also studied piano with Isidor Philipp. In 1922 he married

Guiomar Novães. Villa-Lobos wrote his suite *Prole do bébé* for their children. Pinto publ. a number of effective piano miniatures, of which *Scenas infantis* (1932) and *Children's Festival* (1939) are best known.—NS/LK/DM

Pinza, Ezio (baptized **Fortunio**), celebrated Italian bass; b. Rome, May 18, 1892; d. Stamford, Conn., May 9, 1957. The family moved to Ravenna when he was an infant; he studied engineering. He began to study voice at the age of 18 with Ruzza and Vizzani at the Bologna Cons. He made his operatic debut as Oroveso in *Norma* in Soncino (1914); after military service in World War I, he resumed his career, making his first important appearance as Comte Des Grieux in Rome (1920); then sang at La Scala in Milan (1922–24); was selected by Toscanini for the leading part in the premiere of Boito's *Nerone* (May 1, 1924). He made his American debut at the Metropolitan Opera in N.Y. as Pontifex Maximus in Spontini's *La Vestale* (Nov. 1, 1926), and remained on its staff until 1947; appeared also in San Francisco, Chicago, and other cities in the U.S.; also sang in Europe and in South America. His most celebrated roles were Méphistophélès in Gounod's *Faust*, Don Giovanni, and Boris Godunov. In 1949 he appeared as a musical comedy star in *South Pacific*, and immediately became successful in this new career; also appeared in films.

BIBL.: R. Magidoff, ed., *E. P.: An Autobiography* (N.Y., 1958). —NS/LK/DM

Piozzi, Gabriel(e Mario), lp;16qtalian tenor, keyboard player, teacher, and composer; b. Quinzano, June 8, 1740; d. Dymerchion, North Wales, March 26, 1809. He found a patron in the Marquis d'Araciel of Milan, and subsequently was active as a singer in Europe until settling in England about 1776. In 1784 he married the widow of Henry Thrale. Among his works were string quartets, piano quartets, violin sonatas, and canzonets.—LK/DM

Pipelare, Matthaeus, Flemish composer; b. c. 1450; d. c. 1512. He was active in Antwerp, and was engaged as master of the choristers of the Marian Brotherhood in 's-Hertogenbosch (1498–1500). His style has a certain affinity with that of Pierre de la Rue. His extant works include 9 masses and a number of motets and chansons, which R. Cross ed. in Corpus Mensurabilis Musicae, XXXII/3 (1966–67).—NS/LK/DM

Pipkov, Lubomir, noted Bulgarian composer, son of **Panayot Pipkov**; b. Lovec, Sept. 19, 1904; d. Sofia, May 9, 1974. He studied piano and composition with his father, then entered the Sofia Music School (1919), and completed his training with Boulanger and Dukas (composition) and Lefebure (piano) at the Paris École Normale de Musique (1926–32). Returning to Bulgaria, he occupied several administrative posts, including the directorship of the National Theater in Sofia (1944–47). His style of composition is determined by the inherent asymmetry of Bulgarian folk songs; there is a similarity in his compositions with those of Bartók, resulting from common sources in Balkan and Macedonian music; his harmonic investiture is often polytonal or polymodal.

WORKS: DRAMATIC: Opera: *Yaninite devet bratya* (The 9 Brothers of Yanina; 1929–37; Sofia, Sept. 19, 1937); *Momchil* (1939–44; Sofia, April 24, 1948); *Antigone 43* (1961–62; Ruse, Dec. 23, 1963). ORCH.: Concerto for Winds, Percussion, and Piano (1930); 4 syms.: No. 1 (1939–40), No. 2 (1954), No. 3 for Strings, Trumpet, 2 Pianos, and Percussion (1965), and No. 4 for Strings (1970); *Heroic Overture* (1950); *Journey through Albania*, variations for Strings (1950); Violin Concerto (1951); Piano Concerto (1954); *Symphony-Concerto* for Cello and Orch. (1963; Moscow, April 20, 1964); Concerto for Clarinet and Chamber Orch. (1966); *The Partisan's Grave* for Trombone and Strings (1970). CHAMBER: 3 string quartets (1928, 1948, 1966); 2 violin sonatas (1929, 1969); Piano Trio (1930); Piano Quartet (1939); Sonata for Solo Violin (1969). Piano: *Tableaux et études métrorythmiques* (1972); *Suggestions printanières* (1972). VOCAL: 2 cantatas: *The Wedding* (1934) and *Cantata of Friendship* (1958); *Oratorio for Our Time* (Plovdiv, Dec. 18, 1959); choruses; songs.

BIBL.: K. Iliev, *L. P.* (Sofia, 1958); L. Koen, *L. P.* (Sofia, 1968). —NS/LK/DM

Pipkov, Panayot, Bulgarian composer, father of **Lubomir Pipkov;** b. Plovdiv, Dec. 2, 1871; d. Sofia, Aug. 25, 1942. He studied violin before attending the Milan Cons. (1893–95). After conducting in Rusa, he settled in Sofia in 1905. In addition to his musical career, he also pursued acting and literary activities. He composed 2 children's operettas, many choral works, and piano pieces.—NS/LK/DM

Pirck, Wenzel Raimund (Johann), Austrian organist, teacher, and composer; b. Vienna (baptized), June 27, 1718; d. there, July 17, 1763. He was a Hofscholar (1726–39), and a pupil of Matteo Palotta. From 1739 he was court organist in Vienna, and was also active as a teacher. He composed 25 sinfonias, 12 sonatas for Strings, 16 string quartets, and keyboard music. He also publ. *Trattenimenti per clavicembalo* (Vienna, 1757).—LK/DM

Pires, (Luis) Filipe, Portuguese composer; b. Lisbon, June 26, 1934. He studied piano with Mendes and composition with Croner de Vasconcelos at the Lisbon Cons. (1946–54), and then took courses at the Hannover Hochschule für Musik (1957–60). He taught composition at the Oporto Cons. (1960–70) and at the Lisbon Cons. (1972–75), and subsequently worked in an electronic studio in Paris with Pierre Schaeffer. His music hewed resolutely to the tenets of the cosmopolitan avant-garde.

WORKS: String Quartet (1958); Piano Trio (1960); *Eternal Return* for Baritone and Orch. (1961); *Perspectivas* for 3 Groups of Instruments (1965); *Metromonie* for Flute, Viola, and Harp (1966); *Portugaliae Genesis* for Baritone, Chorus, and Orch. (1968; Lisbon, May 21, 1969); *Homo sapiens* for Magnetic Tape (1972); *Dialogues* for 8 Instrumentalists and Tape (1975).—NS/LK/DM

Pires, Maria-João, Portuguese pianist; b. Lisbon, July 23, 1944. She began piano lessons at a very early age, making her recital debut at 5 and appearing as soloist in a Mozart Concerto when she was 7. She studied piano with Campos Coelho at the Lisbon Academy of Music (1953–60), and concurrently received instruction in composition, theory, and music history from Francine Benoit; then pursued piano training with R. Schmid at the Munich Staatliche Hochschule für Musik and with Karl Engel. She appeared throughout her homeland and in Spain and Germany. After winning 1st prize in the Beethoven Competition in Brussels (1970), she gave concert tours in Europe, Africa, and Japan. In 1986 she made her North American debut as a soloist with the Montreal Sym. Orch., and in 1988 she made her first U.S. tour. In 1993 she was a soloist with Raymond Leppard and the Indianapolis Sym. Orch. on a major tour of Europe. Her readings of Mozart, Beethoven, Schubert, Schumann, and Chopin are finely etched and poetically outlined.—NS/LK/DM

Pirogov, Alexander (Stepanovich), noted Russian bass; b. Novoselki, July 4, 1899; d. Bear's Head Island, June 26, 1964. He studied voice at the Moscow Phil. Inst., and simultaneously attended classes in history and philology at the Univ. of Moscow. In 1924 he joined the Bolshoi Theater in Moscow, remaining on its roster until 1954. He specialized in the Russian operatic repertoire; his performance of the role of Boris Godunov received a prize in 1949; also notable were his interpretations of Méphistophélès in *Faust* and Don Basilio in *Il Barbiere di Siviglia*. His 2 brothers, Grigori (1885–1931) and Mikhail (1887–1933), were also notable basses. —NS/LK/DM

Piron, A(rmand) J(ohn), early jazz violinist, composer; b. New Orleans, La., Aug. 16, 1888; d. there, Feb. 17, 1943. He received a musical tuition from his father, who was an orchestra leader, and began playing professionally in 1904. He first led his own band in 1908, worked in the Peerless Orch. (c. 1912), fronted the Olympia Orch. from 1912. He partnered Clarence Williams in a publishing company, and did promotional tours with Williams, including appearances with W. C. Handy's Orch. (c. 1917). He began working in New Orleans with Papa Celestin (c. 1916). He led his own band from 1918, which played mainly in New Orleans. The band played briefly in N.Y. in 1923 and 1924; during the band's N.Y. bookings, publicity photographs were taken billing them as Williams's Ten Jazz Kings. Piron died in the Charity Hospital, New Orleans. His song, "I Wish I Could Shimmy Like My Sister Kate," has enjoyed several periods of popularity over the decades. Woody Allen borrowed his tune, "The Purple Rose of Cairo," for the title of one of his comedies.

DISC.: *Piron's New Orleans Orchestra* (1923).—JC/LP

Pironkoff, Simeon, Bulgarian composer; b. Lom, June 18, 1927. He took courses in violin, conducting (with A. Dimitrov), and composition (with P. Khadzhiev) at the Bulgarian State Cons. in Sofia (graduated, 1952). He was active as a composer and conductor at Sofia's Youth Theater (1951–61) and served as secretary of the Bulgarian Composer's Union (1966–69). He received the Gottfried von Herder Prize of the Univ. of Vienna (1985). His music is rhythmically animated, harmonically tense, melodically modal, and instrumentally coloristic.

WORKS: DRAMATIC: O p e r a : *A Good Woman from Szechwan* (1965); *The Motley Bird* (1979); *Ah, You, My Dream...* (1985). O t h e r : Film and theater music. ORCH.: Sym. for Strings (1960); *Movements for Strings* (1967); *Night Music* (1968); *Requiem for an Unknown Young Man* for Strings (1968); *A Big Game* for Small Orch. (1970); *Ballet Music in Memory of Igor Stravinsky* for Small Orch. (1972); *Concerto rustico* for Cello and Orch. (1982); *Entrata and Bulgarian Folk Dance* (1983); *Lyric Suite* for Strings (1983); *Symphonic Sketch on a Popular Melody: Rum and Coca-Cola* (1986); Flute Concerto (1987); Violin Concerto (1989); Chamber Sym. (1990); *Passacaglia* (1991); *Bosnian Lullaby* (1993). CHAMBER: 3 trios (1949, 1950, 1987); 3 string quartets (1951, 1966, 1985); Sonata for Solo Violin (1955); *Berceuse* for Clarinet and Piano (1983); *Thema con variationi* for Violin and Piano (1985); *Ecological Trio* for Clarinet, Violin, and Double Bass (1987); *3 Movements* for Harp (1992); piano pieces. VOCAL: *The True Apology of Socrates* for Bass, Strings, and Percussion (1967); *The Life and the Sufferings of the Sinful Sofronii*, oratorio for Narrator, Tenor, Chorus, and Orch. (1976); *In the Eye of the Storm* for Tenor and Orch. (1986); choruses; songs. —NS/LK/DM

Piroye, Charles, French organist, harpsichordist, and composer; b. probably in Paris, c. 1670; d. probably there, after 1717. He was a student of Lully and Lambert, and then an organist of the Jacobins (1690–1712) and at St. Honoré (1708–17) in Paris. He subsequently taught harpsichord.

WORKS: *Jephté*, tragedy (1703); *Cantique pour le temps de noël* for Soprano and Basso Continuo (Paris, 1703); *Messe de M. Biroat*, "plain-chant musical" (n.d.); several instrumental pieces. —LK/DM

Pirro, André (Gabriel Edme), distinguished French musicologist and organist; b. St.-Dizier, Haute-Marne, Feb. 12, 1869; d. Paris, Nov. 11, 1943. He first studied with his father, the local organist, then went to Paris, where he served as organist and maître de chapelle at the Collège Stanislas; also audited the organ classes given by Franck and Widor at the Paris Cons. (1889–91). He studied law at the Sorbonne and continued private studies in music; also studied in the faculty of arts in Nancy (1898–99). He received his doctorat ès lettres from the Sorbonne in 1907 with the diss. *L'Esthétique de Jean-Sébastien Bach* (publ. in Paris, 1907), which was followed that same year by the supplementary diss. *Descartes et la musique* (publ. in Paris, 1907). When the Schola Cantorum was founded in 1896, he was made a member of its board of directors and prof. of music history and organ; was organist at St. Jean-Baptiste de Belleville (1900–1904); lectured on music history at the École des Hautes Études Sociales (1904–14); was prof. of music history at the Sorbonne (1912–37). His outstanding students included Plamenac, Machabey, Rokseth, and Pincherle. In addition to his valuable books, he wrote many important articles on various aspects of music.

WRITINGS: *L'Orgue de Jean-Sébastien Bach* (Paris, 1895; Eng. tr., 1902); *J.-S. Bach* (Paris, 1906; 2nd ed., 1949; Eng. tr., 1957); *Dietrich Buxtehude* (Paris, 1913); *Schütz* (Paris, 1913); *Jean Sébastien Bach auteur comique* (Madrid, 1915); *Les Clavecinistes:*

Étude critique (Paris, 1924); *La Musique a Paris sous le régne de Charles VI, 1380–1422* (Strasbourg, 1930); ed. with A. Gastoué et al., *Bibliothèque nationale: La Musique française du moyen-âge à la Révolution* (Paris, 1934); *Histoire de la musique de la fin du XIVe siècle à la fin du XVIe* (Paris, 1940); *Mélanges: Recueil d'articles publié sous le patronage de la Société française de musicologie* (Geneva, 1971).—NS/LK/DM

Pirrotta, Nino (actually, Antonino), eminent Italian musicologist; b. Palermo, June 13, 1908; d. there, Jan. 15, 1998. He studied at the Cons. Vincenzo Bellini in Palermo; then received a diploma in organ and organ composition at the Florence Cons. (1930) and a liberal arts degree at the Univ. of Florence (1931). He was a lecturer in music history and a librarian at the Palermo Cons. (1936–48); was chief librarian at the Santa Cecilia Cons. in Rome (1948–56); was also a visiting prof. at Princeton Univ. (1954–55), the Univ. of Calif., Los Angeles (summer, 1955), and Columbia Univ. (1955). He then was a prof. at Harvard Univ. (1956–72), where he also was chairman of the music dept. (1965–68); subsequently was prof. of music history at the Univ. of Rome (1972–83). He was made a member of the American Academy of Arts and Sciences (1967) and an honorary member of the American Musicological Soc. (1980). An erudite scholar of wide interests, Pirrotta greatly distinguished himself in the study of Renaissance polyphony and Baroque opera. In addition to his important books, he ed. *The Music of Fourteenth- century Italy* in the Corpus Mensurabilis Musicae series (1954–64), and contributed valuable articles to music journals and other publications.

WRITINGS: With E. Li Gotti, *Il Sacchetti e la tecnica musicale del trecento italiano* (Florence, 1935); *Il codice estense lat.568 e la musica francese in Italia al principio del '400* (Palermo, 1946); *Li due Orfei: Da Poliziano a Monteverdi* (Turin, 1969; 2nd ed., 1975; Eng. tr., 1981); *Music and Culture in Italy from the Middle Ages to the Baroque: A Collection of Essays* (Cambridge, Mass., and London, 1984); *Musica tra Medioevo e Rinascimento* (Turin, 1984); *Scelte poetiche di musicisti: Teatro, poesia e musica da Willaert a Malipiero* (Venice, 1987); *Don Giovanni's Progress: A Rake Goes to the Opera* (N.Y., 1994).

BIBL.: F. Della Seta and F. Piperno, eds., *In Cantu et in sermone: For N. P. on His 80th Birthday* (Florence, 1989). —NS/LK/DM

Pirumov, Alexander, Russian composer; b. Tiflis, Feb. 6, 1930; d. Moscow, July 20, 1995. He studied composition with Kabalevsky at the Moscow Cons. (graduated, 1956). He taught piano first at the music school attached to the Cons. (1956–62), then at the Cons. itself (1962–71; lecturer, from 1971). His *Prelude and Toccata* (1962) and *Scherzo* (1974) were required pieces for the Tchaikovsky Piano Competition.

WORKS: ORCH.: 4 syms. (1956; for Strings and Percussion, 1963; 1965; 1973); *Concert Variations* for Piano and Orch. (1972). CHAMBER: 4 string quartets (1954, 1955, 1959, 1967). KEYBOARD: P i a n o : 2 sonatinas (1961, 1966); *Children's Album* (24 pieces; 1968); *Variations on a Theme of Bartók* (1968); Sonata (1973). O r g a n : 5 Preludes (1967). VOCAL: *October Days*, oratorio (1967); *Requiem in Memory of My Brother* (1975; in memory of his brother, who was killed in World War II). —NS/LK/DM

Pisa, Agostino, Italian music scholar who flourished in the early 17th century. He received a degree in law in Rome (1600). He publ. the earliest known treatise on conducting, *Breve dichiariatione della battuta musicale...* (Rome, 1611), a second augmented ed. of which was publ. in the same year, also in Rome, as *Battuta della musica....*—**NS/LK/DM**

Pisador, Diego, Spanish vihuelist and composer; b. Salamanca, 1509 or 1510; d. probably there, after 1557. In 1526 he took minor orders. In 1552 he publ. in Salamanca *Libro de música de vihuela,* containing madrigals, a set of Spanish ballads, and transcriptions of secular and sacred works by Josquin and others. A. Morphy ed. 14 of Pisador's works in *Les luthistes espagnols du XVIe siècle* (Leipzig, 1902).—**NS/LK/DM**

Pisano (real name, **Pagoli**), **Bernardo,** significant Italian composer; b. Florence, Oct. 12, 1490; d. Rome, Jan. 23, 1548. He studied at the Florence Cathedral school, during which time he sang in the chapel of the church of Ss. Annunziata. He was ordained a priest and made master of the choristers at the cathedral school (1511), and also sang in the chapels of the cathedral and baptistry and became master of the cathedral chapel (1512). He was a singer in the papal chapel in Rome (1514–48), and active at the Medici Chapel in Florence (1515–19). During a visit to Florence in 1529, he became embroiled in a revolt against the Medici Pope Clement VII; accused of being a papal spy, he was arrested, tortured, and expelled from the city by the republican authorities. Pisano was a master of the madrigal, honored as such in his time. He composed both sacred and secular vocal works, the latter represented by his *Musica...sopra le canzone del Petrarcha* (Venice, 1520). Most of his works have been ed. by F. D'Accone in *Music of the Florentine Renaissance,* Corpus Mensurabilis Musicae, XXXII/I (1966).—**NS/LK/DM**

Pisari, Pasquale, Italian singer and composer; b. Rome, c. 1725; d. there, March 27, 1778. He studied voice with Francesco Gasparini and composition with Fiovanni Biordi. From 1752 until his death he was a singer at the Sistine Chapel in Rome. He was admired as a composer of sacred music, including masses, Te Deums, Psalms, and motets.—**LK/DM**

Pisaroni, Benedetta (Rosmunda), Italian soprano, later contralto; b. Piacenza, May 16, 1793; d. there, Aug. 6, 1872. After training in Milan, she made her operatic debut in Mayr's *La rosa biana e la rosa rossa* in Bergamo in Aug. 1813. Upon the advice of Rossini, she turned to contralto roles and sang in Padua (1814), Bologna (1815), and Venice (1816). After singing in the premiere of Meyerbeer's *Romilda e Costanza* (Padua, July 19, 1817), she was called to Naples to create the roles of Zomira in *Riccardo e Zoraide* (Dec. 13, 1818), Andromache in *Ermione* (March 27, 1819), and Malcolm in *La donna del lago* (Sept. 24, 1819), all by Rossini. She appeared as Malcolm in Rome in 1823 and at Milan's La Scala in 1824, and then made her Paris debut as Arsace at the Théâtre-Italien in 1827. In 1829 she sang at the King's Theatre in London. Following further engagements at La Scala in 1831, she retired from the operatic stage.—**NS/LK/DM**

ISBN 0-02-865529-X

90000